CASES AND MATERIALS ON
LAND USE
Sixth Edition

By

Morton Gitelman
Distinguished Professor of Law
University of Arkansas
Fayetteville

John R. Nolon
Charles A. Frueauff Professor of Law
Pace University School of Law
Visiting Professor of Law
Yale University School of Forestry and Environmental Studies

Patricia E. Salkin
Associate Dean and Professor of Government Law
Director, Government Law Center
Albany Law School
Union University

Robert R. Wright
Donaghey Distinguished Professor of Law Emeritus
William H. Bowen School of Law
University of Arkansas
Little Rock

AMERICAN CASEBOOK SERIES®

Mat # 40140010

West, a Thomson business, has created this publication to provide you with accurate and authoritative information concerning the subject matter covered. However, this publication was not necessarily prepared by persons licensed to practice law in a particular jurisdiction. West is not engaged in rendering legal or other professional advice, and this publication is not a substitute for the advice of an attorney. If you require legal or other expert advice, you should seek the services of a competent attorney or other professional.

American Casebook Series and West Group are trademarks registered in the U.S. Patent and Trademark Office.

COPYRIGHT © 1969, 1976, 1982, 1991 WEST PUBLISHING CO.
COPYRIGHT © 1997 By WEST GROUP
© 2004 West, a Thomson business
      610 Opperman Drive
      P.O. Box 64526
      St. Paul, MN 55164–0526
      1–800–328–9352

ISBN 0–314–14602–4

TEXT IS PRINTED ON 10% POST CONSUMER RECYCLED PAPER

**To the memory of Marcia,
November 8, 1937 — January 23, 2003**

I was reminded everywhere I turned of the beauty of this
Earth—its fragility and its enduring strengths. I could see
these same qualities reflected in the human spirit—fragility,
vulnerability, amazing abilities to endure, to adapt, and to overcome.

          Marcia Lynn McIvor, April, 2001

Morton Gitelman
John R. Nolon
Patricia E. Salkin
Robert R. Wright

*

Preface

This sixth edition of the book on land use is a marked departure from previous editions—not so much in coverage—but in a new arrangement of materials. A more logical progression of the materials will, we hope, enable students and instructors to see how the land use system in this country works.

With this edition two new co-editors join the work. Professor Robert Wright has retired and Professors John Nolon and Patricia Salkin have stepped in to bring their unique talents and perspective to the materials. This book originated in the materials put together by Professor Jacob Beuscher at the University of Wisconsin in the 1960's. Professor Wright was at Wisconsin working with Jake Beuscher to help put the mimeographed land use book into shape for publication by West Publishing Co. When Professor Beuscher unexpectedly died, Robert Wright carried on and organized the book for publication. Jake Beuscher was years ahead of the times in his thinking about land use law, and Robert Wright worked diligently for many years to preserve and perpetuate the original vision. We wish to acknowledge the many efforts by Professor Wright to make this book the success it has become.

In thinking about how to preserve the attractions of previous editions and bring into this edition newer thinking about land use problems and solutions, the editors have reorganized the coverage, and while much of what was in the fifth edition has been retained, instructors will find that cases and text are in different places.

Chapter I is entirely new for the sixth edition. This chapter presents a picture of how raw land is turned into a residential subdivision. The scenario covers transactional as well as regulatory considerations and political realities. It is very realistic and typical of what happens constantly in most jurisdictions. References back to this scenario throughout the course will help students understand the concerns and perspectives of the various players in the realm of land development and regulation.

Chapter II presents the common law foundation for land regulation. The first portion is a jurisprudential overview of private property rights and public regulation that impacts those rights. Then, private law doctrines that affect land usage—the law of waste, nuisance, and covenants and servitudes—is covered. These private law devices and actions are still important and form private regimes that can impinge heavily on land use.

Chapter III shifts attention to the subject of public regulation of land usage. In this chapter students are introduced to the history of land use planning, and meet the players in the land use game. New in this edition is an expanded look at ethical considerations that concern the players. Prominent in the ethical material is a close examination of conflict of interest problems, for attorneys, planners, and citizens who serve as planning and zoning commissioners. The chapter ends with material that is familiar from earlier editions—the master plan, state and regional planning, and a look at federal land use regulation (a theme that will reappear in Chapter X).

Chapter IV is entitled The Basics of Zoning, and it offers a compact look at how most zoning ordinances work. New for this edition is more organized coverage of the problems of accessory uses and home occupations. Of course, just as in previous editions, rezonings, variances, special permits, and nonconforming uses are covered.

Chapter V deals with community building and it starts with regulation of subdivisions. In this part of the chapter more coverage of impact fees is offered. The chapter also covers familiar territory such as the official map. We have added a separate section of material on developer agreements and vested rights (as applied to land development projects).

Chapter VI, Smart Growth and Growth Management is mostly new material. Smart growth is at the center of contemporary conversations about how municipalities can and should regulate urban growth. The era of public attempts to halt growth has given way to a multitude of techniques that are used to shape growth and protect critical public resources. This chapter presents several examples from communities around the country that have implemented smart growth techniques and students are enabled to evaluate those ideas and gain perspective on creative thinking in dealing with the problems of urban growth.

Chapter VII is also mostly new material. It deals with local environmental law and covers subject matter that is almost always overlooked in courses on environmental law. Those courses are exclusively directed at federal and some state regulation; they ignore what is happening in the area of local government. Some of the cases presented in this chapter are the same as cases that were presented in earlier editions of the book, but they are put into a new context. Also, the section on resource-specific local regulations is replete with actual programs that are in place in many different localities and how those programs work.

In Chapter VIII coverage of aesthetic regulation, historical preservation, and cultural preservation tracks closely what was in the fifth edition of the book. Of course, the materials have been updated to reflect more recent controversies. Up to this point the book deals with local regulation of land uses, with some coverage of state and federal regulation. The balance of the materials cover restraints on local power to regulate. The editors believe that once the affirmative aspects of the system of American land use regulation are understood, students should look at how that system is kept in proper check.

Chapter IX deals with constitutional limits on local regulation. The chapter concentrates on Supreme Court regulatory takings jurisprudence under the Fifth Amendment injunction that private property cannot be taken for public use without just compensation. After that, coverage turns to the resurgent doctrine of substantive due process and how the lower federal courts and state courts seek to reconcile claims made under this doctrine with takings claims. Also, at the end of the chapter, relevant examples are given of equal protection theory which has received new attention in land use cases.

Chapter X covers statutory and other limitations on local regulation. The material in this chapter deals with federal and state preemption of local power, an area of law that has burgeoned in recent years as more and more federal law has been specifically directed at local land use problems. Logically following preemption issues, the chapter takes up intergovernmental conflicts in land use law, looking at state-local and local-local conflicts.

Chapter XI is entitled "Zoning and Discrimination" and while it is based upon a chapter in the previous edition of the same title, the materials have been organized differently. Instructors will see the same cases for the most part, but in different places. The chapter is no longer divided into exclusionary and inclusionary zoning, but rather takes a more functional and rational approach.

Chapter XII is a reorganized view of how local land use decisions are reviewed. Review by the people, through neighbor consent, initiative, and referendum is mostly the same material that was in the fifth edition. The next section—Mediation—is completely new. The editors have successfully brought together an organized and thorough look at the growing use of mediation to resolve land use disputes. Finally, review by the courts is presented to cover the difficult problem of how courts struggle with various theories dealing with review of local land use decisions.

We think instructors will find the new arrangement of text and cases is more logical and useful in having students understand how the system works, and how government operates in regard to land use regulation—an enterprise that affects almost all citizens. Students will learn where the problems lie and how solutions can be crafted to meet the challenges presented by land use disputes. One housekeeping notice—all court footnotes have been renumbered, so that footnote numbers will run consecutively throughout each chapter.

The authors gratefully acknowledge the reprint permission received for the following new material in the 6th edition:

Fischel, William A. the Economics of Zoning Laws: A Property Rights Approach to American Land Use Controls, pp. 36-37. ©1985 [Copyright Holder]. Reprinted with permission of The Johns Hopkins University Press.

William A. Fischel (2000), "Zoning and Land Use Regulation: Section 6 The Tiebout Model with Zoning Makes Local Taxes More Efficient," in Boudewijn Bouckaert and Gerrit De Geest (eds), Encyclopedia of Law and Economics, Volume II: Civil Law and Economics, Cheltenham, UK and Northampton, MA, USA: Edward Elgar, p. 414-6.

Stuart Meck, Subdivision Control: A Primer for Planning Commissioners, The Commissioner (Fall 1996) (American Planning Association).

Marci Hamilton, "Federalism and the Public Good: The True Story Behind the Religious Land Use and Institutionalized Persons Act, 78 Ind. L.J. 311 (2003) (Copyright 2003 by the Trustees of Indiana University. Reprinted with permission).

Carol Goforth, "A Bad Call: Preemption of State and Local Authority to Regulate Wireless Communication Facilities on the Basis of Radio Frequency Emissions," 44 N.Y.U. L. Rev. 311 (2001) (Copyright 2001 by Carol Goforth. Reprinted with permission).

The current editors of this book have found the preparation of a new, more thoughtfully organized edition to be a labor of love for the subject and its relevance, conducted with remarkable cooperation, unanimity, and amiability. Therefore, it is fitting and proper that we sign this Preface on Labor Day, 2003.

MORTON GITELMAN
JOHN R. NOLON
PATRICIA E. SALKIN

September 1, 2003

Summary of Contents

	Page
PREFACE	v
TABLE OF CASES	xxv

Chapter I. The Many Facets of Land Use Law 1

Chapter II. The Common Law Foundations Underlying Public Regulation of Land Use 15
1. The Nature of Property Rights 16
2. The Law of Nuisance 32
3. Servitudes and Restrictive Covenants 109

Chapter III. Local Land Use Planning and the Regulatory State 195
1. Public Policy and the Economics of Land Use Regulation 195
2. Historical Development of Land Use Planning 200
3. The Players in the Land Use Game 206
4. The Content and Effect of the Master Plan 230
5. State and Regional Planning 252

Chapter IV. The Basics of Zoning 279
1. History of Zoning 279
2. Zoning, Rezoning, and Conformance With the Comprehensive Plan 309
3. Zoning Administration and Flexibility 327
4. Nonconforming Uses 371
5. Accessory Uses 398
6. Home Occupations 408

Chapter V. Community Building: Subdivision Control and Infrastructure 416
1. Regulation of the Subdivision of Land 416
2. The Official Map and Public Streets 522
3. Developer Agreements and Vested Rights 538

Chapter VI. Smart Growth and Growth Management 550
1. Introduction 550
2. Moratoria 564
3. Growth Management 576
4. Centers of Growth and Development 622
5. Smart Growth Techniques 653

	Page
Chapter VII. Local Environmental Law	**699**
1. Historical Overview	699
2. Advent of Local Environmental Law	710
3. Resource–Specific Local Land Use Regulations	736
Chapter VIII. Preserving Aesthetics, Historic Places and Cultural Interests	**825**
1. Aesthetics and Architectural Control	825
2. Historical Landmark and Cultural Preservation	875
Chapter IX. Constitutional Limits on Local Control of Land Uses	**905**
1. Introduction	905
2. Regulatory Takings	911
Chapter X. Statutory Control and Other Limits on Local Land Uses	**1005**
1. Federal Preemption	1005
2. State Preemption	1056
3. Intergovernmental Conflicts	1076
Chapter XI. Zoning and Discrimination	**1101**
1. Discrimination and Housing	1102
2. Discrimination Against Particular Uses	1233
Chapter XII. Review by the People, Parties, and Courts	**1261**
1. Review by the People—Consent, Initiative and Referendum	1261
2. Mediation	1276
3. Review by the Courts	1316
INDEX	1347

Table of Contents

	Page
PREFACE	v
TABLE OF CASES	xxv

Chapter I. The Many Facets of Land Use Law 1
Chapter II. The Common Law Foundations Underlying Public Regulation of Land Use 15

Sec.
1. The Nature of Property Rights 16
    A. The Origins of and Justifications for Private Property 16
    B. The Origins of and Justification for Public Regulation 18
    C. Property Rights Legislation 27
2. The Law of Nuisance 32
    A. Some Important Basic Considerations 32
        (1) Historical Aspects 32
        (2) Public and Private Nuisances 33
        (3) The Duty Not to Interfere Substantially With Your Neighbor 34
        (4) The Restatement's Guides to What Is "Substantial" Harm 34
        (5) Nuisance Per Se and Nuisance Per Accidens 36
        (6) Motive and Nuisance 36
        (7) Doctrinal Versus Functional Approach to Nuisance Cases 37
    B. Conflicting Uses in Open Country 37
        (1) Uses in Conflict With Agricultural, Livestock or Commercial Operations 37
        Hulbert v. California Portland Cement Co. 37
        Notes 40
        McCaw v. Harrison 43
        Notes 44
        (2) Uses in Conflict With Rural Residential Use 46
        State Ex Rel. Cunningham v. Feezell 46
        Friendship Farms Camps, Inc. v. Parson 49
        (3) Uses in Conflict With Part Time, Recreational Residences 52
        Clark v. Wambold 52
        Notes 54
    C. Conflicting Uses on the Rururban Fringe 55
    Maykut v. Plasko 55

Sec.

2. The Law of Nuisance—Continued
    Spur Indus., Inc. v. Del E. Webb Development Co. 57
    Notes 64
    Boomer v. Atlantic Cement Co., Inc. 65
    Notes 69
  D. Conflicting Uses in Older Settled Areas 70
    (1) Residential Areas 70
        Mahoney v. Walter 70
        Notes 74
        Powell v. Taylor 76
        Notes 79
        Wilson v. Handley 80
        Notes 87
        Prah v. Maretti 88
        Notes 93
    (2) Commercial and Industrial Areas 95
        Bove v. Donner–Hanna Coke Corp. 95
        Notes 97
        Hadacheck v. Sebastian 98
        Notes 101
    (3) Areas Adjoining Parks or Recreational Facilities 102
  E. Nuisances in Zoned Areas 104
    Green v. Castle Concrete Co. 104
    Notes 105

3. Servitudes and Restrictive Covenants 109
  A. Defeasible Estates Versus Covenants 111
    City of Idaho Springs v. Golden Sav. & Loan Ass'n 112
    Notes 113
    Severns v. Union Pacific Railroad Company 115
    Notes 121
  B. Restrictive Covenants 123
    (1) Real Covenants 123
        Neponsit Property Owners' Ass'n v. Emigrant Industrial Sav. Bank 124
        Notes 128
        1515–1519 Lakeview Boulevard Condominium Association v. Apartment Sales Corporation 130
    (2) Equitable Servitudes 135
        Tulk v. Moxhay 135
        Notes 137
        Kent v. Koch 137
        Notes 140
        Sanborn v. McLean 141
        Notes 144
    (3) The Nature of the Interest Created: Property or Contract? 147
        Remilong v. Crolla 147
        Notes 150
        Morley v. Jackson Redevelopment Authority 151
        Notes 156

	Page
Sec.	
3. Servitudes and Restrictive Covenants—Continued	
(4) Enforcement	158
Brownfield Subdivision, Inc. v. McKee	160
Notes	163
Hoffman v. Cohen	164
Notes	167
McDonald v. Chaffin	167
Notes	169
Rofe v. Robinson	171
Notes	174
Sills v. Walworth County Land Management Committee	175
Note	178
(5) Alteration and Termination	178
Heffner v. Litchfield Golf Co.	178
Notes	180
West Alameda Heights Homeowners Ass'n v. Board of County Commissioners of Jefferson County	181
Notes	184
(6) Community Associations as Private Governments	187
(7) Drafting Covenants	191
Chapter III. Local Land Use Planning and the Regulatory State	**195**
Sec.	
1. Public Policy and the Economics of Land Use Regulation	195
"Zoning and Land Use Regulation" in Boudewijn, Bouckaert and Gerrit De Geest (Eds). Encyclopedia of Law and Economics, Vol. II. Civil Law and Economics, Cheltenham, Edward, Zelgar	197
Notes	200
2. Historical Development of Land Use Planning	200
A. Standard City Planning Enabling Act	201
B. ALI Model Land Development Code	203
C. Growing Smart Legislative Guidebook	204
Notes	204
3. The Players in the Land Use Game	206
A. Planners	206
B. The Legal Status of Planners	207
New Jersey Chapter, American Institute of Planners v. New Jersey State Bd. of Professional Planners	207
Notes	213
C. Should Planners Be Licensed?	217
Note	218
D. Ethical Conduct of Parties in the Land Use Arena	219
(1) Planners	220
AICP Code of Ethics and Professional Conduct	220
Notes	223
(2) Attorneys	223
Nicholas v. Wilton Zoning Board of Appeals	224
Notes	228

Sec.	Page
3. The Players in the Land Use Game—Continued	
(3) Members of Planning and Zoning Boards	229
4. The Content and Effect of the Master Plan	230
United States Department of Commerce, A Standard City Planning Enabling Act	230
Creative Displays, Inc. v. City of Florence	234
Notes	235
Elysian Heights Residents Association, Inc. v. City of Los Angeles	236
Notes	240
Cochran v. Planning Bd. of City of Summit	243
Bone v. City of Lewiston	249
Notes	251
5. State and Regional Planning	252
A. Federal Land Use Legislation	252
B. State Planning	258
In Re Juster Associates	262
Notes	263
C. Regional Planning	269
Notes	270
D. Interstate Compacts	271
People Ex Rel. Younger v. County of El Dorado	271
Notes	278

Chapter IV. The Basics of Zoning — 279

Sec.	Page
1. History of Zoning	279
A. American Planning and Zoning	279
(1) History of Planning and Zoning	279
(2) History of Local Control of Land Development	281
(3) Defining a Land Use Plan	284
(4) What Is Land Use Law and Practice?	286
(5) Balancing Property Rights and the Public Interest: Limiting Doctrines	286
(6) Zoning Practice	288
(7) Local Boards	290
B. Early Cases	291
Goldman v. Crowther	291
State Ex Rel., Carter v. Harper	296
Village of Euclid v. Ambler Realty Co.	300
Notes	307
2. Zoning, Rezoning, and Conformance With the Comprehensive Plan	309
A Standard State Zoning Enabling Act Under Which Municipalities May Adopt Zoning Regulations	309
Bartram v. Zoning Commission	313
Notes	317
Enterprise Partners v. County of Perkins	318
Notes	322
Osiecki v. Town of Huntington	323

Sec.	Page
2. Zoning, Rezoning, and Conformance With the Comprehensive Plan—Continued	
Notes	325
3. Zoning Administration and Flexibility	327
A. Introduction	327
B. Amendment of Ordinance	332
Church v. Town of Islip	332
Notes	335
Giger v. City of Omaha	337
Montgomery County v. National Capital Realty Corp.	344
Notes	346
C. Administrative Treatment	349
(1) Variance Cases	351
Larsen v. Zoning Board of Adjustment of City of Pittsburgh	351
Notes	355
Sasso v. Osgood	357
Notes	361
McMorrow v. Board of Adjustment for City of Town & Country	361
Notes	363
(2) Special Use Permit Cases	364
City of Chicago Heights v. Living Word Outreach Full Gospel	364
Notes	370
4. Nonconforming Uses	371
A. Expansion or Extension	373
State v. Perry	374
Notes	375
B. Discontinuance	378
State Ex Rel. Morehouse v. Hunt	378
Toys "R" Us v. Silva	380
Notes	387
C. Destruction	388
Moffatt v. Forrest City	388
Notes	389
D. Amortization—Uses and Limitations	390
AVR, Inc. v. City of St. Louis Park	391
Notes	396
5. Accessory Uses	398
Collins v. Lonergan	399
Greentree v. Good Shepherd Episcopal Church	400
Dobo v. Zoning Bd. of Adjustment of City of Wilmington	404
Notes	406
6. Home Occupations	408
Baker v. Posinelli	409
Town of Sullivans Island v. Byrum	411
Notes	414

Chapter V. Community Building: Subdivision Control and Infrastructure 416

Sec.
1. Regulation of the Subdivision of Land 416
   A. The Essential Reasons for and Nature of Subdivision Regulation 416
      Pomeroy, Preface to the Subdivision of Land in San Mateo County, California 11 416
      Melli, Subdivision Control in Wisconsin 416
   B. Role of the Planning Commission 421
      Meck, Subdivision Control: A Primer for Planning Commissioners 421
   C. Governmental Power to Regulate Subdivisions 426
      Ridgefield Land Co. v. Detroit 426
      Notes 430
      Dawe v. City of Scottsdale 434
      Notes 436
      City of Corpus Christi v. Unitarian Church of Corpus Christi 438
      Notes 441
   D. Cluster Zoning 444
      Chrinko v. South Brunswick Twp. Planning Bd. 444
      Orinda Homeowners Committee v. Board of Supervisors 448
      Notes 451
   E. Subdivision Exactions and Other Regulation Issues 452
      (1) Traditional Exactions 453
         Petterson v. City of Naperville 453
         Notes 457
         181 Inc. v. Salem County Planning Bd. 463
         Notes 465
      (2) Off-Site Improvements and Impact Fees 466
         Divan Builders, Inc. v. Planning Bd. of Twp. of Wayne 466
         Notes 474
      (3) Non-traditional Exactions 476
         Pioneer Trust & Sav. Bank v. Village of Mount Prospect 476
         Jordan v. Village of Menomonee Falls 479
         Notes 486
         Nollan v. California Coastal Commission 491
         Notes 496
         Dolan v. City of Tigard 497
         Notes 511
      (4) Denial of Subdivision Approval 513
         Coffey v. Maryland–National Capital Park and Planning Commission 513
         Maryland–Nat'l Capital Park and Planning Comm'n v. Rosenberg 515
         Notes 519
2. The Official Map and Public Streets 522
   Headley v. City of Rochester 524
   Nigro v. Planning Board of Borough of Saddle River 530

Sec.	Page
2. The Official Map and Public Streets—Continued	
Lake City Corporation v. City of Mequon	533
Notes	536
3. Developer Agreements and Vested Rights	538
A. Vested Rights	538
American Planning Association, Growing Smart Legislative Guidebook: Model Statutes for Planning and the Management of Change	538
Avco Community Developers, Inc. v. South Coast Regional Commission	540
B. Developer Agreements	545
American Planning Association, Growing Smart Legislative Guidebook: Model Statutes for Planning and the Management of Change	545
Bollech v. Charles County, Maryland	545
Notes	548

Chapter VI. Smart Growth and Growth Management — 550

Sec.	Page
1. Introduction	550
A. Local Land Use Controls That Achieve Smart Growth	550
Golden v. Planning Board of Town of Ramapo	552
Notes	563
2. Moratoria	564
Maryland–Nat'l Capital Park and Planning Comm'n v. Chadwick	566
Notes	571
New Jersey Shore Builders Association v. Mayor and Township Committee of Township of Middletown	571
Notes	574
3. Growth Management	576
A. Local Regulation of Urban Growth	577
Construction Industry Ass'n of Sonoma County v. City of Petaluma	577
Notes	585
Associated Home Builders of the Greater Eastbay, Inc. v. City of Livermore	586
Notes	596
Steel Hill Development, Inc. v. Town of Sanbornton	597
Notes	602
B. Denial of Access to Infrastructure	603
Dateline Builders, Inc. v. City of Santa Rosa	603
Note	606
Charles v. Diamond	607
Note	610
C. State Growth Management Legislation	610
Haviland v. Land Conservation and Development Commission	613
Residents of Rosemont v. Metro	616
Notes	619

Sec.				Page
4.	Centers of Growth and Development			622
	A.	Introduction		622
	B.	Housing Codes		623
		First National Realty Corp. v. Javins		624
		Notes		628
	C.	Urban Redevelopment Techniques		629
		Matter of Condemnation by Minneapolis Community Development Agency v. Opus Northwest, LLC		630
		Notes		637
	D.	Protecting Growth Districts From Competition		643
		Forte v. Borough of Tenafly		644
		Swain v. County of Winnebago		647
		Notes		650
	E.	Promoting Brownfield Redevelopment		652
5.	Smart Growth Techniques			653
	A.	Post–Euclidian Zoning		653
		Rodgers v. Village of Tarrytown		655
		Notes		663
	B.	Smarter Site Planning: Clustering and Environmental Impact Review		665
	C.	Smarter Patterns of Growth: Flexibility Techniques		668
	D.	Performance Zoning		669
		Notes		673
	E.	Planned Unit Development Zoning		674
	F.	Traditional Neighborhood Districts		676
		Notes		679
	G.	Transfer of Development Rights		680
		Suitum v. Tahoe Regional Planning Agency		682
		Notes		686
	H.	Overlay Zoning Districts		687
		Glisson v. Alachua County		689
		Notes		695
	I.	Incentive Zoning		696
		Notes		698

Chapter VII. Local Environmental Law — 699

Sec.		Page
1.	Historical Overview	699
	De Mars v. Town of Bolton	700
	Notes	702
	Morris County Land Improvement Co. v. Township of Parsippany–Troy Hills	703
	Notes	709
2.	Advent of Local Environmental Law	710
	Just v. Marinette County	711
	Notes	718
	In Re Spring Valley Development	719
	Moviematic Industries Corp. v. Board of County Com'rs	725
	Sun Beach Real Estate Development Corp. v. Anderson	730
	Notes	735

Sec.		Page
3.	Resource–Specific Local Land Use Regulations	736
	A. Water Resource Protection	737
	(1) Aquifer/Groundwater Supplies	738
	Quick v. Austin	739
	Notes	746
	Connecticut Resources Recovery Auth. v. Planning & Zoning Comm'n	746
	Notes	752
	(2) Stormwater Management	752
	Environmental Defense Center, Inc. v. United States Environmental Protection Agency	754
	Notes	757
	(3) Floodplains	758
	April v. City of Broken Arrow	758
	Notes	764
	(4) Wetlands	766
	Fafard v. Conservation Commission of Barnstable	767
	Notes	774
	B. Land Resource Protections	774
	(1) Erosion and Sedimentation Control	774
	Marion Rd. Ass'n v. Westport Planning & Zoning Commission	775
	Notes	777
	(2) Steep Slopes/Ridgeline/Hilltop Protections	777
	Sellon v. City of Manitou Springs	778
	Notes	782
	(3) Scenic Resources	784
	Smith v. Zoning Bd. of Appeals of Town of Greenwich	785
	Notes	797
	(4) Tree and Forest Preservation/Timber Preservation	799
	Echevarrieta v. City of Rancho Palos Verdes	800
	Notes	803
	Rancho Lobo v. Devargas	804
	(5) Fish and Wildlife Protection	809
	Florida Wildlife Federation v. Collier County	811
	Notes	815
	(6) The Public Trust Doctrine	816
	Esplanade v. Seattle	817
	Notes	823

Chapter VIII. Preserving Aesthetics, Historic Places and Cultural Interests — 825

Sec.		Page
1.	Aesthetics and Architectural Control	825
	A. Regulation of Signs and Billboards	826
	State v. Diamond Motors, Inc.	826
	Mayor and City Council of Baltimore v. Mano Swartz, Inc.	829
	Metromedia, Inc. v. City of San Diego	833
	Notes	843
	A Note on the Federal Highway Beautification Act	847

Sec.

1. Aesthetics and Architectural Control—Continued
   B. The Appearance of Structures and Other Aesthetic Regulations 850
      State Ex Rel. Saveland Park Holding Corp. v. Wieland 850
      Note 855
      State Ex Rel. Stoyanoff v. Berkeley 855
      Notes 861
      People v. Stover 863
      Notes 869
      Parking Association of Georgia, Inc. v. City of Atlanta, Georgia 870
   C. Underground Utilities 871
      Union Electric Co. v. City of Crestwood 872
      Notes 874
2. Historical Landmark and Cultural Preservation 875
   A. Federal Government's Role in Historical Landmark and Cultural Preservation 875
   B. The Role of State Governments in Historic and Cultural Preservation 878
   C. Historic Preservation at the Local Government Level 878
      (1) Historic Districts 879
         Opinion of the Justices to the Senate 879
         Notes 882
         South of Second Associates v. Georgetown 884
         Notes 887
      (2) Preserving Landmark Structures 888
         Kent County Council for Historic Preservation v. Romney 888
         Notes 890
         Penn Central Transp. Co. v. City of New York 891
         Notes 895
         Fgl & L Property Corp. v. City of Rye 897
         Notes 900
      (3) Conservation Easements and Land Trusts 902

Chapter IX. Constitutional Limits on Local Control of Land Uses 905

Sec.

1. Introduction 905
   Emmett Mcloughlin Realty, Inc. v. Pima County 906
   Note 910
2. Regulatory Takings 911
   A. The Basic Constitutional Considerations 911
      Mugler v. Kansas 911
      Pennsylvania Coal Co. v. Mahon 913
      Notes 917
      Goldblatt v. Town of Hempstead, N.Y. 920
      Penn Central Transp. Co. v. New York City 923
      Notes 932

Sec.		Page
2. Regulatory Takings—Continued		
	First English Evangelical Lutheran Church v. Los Angeles County	934
	Note	938
	Lucas v. South Carolina Coastal Council	938
	Notes	955
	Palazzolo v. Rhode Island	957
	Tahoe–Sierra Preservation Council, Inc. v. Tahoe Regional Planning Agency	964
B.	Substantive Due Process and Excessive Regulation	978
	First English Evangelical Lutheran Church v. Los Angeles County	978
	Note	980
	Presbytery of Seattle v. King County	980
	Notes	985
	Pearson v. City of Grand Blanc	987
	Notes	996
C.	The Equal Protection Clause	1001
	Village of Willowbrook v. Olech	1002
	Notes	1004

Chapter X. Statutory Control and Other Limits on Local Land Uses 1005

Sec.		
1. Federal Preemption		1005
A.	Religious Land Uses	1010
	Elsinore Christian Center v. City of Lake Elsinore	1010
	Notes	1023
B.	Federal Fair Housing Act Amendments of 1988	1024
	City of Edmonds v. Oxford House, Inc.	1026
	Howard v. City of Beavercreek	1031
C.	Americans With Disabilities Act	1034
	Innovative Health Systems v. City of White Plains	1034
	Notes	1042
D.	Telecommunications Act of 1996	1043
	Sprint Spectrum v. Willoth	1045
	Note	1053
	Further Notes on Federal Preemption	1053
2. State Preemption		1056
A.	Mining	1056
	Gernatt Asphalt Products, Inc. v. Town of Sardinia	1056
B.	Agricultural Uses	1060
	Craig v. County of Chatham	1060
C.	Group Homes for the Mentally Ill	1067
	Jennings v. New York State Office of Mental Health	1067
	Notes	1074
3. Intergovernmental Conflicts		1076
A.	State-Local Conflicts	1076
	Brown v. Kansas Forestry, Fish and Game Comm'n	1076
	Notes	1084

	Page
Sec.	
3. Intergovernmental Conflicts—Continued	
B. Local–Local Conflicts	1086
City of Bridgeton v. City of St. Louis	1086
City of New Rochelle v. Town of Mamaroneck	1090
Notes	1097

Chapter XI. Zoning and Discrimination — 1101

	Page
Sec.	
1. Discrimination and Housing	1102
A. Introduction	1102
B. The Bedroom Suburb	1104
McDermott v. Village of Calverton Park	1104
Notes	1106
C. Non–Traditional Families	1107
Village of Belle Terre v. Boraas	1107
Notes	1111
McMinn v. Town of Oyster Bay	1112
Notes	1114
City of Ladue v. Horn	1116
Notes	1119
City of White Plains v. Ferraioli	1120
Notes	1123
D. Multi–Family Housing	1127
Appeal of Girsh	1127
Notes	1133
McHenry State Bank v. City of McHenry	1135
Notes	1137
E. Mobile Homes And Manufactured Housing	1138
Town of Glocester v. Olivo's Mobile Home Court, Inc.	1138
Notes	1140
Bahl v. City of Asbury	1142
Notes	1151
Marion County v. Department of Community Affairs	1153
Note	1155
F. Racial Discrimination In Housing	1155
United States v. City of Black Jack, Missouri	1155
Note	1160
Village of Arlington Heights v. Metropolitan Housing Development Corp.	1160
Notes	1164
A Note on Gentrification	1167
G. Age Discrimination in Housing	1167
Colony Cove Associates v. Brown	1167
Notes	1172
H. Indirect Housing Discrimination	1173
National Land and Investment Co. v. Kohn	1174
Notes	1179
Ybarra v. Town of Los Altos Hills	1181
Note	1183
Home Builders League of South Jersey, Inc. v. Township of Berlin	1184

Sec.		Page
1. Discrimination and Housing—Continued		
	Notes	1189
I.	Judicial And Legislative Oversight Of Discriminatory Zoning	1192
	Southern Burlington County NAACP v. Township of Mount Laurel	1193
	Note	1201
	Berenson v. Town of New Castle	1201
	Notes	1207
	Toll Brothers, Inc. v. Township of West Windsor	1208
	Note	1217
	Notes	1222
	Home Builders Association of Northern California v. City of NAPA	1223
	Board of Supervisors of Fairfax County v. DeGroff Enterprises, Inc.	1228
	Notes	1231
2. Discrimination Against Particular Uses		1233
A.	Industrial Uses	1233
	General Battery Corp. v. Zoning Hearing Bd. of Alsace Twp.	1233
	Notes	1235
B.	Commercial Uses	1236
	Secret Desires Lingerie, Inc. v. City of Atlanta	1237
	Note	1240
	Voyeur Dorm, L.C. v. City of Tampa	1240
C.	Religious Institutions and Private Schools	1244
	State Ex Rel. Lake Drive Baptist Church v. Village of Bayside	1244
	Notes	1249
	Fifth Avenue Presbyterian Church v. City of New York	1252
	Notes	1256
	State Ex Rel. Wisconsin Lutheran High School Conference v. Sinar	1256
	Notes	1258

Chapter XII. Review by the People, Parties, and Courts 1261

Sec.		
1. Review by the People—Consent, Initiative and Referendum		1261
A.	Introduction	1261
B.	Consent by the Neighbors	1262
	Valkanet v. City of Chicago	1262
	Notes	1266
C.	The Initiative and Referendum Process	1266
	City of Eastlake v. Forest City Enterprises, Inc.	1267
	Notes	1273
2. Mediation		1276
A.	An Introduction to Land Use Mediation	1276
	(1) Land Use Approvals as Negotiations	1278
	(2) Mediators and Facilitators	1279
	(3) Broader Applications	1279
B.	Key Steps in the Mediation Process	1280

Sec.		Page
2. Mediation		1276
C.	Mediation Statutes	1282
	Kucera v. Lizza	1285
	Notes	1287
D.	Mediation Before a Land Use Application Is Made	1288
	Santa Margarita Area Residents v. San Luis Obispo County Board of Supervisors	1288
	Notes	1294
E.	Mediation During the Development Approval Process	1294
	Merson v. McNally	1294
	Notes	1301
	Medeiros v. Hawaii County Planning Commission	1302
	Notes	1308
F.	Mediation After the Development Approval Process	1309
	Scott v. Polk County	1309
	Notes	1311
G.	Mediation and Lawyering	1311
	Wilmington Hospitality v. New Castle County	1311
	Notes	1315
3. Review by the Courts		1316
A.	Introduction	1316
	Fritts v. City of Ashland	1317
	Notes	1320
	Neuzil v. City of Iowa City	1323
	Notes	1331
	Fasano v. Board of County Comm'rs of Washington County	1332
	Notes	1337
	Nova Horizon, Inc. v. City Council of the City of Reno	1339
	Notes	1343
INDEX		1347

Table of Cases

The principal cases are in bold type. Cases cited or discussed in the text are roman type. References are to pages. Cases cited in principal cases and within other quoted materials are not included.

Aaron v. Conservation Commission of Town of Redding, 183 Conn. 532, 441 A.2d 30 (Conn.1981), 718

Aaron v. Target Corp., 269 F.Supp.2d 1162 (E.D.Mo.2003), 642

Abcon, Inc., Appeal of, 35 Pa.Cmwlth. 589, 387 A.2d 1303 (Pa.Cmwlth.1978), 1134

Abel v. Town of Orangetown, 724 F.Supp. 232 (S.D.N.Y.1989), 847

Abram v. City of Fayetteville, 281 Ark. 63, 661 S.W.2d 371 (Ark.1983), 1251

Abrams v. Shuger, 336 Mich. 59, 57 N.W.2d 445 (Mich.1953), 169

Ackerley Communications of Massachusetts, Inc. v. City of Somerville, 878 F.2d 513 (1st Cir.1989), 846

A. Copeland Enterprises, Inc. v. City of New Orleans, 372 So.2d 764 (La.App. 4 Cir.1979), 1236

Ada County v. Henry, 105 Idaho 263, 668 P.2d 994 (Idaho 1983), 1181

Adams County Ass'n for Retarded Citizens, Inc. v. City of Westminster, 196 Colo. 79, 580 P.2d 1246 (Colo.1978), 1125

Admiral Development Corp. v. City of Maitland, 267 So.2d 860 (Fla.App. 4 Dist. 1972), 486

Agins v. City of Tiburon, 157 Cal.Rptr. 372, 598 P.2d 25 (Cal.1979), 932

Agliata v. D'Agostino, 124 N.Y.S.2d 212 (N.Y.Sup.1953), 537

Akron, City of v. Chapman, 160 Ohio St. 382, 116 N.E.2d 697 (Ohio 1953), 106, 396

Alamogordo Improvement Co. v. Prendergast, 43 N.M. 245, 91 P.2d 428 (N.M. 1939), 114

Albany Area Builders Ass'n v. Town of Guilderland, 547 N.Y.S.2d 627, 546 N.E.2d 920 (N.Y.1989), 474

Albino v. Pacific First Federal Sav. & Loan Ass'n, 257 Or. 473, 479 P.2d 760 (Or. 1971), 185

Albright v. City of Portage, 188 Mich.App. 342, 470 N.W.2d 657 (Mich.App.1991), 1275

Alegria v. Keeney, 687 A.2d 1249 (R.I.1997), 956

All American Sign Rentals, Inc. v. City of Orlando, 592 F.Supp. 85 (M.D.Fla.1983), 845

Allen v. Axford, 285 Ala. 251, 231 So.2d 122 (Ala.1969), 174

Allen v. Stockwell, 210 Mich. 488, 178 N.W. 27 (Mich.1920), 460

Alpha Portland Cement Co. v. Missouri Dept. of Natural Resources, 608 S.W.2d 451 (Mo.App. E.D.1980), 371

Alpine Christian Fellowship v. County Com'rs of Pitkin County, 870 F.Supp. 991 (D.Colo.1994), 1252

Alschuler v. Department of Housing and Urban Development, 515 F.Supp. 1212 (N.D.Ill.1981), 1167

American Wildlands v. Browner, 260 F.3d 1192 (10th Cir.2001), 256

Ames, City of v. Story County, 392 N.W.2d 145 (Iowa 1986), 1084

Amoco Oil Co. v. Village of Schaumburg, 277 Ill.App.3d 926, 214 Ill.Dec. 526, 661 N.E.2d 380 (Ill.App. 1 Dist.1995), 465

Anastasio v. Planning Bd. of West Orange Tp., 209 N.J.Super. 499, 507 A.2d 1194 (N.J.Super.A.D.1986), 1001

Anastasio v. Planning Bd. of West Orange Tp., 197 N.J.Super. 457, 484 A.2d 1358 (N.J.Super.L.1984), 1000

Anaya, State ex rel. v. Select Western Lands, Inc., 94 N.M. 555, 613 P.2d 425 (N.M.App.1979), 443

Anderson v. City of Issaquah, 70 Wash.App. 64, 851 P.2d 744 (Wash.App. Div. 1 1993), 861

Anderson v. City of Paragould, 16 Ark.App. 10, 695 S.W.2d 851 (Ark.App.1985), 387

Anello v. Zoning Bd. of Appeals of the Village of Dobbs Ferry, 656 N.Y.S.2d 184, 678 N.E.2d 870 (N.Y.1997), 783

Angell v. Zinsser, 473 F.Supp. 488 (D.Conn. 1979), 1165, 1167
Anshe Chesed Congregation, State ex rel. v. Bruggemeier, 97 Ohio App. 67, 115 N.E.2d 65 (Ohio App. 8 Dist.1953), 1097, 1250
Antioch, City of v. Candidates' Outdoor Graphic Service, 557 F.Supp. 52 (N.D.Cal.1982), 846
Apfelbaum v. Town of Clarkstown, 104 Misc.2d 371, 428 N.Y.S.2d 387 (N.Y.Sup. 1980), 1172
Appalachian Power Co. v. Train, 545 F.2d 1351 (4th Cir.1976), 256
Appeal of (see name of party)
Application of (see name of party)
April v. City of Broken Arrow, 775 P.2d 1347 (Okla.1989), **758**
Ardizzone v. Elliott, 551 N.Y.S.2d 457, 550 N.E.2d 906 (N.Y.1989), 737
Arens v. City of St. Louis, 872 S.W.2d 631 (Mo.App. E.D.1994), 361
Arizona Public Service Co. v. Town of Paradise Valley, 125 Ariz. 447, 610 P.2d 449 (Ariz.1980), 874
Arkansas State Highway Commission v. Cunningham, 239 Ark. 890, 395 S.W.2d 13 (Ark.1965), 571
Arkansas State Highway Commission v. McNeill, 238 Ark. 244, 381 S.W.2d 425 (Ark.1964), 156
Arlington Heights, Village of v. Metropolitan Housing Development Corp., 429 U.S. 252, 97 S.Ct. 555, 50 L.Ed.2d 450 (1977), **1160,** 1164
Arnel Development Co. v. City of Costa Mesa, 126 Cal.App.3d 330, 178 Cal.Rptr. 723 (Cal.App. 4 Dist.1981), 1275
Arnel Development Co. v. City of Costa Mesa, 169 Cal.Rptr. 904, 620 P.2d 565 (Cal.1980), 1275
Arnold v. Mundy, 1821 WL 1269 (N.J.1821), 816
Arrington v. Urban Redevelopment Authority of Pittsburgh, In re, 822 A.2d 135 (Pa.Cmwlth.2003), 1004
Arrowhead Development Co. v. Livingston County Road Com'n, 413 Mich. 505, 322 N.W.2d 702 (Mich.1982), 474
Arthur M. Deck & Associates v. Crispin, 888 S.W.2d 56 (Tex.App.-Hous. (1 Dist.) 1994), 146
Art Piculell Group v. Clackamas County, 142 Or.App. 327, 922 P.2d 1227 (Or. App.1996), 512
Arvidson v. Reynolds Metals Co., 125 F.Supp. 481 (W.D.Wash.1954), 41, 42
Asheville, City of v. Woodberry Associates, Ltd., 114 N.C.App. 377, 442 S.E.2d 328 (N.C.App.1994), 777
Asian Americans for Equality v. Koch, 531 N.Y.S.2d 782, 527 N.E.2d 265 (N.Y. 1988), 698, 1208

Associated Home Builders etc., Inc. v. City of Livermore, 135 Cal.Rptr. 41, 557 P.2d 473 (Cal.1976), **586,** 597
Associated Home Builders etc., Inc. v. City of Walnut Creek, 94 Cal.Rptr. 630, 484 P.2d 606 (Cal.1971), 488
Associated Metals & Minerals Corp. v. Dixon Chemical & Research, Inc., 82 N.J.Super. 281, 197 A.2d 569 (N.J.Super.A.D.1963), 69
Association for Advancement of the Mentally Handicapped, Inc. v. City of Elizabeth, 876 F.Supp. 614 (D.N.J.1994), 1043, 1126
Association of Relatives and Friends of AIDS Patients (A.F.A.P.S.) v. Regulations and Permits Admin. or Administracion de Reglamentos y Permisos (A.R.P.E.), 740 F.Supp. 95 (D.Puerto Rico 1990), 1126
Auburn, Town of v. McEvoy, 131 N.H. 383, 553 A.2d 317 (N.H.1988), 488
Aunt Hack Ridge Estates, Inc. v. Planning Commission of City of Danbury, 160 Conn. 109, 273 A.2d 880 (Conn.1970), 488
Avco Community Developers, Inc. v. South Coast Regional Commission, 132 Cal.Rptr. 386, 553 P.2d 546 (Cal. 1976), **540**
Avenal v. United States, 100 F.3d 933 (Fed. Cir.1996), 956
AVR, Inc. v. City of St. Louis Park, 585 N.W.2d 411 (Minn.App.1998), **391**
AWACS, Inc. v. Zoning Hearing Bd. of Newton Tp., Delaware County, 702 A.2d 604 (Pa.Cmwlth.1997), 408
Ayers v. Porter County Plan Com'n, 544 N.E.2d 213 (Ind.App. 4 Dist.1989), 1125
Ayres v. City Council of City of Los Angeles, 34 Cal.2d 31, 207 P.2d 1 (Cal.1949), 457, 459, 489, 490, 905

Badgett, United States v., 976 F.2d 1176 (8th Cir.1992), 1166, 1173
Baer v. Town of Brookhaven, 540 N.Y.S.2d 234, 537 N.E.2d 619 (N.Y.1989), 1114
Bagko Development Co. v. Damitz, 640 N.E.2d 67 (Ind.App. 4 Dist.1994), 170, 406
Bahl v. City of Asbury, 656 N.W.2d 336 (Iowa 2002), **1142,** 1151
Baker v. Polsinelli, 177 A.D.2d 844, 576 N.Y.S.2d 460 (N.Y.A.D. 3 Dept.1991), **409**
Baker, State v., 81 N.J. 99, 405 A.2d 368 (N.J.1979), 1116
Baldwin v. Barbon Corp., 773 S.W.2d 681 (Tex.App.-San Antonio 1989), 180
Baltica Const. Co., Inc. v. Planning Bd. of Franklin Tp., 222 N.J.Super. 428, 537 A.2d 319 (N.J.Super.A.D.1988), 474
Baltimore, City of v. State Dept. of Health and Mental Hygiene, 38 Md.App. 570, 381 A.2d 1188 (Md.App.1978), 1125

Bannerman v. City of Fall River, 391 Mass. 328, 461 N.E.2d 793 (Mass.1984), 1138
Barber & Sons Tobacco Co., Inc., State ex rel. v. Jackson County, 869 S.W.2d 113 (Mo.App. W.D.1993), 1320
Barger v. Barringer, 151 N.C. 433, 66 S.E. 439 (N.C.1909), 36
Barile v. City of Port Republic, 186 N.J.Super. 587, 453 A.2d 284 (N.J.Super.L.1982), 536
Barnes v. City of Anderson, 642 N.E.2d 1004 (Ind.App. 2 Dist.1994), 1346
Barnes v. Glen Theatre, Inc., 501 U.S. 560, 111 S.Ct. 2456, 115 L.Ed.2d 504 (1991), 1240
Barney v. Burlington Northern R. Co., Inc., 490 N.W.2d 726 (S.D.1992), 122
Barrie v. Kitsap County, 93 Wash.2d 843, 613 P.2d 1148 (Wash.1980), 240
Barrington Hills, Village of v. Village of Hoffman Estates, 81 Ill.2d 392, 43 Ill. Dec. 37, 410 N.E.2d 37 (Ill.1980), 1098
Barsel v. Woodbridge Tp. Zoning Bd. of Adjustment, 189 N.J.Super. 75, 458 A.2d 1303 (N.J.Super.A.D.1983), 536
Bartram v. Zoning Commission of City of Bridgeport, 136 Conn. 89, 68 A.2d 308 (Conn.1949), **313,** 317
Batch v. Town of Chapel Hill, 326 N.C. 1, 387 S.E.2d 655 (N.C.1990), 520
Batchelder v. City of Seattle, 77 Wash.App. 154, 890 P.2d 25 (Wash.App. Div. 1 1995), 798
Baxter v. City of Belleville, Ill., 720 F.Supp. 720 (S.D.Ill.1989), 1125
Bayswater Realty & Capital Corp. v. Planning Bd. of Town of Lewisboro, 560 N.Y.S.2d 623, 560 N.E.2d 1300 (N.Y. 1990), 488
Beach v. Planning and Zoning Commission of Town of Milford, 141 Conn. 79, 103 A.2d 814 (Conn.1954), 520
Beall v. Montgomery County Council, 240 Md. 77, 212 A.2d 751 (Md.1965), 665
Beane v. H.K. Porter, Inc., 280 Mass. 538, 182 N.E. 823 (Mass.1932), 106
Beaver Gasoline Co. v. Zoning Hearing Bd. of Borough of Osborne, 445 Pa. 571, 285 A.2d 501 (Pa.1971), 1235
Beck v. Town of Raymond, 118 N.H. 793, 394 A.2d 847 (N.H.1978), 602
Bedford, Town of v. Village of Mount Kisco, 351 N.Y.S.2d 129, 306 N.E.2d 155 (N.Y. 1973), 620
Begin v. Inhabitants of Town of Sabattus, 409 A.2d 1269 (Me.1979), 585
Bein v. McPhaul, 357 S.W.2d 420 (Tex.Civ. App.-Amarillo 1962), 145
Bellarmine Hills Ass'n v. Residential Systems Co., 84 Mich.App. 554, 269 N.W.2d 673 (Mich.App.1978), 1124
Bella Vista Ranches, Inc. v. City of Sierra Vista, 126 Ariz. 142, 613 P.2d 302 (Ariz. App. Div. 2 1980), 434

Bellemeade Co. v. Priddle, 503 S.W.2d 734 (Ky.1973), 664
Belle Terre, Village of v. Boraas, 416 U.S. 1, 94 S.Ct. 1536, 39 L.Ed.2d 797 (1974), **1107**
Belleville, Town of v. Parrillo's, Inc., 83 N.J. 309, 416 A.2d 388 (N.J.1980), 377
Bellevue Shopping Center Associates v. Chase, 574 A.2d 760 (R.I.1990), 888
Beneficial Development Corp. v. City of Highland Park, 239 Ill.App.3d 414, 179 Ill.Dec. 1005, 606 N.E.2d 837 (Ill.App. 2 Dist.1992), 475
Benjfran Development, Inc. v. Metropolitan Service Dist., 95 Or.App. 22, 767 P.2d 467 (Or.App.1989), 619
Benton v. Kernan, 13 A.2d 825 (N.J.Ch. 1940), 36
Benton v. Pittard, 197 Ga. 843, 31 S.E.2d 6 (Ga.1944), 80
Benzinger v. Union Light, Heat & Power Co., 293 Ky. 747, 170 S.W.2d 38 (Ky. 1943), 874
Berenson v. Town of New Castle, 67 A.D.2d 506, 415 N.Y.S.2d 669 (N.Y.A.D. 2 Dept.1979), **1201**
Berenson v. Town of New Castle, 378 N.Y.S.2d 672, 341 N.E.2d 236 (N.Y. 1975), 1201, 1207, 1208
Berg Development Co. v. City of Missouri City, 603 S.W.2d 273 (Tex.Civ.App.-Hous. (14 Dist.) 1980), 486
Berger v. Board of Sup'rs of Whitpain Tp., 31 Pa.Cmwlth. 386, 376 A.2d 296 (Pa. Cmwlth.1977), 1134
Berger v. State, 71 N.J. 206, 364 A.2d 993 (N.J.1976), 1124
Berkeley, State ex rel. Stoyanoff v., 458 S.W.2d 305 (Mo.1970), **855**
Berman v. Parker, 348 U.S. 26, 75 S.Ct. 98, 99 L.Ed. 27 (1954), 629, 630, 825, 870
Bethlehem, City of v. Druckenmiller, 344 Pa. 170, 25 A.2d 190 (Pa.1942), 80
Bethlehem Evangelical Lutheran Church v. City of Lakewood, 626 P.2d 668 (Colo. 1981), 442
Betsey v. Turtle Creek Associates, 736 F.2d 983 (4th Cir.1984), 1173
Bibber v. Weber, 199 Misc. 906, 102 N.Y.S.2d 945 (N.Y.Sup.1951), 538
Big Sky Hidden Village Owners Ass'n, Inc. v. Hidden Village, Inc., 276 Mont. 268, 915 P.2d 845 (Mont.1996), 129
Bilbar Const. Co. v. Board of Adjustment of Easttown Tp., 393 Pa. 62, 141 A.2d 851 (Pa.1958), 1179
Birmingham, Mich., City of, United States v., 538 F.Supp. 819 (E.D.Mich.1982), 1165
Biske v. City of Troy, 381 Mich. 611, 166 N.W.2d 453 (Mich.1969), 251
Black Jack, Missouri, City of, United States v., 508 F.2d 1179 (8th Cir.1974), **1155**

Blanche Road Corp. v. Bensalem Tp., 57 F.3d 253 (3rd Cir.1995), 999

Bloomingdale, Village of v. CDG Enterprises, Inc., 196 Ill.2d 484, 256 Ill.Dec. 848, 752 N.E.2d 1090 (Ill.2001), 1001

Blue Jeans Equities West v. City and County of San Francisco, 4 Cal.Rptr.2d 114 (Cal.App. 1 Dist.1992), 497

Blue Sky Bar, Inc. v. Town of Stratford, 4 Conn.App. 261, 493 A.2d 908 (Conn.App. 1985), 1236

Board of Adjustment of City of Crestwood, State ex rel. McArthur v., 872 S.W.2d 651 (Mo.App. E.D.1994), 387

Board of Adjustment of City of Dallas v. Patel, 882 S.W.2d 87 (Tex.App.-Amarillo 1994), 397

Board of Adjustment of New Castle County v. Kwik–Check Realty, Inc., 389 A.2d 1289 (Del.Supr.1978), 361

Board of Appeals of Hanover v. Housing Appeals Committee in Dept. of Community Affairs, 363 Mass. 339, 294 N.E.2d 393 (Mass.1973), 1231

Board of County Com'rs of Arapahoe County v. Denver Bd. of Water Com'rs, 718 P.2d 235 (Colo.1986), 606

Board of County Com'rs of Brevard County v. Snyder, 627 So.2d 469 (Fla.1993), 1338

Board of County Com'rs of Cecil County v. Gaster, 285 Md. 233, 401 A.2d 666 (Md. 1979), 520

Board of County Com'rs of Teton County v. Crow, 65 P.3d 720 (Wyo.2003), 1190

Board of County Sup'rs of Fairfax County v. Carper, 200 Va. 653, 107 S.E.2d 390 (Va.1959), 1179

Board of County Sup'rs of Prince William County, Va. v. United States, 48 F.3d 520 (Fed.Cir.1995), 986

Board of Ed. of Community Consol. School Dist. No. 59 of Cook County v. E. A. Herzog Const. Co., 29 Ill.App.2d 138, 172 N.E.2d 645 (Ill.App. 1 Dist.1961), 490

Board of Sup'rs of Arlington County, United States v., 611 F.2d 1367 (4th Cir. 1979), 1097

Board of Sup'rs of Fairfax County v. DeGroff Enterprises, Inc., 214 Va. 235, 198 S.E.2d 600 (Va.1973), **1228**

Board of Sup'rs of West Marlborough Tp. v. Fiechter, 129 Pa.Cmwlth. 537, 566 A.2d 370 (Pa.Cmwlth.1989), 465

Board of Zoning Adjustment for City of Lanett v. Boykin, 265 Ala. 504, 92 So.2d 906 (Ala.1957), 387

Board of Zoning Appeals of Evansville and Vanderburgh County v. Kempf, 656 N.E.2d 1201 (Ind.App.1995), 356

Bob Layne Contractor, Inc. v. Bartel, 504 F.2d 1293 (7th Cir.1974), 1345

Boca Raton, City of v. Boca Villas Corp., 371 So.2d 154 (Fla.App. 4 Dist.1979), 596

Bodor v. East Coventry Tp., 325 F.Supp. 1102 (E.D.Pa.1971), 1001, 1344

Boerne, City of v. Flores, 521 U.S. 507, 117 S.Ct. 2157, 138 L.Ed.2d 624 (1997), 1251

Boland v. City of Great Falls, 275 Mont. 128, 910 P.2d 890 (Mont.1996), 1137

Boles v. City of Chattanooga, 892 S.W.2d 416 (Tenn.Ct.App.1994), 387

Bollech v. Charles County, Maryland, 2003 WL 21546001 (4th Cir.2003), **545**

Bonan v. City of Boston, 398 Mass. 315, 496 N.E.2d 640 (Mass.1986), 1232

Bone v. City of Lewiston, 107 Idaho 844, 693 P.2d 1046 (Idaho 1984), **249**

Booe v. Zoning Bd. of Appeals of City of Shelton, 151 Conn. 681, 202 A.2d 245 (Conn.1964), 356

Boomer v. Atlantic Cement Co., 309 N.Y.S.2d 312, 257 N.E.2d 870 (N.Y. 1970), **65,** 69

Borough of (see name of borough)

Bortz v. Troth, 359 Pa. 326, 59 A.2d 93 (Pa.1948), 76

Bossier City Medical Suite, Inc. v. City of Bossier City, 483 F.Supp. 633 (W.D.La. 1980), 1236

Bove v. Donner–Hanna Coke Corp., 236 A.D. 37, 258 N.Y.S. 229 (N.Y.A.D. 4 Dept.1932), **95**

Boyajian v. Gatzunis, 212 F.3d 1 (1st Cir. 2000), 1024

Boyles v. Hausmann, 2 Neb.App. 388, 509 N.W.2d 676 (Neb.App.1993), 181

Bozeman on Behalf of Dept. of Transp. of State of Mont., City of v. Vaniman, 271 Mont. 514, 898 P.2d 1208 (Mont.1995), 642

Brandt v. Village of Chebanse, Ill., 82 F.3d 172 (7th Cir.1996), 1126, 1165

Bride v. Finegan, 226 Md. 356, 174 A.2d 70 (Md.1961), 180

Bridger Canyon Property Owners' Ass'n, Inc. v. Planning and Zoning Com'n for Bridger Canyon Zoning Dist. and 360 Ranch Corp., 270 Mont. 160, 890 P.2d 1268 (Mont.1995), 674

Bridgeton, City of v. City of St. Louis, 18 S.W.3d 107 (Mo.App. E.D.2000), **1086**

Brier Lake, Inc. v. Jones, 710 So.2d 1054 (La.1998), 200

Bright Development v. City of Tracy, 24 Cal.Rptr.2d 618 (Cal.App. 3 Dist.1993), 874

Brighton by the Sea v. Rivkin, 201 A.D. 726, 195 N.Y.S. 198 (N.Y.A.D. 2 Dept. 1922), 180

Brill, State ex rel. v. Mortenson, 6 Wis.2d 325, 96 N.W.2d 603 (Wis.1959), 387

Britton v. Town of Chester, 134 N.H. 434, 595 A.2d 492 (N.H.1991), 1217

Brous v. Smith, 304 N.Y. 164, 106 N.E.2d 503 (N.Y.1952), 436

TABLE OF CASES

Broward County v. Janis Development Corp., 311 So.2d 371 (Fla.App. 4 Dist. 1975), 488

Brown v. Beuc, 384 S.W.2d 845 (Mo.App. 1964), 355

Brown v. Brown, 2002 WL 1343222 (Tex. App.-Austin 2002), 1316

Brown v. California Dept. of Transp., 321 F.3d 1217 (9th Cir.2003), 845

Brown v. Kansas Forestry, Fish and Game Commission, 2 Kan.App.2d 102, 576 P.2d 230 (Kan.App.1978), **1076**

Brown v. Morris, 279 Ala. 241, 184 So.2d 148 (Ala.1966), 174

Brownfield v. State, 63 Ohio St.2d 282, 407 N.E.2d 1365 (Ohio 1980), 1125

Brownfield Subdivision, Inc. v. McKee, 61 Ill.2d 168, 334 N.E.2d 131 (Ill.1975), **160**

Bruggemeier, State ex rel. Anshe Chesed Congregation v., 97 Ohio App. 67, 115 N.E.2d 65 (Ohio App. 8 Dist.1953), 1097, 1250

Building Industry Assn. v. Superior Court, 211 Cal.App.3d 277, 259 Cal.Rptr. 325 (Cal.App. 4 Dist.1989), 597

Burbridge v. Governing Body of Tp. of Mine Hill, 117 N.J. 376, 568 A.2d 527 (N.J. 1990), 363

Burke v. Smith, 69 Mich. 380, 37 N.W. 838 (Mich.1888), 36

Burma Hills Development Co. v. Marr, 285 Ala. 141, 229 So.2d 776 (Ala.1969), 158

Business Ass'n of University City v. Landrieu, 660 F.2d 867 (3rd Cir.1981), 1167

Cadoux v. Planning and Zoning Commission of Town of Weston, 162 Conn. 425, 294 A.2d 582 (Conn.1972), 1106

California Tahoe Regional Planning Agency v. Jennings, 594 F.2d 181 (9th Cir.1979), 278

Call v. City of West Jordan, 614 P.2d 1257 (Utah 1980), 488

Callahan v. Weiland, 291 Ala. 183, 279 So.2d 451 (Ala.1973), 163

Cameron, State v., 100 N.J. 586, 498 A.2d 1217 (N.J.1985), 1256

Campbell v. Barraud, 58 A.D.2d 570, 394 N.Y.S.2d 909 (N.Y.A.D. 2 Dept.1977), 1172

Campbell v. City Council of Lynn, 415 Mass. 772, 616 N.E.2d 445 (Mass.1993), 1124

Candlestick Properties, Inc. v. San Francisco Bay Conservation etc. Commission, 11 Cal.App.3d 557, 89 Cal.Rptr. 897 (Cal.App. 1 Dist.1970), 718

Cannon v. Coweta County, 260 Ga. 56, 389 S.E.2d 329 (Ga.1990), 1151

Captain Soma Boat Line, Inc. v. City of Wisconsin Dells, 79 Wis.2d 10, 255 N.W.2d 441 (Wis.1977), 45

Card v. Community Redevelopment Agency, 61 Cal.App.3d 570, 131 Cal.Rptr. 153 (Cal.App. 2 Dist.1976), 639

Cardon, State ex rel. Herman v., 112 Ariz. 548, 544 P.2d 657 (Ariz.1976), 103

Carlson v. Town of Smithfield, 723 A.2d 1129 (R.I.1999), 452

Carroll v. Washington Tp. Zoning Commission, 63 Ohio St.2d 249, 408 N.E.2d 191 (Ohio 1980), 1124

Carter v. Adams, 928 S.W.2d 39 (Tenn.Ct. App.1996), 1322

Carter, State ex rel. v. Harper, 182 Wis. 148, 196 N.W. 451 (Wis.1923), **296**

Carthage, Village of v. Central New York Tel. & Tel. Co., 185 N.Y. 448, 78 N.E. 165 (N.Y.1906), 874

Cary v. City of Rapid City, 559 N.W.2d 891 (S.D.1997), 1266

Caserta v. Zoning Bd. of Appeals of City of Milford, 41 Conn.App. 77, 674 A.2d 855 (Conn.App.1996), 388

Casino Reinvestment Development Authority v. Banin, 320 N.J.Super. 342, 727 A.2d 102 (N.J.Super.L.1998), 642

Cassel v. Mayor and City Council of Baltimore, 195 Md. 348, 73 A.2d 486 (Md. 1950), 311

Catholic Bishop of Chicago v. Kingery, 371 Ill. 257, 20 N.E.2d 583 (Ill.1939), 1258

Catholic Family & Children's Services, State ex rel. v. City of Bellingham, 25 Wash.App. 33, 605 P.2d 788 (Wash.App. Div. 1 1979), 1125

Centaur, Inc. v. Richland County, 301 S.C. 374, 392 S.E.2d 165 (S.C.1990), 397

Central Maine Power Co. v. Waterville Urban Renewal Authority, 281 A.2d 233 (Me.1971), 874

Central Management Co. v. Town Bd. of Oyster Bay, 47 Misc.2d 385, 262 N.Y.S.2d 728 (N.Y.Sup.1965), 1172

Cetrulo v. City of Park Hills, 524 S.W.2d 628 (Ky.1975), 664

Charles v. Diamond, 392 N.Y.S.2d 594, 360 N.E.2d 1295 (N.Y.1977), **607**

Charles River Bridge v. Proprietors of Warren Bridge, 36 U.S. 420, 9 L.Ed. 773 (1837), 22

Charleston, City of v. South Carolina State Ports Authority, 309 S.C. 118, 420 S.E.2d 497 (S.C.1992), 1086

Charter Tp. of Delta v. Dinolfo, 419 Mich. 253, 351 N.W.2d 831 (Mich.1984), 1115

Charter Tp. of Harrison v. Calisi, 121 Mich. App. 777, 329 N.W.2d 488 (Mich.App. 1982), 465

Chase, State ex rel. Strother v., 42 Mo.App. 343 (Mo.App.1890), 459

Cherokee Water & Sanitation Dist. v. El Paso County, 770 P.2d 1339 (Colo.App. 1988), 519

Chesterfield Meadows Shopping Center Associates, L.P. v. Smith, 264 Va. 350, 568 S.E.2d 676 (Va.2002), 185

Chiavola, State ex rel. v. Village of Oakwood, 886 S.W.2d 74 (Mo.App. W.D. 1994), 251
Chicago, City of v. Cohen, 49 Ill.App.3d 342, 7 Ill.Dec. 174, 364 N.E.2d 335 (Ill.App. 1 Dist.1977), 387
Chicago, City of v. Sachs, 1 Ill.2d 342, 115 N.E.2d 762 (Ill.1953), 1260
Chicago Heights, City of v. Living Word Outreach Full Gospel Church and Ministries, Inc., 196 Ill.2d 1, 255 Ill.Dec. 434, 749 N.E.2d 916 (Ill.2001), **364,** 370
Children's Home of Easton v. City of Easton, 53 Pa.Cmwlth. 216, 417 A.2d 830 (Pa.Cmwlth.1980), 1116
Chinese Staff and Workers Ass'n v. City of New York, 509 N.Y.S.2d 499, 502 N.E.2d 176 (N.Y.1986), 736
Chokecherry Hills Estates, Inc. v. Deuel County, 294 N.W.2d 654 (S.D.1980), 718
Chrinko v. South Brunswick Tp. Planning Bd., 77 N.J.Super. 594, 187 A.2d 221 (N.J.Super.L.1963), **444**
Christianson v. Gasvoda, 242 Mont. 212, 789 P.2d 1234 (Mont.1990), 520
Christopher Lake Development Co. v. St. Louis County, 35 F.3d 1269 (8th Cir. 1994), 474
Chula Vista, City of v. Pagard, 115 Cal. App.3d 785, 171 Cal.Rptr. 738 (Cal.App. 4 Dist.1981), 1116
Chung v. Sarasota County, 686 So.2d 1358 (Fla.App. 2 Dist.1996), 347
Church v. Town of Islip, 203 N.Y.S.2d 866, 168 N.E.2d 680 (N.Y.1960), **332**
Church of God of Louisiana, Inc. v. Monroe–Ouachita Regional Planning Commission, 404 F.Supp. 175 (W.D.La.1975), 1260
Cimarron Corp. v. Board of County Com'rs of El Paso County, 193 Colo. 164, 563 P.2d 946 (Colo.1977), 488
Citizens Growth Management Coalition of West Palm Beach, Inc. v. City of West Palm Beach, Inc., 450 So.2d 204 (Fla. 1984), 251
Citizens to Preserve Overton Park, Inc. v. Volpe, 401 U.S. 402, 91 S.Ct. 814, 28 L.Ed.2d 136 (1971), 875
Citizens to Preserve Overton Park, Inc. v. Volpe, 432 F.2d 1307 (6th Cir.1970), 875
Citizens to Preserve Overton Park, Inc. v. Volpe, 309 F.Supp. 1189 (W.D.Tenn. 1970), 875
City and County of (see name of city)
City Council of City of Minneapolis, State v., 140 Minn. 433, 168 N.W. 188 (Minn. 1918), 460
City Council of Kirksville, State ex rel. Hickman v., 690 S.W.2d 799 (Mo.App. W.D.1985), 1275
City of (see name of city)
City of Bellingham, State ex rel. Catholic Family & Children's Services v., 25 Wash.App. 33, 605 P.2d 788 (Wash.App. Div. 1 1979), 1125
City of Kansas City, State ex rel. Schneider v., 228 Kan. 25, 612 P.2d 578 (Kan. 1980), 1084
City of Missoula, State ex rel. Thelen v., 168 Mont. 375, 543 P.2d 173 (Mont. 1975), 1125
City of Pevely, State ex rel. Menkhus v., 865 S.W.2d 871 (Mo.App. E.D.1993), 521
City of Tacoma, State ex rel. Craven v., 63 Wash.2d 23, 385 P.2d 372 (Wash.1963), 437
Civic Ass'n of Dearborn Tp., Dist. No. 3 v. Horowitz, 318 Mich. 333, 28 N.W.2d 97 (Mich.1947), 106
Civitans Care, Inc. v. Board of Adjustment of City of Huntsville, 437 So.2d 540 (Ala. Civ.App.1983), 1124
Clackamas County v. Dunham, 30 Or.App. 595, 567 P.2d 605 (Or.App.1977), 1151
Claridge House One, Inc. v. Borough of Verona, 490 F.Supp. 706 (D.N.J.1980), 1137
Clark v. City of Albany, 137 Or.App. 293, 904 P.2d 185 (Or.App.1995), 512
Clark v. Guy Drews Post of Am. Legion No. 88, Dept. of Wis., 247 Wis. 48, 18 N.W.2d 322 (Wis.1945), 145
Clark v. Wambold, 165 Wis. 70, 160 N.W. 1039 (Wis.1917), **52,** 54, 55
Clark v. Winnebago County, 817 F.2d 407 (7th Cir.1987), 1140
Clarkson Valley Estates, Inc. v. Village of Clarkson Valley, 630 S.W.2d 151 (Mo. App. E.D.1982), 1107
C. L. Associates v. Board of Sup'rs of Montgomery Tp., 51 Pa.Cmwlth. 627, 415 A.2d 134 (Pa.Cmwlth.1980), 317
CLEAN v. State, 130 Wash.2d 782, 928 P.2d 1054 (Wash.1996), 640
Cleburne, Texas, City of v. Cleburne Living Center, 473 U.S. 432, 105 S.Ct. 3249, 87 L.Ed.2d 313 (1985), 1004, 1125
Clem v. Christole, Inc., 548 N.E.2d 1180 (Ind.App. 4 Dist.1990), 1124
Cleveland Baptist Ass'n v. Scovil, 107 Ohio St. 67, 140 N.E. 647 (Ohio 1923), 170
Cleveland Elec. Illuminating Co. v. City of Painesville, 10 Ohio App.2d 85, 226 N.E.2d 145 (Ohio App. 7 Dist.1967), 874
Clinkscales v. City of Lake Oswego, 47 Or. App. 1117, 615 P.2d 1164 (Or.App.1980), 317
Clinton v. Summers, 144 A.D.2d 145, 534 N.Y.S.2d 473 (N.Y.A.D. 3 Dept.1988), 497
Cloquet, City of v. Cloquet Sand & Gravel, Inc., 312 Minn. 277, 251 N.W.2d 642 (Minn.1977), 108
Coalition for Responsible Regional Development v. Brinegar, 518 F.2d 522 (4th Cir.1975), 875

TABLE OF CASES

Cochise County v. Broken Arrow Baptist Church, 161 Ariz. 406, 778 P.2d 1302 (Ariz.App. Div. 2 1989), 1256

Cochran v. Planning Bd. of City of Summit, 87 N.J.Super. 526, 210 A.2d 99 (N.J.Super.L.1965), **243**

Coffey v. Maryland–National Capital Park and Planning Commission, 293 Md. 24, 441 A.2d 1041 (Md.1982), **513**

Cohen v. City of Des Plaines, 742 F.Supp. 458 (N.D.Ill.1990), 1260

Colborne v. Village of Corrales, 106 N.M. 103, 739 P.2d 972 (N.M.1987), 460

College Area Renters & Landlord Assn. v. City of San Diego, 50 Cal.Rptr.2d 515 (Cal.App. 4 Dist.1996), 1115, 1192

College Station, City of v. Turtle Rock Corp., 680 S.W.2d 802 (Tex.1984), 488

Collins v. City of Spartanburg, 281 S.C. 212, 314 S.E.2d 332 (S.C.1984), 397

Collins v. Lonergan, 198 A.D.2d 349, 603 N.Y.S.2d 330 (N.Y.A.D. 2 Dept.1993), **399,** 406

Collis v. City of Bloomington, 310 Minn. 5, 246 N.W.2d 19 (Minn.1976), 488

Colony Cove Associates v. Brown, 220 Cal.App.3d 195, 269 Cal.Rptr. 234 (Cal. App. 2 Dist.1990), **1167**

Colorado Manufactured Housing Ass'n v. Pueblo County, 857 P.2d 507 (Colo.App. 1993), 1141

Colorado Springs, City of v. Blanche, 761 P.2d 212 (Colo.1988), 1256

Colts Run Civic Ass'n v. Colts Neck Tp. Zoning Bd. of Adjustment, 315 N.J.Super. 240, 717 A.2d 456 (N.J.Super.L.1998), 407

Columbia County v. Kelly, 25 Or.App. 1, 548 P.2d 163 (Or.App.1976), 1151

Commonwealth v. ———— (see opposing party)

Committee of Seven Thousand v. Superior Court, 247 Cal.Rptr. 362, 754 P.2d 708 (Cal.1988), 461

Committee to Save the Bishop's House, Inc. v. Medical Center Hospital of Vermont, Inc., 137 Vt. 142, 400 A.2d 1015 (Vt. 1979), 902

Commonwealth of (see name of Commonwealth)

Concordia Collegiate Institute v. Miller, 301 N.Y. 189, 93 N.E.2d 632 (N.Y.1950), 1266

Condemnation by Minneapolis Community Development Agency (MCDA), of Certain Lands in City of Minneapolis Situated in Development Dist. No. 57, South Nicollet Mall, Matter of, 582 N.W.2d 596 (Minn.App.1998), **630**

Confederacion de la Raza Unida v. City of Morgan Hill, 324 F.Supp. 895 (N.D.Cal. 1971), 1165

Conforti v. City of Manchester, 141 N.H. 78, 677 A.2d 147 (N.H.1996), 377

Congregation Kol Ami v. Abington Township, 309 F.3d 120 (3rd Cir.2002), 1024

Congregation of St. Rita Roman Catholic Church, In re, 130 So.2d 425 (La.App. 4 Cir.1961), 145

Connecticut Resources Recovery Authority v. Planning and Zoning Com'n of Town of Wallingford, 225 Conn. 731, 626 A.2d 705 (Conn.1993), **746,** 752

Construction Industry Ass'n of Sonoma County v. City of Petaluma, 522 F.2d 897 (9th Cir.1975), **577**

Cooper v. Board of County Com'rs of Ada County, 101 Idaho 407, 614 P.2d 947 (Idaho 1980), 1338

Cornell University v. Bagnardi, 510 N.Y.S.2d 861, 503 N.E.2d 509 (N.Y. 1986), 1259

Cornerstone Bible Church v. City of Hastings, Minn., 740 F.Supp. 654 (D.Minn. 1990), 1250

Corn Ins. Agency, Inc. v. Darby Builders, Inc., 254 Ark. 1004, 497 S.W.2d 260 (Ark.1973), 141

Coronado Development Co. v. City of McPherson, 189 Kan. 174, 368 P.2d 51 (Kan.1962), 486

Corona–Norco Unified Sch. Dist. v. City of Corona, 17 Cal.Rptr.2d 236 (Cal.App. 4 Dist.1993), 519

Corpus Christi, City of v. Unitarian Church of Corpus Christi, 436 S.W.2d 923 (Tex.Civ.App.-Corpus Christi 1968), **438**

Countrywalk Condominiums, Inc. v. City of Orchard Lake Village, 221 Mich.App. 19, 561 N.W.2d 405 (Mich.App.1997), 1106

County Com'rs of Bristol v. Conservation Commission of Dartmouth, 380 Mass. 706, 405 N.E.2d 637 (Mass.1980), 1085

County Com'rs of Queen Anne's County v. Miles, 246 Md. 355, 228 A.2d 450 (Md. 1967), 1180

County of (see name of county)

County of El Dorado, People ex rel. Younger v., 96 Cal.Rptr. 553, 487 P.2d 1193 (Cal.1971), **271**

Courtland Tp. v. Cole, 66 Mich.App. 474, 239 N.W.2d 630 (Mich.App.1976), 1151

Cowart v. City of Ocala, Fla., 478 F.Supp. 774 (M.D.Fla.1979), 1165

Cowboy Country Estates v. Ellis County, 692 S.W.2d 882 (Tex.App.-Waco 1985), 442

Craig v. County of Chatham, 356 N.C. 40, 565 S.E.2d 172 (N.C.2002), **1060**

Craven, State ex rel. v. City of Tacoma, 63 Wash.2d 23, 385 P.2d 372 (Wash.1963), 437

Creative Displays, Inc. v. City of Florence, 602 S.W.2d 682 (Ky.1980), **234**

Creative Environments, Inc. v. Estabrook, 491 F.Supp. 547 (D.Mass.1980), 451, 1346

Creek v. Village of Westhaven, 80 F.3d 186 (7th Cir.1996), 1164

Cresskill, Borough of v. Borough of Dumont, 15 N.J. 238, 104 A.2d 441 (N.J. 1954), 1097

Croteau v. Planning Bd. of Hopkinton, 40 Mass.App.Ct. 922, 663 N.E.2d 583 (Mass.App.Ct.1996), 451

Crowley v. Knapp, 94 Wis.2d 421, 288 N.W.2d 815 (Wis.1980), 1124

Crownhill Homes, Inc. v. City of San Antonio, 433 S.W.2d 448 (Tex.Civ.App.-Corpus Christi 1968), 461

Crozer v. Reichert, 275 Ga. 118, 561 S.E.2d 120 (Ga.2002), 223

CSX Transp., Inc. v. City of Plymouth, Mich., 86 F.3d 626 (6th Cir.1996), 1054

Culp v. City of Seattle, 22 Wash.App. 618, 590 P.2d 1288 (Wash.App. Div. 1 1979), 1126

Cummings v. Dosam, Inc., 273 N.C. 28, 159 S.E.2d 513 (N.C.1968), 129

Cunningham, State ex rel. v. Feezell, 218 Tenn. 17, 400 S.W.2d 716 (Tenn. 1966), **46**

Cutting v. Muzzey, 724 F.2d 259 (1st Cir. 1984), 1001

Cuyahoga Falls, Ohio, City of v. Buckeye Community Hope Foundation, 538 U.S. 188, 123 S.Ct. 1389, 155 L.Ed.2d 349 (2003), 1274

Dadian v. Village of Wilmette, 269 F.3d 831 (7th Cir.2001), 1042

Damascus Community Church v. Clackamas County, 45 Or.App. 1065, 610 P.2d 273 (Or.App.1980), 1251

Daniel v. Kosh, 173 Va. 352, 4 S.E.2d 381 (Va.1939), 70

Danziger v. Conservation Com'n of Town of Newtown, 2001 WL 236758 (Conn.Super.2001), 774

Dateline Builders, Inc. v. City of Santa Rosa, 146 Cal.App.3d 520, 194 Cal.Rptr. 258 (Cal.App. 1 Dist.1983), **603**

Davidson Bros., Inc. v. D. Katz & Sons, Inc., 274 N.J.Super. 159, 643 A.2d 642 (N.J.Super.A.D.1994), 170

Dawe v. City of Scottsdale, 119 Ariz. 486, 581 P.2d 1136 (Ariz.1978), **434**

Day v. Development Authority of City of Adel, 248 Ga. 488, 284 S.E.2d 275 (Ga. 1981), 642

Daytona Rescue Mission, Inc. v. City of Daytona Beach, 885 F.Supp. 1554 (M.D.Fla.1995), 1252

Dearden v. City of Detroit, 403 Mich. 257, 269 N.W.2d 139 (Mich.1978), 1085

DeBeradinis v. Zoning Com'n of City of Norwalk, 228 Conn. 187, 635 A.2d 1220 (Conn.1994), 823

DeBlasio v. Zoning Bd. of Adjustment for Tp. of West Amwell, 53 F.3d 592 (3rd Cir.1995), 1002

DeCoals, Inc. v. Board of Zoning Appeals of City of Westover, 168 W.Va. 339, 284 S.E.2d 856 (W.Va.1981), 674

DeFalco v. Dirie, 923 F.Supp. 473 (S.D.N.Y. 1996), 1345

Del Monte Dunes at Monterey, Ltd. v. City of Monterey, 95 F.3d 1422 (9th Cir. 1996), 1000

Del Oro Hills v. City of Oceanside, 37 Cal. Rptr.2d 677 (Cal.App. 4 Dist.1995), 985

De Mars v. Zoning Commission of Town of Bolton, 142 Conn. 580, 115 A.2d 653 (Conn.1955), **700,** 703

De Mers v. Graupner, 186 Ark. 214, 53 S.W.2d 8 (Ark.1932), 37

Demont v. Abbas, 149 Neb. 765, 32 N.W.2d 737 (Neb.1948), 42

Dennehy v. Department of Revenue, 308 Or. 423, 781 P.2d 346 (Or.1989), 639

Dennis v. Mayor and City Council of Rockville, 286 Md. 184, 406 A.2d 284 (Md. 1979), 252

Denver By and Through Board of Water Com'rs, City and County of v. Board of County Com'rs of Grand County, 782 P.2d 753 (Colo.1989), 1086

Denver, City and County of, United States v., 100 F.3d 1509 (10th Cir.1996), 1054

Department of Community Affairs v. Moorman, 664 So.2d 930 (Fla.1995), 815

DeSisto College, Inc. v. Town of Howey-in-the–Hills, 706 F.Supp. 1479 (M.D.Fla. 1989), 1259

Des Vergnes v. Seekonk Water Dist., 601 F.2d 9 (1st Cir.1979), 1165

Detroit, City of v. Vavro, 177 Mich.App. 682, 442 N.W.2d 730 (Mich.App.1989), 642

DeVita v. County of Napa, 38 Cal.Rptr.2d 699, 889 P.2d 1019 (Cal.1995), 1274

Diakonian Soc. v. City of Chicago Zoning Bd. of Appeals, 63 Ill.App.3d 823, 20 Ill.Dec. 634, 380 N.E.2d 843 (Ill.App. 1 Dist.1978), 1251

Diamond Motors, Inc., State v., 50 Haw. 33, 429 P.2d 825 (Hawai'i 1967), **826,** 844

Diller and Fisher Co., Inc. v. Architectural Review Bd. of Borough of Stone Harbor, 246 N.J.Super. 362, 587 A.2d 674 (N.J.Super.L.1990), 862

Dishler v. Zoning Bd. of Adjustment of Cheltenham Tp., 414 Pa. 244, 199 A.2d 418 (Pa.1964), 356

Divan Builders, Inc. v. Planning Bd. of Wayne Tp., 66 N.J. 582, 334 A.2d 30 (N.J.1975), **466**

Dobo v. Zoning Bd. of Adjustment of City of Wilmington, 356 N.C. 656, 576 S.E.2d 324 (N.C.2003), **404**

Doherty v. Rice, 240 Wis. 389, 3 N.W.2d 734 (Wis.1942), 114

Dolan v. City of Tigard, 512 U.S. 374, 114 S.Ct. 2309, 129 L.Ed.2d 304 (1994), **497,** 511, 512, 513, 1223

TABLE OF CASES xxxiii

Donnelly Advertising Corp. of Maryland v. City of Baltimore, 279 Md. 660, 370 A.2d 1127 (Md.1977), 844

Douglas County, State ex rel. List v., 90 Nev. 272, 524 P.2d 1271 (Nev.1974), 278

Downey v. Incorporated Village of Ardsley, 3 A.D.2d 663, 158 N.Y.S.2d 306 (N.Y.A.D. 2 Dept.1957), 549

Downey Cares v. Downey Community Development Commission, 196 Cal.App.3d 983, 242 Cal.Rptr. 272 (Cal.App. 2 Dist. 1987), 639

Dowsey v. Village of Kensington, 257 N.Y. 221, 177 N.E. 427 (N.Y.1931), 1106

Dreher v. Rana Management, Inc., 493 F.Supp. 930 (E.D.N.Y.1980), 1166

Dreher, State ex rel. v. Fuller, 257 Mont. 445, 849 P.2d 1045 (Mont.1993), 436

Drockton v. Board of Elections of Cuyahoga County, 240 N.E.2d 896 (Ohio Com.Pl. 1968), 1276

Dudding v. Automatic Gas Co., 145 Tex. 1, 193 S.W.2d 517 (Tex.1946), 106

Duffcon Concrete Products v. Borough of Cresskill, 1 N.J. 509, 64 A.2d 347 (N.J. 1949), 1097

Duggins v. Town of Walnut Cove, 63 N.C.App. 684, 306 S.E.2d 186 (N.C.App. 1983), 1141

Duncanson v. Board of Supervisors of Danville Tp., 551 N.W.2d 248 (Minn.App. 1996), 575

Dunedin, City of v. Contractors and Builders Ass'n of Pinellas County, 312 So.2d 763 (Fla.App. 2 Dist.1975), 488

Dunmore v. City of Natchez, 703 F.Supp. 31 (S.D.Miss.1988), 1346

Dur–Bar Realty Co. v. City of Utica, 57 A.D.2d 51, 394 N.Y.S.2d 913 (N.Y.A.D. 4 Dept.1977), 765

Dvorak v. City of Bloomington, 768 N.E.2d 490 (Ind.App.2002), 1115

Eastern Diversified Properties, Inc. v. Montgomery County, 319 Md. 45, 570 A.2d 850 (Md.1990), 489

East Grand County School Dist. No. 2 v. Town of Winter Park, 739 P.2d 862 (Colo.App.1987), 639

Eastlake, City of v. Forest City Enterprises, Inc., 426 U.S. 668, 96 S.Ct. 2358, 49 L.Ed.2d 132 (1976), **1267**

Eaton v. Klimm, 217 Cal. 362, 18 P.2d 678 (Cal.1933), 106

Echevarrieta v. City of Rancho Palos Verdes, 103 Cal.Rptr.2d 165 (Cal.App. 2 Dist.2001), **800,** 803

Edgemont Bank and Trust Co. v. City of Belleville, 85 Ill.App.3d 665, 40 Ill.Dec. 928, 407 N.E.2d 159 (Ill.App. 5 Dist. 1980), 1237

Edmonds, City of v. Oxford House, Inc., 514 U.S. 725, 115 S.Ct. 1776, 131 L.Ed.2d 801 (1995), **1026**

Edwards v. First Bank of Dundee, 393 F.Supp. 680 (N.D.Ill.1975), 890

Ehrlich v. City of Culver City, 50 Cal. Rptr.2d 242, 911 P.2d 429 (Cal.1996), 512

Eichlin v. Zoning Hearing Bd. of New Hope Borough, 671 A.2d 1173 (Pa.Cmwlth. 1996), 1123

Eilers v. Alewel, 393 S.W.2d 584 (Mo.1965), 185

Ellison v. County of Ventura, 217 Cal. App.3d 455, 265 Cal.Rptr. 795 (Cal.App. 2 Dist.1990), 985

El Paso, City of v. El Paso Community College Dist., 729 S.W.2d 296 (Tex. 1986), 639

Elsinore Christian Center v. City of Lake Elsinore, 270 F.Supp.2d 1163 (C.D.Cal.2003), **1010**

Elysian Heights Residents Assn., Inc. v. City of Los Angeles, 182 Cal.App.3d 21, 227 Cal.Rptr. 226 (Cal.App. 2 Dist. 1986), **236**

Emmett McLoughlin Realty, Inc. v. Pima County, 203 Ariz. 557, 58 P.3d 39 (Ariz.App. Div. 2 2002), **906**

Emmington v. Solano County Redevelopment Agency, 195 Cal.App.3d 491, 237 Cal.Rptr. 636 (Cal.App. 1 Dist.1987), 639

Employment Div., Dept. of Human Resources of Oregon v. Smith, 494 U.S. 872, 110 S.Ct. 1595, 108 L.Ed.2d 876 (1990), 1251

Enterprise Partners v. County of Perkins, 260 Neb. 650, 619 N.W.2d 464 (Neb.2000), **318,** 322

Environmental Abatement, Inc. v. Astrum R.E. Corp., 27 S.W.3d 530 (Tenn.Ct.App. 2000), 1316

Environmental Defense Center, Inc. v. United States E.P.A., 319 F.3d 398 (9th Cir.2003), **754,** 757

Environmental Defense Fund v. E.P.A., 167 F.3d 641, 334 U.S.App.D.C. 404 (D.C.Cir.1999), 255

Epicenter of Steubenville, Inc. v. City of Steubenville, 924 F.Supp. 845 (S.D.Ohio 1996), 1126

Erekson v. United States Steel Corp, 260 F.2d 423 (10th Cir.1958), 41, 42

Esplanade Properties, LLC v. City of Seattle, 307 F.3d 978 (9th Cir.2002), **817,** 956

Essex Fells, Borough of v. Kessler Institute for Rehabilitation, Inc., 289 N.J.Super. 329, 673 A.2d 856 (N.J.Super.L.1995), 643

Essick v. Shillam, 347 Pa. 373, 32 A.2d 416 (Pa.1943), 75

Estate of (see name of party)

Ettinger v. City of Lansing, 215 Mich.App. 451, 546 N.W.2d 652 (Mich.App.1996), 1155

Euclid, Ohio, Village of v. Ambler Realty Co., 272 U.S. 365, 47 S.Ct. 114, 71

L.Ed. 303 (1926), 281, 282, **300**, 307, 308, 620, 622, 917, 918, 1133

Evans v. Pollock, 793 S.W.2d 14 (Tex.App.-Austin 1989), 147

Eveline Tp. v. H & D Trucking Co., 181 Mich.App. 25, 448 N.W.2d 727 (Mich. App.1989), 1235

Everett v. Paschall, 61 Wash. 47, 111 P. 879 (Wash.1910), 42

Everett, City of v. Snohomish County, 112 Wash.2d 433, 772 P.2d 992 (Wash.1989), 1084

Evergreen Highlands Ass'n v. West, 73 P.3d 1 (Colo.2003), 129

Ex parte (see name of party)

Exton Quarries, Inc. v. Zoning Bd. of Adjustment of West Whiteland Tp., 425 Pa. 43, 228 A.2d 169 (Pa.1967), 1235

Eyde Const. Co. v. Charter Tp. of Meridian, 149 Mich.App. 802, 386 N.W.2d 687 (Mich.App.1986), 460

Eyerman v. Mercantile Trust Co., N.A., 524 S.W.2d 210 (Mo.App.1975), 80

Fafard v. Conservation Com'n of Barnstable, 432 Mass. 194, 733 N.E.2d 66 (Mass.2000), **767**, 774

Fairfield, Township of v. Likanchuk's, Inc., 274 N.J.Super. 320, 644 A.2d 120 (N.J.Super.A.D.1994), 377

Fallen Leaf Protection Assn. v. South Tahoe Public Utility Dist., 46 Cal.App.3d 816, 120 Cal.Rptr. 538 (Cal.App. 3 Dist. 1975), 520

Familystyle of St. Paul, Inc. v. City of St. Paul, Minn., 728 F.Supp. 1396 (D.Minn. 1990), 1126

Fargo, Cass County, City of v. Harwood Tp., 256 N.W.2d 694 (N.D.1977), 1084

Farhi v. Commissioners of Borough of Deal, 204 N.J.Super. 575, 499 A.2d 559 (N.J.Super.L.1985), 1256

Farley v. Graney, 146 W.Va. 22, 119 S.E.2d 833 (W.Va.1960), 75, 870

Farrell v. Teaneck Tp., 126 N.J.Super. 460, 315 A.2d 424 (N.J.Super.L.1974), 846

Farrior v. Zoning Bd. of Appeals of Black Point Beach Club Ass'n, 70 Conn.App. 86, 796 A.2d 1262 (Conn.App.2002), 163

Fasano v. Board of County Com'rs of Washington County, 264 Or. 574, 507 P.2d 23 (Or.1973), 1308, **1332**, 1337, 1338

Father Ryan High School, Inc. v. City of Oak Hill By and Through Oak Hill Bd. of Zoning Appeals, 774 S.W.2d 184 (Tenn.Ct.App.1988), 1259

Fayetteville, City of v. IBI, Inc., 280 Ark. 484, 659 S.W.2d 505 (Ark.1983), 487

Fayetteville, City of v. McIlroy Bank & Trust Co., 278 Ark. 500, 647 S.W.2d 439 (Ark.1983), 845

Fayetteville, City of v. S & H, Inc., 261 Ark. 148, 547 S.W.2d 94 (Ark.1977), 844

Feezell, State ex rel. Cunningham v., 218 Tenn. 17, 400 S.W.2d 716 (Tenn. 1966), **46**

Feldman v. Zoning Hearing Bd. of City of Pittsburgh, 89 Pa.Cmwlth. 237, 492 A.2d 468 (Pa.Cmwlth.1985), 377

Feldstein v. Kammauf, 209 Md. 479, 121 A.2d 716 (Md.1956), 75

Fernley v. Board of Sup'rs of Schuylkill Tp., 509 Pa. 413, 502 A.2d 585 (Pa.1985), 1208

Ferry v. City of Seattle, 116 Wash. 648, 200 P. 336 (Wash.1921), 42

FGL & L Property Corp. v. City of Rye, 495 N.Y.S.2d 321, 485 N.E.2d 986 (N.Y. 1985), **897**

Fifth Ave. Presbyterian Church v. City of New York, 293 F.3d 570 (2nd Cir. 2002), 1024, **1252**

Finucan v. Coronet Homes, Inc., 259 S.C. 142, 191 S.E.2d 5 (S.C.1972), 181

First Assembly of God of Naples, Florida, Inc. v. Collier County, Fla., 20 F.3d 419 (11th Cir.1994), 1252

First Bet Joint Venture v. City of Central City By and Through City Council, 818 F.Supp. 1409 (D.Colo.1993), 575

First English Evangelical Lutheran Church v. County of Los Angeles, 210 Cal. App.3d 1353, 258 Cal.Rptr. 893 (Cal. App. 2 Dist.1989), 938

First English Evangelical Lutheran Church of Glendale v. Los Angeles County, Cal., 482 U.S. 304, 107 S.Ct. 2378, 96 L.Ed.2d 250 (1987), **934, 978,** 986

First Presbyterian Church of York v. City Council of City of York, 25 Pa.Cmwlth. 154, 360 A.2d 257 (Pa.Cmwlth.1976), 901

First Step, Inc. v. City of New London, 247 F.Supp.2d 135 (D.Conn.2003), 1042

Firth v. Scherzberg, 366 Pa. 443, 77 A.2d 443 (Pa.1951), 106

Fischer v. City of Dover, 131 N.H. 469, 554 A.2d 1293 (N.H.1989), 475

Fischer v. Driesen, 446 N.W.2d 84 (Iowa App.1989), 1151

Fisher v. Viola, 789 A.2d 782 (Pa.Cmwlth. 2001), 783

Fitchburg Housing Authority v. Board of Zoning Appeals of Fitchburg, 380 Mass. 869, 406 N.E.2d 1006 (Mass.1980), 1124

Fitzwater v. Walker, 281 So.2d 790 (La. App. 3 Cir.1973), 145

Fitzwilliam v. Wesley United Methodist Church, 882 S.W.2d 343 (Mo.App. W.D. 1994), 170

Fleming, Appeal of, 44 Pa.Cmwlth. 641, 405 A.2d 1309 (Pa.Cmwlth.1979), 1124

Flores v. City of Boerne, Tex., 73 F.3d 1352 (5th Cir.1996), 1251

Florida East Coast Properties, Inc. v. Metropolitan Dade County, 572 F.2d 1108 (5th Cir.1978), 102

TABLE OF CASES

Florida Land Co. v. City of Winter Springs, 427 So.2d 170 (Fla.1983), 1275

Florida Wildlife Federation v. Collier County, 819 So.2d 200 (Fla.App. 1 Dist. 2002), **811**

Florio v. State ex rel. Epperson, 119 So.2d 305 (Fla.App. 2 Dist.1960), 54

Floyd v. New York State Urban Development Corp., 41 A.D.2d 395, 343 N.Y.S.2d 493 (N.Y.A.D. 1 Dept.1973), 1232

Flying J Travel Plaza v. Commonwealth, Transp. Cabinet, Dept. of Highways, 928 S.W.2d 344 (Ky.1996), 845

Foremost Life Ins. Co. v. Waters, 125 Mich. App. 799, 337 N.W.2d 29 (Mich.App. 1983), 1190

Forest City Enterprises, Inc. v. City of Eastlake., 48 Ohio St.2d 47, 356 N.E.2d 499 (Ohio 1976), 1273

Forte v. Borough of Tenafly, 106 N.J.Super. 346, 255 A.2d 804 (N.J.Super.A.D.1969), **644,** 650

Foster v. Board of Com'rs of Warrick County, Ind., 647 N.E.2d 1147 (Ind.App. 1 Dist.1995), 575

Fournier v. Kattar, 108 N.H. 424, 238 A.2d 12 (N.H.1968), 145

Fox Valley Reproductive Health Care Center, Inc. v. Arft, 446 F.Supp. 1072 (E.D.Wis.1978), 1236

Fralin & Waldron, Inc. v. Henrico County, Va., 474 F.Supp. 1315 (E.D.Va.1979), 1166

Franchise Developers, Inc. v. City of Cincinnati, 30 Ohio St.3d 28, 505 N.E.2d 966 (Ohio 1987), 687

Frandsen v. Mayer, 155 N.W.2d 294 (N.D. 1967), 88

Frank Ansuini, Inc. v. City of Cranston, 107 R.I. 63, 264 A.2d 910 (R.I.1970), 486

Fraser v. Fred Parker Funeral Home, 201 S.C. 88, 21 S.E.2d 577 (S.C.1942), 79

Fred F. French Investing Co., Inc. v. City of New York, 385 N.Y.S.2d 5, 350 N.E.2d 381 (N.Y.1976), 686

Freeborn County v. Claussen, 295 Minn. 96, 203 N.W.2d 323 (Minn.1972), 376

Freedom Baptist Church of Delaware County v. Tp. of Middletown, 204 F.Supp.2d 857 (E.D.Pa.2002), 1023

Freedom Ranch, Inc., Application of, 878 P.2d 380 (Okla.App. Div. 3 1994), 1085

Freeman v. Planning Bd. of West Boylston, 419 Mass. 548, 646 N.E.2d 139 (Mass. 1995), 1000

Frey v. Poynor, 369 P.2d 168 (Okla.1962), 145

Friday, Application of, 33 Pa.Cmwlth. 256, 381 A.2d 504 (Pa.Cmwlth.1978), 1134

Friedberg v. Riverpoint Bldg. Committee, 218 Va. 659, 239 S.E.2d 106 (Va.1977), 129, 144

Friedman v. City of Fairfax, 81 Cal.App.3d 667, 146 Cal.Rptr. 687 (Cal.App. 1 Dist. 1978), 932

Friel v. Triangle Oil Co., 76 Md.App. 96, 543 A.2d 863 (Md.App.1988), 575

Friendship Farms Camps, Inc. v. Parson, 172 Ind.App. 73, 359 N.E.2d 280 (Ind.App. 1 Dist.1977), **49**

Frischkorn Const. Co. v. Lambert, 315 Mich. 556, 24 N.W.2d 209 (Mich.1946), 1190

Fritts v. City of Ashland, 348 S.W.2d 712 (Ky.1961), **1317**

Frost v. Village of Glen Ellyn, 30 Ill.2d 241, 195 N.E.2d 616 (Ill.1964), 1236

Ft. Smith, City of v. Western Hide & Fur Co., 153 Ark. 99, 239 S.W. 724 (Ark. 1922), 97

Fuller, State ex rel. Dreher v., 257 Mont. 445, 849 P.2d 1045 (Mont.1993), 436

Gableman v. Department of Conservation, 309 Mich. 416, 15 N.W.2d 689 (Mich. 1944), 54

Gainesville, City of v. Hope, 377 So.2d 736 (Fla.App. 1 Dist.1979), 317

Galich v. Catholic Bishop of Chicago, 75 Ill.App.3d 538, 31 Ill.Dec. 370, 394 N.E.2d 572 (Ill.App. 1 Dist.1979), 901

Gammons v. Kennett Park Development Corp., 30 Del.Ch. 525, 61 A.2d 391 (Del. Supr.1948), 146

Garcia v. Siffrin Residential Assn., 63 Ohio St.2d 259, 407 N.E.2d 1369 (Ohio 1980), 1125

Gardiner, Town of v. Blue Sky Entertainment Corp., 213 A.D.2d 790, 623 N.Y.S.2d 29 (N.Y.A.D. 3 Dept.1995), 378

Gardiner, Town of v. Stanley Orchards, Inc., 105 Misc.2d 460, 432 N.Y.S.2d 335 (N.Y.Sup.1980), 906, 1266

Gardner v. New Jersey Pinelands Com'n, 125 N.J. 193, 593 A.2d 251 (N.J.1991), 710

Garvin v. Ninth Judicial Dist. Court ex rel. County of Douglas, 59 P.3d 1180 (Nev. 2002), 1275

Gaskin v. Harris, 82 N.M. 336, 481 P.2d 698 (N.M.1971), 187

Gazza v. New York State Dept. of Environmental Conservation, 657 N.Y.S.2d 555, 679 N.E.2d 1035 (N.Y.1997), 956

Geisenfeld v. Village of Shorewood, 232 Wis. 410, 287 N.W. 683 (Wis.1939), 317

General Battery Corp. v. Zoning Hearing Bd. of Alsace Tp., 29 Pa.Cmwlth. 498, 371 A.2d 1030 (Pa.Cmwlth.1977), **1233**

General Elec. Co. v. Maurice Callahan & Sons, Inc., 2 Mass.App.Ct. 124, 309 N.E.2d 209 (Mass.App.Ct.1974), 107

Genusa v. City of Peoria, 475 F.Supp. 1199 (C.D.Ill.1979), 1236

Georgia, State of v. Tennessee Copper Co., 240 U.S. 650, 36 S.Ct. 465, 60 L.Ed. 846 (1916), 41

Georgia, State of v. Tennessee Copper Co., 237 U.S. 474, 35 S.Ct. 631, 59 L.Ed. 1054 (1915), 40

Georgia, State of v. Tennessee Copper Co., 206 U.S. 230, 27 S.Ct. 618, 51 L.Ed. 1038 (1907), 40

Gernatt Asphalt Products, Inc. v. Town of Sardinia, 642 N.Y.S.2d 164, 664 N.E.2d 1226 (N.Y.1996), **1056**

Giger v. City of Omaha, 232 Neb. 676, 442 N.W.2d 182 (Neb.1989), **337**

Gilbert v. State of California, 218 Cal. App.3d 234, 266 Cal.Rptr. 891 (Cal.App. 1 Dist.1990), 575

Girsh, Appeal of, 437 Pa. 237, 263 A.2d 395 (Pa.1970), **1127**, 1133, 1134, 1135

Glassboro, Borough of v. Vallorosi, 117 N.J. 421, 568 A.2d 888 (N.J.1990), 1115

G. L. Cline & Son, Inc. v. Cavalier Bldg. Corp., 213 Va. 557, 193 S.E.2d 693 (Va. 1973), 145

Glisson v. Alachua County, 558 So.2d 1030 (Fla.App. 1 Dist.1990), **689**

Globe Newspaper Co. v. Beacon Hill Architectural Com'n, 100 F.3d 175 (1st Cir. 1996), 888

Glocester, Town of v. Olivo's Mobile Home Court, Inc., 111 R.I. 120, 300 A.2d 465 (R.I.1973), **1138**

Glosemeyer v. Missouri–Kansas–Texas R.R., 879 F.2d 316 (8th Cir.1989), 121

G. M. L. Land Corp. v. Foley, 20 A.D.2d 645, 246 N.Y.S.2d 338 (N.Y.A.D. 2 Dept. 1964), 174

Gold v. Zoning Board of Adjustment, 393 Pa. 401, 143 A.2d 59 (Pa.1958), 414

Goldblatt v. Town of Hempstead, N. Y., 369 U.S. 590, 82 S.Ct. 987, 8 L.Ed.2d 130 (1962), **920,** 932

Golden v. Aldell Realty Corp., 70 N.Y.S.2d 341 (N.Y.Sup.1947), 537

Golden v. City of Overland Park, 224 Kan. 591, 584 P.2d 130 (Kan.1978), 1338

Golden v. Planning Bd. of Town of Ramapo, 334 N.Y.S.2d 138, 285 N.E.2d 291 (N.Y.1972), **552,** 563, 576, 621, 700

Goldman v. Crowther, 147 Md. 282, 128 A. 50 (Md.1925), **291**

Goodman, People v., 338 N.Y.S.2d 97, 290 N.E.2d 139 (N.Y.1972), 844

Gorman Towers, Inc. v. Bogoslavsky, 626 F.2d 607 (8th Cir.1980), 1346

Grace United Methodist Church v. City of Cheyenne, 235 F.Supp.2d 1186 (D.Wyo. 2002), 1024

Grange v. Korff, 248 Iowa 118, 79 N.W.2d 743 (Iowa 1956), 145

Grant v. Seminole County, Fla., 817 F.2d 731 (11th Cir.1987), 1151

Great Atlantic and Pacific Tea Co., Inc. v. Borough of Point Pleasant, 137 N.J. 136, 644 A.2d 598 (N.J.1994), 1276

Great Lakes Motorcycle Dealers Ass'n, Inc. v. City of Detroit, 38 Mich.App. 564, 196 N.W.2d 787 (Mich.App.1972), 88

Green v. Castle Concrete Co., 181 Colo. 309, 509 P.2d 588 (Colo.1973), **104**

Greens at Fort Missoula, LLC v. City of Missoula, 271 Mont. 398, 897 P.2d 1078 (Mont.1995), 1275

Greentree at Murray Hill Condominium v. Good Shepherd Episcopal Church, 146 Misc.2d 500, 550 N.Y.S.2d 981 (N.Y.Sup.1989), **400**

Grendel's Den, Inc. v. Goodwin, 495 F.Supp. 761 (D.Mass.1980), 906, 1266

Griffin v. Tall Timbers Development, Inc., 681 So.2d 546 (Miss.1996), 146

Griffin Development Co. v. City of Oxnard, 217 Cal.Rptr. 1, 703 P.2d 339 (Cal.1985), 1137

Grosso v. Board of Adjustment of Millburn Tp. in Essex County, 61 A.2d 167 (N.J.Sup.1948), 536

Groton, Town of v. Laird, 353 F.Supp. 344 (D.Conn.1972), 1085

Grubbs v. Wooten, 189 Ga. 390, 5 S.E.2d 874 (Ga.1939), 80

Grubel v. MacLaughlin, 286 F.Supp. 24 (D.Virgin Islands 1968), 174

Gruber v. Mayor and Tp. Committee of Raritan Tp., 39 N.J. 1, 186 A.2d 489 (N.J.1962), 436

Grundlehner v. Dangler, 29 N.J. 256, 148 A.2d 806 (N.J.1959), 363

Grupe Development Co. v. Superior Court, 16 Cal.Rptr.2d 226, 844 P.2d 545 (Cal. 1993), 519

Guinnane v. San Francisco City Planning Commission, 209 Cal.App.3d 732, 257 Cal.Rptr. 742 (Cal.App. 1 Dist.1989), 861

Gulest Associates, Inc. v. Town of Newburgh, 25 Misc.2d 1004, 209 N.Y.S.2d 729 (N.Y.Sup.1960), 487

Gumley v. Board of Selectmen of Nantucket, 371 Mass. 718, 358 N.E.2d 1011 (Mass.1977), 883

Gundersen v. Village of Bingham Farms, 372 Mich. 352, 126 N.W.2d 715 (Mich. 1964), 1106

Guttenberg Taxpayers and Rentpayers Ass'n v. Galaxy Towers Condominium Ass'n, 296 N.J.Super. 101, 686 A.2d 344 (N.J.Super.A.D.1995), 190

Guy v. Brandon Tp., 181 Mich.App. 775, 450 N.W.2d 279 (Mich.App.1989), 1141

Hadacheck v. Sebastian, 239 U.S. 394, 36 S.Ct. 143, 60 L.Ed. 348 (1915), **98,** 101, 373

Hagaman v. Board of Ed. of Woodbridge Tp., 117 N.J.Super. 446, 285 A.2d 63 (N.J.Super.A.D.1971), 113

Hagan v. Sabal Palms, Inc., 186 So.2d 302 (Fla.App. 2 Dist.1966), 146

Haghighi v. Russian–American Broadcasting Co., 577 N.W.2d 927 (Minn.1998), 1315

Haines v. City of Phoenix, 151 Ariz. 286, 727 P.2d 339 (Ariz.App. Div. 2 1986), 240

Haldeman v. Teicholz, 197 A.D.2d 223, 611 N.Y.S.2d 669 (N.Y.A.D. 3 Dept.1994), 141

Hall v. Church of the Open Bible, 4 Wis.2d 246, 89 N.W.2d 798 (Wis.1958), 169

Hall v. City of Durham, 323 N.C. 293, 372 S.E.2d 564 (N.C.1988), 337

Hall County Historical Soc., Inc. v. Georgia Dept. of Transp., 447 F.Supp. 741 (N.D.Ga.1978), 888

Halpin v. Poushter, 59 N.Y.S.2d 338 (N.Y.Sup.1945), 114

Hamrick v. Herrera, 744 S.W.2d 458 (Mo. App. W.D.1987), 144

Hanley v. Misischi, 111 R.I. 233, 302 A.2d 79 (R.I.1973), 159

Hansen Brothers Enterprises, Inc. v. Board of Supervisors, 48 Cal.Rptr.2d 778, 907 P.2d 1324 (Cal.1996), 377

Hansman v. Oneida County, 123 Wis.2d 511, 366 N.W.2d 901 (Wis.App.1985), 1151

Hardin County v. Jost, 897 S.W.2d 592 (Ky. App.1995), 332

Hargroder v. City of Eunice, 341 So.2d 463 (La.App. 3 Cir.1976), 187

Harnish v. Manatee County, Florida, 597 F.Supp. 601 (M.D.Fla.1984), 845

Harper, State ex rel. Carter v., 182 Wis. 148, 196 N.W. 451 (Wis.1923), **296**

Harris v. Skirving, 41 Wash.2d 200, 248 P.2d 408 (Wash.1952), 106

Harris v. Zoning Com'n of Town of New Milford, 259 Conn. 402, 788 A.2d 1239 (Conn.2002), 778, 782

Harrisburg, City of v. Capitol Housing Corp., 117 Pa.Cmwlth. 408, 543 A.2d 620 (Pa.Cmwlth.1988), 174

Harris County Flood Control Dist. v. Glenbrook Patiohome Owners Ass'n, 933 S.W.2d 570 (Tex.App.-Hous. (1 Dist.) 1996), 158

Harrison–Rye Realty Corp. v. Crigler, 61 N.Y.S.2d 191 (N.Y.Sup.1945), 130

Harrison–Rye Realty Corp. v. New Rochelle Trust Co., 177 Misc. 776, 31 N.Y.S.2d 1005 (N.Y.Sup.1941), 130

Hart v. Denver Urban Renewal Authority, 551 F.2d 1178 (10th Cir.1977), 890

Hartman v. City of Columbia, 268 S.C. 44, 232 S.E.2d 15 (S.C.1977), 1260

Hasco Elec. Corp. v. Dassler, 144 N.Y.S.2d 857 (N.Y.Sup.1955), 549

Hattiesburg, City of v. Region XII Com'n on Mental Health & Retardation, 654 So.2d 516 (Miss.1995), 1085

Haugen v. Gleason, 226 Or. 99, 359 P.2d 108 (Or.1961), 486, 487

Haviland v. Land Conservation and Development Commission, 45 Or. App. 761, 609 P.2d 423 (Or.App.1980), **613**

Havurah v. Zoning Bd. of Appeals of Town of Norfolk, 177 Conn. 440, 418 A.2d 82 (Conn.1979), 108

Hay, State ex rel. Thornton v., 254 Or. 584, 462 P.2d 671 (Or.1969), 824

Hayes v. Gibbs, 110 Utah 54, 169 P.2d 781 (Utah 1946), 114

Hayes Inv. Corp., State ex rel. Warner v., 13 Wash.2d 306, 125 P.2d 262 (Wash. 1942), 54

Hays v. Hartfield L-P Gas, 159 Ind.App. 297, 306 N.E.2d 373 (Ind.App. 1 Dist. 1974), 70

Headley v. City of Rochester, 272 N.Y. 197, 5 N.E.2d 198 (N.Y.1936), **524**

Heath v. Uraga, 106 Wash.App. 506, 24 P.3d 413 (Wash.App. Div. 2 2001), 178

Heffner v. Litchfield Golf Co., 258 S.C. 447, 189 S.E.2d 3 (S.C.1972), **178**

Hensler v. City of Glendale, 32 Cal.Rptr.2d 244, 876 P.2d 1043 (Cal.1994), 782

Herman, State ex rel. v. Cardon, 112 Ariz. 548, 544 P.2d 657 (Ariz.1976), 103

Hero Lands Co. v. Texaco, Inc., 310 So.2d 93 (La.1975), 69

Herrmann v. Board of County Com'rs of Butler County, 246 Kan. 152, 785 P.2d 1003 (Kan.1990), 1084

Hibbard v. Halliday, 58 Okla. 244, 158 P. 1158 (Okla.1916), 36

Hickman, State ex rel. v. City Council of Kirksville, 690 S.W.2d 799 (Mo.App. W.D.1985), 1275

Hidden Harbour Estates, Inc. v. Basso, 393 So.2d 637 (Fla.App. 4 Dist.1981), 189

Higginbotham v. Barrett, 473 F.2d 745 (5th Cir.1973), 1339

High Ridge Ass'n, Inc. v. County Com'rs of Carroll County, Md., 105 Md.App. 423, 660 A.2d 951 (Md.App.1995), 642

Hill v. Community of Damien of Molokai, 121 N.M. 353, 911 P.2d 861 (N.M.1996), 1126

Hillis Homes, Inc. v. Snohomish County, 97 Wash.2d 804, 650 P.2d 193 (Wash.1982), 488

Hillsborough Ass'n for Retarded Citizens, Inc. v. City of Temple Terrace, 332 So.2d 610 (Fla.1976), 1125

Hills Development Co. v. Township of Bernards, 229 N.J.Super. 318, 551 A.2d 547 (N.J.Super.A.D.1988), 102

Hinman v. Planning and Zoning Commission of Town of Southbury, 26 Conn. Supp. 125, 214 A.2d 131 (Conn.Com.Pl. 1965), 1172

Hobart, Town of v. Collier, 3 Wis.2d 182, 87 N.W.2d 868 (Wis.1958), 1106

Hoboken Environment Committee, Inc. v. German Seaman's Mission of New York, 161 N.J.Super. 256, 391 A.2d 577 (N.J.Super.Ch.1978), 901

Hoffman v. Cohen, 262 S.C. 71, 202 S.E.2d 363 (S.C.1974), **164**

Holiday Pines Property Owners Ass'n, Inc. v. Wetherington, 596 So.2d 84 (Fla.App. 4 Dist.1992), 130, 146

Holmdel Builders Ass'n v. Township of Holmdel, 121 N.J. 550, 583 A.2d 277 (N.J.1990), 1217, 1222

Holmdel Builders Ass'n v. Township of Holmdel, 232 N.J.Super. 182, 556 A.2d 1236 (N.J.Super.A.D.1989), 497

Holy Name Hospital v. Montroy, 153 N.J.Super. 181, 379 A.2d 299 (N.J.Super.L.1977), 1116

Holy Spirit Ass'n for the Unification of World Christianity v. Town of New Castle, 480 F.Supp. 1212 (S.D.N.Y.1979), 1250

Home Builders Ass'n of Cent. Arizona v. City of Scottsdale, 187 Ariz. 479, 930 P.2d 993 (Ariz.1997), 513

Home Builders Ass'n of Greater Kansas City v. City of Kansas City, 555 S.W.2d 832 (Mo.1977), 488

Home Builders Ass'n of Greater St. Louis v. City of St. Peters, 868 S.W.2d 187 (Mo. App. E.D.1994), 164

Home Builders Ass'n of Northern California v. City of Napa, 108 Cal. Rptr.2d 60 (Cal.App. 1 Dist.2001), **1223,** 1231

Home Builders League of South Jersey, Inc. v. Berlin Tp., 81 N.J. 127, 405 A.2d 381 (N.J.1979), **1184**

Hoogasian, People ex rel. v. Sears, Roebuck & Co., 52 Ill.2d 301, 287 N.E.2d 677 (Ill.1972), 107

Hooker v. Weathers, 990 F.2d 913 (6th Cir. 1993), 1173

Hornstein v. Barry, 560 A.2d 530 (D.C. 1989), 1138

Horst v. Housing Authority of Scotts Bluff County, 184 Neb. 215, 166 N.W.2d 119 (Neb.1969), 158

Hospitality Ass'n of South Carolina, Inc. v. County of Charleston, 320 S.C. 219, 464 S.E.2d 113 (S.C.1995), 667

Houghtaling v. Medina Bd. of Zoning Appeals, 134 Ohio App.3d 541, 731 N.E.2d 733 (Ohio App. 9 Dist.1999), 414

Houston, City of v. Emmanuel United Pentecostal Church, Inc., 429 S.W.2d 679 (Tex.Civ.App.-Hous. (14 Dist.) 1968), 169

Howard v. City of Beavercreek, 276 F.3d 802 (6th Cir.2002), **1031**

Howard County v. JJM, Inc., 301 Md. 256, 482 A.2d 908 (Md.1984), 465

H & R Builders, Inc. v. Borough Council of Borough of Norwood, 124 Pa.Cmwlth. 88, 555 A.2d 948 (Pa.Cmwlth.1989), 1135, 1208

Hulbert v. California Portland Cement Co., 161 Cal. 239, 118 P. 928 (Cal.1911), **37**

Hunt, State ex rel. Morehouse v., 235 Wis. 358, 291 N.W. 745 (Wis.1940), **378**

Hunter v. Pillers, 464 S.W.2d 939 (Tex.Civ. App.-Beaumont 1971), 187

Huntington, N.Y., Town of v. Huntington Branch, N.A.A.C.P., 488 U.S. 15, 109 S.Ct. 276, 102 L.Ed.2d 180 (1988), 1164

Hunziker v. State, 519 N.W.2d 367 (Iowa 1994), 955

Hyler v. Town of Blue Hill, 570 A.2d 316 (Me.1990), 443

Hylton Enterprises, Inc. v. Board of Sup'rs of Prince William County, 220 Va. 435, 258 S.E.2d 577 (Va.1979), 465

Idaho Springs, City of v. Golden Sav. & Loan Ass'n, 29 Colo.App. 119, 480 P.2d 847 (Colo.App.1970), **112**

Illinois Cent. R. Co. v. State of Illinois, 146 U.S. 387, 13 S.Ct. 110, 36 L.Ed. 1018 (1892), 816

Inabinet v. Booe, 262 S.C. 81, 202 S.E.2d 643 (S.C.1974), 185

Independent Wireless One Corp. v. Town of Charlotte, 242 F.Supp.2d 409 (D.Vt. 2003), 1053

Infinity Outdoor, Inc. v. City of New York, 165 F.Supp.2d 403 (E.D.N.Y.2001), 844

Innovative Health Systems, Inc. v. City of White Plains, 117 F.3d 37 (2nd Cir. 1997), **1034**

In re (see name of party)

International Funeral Services, Inc. v. DeKalb County, 244 Ga. 707, 261 S.E.2d 625 (Ga.1979), 363

International News Service v. Associated Press, 248 U.S. 215, 39 S.Ct. 68, 63 L.Ed. 211 (1918), 17

Iodice v. City of Newton, 397 Mass. 329, 491 N.E.2d 618 (Mass.1986), 1232

I'On, L.L.C. v. Town of Mt. Pleasant, 338 S.C. 406, 526 S.E.2d 716 (S.C.2000), 1276

Ivy Club Investors Ltd. Partnership v. City of Kennewick, 40 Wash.App. 524, 699 P.2d 782 (Wash.App. Div. 3 1985), 443

Jackson v. City Council of City of Charlottesville, Va., 659 F.Supp. 470 (W.D.Va.1987), 846

Jackson v. New York State Urban Development Corp., 503 N.Y.S.2d 298, 494 N.E.2d 429 (N.Y.1986), 736

Jackson County, State ex rel. Barber & Sons Tobacco Co., Inc. v., 869 S.W.2d 113 (Mo.App. W.D.1993), 1320

Jackson & Morris, People ex rel. v. Smuczynski, 345 Ill.App. 63, 102 N.E.2d 168 (Ill.App. 1 Dist.1951), 460

James v. Valtierra, 402 U.S. 137, 91 S.Ct. 1331, 28 L.Ed.2d 678 (1971), 1274

Javins v. First Nat. Realty Corp., 428 F.2d 1071, 138 U.S.App.D.C. 369 (D.C.Cir.1970), 623, **624,** 628

Jayno Heights Landowners Ass'n v. Preston, 85 Mich.App. 443, 271 N.W.2d 268 (Mich.App.1978), 1124

J. E. D. Associates, Inc. v. Town of Atkinson, 121 N.H. 581, 432 A.2d 12 (N.H. 1981), 487, 488
Jenad, Inc. v. Village of Scarsdale, 38 Misc.2d 658, 238 N.Y.S.2d 156 (N.Y.Sup. 1963), 487
Jennings v. New York State Office of Mental Health, 660 N.Y.S.2d 352, 682 N.E.2d 953 (N.Y.1997), **1067**
Jensen v. City of New York, 399 N.Y.S.2d 645, 369 N.E.2d 1179 (N.Y.1977), 536
Jensen's, Inc. v. City of Dover, 130 N.H. 761, 547 A.2d 277 (N.H.1988), 1141
Jesus Center v. Farmington Hills Zoning Bd. of Appeals, 215 Mich.App. 54, 544 N.W.2d 698 (Mich.App.1996), 1252
Jewell Junction, City of v. Cunningham, 439 N.W.2d 183 (Iowa 1989), 377
Jewish Reconstructionist Synagogue of North Shore, Inc. v. Incorporated Village of Roslyn Harbor, 386 N.Y.S.2d 198, 352 N.E.2d 115 (N.Y.1976), 1250
Jewish Reconstructionist Synagogue of North Shore, Inc. v. Incorporated Village of Roslyn Harbor, 379 N.Y.S.2d 747, 342 N.E.2d 534 (N.Y.1975), 1250
J. & J. Painting, State v., 167 N.J.Super. 384, 400 A.2d 1204 (N.J.Super.A.D.1979), 846
Johnny Cake, Inc. v. Zoning Bd. of Appeals of Town of Burlington, 180 Conn. 296, 429 A.2d 883 (Conn.1980), 363
Johns, State ex rel. State Highway Commission v., 507 S.W.2d 75 (Mo.App.1974), 103
Johnson v. Benbrook Water and Sewer Authority, 410 S.W.2d 644 (Tex.Civ.App.-Fort Worth 1966), 461
Joint Ventures, Inc. v. Department of Transp., 563 So.2d 622 (Fla.1990), 571
Jones v. Herald, 881 P.2d 116 (Okla.App. Div. 3 1994), 141
Jones, State v., 305 N.C. 520, 290 S.E.2d 675 (N.C.1982), 869
Jordan v. Village of Menomonee Falls, 28 Wis.2d 608, 137 N.W.2d 442 (Wis. 1965), **479,** 486, 488
Joseph v. Planning Bd. of Town of Yorktown, 140 A.D.2d 670, 529 N.Y.S.2d 17 (N.Y.A.D. 2 Dept.1988), 487
Joseph Skillken & Co. v. City of Toledo, 380 F.Supp. 228 (N.D.Ohio 1974), 1165
Jurkiewicz v. Butler Cty. Bd. of Elections, 85 Ohio App.3d 503, 620 N.E.2d 146 (Ohio App. 12 Dist.1993), 1274
Just v. Marinette County, 56 Wis.2d 7, 201 N.W.2d 761 (Wis.1972), **711**
Juster Associates, In re, 136 Vt. 577, 396 A.2d 1382 (Vt.1978), **262**
Juster Associates v. City of Rutland, Vt., 901 F.2d 266 (2nd Cir.1990), 263

Kahl v. Consolidated Gas, Elec. Light & Power Co. of Baltimore, 191 Md. 249, 60 A.2d 754 (Md.1948), 874

Ka-Hur Enterprises, Inc. v. Zoning Bd. of Appeals of Provincetown, 40 Mass.App. Ct. 71, 661 N.E.2d 120 (Mass.App.Ct. 1996), 387
Kaiser Hawaii Kai Development Co. v. City and County of Honolulu, 70 Haw. 480, 777 P.2d 244 (Hawai'i 1989), 1276
Kamhi v. Planning Bd. of Town of Yorktown, 465 N.Y.S.2d 865, 452 N.E.2d 1193 (N.Y.1983), 487
Karches v. City of Cincinnati, 38 Ohio St.3d 12, 526 N.E.2d 1350 (Ohio 1988), 765
Kauai County v. Pacific Standard Life Ins. Co., 65 Haw. 318, 653 P.2d 766 (Hawai'i 1982), 1276
Kauffman v. Roling, 851 S.W.2d 789 (Mo. App. W.D.1993), 181
Kawaoka v. City of Arroyo Grande, 17 F.3d 1227 (9th Cir.1994), 575
Kay F. Sterrett v. Loundon County Board of Supervisors, 22 Va.Cir. 148 (1990), 228
KBW, Inc. v. Town of Bennington, 115 N.H. 392, 342 A.2d 653 (N.H.1975), 474
K Care, Inc. v. Town of Lac du Flambeau, 181 Wis.2d 59, 510 N.W.2d 697 (Wis. App.1993), 1127
Kell v. Bella Vista Village Property Owners Ass'n, 258 Ark. 757, 528 S.W.2d 651 (Ark.1975), 130
Keller v. City of Council Bluffs, 246 Iowa 202, 66 N.W.2d 113 (Iowa 1954), 312
Kelley v. John, 162 Neb. 319, 75 N.W.2d 713 (Neb.1956), 1275
Kelly v. Lovejoy, 172 Mont. 516, 565 P.2d 321 (Mont.1977), 187
Kennedy Park Homes Ass'n v. City of Lackawanna, N. Y., 436 F.2d 108 (2nd Cir. 1970), 1165
Kenney, Appeal of, 374 N.W.2d 271 (Minn. 1985), 363
Kent v. Koch, 166 Cal.App.2d 579, 333 P.2d 411 (Cal.App. 1 Dist.1958), **137**
Kent County Council for Historic Preservation v. Romney, 304 F.Supp. 885 (W.D.Mich.1969), **888**
Keshbro, Inc. v. City of Miami, 801 So.2d 864 (Fla.2001), 75
Keystone Bituminous Coal Ass'n v. DeBenedictis, 480 U.S. 470, 107 S.Ct. 1232, 94 L.Ed.2d 472 (1987), 918
Key West, City of v. R.L.J.S. Corp., 537 So.2d 641 (Fla.App. 3 Dist.1989), 488
Khan v. Zoning Bd. of Appeals of Village of Irvington, 639 N.Y.S.2d 302, 662 N.E.2d 782 (N.Y.1996), 372
Kim v. City of New York, 659 N.Y.S.2d 145, 681 N.E.2d 312 (N.Y.1997), 956
King v. City of Bainbridge, 276 Ga. 484, 577 S.E.2d 772 (Ga.2003), 1054
King County v. Rasmussen, 299 F.3d 1077 (9th Cir.2002), 122
Kirkwood, City of v. City of Sunset Hills, 589 S.W.2d 31 (Mo.App. E.D.1979), 1086

Kirsch v. Prince George's County, 331 Md. 89, 626 A.2d 372 (Md.1993), 1115

Kirschenman v. Hutchinson County Bd. of Com'rs, 656 N.W.2d 330 (S.D.2003), 1275

Kit-Mar Builders, Inc., Appeal of, 439 Pa. 466, 268 A.2d 765 (Pa.1970), 1179

Klein v. Baise, 708 F.Supp. 863 (N.D.Ill. 1989), 847

Kode Harbor Development Associates v. County of Atlantic, 230 N.J.Super. 430, 553 A.2d 858 (N.J.Super.A.D.1989), 474

Kola Tepee, Inc. v. Marion County, 99 Or. App. 481, 782 P.2d 955 (Or.App.1989), 1250

Kopietz v. Zoning Bd. of Appeals for City of Village of Clarkston, 211 Mich.App. 666, 535 N.W.2d 910 (Mich.App.1995), 376

Krawski v. Planning and Zoning Com'n of Town of South Windsor, 21 Conn.App. 667, 575 A.2d 1036 (Conn.App.1990), 520

Kroll v. Steere, 60 Conn.App. 376, 759 A.2d 541 (Conn.App.2000), 846

Kuban v. McGimsey, 96 Nev. 105, 605 P.2d 623 (Nev.1980), 102

Kucera v. Lizza, 69 Cal.Rptr.2d 582 (Cal. App. 1 Dist.1997), **1285**

La Crosse, City of v. Wisconsin Dept. of Natural Resources, 120 Wis.2d 168, 353 N.W.2d 68 (Wis.App.1984), 766

Ladue, City of v. Gilleo, 512 U.S. 43, 114 S.Ct. 2038, 129 L.Ed.2d 36 (1994), 846

Ladue, City of v. Horn, 720 S.W.2d 745 (Mo.App. E.D.1986), **1116**, 1119

Ladue, City of v. Zwick, 904 S.W.2d 470 (Mo.App. E.D.1995), 363

Lafayette Park Baptist Church v. Board of Adjustment of City of St. Louis, 599 S.W.2d 61 (Mo.App. E.D.1980), 902

La Fetra v. Beveridge, 199 A. 70 (N.J.Err. & App.1938), 145

Lafferty v. Payson City, 642 P.2d 376 (Utah 1982), 462

Lake Bluff Housing Partners v. City of South Milwaukee, 197 Wis.2d 157, 540 N.W.2d 189 (Wis.1995), 437, 1165

Lake Bluff, Village of v. Jacobson, 118 Ill. App.3d 102, 73 Ill.Dec. 637, 454 N.E.2d 734 (Ill.App. 2 Dist.1983), 442

Lake City Corp. v. City of Mequon, 207 Wis.2d 155, 558 N.W.2d 100 (Wis.1997), **533**

Lake Country Estates, Inc. v. Tahoe Regional Planning Agency, 440 U.S. 391, 99 S.Ct. 1171, 59 L.Ed.2d 401 (1979), 278

Lake Drive Baptist Church, State ex rel. v. Village of Bayside Bd. of Trustees, 12 Wis.2d 585, 108 N.W.2d 288 (Wis.1961), **1244**

Lake Illyria Corp. v. Town of Gardiner, 43 A.D.2d 386, 352 N.Y.S.2d 54 (N.Y.A.D. 3 Dept.1974), 576

Lake Intervale Homes, Inc. v. Parsippany-Troy Hills Tp., Morris County, 28 N.J. 423, 147 A.2d 28 (N.J.1958), 461

Lake Secor Development Co., In re, 141 Misc. 913, 252 N.Y.S. 809 (N.Y.Sup. 1931), 460, 489

Lake Shore Estates, Inc. v. Denville Tp. Planning Bd., 127 N.J. 394, 605 A.2d 1073 (N.J.1992), 783

Lakin v. City of Peoria, 129 Ill.App.3d 651, 84 Ill.Dec. 837, 472 N.E.2d 1233 (Ill. App. 3 Dist.1984), 910, 1266

Lamar Advertising Co. v. City of Douglasville, Georgia, 254 F.Supp.2d 1321 (N.D.Ga.2003), 847

Lambros, Inc. v. Town of Ocean Ridge, Fla., 392 So.2d 993 (Fla.App. 4 Dist.1981), 1235

Lamica v. Gerdes, 270 N.C. 85, 153 S.E.2d 814 (N.C.1967), 174

Lampton v. Pinaire, 610 S.W.2d 915 (Ky. App.1980), 436

Landgrave v. Watson, 593 S.W.2d 875 (Ky. App.1979), 1320

Landmark Land Co., Inc. v. City and County of Denver, 728 P.2d 1281 (Colo.1986), 784

Land/Vest Properties, Inc. v. Town of Plainfield, 117 N.H. 817, 379 A.2d 200 (N.H. 1977), 474

Lane v. Zoning Bd. of Adjustment of City of Talladega, 669 So.2d 958 (Ala.Civ.App. 1995), 1085

Langbein v. Board of Zoning Appeals of Town of Milford, 135 Conn. 575, 67 A.2d 5 (Conn.1949), 1260

Lanier v. Fairfield Communities Inc., 776 F.Supp. 1533 (M.D.Fla.1990), 1173

Laporte, Application of, 2 A.D.2d 710, 152 N.Y.S.2d 916 (N.Y.A.D. 2 Dept.1956), 1251

Larkin v. State of Michigan Dept. of Social Services, 89 F.3d 285 (6th Cir.1996), 1126, 1173

Larsen v. Zoning Bd. of Adjustment of City of Pittsburgh, 543 Pa. 415, 672 A.2d 286 (Pa.1996), **351**

La Salle Nat. Bank v. City of Park Ridge, 74 Ill.App.3d 647, 30 Ill.Dec. 587, 393 N.E.2d 623 (Ill.App. 1 Dist.1979), 1236

Latinos Unidos De Chelsea En Accion (Lucha) v. Secretary of Housing and Urban Development, 799 F.2d 774 (1st Cir. 1986), 1167

Lauderbaugh v. Hopewell Township, 319 F.3d 568 (3rd Cir.2003), 1141

Lawrence v. Harding, 225 Ga. 148, 166 S.E.2d 336 (Ga.1969), 163

Lawson v. City of Kankakee, Ill., 81 F.Supp.2d 930 (C.D.Ill.2000), 847

Lazy Mountain Land Club v. Matanuska-Susitna Borough Bd. of Adjustment & Appeals, 904 P.2d 373 (Alaska 1995), 235

TABLE OF CASES

League of Oregon Cities v. State, 334 Or. 645, 56 P.3d 892 (Or.2002), 29

Leavenworth Properties v. City and County of San Francisco, 189 Cal.App.3d 986, 234 Cal.Rptr. 598 (Cal.App. 1 Dist.1987), 1137

Leaver v. Grose, 563 P.2d 773 (Utah 1977), 187

LeBlanc–Sternberg v. Fletcher, 104 F.3d 355 (2nd Cir.1996), 1256

LeBlanc–Sternberg v. Fletcher, 922 F.Supp. 959 (S.D.N.Y.1996), 1256

LeBlanc–Sternberg v. Fletcher, 67 F.3d 412 (2nd Cir.1995), 1256

Lee County v. New Testament Baptist Church of Fort Myers, Fla., Inc., 507 So.2d 626 (Fla.App. 2 Dist.1987), 465

Legacy Group v. City of Wasco, 131 Cal. Rptr.2d 460 (Cal.App. 5 Dist.2003), 549

Leonard v. City of Bothell, 87 Wash.2d 847, 557 P.2d 1306 (Wash.1976), 1275

Leonard v. Town of Brimfield, 423 Mass. 152, 666 N.E.2d 1300 (Mass.1996), 765, 956

Lesher Communications, Inc. v. City of Walnut Creek, 277 Cal.Rptr. 1, 802 P.2d 317 (Cal.1990), 597

Lesher Communications, Inc. v. City of Walnut Creek, 225 Cal.App.3d 645, 262 Cal.Rptr. 337 (Cal.App. 1 Dist.1989), 240

Lew v. Superior Court, 25 Cal.Rptr.2d 42 (Cal.App. 1 Dist.1993), 75

Lexington–Fayette Urban County Government v. Schneider, 849 S.W.2d 557 (Ky. App.1992), 512

L'Hote v. City of New Orleans, 177 U.S. 587, 20 S.Ct. 788, 44 L.Ed. 899 (1900), 101

Liddy v. Cisneros, 823 F.Supp. 164 (S.D.N.Y.1993), 1043

Lifteau v. Metropolitan Sports Facilities Commission, 270 N.W.2d 749 (Minn. 1978), 640

Lionshead Lake, Inc. v. Wayne Tp., 10 N.J. 165, 89 A.2d 693 (N.J.1952), 1189

List, State ex rel. v. Douglas County, 90 Nev. 272, 524 P.2d 1271 (Nev.1974), 278

Little v. Winborn, 518 N.W.2d 384 (Iowa 1994), 312

Little Rock, City of v. Chartwell Valley Ltd. Partnership by Rodney D. Myers Corp., 299 Ark. 542, 772 S.W.2d 616 (Ark. 1989), 607

Little Rock, City of v. Infant–Toddler Montessori School, Inc., 270 Ark. 697, 606 S.W.2d 743 (Ark.1980), 1260

Little Rock, City of v. Leawood Property Owners' Ass'n, 242 Ark. 451, 413 S.W.2d 877 (Ark.1967), 356

Livingston v. Davis, 243 Iowa 21, 50 N.W.2d 592 (Iowa 1951), 74

Lochwood Meadows, Inc. v. Buck, 416 S.W.2d 623 (Tex.Civ.App.-Dallas 1967), 129

Loggerhead Turtle v. County Council of Volusia County, Fla., 148 F.3d 1231 (11th Cir.1998), 257

Loggerhead Turtle v. County Council of Volusia County, Fla., 92 F.Supp.2d 1296 (M.D.Fla.2000), 257

Long v. Branham, 271 N.C. 264, 156 S.E.2d 235 (N.C.1967), 129

Long Beach Equities, Inc. v. County of Ventura, 231 Cal.App.3d 1016, 282 Cal.Rptr. 877 (Cal.App. 2 Dist.1991), 996

Longboat Key, Town of v. Lands End, Ltd., 433 So.2d 574 (Fla.App. 2 Dist.1983), 487

Long Island Bd. of Realtors, Inc. v. Incorporated Village of Massapequa Park, 277 F.3d 622 (2nd Cir.2002), 844

Longridge Builders, Inc. v. Planning Bd. of Princeton Tp., 52 N.J. 348, 245 A.2d 336 (N.J.1968), 474

Loreto Development Co., Inc. v. Village of Chardon, 119 Ohio App.3d 524, 695 N.E.2d 1151 (Ohio App. 11 Dist.1996), 651

Lorillard Tobacco Co. v. Reilly, 533 U.S. 525, 121 S.Ct. 2404, 150 L.Ed.2d 532 (2001), 845

Loschiavo v. City of Dearborn, 33 F.3d 548 (6th Cir.1994), 1054

Lough v. Zoning Bd. of Review of Town of North Providence, 74 R.I. 366, 60 A.2d 839 (R.I.1948), 371

Louisville Bd. of Zoning Adjustment, City of v. Gailor, 920 S.W.2d 887 (Ky.App.1996), 1085

Love Church v. City of Evanston, 671 F.Supp. 515 (N.D.Ill.1987), 1256

Loveladies Harbor, Inc., Matter of, 176 N.J.Super. 69, 422 A.2d 107 (N.J.Super.A.D.1980), 718

Lowes v. Carter, 124 Md. 678, 93 A. 216 (Md.1915), 145

Lucas v. South Carolina Coastal Council, 505 U.S. 1003, 112 S.Ct. 2836, 120 L.Ed.2d 798 (1992), 719, **938**, 956

Lucas v. South Carolina Coastal Council, 309 S.C. 424, 424 S.E.2d 484 (S.C.1992), 955

Ludlow v. Colorado Animal By–Products Co., 104 Utah 221, 137 P.2d 347 (Utah 1943), 42

Luger v. City of Burnsville, 295 N.W.2d 609 (Minn.1980), 910, 1266

Lutheran High School Ass'n of Greater Detroit v. City of Farmington Hills, 146 Mich.App. 641, 381 N.W.2d 417 (Mich. App.1985), 1259

Luxembourg Group, Inc. v. Snohomish County, 76 Wash.App. 502, 887 P.2d 446 (Wash.App. Div. 1 1995), 465

Lyons, Town of v. Bashor, 867 P.2d 159 (Colo.App.1993), 388

MacDonald v. Board of County Com'rs for Prince George's County, 238 Md. 549, 210 A.2d 325 (Md.1965), 1097, 1322

MacDonald, Commonwealth v., 464 Pa. 435, 347 A.2d 290 (Pa.1975), 108

Macdonald Advertising Co. v. City of Pontiac, 916 F.Supp. 644 (E.D.Mich.1995), 845

Macon–Bibb County Hosp. Authority v. Madison, 204 Ga.App. 741, 420 S.E.2d 586 (Ga.App.1992), 1084

Madison v. Ducktown Sulphur, Copper & Iron Co., 113 Tenn. 331, 83 S.W. 658 (Tenn.1904), 40

Magnolia Development Co. v. Coles, 10 N.J. 223, 89 A.2d 664 (N.J.1952), 460

Maha'ulepu v. Land Use Com'n, 71 Haw. 332, 790 P.2d 906 (Hawai'i 1990), 269

Mahoney v. Walter, 157 W.Va. 882, 205 S.E.2d 692 (W.Va.1974), **70**

Major Media of Southeast, Inc. v. City of Raleigh, 621 F.Supp. 1446 (E.D.N.C. 1985), 846

Malcolm v. Shamie, 95 Mich.App. 132, 290 N.W.2d 101 (Mich.App.1980), 1124

Maldini v. Ambro, 369 N.Y.S.2d 385, 330 N.E.2d 403 (N.Y.1975), 1172

Malm v. Dubrey, 325 Mass. 63, 88 N.E.2d 900 (Mass.1949), 106

Malvern, Borough of v. Jackson, 108 Pa. Cmwlth. 248, 529 A.2d 96 (Pa.Cmwlth. 1987), 1141, 1208

Mandelstam v. City Com'n of City of South Miami, 539 So.2d 1139 (Fla.App. 3 Dist. 1988), 1260

Manders, State ex rel. Miller v., 2 Wis.2d 365, 86 N.W.2d 469 (Wis.1957), 537

Manor Healthcare Corp. v. Lomelo, 929 F.2d 633 (11th Cir.1991), 1345

Mansfield & Swett v. Town of West Orange, 198 A. 225 (N.J.Sup.1938), 431

Maples v. Horton, 239 N.C. 394, 80 S.E.2d 38 (N.C.1954), 180

Marathon Outdoor, LLC v. Vesconti, 107 F.Supp.2d 355 (S.D.N.Y.2000), 844

Marblehead, Town of v. Rosenthal, 316 Mass. 124, 55 N.E.2d 13 (Mass.1944), 317

Marcus v. Baron, 456 N.Y.S.2d 39, 442 N.E.2d 437 (N.Y.1982), 564

Marcus Associates, Inc. v. Town of Huntington, 410 N.Y.S.2d 546, 382 N.E.2d 1323 (N.Y.1978), 1235

Margolis v. District Court, In and For Arapahoe County, 638 P.2d 297 (Colo.1981), 1275

Marion County v. Department of Community Affairs, 817 So.2d 1062 (Fla. App. 5 Dist.2002), **1153**

Marion Road Ass'n, Inc. v. Westport Planning & Zoning Com'n, 1994 WL 592221 (Conn.Super.1994), **775**, 777

Market Square Properties, Ltd. v. Town of Guilderland Zoning Bd. of Appeals, 109 A.D.2d 164, 491 N.Y.S.2d 519 (N.Y.A.D. 3 Dept.1985), 651

Marks v. City Council of City of Chesapeake, Va., 723 F.Supp. 1155 (E.D.Va. 1988), 1236

Marsh v. State of Alabama, 326 U.S. 501, 66 S.Ct. 276, 90 L.Ed. 265 (1946), 191

Marshfield Family Skateland, Inc. v. Town of Marshfield, 389 Mass. 436, 450 N.E.2d 605 (Mass.1983), 1236

Martin v. Beehan, 689 S.W.2d 29 (Ky.App. 1985), 387

Martin v. Williams, 141 W.Va. 595, 93 S.E.2d 835 (W.Va.1956), 75

Martin v. Wray, 473 F.Supp. 1131 (E.D.Wis. 1979), 846

Maryland–National Capital Park and Planning Commission v. Chadwick, 286 Md. 1, 405 A.2d 241 (Md.1979), **566,** 571

Maryland–National Capital Park and Planning Commission v. Rosenberg, 269 Md. 520, 307 A.2d 704 (Md.1973), **515**

Marzocco v. City of Albany, 217 A.D.2d 872, 629 N.Y.S.2d 847 (N.Y.A.D. 3 Dept. 1995), 377

Matter of (see name of party)

Matthews v. Bay Head Imp. Ass'n, 95 N.J. 306, 471 A.2d 355 (N.J.1984), 817

Matthews v. Board of Zoning Appeals of Greene County, 218 Va. 270, 237 S.E.2d 128 (Va.1977), 1106

Matthews v. First Christian Church of St. Louis, 355 Mo. 627, 197 S.W.2d 617 (Mo. 1946), 169

Maxwell v. Land Developers, Inc., 485 S.W.2d 869 (Tenn.Ct.App.1972), 146

Mayhew v. Town of Sunnyvale, 964 S.W.2d 922 (Tex.1998), 996

Maykut v. Plasko, 170 Conn. 310, 365 A.2d 1114 (Conn.1976), **55**

Mayor v. Thomas, 645 So.2d 940 (Miss. 1994), 642

Mayor and City Council of Baltimore v. Mano Swartz, Inc., 268 Md. 79, 299 A.2d 828 (Md.1973), **829,** 844

Mayor and Council of Rockville v. Rylyns Enterprises, Inc., 372 Md. 514, 814 A.2d 469 (Md.2002), 346

McArthur, State ex rel. v. Board of Adjustment of City of Crestwood, 872 S.W.2d 651 (Mo.App. E.D.1994), 387

McBride v. Town of Forestburgh, 54 A.D.2d 396, 388 N.Y.S.2d 940 (N.Y.A.D. 3 Dept. 1976), 326

McCaw v. Harrison, 259 S.W.2d 457 (Ky. 1953), **43**

McClanahan v. Richland County Council, 350 S.C. 433, 567 S.E.2d 240 (S.C.2002), 252

McClure, Appeal of, 415 Pa. 285, 203 A.2d 534 (Pa.1964), 356

TABLE OF CASES

McDermott v. Village of Calverton Park, 454 S.W.2d 577 (Mo.1970), **1104,** 1107

McDonald v. Chaffin, 529 S.W.2d 54 (Tenn.Ct.App.1975), **167**

McGann v. Incorporated Village of Old Westbury, 293 A.D.2d 581, 741 N.Y.S.2d 75 (N.Y.A.D. 2 Dept.2002), 44, 1024

McHenry State Bank v. City of McHenry, 113 Ill.App.3d 82, 68 Ill.Dec. 615, 446 N.E.2d 521 (Ill.App. 2 Dist.1983), **1135**

McKinnon v. Neugent, 225 Ga. 215, 167 S.E.2d 593 (Ga.1969), 114

McMinn v. Town of Oyster Bay, 498 N.Y.S.2d 128, 488 N.E.2d 1240 (N.Y. 1985), **1112**

McMorrow v. Board of Adjustment for City of Town & Country, 765 S.W.2d 700 (Mo.App. E.D.1989), **361**

McNair v. City of Cedar Park, Tex., 993 F.2d 1217 (5th Cir.1993), 462

McNaughton Co. v. Witmer, 149 Pa. Cmwlth. 307, 613 A.2d 104 (Pa.Cmwlth. 1992), 575

McQueen v. South Carolina Coastal Council, 354 S.C. 142, 580 S.E.2d 116 (S.C. 2003), 956

Meat Producers, Inc. v. McFarland, 476 S.W.2d 406 (Tex.Civ.App.-Dallas 1972), 64

Medeiros v. Hawaii County Planning Com'n, 8 Haw.App. 183, 797 P.2d 59 (Hawai'i App.1990), **1302,** 1308

Medinger, Appeal of, 377 Pa. 217, 104 A.2d 118 (Pa.1954), 1189

Mefford v. City of Tulare, 102 Cal.App.2d 919, 228 P.2d 847 (Cal.App. 4 Dist. 1951), 460

Meierhenry v. City of Huron, 354 N.W.2d 171 (S.D.1984), 639

Meighan v. United States Sprint Communications Co., 924 S.W.2d 632 (Tenn. 1996), 985

Memory Gardens Cemetery, Inc. v. Village of Arlington Heights, 250 Ill.App.3d 553, 190 Ill.Dec. 238, 621 N.E.2d 107 (Ill. App. 1 Dist.1993), 378

Menkhus, State ex rel. v. City of Pevely, 865 S.W.2d 871 (Mo.App. E.D.1993), 521

Meredith v. Washoe County School Dist. By and Through Bd. of Trustees, 84 Nev. 15, 435 P.2d 750 (Nev.1968), 158

Merson v. McNally, 665 N.Y.S.2d 605, 688 N.E.2d 479 (N.Y.1997), **1294,** 1301

Merton v. Dolphin, 28 Wis. 456 (Wis.1871), 431

Mesilla, Town of v. City of Las Cruces, 120 N.M. 69, 898 P.2d 121 (N.M.App.1995), 1098

Mesolella v. City of Providence, 439 A.2d 1370 (R.I.1982), 317

Messer v. Town of Chapel Hill, 59 N.C.App. 692, 297 S.E.2d 632 (N.C.App.1982), 488

Metromedia, Inc. v. City of Des Plaines, 26 Ill.App.3d 942, 326 N.E.2d 59 (Ill.App. 1 Dist.1975), 845

Metromedia, Inc. v. City of San Diego, 453 U.S. 490, 101 S.Ct. 2882, 69 L.Ed.2d 800 (1981), **833,** 845

Metromedia, Inc. v. Mayor and City Council of Baltimore, 538 F.Supp. 1183 (D.Md. 1982), 844

Metropolitan Dade County v. Fontainebleau Gas & Wash, Inc., 570 So.2d 1006 (Fla. App. 3 Dist.1990), 348

Metropolitan Dade County Fair Housing and Employment Appeals Bd. v. Sunrise Village Mobile Home Park, Inc., 485 So.2d 865 (Fla.App. 3 Dist.1986), 1172

Metropolitan Housing Development Corp. v. Village of Arlington Heights, 616 F.2d 1006 (7th Cir.1980), 1164

Metropolitan Housing Development Corp. v. Village of Arlington Heights, 558 F.2d 1283 (7th Cir.1977), 1164

Miami Beach, City of v. Rocio Corp., 404 So.2d 1066 (Fla.App. 3 Dist.1981), 1137

Miami Beach Redevelopment Agency, State v., 392 So.2d 875 (Fla.1980), 639

Miami, City of v. Woolin, 387 F.2d 893 (5th Cir.1968), 1344

Middlemist v. City of Plymouth, 387 N.W.2d 190 (Minn.App.1986), 465

Middletown Tp. v. N/E Regional Office, United States Postal Service, 601 F.Supp. 125 (D.N.J.1985), 1085

Midtown Properties, Inc. v. Madison Tp., 68 N.J.Super. 197, 172 A.2d 40 (N.J.Super.L.1961), 487, 490

Miller v. City of Beaver Falls, 368 Pa. 189, 82 A.2d 34 (Pa.1951), 489, 538

Miller v. Covington Development Authority, 539 S.W.2d 1 (Ky.1976), 639

Miller, State v., 83 N.J. 402, 416 A.2d 821 (N.J.1980), 846

Miller, State ex rel. v. Manders, 2 Wis.2d 365, 86 N.W.2d 469 (Wis.1957), 537

Miller-Elston v. Paal, 261 Ark. 644, 550 S.W.2d 771 (Ark.1977), 79

Minshew v. Smith, 380 F.Supp. 918 (N.D.Miss.1974), 1001, 1345

Mira Development Corp. v. City of San Diego, 205 Cal.App.3d 1201, 252 Cal.Rptr. 825 (Cal.App. 4 Dist.1988), 240

Missionaries of Our Lady of La Salette v. Village of Whitefish Bay, 267 Wis. 609, 66 N.W.2d 627 (Wis.1954), 1251

Mitchell v. Hines, 305 Mich. 296, 9 N.W.2d 547 (Mich.1943), 54

M & J Coal Co. v. United States, 47 F.3d 1148 (Fed.Cir.1995), 920

Moffatt v. Forrest City, 234 Ark. 12, 350 S.W.2d 327 (Ark.1961), **388**

Monell v. Department of Social Services of City of New York, 436 U.S. 658, 98 S.Ct. 2018, 56 L.Ed.2d 611 (1978), 1345

Monroe City v. Arnold, 22 Utah 2d 291, 452 P.2d 321 (Utah 1969), 55

Montgomery, City of v. Crossroads Land Co., Inc., 355 So.2d 363 (Ala.1978), 486

Montgomery County v. Citizens Bldg. & Loan Ass'n, Inc., 20 Md.App. 484, 316 A.2d 322 (Md.App.1974), 844

Montgomery County v. Mossburg, 228 Md. 555, 180 A.2d 851 (Md.1962), 371

Montgomery County v. National Capital Realty Corp., 267 Md. 364, 297 A.2d 675 (Md.1972), **344,** 347

Moore v. City of East Cleveland, Ohio, 431 U.S. 494, 97 S.Ct. 1932, 52 L.Ed.2d 531 (1977), 1111

Moore v. Smith, 443 S.W.2d 552 (Tex.1969), 187

Morehouse, State ex rel. v. Hunt, 235 Wis. 358, 291 N.W. 745 (Wis.1940), **378**

Morley v. Jackson Redevelopment Authority, 632 So.2d 1284 (Miss.1994), **151**

Morris County Land Imp. Co. v. Parsippany–Troy Hills Tp., 40 N.J. 539, 193 A.2d 232 (N.J.1963), **703,** 709

Mortenson, State ex rel. Brill v., 6 Wis.2d 325, 96 N.W.2d 603 (Wis.1959), 387

Moschetti v. City of Tucson, 9 Ariz.App. 108, 449 P.2d 945 (Ariz.App.1969), 158

Moskow v. Commissioner of Dept. of Environmental Management, 384 Mass. 530, 427 N.E.2d 750 (Mass.1981), 718

Moss v. Burke & Trotti, 198 La. 76, 3 So.2d 281 (La.1941), 79

Moss v. Town of Winchester, 365 Mass. 297, 311 N.E.2d 555 (Mass.1974), 1135

Mossman v. City of Columbus, 234 Neb. 78, 449 N.W.2d 214 (Neb.1989), 376

Mount Laurel Tp. v. Barbieri, 151 N.J.Super. 27, 376 A.2d 541 (N.J.Super.A.D.1977), 443

Mount Pleasant Realty & Const. Co. v. Zoning Bd. of Review of City of East Providence, 100 R.I. 31, 210 A.2d 877 (R.I. 1965), 355

Moviematic Industries Corp. v. Board of County Com'rs of Metropolitan Dade County, 349 So.2d 667 (Fla.App. 3 Dist.1977), **725,** 746

Mowrer v. Ashland Oil & Refining Co., Inc., 518 F.2d 659 (7th Cir.1975), 69

Mugler v. Kansas, 123 U.S. 623, 8 S.Ct. 273, 31 L.Ed. 205 (1887), **911,** 918

Municipal Art Soc. of New York v. Koch, 137 Misc.2d 832, 522 N.Y.S.2d 800 (N.Y.Sup.1987), 698

Munn v. People of State of Illinois, 94 U.S. 113, 24 L.Ed. 77 (1876), 23

Munoz–Mendoza v. Pierce, 711 F.2d 421 (1st Cir.1983), 1167

Murphey v. Gray, 84 Ariz. 299, 327 P.2d 751 (Ariz.1958), 185

Muskegon Heights, City of v. Moseler, 178 Mich.App. 609, 444 N.W.2d 145 (Mich. App.1989), 1084

NAACP v. Harris, 567 F.Supp. 637 (D.Mass. 1983), 1167

Naegele Outdoor Advertising, Inc. v. City of Durham, 844 F.2d 172 (4th Cir.1988), 846

Nahrstedt v. Lakeside Village Condominium Assn., 33 Cal.Rptr.2d 63, 878 P.2d 1275 (Cal.1994), 188

Napro Development Corp. v. Town of Berlin, 135 Vt. 353, 376 A.2d 342 (Vt.1977), 108

Nassau County v. Kensington Ass'n, 21 N.Y.S.2d 208 (N.Y.Sup.1940), 130

National Advertising Co. v. City of Orange, 861 F.2d 246 (9th Cir.1988), 846

National Advertising Co. v. City of Rolling Meadows, 789 F.2d 571 (7th Cir.1986), 846

National Advertising Co. v. Town of Babylon, 703 F.Supp. 228 (E.D.N.Y.1989), 846

National Land & Inv. Co. v. Kohn, 419 Pa. 504, 215 A.2d 597 (Pa.1965), **1174,** 1179

Naylor v. Township of Hellam, 565 Pa. 397, 773 A.2d 770 (Pa.2001), 576

Nectow v. City of Cambridge, 277 U.S. 183, 48 S.Ct. 447, 72 L.Ed. 842 (1928), 307, 918

Needham Pastoral Counseling Center, Inc. v. Board of Appeals of Needham, 29 Mass.App.Ct. 31, 557 N.E.2d 43 (Mass. App.Ct.1990), 1252

Neighborhood Bd. No. 24 (Waianae Coast) v. State Land Use Commission, 64 Haw. 265, 639 P.2d 1097 (Hawai'i 1982), 269

Neighborhood Committee on Lead Pollution v. Board of Adjustment of City of Dallas, 728 S.W.2d 64 (Tex.App.-Dallas 1987), 397

Neponsit Property Owners' Ass'n v. Emigrant Industrial Sav. Bank, 278 N.Y. 248, 15 N.E.2d 793 (N.Y.1938), **124**

Neptune City, Borough of v. Borough of Avon–By–The–Sea, 61 N.J. 296, 294 A.2d 47 (N.J.1972), 817

Neuberger v. City of Portland, 288 Or. 155, 603 P.2d 771 (Or.1979), 1337

Neuberger v. City of Portland, 37 Or.App. 13, 586 P.2d 351 (Or.App.1978), 1337

Neuzil v. City of Iowa City, 451 N.W.2d 159 (Iowa 1990), **1323,** 1331

New City Office Park v. Planning Bd., Town of Clarkstown, 144 A.D.2d 348, 533 N.Y.S.2d 786 (N.Y.A.D. 2 Dept. 1988), 765

New Hempstead, N.Y., Village of, United States v., 832 F.Supp. 76 (S.D.N.Y. 1993), 1054

New Jersey Builders Ass'n v. Mayor and Tp. Committee of Bernards Tp., Somerset County, 108 N.J. 223, 528 A.2d 555 (N.J.1987), 474

New Jersey Chapter, Am. Institute of Planners v. New Jersey State Bd. of

Professional Planners, 48 N.J. 581, 227 A.2d 313 (N.J.1967), **207**

New Jersey Shore Builders Ass'n v. Mayor and Tp. Committee of Tp. of Middletown, 234 N.J.Super. 619, 561 A.2d 319 (N.J.Super.L.1989), **571**

New London, City of v. University of Connecticut, 1994 WL 65316 (Conn.Super.1994), 1287

New Orleans, City of v. Impastato, 198 La. 206, 3 So.2d 559 (La.1941), 884

New Orleans, City of v. Levy, 223 La. 14, 64 So.2d 798 (La.1953), 884

New Orleans, City of v. Pergament, 198 La. 852, 5 So.2d 129 (La.1941), 884

New Orleans, City of v. State, 364 So.2d 1020 (La.1978), 1085

Newport News, City of v. Hertzler, 216 Va. 587, 221 S.E.2d 146 (Va.1976), 102

New Rochelle, City of v. Town of Mamaroneck, 111 F.Supp.2d 353 (S.D.N.Y.2000), **1090**

Newton v. American Sec. Co., 201 Ark. 943, 148 S.W.2d 311 (Ark.1941), 490

Nicholas v. Wilton Zoning Bd. of Appeals, 2001 WL 1200339 (Conn.Super.2001), **224,** 228

Nigro v. Planning Bd. of Borough of Saddle River, 237 N.J.Super. 305, 567 A.2d 1010 (N.J.Super.A.D.1989), **530**

Noble v. Murphy, 34 Mass.App.Ct. 452, 612 N.E.2d 266 (Mass.App.Ct.1993), 190

Noble State Bank v. Haskell, 219 U.S. 104, 31 S.Ct. 186, 55 L.Ed. 112 (1911), 24

Noghrey v. Acampora, 152 A.D.2d 660, 543 N.Y.S.2d 530 (N.Y.A.D. 2 Dept.1989), 575

Nollan v. California Coastal Com'n, 483 U.S. 825, 107 S.Ct. 3141, 97 L.Ed.2d 677 (1987), **491, 496**

Nonnenmann v. Lucky Stores, Inc., 53 Ill. App.3d 509, 10 Ill.Dec. 714, 368 N.E.2d 200 (Ill.App. 3 Dist.1977), 159

North Cherokee Village Membership v. Murphy, 71 Mich.App. 592, 248 N.W.2d 629 (Mich.App.1976), 1151

Northend Cinema, Inc. v. City of Seattle, 90 Wash.2d 709, 585 P.2d 1153 (Wash. 1978), 1240

Northern Illinois Home Builders Ass'n, Inc. v. County of Du Page, 165 Ill.2d 25, 208 Ill.Dec. 328, 649 N.E.2d 384 (Ill.1995), 513

Northern Maine General Hosp. v. Ricker, 572 A.2d 479 (Me.1990), 1124

North Olmsted Chamber of Commerce v. City of North Olmsted, 86 F.Supp.2d 755 (N.D.Ohio 2000), 847

Northwestern Fertilizing Co. v. Village of Hyde Park, 97 U.S. 659, 24 L.Ed. 1036 (1878), 102

Northwestern Improvement Co. v. Lowry, 104 Mont. 289, 66 P.2d 792 (Mont.1937), 113

Northwestern Laundry v. City of Des Moines, 239 U.S. 486, 36 S.Ct. 206, 60 L.Ed. 396 (1916), 101

Northwest Land and Inv., Inc. v. City of Bellingham, 31 Wash.App. 742, 644 P.2d 740 (Wash.App. Div. 1 1982), 474

Norton v. Randolph, 176 Ala. 381, 58 So. 283 (Ala.1912), 36

Nova Horizon, Inc. v. City Council of the City of Reno, 105 Nev. 92, 769 P.2d 721 (Nev.1989), **1339**

Nucholls v. Board of Adjustment of City of Tulsa, 560 P.2d 556 (Okla.1976), 363

Nussbaum v. Lacopo, 317 N.Y.S.2d 347, 265 N.E.2d 762 (N.Y.1970), 97

Nu–Way Emulsions, Inc. v. City of Dalworthington Gardens, 610 S.W.2d 562 (Tex.Civ.App.-Fort Worth 1980), 377

O'Connor v. City of Moscow, 69 Idaho 37, 202 P.2d 401 (Idaho 1949), 397

O'Connor v. Ryan, 159 S.W.2d 531 (Tex. Civ.App.-San Antonio 1942), 79

Oconomowoc Residential Programs v. City of Milwaukee, 300 F.3d 775 (7th Cir. 2002), 1043

Oklahoma City, Okl. v. Dolese, 48 F.2d 734 (10th Cir.1931), 106

Old Dominion Iron & Steel Corp. v. Virginia Elec. & Power Co., 215 Va. 658, 212 S.E.2d 715 (Va.1975), 187

Oliver, People v., 86 Cal.App.2d 885, 195 P.2d 926 (Cal.App. 1 Dist.1948), 74

Oliver v. Zoning Commission of Town of Chester, 31 Conn.Supp. 197, 326 A.2d 841 (Conn.Com.Pl.1974), 1123

Omnipoint Communications, Inc. v. City of White Plains, 175 F.Supp.2d 697 (S.D.N.Y.2001), 1024

181 Inc. v. Salem County Planning Bd., 133 N.J.Super. 350, 336 A.2d 501 (N.J.Super.L.1975), **463**

1515–1519 Lakeview Boulevard Condominium Ass'n v. Apartment Sales Corp., 146 Wash.2d 194, 43 P.3d 1233 (Wash.2002), **130**

Opinion of the Justices, 139 N.H. 82, 649 A.2d 604 (N.H.1994), 823

Opinion of the Justices, 365 Mass. 631, 313 N.E.2d 561 (Mass.1974), 823

Opinion of the Justices to the Senate, 333 Mass. 773, 128 N.E.2d 557 (Mass. 1955), **879**

Opinion of the Justices to the Senate, 333 Mass. 783, 128 N.E.2d 563 (Mass.1955), 883

Orange Fibre Mills, Inc. v. City of Middletown, 94 Misc.2d 233, 404 N.Y.S 2d 296 (N.Y.Sup.1978), 1098

Orangetown, Town of v. Magee, 643 N.Y.S.2d 21, 665 N.E.2d 1061 (N.Y. 1996), 436

Orinda Homeowners Committee v. Board of Supervisors, 11 Cal.App.3d

768, 90 Cal.Rptr. 88 (Cal.App. 1 Dist. 1970), 448
Osceola County v. Best Diversified, Inc., 830 So.2d 139 (Fla.App. 5 Dist.2002), 31
Osiecki v. Town of Huntington, 170 A.D.2d 490, 565 N.Y.S.2d 564 (N.Y.A.D. 2 Dept.1991), **323**
Ouimette v. City of Somersworth, 119 N.H. 292, 402 A.2d 159 (N.H.1979), 361
Outdoor Systems, Inc. v. City of Merriam, Kan, 67 F.Supp.2d 1258 (D.Kan.1999), 846
Oxford House, Inc. v. Township of Cherry Hill, 799 F.Supp. 450 (D.N.J.1992), 1043

Paladac v. City of Rockland, 558 A.2d 372 (Me.1989), 1152
Palazzolo v. Rhode Island, 533 U.S. 606, 121 S.Ct. 2448, 150 L.Ed.2d 592 (2001), 719, **957**
Palo Alto Tenants Union v. Morgan, 321 F.Supp. 908 (N.D.Cal.1970), 1111
Pan American Health Organization v. Montgomery County, 338 Md. 214, 657 A.2d 1163 (Md.1995), 1085
Park v. Stolzheise, 24 Wash.2d 781, 167 P.2d 412 (Wash.1946), 80
Parkersburg Builders Material Co. v. Barrack, 118 W.Va. 608, 191 S.E. 368 (W.Va.1937), 74, 75
Parking Ass'n of Georgia, Inc. v. City of Atlanta, Ga., 264 Ga. 764, 450 S.E.2d 200 (Ga.1994), **870**
Park Place Home Brokers v. P–K Mobile Home Park, 773 F.Supp. 46 (N.D.Ohio 1991), 1173
Park View Heights Corp. v. City of Black Jack, 454 F.Supp. 1223 (E.D.Mo.1978), 1160
Park View Heights Corp. v. City of Black Jack, 467 F.2d 1208 (8th Cir.1972), 1160
Parma, Ohio, City of, United States v., 494 F.Supp. 1049 (N.D.Ohio 1980), 1165, 1208
Paschen v. Pashkow, 63 Ill.App.2d 56, 211 N.E.2d 576 (Ill.App. 1 Dist.1965), 185
Passaic, City of v. Paterson Bill Posting, Advertising & Sign Painting Co., 62 A. 267 (N.J.Err. & App.1905), 843
Payless ShoeSource, Inc. v. Town of Penfield, N.Y., 934 F.Supp. 540 (W.D.N.Y. 1996), 1054
Pearce v. Scarcello, 920 S.W.2d 643 (Mo. App. W.D.1996), 180
Pearson v. City of Grand Blanc, 961 F.2d 1211 (6th Cir.1992), **987**
Pele Defense Fund v. Puna Geothermal Venture, 8 Haw.App. 203, 797 P.2d 69 (Hawai'i App.1990), 1308
Pelham Esplanade, Inc. v. Board of Trustees of Village of Pelham Manor, 154 A.D.2d 599, 546 N.Y.S.2d 427 (N.Y.A.D. 2 Dept.1989), 389

Pemberton Tp. v. State, 171 N.J.Super. 287, 408 A.2d 832 (N.J.Super.L.1979), 1126
Pengilly v. Multnomah County, 810 F.Supp. 1111 (D.Or.1992), 465
Penn Central Transp. Co. v. City of New York, 438 U.S. 104, 98 S.Ct. 2646, 57 L.Ed.2d 631 (1978), **923**, 932, 955
Penn Central Transp. Co. v. City of New York, 397 N.Y.S.2d 914, 366 N.E.2d 1271 (N.Y.1977), **891**, 895, 896
Penning v. Owens, 340 Mich. 355, 65 N.W.2d 831 (Mich.1954), 312
Pennington v. Rockdale County, 244 Ga. 743, 262 S.E.2d 59 (Ga.1979), 932
Pennsylvania Coal Co. v. Mahon, 260 U.S. 393, 43 S.Ct. 158, 67 L.Ed. 322 (1922), **913**, 917, 918, 933
People v. _____ (see opposing party)
People, By and Through California Dept. of Transp. v. City of South Lake Tahoe, 466 F.Supp. 527 (E.D.Cal.1978), 278
People ex rel. v. _____ (see opposing party and relator)
People of City of Ferndale v. Palazzolo, 62 Mich.App. 140, 233 N.W.2d 216 (Mich. App.1975), 1236
Perry, State v., 149 Conn. 232, 178 A.2d 279 (Conn.1962), **374**, 375
Peter Garrett Gunsmith, Inc. v. City of Dayton, 98 S.W.3d 517 (Ky.App.2002), 1085
Peterman v. State Dept. of Natural Resources, 446 Mich. 177, 521 N.W.2d 499 (Mich.1994), 102
Petruzzi v. Zoning Bd. of Appeals of Town of Oxford, 176 Conn. 479, 408 A.2d 243 (Conn.1979), 376
Petterson v. City of Naperville, 9 Ill.2d 233, 137 N.E.2d 371 (Ill.1956), **453**
Phillips v. Board of Adjustment of Town of Westfield, 44 N.J.Super. 491, 130 A.2d 866 (N.J.Super.A.D.1957), 537
Phillips v. Smith, 240 Iowa 863, 38 N.W.2d 87 (Iowa 1949), 130
Phillips v. Zoning Com'r of Howard County, 225 Md. 102, 169 A.2d 410 (Md.1961), 376
Phillips Petroleum Co. v. Mississippi, 484 U.S. 469, 108 S.Ct. 791, 98 L.Ed.2d 877 (1988), 817
Phoenix, City of v. Beall, 22 Ariz.App. 141, 524 P.2d 1314 (Ariz.App. Div. 1 1974), 1321
Piedmont Triad Airport Auth. v. Urbine, 354 N.C. 336, 554 S.E.2d 331 (N.C. 2001), 643
Piemontese, State v., 282 N.J.Super. 307, 659 A.2d 1385 (N.J.Super.A.D.1995), 869
Pierce v. King County, 62 Wash.2d 324, 382 P.2d 628 (Wash.1963), 311
Pierce Oil Corp. v. City of Hope, 248 U.S. 498, 39 S.Ct. 172, 63 L.Ed. 381 (1919), 102

TABLE OF CASES

Pine Brook Lakes, Inc., Ex parte, 617 So.2d 1014 (Ala.1992), 521

Pinetree Estates Homeowners Ass'n v. First United Lutheran Church of Cobb County, 241 Ga. 228, 244 S.E.2d 856 (Ga.1978), 170

Pioneer Trust and Sav. Bank v. Village of Mount Prospect, 22 Ill.2d 375, 176 N.E.2d 799 (Ill.1961), **476**

Pittsburgh, City of v. Commonwealth of Pennsylvania, 468 Pa. 174, 360 A.2d 607 (Pa.1976), 1085

Planning and Zoning Commission of Town of Westport v. Synanon Foundation, Inc., 153 Conn. 305, 216 A.2d 442 (Conn.1966), 1123

Platte Woods United Methodist Church v. City of Platte Woods, 935 S.W.2d 735 (Mo.App. W.D.1996), 1344

Plum Creek Timber Company, L.P. v. Hillman, 95 Wash.App. 1061 (Wash.App. Div. 1 1999), 1316

Poletown Neighborhood Council v. City of Detroit, 410 Mich. 616, 304 N.W.2d 455 (Mich.1981), 641, 642

Pollard v. Palm Beach County, 560 So.2d 1358 (Fla.App. 4 Dist.1990), 371

Pomona Pointe Associates, Ltd. v. Incorporated Village of Pomona, 185 Misc.2d 131, 712 N.Y.S.2d 275 (N.Y.Sup.2000), 783

Pompano Beach, City of v. Yardarm Restaurant, Inc, 834 So.2d 861 (Fla.App. 4 Dist. 2002), 997

Port of St. Helens v. Land Conservation and Development Com'n, 165 Or.App. 487, 996 P.2d 1014 (Or.App.2000), 619

Portsmouth, City of v. Schlesinger, 140 N.H. 733, 672 A.2d 712 (N.H.1996), 1138

Portsmouth, N.H., City of v. Schlesinger, 82 F.3d 547 (1st Cir.1996), 1138

Potomac Sand & Gravel Co. v. Governor of Md., 266 Md. 358, 293 A.2d 241 (Md. 1972), 718

Powell v. Taylor, 222 Ark. 896, 263 S.W.2d 906 (Ark.1954), **76**

Prah v. Maretti, 108 Wis.2d 223, 321 N.W.2d 182 (Wis.1982), **88,** 93, 94

Prater v. City of Burnside, Ky., 289 F.3d 417 (6th Cir.2002), 1024

Prentiss v. City of South Pasadena, 18 Cal. Rptr.2d 641 (Cal.App. 2 Dist.1993), 902

Presbytery of Seattle v. King County, 114 Wash.2d 320, 787 P.2d 907 (Wash. 1990), **980**

Preseault v. I.C.C., 494 U.S. 1, 110 S.Ct. 914, 108 L.Ed.2d 1 (1990), 122

Preseault v. United States, 100 F.3d 1525 (Fed.Cir.1996), 122

Preston, Town of v. Connecticut Siting Council, 20 Conn.App. 474, 568 A.2d 799 (Conn.App.1990), 271

Prince George's County, Md. v. Sunrise Development Ltd. Partnership, 330 Md. 297, 623 A.2d 1296 (Md.1993), 437

Public Service Elec. & Gas Co., In re, 35 N.J. 358, 173 A.2d 233 (N.J.1961), 874

Puerto Rico, Commonwealth of, United States v., 764 F.Supp. 220 (D.Puerto Rico 1991), 1043

Quadro Stations, Inc. v. Gilley, 7 N.C.App. 227, 172 S.E.2d 237 (N.C.App.1970), 159

Queach Corp. v. Inland Wetlands Com'n of Town of Branford, 258 Conn. 178, 779 A.2d 134 (Conn.2001), 774

Queen City Farms, Inc. v. Central Nat. Ins. Co. of Omaha, 126 Wash.2d 50, 882 P.2d 703 (Wash.1994), 55

Queen Creek Land & Cattle Corp. v. Yavapai County Bd. of Sup'rs, 108 Ariz. 449, 501 P.2d 391 (Ariz.1972), 1276

Quick v. City of Austin, 7 S.W.3d 109 (Tex.1998), **739,** 746

Quirk v. Town of New Boston, 140 N.H. 124, 663 A.2d 1328 (N.H.1995), 490

Rahway, City of v. Raritan Homes, Inc., 21 N.J.Super. 541, 91 A.2d 409 (N.J.Super.A.D.1952), 460

Rajneesh Medical Corp. v. Wasco County, 300 Or. 107, 706 P.2d 948 (Or.1985), 236

Rancho La Costa v. County of San Diego, 111 Cal.App.3d 54, 168 Cal.Rptr. 491 (Cal.App. 4 Dist.1980), 251

Rancho Lobo, Ltd. v. Devargas, 303 F.3d 1195 (10th Cir.2002), **804**

Rebman v. City of Springfield, 111 Ill. App.2d 430, 250 N.E.2d 282 (Ill.App. 4 Dist.1969), 888

Rector, Wardens, and Members of the Vestry of St. Bartholomew's Church v. City of New York, 728 F.Supp. 958 (S.D.N.Y. 1989), 896

Redevelopment Authority of Oil City v. Woodring, 498 Pa. 180, 445 A.2d 724 (Pa.1982), 874

Redfern Lawns Civic Ass'n v. Currie Pontiac Co., 328 Mich. 463, 44 N.W.2d 8 (Mich.1950), 184

Reece, State v., 374 S.W.2d 686 (Tex.Civ. App.-Houston 1964), 158

Reed–Custer Community Unit School Dist. No. 255–U v. City of Wilmington, 253 Ill.App.3d 503, 192 Ill.Dec. 421, 625 N.E.2d 381 (Ill.App. 3 Dist.1993), 639

Regents of University of California v. City of Santa Monica, 77 Cal.App.3d 130, 143 Cal.Rptr. 276 (Cal.App. 2 Dist.1978), 1084

Regional Economic Community Action Program, Inc. v. City of Middletown, 294 F.3d 35 (2nd Cir.2002), 1043

Region 10 Client Management, Inc. v. Town of Hampstead, 120 N.H. 885, 424 A.2d 207 (N.H.1980), 1125

Regus v. City of Baldwin Park, 70 Cal. App.3d 968, 139 Cal.Rptr. 196 (Cal.App. 2 Dist.1977), 639

Reid v. Brodsky, 397 Pa. 463, 156 A.2d 334 (Pa.1959), 106

Reid Development Corp. v. Parsippany-Troy Hills Tp., 31 N.J.Super. 459, 107 A.2d 20 (N.J.Super.A.D.1954), 461

Reid Development Corp. v. Parsippany-Troy Hills Tp., 10 N.J. 229, 89 A.2d 667 (N.J.1952), 461

Reinman v. City of Little Rock, 237 U.S. 171, 35 S.Ct. 511, 59 L.Ed. 900 (1915), 101, 373

Remilong v. Crolla, 576 P.2d 461 (Wyo. 1978), **147**

Renton, City of v. Playtime Theatres, Inc., 475 U.S. 41, 106 S.Ct. 925, 89 L.Ed.2d 29 (1986), 1240

Request for Advisory Opinion on Constitutionality of 1986 PA 281, In re, 430 Mich. 93, 422 N.W.2d 186 (Mich.1988), 639

Reserve, Ltd. v. Town of Longboat Key, 17 F.3d 1374 (11th Cir.1994), 437

R. E. Short Co. v. City of Minneapolis, 269 N.W.2d 331 (Minn.1978), 637, 638

Resident Advisory Bd. v. Rizzo, 564 F.2d 126 (3rd Cir.1977), 1165

Residential Management Systems, Inc. v. Jefferson County Plan Com'n, 542 N.E.2d 227 (Ind.App. 1 Dist.1989), 1127

Residents of Rosemont v. Metro, 173 Or.App. 321, 21 P.3d 1108 (Or.App. 2001), **616**

Resolution Trust Corp. v. Town of Highland Beach, 18 F.3d 1536 (11th Cir.1994), 997

Reynolds Metals Co. v. Yturbide, 258 F.2d 321 (9th Cir.1958), 41

R.G. Moore Bldg. Corp. v. Committee for the Repeal of Ordinance R(C)–88–13, 239 Va. 484, 391 S.E.2d 587 (Va.1990), 1275

Rhema Christian Center v. District of Columbia Bd. of Zoning Adjustment, 515 A.2d 189 (D.C.1986), 1251

Riblet v. Ideal Cement Co., 54 Wash.2d 779, 345 P.2d 173 (Wash.1959), 69

Rice v. Heggy, 158 Cal.App.2d 89, 322 P.2d 53 (Cal.App. 2 Dist.1958), 174

Richards v. City of Muscatine, 237 N.W.2d 48 (Iowa 1975), 638

Richmond Heights, City of v. Richmond Heights Presbyterian Church, 764 S.W.2d 647 (Mo.1989), 1260

Ridgefield Land Co. v. City of Detroit, 241 Mich. 468, 217 N.W. 58 (Mich.1928), **426,** 430

Riegert Apartments Corp. v. Planning Bd. of Town of Clarkstown, 105 Misc.2d 298, 432 N.Y.S.2d 43 (N.Y.Sup.1979), 488

Riter v. Keokuk Electro–Metals Co., 248 Iowa 710, 82 N.W.2d 151 (Iowa 1957), 40

River Park, Inc. v. City of Highland Park, 281 Ill.App.3d 154, 217 Ill.Dec. 410, 667 N.E.2d 499 (Ill.App. 2 Dist.1996), 1001

River Springs Ltd. Liability Co. v. Board of County Com'rs of County of Teton, 899 P.2d 1329 (Wyo.1995), 1074

River Vale Tp. v. Town of Orangetown, 403 F.2d 684 (2nd Cir.1968), 1098

R–N–R Associates v. Zoning Bd. of Review of City of Providence, 100 R.I. 7, 210 A.2d 653 (R.I.1965), 355

Robert E. Kurzius, Inc. v. Incorporated Village of Upper Brookville, 67 A.D.2d 70, 414 N.Y.S.2d 573 (N.Y.A.D. 2 Dept. 1979), 1183

Robinson v. City of Boulder, 190 Colo. 357, 547 P.2d 228 (Colo.1976), 606

Robinson v. City of Raytown, 606 S.W.2d 460 (Mo.App. W.D.1980), 1346

Robinson Brick Co. v. Luthi, 115 Colo. 106, 169 P.2d 171 (Colo.1946), 105

Robinson Tp. v. Knoll, 70 Mich.App. 258, 245 N.W.2d 709 (Mich.App.1976), 1151

Rockenbach v. Apostle, 330 Mich. 338, 47 N.W.2d 636 (Mich.1951), 106

Rodgers v. Village of Tarrytown, 302 N.Y. 115, 96 N.E.2d 731 (N.Y.1951), 317, **655,** 675

Rodrigues v. Village of Larchmont, N.Y., 608 F.Supp. 467 (S.D.N.Y.1985), 1002

Rofe v. Robinson, 415 Mich. 345, 329 N.W.2d 704 (Mich.1982), **171,** 174

Rohn v. City of Visalia, 214 Cal.App.3d 1463, 263 Cal.Rptr. 319 (Cal.App. 5 Dist. 1989), 458

Rohnert Park, City of v. Harris, 601 F.2d 1040 (9th Cir.1979), 1100

Rolling Pines Ltd. Partnership v. City of Little Rock, 73 Ark.App. 97, 40 S.W.3d 828 (Ark.App.2001), 1152

Roman Catholic Welfare Corp. of San Francisco v. City of Piedmont, 45 Cal.2d 325, 289 P.2d 438 (Cal.1955), 1258

Romero–Barcelo v. Brown, 478 F.Supp. 646 (D.Puerto Rico 1979), 890

Rose v. Chaikin, 187 N.J.Super. 210, 453 A.2d 1378 (N.J.Super.Ch.1982), 94

Rosen v. Village of Downers Grove, 19 Ill.2d 448, 167 N.E.2d 230 (Ill.1960), 486

Ross v. City of Rolling Hills Estates, 192 Cal.App.3d 370, 238 Cal.Rptr. 561 (Cal. App. 2 Dist.1987), 799

Ross v. Harootunian, 257 Cal.App.2d 292, 64 Cal.Rptr. 537 (Cal.App. 3 Dist.1967), 145

Rowland v. City of Racine, 223 Wis. 488, 271 N.W. 36 (Wis.1937), 317

Rozes v. Smith, 120 R.I. 515, 388 A.2d 816 (R.I.1978), 355

Ruffinengo v. Miller, 579 P.2d 342 (Utah 1978), 144

Rzadkowolski v. Village of Lake Orion, 845 F.2d 653 (6th Cir.1988), 846

TABLE OF CASES

Sackson v. Zimmerman, 103 A.D.2d 843, 478 N.Y.S.2d 354 (N.Y.A.D. 2 Dept. 1984), 869

Sameric Corp. of Chestnut St., Inc. v. City of Philadelphia, 125 Pa.Cmwlth. 520, 558 A.2d 155 (Pa.Cmwlth.1989), 896

Sanborn v. McLean, 233 Mich. 227, 206 N.W. 496 (Mich.1925), **141, 144**

Sanchez v. City of Santa Fe, 82 N.M. 322, 481 P.2d 401 (N.M.1971), 486

San Diego Gas & Elec. Co. v. City of San Diego, 450 U.S. 621, 101 S.Ct. 1287, 67 L.Ed.2d 551 (1981), 933

Sanibel, City of v. Goode, 372 So.2d 181 (Fla.App. 2 Dist.1979), 240

San Marcos, City of v. R.W. McDonald Development Corp., 700 S.W.2d 674 (Tex. App.-Austin 1985), 782

San Pedro Min. Corp. v. Board of County Com'rs of Santa Fe County, 121 N.M. 194, 909 P.2d 754 (N.M.App.1995), 1074

Sansom Committee by Cook v. Lynn, 735 F.2d 1552 (3rd Cir.1984), 1167

Santa Barbara, City of v. Adamson, 164 Cal.Rptr. 539, 610 P.2d 436 (Cal.1980), 1115, 1116

Santa Fe, City of v. Gamble-Skogmo, Inc., 73 N.M. 410, 389 P.2d 13 (N.M.1964), 884

Santa Margarita Area Residents Together v. San Luis Obispo County, 100 Cal.Rptr.2d 740 (Cal.App. 2 Dist. 2000), 349, **1288**

Sapakoff v. Town of Hague Zoning Bd. of Appeals, 211 A.D.2d 874, 621 N.Y.S.2d 215 (N.Y.A.D. 3 Dept.1995), 387

Sasso v. Osgood, 633 N.Y.S.2d 259, 657 N.E.2d 254 (N.Y.1995), **357**

Saurer v. Board of Zoning Appeals, 629 N.E.2d 893 (Ind.App. 1 Dist.1994), 1346

Saveland Park Holding Corp., State ex rel. v. Wieland, 269 Wis. 262, 69 N.W.2d 217 (Wis.1955), **850,** 870

Sayewich's Estate, In re, 120 N.H. 237, 413 A.2d 581 (N.H.1980), 443

Schanz v. City of Billings, 182 Mont. 328, 597 P.2d 67 (Mont.1979), 1275

Schatz v. Jockey Club Phase III, Ltd., 604 F.Supp. 537 (S.D.Fla.1985), 434

Schaumburg, Village of v. Jeep Eagle Sales Corp., 285 Ill.App.3d 481, 221 Ill.Dec. 679, 676 N.E.2d 200 (Ill.App. 1 Dist. 1996), 845

Schlafly v. Baumann, 341 Mo. 755, 108 S.W.2d 363 (Mo.1937), 114

Schneider v. Fromm Laboratories, 262 Wis. 21, 53 N.W.2d 737 (Wis.1952), 54

Schneider, State ex rel. v. City of Kansas City, 228 Kan. 25, 612 P.2d 578 (Kan. 1980), 1084

Schubach v. Silver, 461 Pa. 366, 336 A.2d 328 (Pa.1975), 108

Schwartz v. Adamson, 1999 WL 170676 (Minn.App.1999), 1315

Schwartz v. City of Flint, 92 Mich.App. 495, 285 N.W.2d 344 (Mich.App.1979), 932

Scott v. Greenville County, 716 F.2d 1409 (4th Cir.1983), 1165

Scott v. Polk County, 793 So.2d 85 (Fla. App. 2 Dist.2001), **1309**

Scott, Estate of v. Victoria County, 778 S.W.2d 585 (Tex.App.-Corpus Christi 1989), 575

Scurlock v. City of Lynn Haven, Fla., 858 F.2d 1521 (11th Cir.1988), 1054

Seabrook, Town of v. Tra-Sea Corp., 119 N.H. 937, 410 A.2d 240 (N.H.1979), 436

Sears, Roebuck & Co., People ex rel. Hoogasian v., 52 Ill.2d 301, 287 N.E.2d 677 (Ill.1972), 107

Seawall Associates v. City of New York, 544 N.Y.S.2d 542, 542 N.E.2d 1059 (N.Y. 1989), 932

Secret Desires Lingerie, Inc. v. City of Atlanta, 266 Ga. 760, 470 S.E.2d 879 (Ga.1996), **1237**

Seekonk, Town of v. Anthony, 339 Mass. 49, 157 N.E.2d 651 (Mass.1959), 376

Seidita v. Board of Zoning Appeals of City of Scranton, 41 Pa.Cmwlth. 340, 399 A.2d 156 (Pa.Cmwlth.1979), 1260

Seifred v. Zabel, 369 N.W.2d 571 (Minn. App.1985), 1172

Selby Realty Co. v. City of San Buenaventura, 109 Cal.Rptr. 799, 514 P.2d 111 (Cal. 1973), 251, 437

Select Western Lands, Inc., State ex rel. Anaya v., 94 N.M. 555, 613 P.2d 425 (N.M.App.1979), 443

Sellon v. City of Manitou Springs, 745 P.2d 229 (Colo.1987), **778,** 782

Semachko v. Hopko, 35 Ohio App.2d 205, 301 N.E.2d 560 (Ohio App. 8 Dist.1973), 185

Severns v. Union Pacific Railroad Co., 125 Cal.Rptr.2d 100 (Cal.App. 2 Dist. 2002), **115**

Seward Chapel, Inc. v. City of Seward, 655 P.2d 1293 (Alaska 1982), 1251

Sheffield Development Co. v. City of Troy, 99 Mich.App. 527, 298 N.W.2d 23 (Mich. App.1980), 1344

Shelton v. City of College Station, 754 F.2d 1251 (5th Cir.1985), 1002

Sher v. Leiderman, 181 Cal.App.3d 867, 226 Cal.Rptr. 698 (Cal.App. 6 Dist.1986), 93

Shifflett v. Baltimore County, 247 Md. 151, 230 A.2d 310 (Md.1967), 107

Shore, Appeal of, 524 Pa. 436, 573 A.2d 1011 (Pa.1990), 1141

Shubert Organization, Inc. v. Landmarks Preservation Com'n of City of New York, 166 A.D.2d 115, 570 N.Y.S.2d 504 (N.Y.A.D. 1 Dept.1991), 902

Signs, Inc. of Florida v. Orange County, Fla., 592 F.Supp. 693 (M.D.Fla.1983), 845

Sills v. Walworth County Land Management Committee, 254 Wis.2d 538, 648 N.W.2d 878 (Wis.App.2002), **175**

Simpson v. City of North Platte, 206 Neb. 240, 292 N.W.2d 297 (Neb.1980), 465

Sinar, State ex rel. Wisconsin Lutheran High School Conference v., 267 Wis. 91, 65 N.W.2d 43 (Wis.1954), **1256,** 1258

Sine v. Western Travel, Inc., 19 Utah 2d 61, 426 P.2d 9 (Utah 1967), 129

Skinner v. Henderson, 556 S.W.2d 730 (Mo. App.1977), 170

Sleepy Hollow Lake, Inc. v. Public Service Commission, 43 A.D.2d 439, 352 N.Y.S.2d 274 (N.Y.A.D. 3 Dept.1974), 874

Sloan v. City of Greenville, 235 S.C. 277, 111 S.E.2d 573 (S.C.1959), 45

Smith v. Fairchild, 193 Miss. 536, 10 So.2d 172 (Miss.1942), 79

Smith v. Independence Tax Increment Finance Com'n, 919 S.W.2d 292 (Mo.App. W.D.1996), 639

Smith, State v., 618 S.W.2d 474 (Tenn. 1981), 869

Smith v. Zoning Bd. of Appeals of Scituate, 347 Mass. 755, 200 N.E.2d 279 (Mass. 1964), 356

Smith v. Zoning Bd. of Appeals of Town of Greenwich, 227 Conn. 71, 629 A.2d 1089 (Conn.1993), **785, 798**

Smuczynski, People ex rel. Jackson & Morris v., 345 Ill.App. 63, 102 N.E.2d 168 (Ill.App. 1 Dist.1951), 460

Smyrna, City of v. Parks, 240 Ga. 699, 242 S.E.2d 73 (Ga.1978), 869

Society for Ethical Culture in City of New York v. Spatt, 68 A.D.2d 112, 416 N.Y.S.2d 246 (N.Y.A.D. 1 Dept.1979), 895

Solid Waste Agency of Northern Cook County v. United States Army Corps of Engineers, 531 U.S. 159, 121 S.Ct. 675, 148 L.Ed.2d 576 (2001), 254

Solomon v. City of Gainesville, 763 F.2d 1212 (11th Cir.1985), 846

Soon Hing v. Crowley, 113 U.S. 703, 5 S.Ct. 730, 28 L.Ed. 1145 (1885), 101

Sosa v. City of West Palm Beach, 762 So.2d 981 (Fla.App. 4 Dist.2000), 31

South Dakota Min. Ass'n, Inc. v. Lawrence County, 155 F.3d 1005 (8th Cir.1998), 1074

Southern Alameda Spanish Speaking Organization v. City of Union City, Cal., 424 F.2d 291 (9th Cir.1970), 1165

Southern Bell Tel. and Tel. Co. v. City of Aiken, 279 S.C. 269, 306 S.E.2d 220 (S.C.1983), 666

Southern Burlington County N.A.A.C.P. v. Mount Laurel Tp., 92 N.J. 158, 456 A.2d 390 (N.J.1983), 1217, 1231

Southern Burlington County N.A.A.C.P. v. Mount Laurel Tp., 67 N.J. 151, 336 A.2d 713 (N.J.1975), **1193,** 1201, 1208, 1217

Southern Cal. Edison Co. v. Bourgerie, 107 Cal.Rptr. 76, 507 P.2d 964 (Cal.1973), 157

Southern Nat. Bank of Houston v. City of Austin, 582 S.W.2d 229 (Tex.Civ.App.-Tyler 1979), 901

Southern Nevada Homebuilders Ass'n, Inc. v. City of North Las Vegas, 112 Nev. 297, 913 P.2d 1276 (Nev.1996), 462

Southern Nevada Homebuilders Ass'n, Inc. v. Las Vegas Valley Water Dist., 101 Nev. 99, 693 P.2d 1255 (Nev.1985), 462

South Fayette Tp. v. Commonwealth, 477 Pa. 574, 385 A.2d 344 (Pa.1978), 1125

South Gwinnett Venture v. Pruitt, 491 F.2d 5 (5th Cir.1974), 1339

South Gwinnett Venture v. Pruitt, 482 F.2d 389 (5th Cir.1973), 1339

South of Second Associates v. Georgetown, 199 Colo. 394, 609 P.2d 125 (Colo.1980), 887

South of Second Associates v. Georgetown, 196 Colo. 89, 580 P.2d 807 (Colo. 1978), **884**

Southview Associates, Ltd. v. Bongartz, 980 F.2d 84 (2nd Cir.1992), 258, 816

Southwestern Illinois Development Authority v. National City Environmental, L.L.C., 199 Ill.2d 225, 263 Ill.Dec. 241, 768 N.E.2d 1 (Ill.2002), 643

Spallone v. United States, 493 U.S. 265, 110 S.Ct. 625, 107 L.Ed.2d 644 (1990), 1208

Spann v. City of Dallas, 111 Tex. 350, 235 S.W. 513 (Tex.1921), 397

Sparks v. Douglas County, 127 Wash.2d 901, 904 P.2d 738 (Wash.1995), 465

Spindler Realty Corp. v. Monning, 243 Cal. App.2d 255, 53 Cal.Rptr. 7 (Cal.App. 2 Dist.1966), 436

Sprenger, Grubb & Associates, Inc. v. City of Hailey, 127 Idaho 576, 903 P.2d 741 (Idaho 1995), 348

Spring Valley Development, In re, 300 A.2d 736 (Me.1973), **719**

Sprint Spectrum L.P. v. Willoth, 176 F.3d 630 (2nd Cir.1999), **1045**

Spur Industries, Inc. v. Del E. Webb Development Co., 108 Ariz. 178, 494 P.2d 700 (Ariz.1972), **57, 64,** 69

S.S. Kresge Co. v. City of New York, 194 Misc. 645, 87 N.Y.S.2d 313 (N.Y.Sup. 1949), 536

St. Agatha Home for Children, People v., 416 N.Y.S.2d 577, 389 N.E.2d 1098 (N.Y. 1979), 1125

Stahl v. Upper Southampton Tp. Zoning Hearing Bd., 146 Pa.Cmwlth. 659, 606 A.2d 960 (Pa.Cmwlth.1992), 1141

Staninger v. Jacksonville Expressway Authority, 182 So.2d 483 (Fla.App. 1 Dist. 1966), 158

Stanton v. Town of Pawleys Island, 317 S.C. 498, 455 S.E.2d 171 (S.C.1995), 389

TABLE OF CASES

State v. _____ (see opposing party)
State, Dept. of Ecology v. Pacesetter Const. Co., Inc., 89 Wash.2d 203, 571 P.2d 196 (Wash.1977), 718
State ex rel. v. _____ (see opposing party and relator)
State Highway Commission, State ex rel. v. Johns, 507 S.W.2d 75 (Mo.App.1974), 103
State of (see name of state)
Steel Hill Development, Inc. v. Town of Sanbornton, 392 F.Supp. 1134 (D.N.H. 1974), 602
Steel Hill Development, Inc. v. Town of Sanbornton, 392 F.Supp. 1144 (D.N.H. 1974), 602
Steel Hill Development, Inc. v. Town of Sanbornton, 469 F.2d 956 (1st Cir. 1972), **597,** 602
Stegeman v. City of Ann Arbor, 213 Mich. App. 487, 540 N.W.2d 724 (Mich.App. 1995), 1115
Steuart Transp. Co. v. Ashe, 269 Md. 74, 304 A.2d 788 (Md.1973), 147
Stevens v. Town of Rye, 122 N.H. 688, 448 A.2d 426 (N.H.1982), 377
Stevenson v. Palmer, 223 Tenn. 485, 448 S.W.2d 67 (Tenn.1969), 371
Stewart B. McKinney Foundation, Inc. v. Town of Fairfield, 790 F.Supp. 1197 (D.Conn.1992), 1043
St. John's Evangelical Lutheran Church v. City of Hoboken, 195 N.J.Super. 414, 479 A.2d 935 (N.J.Super.L.1983), 1252
St. Joseph, City of v. Preferred Family Healthcare, Inc., 859 S.W.2d 723 (Mo. App. W.D.1993), 1127
St. Louis Poster Advertising Co. v. City of St. Louis, 249 U.S. 269, 39 S.Ct. 274, 63 L.Ed. 599 (1919), 845
St. Luke's German Evangelical Lutheran Church v. City of Rochester, 115 Misc.2d 199, 453 N.Y.S.2d 1012 (N.Y.Sup.1982), 536
Stoney-Brook Development Corp. v. Town of Fremont, 124 N.H. 583, 474 A.2d 561 (N.H.1984), 602
Stoney-Brook Development Corp. v. Town of Pembroke, 118 N.H. 791, 394 A.2d 853 (N.H.1978), 602
Stover, People v., 240 N.Y.S.2d 734, 191 N.E.2d 272 (N.Y.1963), **863,** 869
Stoyanoff, State ex rel. v. Berkeley, 458 S.W.2d 305 (Mo.1970), **855**
Strawn v. Canuso, 140 N.J. 43, 657 A.2d 420 (N.J.1995), 252
Strother, State ex rel. v. Chase, 42 Mo.App. 343 (Mo.App.1890), 459
Strykers Bay Neighborhood Council, Inc. v. City of New York, 695 F.Supp. 1531 (S.D.N.Y.1988), 1208
Sturges v. Town of Chilmark, 380 Mass. 246, 402 N.E.2d 1346 (Mass.1980), 602

Suffolk ex rel. Herbert, City of v. Board of Zoning Appeals for City of Suffolk, 266 Va. 137, 580 S.E.2d 796 (Va.2003), 549
Suffolk Housing Services v. Town of Brookhaven, 517 N.Y.S.2d 924, 511 N.E.2d 67 (N.Y.1987), 1208
Sugarman v. Village of Chester, 192 F.Supp.2d 282 (S.D.N.Y.2002), 847
Suitum v. Tahoe Regional Planning Agency, 520 U.S. 725, 117 S.Ct. 1659, 137 L.Ed.2d 980 (1997), **682,** 686
Sullivan v. Board of Sup'rs of Lower Makefield Tp., 22 Pa.Cmwlth. 318, 348 A.2d 464 (Pa.Cmwlth.1975), 1235
Sullivans Island, Town of v. Byrum, 306 S.C. 539, 413 S.E.2d 325 (S C.App. 1992), **411**
Summers v. Acme Flour Mills Co., 263 P.2d 515 (Okla.1953), 69
Sun Beach Real Estate Development Corp. v. Anderson, 98 A.D.2d 367, 469 N.Y.S.2d 964 (N.Y.A.D. 2 Dept.1983), **730**
Sundowner, Inc. v. King, 95 Idaho 367, 509 P.2d 785 (Idaho 1973), 87
Suntide Inn Motel, Oklahoma City, Matter of, 563 P.2d 125 (Okla.1977), 1085
Superior Outdoor Signs, Inc. v. Eller Media Co., 150 Md.App. 479, 822 A.2d 478 (Md. App.2003), 200
Supersign of Boca Raton, Inc. v. City of Fort Lauderdale, 766 F.2d 1528 (11th Cir.1985), 846
Support Ministries for Persons With AIDS, Inc. v. Village of Waterford, N.Y., 808 F.Supp. 120 (N.D.N.Y.1992), 1043, 1126
Surrick v. Zoning Hearing Bd. of Upper Providence Tp., 476 Pa. 182, 382 A.2d 105 (Pa.1977), 1134
Suttle v. Bailey, 68 N.M. 283, 361 P.2d 325 (N.M.1961), 180
Swain v. Winnebago County, 111 Ill. App.2d 458, 250 N.E.2d 439 (Ill.App. 2 Dist.1969), **647,** 651
Swan v. Inhabitants of the Town of Norway, 1989 Me.Super. Lexis 80 (Me.Sup. Ct.1989), 798
Swiss Village Associates v. Municipal Council of Wayne Tp., 162 N.J.Super. 138, 392 A.2d 596 (N.J.Super.A.D.1978), 1135
Sylvia Development Corp. v. Calvert County, Md., 48 F.3d 810 (4th Cir.1995), 1001

Tahoe–Sierra Preservation Council, Inc. v. Tahoe Regional Planning Agency, 535 U.S. 302, 122 S.Ct. 1465, 152 L.Ed.2d 517 (2002), 565, 571, 737, **964**
Tahoe–Sierra Preservation Council, Inc. v. Tahoe Regional Planning Agency, 34 F.Supp.2d 1226 (D.Nev.1999), 738
Tarrytown, Village of v. Planning Board of Village of Sleepy Hollow, 292 A.D.2d

617, 741 N.Y.S.2d 44 (N.Y.A.D. 2 Dept. 2002), 1301

Tate v. Miles, 503 A.2d 187 (Del.Supr.1986), 1343

Tatum v. Clackamas County, 19 Or.App. 770, 529 P.2d 393 (Or.App.1974), 1276

Taub v. City of Deer Park, 882 S.W.2d 824 (Tex.1994), 955

Tax Increment Financing Com'n of Kansas City v. J.E. Dunn Const. Co., Inc., 781 S.W.2d 70 (Mo.1989), 639

Taxpayers Ass'n of Weymouth Tp., Inc. v. Weymouth Tp., 80 N.J. 6, 364 A.2d 1016 (N.J.1976), 1172

Taylor v. Melton, 130 Colo. 280, 274 P.2d 977 (Colo.1954), 144

Taylor v. Shaw and Cannon Co., 236 Va. 15, 372 S.E.2d 128 (Va.1988), 1141

Taylor v. State, Dept. of Rehabilitation and Correction, 43 Ohio App.3d 205, 540 N.E.2d 310 (Ohio App. 10 Dist.1988), 1085

Taylor Home of Charlotte Inc. v. City of Charlotte, 116 N.C.App. 188, 447 S.E.2d 438 (N.C.App.1994), 1126

Taylor, Mich., City of, United States v., 798 F.Supp. 442 (E.D.Mich.1992), 1126

Teachers Ins. and Annuity Ass'n of America v. City of New York, 603 N.Y.S.2d 399, 623 N.E.2d 526 (N.Y.1993), 896

Tennessee Manufactured Housing Ass'n v. Metropolitan Government of Nashville, 798 S.W.2d 254 (Tenn.Ct.App.1990), 1141, 1152

Tentindo v. Locke Lake Colony Ass'n, 120 N.H. 593, 419 A.2d 1097 (N.H.1980), 130

Texas Antiquities Committee v. Dallas County Community College Dist., 554 S.W.2d 924 (Tex.1977), 901

Thelen, State ex rel. v. City of Missoula, 168 Mont. 375, 543 P.2d 173 (Mont. 1975), 1125

Thodos v. Shirk, 248 Iowa 172, 79 N.W.2d 733 (Iowa 1956), 145

Thomas Cusack Co. v. City of Chicago, 242 U.S. 526, 37 S.Ct. 190, 61 L.Ed. 472 (1917), 845

Thornton, City of v. Board of County Com'rs of Adams County, 42 Colo.App. 102, 595 P.2d 264 (Colo.App.1979), 1098

Thornton, State ex rel. v. Hay, 254 Or. 584, 462 P.2d 671 (Or.1969), 824

Thorpe v. Rutland & B.R. Co., 27 Vt. 140 (Vt.1854), 24

Three Guys Real Estate v. Harnett County, 122 N.C.App. 362, 469 S.E.2d 578 (N.C.App.1996), 460

383 Madison Associates v. City of New York, 193 A.D.2d 518, 598 N.Y.S.2d 180 (N.Y.A.D. 1 Dept.1993), 895

Tilles Inv. Co. v. Town of Huntington, 547 N.Y.S.2d 835, 547 N.E.2d 90 (N.Y.1989), 326

T & M Homes, Inc. v. Mansfield Tp., 162 N.J.Super. 497, 393 A.2d 613 (N.J.Super.L.1978), 1346

Toll Bros., Inc. v. Township of West Windsor, 173 N.J. 502, 803 A.2d 53 (N.J.2002), **1208**

Toll Bros., Inc. v. West Windsor Tp., 312 N.J.Super. 540, 712 A.2d 266 (N.J.Super.A.D.1998), 574

Tolman, People v., 110 Cal.App.3d Supp. 6, 168 Cal.Rptr. 328 (Cal.App.Super.1980), 869

Topanga Press, Inc. v. City of Los Angeles, 989 F.2d 1524 (9th Cir.1993), 1240

Towles v. District of Columbia Bd. of Zoning Adjustment, 578 A.2d 1128 (D.C. 1990), 1251

Town of (see name of town)
Township of (see name of township)

Toys R Us v. Silva, 654 N.Y.S.2d 100, 676 N.E.2d 862 (N.Y.1996), **380**

Traveler Real Estate, Inc. v. Cain, 160 A.D.2d 1214, 555 N.Y.S.2d 217 (N.Y.A.D. 3 Dept.1990), 376

Trawalter v. Schaefer, 142 Tex. 521, 179 S.W.2d 765 (Tex.1944), 431

Triplett Grille, Inc. v. City of Akron, 816 F.Supp. 1249 (N.D.Ohio 1993), 1240

Tropic Seas, Inc., United States v., 887 F.Supp. 1347 (D.Hawai'i 1995), 1173

Trudeau, State v., 139 Wis.2d 91, 408 N.W.2d 337 (Wis.1987), 766

Tucker v. Mecklenburg County Zoning Bd. of Adjustment, 148 N.C.App. 52, 557 S.E.2d 631 (N.C.App.2001), 407

Tuftonboro, Town of v. Lakeside Colony, Inc., 119 N.H. 445, 403 A.2d 410 (N.H. 1979), 443

Tulk v. Moxhay, 2 Phillips 774, 41 Eng.Rep. 1143 (English High Court of Chancery, 1848), 135

Tureman v. Ketterlin, 304 Mo. 221, 263 S.W. 202 (Mo.1924), 79

Turner v. City of Spokane, 39 Wash.2d 332, 235 P.2d 300 (Wash.1951), 106

Turner v. County of Del Norte, 24 Cal. App.3d 311, 101 Cal.Rptr. 93 (Cal.App. 1 Dist.1972), 765

Turner v. England, 628 S.W.2d 213 (Tex. App.-Eastland 1982), 164

Turnpike Realty Co. v. Town of Dedham, 362 Mass. 221, 284 N.E.2d 891 (Mass. 1972), 765

Tuxedo Homes, Inc. v. Green, 258 Ala. 494, 63 So.2d 812 (Ala.1953), 459

Udell v. Haas, 288 N.Y.S.2d 888, 235 N.E.2d 897 (N.Y.1968), 279, 325, 326

Underwood v. Webb, 544 S.W.2d 187 (Tex. Civ.App.-Waco 1976), 187

Ungar v. State, 63 Md.App. 472, 492 A.2d 1336 (Md.App.1985), 575

Unification Theological Seminary v. City of Poughkeepsie, 201 A.D.2d 484, 607

TABLE OF CASES

liii

N.Y.S.2d 383 (N.Y.A.D. 2 Dept.1994), 1115

Union City v. Southern Pac. Co., 261 Cal. App.2d 277, 67 Cal.Rptr. 816 (Cal.App. 1 Dist.1968), 106

Union Elec. Co. v. City of Crestwood, 499 S.W.2d 480 (Mo.1973), **872**

United Artists' Theater Circuit, Inc. v. City of Philadelphia, 535 Pa. 370, 635 A.2d 612 (Pa.1993), 896

United Artists Theater Circuit, Inc. v. City of Philadelphia, Philadelphia Historical Com'n, 528 Pa. 12, 595 A.2d 6 (Pa.1991), 896

United Artists Theatre Circuit, Inc. v. Township of Warrington, PA, 316 F.3d 392 (3rd Cir.2003), 996

United States v. _____ (see opposing party)

United States Postal Service v. Town of Greenwich, Conn., 901 F.Supp. 500 (D.Conn.1995), 1085

Uni-Worth Enterprises, Inc. v. City of Cleveland, Mississippi, 412 F.Supp. 349 (N.D.Miss.1976), 1237

Unlimited v. Kitsap County, 50 Wash.App. 723, 750 P.2d 651 (Wash.App. Div. 2 1988), 465

Unruh v. City of Asheville, 97 N.C.App. 287, 388 S.E.2d 235 (N.C.App.1990), 887

USCOC of Virginia RSA# 3 v. Montgomery County Bd. of Supervisors, 245 F.Supp.2d 817 (W.D.Va.2003), 1053

Valatie, Village of v. Smith, 190 A.D.2d 17, 596 N.Y.S.2d 581 (N.Y.A.D. 3 Dept. 1993), 388

Vale Dean Canyon Homeowners Ass'n v. Dean, 100 Or.App. 158, 785 P.2d 772 (Or.App.1990), 462

Valkanet v. City of Chicago, 13 Ill.2d 268, 148 N.E.2d 767 (Ill.1958), **1262**

Van Emburg, Commonwealth v., 467 Pa. 445, 359 A.2d 178 (Pa.1976), 108

Vangellow v. City of Rochester, 190 Misc. 128, 71 N.Y.S.2d 672 (N.Y.Sup.1947), 536

Van Sciver v. Zoning Bd. of Adjustment of Philadelphia, 396 Pa. 646, 152 A.2d 717 (Pa.1959), 371

Varnado v. Southern University at New Orleans, 621 So.2d 176 (La.App. 4 Cir. 1993), 1084

Vartelas v. Water Resources Commission, 146 Conn. 650, 153 A.2d 822 (Conn. 1959), 765

Vella v. Town of Camden, 677 A.2d 1051 (Me.1996), 317

Ventures in Property I v. City of Wichita, 225 Kan. 698, 594 P.2d 671 (Kan.1979), 571

Video Aid Corp. v. Town of Wallkill, 628 N.Y.S.2d 18, 651 N.E.2d 886 (N.Y.1995), 487

Village of (see name of village)

Village of Bayside Bd. of Trustees, State ex rel. Lake Drive Baptist Church v., 12 Wis.2d 585, 108 N.W.2d 288 (Wis.1961), **1244**

Village of Oakwood, State ex rel. Chiavola v., 886 S.W.2d 74 (Mo.App. W.D.1994), 251

Villager Pond, Inc. v. Town of Darien, 56 F.3d 375 (2nd Cir.1995), 1222

Village Square No. 1, Inc. v. Crow-Frederick Retail Ltd. Partnership, 77 Md.App. 552, 551 A.2d 471 (Md.App.1989), 474

Vincent v. Salt Lake County, 583 P.2d 105 (Utah 1978), 102

Virginia Beach, City of v. Virginia Land Inv. Ass'n No. 1, 239 Va. 412, 389 S.E.2d 312 (Va.1990), 332

Visionquest Nat., Ltd. v. Board of Sup'rs of Honey Brook Tp., Chester County, 524 Pa. 107, 569 A.2d 915 (Pa.1990), 1259

Visionquest Nat., Ltd. v. Pima County Bd. of Adjustment Dist. No. 1, 146 Ariz. 103, 703 P.2d 1252 (Ariz.App. Div. 2 1985), 1259

Vlahos Realty Co. v. Little Boar's Head Dist., 101 N.H. 460, 146 A.2d 257 (N.H. 1958), 371

Voyeur Dorm, L.C. v. City of Tampa, Fla., 265 F.3d 1232 (11th Cir.2001), **1240**

Waeckerle v. Board of Zoning Adjustment, 525 S.W.2d 351 (Mo.App.1975), 364

Wagner, United States v., 930 F.Supp. 1148 (N.D.Tex.1996), 1166

Wait v. City of Scottsdale, 127 Ariz. 107, 618 P.2d 601 (Ariz.1980), 1344

Wakelin v. Town of Yarmouth, 523 A.2d 575 (Me.1987), 371

Walden Federal Sav. and Loan Ass'n v. Village of Walden, 212 A.D.2d 718, 622 N.Y.S.2d 796 (N.Y.A.D. 2 Dept.1995), 228

Walker v. State of North Carolina, 262 F.Supp. 102 (W.D.N.C.1966), 1345

Walls v. Planning and Zoning Commission of Town of Avon, 176 Conn. 475, 408 A.2d 252 (Conn.1979), 521

Wal-Mart Stores Inc. v. Planning Bd. of Town of North Elba, 238 A.D.2d 93, 668 N.Y.S.2d 774 (N.Y.A.D. 3 Dept.1998), 651, 797, 798

Walz v. Town of Smithtown, 46 F.3d 162 (2nd Cir.1995), 610

Wambat Realty Corp. v. State, 393 N.Y.S.2d 949, 362 N.E.2d 581 (N.Y.1977), 620

Ward v. Bennett, 583 N.Y.S.2d 179, 592 N.E.2d 787 (N.Y.1992), 536

Warner, State ex rel. v. Hayes Inv. Corp., 13 Wash.2d 306, 125 P.2d 262 (Wash. 1942), 54

Warren County Probation Ass'n v. Warren County Zoning Hearing Bd., 50 Pa. Cmwlth. 486, 414 A.2d 398 (Pa.Cmwlth. 1980), 1125

Washington, City of v. Warren County, 899 S.W.2d 863 (Mo.1995), 1084

Waste Management of New York, LLC v. Doherty, 267 A.D.2d 464, 700 N.Y.S.2d 494 (N.Y.A.D. 2 Dept.1999), 1301

Watchung Lake v. Mobus, 196 A. 223 (N.J.Sup.1938), 54

Waterfront Estates Development, Inc. v. City of Palos Hills, 232 Ill.App.3d 367, 173 Ill.Dec. 667, 597 N.E.2d 641 (Ill. App. 1 Dist.1992), 855

Weatherby Lake, State ex rel. Westside Development Co., Inc. v., 935 S.W.2d 634 (Mo.App. W.D.1996), 251

Webster v. Star Distributing Co., Inc., 241 Ga. 270, 244 S.E.2d 826 (Ga.1978), 159

Weinstein v. Tariff, 356 Mass. 738, 255 N.E.2d 595 (Mass.1970), 187

Weslaco, City of v. Carpenter, 694 S.W.2d 601 (Tex.App.-Corpus Christi 1985), 442

West Alameda Heights Homeowners Ass'n v. Board of County Com'rs of Jefferson County, 169 Colo. 491, 458 P.2d 253 (Colo.1969), **181**

West Beach Marina, Ltd. v. Erdeljac, 94 S.W.3d 248 (Tex.App.-Austin 2002), 1315

Westchester, County of v. Town of Greenwich, Conn., 76 F.3d 42 (2nd Cir.1996), 93

Western Land Equities, Inc. v. City of Logan, 617 P.2d 388 (Utah 1980), 436

Western Presbyterian Church v. Board of Zoning Adjustment of District of Columbia, 862 F.Supp. 538 (D.D.C.1994), 1252

West Greenwich, Town of v. Stepping Stone Enterprises, Ltd., 122 R.I. 132, 416 A.2d 659 (R.I.1979), 108

Westhampton, Inc. v. Kehoe, 227 Ga. 642, 182 S.E.2d 430 (Ga.1971), 151

West Hill Baptist Church v. Abbate, 261 N.E.2d 196 (Ohio Com.Pl.1969), 170

Westside Development Co., Inc., State ex rel. v. Weatherby Lake, 935 S.W.2d 634 (Mo.App. W.D.1996), 251

Westwood Forest Estates, Inc. v. Village of South Nyack, 297 N.Y.S.2d 129, 244 N.E.2d 700 (N.Y.1969), 608

Wetstone v. Cantor, 144 Conn. 77, 127 A.2d 70 (Conn.1956), 54

White Plains, City of v. Ferraioli, 357 N.Y.S.2d 449, 313 N.E.2d 756 (N.Y. 1974), **1120**

Wicker Park Historic Dist. Preservation Fund v. Pierce, 565 F.Supp. 1066 (N.D.Ill.1982), 1167

Wieland, State ex rel. Saveland Park Holding Corp. v., 269 Wis. 262, 69 N.W.2d 217 (Wis.1955), **850,** 870

Wigginess Inc. v. Fruchtman, 482 F.Supp. 681 (S.D.N.Y.1979), 1240

Wildlife Wonderland, Inc., In re, 133 Vt. 507, 346 A.2d 645 (Vt.1975), 263

Wilkins v. City of San Bernardino, 29 Cal.2d 332, 175 P.2d 542 (Cal.1946), 317

William Aldred's Case, 9 Co.Rep. 57b, 77 Eng.Rep. 816 (1610), 54

William C. Haas & Co., Inc. v. City and County of San Francisco, Cal., 605 F.2d 1117 (9th Cir.1979), 932

William J. (Jack) Jones Ins. Trust v. City of Fort Smith, Ark., 731 F.Supp. 912 (W.D.Ark.1990), 465

Williams v. Town of Hilton Head Island, S.C., 311 S.C. 417, 429 S.E.2d 802 (S.C. 1993), 667

Williamson Pointe Venture v. City of Austin, 912 S.W.2d 340 (Tex.App.-Austin 1995), 436

Willistown Tp. v. Chesterdale Farms, Inc., 462 Pa. 445, 341 A.2d 466 (Pa.1975), 1134

Willowbrook, Village of v. Olech, 528 U.S. 562, 120 S.Ct. 1073, 145 L.Ed.2d 1060 (2000), **1002,** 1004

Wilmington Hospitality, L.L.C. v. New Castle County ex rel. New Castle Department of Land Use, 788 A.2d 536 (Del.Ch.2001), **1311**

Wilson v. Handley, 119 Cal.Rptr.2d 263 (Cal.App. 3 Dist.2002), **80**

Wilson v. Key Tronic Corp., 40 Wash.App. 802, 701 P.2d 518 (Wash.App. Div. 3 1985), 70

Wilson v. McHenry County, 92 Ill.App.3d 997, 48 Ill.Dec. 395, 416 N.E.2d 426 (Ill.App. 2 Dist.1981), 323

Wilsonville, Village of v. SCA Services, Inc., 86 Ill.2d 1, 55 Ill.Dec. 499, 426 N.E.2d 824 (Ill.1981), 70

Wiltwyck School for Boys, Inc. v. Hill, 14 A.D.2d 198, 219 N.Y.S.2d 161 (N.Y.A.D. 2 Dept.1961), 1259

Winter v. Hollingsworth Properties, Inc., 777 F.2d 1444 (11th Cir.1985), 434

Wisconsin Lutheran High School Conference, State ex rel. v. Sinar, 267 Wis. 91, 65 N.W.2d 43 (Wis.1954), **1256,** 1258

Wolf v. City of Ely, 493 N.W.2d 846 (Iowa 1992), 236

Wolff v. Mooresville Plan Com'n, 754 N.E.2d 589 (Ind.App.2001), 521

Wolper v. City Council of City of Charleston, 287 S.C. 209, 336 S.E.2d 871 (S.C. 1985), 639

Wood v. City of Madison, 260 Wis.2d 71, 659 N.W.2d 31 (Wis.2003), 520

Woodcrest Investments Corp. v. Skagit County, 39 Wash.App. 622, 694 P.2d 705 (Wash.App. Div. 1 1985), 251

Woodland Beach Property Owners' Ass'n v. Worley, 253 Md. 442, 252 A.2d 827 (Md. 1969), 128, 129

Woodmoor Imp. Ass'n v. Brenner, 919 P.2d 928 (Colo.App.1996), 190

Wright v. City of Lakewood, 43 Colo.App. 480, 608 P.2d 361 (Colo.App.1979), 1275

Wright Development v. City of Wellsville, 608 P.2d 232 (Utah 1980), 461

TABLE OF CASES

Wrigley Properties, Inc. v. City of Ladue, 369 S.W.2d 397 (Mo.1963), 1097

Yanow v. Seven Oaks Park, Inc., 11 N.J. 341, 94 A.2d 482 (N.J.1953), 1260

Ybarra v. Town of Los Altos Hills, 503 F.2d 250 (9th Cir.1974), 602, 1165, **1181**

Yick Wo v. Hopkins, 118 U.S. 356, 6 S.Ct. 1064, 30 L.Ed. 220 (1886), 101

Young v. American Mini Theatres, Inc., 427 U.S. 50, 96 S.Ct. 2440, 49 L.Ed.2d 310 (1976), 1240

Young v. City of Roseville, 78 F.Supp.2d 970 (D.Minn.1999), 847

Young v. St. Martin's Church, 361 Pa. 505, 64 A.2d 814 (Pa.1949), 80

Younger, People ex rel. v. County of El Dorado, 96 Cal.Rptr. 553, 487 P.2d 1193 (Cal.1971), **271**

Zanin v. Iacono, 198 N.J.Super. 490, 487 A.2d 780 (N.J.Super.L.1984), 251

Zavala v. City and County of Denver, 759 P.2d 664 (Colo.1988), 1119

Zelvin v. Zoning Bd. of Appeals of Town of Windsor, 30 Conn.Supp. 157, 306 A.2d 151 (Conn.Com.Pl.1973), 1135

Zoning Bd. of Appeals of Greenfield v. Housing Appeals Committee, 15 Mass. App.Ct. 553, 446 N.E.2d 748 (Mass.App. Ct.1983), 1232

*

CASES AND MATERIALS ON
LAND USE
Sixth Edition

*

Chapter I

THE MANY FACETS OF LAND USE LAW

The study of land use cuts across a number of disciplines and—unlike many legal subjects—deals with a broad range of non-legal problems involving many professions, businesses and players. For example, land use law is important to planners, civil engineers, architects, landscape architects, bankers and other lenders, a wide array of government agencies at every level of government, and an ever-growing multitude of public interest groups. For lawyers and law students, land use problems involve constitutional and administrative law, environmental law, property law, contract law, and other areas of law. The resolution of problems and disputes involving the development of land are rarely simple adversary battles. Almost every dispute that arises about the use of land is polycentric, i.e., one that implicates a number of discrete interests and has multiple centers and multiple parties or stakeholders with very different agendas.

The complexities mentioned also make the subject matter of land development and use a very exciting course of study. Sorting out and solving land use problems exposes the players in the "land use game" to very basic social and political dramas that touch the lives of many people in both urban and rural settings. To understand the "big picture" of land use one must look at many small and discrete portions of the subject matter. This book attempts to provide material on what can only be called the many facets of land use law. We begin by looking at several doctrines of common law that still play an important role in land use, such as nuisance law, the law of waste, and the law relating to private agreements creating servitudes on parcels of land. These private law devices can and do play an important part in regulating land usage and development. Then the book turns to the vast and much more pervasive area of public law—statutes, ordinances, and administrative regulations governing the use of land. These positive law devices can only be understood in the context of the sources of regulatory authority and negative limitations placed on them by constitutional provisions, state and federal. We also offer to students of land use law a look at alternative methods of resolving everyday disputes, such as mediation, arbitration, and how the political process at the state and local government levels operate to deal with the issues.

To grasp the subtleties and complexities of land use problems an outline or flow chart of a typical land development project can provide some insights as to how and when such a project intersects with the material covered in this book. We can use as our example a 40 acre parcel of land located near the western edge of a growing small city and follow the conversion of this piece of land into a residential subdivision containing a number of dwelling units. We will assume that the land is owned by an individual who lives in an old farmhouse on the land and that many years ago it was a farm and more recently used to grow hay and graze some livestock. Once the land was outside the city limits but it was annexed into the city several years ago along with several other parcels to the north, south and east. Most of those other parcels now contain single-family dwellings at a density of three houses per acre. One of the other pieces of land has a small shopping center and some low-rise apartment buildings as well as some single-family houses. We will meet the players in the land use game as we follow the process of development. Note that not all of the problems, issues, and hurdles discussed will impact every such development, but many if not most of them can.

STEP 1. The Farmer and the Developer.

Ms. Developer is in the business of developing and building residential subdivisions. She may live in the city or she may be someone from a different community (more on this later). Having noticed that the city is experiencing significant growth in a westerly direction she undertakes to do a market analysis of the potential for developing a subdivision of fifty or sixty houses. Concluding that the market for homes in the $300,000–$400,000 range is pretty good she looks for land. [Note that this market analysis is a prediction based on many more or less amorphous factors such as population trends in the recent past, industrial and business growth, national and regional economic trends, future prospects for the economy, the possibility of war, pestilence, and political change.] Ms. Developer locates the 40–acre farm and makes a decision that this parcel would be worth developing. Her research indicates that current residential development is getting near to this farm and that city infrastructure is not too remote (streets, water, sewer). Also, the local school district has planned a new elementary school somewhere in the western part of the city. A visit to City Hall indicates that the land in question is currently zoned A–1 a designation that allows agricultural uses and very low density residential uses, and has been zoned for such use ever since it was annexed. The City has a policy of zoning all newly annexed land as A–1. The City's long-range comprehensive land use plan shows that residential uses are planned for that part of the City.

The Farmer is unhappy with the growth of new residential subdivisions in the vicinity of his property. In the past few years his real estate tax assessments have risen and the county assessor has raised the assessment because of nearby development. Also, some of the new residents in fancy houses a quarter mile from the farm have been complaining to the City about strong smells coming from the farm when the wind is from the west. Maybe the time has come to think about selling and retiring.

Our Developer and Farmer are about to meet.

STEP 2. What sort of transaction?

When Ms. Developer (or her agent who may be a realtor in the City) first contacts Farmer and the selling price for the farm is negotiated, the parties verbally agree on $10,000 per acre, or a total price of $400,000. Sometimes a negotiation might offer a price based on the number of buildable lots that a city will allow in a development proposal. At this point, several possibilities emerge. If the Developer has sufficient capital, she may buy the farm outright. Another type of deal could be an offer of an option to pay $25,000 for each housing unit allowed by the City, at the time the development is approved. This could mean more money for Farmer, but a longer wait for a payout. Another possibility is an offer to enter into an arrangement with Farmer to set up a separate entity to develop the land, such as a limited liability company (LLC) or a limited liability partnership (LLP) or a corporation. Farmer would convey the farm to the entity and participate in the profits of the development. This sort of deal, to make Farmer a partner or participant means lower costs at the front end of the development, as the land becomes Farmer's contribution to the entity. This can be significant because Developer knows she (or the entity) will have to borrow considerable amounts of money to prepare the land for any subdivision. On the other hand, once the subdivision is built out, if Farmer is to receive a portion of the profits, Developer's profits might be very slim. This sort of analysis might dictate the percentage of profits for both sides. Farmer must look at this deal from the perspective of how long he must wait to realize any real money from the development (the build-out of the subdivision may take six or seven or more years), whether he assumes any of the risk of failure beyond the land, and whether he wants to become a "businessperson."

Whichever of the options are selected, Ms. Developer must look ahead to the process of land preparation and local government approvals of the development. If Developer is not very well known in the community, or is an "outsider" she will probably want Farmer to be around to seek the most important local approval—a zoning change. If Farmer is not part of the development entity, Developer's purchase of the land might proceed with an option to purchase, contingent upon Farmer securing a zoning change. Why? Cities, especially smaller ones, are friendlier to local residents than to outsiders in zoning requests. Farmer can play the part of a "long-term community resident" who wants to sell the farm and retire and has a buyer, if he can get the land rezoned.

After working through the nature of the transaction, we can proceed on the assumption that Farmer has no desire to become a "partner" in the development and the farm is now in the hands of Developer. She borrowed most of the money from the lending institution, putting as little of her money into the venture as possible. Also, Developer has consulted Attorney to set up a limited liability company to develop the property. Choosing a name for the development, Sunrise Woods Subdivision, Sunrise Woods, LLC is now ready to begin the development process.

STEP 3.   What kind of development?

Developer must make an initial determination of what kind of development to pursue. Should the 40 acres be devoted to single-family homes only? The public street that will provide access to the land is a collector street that will carry more traffic in the future. If the local school district locates the new elementary school along that same street, perhaps even across from her development, that street will carry a great deal of traffic. Developer might consider that the portion of the farm along that street would be less desirable for up-scale homes in the $350,000 category. Maybe a mixed-use development would be better, locating some low-rise luxury condominiums along the street frontage, with the parking in the rear so that the owners would have some insulation from noise. She could also consider a barrier of fencing and vegetation and back yards for single-family homes near the street. Which way to go involves the juggling of several pros and cons. A mixed-use approach would require approval of zoning authorities and might bring out opposition from homeowners in nearby subdivisions who would disparage condominiums as a threat to their property values. Is there a market for condominiums in this area? Would the condos turn away some potential buyers for single-family homes in the subdivision? Should developer perhaps build toward the back of the farm and postpone any decisions about the area along the street? Is there a danger that putting off the decision may harden opposition to the construction of condos at a later time from residents within the subdivision? Suppose Ms. Developer contacts the school board to find out what sites they are considering for the new school. She discovers that the board is thinking about three locations, one of which is right across the street from the farm. A final decision will not be made for a year or so. This information prompts Developer to try for a mixed-use development. She could build the condos first, and use the profits to help finance the houses, thereby reducing her interest load with the bank. A quick market analysis indicates that some condos and amenities like a pool and tennis court could attract young couples and affluent singles, so Developer pursues this plan. Fortunately for Ms. Developer the City has a zoning category that seems just right for Sunrise Woods. PUD, or Planned Unit Development District will allow for mixed types of housing and seems to provide for a great deal of development flexibility. However, Developer sees a few drawbacks. She must present a very detailed plan and if it is approved she cannot deviate from the plan without approval by the Planning Commission. Also, the PUD provisions specify a greater setback from adjacent properties, 200 feet on the north, east and west sides of her land. Those setbacks would eat up several acres. Developer sees more benefits than burdens and decides to seek approval for a PUD rather than two different zoning districts on the farm.

STEP 4. Laying out the subdivision.

At this point Developer makes another financial investment and engages professional help to plan the subdivision. She consults a local civil engineering firm and explains the type of development she envisions. The engineers are knowledgeable about the local government requirements for subdivisions, such as minimum lot sizes and street requirements, utility installations (water, sewer, gas, electricity, telephone), drainage, and a host of other required installations that must be approved by the city and paid for by the developer. Engineer studies the land and works with Developer to draw a rough plan of the layout, showing internal streets and lots and open space. The natural features of the land may inform this preliminary drawing. When Developer and Engineer agree on the essential features and layout a slightly more finished drawing may be prepared. In this City, like most, the subdivision approval process allows a developer to present a "concept plat" that depicts the general idea of the subdivision to the local officials. This saves much expense because if the concept is not acceptable, then money is saved by not surveying lots, streets, and other features of the subdivision. In our case, this first meeting with local planning officials—an informal work session—offers an opportunity to see if the city is amenable to a mixed-use subdivision with condos and houses. To make her concept look good, Developer hires an architect to do a rendering of the concept showing some nice looking condos clustered around a large pool, with some nice looking single-family houses close by. The architect may also have access to previously built similar developments and can provide photographs or slides of up-scale mixed-use projects like that planned by Developer. Even if the concept is accepted informally, all that means is that Developer can proceed to the next step, preparation of a preliminary plat, and initiation of the rezoning process. That next step will be the first inkling to neighbors and nearby property owners that the farm is to be developed. Also, Developer at this time may take her concept and plan to the lending institution to obtain approval of a line of credit for construction loans and other necessary subdivision costs, especially installation of infrastructure—streets, water and sewer, sidewalks.

STEP 5. Preparation of preliminary plat.

Now Ms. Developer must invest a significant amount of money in the preparation of a preliminary plat of her proposed subdivision. Also, preparation must be made to seek a rezoning of the property to allow a Planned Unit Development on the land. Most developers will seek the zoning changes first in order to save money in the event the preliminary plat would have to be revised if the zoning is not approved. However, our Developer decides to work on both at the same time hoping to shorten the approval process and get started sooner on the development, and because she has to have a detailed plan for the PUD, this is no great burden.

The Engineer will work on the plat. The land must be surveyed and proposed lots must be precisely shown. Also, this plat must show land contours, streets within the subdivision, utility easements, and many other details that will be important to the City Planning Commission. In the course of this process Developer may be confronted with problems related to the physical nature of the property. For example, Engineer discovers while surveying the contours that a portion of the land is located in a previously mapped flood plain and may be classified as "wetland." Even if no standing water is visible on that part of the farm, any change in the elevation of that area would require a permit from a federal agency. Likewise, a stand of mature trees covering 8 acres along the north side of the farm might be covered by a city "tree ordinance" that requires a special permit for cutting and removing trees. The land use ordinances of City define residential densities in single-family zoning districts as no more than 4 units per acre. Developer learns early in the platting process that the potential maximum of 160 dwelling units on the 40–acre farm is illusory. Some of the land—especially the stand of trees and the possible wetland—must be subtracted from the development potential. Those problems may also dictate how the internal streets within the subdivision must be laid out to provide proper access to all lots.

Developer may also call in the architect to help design a layout that will be attractive to potential home buyers, maximize the natural features of the land, make the proposed condos fit in nicely with the single-family homes, and make other suggestions for the subdivision. Architect, Engineer, and Developer work together and come up with a plan that places an entrance to the subdivision close to the center of the south frontage along the collector street with an attractive fence (brick pillars and wood) along the street. The entrance would be "gated" and landscaped, following current national trends in upscale subdivisions. Past the entrance, the plat shows a curvilinear street circling through the subdivision with several cul-de-sacs branching off each to have six lots. Just opposite the entrance the plat shows a recreation area with a large swimming pool and clubhouse and several tennis courts. Four low-rise buildings each containing four condos would be located between the street frontage and the curving street. Open space would be preserved around the cul-de-sacs and a nature trail would connect the open space and the stand of trees. This plan would allow for 36 single-family houses and 16 condominiums. However, Developer knows that the approval process for a subdivision plat involves a lot of negotiation with the City Planning Office and the Planning Commission, so she may adopt a strategy of showing more units on slightly smaller lots, so she will have something to "give" to avoid demands by City that she feels would detract from the development.

Developer must now calculate whether the plan would be profitable, predicting the total development costs and the selling price of the proposed units. Obviously, many "unknowns" enter into this calculation. How long will it take to obtain all the approvals and permits? Will the cost of building materials rise in the near future? Will interest rates go up or down (for both future buyers and for Developer)? Will the market stay hot in this part of town? Where will that new school be located? Will property taxes go up or down?

As the preliminary plat takes shape, Developer may consult again with the lending institution to confirm its enthusiasm for the plan. At the same time, Developer prepares for her request to have the property rezoned to allow for her proposal. Engineer might take the lead in this process, or Developer might ask the Attorney who handled the land transaction to help shepherd the rezoning. Sensing that there might be opposition to the condos in the subdivision, Developer decides that her team should include Attorney and Architect as well as Engineer.

STEP 6. Rezoning.

Developer visits City Hall and files an application to rezone the property from A–1, Agricultural to PUD, with single-family and multi-family residential uses. She pays the required fee and is given a set of instructions that include the duty to notify all adjacent property owners of the rezoning request by certified mail. Also, the City will post a sign on the property that is clearly visible from the street. The sign will include a copy of the rezoning request and the time and date for a public hearing before the Planning Commission. Developer may also be required to place a legal notice in the local newspaper conveying the same information. Developer asks the City Planning Office to schedule a subdivision plat submission for Sunrise Woods Subdivision shortly after the hearing on the rezoning petition.

The rezoning petition is to be heard about 30 days after the application is made. This provides some time for the public to take notice of the petition and for members of the Planning Commission to visit the property and the neighborhood. The planning commissioners are local citizens who are volunteers appointed by the City Council. The Commission is empowered by state statute and local ordinance to study land uses, adopt and recommend a comprehensive plan (sometimes called a Master Plan) to the council, to recommend ordinances governing the zoning and development of land, to conduct hearings on requests for zoning changes and to make recommendations on rezonings to the council. A few weeks after making the application, Developer goes to the City Planning Office to ask whether many inquiries from the public have come in. She wants to get a "feel" for potential opposition regarding the condominiums. She learns that a citizens group committed to open space preservation and growth restrictions may oppose Sunrise Woods. She also learns that a dozen telephone calls came in to the office.

Developer decides that she had better be prepared for some vocal opposition at the Planning Commission meeting. She wants Architect and Attorney to be at the meeting and orders renderings and other visual materials that will illustrate the high quality of the proposed units. Also, she might survey people in the neighborhood to explain the project and perhaps find a few supporters of it who will promise to attend the meeting and speak in favor. Developer knows from past experience that rezoning hearings can be contentious and political; she also knows that the Planning Commission only makes a recommendation that then goes forward to the City Council, the legislative body that has sole authority to pass an ordinance amending the zoning map. So, even if the commission is favorably inclined to her proposal and recommends the rezoning, the opponents will have an opportunity to raise all their objections a second time before the City Council. Nevertheless, a favorable recommendation from the commission will carry a lot of weight, and Developer wants to make a very good case for the rezoning. In this City PUDs are treated as a rezoning and must be approved by an ordinance. In some cities, planning commissions can approve a PUD without a change in the underlying zoning category (in our example, the A–1 Agricultural Zone would stay in place and a PUD would be approved). Under either scenario the land would have to be platted and the plat approved.

The day of the Planning Commission hearing arrives and Ms. Developer and her team present the plan. Planning commissioners may have several questions for Developer. One, which troubles some commissioners is that there is only one entrance to Sunrise Woods and that could present traffic flow problems. Developer answers by saying that Sunrise Woods would only have 50 to 60 dwelling units when completed, far less than a "maximum" development of 160 units, and that planning another entrance would mean that residents of Sunrise Woods would drive through other adjacent subdivisions on the east and west to the detriment of those residents, and they would be driving through Sunrise Woods. The Planning Commission then opens the floor to the public and a lively interchange ensues between members of the audience, Ms. Developer, and commissioners. As expected, the presence of condos in the neighborhood concerns many people. Ms. Developer's reassurances that the four condominium structures would be only two stories, expensive, and limited to 16 condos, do not calm the fears. Some speakers state that owners of the condos could rent them out to strangers and neighborhood stability would decline. Ms. Developer tellingly answers by pointing out that owners of single-family houses often rent their houses and further that if people are willing to purchase homes in Sunrise Woods even though condos are part of the development, why should people in nearby subdivisions be concerned. Developer also notes that under the PUD designation she will have to provide a set of covenants protecting the open space and housing densities in Sunrise Woods and that the City would have enforcement powers under the restrictions.

After everyone has had a chance to speak, the public hearing is closed and the commissioners discuss the proposal and vote in an open setting. Ms. Developer is pleased that the commission votes to approve the PUD with only one dissenting vote. A strong recommendation will go to the City Council at its next meeting. Some of the unhappy neighbors attend the City Council meeting and voice their objections to the Sunrise Woods PUD, but there are others whom Ms. Developer has rounded up who speak in favor of the project. The City Council members, seeing no political revolution in the offing, vote for the PUD and cover themselves politically by stating that since the planning commissioners supported it, the City ought to do likewise.

STEP 7. Subdivision plat approval.

Now that the zoning is taken care of, the development process begins to move forward. Engineer prepares a preliminary plat for Planning Commission approval. What is shown on that plat is dictated by the City ordinance that deals with subdivisions. In most cities, that includes precise location of lots, streets, utility easements, land contours and other vital information, including a vicinity map that shows where the subdivision can be found in the City. After submitting the preliminary plat to the City Planning Office a plat review meeting is scheduled far enough in the future to allow for the participation of several different players. The City Engineer studies the plat for compliance with City requirements for lot size, street widths, curb, gutter, and utility lines. The City Street Superintendent also checks the plat for compliance with the Master Street Plan, and that the proposed street names do not conflict with any streets in the City. The local gas, electric and telephone company are notified to check the plat for proper size and location of utility easements. Developer's Engineer may attend these reviews to answer questions and make any necessary changes on the plat.

This review process may take a month to complete. Finally, the plat must be approved by the Planning Commission in a public meeting. Usually, no notification is required to be given to neighbors, but the agenda of the commission is often published in the local newspaper, and some neighbors might notice an agenda item for Sunrise Woods plat approval and come to the meeting to raise once again any concerns they may harbor. The citizens group may monitor plat approvals and several representatives of the group show up to make known that the group opposes the "march of development" at the western edge of City.

In most cases approval of the preliminary plat is pro forma; however the Planning Commission may insist on some revisions. In our case, the Commission wants Developer to "stub out" a street from the curvilinear street to the western edge of the property, so that when a future subdivision is developed to the west of Sunrise Woods, a future street can provide for better traffic management. Developer has little choice.

She can protest, but if the commission is insistent she will have to do what they ask. Attorney informs her that there is no appeal to the City Council from such administrative decisions and no legal basis for a challenge exists. So, that "stub" of a future street is drawn on the plat. Also, the commissioners insist upon a storm drain running along the western edge of the property from the stubbed street to the collector street. Developer protests at the expense and also that when the property to the west is developed, that subdivider will reap the benefit of the drain without having to pay for it. The commissioners agree that the City will pay half the cost of the drain and Developer will pay the other half. When the property to the west is platted, the City will collect half the cost from the new subdivider. Another demand is that Developer create and record conservation easements to protect the wetland area and wooded area in perpetuity in favor of the City. Finally, the commissioners ask for a twenty foot wide strip of land to be dedicated to the City across the entire southern frontage of the land for the purpose of future street widening (the commissioners are concerned that if the new school is built across from Sunrise Woods the collector street will have to be widened, and it would be wise to secure land for the widening at no cost to the City through dedication on the plat). Ms. Developer is very unhappy about this demand and asks Attorney for his opinion. He informs her that courts are not very favorable to requests for dedication in cases where the problem to be addressed is not caused by the developer; however, challenging the City on this could take up to a year or more. Developer decides the costs of challenging the demand are too high and she needs to start building houses as soon as possible, so she has the widening strip designated on the plat as a dedication to City.

Upon approval of the preliminary plat with the changes, Engineer must prepare a final plat. The final plat is the one that is filed in the County Recorder office. The final plat is prepared on special material, in a prescribed size, and must be signed by a number of City officials. After the final plat is recorded, Developer can begin to sell lots and start production.

From the date of the land purchase until recordation of the final plat of Sunrise Woods, 8 months have gone by, and Developer has paid out a lot of money, but has not seen one cent of income. From this moment on, expenses will escalate very rapidly.

STEP 8. The development begins.

Developer decides to begin Sunrise Woods by building one of the condominium structures and one model home on the cul-de-sac nearest the entrance to the subdivision. At the same time a marketing program must begin. Developer decides to work through a local realtor in advertising the condos and homes. The realtor can help work up a feature story in the Sunday newspaper about the homes and also try to get the model home in the next "Parade of Homes" run by the newspaper. By starting at the front part of the subdivision, Developer can put off the cost of paving the entire curvilinear street and the other cul-de-sacs.

Also, the sewer and water connections will not have to run as far from the collector street. Once sales begin to mount money will become available to complete installation of the rest of the infrastructure. The City, like most, requires developers to post a bond for completion of the streets, water and sewer connections, recognizing that an entire subdivision is rarely built at once.

Developer has Architect design the condos and the model home and then, since she has no building crew of her own, arranges with a building contractor to construct the condominium building and the home. Some developers contract with a group of different builders, giving them the exclusive right to build and sell homes in the subdivision. The contract may pass some of the risk to the builders by providing that the builders agree to purchase lots on a fixed time schedule; in an expanding market builders like this arrangement because it protects them from lower quality houses nearby. Another similar arrangement is to form a list of preferred builders and give homebuyers freedom to choose from those on the list.

Developer also consults with Attorney about creating and recording the restrictive covenants. One decision to be made is whether to have a separate set of covenants for the condos and for the single-family homes along with two separate owner associations. Most developers currently use the community association and a declaration of covenants and restrictions to protect the common interest community from undesirable alterations of structures, unsightly fences and other activities detrimental to the integrity of the community. The community association is a "governing body" for the development, empowered to prevent violations of the restrictions and to collect funds to maintain areas such as the swimming pool, tennis courts, nature trails, and other open space. Ms. Developer decides to have one association and treat all of Sunrise Woods as one common interest community. She also wants Attorney to write the covenants in such a manner that she as owner of all unsold lots and condos can have a controlling interest in governing the community, at least until the majority of units are sold.

Aggressive marketing during the first phase of construction, which will take 4 to 6 months, is essential to Developer so that sales will run ahead of construction and a positive cash flow will occur.

STEP 9. Sunrise Woods waxes and wanes.

A development of 52 housing units takes a long time. After two years, Sunrise Woods has six completed houses, one condominium structure fully sold and another begun. Many things can happen to slow or stop the momentum. Suppose a major employer in the City closes down and the housing market suffers; sales in Sunrise Woods may also slow down. Maybe a few "For Sale" signs appear in Sunrise Woods and Ms. Developer is now sort of competing with her own former buyers. On the other hand, suppose the local school board finally decides to build the new elementary school right across the road from Sunrise Woods.

Developer can use this to advertise that children living in the subdivision can walk to and from school; that might spur sales.

If sales slow down too much, Developer may try to raise money by selling a few lots to another builder, even though she will lose control of the design of the houses. Another risk in the early years is that a buyer might want a house on a lot near the back of the subdivision, close to the wooded area, thus forcing Developer to do a lot of paving and run sewer and water to that area prematurely. Development does not usually proceed in a neat and orderly manner.

After a few more years more people in the City are speaking out against "urban sprawl", and are joining a loose coalition of citizen groups that want the Planning Commission to curb growth toward the west; they are lobbying for a moratorium on the issuance of any new building permits until a "slow growth" plan can be adopted and implemented. Ms. Developer joins with a number of other developers to condemn such ideas. After all, the new school is a magnet for residential development and the State is planning to improve a road about a mile west of the current city limits; that will also spur growth. Even though Sunrise Woods is not threatened by the movement to slow or stop westward growth (growth controls might even increase the value of lots in Sunrise Woods), Ms. Developer feels that any interference with natural market forces for development is bad for developers.

Although the City does not change its development ordinances to restrain growth, the pressure of increased population results in the need to upgrade the sewage treatment facilities. The cost of a new treatment plant is beyond the current budget. The Planning Commission recommends the imposition of an "impact fee" on all new residential construction to go toward a new sewage treatment plant. This fee will be scaled to the square footage of new dwelling units and will be collected at the same time building permits are issued. Ms. Developer is worried that she will have to raise the prices of her units and does not like the idea of becoming a "tax collector" for the City. She asks Attorney whether she would be covered by the new impact fee or would be "grandfathered" in because Sunrise Woods was previously approved. Attorney informs Developer that the fee would apply to every new building permit, and that the only way to avoid it would be to secure building permits for undeveloped lots prior to the effective date of the impact fee ordinance. Developer feels like she is being put in a difficult situation. Buying building permits so far in advance of actual construction is costly and unrealistic, so her only option is to either pass the entire cost of the impact fee on to new buyers, or absorb some of the fee herself. She joins a group of developers and lobbies against the new impact fee, arguing that it is really a hidden tax on new homebuyers. The City, however, passes the impact fee ordinance. Council members state publicly that new residents are the "cause" of the problem of sewage treatment and they should pay for the new plant.

Sunrise Woods is now 5 years old. Thirty-three single-family homes and twelve condominiums are built. The development will probably take a few more years to build out, but Ms. Developer is now in a position to look for another property to develop. After counting up all her expenses for Sunrise Woods and the sales figures, she has not made a great deal of profit. [The National Association of Homebuilders 1997 Cost of Doing Business Study pegged the average net profit of builders nationwide at 4.4% before taxes; the average profitability for the top 25 percent of builders was 10.2%.] However, she feels that she has made an important contribution to the City by providing good quality residential living to a number of people, and considers herself a "community builder" as well as a developer. By setting up a separate company for each development she insulates her personal funds from failure of any one subdivision and obtains maximum leverage to engage in the risky business of subdivision development. Meanwhile the political climate in the city has changed. There are now three organized no-growth groups dedicated to preventing any similar rezonings and high density subdivisions. The groups are lobbying for the city council to pass a number of local laws to protect the environment, prevent open space disappearance, and reduce traffic congestion. Developers of the remaining undeveloped parcels are contacting neighbors and concerned stakeholders much earlier in the development process and using mediation to identify affected interests early and to accommodate them in the proposals taken to local land use boards in the first instance.

* * *

The Sunrise Woods scenario is fairly typical. Of course, many subdivisions are much smaller in scope and some much larger, but the problems and process of converting raw land into residential developments are pretty much the same everywhere. As we progress through the materials in this book you will encounter in much greater detail all of the issues raised in the Sunrise Woods story. Some of the questions that might have come to mind as you were reading the scenario are mentioned here, so that you will recognize them later in this course:

1. Where does the city get legal authority to adopt a master plan and zoning ordinance?

2. Under what circumstances can property be rezoned?

3. Don't neighbors have some right to settled expectations about land uses in areas where they have bought homes?

4. What are the legal differences between the local board that amends the zoning ordinance and the one that approves development proposals such as Developer's subdivision request? Is there any significance in these differences?

5. Where are the rules found that the city followed in rezoning and approving the subdivision of Sunrise Woods?

6. What is the role of the land use lawyer in this development process? At what point should Developer consult with her land use attorney?

7. Were the rezoning and the subdivision approval in conformance with the master plan?

8. Were all the required procedural steps followed by the city council and the commission?

9. Once Sunrise Woods is approved, do the neighbors have standing to challenge the approval in court?

10. Would a no-growth citizens association have standing?

11. What could a municipality do to preserve agricultural land and open space if it wanted to?

12. What strategies could municipalities employ to manage growth and development?

13. What standards do the courts use to evaluate challenges of rezoning decisions made by legislative bodies?

14. Are those standards the same as those used to evaluate administrative approvals of subdivision applications?

15. If the rezoning was not awarded or the subdivision not approved, would the developer have any viable legal challenge to bring? What property and due process rights do developers have and how can they be violated in the land use approval process?

16. What do you make of Developer's negotiating process and strategy? Did she involve the neighbors soon enough and give them a meaningful enough role? Note how she responded to some of their concerns. What are the dangers in involving them too much? Not enough? What is the lawyer's role in counseling developer clients regarding these matters?

17. If the covenants recorded with the subdivision and distributed to every purchaser set up an association to enforce the covenants, along with the power to pass rules governing life in the subdivision, what do you think about this sort of "private government"?

Chapter II

THE COMMON LAW FOUNDATIONS UNDERLYING PUBLIC REGULATION OF LAND USE

Today, we deal with land use problems mostly through means of statutes and ordinances and through regulations developed by governmental bodies to which such authority has been entrusted. But this modern methodology should not obscure the fact that there are a number of historic, common law or equitable devices employed not by legislative or regulatory bodies but by private agreements or by courts as a means of controlling the activities of individuals with respect to the use of land. These arose in response to a different situation than that which most commonly troubles us today.

These judge-made concepts were developed to govern situations in which the private rights of one individual impinged upon the rights of others. These were "after the fact" adjudications, for the most part, which determined in a limited context a dispute between individuals who possessed or asserted conflicting rights or in some instances between a single individual and either a large segment of individuals or the public in general. The aims and purposes involved were different from those that surround land use planning and regulation today. The ordered development of a geographical area and the various attributes of social engineering were not present. As in all lawsuits, there were sharply focused issues, and the object was to determine certain facts, apply the law and thereby settle the dispute in question. Nonetheless, the result was to control in a negative way the use of land by an individual or individuals. X could not do something on or with a piece of land because it would interfere with the rights of Y in one way or another in a situation in which law or equity accorded paramount importance to the rights of Y.

Certainly reliance upon judicial interference is not an effective way to promote the rational development of a given geographical area. Yet this form of regulation and of limitation upon the uses to which a particular piece of land might be put is important—not only as an historic method of control—but also because these devices remain available today, although ordinances, statutes or regulations may render such actions unnecessary where a public nuisance results or where the activity in question amounts to a violation of the public interest as expressed in one of the ways mentioned. In many situations, however, the public interest is not at stake, and it is purely a matter of individual versus individual.

Before examining the common law devices that support private regulation of land uses, a brief overview of the origins and modern meaning of the term "property rights" and the history of regulation is appropriate.

SECTION 1. THE NATURE OF PROPERTY RIGHTS

Students of the law learn early on that when we speak of property we refer not to the *res*, the tangible or intangible thing involved, but rather to the rights of persons in the *res*. The English common law as it developed in the centuries following the Norman conquest of 1066 was concerned with disputes that adjudicated superior rights to possess land or other property. Ownership as against the entire world was rarely the concern of the common law courts. This situation resulted in the idea that multiple interests could be created in the same parcel of land. Much of the growth of modern real estate law rests on this idea. Wealth has been based on the imaginative invention of new interests in a piece of land. A modern office building in a city may be viewed in terms of such multiple interests as management leases, ground leases, operating leases and other interests, all the basis of lending and mortgaging. Our study of the common law of property, however, begins with an assumption that rights in land are awarded, conveyed, enfoeffed, or distributed by gift, devise, or intestate succession. For purposes of understanding land use restrictions we want to look more closely at the origins of private property rights.

A. THE ORIGINS OF AND JUSTIFICATIONS FOR PRIVATE PROPERTY

Prior to the age of exploration and colonization, private property was based on customary usage in most primitive societies. An excellent account of how primitive societies viewed property can be found in William Seagle, The History of Law (Tudor Publishing Co., 1946; first published as The Quest for Law, Alfred A. Knopf, 1941) pp. 50–59. In more advanced Western societies, first occupancy was the origin of private property. Occupancy was justified by a natural law outlook based upon Biblical authority wherein the Creator endowed mankind with all the fruits of the Earth for the benefit of man; first discovery or first occupancy was akin to following the maxim that first in time is first in right. In the "Dark Ages" following the decline of the Roman Empire, individual security concerns led to institutions that gave the possessors of land protection in return for a security interest in the land, ultimately leading to Feudalism. Much of western Europe was "governed" by some variant of feudal principles, the most important being possession of land under a reciprocal set of feudal duties, flowing in both directions, *i.e.*, the vassal owed his lord certain duties and the lord had duties toward the vassal-tenant.

As European explorers sailed the seas and "discovered" new lands, first occupancy became a problem as the new lands were populated by indigenous peoples. The explorers and subsequent colonizers claimed the new lands either by arguing that they were "conquerors" having defeated the population, or that the natives were heathens or pagans and thus not entitled to "property rights." The Catholic Church in the sixteenth century attempted to curb these claims by sending priests and others to convert natives to Christianity, and many of the excesses of the colonizers were actively opposed by the Church—without much success as disease and slavery decimated native populations. An excellent account of this period can be found in Robert A. Williams Jr., The American Indian in Western Legal Thought (Oxford Univ. Press 1990).

Gradually, by the seventeenth century—when North America was being colonized—a new theory of property rights emerged. John Locke, who was engaged to prepare a charter for the company that sought to settle what is now South Carolina, confronted the issue of how the company could claim rights in lands occupied by Indians. He rationalized that the settlers had superior rights to possess the land because the natives were merely transients, hunters and gatherers who did not invest labor in clearing the land, planting, tending, and harvesting crops, or building permanent settlements. This was coupled with the idea that private property was a "natural" right. Thus was born, in the early eighteenth century, the labor-natural rights theory of private property, a theory that heavily influenced Thomas Jefferson and other founders of our constitutional republic. The labor theory was much more convenient than Biblical theory in dealing with Indian tribes on the North American continent, even though Indian wars and treaties were common throughout the century. Locke's theory was adopted by the Supreme Court in the "pirated news" case, *International News Service v. Associated Press*, 248 U.S. 215, 236, 39 S.Ct. 68, 63 L.Ed. 211 (1918), where the defendant was copying the plaintiff's news bulletins posted in public venues and selling the news to its own subscribers. The Court used the labor theory to set the foundation for the law of unfair competition, stating:

> And although we may and do assume that neither party has any remaining property interest as against the public in uncopyrighted news matter after the moment of its first publication, it by no means follows that there is no remaining property interest in it as between themselves. For, to both of them alike, news matter, however little susceptible of ownership or dominion in the absolute sense, is stock in trade, to be gathered at the cost of enterprise, organization, skill,

labor, and money, and to be distributed and sold to those who will pay money for it, as for any other merchandise. Regarding the news, therefore, as but the material out of which both parties are seeking to make profits at the same time and in the same field, we hardly can fail to recognize that for this purpose, and as between them, it must be regarded as quasi property, irrespective of the rights of either as against the public.

The labor theory of private property sufficed to explain the origin of property rights as the American republic grew and prospered, especially as that theory was modified by the famous utilitarian philosopher, Jeremy Bentham, who demystified property rights and rejected natural rights theory by means of his aphorism that "Property and Law are born together and die together." Bentham recognized that rights in property can be created by legislatures and courts, and are not natural rights or some beneficence from a Heavenly being. When the age of industrialism exploded in the nineteenth century, Americans and others realized that Locke's labor theory needed modification as capitalism and labor began to clash. Theoretically, we accepted what has come to be called the "social utility" theory of property, looking to the social benefits of creating or destroying rights in property and weighing the claims of competing interests. To put these philosophical ideas into current context, consider, for example, disputes in the field of intellectual property—record companies versus Napster; software companies with so-called "shrink-wrap licenses" versus end-product consumers. Many of the land use controversies encountered later in these materials involve social policy considerations such as environmental protections, social egalitarianism, and other conflicts that engage people and property in a large variety of contexts. For more on the origins of private property rights, see Felix S. Cohen, Dialogue on Private Property, 9 Rutgers L.Rev. 357 (1954).

B. THE ORIGINS OF AND JUSTIFICATION FOR PUBLIC REGULATION

Engrained in Anglo–American juristic thought is the notion that in an open society, each person has a right by virtue of being a person to acquire and hold real estate. This fundamental principle is no weaker today than it was in the time of Locke and Jefferson. But the right to acquire and hold title to land does not necessarily carry with it the right to *use* it in any and every way. At this point, the rights of adjoining landowners and the broader rights of the public in general enter the picture. It would be a mistake, however, to infer that a conflict of interests is the inevitable result or that the posture of the collective mass of the people acting through public agencies is essentially hostile to the rights of individual property owners. This picture of the "public interest" as being in conflict with the property rights of individual citizens is itself a misleading and largely erroneous one, as we shall see. But the first essential to an understanding of the situation is the realization that as civilized society emerged and took shape, certain limitations also developed in the natural course of events, and these limitations applied as much to land as to other aspects of life.

Richard T. Ely, a political economist, in his work Property and Contract in Their Relation to the Distribution of Wealth (N.Y.: The Macmillan Co., 1914), said:

> Furthermore, *Property is exclusive in its nature and not absolute*. A phrase is found in Roman law which, as a definition of property, is misleading. The phrase is, "*Dominium est jus utendi et abutendi re.*" Some have said that it means that the right of property carries with it the right to use or to abuse a thing, and so it has been actually claimed that property is the right to use or misuse a thing, and that the right of property carries with it the right to make a bad use of things. But such an idea comes from bad translation. *Abutendi* means to use up or consume a thing, not to abuse it * * *.
>
> The right of property is an exclusive right, but it has never been an absolute right. In so far as the right of property existed it was an exclusive right, that is, it excluded others; but it was not a right without limitations or qualifications. Notice the distinction between *exclusive* and *absolute*.
>
> The truth is, there are two sides to private property, *the individual side and the social side*. The social side of property finds illustration in the right of eminent domain and in the right of taxation. If there were no such thing as the social side of private property, how could the right of taxation exist? * * *
>
> So also with the right of eminent domain. It is utterly incompatible with the absolute right of private property. *Moreover, this social side of private property is not to be regarded as something exceptional*. On the contrary, it is an essential part of the institution itself. It is just as much a part of private property, as it exists at the present time, as the individual side is a part of it. The two necessarily go together, so that if one perishes the other must perish. The social side limits the individual side, and as it is always present there is no such thing as absolute private property. An absolute right of property, as the great jurist, the late Professor von Ihering says, would result in the dissolution of society.

Vol. 1, pp. 135–137.

In this connection, long before the first faint light of English civilization, the earliest code of Roman law, the Twelve Tables, provided:

> Whoever sets a hedge around his land shall not exceed the boundary; in the case of a wall, he shall leave one foot; in the case of a house, two feet. If a grave or pit, the required depth. If a well, a path, an olive or fig tree, nine feet. Finally, whoever plants other trees shall leave a space of five feet between [his] property and his neighbor's. If there is litigation about boundaries, five feet. (As quoted in Treasury of Law 71 (Nice ed. 1964)).

Limitations on the use of rural and urban land have been grist for the legislative mill for much, if not all, of our legal history. Through the centuries that saw the development of the common law in England dozens, if not hundreds, of statutes placed restrictions on the use of land. When highwaymen were abroad robbing innocent travelers, Parliament enacted a statute requiring property owners to cut down the high hedges along roadways to keep miscreants from "lurking to do hurt." When London suffered the great fire in the seventeenth century, the first set of comprehensive building regulations was enacted in 1666 so that rebuilt London would be safer; a large administrative bureaucracy was established to examine building plans and issue permits. See T. F. Reddaway, The Rebuilding of London After the Great Fire (London: Edward Arnold & Co., 1940).

In colonial times on American shores land use regulations and limitations on the rights of owners were rampant. In the Dutch colonies in what is now New York, immigrants held very fragile title to land that was allotted to them; emerging communities could reallocate land freely. The English colonies also imposed affirmative and negative limitations on private property. In John F. Hart, Colonial Land Use Law and its Significance for Modern Takings Doctrine, 109 Harv. L. Rev. 1252 (1996) the author catalogs a wide variety of colonial laws and rules that regulated the use of land. In Kenney, Forest Legislation in America Prior to March 4, 1789 (Cornell Exp. Sta. Bull., 1916), the author reported at 361:

> * * * The writer soon found that forestry and timber problems had claimed the attention of colonial legislative bodies on many occasions during the seventeenth century, and that hundreds of such laws had been enacted previous to the establishment of the National Government. Long before the Federal Constitution became effective—on March 4, 1789—the legislatures of most of the colonies had realized that forest fires constituted a great menace to the welfare of the people, and modern trespass laws and regulations of the lumber industry have their forerunners in the legislation of the seventeenth and eighteenth centuries. The influence of American forests in the development of the spirit of opposition to Great Britain that culminated in the Revolution of 1776 has not been given its due importance by political and economic writers, nor has it been known that certain developments of forest regulation in the colonies were strikingly anticipatory of recent movements in national forest policy.

An excellent summary of some controls on land use in New York City, spanning three centuries, may be found in McGoldrick et al., Building Regulation in New York City (1944). The introduction to this volume states, at 3–4:

> One need not go very far into the countryside to find areas where one may build his home according to his own notions. But even the earliest experience in tiny New Amsterdam showed that fires from one person's badly built or neglected chimney could menace the

homes and lives of his neighbors, and that, if people were to live in compact communities, some surrender of the individual's right to do as he pleases was essential to the protection of the lives and health of all.

And so we find that three centuries in New York have produced a body of rules regarding buildings scattered among thousands of pages of statutes, local laws and departmental regulations and that there are upwards of ten thousand public employees all or part of whose time is devoted to enforcing them. The development of these rules has been the product of experience, frequently harsh experience, which has demonstrated the need for such rules if life, health and property in a compact community are to be safe. * * *

Also see Theodore Steinberg, God's Terminus: Boundaries, Nature, and Property on the Michigan Shore, 37 Am. J. Legal Hist. 65 (1993).

Although our society thrived, in part, on the inherited English notion of absolute property rights, we know that no such concept really existed because government has always regulated the use of property to some extent. Nevertheless, the concept was an important element in judicial formulation of the concept of the police power, which was regarded as justification for public intervention with property to the extent that governmental action stayed within certain bounds and did not cross that invisible line representing a "taking" of private property for public use. Defining that line has been the central problem in defining the limits of land use regulation.

In the nineteenth century, American courts began to struggle with the problem of reconciling private property rights with the emerging social interests that demanded some sort of land use regulation. Some of the dimensions of this history are illustrated by the following excerpts:

Blackstone, Commentaries on the Law of England * 138:

> III. The third absolute right, inherent in every Englishman, is that of property: which consists in the free use, enjoyment, and disposal of all his acquisitions, without any control or diminution, save only by the laws of the land. * * *
>
> So great moreover is the regard of the law for private property, that it will not authorize the least violation of it; no, not even for the general good of the whole community. If a new road, for instance, were to be made through the grounds of a private person, it might perhaps be extensively beneficial to the public; but the law permits no man, or set of men to do this without consent of the owner of the land. In vain may it be urged, that the good of the individual ought to yield to that of the community; for it would be dangerous to allow any private man, or even any public tribunal, to be the judge of this common good, and to decide whether it be expedient or no. Besides the public good is in nothing more essentially interested, than in the protection of every individual's private rights, as modelled by the municipal law. In this and similar cases the legislature alone can,

and indeed frequently does interpose, and compel the individual to acquiesce. But how does it interpose and compel? Not by absolutely stripping the subject of his property in an arbitrary manner; but by giving him a full indemnification and equivalent for the injury thereby sustained. The public is now considered as an individual, treating with an individual for an exchange. All that the legislature does is to oblige the owner to alienate his possessions for a reasonable price; and even this is an exertion of power, which the legislature indulges with caution, and which nothing but the legislature can perform.

In Charles River Bridge v. Proprietors of Warren Bridge, 36 U.S. (11 Pet.) 420, 9 L.Ed. 773 (1837), Chief Justice Taney identified and recognized the concept of the police power. In this foundation case, the Charles River Bridge had been chartered by the state to operate a toll bridge; subsequently, the state authorized another company to construct and operate a free bridge over the Charles River in close proximity to the plaintiff's bridge. Although the plaintiff's charter did not contain an exclusive grant, it was argued that the state had impaired the charter. Taney, in denying the claim,stated:

"[T]he legislature in the very law extending the charter, asserts its rights to authorize improvements over Charles river which would take off a portion of the travel from this bridge and diminish its profits; and the Bridge Company accept the renewal thus given, and thus carefully connected with this assertion of the right on the part of the state. Can they, when holding their corporate existence under this law, and deriving their franchises altogether from it; add to the privileges expressed in their charter an implied agreement, which is in direct conflict with a portion of the law from which they derive their corporate existence? Can the legislature be presumed to have taken upon themselves an implied obligation, contrary to its own acts and declarations contained in the same law? It would be difficult to find a case justifying such an implication, even between individuals; still less will it be found where sovereign rights are concerned, and where the interests of a whole community would be deeply affected by such an implication. It would, indeed, be a strong exertion of judicial power, acting upon its own views of what justice required, and the parties ought to have done; to raise, by a sort of judicial coercion, an implied contract, and infer it from the nature of the very instrument in which the legislature appear to have taken pains to use words which disavow and repudiate any intention, on the part of the state, to make such a contract.

"Indeed, the practice and usage of almost every state in the Union, old enough to have commenced the work of internal improvement, is opposed to the doctrine contended for on the part of the plaintiffs in error. Turnpike roads have been made in succession, on the same line of travel; the later ones interfering materially with the profits of the first. These corporations have, in some instances, been utterly ruined by the introduction of newer and better modes of transportation, and travelling. In some cases, rail roads have rendered the turnpike roads on the same line of travel so entirely useless, that the franchise of the turnpike corporation is not worth preserving. Yet in none of these cases have the corporations supposed that their privileges were invaded, or any contract violated on the part of the state. Amid the multitude of cases which have occurred, and have been daily occurring for the last forty or fifty years, this is the first instance in which such an implied contract has been contended for, and this Court called upon to infer it from an ordinary act of incorporation, containing nothing more than the usual stipulations and provisions to be found in every such law. The absence of any such controversy, when there must have been so many occasions to give rise to it, proves that neither states, nor individuals, nor corporations, ever imagined that such a contract could be implied from such charters. It shows that the men who voted for these laws, never imagined that they were forming such a contract; and if we maintain that they have made it, we must create it by a legal fiction, in opposition to the truth of the fact, and the obvious intention of the party. We cannot deal thus with the rights reserved to the states; and by legal intendments and mere technical reasoning, take away from them any portion of that power over their own internal police and improvement, which is so necessary to their well being and prosperity."

Although this case is usually studied for its approach to the impairment of contract clause of the Constitution, its preferment of the social good over what the bridge proprietors thought were their vested property rights is what informs our understanding of private property rights. Justice Story's lengthy dissent in the case is based on the labor theory; he was outraged that the investors in the bridge took great risks investing labor and capital in construction of the bridge, risks that no sane investor would take without some understanding that the resulting property rights would be protected from competition.

For a discussion of the Charles River Bridge case, see Stanley I. Kutler, Privilege and Creative Destruction: The Charles River Bridge Case (New York: J. B. Lippincott Co., 1971; paperback reprint, Baltimore: Johns Hopkins Press, 1990). Also see, Wright, The Relation of Law in America to Socio–Economic Change, 28 Ark.L.Rev. 440, 471–474 (1975), and Munn v. Illinois, 94 U.S. (4 Otto) 113, 24 L.Ed. 77 (1876).

Ely, Property and Contract in their Relation to the Distribution of Wealth, pp. 218–221 (1914):

As in the United States all property is held subject to regulations, restrictions, and burdens under the police power, it is appropriate to quote from opinions of the United States Supreme Court giving the views of that high tribunal in noteworthy cases. In the celebrated Slaughter House Cases (1872) we find the following said of the police power:

The power is, and must be from its very nature, incapable of any very exact definition or limitation. Upon it depends the security of the social order, the life and health of the citizen, the comfort of an existence in a thickly populated community, the enjoyment of private and social life, and the beneficial use of property. As says another eminent judge, " * * * Persons and property are subjected to all kinds of restraints and burdens in order to secure the general comfort, health, and prosperity of the State. Of the perfect right of the legislature to do this, no question ever was, or *upon acknowledged general principles, ever can be made*, so far as natural persons are concerned." (Thorpe v. Rutland & Burlington R.R. Co., 27 Vt. 139, 1854).

This is clearly stated by Chief Justice Lemuel Shaw: "All property is acquired and held under the tacit condition that it shall not be used so as to injure the equal rights of others, or to destroy or greatly impair the public rights and interest of the community; under the maxim of the common law, *Sic utere tuo ut alienum non laedas.*" [Commonwealth v. Tewksbury, 11 Metcalf (Mass.), 55 (1846), at p. 57.]

* * *

Still more noteworthy is the opinion of the court as expressed by Mr. Justice Holmes in Noble State Bank v. Haskell [Noble State Bank v. Haskell, 219 U.S. 104, 31 S.Ct. 186, 188, 62 L.Ed. 1006 (1911), p. 111]

The police power extends to all the great public needs. It may be put forth in aid of what is sanctioned by usage, *or held by the prevailing morality or the strong and preponderant opinion to be greatly and immediately necessary to the public welfare.*

Now there is more in this police power than regulation of property relations and contractual relations. But there is no difficulty except where property and economic relations are concerned. No one objects to general benevolence—to doing good without cost—so when we consider police power, its essence is the interpretation of property, and when we consider the real essence of the police power as found in the leading American decisions we find that it is consistent with this concept. *It is that power of the courts committed to them by American Constitutions whereby they must shape property and contract to existing social conditions by settling the question of how far social regulations may, without compensation, impose burdens on property.* It seeks to preserve the satisfactory development of the individual and social sides of private property and thus to maintain a satisfactory equilibrium between them. And it is noteworthy that compensation may be given when property is destroyed under the police power. Tuberculous cows are killed in Wisconsin, but a limited compensation is granted to the owner in pursuance of sound public policy, for it lessens the temptation to conceal disease and it diffuses the loss.

Regulation depends on the past—on what was done in England when the Constitution was framed, that is, precedent but likewise on present conditions and sentiments as seen in the quotation given from Mr. Justice Holmes.

The relationship between the police power of the state, which is the power to regulate for the health, safety, morals and general welfare of the public, and the constitutional prohibition against "taking" private property for public purposes without just compensation, presents the primary problem in understanding the limits of governmental power to regulate the use of land.

The entire scope of eminent domain law as it relates to the regulation of land use is beyond the reach of this course. Some of the more important articles that may be rewarding are: Berger, A Policy Analysis of the Taking Problem, 49 N.Y.U.L.Rev. 165 (1974); Costonis, "Fair" Compensation and the Accommodation Power: Antidotes for the Taking Impasse in Land Use Controversies, 75 Columbia L.Rev. 1021 (1975); Michelman, Property, Utility, and Fairness: Comments on the Ethical Foundations of "Just Compensation" Law, 80 Harv.L.Rev. 1165 (1967); Sax, Takings and the Police Power, 74 Yale L.J. 36 (1963); Van Alstyne, Taking or Damaging by Police Power: The Search for Inverse Condemnation Criteria, 44 So.Cal.L.Rev. 1 (1970). Lengthier treatments which are valuable include, Ackerman, Private Property and the Constitution (1977) and Hagman & Misczynski, Windfalls for Wipeouts: Land Value Capture and Compensation (1978), along with the book from which the following excerpt is taken:

Bosselman, Callies, and Banta, The Taking Issue, pp. 318–322 (1973):

The founding fathers placed in the Constitution the following words:

* * * nor shall private property be taken for public use without just compensation.

Why do these twelve words deserve so much study? Because any system of land use regulation will work only if it satisfies each and every link in a chain of interconnected tests. It must be politically feasible; it must make sense economically; * * * and it must hold up in court. The taking issue is an important link in that chain, because if the courts find the system of regulation so severe that it constitutes a taking, the whole system collapses.

* * *

How did a constitutional clause concerned with the *taking* of land become applicable to the *regulation* of land anyway? Originally it wasn't.

The "taking" clause derived from the English nobles' fear of the King's seizures of land for his own use, a fear that was reflected in the Magna Carta:

> No free man shall be deprived * * * of his freehold * * * unless by the lawful judgment of his peers and by the law of the land.

But the use of land was being regulated—often very severely regulated—throughout English and early American history. Only around the turn of the Twentieth Century did judges and legal scholars popularize the notion that if regulation of the use of land became excessive, it could amount to the equivalent of a taking.

* * *

An examination and analysis of colonial regulations shows that the prevailing pattern of land use regulation was quite similar to that in England. Compensation was generally provided for physical takings of developed property, but literally hundreds of regulations of the use of land were enforced without any compensation to the landowner.

Nor was the issue of compensation for land use regulation raised either during the revolutionary period or in the drafting of the Constitution or Bill of Rights. Rather the draftsmen of the taking clause seem to have carried over the historic British concern over arbitrary seizure of land by the King,—perhaps as reflected in seizures during the then recent revolutionary war—and to have applied that concern to actions of the new Federal Government.

The courts have insisted that the taking clause be strictly observed. Whenever the government has needed land for some public purpose it has either purchased the land on the open market or exercised the power of condemnation, paying the owner the fair market value of his land.

Court decisions during the entire first half of the Nineteenth Century * * * find courts construing the taking clause strictly. To paraphrase a well-known commentator of the period writing in 1857, in order for an owner to be entitled to protection under the taking clause his property must have been actually taken in the physical sense of the word. No indirect or consequential damage, no matter how serious, warranted compensation.

The last half of the Nineteenth Century led to a certain ambivalence on the part of the courts, as the country's tremendous economic expansion inevitably produced conflicts with vested interests. Nonetheless, late in the Nineteenth Century the Supreme Court handed down cases such as Powell v. Pennsylvania and Mugler v. Kansas which denied compensation to the owners of business properties that became virtually valueless because of state regulatory statutes. These statutes were held to be valid police regulations, not takings of property within the meaning of the constitutional prohibition.

But Justice Holmes was soon to change the Court's direction * * * Only two years after Mugler v. Kansas, Holmes wrote from the bench of the Massachusetts Supreme Court in Rideout v. Knox [148 Mass. 368, 19 N.E. 390 (1889)] that the power of eminent domain (the power to acquire land) and the police power (the power to regulate land) differed only in degree and no clear line could be drawn between them. He continued to develop this philosophy in subsequent decisions and influenced a number of leading scholars of the period.

C. PROPERTY RIGHTS LEGISLATION

In March, 1988, the President signed Executive Order 12,630, 53 Fed.Reg. 8859, known as the Federal Takings Executive Order; implementing guidelines were issued by the Attorney General on June 30, 1988 (see Env.L.Rptr.Admin.Materials, p. 35172 (1988)). These federal regulations are discussed in Pollot, The Effect of the Federal Takings Executive Order, Land Use Law, May 1989, p. 3. Also see, Hill, Reflections, Refractions, and Regulations: Variations on the Takings Theme, American Bar Ass'n, Urban, State and Local Law Newsletter, Vol. 12, No. 3 (1989). The thrust of the Executive Order was to require federal agencies to consider the impact of regulations on private property rights. The Executive Order is regarded as the beginning of a movement to provide some sort of statutory protection for property owners against excessive governmental regulation. By 1996, some sort of statutory property rights protection had been introduced in nearly every state and in Congress.

The House of Representatives passed a takings bill in connection with the "Contract for America" movement in 1994–95. That bill languished in the Senate along with a Senate bill that was quite different. The House bill only applied to a select group of federal environmental regulations, while the Senate bill applied to all federal regulations that devalued property. The Senate Bill provided in S. 605, Title V, Section 508 (1995), that property owners are entitled to compensation for reductions of more than one third in market value of land (entirety or a portion) as a consequence of use restrictions imposed under the Endangered Species Act or Section 404 of the Federal Water Pollution Control Act (the wetlands provision). Title II of S. 605 would have gone even further in providing compensation for reductions of one third or more due to any federal statute and also defined property to include all property to which the Fifth Amendment under any circumstances might apply. In May of 1996 a letter was sent to the U.S. Senate, signed by 380 law professors at 125 law schools voicing strong disagreement with S. 605 and urging its defeat.

In 1991 one state enacted takings legislation. In 1992 and 1993 two states in each year enacted takings legislation. In 1994 six states enacted legislation although thirty-one states considered about seventy bills. In 1995 thirty-nine states considered takings bills (about ninety separate bills) and eleven states enacted legislation.

The state legislation that has been enacted falls into two major categories: (1) statutes that require some sort of review of regulations to ascertain or assess the impact on private property, and (2) statutes that require compensation for regulations that devalue private property by a specified amount. A number of variations in these two major categories can be found:

1. In the "assessment" type of legislation, there are variations in the agency that is required to assess. Some acts require the state attorney general to review proposed regulations for impact on property, e.g. West's Ann. Indiana Code § 4–22–2–32, or require the attorney general to promulgate a checklist for agencies to follow, e.g. Idaho Code Ann. § 67–8003, some require the enacting agency to conduct the assessment, e.g. Utah Code Ann. § 63–90–4, and some create a special review agency under legislative auspices, e.g. Mo. Rev. Stat. ch. 536.017. Also, there is variation in what happens after the assessment. Most of the statutes are silent on post-assessment practice; some require reconsideration or modification of regulations that have an effect on private property value.

2. In the "compensation" statutes there is considerable variation on the points of (a) whether the devaluation is measured by the property owner's holdings in their entirety versus segmentation, (b) whether the statute applies to urban zoning regulations, (c) whether compensation can be avoided by "rolling back" the regulation, (d) whether alternative dispute proceedings are required or encouraged.

Five states enacted "compensation" statutes as of January, 1996. Since 1996, the movement for legislative protection against excessive regulation has diminished considerably. A brief description of those statutes follows:

1. Mississippi passed the first compensation statute in 1994. Miss. St. Ann. § 49–33–1, the Mississippi Agricultural and Forestry Activity Act. It provides for compensation whenever timber harvesting regulations devalue private property by 40% or more. In 1995 the statute was amended to include agricultural regulations. It does not apply to urban zoning.

2. Louisiana passed a compensation statute in 1995 that gives property owners a cause of action for compensation in cases of reduction in value of 20% or more. It applies only to agricultural and timber lands and gives agencies the option of avoiding compensation by rescission of the regulations. La. Rev. Stat. § 3:3608 provides:

> To minimize the impact of governmental action affecting private agricultural property and private agricultural property rights, a governmental entity shall:
>
> (1) Avoid imposing an undue burden on the resources of that governmental entity by actions that require compensation of private agricultural property owners under the United States Constitution or the Constitution of Louisiana.
>
> (2) Avoid diminution in value of private agricultural property which is used in agricultural production or which may potentially be used in agricultural production.

(3) Expedite a decision by the entity in cases in which a delay of the decision will substantially interfere with the use or value of private agricultural property rights affected by the provisions of this Part.

(4) Avoid unnecessary delays in compensating owners of private agricultural property when diminution in value occurs by governmental action.

3. Oregon passed a compensation statute applying to "ecotakes" that result in a reduction of 10% or more of property value. Ecotake regulations are defined as those seeking to preserve scenic areas, natural areas, open space, or historical, archeological, cultural properties of significance. Compensation was not in cash, but in credits against personal or corporate income taxes. 1995 Or. Laws S.B. 600. The statute was vetoed by the governor, and the veto sustained. In 2002, Oregon voters approved an initiated amendment to the state constitution to provide compensation for burdensome regulation. It was entitled Measure 7. An immediate appeal to invalidate the measure was brought in the courts and the Oregon Supreme Court, in League of Oregon Cities v. State, 334 Or. 645, 56 P.3d 892 (2002), held the ballot measure invalid because it combined two fundamental changes in the state constitution in one measure.

4. Texas provides for compensation for 25% or more reductions in value of all or part of land or water rights, whether temporary or permanent. It applies to urban regulations. Compensation is not awarded if the agency rescinds or rolls back the challenged regulation. There are many statutory exceptions. Private Real Property Rights Preservation Act, Vernon's Texas Code Ann., Government ch. 2007.

The Texas statute, effective Sept. 1, 1995, defines a "taking" to include (in addition to the traditional constitutional law definitions) a governmental action that:

(i) affects an owner's private real property that is the subject of the governmental action, in whole or in part or temporarily or permanently, in a manner that restricts or limits the owner's right to the property that would otherwise exist in the absence of the governmental action; and

(ii) is the producing cause of a reduction of at least 25 percent in the market value of the affected private property, determined by comparing the market value of the property as if the governmental action is not in effect and the market value of the property determined as if the governmental action is in effect.

The question of whether a governmental action is a taking under the Texas statute is determined by a lawsuit filed by the property owner in district court. If the court finds that a taking has occurred, the remedy is an order to rescind the regulation; if the regulation is not rescinded then the governmental entity must pay the landowner. The Texas statute also has some significant exceptions, including:

(11) an action taken by a political subdivision:

(A) to regulate construction in an area designated under law as floodplain;

(B) to regulate on-site sewage facilities;

(C) under the political subdivisions statutory authority to prevent waste or protect rights of owners of interest in groundwater, or

(D) to prevent subsidence;

* * *

(13) an action that:

(A) is taken in response to a real and substantial threat to public health and safety;

(B) is designed to significantly advance the health and safety purpose; and

(C) does not impose a greater burden than is necessary to achieve the health and safety purpose;

Very few cases under the Texas statute have emerged. In McMillan v. Northwest Harris County Mun. Utility Dist No. 24, 988 S.W.2d 337 (Tex.App.1999), the court held that water, sewer and drainage fees assessed against undeveloped property was fulfillment of a governmental obligation and thus excluded from the act. In Edwards Aquifer Auth. v. Bragg, 21 S.W.3d 375 (Tex.App.2000), the court held that the authority was required to perform a "takings impact assessment" under § 2007.043 of the act before acting on well permit applications. Also see, Anderson, The Texas "Takings" Statute: Ten Basic Facts to Know, 60 Tex.B.J. 12 (1997).

5. Florida provides a compensation remedy for those whose real property has been "inordinately burdened" by government action and also provides for a mediation process to resolve disputes. The Bert J. Harris, Jr., Private Property Rights Protection Act, Fl. Stat. 70.001 et seq. "Inordinate burden" is carefully defined in the statute to track the idea of "investment backed expectations" and "vested property rights."

The Florida statute provides: "When a specific action of a governmental entity has inordinately burdened an existing use of real property or a vested right to a specific use of real property, the property owner of that real property is entitled to relief, which may include compensation for the actual loss to the fair market value of the real property caused by the action of government." The statute also defines inordinate burden, as follows:

The terms "inordinate burden" or "inordinately burdened" mean that an action of one or more governmental entities has directly restricted or limited the use of real property such that the property owner is permanently unable to attain the reasonable, investment-backed expectation for the existing use of the real property or a vested right to a specific use of the real property with respect to the real property as a whole, or that the property owner is left with existing or vested uses that are unreasonable such that the property owner bears permanently a disproportionate share of a burden imposed for the good of the public, which in fairness should be borne by the public at large. The terms "inordinate burden" or "inordinately burdened" do not include temporary impacts to real property; impacts to real property occasioned by governmental abatement, prohibition, prevention, or remediation of a public nuisance at common law or a noxious use of private property; or impacts to real property caused by an action of a governmental entity taken to grant relief to a property owner under this section.

The statute requires landowners who are making a claim to do so within six months after the governmental action and the claim must be accompanied by a written bona fide appraisal that demonstrates the loss in fair market value; after the claim is filed notice must be given to all contiguous property owners and a settlement period begins to run. If no settlement is reached, the property owner may go to circuit court and have a jury trial.

The Florida statute is discussed in Juergensmeyer, Florida's Private Property Rights Protection Act: Does It Inordinately Burden the Public Interest?, 48 U.Fla.L.Rev. 695 (1996); Stroud and Wright, Florida's Private Property Rights Act—What will it mean for Florida's future?, 20 Nova L.Rev. 683 (1996); Monaco, The *Harris* Act: What Relief From Government Regulation Does It Provide for Private Property Owners?, 26 Stetson L. Rev. 861 (1997).

As in Texas, very few cases have been reported under the Florida act. In Sosa v. City of West Palm Beach, 762 So.2d 981 (Fla.App. 2000) the court held that the property owner failed to comply with prerequisites for bringing suit under the act by failing to present to the city any appraisal supporting the claim prior to bringing suit and by presenting his claim less than 180 days before he filed action. In Osceola County v. Best Diversified, Inc., 830 So.2d 139 (Fla.App. 2002) the appellate court held it did not have jurisdiction over an interlocutory appeal by the county and Department of Environmental Protection (DEP) from a trial court order finding that the county and DEP were liable to the property owner for inordinately burdening the owner's property; the county had denied the property owner's zoning application to use property as a landfill, and DEP had refused to issue a general permit to allow property owner to put its property to such use.

6. In the state of Washington a far-reaching compensation statute was subjected to a ballot referendum and defeated by 60% to 40% in November, 1995. See Carol M. Rose, A Dozen Propositions on Private Property, Public Rights, and the New Takings Legislation, 53 Wash. & Lee L. Rev. 265 (1996).

None of the statutes has been in effect long enough to ascertain the fiscal impact of providing compensation to landowners who have been subject to regulations allegedly reducing the fair market value of their land, but short of a constitutional taking. See, generally, Robert Meltz, "Property Rights" Laws in the United States, Congressional Research Service, Library of Congress (Dec. 2, 1996). Also see Organ, Understanding State and Federal Property Rights Legislation, 48 Okla.L.Rev. 191 (1995).

SECTION 2. THE LAW OF NUISANCE

A. SOME IMPORTANT BASIC CONSIDERATIONS

(1) *Historical Aspects*

Long before the modern era of "comprehensive" zoning, courts in the haphazard fashion of our case law and through loose doctrines of private and public nuisance were mitigating against the worst effects of unplanned development of English and American communities. Many thousands of discordant land uses have been reviewed by courts since the law of "nuisance" began to take shape soon after the Norman Conquest. The judge-made criteria for the resolution of land use conflicts show the vagueness and resultant flexibility that one would expect. They display the extreme difficulty of choosing, through the individualized method of the case law process, between clashing land uses that exist in bewildering variety.

In England, at first, such disputes were resolved in local and manorial courts. But after the law reforms of Henry II, in the latter part of the 12th Century, the king's courts began to encroach rapidly into land disputes in general and into nuisance disputes in particular. For private nuisances the royal courts at first gave the dual relief of damages and specific abatement through the assize of novel disseisin and through the assize of nuisance. The ancient overlappings and confusions between these two assizes no longer concern us. Suffice it to say that they were both superseded by trespass on the case, which afforded damages only, so that for specific abatement it became necessary for plaintiffs to petition the Chancery Court for injunctive relief. And today most private nuisance cases "sound" in equity for injunctions, though there may be an incidental prayer for damages.

Avoiding for the moment the difficult problem of drawing the lines of demarcation between "private" nuisances and "public" nuisances, we may look briefly into the ways *public nuisance* cases got into court in times past, and the ways in which they get there today.

A citizen apparently did not, at first, have any judicial remedy when he suffered damages because of a public nuisance. Rather rigorous rules of self-help abatement existed, particularly where the nuisance consisted in interfering with ready passage on a public highway. Presentment and indictment, as for other crimes, seemed to have been the sole early judicial weapon against the public nuisance. The earliest case suggesting that an individual could sue for a public nuisance was in 1535, (Y.B. 27

Hy. VIII 26, 27), but the doctrine that the individual plaintiff must show "special damages" was soon engrafted into the law and flourished like a sturdy weed. Today, if someone can prove "special damages" to the satisfaction of the court, she can not only collect the damages but may also be entitled to an injunction abating the public nuisance. In addition, the community through the municipal, county, or district attorney may also sue to abate the nuisance by injunction. Special statutes often set out conditions that must be met before the prosecuting authority can bring such an action.

(2) Public and Private Nuisances

Public nuisances include a great many interferences with the comfort, moral standards, health, safety and convenience of the community. Included are activities which,

(1) Endanger the health or safety of a considerable number of people, such as discharging fumes from a white lead works or an open pit smelter, polluting a public water supply, or maintaining a breeding place for mosquitoes;

(2) Endanger the property of a considerable number of persons, such as storing explosives in a populous place or keeping diseased animals;

(3) Offend public morals, such as operating a house of prostitution, a gambling house, a disorderly saloon or an indecent exhibition;

(4) Interfere with the comfort of a considerable number of people particularly through odors, dust, smoke, sound or vibrations;

(5) Upset public convenience by obstructing a highway, navigable stream or bridge, or by creating a condition that makes travel unsafe or interferes with the use of a public square or park;

(6) Violate a criminal statute which declares the violation to be a public nuisance, such as permitting black currant plants to grow, failing to drain mosquito breeding waters, eavesdropping on a jury, being a common scold, placing advertising signs along a highway so as to obstruct the view, running dance marathons, using a shanty when fishing through the ice, and a rich variety of unrelated minor offenses.

At common law, a public nuisance was always a crime and punishable as such. Most of our states have enacted very broad criminal statutes, in addition to the specific kinds previously referred to, saying in effect that to maintain a public nuisance is a crime.

A private nuisance is an interference with the use or enjoyment of land, other than by direct physical invasion or trespass. Unlike a public nuisance, a private nuisance normally only affects a limited number of landowners and, perhaps more typically, involves a dispute between adjoining landowners.

Notice that from the point of view of land planning, of closing out or controlling discordant land uses, doctrines evolved in public as in private nuisance cases are in point. As indicated, these doctrines have been kept vague and general and accordingly flexible.

(3) *The Duty Not to Interfere Substantially With Your Neighbor*

The courts have long recognized that give and take in living is unavoidable in an organized society, since almost any use someone may make of her land will interfere to some extent with the free use and undisturbed enjoyment by others of neighboring land. Britton, writing around 1300 A.D., put it this way:

> Sometimes the soil is subject to a servitude by law, although not by any man's appointment, or by the establishment of peaceable seisin, and as, for example, to the obligation that no one shall do anything in his own soil that may be a grievance or annoyance to his neighbor.

Britton 1, 140b, 56 (F.M. Nichols ed. 1901).

Since Britton wrote, Anglo–American courts have said over and over again that the occupancy of neighboring tracts of land by different individuals gives rise to probable conflicts of interests between them, and the interest of each must be reasonably limited so that the interest of the other may have reasonable play.

Aside from statutory controls on land use, then, we have long had as an integral part of our jurisprudence the principle which undergirds the law of nuisance and which finds expression in the maxim, *sic utere tuo ut alienum non laedas*, to the effect that no one may use her property in such a way as to injure the person or property of another. This concept provides a balancing of the legitimate interests of adjoining landowners. Broad generalizations do not carry one very far in the solution of specific conflicts. Other guides which sound more specific, even though in fact they may not be, have been evolved for this reason.

(4) *The Restatement's Guides to What Is "Substantial" Harm*

First, it is said that an essential element is proof of substantial harm, or threat of substantial harm, either to the land as such or to its use and enjoyment.

Next, it is said that the court must weigh the gravity of harm to the plaintiff against the utility of the defendant's use. This is elaborated in the Restatement of Torts 2d (1979) as follows:

> § 827. Gravity of Harm—Factors Involved.
>
> In determining the gravity of harm from an intentional invasion of another's interest in the use and enjoyment of land, the following factors are important:
>
> (a) The extent of the harm involved;

(b) the character of the harm involved;

(c) the *social value* which the law attaches to the type of use or enjoyment invaded;

(d) the *suitability of the particular use or enjoyment invaded* to the character of the locality;

(e) the burden on the person harmed of avoiding the harm.

§ 828. Utility of Conduct—Factors Involved.

In determining the utility of conduct that causes an intentional invasion of another's interest in the use and enjoyment of land, the following factors are important:

(a) the *social value* that the law attaches to the primary purpose of the conduct;

(b) the *suitability* of the conduct to the *character of the locality*; and

(c) the impracticability of preventing or avoiding the invasion. (Emphasis Supplied)

One of the things which you will observe in the nuisance cases that follow in this chapter is the obvious fact that there is no universal standard of "social value" or need. You will also observe that by focusing on the "suitability" of the use for the particular locality judges often find themselves acting something like planning commissions in evaluating facts about the character of the district. (Is there a role for cost-benefit economists and land use planners to play in nuisance actions as expert witnesses?)

Another thing revealed by these cases is that many courts in addition to balancing utility of use against gravity of harm also balance "hardships" or "equities" in determining whether to enjoin the nuisance or just grant judgment for damages.

Further, there is the question of whether nuisance relief should be granted where the plaintiff "came" or "moved" to an activity that was there first. American courts are divided on the point of whether relief should be granted or should be barred on the basis of acquiescence and estoppel. Some courts have held that this defense alone is not sufficient and that there must be other facts present in order to bar the plaintiff. This would seem to be the prevailing view, perhaps based on the idea that otherwise the alleged noxious activity would acquire something in the nature of an easement or servitude over surrounding land. On the other hand, a substantial number of cases have viewed "coming" or "moving" to the nuisance as an absolute defense because of the hardship to the defendant and the fact that the nuisance was self-created by the plaintiff in moving there. A distinction is to be made between a situation in which a plaintiff goes out into an undeveloped area and then sues to abate a noxious activity and a situation in which the noxious activity is gradually approached by the natural outgrowth of the community. The latter is not considered moving to the nuisance.

Somewhat related is the question of whether or not a prescriptive right to maintain a private nuisance can be acquired. The argument would be that the prescriptive right attached when the aggrieved landowner failed to sue within the period of the statute of limitations. The difficulty is in establishing when the statute began to run. No cause of action lies until substantial harm exists or is imminent. Also, some courts state that there is a new cause of action with every day of continuance of the nuisance. Benton v. Kernan, 127 N.J.Eq. 434, 13 A.2d 825 (1940), modified 130 N.J.Eq. 193, 21 A.2d 755 (1941). Other courts call this a permanent nuisance from which the cause of action arises at first occurrence. In that situation, such harmful activity would almost always lead to litigation before the normally long statutory period expired. Consequently, the theoretical ability of a tortfeasor to obtain prescriptive rights to operate a private nuisance is seldom any more than theoretical. Prescriptive rights cannot be obtained in a public nuisance or one designated as a crime under the commonly accepted view.

(5) *Nuisance Per Se and Nuisance Per Accidens*

Courts have made much of two labels: *nuisance per se* and *nuisance per accidens*. In the first category fall immoral activities, some extrahazardous practices, certain court-declared nuisances and clear violations of valid statutes declaring violations to be nuisances. Certain activities which in the haphazard process of the case law have been over and over again declared nuisances may ultimately be said to be nuisances per se. Thus, as we will see, a funeral parlor in a residential area has been held to be a nuisance so often that today courts are apt to declare it a nuisance per se without spending much more time on the case than it takes to pin the label. Proof that a nuisance in fact (per accidens) exists takes more doing. Here the plaintiff must convince the court that the facts she has proved with respect to location, harm and other circumstances merit the relief sought. Her case must stand on its own facts more or less unaided by precedent.

(6) *Motive and Nuisance*

A word about motive in nuisance cases is appropriate. Here one thinks immediately of the spite fence cases, where the objectionable use has no utility, is motivated by malice and fails entirely to offset the harm done with social values. The trend today is in the direction of declaring spite fences actionable nuisances. But in some states the legislature has had to intervene to overcome the effects of "absolute property rights" case law.

To the contrary, some courts acted in the late 19th and early 20th centuries to declare it to be an actionable nuisance to erect or maintain spite fences: E.g., Alabama in Norton v. Randolph, 176 Ala. 381, 58 So. 283 (1912); Michigan in Burke v. Smith, 69 Mich. 380, 37 N.W. 838 (1888); North Carolina in Barger v. Barringer, 151 N.C. 433, 66 S.E. 439 (1909); and Oklahoma in Hibbard v. Halliday, 58 Okl. 244, 158 P. 1158 (1916). Cases of this variety established the modern trend. Of course, as is implicit in the definition of a "spite fence," if it does in fact serve a useful purpose, it is legitimate whatever the inconvenience it may cause. See, e.g., De Mers v. Graupner, 186 Ark. 214, 53 S.W.2d 8 (1932). In such a situation, motivation for the fence is immaterial. Many states have codified the cause of action to enjoin spite fences.

(7) Doctrinal Versus Functional Approach to Nuisance Cases

The cases that follow in this chapter give us an opportunity to see nuisance doctrines at work. But the cases have not been arranged along doctrinal lines. Instead we take up through them typical modern day land use conflicts that arise in the open country, on the rural-urban fringe and in older closely settled areas. Mostly we consider areas that are unzoned, although we also devote attention to some problems that arise in zoned areas.

B. CONFLICTING USES IN OPEN COUNTRY

(1) Uses in Conflict With Agricultural, Livestock or Commercial Operations

HULBERT v. CALIFORNIA PORTLAND CEMENT CO.

Supreme Court of California, 1911.
161 Cal. 239, 118 P. 928.

[Capacity of defendant's mill was 3,000 barrels of cement a day, or around 900,000 barrels a year. The trial court's injunction restricted operations to 88,706 barrels per annum. The defendant is here asking the state supreme court to stay the operation of this injunction pending appeal. Limitations of space require the omission of much of the court's discussion of case law precedents, as well as the concurring opinion of Sloss, J.]

MELVIN, J.

* * *

The salient facts shown by the petitioner are that the California Portland Cement Company is engaged in the manufacture of cement on property situated nearly two miles from the center of the city of Colton in the county of San Bernardino, but not within the limits of said city; that said manufactory is located at Slover Mountain, where the substances necessary to the production of Portland cement are quarried; that long before the surrounding country had been generally devoted to the production of citrus fruits, Slover Mountain had been known as a place where limestone was produced; that quarries of marble and limestone had been established there; that lime kilns had been operated upon said mountain for many years; that in 1891 the petitioner obtained title to said premises and commenced thereon the manufacture of Portland cement; that the said corporation has expended upon said property more than eight hundred thousand dollars; that at the time when petitioner began the erection of the cement plant the land surrounding the plant was vacant and unimproved, except some land lying to the north, which had been planted to young citrus trees; that these trees were first planted about a year before the erection of the cement plant was commenced (but long after the lime kilns and the marble quarries had been operated); that subsequently, other orange groves had been planted in the neighborhood; that petitioner's plant on Slover Mountain has a capacity of three thousand barrels of cement per day; but that by the judgment of the superior court in two certain actions against petitioner entitled Lillie A. Hulbert, Administratrix etc. v. California Portland Cement Company, a Corporation, and Spencer E. Gilbert, plaintiff, v. the same defendant, the corporation aforesaid was enjoined from operating its plant in such a manner as to produce an excess of 88,706 barrels of finished cement per annum; that the regular pay-roll of the company includes the names of about five hundred men who are paid about thirty-five thousand dollars a month; that the fixed, constant monthly expenses for supplies and materials amount to thirty-five thousand dollars; that the California Portland Cement Company employs the best, most modern methods in its processes of manufacture, but that nevertheless there is an unavoidable escape into the air of certain dust and smoke; that petitioner has no other location for the conduct of its business at a profit; that the land of the Hulbert estate is located from fifteen hundred to twenty-five hundred feet from petitioner's cement works and that Spencer E. Gilbert's land is all within one thousand feet therefrom; that petitioner has diligently sought some means of preventing the escape of dust from its factories; that it has consulted the best experts and sought the best information obtainable, and that it is now and has been for a long time conducting experiments along the lines suggested by the most eminent engineering authorities upon this subject, and that as soon as any process can be evolved for preventing the escape of the dust, the petitioner will adopt such process in its works, and it is believed that a process now constructing with all diligence by petitioner will effectually prevent the escape of dust. Petitioner also alleges that it is easily possible to estimate the damages of the plaintiffs in money while it is utterly impracticable to estimate the damage in money which will be caused to the petitioner by the closing of the plant, and that stopping the plant pending the appeals will cause financial ruin to the chief stockholders of the petitioner, and that the elements of loss averred are irreparable on account of the disorganization of petitioner's working force, loss of market, and deterioration of machinery.

* * *

* * * To permit the cement company to continue its operations even to the extent of destroying the property of the two plaintiffs and requiring payment of the full value thereof would be, in effect, allowing the seizure of private property for a use other than a public one—something unheard of and totally unauthorized in the law. *Hennessey v. Carmony*, 50 N.J.Eq. 616, 25 A. 374; *Sullivan v. Jones & Laughlin Steel Co.*, 208 Pa. 540, 57 A. 1065, 66 L.R.A. 712. Nor may we say, as petitioner urges us to declare, that cement dust is not a nuisance and therefore that the restraint imposed is illegal, even though this is one of the first cases, if not the very first, of its kind, in which the emission of cement dust from a factory has been enjoined, for we are bound by the findings of the court in this proceeding and may not consider their sufficiency or lack of it until we take up the appeals on their merits. The court has found that the plaintiffs in the actions tried were specially damaged by a nuisance maintained by the cement company. This entitles the plaintiffs not only to damages, but to such relief as the facts warrant, and the chancellor has determined that limiting the production in the manner selected is a proper form of protection to their rights. It is well settled in California that a nuisance which consists in pouring soot or the like upon the property of a neighbor in such manner as to interfere with the comfortable enjoyment of the premises is a private nuisance which may be enjoined or abated, and for which likewise, the persons specially injured may recover pecuniary damages. Code Civ.Proc., sec. 721; *Fisher v. Zumwalt*, 128 Cal. 493, 61 P. 82; *Melvin v. E.B. & A.L. Stone Co.*, 7 Cal.App. 327, 94 P. 390; *Judson v. Los Angeles Sub. Gas Co.*, 157 Cal. 168, 26 L.R.A., N.S., 183, 106 P. 581. The last-named case was one in which the operation of a gas factory does not constitute a nuisance per se. The manufacture in or near a great city of gas for illuminating and heating is not only legitimate but is very necessary to the comfort of the people. But in this, as in any other sort of lawful business, the person conducting it is subject to the rule *sic utere tuo ut alienum non laedas*, even when operating under municipal permission or under public obligation to furnish a commodity. *Terre Haute Gas Co. v. Teel*, 20 Ind. 131; *Attorney–General v. Gaslight & Coke Co.*, L.R., 7 Ch.Div. 217; *Sullivan v. Royer*, 72 Cal. 248, 13 P. 655. Nor will the adoption of the most approved appliances and methods of production justify the continuance of that which, in spite of them, remains a nuisance. *Evans v. Reading Chemical & Fertilizing Co.*, 160 Pa. 209, 28 A. 702; *Susquehanna Fertilizer Co. v. Malone*, 73 Md. 268, 25 Am.St.Rep. 595, 20 A. 900, 9 L.R.A. 737; *Susquehanna Fertilizer Co. v. Spangler*, 86 Md. 562, 63 Am.St.Rep. 533, 39 A. 270.

Petitioner contends for the rule that the resulting injuries must be balanced by the court and that where the hardship inflicted upon one party by the granting of an injunction would be very much greater than that which would be suffered by the other party if the nuisance were permitted to continue, injunctive relief should be denied. This doctrine of "the balance of hardship" and the associated rule that "an injunction is not of right but of grace" are the bases of petitioner's argument, and many authorities in support of them have been called to our attention.

* * *

* * * We are convinced that upon reason and upon great weight of authority we should deny petitioner's prayer, considering the subject upon the assumption that we have power under the constitution in aid of our appellate jurisdiction in a proper case to suspend the operation of a prohibitory injunction pending an appeal.

Let the temporary order staying the operation of the injunction be dismissed and the petition be denied.

Notes

1. With the California court's refusal to balance hardships, compare §§ 933 and 936 of the Restatement of Torts 2d (1979). Comment (a) to § 933 says:

> The availability of an injunction against a tort * * * depends upon a comparative appraisal of all of the factors in the case. These factors include the relative adequacy to the plaintiff of an injunction and of the other remedies, plaintiff's laches or unclean hands, the relative hardship likely to result to defendant if an injunction should be granted and to plaintiff if it should be denied, the interests of third persons and of the public, and the practicability of framing and enforcing the order or judgment. * * *

And in Comment (c) under § 942 the Restatement says:

> The local community sometimes has a public interest at stake. For example, it will suffer loss of taxes and purchasing power of workers if an industrial plant that has been found to be a nuisance is ordered to be shut down or moved to another location.

For a discussion of the similar provisions of the 1939 Restatement in a nuisance case involving tough "balancing of hardship" problems, see Riter v. Keokuk Electro–Metals Co., 248 Iowa 710, 82 N.W.2d 151 (1957), which essentially embraces the restatement.

2. Other dramatic contests between farmers and country-located industries have involved ore reduction. Some were those involving two great open-air, roast-heap copper smelters in southeastern Tennessee. In Madison v. Ducktown Sulphur, Copper & Iron Co., 113 Tenn. 331, 83 S.W. 658 (1904), the court refused to enjoin "a great and increasing industry" with resulting heavy losses in employment, payrolls, taxes and local business. The court denied injunctive relief to farmers against the devastating effect on crops and other vegetation of sulphurous gases, pointing out that the defendants had spent $200,000 on ineffective experiments to reduce the nuisance. The farmers were relegated to their remedy for damages. Later, the State of Georgia sued on behalf of numerous Georgia landowners whose forests, crops and orchards were being destroyed by the fumes in five Georgia counties. The United States Supreme Court granted an injunction, saying, "It [Georgia] is not lightly to be required to give up quasi-sovereign rights for pay," and "this court has not quite the same freedom to balance the harm that will be done by an injunction against that of which the plaintiff complains, that it would have in deciding between two subjects of a single political power." Georgia v. Tennessee Copper Co., 206 U.S. 230, 237–38, 27 S.Ct. 618, 619, 51 L.Ed. 1038 (1907). Experiments were conducted which led to new production processes and a substantial reduction of harmful fumes. See Georgia v. Tennessee Copper Co., 237 U.S. 474, 35 S.Ct. 631, 59 L.Ed.

1054 (1915), 240 U.S. 650, 36 S.Ct. 465, 60 L.Ed. 846 (1916), and 1 Haynes, American Chemical Industry, A History 263 (1954).

In several cases embattled farmers, at great expense and without marked success, sued ore reduction works claiming damage to cows and other farm animals due to ingestion of fluoride dusts which were carried from defendants' chimneys through the atmosphere and deposited on grass and other vegetation on plaintiffs' farms. See Arvidson v. Reynolds Metals Co., 125 F.Supp. 481 (W.D.Wash.1954), affirmed 236 F.2d 224 (9th Cir.1956), certiorari denied 352 U.S. 968, 77 S.Ct. 359, 1 L.Ed.2d 323 (1957), and Erekson v. United States Steel Corp., 260 F.2d 423 (10th Cir.1958). But see Reynolds Metals Co. v. Yturbide, 258 F.2d 321 (9th Cir.1958), where the attorney for the farmers successfully argued res ipsa loquitur from the law of negligence.

In the Arvidson case, the federal district court said at pages 483, 486 and 488:

> Plaintiffs had the burden of establishing by a preponderance of the evidence that the market value of their farms was depreciated and/or that the physical condition and milk producing capacity of their cattle were damaged by fluorides emanating from defendants' plants. * * *
>
> [After summarizing the testimony of experts called by the company the court concluded:] I have reached the following basic conclusions on the factual issues of the case: Plaintiffs have not sustained the burden of producing a preponderance of credible evidence to establish (a) fluorine content in the forage on their lands in amounts above nontoxic limits; (b) substantial fluorine content in forage attributable to effluence from defendants' plants; or (c) that plaintiffs' lands or cattle sustained fluorine damages in particulars and amounts that can be determined with reasonable or any certainty.
>
> * * * The court is fully satisfied that the utility of defendants' plant operations and their importance to the economy and security of the nation far outweigh any injury to plaintiffs shown by the evidence. Consequently, neither a finding of nuisance nor granting of relief based thereon is justified. * * *

Almost four years after the district judge's decision, it was reported in The Washington Farmer ["Farm Retreat from Industry," The Washington Farmer 5 (June 19, 1958). See also a carefully prepared study finding "excessive fluorides in some areas" and recommending that agricultural enterprises less sensitive to fluorides than dairying be considered. Adams, Miller and Allmendinger, Air Pollution in Cowlitz County 6 (Wash. Ag.Exp.Sta.Circ. 352, Dec. 1959)]:

> Cowlitz county dairymen have been retreating from the vicinity of Longview and Kelso ever since widespread fluorosis was diagnosed * * * in the mid–1940's.
>
> Five dairy farms remain within six miles of the factory complex, embracing an aluminum smelter and a pulp mill, just south of Long-

view. Not long ago there were about 2000 cows. There may be 100 cows left. * * *

Qualified observers say that what is happening and has happened in Cowlitz county is contributing to implications of vast importance to agriculture in Washington, when coexistence with industry becomes a problem in the future.

In the case of Erekson v. United States Steel Corp., 260 F.2d 423 (10th Cir.1958), the farmers were required to attempt to prove their claims "cow by cow" and "sheep by sheep." There was no jury because plaintiffs had started out asking for an injunction and had shifted to damage claims later. Was this good strategy? Also, would it have sufficed in both the Arvidson and the Erekson cases if the plaintiffs had merely proven that even though scientists contended there were not enough fluorides to harm cattle, nevertheless prospective purchasers of farm lands *thought there were* and consequently the marketability of the farms and the values of the farm lands were greatly diminished. Which controls, the common man's assumption or the scientist's knowledge? See Everett v. Paschall, 61 Wash. 47, 111 P. 879 (1910) and Ferry v. City of Seattle, 116 Wash. 648, 200 P. 336 (1921), reversed 116 Wash. 648, 203 P. 40 (1922).

These ore reduction cases involved great expense. Thus, in the Erekson case, an action that involved 300 claims of livestock owners, there were 260 witnesses, 6,622 pages of testimony, 1,267 exhibits, 100,000 chemical analyses of vegetation for fluorine, diagnoses for about 12,000 cattle and thousands of sheep. Counsel presented a special referee with brochures "summarizing" the evidence in 10,000 pages and the referee's report to the court was 347 pages long!

In 2003 several corn farmers joined together to seek substantial damages from the makers of genetically engineered corn, known as Starlink corn. This modified corn has been approved for animal feed, but not for human consumption. The farmers allege that the Starlink corn pollen is blown by the wind and infects corn crops raised for humans, thus rendering that corn unsaleable. A public nuisance theory underlies the lawsuit. See Molly McDonough, "Growing Use of Nuisance," ABA Journal, August 2003, p. 16.

3. Odiferous industrial plants in the open country continue to plague the courts, raising the question whether there is any longer a place for stenchful industry to "hide." A rendering plant in rural rolling farming country was declared a nuisance, but the offender was given a chance to improve conditions by the installation of condensers. Greaser v. Robinson, 54 Montg. 347 (Pa.1938). In Utah, a rendering plant in a rural area was declared a nuisance, damages were given, but an injunction was denied because the embattled neighbors were so late in suing. Ludlow v. Colorado Animal By–Products Co., 104 Utah 221, 137 P.2d 347 (1943). But in Demont v. Abbas, 149 Neb. 765, 32 N.W.2d 737 (1948), the Nebraska court refused to anticipate that the building and operating of a rendering plant in a farming area would necessarily be a nuisance.

McCAW v. HARRISON

Court of Appeals of Kentucky, 1953.
259 S.W.2d 457.

DUNCAN, JUSTICE.

Appellants, who own and operate a dairy farm on land located on each side of the Fayette and Jessamine county line, sought by this action to enjoin appellees from using their adjoining boundary for commercial cemetery purposes. The appeal is from a judgment which denies this relief. The question presented is largely one of fact, the determination of which requires a review of some rather morbid details referred to in the evidence.

Appellants' well, which is the main source of water for stock and family purposes, is located some five hundred feet from the property line of the proposed cemetery. The area embraced by the cemetery site and appellants' land is underlaid with cavernous limestone which contains sinkholes, crevices, channels, and fissures. The overburden of soil is shallow as indicated by rock-sounding maps filed by appellees. Therefore, the burial of bodies will necessarily be on or very close to the underlying rock.

For the appellants, the testimony of an eminent geologist, pathologist, an embalmer, and a cemetery manager indicates some possibility of contamination of the wells and springs in that area. These witnesses, each testifying as to facts within his particular field, describe the process of contamination as follows: (1) harmful disease germs and bacteria are present at death; (2) these organisms survive the embalming process because of the low pressures used to preserve as near as can be, the lifelike appearance of bodies; (3) the water in the area involved will reach these decaying and putrefied bodies because of the shallow overburden of soil and because of the manner of modern day burials; and (4) that the fissures, crevices, channels, and sinkholes in the underlying cavernous limestone will act as a channel and stream for the water carrying these harmful organisms into wells and springs in the area. These witnesses express the view that the contamination resulting from the disease germs and bacteria from the dead human bodies is a definite hazard to appellants' health.

On the other hand, a civil engineer, specializing in sanitary engineering, and a bacteriologist, who has for more than twenty-six years been a professor of bacteriology at the University of Kentucky, testifying for appellees, express the opinion that no contamination of appellants' water supply will result from the proposed use. These witnesses say that the combined factors of the virtual disinfection of the body by embalming, plus the barriers of the casket and vault, make it virtually impossible for the harmful organisms to get into the soil; that even should they reach the soil, they cannot travel a greater distance than fifty feet, which distance is usually considered as affording complete protection to wells and springs from contamination of decaying bodies.

A cemetery does not constitute a nuisance merely because it is a constant reminder of death and has a depressing influence on the minds of persons who observe it, or because it tends to depreciate the value of property in the neighborhood, or is offensive to the aesthetic sense of an adjoining proprietor. 10 Am.Jur., pages 498–499, section 16, Cemeteries. On the other hand, if the location or maintenance of a cemetery endangers the public health, either by corrupting the surrounding atmosphere, or water of wells or springs, it constitutes a nuisance. *Nelson v. Swedish E.L. Cemetery Ass'n*, 111 Minn. 149, 126 N.W. 723, 127 N.W. 626, 34 L.R.A.N.S., 565; *McDaniel v. Forrest Park Cemetery Co.*, 156 Ark. 571, 246 S.W. 874; *Sutton v. Findlay Cemetery Ass'n*, 270 Ill. 11, 110 N.E. 315, L.R.A.1916B,1135; *Hite v. Cashmere Cemetery Ass'n*, 158 Wash. 421, 290 P. 1008.

The parties are in practical agreement concerning the legal principles which control the disposition of this appeal. Their disagreement concerns the question of whether or not the evidence is sufficient to indicate that the maintenance of this cemetery will sufficiently endanger the health of appellants and others so as to bring it within the rule which we have stated.

It hardly needs citation of authority to support the proposition that where the evidence is conflicting and the mind of the reviewing court has no more than a doubt concerning the finding of a Chancellor on a question of fact, the finding will not be disturbed. The evidence in this case deals with a highly technical subject, and although conflicting, does not preponderate greatly in favor of either side. We do not have such a clear conviction of error in the finding of the Chancellor as would justify a reversal.

The contention of appellants that a further hazard to the safety of the residents of the area will be created by possible traffic congestion resulting from slow-moving funeral processions is hardly worthy of note. Funeral processions are an inevitable incident of cemeteries regardless of their location, and to some extent always present a traffic problem. Without reviewing the evidence on this feature of the case, it is sufficient to say that we are not impressed with the argument that the maintenance of the cemetery should be enjoined because of the probability of traffic congestion and possibility of resulting accidents.

For the reasons indicated, the judgment of the lower court is affirmed.

Notes

1. Cemeteries may be considered as religious uses in some cases. Does the fact that a religious body is seeking to use land as a cemetery raise other than nuisance issues? In the case of McGann v. Incorporated Village of Old Westbury, 293 A.D.2d 581, 741 N.Y.S.2d 75, (2002), *appeal dismissed* 98 N.Y.2d 728, 779 N.E.2d 188, 749 N.Y.S.2d 477, the plaintiff Roman Catholic Diocese of Rockville Centre acquired approximately 97 acres of property located within the Incorporated Village of Old Westbury with the intention

of developing and operating a Roman Catholic cemetery on the property. Cemeteries are not a permissible use within the Village, and the subsequent application of the Diocese for a change of zoning was denied. In partially affirming the trial court decision in favor of the diocese the court said:

> The evidence adduced at trial demonstrated that the Roman Catholic Church believes in "the Second Coming of Christ and Resurrection of the Dead," its followers entrust their bodily remains to the Catholic Church in its cemeteries in accordance with that belief, and Catholic cemeteries are a place of worship no different from a church or other similar edifice. Since the proposed use of the subject property involves conduct with a religious purpose, the trial court's determination is supported by the record, and should not be disturbed on appeal unless it could not have been reached upon any fair interpretation of the evidence * * * The defendants' opposing argument is unavailing, since it would otherwise "limit a church to being merely a house of prayer and sacrifice [which] would, in a large degree * * * depriv[e] the church of the opportunity of enlarging, perpetuating and strengthening itself and the congregation." [citation omitted.]
>
> However, the trial court erred in directing the defendant Board of Trustees of the Village (hereinafter the Board) to issue a special permit to the Diocese upon remittitur. In *Cornell Univ. v. Bagnardi,* 68 N.Y.2d 583, 595, 510 N.Y.S.2d 861, 503 N.E.2d 509, the Court of Appeals stated:
>
> "Although the special treatment afforded * * * churches stems from their presumed beneficial effect on the community, there are many instances in which a particular educational or religious use may actually detract from the public's health, safety, welfare or morals. In those instances, the institution may be properly denied. There is simply no conclusive presumption that any religious * * * use automatically outweighs its ill effects [citations omitted]. The presumed beneficial effect may be rebutted with evidence of a significant impact on traffic congestion, property values, municipal services and the like."

2. What about obstructions into roads or navigable streams? It has been stated that "an obstruction placed anywhere within the street limits, even though not on the part of the street ordinarily used for travel, or placed in the air over a street, may constitute a nuisance." Sloan v. City of Greenville, 235 S.C. 277, 111 S.E.2d 573 (1959), and see Annot., 76 A.L.R.2d 896, 898 (1961). In Captain Soma Boat Line, Inc. v. City of Wisconsin Dells, 79 Wis.2d 10, 255 N.W.2d 441 (1977), a tour boat operation sued the city for overhead obstruction of a stream which ran into the Wisconsin River. It was alleged that a street bridge obstructed it at that point in violation of the Northwest Ordinance of 1787, the Wisconsin Constitution, common law, and a state statute declaring obstructions of navigable waters to be public nuisances. The boat line operator lost because, with knowledge of the situation, he had purchased some larger boats. The bridge was not an obstruction to the boats up until then, and the court thought it unreasonable to tear down a public bridge for the benefit of this one entrepreneur.

(2) Uses in Conflict With Rural Residential Use

STATE EX REL. CUNNINGHAM v. FEEZELL

Supreme Court of Tennessee, 1966.
218 Tenn. 17, 400 S.W.2d 716.

[Twenty-six individuals brought suit in the name of the State to enjoin the Defendant from establishing a crematory in a "rural or rural residential" area. The Petitioners alleged that the proposed crematory would constitute a public or private nuisance. Defendant proposed to carry out his operation in a small building which had been converted from a garage and which had a large, protruding smokestack. The petition emphasized the mental anguish of people in the area at the thought that defendant would be burning "dead human bodies." It was alleged that this would "deprive the property owners of the quiet use and enjoyment of their property and endanger their lives and health either by actually rendering them sick mentally and/or physically." It was also contended that the ambulances on these narrow roads would create traffic hazards; that school children and churchgoers would be adversely affected; that dead bodies would have to be stored in the area due to the inadequacy of Defendant's operations; and that there would be pollution resulting from noxious odors, smells, and the emission of vapors. They alleged that no other such establishment was permitted in Tennessee. Defendant's demurrer was sustained by the trial court.]

WHITE, JUSTICE.

* * *

The question presented for determination by the Court is essentially this: Does a cause of action exist to enjoin, as a nuisance, a proposed cremation establishment in a rural or rural residential area under averments of the residents of the area that it will cause mental anguish, depressed feelings, physical discomfort and lower property values? We do not think so.

We believe that for an injunction suit to be sustained prior to the alleged nuisance coming into being, it must be sufficiently shown in the original bill or petition that the proposed establishment is a nuisance *per se*; that is, within itself.

A nuisance at law or a nuisance per se is an act, occupation, or structure which is a nuisance at all times and under any circumstances, *regardless of location or surroundings*. Nuisances in fact or per accidens are those which become nuisances by reason of circumstances and surroundings and an act may be found to be a nuisance as a matter of fact where the natural tendency of the act is to create danger or inflict injury on person or property. 66 C.J.S. Nuisances § 3 (1950). (Emphasis supplied.)

Other definitions are: any act or omission or use of property or thing which is of itself hurtful to the health, tranquility, or morals, or which outrages the decency of the community; that which *cannot* be so *conducted* or *maintained* as to be *lawfully carried on* or *permitted* to *exist*; and, as related to private persons, an act or use of property of a continuing nature, offensive to and legally injurious to health and property, or both. 39 Am.Jur., Nuisances, § 11 (1942). (Emphasis supplied.)

It is perhaps misleading to define a nuisance per se as one which exists "at all times and under any circumstances, regardless of location or surroundings." Actually, a nuisance cannot exist without surrounding circumstances, because it is the surrounding circumstances that determine whether an injury is occasioned; and it is axiomatic that some injury must be occasioned or be at least imminent because of the alleged "nuisance."

There is, in at least one case in this State, an indication that the difference between a nuisance per se, and a nuisance per accidens is that in the former, injury in some form is certain to be inflicted, while in the latter, the injury is uncertain or contingent until it actually occurs. *Pearce v. Gibson County*, 107 Tenn. 224, 64 S.W. 33, 55 L.R.A. 477 (1901). This case held that where injury from a nuisance is not real and immediate and certain to occur, but only uncertain or contingent, the nuisance will not be enjoined anticipatory to its going into operation.

* * *

We do not say that an anticipatory nuisance is not enjoinable under any circumstances. If the injury anticipated is imminent and certain to occur, there may, in fact, be a proper case for immediate abatement, provided, of course the injury is recognized as otherwise actionable at law and equity. We do not say that mental disturbances or "psychic" injuries caused by a nuisance, public or private, are not such as may be actionable at law or equity. They can, in fact, be very real to the complainants. We do say, however, that allegations in the petition must be sufficient, in defining the circumstances and mode of operation surrounding the undertaking, to persuade the court, if they are proved, that injury is imminent and certain. We are convinced that proof of the alleged location of defendant's crematory and the alleged mode of operation and physical appearance of the same will be insufficient to foretell certain injury.

Our research has uncovered no case involving the attempted abatement of a human cremation establishment. Possibly the closest analogy would be the operation of a funeral parlor—at least as regards "psychic" injuries and lowered property values. In a zoning case, *Qualls v. City of Memphis*, 15 Tenn.App. 575 (1932), it was held alternatively that even though a funeral parlor was not a nuisance per se, it could become so with certain facts and circumstances present such as residences nearby, location on a narrow street, and a small lot. The case obviously involves an urban or suburban location, which is not an allegation in the instant case.

* * *

As regards funeral parlors or undertaking establishments, the majority rule in this country, according to an annotation in 39 A.L.R.2d 1000 (1955), is

" * * * that if an undertaking establishment in a purely residential section causes from its normal operations, depressing feelings to families in the immediate neighborhood, and, as a constant reminder of death, appreciably impairs their happiness or weakens their powers of resistance and depreciates the values of their properties, such an establishment constitutes a nuisance."

In the cases that have ruled on this point of equity, the circumstances surrounding the so-called "nuisance" and the anticipated injuries alleged have not followed any exclusive pattern, so some of them merit closer examination. It will be noted that most of these cases rule on the basis of a *proposed* undertaking establishment; the injuries complained of are what *would* occur *if* the business is allowed to begin. * * *

We consider two cases which appear to follow the majority rule, but which apply a certain flexibility to the problem. In *May v. Upton*, 233 Miss. 447, 102 So.2d 339 (1958), it was stated that in an area "essentially" residential, a proposed funeral home should be enjoined as a nuisance but *each case turns on its own facts*, and where an examination of the circumstances, from the evidence presented, indicates otherwise, an injunction should not issue; in this case the funeral home was to be put on the boundary of residential and commercial areas and was *not* enjoined.

In *Jack v. Torrant*, 136 Conn. 414, 71 A.2d 705 (1950), it was the opinion of the court that certain factors regarding the residences in the area should be examined; their extent, kind and location. It is also indicated, as other cases indicate, that the depressed feelings and discomfort must be those that ordinary people sustain in living near an undertaking establishment.

Our holding in the instant case does not, perhaps, coincide precisely with some of the cases following the majority rule. We are not, however, in disagreement with what we think are two of the better reasoned cases aforementioned, i.e., *May v. Upton, supra*, and *Jack v. Torrant, supra*. Nevertheless, we are limited in the instant case to an examination of those factors alleged in the petition, proof of which would not indicate certain injury, either emotional or physical, to petitioners. Residences in a rural area are sparsely situated and there is no allegation in the bill that any residence is in close proximity to the proposed crematory, but that it is to be located in "an entirely rural area."

There is, of course, a minority rule, the gist of which is that mental suffering or depressed feelings are not actionable injuries where funeral parlors are proposed for residential areas. *Stoddard v. Snodgrass*, 117

Or. 262, 241 P. 73, 43 A.L.R. 1160 (1925), is a good example of this line of cases. In *Dawson v. Laufersweiler*, 241 Iowa 850, 43 N.W.2d 726 (1950), the court indicated, in dictum, that no injunction would issue in a strictly residential area; however, the case actually turned on the fact that the neighborhood was "in transition" from a residential to a commercial area. *Bauman v. Piser Undertakers Co.*, 34 Ill.App.2d 145, 180 N.E.2d 705 (1962), apparently follows the minority rule, except that here the section of the street on which a mortuary was to be built was zoned for it, but the total area surrounding the site was predominantly residential.

* * *

Because we find the allegations in the petition insufficient, even if proved, to persuade us that a nuisance is sure to be created by the operation of a crematory in this particular location, we therefore, affirm the ruling of the trial court as set forth in a splendid memorandum opinion.

Affirmed.

FRIENDSHIP FARMS CAMPS, INC. v. PARSON

Appellate Court of Indiana, First District, 1977.
172 Ind.App. 73, 359 N.E.2d 280.

ROBERTSON, CHIEF JUDGE.

Defendants-appellants Friendship Farms Camps, Inc. (Friendship) is appealing the awarding of damages to each of the plaintiffs-appellees, Parsons and Combs, as well as the trial court's granting of an injunction designed to abate a nuisance.

* * *

The record shows that Ronald Gabbard, his wife, and parents orally leased their 80 acres of rural property to Friendship Farms Camps, Inc. for use as a campground. Friendship Farms Camps, Inc. was organized and incorporated by Ronald Gabbard, his wife, and another primarily for the purpose of providing camping facilities on the Gabbard property.

Prior to 1972, youth day camps were held on the property, but beginning in 1972, a number of weekly high school marching band camps were held. The bands would arrive on Sunday afternoon and stay until Friday evening during which time they would practice both marching and playing music. During 1973 and 1974, the band camps use increased, and Friendship proposed to extend the 1975 program to include weekend band camps during football season.

The Parsons and the Combs, whose residences were located across the road from Friendship, brought an action against Friendship to abate an alleged nuisance and for damages. The essence of their testimony at trial was that during the summer months loud band music and electronically amplified voices could be heard from 7:00 or 8:00 A.M. until 9:00 or

10:00 P.M. which interfered with their sleep and use of their property during the evening hours. They had complained to Gabbard and asked that the band music be confined to an earlier hour. Gabbard made an effort to enforce quiet hours. However, the evening noise continued for the reason that the cooler period of the day was better for practice time.

The trial court awarded Parsons and Combs $600 each in damages and permanently enjoined Friendship from permitting music or the use of bull horns on its property between 5:00 P.M. and 8:00 A.M. on weekdays and any time during weekends.

* * *

Friendship's contention that actual physical sickness or illness must result before a nuisance may be found is without merit. This court has repeatedly stated that the essence of a private nuisance is the fact that one party is using his property to the detriment of the use and enjoyment of others. *Stover v. Fechtman* (1966), 140 Ind.App. 62, 222 N.E.2d 281; *Cox v. Schlachter, supra*. While injury to health is a factor to be considered in determining if one's property is being detrimentally used, it is not the only factor to be considered for our legislature has defined a nuisance as:

> "Whatever is injurious to health or indecent or offensive to the senses, or an obstruction to the free use of property, so as essentially to interfere with the comfortable enjoyment of life or property, is a nuisance and the subject of an action." IC 1971, 34–1–52–1 (Burns Code Ed.).

It is settled that noise, in and of itself, may constitute a nuisance if such noise is unreasonable in its degree. *Muehlman v. Keilman* (1971), 257 Ind. 100, 272 N.E.2d 591. Reasonableness is a question for the trier of fact. *Muehlman v. Keilman, supra*.

The evidence at trial shows that the proximity of the band music and amplified voices aggravated existing illnesses of Dr. Parsons and Mrs. Combs. Additionally, the noise interfered with sleep, required windows and doors to be kept closed on summer evenings, prohibited hearing television or conversing with another person in the same room, and made sitting outside unpleasant and visiting with others virtually impossible.

We are of the opinion that there was an adequate evidentiary foundation for the trial court's judgment.

Friendship further argues under this issue that the evidence is not sufficient to support the trial court's restrictive time limitations specified in the injunction. Friendship does not argue that the trial court had no authority to enjoin them but that a time limitation set at 8:30 P.M. should have been imposed.

As previously stated, noise as a nuisance is subject to a test of reasonableness, and reasonableness is to be decided by the trier of fact. *Muehlman v. Keilman, supra*. The record reveals that Parson and Combs complained that the noise interfered with their sleep, prevented them from entertaining friends, and prohibited relaxation.

We are of the opinion that the evidence and reasonable inferences to be drawn therefrom are sufficient to sustain the limited permanent injunction.

Friendship argues that the trial court's decision is contrary to law because there was no finding that its operations produced actual physical discomfort to persons of ordinary sensibilities, tastes, and habits and that the net effect of the injunction was to destroy the operation of a lawful and useful business.

Our previous discussion relating to the sufficiency of the evidence demonstrates that actual physical discomfort is not, necessarily, the sole ingredient of a nuisance. See: IC 1971, 34–1–52–1 (Burns Code Ed.).

As to whether the operation of a lawful and useful business is being destroyed, we agree that curtailment exists, but not its destruction.

* * *

Friendship argues that the trial court's action prevented it from showing that the operation of its business promoted the interests of the surrounding area to an extent outweighing the private inconvenience resulting therefrom. Friendship relies upon *Northern Indiana Public Service Co. v. W.J. & M.S. Vesey* (1936), 210 Ind. 338, 200 N.E. 620, for the proposition that it is a defense to an action to enjoin a nuisance that the act promotes the public convenience and interest to such an extent as to outweigh the private inconvenience. In *Northern Indiana Public Service Co.*, our Supreme Court refused to abate the operation of a gas plant because of the overriding public interest to be served by the continued production of gas for the community's use. While refusing to enjoin the gas plant, the court did award permanent damages.

We feel that in certain circumstances the continued operation of a nuisance creating business is necessary for the benefit and convenience of the community. In these limited situations, less injury would be occasioned by the continued operation of the nuisance than by enjoining it. However, the private injury suffered must be compensated by an award of permanent damages if appropriate.

We believe the trial court was correct in finding that this case does not present a situation where the social utility of the Friendship business greatly outweighed the private harm to the adjoining land owners. Therefore, no error existed in the trial court's ruling.

Friendship finally contends that the monetary damages are excessive and contrary to law. In support of this contention, Friendship argues that no evidence was presented showing a decrease in the fair rental values of the Parsons and Combs properties.

The proper measure of damages in cases of this posture, where the nuisance is found to be abatable, is the injury to the use of the property determined by the depreciation in the fair market rental value during the time the nuisance existed. *Harrison v. Indiana Auto Shredders Co.* (7th Cir.1975), 528 F.2d 1107; *Cox v. Schlachter, supra*; *Davoust v. Mitchell* (1970), 146 Ind.App. 536, 257 N.E.2d 332.

The trial court determined that the fair market rental value of the properties owned by Parsons and Combs depreciated in the amount of six hundred dollars ($600.00) as a result of the Friendship nuisance. Judgment was entered accordingly.

* * *

[Discussion of damages is omitted.]

Affirmed.

(3) Uses in Conflict With Part Time, Recreational Residences

CLARK v. WAMBOLD

Supreme Court of Wisconsin, 1917.
165 Wis. 70, 160 N.W. 1039.

This is an action in equity to enjoin the defendant from maintaining a nuisance consisting of pig pens and pig yards, immediately adjacent to plaintiff's premises on the east shore of Eagle lake in Waukesha county, Wisconsin. The plaintiff owns two acres of land on the shore of the lake, which he purchased in 1905, part of it being purchased from the defendant, and all of which he uses for summer residence purposes. The defendant owns a farm immediately east of the plaintiff's premises and also operates a feed mill thereon. For years before the commencement of this action he has made a business of raising pigs and selling them when about six weeks old, sometimes having eight or nine brood sows at a time. The yards or inclosures in which the pigs are bred are close to the feed mill and also near the plaintiff's property. The brood sows are fed largely with sweepings from the feed mill. There was much evidence to the effect that the pig pens and inclosures were kept in a filthy condition and that the odors arising therefrom and drifting over the plaintiff's premises were very offensive and continuous during the summer months. There was also considerable testimony to the effect that the pens and yards were kept in as clean and sanitary condition as reasonably possible and better than most farmers are accustomed to keep such places. The pig pens and inclosures existed and were in use in 1905, when the plaintiff purchased his property along the lake shore, and at that time the plaintiff bought of the defendant two small parcels along the east side of his property, on which pig pens were situated, in order to remove the pens and keep the defendant's hogs further away from his summer home. The defendant raised more pigs during the years beginning with 1911 or 1912 than before. The court found in substance that the pens and yards were kept in as clean and sanitary condition as can be expected; that there were no odors except such as necessarily exist around well kept pens and yards; and that the effect of such odors is not such as to materially interfere with the enjoyment of plaintiff's premises or materially impair their use by people of ordinary sensibilities. Judgment was entered dismissing the complaint without costs except clerk's fees, and the plaintiff appeals. * * *

WINSLOW, C.J.

The raising of pigs is a perfectly lawful and respectable business. Doubtless it will remain so as long as the human palate craves the thin cut of juicy ham and the crisp slice of breakfast bacon. With all the marvelous advance in the science of animal husbandry which has taken place in recent years we have not yet produced the odorless pig. He may come at some future time in company with the voiceless cat and the flealess dog, but he is not yet in sight. Whenever he comes he will be welcome, but in the meantime pigs will be pigs, and we must put up as best we may with the odorous pig and his still more odorous pen.

Manifestly pigs cannot be raised in the city, hence they must be raised on the farm. If they are raised there under conditions as clean and sanitary as can reasonably be attained considering the characteristics of the animal and the necessity for confinement in close quarters, the fact that odors from those quarters are carried abroad on the summer breeze will not make an actionable nuisance.

It becomes one of those minor discomforts of life which must be borne in deference to the principle that one man's enjoyment of property cannot always be the controlling factor, but must be considered in connection with the reasonable and lawful use of other property by his neighbors.

The trial court in the present case has found upon sufficient evidence that the pens are kept with reasonable cleanliness and we do not find ourselves able to say that the clear preponderance of the evidence is against the finding. It follows that the judgment must be affirmed. Notwithstanding this result, it is not deemed improper to suggest to the respondent that insistence on extreme legal rights is not always good policy, to say nothing of good neighborliness. It is far better to make a friend of one's neighbor by foregoing, at his request, the exercise of some minor right which causes him discomfort, than to make an enemy of him by insisting upon the right simply because the law gives it. It does not appear that it would be difficult, or even inconvenient, to remove the pig yards which are nearest to the plaintiff's property to some other spot upon the farm. Good neighborliness strongly suggests that he ought to do so. A good neighbor is a great treasure. We can generally have such treasures if we are neighborly ourselves. The golden rule is just as good a rule of conduct now as it was nineteen hundred years ago. We are confident that if the defendant acts upon it in the present case he will in the end experience greater satisfaction from that action than he now experiences in the affirmance of this judgment.

By the Court.—Judgment affirmed.

Notes

1. While on the subject of pigs and pig pens, you may care to compare with the Wambold case, William Aldred's Case, 9 Co.Rep. 57b, 77 Eng.Rep. 816 (1610). William Aldred brought trespass on the case against Thomas Benton for erecting a hog sty on Benton's land, near William's house. The trial court found for William, but Benton moved in arrest of judgment, "that the building of the house for hogs was necessary for the sustenance of man: and one ought not to have so delicate a nose, that he cannot bear the smell of hogs; for *lex non favet delicatorum votis*" * * * (the law does not favor the wishes of the dainty). But Benton's motion did not succeed, "for in a house four things are desired *habitio hominis* [habitation by man], *delectatio inhabitantis* [the pleasure of the inhabitant], *necessitas lumines* [necessary light], *et sulubritas aeris* [and wholesome air]." Have our standards of comfort in the home improved or declined in four centuries?

2. On the matter of protecting recreational living (without zoning), consider Schneider v. Fromm Laboratories, Inc., 262 Wis. 21, 53 N.W.2d 737 (1952), where the court, on behalf of four week-end and two permanent residents, refused to enjoin the keeping of between 400 and 900 dogs for the purpose of producing vaccine for dog, fox and horse diseases.

3. Attempts by recreational dwellers to keep out bathing beaches catering to the masses have not been successful. Watchung Lake v. Mobus, 119 N.J.L. 272, 196 A. 223 (1938); State ex rel. Warner v. Hayes Inv. Corp., 13 Wash.2d 306, 125 P.2d 262 (1942). Similarly an attempt to enjoin a public fishing site failed. Gableman v. Department of Conservation, 309 Mich. 416, 15 N.W.2d 689 (1944). Summer dwellers also failed to close up a year-around poultry farm in Wetstone v. Cantor, 144 Conn. 77, 127 A.2d 70 (1956). But shore owners on a 75-acre lake succeeded in enjoining "unreasonable" water skiing in Florio v. State ex rel. Epperson, 119 So.2d 305 (Fla.App.1960), noted in Annot., 80 A.L.R.2d 1117 (1961).

4. Contrasting somewhat with Clark v. Wambold is Mitchell v. Hines, 305 Mich. 296, 9 N.W.2d 547 (1943), which was an action to enjoin a piggery brought by owners of residences in a subdivision in the same general vicinity. The pigs were fed with garbage which was placed in an open field, with the unconsumed portion later being plowed under. Testimony showed that the odors during the spring, summer and fall of 1941 were quite revolting and were reoccurring in the spring of 1942 at the time of trial. The odor had not become objectionable until around 1940, and the plaintiffs and witnesses had lived in that area for from one to twenty-one years. The Michigan court stated that feeding garbage to pigs "is not a new custom nor are the premises where pigs are kept usually odorless." Pig-raising is a lawful business so long as it does not constitute a nuisance because of the means of operation. This was not considered to be a case where newcomers had moved to the nuisance. Said the court: "[R]ather we have a case where for some years the piggery was conducted on a small scale and was not objectionable. Then, either the increased size of the piggery or the condition of the fields through the continued dumping of garbage thereon, or both, created such odors that this suit resulted. The fact that the plaintiffs are home owners and that a residential district has expanded so that it is now in the immediate neighborhood of the piggery is not arguable. If the plaintiffs

were farmers in a rural community and such a condition existed on an adjacent farm, they would still have grounds for complaint." The court concluded that the piggery was a private nuisance and should be enjoined because there was no proof as to how the odors from such a large-scale garbage-feeding operation could be controlled. Can this case be distinguished from Clark v. Wambold because the farm was on the fringe of the subdivision rather than in open country? Consider the language of the court. Whatever the answer, the size of the operation and the methods employed quite obviously had a great deal to do with the decision. Modern day "hog ranches" are mechanized operations raising thousands of pigs in a factory setting. These operations pit farmers and rural residents against the pig factory in nuisance suits and also in enforcement of state environmental regulations. See, e.g., Monroe City v. Arnold, 22 Utah 2d 291, 452 P.2d 321 (1969) (public nuisance); Queen City Farms, Inc. v. Central Nat. Ins. Co., 126 Wash.2d 50, 882 P.2d 703 (1994) (environmental regulations).

C. CONFLICTING USES ON THE RURURBAN FRINGE

MAYKUT v. PLASKO

Supreme Court of Connecticut, 1976.
170 Conn. 310, 365 A.2d 1114.

LONGO, ASSOCIATE JUSTICE.

The defendants, Martin and Mary Plasko, own a twenty-eight acre farm in Trumbull, a portion of which they used to raise corn. To reduce damage to their ripening corn caused by marauding birds, from time to time they used a mechanical noisemaking device known as a "corn cannon" which emitted a noise like a gunshot or explosion. They operated it from 7 a.m. to 8 p.m. and the device sounded at about five-minute intervals. The plaintiff lives in a residence located about 600 feet from the defendants' land, in one of the densely populated areas which border the farm on three sides. The plaintiff complained to the police about the noise of the corn cannon during the summer of 1970; and when he was again disturbed by the cannon in 1971, the plaintiff obtained an ex parte temporary injunction against its continued use. In August of 1972, the plaintiff brought the present action in Circuit Court. After a full hearing, the court granted a permanent injunction against the use of the cannon, and awarded the plaintiff damages in the amount of $25. The court also held that since the use of the cannon constituted a common-law nuisance, it was not necessary to consider claims made by the defendants that a permit for its use had been issued which was valid under the General Statutes and the zoning regulations of the town of Trumbull.

* * *

The law imposes upon every property owner a duty "to make a reasonable use of his own property so as to occasion no unnecessary damage or annoyance to his neighbor." *Nailor v. C.W. Blakeslee & Sons, Inc.*, 117 Conn. 241, 245, 167 A. 548, cited in *Herbert v. Smyth*, 155 Conn. 78, 82, 230 A.2d 235, 237. Determining reasonableness "is essentially a weighing process, involving a comparative evaluation of conflicting interests in various situations." Restatement, 4 Torts § 826, p. 242, cited in *O'Neill v. Carolina Freight Carriers Corporation*, 156 Conn. 613, 617, 618, 244 A.2d 372, and *Nair v. Thaw*, 156 Conn. 445, 452, 242 A.2d 757. The appellate court found no indication that this weighing test had been applied, and therefore dissolved the permanent injunction. We have examined the record in this case and we find that the trial judge did apply the test set out above. Although a memorandum of decision cannot take the place of a finding, it may be consulted "to ascertain the ground on which the court acted." *Ruggles v. Town Plan & Zoning Commission*, 154 Conn. 711, 712, 226 A.2d 108. In its memorandum of decision, the trial court made explicit reference to the weighing test in the following manner: "Determining unreasonableness is essentially a weighing process, involving a comparative evaluation of conflicting interests." The facts outlined in that memorandum of decision and set out in the finding include a consideration not only of the interest of the plaintiff, but of the defendants also. The trial court did apply the proper test.

* * *

The trial and the appellate courts agreed that, if the existence of an enjoinable nuisance was properly found by the trial court, it was not necessary to consider the validity of General Statutes § 26–47a [Use of Noise-making Devices to Repel Marauding Birds and Wildlife] and a provision and amendment of the zoning regulations of the town of Trumbull, both of which the defendants cite as the source of authorization for the use of the corn cannon. We agree with the trial and appellate courts, for "[a]ccording to the weight of authority * * * while what is authorized by law cannot be a public nuisance, it may nevertheless be a private nuisance, and the legislative authorization does not affect any claim of a private citizen for damages * * * or for an injunction." 58 Am.Jur.2d, Nuisances, § 230. This court follows that rule and has upheld the issuance of injunctions against the conduct on one's own property of an otherwise lawful activity. *O'Neill v. Carolina Freight Carriers Corporation*, 156 Conn. 613, 617, 244 A.2d 372; *Nair v. Thaw*, 156 Conn. 445, 451–52, 242 A.2d 757. That a municipality by its zoning regulations condones certain uses is no defense to an unreasonable use constituting a nuisance. *Herbert v. Smyth*, 155 Conn. 78, 83, 230 A.2d 235. The use of the corn cannon was a private nuisance, for it affected a few persons in relation to a right they enjoyed by virtue of their interest in land. 58 Am.Jur.2d, Nuisances, § 9; Prosser, Torts (3d Ed.) § 90. Because the fact that an act may otherwise be lawful does not prevent it from being a private nuisance, it is not necessary to consider the legislative and municipal provisions upon which the defendants seek to rely.

The trial court's conclusion that an enjoinable nuisance existed was arrived at according to law. As to the judgment of the Appellate Division, there is error, the judgment is set aside and the case is remanded to the Appellate Division with direction to affirm the judgment of the Circuit Court.

* * *

SPUR INDUS., INC. v. DEL E. WEBB DEVELOPMENT CO.

Supreme Court of Arizona, 1972.
108 Ariz. 178, 494 P.2d 700.

CAMERON, VICE CHIEF JUSTICE.

From a judgment permanently enjoining the defendant, Spur Industries, Inc., from operating a cattle feedlot near the plaintiff Del E. Webb Development Company's Sun City, Spur appeals. Webb cross-appeals. Although numerous issues are raised, we feel that it is necessary to answer only two questions. They are:

1. Where the operation of a business, such as a cattle feedlot is lawful in the first instance, but becomes a nuisance by reason of a nearby residential area, may the feedlot operation be enjoined in an action brought by the developer of the residential area?

2. Assuming that the nuisance may be enjoined, may the developer of a completely new town or urban area in a previously agricultural area be required to indemnify the operator of the feedlot who must move or cease operation because of the presence of the residential area created by the developer?

The facts necessary for a determination of this matter on appeal are as follows. The area in question is located in Maricopa County, Arizona, some 14 to 15 miles west of the urban area of Phoenix, on the Phoenix–Wickenburg Highway, also known as Grand Avenue. About two miles south of Grand Avenue is Olive Avenue which runs east and west. 111th Avenue runs north and south as does the Agua Fria River immediately to the west. See Exhibits A and B below.

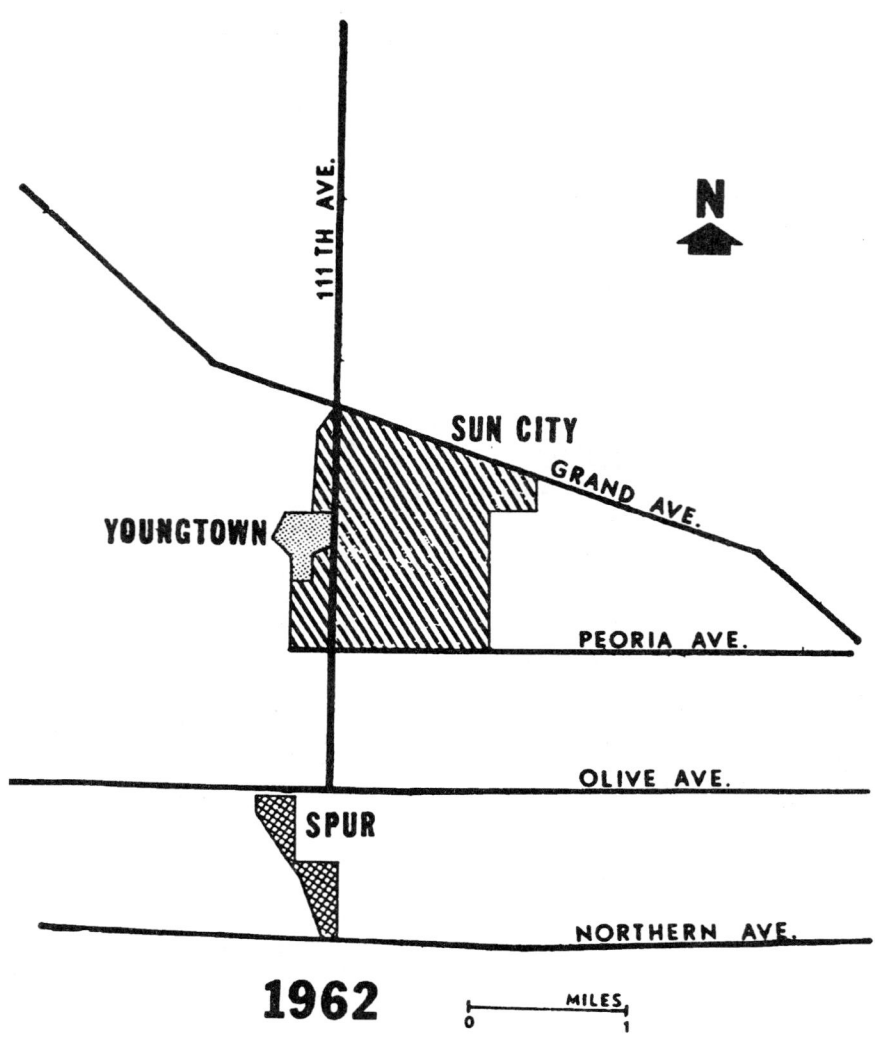

EXHIBIT A

Sec. 2   THE LAW OF NUISANCE   59

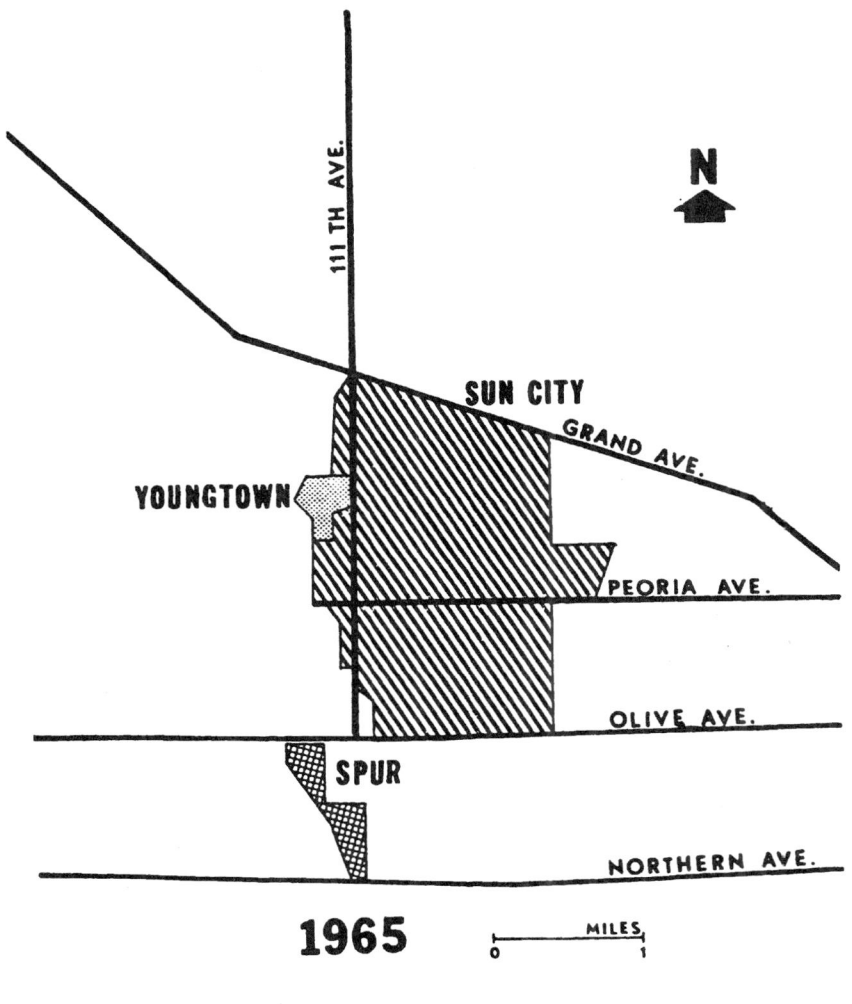

EXHIBIT B

Farming started in this area about 1911. * * * By 1950, the only urban areas in the vicinity were the agriculturally related communities of Peoria, El Mirage, and Surprise located along Grand Avenue. Along 111th Avenue, approximately one mile south of Grand Avenue and 1½ miles north of Olive Avenue, the community of Youngtown was commenced in 1954. Youngtown is a retirement community appealing primarily to senior citizens.

In 1956, Spur's predecessors in interest, H. Marion Welborn and the Northside Hay Mill and Trading Company, developed feedlots, about ½ mile south of Olive Avenue, in an area between the confluence of the usually dry Agua Fria and New Rivers. The area is well suited for cattle feeding and in 1959, there were 25 cattle feeding pens or dairy operations within a 7 mile radius of the location developed by Spur's predecessors. In April and May of 1959, the Northside Hay Mill was feeding between 6,000 and 7,000 head of cattle and Welborn approximately 1,500 head on a combined area of 35 acres.

In May of 1959, Del Webb began to plan the development of an urban area to be known as Sun City. For this purpose, the Marinette and the Santa Fe Ranches, some 20,000 acres of farmland, were purchased for $15,000,000 or $750.00 per acre. This price was considerably less than the price of land located near the urban area of Phoenix, and along with the success of Youngtown was a factor influencing the decision to purchase the property in question.

By September 1959, Del Webb had started construction of a golf course south of Grand Avenue and Spur's predecessors had started to level ground for more feedlot area. In 1960, Spur purchased the property in question and began a rebuilding and expansion program extending both to the north and south of the original facilities. By 1962, Spur's expansion program was completed and had expanded from approximately 35 acres to 114 acres. See Exhibit A above.

Accompanied by an extensive advertising campaign, homes were first offered by Del Webb in January 1960 and the first unit to be completed was south of Grand Avenue and approximately 2½ miles north of Spur. By 2 May 1960, there were 450 to 500 houses completed or under construction. At this time, Del Webb did not consider odors from the Spur feed pens a problem and Del Webb continued to develop in a southerly direction, until sales resistance became so great that the parcels were difficult if not impossible to sell. * * *

By December 1967, Del Webb's property had extended south to Olive Avenue and Spur was within 500 feet of Olive Avenue to the north. See Exhibit B above. Del Webb filed its original complaint alleging that in excess of 1,300 lots in the southwest portion were unfit for development for sale as residential lots because of the operation of the Spur feedlot.

Del Webb's suit complained that the Spur feeding operation was a public nuisance because of the flies and the odor which were drifting or being blown by the prevailing south to north wind over the southern portion of Sun City. At the time of the suit, Spur was feeding between 20,000 and 30,000 head of cattle, and the facts amply support the finding of the trial court that the feed pens had become a nuisance to the people who resided in the southern part of Del Webb's development. The testimony indicated that cattle in a commercial feedlot will produce 35 to 40 pounds of wet manure per day, per head, or over a million pounds of wet manure per day for 30,000 head of cattle, and that despite the admittedly good feedlot management and good housekeeping practices by Spur, the resulting odor and flies produced an annoying if not unhealthy situation as far as the senior citizens of southern Sun City were concerned. There is no doubt that some of the citizens of Sun City were unable to enjoy the outdoor living which Del Webb had advertised and that Del Webb was faced with sales resistance from prospective purchasers as well as strong and persistent complaints from the people who had purchased homes in that area.

* * *

It is noted, however, that neither the citizens of Sun City nor Youngtown are represented in this lawsuit and the suit is solely between Del E. Webb Development Company and Spur Industries, Inc.

* * *

Where the injury is slight, the remedy for minor inconveniences lies in an action for damages rather than in one for an injunction. *Kubby v. Hammond*, 68 Ariz. 17, 198 P.2d 134 (1948). Moreover, some courts have held, in the "balancing of conveniences" cases, that damages may be the sole remedy. See *Boomer v. Atlantic Cement Co.*, 26 N.Y.2d 219, 309 N.Y.S.2d 312, 257 N.E.2d 870, 40 A.L.R.3d 590 (1970), and annotation comments, 40 A.L.R.3d 601.

Thus, it would appear from the admittedly incomplete record as developed in the trial court, that, at most, residents of Youngtown would be entitled to damages rather than injunctive relief.

We have no difficulty, however, in agreeing with the conclusion of the trial court that Spur's operation was an enjoinable public nuisance as far as the people in the southern portion of Del Webb's Sun City were concerned.

* * *

It is clear that as to the citizens of Sun City, the operation of Spur's feedlot was both a public and a private nuisance. They could have successfully maintained an action to abate the nuisance. Del Webb, having shown a special injury in the loss of sales, had a standing to bring suit to enjoin the nuisance. *Engle v. Clark*, 53 Ariz. 472, 90 P.2d 994 (1939); *City of Phoenix v. Johnson, supra*. The judgment of the trial court permanently enjoining the operation of the feedlot is affirmed.

MUST DEL WEBB INDEMNIFY SPUR?

A suit to enjoin a nuisance sounds in equity and the courts have long recognized a special responsibility to the public when acting as a court of equity:

§ 104. Where public interest is involved.

"Courts of equity may, and frequently do, go much further both to give and withhold relief in furtherance of the public interest than they are accustomed to go when only private interests are involved. Accordingly, the granting or withholding of relief may properly be dependent upon considerations of public interest. * * *." 27 Am. Jur.2d, Equity, page 626.

In addition to protecting the public interest, however, courts of equity are concerned with protecting the operator of a lawfully, albeit noxious, business from the result of a knowing and willful encroachment by others near his business.

In the so-called "coming to the nuisance" cases, the courts have held that the residential landowner may not have relief if he knowingly came into a neighborhood reserved for industrial or agricultural endeavors and has been damaged thereby:

> "Plaintiffs chose to live in an area uncontrolled by zoning laws or restrictive covenants and remote from urban development. In such an area plaintiffs cannot complain that legitimate agricultural pursuits are being carried on in the vicinity, nor can plaintiffs, having chosen to build in an agricultural area, complain that the agricultural pursuits carried on in the area depreciate the value of their homes. The area being *primarily agricultural,* any opinion reflecting the value of such property must take this factor into account. The standards affecting the value of residence property in an urban setting, subject to zoning controls and controlled planning techniques, cannot be the standards by which agricultural properties are judged.

> "People employed in a city who build their homes in suburban areas of the county beyond the limits of a city and zoning regulations do so for a reason. Some do so to avoid the high taxation rate imposed by cities, or to avoid special assessments for street, sewer and water projects. They usually build on improved or hard surface highways, which have been built either at state or county expense and thereby avoid special assessments for these improvements. It may be that they desire to get away from the congestion of traffic, smoke, noise, foul air and the many other annoyances of city life. But with all these advantages in going beyond the area which is zoned and restricted to protect them in their homes, they must be prepared to take the disadvantages." *Dill v. Excel Packing Company*, 183 Kan. 513, 525, 526, 331 P.2d 539, 548, 549 (1958). See also *East St. Johns Shingle Co. v. City of Portland*, 195 Or. 505, 246 P.2d 554, 560–562 (1952).

And:

> * * * a party cannot justly call upon the law to make that place suitable for his residence which was not so when he selected it. * * *. *Gilbert v. Showerman*, 23 Mich. 448, 455, 2 Brown 158 (1871).

Were Webb the only party injured, we would feel justified in holding that the doctrine of "coming to the nuisance" would have been a bar to the relief asked by Webb, and, on the other hand, had Spur located the feedlot near the outskirts of a city and had the city grown toward the feedlot, Spur would have to suffer the cost of abating the nuisance as to those people locating within the growth pattern of the expanding city:

"The case affords, perhaps, an example where a business established at a place remote from population is gradually surrounded and becomes part of a populous center, so that a business which formerly was not an interference with the rights of others has become so by the encroachment of the population * * *." *City of Ft. Smith v. Western Hide & Fur Co.*, 153 Ark. 99, 103, 239 S.W. 724, 726 (1922).

We agree, however, with the Massachusetts court that:

"The law of nuisance affords no rigid rule to be applied in all instances. It is elastic. It undertakes to require only that which is fair and reasonable under all the circumstances. In a commonwealth like this, which depends for its material prosperity so largely on the continued growth and enlargement of manufacturing of diverse varieties, 'extreme rights' cannot be enforced. * * *." *Stevens v. Rockport Granite Co.*, 216 Mass. 486, 488, 104 N.E. 371, 373 (1914).

There was no indication in the instant case at the time Spur and its predecessors located in western Maricopa County that a new city would spring up, full-blown, alongside the feeding operation and that the developer of that city would ask the court to order Spur to move because of the new city. Spur is required to move not because of any wrongdoing on the part of Spur, but because of a proper and legitimate regard of the courts for the rights and interests of the public.

Del Webb, on the other hand, is entitled to the relief prayed for (a permanent injunction), not because Webb is blameless, but because of the damage to the people who have been encouraged to purchase homes in Sun City. It does not equitably or legally follow, however, that Webb, being entitled to the injunction, is then free of any liability to Spur if Webb has in fact been the cause of the damage Spur has sustained. It does not seem harsh to require a developer, who has taken advantage of the lesser land values in a rural area as well as the availability of large tracts of land on which to build and develop a new town or city in the area, to indemnify those who are forced to leave as a result.

Having brought people to the nuisance to the foreseeable detriment of Spur, Webb must indemnify Spur for a reasonable amount of the cost of moving or shutting down. It should be noted that this relief to Spur is limited to a case wherein a developer has, with foreseeability, brought into a previously agricultural or industrial area the population which makes necessary the granting of an injunction against a lawful business and for which the business has no adequate relief.

It is therefore the decision of this court that the matter be remanded to the trial court for a hearing upon the damages sustained by the defendant Spur as a reasonable and direct result of the granting of the permanent injunction. Since the result of the appeal may appear novel and both sides have obtained a measure of relief, it is ordered that each side will bear its own costs.

Affirmed in part, reversed in part, and remanded for further proceedings consistent with this opinion.

Notes

1. Does the decision of the Arizona Court amount in effect to a taking of private property for *private* use in contravention of the established eminent domain principle that upon payment of just compensation private property may be taken for *public* use? Or does the result render a certain portion of Spur's property unusable without indemnification, since the only payment by Webb is for the cost of Spur's moving "or shutting down" expenses? Does this decision, which the Court acknowledges "may appear novel," provide a reasonable solution to the problem of "moving to the nuisance" where the activity producing the nuisance is located in a somewhat isolated area? Or should this case be viewed as one in which there was not a true "moving to the nuisance" but as one in which the populated area gradually expanded to encompass or reach the area of the nuisance?

2. In Meat Producers, Inc. v. McFarland, 476 S.W.2d 406 (Tex.Civ.App. 1972), a cattle-feeding operation "of considerable magnitude" was emitting disagreeable odors and permanent damages were sought. At the time of trial, the operations had been suspended, but the Texas Court held it to be a nuisance anyway and granted damages. The plaintiff owned 645 acres adjacent to the Meat Producers' property, and he alleged that the odors had reduced the market value of his property to $335 per acre. The jury found in his favor and assessed a diminution in value of $135 per acre. The defendant argued that any inconvenience from the feed lot was trivial because no one was living on the plaintiff's land when the feed lot was in operation or at the time of trial. The appellate court rejected that argument, saying that the injury is not limited to the actual use of the land. Testimony established that the highest and best use of the land was for residential purposes, "and since there was evidence that odors from the feed lot would substantially interfere with that use, we hold that there was evidence to support the finding that a nuisance existed." The argument that no physical disturbance of the land resulted was also rejected because a "nuisance is by definition a nontrespassory invasion" and it "may be by pollution of the air as well as by disturbance of the soil." Also rejected was the defendant's argument that if a feed lot cannot be operated in a rural area, there are few places where it can be operated inoffensively. The court stated: "For the purpose of determining liability for damages, interference with use of land may be unreasonable, even though utility of the activity causing such interference is great and the harm is relatively small, since it may be reasonable to continue a useful activity causing such interference if payment is made for the harm, but unreasonable to continue it without paying." Various other arguments of the defendant were also rejected. Compare this court's approach with that of the Arizona Court in Spur Industries. Do you think this court would have accepted a "coming to the nuisance" argument by defendant if the plaintiff had begun to develop his land for homesites? By paying permanent damages, is the feed lot operation in effect acquiring something in the nature of an easement or servitude with respect to the land of the plaintiff?

BOOMER v. ATLANTIC CEMENT CO., INC.

Court of Appeals of New York, 1970.
26 N.Y.2d 219, 309 N.Y.S.2d 312, 257 N.E.2d 870.

BERGAN, JUDGE.

Defendant operates a large cement plant near Albany. These are actions for injunction and damages by neighboring land owners alleging injury to property from dirt, smoke and vibration emanating from the plant. A nuisance has been found after trial, temporary damages have been allowed; but an injunction has been denied.

The public concern with air pollution arising from many sources in industry and in transportation is currently accorded ever wider recognition accompanied by a growing sense of responsibility in State and Federal Governments to control it. Cement plants are obvious sources of air pollution in the neighborhoods where they operate.

But there is now before the court private litigation in which individual property owners have sought specific relief from a single plant operation. The threshold question raised by the division of view on this appeal is whether the court should resolve the litigation between the parties now before it as equitably as seems possible; or whether, seeking promotion of the general public welfare, it should channel private litigation into broad public objectives.

A court performs its essential function when it decides the rights of parties before it. Its decision of private controversies may sometimes greatly affect public issues. Large questions of law are often resolved by the manner in which private litigation is decided. But this is normally an incident to the court's main function to settle controversy. It is a rare exercise of judicial power to use a decision in private litigation as a purposeful mechanism to achieve direct public objectives greatly beyond the rights and interests before the court.

Effective control of air pollution is a problem presently far from solution even with the full public and financial powers of government. In large measure adequate technical procedures are yet to be developed and some that appear possible may be economically impracticable.

It seems apparent that the amelioration of air pollution will depend on technical research in great depth; on a carefully balanced consideration of the economic impact of close regulation; and of the actual effect on public health. It is likely to require massive public expenditure and to demand more than any local community can accomplish and to depend on regional and interstate controls.

A court should not try to do this on its own as a by-product of private litigation and it seems manifest that the judicial establishment is neither equipped in the limited nature of any judgment it can pronounce nor prepared to lay down and implement an effective policy for the elimination of air pollution. This is an area beyond the circumference of one private lawsuit. It is a direct responsibility for government and should not thus be undertaken as an incident to solving a dispute between property owners and a single cement plant—one of many—in the Hudson River valley.

The cement making operations of defendant have been found by the court at Special Term to have damaged the nearby properties of plaintiffs in these two actions. That court, as it has been noted, accordingly found defendant maintained a nuisance and this has been affirmed at the Appellate Division. The total damage to plaintiffs' properties is, however, relatively small in comparison with the value of defendant's operation and with the consequences of the injunction which plaintiffs seek.

The ground for the denial of injunction, notwithstanding the finding both that there is a nuisance and that plaintiffs have been damaged substantially, is the large disparity in economic consequences of the nuisance and of the injunction. This theory cannot, however, be sustained without overruling a doctrine which has been consistently reaffirmed in several leading cases in this court and which has never been disavowed here, namely that where a nuisance has been found and where there has been any substantial damage shown by the party complaining an injunction will be granted.

The rule in New York has been that such a nuisance will be enjoined although marked disparity be shown in economic consequence between the effect of the injunction and the effect of the nuisance.

The problem of disparity in economic consequence was sharply in focus in *Whalen v. Union Bag & Paper Co.*, 208 N.Y. 1, 101 N.E. 805. A pulp mill entailing an investment of more than a million dollars polluted a stream in which plaintiff, who owned a farm, was "a lower riparian owner". The economic loss to plaintiff from this pollution was small. This court, reversing the Appellate Division, reinstated the injunction granted by the Special Term against the argument of the mill owner that in view of "the slight advantage to plaintiff and the great loss that will be inflicted on defendant" an injunction should not be granted (p. 2, 101 N.E. p. 805). "Such a balancing of injuries cannot be justified by the circumstances of this case", Judge Werner noted (p. 4, 101 N.E. p. 805). He continued: "Although the damage to the plaintiff may be slight as compared with the defendant's expense of abating the condition, that is not a good reason for refusing an injunction" (p. 5, 101 N.E. p. 806).

Thus the unconditional injunction granted at Special Term was reinstated. The rule laid down in that case, then, is that whenever the damage resulting from a nuisance is found not "unsubstantial", viz., $100 a year, injunction would follow. This states a rule that had been followed in this court with marked consistency * * *

There are cases where injunction has been denied. *McCann v. Chasm Power Co.*, 211 N.Y. 301, 105 N.E. 416 is one of them. There, however, the damage shown by plaintiffs was not only unsubstantial, it was non-existent. Plaintiffs owned a rocky bank of the stream in which defendant had raised the level of the water. This had no economic or other adverse consequence to plaintiffs, and thus injunctive relief was denied. Similar is the basis for denial of injunction in *Forstmann v. Joray Holding Co.*, 244 N.Y. 22, 154 N.E. 652 where no benefit to plaintiffs could be seen from the injunction sought (p. 32, 154 N.E. 655). Thus if, within *Whalen v. Union Bag & Paper Co.*, *supra*, which authoritatively states the rule in New York, the damage to plaintiffs in these present cases from defendant's cement plant is "not unsubstantial", an injunction should follow.

Although the court at Special Term and the Appellate Division held that injunction should be denied, it was found that plaintiffs had been damaged in various specific amounts up to the time of the trial and damages to the respective plaintiffs were awarded for those amounts. The effect of this was, injunction having been denied, plaintiffs could maintain successive actions at law for damages thereafter as further damage was incurred.

The court at Special Term also found the amount of permanent damage attributable to each plaintiff, for the guidance of the parties in the event both sides stipulated to the payment and acceptance of such permanent damage as a settlement of all the controversies among the parties. The total of permanent damages to all plaintiffs thus found was $185,000. This basis of adjustment has not resulted in any stipulation by the parties.

This result at Special Term and at the Appellate Division is a departure from a rule that has become settled; but to follow the rule literally in these cases would be to close down the plant at once. This court is fully agreed to avoid that immediately drastic remedy; the difference in view is how best to avoid it.

One alternative is to grant the injunction but postpone its effect to a specified future date to give opportunity for technical advances to permit defendant to eliminate the nuisance; another is to grant the injunction conditioned on the payment of permanent damages to plaintiffs which would compensate them for the total economic loss to their property present and future caused by defendant's operations. For reasons which will be developed the court chooses the latter alternative.

If the injunction were to be granted unless within a short period— e.g., 18 months—the nuisance be abated by improved methods, there would be no assurance that any significant technical improvement would occur.

The parties could settle this private litigation at any time if defendant paid enough money and the imminent threat of closing the plant would build up the pressure on defendant. If there were no improved techniques found, there would inevitably be applications to the court at Special Term for extensions of time to perform on showing of good faith efforts to find such techniques.

Moreover, techniques to eliminate dust and other annoying by-products of cement making are unlikely to be developed by any research the defendant can undertake within any short period, but will depend on the total resources of the cement industry nationwide and throughout the world. The problem is universal wherever cement is made.

For obvious reasons the rate of the research is beyond control of defendant. If at the end of 18 months the whole industry has not found a technical solution a court would be hard put to close down this one cement plant if due regard be given to equitable principles.

On the other hand, to grant the injunction unless defendant pays plaintiffs such permanent damages as may be fixed by the court seems to do justice between the contending parties. All of the attributions of economic loss to the properties on which plaintiffs' complaints are based will have been redressed.

The nuisance complained of by these plaintiffs may have other public or private consequences, but these particular parties are the only ones who have sought remedies and the judgment proposed will fully redress them. The limitation of relief granted is a limitation only within the four corners of these actions and does not foreclose public health or other public agencies from seeking proper relief in a proper court.

It seems reasonable to think that the risk of being required to pay permanent damages to injured property owners by cement plant owners would itself be a reasonable effective spur to research for improved techniques to minimize nuisance.

* * *

Thus it seems fair to both sides to grant permanent damages to plaintiffs which will terminate this private litigation. The theory of damage is the "servitude on land" of plaintiffs imposed by defendant's nuisance. (See *United States v. Causby*, 328 U.S. 256, 261, 262, 267, 66 S.Ct. 1062, 90 L.Ed. 1206, where the term "servitude" addressed to the land was used by Justice Douglas relating to the effect of airplane noise on property near an airport.)

The judgment, by allowance of permanent damages imposing a servitude on land, which is the basis of the actions, would preclude future recovery by plaintiffs or their grantees (see *Northern Indiana Public Serv. Co. v. W.J. & M.S. Vesey, supra*, p. 351, 200 N.E. 620).

This should be placed beyond debate by a provision of the judgment that the payment by defendant and the acceptance by plaintiffs of permanent damages found by the court shall be in compensation for a servitude on the land.

Although the Trial Term has found permanent damages as a possible basis of settlement of the litigation, on remission the court should be entirely free to re-examine this subject. It may again find the permanent damage already found; or make new findings.

The orders should be reversed, without costs, and the cases remitted to Supreme Court, Albany County to grant an injunction which shall be vacated upon payment by defendant of such amounts of permanent damage to the respective plaintiffs as shall for this purpose be determined by the court.

[Dissenting opinion omitted.]

Notes

1. The Boomer and Spur cases might be compared with some cases in which courts are not as eager to permit the nuisance-like activity to continue. In Mowrer v. Ashland Oil & Refining Co., 518 F.2d 659 (7th Cir.1975), seeping oil from a capped well was held to create a private nuisance despite the fact that the activity causing the seep was conducted with due care. In Associated Metals & Minerals Corp. v. Dixon Chemical & Research, Inc., 82 N.J.Super. 281, 197 A.2d 569 (1963), odors, dusts and fumes produced by defendant and causing a continuous invasion of adjacent property were held to produce a nuisance regardless of considerations of due care or negligence.

2. On the other hand, in Summers v. Acme Flour Mills Co., 263 P.2d 515 (Okl.1953), the court said that it had to be established that the mill was operated in an unreasonable manner in order to establish a nuisance produced by the airborne dust. See also, Riblet v. Ideal Cement Co., 54 Wash.2d 779, 345 P.2d 173 (1959). In that case, incidentally, the plaintiff had been bringing successful nuisance suits every two years against the previous owner of the defendant. The facts of the previous suits were binding against the current owner. A proliferation of lawsuits, of course, was one thing the Boomer majority sought to prevent.

3. One problem which periodically arises with land located on the urban fringe is that relating to ultrahazardous activities. Are these nuisances per se, as they almost certainly would be declared to be if they were located in a settled residential area? The rather dated but still useful American Law of Property § 28.27 (1954) referred to such activity, as well as malicious interference and activities intrinsically detrimental to health and welfare as "hybrid activities" which are not necessarily unreasonable "but which are always unreasonable in certain localities and under certain conditions." The burden is on the plaintiff to establish that the location and conditions are such that these should be enjoined or damages should be awarded or both. This leaves them as something less than nuisances per se, practically speaking, since the facts have to be proven to the court's satisfaction.

The following cases illustrate the problem:

(a) In Hero Lands Co. v. Texaco, Inc., 310 So.2d 93 (La.1975), the question was whether the construction of a hazardous high pressure gas pipeline adjacent to and within fifteen feet of the Hero Lands tract gave rise to an action for damages which impaired the market value and full use of the Hero Lands property. It was concluded that this constituted a dangerous nuisance because it "involved inherent hazards and dangers which are well-known to the public and those purchasing land." Hero was said to have incurred $30,000 in damages.

(b) However, in Hays v. Hartfield L–P Gas, 159 Ind.App. 297, 306 N.E.2d 373 (1974), injunctive relief and damages were sought against Hartfield for the planned operation of a liquid propane bulk plant to be situated near Hays' property. The tank was 300 feet away from Hays' property and had to be set back substantially from a highway so as not to be a traffic hazard. Objection was also made as to anticipated annoyance from dust, noise, lights and odors. These properties were on the fringe of the town limits, but outside of its boundaries. Hays conceded that it was not a nuisance per se, and the court held that evidence was lacking to show that it was a nuisance in fact. There was no proof that it presented a hazard, said the court, and mere fear or apprehension of danger was not enough.

(c) More recent cases involve hazardous wastes, as for example in Wilson v. Key Tronic Corp., 40 Wash.App. 802, 701 P.2d 518 (1985), in which there had been the disposal of hazardous waste on adjoining land, and the plaintiff had had to haul water to his property for months resulting in disruption of family life. Damages were allowed for the annoyance, discomfort and mental anguish accompanying the situation. In Village of Wilsonville v. SCA Services, Inc., 86 Ill.2d 1, 55 Ill.Dec. 499, 426 N.E.2d 824 (1981) the court upheld a permanent injunction against a chemical waste dump and a trial court order for exhumation of all material from the site and reclamation of the land.

(d) In Daniel v. Kosh, 173 Va. 352, 4 S.E.2d 381 (1939), the plaintiff lived near a coal yard and railroad track. The defendant had for some years been unloading gasoline from tank cars into storage tanks for his gasoline business within 100 feet of plaintiff's home. As a result of this, the plaintiff's fire insurance carrier increased his insurance rates to approximately three and one-half times of what they had been. The plaintiff filed suit to enjoin the unloading of gasoline and recover damages. Relief was denied. The court stated that it knew of "no case in which it was held that a mere increase in the insurance rate entitles the plaintiff to redress either in equity or at law. * * * The authorities indeed are to the contrary." It also pointed out that certain other commercial activities, such as a beauty shop, a carpenter shop and a furniture repair shop would also increase the rates.

D. CONFLICTING USES IN OLDER SETTLED AREAS

(1) Residential Areas

MAHONEY v. WALTER

Supreme Court of Appeals of West Virginia, 1974.
157 W.Va. 882, 205 S.E.2d 692.

SPROUSE, JUSTICE:

This case is before the Court upon an appeal from the judgment of the Circuit Court of Marshall County in an action instituted by Raymond Mahoney and fifteen other residents and property owners in Mar–Win Place, a community in Marshall County. The plaintiffs sought to permanently enjoin Eugene A. Walter, Mary A. Walter and Cecil Walter, the defendants, from using their property for the purpose of operating a salvage yard. The defendants were permanently enjoined from operating the salvage yard by the Common Pleas Court of Marshall County, and this judgment was affirmed by an order of the Circuit Court of Marshall County. It is from the judgment of the circuit court that the defendants prosecute this appeal.

* * *

It is apparent from the evidence that Mar–Win Place has been an established community in Marshall County for a number of years and existed as the same type locality for a long time prior to the establishment of the defendants' salvage yard business in 1969. The evidence disclosed that Mar–Win Place is primarily a residential area but was unzoned as to commercial use. Some eight or ten businesses operate in the area including a beauty shop, television repair shop and a tax service. Among the businesses operating in the area, Trenton Construction Company is the largest. It is located on the northern-most edge of the community, but testimony reflected that, because of the topography of the land, the location of the business was neither unsightly nor objectionable. The owner of Trenton Construction Company testified that he had taken great pains to plant trees and foliage to conceal the business from view. The salvage yard was operated primarily as a means of obtaining used parts from wrecked and abandoned automobiles.

The evidence for the plaintiffs revealed the following facts: Approximately one hundred vehicles were stored at random upon the defendants' property. No precaution was taken to drain the vehicles of gasoline or other flammable materials; nor was precaution taken by the defendants to prevent entrance to the yard itself or to the trunks, hoods or interiors of the stored vehicles. A wooden fence had been erected across the front of the property, but no fence had been erected to the sides or rear of the storage area.

The salvage yard is located within a minimum distance of thirty feet to a maximum distance of three hundred feet from adjoining property owners. The yard is open for business six days a week from eight o'clock a.m. to five o'clock p.m. Work was occasionally performed in the yard on Sundays. A four-inch high pressure natural gas line traverses the entire width of the property. A number of wrecked and abandoned vehicles are stacked over the line, undrained of gasoline and other flammable materials. Several of the plaintiffs and their witnesses expressed fear that this situation presented a potential fire hazard.

According to some of the plaintiffs' witnesses a number of rats and snakes had been seen in the vicinity of the salvage yard. Others testified that there were a number of children in the area, and several of the witnesses had observed them playing in or near the salvage yard.

A witness for the plaintiff testified that the noise of the wreckers disturbed her and that she had heard cars being moved in the junk yard between ten and eleven o'clock p.m. Another indicated she was disturbed by the unsightly growth of high weeds in the salvage yard.

Six of the plaintiffs testified that their property values had diminished since the commencement of the operation of the salvage yard. A real estate appraiser in the area stated that he believed that the location of the salvage yard was a deteriorating factor in the value of the Mar–Win property. One plaintiff testified that she had planned to do extensive remodeling to her home but would not do so now because of the salvage yard. Other witnesses for the plaintiff testified that the salvage yard was unsightly, that it disturbed the natural and physical beauty of the neighborhood, and that it presented a threat to the health and safety of the residents of Mar–Win Place.

The principal defense witness, Cecil Walter, testified that the salvage yard could be suitably fenced to prevent entrance of children and to make it more attractive. No action in this respect has been taken by the defendants. Walter stated that he had operated salvage yards for a number of years and had never experienced a fire. He admitted a certain amount of noise was attached to the business of pressing and baling the wrecked cars and abandoned vehicles.

Two residents of Mar–Win testified for the defendants. Neither felt the neighborhood was exclusively residential. * * *

The trial court concluded that the location of the salvage yard is a threat to the health of the residents; that it destroys the natural beauty of the area; that it tends to destroy the residential quality of the area, causing a depreciation of property values; that it causes stress to the residents of the area and interferes with their comfort and enjoyment; that its presence has a deleterious effect on the neighborhood; and that all of this constituted a nuisance which he permanently enjoined.

* * *

The appellant contends that the doctrine of the "balancing of conveniences" should be applied—that is, that when the injury to the defendant in losing its business location is so much greater than the inconvenience to the owners of nearby property, the permanent injunction should be denied or, at the very least, the injunction order should be tailored to permit the continued operation of the salvage yard with appropriate steps being taken to reduce the objectionable features. Considering the relative hardship imposed upon the parties either by granting or denying an injunction is a doctrine that has been in American law for some time. Restatement of Torts, Injunctions, Section 941. However, the balancing of convenience—the disparity of economic consequences is a comparatively new development. 22 Case W.L.Rev. 356; 43 Colo.L.Rev. 225. Under this doctrine, economic consequence to the business owner and the public is compared to the damage to the adjacent property owners who may be compensated by action and damage. The damage to the business owner is normally the loss of investment, loss of profit and the like. The damage to the public is the loss of economic stimuli such as loss of employment.

One of the chief problems with this doctrine is that it compares the general loss to the public, such as loss of jobs, while it only considers specific loss to the private land owner, i.e., the specific money damage to his property, notwithstanding he may be damaged in many general ways which cannot be translated into specific damages. Regardless of the judicial soundness of the doctrine of "balancing conveniences", there was no evidence in this case of a general public economic interest. The only economic interest to be balanced was the private economic interest of the business owner, that is, the loss of this specific locality where he could conduct his business. Admitting this can be, and probably is considerable, Mar–Win Place is not the only locality wherein this type of business can be conducted. The mobility of a business, that is, its adaptability to being conducted in various places rather than in one specific locality is one of the factors to be considered. *Sanders v. Roselawn Memorial Gardens*, 152 W.Va. 91, 159 S.E.2d 784; *Parkersburg Builders Material Company v. Barrack*, 118 W.Va. 608, 191 S.E. 368.

Modern cases litigating alleged nuisances frequently involve the resolution of conflicting interests between business and private residences. This case falls within that pattern.

* * *

While some testimony was conflicting, there was ample evidence upon which the court could conclude that Mar–Win Place was basically a residential area with some unoffensive businesses.

There is likewise evidence to sustain the court's finding that the area, in the immediate vicinity of the salvage yard, was exclusively residential. Facts concerning the activities complained of have been recited. The unsightliness of the yard itself, the noise necessitated by the preparing of the junked automobiles for removal, the possible danger of flammable materials, the possible danger to children from the unprotected nature of the area, and the prevalence of rodents and insects justified the trial court in finding that a nuisance existed regardless of whether the area was exclusively or primarily residential.

The defendants moved that the trial court grant a modified injunction abating the nuisance by permitting them to remedy objectionable features. The trial court overruled that motion and there is ample evidence to sustain this decision that the nuisance could not be abated in this manner.

* * *

Viewing the record as a whole, it is abundantly clear that the trial court had more than sufficient evidence upon which to make a finding that Mar–Win Place was a residential area; that the defendants were conducting their business in the residential area in such a manner as to constitute a nuisance; and that the nuisance could not be abated by anything short of an injunction requiring its removal. The court, having sufficient evidence on which to base its decision of fact and conclusions of law, it cannot be said to have abused its discretion.

* * *

Affirmed.

Notes

1. Parkersburg Builders Material Co. v. Barrack, 118 W.Va. 608, 191 S.E. 368 (1937), concurring opinion 118 W.Va. 608, 192 S.E. 291, 110 A.L.R. 1454 (1937), which is cited in the preceding case, is a leading decision on automobile junkyards. In that case the junkyard property was situated about a thousand feet from the city's eastern boundary near a few residences and several businesses. The court stated that an automobile junkyard was not a nuisance per se, but that it "is not pleasing to the view" and therefore, "should not be located in a community of unquestioned residential character." It did not view the area in question as an established residential area. The principal importance of the Parkersburg case lies in the aesthetic considerations which it took into account. The court pointed out that courts of equity abate nuisances based on noise or on conditions "offensive to the olfactory nerves" but have hesitated to abate nuisances based on visual offensiveness because of the difficulty in creating a standard of measurement. The court stated:

> Happily, the day has arrived when persons may entertain appreciation of the aesthetic and be heard in equity in vindication of their love of beautiful, without becoming objects of opprobrium. Basically, this is because a thing visually offensive may seriously affect the residents of a community in the reasonable enjoyment of their homes, and may produce a decided reduction in property values. Courts must not be indifferent to the truth that within essential limitations aesthetics has a proper place in the community affairs of modern society.

The court recognized that "equity should not be aroused to action merely on the basis of the fastidiousness of taste of complainants." The discussion of aesthetics amounted to dictum in the sense that the junkyard was not enjoined due to its location. But the basis of the holding in the principal case demonstrates the importance of the comments in Parkersburg. Both cases should be remembered in connection with material later on relating to zoning for aesthetic purposes.

2. In 1948 the California Court of Appeals (First District) abated an ugly wooden structure, surrounded by stacks of wooden and paper boxes and waste material, and located in the heart of an attractive residential area, not because it was unsightly, but because it was a fire hazard. People v. Oliver, 86 Cal.App.2d 885, 195 P.2d 926 (1948). And in 1951, the Iowa court was still saying in Livingston v. Davis, 243 Iowa 21, 50 N.W.2d 592 (1951): "That a thing is unsightly or offends the aesthetic sense does not ordinarily make it a nuisance or afford grounds for injunctive relief." And see a long dictum on aesthetics as a basis for nuisance injunctions in a case where the lower court's injunction requiring the screening of a junkyard in a mixed use

neighborhood was annulled. Feldstein v. Kammauf, 209 Md. 479, 121 A.2d 716 (1956).

3. Compare also with the principal case the earlier West Virginia case of Martin v. Williams, 141 W.Va. 595, 93 S.E.2d 835 (1956), annotated in 59 W.Va.L.Rev. 92 (1956). A used car lot on a busy highway was closed by injunction at the behest of homeowners most of whom lived in another municipality across the highway in a residential A zone. The court mentions this zoning but does not stress it. Aesthetics are discussed but the court does not rest the case on this basis. In fact, its statement in this regard is considerably weaker than in that of the Parkersburg case. Bright lights and noise as disturbers of quiet living are stressed. A vigorous dissent argues that a legitimate business should not be closed even though it may be somewhat disturbing. Also, see Farley v. Graney, 146 W.Va. 22, 119 S.E.2d 833 (1960).

5. Notice in the principal case and in other cases in this chapter that the court's determination of how large or how small an area it will look at in evaluating the "character of the locality" may be crucial. See Restatement of Torts 2d § 827 (1979), and Beuscher and Morrison, Judicial Zoning through Recent Nuisance Cases, 1955 Wis.L.Rev. 440, 443–444.

6. In most nuisance cases the injunction is the weapon of choice for those who are offended by the defendant's land use; however, the case of Lew v. Superior Court, 20 Cal.App.4th 866, 25 Cal.Rptr.2d 42 (1993) is certainly an alternative approach for some kinds of nuisances. There, residents of an apartment building sued the owner for damages in small claims court for permitting drug dealers to frequent the building. Several cases of apartment buildings or motels used by drug dealers involve government orders to close the use as a public nuisance, and owners of such properties challenge the orders. In Keshbro, Inc. v. City of Miami, 801 So.2d 864 (Fla. 2001) the court considered two appeals. In one case the owner of a motel with drug and prostitution problems brought an inverse condemnation action against city arising from the six-month closure of his motel pursuant to a nuisance abatement order. The trial court granted the owner's motion for summary judgment and the city appealed. In the other case the owner of an apartment complex in which drug sales occurred brought an inverse condemnation action against the city arising from a one-year prohibition on rental or business activities at the property pursuant to a nuisance abatement order. The trial court granted the owner's motion for summary judgment as to the city's liability and the city appealed. After consolidation of cases, the Supreme Court held that: (1) temporary closure of the motel was not a compensable taking, but (2) temporary closure of the apartment complex was a compensable taking.

7. In Essick v. Shillam, 347 Pa. 373, 32 A.2d 416 (1943) neighbors sought to enjoin the building of a supermarket as a nuisance. The court dissolved the trial court's injunction, stating in part: "Obviously, a community grocery store in a residential district is not such a nuisance per se. It has been held that such stores do not detract from the residential character of the vicinity. * * * Because, however, the establishment here proposed is a supermarket, designed to attract patrons from other communities and having as an adjunct a parking lot for customers, the court below has placed it

in the category of those enterprises which are nuisances as a matter of law when carried on in a residential area. No decision of an appellate court in this Commonwealth has been cited in support of this proposition, and it must be rejected."

In Bortz v. Troth, 359 Pa. 326, 59 A.2d 93 (1948), landowners sued to enjoin the erection and operation of a gasoline station. The case centered around the residential character of the neighborhood. The service station was to be built at the only non-commercial corner of a five-corner intersection. However, the Pennsylvania Court found that to allow the station would be to permit a commercial use to intrude into an exclusively residential area which was not in transition. The nearby commercial uses were not deemed to have altered the character of the residential district. Their proximity did not make it transitional. "To establish that principle as one of law will negative the existence of lines of demarcation dividing commercial, residential and exclusively residential districts. Commercial areas would be moved forward without restraint. * * * Fringe areas would advance so that block after block would steadily succumb to inroads of industrial enterprises."

POWELL v. TAYLOR

Supreme Court of Arkansas, 1954.
222 Ark. 896, 263 S.W.2d 906.

GEORGE ROSE SMITH, JUSTICE.

This is a suit brought by six residents of Gurdon to enjoin the appellees from establishing a funeral home in a residential district within the city. The defendants intend to remodel a dwelling known as the Taylor place and to use it as a combined residence and undertaking parlor. The plaintiffs, who own homes nearby, objected to the proposal and offered to reimburse the defendants for the preliminary expenses already incurred. This effort to dissuade the defendants having failed, the present suit was filed. The chancellor denied relief upon the ground that the neighborhood is not exclusively residential.

On this particular subject the law has undergone a marked change in the past fifty years. Until about the end of the nineteenth century the only limitation upon one's right to use his property as he pleased was the prohibition against inflicting upon his neighbors injury affecting the physical senses. Hence the older cases went no farther than to exclude as nuisances, in residential districts, such offensive businesses as slaughterhouses, livery stables, blasting operations, and the like.

Today this narrow view prevails, if at all, in a few jurisdictions only. It is now generally recognized that the inhabitants of a residential neighborhood may, by taking prompt action before a funeral home has been established therein, prevent its intrusion. In 1952 the Supreme Court of Louisiana reviewed the more recent decisions in twenty-two States and found that nineteen prohibit the entry of a mortuary into a residential area, while only three courts adhered to the older view. *Frederick v. Brown Funeral Homes, Inc.*, 222 La. 57, 62 So.2d 100. In a casenote the matter is summed up in these words: "The modern tendency to expand equity's protection of aesthetics and mental health has led the majority of jurisdictions to bar funeral homes or cemeteries from the residential sanctuaries of ordinarily sensitive people." 4 Ark.L.Rev. 483. These decisions rest not upon a finding that an undertaking parlor is physically offensive but rather upon the premise that its continuous suggestion of death and dead bodies tends to destroy the comfort and repose sought in home ownership.

We have already announced our preference for the view that permits the citizens of a residential district to make timely objection to its invasion by a funeral home. In *Fentress v. Sicard*, 181 Ark. 173, 25 S.W.2d 18, 19, we set aside the chancellor's injunction only because the neighborhood was changing to a business district, having already acquired drugstores, filling stations, grocery stores, etc. In that opinion we said, with reference to the proposed mortuary: "If the district of the location was an exclusively residential one, its intrusion therein would ordinarily constitute a nuisance, and could be prevented by injunction."

It is our conclusion in the case at bar that the neighborhood in question is so essentially residential in character as to entitle the appellants to the relief asked. The Taylor place is situated at the corner of Eighth and East Main Streets, and the testimony is largely directed to the area extending for two blocks in each direction, or a total of sixteen city blocks. In a relatively small city an area of this size may well be treated as a district in itself, else there might be no residential districts in the whole community. Gurdon is a city of the second class, having had a population of 2,390 in the year 1950. It is not shown to have adopted a zoning ordinance.

This square of sixteen blocks is bounded on the west by a public highway which is bordered by commercial establishments, their exact nature not being shown in detail. Otherwise the neighborhood is exclusively residential in appearance and almost so in its actual use. A seamstress living two doors east of the Taylor place earns some income by sewing at home. The couple in the house just south of the Taylor place rent rooms to elderly people and take care of them when they are ill. J.T. McAllister lives diagonally across the intersection from the Taylor place. He is in the wholesale lumber business and uses one room as an office, keeping books there and transacting business by telephone and with persons who call. A photograph of this home shows that there is no sign or anything else to indicate that business is carried on there. Farther up the street an eighty-year-old dentist has a small office in his yard and occasionally treats patients. The testimony discloses no other commercial activity within the area.

On the other hand, the residential quality of the neighborhood is convincingly shown. A real estate dealer describes it as the best residential section in Gurdon. Estimates as to the value of various homes range from $15,000 to $35,000. Many inhabitants of the area confirm its residential character and earnestly protest the entry of the mortuary. One, whose wife suffered a mental illness some years ago, says that he will be forced to move away if the funeral home is established. Another testifies that he will not build a home on his vacant lots across the street from the Taylor place if it is converted to a funeral parlor. A third testifies that she lost interest in buying the house next to the Taylor place when she learned of the defendants' plans. It is true that other witnesses state that they have no objection to the proposal, and the chancellor found that property values will not be adversely affected. But we regard the residential character of the vicinity as the controlling issue, and the evidence upon that question preponderates in favor of the appellants.

Reversed.

MILLWEE, JUSTICE (dissenting).

As I read the opinion of the majority, it is now the law in Arkansas that the operation of a modest undertaking parlor in a mixed residential and business area of a city of the second class constitutes a nuisance per se and may be abated as such by injunction. This holding is so foreign to the traditional attitude of this court and the general legislative policy of this state that I must respectfully dissent.

While the majority conclude that the area in question here is "essentially" residential, they proceed to apply the so-called "modern rule", which is, in those jurisdictions which recognize it, only applicable when the affected area is "exclusively" or "purely" residential. Since this goes far beyond any of the authorities cited by the majority, I suppose it should be dubbed the "ultra modern rule". It is perfectly apparent from the detailed description of the majority that the area affected here is a mixed commercial and residential one and that the chancellor was eminently correct in holding that it was not "exclusively" residential. This determination by the chancellor is in my opinion fully supported by the great preponderance of the evidence.

* * *

About the only businesses or operations which this court has seen fit to enjoin as nuisances per se are: a gaming house, *Vanderworker v. State*, 13 Ark. 700; a bawdy house, *State v. Porter*, 38 Ark. 637; and the standing of a stallion or jackass within the limits of a municipality, *Ex parte Foote*, 70 Ark. 12, 65 S.W. 706. To this select group must now be added the operation of a modest undertaking parlor, where no funerals are to be held, in an area of a city of the second class which is "essentially" but not "actually" or "exclusively" residential.

It should be a matter of common knowledge that there are scores of undertaking establishments located in residential, or mixed residential and commercial, areas of the smaller municipalities in this state with hundreds of thousands of dollars invested in them. Under the rule proclaimed today these enterprises are placed in a most precarious position. And in the future many citizens, such as the appellees, will be denied the privilege of pursuing a dignified and lawful calling in places where their services would be highly welcome and most sorely needed. I cannot agree to this rule.

McFADDIN, J., joins in this dissent.

Notes

1. Compare with the principal case Miller–Elston Mortuary, Inc. v. Paal, 261 Ark. 644, 550 S.W.2d 771 (1977), where the court reversed a trial court finding that a funeral parlor would be a nuisance in a predominantly residential area. The court, in reversing, noted that improper reliance was placed on testimony that allowing the funeral parlor, a black-owned business, to locate in an area that was becoming racially integrated, would discourage further integration.

2. Some samples of language from court opinions serve to illustrate the attitude toward funeral parlors. In Smith v. Fairchild, 193 Miss. 536, 10 So.2d 172 (1942), the Court did not believe that several commercial operations in the area changed the neighborhood from "essentially" residential. The court quoted from Tureman v. Ketterlin, 304 Mo. 221, 263 S.W. 202, 43 A.L.R. 1155 (1924) to this effect: "An undertaking establishment stands on a different footing from that of the occasional corner grocery and oil filling station which have made their appearances there. The latter may offend the aesthetic sense of those living in their proximity; the former would destroy, in an essential respect, the comfort and repose of their home." "The constant going and coming of the hearse; * * * the not infrequent taking in and out of dead bodies; the occasional funeral with its mourners and funeral airs, held in the part of the house designed for a chapel; the unknown dead in the morgue, and the visits of relatives seeking to identify them; the thought of autopsies, of embalming; the dread, or horror, or thought, that the dead are or may be lying in the house next door, a morgue; the dread of communicable disease, not well founded, as we have seen, but nevertheless present in the mind of the normal layman—all of these are conducive to depression of the normal person; each of these is a constant reminder of mortality. These constant reminders, this depression of mind, deprive the home of that comfort and repose to which its owner is entitled." In Fraser v. Fred Parker Funeral Home, 201 S.C. 88, 21 S.E.2d 577 (1942), the Court referred to the need for preservation of the homes of the people as "places of ultimate retreat, security, or release from the cares and struggles for a living" and as having "distinct and necessary characteristics, one of which is cheer." Funeral homes injure this mental health and cheerfulness, said the Court. Indeed: "This is not a case of trying to balance the rights of a home owner with the rights simply of a business operator, and if it were we could not be unmindful that America's future is greatly determined by its homes, and that the 'strength of a nation, especially a republic is in the intelligent and well-ordered homes of the people.'" These two 1942 cases present an almost moralistic defense of good being threatened by evil.

3. For cases permitting the establishment of funeral parlors on the ground, among others, that commercial uses had sufficiently entered the area, see O'Connor v. Ryan, 159 S.W.2d 531 (Tex.Civ.App.1942) and Moss v. Burke & Trotti, Inc., 198 La. 76, 3 So.2d 281 (1941).

Displaying and selling tombstones in a residential section, even though the display was in the form of a mock graveyard, was not enjoined. Grubbs v. Wooten, 189 Ga. 390, 5 S.E.2d 874 (1939). But an injunction was given where stone cutting accompanied the monument sales business in City of Bethlehem v. Druckenmiller, 344 Pa. 170, 25 A.2d 190 (1942).

In Young v. St. Martin's Church, 361 Pa. 505, 64 A.2d 814 (1949), owners of "palatial dwelling houses" in an exclusively residential district failed in their efforts to prevent the establishment of a cemetery nearby. However, efforts to prevent operation of a mental sanitarium and a venereal disease clinic respectively in residential districts succeeded in Park v. Stolzheise, 24 Wash.2d 781, 167 P.2d 412 (1946) and Benton v. Pittard, 197 Ga. 843, 31 S.E.2d 6, 153 A.L.R. 968 (1944).

4. On the subject of permissible activities in a residential area, not involving funeral homes, what about one involving the razing of a nice home? In Eyerman v. Mercantile Trust Co., 524 S.W.2d 210 (Mo.App.1975), the court was confronted with a petition from neighbors to prevent the demolition of a home in a nice, old subdivision. The deceased owner had provided in her will that it be razed. The neighbors alleged that this would harm their property rights, violate the subdivision trust indenture, amount to a private nuisance and violate public policy. Neither the devisees nor the city were parties to the suit. (The devisees presumably could have brought an action for waste. The will may have contained a "no contest" provision.) The court declined to declare this to be a nuisance but enjoined the executor on the basis of public policy, perhaps partially because the subdivision had been designated a landmark by the City (and perhaps unconsciously drawing upon a related concept in the law of trusts).

Eyerman obviously is not a typical nuisance case. It is questionable whether it ought to be considered a nuisance case at all. But how else could the injunction be granted? Is public policy such a broad concept that an injunction can be granted on such a ground? What was actually proposed was an act of waste as to the heirs of the decedent. Where were they and why were they not in court? Does the holding of the majority bear a relationship to the doctrine in the law of trusts that a trust cannot be created to carry out an act such as this because it would be against public policy to enforce the trust?

WILSON v. HANDLEY

Court of Appeal, Third District, California, 2002.
97 Cal.App.4th 1301, 119 Cal.Rptr.2d 263.

ROBIE, J.

"Every body does not see alike.... The tree which moves some to tears of joy is in the Eyes of others only a Green thing that stands in the way." (Blake, The Complete Writings of William Blake (1957) p. 793.)

This private nuisance action embodies the truth of William Blake's observation. Plaintiffs Wendy Wilson and Jane Cassady and defendants Leon and Sue Handley are neighbors in the City of Yreka; the Handleys' property adjoins both plaintiffs' properties. When Wilson began building a two-story log house on her property, the Handleys planted a row of evergreen trees along the property line. Afraid the trees would block their views of Mt. Shasta, plaintiffs brought this action to require the Handleys to remove the trees. Plaintiffs relied in part on California's spite fence statute (Civ.Code, § 841.4), which declares that any "fence or other structure in the nature of a fence" that unnecessarily exceeds 10 feet in height and is maliciously erected or maintained for the purpose of annoying a neighbor is a private nuisance.

The question presented here is whether a row of trees planted parallel to a property line can be a "fence or other structure in the nature of a fence" within the meaning of the spite fence statute. The trial court concluded that, "at least when they grow naturally and are not pruned or trimmed," a row of trees is not within the scope of the spite fence statute because "[t]rees are neither built [n]or constructed." We disagree. Because the spite fence statute must be liberally construed, we conclude a row of trees can be a "fence or other structure in the nature of a fence" and thus can be a spite fence under section 841.4. Whether the row of trees at issue in *this* case is a spite fence is a matter for the trial court to determine in the first instance. Accordingly, we will reverse the judgment and remand the matter for further consideration.

As noted above, plaintiffs and defendants are neighbors in the City of Yreka. Wilson, who is Cassady's daughter, lives next door to her mother, and the Handleys' property is adjacent to both plaintiffs' properties. In the spring of 1997, after learning Wilson planned to build a two-story log home on her property close to their property line, Sue Handley directed a landscape contractor to plant a row of evergreen trees between the Handleys' property and Wilson's property. The trees, which include spruces and Leland cypresses, run parallel to the property line; some of them are within five feet of the line and others are within 10 feet, but most of them are more than 10 feet from the property line. Seventeen of the trees are Leland cypresses, a hybrid specifically designed for screening barriers and windbreaks.

In August 1999, shortly after the completion of Wilson's home, Wilson and Cassady commenced this action against the Handleys by filing a complaint for injunctive relief and damages under several legal theories. The only cause of action at issue in this appeal is the second cause of action, which alleged the trees were a spite fence within the meaning of section 841.4. Plaintiffs claimed that if the trees were allowed to grow unabated, they would eventually block both plaintiffs' views of Mt. Shasta.

Following a court trial on plaintiffs' claim under the spite fence statute, the court found in favor of the Handleys. The court explained its reasoning as follows: "The predicate to the application of th[e] 'spite fence' rule is a determination that the trees are a 'fence or other structure in the nature of a fence'. We do not doubt that trees can be a fence. Here, however, we are concerned with statutory construction. The word 'fence' is qualified or limited by the phrase 'or other structure'.

Trees are neither built [n]or constructed. They grow. This is true at least when they grow naturally and are not pruned or trimmed. At present all of the trees in dispute are in their natural state. [¶] We therefore conclude that plaintiffs can not prevail ... because these trees are not a fence or a structure in the nature of a fence and [we] do not reach the other close and troubling issues relative to maliciousness and intent to annoy."

After the court entered judgment, plaintiffs appealed.

Plaintiffs contend the trial court misinterpreted section 841.4 when it concluded a row of trees in their natural state cannot be a spite fence. Plaintiffs argue "a row of trees planted parallel to a common boundary line" may be a "fence or other structure in the nature of a fence" within the meaning of the spite fence statute.

The Handleys disagree and also contend that, regardless of whether a row of trees can be deemed a "structure in the nature of a fence" under the spite fence statute, plaintiffs' nuisance claim "has no legal substance as a matter of law" because a structure "is not a nuisance solely because it interferes with a view." In other words, the Handleys suggest, a structure the spite fence statute expressly declares to be a private nuisance is nonetheless not actionable as a private nuisance if all it interferes with is light and air.

* * *

The Handleys take the position, which the trial court apparently adopted, that a row of trees cannot be a "structure in the nature of a fence" because "[t]rees are not a 'structure.'" According to the Handleys, "[a] structure, by definition, is a 'thing built or constructed, as a building or dam,'" and trees are grown, not built or constructed. We do not dispute that trees grow. The question, however, is not whether a single growing tree can be a structure, but whether a *row* of growing trees can be a structure. We conclude that it can.

Defined broadly, a "structure" is "something arranged in a definite pattern of organization." (Merriam–Webster's Collegiate Dict. (10th ed.2000) p. 1163, col. 2.) Under this broad definition, a row of trees, arranged in a line by the person who planted them, could easily constitute a "structure." The Handleys would have us apply a narrower definition of the word "structure," as "something constructed or built." (Webster's New International Dict. (2d. ed 1938) p. 2501, col. 1.) Even if we apply that narrower definition, however, we conclude a row of trees may be a "structure."

To "construct" something is to "put together [its] constituent parts ... in their proper place and order." (Webster's New International Dict. (2d. ed 1938) p. 572, col. 3.) Although, to paraphrase a famous poem, only God can construct a tree, any enterprising individual with a shovel and some saplings can construct a *row* of trees by simply planting the saplings in their proper place and order—in other words, in a row. Because a row of trees can be constructed, a row of trees can be a "structure" even within the narrower definition of that word the Handleys advocate.

The question that remains is whether a row of trees can be a structure "in the nature of a fence." The Handleys suggest it cannot because "[a] line of unconnected trees cannot prevent intrusion nor straying from within." While it is true one definition of the word "fence" is "an enclosing structure . . . intended to prevent intrusion from without or straying from within" (Black's Law Dict. (5th ed.1979) p. 556, col. 2), a "fence" can also be a "structure . . . erected . . . to separate two contiguous estates" (*ibid.*) or "a barrier intended . . . to mark a boundary" (Merriam–Webster's Collegiate Dict. (10th ed.2000) p. 428, col. 1). In light of the history and purpose of the spite fence statute, we conclude these latter definitions more accurately express what constitutes a "fence or other structure in the nature of a fence" within the meaning of section 841.4.

The rise of spite fence statutes in the United States stems from the general repudiation in this country of the English doctrine of "ancient lights," under which a landowner could acquire an easement over adjoining property for the passage of light and air. (See *Western etc. Co. v. Knickerbocker* (1894) 103 Cal. 111, 113, 37 P. 192; *Venuto v. Owens–Corning Fiberglas Corp.* (1971) 22 Cal.App.3d 116, 127, 99 Cal.Rptr. 350.) "Such a doctrine was ill-suited to conditions existing in the early part of this century in a new and rapidly growing country. At that time society had a significant interest in encouraging unrestricted land development. Moreover a landowner's rights to use his land were virtually unlimited; it was thought that he owned to the center of the earth and up to the heavens. In contrast, light had little social importance beyond its value for aesthetic enjoyment or illumination." (*Sher v. Leiderman* (1986) 181 Cal.App.3d 867, 876, 226 Cal.Rptr. 698.)

Under American common law, it was said that "a man has a right to build a fence on his own land as high as he pleases, however much it may obstruct his neighbor's light and air." (*Rideout v. Knox* (1889) 148 Mass. 368, 372, 19 N.E. 390, 391.) Thus, in the 1870's, when Charles Crocker sought to purchase an entire city block on San Francisco's Nob Hill on which to build a mansion, and a local undertaker named Yung would not sell his small lot to Crocker, Crocker bought the remainder of the block and built a fence 40 feet high on his property around Yung's lot. (Lewis, The Big Four (1951) pp. 111, 118–119.) Eventually, Yung sold out and Crocker procured the entire block.

In the 1880's, however, courts and legislatures began addressing the issue of whether a fence like Crocker's, built unnecessarily high, simply to spite a neighbor, could be deemed a private nuisance subject to abatement. (See Comment, *Torts: Spite Fence* (1917) 5 Cal. L.Rev. 177.) In 1887, Massachusetts enacted one of the earliest "spite fence" statutes in the United States, expressly declaring such fences a private nuisance. (See *Rideout v. Knox, supra,* 148 Mass. 368, 19 N.E. at p. 391, citing Mass. Gen. Laws ch. 348, § 1 (1887) [now codified as Mass. Ann. Laws ch. 49, § 21] (Law. Co-op 1993).) Other states followed suit. (See, e.g., Ind.Code Ann. § 32–10–10–1 (West 2001); Me.Rev.Stat. Ann. tit. 17, § 2801 (West 1964); N.H.Rev.Stat. Ann. § 476:1 (1955); R.I. Gen. Laws § 34–10–1 (1956); Wis. Stat. Ann. § 844.10 (West 1994).) Meanwhile, beginning in 1888, courts in some states began to hold that a fence erected for no purpose except to harm a neighbor could be abated as a nuisance under the common law. (See *Burke v. Smith* (1888) 69 Mich. 380, 37 N.W. 838; Annot., Spite fences and other spite structures (1941) 133 A.L.R. 691, 692–697, § II.a., and cases cited.)

* * *

Despite the existence of similar spite fence statutes in a number of other states, we have been unable to find any case in which a court has held that a row of trees can be a "fence or other structure in the nature of a fence." The closest case we have found is a decision by the Washington Court of Appeals, in which that court held a row of trees along a property line might be a "fence" within the meaning of a restrictive covenant. (*Lakes at Mercer Island v. Witrak* (1991) 61 Wash. App. 177, 810 P.2d 27.) The absence of any authority directly on point, however, does not mean that a row of trees can never be considered a "structure in the nature of a fence" for purposes of a spite fence statute like section 841.4. As shown by the discussion above, spite fence statutes were enacted to prevent what would otherwise be the lawful practice of a landowner erecting or maintaining an unnecessarily high barrier between his or her property and an adjoining property to annoy the neighboring landowner. In light of this statutory purpose, a structure need not be built to prevent intrusion from without or straying from within to be a "fence or other structure in the nature of a fence" within the meaning of the spite fence statute. Instead, the structure need only be built to separate or mark the boundary between adjoining parcels—albeit, in an unnecessarily high and annoying manner. (See *Lovell v. Noyes* (1898) 69 N.H. 263, 46 A. 25 [noting that a fence, "in the ordinary meaning of the term" is "a structure erected upon or near the dividing line between adjoining owners, for the purpose of separating the occupancy of their lands"].)

Given the purpose of spite fence statutes like section 841.4, and the rule of liberal construction that applies to section 841.4, we conclude a row of trees planted on or near the boundary line between adjoining parcels of land can be a "fence or other structure in the nature of a fence." The Handleys argue, however, that a row of trees cannot be a *spite* fence because it is the "natural condition" of trees to be more than 10 feet high, and a fence must "unnecessarily" exceed 10 feet in height to be a spite fence under section 841.4.

As we read the spite fence statute, the question whether a particular fence or fence-like structure "unnecessarily" exceeds 10 feet in height cannot be answered without reference to the ostensible purpose or purposes the defendant claims for the structure. The spite fence statute expresses the judgment of the Legislature that a fence—that is, a structure built to separate or mark the boundary between two adjoining parcels—does not need to be more than 10 feet high to serve that purpose. However, if a fence or fence-like structure serves some other purpose as well, then its height above 10 feet may be justified by that additional purpose. (See *Rideout v. Knox, supra,* 148 Mass. 368, 19 N.E. at p. 392 ["Even the right to build a fence above [the statutory limit] is not denied when any convenience of the owner would be served by building higher.... If the height above [the statutory limit] is really necessary for any reason, there is no liability"].)

For example, in *Lovell v. Noyes, supra,* 69 N.H. 263, 46 A. at page 25, the Supreme Court of New Hampshire addressed whether a shed that was 15 feet tall and used for storing carriages could be deemed a spite fence. The court acknowledged the structure was "designed to take the place of a 'fence'" and that "[t]here was evidence tending to show that it was erected for the sole purpose of annoying the plaintiff." (*Ibid.*) Nevertheless, the court reversed a verdict in favor of the plaintiff because "[a] building, whether it be a dwelling house, warehouse, stable, or shed for the storage of carriages, etc., must be more than five feet in height, to be of utility." (*Ibid.*)

Here, Sue Handley testified they planted the row of trees for aesthetic purposes and to protect their privacy. If the trial court credits Sue Handley's testimony, then the court could reasonably conclude that the trees—even if they are a "structure in the nature of a fence"—do not exceed 10 feet in height "unnecessarily" if their growth in excess of 10 feet is necessary to maintain their aesthetic qualities or to protect the Handleys' privacy. On the other hand, if the court discredits Sue Handley's testimony and finds that the trees serve no purpose other than to separate or mark the boundary between the adjoining parcels and to annoy plaintiffs, then the court could reasonably conclude that the trees "unnecessarily" exceed 10 feet in height. In any event, this is a determination for the trial court to make in the first instance. It is sufficient for our purposes that we reject the Handleys' suggestion that a row of trees can never "unnecessarily" exceed 10 feet in height for purposes of the spite fence statute.

The Handleys also contend that even if a row of trees can be a spite fence under section 841.4, plaintiffs cannot prevail on their private nuisance claim under the statute because "[t]he *sine qua non* of a private nuisance cause of action is an interference with the use and enjoyment of an interest in private property" and "there is no recognized property right in a view in the State of California." The cases upon which the Handleys rely are inapposite, however, because none of them involved an application of the spite fence statute. It might be true that, absent the spite fence statute, a fence that interfered only with light and air would not be a nuisance under the general definition of a "nuisance" in Civil Code section 3479 ["Anything which is injurious to health, including, but not limited to, the illegal sale of controlled substances, or is indecent or offensive to the senses, or an obstruction to the free use of property, so as to interfere with the comfortable enjoyment of life or property, or unlawfully obstructs the free passage or use, in the customary manner, of any navigable lake, or river, bay, stream, canal, or basin, or any public park, square, street, or highway, is a nuisance." (See *Sher v. Leiderman, supra,* 181 Cal.App.3d at pp. 875–880, 226 Cal.Rptr. 698.) That does not mean, however, that a fence which violates the spite fence statute must interfere with something more than light and air to be a nuisance under *that* statute. Section 841.4 specifically provides that a fence or other structure in the nature of the fence that meets certain requirements "is a private nuisance." Section 841.4 does not specify that the fence must interfere with something more than light and air to be a nuisance, and we are not at liberty to read any such additional requirement into the statute.

* * *

Finally, the Handleys contend that even if a row of trees can be a spite fence within the meaning of section 841.4, the row of trees on their property is not a spite fence because plaintiffs cannot prove the "malice" element of the statute. According to the Handleys, a structure is not a spite fence under section 841.4 unless it "has no utility and was intended solely to annoy the neighbor." They contend there is insufficient evidence in the record to support a finding that their row of trees meets this standard. Plaintiffs dispute the Handleys' formulation of the "malice" element of the statute but offer no alternative formulation.

In upholding the Massachusetts spite fence statute against constitutional challenge more than 100 years ago, the Supreme Judicial Court of Massachusetts explained the "malice" element of the statute as follows: "The fences must be 'maliciously erected, or maintained for the purpose of annoying' adjoining owners or occupiers. This language clearly expresses that there must be an actual malevolent motive, as distinguished from merely technical malice.... [W]e are of opinion that it is not enough to satisfy the words of the act that malevolence was one of the motives, but that malevolence must be the dominant motive,—a motive without which the fence would not have been built or maintained. A man cannot be punished for malevolently maintaining a fence for the purpose of annoying his neighbor merely because he feels pleasure at the thought he is giving annoyance, if that pleasure alone would not induce him to maintain it, or if he would maintain it for other reasons, even if that pleasure should be denied him." (*Rideout v. Knox, supra,* 148 Mass. 368, 19 N.E. at p. 392.)

Under the decision in *Rideout v. Knox, supra,* the intent to annoy the neighbor need not be the *sole* purpose for building or maintaining the fence, as the Handleys suggest, but it must at least be the "dominant" purpose. Courts in other states with similar spite fence statutes have also required a showing that annoyance was the dominant purpose. (See *Lord v. Langdon* (1898) 91 Me. 221, 39 A. 552; *Karasek v. Peier* (1900) 22 Wash. 419, 61 P. 33.)

We likewise adopt the "dominant purpose" test for determining whether the "malice" element of section 841.4 has been satisfied.

Accordingly, the pertinent question is whether the Handleys' dominant purpose in planting the row of evergreen trees along their property line with plaintiffs was to annoy plaintiffs. This is a factual determination to be made by the trial court in the first instance based on the evidence received at trial. If the trial court finds the Handleys planted the trees primarily for reasons other than to annoy plaintiffs—for example, to "beautify" their property or to protect their privacy from the two-story log house looming next door, as the Handleys claimed, then annoyance was not the dominant purpose of the row of trees and the "malice" element of section 841.4 is not satisfied. On the other hand, if the court finds the Handleys planted the trees primarily to annoy plaintiffs, and other purposes such as aesthetics and privacy, if any, were only subordinate to the dominant purpose of annoyance, then the "malice" element has been satisfied.

* * *

The judgment in favor of defendants on plaintiffs' second cause of action is reversed and the case is remanded to the trial court for further proceedings on that cause of action. On remand, the trial court is to apply section 841.4 to the evidence received at trial. In all other respects, the judgment is affirmed. The parties are to bear their own costs on appeal. (Cal. Rules of Court, rule 26(a).).

Notes

1. Spite fence cases are not brought very frequently, but enmity between neighbors can lead to litigation. A leading case from Idaho pitted two adjoining motel owners in a commercial area of Caldwell, Idaho. In Sundowner, Inc. v. King, 95 Idaho 367, 509 P.2d 785 (1973), the facts were:

> In 1966 Robert Bushnell sold a motel to defendants-appellants King. Bushnell then built another motel, the Desert Inn, on property immediately adjoining that sold to the Kings.
>
> The Kings thereafter brought an action against Bushnell (H.J. McNeel, Inc.) based on alleged misrepresentations by Bushnell in the 1966 sale of the motel property. See: King v. H.J. McNeel, Inc., *supra*. In 1968 the Kings built a large structure, variously described as a fence or sign, some 16 inches from the boundary line between the King and Bushnell properties. The structure is 85 ft. in length and 18 ft. in height. It is raised 2 ft. off the ground and is 2 ft. from the Desert Inn building. It parallels the entire northwest side of the Desert Inn building, obscures approximately 80% of the Desert Inn building and restricts the passage of light and air to its rooms.

The defendant argued that the fence was really a "sign" erected for advertising purposes, but the trial court found as a fact, based on testimony of an expert, that the fence had no value for advertising and would be "the largest 'sign' then existing in Oregon, Northern Nevada and Idaho." The appellate court affirmed the holding of the trial court, concluding: "We hold that no property owner has the right to erect and maintain an otherwise useless structure for the sole purpose of injuring his neighbor. The trial court found on the basis of substantial evidence that the structure served no useful purpose to its owners and was erected because of the Kings' ill-will and enmity toward their neighboring competitor. We therefore hold that the trial court did not err in partially abating and enjoining the 'sign' structure as a spite fence."

2. The Idaho case raises the issue of signs as nuisances. Municipalities regularly—by ordinance or administrative action—prohibit signs, permit signs or regulate signs. Later in these materials we will look at signs as First Amendment speech and the aesthetic subject of regulation. At this point, we want to look at signs as nuisances. In Great Lakes Motorcycle Dealers Ass'n, Inc. v. City of Detroit, 38 Mich.App. 564, 196 N.W.2d 787 (1972), the plaintiffs brought a class action to enjoin the erection and enforcement of signs prohibiting the operation of motorcycles on certain streets in the city. The number of these vehicles with the accompanying noise had grown to the point that citizen complaints led the city to accept petitions requesting that they be barred from certain streets. Such signs had been erected over approximately 237 blocks. Although finding that the city had a legitimate interest in regulating traffic so as to eliminate noise and excessive speed, the court held that the blanket exclusion of all such vehicles exceeded reasonable limitations. Said the court: "While some motorcycle riders may well drive vehicles which are excessively noisy at speeds in excess of the posted limits, there is certainly no valid basis for applying the 'Hell's Angels' conception of the motorcycle rider to all motorcycle users." Commercial signs that are not subject to spite fence allegations are sometimes the target of nuisance actions based on other grounds. Frandsen v. Mayer, 155 N.W.2d 294 (N.D. 1967), although it reversed the granting of injunctive relief by the trial judge, stated that under proper circumstances the sign could be enjoined either as a nuisance per accidens or as a public nuisance. Here, the plaintiffs were alleging that the sign was so located that it caused motorists to miss their motel or not to know whether it was a motel, thereby harming business. The court felt that evidence to show harm caused by the sign was lacking.

PRAH v. MARETTI
Supreme Court of Wisconsin, 1982.
108 Wis.2d 223, 321 N.W.2d 182.

ABRAHAMSON, JUSTICE.

This appeal [presents] an issue of first impression, namely, whether an owner of a solar-heated residence states a claim upon which relief can be granted when he asserts that his neighbor's proposed construction of a residence (which conforms to existing deed restrictions and local ordinances) interferes with his access to an unobstructed path for sunlight across the neighbor's property. This case thus involves a conflict between one landowner (Glenn Prah, the plaintiff) interested in unobstructed access to sunlight across adjoining property as a natural source of energy and an adjoining landowner (Richard D. Maretti, the defendant) interested in the development of his land.

The circuit court concluded that the plaintiff presented no claim upon which relief could be granted and granted summary judgment for the defendant. We reverse the judgment of the circuit court and remand the cause to the circuit court for further proceedings.

According to the complaint, the plaintiff is the owner of a residence which was constructed during the years 1978–1979. The complaint alleges that the residence has a solar system which includes collectors on the roof to supply energy for heat and hot water and that after the plaintiff built his solar-heated house, the defendant purchased the lot adjacent to and immediately to the south of the plaintiff's lot and commenced planning construction of a home. The complaint further states that when the plaintiff learned of defendant's plans to build the house he advised the defendant that if the house were built at the proposed location, defendant's house would substantially and adversely affect the integrity of plaintiff's solar system and could cause plaintiff other damage. Nevertheless, the defendant began construction. The complaint further alleges that the plaintiff is entitled to "unrestricted use of the sun and its solar power" and demands judgment for injunctive relief and damages.

After filing his complaint, the plaintiff moved for a temporary injunction to restrain and enjoin construction by the defendant. In ruling on that motion the circuit court heard testimony, received affidavits and viewed the site.

The record made on the motion reveals the following additional facts: Plaintiff's home was the first residence built in the subdivision, and although plaintiff did not build his house in the center of the lot it was built in accordance with applicable restrictions. Plaintiff advised defendant that if the defendant's home were built at the proposed site it would cause a shadowing effect on the solar collectors which would reduce the efficiency of the system and possibly damage the system. To avoid these adverse effects, plaintiff requested defendant to locate his home an additional several feet away from the plaintiff's lot line, the exact number being disputed. Plaintiff and defendant failed to reach an agreement on the location of defendant's home before defendant started construction. The Architectural Control Committee of the subdivision and the Planning Commission of the City of Muskego approved the defendant's plans for his home, including its location on the lot. After such approval, the defendant apparently changed the grade of the property without prior notice to the Architectural Control Committee. The problem with defendant's proposed construction, as far as the plaintiff's interests are concerned, arises from a combination of the grade and the distance of defendant's home from the defendant's lot line.

The circuit court denied plaintiff's motion for injunctive relief, declared it would entertain a motion for summary judgment and thereafter entered judgment in favor of the defendant.

* * *

We consider first whether the complaint states a claim for relief based on common law private nuisance. This state has long recognized that an owner of land does not have an absolute or unlimited right to use the land in a way which injures the rights of others. * * *

* * *

Although the defendant's obstruction of the plaintiff's access to sunlight appears to fall within the Restatement's broad concept of a private nuisance as a nontrespassory invasion of another's interest in the private use and enjoyment of land, the defendant asserts that he has a right to develop his property in compliance with statutes, ordinances and private covenants without regard to the effect of such development upon the plaintiff's access to sunlight. In essence, the defendant is asking this court to hold that the private nuisance doctrine is not applicable in the instant case and that his right to develop his land is a right which is *per se* superior to his neighbor's interest in access to sunlight. This position is expressed in the maxim "cujus est solum, ejus est usque ad coelum et ad infernos," that is, the owner of land owns up to the sky and down to the center of the earth. The rights of the surface owner are, however, not unlimited. *U.S. v. Causby*, 328 U.S. 256, 260–1, 66 S.Ct. 1062, 1065, 90 L.Ed. 1206 (1946). See also 114.03, Stats.1979–80.

The defendant is not completely correct in asserting that the common law did not protect a landowner's access to sunlight across adjoining property. At English common law a landowner could acquire a right to receive sunlight across adjoining land by both express agreement and under the judge-made doctrine of "ancient lights." Under the doctrine of ancient lights if the landowner had received sunlight across adjoining property for a specified period of time, the landowner was entitled to continue to receive unobstructed access to sunlight across the adjoining property. Under the doctrine the landowner acquired a negative prescriptive easement and could prevent the adjoining landowner from obstructing access to light.

Although American courts have not been as receptive to protecting a landowner's access to sunlight as the English courts, American courts have afforded some protection to a landowner's interest in access to sunlight. American courts honor express easements to sunlight. American courts initially enforced the English common law doctrine of ancient lights, but later every state which considered the doctrine repudiated it as inconsistent with the needs of a developing country. Indeed, for just that reason this court concluded that an easement to light and air over adjacent property could not be created or acquired by prescription and has been unwilling to recognize such an easement by implication. *Depner v. United States National Bank*, 202 Wis. 405, 408, 232 N.W. 851 (1930); *Miller v. Hoeschler*, 126 Wis. 263, 268–69, 105 N.W. 790 (1905).

Many jurisdictions in this country have protected a landowner from malicious obstruction of access to light (the spite fence cases) under the common law private nuisance doctrine. If an activity is motivated by malice it lacks utility and the harm it causes others outweighs any social values. VI–A Law of Property sec. 28.28, p. 79 (1954) This court was reluctant to protect a landowner's interest in sunlight even against a spite fence, only to be overruled by the legislature. Shortly after this court upheld a landowner's right to erect a useless and unsightly sixteen-foot spite fence four feet from his neighbor's windows, *Metzger v. Hochrein*, 107 Wis. 267, 83 N.W. 308 (1900), the legislature enacted a law specifically defining a spite fence as an actionable private nuisance. Thus a landowner's interest in sunlight has been protected in this country by common law private nuisance law at least in the narrow context of the modern American rule invalidating spite fences. See, *e.g., Sundowner, Inc. v. King*, 95 Idaho 367, 509 P.2d 785 (1973); Restatement (Second) of Torts, sec. 829 (1977).

This court's reluctance in the nineteenth and early part of the twentieth century to provide broader protection for a landowner's access to sunlight was premised on three policy considerations. First, the right of landowners to use their property as they wished, as long as they did not cause physical damage to a neighbor, was jealously guarded. *Metzger v. Hochrein*, 107 Wis. 267, 272, 83 N.W. 308 (1900).

Second, sunlight was valued only for aesthetic enjoyment or as illumination. Since artificial light could be used for illumination, loss of sunlight was at most a personal annoyance which was given little, if any, weight by society.

Third, society had a significant interest in not restricting or impeding land development. *Dillman v. Hoffman*, 38 Wis. 559, 574 (1875). This court repeatedly emphasized that in the growth period of the nineteenth and early twentieth centuries change is to be expected and is essential to property and that recognition of a right to sunlight would hinder property development.

* * *

Considering these three policies, this court concluded that in the absence of an express agreement granting access to sunlight, a landowner's obstruction of another's access to sunlight was not actionable. *Miller v. Hoeschler, supra*, 126 Wis. at 271, 105 N.W. 790; *Depner v. United States National Bank, supra*, 202 Wis. at 410, 232 N.W. 851. These three policies are no longer fully accepted or applicable. They reflect factual circumstances and social priorities that are now obsolete.

First, society has increasingly regulated the use of land by the landowner for the general welfare. *Euclid v. Ambler Realty Co.*, 272 U.S. 365, 47 S.Ct. 114, 71 L.Ed. 303 (1926); *Just v. Marinette*, 56 Wis.2d 7, 201 N.W.2d 761 (1972).

Second, access to sunlight has taken on a new significance in recent years. In this case the plaintiff seeks to protect access to sunlight, not for aesthetic reasons or as a source of illumination but as a source of energy. Access to sunlight as an energy source is of significance both to the landowner who invests in solar collectors and to a society which has an interest in developing alternative sources of energy.

Third, the policy of favoring unhindered private development in an expanding economy is no longer in harmony with the realities of our society. *State v. Deetz*, 66 Wis.2d 1, 224 N.W.2d 407 (1974). The need for easy and rapid development is not as great today as it once was, while our perception of the value of sunlight as a source of energy has increased significantly.

Courts should not implement obsolete policies that have lost their vigor over the course of the years. The law of private nuisance is better suited to resolve landowners' disputes about property development in the 1980's than is a rigid rule which does not recognize a landowner's interest in access to sunlight. As we said in *Ballstadt v. Pagel*, 202 Wis. 484, 489, 232 N.W. 862 (1930), "What is regarded in law as constituting a nuisance in modern times would no doubt have been tolerated without question in former times." We read *State v. Deetz*, 66 Wis.2d 1, 224 N.W.2d 407 (1974), as an endorsement of the application of common law nuisance to situations involving the conflicting interests of landowners and as rejecting *per se* exclusions to the nuisance law reasonable use doctrine.

* * *

We therefore hold that private nuisance law, that is, the reasonable use doctrine as set forth in the Restatement, is applicable to the instant case. Recognition of a nuisance claim for unreasonable obstruction of access to sunlight will not prevent land development or unduly hinder the use of adjoining land. It will promote the reasonable use and enjoyment of land in a manner suitable to the 1980's. That obstruction of access to light might be found to constitute a nuisance in certain circumstances does not mean that it will be or must be found to constitute a nuisance under all circumstances. The result in each case depends on whether the conduct complained of is unreasonable.

Accordingly we hold that the plaintiff in this case has stated a claim under which relief can be granted. Nonetheless we do not determine whether the plaintiff in this case is entitled to relief. In order to be entitled to relief the plaintiff must prove the elements required to establish actionable nuisance, and the conduct of the defendant herein must be judged by the reasonable use doctrine.

The defendant asserts that even if we hold that the private nuisance doctrine applies to obstruction of access to sunlight across adjoining land, the circuit court's granting of summary judgment should be affirmed.

Although the memorandum decision of the circuit court in the instant case is unclear, it appears that the circuit court recognized that the common law private nuisance doctrine was applicable but concluded that defendant's conduct was not unreasonable. The circuit court apparently attempted to balance the utility of the defendant's conduct with the gravity of the harm. Sec. 826, Restatement (Second) of Torts (1977).

The defendant urges us to accept the circuit court's balance as adequate. We decline to do so.

The circuit court concluded that because the defendant's proposed house was in conformity with zoning regulations, building codes and deed restrictions, the defendant's use of the land was reasonable. This court has concluded that a landowner's compliance with zoning laws does not automatically bar a nuisance claim. Compliance with the law "is not the controlling factor, though it is, of course, entitled to some weight." *Bie v. Ingersoll*, 27 Wis.2d 490, 495, 135 N.W.2d 250 (1965). The circuit court also concluded that the plaintiff could have avoided any harm by locating his own house in a better place. Again, plaintiff's ability to avoid the harm is a relevant but not a conclusive factor. See secs. 826, 827, 828, Restatement (Second) of Torts (1977).

* * *

The judgment of the circuit court is reversed and the cause remanded for proceedings not inconsistent with this opinion.

CECI, J., not participating.

CALLOW, J. dissents [The long dissent is not reproduced due to space limitations.]

Notes

1. In his dissent, Justice Callow argued that the law of private nuisance could not be extended to protect light and air if the obstruction served a useful purpose. He argued that "spite fence" cases are predicated on malice and that the facts of this case do not fit that requirement. He viewed the majority opinion as being in error in dismissing certain rules as being out of date. He thought that policy decisions of this nature should be left to the legislature. He pointed out that the defendant was in conformity with zoning regulations, building codes, deed restrictions and that his use of the land to build a home was reasonable. He viewed the plaintiff's solar system as "an unusually sensitive use." He argued that there was no notice by Prah to Maretti relative to the solar collector. He also points out in an interesting footnote that "Mr. Prah could have avoided this litigation by building his own home in the center of his lot instead of only ten feet from the Maretti lot line and/or by purchasing the adjoining lot for his own protection. Mr. Maretti has already moved the proposed location of his home over an additional ten feet to accommodate Mr. Prah's solar collector, and he testified that moving the home any further would interfere with his view of the lake on which the property faces." With regard to this last point, could it not be urged that Prah in effect moved to the nuisance and should be estopped to complain? What do you think about the other points made by the dissenting justice?

Compare with the Prah case Sher v. Leiderman, 181 Cal.App.3d 867, 226 Cal.Rptr. 698 (1986) where the court ruled against the owner of a passive solar home holding that the neighbors' trees were not a private nuisance. In County of Westchester v. Town of Greenwich, Connecticut, 76 F.3d 42 (2d Cir.1996) a county in New York brought an action against the

Connecticut city and several landowners to obtain a prescriptive easement along a runway approach to the county airport and have the landowners' trees cut as a public nuisance. The court found for the landowners, quoting the trial judge's statement: "If normally unobjectionable land use such as growing trees can be transformed into an 'unreasonable' activity by the act of building an airport that lacks the necessary property rights for full operation, then there would be no reason for airports to ever bother paying for property rights beyond those needed for the the land the airport actually occupies, because the airports could acquire the air easements they needed without cost by bringing nuisance suits against any landowner whose property contained structures blocking, or threatening to block, the airport's runways' clear zones."

2. In Prah v. Maretti, the Wisconsin Court commented approvingly on the fact that solar collectors can provide an important alternative source of energy. In Rose v. Chaikin, 187 N.J.Super. 210, 453 A.2d 1378 (1982), the court thought less of the operation by defendants of a privately owned windmill. The defendants had built the windmill in "an effort to save on electric bills and conserve energy." The noise from the windmill was alleged by plaintiffs to produce "stress-related symptoms, together with a general inability to enjoy the peace of their homes." The court found that the noise levels "are of such a nature that they would be offensive to people of normal sensibilities and, in fact, have unreasonably interfered with plaintiffs' use and enjoyment of their properties." There were certain natural sounds in the area (—the ocean, sea gulls, the wind and distant, occasional boat traffic—), but the windmill produced unnatural sounds which were more or less constant. Witnesses testified that the plaintiffs suffered from nervousness, dizziness, loss of sleep and fatigue and that the sounds interfered with normal home activities such as reading, eating, watching television and general relaxation. The court enjoined the windmill, rejecting a counterclaim by defendants objecting to plaintiffs' heat pump. On the question of the windmill's value as an alternative energy source, the court stated:

> When consideration is given to the social utility of the windmill and the availability of reasonable alternatives, the conclusion supporting an injunction is the same. Defendants' purpose in installing the windmill was to conserve energy and save on electric bills. Speaking to the latter goal first, clearly the court can take judicial notice that alternative devices are available which are significantly less intrusive. Evid.R. 9(1). As to its social utility, a more careful analysis is required. Defendants argue that the windmill furthers the national need to conserve energy by the use of an alternative renewable source of power. See, generally, Wind Energy Systems Act of 1980, 42 U.S.C.A., §§ 9201–13, and Public Utility Regulatory Policies Act of 1978, 16 U.S.C.A., § 824a–3. The social utility of alternate energy sources cannot be denied; nor should the court ignore the proposition that scientific and social progress sometimes reasonably require a reduction in personal comfort. Protokowitz v. Lesofski, *supra* 69 N.J.Super. at 443, 174 A.2d 385; Annotation, "Nuisance—Operation of Air Conditioner," 79 A.L.R.3d 320, 328 (1977). On the other hand, the fact that a device represents a scientific advance and has social utility does not mean that it is permissible at any cost. Such factors must be weighed against the quantum of harm the

device brings to others. Sans v. Ramsey Golf & Country Club, *supra*, 29 N.J. at 448–49, 149 A.2d 599.

Do you think the New Jersey court's conclusions would hold up in light of current public policies emphasizing renewable sources of energy and the current interest in the 21st century regarding wind farms? A proposal in 2003 to locate a wind farm in the ocean off Cape Cod in Nantucket Sound has stirred up a classic confrontation between environmentalists who applaud the energy conservation proposal and residents on Cape Cod who denounce the spoliation of the natural attractions of that coastal area.

(2) Commercial and Industrial Areas

BOVE v. DONNER–HANNA COKE CORP.

Supreme Court of New York, Appellate Division, 1932.
236 App.Div. 37, 258 N.Y.S. 229, motion denied
236 App.Div. 775, 258 N.Y.S. 1075 (1932).

[Plaintiff built a house, the front of which was later converted into a grocery store on two lots in Buffalo, N.Y. Later the defendant's coke plant was built across the street. The plant operates 24 hours a day. Coke is heated to around 2000 degrees Fahrenheit and is taken out of the ovens and run under a "quencher" causing a tremendous cloud of steam, carrying with it minute particles of coke and some gas. Plaintiff claims a private nuisance and sues to enjoin it. The trial court refused the injunction. Plaintiff appealed. On appeal the trial court was affirmed. Only a small part of the opinion is given.]

* * *

It is true that the appellant was a resident of this locality for several years before the defendant came on the scene of action, and that, when the plaintiff built her house, the land on which these coke ovens now stand was a hickory grove. But in a growing community changes are inevitable. This region was never fitted for a residential district; for years it has been peculiarly adapted for factory sites. This was apparent when plaintiff bought her lots and when she built her house. The land is low and lies adjacent to the Buffalo river, a navigable stream connecting with Lake Erie. Seven different railroads run through this area. Freight tracks and yards can be seen in every direction. Railroads naturally follow the low levels in passing through a city. Cheap transportation is an attraction which always draws factories and industrial plants to a locality. It is common knowledge that a combination of rail and water terminal facilities will stamp a section as a site suitable for industries of the heavier type, rather than for residential purposes. In 1910 there were at least eight industrial plants, with a total assessed valuation of over a million dollars, within a radius of a mile from plaintiff's house.

With all the dirt, smoke and gas which necessarily come from factory chimneys; trains and boats, and with full knowledge that this region was especially adapted for industrial rather than residential purposes, and that factories would increase in the future, plaintiff selected this locality as the site of her future home. She voluntarily moved into this district, fully aware of the fact that the atmosphere would constantly be contaminated by dirt, gas and foul odors; and that she could not hope to find in this locality the pure air of a strictly residential zone. She evidently saw certain advantages in living in this congested center. This is not the case of an industry, with its attendant noise and dirt, invading a quiet, residential district. It is just the opposite. Here a residence is built in an area naturally adapted for industrial purposes and already dedicated to that use. Plaintiff can hardly be heard to complain at this late date that her peace and comfort have been disturbed by a situation which existed, to some extent at least, at the very time she bought her property, and which condition she must have known would grow worse rather than better as the years went by.

Today there are twenty industrial plants within a radius of less than a mile and three-quarters from appellant's house, with more than sixty-five smokestacks rising in the air, and belching forth clouds of smoke; every day there are 148 passenger trains, and 225 freight trains, to say nothing of switch engines, passing over these various railroad tracks near to the plaintiff's property; over 10,000 boats, a large portion of which burn soft coal, pass up and down the Buffalo river every season. Across the street, and within 300 feet from plaintiff's house, is a large tank of the Iroquois Gas Company which is used for the storage of gas.

The utter abandonment of this locality for residential purposes, and its universal use as an industrial center, becomes manifest when one considers that in 1929 the assessed valuation of the twenty industrial plants above referred to aggregated over $20,000,000, and that the city in 1925 passed a zoning ordinance putting this area in the third industrial district, a zone in which stockyards, glue factories, coke ovens, steel furnaces, rolling mills and other similar enterprises were permitted to be located.

One has only to mention these facts to visualize the condition of the atmosphere in this locality. It is quite easy to imagine that many of the things of which the plaintiff complains are due to causes over which the defendant has no control. At any rate, if appellant is immune from the annoyance occasioned by the smoke and odor which must necessarily come from these various sources, it would hardly seem that she could consistently claim that her health has been impaired, and that the use and enjoyment of her home have been seriously interfered with solely because of the dirt, gas and stench which have reached her from defendant's plant.

It is very true that the law is no respecter of persons, and that the most humble citizen in the land is entitled to identically the same protection accorded to the master of the most gorgeous palace. However, the fact that the plaintiff has voluntarily chosen to live in the smoke and turmoil of this industrial zone is some evidence, at least, that any annoyance which she has suffered from the dirt, gas and odor which have emanated from defendant's plant is more imaginary and theoretical than it is real and substantial.

I think that the trial court was amply justified in refusing to interfere with the operation of the defendant's coke ovens. No consideration of public policy or private rights demands any such sacrifice of this industry. * * *

Notes

1. Compare Nussbaum v. Lacopo, 27 N.Y.2d 311, 317 N.Y.S.2d 347, 265 N.E.2d 762 (1970) where the plaintiff who lived in a home abutting the thirteenth hole of defendant's golf course, and was hit by a stray golf ball while sitting on his patio sued, alleging nuisance and negligence. The court said:

> The design of the course was not such as to create a cause of action in nuisance or in negligence. "To constitute a nuisance, the use must be such as to produce a tangible and appreciable injury to neighboring property, or such as to render its enjoyment especially uncomfortable or inconvenient." (Campbell v. Seaman, 63 N.Y. 568, 577). But not every intrusion will constitute a nuisance. "Persons living in organized communities must suffer some damage, annoyance and inconvenience from each other. * * * If one lives in the city he must expect to suffer the dirt, smoke, noisome odors and confusion incident to city life" (Campbell v. Seaman, 63 N.Y. 568, 577, *supra*). So, too, one who deliberately decides to reside in the suburbs on very desirable lots adjoining golf clubs and thus receive the social benefits and other not inconsiderable advantages of country club surroundings must accept the occasional, concomitant annoyances (Patton v. Westwood Country Club Co., 18 Ohio App.2d 137, 247 N.E.2d 761 [1969]).
>
> Nuisance imports a continuous invasion of rights, and the occasional—"once or twice a week"—errant golf ball that was found on plaintiff's property does not constitute sufficient impairment of plaintiff's rights (see Bohan v. Port Jervis Gas–Light Co., 122 N.Y. 18, 25–26, 25 N.E. 246, 247–248). There were only, according to plaintiff and his wife, a few golf balls, which were found in the *bushes* and *fence area* of plaintiff's backyard. These minimal trespasses would not warrant the granting of an injunction and cannot sustain a recovery for plaintiff's injuries.

2. Often offensive commercial or industrial uses locate away from other similar uses, and over the years urban expansion results in nuisance litigation against the offender or demands for municipal regulation. In City of Fort Smith v. Western Hide & Fur Co., 153 Ark. 99, 239 S.W. 724 (1922), for example, the city brought a nuisance action against a hide and fur business located near the center of the business district. The court reversed the denial of an injunction, stating: "The case affords, perhaps, an example where a business established at a place remote from population is gradually surrounded and becomes part of a populous center, so that a business which formerly was not an interference with the rights of others has become so by the encroachment of the population. Under these circumstances, private rights must yield to the public good, and a court of equity will afford relief, even where a thing, originally harmless under certain circumstances, has

become a nuisance under changed conditions. Appellee pleads a license from the city in bar of the right to abate the nuisance, but the fact that the city granted a license to operate a hide and fur business does not imply that it could be operated in a manner so as to constitute a public nuisance, or to bar the city from suppressing the nuisance."

More typical than a public nuisance action in such cases is the enacting of an ordinance prohibiting certain commercial or industrial activities within prescribed boundaries. Prior to the widespread adoption of zoning ordinances in the 1920's such ordinances were challenged as "takings" of property without just compensation prohibited by the Fifth Amendment: "Nor shall private property be taken for public use without just compensation." Regulatory takings will be considered at length further in these materials, but some of the early Supreme Court cases relied heavily on nuisance theory to resolve the issue. Consider the following case, and the notes following it.

HADACHECK v. SEBASTIAN

Supreme Court of the United States, 1915.
239 U.S. 394, 36 S.Ct. 143, 60 L.Ed. 348.

MR. JUSTICE MCKENNA delivered the opinion of the court.

Habeas corpus prosecuted in the Supreme Court of the State of California for the discharge of plaintiff in error from the custody of defendant in error, Chief of Police of the City of Los Angeles.

Plaintiff in error, to whom we shall refer as petitioner, was convicted of a misdemeanor for the violation of an ordinance of the City of Los Angeles which makes it unlawful for any person to establish or operate a brickyard or brick kiln, or any establishment, factory or place for the manufacture or burning of brick within described limits in the city. Sentence was pronounced against him and he was committed to the custody of defendant in error as Chief of Police of the City of Los Angeles.

* * *

How the Supreme Court dealt with the allegations, denials and affidavits we can gather from its opinion. The court said, through Mr. Justice Sloss, 165 California, p. 416:

> "The district to which the prohibition was applied contains about three square miles. The petitioner is the owner of a tract of land containing eight acres, more or less, within the district described in the ordinance. He acquired his land in 1902, before the territory to which the ordinance was directed had been annexed to the city of Los Angeles. His land contains valuable deposits of clay suitable for the manufacture of brick, and he has, during the entire period of his ownership, used the land for brickmaking, and has erected thereon kilns, machinery and buildings necessary for such manufacture. The land, as he alleges, is far more valuable for brickmaking than for any other purpose."

The court considered the business one which could be regulated and that regulation was not precluded by the fact "that the value of investments made in the business prior to any legislative action will be greatly diminished," and that no complaint could be based upon the fact that petitioner had been carrying on the trade in that locality for a long period.

And, considering the allegations of the petition, the denials of the return and the evidence of the affidavits, the court said that the latter tended to show that the district created had become primarily a residential section and that the occupants of the neighboring dwellings are seriously incommoded by the operations of petitioner; and that such evidence, "when taken in connection with the presumptions in favor of the propriety of the legislative determination, overcame the contention that the prohibition of the ordinance was a mere arbitrary invasion of private right, not supported by any tenable belief that the continuance of the business was so detrimental to the interests of others as to require suppression."

The court, on the evidence, rejected the contention that the ordinance was not in good faith enacted as a police measure and that it was intended to discriminate against petitioner or that it was actuated by any motive of injuring him as an individual.

The charge of discrimination between localities was not sustained. The court expressed the view that the determination of prohibition was for the legislature and that the court, without regard to the fact shown in the return that there was not another district in which brickmaking was prohibited, could not sustain the claim that the ordinance was not enacted in good faith but was designed to discriminate against petitioner and the other brick yard in the district. "The facts before us," the court finally said "would certainly not justify the conclusion that the ordinance here in question was designed, in either its adoption or its enforcement, to be anything but what it purported to be, viz., a legitimate regulation, operating alike upon all who came within its terms."

We think the conclusion of the court is justified by the evidence and makes it unnecessary to review the many cases cited by petitioner in which it is decided that the police power of a state cannot be arbitrarily exercised. The principle is familiar, but in any given case it must plainly appear to apply. It is to be remembered that we are dealing with one of the most essential powers of government, one that is the least limitable. It may, indeed, seem harsh in its exercise, usually is on some individual, but the imperative necessity for its existence precludes any limitation upon it when not exerted arbitrarily. A vested interest cannot be asserted against it because of conditions once obtaining. *Chicago & Alton R.R. v. Tranbarger*, 238 U.S. 67, 78, 35 S.Ct. 678, 59 L.Ed. 204. To so hold would preclude development and fix a city forever in its primitive conditions. There must be progress, and if in its march private interests are in the way they must yield to the good of the community. The logical result of petitioner's contention would seem to be that a city could not be formed or enlarged against the resistance of an occupant of the ground and that if it grows at all it can only grow as the environment of the occupations that are usually banished to the purlieus.

The police power and to what extent it may be exerted we have recently illustrated in *Reinman v. Little Rock*, 237 U.S. 171, 35 S.Ct. 511, 59 L.Ed. 900. The circumstances of the case were very much like those of the case at bar and give reply to the contentions of petitioner, especially that which asserts that a necessary and lawful occupation that is not a nuisance per se cannot be made so by legislative declaration. There was a like investment in property, encouraged by the then conditions; a like reduction of value and deprivation of property was asserted against the validity of the ordinance there considered; a like assertion of an arbitrary exercise of the power of prohibition. Against all of these contentions, and causing the rejection of them all, was adduced the police power. There was a prohibition of a business, lawful in itself, there as here. It was a livery stable there, a brick yard here. They differ in particulars, but they are alike in that which cause and justify prohibition in defined localities—that is, the effect upon the health and comfort of the community.

The ordinance passed upon prohibited the conduct of the business within a certain defined area in Little Rock, Arkansas. This court said of it: granting that the business was not a nuisance per se, it was clearly within the police power of the State to regulate it, "and to that end to declare that in particular circumstances and in particular localities a livery stable shall be deemed a nuisance in fact and in law." And the only limitation upon the power was stated to be that the power could not be exerted arbitrarily or with unjust discrimination. There was a citation of cases. We think the present case is within the ruling thus declared.

There is a distinction between *Reinman v. Little Rock* and the case at bar. There, a particular business was prohibited which was not affixed to or dependent upon its locality; it could be conducted elsewhere. Here, it is contended, the latter condition does not exist, and it is alleged that the manufacture of brick must necessarily be carried on where suitable clay is found and that the clay on petitioner's property cannot be transported to some other locality. This is not urged as a physical impossibility but only, counsel say, that such transportation and the transportation of the bricks to places where they could be used in construction work would be prohibitive "from a financial standpoint." But upon the evidence the Supreme Court considered the case, as we understand its opinion, from the standpoint of the offensive effects of the operation of a brick yard, and not from the deprivation of the deposits of clay, and distinguished *Ex parte Kelso*, 147 Cal. 609, 2 L.R.A. (N.S.) 796, 109 Am.St.Rep. 178, 82 Pac. 241, wherein the court declared invalid an ordinance absolutely prohibiting the maintenance or operation of a rock or stone quarry within a certain portion of the city and county of San Francisco. The court there said that the effect of the ordinance was "to absolutely deprive the owners of real property within such limits of a valuable right incident to their ownership,—viz., the right to extract therefrom such rock and stone as they might find it to their advantage to dispose of." The court expressed the view that the removal could be regulated but that "an absolute prohibition of such removal under the circumstances," could not be upheld.

In the present case, there is no prohibition of the removal of the brick clay; only a prohibition within the designated locality of its manufacture into bricks. And to this feature of the ordinance our opinion is addressed. Whether other questions would arise if the ordinance were broader, and opinion on such questions, we reserve.

Petitioner invokes the equal protection clause of the Constitution and charges that it is violated in that the ordinance (1) "prohibits him from manufacturing brick upon his property while his competitors are permitted, without regulation of any kind, to manufacture brick upon property situated in all respects similarly to that of plaintiff in error"; and (2) that it "prohibits the conduct of his business while it permits the maintenance within the same district of any other kind of business, no matter how objectionable the same may be, either in its nature or in the manner in which it is conducted."

If we should grant that the first specification shows a violation of classification, that is, a distinction between businesses which was not within the legislative power, petitioner's contention encounters the objection that it depends upon an inquiry of fact which the record does not enable us to determine. It is alleged in the return to the petition that brickmaking is prohibited in one other district and an ordinance is referred to regulating business in other districts. To this plaintiff in error replied that the ordinance attempts to prohibit the operation of certain businesses having mechanical power and does not prohibit the maintenance of any business or the operation of any machine that is operated by animal power. In other words, petitioner makes his contention depend upon disputable considerations of classification and upon a comparison of conditions of which there is no means of judicial determination and upon which nevertheless we are expected to reverse legislative action exercised upon matters of which the city has control.

* * *

Judgment affirmed.

Notes

1. Hadacheck v. Sebastian refers to and was decided in the same year as Reinman v. City of Little Rock, 237 U.S. 171, 35 S.Ct. 511, 59 L.Ed. 900 (1915). In Reinman, a livery stable was eliminated from the downtown area as a result of the ordinance. Other police power ordinances which predated comprehensive zoning were predicated upon nuisance-like situations and drew upon that analogy. Ordinances were upheld which regulated prostitution (L'Hote v. City of New Orleans, 177 U.S. 587, 20 S.Ct. 788, 44 L.Ed. 899 (1900)), Chinese laundries (Soon Hing v. Crowley, 113 U.S. 703, 5 S.Ct. 730, 28 L.Ed. 1145 (1885), but cf. Yick Wo v. Hopkins, 118 U.S. 356, 6 S.Ct. 1064, 30 L.Ed. 220 (1886)), heavy industrial smoke emissions (Northwestern

Laundry v. City of Des Moines, 239 U.S. 486, 36 S.Ct. 206, 60 L.Ed. 396 (1916)), gasoline storage facilities (Pierce Oil Corp. v. City of Hope, 248 U.S. 498, 39 S.Ct. 172, 63 L.Ed. 381 (1919)) and fertilizer operations (Northwestern Fertilizing Co. v. Hyde Park, 97 U.S. (7 Otto) 659, 24 L.Ed. 1036 (1878)). These and the principal case provided, along with some others, the foundation for the suggestion that prohibiting nuisances or activities with nuisance characteristics did not constitute a taking of property even if the property owner was severely limited or even "wiped out." This distinction remains to be of continuing importance. See, e.g., Kuban v. McGimsey, 96 Nev. 105, 605 P.2d 623 (1980), which upheld a county ordinance prohibiting brothels after they had been legally permitted for seven years. The Nevada Court did not view this as resulting in a taking of the property of the owners of "Judy's Ranch" and "Sheri's Ranch."

2. What if a landowner complains that a nearby public land use so devalues his property that a nuisance-like taking has occurred? This, of course, is the other side of the coin, so to speak. For a case in which the property owner claimed that construction of a county jail and work release center on adjacent property amounted to a taking, see Florida East Coast Properties, Inc. v. Metropolitan Dade County, 572 F.2d 1108 (5th Cir.1978). Also see Hills Development Co. v. Township of Bernards, 229 N.J.Super. 318, 551 A.2d 547 (1988), where the court held that rezoning for construction of low and moderate income housing did not deprive adjoining landowners of all or most of their interest in their property and did not constitute a taking. What if the government's alleged nuisance results in a trespass? In Peterman v. State Dept. of Natural Resources, 446 Mich. 177, 521 N.W.2d 499 (1994), the state agency constructed a poorly designed boat launch on its lakefront property that resulted in destruction of a nearby property owner's beach due to sand filtration, and consequent erosion of fast land. The court held that the property owner was entitled to damages for a taking.

(3) Areas Adjoining Parks or Recreational Facilities

In City of Newport News v. Hertzler, 216 Va. 587, 221 S.E.2d 146 (1976), a public park was involved. Hertzler and 31 others alleged that the park had been opened when it was incomplete, unregulated and unsupervised. They complained of erosion of the shore caused by speeding boats launched from the park, health hazards caused by debris, human excrement and stench, annoyance from parties, lack of toilets, lights, trash containers and telephones, and lack of supervision. The trial court granted an injunction which was reversed on appeal. The Virginia Court stated that most of the complaining came from Hertzler and rather cavalierly dismissed his complaints—e.g., (in response to Hertzler's observing human excrement in the park and his viewing a male urinating), this was "not sufficient * * * to show that sanitary facilities were needed or that, if installed, they would be used." The impression provided by this case is that a court will not be inclined to shut down a public park except in an extreme situation.

Certainly, public parks or open space do not represent the only basis for nuisance allegations with regard to public facilities. In Vincent v. Salt Lake County, 583 P.2d 105 (Utah 1978), it was alleged that damages to a privately owned garage had resulted from a leaking county storm drain. The drain had been installed in a subdivision in 1957, and the plaintiffs had constructed their home approximately two years later. The garage wall began to crack in 1971 and widened in 1972. The county stated that an inspection showed no corollary between the drain and the cracks. However, the county failed to reveal that the inspection revealed some unsealed joints in the drain, some of which were grouted at that time. Additional cracks and the eventual sagging of the garage ensued in subsequent years. It was not until August, 1974, when the plaintiffs hired a contractor that they discovered the source of the problem. In affirming a money judgment against the county, the Utah Supreme Court treated the leaking drain as a latent defect unknown to plaintiffs until shortly before they filed suit. The court sustained a trial court instruction that a "nuisance is a condition, not an act or failure to act on the part of the person responsible for the condition."

Can you use "self-help" to abate a nuisance? In State ex rel. Herman v. Cardon, 112 Ariz. 548, 544 P.2d 657 (1976), the State and Gila County, Arizona, sued property owners abutting a highway to recover damages because they had destroyed 29.5 feet of the concrete along the highway which interfered with access to property on which they operated a service station. (The curb had been constructed prior to the time they acquired their lots.) The Arizona Supreme Court stated that public highways were "ways common and free to all persons" and that "a person who suffers injury through a nuisance, here interference with the right of access, may abate it without resort to legal proceedings provided he can do so without bringing about a breach of the peace." The court quoted from Prosser, Law of Torts § 90, p. 605 (4th ed. 1971) to this effect: "Summary abatement of a private nuisance by self-help is open only to those whose interests in the enjoyment of land are interfered with, or in other words, to those to whom it is a nuisance." The court added: "We can conceive of no legal reason why the sovereignty [sic] is immune from this legal principle."

Also, on highways, see State ex rel. State Highway Comm'n v. Johns, 507 S.W.2d 75 (Mo.App.1974), in which an injunction was granted against the encroachment of a building into a street even though the traveled portion of the street was unaffected. The court quoted from cases stating that "any permanent structure or purpresture which materially encroaches upon a public street and impedes travel is a nuisance per se, and may be abated, notwithstanding space is left for the passage of the public."

The Model Airspace Act, adopted by the American Bar Association, provides for a situation in which the state may join with private persons in the joint development and multiple use of the highway rights of way. This would lead to privately owned structures being placed on rights of way or possibly over highways or under elevated highways. This same Act provides that while the state possesses the right to make full use of the airspace over or under a right of way, the residual rights of the owners in fee cannot be additionally burdened without just compensation. See, e.g., 60 Okl.Stat.Ann. §§ 811, 813 (Supp.1974–75). See also, Wright, The Model Airspace Act: Old and New Law for Contemporary Land Use Problems, 1972 Law and the Social Order (Ariz.St.L.J.) 529.

E. NUISANCES IN ZONED AREAS

GREEN v. CASTLE CONCRETE CO.
Supreme Court of Colorado, 1973.
181 Colo. 309, 509 P.2d 588.

[Castle Concrete conducted a mining operation at Snyder Quarry which was enjoined as a public and a private nuisance. Castle was in compliance with state statutes and zoning laws. The issue is whether the operation of a limestone quarry permitted by zoning can be deemed a public nuisance. A further issue is whether the evidence will support a finding of a private nuisance. Castle had been quarrying in the general area for some years and had begun in 1969 to acquire new land, including the Snyder Quarry. Around $250,000 had been invested in land acquisitions. Although a road had been improved preparatory to the quarry operations, little if any of the actual operations had begun when suit was commenced. Seven residents with homes over a mile east of the area filed suit. Their asserted class action was dismissed and only the individual claims remained. Some testimony and a portion of the lower court's opinion dealt with ecological and environmental considerations, but the trial court ruled that this evidence was not considered in granting the injunction. Judicial notice was taken of the value of tourism and the economic loss which might result. Castle argued on appeal that (1) the authority of the trial court was exceeded in enjoining the operations as a public nuisance, and (2) that the finding of a private nuisance was not supported by the evidence.]

DAY, JUSTICE.

* * *

Taking up first the question of the public nuisance, this court very recently discussed the law of public nuisance as pronounced in *Robinson Brick Co. v. Luthi*, 115 Colo. 106, 169 P.2d 171. See *Hobbs v. Smith*, Colo., 493 P.2d 1352, wherein the following was quoted from *Robinson Brick*:

> " 'Where the legislative arm of the government has declared by statute and zoning resolution what activities may or may not be conducted in a prescribed zone, it has in effect declared what is or is not a *public nuisance*. What might have been a proper field for judicial action prior to such legislation becomes improper when the law-making branch of government has entered the field. None of the numerous cases cited appears to go so far as to approve the enjoining of a business operating under valid legislative zoning authority.' " (Emphasis added.)

* * *

Additionally, a reading of the record convinces us that there is not sufficient substantial, competent evidence to support a finding of private nuisance. See *Ryan v. Pitkin Iron Corp.*, 10th Cir., 444 F.2d 717; *Haskell v. Denver Tramway Co.*, 23 Colo. 60, 46 P. 121. The record is devoid of any proof that the quarry has been or *will in fact* be a nuisance. Speculation as to the future harmful effects of blasting and from dust pollution are not based on any actual occurrences other than a test blast. Other blasting complained of was in connection with building the road which would not reoccur. The defendant has not been given an opportunity to show that it can use methods which will remedy the anticipatory nuisance. Plaintiffs have fallen short of discharging the evidentiary burden necessary to entitle them to an injunction on any of the bases asserted. We have stated in other relevant opinions that in such circumstances the trial court should be reversed. See *Mowry v. Jackson*, 140 Colo. 197, 343 P.2d 833; *Hawkins v. Elston*, 58 Colo. 400, 146 P. 254; *Davis v. Pursel*, 55 Colo. 287, 134 P. 107.

* * *

It has been evident to county and state authorities for some years that quarry operations in at least two adjacent areas have been continuing and that large limestone formations abound in this area. Yet no move has been made by the legislature or county or city officials to rezone the area, set it aside for parks and recreation, or to compensate the owners for the taking. Solutions for problems of the magnitude anticipated here may suggest legislative and not judicial action.

We feel compelled to state that, although the goal of creating an aesthetically pleasing environment is clearly laudable, it is equally clear that where the accomplishment of this goal entails the restructuring of societal rights and priorities it cannot be fairly or justly done through a judicially sanctioned private condemnation without compensation under the guise of abating a nuisance. In our populous society, the courts cannot be available to enjoin an activity solely because it causes some aesthetic discomfort or annoyance. Given our myriad and disparate tastes, life styles, mores, and attitudes, the availability of a judicial remedy for such complaints would cause inexorable confusion.

The judgment is reversed, and the cause is remanded with directions to vacate the injunction and dismiss the complaint.

[Concurring and dissenting opinions omitted.]

Notes

1. Robinson Brick Co. v. Luthi, which is cited in the majority opinion was a case where the plaintiff operated a large greenhouse and the defendant mined clay for bricks. The county zoning ordinance did not permit clay mining, but the defendant's activities antedated the ordinance and constituted a non-conforming use. The Colorado court held that the state had "preempted the field of public nuisance as it relates to this case." Nominal damages were allowed in connection with the private nuisance. (Plaintiff testified that the dust from these operations spoiled his plants growing in

the open and caused the need for more cleansing of plants in the greenhouse.)

2. See also Dudding v. Automatic Gas Co., 145 Tex. 1, 193 S.W.2d 517 (1946). Admittedly, the nuisance injunction has been less than successful in eliminating non-conforming uses from zoned areas. On this, see, Noel, Retroactive Zoning and Nuisances, 41 Colum.L.Rev. 457 (1941), and Willis, The Elimination of Nonconforming Uses, 1951 Wis.L.Rev. 685 (1951). Among the cases see, Oklahoma City v. Dolese, 48 F.2d 734 (10th Cir.1931) (failure to remove non-conforming coal yard); Firth v. Scherzberg, 366 Pa. 443, 77 A.2d 443 (1951) (motor terminal); City of Akron v. Chapman, 160 Ohio St. 382, 116 N.E.2d 697 (1953) (reliance solely on retroactive zoning provisions of ordinance and not on nuisance failed to succeed in removal of junk yard). For cases more favorable to the removal or abatement of objectionable nonconforming uses, see Eaton v. Klimm, 217 Cal. 362, 18 P.2d 678 (1933); Malm v. Dubrey, 325 Mass. 63, 88 N.E.2d 900 (1949); and Civic Ass'n of Dearborn Township, Dist. No. 3 v. Horowitz, 318 Mich. 333, 28 N.W.2d 97 (1947) (street carnival can continue, but only if cleaned up).

3. In Rockenbach v. Apostle, 330 Mich. 338, 47 N.W.2d 636 (1951), the question was whether an undertaking establishment could be maintained in a residential district which permitted funeral homes subject to certain requirements. These requirements had been met, but the nuisance question remained. The Michigan Supreme Court stated:

> The weight of authority is to the effect that an ordinance which allows the establishment or maintenance of a funeral home or undertaking establishment in a district zoned either for residential or commercial purposes is permissive only, and not controlling as to whether such undertaking establishment would constitute a nuisance which might be enjoined by an equity court. However, proof of the existence of such a zoning ordinance is admissible as evidence of the character of the district, and bearing on the question of nuisance. A nuisance will not be upheld solely on the ground that it has been permitted by municipal ordinance. Sweet v. Campbell, *supra*; Williams v. Blue Bird Laundry Co., 85 Cal.App. 388, 259 P. 484; Fendley v. City of Anaheim, 110 Cal.App. 731, 294 P. 769; Kosich v. Poultrymen's Service Corp., 136 N.J.Eq. 571, 43 A.2d 15; Perrin's Appeal, 305 Pa. 42, 156 A. 305, 79 A.L.R. 912; White v. Old York Road Country Club, 318 Pa. 346, 178 A. 3. * * *

4. Other cases announcing the doctrine that a permitted use under zoning may be a nuisance include Beane v. H.K. Porter, Inc., 280 Mass. 538, 182 N.E. 823 (1932) (drop forge hammers); Reid v. Brodsky, 397 Pa. 463, 156 A.2d 334 (1959) (a taproom restaurant that attracted delinquents into a resident area zoned "commercial"); and Harris v. Skirving, 41 Wash.2d 200, 248 P.2d 408 (1952) (garbage dump). A nuisance was found to exist in an "unclassified zone" in Turner v. City of Spokane, 39 Wash.2d 332, 235 P.2d 300 (1951) (rock quarry).

5. But compare Union City v. Southern Pacific Co., 261 Cal.App.2d 277, 67 Cal.Rptr. 816 (1968), which relies on a provision of the California Civil Code in stating that no activity which is conducted under the express authority of a statute can be held to be a nuisance.

6. In People ex rel. Hoogasian v. Sears, Roebuck & Co., 52 Ill.2d 301, 287 N.E.2d 677 (1972) the plaintiffs sought to enjoin the continued construction of the Sears Tower, a 110 story, 1350 foot high office building in downtown Chicago:

> Plaintiffs alleged that if construction was allowed to continue the building would interfere with television reception in certain areas. This interference would occur because the broadcasting antennas of Chicago television stations are lower than the contemplated structure which would cause the signals that emanate from these antennas to abnormally reflect from defendant's building thereby allegedly producing distortions on television screens in these areas.
>
> The principal issue in this case is whether defendant has a legal right to use the air space above its property subject only to legislative limitation, or stated conversely, whether an individual or class of individuals has the right to limit the use of such property on the basis that interference with television reception constitutes an actionable nuisance.
>
> * * *
>
> In effect we have competing legitimate commercial interests, both of concern to the public. (See: Richmond Bros., Inc. v. Hagemann (Mass. 1971), 268 N.E.2d 680.) The responsibility in this case for inadequate television reception in certain areas rests more with the broadcaster's choice of location than with the height of defendant's building. Therefore disruption of television signals initiated by totally independent third parties over which defendant has no control cannot be the basis for enjoining the full legal use and enjoyment of defendant's property.
>
> * * *
>
> Considering the foregoing, it is clear to us that absent legislation to the contrary, defendant has a proprietary right to construct a building to its desired height and that completion of the project would not constitute a nuisance under the circumstances of this case. * * *

5. If the Sears case seems somewhat far out in terms of nuisances in zoned areas, let us turn to something more commonplace—billboards. In General Elec. Co. v. Maurice Callahan & Sons, Inc., 2 Mass.App.Ct. 124, 309 N.E.2d 209 (1974), an action was brought to enjoin the erection and maintenance of two billboards. One of the arguments advanced by the defendant was that the billboards were not a nuisance at common law and the plaintiff had no remedy. The court rejected this argument because the plaintiff was basing his action on a statute which allowed restraint of the erection of a billboard or sign which violated any rule or regulation of a statutory board. The billboards violated the rules, and the landowner was not required to exhaust his administrative remedies before suing to enjoin. A final argument was that the adoption of a new zoning ordinance by the city permitting billboards in the area involved rendered the case moot. But the new ordinance also contained a limitation on the size of billboards, and these were about twice that size.

6. Shifflett v. Baltimore County, 247 Md. 151, 230 A.2d 310 (1967) involved another old favorite—junkyards. Testimony adduced at the trial

established what everyone knows—that junkyards are incompatible with residential use. They were not deemed to be nuisances per se, but "courts in other jurisdictions have found * * * that the elimination of junkyards which enjoy the status of a non-conforming use in a residential neighborhood is a reasonable exercise of the police power, because of their nature or the manner in which they are conducted, if the time given for the elimination of the non-conforming use is adequate." The court upheld a zoning ordinance requiring that the junkyards be eliminated within two years of the effective date of the ordinance. Obviously, the junkyards were considered to have nuisance-like characteristics. Moreover, in a residential district, should not a junkyard be regarded as a nuisance per se?

7. What about the operation of a gravel pit in an area zoned for residential use? In City of Cloquet v. Cloquet Sand and Gravel, Inc., 312 Minn. 277, 251 N.W.2d 642 (1977), the gravel pit operators had never secured a conditional use permit to operate in a residential area as required by ordinance, but the trial court held that they need not comply with that requirement because the city was not uniformly enforcing its ordinance. But independent of the ordinance, the court held that defendant's activities, including an excavation that produced a drop-off of 75 to 90 feet, constituted a nuisance. The trial court ordered erection of a fence, the smoothing out of the land contours when the operation ceased, and ordered them to cease operating until the order was complied with. The Minnesota Supreme Court affirmed.

8. Some alleged nuisances in zoned areas present First Amendment considerations. For example, what about statutes or ordinances requiring the licensing and thereby allowing the prohibition of theatrical performances and concerts? See Town of West Greenwich v. Stepping Stone Enterprises, Ltd., 122 R.I. 132, 416 A.2d 659 (1979). In Havurah v. Zoning Board of Appeals, 177 Conn. 440, 418 A.2d 82 (1979), the appellant was a religious organization that argued sleeping accommodations were essential to its religious fellowship. A zoning board of appeals had concluded that unrestricted overnight lodging was a residential use unrelated to the right to worship. See also Napro Development Corp. v. Town of Berlin, 135 Vt. 353, 376 A.2d 342 (1977) involving an adult book store. The Supreme Court of Vermont was cautious to employ the concept of public nuisance in a situation that might intrude on free speech or expression. See also, on adult book stores, Commonwealth v. Van Emburg, 467 Pa. 445, 359 A.2d 178 (1976), and on adult movies, Commonwealth v. MacDonald, 464 Pa. 435, 347 A.2d 290 (1975). Statutes or ordinances regulating such activities have commonly been attacked as being constitutionally vague.

9. What if you have something as beneficial to the public as a nursing home for handicapped children, whose property has been rezoned, but the rezoning has been held invalid? In Schubach v. Silver, 461 Pa. 366, 336 A.2d 328 (1975), neighboring property owners brought suit to enjoin it as a nuisance based upon the earlier decision on the zoning.

SECTION 3. SERVITUDES AND RESTRICTIVE COVENANTS

One cannot efficiently achieve planned land development by relying on the happenstance processes of nuisance law. It is also clear that plans alone are not enough. There must be legally enforceable means to implement or protect plans. In subsequent chapters we deal with legislative and administrative controls designed to accomplish public land use planning. In this section we deal with so-called "private" land use restrictions. These involve typically "a right in the land of another." That is, someone not the owner of land is put in a position in which she can compel the owner to carry out or to refrain from carrying out specified activities on his or her land.

The variety of private law devices available to accomplish land use goals is substantial. The lawyer is faced with a problem of knowledgeable choice. And once she has chosen the device to use, she must know how to create the selected relationship. Then, regardless of the selection made, the lawyer is faced by a formidable challenge to be extraordinarily careful in the language used, because what is written may bind the land for many years. Here we attempt to set up enough guideposts so that a lawyer can at least begin to make intelligent choices.

First, it may help to outline typical functional situations in which the lawyer operates in this area of the law. The list is by no means complete; it is illustrative only

A. Private Arrangements to Implement Private Plans

1. Two or more landowners want to assure that their lands will be kept in open space uses, will be developed for large lot residential use only, or will be subject to a building development scheme.

2. A public utility wants to acquire a right of way across private land for its poles, wires or pipes.

3. Two or more neighbors want to establish a common driveway, or an access way across the land of one or to preserve a scenic view over the land of one for the benefit of another.

4. To implement a subdivision building scheme:

   a. A subdivider wants unilaterally to declare how the land is to be used, that it is to be subject to architectural controls, building setbacks, and the like; or

   b. The subdivider wishes to enter into an agreement with each lot buyer under which the buyer agrees to the building scheme for the lot she is buying and the subdivider agrees to it for all of the unsold lots; or

   c. The subdivider wants each lot buyer to agree that the lot being purchased is subject to the building scheme.

5. The developer of a condominium project wants to place a uniform set of restrictions on the behavior of all unit owners and create a governing mechanism to enforce the restrictions.

6. The developer of a large retirement community that will take many years to fully develop wants to make sure the company can retain sufficient control of land uses and have enough votes to dictate how any set of restrictions are modified in the future.

B. Adaptation of Private Land Planning Tools to Public Planning Ends

1. A city and a developer wish to agree that slum-cleared land will be redeveloped in accordance with a plan made by the city.

2. A city wants to approve a subdivision plat but only on condition that the land will be developed or used in specified ways, subject to access, setback, lot size or other restrictions.

3. A city is willing to approve an amendment rezoning X's land from residential to commercial but only after X has formally agreed that the land will actually be used for only one of many "permitted" commercial purposes.

4. A unit of government wants to acquire from landowner a right preserving an open area, permitting public use, public access to a lake, or similar uses.

5. A unit of government in the course of approving a large-scale planned development incorporating single-family homes, townhouses and condominiums with a set of restrictions wants to insure that the public can, in the future, prevent residents within the development from selling open space or increasing the density of population, or enforce maintenance of the parklands within the development.

6. A unit of government is selling forest land which it owns to a private company. It wants to assure the cutting of sizeable trees only and other desired forestry practices.

[These last six situations suggest that the line between "private" law and "public" law may not always be easy to draw.]

A wide array of legal tools are available to meet the needs of private and public interests. Unfortunately, for most of the past centuries these tools stood alone doctrinally and each tool required very precise legal instruments to further the desired goals. Language in old documents faced strict judicial scrutiny to ascertain just what the parties intended in the past, and many recorded instruments failed, and continue to fail.

In the year 2000 the American Law Institute adopted—after many years of deliberation—the Restatement of Property Third (Servitudes). This new restatement of property law in the area of private arrangements governing the use of land seeks to rationalize most of the common law tools into a seamless whole. State courts in future years will be called upon to use the new restatement principles both to resolve disputes over old language, and to approve of arrangements made by lawyers using the new principles. How readily courts will use the new restatement remains to be seen, but the ALI effort is worthy of close study. Following is an excerpt from the Foreword to the new restatement:

> Professor French's [the Reporter for this work] formulations, approved by the Institute in 1998 and here integrated into the final, official text, are original and important even though they are completely within the canon of modern Property doctrine. They are original and important because much of the law in this field until now has lagged behind social life. Cases and first-year casebooks continue to be mired in easements, covenants, reciprocal easements, and equitable servitudes. Transactions continue to fail because of lack of horizontal privity. Generally developers in particular states have found ways to create the legal arrangements that residents seek, but the law is incoherent when viewed nationally and in many states people pay the price for uncertain doctrine and unnecessary formalities. Meanwhile, a substantial portion of the population has moved to gated communities, to condominiums, and to single-family homes that require membership in private associations. * * *
>
> Professor French begins with the assumption that many of us live in close quarters, that we will give up some of our discretion to obtain limitations on the loud noise and bad taste of our neighbors, and that we are willing to pay for private governance because we believe it to be more efficient than government and because we cannot afford to obtain these amenities—snow shoveling, swimming pool, roadside planting—individually. Therefore this Restatement is enabling toward private governance, so long as there is full disclosure to prospective and current participants and so long as decisions are made according to established and fair procedures. The new work is also attentive to our growing interest in conserving and preserving our natural, historical, and cultural resources and to the increasing use of conservation and preservation servitudes as an important means to that end.

In the materials that follow we have to look at some of the pitfalls and problems associated with the "old" law, but several newer cases are included to present the kinds of problems the new Restatement attempts to avoid.

A. DEFEASIBLE ESTATES VERSUS COVENANTS

One ill-advised way to restrict land use is through the well-established historical device of the defeasible fee. A defeasible fee may be a fee simple determinable or a fee simple upon condition subsequent. In either event, unlike the fee simple absolute, the fee may automatically terminate or be subject to a power of termination at some undetermined future date. In both situations there is a potential for the forfeiture or loss of title and its reinvestiture in the grantor who created the estate.

CITY OF IDAHO SPRINGS v. GOLDEN SAV. & LOAN ASS'N

Colorado Court of Appeals, 1970.
29 Colo.App. 119, 480 P.2d 847.

COYTE, JUDGE.

* * *

The City of Idaho Springs, a second-class city, filed the initial complaint in this suit seeking to quiet title in itself to a certain tract of land located in Clear Creek County. Prior to this suit, the City had determined that a municipal swimming pool was necessary. However, it lacked the proper amount of funds to adequately construct and maintain such a pool. In 1955, the City, in accordance with C.R.S.1953, 139–32–2, had an election to determine whether to sell this particular tract of land to Frank Overturf by warranty deed, subject to the following provision:

> * * * provided, however, that the real property described herein, together with the improvements thereon, shall be used perpetually and solely for the purpose (sic) of the operation of a swimming pool, which said restriction shall run with the land hereby conveyed and in the event of any breach thereof, said property shall forthwith revert to the said party of the first part, its successors and assigns.

The electorate authorized the sale and conveyance and the property was conveyed in accordance therewith.

Defendant Frank Overturf then conveyed the property to Overturf's Park, Inc., which in turn executed a deed of trust to defendant Golden Savings and Loan. Upon default in payment, Golden Savings and Loan foreclosed its deed of trust on the property and acquired a public trustee's deed in January of 1966.

The property was not being used as a swimming pool and, therefore, plaintiff filed suit to enforce the reversion clause contained in the deed and to reaffirm its title to the property. Defendant Golden Savings and Loan Association answered, generally denying the validity of plaintiff's claimed interest, and affirmatively counterclaimed to quiet title in itself to the property in question.

* * *

The sole issue raised by this appeal is the question of whether or not a second-class city may convey property with a possibility of reverter.

Since the trial court based its decision upon C.R.S.1953, 139–32–2 (reenacted as C.R.S.1963, 139–32–2) as interpreted by *Centennial Properties v. Littleton*, 154 Colo. 191, 390 P.2d 471, a full discussion of this case is necessary.

In *Centennial, supra*, the City of Littleton executed a "warranty deed," conveying a certain tract of land to defendant, title to which would automatically revert to the City after ninety-nine years. Holding this "reversion" to be void, the Supreme Court noted that under the applicable statute, C.R.S.1953, 139–32–2, cities and towns (not home rule cities) had the power " * * * to sell and dispose * * * " of real property, but did not have the power to lease property owned by the city. It further held that plaintiff could not convey real property and at the same time retain a present vested interest in the property. Accordingly, the present vested interest retained by the city was declared to be void and title was quieted in the grantee.

The question here, however, is whether a city may properly convey real property, yet retain a possibility of reverter to it. As defined in *School District, etc. v. Russell*, 156 Colo. 75, 396 P.2d 929, a possibility of reverter is merely the *possibility* that the land will come back to the grantor. Frank Overturf and his successors held a fee simple determinable estate, which would last as long as the land was used for the purpose specified in the conveying instrument.

The holder of a bare possibility of reverter does not have a present "vested" interest or "estate" in the land. *United States v. 2,184.81 Acres of Land*, 45 F.Supp. 681. This being so, the City upon delivery of its deed conveyed the entire legal title to the property in question.

The instrument here is in fact a warranty deed granting defendants a fee simple determinable estate in the property so long as it remains in use as a swimming pool. At the time of conveyance, the City of Idaho Springs parted with all present interest in the property, *United States v. 2,184.81 Acres of Land, supra*, retaining only the possibility of regaining title at some indefinite time in the future, if the specified condition under which the property was conveyed should cease to exist.

For this reason, we conclude that there was full compliance with the statute and that the possibility of reverter contained in the warranty deed was valid and enforceable. Judgment is reversed with directions to enter judgment quieting title in the plaintiff in accordance with this opinion.

Notes

1. In Hagaman v. Board of Educ. of Woodbridge Twp., 117 N.J.Super. 446, 285 A.2d 63 (1971), the Appellate Division of the New Jersey Superior Court provided an excellent and well-documented summary of the pertinent points of law relating to defeasible fees. Unlike the principal case, defeasible fees are more commonly employed by private persons rather than by governmental units. They are often related to religion or liquor, although in different ways. One of the classic examples of the fee simple determinable is the conveyance "for as long as St. Paul's Church shall stand." Whether a determinable fee or a fee simple upon condition subsequent, the language often provides for automatic reverter or a right of entry for condition broken in the event "vinous, spirituous or fermented liquors" are sold, or if the premises are used for gambling or some "immoral purpose." (See, e.g., Northwestern Improvement Co. v. Lowry, 104 Mont. 289, 66 P.2d 792, 110 A.L.R. 605 (1937), in which the question was whether a tax deed wiped out the restrictive covenants, and it was held that it did not. The covenants did

not rise to the level of a defeasible fee.) Deeds or wills containing such provisions might be compared to the preoccupation of medieval landowners with benefiting the Church in some manner that would avoid some time in purgatory or otherwise expiate their sins. Provisions against "demon rum" should set well with the Almighty. The problem is that in the absence of statutory limitations, the result is to cloud land titles, promote litigation, deter alienability, and permit the dead hand to rule from the grave. Yet such provisions do not violate the Rule against Perpetuities, nor do restrictive covenants, as revealed in McKinnon v. Neugent, 225 Ga. 215, 167 S.E.2d 593 (1969). In that case, a statute that limited enforceability of covenants in zoned areas to 20 years did not render invalid restrictive covenants which were to run for 25 years.

2. In connection with the tax deed problem in the Lowry case, mentioned in the preceding note, consider the following cases from other jurisdictions:

In Hayes v. Gibbs, 110 Utah 54, 169 P.2d 781 (1946), a general plan of restricted development was found to exist, and the court held that while the authorities "are not uniform on the subject * * * ordinarily a tax sale does not divest easements charged upon the property sold." (169 P.2d at 786.) In Schlafly v. Baumann, 341 Mo. 755, 108 S.W.2d 363 (1937), the Missouri statute was interpreted to mean that a tax sale buyer of a residential lot subject to deed restrictions acquired the lot subject to such restrictions since it was assessed on the basis of the enhanced value produced by the restrictions. In Alamogordo Improvement Co. v. Prendergast, 43 N.M. 245, 91 P.2d 428 (1939), the New Mexico court upheld the power of the seller of lots subject to a restriction against the sale of liquor to enforce the restriction against a tax sale purchaser on the theory that the lot was increased in value by the restriction and that this was considered in assessing the lot for tax purposes.

Whether a tax deed wipes out an equitable servitude imposed by a restrictive covenant may be dependent on judicial interpretation of local tax statutes. Some statutes are "in personam" in that they impose liability on the landowner rather than on the land itself. In that situation, nonpayment results in the sale of the owner's interest only, and the purchaser at the tax sale obtains a derivative title—that is, a title which is encumbered only to the same extent as the delinquent taxpayer. Most states have "in rem" statutes in which the encumbrance attaches to the land itself and the tax sale gives rise to a new title freed of all encumbrances. These statutes often allow room for judicial interpretation. Some statutes expressly save "easements" existing at the time of sale and this term may in its context be held broad enough to include equitable servitudes. See Halpin v. Poushter, 59 N.Y.S.2d 338 (Sup.Ct.1945). Several states expressly provide that restrictions imposed by covenants running with the land survive the tax sale and tax deed. See Wis.Stat. § 75.14(4) (1989), that codified the prior holding in Doherty v. Rice, 240 Wis. 389, 3 N.W.2d 734 (1942).

There is an ancillary—perhaps basic—policy issue involved here: Should other lot owners in a subdivision have to pay delinquent taxes on a lot in order to maintain the restriction and thereby prevent destruction of the restricted character of the neighborhood?

On this subject generally, see 2 American Law of Property § 9.40 at 451–52 (1952).

SEVERNS v. UNION PACIFIC RAILROAD COMPANY

California Court of Appeals, Second District, 2002.
101 Cal.App.4th 1209, 125 Cal.Rptr.2d 100.

VOGEL (C.S.), P.J.

Gary M. Severns (plaintiff) brought a quiet title action against Union Pacific Railroad Company (Union Pacific). The bone of contention was interpretation of a 1901 transaction in which Frederick and Elisabeth Bluemle granted an interest to the California Pacific Railway Company (California Pacific Railway). In essence, plaintiff alleged that the 1901 conveyance transferred only an easement, not a fee interest; that he was the successor in interest to the Bluemles and therefore the owner of the land (servient estate) burdened by the easement; and that the easement had been terminated by abandonment. He therefore sought to quiet title as against Union Pacific, the successor in interest to the California Pacific Railway.

* * *

In 1901 the Bluemles executed the following handwritten deed.

"This indenture, made this 4th day of December A.D.1901 between Frederick Bluemle and Elisabeth Bluemle his wife, of Los Angeles County California, the parties of the first part, and the California Pacific Railway Company, a corporation, the party of the second part.

"Witnesseth: That the said parties of the first part for and in consideration of the sum of five dollars ($5.00) in U.S. Gold Coin, or equivalent to them in hand paid by the said party of the second part, the receipt of which is hereby acknowledged do by these presents grant, bargain, sell, convey, and confirm unto the said party of the second part and to its assigns forever, all that certain lot parcel or tract of land situate in Los Angeles County, California, and more particularly described as follows, viz:

"A strip of land sixty (60) feet wide West of the West line of the Old Tomlinson Stage Road '(also recently, locally called Vermont Avenue'), and West of adjoining parallel to, and along the entire length of the East line of lot three (3) of the Maria Machado de-Rocha Tract–Rancho San Pedro as per map recorded in Book 6 Page 161 of the Miscellaneous Records of Los Angeles County, California and containing in all, two and eighty-six hundredths (2.86) acres, more or less.

"Together with all and singular the tenements, hereditaments and appurtenances thereunto belonging or in anywise appertaining and the reversion and reversions remainder and remainders, rents, issues and profits thereof.

"To Have and to Hold all and singular, the said premises, together with the appurtenances unto the said party of the second part and to its assigns forever.

"Note. [I]t is understood that the above described strip of land herein conveyed, shall be for a right of way, and that said second party, or its assigns shall construct over and along same, a first class electric railway, and will operate said railway with a service of not less than ten daily trains and that local trains or cars, shall stop, for passengers desiring to get on or off the cars at the south line of said right of way.

"Should said railway after being completed and in operation cease thereafter to be operated for a period of six months, then said right of way herein conveyed shall revert to the parties of the first or assigns.

"It is mutually understood and agreed upon by both parties to this indenture, that the existing three wire fence along the east line of said right of way hereunder conveyed shall, for valuable consideration, already received by the said parties of the first part, be move[d] and set up in first class order along the west line of said right of way within thirty days from the date of this indenture by said first parties, their agents or assigns, and free of all expense to the party of the second part, or its assigns, and that the said fence shall, from the date of this indenture belong to the party of the second part or its assigns."

In 1912, the Bluemles conveyed a portion of their land to Lucile Brown, excepting various earlier conveyances. Brown subsequently subdivided her parcel into various lots.

In 1977 and 1978, Frampton Properties, a partnership in which plaintiff held a 25 percent interest, obtained nine of the subdivided lots originally belonging to Brown.

In 1994, Union Pacific commenced removal of the railroad tracks on the right-of-way.

In April 1999, Frampton Properties quitclaimed to plaintiff all of its interest in the nine lots.

In October 1999, plaintiff initiated this quiet title action.

The primary objective in interpreting a deed is to ascertain and carry out the intent of the parties. (*Machado v. Southern Pacific Transportation Co.* (1991) 233 Cal.App.3d 347, 352.) If the deed is ambiguous on its face, extrinsic evidence is admissible to interpret it. (*Baker v. Ramirez* (1987) 190 Cal.App.3d 1123, 1132–1133.) In this case, the trial court found the deed was ambiguous and consequently considered extrinsic evidence to ultimately decide the interest conveyed was an easement.

Union Pacific first contends the use of extrinsic evidence was improper because the 1901 deed is not ambiguous. We agree. The deed is not ambiguous. As we now explain, it is essentially identical to the deed analyzed in *Concord & Bay Point Land Co. v. City of Concord* (1991) 229 Cal.App.3d 289 (*Concord*). Relying upon only the language of the deed and eschewing any statutory presumptions or extrinsic evidence (*id.* at p. 294), the *Concord* court held the deed conveyed a fee subject to a condition subsequent.

In this case, the granting clause recites the Bluemles "grant, bargain, sell, convey, and confirm" the designated parcel. To convey a fee, all that is required is the word "grant." (*Schlageter v. Cutting* (1931) 116 Cal.App. 489, 498.) The language used here is the traditional language for a conveyance of a fee and is identical to the language in the *Concord* deed. (*Concord, supra,* 229 Cal.App.3d at p. 293.) Significantly, the granting clause does *not* restrict the grantee to any particular use. Furthermore, it contains language of inheritance ("to its successors and assigns forever"), language indicating a fee conveyance. (*Id.* at pp. 293–294.)

The next paragraph contains a detailed description of the conveyance. The beginning phrase, "[a] strip of land sixty (60) feet wide"—language virtually the same as that employed in *Concord*—indicates the land itself is being conveyed, not merely a nonpossessory right to use the land. (*Concord, supra,* 229 Cal.App.3d at p. 294.) As our Supreme Court has indicated, "[r]eferences to 'land,' particularly in conjunction with precise and technical designation of the location, generally indicate an intention to transfer the entire estate not just a limited right to pass over the property." (*City of Manhattan Beach v. Superior Court* (1996) 13 Cal.4th 232, 244 (*Manhattan Beach*).)

The following paragraph adds that the grant includes all "tenements, hereditaments and appurtenances thereunto belonging or in anywise appertaining and the reversion and reversions, remainder and remainders, rents, issues and profits thereof." As the *Concord* court noted, this language "is very likely to be surplusage where an easement alone is conveyed." (*Concord, supra,* 229 Cal.App.3d at p. 295; see also *Johnson v. Ocean Shore Railroad Co.* (1971) 16 Cal.App.3d 429, 434.) Hence, it conveys a fee interest.

Next comes the habendum clause ("To Have and to Hold"). This simply repeats the language of inheritance found in the granting clause.

It is not until the following three paragraphs that *any* reference to a "right-of-way" appears. Introduced by the word "Note," the conveyance states the understood purpose of the conveyance: construction of a railroad right-of-way.

Details of the use (number of trains, location of stops) are set forth. These references to a right-of-way do not suggest an easement. They simply describe the purpose to which the land will be put. In this context, the term "right-of-way" describes "that strip of land upon which railroad companies construct their road bed, and, when so used, the term refers to the land itself, not the right of passage over it. [Citation.]" (*Concord, supra,* 229 Cal.App.3d at p. 295; see also *Machado v. Southern Pacific Transportation Co., supra,* 233 Cal.App.3d 347, 359.)

The conveyance then recites what will happen if railroad operations cease for six months: the right-of-way *reverts* to the grantors or their assigns. This reference to a reversion is language normally associated with grant of a fee. "[A]n easement which is abandoned by nonuse or use outside its limitations does not 'revert' to the grantor, it is simply extinguished. [Citation.]" (*Concord, supra,* 229 Cal.App.3d at p. 295.) In other words, this language shows the grantors intended to convey a fee interest subject to a condition subsequent that if the grantee failed to use the land for a railroad right-of-way, the grantors could reclaim the property.

In sum, there is no ambiguity in this conveyance. The *Concord* court's conclusion is equally applicable here. It wrote: "The deed conveys an estate of inheritance in the land itself, unrestricted except for a future condition, upon the failure of which the property conveyed reverts to the grantor. This is a fee simple subject to a condition subsequent; the reversionary interest held by the grantor is a power of termination. [Citations.]" (*Concord, supra,* 229 Cal.App.3d at p. 295.)

* * *

In 1982, the Legislature enacted the Marketable Record Title Act (the Act). (Civ.Code, § 880.020 et seq). It became operative on January 1, 1983. "[T]his comprehensive statute was the product of years of research by the Law Revision Commission. [Citation.]" (*Walton v. City of Red Bluff* (1991) 2 Cal.App.4th 117, 130, fn. 13.)

The California Law Revision Commission surveyed the different statutory schemes enacted in other states requiring recordation of future interests and recommended: "The power of termination should expire after a period of 30 years unless within that time the holder of the power extends the period by recording a notice of intent to preserve the power; an extension should be good for 30 years at a time. There should be a five-year grace period for holders of powers of termination to record a notice of intent to preserve powers that would be immediately or within a short period affected by enactment of the statute. [¶] This scheme will ensure that only those powers of termination will burden property for an extended period that a person has an active interest in preserving. It will also keep record ownership of the power current and help in ascertaining current holders of the power. The scheme has the additional virtue of minimizing potential problems of constitutionality inherent in applying an absolute limitation on powers without the option of extension." (Recommendation Relating to Marketable Title of Real Property (Nov. 1981) 16 Cal. Law Revision Com. Rep. (1981) pp. 421–422, fns. omitted.) The statute would implement the policy that "the public has an interest in free marketability and use of property and in limiting the restricting influence of the 'dead hand' to no more than one generation in the future." (*Id.* at p. 421, fn. omitted.)

The Legislature enacted the recommendation. It expressly declared: "Interests in real property ... created at remote times, whether or not of record, often constitute unreasonable restraints on alienation and marketability of real property because the interests are no longer valid or have been abandoned or have otherwise become obsolete. [¶] Such interests ... produce litigation to clear and quiet titles, cause delays in real property title transactions, and hinder marketability of real property. [¶] Real property title transactions should be possible with economy and expediency. The status and security of recorded real property titles should be determinable to the extent practicable from an examination *of recent records only.*" § 880.020, subds (a)(2), (3), & (4), (italics added.)

To implement this policy, "the Legislature adopted a recordation requirement for certain types of interests, including powers of termination. (§ 885.010 et seq.) Failure to record interests within a given period of time results in expiration of the interest. These times for expiration 'are absolute and apply notwithstanding any disability or lack of knowledge of any person....' (§ 880.250, subd. (a).) [¶] An interest may be preserved by the timely recordation of a notice of intent to preserve the interest and these notices may be given consecutively: Perpetuity of interest is not prohibited. [Citations.] [¶] If the period to record the notice expires within five years after the operative date of the statute, the period is extended until five years after the operative date. (§ 880.370.) A power of termination expires at the later of: (1) 30 years after recordation of the instrument evidencing the power; (2) 30 years after recordation of the last notice of intent to preserve the power. (§ 885.030.)" (*Walton v. City of Red Bluff, supra,* 2 Cal.App.4th 117, 128, fn. omitted.)

The original deed from the Bluemles to California Pacific Railway conveying the fee simple subject to a condition subsequent and creating the power of termination was recorded in 1901. Because the 30 year period to record the intent to preserve the power of termination would have expired long before the statute's enactment, any successor in interest to the Bluemles was entitled to the five-year grace period provided by section 880.370. Because the Act became effective on January 1, 1983, that individual or entity had until January 1, 1988, to record a notice of intent to preserve the future interest (power of termination). It is undisputed that neither plaintiff nor his predecessor(s) in interest recorded a notice of intent. This means the power to terminate has expired so that plaintiff's action is barred. To defeat that result, plaintiff contends: "If the Marketable Record Title Act applies in this case, plaintiff's power of termination expired in 1988, well before the commencement of this action [in 1999]. However, the Act cannot constitutionally be given retroactive application in this case. [¶] Under both state and federal constitutions, the legislature may not enact laws impairing the obligation of contracts or which take property without due process of law. [¶] ... [¶][T]he reverter in this case had not matured as of January 1, 1988, the outside date for recording a notice of intent, nor could anyone have known prior to the cut-off date who would be the parties in interest at the time when the reverter took effect because that event did not occur until November 1994 [when Union Pacific abandoned the right-of-way]." These constitutional arguments have not yet been addressed by a published opinion from a California appellate court. We conclude the arguments lack merit.

Article I, section 10 of the federal Constitution provides in part: "No state shall pass any ... law impairing the obligation of contracts." Article I, section 9 of our state Constitution contains a similar provision: "A ... law impairing the obligation of contracts may not be passed."

The contract clause is triggered in this case because of the dual nature of the 1901 deed. On the one hand, it is a conveyance of a real property interest: a fee simple subject to a condition subsequent. On the other hand, it is a contract: a conveyance supported by consideration which gives the grantors the power of termination upon occurrence of the condition subsequent (failure to use the land for a railroad right-of-way). In essence, plaintiff contends his contractual right to exercise his future interest has been unconstitutionally impaired because the Marketable Record Title Act requires a holder of a future interest to record within a designated time period an intent to preserve it and the failure to timely record results in an expiration of the interest. Plaintiff's contention lacks merit.

For one thing, plaintiff fails to make the distinction between an obligation and a right. The Marketable Record Title Act does not change any obligations in the contract (e.g., convey the land and pay the consideration). Instead, it merely affects the manner in which a party can exercise the right or remedy granted in the form of the future interest. In that regard, Witkin explains: "Parties to a contract have no vested right in the particular remedies or methods of procedure existing at the time of their agreement. The Legislature cannot take away all remedies, nor so substantially restrict the remedies as practically to destroy the right; but an ordinary change in procedure which alters the remedy for breach of a contract is valid though retroactively applied to existing contracts. [Citations.]" (8 Witkin, Summary of Cal. Law (9th ed. 1988) Constitutional Law, § 1081, p. 652.)

At bench, the new law does not abolish or take away the right to exercise a future interest. Instead, it merely adds a procedural requirement to the exercise of that right: timely recordation. The imposition of the requirement will not run afoul of the constitutional provision if it addresses a legitimate state interest and is reasonable and appropriate. (*Home Bldg. & L. Assn. v. Blaisdell* (1934) 290 U.S. 398, 439.) Or stated another way, "a statute limiting the time for assertion even of preexisting property or contract rights is not unconstitutional provided it allows a reasonable time after its enactment for the assertion of those rights. [Citations.]" (*Selectmen of Town of Nahant v. United States* (D.Mass. 1968) 293 F.Supp. 1076, 1078.)

The Law Revision Commission explained the public policy behind requiring a holder of a future interest such as a power of termination to record an intent to preserve it or face its expiration. It wrote that these future interests "seriously impair marketability of property [and] restrain alienability and sometimes the economic use of property as well[.]

Sec. 3   SERVITUDES AND RESTRICTIVE COVENANTS   121

[¶] These problems are aggravated by the fact that there is no limitation on the duration of [a power of termination] as there is on other future interests in property. Because reversionary interests are considered to be 'vested,' the Rule Against Perpetuities does not apply. This feature, combined with the fact that [the power of termination] appear[s] to be devisable and descendable, can result in dispersion of [the power] among unknown or unavailable owners. A person seeking to assemble a marketable title to the property may find that the interests have considerable nuisance value or that it is impossible to obtain quitclaim deeds from all owners of the interests. [¶] ... Legal scholars generally concur that in order to relieve the marketability problems created by [a power of termination], legislation limiting their duration is necessary." (Recommendation Relating to Marketable Title of Real Property (Nov.1981) 16 Cal. Law Revision Com. Rep. (1981) pp. 419–420, fns. omitted.) These are certainly legitimate state interests and plaintiff does not contend to the contrary.

In this case, the statutory scheme gives a holder of a future interest five years from its effective date to record an intent to preserve the power. The burden is minimal: simply record. The time period accorded to complete this minimal task is substantial: five years. Given the state interests furthered by this Act, the recordation requirement is reasonable. This conclusion is consistent with that reached by most other state courts which have considered the constitutionality of very similar statutes.

* * *

Fifty years ago a prominent scholar in this area accurately capsulized the pertinent analysis. He wrote: "[T]hese statutes do not destroy those interests and claims directly; it is the failure on the part of their owners to take the simple and inexpensive step of preserving them by recording a notice of their existence that effects the destruction." (Aigler, *Constitutionality of Marketable Title Acts* (1951) 50 Mich. L.Rev. 185, 199.)

* * *

The judgment is reversed. The parties to bear their own costs on appeal.

Notes

1. Railroad right-of-way cases have become more frequent since the advent of the Rails-to-Trails movement, a federal program to allow conversion of abandoned railroad right of way into hiking or nature trails. The program is administered by the Interstate Commerce Commission and is based on the notion that the railroad right of way should be preserved for future transportation needs of the nation, but in the interim, public use of the right of way should be permitted. Landowners adjacent to railroad right of way frequently object to nature trails and claim a right of reverter. The program has been upheld in the courts. See Glosemeyer v. Missouri–Kansas–Texas R.R., 879 F.2d 316 (8th Cir.1989), cert. denied , 494 U.S. 1003, 110

S.Ct. 1295, 108 L.Ed.2d 473 (1990); Barney v. Burlington Northern Railroad Co., Inc. 490 N.W.2d 726 (S.D.1992); Preseault v. I.C.C., 494 U.S. 1, 110 S.Ct. 914, 108 L.Ed.2d 1 (1990) (the long history of this case in the federal claims court and the Court of Appeals for the Federal Circuit is traced in Preseault v. United States, 100 F.3d 1525 (Fed.Cir.1996)). Also see, Comment, Rails to Trails: Converting America's Abandoned Railroads Into Nature Trails, 22 Akron L.Rev. 645 (1989). The Ninth Circuit Court of Appeals in a case decided just one month prior to the principal case, also wrestled with the easement versus defeasible estate problem. In King County v. Rasmussen, 299 F.3d 1077 (9th Cir. 2002) the original property owner executed a deed to the railroad:

> In consideration of the benefits and advantages to accrue to us from the location construction and operation of the Seattle Lake Shore and Eastern Railway in the County of King in Washington Territory, we do hereby donate grant and convey unto said Seattle Lake Shore and Eastern Railway Company a right of way one hundred (100) feet in width through our lands in said County described as follows to wit:
>
> Lots one (1) two (2) and three (3) in section six (6) township 24 North of Range six (6) East.
>
> Such right of way strip to be fifty (50) feet in width on each side of the center line of the railway track as located across our said lands by the Engineer of said railway company which location is described as follows to wit [legal description inmetes and bounds].
>
> And the said Seattle Lake Shore and Eastern Railway Company shall have the right to go upon the land adjacent to said line for a distance of two hundred (200) feet on each side thereof and cut down all trees dangerous to the operation of said road.
>
> To have and to hold the said premises with the appurtenances unto the said party of the second part and to its successors and assigns forever.

The court said:

> The Railway, and its successor Burlington Northern, built a track on the strip of land and used the track regularly for rail service until approximately 1996. In 1997, Burlington Northern sold its railway corridor, including the Hilchkanum strip, to The Land Conservancy of Seattle and King County ("TLC").
>
> On June 11, 1997, TLC petitioned the United States Surface Transportation Board ("STB") to abandon use of the corridor for rail service under the National Trail System Act, 16 U.S.C. § 1247(d) ("Rails to Trails Act"). The STB approved interim trail use of the corridor—called railbanking—by King County and issued a Notice of Interim Trail Use. The County then purchased the corridor from the TLC and obtained title to the right of way carved from the Hilchkanum property
>
> The Rasmussens oppose King County's efforts to railbank the right of way and claim that King County has no right to use the right of way as a trail because the Railway and its successors held only an easement for railroad purposes. As a result, King County brought this action in

state court to quiet title and to obtain a declaration of its rights in the strip. The Rasmussens removed the action to federal court * * *

King County claims that under Washington state law the Hilchkanum deed conveyed a fee simple estate in the strip of land to the Railway. The Rasmussens argue that, even if Hilchkanum had the power to convey a fee simple estate to the Railway, he intended to convey only an easement. The district court agreed with King County, as do we.

Applying state law to the deed, the court held that: "In conclusion, '[t]he language of the deed, the behavior of the parties, and the circumstances converge to show the Hilchkanums' intent to convey a fee simple.' *Rasmussen,* 143 F.Supp.2d at 1230–31. The underlying facts are undisputed, and, viewing these facts in the light most favorable to the Rasmussens, as we must on summary judgment, we conclude that King County, as the Railway's successor, possesses a fee simple in the strip of land. We, therefore, affirm the district court's summary judgment in favor of King County."

2. The new Restatement of Property Third (Servitudes) § 2.2, Comment g., discusses the problem of right of way instruments and the fee versus easement issue, and points out several of the factors that are used to interpret ambiguous instruments.

3. As we will see, injunctions for the enforcement of restrictive covenants may be refused because of a change in neighborhood conditions. Does the same doctrine apply to rights of entry based on conditions subsequent? See Clark, Real Covenants and Other Interests which "Run with Land" 198 (2d ed. 1947).

B. RESTRICTIVE COVENANTS

(1) Real Covenants

When is a covenant personal in nature, so that it only involves the persons who entered into the covenant, and when is it a covenant that serves to bind successive owners of the land involved? That is the problem that centers about the question of real covenants that "run with the land." A real covenant runs with the land in the sense that it is affixed to the title and is enforceable against the holder of the title even if he or she is a remote grantee and not the original covenantor. In that sense it takes on the qualities of an appurtenant easement.

For a covenant to run with the land and thus continue to impress its requirement against successive titleholders, it must be intended by the original covenantor and covenantee that it not be merely a personal promise and that it continue to be effective as a burden on the title long after the original parties are gone. But intent alone is not enough. It must also be shown that the covenant was intended to "touch and concern" the land—that is, relate to it and affect it as opposed to relating only to the parties agreeing to it. Further, there must be privity of estate between the party seeking to enforce it and the party who is to be bound by it. A real covenant thus becomes an incident to the ownership of the particular land involved, adheres to the title, and derives its vitality from the land itself. That is the result of these ancient requirements of real covenants.

When the first Restatement of Property was drafted, conflicting views over the requirements and nature of real covenants surfaced through the opinions of such scholars as Judge Charles Clark, former dean at Yale, and Dean and Professor Oliver S. Rundell of Wisconsin. These contrasting views are manifested in Clark, Covenants and Interests Running with Land (2d ed. 1947), and Rundell, Judge Clark on the American Law Institute's Law of Real Covenants: A Comment, 53 Yale L.J. 312 (1944). How strictly these ancient requirements should be applied in the modern context formed much of the basis for disagreement, and the case which follows is a leading case that grapples with this problem.

NEPONSIT PROPERTY OWNERS' ASS'N v. EMIGRANT INDUSTRIAL SAV. BANK

Court of Appeals of New York, 1938.
278 N.Y. 248, 15 N.E.2d 793, 118 A.L.R. 973.

LEHMAN, J.

* * *

It appears that in January, 1911, Neponsit Realty Company, as owner of a tract of land in Queens county, caused to be filed in the office of the clerk of the county a map of the land. The tract was developed for a strictly residential community, and Neponsit Realty Company conveyed lots in the tract to purchasers, describing such lots by reference to the filed map and to roads and streets shown thereon. In 1917, Neponsit Realty Company conveyed the land now owned by the defendant to Robert Oldner Deyer and his wife by deed which contained the covenant upon which the plaintiff's cause of action is based.

That covenant provides:

"And the party of the second part for the party of the second part and the heirs, successors and assigns of the party of the second part further covenants that the property conveyed by this deed shall be subject to an annual charge in such an amount as will be fixed by the party of the first part, its successors and assigns, not, however exceeding in any year the sum of four ($4.00) Dollars per lot 20 X 100 feet. The assigns of the party of the first part may include a Property Owners' Association which may hereafter be organized for the purposes referred to in this paragraph, and in case such association is organized the sums in this paragraph provided for shall be payable to such association. The party of the second part for the party of the second part and the heirs, successors and assigns of the party of the second part covenants that they will pay this charge to the party of the first part, its successors and assigns on the first day of May in each and every year, and further covenants that said charge shall on said date in each year become a lien on the land and shall continue to be such lien until fully paid. Such charge shall be payable to the party of the first part or its successors or assigns, and shall be devoted to the maintenance of the roads, paths, parks, beach, sewers and such other public purposes as shall from time to time be determined by the party of the first part, its successors or assigns. And the party of the second part by the acceptance of this deed hereby expressly vests in the party of the first part, its successors and assigns, the right and power to bring all actions against the owner of the premises hereby conveyed or any part thereof for the collection of such charge and to enforce the aforesaid lien therefor.

These covenants shall run with the land and shall be construed as real covenants running with the land until January 31st, 1940, when they shall cease and determine."

Every subsequent deed of conveyance of the property in the defendant's chain of title, including the deed from the referee to the defendant, contained, as we have said, a provision that they were made subject to covenants and restrictions of former deeds of record.

There can be no doubt that Neponsit Realty Company intended that the covenant should run with the land and should be enforceable by a property owners association against every owner of property in the residential tract which the realty company was then developing. The language of the covenant admits of no other construction. Regardless of the intention of the parties, a covenant will run with the land and will be enforceable against a subsequent purchaser of the land at the suit of one who claims the benefit of the covenant, only if the covenant complies with certain legal requirements. These requirements rest upon ancient rules and precedents. The age-old essentials of a real covenant, aside from the form of the covenant, may be summarily formulated as follows: (1) it must appear that grantor and grantee intended that the covenant should run with the land; (2) it must appear that the covenant is one "touching" or "concerning" the land with which it runs; (3) it must appear that there is "privity of estate" between the promisee or party claiming the benefit of the covenant and the right to enforce it, and the promisor or party who rests under the burden of the covenant. Clark on Covenants and Interests Running with Land, p. 74. Although the deeds "contained a provision to the effect that the covenants ran with the land, such provision in the absence of the other legal requirements is insufficient to accomplish such a purpose." *Morgan Lake Co. v. New York, N.H. & H.R.R. Co.*, 262 N.Y. 234, 238, 186 N.E. 685, 686. In his opinion in that case, Judge Crane posed but found it unnecessary to decide many of the questions which the court must consider in this case.

The covenant in this case is * * * an affirmative covenant to pay money for use in connection with, but not upon, the land which it is said is subject to the burden of the covenant. Does such a covenant "touch" or "concern" the land? These terms are not part of a statutory definition, a limitation placed by the State upon the power of the courts to enforce covenants *intended* to run with the land by the parties who entered into the covenants. Rather they are words used by courts in England in old cases to describe a limitation which the courts themselves created or to formulate a test which the courts have devised and which the courts voluntarily apply. Cf. Spencer's Case, Coke, vol. 3, part 5, 16a; *Mayor of Congleton v. Pattison*, 10 East 130. In truth such a description or test so formulated is too vague to be of much assistance and judges and academic scholars alike have struggled, not with entire success, to formulate a test at once more satisfactory and more accurate. * * *

* * * It has been often said that a covenant to pay a sum of money is a personal affirmative covenant which usually does not concern or touch the land. Such statements are based upon English decisions which hold in effect that only covenants, which compel the covenanter to submit to some *restriction on the use* of his property, touch or concern the land, and that the burden of a covenant which requires the covenanter to do an affirmative act, even on his own land, for the benefit of the owner of a "dominant" estate, does not run with his land. *Miller v. Clary*, 210 N.Y. 127, 103 N.E. 1114, L.R.A.1918E, 222, Ann.Cas.1915B, 872. In that case the court pointed out that in many jurisdictions of this country the narrow English rule has been criticized and a more liberal and flexible rule has been substituted. In this State the courts have not gone so far. We have not abandoned the historic distinction drawn by the English courts. * * * *Guaranty Trust Co. of New York v. New York & Queens County Ry. Co.*, 253 N.Y. 190, 204, 170 N.E. 887, 892, opinion by Cardozo, Ch. J.

Both in that case and in the case of Miller v. Clary, *supra*, the court pointed out that there were some exceptions or limitations in the application of the general rule. Some promises to pay money have been enforced, as covenants running with the land, against subsequent holders of the land who took with notice of the covenant. Cf. *Greenfarb v. R.S.K. Realty Corp.*, 256 N.Y. 130, 175 N.E. 649; *Morgan Lake Co. v. New York, N.H. & H.R.R. Co.*, *supra*. It may be difficult to classify these exceptions or to formulate a test of whether a particular covenant to pay money or to perform some other act falls within the general rule that ordinarily an affirmative covenant is a personal and not a real covenant, or falls outside the limitations placed upon the general rule. At least it must "touch" or "concern" the land in a substantial degree, and though it may be inexpedient and perhaps impossible to formulate a rigid test or definition which will be entirely satisfactory or which can be applied mechanically in all cases, we should at least be able to state the problem and find a reasonable method of approach to it. It has been suggested that a covenant which runs with the land must affect the legal relations—the advantages and the burdens—of the parties to the covenant, as owners of particular parcels of land and not merely as members of the community in general, such as taxpayers or owners of other land. Clark, op. cit. p. 76, Cf. Professor Bigelow's article on The Contents of Covenants in Leases, 12 Mich.L.Rev. 639; 30 Law Quarterly Review, 319. That method of approach has the merit of realism. The test is based on the effect of the covenant rather than on technical distinctions. Does the covenant impose, on the one hand, a burden upon an interest in land, which on the other hand increases the value of a different interest in the same or related land?

Even though we accept that approach and test, it still remains true that whether a particular covenant is sufficiently connected with the use of land to run with the land, must be in many cases a question of degree. A promise to pay for something to be done in connection with the promisor's land does not differ essentially from a promise by the promisor to do the thing himself, and both promises constitute, in a substantial sense, a restriction upon the owner's right to use the land, and a burden upon the legal interest of the owner. On the other hand, a covenant to perform or pay for the performance of an affirmative act disconnected with the use of the land cannot ordinarily touch or concern the land in any substantial degree. Thus, unless we exalt technical form over substance, the distinction between covenants which run with land and covenants which are personal, must depend upon the effect of the covenant on the legal rights which otherwise would flow from ownership of land and which are connected with the land. The problem then is: Does the covenant in purpose and effect substantially alter these rights?

* * *

Looking at the problem presented in this case from the same point of view and stressing the intent and substantial effect of the covenant rather than its form, it seems clear that the covenant may properly be said to touch and concern the land of the defendant and its burden should run with the land. True, it calls for payment of a sum of money to be expended for "public purposes" upon land other than the land conveyed by Neponsit Realty Company to plaintiff's predecessor in title. By that conveyance the grantee, however, obtained not only title to particular lots, but an easement or right of common enjoyment with other property owners in roads, beaches, public parks or spaces and improvements in the same tract. For full enjoyment in common by the defendant and other property owners of these easements or rights, the roads and public places must be maintained. In order that the burden of maintaining public improvements should rest upon the land benefitted by the improvements, the grantor exacted from the grantee of the land with its appurtenant easement or right of enjoyment a covenant that the burden of paying the cost should be inseparably attached to the land which enjoys the benefit. It is plain that any distinction or definition which would exclude such a covenant from the classification of covenants which "touch" or "concern" the land would be based on form and not on substance.

Another difficulty remains. Though between the grantor and the grantee there was privity of estate, the covenant provides that its benefit shall run to the assigns of the grantor who "may include a Property Owners' Association which may hereafter be organized for the purposes referred to in this paragraph." The plaintiff has been organized to receive the sums payable by the property owners and to expend them for the benefit of such owners. Various definitions have been formulated of "privity of estate" in connection with covenants that run with the land, but none of such definitions seems to cover the relationship between the plaintiff and the defendant in this case. The plaintiff has not succeeded to the ownership of any property of the grantor. It does not appear that it ever had title to the streets or public places upon which charges which are payable to it must be expended. It does not appear that it owns any other property in the residential tract to which any easement or right of enjoyment in such property is appurtenant. It is created solely to act as the assignee of the benefit of the covenant, and it has no interest of its own in the enforcement of the covenant.

* * *

The corporate plaintiff has been formed as a convenient instrument by which the property owners may advance their common interests. We do not ignore the corporate form when we recognize that the Neponsit Property Owners Association, Inc., is acting as the agent or representative of the Neponsit property owners. * * * Only blind adherence to an ancient formula devised to meet entirely different conditions could constrain the court to hold that a corporation formed as a medium for the enjoyment of common rights of property owners owns no property which would benefit by enforcement of common rights and has no cause of action in equity to enforce the covenant upon which such common rights depend. Every reason which in other circumstances may justify the ancient formula should not be applied in this case. In substance if not in form the covenant is a restrictive covenant which touches and concerns the defendant's land, and in substance, if not in form, there is privity of estate between the plaintiff and the defendant.

* * *

The order should be affirmed, with costs, and the certified questions answered in the affirmative. * * *

Notes

1. In Woodland Beach Property Owners' Ass'n v. Worley, 253 Md. 442, 252 A.2d 827 (1969), the association (Woodland) sought to enforce the annual charge against a lot owner who had failed to pay it. Pursuant to its charter and by-laws, Woodland had improved certain beaches and parks for the use and enjoyment of the property owners and had imposed a small fee to be paid each year by each lot owner. The Maryland Court of Appeals stated:

> The facts as alleged and as appear in the exhibits indicate that Woodland was obligated to maintain the areas in question, and no obligation was placed upon the lot owners to contribute any part of the expense of such maintenance. In some developments, the title instruments impose a specific charge on the individual lots as covenants running with the land to provide for such maintenance. See Wehr v. Roland Park Co., 143 Md. 384, 387–388, 122 A. 363, 364–365 (1923), but

the title instruments in the instant case do not purport to impose such a charge. On the contrary, the obligation to maintain is placed upon Woodland, without any provision giving Woodland the right to collect any sum, equitable or otherwise, from the lot owners. It is clear to us that under these circumstances we should not imply the *existence* of such a covenant and charge on the land.

In line with the Woodland Beach case is Cummings v. Dosam, Inc., 273 N.C. 28, 159 S.E.2d 513 (1968), which invalidated for vagueness restrictions referring to "this Tract and adjoining Tracts being acquired by grantee." The Woodland Beach case required that restrictive covenants be strictly construed, but in Friedberg v. Riverpoint Bldg. Committee, 218 Va. 659, 239 S.E.2d 106 (1977), the court followed the same rule but stated that if it was apparent from the entire instrument that the restrictions must carry a particular meaning by necessary implication, then a use which was denied implicitly must be deemed to be as clearly forbidden as if it had been expressly denied. See similarly, Long v. Branham, 271 N.C. 264, 156 S.E.2d 235 (1967); but compare Lochwood Meadows, Inc. v. Buck, 416 S.W.2d 623 (Tex.Civ.App.1967) (a restriction against a fence or wall would not prohibit a hedge); and Sine v. Western Travel, Inc., 19 Utah 2d 61, 426 P.2d 9 (1967) (restriction against a motel did not prevent construction of a restaurant having no physical connection with a motel on adjacent, unrestricted land). Also see Big Sky Hidden Village Owners Association, Inc. v. Hidden Village, Inc., 276 Mont. 268, 915 P.2d 845 (1996) where the court held that adjoining tracts to the condominium development that were included in the developer's planned unit development plan, were not subject to the restrictions in the original condominium declaration.

The Restatement of Property Third (Servitudes), § 1.3 addresses the problem of the real covenant by declaring that (1) A covenant is a servitude if either the benefit or the burden runs with the land. A covenant that is a servitude "runs with the land." In Comment a., the Restatement explains that not all covenants are servitudes, and a covenant becomes a servitude that runs with the land "if it is intended to do so, if it has been effectively created under the rules stated in Chapter 2, if it is not invalid under the rules set forth in Chapter 3, and if it has not terminated under the rules set forth in Chapter 7." The new Restatement also abandons the difference between affirmative covenants and so-called negative easements (the burdened estate must refrain from doing certain things). § 1.4.

In recent years courts have started relaxing their negative attitudes toward implying affirmative covenants. For example, in Evergreen Highlands Ass'n v. West, 73 P.3d 1 (Colo.2003) the Supreme Court of Colorado, in a case of first impression, said: "We also granted certiorari on the related question of whether, in the absence of a covenant imposing mandatory dues, the homeowners association has the implied power to collect assessments from all lot owners to pay for the maintenance of common areas of the subdivision.... [W]e now hold that the declarations for Evergreen Highlands were sufficient to create a common interest community by implication with the concomitant power to impose mandatory dues on lot owners to pay for the maintenance of common areas of the subdivision."

2. Compare also with Neponsit, Phillips v. Smith, 240 Iowa 863, 38 N.W.2d 87 (1949), where a covenant in deeds to summer resort lots to pay $6.00 a year to the owner of Bluff Park Resort was said to run with the land. But the covenant was held to be "dependent" upon the carrying out of the duty to maintain the resort area. The owner of Bluff Park Resort allowed his horses and pigs to roam at will through the development and did little to maintain it. The action to establish and foreclose liens for the annual assessment failed. See also Nassau County v. Kensington Ass'n, 21 N.Y.S.2d 208 (Sup.Ct.1940). And compare Harrison–Rye Realty Corp. v. Crigler, 61 N.Y.S.2d 191 (1945), affirmed 272 App.Div. 939, 72 N.Y.S.2d 417 (1947), appeal granted 272 App.Div. 976, 73 N.Y.S.2d 636 (1947), affirmed 298 N.Y. 602, 81 N.E.2d 331 (1948) with Harrison-Rye Realty Corp. v. New Rochelle Trust Co., 177 Misc. 776, 31 N.Y.S.2d 1005 (Sup.Ct.1941) reaching opposite results on the same monetary assessment covenant. And see Annot., 23 A.L.R.2d 520 (1952). In Tentindo v. Locke Lake Colony Ass'n, 120 N.H. 593, 419 A.2d 1097 (1980) the court held assessments could not be imposed on lot owners whose membership in the owner's association was involuntary; the association was created by the developer to take over management of common areas, and the deeds of the plaintiff lot owners provided only that an annual $15 premium was to be paid to the developer for benefits provided. Also see Holiday Pines Prop. Owners Ass'n, Inc. v. Wetherington, 596 So.2d 84 (Fla.App.1992).

3. Sometimes the dispute over liability for monetary assessments is between a lot owner and the developer of a sizeable community. Can the development company write the covenants so as to result in lower annual assessments for the lots it retains while purchasers must pay a higher assessment? On this question, see Kell v. Bella Vista Village Property Owners Ass'n, 258 Ark. 757, 528 S.W.2d 651 (1975). One technique that large-scale developers often use is to have two (or more) classes of lot owners with different fees for each class. In large scale retirement communities the problem of inflationary costs of maintenance is especially critical because there may be large numbers of non-resident lot owners scattered around the country who are years away from building their retirement dream homes and who will vote against any increase in maintenance assessments; this group usually outnumbers the current residents who have an interest in raising the assessments to keep the community pleasant and well-maintained.

4. A different sort of real covenant is presented in the next case. How far do you think the type of covenant involved can be used in modern land use regulations?

1515—1519 LAKEVIEW BOULEVARD CONDOMINIUM ASSOCIATION v. APARTMENT SALES CORPORATION

Supreme Court of Washington, En Banc, 2002.
146 Wash.2d 194, 43 P.3d 1233.

CHAMBERS, J.

The 1515—1519 Lakeview Boulevard Condominium Association (homeowners) are the owners of three condominiums that were rendered

Sec. 3   **SERVITUDES AND RESTRICTIVE COVENANTS**   **131**

uninhabitable when the soil underlying the property gave way precipitously during winter storms. The homeowners brought suit against several parties, including the City of Seattle (city). The homeowners argued the city should not have permitted the condominiums to be built due to the latent risk of soil movement, and that the city's storm drains had contributed to the slide. Before allowing the condominiums to be constructed, the city, concerned about the possibility of landslides, had imposed several conditions on the developer. These conditions included a covenant exculpating the city from liability for damages caused by soil movement. In this case, we are asked to determine whether an exculpatory covenant recorded in a deed runs with the land, and whether an action may be maintained against the city for alleged negligence in maintaining storm drains and granting permits. The trial court dismissed all claims against the city at summary judgment. The Court of Appeals agreed that the claims arising from permitting should be dismissed, but reinstated the claims arising from negligently maintained storm drains. We affirm the Court of Appeals dismissal of the negligent permitting claims (though on different grounds), affirm reinstatement of the claims relating to the storm drains, and remand for proceedings consistent with this opinion.

* * *

Apartment Sales Corporation sought and received a permit from the city to build three townhouse condominiums on this site, 1515—1519 Lakeview Boulevard. The site consisted of a small, flat area and a steep slope running down to a section of freeway. Because the sites were in a potential slide area, the developers were required to obtain several zoning variances.

In addition to the variances, the city imposed three specific conditions before it would grant building permits. First, the developers were required to inform all purchasers of the risk of soil movement. Second, continuous insurance was required. Third, the developers were required to grant and record a covenant releasing the city from liability for damages caused by soil movement, except for damages caused by the city's sole negligence. The covenant reads in relevant part:

> * * * 2. Owner(s) on his/her own behalf and on behalf of his/her heirs, successors and assigns hereby waives any right to assert any claim against the City for any loss, or damage to people or property either on or off the site resulting from soil movement by reason of or arising out of the issuance of the permit(s) by the City for development on this property except only for such losses that may directly result from the sole negligence of the City.

* * *

The homeowners received numerous assurances from the developers that the site was stable and the homes would not slip. The homeowners' complaint alleges they were assured the units would be safe, even if the soil slid away. Lakeview was flooded at least four times between November 1992 and November 1996. In each flood, at least a foot of water inundated the garages and basements of the units. Perhaps not coincidentally, the public storm drain system overflowed each time the condominiums flooded. The homeowners provided the declaration of an engineering geologist, Mackey Smith, which stated that failures of the city-maintained public drain system permitted thousands of gallons of water to inundate the condominiums. Smith also stated that these drain overflows were a contributing cause of the soil movement. There was other evidence of infrastructure failure: in November 1996 a city inspector discovered "the pipe leading from the manhole/catch basin of the former Lakeside Boulevard alignment had separated and was blocked.... This break was repaired."

In late December 1996, two severe storms dumped heavy snow onto soils already at or near saturation. Rain followed, saturating the snow because it could not penetrate frozen soil beneath. Then a warm rain quickly melted the saturated snow. Between December 30, 1996 and January 1, 1997 "temperatures rose rapidly and all of the snow was melted by intense warm air. The combination of saturated soil, freezing temperatures, and snow, followed by rapid thaw and warm rain, triggered widespread flooding and landslides throughout the Puget Sound region."

All three townhouses had been occupied about four years when the sites experienced significant soil movement. At approximately 6:00 a.m. on January 3, 1997, early rising homeowners in the Lakeview complex realized they had no running water. This was because the property had moved, breaking the connection with the water main. Water was " 'bubbling out of the ground.' " Within a day, the property had sunk between four and six feet and had moved west two feet. The homes were rendered uninhabitable.

* * *

The city contends innovative land use instruments, such as exculpatory covenants, should be encouraged because the Growth Management Act, chapter 36.70A RCW, is channeling development onto more and more marginal lots. The city is also concerned that if it denies building permits, it runs the risk of committing regulatory takings or inverse condemnation, as well as potentially frustrating the laudable goals of the Growth Management Act. The city argues that requiring the release and requiring the developers to have insurance and inform subsequent purchasers of the danger is a fair way to allow development. This argument suggests that property owners of land marginal for development because of the composition, topography, location, or other characteristic of the property should be free to propose creative solutions, and accept the risks of development.

We hold that a local government and a property owner may reach an arms length, bargained-for agreement which may include waivers of liability for risks created by the proposed use of property because of the shape, composition, location or other characteristic unique to the property sought to be developed. Here we find that the exculpatory language of the covenant was tailored to the specific risks presented by the proposed development of the property and appropriately limited in scope to the danger of soil movement.

* * *

The homeowners argue that this covenant may not be enforced against them on the theory exculpatory waivers do not "run with the land" and therefore cannot bind successors in interest. Accordingly, we turn now to the requirements for a covenant to run.

Covenants are deeply rooted in our law, dating at least to the 14th century. *Restatement (Third) of Prop: Servitudes: Introduction* at 5 (2000). The seminal *Spencer's Case,* 77 Eng. Rep. 72 (Q.B.1583) established the general requirements. *Spencer's Case* involved a covenant by a tenant to build a wall. The tenant covenanted on behalf of himself and his executors, administrators, and assigns to build a brick wall on a leased lot. After executing the covenant, the tenant assigned the property to another. The new tenant refused to build the wall. "Although there is some doubt from the report as to who won, the case is famous because the judges laid down three propositions about the running of the burden of covenants." Jesse Dukeminier & James E. Krier, *Property* 856 (3d ed.1993). There must be intent to bind successors, the obligation must touch and concern the land, and there must be privity of estate. *Id.* Otherwise, the "covenant" is merely a contract and will not bind future possessors of the land. William B. Stoebuck, *Running Covenants: An Analytical Primer,* 52 Wash. L.Rev. 861, 863–64 (1977). Through much of their history, the requirements for a covenant to run varied depending on whether it was "real" (developed and enforced in courts of law) or "equitable" (developed and enforced in the Chancery). However, the distinctions have largely vanished from our law. *See Hollis v. Garwall, Inc.,* 137 Wash.2d 683, 690, 974 P.2d 836 (1999).

Generally, there are five elements required for a covenant to run:

> (1) a promise which is enforceable between the original parties; (2) which touches and concerns; (3) which the parties intended to bind successors; and (4) which is sought to be enforced by an original party or a successor, against an original party or a successor in possession; (5) who has notice of the covenant or has not given value.

Stoebuck, *supra,* at 909–10.

Four of these elements are not seriously disputed by the parties before this Court. The issue before us is whether an exculpatory covenant touches and concerns the land.[1]

* * *

---

1. The recently published *Restatement (Third) of Property* has abolished "touch and concern" as an element of enforceable covenants. In its stead, the *Restatement* provides that a servitude is valid unless it is illegal, unconstitutional, or violates public

This Court has not adopted a strict test for "touch and concern," instead we have established an analytical approach:

> "Generally speaking, a covenant touches or concerns the land if it is such as to benefit the grantor or the lessor, or the grantee or lessee, as the case may be. As the term implies, the covenant must concern the occupation or enjoyment of the land granted or demised and the liability to perform it, and the right to take advantage of it must pass to the assignee. Conversely, if the covenant does not touch or concern the occupation or enjoyment of the land, it is the collateral and personal obligation of the grantor or lessor and does not run with the land."

Rodruck v. Sand Point Maint. Comm'n, 48 Wash.2d 565, 574–75, 295 P.2d 714 (1956), (quoting *City of Seattle v. Fender,* 42 Wash.2d 213, 254 P.2d 470 (1953) (quoting *Pelser v. Gingold,* 214 Minn. 281, 8 N.W.2d 36 (1943))).

It is an open question whether a covenant warning of risk and exculpating liability for that risk touches and concerns the land. The only court to reach whether such covenant would run held, without analysis of touch and concern, that it did run. *Phillips v. Altman,* 1966 OK 46, 412 P.2d 199 (holding that a covenant not to sue for damages arising from oil and gas pollution ran with the land and was not void as against public policy).

* * *

This Court has not relaxed the touch and concern requirement for the enforceability of covenants in settings other than subdivisions and we decline to do so now.

We conclude that this covenant satisfies the touch and concern doctrine as used in this State. Read as a whole, the covenant burdens the use of land, since the covenant is limited to the reasonable enjoyment of the land and limits rights normally associated with ownership. Further, few things touch and concern land more than the soil itself. This is sufficient to meet the requirements of *Rodruck*. The city is exculpated for losses that are not caused by the city's own negligence arising from soil movement, as reasonably contemplated by the parties to the covenant. Therefore, we hold that this covenant runs with the land.

* * *

In summary, we conclude the city is not liable for negligently granting a permit to build on this site. We also hold the exculpatory covenant is valid to the extent it releases the city from liability resulting from soil movement "resulting from . . . the issuance of the permit." The covenant does not, and may not, exculpate the city for soil movement-

---

policy. *Restatement (Third) of Prop: Servitudes* § 3.1 (2000). Whether this Court should adopt the *Restatement* was not raised until the motion for reconsideration to the Court of Appeals opinion, and will not be considered for the first time on review to this Court.

Sec. 3 SERVITUDES AND RESTRICTIVE COVENANTS 135

related losses caused by the city's own negligence. The homeowners may pursue claims against the city arising out of negligent maintenance of the storm and water drain system. Accordingly, we reverse in part, affirm in part, and remand for further proceedings consistent with this opinion.

(2) Equitable Servitudes

Despite some relaxation of the requirements of a real covenant in cases such as Neponsit, the basic requisites for enforcement of a covenant at law remain with us. Equity, of course, by its very nature is different, and the principles or maxims which it has developed often lead to a different result. We see this difference quite vividly in the enforcement of "servitudes" in equity in situations in which the law courts would not enforce a covenant because it did not run with the land, touch or concern the land, or lacked privity.

TULK v. MOXHAY
English High Court of Chancery, 1848.
2 Phillips 774, 41 Eng.Rep. 1143.

In the year 1808 the Plaintiff, being then the owner in fee of the vacant piece of ground in Leicester Square, as well as of several of the houses forming the Square, sold the piece of ground by the description of "Leicester Square Garden or Pleasure Ground, with the equestrian statute then standing in the centre thereof, and the iron railing and stone work round the same," to one Elms in fee: and the deed of conveyance contained a covenant by Elms, for himself, his heirs, and assigns, with the Plaintiff, his heirs, executors, and administrators, "that Elms, his heirs, and assigns should, and would from time to time, and at all times thereafter at his and their own costs and charges, keep and maintain the said piece of ground and Square Garden, and the iron railing round the same in its then form, and in sufficient and proper repair as a Square Garden and Pleasure Ground, in an open state, uncovered with any buildings, in neat and ornamental order; and that it should be lawful for the inhabitants of Leicester Square, tenants of the Plaintiff, on payment of a reasonable rent for the same, to have keys at their own expense and the privilege of admission therewith at any time or times into the said Square Garden and Pleasure Ground."

The piece of land so conveyed passed by divers mesne conveyances into the hands of the Defendant, whose purchase deed contained no similar covenant with his vendor: but he admitted that he had purchased with notice of the covenant in the deed of 1808.

The Defendant having manifested an intention to alter the character of the Square Garden, and asserted a right, if he thought fit, to build upon it, the Plaintiff, who still remained owner of several houses in the Square, filed this bill for an injunction; and an injunction was granted by the Master of the Rolls, to restrain the Defendant from converting or using the piece of ground and Square Garden, and the iron railing round the same, to or for any other purpose than as a Square Garden and Pleasure Ground in an open state, and uncovered with buildings.

On a motion, now made, to discharge that order,

Mr. R. Palmer, for the Defendant, contended that the covenant did not run with the land, so as to be binding at law upon a purchaser from the covenantor, and he relied on the dictum of Lord Brougham C. in *Keppell v. Bayley* (2 M. & K. 547), to the effect that notice of such a covenant did not give a Court of Equity jurisdiction to enforce it by injunction against such purchaser, inasmuch as "the knowledge by an assignee of an estate, that his assignor had assumed to bind others than the law authorized him to affect by his contract,—had attempted to create a burthen upon property which was inconsistent with the nature of that property, and unknown to the principles of the law—could not bind such assignee by affecting his conscience." * * *

The LORD CHANCELLOR (without calling upon the other side.)

That this Court has jurisdiction to enforce a contract between the owner of land and his neighbor purchasing a part of it, that the latter shall either use or abstain from using the land purchased in a particular way, is what I never knew disputed. Here there is no question about the contract: the owner of certain houses in the Square sells the land adjoining, with a covenant from the purchaser not to use it for any other purpose than as a Square Garden. And it is now contended, not that the vendee could violate that contract, but that he might sell the piece of land, and that the purchaser from him may violate it without this Court having any power to interfere. If that were so, it would be impossible for an owner of land to sell part of it without incurring the risk of rendering what he retains worthless. It is said that, the covenant being one which does not run with the land, this Court cannot enforce it; but the question is, not whether the covenant runs with the land, but whether a party shall be permitted to use the land in a manner inconsistent with the contract entered into by his vendor, and with notice of which he purchased. Of course, the price would be affected by the covenant, and nothing could be more inequitable than that the original purchaser should be able to sell the property the next day for a greater price, in consideration of the assignee being allowed to escape from the liability which he had himself undertaken.

That the question does not depend upon whether the covenant runs with the land, is evident from this, that if there was a mere agreement and no covenant, this Court would enforce it against a party purchasing with notice of it; for if an equity is attached to the property by the owner, no one purchasing with notice of that equity can stand in a different situation from the party from whom he purchased. There are not only cases before the Vice-Chancellor of England, in which he considered that doctrine as not in dispute; but looking at the ground on which Lord Eldon disposed of the case of the Duke of Bedford v. The Trustees of the British Museum (2 M. & K. 552), it is impossible to suppose that he entertained any doubt of it. * * *

With respect to the observations of Lord Brougham in *Keppell v. Bayley*, he never could have meant to lay down, that this Court would not enforce an equity attached to land by the owner, unless under such circumstances as would maintain an action at law. If that be the result of his observations, I can only say that I cannot coincide with it.

I think the cases cited before the Vice–Chancellor and this decision of the Master of the Rolls perfectly right, and, therefore, that this motion must be refused with costs.

Notes

1. Tulk v. Moxhay was the landmark case that provided the foundation on which equity erected a set of rules governing the enforcement of negative or restrictive covenants based on the concept of notice. See generally 5 R. Powell, Real Property ¶ 671 (1990).

2. The Restatement of Property, Third (Servitudes) abandons the distinction between real covenants and equitable servitudes. Section 1.4, Comment a., explains that the two branches split in the 19th century and American law became doctrinally confused, concluding: "Because continued use of the terms "real covenant" and "equitable servitude" perpetuates the idea that there is a difference between covenants at law and in equity, which at best tends to generate confusion, and at worst may lead lawyers and judges to focus on irrelevant questions or reach erroneous results, those terms have been dropped in this Restatement in favor of the term "covenant running with land."

KENT v. KOCH

Court of Appeals of California, 1958.
166 Cal.App.2d 579, 333 P.2d 411.

[Defendant was restrained by the trial court from constructing a green fiberglass fence on his premises contrary to a "Declaration of Restrictions, Conditions, Covenants and Agreements." The declaration had been recorded by the plaintiffs in 1936, at which time the plaintiff had begun a large housing development consisting of a number of subdivision units. As each subdivision unit was opened, a declaration of restrictions was recorded, and each declaration, subsequent to subdivision 1, purported to benefit not only the property within that subdivision unit but all of the property within the entire development tract, which was known as "Kent Woodlands." Plaintiffs controlled building applications at first, but then an architectural supervising committee, provided for in declarations other than the subdivision 1 declaration, was appointed by plaintiffs from property owners (none from subdivision 1 owners), and this committee controlled applications. Defendant's property is located in subdivision 1, and plaintiffs have sold all their lots in that subdivision. But plaintiffs had retained "Parcel A," which was an entrance to Kent Woodlands. Defendant, having been turned down in his application to build the green fiberglass fence by the architectural committee, proceeded to file suit. The trial court held that the defendant's lot was subject to the restrictions; that plaintiffs owned a parcel in subdivision 1 known as parcel A as well as other lots in the general tract, Kent Woodlands; and that sales had been in accordance with a general plan of restrictions designed to benefit all lots in the overall tract. After setting out the text of the declaration pertaining to subdivision 1, the appellate court reached the following decision, having earlier stated that the question which was "determinative of the appeal" was the plaintiffs' right to complain in light of the fact that they owned no lots in subdivision 1.]

BRAY, J.

A mere perusal of said agreement shows that it did not intend to make the restrictions for the benefit of any property other than that referred to in it, namely, the lots shown on the map of subdivision 1. It expressly says that it is for the direct benefit of "each and every lot shown on said recorded map." Time and again it refers to "said lots" meaning the lots shown on that map. There is not the slightest ambiguity in the document. It is impossible to read into such clear language any intent to make the restrictions applicable to any other property. Plaintiffs contend that the last line of paragraph 12 above quoted shows such intention. On the contrary it strongly indicates that the restrictions are for the benefit of subdivision 1 lots only. That sentence instead of stating that plaintiffs would subject the new units (the adjoining and contiguous property) to be opened by them to the same restrictions as required of subdivision 1, or would make any restrictions upon the new units applicable to subdivision 1 lots, merely states that plaintiffs will restrict the sale and use of such property "in such a way as, in their opinion shall not impair the value or desirability of the property shown on said map, for residential purposes." This language discloses that plaintiffs intended the new units to be completely independent of the first unit, except only that they would be restricted in such manner as in plaintiffs' opinion not to impair the desirability for residential purposes of the lots in subdivision 1.

It is well settled in this state that restrictive covenants made for the benefit of other property retained by the grantor can not be enforced by the grantor after he no longer owns any of the property benefited. In *Blodgett v. Trumbull,* 1927, 83 Cal.App. 566, 257 P. 199, the grantors deeded to the plaintiff a certain lot subject to certain conditions and restrictions in the deed. Although these were not made for the benefit of the adjoining lots which belonged to the grantors, the court held (83 Cal.App. at page 571, 257 P. at page 202): " * * * the grantors did reserve for themselves, their successors, or assigns the right to enjoin, abate, or remedy by appropriate proceedings any breach of any of the restrictions. The right so reserved would be enforceable, in the absence of fraud, while the defendant Trumbull [the surviving grantor] remained owner of the adjoining lots; but after she had parted with the property which would derive benefit from a continuance of the restrictions, she would have no standing, in a court of equity at least, to complain of a breach." In *Townsend v. Allen,* 114 Cal.App.2d 291, at page 297, 250

P.2d 292, at page 296, 39 A.L.R.2d 1108, the court stated: "However, it does not follow that the grantor retains said right of enforcement even though he has disposed of all land he had retained without making any such restriction. The contrary is shown by cases relating to building and occupation restrictions on subdivisions in which cases the right of enforcement of grantor is considered lost when he has lost all interest in the property to be benefited. In *Firth v. Marovich*, 160 Cal. 257, 260, 116 P. 729, 731 [Ann.Cas.1912D, 1190] it is said (obiter): 'It is not open to question that building restrictions of the kind contained in the deed * * * are valid and enforceable at the suit of the grantor *so long as he continues to own any part of the tract for the benefit of which the restrictions were exacted.*'" (Emphasis ours.)

In *Marra v. Aetna Construction Co.*, 1940, 15 Cal.2d 375, 378, 101 P.2d 490, 492 the court said: "The doctrine of equitable servitudes has been invoked chiefly in cases where uniform building restrictions have been imposed pursuant to a general plan for improving an entire tract or real estate subdivision * * *. It is true, however, that a servitude cannot exist in gross, but must be appurtenant to other benefited property."

* * *

It must be remembered in construing the declaration of restrictions that "any provisions of an instrument creating or claimed to create such a servitude will be strictly construed, any doubt being resolved in favor of the free use of the land." *Wing v. Forest Lawn Cemetery Ass'n*, 1940, 15 Cal.2d 472, 479, 101 P.2d 1099, 1103, 130 A.L.R. 120; *Werner v. Graham*, 181 Cal. 174, 181, 183 P. 945. Thus, plaintiffs having disposed of all the lots in subdivision 1, do not have any property to be benefited by the enforcement of the restrictions and have no standing in a court of equity. Actually, plaintiffs do own a small portion of subdivision 1. However, admittedly this "parcel," so-called on the map, is too small for residence purposes and was reserved for the special purpose of parking for the tract office which adjoins it, as an entrance to the tract, and as a location for the tract's signboard. It is obvious that this parcel would in nowise be benefited by the enforcement of the restrictions. *Blodgett v. Trumbull, supra*, 83 Cal.App. 566, 571, 257 P. 199, points out that after a grantor has parted with the property which would derive benefit from a continuance of the restrictions, such grantor has no standing in court to enforce the restrictions.

Restrictions in a deed cannot be enforced by one lot owner in a tract against another lot owner between whom there is neither privity of contract nor privity of estate. "The leading case on this subject, and the one that is determinative of this appeal, is Werner v. Graham, 181 Cal. 174, 183 P. 945. In that case, among other things, it was specifically held that such servitudes will be enforced only when part of a general plan expressed in the deed, and when the deed expressly provides such restrictions are for the benefit of the other lots in the tract. In other words, unless specifically stated to be for the benefit of other lot owners, such covenants or restrictions are enforceable only as between the original parties to the deed, or their heirs or assigns." *Fees v. Williams*, 212 Cal. 688, 690, 300 P. 30, 31; see also *Townsend v. Allen*, 114 Cal.App.2d 291, 297, 250 P.2d 292, 39 A.L.R.2d 1108.

Plaintiffs' contention that the provision in paragraph 12 to the effect that plaintiffs will restrict the use of property in the units other than subdivision 1 gives them, as owners of property in the other subdivisions, a right to enforce the restrictions on subdivision 1, is answered by *Werner v. Graham, supra*, 1919, 181 Cal. 174, 183 P. 945, which the court says in *Wing v. Forest Lawn Cemetery Ass'n, supra*, 15 Cal.2d 472, 480, 101 P.2d 1099, 130 A.L.R. 120, "has oft been cited as the leading case in this state defining the manner in which an equitable servitude may be established." There restrictive conditions were placed in a deed of one lot in a tract which the owner was subdividing according to a map on file. No express statement was included to the effect that they were for the benefit of the other lots in the tract. In selling these other lots the grantor placed similar restrictions in the deeds thereto. The court held that the failure to state in the deed that the restrictions were for the benefit of the other lots in the tract, although most probably the grantor intended them to be, made the restrictions unenforceable by owners of any other lots. It said (181 Cal. at pages 183–184, 183 P. at page 949): "It is undoubted that, when the owner of a subdivided tract conveys the various parcels in the tract by deeds containing appropriate language imposing restrictions on each parcel as part of a general plan of restrictions common to all the parcels and designed for their mutual benefit, mutual equitable servitudes are thereby created in favor of each parcel as against all the others. The agreement between the grantor and each grantee in such a case as expressed in the instruments between them is both that the parcel conveyed shall be subject to restrictions in accordance with the plan for the benefit of all the other parcels and also that all other parcels shall be subject to such restrictions for its benefit. In such a case the mutual servitudes spring into existence as between the first parcel conveyed and the balance of the parcels at the time of the first conveyance. As each conveyance follows, the burden and the benefit of the mutual restrictions imposed by preceding conveyances as between the particular parcel conveyed and those previously conveyed pass as an incident of the ownership of the parcel, and similar restrictions are created by the conveyance as between the lot conveyed and the lots still retained by the original owner." * * *

As plaintiffs have no interest in any property to be benefited by the restrictions, they may not maintain this action.

The judgment is reversed.

Notes

1. If you represented a real estate developer who wished to sell all of the lots in her subdivision but wished, in the interest of maintaining her business reputation as the developer of high quality subdivisions, to be able to enforce a covenant against landowners in the subdivision, is there any way you could draft a covenant to assure the developer of this right?

2. For an extended discussion of standing to enforce restrictive covenants, see Annot., Who May Enforce Restrictive Covenant or Agreement as to Use of Real Property, 51 A.L.R.3d 556 (1973). On whether an adjacent lot owner in a separate, but adjacent, subdivision has standing to sue, see Corn Ins. Agency v. Darby Builders, 254 Ark. 1004, 497 S.W.2d 260 (1973). Also see Haldeman v. Teicholz, 197 A.D.2d 223, 611 N.Y.S.2d 669 (1994); Jones v. Herald, 881 P.2d 116 (Okl.App.1994).

3. Charles Ascher in Urban Redevelopment: Problems and Practices 226, 237–238 (Woodbury ed. 1953) commented:

> Experience has shown that neither maintenance nor enforcement can be left as responsibility of one or more property owners. In the early years, the developing agency may legitimately take a leading role; indeed it has an obligation to protect the integrity of the scheme against ill-considered acts of the purchasers, however innocent of purpose, until they have time to understand the intentions of the developer. Moreover, in the early years, the developing agency usually has substantial financial interests to protect in unsold land or purchase-money obligations.
>
> But as these financial interests become less and as the attention and energies of the developing agency are focused elsewhere, its readiness to incur expense and trouble on behalf of the scheme weakens. * * *
>
> Effective administration involves some cost and will make claim upon community funds that many residents would prefer to see spent in activities that seem more immediately gratifying, but there is now more than a generation of experience to prove that controls cannot be left to a committee of volunteers. [Copyright 1953 by the University of Chicago. All rights reserved. Published 1953 by the University of Chicago Press. Composed and printed by Kingsport Press, Inc., Kingsport, Tennessee, U.S.A.]

Can Mr. Ascher's concern be met by having local governmental units administer private restrictive covenants? See Susman, Municipal Enforcement of Private Restrictive Covenants: An Innovation in Land–Use Control, 44 Texas L.Rev. 741 (1966).

SANBORN v. McLEAN

Supreme Court of Michigan, 1925.
233 Mich. 227, 206 N.W. 496, 60 A.L.R. 1212.

WIEST, J.

Defendant Christina McLean owns the west 35 feet of lot 86 of Green Lawn subdivision, at the northeast corner of Collingwood avenue and Second boulevard, in the city of Detroit, upon which there is a dwelling house, occupied by herself and her husband, defendant John A. McLean. The house fronts Collingwood avenue. At the rear of the lot is an alley. Mrs. McLean derived title from her husband and, in the course of the opinion, we will speak of both as defendants. Mr. and Mrs. McLean started to erect a gasoline filling station at the rear end of their lot, and they and their contractor, William S. Weir, were enjoined by decree from doing so and bring the issues before us by appeal. Mr. Weir will not be further mentioned in the opinion.

Collingwood avenue is a high-grade residence street between Woodward avenue and Hamilton boulevard, with single, double and apartment houses, and plaintiffs who are owners of land adjoining, and in the vicinity of defendants' land, and who trace title, as do defendants, to the proprietors of the subdivision, claim that the proposed gasoline station will be a nuisance per se, is in violation of the general plan fixed for use of all lots on the street for residence purposes only, as evidenced by restrictions upon 53 of the 91 lots fronting on Collingwood avenue, and that defendants' lot is subject to a reciprocal negative easement barring a use so detrimental to the enjoyment and value of its neighbors. Defendants insist that no restrictions appear in their chain of title and they purchased without notice of any reciprocal negative easement, and deny that a gasoline station is a nuisance per se. We find no occasion to pass upon the question of nuisance, as the case can be decided under the rule of reciprocal negative easement.

This subdivision was planned strictly for residence purposes, except lots fronting Woodward avenue and Hamilton boulevard. The 91 lots on Collingwood avenue were platted in 1891, designed for and each one sold solely for residence purposes, and residences have been erected upon all of the lots. Is defendants' lot subject to a reciprocal negative easement? If the owner of two or more lots, so situated as to bear the relation sells one with restrictions of benefit to the land retained, the servitude becomes mutual, and, during the period of restraint, the owner of the lot or lots retained can do nothing forbidden to the owner of the lot sold. For want of a better descriptive term this is styled a reciprocal negative easement. It runs with the land sold by virtue of express fastening and abides with the land retained until loosened by expiration of its period of service or by events working its destruction. It is not personal to owners but operative upon use of the land by any owner having actual or constructive notice thereof. It is an easement passing its benefits and carrying its obligations to all purchasers of land subject to its affirmative or negative mandates. It originates for mutual benefit and exists with vigor sufficient to work its ends. It must start with a common owner. Reciprocal negative easements are never retroactive; the very nature of their origin forbids. They arise, if at all, out of a benefit accorded land retained by restrictions upon neighboring land sold by a common owner. Such a scheme of restrictions must start with a common owner; it cannot arise and fasten upon one lot by reason of other lot owners conforming to a general plan. If a reciprocal negative easement attached to defendants' lot it was fastened thereto while in the hands of the common owner of it and neighboring lots by way of sale of other lots with restrictions beneficial at that time to it. This leads to inquiry as to what lots, if any, were sold with restrictions by the common owner before the sale of defendants' lot. While the proofs cover another avenue we need consider sales only on Collingwood.

Sec. 3 SERVITUDES AND RESTRICTIVE COVENANTS 143

December 28, 1892, Robert J. and Joseph R. McLaughlin, who were then evidently owners of the lots on Collingwood avenue, deeded lots 37 to 41 and 58 to 62 inclusive, with the following restrictions:

> No residence shall be erected upon said premises, which shall cost less than $2,500 and nothing but residences shall be erected upon said premises. Said residences shall front on Helene (now Collingwood) avenue and be placed no nearer than 20 feet from the front street line.

July 24, 1893, the McLaughlins conveyed lots 17 to 21 and 78 to 82, both inclusive, and lot 98 with the same restrictions. Such restrictions were imposed for the benefit of the lands held by the grantors to carry out the scheme of a residential district, and a restrictive negative easement attached to the lots retained, and title to lot 86 was then in the McLaughlins. Defendants' title, through mesne conveyances, runs back to a deed by the McLaughlins dated September 7, 1893, without restrictions mentioned therein. Subsequent deeds to other lots were executed by the McLaughlins, some with restrictions and some without. Previous to September 7, 1893, a reciprocal negative easement had attached to lot 86 by acts of the owners, as before mentioned, and such easement is still attached and may now be enforced by plaintiffs, provided defendants, at the time of their purchase, had knowledge, actual or constructive, thereof. The plaintiffs run back with their title, as do defendants, to a common owner. This common owner, as before stated, by restrictions upon lots sold, had burdened all the lots retained with reciprocal restrictions. Defendants' lot and plaintiff Sanborn's lot, next thereto, were held by such common owner, burdened with a reciprocal negative easement, and when later sold to separate parties, remained burdened therewith and right to demand observance thereof passed to each purchaser with notice of the easement. The restrictions were upon defendants' lot while it was in the hands of the common owners, and abstract of title to defendants' lot showed the common owners and the record showed deeds of lots in the plat restricted to perfect and carry out the general plan and resulting in a reciprocal negative easement upon defendants' lot and all lots within its scope, and defendants and their predecessors in title were bound by constructive notice under our recording acts. The original plan was repeatedly declared in subsequent sales of lots by restrictions in the deeds, and while some lots sold were not so restricted the purchasers thereof, in every instance, observed the general plan and purpose of the restrictions in building residences. For upward of 30 years the united efforts of all persons interested have carried out the common purpose of making and keeping all the lots strictly for residences, and defendants are the first to depart therefrom.

When Mr. McLean purchased on contract in 1910 or 1911, there was a partly built dwelling house on lot 86, which he completed and now occupies. He had an abstract of title which he examined and claims he was told by the grantor that the lot was unrestricted. Considering the character of use made of all the lots open to a view of Mr. McLean when he purchased, we think he was put thereby to inquiry, beyond asking his grantor whether there were restrictions. He had an abstract showing the subdivision and that lot 86 had 97 companions; he could not avoid noticing the strictly uniform residence character given the lots by the expensive dwellings thereon, and the least inquiry would have quickly developed the fact that lot 86 was subjected to a reciprocal negative easement, and he could finish his house and, like the others, enjoy the benefits of the easement. We do not say Mr. McLean should have asked his neighbors about restrictions, but we do say that with the notice he had from a view of the premises on the street, clearly indicating the residences were built and the lots occupied in strict accordance with a general plan, he was put to inquiry, and had he inquired he would have found of record the reason for such general conformation, and the benefits thereof serving the owners of lot 86 and the obligations running with such service and available to adjacent lot owners to prevent a departure from the general plan by an owner of lot 86.

While no case appears to be on all fours with the one at bar the principles we have stated, and the conclusions announced, are supported by *Allen v. City of Detroit*, 167 Mich. 464, 133 N.W. 317, 36 L.R.A., N.S., 890; *McQuade v. Wilcox*, 215 Mich. 302, 183 N.W. 771, 16 A.L.R. 997; *French v. White Star Refining Co.*, 229 Mich. 474, 201 N.W. 444; *Silberman v. Uhrlaub*, 116 App.Div. 869, 102 N.Y.S. 299; *Boyden v. Roberts*, 131 Wis. 659, 111 N.W. 701; *Howland v. Andrus*, 80 N.J.Eq. 276, 83 A. 982.

We notice the decree in the circuit directed that the work done on the building be torn down. If the portion of the building constructed can be utilized for any purpose within the restrictions it need not be destroyed.

With this modification the decree in the circuit is affirmed, with costs to plaintiffs. * * *

Notes

1. Sanborn v. McLean is a leading case on the equitable interposition of servitudes or reciprocal negative easements based upon a common building scheme. Note that the new Restatement provides that a reciprocal negative easement is to be defined as a covenant. In Ruffinengo v. Miller, 579 P.2d 342 (Utah 1978), the court stated: "It has long been established that if a general scheme for building or development is intended by the original grantor, subsequent grantees may bring action against each other to enforce restrictive covenants, and such intent may be shown by the acts of the grantor and the attendant circumstances." Ruffinengo was allowed to make such a showing over an objection by Miller that he had successfully defended an almost identical lawsuit brought by two other subdivision landowners a short time before, the court stating that he was not in privity with them, not a party, and that there was no collateral estoppel. See also Friedberg v. Riverpoint Bldg. Committee, 218 Va. 659, 239 S.E.2d 106 (1977), upholding a covenant requiring prior approval of construction plans where it applied to all lots as a part of a uniform plan of development. See generally also, Hamrick v. Herrera, 744 S.W.2d 458 (Mo.App.1987); Taylor v.

Melton, 130 Colo. 280, 274 P.2d 977 (1954); Fitzwater v. Walker, 281 So.2d 790 (La.App.1973); La Fetra v. Beveridge, 124 N.J.Eq. 24, 199 A. 70 (1938), and Annot., 4 A.L.R.2d 1364 (1949).

2. A common scheme of development sometimes has to run too many hurdles to prevail. In G.L. Cline & Son, Inc. v. Cavalier Bldg. Corp., 213 Va. 557, 193 S.E.2d 693 (1973), it was held that there was no common scheme developed by a common grantor and that there was no violation of a setback requirement in written restrictive covenants where construction was begun before the effective date of the covenants. See also Ross v. Harootunian, 257 Cal.App.2d 292, 64 Cal.Rptr. 537 (1967), in which a deed restriction did not state that it was part of a general building plan for a tract development and thus no building scheme would be enforced. A somewhat similar case is Fournier v. Kattar, 108 N.H. 424, 238 A.2d 12 (1968). The problem stems from the use of deeds containing restrictions as opposed to filing a plat and restrictive covenants. In Clark v. Guy Drews Post of the American Legion, 247 Wis. 48, 18 N.W.2d 322 (1945), a plat was recorded without restrictions indicated on the plat. A number of deeds were conveyed with restrictions for residential use only. The American Legion's deed contained no restrictive provision of that type. No general scheme of development was found, and the covenants in the other deeds were deemed to be personal covenants. An examination of the record in the case revealed that the subdivider's officer testified that a residential development plan was intended; this was well-known to the townspeople; purchasers were verbally informed of the residential nature of the development; there had been compliance sufficient to indicate a general scheme; all deeds except four contained the restrictions; and even the last deed contained restrictions. The message is thus clear as to the gamble involved in depending on the common scheme of development rule.

3. A Problem of Record Notice: Developer creates and records a subdivision of 100 lots. The first lot sold is lot 89. The deed recites that the buyer will use the lot for single-family residential purposes. It also contains a covenant by Developer that all remaining lots in the subdivision shall also be restricted to single family residences. The deed is recorded. In selling other lots, including lot 25 purchased by your client, no mention is made of the restrictions, either orally or in the instruments of conveyance. Your client knew nothing about the restriction when he purchased. Now he wants to build a four-family apartment building on his lot. Neighbors are protesting and threatening an injunction action. Will you advise him to fight it, and, if so, what are his chances of success?

See Lowes v. Carter, 124 Md. 678, 93 A. 216 (1915) and IV American Law of Property § 17.24 at 601 (1952).

4. Suppose restrictions imposed by a developer are not identical for all lots. Is it possible nevertheless for the court to find and enforce a general building scheme? See Thodos v. Shirk, 248 Iowa 172, 79 N.W.2d 733 (1956) and Grange v. Korff, 248 Iowa 118, 79 N.W.2d 743 (1956). Compare Bein v. McPhaul, 357 S.W.2d 420 (Tex.Civ.App.1962). In Frey v. Poynor, 369 P.2d 168 (Okl.1962), 26 out of 280 lots were not restricted, yet a building scheme was found to exist. But failure to restrict 40% of the lots was fatal to the existence of a building scheme. In re Congregation of St. Rita, 130 So.2d 425

(La.App.1961). In Arthur M. Deck & Associates v. Crispin, 888 S.W.2d 56 (Tex.App.1994) the court held that disparate treatment of some lots did not preclude enforcement of the restrictions because of the unique circumstances of the case (when a set of 1940 single-family only covenants was amended in 1993, two lots were exempted; the court was convinced that those two lots with condominiums on them were physically different).

5. Sometimes a developer acquires a large tract of land that he subdivides piecemeal, one manageable phase at a time. Instead of restricting the whole tract in one fell swoop, he restricts each subdivision phase as he creates it. One of the ablest subdividers in the country, J.C. Nichols of Kansas City, now deceased, strongly urged this procedure. See Urban Land Institute, Community Developer's Handbook (1954 ed.). But suppose the restrictions imposed upon each subdivision are not uniform one set with the other? Do lot owners in subdivision 1 have any standing to enforce restrictions on subdivision 2, etc.? Thus, in Gammons v. Kennett Park Development Corp., 30 Del.Ch. 525, 61 A.2d 391 (1948), Developer acquired a 640 acre tract and created a series of subdivisions, imposing different restrictions upon each. There was nothing in the deeds restricting the first and later subdivisions to suggest a uniform plan for the entire 640 acres. Held: The owner of a lot in subdivision A of the tract had no standing to protest the release, modification or termination of restrictions in accordance with provisions applicable to subdivision B of the tract. Also see Griffin v. Tall Timbers Development, Inc., 681 So.2d 546 (Miss.1996) where the court held covenants giving the original developer of a subdivision the right to form a property owners' association ran with the land and therefore a successor developer had the right to form an association. Compare Holiday Pines Prop. Owners Ass'n, Inc. v. Wetherington, 596 So.2d 84 (Fla.App.1992).

6. Consider the following cases:

In Hagan v. Sabal Palms, 186 So.2d 302 (Fla.App.1966), land was subdivided by a common owner who then sold to different grantees imposing in each deed a restriction limiting the land to use for dwelling purposes. It was held that any grantee might enforce the restrictions against any other grantee on either the basis of mutuality of covenant and consideration or on the basis that reciprocal negative easements had been created. It was considered immaterial as to whether the covenant was one running with the land. The court stated that in a common scheme of development, as here, the burden followed the benefit and became incident to the ownership of the lots.

In Maxwell v. Land Developers, 485 S.W.2d 869 (Tenn.App.1972), the court felt that the restrictions were ambiguous, but stated: "If, however, the seventeen previously executed deeds contained restrictions inserted for the purpose of carrying out a general plan of development of the entire tract, including the remainder thereof retained by the grantor, and the various grantees relied upon this general plan of development and purchased in reliance on the restrictions being made applicable to the entire tract, any party who purchased the remainder of the tract with *actual* knowledge of the general plan of development, and the prior purchases * * * would take the land so purchased subject to those restrictions."

In Steuart Transportation Co. v. Ashe, 269 Md. 74, 304 A.2d 788 (1973), it is emphasized that the establishment of a uniform plan of development "is a matter of intention of the parties." The court found that the similarity in the method of development and applicability of the provisions indicated an intention to continue a uniform plan; that the plat and dedicatory supplement indicated a uniform plan; and that the plan became operative with the first deed.

In Evans v. Pollock, 793 S.W.2d 14 (Tex.App.1989) the court rejected a claim by property owners that all the property in the subdivision was subject to a covenant for residential use. The court held that the residential restriction did not apply to all of the subdivision property at the time the original owners established the subdivision and that a reciprocal negative easement could not be imposed where the restriction did not apply to all subdivision property.

(3) The Nature of the Interest Created: Property or Contract?

REMILONG v. CROLLA
Supreme Court of Wyoming, 1978.
576 P.2d 461.

GUTHRIE, CHIEF JUSTICE.

Appellants prosecute this appeal from a judgment ordering them to remove certain trailers and mobile homes from lands which they own and permanently enjoining them and their successors or assigns from placing, or allowing the placement of, any such trailers or mobile homes upon these lands.

Appellants Remilongs were the original owners of the lands now owned and occupied by appellees Crollas and sold them the tract which they now own and where their home is located, but appellants retained a portion thereof, being an adjoining tract to which this injunctive action was applied. The tract which the Remilongs retained contains 2.9 acres. The adjoining tract sold to the Crollas is one containing approximately .88 acres upon which is located a house which Remilongs sold to Crollas for the sum of $50,000. Crollas assert that a condition of the purchase was that Remilongs would remove all the trailers or mobile homes from the tract which they retained and claim that the fact they have now moved trailers thereon greatly diminishes the value of the lands purchased and that these lands were purchased in reliance upon such promise and agreement. Additionally, they claim damages in the sum of $10,000. * * *

This matter presents two questions upon which our decision must be based, i.e., does an oral contract creating a restrictive covenant come within the statute of frauds? If such agreement is within the prohibition of the statute of frauds, may the effect thereof be avoided by the application of an equitable or promissory estoppel?

It is apparent that if the answer to this first question is in the negative, this judgment should be summarily affirmed. We do not find that this may be so answered, however.

Appellees concede an existent conflict of judicial opinion in this area, and cite authority sustaining their position that such an agreement does not come within the statute. However, in our view, and after examining such authorities, it appears that these opinions are "result oriented" and that the logic upon which they are based is at least questionable. It may be suggested that these opinions ignore certain realities as to the possible effect of such restrictions upon the use, enjoyment, and value of the lands to which they are attached and that the courts may have been more interested in relieving what appeared to be onerous situations than in a proper application of the law. * * *

This court has not heretofore considered the question of whether a restrictive covenant is within the statute of frauds, although an easement for an irrigation ditch has been held to be an interest in real estate within the statute, *Linck v. Brown*, 55 Wyo. 100, 96 P.2d 909, 911. An agreement restricting the use of land is described in many cases and considered to be a negative easement, *Huggins v. Castle Estates, Inc.*, 36 N.Y.2d 427, 369 N.Y.S.2d 80, 330 N.E.2d 48; *Bennett v. Charles Corporation*, W.Va., 226 S.E.2d 559, 563; *Putnam v. Dickinson*, N.D., 142 N.W.2d 111, 124; *Fort Dodge, Des Moines & Southern Railway v. American Community Stores Corporation*, 256 Iowa 1344, 131 N.W.2d 515, 521. When its establishment is sought in equity it has been treated or described as an equitable estate or interest in land, *Turner v. Brocato*, 206 Md. 336, 111 A.2d 855, 861, and cited authorities. However, it is not necessary herein to categorize the nature of the interest created by a restrictive covenant because its real effect upon the use, enjoyment and value of the property to which it may be attached is obvious. A statement appearing in *Wiley v. Dunn*, 358 Ill. 97, 192 N.E. 661, 663, is most applicable in this case:

> " ' * * * The policy of the law requires that everything which affects the title to real estate shall be in writing, and that nothing shall be left to the frailty of human memory or as a temptation to perjury. * * *' " (Quoting from *Stephens v. St. Louis Union Trust Co.*, 260 Ill. 364, 103 N.E. 190, 193; and cited with approval in *Corbridge v. Westminster Presbyterian Church and Society*, 18 Ill.App.2d 245, 151 N.E.2d 822, 831.)

This view is consistent with *Crosby v. Strahan's Estate, supra*, and only serves to implement and strengthen that holding. It may be more desirable, instead of categorizing such restrictive covenant as an equitable interest, equitable servitude, or a negative easement, to frankly recognize that such covenant does affect the title, use, and estate, and recognize it independently for what it is. At best, it could probably be classified as creating a type of equitable ownership or servitude. It would appear of particular importance that such restrictive covenants be classified as interests in land without reference to particular terminology because of their increasing importance and use in our modern-day society. We would then hold that this asserted agreement creating a restrictive covenant upon appellants' land was within the prohibition of the statute of frauds, *Frank v. Visockas*, 356 Mass. 227, 228–229, 249

N.E.2d 1; *Cottrell v. Nurnberger*, 131 W.Va. 391, 47 S.E.2d 454, 456, 5 A.L.R.2d 1298; *Droutman v. E.M. & L. Garage, Inc.*, 129 N.J.Eq. 545, 20 A.2d 75, 76; Annotation 5 A.L.R.2d 1316, 1320–1322; 5 Powell on Real Property, § 672, pp. 152–153 (1976); A.L.I. Restatement of the Law, Property, § 522, p. 3165 (1944). This does not, however, dispose of this case.

In defense of their judgment, appellees raise another proposition, i.e., if the statute of frauds does apply to this case appellants should not be allowed to rely upon it because of fraud or equitable or promissory estoppel, and the trial court apparently recognized that in its findings.

This case poses the direct question of whether equitable, or particularly promissory, estoppel may be used to defeat the statute of frauds and result in the creation of a restrictive covenant, a negative covenant, or equitable servitude upon the lands of the Remilongs. In *Crosby v. Strahan's Estate*, *supra*, this court examined and cited with approval authorities which expressed the view that the statute of frauds was an expression of "fixed legislative policy of the state" and that it was "absolutely necessary to preserve the title to real property from the chances, the uncertainty, and the fraud attending the admission of parol testimony." It further enunciated the caveat that the court should not be tempted to turn aside from its plain provisions merely because of the hardship of a particular case.

Since this is the first case before us involving the avoidance of the statute of frauds to effect the creation of such restrictive covenants, and realizing their increased use, their importance and necessity to present-day society, and the potential number of land titles which could conceivably be affected, this question must be approached with the greatest of caution.

Many authorities, in applying the principle of promissory estoppel, to avoid the provisions of this statute suggest that the purpose of the statute is to prevent suborned perjury in apparent recognition that this was at least one purpose which the statute of frauds no longer subserved. England partially repealed the statute of frauds because this necessity had been removed. See 68 Harv.L.Rev. 383 (1954). It is for this reason your writer finds helpful the application of the rules set out in many cases which involve the application of estoppel in cases which arise other than under paragraph 5 of our statute.

Some courts have met this problem squarely and held they would not by adoption of the doctrine of promissory estoppel avoid the legislative action embraced in the statute of frauds, *Tanenbaum v. Biscayne Osteopathic Hospital, Inc.*, Fla., 190 So.2d 777, 779. If a contract is clearly within the statute, to apply this doctrine of promissory estoppel is to repeal the statute, *Sinclair v. Sullivan Chevrolet Company*, 45 Ill. App.2d 10, 195 N.E.2d 250, 253, affirmed 31 Ill.2d 507, 202 N.E.2d 516. The rule has been recognized that the defense of the statute cannot be raised unless there is a misrepresentation that the requirements of the statute had been complied with or there had been a promise to make a written memorandum, *21 Turtle Creek Square, Ltd. v. New York State Teachers' Retirement System*, 5 Cir. 432 F.2d 64, 65, certiorari denied 401 U.S. 955, 91 S.Ct. 975, 28 L.Ed.2d 239.

Although this court has recognized the almost universal rule that restrictions upon the use of lands are not favored, we have also recognized that equity does have a role to play in limited circumstances, *Kindler v. Anderson*, Wyo., 433 P.2d 268, 271; *Metcalf v. Hart*, 3 Wyo. 513, 27 P. 900, 31 Am.St.Rep. 122, affirmed 31 P. 407; *Vogel v. Shaw*, 42 Wyo. 333, 294 P. 687, 75 A.L.R. 639; *Forde v. Libby*, 22 Wyo. 464, 143 P. 1190. We speak of limited circumstances because the declared legislative policy encompassed in the statute of frauds should be departed from only when such action is necessary to "avoid the fraud, and accomplish what justice and good conscience demand," *Metcalf v. Hart, supra*, 27 P. at 913. Also, see *Roberts Construction Company v. Vondriska*, Wyo., 547 P.2d 1171, 1181. To accomplish the purposes of the statute of frauds, it may be necessary for a court to uphold oral agreements, *Tucker v. Owen*, 4 Cir., 94 F.2d 49, 52.

In light of the fact that appellees could easily have avoided this problem by placing all commitments in writing, they bear a heavy burden to show why the court should come to their rescue, but they have sustained such burden in this case. The trial court's findings that the appellants' promise to remove all the trailers from the remaining property and not permit the further placement of trailers thereon, that the appellants took affirmative action in removing all such trailers at that time, and that the appellees relied thereon, were sustained by the evidence. This is sufficient to apply the doctrine of promissory estoppel, *Hanna State & Savings Bank v. Matson*, 53 Wyo. 1, 77 P.2d 621, 625, wherein this court cites § 90, Restatement of Contracts, and *Vogel v. Shaw, supra*.

* * *

For the reasons stated above, the judgment is affirmed.

Notes

1. It is obvious from the cases that courts encounter difficulty in attempting to decide whether they have under consideration a creature of contract law or a property interest. Clearly, whatever the contract ramifications, under the weight of modern authority, what we call today an "equitable servitude" is a property interest, cognizable and enforceable in equity, which burdens one piece of land to the benefit of another. According to 2 Nichols, Eminent Domain § 5.15(1) Rev.3d ed. 1989, a restrictive covenant constitutes property in the constitutional sense for which compensation must be made if the land in question is taken. These are in the nature of equitable easements, and when land is taken for a public use that will ultimately result in a violation of the restrictions, the landowners who were benefitted by the restrictions are entitled to compensation.

2. The Restatement of Property, Third (Servitudes), § 2.9 provides for an exception to the Statute of Frauds if the beneficiary of the servitude "in

justifiable reliance on the existence of the servitude, has so changed position that injustice can be avoided only by giving effect to the parties' intent to create a servitude."

3. In Westhampton, Inc. v. Kehoe, 227 Ga. 642, 182 S.E.2d 430, 433 (1971), the Georgia court adopted the holding of a trial court that "generally, oral restrictions as to the use of land are valid and enforceable." In that case the purchasers had relied upon the oral representations of the developer as to the quality and size of homes in the subdivision.

MORLEY v. JACKSON REDEVELOPMENT AUTHORITY

Supreme Court of Mississippi, 1994.
632 So.2d 1284.

EN BANC.

SULLIVAN, JUSTICE, FOR THE COURT:

The Jackson Redevelopment Authority (JRA) filed this suit to acquire Morley and Laurence's (owners) property on October 23, 1989, in Hinds County Special Court of Eminent Domain. The owners removed the action to the United States District Court for the Southern District of Mississippi, Jackson Division, and filed an answer on December 20, 1989. The District Court remanded to the state court for failure of complete diversity of citizenship among the parties. Standard Life Insurance Company was also joined as a party to the suit, as it claimed an interest in a restrictive covenant on the property. The trial court held that Standard Life had no compensable interest in the property and granted summary judgment against it, but granted Standard Life leave to appeal. The trial court also granted summary judgment for JRA on the question of public use and necessity. After discovery and a number of pretrial motions and hearings on those motions, the case went to trial on April 17, 1990. The jury awarded the owners $500,000 and the owners have appealed. * * *

The owners purchased the King Edward Hotel property from Standard Life Insurance Company in 1981 for $450,000. The owners had been involved in a number of real estate investments over the years and had a special interest in purchasing historical properties such as the King Edward.

The King Edward Hotel was built in 1923 on a lot of 69,159 square feet in downtown Jackson bounded by West Capitol, Mill and Pearl Streets. The property actually consists of three separate structures. The main hotel tower has 12 floors containing approximately 224,040 square feet of space. Adjacent to the hotel tower is a convention center containing approximately 7,842 square feet and a three-story parking garage which once housed an automobile dealership. The King Edward is on the National Register of Historic Places due to its excellent architectural design and the fact that for many years it served as the center of social and political activity in Jackson.

The King Edward today is a blight on the Jackson skyline. Last occupied in 1967, the building now is home only to a group of pigeons that enter through the numerous broken windows and mark the hotel with great mounds of disease-carrying excrement. Almost all of the witnesses at the trial agreed that the main tower was structurally sound. An expert engineer called by JRA created the most doubt on the soundness of the structure by testifying that two of the 1300 to 1400 steel columns in the building had been exposed and begun to corrode. He stated that tests would have to be made on more of the columns in order to determine the extent of possible corrosion in other parts of the building frame. The owners' expert architect, however, thought that the only reason those columns were deteriorating was the fact that the roof over both of them had holes in it, allowing moisture to seep into those columns. It was generally agreed also that any renovation of the hotel would require "gutting" the entire building, which meant removing all of the finishing material in the hotel and using only the existing structural frame and the facade of the building. Further measures necessary for a renovation were the addition of another stairwell to meet current building codes, removal of asbestos, and removal of the large accumulations of pigeon droppings.

* * *

When the Standard Life Insurance Company sold the King Edward property to Morley and Laurence in 1981, it inserted a covenant, which reads:

> Subject, however, to the following covenants and restrictions, which shall be taken to be covenants running with the land and binding upon the Grantees, their heirs, administrators, executors, assigns and successors in Title: The property shall be used as offices, a hotel, apartments, commercial rental property or a combination of these. No part of the property shall be converted for use as a home for the elderly, a nursing home or as low rent, government subsidized housing.

JRA argues that restrictive covenants such as this are not compensable property interests in an eminent domain action, and that even if they are, this particular one is not compensable because the dominant estate is not identified, no proposed violation of the covenant has been shown and even if a violation is shown, damages are too speculative to allow. Standard Life's position is that their interest is a compensable property interest which has a value which may be determined by the effect on the market value of its own property if it is taken. The owners object to any holding that would diminish their recovery.

State courts are in disagreement over the question of whether compensation is due for the taking of a restrictive covenant and the United States Supreme Court has never decided the question. The majority of states have found such interests to be property for the purposes of the Fifth Amendment and their own takings clauses and thus subject to the due compensation principle. States which deny compensation generally find that restrictive covenants are not interests in land, but merely personal rights not covered by the takings clause. See, Annotation, 4 A.L.R.3rd 1137 (1965); Law of Real Property ¶ 679[4] (Supp.1988). Many opinions which find such interests not compensable mention public policy reasons for the decisions, including the fear that recognition by the public that restrictive covenants are property interests would result in greater costs for government to acquire property and widespread proliferation of the covenants in order to thwart attempts by the sovereign to take property for public use. Stoebuck, Condemnation of Rights the Condemnee Holds in Lands of Another, 56 Iowa L.Rev. 293, 306–307 (1970); *Anderson v. Lynch*, 188 Ga. 154, 3 S.E.2d 85 (Ga.1939).

We view as better reasoned those opinions that find such interests to be interests in real property for which due compensation must be paid upon a taking by the exercise of eminent domain powers.

These courts take a different view of the meaning of property. For example, in finding the taking of a right to assess fees against a parcel of property a right for which compensation was due, one federal appeals Court quoted an earlier U.S. Supreme Court decision:

> It is conceivable that the [term "property"] was used in its vulgar and untechnical sense of the physical thing with respect to which the citizen exercises rights recognized by law. On the other hand, it may have been employed in a more accurate sense to denote the group of rights inhering in the citizen's relation to the physical thing, as the right to possess, use and dispose of it. In point of fact, the construction given the phrase has been the latter.

Adaman Mutual Water Company v. United States, 278 F.2d 842, 845 (9th Cir.1960) (quoting *United States v. General Motors Corp.*, 323 U.S. 373, 377–380, 65 S.Ct. 357, 359–361, 89 L.Ed. 311 (1945)).

In a similar description of the scope of what constitutes "property" for purposes of the takings clause, Professor Stoebuck wrote:

> For every burden on your land, someone else enjoys a corresponding benefit or right. Physicists tell us that matter may not be destroyed—altered in form or transformed into energy, but not destroyed. And so with the interests in land; they may be redistributed, but the totality of absolute ownership will always exist somewhere, though scattered among the state and various individuals.... If your land is burdened by private restrictions known as restrictive covenants, servitudes, or negative easements [your neighbor] still has a property interest, though of a negative rather than positive sort. Matter has simply been altered in form.

Stoebuck, Condemnation of Rights the Condemnee Holds in Lands of Another, 56 Iowa L.Rev. 293, 293 (1970).

Both Professor Stoebuck and the Court in *Adaman* note that restrictive covenants have more in common with other interests accepted as property than not. Restrictive covenants generally must be created by a deed, be properly recorded, pass the Statute of Frauds and, once created, they run with the land. They, therefore, have more in common with real property than with property outside that rubric. *Adaman*, 278 F.2d at 849; Stoebuck 56 Iowa L.Rev. at 305. "Because the transfer of these rights and duties are subject to legal principles different from those which concern the passing of other interests, a unique, direct connection with the land is established. This connection justifies the distinction [between property and other rights]." *Adaman*, 278 F.2d at 849. The *Adaman* Court finally compared restrictive covenants to easements, which universally require compensation when taken, and concluded, "[b]oth interests are directly connected to the land and we are unable to find a distinction between them which will justify dissimilar treatment at the hands of the condemning authority." Id. at 849.

Clearly, Standard Life kept one of the "bundle of rights" which made up the complete estate when they sold the King Edward to Morley and Laurence. For this reason JRA's argument that only where the dominant estate is mentioned in the instrument containing the covenant may the owner of the dominant estate be entitled to compensation [is] unpersuasive. The "stick" Standard Life kept is the right of Morley and Laurence or their successors in title to build housing for the elderly, a nursing home, or government subsidized housing on the property. In order for the owners or their successors to use the property for any of these purposes, they would have to buy this right back from Standard Life. Would any prudent buyer seeking to purchase the property for one of those uses do so without purchasing this right? Would they not want, indeed, need a deed showing that Standard Life had sold the rights back to the owners? Certainly. To do otherwise would be to buy a lawsuit. Without a repurchase of the rights, the title to the property would be unmarketable.

Therefore, this Court finds that the restrictive covenant in favor of Standard Life is an interest in land subject to the due compensation principle under Section 17 of our Constitution.

Having found the restrictive covenant is an interest in land subject to compensation, it is necessary to discuss the method of calculating that compensation.

We have heretofore strictly adhered to the "unit rule." We set out the basis and application of the rule in *Lennep v. Mississippi State Highway Commission*, 347 So.2d 341 (Miss.1977), quoted in *Mississippi State Highway Commission v. Daughtrey–Hughes, Inc.*, 375 So.2d 413, 414 (Miss.1979).

> It is clear that the legislature intended for the unit valuation method to be applied in determining compensation in eminent domain cases. Mississippi Code Annotated, Section 11–27–5 (1972). We have consistently followed the statutory mandate and use the unit valuation method for determining compensation where property sought to be condemned involves a leasehold interest. In Lee v. Indian Creek Drainage District, 246 Miss. 254, 148 So.2d 663, 666 (1963), we stated Where there are different interests or estates in

Sec. 3 **SERVITUDES AND RESTRICTIVE COVENANTS** **155**

the property acquired by condemnation, the proper course is to ascertain the entire compensation to be awarded as though the property belonged to one person and then apportion this sum among the different parties according to their respective rights.

Accord, *State Highway Comm. v. Rankin County Board of Ed.*, 531 So.2d 612 (Miss.1988).

Nichols' The Law of Eminent Domain, Sackman (3rd Ed.1990) points out the difficulty of valuation of restrictive covenants by the traditional unit rule:

> There is no doubt a property may be restricted by means of a covenant running with the land to a use which is quite consistent with its highest and best use on the date of the condemnation. Thus, a servient tenement will have a value at least in theory equaling its value as unencumbered. Yet, the restriction imposed in favor of one or more other properties may be of substantial value to those properties. Thus, the "unit rule" has no application.

Id. at s 12.05[4][h], p. 129.

The proper method of valuation is the difference between the market value of the dominant estate before and after the taking. Standard Life urges the Court to adopt this view.

However, that view is fundamentally incompatible with the reality that the covenant gives Standard Life an interest in the King Edward property. The unit rule requires that in this case, a value be assessed on the fee simple interest in the King Edward, then that amount be apportioned among the owners and Standard Life, according to their respective interests.

JRA insists that any damages to Standard Life's covenant are purely speculative and thus should not be compensable. However, Standard Life's covenant is plainly being extinguished. We recently stated that:

> Because our constitution requires "due compensation" the presumption is that the construction will be of such character as to do the most injury to the remaining property of the landowner. 4 Nichols, The Law of Eminent Domain § 14.15, pp. 14–327 thru–329 (Rev. 3d Ed.1990). This view is a function of the policy imperative that compensation and damages be payable once and for all and not piecemeal. One policy imperative of the before-and-after rule for more than half a century has been that the landowner's entire right and the Commission's entire liability will be resolved in a single action. That rule gives the landowner substantial incentive to discover and show all special damages.

King v. Miss. State Highway Commission, 609 So.2d 1251, 1254 (Miss. 1992) (footnote omitted).

Although we made these statements in an inverse condemnation case, the rationale applies equally to the facts in this case. The lower court was presented with ample evidence that the restrictive covenant had value. Therefore, it erred in granting summary judgment against Standard Life.

AFFIRMED IN PART; REVERSED IN PART AND REMANDED TO THE SPECIAL COURT OF EMINENT DOMAIN OF HINDS COUNTY, MISSISSIPPI.

Notes

1. The minority view on compensation for a restrictive covenant has some strong adherents. Consider the following statements from the case of Arkansas State Highway Comm'n v. McNeill, 238 Ark. 244, 381 S.W.2d 425 (1964):

> The McNeills own a residence in Crestview Estates, an addition to Fort Smith. The Crestview bill of assurances provides that property in the addition shall be used only for residential purposes. The highway department does not propose to take any of the appellees' land. It is, however, acquiring a tract that is comprised of eleven lots within the addition and that abuts the appellees' north boundary line. When the interchange is completed the area behind the McNeills' home will be a busy highway instead of a quiet residential district. Expert witnesses testified that this transition will diminish the value of the plaintiffs' property by $10,000 or more. * * *
>
> Does the fact that the proposed interchange will violate the restrictive covenant render the appellant liable for the decrease in the market value of the McNeills' property? This problem has arisen in some twenty jurisdictions, with the decisions about equally divided between the allowance of compensation and its denial. The cases are discussed in Nichols, Eminent Domain (3d Ed.), § 5.73, and in a Comment, 53 Mich.L.Rev. 451. When compensation is allowed it is ordinarily measured by the diminution in market value. United States v. Certain Land in City of Augusta, D.C.Maine, 220 F.Supp. 696; United States v. 11.06 Acres, D.C.Mo., 89 F.Supp. 852; Town of Stamford v. Vuono, 108 Conn. 359, 143 A. 245; Johnstone v. Detroit, G.H. & M.R.R., 245 Mich. 65, 222 N.W. 325, 67 A.L.R. 373.
>
> Many of the decisions denying compensation are discussed in Anderson v. Lynch, 188 Ga. 154, 3 S.E.2d 85, 122 A.L.R. 1456. The courts seem to have had some difficulty in finding a sound basis for refusing an award, some saying that the plaintiff has no property interest in the land being taken, others that the restrictive covenant does not confer a property right, and still others that the public power of eminent domain should not be impaired by private contract. * * *
>
> In those jurisdictions where, as here, compensation would be denied in the absence of a restriction, the decisions approving an award on the basis of the restriction alone are, in our opinion, demonstrably wrong. We need not, however, adopt the somewhat dubious reasons that have been given for the denial of compensation. We think the problem is essentially a simple one in causation.
>
> It seems almost too plain for argument that the reduction in the value of the McNeills' property is attributable not to the breach of the

restriction but rather to the fact that a highway is about to pass through a residential district. Suppose, for example, that this addition, Crestview Estates, had been developed in exactly the same way that it was actually developed, as a residential district, but without any such restriction in the bill of assurances. If the interchange had then been constructed the McNeills' damage, as far as the pleadings and proof indicate, would have been the same to the penny as if the restriction had existed. Yet it would not have been compensable. Thus it is illogical to permit a recovery upon the theory that the breach of covenant is the proximate cause of the injury.

Another illustration to demonstrate the fallacy in the decisions allowing compensation: Assume the existence of a purely residential area that is in part restricted and in part unrestricted. If a highway should be constructed just within the restricted section the landowners on that side of the highway would receive compensation while those on the other side, although suffering identical damage, would be without a remedy. Under such a rule it is evident that whenever the owners of property in an unrestricted neighborhood learn that a throughway is coming in their direction it is to their advantage to enter into an agreement imposing restrictions. In that way, by merely signing a piece of paper which they may destroy at will, they are able to pluck valuable causes of action from the thin air.

We do not deny the existence of a property right in the appellees. It may be that the restrictive covenant gave added value to their land when they bought it. But it is not the breach of the covenant alone that is causing their damage. This same tract, instead of being taken for a highway, might have been condemned by the city as a site for a public park. That too would have involved a breach of covenant, but the value of the appellees' property might actually have been enhanced. Thus there is no logical basis for attributing the appellees' present damage to the naked breach of covenant. Even without the restriction their injury would still have occurred. We cannot permit an irrelevant clause in the bill of assurances to create a fictitious cause of action.

2. The majority view is explained in these comments by the Supreme Court of California in Southern California Edison Co. v. Bourgerie, 9 Cal.3d 169, 107 Cal.Rptr. 76, 79, 507 P.2d 964, 967 (1973):

We need not contemplate in depth the somewhat esoteric dialogue on the appropriate characterization of a building restriction. One writer has perceptively declared that the 'no-property-interest argument is less the motivation for denial of compensation than it is a rationalization for a result desired for other reasons' (Stoebuck, op. cit. *supra*, 56 Iowa L.Rev. at p. 306). An objective analysis reveals the real basis for the decisions which deny compensation for the violation of building restrictions by a condemner relates to pragmatic considerations of public policy rather than abstract doctrines of property law, and it is upon these issues of policy that jurisdictions choose between the minority and majority views. * * * Denial of compensation has been justified upon the ground that the cost of constructing public projects will be substantially increased if compensation must be provided by a condemner for the violation of a restriction. In addition, it is asserted that a condemner might be required to join a large number of landowners as defendants in cases where the benefit of the restriction runs to numerous lots, and that this could result in inhibiting the condemner's ability to acquire essential property. Finally, it has been suggested that landowners might 'pluck valuable causes of action from the thin air' by entering into agreements imposing restrictions whenever condemnation proceedings are on the horizon. (Arkansas State Highway Comm'n v. McNeill, 238 Ark. 244, 381 S.W.2d 425, 427 (1964).) We find these reasons for denying compensation to be unpersuasive. Conceding the possibility that the cost of condemning property might be increased somewhat by awarding compensation for the violation of building restrictions, we cannot conclude that such increases will significantly burden exercise of the power of eminent domain. As a practical matter some takings would result in negligible damage to the owners * * *; if the character of the improvement were such that damage to some landowners would result * * *, it is likely that only those immediately adjoining or in close proximity to the improvement would suffer substantial injury, even in highly restricted areas.

See also: Horst v. Housing Auth., 184 Neb. 215, 166 N.W.2d 119, 121 (1969) ("We therefore hold that lawful covenants restricting the use of land and binding upon successors in title constitute an interest in the land, and property in the constitutional sense. Where the taking of the land by eminent domain permits a use violative of the restrictions and extinguishes such interest, there is a taking of the property of the owners of the land for whose benefit the restrictions were imposed, and such owner is entitled to compensation for the damage * * * "); Meredith v. Washoe County School District, 84 Nev. 15, 435 P.2d 750 (1968) ("The basic question, then, is whether an equitable servitude, or easement, such as here, a restrictive covenant, is deemed to be 'property' in a constitutional sense, for which just compensation must be paid. To a 'majority' of jurisdictions this has been the question and has been answered in the affirmative."); Moschetti v. Tucson, 9 Ariz.App. 108, 449 P.2d 945 (1969); Staninger v. Jacksonville Expressway Auth., 182 So.2d 483 (Fla.App.1966); and State v. Reece, 374 S.W.2d 686 (Tex.Civ.App.1964). Compare Burma Hills Development Co. v. Marr, 285 Ala. 141, 229 So.2d 776 (1969), in which after considering the statement of the "majority" and "minority" views, Alabama decided to adhere to the minority.

3. In Harris County Flood Control District v. Glenbrook Patiohome Owners Ass'n, 933 S.W.2d 570 (Tex.App.1996) the court held that the homeowners association had a cause of action in inverse condemnation for a taking of its property right to collect assessment fees for the period of time from when the government entity purchased 20 homes to widen a bayou until the entity brought an action to condemn the covenants. (The flood control district refused to pay the monthly fees required by the covenants after it purchased the homes.)

(4) Enforcement

Problems relating to enforcement are diverse. The basic rule is that any person owning a lot in the subdivision may enforce the restrictive covenants against any other landowner in the subdivision. Each lot is at one and the same time both a dominant and servient tenement; each lot is burdened by the covenants and each is benefited.

But a variety of questions may arise relative to enforcement. Some of those questions arise in relation to termination, such as whether the change of conditions and circumstances in the subdivision and its environs would render it inequitable to enforce the covenants. Some questions relate to the propriety of enforcing the covenants. Has there been such a waiver of them in similar situations that it would not be equitable to enforce them in this one? Has there been laches on the part of the plaintiff? Should principles of equitable estoppel apply?

Sometimes the issue is the validity of the covenants themselves. Are they even-handed in their operation, and are they reasonable? Are they constitutional?

Some cases involve rather unusual arguments insofar as the typical restrictive covenant situation is concerned. In Quadro Stations, Inc. v. Gilley, 7 N.C.App. 227, 172 S.E.2d 237 (1970), about four acres adjoining property which was sold was restricted from use in the sale of petroleum products for a period of 25 years. The court held this not to be unreasonable as to the area involved, and, it did not accept the argument of the defendants that the covenant was illegal as being in restraint of trade. The same issue arose in Webster v. Star Distributing Co., Inc., 241 Ga. 270, 244 S.E.2d 826 (1978), in which the lease of the Websters contained a restrictive covenant limiting the use of the premises to professional dry cleaning and laundering, but prohibited coin-operated laundering, while Star's lease limited use to coin-operated laundering and dry cleaning. When Star began engaging in "drop-off" laundry business, the Websters sued. The covenant was upheld as not being in restraint of trade.

Standing may sometimes also be a factor. In Nonnenmann v. Lucky Stores, Inc., 53 Ill.App.3d 509, 10 Ill.Dec. 714, 368 N.E.2d 200 (1977), the plaintiff had violated the covenants (although not the zoning which accompanied annexation of the subdivision) by building apartment houses on two lots in the subdivision. The court held that he still had standing to seek injunctive relief based upon the defendant's violation of the covenants. Probably not all courts would have permitted him to come into equity under the circumstances.

The single-family classification often gives rise to enforcement questions, as some of the cases later on will illustrate, as does the vague "residential use" classification. In Hanley v. Misischi, 111 R.I. 233, 302 A.2d 79 (1973), a landowner was not permitted to construct a street across her lot to give access to houses to be constructed on a new plat because the proposed street was not a single family home and was not of benefit or incidental to residential use in the subdivision.

The cases that follow illustrate some of the conflicts that arise in connection with single-family limitations.

BROWNFIELD SUBDIVISION, INC. v. McKEE
Supreme Court of Illinois, 1975.
61 Ill.2d 168, 334 N.E.2d 131.

WARD, JUSTICE.

Acting on the complaint of Brownfield Subdivision, Inc., a not-for-profit corporation, and E.J. Buras, the plaintiffs, the circuit court of Champaign County entered an order of injunction prohibiting the defendants, Robert and Mary Ann Collenberger, from occupying what was described as a sectional home in the Brownfield subdivision as a residence. The ground for the order was the court's finding that the structure was a mobile home, a type of structure prohibited in the subdivision by an applicable restrictive covenant. The appellate court affirmed (19 Ill.App.3d 374, 311 N.E.2d 194), and we granted a petition for leave to appeal filed by the defendants.

The restrictive covenant provides in part:

"No building shall be erected on any lot except a one family dwelling house, a garage and one service building and used exclusively as such. Buildings shall be permanent structures of an attractive design. Duplexes may be built on Lots 34, 35, 36, 37 and 38.

"No structure of a temporary character, trailer, basement, tent, shack, mobile home or garage shall be used on any Lot, at any time, as a residence, either temporarily or permanently."

The Collenbergers purchased a structure described as an "Armor Home" and a lot in the Brownfield subdivision from Rex McKee, another defendant, who is the president of Illinois Mobile Homes, Inc. A retail installment contract was used by the parties in the sale of the structure. It described the Armor Home as a mobile home and provided that title should remain vested in the seller until full payment was made. The Collenbergers were given a certificate of title which also referred to the Armor Home as a mobile home and stated its year of manufacture, its style or model and its serial number.

The Armor Home here is 52 feet long, 24 feet wide and has a total living area of 1,460 feet. It is manufactured in two separate sections which, when joined, provide three bedrooms, a living room, dining room, kitchen, a utility room and 1½ baths. The sections are built upon detachable running gears, i.e., upon undercarriages, springs, axles, wheels and hitches, which are designed to permit their removal at the location where the structure is to be installed.

Prior to installing the Armor Home on their lot, the Collenbergers constructed a concrete foundation 52 feet long, 24 feet wide and 36 inches deep. Stacks of concrete blocks were placed on top of the foundation. Then, three steel I-beams were placed on top of the stacks. When the two sections were delivered at the lot, they were set on jacks which had been placed on the four corners of the foundation. Workmen then removed the detachable running gears from the two sections and lowered the two sections onto the I-beams. The sections were fastened together by angle irons and 16–penny nails.

After the sections were connected, a mason cemented the ends of the beams and the stacks of concrete blocks to the foundation. The mason also built a perimeter wall of building blocks which was cemented to the foundation. However, the bottom of the Armor Home was not cemented, welded or attached in any way to the I-beams or to the perimeter wall. The structure simply rested on the three I-beams. After the sections were joined aluminum enamel siding was installed on the sides of the structure. A family room was added connecting the Armor Home to a previously constructed garage.

Robert Collenberger testified that he knew of the covenant's restrictions when he bought the lot. He said that although the Armor Home after installation could be transported to another location by reattaching the running gear to the bottom of each section, the structure would first have to be dismantled. This would require removing the aluminum siding, removing the bolts from the angle irons and the nails connecting the two sections, removing the shingles from the roof and disconnecting all the utilities.

Rex E. McKee testified that he sold the sectional home to the Collenbergers. He said that there is a difference between a double-wide mobile home and a sectional home. A double-wide home is two mobile homes constructed so that they may be fitted together to make a large mobile home, and it is portable, he said. A sectional home is designed to be a single dwelling with a single roof, and though it is constructed in two sections, it is not portable, he testified. He said that in his opinion the Collenberger's house was a permanent single house and not a mobile home.

He did admit, on cross-examination, that he had advertised the Armor Home as a "double wide mobile home." * * *

Warren Huddleston, the president of Countryside Mobile Homes, Inc., testified that the difference between mobile homes and sectional homes is that a mobile home's running gear is designed to be a permanent part of the unit. He said that a sectional home's running gear is designed to be detached, that is, it is designed to be removed from the housing unit when the unit is placed on a foundation. He stated that the Collenbergers' house in his opinion is a permanent family dwelling and not a mobile home.

The defendants' contention is that their Armor Home is a sectional home and therefore not a mobile home. This contention relies upon the testimony of Rex McKee and Warren Huddleston that sectional homes and mobile homes have important differences. The defendants alternatively argue that even if the structure was a mobile home, it became a permanent structure when it was placed in the foundation.

* * *

There is authority that modular and sectional homes are considered to be in the mobile-home category. B. Hodes and G. Roberson, The Law of Mobile Homes 4 (3d ed. 1974) states:

* * *

"4. A *Modular Unit* is a factory fabricated transportable building unit designed to be used by itself or to be incorporated with similar units at a building site into a modular structure to be used for residential, commercial, educational or industrial purposes.

"5. A *Sectional Home* is a dwelling made of two or more modular units factory fabricated and transported to the home site where they are put on a foundation and joined to make a single house."

We consider the structure here must be deemed to be within the prohibitory language of the covenant, "no structure of a temporary character, trailer * * *."

It was advertised as a double-wide mobile home in the installment contract under which it was purchased. Photographs in evidence show it to have the superstructure and appearance of a mobile home. In Hodes and Roberson, The Law of Mobile Homes, which we have cited, it is said that sectional homes are regarded as within the mobile-homes category. There was a concrete foundation here but the structure was in no way attached to it or to the three I-beams on which the structure simply rested. The structure can be transported to another location after the two sections have been separated and the removable undercarriages reattached to the bottoms of the sections. One of the exhibits (an article from a trade journal) attached to the defendants' brief in this court refers to a modular unit's portability as a difference from and an advantage over the conventional home.

The majority of courts considering the question have held that removing the wheels or running gear of a mobile home and placing it on a permanent foundation does not convert the home into a permanent structure. In addition to *Timmerman v. Gabriel and Town of Manchester v. Phillips*, which we described above, such holdings include: *Town of Brewster v. Sherman* (1962), 343 Mass. 598, 180 N.E.2d 338; *Town of Greenland v. Hussey* (1970), 110 N.H. 269, 266 A.2d 122; *Bullock v. Kattner* (Tex.Civ.App.1973), 502 S.W.2d 828; *Jones v. Beiber* (1960), 251 Iowa 969, 103 N.W.2d 364. See also *City of Astoria v. Nothwang* (1960), 221 Or. 452, 351 P.2d 688.

There is some contrary authority: *Anstine v. Zoning Board of Adjustment* (1963), 411 Pa. 33, 190 A.2d 712; *Lescault v. Zoning Board of Review* (1960), 91 R.I. 277, 162 A.2d 807; *In re Willey* (1958), 120 Vt. 359, 140 A.2d 11. However, we consider the position taken in the majority of holdings is to be preferred.

For the reasons given, the judgment of the appellate court is affirmed.

Notes

1. Compare with the principal case, Farrior v. Zoning Board of Appeals of the Black Point Beach Club Association, 70 Conn.App. 86, 796 A.2d 1262 (2002), where the court held that a motor home (RV) parked at Farrior's beachfront property did not violate a covenant against mobile homes. The problem of mobile homes, modular units, sectional units, prefabricated homes and the like are problems of the modern era and the high cost of single-family units of the traditional type. The law wrestles with these problems in the context of zoning ordinances as well as in regard to restrictive covenants. Socio-economic considerations, as well as legal principles and interpretations, are involved whether the courts mention them or not. Ironically perhaps, in the 21st century Armor homes are considered desirable historic treasures, because few of them have survived.

2. A related situation was considered in Lawrence v. Harding, 225 Ga. 148, 166 S.E.2d 336 (1969). The restrictive covenant provided that a "building" with metal siding or metal roofing was prohibited. The mobile home was placed on a permanent foundation, was completely enclosed, had an attached porch, had concrete underpinnings, had a metal roof, and had a septic tank, gas line, water line, and electric lines. It was held to be a building for purposes of the restrictive covenant and thus violative of the covenant. The Georgia Court, by holding it to be a "building", declined to accept the argument of the defendants that if the covenants had sought to forbid mobile homes, they could have so stated. While the reasoning process may be different from that in the preceding cases, the result was the same—the mobile home or "building" or whatever had to go.

3. Aside from the question of mobile homes or modular structures, what about condominiums? When many sets of restrictive covenants were drafted, the concept of the condominium involving ownership of airspace and joint ownership of common areas was unknown. Yet as far as ownership of the condominium itself is concerned, it is arguably a single unit in the sense that it is an owned dwelling housing a single family. In Callahan v. Weiland, 291 Ala. 183, 279 So.2d 451 (1973), the Alabama Supreme Court was confronted with a situation involving deed restrictions which prevented maintaining an apartment house on the premises. Callahan wanted to construct a ten-story condominium on five lots in the subdivision. The provision also stated that "a single dwelling house with necessary outbuildings" was all that could be erected. The court held the proposed condominium to be an apartment house within the intent of the provisions since condominiums were unknown when the restrictions were written. The Alabama court was fully aware of the difference between a condominium and an apartment house but felt that any multi-unit dwelling was contrary to the intent of the restrictions. On this subject generally, see Annot., Use of Property for Multiple Dwellings as Violating Restrictive Covenant Permitting Property to Be Used for Residential Purposes Only, 99 A.L.R.3d 985 (1980); Annot., Erection of Condominium as Violation of Restrictive Covenant Forbidding Erection of Apartment Houses, 65 A.L.R.3d 1212 (1975); and Annot., Zoning or Building Regulations as Applied to Condominiums, 71 A.L.R.3d 866 (1976).

4. Enforcement cases quite often deal with definitions. In Turner v. England, 628 S.W.2d 213 (Tex.App.1982), the question was whether a concrete slab was a "structure" which the covenants prohibited. The concrete slab was actually a tennis court. After stating the settled law in Texas that restrictive covenants are to be strictly construed, and after citing cases from Utah, Pennsylvania and Massachusetts to the effect that tennis courts are not prohibited structures, the court held that a concrete slab for a tennis court would not violate the restrictive covenants.

5. Can or should the public get involved in how the covenants are enforced? In Home Builders Ass'n of Greater St. Louis v. City of St. Peters, 868 S.W.2d 187 (Mo.App.1994) the court upheld a city ordinance that required any new residential subdivision be encumbered by an indenture containing several minimum requirements, including that any subdivision have at least three subdivision managers, that subdivisions with covenants must assess a fee sufficient to enforce the covenants, and that each developer at the outset of his subdivision establish a trust account at a bank, deposit at least $2,000 in the account, and that after ten or more lots are sold a majority of the lot owners, other than the developer, may require the trustee of the trust account to reimburse them for the costs of enforcing covenants not enforced by the subdivision managers. What policy considerations do you discern behind such an ordinance?

HOFFMAN v. COHEN

Supreme Court of South Carolina, 1974.
262 S.C. 71, 202 S.E.2d 363.

LITTLEJOHN, JUSTICE:

This class action was instituted by the respondent, Ralph Hoffman, as Trustee, for a declaratory judgment holding that the proposed construction of a high-rise condominium apartment building, containing 62 dwelling units, upon certain lands owned by him in the Forest Dunes Subdivision of Myrtle Beach would not violate the restrictive covenants imposed upon that subdivision by its original developer. The defendants-appellants are lot owners in the subdivision and were made parties individually and as representatives of all other lot owners.

The issues were referred to the Master in Equity for Horry County, who recommended that the court declare that such a condominium is permissible under the applicable restrictions. His recommendation was accepted by the circuit court and incorporated into its order, from which this appeal is prosecuted by the defendants.

The Forest Dunes Subdivision was originally developed by Myrtle Beach Farms Company in 1941. It fronts on the Atlantic Ocean approximately 1900 feet, with a depth, running back to U.S. Highway No. 17, of approximately 1550 feet. A map of the subdivision indicates that there are approximately 185 lots, nearly all of which have a width of 75 feet and a depth of 150 feet. All but three of the 20 lots which front on the Atlantic Ocean have a width of 75 feet and a depth of approximately 260 feet. The property upon which the respondent proposes to build the

Sec. 3 **SERVITUDES AND RESTRICTIVE COVENANTS** **165**

condominium is composed of two beach-front lots, each 75 feet by 260 feet, plus an adjoining area designated "reserved", which is slightly larger than one of the platted lots. They lie in the southeastern corner of the subdivision, facing the strand and fronting on the ocean. It is uncontradicted that all deeds executed by the developer to all lots in Forest Dunes, including those owned by the respondent, contain the same restrictive covenants which provide in pertinent part as follows:

"a. No lot shall be subdivided and no residence or building, including porches and projections of any kind, shall be erected so as to extend beyond, over or across any of the building lines relating to said lot.

* * *

"c. This property shall be used for residential purposes only and any residence erected on the lot herein conveyed is to cost not less than Six Thousand ($6,000.00) Dollars or to be built according to plans and specifications approved by grantor hereof in writing by its proper officers.

* * *

"g. No lot shall be subdivided, or its boundary lines changed except with written consent of the grantor endorsed on the deed of conveyance thereof.

"h. The conditions, limitations, and restrictions hereinabove made shall be deemed covenants running with the land binding on both the grantor and grantee, their heirs, successors and assigns."

Single-family residences are the rule in the subdivision, the principal exception being a two-story building containing five separate dwelling units constructed upon the lot which lies immediately to the north of the respondent's property.

The respondent proposes to construct a building estimated to cost $3,000,000.00. The first floor would be partially underground and used for parking; the main, or ground floor, would have two apartments and a recreation room, manager's quarters and service areas. Above that would be 15 floors composed of four apartment units each. There would be two elevators in the building. Common facilities for the unit owners include a lobby, a recreation room, parking garage, elevators, hallways, foyer, utility rooms, swimming pool, shuffleboard courts and other related recreational facilities.

The appellants submit four questions for our determination. Under the view we take, we need answer only one basic inquiry: Would the proposed condominium violate the restrictions quoted hereinabove? We think that it would and, accordingly, reverse the order of the trial court.

Restrictive covenants are contractual in nature. The cardinal rule of construction in interpreting any contract is to ascertain and give effect to the intention of the parties. Such intent should, as nearly as possible, be gleaned from the instrument itself. *Nance v. Waldrop*, 258 S.C. 69, 187 S.E.2d 226 (1972).

The respondent asserts that the language in the restrictions in question is unambiguous. Because multi-family dwellings, including condominiums, clearly constitute a permissible use, his argument continues, there is no room for construction and no need to resort to matters outside the restrictions themselves. We disagree. We cannot say that reasonable men could not differ as to the meaning of the language employed.

The respondent argues that conventional apartment-type buildings are permitted under the restrictions and that the only difference between a conventional apartment house and a condominium-type of apartment building lies in the fact that normally an apartment building has one owner, whereas a condominium-type apartment building has many owners. He further urges that some three owners have built two living units on their lots and that one has built five units on his lot. The question of whether a conventional apartment-type building would be permitted in this subdivision is not before the Court at this time, but we cannot agree that there are no basic differences between a conventional apartment building and a condominium apartment building. We think that the building of 62 dwelling units on what amounts to approximately three building lots is entirely inconsistent with the overall scheme of the subdivision. Though a condominium is not strictly speaking a commercial project, it involves congestion and many of the undesirable characteristics incident to a commercial undertaking such as a hotel. It is common knowledge that beach residences, especially apartments (conventional or condominium), are often rented to temporary guests at least a part of the year. When so used in a building of this type, the property would become a commercial-type operation, inconsistent, we think, with the whole tenor of the restrictions.

The respondent correctly relies upon *Sprouse v. Winston*, 212 S.C. 176, 46 S.E.2d 874 (1948), for the proposition that restrictive covenants are to be construed most strictly against the grantor and persons seeking to enforce them. However, it was also held therein that "the rule will not be applied to defeat the obvious purpose of the restriction" and, before giving it effect, "the court will have recourse to every aid, rule, or canon of construction to ascertain the intention of the parties * * *." See also *Edwards v. Surratt*, 228 S.C. 512, 90 S.E.2d 906 (1956).

In construing covenants the circumstances surrounding their origin are proper considerations for a court when the language used is susceptible of more than one reasonable interpretation. * * * The concept of condominiums is relatively new to South Carolina; in fact, it was only eleven years ago that the "Horizontal Property Act" was enacted by our legislature. See 11 S.C.Code § 57–494 et seq. (Cum.Supp.1971). It is a virtual certainty that the question of whether condominiums should be permitted on this property was not even considered by the developer in 1941 when these restrictions were whelped. * * *

The Forest Dunes Subdivision is now a rather fully developed subdivision consisting almost exclusively of single-family residences. So far as the record shows no contest has been made concerning those lots whereon more than one residential unit has been constructed. The houses that have been constructed therein are rather substantial in size, with an average value of approximately $50,000.00.

The evidence warrants the conclusion that a general building scheme or plan of development founded on these restrictions has evolved in the area here in question. The [appellants] in this action and their predecessors in title have obviously relied upon the restrictions in buying and developing the property. The circumstances surrounding the inception of the restrictions and the developments subsequent thereto enforce the argument that the restrictions as drawn were designed and intended to prevent such uses as the [respondent proposes to make of his lots]. *Nance v. Waldrop, supra.*

Reversed.

Moss, C.J., and Lewis, J., concur.

Bussey and Brailsford, JJ., dissent. [Dissenting opinion omitted.]

Notes

1. Consider this: The covenants provided that no lot could be subdivided. In a condominium, there is a division of ownership with each landowner holding title to the airspace which constitutes his living area and with common ownership in such areas as the walls, the roof, the foundation, the elevators, stairs, recreation rooms, and so on. Could it be said that the nature of a condominium in and of itself produces divided ownership and thus "subdivides" the total landscape parcel? See Wright, The Law of Airspace 87–98 (1968).

2. Note that the City of Myrtle Beach had zoned this area so as to permit multiple-family dwellings, including condominiums. The question of conflicts or inconsistencies between zoning regulations and restrictive covenants is considered, infra. Recall this case when you arrive at that material.

3. If you owned a large lot in an exclusive residential area, which lot was irregularly shaped and situated on rugged terrain, and the area was limited by restrictive covenants to single-family dwellings, could you build a cluster of condominium townhouses on the property which were separated by an airspace in between each townhouse? Assume that the townhouses are quite attractive and that each sells at a price comparable to houses in the area. Assume also that this particular construction can make the most effective use of the land in question. What is the answer?

McDONALD v. CHAFFIN

Court of Appeals of Tennessee, Middle Section, 1975.
529 S.W.2d 54.

[Trustees of the West Meade Church of Christ purchased property in the West Meade Farms subdivision subject to the restrictive covenants filed of record. The covenants provided that only "a private dwelling house, or improvement in connection therewith" could be erected on the premises and specifically excluded certain uses, such as apartment houses and business structures and places "of public gathering." The plaintiffs, owners of property in the subdivision, alleged that defendants were using the property for church services and sought injunctive relief. Defendants admitted that they had met on the premises "in a private religious gathering." The Chancellor enjoined the defendants from using their property as a church on the basis that the premises were not being used as a private dwelling and were being used as a place of public gathering. The defendants appealed, alleging a violation of the First Amendment to the United States Constitution.]

DROWOTA, JUDGE.

Restrictive covenants are to be strictly construed. That is, they are to be read without the drawing of unnecessary implications and will not be taken to preclude that which is not plainly prohibited. *Shea v. Sargent*, 499 S.W.2d 871, 873 (Tenn.1973). But in reading the covenant we should give the words a fair and reasonable meaning in order to effectuate its purpose. *Hamilton v. Broyles*, 57 Tenn.App. 116, 415 S.W.2d 352 (1966).

We agree that any use of the subject property as a church building would constitute a violation of the applicable restrictive covenant. Such use is not for residential purposes, and we take judicial notice that such use would ordinarily entail regular public gatherings. This result is mandated by the plain meaning of the covenant and is consistent with the "complete accord" reached by the many other courts that have considered the question of the applicability to churches of covenants restricting property to residential use. See Annot., 13 A.L.R.2d 1239.

There is no bill of exceptions in this case and we find no proof in the record to contradict the Chancellor's finding that the building on the subject property was in fact used as a church and not as a residence, or that the worship services were public gatherings. It was conceded by appellants in oral argument that no one resides in the structure. Thus we are not faced with any issue involving the applicability of such restrictive covenants to persons conducting private religious worship services in their homes.

The remaining question is whether federal constitutional restrictions exist on the power of the Chancery Court to enforce the restrictive covenant in this case. The restrictive covenant here involved was expressly incorporated by reference into the deed conveying the property to defendants. As such the restriction originated purely in private conduct. It is not clear whether judicial enforcement of the private agreement, *in such a case as this*, ought to trigger constitutional restrictions designed to restrain action by the federal and state governments. Of course, the agreement rests upon state law recognizing the validity of such limitations on land use and requires for its effectiveness enforcement by the state. See *Shelley v. Kraemer*, 334 U.S. 1, 68 S.Ct. 836, 92 L.Ed. 1161

(1948) (court enforcement of a restrictive covenant excluding persons of designated race or color from the ownership or occupancy of real property constitutes state action).

Assuming, *arguendo*, the presence of state action, we find that court enforcement of the restrictive covenant does not violate the first amendment. Enforcement of a facially neutral restriction on the use of land for other than residential purposes works only an incidental or indirect burden on appellants no different from that borne by other property owners and does not rise to the level of a violation of their rights of assembly or free exercise of religion. See *Braunfeld v. Brown*, 366 U.S. 599, 81 S.Ct. 1144, 6 L.Ed.2d 563 (1961). In this circumstance, churches are on the same plane as other property owners with respect to the use of land. Because of the incidental nature of the restriction, we are not obligated to find a "compelling" state interest to support the restriction. Compare *Braunfeld v. Brown, supra*, with *Sherbert v. Verner*, 374 U.S. 398, 83 S.Ct. 1790, 10 L.Ed.2d 965 (1963).

We are not here faced with a situation in which persons are effectively restricted from establishing a place of worship due to a pervasive system of restrictive covenants or zoning throughout the area. Nor are we confronted with an attempt to secure the assistance of the state in the discriminatory enforcement of restrictions as between religions. The first amendment does not preclude reasonable regulation of the time, place, or manner of the exercise of constitutionally protected activities. *Jones v. Opelika*, 316 U.S. 584, 62 S.Ct. 1231, 86 L.Ed. 1691 (1942).

* * *

Affirmed.

Notes

1. Restrictive covenants, which expressly or by necessary implication exclude churches, have been upheld in the vast majority of cases. See, e.g., Hall v. Church of the Open Bible, 4 Wis.2d 246, 89 N.W.2d 798 (1958). This would also apply if an existing residence were altered in such a way as to provide for the conduct of church services. Matthews v. First Christian Church, 355 Mo. 627, 197 S.W.2d 617 (1946). For a discussion of some of the cases, see Note, Restrictive Covenants as a Device to Control Religious Uses, 12 Syracuse L.Rev. 347 (1961). Such a covenant has been enforced even though the zoning ordinance expressly permits churches. Abrams v. Shuger, 336 Mich. 59, 57 N.W.2d 445 (1953).

Sometimes the exclusion of churches is inadvertent as where a hasty draftsman writes "single family residential use only" without realizing that if the people who come to live in the new neighborhood later want a church there, releases will have to be obtained from possibly dozens of lot owners. Moreover, some of the owners may be infants, mental incompetents or absentee landlords. For a case which gets into this subject along with questions of changed conditions and acquiescence, see City of Houston v. Emmanuel United Pentecostal Church, 429 S.W.2d 679 (Tex.Civ.App.1968).

Also see Fitzwilliam v. Wesley United Methodist Church, 882 S.W.2d 343 (Mo.App.1994) where the words "residential use" in the restrictions were interpreted to allow a church that had purchased a lot with a house on it in the subdivision to tear down the house and put in a parking lot. A very similar case is Bagko Development Co. v. Damitz, 640 N.E.2d 67 (Ind.App. 1994) which interpreted "residential purposes" to allow a Little League practice field.

2. Occasional cases challenge such covenants as being violative of the First Amendment as did the principal case. In West Hill Baptist Church v. Abbate, 24 Ohio Misc. 66, 261 N.E.2d 196 (1969), a restrictive covenant was challenged on that basis. This court compared covenants to zoning and concluded that this was simply "private zoning or zoning by contract." It concluded that if a zoning ordinance is unconstitutional, then a restrictive covenant in the same area and to the same effect would be unconstitutional. It cited Shelley v. Kraemer with regard to state action and concluded that enforcement of the covenants against the church would violate the religious freedom guaranteed by the First Amendment. But unlike the Shelley case, which held it to be invalid to exclude people on the basis of race, this type of covenant does not seek to keep people out on any basis. It simply limits the *uses* in the subdivision. Moreover, it is fallacious to equate zoning (—a public exercise of the police power—) with private restrictive covenants which are a matter of contract and are non-discriminatory use limitations. The Abbate case was contrary to prior Ohio case law. Cleveland Baptist Association v. Scovil, 107 Ohio St. 67, 140 N.E. 647 (1923). On September 22, 2000, the President signed the Religious Land Use and Institutionalized Persons Act of 2000, Pub.L. No. 106–274, 42 U.S.C. § 2000 cc, et seq. which Congress enacted in order "[t]o protect religious liberty, and for other purposes." This statute, RLUIPA, limits governmental land use restrictions of religious uses to cases where there is a compelling public interest in the limitation. The lower federal courts, as of 2003, are divided on the constitutionality of the act. If it is ultimately upheld by the Supreme Court, do you think there would be a "spillover" effect to covenant cases?

3. Shelley v. Kraemer invalidated a racial restrictive covenant. The unenforceability and invalidity of racial restrictive covenants does not serve to invalidate the other covenants because they are severable. See, e.g., Skinner v. Henderson, 556 S.W.2d 730 (Mo.App.1977).

4. Enforcement of restrictive covenants to enjoin the building of a church can fail for reasons similar to those involving other, non-church situations. In Pinetree Estates Homeowners Association v. First United Lutheran Church, 241 Ga. 228, 244 S.E.2d 856 (1978), the homeowners were unable to enforce restrictive covenants against the church because they could not show that the church and any one of them had a common grantor bound by the covenants. The homeowners contended that the church had constructive notice. Could not the argument of the common scheme of development have been applied on behalf of the homeowners? The court does not discuss it.

5. Only rarely do courts have to consider whether a covenant is violative of public policy and thus unenforceable. One interesting case along this line is Davidson Bros., Inc. v. D. Katz & Sons, Inc., 274 N.J.Super. 159,

643 A.2d 642 (1994). The court found that a covenant prohibiting the use of the property for a supermarket was contrary to public policy because to enforce the covenant would reduce the necessary shopping services available to a large population of disadvantaged persons in New Brunswick, New Jersey.

ROFE v. ROBINSON
Supreme Court of Michigan, 1982.
415 Mich. 345, 329 N.W.2d 704.

LEVIN, JUSTICE.

This action concerns the enforceability of deed restrictions. Plaintiffs and defendants are property owners in the Hickory Knolls Subdivision. The deed restrictions provide that all buildings in the subdivision are to be restricted to residential, single-family use. Defendants, however, seek to construct three one-story office buildings on two of the lots in this subdivision. The front of these buildings would face plaintiffs' adjoining lots. Defendants, under the zoning ordinance, are required to build a six-foot wall along the border separating office use from residential use. Defendants' proposed site plans provide for parking along this wall. Plaintiffs brought this action seeking a permanent injunction enjoining defendants from developing their lots as office sites.

The trial court upheld the restrictions and issued the permanent injunction plaintiffs requested. The Court of Appeals reversed, finding a change in the character of the subdivision. We reverse the decision of the Court of Appeals, 99 Mich.App. 404, 298 N.W.2d 609, and remand for consideration of the issues the Court of Appeals found unnecessary to address.

Hickory Knolls Subdivision is triangular and consists of 45 lots. The subdivision is bounded by Telegraph Road on the east, Franklin Road on the west, and Hickory Grove Road on the south. Lots 1 through 12 are accessible only from Telegraph Road and comprise the eastern side of the triangle. Each of lots 1 to 12 is vacant, except lot 2. Until 1971, no commercial development occurred on any of the lots in the subdivision. However, in 1971, the residence on lot 2 was converted to office use. There has been no objection by the residents of the subdivision to the use of the building on lot 2 as an office.

In 1956, the subdivision was zoned for single-family residential use. In 1968, Bloomfield Township changed the zoning on lots 1 to 12 to the 0–1 classification, limiting construction to office buildings and prohibiting the construction of single-family residences.

* * *

Across from the Hickory Knolls Subdivision, on the other side of Telegraph Road, is the Hickory Grove Subdivision, a residential area. There is a berm separating this subdivision from Telegraph Road. The area along Telegraph Road north of Franklin Road is zoned for office development and consists of several office buildings. The land along

Telegraph Road south of Hickory Grove Road is vacant for some distance.

Plaintiffs argue that the deed restrictions should be enforced because the restrictions constitute a valuable property right and because there have been no changes in the subdivision to render enforcement of the restrictions inequitable.

Defendants contend that the restrictions are unenforceable because it is illegal (due to the rezoning) and impractical to build residences on lots 7 and 8. Defendants further contend that the character of the subdivision has changed so that it is inequitable to enforce the restrictions, citing factors such as rezoning, the use of the building on lot 2 as an office, the evolution of Telegraph Road, and the condemnation of 54 feet of lots 7 and 8 for the widening of Telegraph Road. We are not persuaded by these arguments.

Deed restrictions are property rights. The courts will protect those rights if they are of value to the property owner asserting the right and if the owner is not estopped from seeking enforcement.

Defendants argue that it is impractical to build residences on lots 7 and 8. They contend that a residence cannot be economically built or sold and that the deed restrictions will require the lots to remain permanently vacant and useless. Plaintiffs' witness testified that there is always a market for any property with appropriate price adjustments and lots 1 through 12 could be sold as residential lots.

Economic impracticability does not itself justify lifting building restrictions. Plaintiffs purchased their property, in apparent reliance on the deed restrictions, and defendants were on notice of the restrictions when they purchased their lots. This Court has long recognized that such restrictions create valuable property rights. "The right, if it has been acquired, to live in a district uninvaded by stores, garages, business and apartment houses is a valuable right." In *Cooper v. Kovan*, 349 Mich. 520, 530–531, 84 N.W.2d 859 (1957), this Court said:

> "Home owners seek, by purchasing in areas restricted to residential building, freedom from noise and traffic which are characteristic of business areas. How much in dollars the peace and quiet of this neighborhood is worth, or how much the contemplated major business invasion would diminish that value, would be hard to establish. But it is clear in our mind that residential restrictions generally constitute a property right of distinct worth."

The change in zoning does not support defendants' challenge to the validity of the deed restriction. If, as the defendants contend, the property as restricted is substantially valueless regardless of the zoning, then it is the deed restriction and not the zoning which brought about the loss of value.

Even if the zoning were relevant, it is well established in this state that a change in zoning cannot, by itself, override prior restrictions placed in deeds. Zoning laws determine property owners' obligations to the community at large but do not determine the rights and obligations of parties to a private contract. These are separate obligations, both of which may be enforceable.

Defendants next argue that the character of the subdivision has changed so that enforcement of the restrictions would be inequitable. In support of this claim, defendants cite factors such as rezoning, the use of lot 2 for business purposes, and the evolution and widening of Telegraph Road. However, the restrictions will not be lifted unless the character of the subdivision has changed in such a way as to subvert the original purpose of the restrictions. Because the character of the subdivision has not so changed, defendants are not entitled to relief on these grounds.

A change in zoning is not sufficient evidence of a change in the character of an area to require lifting residential restrictions. In *Brideau v. Grissom*, 369 Mich. 661, 668, 120 N.W.2d 829 (1963), this Court said that "[t]he change in the zoning ordinance cannot operate to destroy the obligations involved in the restrictions. * * * Such change is only a factor to be considered in determining whether a change of circumstances has occurred that an equity court will not enforce the restriction." In *Brideau*, this Court found the restriction to be enforceable in spite of the zoning change, because this Court was "unable to say that the original plan of development [had] been subverted by a change in the character and usage of the neighborhood." A change in zoning is thus only relevant if it is indicative of a change in the character of the area. Rezoning itself is not such a change.

We are also unpersuaded that use of one of the 45 lots for office purposes so changes the character of the subdivision as to render the restrictions inequitable. This structure was built as a residence and previously used as such, although now it is used for business purposes. The use of this building for office purposes has not materially changed the character of the subdivision. The subdivision has remained substantially residential.

Likewise, the evolution and widening of Telegraph Road does not justify lifting the restrictions. The widening of Telegraph Road has not changed the character of the subdivision. The subdivision is still substantially residential. Similarly, the evolution of Telegraph Road into a business district has not rendered enforceability of the restrictions inequitable, because the subdivision has not lost its character as a residential area. "The fact that substantial changes in the character of the neighborhood outside of the subdivision have taken place does not make it inequitable to enforce the restrictions." Furthermore, as this Court said in *Redfern Lawns Civic Ass'n. v. Currie Pontiac Co.*, 328 Mich. 463, 470, 44 N.W.2d 8 (1950), "there must of necessity be a dividing line somewhere".

Although there has been a change in the character of Telegraph Road, this change has not subverted the purpose of the residential restrictions so as to render enforcement of the restrictions inequitable.

We therefore reverse the decision of the Court of Appeals and remand for consideration of the issues regarding laches, waiver, and interpretation of the deed restrictions, which it found unnecessary to consider.

[The extensive footnotes of the court have been omitted.]

Notes

1. Also see Brown v. Morris, 279 Ala. 241, 184 So.2d 148 (1966). Unlike Rofe v. Robinson, this case involved a situation in which the land had been zoned commercial prior to imposition of the restrictive covenants. The result is the same. There is nothing to prevent a developer from imposing more restrictive limitations upon the use of his land than those imposed by the local government. Basically, restrictive covenants do not supersede zoning, nor does zoning by itself vitiate the restrictive covenants. Probably a fair approximation of the majority view is that if the covenant is less restrictive, the ordinance will prevail and if the covenant is more restrictive, the covenant will prevail. Neither is superseded nor eliminated; the more restrictive prevails.

As Rofe v. Robinson indicates, however, a carefully considered zoning amendment that is less restrictive than the covenants is some indication that the conditions in the restricted area may have changed to the point that the covenants should no longer be enforced in equity.

2. Compare the language in Rice v. Heggy, 158 Cal.App.2d 89, 322 P.2d 53 (1958): "Appellants stress the point that some of the property in question has been rezoned * * * since the making of the deed restrictions, and argue that this rezoning should override the restrictions. The contention is untenable and such rezoning by no means compelled the trial court to declare that appellants were entitled to construct multiple unit dwellings which would violate the deed restrictions." Does this mean that the deed restrictions take precedence or that the more restrictive of the two, whether zoning or the covenants, takes precedence?

3. In Grubel v. MacLaughlin, 286 F.Supp. 24 (D.V.I.1968), the court held that "the obligation of the plaintiffs under the restrictive covenant to use their land for residential purposes only has been extinguished by the zoning regulation which makes that use unlawful. Since * * * the zoning regulation is valid, it necessarily follows that the restrictive covenant in the plaintiffs' deed is unenforceable * * *." That does not find support in more than a handful of cases. The general rule is that zoning regulations do not supersede or vitiate lawful restrictive covenants in situations in which the restrictive covenants are more restrictive. See generally Allen v. Axford, 285 Ala. 251, 231 So.2d 122 (1969); G.M.L. Land Corp. v. Foley, 20 A.D.2d 645, 246 N.Y.S.2d 338 (1964), affirmed 14 N.Y.2d 823, 251 N.Y.S.2d 472, 200 N.E.2d 455 (1964). A zoning ordinance, in and of itself, does not render null and void an otherwise valid restrictive covenant or building limitation. Lamica v. Gerdes, 270 N.C. 85, 153 S.E.2d 814 (1967). See generally, Church, The Effect of Private Restrictive Covenants on Exercise of the Public Powers of Zoning and Eminent Domain, 1963 Wis.L.Rev. 321.

4. In City of Harrisburg v. Capitol Housing Corp., 117 Pa.Cmwlth. 408, 543 A.2d 620 (1988), a redevelopment contract was incorporated into a

vendor's deed restricting the use of the land in question to "residential private housing" for a period of forty years. Because of that, it was held that a proposed conveyance of the apartment building on the land to a nontaxable, governmental entity (the Pennsylvania Higher Education Assistance Agency) would violate such restriction and the sale was enjoined. The Commonwealth Court stated that the state agency did not have the authority to override a land use restriction incorporated into a deed.

5. The Restatement of Property, Third (Servitudes), § 7.10 takes a fairly liberal position on changed conditions, using the language, "When a change has taken place since the creation of a servitude that makes it impossible as a practical matter to accomplish the purpose for which the servitude was created, a court may modify the servitude ..." The Reporter's Note to that section catalogs a large number of cases dealing with the modification issue.

SILLS v. WALWORTH COUNTY LAND MANAGEMENT COMMITTEE

Court of Appeals of Wisconsin, 2002.
254 Wis.2d 538, 648 N.W.2d 878.

BROWN, J.

A group of neighborhood citizens appeals from a circuit court certiorari review upholding the grant of a conditional use permit (CUP) for the creation and operation of a public museum at Black Point Estate, a historic residence located on Geneva Lake. The neighbors contend that the Walworth County Land Management Committee erred as a matter of law by failing to consider the potential application of restrictive covenants limiting the use of the Black Point property as "first class residence property." This is an issue of first impression in Wisconsin. We share the view of other jurisdictions, however, that private contracts restricting the use of land are not grounds for denial of a CUP. While the Committee may, in its discretion, consider the potential application of private agreements, it is not under an obligation to do so.

* * *

The Black Point Estate is a well-preserved, thirteen-bedroom Queen Anne-style residence built in 1888, housing a valuable collection of period furnishings and art. The property was constructed as a family summer home by the great-grandfather of the current owner, William Petersen. The residence is listed on the National Register of Historic Places and the Wisconsin State Register. Described in testimony as a "time capsule," the residence today is in virtually the same condition as it was in the 19th century.

The Petersen family's plan to preserve the estate led to a proposal under which the State of Wisconsin would own Black Point, and a local nonprofit organization, Black Point Historic Preserve, Inc., would manage the site. To implement the plan, Petersen, the State of Wisconsin and the Black Point Historic Preserve, Inc., submitted an application for a CUP to the Committee. The Committee held two days of public hearings to consider the application. The record of the Committee's proceedings consists of nearly 2000 pages of reports, transcripts, letters and other correspondence. Much of the testimony concerned traffic safety, property values and conservation issues. The Committee approved the CUP application on May 23, 2000, subject to several conditions.

* * *

We begin our analysis with the neighbors' contention that the Committee erred by considering the historic benefit of Black Point Estate because the ordinance does not explicitly mention historic preservation in its statements of purpose and intent. * * * Therefore, according to the neighbors, preservation or historic benefit is not a valid criterion for evaluating a CUP application. However, the appropriateness of the Committee considering the preservation of Black Point as a historical site and as a museum is strongly supported by the ordinance, case law and statutes. * * *

[W]e are persuaded that the general welfare is promoted by the preservation of historical sites and maintenance of museums to educate the public and to inspire patriotism and respect for our history. Since this is an aspect of general welfare, the ordinance recognizes preservation or historic benefit as a valid criterion for evaluating a CUP application.

* * *

The neighbors contend that there is no assurance that the conditions governing the CUP will be enforced once the State takes ownership of the property since the State is not bound by local zoning. *See Green County v. City of Monroe,* 3 Wis.2d 196, 198, 87 N.W.2d 827 (1958). The Committee cites Wis. Stat. § 13.48(13) as a statutory exception to the common law rule that the State is not subject to local zoning. Relying on an attorney general's opinion, the neighbors respond that the statute applies only to property directly used by the State, such as office buildings, and not property held by the State for recreational purposes for the general public. *See* 81 Op. Att'y Gen. 9–93 at 58 (1993). We do not rule on the correct interpretation of § 13.48(13). Even if the neighbors are correct that the State is not subject to local zoning laws, we view this issue as an evidentiary matter for the Committee in its consideration of whether the evidence suggests that the State would not administer or oversee the property in a responsible manner. Our review of the record reveals no evidence that the State intends to back away from its commitment to the proposed use. * * *

The neighbors allege that Black Point Estate is subject to a private restrictive covenant that effectively trumps the County's authority to issue the CUP. The restrictive covenant dates back to 1910 and states in relevant part:

[T]hat no part or portion of the real estate herein before described ... shall at any time be occupied, sold or used by ... their heirs, executors, administrators, successors or assigns, for [a list of specified prohibited uses] any other use or purpose inconsistent with the maintenance and preservation of all and each and every part of said real estate herein before described, as first class residence property.

The Committee determined that it was not allowed as a matter of law to consider the restrictive agreement as part of the review process. The neighbors claim that this determination violated ORDINANCE § 1.5 which provides:

Except for the provisions of any ordinance enacted under Section 59.69, Wisconsin Statutes, relating to shorelands which are hereby superseded, it is not intended that this Ordinance repeal, abrogate, annul, impair or interfere with any existing easements, covenants, deed restrictions, agreements, ordinances, rules, regulations, or permits previously adopted or issued pursuant to law. However, wherever this Ordinance imposes greater restrictions, the provisions of this Ordinance shall govern.

According to the neighbors, ORDINANCE § 1.5 required the Committee to consider whether its approval of the CUP application effectively repealed, abrogated, annulled, impaired or interfered with the restrictive agreement and its prohibition against the use of Black Point estate for any purpose other than "first class residence property." This argument raises a broader issue of how the existence of private covenants impacts the administration of county zoning ordinances. We have not found a case in Wisconsin that directly addresses this point of law; however, the Committee has presented us with persuasive authorities supporting the principle that restrictive private covenants have no relevance to proceedings under the zoning laws.

* * *

The rule which we recognize here, that a private restrictive covenant is not grounds for denial of a proposed use, does not mean that parties to the covenant are without a remedy. When the terms of a zoning law conflict with those contained in restrictive covenants, the remedy for the breach is not through the zoning process but rather by an action for breach of covenant. * * *

We also agree with the Committee's position that enforcement of private restrictions via the county's zoning authority would constitute an impermissible delegation of the police power to private entities. In this case, the neighbors in effect are seeking to have the zoning committee apply the ordinance to prohibit an alleged violation of a restrictive covenant entered into by private parties back in 1910. If the Committee refused to grant the permit because of the restrictive agreement, the agreement would then have the force of law. The Committee has no authority to enforce private covenants in this manner; to do so would involve an improper delegation of the municipality's police power to private individuals. *See State ex rel. Sims v. Eckhardt,* 322 S.W.2d 903, 909–10 (Mo.1959) (discussing examples where ordinances which attempted to enforce private agreements were held to be void). To reiterate, the parties to a private restriction may challenge a use claimed to violate the restriction, even though that use may be permitted under the zoning ordinance, but they cannot ask the Land Management Committee to act as the enforcer.

* * *

To summarize, we conclude that the decision of the Committee in granting the CUP to Black Point Estate was based on substantial evidence. The Committee was not required to consider the applicability of the restrictive covenant in evaluating the CUP application. Finally, the neighbors failed to make a prima facie showing of an impermissibly high risk of bias to justify allowing additional discovery to supplement the certiorari record. We therefore affirm the circuit court's order and sustain the Committee's action in issuing a CUP to Black Point Estate.

Order affirmed.

Note

The cases you have seen in this section all involve judicial determinations on the validity or interpretation of restrictions. Another, more dramatic, enforcement issue arises when a property owner builds a structure and the neighbors seek to have it torn down because it violates a restriction. If the neighbors can get past equitable defenses, especially laches, the courts almost always enforce the covenant even if a new house has to be destroyed. See, for example, Heath v. Uraga, 106 Wash.App. 506, 24 P.3d 413 (2001) where a lot owner's house plans were rejected by the homeowner association as violative of a restriction on height, roof pitch, and interference with views. The lot owner built anyway and the trial court ordered the house torn down; the court of appeals affirmed.

(5) *Alteration and Termination*

HEFFNER v. LITCHFIELD GOLF CO.

Supreme Court of South Carolina, 1972.
258 S.C. 447, 189 S.E.2d 3.

BRAILSFORD, JUSTICE:

This is an appeal from an order of the circuit court denying an injunction against the proposed construction of tennis courts on two lots owned by the respondent, Litchfield Golf Company, Inc., hereinafter called Litchfield.

In 1969 the appellant purchased from Litchfield lot number 33, section E, as shown on the recorded plat of Litchfield Golf Club and subdivision. The recorded plat contained no restrictions on land use within the subdivision, which consists of 580 lots laid out with maximum exposure to the eighteen hole golf course and related facilities. However,

Sec. 3   **SERVITUDES AND RESTRICTIVE COVENANTS**   **179**

all conveyances of lots within the subdivision, including the conveyance to appellant, have contained identical provisions, twenty in number, which impose limitations on the use of the lot conveyed. The first provision restricts the lot to residential use. The twentieth provision, at the heart of the case, reads:

> It is understood and agreed that these covenants, conditions and restrictions are made solely for the benefit of the Grantor and Grantee herein and may be changed at any time by mutual consent in writing of the parties hereto, their heirs, successors or assigns.

Lots 30, 31 and 32 of section E had been sold by Litchfield before the appellant purchased lot 33. These four lots front on serpentine Eagle Avenue which meanders between the eighth and ninth holes, the club-house area, the fifth, sixth and seventh holes, the practice range and the tennis court area. A total of thirty-three lots front on this street. Twenty-eight of these, including lots 30–33, abut directly on the golf course. Lot 30 is the westernmost of the four lots, and it is bounded by the tennis court area on the west. Sometime after the appellant completed construction of an expensive home on his lot, Litchfield reacquired lots 30 and 31 and made known its intention to expand the club's tennis court area by utilizing lots 30 and 31. The appellant, whose home is separated from the existing courts by lots 30–32, each fronting one hundred feet on Eagle Avenue, contends that these lots are burdened with restrictions which preclude the intended use.

Because of the express limitation contained in the above quoted provision of the indenture, appellant has no standing to enforce the restrictive covenants imposed upon lots 30 and 31 on the occasion of their original sale by Litchfield. Litchfield and the grantees in that deed reserved to themselves the right to modify the restrictions imposed on the use of the lots, and Litchfield presently stands simultaneously as original grantor and as successor to the original grantees of those lots. Hence, the covenant, as such, does not bar the intended use of the premises by Litchfield.

Appellant's suit must fail unless it is supported by the doctrine of reciprocal negative easements by implication, which has been expounded in a number of our decisions * * *.

* * *

Mutuality of covenant and consideration, which are essential to the existence of a general scheme of development enforceable, inter se, by the purchasers of lots in a subdivision, may be implied only when the common grantor manifests his intention to subject the parcels conveyed to common restrictions for the benefit of all grantees. By the express terms of the twentieth provision, uniformly included in the Litchfield deeds, the benefit of the restrictions in each is limited to the parties thereto, who reserve the right to modify or abrogate by mutual assent. This directly precludes an implication that the grantor intended to create restrictions for the benefit of all purchasers in the subdivision. By near unanimous authority, no enforceable general scheme of development is inferable in the face of a provision of this tenor. See the cases collected at 19 A.L.R.2d 1274, 1282 (1951), and 4 A.L.R.3d 570, 573 (1965); 26 C.J.S. Deeds § 167(2) at 1145 (1956); 20 Am.Jur.2d, Covenants, Conditions, and Restrictions, Sec. 178 (1965); *Humphrey v. Beall*, 215 N.C. 15, 200 S.E. 918 (1939); *Brighton by the Sea, Inc. v. Rivkin*, 201 App.Div. 726, 195 N.Y.S. 198 (1922).

* * *

Affirmed.

Notes

1. Regardless of whether both parties have the power to release the lots from the restriction or the subdivider reserves the right to release remaining lots from the burden, the courts generally have been quick to say that there is no general plan and the restriction may not be enforced. See Suttle v. Bailey, 68 N.M. 283, 361 P.2d 325 (1961); and Maples v. Horton, 239 N.C. 394, 80 S.E.2d 38 (1954). And see Bride v. Finegan, 226 Md. 356, 174 A.2d 70 (1961) refusing to find a general development plan where covenants said the subdivider must consent to further subdivision of parcels. In Brighton by the Sea v. Rivkin, 201 App.Div. 726, 195 N.Y.S. 198 (1922), the plaintiff, who owned 10 blocks of land, developed it by erecting 300 dwellings. The deeds to each lot, including the one to the defendant, bound the grantee not to conduct any trade or business on the lot. But the grantor was not bound by the covenants in these deeds to restrict all of the lots in like manner. Further, power to alter or modify or annul any of the restrictions by agreement with the owner of the particular lot was expressly reserved in the grantor. The grantor sought to enjoin defendant from conducting a business on her lot without grantor's consent. The court said: "The provisions reserving grantor control over the restrictions prevented any mutuality of covenant and consideration between the grantees, and marked the covenant as being for the benefit of the grantor." The court held that there should be no interim decree of specific performance, and that whether one should ultimately issue or not should await full trial of the action so the court could determine whether specific performance was "equitable" under all the circumstances. In Baldwin v. Barbon Corp., 773 S.W.2d 681 (Tex.App.1989) the court held that a developer who had expressly reserved the right to amend or alter the covenants was authorized to remove residential restrictions on some of the lots (he still owned several lots in the subdivision).

2. It is not uncommon to find a provision in the restrictive covenants stating that provisions in them may be amended or modified by a writing signed by a substantial percentage of the lot owners in the subdivision (normally anywhere from 60% to 75%). Of course, these are sometimes written in an ambiguous way. See Pearce v. Scarcello, 920 S.W.2d 643 (Mo.App.1996). The original covenants required wooden shingles on roofs. Seven houseowners replaced their shingles with non-wooden material, after a majority of the homeowners filed amended covenants with the Recorder of Deeds. The court said the covenant had not been properly amended and ordered the removal of the shingles. Poor drafting creates most of the

ambiguity problems; for example, the covenants state that they are to run for 30 years, after which time they shall be automatically extended for 10 year periods unless a majority of the owners record an agreement to change the covenants. This fairly common language creates a problem of interpretation, i.e., can the owners modify the covenants during the first 30 years, or only during the 10 year periods? In several cases the courts have said that the covenants cannot be changed during the initial period, even though that may not be what the grantor contemplated. See, e.g., Boyles v. Hausmann, 2 Neb.App. 388, 509 N.W.2d 676 (Neb.App.1993) and Kauffman v. Roling, 851 S.W.2d 789 (Mo.App.1993).

If restrictive covenants serve to create an interest in land, how can that interest be violated or limited by a majority vote of the landowners? Once a property interest has been created, even if there is only one dissenter to some change affecting that interest, is it not a taking of his property to make the change? Obviously, the concept that the change may be made, based upon provisions in the restrictive covenants, draws upon their contractual heritage.

3. In Finucan v. Coronet Homes, Inc., 259 S.C. 142, 191 S.E.2d 5 (1972), the South Carolina Supreme Court reversed a lower court ruling that held that owners of lots in the original 1957 subdivision had no standing to enforce covenants pertaining to a 1960 addition to the subdivision. The 1957 subdivision had 38 lots in it, and the covenants were subject to change by a majority of the lot owners. The 1960 addition had identical restrictive covenants, and the court believed that the 1960 plat plus the original 38 lots constituted one subdivision, and that change could be effected only by a majority of the entire (1957 and 1960) subdivision.

WEST ALAMEDA HEIGHTS HOMEOWNERS ASS'N v. BOARD OF COUNTY COMMISSIONERS OF JEFFERSON COUNTY

Supreme Court of Colorado, 1969.
169 Colo. 491, 458 P.2d 253.

[This was a class action by the homeowners association and certain individuals to enjoin the construction of two large shopping facilities on the property in question by Woolworth and Safeway. The covenants restricted the use of the land to residential, and the trial court declared the covenants null and void. The subdivision was a large one of over 350 lots, only 80 to 85 of which were undeveloped. The only commercial uses were a service station and a garden center located on land originally reserved in the plat for commercial use. Apartments were on other land set aside for commercial purposes. The proposed shopping facilities would be on residential land as restricted by the covenants. The action was precipitated by an application by George Newton, the original developer, to re-zone part of the blocks retained by him which front on a four-lane highway. Outside of the subdivision and close by, there had been extensive commercial development. The trial court invalidated the covenants on the basis that the character of the area had changed and that the subject land was not suitable for residential use and thus enforcement of the covenants would not be equitable.]

DAY, JUSTICE

* * *

The pertinent rule of law applicable to this case is most recently set out in *Zavislak v. Shipman*, 147 Colo. 184, 362 P.2d 1053, wherein this court adopted the language of *McArthur v. Hood Rubber Co.*, 221 Mass. 372, 109 N.E. 162, as follows:

> " ' * * * When the purpose for which the restriction was imposed has come to an end, and where the use of the tract of land for whose benefit it was established has so utterly changed that no party to the bill could be heard to enforce it in equity or would suffer any damage by its violation, * * * a proper case is made out for equitable relief. * * * ' "

Parties plaintiffs and defendants all rely on our pronouncement in *Zavislak*. The court, in striking down the covenants, attempted to apply the same rule of law. We hold, however, that the court misconceived and misapplied the rule to changes and developments outside of and beyond the subdivision itself. This is made evident by the court's reference to the changed traffic patterns on Wadsworth and Alameda and the development of Villa Italia Shopping Center and other developments east of the Alameda and Wadsworth intersection.

The true test here, however, as to whether the purpose of the restrictions has come to an end, is the development of the subdivision which is the subject of the covenants subsequent to their creation. Thus the courts look to whether the original purposes of insuring maintenance of residential character for the subdivision has been abandoned or changed by acquiescence or passiveness of the subdivision residents.

Newton, in planning the property with the restrictions which he imposed, intended to insure the maintenance of the residential character for the subdivision. That purpose has continued to the present time, and the effect of it is demonstrated by what has happened to land outside of its perimeter over which the West Alameda Heights residents had no control. It is undisputed that in the subdivision wherein the covenants did control no change of the use contemplated when the plat was filed has occurred. Only the property originally platted for use of commercial enterprises thereon has been occupied as such.

Another test announced in the *Zavislak* case is whether the parties would suffer any damage by the removal of the covenant. Touching on this phase the testimony of the individual plaintiffs was that their property would be subject to substantial decrease in value. One of plaintiffs' witnesses—a professional land planner—depicted the foreseeable increase in traffic to and from the proposed shopping facility with concomitant increase in noise, fumes, and hazard to children. The Traffic and Safety Engineer for Jefferson County stated that although he probably could control increased traffic through the residential area by the use of traffic signals and one-way streets, he candidly admitted that such a traffic pattern would inconvenience the homeowners as much as it might deter shoppers from driving through the area. There was testimony as to the present pleasant aspects of the neighborhood, undisturbed by the commercial activity beyond the borders.

Contrariwise, the defendants did not prove that the purpose of the protective covenants had come to an end; that the land use within the tract had changed from what it was intended to be at the time the plat was filed; and that no person would suffer any damage by its violation. The evidence therefore is contrary to the court's finding that plaintiffs will suffer no damage from commercial use of the subject property.

Cases are numerous from other jurisdictions wherein covenants have been sought to be removed because subject lands would be more valuable for commercial than for residential purposes, and wherein there were conditions such as the presence of commercial uses nearby, heavy street traffic on the perimeter of the tract, and some commercial property within a primarily residential subdivision. But the weight of authority supports the view that *changes outside* of the tract will not warrant the lifting of restrictive covenants affecting property within the subdivision if the covenants are still a benefit to the owners of the property under the restrictions. *Robertson v. Nichols*, 92 Cal.App.2d 201, 206 P.2d 898; *Batman v. Creighton*, 101 So.2d 587 (Fla.App.); *Cawthon v. Anderson*, 211 Ga. 77, 84 S.E.2d 66; *Redfern Lawns Civic Ass'n, et al. v. Currie Pontiac Co.*, 328 Mich. 463, 44 N.W.2d 8; *Weinstein v. Swartz*, 3 N.J. 80, 68 A.2d 865; *Chuba v. Glasgow*, 61 N.M. 302, 299 P.2d 774; *Frey v. Poynor*, 369 P.2d 168 (Okla.); *Pitts v. Brown*, 215 S.C. 122, 54 S.E.2d 538; *Bullock v. Steinmil Realty, Inc.*, 1 Misc.2d 46, 145 N.Y.S.2d 331, aff'd 3 A.D.2d 806, 161 N.Y.S.2d 602.

Normal growth and change and the possibility of encroachment of commercial uses, we can infer, were contemplated when the covenants and the master plan of development were created by the original owner and platter. There would be no need for the covenants to protect the subdivisions from inroads of commercial expansion if it were not expected that such might take place. As long as the original purpose of the covenants can still be accomplished and substantial benefit will inure to the restricted area by their enforcement, the covenants stand even though the subject property has a greater value if used for other purposes. See 4 A.L.R.2d 1111.

A comment in *Cowling v. Colligan*, 158 Tex. 458, 312 S.W.2d 943, appeals to us:

"The reasoning of the courts is that if because of changed conditions outside the restricted area one lot or tract were permitted to drop from under the protective cover of residential-only restrictions, the owner of the adjoining lot would then have an equal claim on the conscience of the court, and, in due course, all other lots would fall like tenpins, thus circumventing and nullifying the restriction and destroying the essentially residential character of the entire area."

In the case of protective covenants, it has sometimes been held that changes within the affected area may result in modification or removal of the covenant because the changes were within the control of those entitled to enforce the covenant. In other words, the doctrines of abandonment, estoppel and waiver are applicable. *See Thodos v. Shirk*, 248 Iowa 172, 79 N.W.2d 733; *Mechling v. Dawson*, 234 Ky. 318, 28 S.W.2d 18; *Greer v. Bornstein*, 246 Ky. 286, 54 S.W.2d 927; *Tull v. Doctors Bldg. Inc.*, 255 N.C. 23, 120 S.E.2d 817. However, as to changes in conditions occurring outside the area restricted, the parties affected have no control whatever, and the doctrines of waiver, abandonment and estoppel are not applicable. Here, the problem presents itself as to whether the outside conditions affect the entire subdivision in a way that the restrictive purposes of the protective covenants would be defeated. As stated in *Thodos v. Shirk, supra*:

> "In both cases the factual situation largely governs as to whether or not equity will refuse to enforce the restrictions for the reason that by so doing the result would be oppressive and inequitable without any appreciable value to other property in the restricted area. It has been said that in order for this equitable defense of change of conditions to arise, there must be a change in the character of the surrounding neighborhood sufficient to make it impossible any longer to secure in substantial degree the benefits sought to be realized through the performance of the building restriction."

The construction of Villa Italia Shopping Center and of other commercial properties outside of West Alameda Heights, but in close proximity to it, have not changed the residential character of the subdivision. If the changed conditions outside the tract have made the particular property held by the owner since the original platting less desirable for residential use than it previously was, this is not to say that the whole tract has been made unfit for residential use. On the contrary, the evidence shows that the subdivision is a residential area of high quality, with expensive homes and quiet streets. The construction of commercial facilities nearby are all the more reason why the covenants for West Alameda Heights must be strictly enforced. The covenants have no meaning if external forces and pressures result in their removal.

The judgment is reversed and the cause remanded to the trial court with directions to enter a permanent injunction as prayed for in the complaint.

Notes

1. In Redfern Lawns Civic Ass'n v. Currie Pontiac Co., 328 Mich. 463, 44 N.W.2d 8 (1950), cited in the principal case, the Michigan court said: "The only equitable consideration in the case at bar appears to be the undesirability of using the lots in question for resident purposes. On this point it may be observed that there must of necessity be a dividing line somewhere. The original subdividers made no provision for possible business lots along Grand River avenue. It is inevitable that all lots on the fringe of a residential district may, with the changes of the surrounding neighborhood,

become a buffer between the residential area and a business or commercial area. It is one of the factors inherent in considering the nature and value of such property. To lift the restriction under consideration here on the lots in question would only cut down this desirable residential area and create another buffer area. To permit the dividing line to be moved in the case at bar thereby creating another buffer district, now composed of both residences and vacant property, does not present sufficiently strong equitable considerations."

2. There have been a good many of these change of character cases in recent years, and the problem usually comes from the effect of the commercialization of nearby property on border or buffer lots (as illustrated by the principal case). What if reasonable minds might differ on whether a change in character has occurred? In Semachko v. Hopko, 35 Ohio App.2d 205, 301 N.E.2d 560 (1973), the court stated that "reasonable minds can come to different conclusions whether there was a substantial change in the character of the neighborhood * * * so as to nullify the deed restrictions * * *. Under such circumstances, a court of equity will not enforce such restriction." Do you agree? In Albino v. Pacific First Fed. Sav. and Loan Ass'n, 257 Or. 473, 479 P.2d 760 (1971), the Oregon court said that in order to refuse to enforce the restrictions "the effect of the change upon the restricted area" must be "such as to 'clearly neutralize the benefits of the restrictions to the point of defeating the object and purpose of the covenant' " and that it is not enough that because of external changes the restricted residential area may now be more valuable for commercial purposes. In Inabinet v. Booe, 262 S.C. 81, 202 S.E.2d 643 (1974), it was stated that the changes must be "so radical as to practically destroy the essential objectives and purposes of the agreement." See similarly, Murphey v. Gray, 84 Ariz. 299, 327 P.2d 751 (1958); Eilers v. Alewel, 393 S.W.2d 584 (Mo.1965); and Paschen v. Pashkow, 63 Ill.App.2d 56, 211 N.E.2d 576 (1965). In Chesterfield Meadows Shopping Center Associates, L.P. v. Smith, 264 Va. 350, 568 S.E.2d 676 (2002), a covenant drawn to protect an historic house was terminated. The court stated: " * * * the chancellor, relying particularly upon the testimony of Judge Gates, found that the primary purpose of the 1979 restrictive covenant was to protect Wrexham Hall against commercial development of property in the area in which it was then located and 'to some extent' to protect one other historic property. After noting that Wrexham Hall had been relocated and replaced by Chesterfield's shopping center, the chancellor further found that much of the surrounding area had been 'transformed [from] once serene farmland, to a thriving commercial area.' Based upon this change in local conditions, the chancellor concluded that 'the essential objects and purposes of the [covenant] are practically destroyed, and the covenant is null and void.' " The supreme court affirmed.

3. How long will a restrictive covenant endure, assuming no express time limitation, no change in the character of the neighborhood or other reason for denial of judicial enforcement? The rule against restraints on alienation is chiefly concerned with limitations on *estates* in land, not with promises respecting the use of land. See Restatement of Property § 394 (1944). And the same can be said of the Rule against Perpetuities. A comment under section 399 of the Restatement says that any "undesirable freezing of a locality into a mode of use unsuited to social interests" can be

prevented by rules developed in equity without calling on the Rule against Perpetuities. The common assumption that covenants are limited to 25, or 30, or 99 years or some other magical period is not justified as a matter of case law. There are so-called "clearing statutes" in some states. In Wisconsin, for example, Wis.Stat.Ann. § 893.15(5) (1966) limits such restrictions to 60 years, unless renewed by fresh recording. Some states limit the duration to 20 or 30 years. Ga.Code Ann. § 29–301 (1980) and Minn.Stat.Ann. § 500.20 (1947). See also N.Y.Law Revision Commissioners Report 691–780 (1951). And recall the Uniform Act Relating to Reverter of Realty previously noted. Clearing statutes are discussed in Ascher, Urban Redevelopment: Problems and Practices 258–260 (1953), and Clark, Real Covenants and Other Interests Which "Run with Land" 199 (2d ed. 1947).

4. But quite apart from the maximum legal life of a restriction on the use of land, there is the practical problem of the draftsman—should he impose on the land a restriction for the indefinite future? Or should he place an express time limitation on the restriction? Or should he provide for a community association and either give it power to renew the restriction at the end of a designated period by affirmative action, or power to permit the restriction automatically to renew itself by non-action? Note the technique suggested in the FHA outline of protective covenants. The nature of the restriction is of major importance in considering questions like this. Imposing the "wrong kind" of restrictions on land for the indefinite future has often brought criticism of all restrictions and explains the movement for clearing statutes. Yet a lot owner may want the "right kind" of restrictions to continue indefinitely. The resolution of this conundrum may lie not in clearing statutes or even in case law, but in governmental administrative or judicial review procedures yet uninvented. One other thing about clearing statutes: When does the clearing period start? If it starts with the imposition of restrictions on the particular lot, then it may happen that restrictions expire on your lot long before they do on your neighbor's.

In England and in at least one American state, statutes provide for special actions for removal of restrictions imposed by covenants. The English statute permits an action in the Lands Tribunal and discharge or modification of a restrictive covenant on (1) a showing of change in character of the property or the neighborhood, or (2) a showing that the proposed discharge or modification will not injure the persons entitled to the benefit of the restriction. Volume 7 of the Planning and Compensation Reports of the Land Tribunal (1957) reports numerous cases on discharge and modification of covenants under Subsection (1) of section 84 of the Law of Property Act of 1925. See Preston and Newsom, Restrictive Covenants Ch. 7 (3d ed. 1960); N.Y.Real Property Actions & Proc.Law § 1951 (McKinney 1979); and Abbott, Statutory Provisions for the Modification and Discharge of Restrictive Covenants Affecting Freehold Lands, 18 Faculty L.Rev. 141 (1958). See also an article in 110 Solicitors' Journal 521 (1966) on The Law Commission and Restrictive Covenants.

An annotation discussing the validity and effect of *contractual* provisions relating to the revocation or modification of covenants is found in Annot., 4 A.L.R.3d 570 (1965). These contractual provisions may place the power to revoke or modify in the original owner or subdivider, the grantees or lot owners, or revocation or modification may be dependent on the happening of certain described occurrences. The annotator notes a trend toward the vesting of such powers in the owners or toward allowing the lot owners to participate with the developer in this process.

5. Equitable defenses can be employed in modification or termination cases, such as acquiescence, waiver and laches. In Underwood v. Webb, 544 S.W.2d 187 (Tex.Civ.App.1976), a violation on two lots in a 493 lot development was considered insufficient to eliminate the restriction. In Hargroder v. City of Eunice, 341 So.2d 463 (La.App.1976), there was no waiver of the limitation to residential use by the erection of numerous storage sheds in violation of the restriction. On the other hand, if landowners stand by for an unreasonable length of time while erection of the violating structure takes place, laches may preclude them from suing. Weinstein v. Tariff, 356 Mass. 738, 255 N.E.2d 595 (1970). Estoppel may also apply, as it did in Kelly v. Lovejoy, 172 Mont. 516, 565 P.2d 321 (1977), where the landowners purchased their land knowing that their neighbors were keeping horses in violation of the restrictions. (It was also deemed that they acquiesced in the horses being there.)

6. There may also be termination based on relative hardship, although the covenant will be enforced if the community benefits derived are deemed to be greater. Gaskin v. Harris, 82 N.M. 336, 481 P.2d 698 (1971).

7. The question of the monetary value of the property with and without the restrictions may enter in, as it did in Hunter v. Pillers, 464 S.W.2d 939 (Tex.Civ.App.1971), in which the appraised value of residential property of $52,800 was lowered to $7,800 due to the construction of an interstate highway adjacent to the land and the owner had an offer to sell at $85,000 if the restrictions were cancelled.

8. Duration of the restrictive covenants is obviously a problem (which leads to "change in circumstances" cases), and in states in which no statutory provisions limit the duration and the covenants themselves do not limit the duration, the indefinite duration of the restrictions is not deemed unreasonable and unenforceable per se. See Moore v. Smith, 443 S.W.2d 552 (Tex.1969). It is a better practice in such states to provide for automatic expiration of the covenants after a period of years, such as 25, or to provide for automatic extension for successive periods after that unless cancelled by a majority of the landowners. Care to avoid ambiguities in drafting is essential, however, as illustrated by Leaver v. Grose, 563 P.2d 773 (Utah 1977).

9. If there is a division of a benefited estate, is the covenant destroyed? See Old Dominion Iron & Steel Corp. v. Virginia Elec. and Power Co., 215 Va. 658, 212 S.E.2d 715 (1975).

(6) Community Associations as Private Governments

The popularity of condominium developments, retirement communities, planned unit developments and even new towns has created a number of legal issues, some of which have already been touched on in this chapter. All of these modern types of large scale residential developments utilize restrictive covenants to set the parameters of land uses, and most of them rely on a property owners association or community association to govern the rules created by the covenants, and to make new rules through a procedure set forth in the covenants. Frequently, conflict arises where the association is seeking to enforce the covenant against one owner. In some respects, especially in larger covenant-ruled communities, the association takes on the role of a private government with many powers; and, in running the association, the question of such niceties as "constitutional rights" is often invoked.

In an article in the Wall Street Journal, Sept. 22, 1994, p. 1, Mitchell Pacelle, a staff reporter for the newspaper, reports on a number of disputes between owners and associations and also on the spread of this sort of private government: "About 100,000 of the roughly 300,000 dwelling units in Montgomery County, an affluent expanse of suburban Washington that includes Rockville, are ruled by community associations, including nearly all newly built homes. * * * [An owner's] yard and home are very much the business of the association, a private, government-like body that enforces strict rules about everything from paint and storm doors to sandboxes and birdhouses." In 2003 an article by Associated Press reporter Jim Wasserman reported that some 249,000 homeowners associations with an estimated 50 million people exist nationally, and up to 8,000 new associations are created each year. Wasserman's article described a dispute between a homeowner in Gold River, California who took down his American flag and raised a United Nations flag to protest the war in Iraq, and the homeowners association that ordered him to remove it. http://beta.kpix.com/news/ap/APTV/State/CA/n/CA-HomeownerAssociati-kn.html.

Lawyers consulted on disputes between owners and associations often turn to the Community Associations Institute, an organization that provides publications and a great deal of information. See the Institute website: http://www.caionline.com/.

Many of the disputes over covenant enforcement stem from antagonisms among neighbors and only occasionally are those antagonisms strong enough that a client will invest in legal fees and court costs in an attempt to challenge the association. However, the number of people willing to do so is growing steadily. The lawyer's role in these battles should go beyond counseling about the law of covenants; she should look to the real issues of life that led to the standoff and be willing to counsel clients thoughtfully about matters other than legalities.

One case that generated much comment was Nahrstedt v. Lakeside Village Condominium Association, Inc., 8 Cal.4th 361, 33 Cal.Rptr.2d 63, 878 P.2d 1275 (1994). A homeowner in a 530-unit condominium complex sued to prevent the association from enforcing a restriction against the keeping of animals in any unit in the development. She alleged that the restriction was unreasonable as applied to her because she kept her three cats indoors, they made no noise, and were in no way a nuisance; she also sought damages for invasion of privacy and emotional distress. The intermediate appellate court divided, as did the California Supreme

Court. The majority opinion contains an extensive guide to the history of associations, now generally called "common interest developments." The opinion concluded that as a matter of policy it would be unwise for courts to review restrictions on a case-by-case "as applied" basis because that "would impose substantial litigation costs on the owners through their homeowners association, which would have to defend not only against owners contesting the application of the [covenants] to them, but also against owners contesting any case-by-case exceptions the homeowners association might make. In short, it is difficult to imagine what could more disrupt the harmony of a common interest development than the course proposed by the dissent." The dissenting opinion stressed the values of pet ownership, the fact that the plaintiff's cats were never outside her unit (they were only discovered by neighbors peering into her window), and said this about the underlying issues of private government:

> Our true task in this turmoil is to strike a balance between the governing rights accorded a condominium association and the individual freedom of its members. To fulfill that function, a reviewing court must view with a skeptic's eye restrictions driven by fear, anxiety, or intolerance. In any community, we do not exist in vacuo. There are many annoyances we tolerate because not to do so would be repressive and place the freedom of others at risk.
>
> In contravention, the majority's failure to consider the real burden imposed by the pet restriction unfortunately belittles and trivializes the interest at stake here. Pet ownership substantially enhances the quality of life for those who desire it. When others are not only undisturbed by, but completely unaware of, the presence of pets being enjoyed by their neighbors, the balance of benefit and burden is rendered disproportionate and unreasonable, rebutting any presumption of validity. Their view, shorn of grace and guiding philosophy, is devoid of the humanity that must temper the interpretation and application of all laws, for in a civilized society that is the source of their authority. As judicial architects of the rules of life, we better serve when we construct halls of harmony rather than walls of wrath.

The court remanded the case to the court of appeals to determine whether the covenant was reasonable, "not by reference to facts that are specific to the objecting homeowner, but by reference to the common interest development as a whole." The court also said that the recorded covenant is presumed reasonable "and will be enforced uniformly against all residents of the common interest development unless the restriction is arbitrary, imposes burdens on the use of lands it affects that substantially outweigh the restriction's benefits to the development's residents, or violates a fundamental public policy."

Some other cases in the same vein are Hidden Harbour Estates v. Basso, 393 So.2d 637 (Fla.App.1981) (the court drew a distinction between association rules in the recorded covenants and those imposed by the association board of directors, according more judicial review to rules not in the covenants); Noble v. Murphy, 34 Mass.App.Ct. 452, 612 N.E.2d 266 (1993). In Woodmoor Improvement Association v. Brenner, 919 P.2d 928 (Colo.App.1996) the court held that a homeowner could keep his satellite dish despite a covenant against outside aerials or antennas, because the architectural committee of the association had approved his plans, thus creating an estoppel against the association. Also see, Uriel Reichman, Residential Private Governments: An Introductory Survey, 43 U. Chi. L. Rev. 253 (1976); Robert G. Natelson, Consent, Coercion, and "Reasonableness" in Private Law: The Special Case of the Property Owners Association, 51 Ohio State L. J. 41 (1990); Comment, Beyond Nahrstedt: Reviewing Restrictions Governing Life in a Property Owner Association, 42 UCLA L. Rev. 837 (1995).

Chapter 6 of the Restatement of Property, Third (Servitudes) is entitled Common–Interest Communities. Sections 6.1 to 6.21 of the Restatement are devoted to the topic. In the Introductory Note, the Restatement says:

> This Chapter covers the increasingly important body of law governing residential common-interest communities and their associations. This relatively new and rapidly growing body of law, known to specialists in the field as "community association law," applies to a significant percentage of American housing.

> * * *

> There are important public interests at stake in the law governing common-interest communities. They provide an increasing share of the housing available to Americans at all income levels. * * *

> The law of residential common-interest communities reflects these tensions between protecting freedom of contract, protecting private and public interests in security of the home both as a personal base and as a financial asset, and protecting the public interest in the ongoing financial stability of common-interest communities. It also reflects the tensions between protecting the democratic process at work in common-interest communities and protecting the interests of individual community members from imposition by those who control the association.

Are homeowners in condominiums immune from those who would assert constitutional rights, if doing so would violate a covenant? This interesting question was presented in a New Jersey case, Guttenberg Taxpayers and Rentpayers Association v. Galaxy Towers Condominium Association, 296 N.J.Super. 101, 686 A.2d 344 (1995) affirmed, after remand 297 N.J.Super. 309, 688 A.2d 108 (1996). The covenant in this case seemed to bar distribution of political literature in a three-building, 1015 unit condominium complex. The plaintiffs sought a declaratory judgment and injunction to allow distribution of information about an upcoming school board election by slipping literature under doors. The plaintiffs alleged that the condominium complex was in essence the functional equivalent of a company town, citing Marsh v. Alabama, 326 U.S. 501, 66 S.Ct. 276, 90 L.Ed. 265 (1946). The court remanded to the trial court for a full hearing, stating that the case involved balancing of property rights and free speech rights. The trial court held for the plaintiffs, finding that they had no meaningful alternative method of access to the large number of registered voters who lived in the complex (mailing literature could not be accomplished in time to provide information about the election). The injunction was affirmed without opinion. Also see David J. Kennedy, Residential Associations as State Actors: Regulating the Impact of Gated Communities on Nonmembers, 105 Yale L.J. 761 (1995).

In the planned community or new town situation, where the only government is the association, the issue of incorporation is frequently raised. The movement to incorporate may be based on democratic ideals or it may be fueled by economic concerns (a desire to relieve the burden of assessments by securing state turnback revenues). The largest new town in America, Columbia, Maryland, has been caught up in this issue. See Michael Janofsky, Citizens Debate Change in a Maryland Suburb, New York Times, Feb. 26, 1995, p. 11.

(7) Drafting Covenants

In Zile, Private Restrictions on Residential Subdivisions: Some Drafting Suggestions, 32 Wis.Bar Bull. 26 (1959), may be found some valuable comments on considerations which enter into the preparation of documents of this type. Reference should be had, in that connection, to the 1959 Wis.L.Rev., containing discussion of the description of the area and the establishment of a general plan or scheme, the legal effect and enforcement of private restrictions, the definition of "building" or "structure" and problems associated with man-made objects primarily in the ground rather than above it, the type of dwelling to be allowed, the building location, the lot size, the dwelling size, height restrictions, cost considerations, building materials, architectural or design control, temporary structures, time for completion of construction, utility easements, miscellaneous restrictions, lifetime of restrictions and renewal provisions, substantive regulatory provisions, amending procedures, and land use problems and concepts generally. Also available are checklists from the FHA, and other governmental agencies that are involved in the many mortgage subsidization programs. Generally speaking, some of the aspects to be considered and properly developed in such a drafting process are these:

A. The area should be clearly described by use of the subdivision name (assuming the entire area is to be restricted); otherwise, the area must be described specifically by lots and blocks or in metes and bounds.

B. The intent to establish a general plan of development should be clearly expressed.

C. Certain words (such as "structure," "family" and "building") should be defined at the outset and later used as defined.

D. The general nature of the land use should be specified, as for example, "for residential purposes only," perhaps excluding also all but single-family residential uses or exempting from the exclusion certain named professional businesses.

E. The buildings permissible on each lot should be stated, as for example, a dwelling house with attached garage. Some statement may be desired to make it clear that churches, etc., are not excluded.

F. The type of dwelling may be specified—as, for example, a dwelling for a single family.

G. Setback lines from streets, sides of the lot, and the rear boundary should be provided for. In this connection, it must be determined whether only minimal requirements are to be provided or whether it is deemed desirable to have all houses a uniform distance from the street. Corner lots, irregular lots and lots with unusual topography must be considered, along with the desired size of yards. Aesthetic considerations may also enter into the provisions, and it may be well to provide that interior side yard lines or rear yard lines are inapplicable where lots are consolidated.

H. Provision should be made so that a minimum lot size is maintained (as through provisions against the division of single, unconsolidated lots). This is somewhat tricky, however, as, for example, the prohibition should not prevent the division of three regular lots into two lots (each of which would be larger than a single lot).

I. Provision should be made for a minimum building size, which presumably would bear some relationship to the lot size. The reference might be to the total square footage of inside living space, or to ground floor area (making provision for a larger ground floor area in the case of one-story dwellings than in the case of two-story dwellings), etc. Garages, breezeways, porches, carports, attics and utility rooms should (or for the most part would be) excluded from such computation. If such words as "living area" or "ground floor space" are employed, these should be clearly defined in the definitions section. Depending upon the area of the country, some provision may be made with respect to basements (which would usually be less common in the South and Southwest, for example, than in the East or Middle West).

J. Height limitations may be desirable, depending upon the type of development involved. This might be expressed either in feet or in stories. Chimneys, TV antennas or the like would normally be excluded from consideration in situations in which the height is measured in feet. In hilly areas, split levels may present some particular problems both as to height provisions measured in feet and in number of stories.

K. In addition to provisions pertaining to size, it may be desirable to provide for structures costing a minimum amount in order to preserve the high quality of the area. This opens something of a Pandora's box, however, unless dealt with clearly. The cost figure might be based on the evaluation of the structure by the lending agency or the sales price of the contractor or the builder's cost. A greater difficulty arises from the tendency of real estate to appreciate in dollar value over a long period of time, with the result that a new "$30,000 house" of today may amount essentially to what would have been classified as a new "$15,000 house" only a relatively few years ago. This is probably a continuing trend. If cost figures are used, it may be desirable to accelerate them in accord with some recognized price index on building costs, such as that published by the Bureau of Standards, but that may create or lead to more difficulty than is merited. Another consideration on cost figures is whether the architects' fee, legal fees, landscaping costs and the like are included.

L. Provisions relating to building materials may be desirable. For example, a sanction against pre-fabricated homes might be inserted; or it might be provided that a given percentage of the outside walls must be covered with brick or stone; exposed cement blocks, stucco or plywood exteriors or fake siding might be prohibited; and buildings moved onto the lot from elsewhere might be ruled out. Other provisions (perhaps taken care of by city codes) might be added to require insulation in the outer walls and roof, to require certain types of foundations, or to require the use of certain grades or types of lumber or other construction or engineering specifications.

M. Architectural or design control provisions may be desirable—as, for example, providing for plans to be approved in advance in writing by the developer or by a subsequently elected committee of property owners in the area. Such provisions, of course, require specificity if they are to be effective and if confusion is to be avoided.

N. Limitations on occupancy or use, other than as dwellings, may be desirable.

O. Occasionally, the developer may wish to provide that construction work must be completed within a given period of time, although this would normally be left to private contract.

P. Unsightly fences and signs in many instances will be prohibited, although decorative fences (and this must be clearly defined) may serve a useful purpose and thus be permitted. Location, height, materials and the like are aspects to be considered in connection with "decorative" fences.

Q. The developer may wish to provide for limitations on highway or street access or which direction houses built on corners will face. Normally, these considerations would be of little or no import, however.

R. Various provisions relating to utilities usually are provided. It may be desirable to provide altogether for underground utilities (or for a portion of the utilities to be underground). Minimally, some provision should be made which will confine the utilities to a given area (such as a five-foot easement for utility purposes over the rear of each lot).

S. It may be desirable to incorporate some provisions relating to landscaping, yards, the alteration of natural flow of ground water, the preservation of trees, or the like.

T. Enforcement provisions are not essential, but it may be desirable (due to the natural reluctance or inertia of people in acting) to designate a person, persons or a committee empowered to act on behalf of all property owners in enforcing the building scheme. This would be in addition to, and not in limitation of, the right of any individual property owner to take action unilaterally; or it could be exclusive. The former would seem to be preferable.

U. Provisions might shorten the statute of limitations. The end result would be to force offended property owners to act within a somewhat more reasonable period of time or be barred.

V. Provisions causing the restrictions to expire after a given time might be desirable. As an alternative, it might be provided that the restrictions would be automatically extended unless a majority of the owners abolished or modified them in writing (with the same being filed of record). Such provisions might be varied in several other ways. Of course, a change in conditions in the area or the changed nature of the neighborhood may lay the basis for terminating the restrictions through an adjudication that it would be inequitable to enforce them.

W. An amending procedure should be provided for in order that a majority or more of the property owners may make such modifications when necessary. Presumably, the "majority" (or whatever figure might be used) would be a majority of the owners of lots in the subdivision. Moreover, the "owner" should normally be defined as the holder of the fee simple title, not the lessee. The statement might be made that amendments would be in keeping with the general plan of development and could not be such as to alter the basic scheme.

X. A severability clause might be inserted, although its insertion or deletion is probably of little legal consequence. Invalidation of one of the provisions would normally leave the general plan unaffected anyway, and if the invalidation destroyed the general plan, then the severability clause could not save what was left.

Restrictive covenants designed to promote an ordered, desired development of a given land area are of no value unless they are observed and unless they are enforced when violated. The developer should take pains, therefore, to call the covenants to the attention of lot purchasers—not just so they will observe them, but also in order that they will make an effort to see that others observe them. A separate printed sheet containing the covenants and delivered at the time of sale would be helpful.

Chapter III

LOCAL LAND USE PLANNING AND THE REGULATORY STATE

This chapter introduces legal and policy debates that are central to the ability and power of local governments to regulate land uses. A brief discussion of the importance of economics in land use controls may explain the historical interests of the federal and state governments in regulating and attempting to regulate land use decisionmaking. The focus then shifts to an examination of the players in the land use game, exploring who these people are, how they are regulated and what basic powers and duties they possess. The historical development of planning and the comprehensive plan are then discussed to set the stage for the next chapter describing the legal techniques to implement the plan. The chapter concludes with consideration of the intergovernmental dynamics of planning.

SECTION 1. PUBLIC POLICY AND THE ECONOMICS OF LAND USE REGULATION

A recurring tension in the regulation of land use is the economic impact of the decisions regarding how a particular parcel of land may or may not be used. Understanding the economic dilemma and the demands of the market forces is key to appreciating the political realities that challenge the government's use of the police power to decide how private citizens can use their private property in an appropriate manner to benefit collectively the community as a whole.

Consider the following scenario:

John Jones has recently sold his home in the big city and purchased approximately 10 acres of land in a suburban community where he is semi-retired. On the land is an old farmhouse that he has started to renovate while he resides in the dwelling. Renovation plans include remodeling the kitchen, replacing the wrap-around porch and adding a new master bedroom off of the back of the house. John decided that in addition to renovating the house, he would construct a barn wherein he would make and sell wooden toy cars, trains and planes, thereby turning his hobby into a part-time business venture. He also purchased a large satellite dish to get better television reception. He placed the dish in front of his house, and painted on it the following message: "Welcome to J.J.'s World of Wooden Toys."

Due in large part to growing development pressures in the community, about a year ago the community adopted a comprehensive land use plan and implemented a series of land use laws designed to protect the character of the community. Among the regulations that apply to Jones' land are restrictions on the siting of satellite dishes, home occupations and commercial/business use of residentially zoned property, and sign laws. Building permit applications, with the accompanying required fee, must also be submitted to the community's planning department for approval prior to any renovations and new construction taking place.

Jones knew nothing about the land use laws in the community and he is outraged when visited by the local zoning enforcement officer who issues a "stop work" order for the renovations. She ordered that the newly constructed barn be torn down since it fails to comply with set-back restrictions in the zoning ordinance, and she cited Jones for placing the satellite dish in the front of his house, rather than in the back, as also required by the zoning ordinance.

Questions:

1. Should government control the way in which Jones desires to use his 10 acres of private property? What are the arguments in support and opposition to regulating the use of private property?

2. Should government restrict Jones from turning his "home hobby" into a small business on his property? What types of legitimate considerations should government apply when determining the allowed level of intensity of home occupations? Can government adopt home occupation laws that apply just to Jones' business or must they be broad enough to capture all imaginable home occupations? Why?

3. Should government regulate the placement of a satellite dish on private property?

4. Do land use regulations such as those described in the scenario above have a positive or a negative effect on the value of privately owned property?

5. Does government regulation of land use impact the market value of land? If so, at what points? If some regulations enhance the value of some property while at the same time decreasing the value of other property, is government responsible for compensating private property owners for a market loss? Would the property owners who

obtained an increase in value be responsible for paying the government or other landowners as a result of their windfall?

The following excerpt is from William A. Fischel's 1985 book, The Economics of Zoning Laws: A Property Rights Approach to American Land Use Controls (reprinted with permission):

> It is a truism in zoning law that no individual property owner or resident has a legal right to a particular zoning ordinance. Zoning is not a personal property right; it is a community property right. * * * It is not the same as owning one's car or home or personal effects, but there are enough similarities to draw some analogies.
>
> No zoning law says that the community has a legal right to control undeveloped land or to prevent redevelopment. The very broad, vague, and difficult-to-monitor purposes of zoning nonetheless provide an effective arsenal to accomplish as much. No law allows the community to sell this property right in the way one might sell his house. It is clear, though, that zoning can be changed at the discretion of community authorities. Zoning laws nominally vest authority in elected officials and hope that they will pay attention to planners, but every zoning procedure guarantees a great deal of public participation, especially by neighbors. Thus even though resident homeowners have no vested right to zoning, they appear to have a reliable political entitlement to the status quo in land use.
>
> The major difference between these public rights (zoning) and their closest private analog, private homeowners' associations, is that the latter do not include any property owners who have not agreed to the rules in advance (Ellickson 1982). Zoning is enacted by a local government, which usually has some involuntary members. The one-resident, one-vote rule and majority voting procedures open the possibility that public property rights might be expanded at the expense of politically effete members of the community. * * *

An excerpt from Fischel's chapter in the Encyclopedia of Law and Economics (see: http://www.dartmouth.edu/~wfischel/Papers/WAF-zoningËLEpdf.pdf) appears below:

"ZONING AND LAND USE REGULATION" IN BOUDEWIJN, BOUCKAERT AND GERRIT DE GEEST (EDS). ENCYCLOPEDIA OF LAW AND ECONOMICS, VOL. II. CIVIL LAW AND ECONOMICS, CHELTENHAM, EDWARD, ZELGAR

2000.

6. THE TIEBOUT MODEL WITH ZONING MAKES LOCAL TAXES MORE EFFICIENT

Land use controls in the US are regarded as a necessary condition for the model of local government embraced by the economics profession. Tiebout (1956) suggested that the free-rider problem could be overcome for public goods that are confined to small geographic areas. For local public goods, Tiebout argued that preferences could be truly revealed if households could select among many geographically contiguous communities assumed to provide a wide range of public services. Because most large US metropolitan areas—in which most Americans live—have scores if not hundreds of municipalities, and because most people move several times during their lives, American cities approximate the necessary conditions for Tiebout's model.

Hamilton (1975, 1976) added the local property tax and 'fiscal' zoning to Tiebout's model. A criticism of Tiebout holds that the property tax system—the mainstay of American local government—encourages developers to build low-value housing in communities with high levels of public services. This creates two kinds of deadweight loss. The property tax itself discourages housing consumption, since a larger house increases one's tax bill but usually not one's benefits from public services. Second, willingness to pay for local services is not accurately revealed, since some low-demand immigrants can receive higher levels of local services than they are willing to pay for in property taxes. As a result, the Tiebout model's efficiency advantages are undermined.

Hamilton showed that both of these inefficiencies could be overcome if the original residents (or developers) of the community established a zoning regime that required subsequent development to generate property tax revenues that covered each household's expected cost of local public services. Such zoning is called 'fiscal zoning', though it is empirically indistinguishable from any other brand (Bogart, 1993). In the Tiebout–Hamilton system, the property tax has no deadweight loss, and the level of public services is efficient because mobility by households among communities allows them to choose a known level of public services for which they must pay. Mobility allows households to choose the mix of services and housing they prefer and also encourages communities to keep costs down (Martinez–Vazquez and Sjoquist, 1988).

In proposing this model, Hamilton implicitly embraced the view of zoning as a municipal property right. Economists often view the local government fisc in the same terms as the national fisc. Levels of spending and taxes are, in the conventional view, determined by an entirely political process. But in the Tiebout–Hamilton world, local governments are much different; they must respond as purveyors of public services to the regional property market. As Oates (1969) first showed, if local governments provide high-quality local services at a lower level of property taxes—that is, if they operate like efficient firms—they reward their established residents with higher owner-occupied housing values. (Oates's study has been replicated many times; a survey and additional evidence on capitalization of local fiscal variables in home values is Yinger et al., 1988).

The same incentive that homeowner-voters have for supporting efficient levels of taxes and spending—maximizing the value of their own homes—also influences their support for local zoning. Zoning laws (and changes in zoning) that increase resident homeowners' net worth will be favored, assuming residents control the local political process, and policies that decrease it will be opposed. Zoning is also a means of controlling other municipal costs by limiting the types of development that may raise taxes or require public expenditures (Oates, 1977).

There is ample evidence that owner-occupied housing in well-planned communities is more valuable than similar units in poorly controlled areas. For example, Lafferty and Frech (1978) found that suburban communities in the Boston area that kept their commercial areas within closely contiguous zones rather than letting them scatter about had higher single-family home values (see also Burnell, 1985). Speyrer (1989) found that houses protected either by covenants or by zoning in the Houston, Texas, area were more valuable than houses in sections of Houston that were both unzoned and uncovenanted. (Sprawling Houston, which is unzoned and has areas in which covenants have lapsed or were never established, surrounds two small cities that do have zoning.)

The fact that more stringent zoning restrictions can increase housing values raises the question of why all communities do not zone to the most restrictive degree possible. One reason is that zoning may be sufficiently fungible that homeowners can be compensated for devaluations of their property. Suppose a proposed office building is opposed by nearby homeowners, who credibly complain that their property will be devalued by the traffic, the building's shadow and other spillovers (Thibodeau, 1990). If the developer can compensate them with cash or in-kind payments, the existing residents may 'take the money and run', leaving behind houses that are devalued but neighborhoods whose aggregate property values (for both housing and office buildings) are higher. Thus the finding that spillovers devalue nearby housing is consistent with efficient land use.

The implication of the foregoing is that the efficiency of land-use controls is best evaluated by looking at aggregate land values, not simply owner-occupied houses (Lind, 1973; Sonstelie and Portney, 1978; Brueckner, 1990). But even this standard must be qualified. If the municipality possesses some monopoly power (vis-à-vis other communities) in its provision of developable land, maximization of aggregate land value may be inconsistent with Pareto efficiency (M. White, 1975; Pines and Weiss, 1976). While there is empirical evidence in support of the 'monopoly zoning' hypothesis (L. Rose, 1989; Thorson, 1996; Bates, 1993), it is nonetheless impressive how many local jurisdictions there are in US metropolitan areas (Fischel, 1981). At any rate, Congress in 1984 specifically exempted local governments from financial liability under the Sherman Act, thus staunching anti-monopoly litigation against municipalities (Deutsch and Butler, 1987).

* * *

Notes

1. Should zoning and local land use controls be used to regulate the housing market to the extent that it protects the value of investments in homeownership? For a discussion of this issue, see Edward C. Glaeser and Joseph Gyourko, "The Impact of Zoning on Housing Affordability," Harvard Institute of Economic Research, Discussion Paper Number 1948 (March 2002). This paper can be accessed at the following website: http://post.economics.harvard.edu/hier/2002papers/HIER1948.pdf. See also, William A. Fischel, "An Economic History of Zoning and a Cure for its Exclusionary Effects," (2001) available at http://www.dartmouth.edu/~wfischel/Papers/02–03.pdf; Andrew G. Dieterich, "An Egalitarian's Market: The Economics of Inclusionary Zoning Reclaimed," 24 Ford. Urb. L.J. 231 (1996) and Allan Mallach, "The Tortured Reality of Suburban Exclusion: Zoning, Economics and the Future of the Berenson Doctrine," 4 Pace Envtl. L. Rev. 37 (1986).

2. What considerations, if any, should be given to economic impacts of local land use controls on property values when laws are designed to protect and preserve environmental interests? Is protection of the environment a significant community property interest? See, Nancy E. Bockstael and Elena G. Irwin, "Economics and the Land Use–Environment Link," *The International Yearbook of Environmental and Resource Economics*, Edward Elgar Publishing, H. Folmer and T. Tietenberg, ed. (2000). What are the economic impacts of land use controls on agriculture and farming? Can and should local governments impact the economic value of land used for agricultural purposes? Is this is a local, state or federal government issue?

3. Should land use controls be used to protect investments in commercial businesses? See, Superior Outdoor Signs, Inc. v. Eller Media Co., 150 Md.App. 479, 822 A.2d 478 (2003) (The Maryland Court said, "It is not the function of county zoning ordinance to provide economic protection for existing businesses.") Also see, Brier Lake, Inc. v. Jones, 710 So.2d 1054 (La.1998) where the Louisiana Supreme Court required a landowner to remove a satellite dish for failure to comply with local regulations.

SECTION 2. HISTORICAL DEVELOPMENT OF LAND USE PLANNING

The historical foundation for local planning and land use controls is found in the 1922 and 1928 model planning and zoning enabling acts published by the U.S. Department of Commerce. The Standard State Zoning Enabling Act is discussed later in this Chapter, but a brief mention of the Acts and subsequent national efforts to modernize these model laws is offered below since by 1930 most states had adopted, in whole or in part, the standard acts and as we begin the 21st century roughly half of the states still follow these models. See, Stuart Meck, "Executive Summary Status of State Planning Reform," in *Planning Communities for the 21st Century* (American Planning Association 1999).

A. STANDARD CITY PLANNING ENABLING ACT

The following is excerpted from, American Law Institute, A Model Land Development Code: Proposed Official Text and Commentary (1975) at 1.

For many years the Standard State Zoning Enabling Act prepared by the U.S. Department of Commerce in 1922 (referred to as SZEA) and the Standard City Planning Enabling Act prepared by the U.S. Department of Commerce in 1928 (referred to as SPEA) reflected with remarkable accuracy the existing state legislation regulating land development in almost all of the 50 states. The SPEA covered six subjects: (1) the organization and power of the plan commission which was directed to prepare and adopt a "master plan"; (2) the content of the master plan for the physical development of the territory governed by one of the class of local governments authorized to plan; (3) provision for adoption by the governing body of master street plan for the community and the control thereafter of private building in the bed of mapped but opened streets and of public building in unofficial or unapproved streets; (4) provision for approval by the plan commission, before approval by the governing body, of all public improvements (legislative override of commission veto was provided); (5) control of private subdivision of land into building parcels and accompanying streets and other open spaces; (6) provision for the establishment of a region, for the making of a plan for the region and for adoption of the regional plan by any municipality in the region that desired to do so.

* * *

The SZEA and the SPEA were based on two important assumptions: (1) the "owner" of land (private person or governmental agency) has the power to use or develop his land as he wishes except as specifically restricted in state and local legislation; (2) The public interest of the state lies in *authorizing* local government to control the development of decisions of an owner of land within the borders of the local government. There was no affirmative authorization to an owner to undertake development not expressly prohibited by local ordinances and there was no authority granted to a private person or government organization to acquire land by purchase or eminent domain. The SPEA and the SZEA and the state statutes modeled after them assume that the decision to acquire land for development and the decision to develop are made independently of the planning laws and that the purpose of local laws which they authorize is to *prohibit* undesirable development and not to encourage desirable development.

Furthermore, as far as these enabling acts were concerned, it appears to have been immaterial to the broader public interest of the state whether any local government actually engaged in planning, whether development actually took place in accordance with a plan, whether the plan, if any, produced by the local government in fact promoted the public interest of the local community, and even whether the plan of the local government adversely affected the public interest of a larger area such as a region or the state as a whole. The purpose for which the local government could act under the SPEA and the SZEA were the full inventory of constitutionally permissible purposes—promotion of health, safety, moral, and general welfare—but the purely local public interest was dominant.

These early model acts were criticized by the drafters of the ALI Model Land Development Code as unable to meet the challenges of society fifty years later. They pointed to the outpouring of environmental legislation at the federal and state levels that had begun to place significant constraints on the use of land, including measures to protect clean air, clean water, coastal resources, wetlands, solid waste disposal, disposal of radioactive waste and other measures.

The Preface to the American Planning Association's 2002 Growing Smart Legislative Guidebook, provides the following reflection on the early model acts:

> The planning approaches of the 1920s are incapable of meeting the challenges of the twenty-first century. There are at least four reasons for this deficiency:
>
> **(1) A more significant governmental dimension for planning.** In the 1920s, government was simpler, and there were fewer governmental units. Planning was a local activity, not something that was expected of all levels of government. Indeed, the role of the federal and state governments in shaping our urban and rural areas ranged from minimal to nonexistent. Beginning in the 1950s, the federal government created programs addressing transportation, environment, and other functional areas that had statewide or regional significance. Increasingly, the federal government devolved or placed greater responsibility on the state and local governments for making transportation, environmental, and public facilities planning decisions when federal monies were involved. Moreover, the repercussions of decisions on development whose impacts spill over jurisdictional boundaries are no longer ignored. States recognized this concern and state legislatures responded. In some parts of the country, states now take an active role in managing this intergovernmental dimension to ensure uniformity, fairness, and the advancement of state interests.
>
> **(2) A marked shift in society's view of land.** People no longer believe, as they did in the nineteenth century, that land is something merely to be bought and sold. We now regard land as a resource. Where we once encouraged the filling in and development of swamps, we now regard those same wetlands as a vital part of nature's system of flood control and important for wildlife and their habitats that should be protected for the benefit of future generations. Where we once built without

concern for scenic protection, we now value scenic beauty as an irreplaceable regional asset. We see vacant, developable land as having competing social values—it can be used for the construction of affordable housing or for the continuation of agriculture. We recognize that how we develop our land—at what density or intensity—will have consequences for the form and relative compactness of metropolitan areas, which in turn will affect how much we have to travel to conduct our lives and what consequences that has for the air we breathe.

(3) A more active citizenry. In the 1920s, community plans tended to be prepared by consultants working for business elites who sought little broad-based public support or involvement. What opportunities there were for citizen participation were rudimentary and perfunctory—a single public hearing after the major planning decisions had already been made. As a consequence, such plans were not often implemented. Although many planning statutes are silent on the tools and techniques of participation, citizens now expect to be engaged in the community planning processes, and, when they participate, they expect to see results from their efforts. The existence of the Internet, on which plans and information about development can be placed as part of a government's home page, also opens up new options for citizen involvement.

(4) A more challenging legal environment. Land-use controls are being employed to solve or prevent environmental problems, maintain open space, exact public improvements for schools and roads, and preserve agricultural land. The line between protecting the public from nuisances—the focus of the 1920s—and securing public benefits has blurred over the past 70 years. In response, courts have begun to require government to compensate land owners for regulations that result in either a permanent or temporary taking of private property, that go "too far" in pushing the envelope in protecting the public health, safety, and welfare—the traditional police power objectives of land use controls. Thus, the planning basis for our development decisions becomes even more significant as the justification for the regulatory and public expenditure systems it underpins.

B. ALI MODEL LAND DEVELOPMENT CODE

In 1975, after many years of effort and many drafts reviewed, debated and re-written, the American Law Institute published a Model Land Development Code. Much more sophisticated than its predecessor models, the Model Land Development Code was organized into the following twelve sections: General Provisions, Local Land Development Regulation, Local Land Development Planning, Discontinuance of Existing Land Use, Acquisition and Disposition of Land, Land Banking, State Land Development Regulation, State Land Development Planning, Judicial Review of Orders, Rules and Ordinances, Enforcement of Local Land Development Regulations, Public Records of Development Regulations, and Financial Coordination of Governmental Development.

By all accounts, the Model Land Development Code was a failure. With the exception of the State of Florida that based its development of regional impacts law on the relevant provisions of this Code, no other state used the document in any meaningful way to make reforms to its state enabling statutes. This left a void for reformers who needed fresh ideas and perspectives to assist in modernizing individual state planning and zoning statutes, creating the need for the American Planning Association's contribution discussed next.

C. GROWING SMART LEGISLATIVE GUIDEBOOK

The most recent chapter in the history of the evolution of land use planning and zoning is the 2002 American Planning Association *Growing Smart Legislative Guidebook* which offers the following view on the 1920's standard acts:

> Most states' planning statutes are the offspring of the two model statutes drafted by an advisory committee of the U.S. Department of Commerce in the 1920s. For many states, the *Standard City Planning and Zoning Enabling Acts* still supply the institutional structure for planning (such as the establishment of planning commissions and boards of adjustment or appeals), although some procedural and substantive components have changed over time.
>
> These acts regarded planning and zoning as matters of purely *local* and, more particularly, *urban* concern. The acts were intended to provide clear delegation of the state's police power authority to local government, which is the fundamental reason enabling legislation exists. They were also intended to preserve private property rights and to protect cities against slums, blight, congestion, and loss of amenities.
>
> Their drafters also wanted to ensure that private investments and the value they produce could be protected from nuisances and other incompatibilities from neighboring properties. They also wanted to establish a uniform national framework of planning and zoning that could survive challenges in state and federal courts.

Notes

1. Were the economic considerations of land use controls, based upon the early enabling acts designed to protect the property interests of the community as a whole? How can local governments ensure that local land use controls protect private investments in property? Should this be a leading consideration in adopting new plans and zoning laws? Can this be accomplished equitably?

2. For further explanations and critiques of the *Growing Smart Legislative Guidebook* see, Patricia E. Salkin, "The Next Generation of Planning & Zoning Enabling Acts Is on the Horizon: 2002 Growing Smart Legislative

Guidebook Is a Must–Read for Land Use Practitioners," 30 Real Estate L. J. 353 (2002), and Edward J. Sullivan, "Out of the Chaos: Towards a National System of Land–Use Procedures," 34 The Urban Lawyer 449 (2002). Not all stakeholders believe that the most recent effort offers effective guidance on all issues. See, for example, John J. Delaney, Esq. "APA's Growing Smart Legislative Guidebook: Will it Promote "Smart Process?" " and Robert Liberty, "Heart and Teeth to Go with the Brains of Smart Growth: Comments on the American Planning Association's Growing Smart Legislative Guidebook." Stuart Meck, AICP, editor of the Guidebook provides a response in "Growing Smart: Drafting the Next Generation of Model Planning and Zoning Enabling Legislation for the United States (and Responding to Its Critics)." All three papers are available at http://www.smart-growth.umd.edu/publications/Guidebook.html.

3. The federal government has also played a role in influencing the way in which state and local governments control the use of land. For example, The National Commission on Urban Problems recommended that state governments enact legislation enabling appropriate governmental agencies to acquire land in advance of development for the following purposes: (a) assuring the continuing availability of sites needed for development; (b) controlling the timing, location, type and scale of development; (c) preventing urban sprawl; and (d) reserving to the public gains in land values resulting from the action of government in promoting and servicing development. National Commission on Urban Problems, Building the American City 251 (1968).

In 1974 Congress responded by providing specific legislative authority in the Community Development Act of 1974 for the allocation of funds under the special revenue sharing program for "community development" grants to local governments for "the acquisition of real property * * * which is (a) blighted, deteriorated, deteriorating, undeveloped or inappropriately developed from the standpoint of sound community development and growth; (b) appropriate for rehabilitation or conservation activities; (c) appropriate for the preservation or restoration of historic sites, the beautification of urban land, the conservation of open spaces, natural resources, and scenic areas, the provision of recreational opportunities, or the guidance of urban development; (d) to be used for the provision of public works, facilities, and improvements eligible for assistance under this title; or (e) to be used for other public purposes." 42 U.S.C.A. 5305(a)(1) (1974).

For an historical examination of the extent of federal influence on state and local planning, See, Patricia E. Salkin, "Smart Growth and Sustainable Development: Threads of a National Land Use Policy," 36 Valparaiso U. L. Rev. 381 (2002); Robert I. McMurry, "Using Federal Laws and Regulations to Control Local Land Use," SG ALI–ABA 357 (2001); Shelby D. Green, "The Search for a National Land Use Policy: For the Cities' Sake," 26 Fordham Urb. L. J. 69 (1998); and John R. Nolon, "The National Land Use Policy Act," 13 Pace Envtl. L. Rev. 519 (1996). Professor Kayden argues that the U.S. does not have a national land use policy per se, and that it is unlikely that Congress will produce such legislation. See, Jerold S. Kayden, "National Land–Use Planning in America: Something Whose Time Has Never Come," 3 Wash. U.J.L. & Pol'y 445 (2000).

SECTION 3. THE PLAYERS IN THE LAND USE GAME

In his book, *The Zoning Game: Municipal Practices and Policies*, Richard F. Babcock identifies the following "players" in the zoning game: local decisionmakers (e.g., members of local legislative bodies, planning boards and zoning boards), planners, lawyers and judges. Code enforcement officers, engineers, architects and members of the public may also participate in the process. This section offers insights into the legal status of planners who are key participants in the process, and it focuses on ethical considerations of parties involved.

A. PLANNERS

Bureau of Labor Statistics, U.S. Department of Labor, *Occupational Outlook Handbook, 2002–03 Edition*, Urban and Regional Planners, http://www.bls.gov/oco/ocos057.htm:

> Planners develop long- and short-term land use plans to provide for growth and revitalization of urban, suburban, and rural communities, while helping local officials make decisions concerning social, economic, and environmental problems. Because local governments employ the majority of urban and regional planners, they often are referred to as community, regional, or city planners.
>
> Planners promote the best use of a community's land and resources for residential, commercial, institutional, and recreational purposes. Planners may be involved in various other activities, including decisions on alternative public transportation system plans, resource development, and protection of ecologically sensitive regions. They address issues such as traffic congestion, air pollution, and the effect of growth and change on a community. They may formulate plans relating to the construction of new school buildings, public housing, or other infrastructure. Some planners are involved in environmental issues ranging from pollution control to wetland preservation, forest conservation, or the location of new landfills. Planners also may be involved with drafting legislation on environmental, social, and economic issues, such as sheltering the homeless, planning a new park, or meeting the demand for new correctional facilities.
>
> Planners examine proposed community facilities such as schools to be sure these facilities will meet the changing demands placed upon them over time. They keep abreast of economic and legal issues involved in zoning codes, building codes, and environmental regulations. They ensure that builders and developers follow these codes and regulations. Planners also deal with land use issues created by population movements. For example, as suburban growth and economic development create more new jobs outside cities, the need for public transportation that enables workers to get to these

jobs increases. In response, planners develop transportation models for possible implementation and explain their details to planning boards and the general public.

Before preparing plans for community development, planners report on the current use of land for residential, business, and community purposes. These reports include information on the location and capacity of streets, highways, airports, water and sewer lines, schools, libraries, and cultural and recreational sites. They also provide data on the types of industries in the community, characteristics of the population, and employment and economic trends. With this information, along with input from citizens' advisory committees, planners design the layout of land uses for buildings and other facilities such as subway lines and stations.

* * *

Planners prepare reports showing how their programs can be carried out and what they will cost. Urban and regional planners often confer with land developers, civic leaders, and public officials. They may function as mediators in community disputes and present alternatives acceptable to opposing parties. Planners may prepare material for community relations programs, speak at civic meetings, and appear before legislative committees and elected officials to explain and defend their proposals. In large organizations, planners usually specialize in a single area such as transportation, demography, housing, historic preservation, urban design, environmental and regulatory issues, or economic development. In small organizations, planners must be able to do various kinds of planning.

B. THE LEGAL STATUS OF PLANNERS

NEW JERSEY CHAPTER, AMERICAN INSTITUTE OF PLANNERS v. NEW JERSEY STATE BD. OF PROFESSIONAL PLANNERS

Supreme Court of New Jersey, 1967.
48 N.J. 581, 227 A.2d 313, appeal dismissed, certiorari denied
389 U.S. 8, 88 S.Ct. 70, 19 L.Ed.2d 8 (1967).

FRANCIS, J. In this declaratory judgment proceeding the Chancery Division of the Superior Court declared unconstitutional a portion of section 11 of the professional planners licensing act, L.1962, c. 109; N.J.S.A. 45:14A–11. The condemned portion exempted duly licensed professional engineers, licensed land surveyors and registered architects of this State from the requirement, imposed by the statute on all other persons, to take and pass an examination for a planner's license, and it directed the State Board of Professional Planners (which was created by the same statute) to issue such a license on application therefor and payment of fee by any such exempted person. The trial court also held that the invalid portion of section 11 was severable, and not so intimately connected with the statute as to indicate that the Legislature would not have adopted the remainder without it. The Board was restrained from issuing licenses to persons who sought to qualify under the offending exemption. An appeal was taken to the Appellate Division, where the restraint was continued until final judgment. Thereafter, before the matter was reached for argument there, all parties moved for certification pursuant to R.R. 1:10–3, and we granted the motion.

The action was instituted by the New Jersey Chapter, American Institute of Planners, an unincorporated association of the State of New Jersey. The association is a professional society created to study and advance the art and science of city, regional, state and national planning.
* * *

Prior to 1962 unsuccessful attempts were made under the sponsorship of the American Institute of Planners to obtain passage by the Legislature of a so-called professional planners licensing act. The proposal encountered opposition from other established professional groups, principally engineers, land surveyors and architects, who were already subject to separate licensing statutes and who had qualified for licenses by meeting the conditions imposed thereby. Finally in 1962 the act in question, obviously a compromise measure (more of this later) was adopted with the acquiescence of the competing interests, as chapter 109 of the Laws of 1962.

The act provided that after July 10, 1962 no person could practice or offer to practice professional planning in this State unless he were licensed to do so under its provisions. The practice of professional planning is defined in most general terms in section 2 as "the administration, advising, consultation or performance of professional work in the development of master plans in accordance with the provisions of chapters 27 and 55 of Title 40 of the Revised Statutes, as amended and supplemented; and other professional planning services related thereto intended primarily to guide governmental policy for the assurance of the orderly and co-ordinated development of municipal, county, regional and metropolitan land areas, and the State or portions thereof." N.J.S.A. 45:14A–2.

Chapters 27 and 55 of Title 40 provide for the creation of county, regional and municipal planning boards to make and adopt master plans for the physical development of the political unit involved. * * *

In order to become licensed as a professional planner, a candidate must file an application under oath showing that he has the minimum educational qualifications. They are:

> (a) A graduate degree in professional planning from an accredited college or university in a curriculum in recognized planning subjects as shall be approved by the State Board of Professional Planners, plus a minimum of three years experience in the full-time practice of professional planning; or (b) an undergraduate degree from an accredited college or university in a curriculum offering a major or option comprising a minimum of 21 credit hours in such

recognized planning subjects as shall be approved by the board, with a minimum of four years experience in the full-time practice of professional planning; or (c) graduation from a secondary school and at least 12 years of professional planning experience acceptable to the board; or, (d) for a period of eight years only subsequent to July 1, 1963, a degree in a *closely related course of study such as architecture, landscape architecture, engineering,* law, sociology, geography, public administration, political science or economics, with a minimum of 18 credit hours in recognized planning subjects included as part of or in addition to such courses of study in an accredited college or university, plus a minimum of five years experience in the full-time practice of professional planning. (Emphasis ours) In addition the applicant must obtain a passing grade as determined by the board upon a qualifying examination to be prepared by the board or by experts chosen by it, and given annually. * * *

When the statute was adopted by the Legislature it contained section 11 consisting of five paragraphs dealing generally with the license-qualifying examinations. The fourth paragraph provides:

> The board upon application therefor and the payment of the application and license fees fixed by this act shall issue a certificate of license as a professional planner to any duly licensed professional engineer, licensed land surveyor or registered architect of New Jersey.

This paragraph was not included in the bill, A 546, as introduced in 1961 under the sponsorship of the New Jersey Chapter of the American Institute of Planners. It was inserted however, (along with section 3, N.J.S.A. 45:14A–3, and part of section 17, N.J.S.A. 45:14A–17, to be more specifically referred to hereafter in connection with the discussion of severability of section 11), in order to exempt the described engineers, land surveyors and architects from the obligation of satisfying the qualifications required of other aspiring planners and from the burden of taking and passing the licensing examination.

Plaintiffs challenge the validity of the fourth paragraph, saying it denies them equal protection of the law contrary to the guaranties of the Federal Constitution and the New Jersey Constitution. More specifically they say that by requiring all persons except licensed professional engineers, licensed land surveyors and registered architects of this State to possess certain educational qualifications and experience in the field of planning, and to take and pass an examination on subjects related to that field in order to be licensed as a practitioner of planning, the legislation violates the cited constitutional strictures against discrimination.

* * *

In this instance we are satisfied from the legislative history and from an examination of the statute as a whole that the Legislature would not have adopted it without the exemption provision contained in the fourth paragraph of section 11.

The first proposed planners' licensing act * * * did not contain an exemption for engineers, land surveyors and architects. There is no doubt it encountered opposition from those groups, particularly from the New Jersey Society of Professional Engineers. It was not adopted. Thereafter futile attempts were made in 1959 and 1960 to procure passage of such legislation. Then in 1961 two bills were introduced, one sponsored by the Society of Professional Engineers (A 483), and the other by the Institute of Planners. (A 546). The bills continued the conflict between the professions. The engineers' bill provided for the registration and licensing of professional planners, and created an administrative and examining board to carry out its provisions. The board was to consist of five engineers, one of whom would also be a licensed land surveyor, and one a licensed professional planner. The planners' bill called for establishment of a separate board of licensed professional planners. The statement originally attached said among other things:

> "Planning is a distinct, separate profession, which requires specialized training. It is not a branch of engineering, architecture, or any other profession. Thirty leading colleges and universities award degrees in planning, and more than 400 New Jersey municipalities and 15 counties have planning boards."

As we were advised at oral argument, it became apparent that neither bill could pass to the exclusion of the other. The engineers, land surveyors and architects seemed to feel there was no need at all to regard planning as a distinct profession and to require licenses for planners as such. But if the Legislature disagreed and found justification for such regulation, then they felt that persons in their professions who took and passed the examinations for licenses to practice in their respective fields, as already required by separate statutes, ought to receive automatic licensure under the planners' act. In 1962 an obvious compromise in the form of the present statute was submitted and adopted. It became chapter 109, L.1962.

* * *

The history of the act and its evolution into the form which made it acceptable legislatively demonstrate plainly that the establishment of prerequisites for licensing planners, and the provisions for exemption therefrom of licensed engineers, land surveyors and registered architects were intended to be interdependent and to exist as a whole or not at all. * * * We are satisfied that if the exemption provision were invalid, it would be usurpation of the legislative province for a court to allow the remainder of the enactment to stand without it. Washington National Ins. Co. v. Board of Review, 1 N.J. 545, 556, 64 A.2d 443 (1949). Therefore whether the entire act here shall stand or fall depends upon our determination of the constitutionality of the fourth paragraph of section 11, to which we now turn.

* * *

The more specific issue vigorously argued by plaintiffs is that by exempting licensed professional engineers, land surveyors and registered architects from the educational requirements and examination for a planner's license, while requiring all other persons, particularly those educated for and trained in planning to satisfy the requirements, the statute transgresses the constitutional mandate for equal protection of the law. They urge that all persons have a common right to aspire to and qualify for the practice of a profession or occupation, and are entitled to be treated equally with respect to State-imposed tests for license to do so. And they contend that creation of the exempt separate class of engineers, land surveyors and architects, and authorizing automatic licensure for such persons violates the basic charter right of all other persons not to be treated in discriminatory fashion.

* * *

There is no substantial dispute in the testimony of the expert witnesses who appeared on both sides of the case that there is a definite interrelationship among the disciplines of engineering, architecture, landscape architecture, land surveying and planning. * * *

Plaintiffs' experts concede that historically city planning had its origin and its early development "with architects, engineers and landscape architects. That is where we got our original planners"; "they were really planners"; they "came out of" architecture, engineering and landscape architecture. * * *

The text writers support the view that city planning had and has its roots in the three professions recognized by our Legislature. For example, McQuillin, in 1 Municipal Corporations 432 (1949) says:

> "The first instance of a comprehensive city plan was that of Christopher Wren for London following the destructive fire of 1666, but it was never adopted. In 1682 a plan for Philadelphia was drafted by civil engineers and surveyors appointed by William Penn. The plan adopted for the national capital was prepared by Major Pierre Charles L'Enfant, a French army engineer employed by Washington, who presented a scheme at once comprehensive and attractive, and the observance of which in the main has enabled the national capital to develop as one among the beautiful cities of the world."

Further:

> "As knowing how to do a thing before it is attempted is needed, it is plain that satisfactory city planning and zoning must be the result of the united efforts of the applied talents working in harmony of the various professions, arts and sciences, particularly that of the civil engineer, the architect, the landscape architect, or designer, the economist and the lawyer." Id., at pp. 434–435.

See also, James, Land Planning in the United States for the City, State and Nation (1926), where it is pointed out in chapter 3 that the concept of city planning in the modern sense was first introduced at the Chicago World's Fair in 1893, and that the exposition was the joint effort of architects, landscape architects and engineers.

Plaintiffs' witnesses assert that the modern "new breed" planner is one step removed from the engineers, architects and land surveyors. His claimed separate expertise in the preparation of master plans, they say, comes from knowledge of and training in community studies, which include preparation of base maps, land use surveys, housing conditions, review of business uses, environmental studies in neighborhoods, community facilities, population and economic surveys. This expertise is applied to the conditions and circumstances of a particular community, and a master plan for its physical development is evolved. Thus, plaintiffs say, planners operate on the top-most echelon of the process which in the ultimate produces the comprehensive master plan; at that level they apply their understanding of the operation of socio-economic forces to the component data prepared or compiled by the other professional groups such as engineers, architects and land surveyors, as well as lawyers, financial experts, and experienced men of public affairs, in order to fashion what they believe is the appropriate master plan.

There is no doubt that in more recent years community planning has drawn into its creative work social and economic considerations to a greater extent than in its formative period. And it may be that in the course of time the Legislature will conclude that such a high degree of specialized expertise has come into being in planning that the practice ought to be treated as uniquely separate from and independent of all other professional disciplines. * * * In this connection, however, the evidence is uncontradicted that at present there is a shortage of persons engaging in planning, whatever may be their professional, educational or experiential background. According to the Executive Director of the American Society of Planning Officials, the Society advertised about 1300 professional planning jobs during 1965, and at the end of the year about 400 of them were open and unfilled. That number was higher than at the end of 1964, which in turn was higher than in 1963. It may well be that the Legislature felt the need could be alleviated by admitting to the practice of planning without examination those persons who had already qualified for licenses in the related professional fields of engineering, land surveying and architecture. Under all of the circumstances it cannot be said reasonably that planning did not have its gestative stirrings and its early and continued practice in the three exempted disciplines, particularly in engineering and architecture. Nor can it be said on the record before us that it was wholly arbitrary and without reasonable basis for the Legislature to regard licensed members of the three professions as possessing sufficient minimal qualifications for planning to warrant treatment as a distinct class and to grant them exemption from the licensing requirements of the professional planners act, if they wish to practice in that field.

The notion that the lawmakers felt the desirability of some control of the developing practice of community planning must be accepted. It is reasonable also to conclude from the record that an awareness existed of the present shortage of persons engaged in the practice. Further, the evidence submitted warrants the inference that the legislators were aware of the historical part played by the engineers, land surveyors and architects in the development of community planning, and the continuing practice of such planning as an incident of their professional work. All of these circumstances suggest the view that the Legislature felt the current need in the field of community planning was for regulation of those persons who wished to engage in the practice but who had not demonstrated to any public agency that they had sufficient qualifications to do so. The circumstances suggest also satisfaction on the part of the lawmakers that achievement of licensure in one of the three named professions demonstrates possession of sufficient minimal competence to engage in planning to warrant treating such license holders as a separate class and exempting them from the requirements imposed upon those who have no license of any kind to practice planning. Under the principles of law laid down for the control of judicial review, we cannot say that the exempt class created by the fourth paragraph of section 11 is purely arbitrary and without any rational relation to the statutory objective of regulation of the planning profession.

Accordingly the challenged portions of the professional planners act cannot be declared violative of the constitutional mandate for equal protection of the laws. The judgment of the trial court is reversed, and the restraint imposed upon the New Jersey State Board of Professional Planners respecting the issuance of planners' licenses to those licensed in the exempt professions is vacated.

[A partial dissent is omitted.]

Notes

1. Michigan statutes define "community planner" as "a person qualified to prepare comprehensive community plans * * *" MI ST. 339.2301, and further provide that "A community planner shall not engage in the practice of architecture, engineering, or land surveying * * * unless licensed * * * as an architect, professional engineer, or land surveyor." MI ST 339.2304. In New Jersey, the "practice of professional planning" is defined to include "* * * the administration, advising, consultation or performance of professional work in the development of master plans * * * and other professional planning services related thereto intended primarily to guide governmental policy for the assurance of the orderly and coordinated development of municipal, county, regional, and metropolitan land areas, and the State or portions thereof. The work of the professional planner shall not include or supercede any of the duties of an attorney at law, a licensed professional engineer, land surveyor or registered architect * * *" N.J.S.A. 45:14A–2(c).

2. In addition to the problem of the principal case, defining the "planner," the type of work done by the planner, whoever she may be, can

raise serious questions. Planners frequently participate in the drafting of land use ordinances, and may also appear before some governmental agency as an advocate. Do these activities constitute unauthorized practice of law? Consider the following excerpts from an article, Care, The City Planner and the Unauthorized Practice of Law, 2 Land Use Controls Q. No. 4, pp. 23–30 (1968):

> A zoning ordinance is a complicated, highly technical, legal instrument which is, or should be, related in some way to a comprehensive plan. Few attorneys are capable of preparing a zoning ordinance. Probably even fewer members of the planning profession have the experience and legal knowledge for such work despite the fact that many planners do prepare zoning ordinances as well as amendments to ordinances. In the past, planners have tended to utilize a "cut and paste" technique, with the almost verbatim transfer of language or standards from other zoning ordinances to their own. As a result, many communities are now saddled with zoning ordinances that are outmoded and inappropriate and which, in general, reflect the concepts and personal prejudices of the person or persons who prepared the original text. * * *
>
> Although it is sometimes difficult to establish a line of demarcation between the functions of the planner and those of the municipal attorney during the preparation of a zoning ordinance, guidelines have been established by the professional legal and planning organizations. The American Institute of Planners has adopted a statement of principles of responsibility relating to the preparation of land-use control and other planning regulations which attempts to delineate the area of responsibility of both the planner and the attorney. This statement acknowledges the contribution of the legal profession to the planning process in these words:
>
>> Attorneys contribute significantly to the substantive portion of planning and to the application of planning concepts. They assist in developing and clarifying the relationship of planning to government, and to the means of applying planning processes and proposals to public policy and private activity * * *.
>
> This statement of principles also admits that "a planner, unless he is also an attorney and member of the Bar, *does not have the professional competence to put the technical provisions of an ordinance into suitable final legal form.*" (Emphasis added.) There are perhaps no more than a dozen planners in this country who can satisfy this requirement. There are a great many more practicing attorneys with some expertise in zoning enactments and litigation, but few of them have any practical experience in the technical phases of plan preparation. (There is a need for individuals with such dual competence within both professions.) It is apparent that the planners' professional organization is aware of the need for coordination of the activities of both the planner and the municipal attorney during the preparation of a zoning enactment. It is clear, also, that this organization realizes that the professional planner is not competent to relate the concepts of due process, private property rights, and other constitutional guarantees to planning proposals and land-use control regulations. It is unfortunate that many practicing

planners recognize neither this limitation on their part nor the importance of preserving the constitutional guarantees with respect to the rights of individual property owners.

* * *

There is literally no case law relating to this subject, although in 1964 the Illinois State Bar filed suit against Evert Kinkaid and Associates, Inc., a planning consulting firm located in Chicago, alleging that the firm was in the business of drafting zoning ordinances for various municipalities in Illinois and that such activity constituted the unauthorized practice of law. The Circuit Court of Madison County, Illinois, entered a consent decree which enjoined the defendant from drafting zoning ordinances and which read in part as follows:

> "That the Defendant shall not prepare or purport to prepare any legal documents in a form which may be adopted as an ordinance or resolution by the legislative body of the County of Madison. That the Defendant and its agents and employees shall in connection with providing professional planning consultant services to the County of Madison restrict themselves solely and completely to the preparation and recommendation of technical planning standards which may be embodied in a subsequent draft of a zoning ordinance, it being understood that the preparation of the draft of such zoning ordinance shall be the responsibility of a member of the Bar of the State of Illinois to be designated by the Board of Supervisors of Madison County."

It has been well established in the majority of states that representation before state agencies conducting adversary administrative proceedings constitutes the practice of law and that laymen may not appear in such proceedings in a representative capacity nor may they do the necessary preparatory work. The practice of law has been broadly defined as including not only proceedings where trial work is involved but also "the preparation of legal documents, their interpretation, the giving of legal advice, or the *application of legal principles to problems of any complexity* * * *."

* * *

In Liebtag v. Dilworth [Ct. of Common Pleas, 1st Dist., Philadelphia (1961)] the Philadelphia Zoning Board of Adjustment had adopted a rule which prohibited non-lawyers from practicing before that body. The plaintiff, a planner, filed a mandamus suit, complaining that he had been unlawfully and improperly deprived of his right to earn a livelihood. The court not only held the rule to be valid and enforceable, but that such practice constituted the practice of law and that those sections of the city's zoning ordinance which related to the operation of the Zoning Board of Adjustment were invalid, null, and void to the extent that they purported to authorize any lay person to engage in the practice of law before that body. Thus the court indicated in no uncertain terms that the representation of an applicant before an administrative body of this nature by a non-lawyer—even a planner who may have specialized training in a related field—constitutes the unauthorized practice of law.

Liebtag relates only to lay practice before a board of appeals, at least that was the only body directly involved in the case. It is suggested here that because of differences between the nature of the activities of a planning commission and a board of appeals, representation before a commission is not necessarily the practice of law although practice before a board may well be so.

* * *

It would appear, then, that whereas practice before a board of appeals may very well constitute the practice of law as defined by the court in Liebtag v. Dilworth, practice before a planning commission may not necessarily be considered as such. The legal elements of a proceeding before a board of appeals are obvious and inescapable, while proceedings before a planning commission may be entirely without legal significance. A final determination as to whether the practice of law is involved depends to a large extent upon the nature of the proceedings before the planning commission and the type of presentation made by the individual involved. If the proceedings before a planning commission require the application of case law and legal principles, or an understanding of the rules of evidence and the historical development of property rights, the practice of law is involved, and it would be improper for a planner to appear in any capacity other than as an expert witness.

Thus far we have considered only the status of the planning consultant or privately employed planner practicing before a board of appeals and, under certain conditions, before a planning commission. A more complex, and perhaps more important, problem is raised by planners employed by public agencies. * * *

It is customary for planners employed by a planning commission or board of appeals to prepare a written analysis of each application considered by that agency. Such reports are frequently legally oriented and may recommend denial of a specific application because it constitutes a "spot zone" or a "strip zone," both of which are terms that require legal interpretation, or because the applicant is unable to satisfy certain legal criteria established by the courts or by enabling statutes. These comments may then be reiterated or even amplified during a verbal presentation of the staff recommendation, so that the planner is, in effect, using conclusions of law to influence the decision of an administrative agency. Such a situation is particularly unfair and inappropriate in view of the fact that, once a request for an ordinance amendment or a variance has been denied, there is a presumption that the legislative or administrative body involved has acted properly, and the courts will generally be loath to overturn such a decision.

The question, then, appears to be whether the public, and, more particularly, an applicant appearing before a planning commission or board of appeals, is being deprived of the proper determination of substantial rights in an instance where a publicly employed planner, acting in an advisory capacity, is able to convince such body that the applicant cannot legally substantiate his request. Is such an individual qualified to interpret the law, to quote legal precedent, and to relate precedent to the application under consideration? Under the circumstances, it is logical to conclude that this individual is performing much the same type of service that the court considered the practice of law in Liebtag v. Dilworth, the only distinction being that he is a public employee and his "client" is the administrative body rather than an individual appearing before the body.

Even more significant is the fact that many city planners, dissatisfied with "Euclidean" zoning because it does not provide either the amount of flexibility or the control felt necessary to achieve certain planning goals, are experimenting with new methods of land-use control—frequently without professional counsel and sometimes without the actual knowledge of the administrative agency involved. This is often accomplished by establishing requirements for the submission of so-called development plans, which may or may not contain restrictive covenants or be required to be filed of record. This is, however, only one of the methods being used to overcome the shortcomings of "Euclidean" zoning. Another method is to prepare and recommend the adoption of bylaws or rules of procedure that substantially affect the rights of the public, or suggest the use of restrictive methods of processing applications.

The most unfortunate aspect of this effort on the part of the planner is that, in most cases, he has little or no appreciation of the legal significance of some of the procedures and requirements that he has helped to establish. His concern is not with the property rights of individuals but with how to overcome such rights—rights he sometimes considers to be an impediment to the public welfare—in order to achieve the above-mentioned "goals." This is not to say that there is no need for an improvement in the existing land-use control system, but only that we should move in that direction only with the advice and assistance of legal counsel and only after the administrative body involved and the general public have been apprised of the rights they may be surrendering in the process.

C. SHOULD PLANNERS BE LICENSED?

This article by Joseph A. Pobiner, AICP is excerpted from the April/May 1994 issue of Texas Planning Review, the newsletter of the Texas Chapter of the American Planning Association. Copyright by Joseph A. Pobiner.

At present, only Michigan and New Jersey regulate the practice of planning at the state level through a process of certification and licensure. Hawaii has considered similar legislation, and other states are likely to follow. Licensing probably won't solve any problems related to the practice of planning, but it might give planners a way to improve the quality of such practice. Many associated disciplines—engineers, landscape architects, architects, lawyers—offer professional planning consulting services. The discipline of planning sprang from these (and other) professions. Yet all of these professions are strictly regulated. By law, a certified planner cannot legally call him/herself an engineer, architect, and so on. With planning becoming increasingly specialized, would licensing ensure the quality of work from those calling themselves "planners"?

How would such a system work? Probably planning would copy the certification processes of other professions. An overall national exam with sections of state-specific questions could be administered. The exam used by the American Institute of Certified Planners (an institute of the American Planning Association) seems to be the logical vehicle for such a test. But since APA is composed of professional and citizen planners, would/should the "lay planners" be allowed to take the exam or not? Would such a distinction alienate a large segment of APA's membership? Grandfathering all existing practicing planners, regardless of certification or education, would also undoubtedly be required. That means, in effect, that it would take quite some time to ensure that all "licensed" practicing planners had gone through the certification process. One solution might be the introduction of a system for naming AICP "fellows," similar to the system used by the American Society of Landscape Architects and the American Institute of Architects. If planners were certified, perhaps there would be a provision in the state procurement code that would exempt planning proposals from competitive bids. That would assure public clients that planning services were selected based on merit and experience, not merely price.

Note

1. To be licensed in Michigan, planners must meet the following statutory requirements:

(a) Has passed an examination approved by the department and the board.

(b) Is of good moral character.

(c) Has had not less than 6 years of planning experience in the type of work necessary to the preparation or implementation of comprehensive community plans, not less than 2 years of which shall have been in the United States. However, only 2 years of planning experience is mandatory. A maximum waiver of 4 years may be allowed for 1 degree only as follows:

  i. Doctorate or master's degree in planning, 4 years' credit.

  ii. Bachelor's degree in planning, 3 years' credit

  iii. Doctorate or master's degree in a related field including architecture, landscape architecture, civil engineering, sociology, economics, geography, political science, or public administration, 3 years' credit.

  iv. Any other degree in a related field, 2 years' credit.

MI St. 339.2306.

New Jersey's licensure requirements provide in part that it " ... shall be unlawful for any person to practice or to offer to practice professional planning in this State, or to use the title 'professional planner' or any other title, sign, card or device in such manner as to tend to convey the impression that such person is practicing professional planning or is a professional planner, unless such person is duly licensed ..." N.J.S.A. 45:14A–1. Similar to the qualifications for licensure in Michigan, New Jersey requires at a minimum that applicants for a professional planner license:

(1) Be of good moral character;

(2) Be a citizen of the United States or have declared his intention to become a citizen of the United States;

(3) Pass the required examinations.

* * *

The applicant for license as a professional planner shall submit the following minimum educational and experience qualifications:

(1) A graduate degree in professional planning from an accredited college or university in a curriculum offering instruction in such recognized planning subjects as principles of land use planning, history of city planning, planning project design, and planning law and administration * * * with a minimum of two years' experience in the full-time practice of professional planning * * *; or

A graduate degree in a field other than professional planning from an accredited college or university with a minimum of four years' experience in the full-time practice or professional planning * * *; or

(2) An undergraduate degree in professional planning from an accredited college or university; or curriculum offering a major or option comprising a minimum of 21 credits in such recognized planning subjects * * * with a minimum of three years' experience in the full-time practice of professional planning * * *; or

An undergraduate degree in a field other than professional planning from an accredited college or university with a minimum of four years' experience * * *

(3) Graduation from a secondary school and at least 8 years of professional planning experience * * *;

N.J.S.A. 45:14A–9.

D. ETHICAL CONDUCT OF PARTIES IN THE LAND USE ARENA

Ethical dilemmas in the land use arena can be categorized into (1) conflicts of interest; (2) compatibility of dual office holding; and (3) bias and prejudgment. By far, the overwhelming amount of litigation centers on alleged conflicts of interest on the part of planners, attorneys, members of planning and zoning boards, and other participants in the planning and land use regulation process. This section examines relevant regulations and explores, through cases and notes, a variety of ethics issues that have captured the public's attention. Attorneys must be conversant with ethical challenges facing all of the parties in the land use game so that municipal attorneys can provide guidance to their government clients and so that attorneys representing private client interests before government can ensure that there is integrity in the land use planning and decisionmaking processes.

(1) Planners

Professional planners who are members of the American Institute of Certified Planners, a voluntary membership organization that requires successful completion of a written examination as a condition of membership, and requires its members to adhere to a written code of ethics. Excerpts from this code are reprinted below:

AICP CODE OF ETHICS AND PROFESSIONAL CONDUCT
(Adopted October 1978—as amended October 1991).

This Code is a guide to the ethical conduct required of members of the American Institute of Certified Planners. The Code also aims at informing the public of the principles to which professional planners are committed. * * *

The Code's standards of behavior provide a basis for adjudicating any charge that a member has acted unethically. However, the Code also provides more than the minimum threshold of enforceable acceptability. It sets aspirational standards that require conscious striving to attain.

The principles of the Code derive both from the general values of society and from the planning profession's special responsibility to serve the public interest. As the basic values of society are often in competition with each other, so also do the principles of this Code sometimes compete. For example, the need to provide full public information may compete with the need to respect confidences. Plans and programs often result from a balancing among divergent interests. An ethical judgment often also requires a conscientious balancing, based on the facts and context of a particular situation and on the precepts of the entire Code. * * *

The Planner's Responsibility to the Public

A. A planner's primary obligation is to serve the public interest. While the definition of the public interest is formulated through continuous debate, a planner owes allegiance to a conscientiously attained concept of the public interest, which requires these special obligations:

(1) A planner must have special concern for the long range consequences of present actions.

(2) A planner must pay special attention to the interrelatedness of decisions.

(3) A planner must strive to provide full, clear and accurate information on planning issues to citizens and governmental decision-makers.

(4) A planner must strive to give citizens the opportunity to have a meaningful impact on the development of plans and programs. Participation should be broad enough to include people who lack formal organization or influence.

(5) A planner must strive to expand choice and opportunity for all persons, recognizing a special responsibility to plan for the needs of disadvantaged groups and persons, and must urge the alteration of policies, institutions and decisions which oppose such needs.

(6) A planner must strive to protect the integrity of the natural environment.

(7) A planner must strive for excellence of environmental design and endeavor to conserve the heritage of the built environment.

The Planner's Responsibility to Clients and Employers

B. A planner owes diligent, creative, independent and competent performance of work in pursuit of the client's or employer's interest. Such performance should be consistent with the planner's faithful service to the public interest.

(1) A planner must exercise independent professional judgment on behalf of clients and employers.

(2) A planner must accept the decisions of a client or employer concerning the objectives and nature of the professional services to be performed unless the course of action to be pursued involves conduct which is illegal or inconsistent with the planner's primary obligation to the public interest.

(3) A planner shall not perform work if there is an actual, apparent, or reasonably foreseeable conflict of interest, direct or indirect, or an appearance of impropriety, without full written disclosure concerning work for current or past clients and subsequent written consent by the current client or employer. A planner shall remove himself or herself from a project if there is any direct personal or financial gain including gains to family members. A planner shall not disclose information gained in the course of public activity for a private benefit unless the information would be offered impartially to any person.

(4) A planner who has previously worked for a public planning body should not represent a private client, for one year after the planner's last date of employment with the planning body, in connection with any matter before that body that the planner may have influenced before leaving public employment.

(5) A planner must not solicit prospective clients or employment through use of false or misleading claims, harassment or duress.

(6) A planner must not sell or offer to sell services by stating or implying an ability to influence decisions by improper means.

(7) A planner must not use the power of any office to seek or obtain a special advantage that is not in the public interest nor any special advantage that is not a matter of public knowledge.

(8) A planner must not accept or continue to perform work beyond the planner's professional competence or accept work which cannot be performed with the promptness required by the prospective client or employer, or which is required by the circumstances of the assignment.

(9) A planner must not reveal information gained in a professional relationship which the client or employer has requested to be held inviolate. Exceptions to this requirement of non-disclosure may be made only when (a) required by process of law, or (b) required to prevent a clear violation of law, or (c) required to prevent a substantial injury to the public. Disclosure pursuant to (b) and (c) must not be made until after the planner has verified the facts and issues involved and, when practicable, has exhausted efforts to obtain reconsiderations of the matter and has sought separate opinions on the issue from other qualified professionals employed by the client or employer.

The Planner's Responsibility to the Profession and to Colleagues

C. A planner should contribute to the development of the profession by improving knowledge and techniques, making work relevant to solutions of community problems, and increasing public understanding of planning activities. A planner should treat fairly the professional views of qualified colleagues and members of other professions.

(1) A planner must protect and enhance the integrity of the profession and must be responsible in criticism of the profession.

(2) A planner must accurately represent the qualifications, views and findings of colleagues.

(3) A planner who reviews the work of other professionals must do so in a fair, considerate, professional and equitable manner.

(4) A planner must share the results of experience and research which contribute to the body of planning knowledge.

(5) A planner must examine the applicability of planning theories, methods and standards to the facts and analysis of each particular situation and must not accept the applicability of a customary solution without first establishing its appropriateness to the situation.

(6) A planner must contribute time and information to the professional development of students, interns, beginning professionals and other colleagues.

(7) A planner must strive to increase the opportunities for women and members of recognized minorities to become professional planners.

(8) A planner shall not commit an act of sexual harassment.

The Planner's Self–Responsibility

D. A planner should strive for high standards of professional integrity, proficiency and knowledge.

(1) A planner must not commit a deliberately wrongful act which reflects adversely on the planner's professional fitness.

(2) A planner must respect the rights of others and, in particular, must not improperly discriminate against persons.

(3) A planner must strive to continue professional education.

(4) A planner must accurately represent professional qualifications, education and affiliations.

(5) A planner must systematically and critically analyze ethical issues in the practice of planning.

(6) A planner must strive to contribute time and effort to groups lacking in adequate planning resources and to voluntary professional activities.

Notes

1. Planners are members of the community too, and occasionally their personal needs and interests could present a potential for conflicts of interest. Should planners live in the community where they work? What should planners do when confronted with "investment" opportunities in their community to participate in a small development project? Should they be able to invest in real estate development in the same municipality where they work? Can their spouse? Is disclosure enough? See Advisory Opinion, American Institute of Certified Planners at http://www.planning.org/ethics/rulings.html. In a case decided on procedural grounds (reversal of a summary judgment order) the court found that more information was needed to determine whether a conflict of interest existed where the property-owner applicant was the director of the county planning and zoning department since he submitted an application for a conditional use permit (needed in order to lease his property for the installation of a telecommunications tower) to his own office for review. Crozer v. Reichert, 275 Ga. 118, 561 S.E.2d 120 (2002).

2. In 2000, the American Institute of Certified Planners commissioned an independent critique of the Code of Ethics for Planners. Among the purposes of the critique was an assessment of whether the language of the Code was clear and enforceable. The assessment is available at http://www.planning.org/ethics/salkin.htm.

(2) Attorneys

Although lawyers do have a professional code of ethics to follow, there is no code of ethics or professional conduct that specifically covers lawyers who participate in land use matters. Consider the following ethics questions:

1. A lawyer sits as a member if the planning board. May she step down to represent a client before the board and then return to her seat after the matter is presented and/or resolved?

2. A lawyer in private practice who advised the zoning board for five years was recently replaced with another attorney when the new mayor took office. Can he now represent an applicant before that same board?

3. When a full-time city attorney is assigned to review a matter pending before the planning and zoning boards and to advise them on appropriate action(s), who is the client of the city attorney? Does it make a difference if the various offices and divisions within the government have different ideas on how to proceed?

4. May an attorney who serves as counsel to the municipal water supply board represent a developer in applications for subdivision approval before the city planning and zoning commission?

5. What is the appropriate conduct for a lawyer-member of the planning commission when a partner or associate in her law firm appears before the commission? Who should be disqualified—the attorney-commission member or the law firm? Why?

6. What is the appropriate ethical conduct where the planning commissioner's daughter is a member of a law firm appearing before the board? Does it make a difference whether her daughter is the attorney of record in the matter?

NICHOLAS v. WILTON ZONING BOARD OF APPEALS

Superior Court of Connecticut, 2001.
2001 WL 1200339, 30 Conn. L. Rptr. 386.

MEMORANDUM OF DECISION RE MOTION TO DISQUALIFY #109

HICKEY, J.

The defendant, the Zoning Board of Appeals of the town of Wilton, has moved to disqualify Robert A. Fuller (Fuller) from representing the plaintiff in this case on the grounds that: (1) the representation violates Rule 1.9 of the Rules of Professional Conduct because Fuller formerly represented the town of Wilton, as town counsel, in connection with the same property and same issue involved in this case, and the town of Wilton has not consented to Fuller's representation of the plaintiff in this case; and (2) the documents and/or testimony arising from Fuller's prior representation may be presented in the trial of this case, in violation of Rules 1.6 and 3.7 of the Rules of Professional Conduct. On September 11, 2001, during a hearing held by this court, the parties were provided with an opportunity to present oral arguments and evidence in support of their respective positions.

A brief summary of the background of this case is useful to an understanding of the issues raised by the motion presently before this court. The plaintiff, Nick P. Nicholas, is the owner of a parcel of land located at 92 Hulda Hill Road in Wilton, Connecticut. The subject property contains 2.104 acres located in a two-acre residential zone, and is shown as Lot No. 1 on the subdivision map #2829, approved by Planning and Zoning Commission for the town of Wilton in 1969. On September 20, 1999, the plaintiff applied for a zoning permit to build a single-family residence on the subject property. On September 23, 1999, the zoning enforcement officer, relying on a legal opinion provided by the town's land use counsel, denied the application on the ground that the parcel was not a valid building lot.

Prior to the plaintiff's purchase of Lot No. 1, however, in an opinion letter drafted in 1975, the plaintiff's present attorney, Robert A. Fuller, then town counsel, advised the town planner that a permit could be issued on the lot in accordance with various sections of the zoning regulations in effect at that time, and furthermore, advised the town planner that if it was impossible for the property owner to comply with certain regulations, the town could not validly deny the owner use of the property. In July of 1986, Fuller resigned from his position as town counsel for the town of Wilton and has not since represented the town of Wilton in any capacity.

On October 21, 1999, the plaintiff filed an appeal of the zoning enforcement officer's decision with the Zoning Board of Appeals of the town of Wilton. A public hearing was held on December 20, 1999. Fuller was present at the hearing and provided testimony in relation to the 1975 opinion letter he rendered while serving as town counsel. On January 19, 2000, the board denied the appeal on the ground that the subdivision lot was not a valid lot. The plaintiff now appeals the decision of the board, the defendant herein, and asserts that it acted illegally, arbitrarily, and in abuse of its discretion. Fuller is the plaintiff's counsel in this case, the appeal of the board's decision.

In its memorandum, the defendant argues that the plaintiff's interests are adverse to Fuller's former client's interests. Moreover, the defendant argues that the present matter is the same or at least substantially related to Fuller's prior representation, inasmuch as this case and Fuller's 1975 opinion letter both deal with the same piece of property and the same issue of whether or not that property is a buildable lot. Furthermore, the defendant argues that the scope of Rule 1.9 of the Rules of Professional Conduct is not limited to situations where the lawyer might disclose privileged information received from the former client. Rather, the defendant contends that unless the former client consents, Rule 1.9 is a blanket prohibition that applies regardless of whether the lawyer now states that he relied on public records or documents. Consequently, the defendant requests that Fuller be disqualified from serving as the plaintiff's counsel in this case.

In response, Fuller argues that the similarity in the subject matter of the present litigation and the 1975 opinion letter is insufficient, by itself, to provide a basis for his disqualification. Fuller contends that the 1975 opinion letter was not a confidential document and has been part of the public record since it was rendered, and was not based on any confidential information obtained by him while serving as town counsel. Fuller also maintains that Rule 1.9 is not as sweeping as the defendant contends and requires the court to make its determination based on the facts of each case. Thus, Fuller concludes that the facts of this case do not warrant his disqualification.

"The trial court has the authority to regulate the conduct of attorneys and has a duty to enforce the standards of conduct regarding attorneys * * * Since October 1986, the conduct of attorneys has been regulated also by the Rules of Professional Conduct, which were approved by the judges of the Superior Court and which superseded the Code of Professional Responsibility * * * The trial court has broad discretion to determine whether there exists a conflict of interest that would warrant disqualification of an attorney." Bergeron v. Mackler, 225 Conn. 391, 397, 623 A.2d 489 (1993). "Disqualification of counsel is a remedy that serves to enforce the lawyer's duty of absolute fidelity and to guard against the danger of inadvertent use of confidential information * * * In disqualification matters, however, we must be solicitous of a client's right freely to choose his counsel, * * * mindful of the fact that a client whose attorney is disqualified may suffer the loss of time and money in finding new counsel and may lose the benefit of its longtime counsel's specialized knowledge of its operations * * * The competing interests at stake in the motion to disqualify, therefore, are: (1) the defendant's interest in protecting confidential information; (2) the plaintiffs' interest in freely selecting counsel of their choice; and (3) the public's interest in the scrupulous administration of justice." The mere appearance of impropriety, however, "will not stand alone to disqualify an attorney in the absence of any indication that the attorney's representation risks violating the Rules of Professional Conduct."

Rule 1.9 of the Rules of Professional Conduct governs disqualification of counsel for a conflict of interest relating to a former client. The rule states, in relevant part, that: "A lawyer who has formerly represented a client in a matter shall not thereafter: (1) Represent another person in the same or a substantially related matter in which that person's interests are materially adverse to the interests of the former client unless the former client consents after consultation * * *" Furthermore, the Commentary to Rule 1.9 states, in relevant part, "The scope of a 'matter' for purposes of subdivision (1) may depend on the facts of a particular situation or transaction. The lawyer's involvement in a matter can also be a question of degree * * * The underlying question is whether the lawyer was so involved in the matter that the subsequent representation can be justly regarded as a changing of sides in the matter in question * * * Information acquired by the lawyer in the course of representing a client may not subsequently be used by the lawyer to the disadvantage of the client. However, the fact that a lawyer has once served a client does not preclude the lawyer from using generally known information about that client when later representing another client."

In the present case, this court has considered the relationship between Fuller's representation of the defendant as town counsel for the town of Wilton several years ago, and his representation of the plaintiff against the defendant, the Zoning Board of Appeals of the town of Wilton, in this appeal. In balancing the competing interests at stake in this case, this court notes that the defendant does not allege that it divulged any confidential information to Fuller. This court finds that twenty-six years have passed since Fuller authored the opinion letter for the town of Wilton, at a time when the town was not in an adversarial position with respect to the subject property. This court finds that fifteen years have gone by since Fuller severed his relationship with the defendant. Furthermore, this court finds that the public's interest in the scrupulous administration of justice will not be compromised by Fuller's continued representation of the plaintiff in this case. Consequently, this court finds that in this case, the plaintiff's interest in the free selection of the counsel of his choice outweighs the defendant's interest in protecting confidential information. * * * Accordingly, this court finds that Fuller's prior representation of the defendant does not provide a sufficient relationship to the facts surrounding this present matter to warrant his disqualification pursuant to Rule 1.9.

Next, the defendant asserts that Rule 3.7 prohibits a lawyer from acting as an advocate at trial where the lawyer is likely to be a necessary witness, except under limited circumstances not applicable here. The defendant asserts that Fuller has already provided testimony in relation to this matter in the past, on December 20, 1999, at the public hearing held by the Zoning Board of Appeals of the town of Wilton. The defendant argues that Fuller's continued representation of the plaintiff may result in a violation of Rule 3.7 of the Rules of Professional Conduct.

In response, Fuller argues that speculation as to a possible future violation of Rule 3.7 is not a valid ground for his disqualification. Fuller maintains that Rule 3.7 is not applicable in this case, as he does not intend to testify on any issue in this case. Rule 3.7 provides the framework for disqualification where counsel is likely to be called as a necessary witness in the present litigation. * * * Nevertheless, "[t]estimony may be relevant and even highly useful but still not strictly necessary * * * A finding of necessity takes into account such factors as the significance of the matters, weight of the testimony and availability of other evidence * * * [T]he mere statement that the attorney will be a necessary party witness [would] not support [the] motion." (Brackets in original; citations omitted; internal quotation marks omitted.) Somers & Associates v. Kendall, supra, Superior Court, Docket No. 064478; Bopko v. Bopko, supra, 28 Conn. L. Rptr. 557. A strong showing that the testimony of the opposing attorney is truly necessary is required before the court may grant a motion to disqualify opposing counsel. Somers & Associates v. Kendall, supra, Docket No. 064478; DeMarco v. Fire Command, Inc., Superior Court, judicial district of New Haven at New Haven, Docket No. 297381 (July 27, 1990) (Downey, J.) (2 Conn. L. Rptr. 101). In this case, the defendant simply fails to persuade this court that Fuller's testimony will truly be necessary, in violation of Rule 3.7.

Accordingly, for the foregoing reasons, the defendant's motion to disqualify is denied without prejudice.

Notes

1. A case somewhat contrary to the Wilton case is Walden Federal Sav. and Loan Ass'n v. Village of Walden, 212 A.D.2d 718, 622 N.Y.S.2d 796 (2d Dept. 1995), leave to appeal dismissed, 86 N.Y.2d 777, 631 N.Y.S.2d 603, 655 N.E.2d 700 (1995), where a law firm represented a municipality at various times for approximately 30 years, and during the scope of that representation the law firm, among other things, worked on the drafting of a local site plan law. The New York appellate court held that six years after the last representation, the law firm was prohibited under the applicable Code of Professional Responsibility from appearing before the municipality on behalf of another client requesting site plan review. This case has chilling implications for land use attorneys who represent municipal clients as part of their private practice. But see, Kay F. Sterrett v. Loundon County Board of Supervisors, 22 Va. Cir. 148 (1990) where the Virginia Court held that a law firm would not be disqualified where the firm employs a former county attorney who was involved in land-use matters during her employ as a county attorney.

2. For a review of legal ethical dilemmas in land-use planning and zoning see, Eric Dyas, "Conflicts of Interest in Planning and Zoning Cases," 17 J. Legal Prof. 219 (1992); Mark W. Cordes, "Policing Bias and Conflicts of Interest in Zoning Decisionmaking," 65 N.D.L.Rev. 161 (1989); Patricia E. Salkin, "Legal Ethics and Land–Use Planning," 30 The Urban Lawyer 383 (Spring 1998); Salkin, "1998 Survey of Ethics in Land Use Law," 26 Fordham Urb. L.J. 1393 (1999); and Salkin, "Ethics Allegations in Land Use Continue to Fill the Court Dockets," Zoning and Planning Law Report (April 2003).

3. In addition to planners and lawyers, there are other professionals who are involved in the land use arena. For example, the American Association of Engineering Societies represents over 500,000 engineers and in 1984 they issued a Model Guide for Professional Conduct. The National Society for Professional Engineers represents over 75,000 engineers and in 1993 they issued a revised Code of Ethics for Engineers. The National Association of Realtors represents more than 750,000 realtors and in 1994 they issued a revised Code of Ethics and Standard of Practice. In a recent opinion, the New York Attorney General found that a member of a village design review board who is a professional architect need not resign from the board although he is a partner in a firm that about once a year accepts projects over which the board has jurisdiction. However, the Attorney General advised that the board member should "unquestionably" recuse himself from any consideration of a project or matter involving his firm. While

noting that "to maintain public confidence in the integrity of government, public officials must avoid even the appearance of impropriety," the opinion concludes that, "* * * if resignation and not recusal was the appropriate remedy in every instance where a local official's private endeavors raised a potential conflict of interest * * * local units of government would have difficulty finding qualified individuals to serve the public interest." See, Op. N.Y. Atty. Gen. 2002–8 (March 4, 2002).

(3) Members of Planning and Zoning Boards

Individuals who serve on planning boards and zoning boards are typically community volunteers who receive little or no financial remuneration for their service. Membership on these boards is most often left to the discretion of the appointing authority, which may be the chief elected official or the local legislative body. What sparse limitations there may be on membership qualifications, board members usually reside within the community they serve. This very fact raises ethics questions with some degree of frequency. Consider the following:

1. Can or should a member of a planning board discuss and vote on an application involving her neighbor's property? What if it is an application of a landowner within her development? Can a board member leave her seat on the board during a public hearing to speak in favor or in opposition to the application before the board where the board member has a personal interest in the matter? If it is permissible for the board member to do this, must she recuse herself from voting? How about her ability to discuss and debate the matter with her colleagues on the board? May she question the applicant or the applicant's representative(s)?

2. Can or should individuals in the following professions serve on planning board and zoning boards: engineers, architects, lawyers, planners, realtors, land surveyors, bankers, developers? Does their potential expertise in land use planning and zoning matters make them more suitable candidates for membership on the boards? When might they be confronted with ethical dilemmas?

3. Can or should board members vote on matters that could impact members of their immediate family? How significant would the impact need to be? Must it be financial?

Few states provide statutory guidance for members of planning and zoning boards who may find themselves in a conflict of interest situation. For example, Connecticut General Statutes provides in part: "No member of any zoning commission or board and no member of any zoning board of appeals shall participate in the hearing or decision of the board or commission of which he is a member upon any matter in which he is directly or indirectly interested in a personal or financial sense." Conn. Gen. Stat. § 8–11, see also § 8021 for similar language for members of planning commissions.

SECTION 4. THE CONTENT AND EFFECT OF THE MASTER PLAN

UNITED STATES DEPARTMENT OF COMMERCE, A STANDARD CITY PLANNING ENABLING ACT
(1928).

Sec. 6. General Powers and Duties—It shall be the function and duty of the commission to make and adopt a master plan for the physical development of the municipality, including any areas outside of its boundaries which, in the commission's judgment, bear relation to the planning of such municipality. Such plan, with the accompanying maps, plats, charts, and descriptive matter, shall show the commission's recommendations for the development of said territory, including, among other things, the general location, character, and extent of streets, viaducts, subways, bridges, waterways, water fronts, boulevards, parkways, playgrounds, squares, parks, aviation fields, and other public ways, grounds and open spaces, the general location of public buildings and other public property, and the general location and extent of public utilities and terminals, whether publicly or privately owned or operated, for water, light, sanitation, transportation, communication, power, and other purposes; also the removal, relocation, widening, narrowing, vacating, abandonment, change of use or extension of any of the foregoing ways, grounds, open spaces, buildings, property, utilities, or terminals; as well as a zoning plan for the control of the height, area, bulk, location, and use of buildings and premises. As the work of making the whole master plan progresses, the commission may from time to time adopt and publish a part or parts thereof, any such part to cover one or more major sections or divisions of the municipality or one or more of the aforesaid or other functional matters to be included in the plan. The commission may from time to time amend, extend, or add to the plan.

Sec. 7. Purposes in View—In the preparation of such plan the commission shall make careful and comprehensive surveys and studies of present conditions and future growth of the municipality and with due regard to its relation to neighboring territory. The plan shall be made with the general purpose of guiding and accomplishing a coordinated, adjusted, and harmonious development of the municipality and its environs which will, in accordance with present and future needs, best promote health, safety, morals, order, convenience, prosperity, and general welfare, as well as efficiency and economy in the process of development; including, among other things, adequate provision for traffic, the promotion of safety from fire and other dangers, adequate provision for light and air, the promotion of the healthful and convenient distribution of population, the promotion of good civic design and arrangement, wise and efficient expenditure of public funds, and the adequate provision of public utilities and other public requirements.

See Knack, Meck and Stollman, The Real Story Behind the Standard Planning and Zoning Acts of the 1920's, Land Use Law (Feb. 1996) p. 3. The Model Land Development Code provides model enabling legislation for planning that differs considerably from the Standard Act. Some excerpts from Article 3 of the Code and the commentary follow:

* * *

Two key issues need to be resolved in regard to the content of the plan: First, to what extent should the plan concentrate on physical development? Second, should the plan emphasize long term goals or continuing processes?

1. The Role of Physical Planning

Traditional urban planning based on the SPEA has concentrated on (a) the proper location and intensity of activities which use land, and (b) the type, design, and location of physical structures and facilities that serve these activities. The planner has examined the present physical setting, made long range projections of population and employment, and forecasted land and facility demands to be generated. Then, applying professional judgments as to desired future conditions, he has prepared a plan locating activities and specified facilities.

This planning process has a number of objectives. (See, e.g., Mocine, Urban Physical Planning and the "New Planning," 32 J.A.I.P. 234 (July 1966).) One is to maximize economic efficiency by predicting physical facility needs and coordinating the size and location of such facilities with activity locations. Thus, for example, the process should lead to acquiring land and building schools near planned residential locations, constructing sewer lines large enough to serve adjacent activities, and locating expressways to connect places of residence and employment. This objective recognizes the long lead time required for major public improvements and the desirability of employing these improvements efficiently over their lifetimes to justify the original expense.

A second objective is to maximize desired relationships between different land use activities and their attendant physical structures. For example, a plan may call for areas exclusively developed for single family residences, but with provision for nearby shopping centers. Or it may seek to stimulate mixed residential densities and certain commercial activities. This objective assumes that the market is deficient in creating desired mixes of uses. It also assumes that without governmental intervention individual landowners will create external costs, and environments of maximum desirability will be largely unobtainable.

A third objective is to allocate land (a scarce resource in a locational sense) to desired activities. For instance, the city may decide that it wants to encourage only single family houses, but the market unhindered would result in numerous multiple dwellings.

Or, the city may desire to encourage industrial investment and seek to preserve adequate space for new factories. This objective, like the second, assumes an imperfect market and the necessity of governmental intervention to stimulate private investment towards desired goals.

A fourth objective is to provide a general urban design which is pleasing. For instance, a plan might call for the preservation of open space for recreation and appearance, require tree planting and setbacks, attempt to order the three-dimensional design of areas, or group leisure activities in specified locations.

A growing number of planners reject this traditional approach. They argue that planning for physical development is based on insufficient information, has too limited a focus, and is unrelated to desirable economic and social goals. In addition, as explored below, they believe that long-range (end-state) planning is not effective; rather the planner should concentrate his efforts on short term programs to realize specific objectives.

* * *

The Code can take any of four major positions: (1) A plan should deal only with physical development without consideration of economic and social data and consequences. (This basically is the approach of the SPEA.) (2) The plan should have a physical development nucleus but should require that specified economic and social data be taken into consideration in its preparation and consideration. (This is the approach adopted.) (3) The plan should have a development focus and speak primarily in terms of economic and social objectives and means for their attainment including physical development. (This path is largely uncharted.) (4) There should be no section on planning because there is no solid urban planning theory at present.

Alternative (2) has been chosen for several reasons. First, the Model Land Development Code encompasses a variety of laws relating to the physical development of land but does not attempt direct regulation of social and economic affairs outside the sphere of land development. It is appropriate, therefore, that the planning powers authorized by the Code be limited to those that parallel its other Articles. Second, we have existing institutions of land planning which need a framework. The present statutory framework, built on the SPEA, is inadequate in a number of respects. We are beginning to appreciate better than before that we cannot realistically determine patterns and characteristics of physical development mainly on the basis of design and appearance. Rather, how and where development takes place relates more importantly to social and economic values and objectives. Therefore, we should require explicit analysis and disclosure to the greatest extent possible of a variety of social and economic consequences of planned physical development. Otherwise we hide such policy judgments, make them implicitly rather than explicitly, or, as often occurs, design a plan which will never be carried out because the implementing decisions will be politically unfeasible.

* * *

Most master plans have been of the long-range (end-state) type. They have sought to present a "picture" of what the planning area should look like some twenty or twenty-five years in the future. In the view of many planners, however, few of these plans have had a demonstrable impact on development. (See, e.g., Meyerson, Building the Middle–Range Bridge for Comprehensive Planning, 22 J.A.I.P. 58 (1956); Webber, Prospects for Policies Planning, in Duhl (ed.) The Urban Condition (1963), 319; Robinson, Beyond the Middle–Range Planning Bridge, 31 J.A.I.P. 304 (Nov. 1965); Mitchell, The New Frontier in Metropolitan Planning, 27 J.A.I.P. 169 (Aug. 1961).)

* * *

This Article provides for long-term goal setting. The goals, however, are to be put in terms of nature and rate of change rather than in static form. Further, the goals are primarily important as a framework for the short-term programming required by Section 3–105 and they are expected to change. In addition, the Code makes numerous references to the identification and treatment of major problems of physical development. These are the basic departure points for the programming. Thus the Article provides for a broad framework of objectives, but is concerned mainly with the preparation and evaluation of specific programs of public action.

* * *

The relationship between planning and regulation has been the subject of discussion for many years. Two articles debating the subject are Sullivan and Kressel, Twenty Years After—Renewed Significance of the Comprehensive Plan Requirement, 9 Urban Law Ann. 33 (1975) and Tarlock, Consistency with Adopted Land Use Plans as a Standard of Review: The Case Against, 9 Urban Law Ann. 69 (1975). For a more recent updates on the evolving role of the comprehensive plan, see, Sullivan and Pelham, "The Evolving Role of the Comprehensive Plan," 29 The Urban Lawyer 363 (1997) and Sullivan, "The Role of the Comprehensive Plan," 31 The Urban Lawyer 915 (1999). In this last article, Sullivan discusses the organization of caselaw into three major categories: 1) the traditional approach which gives no significance to the plan; 2) the "planning factor" approach, which gives the plan a role in such determinations; and 3) the "planning mandate" approach which treats the plan as a dispositive standard for land-use regulations and standards.

CREATIVE DISPLAYS, INC. v. CITY OF FLORENCE

Supreme Court of Kentucky, 1980.
602 S.W.2d 682.

STEPHENS, JUSTICE.

The issue before the court is whether Boone County and Florence, Kentucky, have properly enacted planning and zoning ordinances, pursuant to KRS chapter 100 (1966).

* * *

Until 1966, the City of Florence and Boone County fiscal court were separate planning bodies. The record shows that Florence adopted its zoning ordinance in December of 1962, and Boone County adopted its in February of 1966. In September of 1966, a county-wide planning unit was formed, encompassing Florence, Walton, Hopeful Heights, and Boone County, and known as the Boone County Planning and Zoning Commission. This entity was created in response to House Bill 390, which passed the Kentucky Legislature and became effective on June 16, 1966, and is presently contained in KRS chapter 100.

In October, 1966, the Boone County Planning and Zoning Commission adopted its "comprehensive plan," pursuant to KRS 100.183. This plan consisted solely of the already existing plans of Florence and Boone County. The statute provides that the minimum requirements for the plan include a statement of goals and objectives, a land use plan, a transportation plan, and a community facilities plan. KRS 100.187. It is not argued that the comprehensive plan adopted by the Commission did not contain these elements. On the contrary, it is admitted that the individual plans of Florence and Boone County comply in every respect with the substantive requirements of chapter 100. Yet, Creative Designs still challenges the plan adopted by the Commission as invalid under the statute, and we agree.

* * *

The actions of the Boone County Planning and Zoning Commission in *pro forma* adopting the pre-existing plans of Florence and Boone County do not constitute the "preparation" of a comprehensive plan for the newly created unit.

Further, although the plan adopted by the Commission contains all the elements listed in KRS 100.187, that section requires "a statement of goals and objectives, principles, policies, and standards, which shall serve as a guide for the physical development and economic and social well-being *of the planning unit*." (emphasis added). In this instance the planning unit includes Florence, Walton, Hopeful Heights, and Boone County. The goals and objectives expressed by Florence and Boone County in their individual plans in no way address the question of the proper goals for the new, county-wide planning unit. The same is true of the specialized research, analysis, and projections which are required to support the elements of the comprehensive plan. KRS 100.191. Research into population distribution, economic and business activity, and transportation and community facility needs, done in advance of the local plans, will not suffice as the basis for the county-wide plan.

Finally, and probably most significantly, the statutory scheme set out in KRS 100.197 requires the planning commission to hold a public hearing before adoption of the comprehensive plan. Florence and Boone County admit that no hearing was held to consider the county-wide plan. They argue that the prior hearings held with regard to the individual plans of Florence and Boone County are sufficient to satisfy the mandates of the statute. We disagree. The citizens of Florence, the largest population center in the county, have never had the opportunity to express their opinions about the future planning and zoning of the rest of Boone County. Residents of Hopeful Heights, Walton, and rural areas of the county have not been able to voice their concerns about the same issues in Florence. And none of the people of Boone County have been allowed to speak their minds with regard to the comprehensive plan for the county-wide planning unit in which they now live. For this reason, we hold that the comprehensive plan adopted by the Boone County Planning and Zoning Commission does not comply with the requirements of KRS 100.183, et seq.

KRS 100.367 provides that all plans in existence on the effective date of KRS chapter 100 (June 16, 1966), may continue in effect until they are superseded by new plans or until five years have passed. Thus, all plans which did not conform to the new law on June 16, 1971, ceased to exist on that date. Regrettably, the comprehensive plan in the case at bar falls into that category. The comprehensive plan of the Boone County Planning and Zoning Commission, and any zoning ordinances adopted pursuant thereto, are void.

* * *

The decision of the Court of Appeals is reversed and the case is remanded to the trial court for entry of a judgment consistent with this opinion.

* * *

Notes

1. Compare with the principal case Lazy Mountain Land Club v. Matanuska–Susitna Borough Bd. of Adjustment and Appeals, 904 P.2d 373 (Alaska 1995) where the court rejected a developer's argument that piecemeal adoption of various planning documents and incorporation by reference of a previous document evidenced the lack of a comprehensive plan.

2. Courts have had very little concern with the question of adequacy of the plan. The enabling legislation for planning rarely makes provision for judicial (or any other) review of the finished product. One notable exception to this state of affairs is found in the State of Oregon. In 1973, Oregon amended its planning enabling statute to make land use planning mandatory

for local government units, and created a state level administrative agency, the Land Conservation and Development Commission (LCDC), which has power to establish statewide planning "goals" and to review local plans for consistency with the established "goals." Since 1975, when the 14 statewide "goals" were promulgated, several hundred contested disputes concerning the consistency of local land use decisions with the "goals" have been adjudicated by LCDC. For three divergent views on the efficacy of this approach, see Comprehensive Plans and the Law: The Oregon Experience, 32 Land Use Law & Zoning Digest 6 (Sept. 1980). Also see Rajneesh Medical Corp. v. Wasco County, 300 Or. 107, 706 P.2d 948 (1985).

3. The Creative Displays case is one of the few that looks at the process of adopting and evaluating the comprehensive plan. In many states the enabling legislation for zoning, subdivision regulations and other land use regulations specifies that these regulations may be adopted or enacted only after the adoption of a comprehensive plan. In a later chapter the question of the validity of regulations where the comprehensive planning process was insufficient will be taken up in greater detail. In Wolf v. City of Ely, 493 N.W.2d 846 (Iowa 1992) the court held a zoning ordinance invalid because the town had not adopted a comprehensive plan; the court acknowledged that "A majority of courts in states where zoning must be 'in accordance with a comprehensive plan' hold a plan external to the zoning ordinance is not required." However, the court stated that the trend of decisions is in the other direction and aligned Iowa with the trend.

ELYSIAN HEIGHTS RESIDENTS ASSOCIATION, INC. v. CITY OF LOS ANGELES

California Court of Appeal, Second District, 1986.
182 Cal.App.3d 21, 227 Cal.Rptr. 226.

COMPTON, ACTING PRESIDING JUSTICE.

Elysian Heights Residents Association, Inc., et al., hereinafter appellants, appeal from a judgment of the superior court denying their petition for administrative mandamus. (See Code Civ.Proc., § 1094.5.) By way of this petition, appellants sought the revocation of a building permit issued by respondents City of Los Angeles, et al. to Morton Park Associates [Morton] for the construction of a three story, 45–unit apartment complex. Pursuant to appellants' request, and in order to preserve the status quo, we stayed further development of the project pending the outcome of this appeal. We now affirm the judgment and vacate the stay order.

* * *

In December 1984, while the administrative appeal was still pending, the Department of Building and Safety, pursuant to the terms of an ordinance imposing a moratorium on all projects which exceeded the zoning and height requirements of the District Plan, ordered Morton to immediately cease all construction work. At approximately the same time various homeowner associations filed an action in superior court, entitled *Federation of Hillside Canyon Associations, Inc. et al. v. City of*

Los Angeles (Los Angeles Sup.Ct. No. 526,616), to prevent the City from issuing building permits for development of property inconsistent with the General Plan. * * *

[The court found that the existing plan would have permitted a 12-unit apartment building.]

In January 1985, the superior court, in ruling on the *Federation* case, issued a writ of mandate requiring the City to bring its zoning ordinances into conformity with the General Plan, but denied the petitioners' request for an injunction against the issuance of building permits for inconsistent development. * * *

We first consider appellants' contention that the disputed building permit was issued in violation of state statute and was thus void *ab initio* and must be revoked. The major thrust of appellants' argument in this regard is that building permits, to be validly issued, must be consistent with a municipality's general plan. It is, therefore, necessary to determine whether Government Code section 65860 mandates such conformity.

* * *

[W]e first note that in recent years the Legislature has enacted a number of statutes as part of the State Planning & Zoning Law (Gov. Code, § 65000, et seq.), the combined effect of which is to require that cities and counties adopt a general plan for the future development, configuration, and character of a city and county and require that future land use decisions be made in harmony with that general plan. (*City of Los Angeles v. State of California* (1982) 138 Cal.App.3d 526, 530, 187 Cal.Rptr. 893; *Bownds v. City of Glendale* (1980) 113 Cal.App.3d 875, 880, 170 Cal.Rptr. 342.) These requirements, forming what is generally referred to as the consistency doctrine, promote a particular nexus between land-use plans and government regulation of land use, such as zoning and subdivision map approval.

The doctrine has its roots in the language of the Standard Zoning Enabling Act (U.S. Dept. of Commerce, The Standard State Zoning Enabling Act, 1922 [rev. ed., 1926.]), which provides that zoning shall be done "in accordance with" a comprehensive plan. (See DiMento, *Improving Development Control through Planning: The Consistency Doctrine* (1978) 5 Colum.J.Envt'l L. 1.) Under this historical antecedent of the consistency doctrine, violations of the "in accordance with" language were found when (1) only selected areas within a municipality were regulated by zoning; (2) zoning was done by means of an interim ordinance that was enacted by legally questionable government practices; or (3) the zoning ordinance failed to control one or more of the factors it was intended to regulate. (See DiMento, *Developing the Consistency Doctrine: The Contribution of the California Courts* (1980) 20 Santa Clara L.Rev. 285, 286.)

California's state planning laws took what some may consider a giant step forward when the Legislature, in 1973, mandated that zoning changes and subdivision approvals be consistent with the local general plan, and that the plan itself be internally consistent. (Lefcoe, *California's Land Planning Requirements: The Case for Deregulation* (1981) 54 So.Cal.L.Rev. 447, 488.) Although the Planning and Zoning Law establishes the authority of most local government entities to regulate the use of land (*Topanga Assn. for the Scenic Community v. County of Los Angeles* (1974) 11 Cal.3d 506, 518–519, fn. 18, 113 Cal.Rptr. 836, 522 P.2d 12), it commands municipalities to adopt "a comprehensive, long-term general plan for the physical development of the county or city...." (Gov.Code, § 65300.) The plan itself must include, inter alia, a statement of policies, and nine specified elements: land use, circulation, housing, conservation, open-space, seismic safety, noise, scenic highway, and safety. (Gov.Code, § 65302.) Section 65566 requires that acquisition, regulation, and any other actions of the local government related to open space conform to the local open-space plan. Under section 65567, building permits, subdivision maps, and zoning ordinances affecting *open space* must be consistent with the *open space* plan. Section 65803 exempts charter cities from the consistency statutes unless they adopt these requirements or fall within the provisions of section 65860. And, sections 66473 and 66474 set forth various requirements for attaining subdivision consistency with general and specific plans.

Most relevant here, of course, is section 65860, which generally requires that county or city zoning ordinances be consistent with the general plan of the county or city, and allows private citizens to bring suit to enforce consistency of zoning with the general plan. Subdivision (d) specifically makes the statute applicable to Los Angeles and establishes a time table for bringing the City's zoning ordinances into conformity with the general plan.

As can be seen, neither the language of section 65860 nor the statutory scheme in general mandates that building permits be scrutinized for plan consistency. Indeed, had the Legislature intended to fashion such a requirement, it clearly had the power to do so. In this regard, the State Planning and Zoning Law specifically prohibits the adoption or issuance of permits, subdivision maps, or zoning ordinances that are inconsistent with *open space* plans; requires that tentative subdivision tract maps be drawn in conformity with the general plan (Gov.Code, § 66474.61, subd. (a)); and allows a court to enjoin issuance of all permits where a *general plan* is found to be inadequate. (Gov.Code, § 65755.) There is, however, nothing in the legislative history of section 65860 to suggest that the Legislature intended to prohibit the issuance of building permits for projects consistent with the zoning of a particular community but not the general plan. Moreover, there is no mention of any remedies available to halt construction of projects which are not in conformity with the general plan, and no sanctions are provided for noncompliance with section 65860, subdivision (d).

* * *

Generally, the enumeration of acts or things as coming within the operation of a statute precludes the inclusion by implication of other acts or things not listed. (*Western Pioneer Insurance Co. v. Estate of Taira* (1982) 136 Cal.App.3d 174, 181, 185 Cal.Rptr. 887.) Applying this rule to the instant case, we think it clear that the Legislature has purposefully failed to prohibit the issuance of building permits while the consistency process is being implemented. In the absence of any such provision it would ill-behoove any court to indirectly mandate the withholding of permits that are not in conformity with a municipality's general plan. If the Legislature desires such consistency, it should specifically say so.

Recognizing that amending zoning ordinances to make them consistent with a general plan would take time, the Legislature added subdivision (c) to section 65860 which states: "In the event that a zoning ordinance becomes inconsistent with a general plan by reason of amendment to such plan, or to any element of such plan, such zoning ordinance *shall be amended within a reasonable time* so that it is consistent with the general plan as amended." (Emphasis added.) The trial court had before it evidence that in 1982 the City had approximately 200,000 lots which had zoning inconsistent with the applicable General Plan. If appellants' contentions were correct, no new building permits could be issued until all inconsistently-zoned lots were made to conform to the provisions of the General Plan. This would bring new construction in the City to a grinding halt and cause economic havoc. As one commentator has aptly observed, "Halting construction for the years it takes to adopt a general plan [or amend zoning ordinances] works great hardship. During those years of delay, some projects that were once economically feasible will become impracticable. Even those projects that survive the de facto moratorium will be costly to consumers if developers are able to recoup their increased land holding, construction, and borrowing costs through higher prices. For buyers priced out of the market by these delays, the loss may be irretrievable; anyone who doubts it should talk to a renter who could have afforded a house some years ago, but who had been left behind by rising prices. Neither the courts nor the Legislature seem to have understood who really pays the price when zone changes, building permits, and subdivision approvals are withheld pending the adoption of a general plan." (Lefcoe, *California's Land Planning Requirements: The Case for Deregulation, supra,* 54 So.Cal.L.Rev. 447, 489.)

* * *

The City's Interim Ordinance, which does require permit/plan consistency, was given only prospective application and thus did not affect the validity of Morton's permit. After balancing competing interests, the City Council properly determined that projects which had been approved prior to the ordinance's effective date, and did not vary from their originally approved plans, were entitled to go forward. As found by the trial court in the *Federation* case, the enactment of the Interim Ordinance represented a good faith effort by the City to bring its regulations into substantial compliance with state law. Zoning ordinances are, of course, presumed to be a valid exercise of the police power with every intendment in favor of their validity. "The wisdom of the prohibitions and restrictions is a matter for legislative determination, and even though a court may not agree with that determination it will not substitute its judgment for that of the zoning authorities if there is any reasonable justification for their action." (*Lockard v. City of Los Angeles* (1949) 33 Cal.2d 453, 461, 202 P.2d 38.) We agree with respondents that for this court to now say that the issuance of Morton's building permit constituted an abuse of discretion would seriously undermine the City Council's authority to enact land-use regulations and invite a further, unending spiral of litigation. It must be remembered that the Plan which appellants view as sacrosanct was itself a creature of the City and presumptively can be changed by the City.

Having concluded that the State Planning and Zoning Law does not preclude issuance of permits which may be inconsistent with a community's general plan, and that Morton's building permit was issued in compliance with City ordinances, we need not discuss appellants' remaining contentions.

The judgment is affirmed and the stay order is vacated.

[Dissenting opinion omitted.]

Notes

1. Assuming that the plan is valid, how should a court view a land use regulation that is not consistent with the plan? See DiMento, The Consistency Doctrine: Continuing Controversy, 4 Zoning and Planning Law Report No. 1 (Jan. 1981). The author points out that only a few states have accepted the principle that a regulation must either be consistent with the plan or valid despite the plan because of changed circumstances. The majority of jurisdictions still view the plan as advisory to local officials. See, e.g., Barrie v. Kitsap County, 93 Wash.2d 843, 613 P.2d 1148 (1980), holding that a land use decision was not invalid because of inconsistency with the plan, and City of Sanibel v. Goode, 372 So.2d 181 (Fla.App.1979), holding a decision invalid despite its consistency with the plan.

2. In Haines v. City of Phoenix, 151 Ariz. 286, 727 P.2d 339 (1986), the appellate court held that the city council could rationally have found consistency with the general plan in allowing a 500 foot building to be constructed, despite the plan's 250 foot height limit!

3. Some other California cases that explore the consistency doctrine at length are Lesher Communications, Inc. v. City of Walnut Creek, 262 Cal.Rptr. 337 (Cal.App.1989), reversed 52 Cal.3d 531, 277 Cal.Rptr. 1, 802 P.2d 317 (1990), and Mira Development Corp. v. City of San Diego, 205 Cal.App.3d 1201, 252 Cal.Rptr. 825 (1988).

4. In his recent article, 3 Wash. U.J.L. & Pol'y 295 (2000), addressing the legislative requirement that zoning and local land use controls be consistent with an independently adopted local comprehensive plan, Stuart Meck, AICP offers the following model statute:

CONSISTENCY OF LAND DEVELOPMENT REGULATIONS AND LAND USE ACTIONS WITH A LOCAL COMPREHENSIVE PLAN: A MODEL ACT

(1) Land development regulations and amendments thereto, including amendments to the zoning map, and any land use actions shall be consistent with the local comprehensive plan that has been adopted by the legislative body of a local government, provided that in the event the land development regulations, as amended, become inconsistent with the local comprehensive plan by reason of amendment to the plan or adoption of a new plan, the regulations shall be amended within [6] months of the date of amendment or adoption so they are consistent with the local comprehensive plan, as amended.

(a) Except as provided in paragraph (1) above, any land development regulations and amendments thereto and any land use actions that are not consistent with the local comprehensive plan shall be voidable.

(b) Any land development regulations and amendments thereto shall be void [6] months from the date on which a local comprehensive plan is required to be adopted, if a comprehensive plan must be adopted pursuant to [cite to section in statute] but no comprehensive plan has been adopted.

(c) As used in this Section, "land use action" means: preliminary or final approval of a subdivision plat; approval of a planned unit development [or similar site-specific development plan]; approval of a conditional use; granting of a variance; or a decision by the local government to construct a capital improvement and/or acquire land for community facilities, including transportation facilities.

(2) A local government shall determine, in the manner prescribed in this Section, whether such land development regulations, amendments thereto, and land use actions are consistent with the local comprehensive plan. Before the legislative body of a local government may enact or amend land development regulations and before the legislative body, the local planning commission, the hearing examiner, the Land Use Board of Review, any other body with administrative authority may take any land use action, the local planning agency shall prepare a written report to the legislative or administrative body regarding the consistency with the local comprehensive plan of: the proposed land development regulations; a proposed amendment to existing land development regulations; or a proposed land use action. The written report shall be advisory to the legislative or administrative body. Pursuant to paragraph (3) below, the written report shall state whether or not, in the opinion of the local planning agency, the regulations, amendment, or action is consistent with the local comprehensive plan. The written report shall also contain recommendations pursuant to paragraph (4) below as to whether or not to approve, deny, substantially change, or revise the regulations, amendment, or action. The local planning agency shall make the written report available to the public at least [7] days prior to any public hearing or meeting on the regulations, amendment, or action that is the subject of the report.

(3) The local planning agency shall find that proposed land development regulations, a proposed amendment to existing land development regula-

tions, or a proposed land use action is consistent with the local comprehensive plan when the regulations, amendment, or action:

(a) furthers, or at least does not interfere with, the goals and policies contained in the local comprehensive plan;

(b) is compatible with the proposed future land uses and densities and/or intensities contained in the local comprehensive plan; and

(c) carries out, as applicable, any specific proposals for community facilities, including transportation facilities, other specific public actions, or actions proposed by nonprofit and for-profit organizations that are contained in the local comprehensive plan.

In determining whether the regulations, amendment, or action satisfies the requirements of subparagraph (a) above, the local planning agency may take into account any relevant guidelines contained in the local comprehensive plan.

(4) If the local planning agency determines that the regulations, amendment, or action is not consistent with the local comprehensive plan, it:

(a) shall state in the written report what changes or revisions in the regulations, amendment, or action are necessary to make it consistent; and

(b) may state in the written report what amendments to the local comprehensive plan are necessary to eliminate any inconsistency between the plan and the regulations, amendment, or action.

(5) The legislative or administrative body shall, upon receipt of the written report of the local planning agency, review it and, giving the report due regard, shall in the written minutes of its deliberations:

(a) adopt the report;

(b) reject the report; or

(c) adopt the report in part and reject it in part.

(6) If the legislative or administrative body rejects the report in part or in whole, in the written minutes of its deliberations:

(a) it shall state whether the proposed land development regulations, a proposed amendment to existing land development regulations, or a proposed land use action is consistent with the local comprehensive plan pursuant to paragraph (3) above; and/or

(b) if the legislative or administrative body determines that the regulations, amendment, or action is not consistent with the local comprehensive plan:

1. it shall state what changes or revisions in the regulations, amendment, or action are necessary to make it consistent; and/or

2. it may state what amendments to the local comprehensive plan may be necessary to eliminate any inconsistency between the plan and the regulations, amendment, or action.

5. If regulatory decisions are not readily subject to attack by way of the consistency doctrine, can citizens attack the plan itself prior to the issuance

Sec. 4　　CONTENT & EFFECT OF THE MASTER PLAN　　243

of building permits or the rendering of zoning decisions? Consider the following materials.

COCHRAN v. PLANNING BD. OF CITY OF SUMMIT

Superior Court of New Jersey, Law Division, 1965.
87 N.J.Super. 526, 210 A.2d 99.

FELLER, J.S.C.

This is an action * * * challenging the adoption of a master plan by the Planning Board of the City of Summit and seeking to enjoin the city and its agencies, boards, and officials from implementing the master plan in any way. In particular, plaintiffs object to that part of the plan which would permit an expansion of the Ciba Corporation's parking area and research and office space into the residential area which adjoins the rear of plaintiffs' property.

Plaintiffs are citizens, taxpayers and owners of lands located at 249 Kent Place Boulevard in Summit. Their property is adjacent and contiguous to property owned by the Ciba Corporation (hereinafter Ciba). Plaintiffs' premises and that portion of the Ciba tract in question are presently in the A–15 zoning district, which is limited to one-family residences with a minimum lot area of 15,000 square feet. Prior to 1958 the Ciba tract was in an A–10 zone, which was limited to one-family residences with a minimum lot area of 10,000 square feet. The tract is bordered on three sides by one-family residences and is presently subject to enforceable deed restrictions which limit the use of the tract to the erection of one-family residences until 1975.

On December 9, 1963 defendant planning board adopted a master plan for the city, which provided in part that the Ciba tract, namely, 63½ acres in the A–15 zone, should be rezoned for parking areas and research and office building use. This rezoning is for the purpose of providing for the eventual expansion therein of Ciba's existing operations. The plan requires a 125–foot buffer zone, which would separate the rear line of plaintiffs' property from the proposed Ciba construction. This zone would contain trees, shrubs and a screen, all of them calculated to preserve the existing residential atmosphere of the area.

Plaintiffs claim that the adoption of the master plan is arbitrary, discriminatory, capricious, unreasonable and an abuse of the planning board's discretion; * * * that it was procedurally defective because it was adopted on improper notice, ten days' notice not having been given of the December 9, 1963 hearing at which the plan was adopted, as required by the act, and that the planning board was illegally constituted. Plaintiffs further contend that the master plan was an abuse of discretion in that it was contrary to the expressed wishes of the citizens of the city made known at the hearings thereon and prior thereto; was contrary to the purpose of the plan to preserve the already established pattern of the better single-family areas of Summit; was contrary to the general welfare and health of the citizens; was *ultra vires* the planning board's power, and did not conform to the character of the neighborhood.

Plaintiffs also contend that the * * * action of the board was allegedly based on insufficient and incompetent facts and findings and on insufficient surveys and studies, in violation of N.J.S.A. 40:55–1.12.

* * *

Defendants contend that the master plan was properly adopted at a meeting held on December 9, 1963; insist there was proper notice of the meeting, and that the meeting was a continuance of a previous one held on November 26, 1963. * * *

Defendants further contend that the plan was the result of a comprehensive study by the planning board which commenced in January 1962 and terminated on December 9, 1963, after an average of a meeting every two weeks with interested persons and citizens. They say that all the work and the final plan are in accordance with the requirements of N.J.S.A. 40:55–1.1 et seq.

A review of the evidence indicates that the following questions should be resolved: whether the planning board had the authority or power to adopt a master plan under the ordinance setting up the board; whether the plaintiffs' property has been harmed or damaged by the adoption of the plan or whether their suit is premature; whether the plan is arbitrary, capricious, unreasonable, or an abuse of discretion * * *.

I

Initially, plaintiffs contend that the ordinance of March 16, 1954, which created the Planning Board of the City of Summit, did not give the board the power to prepare and adopt a master plan; furthermore, they contend that since no other ordinance granted this power to the board, the provisions of N.J.S.A. 40:55–1.3 have been violated by such preparation and adoption, and that the master plan should be set aside as *ultra vires* the power of the planning board. N.J.S.A. 40:55–1.3 provides in relevant part that:

> "The governing body may by ordinance grant any of the powers exercisable by a planning board to a planning board continued by section twenty-seven of this act or to be created under section four of this act, *but no particular power may be exercised until expressly granted by ordinance* and until compliance is made with the conditions, standards, procedures and regulations enumerated in the sections describing such power." (Emphasis added).

The defendants rely in part on the passage of an ordinance by the Summit governing body on December 19, 1961, which made an appropriation for the engagement of special consultants for the preparation of a master plan. It is argued that this ordinance is sufficient to satisfy the demands of N.J.S.A. 40:55–1.3. The ordinance provided:

Section 1. That pursuant to Chapter 48, P.L.1956, the sum of $24,000 is hereby appropriated for the engagement of special consultants for the preparation and the preparation, of a master plan or plans, when required in order to conform to the planning laws of the State, and shall be deemed an emergency appropriation as defined and provide [sic] for in R.S. 40:50–12.

Such appropriation and/or the 'special emergency notes' authorized to finance the appropriation shall be provided for in succeeding annual budgets by the inclusion of at least ⅕ of the amount authorized pursuant to this act.

Section 2. This ordinance shall take effect immediately after final passage and publication as provided by law.

If the above ordinance does not by implication grant the planning board power to prepare and adopt a master plan, then the other sections of the Planning Act do. * * *

For the above reasons, and specifically because of the legislative expression in N.J.S.A. 40:55–1.10, this court is of the opinion that the Summit Planning Board had the power to enact a master plan and that such action by the board was not *ultra vires.*

II

The second question is whether plaintiffs' property has been harmed or damaged by the adoption of the master plan and whether their suit is premature. If the action is premature, they have sustained no damage or harm to their property, and a determination of the procedural inadequacies and conflicts of interest alleged by plaintiffs would be unnecessary.

Plaintiffs request the court to declare the master plan null and void because it represents a taking of private property for public use without just compensation. * * *

Defendants contend that plaintiffs' failure to allege and prove injury to their property rights results in the presentation of legal questions which are premature and which do not present justiciable controversies. This court agrees that such allegations and proof of injury to private property rights are necessary before the requested relief may be considered and granted by this court. Plaintiffs have not demonstrated that degree of injury which would entitle them to relief.

* * *

If plaintiffs cannot demonstrate injury, then they may not obtain relief; if their claims are based upon assumed potential invasions of rights, then these are not enough to warrant judicial intervention. See Ashwander v. T.V.A., 297 U.S. 288, 56 S.Ct. 466, 80 L.Ed. 688 (1936).

The crux of this problem is clear when it is remembered that a master plan is of no force and effect until it is adopted by the governing body of the municipality. Thus, the master plan under consideration in the City of Summit is of no effect until it is adopted by the municipal governing body.

The master plan represents at a given time the best judgment of the planning agency as to the proper course of action to be followed. In this stage the plan for community development remains flexible and is not binding, either on government or individual. See Webster, Urban Planning & Municipal Policy 265 (1958). A master plan is not a straitjacket delimiting the discretion of the legislative body, but only a guide for the city, Rhyne, Municipal Law, sec. 32–59, p. 977 (1957); furthermore, a master plan is nothing more than the easily changed instrumentality which will show a commission from day to day the progress it has made. Haar, Land Use Planning 693 (1959).

The mere adoption and recording of a master plan has no legal consequence. The plan is merely a declaration of policy and a disclosure of an intention which must thereafter be implemented by the adoption of various ordinances. Horack & Nolan, Land Use Controls 36 (1955).

In New Jersey the fact that a master plan adopted by a planning board has no legal consequences is substantiated, not only by the absence of statutory language to that effect, but also by the necessity of a municipality's adoption of the master plan by the governing body before the plan takes effect. See N.J.S.A. 40:55–1.13; Wollen v. Fort Lee, 27 N.J. 408, 424, 142 A.2d 881, 890 (1958), where the court said that "the master plan is not conclusive on the governing body." Moreover, it is not mandatory for a township to create a planning board, and a governing body could assume directly the duties of a planning board. Jones v. Zoning Bd. of Adjustment of Long Beach Tp., 32 N.J.Super. 397, 406, 108 A.2d 498 (App.Div.1954).

* * *

It is clear that a master plan is only a plan, and that it requires legislative implementation before its proposals have binding effect and legal consequences. If the necessary legislative implementation is taken—and, of course, such implementation must be taken according to the applicable statutes—then a zoning ordinance and not a master plan would be before the court. Until appropriate municipal legislative action is taken, however, the municipality has only a dormant plan which differs from proposals that may be under consideration by any municipal board or citizen of the municipality in that it is comprehensive and has been reduced to printed form. Indeed, a master plan is not even a statutory prerequisite to zoning action. Kozesnik v. Montgomery Township, 24 N.J. 154, 165, 131 A.2d 1 (1957).

The issue here is whether a plan for municipal development, not yet implemented by the necessary legislative action, may be legally considered to deprive one of the enjoyment of his property, contrary to the United States and New Jersey Constitutions. The statutes providing for the adoption of a master plan were upheld as constitutional in Mansfield & Swett, Inc. v. West Orange, 120 N.J.L. 145, 198 A. 225 (Sup.Ct.1938).

The court, in the course of its opinion, said that the State possesses the inherent authority to resort, in the building and expansion of its community life, to such measures as may be necessary to secure the essential common material and moral needs. The public welfare is of prime importance, and the correlative restrictions upon individual rights, either of person or of property, are considered a negligible loss compared with the resultant advantages to the community as a whole. Municipal planning confined to the common need is inherent in the authority to create the municipality itself. It is as old as government itself; it is of the very essence of civilized society. A comprehensive scheme of physical development is requisite to community efficiency and progress.

* * * The principle is firmly established in our federal jurisprudence that injury to private property ensuing from governmental action in a proper sphere, reasonably taken for the public good, and for no other purpose, is not necessarily classable as a "taking" of such property within the intendment of the constitutional guaranties against the deprivation of property without due process of law, or the taking of private property for public use without compensation.

* * *

Attention is also called to the following cases: Headley v. City of Rochester, 272 N.Y. 197, 5 N.E.2d 198 (Ct.App.1936); Reopening of Philadelphia Parkway Between Twentieth and Twenty–Second Street, 295 Pa. 538, 145 A. 600, 64 A.L.R. 542 (Sup.Ct.1929); Windsor v. Whitney, 95 Conn. 357, 111 A. 354, 12 A.L.R. 669 (Sup.Ct.Err.1920); Harrison v. City of Philadelphia, 217 F. 107 (E.D.Pa.1914); Bauman v. Ross, 167 U.S. 548, 17 S.Ct. 966, 42 L.Ed. 270, 64 A.L.R. 542 (1897). These authorities indicate that the power of a municipality to plan for the future is part of the police power. The adoption of maps and/or reports, commonly called a "master plan," does not result in a "taking" of property in violation of our Federal and State Constitutions.

The plaintiffs have alleged that the adoption of the master plan destroys property values. To support this thesis they called as witnesses George Goldstein, who is a real estate appraiser and a consultant for the Federal Government and many public agencies, as well as for many of the largest industrial companies in the country, and Norman Lemcke, who is a retired vice-president of the Prudential Mortgage Loan Department. Goldstein testified that the adoption of the master plan had diminished adjacent property values up to 25%, as in the case of plaintiffs' home. Lemcke testified that before the plan he would have granted a 66% mortgage on the plaintiffs' house, but after its adoption he would only grant a 50% mortgage. He further testified that for financing purposes lending institutions take into account whether there is a master plan affecting the property, and the manner in which it is affected. Plaintiffs also rely upon N.J.S.A. 40:55–1.12, which requires, among other things, that a master plan be made with the general purpose of the maintenance of property values previously established.
* * *

The contentions of plaintiffs' two experts are disputed by several witnesses for the defense; but without considering the relative merits of the contentions raised by the conflicting views, this court feels that the testimony, taken in the light most favorable to plaintiffs, is at best mere conjecture. There has been no attempted sale by plaintiffs of their property, and the damages which they claim they will sustain if and when they do try to sell their property, is at this point a matter of speculation. * * *

It is the opinion of this court that plaintiffs' suit is premature. Not until their property is actually taken or damaged will they be in a position to establish that its value will be destroyed or diminished.

III

Plaintiffs question the soundness of the master plan on the ground that it is arbitrary, capricious and unreasonable. In view of the position taken by this court that plaintiffs are premature in their suit, it is not necessary to discuss this issue. However, the court feels that even if the reasonableness of the master plan were properly before it, the result would be the same. The action of a planning board is only an initial step; it is not even required by law, Kozesnik v. Montgomery Township, supra; it is only the manifestation of an advisory step in connection with *quasi*-judicial action the board may take in the future. As stated by Horack and Nolan, Land Use Controls 36 (1955):

> [The master plan] is merely a declaration of policy and a disclosure of an intention which must thereafter be implemented.

Since this master plan may never be adopted by the governing body of Summit, there is at present no justiciable controversy before the court. There may be such a controversy if and when the proposed plan is adopted by the governing body. Until implementation of the proposal is attempted, there can be no purpose in an adjudication by this court at this time.

If the court, for example, declared the master plan or any portion thereof arbitrary, capricious, and/or unreasonable, would a property owner be permitted to make use of his property other than in a manner now permitted or other than in a manner that would be permitted if the plan were sustained? Would the governing body be limited in the adoption of land use ordinances other than as they are at the moment if the plan were stricken by this court? The answers to these questions appear obvious.

This suit to test the reasonableness of the master plan is premature, and the issues involved are clearly not ready for judicial determination. Furthermore, should the plaintiffs follow the normal administrative pattern of going first to the planning board and then, if necessary, to the governing body, they may very well be able to persuade these bodies to compromise their differences in connection with the master plan, in which case they would be able to avoid further litigation.

* * *

Complaint dismissed and judgment for defendants.

BONE v. CITY OF LEWISTON

Supreme Court of Idaho, 1984.
107 Idaho 844, 693 P.2d 1046.

BISTLINE, JUSTICE.

On February 9, 1982, Mr. John Bone filed an application with the City of Lewiston Planning and Zoning Commission requesting that his land be rezoned from a low-density residential use to a limited commercial use. The City's land use plan map shows Mr. Bone's land as being zoned for commercial use.

The Commission recommended to the City Council that Mr. Bone's request be denied for the following reasons: (1) The uses allowed in the zoning classification Mr. Bone seeks would not be compatible with the established low-density residential uses of the various properties bordering Mr. Bone's land; and (2) Lewiston has an over-abundance of unused commercial properties. No need presently exists for further classification of property for commercial use. The City Council, without adopting any findings of fact and conclusions of law, agreed with the Commission's recommendation and denied Mr. Bone's application.

Mr. Bone subsequently filed suit in district court against the City, requesting declaratory relief and a writ of mandamus forcing the City to enact a zoning ordinance in conformity with its comprehensive plan pursuant to I.C. § 67–6511. * * *

[The Court first disposes of a procedural issue and then moves to discuss the question of conformity with the comprehensive plan.]

Mr. Bone argues that he is entitled to have his property zoned in conformance with the City's land use map. He cites I.C. § 67–6511 as support for his position. That section states that zoning ordinances shall be "in accordance with" a comprehensive plan. For Mr. Bone, § 67–6511's terminology "in accordance with" means as a matter of law that a zoning applicant is entitled to have his or her property zoned exactly as the City's land use map shows it to be zoned. We do not agree with such a proposition for two reasons.

First, construing § 67–6511 as Mr. Bone would have us read it results in an interpretation of the section that contradicts itself. Subsections 67–6511(a) and (b) discuss the amendment process of zoning districts. In subsection (b) it states that if a rezone request is in accordance with the applicable comprehensive plan, the planning and zoning commission "*may* recommend and the governing board *may* adopt or reject the [zoning] amendment [request]" as proposed. (Emphasis added.)

Requiring all rezone applications to be granted when they agree with the land use map's designation of the property ignores the permissive language used in subsection (b). Had the legislature intended the result Mr. Bone proposes, they would have used the word "shall" instead of "may" and not used the words "or reject."

* * *

Second, adopting Mr. Bone's interpretation would elevate the comprehensive plan and land use map to the status of a zoning ordinance. This result finds no basis in law or reason, for the three—the comprehensive plan, the land use map, and the zoning ordinances—serve different purposes. The City of Lewiston's land use map, as § 67–6508(c) indicates, is a map displaying *"suitable projected* land uses for the jurisdiction." (Emphasis added.) It is not a map of how the City should presently be zoned, but a map of projected uses in the year 2000. In fact, the City's comprehensive plan describes the City's land use map as depicting "the projected structure and land use interrelationships for the City in the year 2000." It goes on further to say, "This map is not an attempt to show precise boundaries or locations, but is a general representation of the relative extent and patterns of *projected land uses."* (Emphasis added.) Thus, the land use map, in essence, is a goal or forecast of future development in the City. This is contrasted with zoning ordinances, which represent the present uses allowable for the various pieces of property in the City.

It is illogical to say that what has been projected as a pattern of projected land use is what a property owner is entitled to have zoned today. The land use map is not intended to be a map of present zoning uses, nor even a map which indicates what uses are presently appropriate. Its only purpose is that which I.C. § 67–6508(c) mandates—to indicate "suitable projected land uses." Therefore, we hold that a city's land use map does not require a particular piece of property, as a matter of law, to be zoned exactly as it appears on the land use map.

Our holding is supported by a large body of case law which states that comprehensive plans do not themselves operate as legally controlling zoning law, but rather serve to guide and advise the various governing bodies responsible for making zoning decisions. *See Theobald v. Board of County Commissioners, Summit County,* 644 P.2d 942, 949 (Colo.1982); *Barrie v. Kitsap County,* 613 P.2d 1148, 1152 (Wash.1980); *Holmgren v. City of Lincoln,* 199 Neb. 178, 256 N.W.2d 686, 690 (1977); 82 Am.Jur.2d, Zoning and Planning, § 69; 3 Anderson, *American Law of Zoning* 609.

Our holding that "in accordance with" does not require that governing bodies, as a matter of law, zone their land as it appears on their land use maps does not mean that such bodies can ignore their comprehensive plans when adopting or amending zoning ordinances. Section 67–6511 requires governing bodies to zone in accordance with their comprehensive plan. We hold that "in accordance with" is a question of fact. What a governing body charged to zone "in accordance with" under § 67–6511 must do is make a factual inquiry into whether the requested zoning ordinance or amendment reflects the goals of, and takes into account those factors in, the comprehensive plan in light of the present factual circumstances surrounding the request.

Here, the district court found that Mr. Bone's rezone application was in accordance with the City's comprehensive plan without having before it the record of either the planning and zoning commission or the City Council. The district court furthermore refused to allow the City to submit evidence of whether Mr. Bone's rezone application was factually in accordance with its comprehensive plan and the present circumstances surrounding the application. Thus, the district court erred in reaching its conclusion by failing to have before it the necessary information upon which to decide the case.

For the foregoing reasons we reverse and remand this case to the district court with directions for that court to remand to the City Council for the adoption of findings of fact and conclusions of law.

* * *

DONALDSON, C.J., and SHEPARD, BAKES AND HUNTLEY, JJ., concur.

Notes

1. In Selby Realty Co. v. City of San Buenaventura, 10 Cal.3d 110, 109 Cal.Rptr. 799, 514 P.2d 111 (1973), the court held that adoption of a comprehensive plan that showed proposed streets crossing the landowner's property did not amount to a taking of the property. The court said: "The fact that some of the proposed streets, if ultimately constructed, will cross plaintiff's property gives this plaintiff no greater right to secure a declaration as to the validity of the plan or its effect upon his land than that available to any other citizen whose property is included within the plan. The plan is by its very nature merely tentative and subject to change. Whether eventually any part of plaintiff's land will be taken for a street depends upon unpredictable future events." Also see Biske v. City of Troy, 381 Mich. 611, 166 N.W.2d 453 (1969); Rancho La Costa v. County of San Diego, 111 Cal.App.3d 54, 168 Cal.Rptr. 491 (1980); Zanin v. Iacono, 198 N.J.Super. 490, 487 A.2d 780 (1984); Woodcrest Investments Corp. v. County of Skagit, 39 Wash.App. 622, 694 P.2d 705 (1985); Callies, Land Use: Herein of Vested Rights, Plans, and the Relationship of Planning and Controls, 2 U.Hawaii L.Rev. 167, 182–92 (1979).

2. In Citizens Growth Management Coalition of West Palm Beach, Inc. v. City of West Palm Beach, 450 So.2d 204 (Fla.1984), the court held that a citizen association lacked standing to challenge the validity of a downtown large-scale redevelopment. And, in State ex rel. Chiavola v. Village of Oakwood, 886 S.W.2d 74 (Mo.App.1994) the court held that a zoning ordinance satisfied the statutory requirement despite the lack of a separate comprehensive plan, given the comprehensive scope of the ordinance and the nature of the village as a small suburb of a large city. Accord: State ex rel. Westside Development Co., Inc. v. Weatherby Lake, 935 S.W.2d 634 (Mo. App.1996).

3. The most acute everyday problem in assessing the legal effect of the plan is the usual lack of public interest or participation in the adoption of the plan, especially in the undeveloped parts of the community. Some years after the adoption of the plan a developer may seek a zoning change or development approval on a vacant parcel which is designated as, say, multi-family. Nearby neighbors living in recently developed single-family subdivisions will be vociferous objectors to the implementation of the plan. Of course they were not participants in the adoption of the plan and probably never knew of its existence. Is there a solution to this problem? One possibility is suggested by the case of Dennis v. Mayor and City Council of Rockville, 286 Md. 184, 406 A.2d 284 (1979), where the city had enacted an ordinance requiring all sellers of property to either provide purchasers with a copy of the master plan or to escort them to a place where the plan could be inspected. Violation of the duty imposed on sellers gives the purchaser a right to terminate the sales agreement prior to conveyance. The Court of Appeals of Maryland upheld the ordinance against arguments that it works a forfeiture of property and interferes with contractual rights. Do you think the Rockville ordinance is a more effective means of promulgating the plan than the typical public hearings held by a planning commission attended by a handful of developers and real estate brokers?

Also see Nev. Rev. Stat. § 113.070 requiring sellers of residences to provide the buyer with a written document disclosing "the zoning designations and the designations in the master plan regarding land use * * * for the adjoining parcels of land."

Somewhat related is the problem of whether purchasers of homes in subdivisions must be given notice of off-site environmental hazards. See, in this regard, Strawn v. Canuso, 140 N.J. 43, 657 A.2d 420 (1995) where the court stated that a broker-developer of residential real estate may be liable for nondisclosure of off-site physical conditions known to it and unknown and not readily observable by the purchaser, if those conditions may affect the habitability, use, or enjoyment of the property; in this case the off-site condition was a closed toxic landfill near a residential development.

4. See McClanahan v. Richland County Council, 350 S.C. 433, 567 S.E.2d 240 (2002) where the Court found no due process violation where the plan was ignored, stating "the Plan is only a guideline and that there had not been an impairment of the appellant's rights." For a discussion of this case and its implications for community planning and smart growth, see David J. Harmon, Comment: Problems and Opportunities for Progressive Comprehensive Land Use Planning in Richland County, South Carolina After McClanahan v. Richland City Council, 54 S.C.L.Rev. 837 (2003).

SECTION 5. STATE AND REGIONAL PLANNING

A. FEDERAL LAND USE LEGISLATION

The history of land use controls in the United States has primarily been one of delegation of the power to plan to local governments along with the power to implement the plans at that level of government. One major effect of localizing land use controls has been the fostering of parochialism and the avoidance of a rational basis for dealing with regional problems. Beginning in the late 1960's and accelerating in the 1970's, states and to some degree the federal government began to demonstrate greater interest in intervening in the local planning process. This was likely spurred in part by the increasing emphasis on environmental controls, in part by federal transportation, housing and urban redevelopment programs, and in part by a concern over the problems created by "urban sprawl" and the proliferation of local, largely uncoordinated controls over a widespread metropolitan area encompassing a multiplicity of municipalities. The energy crisis of the late 1970's has also been a factor. The movement toward state and regional planning has been in four directions:

(1) Federal land use legislation that would spur state level planning;

(2) Removal of some planning decisions from local to regional or state political jurisdiction;

(3) Efforts to modernize or reform state planning and zoning enabling acts; and

(4) Interstate compacts.

Federal impact on land use planning has been evident for several years. The millions of acres still in the public domain have required, in addition to management, some thought devoted to planning for the future. Also, some of the massive federal spending programs that have land use impacts have led to requirements of planning by state agencies charged with operations. In addition to urban redevelopment, typical in this respect is the federal highway program (see, e.g., the Highway Act of 1962, 76 Stat. 1145). Much federal money has gone into education about planning as well as research and public dissemination of planning materials. In other words, there has been and continues to be pervasive federal influence on land use planning, albeit in a non-coordinated fashion. The influences just described, however, have been of low visibility.

However, when considering the influence of federal environmental regulations on state and local land use planning, a more noticeable pattern emerges. This is particularly evident in the efforts of the Environmental Protection Agency ("EPA") to control air and water pollution.

Early attempts by EPA to reduce air pollution by intervening in local development matters were recognized as a threat to the power of the states to control land use, secured by the Tenth Amendment: "The powers not delegated to the United States by the Constitution, nor prohibited by it to the States, are reserved to the States respectively, or to the people." These attempts were met with amendments to the Clean Air Act in 1977 that expressly prohibited federal requirements aimed directly at land use control. 42 U.S.C. § 7431 (1994) (stating that "[n]othing in this chapter constitutes an infringement on the existing authority of counties and cities to plan or control land use, and nothing in this chapter provides or transfers authority over such land use").

The 1977 Clean Air Act Amendments were not an isolated example of the reluctance of the federal government to interfere with the plenary land use authority of the states. More recently, the efforts of the Army Corps of Engineers to prevent the construction of a landfill by a consortium of municipalities in the Chicago area were struck down by the U.S. Supreme Court. In Solid Waste Agency of Northern Cook County v. United States Corps of Engineers, 531 U.S. 159, 121 S.Ct. 675, 148 L.Ed.2d 576 (2001) the Court held that the Corps lacked jurisdiction under the Clean Water Act to regulate development in intrastate, non-navigable waters solely on the basis of the presence of migratory birds. The jurisdictional limits of federal agencies to protect the environment, resting in part on the Interstate Commerce Clause of the federal Constitution, were at issue in this case. Such jurisdictional limits, of course, do not constrain state governments or their localities in regulating wetland disturbances or other private land uses.

These jurisdictional, constitutional, and political obstacles have redirected federal energies from regulating land use to influencing state land use regulation. The Clean Water Act provides states with federal funds to encourage land use planning to prevent nonpoint source pollution. 33 U.S.C. § 1281(g)(1) (1994). State and local governments are encouraged under the federal Coastal Zone Management Act to adopt plans to preserve coastal areas. The Act provides grants to coastal states to develop management programs for their coastal zones. 16 U.S.C. §§ 1451–1465 (1994). State programs must meet several requirements, including providing for management of land uses having a significant impact on coastal waters and making a clear statement of which agencies and officials are to take action to implement the program. See Linda A. Malone, The Coastal Zone Management Act and the Takings Clause in the 1990's: Making the Case for Federal Land Use to Preserve Coastal Areas, 62 U. Colo. L. Rev. 711, 727 (1991) (stating that "[if] the requirements for state programs were more specific, the CZMA could come close to the most controversial form of land control—federal land control. The passage of the CZMA was possible because the Act required state programs to implement federal policy rather than federal regulations."). Federal financial aid is denied for developments in sensitive coastal areas under the Coastal Barrier Resources Act. 16 U.S.C. § 3501 (1994 & Supp. V 1999).

The modification of habitats that may harm endangered species is prohibited under the Endangered Species Act ("ESA") unless the modification is allowed by a permit issued pursuant to an approved habitat conservation plan. 16 U.S.C. § 1539 (1994). The ESA is an example of a federal environmental law that pursues objectives other than the prevention of nonpoint source pollution and illustrates how federally prescribed standards and procedures may interfere with the prerogatives of local governments to control land use. Under the ESA, landowners and developers may prepare Habitat Conservation Plans ("HCPs") that fully describe proposed land development activities and demonstrate measures that will mitigate their adverse impact on endangered or threatened species. § 1539(a)(2)(A). An approved HCP is a prerequisite for the issuance of a permit for land development activities that result in an incidental taking of a protected species. § 1539(a). This regulatory regime is based on the ESA's ban on taking of endangered species by any person subject to the jurisdiction of the United States. § 1538(a)(1). "Persons" subject to the Act include private citizens and entities such as local governments and officials. § 1532(13). The process of preparing and reviewing an HCP is somewhat redundant of local requirements contained in site plan or subdivision regulations that require developers to prepare detailed development plans and submit them to local administrative agencies for review and approval.

Similar efforts to influence state and local action are evident in federal transportation policies. Regional transportation planning must conform to State Implementation Plans that meet national ambient air quality standards under the Clean Air Act. 42 U.S.C. § 7506(i) (1994). Federal funding can be denied to any development project that does not conform to the State Implementation Plan. Envtl. Def. Fund v. EPA, 167 F.3d 641, 644 (D.C.Cir.1999). A tepid attempt is made under this scheme to conform federal transportation planning to local land use planning, recognizing that land use planning is done, in most states, at the local rather than the regional level. Under the Intermodal Surface Transportation Efficiency Act, regional transportation planning agencies known as Metropolitan Planning Organizations ("MPOs") must develop long- and short-term transportation plans that consider "the likely effect of transportation policy decisions on land use and development and the consistency of transportation plans and programs with the provisions of all applicable short and long-term land use and development plans." 23 U.S.C. § 134(f)(4) (1994). The enigma embodied in this requirement is easily described: it requires regional transportation agencies to achieve consistency with land use plans that are predominantly local in nature and not consistent with one another at the regional level. The federal Transportation Equity Act for the 21st Century provides regional transportation planning agencies with the authority to fund projects that reduce traffic congestion and to acquire scenic easements and create bicycle trails. Transportation Equity Act for the 21st Century, Pub. L. No. 105–178, 112 Stat. 107 (1998). It also provides tax breaks for employers who subsidize employees' use of mass transit.

These are but a few of many federal actions that are aimed at stemming air and water pollution, but that recognize that the direct power to regulate land use for such purposes is not within the legal authority of federal agencies. These efforts are nonetheless a heroic effort on the part of the federal government to reach down to the local level and directly influence the effects that land use has on air and water quality and on natural resources.

A manifestation of this struggle is seen in the EPA proposal to delay a Clean Water Act rule that revises the federal impaired waters program. Susan Bruninga, EPA Moves to Delay Action on TMDL Rule; Rule Changes May Be Proposed in Spring, 32 Env't Rep. (BNA) 1415 (2001). The Total Maximum Daily Load ("TMDL") program established under section 303(d) of the Clean Water Act requires states to identify and list waters not meeting federally established water quality standards. States are required to allocate the quantities of particular pollutants among the sources that discharge into impaired waters, to ensure that pollutants do not exceed federal standards, and to provide reasonable assurances to EPA that their allocations will be enforced. On July 16, 2001, EPA filed its proposal in the U.S. Court of Appeals for the District of Columbia to delay by eighteen months the effective date of its final rule under the TMDL program. Id. at 1415.

The acronyms and technical vocabulary should not mask the simple reality of the TMDL program: the pollutants it regulates emanate largely from development projects and land uses that are regulated by local and state agencies. The type of nonpoint source pollution of water affected by the TMDL program includes the runoff from impervious surfaces such as roofs, driveways, parking lots, and roads; erosion and sedimentation caused by development activities, including the removal of vegetation and site disturbance; and the movement into water bodies of fertilizer, pesticides, and herbicides from lawns, golf courses, and farms. While federal authority to regulate point source discharges from air stacks, effluent pipes, and other discernable, discrete conveyances has been established, federal power to regulate nonpoint source pollution is far from clear, in part because of the independent authority of state governments to regulate the land uses that cause such pollution. The Tenth Circuit Court of Appeals held that the Clean Water Act does not give EPA the authority to regulate nonpoint source pollution. American Wildlands v. Browner, 260 F.3d 1192, 1198 (10th Cir. 2001); see also Appalachian Power Co. v. Train, 545 F.2d 1351, 1373 (4th Cir. 1976) (stating that "Congress consciously distinguished between point source and nonpoint source discharges, giving EPA authority under the [Clean Water] Act to regulate only the former."). The American Wildlands case made it clear, however, that the TMDL Program established under 33 U.S.C. § 1313 requires states to "assure that there shall be achieved * * * cost-effective and reasonable best management practices for nonpoint source control." American Wildlands, 260 F.3d at 1198 (quoting 40 C.F.R. § 131.112(a)(2)).

It is interesting to ask what recourse EPA has, assuming its authority to enforce TMDL standards, if a state refuses to cooperate or fails to do an adequate job of preventing the nonpoint source pollution of waters that are designated as impaired under the TMDL program. The circuitous route traveled by EPA to influence local land use regulation under the TMDL program is being tracked by the National Marine Fisheries Service ("NMFS") in its attempt to protect seasonal species of Pacific Northwest Salmon listed as threatened under the ESA. Under § 4(d) of the Act, NMFS has issued regulations requiring states and municipalities to adopt protective regulations. NMFS issued these regulations under authority of 16 U.S.C. § 1533 (1994). Since local governments in northwest states regulate and permit land use activities in watersheds that contain salmon habitat, localities that fail to adopt protective standards can be said to have neglected their duties under the ESA.

An emerging legal theory posits that local governments are liable for third party developer and landowner actions that endanger protected species. This is implicit in the NMFS rules that grant immunity from such liability for local governments that adopt regulations to protect salmon and for third parties acting under approved local regulations. In Loggerhead Turtle v. County Council, 148 F.3d 1231 (11th Cir.1998), the Eleventh Circuit held that an environmental plaintiff had standing to challenge a Florida county for failing to regulate beachfront lighting when that lighting was shown to be the proximate cause of the disorientation and death of turtle hatchlings in their attempt to return to the sea. This injury to a protected species was found to be "fairly traceable" to the actions of the county. Id. at 1249. On remand, it was found that the county's regulations did not cause the taking of an ESA-protected species. Loggerhead Turtle v. County Council, 92 F.Supp.2d 1296 (M.D.Fla.2000). This specific holding, however, did not negate the general principle of the circuit court's decision that local governments may be liable for third party actions taken under their regulations. Hypothetically, EPA could assume the state's role, classify its waters, and issue, condition, or deny permits for proposed land uses under a pollution prevention system of federal design. Because of the cost and controversy involved in making EPA responsible for the regulation of nonpoint source pollution, this threat may be illusory. There are, however, precedents for this type of EPA preemptive strike and penalties within EPA's control for state noncompliance, such as withholding discretionary funding or denying point source permit applications that would further degrade impaired waters.

Assuming that states wish to comply with the TMDL program, classify their waters as required, and establish allocation systems for the loading of pollutants within each water source, how is the program to be implemented? To act effectively, the states inevitably must require their local governments to amend their land use controls to meet TMDL standards or preempt local authority to the extent necessary to meet those standards through more direct state action. Simply stating this proposition reveals the depth of the problem.

Since 1972 an intense public debate has emerged, centered around a bill passed by the Senate (S. 632, 92d Cong.), known colloquially as the Jackson bill, and officially as the Land–Use Policy and Planning Assistance Act of 1972. That bill never passed the House, nor did any of the similar bills introduced in the House. A federal land use bill has, however, been an idea still raised in congressional sessions since. Strong forces have been aligned on both sides of the debate about the propriety and wisdom of a federal land use bill. So far, the forces of opposition to such legislation have prevailed. See John R. Nolon, National Land Use Planning: Revisiting Senator Jackson's 1970 Policy Act, Land Use Law, May, 1996, p. 3. The House and the Senate again revisited federal assistance for state and local planning with the introduction and subsequent Senate Hearings on the Community Character Act. See Patricia E. Salkin, Congress Misses Twice with the Community Character Act: Will Three Times Be a Charm?, 31 Real Estate L.J. 167 (Fall 2002).

The proponents of federal intervention into the land use planning process base their case mainly on the failure of widespread planning on the state and regional levels, which is blamed for much of the preventable environmental damage occurring daily; also, leaving planning to local initiative is seen as no solution to regional problems. The opponents see federal support of state land use planning as the first step in a process that would lead next to federal demands for such planning and eventually to federal takeover of planning and even worse, federal implementation of plans through controls administered by a federal agency.

B. STATE PLANNING

Even apart from any handwriting on the federal wall, some states have already taken steps to provide for state agencies not only to engage in land use planning, but to regulate the development of land under the auspices of a state plan. The two leading states are Vermont and Hawaii. Consider the utility of these models in states with greater geographical area than Hawaii or Vermont.

In Vermont, Act 250 removed from local control certain large-scale developments. A state level agency was created to issue permits for developments within the definitions of the Act. A good description of Act 250 can be found in a federal case brought by a developer who was denied a permit to develop near a ski resort because the state agency found that a large part of the proposed development contained a deeryard (winter habitat for white-tailed deer). In Southview Associates, Ltd. v. Bongartz, 980 F.2d 84 (2d Cir.1992) Chief Judge Oakes wrote:

> Act 250 has been a major feature of the Vermont legal landscape for over twenty years. Its enactment represented the culmination of an effort to create a process that would subject subdivisions and other large developments in Vermont to administrative review so as to ensure economic growth without environmental catastrophe. See Governor's Commission on Environmental Control, Reports to Governor 2 (January 1970; May 1970). A brief discussion of the backdrop to the statute's enactment underscores its purpose.
>
> Beginning in the mid–1960s, Vermont experienced a massive increase in second-home construction and other recreational development, particularly in the southern portion of the state and around ski areas. Robert K. Reis, *Vermont's Act 250: Reflections on the First Decade and Recommendations for the Second* 9 (1980); David G. Heeter, *Almost Getting it Together in Vermont, in Environmental and Land Controls Legislation* 323, 326 (David R. Mandelker ed.

1976); Fred Bosselman & David Callies, *The Quiet Revolution in Land Use Control* 54 (1971) (prepared for the Executive Office of the President, Council on Environmental Quality); Erickson, *The Vermont Environmental Protection Act of 1970, in Environmental Protection* 678, 679 (Louis L. Jaffe & Laurence H. Tribe, eds. 1971). These developments shifted economic activity away from agriculture and forestry—the traditional mainstays of the region. Erickson, supra, at 679. The Town of Dover, located in Southern Vermont, provides an example. As one writer explained, in Dover, in 1969, developers were completing, building or planning 19 vacation home subdivisions. According to a regional planner, if all the planned lots had been improved and occupied, the town's population would have increased from 370 to 16,000 within a few years. Id.

This spate of development was fueled by several factors, including the construction of interstate highways, the increased popularity of skiing and other outdoor activities, and what might be termed America's fascination with "the country life." See Reis, supra, at 9. Although the development yielded considerable tax revenue and increased property values, at times it threatened to destroy the very base of its existence: Vermont's relatively unspoiled environment. Poorly planned vacation home subdivisions in mountainous areas—typified by steep slopes and thin soil cover—caused soil erosion, water pollution from sewage systems, and a decline in the aesthetic quality of the land. Erickson, supra, at 680; Bosselman & Callies, supra, at 54–55; Heeter, supra, at 327. Public concern over the side-effects of this new and rapid growth reached the high water mark when, in the summer of 1968, the International Paper Company proposed to construct a huge recreational and vacation home development on 20,000 acres of wilderness in the towns of Stratton and Winhall. Governor's Commission on Environmental Control, supra, at 3; Bosselman & Callies, supra, at 54; Heeter, supra, at 328.

In May of 1969, then Governor Deane C. Davis responded by creating the Governor's Commission on Environmental Control. Governor Davis charged the Commission with determining how economic growth could be attained without environmental destruction. Heeter, supra, at 329 (quoting opening remarks by Governor Deane C. Davis, *Proceedings of the Governor's Conference on Natural Resources* 1 (May 14, 1969)). The Commission's recommendations included the enactment of a land use law that would require large developments, including subdivisions, to undergo administrative review prior to construction. Governor's Commission on Environmental Control, supra, at 3–4. This proposal formed the basis of Act 250, enacted by the Legislature in 1970.

Not all development projects are subject to Act 250 review. Essentially, an Act 250 permit is required if a person wishes to construct (1) improvements on a parcel or parcels involving more than ten acres located within a radius of five miles; (2) housing projects with 10 or more units located on land owned or controlled by that person within a radius of 5 miles; (3) a subdivision partitioned for resale into ten or more lots within a radius of 5 miles; and (4) improvements above the elevation of 2500 feet. No permit is necessary for construction required for farming, logging or forestry purposes below the elevation of 2500 feet. 10 V.S.A. §§ 6001, 6081(a) (1984 & Supp.1991).

A person whose project is subject to Act 250 jurisdiction must file an application with the regional three-person district commission. 10 V.S.A. §§ 6026, 6083 (1984 & Supp.1991). The district commission evaluates the project according to ten criteria relating to: (1) water and air pollution that will result; (2) availability of water to meet the project's needs; (3) the project's burden on the existing water supply; (4) soil erosion that will result; (5) the project's effect on congestion and safety of transportation routes; (6) the burden the project will place on municipal and local government provision of educational and other services; (7) whether the project will have an undue adverse effect on "the scenic or natural beauty of the area, aesthetics, historic sites or rare and irreplaceable natural areas"; and (8) whether the project conforms with various state, regional and local development plans. 10 V.S.A. § 6086 (1984 & Supp.1991). If the district commission grants the application for a permit, it may attach conditions to it to assure compliance with the criteria for permit issuance. 10 V.S.A. § 6086(c) (1984).

A permit applicant may appeal the decision of the district commission to the nine-member Vermont Environmental Board. 10 V.S.A. §§ 6021(a), 6089(a) (1984 & Supp.1991). The Board reviews challenged findings de novo. 10 V.S.A. § 6089(a) (Supp.1991). The permit applicant may, in turn, appeal the Board's decision to the Supreme Court of Vermont, 10 V.S.A. § 6089(b) (Supp.1991), which will uphold the Board's findings of fact "if supported by substantial evidence in the record as a whole." 10 V.S.A. § 6089(c) (Supp.1991); see In re Southview Associates, 153 Vt. 171, 177, 569 A.2d 501, 504 (1989).

The Vermont Legislature accompanied the enactment of Act 250 with a statement of legislative intent, which provides, in part:

[T]he unplanned, uncoordinated and uncontrolled use of the lands and the environment of the state of Vermont has resulted in usages of the lands and the environment which may be destructive to the environment and which are not suitable to the demands and needs of the people of the state of Vermont * * *.

* * *

* * * it is necessary to regulate and control the utilization and usages of lands and the environment to ensure that, hereafter, the only usages which will be permitted are not unduly detrimental to the environment, [and] will promote the general welfare through orderly growth and development * * *.

Findings and declaration of intent, 1969, No. 250 (Adj.Sess.), § 1, in 10 V.S.A. annotations following § 6001 (1984).

Subsequently, in 1973, the legislature further clarified the purpose of the act by adopting a "Capability and Development Plan" to guide the implementation of Act 250. 1973 Capability and development plan; statement of intent and findings, 1973 No. 85, § 7, in 10 V.S.A. annotations following § 6042 (1984). See Norman Williams & Tammara Van Ryn–Lincoln, *The Aesthetic Criterion in Vermont's Environmental Law*, 3 Hofstra Prop.L.J. 89, 94–95 (1990). The plan states, in relevant part:

(2) Utilization of Natural Resources [C]onservation of the recreational opportunity afforded by the state's hills, forests, streams and lakes * * * are matters of public good. Uses which threaten or significantly inhibit these resources should be permitted only when the public interest is clearly benefited thereby.

* * *

(6) General Policies for Economic Development In order to achieve a strong economy * * * economic development should be pursued selectively so as to provide maximum economic development with minimal environmental impact.

* * *

(10) Recreational Resources The use and development of land and waters should occur in such a way as not to significantly diminish the value and availability of outdoor recreational activities to the people of Vermont, including hunting * * *.

* * *

(11) Special Areas Lands that include or are adjacent to sites or areas of historical, cultural, scientific, architectural, or archeological value * * * should only be developed in a manner that will not significantly reduce that value of the site or area.

Thus, the Legislature intended Act 250 to protect Vermont's environmental resources with an eye towards maintaining, among other things, existing recreational uses of the land—such as hunting, for example—and preserving lands, when possible, that have special values to the public. In recognition of the importance of economic growth, however, the focus of the Act is not on barring development but on molding it to minimize its environmental impact. And in practice, one commentator has stated that "[t]he statute has * * * been administered not as a 'no-growth' law, but as a law designed to improve the quality of growth." Williams & Van Ryn–Lincoln, supra, at 94.

IN RE JUSTER ASSOCIATES

Supreme Court of Vermont, 1978.
136 Vt. 577, 396 A.2d 1382.

[Juster Associates had previously received a permit from the Vermont Environmental Conservation Board for a 31 acre shopping center in the Town of Rutland. After construction was completed and the center was in operation, the septic tank sewage disposal system failed. Several alternatives also failed and Juster Associates returned to the Board seeking an amendment of its original permit to allow installation of a new system on a 4 acre site near, but not abutting the shopping center. The Board granted the new permit and an appeal was taken by the city and downstream riparian owners.]

DALEY, JUSTICE.

* * *

No one questions the applicability of our so-called Act 250, found in 10 V.S.A. chapter 151. The project in question is to be located on more than one acre of land within a municipality which has not adopted permanent zoning and subdivision bylaws * * * and therefore comes within the scope of the statute. The initial issue * * * is whether the Board had jurisdiction over Juster's application for a permit to develop the four acre tract as a sewage disposal facility. * * *

The purpose of Act 250 is to protect and conserve the environment of the state and to insure that lands slated for development are devoted to uses which are not detrimental to the public welfare and interest. 1969 No. 250 (Adj.Sess.), § 1; In re Great Eastern Building Co., 132 Vt. 610, 614, 326 A.2d 152, 154 (1974). These ends are served by a system of land use permits established by the Legislature. Where the Act applies, property may not be developed without a permit. 10 V.S.A. § 6081. An application for a permit must be made to a District Commissioner. 10 V.S.A. § 6083. The District Commission must provide general notice, by newspaper publication, and notice to certain persons designated by statute and by Board rule. 10 V.S.A. § 6084. After hearing, the District Commission may approve the application and issue a permit. 10 V.S.A. § 6086. Within this framework, the Board acts as a quasi-judicial appellate body, to hear appeals from commission decisions. Environmental Board Regulations, Rule 1(C)(1).

Notwithstanding the statutory procedure of hearings at the District Commission level with appeals to the Board, the Board seeks, by granting an amendment to an outstanding permit, to allow a four acre tract of land to be developed without proceedings before the District Commission. It contends that its power to do so lies in its jurisdiction to enforce the permits that it issues. The Board argues that it has jurisdiction because the land is to be used to fulfill a condition attached to an existing permit. We cannot agree.

We do not dispute the Board's authority to police its permits. It may, under the statute, revoke a permit if the conditions attached to the permit are violated. 10 V.S.A. § 6090. But we cannot allow it, under the guise of permit enforcement, to subvert the protective scheme ordained by the Legislature. The statute is intended, by a system of notice and hearings, to assure full consideration of land use proposals for all parcels of land. In bypassing the District Commission, the Board precluded a complete discussion of the issues involved in constructing a waste disposal facility on new acreage. This land was not considered in the previous hearings. When the original permit was issued, the matters now under discussion were not even contemplated. Development of the four acre plot may affect persons other than those who participated in the hearings that were conducted on the shopping center. However, the public was not notified that the land was to be developed, thus circumventing its participation.

* * * To accept the Board's rationale is to diminish the scrutiny given to land use under the statutory framework, because it allows for approval of a development without the discussion provided for by the statute.

Our review of the record convinces us that the Board lacked authority to entertain the application filed by Juster. Initial consideration of a land use proposal is a function assigned by the Legislature to the District Commission. The Board is not vested with concurrent jurisdiction to hear and decide the same matters.

* * *

Notes

1. This case gives some illustration of how the Vermont system operates. Also see In re Wildlife Wonderland, Inc., 133 Vt. 507, 346 A.2d 645 (1975), where the court upheld the environmental board's denial of a permit to construct and operate a game farm where some 300 wild and domestic animals could be viewed by the paying public.

The Juster case has been one long saga illustrating a dispute between developer and city. Another round in that dispute is Juster Associates v. City of Rutland, 901 F.2d 266 (2d Cir.1990), which involves an antitrust challenge against the city.

2. In 1988 the Vermont legislature adopted Act 200, which has been referred to as a growth control law. The statute is designed to encourage towns to adopt comprehensive growth control regulations by offering state funds to pay for the planning; towns that do not elect to participate are disabled from participating in regional planning. Act 200 fostered a bitter fight in Vermont. At least 51 towns rejected the Act in 1990 town meeting elections. Also, some towns returned money to the state and backed out of the program. The opposition to Act 200 appeared to focus on the loss of local control of land use regulation and a perceived threat to property rights. The future of the program is in some doubt.

In Hawaii the state has preempted a sizeable amount of what would normally be considered local zoning authority. The Hawaii statutory framework is set forth here:

Hawaii Revised Statutes (1968):

§ 205–1 Establishment of the commission. There shall be a state land use commission, hereinafter called the commission. The commission shall consist of nine members who shall hold no other public office and shall be appointed in the manner and serve for the term set forth * * *

§ 205–2 Districting and classification of lands. (a) There shall be four major land use districts in which all lands in the State shall be placed: urban, rural, agricultural, and conservation. The land use commission shall group contiguous land areas suitable for inclusion in one of these four major districts. The commission shall set standards for determining the boundaries of each district, provided that:

(1) In the establishment of boundaries of urban districts those lands that are now in urban use and a sufficient reserve area for foreseeable urban growth shall be included;

(2) In the establishment of boundaries for rural districts, areas of land composed primarily of small farms mixed with very low density residential lots, which may be shown by a minimum density of not more than one house per one-half acre and a minimum lot size of not less than one-half acre shall be included, except as herein provided;

(3) In the establishment of the boundaries of agricultural districts the greatest possible protection shall be given to those lands with a high capacity for intensive cultivation; and

(4) In the establishment of the boundaries of conservation districts, the "forest and water reserve zones" provided in Act 234, section 2, Session Laws of Hawaii 1957, are renamed "conservation districts" and, effective as of July 11, 1961, the boundaries of the forest and water reserve zones theretofore established pursuant to Act 234, section 2, Session Laws of Hawaii 1957, shall constitute the boundaries of the conservation districts; provided that thereafter the power to determine the boundaries of the conservation districts shall be in the commission.

In establishing the boundaries of the districts in each county, the commission shall give consideration to the master plan or general plan of the county.

(b) Urban districts shall include activities or uses as provided by ordinances or regulations of the county within which the urban district is situated.

(c) Rural districts shall include activities or uses as characterized by low density residential lots of not more than one dwelling house per one-half acre, except as provided by county ordinance pursuant to section 46–

4(c), in areas where "city-like" concentration of people, structures, streets, and urban level of services are absent, and where small farms are intermixed with low density residential lots except that within a subdivision, as defined in section 484–1, the commission for good cause may allow one lot of less than one-half acre, but not less than 18,500 square feet, or an equivalent residential density, within a rural subdivision and permit the construction of one dwelling on such lot, provided that all other dwellings in the subdivision shall have a minimum lot size of one-half acre or 21,780 square feet. Such petition for variance may be processed under the special permit procedure. These districts may include contiguous areas which are not suited to low density residential lots or small farms by reason of topography, soils, and other related characteristics.

(d) Agricultural districts shall include activities or uses as characterized by the cultivation of crops, orchards, forage, and forestry; farming activities or uses related to animal husbandry, aquaculture, game and fish propagation; aquaculture, which means the production of aquatic plant and animal life for food and fiber within ponds and other bodies of water; wind generated energy production for public, private and commercial use; bona fide agricultural services and uses which support the agricultural activities of the fee or leasehold owner of the property and accessory to any of the above activities, whether or not conducted on the same premises as the agricultural activities to which they are accessory, including but not limited to farm dwellings as defined in section 205–4.5(a)(4), employee housing, farm buildings, mills, storage facilities, processing facilities, vehicle and equipment storage areas, and roadside stands for the sale of products grown on the premises; wind machines and wind farms; small-scale meteorological, air quality, noise and other scientific and environmental data collection and monitoring facilities occupying less than one-half acre of land, provided that such facilities shall not be used as or equipped for use as living quarters or dwellings; agricultural parks; and open area recreational facilities, including golf courses and golf driving ranges, provided that they are not located within agricultural district lands with soil classified by the land study bureau's detailed land classification as overall (master) productivity rating class A or B.

These districts may include areas which are not used for, or which are not suited to, agricultural and ancillary activities by reason of topography, soils, and other related characteristics.

(e) Conservation districts shall include areas necessary for protecting watersheds and water sources; preserving scenic and historic areas; providing park lands, wilderness, and beach reserves; conserving indigenous or endemic plants, fish, and wildlife, including those which are threatened or endangered; preventing floods and soil erosion; forestry; open space areas whose existing openness, natural condition, or present state of use, if retained, would enhance the present or potential value of abutting or surrounding communities, or would maintain or enhance the conservation of natural or scenic resources; areas of value for recreational purposes; other related activities; and other permitted uses not detrimental to a multiple use conservation concept.

§ 205–3.1 Amendments to district boundaries. (a) District boundary amendments involving land areas greater than fifteen acres shall be processed by the land use commission pursuant to section 205–4.

(b) Any department or agency of the State, and department or agency of the county in which the land is situated, or any person with a property interest in the land sought to be reclassified may petition the appropriate county land use decision-making authority of the county in which the land is situated for a change in the boundary of a district involving lands less than fifteen acres presently in the agricultural, rural, and urban districts.

(c) District boundary amendments involving land areas of fifteen acres or less, except in conservation districts, shall be determined by the appropriate county land use decision-making authority for said district and shall not require consideration by the land use commission pursuant to section 205–4. District boundary amendments involving land areas of fifteen acres or less in conservation districts shall be processed by the land use commission pursuant to section 205–4. The appropriate county land use decision-making authority may consolidate proceedings to amend state land use district boundaries pursuant to this subsection, with county proceedings to amend the general plan, development plan, zoning of the affected land or such other proceedings. Appropriate ordinances and rules to allow consolidation of such proceedings may be developed by the county land use decision-making authority.

(d) The county land use decision-making authority shall serve a copy of the application for a district boundary amendment to the land use commission and the department of business, economic development and tourism and shall notify the commission and the department of the time and place of the hearing and the proposed amendments scheduled to be heard at the hearing. A change in the state land use district boundaries pursuant to this subsection shall become effective on the day designated by the county land use decision-making authority in its decision. Within sixty days of the effective date of any decision to amend state land use district boundaries by the county land use decision-making authority, the decision and the description and map of the affected property shall be transmitted to the land use commission and the department of planning and economic development, and tourism by the county planning director. [L 1985, c 230, § 3]

§ 205–4 Amendments to district boundaries involving land areas greater than fifteen acres. (a) Any department or agency of the State, any department or agency of the county in which the land is situated, or any person with a property interest in the land sought to be reclassified, may petition the land use commission for a change in the boundary of a district. This section applies to all petitions for changes in district boundaries of lands within conservation districts and all petitions for changes in district boundaries involving lands greater than fifteen acres in the agricultural, rural, and urban districts, except as provided in section 201E–210. * * *

(e) * * *

(2) All departments and agencies of the State and of the county in which the land is situated shall be admitted as parties upon timely application for intervention.

(3) All persons who have some property interest in the land, who lawfully reside on the land, or who otherwise can demonstrate that they will be so directly and immediately affected by the proposed change that their interest in the proceeding is clearly distinguishable from that of the general public shall be admitted as parties upon timely application for intervention.

(4) All other persons may apply to the commission for leave to intervene as parties. Leave to intervene shall be freely granted, provided that the commission or its hearing officer if one is appointed may deny an application to intervene when in the commission's or hearing officer's sound discretion it appears that: (A) the position of the applicant for intervention concerning the proposed change is substantially the same as the position of a party already admitted to the proceeding; and (B) the admission of additional parties will render the proceedings inefficient and unmanageable. A person whose application to intervene is denied may appeal such denial to the circuit court pursuant to section 91–14.

* * *

§ 205–6 Special permit. The county planning commission may permit certain unusual and reasonable uses within agricultural and rural districts other than those for which the district is classified. Any person who desires to use his land within an agricultural or rural district other than for an agricultural or rural use, as the case may be, may petition the planning commission of the county within which his land is located for permission to use his land in the manner desired. Each county may establish the appropriate fee for processing the special permit petition.

The planning commission, upon consultation with the central coordinating agency, except in counties where the planning commission is advisory only in which case the central coordinating agency, shall establish by rule or regulation, the time within which the hearing and action on petition for special permit shall occur. The county planning commission shall notify the land use commission and such persons and agencies that may have an interest in the subject matter of the time and place of the hearing.

The county planning commission may under such protective restrictions as may be deemed necessary, permit the desired use, but only when the use would promote the effectiveness and objectives of this chapter. A decision in favor of the applicant shall require a majority vote of the total membership of the county planning commission.

Special permits for land the area of which is greater than fifteen acres shall be subject to approval by the land use commission. The land use commission may impose additional restrictions as may be necessary or appropriate in granting such approval, including the adherence to representations made by the applicant.

A copy of the decision together with the complete record of the proceeding before the county planning commission on all special permit requests involving a land area greater than fifteen acres shall be transmitted to the land use commission within sixty days after the decision is rendered. Within forty-five days after receipt of the complete record from the county planning commission, the land use commission shall act to approve, approve with modification, or deny the petition. A denial either by the county planning commission or by the land use commission, or a modification by the land use commission, as the case may be, of the desired use shall be appealable to the circuit court of the circuit in which the land is situated and shall be made pursuant to the Hawaii Rules of Civil Procedure.

* * *

§ 205-18 Periodic review of districts. The office of state planning shall undertake a review of the classification and districting of all lands in the State, within five years from December 31, 1985, and every fifth year thereafter. The office, in its five-year boundary review, shall focus its efforts on reviewing the Hawaii state plan, county general plans, and county development and community plans. Upon completion of the five-year boundary review, the office shall submit a report of the findings to the commission. The office may initiate state land use boundary amendments which it deems appropriate to conform to these plans. The office may seek assistance of appropriate state and county agencies and may employ consultants and undertake studies in making this review.

One notable feature of the Hawaii statute is the provision for a review of district boundaries and regulations each five years after the adoption of the first district boundaries (which occurred in 1964). The second review was completed in 1974, and published in February, 1975. See Report to the People (Hawaii Land Use Commission, 1975). The report indicates that during the 1969-1974 period proposals were made to change the district classification of 133,438 acres of land. Approved changes in that period totaled 66,670 acres. Id., at p. 25. Out of the approved changes, a total of 5,438 acres were placed in the urban district while 4,056 acres were removed from the urban district. Ibid. See, generally, P. Myers, Zoning Hawaii: An Analysis of the Passage and Implementation of Hawaii's Land Classification Law (1975) and Mandelker & Kolis, Whither Hawaii: Land Use Management in an Island State, 1 U.Hawaii L.Rev. 48 (1979). In 1978, Hawaii adopted a new state planning act, Hawaii Rev.Stat. § 226–1 et seq. The reviews have been sporadic in recent years, with the latest in the early 1990's.

For a case interpreting the Hawaiian classifications in relation to the special permit procedures, see Neighborhood Bd. No. 24 (Waianae Coast) v. State Land Use Comm'n, 64 Hawaii 265, 639 P.2d 1097 (1982). A developer sought and received a special permit to construct an amusement park on a 103–acre parcel of land in the agricultural district. The court held that the special permit was improper and that the developer should have sought a district boundary amendment; use of the special permit procedure would, in this type of large-scale development, allow ad hoc infusion of major urban uses into agricultural districts. Compare Maha'ulepu v. Land Use Comm'n, 71 Hawaii 332, 790 P.2d 906 (1990) where the court held that the commission could issue special permits for golf courses on prime agricultural land. (In 1985 the legislature amended the definition of permitted uses in agricultural districts (Section 205–2, supra) to include golf courses.) See Comment, *Maha'ulepu v. Land Use Commission*: A Symbol of Change; Hawaii's Land Use Law Allows Golf Course Development on Prime Agricultural Land by Special Use Permit, 13 Haw. L. Rev. 205 (1991).

C. REGIONAL PLANNING

The political culture in most states automatically rejects any notion of "regional" government; the rules governing life are either local or at the state level. Even at the local level, in many states cities view county government with suspicion and vice versa. One state that has a history of regional approaches to problem solving is Minnesota. Statutes in that state seek to promote regional land use problem solving. Some excerpts from Minnesota Statutes Annotated (1963):

462.383

The legislature finds that problems of growth and development in urban and rural regions of the state so transcend the boundary lines of local government units that no single unit can plan for their solution without affecting other units in the region; that various multi-county planning activities conducted under various laws of the United States are presently being conducted in an uncoordinated manner; that intergovernmental cooperation on a regional basis is an effective means of pooling the resources of local government to approach common problems; and that the assistance of the state is needed to make the most effective use of local, state, federal, and private programs in serving the citizens of such urban and rural regions.

It is the purpose of sections 462.381 to 462.398 to facilitate intergovernmental cooperation and to insure the orderly and harmonious coordination of state, federal, and local comprehensive planning and development programs for the solution of economic, social, physical, and governmental problems of the state and its citizens by providing for the creation of regional development commissions.

Laws 1969, c. 1122, § 3, eff. June 1, 1969.

* * *

462.387

Any combination of counties or municipalities representing a majority of the population of the region for which a commission is proposed may petition the commissioner by formal resolution setting forth its desire to establish, and the need for, the establishment of a regional development commission. For purposes of this section the population of a county does not include the population of a municipality within the county.

462.39

The commission shall prepare and adopt, after appropriate study and such public hearings as may be necessary, a comprehensive development plan for the region. The plan shall consist of a compilation of policy statements, goals, standards, programs, and maps prescribing guides for an orderly and economic development, public and private, of the region. The comprehensive development plan shall recognize and encompass physical, social, or economic needs of the region, and those future developments which will have an impact on the entire region including but not limited to such matters as land use, parks and open space land needs, access to direct sunlight for solar energy systems, the necessity for and location of airports, highways, transit facilities, public hospitals, libraries, schools, public and private housing, and other public buildings. In preparing the development plan the commission shall use to the maximum extent feasible the resources, studies and data available from other planning agencies within the region, including counties, municipalities, special districts, and subregional planning agencies, and it shall utilize the resources of the director to the same purpose. No development plan or portion thereof for the region shall be adopted by the commission until it has been submitted to the director for review and comment and a period of 60 days has elapsed after such submission. When a development plan has been adopted, the commission shall distribute it to all local government units within the region.

* * *

462.391

The commission may participate as a party in any proceedings originating before the Minnesota municipal board under chapter 414, if the proceedings involve the change in a boundary of a governmental unit in the region.

Notes

1. What major differences do you see between the Vermont approach, the Hawaii approach, and the Minnesota approach? Which model do you think affords the best accommodation between regional concerns and the

"rights" of local property owners? Are there practical considerations that commend one approach over the other?

2. The approaches described above were hailed in the early 1970's as the "wave of the future." See Bosselman and Callies, The Quiet Revolution in Land Use Control (Council on Environmental Quality 1971). Statewide planning control as in Vermont and Hawaii did not spread to other states and regional planning has been utilized only in special circumstances. See, e.g., Booth, Developing Institutions for Regional Land Use Planning and Control—The Adirondack Experience, 28 Buffalo L.Rev. 645 (1979). See generally, Callies, The Quiet Revolution Revisited, American Planning Association J. 135 (Apr. 1980). Also see Marie L. York, Regions: Blind Isolation or Shared Vision?, Land Use Law, April, 1995, p. 3.

3. Several states have adopted planning enabling legislation which is somewhere in between state level control and local autonomy. In Florida, for example, areas that have been designated as of "critical environmental concern" are subject to planning and regulation at the state level; this approach can be viewed as a partial preemption of the traditional planning function. Some states have opted for mandatory local planning with the state (either by statute or administrative regulation) mandating particular elements of the plans. See, e.g., Cal.Govt.Code § 65101; Or.Rev.Stat. § 215.505 et seq.; Rev.Code Wash.Ann. § 36.70.010. Many states have preempted local planning and regulation of particular types of activities that have a widespread impact, such as power plant sitings. See, e.g., Town of Preston v. Connecticut Siting Council, 20 Conn.App. 474, 568 A.2d 799 (1990). Industrial pollution has also engendered preemption of local control. See, e.g., Niro, Illinois Environmental Law—State Preemption of Local Governmental Regulation of Pollution Related Activities, 67 Ill.Bar J. 118 (1978).

D. INTERSTATE COMPACTS

PEOPLE EX REL. YOUNGER v. COUNTY OF EL DORADO

Supreme Court of California, In Bank, 1971.
5 Cal.3d 480, 96 Cal.Rptr. 553, 487 P.2d 1193.

SULLIVAN, JUSTICE.

The Attorney General, on behalf of the People of the State of California, seeks a writ of mandate commanding the Counties of El Dorado and Placer to pay to the Tahoe Regional Planning Agency (Agency) the amounts of money respectively allotted to them by the Agency as being necessary to support its activities. We issued an alternative writ of mandate to which respondents have made return by answer. The issues thus presented to us are of great concern to California, to its neighbors and, indeed, to the entire country.

The controversy which we are required to review focuses upon the Lake Tahoe Basin—an area of unique and unsurpassed beauty situated high in the Sierras along the California–Nevada border. Mark Twain, an early visitor to the region, viewed the lake as "a noble sheet of blue water lifted six thousand three hundred feet above the level of the sea * * * with the shadows of the mountains brilliantly photographed upon its still surface * * * the fairest picture the whole earth affords." Year after year the lake and its surrounding mountains have attracted and captivated countless visitors from all over the world.

However, there is good reason to fear that the region's natural wealth contains the virus of its ultimate impoverishment. A staggering increase in population, a greater mobility of people, an affluent society and an incessant urge to invest, to develop, to acquire and merely to spend—all have combined to pose a severe threat to the Tahoe region. Only recently has the public become aware of the delicate balance of the ecology, and of the complex interrelated natural processes which keep the lake's waters clear and fresh, preserve the mountains from unsightly erosion, and maintain all forms of wildlife at appropriate levels. Today, and for the foreseeable future, the ecology of Lake Tahoe stands in grave danger before a mounting wave of population and development.

In an imaginative and commendable effort to avert this imminent threat, California and Nevada, with the approval of Congress (Pub.Law 91–148, 83 Stat. 360), entered into the Tahoe Regional Planning Compact (Compact) the provisions of which are found in Government Code section 66801. The basic concept of the Compact is a simple one—to provide for the region as a whole the planning, conservation and resource development essential to accommodate a growing population within the region's relatively small area without destroying the environment.

To achieve this purpose, the Compact establishes the Tahoe Regional Planning Agency with jurisdiction over the entire region. (§ 66801, art. III, subd. (a).) The Agency has been given broad powers to make and enforce a regional plan of an unusually comprehensive scope. This plan, to be adopted on or before September 1, 1971, must include, as correlated elements, plans for land-use, transportation, conservation, recreation, and public services and facilities. (§ 66801, art. V, subd. (b).) The Compact emphasizes that in formulating and maintaining this regional plan, the Agency "shall take account of and shall seek to harmonize the needs of the region as a whole * * *." (Id.)

The Agency is given the power to "adopt all necessary ordinances, rules, regulations and policies to effectuate the adopted regional * * *" plan. (§ 66801, art. VI, subd. (a).) While ordinances so enacted establish minimum standards applicable throughout the region, local political subdivisions may enact and enforce equal or higher standards. "The regulations shall contain general, regional standards including but not limited to the following: water purity and clarity; subdivision; zoning; tree removal; solid waste disposal; sewage disposal; land fills, excavations, cuts and grading; piers, harbors, breakwaters; or channels and other shoreline developments; waste disposal in shoreline areas; waste disposal from boats; mobile-home parks; house relocation; outdoor advertising; flood plain protection; soil and sedimentation control; air pollution; and watershed protection. Whenever possible without diminishing the effectiveness of the * * * general plan, the ordinances, rules, regulations and policies shall be confined to matters which are general and regional in application, leaving to the jurisdiction of the respective states, counties and cities the enactment of specific and local ordinances, rules, regulations and policies which conform to the * * * general plan." (Id.) The Compact also provides that "[v]iolation of any ordinance of the [A]gency is a misdemeanor." (§ 66801, art. VI, subd. (f).) Finally, it states that "all public works projects shall be reviewed prior to construction and [except for certain state public works projects] approved by the [A]gency as to the project's compliance with the adopted regional general plan." (§ 66801, art. VI, subd. (c).) * * *

The Compact permits the Agency to receive fees for its services, gifts, grants and other financial aids. It also provides for Agency financing as follows: "Except as provided in subdivision (e), on or before December 30 of each calendar year the agency shall establish the amount of money necessary to support its activities for the next succeeding fiscal year commencing July 1 of the following year. The agency shall apportion not more than $150,000 of this amount among the counties within the region on the same ratio to the total sum required as the full cash valuation of taxable property within the region in each county bears to the total full cash valuation of taxable property within the region. Each county in California shall pay the sum allotted to it by the agency from any funds available therefor and may levy a tax on any taxable property within its boundaries sufficient to pay the amount so allocated to it. Each county in Nevada shall pay such sum from its general fund or from any other moneys available therefor." (§ 66801, art. VII, subd. (a).)

After ratification of the Compact by Congress and upon proclamation of the Governors of California and Nevada, the Agency came into existence on March 19, 1970. It adopted a budget, pursuant to section 66801, article V, subdivisions (a) and (e), for the fourth quarter of the fiscal year 1969–1970—that is, for the months April through June 1970. Of the total budget of $81,770.85, $22,344.68 was allotted to El Dorado County, and $10,322.98 to Placer County. However, no specific demand was made upon the counties to pay the amounts apportioned to them, and they have consistently refused to do so.

The Agency has also adopted a budget of $180,000 for the fiscal year 1970–1971. Of this sum, the amount apportioned to El Dorado County is $60,150 and that allotted to Placer County is $33,600. No demand was made upon either county for such sums until December 29, 1970. The counties have refused to pay the above sums or any part of them.

For the fiscal year 1971–1972, the Agency has adopted a budget of $222,400, of which El Dorado County's share is $54,450, and Placer County's share is $40,350. The Attorney General asserts that, absent an order of this court, the counties will refuse to pay these sums.

The positions of the parties before us may be summarized as follows: the Attorney General contends that the respondent counties have a clear duty, imposed by the Compact, to pay their share of the funds necessary to support the activities of the Agency and that we should compel the performance of this duty by a writ of mandate. The counties contend first, that they are not required to make any payments to the Agency because the Compact is unconstitutional and void and, secondly, that the remedy here sought is inappropriate because the People have a plain, speedy and adequate remedy at law. * * *

We turn to the merits. The counties first contend that the Compact violates former sections 11, 12 and 13 of article XI of the California Constitution * * * Generally speaking, these sections confer upon specified local governmental bodies broad powers over purely local affairs. But, as we shall point out, the Compact is unaffected by any of the above provisions since its subject matter is of regional, rather than local, concern.

The regional nature of the Compact is manifest from the express language of the legislation. Article I of the Compact which sets forth legislative findings and declarations of policy, provides in relevant part: "It is found and declared that the waters of Lake Tahoe and other resources of the Lake Tahoe region are threatened with deterioration or degeneration. [Par.] It is further declared that by virtue of the special conditions and circumstances of the natural ecology, developmental pattern, population distribution and human needs in the Lake Tahoe region, the region is experiencing problems of resources use and deficiencies of environmental control." The same article further declares the "need to maintain an equilibrium between the region's natural endowment and its manmade environment," and specifically recognizes "that for the purpose of enhancing the efficiency and governmental effectiveness of the region, it is imperative that there be established an areawide planning agency with power to adopt and enforce a regional plan of resource conservation and orderly development, to exercise effective environmental controls and to perform other essential functions * * *." Of course, such findings and declarations of policy are entitled to great weight. (Bishop v. City of San Jose (1969) 1 Cal.3d 56, 63, 81 Cal.Rptr. 465, 460 P.2d 137; Housing Authority v. Dockweiler (1939) 14 Cal.2d 437, 449–450, 94 P.2d 794; Wilson, Consideration of Facts in Constitutional Cases (1944) 17 So.Cal.L.Rev. 335.)

Even without such explicit findings we could hardly avoid a conclusion that the purpose of the Compact is to conserve the natural resources and control the environment of the Tahoe Basin as a whole through area-wide planning. Lake Tahoe itself is an interstate body of water; the surrounding region, defined by the Compact, is also interstate, since it includes not only the lake but the adjacent parts of three counties of Nevada and two counties of California. (§ 66801, art. III, subd. (a).) The water that the Agency is to purify cannot be confined within one county or state; it circulates freely throughout Lake Tahoe. The air which the Agency must preserve from pollution knows no political boundaries. The wildlife which the Agency should protect ranges freely from one local jurisdiction to another. Nor can the population and explosive development which threaten the region be contained by any of the local authorities which govern parts of the Tahoe Basin. Only an agency transcending local boundaries can devise, adopt and put into operation solutions for the problems besetting the region as a whole. Indeed, the fact that the Compact is the product of the cooperative efforts and mutual agreement of two states is impressive proof that its subject matter and objectives are of regional rather than local concern. * * *

Furthermore, problems which exhibit exclusively local characteristics at certain times in the life of a community, acquire larger dimensions and changed characteristics at others. "It is * * * settled that the constitutional concept of municipal affairs is not a fixed or static quantity. It changes with the changing conditions upon which it is to operate." (Pac. Tel. & Tel. Co. v. City & County of S.F. (1959) 51 Cal.2d 766, 771, 336 P.2d 514, 517.) When the effects of change are felt beyond the point of its immediate impact, it is fatuous to expect that controlling such change remains a local problem to be solved by local methods. Old attitudes confer no irrevocable license to continue looking with unseeing eyes. The Compact gives the Agency power to adopt regional planning and regional zoning ordinances to solve regional problems of resource management; it does not delegate to the Agency the same powers granted to the counties.

In short, since the powers conferred upon the Agency are for regional purposes, not local purposes, and since no power to enact penal legislation has been delegated to the Agency, former section 11 is not violated.

* * *

The Counties of El Dorado and Placer also contend that the Compact is void because it denies their residents equal protection of the laws in violation of sections 11 and 21 of article I of the California Constitution and of the Fourteenth Amendment to the United States Constitution. Such violation of equal protection is asserted on two separate grounds: (1) That the Compact by failing to provide therefor denies to the citizens of the Tahoe Basin their right of initiative, referendum and recall; and (2) that the method of selecting the governing body of the Agency violates the "one person, one vote" rule.

The counties' first argument is essentially this: Since the Legislature has provided for initiative, referendum and recall for counties but has made no such provision for the Agency, there is an unreasonable and arbitrary classification "[d]enying the citizens of the Tahoe Basin such basic rights * * *." The point seems to be that although the citizens of El Dorado and Placer Counties do have such rights in respect to their counties, they are constitutionally entitled to an additional bundle of similar rights in respect to the Agency. We can discern no merit in this line of argument.

As we recently said, the concept of equal protection of the laws means simply "that persons similarly situated with respect to the legitimate purpose of the law receive like treatment." (Purdy & Fitzpatrick v. State of California (1969) 71 Cal.2d 566, 578, 79 Cal.Rptr. 77, 85, 456 P.2d 645, 653.) So far as the procedures of the initiative, referendum and recall are concerned, the Agency is treated no differently than other districts in California. All districts, including regional agencies such as the present one, are excluded from the initiative, referendum and recall provisions of the Elections Code where, as here, the district has been "formed under a law which does not provide a procedure for elections * * *." (Elec.Code, § 5150.) Since the residents of the Tahoe Basin are thus treated in the same way as those of other districts created under similar laws, they have suffered no denial of equal protection.

Nor can we discern any constitutional infirmity in the appointment, rather than the election of the governing body of the Agency. (See § 66801, art. III, subd. (a).) Certainly such a scheme of organization is not without precedent. (See, for example, the San Francisco Bay Conservation and Development Commission; Gov.Code, § 66620; see also Gov. Code, § 66400 et seq.; § 65063 et seq.; § 66500 et seq.) Indeed, in the instant case, the selection of the governing body by appointment would appear to be a necessary consequence of the interstate nature of the Agency. * * *

The counties' "one person, one vote" argument is also lacking in merit. They urge that the Agency exercises "general governmental powers" and that, therefore, under Avery v. Midland County (1968) 390 U.S. 474, 88 S.Ct. 1114, 20 L.Ed.2d 45 and its progeny, the governing board of the Agency must be apportioned in a manner which conforms with the "one person, one vote" requirement of the Fourteenth Amendment.

Clearly the members of the governing board of the Agency do not represent equal numbers of residents of the region. The United States census for 1970 gives the following populations for the counties here involved: Placer, 76,218; El Dorado, 41,704; Washoe, 119,965; Ormsby, 15,264; and Douglas, 6,046. Since one member of the Agency's governing board represents each of these counties some members of the board represent far more residents than do others. Furthermore, the 11,998 residents of the City of South Lake Tahoe are, in a sense, represented twice, since both that city and El Dorado County within which it is located have a member on the Agency. Finally, the *ex officio* members and the members appointed by the governors do not represent residents at all, but rather "the public at large." If the Agency's governing board must be selected on a "one person, one vote" basis, it obviously fails the test. (See Calderon v. City of Los Angeles (1971) 4 Cal.3d 251, 93 Cal.Rptr. 361, 481 P.2d 489.)

However, the members of the Agency's governing board are appointed, not elected. In Sailors v. Board of Education (1967) 387 U.S. 105, 87 S.Ct. 1549, 18 L.Ed.2d 650, the United States Supreme Court upheld a similar system of appointing members of a county school board over the objection that it violated the "one person, one vote" principle. There, the residents of each local school board district elected a local school board. Each of these boards, in turn, selected a delegate to a biennial meeting at which the delegates elected a five-member county board.

The court stated: "Viable local governments may need many innovations, numerous combinations of old and new devices, great flexibility in municipal arrangements to meet changing urban conditions. We see nothing in the Constitution to prevent experimentation. At least as respects nonlegislative officers, a State can appoint local officials or elect them or combine the elective and appointive systems as was done here. * * * Since the choice of members of the county school board did not involve an election and since none was required for these nonlegislative offices, the principle of 'one man, one vote' has no relevancy." (387 U.S. at pp. 110–111, 87 S.Ct. at p. 1553.)

* * *

The members of the Agency's governing board are appointed; consequently, the fact that they do not "represent" equal numbers of people does not deny those who are "underrepresented" equal protection of the laws.

Furthermore, we perceive significant state interests which justify the Compact's provisions for appointment of the Agency's governing board. In the first place, the Agency presents unique problems because of its interstate nature. If the board were apportioned on the basis of population within the region, Nevada would be accorded more votes than California, since the population of Washoe, Ormsby and Douglas Counties is 141,275 whereas the population of El Dorado and Placer Counties is 117,922. California, whose concurrence was essential to the formation of the Agency, would be less interested in the Agency if its vote were less than equal to Nevada's. Secondly, persons not residing within the Tahoe Basin have a very real and direct interest in the actions of the Agency. Aside from the general interest of the people of this state, including its vacationers, in the preservation of Lake Tahoe, it is common knowledge that many nonresidents own vacation homes and other property within the region. They will, of course, be directly affected by any planning or zoning by the Agency. Finally, the Compact represents an innovative attempt to deal with a problem directly affecting nonresidents of the Tahoe Basin, as well as residents. The Compact gives to the residents of the region a clear majority of the representation on the governing board, since such residents are the persons most intimately involved with the Agency. Yet, as we have seen, the general population of the state has a very substantial, if lesser, interest in the Agency. The public at large is represented by the two members sitting *ex officio* and by the two members appointed by the governors.

* * *

We, therefore, reach these final conclusions: Section 66801 of the Government Code, which constitutes the enactment by the California

Legislature of the Tahoe Regional Planning Compact, is constitutional. The Compact imposes on respondent counties a clear and present duty to pay to the Tahoe Regional Planning Agency the sums heretofore and hereafter allotted to them by the Agency as representing their respective shares of the amount of money necessary to support the Agency's activities. Respondents have consistently failed and refused to perform their duty enjoined on them by said law. The performance of respondents' duty properly can and should be compelled by issuance of a peremptory writ of mandate.

* * *

Let a peremptory writ of mandate issue as prayed.

Notes

1. The Supreme Court of Nevada also ordered a county to pay its share of the expenses of the agency. State ex rel. List v. County of Douglas, 90 Nev. 272, 524 P.2d 1271 (1974). The exact governmental nature of the Tahoe agency has inspired a considerable amount of litigation. See, e.g., Lake Country Estates, Inc. v. Tahoe Regional Planning Agency, 440 U.S. 391, 99 S.Ct. 1171, 59 L.Ed.2d 401 (1979); California Tahoe Regional Planning Agency v. Jennings, 594 F.2d 181 (9th Cir.1979).

2. In the Lake Country Estates case, supra, the Supreme Court was asked to decide whether the Tahoe Agency was protected by sovereign immunity under the Eleventh Amendment. The agency argued that any agency that is so important that it could not even be created by the States without a special act of Congress should receive the same immunity that is accorded to the States themselves. The majority rejected the argument finding that the tenor of the interstate compact and the understanding of both states all indicated that the agency was a "political subdivision" like a county or municipality, and not an "arm of the State."

3. In People, California Dept. of Transportation v. City of South Lake Tahoe, 466 F.Supp. 527 (E.D.Cal.1978), the court held that the interstate agency could be held to the higher environmental standards of either state agency. The California Tahoe Regional Planning Agency had adopted a transportation plan which did not show a "loop road" extending from the City of South Lake Tahoe, California to an existing casino area in Nevada. The Tahoe Regional Planning Agency had adopted a plan showing such a road and authorized construction without submitting its plan or proposal to the California Tahoe Regional Planning Agency. Although the court held that both the city and the Tahoe Regional Planning Agency were bound to comply with the California requirements, an injunction against construction was denied because the project only involved a few thousand dollars and if it was ultimately disapproved by the California agency, the road could be blocked off.

Chapter IV

THE BASICS OF ZONING

SECTION 1. HISTORY OF ZONING

A. AMERICAN PLANNING AND ZONING

(1) History of Planning and Zoning

Land use in this country is determined by zoning ordinances adopted by local governments. Their provisions dictate the types of uses to which land may be put, the density at which development may occur, the height, size, and shape of buildings, and the mix of commercial, residential, public, and other land uses in each locality. Zoning is a key method by which society marshals market forces to locate houses, manufacturing, and offices, protects local natural resources and the environment, and defines the character of its communities.

The law of most states stipulates that zoning is valid only if it is in accordance with a comprehensive land use plan. Planning "is the essence of zoning" says the judiciary in New York State. [See, e.g., Udell v. Haas, 21 N.Y.2d 463, 469, 235 N.E.2d 897, 900–01, 288 N.Y.S.2d 888, 893 (1968)] Comprehensive planning is society's insurance that the public welfare is served by land use regulation.

As the predicate for zoning, comprehensive planning is a critical public function. What constitutes comprehensive planning and how planning is done are determined by state legislatures. Given the importance of land use and the central legal role of comprehensive planning, one would expect state statutes to carefully define a comprehensive land use plan and to provide a predictable, reliable, and effective method of land use planning. Surprisingly, this is not the case in the majority of states.

This is demonstrated by reviewing the requirements in the adjacent New England states of Connecticut and New York. New York's statutes are typical of those of nearly half of the states in this country. They define very generally what a land use plan is and illustrate what a plan may include. There is no requirement that plans be kept up-to-date. New York law does not require municipalities to adopt such plans before they enact zoning ordinances. Where a land use plan and a zoning ordinance are adopted by a community, the statutes do not specify how they are to be interrelated. Legislation is adopted by a single legislative body, which is charged with adopting the comprehensive plan, the zoning ordinance, and all other land use regulations. There is no requirement in New York law for the development of regional land use plans, although local plans are encouraged to meet regional needs.

Connecticut's law is somewhat more directive. Zoning regulations must conform to a comprehensive plan and consider the local plan of conservation and development. The comprehensive plan is deemed to be implied from the zoning regulations themselves while the plan of conservation and development is a separate document adopted by the local planning commission. Towns and cities must adopt a plan and must update the plan at least every 10 years, although the state lacks a clear and effective method of enforcing these mandates. In enacting and amending zoning provisions, the local zoning commission must take the plan of conservation and development into consideration. In Connecticut, the matters that must be included in a local plan lack specificity. [Connecticut General Statutes § 8–23, for example, states that a local plan of conservation and development shall promote with the greatest efficiency and economy the coordinated development of the community and promote housing choice and economic diversity.] Local zoning commissions in Connecticut adopt zoning laws. Planning commissions adopt the plan of conservation and development. Wetlands agencies adopt local wetlands laws that must be as specific as state-promulgated wetlands regulations. Connecticut law provides for the creation of regional planning agencies that are charged with the adoption of regional plans of conservation and development, but there is little provision for the coordination or consistency of local and regional plans.

The benefit of this legal dissonance is flexibility. Since plans can be whatever localities want them to be, zoning is also malleable, since its purpose is to accomplish the objectives of the comprehensive plan. In this, danger lurks. Judicial decisions make it clear that land use regulations will not be sustained if they are ad hoc, arbitrary, capricious, unjust, unfair or irrational—characteristics they risk assuming if not demonstrably in conformance with a discrete and well considered plan.

The legal underpinnings of the current land use system were set nearly 80 years ago. They were designed in a different era to meet different challenges. In those days, "comprehensive planning" referred to "city-wide" planning because developing communities were separated by open spaces and land development impacts were local in character. At that time, conformance with a comprehensive plan was defined very loosely. Localities were not required to adopt discrete land use plans. It was enough that zoning ordinances contained some evidence of comprehensive planning.

In today's more complex and interrelated regions, "comprehensive" planning, in effect, means "regional" planning. Decisions made in one municipality affect regional air quality, the water quality of others in a watershed, and the cost and availability of housing and commercial real estate in the market area. Without laws that require the adoption of discrete land use plans, that tie zoning ordinances directly to the accomplishment of the provisions of those plans, and that require some relationship among local plans in the larger region, we are doomed to have no way of knowing where we are going and, worse, no method of getting there should we somehow decide how and where we want to use and conserve the land. How we got so lost on our road to comprehensive land use planning and how to find the road to a mutually satisfactory destination are the keenest questions facing land use regulators today.

(2) *History of Local Control of Land Development*

A vigorous debate over the wisdom of conforming market forces to a public plan for orderly development took place during the early part of this century. Zoning was "seen either as a protection of the suburban American home against the encroachment of urban blight and danger, or as the unrestrained caprice of village councils claiming unlimited control over private property in derogation of the Constitution." Arthur V. N. Brooks, *The Office File Box—Emanations from the Battlefield*, in Zoning and the American Dream 3, 7 (Charles M. Haar & Jerold S. Kayden eds.,1989). The acceptance of comprehensive zoning spread quickly as landowners began to realize that reasonable restrictions—public control of the landowner's and neighboring property for the public good—would tend to stabilize and preserve the value of all property. Harold M. Lewis, Planning The Modern City 255 (1949). It culminated decisively in 1926 in favor of comprehensive control of development in the United States Supreme Court decision, Village of Euclid v. Ambler Realty Co., 272 U.S. 365, 47 S.Ct. 114, 71 L.Ed. 303 (1926). Justice Sutherland's opinion reflected a gathering consensus among state supreme court judges that public guidance of private development was within the police power of the states.

The evolution of public control of land development started centuries before the beginning of the Christian era. As an example, a Roman commission in 451–450 B.C.E. adopted building regulations that resemble the setback requirements found in today's zoning ordinances. Robert R. Wright & Morton Gitelman, Cases and Materials on Land Use, 2 (3d ed. 1982). In 1581, certain noxious property uses were banned "within the compass and precinct of two and twenty miles from the City of London." Similar laws were passed by the early American colonies. For example, in 1692, certain business uses, deemed "offensive" by the Province of Massachusetts Bay were limited to certain locations. Violations were punishable by fines, a portion of which were given to the informer. A bulletin for the United States Department of Agriculture states that zoning regulations have been in use in various and sporadic ways for several centuries, beginning in this country long before we were one nation in the settlement along the Atlantic seaboard. Solberg, "Rural Zoning in the United States" (Ag.Info.Bull. 59, U.S.D.A., 1952). These early precursors of modern zoning regulated gunpowder mills and storehouses; and later on, fire districts were established in some cities with wooden buildings being prohibited in certain areas. As early as 1692, Massachusetts' authorization of certain market towns to assign places for slaughterhouses and similar noxious businesses constituted zoning of a sort. In 1889, a Wisconsin statute permitted municipalities to designate fire zones and control buildings erected therein. Prior to the enactment of comprehensive zoning ordinances, some municipalities separately enacted use, area, and height restrictions on building development. Harold M. Lewis, Planning The Modern City 258 (1949).

During the first 25 years of the twentieth century, local officials came to realize that narrowly focused, nuisance preventing legislation was not sufficient to address the needs of the nation's increasingly complex urban areas. James Metzenbaum, The Law of Zoning, 14–15 (2d ed. 1955). In 1916, New York City passed the first comprehensive zoning ordinance in the United States; other cities soon followed.

In 1922, the U.S. Department of Commerce published a model statute, the Standard State Zoning Enabling Act, to promote zoning. Standard State Zoning Enabling Act (U.S. Dep't of Commerce 1926) reprinted in 5 Edward H. Ziegler, Jr., Rathkopf's The Law of Zoning and Planning app. A. (2002). The model act, with certain variations, was adopted by most states as a method of encouraging and guiding their municipalities in adopting zoning ordinances. [Richard P. Fishman, ed., Housing for All Under Law 331 (1978).]. So great was the perceived need for the regulation of land development, that by the time the Euclid case was decided in 1926, 43 states had passed enabling statutes and 500 municipalities had adopted local zoning ordinances. In this way, public control of market forces in land development was codified.

Zoning, according to one view, was intended to be an end in itself. The "unitary" view of zoning holds that the zoning ordinance itself contains comprehensive planning principles and can exist independently from a comprehensive plan without violating the legal requirement that zoning be "in accordance with" a comprehensive plan. Housing for All Under Law, supra, at 332. The historical reason that zoning came before planning in the United States is said to be the urgent need for its adoption to protect single-family districts, the local tax-base, and property values. See Jerry Mitchell, In Accordance with a Comprehensive Plan: The Rise of Strict Scrutiny in Florida, 6 J. Land Use & Envtl. L. 79, 81 (1990). In part, the urgency for promoting zoning before planning resulted from Herbert Hoover's effort to relieve housing shortages through "the adoption of zoning plans which would protect residential districts * * *. [W]ith such protection assured, real estate owners would be more likely to resume the building of houses." Harold M. Lewis, Planning The Modern City 262 (1949). There is evidence that early proponents of zoning were also motivated by public health and safety matters, traffic congestion, and the like. Norman Williams, Jr. & John M. Taylor, American Planning Law 311 (1988).

However, the drafters of the enabling acts thought that more was needed. A second model act, the Standard City Planning Enabling Act, Standard City Planning Enabling Act (U.S. Dep't of Commerce 1928) promulgated in 1928, promoted the adoption of a local comprehensive land use plan as a document separate and distinct from zoning. The Practice of Local Government Planning 40 (David S. Arnold et al. eds., 1979). This act, and its adoption by the states, gave rise in some quarters to the notion that comprehensive land use planning should precede the zoning ordinance and serve as its predicate. Lewis wrote that: "The danger is that [zoning] may be considered a substitute for city planning and that, a zoning plan having been adopted, enthusiasm and interest may die out. Zoning is not a substitute for a city plan; it is an essential part of a comprehensive plan." 1 Harold M. Lewis, Planning The Modern City 261–262 (1949).

In the promulgation of the model acts and the progress of local land use regulation, however, zoning came first. Many states adopted the Standard City Planning Enabling Act, but after they had created the legal framework for zoning. Most failed in any meaningful way to prescribe how zoning and planning were to be integrated. This fissure remains today, narrowed by provisions in most states that require zoning to be in accordance with the comprehensive land use plan and by reforms in others that require a plan to be adopted before land use is regulated. Language in the Standard City Planning Enabling Act that defines the content and role of the comprehensive plan throws further light on the legal effect of the plan. The Standard City Planning Enabling Act defined the purpose of the master plan as:

> Guiding and accomplishing a coordinated, adjusted, and harmonious development of the municipality and its environs which will, in accordance with present and future needs, best promote health, safety, order, morals, convenience, prosperity, and general welfare as well as efficiency and economy in the process of development, including, among other things, adequate provision for traffic, the provision of safety from fire and other dangers, adequate provisions for light and air, the promotion of good civic design, wise and efficient expenditure of public funds, and the adequate provision of public utilities and other public requirements. Richard P. Fishman, ed., Housing for All Under Law, 329 (1978) (quoting SPEA § 7).

Because zoning preceded planning in both the Hoover Commission and in most state legislatures, the enigma of conforming zoning to planning is as old as comprehensive land use regulation itself.

The Standard City Planning Enabling Act recommended that plans be adopted by planning boards while zoning ordinances were to be adopted by the local legislative bodies. Edward M. Bassett, The Master Plan 83–84 (1938). This separation of responsibility for the preparation of zoning ordinances and land use plans renders the local land use system more enigmatic; in practice, how can a local legislative body be bound by a plan adopted by a lay board that is advisory in function? This division of authority has a certain logic, however. A visionary, long-term plan for the community does not have short-term impacts on property values and neighborhood character, and is less likely to arouse impassioned resistance. "It is of the essence of zoning, therefore, that it regulates development. Planning does not involve this coercive control, although zoning ordinances are the means whereby planning goals are achieved." Beverly J. Pooley, Planning and Zoning in the United States 4–5 (1982). Since a planning board or commission, in most states, is composed of appointed, rather than elected, members, the pressure of the electorate is felt less in its deliberations. In these ways, long-term community planning is immunized from short-term political considerations. To the extent that the zoning ordinance, although adopted by the local legislature, an elected body, is required to conform to the comprehensive land use plan, it enjoys a degree of immunization from such pressures as well.

(3) *Defining a Land Use Plan*

As this land use system evolved, basic concepts were left undefined, not the least of which was the definition of a comprehensive land use plan itself. A leading contemporary textbook on planning published by the American Planning Association defines a land use plan as having the following characteristics:

- It is primarily a physical plan, although it may incorporate social and economic objectives.
- It is long-range, slightly utopian, inspired by a vision of the future, and provides guidance as to how to get there.
- It is comprehensive, dealing with the entire community and its major development issues: transportation, housing, land use, utilities, recreation and their interrelationships.
- The plan contains a statement of policy and is a guide to the land use actions of local legislators and other decision-makers. The Practice of Local Government Planning.

The definitions of a comprehensive land use plan used during the formative period of this century are as numerous as are the terms used to describe such a plan. George McAneny, who was Chairman of the Board of the Regional Planning Association, defined city planning as:

> getting ready for the future * * * growth. It is the guidance into proper channels of a community's impulses towards a larger and broader life. On the face it has to do with things physical—the laying out of streets and parks and rapid-transit lines. But its real significance is far deeper; a proper city plan has a powerful influence for good upon the mental and moral development of the people. It is the firm base for the building of a healthy and happy community. 1 Harold M. Lewis, Planning The Modern City 7–8 (1949).

Earle S. Draper defined city planning as:

a great number of things. Careful surveys and inventories of resources are necessarily the first requirement. The deliberative process which we call planning consists of an analysis of the facts, of an appraisal of the situation, and of the resulting considered opinion which comes forth as a plan presented in the proper garb, whether it be pictures, charts, maps, verbal descriptions, or a combination of all of these.

Nelson P. Lewis defined it as "simply the exercise of such foresight as will promote the orderly and sightly development of a city and its environs along rational lines with due regard for health, amenity, and convenience and for its commercial and industrial advancement."

The document itself is called, variously, a master plan, a comprehensive plan, a comprehensive master plan, a land use plan, a comprehensive land use plan, an official master plan, and so on. Beverly J. Pooley, Planning and Zoning in the United States 14–15 (1982). There was no clear agreement as to whether this document should limit itself to physical phenomena, or should include economic, demographic, and social matters. The evolution of planning science is influenced in part by the following: (1) demographics; (2) economics; (3) views of government responsibility; (4) planning theories; and (5) the ever emerging stressors in our developed and developing regions. Richard P. Fishman, ed., Housing for All Under Law, 325.

What is meant by comprehensive itself is unclear. Most definitions presuppose a local focus, but some include regional and state-wide considerations. The expanding scope of city planning is indicated by the statement of purposes in the constitution of the American Institute of Planners originally the American City Planning Institute, as amended in 1946. It reads: "Its particular sphere of activity shall be the planning of the unified development of urban communities and their environs, and of states, regions, and the nation, as expressed through determination of the comprehensive arrangement of land uses and land occupancy and the regulation thereof." 1 Harold M. Lewis, Planning The Modern City 6 (1949).

The elements of a plan, that is, the subjects to be covered in it, have been described in numerous ways as well. Lewis divided the comprehensive plan into six principal, non-exclusive elements that included: (1) "The pattern of land uses;" (2) the mass-transportation system; (3) public facilities for the fast movement of passengers and goods; (4) "the street system;" (5) the park and recreational system; and (6) "the location of public buildings." In 1928, the Standard City Planning Enabling Act set forth suggested elements of comprehensive plans. Edward M. Bassett listed zoning districts, streets, public building sites, public reservations, parks, public utility routes, and bulkhead and pierhead lines as elements of planning. One architect categorized the comprehensive plan into twelve areas of study: "streets; transportation of people; transportation of goods; factories and warehouses; food supply and markets; water supply and sanitation; housing; recreation; parks;

boulevards and tree planting; architecture; laws and financing." [1 Harold M. Lewis, Planning The Modern City 54–55 (1949).]

This review of the creation and early evolution of the land use system establishes that it was enigmatic at inception. There was little agreement as to most of its critical details. One clear conclusion emerges, however. The framers of the system wanted those involved in its implementation to carry on a conversation about the goals and objectives of land use regulation. This conversation was to touch on, at a minimum, the major public interest issues affected by land use. It was to be carried on at the appropriate level and in requisite detail to confront the challenges of the day. This conversation—call it comprehensive land use planning—can be civil and productive because it is removed from the rancorous debate over specific regulations and particular projects. Whether we are abiding by this vision of land use planning is a key question for students of this legal system to consider.

(4) *What Is Land Use Law and Practice?*

Land use law, broadly defined, encompasses the full range of laws and regulations that influence or affect the development and conservation of the land. This law is intensely intergovernmental and interdisciplinary. In land use law there are countless intersections among federal, state, regional, and local statutes. It is significantly influenced by other legal regimes such as environmental, administrative, and municipal law, to name a few.

By dividing their jurisdictions into zoning districts and prescribing the specifications for land development pertaining to each district, local governments create a blueprint for the future development of each community. The aggregate result of these blueprints, when aligned on an intermunicipal basis, is a plan for the future development of the region. These patterns evolve as local boards and agencies review, approve, and condition applications for site plans, subdivisions, and special permits; they change as the local legislature rezones discrete areas and as property owners are awarded variances from the strict application of the zoning law.

Many of the intersecting laws and regulations of higher levels of government are adopted, in the first instance, either to influence or remedy to the consequences of local land use planning and regulation. This is true particularly in the area of environmental law where state and federal agencies shape and sometimes preempt local decision-making in the interest of protecting endangered natural resources such as rivers and aquifers. Nonetheless, it is the decisions made by boards and agencies at the municipal level that constitute the primary regulatory influence on the land.

(5) *Balancing Property Rights and the Public Interest: Limiting Doctrines*

The critical role given to local governments in regulating land use involves them in a delicate act of balancing private property rights with the greater public interest. Local land use decisions affect the right of landowners to use their land in the interest of protecting the health, safety, welfare, and morals of the public as a whole. Citizen groups of all kinds and landowners have a coequal interest in what local governments do in the land use area. Where it serves their interests, they are vigilant in employing the legal doctrines that limit the government's authority to regulate land use. These limitations are several:

- The first is the doctrine of substantive due process that requires land use regulations to serve a legitimate public purpose.
- Secondly, the administrative process by which regulations are adopted and enforced must follow the procedural requirements of state statutes and meet the fairness requirements of procedural due process.
- Third, localities must avoid improperly discriminating among similar parcels or against types of land users in violation of equal protection guarantees.
- Fourth, since local governments can exercise only those powers delegated to them by the state legislature, land use regulations cannot be *ultra vires*—beyond the scope of local authority. The action of the municipality must be undertaken pursuant to legislative power that has been delegated to it.
- Fifth, local land use regulations must not effect a taking of private property for a public purpose without just compensation in violation of the takings provisions of the state and federal constitutions.
- Sixth, the doctrine of vested rights limits the authority of municipalities in certain cases to impose significant new regulations on existing investments in land, such as completed structures, projects under construction, or projects already approved.
- Seventh, local land use regulations are not permitted to control matters whose regulation has been preempted by the state legislature.
- Finally, local regulations must not abridge freedoms of speech, expression and the exercise of religion protected by the state and federal constitutions.

Local land use authority is also limited by the power of state and federal legislatures and rights created by constitutional provisions. A number of these are based in equity. For example, a local zoning law that excludes all growth or types of housing affordable to lower income people is said to be unconstitutionally exclusionary. The police power is to be exercised in the interests of all the people of the state and cannot, by definition, be used for exclusionary purposes, an inherent constitutional principle. In some states, statutes provide that housing for groups of developmentally disabled individuals or substance abusers must be considered single-family housing and allowed in single-family zoning districts. The courts have found either an express or implied intention in these statutes to preempt local government's authority to exclude these types of group residences from single-family districts, the predominant residential zoning district in most communities.

Other types of preemptive effects are found in federal statutes that provide for the exclusive licensing of public utilities, which serve the public's interest in the utility's service. Such statutes can preempt or partially preempt local governments' authority to regulate public utilities, which may not be excluded from the municipality or unduly constrained.

(6) Zoning Practice

Zoning practice varies from state to state. The configuration of local legislative and administrative bodies and the nomenclature may be different. No central standard-setting agency has drafted the model zoning law, named and labeled the types of permissible zoning districts, or dictated the terms used in local zoning practice. Despite this lack of central control, much about the practice is the same in many states. Under the typical local zoning law, private land use is governed by five basic techniques. Each triggers a different procedure and is governed by different substantive standards. These five categories are as follows:

1. As–of–Right Uses and Their Accessory Uses

In each zoning district, certain land uses are permitted as the principal and primary uses of land. Accessory uses that are customarily found in association with these principal uses, but which are incidental and subordinate to them, are also permitted as-of-right. In a single-family zoning district, a single-family home is the principal use and a garage or shed is allowed as an accessory use. In most cases, the owner of an individual lot who proposes an as-of-right use of that lot need only submit construction drawings and secure a permit from the building inspector or department. Typically, no administrative agency decisions are involved in such an application.

2. Nonconforming Uses

A use of land that was in existence when a zoning restriction was adopted and that is prohibited by that restriction is called a nonconforming use. Because of the landowner's investment in that use, most zoning laws permit nonconforming uses to continue but not to be expanded or enlarged. Typically, nonconforming uses may not be reestablished after they have been abandoned or reconstructed after serious damage. Where certain nonconforming uses are particularly inconsistent with the as-of-right uses permitted in a district, the zoning law can require the nonconforming uses to be terminated, or amortized, after a specified number of years. Nonconforming uses that are considered threats to public health or safety can be required to cease immediately. The local zoning administrator must decide questions raised as to whether a use is nonconforming or conforming, whether it has been abandoned, or whether proposed improvements constitute a prohibited expansion or enlargement. The administrator's decision on these matters can be appealed to a board of appeals that handles zoning matters.

3. Variances

If a proposed use of property does not conform to applicable zoning restrictions, it can be authorized by a use or area variance awarded by a board of appeals in certain circumstances. Use variances allow property owners to use their buildings and parcels for purposes otherwise prohibited by the zoning law. Since use separation is the fundamental characteristic of zoning, this is precariously close to a legislative determination, and boards of appeal are limited in their discretion to award use variances. Often they are limited to parcels of land which can not be used profitably under any of the use categories allowed in their zoning district. An area variance is given because of practical difficulties encountered by property owners in complying with the dimensional or physical requirements of the applicable zoning regulations, such as height or setback requirements. In most states, boards of appeal are allowed to impose limiting conditions on variances as corrective measures designed to protect neighboring properties against the possible adverse effects of the use of the property benefited by the variance.

4. Special Use Permits

In addition to permitting certain land uses as-of-right in zoning districts, the zoning law can authorize other uses to be made of the land, but only if they receive a special—or conditional—use permit issued by a local administrative agency such as the board of appeals or the planning board. Typical land uses that are permitted by special or conditional permits include religious institutions, nursing homes, and day care centers. In most states, when such uses are listed as specially permitted uses in the zoning law, they are declared by the local legislature to be uses that are harmonious with as-of-right uses, in general, with the recognition that, in a specific location, they can negatively impact adjacent properties and need to be limited or conditioned to mitigate such impacts. If an applicant for a special use permit can demonstrate conclusively that no such impacts will result, or that the proposal mitigates those impacts effectively, the special use permit will usually be granted.

5. Rezoning

Finally, where a proposed use is not permitted by one of the above devices, the property owner may request that the local government rezone the property, making the proposed activity an as-of-right use under that zoning amendment. Alternatively, the local legislature, at its initiative, can rezone a parcel or area in the public interest. In most cases, the local legislature is not required to entertain a single owner's rezoning petition.

What constitutes a valid zoning regulation has been the subject of much debate. The restrictive view is that zoning is a rigid, district bound technique and that the locality is constrained by a literal reading of the enabling statutes. This view asserts, additionally, that zoning can regulate only the "use," not the "user" of property. The breadth of the statutes delegating zoning authority to local governments and the presumption of validity accorded zoning regulations by the courts have made it possible, in most states, for localities to create a variety of zoning mechanisms not referred to in the statutes but upheld by the courts as within the locality's implied authority to legislate to achieve the most appropriate use of the land.

(7) *Local Boards*

Land use law is interesting, in part, because it involves practice before a variety of public bodies. These include legislatures, administrative bodies and their ministerial officers, quasi-judicial bodies such as boards of appeals, and courts to which final decisions of local land use boards may be appealed. In most municipalities, the most critical land use decisions are made by the legislative body, which adopts the zoning law and other land use regulations, and the planning board, board of appeals, and the zoning enforcement officer which are charged with reviewing development proposals and enforcing the zoning law's provisions. The procedures that must be followed by the legislature in adopting laws and by these administrative agencies in reviewing and approving project proposals are contained in specific enabling statutes adopted by the state legislature as supplemented by the provisions of local law.

In the typical community, when an application for a building permit is submitted to the local building inspector or zoning enforcement officer, the administrator must ascertain before issuing the permit that the proposed construction is in compliance with the zoning law and other land use regulations. If the proposed development is not in compliance with the use and dimensional requirements of the zoning law, then the permit must be denied. This denial can be appealed to the board of appeals, which can reverse the officer's interpretation of zoning provision if in error or issue a use or area variance in conformance with the standards of state law.

If, on the other hand, the proposed development complies with the zoning provisions, but requires subdivision, site plan, special permit, or other approval, the applicant will be referred to the appropriate administrative agency for its review and determination. The decision-making process must follow prescribed time periods, honor requirements to provide public notice of the matter and hold public hearings, maintain a record of the agency's deliberations, and file and circulate its final determination on the matter. Most states have laws requiring that local agency meetings be open to the public and that copies of local records be provided to the public upon request.

Only if the standards of local land use regulations are met and the proposal is approved by the administrative agency can a building permit be issued. In most communities, one may not commence construction without a building permit and may not occupy buildings without a certificate of occupancy. To qualify for a building permit and certificate of occupancy, the property owner must honor any conditions imposed by the approving agency and construction plans for the development must conform to the requirements of the applicable building codes.

B. EARLY CASES

Our unique land use system could have evolved differently. When local governments began adopting zoning regulations, it was by no means clear that the public sector had such extensive power. Private property owners were accustomed to doing what they wished with their land, so long as their activities were not injurious to the public. It was settled that local statutes could proscribe potentially injurious or dangerous activity on the land, but not that whole sections of a community could be limited to single-family residential use where two-family homes, shops, and multi-family buildings were prohibited. In the early days of reviewing challenges to comprehensive zoning, the state courts split. The majority deferred to the wisdom of comprehensive zoning while a significant number of courts believed that separating land uses in designated districts was not within the power of local governments to protect the health, safety, and welfare of the public.

GOLDMAN v. CROWTHER
Court of Appeals of Maryland, 1925.
147 Md. 282, 128 A. 50, 38 A.L.R. 1455.

[Only a small part of the lengthy opinion is given.]

OFFUTT, J.

Daniel Goldman and his wife, as tenants by the entireties, own the property known as 1513 Park Avenue in a part of Baltimore City, which, under Ordinance No. 922 of the Mayor and City Council of Baltimore City, known as the "zoning ordinance," is classified as a residence district. In May, 1923, Goldman undertook to use the basement of a four story dwelling on that property for repairing, by hand and an ordinary sewing machine, for hire, used clothing for such patrons as had occasions to require his services. The business which he thus carried on required no alteration or repair of the building, and in the opinion of Goldman no permit was necessary to use it for that purpose. He was however informed that by so using it without a permit he was violating certain ordinances of the Mayor and City Council of Baltimore and shortly thereafter he was arrested for such violation, and while that complaint against him was pending he applied to the inspector of buildings of Baltimore City for a permit to use the premises for the purposes referred to. The inspector of buildings refused to grant the permit, partly at least on the ground that he was compelled under the zoning law to disapprove applications for such a use of property in a residence district. Goldman then filed in the Superior Court of Baltimore City a petition in which he asked that a writ of mandamus be issued against the building inspector of Baltimore City and the mayor of said city, directing them to issue to him a permit for the use of his premises for the purposes referred to above. The defendants answered that petition, and in their answer they averred that the permit was refused not only upon the authority of the zoning ordinance, but as well, upon the authority of other ordinances of the City of Baltimore vesting a discretion in the building inspector as to the issuance of permits in such cases, and that in refusing the permit in this case the building inspector acted in the exercise of that discretion. In connection with such issues of fact as were presented by the petition and the answer thereto, an agreed statement of facts was filed, and from that statement and the admissions found in the pleadings it further appears that the real and substantial reason for refusing the permit was that Goldman's property is located in a residence district of Baltimore City, the outlines of which are fixed by the zoning ordinance referred to. The verdict of the trial court was in favor of the defendants and the writ of mandamus refused, and from the judgment on that verdict this appeal was taken.

The important and controlling, and indeed under the agreed statement of fact the only question presented by the appeal is whether the zoning ordinance of Baltimore City, known as Ordinance No. 922, in so far as it affects the right of the appellant to use his property in the manner we have described, is a valid and an enforceable enactment, and in dealing with that question it can be said that there is nothing in the record from which it can be inferred that such use is offensive to the eye, the ear, or the nose of a person of ordinary sensibilities, or that it imperils the public health, welfare or safety, any more than would the same character of work if done by Goldman for himself and his family, except that possibly more of it is done.

This question can be approached by either of two avenues: One legal; the other political and sociological. If approached by the former the validity of the restraints and prohibitions of the ordinance must depend upon whether they violate certain definite guaranties and assurances found in the Federal and State Constitutions and the law of the land. If approached by the latter, the question is to an extent freed from the embarrassment of harmonizing any apparently repugnant provisions of the act with those guaranties, since in such case the end to be accomplished and the benefit to be derived are the main factors to be considered, and the rights of mere individuals may be subordinated to the public convenience, upon the principle that such rights are always subject to the paramount authority of the State to subordinate them to what is conceived by those speaking for it to be for the benefit of the State, as representing all the citizens.

Which one of these two methods of approach should be used in this case is a question which goes to the root of our system of government, but without referring further to that, it is sufficient to say that in our opinion, we are not at liberty to examine the question from any other than a legal standpoint, and therefore we cannot be controlled in our consideration of the validity of this ordinance by its possible benefit to the public, if in point of fact that benefit is purchased by appropriating the rights and property of individuals to the public use without just compensation, and by the violation of the guaranties of the State and Federal Constitutions.

* * *

By this ordinance all the land in the city of Baltimore is subjected to restrictions which limit the number of families who may dwell on it, the use to which it may be put, the height of buildings which may be constructed on it, and the proportion of each lot of ground which a building may occupy, except that in the "industrial use district" the land or structures thereon may be used for any lawful purpose. Many of these restrictions relating to the use of property bear no apparent relation to the public health, safety or welfare, nor does the ordinance contain any definite or fixed standards by which the reasonableness or the necessity for the restrictions may be measured or determined, nor are they necessarily uniform or definite in their application. For after specifying with the most meticulous particularity the nature, extent and application of the restrictions, the board of zoning appeals is authorized in its discretion to disregard the "strict letter" of the ordinance, and to vary or modify any of the regulations or provisions contained in it relating to "the use, construction or alteration of buildings or structures or the use of land, so that the spirit of the ordinance shall be observed, public safety and welfare secured and substantial justice done." This sonorous but vague and cloudy formula is to say the least of it a poor and uncertain substitute for those guaranties of the State and Federal Constitutions which assure to every citizen the right to hold and enjoy and use his property in any manner he pleases so long as he does not thereby injuriously affect the health, security or welfare of his neighbor or the public, as the words health, security and welfare have hitherto been understood in this State. There may also be an appeal from the board of zoning appeals to the Baltimore City Court, but that remedy, if anything, increases rather than lessens the difficulty and hardship which the ordinance inflicts upon the landowner, for it only transfers the discretion from the board of zoning appeals, which would presumably have some special knowledge and training, to a jury which might have none and who, in the absence of any fixed or definite rules or standards to guide them, would naturally exercise that discretion varyingly in accordance with the views of different juries.

Before dealing with the constitutionality of the ordinance in whole or in part, we will refer briefly to the territory upon which it is to operate.

From a small village containing a few scattered houses on the shores of the Patapsco in 1729, Baltimore City has grown into a great maritime city, with a population currently estimated in round numbers at eight hundred thousand, occupying over eighty square miles. Within its confines are found an infinite variety of commercial and industrial enterprises and activities. Its commerce is borne over the world by great land

and water transportation systems which serve its people. It includes within its boundaries property devoted to every variety of use, including residential, commercial, agricultural, industrial, maritime and recreational. It is constantly expanding and constantly with its growth and changing conditions the use of property in it changes, so that what was formerly residential property has become commercial property, and property which was at one time most useful for commercial or agricultural purposes is now most valuable for industrial purposes. Heretofore these changes have been in response to conditions created by the growth of the city, the increase of its population, the demands of new enterprises, changes in transportation facilities, changing markets, and various other factors which cannot be readily anticipated or controlled. This ordinance at a stroke arrests that process of natural evolution and growth, and substitutes for it an artificial and arbitrary plan of segregation, under which the landowner may only use his property for certain designated purposes, and under which he may be forbidden to use it for the only purpose for which it is adapted and most valuable.

* * *

There is a theory which has obtained some recognition, that the guaranties of written constitutions are not inflexible, and that the decisions construing them at one period of the state's history, under conditions existing then, ought not to bind the courts at some later period when conditions have changed, and when from economic, sociological or political considerations it is desirable that a different or more liberal construction be given. That theory is based upon the conception that any constitutional guaranty, no matter how plain and clear it may be, can be dissolved and avoided by the application of the police power of the state. That the police power is a real and essential element in the sovereignty of the state cannot be questioned or denied, and that written constitutions are presumed to have been made with conscious knowledge of that fact must be admitted. But it has never been supposed in this State that the police power is a universal solvent by which all constitutional guaranties and limitations can be loosed and set aside regardless of their clear and plain meaning, nor that it is a substitute for those guaranties, for far-reaching and powerful as it is, it has its limitations. Just what those limits are have not been, and in the nature of things, cannot be clearly and definitely marked, except that any exercise of the power which interferes with some right protected by the letter of the Constitution must bear some substantial relation to the public health, morals, safety, comfort or welfare. For while the existence of the police power may be invoked to determine what rights are guaranteed by the Constitution, it can never be invoked to justify an invasion of those rights once they have been ascertained. * * *

One of the most striking manifestations of this tendency [to encroach on individual rights] is the great volume of so-called zoning legislation which has in recent years been written into the laws of the several states, of which the ordinance before us is an apt illustration and which subject private property to an infinite variety and number of restrictions limiting its use, many of which rest for sanction upon no more definite or substantial foundation than that they are supposed to be in the interest of general prosperity or the public convenience. That the right to hold, enjoy and use property is not absolute but subject to the police power of the State is axiomatic (6 R.C.L. 194), and that that power may be affected by changing conditions is inevitable and unquestionable, for a use which at one time may be inoffensive and harmless may at another affect the security or the welfare of others with equal rights, and one of the sources of the police power is the maxim, "Sic utere tuo ut alienum non laedas." So, property in a populous urban community may be properly subjected to restrictions which would be unreasonable and arbitrary in a thinly settled rural community, so long as the restrictions bear some definite relation to the protection of the public health, morals, safety or comfort. These principles are self evident and are almost universally accepted. But the question before us goes much further than that. It is whether the power to hold, use and enjoy property can be restricted or taken away by the State under the guise of the police power for purely aesthetic reasons or for any such elastic and indeterminate object as the general prosperity without compensation.

* * *

From an examination of the maps which form a part of the ordinance, it appears that the residence zones or districts of Baltimore City comprise a number of separated areas varying in extent, irregular in outline, and located without apparent reference to any definite plan, but which nevertheless in the aggregate include a very large part of the total area of that city. And by reference to the ordinance it appears that in those districts no land or building can be used and no buildings erected except for one of fifteen specified uses, to which reference has already been made, unless specially authorized by the board of zoning appeals. These restrictions are wholly arbitrary and have no logical relation to the public welfare, but rest solely upon aesthetic grounds. Under the provisions of sections 3 and 7d and 7g of article 3 of the ordinance, a neighborhood drug store might be forbidden, and a crematory permitted, a bakery forbidden and a sewage disposal plant permitted, an office building prohibited and a refuse dump permitted, a grocery store forbidden and an amusement park allowed. Nor is there any rule or standard prescribed to guide the discretion of those entrusted with the administration of the ordinance in deciding what shall be allowed or what forbidden any more definite than that, in any departure from the letter of the law, the spirit of the ordinance shall be preserved, public safety and welfare secured, and substantial justice done. But as the ordinance itself is based upon the theory that its prescriptions are in the interest of the public welfare, it is not clear how any departure from them can be justified on that ground, for if the restrictions are not necessary to the public welfare, there can be no justification for them at all, and in fact there is none. Their only apparent purpose was to prevent the encroachment of business establishments of any kind upon residential territory, regardless of whether they affected in any degree the public health, morals, safety, or welfare. In effecting that purpose they take from the property owner the right to use his property for any purpose not sanctioned by the letter of the ordinance or allowed by the practically unfettered discretion of the board of zoning appeals, and deprive him of privileges guaranteed by the twenty-third article of the Maryland Bill of Rights.

We have reached the conclusion, therefore, that so much of the ordinance as attempts to regulate and restrict the use of property in Baltimore City is void: first, because it deprives property owners of rights and privileges protected by the Constitution of the State; second, because such deprivation is not justified by any consideration for the public welfare, security, health, or morals apparent in the ordinance itself; and third, because it does not require that the restrictions shall in fact be based upon any such consideration. But in reaching this conclusion we do not hold that the use of property in Baltimore City may not be regulated or restricted where such regulation or restriction is based upon such consideration. * * *

STATE EX REL., CARTER v. HARPER

Supreme Court of Wisconsin, 1923.
182 Wis. 148, 196 N.W. 451, 33 A.L.R. 269.

Mandamus to compel the issuance of a building permit. The relator is in the wholesale and retail milk and dairy products business in the city of Milwaukee. In September, 1919, he purchased a lot and erected thereon a building which he is using as a dairy and milk pasteurizing plant. During the summer of 1921 he found that his business had outgrown the capacity of his plant to such an extent that it became impossible for him to conduct his business in said building in accordance with city and state health regulations. He made application to the inspector of buildings of the city of Milwaukee for a permit to erect an addition to the present building. The application was denied for the reason that the proposed addition to the building was in violation of the terms of the so-called zoning ordinance of the city of Milwaukee, adopted pursuant to authority conferred by sec. 62.23, Stats.

An alternative writ of mandamus issued out of the circuit court for Milwaukee county in the usual form, addressed to the inspector of buildings of the city of Milwaukee, to compel the issuance of said permit. The respondent made return setting forth the so-called zoning ordinance, to which return the relator demurred. The demurrer was overruled, and judgment ordered quashing the alternative writ and dismissing the petition. From the judgment thus entered this appeal is taken.

OWEN, J. The so-called zoning ordinance of the city of Milwaukee established within said city four classes of use districts designated: residence districts, local business districts, commercial and light manufacturing districts, and industrial districts. Relator's property is within a residence district. The ordinance then prescribes the uses to which property within the districts so created may be devoted. The present use of relator's property does not conform to the use permitted by the ordinance in residence districts. The ordinance further provides that no building within a residence district devoted to a non-conforming use shall be enlarged unless the use is changed to a conforming use.

This is a brief statement of the provisions of the ordinance upon which the building inspector relies as a justification for the denial of the permit. That the terms of the ordinance do furnish such justification, if the ordinance is a valid regulation, is not denied by the appellant. He claims, however, that the ordinance is unreasonable and oppressive, that it deprives him of the equal protection of the laws, and takes his property without due process of law and without just compensation.

The constitution of this state, sec. 13, art. I, provides that the property of no person shall be taken for public use without just compensation therefor, and the Fourteenth amendment of the federal constitution provides that no person shall be deprived of his property without due process of law. These provisions are intended to secure the enjoyment of most substantial and fundamental rights, and the allegation that one is being deprived of his property without just compensation or without due process of law calls for most serious consideration. It has long been settled, however, that these constitutional provisions interpose no barrier to the exercise of the police power of the state. Thus it was said in *State ex rel. Kellogg v. Currans*, 111 Wis. 431, 87 N.W. 561, at page 435, speaking of constitutional limitations upon legislative power:

> "These limitations, however, according to all the authorities, state and federal, are to be read as not extending so far as to deprive the states of their power to so control the conduct of individuals as to protect the welfare of the community—a power commonly described as the 'police power.'"

Many declarations appear in our Reports, coming from the pen of Mr. Justice Marshall, tending to create the impression that there are constitutional limitations upon the exercise of this power. *State ex rel. Milwaukee Med. Coll. v. Chittenden*, 127 Wis. 468, 107 N.W. 500; *Bonnett v. Vallier*, 136 Wis. 193, 116 N.W. 885; *Mehlos v. Milwaukee*, 156 Wis. 591, 146 N.W. 882. A careful reading of these cases, however, will indicate that the constitutional limitations which were there in the mind of the court were either some express constitutional provision prohibiting certain specified legislation, or the line of reasonableness beyond which the legislature could not go. * * *

It is thoroughly established in this country that the rights preserved to the individual by these constitutional provisions are held in subordination to the rights of society. Although one owns property he may not do with it as he pleases, any more than he may act in accordance with his personal desires. As the interest of society justifies restraints upon individual conduct, so also does it justify restraints upon the use to which property may be devoted. It was not intended by these constitutional provisions to so far protect the individual in the use of his property as to enable him to use it to the detriment of society. By thus protecting individual rights, society did not part with the power to protect itself or to promote its general well-being. Where the interest of the individual conflicts with the interest of society, such individual interest is subordinated to the general welfare. If in the prosecution of governmental functions it becomes necessary to take private property, compensation must be made. But incidental damage to property resulting from governmental activities, or laws passed in the promotion of the public welfare, is not considered a taking of the property for which compensation must be made. * * *

The legislation authorizing so-called zoning ordinances is of comparatively recent origin, and it is not unnatural that those adversely affected shall regard them as an unjust and unwarranted interference with their property rights. The question of whether such ordinances fall legitimately within the realm of the police power has been considered by a few courts, presently to be noted, with conflicting results. The pioneer nature of the legislation requires that it have careful consideration, tested by the fundamental principles to which we have alluded. We are required to consider whether such ordinances have any reasonable tendency to promote the public morals, health, or safety or the public comfort, welfare, or prosperity.

The purpose of the law is to bring about an orderly development of our cities; to establish residence districts into which business, commercial, and industrial establishments shall not intrude; and to fix business districts and light industrial districts upon which heavy industrial concerns may not encroach. This is no new idea, although it has but recently taken the form of legislation. Everyone who has observed the haphazard development of cities, the deterioration in the desirability of certain residential sections by the encroachment of business and industrial establishments upon and into such sections, resulting in the consequent destruction of property values and in the ultimate abandonment of such sections for residential purposes, has appreciated the desirability of regulating the growth and development of our urban communities. The homeseeker shuns a section of a city devoted to industrialism and seeks a home at some distance from the business center. A common and natural instinct directs him to a section far removed from the commerce, trade, and industry of the community. He does this because the home instinct craves fresh air, sunshine, and well-kept lawns—home association beyond the noise of commercial marts and the dirt and smoke of industrial plants. Fresh air and sunshine add to the happiness of the home and have a direct effect upon the well-being of the occupants. It is not uncommon to witness efforts of promoters to preserve the residential character of their additions by placing covenants in their deeds restricting the use of the property to residential purposes and, in some instances, requiring the erection of a home according to specified standards. It cannot be denied that a city systematically developed offers greater attractiveness to the homeseeker than a city that is developed in a haphazard way. The one compares to the other about as a well-ordered department store compares to a junk-shop. If such regulations stabilize the value of property, promote the permanency of desirable home surroundings, and if they add to the happiness and comfort of the citizens, they thereby promote the general welfare.

When we reflect that one has always been required to so use his property as not to injure his neighbors, and that restrictions against the use of property in urban communities have increased with changing social standards, and that the luxuries of one decade become the necessities of another, can it be said that an effort to preserve various sections of a city from intrusion on the part of institutions that are offensive to and out of harmony with the use to which such sections are devoted is unreasonable? The present standards of society prompt a revolt against such unbecoming intrusions, and they constitute such a recognized interference with the rights of the residents of such sections as to justify regulation.

The benefits to be derived by cities adopting such regulations may be summarized as follows: They attract a desirable and assure a permanent citizenship; they foster pride in and attachment to the city; they promote happiness and contentment; they stabilize the use and value of property and promote the peace, tranquility, and good order of the city. We do not hesitate to say that the attainment of these objects affords a legitimate field for the exercise of the police power. He who owns property in such a district is not deprived of its use by such regulations. He may use it for the purposes to which the section in which it is located is dedicated. That he shall not be permitted to use it to the desecration of the community constitutes no unreasonable or permanent hardship and results in no unjust burden.

* * *

There remains a further question to be considered. Appellant claims that the ordinance is unreasonable in that it prohibits him from enlarging the business to which his property was devoted prior to the passage of the ordinance. The reasonableness of this feature of the ordinance, as well as its main purpose, is subject to judicial review. Where, however, a given situation is conceded to present a proper field for the exercise of the police power, the extent of the interference is a matter which lies very greatly in legislative discretion. *Mehlos v. Milwaukee*, 156 Wis. 591, 146 N.W. 882. If the appellant has acquired a vested right to enlarge his business, then every other person having an embryo business in a residential section must be accorded the same privilege, and an infant industry may grow to mammoth proportions, thereby to a very large extent defeating the purposes of the regulation.

In *Hadacheck v. Sebastian*, 239 U.S. 394, 36 S.Ct. 143, 60 L.Ed. 348, a brickyard of the value of $800,000, situated far outside the city limits when acquired, was suppressed after it had been included in the city limits. If property of that nature and of that value must yield to the supremacy of the police power, it is difficult to see how a regulation prohibiting appellant's enlargement of his business can be held unreasonable. Then, too, it may be remarked that an ordinance permitting those already engaged in business to enlarge the same while prohibiting all others from engaging therein, would not tend to make the ordinance less vulnerable. *See People ex rel. Roos v. Kaul*, 302 Ill. 317, 134 N.E. 740, and cases there cited.

It is further contended that the ordinance amounts to class legislation by reason of the provisions of sec. 26.46, Milwaukee Code, 1921 Supp., which provides that "A structure or premises may be erected or used in any location by a public-service corporation for any purpose which the railroad commission decides is reasonably necessary for the public convenience or welfare." When it is remembered that such buildings are erected to promote the comfort and convenience of the public and that it is within the power of the state to compel such erection, it would appear that this constitutes a reasonable and valid classification. It must be apparent that an ordinance enacted pursuant to state authority which prevents the erection of buildings or the conduct of business deemed inimical to public interest need not also prohibit the erection of buildings or the conduct of business which is essential to the comfort and convenience of the public and which the duly constituted authority of the state determines to be necessary for the public service which a public utility is required to render. A similar provision received the consideration of the court in *Opinion of the Justices*, 234 Mass. 597, 127 N.E. 525, concerning which it was said (p. 606) that the provision "is within settled principles touching legislative control over property devoted to that use."

It is our conclusion that the ordinance is, in the respects here considered, a reasonable, valid, and constitutional enactment. It is appreciated that there are other provisions of the ordinance the validity of which may be the subject of future challenge. It is to be understood that no opinion is expressed with reference to any features of the ordinance except such as are herein treated. So far as the ordinance affects the rights of appellant, it fully authorizes the denial of a building permit the issuance of which he seeks to coerce.

Judgment affirmed.

VILLAGE OF EUCLID v. AMBLER REALTY CO.

Supreme Court of the United States, 1926.
272 U.S. 365, 47 S.Ct. 114, 71 L.Ed. 303, 54 A.L.R. 1016.

MR. JUSTICE SUTHERLAND delivered the opinion of the court.

The village of Euclid is an Ohio municipal corporation. It adjoins and practically is a suburb of the city of Cleveland. Its estimated population is between 5,000 and 10,000, and its area from 12 to 14 square miles, the greater part of which is farm lands or unimproved acreage. It lies, roughly, in the form of a parallelogram measuring approximately 3 1/2 miles each way. East and west it is traversed by three principal highways: Euclid avenue, through the southerly border,

St. Clair avenue, through the central portion, and Lake Shore boulevard, through the northerly border, in close proximity to the shore of Lake Erie. The Nickel Plate Railroad lies from 1,500 to 1,800 feet north of Euclid avenue, and the Lake Shore Railroad 1,600 feet farther to the north. The three highways and the two railroads are substantially parallel.

Appellee is the owner of a tract of land containing 68 acres, situated in the westerly end of the village, abutting on Euclid avenue to the south and the Nickel Plate Railroad to the north. Adjoining this tract, both on the east and on the west, there have been laid out restricted residential plats upon which residences have been erected.

On November 13, 1922, an ordinance was adopted by the village council, establishing a comprehensive zoning plan for regulating and restricting the location of trades, industries, apartment houses, two-family houses, single family houses, etc., the lot area to be built upon, the size and height of buildings, etc.

The entire area of the village is divided by the ordinance into six classes of use districts, denominated U-1 to U-6, inclusive; three classes of height districts, denominated H-1 to H-3, inclusive; and four classes of area districts, denominated A-1 to A-4, inclusive. The use districts are classified in respect of the buildings which may be erected within their respective limits, as follows: U-1 is restricted to single family dwellings, public parks, water towers and reservoirs, suburban and interurban electric railway passenger stations and rights of way, and farming, noncommercial greenhouse nurseries and truck gardening; U-2 is extended to include two-family dwellings; U-3 is further extended to include apartment houses, hotels, churches, schools, public libraries, museums, private clubs, community center buildings, hospitals, sanitariums, public playgrounds and recreation buildings and a city hall and courthouse; U-4 is further extended to include banks, offices, studios, telephone exchanges, fire and police stations, restaurants, theaters, and moving picture shows, retail stores and shops, sales offices, sample rooms, wholesale stores for hardware, drugs and groceries, stations for gasoline and oil (not exceeding 1,000 gallons storage) and for ice delivery, skating rinks and dance halls, electric sub-stations, job and newspaper printing, public garages for motor vehicles, stables and wagon sheds (not exceeding five horses, wagons or motor trucks) and distributing stations for central store and commercial enterprises; U-5 is further extended to include billboards and advertising signs (if permitted), warehouses, ice and ice cream manufacturing and cold storage plants, bottling works, milk bottling and central distribution stations, laundries, carpet cleaning, dry cleaning and dyeing establishments, blacksmith, horseshoeing, wagon and motor vehicle repair shops, freight stations, streetcar barns, stables and wagon sheds (for more than five horses, wagons or motor trucks), and wholesale produce markets and salesrooms; U-6 is further extended to include plants for sewage disposal and for producing gas, garbage and refuse incineration, scrap iron, junk, scrap paper and rag storage, aviation fields, cemeteries, crematories, penal and correctional institutions, insane and feeble minded institutions, storage of oil and gasoline (not to exceed 25,000 gallons), and manufacturing and industrial operations of any kind other than, and any public utility not included in, a class U–1, U–2, U–3, U–4 or U–5 use. There is a seventh class of uses which is prohibited altogether.

Class U–1 is the only district in which buildings are restricted to those enumerated. In the other classes, the uses are cumulative; that is to say, uses in class U–2 include those enumerated in the preceding class, U–1; class U–3 includes uses enumerated in the preceding classes, U–2 and U–1; and so on. In addition to the enumerated uses, the ordinance provides for accessory uses, that is, for uses customarily incident to the principal use, such as private garages. Many regulations are provided in respect of such accessory uses.

The height districts are classified as follows: In class H–1, buildings are limited to a height of two and one-half stories or thirty-five feet; in class H–2, to four stories or fifty feet; in class H–3, to eighty feet. To all of these, certain exceptions are made, as in the case of church spires, water tanks, etc.

The classification of area districts is: In A–1 districts, dwellings or apartment houses to accommodate more than one family must have at least 5,000 square feet for interior lots and at least 4,000 square feet for corner lots; in A–2 districts, the area must be at least 2,500 square feet for interior lots, and 2,000 square feet for corner lots; in A–3 districts, the limits are 1,250 and 1,000 square feet, respectively; in A–4 districts, the limits are 900 and 700 square feet, respectively. The ordinance contains, in great variety and detail, provisions in respect of width of lots, front, side and rear yards, and other matters, including restrictions and regulations as to the use of billboards, sign boards and advertising signs.

A single family dwelling consists of a basement and not less than three rooms and a bathroom. A two-family dwelling consists of a basement and not less than four living rooms and a bathroom for each family; and is further described as a detached dwelling for the occupation of two families, one having its principal living rooms on the first floor and the other on the second floor.

Appellee's tract of land comes under U–2, U–3 and U–6. The first strip of 620 feet immediately north of Euclid avenue falls in class U–2, the next 130 feet to the north, in U–3, and the remainder in U–6. The uses of the first 620 feet, therefore, do not include apartment houses, hotels, churches, schools, or other public and semi-public buildings, or other uses enumerated in respect of U–3 to U–6, inclusive.

Annexed to the ordinance, and made a part of it, is a zone map, showing the location and limits of the various use, height and area districts, from which it appears that the three classes overlap one another; that is to say, for example, both U–5 and U–6 use districts are in A–4 area districts, but the former is in H–2 and the latter in H–3 height districts. The plan is a complicated one and can be better understood by an inspection of the map, though it does not seem necessary to reproduce it for present purposes.

The lands lying between the two railroads for the entire length of the village area and extending some distance on either side to the north and south, having an average width of about 1,600 feet, are left open, with slight exceptions, for industrial and all other uses. This includes the larger part of appellee's tract. Approximately one-sixth of the area of the entire village is included in U-5 and U-6 use districts. That part of the village lying south of Euclid avenue is principally in U-1 districts. The lands lying north of Euclid avenue and bordering on the long strip just described are included in U-1, U-2, U-3, and U-4 districts, principally in U-2.

The enforcement of the ordinance is entrusted to the inspector of buildings, under rules and regulations of the board of zoning appeals. Meetings of the board are public, and minutes of its proceedings are kept. It is authorized to adopt rules and regulations to carry into effect provisions of the ordinance. Decisions of the inspector of buildings may be appealed to the board by any person claiming to be adversely affected by any such decision. The board is given power in specific cases of practical difficulty or unnecessary hardship to interpret the ordinance in harmony with its general purpose and intent, so that the public health, safety and general welfare may be secure and substantial justice done. Penalties are prescribed for violations, and it is provided that the various provisions are to be regarded as independent and the holding of any provision to be unconstitutional, void or ineffective shall not affect any of the others.

The ordinance is assailed on the grounds that it is in derogation of Sec. 1 of the 14th Amendment to the Federal Constitution in that it deprives appellee of liberty and property without due process of law and denies it the equal protection of the law, and that it offends against certain provisions of the Constitution of the state of Ohio. The prayer of the bill is for an injunction restraining the enforcement of the ordinance and all attempts to impose or maintain as to appellee's property any of the restrictions, limitations or conditions. The court below held the ordinance to be unconstitutional and void, and enjoined its enforcement. 297 F. 307.

Before proceeding to a consideration of the case, it is necessary to determine the scope of the inquiry. The bill alleges that the tract of land in question is vacant and has been held for years for the purpose of selling and developing it for industrial uses, for which it is especially adapted, being immediately in the path of progressive industrial development; that for such uses it has a market value of about $10,000 per acre, but if the use be limited to residential purposes the market value is not in excess of $2,500 per acre; that the first 200 feet of the parcel back from Euclid avenue, if unrestricted in respect of use, has a value of $150 per front foot, but if limited to residential uses, and ordinary mercantile business be excluded therefrom, its value is not in excess of $50 per front foot.

It is specifically averred that the ordinance attempts to restrict and control the lawful uses of appellee's land so as to confiscate and destroy a great part of its value; that it is being enforced in accordance with its terms; that prospective buyers of land for industrial, commercial and residential uses in the metropolitan district of Cleveland are deterred from buying any part of this land because of the existence of the ordinance and the necessity thereby entailed of conducting burdensome and expensive litigation in order to vindicate the right to use the land for lawful and legitimate purposes; that the ordinance constitutes a cloud upon the land, reduces and destroys its value, and has the effect of diverting the normal industrial, commercial and residential development thereof to other and less favorable locations.

The record goes no farther than to show, as the lower court found, that the normal, and reasonably to be expected, use and development of that part of appellee's land adjoining Euclid avenue is for general trade and commercial purposes, particularly retail stores and like establishments, and that the normal, and reasonably to be expected, use and development of the residue of the land is for industrial and trade purposes. Whatever injury is inflicted by the mere existence and threatened enforcement of the ordinance is due to restrictions in respect of these and similar uses; to which perhaps should be added—if not included in the foregoing—restrictions in respect to apartment houses. Specifically, there is nothing in the record to suggest that any damage results from the presence in the ordinance of those restrictions relating to churches, schools, libraries and other public and semi-public buildings. It is neither alleged nor proved that there is or may be a demand for any part of appellee's land for any of the last named uses; and we cannot assume the existence of facts which would justify an injunction upon this record in respect of this class of restrictions. For present purposes the provisions of the ordinance in respect of these uses may therefore be put aside as unnecessary to be considered. It is also unnecessary to consider the effect of the restrictions in respect of U–1 districts, since none of the appellee's land falls within that class.

* * *

Building zone laws are of modern origin. They began in this country about twenty-five years ago. Until recent years, urban life was comparatively simple; but with the great increase and concentration of population, problems have developed, and constantly are developing, which require, and will continue to require, additional restrictions in respect of the use and occupation of private lands in urban communities. Regulations, the wisdom, necessity and validity of which, as applied to existing conditions, are so apparent that they are now uniformly sustained, a century ago, or even half a century ago, probably would have been rejected as arbitrary and oppressive. Such regulations are sustained, under the complex conditions of our day, for reasons analogous to those which justify traffic regulations, which, before the advent of automobiles and rapid transit street railways, would have been condemned as fatally arbitrary and unreasonable. And in this there is no inconsistency, for while the meaning of constitutional guaranties never varies, the scope of their application must expand or contract to meet the new and different conditions which are constantly coming within the field of their operation. In a changing world, it is impossible that it should be otherwise. But although a degree of elasticity is thus imparted, not to the *meaning*, but to the *application* of constitutional principles, statutes and ordinances, which, after giving due weight to the new conditions, are found clearly not to conform to the Constitution, of course, must fall.

The ordinance now under review and all similar laws and regulations must find their justification in some aspect of the police power, asserted for the public welfare. The line which in this field separates the legitimate from the illegitimate assumption of power is not capable of precise delimitation. It varies with circumstances and conditions. A regulatory zoning ordinance, which would be clearly valid as applied to the great cities, might be clearly invalid as applied to rural communities. In solving doubts, the maxim "sic utere tuo ut alienum non laedas," which lies at the foundation of so much of the common law of nuisances, ordinarily will furnish a fairly helpful clew. And the law of nuisances, likewise, may be consulted, not for the purpose of controlling, but for the helpful aid of its analogies in the process of ascertaining the scope of, the power. Thus the question whether the power exists to forbid the erection of a building of a particular kind or for a particular use, like the question whether a particular thing is a nuisance, is to be determined, not by an abstract consideration of the building or of the thing considered apart, but by considering it in connection with the circumstances and the locality. * * *

* * *

We find no difficulty in sustaining restrictions of the kind thus far reviewed. The serious question in the case arises over the provisions of the ordinance excluding from residential districts, apartment houses, business houses, retail stores and shops, and other like establishments. This question involves the validity of what is really the crux of the more recent zoning legislation, namely, the creation and maintenance of residential districts, from which business and trade of every sort, including hotels and apartment houses, are excluded. Upon that question this court has not thus far spoken. The decisions of the state courts are numerous and conflicting; but those which broadly sustain the power greatly outnumber those which deny it altogether or narrowly limit it; and it is very apparent that there is a constantly increasing tendency in the direction of the broader view. * * *

The matter of zoning has received much attention at the hands of commissions and experts, and the results of their investigations have been set forth in comprehensive reports. These reports, which bear every evidence of painstaking consideration, concur in the view that the segregation of residential, business and industrial buildings will make it easier to provide fire apparatus suitable for the character and intensity of the development in each section; that it will increase the safety and security of home life; greatly tend to prevent street accidents, especially to children, by reducing the traffic and resulting confusion in residential sections; decrease noise and other conditions which produce or intensify nervous disorders; preserve a more favorable environment in which to rear children, etc. With particular reference to apartment houses, it is pointed out that the development of detached house sections is greatly retarded by the coming of apartment houses, which has sometimes resulted in destroying the entire section for private house purposes; that in such sections very often the apartment house is a mere parasite, constructed in order to take advantage of the open spaces and attractive surroundings created by the residential character of the district. Moreover, the coming of one apartment house is followed by others, interfering by their height and bulk with the free circulation of air and monopolizing the rays of the sun which otherwise would fall upon the smaller homes, and bringing, as their necessary accompaniments, the disturbing noises incident to increased traffic and business, and the occupation, by means of moving and parked automobiles, of larger portions of the streets, thus detracting from their safety and depriving children of the privilege of quiet and open spaces for play, enjoyed by those in more favored localities,—until, finally, the residential character of the neighborhood and its desirability as a place of detached residences are utterly destroyed. Under these circumstances, apartment houses, which in a different environment would be not only entirely unobjectionable but highly desirable, come very near to being nuisances.

If these reasons, thus summarized, do not demonstrate the wisdom or sound policy in all respects of those restrictions which we have indicated as pertinent to the inquiry, at least, the reasons are sufficiently cogent to preclude us from saying, as it must be said before the ordinance can be declared unconstitutional, that such provisions are clearly arbitrary and unreasonable, having no substantial relation to the public health, safety, morals, or general welfare. * * *

It is true that when, if ever, the provisions set forth in the ordinance in tedious and minute detail, come to be concretely applied to particular premises, including those of the appellee, or to particular conditions, or to be considered in connection with specific complaints, some of them, or even many of them, may be found to be clearly arbitrary and unreasonable. But where the equitable remedy of injunction is sought, as it is here, not upon the ground of a present infringement or denial of a specific right, or of a particular injury in process of actual execution, but upon the broad ground that the mere existence and threatened enforcement of the ordinance, by materially and adversely affecting values and curtailing the opportunities of the market, constitute a present and irreparable injury, the court will not scrutinize its provisions, sentence by sentence, to ascertain by a process of piecemeal dissection whether there may be, here and there, provisions of a minor character, or relating to matters of administration, or not shown to contribute to the injury complained of, which, if attacked separately, might not withstand the test of constitutionality. In respect of such provisions, of which specific complaint is not made, it cannot be said that the landowner has suffered or is threatened with an injury which entitles him to challenge their constitutionality. * * *

* * * Under these circumstances, therefore, it is enough for us to determine, as we do, that the ordinance in its general scope and dominant features, so far as its provisions are here involved, is a valid exercise of authority, leaving other provisions to be dealt with as cases arise directly involving them.

And this is in accordance with the traditional policy of this court. In the realm of constitutional law, especially, this court has perceived the embarrassment which is likely to result from an attempt to formulate rules or decide questions beyond the necessities of the immediate issue. It has preferred to follow the method of a gradual approach to the general by a systematically guarded application and extension of constitutional principles to particular cases as they arise, rather than by out of hand attempts to establish general rules to which future cases must be fitted. This process applies with peculiar force to the solution of questions arising under the due process clause of the Constitution as applied to the exercise of the flexible powers of police, with which we are here concerned.

Decree reversed.

Notes

1. A year and a half after the Euclid decision, the U.S. Supreme Court, again speaking through Mr. Justice Sutherland, summarily declared a zoning ordinance unreasonable and unconstitutional as applied to the plaintiff's particular tract of land. Nectow v. Cambridge, 277 U.S. 183, 48 S.Ct. 447, 72 L.Ed. 842 (1928). In Nectow, the property owner showed that the local zoning law permitted only residential uses and that there was no market for residential uses in the neighborhood. The owner's argument was that the zoning law, as applied to the parcel, did not accomplish a public purpose because of market conditions. In essence, the law allowed the owner no economical use of the land. Nectow won, and then the U.S. Supreme Court handed down no significant decisions implicating local land use matters for the next four decades. Nectow's claim is called an "as applied" challenge to local zoning authority, while Ambler Realty's is called a "facial" attack. Can you tell the difference? What exactly is being challenged in the Euclid case and what would the consequence have been if the court had found for the plaintiff? Which type of challenge do you think it is easier to win? Why?

2. Although the Euclid case was hailed as a great legal victory for the concept of zoning, in recent years a more critical re-analysis of Euclid has emerged. Today, there are many who question the wisdom of the strict segregation of uses with protection of single-family dwellings as the highest purpose of zoning. For example, Jane Jacobs, the urban economist, in her book, The Death and Life of Great American Cities, points out that in an

earlier era the mixture of apartments, stores, and small industrial uses promoted safety and vitality, as well as a sense of neighborhood and community, which is lacking in newer communities that comply with zoning's philosophy of separated uses. Some developers are harking back to that earlier era. See Maureen Milford, New Village with a 16th–Century Concept, N.Y. Times, Dec. 3, 1995, p. 31. The article describes a 30 million dollar development in rural Pennsylvania, Stoudtburg Village, where the homeowners live over their shops. In Chapter VI, we explore a number of innovative zoning techniques that promote mixed-use and traditional neighborhood developments that are being used to add vitality to newly constructed neighborhoods.

3. Pay close attention to the substantive legal claims that are made by the plaintiffs in these and subsequent cases. What legal rights do the plaintiffs have that they claim have been violated? What remedies are they asking for? What standards do the courts use to review the municipal actions challenged? We explore these issues in depth in Chapter XII.

4. In Chapter II, we reviewed the principles of common law nuisance law. Consider the use of the Court in Euclid of these principles in determining that it is within the local police power to separate land uses, particularly to keep apartments out of single-family neighborhoods. How close is the analogy between what is accomplished by zoning and nuisance law?

5. What do you make of the following statement by the court in Euclid: "But the village, though physically a suburb of Cleveland, is politically a separate municipality, with powers of its own and authority to govern itself as it sees fit * * * "? Consider, for example, the problem of urban sprawl which is a contemporary manifestation of the suburban growth that was being experienced by the Cleveland suburbs in the 1920s. Is sprawl a local or a regional problem? Can the problem be solved if this judicial statement regarding local self-determination in land use matters remains true today? If municipalities are creatures of state governments, is it theoretically within the power of state legislatures to address the problems of uncontrolled metropolitan growth? How?

6. From the beginning of the modern era, the work of competent and dedicated attorneys has shaped how American jurisdictions have decided to control the use of privately owned land. Consider the career of Alfred Bettman, a corporate lawyer in Cincinnati who submitted an amicus brief to the U.S. Supreme Court supporting the village of Euclid's position, arguing for the constitutionality of zoning. It is reported that Justice Sutherland had determined to write an opinion for the majority holding Euclid's ordinance unconstitutional when he read Bettman's brief and changed his mind. Bettman also drafted the first adopted planning enabling act in the nation for Ohio. He also served on the Hoover Commission and assisted in the creation of the Standard City Planning Enabling Act. See Amicus Curiae: The American Planning Association in the Courtroom, Lora A. Lucero, Zoning and Planning Law Report, vol. 26, no. 2, Feb. 2003.

SECTION 2. ZONING, REZONING, AND CONFORMANCE WITH THE COMPREHENSIVE PLAN

Local governments are municipal corporations that obtain their legal authority from their charters, home rule authority, and from state enabling acts. In the land use field, municipal authority comes primarily from discrete enabling acts adopted by the state legislatures modeled after the standard zoning and planning enabling acts described in Section One. If a local legislative body attempts to adopt or amend zoning laws in a manner that is inconsistent with the enabling laws, that attempt may be challenged successfully as *ultra vires*: beyond the corporate authority of the municipality. State statutes prescribe both the subject matter of local land use laws and their mode of adoption, for example, by requiring public notice of a zoning amendment and public hearing prior to its adoption. Attempts to adopt or amend zoning that do not follow prescribed procedures are described as being jurisdictionally defective or *ultra vires*.

Municipal attorneys examine closely the content of state enabling acts to confirm that zoning laws are within their client's municipal authority. Developers' attorneys need the same assurance so that their clients' approved projects are immunized from attack. Citizens and environmental groups that scrutinize local land use actions for validity employ attorneys who need to know if the local law their clients find objectionable was properly adopted and within the locality's power. Since the majority of state zoning enabling acts were patterned after the Standard Zoning Enabling Act promulgated by the Hoover Commission in the 1920s, it provides a proper place to begin our inquiry into the range of authority of local governments to adopt zoning and other land use laws. In its original form, the first three sections of the standard act read as follows:

A STANDARD STATE ZONING ENABLING ACT UNDER WHICH MUNICIPALITIES MAY ADOPT ZONING REGULATIONS

(Recommended by the U.S. Department of Commerce, 1926).

A STANDARD STATE ZONING ENABLING ACT

Section 1. Grant of Power. For the purpose of promoting health, safety, morals, or the general welfare of the community, the legislative body of cities and incorporated villages is hereby empowered to regulate and restrict the height, number of stories, and size of buildings and other structures, the percentage of lot that may be occupied, the size of yards, courts, and other open spaces, the density of population, and the location and use of buildings, structures, and land for trade, industry, residence or other purposes.

Section 2. Districts. For any or all of said purposes the local legislative body may divide the municipality into districts of such number, shape, and area as may be deemed best suited to carry out the purposes of this act; and within such districts it may regulate and restrict the erection, construction, reconstruction, alteration, repair, or use of buildings, structures, or land. All such regulations shall be uniform for each class or kind of buildings throughout each district, but the regulations in one district may differ from those in other districts.

Section 3. Purpose in View. Such regulations shall be made in accordance with a comprehensive plan and designed to lessen congestion in the streets; to secure safety from fire, panic, and other dangers; to promote health and the general welfare; to provide adequate light and air; to prevent the overcrowding of land; to avoid undue concentration of population; to facilitate the adequate provision of transportation, water, sewerage, schools, parks, and other public requirements. Such regulations shall be made with reasonable consideration, among other things, to the character of the district and its peculiar suitability for particular uses, and with a view to conserving the value of buildings and encouraging the most appropriate use of land throughout such municipality.

In Chapter VII, we explore the advent of local environmental law. That chapter explains how local legislatures have amended their zoning and other land use laws to protect natural resources such as ridgelines, watercourses, and habitats. Can you spot any possible authority in the standard act above that supports the adoption of such laws? Do such laws have anything to do with location and use of buildings, structures, and land; in other words, are they within the grant of power? If the local environmental law singles out just properties that contain ridges, streams and rivers, and habitats and subjects them to stricter standards, would the law violate the uniformity requirement: that all regulations shall be uniform for each kind or class of buildings throughout the zoning district? Are buildings that encroach on critical environmental areas themselves a separate class as to which standards must be uniform?

What if the local government has no formally adopted comprehensive plan and then adopts a zoning law or amendment? What if the comprehensive plan is fairly old and a zoning amendment itself contains findings that explain the planning rationale for the amendment? What if the local legislature wishing to add environmental standards to its zoning laws finds that its comprehensive plan has no findings, goals, or objectives that address themselves to environmental protection? In other words, what does it mean that zoning laws must be "made in conformance with the comprehensive plan?

In the decades since the adoption of zoning enabling acts by the fifty states, many amendments have been made and new laws passed that enable local governments to meet modern land use challenges. In Chapter V, we look at the delegation of the power to adopt regulations controlling the subdivision of land and development of individual sites; these laws contain standards that are more detailed than those of zoning laws. As times mature, state legislatures add provisions to their enabling laws, or pass new ones, that allow local governments to promote energy conservation, affordable housing, traditional neighborhood development, or the transfer of density from one district to another. These laws raise many issues for lawyers in the land use field to identify, analyze, and explain to their clients. In this section, we examine in some detail the issue of whether a zoning law is made in conformance with the comprehensive plan.

"Spot zoning" in many jurisdictions is a shorthand description of the legal flaw that exists when a zoning amendment does not conform to the comprehensive plan. In a broad sense, spot zoning is any change that departs from the comprehensive plan. More specifically, it is the singling out by a zoning amendment of a small parcel of land and permitting the owner to use it in a manner inconsistent with the permissible uses in the area. Some courts, in discussing it, apply the terms "arbitrary," "capricious," "unreasonable," and similar adjectives. See, e.g., Cassel v. Mayor and City Council of Baltimore, 195 Md. 348, 73 A.2d 486 (1950); and Pierce v. King County, 62 Wash.2d 324, 382 P.2d 628 (1963). In the oft-cited Cassel case, the court stated:

> Spot zoning, the arbitrary and unreasonable devotion of a small area within a zoning district to a use which is inconsistent with the use to which the rest of the district is restricted, has appeared in many cities in America as a result of pressure put upon councilmen to pass amendments to zoning ordinances solely for the benefit of private interest. * * * It is, therefore, universally held that a 'spot zoning' ordinance, which singles out a parcel of land within the limits of a use district and marks it off with a separate district for the benefit of the owner, thereby permitting a use of that parcel inconsistent with the use permitted in the rest of the district, is invalid if not in accordance with the comprehensive plan and is merely for private gain. (195 Md. at 355, 73 A.2d at 488–489.)

Another way of analyzing a zoning amendment that applies to a relatively small area is to ask whether it is *ultra vires*; if zoning must conform to the comprehensive plan, does this rezoning violate that statutory requirement? Or, the inquiry could be whether the amendment is a violation of substantive due process: if the only objective of a zoning amendment is to further private landowner interests, it is void, constitutionally, since it does not promote the public health, safety, or welfare. The state enabling acts delegate a portion of the state legislature's power to act in the public interest—its police power—to local governments; all such laws must promote the public interest in some demonstrable way.

To put the issue differently, imagine that you live in a quiet residential district, protected by the zoning district's proscription of all land uses save single-family residential. You learn that a neighbor has entered into a contract to sell her two acres to a developer, contingent on the ability of the purchaser to secure a zoning amendment allowing the land to be used for a small shopping center, offering many needed goods and services to the neighbors. Your sense of justice is offended! After all, you bought your home with the expectation that the zoning laws in the area would be enforced. You fear that your property values will be lowered. The customers of the businesses proposed will be parking, walking, talking, and carrying on unpredictably within earshot of your front door. Surely this cannot be legal. The developer makes a strong case to the zoning authorities. National studies decry the monotony of suburban neighborhoods. Health scholars tie the increasing obesity of Americans to urban sprawl—the car-dependent life induced by single-use zoning districts; they prescribe mixed land uses within neighborhoods: walkable communities. Certainly it makes sense to have a few places to shop within walking distance of the hundreds of homes in this zoning district? Would this zoning amendment be within the power of the local legislature to adopt? Do the nearby neighbors have a right to the investment-backed expectations in the zoning that existed when they bought?

Obviously, every departure from the plan that was originally instituted for a district does not constitute illicit spot zoning. Otherwise zoning would rigidify permissible land uses within the district to the point that no changes—not even variances or special permits—could be made without a general overhaul. In Penning v. Owens, 340 Mich. 355, 65 N.W.2d 831 (1954), the court said that the inconsistent zoning of a small area must be carefully scrutinized and can be sustained only when the circumstances are such as to warrant the action taken. In Little v. Winborn, 518 N.W.2d 384 (Iowa 1994), the court held that rezoning of agricultural property from "agricultural protection district" to "agricultural" in order to allow the owner to use his property for a shooting range was invalid spot zoning. Its purpose was to benefit the owner, not the public.

Whatever courts may purport to be doing in the spot zoning cases, much of it comes back to the adjectives previously mentioned: Is the action taken arbitrary and unreasonable? Did the zoning ordinance or amendment that singled out this parcel make good sense in the light of the facts involved? As the Iowa court said in Keller v. City of Council Bluffs, 246 Iowa 202, 209–210, 213–214, 66 N.W.2d 113, 117–118, 120, 51 A.L.R.2d 251 (1954):

> The spirit of a zoning ordinance is not violated nor is it inconsistent with a comprehensive zoning ordinance to grant a just and reasonable exception by amendment based upon the character and use of property not similar to other property in the district, but [which] is now and was distinguishable before the adoption of the comprehensive zoning ordinance. * * * "Spot zoning" when construed to mean reclassification of one or more *like tracts* or *similar lots* for a use prohibited by the original zoning ordinance and out of harmony therewith is illegal. When done under certain other conditions and circumstances in accordance with a comprehensive zoning

plan, such action will not be declared void. It depends upon the circumstances of each case.

One of the objectives of the "in conformance with" requirement is to prevent the local legislature from using its power to benefit private property interests in ways that are counter to the public interest. Where the locality has a detailed, comprehensive, up-to-date, separately adopted comprehensive, or master, plan, it is easier to determine how, precisely, a zoning amendment advances the public interest. What happens where there is no adopted comprehensive plan at all, or where the plan is not specific or is out of date? The answer depends on what the modern planning and zoning enabling acts say in the state and the attitude of the state courts about the requirement that zoning must be consistent with the plan.

BARTRAM v. ZONING COMMISSION

Supreme Court of Errors of Connecticut, 1949.
136 Conn. 89, 68 A.2d 308.

MALTBIE, CHIEF JUSTICE.

This is an appeal by the defendants from a judgment sustaining an appeal from a decision of the zoning commission of the city of Bridgeport taken in accordance with the provisions of sec. 845 of the General Statutes. The commission changed the classification of a Sylvan Avenue lot, with a frontage of 125 feet and a depth of 133 feet, from a residence zone to a business No. 3 zone.

With some corrections to which the defendants are entitled, the controlling facts found by the court are these: Zoning regulations became effective in Bridgeport on June 1, 1926. They provided for three classes of residence zones, two classes of business zones, and two classes of industrial zones. In 1937 the regulations were amended to establish business zones No. 3 and special regulations were adopted as to them. These regulations, as further amended, contain provisions as to the type of construction of buildings and require open yards about them, a setback of thirty feet from the street and parking facilities for cars on private property; the sale of liquors was originally restricted but this provision was amended to forbid sales of liquor under any permit for a tavern, restaurant or all-liquor package store. The territory surrounding the lot in question is contiguous to the northern boundary of the city and quite a distance from its shopping and business center. Previous to 1936, both sides of Sylvan Avenue to a depth of 100 feet had for a considerable distance been in a business No. 1 zone, but in that year the classification was changed to residence A; and since that date, as before, a considerable territory in the neighborhood of the premises in question has been in residential zones. When zoning was originally adopted, the area was sparsely built up and contained much farm land. Beginning before 1936, people desiring to get away from the noise and congestion of the center of the city began to build homes there; at present it is quite generally built up with residences, at least 40 per cent of which have been constructed since 1936. Most of the houses in the immediate vicinity of the premises in question are comparatively new; they are neat, one-family homes, with well-kept lawns and attractive plantings; and they give every indication that a self-respecting community of people of moderate means have moved to this outlying section of the city. In the vicinity of the premises in question there exist as nonconforming uses four stores, three selling groceries or meat and one a liquor package store. One of the former is a small store in a building almost opposite the premises in question, the second floor of which is occupied as a residence. There is no drug store in the vicinity. There is also, near the premises in question, a small church. Sylvan Avenue is a street sixty feet wide and it is a principal traffic artery to and from the section surrounding it.

The application for the change of zone was made by the defendant Rome. He presented to the commission at the hearing plans for a building he proposes to erect, which in all respects would comply with the regulations for a business No. 3 zone, which would contain provision for five places of business—a drug, a hardware and a grocery store, a bakeshop and a beauty parlor—and which would provide for the parking of cars in the rear of the building, and between it and the street line. Aside from Rome, no one appeared to support his application, but ten residents and property owners in the neighborhood opposed it. They gave various reasons for the position they took, among them these: They desired to have the residential character of the section preserved from business development; in many instances they had purchased or developed their properties in reliance upon the residence zoning of the area and in the expectation that this zoning status would remain unchanged; they were fearful that the business zoning of any portion of the area would be destructive of the peace and quiet they desired to have preserved; they believed that the business zoning of any part of it, however small and wherever located, would have a tendency to break down the residence zoning of the area by making further business zoning in it more likely; and there was no present need for further and more adequate shopping facilities in the neighborhood. A remonstrance against granting the application signed by more than seventy residents in the neighborhood was also filed with the commission; but only some forty-six different addresses of the signers appear on it; in a number of instances the signers were husband and wife or two or more residing in the same house; and many of them lived at a considerable distance from the premises in question. Within a radius no longer than the distance to the addresses given by some of the signers are more than 200 residences.

The commission gave the following reasons for its decision: 1. The location is on Sylvan Avenue, a sixty-foot street, and there is no shopping center within a mile of it. To the north of this tract there is a very large development but only small nonconforming grocery stores to serve the people. 2. There is practically only one house, adjacent to this tract on the north, which will be directly affected by this change of zone. 3. Business No. 3 regulations, with their thirty-foot setback and liquor restrictions, were designed to meet conditions like this and help alleviate the great congestion in the centralized shopping districts. The court also found that a member of the commission testified that it was its policy to encourage decentralization of business in order to relieve traffic congestion and that, as part of that policy, it was considered desirable to permit neighborhood stores in outlying districts; and nowhere in the record is there any suggestion that this testimony is not true.

The trial court concluded that the change was an instance of "spot zoning." A limitation upon the powers of zoning authorities which has been in effect ever since zoning statutes were made applicable generally to municipalities in the state is that the regulations they adopt must be made "in accordance with a comprehensive plan." Public Acts, 1925, c. 242, sec. 3 (Rev.1949, sec. 837). "A 'comprehensive plan' means 'a general plan to control and direct the use and development of property in a municipality or a large part of it by dividing it into districts according to the present and potential use of the properties.'" *Bishop v. Board of Zoning Appeals*, 133 Conn. 614, 618, 53 A.2d 659; *State ex rel. Spiros v. Payne*, 131 Conn. 647, 652, 41 A.2d 908. Action by a zoning authority which gives to a single lot or a small area privileges which are not extended to other land in the vicinity is in general against sound public policy and obnoxious to the law. It can be justified only when it is done in furtherance of a general plan properly adopted for and designed to serve the best interests of the community as a whole.

The vice of spot zoning lies in the fact that it singles out for special treatment a lot or a small area in a way that does not further such a plan. Where, however, in pursuance of it, a zoning commission takes such action, its decision can be assailed only on the ground that it abused the discretion vested in it by the law. To permit business in a small area within a residence zone may fall within the scope of such a plan, and to do so, unless it amounts to unreasonable or arbitrary action, is not unlawful. *Bishop v. Board of Zoning Appeals*, supra; see *Parsons v. Wethersfield*, 135 Conn. 24, 29, 60 A.2d 771. The zoning regulations of Bridgeport were adopted under the provisions of the General Statutes which gave the commission power to divide the municipality into districts and in each district to regulate the construction and use of buildings and land, and to change the regulations from time to time. General Statutes, Rev.1930, secs. 424, 425, as amended (Rev.1949, secs. 837, 838); see *De Palma v. Town Plan Commission of Greenwich*, 123 Conn. 257, 265, 193 A. 868. The commission might be guilty of spot zoning either in the original regulations it made or in later amendments, but, if in one or the other it decides, on facts affording a sufficient basis and in the exercise of a proper discretion, that it would serve the best interests of the community as a whole to permit a use of a single lot or small area in a different way than was allowed in surrounding territory, it would not be guilty of spot zoning in any sense obnoxious to the law. That was the situation in this case, and we cannot sustain the conclusion of the trial court that the action of the commission was improper as an instance of spot zoning.

The trial court also concluded that the change in zoning was in violation of the declared objects of the zoning regulations of Bridgeport, as stated in their first section. That section states among the purposes to be served by them the promotion of the health, safety, morals and general welfare of the community and the lessening of congestion in streets. The reasons which led the commission to take the action it did, as we have stated them above, fall well within the scope of these purposes. The fact that the change was advocated only by Rome at the hearing and was opposed by numerous property owners and residents in the neighborhood did not, as the trial court concluded, deprive the commission of power to make it. It does not appear that there was anything like unanimous opposition to the change of property owners in the surrounding territory; but, even if there had been, it was the duty of the commission to look beyond the effect of the change upon them to the general welfare of the city. The reasons given before the commission by those who opposed the change were quite largely based on fear that other like changes might be made rather than upon the effect of the particular one in question. The property of no one was taken by the commission's decision; nor is there any finding or, indeed, evidence that property values would be affected; and no such situation is before us as was presented in *Strain v. Mims*, 123 Conn. 275, 193 A. 754, where, in speaking of a change in zoning from business to residence which practically affected only a single property, we said (p. 286): "However, where the value of property of an individual is seriously affected by a zoning regulation especially applicable to it, this fact imposes an obligation carefully to consider the question whether the regulation does in fact tend to serve the public welfare and the recognized purposes of zoning." Property owners in the neighborhood had no right to a continuation of the existing situation which could be effective against a decision by the commission reached legally and properly. The state, through the authority it vests in zoning authorities, "may regulate any business or the use of any property in the interest of the public health, safety or welfare, provided this be done reasonably. To that extent the public interest is supreme and the private interest must yield." *Windsor v. Whitney*, 95 Conn. 357, 366, 111 A. 354, 356, 12 A.L.R. 669; *Strain v. Mims*, supra. The commission could not properly be held, upon the record in this case, to have acted in violation of law in making the change it did.

How best the purposes of zoning can be accomplished in any municipality is primarily in the discretion of its zoning authority; that description is a broad one; and unless it transcends the limitations set by law its decisions are subject to review in the courts only to the extent of determining whether or not it has acted in abuse of that discretion. *First Nat. Bank & Trust Co. v. Zoning Board of Appeals*, 126 Conn. 228, 237, 10 A.2d 691. A court is without authority to substitute its own judgment for that vested by the statutes in a zoning authority. *Piccolo v. West Haven*, 120 Conn. 449, 455, 181 A. 615; *Mrowka v. Board of Zoning Appeals*, 134 Conn. 149, 155, 55 A.2d 909. In view of the facts presented in this case, the trial court could not properly find that the policy which determined the decision of the commission would so clearly fail to serve the proper purposes of zoning in the city that the court might set aside that decision; nor do the facts show that it was unreasonable to apply that policy in the situation before us. This is illustrated by the fact that, had this lot been placed in a business No. 3 zone as an incident to the adoption of an original plan for zoning the city as a whole, that action could not on this record be held an unreasonable exercise by the commission of its powers.

There is error, the judgment is set aside and the case is remanded with direction to enter judgment dismissing the appeal. * * *

[Dissenting opinion omitted.]

Notes

1. Although the Bartram case is rather old, the approach taken by the court in that case is still the prevailing approach in most jurisdictions. For another example, see Vella v. Town of Camden, 677 A.2d 1051 (Me.1996), where the owner of an inn sued to set aside zoning amendments that favored a competing innkeeper on grounds of spot zoning inconsistent with the comprehensive plan.

2. Compare spot zoning which creates a small residential district in the heart of a commercial district, Geisenfeld v. Shorewood, 232 Wis. 410, 287 N.W. 683 (1939) and Rowland v. City of Racine, 223 Wis. 488, 271 N.W. 36 (1937), with spot zoning which creates a small business district in the heart of a residential district, as in the principal case. See also Town of Marblehead v. Rosenthal, 316 Mass. 124, 55 N.E.2d 13 (1944); Wilkins v. San Bernardino, 29 Cal.2d 332, 175 P.2d 542 (1946); C.L. Associates v. Board of Supervisors of Montgomery Twp., 51 Pa.Cmwlth. 627, 415 A.2d 134 (1980); Mesolella v. City of Providence, 439 A.2d 1370 (R.I.1982). For further discussion of the principal case, see 1 Williams, American Land Planning Law § 26.05 (1988).

3. Is a decision refusing to rezone a parcel to a classification called for by the comprehensive plan presumptively invalid? See City of Gainesville v. Hope, 377 So.2d 736 (Fla.App.1979), and Clinkscales v. City of Lake Oswego, 47 Or.App. 1117, 615 P.2d 1164 (1980).

4. In Rodgers v. Village of Tarrytown, 302 N.Y. 115, 96 N.E.2d 731 (1951), the New York Court of Appeals held that a village planning board had the authority to create a new, flexible zoning mechanism: a floating zoning district. The plaintiff argued that the floating zone that allowed multi-family buildings in a single-family zoning district on 15–acre or larger parcels violated the uniformity requirement of zoning districts or constituted illegal spot zoning. The court disagreed and sanctioned the novel concept of first creating a floating zoning district and later affixing it to a specific parcel upon the application of the landowner. In sustaining such techniques as within the locality's implied zoning power, the court noted that a "decision as to how a community shall be zoned or rezoned, as to how various properties shall be classified or reclassified, rests with the local legislative body; its judgment and determination will be conclusive, beyond interference from the courts, unless shown to be arbitrary."

ENTERPRISE PARTNERS v. COUNTY OF PERKINS

Supreme Court of Nebraska, 2000.
619 N.W.2d 464, 260 Neb. 650.

McCormack, J.

* * *

In April 1998, the Board became aware of proposals to build hog confinement facilities in Perkins County. At subsequent meetings of the Board, individuals and public groups expressed concerns about the effect these types of facilities would have on the environment, on the health of the citizens of Perkins County, and the need to prevent these facilities from being built. The Board sent a letter to the Nebraska Department of Environmental Quality (DEQ) voicing its concerns and going on record as opposing the approval of a permit to allow Enterprise to construct a hog confinement facility in Perkins County.

DEQ responded in a letter addressing the Board's concerns and explaining evaluation procedures and the requirements that needed to be met in order for a permit to be issued. DEQ also pointed out that two of the Board's concerns could not be addressed by DEQ as it did not have the authority to regulate those issues. These issues were the odor and insects and the impact on county roads. DEQ stated that "[t]he Legislature has given counties the authority to implement land use planning and adopt zoning regulations which could govern the location of livestock facilities. Odors, dust and insects are considered to be nuisances and are not regulated by the DEQ." With regard to the impact on county roads, DEQ stated that "[t]his is not an issue which DEQ can address, but as a local issue it may possibly be addressed through load limit restrictions."

Proposed ordinances were submitted to the Board, and discussion was held on December 21, 1998. Ordinance 98–1 attempts to locally regulate livestock confinement facilities by regulating odor emanating from the facility by requiring that certain parts of the facility be covered. By controlling odor, other problems with flies would be avoided. Ordinance 98–2 requires large-scale livestock operations to demonstrate that no livestock waste, liquid or solid, would be carried or washed onto or into county roads, ditches, or properties adjacent to the facility during or following a 25–year storm. This demonstration must also be updated on a yearly basis through inspections by the county. The Board passed both ordinances and increased the civil penalty contained in them from $200 to $5,000 per day for each violation.

Enterprise filed a petition for declaratory judgment arguing that the ordinances are zoning ordinances and were passed in violation of Neb. Rev.Stat. § 23–114.03 (Reissue 1997) which requires the Board to have a county comprehensive development plan before the adoption of zoning regulations. The Board stipulated that it had not adopted a comprehensive zoning plan pursuant to § 23–114.03. Enterprise also asserted that Ordinances 98–1 and 98–2 contain environmental requirements that are specifically reserved for the state. Enterprise also argued that these ordinances deprived it of property without due process of law and that the Board lacked the authority to impose civil penalties.

The trial court ruled that the ordinances were not zoning ordinances but fell within the exercise of police powers granted to the counties by the Legislature, that no preemption or conflict existed between the ordinances and state statutes, and that the ordinances were not arbitrary or unreasonable and did not violate the constitution. The trial court found generally for the Board and found that both ordinances were valid and enforceable.

* * *

Enterprise assigns that the trial court erred in not finding that Ordinances 98-1 and 98-2 were zoning ordinances. Enterprise asserts that the ordinances are zoning ordinances and were passed by the Board in violation of § 23-114.03. Section 23-114.03 provides that "[z]oning regulations shall be adopted or amended by the county board only after the adoption of the county comprehensive development plan by the county board * * *." Both Enterprise and the Board stipulated that "Perkins County, Nebraska, has not adopted a comprehensive zoning plan pursuant to Neb.Rev.Stat. § 23-114, et seq." Therefore, Enterprise concludes that Ordinances 98-1 and 98-2 are invalid because the Board does not have a comprehensive development plan. We agree.

A county is a political subdivision of the state having subordinate powers of sovereignty conferred by the Legislature. *Hoiengs v. County of Adams*, 245 Neb. 877, 516 N.W.2d 223 (1994). A political subdivision has only that power delegated to it by the Legislature; a grant of power to a political subdivision is to be strictly construed. *Metropolitan Utilities Dist. v. Twin Platte NRD*, 250 Neb. 442, 550 N.W.2d 907 (1996).

Counties have the statutory authority to regulate the use of lands within their jurisdiction to promote the public health, safety, and welfare pursuant to § 23-114.03 and Neb.Rev.Stat. § 23-174.10 (Reissue 1997). * * * Section 23-114.03 states:

> Zoning regulations shall be adopted or amended by the county board only after the adoption of the county comprehensive development plan by the county board and the receipt of the planning commission's specific recommendations. Such zoning regulations shall be consistent with the comprehensive development plan and designed for the purpose of promoting the health, safety, morals, convenience, order, prosperity, and welfare of the present and future inhabitants of Nebraska, including, among others, such specific purposes as:
>
> > (1) Developing both urban and nonurban areas;
> >
> > (2) Lessening congestion in the streets or roads;
> >
> > (3) Reducing the waste of excessive amounts of roads;
> >
> > (4) Securing safety from fire and other dangers;

(5) Lessening or avoiding the hazards to persons and damage to property resulting from the accumulation or runoff of storm or flood waters;

(6) Providing adequate light and air;

(7) Preventing excessive concentration of population and excessive and wasteful scattering of population or settlement;

(8) Promoting such distribution of population, such classification of land uses, and such distribution of land development as will assure adequate provisions for transportation, water flowage, water supply, drainage, sanitation, recreation, soil fertility, food supply, and other public requirements;

(9) Protecting the tax base;

(10) Protecting property against blight and depreciation;

(11) Securing economy in governmental expenditures;

(12) Fostering the state's agriculture, recreation, and other industries;

(13) Encouraging the most appropriate use of land in the county; and

(14) Preserving, protecting, and enhancing historic buildings, places, and districts.

Within the area of jurisdiction and powers established by section 23–114, the county board may divide the county into districts of such number, shape, and area as may be best suited to carry out the purposes of this section and regulate, restrict, or prohibit the erection, construction, reconstruction, alteration, or use of nonfarm buildings or structures and the use, conditions of use, or occupancy of land. All such regulations shall be uniform for each class or kind of land or buildings throughout each district, but the regulations in one district may differ from those in other districts. An official map or maps indicating the districts and regulations shall be adopted, and within fifteen days after adoption of such regulations or maps, they shall be published in book or pamphlet form or once in a legal newspaper published in and of general circulation in the county or, if none is published in the county, in a legal newspaper of general circulation in the county. Such regulations shall also be spread in the minutes of the proceedings of the county board and such map or maps filed with the county clerk. Nonfarm buildings are all buildings except those buildings utilized for agricultural purposes on a farmstead of twenty acres or more which produces one thousand dollars or more of farm products each year.

Section 23–174.10 states:

In any county which has adopted county zoning regulations, the county board, by resolution, may make regulations as may be necessary or expedient to promote the public health, safety, and welfare, including regulations to prevent the introduction or spread of contagious, infectious, or malignant diseases; to provide rules for the prevention, abatement, and removal of nuisances, including the pollution of air and water; and make and prescribe regulations for the construction, location, and keeping in order of all slaughterhouses, stockyards, warehouses, sheds, stables, barns, commercial feedlots, dairies, junk and salvage yards, or other places where offensive matter is kept, or is likely to accumulate. Such regulations shall be not inconsistent with the general laws of the state and shall apply to all of the county except within the limits of any incorporated city or village, and except within the unincorporated area where a city or village has been granted zoning jurisdiction and is exercising such jurisdiction.

The statutory language in these sections grants extensive powers to counties to regulate their lands. These powers, however, are rooted in zoning, and zoning regulations can be enacted only after adoption of a county comprehensive development plan by a county board. § 23–114.03.

Zoning is "the process that a community employs to legally control the use which may be made of property and the physical configuration of development upon the tracts of land located within its jurisdiction." *Ford v. Bd. of Cty. Com'rs of Converse*, 924 P.2d 91, 94 (Wyo.1996). According to this definition Ordinances 98–1 and 98–2 are zoning regulations.

* * *

Ordinance 98–1, regarding fly and odor control, states in pertinent part:

The Commissioners of Perkins County find that large livestock confinement facilities use lagoons to store and treat waste produced by animals in confinement. These lagoons produce odor. The odor is made up of many different kinds of volatile compounds including ammonia, phenol, cresol, volatile fatty acids, aldehydes, bezene, xylene and hydrogen sulfide. The Commissioners find that there has [sic] been reports of adverse health effects to citizens of other jurisdictions from exposure to the odor. By controlling odors, other problems such as flies can also be avoided.

* * *

SECTION 2: COVERS REQUIRED

2.01 An owner or operator of a large livestock confinement facility shall not operate a facility in Perkins County unless the following are covered: livestock waste storage containment structures that receives [sic] livestock waste on a regular basis and permanent livestock waste containment structures in which an anaerobic pool is maintained. Facilities that have structures that receive livestock waste only on an [sic] sporadic baisis [sic] due to storm runoff are not required to have covers on their livestock waste containment structures.

SECTION 3: INSPECTIONS

    3.01 The County shall have the right to inspect the site to insure [sic] compliance with the provisions of this regulation.

Ordinance 98–1 attempts to legally control the use and development of property by requiring covers to be used for certain land uses and by restricting land use until inspection by the county. Ordinance 98–1 is therefore a zoning regulation.

The Board has been given the power by the Legislature to regulate through the use of zoning but, pursuant to § 23–114.03, zoning regulations shall be adopted only after the adoption by the Board of a comprehensive development plan. Why the Board has never adopted a comprehensive development plan is not apparent from the record. Because of the failure of the Board to adopt such a plan, these ordinances are not valid as to Enterprise's hog confinement facilities.

* * *

[Using similar logic, the court finds that Perkins County Ordinance 98–2 is also a zoning regulation.]

Counties in Nebraska have been delegated the power to regulate the use of lands within their jurisdiction to promote the public health, safety, and welfare pursuant to §§ 23–114.03 and 23–174.10 since 1967. A county board may by resolution make regulations as may be necessary to promote the health, safety, and welfare of its public if it has adopted a comprehensive development plan as required by § 23–114.03. Since the Board has failed to adopt a comprehensive development plan, the Board does not have the authority to pass Ordinances 98–1 and 98–2, as they are clearly zoning-related regulations. We therefore conclude that Ordinances 98–1 and 98–2 are invalid.

    REVERSED.

Notes

    1. The principal case involves an "evolved" enabling act, patterned after the standard enabling act but revised to meet the needs of a rural state and to comport with other legal norms held by the state legislature. Can you spot the similarities and differences between Section 23–114.03 and the standard act? What about the in conformance with language? Is it different? The Nebraska zoning enabling act contains this provision: "Zoning regulations shall be adopted or amended by the county board only after the adoption of the county comprehensive development plan * * *." Can you find that language in the standard act? Why was this language added by the Nebraska legislature? What does this addition mean? Given this language in the act, could the court have come to any other conclusion?

    2. The Perkins County case raises a key question: when does a law constitute zoning? Note that the county did not adopt zoning wholesale, it simply passed a law regulating a uniquely modern phenomenon: the spread of concentrated animal feeding facilities across the rural landscape. If this is a zoning law, it is subject to the jurisdictional limitations of the zoning

enabling act. If it is not, its authority must reside in another state enabling act. Some states have adopted municipal home rule statutes giving local governments the authority to adopt local laws to regulate municipal property, affairs, and government or, in some cases, to protect the physical environment. Would such an enabling law provide a separate source of authority for counties to regulate the environmental impacts of pig farms and feed lots? Or because the law controls the "use which may be made of property and the physical configuration of development," in the court's words, would it still be zoning and subject to the comprehensive plan requirement? How onerous is it to require a local government to adopt a comprehensive plan? How big is Perkins County? Why isn't it zoned? Does the county have a professional planner on staff or on retainer?

3. In a case where two property owners sought to declare a county zoning ordinance establishing agricultural zoning classification unconstitutional, the Appellate Court of Illinois ruled that the ordinance was constitutional and looked to the comprehensive plan for guidance. Wilson v. County of McHenry, 92 Ill.App.3d 997, 48 Ill.Dec. 395, 416 N.E.2d 426 (2d Dist. 1981). The county zoning ordinance was amended on November 1, 1979, to provide a 160-acre lot minimum in agricultural zones pursuant to the McHenry County Year 2000 plan. The plan attempted to channel development toward existing urban centers; particularly recognizing prime agricultural land as a primary, finite material resource. The Wilsons, the property owners, argued that by classifying their land as agricultural, they would lose substantial value in their property ($4,000 per acre as zoned agriculture versus $18,000 to $20,000 per lot as zoned one-acre residential). The Wilsons alleged that 37.4 percent of their land was not prime farm land and that the average yield was only 95 bushels of corn per acre. The court noted that "a significant aspect in the case is the county's adoption of a comprehensive plan for the area." The court stated that the adoption of a comprehensive pan which incorporates valid zoning goals increases the likelihood that the zoning of a particular parcel in conformity with the plan is not arbitrary or unrelated to the public interest. The Illinois courts have placed increasing importance on the existence of a comprehensive plan in reviewing zoning cases. The court also ruled that lower property values by themselves were insufficient to overcome the presumption of validity of the ordinance.

OSIECKI v. TOWN OF HUNTINGTON

New York Appellate Division, Second Department (1991).
170 A.D.2d 490, 565 N.Y.S.2d 564.

MEMORANDUM BY THE COURT.

In an action for a judgment declaring, inter alia, that the one-acre residential zoning classification of the plaintiffs' property is invalid because it does not comply with a comprehensive plan, the plaintiffs appeal from a judgment of the Supreme Court, Suffolk County (Seidell, J.), dated December 20, 1988, which, after a nonjury trial, inter alia, declared the one-acre residential zoning classification valid.

ORDERED that the judgment is reversed, on the law, without costs or disbursements, and it is declared that the one-acre residential zoning classification of the plaintiffs' property is invalid because it does not comply with a comprehensive plan.

The plaintiffs own an approximately five and one-half acre parcel at the northwest corner of Old Country Road and Old New York Avenue in the Town of Huntington (hereinafter the Town). It is zoned for low density residential use (one-acre plots). Two other parcels to the west, on the north side of Old Country Road have been zoned for commercial office buildings and have been developed as such. The properties to the south and east of the subject property, across Old County Road and Old New York Avenue are zoned for one-acre residential use, but are respectively in current use as a farm and for water district purposes by the Town of Huntington. To the north of the subject property is the Northern State Parkway. North of the Parkway is a Town Park also zoned one-acre residential.

The plaintiffs commenced this action for a judgment declaring the one-acre residential zoning of their property invalid as (1) inconsistent with the Town's comprehensive zoning plan, or (2) a violation of equal protection of the law in relation to the other commercially zoned property adjacent to it. After a nonjury trial, the court rejected the plaintiffs' assertions that the residential zoning of their property was invalid. We disagree.

Town Law § 263 provides that zoning ordinances must be made in accordance with a comprehensive plan. A comprehensive plan is a compilation of land use policies that may be found in any number of ordinances, resolutions, and policy statements of the town (*see, Curtiss–Wright Corp. v. Town of East Hampton*, 82 A.D.2d 551, 557, 442 N.Y.S.2d 125). As the Court of Appeals noted in *Udell v. Haas*, 21 N.Y.2d 463, 472, 288 N.Y.S.2d 888, 235 N.E.2d 897), "[t]hese policies may be garnered from any available source, most especially the master plan of the community, if any has been adopted, the zoning law itself and the zoning map".

Town Law § 272–a gives the planning board the authority to prepare a master plan for the development of the entire area of a town. The planning board of the Town adopted such a plan in 1965 and it was amended in 1966. The master plan designated the entire block, of which the subject parcel is a part, for commercial development and a large number of zoning changes and Town actions have been consistent with the master plan (see, *Tilles v. Town of Huntington*, 74 N.Y.2d 885, 547 N.Y.S.2d 835, 547 N.E.2d 90, *affg.* 137 A.D.2d 118, 528 N.Y.S.2d 386). In addition, as recently as 1986 the Town Planning Board and Planning Department recommended that the subject parcel be developed commercially. Unrefuted expert testimony indicated that the Town's action constituted comprehensive planning that the block be commercially developed. Indeed, the Town acknowledges that the numerous rezonings in the area show that it followed the master plan to a large extent.

Nevertheless, the Town maintains that it is not obliged to slavish servitude to the master plan and that it was free, in 1989, to determine that the master plan should not be followed with regard to this property (see, *Town of Bedford v. Village of Mount Kisco*, 33 N.Y.2d 178, at 188, 351 N.Y.S.2d 129, 306 N.E.2d 155; *Tilles v. Town of Huntington*, 137 A.D.2d 118, 528 N.Y.S.2d 386, *affd.* 74 N.Y.2d 885, 547 N.Y.S.2d 835, 547 N.E.2d 90, *supra*). However, the Town makes no attempt to justify its "determination" that disregarding the Town's specific master plan is not inconsistent with a comprehensive zoning plan for the area rather than an entirely ad hoc decision (cf., *Town of Bedford v. Village of Mount Kisco, supra*). To accept the Town's contention that it is free to determine that the master plan should no longer be followed, without articulating a reason for that determination, would invite the kind of ad hoc and arbitrary application of zoning power that the comprehensive planning requirement was designed to avoid (see, *Town of Bedford v. Village of Mount Kisco, supra*, 33 N.Y.2d at 187, 188, 351 N.Y.S.2d 129, 306 N.E.2d 155).

We find that the record establishes that the commercial development of the subject parcel was part of the Town's comprehensive development plan. The Town does not articulate any basis for changing that plan at the present time and we can find none. Thus, the residential zoning of the subject parcel is void as it fails to comport with the Town's comprehensive plan (see, *Udell v. Haas*, 21 N.Y.2d 463, 288 N.Y.S.2d 888, 235 N.E.2d 897, *supra*; *cf., Tilles v. Town of Huntington*, 74 N.Y.2d 885, 547 N.Y.S.2d 835, 547 N.E.2d 90, *supra*).

Notes

1. Separate provisions of the Town Law in New York authorize, but do not require, towns to adopt comprehensive plans and zoning laws. Parallel provisions are found in the Village Law and the General City Law so that all three types of municipalities in the state (towns, villages, and cities) have the same authority to control land use. These laws follow closely the pattern of the standard zoning enabling act. Section 263 of the Town Law states that "such regulations shall be made in accordance with a comprehensive plan." Section 272–a of the Town Law states that town boards "may" adopt a comprehensive plan, specifies fifteen subjects that a comprehensive plan "may" include, and ends by stating that "all town land use regulations must be in accordance with a comprehensive plan adopted pursuant to this section."

2. Dealing with slightly different language in these enabling acts at an earlier time, New York's highest court struck down a village zoning amendment because it failed to conform to the comprehensive plan requirement even though the village had now adopted a comprehensive plan. Udell v. Haas, 21 N.Y.2d 463, 235 N.E.2d 897, 288 N.Y.S.2d 888 (1968). In 1951, when the plaintiff bought the property, it was zoned Business A, allowing for retail, office, and laboratory uses. Nine years later, the plaintiff's representative presented building plans to the village for a business development. That same night, the planning board recommended that the area where the plaintiff's property was located be changed from business to residential. The local legislature rezoned the land shortly thereafter but failed to articulate the comprehensive planning objectives achieved by the rezoning. The court

concluded that the "vague desires of a segment of the public were not a proper reason to interfere with the [plaintiff's] right to use his property in a manner which for some 20 odd years was considered perfectly proper. If there is to be any justification for this interference with [plaintiff's] use of his property, it must be found in the needs and goals of the community as articulated in a rational statement of land use control policies known as the comprehensive plan." In the absence of a formally adopted comprehensive plan, the court examined "all relevant evidence," including the zoning map and law, for evidence of comprehensive planning. The court also reviewed a 1958 zoning amendment entitled Development Policy for the Village. This amendment envisioned the village as a low-density, single-family community with commercial development limited to outlying areas. The court noted that the plaintiff's land was located in that commercial area prior to the 1960 rezoning. The court reasoned that a "comprehensive plan requires that the rezoning should not conflict with the fundamental land use policies and development plans of the community" and invalidated the rezoning.

3. An interpretation of the Udell decision is found in McBride v. Town of Forestburgh, 54 A.D.2d 396, 388 N.Y.S.2d 940 (3d Dep't 1976). Here, the court wrote that "[i]t would appear that neither a master plan nor even a written plan is necessary." In the court's view, "the requirements of the enabling statute are met if implicit in the [zoning] law there is the element of planning which is both rational and consistent with the basic land use policies of the community." The court further held that there was a sufficient showing of a comprehensive plan based on the small size of the community and the planning done before the adoption of the law.

4. Do New York communities have an obligation to formally adopt a comprehensive plan today, like Perkins County in Nebraska? The language quoted in note 1 above from § 272–a raises an untested issue in the state on this point. If not, how will a court find the comprehensive plan to which all land use regulations must conform? If a community adopts a new zoning regulation but does not have a comprehensive plan, how would it demonstrate that the regulation is in conformance with the comprehensive plan? Is Udell v. Haas still good law?

5. How difficult would it have been for the town board in Osieki to articulate a rationale for departing from the comprehensive plan in the adoption of the zoning amendment that is the subject of the plaintiff's suit? Depending on your answer, what kind of assurance does the comprehensive plan give to citizens that its provisions will be followed? Does a rationale articulated in adopting a rezoning amendment constitute an amendment of the comprehensive plan?

6. Also see Tilles Investment Co. v. Town of Huntington, 74 N.Y.2d 885, 547 N.Y.S.2d 835, 547 N.E.2d 90 (1989), where the owner of 52 acres zoned residential challenged the town's refusal to rezone his land for commercial (two other parcels had been rezoned). The court held that the decision was in accord with the comprehensive plan, stating that the statute mandated comprehensive planning, not slavish servitude to any particular comprehensive plan.

SECTION 3. ZONING ADMINISTRATION AND FLEXIBILITY

A. INTRODUCTION

How much flexibility do enabling acts provide local governments? What restrictions are there on localities that wish to change the rules by amending their zoning ordinances, or by giving their administrative boards discretionary authority to interpret the rules to effect desirable results in individual circumstances? The power to amend the zoning ordinance and change district lines and designations on the zoning map provides a degree of flexibility. In some states, localities are required to show that circumstances have changed which necessitate the amendment. When changing district lines or applying an existing zoning district to a new area, does the local government have the authority to impose conditions on development in the expanded or new area that do not apply in the other areas to which that district designation applies? Is this a violation of equal protection guarantees or at odds with the uniformity requirement in the zoning enabling act? How can the local government provide relief to single parcel owners who suffer practical difficulties or economic hardships when zoning standards are applied to their particular properties? Can local governments designate certain land uses, such as religious institutions or junkyards, as special uses and impose conditions on them to mitigate their adverse impacts on surrounding neighborhoods?

Let's begin with a review. The zoning ordinance establishes a number of zoning districts and contains a map indicating which parts of the community are within each district. Technical terms are defined, as-of-right uses permitted in each district, accessory uses are allowed, and a variety of dimensional requirements are applied to land development with the dimensions changing from district to district. Examples of area and bulk standards include maximum height of buildings, minimum width of lots, maximum area of lot that buildings can cover, minimum setback requirements from the lot lines, etc.

Zoning provisions are adopted in the first instance by the local legislative body after being drafted by a zoning commission or planning body and subjected to public scrutiny. Where local laws are codified, the zoning provisions become part of the municipal code. The code might be organized alphabetically by chapters and Zoning might be Chapter 40 of the code since it comes near the end of the alphabet. This Zoning Chapter is further subdivided into various articles. A typical chapter will have a variety of titles including, among others, the following:

Article I: General Provisions

A. Title—states the title.

B. Scope—establishes the breadth of issues to be covered by the chapter or law.

C. Statutory Authority—states the legal authority for enacting a zoning law.

D. Purposes—lists the reasons for adopting the zoning law.

Article II: Definitions

A. Definitions—defines words in the chapter that have substantive importance.

B. Word Usage—often explains that the normal dictionary definition of words shall be used where the words are not specifically defined.

Article III: Zoning Districts and Map

A. Districts Enumerated—sets forth the various use districts established by the chapter. Examples of district types include single-family residential, multi-family residential, commercial, light industrial, conservation, and agricultural. There are few limits on the types and number of districts that a community may establish.

B. Zoning Map—explains that the location and boundaries of the enumerated districts are shown on the zoning map and that the map, together with any amendments to it, if not appended to the chapter itself, is available in the municipal clerk's office.

Article IV: District Regulations

A. Application of Regulations—states that no building, structure, or land shall be used and no building, structure or part thereof shall be erected, moved, or altered unless for a use expressly permitted by and in conformance with the regulations for the district in which the building, structure, or land is located.

B. General Regulations—contains regulations that are applicable to all districts, including specifications regarding irregularly shaped lots, building height, minimum lot area, uses of yards, frontage, and driveways, roof structures, and easements.

C. Schedule of Permitted Uses (Schedule A)—lists the types of land uses permitted in particular districts. Where a use is not listed, it is prohibited.

D. Schedule of Area and Bulk Requirements (Schedule B)—defines the area and bulk requirements for each of the enumerated districts. Includes regulations governing minimum lot area, minimum lot width, minimum front and side yard setbacks, minimum rear yard, minimum road frontage, maximum lot coverage, maximum height, parking setback, and floor area ratio.

E. Off–Street Parking and Loading Regulations—sets forth the required number of parking spaces, and their dimensions, for a given use district and particular use.

Article V: Supplementary Regulations—Land Activities

A. Accessory Uses and Structures—establishes regulations governing land uses and structures incidental to the district's primary permitted uses, dwelling units, and structures.

B. Cemeteries—establishes minimum lot size and setback requirements from any street, right-of-way, or property line. May also require site plan approval.

C. Communications Antenna or Tower; Satellite Dishes—regulates the location, placement and appearance of communication facilities. Under the Federal Telecommunications Act of 1996, municipalities are prohibited from excluding such facilities from their jurisdictions.

D. Home Occupations—provides for the regulation of home occupations such as professional offices, day-care facilities, and dance studios. May be included under the section on accessory uses.

E. Hotel or Motel—establishes requirements for the location of hotels and motels in particular districts. Sets forth a minimum lot size and required road frontage and side and rear yard setbacks.

F. Mobile Homes—establishes regulations controlling the location and appearance of individual mobile homes as well as mobile home developments within a community. Also establishes bulk and area requirements for such dwellings.

G. Places of Worship—in addition to regulating the placement of such facilities within particular zones and establishing minimum lot sizes and setbacks, many zoning laws also provide that places of worship are subject to a special permit and site plan approval. Some laws also require a design that is compatible with the existing neighborhood character.

H. Planned Unit Development—regulations designed to promote variety and flexibility in land development while stressing the efficient use of open space and public facilities. May provide for the type and number of residential and commercial uses allowed, as well as for bulk and area requirements and design of buildings.

I. Prohibitions—general categories of activities or uses that are prohibited in all districts.

Article VI: Special Use Permits

A. Purpose—sets forth the reasons for allowing special uses in a given district. Generally, because of their characteristics or the unique characteristics of the area in which they are to be located, special uses require careful consideration so that they may be properly located. Chapter will designate the planning board/commission or another administrative body to issue special use permits.

B. Submission of Application—may state that an application for a special use must be submitted to the zoning administrator along with the proper fee.

C. General Standards—establishes requirements applicable to all special uses. To grant a special use permit, the board must find:

    1. that the proposed use is in harmony with the general purpose and intent of the land use chapter;

    2. that there will be adequate access for fire and police protection;

    3. that the streets serving the proposed use are adequate to carry prospective traffic and will not cause a traffic hazard or undue traffic congestion;

    4. that the lot on which the use is to be located is of sufficient size and adequate dimension to permit the use in a manner not detrimental to surrounding property;

    5. that the buildings, structures, facilities, and site layout will be adequately landscaped and maintained; and

    6. that the proposed use, buildings and structures will not be detrimental to the public health, and safety, or to property values of the neighborhood.

Article VII: Planning Board/Commission

A. Establishment—authorizes the municipal legislature to create a planning board or commission. May also establish terms of office and eligibility for service.

B. Powers and Duties—sets forth the board's responsibilities, including the review of applications for certain land use approvals such as land subdivision, site plan approval, or special use permit applications.

C. Procedure—establishes the procedure for planning board review of various actions. May also provide procedure for referral of certain land use decisions to the county planning board.

D. Public Notice and Hearing—details the procedure utilized by the planning board to notify the public of hearings, meetings, and other actions.

Article VIII: Zoning Board of Appeals

A. Establishment—creates a zoning board of appeals, specifying the number of members who may serve. May also establish terms of office and eligibility for service.

B. Powers and Duties—sets forth the board's responsibilities, including hearing and reviewing appeals from any order, requirement, decision, or determination made by the zoning administrator. May provide that the board shall hear and decide applications for certain types of land use approvals and issue variances. Grants the board the authority to interpret the zoning law; many communities also provide the board with the authority to prescribe conditions in the granting of any special use permit or variance to preserve the general purpose and intent of the land use chapter.

C. Procedure—establishes the procedural requirements for actions before the board. Requires applications be in writing and to refer to the specific provisions of the law involved. Requires referral of applications to the local planning board and in certain instances to the county or regional planning board.

D. Public Notice and Hearing—requires that the zoning board of appeals to provide proper public notice. Fixes a reasonable time for a public hearing of any appeal or other matter referred to it.

Article IX: Administration and Enforcement

A. Zoning Administrator—establishes an administrative officer who has the authority and responsibility to administer and enforce the provisions of the zoning and land use chapter or law. Duties generally include the review and approval of all development permits (building permits, certificates of occupancy, wetland permits, etc.), the issuance of stop-work orders, and the maintenance of records and site inspection. Some communities charge the municipal building inspector with the administration of the zoning and land use chapter or law.

B. Building Permits—establishes that no building or structure in any district shall be erected, reconstructed or restored, structurally altered, or used without a building permit. Requires that the proposed construction conform to the provisions of the zoning and land use chapter before a building permit will be issued. Also establishes the information to be included in the application and application procedure.

C. Certificates of Occupancy—explains that a certificate of occupancy must be received before a structure is used or occupied. Attests to the fact that the actual construction is in conformance with the Uniform Fire Prevention and Building Code and is satisfactory for occupancy or use.

D. Penalties for Offenses—sets forth the penalties that may be levied for violations of the land use chapter or law, including fines and jail sentences.

E. Schedule of Fees—establishes that fees shall be paid on the filing of any application, in accordance with the fee schedule established by the municipal legislature.

Article X: Amendments

Amendment Procedure—sets forth the procedural requirements for amending the land use chapter or law. Generally states that the chapter or law may be amended, changed, modified, or repealed by the local legislature on its own initiative, on recommendation of the planning board, or on petition. Proposed amendments are subject to public notice and hearing requirements and must also be referred to the planning board for its recommendations.

By reference to the particular zoning chapter, the interested attorney can understand the standards and steps required for amending the zoning ordinance, the issuance of special or conditional permits, the award of use and area variances, the extent to which accessory uses or home occupations are permitted, whether and for how long uses that do not conform to new zoning standards can be continued, and other flexibility devices, such as the Planned Unit Development device, that can be employed to breathe flexibility into zoning administration. The attorney can also learn about the ministerial officers and administrative boards that play central roles in the execution of the zoning policies and procedures of the community. The zoning enforcement officer can interpret zoning provisions and issue rulings regarding the ordinance, these may be appealed to the board of appeals, and administrative agencies may be designated to decide on applications by landowners for variances, special or conditional permits, or approval to subdivide land or develop individual parcels.

In drafting and adopting zoning provisions, the local legislature must establish sufficient standards to guide the administrative review boards. In Hardin County v. Jost, 897 S.W.2d 592 (Ky.App.1995), the entire county was placed in one zone and every land use, except agriculture, was designated as a conditional use. To determine if a conditional use permit would issue, a point system under a "growth guidance assessment" scheme was utilized. The court found the entire ordinance invalid in that sufficient standards were not set forth, and the ordinance left land use "to the subjective whim and caprice of the zoning authority." In City of Virginia Beach v. Virginia Land Investment Ass'n No. 1, 239 Va. 412, 389 S.E.2d 312 (1990), the court held that the rezoning of some 400 acres of land from planned unit development to agricultural was invalid as piecemeal downzoning not justified by change in circumstances or prior mistake.

B. AMENDMENT OF ORDINANCE

CHURCH v. TOWN OF ISLIP
Court of Appeals of New York, 1960.
8 N.Y.2d 254, 203 N.Y.S.2d 866, 168 N.E.2d 680.

CHIEF JUDGE DESMOND.

Neighboring property owners brought this declaratory judgment suit against the Town of Islip in Suffolk County and against its Town Board and the owners of the involved property to have declared unconstitutional and void a 1954 zoning change (from Residence A to Business) of defendants Housler's corner lot in Islip, irregular in shape and about 210 feet on Bay Shore Road and 230 feet on Udall's Road. The complaint charged that the amendment was not in conformity with a comprehensive plan, that it was passed arbitrarily after a contrary recommendation by the Town Planning Board, that it arbitrarily singled out this one tract for business zoning, and that it was illegal as "contract zoning" because the Town Board's consent to the change of zone was subject to the condition that defendants owners Housler agree to the following:

Sec. 3   ZONING ADMINISTRATION AND FLEXIBILITY   333

1. The building shall not total more than 25% of the area.

2. An anchor post fence, or equal, six feet high, is to be erected five feet within the boundary line of the property.

3. Live Shrubbery, 3 feet high either within or outside of the fence is to be planted, and allowed to grow to the height of the fence and after that, to be maintained at the height of the fence.

4. The above must be performed or put in operation before carrying on any retail business on the property.

The trial was before an Official Referee who at the request of counsel inspected the properties of plaintiffs and defendants. He found for plaintiffs. He described the neighborhood as residential in use and zoning except for a substantial business zone on Bay Shore Road, one block east of the Housler property. He wrote that there were a number of unoccupied stores in that nearby business section, that there was not shown any need for rezoning the Housler lot for business, that the change was illegal "spot zoning", and that the imposition by the Town Board of conditions was illegal "contract zoning".

Defendants appealed to the Appellate Division which by a divided vote reversed on the law and facts and gave judgment declaring the amendment to be valid. The majority pointed out that this was a statutory change by the town's legislative body, that the Referee's finding of no public need or convenience was contrary to the evidence and that in any event the Town Board's legislative finding was conclusive since supported by a factual basis, that the evidence showed the Housler parcel to be located on a main traffic artery, that community growth pressures forcing zoning changes negatived the idea that the Town Board's action was arbitrary or without reason, and that there was nothing illegal about the Town Board's subjecting the new district to uses more restricted than customarily permitted in a business district. The court took notice of the recent enormous population increases in Nassau and Suffolk Counties and of the "consequent multiplication of practical problems presented to local legislative bodies by a deluge of applications for zoning district changes which are prompted by the necessities of such growth". Continuing, the Appellate Division said that "It is understandable that in the public interest and in the interest of practical expediency the practice of granting zoning changes and conditioning their uses by means of privately imposed restrictive covenants has seemingly become widespread [citing cases]." The majority denied that "such practice is contrary to the spirit of zoning ordinances" or "beyond the statutory powers of local legislative bodies".

The dissent, citing sections 262–265 of the Town Law, said that changes in zones by the Town Board could be made only according to a comprehensive plan, whereas this change was subject to special conditions imposed on this property only. The Presiding Justice thought this to be illegal and that it amounted to zoning by contract. He thought, further, that the owners had not complied with the conditions and that they are unenforcible [sic] anyhow since they were either invalidly agreed to in consideration of the zoning change or were not supported by any consideration. In this connection, see the reply brief where plaintiffs expressly concede that the owners Housler have complied with the conditions by recording an appropriate agreement.

We start with the proposition that this zoning being a legislative act (not a variance) is entitled to the strongest possible presumption of validity and must stand if there was any factual basis therefore (*Shepard v. Village of Skaneateles,* 300 N.Y. 115; *Wiggins v. Town of Somers,* 4 N.Y.2d 215). The Town Board's action in this instance was unanimous. Appellants do not seem to question the Appellate Division's fact findings. It is undisputed that Bay Shore Road has become a busy arterial highway with a traffic light at this corner and that the very Town Planning Board which recommended against this zoning change recommended a shopping area (now established) only 600 feet from this parcel on Bay Shore Road. On the issue of arbitrariness, there was reliable testimony that all of Bay Shore Road would be eventually zoned for business and that this trend could not be stopped, that the subject property is more desirable for business use than for residential, and that there was nothing arbitrary, preferential or discriminatory about the Town Board action, unanimously voted after hearing and deliberation.

Appellants' arguments all revolve about the idea that this is illegal as "contract zoning" because the Town Board, as a condition for rezoning, required the owners to execute and record restrictive covenants as to maximum area to be occupied by buildings and as to a fence and shrubbery. Surely these conditions were intended to be and are for the benefit of the neighbors. Since the Town Board could have, presumably, zoned this Bay Shore Road corner for business without any restrictions, we fail to see how reasonable conditions invalidate the legislation. Since the owners have accepted them, there is no one in a position to contest them. Exactly what "contract zoning" means is unclear and there is really no New York law on the subject. All legislation "by contract" is invalid in the sense that a Legislature cannot bargain away or sell its powers. But we deal here with actualities, not phrases. To meet increasing needs of Suffolk County's own population explosion, and at the same time to make as gradual and as little of an annoyance as possible the change from residence to business on the main highways, the Town Board imposes conditions. There is nothing unconstitutional about it. Incidentally, the record does not show any agreement in the sense that the owners made an offer accepted by the board.

The judgment should be affirmed, without costs.

FROESSEL, J. (Dissenting).

I dissent and vote to reverse for the reasons stated in Presiding Justice Nolan's dissenting opinion below with respect to the Town Board's lack of power. The board is authorized by the Town Law to create districts subject to this condition: "All such regulations [within a district] shall be *uniform* for each class or kind of buildings, throughout such district" (§ 262), and "shall be made in accordance with a *compre-*

hensive plan" (§ 263: emphasis supplied). The purpose of a plan is to look ahead. Piecemeal, parcel by parcel, conditional zoning pending the adoption of a plan is unauthorized. Variances in appropriate situations may be granted by Zoning Boards of Appeal but only under prescribed safeguards (§§ 261, 267). The power exercised by the Town Board is without warrant in law.

JUDGES DYE, FULD, BURKE and FOSTER concur with CHIEF JUDGE DESMOND; JUDGE FROESSEL dissents in an opinion in which JUDGE VAN VOORHIS concurs.

Judgment affirmed.

Notes

1. Conditional zoning, in the sense that certain conditions are "unilaterally" imposed on the premises by the city in order for rezoning to become effective, or in the sense that the land is rezoned conditionally and subject to revocation of the action if the conditions are not met, has been upheld in Wisconsin, Kansas, Nebraska, Massachusetts, New York, North Carolina, and some other jurisdictions. But a number of jurisdictions, particularly in the South, have rejected conditional rezoning as being the same as contract rezoning or as amounting to spot zoning. A key issue is whether there is really a distinction and whether conditions are in fact imposed unilaterally by the city without there first having been a bargaining or negotiating process. A further question might be whether it should matter as to whether there is a discussion process which takes on the colorations of negotiation or bargaining.

2. Consider the following explanation of conditional rezoning excerpted from Stefaniak, The Status of Conditional Rezoning in Illinois—An Argument to Sustain a Flexible Zoning Tool, 63 Ill.Bar J. 132 (1974):

> The concept of conditional rezoning has been the subject of much confusion, and the terms "conditional rezoning" and "contract zoning" are often used interchangeably. The term "conditional rezoning" has been utilized here and it is utilized to denote a broad concept with express contractual agreements and the unilateral imposition of conditions being forms of the larger concept. Conditional rezoning occurs whenever a municipal authority reclassifies land with the reclassification being subject to special limitations on the use of the rezoned property not imposed upon other lands in the same classification or where the reclassification requires the landowner to perform some act such as making improvements on the rezoned property or paying money to meet community expenses incurred as a result of the reclassification. The special limitations on use or the acts required can be brought about through either the unilateral imposition of conditions or an express agreement between the landowner and the municipality or rezoning authority. The unilateral imposition of conditions most commonly takes one of two forms:
>
>> "Where a landowner requests that his property be rezoned to allow a use not permitted under existing restrictions, he may be advised that his land will be reclassified if he first executes and files a

covenant which limits the use of his parcel in specific ways not common to other property similarly classified. * * * [or] * * * Land may be reclassified subject to conditions not applicable to other property in the same or similar districts."

The form of conditional rezoning typically referred to as contract zoning occurs when the municipality and the landowner enter into an express agreement in which both undertake reciprocal obligations. Any distinction between the two forms is tenuous and of no real import because both bring about the same result. Conditional rezoning in either of its forms is intended to reclassify land to allow a more beneficial use while imposing conditions ameliorating any hardships that the reclassification may impose on adjoining property owners or the community as a whole. The same arguments are lodged against the validity of both forms of conditional rezoning, except that contract zoning is subject to the further criticism that it constitutes a bargaining away of the police power. Dealing with conditional rezoning as a broader concept encompassing two forms is more precise and does away with nebulous distinctions. * * *

3. Neither the Standard Zoning Enabling Act nor the enabling legislation of most states contemplated the problem of contract or conditional rezoning. Some state legislatures have sought to provide authority for this device in order to promote flexibility in rezoning. In 1973, for example, the Indiana legislature amended its enabling legislation (Public Law No. 185, April 23, 1973):

Section 1 IC 1971, 18–7–2–20 is amended to read as follows: Sec. 20. To effectuate the purposes of this chapter, the metropolitan plan commission shall have the power and duty to:

* * *

17. If deemed advisable by the commission, require or allow the owner of any parcel of property, in connection with any petition for amendment to the zoning ordinance changing the zoning classification of that parcel, to make written commitments relative to the use or development of that parcel of property. The commission shall have power to establish rules and regulations governing the creation, form, and recording of commitments and the designation of specially affected persons and categories of specially affected persons entitled to enforce commitments. Commitments shall be recorded in the office of the County Recorder and shall be effective upon adoption of the amendment to the zoning ordinance. Commitments, unless modified or terminated by the commission as hereinafter provided, shall be binding on the owner, subsequent owners of the parcel of property and other persons acquiring an interest therein. Commitments may be modified or terminated by the decision of the commission made at a public hearing after notice as provided by the rules and regulations. The requiring or allowing of such commitments shall not obligate the commission to take any official action nor shall it limit the power of the commission to take any official action regarding the parcel of property. The provisions of this subsection shall not affect the validity of any covenant, easement,

equitable servitude or other land use restriction which is presently in effect or may be created in accordance with law.

4. Consider the following definitions of conditional zoning and contract zoning. Conditional zoning is a device employed to bring some flexibility of use to an otherwise rigid system of control. "Conditional Zoning" involves ordinances which provide either that rezoning becomes effective immediately with an automatic repealer if the specified conditions are not met, or that the zoning become effective only upon conditions' being met within a certain time. This type of zoning seeks to minimize the potentially deleterious effect of a zone change on neighboring properties through reasonably conceived conditions which harmonize the landowner's need for rezoning with the public interest. 83 Am. Jur. 2d Zoning and Planning § 162. On the other hand, illegal contract zoning properly connotes a transaction wherein both the landowner who is seeking a certain zoning action and the zoning authority itself undertake reciprocal obligations in the context of a bilateral contract. See Hall v. City of Durham, 323 N.C. 293, 372 S.E.2d 564 (1988).

GIGER v. CITY OF OMAHA

Supreme Court of Nebraska, 1989.
232 Neb. 676, 442 N.W.2d 182.

WHITE, JUSTICE.

This appeal involves two lawsuits relating to a development known as One Pacific Place. The development is being constructed on an 84-acre tract of land formerly owned by Carl Renstrom located in southwest Omaha. The land, hereafter the Renstrom property, is approximately triangular in shape, bordered on the north by Pacific Street, on the east by the Happy Hollow and Sunset Hills residential developments, on the southwest by the Big Papillion Creek, and on the west by 105th Street.

In March 1983, appellee Midlands Development Company (Midlands) entered into a real estate purchase agreement with the Renstrom estate for the purchase of the property. Midlands then applied to the city to have the Renstrom property rezoned to permit the construction of a mixed-use development consisting of retail, office, and residential buildings. As part of the application process, Midlands submitted several development plans. A final plan was developed which indicated the following uses for 48 acres of the tract: 112,000 square feet of retail space, 390,000 square feet of office space, 558,000 square feet of parking space, 300 residential units, a private lake, and a planned unit development (PUD). The plan also called for the construction of a public park on the remaining 36 acres to be deeded by Midlands to the city. In a "new procedure," Midlands and the city entered into four agreements incorporating the plan. The four agreements, collectively known as the development agreement, were submitted to the city for approval. In February 1985, the city passed an ordinance approving the development agreement, incorporating it as part of the ordinance, and passed five separate ordinances rezoning the Renstrom property. Building permits were then issued, including a permit allowing Midlands to fill in the flood plain of the Big Papillion Creek located on the land and to make modifications to the creek channel.

Construction on the site began approximately in September of 1985. Thereafter, two lawsuits were filed in the district court for Douglas County: *Giger et al. v. City of Omaha et al.,* filed by neighboring property owners, and *Witherspoon et al. v. City of Omaha et al.,* filed by downstream riparian property owners living along the Big Papillion Creek. The two petitions requested an order declaring the city's rezoning ordinance and accompanying building permits void, and an injunction to enjoin Midlands from developing the property in any manner inconsistent with prior zoning ordinances. The suits were ordered consolidated for trial. After a lengthy trial, the trial court denied the plaintiffs' requested relief.

Though the plaintiffs-appellants assign a total of 15 errors, these errors are consolidated into three issues for consideration on appeal. The first two issues relate to appellants' contention that the trial court erred in not finding that the Omaha City Council acted in an arbitrary, capricious, and unreasonable manner in adopting the rezoning ordinance. Specifically, the appellants allege that the city entered into a development agreement with Midlands, adopted a rezoning ordinance which incorporated that agreement, and rezoned the Renstrom property pursuant to that agreement and that the city adopted the rezoning ordinance without giving adequate consideration to the risk of flood created by the project. The last issue involves appellants' claim that the trial court erred in not granting a permanent injunction enjoining Midlands from filling the flood plain on the Renstrom property and altering the channel of the Big Papillion Creek.

* * *

The first argument raised by the appellants is that the city, by adopting a rezoning ordinance pursuant to an agreement between itself and Midlands, acted in an arbitrary, capricious, and unreasonable manner. In support of this argument, the appellants challenge the validity of the rezoning ordinance on two grounds. They assert, first, that rezoning by agreement is invalid per se and, second, that the rezoning ordinance violates the substantive standards set out in §§ 14–402 and 14–403.

Specifically, the appellants contend that because rezoning by agreement is illegal contract rezoning, it is invalid per se, is an ultra vires act, and fosters an "appearance of evil." They allege illegal contract rezoning occurred because the city bargained away and sold its police power. The appellants do not cite any Nebraska authority for this proposition and claim that this court has never faced a true contract zoning situation. However, we note that *Bucholz v. City of Omaha, supra,* a case where the city conditioned its granting of a rezoning ordinance on the developer's entering into a protective covenant, has been characterized as an example of contract rezoning. 2 R. Anderson, American Law of Zoning § 9.21 (3d ed. 1986); 1 N. Williams & J. Taylor, American Planning Law, Land Use and the Police Power § 29.03 (rev. 1988). Yet, *Bucholz* has also been labeled as an example of a conditional rezoning. Annot., 70 A.L.R.3d 125, 162 (1976); 2 A. Rathkopf & D. Rathkopf, Rathkopf's the Law of Zoning and Planning § 27.05 (rev. 1989); Note, *The Validity of Conditional Zoning: a Florida Perspective,* 31 U.Fla.L.Rev. 968, 971 n. 21 (1979); Comment, *Land Use—Goffinet v. County of Christian: New Flexibility in Illinois Zoning Law,* 8 Loy.U.Chi.L.J. 642, 643 n. 15 (1977). This distinction is academic because our scope of review, as explained below, is limited to determining whether the conditions imposed by the city for rezoning are reasonably related to the interest of public health, safety, morals, and the general welfare.

This court realizes that in the development of a project such as One Pacific Place there are negotiations between the developer and the city. We are also aware that a city rezones property based on representations made and plans submitted by the developer. However, once a parcel of land has been rezoned, there is no guarantee the developer will follow through on the plans submitted to the city. Legally, the developer is entitled to use his or her land in any manner permitted by the zoning classification. Of course, the city would not be without a remedy if the land was used in a manner not contemplated in the original plans submitted by the developer. The city could rezone the property to another designation and then institute the appropriate proceedings to prevent the unwanted development. See Neb.Rev.Stat. § 14–415 (Reissue 1987).

However, as *Cummings Enterprises v. Shukert,* 231 Neb. 370, 436 N.W.2d 199 (1989), indicates, this is not always an effective remedy. In *Cummings Enterprises,* the developer's land was rezoned from second suburban district to first commercial. He applied for a building permit for a carwash, a permissible use under that classification, and his request was denied. Subsequently, the city rezoned the developer's property to a classification which excluded carwashes. The developer successfully sued for a writ of mandamus ordering the issuance of the building permit. The city issued the permit, and the developer built the carwash. We held that the city had waived its right to appeal the order, since it voluntarily complied with the order instead of obtaining a supersedeas.

In addition, this court gives great deference to the city's determination of which laws should be enacted for the welfare of the people. *Wolf v. City of Omaha, supra; City of Omaha v. Glissmann, supra.* When the city rezones a parcel of property, we presume the validity of that action absent clear and satisfactory evidence to the contrary. *Bucholz v. City of Omaha,* 174 Neb. 862, 120 N.W.2d 270 (1963); *Davis v. City of Omaha,* 153 Neb. 460, 45 N.W.2d 172 (1950). Therefore, when the city considers a request for rezoning based upon a plan or representation by the developer, it is presumed that the city grants the request after making the determination that the plan as represented is in the interest of public health, safety, morals, and the general welfare. We do not think a developer should be allowed to develop property in a manner inconsistent with the plan or representation on which the rezoning was based, despite the fact that the inconsistent use may be permissible under the new zoning classification. By developing the property in a manner not contemplated by the city in granting the rezoning classification, the developer contravenes a decision made by the city pursuant to its police power for the benefit of the community. If the city is limited to only enacting bare zoning ordinances and is not permitted to insist that developers construct buffer zones or make other changes in order to blend the development into the surrounding community, the city will be stripped of the power to act for the benefit of the general welfare. Accordingly, the city should be permitted to condition rezoning ordinances on the adoption of an agreement between the developer and the city, or any other means assuring the developer builds the project as represented. A t the risk of confusion, but for the sake of convenience, we will refer to this zoning arrangement as conditional zoning. As Rathkopf notes:

> The purpose [of conditional rezoning] is to minimize the negative externalities caused by land development which otherwise benefits the community. The developer may agree to restrict development of its property, make certain improvements, dedicate a portion of land to the municipality, or make payments to the government. Conditional rezoning is valuable as a planning tool because it permits a municipality greater flexibility in balancing developmental demands against fiscal and environmental concerns. It also provides a municipality with flexibility to meet specific rezoning requests while preserving the integrity of adjacent property. For instance, the agreement can mitigate the harshness of commercial or industrial rezoning on neighboring residential property by requiring a buffer on the zone boundaries. Finally, conditional rezoning allows a municipality to maintain greater control over the development process.

2 A. Rathkopf & D. Rathkopf, Rathkopf's the Law of Zoning and Planning § 27.05 at 27–45 to 27–46 (rev. 1989). Thus, this device allows the city flexibility to extract improvements that bare zoning ordinances do not provide, grants a greater means of control over the development to the city, and gives the city a remedy to enforce the developer's plans and representations. Theoretically, if the rezoning ordinance adopts the plan, as in this case, the city could institute legal proceedings if the developer builds a project inconsistent with the plans without resorting to rezoning the property. For the foregoing reasons we hold conditional rezoning to be valid. Our holding today is a reflection of the trend started in this jurisdiction by *Bucholz* and the growing movement in this country permitting conditional rezonings. 2 A. Rathkopf & D. Rathkopf, *supra.*

However, our holding recognizing the validity of conditional rezoning is not without limitation. Conditional rezoning is a legislative function and therefore must be within the proper exercise of the police power. Accordingly, the conditions imposed by the city for the rezoning must be reasonably related to the interest of public health, safety, morals, and the general welfare. See, e.g., *Treme v. St. Louis County,* 609 S.W.2d 706 (Mo.App.1980) (where offer made or exaction demanded for rezoning bears no reasonable relationship to activities of developer, action of county or municipality in rezoning property in exchange for such offer or exaction is contracting away of police power, which is forbidden); *State ex rel. Myhre v. Spokane,* 70 Wash.2d 207, 422 P.2d 790 (1967) (amendment to zoning ordinance and concomitant agreement should be declared invalid only if it can be shown that there was no valid reason for change, that they are clearly arbitrary and unreasonable and have no substantial relation to public health, safety, morals, and general welfare, or that city is using concomitant agreement for bargaining and sale to highest bidder or solely for the benefit of private speculators). See 2 A. Rathkopf & D. Rathkopf, *supra.* Hence, to successfully challenge the validity of conditional rezoning, the appellants must prove that the conditions imposed by the city in adopting the rezoning ordinance were unreasonable, discriminatory, or arbitrary, and that the regulation bears no relationship to the purpose or purposes sought to be accomplished by the ordinance. This is the same test used for testing the validity of zoning ordinances in this jurisdiction. See, *Wolf v. City of Omaha,* 177 Neb. 545, 129 N.W.2d 501 (1964); *Bucholz v. City of Omaha,* 174 Neb. 862, 120 N.W.2d 270 (1963); *City of Omaha v. Cutchall,* 173 Neb. 452, 114 N.W.2d 6 (1962); *City of Omaha v. Glissmann,* 151 Neb. 895, 39 N.W.2d 828 (1949); *Cassel Realty Co. v. City of Omaha,* 144 Neb. 753, 14 N.W.2d 600 (1944). "The validity of a zoning ordinance will be presumed in the absence of clear and satisfactory evidence to the contrary." *Bucholz v. City of Omaha, supra* 174 Neb. at 865–66, 120 N.W.2d at 273, citing *Davis v. City of Omaha,* 153 Neb. 460, 45 N.W.2d 172 (1950).

The appellants argue that by entering into the development agreement the city has curtailed or bargained away its police powers because (1) the agreement prohibits amendment without the consent of the developer; (2) the city is committed to approve a PUD "without any present indication as to what such PUD's might contain"; (3) the city is obligated to issue building permits "without regard to compliance with other building codes, rules and regulations of the City"; (4) the city is required to spend $64,700 for offsite improvements; (5) the agreement mandates the manner in which the city is to levy special assessments for the payments of these improvements; and (6) "[t]hroughout the Subdivision Agreement [one of the agreements in the development agreement], the City obligates itself to deal in many ways involving its legislative and administrative authority with a *non-existent* Sanitary and Improvement District to be created in the future." Brief for appellants Witherspoon et al. at 18–19. However, the plain language in the provisions of the development agreement contradict appellants' contentions.

* * *

Simply stated, the agreement expressly provides that Midlands may vary the development only if the city does not find the variation deviates from the development plan and the variations do not violate any provision of the Omaha Municipal Code. Clearly, under this agreement, the powers of the city are unchanged. We fail to see how the development agreement can be construed as bargaining away the city's police power.

In fact, this agreement is in reality an enhancement of the city's police power. An examination of the development agreement and the evidence at trial establishes that the agreement provides more restrictive ceilings and development regulations than the current underlying zoning regulations. For example, a portion of the development, where the office buildings will be located, has been rezoned to ninth residence district (R–9). Absent the agreement, according to Omaha Mun.Code, ch. 55, art. XV, §§ 55–311 et seq. (1983), under the R–9 classification Midlands is free to erect any number of office buildings with no real limitations on the amount of square footage. Here, the agreement restricts Midlands to a maximum of three office buildings and a total of 390,000 square feet of office space.

In sum, we find that there is not clear and satisfactory evidence to support the appellants' contention that the city has bargained away its police power. The evidence clearly shows that the city's police powers are not abridged in any manner and that the agreement is expressly subject to the remedies available to the city under the Omaha Municipal Code. Further, we find that the agreement actually enhances the city's regulatory control over the development rather than limiting it.

The appellants' second contention is that the city engaged in an ultra vires act because there is no statutory enabling act permitting conditional rezoning. * * * In addition to having the power to enact zoning regulations, the city also has the power to amend, supplement, change, modify, or repeal those regulations. § 14–405. Further, § 14–403 in part provides:

> Whenever the City council shall determine that the use or contemplated use of any building, structure or land will cause congestion in the streets, increase danger from fire or panic, imperil public safety, cause undue concentration or congregation of people, or impede transportation, the council may include in such regulations requirements for alleviating or preventing such conditions when any change in use or zoning classification is requested by the owner.

It is axiomatic that zoning is a local concern. In light of this, plus the fact that the Legislature has used the general term "regulations" without explicitly delineating what regulations the city is permitted to use, coupled with a grant of power to the city to implement, amend, supplement, change, modify, or repeal those regulations, it is clear that the Legislature has given the city broad powers to regulate land uses within its jurisdiction as long as those regulations are within the police power. Thus, we find in chapter 14 of the Nebraska Revised Statutes an implied grant of power to the city to enact all necessary zoning regulations, including conditional rezoning, as long as those regulations are within the proper exercise of the police power.

Sec. 3 ZONING ADMINISTRATION AND FLEXIBILITY

The third contention by the appellants is that the city fostered an "appearance of evil" by engaging in conditional rezoning. They allege that conditional rezoning could result in corruption of officials and that if the practice is permitted, officials will concentrate more on what they can extract from the developer than on proper rezoning criteria. This argument lacks merit. The appellants admit there is no evidence of graft or corruption in the case at bar, and we believe our holding is more than adequate to protect against any alleged abuse of this type. We will not strike down a conditional zoning because it looks evil, but only if its application is evil. Accordingly, appellants' challenge to this conditional rezoning as invalid fails.

* * *

The appellants assert that the rezoning ordinance violates the uniformity provision in § 14–402 because the agreement results in concessions for both the city and Midlands which are not allowed to other developers. As an example, appellants state in their brief that " '[n]o other developers in the City' have 'been required to give a park for free to the City in exchange for rezoning.' " Brief for appellants Witherspoon et al. at 14. We note that the uniformity requirement in § 14–402 is derived from § 2 of the Standard State Zoning Enabling Act and that almost every jurisdiction has incorporated this limitation into its state zoning enabling legislation. 1 R. Anderson, American Law of Zoning § 5.25 (3d ed. 1986). In his treatise on zoning, Anderson states that there have been few cases interpreting the uniformity requirement and that attacks on conditional rezoning as being violative of the uniformity requirement have "not been notably successful." 2 R. Anderson, American Law of Zoning § 9.20 at 164 (3d ed. 1986); 1 R. Anderson, *supra,* § 5.25. The jurisdictions that have addressed the uniformity requirement have analyzed the challenged ordinances to see if they are reasonable and not discriminatory. 1 R. Anderson, *supra,* § 5.25. For instance, in *Mont. Co. v. Woodward & Lothrop,* 280 Md. 686, 719–20, 376 A.2d 483, 501 (1977), the court, construing a uniform provision comparable to Nebraska's, said:

> The uniformity provision contained in Art. 66D, § 8–102 was derived from § 2 of the Standard State Zoning Enabling Act, as to which it was said in 1 Anderson, *American Law of Zoning,* § 5.22 (2d ed. 1976), that the purpose of the provision was mainly a political rather than a legal one, *i.e.,* to give notice to property owners that there shall be no improper discriminations. [Citations omitted.] We have also recognized that invidious distinctions and discriminations in applying the uniformity requirement are impermissible. [Citations omitted.] The uniformity requirement does not prohibit classification within a district, so long as it is reasonable and based upon the public policy to be served.

See, *Oshtemo Twp v. Central Ad. Co.,* 125 Mich.App. 538, 336 N.W.2d 823 (1983) (township rural zoning act, providing that zoning ordinance provisions must be uniform for each class of land, buildings, dwellings, and structures throughout the district, is subject to "reasonableness" exception, allowing reasonable restrictions based upon different conditions within the zone); *Quinton v. Edison Park Development Corp.*, 59 N.J. 571, 285 A.2d 5 (1971) (statute which required that zoning regulations be uniform for each class or kind of buildings or other structures or uses of land throughout each district does not prohibit classifications within a district so long as they are reasonable).

We think allowing reasonable classifications within a district is a good rule, especially in view of the broad delegation of authority given by the Legislature to the city in making zoning regulations, as set forth above. Accordingly, the uniformity requirement in § 14–402 does not prohibit reasonable classifications within a district. To successfully challenge the rezoning ordinance on the grounds it violates the uniformity requirement of § 14–402, the appellants must prove that the actions of the city in adopting the rezoning ordinance were unreasonable, discriminatory, or arbitrary, and that the regulation bears no relationship to the purpose or purposes sought to be accomplished by the ordinance.

Other than pointing to the provisions of the agreement itself, the appellants cite no evidence in support of their claim that the rezoning action violates the uniformity requirement. Implicit in appellants' proposition is the assumption that no other developer will be able to take advantage of conditional rezoning. Today's holding clearly refutes that assumption. The appellants have failed to show by clear and satisfactory evidence, *Bucholz v. City of Omaha,* 174 Neb. 862, 120 N.W.2d 270 (1963), and *Davis v. City of Omaha,* 153 Neb. 460, 45 N.W.2d 172 (1950), that the city acted in an unreasonable, discriminatory, or arbitrary manner, and that the regulation bears no relationship to the purpose sought to be accomplished by the ordinance.

* * *

[Significant portions of the case dealing with whether the rezoning is invalid because it devalues nearby properties or fails to meet the "in conformance with the comprehensive plan" requirement are omitted. The court determined that it was not invalid for these reasons.]

MONTGOMERY COUNTY v. NATIONAL CAPITAL REALTY CORP.

Court of Appeals of Maryland, 1972.
267 Md. 364, 297 A.2d 675.

[The property owner sought rezoning from C–O, commercial office building, to C–2, general commercial. The planning staff recommended disapproval of the application, primarily on grounds of the height and ground coverage permissible in the C–2 zone. The Planning Board rejected the staff recommendation and approved the application after the applicant submitted a set of covenants, conditions and restrictions which would "become effective upon the approval" of the zoning application. The local legislative body reversed the Planning Board, relying on a memorandum from the County Attorney to the effect that conditional zoning was not allowed in Montgomery County. The trial court reversed and ordered approval of the application, and the county appealed.]

LEVINE, JUDGE.

* * *

Entirely apart from the "change" argument, we think resolution of the question whether the covenants constituted a form of impermissible conditional zoning is decisive of this case. For, as we have seen, by a determination of that point in appellant's favor, two of the main props to appellee's case would topple, i.e., the favorable recommendations of the Planning Board and Mr. Hussmann, respectively. This would then confront appellee with unfavorable positions of the staff and Hussmann and without any public agency support.

We think it clear that the covenants, coupled with the site plan attached thereto, if adopted as a basis for the requested reclassification, would have produced a form of conditional zoning. If recorded, the covenants would have bound appellee to compliance only on the condition that the C–2 classification first had been granted. Had the Council then granted the application on the strength of the covenants, as encouraged to do so by Mr. Hussmann and the Planning Board it would have committed what we believe would have been a classic illustration of conditional zoning. The invalidity of conditional zoning in Maryland is not seriously open to question. Citizens Ass'n v. Pr. Geo. County, 222 Md. 44, 158 A.2d 663 (1960); Rose v. Paape, 221 Md. 369, 376–377, 157 A.2d 618 (1960); Baylis v. City of Baltimore, 219 Md. 164, 169–170, 148 A.2d 429 (1959). It is interesting to note that in none of those cases was there cited a provision comparable to § 111–48(d) of the Montgomery County Zoning Ordinance also codified by that same designation in the Montgomery County Code, 1965, which provides:

"No application for a local or a sectional or District plan map amendment shall be approved conditionally for the erection on the land of a structure at a particular location, or within a particular time, or by a particular person, or of a particular type, or for the subdivision of the land in a particular manner, or on any other condition."

In 3 Rathkopf, Zoning and Planning 74–9, it is stated:

" * * * The general rule in these jurisdictions in which the validity of such covenants has been litigated is that they are illegal. The basis of such rule is that the rezoning of a particular parcel of land upon conditions not imposed by the zoning ordinance generally in the particular district into which the land has been rezoned is prima facie evidence of 'spot zoning' in its most maleficent aspect, is not in accordance with a comprehensive plan and is beyond the power of the municipality."

"Legislative bodies must rezone in accordance with a comprehensive plan, and in amending the ordinance so as to confer upon a particular parcel a particular district designation, it may not curtail or limit the uses and structures placed or to be placed upon the lands so rezoned differently from those permitted upon other lands in the same district. Consequently, where there has been a concatenated rezoning and filing of a 'declaration of restrictions' the general view (where the question has been litigated) is that both the zoning amendment and the restrictive covenant are invalid for the reasons expressed above."

Although the rule followed in Maryland has undergone erosion in some states we believe that it continues to be supported by the weight of authority.

Nor is appellee helped by our decisions in Funger v. Mayor of Somerset, 249 Md. 311, 328, 239 A.2d 748 (1968) and Greenbelt v. Bresler, 248 Md. 210, 215–216, 236 A.2d 1 (1967). What distinguishes those cases from those we have cited earlier is that in each, the municipality within which the subject land was located agreed to support the rezoning application before the respective county legislative body in exchange for certain commitments entered into by the applicant. Thus, since in both cases the legislative body was not a party to the agreement, neither the rezoning nor the agreement was invalidated. For the reasons we have stated, the Council was correct in refusing to grant the rezoning upon the conditions expressed in the Declaration of Covenants and the attached site plan.

Nothing we have said in distinguishing *Funger* and *Greenbelt* from the cases involving agreements entered into by legislative bodies supports enforceability of the covenants here by the Planning Board, since, as we have noted, the covenants were to become binding on appellee only if the Council granted the application. In short, we are concerned here merely with the fact that the Planning Board's favorable report was predicated solely on the existence of covenants which, in light of our holding, were worthless. Thus, they imparted the same value to the recommendation of the Board. What we have just said doubtlessly applies with greater force to Mr. Hussmann's recommendation, as he, being a county employee and in no respect a party to the covenants, gratuitously considered them in arriving at his favorable conclusion. Thus, we think the Council was correct in refusing to rely upon the covenants while deciding the zoning application, and the favorable recommendation of the Planning Board and Mr. Hussmann were entitled to no weight.

* * *

Order reversed.

Notes

1. Some state legislatures have sought to relax the prohibition of conditional zoning by providing statutory authority. Note that the principal case was superseded by statute as stated in Mayor and Council of Rockville v. Rylyns Enterprises, Inc., 372 Md. 514, 814 A.2d 469 (2002). In 1970,

Maryland's state legislature amended the zoning enabling authority by enacting Section 4.01 of Article 66B which states:

> (B) The local legislative body of a county or municipal corporation, upon the zoning or rezoning or any land * * * may impose such additional restrictions, conditions, or limitations as may be deemed appropriate to preserve, improve, or protect the general character and design of the lands and improvements being zoned or rezoned, or of the surrounding or adjacent lands and improvements, and may, upon the zoning or rezoning or any land or lands, retain ore reserve the power and authority to approve or disapprove the design or buildings, construction, landscaping or other improvements, alterations, and changes made or to be made on the subject land or lands to assure conformity with the intent and purpose of this article and of the jurisdiction's zoning ordinance. The powers provided in 4.01(B) shall be applicable only if the local legislative body adopts an ordinance which shall include enforcement procedures and requirements for adequate notice of public hearing and conditions sought to be imposed.

This recodification "in effect authorized 'conditional zoning' in certain circumstances," so long as local governments meet the statutory requirements and adopt the proper ordinances. 814 A.2d at 498. Curiously, this statute was adopted before the Montgomery case was decided but was not called to the attention of the court, which relied on previous judicial interpretations of local authority to impose conditions on zoning.

2. In Y. Chung v. Sarasota County, 686 So.2d 1358 (1996), a rezoning petition was denied, litigated, and, in settlement, the county agreed to rezone Chung's property subject to numerous stipulations and conditions. Based on the settlement, the trial court entered a stipulated final judgment, and retained jurisdiction over its enforcement. Adjacent neighbors intervened, claimed the settlement constituted illegal contract zoning, and the District Court agreed. The court noted:

> Contracts have no place in a zoning plan and a contract between a municipality and a property owner should not enter into the enactment or enforcement of zoning regulations * * * One of the reasons contract zoning is generally rejected is because "[t]he legislative power to enact and amend zoning regulations requires due process, notice, and hearings." Terry Lewis et al., Spot Zoning, Contract Zoning, & Conditional Zoning, in 2 Florida Environmental & Land Use Law 9–1, 9–13 (James J. Brown, ed., 2d ed. 1994). Assuming that the developer and municipality bargain for a rezoning ordinance that is fairly debatable and nondiscriminatory, contract zoning is nevertheless illegal when they enter into a bilateral agreement involving reciprocal obligations. By binding itself to enact the requested ordinance (or not to amend the existing ordinance), the municipality bypasses the hearing phase of the legislative process. * * * If each parcel of property were zoned on the basis of variables that could enter into private contracts then the whole scheme and objective of community planning and zoning would collapse. The residential owner would never know when he was protected against commercial encroachment * * *. The adoption of an ordinance is the exercise of municipal legislative power. In the exercise of this govern-

mental function a city cannot legislate by contract. If it could, then each citizen would be governed by an individual rule based upon the best deal that he could make with the governing body. We conclude that the County's settlement agreement here presents a case of improper contract zoning. Although the County Commission approved the settlement at its regular meetings, it bypassed the more stringent notice and hearing requirements for a rezoning. When it entered into the settlement agreement that obligated it to rezone Chung's property, the County contracted away the exercise of its police power, which constituted an ultra vires act.

3. What should happen if the city breaches its part of the agreement? In Sprenger, Grubb & Associates v. City of Hailey, 127 Idaho 576, 903 P.2d 741 (1995) a developer with a 654–acre parcel entered into a development agreement with the city that provided for a master residential-business plan and annexation into the city. After the annexation in 1973, the city zoned 12.6 acres of the land for business. From 1973 to 1993, the developer gradually built out the plan. The city, at the behest of the mayor and with a great deal of public support, pushed for rezonings to protect the core downtown business area that resulted in downzoning the developer's 12.6 acre parcel from business to "limited business." (The mayor had wanted downzoning to residential, but settled for the limited business designation.) The developer sued alleging that the downzoning devalued the property by $800,000, that the city was estopped from rezoning in breach of the development agreement, and that the downzoning was a taking. The Idaho Supreme Court held for the city, noting that under some circumstances a city might be estopped from breaching a development agreement, but that in this case the downzoning was not a breach because the limited business designation was in substantial compliance with the agreement. The court also found that the devaluation was not a taking because the developer still had residual economic value in the land.

4. Another case with a cautionary message for developers is Metropolitan Dade County v. Fontainebleau Gas & Wash, Inc., 570 So.2d 1006 (Fla.App.1990). In 1975, a developer sought rezoning of a parcel from professional office to limited business and, in a letter accompanying the application, indicated that the company would offer a written covenant restricting use of the property to a bank. The county granted the rezoning, expressing in the resolution that the use would be limited to a bank, but the covenant was never recorded. The bank was never built and the property changed hands many times. Fifteen years after the rezoning, the present owner received a building permit and built a gas station. Just before the station was finished the county discovered the old restriction and issued a stop work order. In a suit by the developer, the court held for the county stating that owners are deemed to purchase property with constructive knowledge of applicable land use regulations, the county applies the zoning code by resolution, and the resolutions that are passed subsequent to public hearings can modify districts and restrict property use. "Anyone attempting to learn what, if any, use limitations apply to his property need only turn to the applicable resolution." The court went on to hold that the owner could not claim detrimental reliance on the permit inadvertently issued by the county.

5. However, in Santa Margarita Area Residents Together v. San Luis Obispo County Board of Supervisors, 84 Cal.App.4th 221, 100 Cal.Rptr.2d 740 (2000), the Second Appellate District upheld a development agreement that freezes zoning on the project property in return for the developer's commitment to submit a specific plan for construction in compliance with county land use requirements. Contingencies and further approvals remain, but the agreement commits the county and the builder to the project, including its public improvements and amenities. The court reasoned that a "[g]overnmental entity does not contract away its police power unless the contract amounts to the 'surrender' or 'abnegation' of a proper governmental function." The zoning freeze in the agreement was not a surrender or abnegation because it was not of unlimited duration. The county's action was described as a legitimate exercise of governmental police power in the public interest and not a surrender of police power to a special interest.

C. ADMINISTRATIVE TREATMENT

Lawyers are often engaged to secure or oppose variances from the local zoning board of appeals or a special use permit from a local administrative agency. Variances and special, or conditional, use permits provide flexibility in local zoning practice and provide relief for individual parcel owners while protecting the surrounding neighborhood. Municipal attorneys advise these boards and the local legislative bodies that design the local zoning apparatus. Local legislatures create the board of appeals and other administrative agencies, delegate authority to them, and prescribe the procedures that they must follow. Local legislatures are directed and limited by state statutes in establishing the local administrative regime and, as they adopt laws, their local boards and administrators are required to comply with the standards and procedural steps contained in them.

In most states, when a locality adopts a zoning ordinance, the state enabling statute requires that it establish a zoning board of appeals, which may be called a board of standards or board of adjustment. Typically these boards serve in a review—or appellate—capacity. If an interpretation of the meaning and applicability of the zoning ordinance is rendered by the zoning administrative officer, that interpretation may be appealed to the board of appeals. If the administrative officer informs a property owner that her construction plans do not conform with the strict use or dimensional requirements of the zoning ordinance, she may appeal to the board for a variance.

A variance allows the owner of a particular parcel that is uniquely situated to prove that relief is needed but will not be detrimental to the integrity of the ordinance or the character of the surrounding neighborhood. Variances provide relief from unnecessary hardships that arise because of special conditions applicable to the affected parcel. They provide a safety valve that responds to unique circumstances, avoids as applied legal challenges by property owners, and preserves the spirit of the ordinance as drafted by the legislature.

It is said that the board of appeals, in this review capacity, serves as a quasi-judicial agency and operates as such. When the decisions of a board of appeals are appealed to a court, the court can certify the record of the quasi-judicial body and, in most states, does not conduct a de novo trial on the facts determined by the board. Boards of appeals conduct their proceedings in a formal fashion, allow evidence to be presented and confronted, create a record, and make fact-based decisions that are supported by that record. These decisions must be filed in a timely manner with the municipal clerk or in another office, and aggrieved parties are allowed to appeal them to the courts within a prescribed time after the date of the filing. Courts in most states defer to the discretion of boards of appeals and affirm their decisions unless the appellant can prove affirmatively that the decision is arbitrary or unreasonable, not based on facts on the record, or does not conform to applicable standards.

Section 7 of the Standard Zoning Enabling Act empowered the board of appeals:

* * *

(b) to hear and decide special exceptions of the ordinance upon which such board is required to pass under such ordinance: and

(c) to authorize upon appeal in specific cases such variance from the terms of the ordinance as will not be contrary to the public interest, where, owing to special conditions, a literal enforcement of the provisions of the ordinance will result in unnecessary hardship, and so that the spirit of the ordinance shall be observed and substantial justice done.

These or similar words are contained in most of the state zoning enabling laws today.

Boards of appeals may also be used for other functions. They may be assigned the task, for example, of issuing special use permits, known in some jurisdictions as conditional use permits or special exceptions. In hearing and determining applications for special use permits, the board is said to serve in an administrative capacity and to be exercising original jurisdiction. If an article of the zoning ordinance provides that a house of worship is permitted, subject to the issuance of a special use permit, the religious institution applies directly to the board of appeals for that permit. It is a matter of state law and local practice whether the board of appeals, planning board or commission, or other administrative agency is charged with the issuance of special permits.

Special land uses, such as gasoline stations, certain utilities, clubs, hospitals, sanatoria, junkyards, mobile home parks, and houses of worship are permitted in designated zoning districts, but are subject to the imposition of certain conditions that protect surrounding properties from adverse impacts. Conditional uses are different from the as-of-right uses permitted in each zoning district. They are declared to be harmonious with the zoning district in which they are allowed, by permit, but it is recognized that they are sufficiently different that special conditions on construction and use may be needed to prevent adverse impacts on the district. This allows the administrative body to consider in detail the physical conditions in the area, the nature of the proposed conditional use, and to tailor the proposed use to its surroundings.

The essential difference, in most ordinances, is that a variance allows a property owner to use her land or buildings in a manner that is prohibited by the ordinance, while a special use permit authorizes uses that are allowed and encouraged by the ordinance and declared to be harmonious with the applicable zoning district. This distinction between these two forms of providing zoning fairness and flexibility is illustrated by judicial decisions. In most states, there is a brisk pace of litigation that results from the impact of board decisions regarding variances and special use permits on the property values and the daily lives of the affected parties.

(1) Variance Cases

LARSEN v. ZONING BOARD OF ADJUSTMENT OF CITY OF PITTSBURGH

Supreme Court of Pennsylvania, 1996.
543 Pa. 415, 672 A.2d 286.

[The owners of a house with a very steep back yard sloping toward the Ohio River sought and received a variance to add a 20–by–20–foot deck off the rear of the house to provide their two-year-old child with an outside play area. A neighbor residing in a multi-unit condominium next door appealed the grant of a variance. The trial court ruled that the house owners had failed to satisfy the criteria needed to support a variance, and the house owners appeal.]

CASTILLE, JUSTICE.

* * *

There are essentially four factors that appellants must prove to be entitled to a variance under the applicable statute and ordinance. The factors are:

(1) that an unnecessary hardship exists which is not created by the party seeking the variance and which is caused by unique physical circumstances of the property for which the variance is sought;

(2) that a variance is needed to enable the party's reasonable use of the property;

(3) that the variance will not alter the essential character of the district or neighborhood, or substantially or permanently impair the use or development of the adjacent property such that it is detrimental to the public's welfare; and

(4) that the variance will afford the least intrusive solution.

53 P.S. § 10910.2; § 909.05 of the Pittsburgh Code of Ordinance ("PCO"). * * * The failure of a zoning board to consider each requirement of a zoning ordinance prior to granting a variance is an error of law. * * * Here, the zoning board failed to consider each of these requirements. Furthermore, the record reveals that appellants failed to provide evidence that would satisfy even the first criteria. Accordingly, appellants' claim must fail.

1. HARDSHIP CAUSED BY UNIQUE PHYSICAL CHARACTERISTICS

(a) Unnecessary Hardship

In order to satisfy the first prong under both the statute and PCO, appellants must prove: (1) that the variance is needed to avoid an "unnecessary hardship;" (2) that the "unnecessary hardship" was not created by them; and (3) that the "unnecessary hardship" was caused by unique physical circumstances of the property for which the variance is sought. With respect to the first factor, in determining whether the denial of the variance would cause the level of hardship needed to warrant a variance, this Court held in *Richman v. Zoning Board of Adjustment*, 391 Pa. 254, 259–60, 137 A.2d 280, 283 (1958), that the hardship must truly be an "unnecessary" one, and not simply a " 'mere' hardship." Furthermore, the "unnecessary" hardship must be one that is "unique or peculiar" to the property. *Id.*

Here, the Board found that appellants would suffer an "unnecessary hardship" from a denial of the variance because they would be denied the reasonable use of their land if they could not provide a play area for their child. However, the mere desire to provide more room for a family member's enjoyment fails to constitute they type of "unnecessary hardship" required by the law of this Commonwealth.

In the matter of *In re Kline Zoning Case*, 395 Pa. 122, 124, 148 A.2d 915, 916 (1959), a property owner sought a variance from a thirty-foot setback requirement in order to enclose his front porch. The basis for his variance request was that his wife suffered from asthma and hay fever, and that his son suffered from a severe respiratory ailment as well as hay fever. The enclosure of the porch would have allowed his family to have additional room in which to habitate. This Court, applying the test set forth by Richman, supra, upheld the zoning board's denial of the variance finding that the owner's need for additional room for his family failed to establish an unnecessary hardship justifying the variance.

The circumstances of *In re Kline Zoning Case* are analogous to the circumstances at hand. In both cases, the property owners sought variances to modify their homes to add a greater area for the family members to play in or to use. Thus, under *In re Kline Zoning Case*, we find that the Zoning Board erred as a matter of law in granting the variance based simply upon appellants' need to provide a greater play area for their child. Variances are meant to avoid "unnecessary" hardships; the granting of relief cannot be done simply to accommodate the changing needs of a growing family.

(b) Creation of Hardship

Notwithstanding appellants' failure to establish an unnecessary hardship, appellants further failed to establish that the physical circumstances allegedly causing the unnecessary hardship were not created by them. * * * Section 909.05(a)(1)(A) of the Pittsburgh Code of Ordinances expressly provides that parties are not entitled to a variance for circumstances which are the result of "any act of the appellant or his predecessors in title subsequent to the adoption of this Zoning Ordinance, whether in violation of the provisions hereof or not." See also, 53 P.S. § 10910.2(a)(3). To the extent that the hardship found by the zoning board was the result of the fact that appellants' first addition to their residence covered 75% of the property, thereby precluding any additional building absent a variance, appellants themselves created the complained of hardship. When appellants purchased the property, the house had a seventy-six foot setback from the rear property line. It was appellants themselves who built the forty-four foot deep addition which left them with insufficient space to erect an outside deck that would have complied with the ordinance at issue without the need for a variance. Therefore, appellants failed to prove that the "unnecessary hardship" was not caused by their own making.

(c) Unique Physical Circumstances

Appellants also failed to demonstrate that the "unique physical circumstances" of their property caused the hardship. In order to prove that the physical circumstances of a property justify a variance, the party seeking the variance must demonstrate that the circumstances are unique or peculiar to the property in question and not a condition common to the neighborhood or zoning district. * * * Here, the record establishes that the physical circumstances were in fact not unique to appellants' property and that most of the properties along Grandview Avenue had similar precipitously steep backyards. This Court has held that a condition which affects only a small portion of a district is not sufficiently unique to warrant a variance, but rather should be remedied by re-zoning. *English v. Zoning Board of Adjustment of Norristown*, 395 Pa. 118, 120–21, 148 A.2d 912, 914 (1959) (where zoning board grants a variance where neighborhood changes affect a small group of properties on one street, it is "virtually enacting zoning legislation instead of merely performing its function of administering the zoning law prescribed by the governing body of the municipality"). See also, *Walter v. Zoning Board of Adjustment*, 437 Pa. 277, 280, 263 A.2d 123, 126 (1970) (party seeking variance cannot complain of hardship existing at time the land was purchased). Thus, the condition which gave rise to appellants' alleged "unnecessary hardship" was not unique or peculiar to their property.

2. VARIANCE NEEDED TO ENABLE REASONABLE USE OF PROPERTY

Even if appellants had established the existence of an unnecessary hardship, they would be entitled to a variance only if they could establish that the variance was necessary for the reasonable use of the land. * * * At the outset, the Zoning Board's failure to address this issue is an error of law. Furthermore, in order to meet this requirement, appellants would have to show that a denial of the requested variance would make the property practically useless. *Abe Oil Co. v. Zoning Hearing Board of Richmond Twp.*, 168 Pa.Commw. at 120, 125, 649 A.2d 182, 185 (1994) (variance for construction of gas station not justified where property was amenable to "any number" of uses) * * * Because appellants' property can be used as a residential dwelling absent the 400–square foot deck, they have failed to meet this requirement for a grant of a variance.

3. Variance's Impact Upon Neighborhood

Appellants also had to establish that the variance would "not alter the essential character of the neighborhood or district in which the property is located" or be contrary to the public interest. Although the zoning board found that the variance would not be contrary to the public interest, the only factual finding on which that conclusion was based was that the objections to the variance were related to "precedence and aesthetics."

Appellee stated in his appeal that the variance would permit the construction of a deck further out over the hillside than any other property in the neighborhood, thereby obstructing the view of the Ohio River from other properties along the street and substantially altering the character of the neighborhood. Appellee's concerns that the variance will set a precedent for the granting of future variances which will result in an obstruction of the view of the Ohio River afforded from the properties along Grandview Avenue is a concern that the "essential character" of the neighborhood will be altered as a result of the variance. The zoning board's failure to consider appellee's concerns or otherwise address the effect of the variance on the neighborhood was a failure to address a requirement of the statute. * * *

4. Variance Must Be the Least Intrusive Solution

Finally, once the zoning board determines that a variance is justified, the variance granted must be the minimum variance necessary to afford relief, resulting in the least modification of the regulation at issue. No testimony was heard by the zoning board as to the possibility of less drastic alternatives. * * *

Because the zoning board committed both a manifest abuse of discretion in determining that appellants had established an unnecessary hardship and numerous errors of law in failing to address the majority of the requirements under both the state and local zoning laws, the Commonwealth Court did not exceed its standard of review in reversing the order. * * *

For the foregoing reasons, the order of the Commonwealth Court is affirmed.

[Concurring opinion omitted.]

Notes

1. The universal standard for granting a variance from the literal terms of the zoning ordinance is hardship. As you might expect, defining that term has been anything but simple for the courts. Consider the following examples:

(a) R–N–R Associates v. Zoning Board of Review, 100 R.I. 7, 210 A.2d 653 (1965), mentioned in Bryden, Zoning: Rigid, Flexible or Fluid?, 44 J. Urban L. 287, 308 (1967), illustrates the showing which one court required to be made by an applicant for a variance in order to demonstrate sufficient hardship. How "hard" should the "hardship" be? This case involved an application for a variance to allow the operation of a laundromat in a C–1 district when the zoning provisions only permitted the operation of laundromats in C–2 districts. The court in affirming a denial of the variance, stated that "it is the purpose of the variance to immunize zoning legislation against attack on the ground that it may in some instances operate to effect a taking of property without just compensation." The court added: "It is important, in our opinion, that zoning boards of review be informed that the right of a landowner to a variance turns upon a showing of unnecessary hardship, that is, a showing that an ordinance restriction deprives him of all beneficial use of his land. When such is established, confiscation must be avoided by the grant of some alternate use by way of a variance. The provision of the statute that such use, when granted by way of variance, be not contrary to the public interest does not operate to negative a landowner's right to a variance in a proper case. It simply restricts the board as to the scope and character of the use that may be allowed by way of variance in order to relieve a landowner from the confiscatory effect of a literal enforcement of the pertinent provision of the ordinance." Does this statement go too far? Must there be the equivalent of a taking or confiscation of the property or its beneficial use before a variance may be granted? See similarly, Mount Pleasant Realty & Constr. Co. v. Zoning Bd. of Review, 100 R.I. 31, 210 A.2d 877 (1965), in which the Rhode Island court affirmed a denial of an application for a variance to the zoning ordinance to allow petitioner to build a store building in a residential area, the court stating that there was no proof that "devoting the property to residential purposes would result in a loss of all beneficial use." Also see Rozes v. Smith, 120 R.I. 515, 388 A.2d 816 (1978).

(b) Compare with the Rhode Island cases cited previously, Brown v. Beuc, 384 S.W.2d 845 (Mo.App.1964), in which it was held that a lack of parking facilities was not a sufficient ground to prevent the enforcement of a provision requiring a front yard of not less than 25 feet in a multiple family dwelling district. The court stated that "the practical difficulty or undue hardship relied on as a ground for variance must be unusual or peculiar to the property involved and must be different from that suffered throughout the zone or neighborhood." The court added: "When we say inherent in the land and that the hardship must be due to conditions not personal to the owner, but rather to conditions affecting the land, we mean such hardships as result from the peculiar topography or condition of the land which makes the land unsuitable for the use permitted in the zone in which it lies." Although the variance was denied, the test seems to be less stringent than that employed in Rhode Island. Of course, as the Missouri case indicates, an applicant must do more than establish economic or financial hardship; he must establish a hardship which is unique or peculiar to the property involved. See Dishler v. Zoning Bd. of Adjustment, 414 Pa. 244, 199 A.2d 418 (1964); and Appeal of McClure, 415 Pa. 285, 203 A.2d 534 (1964). In the McClure case, the land zoned for residential purposes was apparently no longer suitable for residential use, but the court held that this did not require that a variance be granted to permit the erection of a branch bank, since the answer lay in rezoning rather than in seeking a variance.

(c) One consideration which arises is illustrated by Booe v. Zoning Bd. of Appeals, 151 Conn. 681, 202 A.2d 245 (1964), in which the court stated: "We have repeatedly held that the hardship which justifies a board of appeals in granting a variance must be one which originates from the zoning ordinance. When the claimed hardship arises because of the actions of the applicant, the board is without power to grant a variance." In this case the landowner had created his own difficulty by conveying away a substantial amount of land, while retaining only a four-acre parcel, which he sought to use for a hotel in contravention of a five-acre requirement in the zoning ordinance. See also Appeal of McClure, supra; and Smith v. Zoning Bd. of Appeals, 347 Mass. 755, 200 N.E.2d 279 (1964).

(d) If the variance involved the construction of a swimming pool and related recreational facilities in an area zoned residential, could this be justified as being in keeping with the spirit and intent of the zoning ordinance and as enhancing rather than adversely affecting the character of the neighborhood? Or should the "unnecessary hardship" doctrine be applied? See City of Little Rock v. Leawood Property Owners' Ass'n, 242 Ark. 451, 413 S.W.2d 877 (1967).

If anything, the foregoing cases seem to suggest that policies relative to variances differ from state to state even when the same general "unnecessary hardship" principle is expressly followed in one way or another. Yet facts and figures available suggest that a substantial majority of all applications for departures from zoning requirements are approved in locations that are widely separated geographically. (See Note, Administrative Discretion in Zoning, 82 Harv.L.Rev. 668, 673 (1969), which concludes that if the test of a system is the number of departures from it, zoning is a spectacular failure.)

2. In most jurisdictions, the requirement for obtaining a variance also states that the problem causing the need comes from the property and not from any act of the owner. Not too many cases present this issue, but one interesting example can be found in Board of Zoning Appeals of Evansville and Vanderburgh County v. Kempf, 656 N.E.2d 1201 (Ind.App.1995). In this case, the property owner had his development plat approved on condition that he install a 10–foot wide greenspace across the front of his property. After the property was developed, the city discovered that the owner had paved over the 10–foot area where the green space was to have been installed. The owner then sought a variance on the ground that none of the other adjacent business had green space and that economic necessity established a hardship. The court held for the city, stating: "The Board concluded that Kempf was not entitled to the requested variance because he himself had created the need for the variance by paving over the area in question. We hold this requirement advances a legitimate governmental interest in

preventing the type of 'end run' around the zoning ordinances and procedures employed in the present case."

SASSO v. OSGOOD

Court of Appeals of New York, 1995.
86 N.Y.2d 374, 633 N.Y.S.2d 259, 657 N.E.2d 254.

[The owner of a waterfront parcel of land containing a boathouse sought a variance to allow him to demolish the existing structure and build a larger boathouse. Neighbors objected to the application on the ground that the proposed boathouse would obstruct their access to light, air, and view, and that the foundations of their boathouses and septic systems would be damaged by construction and altered drainage patterns. The zoning board granted the variance and the neighbors appealed; the intermediate appellate court determined that the applicant had failed to show "practical difficulties sufficient to justify an area variance" primarily because he had not shown that strict enforcement of the ordinance would cause him a significant economic injury.]

SIMONS, JUDGE

* * *

Prior to July 1, 1992, the authority of town zoning boards of appeal to grant variances from local zoning ordinances was defined in former Town Law § 267. Zoning boards were authorized to grant variances "[w]here there are practical difficulties or unnecessary hardships in the way of carrying out the strict letter of [local] ordinances" provided that "the spirit of the ordinance shall be observed, public safety and welfare secured and substantial justice done" (former Town Law § 267[5]). Although the former statute did not distinguish between "use" and "area" variances or assign the specific tests to them, court decisions generally applied the "unnecessary hardship" test in use variance cases, while requiring a demonstration of "practical difficulties" in area variance cases (*see, Matter of Village of Bronxville v. Francis*, 1 A.D.2d 236, 238, aff'd 1 N.Y.2d 839; *see also, Matter of Hoffman v. Harris*, 17 N.Y.2d 138, 144; *Dauernheim, Inc. v. Town Bd. of Town of Hempstead*, 33 N.Y.2d 468, 471; *Matter of Off Shore Rest. Corp. v. Linden*, 30 N.Y.2d 160, 168).

A three-pronged test of "unnecessary hardship" was clearly articulated more than fifty years ago (*see, Matter of Otto v. Steinhilber*, 282 N.Y. 71, 76) and that test, now embodied in Town Law § 267–b(2), has been applied in use variance cases without substantial difficulty. * * * The definition and application of the "practical difficulties standard" has proven far more troublesome.

Lacking a statutory definition, we have recognized the existence of "practical difficulties" where the unusual topography of the subject parcel interfered with construction of a building (*see, Matter of Wilcox v. Zoning Bd. of Appeals of City of Yonkers*, 17 N.Y.2d 249, 255), and where area variances were required to build a house on an amply sized but oddly shaped parcel that did not meet frontage and side yard requirements (*Conley v. Town of Brookhaven Zoning Bd. of Appeals*, 40 N.Y.2d 309, 316). We have also suggested that an area variance could be granted upon a showing of "significant economic injury" (*Matter of Fulling v. Palumbo*, 21 N.Y.2d 30, 33; see also, *Matter of Cowan v. Kern*, 41 N.Y.2d 591, 596). In *Matter of National Merritt v. Weist* (41 N.Y.2d 438) we considered both unique topography and economic injury relevant to the application for an area variance. We have noted several times, however, that there is no precise definition of the term "practical difficulties" (*Matter of Doyle v. Amster*, 79 N.Y.2d 592, 595; *Matter of Fuhst v. Foley*, 45 N.Y.2d 441, 445), observing that "[t]he basic inquiry at all times is whether strict application of the ordinance in a given case will serve a valid public purpose which outweighs the injury to the property owner" (*Matter of De Sena v. Board of Zoning Appeals of Inc. Vil. of Hempstead*, 45 N.Y.2d 105, 108).

Without any legislative guidance defining the requirements for an area variance, the courts began to develop a list of criteria to be applied under former Town Law § 267 (*see, Matter of Wachsberger v. Michalis*, 19 Misc.2d 909, aff'd 18 A.D.2d 921; see also, *Matter of Friendly Ice Cream Corp. v. Barrett*, 106 A.D.2d 748; *Matter of Human Dev. Servs. of Port Chester v. Zoning Bd. of Appeals of Vil. of Port Chester*, 110 A.D.2d 135, aff'd 67 N.Y.2d 702). Although originally offered as guidance for determining whether "the spirit of the ordinance is observed, public safety and welfare secured and substantial justice done" (*see, Wachsberger v. Michalis, supra*, 19 Misc.2d, at 912 [Meyer, J.]), these criteria came to be known as the "practical difficulties" test (see, 2 Anderson, New York Zoning Law and Practice, § 23.34, at 208–209 [3d ed.]). These criteria notwithstanding, precise and concise definition of "practical difficulties" never emerged from the case law. In particular, it remained unclear whether a showing of "significant economic injury" was part of the "practical difficulties" test.* * *

Effective July 1, 1992, the Legislature repealed former Town Law § 267, and enacted comprehensive provisions governing zoning boards of appeals. Unlike former Town Law § 267, the new statute defines "use" and "area" variances, as well as the criteria to be evaluated in determining applications for each. Use variances may be granted upon an applicant's showing "that applicable zoning regulations and restrictions have caused unnecessary hardship," expressly incorporating that phrase as it existed in former Town Law § 267. The statute defines the elements of proof necessary to establish unnecessary hardship, essentially codifying the criteria originally set forth in *Matter of Otto v. Steinhilber* (282 N.Y. 71, 76, *supra*), with the added requirement that the applicant prove that "the alleged hardship has not been self-created" (Town Law § 267–b[2][b][4]).

The standard for area variances is governed by Town Law § 267–b(3) in a provision that does not expressly require the applicant to prove "practical difficulties". It states:

In making its determination [whether to grant an area variance], the zoning board of appeals shall take into consideration *the benefit to the applicant if the variance is granted, as weighed against the detriment to the health, safety and welfare of the neighborhood or community by such grant.* In making such determination the board shall also consider: (1) whether an undesirable change will be produced in the character of the neighborhood or a detriment to nearby properties will be created by the granting of the area variance; (2) whether the benefit sought by the applicant can be achieved by some other method, feasible for the applicant to pursue, other than an area variance; (3) whether the requested area variance is substantial; (4) whether the proposed variance will have an adverse effect or impact on the physical or environmental conditions in the neighborhood or district; and (5) whether the alleged difficulty was self-created, which consideration shall be relevant to the decision of the board of appeals, but shall not necessarily preclude the granting of the area variance. (Town Law § 267–b[3][b] [emphasis added]).

The five factors listed parallel the criteria previously used by the lower courts and identified by Professor Anderson as the "practical difficulties" test. * * *

The precise question posed on this appeal is whether by failing to include the phrase "practical difficulties" in the new statute, the Legislature has eliminated the requirement that the applicant for an area variance make that showing.

* * *

Reference to the bill jacket for chapter 692 of the Laws of 1991 supports intervenor's contention that an applicant for an area variance need not show "practical difficulties" as required under former Town Law § 267 and prior case law. The Legislature enacted the statute to clarify existing law by setting forth readily understandable guidelines for both zoning boards of appeal and applicants for variances and to eliminate the confusion that then surrounded applications for area variances. As one memorandum in the bill jacket states:

The rules governing the granting of area variances that have been established by the courts are not nearly as clear as those governing use variances, and the result has been a great deal of confusion by boards of appeals, with a high degree of potential exposure to litigation. The new Town Law, section 267–b(3) and Village Law, section 7–712–b(3) resolve this problem by establishing a statutory test for the issuance of area variances which is flexible and which incorporates what we believe are the best features of the court decisions in order to protect the community (Bill Jacket, L 1991, ch 692, at 26, Memorandum of Executive Deputy Secretary of State James Baldwin).

The same intent may be found in several other memoranda and establish that the legislation was enacted to aid laypersons—both applicants and lay members of zoning boards of appeal—in understanding and implementing the existing case-law; it was intended to have "little impact on existing laws since the main thrust of the legislation is to clarify and establish, in statute, the powers of the Zoning Board as already defined by jurisprudence." * * *

We conclude Town Law § 267–b(3)(b) requires the Zoning Board to engage in a balancing test, weighing "the benefit to the applicant" against "the detriment to the health, safety and welfare of the neighborhood or community" if the area variance is granted, and that an applicant need not show "practical difficulties" as that test was formerly applied.

Applying the new statute we conclude that the action of the Henderson Zoning Board was rational and not arbitrary and capricious. * * * As required by Town Law § 267–b(3)(b), the Zoning Board addressed five specific criteria. First, it determined that no undesirable change would be produced in the character of the neighborhood, because Graham's Creek serves primarily as a site for boathouses and commercial marinas, and that the addition of intervenor's proposed three-slip boathouse will not result in a significant increase in boat traffic or noise. The Zoning Board's conclusion that the variance will have minimal impact on nearby properties is supported by evidence that intervenor's boathouse will comply with all setback and height restrictions imposed by local ordinances. In making this finding, the Board had before it and considered the conditions imposed on intervenor's construction by the Town Planning Board which mitigated concerns voiced by petitioners (see, Town Law § 267–b[3][b][1]).

Next, the Zoning Board concluded that no alternatives other than the grant of area variances existed, because intervenor's lot is of substandard size, and no improvement to the property could be made without the requested lot size and width variances. The Zoning Board then acknowledged that the variances sought were substantial, but that there was no available adjacent land for intervenor to purchase so that he could meet the zoning requirements, and granting the variances would merely permit intervenor to use his property for a permitted use equal to all other neighboring lots. The Zoning Board's conclusion under subdivision (4) that granting the variances would lead to no adverse effect or impact on the neighborhood other than the previously discussed effect on petitioners is also supported by the record.

The only determination of the Zoning Board not supported by the record is its conclusion that intervenor's difficulty was not self-created. The record reveals that the parcel was of substandard lot size when intervenor purchased it in 1989 and it is well established that, in such circumstances, the variance applicant's difficulty or hardship is self-created. Nevertheless, the statute expressly states that the fact that the applicant's difficulty was self-created does not necessarily preclude the granting of the area variance. Under all the circumstances presented, the

Board did not act arbitrarily in granting a variance notwithstanding the applicant's self-created difficulty.

In sum, the Zoning Board weighed the benefit to intervenor—the opportunity to fully use his property for a permitted use—against any detriment to the health, safety and welfare of the neighborhood or community, and determined to grant the variance. Its conclusions find ample support from the photographs and other materials in the record, and its determination was not irrational, arbitrary or capricious. Thus, the Appellate Division erred in reversing the order of Supreme Court confirming the determination.

Accordingly, the order of the Appellate Division should be reversed, with costs to intervenor against petitioners, and the judgment of Supreme Court, Jefferson County reinstated.

Order reversed, with costs to intervenor against petitioners, and judgment of Supreme Court, Jefferson County, reinstated.

Notes

1. Other jurisdictions have recognized a different standard of hardship for area variances as opposed to use variances. See, e.g., Board of Adjustment v. Kwik–Check Realty, Inc., 389 A.2d 1289 (Del.1978); Arens v. City of St. Louis, 872 S.W.2d 631 (Mo.App.1994). But see Ouimette v. City of Somersworth, 119 N.H. 292, 402 A.2d 159 (1979), where the court held that the standard of proof is the same for both area and use variances.

2. In a jurisdiction applying the law of this case, would the result have differed if the facts were those of the Larsen case?

McMORROW v. BOARD OF ADJUSTMENT FOR CITY OF TOWN & COUNTRY

Missouri Court of Appeals, Eastern District, 1989.
765 S.W.2d 700.

SMITH, PRESIDING JUDGE.

Petitioners appeal from a judgment of the trial court which upheld the action of the Board of Adjustment of the City of Town and Country refusing to grant variances from the zoning ordinances to petitioners. We affirm.

Petitioners' lot is slightly over an acre in area. It is shaped, however, like an anteater's snout, with widths of 31.25 feet and 193.04 feet on the ends and lengths of 523.65 feet and 562.87 feet on the sides. Because of setback and building lines established by the Town and Country ordinances, the area on which structures are permitted on the lot is quite restricted. In fact the single family residence on the property is nonconforming because it infringes upon both set-back and building lines. The residence was built prior to annexation of the property by Town and Country. The area is zoned Suburban Estate which is single family residential with a one acre minimum lot size. The McMorrows desire to build an in-ground swimming pool on the lot. The only feasible location, because of the lot configuration and topography, would require substantial variance from the set-back and building line requirements of the ordinances. In addition, a variance would be required for expansion of what is already a non-conforming structure, the residence. The Board denied the variances requested on the basis that there was no showing of "practical difficulties or unnecessary hardships" requiring granting of the variances.

It is petitioners' position that by establishing that the configuration and topography of their lot makes construction of the pool impossible without the variances they have carried their burden for obtaining the variances. We disagree.

The authority to grant a variance should be exercised sparingly and only under exceptional circumstances. *Matthew v. Smith,* 707 S.W.2d 411 (Mo. banc 1986) l.c. 413. Otherwise continued viability of the zoning code is compromised. *Ogawa v. City of Des Peres,* 745 S.W.2d 238 (Mo.App. 1987) [8]. The statutory authorization for granting variances is found in Sec. 89.090(3) RSMo 1986, and occurs upon a finding of "practical difficulties or unnecessary hardship." The Town and Country ordinances parallel this statutory mandate. In *Matthew v. Smith, supra,* [2], the court indicated that "practical difficulties" was a slightly less rigorous test than "unnecessary hardship" and then stated:

"To obtain a use variance, an applicant must demonstrate, *inter alia,* unnecessary hardship; and to obtain an area variance, an applicant must establish, *inter alia,* the existence of conditions *slightly* less rigorous than unnecessary hardship." (Emphasis in original).

Petitioners seek area variances. "Unnecessary hardship" has been considered in this state as involving circumstances where the refusal to grant the variance would amount to a denial of any permitted use under the ordinances. *Ogawa v. City of Des Peres, supra,* [13]; *Conner v. Herd,* 452 S.W.2d 272 (Mo.App.1970) [14]; *Brown v. Beuc,* 384 S.W.2d 845 (Mo.App.1964) [9]. Such denial may include not only the impossibility of use but unwarranted economic hardship in achieving a permitted use. *Conner v. Herd, supra* [10, 11]. It is clear from the cases that variances are to be granted only for severe interferences with the ability of the landowner to use his land and not for "mere inconvenience." *Volkman v. City of Kirkwood,* 624 S.W.2d 58 (Mo.App.1981) [5, 6].

The record does not establish that petitioners have carried their burden to justify the variances sought. The land is useable, and is being used, for the use permitted by the zoning ordinances as a single family residence. Petitioners want to add to that residential complex a swimming pool, a permitted structure in the district. They have failed to establish that a swimming pool is a necessity, that they will suffer undue financial burdens if one is not built, or that their satisfactory residential use of the property is impossible without a pool. Throughout the hearing the Board sought petitioners' explanation of why the absence of a pool constituted a "practical difficulty" or "unnecessary hardship." No explanation was advanced other than that the configuration and topography made construction of a pool impossible without the variances. That a structure permitted in the area cannot be built because of the zoning restrictions does not alone establish that a variance must be granted. Even under the "slightly less rigorous" test of area variances set forth in *Matthew v. Smith,* the record does not authorize the variances sought.

Judgment Affirmed.

Notes

1. Also see City of Ladue v. Zwick, 904 S.W.2d 470 (Mo.App.1995), where the property owner was denied a variance to build a tennis court. The property owner argued that a tennis court must be located on a north/south axis and that such orientation was precluded by the hilly topography and odd shape of his lot. The court said: "[N]ot every lot, even in Ladue, is a buildable lot. It is elementary that not every odd scrap of land in an unrestricted commercial district is suitable for a skyscraper, even though a skyscraper may be a 'permitted use.' Likewise, even though [the ordinance] permits tennis courts in residential districts, it is the proposed owner's burden to find a buildable lot. To take advantage of the City's permitted use, a tennis enthusiast must find a lot with less hills, larger acreage, or a more conventional shape."

2. Many states, in their zoning enabling legislation, prohibit the granting of use variances. In these states, the distinction between unnecessary hardship for use variances and practical difficulties for area variances is meaningless. Should hardship be construed strictly in states that do not allow use variances? See International Funeral Services v. DeKalb County, 244 Ga. 707, 261 S.E.2d 625 (1979). Also see Nucholls v. Board of Adjustment of City of Tulsa, 560 P.2d 556 (Okl.1976), where the court held that the city zoning ordinance was unconstitutional insofar as it prohibited the granting of use variances.

3. Should a court be more or less ready to permit a variance where expansion of a non-conforming use is involved? See Grundlehner v. Dangler, 29 N.J. 256, 148 A.2d 806, 812 (1959). Compare Johnny Cake, Inc. v. Zoning Bd. of Appeals of Burlington, 180 Conn. 296, 429 A.2d 883 (1980), with In re Kenney, 374 N.W.2d 271 (Minn.1985). In the Connecticut case, the court held that the zoning board had no authority to grant a variance extending a nonconforming use; the applicant, a seminary, wanted to convert an old fire watchtower to an FM radio transmitter. In the Minnesota case, the court held that the board of adjustment had the authority to issue a variance that would expand a nonconforming boathouse, despite language in the enabling act stating that "no variance may be granted that would allow any use that is prohibited in the zoning district." Also see Burbridge v. Governing Body of the Twp. of Mine Hill, 117 N.J. 376, 568 A.2d 527 (1990), where the court held that a variance to expand a nonconforming use could be granted on the ground that the final result would be more aesthetic (the nonconforming use was an auto body repair shop).

4. On the relationship between variances and special use permits, see Dallstream and Hunt, Variations, Exceptions and Special Uses, 1954 U.Ill.

L.F. 213, and for a case illustration, see Waeckerle v. Board of Zoning Adjustment, 525 S.W.2d 351 (Mo.App.1975).

5. On the problem of notice in the variance procedure, see the exhaustive annotation, "Construction and Application of Statute or Ordinance Provisions Requiring Notice as Prerequisite to Granting Variance or Exception to Zoning Requirement," 38 A.L.R.3d 167 (1971).

6. Several interesting and instructive articles describe the results of empirical observation of particular zoning boards of adjustment in the handling of variance cases. See Dukeminier and Stapleton, The Zoning Board of Adjustment: A Case Study of Misrule, 50 Ky.L.J. 273 (1962); Note, Zoning Variances and Exceptions: The Philadelphia Experience, 103 U.Pa. L.Rev. 516 (1955); Comment, Zoning: Variance Administration in Alameda County, 50 Calif.L.Rev. 101 (1962). Dukeminier and Stapleton conclude that (1) the issues are not made clear; (2) the board frequently does not follow the law or find facts or state reasons, or have a correct view of its function; and (3) that Euclidean zoning after 75 years has hardening of the arteries that even massive doses of Geritol might not cure. Newer land use control techniques, perfected in the 40 years since this article was written, have possibly aided somewhat in reducing the reliance on traditional administrative forms of relief. These techniques, such as cluster zoning, zero lot line development, or the planned unit development, however, are customarily applied to larger tracts of land and do not address themselves to the problem of abuses relating to one or two lots—which is where the abuses generally occur.

(2) Special Use Permit Cases

CITY OF CHICAGO HEIGHTS v. LIVING WORD OUTREACH FULL GOSPEL

Supreme Court of Illinois, 2001.
196 Ill.2d 1, 749 N.E.2d 916, 255 Ill.Dec. 434.

JUSTICE MCMORROW delivered the opinion of the court:

* * *

Under the City's zoning ordinance, the authority to grant or deny an application for a special use permit is reserved to the city council. Prior to the council taking action on an application for a special use permit, the City's zoning board of appeals and the City's plan commission must review the application and make a recommendation. These recommendations are forwarded to the city council, which then decides whether to approve or deny the application. The City's zoning ordinance states that the zoning board of appeals may recommend to the city council that a special use be allowed only if the following six criteria are satisfied:

> "(a) That the establishment, maintenance or operation of the special use will not be unreasonably detrimental to or endanger the public health, safety, morals, comfort or general welfare;
>
> (b) That the special use will not be injurious to the use and enjoyment of other property in the immediate vicinity for the

purposes already permitted nor substantially diminish and impair property values within the neighborhood;

(c) That the establishment of the special use will not impede the normal and orderly development and improvement of surrounding property for uses permitted in the district;

(d) That adequate utilities, access roads, drainage and/or other necessary facilities have been or are being provided;

(e) That adequate measures have been or will be taken to provide ingress and egress so designed as to minimize traffic congestion in public streets;

(f) That the special use shall in all other respects conform to the applicable regulations of the district in which it is located, except as such regulations may in each instance be modified by the city council pursuant to the recommendations of the zoning board of appeals." Chicago Heights Municipal Code, app. A, Zoning, § 12–6.6 (1973).

In January 1996, after taking possession of the property at 400 West Lincoln Highway, Living Word submitted an application to the City for a special use permit. A public hearing was held before the City's zoning board of appeals on March 13, 1996. After the hearing, the board forwarded Living Word's application to the City's plan commission. On March 27, 1996, the plan commission recommended that Living Word's application for a special use permit be denied. On April 3, 1996, the zoning board of appeals also recommended that the application be denied. Finally, on April 15, 1996, the city council agreed with the recommendations of the plan commission and the zoning board of appeals and denied Living Word's application for a special use permit.

The city council ultimately denied Living Word's application based upon a comprehensive development plan adopted by the City in December 1995. This plan targeted West Lincoln Highway, the area in which the church is located, for development as a commercial corridor. The concern of the council was that granting a special use permit for a noncommercial use, such as a church, would be at odds with the goals of the comprehensive plan.

Although the city council denied Living Word's application for a special use permit, the church continued to hold services in the building at 400 West Lincoln Highway. Eventually, the City filed suit in the circuit court of Cook County, seeking to permanently enjoin the church from continuing its services. Living Word responded with 14 affirmative defenses which were later refiled in a 14–count counterclaim. Three of the counts in the counterclaim are relevant here. Count VI of the counterclaim alleged that the city council's denial of Living Word's application for a special use permit violated Living Word's right to the free exercise of religion under the first and fourteenth amendments of the United States Constitution. Count XIII alleged that Living Word was merely continuing the Masons' permitted nonconforming use of the property. Count XIV alleged that the city council's denial of Living Word's application for a special use permit was "arbitrary, capricious and unreasonable in light of [sic] fact that use of the property by [Living Word] meets standards (a) through (f) of section 12–6.6 of the zoning code of the City."

A bench trial was held in December 1997. During this trial, the court heard testimony from several witnesses, including Maria Arbeen, a real estate appraiser. Arbeen testified that, in her opinion, Living Word had satisfied all the criteria for obtaining a special use permit listed in the City's zoning ordinance.

The court also heard testimony from Joseph Christofanelli, the city planner for the City of Chicago Heights. Christofanelli stated that the City was suffering economic problems and was approximately $57 million in debt. Because of this, Christofanelli explained, the City needed to concentrate on developing commercial areas that would generate real estate and sales taxes. The West Lincoln Highway corridor was of particular importance to the City because that corridor was the City's best commercial, tax-revenue-generating area. Christofanelli stated that permitting any noncommercial use within the West Lincoln Highway corridor would be detrimental to surrounding commercial properties because these properties would miss out on the "spill-over effect" whereby customers patronize more than one business in an area. Christofanelli stated that Living Word's application for a special use permit was denied because "the church was something we had not envisioned for that particular corridor, and here, again, that's based upon the Comprehensive Plan."

The court heard testimony similar to Christofanelli's from Steven Albert, a real estate appraiser. Albert stated that any noncommercial use in the West Lincoln Highway corridor would be incompatible with, and detrimental to, the goals of the City's comprehensive plan. In addition to the foregoing testimony, the circuit judge also reviewed several exhibits, including the City's zoning ordinance, the City's comprehensive plan, the City's official zoning map, Living Word's special use application, minutes from city council meetings, minutes from meetings of the City's zoning board of appeals, minutes from a meeting of the City's plan commission, and numerous diagrams and letters.

* * *

[The trial court denied the city's request for a permanent injunction against the church, finding that the church had met all applicable standards for the special use permit. This ruling was vacated for jurisdictional reasons by the appellate court which then decided the case in the city's favor under the Illinois Religious Freedom Restoration Act, finding that the Act was not violated by the denial of the permit. The church appealed on several grounds including that the city's denial of its application was arbitrary and capricious as a matter of general zoning law. Portions of the case applicable to other claims of the church are omitted.]

ADMINISTRATIVE ACTION

In general, a "special use" is a type of property use that is expressly permitted within a zoning district by the controlling zoning ordinance so long as the use meets certain criteria or conditions. "The purpose of special uses is to provide for those uses that are either necessary or generally appropriate for a community but may require special regulation because of unique or unusual impacts associated with them." S. Connor, *Zoning,* in Municipal Law & Practice § 13.17 (Ill. Inst. for Cont. Legal Educ. 2000). A church may be an appropriate special use because, depending upon its size and location, it may create traffic or parking problems within the neighborhood in which it is located. For example, the number of parking spaces needed by a church may vary considerably depending upon the availability of parking spaces in the neighborhood at the time the church holds services. Thus, although a church might be considered a desirable and appropriate use within a zoning district, the municipality may classify it as a special use and may require, for example, that parking problems be resolved before granting a special use permit to a property owner that would allow the owner to use the property as a church. See generally 3 E. Ziegler, Rathkopf's Law of Zoning & Planning, ch. 41 (4th ed. 1992); 3 K. Young, Anderson's American Law of Zoning, ch. 21 (4th ed. 1996). In Illinois, municipal special uses are authorized by section 11–13–1.1 of the Illinois Municipal Code (65 ILCS 5/11–13–1.1 (West 1994)).

Special uses must be clearly distinguished from use variances. "[A] variance is 'authority extended to a property owner to use his property in a manner forbidden by the zoning enactment,' " generally upon a showing of hardship. 3 K. Young, Anderson's American Law of Zoning § 20.03, at 416 (4th ed. 1996), quoting *Mitchell Land Co. v. Planning & Zoning Board of Appeals,* 140 Conn. 527, 532, 102 A.2d 316, 319 (1953). A special use, on the other hand, " 'allows [a property owner] to put his property to a use the enactment expressly permits.' " 3 K. Young, Anderson's American Law of Zoning § 20.03, at 416 (4th ed. 1996), quoting *Mitchell Land Co. v. Planning & Zoning Board of Appeals,* 140 Conn. 527, 532–33, 102 A.2d 316, 319 (1953). In sharp contrast to a variance, the inclusion of a special use within a zoning ordinance " 'is tantamount to a legislative finding that the permitted use is in harmony with the general zoning plan and will not adversely affect the neighborhood.' " 3 K. Young, Anderson's American Law of Zoning § 21.13, at 126 (4th ed. 1999 Supp.), quoting *Twin County Recycling Corp. v. Yevoli,* 90 N.Y.2d 1000, 1001, 665 N.Y.S.2d 627, 688 N.E.2d 501, 502 (1997). "A special exception use is a 'permitted use' when allowed under a special permit. Thus, there has been a local legislative determination that the use, as such, is neither inconsistent with the public's health, safety, morals or general welfare, nor out of harmony with the town's general zoning plan." 3 E. Ziegler, Rathkopf's Law of Zoning & Planning § 41.08, at 41–34 (4th ed. 1992); see also 83 Am.Jur.2d *Zoning & Planning* § 974, at 814 (1992) ("Where a zoning ordinance authorizes a business as a special use, such authorization is tantamont [sic] to a legislative conclusion that the use is appropriate in the district"). Thus, in the instant case, the City zoning ordinance's authorization of churches as a special use along West Lincoln Highway constitutes a legislative finding that churches, as such, are compatible with the surrounding property uses in that area.

In the case at bar, the city council's reason for denying Living Word's application for a special use permit is not in dispute. Stated simply, the city council denied Living Word's application because it believed that all noncommercial uses were incompatible uses along West Lincoln Highway. The council based this belief on the City's then recently adopted comprehensive development plan. This plan, adopted by the City approximately one month before Living Word submitted its application for a special use permit, addresses many areas of concern for the City, including demographic and economic trends occurring within the City. One portion of the plan is devoted to land use and highlights the West Lincoln Highway corridor as an area that should be "improved as an auto commercial area oriented to a regional clientele." Relying on this stated goal, the city council concluded that to grant a special use permit for any noncommercial use, including churches, along West Lincoln Highway would frustrate the plan to develop that area as a strong commercial corridor. For this reason, the council denied Living Word's application.

It must be emphasized that the city council's objection to Living Word's application for a special use permit did not center on any attribute of Living Word that is unique to this particular church or its facilities. The council did not conclude, for example, that the church will impede the orderly development of surrounding properties or lower their value because the church building is unusually large, or because the church's congregation generates traffic problems along West Lincoln Highway. Instead, Living Word's application was denied because the council believed that any noncommercial use of property located in the West Lincoln Highway corridor would have a negative effect on the commercial development of that corridor and, therefore, that all noncommercial uses should be completely excluded.

It is clear that the city council's rationale for denying Living Word's special use permit application is at odds with the legislative intent expressed in the City's zoning ordinance. According to the zoning ordinance, and in contrast to the council's explanation for denying Living Word's application, churches are not a *per se* incompatible use along Lincoln Highway. Quite the contrary, the City zoning ordinance's inclusion of churches as a special use in the West Lincoln Highway corridor "is equivalent to a legislative finding that [such a] use is one that is in harmony with the other uses permitted in the district." 3 E. Ziegler, Rathkopf's Law of Zoning & Planning § 41.05, at 41–21 through 41–22 (4th ed. 1992).

In light of the above, the question arises as to whether the city council, in denying Living Word's application for a special use permit, could legitimately set the legislative intent expressed in the zoning ordinance to one side and, instead, rely upon the developmental goals expressed in the comprehensive plan as the basis for its decision. For the following reasons, we believe the answer to this question is no.

* * *

There is nothing of record in this case which would indicate that Living Word's use of its property as a church would have any adverse effects on surrounding properties above and beyond those that would inherently be associated with any church located in the West Lincoln Highway corridor. Accordingly, in the case at bar, if the city council's denial of the permit application is considered an administrative decision, it cannot be upheld.

The existence of the comprehensive plan, and the council's reliance upon that plan, does not alter this conclusion. The special use criteria in the City's zoning ordinance do not include conformance with the comprehensive plan as a requirement that must be met before a special use permit may be granted. See E. Ziegler, Rathkopf's Law of Zoning & Planning § 41.08, at 41–37 (4th ed. 1992) ("Zoning ordinances may expressly provide as a standard for issuance of a special permit that the proposed use at the particular location be compatible with or not negatively impact the local comprehensive zoning plan"). Moreover, the City's zoning ordinance is law; the comprehensive plan is not. As our Municipal Code explains, "[an official comprehensive] plan shall be advisory and in and of itself shall not be construed to regulate or control the use of private property in any way, except as to such part thereof as has been implemented by ordinances duly enacted by the corporate authorities." 65 ILCS 5/11-12-6 (West 1994); see also *Chase v. City of Minneapolis,* 401 N.W.2d 408, 413 (Minn.App.1987) (incompatibility with comprehensive plan insufficient basis for denying conditional use permit); *Amoco Oil Co. v. City of Minneapolis,* 395 N.W.2d 115, 118 (Minn.App.1986) (same). Acting administratively, the city council is bound by the City's zoning ordinance, not the comprehensive plan. Thus, the city council's reliance on the comprehensive plan could not justify the decision to deny Living Word's application for a special use permit.

LEGISLATIVE ACTION

Even if one views the city council's decision to deny Living Word's application as a purely legislative act, that decision cannot be sustained under the justification offered by the city council. The City has emphasized that the council's decision to deny Living Word's application for a special use permit was based on a desire to exclude all noncommercial uses from the West Lincoln Highway corridor and not on any objection or ill-will directed to Living Word in particular. Further, as the City has made clear on appeal, the city council does not intend to apply this policy of excluding noncommercial uses from the West Lincoln Highway corridor on an *ad hoc* basis, but will, instead, consistently deny all noncommercial applications for special use permits. It is clear, therefore, that to uphold the rationale offered by the council for denying Living Word's application for a special use permit would result in the effective amendment of the City's zoning ordinance. Adopting the council's reasoning would completely remove churches from the list of special uses set forth in the City's zoning ordinance. Other noncommercial uses which are listed as special uses under the zoning ordinance, such as public parks and public libraries, would also be eliminated. A new zoning district, one exclusively commercial in character, would thus be created in the West Lincoln Highway corridor. Under the present circumstances, this *de facto* amendment of the City's zoning ordinance cannot be allowed.

* * *

In so holding, we do not mean, in any way, to diminish the severity of the economic problems facing the City or the City's need to address these problems by changing its zoning regulations. Our holding is simply that, if the city council wishes to unconditionally remove all noncommercial uses from the West Lincoln Highway corridor, it must amend the City's zoning ordinance to reflect that intent, and it must do so according to the amendment procedures set forth within the zoning ordinance.

* * *

For the foregoing reasons, the appellate court's vacation of the February 26, 1998, order is affirmed; the judgment of the appellate court that the trial court grant the injunctive relief sought by the City is reversed. The judgment of the circuit court denying the City's request for a permanent injunction against Living Word is affirmed; the circuit court's entry of its February 26, 1998, order is reversed, and that order is vacated. The cause is remanded to the circuit court to enter judgment ordering the City to grant Living Word's application for a special use permit.

Appellate court affirmed in part and reversed in part; circuit court vacated in part and affirmed in part; cause remanded.

Notes

1. In the Living Word case, we encounter a city whose zoning ordinance reserves to the city council the power to issue special use permits. This evidences a decision by the legislative body not to delegate this important function to the board of appeals, the planning board or commission, or other administrative agency. State law in Illinois did not provide the court sufficient guidance to determine whether the city council, in exercising this reserved authority, was acting in a legislative or an administrative capacity. It avoided the issue by finding that the denial was invalid either as an administrative or a legislative act. This illustrates the importance of identifying the capacity in which a local board is acting and determining whether it followed the applicable requirements. The court found that the city council, as a legislative body, could have changed the law and made the church ineligible for the permit, but that it would have had to follow the prescribed rules for amending the zoning ordinance, which it did not.

2. One constitutional principle which is particularly important in conditional use and special permit cases is the principle that the ordinance contain adequate standards for the issuance of the permit so that a reviewing court may ascertain whether the decision-maker stayed within the bounds of delegated authority. See, e.g., Alpha Portland Cement Co. v. Missouri Dept. of Natural Resources, 608 S.W.2d 451 (Mo.App.1980). The absence of standards would make the grant of a special permit or conditional use wholly discretionary with the agency. In Wakelin v. Town of Yarmouth, 523 A.2d 575 (Me.1987), the court struck down an ordinance which specified that the zoning board should grant a special exception if the proposed use is "compatible with existing uses" defining compatible "with respect to size, visual impact, intensity of use, proximity to other structures, and density of development." The court held that the definition was unconstitutionally vague and constituted an unlawful delegation of authority.

3. A question that arises frequently is whether the planning commission or zoning board can impose special conditions or restrictions on the special permit or conditional use. In Montgomery County v. Mossburg, 228 Md. 555, 180 A.2d 851 (1962), the court upheld the authority of the county to condition a special exception allowing a night club on the applicant's agreement to observe closing hours more restrictive than allowable under the state alcoholic beverage license. The court indicated that the reason for the special exception device was to enable the local authority to protect nearby properties and to tailor the scope of permission so as to strike a reasonable balance. Also see Stevenson v. Palmer, 223 Tenn. 485, 448 S.W.2d 67 (1969) (upholding a condition requiring an apartment complex developer to construct a brick wall around three sides of the complex); Vlahos Realty Co. v. Little Boar's Head Dist., 101 N.H. 460, 146 A.2d 257 (1958) (upholding an 11:00 p.m. closing hour as a condition to a variance); Van Sciver v. Zoning Bd. of Adjustment, 396 Pa. 646, 152 A.2d 717 (1959) (overruling a restriction on the hours of operation of a laundromat on the grounds that the restriction was erroneous, arbitrary and unreasonable); and Lough v. Zoning Bd. of Review, 74 R.I. 366, 60 A.2d 839 (1948) (sustaining the zoning board in granting an exception allowing a gasoline station and garage to be constructed at an intersection, since the zoning board attached nine conditions for the protection of neighboring property owners). Generally, see Strine, The Use of Conditions in Land–Use Control, 67 Dick.L.Rev. 109 (1963).

4. In Pollard v. Palm Beach County, 560 So.2d 1358 (Fla.App.1990), the court held that an applicant for a special exception who met all the standards specified in the ordinance could not be denied the exception because of neighbors' objections. (The exception was for an adult congregate living facility for the elderly.)

SECTION 4. NONCONFORMING USES

The policy of allowing nonconforming uses to continue originated in concerns that the application of zoning regulations to uses existing prior to the regulations' enactment might be construed as confiscatory and unconstitutional. It was assumed that, by limiting the enlargement and reconstruction of nonconforming uses, they would disappear over time. The allowance of nonconforming uses has been characterized by the courts as a grudging tolerance of them. The right of municipalities to adopt reasonable measures to eliminate them has been recognized. The ultimate goal of the zoning law is to achieve uniformity of property uses within each zoning district which can only be accomplished by the elimination of uses that do not conform to the specifications of district regulations.

A nonconforming use is created when existing land uses, valid when established, are prohibited by a new or amended zoning law. Nonconforming land uses are defined and regulated in most local zoning laws. A typical local ordinance may state, for example: "A nonconforming use is any use, whether of a building or tract of land or both, existing on the effective date of this chapter, which does not conform to the use regulations of the district in which it is located." Nonconforming use issues arise when the zoning law is first adopted. When a district is zoned residential, for example, all existing nonresidential uses in that district are rendered nonconforming. Later amendments to the zoning ordinance may have the same effect.

Often, zoning ordinances will provide automatic relief to owners of vacant residential lots that become nonconforming due to increased minimum area requirements, or upzoning. But see Khan v. Zoning Bd. of Appeals of Village of Irvington, 87 N.Y.2d 344, 639 N.Y.S.2d 302, 662 N.E.2d 782 (1996), where the court refused to adopt a so-called "single and separate ownership" rule as matter of common law; this rule states that one who owns property in single and separate ownership prior to enactment of the ordinance rendering it nonconforming has a vested right to use the property for residential purposes.

When property owners propose the improvement, expansion, rebuilding, or other change in their nonconforming property use, they must be certain to comply with local regulations governing those matters. Normally, these regulations are found in a discrete article of the local zoning law, entitled Nonconforming Uses. The nonconforming use article of the zoning law will prohibit or limit changes in buildings and lot uses that are nonconforming and provide in a variety of ways for the termination of nonconforming uses, such as limiting their expansion or enlargement, prohibiting the reconstruction of damaged structures, disallowing the reestablishment of nonconforming uses after they have been discontinued for a time, or simply terminating them after the passage of a stipulated amount of time.

This section will present the salient considerations developed by the courts in dealing with nonconforming uses and related regulations and the legitimacy of efforts to dispose of such uses. In this connection, several questions most commonly arise in the various cases:

1. Was there an established use at the time of zoning? (In that regard, what if the site for the structure had been surveyed, or an architect employed, or the site graded, or the basement or foundation

dug, or construction begun, and so on?) In short, what was the existing situation when zoning was instituted? The question of change of position and good faith by the landowner often enters in.

2. What is the extent of the nonconforming use, and will the terms of the ordinance permit expansion or a change of some sort with respect to such use?

3. Has there been a termination of the nonconforming use due to substantial destruction of the building in which it is housed, or abandonment of the use, or legislative action of one type or another (including the amortization process)?

4. Is the nonconforming use subject to termination as a nuisance through the granting of injunctive relief? In connection with this latter question, some cases (particularly some of the earlier ones) removed noxious uses which amounted to nuisances or were nuisance-like in character. This was basically the reasoning and result of Hadacheck v. Sebastian and Reinman v. Little Rock.

A. EXPANSION OR EXTENSION

Local laws often prohibit the enlargement, alteration, or extension of a nonconforming use. To allow the expansion of nonconforming uses, which the zoning law wishes to eliminate over time, would defeat that underlying policy. Normally, the law allows the owners of nonconforming land uses to perform property repairs, conduct normal maintenance, and complete internal alterations that do not increase the degree of, or create any new, noncompliance with the locality's zoning regulations. Courts have upheld prohibitions on the construction of an awning over a courtyard outside a restaurant, on the theory that it would create additional space for patrons to congregate and, in this sense, increase the degree of the nonconforming use. Similarly, the prohibition of the conversion of seasonal bungalows to year-round residences has been upheld as an acceptable method of preventing the enlargement of a nonconforming use.

Where nonconforming business operations are proposed to be expanded, the case law is somewhat less clear. Where roads and structures built on a parcel used as a gravel mining operation exhibited the owner's intention to use the entire parcel, the court held that expanding the mining operation to another location on the property was permitted. The addition of a body-toning operation to the premises containing a nonconforming beauty parlor, however, was considered a prohibited extension of the prior nonconforming use. The court's interest in protecting the owner's demonstrated investment in the gravel mining operation could explain the difference between these cases.

Nonconforming use provisions in zoning laws vary considerably from one locality to another. A municipality particularly intent on eliminating nonconforming uses may prohibit any physical expansion of a building; another may favor property use by allowing, for example, the construction of an additional story because it does not increase the footprint, or lot coverage, of the structure.

STATE v. PERRY

Supreme Court of Errors of Connecticut, 1962.
149 Conn. 232, 178 A.2d 279.

SHEA, ASSOCIATE JUSTICE.

The defendant was convicted, after a trial, to the court, of a violation of the zoning regulations of Stamford. He has appealed, claiming that the court erred in finding on all the evidence that he was guilty of the crime charged beyond a reasonable doubt.

The material facts are not disputed. The defendant is president of the Pickwick Ice Cream Company, which has manufactured ice cream for over twenty-five years on premises located on Newfield Avenue in Stamford. Prior to 1951 the premises were in an industrial zone. In that year, the property was rezoned to a commercial neighborhood zone, and the industrial use by the ice cream company became a nonconforming use. Before this change of zone, all of the property was used in connection with the ice cream business, either for manufacture or storage or for the parking of trucks. In January, 1959, the defendant brought to the property a large trailer which was later insulated and equipped with a blower unit. A rubber hose attached to the trailer was connected to pipes leading from the manufacturing plant. Through these pipes, ammonia, as a cooling agent, was conducted to the trailer to refrigerate it. The trailer was kept at a freezing temperature all of the time and was used to store materials connected with the production of ice cream. The company owned a tractor to which it could connect the trailer for transportation purposes. The trailer is roadworthy, has no foundation and may be moved within a few minutes by hooking it up to the tractor. The trailer is not permanently registered with the commissioner of motor vehicles. Temporary registrations have been issued for it, but the last one expired December 24, 1959. Since then, the trailer has remained on the premises, constantly hooked up to the plant. In February, 1959, the zoning enforcement officer in writing, requested the defendant to discontinue the use of the trailer.

The Stamford zoning regulations provide that a nonconforming use may be continued but may not be extended or expanded, or changed to a less restrictive use. Stamford Zoning Regs. § 9(A) (1951, as amended).[1] The intention of the regulations is to abolish nonconforming uses, or to reduce them to conformity, as speedily as justice will permit. This is in

---

1. "Section 9—Non-conforming Uses A—Any building or use of land or building legally existing at the time of enactment of this regulation, or of any amendments thereto, or authorized lawful permit issued prior to the adoption of these regulations which does not conform to the provisions of these regulations for the Use Districts in which it is located, shall be designated a non-conforming use. Such use may be continued but may not be extended or expanded, or changed to a less restrictive use as listed in Section 5—Land Use Schedule."

accordance with the policy of the law and the spirit of zoning. *Town of Guilford v. Landon*, 146 Conn. 178, 182, 148 A.2d 551; *Salerni v. Scheuy*, 140 Conn. 566, 570, 102 A.2d 528. It is apparent from the evidence that the defendant attempted to provide, through the use of the trailer, additional enclosed space for his freezing and storing operations. Had he attempted to add to the existing building or to erect a new building for these purposes, he could not have done so, because this would have constituted, beyond question, an extension of a nonconforming use. What he cannot do directly he has attempted to do indirectly by the importation of the trailer. The facts clearly show that the trailer, because of its makeup, location and long continued attachment to the pipes leading from the plant, is intended, designed and arranged to be used to expand, enlarge and extend the nonconforming use conducted in the building on the premises. This is a clear violation of the regulation. *Beerwort v. Zoning Board of Appeals*, 144 Conn. 731, 734, 137 A.2d 756; *Burmore Co. v. Smith*, 124 N.J.L. 541, 547, 12 A.2d 353; 2 Rathkopf, Law of Zoning and Planning (3d Ed.) p. 59–6. It is not a simple case of increasing the size of the defendant's business. Rather, it is an expansion and extension of the use of the premises by adding facilities for storage and the freezing of commodities where such accommodations had not previously existed *Grundlehner v. Dangler*, 51 N.J.Super. 53, 59, 143 A.2d 192, modified on other grounds, 29 N.J. 256, 148 A.2d 306.

There is no error.

In this opinion the other Judges concurred.

Notes

1. There are many interesting cases involving the general subject-matter presented in Perry. Generally speaking, there seems to be no right to expand or enlarge a nonconforming use regardless of whether the local ordinance prohibits it. The theory behind this is readily apparent—the nonconforming use, as such, is contrary to the intent and purposes of zoning.

The problems arise, however, in distinguishing between the extension or enlargement of a nonconforming use and its repair, in determining whether the construction of a new building is permissible, in deciding whether the addition of new equipment amounts to an extension, whether some new service or product is such an addition as to constitute an extension, or whether an increase in the intensity of use or volume of business amounts to a violation. These are only a few of the multitude of problems that arise in regard to changes in nonconforming uses.

Consider these situations:

(a) Before the town adopted its zoning ordinance, Anthony had been removing and processing sand and gravel from the land in question and had developed an operation whereby he could load the ingredients for concrete on dump trucks and take the loaded material to the customer. Some years later, after zoning had made his use nonconforming, he erected more modern facilities that could be used in connection with more complicated vehicles. The wooden platform that had previously been used for loading and storing materials was replaced by a steel bin and accessories, and new small buildings and a heating plant were constructed. Where dump trucks had been serviced by the earlier arrangement, the new facilities serviced cement mixer trucks. The town sought an injunction. What result? See Seekonk v. Anthony, 339 Mass. 49, 157 N.E.2d 651 (1959).

(b) At the time of the adoption of the zoning ordinance, the land in question was used as a used car lot and a store or warehouse for the storage and sale of second-hand furniture and other used articles. This was a nonconforming use. Over a 12–year period, this developed "by some sort of 'creeping' process" into a "full-fledged junkyard and shop, where, among other things, large numbers of worn out and wrecked motor vehicles were junked and burned." Was this an enlargement and extension, or was it only the intensification of a pre-existing nonconforming use? (The latter, said the court, would be permissible, while the former would not be.) See Phillips v. Zoning Comm'r, 225 Md. 102, 169 A.2d 410 (1961). In Traveler Real Estate, Inc. v. Cain, 160 A.D.2d 1214, 555 N.Y.S.2d 217 (1990), the court held that a beauty parlor operating on the first floor of a two-story building could be denied a permit to install tanning beds on the second floor because that would be an expansion.

(c) At the time of the zoning ordinance, defendant was using the property for outdoor storage of earthmoving equipment along with some repair and maintenance. Now defendant wishes to build a structure to enclose his operation. The Supreme Court of Minnesota, in a case of first impression, held that the structure would be an expansion or extension of the nonconforming use: "An addition to an existing building is clearly an extension or expansion of a prior nonconforming use. In our judgment, construction of a building where none existed before constitutes an expansion of a nonconforming use in the same manner as an addition to an existing building. Furthermore, the building will prolong the continuation of the nonconforming use and considerably lessen the likelihood that it will be eliminated in the foreseeable future." County of Freeborn v. Claussen, 295 Minn. 96, 203 N.W.2d 323 (1972). Also see Mossman v. City of Columbus, 234 Neb. 78, 449 N.W.2d 214 (1989), where the court interpreted a provision in the ordinance allowing alteration of nonconforming uses, only if no "structural alterations" were made, to prohibit a mobile home owner to replace his mobile home with another one.

(d) The purchasers of a nonconforming church building were denied permission to convert it into a single-family residence which would also be nonconforming because of lot frontage and area requirements. The town invoked a regulation which prohibited conversion of one nonconforming use to another nonconforming use. In Petruzzi v. Zoning Bd. of Appeals, 176 Conn. 479, 408 A.2d 243 (1979), the court held that the permit had been improperly denied because the church structure had preceded the enactment of the first zoning ordinance making its nonconformity a vested right. Also, the court noted that only interior alteration of the structure was involved. Also see Kopietz v. Zoning Bd. of Appeals, 211 Mich.App. 666, 535 N.W.2d 910 (1995), where the court reversed the denial of a permit to convert a nonconforming funeral home into a nonconforming bed-and-breakfast. The court held that the board abused its discretion by failing to make a determination whether the proposed nonconforming use moved in the direction of diminishing the nonconformity.

(e) An asphalt company sought permission to construct a 1000–barrel capacity asphalt storage tank to replace two 400–barrel underground tanks which had developed leaks. In Nu–Way Emulsions, Inc. v. City of Dalworthington Gardens, 610 S.W.2d 562 (Tex.Civ.App.1980), the court held that the proposal amounted to enlargement and alteration of a nonconforming use rather than repair of an existing use as alleged by the plaintiff. Cf. Feldman v. Zoning Hearing Bd. of City of Pittsburgh, 89 Pa.Cmwlth. 237, 492 A.2d 468 (1985), where the property owner sought to convert an auto repair shop into a convenience store/gas station; Stevens v. Town of Rye, 122 N.H. 688, 448 A.2d 426 (1982), involving conversion of an auto garage into a showroom for plumbing supplies and bath fixtures.

(f) Conversion of an existing nonconforming restaurant into a discotheque was held to be a substantial alteration of the use in Town of Belleville v. Parrillo's, Inc., 83 N.J. 309, 416 A.2d 388 (1980). The court stressed the factors of the changes in hours of operation, clientele, admission policies, facilities, and music. Similarly, conversion of a movie theater to live entertainment was held to be an impermissible expansion of a nonconforming use in Conforti v. City of Manchester, 141 N.H. 78, 677 A.2d 147 (1996). A little closer to the line, perhaps, is Marzocco v. City of Albany, 217 A.D.2d 872, 629 N.Y.S.2d 847 (1995), where the owner of a nonconforming tavern/restaurant catering to the gay population and featuring male strippers changed the character of his business to one offering topless female dancers as entertainment, then giving up his liquor license and establishing a "juice bar" offering totally nude female dancers and "erotic entertainment." The court found that a significant change in use was involved.

(g) A private care facility operated for about four years in a residential zone which permitted nursing homes, but excluded facilities that care for "insane or other mental cases." The facility cared for eight elderly people with mental problems as a nonconforming use. When the facility changed to one which cared for young people with mental problems the city charged the operator with violating the zoning ordinance. Although the city argued that young people with mental problems are more apt to be violent than elderly people with such infirmities and that the facility was expanding the nonconforming use, the court reasoned that the intensification was permissible because the nature and character of the use remained substantially the same. The court analogized the change as similar to a store which changes its inventory or a factory which changes its product. City of Jewell Junction v. Cunningham, 439 N.W.2d 183 (Iowa 1989).

2. In Hansen Brothers Enterprises, Inc. v. Board of Supervisors of Nevada County, 12 Cal.4th 533, 48 Cal.Rptr.2d 778, 907 P.2d 1324 (1996), the court held that the diminishing asset doctrine required that a mining company be allowed expand its rock quarrying and aggregate production into other areas of its property. The court said that under the diminishing asset doctrine quarrying cannot be limited to land actually excavated at the time of enactment of a restrictive ordinance because to do so would deprive the landowner of his use of the property as a quarry. Contra: Township of Fairfield v. Likanchuk's, Inc., 274 N.J.Super. 320, 644 A.2d 120 (App.Div. 1994) (diminishing asset doctrine not applicable unless owner can show that the entire tract was dedicated by the owner to the mining activity).

3. In Memory Gardens Cemetery, Inc. v. Village of Arlington Heights, 250 Ill.App.3d 553, 190 Ill.Dec. 238, 621 N.E.2d 107 (1993), a nonconforming cemetery sought a permit to construct an additional mausoleum. (Twelve mausoleums were already on the cemetery property.) After the city denied the permit, the cemetery sought a declaratory judgment that it did not need a permit on the theory that a mausoleum in a cemetery is not a change in use. The plaintiffs put on the testimony of several expert witnesses who all defined a cemetery as including in-ground internment, mausoleum entombment, and inurnment of cremated remains. The court found, however, that under Illinois law, mausoleums are treated distinctly and thus the construction of a mausoleum would be an expansion or enlargement of a nonconforming use (although, apparently, internment of additional bodies in gravesites would not be an expansion or enlargement). Compare Town of Gardiner v. Blue Sky Entertainment Corp., 213 A.D.2d 790, 623 N.Y.S.2d 29 (1995), where the town sought to close down a nonconforming tourist camp that had been used for sky diving, parachuting, and other recreational aviation activities. The court held that an increase in the volume of skydivers, pilots, and campers was not an improper extension of the nonconforming use because there was no change in the nature of the use, just the volume.

B. DISCONTINUANCE

A property owner's right to continue a nonconforming use may be lost by abandonment. Originally, this required a voluntary, completed act of abandonment by the owner. It was said that there must be the concurrence of an intention to abandon and some act, or failure to act, which implies a lack of interest on the part of the owner to retain the use. Time was considered relevant to the issue of abandonment, but not enough, alone, to establish it. Furthermore, the mere failure to continue the nonconforming use was not sufficient to establish abandonment. Although these rules still exist in some jurisdictions, modern zoning laws frequently stipulate that any discontinuance of the nonconforming use for a specified period constitutes abandonment. Courts hold that such provisions are sufficient to establish the owner's intent to abandon the nonconforming use as a matter of law. Where the established period is reasonable, discontinuance of the use for that time amounts to an abandonment of the use. It has been held that local discontinuance periods apply even when the owner can prove that he did not actually intend to abandon the nonconforming use.

STATE EX REL. MOREHOUSE v. HUNT

Supreme Court of Wisconsin, 1940.
235 Wis. 358, 291 N.W. 745.

[A building which could accommodate 20 to 25 students, in the University Heights area of Madison, was used as a fraternity house before the district was zoned for single family residences. The fraternity in the early 1930's deeded the building to its mortgagee. It was then used as a rooming house for over two years. In 1934, it was leased to

Dean Garrison of the law school "to be used for the purpose of residence only." Dean Garrison and his family lived in the structure for the initial two year lease period and then for three more years under successive one year leases. Two servants and a student who tended the furnace lived with the Garrisons. From September, 1935, Dean Garrison subleased some extra rooms as a separate apartment.

After Dean Garrison moved out the mortgagee-owner sought a nonconforming use permit permitting renewed use as a fraternity house. The building commissioner refused, but this was reversed by the board of zoning appeals, which wrote an elaborate decision.

Certiorari was brought by neighbors. The circuit judge reversed the zoning board.]

FOWLER, JUSTICE.

* * * The case is certiorari. When certiorari is invoked to review the action of an administrative board, the findings of the board upon the facts before it are conclusive if in any reasonable view the evidence sustains them. *Wisconsin Labor R. Board v. Fred Rueping L. Co.*, 228 Wis. 473, 493, 279 N.W. 673, 117 A.L.R. 398. Under this rule the appeal board's view of the facts, so far as they appear from its decision, must be accepted as final and conclusive upon the trial court and upon us. The statutory provision for review by certiorari of the board's action, to the effect that the court may take further evidence and may consider it in reaching its determination, may warrant the court's overriding the board's findings of fact if the additional evidence received shows them to be erroneous, but where as here the additional evidence is incompetent it cannot be given that effect however it might be if it were competent. The view of the board that the owner did not intend to abandon the right of use of the building as a fraternity house but that the use of it for a residence was intended to be only temporary until opportunity should arise to sell it for that purpose, must therefore be upheld and given whatever legal effect it has.

* * *

The quotations from the decision of the board above given show that the board concluded as fact that lapse for a year of the nonconforming use before resuming or adopting another lawful nonconforming use, was a reasonable time in which to resume or adopt a lawful nonconforming use; that lapse of the conforming use under either of the above situations is consistent with and does not constitute an abandonment of the nonconforming use, and that under the facts of the instant case the owner by leasing the premises to Dean Garrison and permitting him to use them as a one-family residence for one year did not intend to abandon or discontinue Class B use.

The question remains whether the owner's intent in respect above stated operates to avoid the language of the ordinance declaring that discontinuance of a nonconforming use prevents resumption of that use.

Although the letter of the ordinance is as stated the letter need not necessarily be applied. *State ex rel. Schaetz v. Manders, supra.* "The letter killeth but the spirit giveth life." If the resumption of the nonconforming use is within the spirit of the ordinance, although contrary to its letter, the spirit rather than the letter governs.

That mere cessation of a nonconforming use under the terms of a zoning ordinance does not destroy the right to continue it or prevent resumption of it was held in the *Manders* case, supra. Under the rule of that case, discontinuance involves more than mere cessation. It involves abandonment. Under that rule, had the owner kept the premises vacant, waiting opportunity to rent or sell to a fraternity, the nonconforming use would have continued. Under the reason of that rule, had the owner, under the finding of fact as to the owner's intention, employed a caretaker for the house this would not have operated as a discontinuance. * * *

* * * But the reservation of right to cancel the lease on sale of the premises is indicative of intent to sell for a fraternity house if opportunity arose. Putting in the lease for "residence only" indicates that the lessee should not turn the house into a tearoom or restaurant or a boardinghouse, but it does preclude the idea of making it a two-family residence, as later was done, to the knowledge and with the implied assent of the owner, and as might have been done forthwith without violating of the ordinance. Whether under all the circumstances the owner's acts constituted a "voluntary relinquishment or abandonment" of the right to devote the premises to a Class B use depends on whether the use of the building as a single-family residence for a year was a reasonable time under all the circumstances, to allow the owner to devote the premises to the Class B use of a two-family residence. The appeal board thought it was. This was a question for the board to decide and its decision should be sustained. * * *

* * * We are of opinion that the judgment of the circuit court should be reversed, and the record remanded with directions to enter judgment affirming the ruling of the board of zoning appeals. * * *

[The dissenting opinion of Wickhem, J., in which two other justices concurred, is not given.]

TOYS "R" US v. SILVA

Court of Appeals of New York, 1996.
89 N.Y.2d 411, 654 N.Y.S.2d 100, 676 N.E.2d 862.

KAYE, CHIEF JUDGE.

(1) The New York City zoning laws prohibit continuation of a nonconforming use if, during a two-year period, "the active operation of substantially all the non-conforming uses * * * is discontinued" (New York City Zoning Resolution § 52–61). This case presents a novel question of statutory construction: what is the appropriate legal standard to determine whether a nonconforming use has been discontinued under

the Zoning Resolution? Contrary to the trial court and Appellate Division, we conclude that substantial—rather than complete—discontinuation of the active, nonconforming activity forfeits the nonconforming use, and that the good faith of the owner is irrelevant to that determination.

(2) Here, the Board of Standards and Appeals (BSA) on the facts found minimal warehouse activity following the complete stoppage of operations for 20 months, which failed to preserve nonconforming use status, and it revoked the building permit allowing petitioner to maintain a nonconforming use on the premises. Because the BSA determination was supported by substantial evidence, we reverse the trial court and Appellate Division decisions reinstating the building permit.

1. FACTS

At issue here is a portion of a 16–story building located at the northeast corner of Third Avenue and East 80th Street in Manhattan. Built in 1926, the entire premises were situated in a retail zoning district and, in compliance with the certificate of occupancy and applicable zoning regulation, served as a storage and warehouse facility. When Morgan Manhattan Storage and Warehouse Company purchased the building in 1956, it continued to use the structure exclusively as a warehouse.

The 1961 New York City Zoning Resolution changed the neighborhood from a retail zoning district to residential districts overlaid with strips of commercial districts on the avenue (rather than street) blocks. As a result, that portion of the building on Third Avenue presently remains in a commercial (C1–9) zoning district. The portion fronting on 80th Street, however, is now in a residential (R8B) zone. Because warehouse use is no longer permitted as of right in either the commercially or the residentially zoned areas (see, Zoning Resolution art II; §§ 32–00, 32–25), use of the building as a warehouse could continue under the Zoning Resolution only as a nonconforming use (see, Zoning Resolution §§ 12–10, 52–11).

Morgan continued to use the building as a warehouse until August 1989, when it contracted to sell the premises to a real estate developer. At that time, Morgan emptied the building and for the next 20 months ceased all warehouse operations. The sale fell through, and in April 1991 Morgan transferred a limited amount of goods stored in its other warehouses to the 80th Street facility and assigned a property manager there, in an effort to resume nonconforming warehouse use and thereby maintain the value of its property.

In June 1992, Chase Manhattan Bank acquired the premises from Morgan by way of deed in lieu of foreclosure. In response to a request by Chase for advice as to whether nonconforming warehouse use was permissible, the New York City Department of Buildings (DOB) issued an informal opinion that the nonconforming use at the premises had been re-established in April 1991 and could lawfully continue.

Petitioner Toys "R" Us purchased the basement, first and second floors of the building from a subsidiary of Chase in March 1994. Three months later, petitioner filed an application with DOB to convert the purchased premises into a retail toy store. DOB approved the application and in September 1994 issued a building permit authorizing the conversion.

The 38,000 square foot premises occupy both commercially and residentially zoned space. A toy store is permitted as of right in the commercially zoned portion of the premises on Third Avenue but not in the residentially zoned section fronting on 80th Street, which includes the building's loading docks (see, Zoning Resolution art II; §§ 32–00, 32–15). The instant dispute arises out of the DOB authorization to develop and operate this latter segment of the property situated in the residential zoning district as a retail toy store—a nonconforming use.

Respondent-intervenor "Neighbors–R–Us," a coalition of neighborhood and block associations, objected to the building permit and sought its revocation. In October 1994, DOB denied the request. Respondent-intervenor then challenged the issuance of the building permit by way of an administrative appeal to the BSA. It urged that the nonconforming warehouse use had been discontinued during the two-year period from August 1989 to July 1991 and, therefore, the Zoning Resolution only allowed the property to be developed in furtherance of a permitted use.

The BSA held public hearings during a five-month period concerning the nature and extent of warehouse operations during the period between April and July 1991 and conducted a site inspection of the building and the surrounding area.

After reviewing hundreds of pages of documents and hearing testimony from all sides, the BSA, "based on the totality of the evidence presented," found the warehouse activity between April and July 1991 minimal. Concluding that the Zoning Resolution did not require complete cessation of the nonconforming use as a precondition to termination, the BSA determined that the insignificant level of warehouse activity during that period failed to perpetuate the nonconforming warehouse use. Deeming Morgan's clear intent to resume warehouse operations insufficient to preserve the nonconforming use, the BSA revoked petitioner's building permit.

Petitioner commenced a CPLR article 78 proceeding seeking to reinstate the permit. Supreme Court held that the storage of some goods in the warehouse during April to July 1991, coupled with the absence of any bad faith or fraud by Morgan, sufficiently continued the nonconforming use. It thus granted the petition and annulled the BSA determination, allowing petitioner to maintain a nonconforming retail use in the residentially zoned space.

The Appellate Division affirmed, one Justice dissenting. Like the trial court, the Appellate Division applied a good-faith standard and concluded that the concededly minimal storage activity from April to July 1991 sufficed to preserve nonconforming use status under the

Zoning Resolution. The Appellate Division granted leave to appeal to this Court, and we now reverse.

* * *

Whether petitioner can use the residential portion of the premises at issue here for nonconforming toy store use depends on whether its predecessor, Morgan, discontinued its nonconforming warehouse operations for two years within the meaning of section 52–61. This Court has never considered the proper legal standard for determining when a nonconforming use is abandoned under this zoning ordinance. In revoking petitioner's building permit, the BSA construed section 52–61 as requiring substantial discontinuation, rather than complete cessation, of the nonconforming use by the property owner for two consecutive years, irrespective of any intent to preserve nonconforming use status.

The BSA, comprised of five experts in land use and planning, is the ultimate administrative authority charged with enforcing the Zoning Resolution (see, NY City Charter §§ 659, 666). Consequently, in questions relating to its expertise, the BSA's interpretation of the statute's terms must be "given great weight and judicial deference, so long as the interpretation is neither irrational, unreasonable nor inconsistent with the governing statute" (*Matter of Trump–Equitable Fifth Ave. Co. v. Gliedman*, 62 N.Y.2d 539, 545; *see, Appelbaum v. Deutsch*, 66 N.Y.2d 975, 977). Its determination, moreover, must be sustained if it has a rational basis and is supported by substantial evidence (*see, Appelbaum v. Deutsch*, 66 N.Y.2d at 977, supra; *Matter of Fuhst v. Foley*, 45 NY2d 441, 444). Where, however, the question is one of pure legal interpretation of statutory terms, deference to the BSA is not required (*see, Matter of Teachers Ins. & Annuity Assn. v. City of New York*, 82 N.Y.2d 35, 41–42).

Here, we must resolve two questions. First, we must determine the appropriate legal standard for abandonment under Zoning Resolution § 52–61—a pure legal question that does not mandate deference to the BSA. We must then decide whether the BSA's conclusion that Morgan abandoned nonconforming warehouse use was supported by substantial evidence.

* * *

According to petitioner, New York courts have uniformly required proof that the entire nonconforming use was discontinued as a precondition to termination. Petitioner points to *Matter of Marzella v. Munroe* (69 N.Y.2d 967) in support of this contention. In *Marzella*, the property owner used a parcel of land that had been rezoned to permit only one two-family structure to house four families in two dwellings. When one house remained vacant for 15 years, so that three families rather than four resided on the property, the local zoning board concluded that nonconforming use of the property for four families had been abandoned. This Court disagreed, finding insufficient evidence to establish that the entire nonconforming use had been abandoned (*id.*, at 968).

In doing so, we explained that "[a]bandonment does not occur unless there has been a complete cessation of the nonconforming use" (*id.*, at 968). Notably, however, the local zoning ordinance in Marzella broadly prohibited resumption of any "nonconforming use which has been abandoned" (*see*, Village of Dobbs Ferry Code § 300–81B). The term "abandoned" was not qualified in any way; the statute therefore gave no indication that anything less than complete discontinuation of the nonconforming use would suffice to surrender it.

Similarly, in *Town of Islip v. P.B.S. Marina* (133 A.D.2d 81), also relied upon by petitioner, the relevant zoning ordinance contained absolute terms, providing that "discontinuance of any non[-]conforming use for a period of one year or more terminates such non-conforming use." The Appellate Division thus concluded that " 'discontinuance connotes a complete cessation * * * so that a minimal nonconforming function, of itself, would not constitute an abandonment' " (*id.*, quoting *Baml Realty v. State of New York*, 35 A.D.2d 857). Indeed, in each of the cases cited by petitioner adopting the complete cessation standard, the statutes spoke exclusively in terms of discontinuance, failing to qualify that requirement in any way (*see, e.g., Baml Realty v. State of New York*, 35 A.D.2d 857, *supra*; *City of Binghamton v. Gartell*, 275 App. Div. 457, 459).

Unlike the statutes in these prior cases, however, Zoning Resolution § 52–61 explicitly equates abandonment with something less than discontinuation of the entire nonconforming use. Section 52–61 specifically terminates any further nonconforming use when "the active operation of substantially all the non-conforming uses * * * is discontinued" for a continuous two-year period (emphasis added). To construe this statute as requiring the property owner to discontinue all nonconforming operations—as the courts below did—simply ignores the plain language of the ordinance requiring that the owner merely cease "substantially" all of the nonconforming use.[2] Allowing the slightest nonconforming function to preserve the nonconforming use, moreover, would eliminate the specific language requiring "active" operations to avoid termination.

The carefully chosen words of section 52–61 thus impose a standard of substantial rather than complete cessation.[3] The language of the

---

2. Tellingly, the drafters of section 52–61 rejected a proposed termination provision that omitted the qualifying language "substantially all." In a Zoning Resolution submitted to the City Planning Commission pursuant to a contract with the City of New York, a special planning staff of architects suggested the following regarding termination of nonconforming uses: "If a nonconforming use *discontinues active or continuous operations* for a continuous period of one year, the building or other structure or tract of land where such non-conforming use previously existed shall thereafter be occupied and used only for a conforming use. Intent to resume active operations shall not affect the foregoing" (Voorhees, Walker, Smith and Smith, Report to NY City Planning Commn, Proposed Zoning Resolution § 51–31 [Aug. 1958] [emphasis added]).

3. Petitioner alternatively urges that, because section 52–61 refers to discontinuation of "substantially all the non-conforming uses" —emphasizing the plural "uses"—discontinuation should be measured by whether a majority of the number of nonconforming uses is maintained, regardless of the level of activity devoted to each use. Petitioner, however, overlooks the

statute also contradicts the conclusion of both the trial court and Appellate Division that section 52–61 implicitly contains a good-faith standard, allowing nonconforming activity to continue upon a showing that a property owner, in the absence of bad faith or fraud, intended to resume nonconforming use.

Generally, abandonment of a nonconforming use requires both an intent to relinquish and some overt act or failure to act, indicating that the owner neither claims nor retains any interest in the subject matter of the abandonment (*see*, 1 Anderson's American Law of Zoning § 6.65, at 678 [Young 4th ed]). In New York, however, the inclusion of a lapse period in the zoning provision removes the requirement of intent to abandon—discontinuance of nonconforming activity for the specified period constitutes an abandonment regardless of intent (*see*, *Matter of Prudco Realty Corp. v. Palermo*, 60 N.Y.2d 656, 657–658).

Zoning Resolution § 52–61 provides a specific lapse period—two years—thereby rendering the owner's intent irrelevant to abandonment. Indeed, section 52–61 goes even one step further, expressly stating that "[i]ntent to resume active operations shall not affect" the determination whether a nonconforming use has been discontinued.

Notwithstanding the unique language of this particular zoning provision, petitioner urges that section 52–61 must be interpreted in its favor as the landowner. To be sure, zoning restrictions, being in derogation of common-law property rights, should be strictly construed and any ambiguity resolved in favor of the property owner (*see*, *Matter of Allen v. Adami*, 39 N.Y.2d 275, 277). Zoning Resolution § 52–61, however, is not ambiguous—its clear language prohibits additional nonconforming activity when "substantially all" of the "active" nonconforming operations are discontinued, and deems the owner's intent irrelevant. Furthermore, public policy specifically supports termination of nonconforming uses, and the Zoning Resolution itself seeks to achieve "a gradual remedy" for "incompatible" nonconforming uses (Zoning Resolution § 51–00). * * *

The Appellate Division's concern that anything less than complete cessation under section 52–61 will lead to arbitrary results warrants comment. Section 52–61 imposes an objective, not subjective, standard: substantial discontinuation of active, nonconforming operations. Stated otherwise, section 52–61 terminates a nonconforming use when only minimal nonconforming activity continues. Whether this standard has been satisfied will, of course, turn on the peculiar facts of each case. All zoning cases are by their nature fact specific, and as a leading authority recognizes, the right to a nonconforming use must necessarily be decided "on a case-by-case basis" (1 Anderson's American Law of Zoning § 6.23, at 553 [Young 4th ed]). Certainly, the DOB and BSA, comprised of qualified experts, are capable of making these determinations.

* * *

basic rule of statutory construction that "[w]ords in the singular number include the plural, and in the plural number include the singular" (General Construction Law § 35).

The BSA's determination that Morgan substantially discontinued nonconforming warehouse use of the property for 24 months must be confirmed if it has a rational basis and is supported by substantial evidence (*Matter of Cowan v. Kern*, 41 N.Y.2d 591, 598). And where substantial evidence exists, a reviewing court may not substitute its judgment for that of the BSA—even if the court might have decided the matter differently (*Matter of Cowan v. Kern*, 41 N.Y.2d at 599, *supra*; *Matter of Collins v. Codd*, 38 N.Y.2d 269, 270). In reaching its conclusion, moreover, the BSA had de novo review power and was not bound by the findings of the DOB (*see*, Zoning Resolution § 72–11).

The BSA's review of warehouse logs for the contested four-month period revealed only eight customer accounts, compared to the 1,500 accounts previously maintained by the company. It further revealed that approximately 19 crates were shipped to the warehouse at that time, which would have occupied only one-tenth of one percent of the entire volume of the building. This extremely low level of activity was corroborated by testimony of the following: an Enviropact employee who, after examining every lobby floor and 75% of the storage lockers, saw only 12 to 15 crates and a few cardboard files; a Chase loan officer who walked through the building and observed about 20 large storage crates; various neighborhood residents who noticed that the building was vacant and unused; and a local real estate agent who found the warehouse to be completely empty, unheated, unlit and infested with pigeons. Based on this evidence, the BSA rejected the testimony of Morgan's president, Jeffrey Morgan, that five percent of the building was used to maintain 40 to 50 customer accounts from April to July 1991.

The BSA's conclusion, however, was premised on more than the drastic reduction in the volume of storage activity. The BSA specifically noted the absence of any standard evidence for the critical four-month period typically available to document a legitimate business operation, such as insurance records, tax documents, advertisements, liability coverage, customer records, employee records, certain directory listings, telephone records or sales receipts. Jeffrey Morgan even acknowledged that the company failed to renew the requisite Department of Consumer Affairs license after it expired in April 1991.

The BSA thus properly considered objective factors regarding the nature and degree of nonconforming warehouse use, and its determination that Morgan's level of warehouse operations from April to July 1991 was too insignificant to preserve nonconforming use status under section 52–61 was supported by substantial evidence. That conflicting inferences may have been drawn from this evidence is of no moment. "[T]he duty of weighing the evidence and making the choice rests solely upon the [administrative agency]. The courts may not weigh the evidence or reject the choice made by [such agency] where the evidence is conflicting and room for choice exists" (*Matter of Stork Rest. v. Boland*, 282 N.Y. 256, 267).

* * *

Accordingly, the order of the Appellate Division should be reversed, with costs, and the petition dismissed.

JUDGES SIMONS, TITONE, BELLACOSA, SMITH, LEVINE and CIPARICK concur.

Notes

1. There is no uniformity of interpretation in situations in which the use has been discontinued and resumption of it is attempted. Some ordinances attempt to spell out specific time periods and provide that the use cannot be resumed after a given period of non-use has elapsed. A Wisconsin provision stated that if the nonconforming use were "*discontinued* for a period of 12 months, any future use of the building and premises shall conform to the ordinance." Did the word, "discontinued," mean a "voluntary abandonment" in the sense of an *intent* to discontinue? In State ex rel. Brill v. Mortenson, 6 Wis.2d 325, 96 N.W.2d 603 (1959), the Wisconsin court answered in the negative. Board of Zoning Adjustment v. Boykin, 265 Ala. 504, 92 So.2d 906 (1957), states, however, that "the word discontinuance, as used in a zoning ordinance, is equivalent to abandonment" and adds that "discontinuance results from the concurrence of an intent to abandon and some overt act or failure to act which carries the implication of abandonment."

2. The construction by courts of "discontinued" as implying the requirement of an intent to abandon the nonconforming use is rather odd in view of the purpose of zoning. It exacerbates the problem caused by the nonconforming use and increases the difficulty in dealing with it. Some courts look at the fact of discontinuance and ignore the intent of the owner. Thus in City of Chicago v. Cohen, 49 Ill.App.3d 342, 7 Ill.Dec. 174, 364 N.E.2d 335 (1977), the nonconforming use was terminated even though the owner testified he had no intention of abandoning but rather was actively seeking a tenant during the six-month period. Also see Martin v. Beehan, 689 S.W.2d 29 (Ky.App.1985), where the court found a nonconforming hotel abandoned despite intermittent attempts to sell the hotel over a 10-year period. The court said the intent of the owner was immaterial, as did the courts in Anderson v. City of Paragould, 16 Ark.App. 10, 695 S.W.2d 851 (1985), and Ka–Hur Enterprises, Inc. v. Zoning Bd. of Appeals of Provincetown, 40 Mass.App.Ct. 71, 661 N.E.2d 120 (1996).

An unusual situation was presented in Sapakoff v. Town of Hague Zoning Bd. of Appeals, 211 A.D.2d 874, 621 N.Y.S.2d 215 (1995), where a nonconforming restaurant and bar was forfeited to the federal government under the drug laws, and the government sold the property at auction to Sapakoff who sought to reinstitute the nonconforming use. The court held that the two-year discontinuance provision was not tolled by virtue of the federal seizure and the permit to resume the previous use was revoked.

3. In Boles v. City of Chattanooga, 892 S.W.2d 416 (Tenn.App.1994), the court held that discontinuance of an adult-oriented establishment while a temporary restraining order was in effect was involuntary, and thus did not constitute discontinuance of a nonconforming use; and, in State ex rel. McArthur v. Board of Adjustment of City of Crestwood, 872 S.W.2d 651 (Mo.App.1994), the court held that the city could not terminate nonconforming use rights of six spaces in a mobile home park that had been vacant for a

period of time, because the individual spaces were not lots or parcels, and thus the owner's inability to rent the individual spaces in the park was not a discontinuance.

4. Can a city treat a change of ownership as a discontinuance or termination-triggering event? In Village of Valatie v. Smith, 190 A.D.2d 17, 596 N.Y.S.2d 581 (1993), the court held that a provision in the village code terminating a nonconforming use upon a change in ownership of the property was unconstitutional on its face. The court stated: "[T]he provision at issue appears to run afoul of fundamental rule that zoning deals basically with land use rather than the person who owns or occupies the land." In Caserta v. Zoning Bd. of Appeals of City of Milford, 41 Conn.App. 77, 674 A.2d 855 (1996), the court held that after a change in ownership and an attempt by the new owner to reestablish a discontinued use, reference must be made to the previous owner's intent to reestablish the use. And, in Town of Lyons v. Bashor, 867 P.2d 159 (Colo.App.1993), the court held that the right to maintain a prior nonconforming use of two houses on one lot ran with the land (the lot was put up for sale after a court ordered dissolution of a marriage and had partitioned the land).

5. See Eric J. Strauss and Mary M. Giese, Elimination of Nonconformities: The Case of Voluntary Discontinuance, 25 The Urban Lawyer 159 (1993).

C. DESTRUCTION

MOFFATT v. FORREST CITY

Supreme Court of Arkansas, 1961.
234 Ark. 12, 350 S.W.2d 327.

McFADDIN, JUSTICE.

This litigation involves the application of the Zoning Ordinance of Forrest City, Arkansas. Appellants, Mr. and Mrs. Louie Moffatt, purchased a home in the residential district of Forrest City in 1951. In 1954 they made additions to the home and began operating a meat market and meat processing plant in said additions; and, as business improved, they made other additions and enlargements to the meat market portion of the premises. In 1959, Forrest City adopted a zoning ordinance which classified the area in which the Moffatt premises are located as entirely residential. Moffatt's market was a nonconforming use. The Zoning Ordinance provided: "If a building occupied by a non-conforming use is damaged to the extent of 60 per cent or more of its reproduction value exclusive of foundations, such building may not be restored for any non-conforming use."

On July 20, 1960, there was a fire in which the Moffatt residence quarters were almost entirely destroyed, and the market portion was considerably damaged. When the Moffats undertook to repair the market in order to resume business, the municipality filed this suit in Chancery Court to enjoin them from any reconstruction. The city alleged that the building was more than 60 per cent destroyed, exclusive of foundations, and that because of the Zoning Ordinance the owners could not restore the property for use as a meat market, such being a nonconforming use. The Moffatts resisted the city's claim. There were several hearings in the Chancery Court, and the Chancellor personally viewed the premises. The Chancery decree sustained the city's claim and enjoined the reconstruction of the building, or any building on the premises, for use as a meat market. The Moffatts have appealed. * * *

We agree with the appellants that a zoning ordinance is to be strictly construed in favor of the property holders, since the ordinance is in derogation of the common law and operates to deprive the owner of the property of a use which would otherwise be lawful. *City of Little Rock v. Williams*, 206 Ark. 861, 177 S.W.2d 924, and cases and authorities there cited; see, also *City of West Helena v. Bockman*, 221 Ark. 677, 256 S.W.2d 40. But even giving the Zoning Ordinance of Forrest City a strict construction in favor of the property holders, we must decide the fact question: whether the building on the premises was damaged "to the extent of 60 per cent or more of its reproduction value exclusive of foundations."

The residence and the meat market were housed in one structure. This is shown by the plats and pictures in the transcript. Regardless of the fact that there were additions to the market side of the house, there was only one overall building; and appellants could not have successfully claimed that the market was one building and the residence was another. Such a theory was originally urged, but with becoming candor appellants' learned counsel conceded: " * * * the cause was ultimately submitted on the theory that the market and the residence constituted one structure and that the issue before the Court was 60% destruction of it exclusive of foundations."

There was evidence that the total value of the building before the fire was approximately $15,000; and that to restore the building after the fire would cost approximately $12,000. Five witnesses—some of them building contractors—testified that the damage exceeded 60 per cent. Mr. Moffatt did not dispute the fact that the residence portion of the structure was a total loss; and there was other evidence that the residence portion was 10/15ths of the total value. While there is evidence to the contrary, we cannot say that the preponderance of the evidence is contrary to the Chancellor's conclusions as to the percentage of damage.

Affirmed.

Notes

1. In Stanton v. Town of Pawleys Island, 317 S.C. 498, 455 S.E.2d 171 (1995), the court reversed the denial of a permit to repair a home that had been substantially damaged in a hurricane. The zoning ordinance prohibited ground level living quarters in coastal high hazard areas. Thus Stanton's house was nonconforming. The court held that, as a whole, the house was not more than 50 percent destroyed. Compare Pelham Esplanade v. Village of Pelham Manor Board of Trustees, 154 A.D.2d 599, 546 N.Y.S.2d 427

(1989), where the owner of two apartment buildings sought a permit to rebuild one of the buildings that had undergone fire damage greater than 50 percent. The court held that looking at the "apartment complex as a whole," less than 50 percent was destroyed and the owner was entitled to the permit.

2. In the absence of an ordinance provision to the contrary, the general rule is that a discontinuance of use caused by a fire on the premises does not amount to an abandonment and the building may be repaired and the use resumed. What about discontinuance of the use due to repair of the building, acts of war, government restrictions, foreclosure or condemnation actions, or injunctive relief granted by a court having equity powers?

D. AMORTIZATION—USES AND LIMITATIONS

Some local zoning ordinances require certain nonconforming uses to be amortized over a specified period at the end of which they must be terminated. The term "amortization" is used to describe these provisions because they allow the owner some time during which to recoup his investment in the nonconforming use. Courts may uphold such provisions where the benefit to the public has been deemed of greater moment than the detriment to the property owner and where the property owner's investment is fairly recognized. When an amortization period is reasonable is a question that is answered, typically, in the light of the facts of each particular case. Certainly, a critical factor is the length of the amortization period in relation to the investment. The critical question, however, is whether the public gain achieved by the exercise of the police power outweighs the private loss suffered by the owners of the nonconforming uses. Some state courts take a more expansive view of property rights and make local regulators work harder to allow significant owner investments to be recouped.

Contexts in which amortization provisions are likely to be upheld are:

1. When the common law of nuisance would allow neighboring property owners to enjoin the continuation of the nonconforming use. For example, a gravel pit, auto wrecking operation, or junkyard, harmful to children in a developing residential area, might be enjoined under a private nuisance action. If an amortization provision is challenged, the municipality can show that the owner's property interest is slight because of her vulnerability to a nuisance action. In this context, however, the label "amortization" is inappropriate. The grace period, if any, allowed by the local statute is gratuitous if, in fact, the owner's use may be enjoined as a nuisance.

2. When the nonconforming use is somewhat noxious and the owner has little investment in it. For example, a provision requiring the owner to cease raising pigeons on the roof or to remove an old outdoor sign might withstand challenge because of the minimal nature of the owner's investment and the significant harm done to the zoning scheme if the owner's activity is allowed to continue. Harder cases are presented when the owner has a significant investment in the use and the public

interest in removing it is clear but where the threat to public health and safety is not imminent.

AVR, INC. v. CITY OF ST. LOUIS PARK
Court of Appeals of Minnesota, 1998.
585 N.W.2d 411.

WILLIS, JUDGE.

* * *

AVR owns and operates a ready-mix concrete plant in the City of St. Louis Park. The plant was constructed in 1954. In 1959, the city passed a zoning ordinance permitting ready-mix plants in the area of the city zoned for industrial use but only pursuant to a special use permit. The city did not grant a special use permit to the then-owners of this ready-mix plant, but rather classified the plant as a preexisting nonconforming use, because it was within 400 feet of a residential district.

In 1973, the city amended its zoning code to eliminate ready-mix and concrete block plants as permitted uses in the city. AVR purchased the ready-mix plant in 1974 for $260,000. In May 1980, the city adopted a new comprehensive plan and put AVR on notice that the city intended to phase out the plant and rezone the site for commercial or office use or "as a second choice high density residential use." AVR commenced a declaratory judgment action seeking to invalidate the 1973 zoning ordinance on the ground that it wrongfully eliminated ready-mix plants as permitted uses in industrial zones. The district court declared the ordinance void as applied to AVR, and the city appealed. This court concluded that because the plant was not a public nuisance or a nuisance per se, the city could not legislate it out of existence. *Apple Valley Red–E–Mix v. City of St. Louis Park*, 359 N.W.2d 313, 315 (Minn.App.1984), review denied (Minn. Mar. 21, 1985).

In 1990, the city adopted another new comprehensive plan, which provides that, in the area where the AVR plant is located,

> [h]eavy industrial uses including a concrete ready mix plant and outdoor storage of heavy equipment are to be phased out, and the sites are to be used for high density residential use.

St. Louis Park, Minn., Comprehensive Plan 1990–2010 § 16, at 16–5 (1990). In 1992, the city rezoned AVR's property from I–4 Industrial to R–4 Multifamily Residential. The ordinance provides that the city council

> shall by ordinance amend the Zoning Ordinance to establish an amortization period for individual land uses not permitted in the City. The amortization period shall commence upon publication of the ordinance establishing the length of amortization period.

St. Louis Park, Minn., Code of Ordinances § 14:7–4(D)(4) (1992). The 1992 ordinance required the owners of all properties "that contain a use not permitted in any zoning district [to] register their non-conforming use with the City" within one year of the adoption of the ordinance. *Id.* § 14:7–4(B). The ordinance also required the zoning administrator to meet with such property owners, review each registration application, and determine a reasonable amortization period for each nonconforming use. In determining the length of a reasonable amortization period, the zoning administrator was to consider, at a minimum, the following factors:

> a. Information relating to the structure located on the property;
>
> b. Nature of the use;
>
> c. Location of the property in relation to surrounding uses;
>
> d. Description of the character of and uses in the surrounding neighborhood;
>
> e. Cost of the property and improvements to the property;
>
> f. Benefit to the public by requiring the termination of the non-conforming use;
>
> g. Burden on the property owner by requiring the termination of the non-conforming use;
>
> h. The length of time the use has been in existence and the length of time the use has been non-conforming.

Id. § 14:7–4(D)(2). The city council accepted AVR's registration of the plant property as substantially complete on June 29, 1995.

On July 11, 1995, the city council and planning commission held a joint public hearing for the purpose of adopting an amortization ordinance relating to the AVR plant. City staff presented to the council and planning commission the report and recommendation required by the 1992 ordinance. AVR presented information supporting its position that the plant has an indefinite remaining physical life.

On October 2, 1995, the city amended its zoning ordinance by adopting the following provision:

> The reasonable amortization period applicable to the ready-mix facility owned and operated by [AVR] * * * shall be two (2) years, commencing upon publication of this ordinance. At the conclusion of the two-year amortization period, [AVR's] nonconforming ready-mix use shall terminate and cease to operate.

Id. § 14:7–4.1 (1995). In conjunction with the adoption of section 14:7–4.1, the city council adopted a resolution that contained 42 findings of fact supporting the ordinance and that stated:

> The Minnesota Supreme Court has directed, in the *Naegele Outdoor Advertising Co. of Minn. v. Village of Minnetonka* decision, that any amortization period must be "reasonable." Courts in other jurisdictions have identified at least seven (7) factors by which the reasonableness of an amortization period may be evaluated. The St. Louis

Park Code of Ordinances incorporates those specific factors in its Amortization Ordinance.

St. Louis Park, Minn., Res. No. 95-131, p. 3 (1995) (citing St. Louis Park, Minn., Code of Ordinances § 14:7-4(D)(2)(a-h) (1992)). The city addressed the factors identified in its amortization ordinance in making findings to support its determination of the length of the amortization period for AVR's plant.

The city also considered the useful life of the plant. To assist it in making that determination, the city retained an accounting firm and a real estate appraisal firm. The accounting firm advised the city that, based on generally accepted accounting principles, the plant's "useful life expired no later than 1994" and that AVR had not only recovered its investment but also had earned a return of approximately 560 percent on its investment. *Id.* p. 37. The city council found that

> [b]ased upon the expert opinions of Arthur Andersen and Patchin, the age of [AVR's] St. Louis Park Facility, AVR's proposal to the City nine years ago to replace the existing St. Louis Park structure, AVR's testimony regarding necessary size of potential relocation sites, and the voluntary relocation and/or new construction actions of other ready-mix businesses in the Twin Cities area, AVR's St. Louis Park Facility has passed its useful life and AVR has had a reasonable opportunity to recover its economic investment.

Id. p.39.

In December 1995, AVR commenced an action seeking a declaration that the city's adoption of the amortization ordinance and the ordinance establishing a two-year amortization period for AVR's plant (1) violate AVR's right to due process of law; (2) violate AVR's right to equal protection of the laws; (3) violate AVR's vested rights by eliminating concrete ready-mix plants as a special or permitted use; and (4) constitute an unconstitutional taking of AVR's property without just compensation. AVR and the city made cross-motions for summary judgment. On January 15, 1998, the district court granted summary judgment to the city and dismissed AVR's complaint. This appeal followed.

* * *

AVR contends that the city's adoption of an amortization ordinance for AVR's plant is equivalent to a decision to grant or deny a variance or special use permit. Therefore, AVR argues, the city's decision is quasi-judicial and the courts should afford it less deference than they would give a legislative zoning decision. Minnesota courts have distinguished

> between zoning matters which are legislative in nature (rezoning) and those which are quasi-judicial (variances and special use permits). Even so, the standard of review is the same for all zoning matters, namely, whether the zoning authority's action was reasonable. Our cases express this standard in various ways: Is there a "reasonable basis" for the decision? or is the decision "unreason-

able, arbitrary or capricious'"? or is the decision "reasonably debatable"?

Honn v. City of Coon Rapids, 313 N.W.2d 409, 416–17 (Minn.1981). But application of the reasonableness standard depends on the zoning action at issue:

> [I]n legislative zoning, the municipal body is formulating public policy, so the inquiry focuses on whether the proposed use promotes the public welfare. In quasi-judicial zoning, public policy has already been established and the inquiry focuses on whether the proposed use is contrary to the general welfare as already established in the zoning ordinance. Consequently, the reviewing courts, in determining what is reasonable, should keep in mind that the zoning authority is less circumscribed by judicial oversight when it considers zoning or rezoning than when it considers a special use permit or a variance.

Id. at 417. AVR argues that because the amortization ordinance "does not effect a zoning change to unimproved property" but rather "terminat[es] AVR's use of the property" as a ready-mix plant, it is "equivalent to the grant or denial of a special use permit." We disagree. *See Naegele Outdoor Adver. Co. v. Village of Minnetonka*, 281 Minn. 492, 501, 503, 162 N.W.2d 206, 213, 215 (1968) (identifying ordinance establishing amortization period as legislative device and stating power to enact "this type of zoning requirement" is implied); *DI MA Corp. v. City of St. Cloud*, 562 N.W.2d 312, 319–20 (Minn.App.1997) (analyzing validity of amortization ordinance under statute that establishes requirements for amendments to zoning ordinances).

Because zoning or rezoning classifications are legislative acts, courts must uphold them unless

> [their] opponents prove that the classification is unsupported by any rational basis related to promoting the public health, safety, morals, or general welfare, or that the classification amounts to a taking without compensation. This rule applies regardless of the size of the tract of land involved.

State by Rochester Ass'n of Neighborhoods v. City of Rochester, 268 N.W.2d 885, 888 (Minn.1978).

AVR has not shown that the city's adoption of the ordinance establishing an amortization period for AVR's plant is unsupported by any rational basis related to the promotion of the public health, safety, morals, or general welfare. Because the city's establishment of an amortization period for a preexisting nonconforming use was a legislative act, we conclude that the district court did not err in deferring to the city's broad discretion.

AVR contends that the two-year amortization period for its plant is unreasonable. In establishing the length of the amortization period, the city considered the plant's "useful life," a term the Minnesota Supreme Court has used but has not defined. *Naegele*, 281 Minn. at 501, 162

N.W.2d at 213 (stating only "that the useful life of the nonconforming use corresponds roughly to the amortization period"). The city based its determination of useful life on its conclusion that AVR had recouped its original investment and, to a lesser extent, on the fact that the property has been fully depreciated for income tax purposes. In addition, the city considered the other factors it had adopted by ordinance.

AVR argues that the city acted unreasonably in failing to consider "the remaining useful economic or expected life" in determining the length of the amortization period. *See, e.g., City of La Mesa v. Tweed & Gambrell Planing Mill*, 146 Cal.App.2d 762, 304 P.2d 803, 808 (Cal.Dist. Ct.App.1956) (noting estimated 21 years of remaining economic life as one reason for holding five-year amortization period arbitrary and unreasonable). In *Naegele*, the supreme court stated only that the underlying issue in determining the length of an amortization period is whether it is reasonable. 281 Minn. at 501, 162 N.W.2d at 213.

In analyzing the reasonableness of an amortization period, courts in some jurisdictions have considered the property owner's recoupment of its original investment. *See, e.g., Rives v. City of Clarksville*, 618 S.W.2d 502, 510 (Tenn.Ct.App.1981) (considering length of amortization period in relation to property owner's investment); *Town of Islip v. Caviglia*, 73 N.Y.2d 544, 542 N.Y.S.2d 139, 540 N.E.2d 215, 224 (N.Y.1989) (determining reasonableness by examining all facts, including length of amortization period in relation to investment); *City of University Park v. Benners*, 485 S.W.2d 773, 777 (Tex.1972) (noting that termination of nonconforming use after amortization period allowing recoupment of investment is not unconstitutional taking).

Courts also have considered whether the property in question has been fully depreciated for income tax purposes in reviewing the reasonableness of an amortization period, although this factor alone has not been held to be determinative. *See, e.g., Art Neon Co. v. City & County of Denver*, 488 F.2d 118, 122 (10th Cir.1973) (considering depreciation for tax purposes); National Adver. Co. v. County of Monterey, 1 Cal.3d 875, 83 Cal.Rptr. 577, 464 P.2d 33, 35–36 (Cal.1970) (holding that where billboards have been fully depreciated for tax purposes, amortization period was not unreasonable); *Village of Skokie v. Walton on Dempster, Inc.*, 119 Ill.App.3d 299, 74 Ill.Dec. 791, 456 N.E.2d 293, 297 (Ill.App.Ct. 1983) (concluding that amortization period was reasonable where property was completely depreciated for tax purposes); *Philanz Oldsmobile, Inc. v. Keating*, 51 A.D.2d 437, 381 N.Y.S.2d 916, 920 (N.Y.App.Div.1976) (stating that where signs had been fully depreciated for tax purposes, financial loss is nonexistent).

To the extent AVR's contention that the city should have considered the "remaining useful economic or expected life" of AVR's plant is another way of saying that the amortization period should be based on the plant's fair market value or its replacement cost, the argument leads to illogical and contradictory consequences. As one court has recognized:

[A]pplication of the market-value standard would result in a vicious circle: market value depends on the period of expected nonconforming use, and the period of nonconforming use allowed depends on market value. * * *

Cost of replacing the nonconforming structure, even with an allowance for depreciation, would also provide an unsatisfactory measure of recoupment. A landowner is not permitted to extend the period of nonconforming use by replacements or improvements because [the owner] would be able to extend the nonconforming use indefinitely * * *. To allow replacement cost as a measure of the recoupment allowed would thus allow unjustified extension of the nonconforming use. Moreover, [it] would ignore the factor of obsolescence, which might be substantial * * *.

Murmur Corp. v. Board of Adjustment, 718 S.W.2d 790, 796–97 (Tex. App.1986) (citations omitted).

Here, the city used a combination of recoupment of investment and tax depreciation status as factors in determining the useful life for AVR's plant. The record shows that over the past 23 years the plant provided AVR a return of approximately 560% on its investment and that the plant has been fully depreciated for income tax purposes. These two factors provided the city with a reasonable basis to determine the plant's useful life for purposes of establishing an amortization period.

* * *

Because the ordinance establishing a two-year amortization period for AVR's plant reflects the city's consideration of the plant's useful life and an analysis of other relevant factors adopted by the city, the district court did not err in upholding the city's two-year amortization period.

* * *

Because the city's action was a legislative decision, the district court did not err in deferring to the city's broad discretion to adopt an ordinance establishing a two-year amortization period for AVR's plant. Additionally, because the ordinance establishing an amortization period for AVR's plant is based on the city's consideration of the plant's useful life and application of other relevant factors, the district court did not err in upholding the city's establishment of a two-year amortization period. Finally, because AVR did not demonstrate disparate treatment of similarly situated property owners resulting from the enactment of the amortization ordinance and the ordinance establishing a two-year amortization period for AVR's plant, the district court did not err in concluding that there is no equal protection violation.

Affirmed.

Notes

1. In Akron v. Chapman, 160 Ohio St. 382, 116 N.E.2d 697, 42 A.L.R.2d 1140 (1953), the city required the defendant's nonconforming

junkyard to comply with the requirements of the new residential classification specified in the zoning ordinance. The defendant continued to operate his junkyard and the city brought an action to close his business. In holding for the property owner, the court wrote: "What is property? It has been defined as not merely the ownership and possession of lands or chattels but the unrestricted right of their use, enjoyment and disposal. Anything which destroys any of these elements of property, to that extent destroys the property itself. The substantial value of property lies in its use. If the right of use is denied, the value of the property is annihilated and ownership is rendered a barren right. See Spann v. City of Dallas, 111 Tex. 350, 235 S.W. 513, 19 A.L.R. 1387, and O'Connor v. City of Moscow, 69 Idaho 37, 202 P.2d 401, 9 A.L.R.2d 1031. The right to continue to use one's property in a lawful business and in a manner which does not constitute a nuisance and which was lawful at the time it was acquired is within the protection of Section 1, Article XIV, Amendments, Constitution of the United States, and Section 16, Article I of the Ohio Constitution, which provide that no person shall be deprived of life, liberty or property without due process of law."

2. For a case with facts similar to the Akron case but an opposite result, see Collins v. City of Spartanburg, 281 S.C. 212, 314 S.E.2d 332 (1984). The court upheld an ordinance imposing a five-year amortization period on junkyards, auto wrecking yards and auto storage yards, balancing the large public gain from elimination of eyesores against the small private loss. Also see Neighborhood Committee on Lead Pollution v. Board of Adj. of City of Dallas, 728 S.W.2d 64 (Tex.App.1987), where the court upheld a six-year amortization period for a lead smelting and plating operation. Under Texas law, the Board of Adjustment may determine the termination date for nonconforming uses, under the standard of examining the capital investment in the structure by the person owning the land at the time the use became nonconforming. Board of Adjustment of Dallas v. Patel, 882 S.W.2d 87 (Tex.App.1994).

3. The amortization technique has been widely discussed in the literature, and has found its way into the text of a large number of zoning ordinances. Despite the attention given, very few significant land uses have been eliminated as a result of amortization. In 1971, the American Society of Planning Officials polled its membership to determine the extent to which amortization was being used to eliminate nonconforming uses. Out of 489 cities and counties responding, 159 reported that their zoning ordinances contained amortization provisions, but only 27 communities reported use of the technique against buildings and structures. Where amortization has been used it has usually been against billboards or other uses involving a negligible capital investment. In general, most zoning administrators who were surveyed expressed dissatisfaction with the amortization technique. See Robert Scott, The Effect of Nonconforming Land–Use Amortization, (Planning Advisory Service Report No. 280, May, 1972).

4. In Centaur, Inc. v. Richland County, 301 S.C. 374, 392 S.E.2d 165 (1990), the court upheld a two-year amortization period for sexually-oriented business and limiting their relocation to 16 specified areas in the county.

SECTION 5. ACCESSORY USES

Accessory uses are those uses of land found on the same lot as the principal use and that are subordinate, incidental to, and customarily found in connection with the principal use. For example, a garage is accessory to a residential use of a property because it is customarily found in connection with and is incidental and subordinate to the principal residential use. Generally, zoning laws permit lot owners to use their land for a permitted principal use as well for activities that are accessory to that use.

In order to qualify as accessory, a use must also be incidental and subordinate to the principal use. To be incidental, an accessory use must be reasonably related to the principal use. For instance, a garage or recreational use is reasonably related to the principal residential use and thus deemed incidental. To be subordinate, the accessory use must be proportionately smaller than the principal use. The garage is generally smaller than the house, for instance. An accessory use must also be customarily found in conjunction with its principal use. A use is customary if it commonly, habitually, and by long practice has been reasonably associated with a principal use. A most common example of this is vehicle parking for a residence or business.

Accessory use provisions in zoning laws allow a range of incidental uses of property that owners expect to engage in when they purchase their property for its principal use. By permitting uses customarily incidental and subordinate to the principal activity, zoning ordinances allow property owners additional beneficial use of their property. Regulations which limit the accessory uses allowed in a district also recognize that some neighborhoods should be protected from accessory uses that are not consistent with the expectations of the property owners. This separation of inconsistent uses into zoning districts is part of the original purpose of zoning.

Local ordinances regulate accessory uses in a variety of ways. Within the local zoning law language regulating accessory uses may be found in the definitions of "accessory," "lot," or "use," in separate sections, or in the schedule of regulations for individual districts. There are at least five different approaches a municipality can utilize to regulate accessory uses in its zoning law.

- First, a municipality may simply permit accessory uses by accepting those uses that meet the qualifications of what is customary and incidental. In this case the ordinance does not provide guidelines or expressly state what is or is not an accessory use. Rather, the ordinance simply defines accessory uses as customary, incidental, and subordinate in the definition section and then permits these uses in each district.

- Second, a zoning law may permit certain accessory uses and prohibit all others. The legislature can do this by listing which accessory uses are allowed in each use district. As a matter of statutory construction, those uses not expressly permitted in the list are prohibited unless clearly stated otherwise. This is the most restrictive means of regulation because it limits what qualifies as an accessory use to the legislature's list. It could result in denial of a use that is otherwise incidental, subordinate, and customary to the principal use.

- A more flexible approach is to list and prohibit only problematic accessory uses. This eliminates foreseeable problems with the listed uses while permitting all other accessory uses that are customary, incidental, and subordinate.
- A fourth approach is to provide guidelines that can assist the zoning enforcement officer and zoning board of appeals in interpreting what is an accessory use and by adopting a nonexclusive, illustrative list of acceptable uses. If this approach is used, it is crucial that the law explicitly state that the list is nonexclusive.
- A final regulatory approach is to list some accessory uses that are allowed by special use permit and subject them to certain requirements. This approach can be used by itself or in conjunction with any of the other four approaches.

Permitting accessory uses creates needed flexibility, but can also create problems both for landowners and the municipality. A municipality must be careful when enforcing accessory use regulations against educational institutions and religious organizations. Accessory uses connected to these principal uses are presumed to serve the public interest if they are incidental to the principal use. Although originally intended to permit landowners to use their property fully, the accessory use device is sometimes used to expand greatly the intensity of use, establish a unique or novel use, to expand a nonconforming use, or to change the use of a property when a variance cannot be obtained. A municipality drafting and enforcing an accessory use provision should be careful to avoid these concerns.

COLLINS v. LONERGAN

New York Appellate Division, Second Department, 1993.
198 A.D.2d 349.

MEMORANDUM BY THE COURT.

In a proceeding pursuant to CPLR article 78 to review a determination of the Zoning Board of Appeals of the Town of Lewisboro dated June 28, 1991, which, after a hearing, granted the appellants a permit to construct a skateboard ramp upon certain conditions, the appeal is from a judgment of the Supreme Court, Westchester County (Herold, J.), entered August 27, 1991, 151 Misc.2d 994, 574 N.Y.S.2d 495, which granted the petition and annulled the determination.

ORDERED that the judgment is reversed, on the law, with costs payable by the petitioners to the appellants, the determination is confirmed, and the proceeding is dismissed on the merits.

A zoning board determination should not be set aside unless there is a showing of illegality, arbitrariness, or abuse of discretion (see, *Matter of Fuhst v. Foley*, 45 N.Y.2d 441, 444, 410 N.Y.S.2d 56, 382 N.E.2d 756, *Conley v. Town of Brookhaven Zoning Bd. of Appeals*, 40 N.Y.2d 309, 386 N.Y.S.2d 681, 353 N.E.2d 594). Therefore, "the determination of responsible local officials * * * will be sustained if it has a rational basis and is supported by substantial evidence" (see, *Matter of Fuhst v. Foley,* supra, 45 N.Y.2d at 444, 410 N.Y.S.2d 56, 382 N.E.2d 756). We find that the Supreme Court erred in annulling the determination of the Zoning Board. The Board's determination that a skateboard ramp is a permitted accessory use because it is customarily incidental to the primary use, had a rational basis, and was not illegal, or arbitrary and capricious.

GREENTREE v. GOOD SHEPHERD EPISCOPAL CHURCH

Supreme Court, New York County, New York, 1989.
550 N.Y.S.2d 981, 146 Misc.2d 500.

LEONARD N. COHEN, JUSTICE:

" * * * [T]HERE WAS NO ROOM FOR THEM IN THE INN." (LUKE 2:7)

This is a motion by plaintiffs, a unit owner and President of the Board of Managers of a condominium known as Greentree At Murray Hill, located at 248 East 31st Street, New York, New York (the "Condominium") to temporarily enjoin defendants from operating a homeless shelter at Good Shepherd Episcopal Church (the "Church") adjacent to the condominium. By separate notices of cross-motion, the defendant Church, the defendant The Partnership for the Homeless, Inc. (the "Partnership"), and the City defendants, seek dismissal of the complaint for failure to state a cause of action.

"AM I MY BROTHER'S KEEPER?" (GENESIS 4:9)

This action involves important questions regarding who shall be responsible for our less fortunate brothers and sisters. Specifically, the action concerns the extent, if any, to which the court may or should be brought in as arbiter of a dispute involving the right of a church and its parishioners to exercise their religion and to practice Christian charity by temporarily sheltering the homeless and the rights of some of the adjacent property-owning residents who fear crime, drug sales, prostitution and a diminution of property values.

In June 1989, in response to the citywide need for emergency shelters for the thousands of homeless, the Church opened its doors to groups of ten (10) homeless men for temporary emergency shelter three (3) nights a week, in cooperation with the defendant Partnership. The Partnership, a not-for-profit corporation, was founded in August 1982, by lay persons from various religious congregations with leaders of the major religious faith denominations, to provide the major interfaith response to the growing problem of homelessness in New York City. The

Partnership presently includes a network of over 380 churches and synagogues in all five boroughs, as well as programs in other major cities across the nation. The Partnership's temporary homeless shelter city network currently embraces 147 church/synagogue shelters, including this Church, providing up to 1600 homeless beds at the height of the winter and over 400,000 individual nights of temporary shelter annually.

Although the Partnership has a contractual relationship with defendant New York City Human Resources Administration ("HRA"), which provides approximately 17 percent of its operating budget, and less than 3 percent of its total budget, the bulk of its operating budget is funded from the private sector. The City, through HRA's contract with the Church, provides only beds, linens, clothing, toiletries and cleaning supplies. The City's Department of Buildings periodically inspects the space for compliance with relevant health and safety regulations. The City does not pay either the Partnership or the Church for its temporary sheltering of the homeless, nor does the City provide for any siting control. Sites for temporary shelters are selected by the Partnership in cooperation with participating churches and/or synagogues. The homeless men who are afforded temporary shelter at the Church are transported there by the City from the John Heuss Center, a drop-in center on Beaver Street in lower Manhattan, established by Trinity Parish. The men arrive between 9:15–9:45 p.m., and are picked up by bus the following morning at approximately 6:00 a.m. From the time of their arrival until their departure the following morning, the men are continually supervised and are not allowed to congregate in the street. The court notes that the Church also has a program which provides food for the hungry on Sundays (following the morning service) and on Fridays at lunchtime. That program—which is not the subject of this lawsuit—distributes bag lunches to approximately 100 guests on Sunday and between 50–75 on Friday. The funds are provided entirely by the Parish and the work is done entirely by parishioners.

In opposition to plaintiff's motion to temporarily enjoin operation of its homeless shelter, and in support of its cross motion to dismiss the complaint, the Church has submitted affidavits by The Right Reverend Richard F. Grein, and Bishop Coadjutor and acting Ecclesiastical Authority of the Diocese of New York of the Episcopal Church, and by the Reverend Vincent Ioppolo, Rector of the Church, attesting to their deep and sincere religious convictions underlying their participation in the homeless shelter program. They cite the teachings of Jesus and the Holy Scriptures and resolutions adopted by the Diocese at its conventions in 1973, 1981, 1983, 1984, 1985 and 1986.

The Bishop states:

"While others may debate the root causes of hunger and homelessness and who should bear the ultimate responsibility for feeding and housing the victims, as Christians, we do not believe we have the leisure to turn our backs in the meantime on those in our midst who hunger, thirst or have no place to lay their heads."

The Rector of the Church states that:

> "[C]aring for the poor and sheltering the homeless has consistently been part of religion in the Judeo–Christian tradition. The mandate to embrace and to minister to society's outcasts is a lesson learnt [sic] from the Bible."

The Bishop and Rector cite Bible chapter and verse in support of their position that sheltering the homeless is a religious obligation and an important outlet for its ministry.

The Reverend Ioppolo also states that "the religious tradition of giving refuge to persons in need has its roots in Roman, medieval European and English common law. During the Middle Ages every church was a potential sanctuary. Religious sanctuary is an equally well-established practice in this country."

Plaintiffs do not seriously question the sincerity of the religious convictions of the defendant Church or ascribe any but honorable motivations to its conduct in opening up its doors to the handful of homeless men three nights a week. However, they assert that the Church may not house the ten homeless men because such use of the Church would constitute a violation of the applicable Zoning Resolution and the Church's Certificate of Occupancy. Plaintiffs also claim that such use constitutes a public and private nuisance.

* * *

[Portions of the case dealing with other claims of the plaintiffs are omitted]

The plaintiffs argue as to the first and second causes of action that the Church is currently classified as a "Place of Assembly," pursuant to Subchapter 3, § 27–254 of the New York City Charter, and, as such, it may only be used "for religious, recreational, political or social purposes, or for the consumption of food or drink or for similar group activities * * *." They argue that for the premises to be used legally as a shelter, it would have to be classified for "residential use," pursuant to subchapter 3, § 27–264 of the New York City Charter, which applies to "buildings and spaces that are primarily occupied for the shelter and sleeping accommodations of individuals on a day-to-day or week-to-week basis" (emphasis added). Plaintiffs further argue that a new Certificate of Occupancy is required "to ensure that the premises are safe for their intended use" and that the Church is being used as a hotel or motel contrary to the Certificate of Occupancy. They state that a new Certificate of Occupancy is therefore required because such "unauthorized and illegal use threatens not only the people staying within the Church but the adjoining property owners such as the plaintiffs herein."

It has long been held that a church or synagogue may be used for accessory uses and activities which go beyond just prayer and worship (*Community Synagogue v. Bates*, 1 N.Y.2d 445, 453, 154 N.Y.S.2d 15, 136 N.E.2d 488 [1956]). Section 12–10 of the Zoning Resolution defines the term "accessory use" and relevantly states that such use:

"(a) Is a use conducted on the same zoning lot as the principal use to which it is related (whether located within the same accessory building or other structure, or as an accessory use of land), * * * and

(b) Is a use which is clearly incidental to, and customarily found in connection with, such principal use; and

(c) Is either in the same ownership as such principal use, or is operated and maintained on the same zoning lot substantially for the benefit or convenience of the owner, occupants, employees, customers, or visitors of the principal use."

Such permissible "accessory uses" for a church or synagogue include a Sunday school, men's and women's clubs, youth and community centers (*Id*); a guest house for a Rabbi (*Jewish Reconstructionist Synagogue v. Incorporated Village of Roslyn Harbor*, 38 N.Y.2d 283, 379 N.Y.S.2d 747, 342 N.E.2d 534 [1975], rearg. denied, 39 N.Y.2d 743, 384 N.Y.S.2d 1029, 349 N.E.2d 892 [1976], cert. denied, 426 U.S. 950, 96 S.Ct. 3171, 49 L.Ed.2d 1187); a school and meeting room at a church (*Diocese of Rochester v. Planning Bd. of Town of Brighton*, 1 N.Y.2d 508, 154 N.Y.S.2d 849, 136 N.E.2d 827 [1956]); a day care center (*Unitarian Universalist Church v. Shorten*, 63 Misc.2d 978, 314 N.Y.S.2d 66 [Sup. Ct., Nassau Co 1970]); a drug program (*Slevin v. Long Island Jewish Med. Center*, 66 Misc.2d 312, 319 N.Y.S.2d 937 [Sup.Ct. Nassau Co.1971]) as well as a temporary shelter for the homeless operated by a church, such as in the case at bar (*St. John's Evangelical Lutheran Church v. City of Hoboken*, 195 N.J.Super. 414, 479 A.2d 935 [Hudson Co.1983]).

Therefore, it is clear that the Church's temporary homeless shelter sanctuary program is, as a matter of law, a permissible "accessory use" of the Church which is a protected activity under § 12–10 of the Zoning Resolution and under the Church's current Certificate of Occupancy. Accordingly, plaintiffs' argument that the use of Church property as an emergency temporary shelter for the homeless violates the applicable Zoning Resolution and its Certificate of Occupancy is without merit.

Plaintiffs' argument that the Church is operating a "hotel or motel for transients," contrary to its Certificate of Occupancy and requiring a zoning variance, is also without merit. There is no allegation that living or sleeping accommodations are being rented, or that provisions exist for a 24 hour desk, bellboy or telephone service. Under Zoning Resolution § 12–10, such factors are the sine qua non of a "hotel" (See also, Black's Law Dictionary [rev. 4th ed.], which defines a "hotel" as "a house which is held out to well-behaved members of the traveling public, *who are willing to pay reasonable rates for accommodations*, as a place where they will be received and entertained *as guests for compensation*, and will be furnished with food, drink, and lodging, and everything which they have occasion for while on their way" [emphasis added]).

To the extent that the first and second causes of action allege violations of the Zoning Resolution and Certificate of Occupancy, the court finds, as a matter of law, that such allegations fail to state causes of action. Accordingly, the defendants' cross motions to dismiss those branches of the first and second causes of action are granted.

* * *

DOBO v. ZONING BD. OF ADJUSTMENT OF CITY OF WILMINGTON

Supreme Court of North Carolina, 2003.
576 S.E.2d 324, 356 N.C. 656.

PER CURIAM.

For the reasons stated in the dissenting opinion, the decision of the Court of Appeals is reversed and the case is remanded to the Court of Appeals for further remand to the Superior Court, New Hanover County, for proceedings not inconsistent with the dissenting opinion. REVERSED AND REMANDED; DISCRETIONARY REVIEW IMPROVIDENTLY ALLOWED.

TYSON, JUDGE, * * * I respectfully dissent from part IIA of the majority's opinion as I would hold that petitioners' actual use of the Wood–Mizer portable band saw does not violate the Zoning Ordinance.

IIA.

Petitioners argue that the Board's decision was not supported by competent evidence, and is arbitrary and capricious. I agree. Section 19–6 of the Zoning Ordinance defines the term "accessory use": Accessory use or structure: A use or structure on the same lot with, and of a nature customarily incidental and subordinate to, the principal use or structure (i.e. pump house, home occupation, tool shed, detached garage, storage shed, garage apartment, and other uses as determined by the Code Enforcement Officer).

All of the evidence presented shows that petitioners used the Wood-Mizer saw for non-commercial and non-industrial purposes, as well as for the construction of a fully permitted hobby woodworking shop to be located on their property. I disagree with the majority that because the saw is powered by a forty-horsepower diesel engine; is twenty-six feet four inches in length, six feet six inches wide, seven feet seven inches high; includes the use of a trailer, backhoe, front-end loader, and dump truck; and is capable of cutting logs twenty-one feet long by three inches in diameter automatically converts the use of the Wood–Mizer saw into an industrial use or involves a manufacturing process. Adopting the reasoning of the majority would allow the City to prohibit petitioners' private automobile, with a 200 horsepower engine and a twenty gallon gas tank, because it could be used as a commercial taxicab.

Construction necessarily requires heavy equipment to complete the improvements, such as bulldozers, dump trucks, and front-end loaders for clearing and grading of the land, as well as cranes to set trusses on the structure. Here, the record shows that the backhoe, front-end loader, and dump truck were also legally located on petitioners' 3.2 acre tract, as petitioners legally operate a well drilling business on their property. The Board's and majority's focus is solely on the size and possible uses of the saw, not its actual use by petitioners. Their assertions are insufficient to prohibit petitioners' non-industrial use of their saw.

The conclusion of the Board that "[t]he use of the sawmill on the Dobo property is not a permitted use during the construction of the accessory structure on the property" is not supported by substantial, competent evidence. There is no evidence in the record that petitioners' use of the Wood–Mizer saw to construct a fully permitted woodworking hobby shop is not a permitted use during construction. Testimony by the Code Enforcement Officer that the use of the saw would not be customary is speculative as he further testified that he does not enforce the building code. *See C.C. & J. Enter., Inc. v. City of Asheville*, 132 N.C.App. 550, 553, 512 S.E.2d 766, 769, *disc. review improvidently allowed*, 351 N.C. 97, 521 S.E.2d 117 (1999) (speculative assertions or mere expression of opinion about the possible effects of granting a permit are insufficient to support the findings of a quasi-judicial body).

This Court in *Tucker v. The Mecklenburg Cty. Zoning Bd. of Adjust.*, 148 N.C.App. 52, 557 S.E.2d 631 (2001), addressed a similar issue involving the operation of a dog kennel by respondents on their residentially zoned property. The zoning ordinance in *Tucker* permitted the operation of a private kennel as an accessory use and prohibited the operation of a commercial kennel. While in all respects the kennel operated by respondents could have been used as a commercial kennel, the Board of Adjustment found that because the dogs were adopted and not sold, the kennel was not a commercial kennel but a private kennel permitted as an accessory use under the zoning ordinance. *Id.* at 57–59, 557 S.E.2d at 635–36. This Court agreed and reversed the trial court's order finding the kennel to be a commercial kennel in violation of the zoning ordinance. *Id.* at 57–59, 557 S.E.2d at 636.

Here, the evidence clearly establishes that petitioners used the saw primarily for the construction of a permitted and allowed hobby woodworking shop behind their home and occasionally for the cutting of lumber for friends without charge. There is no evidence that the actual use of the saw by petitioners is for industrial or manufacturing purposes nor that it is not "of a nature that is customarily incidental and subordinate to" the residential use of their property. The actual use of the saw in this case is an accessory use and does not violate the Zoning Ordinance. Counsel for respondent conceded that the construction of the hobby shop is fully permitted and is an allowed accessory use of petitioners' residentially zoned property. Accordingly, I would hold that the Board's decision was not supported by substantial, competent evidence and was arbitrary and capricious.

Petitioners argue that if we scratch the surface facts, it is readily apparent that this action is a thinly veiled attempt by the residents of the adjoining subdivision to impose *de facto* restrictive covenants onto petitioners' property that were never bargained for nor agreed to by petitioners.

The general rule is that a zoning ordinance, being in derogation of common law property rights, should be construed in favor of the free use of property. *See Yancey v. Heafner,* 268 N.C. 263, 266, 150 S.E.2d 440, 443 (1966); *City of Sanford v. Dandy Signs, Inc.,* 62 N.C.App. 568, 569, 303 S.E.2d 228, 230 (1983). Zoning regulations are not a substitute for private restrictive covenants. If the subdivision residents believe that petitioners' use of their property is unreasonable, their remedy is an action in nuisance, not to enlist the City as an accomplice by incessant complaints about their neighbor.

The record shows that petitioners have owned, used, and lived on their property for half a century. The recent addition of an exclusive, walled, and gated subdivision on adjoining property does not convert petitioners' lawful use into an illegal one, simply because petitioners' use is inconsistent with the permitted uses within the adjoining subdivision. Purchasers of lots in a subdivision development, located in formerly rural areas that are rapidly urbanizing, have the duty to inform themselves of uses on adjoining, but unrestricted, property that may not compliment the restrictions and uses that subdivision residents privately covenant among themselves and that apply solely within the confines of their development.

Petitioners further object to the irrelevant statements made by the adjoining neighbors to the Board as to noise and smell from petitioners' property, burning by petitioners on their property, and junk on petitioners' property. The record clearly shows and counsel for respondent conceded that despite numerous visits to petitioners' property, no violation of the penal noise ordinance was found or other ordinances. While there is no indication that the Board's decision was based on this testimony, speculative opinions such as these fail to constitute substantial competent evidence to support a finding that the petitioners' use was not an accessory use. *See C.C. & J.,* 132 N.C.App. at 553, 512 S.E.2d at 769. There is no competent evidence in the record that petitioners' actual use of the Wood–Mizer saw did not constitute an accessory use under the Zoning Ordinance. I would reverse the superior court's order, affirming the 3–2 decision of the Board, and dissent from part IIA of the majority's opinion.

Notes

1. In the Collins case, how do you imagine the matter got to the Zoning Board of Appeals in the first place? If the zoning code simply allows accessory uses that are incidental, subordinate, and customary, then how would a homeowner proceed to get permission to construct a skateboard ramp? Since the jurisdiction of the Zoning Board of Appeals is appellate only with regard to such matters, what decision must have been appealed to it to give it jurisdiction to determine whether the ramp was a permissible accessory use? See Bagko Development Co. v. Damitz, 640 N.E.2d 67 (Ind.App. 4

Dist., 1994), where the court upheld a property owner's development and use of Little League practice facility. The facility was built on a lot adjoining the lot containing their home and did not violate the zoning ordinance. The primary use of double lot was residential, and use of practice facility for approximately 8.7 hours per week for about 10 weeks of the year was a subordinate "accessory recreational use" of property.

2. Is a skateboard ramp in 1993 truly a use customarily found in connection with the use of a single-family home? If the Zoning Board of Appeals decided that it was not and, for that reason, denied the homeowner's appeal, what would the effect of that decision be on the ability of homeowners to adopt new recreational uses that evolve with inventions in the recreational segment of the economy? When the ZBA found that skateboard ramps are customarily found in connection with single-family use was it finding that in a literal sense or that recreational uses of this type and intensity are customary in single-family neighborhoods? If you owned the house adjacent to the Collins' home and you had a tennis court in your yard, could you explain the difference in intensity of use between your recreational use and that proposed by your neighbors? What facts would the building inspector need to gather regarding a proposed skateboard ramp to determine whether it met the standards for an accessory use?

3. In Tucker v. Mecklenburg County Zoning Bd. of Adjustment, 557 S.E.2d 631 N.C.App. (2001), the North Carolina Court of Appeals held that respondent's kennel was a permitted accessory use. Respondents established Project HALO Corporation (HALO) as a non-profit organization with the primary goal being the rescue of stray and unwanted dogs. Respondents pay the county licensing and registration fees and taxes. HALO then pays all expenses associated with caring for the dogs. On average, respondents keep approximately 10 to 15 dogs in pens located between their residence and the rear lot line. The animals were not sold, but were either adopted or kept by homeowners, and all animals were owned and licensed by homeowners.

4. Similar to Tucker, the N.J. Superior Court found that a pigeon coop was an accessory use under the zoning code. See Colts Run Civic Ass'n v. Colts Neck Tp. Zoning Board of Adjustment, 315 N.J.Super. 240, 717 A.2d 456 N.J.Super.L. (1998). The question before the N.J. Superior Court was whether the maintenance of a "domestic animal shelter," in this case a pigeon coop, as a hobby activity is a permitted accessory use. The zoning district provided for a mixture of residential and agricultural uses. The stated purpose of the zoning plan for this district includes the "continuation of farming." The defendant represented that he raises, trains, and breeds racing pigeons only as a hobby. The pigeons would not be used for business or commercial purposes, and would not be sold, bred, shown, or raced for profit. Ultimately, defendant Board concluded that while the raising of racing pigeons does not serve agricultural purposes in this agriculturally sensitive zoning district, the proposed use is "subordinate" and "incidental" as an accessory use. The defendant Board reasoned that the raising of racing pigeons "while perhaps not a widely popular hobby, is nevertheless a hobby which is incidental to the residential use of the property in question and is the type of hobby which would customarily be associated with a residential use."

5. An antenna for a wireless mobile telephone system was not a permitted "accessory use" on the top of an apartment building. The court found that the principal use of apartment building was residential, while use of antennae was commercial. The antennae would serve only non-residents and those residents who subscribed to the provider's telephone services. See AWACS, Inc. v. Zoning Hearing Bd. of Newton Tp., Delaware County, 702 A.2d 604 (Pa.Cmwlth.1997).

SECTION 6. HOME OCCUPATIONS

Historically, single-family homes have been used by their occupants for a variety of occupational uses such as beauty parlors, dressmaking, laundries, and day care. Zoning limits single-family homes to residential uses and to those uses that are customarily associated with residential use and incidental and subordinate to that residential use. Does this mean that a single-family homeowner can conduct a particular business in a particular neighborhood, as an accessory use, or is the occupational use prohibited?

In some communities, this question is answered on a case-by-case basis without benefit of any special regulations. The zoning authorities examine the proposed occupational use and determine whether it is customary, incidental, and subordinate to the residential use. Other municipalities define "home occupations" more specifically in their zoning laws, requiring homeowners to conform their occupational uses to those definitions. Some adopt a list of permitted occupational uses of homes while others prohibit a specific list of occupations, while some use a standards approach using signs, traffic, and other activities more in keeping with commercial districts. Thus, a homeowner who trades stocks over the internet from her den does not need a permit while the next door neighbor who takes in children for day care does.

Permitting occupations to be conducted in single-family zoned neighborhoods honors expectations of homeowners that such uses have been permitted historically and are within the bundle of rights purchased with the single-family home. Zoning restrictions limiting the occupational use of homes recognize that residential districts must be protected from home occupations that are out of character with the neighborhood and are not uses that homeowners expect to be affected by when they purchase a home in a single-family area. One of the original purposes of zoning is to separate uses that are inconsistent with one another into distinct zoning districts.

Municipalities use a variety of techniques that municipalities use to regulate home occupations and professional offices:

1. They may let their definition of accessory uses govern the matter, leaving it to the zoning enforcement official to determine, in a given instance, whether a proposed occupational use is customary, incidental, and subordinate to the principal permitted use of a parcel as a single-family home.

2. Local legislatures may adopt a general definition of a home occupation to provide some guidance to enforcement officials to aid their determinations in these matters.

3. They may supplement their general definition of home occupation with a list of permitted occupations, a list of prohibited occupations, and a definition of permitted professional offices.

4. Specified home occupations may be permitted only upon the issuance of a special use permit by a designated reviewing board.

5. Local legislatures may include specific standards that certain occupational uses must meet, such as limiting the percentage of floor area that may be used, prohibiting carrying or selling of merchandise, prohibiting any alteration of the exterior of the building, limiting businesses to those conducted by occupants of the residence, and limiting the number of associates, partners, and employees.

BAKER v. POSINELLI

New York Appellate Division, Third Department, 1991.
177 A.D.2d 844, 576 N.Y.S.2d 460.

LEVINE, JUSTICE.

Appeal from a judgment of the Supreme Court (Doran, J.), entered September 10, 1990 in Schenectady County, which granted petitioner's application, in a proceeding pursuant to CPLR article 78, to annul a determination of respondent Town of Glenville Zoning Board of Appeals denying petitioner's request to use her home as a dance studio.

Petitioner is the owner of a residence on Kile Drive in the Town of Glenville, Schenectady County. The house is located in a residentially zoned district where, pursuant to Town of Glenville Zoning Ordinance § 6.2, home occupations are permitted under certain circumstances. Petitioner purchased the residence in late 1983 and began conducting dance classes in her home shortly thereafter. In September 1989, petitioner was served by respondent Town Building Inspector with a notice of violation of Town of Glenville Zoning Ordinance § 6.2. Petitioner then appealed to respondent Town Zoning Board of Appeals (hereinafter the Board) seeking a determination that her dance instruction was a permitted home occupation under § 6.2. After a public hearing, the Board voted to interpret the ordinance as not permitting the dance classes as a home occupation. The reasons of three of the four Board members who voted against petitioner's application were set forth in the minutes of the Board's April 1990 meeting. Subsequently, petitioner commenced the instant CPLR article 78 proceeding to annul the Board's determination. Supreme Court granted the petition, concluding that petitioner's dance studio was a permitted home occupation under the ordinance. This appeal ensued.

Section 6.2.1 of the Town's zoning ordinance governing home occupations provides that a home occupation is permitted in a residential district as a matter of right so long as it meets seven specified conditions.

Three of the conditions are relevant herein in requiring that the occupation be one which "[i]s customarily carried on in a dwelling unit or a building or other structure accessory to a dwelling unit", "[i]s clearly incidental and accessory or secondary to the use of the dwelling unit or residential purposes" and "[d]oes not produce offensive noise, odor, vibration, smoke, dust, heat or glare." In voting to disallow petitioner's dance studio as a permitted home occupation under the ordinance, the Board members who opposed petitioner's application relied on the foregoing provisions, reasoning essentially that (1) a dance studio of the size of petitioner's is not customarily carried on in a dwelling unit, (2) the use of petitioner's home as a dance studio was not clearly incidental to its use as a residence, and (3) the increased traffic on Kile Drive generated by the dance studio may produce offensive noise, odor, smoke, dust and vibration.

Initially, we note that the latter two reasons set forth by the Board are without factual support in the record. There was no evidence presented to the Board which would indicate that petitioner's use of the house for dance instruction was anything but incidental to its primary use as a residence. Nor was there sufficient proof that the increased traffic on Kile Drive, which was conceded by petitioner, had produced or would produce offensive noise, odor, smoke, dust or vibration.

We reach a different conclusion, however, with regard to the primary ground set forth by the Board that petitioner's dance studio, because of its size, was not an occupation "customarily carried on in a dwelling unit" and, hence, did not constitute a home occupation within the meaning of the ordinance. The evidence before the Board was that petitioner instructed approximately 160 dance students per week, holding classes 30 weeks out of the year, five days per week for 3 1/2 to 5 hours per day. The average size of petitioner's classes was eight students. "[T]he Board's interpretation of the home occupation provisions of the [z]oning [o]rdinance must be upheld if it is neither irrational nor unreasonable" (*Matter of Criscione v. Wallace*, 145 A.D.2d 697, 698, 535 N.Y.S.2d 238; *see, Matter of Aboud v. Wallace*, 94 A.D.2d 874, 875, 463 N.Y.S.2d 572). In view of the proof here, we cannot say that it was irrational for the Board to find that petitioner's operation was more extensive than what was intended to be permitted under the ordinance as a home occupation *(see, Matter of Aboud v. Wallace, supra; see also, Draving v. Lower Southampton Twp. Zoning Hearing Bd.*, 40 Pa. Commw. 243, 397 A.2d 54; *City of Florence v. Turbeville*, 239 S.C. 126, 121 S.E.2d 437). Accordingly, the Board's determination should be sustained. Because it is clear that the Board would have denied petitioner's application to use her home as a dance studio solely upon the foregoing basis, the invalidity of the other two grounds set forth by the Board is of no consequence (*cf., Matter of Van Euclid Co. v. Sargent*, 97 A.D.2d 913, 915, 470 N.Y.S.2d 750).

ORDERED that the judgment is reversed, on the law, with costs, determination confirmed and petition dismissed.

Mahoney, P.J., and Casey, Mercure and Harvey, JJ., concur.

TOWN OF SULLIVANS ISLAND v. BYRUM
Court of Appeals of South Carolina, 1992.
413 S.E.2d 325, 306 S.C. 539.

Per Curiam

The Plaintiff, Town of Sullivans Island (Town), sought to enjoin the Defendants, Byrums, from using part of their residence as a "Bed & Breakfast" boarding house. The Town also sought to enjoin the Byrums' use of a garage apartment for human habitation. The Town argued that both uses violated the applicable zoning ordinances. The trial judge refused the requested injunctions, and the Town appealed. We reverse and remand for the entry of an order granting both injunctions.

A fire damaged the Byrums' residence in 1983. The Byrums decided to renovate the house and use part of it as a Bed & Breakfast. As a result, the repair work went far beyond the fire damage, including the development of six separate bedrooms and baths. Nothing indicates that the Byrums told the Town of their intended use during the repair process.

At the time of the renovations, § 21-3 of the Town's zoning ordinances defined "permitted home occupation uses" as follows:

> Any use conducted entirely within a dwelling and carried on by the occupants thereof, which use is clearly incidental and secondary to the use of the dwelling for residential purposes and does not change the character thereof, and no person, not a resident of the premises is employed specifically in connection with the activity. Provided, further, that no mechanical equipment is installed or used except such as is normally used for domestic or professional purposes, and that not over twenty-five (25%) percent of the total floor space of any structure is used for home occupation.

This is the second time these parties have been before this Court regarding the Byrums' Bed & Breakfast operation. In the first case, the Byrums' sought a variance from the twenty-five (25%) per cent limitation on "home occupation" uses. The Board of Adjustment denied the variance on two grounds: (1) a Bed & Breakfast is not a home occupation; and (2) the operation exceeded the twenty-five (25%) per cent limitation on structural usage for home occupations. The Circuit Court reversed both findings on appeal. This Court reversed the Circuit Court and reinstated the Board's denial of the variance, concluding that the Bed & Breakfast operation exceeded the twenty-five (25%) per cent limitation. *Byrum v. Board of Adjustment*, 294 S.C. 114, 362 S.E.2d 890 (Ct.App.1987) (*Byrum* I). This Court did not discuss the first issue.

During the pendency of the appeal before the Circuit Court in *Byrum* I, the Town amended its "home occupation" ordinance and specifically prohibited the use of a residence as a boarding house. At the time of this amendment, the Byrums continued to use more than twenty-five (25%) per cent of the residence in the Bed & Breakfast operation contrary to both the original and the amended ordinance.

After this Court's decision in *Byrum* I, the Byrums continued to operate the Bed & Breakfast but allegedly reduced the structure usage to less than twenty-five (25%) per cent. They applied to the Town for a license, and the Town denied their application. They continued to operate the Bed & Breakfast, and the Town commenced the present action.

* * *

The zoning ordinance defined home occupation as quoted herein above. We conclude that the Bed & Breakfast operation is not "clearly incidental and secondary" to the residential use of the property, and that it changed the character of the residence. The Byrums' renovation of the property included the construction of an apartment within the house where Mr. and Mrs. Byrum would live. This apartment had its own kitchen, bathroom, bedroom, and a small living room. After the renovation, there were five other bedrooms which were used for the Bed & Breakfast. Each bedroom had its own bathroom, water heater, air conditioner, and heater. The second (large) kitchen was used primarily for the preparation of continental breakfasts for the boarders. Under these facts, it is clear that the Bed & Breakfast operation dominated the character and use of the residence and, therefore, it is not a home occupation. It is more like a boarding house than a traditional home occupation, such as a craft shop or dressmaker. The Pennsylvania Commonwealth Court recently reached the same result in a remarkably similar case. *Reynolds v. Zoning Hearing Board of Abington Township*, 134 Pa.Commw. 382, 578 A.2d 629 (1990).

In calculating the percentage of use, the trial judge erred in excluding the square footage of the upstairs hallway or foyer. The record clearly demonstrates that all of the upstairs rooms are part of the present Bed & Breakfast operation. Thus, the only use of the hallway is for the Bed & Breakfast operation. When the square footage of the hallway is added into the trial judge's calculations, the present use clearly exceeds the twenty-five (25%) per cent limitation.

Even if the Bed & Breakfast operation is a home occupation as contemplated by the original ordinance, and the present operation does not exceed the twenty-five (25%) per cent limitation, the amended ordinance is applicable and prohibits any Bed & Breakfast operation. The operation is not a non-conforming use under the amended ordinance, because it was not a conforming use at the time of the amendment, *i.e.*, the Byrums were in violation of the twenty-five (25%) per cent limitation at the time of the amendment. *See Troutman v. Aiken*, 213 Ga. 55, 96 S.E.2d 585 (1957) (A use cannot be a non-conforming use if it was unlawful at the time of the amendment of the ordinance to prohibit the use). This ruling conforms to the law's general disfavor of nonconforming uses.

Nor should the Byrums be entitled to prevail by reason of the law of estoppel.

As a general rule, estoppel does not lie against the government to prevent the due exercise of its police power or to thwart the application of public policy. *South Carolina Dept. of Social Servs. v. Parker,* 275 S.C. 176, 268 S.E.2d 282 (1980). The acts of government agents acting within the scope of their authority can give rise to estoppel against the government, but unauthorized conduct or statements do not give rise to estoppel. *South Carolina Coastal Council v. Vogel,* 292 S.C. 449, 357 S.E.2d 187 (Ct.App.1987), *appeal dismissed,* 294 S.C. 80, 362 S.E.2d 646 (1987). To prove estoppel against the government, the claiming party must show (1) a lack of knowledge and the means of knowledge about the truth of the matter in question, (2) justifiable reliance on the government's conduct, and (3) a prejudicial change in position. *Midlands Utility, Inc. v. South Carolina Dept. of Health and Envtl. Control,* 298 S.C. 66, 378 S.E.2d 256 (1989). When a landowner has actual or constructive notice of a matter, and does not show any misrepresentation or concealment by the government, estoppel will not lie against the government. *South Carolina Pub. Serv. Auth. v. Ocean Forest, Inc.,* 275 S.C. 552, 273 S.E.2d 773 (1981) (power company's easement to cut "danger trees"); *South Carolina State Highway Dept. v. Metts,* 270 S.C. 73, 240 S.E.2d 816 (1978) (right of way over property); *City of Myrtle Beach v. Parker,* 260 S.C. 475, 197 S.E.2d 290 (1973) (existence of a public street).

The Town is not estopped from raising the non-conforming use issue. The record clearly demonstrates that the Town objected to the operation on two grounds at all relevant times. First, it contended that the operation was not a home occupation. Second, it contended that the operation, if permitted as a home occupation, exceeded the twenty-five (25%) per cent limitation on home occupations. Moreover, the Byrums clearly knew at all relevant times that their use exceeded the twenty-five (25%) per cent limitation; that is why they sought a variance in *Byrum* I. Thus, they could not have detrimentally relied on the position taken by the Town, and reliance is a necessary element of estoppel. In addition, nothing indicates that the Byrums changed their position in reliance on any statement or conduct by the Town.

The cases relied upon by the trial judge and the Byrums are not applicable. They involve situations where an official told a property owner that a use was permitted but later reversed that position. Here, the Town never told the Byrums that their Bed & Breakfast operation was a permitted use.

The Town is not estopped from challenging the use of the garage as an apartment. There is no evidence of any statement or conduct by Town that reasonably misled the Byrums into believing the garage apartment was a permitted use, or that the Town would not contest the use. The trial judge found that the Town's building inspector must have known about the construction of the garage apartment. He based this finding on the fact that the inspector visited the residence during the construction. He concluded the inspector must have seen the garage apartment construction and must have had plans showing the garage construction. There is no evidence to support these conclusions.

The building inspector testified he never inspected the garage, never saw any plans, and never knew of the garage apartment construction. No one testified that they showed the garage apartment to the inspector or told him about it.

The Town's administrator testified his search of the Town's records did not reveal any plans on file. He also testified that the Town did not uniformly require plans at the time of the construction. The building permits do not indicate that plans were filed by anyone. No one testified that they submitted any plans. One of the Byrums testified that he assumed the contractor submitted plans, but the contractor did not testify.

Assuming that the building inspector knew of the garage apartment construction, nothing indicates that he had authority to allow such construction or grant a variance to the zoning ordinances.

In summary, we hold the injunctions should be granted. The case is remanded to the Circuit Court of Charleston County for the entry of judgment in accordance with this decision.

REVERSED AND REMANDED.

Notes

1. Whether a particular home occupation is permitted depends entirely on the exact language of the zoning provisions adopted by the local legislature in each community. Most judicial decisions on the subject involve an attempt on the court's part to determine what types of home occupations are permitted by the specific language of the zoning law and whether that language was interpreted reasonably by the local official or board with delegated authority to make decisions on home occupations. Since zoning regulations are deemed by the courts to be in derogation of common law property rights, they are subject to strict interpretation. Local officers and review boards that decide to deny a property owner the right to an occupational use should base their decisions on specific language in the zoning law and on facts that justify those decisions.

2. In Houghtaling v. Medina Bd. of Zoning Appeals, 134 Ohio App.3d 541, 731 N.E.2d 733 (9th Dist. 1999), the Ohio Court of Appeals held that a seven-and-one-half-foot tall anchor erected on front lawn of residence was not considered a "sign" pursuant to a provision of the zoning code that banned signs advertising home occupations. The homeowners operated a travel business that was a permissible home occupation. The court found that the anchor did not "advertise" a home occupation despite evidence showing that the owners used the anchor as a reference point for people who came to their home for business purposes.

3. In Gold v. Zoning Board of Adjustment, 1958, 393 Pa. 401, 143 A.2d 59, the Supreme Court of Pennsylvania held that a one-chair barber shop

conducted in the basement of premises located in a Residential District in Philadelphia was not a home occupation and, therefore, was not permitted as an accessory use. The court stated that the use must not only be incidental to, but must also be customarily conducted in, a dwelling. "Thus, that it might be incidental to his living in the home is not sufficient, and merely because he would have only one chair, operate only by appointment, or display no signs, would not determine the matter. A practical and sensible approach to the question leaves no doubt that this is not a customary use of a dwelling, such as sewing or cooking might be. Barbering is a commercial use, and not ordinarily or customarily conducted in a home. It is a business ordinarily conducted in a business shop or building."

4. Do you recall the plight of poor Daniel Goldman in the first case presented in this Chapter, Goldman v. Crowther? He was arrested "for repairing, by hand, on an ordinary sewing machine, for hire, used clothing for such patrons as had occasions to require his services," in violation of the use prescriptions of Baltimore's zoning ordinance. The work was done in a four-story residential building that the Goldmans owned and that was located in a zone limited to residential use. Assuming that the Goldmans lived in the building, do you think that this tailoring business should have been allowed as an accessory use? Under modern zoning ordinances, would the business be allowed as a permitted home occupation? How much was the city's zoning scheme benefited by the restriction on tailoring? Was that benefit worth the price of litigation? Is the Goldman v. Crowther case an example of bad facts creating bad law?

Chapter V

COMMUNITY BUILDING: SUBDIVISION CONTROL AND INFRASTRUCTURE

SECTION 1. REGULATION OF THE SUBDIVISION OF LAND

A. THE ESSENTIAL REASONS FOR AND NATURE OF SUBDIVISION REGULATION

POMEROY, PREFACE TO THE SUBDIVISION OF LAND IN SAN MATEO COUNTY, CALIFORNIA 11
(1932).

A subdivision is not merely a means of marketing land; it is far more, a process of community building. All the flurry of subdivision sales, all the financial considerations involved at the time, all the huge importance of immediate details—these are infinitesimal factors in the ultimate result, which is the addition of an integral part of the community, a part, which, once established in the comparatively short flash of time involved, is fixed as to its physical framework and permanently marked in its character. The fleeting economic effect of the act of subdividing gives way to the permanent, inexorable economic and social effect of the subdivision as a part of the form and life of the community. No subdivision is too small to have character. It may be no more than a particular curve to a street, or the placing of the lots, or the skillful use of setbacks, or the planting plan; but it may give to a mere linear design the impulse of life and set it throbbing with vitality.

MELLI, SUBDIVISION CONTROL IN WISCONSIN
1953 Wis.L.Rev. 389.

Subdivision control, the regulation of the division of raw land into building lots, is a vital component of land-use control. It has become particularly important in the post World War II period as communities have sprung up in previously rural areas. Its importance is not limited to urban communities and their immediate environs. The trend to country living has turned whole sections some distance from large cities into semi-urban areas. The tremendous expansion of recreational areas has created numerous communities along the shores of lakes and rivers. Fortunately, after the ill-fated experience with uncontrolled subdivision in the 1920's, control of that process has become recognized as an integral part of any land-use planning scheme and the statutes of all states, except one, make some sort of provisions for it.

Subdivision control is, of course, only one of the instruments used by a community to regulate the use of privately owned land in the public interest. It is closely related to zoning control in that both are preventive measures intended to avert community blight and deterioration by requiring that new development proceed in defined ways and according to prescribed standards. Zoning relates to the type of building development which can take place on the land; subdivision control relates to the way in which the land is divided and made ready for building development. The two are mutually dependent because the layout of an area is inseparable from the character of the use to be made of the land. * * *

I. WHY HAVE SUBDIVISION CONTROLS?

One of the basic problems involved in any type of governmental control is the justification for that control. Just why, many people ask, should a land owner be compelled to obtain the approval of a governmental agency when he is going to divide a parcel of his land into lots for sale. The answer to this question is not simple because the subdividers are not the only group involved. The home buyer, the mortgage lender and, more importantly, the community as a whole are vitally concerned in the process of subdivision. It is only by understanding the relationship of all of these groups to subdivision control that its validity can be determined.

(1) *The Community.* The most important reason for having subdivision control is to provide an effective instrument for land-use control by the community. The community has a legitimate interest in any new subdivision for a number of reasons.

Permanence of development. The original layout of an area will determine its character for an indefinite period of time. Even though another plan may be clearly more desirable, the cost of changing it once the area has been built up is almost prohibitive. Therefore, whether he realizes it or not the subdivider is setting the pattern for the future community. Many of the perplexing problems facing communities today—traffic congestion, high maintenance costs, cramped school areas, slums—are directly traceable to the manner in which they were originally laid out. Obviously the most practical and economical way of meeting these problems is to provide some method by which the original subdivision of raw land can be suited to the needs of the developing community. The alternative to governmental supervision of the private subdivider is municipal ownership and development of outlying areas. This method has been used successfully by a number of European cities and is sometimes advocated as the solution to the problems of American communities. Whether or not it would be an effective solution is difficult to determine in the absence of experience, but traditionally Americans have preferred the first alternative.

Future services. As society becomes more complex the community is called upon to furnish more services to its residents. Because such services will have to be furnished to any new area the community should have an opportunity to consider each new subdivision in relation to the services it is expected to provide. For example, the community will have to furnish schools and recreational facilities to the area, and it should have notice of where an increase in population is expected so that it can plan accordingly.

Safety considerations. The community will have to provide police and fire protection to the new area. It should have an opportunity to make sure that the streets are wide enough to get fire-fighting apparatus in and that the lots are of sufficient size for safety from fire hazards. It will want to check the layout of the area for traffic control and parking problems. The streets must be adequate for modern traffic. The main thoroughfares should be wide and should link with existing main thoroughfares; there should not be too many streets at an intersection and they should intersect at right angles, particularly on main thoroughfares; the street grades and curves should be safe for modern traffic; adequate off-street parking should be provided for commercial and industrial areas. From the safety angle the community will also want to check the subdivision to be sure that there are adequate places for children to play so that they will not have to play in the streets.

Health considerations. Health is another community consideration. The governing unit will want to be sure that the area is one which will be safe for people to live in. For example, the drainage should be checked to be sure that basements will not flood; an investigation should be made to determine whether the sewage disposal plant of the community is adequate to take care of the new area and, if the area is one which cannot be served by public sewer and water, the community will want to be sure that the lots are of a sufficient size so that private disposal of waste will not create a health problem.

Fiscal considerations. In addition to the services which it is called upon to furnish, the community must always keep in mind the pocketbooks of its citizens and must consider each new development in relation to tax revenues. From this standpoint the community is vitally interested in making sure that new subdivisions will not become blighted areas. Blighted areas from which the tax return is low are one of the biggest problems facing communities today because such areas are unable to pay their way. The cost of services furnished by the community—fire and police protection, schools, recreation facilities, sewage disposal, street repairs—exceeds the revenues obtained from them, and the cost of their services must be borne by higher tax rates which bear heavily on those in the more desirable areas. It is generally agreed that the best means of dealing with blighted areas is to prevent them from developing in the first place by insisting on a desirable layout. Areas with narrow streets and lots and inadequate play space for children deteriorate much more rapidly than others.

Just as important, from a fiscal viewpoint, as the layout of the subdivision is the question of whether it should ever have been subdivided in the first place. The scattering of subdivisions too far from community services such as water and sewer, fire protection, public transportation and schools should be prevented if possible. Subdivisions which are not within reasonable reach of all these services will not only be less desirable places for people to live, but will also tax the resources of the community in attempting to furnish the services. For example, the necessity of extending sewer and water mains a great distance may make the lots so expensive that they will not sell and the community—the taxpayers—will have to shoulder the cost of useless improvements.

Another important question in the determination of whether an area should be subdivided is the problem of whether there are too many lots already available for the demand. An excess of subdivided lots may mean not only that whole areas will end up as dead-land, undeveloped but useless as agricultural land because of divided ownerships, confused titles and high tax assessments, but also that areas will be left only partially developed. This means that in order to furnish the necessary services to the developed lots the community will have to extend sewers, water mains and streets past many vacant lots. Of course, it may be both undesirable and unconstitutional to give a community absolute power to prohibit subdivision only because it may create an excess of subdivided lots. For one thing, the basis for such prohibition is not too sound. Predictions about population trends and economic prosperity have been known to err sadly. But the approving authorities should point out the disadvantages to the subdivider in situations like this.

Accurate records. There is one other reason clearly behind many statutory provisions controlling the subdivision of land. This is the necessity of having a clear and accurate description of the subdivided lots. When land is divided into such small parcels, the awkward and frequently inaccurate metes and bounds description is undesirable. Very early in the history of many states a survey and plat of new subdivisions was required. For example, in Wisconsin the original statutes of 1849 made such a requirement. This means that for purposes of transfer and taxes the parcels can be referred to by block and lot in the subdivision.

(2) *The Home Buyer and Mortgage Lender*

In addition to protecting the community interests subdivision control protects the lot purchaser or home buyer and his mortgage lender. Actually much of his protection arises as an incident of the community supervision because any scheme for orderly land-use development will benefit individuals who have invested in the subdivided lots. For example, subdivisions located too far from fire protection, public transportation and schools are a poor investment for the average home owner. Areas so far from public water and sewer that the cost of extending those services is prohibitive should also be avoided. This is true of subdivisions which, because of an excess of subdivided lots, may never be fully built up. In discouraging the subdivision of these areas the community is protecting the potential buyer.

The purchase of a home is a major investment for the average citizen which he usually amortizes over many years. By requiring that the original layout be of a type that will maintain its character for a long period of years, the community is protecting his investment. Aesthetic considerations, such as the orientation of the subdivision away from near-by areas which are undesirable and the requirement of a certain percentage of curved streets and of planting strips along major traffic ways, are of vital importance here. Any study of real estate values will show that these requirements are not for aesthetic purposes only. They prevent deterioration of the area and preserve property values. They are probably the best protection the home owner has for his investment.

In protecting the investment of the home owner, the mortgage lender and the seller under a land contract are also protected. The great interest shown by the FHA in the original planning of subdivisions in which it may be insuring the mortgages is ample evidence of the fact that the original layout of the subdivision affects the investment of the mortgage lender.

Besides protecting his investment from early obsolescence, community control of subdivision also benefits the home owner in other ways. By requiring a survey and plat of the planned area for official scrutiny, the community provides the buyer with accurate boundary lines thus eliminating costly boundary disputes. In addition when the buyer is purchasing in an undeveloped area the plat gives him an idea of what the area will be like when it is fully developed. For example, the plat shows him what the subdivider's plans are as to street layout, location of commercial and recreational areas, if any, and size of other lots. To a certain extent it also protects him from changes in that development plan. The majority rule is that the sale of lots by reference to a plat showing certain streets and public places estops the subdivider from later changing those streets and public places. There is a possibility that the sale of lots by reference to a plat may also estop the subdivider from later lowering the size of the lots shown on the plat although the majority rule is contra.

(3) *The Subdivider*

Subdivision control by the community also benefits the subdividers themselves. Excessive subdivision and the platting of areas which are too far from community services or which are not good for development frequently spell financial ruin for the subdivider. In discouraging this type of subdivision, the community is therefore protecting his interests as well as those of the public and of potential buyers.

By requiring that the subdivider comply with certain standards, the subdivision control law protects the honest subdivider from the fly-by-night operator. The subdivider who invests the money and time necessary to comply with these requirements is not a speculator who is out to make a quick profit and move on to greener fields. Furthermore, while one subdivider may lay out a very desirable subdivision without any community control, he is being protected from subdividers who without such supervision might surround his development with very undesirable areas which would decrease the value of his subdivision.

This does not mean to say that the subdivider receives only benefit from governmental supervision of subdivision. There are many areas where his interests conflict with the other interests involved. While recognizing that there is legitimate need for control of his business, the fact that certain types of requirements may bear too heavily on him cannot be overlooked. Because the subdivider is so important to the development of the community and because it is so necessary that he be encouraged to develop his land in compliance with the platting laws, a complete discussion of the subdivider and his problems is included in this report. * * *

B. ROLE OF THE PLANNING COMMISSION

The previous reading explains the need for a land use control technique that will help to ensure the orderly growth and development of communities. The following article provides the details on how subdivision controls accomplish these goals, and it also discusses the roles of various players in the land use arena with respect to the review and approval of a subdivision.

MECK, SUBDIVISION CONTROL: A PRIMER FOR PLANNING COMMISSIONERS

The Commissioner (Fall 1996).

Subdivision regulations are land-use controls that govern the division of land into two or more lots, parcels, or sites for building. They provide criteria for the internal design of a land development as well as the standards by which the public improvements in the subdivision are constructed. They protect purchasers of land by ensuring that public improvements are available when it is time to build on the lots and by providing a mechanism for the official recording of lots with the appropriate governmental agency.

State enabling acts or municipal charters give local planning commissions a pivotal role in overseeing subdivision review. Procedures discussed below may vary from state to state and even within states, depending on local practices.

The state enabling legislation or municipal charter will outline the basic steps in processing a subdivision. The legislation may also exempt certain types of land subdivision from detailed local review; this typically occurs when no public improvements or land dedication is required and/or when only two to three lots are created (these are called minor subdivisions or lot splits and an abbreviated approval process will apply to them). The statutes will authorize the local government to adopt the regulations, including design criteria and specific engineering standards. The regulations govern the manner in which the developer submits the subdivision and defines the criteria against which the subdivision will be judged.

In most communities, subdivision review is a two-part process. First, the developer submits a preliminary plan or plat for the initial planning and layout of streets and lots, and type, size, and placement of utilities (water, sanitary and storm sewers, gas, electric, and cable). The preliminary plat shows topographic contour lines—the result of a survey of the site and/or aerial photography—and other site features such as streams and ponds, large trees and other vegetation, flood hazard areas, and existing buildings. Contour lines, typically shown at two-foot intervals, are important because they illustrate land forms such as hills or ravines. By understanding the topography of the site, you can determine whether there will need to be grading changes to ensure that lots will be well-drained and buildable. In addition, you will understand whether or not the streets are laid out to blend with the site's inherent amenities, and whether utilities, such as sanitary sewers, are designed to depend on natural gravity to work.

Often the preliminary plan will cover an area that is larger than the portion that will be initially developed. A developer may wish to improve only that portion of the site that may be sold as lots within one to two years. Consequently, the preliminary plan may show the phasing of the subdivision over a period of several years.

The planning commission is the first governmental agency to officially review the preliminary plan, although the developer may have contacted other agencies before the submission, such as the local government's planning director or professional engineer, and public utility providers. The planning director, if there is one, will have circulated copies of the preliminary plan to other local government agencies for comments, thus ensuring coordination. The planning director will typically submit these comments, along with an analysis of whether the plan meets the design and informational requirements contained in the subdivision regulations and an identification of issues related to the community's comprehensive and functional plans, in a written report to the planning commission. Sometimes a checklist of requirements accompanies the report.

In the preliminary plan stage of review, the basic design issues for the subdivision are resolved. Here are some items a planning commission member should look for in this part of the process:

- Whether the information required by the subdivision regulations is shown on the preliminary plat.

- Whether proposed streets are properly oriented and integrated with existing streets and are of adequate width.
- Whether street intersections are safe and avoid dog-legs that create dangerous jogs.
- Whether proposed lots satisfy area and other dimensional requirements of the zoning code.
- Whether lot layout is sound. For example, odd-angled lots may make it difficult to site a building and still meet yard requirements. Extra-deep lots may need to be provided at corners, in order to satisfy setback and sight distance requirements across intersections, or for sites traversed by ravines or stream valleys, or prone to flooding.
- Whether sites have been dedicated or reserved for parks, or for other public facilities such as schools. Some communities may have mandatory parkland dedication provisions, requiring the dedication of a certain amount of land, or payment of a fee in lieu of dedication, for each lot or dwelling unit, based on a formula in the subdivision regulations. Other communities handle these facilities in a different manner. For example, the local government or school system may decide to purchase land in the proposed subdivision within a certain period of time.
- Whether the plan shows proposed utility easements, such as those for electricity and gas, and whether they are of sufficient depth, located at lot edges if possible, and split between adjoining lots.
- Whether street names are consistent with the local governments policies. For example, it is a good idea to avoid similar street names like Maple Street when there is a "Maple Avenue" that may be confusing to emergency and fire service personnel, as well as the U.S. Postal Service.
- Whether block lengths are excessively long, resulting in uninterrupted straight stretches of road that encourage speeding.
- Whether stormwater detention or retention facilities should be provided onsite or as part of a larger regional facility located offsite. Often, an offsite facility is a better solution to stormwater problems than a smaller, privately owned facility because it will be maintained by the local government.
- Whether the preliminary plan reflects thoroughfares that are proposed in the community's major thoroughfare plan. If the thoroughfare plan calls for a wider right-of-way than a typical residential street to meet community-wide needs (as opposed to those resulting from development of the subdivision), the local government may need to acquire the additional right-of-way to permit future road widenings.

The planning commission will review the proposed subdivision at a public meeting or hearing, listen to the comments of the developer, staff, and interested citizens, and recommend to the legislative body whether to approve, approve with conditions, or deny the preliminary plat. When the recommendation is to approve with conditions, the developer should be required to make changes on the preliminary plan before action by the local legislative body. When the planning commission finds it cannot recommend approval, it should indicate in writing what changes need to be made on the plan before a recommendation for approval can go forward.

The legislative body will take some formal action, such as enactment of an ordinance or resolution, approving the preliminary plan. When that happens, the developer goes ahead with preparation of the final plat, prepared by a surveyor. The final plat is a precise drawing that contains the necessary information that will fix the location of lots and streets with reference to survey markers, such as iron pins driven deep into the ground, and concrete monuments. This information—measurements in tenths of a foot, and angles and bearings—will create the legal land title record for locating the lots. It will also be the means by which the streets and other proposed public improvements are conveyed to and accepted by the local government after the developer constructs them to the government's standards. The final plat is accompanied by engineering drawings and supporting technical analyses, such as those dealing with stormwater or water pressure. These drawings describe the installation of public and private improvements, and other site development modifications such as site grading. Some plats may be accompanied by plans to control erosion and sedimentation during site development, or to address specialized issues such as impact on existing wetlands and their protection or restoration.

The engineering drawings will show proposed vertical and horizontal profiles of streets, water and sewer lines, location of street lights and fire hydrants, sidewalks, design of detention and retention basins, and construction specifications, such as type of concrete or asphalt used and depth of pavement and aggregate base.

The planning commission is again the initial review body, with the staff providing similar backup as in the earlier review stage. In this case, however, the local government's engineer performs a detailed examination of the engineering drawings to ensure that the improvements are properly designed and meet the adopted design and construction standards.

If the final plat is consistent with the approved preliminary plat and any conditions imposed upon it, then the basic design and layout of the subdivision will be agreed upon. Still, the final plat must be checked once again against the requirements in the subdivision regulations and the zoning code for compliance. At this point, the planning commission may find other details that need attention. For example:

- Has the developer provided sidewalks throughout the subdivision that connect with other sidewalks in the area? Sometimes developers resist sidewalk installation, claiming they are not needed or add unnecessarily to a lots costs. But once a subdivision is completed, it is a difficult matter for the local government to construct sidewalks because it must resort to a complicated, often contentious process of special assessments to individual property owners.

- Are curb radii appropriate to the function of the street? The final plat will show the curb radii, which can range anywhere from five to 35 feet, depending on the roads classification. There can be a fair degree of debate about what size radius should be employed and its impact. The larger the curb radius, the faster a vehicle can negotiate a turn. By contrast, the smaller the radius, the slower a vehicle moves, making the intersection safer for a pedestrian.
- Are street lights provided at intersections and, preferably, spaced at regular intervals along streets?
- When a lot is near a flood hazard area or an area with stormwater problems, will the buildable portion of the lot be above the flood elevation? Some final plats specify a pad elevation for the ground floor of the building to ensure that the building will be constructed at a level high enough to prevent flooding.
- Will water pressure be adequate throughout the subdivision? For example, many communities require looped water lines to minimize loss of pressure during large flows of water.
- Will natural areas and stands of old, larger trees that meet certain circumference standards be maintained, albeit in private ownership? Many communities have adopted ordinances to ensure the preservation of mature trees during the subdivision process.
- Are street stubs provided to adjoining vacant tracts of land to allow the future continuation of the internal street system?

The planning commission then reviews the final plat, often along with the engineering plans, at another public meeting and recommends action on it to the local legislative body. Once the local legislative body approves the final plat and the developer makes any additional changes that may be required, the plat is almost ready for recording. However, before the plat may be recorded—at this point it is in the form of a reproducible mylar or linen drawing (although some local governments are requiring that it also be submitted in a computerized format as well)—the developer must either construct the required improvements or post a performance bond to ensure that the improvements will be constructed within the next one or two years. Should the developer fail to complete the improvements within a certain period, the local government may use the performance bond, usually set at 110 to 120 percent of the estimated costs of the improvements, to pay for the installation itself.

If the developer completes the improvements or posts the performance bond, the plat is recorded. Site development work commences and individual lots are ready to be sold. The local government, through its professional engineer, inspects the improvements as they are being constructed. When site development work is completed, the developer requests a release of the performance bond and, if the improvements have been installed properly, the local government releases the bond and accepts responsibility for the improvements. Some communities may also require a maintenance bond for a portion of the cost of the improvements (a figure of around 10 percent) to ensure that the infrastructure will survive one additional building season. The developer may also be required to supply as-built engineering plans, showing the exact location of improvements as they were constructed on the site, so there is a permanent record of the infrastructure. This is especially important as a record for locating underground utilities.

C. GOVERNMENTAL POWER TO REGULATE SUBDIVISIONS

RIDGEFIELD LAND CO. v. DETROIT

Supreme Court of Michigan, 1928.
241 Mich. 468, 217 N.W. 58.

MCDONALD, J.

The plaintiff has brought certiorari to review the action of the Wayne circuit court in denying a writ of mandamus to compel the defendants to approve a plat. The proposed plat, known as Ridgefield subdivision No. 1, contains 80 acres of land, and is bounded on the north by Pembroke avenue and on the east by Livernois avenue. To conform to the general plan for streets adopted by the city of Detroit, Pembroke avenue ought to be 86 feet wide and Livernois avenue 120 feet wide. In respect to the width of these two streets, the plat did not conform to the general plan. It was submitted to the city plan commission on several occasions, and finally was conditionally approved as follows:

"In order that Mr. Fry may be able to file a plat on the property in question and have his property assessed by lot numbers, the commission agrees to make certain concessions and to approve the plat providing the following changes are made:

1. A 10 foot building line is to be established on Pembroke avenue to conform with property platted to the west.

2. Seventeen feet is to be dedicated for Livernois avenue in addition to the regular 33-foot dedication."

The plaintiff refused to accept the changes, and began this proceeding to compel the approval of the plat as offered.

It is first contended that there is no statute or ordinance authorizing the city plan commission or the city council to require the dedication of an additional 17 feet on Livernois avenue and the establishment of a 10 foot building line on Pembroke avenue as conditions precedent to the approval of this plat.

Under authority of Act No. 279, Pub.Act 1909, as amended (1 Comp.Laws 1915, sec. 3304 et seq.), the city of Detroit provided in its

Sec. 1   REGULATION OF THE SUBDIVISION OF LAND   427

charter for the appointment of a city plan commission of nine members with "power to pass upon the acceptance of all plats of land within and for a distance of three miles beyond the limits of the city."

The authority of the common council with reference to the approval of plats is derived from Act No. 360, Pub.Acts 1925, the applicable portion of which reads as follows:

> "The governing body shall determine as to whether such lands are suitable for platting purposes and shall have the right to require that all streets and private roads shall be graveled or cindered and properly drained, and bridges and culverts installed where necessary, and where lots are platted of a width of 60 feet or less, may require that concrete or gravel walks shall be built and that all highways, streets and alleys conform to the general plan that may have been adopted by the governing body of the municipality for the width and location of highways, streets and alleys; * * * The governing body shall reject said plat if the same does not conform to the provisions of this act."

It thus appears that the common council, which is the governing body referred to in the statute, has power to adopt a general plan for the width of streets and to refuse to approve any plan which does not conform thereto. It adopted such a plan. This plan called the "master plan" was prepared by the city plan commission and rapid transit commission in collaboration with the road commissions of Wayne, Oakland, and Macomb counties and the authorities of the included municipalities. It was adopted by resolution of the common council of the city of Detroit on April 14, 1925. As to width and location, it classifies streets as super-highways, major highways, and secondary thoroughfares. Super-highways are required to be 204 feet wide, major highways are section line roads 120 feet in width, and secondary thoroughfares are quarter section lines 86 feet wide. Livernois avenue is a section line road and Pembroke avenue is a quarter section line road. The proposed plat gives these two streets a width of 66 feet each. The plaintiff concedes that in this respect its plat does not conform to the general street plan but it contends that it does conform to the width of Pembroke and Livernois avenues as dedicated in other plats; that the statute gives the city no power to require a greater width as a condition to the approval of the plat and that if it can be interpreted as conferring such power, it is an infringement on the constitutional rights of the plaintiff in that it compels the dedication of private property for public use without compensation therefor. There is no merit to this contention. The other plats referred to were approved and recorded before the present general street plan was adopted; so it cannot be said that it was not made applicable alike to all persons.

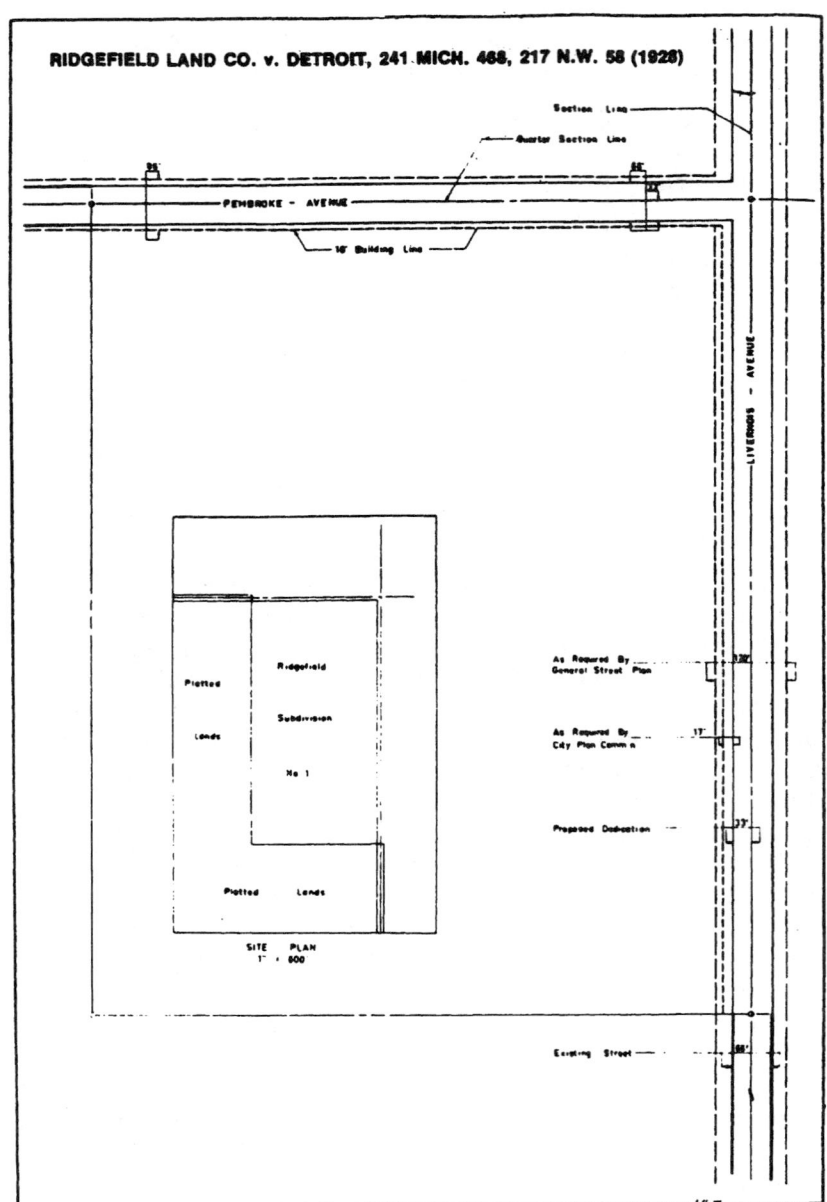

The streets in the city of Detroit, as elsewhere, were originally laid out for the horse and buggy age. They are too narrow for the present traffic conditions. It has become necessary for the general convenience and the public safety to widen them and to prevent others of the same kind from being established. Because of this necessity, there is nothing unreasonable in the demand of the city that the streets designated in the plaintiff's plat shall be of such a width as to conform to the general street plan. It has been determined that streets of a certain width are necessary to accommodate the traffic. They are necessary for the public safety and therefore the right to provide for them is within the police power of the city.

The error in plaintiff's position is the assumption that in requiring an additional dedication and the establishment of a building line to conform to its general plan, the city is exercising power of eminent domain. Its argument would have merit and the authorities cited would have application if this were a case where the plat had been recorded and the city were undertaking to widen the streets or to establish a building line. But this is not such a case. Here the city is not trying to compel a dedication. It cannot compel the plaintiff to subdivide its property or to dedicate any part of it for streets. It can, however, impose any reasonable condition which must be complied with before the subdivision is accepted for record. In theory, at least, the owner of a subdivision voluntarily dedicates sufficient land for streets in return for the advantage and privilege of having his plat recorded. Unless he does so, the law gives him no right to have it recorded. In Ross v. Goodfellow, 7 App.Cas.D.C. 1, 10, 11, it is said:

> It must be remembered that each owner has the undoubted right to lay off his land in any manner that he pleases, or not to subdivide it at all. He cannot be made to dedicate streets and avenues to the public. If public necessity demands parts of his lands for highways, it can be taken only by condemnation and payment of its value. But he has no corresponding right to have his plat of subdivision so made admitted to the records.
>
> In providing for public record, congress can accompany the privilege with conditions and limitations applicable alike to all persons. In providing for such record in the act of 1888, congress sought to conserve the public interest and convenience by requiring practical conformity in all subdivisions of land into squares, streets, and avenues, with the general plan of the city as originally established, and this, regardless of the fact that it might in instances practically coerce the dedication of streets to public use which would otherwise have to be paid for.

In the instant case, the defendants have imposed two conditions with which the plaintiff is required to comply for the privilege of having its plat recorded. They are reasonable and necessary for the public welfare. In the exercise of its power under the statute and its charter, the city had a right to impose them. They do not constitute the taking of private property for public use, and are not an infringement on plaintiff's constitutional rights. The circuit judge was right in holding that the statute conferred power upon the city of Detroit to adopt its present general street plan and to refuse to approve and record all plats that did not conform thereto.

The order is affirmed, with costs to the defendants. * * *

Notes

1. The Ridgefield case has been cited in many jurisdictions over the years for the proposition that subdivision regulation is a fair exchange for the privilege of recording the plat and enabling the subdivider to sell lots by number rather than legal description. Other rationales for subdivision regulation can be found in earlier materials:

A. Consider the following description of the District of Columbia program which ties regulation to public acceptance for maintenance of streets that the subdivider delineates on the proposed plat and offers to dedicate to the public:

Tooke, Methods of Protecting the City Plan in Outlying Districts, 15 Geo.L.J. 127, 137 (1927):

* * * This third method of protecting the city plan is by a control of the privilege of the owner to dedicate streets and highways in making a subdivision for residential or business purposes. * * * The Act of August 27, 1888, "to regulate the subdivision of land within the District of Columbia" authorized the Commissioners to promulgate general orders regulating the platting and subdividing of all lands within the District and provided that such plats must be approved by them before being admitted to record. Section 5 of the Act laid down that "no future subdivision of land in the District of Columbia, without the limits of the cities of Washington and Georgetown, shall be recorded in the Surveyor's office of the said District, unless made in conformity with the general plan of the city of Washington." In 1893, in order to carry out more completely the same object, Congress passed a supplemental Act providing for a plan for the extension of a permanent system of highways throughout that part of the District lying outside of Washington and Georgetown, which system was to be made as nearly in conformity with the street plan of the city of Washington as the Commissioners should deem advisable and practicable.

The provisions of the second * * * section were as follows:

"Sec. 2. And after any such map shall have been so recorded, no further subdivision of any land included therein shall be admitted to record in the office of the surveyor of said district, or in the office of the recorder of deeds thereof, unless the same be first approved by the Commissioners, and be in conformity to such map. Nor shall it be lawful, when any such map shall have been so recorded, for the Commissioners of the District of Columbia, or any other officer or person representing the United States or the District of Columbia, to thereafter improve, repair or assume any responsibility in regard to any abandoned highway within the area covered by such map, or to accept, improve, repair or assume any responsibility in regard to any highway that any owner of land in such area shall thereafter attempt to lay out or establish, unless such landowner shall first have submitted to the Commissioners a plat of such proposed highway, and the Commissioners shall have found the same to be in conformity to such map, and shall have approved such plat, and caused it to be recorded in the office of said surveyor."

* * *

The constitutionality of this Act came before the Supreme Court of the United States in 1896 in the case of Bauman v. Ross, 167 U.S. 548, 17 S.Ct. 966, 42 L.Ed. 270, and was unanimously upheld by the Court. The opinion of Gray, J., reviewed not only the history of the legislation on the condemnation of lands for public purposes in the District, but also the adjudications of the Courts of the several States upon similar statutory provisions for the taking of lands by eminent domain. As to section 2, the Court said:

"The recording of the map under section 2 does not constitute a taking of any land, nor in any way interfere with the owner's use and enjoyment thereof. The provision of that section that after the map has been recorded, no further subdivision, not in conformity with the map, shall be admitted to record, goes no further than the earlier acts of Congress of January 12, 1809, c. 8, and August 27, 1888, c. 916, cited at the beginning of this opinion; and is clearly within the authority of Congress to prevent anything being placed upon the public records, which may tend to defeat its object of securing uniformity in the entire system of highways in the District. The provision of section 3, giving to any deed or will, duly recorded, which refers to the subdivision made by the map, the same effect as if such subdivision had been made and recorded by the grantor or testator, tends to promote the same object and benefits rather than injures owners of lands. The provision of section 2, forbidding the Commissioners of the District of Columbia and all other public officers or agents to accept, improve, repair, or assume any responsibility in regard to highways not in conformity with the map, does not touch the rights of owners of lands; but was evidently intended to prevent the District of Columbia from being held responsible to travelers upon such highways, under the law prevailing in the District, as declared by this Court, and suffered to remain unchanged by Congress. The object of the recording of the map is to give notice to all persons of the system of highways proposed to be established by subsequent proceedings of condemnation. It does not restrict in any way the use or improvement of lands by their owners before the commencement of proceedings for condemnation of lands for such highways; nor does it limit the damages to be awarded in such proceedings. The recording of the map, therefore, did not of itself entitle the owners of lands to any compensation or damages."

B. In Trawalter v. Schaefer, 142 Tex. 521, 179 S.W.2d 765 (1944), The Texas Supreme Court upheld the requirement of approval of proposed subdivisions on the theory that such approval was necessary to enable tax assessors to properly locate the newly created lots. Also see Merton v. Dolphin, 28 Wis. 456 (1871).

C. In many jurisdictions the rationale for subdivision regulation is founded on an expansive and general view of the police power. One of the most sweeping statements can be found in Mansfield & Swett, Inc. v. West Orange, 120 N.J.L. 145, 198 A. 225 (1938):

The state possesses the inherent authority—it antedates the constitution—to resort, in the building and expansion of its community life, to such measures as may be necessary to secure the essential common material and moral needs. The public welfare is of prime importance; and the correlative restrictions upon individual rights—either of person or of property—are incidents of the social order, considered a negligible loss compared with the resultant advantages to the community as a whole. Planning confined to the common need is inherent in the authority to create the municipality itself. It is as old as government itself; it is of the very essence of civilized society. A comprehensive scheme of physical development is requisite to community efficiency and progress.

To particularize, the public health, safety, order and prosperity are dependent upon the proper regulation of municipal life. The free flow of traffic with a minimum of hazard of necessity depends upon the number, location and width of streets, and their relation to one another, and the location of building lines; and these considerations likewise enter into the growth of trade, commerce and industry. Housing, always a problem in congested areas affecting the moral and material life of the people, is necessarily involved in both municipal planning and zoning. And it is essential to adequate planning that there be provision for future community needs reasonably to be anticipated. We are surrounded with the problems of planless growth. The baneful consequences of haphazard development are everywhere apparent. There are evils affecting the health, safety and prosperity of our citizens that are well-nigh insurmountable because of the prohibitive corrective cost. To challenge the power to give proper direction to community growth and development in the particulars mentioned is to deny the vitality of a principle that has brought men together in organized society for their mutual advantage. A sound economy to advance the collective interest in local affairs is the primary aim of municipal government.

The police power of the state may be delegated to the state's municipal subdivisions created for the administration of local self-government, to be exerted whenever necessary for the general good and welfare. It reaches to all the great public needs; and the right of property yields to the exercise of this reserve element of sovereignty. The authority is of the essence of the social compact. The genius of organized government is the subordination of individual personal and property rights to the collective interest. In Commonwealth v. Alger, 61 Mass. (7 Cush.) 53, 84, Chief Justice Shaw spoke thus: "We think it is a settled principle, growing out of the nature of well-ordered civil society, that every holder of property, however absolute and unqualified may be his title, holds it under the implied liability that his use of it may be so regulated, that it shall not be injurious to the equal enjoyment of others having an equal right to the enjoyment of their property, not injurious to the rights of the community. All property in this commonwealth is * * * held subject to those general regulations which are necessary to the common good and general welfare. Rights of property, like all other social and conventional rights, are subject to such reasonable limitations in their enjoyment, as shall prevent them from being injurious, and to

such reasonable restraints and regulations established by law, as the legislature, under the governing and controlling power vested in them by the constitution, may think necessary and expedient. This is very different from the right of eminent domain, the right of a government to take and appropriate private property to public use, whenever the public exigency requires it; which can be done only on condition of providing a reasonable compensation therefor. The power we allude to is rather the police power, the power vested in the legislature by the constitution, to make, ordain and establish all manner of wholesome and reasonable laws, statutes and ordinances, either with penalties or without, not repugnant to the constitution, as they shall judge to be for the good and welfare of the commonwealth, and of the subjects of the same. It is much easier to perceive and realize the existence and sources of this power, than to mark its boundaries, or prescribe limits to its exercise."
* * *

2. An important area of federal regulation that has a great impact on land subdivision is The Interstate Land Sales Full Disclosure Act, 15 U.S.C.A. §§ 1701–1720, which requires developers of residential subdivisions of fifty or more lots to register the subdivision with the Department of Housing and Urban Development, prepare a detailed "property report" which must be provided to every would-be purchaser of a lot, and refrain from certain advertising practices. A cause of action for damages for misrepresentation or omission in the property report is given to the purchaser (§ 1709), and a limited right to revoke a purchase agreement is provided (§ 1703(b)). Among other information required in the property report, is

"(5) a statement of the present condition of access to the subdivision, the existence of any unusual conditions relating to noise or safety which affect the subdivision and are known to the developer, the availability of sewage disposal facilities and other public utilities (including water, electricity, gas, and telephone facilities) in the subdivision, the proximity in miles of the subdivision to nearby municipalities, and the nature of any improvements to be installed by the developer and his estimated schedule for completion."

The coverage provisions of the act, § 1702, exempt many of the typical urban and suburban subdivisions of more than 50 lots; however, the coverage of the act is still widespread. An indication of the importance and implications of the act can be gathered from the letter that was widely circulated in 1973 by the Office of Interstate Land Sales Registration of the U.S. Department of Housing and Urban Development (HUD):

Re: Interstate Land Sales Full Disclosure Act

Dear Member:

The purpose of this letter is to alert you to consequences which may ensue from your failure to understand fully the Interstate Land Sales Full Disclosure Act and its implementing regulations.

The 1968 Interstate Land Sales Full Disclosure Act became effective April 28, 1969, and has now been operative for nearly four years. Although the Office of Interstate Land Sales Registration (OILSR) has processed thousands of registrations on both domestic and foreign subdivisions, it is nevertheless likely that an even larger number of subdivisions covered by this Act are still unregistered.

Unless exempt, any developer having 50 or more lots or parcels of subdivided land who sells these lots by using the U.S. mails or any other instruments of interstate commerce, without first registering with OILSR and providing the purchaser in advance of sale with an approved property report, is in violation of the law and may be sentenced to a jail term of 5 years or a $5,000 fine, or both.

In addition, all such contracts are voidable at the absolute and unconditional election of the purchaser. Besides refunding the purchase price of the lot, the developer may be required to pay the reasonable costs of all improvements on the lot or lots. Once an unregistered developer is faced with the wholesale repurchasing of properties previously sold, many of which have already been improved, his bankruptcy is more than a remote possibility. All developers should be forewarned to reassess their positions on the need for registration before it is too late. Attorneys who have developers as clients have a professional responsibility to familiarize themselves with the provisions of the Interstate Land Sales Full Disclosure Act and its implementing regulations, and to advise their clients accordingly.

In addition to the direct penalties that the developer may face, there may be serious derivative consequences for the accountants, bankers and title companies, and even the real estate brokers of unregistered developers under certain circumstances.

We urge you to read and study the Interstate Land Sales Full Disclosure Act and the OILSR Regulations. We are ready at all times to answer any questions from concerned parties.

> Sincerely,
> George K. Bernstein
> Interstate Land Sales Administrator

The Interstate Land Sales Full Disclosure Act has been held to apply to condominium developments. See Winter v. Hollingsworth Properties, Inc., 777 F.2d 1444 (11th Cir.1985) and Schatz v. Jockey Club Phase III, Ltd., 604 F.Supp. 537 (S.D.Fla.1985).

3. The preceding materials all deal with the question of the validity and scope of enabling legislation authorizing municipal regulation of the subdivision of land. In the absence of enabling legislation, could a city regulate subdivisions? See Bella Vista Ranches, Inc. v. City of Sierra Vista, 126 Ariz. 142, 613 P.2d 302 (App.1980) where the court held that a 1966 subdivision ordinance was invalid because the state did not enact enabling legislation until 1974.

DAWE v. CITY OF SCOTTSDALE

Supreme Court of Arizona, In Banc, 1978.
119 Ariz. 486, 581 P.2d 1136.

STRUCKMEYER, VICE CHIEF JUSTICE.

This is an action by appellants to have the recorded plat of the Palo Verde Terrace declared a legally existing subdivision, for a declaration

Sec. 1   REGULATION OF THE SUBDIVISION OF LAND   435

that the City of Scottsdale's annexation of the property covered by the plat and its ordinance adopted after the plat was recorded did not affect the validity of the subdivision plan or the owners' right to develop the property, and to compel Scottsdale to issue certain construction permits. The Superior Court entered a judgment in favor of Scottsdale, declaring Scottsdale's zoning applicable to the Palo Verde Terrace and denying appellants' construction permits. The Court of Appeals reversed, 119 Ariz. 493, 581 P.2d 1143 (App.1978). We accepted review. Opinion of the Court of Appeals vacated. Judgment of the Superior Court affirmed.

* * *

* * * During the time when the county was without any zoning, appellants' predecessors in interest, in order to avoid the 35,000 square-foot minimum lot size requirements of the prior zoning ordinance and the ordinance adopted on February 27, 1960, recorded the Palo Verde Terrace subdivision plat. This plat provided for 120 lots of a maximum 10,000 square feet each. No attempt was made to improve the property and it has remained vacant and unimproved from the date the subdivision was recorded in 1960 through the date of the filing of this action, January 17, 1975. In the year 1963, Scottsdale annexed an area which included the Palo Verde Terrace. Scottsdale's zoning permitted a minimum size of 35,000 square feet per lot in the annexed area.

The principal question at issue is whether the appellants have had since 1963 a vested right to develop substandard lots within the City of Scottsdale because of the recording of their plat. We think not.

It has been repeatedly held that subdivision ordinances apply to lots on prior recorded maps which were unsold at the time of the ordinance's enactment. Ziman v. Village of Glencoe, 1 Ill.App.3d 912, 275 N.E.2d 168 (1971); Sherman–Colonial Realty Corp. v. Goldsmith, 155 Conn. 175, 230 A.2d 568 (1967); Blevens v. City of Manchester, 103 N.H. 284, 170 A.2d 121 (1961); State ex rel. Mar–Well, Inc. v. Dodge, 113 Ohio App. 118, 177 N.E.2d 515 (1960); Caruthers v. Board of Adjustment, 290 S.W.2d 340 (Tex.Civ.App.1956).

* * *

Appellants, however, argue that the case of Robinson v. Lintz, 101 Ariz. 448, 420 P.2d 923 (1966), holds that a subdivision lot becomes legally established as to size and description when it is properly recorded and that it is unaffected by subsequent zoning enactments or amendments. Robinson v. Lintz is authority for the proposition that a subdivision lot becomes legally established as to size and description when a plat containing it is recorded. But it does not hold that such a lot is unaffected by subsequent zoning enactments.

* * *

* * * *Robinson* did not concern itself with the problem we must decide here; namely, whether the filing of a plat immunizes a parcel of real estate from subsequent zoning regardless of how urgent the need for regulation might be.

A. Rathkopf, in The Law of Zoning and Planning, Ch. 71, § 11, page 93 (4th ed. 1978), states:

> "* * * whether the subdivider has the right to continue the development of his subdivision as planned in the face of changed rules and regulations of the planning board, or an amendment to the zoning ordinance which changes the permitted uses or the nonuse restrictions of land covered by the plat, is in great measure governed by the same considerations which determine vested rights under a building permit."

We have held that where the amount of work which was done toward the construction of a service station was of small consequence, the permittee acquired no vested right to complete the construction of the building if the board of supervisors exercised its power to rezone the property and revoked the building permit. Verner v. Redman, 77 Ariz. 310, 271 P.2d 468 (1954).

* * *

Judgment of the Superior Court affirmed.

Notes

1. Does this case indicate that any new subdivision requirement may be applied retroactively to the development of land that was platted at an earlier time? The problem of retroactive subdivision regulation is not unusual, but the case law is sparse. See Brous v. Smith, 304 N.Y. 164, 106 N.E.2d 503 (1952); Town of Seabrook v. Tra–Sea Corp., 119 N.H. 937, 410 A.2d 240 (1979); Lampton v. Pinaire, 610 S.W.2d 915 (Ky.App.1980); Williamson Pointe Venture v. City of Austin, 912 S.W.2d 340 (Tex.App.1995); State ex rel. Dreher v. Fuller, 257 Mont. 445, 849 P.2d 1045 (1993).

Presumably, if the new requirements are within the police power, the community may impose them through the building permit or similar administrative process as well as by way of subdivision plat approval. However, if the landowner has changed his position in reliance on old requirements or the absence of requirements, some courts might approach the problem by finding a vested right in the landowner to proceed without meeting the new conditions. Some cases which shed light on the vested right theory are Gruber v. Mayor and Twp. Committee of Raritan Twp., 39 N.J. 1, 186 A.2d 489 (1962); Spindler Realty Corp. v. Monning, 243 Cal.App.2d 255, 53 Cal.Rptr. 7 (1966), certiorari denied 385 U.S. 975, 87 S.Ct. 515, 17 L.Ed.2d 437 (1966) and Western Land Equities, Inc. v. City of Logan, 617 P.2d 388 (Utah 1980).[1] In Town of Orangetown v. Magee, 88 N.Y.2d 41, 643 N.Y.S.2d

---

1. In California, where judicial rulings have consistently rejected the vested right argument, the legislature, in 1979, enacted a provision authorizing cities and developers to enter into development agreements. Cal.Govt.Code § 65864 et seq. For analysis of this legislation, see Hagman, Development Agreements, 3 Zoning and Planning Law Report Nos. 9 and 10 (Oct., Nov.1980). In the Utah case the court held that a developer's rights should vest at the time of application for a building permit; the court discusses several alternative theories in the opinion.

Sec. 1 REGULATION OF THE SUBDIVISION OF LAND 437

21, 665 N.E.2d 1061 (1996) the court upheld a $5 million dollar verdict for a developer whose building permit was wrongfully revoked in mid-project. The trial court found that the developer had spent over $4 million on preparation and land clearing before work was halted by the town. A similar case is Reserve, Ltd. v. Town of Longboat Key, 17 F.3d 1374 (11th Cir.1994) where after spending $6 million the developer's permit was revoked under an ordinance provision providing for revocation of a permit if, after construction was commenced, no substantial work was accomplished in any 30–day period.

2. In Prince George's County v. Sunrise Development Limited Partnership, 330 Md. 297, 623 A.2d 1296 (1993) the court set out the following factual situation:

> In this case the developer of a proposed twelve-story apartment building contends that the project was sufficiently advanced on May 1, 1990, to prevent downzoning. The developer's vested rights argument ultimately rests on a single footing, one that was placed in the ground during the preceding December for a proposed column at a proposed outside corner of a proposed portico.
>
> * * *
>
> [The court accepted the Maryland rule as embodying a two-prong test, (1) a manifest commencement of labor on the ground which everyone can readily see and recognize as the commencement of a building, and (2) the work must have been begun with the intention to continue the work until completion of the building.]
>
> Turning from semantics to the merits of this controversy, the question is whether the Board acted arbitrarily, capriciously or without substantial evidence in concluding that the footing in the middle of the 9.9591 acre site was not readily visible or recognizable on May 1, 1990, as the commencement of a highrise apartment building. The footing's dimensions, as reflected by the Board, result in an area of four square feet. A four square foot footing occupies 9/1,000,000 of the R–10 zone, considered in two dimensions. The footing occupies none of the air space of the R–10 zone, if it is considered in three dimensions. The Board did not err in declining to conclude that this swatch of cement would alert persons who came on the property that construction of a building had begun under the R–10 use.

Also see Lake Bluff Housing Partners v. South Milwaukee, 197 Wis.2d 157, 540 N.W.2d 189 (1995) holding that a change in zoning during the developer's activities did not upset the developer's vested rights. The state bar association is apparently drafting legislation to provide for development agreements in Wisconsin in order to overcome the uncertainties created by the case.

3. With the principal case, compare Selby Realty Co. v. City of San Buenaventura, 10 Cal.3d 110, 109 Cal.Rptr. 799, 514 P.2d 111 (1973). Also see State ex rel. Craven v. City of Tacoma, 63 Wash.2d 23, 385 P.2d 372 (1963).

4. Does the reasoning in the principal case suggest that compulsory subdivision is within the police power? If so, what becomes of the theory that subdivision is a privilege that can be conditioned on the dedication of land for streets and other amenities? Should the classic theory be modified to one which allows any kind of land development to be subjected to conditions and permits? Consider the following case and the notes thereafter.

CITY OF CORPUS CHRISTI v. UNITARIAN CHURCH OF CORPUS CHRISTI

Court of Civil Appeals of Texas, 1968.
436 S.W.2d 923, refused n.r.e.

NYE, JUSTICE.

The Unitarian Church of Corpus Christi as the owner of certain property, applied to the City of Corpus Christi for a building permit to improve its property for church purposes. The church was told by a city department employee that the church property would have to be platted prior to the issuance of the permit. The church prepared a plat of the property, outlining the boundaries of its lot, designating utility easements and submitted it to the City Planning Commission for approval. After a hearing on the church's application, the Commission conditionally approved the church's plat. Approval was subject to the church dedicating a strip of their land, 25 feet by 630 feet for the purpose of widening an easement so that an existing street could be extended. The church was dissatisfied and appealed this decision to the City Council seeking approval of their plat without the requirement of street dedication. After a hearing, the City Council denied the relief sought by the church. The church then filed suit in the district court seeking a declaratory judgment: that the City had no authority under the applicable statutes, charters, and ordinances to require the church to file a map or plat of its property as a condition to granting the building permit. The church sought additionally, the issuance of a writ of mandamus to compel the City to approve their submitted plat. The trial was had before the court without a jury, resulting in a judgment granting the writ of mandamus against the City and ordering approval of the plat as submitted by the church. * * *

The church's lot faces a major dedicated city street (Carroll Lane) on the southeast side. The lot was and is presently served with public utilities. Adjoining the church's property on the northeast side is a tract of land (also 2½ acres) called the Hancock Tract which has heretofore been platted. The owners of the Hancock Tract had dedicated to the City a strip of land 25 feet by 630 feet, being one half of the proposed extension of Kay Street. The City by its present action would require the church to dedicate the other half of the Kay Street extension as a condition to the approval of the plat and the subsequent granting of a building permit. See the following diagram.

The church is the owner of the property within the City that is not now platted into lots and blocks. The charter of the City of Corpus Christi provides that the City " * * * shall never grant any permit to construct or repair any house or structure within such area (unplatted property) until such map shall be so approved and filed * * *." It follows as we discuss this point in more detail later, that it would be necessary that as a condition precedent to the granting of a building permit by the City, that the church must file a plat of its unplatted property. It is likewise proper for a city to require a property owner to obtain a building permit prior to the erection of a building. This requirement is a valid exercise of a municipality's police power. * * *

This is a limited type law suit involving a single lot owner whose unplatted property was annexed into the City. The property owner wishes to obtain a building permit to build in connection with the entire lot, understanding that such lot would not now or ever, under its proposed plat, be subdivided into two or more lots.

If the statutes, charter provisions or ordinances pertaining to the City of Corpus Christi do not impose upon the church a legal obligation to dedicate a portion of its land for street purposes under these facts, or if such statutes, charter provisions or ordinances do not authorize the City to require a property owner to make such dedication, then the issuance of a mandamus will be proper. Where the church has done all that the statutes and law demands, the authorized granting of a building permit becomes a mere ministerial duty, the performance of which may be compelled by mandamus. Thus where the City itself or by and through its planning commission, in its construction of the law, deprives a citizen of an unquestionable legal right and there is no other adequate remedy, the court having power to issue mandamus may review the matter. Commissioners' Court v. Frank Jester Development Co., 199 S.W.2d 1004 (Tex.Civ.App.—Dallas 1947, n.r.e.)

* * * Article V, Section 6 of the charter of the City of Corpus Christi provides in part as follows:

"Any property within the City * * * *not now platted into blocks and lots,* shall be platted * * * to conform to the requirements of * * * (the) * * * Department of Public Works and Zoning and Planning Commission. Its owners, before such property is laid off and *subdivided* shall file * * * a correct map thereof. The City shall never pay for the property used for streets * * * within any such subdivision, * * * "(emphasis supplied)

" * * * After approval such map shall be filed in the office of the County Clerk in the manner provided by law. The head of the engineering * * * (Department) * * * shall never grant any permit to construct or repair any house or structure within such area until such map shall be so approved and filed * * *."

The City, by ordinance adopted in part the rules and regulations governing the platting of land into subdivisions as provided in Art. 974a, Vernon's Ann.Civ.St. Section 1 of such article provides in part as follows:

"Hereafter every owner of any tract of land situated within the corporate limits * * * who may hereafter *divide* the same in two or more parts *for the purpose of laying out any subdivision* of any tract of land or any addition to any * * * city, or for laying out suburban lots or building lots, * * * shall cause a plat to be made thereof * * *." (emphasis supplied).

The City's ordinance above referred to a defined a subdivision as follows:

"C. *SUBDIVISION.* A subdivision *is the division* of any lot, tract or parcel of land *into two or more parts,* lots or sites, *for the purpose,* whether immediate or future *of sale or division of ownership.* This definition also includes the resubdivision of land or lots which are a part of a previously recorded subdivision * * *." (emphasis supplied).

"D. *SUBDIVIDER AND/OR DEVELOPER.* The terms 'subdivider' and 'developer' are synonymous and used interchangeably, and shall include any person, * * * who does, or participates in the *doing of, any act toward the subdivision of land* within the intent, scope, and purview of this ordinance. The singular shall include the plural, and the plural shall include the singular." (emphasis supplied).

The language of Section 1 of Art. 974 is plural and relates to a division of property into parts. The same is true of the City charter and the applicable provisions of its ordinances. It contemplates subdivision for subdivision development purposes. The City's argument that the singular and plural include each other is not applicable to the provisions. A municipal charter is to be read as a whole and every word, phrase, and expression must be considered and interpreted as if deliberately chosen and used for a purpose. 39 Tex.Jur.2d, § 45, Municipal Corporations, p. 397. The church does not propose to divide its property into two or more parts or to lay out a subdivision as stated in Art. 974a and the City's charter.

We believe that the applicability of the language in Art. 974a is controlled by the word "divide". The statute states that "every owner of any tract of land * * * who may hereafter *divide* the same in two or more parts * * * " controls the disposition of those who are affected thereby.

The City relies upon the case of Ayres v. City Council of Los Angeles, 34 Cal.2d 31, 207 P.2d 1, 11 A.L.R.2d 503 (1949) and Southern Pacific Company v. City of Los Angeles, 242 Cal.App.2d 38, 51 Cal.Rptr. 197 (1966). However, in each of these cases an ordinance or statute gave the authority required of them.

It is urged upon us that since the City's platting ordinance provides that whenever a half street has already been provided for, adjacent to a tract "*to be subdivided,*" the other remaining half street shall be platted in such *subdivision* in accordance with Section VI–A of the ordinance. (emphasis supplied). This platting ordinance refers to subdivisions and the emphasis is on "subdivide". The City summarizes the record and contends that the overwhelming evidence shows that the trial court erred and abused its discretion in ordering a writ of mandamus to issue against the City to approve the church's plat in the face of the statutes, charter and ordinance which govern the approval of such plats. This is not a discretionary matter. There is no statute, charter or ordinance which would require the church as a single lot owner to dedicate a portion of its property for streets in order to get approval of its plat to obtain a building permit, where the church does not propose to subdivide the lot into smaller lots or otherwise divide it into a subdivision.

We have no quarrel with the trial court's judgment that the various articles and ordinances make the reasonable requirement that the church must file a plat of its unplatted lot. However, the withholding of a building permit upon the condition that a portion (amounting to 15%) of the church's property be dedicated to public use as a condition for the approval of such plat, is not by law authorized in this case.

* * *

We have considered all of appellant's points of error and they are overruled.

The judgment of the trial court is affirmed.

Notes

1. Is the problem in the principal case that the city had geared all of its required exactions to the concept of "subdivision" and failed to anticipate

the problem of "development" of a large parcel without dividing it into two or more lots? Is the cure for the problem to define the city's power in a way which would include more than just the division of land? Some enabling statutes do just that. The Arkansas statute, for example, provides in Ark. Code Ann. § 14–56–417: "Following adoption and filing of a master street plan, the planning commission may prepare and shall administer, after approval of the legislative body, regulations controlling the development of land. The development of land includes, but is not limited to the provision of access to lots and parcels, the extension or provision of utilities, the subdividing of land into lots and blocks, and the parceling of land resulting in the need for access and utilities." Compare with the principal case Bethlehem Evangelical Lutheran Church v. City of Lakewood, 626 P.2d 668 (Colo.1981).

In Village of Lake Bluff v. Jacobson, 118 Ill.App.3d 102, 73 Ill.Dec. 637, 454 N.E.2d 734 (1983), the court held that a village could enforce its subdivision ordinance to enjoin construction of an apartment building on non-subdivided property outside the city limits but within the statutory planning jurisdiction.

Two Texas decisions in 1985 held that development of mobile home parks, with spaces leased to individual mobile home owners, constituted subdivisions. See Cowboy Country Estates v. Ellis County, 692 S.W.2d 882 (Tex.App.1985) and City of Weslaco v. Carpenter, 694 S.W.2d 601 (Tex.App. 1985).

2. In those states where the enabling legislation is tied to the subdivision plat as the triggering event for regulation or exactions, the problem of how to deal with avoidance of regulation through metes and bounds sales arises. By not subdividing into lots and blocks, can the developer avoid all regulation?

The metes and bounds problem plagues land planners almost everywhere. By selling off individual parcels without benefit of recorded plat, the subdivider avoids meeting the conditions that he knows would be imposed if he presented a formal plat for approval. If a great many metes and bounds parcels are created, attempts at public planning of land development are frustrated, and prospective subdividers become less and less willing to subject themselves to regulations which so many neighbors have escaped. One approach to the problem is that of a statute which would refuse a building permit to the metes and bounds owner, unless reasonable planning conditions (like construction of a road) are met. Of course this may penalize the innocent purchaser instead of the fellow who schemed to avoid the law. What about providing by law for a right to avoid the sale?

Another approach is to define "subdivision" as including 2 or more lots. Then every land division (a division always produces at least two parcels) means a survey, a plat, and plat approval. The expense and delay for the man who has only a few lots to dispose of make this difficult to sell to local municipal governing bodies or to state legislatures. And even if sold it must be carefully policed, by inadequately manned staffs.

A further approach is not to require a formal survey or plat, for divisions into just a few lots, but to insist nevertheless on planning commis-

Sec. 1 **REGULATION OF THE SUBDIVISION OF LAND** 443

sion approval on the deeds of transfer. This approach is evidenced by the following Oklahoma statute:[2]

" * * * [W]hoever, being the owner or agent of the owner of any parcel of ground, transfers, or sells, or agrees to sell, or negotiates to sell any tract of land of two and one half (2½) acres or less where such tract was not shown of record in the office of the County Clerk as separately owned at the effective date of the regulations hereinafter provided for and not located within a subdivision approved according to law and filed of record in the office of the County Clerk, or if so located, not comprising at least one (1) entire lot as recorded, without first obtaining the written approval of the Commission by its endorsement on the instrument of transfer, shall be subject to the penalties of this Act provided; and such transaction shall be unlawful and the deed or other instrument of transfer shall not be valid, and if recorded, shall not import notice; and the description of such lot or parcel by metes and bounds, in the instrument of transfer or other document used in the process of selling or transferring, shall not exempt the transaction or the parties from such penalties or from the remedies in this Act provided.

"In its consideration of such transfers, referred to as 'lot-splits', the Commission shall apply the same regulations as are applied to subdivisions in order to accomplish the purposes of planning as herein provided."[3]

Compare with this approach the case of State ex rel. Anaya v. Select Western Lands, Inc., 94 N.M. 555, 613 P.2d 425 (App.1979).

3. Can a testamentary devise establish a subdivision? See In re Estate of Sayewich, 120 N.H. 237, 413 A.2d 581 (1980). How about a judicial partition of land? See Mount Laurel Twp. v. Barbieri, 151 N.J.Super. 27, 376 A.2d 541 (1977). A Minnesota statute enables counties with subdivision regulations to require review of all real estate transfer agreements for compliance with subdivision regulations. 1977 Minn.Laws Ch. 189. Is this a workable solution to the metes and bounds problem? In Hyler v. Town of Blue Hill, 570 A.2d 316 (Me.1990) the court found that execution of seven deeds dividing a parcel of land among family members, after the grantor had failed to get a subdivision approved, was an attempt to evade the subdivision ordinance. (Maine has a statute exempting gifts to family members from subdivision regulation).

4. In Town of Tuftonboro v. Lakeside Colony, Inc., 119 N.H. 445, 403 A.2d 410 (1979), the court held that conversion of an existing colony of rental cottages to a condominium development constituted a subdivision requiring the developer to comply with the subdivision ordinance.

Compare Ivy Club Investors v. City of Kennewick, 40 Wash.App. 524, 699 P.2d 782 (1985), where the court held that the city could not condition approval of a conversion of apartments to condominiums upon the payment of park fees as prescribed in the subdivision ordinance.

2. Okl.Stat. Tit. 19, § 863.10 (1962).

3. Little seems to be known about the actual operation of this statute. See 19 Okl. Bar J. 933 (1948).

D. CLUSTER ZONING

CHRINKO v. SOUTH BRUNSWICK TWP. PLANNING BD.

Superior Court of New Jersey, Law Division, 1963.
77 N.J.Super. 594, 187 A.2d 221.

FURMAN, J.S.C.

This prerogative writ action contests the validity of two ordinances of South Brunswick Township in Middlesex County permitting cluster or open space zoning. By their terms a subdivision developer may reduce minimum lot sizes by 20% or 30% and minimum frontages by 10% or 20% upon his concurrently deeding 20% or 30% of the subdivided tract for parks, school sites and other public purposes, with the approval of the planning board.

South Brunswick Township is in the western section of Middlesex County abutting Somerset and Mercer Counties. Its land area is over 41 square miles. The New Jersey Turnpike, three main arterial highways and the main line of the Pennsylvania Railroad bisect the township. Once predominantly agricultural, with settled communities at Kingston, Dayton, Monmouth Junction and Deans, South Brunswick has experienced an estimated doubling of its population in the three years between 1957 and 1960 and an onrush of new industry and commercial establishments, particularly along the highways.

Downtown New York and downtown Philadelphia are within a radius of 35 miles, drawn from South Brunswick Township. The urban sprawl from the New York metropolitan area reaches within a few miles of the township on the north and east. Residential developments for the wage earners of Philadelphia, Trenton and vicinity are pushing towards South Brunswick from the south and west. Kendall Park, which was developed recently for one-family housing on lots approximating 13,500 square feet, now holds about 40% of the population of South Brunswick Township in an area slightly over one square mile along the northern boundary.

A similar project, Brunswick Acres, is proposed for a 235–acre tract in the Residential 20 Zone in the northeast corner of the township. This development is intertwined with the legal and factual issues before the court. The plaintiffs contend that the cluster or open space ordinances were enacted for the special benefit of the owner, Yenom Corporation. The defendants' position is that they responded with reasonable legislation, general in effect, to the problem of large subdivision developments without land areas available for schools, recreation areas and green spaces.

Facing multiple housing developments and a population upsurge, the South Brunswick Planning Board authorized a master plan report from a firm of planning consultants in 1960. The master plan report, which recommended balanced growth, was submitted in late 1961. No master plan has been adopted. On the subject of cluster or open space zoning, the master plan report suggested an optional system parallel to that enacted in the zoning ordinances under attack here, but applicable only in zones with a minimum lot size of 45,000 square feet and allowing reductions of minimum lot sizes but not minimum frontages. The planning consultants label this recommended scheme "density zoning," stressing that no more homes can be built in a subdivision despite smaller size lots, because the land thus saved must be deeded to the municipality.

The need for preserving woods and parklands in a natural state, as well as lands adequate for other public purposes, is widely recognized. The voters of this State approved by referendum in 1961 the expenditure of $60,000,000 for the acquisition of so-called "green acres" by the State or political subdivisions. L.1961, c. 45, N.J.S.A. 13:8A–1 et seq. Technical Bulletin 42 of the Urban Land Institute, published in 1961, endorses density zoning, which it designates as organic zoning for planned residential developments. Other discussions of the various governmental techniques for acquiring or maintaining recreation and park areas are found in Krasnowiecki & Paul, "Preservation of Open Space in Metropolitan Areas," 110 U.Pa.L.Rev. 179 (1961); Comment, "Techniques for Preserving Open Spaces," 75 Harv.L.Rev. 1622 (1962); Comment, "Control of Urban Sprawl or Securing Open Space: Regulation by Condemnation or by Ordinance?" 50 Cal.L.Rev. 483 (1962).

The cluster or open space zoning ordinance of South Brunswick Township was adopted as No. 19–62, an amendment to the zoning ordinance of 1958. Its main pertinent provisions are as follows:

"Section 2. The purpose of this subsection is to provide a method of development of residential land which will nevertheless preserve desirable open spaces, school sites, recreation and park areas and lands for other public purposes.

"Section 3. At the discretion of the Planning Board, a subdivider may be allowed to reduce the minimum lot size and dimension requirements in accordance with the provisions of this Ordinance, provided the following conditions are met:

(a) The resulting net lot density of the area to be subdivided shall be no greater than the net lot density of the said area without regard to the provisions of this Ordinance.

(b) All lands within the subdivision other than streets, building lots and private recreational areas shall be deeded to the Township for public purposes simultaneously with the granting of final subdivision approval.

(c) The lands to be deeded for public purposes shall be located, shaped and improved as required by the Planning Board, which shall consider the suitability, physical condition and location of the lands with regard to its proposed uses and to the needs of the Township, in reaching its determination. The

Planning Board shall, prior to reaching its determination, cause at least one of its members to confer with the Board of Education, Recreation Commission, Shade Tree Commission, Municipal Utilities Authority, Engineer and other interested municipal agencies as to the potential uses and advisability of accepting the lands offered to be donated.

(d) A portion of the land to be donated for public purposes shall be at least a usable single five acre tract.

(e) With the exception of minimum lot sizes and lot dimension requirements, the subdivision must comply with all other provisions of the Zoning Ordinance, such as front, rear and side setbacks, size of buildings, etc.

(f) There must exist approved plans for public water and public sewer systems which shall be available to all lots in the subdivision prior to the issuance of any Certificates of Occupancy.

(g) A developer may apply to the Planning Board for permission to reduce lot sizes and donate lands to the Township in accordance with this Ordinance at any time prior to applying for final subdivision approval.

"Section 4. If the tract to be subdivided is located in a zone which requires a minimum lot size of 20,000 square feet or less, the developer must donate, exclusive of open drainage water courses, 20% of the tract to the Township; if the tract to be subdivided is located in a zone which requires a minimum lot size in excess of 20,000 square feet, the developer must donate, exclusive of open drainage water courses, 30% of the tract to the Township. The area of the tract shall be determined from a certified outline survey submitted by the subdivider.

"Section 5. If the minimum lot size requirement of the tract to be subdivided be 20,000 square feet or less, the minimum lot size requirement shall be reduced 20% and the minimum frontage requirement shall be reduced 10%. If the minimum lot size requirement of the tract to be subdivided be in excess of 20,000 square feet, the minimum lot size requirement shall be reduced 30% and the minimum frontage requirement shall be reduced 20%."

A companion zoning ordinance amendment, No. 20–62, also challenged in this litigation, amplifies previous requirements concerning performance guarantees by developers to cover specifically improvements to lands to be deeded to the township for public purposes.

* * *

Although the state zoning law does not in so many words empower municipalities to provide an option to developers for cluster or density zoning, such an ordinance reasonably advances the legislative purposes of securing open spaces, preventing overcrowding and undue concentration of population, and promoting the general welfare. Nor is it an objection that uniformity of regulation is required within a zoning district. N.J.S.A. 40:55–31. Such a legislative technique accomplishes uniformity because the option is open to all developers within a zoning district, and escapes the vice that it is compulsory. Midtown Properties, Inc. v. Madison Tp., 68 N.J.Super. 197, 210, 172 A.2d 40 (Law Div.1961).

Zoning ordinances in rapidly growing municipalities may be founded on an outmoded concept that houses will be built one at a time for individual owners in accordance with zoning regulations, with latitude for variances in hardship or other exceptional cases, and that the municipality can take steps whenever warranted to acquire school, park and other public sites. Such a gradual and controlled development is not practicable in many municipalities today. Confronted with a subdivision plan for several hundred homes in a tract meeting all water drainage, sanitation and other conditions, a municipality must anticipate school needs but without lands set aside for that purpose; it must anticipate a large population concentration without recreation areas, parks or green spaces, or lands for firehouses or other public purposes. Cluster or density zoning is an attempted solution, dependent, as set up in the South Brunswick zoning ordinance, upon the agreement of the large-scale developer whose specific monetary benefit may be only that he saves on street installation costs.

* * *

The benefits to Yenom Corporation, other than a saving in street construction costs, are obscure. The same number of homes may be constructed, but on smaller lots. Lands acceptable to the planning board, including at least one five-acre parcel, must be deeded to the municipality. The paramount concern of the municipal officials, as one of them graphically described, was to avoid a "bad deal," the Brunswick Acres plan for 526 homes on 13,500–square–foot lots with only ten acres reserved for public use. Such an objective is valid, if enacted as ordinance No. 19–62 was enacted, as general, not special legislation.

* * *

The proofs in this litigation establish adequate consideration of cluster or density zoning by the South Brunswick Township Planning Board, including four new members who took office on July 1, 1962; specific approval of the concept in the resolutions dated August 25 and September 11, 1962; and endorsement of the ordinances under attack on September 18, 1962, within two weeks of their final adoption.

* * *

For all the foregoing reasons decision is in favor of the defendants.

ORINDA HOMEOWNERS COMMITTEE v. BOARD OF SUPERVISORS

California Court of Appeals, 1970.
11 Cal.App.3d 768, 90 Cal.Rptr. 88.

DEVINE, PRESIDING JUSTICE.

Appellants sought unsuccessfully to gain invalidation by the superior court of a rezoning ordinance of Contra Costa County, in the unincorporated Orinda area. Injunction and writ of mandate were denied and judgment was rendered against plaintiffs. Although a question of standing exists as to some of the plaintiffs, we have no doubt that three of the plaintiffs, homeowners, are qualified because Contra Costa County Ordinance No. 1975, section 2205.10, gives standing to appeal from decisions of the County Planning Commission to anyone whose property rights are adversely affected. It seems to have been taken for granted in the trial court, and understandably so, that the property rights of the homeowners would be adversely affected to a certain extent by the rezoning of the adjacent property, and the question whether rezoning conformed with the general plan was an issue in the case. There is no need, therefore, to make a problem of this matter, and when we refer to plaintiffs, or appellants, herein, we mean the three property owners. We take note, however, of the fact that the litigation is of personal interest to many others in the Orinda area.

Plaintiffs are homeowners upon lands adjacent to a parcel of 187 acres which is owned by real party in interest. The Board of Supervisors of Contra Costa County, on recommendation of the County Planning Commission, rezoned the 187-acre parcel from R-20 (single family residential) to P-1 (planned unit development). The plan called for development of "residential clusters" as well as single family residential lots. The maximum density of the clusters would be eight units per acre. Approximately 345 dwelling units would be constructed, of which about 236 would be located in clusters. The actual number of units is subject to change, but "in no case shall the total number of dwelling units exceed 368." The density of the entire property would not exceed two residential units per acre, which is within the density requirements of the master plan previously adopted by the county. The plan provided for approval by the County Director of Planning of the design of all clusters.

PLANNED UNIT DEVELOPMENT

In Hagman, Larson & Martin, California Zoning Practice (Cont.Ed.Bar) p. 236, it is said that a "planned unit development might be described as a tract of land absolved from conventional zoning to permit clustering of residential uses and perhaps compatible commercial and industrial uses, and permitting structures of differing heights." Although planned unit development (which in professional zoning circles has attained the dignity of alphabetical titles—PD or PUD) is often regarded as synonymous with cluster development, "[i]t is more accurate to define cluster development as a device for grouping dwellings to increase dwelling densities on some portions of the development area in order to have other portions free of buildings." (Id., at p. 240.) Since the ordinance in the present case permits as well as regulates residential units only, the term "cluster development" probably fits the situation better than the broader term "planned unit development." But whatever title be given to the concept, the plan is to devise a better use of undeveloped property than that which results from proceeding on a lot-to-lot basis. Control of density in the area to be developed is an essential part of the plan. The reservation of green, or at least open, spaces in a manner differing from the conventional front or back yard is another ingredient. Conformity to good landscaping, as the planners devise it, is also an objective. We do not mean to give a treatise on the subject of planned unit development, however. An excellent description of this species of zoning and a compendium of the literature on the subject is to be found in 114 Pa.L.Rev. 3–170.

Government Code, Section 65852

Appellants contend that the planned unit development or cluster development, as enacted by the ordinance, conflicts with Government Code, section 65852, which provides: "All such regulations shall be uniform for each class or kind of building or use of land throughout each zone, but the regulation in one type of zone may differ from those in other types of zones." It is remarked in Hagman, Larson & Martin, California Zoning Practice (Cont.Ed.Bar) p. 237, that no California court has passed on the validity of the planned unit development, although it was presumed to be valid in Millbrae Ass'n for Residential Survival v. City of Millbrae, 262 Cal.App.2d 222, 69 Cal.Rptr. 251, and the authors cite possible nonconformity with Government Code, section 65852.

We hold that a residential planned unit development (a cluster development) does not conflict with section 65852 merely by reason of the fact that the units are not uniform, that is, they are not all single family dwellings and perhaps the multi-family units differ among themselves. Section 65852 provides that the *regulations* shall be uniform for each class or kind of building or use of land through-out the zone. It does not state that the units must be alike even as to their character, whether single family or multi-family. In conventional zoning, where apartment houses are permitted in a particular zone, single family dwellings, being regarded (whether rightly or wrongly) as a "higher" use, are also allowed. This causes no conflict with section 65852.

We find nothing to indicate that the Legislature's policy, as expressed in the section, was to prevent county planning agencies and boards of supervisors from applying the concept of planned unit development for the use that is best and most harmonious for the area as the planners and the county legislators conceive it to be. In Cheney v. Village 2 at New Hope, Inc., 429 Pa. 626, 241 A.2d 81, a leading case sustaining planned unit development, it was observed that large scale residential developments, particularly in suburban areas, have resulted in more efficient and aesthetic use when there are not inflexible rules applying to individual lots.

In fact, section 65852 seems to have been discussed but once, in Scrutton v. County of Sacramento, 275 Cal.App.2d 412, 417, 79 Cal.Rptr. 872, 877. In that case, appellant contended that rezoning of her property from agricultural to multiple family residential use, upon condition that she pave an adjoining street at her own expense, violated the section. But the court rejected this, holding that section 65852 "aims at the general objective of uniform land use within each land zone," and that the conditional zoning which had been enacted did not conflict with the code section. In Desert Outdoor Advertising, Inc. v. County of San Bernardino, 255 Cal.App.2d 765, 63 Cal.Rptr. 543, an ordinance which prohibited billboards, except in certain areas and under certain conditions, was upheld because it was uniform in application wherever equal conditions existed. It had been contended by appellant in that case that former section 65802, the predecessor to present section 65852, of the Government Code had been violated. No other cases involving these sections (or their predecessor, Government Code, section 38697) have been found. These sections were derived from section 2 of the Standard State Zoning Enabling Act, and it is said in 1 Anderson, American Law of Zoning, § 5.17, p. 288, that the purpose of the section was mainly a political rather than a legal one, namely, to give notice to property owners that there shall be no improper discriminations. This was useful in the early days of zoning. Professor Anderson suggests that the fact that the section is an expression of policy may be the reason for the scarcity of judicial construction of the uniformity requirement.

* * *

Appellants complain that the ordinance leaves to the Planning Agency the matter of density within a zone. But the rezoning resolution provides, in paragraph 10, for the maximum number of dwelling units for the entire property. Although variations from the estimated number of dwelling units are permissible within the maximum, these are not to be made by the Planning Director solely, but only upon approval by the Planning Commission after a hearing. We discern no unlawful delegation of legislative power.

The case is different from that of People v. Perez, 214 Cal.App.2d Supp. 881, 882, 29 Cal.Rptr. 781, cited by appellants, in which a zone was created which nominally was for agricultural use, but which was made subject to varying types of residential use by special permit, no guides being given to the planning body save the most general (the identical standards given to the city council by the Government Code). In the case before us, a single use, residential, is projected.

* * *

The judgment is affirmed.

Notes

1. See Creative Environments, Inc. v. Estabrook, 491 F.Supp. 547 (D.Mass. 1980) where the court held that plaintiff had no constitutional right to construct a development utilizing the cluster concept; Croteau v. Planning Bd. of Hopkinton, 40 Mass.App.Ct. 922, 663 N.E.2d 583 (1996) where the court upheld denial of a cluster development plan because the open space would not be of public significance.

2. The basic aim of the cluster plan is to make suburbia more attractive by eliminating row on row of blocks of similar houses, located on lots of similar size, each an equal distance from the street and approximately an equal distance from one another. This type of suburban planning creates something that has all the charm of a high-rent army camp. The cluster type of planning seeks to retain the attractiveness of country living in urban or semi-urban areas by eliminating conformity and standardization and by placing a high priority on diversity of lot sizes, house locations and by placing a premium on open spaces, trees and natural beauty.

3. New Hampshire, like many other states, permits cluster development and encourages its use as an innovative land use control. N.H. Rev.Stat.Ann. § 674:21. Under this authority, the Town of Peterborough, New Hampshire adopted a cluster development provision in its zoning code which seeks to "permit greater flexibility in the design of housing projects; discourage development sprawl; facilitate the economical and efficient provision of public services; [and] preserve more usable space, agricultural land, recreational areas, and scenic vistas." Code of the Town of Peterborough, New Hampshire, § 245–26(A). Peterborough permits residential clustering as a special exception in its General Residence and Rural Districts and as-of-right in its Retirement Community District. The maximum number of dwelling units permitted in a clustered development may not exceed the density allowed in the zoning district where the parcel is located. The town's cluster development provision requires that a minimum of 30% of the total land area be dedicated as common open space. Code of the Town of Peterborough, New Hampshire, § 245–26(C)(8). To insure that the open space remains undeveloped, title to the open space must be deeded to a neighborhood association or to the town or to a conservation organization. The regulations require that the development be situated so as to minimize alteration of the parcel's natural features and to protect the surrounding landscape and the character of adjacent development. Code of the Town of Peterborough, New Hampshire, § 237–22.

Montana enacted provisions to encourage cluster development based on findings that agricultural land is being taken out of production; farmers are being forced to sell their land to generate income; and that cluster development could facilitate farmland preservation while reducing government infrastructure and services. See Mont. Code Ann., § 76–3–509 (2002) which provides:

(1) If the governing body has adopted a growth policy that meets the requirements of 76–1–601, the governing body may adopt regula-

tions to promote cluster development and preserve open space under this section.

4. Carlson v. Town of Smithfield, 723 A.2d 1129, (R.I. 1999) held that a statute allowing, but not obligating, municipalities to provide for cluster development did not prevent an ordinance from requiring approval of both planning board and zoning board for cluster developments. In this case the Carlsons argued that the zoning ordinance, which required approval of both the planning and zoning boards, violated the enabling statute, R.I. Gen. 1956, § 45-24-47(B), which provides that the planning board must approve any land developments. The Carlsons unsuccessfully argued that this gave the planning board exclusive jurisdiction to approve cluster developments (the planning board had approved the development while the zoning board had not). The court further held that the Carlsons had not exhausted their administrative remedies.

5. Consider how the Planned Unit Development (PUD) and the cluster development are different and similar. Although the terminology is sometimes used interchangeably and there is an obvious relationship, they are different planning and land use control techniques.

E. SUBDIVISION EXACTIONS AND OTHER REGULATION ISSUES

Can a local unit require as a condition to subdivision plat approval:

    a. Installation of public improvements such as street grading, street surfacing, sanitary and storm sewers, water mains, curb and gutter, sidewalks, street trees and street signs; or

    b. Dedication of subdivision streets and widening strips along existing boundary streets; or

    c. Imposition of restrictive covenants dictated by the local unit but promised by the developer; or

    d. Dedication of land (or first rights of purchase) for park, playground, school, police or fire station, sites; or

    e. Payment of fees in lieu of such dedication; or

    f. Written findings by the local school board that school facilities will be adequate to take care of the children from the proposed subdivision; or

    g. A "contract" by the developer to contribute a substantial sum for school construction, a water or sewerage or other public facility?

These pose issues faced by developers on the growth fringes of many of America's urban areas. Obviously, answers to many if not most of the questions may turn on factual variables, not stated. How wide a widening strip? What restrictive covenants? Is the fee for a neighborhood park or one that is city-wide? Clearly also, in analyzing such issues in particular cases, a first step is to ascertain whether the applicable enabling statute authorizes the action taken. Here, admittedly, the attitude a court brings to the task of construing the statute may make a major difference. But also, the action may be ultra vires and void even on the most liberal construction. Thus, to get to issues of constitutionality, we must assume sufficient enabling delegation. Notice that we talk about what would happen if the particular action were reviewed in a court. Actually, dozens of conditions of doubtful validity imposed on developers are as a practical fact accepted by them and not contested in court. The developer is after all a businessperson anxiously awaiting the day when she can begin realizing on her substantial investment by selling lots or lots and houses. A court review may delay that day for a long time. In addition, she may be quite anxious not to arouse the antagonism of the very local officials before whom she may again be shortly reappearing and asking approval for another subdivision. Finally, she may be able to pass the additional cost of the imposed condition on to her customer. In fact, the developer may even be able to charge a profit on the additional cost.

An undeniable fact stands out. The subdivider is in a business that places costs (externalities) onto the community at large. How do we measure these costs? And once measured can they be charged back, regardless of the manner of charge? And can the charging back be premised on rough and ready estimates or must there be precise cost-benefit analyses? What if any role does municipal past practice play? Police stations have always been paid for out of general taxes; small parks are sometimes paid for through special assessments. Are such facts significant?

(1) Traditional Exactions

PETTERSON v. CITY OF NAPERVILLE
Supreme Court of Illinois, 1956.
9 Ill.2d 233, 137 N.E.2d 371.

[The plaintiff obtained a declaratory judgment from the trial court declaring the city of Naperville's subdivision control ordinance void. The case is up on direct appeal from this judgment. Plaintiff's land is located in Du Page County outside Naperville but within its 1½ mile extraterritorial plat approval jurisdiction. Du Page County approved the plat under its subdivision control ordinance requiring bituminous streets only 20 feet wide, without curbs and gutters. On its review the Naperville city planning commission under the city's ordinance required bituminous streets 25 feet wide and plaintiffs agreed to provide these. But the planning commission also required curbs and gutters and suitable storm water drainage facilities. These it was estimated, would cost $19,000 more than the county approved scheme, and the plaintiff refused to provide them. The planning commission then refused to approve the plat. Plaintiff claims the commission's action is (1) ultra vires as to the enabling statutes and (2) arbitrary and unreasonable and therefore unconstitutional.]

MR. JUSTICE DAVIS [after reviewing the facts and analyzing the applicable Illinois statutes]:

* * * A consideration of the above statutes and their amendatory provisions reveals the clear intention of our legislature to grant to municipalities adopting an official plan exclusive control and jurisdiction over the subdivision of lands located not more than one and one-half miles beyond the corporate limits of the municipality. Cities ordinarily have no jurisdiction beyond their corporate limits, and municipal ordinances are confined in their application to the territory of the municipality adopting them. Dean Milk Co. v. City of Elgin, 405 Ill. 204, 90 N.E.2d 112; City of Rockford v. Hey, 366 Ill. 526, 9 N.E.2d 317. But the legislature may, if it sees fit, confer special extraterritorial powers on municipalities, and when it does so the courts recognize and give effect to them. City of West Frankfort v. Fullop, 6 Ill.2d 609, 129 N.E.2d 682; Chicago Packing and Provision Co. v. City of Chicago, 88 Ill. 221. The exercise of such extraterritorial powers by a municipality is, of course, always subject to the requirement that the ordinance passed pursuant to legislative authority constitutes a valid exercise of the police power, and bears a reasonable and substantial relation to the public health, safety or general welfare. City of Park Ridge v. American Nat. Bank and Trust Co., 4 Ill.2d 144, 122 N.E.2d 265, 50 A.L.R.2d 900. It is true that the legislature has given to counties certain powers relative to maps, plats and subdivisions. This power was first conferred in 1915 (Laws of 1915, p. 334–335) and enlarged in 1949. (Ill.Rev.Stat. 1949, ch. 34, par. 25.09.) However, there is nothing in these legislative provisions relative to the powers of counties which indicates that it was not the intention of the legislature to give exclusive control in those areas within one and one-half miles outside the territorial limits of a municipality to municipalities which have an official plan in effect in such territory. Thus, even though the county of Du Page adopted a resolution regulating subdivisions in the county, the lands in question here, being within the limits prescribed by the City Plan Commission Act and the subdivision control ordinance, are subject to the exclusive control and jurisdiction of the city of Naperville so far as the subdivision of lands and the approval of maps and plats of such subdivisions are concerned.

Plaintiffs contend that the ordinance as drawn is void as an exercise of power by the defendant beyond the grant of the statute; that the statute by granting the right to include "reasonable requirements with reference to streets, alleys, and public grounds," does not contemplate that a city may include such requirements as curbs and gutters or the other improvements prescribed by the ordinance. In this connection the plaintiffs rely on those cases which hold that the legislative powers of cities are strictly construed, and if there is any reasonable doubt as to the existence of the power, the doubt must be resolved against the municipality. But the primary object of statutory construction is to ascertain and give effect to legislative intent. In ascertaining legislative intent, the courts should consider the reason or necessity for the enactment and the meaning of the words, enlarged or restricted, according to their real intent. Likewise the court will always have regard to existing circumstances, contemporaneous conditions, and the object sought to be

Sec. 1   REGULATION OF THE SUBDIVISION OF LAND   455

obtained by the statute. People ex rel. Holvey v. Kapp, 355 Ill. 596, 189 N.E. 920; Chicago Packing and Provision Co. v. City of Chicago, 88 Ill. 221.

Subsection 2 of section 2 of the City Plan Commission Act (Ill.Rev. Stat.1953, ch. 24, par. 53–2(2)) in force at the time of the adoption of the subdivision control ordinance, grants to planning commissions in municipalities of more than 500,000 inhabitants, or in municipalities lying wholly or partly within a radius of thirty miles from the corporate limits of municipalities of more than 500,000 inhabitants, the power to recommend to the corporate authorities a plan or plans for the development and redevelopment of the municipality and contiguous unincorporated territory not more than one and one-half miles beyond the corporate limits of the municipality, and further empowers the commission "To provide for the health, safety, comfort and convenience of the inhabitants of the municipality and contiguous territory, such plan or plans may establish reasonable standards of design for subdivisions and for resubdivisions of unimproved land and of areas subject to redevelopment, including reasonable requirements for public streets, alleys, ways for public service facilities, parks, playgrounds, school grounds, and other public grounds." We believe that the power to prescribe reasonable requirements for public streets in the interest of the health and safety of the inhabitants of the city and contiguous territory includes more than a mere designation of the location and width of streets as plaintiffs seem to contend. The legislature undoubtedly had in mind the complex problems connected with the development of territory contiguous to cities as bearing on the health and safety of all inhabitants within and without the municipality; that in such territory, in the interest of uniformity, continuity, and of public health and safety, the streets should be constructed in such a way as to afford reasonably safe passage to the traveling public and provide reasonable drainage in the interests of health. Plaintiffs made no objection to the paving requirements set forth in the ordinance and agreed to comply with those provisions, apparently considering them to be within the powers granted. Considering the expressed object and purpose of the legislation, it is our conclusion that the provisions of the ordinance requiring curbs and gutters and proper drainage are within the powers conferred by the statute.

The trial court found that the ordinance, as applied to plaintiffs and their property, was arbitrary, unreasonable and discriminatory and had no reasonable relation to the public health, safety or general welfare, and that it was therefore unconstitutional and void. The only proof offered to sustain this finding was evidence which compared the cost of complying with the county regulations and the cost of complying with the requirements of the subdivision control ordinance, together with some testimony that the surface waters drained westward to the river and not toward the city. The fact alone that the cost of curbs and gutters and the drainage facilities prescribed by the subdivision control ordinance would be greater than the cost of open ditches and culverts forms no basis for the finding that the ordinance is arbitrary, unreasonable or discriminatory. There is no proof whatever to show that the ordinance affects plaintiffs' property any differently than other property within the area in question or that it imposes unreasonable or excessive burdens upon the plaintiffs. One who challenges the validity of an ordinance as arbitrary and unreasonable must prove by clear and affirmative evidence that the ordinance constitutes arbitrary, capricious and unreasonable municipal action; that there is no permissible interpretation which justified its adoption, or that it will not promote the safety and general welfare of the public. First Nat. Bank of Lake Forest v. County of Lake, 7 Ill.2d 213, 130 N.E.2d 267. The fact alone that the ordinance may operate to impose burdens or restrictions on the property which would not have existed without the enactment of the ordinance is never determinative of the question of validity. Miller Brothers Lumber Co. v. City of Chicago, 414 Ill. 162, 111 N.E.2d 149. The privilege of the individual to use his property as he pleases is subject always to a legitimate exercise of the police power under which new burdens may be imposed upon property and new restrictions placed upon its use when the public welfare demands. 2700 Irving Park Bldg. Corp. v. City of Chicago, 395 Ill. 138, 69 N.E.2d 827. Plaintiffs offered no convincing proof to support their contention that the ordinance bears no reasonable relation to the public health, safety or general welfare. Such proof as was adduced on this question was introduced by defendant and supports the opposite conclusion. The trial court erred in holding the ordinance unconstitutional on the ground that it was arbitrary, unreasonable and confiscatory and without proper relation to the legitimate objects of the police powers.

* * *

Plaintiffs further urge that the subdivision control ordinance is unconstitutional because it amounts to either taxation without the consent of the taxpayers, or to an exercise of the power of eminent domain without providing compensation to the property owner for the property taken for public use; that if the statute is construed as providing for a form of taxation or special assessment for local improvements, it is void as violating the constitutional provision for uniformity of taxation; and that if the power exercised thereunder is a power of eminent domain, it violates the constitutional requirement that private property shall not be taken for public use without just compensation. This argument ignores the fact that this is not a proceeding initiated by the city for the construction of a local improvement, or to take property under the law of eminent domain. It is a lawsuit in which the plaintiffs seek approval of a proposed plat of a subdivision under an ordinance which exacts compliance with certain requirements as a condition precedent to approval. They cite in support of this contention the case of City of Chicago v. Larned, 34 Ill. 203, followed in 34 Ill. 283, which involved an assessment for improvements made by the city council on the basis of the frontage of the lots upon the street to be improved. There the court held that under the provisions of the constitution of 1848, then in effect, all taxes were subject to the principles of equality and uniformity, and since this special assessment violated these constitutional provisions, it was not a tax, but an exercise of the power of eminent domain for which just compensation must be made; that though compensation could be made by benefits, when these were exhausted it then became a question of taxation, and the principles of equality and uniformity must apply; that the assessment of injuries and benefits is a judicial proceeding not to be made by a city council and that the purported assessment was void. Since the adoption of our present constitution, however, the power to levy and collect special assessments is regarded as a branch of the taxing power and the assessment is regarded as a species of taxation. Chicago and Alton Railroad Co. v. City of Joliet, 153 Ill. 649, 654, 39 N.E. 1077. The case at bar does not involve the imposition of a tax by the municipal authorities, but rather involves the imposition of regulatory provisions by way of the exercise of the police power through an ordinance requiring certain conditions precedent to the subdivision of lands and the approval of plats thereof. The validity of the ordinance is to be tested, neither by the principle of uniformity of taxation nor by the law of eminent domain, but rather by the settled rules of law applicable to cases involving the exercise of police powers. The fact that the exercise of such powers imposes certain burdens, or prevents the most profitable use of the property in private hands, does not of itself render the legislation invalid as a taking of the property without just compensation. City of West Frankfort v. Fullop, 6 Ill.2d 609, 129 N.E.2d 682. The imposition of reasonable regulations as a condition precedent to the subdivision of lands and the recording of plats thereof is not a violation of the constitutional requirement of uniformity of taxation or tantamount to the taking of private property for public use without just compensation.

We find that the judgment of the circuit court of Du Page County was erroneous and it must be reversed.

Notes

1. With the principal case compare, Ayres v. City Council of City of Los Angeles, 34 Cal.2d 31, 207 P.2d 1, 11 A.L.R.2d 503 (1949). The court upheld as valid conditions to the approval of a 13 acre subdivision:

(1) Dedication of a 10 foot strip, 1500 feet along an important traffic artery;

(2) Reservation of an additional 10 foot strip along the same street for trees and shrubs to assure non-access to the artery;

(3) Dedication of an 80 foot, rather than a proffered 60 foot, width for a new street across the subdivision; and,

(4) Dedication of a triangular shaped parcel 12½ x 75 feet to eliminate a traffic hazard.

(With regard to the first two conditions, similar dedications and reservations had been required of earlier subdivisions along the artery.)

The state legislature had given the city of Los Angeles subdivision control powers in its city charter and had by the so-called "Map Act" also empowered cities generally to control subdividing. The city had enacted a subdivision ordinance, but the subdivider contended the conditions, particularly the one requiring dedication of land along an existing street, were not expressly provided for either in the state legislation or in the local ordinance. Said the California court (two judges dissenting):

> The status of an autonomous city, Const. Art. XI, sec. 6; West Coast Advertising Co. v. San Francisco, 14 Cal.2d 516, 95 P.2d 138 (1939); City of Oakland v. Williams, 15 Cal.2d 542, 103 P.2d 168 (1940), is recognized by express references to city ordinances in the Subdivision Map Act. Where as here no specific restriction or limitation on the city's power is contained in the Charter, and none forbidding the particular conditions is included either in the Subdivision Map Act, or the city ordinances, it is proper to conclude that conditions are lawful which are not inconsistent with the Map Act and the ordinances and are reasonably required by the subdivision type and use as related to the character of local and neighborhood planning and traffic conditions.

Compare Rohn v. City of Visalia, 214 Cal.App.3d 1463, 263 Cal.Rptr. 319 (1989) where the court held that a required dedication of 14 per cent of the land to correct a street alignment was an invalid taking.

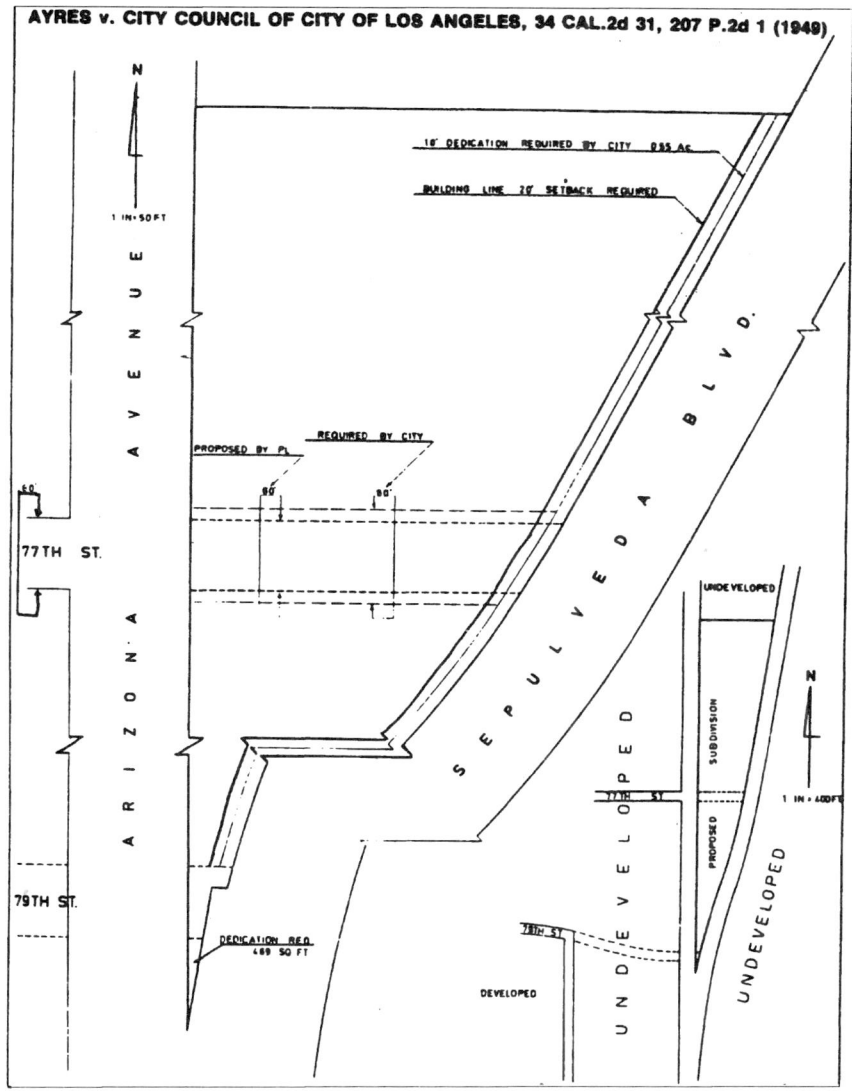

2. The Ayres case involves a "home rule" municipality in a state with a strong tradition of municipal home rule. In states where the powers of municipal corporations are strictly construed, the question of whether the requirements imposed on subdivision approval are *ultra vires* with regard to the enabling legislation is frequently litigated. For example, in State ex rel. Strother v. Chase, 42 Mo.App. 343 (1890), the court held that the city could not require the subdivider to plat an alley extension through his adjacent unplatted land as a condition of subdivision approval. For other cases strictly limiting the approving body to the standards or conditions specified in the enabling legislation, see Tuxedo Homes v. Green, 258 Ala. 494, 63 So.2d 812 (1953) (City engineer in absence of statutory authorization could not require

installation of a lift pump for sewage, but the city might later refuse street dedications); People ex rel. Jackson & Morris, Inc. v. Smuczynski, 345 Ill.App. 63, 102 N.E.2d 168 (1951) (Village, having failed to adopt a subdivision ordinance for its guidance as required by statutes, must approve plat as a "ministerial" act); State ex rel. Lewis v. City Council of Minneapolis, 140 Minn. 433, 168 N.W. 188 (1918) (Could not require grading under a statute referring only to direction and width of streets); Rahway v. Raritan Homes Inc., 21 N.J.Super. 541, 91 A.2d 409 (1952) (No power to regulate subdividing until city complied with state statute requiring appointment of planning board and adoption of local ordinance); Magnolia Development Co. v. Coles, 10 N.J. 223, 89 A.2d 664 (1952) (No power to require sidewalks, curbs, gutters and gravel roadway in absence of enabling authority); In re Lake Secor Development Co., 141 Misc. 913, 252 N.Y.S. 809 (1931) (Could not force installation of water system under statute referring only to streets, light and air); Eyde Const. Co. v. Charter Twp. of Meridian, 149 Mich.App. 802, 386 N.W.2d 687 (1986) (Township lacked authority to condition plat approval on provision of recreational facilities). See also Annot., Validity and Construction of Regulations as to Subdivision Maps or Plats, 11 A.L.R.2d 524, 535 (1950).

3. Assuming a carefully worded enabling act, and a local subdivision ordinance based on it, there is little doubt that "reasonable" improvements can be required. Mefford v. City of Tulare, 102 Cal.App.2d 919, 228 P.2d 847 (1951) upheld as valid requirements that a profile map be furnished and sewer and water installed. Allen v. Stockwell, 210 Mich. 488, 178 N.W. 27 (1920) upheld ordinance provisions requiring grading and graveling of streets; sidewalks; installation of surface drains and sanitary sewers, apparently under general home rule delegations. Also see Colborne v. Village of Corrales, 106 N.M. 103, 739 P.2d 972 (1987). In Three Guys Real Estate v. Harnett County, 122 N.C.App. 362, 469 S.E.2d 578 (1996) the court held that the county was entitled to deny approval of a subdivision plat because the proposed development did not show any public roads, only private easements along logging trails.

Bolstering the position these courts have taken are (1) widespread use of requirements for installation of improvements or submission of a bond for their installation and (2) the findings of many of the studies of free and easy subdividing in the roaring 20's when to "develop" a subdivision one drove a few stakes, mounted some flags, and perhaps erected a pair of grotesque gate posts.[4]

4. Reference may be had, in this regard, to the following:

Adams, VII Regional Survey of New York and Environs (1929);

Cornick, Premature Subdivision and Its Consequences (1938)—Also published by N.Y. Division of State Planning under title "Problems created by premature Subdivision of Urban Lands in Selected Metropolitan Districts";

Fisher, Real Estate Subdividing Activity and Population Growth in Nine Urban Areas (1928)—Deals with Detroit, Cleveland, Milwaukee, Toledo, Birmingham, Grand Rapids, Flint and Ann Arbor areas;

Monchow, Seventy Years of Real Estate Subdividing in the Region of Chicago (1939);

Smith and Fisher, Land Subdividing and the Rate of Utilization (1932)—Intensive study of Grand Rapids area making use of techniques learned in previous study; Whitten, A Research into the Economics of Land Subdivision (1927); New Jersey

Usually the developer is offered the following alternatives:

(1) Install the improvements before the final plat approval—(usually here he will be relying on approval of his preliminary plat); or,

(2) Furnish escrow money to cover the cost of the improvements; i.e., the plat is approved, and the escrow money is released in installments as the improvements are put in; or

(3) Furnish a surety bond guaranteeing installation of improvements.

Small developers complain about the additional capital required to be risked where improvements must be installed. Large developers know that improvements make lots and houses more saleable and are quite willing to install them, particularly in the typical modern development which involves mass production of houses on the subdivided land. Their complaint is that often the municipal requirements are unreasonable in that the streets required are too wide, the pavement too thick, the sewer too big, etc. See Urban Land Institute, The Community Builders Handbook 39–40 (1954 ed.). We have little or no case law on such questions as these:

(1) Considering the subdivision alone a 10 inch sewer would be adequate, but considering probable development on other lands further out, the developer is required to install and pay for a 15 inch sewer. Is this a valid requirement? See Wright Development, Inc. v. City of Wellsville, 608 P.2d 232 (Utah 1980).

(2) How wide should the roadway of a minor residential street be? The developer says 26 feet, the city says 33 feet?

(3) Is a sidewalk on one side of the street enough?

Improvement requirements should vary with density, topography, soil and whether or not the subdivision is a quiet backwater or is in the mainstream of development. In addition, as we cease to be exclusively concerned with residential subdivisions and begin to regulate subdivisions for commercial and industrial uses, we recognize that improvement requirements must differ. In California, for example, exactions for major thoroughfares is a problem. See Committee of Seven Thousand v. Superior Court, 45 Cal.3d 491, 247 Cal.Rptr. 362, 754 P.2d 708 (1988).

4. The question of what is a "reasonable" improvement, especially in regard to expensive utility or drainage installations, is sometimes litigated. In Texas, for example, subdividers may be required to pay the entire cost of installing water mains which must subsequently be donated to the city water and sewer authority. See Crownhill Homes, Inc. v. City of San Antonio, 433 S.W.2d 448 (Tex.Civ.App. 1968) and Johnson v. Benbrook Water and Sewer Auth., 410 S.W.2d 644 (Tex.Civ.App. 1966). Compare Reid Development Corp. v. Parsippany–Troy Hills Twp., 10 N.J. 229, 89 A.2d 667 (1952); Reid Development Corp. v. Parsippany–Troy Hills Twp., 31 N.J.Super. 459, 107 A.2d 20 (1954); Lake Intervale Homes, Inc. v. Parsippany–Troy Hills, 28 N.J. 423, 147 A.2d 28 (1958).

State Planning Board, Land Subdivision in New Jersey (1938); and, New Jersey State Planning Board, Premature Land Subdivision a Luxury (1941)—Tax Delinquency, Municipal Debt and Premature Subdivision in New Jersey.

5. If the developer pays his fair share of fees for the water and sewer system and then is forced to abandon his project because of financial difficulties, can the developer get a refund? In McNair v. City of Cedar Park, Texas, 993 F.2d 1217 (5th Cir.1993) the city determined that a major capital expansion of its water system was necessary to accommodate any new development. It imposed a community impact fee of $2,400 per living unit, payable by developers at the time of obtaining subdivision approval. The city, in turn, obligated itself to provide water and sewer services to all new developments. McNair had 100 acres of land, purchased for $1.65 million; he planned an upscale trailer park for 1,600 new residents. After some negotiation with the city, McNair paid the city $1.3 million based on the $2,400 fee for 542 units. Subsequently, McNair abandoned his project and sought a refund of the water fee, plus accrued interest, but by that time, Cedar Park was well into a five-year plan to construct a new system, having already spent $2 million and committed an additional $8 million. The city refused the refund and McNair sued the city alleging unjust enrichment and assumpsit; the case was removed to federal court after McNair added federal law claims. The court held for the city: "The City's retention of the fee is fundamentally fair when one considers that McNair received exactly what he bargained for. He has paid his share of the systemic water and sewer expansion costs and cannot be asked to pay same again. His tract of land is entitled to those city services. At the same time, the City has incurred a substantial expense and obligation. Equity and the controlling law demand that the agreement between the City and McNair be honored. Nothing more; nothing less."

6. What if the developer fails to install the improvements? In Vale Dean Canyon Homeowners Ass'n v. Dean, 100 Or.App. 158, 785 P.2d 772 (1990) the court held that lot owners were third-party beneficiaries of the contract to install roadway improvements made between the developer and the county, and could bring a breach of contract action against the developer.

7. Expensive water and sewer facilities may, however, give rise to a challenge that the city is using the exaction for revenue raising purposes or that the fees are not based on an equitable formula. In Lafferty v. Payson City, 642 P.2d 376 (Utah 1982), the court held that a $1,000 impact fee imposed on a single family dwelling was out of line with the actual costs and was really a revenue raising device. In Southern Nevada Homebuilders Ass'n, Inc. v. Las Vegas Valley Water Dist., 101 Nev. 99, 693 P.2d 1255 (1985) the court struck down a fee imposed on new customers to expand the sewer system because a portion of the fee was used to make improvements in the existing system. Also see Southern Nevada Homebuilders Ass'n v. City of North Las Vegas, 112 Nev. 297, 913 P.2d 1276 (1996) where the court held that imposition of money exactions for expansion of fire and emergency medical services was ultra vires. The enabling statute permitted exactions only for capital improvements or facility expansion necessitated by and attributable to new development.

181 INC. v. SALEM COUNTY PLANNING BD.
Superior Court of New Jersey, Law Division, 1975.
133 N.J.Super. 350, 336 A.2d 501, modified on appeal
140 N.J.Super. 247, 356 A.2d 34 (1976).

MILLER, J.C.C., Temporarily Assigned.

Plaintiff challenges, as unconstitutional, actions of the Salem County Planning Board compelling it to dedicate to the county a portion of land, owned by it, bordering upon a county road, as a condition precedent to approval by the county of a site plan submitted for the construction of a law office. * * *

Plaintiff is the owner of a tract of land in Woodstown, Salem County. The tract abuts on Elm Street (County Road 40) and on U.S. 40 and is irregular in shape. Following its purchase in December 1971 plaintiff applied to the Salem County Planning Board for site plan approval. The site plan review committee recommended approval subject, among other things, to the dedication of 8.25' along its border on Elm Street, to be used for a proposed widening of Elm Street from 49.5' to 66' pursuant to the official map. The time of such widening is indefinite.

* * *

The original site plan review resolution was adopted January 21, 1970 by the board of freeholders pursuant to N.J.S.A. 40:27–6.6. It provided in § 8 that, "As a condition to the approval of a site plan, the planning board *shall* require the dedication of additional right of way * * *" (emphasis supplied). It was this mandatory feature to which plaintiff objected. * * *

* * *

The vice in the county's resolution is that it sets up a blanket policy of taking frontage along every county road without regard to present need, imminency of proposed use or, indeed, of any standard whatsoever. To then expect a landowner to prove himself outside the perimeter of so nebulously defined an area makes it impossible for him to meet his burden. A perusal of the record in this case and an analysis of the testimony which was necessarily adduced by the plaintiff illustrates the predicament of the landowner.

In order, therefore, for the county to place upon the landowner the burden of proof * * * the county must first make its position clear. This must be done, not in generalities, but in specifics applicable to the land sought to be obtained. While obviously there should be the adoption of an official map and a master plan, this is not enough. There should be, at the bare minimum, a proposal for the imminent use of the land, not a mere "banking" for unscheduled future use. While it is true that road appropriations are made on an annual basis it is also true that plans for road work involve "lead time." If the county does not intend to use the land proposed to be taken within such "lead time," to take it without compensation merely because opportunity presents itself runs afoul of the Constitution.

The planning board felt that there was a sufficient rational *nexus* between the proposed use and the widening *in futuro* of Elm Street to justify the requirement of a compulsory dedication. This finding constitutes error.

* * *

In Brazer v. Mountainside, 55 N.J. 456, 465–466, 262 A.2d 857 (1970), the court said that statutory and ordinance provisions for a compulsory dedication could only be valid where the proposed street bears a realistic relation to or is reasonably made necessary by the subdivision. See also Princeton Res. Lands v. Princeton Tp., 112 N.J.Super. 467, 474, 475, 271 A.2d 719 (App.Div.1970), holding that a developer may not be compelled to donate land to increase the width of an existing abutting street.

The constitutional basis of the nexus requirement is neither strange nor novel. It appears in the earlier zoning cases, for instance, Grosso v. Millburn Tp. Adjustment Bd., 137 N.J.L. 630, 633, 61 A.2d 167 (Sup.Ct. 1948), which held that "lands may not be taken for highway use, presently or in futuro, without just compensation." Grosso, supra at 633, 61 A.2d at 169. See also Lomarch Corp. v. Mayor of Englewood, 51 N.J. 108, 237 A.2d 881 (1968). And Battaglia v. Wayne Tp. Planning Board, 98 N.J.Super. 194, 236 A.2d 608 (App.Div.1967), is particularly apposite since, like the instant case, it involved a site plan approval:

> Unlike the case of a land subdivision, no new streets are necessitated by the plaintiff's planned use; there are no purchasers to whom the cost of the improvements can be passed, and plaintiff's land receives no discernible benefit from compliance with the imposed conditions. [at 200, 236 A.2d at 611]

Had Battaglia not applied for official action, Wayne Township could not have imposed upon him the obligations sought to be imposed. The same logic is inescapable here.

* * *

Since the case must go back, the board of freeholders should revise the site plan (and subdivision) standards, eliminating automatic dedication and limiting compulsory taking to those occasions when it meets the rational nexus test and the county's proposed use is specific and imminent. For example, most (although certainly not all) minor subdivisions will probably be found not to meet the rational nexus test as defined herein.

The actions of the planning board are reversed. The case is remanded to the planning board * * *. Jurisdiction is retained. No costs.

Notes

1. Compare with the principal case Sparks v. Douglas County, 127 Wash.2d 901, 904 P.2d 738 (1995). In this case the developer sought approval for four separate small plats in an "in-fill" situation. The county planning commission found that the existing road abutting the proposed developments was substandard and would, after the developer's building, require widening and structural rebuilding; the county asked for dedication of right-of-way for the future widening of the streets. The developer appealed and ultimately the Supreme Court of Washington held that the facts established a sufficient nexus between the developer's activity and the need for road improvements; even though the maximum possible development proposed would be sixteen houses or thirty-two duplex units, that amount of development would nearly double the amount of traffic on the road and would accelerate the need for widening and rebuilding. Also see Pengilly v. Multnomah County, 810 F.Supp. 1111 (D.Or.1992) where the court upheld a county requirement that home builders dedicate several feet of additional right-of-way as a condition of receiving a building permit on the ground that the requirement promoted aesthetics and traffic efficiency.

2. Similar to the principal case are Simpson v. City of North Platte, 206 Neb. 240, 292 N.W.2d 297 (1980); Howard County v. JJM, Inc., 301 Md. 256, 482 A.2d 908 (1984); Lee County v. New Testament Baptist Church, 507 So.2d 626 (Fla.App. 2 Dist.1987); Middlemist v. City of Plymouth, 387 N.W.2d 190 (Minn.App.1986); Unlimited v. Kitsap County, 50 Wash.App. 723, 750 P.2d 651 (1988); Board Of Supervisors of West Marlborough Twp. v. Fiechter, 129 Pa.Cmwlth. 537, 566 A.2d 370 (1989).

3. In addition to holding that compulsory dedications of portions of the landowner's property for future widening is invalid, courts have utilized the same reasoning when the governing entity seeks to require the landowner to improve an existing road which abuts his property. See Hylton Enterprises v. Board of Supervisors, 220 Va. 435, 258 S.E.2d 577 (1979); Charter Twp. of Harrison v. Calisi, 121 Mich.App. 777, 329 N.W.2d 488 (1982). In Luxembourg Group, Inc. v. Snohomish County, 76 Wash.App. 502, 887 P.2d 446 (1995) the court held that requiring a landowner to dedicate an access road not necessary for his development in order to provide access to a neighbor's landlocked parcel was a taking without compensation.

4. Several right-of-way dedication cases involve the conversion of existing gasoline service stations into the ubiquitous and fast-spreading combination convenience store/gasoline station type of business. In Amoco Oil Co. v. Village of Schaumburg, 277 Ill.App.3d 926, 214 Ill.Dec. 526, 661 N.E.2d 380 (1995), app. denied 167 Ill.2d 549, 217 Ill.Dec. 662, 667 N.E.2d 1055, cert. denied 519 U.S. 976, 117 S.Ct. 413, 136 L.Ed.2d 325 (1996) the court held that a demanded dedication of a 40 by 40 foot triangular section of the landowner's property to rebuild and improve traffic safety at a busy intersection constituted a taking. The dedication would have amounted to about twenty percent of the owner's property and the current defects in the intersection were due to poor original design, not the gas station's activities. Also see William J. (Jack) Jones Insurance Trust v. City of Fort Smith, 731 F.Supp. 912 (W.D.Ark.1990).

(2) *Off–Site Improvements and Impact Fees*

DIVAN BUILDERS, INC. v. PLANNING BD. OF TWP. OF WAYNE

Supreme Court of New Jersey, 1975.
66 N.J. 582, 334 A.2d 30.

PASHMAN, J.

* * *

* * * Divan's proposal contemplated the construction of 31 single family dwellings in a residential zone of the Township. Because a substantial portion of the building site was covered by a pond, the developer's plan called for its draining and the construction of a conduit which would pipe the water from its upstream source through the development and into an existing drainage facility on the downstream border of the site.

* * *

On June 21, 1972, the Wayne governing body amended its subdivision ordinance by adopting Ordinance No. 69–1972. The ordinance establishes procedures to be followed when off-site improvements are deemed necessary to service a subdivision. The ordinance provides in part that:

> "Prior to the granting of final approval of all subdivisions hereafter submitted to the Planning Board, and prior to the issuance of any building permits for any land use, including land uses which require site plan approval * * * and any residence or other use of property on an unimproved street or where any off-site improvements have not then been installed, the subdivider or other named type of applicant * * * shall have installed, posted a performance bond, or made cash payments, in the manner provided in Section 5 below, with respect to the immediate or ultimate installation of any required off-site improvements."

Off-site improvements include the installation of new, or the extension or modification of existing improvements made necessary in whole or in part by the subdivision which will be benefited by the improvement. The ordinance also provides that the cost of off-site improvements shall be allocated between the applicant, other property owners, or any one or more of them. The cost allocation is based upon such factors as the benefit conferred upon the subdivision, the cost of the improvement, and the extent to which the improvement is necessary to protect neighboring property under the proposed plan.

On June 26, 1972, the Planning Board recommended final approval of plaintiff's remaining 26 lots subject to certain conditions, including the following:

[T]hat the applicant contribute to the Township of Wayne a sum of $20,000 as their share of improving the downstream conditions of the stream which carries the drainage from the subdivision.

In July 1972 plaintiff received final approval for the remaining portion of its subdivision on the condition that it pay the Township $20,000. This sum represented approximately 8% of the estimated $250,000 cost of the off-site improvement deemed necessary to serve the entire drainage basin. Only one other developer, however, was required to contribute a similar sum pursuant to the ordinance.

* * *

It is clear * * * that a municipality may condition subdivision approval upon the developer's installation of those improvements which the local governing body finds necessary for the protection of the public interest. The problem, of course, is that the statutory scheme makes no specific reference to off-site improvements in this context.

In our view, however, this omission does not preclude a determination that the Planning Act authorizes municipalities to adopt both on-site and off-site improvement ordinances. * * * In our judgment, the constitutional and legislative direction to resolve questions of municipal authority broadly in favor of the local unit, compels the conclusion that, by necessary implication, N.J.S.A. 40:55–1.21 empowers a planning agency to require both on-site and off-site improvements of the physical character and type referred to in N.J.S.A. 40:55–1.20 and N.J.S.A. 40:55–1.21, including off-site improvements made necessary by reason of the subdivision's effect on lands other than the subdivision property, provided that the agency acts pursuant to a valid local ordinance containing suitable standards governing construction and installation of improvements. See Deerfield Estates v. Twp. of East Brunswick, 60 N.J. 115, 286 A.2d 498 (1972).

* * *

We have heretofore recognized that a municipality may utilize three principal ways to finance an off-site improvement. In Deerfield Estates, supra, the defendant municipality refused to install water mains to serve plaintiff's lots. As a threshold question, the Court held that a municipality which had created a planning board and adopted an adequate subdivision ordinance could validly condition subdivision approval upon installation of necessary water mains. 60 N.J. 122, 286 A.2d 498.

Proceeding to the question of financing the water main extension, Justice Mountain set forth three principal ways in which the municipality could defray the cost of the improvements:

> "First, it may be undertaken entirely at municipal cost and expense. * * * In the second place the municipality may undertake the project as a local improvement and assess the cost against the owners of the properties benefited pursuant to the procedure outlined in N.J.S.A. 40:56–1, et seq.

"The third course is to require that the work be done at the expense of the developer either with or without a formula providing for partial or total reimbursement. Recourse to this third alternative, as to which there has hitherto existed some question, may be had only where appropriate local legislation permits the imposition and when it is fair and equitable that this be done." [60 N.J. at 131, 286 A.2d at 507; footnote omitted].

* * *

Because the need for the off-site improvement was so created, the municipality in recognition of that fact may, in any event, fairly and properly call upon the subdivider to pay the difference between the cost of the improvement and the total amount by which all properties served thereby, including the subdivision, have been specially benefited by the improvement.

Further, but only if the off-site improvement is to be constructed as a "local improvement," * * * with all properties specially benefited thereby to be assessed for the amount of special benefits accruing to each—the subdivider may be called upon to pay in addition to the amount above set forth the amount by which the subdivision property was specially benefited by the improvement.

If the off-site improvement is to be constructed by the municipality as a general improvement—no part of the cost of which may be specially assessed on properties specially benefited thereby—or if the off-site improvement is to be constructed by the subdivider with a provision for later reimbursement by the municipality, then the subdivider may not be charged with the amount by which the subdivision property was specially benefited. To do so would result in patent discrimination in the treatment afforded the subdivision property as contrasted with the other properties specially benefited by the improvement. * * *

We pass now from the question of cost allocation to a consideration of how provision therefor may be made at the time subdivision approval is granted, a date antecedent to the actual construction of the improvement.

It is at once apparent that before the stated conditions are actually imposed on the applicant for subdivision approval, the governing body must decide whether the off-site improvement is to be constructed (1) by the municipality as a general improvement or (2) as a local improvement or (3) whether it is to be done by the developer with a formula providing for partial reimbursement if the improvement specially benefits properties other than the subdivision.

Once that decision has been made, the planning agency should be required to estimate, with the aid of the municipal engineer and such other persons having pertinent information or expertise (a) the cost of the improvement and (b) the amount by which all properties to be serviced thereby, including the subdivision property, will be specially benefited therefrom.

Sec. 1   REGULATION OF THE SUBDIVISION OF LAND   469

When that has been determined, the subdivider may be required to provide, as a condition for approval of his subdivision application, a bond (or a cash deposit, in lieu thereof) to insure payment to the municipality of one of the following amounts:

(a) If the improvement is to be constructed by the municipality as a general improvement, an amount equal to the difference between the estimated cost of the improvement and the estimated total amount by which all properties to be serviced thereby, including the subdivision property, will be specially benefited by the improvement;

(b) If the improvement is to be constructed by the municipality as a local improvement, then in addition to the amount referred to in (a) the estimated amount by which the subdivision property will be specially benefited by the improvement; or

(c) If the improvement is to be constructed by the subdivider, an amount equal to the estimated cost of the improvement.

If the subdivider should deem that any of the amounts so estimated by the planning agency are unreasonable, it may challenge them and seek to have them revised in appropriate proceedings brought to compel subdivision approval.

Further, since the amounts are only estimated amounts, they should be redetermined once the improvement is completed to the end that the subdivider will be required to pay his appropriate and only his appropriate share of the cost thereof. If the municipality and the subdivider cannot agree with respect thereto, the dispute will have to be decided in a judicial proceeding or proceedings. * * *

It is evident that neither Ordinance 69–1972 nor the action taken by the municipality here conformed to the controlling principles herein set forth. Further, it *prima facie* appears—although defendants deny it—that there has been a disregard of the fundamental principle prohibiting discrimination in cost apportionment in requiring plaintiff to pay $20,000 and allocating no part of the cost to the other properties allegedly specially benefited by [the] improvement, which was constructed as a general improvement.

* * *

To that end, since the improvement was constructed by the municipality as a general improvement, the judgment is reversed and the cause remanded to the trial court for a determination at a trial, following appropriate discovery proceedings and a pretrial conference, of the difference between the cost of the improvement and the total amount by which all properties served thereby were specially benefited therefrom. That difference is fairly chargeable, under the circumstances indicated by the record, in equal shares to plaintiff and the other developer who made a $20,000 payment since their subdivisions created the need for the off-site improvement. Plaintiff will then be entitled to recover from the municipality only that portion, if any of the $20,000 it paid which exceeds the amount fairly chargeable to it.

Reversed and remanded.

POLICY GUIDE ON IMPACT FEES

(ratified by the Board of Directors of the American Planning Association in October 1988 (see, www.planning.org))

Impact fees are payments required by local governments of new development for the purpose of providing new or expanded public capital facilities required to serve that development. The fees typically require cash payments in advance of the completion of development, are based on a methodology and calculation derived from the cost of the facility and the nature and size of the development, and are used to finance improvements offsite of, but to the benefit of the development.

Local governments throughout the country are increasingly using impact fees to shift more of the costs of financing public facilities from the general taxpayer to the beneficiaries of those new facilities. As a general matter, impact fees are capitalized into land values, and thus represent an exaction on the incremental value of the land attributable to the higher and better use made possible by the new public facilities. Some commentators have argued that, under certain circumstances, others may instead bear the incidence of the fee (these may include the original landowner, the developer, or the consumer). There has been little to demonstrate that the imposition of a fee system has stifled development. The fees supplement local government resources that otherwise have decreased because of diminished state and federal transfers of funds. Local governments have also used impact fees to delay or as a substitute for general property tax increases.

Impact fees, when based on a comprehensive plan and used in conjunction with a sound capital improvement plan, can be an effective tool for ensuring adequate infrastructure to accommodate growth where and when it is anticipated. It is important that communities rely on zoning and other land use regulations, consistent with a comprehensive plan, to influence patterns of growth and to more accurately predict new infrastructure needs. However, in areas facing development moratoria because of the lack of adequate public facilities, impact fees may be viewed not as growth stopping measures, but rather as growth facilitators. Impact fees should not be considered a panacea for the funding of general capital improvements, nor should they be used to "stop growth." They can do neither.

Local government experimentation with impact fees has been paralleled by increasing state court involvement in the review of these fees. A general trend in the state courts has been to require a "rational nexus" between the fee and the needs created by development and the benefits incurred by the development. This analysis is a moderate position between a standard that requires that the fee be "specifically and uniquely attributable" to the needs created by new development, and the relaxed standard that the fee be "reasonably related" to the needs created by development.

Impact fees have been criticized as being an inequitable means to finance public facilities. By requiring new development to pay for new facilities without benefiting from existing facility capacity, local governments may be bypassing the traditional practice of intergenerational contribution toward public facilities. Some commentators have argued that, when set at high levels, impact fees may also tend to be regressive. Certain public facilities may be considered "public goods" that should be financed by the entire community, such as general government, police, or schools. To the extent that impact fees are paid by those who are most likely to benefit from the public facilities provided therefrom, however, impact fees are equitable.

Many local communities have expanded the use of impact fees to finance a wide variety of public facilities. The most widespread use of these fees is for sewer and water facilities, parks, and roads. Impact fees are also being used for schools, libraries and public facilities. In recent years, rulings at the state court level have defined how impact fees may be applied and utilized. Thus, there are numerous standards and guidelines available to assist local and regional governmental agencies on the planning processes that must be undertaken to develop a legally defensible impact fee program. Approximately half the states have enacted enabling legislation for impact fees, some of which have specifically included language that governs how these programs are to be implemented. To be most effective and legally valid, impact fees must be carefully designed and documented.

Based on these findings, the American Planning Association adopted the following policies:

1. Support state enabling legislation that establishes clear and concise standards for the adoption and use of impact fees consistent with this policy.

2. Encourage consideration of the use of impact fees as a means to provide additional resources for an adequate public infrastructure and services only as they relate to the needs of new development.

3. Support the use of impact fees as a standardized method for ensuring that new development pays its fair share of the cost of public infrastructure.

4. Encourage the use of impact fees to pay for facilities where a rational nexus can be established.

5. Impact fees should be used in the context of community-wide plans and programs for financing public facilities and services, and ensure the adequacy of public facilities to serve future development.

6. Oppose requiring voter approval to establish fees for mitigation of impacts on public facilities and services where such fees are imposed pursuant to a legislatively approved program in compliance with APA standards for the adoption and use of impact fees.

7. Support continued dialogue between local planning agencies, the general public, and the development community to discuss the public costs associated with new development, reaching an understanding on the calculation of such costs, and establishing alternative means for financing these costs, including the use of impact fees.

8. As a framework for imposing fees, local jurisdictions are encouraged to develop, adopt, and implement capital improvement programs consistent with an adopted comprehensive plan with consideration given to other funding alternatives.

IMPACT FEE STANDARDS

- The imposition of a fee must be rationally linked (the "rational nexus") to an impact created by a particular development and the demonstrated need for related capital improvements pursuant to a capital improvement plan and program.
- Some benefit must accrue to the development as a result of the payment of a fee.
- The amount of the fee must be a proportionate fair share of the costs of the improvements made necessary by the development and must not exceed the cost of the improvements.
- A fee cannot be imposed to address existing deficiencies except where they are exacerbated by new development.
- Funds received under such a program must be segregated from the general fund and used solely for the purposes for which the fee is established.
- The fees collected must be encumbered or expended within a reasonable timeframe to ensure that needed improvements are implemented.
- The fee assessed cannot exceed the cost of the improvements, and credits must be given for outside funding sources (such as federal and state grants, developer initiated improvements for impacts related to new development, etc.) and local tax payments which fund capital improvements, for example.
- The fee cannot be used to cover normal operation and maintenance or personnel costs, but must be used for capital improve-

ments, or under some linkage programs, affordable housing, job training, child care, etc.

- The fee established for specific capital improvements should be reviewed at least every two years to determine whether an adjustment is required, and similarly the capital improvement plan and budget should be reviewed at least every 5 to 8 years.
- Provisions must be included in the ordinance to permit refunds for projects that are not constructed, since no impact will have manifested.
- Impact fee payments are typically required to be made as a condition of approval of the development, either at the time the building or occupancy permit is issued.

Compare the position of the American Planning Association to that of the National Association of Homebuilders below (available at www.nahb.org):

Impact Fee Policy

The financing of off-site infrastructure that serves or has the potential for serving more than one project should be based on community-wide or broader funding sources, rather than impact fees/taxes on new housing.

Background

Federal funding of infrastructure—for new roads, highways, sewer and water, other facilities and federal assistance for maintaining old infrastructure—has steadily decreased. This has significantly increased pressure on local governments to find alternative sources of funding. More and more jurisdictions are imposing impact fees on developers and, through developers, on new housing consumers, as a way to pay for improvements beyond that necessary for new development. These exactions, which now exceed $15,000 per home in many areas and even more in some areas, have worsened the nation's housing affordability problems. A more equitable and affordable approach to infrastructure financing assures that impact fees cover only costs that are directly attributable or beneficial to new home construction. Credits for other fees and revenues, such as permit fees, connection fees and sales, income and property taxes, as the result of new home building must be accounted for before imposing new fees and taxes. Costs of facilities that serve the entire community should be spread over the entire community.

Solutions

- Seek and support legislation to provide mechanisms for facilitating broad-based infrastructure finance.
- Support the use of community-wide resources such as property taxes, sales taxes, transfer taxes, and income taxes to support infrastructure finance.

- Encourage government accountability of current and available funding sources before assessing any fee.

Notes

1. The rational nexus test has been utilized by most jurisdictions facing the problem of imposing on developers the requirement of dedicating land outside the proposed subdivision for future improvements or the actual construction of improvements outside the boundaries of the subdivision. As in the principal case, courts are suspicious of schemes that require a developer to pay the total cost of an off-site improvement. See Baltica Construction Co., Inc. v. Planning Board of Franklin Twp., 222 N.J.Super. 428, 537 A.2d 319 (1988); Longridge Builders, Inc. v. Planning Board of Princeton Twp., 52 N.J. 348, 245 A.2d 336 (1968); Kode Harbor Dev. Assoc. v. County of Atlantic, 230 N.J.Super. 430, 553 A.2d 858 (1989); Christopher Lake Development Co. v. St. Louis County, 35 F.3d 1269 (8th Cir.1994).

2. Even where developers are asked only to pay a pro rata share of necessary off-site improvements, the rational nexus test must be carefully applied. In New Jersey Builders Association v. Mayor and Twp. Committee of Bernards Twp., 108 N.J. 223, 528 A.2d 555 (1987), the court held requiring new developments to pay a pro rata share of the township's long-range $20 million road improvement plan was ultra vires. Also see Albany Area Builders Association v. Town of Guilderland, 74 N.Y.2d 372, 547 N.Y.S.2d 627, 546 N.E.2d 920 (1989), where the town's Transportation Impact Fee Law was held to have been preempted by the state statutes dealing with road improvements and financing. In Land/Vest Properties, Inc. v. Town of Plainfield, 117 N.H. 817, 379 A.2d 200 (1977), the court upheld the theory of off-site road improvements, but struck down the proposed exaction for failure to establish the rational nexus. Compare KBW, Inc. v. Town of Bennington, 115 N.H. 392, 342 A.2d 653 (1975).

3. In Arrowhead Development Co. v. Livingston County Road Commission, 413 Mich. 505, 322 N.W.2d 702 (1982), the court found that a requirement that the developer regrade an existing county road to eliminate a dangerous condition which would be exacerbated by the development exceeded the commission's statutory powers.

4. In Northwest Land and Investment, Inc. v. City of Bellingham, 31 Wash.App. 742, 644 P.2d 740 (1982), the developer brought a tort action against the city for unlawfully requiring him to install off-site improvements; the court denied relief because the developer did not pursue a challenge to the requirement, and thus, the proximate cause of his loss was his compliance.

Village Square No. 1, Inc. v. Crow–Frederick, 77 Md.App. 552, 551 A.2d 471 (1989) was a case involving a "recapture agreement," a common device used in off-site or in oversized on-site improvements that will, in the future, benefit subsequent developers. The usual agreement provides for the city to calculate how much of the improvement installed by a developer will benefit future nearby developments, a provision that the city will charge the future development(s) that portion of previously installed improvement that benefits the new development, and a promise to reimburse the original developer that amount. As you might expect, a lot of guesswork goes into this process, and there is no guarantee that the original developer will ever see any money. In addition to the Maryland case, where the original developer lost, see Beneficial Development Corp. v. City of Highland Park, 239 Ill.App.3d 414, 179 Ill.Dec. 1005, 606 N.E.2d 837 (1992). In this case, the court upheld the recapture agreement, but the amount obtained by the developer was minimal. Also see Fischer v. Dover, 131 N.H. 469, 554 A.2d 1293 (1989), cert. denied 502 U.S. 899, 112 S.Ct. 276, 116 L.Ed.2d 228, where a developer who had installed a road with a recapture agreement received $8,000 10 years later when another developer came along. The installing developer argued, without success, that he should receive an additional sum to represent the inflation in road costs over the 10–year period.

5. Put yourself in the position of a planning commissioner or other local official of a unit on the growth fringe of an urban area. Yours is one of the toughest jobs in government. Your town or borough, or village, or satellite city is perhaps reasonably well-equipped with "paper" legal powers. But it is woefully weak in terms of revenue sources and technical competence to wrestle with the problems of urban growth that plague it. There are pressures on you to slow down development so it will not outstrip the community's ability to finance demanded services, especially schools. Other pressure from "old timers" push for preservation of neighborhood "amenities" and the character of the community, by which may be meant, "Keep the little houses with their swarms of kids out" or "Let's have big lots and big houses only and, for goodness sakes, no trailer camps." Other strong-minded citizens will be pushing hard for "getting some industry in to take some of the property tax load off us householders." And every citizen, even the one who has just moved in last week, will agree that in the future you should make all newcomers "pay their own way." There will be little pressure on you to do what is best in terms of the needs of the metropolitan region; instead you will be asked to wear intellectual blinders and do what is "best" for your political entity and let neighboring units take the consequences.

So, for example, who should pay for the increased costs of public infrastructure related to the new development? Should the cost of a new water filtration system necessitated by the increased number of houses on the system be borne by the community as a whole since each resident will benefit, or should the costs be borne solely by the new residents/homeowners who created the need for the upgrade? Impact fees, or development fees to fund certain off-site improvements, have been a controversial source of revenue for local governments over the last ten years as evidenced in the policy positions of the American Planning Association and the National Association of Home Builders set forth above. With approximately half of the states providing statutory authorization and guidelines for the adoption of local impact fee laws, the American Planning Association's Legislative Guidebook offers model state statutory language as well as a discussion of elements of a good impact fee statute. See, American Planning Association, *Growing Smart Legislative Guidebook: Model Statutes for Planning and the Management of Change* (Stuart Meck, ed.) (2002) at Chapter 8 (available at www.planning.org).

(3) Non-traditional Exactions

PIONEER TRUST & SAV. BANK v. VILLAGE OF MOUNT PROSPECT

Supreme Court of Illinois, 1961.
22 Ill.2d 375, 176 N.E.2d 799.

MR. JUSTICE HERSHEY delivered the opinion of the court:

Plaintiffs brought a mandamus proceeding in the circuit court of Cook County to compel the corporate authorities of the village of Mount Prospect to approve a plat of subdivision which complied with all the provisions of the official plan of the municipality except that requiring a dedication of land for public use. The case was submitted to the court on an agreed statement of facts. The court entered an order finding the land dedication requirements of the village's official plan invalid and directed the issuance of a writ of mandamus commanding the corporate authorities to approve the plat. The trial court has certified that the validity of a municipal ordinance is involved and that the public interest requires a direct appeal.

Article 53 of the Revised Cities and Villages Act authorizes municipalities to establish plan commissions with authority to recommend to the corporate authorities the adoption of an official plan. Section 53–2 (Ill.Rev.Stat.1959, c. 24, par. 53–2) provides that the plan may "establish reasonable standards of design for subdivisions and for resubdivisions of unimproved land and of areas subject to redevelopment, including reasonable requirements for public streets, alleys, ways for public service facilities, parks, playgrounds, school grounds, and other public grounds." Section 53–3 provides that no plat of subdivision "shall be entitled to record or shall be valid unless the subdivision shown thereon provides for streets, alleys, * * * and public grounds in conformity with the applicable requirements of the official plan."

The village of Mount Prospect has established a plan commission and has adopted by ordinance an official plan as recommended by the commission. Section 6 of article II of that plan contains a requirement for the dedication of public grounds as follows:

> "Dedication of Lands for Public Use: The plat shall have lettered upon it a statement of dedications properly conveying all usable lands dedicated for such public uses as streets, public schools, parks or any other public use, and there shall be attached to the plat a certificate of title certifying the ownership of all such lands to be so dedicated by said plat. Public grounds, other than streets, alleys and parking areas, shall be dedicated in appropriate locations by the plat (a) at the rate of at least one (1) acre for each sixty (60) residential building sites or family living units, which may be accommodated under the restrictions applying to the land; or (b) at the rate of at least one-tenth (1/10) acre for each one (1) acre of

Sec. 1 REGULATION OF THE SUBDIVISION OF LAND

business or industrial building sites which may be accommodated under the restrictions applying to the land."

Plaintiff Salvatore Dimucci is engaged in the business of subdividing real estate for residential purposes and caused a plat of the subdivision to be submitted to the plan commission for approval which complied in all respects with the aforesaid ordinance except as to the dedication of some 6.7 acres of land which would be required under the language of section 6 of article II quoted above. The plaintiffs have refused to dedicate land, and, in view of that refusal, the village board has refused to approve the plat of the subdivision. It is established in the record that the 6.7 acres of land sought to be required to be dedicated or donated would be for the use of an elementary school and for the use of the Mount Prospect Park District as an elementary school site and a secondary use as a playground. The proposed subdivision shows some 250 residential units.

The issue here presented for determination is the validity of the quoted section of the ordinance, and no provision of the ordinance other than that requiring the dedication is under attack by the plaintiffs in this proceeding.

The statute from which the village derives its authority has been before us on two previous occasions. Petterson v. City of Naperville, 9 Ill.2d 233, 137 N.E.2d 371; Rosen v. Village of Downers Grove, 19 Ill.2d 448, 167 N.E.2d 230. In each of these cases the issue presented for decision was narrowly circumscribed, and in neither case did we pass upon the precise point that is involved here. The Petterson case did not involve any question of required dedication of land, but rather concerned the reasonableness of a requirement that the subdivider provide curbs and gutters for the streets of the subdivision. We sustained the validity of such a requirement, stating that "the power to prescribe reasonable requirements for public streets in the interest of the health and safety of the inhabitants of the city and contiguous territory includes more than a mere designation of the location and width of streets." The Rosen case involved a portion of an ordinance of the village of Downers Grove which required subdividers to dedicate land for educational facilities but also provided that if the plan commission should deem that the dedication of such land would not of itself meet the reasonable requirements of providing educational facilities for the proposed subdivision, then the plan commission might require any additional means for providing reasonable facilities. Acting under this ordinance, the municipality attempted to require subdividers to pay a certain sum per lot for educational purposes. We held this attempt invalid because the specific technique employed was not authorized by the statute, and also because the term "educational purposes" was broader than the language of the statute. The Downers Grove ordinance did contain a paragraph, similar to that involved in the instant case, requiring the dedication for public grounds of at least one acre of land for each 75 family living units; but this particular provision was not directly involved in the litigation and we refused to pass on its validity.

Our opinion in the Rosen case thus specifically left undecided the question that is now presented for decision. It did, however, suggest some basic principles for distinguishing between permissible and forbidden requirements. We stated in the Rosen case that the statutory provisions with respect to reasonable requirements for streets and public grounds were based upon the theory that "the developer of a subdivision may be required to assume those costs which are specifically and uniquely attributable to his activity and which would otherwise be cast upon the public." We further observed: "But because the requirement that a plat of subdivision be approved affords an appropriate point of control with respect to costs made necessary by the subdivision, it does not follow that communities may use this point of control to solve all of the problems which they can foresee. The distinction between permissible and forbidden requirements is suggested in Ayres v. The City Council of Los Angeles, 34 Cal.2d 31, 207 P.2d 1, 11 A.L.R.2d 503, which indicates that the municipality may require the developer to provide the streets which are required by the activity within the subdivision but can not require him to provide a major thoroughfare, the need for which stems from the total activity of the community." It is in the light of these basic principles that the reasonableness of the requirement sought to be imposed by the defendant village must be determined. If the requirement is within the statutory grant of power to the municipality and if the burden cast upon the subdivider is specifically and uniquely attributable to his activity, then the requirement is permissible; if not, it is forbidden and amounts to a confiscation of private property in contravention of the constitutional prohibitions rather than reasonable regulation under the police power.

* * *

There can be no controversy about the obvious fact that the orderly development of a municipality must necessarily include a consideration of the present and future need for school and public recreational facilities. Neither the plaintiffs nor the defendants in this case take the negative side of the question as to the desirability either of education or recreation. The question is not one of the desirability of education or recreation, nor of the desirability to improve the public condition, but, rather, the question presented here is one of determining who shall pay for such improvements. Is it reasonable that a subdivider should be required under the guise of a police power regulation to dedicate a portion of his property to public use; or does this amount to a veiled exercise of the power of eminent domain and a confiscation of private property behind the defense of police regulations?

That the addition by this subdivision of some 250 residential units to the municipality would of course aggravate the existing need for additional school and recreational facilities is admitted by the parties to this cause. No complaint is made by the plaintiff in this cause that the land required to be dedicated for such purposes by subdivision control ordinance is unnecessary. The sole question thus presented here is whether the state of law is such that a mandatory dedication of the land without cost to the public may be sustained in the regulation of proposed subdivision when it is admitted that such land may well be needed.

However, this record does not establish that the need for recreational and educational facilities in the event that said subdivision plat is permitted to be filed, is one that is specifically and uniquely attributable to the addition of the subdivision and which should be cast upon the subdivider as his sole financial burden. The agreed statement of facts shows that the present school facilities of Mount Prospect are near capacity. This is the result of the total development of the community. If this whole community had not developed to such an extent or if the existing school facilities were greater, the purported need supposedly would not be present. Therefore, on the record in this case the school problem which allegedly exists here is one which the subdivider should not be obliged to pay the total cost of remedying, and to so construe the statute would amount to an exercise of the power of eminent domain without compensation. Sanitary District of Chicago v. Chicago and Alton R. Co., 267 Ill. 252, 108 N.E. 312, and cases there cited; Ridgemont Develop. Co. v. City of East Detroit, 358 Mich. 387, 100 N.W.2d 301.

Section 6 of article II of the defendant village ordinance imposes an unreasonable condition precedent for the approval of a plat of a subdivision and purports to take private property for public use without compensation. The circuit court of Cook County was correct in so holding, and the judgment of that court is affirmed.

JORDAN v. VILLAGE OF MENOMONEE FALLS

Supreme Court of Wisconsin, 1965.
28 Wis.2d 608, 137 N.W.2d 442, appeal dismissed
385 U.S. 4, 87 S.Ct. 36, 17 L.Ed.2d 3 (1966).

Action by plaintiffs Martin A. Jordan and James F. McMicken and their wives against defendant village to recover $5,000 paid by plaintiffs as an equalization fee in lieu of dedicating land as required by defendant's ordinance governing the subdivision of lands within the village.

In October, 1959, Jordan and McMicken (hereinafter "plaintiffs") commenced negotiations for the purchase of a 7.85 acre tract of land in defendant village for the purpose of subdividing it into lots and selling the lots. While negotiating, plaintiffs became aware that defendant had enacted an ordinance in March, 1959, which required subdividers to either dedicate a portion of their land or pay a fee in lieu thereof. Pertinent sections of the ordinance are:

> "In order that adequate open spaces and sites for public uses may be properly located and preserved as the community develops; and in order that the cost of providing the public school, park, and recreation sites and facilities necessary to serve the additional families brought into the community by subdivision development may be most equitably apportioned on the basis of the additional need

created by the individual subdivision development, the following provisions are established:

"8.01. Reservation of Potential Sites.

"(1) In the design of the plat, consideration shall be given to the adequate provision of and correlation with such public sites or open areas.

"(2) Where it is determined by the plan commission that a portion of the plat is required for such public sites or open spaces, the subdivider may be required to reserve such area for a period not to exceed three years, after which the Village shall either acquire the property or release the reservation.

"8.02. Dedication of Sites.

"(1) Within the corporate limits of the Village, where feasible and compatible with the comprehensive plan for development of the community, the subdivider shall provide and dedicate to the public adequate land to provide for the school, park and recreation needs of the subdivision.

"(2) The amount of land to be provided shall be determined on the basis of an amount equal in value to $200.00 per residential lot created by the subdivision. Such value shall be determined by the Village assessor on the basis of full and fair market value of the land. If the owner is not satisfied with such appraisal, he may appeal such determination, in which case an appraisal board consisting of one appraiser selected by the Village at its own expense, one selected by the property owner at his own expense and a third selected by the two other appraisers at Village expense, shall determine the value.

"8.03. Proportionate Payment in Lieu of Dedication.

"(1) Where such dedication is not feasible or compatible with the comprehensive plan, the subdivider shall in lieu thereof pay to the Village a fee equivalent to the value of the required dedication. Such fee shall be distributed as follows:

'A. $120.00 per residential lot created by the subdivision to be held in a non-lapsing fund for the benefit of the school district or districts in which the plat lies, on the basis of proper apportionment between districts where the plat is in more than one district, and to be made available to the appropriate district or districts upon their request.

'B. $80.00 per residential lot created by the subdivision to be placed in a non-lapsing fund to be used for park and recreation area development.'

"(2) Such fees shall be used exclusively for immediate or future site acquisition or capital improvement. * * *

"8.05. Determination of Feasibility.

"The determination as to the feasibility of dedication shall be made by the Village Plan Commission. The subdivider shall however have the option of choosing to make payment in lieu of dedication."

With full knowledge of the ordinance, plaintiffs purchased the property for $22,000. Plaintiff Jordan did once voice an informal objection to Gottlieb, village commissioner, stating that he thought the ordinance was unconstitutional. Because of the small area and the particular layout of the subdivision planned, it did not occur to plaintiffs to dedicate any land for school or park sites. They proceeded on the assumption that they would pay the $5,000 equalization fee in lieu of land dedication, which fee they paid by check September 12, 1960, and typed "paid under protest" on the check. Plaintiffs then proceeded to complete the subdivision at a total cost of $73,896.98, including the $5,000 platting fee. All 25 lots were sold between September, 1961, and April, 1963, for a total sum of $100,000.

On October 26, 1962, plaintiffs served on defendant a formal demand and claim for return of the payment, which was denied by defendant.

Plaintiffs alleged that the payment was a tax which the village could not levy because (1) it did not have authorization from the legislature and (2) it was an unconstitutional taking of property without just compensation. Trial was to the court and judgment was entered February 12, 1965, for plaintiffs, requiring defendants to repay to plaintiffs the $5,000 plus interest from September 12, 1960.

Defendant has appealed.

* * *

CURRIE, CHIEF JUSTICE.

The issue on this appeal is the constitutionality of the ordinance pursuant to which the $5,000 equalization fee was paid. Defendant asserts that the ordinance is a valid exercise of its police power in controlling subdivision development to assure its burgeoning population adequate parks and schools. Plaintiffs contend that section 8.03 of the ordinance levies a tax which is not authorized by the legislature and unconstitutional.

* * *

Preliminary to considering the constitutionality of the equalization fee provisions of the ordinance, we deem it advisable to pass on the requirement that the subdivider, where practicable, be required to dedicate a portion of the subdivision for sites for school, park and recreational needs of a value of $200 per residential lot. If this provision of the ordinance is unconstitutional, then of course the provision for payment of a cash fee in lieu of dedicating land for school, park and recreational sites would of necessity also be unconstitutional.

No claim has been asserted in this litigation that the $200 per lot value of land required to be dedicated by the subdivision owner is unreasonable in amount. Nelson, defendant's municipal planning expert, testified that the experience of municipal planners throughout the country has shown that for a good environment for human habitation, for each family in the area, there must be a minimum of 3,000 square feet of land devoted to park and school purposes. After some study of average land values in the village, the village planning commission and the village board determined that land valued at $200 would by and large provide the added park and school lands required for each family brought into the village by creation of the subdivision.

The grounds of the attack upon the land dedication requirement is that it is not authorized by statute and is an unconstitutional taking of private property for public use without just compensation.

Upon careful analysis of sec. 236.45, Stats., we conclude that it does authorize the land dedication requirement of the instant ordinance. Sub. (1) of this statute declares that the purposes of the statute include facilitating "adequate provision for transportation, water, sewerage, schools, parks, playgrounds and other public requirements." The common practice of providing for transportation in a subdivision is for municipal platting ordinances to require dedication of land for streets by the subdivider. Likewise the accepted way to provide water and sewerage facilities for a proposed subdivision is to require the subdivider to provide the same as a condition to the municipality approving the proposed plat. In Zastrow v. Village of Brown Deer[5] this court stated:

> "The Village could require as a condition of its approval of a plat that the subdivider make and install any public improvements reasonably necessary, including a water system, and it could require as a condition for accepting the dedication that the designated facilities previously constructed and provided be without cost to the Village, and that such facilities be according to the Village's specifications and under its inspection, including water mains and laterals."

Similarly it would seem to follow that the way to facilitate provision for schools, parks, and playgrounds to serve the subdivision would be to require the subdivider to dedicate a portion of the subdivision for such purposes. Sec. 236.13(2)(a) and (b), Stats.,[6] which apply statewide to all

---

5. 9 Wis.2d 100, 100 N.W.2d 359 (1960).

6. These subsections provide: "(a) As a further condition of approval, the governing body of the town or municipality within which the subdivision lies may require that the subdivider make and install any public improvements reasonably necessary or that he execute a surety bond to insure that he will make those improvements within a reasonable time.

"(b) Any city or village may require as a condition for accepting the dedication of public streets, alleys or other ways, * * * that designated facilities shall have been previously provided without cost to the municipality, * * *"

municipalities, irrespective of whether they have planning commissions, grants to municipalities the right to require the subdivider to pay for such public improvements as water and sewer mains, and to dedicate land for public streets, as a condition to the municipality approving the proposed subdivision plat. Sec. 236.45 was intended by the legislature to vest additional authority in those municipalities which had created planning commissions to impose further requirements upon the subdivider. In addition to the aforequoted language spelling out legislative purpose in sub. (1) of this statute, the first sentence of sub. (2)(a), of sec. 236.45, makes clear this intent. The third sentence of this subsection reads, "Such ordinances may make applicable to such divisions any of the provisions of this chapter, or may provide other surveying, monumenting, mapping and approving requirements for such division." Standing alone the statutory words "other * * * approving requirements" would normally be confined to requirements of the same general nature as the antecedent enumerated specific words "surveying, monumenting, mapping." We reject such a restrictive interpretation in favor of the broader one which will encompass the objectives stated in sub. (1). We are further motivated in favor of such a broad interpretation by the direction of sub. (2)(b) requiring a liberal construction of sec. 236.45.

Having concluded that sec. 236.45, Stats., does authorize the land dedication provisions of the instant ordinance, we turn now to the question of whether they constitute an unconstitutional taking of private property for a public purpose. The Illinois supreme court in Pioneer Trust & Sav. Bank v. Village of Mt. Prospect laid down this test of the constitutionality of a requirement placed upon a subdivider, as a condition for approval of the subdivision plat:

> "If the requirement is within the statutory grant of power to the municipality and if the burden cast upon the subdivider is specifically and uniquely attributable to his activity, then the requirement is permissible; if not, it is forbidden and amounts to a confiscation of private property in contravention of the constitutional prohibitions rather than reasonable regulation under the police power."

We deem this to be an acceptable statement of the yardstick to be applied, provided the words "specifically and uniquely attributable to his activity" are not so restrictively applied as to cast an unreasonable burden of proof upon the municipality which has enacted the ordinance under attack. In most instances it would be impossible for the municipality to prove that the land required to be dedicated for a park or a school site was to meet a need solely attributable to the anticipated influx of people into the community to occupy this particular subdivision. On the other hand, the municipality might well be able to establish that a group of subdivisions approved over a period of several years had been responsible for bringing into the community a considerable number of people making it necessary that the land dedications required of the subdividers be utilized for school, park and recreational purposes for the benefit of such influx. In the absence of contravening evidence this would establish a reasonable basis for finding that the need for the acquisition was occasioned by the activity of the subdivider. Possible contravening evidence would be a showing that the municipality prior to the opening up of the subdivisions, acquired sufficient lands for school, park and recreational purposes to provide for future anticipated needs including such influx, or that the normal growth of the municipality would have made necessary the acquisition irrespective of the influx caused by opening up of subdivisions.

There also may be situations, unlike the instant one, where there is no substantial influx from the outside and the proposed subdivision only fulfills a purely local need within the community. In those situations it may be more difficult to adduce proof sufficient to sustain a land dedication requirement.

We conclude that a required dedication of land for school, park or recreational sites as a condition for approval of the subdivision plat should be upheld as a valid exercise of police power if the evidence reasonably establishes that the municipality will be required to provide more land for schools, parks and playgrounds as a result of approval of the subdivision.

* * *

We do not consider the fact that other residents of the village as well as residents of the subdivision may make use of a public site required to be dedicated by subdivider for school, park or recreational purposes is particularly material to the constitutional issue. This is also true of land required to be dedicated for public street purposes.

* * *

We turn now to the issue of the constitutionality of the equalization fee provision contained in section 8.03 of the ordinance whereby the subdivider is required to pay a total of $200 per lot in lieu of dedicating land of that value for school, park or recreational needs where the village planning commission finds dedication of land for such purposes is not feasible. In respect to this provision, the question which poses the greater difficulty is not whether there is an attempted illegal taking which cannot be justified as a reasonable exercise of the police power, but whether the legislature has authorized such a provision.

* * *

Is the equalization fee such a concomitant of the land dedication provision of the ordinance that its authorization can be found in the language of subs. (1) and (2) of sec. 236.45 hereinbefore relied upon to sustain the land dedication requirement of the ordinance? We conclude that it is.

Where a comparatively small tract of land is subdivided, as in the instant situation, and there is no adjoining land already devoted to school park, or playground purposes to which a portion of the proposed subdivision might be attached, it usually would be impracticable to require dedication of any land of the subdivision. The two alternatives are either to relieve the subdivider from any obligation whatever in this direction, or to require payment of an equalization fee of the nature of that here imposed. The latter is in keeping with the stated purpose of the statute.

While section 8.03(2) of the ordinance permits use of the proceeds of the equalization fee for capital improvement of schools, parks and recreation areas in addition to site acquisition, nevertheless the making of these capital improvements is encompassed by the words of sub. (1) of sec. 236.45 which declare that the purposes of the statute include facilitating "adequate provision for * * * schools, parks, playgrounds and other public requirements."

The equalization fee exacted pursuant to the ordinance is not a property tax. It is not imposed upon the land in the subdivision as such but is imposed on the transaction of obtaining approval of the plat. Thus, if a tax, it partakes of the nature of an excise tax and does not violate the uniformity clause found in sec. 1, art. VIII of the Wisconsin constitution.

While plaintiffs do not openly contend that the equalization fee is in the nature of a special assessment, they employ arguments that tend in that direction. Thus they point to the fact that the ordinance does not require that park and school sites purchased with funds paid in lieu of dedication bear any relationship to the subdivision providing the funds. This argument would be pertinent if the equalization fee's validity were dependent on justifying it as a special assessment. The argument, however, does have some pertinency on the previously considered issue of unconstitutional taking of private property for a public purpose as opposed to a reasonable exercise of police power.

To conclude, we determine that the imposition of the instant $5,000 equalization fee is not invalid as unconstitutional. In so holding we are cognizant that this result is contra to the conclusions reached by the Illinois and Kansas courts in the well considered cases of Rosen v. Village of Downers Grove[7] and Coronado Development Co. v. City of McPherson[8] with respect to the issue of the validity of the attempted exercise of the police power. While we have great respect for these courts, we believe that there is a reasonable basis for upholding the exercise of the police power voiced in the instant ordinance.

Judgment reversed and cause remanded with directions to dismiss the complaint.

HALLOWS, JUSTICE (dissenting).

* * *

By analogy, any dedication of land for parks and school purposes or money in lieu thereof should be governed by the same rules which apply to public roads and sewer and water in the subdivision. When land is dedicated for public streets or for the furnishing of water mains and

7. 19 Ill.2d 448, 167 N.E.2d 230 (1960). 8. 189 Kan. 174, 368 P.2d 51 (1962).

sewers, their location insures some definite benefit to the rest of the land in the plat. While these are of special benefit to the lots, they are, of course, incidentally of benefit to the community at large.

In respect to the alternative provision for the payment of money in lieu of land for school and park purposes, I find no authority for the municipality to enact such an alternative and no restriction or requirement that the money be used for parks and schools in the vicinity of the subdivision. The money may be used anywhere in the municipality and is not restricted for the direct benefit of the subdivision. Consequently, this requirement of the payment of a fee which a municipality has the option to demand in lieu of land is nothing more than a revenue-raising device for the general welfare of the municipality and as such is in the nature of a tax and cannot be justified as an exercise of the police power. City of Milwaukee v. Milwaukee & S.T. Corp., 6 Wis.2d 299, 94 N.W.2d 584 (1959); 51 Am.Jur., Taxation, p. 35, sec. 3, and p. 46, sec. 12. I think the trial court was correct in finding the requirement to be in the nature of a tax and the village had no power and was not authorized by the legislature to impose it. Whitney v. Department of Taxation, 16 Wis.2d 274, 114 N.W.2d 445 (1962). There is no implementing authorization conferring the power to impose such a tax nor does the Home–Rule Amendment (sec. 3, Art. XI, Wis. Const.) authorize it since a tax is not a local matter. City of Plymouth v. Elsner, 28 Wis.2d 102, 135 N.W.2d 799 (1965). Being in the nature of a tax it makes no difference whether the tax is a property tax bound by the uniformity requirement or an excise tax not so restricted.

It is quite apparent the so-called equalizing fee bears no reasonable relationship to the subdivision since it is not restricted to its benefit. The placing of such payments in the general treasury of the municipality cannot be justified on the theory that parks and schools will eventually be built or have been built in the subdivision area out of the general fund. Such a view ignores the vital distinction between the taxing power and the police power.

* * *

I would affirm.

Notes

1. For cases holding park or school site dedications or fees in lieu of dedications invalid because unauthorized by enabling statutes see: Rosen v. Village of Downers Grove, 19 Ill.2d 448, 167 N.E.2d 230 (1960); Coronado Development Co. v. City of McPherson, 189 Kan. 174, 368 P.2d 51 (1962); and Haugen v. Gleason, 226 Or. 99, 359 P.2d 108 (1961), all of which are cited in support of the dissent in the Jordan case. Other cases striking down such exactions include City of Montgomery v. Crossroads Land Co., Inc., 355 So.2d 363 (Ala.1978); Admiral Development Corp. v. City of Maitland, 267 So.2d 860 (Fla.App.1972); Sanchez v. City of Santa Fe, 82 N.M. 322, 481 P.2d 401 (1971); Frank Ansuini, Inc. v. City of Cranston, 107 R.I. 63, 264 A.2d 910 (1970); Berg Development Co. v. City of Missouri City, 603 S.W.2d

273 (Tex.Civ.App.1980); J.E.D. Associates, Inc. v. Town of Atkinson, 121 N.H. 581, 432 A.2d 12 (1981); Kamhi v. Planning Bd. of Yorktown, 59 N.Y.2d 385, 465 N.Y.S.2d 865, 452 N.E.2d 1193 (1983); City of Fayetteville v. IBI, Inc., 280 Ark. 484, 659 S.W.2d 505 (1983); and Town of Longboat Key v. Lands End, Ltd., 433 So.2d 574 (Fla.App.1983). Compare Gulest Associates v. Town of Newburgh, 25 Misc.2d 1004, 209 N.Y.S.2d 729 (1960) and Midtown Properties v. Township of Madison, 68 N.J.Super. 197, 172 A.2d 40, 47 (1961), affirmed 78 N.J.Super. 471, 189 A.2d 226 (1963). See also Reps and Smith, Control of Urban Land Subdivision, 14 Syracuse L.Rev. 405, 411 (1963), and Comment, Requiring Dedication of Park Land, 1961 Wis.L.Rev. 310.

In Haugen v. Gleason, supra, the court reversed the lower court and invalidated a $37.50 per lot fee for park purposes. It treated the fee as a tax upon subdividers for public purposes and held that such a tax was not authorized by any enabling legislation.

In Gulest, supra, the enabling act expressly authorized fees in an amount to be determined by the town board, "which amount shall be available for use by the town for neighborhood park, playground or recreation purposes including the acquisition of property." Nevertheless, the Supreme Court of Orange County, New York annulled a $50.00 per lot fee because (1) the fee could be used in any section of the town and thus was for the benefit, not of subdivision residents, but of the town as a whole, and (2) the statute failed to set out standards or tests.

On the basis of the Gulest case, the developer in Jenad, Inc. v. Village of Scarsdale, 38 Misc.2d 658, 238 N.Y.S.2d 156 (1963) tried unsuccessfully to recover fees he had paid voluntarily in lieu of land dedications. "Plaintiff had a preliminary remedy had it felt aggrieved * * * and no facts have been presented to the court to indicate that plaintiff would have been deprived of the reasonable use of its lands during the pendency of a lawsuit to attack the legality or constitutionality of the Scarsdale regulation before it paid the money in question. Everything before the court points to a business arrangement entered into between plaintiff and the village, and concluded in an amicable fashion resulting in plaintiff thanking the Village Attorney for his 'cooperation' in the matter." Also see Joseph v. Yorktown Planning Bd., 140 A.D.2d 670, 529 N.Y.S.2d 17 (1988). In Video Aid Corp. v. Town of Wallkill, 85 N.Y.2d 663, 628 N.Y.S.2d 18, 651 N.E.2d 886 (1995), a developer paid a $27,000 sewer and water connection fee only after the town indicated it would not grant a building permit unless the fee was paid; the developer then contested the fee as an unconstitutional exaction and sought reimbursement. The New York Court of Appeals held, in a four to three decision that even though the exaction was unconstitutional, the developer could not claim coercion and obtain a refund. The majority concluded that the developer had not even taken the simple step of making a notation on the check that the payment was under protest, and that some indication of protest is necessary when making such payments in order to permit public agencies to operate on a sound fiscal basis and that such agencies need to made aware when collected funds may have to be refunded. The majority also indicated that an exception to the rule would be recognized in cases where payments are made under duress, but that exception would be applied very narrowly. The message of this case is that in every case where a developer may think that an exaction is excessive, exaction payments should be made under protest; such a practice might also be wise in jurisdictions other than New York.

On the other hand, several cases have followed the holding in the Jordan case and have upheld equalization assessments or dedications for park purposes. See Aunt Hack Ridge Estates, Inc. v. Planning Comm'n of the City of Danbury, 160 Conn. 109, 273 A.2d 880 (1970); Associated Home Builders of Greater East Bay, Inc. v. City of Walnut Creek, 4 Cal.3d 633, 94 Cal.Rptr. 630, 484 P.2d 606 (1971), appeal dismissed 404 U.S. 878, 92 S.Ct. 202, 30 L.Ed.2d 159 (1971); Cimarron Corp. v. Board of County Comm'rs, 193 Colo. 164, 563 P.2d 946 (1977); Collis v. City of Bloomington, 310 Minn. 5, 246 N.W.2d 19 (1976); Home Builders Ass'n of Greater Kansas City v. City of Kansas City, 555 S.W.2d 832 (Mo.1977); Call v. City of West Jordan, 614 P.2d 1257 (Utah 1980); Town of Auburn v. McEvoy, 131 N.H. 383, 553 A.2d 317 (1988) (overruling the J.E.D. Associates case, supra); Messer v. Town of Chapel Hill, 59 N.C.App. 692, 297 S.E.2d 632 (1982), appeal dismissed 307 N.C. 697, 301 S.E.2d 390 (1983); City of College Station v. Turtle Rock Corp., 680 S.W.2d 802 (Tex.1984); and Bayswater Realty and Capital Corp. v. Planning Bd., 76 N.Y.2d 460, 560 N.Y.S.2d 623, 560 N.E.2d 1300 (1990). Also see the annotation in 43 A.L.R.3d 862. In the Walnut Creek case, the court rejected arguments that: (1) the exaction discriminated in favor of apartment builders (the court said that apartment development does not diminish the available supply of open land to the same extent as the activity of subdividers); (2) the exaction amounted to double taxation, once in the higher cost to the lot purchaser, and again in subsequent property taxes to maintain the parks.

Two cases from Florida, both intermediate appellate court decisions, reached opposite conclusions on the validity of money exactions. Compare Broward County v. Janis Development Corp., 311 So.2d 371 (Fla.App.1975) with City of Dunedin v. Contractors and Builders Ass'n of Pinellas County, 312 So.2d 763 (Fla.App.1975) quashed 329 So.2d 314 (1976). See Rhodes, Impact Fees: The Cost–Benefit Dilemma in Florida, 27 Land Use Law & Zoning Dig. 7 (No. 10, 1975). Also see City of Key West v. R.L.J.S. Corp., 537 So.2d 641 (Fla.App.1989), review denied 545 So.2d 1367 (1989) where the court upheld retroactive sewer impact fees for units already sold by a condominium developer (the city had held back occupancy permits for newly-sold units until the fees were paid for units previously sold).

In Riegert Apartments Corp. v. Planning Bd., 105 Misc.2d 298, 432 N.Y.S.2d 43 (1979), a trial court upheld a money exaction in addition to a compulsory land dedication for flood control purposes. The Court of Appeals reversed. 57 N.Y.2d 206, 455 N.Y.S.2d 558, 441 N.E.2d 1076 (1982). Compare Hillis Homes, Inc. v. Snohomish County, 97 Wash.2d 804, 650 P.2d 193 (1982).

2. For a comprehensive discussion of the rationale of exactions see, Heyman and Gilhool, The Constitutionality of Imposing Increased Community Costs on New Suburban Residents Through Subdivision Exactions, 73 Yale L.J. 1119 (1964) and Johnston, Constitutionality of Subdivision Control Exactions: The Quest for a Rationale, 52 Cornell L.Q. 871 (1967). For a practical overview, see Delaney and Smith, Development Exactions: Winners

and Losers, Land Use Law, Nov. 1989, p. 3. A review of state enabling legislation regarding impact fees is found in Morgan, State Impact Fee Legislation: Guidelines for Analysis, Land Use Law, Mar. 1990, p. 3 (Part I) and Apr. 1990, p. 3 (Part II). Also see Eastern Diversified Properties, Inc. v. Montgomery County, 319 Md. 45, 570 A.2d 850 (1990); Blaesser & Kentopp, Impact Fees: The "Second Generation," 38 Wash.U.J.Urb. & Contemp.L. 55 (1990). For interesting examples of impact fee enabling legislation, see Va.Code Ann. § 15.1–498.1 et seq. (effective July 1, 1990); N. Mex. St. § 5–8–1 et seq. (1993); Idaho Rev. Stat. §§ 67–8201 to 67–8216 (1992). In Idaho Bldg. Contractors Ass'n v. Coeur d'Alene, 126 Idaho 740, 890 P.2d 326 (1995) the court struck down an ordinance imposing a development impact fee on all new construction, holding that the act was inapplicable and the city was really using the fee as a revenue raising device. Also see, Arthur C. Nelson, Development Impact Fees: The Next Generation, 26 The Urban Lawyer 541 (1994).

3. Compare Miller v. City of Beaver Falls, 368 Pa. 189, 82 A.2d 34 (1951) with In re Lake Secor Development Co., 141 Misc. 913, 252 N.Y.S. 809 (1931). In Miller an attempt to require the subdivider in effect to grant the city a three year first right of purchase of park land was declared invalid. The city did not pass the contested ordinance until after the council knew of the intention to subdivide, and the ordinance applied to 4½ acres of the subdivider's total of 16 acres. Construction of 12 houses had been commenced prior to the ordinance on part of the 16 acres, but not on the 4½ acre portion. Said Justice Bell for the Pennsylvania Court:

> "The city is not without remedy, but cannot eat its cake and have its penny too. If it desires plaintiff's land for a park or playground which it considers desirable or necessary for its future progress, it can readily and lawfully obtain this land in accordance with the Constitution which, we repeat, is the Supreme Law of the land * * * All that is required is that just compensation be paid therefor."

In the Secor case the planning board denied approval of a 138–acre (2000 lot) subdivision for several reasons, among them "insufficient park area." There is no indication how large a dedication the planning board demanded. The court, after first holding that the planning board had exceeded its enabling authority by insisting on a water system, said at page 812:

> "The demand of the planning board for additional park area is reasonable. The argument that 'all Putnam County is a park' advanced by the petitioner is without merit. The apparent purpose of the petitioner is to establish a summer colony. It must dedicate to public use sufficient area to provide for the ultimate use to be made of this plat. It argues that the residents there can trespass upon other lands for recreational purposes. The mere statement of the proposition is its answer."

4. In connection with park and school site dedication problems recall that it is constitutional under appropriate legislation to require the subdivider to dedicate, free of charge, all land needed for new streets of ordinary width within the subdivision. (Recall the cross street in the Ayres case, supra.) And the requirement seems universal even though the land may

amount to 20 or 25% of the total area, where a gridiron street pattern is used.

As was seen from the Ridgefield case and the Ayres case, supra, there is also authority sustaining required dedications of strips for the purpose of widening existing streets abutting in the subdivision. See also Newton v. American Sec. Co., 201 Ark. 943, 148 S.W.2d 311 (1941).

5. Consider Board of Educ. of Community Consol. Sch. Dist. No. 59 v. E.A. Herzog Constr. Co., 29 Ill.App.2d 138, 172 N.E.2d 645 (1961). Herzog on May 9, 1957 in writing agreed to pay $95,000 toward the cost of a school and the board of education agreed to hold a special referendum to approve the school and to begin construction no later than July 15, 1958. Next day, on May 10, 1957, the county commissioner rezoned Herzog's land and authorized his project. On August 27, 1958, the original agreement was amended with the board of education acknowledging that its delay in commencing construction had undoubtedly affected Herzog's sales and consequently his revenues. Herzog's commitment to pay the $95,000 was restated but the time for payment was postponed until completion of the school. The school was completed. Herzog refused to pay and the board sued. Herzog claimed the agreements void as against public policy as contracts "for the purchase of influence upon the action of public officers." He also charged that the board of education conspired with members of the county board to withhold rezoning until Herzog agreed to contribute to the cost of the school. The court took judicial notice that the school district has no control over the actions of the county board, brushed aside "these wild and irresponsible charges" and affirmed judgment against Herzog. Said the court:

> "The defendant voluntarily agreed to pay the $95,000 toward construction of the building, as it realized that the proposed school building was essential to its sales program. Having accepted the benefits of the agreement, it is now attempting to renege on its voluntary agreement to contribute money to the school board. It will not be permitted to do so."

Compare Midtown Properties v. Township of Madison, 68 N.J.Super. 197, 172 A.2d 40 (1961), affirmed 78 N.J.Super. 471, 189 A.2d 226 (1963) where a detailed contract between subdivider and a local unit was set aside as an attempt to do by contract what can only be done by following statutory procedures.

6. In Quirk v. Town of New Boston, 140 N.H. 124, 663 A.2d 1328 (1995) the court upheld a requirement that campground developments provide a 200 foot buffer zone around the perimeter of the property. The owner of an existing campground who had invested considerably in installation of oversized septic systems was denied a permit for a new recreation hall that would have encroached on the buffer zone. The court found that the regulation was akin to a setback requirement, that it was not arbitrary, and that the campground owner had not suffered a taking.

Sec. 1 REGULATION OF THE SUBDIVISION OF LAND 491

NOLLAN v. CALIFORNIA COASTAL COMMISSION
Supreme Court of the United States, 1987.
483 U.S. 825, 107 S.Ct. 3141, 97 L.Ed.2d 677.

JUSTICE SCALIA delivered the opinion of the Court.

The Nollans own a beachfront lot in Ventura County, California. A quarter-mile north of their property is Faria County Park, an oceanside public park with a public beach and recreation area. Another public beach area, known locally as "the Cove," lies 1,800 feet south of their lot. A concrete seawall approximately eight feet high separates the beach portion of the Nollans' property from the rest of the lot. The historic mean high tide line determines the lot's oceanside boundary.

The Nollans originally leased their property with an option to buy. The building on the lot was a small bungalow, totaling 504 square feet, which for a time they rented to summer vacationers. After years of rental use, however, the building had fallen into disrepair, and could no longer be rented out.

The Nollans' option to purchase was conditioned on their promise to demolish the bungalow and replace it. In order to do so, under California Public Resources Code §§ 30106, 30212, and 30600 (West 1986), they were required to obtain a coastal development permit from the California Coastal Commission. On February 25, 1982, they submitted a permit application to the Commission in which they proposed to demolish the existing structure and replace it with a three-bedroom house in keeping with the rest of the neighborhood.

The Nollans were informed that their application had been placed on the administrative calendar, and that the Commission staff had recommended that the permit be granted subject to the condition that they allow the public an easement to pass across a portion of their property bounded by the mean high tide line on one side, and their seawall on the other side. This would make it easier for the public to get to Faria County Park and the Cove. The Nollans protested imposition of the condition, but the Commission overruled their objections and granted the permit subject to their recordation of a deed restriction granting the easement.

On June 3, 1982, the Nollans filed a petition for writ of administrative mandamus asking the Ventura County Superior Court to invalidate the access condition. They argued that the condition could not be imposed absent evidence that their proposed development would have a direct adverse impact on public access to the beach. The court agreed, and remanded the case to the Commission for a full evidentiary hearing on that issue.

On remand, the Commission held a public hearing, after which it made further factual findings and reaffirmed its imposition of the condition. It found that the new house would increase blockage of the view of the ocean, thus contributing to the development of "a 'wall' of residential structures" that would prevent the public "psychologically * * * from realizing a stretch of coastline exists nearby that they have every right to visit." The new house would also increase private use of the shorefront. These effects of construction of the house, along with other area development, would cumulatively "burden the public's ability to traverse to and along the shorefront." Therefore the Commission could properly require the Nollans to offset that burden by providing additional lateral access to the public beaches in the form of an easement across their property. The Commission also noted that it had similarly conditioned 43 out of 60 coastal development permits along the same tract of land, and that of the 17 not so conditioned, 14 had been approved when the Commission did not have administrative regulations in place allowing imposition of the condition, and the remaining 3 had not involved shorefront property.

The Nollans filed a supplemental petition for a writ of administrative mandamus with the Superior Court, in which they argued that imposition of the access condition violated the Takings Clause of the Fifth Amendment, as incorporated against the States by the Fourteenth Amendment. The Superior Court ruled in their favor on statutory grounds, finding, in part to avoid "issues of constitutionality," that the California Coastal Act of 1976, Cal.Pub.Res.Code Ann. § 30000 et seq., authorized the Commission to impose public access conditions on coastal development permits for the replacement of an existing single-family home with a new one only where the proposed development would have an adverse impact on public access to the sea. In the Court's view, the administrative record did not provide an adequate factual basis for concluding that replacement of the bungalow with the house would create a direct or cumulative burden on public access to the sea. Accordingly, the Superior Court granted the writ of mandamus and directed that the permit condition be struck.

The Commission appealed to the California Court of Appeal. * * *

The Court of Appeal reversed the Superior Court. 177 Cal.App.3d 719, 223 Cal.Rptr. 28 (1986). It disagreed with the Superior Court's interpretation of the Coastal Act, finding that it required that a coastal permit for the construction of a new house whose floor area, height or bulk was more than 10% larger than that of the house it was replacing be conditioned on a grant of access. Id., at 723–724, 223 Cal.Rptr., at 31; see Cal.Pub.Res.Code § 30212. It also ruled that the requirement did not violate the Constitution under the reasoning of an earlier case of the Court of Appeal, Grupe v. California Coastal Comm'n, 166 Cal.App.3d 148, 212 Cal.Rptr. 578 (1985). In that case, the court had found that so long as a project contributed to the need for public access, even if the project standing alone had not created the need for access, and even if there was only an indirect relationship between the access exacted and the need to which the project contributed, imposition of an access condition on a development permit was sufficiently related to burdens created by the project to be constitutional. * * * The Court of Appeal ruled that the record established that that was the situation with respect to the Nollans' house. * * * It ruled that the Nollans' taking claim also failed because, although the condition diminished the value of the Nollans' lot, it did not deprive them of all reasonable use of their property. * * * Since, in the Court of Appeal's view, there was no statutory or constitutional obstacle to imposition of the access condition, the Superior Court erred in granting the writ of mandamus. The Nollans appealed to this Court, raising only the constitutional question.

II

Had California simply required the Nollans to make an easement across their beachfront available to the public on a permanent basis in order to increase public access to the beach, rather than conditioning their permit to rebuild their house on their agreeing to do so, we have no doubt there would have been a taking. To say that the appropriation of a public easement across a landowner's premises does not constitute the taking of a property interest but rather, (as Justice Brennan contends) "a mere restriction on its use," is to use words in a manner that deprives them of all their ordinary meaning. Indeed, one of the principal uses of the eminent domain power is to assure that the government be able to require conveyance of just such interests, so long as it pays for them. Perhaps because the point is so obvious, we have never been confronted with a controversy that required us to rule upon it, but our cases' analysis of the effect of other governmental action leads to the same conclusion. We have repeatedly held that, as to property reserved by its owner for private use, "the right to exclude [others is] 'one of the most essential sticks in the bundle of rights that are commonly characterized as property.'" *Loretto v. Teleprompter Manhattan CATV Corp.*, 458 U.S. 419, 433, 102 S.Ct. 3164, 3175, 73 L.Ed.2d 868 (1982), quoting *Kaiser Aetna v. United States,* 444 U.S. 164, 176, 100 S.Ct. 383, 391, 62 L.Ed.2d 332 (1979). In *Loretto* we observed that where governmental action results in "[a] permanent physical occupation" of the property, by the government itself or by others, "our cases uniformly have found a taking to the extent of the occupation, without regard to whether the action achieves an important public benefit or has only minimal economic impact on the owner." We think a "permanent physical occupation" has occurred, for purposes of that rule, where individuals are given a permanent and continuous right to pass to and fro, so that the real property may continuously be traversed, even though no particular individual is permitted to station himself permanently upon the premises.[9]

* * *

9. The holding of *PruneYard Shopping Center v. Robins,* 447 U.S. 74, 100 S.Ct. 2035, 64 L.Ed.2d 741 (1980), is not inconsistent with this analysis, since there the owner had already opened his property to the general public, and in addition permanent access was not required. The analysis of *Kaiser Aetna v. United States,* 444 U.S. 164, 100 S.Ct. 383, 62 L.Ed.2d 332 (1979), is not inconsistent because it was affected by traditional doctrines regarding navigational servitudes. Of course neither of those cases involved, as this one does, a classic right-of-way easement.

Given, then, that requiring uncompensated conveyance of the easement outright would violate the Fourteenth Amendment, the question becomes whether requiring it to be conveyed as a condition for issuing a land use permit alters the outcome. We have long recognized that land use regulation does not effect a taking if it "substantially advance[s] legitimate state interests" and does not "den[y] an owner economically viable use of his land," *Agins v. Tiburon,* 447 U.S. 255, 260, 100 S.Ct. 2138, 2141, 65 L.Ed.2d 106 (1980). See also *Penn Central Transportation Co. v. New York City,* 438 U.S. 104, 127, 98 S.Ct. 2646, 2660, 57 L.Ed.2d 631 (1978) ("a use restriction may constitute a 'taking' if not reasonably necessary to the effectuation of a substantial government purpose"). Our cases have not elaborated on the standards for determining what constitutes a "legitimate state interest" or what type of connection between the regulation and the state interest satisfies the requirement that the former "substantially advance" the latter. They have made clear, however, that a broad range of governmental purposes and regulations satisfies these requirements. * * * The Commission argues that among these permissible purposes are protecting the public's ability to see the beach, assisting the public in overcoming the "psychological barrier" to using the beach created by a developed shorefront, and preventing congestion on the public beaches. We assume, without deciding, that this is so—in which case the Commission unquestionably would be able to deny the Nollans their permit outright if their new house (alone, or by reason of the cumulative impact produced in conjunction with other construction) would substantially impede these purposes, unless the denial would interfere so drastically with the Nollans' use of their property as to constitute a taking.

The Commission argues that a permit condition that serves the same legitimate police-power purpose as a refusal to issue the permit should not be found to be a taking if the refusal to issue the permit would not constitute a taking. We agree. Thus, if the Commission attached to the permit some condition that would have protected the public's ability to see the beach notwithstanding construction of the new house—for example, a height limitation, a width restriction, or a ban on fences—so long as the Commission could have exercised its police power (as we have assumed it could) to forbid construction of the house altogether, imposition of the condition would also be constitutional. Moreover (and here we come closer to the facts of the present case), the condition would be constitutional even if it consisted of the requirement that the Nollans provide a viewing spot on their property for passersby with whose sighting of the ocean their new house would interfere. Although such a requirement, constituting a permanent grant of continuous access to the property, would have to be considered a taking if it were not attached to a development permit, the Commission's assumed power to forbid construction of the house in order to protect the public's view of the beach must surely include the power to condition construction upon some concession by the owner, even a concession of property rights, that serves the same end. If a prohibition designed to accomplish that purpose would be a legitimate exercise of the police power rather than a taking, it would be strange to conclude that providing the owner an alternative to that prohibition which accomplishes the same purpose is not.

The evident constitutional propriety disappears, however, if the condition substituted for the prohibition utterly fails to further the end advanced as the justification for the prohibition. When that essential nexus is eliminated, the situation becomes the same as if California law forbade shouting fire in a crowded theater, but granted dispensations to those willing to contribute $100 to the state treasury. While a ban on shouting fire can be a core exercise of the State's police power to protect the public safety, and can thus meet even our stringent standards for regulation of speech, adding the unrelated condition alters the purpose to one which, while it may be legitimate, is inadequate to sustain the ban. Therefore, even though, in a sense, requiring a $100 tax contribution in order to shout fire is a lesser restriction on speech than an outright ban, it would not pass constitutional muster. Similarly here, the lack of nexus between the condition and the original purpose of the building restriction converts that purpose to something other than what it was. The purpose then becomes, quite simply, the obtaining of an easement to serve some valid governmental purpose, but without payment of compensation. Whatever may be the outer limits of "legitimate state interests" in the takings and land use context, this is not one of them. In short, unless the permit condition serves the same governmental purpose as the development ban, the building restriction is not a valid regulation of land use but "an out-and-out plan of extortion." *J.E.D. Associates, Inc. v. Atkinson,* 121 N.H. 581, 584, 432 A.2d 12, 14–15 (1981); * * *

III

The Commission claims that it concedes as much, and that we may sustain the condition at issue here by finding that it is reasonably related to the public need or burden that the Nollans' new house creates or to which it contributes. We can accept, for purposes of discussion, the Commission's proposed test as to how close a "fit" between the condition and the burden is required, because we find that this case does not meet even the most untailored standards. The Commission's principal contention to the contrary essentially turns on a play on the word "access." The Nollans' new house, the Commission found, will interfere with "visual access" to the beach. That in turn (along with other shorefront development) will interfere with the desire of people who drive past the Nollans' house to use the beach, thus creating a "psychological barrier" to "access." The Nollans' new house will also, by a process not altogether clear from the Commission's opinion but presumably potent enough to more than offset the effects of the psychological barrier, increase the use of the public beaches, thus creating the need for more "access." These burdens on "access" would be alleviated by a requirement that the Nollans provide "lateral access" to the beach.

Rewriting the argument to eliminate the play on words makes clear that there is nothing to it. It is quite impossible to understand how a requirement that people already on the public beaches be able to walk across the Nollans' property reduces any obstacles to viewing the beach created by the new house. It is also impossible to understand how it lowers any "psychological barrier" to using the public beaches, or how it helps to remedy any additional congestion on them caused by construction of the Nollans' new house. We therefore find that the Commission's imposition of the permit condition cannot be treated as an exercise of its land use power for any of these purposes. Our conclusion on this point is consistent with the approach taken by every other court that has considered the question, with the exception of the California state courts. * * * We view the Fifth Amendment's property clause to be more than a pleading requirement, and compliance with it to be more than an exercise in cleverness and imagination. As indicated earlier, our cases describe the condition for abridgement of property rights through the police power as a "*substantial* advanc[ing]" of a legitimate State interest. We are inclined to be particularly careful about the adjective where the actual conveyance of property is made a condition to the lifting of a land use restriction, since in that context there is heightened risk that the purpose is avoidance of the compensation requirement, rather than the stated police power objective.

We are left, then, with the Commission's justification for the access requirement unrelated to land use regulation:

> "Finally, the Commission notes that there are several existing provisions of pass and repass lateral access benefits already given by past Faria Beach Tract applicants as a result of prior coastal permit decisions. The access required as a condition of this permit is part of a comprehensive program to provide continuous public access along Faria Beach as the lots undergo development or redevelopment." App. 68.

That is simply an expression of the Commission's belief that the public interest will be served by a continuous strip of publicly accessible beach along the coast. The Commission may well be right that it is a good idea, but that does not establish that the Nollans (and other coastal residents) alone can be compelled to contribute to its realization. Rather, California is free to advance its "comprehensive program," if it wishes, by using its power of eminent domain for this "public purpose," see U.S. Const., Amdt. V; but if it wants an easement across the Nollans' property, it must pay for it.

Reversed.

[Dissenting opinions omitted.]

Notes

1. Is the "nexus" test articulated by Justice Scalia in the Nollan case the same as the "rational nexus" test used in the off-site improvement cases? How does the Nollan case impact on traditional exactions? See,

generally, Lemon, Feinland & Deihl, The First Applications of the Nollan Nexus Test: Observations and Comments, 13 Harv.Env.L.Rev. 585 (1989); Comment, The Future of Municipal Parks in a Post–Nollan World: A Survey of Takings Tests as Applied to Subdivision Exactions, 8 Va.Nat.Resources L. 141 (1988). Also see, Sterk, Nollan, Henry George, and Exactions, 88 Colum.L.Rev. 1731 (1988); Karlin, Back to the Future: From Nollan to Lochner, 17 Southwest. U.L.Rev. 627 (1988).

2. Does the "heightened scrutiny" rule of Nollan apply to non-possessory exactions, such as impact fees? The California Court of Appeal said "no" in Blue Jeans Equities West v. City and County of San Francisco, 3 Cal.App.4th 164, 4 Cal.Rptr.2d 114, cert. denied 506 U.S. 866, 113 S.Ct. 191, 121 L.Ed.2d 135 (1992), a case involving a traffic impact fee imposed on developers of office buildings in downtown San Francisco. Even if "heightened scrutiny" should be given to money exactions, does the rationale in Nollan doom any impact fee which is not earmarked for an improvement which would specifically benefit the proposed development? In Holmdel Builders Association v. Township of Holmdel, 232 N.J.Super. 182, 556 A.2d 1236 (1989), the court held that a mandatory development fee imposed for the purpose of aiding the municipality to provide realistic opportunities for affordable housing was invalid as nothing more than a revenue raising device and illegal tax. The court, however, also said that if developers were given something in return, such as an opportunity to build at higher densities if they paid the fee, such a fee might be valid. The New Jersey Supreme Court partially reversed (see the opinion in the next chapter). Also consider, in light of Nollan, a measure adopted by the voters of San Francisco which imposes an impact fee on developers of office towers in the downtown district for the purpose of providing housing and day care opportunities. A case similar to Nollan, but without constitutional issues is Clinton v. Summers, 144 A.D.2d 145, 534 N.Y.S.2d 473 (1988).

DOLAN v. CITY OF TIGARD

Supreme Court of the United States, 1994.
512 U.S. 374, 114 S.Ct. 2309, 129 L.Ed.2d 304.

CHIEF JUSTICE REHNQUIST delivered the opinion of the Court.

Petitioner challenges the decision of the Oregon Supreme Court which held that the city of Tigard could condition the approval of her building permit on the dedication of a portion of her property for flood control and traffic improvements. 317 Ore. 110, 854 P. 2d 437 (1993). We granted certiorari to resolve a question left open by our decision in Nollan v. California Coastal Comm'n, 483 U. S. 825 (1987), of what is the required degree of connection between the exactions imposed by the city and the projected impacts of the proposed development.

I

The State of Oregon enacted a comprehensive land use management program in 1973. Ore. Rev. Stat. §§ 197.005–197.860 (1991). The program required all Oregon cities and counties to adopt new comprehensive land use plans that were consistent with the statewide planning goals. §§ 197.175(1), 197.250. The plans are implemented by land use regulations which are part of an integrated hierarchy of legally binding goals, plans, and regulations. §§ 197.175, 197.175(2)(b). Pursuant to the State's requirements, the city of Tigard, a community of some 30,000 residents on the southwest edge of Portland, developed a comprehensive plan and codified it in its Community Development Code (CDC). The CDC requires property owners in the area zoned Central Business District to comply with a 15% open space and landscaping requirement, which limits total site coverage, including all structures and paved parking, to 85% of the parcel. CDC, ch. 18.66, App. to Pet. for Cert. G16–G17. After the completion of a transportation study that identified congestion in the Central Business District as a particular problem, the city adopted a plan for a pedestrian/bicycle pathway intended to encourage alternatives to automobile transportation for short trips. The CDC requires that new development facilitate this plan by dedicating land for pedestrian pathways where provided for in the pedestrian/bicycle pathway plan.

The city also adopted a Master Drainage Plan (Drainage Plan). The Drainage Plan noted that flooding occurred in several areas along Fanno Creek, including areas near petitioner's property. The Drainage Plan also established that the increase in impervious surfaces associated with continued urbanization would exacerbate these flooding problems. To combat these risks, the Drainage Plan suggested a series of improvements to the Fanno Creek Basin, including channel excavation in the area next to petitioner's property. Other recommendations included ensuring that the floodplain remains free of structures and that it be preserved as greenways to minimize flood damage to structures. The Drainage Plan concluded that the cost of these improvements should be shared based on both direct and indirect benefits, with property owners along the waterways paying more due to the direct benefit that they would receive. * * *

Petitioner Florence Dolan owns a plumbing and electric supply store located on Main Street in the Central Business District of the city. The store covers approximately 9,700 square feet on the eastern side of a 1.67–acre parcel, which includes a gravel parking lot. Fanno Creek flows through the southwestern corner of the lot and along its western boundary. The year-round flow of the creek renders the area within the creek's 100–year floodplain virtually unusable for commercial development. The city's comprehensive plan includes the Fanno Creek floodplain as part of the city's greenway system.

Petitioner applied to the city for a permit to redevelop the site. Her proposed plans called for nearly doubling the size of the store to 17,600 square feet, and paving a 39–space parking lot. The existing store, located on the opposite side of the parcel, would be razed in sections as construction progressed on the new building. In the second phase of the project, petitioner proposed to build an additional structure on the northeast side of the site for complementary businesses, and to provide more parking. The proposed expansion and intensified use are consistent with the city's zoning scheme in the Central Business District.

The City Planning Commission granted petitioner's permit application subject to conditions imposed by the city's CDC. The CDC establishes the following standard for site development review approval:

"Where landfill and/or development is allowed within and adjacent to the 100–year floodplain, the city shall require the dedication of sufficient open land area for greenway adjoining and within the floodplain. This area shall include portions at a suitable elevation for the construction of a pedestrian/bicycle pathway within the floodplain in accordance with the adopted pedestrian/bicycle plan."

Thus, the Commission required that petitioner dedicate the portion of her property lying within the 100–year floodplain for improvement of a storm drainage system along Fanno Creek and that she dedicate an additional 15-foot strip of land adjacent to the floodplain as a pedestrian/bicycle pathway. The dedication required by that condition encompasses approximately 7,000 square feet, or roughly 10% of the property. In accordance with city practice, petitioner could rely on the dedicated property to meet the 15% open space and landscaping requirement mandated by the city's zoning scheme. The city would bear the cost of maintaining a landscaped buffer between the dedicated area and the new store.

Petitioner requested variances from the CDC standards. Variances are granted only where it can be shown that, owing to special circumstances related to a specific piece of the land, the literal interpretation of the applicable zoning provisions would cause "an undue or unnecessary hardship" unless the variance is granted. Rather than posing alternative mitigating measures to offset the expected impacts of her proposed development, as allowed under the CDC, petitioner simply argued that her proposed development would not conflict with the policies of the comprehensive plan. The Commission denied the request.

The Commission made a series of findings concerning the relationship between the dedicated conditions and the projected impacts of petitioner's project. First, the Commission noted that "[i]t is reasonable to assume that customers and employees of the future uses of this site could utilize a pedestrian/bicycle pathway adjacent to this development for their transportation and recreational needs." The Commission noted that the site plan has provided for bicycle parking in a rack in front of the proposed building and "[i]t is reasonable to expect that some of the users of the bicycle parking provided for by the site plan will use the pathway adjacent to Fanno Creek if it is constructed." In addition, the Commission found that creation of a convenient, safe pedestrian/bicycle pathway system as an alternative means of transportation "could offset some of the traffic demand on [nearby] streets and lessen the increase in traffic congestion."

The Commission went on to note that the required floodplain dedication would be reasonably related to petitioner's request to intensify the use of the site given the increase in the impervious surface. The Commission stated that the "anticipated increased storm water flow from the subject property to an already strained creek and drainage basin can only add to the public need to manage the stream channel and floodplain for drainage purposes." Based on this anticipated increased storm water flow, the Commission concluded that "the requirement of dedication of the floodplain area on the site is related to the applicant's plan to intensify development on the site." The Tigard City Council approved the Commission's final order, subject to one minor modification; the City Council reassigned the responsibility for surveying and marking the floodplain area from petitioner to the city's engineering department.

Petitioner appealed to the Land Use Board of Appeals (LUBA) on the ground that the city's dedication requirements were not related to the proposed development, and, therefore, those requirements constituted an uncompensated taking of their property under the Fifth Amendment. In evaluating the federal taking claim, LUBA assumed that the city's findings about the impacts of the proposed development were supported by substantial evidence. * * * Given the undisputed fact that the proposed larger building and paved parking area would increase the amount of impervious surfaces and the runoff into Fanno Creek, LUBA concluded that "there is a 'reasonable relationship' between the proposed development and the requirement to dedicate land along Fanno Creek for a greenway." With respect to the pedestrian/bicycle pathway, LUBA noted the Commission's finding that a significantly larger retail sales building and parking lot would attract larger numbers of customers and employees and their vehicles. It again found a "reasonable relationship" between alleviating the impacts of increased traffic from the development and facilitating the provision of a pedestrian/bicycle pathway as an alternative means of transportation.

The Oregon Court of Appeals affirmed, rejecting petitioner's contention that in Nollan v. California Coastal Comm'n, 483 U. S. 825 (1987), we had abandoned the "reasonable relationship" test in favor of a stricter "essential nexus" test. 113 Ore. App. 162, 832 P. 2d 853 (1992). The Oregon Supreme Court affirmed. 317 Ore. 110, 854 P. 2d 437 (1993). The court also disagreed with petitioner's contention that the *Nollan* Court abandoned the "reasonably related" test. Id., at 118, 854 P. 2d, at 442. Instead, the court read *Nollan* to mean that an "exaction is reasonably related to an impact if the exaction serves the same purpose that a denial of the permit would serve." Id., at 120, 854 P. 2d, at 443. The court decided that both the pedestrian/bicycle pathway condition and the storm drainage dedication had an essential nexus to the development of the proposed site. Id., at 121, 854 P. 2d, at 443. Therefore, the court found the conditions to be reasonably related to the impact of the expansion of petitioner's business. * * *

II

* * *

Petitioner contends that the city has forced her to choose between the building permit and her right under the Fifth Amendment to just compensation for the public easements. Petitioner does not quarrel with the city's authority to exact some forms of dedication as a condition for the grant of a building permit, but challenges the showing made by the city to justify these exactions. She argues that the city has identified "no special benefits" conferred on her, and has not identified any "special quantifiable burdens" created by her new store that would justify the particular dedications required from her which are not required from the public at large.

III

In evaluating petitioner's claim, we must first determine whether the "essential nexus" exists between the "legitimate state interest" and the permit condition exacted by the city. *Nollan*, 483 U. S., at 837. If we find that a nexus exists, we must then decide the required degree of connection between the exactions and the projected impact of the proposed development. We were not required to reach this question in *Nollan*, because we concluded that the connection did not meet even the loosest standard. 483 U. S., at 838. Here, however, we must decide this question.

A

We addressed the essential nexus question in *Nollan*. * * * We resolved, however, that the Coastal Commission's regulatory authority was set completely adrift from its constitutional moorings when it claimed that a nexus existed between visual access to the ocean and a permit condition requiring lateral public access along the Nollan's beachfront lot. How enhancing the public's ability to "traverse to and along the shorefront" served the same governmental purpose of "visual access to the ocean" from the roadway was beyond our ability to countenance. The absence of a nexus left the Coastal Commission in the position of simply trying to obtain an easement through gimmickry, which converted a valid regulation of land use into "an out-and-out plan of extortion."

No such gimmicks are associated with the permit conditions imposed by the city in this case. Undoubtedly, the prevention of flooding along Fanno Creek and the reduction of traffic congestion in the Central Business District qualify as the type of legitimate public purposes we have upheld. It seems equally obvious that a nexus exists between preventing flooding along Fanno Creek and limiting development within the creek's 100–year floodplain. Petitioner proposes to double the size of her retail store and to pave her now-gravel parking lot, thereby expanding the impervious surface on the property and increasing the amount of stormwater run-off into Fanno Creek.

The same may be said for the city's attempt to reduce traffic congestion by providing for alternative means of transportation. In theory, a pedestrian/bicycle pathway provides a useful alternative means of transportation for workers and shoppers: "Pedestrians and bicyclists occupying dedicated spaces for walking and/or bicycling * * * remove potential vehicles from streets, resulting in an overall improvement in total transportation system flow." A. Nelson, Public Provision of Pedestrian and Bicycle Access Ways: Public Policy Rationale and the Nature of Private Benefits 11, Center for Planning Development, Georgia Institute of Technology, Working Paper Series (Jan. 1994). See also, Intermodal Surface Transportation Efficiency Act of 1991, Pub. L. 102–240, 105 Stat. 1914; (recognizing pedestrian and bicycle facilities as necessary components of any strategy to reduce traffic congestion).

B

The second part of our analysis requires us to determine whether the degree of the exactions demanded by the city's permit conditions bear the required relationship to the projected impact of petitioner's proposed development. * * *

The city required that petitioner dedicate "to the city as Greenway all portions of the site that fall within the existing 100–year floodplain [of Fanno Creek] ... and all property 15 feet above [the floodplain] boundary." In addition, the city demanded that the retail store be designed so as not to intrude into the greenway area. The city relies on the Commission's rather tentative findings that increased stormwater flow from petitioner's property "can only add to the public need to manage the [floodplain] for drainage purposes" to support its conclusion that the "requirement of dedication of the floodplain area on the site is related to the applicant's plan to intensify development on the site."

The city made the following specific findings relevant to the pedestrian/bicycle pathway:

> "In addition, the proposed expanded use of this site is anticipated to generate additional vehicular traffic thereby increasing congestion on nearby collector and arterial streets. Creation of a convenient, safe pedestrian/bicycle pathway system as an alternative means of transportation could offset some of the traffic demand on these nearby streets and lessen the increase in traffic congestion."

The question for us is whether these findings are constitutionally sufficient to justify the conditions imposed by the city on petitioner's building permit. Since state courts have been dealing with this question a good deal longer than we have, we turn to representative decisions made by them.

In some States, very generalized statements as to the necessary connection between the required dedication and the proposed development seem to suffice. See, e.g., Billings Properties, Inc. v. Yellowstone County, 144 Mont. 25, 394 P. 2d 182 (1964); Jenad, Inc. v. Scarsdale, 18 N. Y. 2d 78, 218 N. E. 2d 673 (1966). We think this standard is too lax to adequately protect petitioner's right to just compensation if her property is taken for a public purpose.

Other state courts require a very exacting correspondence, described as the "specifi[c] and uniquely attributable" test. The Supreme Court of Illinois first developed this test in Pioneer Trust & Savings Bank v. Mount Prospect, 22 Ill. 2d 375, 380, 176 N. E. 2d 799, 802 (1961). Under this standard, if the local government cannot demonstrate that its exaction is directly proportional to the specifically created need, the exaction becomes "a veiled exercise of the power of eminent domain and a confiscation of private property behind the defense of police regulations." Id., at 381, 176 N.E. 2d, at 802. We do not think the Federal Constitution requires such exacting scrutiny, given the nature of the interests involved.

A number of state courts have taken an intermediate position, requiring the municipality to show a "reasonable relationship" between the required dedication and the impact of the proposed development. Typical is the Supreme Court of Nebraska's opinion in Simpson v. North Platte, 206 Neb. 240, 245, 292 N. W. 2d 297, 301 (1980), where that court stated:

"The distinction, therefore, which must be made between an appropriate exercise of the police power and an improper exercise of eminent domain is whether the requirement has some reasonable relationship or nexus to the use to which the property is being made or is merely being used as an excuse for taking property simply because at that particular moment the landowner is asking the city for some license or permit."

Thus, the court held that a city may not require a property owner to dedicate private property for some future public use as a condition of obtaining a building permit when such future use is not "occasioned by the construction sought to be permitted." Id., at 248, 292 N. W. 2d, at 302.

Some form of the reasonable relationship test has been adopted in many other jurisdictions. See, e.g., Jordan v. Menomonee Falls, 28 Wis. 2d 608, 137 N. W. 2d 442 (1965); Collis v. Bloomington, 310 Minn. 5, 246 N. W. 2d 19 (1976) (requiring a showing of a reasonable relationship between the planned subdivision and the municipality's need for land); College Station v. Turtle Rock Corp., 680 S. W. 2d 802, 807 (Tex.1984); Call v. West Jordan, 606 P. 2d 217, 220 (Utah 1979) (affirming use of the reasonable relation test). Despite any semantical differences, general agreement exists among the courts "that the dedication should have some reasonable relationship to the needs created by the [development]." Ibid. See generally, Morosoff, Take My Beach Please!: Nollan v. California Coastal Commission and a Rational–Nexus Constitutional Analysis of Development Exactions, 69 B. U. L. Rev. 823 (1989); see also Parks v. Watson, 716 F. 2d 646, 651–653 (C.A.9 1983).

We think the "reasonable relationship" test adopted by a majority of the state courts is closer to the federal constitutional norm than either of those previously discussed. But we do not adopt it as such, partly because the term "reasonable relationship" seems confusingly similar to the term "rational basis" which describes the minimal level of scrutiny under the Equal Protection Clause of the Fourteenth Amendment. We think a term such as "rough proportionality" best encapsulates what we hold to be the requirement of the Fifth Amendment. No precise mathematical calculation is required, but the city must make some sort of individualized determination that the required dedication is related both in nature and extent to the impact of the proposed development.

* * *

We turn now to analysis of whether the findings relied upon by the city here, first with respect to the floodplain easement, and second with respect to the pedestrian/bicycle path, satisfied these requirements.

It is axiomatic that increasing the amount of impervious surface will increase the quantity and rate of storm-water flow from petitioner's property. Therefore, keeping the floodplain open and free from development would likely confine the pressures on Fanno Creek created by petitioner's development. In fact, because petitioner's property lies within the Central Business District, the Community Development Code already required that petitioner leave 15% of it as open space and the undeveloped floodplain would have nearly satisfied that requirement. But the city demanded more—it not only wanted petitioner not to build in the floodplain, but it also wanted petitioner's property along Fanno Creek for its Greenway system. The city has never said why a public greenway, as opposed to a private one, was required in the interest of flood control.

The difference to petitioner, of course, is the loss of her ability to exclude others. As we have noted, this right to exclude others is "one of the most essential sticks in the bundle of rights that are commonly characterized as property." Kaiser Aetna, 444 U. S., at 176. It is difficult to see why recreational visitors trampling along petitioner's floodplain easement are sufficiently related to the city's legitimate interest in reducing flooding problems along Fanno Creek, and the city has not attempted to make any individualized determination to support this part of its request.

The city contends that recreational easement along the Greenway is only ancillary to the city's chief purpose in controlling flood hazards. It further asserts that unlike the residential property at issue in *Nollan*, petitioner's property is commercial in character and therefore, her right to exclude others is compromised. * * *

Admittedly, petitioner wants to build a bigger store to attract members of the public to her property. She also wants, however, to be able to control the time and manner in which they enter. The recreational easement on the Greenway is different in character from the exercise of state-protected rights of free expression and petition that we permitted in *PruneYard*. In *PruneYard*, we held that a major private shopping center that attracted more than 25,000 daily patrons had to provide access to persons exercising their state constitutional rights to distribute

Sec. 1 REGULATION OF THE SUBDIVISION OF LAND 505

pamphlets and ask passersby to sign their petitions. We based our decision, in part, on the fact that the shopping center "may restrict expressive activity by adopting time, place, and manner regulations that will minimize any interference with its commercial functions." By contrast, the city wants to impose a permanent recreational easement upon petitioner's property that borders Fanno Creek. Petitioner would lose all rights to regulate the time in which the public entered onto the Greenway, regardless of any interference it might pose with her retail store. Her right to exclude would not be regulated, it would be eviscerated.

If petitioner's proposed development had somehow encroached on existing greenway space in the city, it would have been reasonable to require petitioner to provide some alternative greenway space for the public either on her property or elsewhere. * * * But that is not the case here. We conclude that the findings upon which the city relies do not show the required reasonable relationship between the floodplain easement and the petitioner's proposed new building.

With respect to the pedestrian/bicycle pathway, we have no doubt that the city was correct in finding that the larger retail sales facility proposed by petitioner will increase traffic on the streets of the Central Business District. The city estimates that the proposed development would generate roughly 435 additional trips per day. Dedications for streets, sidewalks, and other public ways are generally reasonable exactions to avoid excessive congestion from a proposed property use. But on the record before us, the city has not met its burden of demonstrating that the additional number of vehicle and bicycle trips generated by the petitioner's development reasonably relate to the city's requirement for a dedication of the pedestrian/bicycle pathway easement. The city simply found that the creation of the pathway "could offset some of the traffic demand * * * and lessen the increase in traffic congestion."

As Justice Peterson of the Supreme Court of Oregon explained in his dissenting opinion, however, "[t]he findings of fact that the bicycle pathway system '*could* offset some of the traffic demand' is a far cry from a finding that the bicycle pathway system *will*, or is *likely to*, offset some of the traffic demand." 317 Ore., at 127, 854 P. 2d, at 447 (emphasis in original). No precise mathematical calculation is required, but the city must make some effort to quantify its findings in support of the dedication for the pedestrian/bicycle pathway beyond the conclusory statement that it could offset some of the traffic demand generated.

IV

Cities have long engaged in the commendable task of land use planning, made necessary by increasing urbanization particularly in metropolitan areas such as Portland. The city's goals of reducing flooding hazards and traffic congestion, and providing for public greenways, are laudable, but there are outer limits to how this may be done. "A strong public desire to improve the public condition [will not] warrant achieving the desire by a shorter cut than the constitutional way of paying for the change." *Pennsylvania Coal*, 260 U. S., at 416.

The judgment of the Supreme Court of Oregon is reversed, and the case is remanded for further proceedings consistent with this opinion.

JUSTICE STEVENS, with whom JUSTICE BLACKMUN and JUSTICE GINSBURG join, dissenting.

The record does not tell us the dollar value of petitioner Florence Dolan's interest in excluding the public from the greenway adjacent to her hardware business. The mountain of briefs that the case has generated nevertheless makes it obvious that the pecuniary value of her victory is far less important than the rule of law that this case has been used to establish. It is unquestionably an important case.

* * *

I

Candidly acknowledging the lack of federal precedent for its exercise in rulemaking, the Court purports to find guidance in 12 "representative" state court decisions. To do so is certainly appropriate. The state cases the Court consults, however, either fail to support or decidedly undermine the Court's conclusions in key respects.

First, although discussion of the state cases permeates the Court's analysis of the appropriate test to apply in this case, the test on which the Court settles is not naturally derived from those courts' decisions. The Court recognizes as an initial matter that the city's conditions satisfy the "essential nexus" requirement announced in Nollan v. California Coastal Comm'n, 483 U. S. 825 (1987), because they serve the legitimate interests in minimizing floods and traffic congestions. The Court goes on, however, to erect a new constitutional hurdle in the path of these conditions. In addition to showing a rational nexus to a public purpose that would justify an outright denial of the permit, the city must also demonstrate "rough proportionality" between the harm caused by the new land use and the benefit obtained by the condition. The Court also decides for the first time that the city has the burden of establishing the constitutionality of its conditions by making an "individualized determination" that the condition in question satisfies the proportionality requirement.

Not one of the state cases cited by the Court announces anything akin to a "rough proportionality" requirement. For the most part, moreover, those cases that invalidated municipal ordinances did so on state law or unspecified grounds roughly equivalent to *Nollan's* "essential nexus" requirement. See, e.g., Simpson v. North Platte, 206 Neb. 240, 245–248, 292 N. W. 2d 297, 301–302 (1980) (ordinance lacking "reasonable relationship" or "rational nexus" to property's use violated Nebraska constitution); J. E. D. Associates, Inc. v. Town of Atkinson, 121 N. H. 581, 583–585, 432 A. 2d 12, 14–15 (1981) (state constitutional grounds). One case purporting to apply the strict "specifically and uniquely attributable" test established by Pioneer Trust & Savings Bank v. Mount Prospect, 22 Ill. 2d 375, 176 N. E. 2d 799 (1961), nevertheless found that test was satisfied because the legislature had decided that the subdivision at issue created the need for a park or parks. Billings Properties, Inc. v. Yellowstone County, 144 Mont. 25, 33–36, 394 P. 2d 182, 187–188 (1964). In only one of the seven cases upholding a land use regulation did the losing property owner petition this Court for certiorari. See Jordan v. Village of Menomonee Falls, 28 Wis. 2d 608, 137 N. W. 2d 442 (1965), appeal dism'd, 385 U. S. 4 (1966) (want of substantial federal question). Although 4 of the 12 opinions mention the Federal Constitution—two of those only in passing—it is quite obvious that neither the courts nor the litigants imagined they might be participating in the development of a new rule of federal law. Thus, although these state cases do lend support to the Court's reaffirmance of *Nollan's* reasonable nexus requirement, the role the Court accords them in the announcement of its newly minted second phase of the constitutional inquiry is remarkably inventive.

In addition, the Court ignores the state courts' willingness to consider what the property owner gains from the exchange in question. The Supreme Court of Wisconsin, for example, found it significant that the village's approval of a proposed subdivision plat "enables the subdivider to profit financially by selling the subdivision lots as home-building sites and thus realizing a greater price than could have been obtained if he had sold his property as unplatted lands." Jordan v. Village of Menomonee Falls, 28 Wis. 2d 608, 619–620; 137 N. W. 2d 442, 448 (1965). The required dedication as a condition of that approval was permissible "[i]n return for this benefit." Ibid. See also Collis v. Bloomington, 310 Minn. 5, 11–13, 246 N. W. 2d 19, 23–24 (1976) (citing Jordan); College Station v. Turtle Rock Corp., 680 S. W. 2d 802, 806 (Tex.1984) (dedication requirement only triggered when developer chooses to develop land). In this case, moreover, Dolan's acceptance of the permit, with its attached conditions, would provide her with benefits that may well go beyond any advantage she gets from expanding her business. As the United States pointed out at oral argument, the improvement that the city's drainage plan contemplates would widen the channel and reinforce the slopes to increase the carrying capacity during serious floods, "confer[ring] considerable benefits on the property owners immediately adjacent to the creek."

The state court decisions also are enlightening in the extent to which they required that the entire parcel be given controlling importance. All but one of the cases involve challenges to provisions in municipal ordinances requiring developers to dedicate either a percentage of the entire parcel (usually 7 or 10 percent of the platted subdivision) or an equivalent value in cash (usually a certain dollar amount per lot) to help finance the construction of roads, utilities, schools, parks and playgrounds. In assessing the legality of the conditions, the courts gave no indication that the transfer of an interest in realty was any more objectionable than a cash payment. See, e.g., Jenad, Inc. v. Scarsdale, 18

N. Y. 2d 78, 218 N. E. 2d 673 (1966); Jordan, supra; Collis, supra. None of the decisions identified the surrender of the fee owner's "power to exclude" as having any special significance. Instead, the courts uniformly examined the character of the entire economic transaction.

II

It is not merely state cases, but our own cases as well, that require the analysis to focus on the impact of the city's action on the entire parcel of private property. In Penn Central Transportation Co. v. New York City, 438 U. S. 104 (1978), we stated that takings jurisprudence "does not divide a single parcel into discrete segments and attempt to determine whether rights in a particular segment have been entirely abrogated." Id., at 130–131. Instead, this Court focuses "both on the character of the action and on the nature and extent of the interference with rights in the parcel as a whole." Ibid. Andrus v. Allard, 444 U. S. 51 (1979), reaffirmed the nondivisibility principle outlined in Penn Central, stating that "[a]t least where an owner possesses a full 'bundle' of property rights, the destruction of one 'strand' of the bundle is not a taking, because the aggregate must be viewed in its entirety." Id., at 65–66. As recently as last Term, we approved the principle again. See Concrete Pipe & Products, Inc. v. Construction Laborers Pension Trust, 508 U.S. 602 (1993) (explaining that "a claimant's parcel of property [cannot] first be divided into what was taken and what was left" to demonstrate a compensable taking). Although limitation of the right to exclude others undoubtedly constitutes a significant infringement upon property ownership, Kaiser Aetna v. United States, 444 U.S. 164, 179–180 (1979), restrictions on that right do not alone constitute a taking, and do not do so in any event unless they "unreasonably impair the value or use" of the property. PruneYard Shopping Center v. Robins, 447 U.S. 74, 82–84 (1980).

The Court's narrow focus on one strand in the property owner's bundle of rights is particularly misguided in a case involving the development of commercial property. As Professor Johnston has noted:

> "The subdivider is a manufacturer, processer, and marketer of a product; land is but one of his raw materials. In subdivision control disputes, the developer is not defending hearth and home against the king's intrusion, but simply attempting to maximize his profits from the sale of a finished product. As applied to him, subdivision control exactions are actually business regulations." Johnston, Constitutionality of Subdivision Control Exactions: The Quest for A Rationale, 52 Cornell L. Q. 871, 923 (1967).

The exactions associated with the development of a retail business are likewise a species of business regulation that heretofore warranted a strong presumption of constitutional validity.

In Johnston's view, "if the municipality can demonstrate that its assessment of financial burdens against subdividers is rational, impartial, and conducive to fulfillment of authorized planning objectives, its

Sec. 1 REGULATION OF THE SUBDIVISION OF LAND 509

action need be invalidated only in those extreme and presumably rare cases where the burden of compliance is sufficiently great to deter the owner from proceeding with his planned development." Id., at 917. The city of Tigard has demonstrated that its plan is rational and impartial and that the conditions at issue are "conducive to fulfillment of authorized planning objectives." Dolan, on the other hand, has offered no evidence that her burden of compliance has any impact at all on the value or profitability of her planned development. Following the teaching of the cases on which it purports to rely, the Court should not isolate the burden associated with the loss of the power to exclude from an evaluation of the benefit to be derived from the permit to enlarge the store and the parking lot.

The Court's assurances that its "rough proportionality" test leaves ample room for cities to pursue the "commendable task of land use planning,"—even twice avowing that "[n]o precise mathematical calculation is required,"—are wanting given the result that test compels here. Under the Court's approach, a city must not only "quantify its findings," and make "individualized determination[s]" with respect to the nature and the extent of the relationship between the conditions and the impact, but also demonstrate "proportionality." The correct inquiry should instead concentrate on whether the required nexus is present and venture beyond considerations of a condition's nature or germaneness only if the developer establishes that a concededly germane condition is so grossly disproportionate to the proposed development's adverse effects that it manifests motives other than land use regulation on the part of the city. The heightened requirement the Court imposes on cities is even more unjustified when all the tools needed to resolve the questions presented by this case can be garnered from our existing case law.

III

Applying its new standard, the Court finds two defects in the city's case. First, while the record would adequately support a requirement that Dolan maintain the portion of the floodplain on her property as undeveloped open space, it does not support the additional requirement that the floodplain be dedicated to the city. Second, while the city adequately established the traffic increase that the proposed development would generate, it failed to quantify the offsetting decrease in automobile traffic that the bike path will produce. Even under the Court's new rule, both defects are, at most, nothing more than harmless error.

In her objections to the floodplain condition, Dolan made no effort to demonstrate that the dedication of that portion of her property would be any more onerous than a simple prohibition against any development on that portion of her property. Given the commercial character of both the existing and the proposed use of the property as a retail store, it seems likely that potential customers "trampling along petitioner's floodplain," are more valuable than a useless parcel of vacant land. Moreover, the duty to pay taxes and the responsibility for potential tort liability may well make ownership of the fee interest in useless land a liability rather than an asset. That may explain why Dolan never conceded that she could be prevented from building on the floodplain. The City Attorney also pointed out that absent a dedication, property owners would be required to "build on their own land" and "with their own money" a storage facility for the water runoff. Dolan apparently "did have that option," but chose not to seek it. If Dolan might have been entitled to a variance confining the city's condition in a manner this Court would accept, her failure to seek that narrower form of relief at any stage of the state administrative and judicial proceedings clearly should preclude that relief in this Court now.

The Court's rejection of the bike path condition amounts to nothing more than a play on words. Everyone agrees that the bike path "could" offset some of the increased traffic flow that the larger store will generate, but the findings do not unequivocally state that it will do so, or tell us just how many cyclists will replace motorists. Predictions on such matters are inherently nothing more than estimates. Certainly the assumption that there will be an offsetting benefit here is entirely reasonable and should suffice whether it amounts to 100 percent, 35 percent, or only 5 percent of the increase in automobile traffic that would otherwise occur. If the Court proposes to have the federal judiciary micromanage state decisions of this kind, it is indeed extending its welcome mat to a significant new class of litigants. Although there is no reason to believe that state courts have failed to rise to the task, property owners have surely found a new friend today.

IV

The Court has made a serious error by abandoning the traditional presumption of constitutionality and imposing a novel burden of proof on a city implementing an admittedly valid comprehensive land use plan. Even more consequential than its incorrect disposition of this case, however, is the Court's resurrection of a species of substantive due process analysis that it firmly rejected decades ago.

* * *

This case inaugurates an even more recent judicial innovation than the regulatory takings doctrine: the application of the "unconstitutional conditions" label to a mutually beneficial transaction between a property owner and a city. The Court tells us that the city's refusal to grant Dolan a discretionary benefit infringes her right to receive just compensation for the property interests that she has refused to dedicate to the city "where the property sought has little or no relationship to the benefit." Although it is well settled that a government cannot deny a benefit on a basis that infringes constitutionally protected interests "—especially [one's] interest in freedom of speech," Perry v. Sindermann, 408 U.S. 593, 597 (1972)—the "unconstitutional conditions" doctrine provides an inadequate framework in which to analyze this case. Dolan has no right to be compensated for a taking unless the city acquires the property interests that she has refused to surrender. Since no taking has yet occurred, there has not been any infringement of her constitutional right to compensation. * * *

Even if Dolan should accept the city's conditions in exchange for the benefit that she seeks, it would not necessarily follow that she had been denied "just compensation" since it would be appropriate to consider the receipt of that benefit in any calculation of "just compensation." See Pennsylvania Coal Co. v. Mahon, 260 U.S. 393, 415 (1922) (noting that an "average reciprocity of advantage" was deemed to justify many laws); Hodel v. Irving, 481 U.S. 704, 715 (1987) (such " 'reciprocity of advantage' " weighed in favor of a statute's constitutionality). Particularly in the absence of any evidence on the point, we should not presume that the discretionary benefit the city has offered is less valuable than the property interests that Dolan can retain or surrender at her option. But even if that discretionary benefit were so trifling that it could not be considered just compensation when it has "little or no relationship" to the property, the Court fails to explain why the same value would suffice when the required nexus is present. In this respect, the Court's reliance on the "unconstitutional conditions" doctrine is assuredly novel, and arguably incoherent. The city's conditions are by no means immune from constitutional scrutiny. The level of scrutiny, however, does not approximate the kind of review that would apply if the city had insisted on a surrender of Dolan's First Amendment rights in exchange for a building permit. * * *

In our changing world one thing is certain: uncertainty will characterize predictions about the impact of new urban developments on the risks of floods, earthquakes, traffic congestion, or environmental harms. When there is doubt concerning the magnitude of those impacts, the public interest in averting them must outweigh the private interest of the commercial entrepreneur. If the government can demonstrate that the conditions it has imposed in a land-use permit are rational, impartial and conducive to fulfilling the aims of a valid land-use plan, a strong presumption of validity should attach to those conditions. The burden of demonstrating that those conditions have unreasonably impaired the economic value of the proposed improvement belongs squarely on the shoulders of the party challenging the state action's constitutionality. That allocation of burdens has served us well in the past. The Court has stumbled badly today by reversing it.

I respectfully dissent.

JUSTICE SOUTER, dissenting. [Dissenting opinion omitted.]

Notes

1. Does the Dolan case really change the burden of proof in exaction cases, requiring the city to justify its subdivision demands? If so, what impact would this decision have on traditional exactions? Could a developer protest that the subdivision requirement of thirty-foot-wide streets is a taking because the number of houses he intends to build does not justify a

street wider than, say, twenty feet? Consider the case, Lexington–Fayette Urban County Government v. Schneider, 849 S.W.2d 557 (Ky.App.1992), where a developer who had built 200 homes in a subdivision sought a rezoning in order to develop an additional 33 lots on an 18–acre tract at the southern end of his property. The planning commission conditioned approval upon the construction of a bridge over the creek that ran through the existing subdivision to connect two portions of a boulevard that had not been in existence when the developer began his subdivision. Arguing that the boulevard was not needed to provide access or regular traffic to the proposed 33 new homes, developer refused to bear the cost of the bridge (between $125,000 and $250,000). The Court of Appeals held that the bridge was an unreasonable burden on the developer when viewed in relation to the development of 33 lots. Also see Art Piculell Group v. Clackamas County, 142 Or.App. 327, 922 P.2d 1227 (1996) where the court discussed how to determine rough proportionality in a case where a subdivider was asked to construct a road to collector standards at the edge of his subdivision; to the east and west of the proposed subdivision the collector road already was built. The subdivider argued that his subdivision would contribute a small percentage of future traffic on the road and that, under Dolan, he should not have to pay more than his fair share for an improvement that would benefit the public at large and his subdivision at small.

2. One result of the Dolan case was to require a closer look at just what are exactions. In Clark v. City of Albany, 137 Or.App. 293, 904 P.2d 185 (1995), rev. denied 322 Or. 644, 912 P.2d 375 (1996) the court reviewed seven separate conditions imposed on a developer's plan for a fast food restaurant. The court held that a condition requiring the developer to design and construct off-site street improvements was an exaction, and that a condition requiring a sidewalk was an exaction; however, conditions that the developer designate an on-site area as traffic-free and that he provide a storm drainage plan and construct a storm drain were not exactions. The court remanded for a determination of rough proportionality of those conditions found to be exactions.

3. Another issue left open by the Dolan decision is whether the analysis applies to exactions other than land dedications. Does Dolan apply to money exactions? The California Supreme Court has held that it does apply in money exaction cases. In Ehrlich v. City of Culver City, 12 Cal.4th 854, 50 Cal.Rptr.2d 242, 911 P.2d 429 (1996), the court, applying Dolan, held that a $280,000 fee imposed on a developer to mitigate the loss of community recreational facilities (the proposed development would replace a failed private tennis club with luxury condominiums), was not shown by the city to be roughly proportional to the impact of the proposed development; on the other hand, a requirement that the developer provide for art reasonably accessible to the public in connection with a generally applicable exaction requirement was upheld in the case. The court said:

> [I]t is not at all clear that the rationale (and the heightened standard of scrutiny) of Nollan and Dolan applies to cases in which the exaction takes the form of a generally applicable development fee or assessment * * * But when a local government imposes special, discretionary permit conditions on development by individual property owners—as in the case of the recreational fee at issue in this case—Nollan and Dolan

require that such conditions, whether they consist of possessory dedications or monetary exactions, be scrutinized under the heightened standard.

Compare with the California case, Home Builders Ass'n of Central Arizona v. City of Scottsdale, 233 Ariz. Adv. Rep. 23, 187 Ariz. 479, 930 P.2d 993 (1997) where the plaintiffs challenged a water resources development fee imposed by the city in order to obtain new water in the future. The court considered the Dolan case and found it inapplicable because under the Arizona enabling act a reasonable relationship between the fee and the public burden is required and that standard was met in this case. Also, the court said that a money exaction is a considerably more benign form of regulation than a demand that land be ceded to the city. In Northern Illinois Home Builders Ass'n, Inc. v. County of Du Page, 165 Ill.2d 25, 208 Ill.Dec. 328, 649 N.E.2d 384 (1995) the court upheld one of two state enabling statutes that authorized counties to create schedules of exactions for transportation impacts. The court found that Dolan was no impediment to the imposition of transportation impact fees because of the state police power concern over traffic congestion and the continued adherence of Illinois to the "specifically and uniquely attributable" test for exactions.

4. On the federalism aspects of Dolan see Matthew J. Cholewa and Helen L. Edmonds, Federalism and Land Use After *Dolan*: Has the Supreme Court Taken Takings from the States?, 28 The Urban Lawyer 401 (1996).

(4) Denial of Subdivision Approval

COFFEY v. MARYLAND–NATIONAL CAPITAL PARK AND PLANNING COMMISSION

Court of Appeals of Maryland, 1982.
293 Md. 24, 441 A.2d 1041.

SMITH, JUDGE.

* * *

Appellant, Wade S. Coffey, owns 15.85 acres of land on Riverdale Road in Prince George's County, located approximately 1,800 feet east of that road's intersection with the Baltimore–Washington Parkway. The land is zoned R–T (Townhouse Development). This permits a maximum development density of 8.0 to 11.9 units per acre. The master plan for that area, approved in December 1980 by the District Council for Prince George's County, restricts density to 2.7 to 3.5 dwelling units per acre. Almost immediately after adoption of the plan, in January 1981, Coffey submitted an application for approval of a preliminary plan of subdivision. The planning for the subdivision had been in progress for some time. He proposed 117 townhouse units on the tract, a density of 7.38 dwelling units per acre.

Prince George's County Code § 24–103(a)(1) requires subdivision plats to conform to the master plan. Relying upon our decision in *Board of County Comm'rs v. Gaster,* 285 Md. 233, 401 A.2d 666 (1979), the Prince George's County Planning Board of the Maryland–National Capital Park and Planning Commission (the Commission) rejected the proposed subdivision because of noncompliance with the master plan. The Circuit Court for Prince George's County affirmed. Coffey then appealed to the Court of Special Appeals. Because we have not previously addressed such an issue under Art. 66D, we issued the writ of certiorari ex mero motu prior to consideration of the appeal by the intermediate appellate court.

* * *

Coffey's argument runs that prior to *Gaster* planning boards regarded master plans as only a set of recommendations, that *Gaster* was the first case where noncompliance with a master plan caused rejection of a proposed subdivision, and that noncompliance with the master plan constituted insufficient grounds for disapproval of a proposed subdivision. Cases making statements relative to master plans being guides have arisen in the context of an attempted piecemeal change in zoning. For instance, in *Chapman v. Montgomery County,* 259 Md. 641, 643, 271 A.2d 156 (1970), Judge Finan said for the Court, "A 'Master Plan' is not to be confused as a substitute for a comprehensive zoning or rezoning map, nor may it be equated with it in legal significance." No opinion of this Court has made a statement relative to master plans acting only as guides in the context of the facts here involved.

At oral argument, counsel for the Commission said that its past practice had been to treat the master plan as a guide in zoning matters. Counsel further stated, however, that the Commission regarded the master plan as binding in subdivision matters subsequent to the enactment of the regulation requiring proposed subdivisions to conform to the master plan.

* * *

As the author points out in 4 R. Anderson, *American Law of Zoning 2d* § 23.20, at 89 (1977), "Subdivision controls are imposed for the purpose of implementing a comprehensive plan for community development. To achieve this end, plats submitted to a planning commission for approval must be examined in relation to the official map and the master plan." Moreover, as the court observed in *Popular Refreshments, Inc. v. Fuller's Milk Bar, etc.,* 85 N.J.Super. 528, 537, 205 A.2d 445 (1964), petition for certification denied, 44 N.J. 409, 209 A.2d 143 (1965), "If planning boards had no alternative but to rubber-stamp their approval on every subdivision plat which conformed with the zoning ordinance, there would be little or no reason for their existence. While planning and zoning complement each other and serve certain common objectives, each represents a separate municipal function and neither is a mere rubber-stamp for the other," citing *Levin v. Livingston Tp.,* 35 N.J. 500, 506, 173 A.2d 391 (1961).

In this regard, the language used by the court in *Shoptaugh v. County Comm.,* 37 Colo.App. 39, 543 P.2d 524 (1975), *cert. denied* (1976), is significant here. The court there said:

"Here, the landowner argues that since the proposed use of the land was a use of right under the zoning laws, the Board had no alternative but to either change the zoning or approve the plat. This argument fails to take into consideration that a subdivider must first meet the zoning regulations and then additionally must comply with the state and county subdivision regulations." 37 Colo.App. at 41–42, 543 P.2d 524.

The process of comprehensive zoning or rezoning is a time consuming one. It would be virtually impossible to adopt comprehensive rezoning changes calculated to impose the same density requirements as the master plan which would become effective simultaneously with the adoption of a new master plan that called for lower density development than the preceding plan.

Here we have a regulation duly enacted by the legislative body for Prince George's County which specifies that the planning board shall not approve a subdivision plat not in compliance with the master plan. This subdivision regulation is as much entitled to obedience as any other legislative enactment. The need for the regulation specifying that a subdivision plan must conform to the master plan can be illustrated by comparison to the putting of water in a teacup drop by drop. After a period of time there comes the drop which will cause the cup to overflow. By analogy, developing some of the lots in conformity with the existing zoning will not disrupt the master plan. Concentrated use and development, however, will disrupt it. The legislative body wished to avoid this when it specified that subdivisions must comply with the master plan. Accordingly, the Commission was justified in rejecting Coffey's proposed subdivision for his failure to conform that proposal with the master plan.

Judgment affirmed; Appellant to pay the costs.

MARYLAND–NAT'L CAPITAL PARK AND PLANNING COMM'N v. ROSENBERG

Court of Appeals of Maryland, 1973.
269 Md. 520, 307 A.2d 704.

McWILLIAMS, JUDGE.

In this appeal, stemming from the confrontation of a landowner and the appellant (the Commission), we are asked to consider what is known in Prince George's County as the "Adequate Public Facilities Ordinance." * * * As we see this case the single issue is whether the action of the Commission was arbitrary and capricious. We think it was. However, before we undertake to relate the facts, we shall set forth the pertinent parts of both the enabling act (Code of Public Local Laws of Prince George's County, § 59–76 (1963)), and the ordinance (Code of Ordinances and Resolutions of Prince George's County, § 3(a) 16 (1967)):

"* * * The regulations may provide for (1) the harmonious development of the district; (2) the coordination of roads within the subdivision with other existing, planned or platted roads or with other features of the district or with the commission's general plan or with any road plan adopted or approved by the commission as part of the commission's general plan; (3) adequate open spaces for traffic, recreation, light, and air by dedication or otherwise, and the dedication to public use or conveyance of areas designated for such dedication under the provisions of zoning regulations relating to average lot size or planned community subdivision and for the payment of a monetary fee in lieu of dedication, not to exceed five percent of the total assessed value of the land, to be used by the commission to purchase such open spaces for the use and benefit of the subdivision in cases where dedication would be impractical; (4) the reservation of lands for schools and other public buildings and for parks, playgrounds, and other public purposes, provided no reservation of land for traffic, recreation or any other public purposes as herein provided shall continue for longer than three (3) years without the written approval of all persons holding or otherwise owning any legal or equitable interest in said property; and provided further that such properties so reserved for public use as hereinbefore provided shall be exempt from all state, county and local taxes during such period; (5) the conservation of or production of adequate transportation, water, drainage and sanitary facilities; (6) the preservation of the location of and the volume and flow of water in and other characteristics of natural streams and other waterways; (7) the avoidance of population congestion; (8) the avoidance of such scattered or premature subdivision of land as would involve danger or injury to health, safety or welfare by reason of the lack of water supply, drainage, transportation or other public services or necessitate an excessive expenditure of public funds for the supply of such services; (9) conformity of resubdivided lots to the character of lots within the existing subdivision with respect to area, frontage and alignment to existing lots and streets; (10) control of subdivision or building (except for agricultural or recreational purposes) in flood plain areas or streams and drainage courses, and on unsafe land areas; (11) preservation of outstanding natural or cultural features and historic sites or structures; or (12) other benefits to the health, comfort, safety or welfare of the present and future population of the regional district."

"16. Before preliminary approval may be granted for any subdivision plat the Planning Board must find that: sufficient public facilities and services exist or are programmed for the area. It is the intent of this section that public facilities and services should be adequate to preclude danger or injury to the health, safety and welfare and excessive expenditure of public funds.

"i. The Planning Board shall give due weight to the potential of the proposed subdivision in relation to the surroundings, including the nature, extent and size of the proposed subdivision; the estimated increase in population; the anticipated timing of the

Sec. 1   REGULATION OF THE SUBDIVISION OF LAND   517

development of the land proposed for subdivision; and the degree of urbanization or development within a reasonable distance of the subject property; and the following factors:

"The availability of existing or programmed sewerage or water mains.

"The potential effect of the proposed subdivision on the efficient and economic operation of existing or programmed public facilities.

"The distance of any necessary extension of sewerage and water facilities through unsubdivided lands which are indicated for eventual development on an approved plan.

"The location of the proposed subdivision in respect to the approved Ten Year Water and Sewerage Plan, or in any future plan which designated the timing of construction of facilities.

"The availability of access roads adequate to serve traffic which would be generated by the subdivision, or the presence of a proposal for such road(s) on an adopted Master Plan and in the current Capital Improvement Program or the State Roads Commission program.

"The availability within a reasonable distance, and the adequacy of school, fire, police, utility, and park and recreation services."

The 31 acre tract of land (the property) with which we shall be concerned abuts the northwest side of the Pennsylvania Railroad which at that point serves also as one side of an equilateral triangle; the northeast side is the Capital Beltway (Interstate Rte 495); the south side is the John Hanson Highway (U.S. Rte 50). The property lies within the development known as West Lanham Hills which is about four miles northeast of the District line. Except for the land inside the triangle one can safely say the area surrounding the property is fully developed. Since 1964 the zoning classification of the property has been R–18 (Multiple Family, Medium Density, Residential), a classification with which the owner (appellee) seems content. It is said that a six acre strip has been or will be acquired to serve as the site for the Metro's Ardmore station.

In June 1971 the appellee submitted to the Commission for its approval, as required by the subdivision regulations, a preliminary plan for the subdivision of two parcels of the property. The Commission referred the application to its staff which, in turn, sent it to various county agencies for review and comment. The Board of Education was one of the agencies whose comment was solicited. It referred the matter to its Office of Population Analysis. On 16 June the Office of Population Analysis sent a memorandum to F. Harris Allen, Principal Development Coordinator of the Commission. The memorandum indicated a "Projected Pupil Yield" of 134 for the West Lanham Hills Elementary School, the capacity of which was 640 and which, at the time, had an actual enrollment of 657.

Several weeks later there came into existence an "adequate public facilities check sheet" apparently prepared by someone on the Commission's technical staff. Allen said he used this "in the course of the review of preliminary plans." This check sheet, dated 6 July 1971, indicates that the property had a "potential" of 651 units and that, fully developed and occupied, it would yield 175.8 pupils. The Office of Population Analysis, it will be recalled, developed a figure of 134. The September 1970 enrollment at the West Lanham Hills Elementary School was stated, in the check sheet, to be 668 pupils or 11 more than the enrollment reported by the Office of Population Analysis. There appears also, in the check sheet, the following notation:

> There are no additions in the CIP [Capital Improvement Program] which would increase the capacity of this school *or any other elementary schools in the vicinity*. (Emphasis added.)

It is conceded that the technical staff of the Commission recommended approval of the appellee's application. It was considered by the Prince George's County Planning Board of the Commission on 9 August and disapproved the same day. A letter from Allen to the appellee, dated 13 August, states, in part:

> " * * * West Lanham Hills Elementary School which would serve this property is currently operating over its listed capacity and there are no plans for any elementary schools in the Capital Improvements Program which would relieve this situation. The property, if developed in accordance with the allowable density, would generate approximately 134 elementary school children which would further overload the existing school.
>
> "It was therefore the opinion of the Planning Board that since adequate public facilities are neither existing or programmed to serve the area the proposed subdivision should be denied."

* * *

Nothing in the record suggests the Board held any kind of a hearing and Allen's testimony makes it quite clear that the only evidence or information before the Board when it denied the appellee's application was the check sheet sent up from the technical staff. All the Board could have learned from the check sheet was that last year's (September 1970) enrollment at West Lanham Hills Elementary was 28 pupils in excess of its capacity and that the property could yield 651 dwelling units. * * * The Board could also have learned that an increase in the capacity of West Lanham Hills *"or any other elementary schools in the vicinity"* was not contemplated. What is meant by "vicinity" or which "other elementary schools" the staff had in mind is anyone's guess. We are not to be persuaded that the Board could have given "due weight * * * [to] [t]he availability within a reasonable distance, and the adequacy of school * * * services," in the light of such trivial and inaccurate evidence.

In Baltimore Planning Commission v. Victor Development Co., 261 Md. 387, 275 A.2d 478 (1971), we chose not to deal with the question whether the (Baltimore) Commission had "the power to formulate a rule dealing with the effect of subdivisions upon schools," although we hinted

Sec. 1 REGULATION OF THE SUBDIVISION OF LAND 519

there might be some question about it. Here we choose not to deal with the question whether public schools are "public services" as that expression is used in the enabling act. The appellee urges that the principle of ejusdem generis should apply because of the juxtaposition of "public services" with "lack of water supply, drainage, transportation, or other public services," and it is, to be sure, not a wholly unattractive argument.

The subdivision regulation does not undertake to restrict pupils to the school within the boundaries of the service area in which they reside. The only limitation is that there must be an adequate school available "within a reasonable distance." Nor do the school authorities consider the boundaries of the service areas to be static and inflexible. Panor, it will be recalled, testified that they have "from year to year changed literally—practically all service areas of all existing schools." Reflecting upon Panor's testimony that the schools in the four contiguous areas have a capacity of 2,300 pupils and that the enrollment as of September 1972 was 251 less than capacity, one need not be especially perceptive to suppose that the area boundaries could readily be adjusted to take care of the 45 pupils said to be in excess of the capacity of West Lanham Hills Elementary School. One must, of course, assume the instant development and occupancy of the appellee's project, but one need not assume that it has been in the R–18 classification since 1964. That is a fact. The regulation does not define "reasonable distance" but we do not think the Board can be heard to say that a mile, or even a mile and one-half, is not a "reasonable distance."

Since we are fully persuaded that the Board's refusal to approve the appellee's preliminary plan was arbitrary and capricious the order of the trial court will be affirmed.

Order affirmed. Costs to be paid by the appellant.

Notes

1. In Corona–Norco Unified School Dist. v. City of Corona, 13 Cal. App.4th 1577, 17 Cal.Rptr.2d 236 (1993) the court held that a school district could not enjoin a city from giving subdivision approval for two projects on the ground of inadequate school facilities. The court based its decision on state statutes that allow school districts to impose exactions of developments for school purposes and concluded that the complex statutory scheme precluded denial of subdivision approval. Also see Grupe Development Co. v. Superior Court, 4 Cal.4th 911, 16 Cal.Rptr.2d 226, 844 P.2d 545 (1993).

In Cherokee Water & Sanitation Dist. v. El Paso County, 770 P.2d 1339 (Colo.App.1988), the court upheld a county regulation requiring all developers to demonstrate a 300 year water supply prior to subdivision approval. The case was a declaratory judgment action presenting a facial challenge to the regulation. The court said:

> Nor have the plaintiffs shown an unconstitutional taking of property. As the challenge is facial, plaintiffs must prove that the mere enactment deprived them of all reasonable use of their property. Land-

mark Land Co. v. City & County of Denver, 728 P.2d 1281 (Colo.1986), appeal dismissed sub nom., Harsh Investment Corp. v. City & County of Denver, 483 U.S. 1001, 107 S.Ct. 3222, 97 L.Ed.2d 729 (1987). Plaintiffs were unable to demonstrate that the regulation will prevent even residential development on their property, let alone any other reasonable use. Thus, no taking occurred by enactment of the regulation.

Nor are we convinced that the regulation is arbitrary or capricious. Plaintiffs bore the burden of proving beyond a reasonable doubt that the regulations are not rationally and reasonably related to a valid governmental interest. Sellon v. City of Manitou Springs, 745 P.2d 229 (Colo. 1987). The evidence presented by the county demonstrates that the regulation is designed to insure that no development take place where there are not adequate water supplies for the future. Such an interest is valid, and the regulation is rationally and reasonably related thereto, thus satisfying both the federal and state constitutional requirements.

Also see Christianson v. Gasvoda, 242 Mont. 212, 789 P.2d 1234 (1990) where the court upheld denial of a subdivision because it would exacerbate drainage and flooding problems in flatlands below the developer's land. The same developer had previously developed three subdivisions in the uplands area, and the court said the problems created by previous development justified rejection of the proposed subdivision. A similar case from Connecticut involved a steep slope development. Krawski v. Planning and Zoning Comm'n of Town of South Windsor, 21 Conn.App. 667, 575 A.2d 1036 (1990). And in Wood v. City of Madison, 260 Wis.2d 71, 659 N.W.2d 31 (2003) the court upheld denial of a subdivision because the commercial portion was incompatible with nearby agricultural uses, rejecting the argument that plat approval was being used to perform a zoning function.

In Beach v. Planning and Zoning Comm'n, 141 Conn. 79, 103 A.2d 814 (1954), the commission denied subdivision plat approval for a 145–lot subdivision for the following reasons: "(1) This land is adjacent to a new development which will contain 79 homes. (2) The Council has stated that the financial situation of the town is such that no schools could be built in this area for some time. (3) The additional Police and Fire protection which would be needed in this area cannot now be provided due to the financial situation of the town. (4) The report of the school superintendent shows that the new school in this area will be inadequate to provide for the children already living in this area soon after it opens." The court held that neither the enabling statute nor the subdivision ordinance authorized rejection of plat approval on those grounds and that the rejection was ultra vires. Compare Fallen Leaf Protection Ass'n v. South Tahoe Public Utility Dist., 46 Cal.App.3d 816, 120 Cal.Rptr. 538 (1975) which upheld an absolute prohibition of septic tanks and cesspools for waste disposal. Also compare Board of County Comm'rs of Cecil County v. Gaster, 285 Md. 233, 401 A.2d 666 (1979), where the court upheld denial of a subdivision because of traffic congestion in an area not programmed for new roads until 1990. And see Batch v. Town of Chapel Hill, 326 N.C. 1, 387 S.E.2d 655 (1990) where the court upheld denial of a subdivision plat for failure to coordinate with the town's transportation plan.

In Wolff v Mooresville Plan Comm'n, 754 N.E.2d 589 (Ind.App.2001), the Court upheld the planning commission's denial of preliminary primary plat approval for a single-family residential subdivision of approximately 278 lots based upon the following findings: that the Plat as filed "failed to address issues concerning the treatment of sanitary waste in a sufficient manner to guarantee that there is a capacity to serve the proposed number of homes on the initial Plat; the applicant failed to provide sufficient information on drainage issues relating to the topography of the ground; health and safety issues concerning roadways and entryways due to topography (evidence presented that the Plat is not suitable due to topography problems, roadway problems and healthy and safety issues concerning sewer and water); and problems with access, sight distances and County approval of the access."

2. In Walls v. Planning and Zoning Comm'n, 176 Conn. 475, 408 A.2d 252 (1979), the court held that adjacent property owners had no standing to challenge the approval of a subdivision. In State ex rel. Menkhus v.City of Pevely, 865 S.W.2d 871 (Mo.App.1993) the court held a property owner whose subdivision plat met all the requirements of the ordinance could not be denied approval, and in Ex Parte Pine Brook Lakes, Inc., 617 So.2d 1014 (Ala.1992) the court held that the county board improperly denied subdivision approval by merely referring to some possible future road construction in the area.

3. In the 1980's two developments made an impact on the conventional wisdom surrounding subdivision exactions. The twin forces of rapid inflation and the property tax revolt made more people aware of the fact that subdivision exactions have a powerful role in the cost of housing. In those states that have adopted limitations on the property tax, notably California through Proposition 13, one result was an increase in subdivision exactions and permit fees. Cities saw the loss of property tax revenues as reducing funding for municipal services that could be made up only by increasing revenues from other sources. Subdivision exactions, in this sense, would be a hidden tax imposed on new residents, reflected in the cost of housing. However, when coupled with rapid inflation, the increase in exactions became a more visible factor in housing costs. In some communities estimates were that exactions and other development regulations accounted for as much as twenty-five percent of the cost of a single-family dwelling. One result of this problem has been increased attention to ways in which the cost of housing can be lowered. See U.S. Dept. Housing and Urban Development, Reducing the Development Costs of Housing: Actions for State and Local Governments (1979); Ellickson, Suburban Growth Controls: An Economic and Legal Analysis, 66 Yale L.J. 385 (1977). In many communities, even in states without property tax revolt problems, inflationary forces have induced developers to seek reductions in exactions in order to keep the cost of housing down. Even traditional exactions have come under attack. Developers are questioning the necessity of sidewalks in residential subdivisions and the established street widths. They may ask for elimination of curb and gutter requirements, reduction of minimum lot sizes, and revision of building codes, all in the name of making housing affordable (and, incidentally, keeping them in business). In some cities developers are seeking permission to develop single-family and multi-family areas with private drives, rather

than streets constructed to city standards and dedicated to the public. If a community resists the pressure for reduction of exactions, developers will frequently raise the spectre that they will pick up and move their operations to nearby cities where the regulatory costs are lower, leaving the community without a housing industry. No easy answers to these problems are available. However, some questions may be posed. Should exactions be standardized at the state level, rather than delegated to local government as is the present practice? Presumably, exactions are a result of the police power, delegated in the enabling legislation. Does the health, safety, morals and general welfare of the public justify thirty-foot wide streets with curb and gutter in the residential subdivisions of City A and twenty-five foot wide streets without curb or gutter in City B? Would it be better and cheaper to have a standard set of exactions and codes for the entire state? Would such a change be politically feasible? Further, what is the relationship, if any, between growth controls, exactions, inflation and the cost of housing? See Patricia E. Salkin, Barriers to Affordable Housing: Are Land–Use Controls the Scapegoat?, Land Use Law (April 1993) p. 3. Also see Jerry Cheslow, Impact Fees Reexamined in California, N.Y. Times, Apr. 4, 1993, p. 31; this article discusses how impact fees can stunt growth in a financial recession.

SECTION 2. THE OFFICIAL MAP AND PUBLIC STREETS

In 1925, Philip Nichols and Frank B. Williams debated whether to use eminent domain or the police power to prevent building in officially mapped streets. See the 1925 Proceedings, National City Planning Conference 378 and following. Mr. Nichols argued for eminent domain pointing to the quaint Yankee custom of exactly off-setting damages for eminent domain taking with the special benefits to the rest of the land. Mr. Williams took the police power position urging a board of adjustment to take care of hardship cases. It was pointed out that William Penn laid out a system of checkerboard streets for Philadelphia and that the official map has been popular in Pennsylvania ever since. The Randall map for New York City was authorized in 1807, and an official map for Baltimore in 1817. Mr. Williams said (at 396):

> The age of Washington was the age of city planning. The street plan of New York City, [way out to 155th street] already referred to, was protected by a state law providing that a property owner, when the city was ready to lay out the street and took the land necessary for the purpose, could recover no damages for improvements which he had made in the bed of a mapped street; and there were similar laws in other states. For many years these laws remained unchallenged in our statute books and were generally regarded as valid. But, before our Civil War, in 1861, a change of attitude occurred, and today except in the State of Pennsylvania, all these laws are, under decisions of our highest state courts, held to be a taking of property rights without compensation contrary to our state constitutions.

Kucirek and Beuscher, Wisconsin's Official Map Law, 1957 Wis. L.Rev. 176, 177, state:

In essence the official map is a simple device. It is one way, but not the only way, to fix building lines. The official map may plat future as well as existing streets. Where future streets are mapped, subdividers must conform to the mapped street lay-out, unless they can prevail upon the proper officials to amend the map. Public sewer and water will be installed only in the bed of the mapped streets. Even more important, a landowner who builds in the bed of the mapped street may be refused compensation for his building when the street is ultimately opened and the mapped land taken. To guard against this drastic consequence, official map laws now customarily require the landowner to obtain a building permit before proceeding with construction.

The official map of future streets has obvious advantages in terms of the public coffers. It assures that land needed for future streets will be available at bare land prices. Mapping of future streets also gives direction and pattern to future growth of the community, though some feel that the map casts the mold too inflexibly, especially if minor as well as major streets are mapped.

Where existing streets have been officially mapped, the map will often set widening lines (set-backs) warning that new structures must be located in conformance with their lines, and these also have obvious advantages in cutting costs of street widening. Again, a building permit is usually used to assure compliance.

The official map is not the only means of establishing building lines. Other familiar methods are:

(1) Set-back provisions in zoning ordinances;

(2) Set-back ordinances as such—ordinances stating that for prescribed streets no buildings are to be built any closer to the street line than a specified distance;

(3) Set-backs established on plats as a condition to subdivision approval;

(4) Set-back provisions in privately established deed restrictions (restrictive covenants);

(5) The now virtually obsolete method of purchasing set-back easements through eminent domain proceedings.

(6) In the subdivision process, as we have already seen, subdividers may be required to honor the master street plan insofar as that plan indicates street locations; and, of course, the subdivider may be required to install the street at his expense and in compliance with published standards.

The name "official map" is not universal. In Pennsylvania and California for instance, the same planning device is there referred to as "confirmed map" and "precise map" respectively. The name "official map" seems to have originated with Edward M. Bassett and Frank B. Williams, who wrote New York's 1926 act and in 1935 published a model official map act. They distinguished the "official map" sharply from the "master plan":

> A master plan embraces many features not included in an official map. The master plan, therefore, does not usually show precise data founded in careful surveys, while the official map, upon which the details of both public and private works must be based, should be capable of accurate interpretation. The master plan, therefore, may be characterized as plastic, the official map as rigid.

In other words under the Bassett–Williams scheme, the master plan is not binding upon landowners; the official map is. The master plan is the general formulation, often reflected by non-precise maps, of the results of planning studies—studies not only of the circulatory system, but also of land use districts, location of parks and recreation areas, sites for public buildings and facilities, location of public utilities and other matters. The official map is intended to reflect some aspects of the master plan in a precise, accurate and legally binding manner.

Nonetheless, it is easy to overemphasize in practical terms the differences to the landowner between the officially enacted map on one hand and the commission-approved "unofficial" street plan on the other. Knowledgeable landowners are not apt to build in the bed of an "unofficially" mapped street or other proposed public site. True, the owner may know that he is entitled to compensation for his building when the land is ultimately taken for the public purpose. But he knows of the vagaries of valuation juries and in any case, compensation or no compensation, he does not want to build a structure only to have it torn down, perhaps only a short time later. Consequently many cities successfully guide development along future streets through master street plans, not backed by any legal sanctions except subdivision plat approval. Such plans are less successful in achieving voluntary set-backs along existing streets. Here the legal sanctions of a set-back ordinance or a precise official map are needed to keep the uncooperative owner "in line."

Another point of comparison between a master plan and an official map needs to be made. Even though the master plan is not backed by legal sanctions, it may blight the market for mapped real estate quite as effectively as an official map. If a would-be buyer learns that the land has been marked with a "green spot" on the master plan for a park or has been "master planned" as the bed of a proposed street or thoroughway, he will be as reluctant to buy as if the land had been officially mapped. He does not want to buy and develop land for his private use when he knows that it is earmarked for public taking.

HEADLEY v. CITY OF ROCHESTER

Court of Appeals of New York, 1936.
272 N.Y. 197, 5 N.E.2d 198.

LEHMAN, J.

The plaintiff since 1918 has been the owner of premises in the city of Rochester which are bounded on the south by East avenue and on the west by North Goodman street. East avenue and North Goodman street have been, for more than twenty years, public streets or highways. In 1931, pursuant to article 3 of the General City Law (Cons.Laws, ch. 21), the Council of the city of Rochester passed an ordinance which amended, changed and added to an official map or plan previously adopted by the Council "so as to correct and revise said established Official Map or Plan and to lay out new streets and highways and to widen existing highways." In that map or plan the southerly twenty-five feet of plaintiff's said premises are included in East avenue, as widened, and a strip of plaintiff's premises extending along its westerly edge is included in North Goodman street, as widened. The plaintiff has brought an action to obtain a judgment declaring "that the ordinance and map and plan adopted by the said City of Rochester as aforesaid is unconstitutional and void." At Special Term the complaint was dismissed. The Appellate Division reversed and granted judgment "declaring that the ordinance, map and plan herein involved, are void and ineffectual to create any limitations or restrictions upon the use or conveyance of plaintiff's property."

By chapter 690 of the Laws of 1926 the Legislature added article 3, entitled "Official Maps and Planning Boards," to the General City Law. That article empowers the legislative body of every city to establish an official map or plan of the city showing the streets, highways and parks theretofore laid out and established by law. (Sec. 26.) It empowers such legislative body "whenever and as often as it may deem it for the public interest, to change or add to the official map or plan of the city so as to lay out new streets, highways or parks, or to widen or close existing streets, highways or parks." (Sec. 29.) It further empowers the legislative body of the city to create a planning board of five members and it requires that before making any addition or change in an official map in accordance with section 29 "the matter shall be referred to the planning board for report thereon." The planning board is given "power and authority to make such investigations, maps and reports and recommendations in connection therewith relating to the planning and development of the city as to it seems desirable." (Sec. 31.)

The adoption or revision of a general map pursuant to the provisions of the General City Law does not have the effect of divesting the title of the owner of land in the bed of a street as shown on the map; it does not have the effect of placing upon the city a duty to begin, presently, condemnation proceedings to acquire such land. Article 3 of the statute provides the machinery for intelligent planning in advance for the needs of the city as the city is expected to grow in the future. Only time can prove whether the city has wisely gauged the future, and the city is under no compulsion to open any street shown on the map unless and until the legislative body of the city decides that it is actually needed.

The mere adoption of a general plan or map showing streets and parks to be laid out or widened in the future, without acquisition by the city of title to the land in the bed of the street, can be of little benefit to the public if the development of the land abutting upon and in the bed of the proposed streets proceeds in a haphazard way, without taking into account the general plan adopted and, especially, if permanent buildings are erected on the land in the bed of the proposed street which would hamper its acquisition or use for its intended purpose. So long as the owners of parcels of land which lie partly in the bed of streets shown on such a map are free to place permanent buildings in the bed of a proposed street and to provide private ways and approaches which have no relation to the proposed system of public streets, the integrity of the plan may be destroyed by the haphazard or even malicious development of one parcel or tract to the injury of other owners who may have developed their own tracts in a manner which conforms to the general map or plan.

A statutory requirement that a city must acquire title to the land in the bed of the streets shown on the general map or plan, and to provide compensation for the land taken, would create practical difficulties which would drastically limit, if, indeed, they did not render illusory, any power conferred upon the city to adopt a general map or plan which will make provision for streets which will be needed only if present anticipations of the future development of the city are realized. On the other hand, to leave the land in private ownership, and, without compensation to the owner, incumber it with restrictions upon its use which would result in diminution in its value might be inequitable and perhaps even beyond the power of the State. To meet the difficulty, the Legislature has provided in section 35 of the General City Law that "for the purpose of preserving the integrity of such official map or plan no permit shall hereafter be issued for any building in the bed of any street or highway shown or laid out on such map or plan, provided, however, that if the land within such mapped street or highway is not yielding a fair return on its value to the owner, the board of appeals or other similar board in any city which has established such a board having power to make variances or exception in zoning regulations shall have power in a specific case * * * to grant a permit for a building in such street or highway which will as little as practicable increase the cost of opening such street or highway, or tend to cause a change of such official map or plan, and such board may impose reasonable requirements as a condition of granting such permit, which requirements shall inure to the benefit of the city." The sole complaint of the plaintiff is that so long as that section remains in force the effect of the ordinance adopted by the city is to restrict the use to which the plaintiff may put his land in the bed of the street and to that extent constitutes a taking of his property, and that, since the city is not required to pay any compensation to him unless or until at some time in the indefinite future it may choose to take title to the land, the effect of the ordinance is to deprive him of his property without due process of law.

Not every restriction placed by authority of the State upon the use of property for the general welfare of the State, without payment of compensation, constitutes a deprivation of property without due process of law. This court has sustained a reasonable restriction upon the height of signs on roofs, saying: "Compensation for such interference with and restriction in the use of property is found in the share that the owner enjoys in the common benefit secured to all."

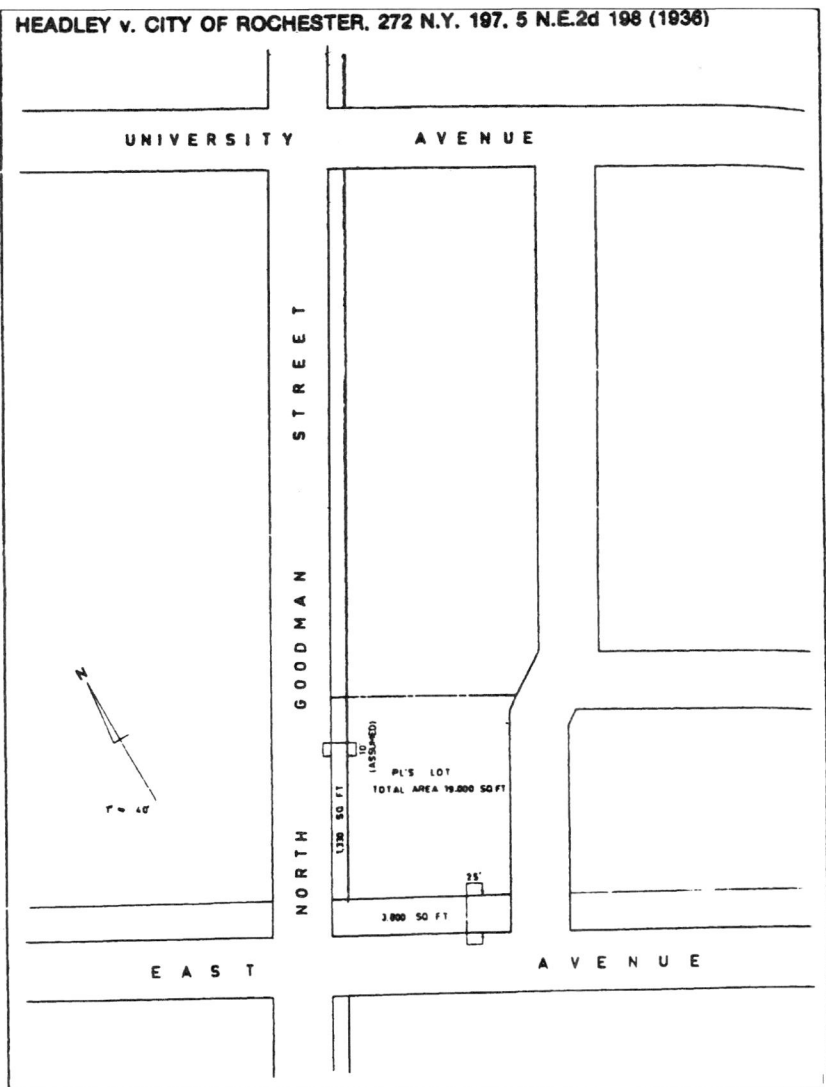

People ex rel. M. Wineburgh Adv. Co. v. Murphy, 195 N.Y. 126, 131, 88 N.E. 17. Under the provisions of the General City Law the owner of land in the bed of the street shown in a map remains as free to alien the land or to use it as he sees fit as he was before the map was adopted, except in one respect. If he desires to improve the property by erecting a building for which a permit is required, the grant of such a permit is surrounded by drastic conditions or restrictions which will in many cases act as an obstacle to such use of the land.

* * *

* * * The complaint alleges only the conclusion of the pleader that by reason of the filing of the ordinance and map or plan "the plaintiff has been, and is, deprived of his property without the payment of compensation therefor." The complaint is silent as to how the plaintiff is injured by the ordinance and the map. The stipulation of facts upon which the case was submitted for decision again fails to indicate in what manner the ordinance has caused damage to the plaintiff or interferes with any use to which the plaintiff desires to put the land. On the contrary, it appears from the stipulated facts that "the plaintiff has at present no plans for the use of said premises nor any particular desire as to the purposes for which he expects to use the same" and "that the plaintiff, because of the claim of the defendant under said ordinance and map, is undecided as to whether he shall endeavor to build upon said premises or endeavor to sell the same." It may be added, incidentally, that the stipulated facts fail to show that there is at present any actual controversy with the city as to the use to which the property may be put, and it appears "that the plaintiff has made no application to the Planning Board, Board of Appeals or Supervisor of Zoning of the City of Rochester for a permit to use those portions of his property included in said map as widened streets or to build thereon or to alter any existing structures therein."

Regardless of the form of action in which relief is sought, the courts will not declare a statute unconstitutional unless and until such relief is necessary for the protection of some right of the suitor guaranteed by the Constitution. * * *

The opinion of the Appellate Division leans heavily upon Forster v. Scott, 136 N.Y. 577, 32 N.E. 976, as authority for its decision. The analogy between the cases is quite illusory and the principles here involved are not touched by that case. There the city of New York, in accordance with the provisions of chapter 681 of the Laws of 1886, filed a map of a proposed street or avenue which as the court pointed out *"covers the entire lot"* of the plaintiff. The statute provided that "no compensation shall be allowed for any building, erection or construction which at any time, subsequent to the filing of the maps, plans, or profiles mentioned in section six hundred and seventy-two of the act, may be built, erected or placed in part or in whole upon or through any street, avenue, road, public square or place exhibited upon such maps, plans or profiles." (p. 582.) The plaintiff made a contract to sell his land to the defendant. He agreed to convey a good title to the land "in fee simple free from any lien or encumbrance." The defendant refused the title, claiming that the filing of the map created an incumbrance upon the property. The validity of the title was submitted to the court upon stipulated facts. It appeared from them that no building was erected on the plaintiff's land and "the same is a vacant lot which derives almost its

Sec. 2   THE OFFICIAL MAP AND PUBLIC STREETS   529

entire value from the possibility of being used for building purposes. If the lot cannot now be built upon without the house being destroyed, without compensation in the event of the street being opened as prescribed by the statutes above set forth, the lot is not worth what defendant agreed to pay, whereas if it can be used for building purposes it is worth at least $5,000." In other words, the statute purported to give the city the right at some indefinite time in the future to appropriate the land of the plaintiff shown on the map without paying for it the value it would then have if, pending such appropriation, its owner chose to improve it for the only purpose for which it had substantial value.

The court there said: "An encumbrance is said to import every right to or interest in the land, which may subsist in another, to the diminution of the value of the land, but consistent with the power to pass the fee by a conveyance." (p. 582.) If the statute was valid the land "could not be used for building purposes, except at the risk to the owner of losing the cost of the building at some time in the future." (p. 583.) The value of the land was derived from its availability for building purposes and that value would be drastically reduced if the owner could not obtain compensation for the improvements put upon the land. Since these facts were stipulated it could hardly be doubted that the statute attempted to create a public right or interest in the land which diminished its value and would, therefore, constitute an incumbrance as defined by the court. Then in an action between vendor and vendee under a contract of sale, the court was bound to pass upon the validity of the statute.

Every element which led the court to find in that case that the filing of the map, in accordance with the statute there challenged, created, if the statute were valid, an incumbrance upon the property, is wanting in the case now under review. The statute here does not purport to give to the city the right to appropriate the plaintiff's land or any part of it for less than the full value of the lands with the improvements thereon erected at the time of such appropriation. The only restrictions upon the use of any part of the plaintiff's land while title thereto remains in the plaintiff result indirectly from the conditions which the statute attaches to the grant thereafter of a permit to erect a building upon the small portion of plaintiff's land which, as shown on the map, will lie in the bed of the street on which the plaintiff's land abuts, if or when at some time in the future the city may desire to carry out its intention to widen the street. Since it is affirmatively shown that the plaintiff has no plans at present for the use of the premises it seems plain that what this court said and decided in the case of Forster v. Scott (supra) cannot possibly be regarded as any precedent, for the grant of a judgment declaring the statute invalid, unless from the facts here presented the court as matter of law would be constrained to draw the inference that the conditions which the Legislature has sought to impose upon the grant of a permit for the use of a small part of plaintiff's land, creates a limitation upon its use "to the diminution of the value of the land."

No inference of law, indeed no inference of fact, that the attempted condition has affected or will affect the use to which the plaintiff's land will be put or has diminished the value of the land, may be drawn from the stipulated facts. There is no suggestion that a plot of nineteen thousand square feet cannot be suitably improved and put to the most profitable use by the erection of a building which does not encroach upon the small portions which may be used hereafter to widen the street. Sometimes land owners in a particular district assume mutual obligations to set back buildings some distance from the streets. Sometimes such obligations are imposed by zoning ordinance. Sometimes an owner does so voluntarily because he believes that such a setback is the best use for the land immediately abutting on the street. The plaintiff or any successor in title to the property could use the land within the bed of the widened street for such purpose even without a permit. It may be the best use to which that land could be put, even if no map had been adopted, and there were no probability that the city would in time widen the street. Certainly it cannot be said that owners of property do not receive any benefit from the adoption of general maps or plans for the development of city streets, if they can develop their land with some assurance that other owners will not be permitted to frustrate the plan, maliciously or unreasonably. Whether the State may impose conditions for the issuance of permits in order to protect the integrity of the plan of a city where it appears that such conditions interfere with a reasonable use to which the land would otherwise be put or diminishes the value of the land, should not now be decided. Without proof that the imposition of such conditions has deprived an owner of land of some benefit he would otherwise derive from the land, there can be no deprivation of property for which compensation should be made.

Solicitude for the protection of the rights of private property against encroachment by government for a supposed public benefit does not justify the courts in declaring invalid a public law which serves a public purpose, because ten years after it has been on the statute books a single owner, without proof, or even claim, of actual injury, asserts that he has been deprived of his property.

The judgment of the Appellate Division should be reversed and that of the Special Term affirmed, with costs in this court and in the Appellate Division.

NIGRO v. PLANNING BOARD OF BOROUGH OF SADDLE RIVER

Superior Court of New Jersey, Appellate Division, 1989.
237 N.J.Super. 305, 567 A.2d 1010.

PER CURIAM.

This is an appeal by a planning board from a final judgment of the Law Division reversing its denial of an application for preliminary subdivision approval as unreasonable, arbitrary and capricious. Defendant Saddle River Planning Board contends the street layout of the proposed subdivision did not conform to the officially adopted official map; that the official map was statutorily conclusive with respect to the street location; that it therefore could not lawfully approve a proposal that failed to conform to the official map; and that *ergo,* of necessity, its action could not have been unreasonable, arbitrary or capricious. We agree.

This litigation involves a 25.5 acre tract in Saddle River which is still devoted to farming. It is essentially surrounded by the rear lots of developed residential properties containing at least two acres. Importantly to this case, it is bounded to the north by lots facing Glenwood Drive and to the south by lots facing Twin Brooks Road.

Plaintiff James Nigro is the contract purchaser of some eight acres on the western side of the undeveloped tract. The present owners, the Demarests, are unwilling to sell the remaining 17.5 acres upon which they plan to continue their farming operation. Nigro applied to the Planning Board for preliminary approval of a major subdivision in which four new residential lots would be created in the western part of the Demarest tract. The lots in the proposed subdivision conform with the required areas and frontages but the proposed street access does not conform to that shown in the existing master plan and official map. Nigro proposes to provide access by the construction of a new street running north from Twin Brooks Road; the official map shows access to the Demarest tract will be provided by a proposed street running south from Glenwood Drive. * * *

The Planning Board denied the application upon findings, *inter alia,* that the proposed subdivision was inconsistent with the master plan and the official map. In its conclusions, it properly identified the basic issue.

> The basic problem arises in that the property owner wishes to develop the property in a manner different than that recognized in the Master Plan and Official Map of the municipality. Those documents provide for development of the tract from Glenwood Drive. The property owner has chosen to sell off the portion of the property in question which is located some distance from the roadway access to the property at Glenwood Drive. The applicant has been able to acquire property on Twin Brooks Road and provide an area of access by way of public street. The basic conflict arises in creating a public street in an area where single family residential homes exist where no street was ever contemplated, and in a location not conforming to the planning process of the municipality which clearly contemplated development from Glenwood Drive.

The trial judge considered the street locations as shown in the master plan and official map as proposed locations—merely tentative proposals for later discussion and consideration. They were, she concluded, nonbinding. In her view, the evidence showed good planning reasons for the development of the property from the south. She found the action of the Planning Board to be arbitrary and capricious and remanded the matter with directions to grant the requested subdivision approval.

We are satisfied that the trial judge's action in treating the official map as tentative—as merely showing a nonbinding proposed rights-of-way—was error. Such is not the law. The legislature has decreed to the contrary.

> The official map shall be deemed conclusive with respect to the location and width of streets and public drainage ways and the location and extent of flood control basins and public areas, whether or not such streets, ways, basins or areas are improved or unimproved or are in actual physical existence.
>
> [*N.J.S.A.* 40:55D–32]

The language is clear and unambiguous. We are not at liberty to construe it otherwise. *See Service Armament Co. v. Hyland,* 70 *N.J.* 550, 556, 362 A.2d 13 (1976); *Gangemi v. Berry,* 25 *N.J.* 1, 10, 134 A.2d 1 (1957).

Moreover, this clear meaning construction is supported by an examination of the nature of an official map. New Jersey early accepted the notion of planning the systematic physical development of a community. *See Kligman v. Lautman,* 53 *N.J.* 517, 534, 251 A.2d 745 (1969); Cunningham, *Control of Land Use in New Jersey,* 15 *Rut.L.Rev.* 1, 2–3 (1960). Municipal planning has been authorized since 1930. *Ibid.* And from the beginning New Jersey permitted the adoption, by ordinance, of an official map to be deemed conclusive with respect to the location and width of streets, parks and playgrounds; *Mansfield & Swett v. West Orange,* 120 *N.J.L.* 145, 149, 198 A. 225 (Sup.Ct.1938). This concept has been continued and is presently contained in Article 5 of the Municipal Land Use Law. *N.J.S.A.* 40:55D–32 to 34. Unlike other planning devices, the official map forecasts with precision the location of streets, drainage ways, parks and playgrounds so as to provide some continuity in the planning process. *See* 5 Williams, *American Planning Law* § 155 (1985) at 325–326. It not only provides a blueprint of the size and location of such existing and proposed public uses but protects proposed sites from other use and guides the development of land in accordance with the preconceived lines for sound and orderly growth. *See* 4 Anderson, *American Law of Zoning 2nd* § 24.02 (1977). It has been described as "a device for putting some teeth on the otherwise advisory effect of certain aspects of a master plan." *See Kligman v. Lautman, supra,* 53 *N.J.* at 535, n. 2, 251 A.2d 745. Unlike other planning devices, the official map represents solemn action by the governing body which adopts it by ordinance after public hearing. *See* Bernstein, *The Impact of the New Official Map on Municipalities,* New Jersey Municipalities (February 1955) 23. It can be fairly characterized as the skeletal framework upon which the community can develop and grow.

The integrity of this framework is a repeated theme. No structures can be built on the bed of a proposed street. *N.J.S.A.* 40:55D–34. In general, buildings must be on lots which abut streets appearing on the official map. *N.J.S.A.* 40:55D–35. *See also* Bernstein, *supra.* This is not to say that lots cannot be developed which do not abut such a street.

Streets which appear on a planning board approved plat are sufficient, *ibid.*, but by implication such streets are intended to fill out the skeleton, not conflict with it. *See Levin v. Livingston Tp.*, 35 *N.J.* 500, 511, 173 *A.*2d 391 (1961). It is significant that the legislature provided hardship relief from the bar to construction in the bed of a proposed street. *N.J.S.A.* 40:55D–34, but made no similar provision for street alignment. In the case of construction in a proposed street bed, the relief must interfere with the planned street as little as practicable. *N.J.S.A.* 40:55D–34. Amendments, *i.e.*, a restructuring of the skeleton, are for the governing body. *N.J.S.A.* 40:55D–32. Whether the official map should be amended to provide access to the tract which plaintiff seeks to develop is a matter for the governing body.

In sum, we are satisfied that the Planning Board could not lawfully approve plaintiff's application because it conflicted with the official map. Its action was proper and must be sustained.

Reversed.

LAKE CITY CORPORATION v. CITY OF MEQUON

Supreme Court of Wisconsin, 1997.
207 Wis.2d 155, 558 N.W.2d 100.

N. PATRICK CROOKS, J.

The City of Mequon (Mequon) seeks review of a published decision of the court of appeals, which reversed and remanded a judgment of the Circuit Court for Ozaukee County, Joseph D. McCormack, Judge. The court of appeals held that, under Wis. Stat. § 236.13(1)(c) (1991–92) a local master plan is consistent with an official map only to the extent the master plan reflects issues encompassed in the official map. Accordingly, the court of appeals held that Mequon's Plan Commission (Plan Commission) improperly denied preliminary plat approval to Lake City Corporation (Lake City) on the grounds that the plat conflicted with an element contained only in the master plan. We conclude that, under § 236.13(1)(c), a master plan is consistent with an official map if any common elements contained in both the master plan and official map are not contradictory. We further conclude that a master plan is consistent with an official map even if the master plan contains additional elements that the official map does not. We therefore hold that a city plan commission may rely on an element contained solely in a master plan to reject plat approval. Thus, we reverse the decision of the court of appeals.

However, it does not necessarily follow that a master plan is inconsistent with an official map if the master plan contains elements that the official map does not. A master plan, pursuant to Wis. Stat. § 62.23(2), is likely to contain additional elements. Yet, a master plan is not incompatible with an official map simply because the master plan contains additional elements. So long as any issues addressed in both a master plan and an official map are not contradictory, the master plan is consistent with the official map.

We additionally accept Mequon's interpretation because it gives effect to the words "master plan" in Wis. Stat. § 236.13(1)(c), whereas Lake City's interpretation does not. Under Lake City's interpretation, a plan commission can rely on a master plan only to the limited extent that it reflects issues contained in an official map. Accordingly, the words "master plan" are rendered superfluous, because the master plan serves as nothing more than a conduit to the official map. If the legislature had intended such a result, it need not have included the words "master plan" in the statute; it could have simply included the words "official map."

We further reject Lake City's proffered interpretation because it leads to an illogical result. Under Wis. Stat. § 236.11, a final plat is entitled to approval only if it "conforms substantially ... to local plans ... adopted as authorized by law...." The reference in § 236.11 to local (master) plans is not qualified by reference to an official map. Accordingly, if we were to accept Lake City's interpretation, this would result in the following: under § 236.11 a plan commission would have authority to deny final plat approval based on any element contained in a master plan, whereas under § 236.13(1)(c) it would have authority to deny preliminary plat approval based on an element contained in a master plan only if the element was similarly contained in an official map. Not only is this result absurd, but it also directly contradicts § 236.13(1)(c). Section 236.13(1)(c) explicitly applies to preliminary and final plats, and therefore indicates that a plan commission's authority to review both preliminary and final plats under ch. 236 should be substantially similar.

Application of Lake City's interpretation would lead to an additional illogical result. Pursuant to Wis. Stat. §§ 62.23(2), (3), and (6)(b), a city is not required to have an official map, nor is a municipality prohibited from having a master plan in the absence of an official map. Under Lake City's interpretation of Wis. Stat. § 236.13(1)(c), if a municipality has only a master plan, then the master plan could never serve as the basis for the denial of preliminary plat approval, since none of the issues addressed in the master plan would be similarly addressed in the (non-existent) official map. Therefore, in these circumstances, § 236.13(1)(c) would be rendered a nullity. Again, this result defies common sense, because the plan commission could then deny final plat approval based upon any element contained in the master plan under Wis. Stat. § 236.11. * * *

Finally, we conclude that the 1957 interpretive commentary to Wis. Stat. § 236.13 supports Mequon's interpretation of this statute. The interpretive commentary states: "The master plan standing alone has no legal teeth. But for plat approval purposes 236.13(1) puts legal teeth into the relatively few master plans that do exist in this state." Jacob H. Beuscher, Interpretive Commentary [1957], Wis. Stat. Ann. § 236.13 (West 1987 & Supp.1996). Mequon's interpretation is consistent with the legislature's intent to put "legal teeth" into master plans, because it allows city plan commissions to continue to rely on master plans to deny plat approval. * * *

III.

In Chapter 236, the legislature has delegated the power to approve subdivision plats to municipalities. * * * In particular, the legislature has given municipalities the discretion to delegate their plat approval power to city plan commissions. Where a municipality has delegated such power, as is the case here, the city plan commission has the power to deny plat approval based on an element contained in a master plan under Wis. Stat. § 236.13(1)(c).

However, in Wis. Stat. § 236.13(1)(c), the legislature did not indicate that a plan commission's ability to rely on a master plan is limited by zoning ordinances. If the legislature had intended this, it could have easily qualified the language in § 236.13(1)(c) by requiring that a master plan be consistent with zoning ordinances in order to serve as a basis for denial of plat approval. It is clear that the legislature knew how to accomplish this goal, since it included similar qualifying language in this very same statute. See § 236.13(1)(c). Furthermore, the legislature also has specified that its grant of zoning power to city councils "may not be deemed a limitation on any power granted elsewhere." Wis. Stat. § 62.23(7)(a). Thus, because the statutes do not indicate that the legislature intended zoning ordinances to limit a city plan commission's authority to deny plat approval based on a master plan, we are not persuaded by Lake City's argument.

* * *

Zoning regulations and subdivision controls are not only adopted and administered by separate agencies, but are authorized by separate enabling acts which may be unlike in their requirements for enactment of regulations and their procedure for enforcement or relief. Thus, the authority of the agency assigned to plat review may not be limited by the zoning regulations.

Accordingly, the court held that "[a]s long as the regulation is authorized by and within the purposes of ch. 236, the fact that it may also fall under the zoning power does not preclude a local government from enacting the regulation pursuant to the conditions and procedures of ch. 236." Thus, * * * the power of a plan commission which is authorized to review plats is not limited or detracted by zoning regulations. * * *

In summary, we hold that Wis. Stat. § 236.13(1)(c) authorizes a city plan commission to deny approval of a plat that conflicts with a local master plan, so long as any common elements contained in both the master plan and official map are not contradictory. We further conclude that a master plan is consistent with an official map even if the master plan contains additional elements that the official map does not. We therefore hold that a city plan commission may rely on an element contained solely in a master plan to reject plat approval. Applying this holding to the present case, we conclude that the Plan Commission had the authority to deny approval of Lake City's proposed preliminary plat, because this plat conflicted with Mequon's newly revised master plan. The cause is remanded to the circuit court for the purpose of reinstatement of its judgment

The decision of the court of appeals is reversed and cause remanded.

Notes

1. The Bartholomew street map for Rochester, N.Y., was involved in Vangellow v. City of Rochester, 190 Misc. 128, 71 N.Y.S.2d 672 (Sup.Ct. 1947). There, old buildings were built right up to the street line. The map required a 10-foot setback. Plaintiffs, who proposed to tear down and reconstruct the buildings, wanted to build showrooms right up to the street line. They brought this action for a declaratory judgment declaring the map invalid as applied to the plaintiffs. Held: The official map as applied to the plaintiffs is not totally void and the court has no jurisdiction until the plaintiffs have exhausted their administrative review remedy before the Rochester zoning board of appeals.

See also S.S. Kresge Co. v. City of New York, 194 Misc. 645, 87 N.Y.S.2d 313 (Sup.Ct.1949); Jensen v. City of New York, 42 N.Y.2d 1079, 399 N.Y.S.2d 645, 369 N.E.2d 1179 (1977); St. Luke's German Evangelical Lutheran Church v. City of Rochester, 115 Misc.2d 199, 453 N.Y.S.2d 1012 (1982).

In Ward v. Bennett, 79 N.Y.2d 394, 583 N.Y.S.2d 179, 592 N.E.2d 787 (1992) the New York Court of Appeals held that a landowner denied a building permit to construct a single-family house in the bed of a mapped but unopened street could bring a takings claim for compensation even though the city argued that the owner had not exhausted the available remedy of seeking to have the street de-mapped; the court said that the case was "ripe" for judicial review. This holding seems inconsistent with that in the Vangellow case, supra.

2. In Grosso v. Board of Adjustment, 137 N.J.L. 630, 61 A.2d 167 (1948) the official map as hastily amended after the plaintiff applied for a building permit placed plaintiff's entire property in the bed of a proposed street. The court had little difficulty holding that the map was invalid as applied to the plaintiff. Compare Barsel v. Woodbridge Twp. Zoning Bd. of Adjustment, 189 N.J.Super. 75, 458 A.2d 1303 (1983). Also see Barile v. City of Port Republic, 186 N.J.Super. 587, 453 A.2d 284 (1982).

3. In a report prepared for the U.S. Bureau of Public Roads, Professors Daniel Mandelker and Graham Waite summarize official map enabling acts for the 28 states that have such statutes. (Mandelker and Waite, A Study of Future Acquisition and Reservation of Highway Rights-of-Way (Mimeo prepared under Contract CPR 11–8006, 1963) Charts 2 and 3, Part I, Appendix). In general these statutes are built on one of three models: (1) the so-called Standard Act; (2) the Bettman model; and (3) the Bassett–Williams model.

The Standard Act calls for payment for the reserved rights-of-way from the time of reservation. As might be expected, little use has been made of this procedure in the four states that have enacted it into law.

Both the Bettman and Bassett–Williams acts authorize the mapping of future streets and widening lines through exercise of the police power. Both include provisions intended to take care of hardship cases, but hardship is defined differently in the two acts.

The Bettman act requires a showing (1) that a reasonable return cannot be earned from the property including the mapped part, or (2) that balancing the interests of the municipality against the interests of the owner, considerations of equity and justice dictate the grant of a permit.

The Bassett–Williams model requires not only a showing that the land in the bed of the mapped street is not yielding a fair return, but it also authorizes refusal of a building permit where the applicant will not be substantially damaged by placing his building outside the mapped street. See, for example, State ex rel. Miller v. Manders, 2 Wis.2d 365, 86 N.W.2d 469 (1957).

These hardship standards should be compared with the standards for zoning variances taken up in Chapter VII. It may be that a city is well advised to use its zoning power to establish set-back lines, rather than establish widening lines under the official map act. See Kucirek and Beuscher, Wisconsin's Official Map Act, 1957 Wis.L.Rev. 176, 196–197 and Phillips v. Board of Adjustment, 44 N.J.Super. 491, 130 A.2d 866 (1957).

Notice the hardship provisions of the Bettman and the Bassett–Williams acts are phrased in terms of *new* buildings. Nothing is said about alterations of buildings which were already in place when the land was mapped. See Golden v. Aldell Realty Corp., 70 N.Y.S.2d 341 (Sup.Ct.Queens 1947); Agliata v. D'Agostino, 124 N.Y.S.2d 212 (Sup.Ct.Queens 1953); and Kucirek and Beuscher, Wisconsin's Official Map Law, 1957 Wis.L.Rev. 176, 208–210.

Though based generally on the Bassett–Williams or Bettman models the following states have enabling acts which do not classify neatly under one or the other: California, Connecticut, Kentucky (Jefferson County), Maine, Michigan, Minnesota, Missouri, North Carolina, Oklahoma, South Carolina, Texas and Washington. Other states' enabling acts can be grouped as follows:

Standard Act	Bettman	Bassett–Williams
Alabama	Alabama (for counties over 400,000)	Delaware
Colorado		Massachusetts
Kentucky	Georgia	New Jersey
Maryland	New Hampshire	New York
	New Mexico	Pennsylvania (for 2nd class townships)
	Tennessee	Wisconsin
	Utah	
	Wyoming	

Instead of providing variance procedures for hardship cases, it is also possible to map future streets and widening lines and protect them by a "first right of refusal." Such statutes exist in at least 12 states and unlike hardship laws several of them apply to the mapping of major highways in the open country. Under right of refusal statutes, the governing unit has a specified period of time, 30, 60 or 90 days, for example, after the owner seeks a building permit or indicates an intention to sell within which to buy him out on a voluntary basis or bring condemnation. See Mandelker and Waite, "A Study of Future Acquisition and Reservation of Highway Rights-of-Way" (Mimeo, prepared under Contract CPA 11–8006, 1963) Chart 3, Appendix I. For an illustrative statute of this type, see Wis.Stat. § 84.295 (1961); and see Miller v. City of Beaver Falls, 368 Pa. 189, 82 A.2d 34 (1951).

4. Is a person suing for breach of covenants in a warranty deed charged with knowledge or notice of the official map? See Bibber v. Weber, 199 Misc. 906, 102 N.Y.S.2d 945 (1951), affirmed 278 App.Div. 973, 105 N.Y.S.2d 758 (1951).

5. In 2000, the Utah Legislature adopted H.B. 165, the "Transportation Corridor Preservation Act." Among other things, the Act authorizes the adoption of official maps as part of the previously required general plans. The statute defines "official map" as "a map, drawn by government authorities and recorded in county recording offices that ... shows actual and proposed rights-of-way, centerline alignments, and setbacks for highways and other transportation facilities." Utah Code Ann. Sec. 72–5–401 (4). Why did it take so long for Utah to recognize the "official map" for transportation planning purposes? See, Recent Legislative Development VI. Governmental Law, 2000 Utah L. Rev. 953 (2000).

SECTION 3. DEVELOPER AGREEMENTS AND VESTED RIGHTS

A. VESTED RIGHTS

American Planning Association, Growing Smart Legislative Guidebook: Model Statutes for Planning and the Management of Change

(Stuart Meck, ed.) (2002).

EXCERPT FROM CHAPTER 8

Several states have "vesting" statutes intended to protect the legal status of rights obtained at various points in the development review process. Vesting statutes are laws that create criteria for determining when a landowner has achieved or acquired a right to develop his or her property in a particular manner, which cannot be abolished or restricted by regulatory provisions subsequently enacted. This is called a vested right because it is a right that has become fixed ("vested") and cannot be eliminated or amended. Such laws are not the same as "takings" or "property rights" statutes, which either provide for review of regulatory statutes for potential taking effects or lower the threshold amount by which property must be diminished in value by enforcement of a regulation for there to be a compensable taking.

Sec. 3 DEVELOPER AGREEMENTS AND VESTED RIGHTS   539

Vesting statutes are also not the same as development agreement statutes. Though the effect of a development agreement is to fix the government's right to regulate the property in question, the method used is an agreement in which the landowner typically agrees to at least some restrictions that the government could not generally obtain in exchange for his or her obligations becoming fixed (and for other favorable variances from land development regulations). Vesting statutes, in contrast, apply to the generally applicable regulations of land use, and no agreement is needed for the landowner to be able to assert a vested right to develop.

There is a common thread through most existing vesting statutes. For the development rights to be vested, the government must have made a decision and the landowner must have, in good faith, relied, to his or her detriment, on that decision by making some improvement to the land or some other commitment of resources. It is not surprising that these elements are found so frequently, either expressly or implicitly, for the common law has for hundreds of years included the doctrine of estoppel. Estoppel means that when someone does something with the intent that you will rely on their action or statement, and you indeed rely in good faith on that action or statement demonstrate that reliance by some action to your detriment (not a mere statement that you will rely on it), the original party is legally bound by that action or statement. While the doctrine of estoppel is most commonly applied in private disputes, it has also been used by some courts in land-use cases to create a vested right to develop which is protected by the federal and state constitutions. However, some state courts have restricted or denied the applicability of the estoppel doctrine to land-use cases. In some cases, these courts have stated that granting vested rights at all would be an improper restriction on the police power. In other cases, they have ruled that the landowner must demonstrate that the local official upon whose statement or decision he or she relied was within authority to make the statement or decision, as the government is not bound by an official's unauthorized acts. Even where estoppel is applied to land-use decisions and a vested right was recognized, there is a difference of opinion on what sort of government acts and what level of reliance triggers estoppel. It is almost universal across the case law that the reliance must be in the form of "substantial" or "extensive" expenditures or actual construction, but these terms are rarely defined, instead being left to a case-by-case analysis. Also decided on an ad-hoc basis is the more fundamental issue of what sort of government statement, action, or decision could be the basis of estoppel. Is a statement by an official that one will receive approval sufficient? Preliminary approval of a site plan? Final approval of a site plan? Issuance of a building permit?

Further confusing an examination of the case law is the issue of "last-minute" amendments to land development regulations. Some state courts have decided that a development permit application may be subject to an ordinance that was pending in the local legislative process at the time the application was submitted. Courts in some other states have applied estoppel to such pending ordinances, and have not allowed a new or amended regulation to apply to a development permit application where the applicant had made a substantial investment in good-faith reliance on the ordinances in place at the time of application. And some state courts have found that an applicant who was entitled to a development permit under the regulations in place at the time of application could not be denied a permit based on amended regulations even where there was no substantial investment or reliance by the applicant landowner. "Where a project is caught in a change in the law due to denials of successive applications or delays in processing, the court might look askance at a denial based exclusively on the new law." In such states, courts are especially willing to ignore post-application amendments where the court finds that the local government amended its regulations after the application, or delayed the application until the ordinance became effective, with the intent of barring the application.

AVCO COMMUNITY DEVELOPERS, INC. v. SOUTH COAST REGIONAL COMMISSION

Supreme Court of California, 1976.
17 Cal.3d 785, 132 Cal.Rptr. 386, 553 P.2d 546.

Mosk, J.

We are confronted with the apparently irreconcilable conflict between the interests of a land developer who seeks to avoid compliance with a recently enacted law regulating its project, and the interests of the public in assuring development of the property in a manner consistent with the requirements of current law. Specifically, we must decide whether the developer of a subdivision may acquire a vested right to construct buildings on its land without a permit from the California Coastal Zone Commission (the commission) if it has subdivided and graded the property and made certain improvements on the land, such as installing utilities, but had not applied for or received a building permit for any structures on the land before February 1, 1973.

Section 27400 of the California Coastal Zone Conservation Act of 1972 hereinafter called the Act, provides that on or after February 1, 1973, any person desiring to perform any development within the coastal zone must obtain a permit from the commission. Section 27404, at the time relevant to the events in the present case, qualified this requirement by allowing a builder to proceed after February 1 if he had obtained a vested right to do so by having secured a building permit and in good faith diligently commenced construction and performed substantial work in reliance thereon before the effective date of the Act.

Petitioner, Avco Community Developers, Inc. (Avco) owns 7,936 acres of land in Orange County which it is developing as the Laguna Niguel Planned Community. Of this total, 836 acres, known as the Capron property, was purchased by Avco in 1968. Approximately 473 acres of the Capron property lies within the coastal zone. Our concern in this proceeding is with 74 acres of the land within the permit area, designated as tract 7479.

In 1971, the county, at the instance of Avco, zoned 5,234 acres of the Laguna Niguel project, including tract 7479, as a "Planned Community Development" containing a total of 18,925 residential units. The development was to proceed according to "Planned Community District Regulations" enacted by the county. In 1972, a final map was approved for tract 7479, dividing it into 27 parcels, devoted largely to multiple residential uses. In that year the county issued a rough grading permit which did not refer to grading for any specific building site.

Avco undertook a number of studies for the development of the tract, and proceeded to subdivide and grade the property. By February 1, 1973, pursuant to approvals issued for such purposes by the county, Avco had completed or was in the process of constructing storm drains, culverts, street improvements, utilities, and similar facilities for the tract as well as for the remainder of the Capron property. Under the county's building code, a permit could not be obtained until grading had been completed. Avco had not completed the rough grading by February 1, 1973, and it neither submitted building plans for the tract nor obtained a permit to construct any structures. Before that date, the company had spent $2,082,070 and incurred liabilities of $740,468 for the development of the tract; it is losing $7,113.46 a day, largely due to loss of anticipated rental value, as a result of its inability to proceed with construction of buildings on the tract.

Avco applied to the commission for an exemption from the permit requirements of the Act, claiming that it had a vested right to complete development, and, when its application was denied, sought a writ of mandate to compel the commission to grant the exemption. The trial court, after a hearing in which the evidence consisted entirely of the record of the proceedings before the commission, declined to issue the writ.

The court found that the approvals granted by the county for the development of tract 7479 led Avco to reasonably expect that it would be allowed to construct buildings on the tract "without further discretionary governmental approval," and that the subdivision improvements were installed in good faith reliance upon the county's actions. The court also found that Avco had a detailed plan for the buildings to be constructed on the tract. A model of the structures intended to be built on the tract had been completed in July 1971, and the court found that the maximum number, size and type of buildings "allowable" on the tract could be ascertained by reference to the tract map, the planned community district regulations, and the model.

Although the court opined that fairness suggested Avco be allowed to complete development of the tract in accordance with the map, the regulations and the model, nevertheless because Avco did not have a building permit the trial court felt compelled to hold that it did not have a vested right to construct the buildings, and thus was not exempt from the permit requirement of the Act. Avco asserts that it had a vested right to construct buildings on tract 7479, that the commission is estopped to claim otherwise, and that the Act is unconstitutional.

Vested Rights

It has long been the rule in this state and in other jurisdictions that if a property owner has performed substantial work and incurred substantial liabilities in good faith reliance upon a permit issued by the government, he acquires a vested right to complete construction in accordance with the terms of the permit. Once a landowner has secured a vested right the government may not, by virtue of a change in the zoning laws, prohibit construction authorized by the permit upon which he relied. Here Avco asserts that it had a vested right to construct buildings on tract 7479 without permission from the commission because prior to February 1, 1973, when the coastal permit requirement took effect, it spent large sums of money to construct subdivision improvements and grade the tract, in reliance on several county authorizations, and that these improvements were undertaken and approvals issued for the purpose of constructing buildings. Thus, Avco relies upon the doctrine of vested rights as defined in the common law and in the Act itself.

Vested Rights Under Common Law

Evaluation of this claim requires a determination of the point in the development process at which a landowner can be said to have acquired a vested right to construct buildings on his land. The commission contends, subject to an exception to be discussed infra, that a builder may not acquire a vested right prior to the issuance of a building permit, whereas Avco asserts that in the context of a subdivision a developer's right to construct buildings vests when it has subdivided the land and installed subdivision improvements such as roads and utilities pursuant to governmental authorization. * * *

[N]either the existence of a particular zoning nor work undertaken pursuant to governmental approvals preparatory to construction of buildings can form the basis of a vested right to build a structure which does not comply with the laws applicable at the time a building permit is issued. By zoning the property or issuing approvals for work preliminary to construction the government makes no representation to a landowner that he will be exempt from the zoning laws in effect at the subsequent time he applies for a building permit or that he may construct particular structures on the property, and thus the government cannot be estopped to enforce the laws in effect when the permit is issued.

With commendable candor, the commission concedes that it does not deem a building permit to be an absolute requirement under all circumstances for acquisition of a vested right. It suggests that in rare situations the government may grant another type of permit, such as a conditional use permit, which affords substantially the same specificity and definition to a project as a building permit, and that in such instances a builder might acquire a vested right even though the document was not designated a "building permit." * * * Not only had Avco failed to apply to the county for permits for specific buildings by the date the requirements of the Act became effective, but the county was not advised of such elementary details as the dimension or height of the buildings to be constructed on tract 7479. The trial court's finding that "the maximum number, size and type of buildings that would be allowable to be constructed upon Tract 7479" could be ascertained by reference to the tract map, the regulations, and the model of the buildings does not support a conclusion to the contrary.

The model was prepared by Avco for its own use and was not submitted to the county. An examination of the tract map and the regulations fails to disclose the number and size of the buildings to be constructed on the tract. The map merely designates certain areas for multiple residential use; the regulations for multiple residential structures are stated in the most general terms, and they do not refer to any identifiable buildings to be constructed on any specific lots.

Thus, on the date the Act became effective, the county did not know, much less had it approved, plans indicating such matters as the placement of the buildings to be built on the tract, the size of the proposed buildings, the number of apartments of specified size, or how high the buildings would rise, there being no legal height limitation for multiple residential units. Indeed, it was not even clear how many units would be built on the tract.

Under these circumstances, it would be impossible to determine the precise scope of any purported right to construct buildings on the tract, and we would be compelled to deny the claim of a common law vested right * * *

* * *

The contention that Avco was entitled to a building permit because the county would have been compelled to issue it upon mere application has no merit. The Orange County Building Code (§ 302(a)) provides that a building permit may not issue unless the plans conform not only to the structural requirements of the code but to "other pertinent laws and ordinances." This provision codifies the general rule that a builder must comply with the laws which are in effect at the time a building permit is issued, including the laws which were enacted after application for the permit. A landowner which has not even applied for a permit cannot be in a better position merely because it had previously received permission to subdivide its property and made certain improvements on the land.

* * *

Avco insists that the existence and scope of vested rights is a question of fact for the trial court, that we must accept the court's findings as true, and that they lead inevitably to the conclusion that it has acquired a vested right to construct buildings on tract 7479 without a permit from the commission.

Even if we assume arguendo that a building permit is not required in order to acquire a vested right to construct particular buildings in every case, Avco cannot prevail. As we have seen, although the trial court found that Avco had a detailed plan for the buildings to be erected on the tract, the county was not aware of and had not approved such a plan, and the preliminary approvals which it did grant did not refer to any identifiable buildings. In view of this central premise, the further findings of the trial court that Avco reasonably expected that it would be allowed to construct "buildings" on the tract "without further discretionary governmental approval" and that by granting the preliminary approvals the county represented to Avco that it would be permitted to construct "buildings ... upon obtaining building permits" are not sufficient to sustain a conclusion that Avco had secured a vested right to build structures which the county did not approve and as to which it had no detailed information. * * *

If we were to accept the premise that the construction of subdivision improvements or the zoning of the land for a planned community are sufficient to afford a developer a vested right to construct buildings on the land in accordance with the laws in effect at the time the improvements are made or the zoning enacted, there could be serious impairment of the government's right to control land use policy. In some cases the inevitable consequence would be to freeze the zoning laws applicable to a subdivision or a planned unit development as of the time these events occurred.

Thus tracts or lots in tracts which had been subdivided decades ago, but upon which no buildings have been constructed could be free of all zoning laws enacted subsequent to the time of the subdivision improvement, unless facts constituting waiver, abandonment, or opportunity for amortization of the original vested right could be shown. In such situations, the result would be that these lots, as well as others in similar subdivisions created more recently or lots established in future subdivisions, would be impressed with an exemption of indeterminate duration from the requirements of any future zoning laws. To illustrate: let us hypothesize that because of mounting costs, decreasing demand or innumerable other potential causes, Avco does not build multiple residential units on tract 7479 for a number of years. If we were to accept its premise, the tract would be exempted not only from the current requirements of the Act, but from all zoning laws enacted for an indefinite period in the future. It is no response to these inherent evils to assert that this builder presently intends to construct its multiple residential units expeditiously.

* * *

The judgment is affirmed.

B. DEVELOPER AGREEMENTS

American Planning Association, Growing Smart Legislative Guidebook: Model Statutes for Planning and the Management of Change

(Stuart Meck, ed.) (2002).

EXCERPT FROM CHAPTER 8

A development agreement is "a statutorily authorized, negotiated agreement between a local government and a private developer that establishes the respective rights and obligations of each party with respect to certain planning issues or problems related to a specific proposed development or redevelopment project." (Erin J. Johnson, "Development Agreements: Planning Perspectives," in Development Agreements: Analysis, Colorado Case Studies, Commentary, 3) There are times when a local government and a developer may both wish to vary in some way from the development and land use choices possible under the existing land development regulations and have those variations be fully enforceable. A development agreement allows both flexibility and certainty. It permits flexibility by allowing terms and conditions that are different from and more detailed than the requirements of land development regulations and the statutes authorizing them. It brings certainty by making all elements of the agreement enforceable, against the local government as well as the developer. Thus, it is superior to informal agreements that are only worth as much as the good faith of the parties.

BOLLECH v. CHARLES COUNTY, MARYLAND

United States Court of Appeals, Fourth Circuit, 2003.
69 Fed.Appx. 178 (unpublished).

PER CURIAM.

Appellants Bollech, Haapala, Mesisinger and Winson (the "Trustees") own land on which they planned to develop residential units. In 1989, the Trustees entered into a Development Agreement with Charles County and the Cliffton Potomac Associates Ltd. Partnerships I–X (the "Newburg Station Owners") for the residential development of land.

The Development Agreement's purpose was to assure the timely and orderly provision of water and sanitary sewer facilities to support (1) the proposed residential development on the Trustees' land (the "Potomac Cliffs") and land owned by the Newburg Station Owners (the "Newburg Station"), and (2) a portion of existing developments on adjacent land. The Trustees and the Newburg Station Owners (collectively, the "Property Owners") were allowed under the Development Agreement to develop residential units in prescribed stages. In return, the Property Owners agreed to construct, within a certain amount of time, adequate public facilities (including upgrading, repairing and expanding the existing sewer plant) to serve the proposed residential development and a portion of the existing development on adjacent property.

In 1999, the Trustees submitted an application for a preliminary plan for development. The County refused to accept the application because amendments to the local zoning regulations prevented the County from approving the application. The Trustees claim the Development Agreement provides that the Trustees may develop the residential units on their land irrespective of changes in County land use regulations. In response, the County claims that the County is no longer obligated under the Development Agreement to approve the Trustees' development applications for building permits.

The Trustees brought suit against the County for (1) impairment of the obligation of contract in violation of the Contracts Clause, U.S. Const. Art. I, § 10, cl. 1; and (2) breach of contract. The district court entered an order granting the County's motion for summary judgment and denying the Trustees' cross-motion for summary judgment. In a memorandum opinion, the district court stated that the Development Agreement no longer imposed an enforceable obligation on the County because the Trustees did not ensure the provision of adequate sewer and water facilities within the time period required by the Development Agreement.

* * *

The Contracts Clause states that "No State shall . . . pass any . . . Law impairing the Obligation of Contracts." U.S. Const. Art. I, § 10, cl. 1. In order to prove a violation of the Contracts Clause, a plaintiff must first prove that there is an enforceable contract that the government has impaired in some manner. in order to prove that there is an enforceable contract, there is no violation of the Contracts Clause.

If there is an enforceable contractual obligation that has been impaired, the plaintiff must prove that the impairment was substantial. If the impairment is substantial, the court then determine if the government action giving rise to the substantial impairment was reasonable and necessary to protect an important public interest.

The County claims there was no enforceable contractual obligation to the Trustees at the time of the alleged impairment, 1999. * * * The language of the Development Agreement indicates (1) that the Trustees had an obligation to expand and repair the existing sewage treatment plant as a predicate for development of the proposed residential units and (2) that the development of Potomac Cliffs was to take place by a specified date in 1994. In return, the County promised, among other things, to issue building permits upon application and upon compliance with applicable regulations, in accordance with the schedule set out in the Development Agreement.

The Development Agreement unambiguously imposes obligations on the Trustees. For instance, the Development Agreement states in § 4 .1:

Sec. 3 **DEVELOPER AGREEMENTS AND VESTED RIGHTS** 547

The development of the property shall be supported by adequate levels of public facilities, including sanitary sewer facilities, water facilities, roadway facilities, stormwater management facilities.... All public facilities necessary to meet adequacy requirements shall be provided and initially financed by the property owners. Owners ... of the Potomac Cliffs Tract generally are responsible for providing public facilities to be situated on that tract.

Under § 4.2.3 of the Development Agreement, the Newburg Station Owners had primary responsibility for the construction of sewer and water facilities, but § 4.2.2(c) states that the Trustees had responsibility for the construction of the facilities if the Newburg Station Owners failed to construct the facilities and the Trustees still planned to develop Potomac Cliffs.

In addition, § 3.2 of the Development Agreement requires the property owners to develop their property in phases. Section 3.2(a) details the schedule of construction phases in which Potomac Cliffs was to be developed. Full development of Potomac Cliffs by the Trustees was scheduled to be completed in 1994.

There is no factual dispute as to whether the Trustees developed Potomac Cliffs by 1994; not only had the Trustees failed to develop Potomac Cliffs by the specified date, but the Trustees failed to ensure the development of adequate sewer and water facilities as required by the Development Agreement in Section 4.2.6(a), which states, in part: "Construction of the additional capacity [to the existing sewer facility] shall be pursued in a timely and reasonable manner, subject to timely approval by the appropriate authorities, so as to meet the schedule for development set forth in Section 3.2 of this Agreement."

The Trustees' failure to meet their obligation under the Development Agreement released the County from the County's obligations under the Agreement. * * * A material failure to perform by one party "prevents performance of [the other party's remaining duties] from becoming due, at least temporarily, and it discharges those duties if it has not been cured during the time in which performance can occur." Restatement (Second) of Contracts § 237 cmt. a. The County was discharged from any enforceable contractual obligation after the Trustees failed to perform within the time period specified in the Development Agreement. * * *

The Trustees argue that the district court erred in finding that the Development Agreement imposes a six-year termination date. The Trustees point out that the Development Agreement expressly required construction to extend over a period of ten years. In addition, the Trustees argue that because the Development Agreement had no express termination date, the Development Agreement is valid for a reasonable amount of time.

The district court did not find that the Development Agreement terminated after six years. The district court recognized that the Trustees were obligated to develop the residential units on their property within the time specified in the Development Agreement under § 3.2. Section 3.2(a) requires that the Potomac Cliffs area be developed by August 12, 1994. In addition, § 4.2.6(a) requires the construction of additional capacity at the existing sewer facility in time to meet the schedule in Section 3.2. Section 4.2.6(a) also requires that the design documents for the construction of additional capacity be submitted for approval to the appropriate authorities no later than six months after the effective date of the Agreement. The Trustees did not meet their obligations within the specified time periods. The Trustees' failure to perform released the County from the County's obligations after the specified time periods elapsed.

The reference to the ten year construction period does not extend the period in which the Trustees can perform. Section 3.2 states that "[t]he construction schedule shall extend over a period of a minimum of ten (10) years, commencing, for the purpose of this Agreement, August 12, 1988." This language applies to the development of both Potomac Cliffs and Newbury Station as a unit. Section 3.2 lays out the phases, within the ten year period, in which each property must be developed. Section 3.2(a) lays out the plan for Potomac Cliffs, which involves five phases, the last ending in August 1994. Section 3.2(b) lays out the plan for Newbury Station, which involves nine phases, the last ending in August 1998.

The County's obligation to the Trustees were discharged after August 1994. The district court correctly held that there was no enforceable contract obligation between the County and the Trustees at the time the alleged violation occurred.

* * *

The district court held that there was no breach of contract for the same reason there was no Contracts Clause violation: at the time of the alleged violation, there was no enforceable contractual obligation against the County. The above analysis validates the district court's decision.
* * *

AFIRMED.

Notes

1. Developers typically invest a substantial amount of capital into subdivisions and other types of developments. Is it appropriate at any point in the land development process—which can take years from initial preliminary and final plat approvals to application for the last of the building permits—for developers to know for certain that they will be able to fully build-out their project as envisioned? Why or why not? See, Terry D. Morgan, "Vested Rights Legislation," 34 The Urban Lawyer 131 (Winter 2002).

2. A number of states have adopted statutes to grant vested rights to developers at various stages in the approval process. A key issue is to determine what permit(s) and/or what type of approval(s) will trigger a vested right. For examples of different approaches, see, Ariz. Rev. Stat. § 9–

1201, et. seq.; Cal. Gov't Code § 66498; Colo. Rev. Stat. § 24–68–102, et. seq.; Kan. Stat. § 12–764; N.J. Stat. § 40:55D–49; Or. Rev. Stat. § 227.178; and Va. Code § 15.2–2307. For many states, the answer to this question is found in the common-law of the state. States approaches typically categorized as either "early vesting" or "late vesting" depending upon when in the process the right to develop vests. Some states, such as New York, require that substantial work be completed, e.g., "having the shovel in the ground." See, Downey v. Incorporated Village of Ardsley, 3 A.D.2d 663, 158 N.Y.S.2d 306 (1957) and Hasco Electric Corp. v. Dassler, 144 N.Y.S.2d 857, aff'd 1 A.D.2d 889, 150 N.Y.S.2d 552 (1956). See also, City of Suffolk ex rel. Herbert v Board of Zoning Appeals for the City of Suffolk, 266 Va. 137, 580 S.E.2d 796 (2003).

3. Because of the uncertainties of vested rights, beginning with California in 1979 states began to enact statutes authorizing local governments to enter into developer agreements. California's statute followed on the heels of the decision in Avco Community Developers, Inc. v South Coast Regional Commission. For a fuller discussion of the policy issues surrounding developer agreements, see, Douglas R. Porter and Lindell L. Marsh, eds., *Development Agreements: Practice, Policy, and Prospects* (the Urban Land Institute, 1989). See also, David L. Callies and Julie A. Tappendorf, "Unconstitutional Land Development Conditions and the Development Agreement Solution: Bargaining for Public Facilities After Nollan and Dolan," 51 Case W. Res. L. Rev. 663 (2001) for an excellent discussion legal and constitutional challenges of using developer agreements. For a specific case study on Maryland, see, John J. Delaney, "The Maryland Experience," SH018 ALI–ABA 585 (ALI–ABA Land Use Institute: Planning, Regulation, Litigation, Eminent Domain, and Compensation, August 2002). In Legacy Group v. City of Wasco, 106 Cal.App.4th 1305, 131 Cal.Rptr.2d 460 (2003) the court held that a claim for breach of a development agreement was subject to the same statute of limitations as for contract claims.

Chapter VI

SMART GROWTH AND GROWTH MANAGEMENT

SECTION 1. INTRODUCTION

A. LOCAL LAND USE CONTROLS THAT ACHIEVE SMART GROWTH

"Smart Growth" admits of no clear definition. It provides a popular label for a growth strategy that addresses current concerns about traffic congestion, disappearing open space, non-point source pollution, the high cost of housing, increasing local property taxes, longer commutes, and the diminishing quality of community life. To accomplish smart growth, government must take two related actions. The first is the designation of discrete geographical areas into which private market growth pressures are directed. The second is the designation of other areas for recreation, conservation, and environmental protection. This reduces a complicated subject to its two most essential features and leaves much for further discussion. This focus, however, permits a precise description of how smart growth can be implemented, if a consensus for it is developed.

The balance between land development and conservation that is a standard component of most smart growth and growth management strategies is reflected in this chapter and Chapter VII which discusses local environmental law. In Chapter VI, we touch on the imposition of moratoriums on development, which create time to think under pressure and revise the local land use regime; local and statewide growth management strategies; efforts to preserve agricultural land in rural areas; initiatives to expand or revitalize existing urban and suburban centers; and a few of the more popular innovative land use tools such as floating zones, planned unit development districts, overlay zones, incentives, and performance zoning. These latter techniques are sometimes referred to as neo-Euclidian measures: designed to breathe flexibility into the rigid uniformity of the district-bound zoning approved in Euclid v. Ambler Realty. Chapter VII covers the many types of laws localities are adopting to protect natural resources from the adverse impacts of development. Together, these chapters give the student an introduction to the full range of techniques being used to achieve smart growth objectives.

What is accomplished by directing development to growth areas? The aspiration is to create a sense of community, promote economically viable development, ensure the ease of movement and safety of residents, and preserve open space, natural resources, and sustainable habitats. In 1979, a growth boundary encompassing Portland and 23 surrounding towns was established to comply with Oregon's innovative growth management law.[1] Fifteen miles from city hall, outside the bounded growth area, is the Willamette River Valley, where growth is limited to small-scale development consistent with the predominately agricultural use of the land. Maryland's novel smart growth spending law directs state infrastructure improvements into settled communities and "priority funding areas," which are growth areas designated by county governments.[2]

Concentrating development in designated growth areas, bounded in some specific way, is a necessary factor in the smart growth equation. Bounded growth, however, is not a novel concept. Local governments have traditionally drawn blueprints for growth in the design of their zoning codes. Zoning's primary characteristic is the creation of hard-edged districts that separate land uses into residential, commercial, and industrial zones. Traditional zoning districts separate land uses to advance a number of public purposes. The architects of zoning thought that this approach to community planning protected children in residential districts from commercial and industrial traffic, for example, and protected residential property values by placing noxious and inconsistent uses in distant locations. The zoning enabling acts in most states enable local governments to divide the community into zoning districts and to regulate the density of population, the use of land, and the size, shape, and location of buildings within each district. Although this authority has been used in some communities to impose a grid type of development pattern on the land, with residences separated from retail and commercial areas, zoning itself may be used to designate a variety of growth districts to carry out a local smart growth agenda. Municipalities have designated large parcels of land for mixed-use zones, planned unit development districts, planned residential development areas, and floating zones, as well as conservation areas.

1. American Planning Association, Planning Communities for the 21st Century 49–50 (1999). In 1973, the Oregon legislature passed Senate Bill 10, Or. Rev. Stat. §§ 197.000—197.860 (1991), requiring municipal and county governments to adopt comprehensive plans consistent with state goals. Id. at §§ 197.005(3), 197.010. The growth management objectives of the state's plan are to "geographically bound urban development, provide adequate housing and urban development within the boundaries, and prevent urban encroachment on important natural resource lands outside the boundaries." John M. DeGrove, Lincoln Inst. of Land Policy, Planning & Growth Management in the States 117–120 (1993).

2. Md. Code Ann., State Fin. & Proc. § 5–7B–01 (1995 & Supp. 2000). This legislation (Smart Growth and Neighborhood Conservation Act) encourages bounded development by pledging the state to concentrate its infrastructure and development project funding in "priority funding areas" to ensure that growth occurs in and around existing and carefully planned growth areas. This is balanced by the Rural Legacy Program, Md. Code Ann., Nat. Res. § 5–9A–01 (2000), which directs other state resources to protect agricultural, forest, and natural resource lands.

Perhaps we are moving into an era of "smarter growth," where public policy encourages more compact and integrated land uses to accomplish a number of contemporary public interests, such as the reduction of car travel and air pollution and the rate of consumption of farmland, natural resources, and environmentally sensitive areas. Smart growth advocates see the designation of areas for more compact, mixed-use development as a present imperative, a necessary change in the zoning blueprint needed to address the concerns addressed by the Oregon and Maryland growth management initiatives.

If local governments are to design the basic blueprint for smart growth, how should they proceed? State law provides numerous planning tools for municipalities to use in designating growth and conservation areas. The principal among these, of course, is the comprehensive plan, the ideal document to account for the rational allocation of land use. Local comprehensive plans usually include a statement of goals and objectives regarding the community's physical development and describe the specific actions to be taken to provide for the long-range growth and development of the locality.

Comprehensive plans can, in fact, be quite detailed, incorporating maps, graphs, and studies that can precisely locate designated growth areas and spell out the techniques to be used to encourage development in those areas. This authority is highly elastic, and can be stretched to fit all development contexts, from urban and suburban to rural, where communities wish to control growth. Growth control measures, including goals, objectives, and techniques contained in the comprehensive plan—then adopted into a variety of local laws—were validated over thirty years ago by the Court of Appeals in Golden v. Ramapo.

GOLDEN v. PLANNING BOARD OF TOWN OF RAMAPO

Court of Appeals of New York, 1972.
30 N.Y.2d 359, 334 N.Y.S.2d 138, 285 N.E.2d 291, appeal dismissed
409 U.S. 1003, 93 S.Ct. 440, 34 L.Ed.2d 294.

SCILEPPI, JUDGE.

Both cases arise out of the 1969 amendments to the Town of Ramapo's Zoning Ordinance. * * *

Experiencing the pressures of an increase in population and the ancillary problem of providing municipal facilities and services, the Town of Ramapo, as early as 1964, made application for grant under section 801 of the Housing Act of 1964 (78 U.S.Stat. 769) to develop a master plan. The plan's preparation included a four-volume study of the existing land uses, public facilities, transportation, industry and commerce, housing needs and projected population trends. The proposals appearing in the studies were subsequently adopted pursuant to section 272–a of the Town Law, Consol.Laws, c. 62, in July, 1966 and implemented by way of a master plan. The master plan was followed by the adoption of a comprehensive zoning ordinance. Additional sewage district and drainage studies were undertaken which culminated in the adoption of a capital budget, providing for the development of the improvements specified in the master plan within the next six years. Pursuant to section 271 of the Town Law, authorizing comprehensive planning, and as a supplement to the capital budget, the Town Board adopted a capital program which provides for the location and sequence of additional capital improvements for the 12 years following the life of the capital budget. The two plans, covering a period of 18 years, detail the capital improvements projected for maximum development and conform to the specifications set forth in the master plan, the official map and drainage plan.

Based upon these criteria, the Town subsequently adopted the subject amendments for the alleged purpose of eliminating premature subdivision and urban sprawl. Residential development is to proceed according to the provision of adequate municipal facilities and services, with the assurance that any concomitant restraint upon property use is to be of a "temporary" nature and that other private uses, including the construction of individual housing, are authorized.

The amendments did not rezone or reclassify any land into different residential or use districts, but, for the purposes of implementing the proposals appearing in the comprehensive plan, consist, in the main, of additions to the definitional sections of the ordinance, section 46-3, and the adoption of a new class of "Special Permit Uses", designated "Residential Development Use." "Residential Development Use" is defined as "The erection or construction of dwellings on any vacant plots, lots or parcels of land" (§ 46-3, as amd.); and, any person who acts so as to come within that definition, "shall be deemed to be engaged in residential development which shall be a separate use classification under this ordinance and subject to the requirement of obtaining a special permit from the Town Board" (§ 46-3, as amd.).

The standards for the issuance of special permits are framed in terms of the availability to the proposed subdivision plat of five essential facilities or services: specifically (1) public sanitary sewers or approved substitutes; (2) drainage facilities; (3) improved public parks or recreation facilities, including public schools; (4) State, county or town roads—major, secondary or collector; and, (5) firehouses. No special permit shall issue unless the proposed residential development has accumulated 15 development points, to be computed on a sliding scale of values assigned to the specified improvements under the statute. Subdivision is thus a function of immediate availability to the proposed plat of certain municipal improvements; the avowed purpose of the amendments being to phase residential development to the Town's ability to provide the above facilities or services.

Certain savings and remedial provisions are designed to relieve of potentially unreasonable restrictions. Thus, the board may issue special permits vesting a present right to proceed with residential development in such year as the development meets the required point minimum, but in no event later than the final year of the 18–year capital plan. The approved special use permit is fully assignable, and improvements scheduled for completion within one year from the date of an application are to be credited as though existing on the date of the application. A prospective developer may advance the date of subdivision approval by agreeing to provide those improvements which will bring the proposed plat within the number of development points required by the amendments. And applications are authorized to the "Development Easement Acquisition Commission" for a reduction of the assessed valuation. Finally, upon application to the Town Board, the development point requirements may be varied should the board determine that such a variance or modification is consistent with the on-going development plan.

The undisputed effect of these integrated efforts in land use planning and development is to provide an over-all program of orderly growth and adequate facilities through a sequential development policy commensurate with progressing availability and capacity of public facilities. While its goals are clear and its purposes undisputably laudatory, serious questions are raised as to the manner in which these ends are to be effected, not the least of which relates to their legal viability under present zoning enabling legislation, particularly sections 261 and 263 of the Town Law. The owners of the subject premises argue, and the Appellate Division has sustained the proposition, that the primary purpose of the amending ordinance is to control or regulate population growth within the Town and as such is not within the authorized objectives of the zoning enabling legislation. We disagree.

In enacting the challenged amendments, the Town Board has sought to control subdivision in all residential districts, pending the provision (public or private) at some future date of various services and facilities. A reading of the relevant statutory provisions reveals that there is no specific authorization for the "sequential" and "timing" controls adopted here. That, of course, cannot be said to end the matter, for the additional inquiry remains as to whether the challenged amendments find their basis within the perimeters of the devices authorized and purposes sanctioned under current enabling legislation. Our concern is, as it should be, with the effects of the statutory scheme taken as a whole and its role in the propagation of a viable policy of land use and planning.

* * *

Of course, zoning historically has assumed the development of individual plats and has proven characteristically ineffective in treating with the problems attending subdivision and development of larger parcels, involving as it invariably does, the provision of adequate public services and facilities. To this end, subdivision control (Town Law, §§ 276, 277) purports to guide community development in the directions outlined here, while at the same time encouraging the provision of adequate facilities for the housing, distribution, comfort and convenience of local residents (*Village of Lynbrook v. Cadoo*, 252 N.Y. 308, 314, 169 N.E. 394, 396). It reflects in essence, a legislative judgment that the development of unimproved areas be accompanied by provision of essential facilities (*Matter of Brous v. Smith*, 304 N.Y. 164, 106 N.E.2d 503; see, also, 3 Rathkopf, The Law of Zoning and Planning [3d ed.], pp. 71–1 to 71–7; Cutler, Legal and Illegal Methods for Controlling Community Growth on the Urban Fringe, 1961 Wis.L.Rev. 370). And though it may not, in a definitional or conceptual sense be identified with the power to zone, it is designed to complement other land use restrictions, which, taken together, seek to implement a broader, comprehensive plan for community development (see Haar, The Master Plan: An Impermanent Constitution, 20 Law & Contemp.Probs. 353).

It is argued, nevertheless, that the timing controls currently in issue are not legislatively authorized since their effect is to prohibit subdivision absent precedent or concurrent action of the Town, and hence constitutes an unauthorized blanket interdiction against subdivision.

It is, indeed, true that the Planning Board is not in an absolute sense statutorily authorized to deny the right to subdivide. That is not, however, what is sought to be accomplished here. The Planning Board has the right to refuse approval of subdivision plats in the absence of those improvements specified in section 277, and the fact that it is the Town and not the subdividing owner or land developer who is required to make those improvements before the plat will be approved cannot be said to transform the scheme into an absolute prohibition any more than it would be so where it was the developer who refused to provide the facilities required for plat approval.[3] Denial of subdivision plat approval,

---

3. The difference between the ordinary situation and the situation said to subsist here resides in the fact that where plat approval is denied for want of various improvements, the developer is free to provide those improvements at his own expense. In the ordinary case where the proposed improvements will not be completed before the plat is filed the developer's obligation is secured by a performance bond (Town Law, § 277; see, also, Control of Land Subdivision, Office of Planning Coordination [1968 ed.], p.32). On the other hand, in the present case, plat approval is conditioned upon the Town's obligation to undertake improvements in roads, sewers, and recreational facilities. As the town may not be held to its program, practices do vary form year to year "and fiscal needs cannot be frozen beyond review and recall" (concurring opn. Hopkins, J. 37 A.D.2d 244, 324 N.Y.S.2d 187), the "patient owner" who relied on the capital program for qualification then is said to face the prospect that the improvements will be delayed and the impediments established by the ordinance further extended by the Town's failure to adhere to its own schedule.

The reasoning, as far as it goes, cannot be challenged. Yet, in passing on the validity of the ordinance on its face, we must assume not only the Town's good faith, but its assiduous adherence to the program's scheduled implementation. We cannot, it is true, adjudicate in a vacuum and we would be remiss not to consider the substantial risk that the Town may eventually default in its obligations. Yet, those are future events, the staple of clairvoyant, not of court deliberations. The threat of default is not so imminent or likely that it would warrant our prognosticating and striking down these amendments as invalid on their face. When and if the danger should materialize, the aggrieved landowner can seek relief by way of an article 78 proceeding, declaring the ordinance unconstitutional as applied to his property. Alternatively, should it arise at some future point in time that the Town must fail in its enterprise, an action for a declaratory judgment will indeed prove the most effective vehicle for relieving property owners of what would constitute absolute prohibitions.

invariably amounts to a prohibition against subdivision, albeit a conditional one (Real Property Law, Consol.Laws, c. 50, §§ 334–a, 335; see, also, 3 Rathkopf, Law of Zoning and Planning [3d ed.], pp. 71–122, supra); and to say that the Planning Board lacks the authority to deny subdivision rights is to mistake the nature of our inquiry which is essentially whether development may be conditioned pending the provision by the municipality of specified services and facilities. Whether it is the municipality or the developer who is to provide the improvements, the objective is the same—to provide adequate facilities, off-site and on-site; and in either case subdivision rights are conditioned, not denied.

* * *

Recognition of communal and regional interdependence, in turn, has resulted in proposals for schemes of regional and State-wide planning, in the hope that decisions would then correspond roughly to their level of impact (see, e.g., Proposed Land Use and Development Planning Law, §§ 2–101, 4–101, 4–102; ALI, A Model Land Development Code, art. 7). Yet, as salutary as such proposals may be, the power to zone under current law is vested in local municipalities, and we are constrained to resolve the issues accordingly. What does become more apparent in treating with the problem, however, is that though the issues are framed in terms of the developer's due process rights, those rights cannot, realistically speaking, be viewed separately and apart from the rights of others " 'in search of a [more] comfortable place to live.' " (*Concord Twp. Appeal*, 439 Pa. 466, 474, n. 6, 268 A.2d 765, 768, supra; *National Land & Inv. Co. v. Easttown Twp. Bd. of Adj.*, 419 Pa. 504, 527–528, 215 A.2d 597, supra; see, generally, Sager, Tight Little Islands: Exclusionary Zoning, Equal Protection and the Indigent, 21 Stan.L.Rev. 767; Roberts, Demise of Property Law, 57 Cornell L.Rev. 1).

There is, then, something inherently suspect in a scheme which, apart from its professed purposes, effects a restriction upon the free mobility of a people until sometime in the future when projected facilities are available to meet increased demands. Although zoning must include schemes designed to allow municipalities to more effectively contend with the increased demands of evolving and growing communities, under its guise, townships have been wont to try their hand at an array of exclusionary devices in the hope of avoiding the very burden which growth must inevitably bring (*see National Land & Inv. Co. v. Easttown Twp. Bd. of Adj.*, 419 Pa. 504, 532, 215 A.2d 597, supra; *Girsh Appeal*, 437 Pa. 237, 263 A.2d 395; *Concord Twp. Appeal*, 439 Pa. 466, 268 A.2d 765, supra; see, also, Roberts, Demise of Property Law, 57 Cornell L.Rev. 1, 5). Though the conflict engendered by such tactics is certainly real, and its implications vast, accumulated evidence, scientific and social, points circumspectly at the hazards of undirected growth and the naive, somewhat nostalgic imperative that egalitarianism is a function of growth. (See, generally, Lewis, Ecology and Politics: II, *New York Times*, March 6, 1972, p. 33, cols. 1, 2).

Of course, these problems cannot be solved by Ramapo or any single municipality, but depend upon the accommodation of widely disparate interests for their ultimate resolution. To that end, Statewide or regional control of planning would insure that interests broader than that of the municipality underlie various land use policies. Nevertheless, that should not be the only context in which growth devices such as these, aimed at population assimilation, not exclusion, will be sustained; especially where, as here, we would have no alternative but to strike the provision down in the wistful hope that the efforts of the State Office of Planning Coordination and the American Law Institute will soon bear fruit.

Hence, unless we are to ignore the plain meaning of the statutory delegation, this much is clear: phased growth is well within the ambit of existing enabling legislation. And, of course, it is no answer to point to emergent problems to buttress the conclusion that such innovative schemes are beyond the perimeters of statutory authorization. These considerations, admittedly real, to the extent which they are relevant, bear solely upon the continued viability of "localism" in land use regulation; obviously, they can neither add nor detract from the initial grant of authority, obsolescent though it may be. The answer which Ramapo has posed can by no means be termed definitive; it is, however, a first practical step toward controlled growth achieved without forsaking broader social purposes.

* * *

The subject ordinance is said to advance legitimate zoning purposes as it assures that each new home built in the township will have at least a minimum of public services in the categories regulated by the ordinance. The Town argues that various public facilities are presently being constructed but that for want of time and money it has been unable to provide such services and facilities at a pace commensurate with increased public need. It is urged that although the zoning power includes reasonable restrictions upon the private use of property, exacted in the hope of development according to well-laid plans, calculated to advance the public welfare of the community in the future (*Arverne Bay Constr. Co. v. Thatcher*, 278 N.Y. 222, 229, 15 N.E.2d 587, 590; *Hesse v. Rath*, 249 N.Y. 436, 438, 164 N.E. 342), the subject regulations go further and seek to avoid the increased responsibilities and economic burdens which time and growth must ultimately bring (see *National Land & Inv. Co. v. Easttown Twp. Bd. of Adj.*, 419 Pa. 504, 532, 215 A.2d 597, supra; *Girsh Appeal*, 437 Pa. 237, 263 A.2d 395, supra; *Concord Twp. Appeal*, 439 Pa. 466, 268 A.2d 765, supra).

* * *

What we will not countenance, then, under any guise, is community efforts at immunization or exclusion. But, far from being exclusionary, the present amendments merely seek, by the implementation of sequential development and timed growth, to provide a balanced cohesive community dedicated to the efficient utilization of land. The restrictions conform to the community's considered land use policies as expressed in its comprehensive plan and represent a bona fide effort to maximize population density consistent with orderly growth. True other alternatives, such as requiring off-site improvements as a prerequisite to subdivision, may be available, but the choice as how best to proceed, in view of the difficulties attending such exactions (see Heyman & Gilhool, The Constitutionality of Imposing Increased Community Costs on New Suburban Residents through Subdivision Exactions, 73 Yale L.J. 1119; see, also, ALI, A Model Land Development Code, § 3–104, subd. [6]), cannot be faulted.

Perhaps even more importantly, timed growth, unlike the minimum lot requirements recently struck down by the Pennsylvania Supreme Court as exclusionary, does not impose permanent restrictions upon land use (see *National Land & Inv. Co. v. Easttown Twp. Bd. of Adj.*, 419 Pa. 504, 215 A.2d 597, supra; *Concord Twp. Appeal*, 439 Pa. 466, 268 A.2d 765, supra). Its obvious purpose is to prevent premature subdivision absent essential municipal facilities and to insure continuous development commensurate with the Town's obligation to provide such facilities. They seek, not to freeze population at present levels but to maximize growth by the efficient use of land, and in so doing testify to this community's continuing role in population assimilation. In sum, Ramapo asks not that it be left alone, but only that it be allowed to prevent the kind of deterioration that has transformed well-ordered and thriving residential communities into blighted ghettos with attendant hazards to health, security and social stability—a danger not without substantial basis in fact.

* * *

The proposed amendments have the effect of restricting development for onwards to 18 years in certain areas. Whether the subject parcels will be so restricted for the full term is not clear, for it is equally probable that the proposed facilities will be brought into these areas well before that time. Assuming, however, that the restrictions will remain outstanding for the life of the program, they still fall short of a confiscation within the meaning of the Constitution.

An ordinance which seeks to permanently restrict the use of property so that it may not be used for any reasonable purpose must be recognized as a taking: The only difference between the restriction and an outright taking in such a case "is that the restriction leaves the owner subject to the burden of payment of taxation, while outright confiscation would relieve him of that burden" (*Arverne Bay Constr. Co. v. Thatcher*, 278 N.Y. 222, 232, 15 N.E.2d 587, 592, supra). An appreciably different situation obtains where the restriction constitutes a *temporary* restriction, promising that the property may be put to a profitable use within a reasonable time. The hardship of holding unproductive property for some time might be compensated for by the ultimate benefit inuring to the individual owner in the form of a substantial increase in valuation; or, for that matter, the landowner might be compelled to chafe under the temporary restriction, without the benefit of such compensation, when that burden serves to promote the public good (*cf. Arverne Bay Constr. Co. v. Thatcher*, 278 N.Y. 222, 232, 15 N.E.2d 587, 592, supra).

We are reminded, however, that these restrictions threaten to burden individual parcels for as long as a full generation and that such a restriction cannot, in any context, be viewed as a temporary expedient. The Town, on the other hand, contends that the landowner is not deprived of either the best use of his land or of numerous other appropriate uses, still permitted within various residential districts, including the construction of a single-family residence, and consequently, it cannot be deemed confiscatory. Although no proof has been submitted on reduction of value, the landowners point to obvious disparity between the value of the property, if limited in use by the subject amendments and its value for residential development purposes and argue that the diminution is so considerable that for all intents and purposes the land cannot presently or in the near future be put to profitable or beneficial use, without violation of the restrictions.

* * *

Without a doubt restrictions upon the property in the present case are substantial in nature and duration. They are not, however, absolute. The amendments contemplate a definite term, as the development points are designed to operate for a maximum period of 18 years and during that period, the Town is committed to the construction and installation of capital improvements. The net result of the on-going development provision is that individual parcels may be committed to a residential development use prior to the expiration of the maximum period. Similarly, property owners under the terms of the amendments may elect to accelerate the date of development by installing, at their own expense, the necessary public services to bring the parcel within the required number of development points. While even the best of plans may not always be realized, in the absence of proof to the contrary, we must assume the Town will put its best effort forward in implementing the physical and fiscal timetable outlined under the plan. Should subsequent events prove this assumption unwarranted, or should the Town because of some unforeseen event fail in its primary obligation to these landowners, there will be ample opportunity to undo the restrictions upon default. For the present, at least, we are constrained to proceed upon the assumption that the program will be fully and timely implemented (n. 7, p. 373, 334 N.Y.S.2d p. 148, 285 N.E.2d p. 298, supra).

* * *

In sum, where it is clear that the existing physical and financial resources of the community are inadequate to furnish the essential services and facilities which a substantial increase in population requires, there is a rational basis for "phased growth" and hence, the challenged ordinance is not violative of the Federal and State Constitutions. Accordingly, the order appealed from should be reversed and the actions remitted to Special Term for entry of a judgment declaring section 46–13.1 of the Town Ordinance constitutional.

BREITEL, JUDGE (dissenting). The limited powers of district zoning and subdivision regulation delegated to a municipality do not include the power to impose a moratorium on land development. Such conclusion is dictated by settled doctrine that a municipality has only those powers, and especially land use powers, delegated or necessarily implied.

But there is more involved in these cases than the arrogation of undelegated powers. Raised are vital constitutional issues, and, most important, policy issues trenching on grave domestic problems of our time, without the benefit of a legislative determination which would reflect the interests of the entire State. The policy issues relate to needed housing, planned land development under government control, and the exclusion in effect or by motive, of walled-in urban populations of the middle class and the poor. The issues are raised by a town ordinance, which, as one of the Appellate Division Justices noted below, reflect a parochial stance without regard to its impact on the region or the State, especially if it becomes a valid model for many other towns similarly situated.

* * *

It is important to note how radically the Ramapo scheme differs from those used and adopted under existing enabling acts. The zoning acts, starting from 50 years ago, based on national models, provided simply for district zoning to control population density and some planning to protect preferred uses of land, such as single-family dwellings, from other uses considered less desirable or even harmful to residential living or environmental balance. Since the beginning, in this State and elsewhere, by amendment to the enabling acts by the Legislature, provision has been made for subdivision planning and, in some instances, planned unit development, to prevent large-scale developers from dumping homes wholesale in raw land areas without private and, to some extent, public facilities essential to the use of the homes. In more recent years, since World War II, the need for a much enlarged kind of land planning has become critical. The evils of uncontrolled urban sprawl on the one hand, and the suburban and exurban pressure to exclude urban population on the other hand, have created a massive conflict, with social and economic implications of the gravest character. Throughout the nation the conflict has risen or threatened and solutions are being sought in careful intensive examination of the problem affecting those within and those without the localities to be regulated.

* * *

Decisive of the present appeals, however, is the absence in the town of legislative authorization to postpone growth, let alone to establish unilaterally phased population levels, through the expedient of barring residential development for scheduled periods of up to 18 years. It has always been the rule that a municipality has only those land use powers delegated or necessarily implied (1 Anderson, American Law of Zoning, § 3.10). Existing enabling legislation does not grant the power upon which the Ramapo ordinance rests. And for policy reasons, one should not strain the reading of the enabling acts, even if straining would avail, to distort them, beyond any meaning ever attributed to them, except by the ingenious draftsmen of the Ramapo ordinance.

* * *

Going beyond district zoning, the statute provides for subdivision platting (§ 276 et seq.). It does not provide support for the procedures essayed in the Ramapo ordinance. But what is important is that even intensive subdivision regulation was required to be authorized by statute before towns could control subdivision developers. Statutory authorization was all the more important because the then drastic regulation required the developers to provide private and public facilities for the wholesale distribution of homes and to provide moneys and bonds to make sure that they performed as promised. Notably, no developer is forbidden to develop for a period of years.

The urgent need to control the tempo and sequence of land development has been recognized by courts, government commissions, and commentators (see Cutler, Legal and Illegal Methods of Controlling Community Growth, 1961 Wis.L.Rev. 370; Fagin, Regulating the Timing of Urban Development, 20 Law & Contemp.Prob. 298; Report of National Commission on Urban Problems, pp. 245, 251; New York State, Office of Planning Coordination, Planning Law Revision Study, Draft Outline, pp. 13, 17). Techniques to control the rate, nature and sequence of community development are plentiful although not all are presently authorized or comport with constitutional limitations. Thus, in *Albrecht Realty Co. v. Town of New Castle*, 8 Misc.2d 255, 167 N.Y.S.2d 843, the Town of New Castle in Westchester County sought to control growth by placing a moratorium on the issuance of building permits for unspecified periods and with no apparent object other than controlling growth. The measure was voided because the enabling act did not authorize "a direct regulation of the rate of growth" (at p. 256, 167 N.Y.S.2d at p. 844). For another technique, in California the purchase of "development rights" or a time-limited easement by the local government reportedly has been employed. The community is saved the expense of purchasing the fee simple of the owner. It obtains flexibility by the power to release land for development while landowners are compensated. The method is also said to justify assessing or taxing the owner at a lower rate (see Cutler, op. cit., supra, at p. 394). A similar approach is followed in England and has been recently recommended by the President's National Commission on Urban Problems (Report, at p. 251; Mandelker, Notes from the English: Compensation in Town and County Planning, 49 Cal.L.Rev. 699; see, also, Ann., Zoning—With Compensation, 41 ALR3d 636).

* * *

The exclusionary effect of local efforts to preserve the country's Edens has been largely noted. Professor Roberts, in an important essay, explores the conditions bedevilling places like Ramapo but also assesses the calamitous effects of ill-advised parochial devices (E.F. Roberts, The Demise of Property Law, 57 Cornell L.Rev. 1). The problems of development of the larger community run so deep, he suggests that: " 'Snob zoning,' of course, may best be 'solved' by the legislature. This really is the lesson contained in *Girsh* which seems, moderately enough, to suggest that a regional planning mechanism should be devised to create a pluralist suburbia in which each class could find its proper place. More interest, however, is being generated by the notion of statewide land-use planning which presumably would allow each class its niche outside center city. Whether this interest in formulating state planning derives from a concern for the lower orders or reflects instead an irritation at the lack of order when a multitude of tiny hamlets makes any planning impossible, is difficult to tell." (at p. 37). To leave vital decisions controlling the mix and timing of development to the unfettered discretion of the local community invites disaster.

* * *

A glance at history suggests that Ramapo's plan to have public services installed in advance of development is unrealistic. Richard Babcock, the distinguished practitioner in land development law, some years ago addressed himself to the natural desire of communities to stay development while they caught up with the inexorable thrust of population growth and movement. He observed eloquently that this country was built and is still being built by people who moved about, innovated, pioneered, and created industry and employment, and thereby provided both the need and the means for the public services and facilities that followed (Babcock, The Zoning Game, at pp. 149–150). Thus, the movement has not been in the other direction, first the provision of public and utility services and then the building of homes, farms, and businesses. This court has said as much, in effect, in *Westwood Forest Estates v. Village of South Nyack*, 23 N.Y.2d 424, 297 N.Y.S.2d 129, 244 N.E.2d 700, supra, unanimously and in reliance on commonplace authority and precedent.

As said earlier, when the problem arose outside the State the judicial response has been the same, frustrating communities, intent on walling themselves from the mainstream of development, namely, that the effort was invalid under existing enabling acts or unconstitutional (*National Land & Inv. Co. v. Easttown Twp. Bd. of Adj.*, 419 Pa. 504, 215 A.2d 597, supra; Girsh Appeal, 437 Pa. 237, 263 A.2d 395, supra; *Bristow v. City of Woodhaven*, 35 Mich.App. 205, 192 N.W.2d 322, supra; *Lakeland Bluff v. County of Will*, 114 Ill.App.2d 267, 252 N.E.2d 765, supra; *Concord Twp. Appeal*, 439 Pa. 466, 268 A.2d 765, supra; *Oakwood at Madison v. Township of Madison*, 117 N.J.Super. 11, 283 A.2d 353 supra). The response may not be charged to judicial conservatism or self-restraint. In short, it has not been illiberal. It has indeed reflected the larger understanding that American society is at a critical crossroads in the accommodation of urbanization and suburban living, with effects that are no longer confined, bad as they are, to ethnic exclusion or "snob" zoning (see Roberts, op. cit., supra, at pp. 36–49). Ramapo would preserve its nature, delightful as that may be, but the supervening question is whether it alone may decide this or whether it must be decided by the larger community represented by the Legislature. Legally, politically, economically, and sociologically, the base for determination must be larger than that provided by the town fathers.

Accordingly, I dissent and vote to affirm the orders in both cases.

FULD, C.J., and BURKE, BERGAN and GIBSON, JJ., concur with SCILEPPI, J.

BREITEL, J., dissents and votes to affirm in a separate opinion in which JASEN, J., concurs.

Notes

1. Golden is the seminal case establishing the authority of local governments to adopt phased growth control ordinances. What are the elements of the Ramapo strategy that achieved its objective of phased growth?

2. What is the majority's thinking as it traces the delegated authority of the Town of Ramapo and concludes that the authority includes growth control measures? What statutes does it point to in coming to this conclusion? What do these statutes provide that justify the court's conclusion?

3. Golden is one of the first cases to examine the issue of urban sprawl and its antidote: managed growth, currently called smart growth. With 1600 local governments in New York alone, how can individual municipalities, acting independently and in a policy vacuum, establish growth control systems that properly direct regional marketplace and population pressures? Is the court content to leave this issue in the hands of municipal governments? What are its options?

4. Does Golden articulate the view that communities must accept population growth subject only to reasonable restrictions that phase that growth so that municipal services may be provided? How does that square with the views of those who argue that, in the interest of protecting biodiversity and the environmental context of natural resources, localities should prevent the development of large-scale landscapes rich in habitat, wetlands, woods, and water resources? How should advocates of natural resource preservation or conservation, or adherents to the deep ecology movement, respond?

5. The Ramapo case has spawned a great deal of literature. Some of the more interesting articles on the case and its implications are Bosselman. Can the Town of Ramapo Pass a Law to Bind the Rights of the Whole World? 1 Fla.St.U.L.Rev. 234 (1973) and O'Keefe, Time Controls on Land Use: Prophylactic Law for Planners, 57 Cornell L.Rev. 827 (1972). Also see Freilich and Greis, Timing and Sequencing Development: Controlling Growth, in Burchell and Listokin (ed.), Future Land Use, p. 59 (1975). A

comprehensive treatment of the problem is found in Management & Control of Growth (Urban Land Institute 1975). A collection of articles presented on the 25th anniversary of the Golden case is contained in the Urban Lawyer, Vo. 35, No. 1, Winter 2003.

6. The local officials in Ramapo responsible for the town's growth control laws knew they were vulnerable. If small groups of residents in discrete parts of town grew discontent with the town's land use laws, they had the power to form their own villages, adopt their own land use laws, and abandon the carefully sculpted town-wide approach. At the time the growth control law was adopted, there were six independent villages within the town and their growth and zoning were carefully incorporated into the town's proposals.[4] In 1967, the town board adopted a local law that limited the creation of villages under New York's law that allowed village secession from towns. This law provided that every petition for the incorporation of additional villages within town boundaries should comply with all the requirements of the applicable provisions of the state's village incorporation law and contain allegations that the proposed incorporation was in the overall public interest of the proposed village, the rest of the town, and any school or fire district affected by the incorporation.

The constitutionality of this law was challenged in Marcus v. Baron, 57 N.Y.2d 862, 456 N.Y.S.2d 39, 442 N.E.2d 437 (1982). The petitioners claimed that the law was inconsistent with the state-adopted village incorporation law. The New York Court of Appeals found nothing in state law to sustain town authority to govern village secession: no express or implied authority, no legislative intent, and no evidence of this authority in the constitution or other municipal statute. The result was the invalidation of the controlled secession law. Since the Marcus v. Baron decision, another six villages have been formed and more areas each year threaten to follow suit. In the last two months of 2002, residents within another three areas in the town have initiated petitions to incorporate. As a result, there is today very little contiguous land left in Ramapo for the town's comprehensive plan and inventive zoning controls to regulate.

SECTION 2. MORATORIA

A moratorium on development suspends the right of property owners to obtain development approvals while the community takes time to consider, draft, and adopt land use plans or rules to respond to new or changing circumstances not adequately dealt with by its current laws. At the local level, moratoria figure into growth management and smart growth by giving communities experiencing growth pressures time to rethink their land use plan and laws and adopt a new, smarter approach that more properly manages growth.

A moratorium is sometimes used, for example, by a community just prior to adopting its first comprehensive plan and zoning law or under-

---

4. These six villages were: Suffern, Spring Valley, Hillburn, Sloatsburg, New Square, and Pomona.

taking a comprehensive revision of its plan and zoning. The moratorium prevents developers and property owners from rushing to develop their land under current land use rules that the community is in the process of changing. By so doing, it helps to accomplish the purpose of the new rules by giving them the broadest possible applicability and preventing development that is inconsistent with them. Moratoria are also used to prevent development for a time while the government agency decides whether to acquire land for a public use or until capital improvements are made, as in the Golden case.

A moratorium can be seen as the most extreme land use action that a regulatory agency can take, because it suspends completely the rights of owners to use their property. In this light, regulators are advised to precede the adoption of a moratorium by findings that confirm the necessity of this action. What are the conditions that mandate the imposition of a moratorium? Are there no available alternatives less burdensome on property rights? Why are the existing land use plans and ordinances not adequate? What recent circumstances have occurred that justify the adoption of the moratorium? How serious and urgent are these circumstances? What hard evidence is there to document the necessity of the moratorium? Does the regulatory agency, in fact, have the legal authority to declare a moratorium? For how long? Under what circumstances?

In the case of Tahoe–Sierra Preservation Council, Inc. v. Tahoe Regional Planning Agency, 535 U.S. 302, 122 S.Ct. 1465, 152 L.Ed.2d 517 (2002), the U.S. Supreme Court held that a moratorium on all development lasting 32 months was not, by itself, a regulatory taking. At issue in the Tahoe case was the validity of a moratorium on development adopted by the Tahoe Regional Planning Agency to protect the unique environment and tourist-based economy of the Lake Tahoe region. The purpose of the moratorium was to give the Agency time to deal with the threat posed by construction and land development to the clarity of Lake Tahoe, which had begun to cloud as early as the late 1950's. The problem addressed was the construction of buildings, mostly homes, in the steeper drainage areas near streams and wetlands. These resources act as filters for much of the nitrogen, phosphorous, and other pollution that water runoff carries.

By 1980, it was obvious that the initial land use regulations adopted by the Agency had failed. After the withdrawal of support by the State of California, the Agency's structure was redefined by amendments to the compact law in that year. The Agency was directed by the two states to develop environmental threshold carrying capacities including standards for air quality, water quality, soil conservation, vegetation preservation, and noise. This new legislation halted temporarily all development in critical environmental areas in the region, giving the Agency the time it required to consider, draft, adopt, and implement needed new regulations. That moratorium lasted for 32 months.

The legal challenge to this moratorium was launched by a nonprofit corporation representing 400 owners of land in the critical environmental areas of the Basin who had purchased their parcels prior to the 1980 changes in the compact legislation. They claimed that the moratorium on the development of their properties was a regulatory taking. Their essential argument was that, even though the regulation does not take the future right to develop, the temporary taking of all development rights, for the 32-month period, itself violates the Constitution. The landowners argued for a categorical rule which would classify a development moratorium as a taking without considering the moratorium's length, the severity of the problems addressed, the good faith of the agency involved, or what it did to conduct the required studies, analyze the underlying problems, and draft appropriate new regulations.

The U.S. Supreme Court rejected the plaintiffs' arguments and refused to declare that a moratorium is a categorical taking, regardless of the circumstances. It held that a moratorium, like most other land use regulations, is subject to an ad hoc inquiry that considers the circumstances of the case such as the character of the regulation, the public interest to be achieved, the extent to which it interferes with the owner's investment-backed expectations, and how severely they are affected by the regulation. In other words, a moratorium may be a taking, under the circumstances of a particular case, but is not categorically so. In the Tahoe case, the Court noted that the lower federal courts had concluded that the 32-month period was not unreasonable and that the Agency had acted in good faith during that time to do what needed to be done before the moratorium could be lifted. It further recognized that the consensus of land use planners is that moratoria are an essential tool of successful development.

Moratoria, the Court noted, prevent landowners from rushing to develop, causing inefficient and ill-conceived growth before a comprehensive plan can be adopted. They prevent regulators from making hasty decisions which would disadvantage landowners as well as the public. The Court recognized that land values can actually increase during a moratorium and that the public and all landowners are reciprocally benefited by moratoria because they protect everyone's interest against immediate construction that might be inconsistent with the provisions of the plan that is ultimately adopted. Of course, moratoria can be enacted that are not reasonable in these ways and they are vulnerable, under Tahoe, to challenge.

MARYLAND–NAT'L CAPITAL PARK AND PLANNING COMM'N v. CHADWICK

Court of Appeals of Maryland, 1979.
286 Md. 1, 405 A.2d 241.

MURPHY, CHIEF JUDGE.

The central issue in this case is whether the appellant, Maryland–National Capital Park and Planning Commission (the Commission), by placing the appellees' land in public "reservation" without their consent for a period not to exceed three years, as authorized by * * * the Montgomery County Code * * *, unconstitutionally deprived the landowners of the use of their property without payment of just compensation.

* * *

Under § 7–115(a), the Commission's approval is required before any subdivision plat within the regional district may be recorded in the land records of Montgomery or Prince George's Counties. The Commission is empowered under § 7–116(a)(4) to prepare subdivision regulations which may provide for

> "the reservation of lands for schools and other public buildings and for parks, playgrounds, and other public purposes, provided no reservation of land for traffic, recreation or any other public purposes as herein provided shall continue for longer than three years without the written approval of all persons holding or otherwise owning any legal or equitable interest in the property; and provided further that the properties reserved for public use shall be exempt from all State, county, and local taxes during the period."

Pursuant to the state enabling legislation, Montgomery County adopted an ordinance authorizing the placement of land in public reservation. Under the provisions of the ordinance * * * the Commission's Planning Board for Montgomery County, which is authorized to administer subdivision regulations in that jurisdiction, is required to "refer all preliminary subdivision plans to the general plan or parts thereof, adopted or proposed or studies related thereto, or shall otherwise determine the need for reserving for public use any of the land included in the preliminary subdivision plan." The ordinance specifies that reservations "for a period of three years may be required for road or street rights of way, public school and building sites, parks, playgrounds or other recreational areas or other public purposes." The ordinance also provides that placement of land in public reservation shall be by resolution of the Commission, which shall state the time, not over three years, that the reservation will be effective.

Under the provisions of the ordinance, property in reservation is exempt from all state, county and local taxes * * *. It is also subject to restrictions on its use, as detailed in § 50–31(a)(5):

> "(5) PRESERVATION. During the reservation period, no building or structure shall be erected upon the land so reserved. No trees, topsoil or cover shall be removed or destroyed; no grading shall be done; no storm drainage structure shall be so built as to discharge water on the reservation except for storm drainage construction in accordance with a storm drainage plan approved by the department of public works or the Washington Suburban Sanitary Commission; *nor shall any land so reserved be put to any use whatsoever, except upon written approval of the board.* Nothing in this section shall be

construed as prohibiting the owner from removing weeds or trash from property so reserved, nor from selling when approved by the board such parts of the land as may be necessary for water, sewer or road right of way for public agencies." (Emphasis added.)

Nothing in the state enabling act, or in Montgomery County's implementing ordinance, obligates the Commission to acquire property placed by it in reservation, either during or at the expiration of the reservation period. No provision is made for payment of compensation to the property owner for the time that his property is held in reservation, whether or not it is ultimately acquired by the Commission.

* * *

On April 25, 1978, the Chadwicks filed suit in the Circuit Court for Montgomery County, seeking the issuance of a writ of mandamus directing the Commission to approve their preliminary subdivision plan, and requesting a declaratory judgment that the reservation of their property and any statute requiring such reservation were unconstitutional as a taking of property without payment of just compensation. The court (McAuliffe, J.) held that the Commission's resolution placing the Chadwicks' property in public reservation under § 50–31 of the County Code was unconstitutional and it ordered the Commission to approve the preliminary subdivision plan. * * *

* * * Our cases have recognized and applied the distinction between a compensable taking under the eminent domain power and a noncompensable regulation under the police power. * * * We have consistently upheld regulations which may have, as an incidental effect, the diminution of value of property, so long as those regulations have been shown to be fair exercises of the police power. * * * A regulation which prohibits a beneficial use of private property constitutes a fair exercise of the police power if the public interest generally requires it and the regulation is reasonably necessary to achieve the public goal without being unduly oppressive upon individuals. * * * However, we have recognized that a governmental action, while not rising to the status of a compensable "taking" of property, may amount to an invalid deprivation of property rights without due process of law, either because the purpose of the action was improper, see, e.g., *Hoyert v. Bd. of County Comm'rs*, 262 Md. 667, 278 A.2d 588 (1971) (attempt to depress value of property in anticipation of subsequent condemnation); *Carl M. Freeman, Inc. v. St. Rds. Comm'n*, 252 Md. 319, 250 A.2d 250 (1969) (sole purpose of ordinance is to freeze land values) or because the means chosen were too burdensome on the individual property owner. See, e.g., *Spaid v. Board of Co. Comm'rs*, 259 Md. 369, 269 A.2d 797 (1970) ("buffer zoning" to establish a border of vacant property around a residential neighborhood). * * *

* * *

The present case does not involve a valid exercise of the police power regulating, in the public interest, a mere beneficial use of private property for which compensation need not be paid to the affected landowner. On the contrary, we think the Commission's resolution placing appellees' land in reservation for a period up to three years stripped the landowners, for that extended period of time, of all reasonable use of their property and was tantamount to a "taking" without compensation as the lower court declared. In so concluding, we recognize the commendable governmental objective sought to be achieved by placing the land in reservation but, as was said in *Pennsylvania Coal Co. v. Mahon,* supra (260 U.S. at 416, 43 S.Ct. at 160), "a strong public desire to improve the public condition is not enough to warrant achieving the desire by a shorter cut than the constitutional way of paying for the change."

We construe the ordinance under which the Commission acted as not permitting the landowner to make, as a matter of right, any use of the property placed in reservation (other than to remove trash and weeds). We further construe the ordinance as not authorizing the planning board to permit, upon the landowner's application, any use of the reserved property which conflicts with the flat prohibition contained in the ordinance against grading the land, erecting any structures thereon, or removing trees, top soil or other cover. Restrictions of such totality upon the use of property placed in reservation *for a three-year period* bring this case within the principle, so well illustrated in *Pennsylvania Coal,* that a governmental restriction imposed on the use of land may be so onerous as to constitute a taking which constitutionally requires the payment of just compensation.

* * *

Considered together, *Pennsylvania Coal* and *Penn Central* provide ample guidance for determining whether a governmental restriction on the use of land, sought to be imposed under the police power, is of such magnitude as to constitute a taking in the constitutional sense. As we have indicated, the Commission's resolution placing appellees' land in reservation for a period of up to three years, with no reasonable uses permitted, amounts to a virtual "freeze" on the use of the property in its entirety. The resolution does not merely circumscribe a beneficial use of the property; it inhibits all beneficial use for up to three years, without any guarantee that the property will be acquired in the future. That the Commission's resolution is tantamount to a taking is, we think, clearly buttressed by cases in other jurisdictions.

In *Miller v. Beaver Falls,* 368 Pa. 189, 82 A.2d 34 (1951), Pennsylvania's Supreme Court invalidated a state law and implementing city ordinance which allowed a municipality to designate private property as parklands for up to three years, but which imposed no duty upon the municipality to acquire the designated property. The enactments provided that no compensation for improvements located on the property after notice was given of its placement in reservation would be paid if the property was subsequently acquired for public use. While the court conceded the desirability of the purpose to be achieved (establishment of parks for public use), it said that the city's action "in plotting [the] ground for a park or playground and freezing it for three years is, in reality, a taking of property by possibility, contingency, blockade and subterfuge, in violation of the clear mandate of our Constitution that property cannot be taken * * * without just compensation having been first made and secured." 82 A.2d at 37.

* * *

* * * See also *Gordon v. City of Warren Plan. & Urb. Renew. Comm'n*, 388 Mich. 82, 199 N.W.2d 465 (1972); *Peacock v. County of Sacramento*, 271 Cal.App.2d 845, 77 Cal.Rptr. 391 (1969). Compare *Washington Sub. San. Comm'n v. Nash*, 284 Md. 376, 396 A.2d 538 (1979); *Hoyert v. Bd. of County Comm'rs*, 262 Md. 667, 278 A.2d 588 (1971); *Carl M. Freeman, Inc. v. St. Rds. Comm'n*, 252 Md. 319, 250 A.2d 250 (1969).

The Commission, supported by a well-prepared amicus curiae brief filed by the Attorney General, urges that we apply the rationale of cases like *Headley v. City of Rochester*, 272 N.Y. 197, 5 N.E.2d 198 (1936), and *State v. Manders*, 2 Wis.2d 365, 86 N.W.2d 469 (1957), sustaining the constitutionality of so-called official map laws—statutes which establish the location of existing and planned streets and place restrictions on the issuance of permits to build structures in the bed of proposed roadways. These statutes restricting development in the bed of mapped streets contained provisions for variances to assure the landowner of a reasonable return on affected property, including the granting of a building permit to prevent substantial damage accruing to the owner where that course of action is required by justice and equity. Maryland's statute controlling development in mapped streets is similar to those involved in *Headley* and *Manders*. * * *

The facts of the present case clearly distinguish it from the cited cases involving the reservation of street locations. As in those cases, we recognize the need to promote intelligent planning by placing reasonable restrictions on the improvement of land scheduled to be acquired for public use. We do not, therefore, condemn as beyond the police power the enactment of reservation statutes which are reasonable in their application both as to duration and severity. Our holding today is a narrow one, limited to the facts before us. We conclude only that the Commission's resolution passed pursuant to * * * the County Code, placing appellees' land in reservation for up to three years, without any reasonable uses permitted as of right, was tantamount to a "taking" in the constitutional sense. Because the Commission's resolution did not provide for the payment of just compensation, it was unconstitutional as applied to the appellees' property and was thus of no effect. Consequently, the trial judge correctly ruled, in accordance with the requested prayer for relief, that the Commission's resolution was a nullity and that the Commission was required to forthwith approve appellees' preliminary subdivision plan.

JUDGMENT AFFIRMED WITH COSTS.

Notes

1. Was Chadwick overruled by Tahoe? The plaintiff's argument in Tahoe was that a moratorium suspending all development rights applied to a large area of environmental significance was, *per se*, a regulatory taking. Did the Court in Tahoe hold that moratoria cannot be takings? Are the circumstances in the Chadwick case sufficiently different from those in Tahoe to merit a different result, as applied to that situation?

2. Regulations that have the effect of preventing any development of land so as to make future acquisition by condemnation less costly are almost invariably held to be takings. One example is Ventures in Property I v. City of Wichita, 225 Kan. 698, 594 P.2d 671 (1979), where the city denied the property owner permission to plat his property preparatory to development because a future highway was scheduled to be built on a portion of the land. Also see Joint Ventures, Inc. v. Department of Transportation, 563 So.2d 622 (Fla.1990).

3. Many land use enabling statutes have provisions similar to the one litigated in the principal case. However, most such statutes provide for a shorter period of time for the public to decide whether or not to condemn. The typical time period is one year. Would such a provision have saved the Maryland scheme? The court in Chadwick acknowledged a distinction between temporary restrictions on development (valid regulation) and tying up land for a long period (taking), but relied in part on a New Jersey case invalidating a one-year reservation scheme. Perhaps one reason for judicial mistrust of reservation schemes is that the way they typically work in practice is that just when the landowner is ready to develop, his land is put into limbo while the public decides whether it can afford to buy him out.

4. Closely related to reservation schemes and efforts to keep land undeveloped so that it may be condemned at lower cost are situations where the public, through the condemning agency, engages in improper behavior. Consider the following: A farmer is approached by state highway commission employees seeking right of way for a road across the farmer's land. The farmer, a benevolent person and good citizen, says he will give the land for the road if the highway commission will in turn pave another road leading into a nearby town. The highway commission makes such a verbal promise but fails to perform. Does the farmer have any remedy? See, Arkansas State Highway Comm'n v. Cunningham, 239 Ark. 890, 395 S.W.2d 13 (1965).

NEW JERSEY SHORE BUILDERS ASSOCIATION v. MAYOR AND TOWNSHIP COMMITTEE OF TOWNSHIP OF MIDDLETOWN

Superior Court of New Jersey, Law Division, 1989.
234 N.J.Super. 619, 561 A.2d 319.

PESKOE, J.S.C.

In this action in lieu of prerogative writs, plaintiff attacks the validity of the Middletown Township moratorium ordinance adopted pursuant to *N.J.S.A.* 40:55D–90b. For reasons set forth below, this court concludes that the ordinance is invalid because it was based on a health officer's opinion that lacked the factual basis to demonstrate the existence of a "clear imminent danger to the health of the inhabitants." No published opinion has yet addressed what constitutes the statutorily required demonstration that a municipality must consider. I hold that a moratorium ordinance is not tested by the usual standard applied to a municipal land use ordinance. Rather, the statute requires that municipal action have clear and specific factual support.

* * *

The Municipal Land Use Law (MLUL) governs land use in this State. It delegates to each municipality significant and specific powers to control the use of land within its boundaries. *N.J.S.A.* 40:55D–1 *et seq.* Among these is the power to impose a moratorium on all development. *N.J.S.A.* 40:55D–90b, effective March 21, 1986, sets forth the applicable standards. Prior to the passage of this MLUL amendment, courts had disagreed about a municipality's power to enact moratoriums and, if there was such power, under what circumstances it could be exercised. *N.J. Shore Builders Ass'n v. Dover Tp. Committee,* 191 N.J.Super. 627, 468 A.2d 742 (Law Div.1983). There is no longer any doubt about the power or the legislative intent strictly to limit the use of that power.

The power to impose any moratorium may be exercised only upon the determination that there exists "a clear imminent danger to the health of the inhabitants" and the moratorium may endure only for a maximum of six months. In exercising the moratorium power, the municipality is held to a strict necessity test that contrasts strikingly with the general judicial respect accorded municipal land use legislation.

* * *

* * *

Middletown enacted a moratorium applicable only to major site plan and subdivision applications on October 17, 1988. Applications for other development were not affected in any way. The moratorium ordinance was introduced and had a first reading on July 25, 1988. At that time no qualified health officer had submitted a written (or any other) opinion that there existed a clear imminent danger to the inhabitants' health. Earlier that month some residents of Middletown had experienced low water pressure and at its July 18 meeting the township committee discussed the possibility of a building moratorium to alleviate water problems.

* * *

The moratorium ordinance restricts planning board consideration of major subdivisions for six months. It expires in March 1989. The municipal governing body had been considering the moratorium since at least July 25, 1988 and had heard many statements from those attending the hearings prior to adoption of the ordinance. The information provided by the representatives of the water companies was to be considered, as was all other information bearing on the committee's concern, whether given under oath or not. The water company speakers explained in detail the utility's planned augmentation of the pumping system. They explained carefully the status of the raw water supply and the irrelevance of the reservoir level at that time to the problems experienced in Middletown. The relevant concern, in order to increase the water supply, was the pumping and treatment capacity of the system. They pointed out that the failure to approve requests to build pumping stations and water towers had led to the inadequacy of water pressure during peak demand periods in certain locations and from time to time otherwise. There was no raw water shortage in view of the rate by which the reservoirs are naturally replenished. * * *

* * *

The evidence provided by the water company officers was overwhelming that the emergency, if any, was not caused by a shortage of raw water but by an inadequate distribution system. The utility's capacity to pump water was shown to be sufficient to meet the usual level of demand and to meet increased seasonal demand on a short-term basis. If improvements underway were completed on schedule the capacity would soon be adequate for all purposes.

No evidence was presented to the Middletown governing body by fire protection experts or others qualified to evaluate the existence of dangers from inadequate fire protection. The complaints regarding low pressure in particular areas of the township were recurring and were not new, nor were they related to the level of raw water in reservoirs. Those complaints concerned mainly the areas long known to the water company as requiring water towers or similar means to improve the condition.

There was no indication that businesses requiring abundant water were unable to operate. Voluntary conservation measures urged by the water company had apparently resulted in some thirsty lawns but no particular hazard otherwise. Those measures caused the water demand to drop sufficiently so that the water distribution system was no longer overburdened. No witness showed any facts from which the township committee reasonably could find that an imminent health hazard threatened Middletown Township.

The statute requires "a written opinion by a qualified health professional that a clear imminent danger to the health of the inhabitants of the municipality exists." It must be inferred that the Legislature intended that the opinion on which the municipality is to rely has an adequate and fully disclosed factual basis.

The statute requires the municipality to *demonstrate* on the basis of a health expert's opinion that a hazard exists. "Demonstrate" is not defined in the statute. *The Random House Dictionary of the English Language* (1967), unabridged, defines it as "to make evident or establish by arguments or reasoning; prove; to describe, explain or illustrate by examples, specimens, experiments or the like." No such demonstration occurred so as to warrant Middletown's moratorium. The recitation of findings incorporated in ordinance #2061 refers to an exploration of less restrictive measures, but does not enumerate them. No evidence of such exploration was set forth at the hearings. The six findings of fact set forth are not supported by the record.

* * *

Clearly the Legislature did not regard a moratorium as a device to be utilized casually. There are only two provisions in the MLUL dealing with moratoriums. One forbids a municipality's utilization of a moratorium for the purpose of developing and adopting a master plan. The other permits a moratorium solely where the municipality demonstrates a clear imminent danger to the community and requires a health expert's written opinion as a basis for the demonstration.

The Legislature used the word "clear" as to the imminence of danger to be found by the municipality. The word does not appear anywhere else in the MLUL as a basis for decision. Although I am reluctant to enunciate a standard by which to measure the municipality's duty to weigh facts in relation to a legislative act in terms ordinarily relevant to a decision between adversaries, it appears that the Legislature intended that a clear and convincing need for a moratorium be shown before one is enacted.

It is evident that the Legislature intended to set a high standard for the showing that would justify a moratorium. This court infers that had the Legislature specifically addressed the issue, it would have required, at least, that the expert explain in full the reasons for the opinion and that the municipal governing body weigh available credible evidence and consider the adequacy of the reasons in light of all the circumstances. Had the municipality adhered to such a standard, it could not rationally and reasonably have enacted the moratorium ordinance on October 17, 1988.

* * *

* * * Although it is not necessary that I reach this issue, I deem it helpful to state that I conclude further, even if the moratorium had had an adequate statutory basis, its terms were not rationally designed to meet the hazard as defined.

Notes

1. In Toll Brother's Inc. v. West Windsor Township, 712 A.2d 266, 312 N.J.Super. 540 (1998), the Township of West Windsor adopted an ordinance that created timed growth districts, the purpose of which was to slow growth. New Jersey's Municipal Land Use Law (N.J. Stat. Ann. § 40:55D–90) prohibits "the prohibition of development in order to prepare a master plan and development regulations" in addition to moratoria on applications for development or interim zoning ordinance * * * except * * * where the municipality demonstrate * * * clear imminent danger to the health of inhabitants * * *and in no cases shall exceed a six-month term." The court held that the township's timed growth controls constituted a prohibited

moratorium because in order to immediately develop, 40 percent of the allowable density was foregone. The state supreme court decision in this case is in Chapter XI. For additional background, see Peter A. Buchsbaum, Timed Growth Ordinances Rejected in New Jersey, 31 The Urban Lawyer 823 (1999).

2. Most situations involving moratoria on development because of water or sewer system emergencies pit developers against a state-level agency, usually an environmental agency. This type of moratorium is not litigated frequently because the state's police power interest in public health and safety is easily defended. See, e.g., Ungar v. State, 63 Md.App. 472, 492 A.2d 1336 (1985); Friel v. Triangle Oil Co., 76 Md.App. 96, 543 A.2d 863 (1988). In Estate of Scott v. Victoria County, 778 S.W.2d 585 (Tex.App.1989), the property owner sought compensation for a taking due to a sewer moratorium. The court held that a property owner has no property right in sewer extensions, merely an expectancy of service. In Foster v. Board of Comm'rs of Warrick County, 647 N.E.2d 1147 (Ind.App.1995), the court upheld a moratorium on further building permits in a previously approved subdivision because earlier construction by the developer caused severe drainage problems affecting nearby residents; the county board imposed the moratorium until the inadequate drainage system previously installed by the developer was corrected. And in McNaughton Co. v. Witmer, 149 Pa.Cmwlth. 307, 613 A.2d 104 (1992), the court held that a developer could not recover damages for delay in his project for the period during which a validly enacted sewer connection moratorium was in effect.

The New York Times reported on November 20, 1989 (page B 6), a two-year-old moratorium on all new sewer mains from Mt. Kisco to Yonkers, New York: "Much of the county's new construction has come to a halt. Although individual home builders can still hook up to existing sewer mains, dozens of developers, who must extend the mains before erecting homes now own land they can neither build on nor sell." Also see Kawaoka v. City of Arroyo Grande, 17 F.3d 1227 (9th Cir.1994), where the court upheld a city's temporary water moratorium against charges of spot zoning, differential treatment, and racial bias against persons of Japanese ancestry; Gilbert v. State, 218 Cal.App.3d 234, 266 Cal.Rptr. 891 (1990), upholding a moratorium on new water connections.

3. Sometimes a moratorium is enacted specifying one particular land use. In Duncanson v. Board of Supervisors of Danville Twp., 551 N.W.2d 248 (Minn.App.1996), the court upheld a moratorium on feedlots despite the fact that the plaintiff's proposed feedlot was the only project known to be affected by the moratorium. And in First Bet Joint Venture v. City of Central City, 818 F.Supp. 1409 (D.Colo.1993), a moratorium on zoning permits for future gaming facilities was upheld (the plaintiff's taking claim was held not ripe). See Wendy U. Larsen and Marcella Larsen, Moratoria as Takings Under Lucas, Land Use Law (June 1994), p. 3.

4. Another type of moratorium is one that halts development for a temporary period pending adoption of a new comprehensive plan or new zoning ordinance. The validity of this type of moratorium depends upon interpretation of the state's enabling statutes, which may or may not expressly grant such power to municipalities. See, e.g., Noghrey v. Acampo-

ra, 152 A.D.2d 660, 543 N.Y.S.2d 530 (1989). In Naylor v. Township of Hellam, 773 A.2d 770, 565 Pa. 397 (2001), the Supreme Court of Pennsylvania held that the municipality lacked the authority to impose a moratorium on subdivision approvals while revising its comprehensive plan because the Municipal Planning Code (MPC) 53 §§ 10101–11202 does not expressly authorize moratoria and therefore the power to suspend development is not implicit or incidental to the powers expressly conferred. This case demonstrates that the outcome of a moratorium is closely related to a municipality's home rule authority.

Where municipalities do have the power to adopt moratoria while creating or revising their comprehensive plan or zoning law, moratoria may be invalid because of their duration or other defect. In Lake Illyria Corporation v. Town of Gardiner, 43 A.D.2d 386, 352 N.Y.S.2d 54 (3rd Dep't 1974), for example, a moratorium was declared invalid that lasted for four years and where the town did not show adequate progress in concluding its planning process. In Gardiner the court wrote: "The purpose of 'stop-gap' zoning is to allow a local legislative body, pending decision upon the adoption of a comprehensive zoning ordinance, to take reasonable measures temporarily to protect the public interest and welfare until an ordinance is finally adopted. Otherwise, the eventual comprehensive zoning ordinance might be of little avail. While it might be deemed a proper exercise of power for the Town to freeze building uses when the Town is actively engaged in the enactment of a comprehensive zoning law, the present case demonstrates the potential abuse of such a process by long delay and the inevitable spot zoning resulting from a variance procedure. The ordinance in question (1972) represents the fourth consecutive yearly enactment that provided for the same interim or 'stop-gap' zoning, and throughout this period of time the only meaningful progress towards the preparation of a comprehensive plan has taken place relatively recently, since the appointment of a Zoning Commission on July 11, 1972. This appointment followed by almost four months the commencement of the instant lawsuit. A course of conduct such as that followed by the Town herein is plainly contrary to the purpose of interim or 'stop-gap' zoning. Under the present circumstances, the absence of justification for such an exercise of power renders this four-year delay unreasonable."

SECTION 3. GROWTH MANAGEMENT

INTRODUCTION: WHO SHOULD DECIDE?

The case of Golden v. Ramapo, 30 N.Y.2d 359, 334 N.Y.S.2d 138, 285 N.E.2d 291 (1972), which began this chapter on smart growth and growth management, set in motion three decades of debate over which level of government should dictate such matters. In Golden, the court's ambivalence over the predominant authority of local governments in land use was palpable: New York's zoning regime, it said, "is burdened by the largely antiquated notion which deigns that the regulation of land use and development is uniquely a function of local government* * *." [5]

---

5. Golden, 30 N.Y.2d 359, 334 N.Y.S.2d 138, 285 N.E.2d at 299.

At precisely the same time, a revolution to wrest land use control from local governments was begun. It was fueled by the understanding that local control of land use creates serious inefficiencies and inequities. A report entitled The Quiet Revolution, prepared for the Council of Environmental Quality in 1971, contained a powerful statement of the problems caused by the delegation of land use control to towns, villages, boroughs, cities, and townships: "This country is in the midst of a revolution in the way we regulate land * * *. The *ancien regime* being overthrown is the feudal system under which the entire pattern of land development has been controlled by thousands of individual local governments, each seeking to maximize its tax base and minimize its social problems, and caring less what happens to all the others."[6]

The revolution has not succeeded, despite all the attention given to the efforts of states to create statewide counter-regimes under the rubrics of growth management, sustainable development, and, recently, smart growth. After analyzing recent state planning and smart growth legislation, a preeminent practitioner and scholar concludes that one of the major problems in fighting sprawl today is "the states' failure to reclaim some of their authority delegated early on to localities in the land use field * * *."[7]

In this section, we examine a number of cases challenging the attempts of single municipalities in burgeoning regions to control growth, and then turn to the efforts of state legislatures to guide and direct local prerogatives in the interests of growth management.

A. LOCAL REGULATION OF URBAN GROWTH

CONSTRUCTION INDUSTRY ASS'N OF SONOMA COUNTY v. CITY OF PETALUMA

United States Court of Appeals, Ninth Circuit, 1975.
522 F.2d 897, certiorari denied 424 U.S. 934,
96 S.Ct. 1148, 47 L.Ed.2d 342 (1976).

CHOY, CIRCUIT JUDGE:

The City of Petaluma (the City) appeals from a district court decision voiding as unconstitutional certain aspects of its five-year housing and zoning plan. We reverse.

---

6. Fred Bosselman & David Callies, Council on Envtl. Quality, The Quiet Revolution in Land Use Control 1 (1972). See also Michael Allan Wolf, The Prescience and Centrality of Euclid v. Ambler, in Zoning and The American Dream: Promises Still to Keep 252, 253 (Charles M. Haar & Jerold S. Kayden eds., 1989) (specifying the problems identified in Euclid of assigning control over land use to local governments as "exclusion, anti-competitiveness, parochialism, and aestheticism"). To these must be added the propensity of local governments, most of which rely heavily on local property taxes, to favor economic development over environmental protection. See Paul E. Peterson, The Price of Federalism 36–37, 69–75 (Brookings, 1995).

7. Robert H. Freilich, From Sprawl to Smart Growth 240 (A.B.A. 1999).

STATEMENT OF FACTS

The City is located in southern Sonoma County, about 40 miles north of San Francisco. In the 1950's and 1960's, Petaluma was a relatively self-sufficient town. It experienced a steady population growth from 10,315 in 1950 to 24,870 in 1970. Eventually, the City was drawn into the Bay Area metropolitan housing market as people working in San Francisco and San Rafael became willing to commute longer distances to secure relatively inexpensive housing available there. By November 1972, according to unofficial figures, Petaluma's population was at 30,500, a dramatic increase of almost 25 per cent in little over two years.

The increase in the City's population, not surprisingly, is reflected in the increase in the number of its housing units. From 1964 to 1971, the following number of residential housing units were completed:

Year	Units	Year	Units
1964	270	1968	379
1965	440	1969	358
1966	321	1970	591
1967	234	1971	891

In 1970 and 1971, the years of the most rapid growth, demand for housing in the City was even greater than above indicated. Taking 1970 and 1971 together, builders won approval of a total of 2000 permits although only 1482 were actually completed by the end of 1971.

Alarmed by the accelerated rate of growth in 1970 and 1971, the demand for even more housing, and the sprawl of the City eastward, the City adopted a temporary freeze on development in early 1971. The construction and zoning change moratorium was intended to give the City Council and the City planners an opportunity to study the housing and zoning situation and to develop short and long range plans. The Council made specific findings with respect to housing patterns and availability in Petaluma, including the following: That from 1960–1970 housing had been in almost unvarying 6000 square-foot lots laid out in regular grid patterns; that there was a density of approximately 4.5 housing units per acre in the single-family home areas; that during 1960–1970, 88 per cent of housing permits issued were for single-family detached homes; that in 1970, 83 per cent of Petaluma's housing was single-family dwellings; that the bulk of recent development (largely single-family homes) occurred in the eastern portion of the City, causing a large deficiency in moderately priced multi-family and apartment units on the east side.

To correct the imbalance between single-family and multi-family dwellings, curb the sprawl of the City on the east, and retard the accelerating growth of the City, the Council in 1972 adopted several resolutions, which collectively are called the "Petaluma Plan" (the Plan).

The Plan, on its face limited to a five-year period (1972–1977),[8] fixes a housing development growth rate not to exceed 500 dwelling units per

---

8. The district court found that although the Plan is ostensibly limited to a five-year period, official attempts have been made to perpetuate the Plan beyond 1977.

year.[9] Each dwelling unit represents approximately three people. The 500–unit figure is somewhat misleading, however, because it applies only to housing units (hereinafter referred to as "development-units") that are part of projects involving five units or more. Thus, the 500–unit figure does not reflect any housing and population growth due to construction of single-family homes or even four-unit apartment buildings not part of any larger project.

The Plan also positions a 200 foot wide "greenbelt" around the City,[10] to serve as a boundary for urban expansion for at least five years, and with respect to the east and north sides of the City, for perhaps ten to fifteen years. One of the most innovative features of the Plan is the Residential Development Control System which provides procedures and criteria for the award of the annual 500 development-unit permits. At the heart of the allocation procedure is an intricate point system, whereby a builder accumulates points for conformity by his projects with the City's general plan and environmental design plans, for good architectural design, and for providing low and moderate income dwelling units and various recreational facilities. The Plan further directs that allocations of building permits are to be divided as evenly as feasible between the west and east sections of the City and between single-family dwellings and multiple residential units (including rental units),[11] that the sections of the City closest to the center are to be developed first in order to cause "infilling" of vacant area, and that 8 to 12 per cent of the housing units approved be for low and moderate income persons.

In a provision of the Plan, intended to maintain the close-in rural space outside and surrounding Petaluma, the City solicited Sonoma County to establish stringent subdivision and appropriate acreage parcel controls for the areas outside the urban extension line of the City and to limit severely further residential infilling.

Such attempts include the urban extension line (see text infra) and the agreement to purchase from the Sonoma County Water Agency only 9.8 million gallons of water per day through the year 1990. This flow is sufficient to support a population of 55,000. If the City were to grow at a rate of about 500 housing units per year (approximately three persons per unit), the City would reach a population of 55,000 about the year 1990. The 55,000 figure was mentioned by City officials as the projected optimal (and maximum) size of Petaluma. See, e.g., R.T. at 135–43, 145–46.

9. The allotment for each year is not an inflexible limitation. The Plan does provide for a 10 percent variance (50 units) below or above the 500 unit annual figure, but the expectation of the Council is that not more than 2500 units will be constructed during the five-year period.

10. At some points this urban extension line is about one-quarter of a mile beyond the present City limits.

11. By providing for the increase of multi-family dwellings (including townhouses as well as rental apartments), the Plan allows increased density. Whereas, during the years just preceding the Plan, housing density was about 4.5 units per acre, under the Plan single-family housing will consist of not only low (4.5 units per acre) but also medium density (4.5 to 10 units per acre). And multi-family housing, to comprise about half of the housing under the Plan, will be built at a density of 10 or more units per acre.

Purpose of the Plan

The purpose of the Plan is much disputed in this case. According to general statements in the Plan itself, the Plan was devised to ensure that "development in the next five years will take place in a reasonable, orderly, attractive manner, rather than in a completely haphazard and unattractive manner." The controversial 500–unit limitation on residential development-units was adopted by the City "[i]n order to protect its small town character and surrounding open space."[12] The other features of the Plan were designed to encourage an east-west balance in development, to provide for variety in densities and building types and wide ranges in prices and rents, to ensure infilling of close-in vacant areas, and to prevent the sprawl of the City to the east and north. The Construction Industry Association of Sonoma County (the Association) argues and the district court found, however, that the Plan was primarily enacted "to limit Petaluma's demographic and market growth rate in housing and in the immigration of new residents." *Construction Industry Ass'n v. City of Petaluma*, 375 F.Supp. 574, 576 (N.D.Cal.1974).

Market Demand and Effect of the Plan

In 1970 and 1971, housing permits were allotted at the rate of 1000 annually, and there was no indication that without some governmental control on growth consumer demand would subside or even remain at the 1000–unit per year level. Thus, if Petaluma had imposed a flat 500–unit limitation on *all* residential housing, the effect of the Plan would clearly be to retard to a substantial degree the natural growth rate of the City. Petaluma, however, did not apply the 500–unit limitation across the board, but instead exempted all projects of four units or less. Because appellees failed to introduce any evidence whatsoever as to the number of exempt units expected to be built during the five-year period, the effect of the 500 *development-unit* limitation on the natural growth in housing is uncertain. For purposes of this decision, however, we will assume that the 500 development-unit growth rate is in fact below the reasonably anticipated market demand for such units and that absent the Petaluma Plan, the City would grow at a faster rate.

According to undisputed expert testimony at trial, if the Plan (limiting housing starts to approximately 6 per cent of existing housing stock each year) were to be adopted by municipalities throughout the region, the impact on the housing market would be substantial. For the decade 1970 to 1980, the shortfall in needed housing in the region would be about 105,000 units (or 25 per cent of the units needed). Further, the aggregate effect of a proliferation of the Plan throughout the San Francisco region would be a decline in regional housing stock quality, a loss of the mobility of current and prospective residents and a deterioration in the quality and choice of housing available to income earners

---

12. After the appellees initiated this suit, the City attempted to show that the Plan was implemented to prevent the overtaxing of available water and sewage facilities. We find it unnecessary, however, to consider the claim that sewage and water problems justified implementation of the Plan.

with real incomes of $14,000 per year or less. If, however, the Plan were considered by itself and with respect to Petaluma only, there is no evidence to suggest that there would be a deterioration in the quality and choice of housing available there to persons in the lower and middle income brackets. Actually, the Plan increases the availability of multi-family units (owner-occupied and rental units) and low-income units which were rarely constructed in the pre-Plan days.

COURT PROCEEDINGS

Two landowners (the Landowners) and the Association instituted this suit under 28 U.S.C.A. §§ 1331, 1343 and 42 U.S.C.A. § 1983 against the City and its officers and council members, claiming that the Petaluma Plan was unconstitutional. The district court ruled that certain aspects of the Plan unconstitutionally denied the right to travel insofar as they tended "to limit the natural population growth of the area." 375 F.Supp., at 588. The court enjoined the City and its agents from implementing the unconstitutional elements of the Plan, but the order was stayed by Justice Douglas pending this appeal.

* * *

Appellees claim that the Plan is arbitrary and unreasonable and, thus, violative of the due process clause of the Fourteenth Amendment. According to appellees, the Plan is nothing more than an exclusionary zoning device,[13] designed solely to insulate Petaluma from the urban complex in which it finds itself. The Association and the Landowners reject, as falling outside the scope of any legitimate governmental interest, the City's avowed purposes in implementing the Plan—the preservation of Petaluma's small town character and the avoidance of the social and environmental problems caused by an uncontrolled growth rate.

In attacking the validity of the Plan, appellees rely heavily on the district court's finding that the express purpose and the actual effect of the Plan is to exclude substantial numbers of people who would otherwise elect to move to the City. 375 F.Supp. at 581. The existence of an exclusionary purpose and effect reflects, however, only *one* side of the

---

13. "Exclusionary zoning" is a phrase popularly used to describe suburban zoning regulations which have the effect, if not also the purpose, of preventing the migration of low and middle-income persons. Since a large percentage of racial minorities fall within the low and middle income brackets, exclusionary zoning regulations may also effectively wall out racial minorities. See generally Aloi, Goldberg & White, Racial and Economic Segregation by Zoning: Death Knell for Home Rule?, 1969 U.Tol.L.Rev. 65 (1969); Bigham & Bostick, Exclusionary Zoning Practices: An Examination of the Current Controversy, 25 Vand.L.Rev. 1111 (1972); Davidoff & Davidoff, Opening the Suburbs: Toward Inclusionary Land Use Controls, 22 Syracuse L.Rev. 509 (1971); Note, Exclusionary Zoning and Equal Protection, 84 Harv.L.Rev. 1645 (1971).

Most court challenges to and comment upon so-called exclusionary zoning focus on such traditional zoning devices as height limitations, minimum square footage and minimum lot size requirements, and the prohibition of multi-family dwellings or mobile homes. The Petaluma Plan is unique in that although it assertedly slows the growth rate it replaces the past pattern of single-family detached homes with an assortment of housing units, varying in price and design.

zoning regulation. Practically all zoning restrictions have as a purpose and effect the *exclusion* of some activity or type of structure or a certain density of inhabitants. And in reviewing the reasonableness of a zoning ordinance, our inquiry does not terminate with a finding that it is for an exclusionary purpose. We must determine further whether the *exclusion* bears any rational relationship to a *legitimate state interest.* If it does not, then the zoning regulation is invalid. If, on the other hand, a legitimate state interest is furthered by the zoning regulation, we must defer to the legislative act. Being neither a super legislature nor a zoning board of appeal, a federal court is without authority to weigh and reappraise the factors considered or ignored by the legislative body in passing the challenged zoning regulation. The reasonableness, not the wisdom, of the Petaluma Plan is at issue in this suit.

In determining whether the City's interest in preserving its small town character and in avoiding uncontrolled and rapid growth falls within the broad concept of "public welfare," we are considerably assisted by two recent cases. *Belle Terre,* supra, and *Ybarra v. Town of Los Altos Hills*, 503 F.2d 250 (9th Cir.1974) each of which upheld as not unreasonable a zoning regulation much more restrictive than the Petaluma Plan, are dispositive of the due process issue in this case.

In *Belle Terre* the Supreme Court rejected numerous challenges to a village's restricting land use to one-family dwellings excluding lodging houses, boarding houses, fraternity houses or multiple-dwelling houses. By absolutely prohibiting the construction of or conversion of a building to other than single-family dwelling, the village ensured that it would never grow, if at all, much larger than its population of 700 living in 220 residences. Nonetheless, the Court found that the prohibition of boarding houses and other multi-family dwellings was reasonable and within the public welfare because such dwellings present urban problems, such as the occupation of a given space by more people, the increase in traffic and parked cars and the noise that comes with increased crowds. According to the Court,

> "A quiet place where yards are wide, people few, and motor vehicles restricted are legitimate guidelines in a land-use project addressed to family needs. This goal is a permissible one within Berman v. Parker, supra. The police power is not confined to elimination of filth, stench, and unhealthy places. It is ample to lay out zones where family values, youth values, and the blessings of quiet seclusion, and clean air make the area a sanctuary for people."

416 U.S. at 9, 94 S.Ct. at 1541. While dissenting from the majority opinion in *Belle Terre* on the ground that the regulation unreasonably burdened the exercise of First Amendment associational rights, Mr. Justice Marshall concurred in the Court's express holding that a local entity's zoning power is extremely broad:

> "[L]ocal zoning authorities may properly act in furtherance of the objectives asserted to be served by the ordinance at issue here: *restricting uncontrolled growth,* solving traffic problems, keeping

rental costs at a reasonable level, and making the community attractive to families. The police power which provides the justification for zoning is not narrowly confined. And, it is appropriate that we afford zoning authorities *considerable latitude in choosing the means by which to implement such purposes."*

416 U.S. at 13–14, 94 S.Ct. at 1543 (Marshall, J., dissenting) (emphasis added) (citations omitted).

Following the *Belle Terre* decision, this court in *Los Altos Hills* had an opportunity to review a zoning ordinance providing that a housing lot shall contain not less than one acre and that no lot shall be occupied by more than one primary dwelling unit. The ordinance as a practical matter prevented poor people from living in Los Altos Hills and restricted the density, and thus the population, of the town. This court, nonetheless, found that the ordinance was rationally related to a legitimate governmental interest—*the preservation of the town's rural environment*—and, thus, did not violate the equal protection clause of the Fourteenth Amendment. 503 F.2d at 254.

Both the Belle Terre ordinance and the Los Altos Hills regulation had the purpose and effect of permanently restricting growth; nonetheless, the court in each case upheld the particular law before it on the ground that the regulation served a legitimate governmental interest falling within the concept of the public welfare: the preservation of quiet family neighborhoods (Belle Terre) and the preservation of a rural environment (Los Altos Hills). Even less restrictive or exclusionary than the above zoning ordinances in the Petaluma Plan which, unlike those ordinances, does not freeze the population at present or near-present levels.[14] Further, unlike the Los Altos Hills ordinance and the various zoning regulations struck down by state courts in recent years, the Petaluma Plan does not have the undesirable effect of walling out any particular income class nor any racial minority group.[15]

14. Under the Petaluma Plan, the population is expected to increase at the rate of about 1500 persons annually. This rate approximates the rate of growth in the 1960's and represents about a 6 per cent increase per year over the present population.

15. Although appellees have attempted to align their business interests in attacking the Plan with legitimate housing needs of the urban poor and racial minorities, the Association has not alleged nor can it allege, based on the record in this case, that the Plan has the purpose and effect of excluding poor persons and racial minorities. Cf. Board of County Supervisors of Fairfax County v. Carper, 200 Va. 653, 107 S.E.2d 390 (1959). Contrary to the picture painted by appellees, the Petaluma Plan is "inclusionary" to the extent that it offers new opportunities, previously unavailable, to minorities and low and moderate-income persons. Under the pre-Plan system single family, middle-income housing dominated the Petaluma market, and as a result low and moderate income persons were unable to secure housing in the area. The Plan radically changes the previous building pattern and requires that housing permits be evenly divided between single-family and multi-family units and that approximately eight to twelve per cent of the units be constructed specifically for low and moderate income persons.

In stark contrast, each of the exclusionary zoning regulations invalidated by state courts in recent years impeded the ability of low and moderate income persons to purchase or rent housing in the locality. See, e.g., Southern Burlington County NAACP v. Township of Mount Laurel, 67 N.J. 151, 336 A.2d 713 (Mar. 24, 1975) (zoned exclusively for single-family detached dwellings

Although we assume that some persons desirous of living in Petaluma will be excluded under the housing permit limitation and that, thus, the Plan may frustrate some legitimate regional housing needs, the Plan is not arbitrary or unreasonable. We agree with appellees that unlike the situation in the past most municipalities today are neither isolated nor wholly independent from neighboring municipalities and that, consequently, unilateral land use decisions by one local entity affect the needs and resources of an entire region. See, e.g., *Golden v. Planning Board of Town of Ramapo*, 30 N.Y.2d 359, 334 N.Y.S.2d 138, 285 N.E.2d 291, appeal dismissed, 409 U.S. 1003, 93 S.Ct. 436, 34 L.Ed.2d 294 (1972); *National Land & Investment Co. v. Kohn*, 419 Pa. 504, 215 A.2d 597 (1965); Note, Phased Zoning: Regulation of the Tempo and Sequence of Land Development, 26 Stan.L.Rev. 585, 605 (1974). It does not necessarily follow, however, that the *due process* rights of builders and landowners are violated merely because a local entity exercises in its own self-interest the police power lawfully delegated to it by the state. See *Belle Terre,* supra; *Los Altos Hills,* supra. If the present system of delegated zoning power does not effectively serve the state interest in furthering the general welfare of the region or entire state, it is the state legislature's and not the federal courts' role to intervene and adjust the system. As stated supra, the federal court is not a super zoning board and should not be called on to mark the point at which legitimate local interests in promoting the welfare of the community are outweighed by legitimate regional interests. See Note, supra, at 608–11.

We conclude therefore that under *Belle Terre* and *Los Altos Hills* the concept of the public welfare is sufficiently broad to uphold Petaluma's desire to preserve its small town character, its open spaces and low density of population, and to grow at an orderly and deliberate pace.[16]

and multi-family dwellings designed for middle and upper income persons); Oakwood at Madison, Inc. v. Township of Madison, 117 N.J.Super. 11, 283 A.2d 353 (1971) (minimum one or two acre requirement and severe limitation on multi-family units); Appeal of Kit–Mar Builders, Inc., 439 Pa. 466, 268 A.2d 765 (1970) (two to three acre minimum lot size); Appeal of Girsh, 437 Pa. 237, 263 A.2d 395 (1970) (prohibition of apartment buildings); National Land & Investment Co. v. Kohn, 419 Pa. 504, 215 A.2d 597 (1965) (four acre minimum lot); Board of County Supervisors of Fairfax County v. Carper, 200 Va. 653, 107 S.E.2d 390 (1959) (rezoning to minimum two acre lots with the effect of keeping poor in another section of municipality).

16. Our decision upholding the Plan as not in violation of the appellees' due process rights should not be read as a permanent endorsement of the Plan. In a few years the City itself for good reason may abandon the Plan or the state may decide to alter its laws delegating its zoning power to the local authorities; or to meet legitimate regional needs, regional zoning authorities may be established. See, e.g., Cal.Gov.Code §§ 66600 et seq. (San Francisco Bay Conservation and Development Commission); Cal.Gov.Code §§ 66801, 67000 et seq. (Tahoe Regional Planning Agency); Public Resources Code §§ 27000 et seq. (California Coastal Zone Conservation Commission). To be sure, housing needs in metropolitan areas like the San Francisco Bay Area are pressing and the needs are not being met by present methods of supplying housing. However, the federal court is not the proper forum for resolving these problems. The controversy stirred up by the present litigation, as indicated by the number and variety of amici on each side, and the complex economic, political and social factors involved in this case are compelling evidence that resolution of the important housing and environmental issues raised here is exclusively the domain of the legislature.

COMMERCE CLAUSE

The district court found that housing in Petaluma and the surrounding areas is produced substantially through goods and services in interstate commerce and that curtailment of residential growth in Petaluma will cause serious dislocation to commerce. 375 F.Supp. at 577, 579. Our ruling today, however, that the Petaluma Plan represents a reasonable and legitimate exercise of the police power obviates the necessity of remanding the case for consideration of appellees' claim that the Plan unreasonably burdens interstate commerce.

It is well settled that a state regulation validly based on the police power does not impermissibly burden interstate commerce where the regulation neither discriminates against interstate commerce nor operates to disrupt its required uniformity. *Huron Cement Co. v. Detroit*, 362 U.S. 440, 448, 80 S.Ct. 813, 4 L.Ed.2d 852 (1960). * * *

* * *

Consequently, since the local regulation here is rationally related to the social and environmental welfare of the community and does not discriminate against interstate commerce or operate to disrupt its required uniformity, appellees' claim that the Plan unreasonably burdens commerce must fail.[17]

Reversed.

Notes

1. The courts, in growth regulation cases, frequently refer to the exclusionary effects of certain zoning practices as being part of the issue of growth regulation. See, e.g., Begin v. Inhabitants of Sabattus, 409 A.2d 1269 (Me.1979). This particular aspect of the problem is taken up in a subsequent chapter in some detail. For our purposes at this point, it is sufficient to note that zoning usually deals with the permitted uses on a parcel of land or within a geographic district, and that although zoning regulations may have a very real impact on population densities and housing types, the problem of regulating growth is more closely tied to land subdivision regulations, provision of municipal facilities, and rationing of building permits.

2. Local governments have invented many ways to manage growth while preserving the community character or natural resources. The City of Aspen, Colorado, Growth Management Quota System (Aspen Municipal Code Chapter 26.470) is designed to limit growth to 30,000 people, including visitors, in order to protect community character and ensure adequate delivery of municipal services. To accomplish this, the Growth Management Quota System allows a maximum annual growth rate of 2 percent per year, which limits the amount of development of residential housing, tourist

---

17. Our decision today conforms with others which have upheld reasonable state environmental legislation despite some burden incidentally placed on interstate commerce. See, e.g., *Huron Cement Co. v. Detroit*, supra (air pollution statute); *Procter & Gamble Co. v. City of Chicago*, 509 F.2d 69 (7th Cir.), certiorari denied, 421 U.S. 978, 95 S.Ct. 1980, 44 L.Ed.2d 470 (1975) (ban on phosphate detergents); *American Can Co. v. Oregon Liquor Control Commission*, 15 Or.App. 618, 517 P.2d 691 (1973) (ban on non-returnable beverage containers).

accommodations, and commercial and office development. A scoring system that includes bonus points for affordable housing among other amenities is used to determine which development projects will be granted a permit in a given year.

3. The Ramapo and Petaluma cases focused nationwide interest on the techniques of growth control. Despite the concerns expressed in the dissenting opinion in Ramapo and the district court opinion in Petaluma about local parochialism and the need for addressing the problem on a regional or statewide basis, most of the development in the area has continued to focus on individual communities and local plans. As you read the next principal case, determine whether the majority adequately deals with the issue of local parochialism in the context of regional housing needs and regional welfare.

ASSOCIATED HOME BUILDERS OF THE GREATER EASTBAY, INC. v. CITY OF LIVERMORE

Supreme Court of California, 1976.
18 Cal.3d 582, 135 Cal.Rptr. 41, 557 P.2d 473.

TOBRINER, JUSTICE.

We face today the question of the validity of an initiative ordinance enacted by the voters of the City of Livermore which prohibits issuance of further residential building permits until local educational, sewage disposal, and water supply facilities comply with specified standards. Plaintiff, an association of contractors, subdividers, and other persons interested in residential construction in Livermore, brought this suit to enjoin enforcement of the ordinance. The superior court issued a permanent injunction, and the city appealed.

* * *

[At this point the court reversed the trial court in holding that notice and hearing requirements in the zoning enabling legislation also applied to initiatives. These were held to be inapplicable to enactments by the voters. The court also reversed a trial court finding that the ordinance was unconstitutionally vague.]

Finally, we reject plaintiff's suggestion that we sustain the trial court's injunction on the ground that the ordinance unconstitutionally attempts to bar immigration to Livermore. Plaintiff's contention symbolizes the growing conflict between the efforts of suburban communities to check disorderly development, with its concomitant problems of air and water pollution and inadequate public facilities, and the increasing public need for adequate housing opportunities. We take this opportunity, therefore, to reaffirm and clarify the principles which govern validity of land use ordinances which substantially limit immigration into a community; we hold that such ordinances need not be sustained by a compelling state interest, but are constitutional if they are reasonably related to the welfare of the region affected by the ordinance. Since on the limited record before us plaintiff has not demonstrated that the Livermore ordinance lacks a reasonable relationship to the regional welfare, we cannot hold the ordinance unconstitutional under this standard.

1. SUMMARY OF PROCEEDINGS

The initiative ordinance in question was enacted by a majority of the voters at the Livermore municipal election of April 11, 1972, and became effective on April 28, 1972. The ordinance, set out in full in the margin,[18] states that it was enacted to further the health, safety, and welfare of the citizens of Livermore and to contribute to the solution of air pollution. Finding that excessive issuance of residential building permits has caused school overcrowding, sewage pollution, and water rationing, the ordinance prohibits issuance of further permits until three standards are met: "1. EDUCATIONAL FACILITIES—No double sessions in the schools nor overcrowded classrooms as determined by the California Education Code. 2. SEWAGE—The sewage treatment facilities and capacities meet the standards set by the Regional Water Quality Control Board. 3. WATER SUPPLY—No rationing of water with respect to human consumption or irrigation and adequate water reserves for fire protection exist."

Plaintiff association filed suit to enjoin enforcement of the ordinance and for declaratory relief. After the city filed its answer, all parties moved for judgment on the pleadings and stipulated that the court, upon the pleadings and other documents submitted, could determine the merits of the cause. On the basis of that stipulation the court rendered findings and entered judgment for plaintiff. The city appeals from that judgment.

* * *

---

18. The initiative provides as follows: "INITIATIVE ORDINANCE RE BUILDING PERMITS

"An ordinance to control residential building permits in the City of Livermore:

"A. The people of the City of Livermore hereby find and declare that it is in the best interest of the City in order to protect the health, safety, and general welfare of the citizens of the city, to control residential building permits in the said city. Residential building permits include single-family residential, multiple residential, and trailer court building permits within the meaning of the City Code of Livermore and the General Plan of Livermore. Additionally, it is the purpose of this initiative measure to contribute to the solution of air pollution in the City of Livermore.

"B. The specific reasons for the proposed position are that the undersigned believe that the resulting impact from issuing residential building permits at the current rate results in the following problems mentioned below. Therefore no further residential permits are to be issued by the said city until satisfactory solutions, as determined in the standards set forth, exist to all the following problems:

"1. EDUCATIONAL FACILITIES—No double sessions in the schools nor overcrowded classrooms as determined by the California Education Code.

"2. SEWAGE—The sewage treatment facilities and capacities meet the standards set by the Regional Water Quality Control Board.

"3. WATER SUPPLY—No rationing of water with respect to human consumption or irrigation and adequate water reserves for fire protection exist.

"C. This ordinance may only be amended or repealed by the voters at a regular municipal election.

"D. If any portion of this ordinance is declared invalid the remaining portions are to be considered valid."

[The portion of the decision dealing with the conflict between the notice and hearing provisions of the zoning enabling act and the initiative procedures act is omitted.]

3. THE LIVERMORE ORDINANCE IS NOT VOID FOR VAGUENESS

The trial court found the ordinance unconstitutionally vague on two grounds: (1) that the ordinance did not contain sufficiently specific standards for the issuance or denial of building permits, and (2) that it did not specify what person or agency was empowered to determine if the ordinance's standards have been met. We disagree with both rationales and find the ordinance sufficiently specific to fulfill constitutional requirements.

The controversy concerning the specificity of the ordinance centers upon the standard as to education. The ordinance prohibits issuance of residential building permits until a "satisfactory solution" has been evolved to the problem of "Educational Facilities"; it defines a satisfactory solution as one characterized by "No double sessions in the schools nor overcrowded classrooms as determined by the California Education Code."

The term "double sessions" is sufficiently specific; as stated by Professor Deutsch, it "can be defined by reference to common practice, since the term is frequently used to refer to a situation where different groups of students in the same grade are attending the same school at different times of the day because of a lack of space." (Deutsch, op. cit., supra, pp. 22–23.) The phrase "overcrowded classrooms as determined by the California Education Code," however, is less clear, since nowhere in the Education Code does there appear a definition of "overcrowded classrooms."

The City of Livermore, however, points out that the ordinance does not refer to a definition of "overcrowded classrooms" contained in the Education Code, but to a determination of that subject. The language, it contends—and plaintiff does not dispute the contention—was intended to refer to resolution 3220, adopted by the board of the Livermore Valley Joint School District on January 18, 1972, in which that board, pursuant to authority granted it by Education Code section 1052, established clear and specific standards for determining whether schools are overcrowded.[19]

19. Board Resolution 3220 provides as follows:

"ADEQUACY OF SCHOOLS

"1. Sufficient instructional space shall be determined to exist when:

  a. For elementary schools:

  (1) All students can be housed in single session classes in affected schools.

  (2) At least 900 square feet of functional instructional area are available for each classroom or teaching station.

  (3) Class sizes average 30 students or less throughout the District.

  b. For secondary schools:

  (1) All students can be housed within the capacity of existing schools on regular day session. Capacity will be determined by applying State Department of Education criteria in keeping with maximum class size.

"2. Minimum support services exist when:

Rather than interpret the ordinance in a manner which would expose it to the charge of unconstitutional vagueness, we adopt the suggestion of the city and construe the ordinance's standard on education to incorporate the specific guidelines established in board resolution 3220. In so doing we conform to the rule that enactments should be interpreted when possible to uphold their validity * * * and the corollary principle that courts should construe enactments to give specific content to terms that might otherwise be unconstitutionally vague. * * *

* * *

The ordinance's standards relating to sewage and water supply present no constitutional difficulties. The sewage provision incorporates the "standards set by the Regional Water Quality Control Board"; that agency has in fact established specific and detailed standards of water purification and sewage disposal. The water supply provision describes a "satisfactory solution" as one in which water is not rationed, and "adequate water reserves for fire protection exist." The existence of rationing is an objective fact which can be ascertained by inquiry to the agencies having authority to ration. Although individuals may differ as to the adequacy of reserves for fire protection, the considered judgment of the agencies responsible for fire protection would provide a reliable guide.

Although we have determined that the ordinance's standards meet constitutional requirements of certainty, plaintiff argues, and the trial court held, that the ordinance is void because it fails to designate what agency or person determines whether these standards have been achieved. We question plaintiff's underlying assumption that an ordinance or statute is void if it does not specify on its face the agency that is to adjudge disputes concerning its application; by such a test most of the civil and criminal laws of this state would be invalidated. In any event, we believe that the Livermore ordinance, read in the light of the structure of Livermore's city government and the applicable judicial decisions, does indicate the method by which disagreements concerning the ordinance's standards are resolved.

The Livermore ordinance establishes standards to govern the issuance or denial of residential building permits. These standards must be

a. Sufficient shelf and cabinet space is provided to accommodate books and equipment normally associated with a classroom.

b. A faculty workroom exists.

c. Off-street parking for each teaching station is provided.

d. Sufficient playground area and playground equipment is provided to support outdoor play activity.

e. Sufficient furniture and equipment for each classroom to accommodate all students and teachers.

f. A library is established equivalent to at least one classroom for each 600 students.

"3. School construction and outfitting, in terms of classroom space, architectural layout, space relationship, outdoor facilities, utilities, grounds development, and furniture and equipment, shall meet or exceed State Bureau of Education standards."

directed in the first instance to the city building inspector, the official charged with the duty of issuing or denying such permits. Since the duties of this official are ministerial in character, his decisions can be reviewed by writ of mandamus. * * * Thus the ultimate decision as to compliance with the standards will be rendered by the courts. * * *

4. On the Limited Record Before Us, Plaintiff Cannot Demonstrate That the Livermore Ordinance Is Not a Constitutional Exercise of the City's Police Power

Plaintiff urges that we affirm the trial court's injunction on a ground which it raised below, but upon which the trial court did not rely. Plaintiff contends that the ordinance proposes, and will cause, the prevention of nonresidents from migrating to Livermore, and that the ordinance therefore attempts an unconstitutional exercise of the police power, both because no compelling state interest justifies its infringement upon the migrant's constitutionally protected right to travel, and because it exceeds the police power of the municipality.

The ordinance on its face imposes no absolute prohibition or limitation upon population growth or residential construction. It does provide that no building permits will issue unless standards for educational facilities, water supply and sewage disposal have been met, but plaintiff presented no evidence to show that the ordinance's standards were unreasonable or unrelated to their apparent objectives of protecting the public health and welfare. Thus, we do not here confront the question of the constitutionality of an ordinance which limits or bars population growth either directly in express language or indirectly by the imposition of prohibitory standards; we adjudicate only the validity of an ordinance limiting building permits in accord with standards that reasonably measure the adequacy of public services.

* * * [T]he limited record here prevents us from resolving that constitutional issue. We deal here with a case in which a land use ordinance is challenged solely on the ground that it assertedly exceeds the municipality's authority under the police power; the challenger eschews any claim that the ordinance discriminates on a basis of race or wealth. Under such circumstances, we view the past decisions of this court and the federal courts as establishing the following standard: the land use restriction withstands constitutional attack if it is fairly debatable that the restriction in fact bears a reasonable relation to the general welfare. For the guidance of the trial court we point out that if a restriction significantly affects residents of surrounding communities, the constitutionality of the restriction must be measured by its impact not only upon the welfare of the enacting community, but upon the welfare of the surrounding region. We explain the process by which the court can determine whether or not such a restriction reasonably relates to the regional welfare. Since the record in the present case is limited to the pleadings and stipulations, and is devoid of evidence concerning the probable impact and duration of the ordinance's restrictions, we conclude that we cannot now adjudicate the constitutionality of the ordi-

nance. Thus we cannot sustain the trial court judgment on the ground that the ordinance exceeds the city's authority under the police power; that issue can be resolved only after trial.

* * *

We therefore reaffirm the established constitutional principle that a local land use ordinance falls within the authority of the police power if it is reasonably related to the public welfare. Most previous decisions applying this test, however, have involved ordinances without substantial effect beyond the municipal boundaries. The present ordinance, in contrast, significantly affects the interests of nonresidents who are not represented in the city legislative body and cannot vote on a city initiative. We therefore believe it desirable for the guidance of the trial court to clarify the application of the traditional police power test to an ordinance which significantly affects nonresidents of the municipality.

When we inquire whether an ordinance reasonably relates to the public welfare, inquiry should begin by asking *whose* welfare must the ordinance serve. In past cases, when discussing ordinances without significant effect beyond the municipal boundaries, we have been content to assume that the ordinance need only reasonably relate to the welfare of the enacting municipality and its residents. But municipalities are not isolated islands remote from the needs and problems of the area in which they are located; thus an ordinance, superficially reasonable from the limited viewpoint of the municipality may be disclosed as unreasonable when viewed from a larger perspective.

These considerations impel us to the conclusion that the proper constitutional test is one which inquires whether the ordinance reasonably relates to the welfare of those whom it significantly affects. If its impact is limited to the city boundaries, the inquiry may be limited accordingly; if, as alleged here, the ordinance may strongly influence the supply and distribution of housing for an entire metropolitan region, judicial inquiry must consider the welfare of that region.

* * *

We explain the process by which a trial court may determine whether a challenged restriction reasonably relates to the regional welfare. The first step in that analysis is to forecast the probable effect and duration of the restriction. In the instant case the Livermore ordinance posits a total ban on residential construction, but one which terminates as soon as public facilities reach specified standards. Thus to evaluate the impact of the restriction, the court must ascertain the extent to which public facilities currently fall short of the specified standards, must inquire whether the city or appropriate regional agencies have undertaken to construct needed improvements, and must determine when the improvements are likely to be completed.

The second step is to identify the competing interests affected by the restriction. We touch in this area deep social antagonisms. We allude to the conflict between the environmental protectionists and the egalitarian humanists; a collision between the forces that would save the benefits of nature and those that would preserve the opportunity of people in general to settle. Suburban residents who seek to overcome problems of inadequate schools and public facilities to secure "the blessing of quiet seclusion and clean air" and to "make the area a sanctuary for people" (*Village of Belle Terre v. Boraas*, supra, 416 U.S. 1, 9, 94 S.Ct. 1536, 1541, 39 L.Ed.2d 797) may assert a vital interest in limiting immigration to their community. Outsiders searching for a place to live in the face of a growing shortage of adequate housing, and hoping to share in the perceived benefits of suburban life, may present a countervailing interest opposing barriers to immigration.

Having identified and weighed the competing interests, the final step is to determine whether the ordinance, in light of its probable impact, represents a reasonable accommodation of the competing interests. We do not hold that a court in inquiring whether an ordinance reasonably relates to the regional welfare, cannot defer to the judgment of the municipality's legislative body. But judicial deference is not judicial abdication. The ordinance must have a *real and substantial* relation to the public welfare. (*Miller v. Board of Public Works*, supra, 195 Cal. 477, 490, 234 P. 381.) There must be a reasonable basis in fact, not in fancy, to support the legislative determination. (*Consolidated Rock Products Co. v. City of Los Angeles* (1962) 57 Cal.2d 515, 522, 20 Cal.Rptr. 638, 370 P.2d 342.) Although in many cases it will be "fairly debatable" (*Euclid v. Ambler Co.*, supra, 272 U.S. 365, 388, 47 S.Ct. 114, 71 L.Ed. 303) that the ordinance reasonably relates to the regional welfare, it cannot be assumed that a land use ordinance can *never* be invalidated as an enactment in excess of the police power.

The burden rests with the party challenging the constitutionality of an ordinance to present the evidence and documentation which the court will require in undertaking this constitutional analysis. Plaintiff in the present case has not yet attempted to shoulder that burden. Although plaintiff obtained a stipulation that as of the date of trial the ordinance's goals had not been fulfilled, it presented no evidence to show the likely duration or effect of the ordinance's restriction upon building permits. We must presume that the City of Livermore and appropriate regional agencies will attempt in good faith to provide that community with adequate schools, sewage disposal facilities, and a sufficient water supply; plaintiff, however, has not presented evidence to show whether the city and such agencies have undertaken to construct the needed improvements or when such improvements will be completed. Consequently we cannot determine the impact upon either Livermore or the surrounding region of the ordinance's restriction on the issuance of building permits pending achievement of its goals.

With respect to the competing interests, plaintiff asserts the existence of an acute housing shortage in the San Francisco Bay Area, but presents no evidence to document that shortage or to relate it to the probable effect of the Livermore ordinance. Defendants maintain that Livermore has severe problems of air pollution and inadequate public facilities which make it reasonable to divert new housing, at least temporarily, to other communities but offer no evidence to support that claim. Without an evidentiary record to demonstrate the validity and significance of the asserted interests, we cannot determine whether the instant ordinance attempts a reasonable accommodation of those interests.

In short, we cannot determine on the pleadings and stipulations alone whether this ordinance reasonably relates to the general welfare of the region it affects. The ordinance carries the presumption of constitutionality; plaintiff cannot overcome that presumption on the limited record before us. Thus the judgment rendered on this limited record cannot be sustained on the ground that the initiative ordinance falls beyond the proper scope of the police power.

* * *

The judgment of the superior court is reversed, and the cause remanded for further proceedings consistent with the views expressed herein.

WRIGHT, C.J. and MCCOMB, SULLIVAN and RICHARDSON, JJ., concur.

* * *

[A dissenting opinion by JUSTICE CLARK is omitted.]

MOSK, JUSTICE (dissenting).

I dissent.

Limitations on growth may be justified in resort communities, beach and lake and mountain sites, and other rural and recreational areas; such restrictions are generally designed to preserve nature's environment for the benefit of all mankind. They fulfill our fiduciary obligation to posterity. As Thomas Jefferson wrote, the earth belongs to the living, but in usufruct.

But there is a vast qualitative difference when a suburban community invokes an elitist concept to construct a mythical moat around its perimeter, not for the benefit of mankind but to exclude all but its fortunate current residents.

* * * Where I part company with the majority is in its substantive holding that a total exclusion of new residents can be constitutionally accomplished under a city's police power.

The majority, somewhat desultorily, deny that the ordinance imposes an absolute prohibition upon population growth or residential construction. It is true that the measure prohibits the issuance of building permits for single-family residential, multiple residential and trailer residential units until designated public services meet specified standards. But to see such restriction in practicality as something short of total prohibition is to employ ostrich vision.

First of all, the ordinance provides no timetable or dates by which the public services are to be made adequate. Thus the moratorium on permits is likely to continue for decades, or at least until attrition ultimately reduces the present population. Second, it is obvious that no inducement exists for *present* residents to expend their resources to render facilities adequate for the purpose of accommodating *future* residents. It would seem more rational, if improved services are really contemplated for any time in the foreseeable future, to admit the new residents and compel them to make their proportionate contribution to the cost of the educational, sewage and water services. Thus it cannot seriously be argued that Livermore maintains anything other than total exclusion.

The trial court found, inter alia, that the ordinance prohibited the issuance of building permits for residential purposes until certain conditions are met, but the measure does not provide that any person or agency is required to expend or commence any efforts on behalf of the city to meet the requirements. Nor is the city itself obliged to act within any specified time to cure its own deficiencies. Thus, in these circumstances procrastination produces its own reward: continued exclusion of new residents.

The significant omissions, when noted in relation to the ordinance preamble, reveal that the underlying purpose of the measure is "to control residential building permits in the City of Livermore"—translation: to keep newcomers out of the city—and not to solve the purported inadequacies in municipal educational, sewage and water services. Livermore concedes no building permits are now being issued and it relates no current or prospective schedule designed to correct its defective municipal services.

A municipal policy of preventing acquisition and development of property by nonresidents clearly violates article I, sections 1 and 7, subdivisions (a) and (b), of the Constitution of California.

Exclusion of unwanted outsiders, while a more frequent phenomenon recently, is not entirely innovative. The State of California made an abortive effort toward exclusivity back in the 1930s as part of a scheme to stem the influx of poor migrants from the dust bowl states of the southwest. The additional burden these indigent new residents placed on California services and facilities was severely aggravated by the great depression of that period. In *Edwards v. California* (1941) 314 U.S. 160, 62 S.Ct. 164, 86 L.Ed. 119, the Supreme Court held, however, that the nature of the union established by the Constitution did not permit any one state to "isolate itself from the difficulties common to all of them by restraining the transportation of persons and property across its borders." The sanction against immigration of indigents was invalidated.

If California could not protect itself from the growth problems of that era, may Livermore build a Chinese Wall to insulate itself from growth problems today? And if Livermore may do so, why not every municipality in Alameda County and in all other counties in Northern California? With a patchwork of enclaves the inevitable result will be creation of an aristocracy housed in exclusive suburbs while modest wage earners will be confined to declining neighborhoods, crowded into sterile, monotonous, multi-family projects, or assigned to pockets of marginal housing on the urban fringe. The overriding objective should be to minimize rather than exacerbate social and economic disparities, to lower barriers rather than raise them, to emphasize heterogeneity rather than homogeneity, to increase choice rather than limit it.

* * *

One thing emerges with clarity from the foregoing and from numerous related cases: access to housing is regarded by the Supreme Court as a matter of serious social and constitutional concern. While this interest has generally been manifest in the context of racial discrimination, there is no valid reason for not invoking the principle when persons of all races and of all economic groups are involved. There are no invariable racial or economic characteristics of the goodly numbers of families which seek social mobility, the opportunities for the good life available in a suburban atmosphere, and access to types of housing, education and employment differing from those indigenous to crowded urban centers.

There is a plethora of commentary on efforts, in a variety of contexts, of local communities to discourage the influx of outsiders. In virtually every instance, however, the cities limited availability of housing; until now it has never been seriously contemplated that a community would attempt total exclusion by refusing all building permits. * * *

* * *

In sum, I realize the easiest course is for this court to defer to the political judgment of the townspeople of Livermore, on a they-know-what's-best-for-them theory (*Eastlake v. Forest City Enterprises, Inc.* (1976) 426 U.S. 668, 96 S.Ct. 2358, 49 L.Ed.2d 132; *James v. Valtierra* (1971) 402 U.S. 137, 91 S.Ct. 1331, 28 L.Ed.2d 678). But conceptually, when a locality adopts a comprehensive, articulated program to prevent any population growth over the foreseeable future, it places its public policy intentions visibly on the table for judicial scrutiny and constitutional analysis.

Communities adopt growth limits from a variety of motives. There may be conservationists genuinely motivated to preserve general or specific environments. There may be others whose motivation is social exclusionism, racial exclusion, racial discrimination, income segregation, fiscal protection, or just fear of any future change; each of these purposes is well served by growth prevention.

Whatever the motivation, total exclusion of people from a community is both immoral and illegal. (Cal. Const. art. I, §§ 1, 7, subds. (a) & (b).) Courts have a duty to prevent such practices, while at the same time recognizing the validity of genuine conservationist efforts.

The problem is not insoluble, nor does it necessarily provoke extreme results. Indeed, the solution can be relatively simple if municipal agencies would consider the aspirations of society as a whole, rather than merely the effect upon their narrow constituency. (See, e.g., A.L.I. Model Land Development Code, art. 7.) Accommodation between environmental preservation and satisfaction of housing needs can be reached through rational guidelines for land-use decision-making. Ours, of course, is not the legislative function. But two legal inhibitions must be the benchmark of any such guidelines. First, any absolute prohibition on housing development is presumptively invalid. And second, local regulations, based on parochialism, that limit population densities in growing suburban areas may be found invalid unless the community is absorbing a reasonable share of the region's population pressures.

Under the foregoing test, the Livermore ordinance is fatally flawed. I would affirm the judgment of the trial court.

Notes

1. In light of the decision in the principal case, how might a court would respond to a local referendum or initiated ordinance expressing either an absolute cap on population or a specific limit on the number of building permits to be issued? In City of Boca Raton v. Boca Villas Corp., 371 So.2d 154 (Fla.App.1979), certiorari denied 449 U.S. 824, 101 S.Ct. 86, 66 L.Ed.2d 27 (1980), the court affirmed a trial court judgment holding invalid an initiated ordinance adopted by the citizens of Boca Raton establishing a limit of 40,000 dwelling units in the city. The court stated that a determination that the ordinance was confiscatory was not necessary in that the trial court found that the ordinance bore no rational relationship to the general welfare. The court stated:

> Our study of the briefs and record convinces us that there is substantial competent evidence to support the finding of an absence of a rational relationship regarding the charter amendment and zoning ordinance. That being the case, we need not reach the question of confiscation vel non because the finding that there is no compelling need justifying an exercise of the police power burdening private property is sufficient to warrant striking down the legislative act. * * * That is not to say there must be an absolute necessity requiring the enactment of certain zoning restrictions before they can be tolerated as a proper exercise of the police power. But, as here, an excessive restriction on the use of private property which does not contribute substantially to the public health, morals, safety and welfare is arbitrary and unreasonable and thus unconstitutional. * * * The trial court found, and the record supports such finding, that the charter amendment and implementing ordinances bore no such rational relationship to the requisite purposes.

> We would concede that most of the cases where judicial invalidation of zoning laws has been upheld have in some measure involved the issue of confiscation. Those cases hold that as applied to the property involved the zoning ordinance was unreasonable because it deprived a property owner of the beneficial use of his property. We suggest the reason that the confiscation issue is so pervasive in the case law on this subject is because someone's ox is getting gored. Who is going to institute litigation but the person who feels his property rights infringed upon by excessive restrictions upon the use thereof?

There are cases, however, which support the principle that zoning which unnecessarily restricts property, zoning which bears no rational relationship to the public health, safety, morals and welfare is unconstitutional without raising the confiscation issue.

* * *

In view of our conclusion that an otherwise valid attack may be made upon the charter amendment and implementing ordinances, we need not consider the trial judge's findings that the cap and implementing ordinances are so drastic and restrictive as to be confiscatory as applied to appellees' property.

2. In 1971, in Boulder, Colorado, local citizens led by the Zero Population Growth group, placed a 100,000 resident population cap measure on the ballot; the measure was defeated, but an alternative measure sponsored by the city council directed toward studying means of limiting growth, passed handily. See, Godschalk, Brower, McBennett, Vestal & Herr, Constitutional Issues of Growth Management 255–66 (1979).

3. After the decision in the Livermore case, several California cities and towns experienced initiated growth limitation ordinances. In 1987, the California Evidence Code § 669.5 was amended to provide that—in cases involving an ordinance which numerically limits residential construction permits—the city "shall bear the burden of proof that the ordinance is necessary for the protection of the public health, safety, or welfare of the population * * *" This provision is discussed in Building Industry Ass'n of San Diego v. Superior Court, 211 Cal.App.3d 277, 259 Cal.Rptr. 325 (1989). Also see Lesher Communications, Inc. v. City of Walnut Creek, 52 Cal.3d 531, 277 Cal.Rptr. 1, 802 P.2d 317 (1990), where the court struck an initiated growth control ordinance challenged as inconsistent with the existing general plan, finding that the ordinance was not labeled as, or intended to be viewed as, an amendment to the plan.

STEEL HILL DEVELOPMENT, INC. v. TOWN OF SANBORNTON

United States Court of Appeals, First Circuit, 1972.
469 F.2d 956.

COFFIN, CHIEF JUDGE.

Located in the rolling hills of Belknap County, New Hampshire is the tiny town of Sanbornton with a year-round population of approximately 1,000 persons living in some 330 regular homes. Long popular as a major recreational and resort area, Belknap County commenced to share its rural beauty with visitors in considerably greater degree with the opening in the 1960's of Interstate Highway 93 which funneled droves of touring urbanites from the Boston area, one hundred miles away, into towns like Sanbornton. Since Sanbornton borders Lake Winnisquam, is within easy reach of Lake Winnipesaukee and affords simple access to most New Hampshire ski areas, it is no surprise that its summer population is about 2,000 persons, that it has around 400 seasonal homes, and now is afforded the unique opportunity to serve as a seasonal second home paradise for persons who would buy the proposed 500 to 515 family units planned by appellant Steel Hill Development, Inc. In short, as the district court stated, "this case reflects the current clash between those interested in opening up new and hitherto undeveloped land for sale and profit and those wishing to preserve the rural character of Northern New England and shield it from the relentless pressure of an affluent segment of our society seeking new areas for rest, recreation and year round living." *Steel Hill Development, Inc. v. Town of Sanbornton*, 338 F.Supp. 301, 302 (D.N.H.1972).

Steel Hill acquired its 510 acres in December 1969 and immediately began surveying the land, mapping the topography and creating plans for conventional and "cluster" development. At that time, and until March 9, 1971 the entire Steel Hill tract was zoned as General Residence and Agricultural, requiring a minimum lot size of 35,000 square feet, or about three-fourths of an acre. Desirous of effectuating the "cluster" plan which appellant knew would require amending the zoning ordinance, appellant engaged in extensive and cordial negotiations with the town planning board during 1970. In order to permit some development while the "cluster" concept was under consideration, the board accepted a plan for 50 conventional lots meeting the 35,000 square feet requirement and scheduled, according to usual practice, a public hearing on the matter. About one hundred townsfolk attending the meeting on November 13, 1970 expressed opposition to any development by Steel Hill. Nevertheless, the planning board later approved the subdivision plan for thirty-seven lots, in the face of a petition, presented by about thirty town residents, for zoning the entire town as six acre minimum lots. Because public interest had been heightened in preserving Sanbornton's "charm as a New England small town", the planning board then proposed amendments to the zoning ordinance designed to enlarge the Forest Conservation areas, and to establish separate General Residential Districts and Agricultural Districts, with increased minimum acreage requirements in these districts and in the Historical Preservation and the Recreational Districts. These were passed.

As a result of the re-zoning, approximately 70 per cent of appellant's land is in the Forest Conservation District and 30 per cent in the Agricultural District. Clearly, its plans for "cluster" or conventional development are inconsistent with the new zoning ordinance. Appellant filed suit in the district court alleging that the three and six acre minimum lot size requirements are unconstitutional because they bear no rational relationship to the health, safety, morals or general welfare of the community and are therefore violative of N.H. R.S.A. 31:60 and the due process clause of the Fourteenth Amendment; that the rezoning greatly reduced the value of its land so as to constitute a taking without compensation; and that the classification of its land was violative of the equal protection clause of the Fourteenth Amendment because it was arbitrary and discriminatory in the restrictions imposed on development. The district court found adversely to appellant on all counts.

* * *

New Hampshire, like most states, has granted authority to localities to zone in order to promote public health, safety, morals and general welfare. N.H. R.S.A. 31:60. A zoning ordinance under such a statute may not be declared unconstitutional unless its "provisions are clearly arbitrary and unreasonable, having no substantial relation to the public health, safety, morals, or general welfare." *Village of Euclid v. Ambler Realty Co.*, 272 U.S. 365, 47 S.Ct. 114, 71 L.Ed. 303 (1926); *Gorieb v. Fox*, 274 U.S. 603, 47 S.Ct. 675, 71 L.Ed. 1228 (1927). Thus a court does not sit as a super zoning board with power to act *de novo,* but rather has, in the absence of alleged racial or economic discrimination, a limited role of review.

The district court found that, as the Sanbornton Planning Board had itself determined, topography and soil conditions posed severe problems of pollution, improper sewage disposal, poor drainage and erosion to large-scale development of the Steel Hill Tract, justifying imposition of the three-acre minimum lot size requirement in accordance with the public health. We have carefully read the conflicting trial testimony of the various experts who expressed an opinion on these matters and cannot say that the court's finding is clearly erroneous. In any event, appellant does not seem to challenge that ruling, but rather directs its argument to the unreasonableness of the six acre lot requirement.

The district court stated that it could not find the six acre requirement reasonable if only health and safety were considered, but that such requirement was reasonably related to the promotion of the general welfare of the community. N.H. R.S.A. 31:60. The court considered the pollution of Lake Winnisquam, possible interference with smelt spawning in Black Brook, increased traffic problems inherent in large-scale development, and increased air pollution. Testimony of planning board members and citizens opposed to Steel Hill's plans additionally reveals a desire to discourage density of population, and most importantly, a fear of premature development which was manifested in this effort to provide for orderly growth of the unspoiled areas of the town in a logical way. Several witnesses testified that not only would the town's rural character be destroyed by Steel Hill's massive plans, which would, in effect, double the town's population, but that there could be immeasurable ecological harm.

* * * [A]ppellant here does not seek to satisfy an already existing demand for suburban expansion, but rather seeks to create a demand in Sanbornton on behalf of wealthy residents of Megalopolis who might be willing to invest heavily in time and money to gain their own haven in bucolic surroundings. Note, 57 Iowa L.Rev. 126, 127 (1972). These different problems of suburban and rural expansion, their scientific and legal analyses, and their appropriate solutions cannot so easily be equated.

More appropriate to appellant's argument, and not cited to us, is *Kavanewsky v. Zoning Board of Appeals of Town of Warren*, 160 Conn. 397, 279 A.2d 567 (1971), where the town, when threatened with rapid development, increased minimum lot size requirements from one to two acres, an increase which the court found motivated by a "demand of the people to keep Warren a rural community with open spaces and keep undesirable businesses out", id. at 570, a goal not within the general welfare. In contrast, perhaps, is *Confederacion de la Raza Unida v. City of Morgan Hill*, 324 F.Supp. 895 (N.D.Cal.1971), which permitted a restriction, imposed by a zoning ordinance, on the development of a charming mountainous area of a city because of esthetic and environmental concerns. Yet even *Kavanewsky*, so far as appears, was dealing with an effort to keep out permanent residents and businesses, not to damp down a promoter's goal of doubling the housing in a small town by its large-scale second home plans. If, however, appellant has failed to present us with any controlling authority, neither have appellees. *Morgan Hill* involved a more detailed ordinance regulating density which resulted in a minimum lot size of only one half acre on the average. *County Commissioners of Queen Anne's County v. Miles*, 246 Md. 355, 228 A.2d 450 (1967), involved the upholding of a five acre minimum lot size requirement. The affected land comprised only 6.7 per cent of the county and the zoning was done pursuant to a long-range plan to preserve an unusually beautiful country estate section of a river. While we note that it is not within judicial competence to say that the forests in Sanbornton are any less worth preserving than country river estates, we do find it significant that the six acre requirement extends to approximately 50 per cent of the town, including the only area currently under any sort of development.

In short, no precedent compels its application to the case before us. We are faced with "a local legislative determination that the general welfare will be promoted by exclusion of an unwanted use from a nonmetropolitan community [which exclusion] is not likely to conflict with a regional need for local space for that use." 57 Iowa L.Rev. at 140. We recognize, as within the general welfare, concerns relating to the construction and integration of hundreds of new homes which would have an irreversible effect on the area's ecological balance, destroy scenic values, decrease open space, significantly change the rural character of this small town, pose substantial financial burdens on the town for police, fire, sewer, and road service, and open the way for the tides of weekend "visitors" who would own second homes. If the federal government itself has thought these concerns to be within the general welfare, see, e.g., 42 U.S.C.A. § 4321, et seq., we cannot say that Sanbornton cannot similarly consider such values and reflect them in its zoning ordinance. Though some courts may have rejected them within the suburban zoning context, as in *Kohn*, and its progeny, or where permanent first homes are involved, as in *Kavanewsky*, but cf. *Morgan Hill*, we think they are persuasive in the case before us. "Many environmental and social values are involved in a determination of how land would best be used in the public interest. The choice of the voters of [the city] is not lacking in support in this regard." *Southern Alameda Spanish Speaking Organization v. City of Union City*, 424 F.2d 291 (9th Cir.1970).

Yet, though it may be proper for Sanbornton to consider the foregoing factors, we think the town has done so in a most crude manner. We are disturbed by the admission here that there was never any professional or scientific study made as to why six, rather than four or eight, acres was reasonable to protect the values cherished by the people of Sanbornton. On reviewing the record, we have serious worries whether the basic motivation of the town meeting was not simply to keep outsiders, provided they wished to come in quantity, out of the town. We cannot think that expansion of population, even a very substantial one, seasonal or permanent, is by itself a legitimate basis for permissible objection. Were we to adjudicate this as a restriction for all time, and were the evidence of pressure from land-deprived and land-seeking outsiders more real, we might well come to a different conclusion. Where there is natural population growth it has to go somewhere, unwelcome as it may be, and in that case we do not think it should be channelled by the happenstance of what town gets its veto in first. But, at this time of uncertainty as to the right balance between ecological and population pressures, we cannot help but feel that the town's ordinance, which severely restricts development, may properly stand for the present as a legitimate stop-gap measure.

In effect, the town has bought time for its citizens not unlike the action taken in referendum by the City of Boulder, Colorado to restrict growth on an emergency basis until an adequate study can be made of future needs. 60 Georgetown L.J. 1363 (1972). *See also Golden v. Planning Board of Town of Ramapo*, 30 N.Y.2d 359, 334 N.Y.S.2d 138, 285 N.E.2d 291 (1972), appeal dismissed 409 U.S. 1003, 93 S.Ct. 440, 34 L.Ed.2d 294 (1972). It was evident to the zoning board, and the district court, that haphazard and uncontrolled development of the town's hill areas would be inimical to present and future Sanbornton residents, *see Candlestick Properties, Inc. v. San Francisco Bay Conservation & Development Comm.*, 11 Cal.App.3d 557, 89 Cal.Rptr. 897 (1970), and that if the zoning laws do become "permanent barriers", then as the district court said, resort to the courts is always possible. *Steel Hill Development*, supra, 338 F.Supp. at 307. The zoning ordinance here in question has been in existence less than two years. Hopefully, Sanbornton has begun or soon will begin to plan with more precision for the future taking advantage of numerous federal or state grants for which it might qualify. Additionally, the New Hampshire legislature, to the extent it expects small towns like Sanbornton to cope with environmental problems posed by private developments, might adopt legislation similar to the federal National Environmental Policy Act, 42 U.S.C.A. § 4321 et seq. and thereby require developers to submit detailed environmental statements, if such power does not already reside within the town's arsenal of laws. Thus, while we affirm the district court's determination at the present time, we recognize that this is a very special case which cannot be read as evidencing a general approval of six-acre zoning, and that this requirement may well not indefinitely stand without more homework by the concerned parties.

Lastly, we find little merit to appellant's contentions that the zoning ordinance has resulted in a taking of appellant's property without just compensation or that it is discriminatory. As the district court found, appellant still has the land and buildings for which it paid $290,000. The estimated worth, had Steel Hill's original plans been approved, is irrelevant. Though the value of the tract has been decreased considerably, it is not worthless or useless so as to constitute a taking. *Hadacheck v. Sebastian,* 239 U.S. 394, 36 S.Ct. 143, 60 L.Ed. 348 (1915); *Sibson v. State, N.H.,* 282 A.2d 664 (1971). *Cf. State v. Johnson,* 265 A.2d 711 (Me.1970); *Bartlett v. Zoning Comm. of Town of Old Lyme,* 161 Conn. 24, 282 A.2d 907 (1971). As to appellant's claim of discrimination, we note that its land, like all other land zoned six acres, is essentially virgin forest. It is adjacent to, and its March 1971 re-zoning represented an extension of, the Forest Conservation District created in 1970. Thus the ordinance cannot be said to discriminate unreasonably against Steel Hill, be it the only developer in the town.

Affirmed.

Notes

1. For the subsequent history of the Steel Hill case, see Steel Hill Development, Inc. v. Town of Sanbornton, 392 F.Supp. 1134, and 392 F.Supp. 1144 (D.N.H.1974).

2. Do you think that a rural community far from the expanding metropolis is in a better legal position to preserve its "way of life" by preventing virtually all large developments than a rural community right in the path of the growing urban area? See Ybarra v. Town of Los Altos Hills, 503 F.2d 250 (9th Cir.1974), and Sturges v. Town of Chilmark, 380 Mass. 246, 402 N.E.2d 1346 (1980).

3. In New Hampshire, the courts have held that growth control ordinances must comply with the zoning enabling statutes. See Beck v. Town of Raymond, 118 N.H. 793, 394 A.2d 847 (1978), and Stoney–Brook Development Corp. v. Town of Pembroke, 118 N.H. 791, 394 A.2d 853 (1978). After these decisions the legislature passed enabling legislation authorizing towns and cities to enact growth control ordinances. See N.H.Rev.Stat.Ann. 31:62–a and 31:62–b.

In Stoney–Brook Development Corp. v. Town of Fremont, 124 N.H. 583, 474 A.2d 561 (1984), the town had set a three percent growth rate which was challenged by the developer (who had received only three of the four building permits it sought). The court ruled for the developer holding that growth controls must be the product of careful study and must be constantly reviewed with a general view of relaxing the controls. Under this test, the court found the town's three percent figure to be arbitrary and artificial.

B. DENIAL OF ACCESS TO INFRASTRUCTURE

DATELINE BUILDERS, INC. v. CITY OF SANTA ROSA

California Court of Appeal, First District, 1983.
146 Cal.App.3d 520, 194 Cal.Rptr. 258.

WHITE, PRESIDING JUSTICE.

On this appeal by Dateline Builders, Inc. (Builders) from a judgment in favor of the City of Santa Rosa (City), the major question is whether the City was required to connect its existing sewer trunk line to Builders' proposed "leap frog" housing development beyond the City's boundaries. For the reasons set forth below we have concluded that the City reasonably exercised its police power because Builders' proposed housing development was not consistent with the City's compact land use and development policy as set forth in the City and County's previously adopted General Plan.

The pertinent facts substantially as found below and revealed by the record are as follows: Builders, a California corporation, held an option on a parcel of real property located beyond the limits of the city boundary, on Todd Road in an undeveloped rural area known as the Santa Rosa Plain. The City is a charter city located in Sonoma County (County).

The County Board of Supervisors determined that: 1) there was a need for development of sewer facilities in the Santa Rosa Plain; 2) it was in the public interest to avoid the proliferation of small and scattered un-unified sewer treatment facilities by a cooperative effort with the City to create a single regional facility to be owned and operated by the City. On October 17, 1964 the City and County entered into the "Plains Agreement," a mutual expression of policy and intent to exercise their police powers cooperatively for the orderly development of the Santa Rosa Plain, and to prevent a proliferation of fragment sewer districts and systems.

Paragraph 10 of the Plains Agreement provided that both the City and County would adopt a policy that the areas in the Santa Rosa Plain adaptable to urban type development, would be developed consistent with the City and County's General Plan and with the development standards of the City. To implement this policy the City and County agreed to enact subdivision, building, zoning and other property development regulations "to prevent haphazard or substandard property development." Paragraph 10 further provided that any development proposal in the Santa Rosa Plain be accompanied by proof that the proposed development was consistent with the City and County's joint General Plan and consistent with the City's development standards and regulations.

To implement one of the policies of the Plains Agreement the City Council adopted a procedure that required the proponent of a development to apply for and receive a certificate of compliance (certificate) prior to the extension of new service outside the city; the certificate then served as proof of compliance with the city's development standards.

* * *

Builders' application for a certificate was reviewed by the City for consistency with its plan, and development policies and standards. The City determined that Builders' proposed development in an agricultural area well beyond the city boundaries represented "leap-frog" development inconsistent with the city's plans, policies and standards. On December 9, 1971, the City denied the request without prejudice; Builders never submitted a subsequent or renewed application for a certificate. Builders appealed the determination to the City Council. On January 4, 1972 the City Council heard the appeal and refused to issue the certificate, on the same grounds, i.e., inconsistent with the City's General Plan and standards for compact development.

* * *

Builders rely on and urge us to follow, *Robinson v. City of Boulder* (1976) 190 Colo. 357, 547 P.2d 228 and *Delmarva Enterprises, Inc. v. Mayor and Council of the City of Dover* (Del.1971) 282 A.2d 601. In both *Robinson* and *Delmarva, supra,* the owners of property outside of the city limits successfully argued that each city had unlawfully discriminated against them by refusing to hook up their properties to the city's exclusive water and sewer services. Both the Delaware and Colorado courts reasoned that: 1) as the exclusive supplier of these services, each city acting in a proprietary capacity as a public utility, was held to the same standards as a private utility, and therefore could refuse to do so only for utility-based reasons, such as insufficient capacity; and 2) each city was bound by the rule that a municipality is without jurisdiction over territory beyond its limits in the absence of legislation. In *Boulder, supra,* 547 P.2d at 230–231, however, the court did not reach the City's argument that the rules applicable to private utilities should not apply to a governmental utility authorized to implement governmental objectives such as the adoption of a Master-plan. The City of Boulder and the county in which it was located had jointly developed and adopted a Boulder Valley comprehensive plan to provide for discretionary land use decisions. The court specifically noted that the proposed Boulder development complied with the county zoning regulations and that the county, rather than the city, had the ultimate responsibility for the approval of the proposed development.

Builders argue that the *Boulder* case, *supra,* is on all fours with the facts of the instant case. Builders, however, ignore the fact that its Todd Road project had the tentative approval of the county conditioned, inter alia, upon a change in zoning and other conditions with which Builders admittedly did not attempt to comply. However, we do not base our holding only on this factual distinction. By failing to seek rezoning from the County or meet the other 23 conditions imposed by the County in its tentative approval of the subdivision map, and then pursuing this action against the City, Builders was trying to play off against each other, the City and County who had agreed to cooperative planning. Basically, Builders argues that because a City cannot exercise its police power beyond its boundaries, the City was prevented from using the denial of the sewer hookup as a planning tool.

Builders ignores the joint policy of the City and County as expressed in the Plains Agreement, for orderly growth in conformance with the guidelines of the jointly adopted General Plan. Agreements such as that here in issue that lead to joint planning by cities and counties should and have been encouraged by the Legislature. The complex economic, political and social factors involved in land use planning are compelling evidence that resolution of the important housing and environmental issues raised here, is the domain of the Legislature. (Cf. *Construction Ind. Ass'n, Sonoma Co. v. City of Petaluma, supra,* 522 F.2d fn. 17 at 909.) Unfortunately, the experience of many communities in this state has been that when planning is left to developers, the result is urban sprawl. The City's express and reiterated reason for denying the certificate was that Builders' proposed development violated its policy of orderly compact development from the urban core, and would result in a "leap-frog" development and "urban sprawl." A municipality cannot be forced to take a stake in the developer's success in the area. (Cf. *Reid Dev. Corp. v. Parsippany–Troy Hills Tp.* (1954) 31 N.J.Super. 459, 107 A.2d 20, at 23.) Neither common law nor constitutional law inhibits the broad grant of power to local government officials to refuse to extend utility service so long as they do not act for personal gain nor in a wholly arbitrary or discriminatory manner. (See authorities cited in *Control of the Timing and Location of Government Utility Extensions* (1974) 26 Stanford L.Rev. 945–963.)

Builders rely on the line of California authorities holding that where a municipality provides a public utility service "[g]enerally it is true that where the scope of a project transcends the boundaries of a municipality it ceases to be for a municipal purpose." (*Santa Barbara etc. Agency v. All Persons* (1957) 47 Cal.2d 699, 710, 306 P.2d 875, revd. on other grounds (1958) 357 U.S. 275, 78 S.Ct. 1174, 2 L.Ed.2d 1313, dealing with a county water agency.) The California Supreme Court in upholding the right of a charter city to issue notices of sale for revenue bonds for sewerage improvements applied the above principle to sewer systems: " * * * sewer projects may transcend the boundaries of one or several municipalities * * *. In such circumstances the project 'ceases to be a municipal affair and comes within the proper domain and regulation of the general laws of the state.' (*Wilson v. City of San Bernadino* (1960) 186 Cal.App.2d 603, 604, 611 [9 Cal.Rptr. 431] * * *)" (*City of Santa Clara v. Von Raesfeld* (1970) 3 Cal.3d 239, 246, 90 Cal.Rptr. 8, 474 P.2d 976; see also *Pixley v. Saunders* (1914) 168 Cal. 152, 160, 141 P. 815.) These authorities, of course, predate *Associated Home Builders etc., Inc. v. City of Livermore, supra,* 18 Cal.3d 582, 601, 135 Cal.Rptr. 41, 557 P.2d 473. We agree with the City that unlike the situation in the past, most municipalities today are neither isolated nor wholly independent from neighboring entities, and consequently, land use decisions by one local unit affect the needs and resources of the entire region. The Plains Agreement and the General Plan demonstrate that the City and County were aware of these realities.

Builders recognize that in this state, as elsewhere, publicly owned municipal utilities are not regulated by the Public Utilities Commission (PUC) or any other supervisory agency in the absence of a legislative grant of authority while privately owned utilities are. (*American Microsystems, Inc. v. City of Santa Clara* (1982) 137 Cal.App.3d 1037, 1042–1043, 187 Cal.Rptr. 550.) It has long been the rule in this state that when operating a municipal utility, a city retains its character as a municipal corporation. Reasons must be found for holding it liable to the same extent as a private utility corporation. (*Pasadena v. R.R. Com.* (1920) 183 Cal. 526, 530, 192 P. 25.) Builders here argue that there were sufficient reasons here because the City was the only supplier, could not act beyond its boundaries and could not use sewer hookup as a planning device. We do not agree.

In *Associated Home Builders, etc., Inc. v. City of Livermore, supra,* 18 Cal.3d 582, 601, 135 Cal.Rptr. 41, 557 P.2d 473, our Supreme Court intimated that in California a city may enact restrictions that are effective beyond its boundaries. *Associated Home Builders* also reiterated the desirability of regional planning. As to a city's alleged inability to act beyond its boundaries, we note that Government Code section 65859 set forth below, a part of the same enactment as Government Code section 65300 and 65302 * * * expressly provides otherwise.

Builders' contention that denial of the certificate could not be used as a planning device overlooks a fundamental distinction between such a decision as an improper initial use of the police power, and as here, a necessary and proper exercise of the power once the planning decision had been made. Here, of course, the adoption of the General Plan with its policy of orderly and compact growth to avoid urban sprawl was made in 1967. The policy was a proper exercise of the police power for the general welfare (*Associated Home Builders, supra,* 18 Cal.3d 601, 135 Cal.Rptr. 41, 557 P.2d 473; cf. *Wilson v. Hidden Valley Mun. Water Dist.* (1967) 256 Cal.App.2d 271, 288, 63 Cal.Rptr. 889) previously adopted by the City Council and the County. (Cf. *Golden v. Ramapo* (1972) 30 N.Y.2d 359, 334 N.Y.S.2d 138, 285 N.E.2d 291, app. dism. 409 U.S. 1003, 93 S.Ct. 440, 34 L.Ed.2d 294.) Builders' argument that only zoning may be used for planning sits poorly in its mouth as they never sought to rezone the property or meet any of the County's other conditions.

The judgment is affirmed.

Note

The Robinson v. City of Boulder case discussed in the principal case was overruled in 1986. Board of County Commissioners v. Denver Board of Water Commissioners, 718 P.2d 235 (Colo.1986). For discussion of the problems of regulating growth by controlling access to water service see Kelly, Piping Growth: The Law, Economics, and Equity of Sewer and Water Connection Policies, Land Use Law (July 1984) p. 3; Biggs, No Drip, No Flush, No Growth: How Cities Can Control Growth Beyond Their Boundaries by Refusing to Extend Utility Services, 22 The Urban Lawyer 285 (1990). Also see City of Little Rock v. Chartwell Valley Ltd., 299 Ark. 542, 772 S.W.2d 616 (1989).

CHARLES v. DIAMOND
Court of Appeals of New York, 1977.
41 N.Y.2d 318, 392 N.Y.S.2d 594, 360 N.E.2d 1295.

JASEN, JUDGE.

Petitioner, a landowner in the Village of Camillus, planned to construct three apartment buildings, totaling 36 units, on his property. Village law required that such buildings had to be connected to the village sewage system. On May 9, 1972, the village board authorized issuance of a building permit. However, on May 22, 1972, the State Department of Environmental Conservation informed petitioner that he could not connect into the village sewage system until "the Village undertakes a program to correct the deficiencies of their sewage system". The State likewise directed the Onondaga County Health Department not to authorize the petitioner to connect into the existing system until the present deficiencies were corrected. Thereafter, in June, 1972, petitioner commenced this article 78 proceeding against the State Commissioner of Environmental Conservation, the Deputy Commissioner, Onondaga County Department of Health, and the Village of Camillus, contending that the actions of the State, county and village were arbitrary and capricious, resulting in an unconstitutional appropriation of his property without compensation. Petitioner sought a judgment directing the respondents to approve the village connection to his property, requiring the village to take appropriate steps so that the State and county would allow petitioner to use the village sewer system and awarding damages in the amount of $50,000 for damages already sustained. Alternatively, petitioner sought damages in the amount of $100,000 for the appropriation of his property in the event "that sewers are not approved * * * and he is not allowed to build the apartments on his property".

* * *

At the threshold, we note that this case does not involve the potentially troublesome issue of whether mere failure to provide municipal services can result in an inverse condemnation for which the municipality must pay compensation. Much more is involved here than merely an asserted failure to provide a service due equally to all members of the community. It is, of course, old law that a municipality is under no obligation to furnish sewers to particular property owners. Municipal corporations have ample opportunity to provide sewers "but it is not their duty to make every sewer or drain which may be desired by individuals, or which a jury might even find to be necessary and proper." * * * Although municipal sewage disposal obligations have been discussed at great length in the tort realm, and little mentioned elsewhere, it is virtually beyond question that an individual property owner has no right to insist that the municipality provide him with a system, at least where the problem is unique to his land and can be remedied at his expense. Article 14 of the Village Law provides for the optional construction of sewers in a village, with the cost to be borne entirely by the village, entirely by the owners of the property benefited or by the village and the property owners jointly, at the option of the village. It is also old law that once a municipality has acted to provide a sewer and its improvement causes damage, the municipality is liable to compensate for the injuries sustained. * * *

In this case, it is undisputed that the village provided a sewage disposal system and that local law requires that if a sewer is provided, it must be used. Moreover, the local law requires sewer-connected toilet facilities if the property is intended for any human use. The vice of the situation is that the municipality requires the use of public sewers if the property is to be developed for human use and yet has not provided an adequate system for meeting the requirement imposed by the ordinance. Hence, the claim is more than an undifferentiated demand for municipal service due to all citizens equally. The contention, stripped to its essence, is that the sewer ordinance is being applied unconstitutionally to petitioner's property, thereby frustrating nearly all reasonable development.

* * *

A police power regulation to be reasonable must be kept within the limits of necessity. * * * In *Matter of Belle Harbor Realty Corp. v. Kerr*, 35 N.Y.2d 507, 364 N.Y.S.2d 160, 323 N.E.2d 697, we established a three-pronged test for measuring whether necessity limits have been exceeded. "To justify interference with the beneficial enjoyment of property the municipality must establish that it has acted in response to a dire necessity, that its action is reasonably calculated to alleviate or prevent the crisis condition, and that it is presently taking steps to rectify the problem." * * * In that case, the municipality revoked a building permit on the ground that evidence uncovered since the issuance of the permit revealed that sewers were "grossly inadequate" for present use and new sewer connections were not advisable. The builder contended that the city had not acted because of sewer inadequacy but in response to community opposition to the planned development. We authorized the commencement of a proceeding to determine whether the revocation was a necessary health measure or was, in fact, motivated by political considerations. However, there was no contention that the developer would be entitled to money damages for any delay, whether justified by health requirements or not.

Similarly, in [*Westwood Forest Estates v. Village of South Nyack*, 23 N.Y.2d 424, 297 N.Y.S.2d 129, 244 N.E.2d 700 (1969)], we struck down a village zoning ordinance that prohibited all apartment house construction. The ordinance was purportedly justified by the fact that the village had inadequate sewage treatment facilities and new multiple dwellings would increase pollution of the Hudson River. Yet the sewage problem was not caused by the nature of the plaintiff's land but was general to the community. It was, we concluded, impermissible to single out one landowner to bear a heavy financial burden caused by a general community condition. * * * We were careful to note that the village, while it could not blanketly prohibit development, could impose moratoriums or other temporary measures in order to deal with the problem. * * * Indeed, we have sustained development restrictions, pursuant to a general community plan, for periods as long as 18 years. (See *Matter of Golden v. Planning Bd. of Town of Ramapo*, 30 N.Y.2d 359, 334 N.Y.S.2d 138, 285 N.E.2d 291, app. dsmd., 409 U.S. 1003, 93 S.Ct. 436, 34 L.Ed.2d 294.) However, the crucial factor, perhaps even the decisive one, is whether the ultimate economic cost of the benefit is being shared by the members of the community at large, or, rather, is being hidden from the public by the placement of the entire burden upon particular property owners. (See *French Investing Co. v. City of New York*, 39 N.Y.2d 587, 596–597, 385 N.Y.S.2d 5, 10–11, 350 N.E.2d 381, 386–387, *supra.*)

* * *

In this case, the delay, as measured from the time the difficulty first surfaced, has been substantial. Petitioner has been through a tortured course of litigation and appeal. Yet the reasons, if any, for apparent municipal inactivity in the face of sewage difficulties have never been explained. The present record, even after two appeals to the Appellate Division, is woefully silent. While it is true that the municipality has not submitted any justification for the delay, we also note that the property owner has not submitted any proof, apart from his conclusory allegations, that the municipal delay has exposed him to, or has caused him, significant economic injury of some sort. It is, of course, the property owner that must come forward with such proof in support of the claim that the zoning ordinance is being applied to the property unconstitutionally, in order to put the municipality to the task of justifying its action. * * * On this inadequate record, it would be inappropriate for us to determine the constitutionality of the municipal action. Both parties have not submitted the proof necessary for an intelligent and conclusive judicial evaluation of their respective claims. Since the parties should be given an opportunity, which neither has yet had, to submit their proof on trial, any temporary relief, short of a final declaration on the constitutionality of the village action, would be an idle gesture.

* * *

Assuming that the landowner has been prejudiced by an unreasonable delay on the part of the municipality, the question of proper constitutional remedy is reached. Of course, in the event that unreasonable delay is established, the landowner is entitled to a declaration that the ordinance, insofar as it requires the use of public sewers, may not be constitutionally applied to him. * * * Thus, this petitioner would be constitutionally free from the requirement that his property be tied into the public sewer system. The property could be developed by the use of private sewer disposal systems, provided compliance is made with pertinent provisions of local law. He should have that option.

A permit for the construction of a private sewage disposal system may be obtained by the owner. Of course, the proposed facility must comply with all relevant State health and sanitary requirements and is subject to village inspection. In addition, the property owner would be required to operate and maintain the facility in a sanitary manner at all times.

* * *

The order of the Appellate Division should be modified and, as modified, affirmed, without costs.

Order modified, without costs, and the matter remitted to Supreme Court, Onondaga County, for further proceedings in accordance with the opinion herein and, as so modified, affirmed.

BREITEL, C.J., and GABRIELLI, JONES, WACHTLER, FUCHSBERG and COOKE, JJ., concur.

Note

Also see Walz v. Town of Smithtown, 46 F.3d 162 (2d Cir.1995), where homeowners brought a successful civil rights action against the town and the town's superintendent of highways for denial of a permit to connect their home to the public water system after the failure of their well. The court upheld a jury verdict of $102,000 in compensatory damages against the town, $9,500 in punitive damages against the superintendent, and over $48,000 in attorney's fees.

C. STATE GROWTH MANAGEMENT LEGISLATION

The legislatures of all 50 states have developed statewide approaches to growth management. The adoption of the zoning and planning enabling acts, in the first instance, evidences a policy of delegating much of the responsibility for managing private land development to the local or county level of government. What is known as state growth management legislation refers to additional statutes that provide further guidance to, or impose limitations on, local land use authority. Even under these statutes, local governments play a significant, if somewhat more tethered, role in land use regulation.

Growth management statutes have been enacted to create fairer, more efficient, or more environmentally sound land use patterns. Much of the attention in the literature is focused on state statutes that define urban growth boundaries or that provide for state or regional plans which local comprehensive plans must consider or with which they must conform. But other approaches exist that guide or limit local land use authority in the interest of achieving better results. These include, for example, statutes that create regional land use review boards to which specified local decisions can be referred, affordable housing goals and mandates, regional agencies that exercise extraordinary power over a single area, state agency power over regional impact projects, and programs designed to obtain local compliance with one or more state growth management objectives. With continuing population pressures and the persistence of urban sprawl, it is likely that state statutes will continue to be adopted that attempt to influence, if not replace, local hegemony in this field. For the foreseeable future, however, it is not likely that the central role of local governments will be replaced.

An interesting example of a law that limits local land use authority is Connecticut's Affordable Housing Appeals Act. The Act makes it difficult for town land use commissions to turn down an affordable housing proposal unless ten percent of their housing stock is already affordable to low and moderate income households. (See Conn. Gen. Stat. § 8–30g). The Act requires the municipality to carry the burden of proving that the denial is in the public interest. This reverses the presumption of validity used by the courts to review challenges to other local land use decisions. The local commission must show that its decision was supported by substantial evidence on the record, that the rejection was necessary to protect substantial public interests in health or safety, and that those interests clearly outweigh the need for affordable housing and cannot be protected by reasonable changes to the proposed affordable housing development.

The positions of scholars and advocates on the issue of regional planning differ greatly. Three popular views are that regional planning agencies should preempt local land use authority to the extent necessary to serve regional interests; that regional agencies should be set up to mediate inter-local matters in the region's best interest; and that localities should be encouraged to form intermunicipal land use compacts to meet their own needs, which are increasingly interdependent and regional in nature. Some states have adopted enabling acts to form regional agencies which may or may not preempt some aspect of local control. Others provide funding or assistance to facilitate the formation of voluntary regional councils or agencies, often for the purpose of securing federal transportation or planning funds.

The Standard City Planning Enabling Act, promulgated by the Hoover Commission in 1928, provided for regional planning by authorizing local planning commissions to petition the governor to establish a regional planning commission and to prepare a master plan for the region's physical development. Provisions were included in the planning enabling act for communication between the regional and municipal planning commissions with the objective of achieving a certain degree of consistency between local and regional plans. In 1968, the Douglas Commission, appointed by President Johnson, issued its Report on Urban Problems, Building the American City, which reinforced regional planning. The Commission recommended that each state create a state agency for land use planning and prepare state and regional land use plans. In other words, regional consciousness has been with us since the early days of American zoning.

Much of the country, at one time or another, has been brought within the jurisdiction of some form of regional planning organization due to a variety of influences. The most powerful of these was the promise of funding for regional efforts under housing, water, and public works programs of the federal government. Predominant among these organizations were voluntary area-wide regional councils of government, multi-state river basin compacts, and regional economic development organizations.

With few exceptions, these regional bodies have stopped far short of preemptive land use planning and regulation. They have become, however, effective vehicles for communication, education, collaboration, and networking. Among their most significant contributions is the effect they have of educating local land use officials. In these regional bodies, local representatives learn about the common problems and mutual dependence of localities that share the same economic or housing market area or that have regulatory power over river basins and watersheds that cannot be protected without intermunicipal cooperation.

Several states have adopted statutes that create urban growth areas. These statutes aim to achieve the essential goal of smart growth: to contain growth in defined and serviceable districts. They are guided by various objectives, including the creation of cost-effective centers, preservation of agricultural districts, promotion of affordable housing, protection of significant landscapes containing critical environmental assets, and the preservation of open lands for the future. Not all of these state growth management statutes are regional in nature. Maine requires local land use plans to identify areas suitable for absorbing growth and other areas for open space protection. Minnesota authorizes, but does not require, localities to designate urban growth areas in local and county comprehensive plans. Oregon and Maryland take a more direct approach, requiring the creation of growth and preservation districts and taking effective action to see that local governments conform their regulatory activities to established state land use objectives.

The Maryland statute, adopted in 1997, establishes priority funding areas and denies state agency funding for growth-related projects outside those designated areas. The state makes it clear that it will not fund growth inducing projects in rural areas not served by water and sewer systems. This is an incentive based program intended to slow down the conversion of agricultural and rural lands and to create growth areas that are serviceable in a cost-effective manner.

The Oregon growth management statute, adopted in 1973, is the most directive of its kind. It creates a state agency known as the Land Conservation and Development Commission (LCDC), articulates a number of statewide land use planning goals, requires local governments to adopt comprehensive plans that contain urban growth boundaries, and requires local plans to be approved by the Commission. The statute also created the Metropolitan Service District (Metro) to supervise the intermunicipal urban growth boundary in the greater Portland area. In 1979, the statute was amended to create the Land Use Board of Appeals (LUBA) to review local land use decisions. Litigation under this regime has not attacked its legality, but mainly the validity of particular planning decisions that affect individual parcels.

Goal 14 of the Oregon land use planning statute—the urbanization goal—classifies land into three categories: rural, urbanizable, and urban. Rural lands are agricultural, forest, or open space lands, or other land suitable for sparse settlement, with few public services. Urbanizable lands are to be contained within an urban growth boundary and are deemed suitable for future urban uses: lands that can be served by infrastructure and that are needed for the expansion of an urban area. Urban areas are within or adjacent to existing cities with concentrations of population and supporting public facilities and services. The statute provides for the orderly conversion of rural land to urban, based on the consideration of a number of factors including the need to accommodate population growth through the provision of housing, jobs, and infrastructure.

HAVILAND v. LAND CONSERVATION AND DEVELOPMENT COMMISSION

Court of Appeals of Oregon, 1980.
45 Or.App. 761, 609 P.2d 423.

BUTTLER, PRESIDING JUDGE.

Petitioners appeal from an order of the Land Conservation and Development Commission (LCDC or Commission) in which that agency concluded that the City of Medford and Jackson County had not violated statewide planning goals in establishing the urban growth boundaries of Medford which excluded petitioners' property.

In Spring, 1978, the city and county amended their comprehensive plans, which have not yet been acknowledged by LCDC, by passing ordinances each establishing an urban growth boundary around the city of Medford. The boundaries were drawn in order to comply with LCDC Statewide Planning Goal 14. To the end of providing for "an orderly and efficient transition from rural to urban land use," Goal 14 requires that "urban growth boundaries shall be established to identify and separate urbanizable land from rural land."

The ordinances adopted by the city and county differ; the city urban growth boundary is more inclusive than that of the county but both versions exclude petitioners' property.

Petitioners sought review of the ordinances by LCDC, as authorized by former ORS 197.300(1)(d),[20] which requires the Commission to re-

20. ORS 197.300, 197.305, 197.310 and 197.315 were repealed by Oregon Laws 1979, chapter 772, section 26, effective November 1, 1979. That chapter establishes a

view, upon "(p)etition by any person or group of persons whose interests are substantially affected, a comprehensive plan provision * * * or other ordinance or regulation alleged to be in violation of statewide planning goals * * *." The LCDC properly limited its review to consideration of whether the local planning authority properly applied the Commission's goals in light of facts found by it and supported by the record. Former ORS 197.305.

That section limits the Commission's review to the record, and former ORS 197.310(3) directs the Commission to enter a final order which must include "a clear statement of findings setting forth the basis for the commission's determination in the proceeding." Under former ORS 197.310(5) the order of the commission may be appealed in the manner provided in ORS 183.480 for appeals from final orders in contested cases. Subsection (2) of that section provides that our review of such orders shall be solely as provided in ORS 183.482 (among other sections).

Our review, then, is of the Commission's order, including the findings and conclusions supporting it. If those findings are supported by the evidence from the record on which the Commission relied, and the conclusions are supported by those findings, we may not disturb the order solely because we might reach a different conclusion. See ORS 183.482(8)(a) (supra, note 1).

On this appeal, petitioners contend that there are inadequate facts in the record to support the population projection arrived at by the planning staffs, that the city and county erred in failing to adopt site-specific findings explaining why petitioners' land was excluded from the urban growth boundary, that petitioners' land had been committed to urbanization and therefore should have been included within the boundary and that inadequate consideration had been given to Goal 14, the urbanization goal of the statewide planning goals, and also Goals 2, 3, 5, 6, 9, 10, 11 and 12.

Taking the last contention first, the Commission, in its opinion and final order, determined that in establishing an urban growth boundary, which is only a preliminary step in adopting a comprehensive plan, only Goal 14 need be directly considered. When a comprehensive plan is adopted and submitted to the Commission for acknowledgment the other goals must be addressed. Until that time, the other planning goals apply only indirectly through the seven factors of Goal 14.[21]

Land Use Board of Appeals and provides new procedures for the review of land use decisions. The extent to which the appealability of local decisions, or the scope of review by the board, the commission and this court, must abide the event.

21. Goal 14 requires that "(e)stablishment and change of the boundaries shall be based upon consideration of the following factors:

"(1) Demonstrated need to accommodate long-range urban population growth requirements consistent with LCDC goals;

"(2) Need for housing, employment opportunities, and livability;

"(3) Orderly and economic provision for public facilities and services;

We accept the agency's determination on the scope and applicability of the goals drafted by it, as we would accept as authoritative an agency's interpretation of a regulation promulgated by it. See *McPherson v. Employment Division*, 285 Or. 541, 549, n. 6, 591 P.2d 1381 (1979).

The Commission properly viewed a challenge to an urban growth boundary under former ORS 197.300(1)(d) in limiting its role to consideration of whether the local planning authorities had properly applied Goal 14 in light of facts found by the planning authorities and supported in the record. The Commission viewed Goal 14 criteria as "accountability safeguards" to provide a means for assessing urbanization decisions, stating that if it appears that

> "the planning body fully considered all of the urbanization criteria, and the facts pertinent to the application of those criteria, and if the facts reported have support in the record, the local decision should be upheld even though the Commission or a court might have balanced the criteria differently or drawn a different conclusion from the facts presented."

The Commission proceeded to review each of the Goal 14 criteria in light of the record and found that each of them was considered and that the findings relating to those criteria are supported by the record. Based on that review, the Commission entered its own findings with specific reference to the record supporting them. Those findings are supported by the record and support the Commission's order. No useful purpose would be served by detailing them here, except to note the disposition of the specific contentions made by petitioners here.

The LCDC found that petitioners' challenge to the population projection did not manifest a violation of Goal 14. The first two criteria of Goal 14, consideration of "(d)emonstrated need to accommodate long-range urban population growth requirements consistent with LCDC goals" and of "(n)eed for housing, employment opportunities and livability" necessitate an estimation of the area's future population. Petitioners contend that the city and county population projections for the year 2000 are too low and that more land will be needed to meet the criteria than found by the city and county. The Commission, however, found that there was substantial evidence in the record to support the conclusion that, if anything, the amount of land included within the urban growth boundary exceeded the needs of the future population as estimated by the city and county, and, in fact, was in excess of the needs of the future population as projected by petitioners.[22] There is substantial evidence in the record to support this finding.

"(4) Maximum efficiency of land uses within and on the fringe of the existing urban area;

"(5) Environmental, energy, economic and social consequences;

"(6) Retention of agricultural land as defined, with Class I being the highest priority for retention and Class VI the lowest priority; and,

"(7) Compatibility of the proposed urban uses with nearby agricultural activities."

22. The hearings officer calculated that the amount of vacant land included within the urban growth boundary would support

Petitioners next argue that site-specific findings should have been made to explain the exclusion of their land because of their extensive participation, including attendance at all planning commission hearings and presentation of oral and written testimony, which made them parties to the proceeding. Although decisions that result from judicial or quasi-judicial proceedings may require specific findings relating to each party involved, the Commission properly concluded that these proceedings were essentially legislative and do not require findings regarding the specific property of each landowner affected. See *Culver v. Dagg*, 20 Or.App. 647, 532 P.2d 1127, rev. den. (1975).

Moreover, LCDC points out that the record does contain findings with respect to the area of land which includes petitioners' property, which findings refute petitioners' additional contention that their property must be included because of its commitment to urbanization. The city and county considered that criterion for inclusion of property, but were aware that the drawing of an urban growth boundary involved, in addition, consideration of the seven Goal 14 criteria. A certain amount of land was included based upon an estimate of the future need for urban land and the findings reflect a concern that the inclusion of more land, including the area in which petitioners' property is located, within the boundary would violate Goal 14 by including more land than was warranted by that estimate. Absent evidence that the need for urbanizable land cannot be filled without including either committed lands or, for example, class I–IV agricultural lands, there is no reason why land committed to urban use may not be excluded for reasons which outweigh the commitment factor. The judgment is essentially a legislative one, subject to compliance with Goal 14.

The Commission's findings that the city and county considered Goal 14 are supported by substantial evidence in the record. We affirm its conclusion and final order.

Affirmed.

RESIDENTS OF ROSEMONT v. METRO

Court of Appeals of Oregon, 2001.
173 Or.App. 321, 21 P.3d 1108.

DEITS, C.J.

Petitioners Rosemont Property Owners Assoc., Kuhl and Eiselius (petitioners) seek review of, and respondents City of Lake Oswego and City of West Linn (cities) cross-petition from, LUBA's decision remanding Metro's decision that amended its urban growth boundary (UGB) to add an 830–acre area. We affirm on the petition and reverse and remand on the cross-petition.

The parties agree that the facts are correctly stated in LUBA's opinion:

a growth rate of 4.3%, a higher rate "than seriously contended for by any of the petitioners."

"On March 6, 1997, Metro designated 18,579 acres of land as urban reserves pursuant to OAR chapter 660, division 21, including lands in the Stafford area of Clackamas County. That area included five urban reserve study areas (URSAs) numbered 30, 31, 32, 33 and 34. On February 25, 1999, LUBA remanded Metro's decision in *D.S. Parklane Development, Inc. v. Metro*, 35 Or. LUBA 516 (1999) (*Parklane I*), aff'd 165 Or.App. 1, 994 P.2d 1205 (2000) (*Parklane II*).

"In 1998, Metro began proceedings to consider expanding its UGB in order to comply with a state mandate to provide a 20-year supply of residential land within the UGB. ORS 197.296. Pursuant to ORS 197.299, Metro was required to add to the UGB half of the amount of land needed to comply with ORS 197.296 by December 1998. Metro planning staff conducted various analyses that narrowed potential expansion sites to 26 URSAs, and then conducted further analyses that ranked those 26 URSAs as candidates for urbanization."

"On December 3, 1998, while the decision appealed in *Parklane I* was before LUBA, the Metro Council considered proposals to expand the UGB to include all of URSAs 31, 32, 33 and 34. The Council voted to remove more than half of the land in those URSAs from consideration, and approved an expansion of the UGB to include 830 acres of land in URSAs 31, 32 and 33, hereafter the 'expansion area' or the 'Rosemont area.' Proponents of including the Rosemont area in the UGB had developed a concept plan, the Rosemont Village Concept Plan (RVCP), proposing development in accordance with the requirements of Metro's 2040 Growth Concept. The 830–acre expansion area includes approximately 762 acres of land zoned for exclusive farm use (EFU), with the remainder consisting of exception lands, *i.e.*, lands for which an exception to Statewide Planning Goal 3 (Agricultural Lands) had previously been taken. The soils on the EFU-zoned lands are predominantly Class III and IV soils.

"On December 17, 1998, the Council adopted Ordinance No. 98–782C, approving the challenged UGB expansion." (Footnotes omitted.)

The cities, among others, brought these consolidated appeals to LUBA, challenging various aspects of Metro's decision. Petitioners intervened in the LUBA proceeding to assert positions that generally supported the local decision. Although LUBA resolved many of the cities' critical arguments in their favor, it rejected their contention that Metro erred in basing the LUBA amendment on a "subregional need" for "affordable housing" in the general area of the cities and the proximate Stafford area, rather than determining the need for urban land by reference to the entire Metro region. In their cross-petition, which we address first, the cities' only assignment of error challenges that adverse ruling by LUBA.

The cities argue that it is inconsistent with Statewide Planning Goal 14 for a planning body to expand its UGB based on a need for housing or other urban facilities in only a part of its territory, at least without considering "whether that need could be accommodated outside of the identified subregion."[23] This court has not previously decided the question that the cities raise. However, in *1000 Friends of Oregon v. Metro Service Dist.*, 18 Or. LUBA 311, 324 (1989), LUBA was presented with at least part of the question and concluded that,

> "within the Metro UGB a subregional need could also constitute a regional need for purposes of Goal 14 factors 1 and 2. * * * [W]e reject petitioner's contention that, as a matter of law, a subregional need could never provide a basis for amending Metro's regional UGB."

For the reasons that follow, we agree with LUBA that a subregional need may, in some circumstances, constitute need for purposes of satisfying factors 1 and 2 of Goal 14. We also conclude, however, that LUBA erred in affirming Metro's decision here, because, in deciding that factors 1 and 2 of Goal 14 were satisfied, Metro focused solely on what it identified as a subregional need without any consideration of this need in the regional context or any explanation of how this area was identified as a subregion or why the needs of this area should be viewed in isolation.

* * *

Considering the text and context of the pertinent laws, we believe that LUBA was correct in holding that it cannot be said, as a matter of law, that a subregional need will *never* satisfy the need factors of Goal 14. However, we also conclude that there is nothing in the text or context of Goal 14 or those portions of the Metro Code implementing Goal 14 that provides authority for a subregional need alone to serve as the basis for a UGB expansion without consideration being given to the "regional context." As LUBA explained in an early decision on this subject:

> "As a regional urban growth boundary, Metro's boundary looks to growth trends on a regional basis and is designed to accommodate regional growth. Changes within jurisdictions served by Metro may be necessary to accommodate that regional growth, *but the Board does not agree with the petitioner that only the growth in Clackamas County is relevant in deciding whether the urban growth boundary in Clackamas County needs to be amended*. Without a showing by petitioner as to how the Clackamas County urban growth boundary is critical to the regional urban growth boundary in some manner requiring it to be viewed by itself, we believe we would be doing

---

23. The cities also make arguments that, even assuming our rejection of their underlying contention, the "factual base" for and evidence supporting Metro's designation of the Stafford–Rosemont subregion were inadequate and that the Rosemont Village Concept Plan was insufficient to ensure that the subregional need would be met. We do not reach those secondary arguments. As the parties and LUBA do, we will use the term "subregion" to refer to localized areas within a planning jurisdiction, as distinct from the "region" that constitutes all of the planning body's territory.

more harm than good by accepting petitioner's proposition." *Home Builders Ass'n v. Metropolitan Service District*, 2 Or LUBA 25, 30 (1980) (emphasis added).

In order to satisfy the need factors of Goal 14, a subregional need must be identified and evaluated in the context of the regional needs. *See 1000 Friends of Oregon v. Metro*, 38 Or. LUBA 565 (2000) (slip op at 3–14) (LUBA concluded that Metro properly identified a subregional need for housing and considered the role that need plays in the context of the entire UGB and regional need).

Here, Metro's decision to expand the UGB in the Stafford–Rosemont area appears to have been based *solely* on subregional considerations of the kind reflected in factor 2. As the cities argue:

> "Metro's decision in this case was based solely on a determination of need for affordable housing within three or six miles of the Stafford and Rosemont intersection, and did not consider whether that need could be accommodated outside of the identified subregion." (Footnotes omitted.)

We agree with the cities that Metro erred in that respect and that LUBA accordingly erred in affirming that aspect of Metro's decision. To illustrate, there might be some *a priori* logic to the proposition that persons employed on the rural fringe of Clackamas County cannot be adequately accommodated by housing on the urban fringes of Multnomah and Washington Counties. However, there is no corresponding logic to the proposition that Metro appears to have found decisive here, *i.e.*, that a determinative housing need could be established solely by reference to areas in close proximity to the preselected site of the proposed UGB expansion and without *any* consideration of other parts of the regional planning territory. Metro's decision does not explain why the affordable housing must lie within a six-mile radius of the Stafford–Rosemont intersection, let alone why that intersection may appropriately be treated as the nucleus of an identifiable subregion or of the subregion to which virtually exclusive consideration was given as the site of the expansion. We hold that Metro's present supportive showing for its decision does not satisfy Goal 14 in this regard.

* * *

Notes

1. In Benjfran Development Inc. v. Metropolitan Service Dist., 95 Or.App. 22, 767 P.2d 467 (1989), landowners challenged the refusal of the Metropolitan Service District to allow 500 acres to be developed as an industrial park. The District was created to administer the urban growth boundary program in the greater Portland area. The landowner's argument was that the state economic development planning goal—Goal 9—and another parallel state statute should be given precedence over the urbanization goal—Goal 14. The court deferred to the decision of the District to disallow the development of the acreage for industrial purposes. See also Port of St.

Helens v. Land Conservation & Development Comm'n, 165 Or.App. 487, 996 P.2d 1014 (2000).

2. Consider how radically the Oregon growth management statute changed the historical balance of power between local, regional, and state agencies regarding the regulation of land use. Is there something unique about the legal system or the political culture in Oregon that enabled state lawmakers to effect such a drastic change? If local governments are created by the states and given their legislative authority primarily through state enabling acts, why can't their land use authority be taken away in the interest of achieving statewide or regional objectives?

3. In 1973, in Bedford v. Mount Kisco, 33 N.Y.2d 178, 351 N.Y.S.2d 129, 306 N.E.2d 155 (1973), the Court of Appeals heard the Town of Bedford's complaint that a rezoning by the Village of Mount Kisco from single-family to multi-family use of a parcel bounded on three sides by the town would have an undue impact on the town. The Court of Appeals found for Mount Kisco noting that "the [village] Board of Trustees considered the welfare and economic stability of Mount Kisco, as its first concern * * *. Bedford understandably differed from the conclusion reached, but that difference must be regarded as the necessary result of conflicting zoning policies that are confronted at the edge of every municipality." Bedford v. Mount Kisco represents the settled judicial doctrine in New York: that the state courts will not serve as the mediating mechanism for these border disputes in the ordinary circumstance.

4. Local sovereignty in land use matters has been established and generally reinforced since zoning was declared constitutional. In Euclid v. Ambler Realty Co., the court recognized the principle of local self-determinism in land use control with these words: "although physically a suburb of Cleveland, Euclid has powers of its own." However, federal and state preemption of local control does limit local sovereignty regarding particular matters of concern to these higher levels of government. See Chapter X.

5. In Wambat Realty Corp. v. State of New York, 41 N.Y.2d 490, 362 N.E.2d 581, 393 N.Y.S.2d 949 (1977), the Court of Appeals upheld the Adirondack Park Agency Act. The Adirondack Park Agency was authorized to govern land use decisions in 12 counties containing 105 local towns and villages. Its jurisdiction contains six million acres of private land, over 20 percent of the state. It is a classic example of top-down regionalism. The statute creating the APA allows local control over land use only after communities adopt land use plans and regulations that conform to the Agency's plan and regulatory regime, which preempted the land use authority of localities in the Adirondack region to various degrees. The plaintiff in Wambat claimed that the Act, "which set forth a comprehensive zoning and planning program for all of the public and private lands within the park, together with other restrictions on local land use contained in the act, unconstitutionally deprive[d] the Town of Black Brook of its own zoning and planning powers." The court disagreed, holding that the preservation of the area was a paramount state concern.

6. In 1970, the New York legislature was presented with the Statewide Comprehensive Planning Act, which provided for the creation of state, regional, county, and local plans—all cross certified and consistent, another

classic top-down approach. At the time, this was the nation's most far-reaching attempt to guide and constrain the parochial effects of local land use decision-making. The perceived threat to local control was clear, and the political reaction was predictable, swift, and definitive. The bill was withdrawn, and the New York Office of Planning Coordination—the agency that proposed it—was voted out of existence by the state legislature.

7. Despite this stunning political defeat, the state's highest court, the Court of Appeals, took a remarkably strong position regarding the need for regional mechanisms to make sense out of "insular" land use decisions. Refer back to Golden v. Town of Ramapo, 30 N.Y.2d 359, 334 N.Y.S.2d 138, 285 N.E.2d 291 (1972), where the court upheld the Town of Ramapo's novel growth management legislation. In so doing, it recognized the limitations of planning a region one community at a time, stating that "only at the regional level can the pitfall of idiosyncratic municipal action be avoided." The court called for a system of "statewide or regional control of land use planning" to "insure that interests broader than that of the municipality underlie various land use policies." It went on to say that "zoning enabling legislation is burdened by the largely antiquated notion which deigns that the regulation of land use and development is uniquely a function of local government." It found that this system suffers from "pronounced insularism" and that "questions of broader public interest have commonly been ignored" by it. In the absence of any regional or statewide planning framework, however, the decision simply sanctioned local growth management, allowing one suburb in the path of metropolitan development to adopt an ordinance in a contextual vacuum.

8. Since the creation of the Adirondack Park Agency and the Golden decision, nine voluntary, relatively weak regional councils, organized by local governments, focusing mostly on data gathering, research, grant getting, and technical assistance to local communities, have been New York's approach to regionalism in land use planning in most of the state. These regional councils are not guided by any statewide plan or development and conservation guidelines, paralleling the situation in most states. After a 20-year respite from regional legislation, the state legislature adopted the Hudson River Greenway Act in 1991, creating the Hudson River Greenway Communities Council and providing for a voluntary regional planning process based on local plans and county compacts that adhere to a few greenway planning principles. The Greenway is enjoying some success with a majority of the 242 communities in the regions voting to become participating localities in the Greenway compact.

9. Strong regionalism has not prevailed in New York for the same reason it has not prevailed in the majority of states. Former Speaker of the House Thomas P. O'Neill Jr., once quipped that "all politics is local." All reform efforts aimed at constraining local control must overcome this political reality. The danger in advocating top-down, statewide land use solutions is that it identifies local control as the problem to be solved, rather than the base on which to build an intermunicipal process, responsive to regional needs. The challenge for advocates of a regional approach to land use planning and control is to identify effective regional processes that respect the critical role that local governments play in land use decision-making. To be politically palatable, these solutions must be perceived not as

methods of imposing a state or regional body's will on local governments but as means of communicating effectively about regional and local needs, balancing those interests, and arriving at mutually beneficial decisions over time.

SECTION 4. CENTERS OF GROWTH AND DEVELOPMENT

A. INTRODUCTION

State growth management statutes, such as the Maryland and Oregon acts discussed in Section 3, reinforce the notion that development should be concentrated in serviceable centers. What is accomplished by centering growth in this way? The goal is to create a sense of community, promote economically viable development, ensure the ease of movement and safety of residents, and preserve open space, natural resources, and sustainable habitats.

The urban growth boundary in the greater Portland area encompasses the city and 23 surrounding towns. The growth management objectives of the state's plan are to concentrate urban development in districts, provide adequate housing and economic development within the boundaries, and prevent urban encroachment on important natural resource lands outside the boundaries. Maryland's novel smart growth spending law directs state infrastructure improvements into settled communities and "priority funding areas," which are growth areas designated by the state and county governments.

Local legislatures through their adopted zoning laws and maps have been designing growth districts since zoning was first adopted in New York City in 1916. Choices were made about how to draw the district lines and what uses to allow within each district and what densities to permit. The *sine qua non* of zoning, of course, was use separation. Historically, zoning concentrated on separating uses within zoning districts. The classic separation of use approach employs single-family districts here and industrial zones there. Citing expert reports to sustain the constitutionality of zoning, the U.S. Supreme Court's decision in Village of Euclid v. Ambler Realty Co., 272 U.S. 365, 47 S.Ct. 114, 71 L.Ed. 303 (1926), stated:

> These reports, which bear every evidence of painstaking consideration, concur in the view that the segregation of residential, business and industrial buildings will make it easier to provide fire apparatus suitable for the character and intensity of the development in each section; that it will increase the safety and security of home life; greatly tend to prevent street accidents, especially to children, by reducing the traffic and resulting confusion in residential sections; decrease noise and other conditions which produce or intensify nervous disorders; preserve a more favorable environment in which to raise children, etc.

Id. at 394.

Authority to regulate subdivision and site plan development was delegated to local governments to complement zoning and help localities implement their physical plans. (See Chapter V.) Such regulations initially concentrated on the creation of safe intersections; the fluid movement of vehicles; the adequacy of road width, curbs, and sidewalks; the siting of buildings; and the prevention of off-site impacts such as flooding. This type of conventional land use regulation gives local regulators and developers very little leeway in subdivision design, lot layouts, or the placement of buildings on the lot and, combined with strict use separation among zoning districts, becomes a blueprint for sprawl.

According to some experts, a more compact, mixed-use community that incorporates a diversity of housing, public and open spaces, and interconnected street patterns "directly conflicts with current zoning theory and local planning practice."[24] This view is supported by a national survey of developers and planners who "report that nearly all local zoning codes in their region continue to mandate or allow by right only conventional suburban development."[25] Ironically, many existing urban cities already exhibit the type of mixed use, diverse development pattern that planners strive to create in newer suburbs. The problem, in some older cities, is that they have been emptying out for decades and, despite recent evidence of an increase in urban populations, severe problems attend the efforts of urban communities to redevelop their aging neighborhoods and infrastructure.

The big picture here focuses on metropolitan area settlement patterns. How do cities become more livable, attract back the affluent households they have lost, and develop the tax base they need to support their diverse populations and the cultural, civic, educational, and governmental services they provide their regions? How do older suburbs protect and enhance their aging residential and commercial neighborhoods? How do cities and established suburbs deal with the competition for economic development and high end residential projects coming from communities on the fringe? How do these fringe communities ensure that cost-effective land patterns are created as they develop and change? It is one thing to designate urban growth districts or boundaries in cities, older suburbs, and the developing fringe, another to understand how to attract needed development to appropriate areas.

The cases in this section illustrate the complexity of these questions while describing some of the legal authority that localities have to deal with these persistent challenges. They point out the opportunities and difficulties of ordering development. They also raise serious questions about how the legal authority given to localities can be used effectively.

B. HOUSING CODES

Many students will recognize the next case, First National Realty Corp. v. Javins, from their first year property class. Justice Wright held

---

24. See Eric M. Braun, *Growth Management and New Urbanism: Legal Implications*, The Urban Lawyer 817, 818 (Fall 1999).

25. Edward H. Zeigler, *Zoning for New Urbanist Development: Lessons Learned from a Recent Survey*, Land Development (Fall 1998), at 27

that a warranty of habitability should be implied in multi-family residential leases when evidence showed serious violations of the District of Columbia's housing maintenance code. The case is presented here stripped of most of the rationale that led the court to imply the warranty, leaving those portions that reflect on the realities of urban living for low and moderate income families and the efficacy of legal tools such as housing codes to maintain the quality of life in the urban core.

New York City adopted the first urban housing code in 1901—the Tenement House Act. Housing codes aim to ensure that multi-family buildings are safe, sanitary, and efficient. The housing code, like a number of other techniques used to maintain livability and redevelop cities, is not traditionally thought of as a land use technique, but is one of a growing list of tools that community leaders use to accomplish their land use planning objectives. The Javins case illustrates that urban cities, in their struggle to remain livable, do have authority to regulate housing conditions, to enforce housing code standards, and to force building owners to repair, where the funds are available.

FIRST NATIONAL REALTY CORP. v. JAVINS

United States Court of Appeals, District of Columbia Circuit.
428 F.2d 1071 (D.C.Cir.1970).

J. SKELLY WRIGHT, Circuit Judge.

These cases present the question whether housing code violations which arise during the term of a lease have any effect upon the tenant's obligation to pay rent. The Landlord and Tenant Branch of the District of Columbia Court of General Sessions ruled proof of such violations inadmissible when proffered as a defense to an eviction action for nonpayment of rent. The District of Columbia Court of Appeals upheld this ruling. *Saunders v. First National Realty Corp.*, 245 A.2d 836 (1968).

Because of the importance of the question presented, we granted appellants' petitions for leave to appeal. We now reverse and hold that a warranty of habitability, measured by the standards set out in the Housing Regulations for the District of Columbia, is implied by operation of law into leases of urban dwelling units covered by those Regulations and that breach of this warranty gives rise to the usual remedies for breach of contract.

The facts revealed by the record are simple. By separate written leases, each of the appellants rented an apartment in a three-building apartment complex in Northwest Washington known as Clifton Terrace. The landlord, First National Realty Corporation, filed separate actions in the Landlord and Tenant Branch of the Court of General Sessions on April 8, 1966, seeking possession on the ground that each of the appellants had defaulted in the payment of rent due for the month of April. The tenants, appellants here, admitted that they had not paid the landlord any rent for April. However, they alleged numerous violations of the Housing Regulations as 'an equitable defense or (a) claim by way of recoupment or set-off in an amount equal to the rent claim,' as provided in the rules of the Court of General Sessions. They offered to prove

> 'that there are approximately 1500 violations of the Housing Regulations of the District of Columbia in the building at Clifton Terrace, where Defendant resides some affecting the premises of this Defendant directly, others indirectly, and all tending to establish a course of conduct of violation of the Housing Regulations to the damage of Defendants * * *.'

Settled Statement of Proceedings and Evidence, p. 2 (1966). Appellants conceded at trial, however, that this offer of proof reached only violations which had arisen since the term of the lease had commenced. The Court of General Sessions refused appellants' offer of proof and entered judgment for the landlord. The District of Columbia Court of Appeals affirmed, rejecting the argument made by appellants that the landlord was under a contractual duty to maintain the premises in compliance with the Housing Regulations. *Saunders v. First National Realty Corp., supra*, 245 A.2d at 838.

Since, in traditional analysis, a lease was the conveyance of an interest in land, courts have usually utilized the special rules governing real property transactions to resolve controversies involving leases. However, as the Supreme Court has noted in another context, 'the body of private property law * * *, more than almost any other branch of law, has been shaped by distinctions whose validity is largely historical.' Courts have a duty to reappraise old doctrines in the light of the facts and values of contemporary life—particularly old common law doctrines which the courts themselves created and developed. As we have said before, 'The continued vitality of the common law * * * depends upon its ability to reflect contemporary community values and ethics.'

* * *

A. In our judgment the common law itself must recognize the landlord's obligation to keep his premises in a habitable condition. This conclusion is compelled by three separate considerations. First, we believe that the old rule was based on certain factual assumptions which are no longer true; on its own terms, it can no longer be justified. Second, we believe that the consumer protection cases discussed above require that the old rule be abandoned in order to bring residential landlord-tenant law into harmony with the principles on which those cases rest. Third, we think that the nature of today's urban housing market also dictates abandonment of the old rule.

* * *

It is overdue for courts to admit that these assumptions are no longer true with regard to all urban housing. Today's urban[26] tenants,

---

26. In 1968 more than two thirds of America's people lived in the 228 largest metropolitan areas. Only 5.2% lived on farms. The World Almanac 1970 at 251 (L.

the vast majority of whom live in multiple dwelling houses, are interested, not in the land, but solely in 'a house suitable for occupation.' Furthermore, today's city dweller usually has a single, specialized skill unrelated to maintenance work; he is unable to make repairs like the 'jack-of-all-trades' farmer who was the common law's model of the lessee. Further, unlike his agrarian predecessor who often remained on one piece of land for his entire life, urban tenants today are more mobile than ever before. A tenant's tenure in a specific apartment will often not be sufficient to justify efforts at repairs. In addition, the increasing complexity of today's dwellings renders them much more difficult to repair than the structures of earlier times. In a multiple dwelling repair may require access to equipment and areas in the control of the landlord. Low and middle income tenants, even if they were interested in making repairs, would be unable to obtain any financing for major repairs since they have no long-term interest in the property.

* * *

Thus we are led by our inspection of the relevant legal principles and precedents to the conclusion that the old common law rule imposing an obligation upon the lessee to repair during the lease term was really never intended to apply to residential urban leaseholds. Contract principles established in other areas of the law provide a more rational framework for the apportionment of landlord-tenant responsibilities; they strongly suggest that a warranty of habitability be implied into all contracts for urban dwellings.

B. We believe, in any event, that the District's housing code requires that a warranty of habitability be implied in the leases of all housing that it covers. The housing code—formally designated the Housing Regulations of the District of Columbia—was established and authorized by the Commissioners of the District of Columbia on August 11, 1955. Since that time, the code has been updated by numerous orders of the Commissioners. The 75 pages of the Regulations provide a comprehensive regulatory scheme setting forth in some detail: (a) the standards which housing in the District of Columbia must meet; (b) which party, the lessor or the lessee, must meet each standard; and (c) a system of inspections, notifications and criminal penalties. The Regulations themselves are silent on the question of private remedies.

* * *

The District of Columbia Court of Appeals gave further effect to the Housing Regulations in *Brown v. Southall Realty Co.*, 237 A.2d 834 (1968). There the landlord knew at the time the lease was signed that housing code violations existed which rendered the apartment 'unsafe and unsanitary.' Viewing the lease as a contract, the District of Columbia Court of Appeals held that the premises were let in violation of

Long ed.). More than 98% of all housing starts in 1968 were non-farm. Id. at 313.

Sections 2304[27] and 2501[28] of the Regulations and that the lease, therefore, was void as an illegal contract. In the light of Brown, it is clear not only that the housing code creates privately enforceable duties as held in Whetzel, but that the basic validity of every housing contract depends upon substantial compliance with the housing code at the beginning of the lease term. The Brown court relied particularly upon Section 2501 of the Regulations which provides:

> 'Every premises accommodating one or more habitations shall be maintained and kept in repair so as to provide decent living accommodations for the occupants. This part of this Code contemplates more than mere basic repairs and maintenance to keep out the elements; its purpose is to include repairs and maintenance designed to make a premises or neighborhood healthy and safe.'

By its terms, this section applies to maintenance and repair during the lease term. Under the Brown holding, serious failure to comply with this section before the lease term begins renders the contract void. We think it untenable to find that this section has no effect on the contract after it has been signed. To the contrary, by signing the lease the landlord has undertaken a continuing obligation to the tenant to maintain the premises in accordance with all applicable law.

This principle of implied warranty is well established. Courts often imply relevant law into contracts to provide a remedy for any damage caused by one party's illegal conduct. In a case closely analogous to the present ones, the Illinois Supreme Court held that a builder who constructed a house in violation of the Chicago building code had breached his contract with the buyer:

> ' * * * The law existing at the time and place of the making of the contract is deemed a part of the contract, as though expressly referred to or incorporated in it. * * *'

> 'The rationale for this rule is that the parties to the contract would have expressed that which the law implies 'had they not supposed that it was unnecessary to speak of it because the law provided for it.' * * * Consequently, the courts, in construing the existing law as part of the express contract, are not reading into the contract provisions different from those expressed and intended by the parties, as defendants contend, but are merely construing the contract in accordance with the intent of the parties.'

We follow the Illinois court in holding that the housing code must be read into housing contracts—a holding also required by the purposes and the structure of the code itself.[29] The duties imposed by the Housing

---

27. 'No person shall rent or offer to rent any habitation, or the furnishings thereof, unless such habitation and its furnishings are in a clean, safe and sanitary condition, in repair, and free from rodents or vermin.'

28. 'The housing and sanitary codes, especially in light of Congress' explicit direction for their enactment, indicate a strong and pervasive congressional concern to secure for the city's slum dwellers decent, or at least safe and sanitary, places to live.' *Edwards v. Habib,* supra Note 44, 130 U.S.App.D.C. at 139, 397 F.2d at 700.

29. 'The housing and sanitary codes, especially in light of Congress' explicit direction for their enactment, indicate a strong and pervasive congressional concern

Regulations may not be waived or shifted by agreement if the Regulations specifically place the duty upon the lessor. Criminal penalties are provided if these duties are ignored. This regulatory structure was established by the Commissioners because, in their judgment, the grave conditions in the housing market required serious action. Yet official enforcement of the housing code has been far from uniformly effective.[30] Innumerable studies have documented the desperate condition of rental housing in the District of Columbia and in the nation. In view of these circumstances, we think the conclusion reached by the Supreme Court of Wisconsin as to the effect of a housing code on the old common law rule cannot be avoided:

> ' * * * The legislature has made a policy judgment—that it is socially (and politically) desirable to impose these duties on a property owner—which has rendered the old common law rule obsolete. To follow the old rule of no implied warranty of habitability in leases would, in our opinion, be inconsistent with the current legislative policy concerning housing standards. * * * '

We therefore hold that the Housing Regulations imply a warranty of habitability, measured by the standards which they set out, into leases of all housing that they cover.

* * *

The judgment of the District of Columbia Court of Appeals is reversed and the cases are remanded for further proceedings consistent with this opinion.

So ordered.

Notes

1. What are the economic consequences of the Javins decision? When landlords defer maintenance and housing code violations occur, what will tenants do with the rent if they know about Javins? Will they pay it? Will they put it in escrow? Will they join forces and contract to make repairs, pay for them with withheld rents, and offset that amount in any non-payment action? How are rents in inner city apartment buildings set? What is their market value? Are these rents enough to pay utilities, insurance, mortgage principal and interest, property taxes, building maintenance personnel and materials, and make capital improvements? If not, can landlords raise rents to cover recurring expenses and needed improvements?

2. The conditions of low and moderate income housing in the District of Columbia and many other cities continued to decline even after the judicially-created warranty of habitability was codified in state statutes. During this same time, more affluent residents were pouring out into the

---

to secure for the city's slum dwellers decent, or at least safe and sanitary, places to live.' *Edwards v. Habib,* supra Note 44, 130 U.S.App.D.C. at 139, 397 F.2d at 700.

30. See Gribetz & Grad, Housing Code Fnforcement: Sanctions and Remedies, 66 Colum.L.Rev. 1254 (1966); Note, Enforcement of Municipal Housing Codes, 78 Harv. L.Rev. 801 (1965).

developing suburbs with modern housing in single-family subdivisions—communities with low crime rates and higher quality schools.

3. Housing codes should not be confused with building codes. Building codes, including separate provisions for fire prevention, plumbing, and electrical improvements, contain standards that must be met when buildings are newly constructed or substantially rehabilitated. The local building inspector must review the developer's construction drawings and certify that building code standards are met before a building permit may be issued. Without a building permit, no construction can be commenced legally. After construction is completed, the inspector certifies that it conforms with the approved drawings and then issues the owner a certificate of occupancy. Without this certificate, a building may not be occupied. When a building is sold, the buyer's attorney will insist that a valid certificate of occupancy be delivered before the closing of title. This certificate represents the finish line in the long journey that developers make from buying vacant land to obtaining land use approvals, constructing the buildings, and selling or renting the final product.

C. URBAN REDEVELOPMENT TECHNIQUES

One of the most intriguing questions in municipal law is why one person's private property can be taken under the power of eminent domain to allow another private party to redevelop an area. In Berman v. Parker, 348 U.S. 26, 75 S.Ct. 98, 99 L.Ed. 27 (1954), the U.S. Supreme Court noted that the public uses for which property may be taken under the power of eminent domain are coextensive with the police power of the state. Since the public welfare is broad and inclusive, the ends that may be achieved by using the power to condemn title to land may include stemming blight and deterioration, redeveloping underdeveloped areas, and increasing the economic productivity of an area. The Berman court noted that the role of the judiciary in determining whether that power of eminent domain is being exercised for a public purpose is an extremely narrow one.

The plaintiffs in Berman complained that their property, which contained a department store, could not be taken for a slum clearance project aimed at the elimination of squalid housing conditions. How, the plaintiffs asked, does it serve the public interest in stemming housing blight to condemn a commercial building? The court deferred to the urban renewal authority in the District which had decided that area-wide blight could only be cured by an area-wide solution and, thus, it was necessary to take the plaintiffs' building whose existence and use did not conform to the urban renewal plan for the area.

The advocates of urban renewal won a short-lived victory in Berman. The questionable results of slum clearance and redevelopment came under fierce attack only a few years after the decision. The critics held that urban renewal was fostering segregation, was responsible for the demolition of historic buildings, was dislocating the urban poor, and was wasting government resources. With the passage of the Housing and Community Development Act of 1974, federal urban renewal planning and project grants were folded into the special revenue sharing formula of the Community Development Block Grant program. The disappearance of dedicated urban renewal funding and a number of other categorical funding programs for urban areas added to the sense of ambivalence about the ability of cities to revitalize themselves.

This ambivalence has not curtailed the use of the power of eminent domain to take "blighted" property and commit it to redevelopment. Many challenges have been brought against condemnation schemes that take title to moderately blighted or underdeveloped properties so that commercial or industrial developers can acquire title to the land and develop commercial centers, mixed-use marina complexes, shopping plazas, light industrial parks, and other, more intensive, job-producing developments.

Courts have not set aside these arrangements even when the funds used to pay the owners of the condemned land come from the private company that is selected to redevelop the area. The fact that numerous property owners are displaced by such arrangements and are not able to find suitable locations to live or reestablish their businesses has not altered the favorable judicial attitude toward the use of eminent domain in the interest of renewal, redevelopment, higher tax bases, and more jobs for struggling cities and older suburbs.

The role of the courts in reviewing the propriety of land condemnations is threefold: to be sure the condemning authority followed the procedures required by the state eminent domain law; to be sure the purpose for which the property is taken is a public one—which, under Berman, is broadly defined; and to see that just compensation is paid. Condemning authorities do not have to demonstrate that their proposed redevelopment plans, in fact, will be beneficial. "Just" compensation does not mean enough money to reestablish your home or business; the standard is whether the authority paid the price that a willing buyer would pay a willing seller at the time of the condemnation. Since the properties taken are often in declining or underdeveloped areas, this price is sometimes quite modest.

MATTER OF CONDEMNATION BY MINNEAPOLIS COMMUNITY DEVELOPMENT AGENCY v. OPUS NORTHWEST, LLC

Court of Appeals of Minnesota, 1998.
582 N.W.2d 596.

SCHUMACHER, JUDGE.

The city seeks to invoke the power of eminent domain to take two parcels of property located on Nicollet Mall in downtown Minneapolis. The condemnation is being undertaken to serve the city's desire to locate a mid-priced retail store, parking complex, extended skyway access, and an office building in the south Nicollet Mall area. Due to the high cost of downtown property, the city has used tax increment financing to attract a mid-priced retailer to locate downtown.

The city has been unsuccessful for a number of years in bringing development projects to south Nicollet Mall. There has been no large-scale development in the area for a number of years, and the city complains that a lack of skyway connections, insufficient parking, and parcelization of land ownership prevents projects that could improve the tax base and economy of the area. In the mid–1980s, the city designated the area as a redevelopment district and a tax increment financing district. At that time, it made detailed findings supporting those designations. In 1996, before commencing the Ryan–Dayton Hudson project, the city updated and confirmed its earlier findings.

The city is contracting with Ryan Corporation for the development, construction, and eventual ownership of much of the project. The retail store will be owned and operated by the Dayton Hudson Corporation, which will place a Target store on the first and second floors of the building (hereinafter Dayton Hudson and Target collectively referred to as Dayton Hudson).

Opus is the owner of the two parcels being condemned. Before the city and Dayton Hudson chose Ryan, Opus also bid on the project, but it was not chosen because, among other reasons, Opus could not secure a mid-priced retailer as an anchor tenant. Opus now proposes to build a $120 million office building on its property without any government subsidies, however, its current proposal still does not contain a mid-priced anchor retailer. Opus objected to the condemnation proceedings.

Minneapolis ordinances require contractors to file affirmative action plans before doing business with the city. Dayton Hudson has not filed an affirmative action plan with the city. Opus, as a private taxpayer under the tax increment financing statutes, challenges the legality of the overall project.

* * *

From the 19th century to the present, the judiciary's review of condemnation proceedings has remained "very narrow." *State ex rel. Simpson v. Rapp*, 39 Minn. 65, 67, 38 N.W. 926, 928 (1888); *County of Dakota (C.P.46–06) v. Lakeville*, 559 N.W.2d 716, 719 (Minn.App.1997). We review only whether the taking serves a public purpose and is necessary. *City of Duluth v. State*, 390 N.W.2d 757, 763, 764 (Minn. 1986).

> Great weight must be given to the determination of the condemning authority, and the scope of review is narrowly limited. If it appears that the record contains some evidence, however informal, that the taking serves a public purpose, there is nothing left for the courts to pass upon. * * * The court is precluded from substituting its own judgment for that of the [public body] as to what may be necessary and proper to carry out the purpose of the plan.

Id. at 763 (quoting *Housing & Redev. Auth. v. Minneapolis Metro. Co.*, 259 Minn. 1, 15, 104 N.W.2d 864, 874 (1960)). Public purpose and necessity are questions of fact, and the district court's decisions on these matters will not be reversed on appeal unless clearly erroneous. *State by Humphrey v. Byers*, 545 N.W.2d 669, 672 (Minn.App.1996).

Opus admits that this court should show deference to the city's legislative condemnation findings but contends that the deference should not be "slavish." Opus argues that "substantial authority" requires that we apply a "heightened scrutiny" to any condemnation that benefits private interests. Opus's foreign authority, however, is distinguishable. *See Wilmington Parking Auth. v. Land With Improvements*, 521 A.2d 227, 230–31 (Del.1986) (government parking authority acted outside its narrow statutory parking power when underlying purpose of condemnation was to benefit newspaper, not create parking); *City of Lansing v. Edward Rose Realty, Inc.*, 442 Mich. 626, 502 N.W.2d 638, 645 (1993) (city sought to condemn apartment building because owner refused to use city's franchised cable company; court held condemnation served no public purpose because there was no statutory grant of power to allow access for cable T.V., and public benefit was not clear and predominant); *Poletown Neighborhood Council v. City of Detroit*, 410 Mich. 616, 304 N.W.2d 455, 457, 459 (1981) (court, despite announcing it was using heightened standard, affirmed Detroit's condemnation of land to allow General Motors to construct assembly plant to increase employment and revitalize economic base of community); *City of Ctr. Line v. Chmelko*, 164 Mich.App. 251, 416 N.W.2d 401, 402 (1987) (city's condemnation was "complete fiction" because city acted as agent for local car dealer and alleged public purposes were not supported by the evidence); *City of Jamestown v. Leevers Supermarkets, Inc.*, 552 N.W.2d 365, 372, 374 (N.D.1996) (case remanded for court to determine if "primary object" was public; court noted trend is to allow broad legislative discretion to use powers of eminent domain for variety of economic development purposes).

Unlike the condemnations criticized in *City of Lansing* and *Wilmington Parking*, the condemnation of Opus's property falls within the city's prescribed authority. Additionally, it appears that the application of a heightened level of scrutiny to review condemnation proceedings, for which Opus cites these foreign cases, is out of touch with the national trend. 2A *Nichols on Eminent Domain*, § 7.06[24][c], at p. 7–242 (Matthew Bender revised 3d ed.1998) (trend is to sanction "broad legislative discretion to use eminent domain for a variety of economic development purposes.").

Finally, Opus's foreign authority is inconsistent with Minnesota caselaw. Minnesota courts have not employed a heightened standard of review in appeals involving governmental condemnation benefiting private parties. *See, e.g., City of Duluth*, 390 N.W.2d at 763–64 (condemnation of Jeno Paulucci's Chun King plant to allow a paper mill to be built); *City of Minneapolis v. Wurtele*, 291 N.W.2d 386, 390 (Minn.1980) (condemnation of private property to construct City Center in downtown Minneapolis). We reject the invitation to change our well-established and limited standard of review.

What constitutes a "public use" or "public purpose" is broadly defined. *City of Duluth*, 390 N.W.2d at 763. As noted, it includes a city's acquisition of private property for use by a different private entity. *Id.* at 763–64. If there is some evidence in the record that the taking serves a public purpose, there is nothing left for the court to decide. *Id.*

Condemnation efforts undertaken to enhance deteriorating urban areas and to create jobs satisfy the public purpose aspect of a condemnation proceeding. *Id.* at 763; *see also Wurtele*, 291 N.W.2d at 390. The legislature has recognized that actions taken to foster new development, including the financing thereof, "in areas of a city that are already built up in order to provide employment opportunities, to improve the tax base, and to improve the general economy of the state * * * are [examples of] a public purpose." Minn.Stat. § 469.124 (1996). In this case, the city presented testimony that the proposed project will have the following benefits: a mid-priced retail store, increased parking, increased employment, increased tax base, extension of the skyway system, unification of the multiple-ownership/parcelization of the area, modernization of outdated and incompatible buildings, and furtherance of the city's ultimate objective of creating an economically viable retail corridor between downtown businesses and the convention/hospitality district. The city also presented evidence that these objectives will not be met by Opus's proposal or without the city's involvement. The finding of public purpose in this case is consistent with the authority granted by the legislature in section 469.124, and it is not clearly erroneous.

Absolute necessity is not required for a finding of public purpose, rather "[i]t is enough to find that 'the proposed taking is *reasonably necessary* or *convenient* for the furtherance of a proper purpose.'" *City of Duluth*, 390 N.W.2d at 764–65 (quoting *City of Pipestone v. Halbersma*, 294 N.W.2d 271, 274 (Minn.1980)) (emphasis added). A party challenging the necessity of the condemnation of a parcel will not succeed by merely suggesting alternatives to the government's plan. *Id.* at 766. Accordingly, Opus's argument, to the extent that it relies on Opus's own plan to build an alternative tower, is not persuasive.

The heart of Opus's appeal involves challenges to the legality and attainability of the city's condemnation. Any corporation contracting with the City of Minneapolis must have an affirmative action plan filed with the city. Minneapolis, Minn., Code of Ordinances (hereinafter MCO) § 139.50(b), (c) (1997). The city ordinance applies specifically to tax increment financing contracts and to owner-occupants of any project financed through tax increment financing. MCO § 139.50(d) (1997) (citing Minnesota Tax Increment Financing Act). Dayton Hudson will be the eventual owner occupant of the tax-increment-financed, mid-priced retail store. Dayton Hudson, however, does not have an affirmative action plan on record with the city and is not currently permitted to contract with the city for that reason. Opus contends that the condemnation is, therefore, illegal.

Opus relies on three early Minnesota Supreme Court cases in support of its argument. In each of those cases, the supreme court found that the proposed condemnation of rivers and lakes to create a utility plant was illegal and, therefore, the condemnations could not go forward. See *Minnesota Canal & Power Co. v. Fall Lake Boom Co.*, 127 Minn. 23, 31–32, 148 N.W. 561, 564 (1914) (condemnation denied, despite approval by U.S. government, because Minnesota Canal, in order to make its plant work, would need to obtain greater amounts of navigable water than allowed by state statute); *Minnesota Canal & Power Co. v. Pratt*, 101 Minn. 197, 222–23, 112 N.W. 395, 401–02 (1907) (condemnation prohibited because, despite change in state laws, waters in question were also federal and Minnesota Canal did not receive permission from U.S. government); *Minnesota Canal & Power Co. v. Koochiching Co.*, 97 Minn. 429, 443, 107 N.W. 405, 410 (1906) (condemnation prohibited due to absence of state and federal laws allowing alienability of navigable waters).

In sum, the *Minnesota Canal* trilogy stands for the proposition that a condemning authority cannot undertake a public project if the project itself is not permitted by law. The public purposes for the present condemnation (obtaining a mid-priced retail store, increased public parking and employment, etc.) and the means of accomplishment (through tax increment financing for Ryan) are all legal. In the *Minnesota Canal* cases, however, the diversion of lakes and rivers, no matter how attempted, was not permitted by law.

In addition, Opus's challenge to the legality of Dayton Hudson's occupancy is anticipatory. The ordinance requires an owner-occupant of a tax-increment-financed project to file an affirmative action plan with the city. It is contemplated that Dayton Hudson will be the *eventual* owner-occupant of the mid-priced retail store included in this project, but Dayton Hudson is not a *current* owner-occupant and is not now in violation of MCO § 139.50. In its brief and at oral argument, the city argued that the goals for which condemnation was initiated are not dependent on a specific retailer or developer. To date, the city has signed a development contract with Ryan; neither that agreement nor the contemplated building of a mid-priced retail store is illegal. In the event Dayton Hudson violates the city ordinance, a controversy will exist upon which a court can pass judgment. *See Izaak Walton League of Am. Endowment, Inc. v. State, Dep't of Natural Resources*, 312 Minn. 587, 589, 252 N.W.2d 852, 854 (1977) ("The existence of a justiciable controversy is prerequisite to adjudication. The judicial function does not comprehend the giving of advisory opinions."). Because there is no existing illegality affecting the project as a whole, we decline to speculate on the likelihood of a future violation of MCO § 139.50. The condemnation is not barred by the fact that Dayton Hudson does not have an affirmative action plan on file with the city.

Opus also argues that there can be no proper or necessary purpose if the project for which property is condemned is too speculative, relying on a Wisconsin case holding that a private owner is "entitled to have it shown that the taking is for a public use definite and certain of attainment." *Schumm v. Milwaukee County*, 258 Wis. 256, 45 N.W.2d 673, 676 (1951). In *Schumm*, a non-profit group and the county entered into negotiations for condemnation of property upon which the non-profit group intended to construct war memorials. *Id.*, 45 N.W.2d at 674. Without any of the necessary resolutions, the county instructed its counsel to commence condemnation proceedings. *Id.*, 45 N.W.2d at 675. There was no valid contract between the county and the non-profit group. *Id.*, 45 N.W.2d at 676. There were numerous details to be resolved, including the specifications for the memorials, the amount of money required, whether resolutions would be passed, and whether the city in which the proposed memorials were to be placed would grant permission to the county. *Id.*, 45 N.W.2d at 677. The county's agreement with the group was too riddled with uncertainty to justify the taking of private property. *Id.*

Opus suggests that the lack of finality to some details of the development agreement between the city and Ryan render the project similar to that in *Schumm* and too speculative to justify condemnation. This case differs substantially and significantly from *Schumm*. First, the city supports and has passed resolutions directing the project to go forward. Second, there is a written contract between the city and Ryan and Dayton Hudson is committed to the project, assuming that this litigation can be resolved. Third, funding is in place through the tax increment financing plan and Ryan. Fourth, while there have been no negotiations with owners on block 34, this is within the city's control, and there is no need to secure the approval of a distinct governing authority. Finally, the contingencies that exist appear to be normal for this stage and type of development, and Opus has presented no evidence that the Ryan-city contract is out of the ordinary.

The trial court concluded that there was no evidence to suggest that the project would not be completed once the cloud of litigation was removed. The relative certainty of this project stands in marked contrast to the ambiguity and uncertainty of the plans for the property to be condemned by the county in *Schumm*. Considering our standard of review, the trial court's finding that the public purpose of the project is proper and not speculative is supported by the evidence and is not clearly erroneous.

Opus challenges the use of tax increment financing money in this project as a private taxpayer under Minn.Stat. § 469.1771, subd. 1(a) (1996). The statute provides:

> The owner of taxable property located in the city, town, school district, or county in which the tax increment financing district is located may bring suit for equitable relief or for damages, as provided in subdivisions 3 and 4, arising out of a failure of a municipality or authority to comply with the provisions of sections 469.174 to 469.179, or related provisions of this chapter.

Id. This court reviews statutory construction de novo. *Hibbing Educ. Ass'n v. Public Employment Relations Bd.*, 369 N.W.2d 527, 529 (Minn. 1985). Findings of fact and credibility determinations, upon which the trial courts base legal conclusions, will not be set aside unless clearly erroneous. Minn. R. Civ. P. 52.01.

In 1983, the city declared the area in question on the south Nicollet Mall to be a redevelopment district. In 1985, the area in question was designated as tax increment financing District 63. Opus has not challenged the findings supporting either decision. In 1996, before the city condemned Opus's property, it made new, summary findings that updated and confirmed the findings made in 1983 and 1985. At issue is whether the tax increment financing statute required the city's 1996 findings and, if so, whether they were sufficiently detailed. The city's 1996 findings concluded that private investment would not be forthcoming and that tax increment financing would generate higher property values than any purely private investment.

Before a tax increment financing district can be created, a municipality must make the necessary findings. Minn.Stat. § 469.175, subd. 3 (1996). Once the district is properly created, however, a municipality may *modify* a tax increment financing plan with *no specified procedure or findings* unless modification includes an increase in the bonded indebtedness or there are other circumstances identified in the statute and not present here. Minn.Stat. § 469.175, subd. 4 (1996). Specifically, in the absence of changes specified in Minn.Stat. § 469.175, subd. 4, changes to an existing tax increment financing plan constitute "modification" for which no new findings are required and no procedure is prescribed by the statute.

Under Minn.Stat. § 469.175, subd. l(a)(5)(ii) (1996), an original tax increment financing district plan must include an estimate of the "amount of bonded indebtedness to be incurred." The original tax increment financing plan for this area anticipated that $157 million of indebtedness would be incurred. It appears that only two projects financed by tax increment financing ever drew on the authorized total indebtedness. These projects total $36.4 million. Because the current project is estimated to cost $62 million, the three projects do not exceed the total estimated indebtedness. Accordingly, since the "amount of bonded indebtedness" is not being increased, the 1996 decision is a mere modification of the existing plan and Minn.Stat. § 469.175, subd. 4 does not require the city to issue new, detailed findings. We affirm the trial court's conclusion that Opus failed to establish the existence of a statutory violation.

The trial court's findings of public purpose and necessity are supported by the evidence and are not clearly erroneous. The failure of Dayton Hudson to file an affirmative action plan does not render the project illegal. Further, because the project is supported by the city and is the subject of a contract between the city and Ryan, the condemnation is not based on speculation. Finally, the city was not required to make new findings because the current project does not require an increase in the amount of bonded indebtedness authorized in the original tax increment financing plan.

Affirmed.

Notes

1. Note that Minneapolis designated the Nicollet Mall area a redevelopment district in 1983 and an area eligible for tax increment financing in 1985, in the waning years of federal urban renewal funding. Tax increment financing statutes were adopted in many states to provide an alternative method of financing redevelopment. Earlier Minnesota cases had consistently upheld the tax increment financing approach to redevelopment. In R.E. Short Co. v. City of Minneapolis, 269 N.W.2d 331 (1978), the first Minnesota opinion on tax increment financing, the court stated:

> The purpose of tax-increment financing of urban redevelopment is to create economically productive property where none presently exists by providing inducements to private commercial development. The municipality, either with or without the power of eminent domain, acquires all the property in an area in which the value of real estate is declining or there is a high proportion of underutilized or tax-delinquent land. Pursuant to a development plan for the area, the municipality then delineates a number of new disposition parcels which it markets to private developers. Inducements to such private development include promises to construct certain support facilities or various other types of incentives affording substantial savings to the developer. Once the land becomes productive, the increment over the prior tax revenues is utilized to pay off the interest and principal on the bonds issued to finance the redevelopment, and the municipality retains in its general treasury the amount equal to the former tax revenue from the area. After the bonds are paid off, the area is expected to remain economically productive, providing substantially increased tax revenues for municipal government.

This philosophy of development financing underlays the decision to create the Loring Park Development District just south of downtown Minneapolis. Acting pursuant to L.1971, c. 677, the city council established this district by a resolution dated June 9, 1972. At that time, there were 58 privately owned land parcels, many of which were economically unproductive. The goal of the Loring Park Development District was to renew the area by the private construction of additional residential units, convention and hotel facilities, and various other commercial enterprises. The city also planned to upgrade the public works and beautify the district by constructing the Loring Greenway. All of this development, the city council determined, would provide not only employment during the construction phase of the project but also additional permanent employment, increased tax revenues, and a more productive tax base for the district and the city. In April 1973, the city held the first of four bond sales, and in August it began acquisition of the land, first by purchase and, after April 1974, by eminent domain proceedings. The district was then replatted into 14 disposition parcels which were to be offered to developers willing to construct structures that would conform to the alternative land uses outlined in the development program.

* * *

In 1976, Convention Hotel Associates, the predecessor of appellant Mart Plaza Hotel, Inc., proposed to construct a hotel and trade mart on parcel 2D if the city would build a 750–car, public parking ramp on parcel 2E. In October 1976, the city council issued to it a letter of intent, which was renewed in July 1977. The proposal and the development contract were discussed in two city council committees in December 1977, and the contract was unanimously approved by the council on December 16, 1977. After Mayor Stenvig vetoed this resolution, all interested parties were permitted to present their positions on the proposal to the full city council. The council then weighed the testimony and overrode the veto on December 30, 1977.

Among its terms the contract provided that the city would construct a public parking facility, the lower level of which would be rented by the developer for use as a convention hall. The city also agreed to design the parking ramp to be compatible with the hotel and to ensure that tennis facilities for hotel guests could be erected by the developer on its roof. Another part of the contract contained a management agreement under which the developer was to manage the parking ramp for a term of 20 years, and the developer was granted a 50–year exclusive option to purchase the parking ramp and convention hall. The city, however, retained exclusive control over the ramp. The rates, hours, and methods of operation were to be set by the city, and the hotel, the trade mart, and their customers would receive no preferential treatment. All income from the ramp would go directly to the city, and the entire agreement could be canceled by the city if the developer did not perform in a satisfactory manner. Finally, the ramp and the land upon which it would be constructed were in no way made subordinate to the mortgage that the developer secured to finance the construction of the hotel.

2. Tax increment financing statutes allow cities or redevelopment authorities to issue bonds secured by the increase in property tax revenues that the newly redeveloped land will generate for the city. This projected increase in taxes becomes the revenue stream used to pay the principal and interest on bonds sold to private investors. Because these are considered public bonds, the interest paid to investors is tax exempt and therefore lower than interest paid on private financing from commercial lenders. By issuing and selling these bonds, the authority secures the capital needed, up front, to purchase land, install infrastructure, or lower the cost of the enterprise so that it becomes economically feasible. Often, the TIF program is entwined with a state statutory enterprise zone enabling act that allows cities to offer zoning and tax incentives for redevelopment in the poorest areas of cities.

3. In accord with the R.E. Short case is Richards v. Muscatine, 237 N.W.2d 48 (Iowa 1975) which upheld tax increment financing against an attack that alleged a disparate burden on taxpayers outside the redevelopment area for the duration of the project; the court also rejected an argument that the scheme violated a constitutional provision on uniformity

of taxation, holding that the private developer pays taxes on his development at the same rate as all other taxpayers. Compare Miller v. Covington Development Auth., 539 S.W.2d 1 (Ky.1976) where the court held tax increment financing violative of the state constitution and struck down the statute with State v. Miami Beach Redevelopment Agency, 392 So.2d 875 (Fla.1980), upholding the Florida statute.

Most of the cases that present a broad constitutional attack on the tax increment financing programs have upheld the theory of the device. In addition to the principal case and those cited above, see Tax Increment Financing Comm'n of Kansas City v. J.E. Dunn Construction Co., Inc., 781 S.W.2d 70 (Mo.1989); Dennehy v. Department of Revenue, 308 Or. 423, 781 P.2d 346 (1989); In re Request for Advisory Opinion on Constitutionality of 1986 Pa. 281, 430 Mich. 93, 422 N.W.2d 186 (1988); City of El Paso v. El Paso Community College Dist., 729 S.W.2d 296 (Tex.1986); Wolper v. City Council of City of Charleston, 287 S.C. 209, 336 S.E.2d 871 (1985); Meierhenry v. City of Huron, 354 N.W.2d 171 (S.D.1984); Kuehn, Tax Increment Financing, Land Use Law (May, 1985) p. 3.

4. Even in states that have upheld tax increment financing, courts may give close scrutiny to the specific projects proposed. See, e.g., Downey Cares v. Downey Community Development Comm'n, 196 Cal.App.3d 983, 242 Cal.Rptr. 272 (1987) (ordinance invalidated because one city council member owned property and a real estate business within the redevelopment area); Emmington v. Solano County Redevelopment Agency, 195 Cal.App.3d 491, 237 Cal.Rptr. 636 (1987) (occasional flooding and lack of infrastructure insufficient to support a finding that the area was blighted); East Grand County School Dist. No. 2 v. Town of Winter Park, 739 P.2d 862 (Colo.App. 1987) (failure to hold required public meetings not cured by submitting proposal to voters); Card v. Community Redevelopment Agency of South Pasadena, 61 Cal.App.3d 570, 131 Cal.Rptr. 153 (1976) (taxpayers successfully challenged a project that made no provision for relocation of displaced citizens); Regus v. City of Baldwin Park, 70 Cal.App.3d 968, 139 Cal.Rptr. 196 (1977) (evidence failed to show that the redevelopment area was blighted). Compare Smith v. Independence Tax Increment Finance Comm'n, 919 S.W.2d 292 (Mo.App.1996). The Regus case illustrates one of the frequently heard criticisms of tax increment financing, that the scheme provides more benefits for the private developer than for the public. Do you think the principal case provides a sufficient answer to that criticism? Another criticism of such redevelopment programs is that the city chooses redevelopment projects which are most likely to generate tax increments, e.g., shopping centers and office buildings, rather than housing projects for low-income or even moderate-income persons. In Reed–Custer Community Unit School Dist. No. 255–U v. City of Wilmington, 253 Ill.App.3d 503, 192 Ill.Dec. 421, 625 N.E.2d 381 (1993) the court struck down a proposed TIF district. The plaintiffs, a local school district, a library district and a mosquito abatement district claimed that the defective TIF District would eat into their property tax revenues. The court found that a prerequisite for a TIF district under Illinois law was that the land be substantially vacant. Here the 600–acre proposed district, a former strip mine area, was occupied by a sales office, a beach house, maintenance and storage buildings, and twelve permanent

homes. (Also, more than 100 recreational vehicles were parked in the area, although the court could not clarify their status under the statute).

5. The "public purpose" doctrine was held to include a sports stadium in Lifteau v. Metropolitan Sports Facilities Comm'n, 270 N.W.2d 749 (Minn. 1978). Also see CLEAN v. State, 130 Wash.2d 782, 928 P.2d 1054 (Wash. 1996) where the court found the state's stadium act consistent with the public purpose provision of the Washington constitution. The sports stadium problem is rather common in recent years. Should the public extend its credit to the development of an expensive stadium either to satisfy a local sports franchise or to lure one? Is it a good deal for the public? See Ronald Smothers, Cities Warned the Odds Aren't Good in Sports Deals, N.Y. Times, Sept. 18, 1995, p. A 7.

6. The Opus decision pinpoints a critical and ubiquitous problem: parcelization. This term refers to the problem caused by the multiple ownership of many small parcels in a proposed redevelopment area. By using eminent domain and working with a qualified and eligible redeveloper, cities can unify parcel ownership, create an efficient scale of operations, and hope to attract investment capital and project funding for truly viable projects. When aided by techniques such as tax increment financing, projects become even more feasible. Is there real hope for urban areas in this blueprint for redevelopment? As land values rise in suburban and fringe areas and as the population sprawls out with attendant property tax increases, open space disappearance, and traffic congestion, do opportunities arise to reinvest in existing urban areas, using these and other revitalization techniques? If the answer is no, then where will new households formed as the population increases settle? How much of the projected increase in the nation's population can be counted on to locate in urbanized areas as opposed to the greenfields farther out? In attempting to answer these questions, one can see more clearly the connection between urban revitalization and suburban settlements and between the forces of economic development and environmental conservation.

7. Local political officials seem always to view the prospect of jobs and economic growth as outweighing private property rights. This situation often leads to what many characterize as misuse of TIF and enterprise zone projects. Consider the following:

a. Wilkerson, "What Illinois Gave to Keep Sears," New York Times, Aug. 27, 1989:

Amid reports that Sears was planning to move from the Chicago Loop to Texas or North Carolina, state officials suggested that there was a suitable site in the suburb of Hoffman Estates, 35 miles northwest of the city. The officials not only offered $61 million to prepare the location and build highways near it, but also pledged that the town would be designated an enterprise zone, making Sears eligible for a host of incentives normally used to attract businesses to depressed areas.

* * *

Hoffman Estates, a community where houses cost as much as $300,000 and unemployment is 3.2 percent, would not normally qualify as an enterprise zone. With Sears promising thousands of jobs, the State Legislature changed the law so that Hoffman Estates would qualify.

Meanwhile, vast stretches of Chicago's rundown West Side that were already designated as enterprise zones remained abandoned, and legislators from the area opposed the Hoffman Estates deal. But the critics were even angrier about the approval of a second measure allowing Sears to qualify for another incentive. The benefit, called tax increment financing, is essentially a giveaway program usually reserved for companies willing to locate in bleak neighborhoods. Extending this incentive to the Sears–Hoffman Estates deal—and to other potential arrangements in which 2,000 or more jobs are gained—means Sears will acquire an 800–acre site valued at $100 million in exchange for agreeing to pay property taxes on the land.

State officials argued that the arrangement would leave Hoffman Estates "less blighted."

b. In 1995 the Colorado state auditor reported that the state's enterprise zone program had failed to help blighted communities, and he cited national research to the effect that tax incentives do not necessarily create jobs. The Denver Post, Dec. 26, 1995, p. 1. On the following day the newspaper continued its exposé with a front-page article describing how $12.5 million of enterprise zone funds since 1989 went to help all sorts of charities and non-profits rather than poor areas; some of the recipients named were the Potato Administrative Committee in Monte Vista, Colorado; the Southeast Game and Fish Club in Lamar, Colorado; the University of Southern Colorado Sports Complex. The Denver Post, Dec. 27, 1995 p. 1.

7. When the redevelopment efforts include use of the eminent domain power to condemn private property that is designated for a private entity the courts are required to focus closely on just what is a public purpose. Examples of this problem start with the famous Poletown case from Michigan. Poletown Neighborhood Council v. City of Detroit, 410 Mich. 616, 304 N.W.2d 455 (1981). Poletown arose out of the economic crisis that faced Detroit and its most significant economic buttress, the automobile industry, in the 1970's and early 1980's. In 1981, unemployment in the City of Detroit reached eighteen percent. In 1980 General Motors entered discussions with the city to build a "new generation facility" in Detroit if a suitable site could be found to replace its aging Cadillac and Fisher Body facilities. Underlying the discussions was the threat that if no such site could be found, taken and made available to General Motors, it would close its plant, take the six thousand jobs those plants represented and go elsewhere. Reacting to the dismal economic climate and the steady loss of manufacturing facilities in Michigan, the Michigan Legislature had previously passed the Economic Development Corporations Act, 1974 P.A. 338, M.C.L. § 125.1601 et seq.; M.S.A. § 5.3520(1) et seq. The act provided that in order to "alleviate and prevent conditions of unemployment" municipalities were granted the power to assist "industrial and commercial enterprises" to revitalize their facilities. M.C.L. § 125.1602; M.S.A. § 5.3520(2). To further this objective, the Legislature authorized municipalities to acquire property by condemnation in order to provide industrial and commercial sites and the means of transfer from

the municipality to private users. M.C.L. § 125.1622; M.S.A. § 5.3520(22). The Supreme Court deferred to the legislative determination of public purpose, and concluded that the benefit to the city was "clear and significant" and therefore sufficient to satisfy the Court that this "project was an intended and a legitimate object of the Legislature" even though "a private party will also * * * receive a benefit as an incident thereto." Poletown at 634, 304 N.W.2d 455. The court also stated that in cases where private property is taken for private redevelopment the courts will apply a "heightened scrutiny" standard to determine the validity of the taking. Poletown was a viable ethnic community that was destroyed by the new General Motors plant and the case was the subject of a critical film documentary.

In the years after Poletown courts have sometimes taken a position in favor of the private property owner who resists condemnation. Even in Michigan, the intermediate court of appeals wrote that Poletown should be overruled. In City of Detroit v. Vavro, 177 Mich.App. 682, 442 N.W.2d 730 (1989), the Court of Appeals upheld a condemnation for the benefit of Chrysler Corp.; the court, however, stated:

> In sum, we believe that plaintiff is permitted to take the defendants' property and turn it over to Chrysler Corporation in light of the decision in Poletown, supra, and that the procedures employed in doing so met the minimum legal requirements. However, we do agree with defendants that the Poletown decision was incorrect and we urge the Supreme Court to take this matter up and overrule Poletown and restore the constitutional protections of private property.

Some other cases that raise the same issue as Poletown are Day v. Development Authority of City of Adel, 248 Ga. 488, 284 S.E.2d 275 (1981) (public development of facility to be used as a retail grocery store by a private corporation); Mayor v. Thomas, 645 So.2d 940 (Miss.1994) (city could not condemn riverfront property for purpose of private development of riverboat gaming enterprise); High Ridge Ass'n, Inc. v. County Comm'rs of Carroll County, 105 Md.App. 423, 660 A.2d 951 (1995) (city could not condemn a 50 foot strip of land so as to make it easier for an adjacent property owner to develop his land); Aaron v. Target Corporation, 269 F.Supp.2d 1162 (E.D.Mo. 2003) (Target store that was leasing premises enlisted city to aid in condemning its store and conveying the land to Target as redeveloper; federal court issued temporary restraining order to prevent condemnation); City of Bozeman, Dept. of Transportation of State of Montana v. Vaniman, 271 Mont. 514, 898 P.2d 1208 (1995) (the court held that plans for a highway interchange complex improperly included a provision for a private Chamber of Commerce to occupy 40 percent of the proposed offices; however, excluding the chamber from the plan was a sufficient remedy and the remainder of the proposal met the public purpose test); Casino Reinvestment Development Auth. v. Banin, 320 N.J.Super. 342, 727 A.2d 102 (1998) (acquisition of private property by eminent domain to enable casino hotel developer to build project held to be for a private rather than public purpose). The developer in the New Jersey case was Donald Trump, and his efforts to acquire the private holdings were satirized in the "Doonesbury" comic strip by Garry Trudeau on April 20, 1997.

These cases are usually fact-specific and state courts differ considerably in resolving the struggle over the meaning of public purpose. Two cases that offer extensive discussion of the problem are Southwestern Ill. Dev. Auth. v. National City Environmental, L.L.C. 199 Ill.2d 225, 768 N.E.2d 1, 263 Ill.Dec. 241 (2002) and Piedmont Triad Airport Auth. v. Urbine, 354 N.C. 336, 554 S.E.2d 331 (2001). In the Illinois case a divided court struck down condemnation of a large parcel of land containing an automobile scrap recycling facility that was located across the road from a recently constructed automobile racing venue that was seeking to become the leading NASCAR track in the Midwest. The track was going to redevelop the land for a parking garage for track patrons. The court majority was not impressed with arguments that the parking garage would enhance the track's attractiveness for national NASCAR events and would alleviate the dangers of track patrons parking on the other side of the road and having to cross on foot in heavy traffic. In the North Carolina case the court upheld agency condemnation of more than a thousand acres of land near the airport that was alleged to be for the sole purpose of allowing Federal Express to expand its airport facilities through a new hangar and other buildings. The court was impressed by the fact that the land would not be turned over to Federal Express, but would be owned by the airport authority and leased to the company.

The other side of the coin is represented by Borough of Essex Fells v. Kessler Institute for Rehabilitation, Inc., 289 N.J.Super. 329, 673 A.2d 856 (1995) where the local government stated it was taking property for a park, but the court found that was a cover for the real purpose which was to prevent the private corporation from building a rehabilitation facility. The court said: "[W]here a condemnation is commenced for an apparently valid, stated purpose but the real purpose is to prevent a proposed development which is considered undesirable, the condemnation may be set aside."

D. PROTECTING GROWTH DISTRICTS FROM COMPETITION

The cases in this section raise questions about the ability of local governments and their citizens to contain growth in established centers. Market pressures sometimes operate as a centrifugal force: the conditions at the urban core repel capital investment outward. The underlying tension in land use policy and lawmaking is the tension between the principle of centered growth and the realities of the market. Can localities use their land use authority to tug at the momentum of the market? Can zoning be used to prevent competition with businesses in designated growth districts or to keep people from moving far away from established commercial centers? Do commercial property owners in developed districts have standing to sue adjacent municipalities for zoning land to accommodate their competitors? How much control do individual localities have over external market and political forces that frustrate their carefully conceived land use plans?

FORTE v. BOROUGH OF TENAFLY
Superior Court of New Jersey, Appellate Division, 1969.
255 A.2d 804, 106 N.J.Super. 346.

GAULKIN, S.J.A.D.

Defendants (hereafter Tenafly) appeal from a judgment declaring Tenafly's amended zoning ordinance unconstitutional insofar as it forbade the construction of a supermarket upon plaintiffs' lands.

Prior to August 1967 the zoning ordinance permitted such a use in the zone in which plaintiffs' lands were situated. Early in 1967 plaintiffs applied to the building inspector for a permit to build the building, and to the planning board (board) for approval of its site plan and parking area. The board, aided by Kendree and Shepherd, planning consultants, was then engaged in a planning study of the borough with a view toward a comprehensive master plan. The consultants had recommended and the board agreed that the 'central business core' of the borough should not only be preserved as the borough's retail shopping area, but strengthened and improved. This was to be done principally by improving the roads and the traffic pattern in said core to eliminate through-traffic and traffic congestion, and by forbidding retail businesses in the rest of the borough. This the board and its advisers felt would encourage retail businesses in the area to remain and improve and expand their properties, thus improving the appearance and enhancing the value of all properties in the business area, and providing the borough with an inviting 'downtown' center. If retail businesses were allowed to spread along the roads throughout the borough, it was believed the central business area would deteriorate and decay. Therefore, instead of approving plaintiffs' application, the board adopted a resolution asking 'that an interim zoning ordinance amendment be adopted in order to create a new district known as the C–2 District in order to discourage and restrict the spread of retail business beyond the downtown business core * * *.' Shepherd, the borough's planning consultant, testified that 93% of all of the borough's retail business establishments were in the central business core.

The governing body agreed and, on November 28, 1967, passed ordinance #939. The ordinance recited the resolution of the planning board and created the C–2 District, stating

'A. Intent—This district is intended for commercial and wholesale services and small local convenience neighborhood service establishments and other businesses not suited to the general retail business zone, and to provide uses which will not have an adverse effect upon the downtown business core.'

The C–2 District included plaintiffs' property.

That portion of the C–2 zone here involved included all the lands previously contained in the business zone on the west side of County Road north of Mahan Street to the Cresskill border. Plaintiffs' lands were on said side of County Road, beginning at Prospect Terrace, the street north of and parallel to Mahan Street. At the time of the passage of the amendment there were a number of businesses in the new C–2 zone. Coming south from the Cresskill border on said side of County Road there was a Robert Hall clothing store. In the next block, between Summit Street and Hudson Avenue there was an Esso Service Station, Midtown County Rambler (selling new and used cars), County Auto Parts, an unoccupied but recently renovated business building and a funeral home. Continuing south, in the next block there was Lamb Studios (manufacturers of ceramics) and property occupied jointly by Stryker Drafting and Manufacturing Company and Poretta Plumbing and Heating Company. Then came plaintiffs' lots. Below Prospect Terrace there was a barber and beauty shop, a tavern with a catering service, a TV repair shop and a small grocery store with living quarters on the second floor. On the easterly side of County Road, opposite the premises in question, (zoned residential), there is a Ford automobile agency at the corner of Summit Street, a gasoline station at the corner of Hudson Avenue, between Hudson and Prospect a dance school and studio, and on the corner of Prospect and County Road a cocktail lounge. The land abutting plaintiffs' property to the rear is in the M–1 industrial zone.

Plaintiffs immediately instituted this action to have the ordinance declared invalid. Defendants contend that the action should have been dismissed because plaintiffs failed to first apply for a variance. Under the circumstances here presented, it would have been futile to apply for a variance and therefore it was proper for plaintiffs to proceed as they did.

After a full trial, the trial court entered the judgment appealed from.

Defendants made some effort before the trial court to justify the elimination of retail stores in the C–2 zone on the ground that such uses would increase traffic on County Road, and so forth. The trial judge ruled, in effect, that since the true reasons were those expressed in the ordinance itself, it was not necessary to pass on the other alleged justifications. We agree, but add that the evidence does not establish any other justification. In other words, if the intention to preserve, rehabilitate and improve the central business area does not sustain the ordinance, it must fall.

The first question, then, is this: May a municipality which wishes to preserve, rehabilitate and improve an established business area devoted chiefly to retail stores, zone the rest of the municipality against retail sales? We hold that it may.

Plaintiffs admit that if Tenafly were writing on a clean slate it could zone one part of the borough for retail stores and forbid all but residential use in the remainder of the borough. However, they argue that here Tenafly did not write on a clean slate; before the amendment of the ordinance they were in the same zone and had the same rights as those in the so-called central business core; much of the land in the C–2 District was already devoted to commercial uses, including retail, and since the ordinance was tailored to permit nearly all of them to continue as nonconforming uses, the amendment was a sham directed against them alone, solely because they wanted to build a supermarket. Plaintiffs insist it was passed for the sole benefit of the merchants in the central business core; therefore it was unlawfully oppressive, discriminatory and unconstitutional. Furthermore, even assuming that Tenafly would have had the right to forbid retail stores in an area not already commercial, it was arbitrary and unreasonable to do so in this area, already largely commercial (including retail) and abutting commercial and industrial zones. They point out that the Robert Hall store sells only at retail, the gas station and the auto parts store are of course retail, and the manufacturers of ceramics may be selling at retail, as may the plumbing and heating and the barber and beauty shops, the tavern and the TV repair store. The small grocery store admittedly sells only at retail.

The trial judge ruled, in effect, that since the avowed purpose of the ordinance was 'to protect the business district' it was invalid. We think that was too narrow a view. Zones are often created or uses therein curtailed in a manner which benefits other zones. The mere fact that this is one of the purposes of the ordinance does not make it invalid. An area desirable for industry may be zoned otherwise because industry would damage a nearby residential or business zone. Conversely, residential uses may be forbidden in or near industrial areas to encourage the full expansion of industrial plants therein without fear of complaint of nuisance. It is true that a municipality may not, by zoning or otherwise, exclude a particular use only because it will compete with an existing business or businesses (*179 Duncan Ave. v. Jersey City*, 122 N.J.L. 292, 5 A.2d 68 (Sup.Ct.1939)), but if the exclusion of competition happens to be an incident or effect of otherwise valid zoning, it does not invalidate it.

Tenafly has what it considers to be a decaying central business core, choked by poor parking and traffic facilities. We take judicial notice that this is a problem which today faces many municipalities. Tenafly could have permitted the deterioration to continue into blight, hoping that new and desirable retail business areas would develop elsewhere. Instead, it appears that it wishes to make a strong effort to revitalize the present area. It elected to do so upon the recommendation of the planning consultants and the planning board. We hold that it has the right to do so, and the fact that the ordinance may give the central area a virtual monopoly over retail business does not invalidate it.

There is no evidence that Tenafly is trying to keep out supermarkets, or to benefit any particular business or businesses in the central business core. Tenafly is perfectly willing for supermarkets to open in C–1 zones, where such uses are permitted, although it concedes that there may be difficulty in finding or assembling therein the necessary land.

Assuming that the ordinance is generally valid, it leaves the question whether it is unreasonable and therefore invalid insofar as it applies to plaintiffs' property. Plaintiffs contend that it is unreasonable for the ordinance to take away from them the right to sell at retail because nearly every one of their neighbors in the C–2 zone sells at retail—some, like Robert Hall and the grocery, only at retail. They argue that the neighbors will continue to sell at retail either as permitted, accessory or nonconforming uses; hence it is discriminatory, arbitrary and unreasonable not to let them do likewise. But plaintiffs may use their property for the many purposes allowed by the ordinance. If they do, they will have the same rights to make incidental or accessory retail sales as those already carrying on similar businesses in the C–2 zone. The nonconforming retail stores are not so numerous as to make the ordinance unreasonable.

The judgment is reversed.

SWAIN v. COUNTY OF WINNEBAGO

Appellate Court of Illinois, Second District, 1969.
250 N.E.2d 439, 111 Ill.App.2d 458.

DAVIS, ACTING PRESIDING JUSTICE.

This is a declaratory judgment action brought to challenge the validity of a zoning ordinance adopted by the Winnebago County Board of Supervisors, which ordinance rezoned the property of the defendants, David W. Johnson, Helga S. Johnson, Gunnard R. Olson and Myrtle A. Olson, to permit the construction of a shopping center. The plaintiffs' amended complaint was dismissed and they have appealed.

The defendants' property consists of 145 acres of unimproved land located in Winnebago County on East State Street Road, approximately one mile east of Mulford Road. The land had been zoned for agricultural use, and was changed by the ordinance in question to a business zoning classification to permit the development of a regional shopping center. This land is a substantial distance from the downtown Rockford area, and it is outside of the corporate limits of the City of Rockford.

* * *

The plaintiffs challenge the zoning ordinance on two grounds: first, that it did not receive the required vote of the County Board of Supervisors; and second, on the standard constitutional ground that the rezoning was arbitrary and bears no reasonable relationship to the public health, safety and general welfare, and, thus, is void. They concede that their attack is not based upon any statutory remedy, such as a quo warranto; and they assert that they brought this action, as residents, citizens and taxpayers of Winnebago County, and challenge an amendatory zoning ordinance on the grounds above specified.

The plaintiffs are not the owners of the real estate which was rezoned. To have standing to sue, under the circumstances, they have the burden of alleging facts which show that they have suffered special damage as a result of the ordinance, which differ from that suffered by the general public. *Garner v. County of Du Page*, 8 Ill.2d 155, 158, 159, 133 N.E.2d 303 (1956); *Bullock v. City of Evanston*, 5 Ill.2d 22, 33, 34, 123 N.E.2d 840 (1955); *Hughes v. City of Peoria*, 80 Ill.App.2d 392, 394, 395, 225 N.E.2d 109 (1967).

The necessity of showing special damage extends generally to the plaintiffs' right to challenge the validity of the zoning ordinance and not to any particular ground on which the validity is challenged. The special interest that must be shown before a taxpayer may challenge the act of a corporate body is not limited to ordinances affecting zoning. The financial or administrative affairs of the county are not subject to question by the suit of a taxpayer unless his taxes are directly to be affected, or unless he, as opposed to the general public, has some special or distinct interest affected. *Bistor v. Board of Assessors*, 346 Ill. 362, 372, 373, 179 N.E. 120, 78 A.L.R. 686 (1931); 14 I.L.P. Counties s 87, p. 157; 20 C.J.S. Counties s 288.

The reason for such a rule is well stated in *Garner v. County of Du Page, supra*, where the court, on page 159, 133 N.E.2d page 304, said:

> "As stated in 43 C.J.S. Injunctions s 22B, Where a similar rule is expressed in connection with the right of a private individual to seek injunctive relief for a public injury, 'The rule is not a technical and arbitrary one, but has a solid foundation in principle and is sustained by very sound reasons of public policy, its object being to protect defendant against a multiplicity of suits and to secure him in one suit a final determination of all the controverted questions involved.'"

We do not find the allegations in the complaint sufficient to establish the plaintiffs' standing to sue. There is no allegation, and it would seem that there could be none, that the general tax burden would be increased as a result of the rezoning. See: *Garner v. County of Du Page*, supra, 159, 133 N.E.2d 303. The allegations in regard to increased traffic and the use and development of public facilities are not special damages peculiar to the plaintiffs, as opposed to the general public. The remainder of the plaintiffs' allegations, insofar as special damages are concerned, amount to no more than allegations, differently stated, that the plaintiffs will suffer losses by reason of increased competition which will result from the new shopping center.

The property in question is distant from the business properties of the plaintiffs. There is no factual basis in the complaint for assuming that the allegations of loss and depreciation in business interests and value of business properties could result from anything other than the new and increased competition which may result from this zoning.

The plaintiffs contend, however, that *Hughes v. City of Peoria, supra*, establishes their standing to sue in this case. In Hughes, the plaintiffs claimed to represent a number of persons operating businesses in the central business district of Peoria. The land, which had been rezoned to permit a shopping center, was three or four miles from the plaintiffs' businesses and properties. The plaintiffs alleged that they had invested large sums of money in their businesses and properties in reliance upon the existing zoning classifications; and that as a result of the rezoning, their businesses and properties would be greatly depressed and depreciated in value. The trial court found for the defendants on summary judgment.

The Appellate Court acknowledged, on pages 394 and 395, 225 N.E.2d 109, that the plaintiffs had the burden of establishing that they would suffer a special damage by reason of the new use, which would differ from that suffered by the general public, and at page 395, 225 N.E.2d at page 110, the court stated: 'The allegations in the complaint of damages to plaintiffs' businesses and properties are allegations of special damage, *Brown v. County of Lake*, 67 Ill.App.2d 144, 213 N.E.2d 790, * * *.' Thus, the Appellate Court concluded that there was no basis for the trial court's finding that the properties of the plaintiffs were located so far distant from the rezoned properties so as to preclude any damage to the plaintiffs.

It is interesting to note, however, that the Appellate Court, at pages 396 and 397, 225 N.E.2d 109, referred to an allegation in the complaint that the plaintiffs would be 'greatly disadvantaged in competition with the new proposed shopping center,' and conceded that such an allegation is not a recognizable special damage. The court further stated that all of the cases which were called to its attention clearly held that increased business competition provides no standing to complain of a zoning change, and at page 397, 225 N.E.2d 109, it cited a number of such cases.

The case of *Brown v. County of Lake*, 67 Ill.App.2d 144, 213 N.E.2d 790 (1966), is not authority for the proposition that losses resulting to businesses and business properties from the increase in competition permitted by a zoning change are special damages giving the injured party standing to sue. Yet, this is what we read the statement in Hughes to mean.

In both Hughes and the case at bar, the general allegations of depreciation and loss in value of the plaintiffs' businesses and business properties are mere conclusions which must be supported by specific allegations of fact which show a special damage. *Winston v. Zoning Board of Appeals*, 407 Ill. 588, 594, 95 N.E.2d 864 (1951).

Realistically, however, the only factual basis that can be found (or assumed) to support the conclusions of damage, in both Hughes and the case at bar, is that the new competition will cause the plaintiffs' businesses to suffer.

* * *

From the allegations in the complaint in the case at bar, we do not believe—as apparently the court did in Hughes—that there is any valid basis for a finding of damage to the plaintiffs' businesses or properties, other than as a result of increased competition. It is not the function of the county zoning ordinances to provide economic protection for existing businesses. *Exchange Nat. Bank of Chicago v. Village of Skokie*, 86

Ill.App.2d 12, 21, 229 N.E.2d 552 (1967). Neither the fact that parties may suffer reduced incomes or be put out of business by more vigorous or appealing competition, nor the fact that properties on which such businesses are operated would thus depreciate in value, give rise to a standing to sue. *Cord Meyer Development Company v. Bell Bay Drugs, Inc.*, 20 N.Y.2d 211, 282 N.Y.S.2d 259, 229 N.E.2d 44, 46, 47 (1967); *Whitney Theatre Co. v. Zoning Board of Appeals,* 150 Conn. 285, 189 A.2d 396, 398 (1963); *London v. Planning and Zoning Com'n. of Town of Stratford*, 149 Conn. 282, 179 A.2d 614, 616 (1962); *Kreatchman v. Ramsburg*, 224 Md. 209, 167 A.2d 345, 351 (1961).

Free and open competition has always been a strong pillar in the foundation of our society. A person can have no vested or special property right in either the monopoly or competitive advantage accorded by zoning restrictions at a given time. It is the philosophy of our society that any increased competition which may result from a change in the zoning restrictions will ultimately be beneficial. A competitor who may suffer has no actionable injury. Whether or not the particular zoning is in the best interest of the orderly development of the community is a determination to be made by the legislative body—the Winnebago County Board of Supervisors.

The plaintiffs do not claim a right to represent or speak for the people of the entire county. They claim a special interest in the zoning in question because of their particular properties which are located in a rather small, specified area in the City of Rockford and within the county. The factual allegations of their complaint, however, do not warrant concluding that they have suffered any special damage from the change of zoning, which differed from that of the general public, other than that resulting from the potential increased competition. We deem this insufficient to accord them standing to maintain this suit. See: *Garner v. County of Du Page, supra,* 8 Ill.2d 160, 133 N.E.2d 303.

* * *

For the reasons stated herein, the judgment of the trial court dismissing the complaint is affirmed.

Judgment affirmed.

Notes

1. Plaintiffs in Forte concede that if Tenafly were writing on a clean slate it could create any development pattern it chose in the interest of creating viable economic, mixed-use centers. They urge the court to use the existence of nonconforming uses in the area of their proposed supermarket to hold the denial of their proposal unreasonable, motivated solely to prevent economic competition with stores in the central district. Since the court disagreed and upheld the denial, does the decision support the creation of zoning centers in newly developing communities, older suburbs, and developed urban areas? If comprehensive plans may include objectives and strategies for the proper economic development of communities, how are such

strategies to be implemented if zoning is prohibited from marshalling market forces?

2. Who are the combatants in the Swain? Are they proxies for those engaged in the ongoing struggle to create rational land development patterns? The City of Rockport and the plaintiff merchants in this sense represent older cities with existing centers and supportive infrastructure. Winnebago County is the outlying suburban jurisdiction seeking desirable tax ratables: projects that bring in more property tax revenue than they cost the municipality in the provision of services. While cost of service studies often demonstrate that agricultural land pays more in property taxes than it costs the municipality in services, how does the county compare the economics of 145 agriculturally zoned acres with the cost-benefit of a regional shopping center? What incentive is there for the county to disapprove the proposed development? Is it enough to say that it will add to the forces of sprawl and hasten the decline of Rockport? Do your answers argue for state intervention in local land use decision-making?

3. Wal–Mart v. Town of North Elba, 238 A.D.2d 93, 668 N.Y.S.2d 774 (1998), is a case in which the court upheld the denial of a permit to build a big box retail outlet outside the town's core commercial district because of its negative impact on the general character and ambience of the community. The petitioner, Wal–Mart, contended that the town had improperly and erroneously come to that conclusion. The court held that the data documenting the decline of the downtown and estimating the store's further adverse influence on that decline were reasonable and sustainable. It held that it was not irrational to conclude that the use, though permitted, is not desirable at the particular location. (Matter of Market Sq. Props. v. Town of Guilderland Zoning Bd. of Appeals, 109 A.D.2d 164, 166, 491 N.Y.S.2d 519, affd. 66 N.Y.2d 893, 498 N.Y.S.2d 772, 489 N.E.2d 741, (1985)) The court stated that while the town's decision refers to the economic effect the proposed store would be expected to have upon other local businesses, it does so in the context of assessing the probability and extent of the change it would work upon the overall character of the community, as a result of an increased vacancy rate among commercial properties in the downtown area—an entirely proper avenue of inquiry.

4. Wal–Mart was also denied a permit to build a retail outlet in the village of Chadron, Ohio, on 23 acres that were zoned C–1: local retail business. The zoning code defined local retail business to include businesses that normally employ fewer than 10 people and occupy less that 10,000 square feet. Wal–Mart contended that these provisions failed to advance a legitimate public interest. In Loreto Development Co. v. Village of Chardon, 119 Ohio App.3d 524, 695 N.E.2d 1151 (1996), the Court of Appeals of Ohio upheld the ordinance and the denial. Because of the great deference that courts give to determinations of legislative bodies, the court held that the plaintiff had not carried its burden of proving that no legitimate public purpose was served by the ordinance. The fact that the legislature wished to protect the residential, small-town character of this part of town was clearly a legitimate interest to be advanced by zoning.

5. The Village Districts Act (Conn. Gen. Stat. § 8–2j) was signed into law on May 22, 1998, as Public Act 98–116, "An Act Authorizing the

Establishment of Village Districts" effective October 1, 1998. The Act, an amendment to Connecticut's zoning enabling legislation, authorizes local zoning commissions to protect the distinctive character, landscape, and historic value of the areas under their jurisdiction. The Pennsylvania Municipalities Planning Code (MPC) states that zoning ordinances may permit the preservation of "natural and historic resources and prime agricultural land and activities." 53 PA. Stat. § 10603(b)(5).

E. PROMOTING BROWNFIELD REDEVELOPMENT

Another method of keeping density in the right place and preventing urban sprawl is brownfield redevelopment. In many communities, former industrial properties blight the landscape and remain unrealized economic opportunities. Generally known as "brownfields," these properties are abandoned, idled, or under-used industrial and commercial facilities where expansion or redevelopment is complicated by real or perceived environmental contamination. Nationwide, there are over 450,000 brownfields.

Because brownfields are often contaminated from past operations, they present economic and public policy challenges to their host communities. Developers are often reluctant to engage in redevelopment efforts because of the liability that may be imposed upon them under the Comprehensive Environmental Response, Compensation and Liability Act (CERCLA, 42 U.S.C. § 9601 *et seq.*). CERCLA and similar laws adopted by many states impose strict, joint, and several liability upon an owner or operator of a site where contamination is present, regardless of whether that person caused the pollution. Consequently, a developer could be liable for millions of dollars of remediation costs simply by purchasing a site with hazardous contamination. This potential liability causes most brownfield sites to lie fallow. As a means to encourage the redevelopment of brownfields, a number of states have enacted statutes to reduce liability and have created programs that provide financial incentives to redevelopers.

Brownfield redevelopment is an important smart growth technique for a variety of reasons. First, by remediating contaminated properties, the environmental threat presented by these sites is eliminated, thereby protecting the health of the community. Second, when redeveloped, the formerly abandoned sites generate tax revenue for the community. Third, by developing brownfield sites, which are typically located in more urbanized areas, some development pressure is removed from outlying greenfields. Fourth, communities can use brownfields to meet various planning objectives such as the creation of affordable housing or additional commercial development.

Under its Land Recycling Program, the State of Pennsylvania provides grants to communities to create inventories of their brownfields. This program provides up to $50,000 to municipalities for this purpose. Brownfield sites that are available for redevelopment and the information gathered about them are posted on the state's Brownfields Directory, known as "PA SiteFinder." For each site that is posted on the directory, the municipality receives $1,000 up to a maximum of $50,000. Pennsylvania Dept. of Environmental Protection Brownfields Inventory Program, http://www.dep.state.pa.us/dep/deputate/airwaste/wm/landrecy/Inventory/BIG.htm.

In 1993, the New Jersey state legislature enacted the Environmental Opportunity Zone Act (EOZA), N.J. Stat. Ann. §§ 54.4–3.150 *et seq.* which permits municipalities to designate certain contaminated properties as environmental opportunity zones. N.J. Stat. Ann. § 54.4–3.153. Once such properties are designated, they are eligible for the abatement of local real property taxes for up to 15 years. To receive this tax advantage, the owner must agree to remediate the property. Municipalities may be eligible for grants to offset the remediation costs of brownfields they have acquired by tax foreclosure or private conveyance. In New Jersey, municipal governments may undertake the remediation of brownfields without fear that the state will impose liability upon them where the municipality enters into a remediation agreement with the state Department of Environmental Protection (DEP). N.J. Stat. Ann. § 58:10–23.11(g)(d)(2)(e). Localities are eligible to receive up to $2 million per year for investigation and cleanup activities. Using these liability protection and funding mechanisms, a number of New Jersey municipalities are remediating and redeveloping brownfield sites. For example, the Borough of Northvale received $376,372 for the remedial investigation of a two-acre site that the borough intended to redevelop for light industrial or commercial use. The site has confirmed soil contamination believed to be the result of buried drums and has been the subject of prior grants totaling $1.2 million. The Township of Willingboro received $76,751 for remedial work it performed at Willingboro Plaza, a 56–acre former commercial shopping mall located along New Jersey Route 130 that was plagued by the presence of underground storage tanks, soil contamination, and asbestos. Merck–Medco constructed a 240,000 square-foot mail-order pharmacy distribution facility on 17 acres of the site. The project developer, ReNEWal, will also construct a 40,000 square-foot library on the site for the township. The next stage of the brownfield redevelopment project is the creation of a Willingboro Town Center, an approximately 700,000 square-foot mixed-use community. The Township of West Deptford received $96,308 for remedial investigation of a 600–acre site on Jobstown Road that is part of River Winds at West Deptford. The township's development plans include assisted living facilities, an indoor community center, an aquatic facility, a golf course, marina, hotel conference center, and restaurants and shops. New Jersey Department of Environmental Protection, Site Remediation Program, "New Jersey Brownfields Redevelopment Update 2001," at xxviii and xxxi (October 2001).

SECTION 5. SMART GROWTH TECHNIQUES

A. POST–EUCLIDIAN ZONING

The essence of traditional zoning is the division of the community into zoning districts and the separation of land uses among those districts. In Euclid v. Ambler Realty, the 1926 U.S. Supreme Court case which upheld the constitutional validity of zoning, the key question was whether the separation of uses served a legitimate public purpose. The Court held that it did and traditional, or Euclidian, zoning has been characterized ever since as zoning that mandates the separation of residential, retail, commercial, and industrial land uses among zoning districts.

Post–Euclidian, or Neo–Euclidian, zoning encompasses a variety of techniques designed to allow regulatory flexibility that some suggest is not permitted under the Euclidian approach. That use separation is a valid police power objective does not mean that mixed-use zoning is not. That Euclidian zoning prescribed uniform height, lot coverage, and setback standards does not mean that localities may not waive those bulk and area restrictions to serve sound community planning objectives. For decades, localities have been inventing techniques that provide them more flexibility in placing development on the land. Since these newer techniques tend to use higher densities, mixed-uses, and cost-effective design, they may also be called smart growth techniques. What smart growth aspires to do is to aggregate development in more cost-effective arrangements so that it is more cost and energy efficient, more affordable, and more environmentally sound. To accomplish these objectives is difficult in some states using the prescriptions of Euclidan zoning.

Breaking out of the mold, however, has not been easy. The local governments that have invented smart growth techniques, and the courts that have reviewed their validity when challenged, have had to examine whether the enabling acts of the states permitted such flexibility. The original zoning enabling act, which was followed often literally in the original acts adopted by the states, delegated permission to localities to "divide the municipality into districts of such number, shape, and area as may be deemed best suited to carry out the purposes of this act." It further specified that "all such regulations shall be uniform for each class or kind of buildings throughout each district." (See Chapter IV) The purposes of zoning originally included accomplishing the objectives of the comprehensive plan, promoting the general welfare, preventing the overcrowding of land, avoiding undue concentration of population, and facilitating the adequate provision of service and infrastructure. The standard zoning enabling act ended its purpose clause with these critical words: "Such [zoning] regulations shall be made with reasonable consideration, among other things, the character of the district and its peculiar suitability for particular uses, and with a view to conserving the value of buildings and encouraging the most appropriate use of land throughout such municipality."

Do these words allow local governments to adopt techniques such as floating zones, overlay districts, clustered subdivisions, bonus or incentive zoning, transfer of development rights, or performance zoning? These and similar techniques have been adopted by localities to do a better job of arranging permitted densities on individual sites and to create a better overall pattern of land development in the community. In some states, whether localities have the legal authority to adopt smart growth techniques depends on how expansively the courts view the delegation of zoning authority to local governments. Localities, it is said, have only those powers expressly delegated to them or those necessarily implied to accomplish the stated legislative goals. So, for example, can a local legislature authorize its planning board to cluster the density permitted under the zoning applicable to a particular parcel on 70 percent of the land in order to preserve open space and protect the community's character? Would this violate the uniformity requirement of the zoning enabling act? Is this the creation of a new district that amounts to illegal spot zoning? Does it serve any of the purposes for which zoning may be adopted?

Why do neighboring property owners object when a locality, using a smart growth zoning technique, permits a mixed-use development or a clustered development in a single-family residential zone? What are the investment-backed expectations of a home purchaser who buys a home in a Euclidian zoning district? Do purchasers have vested rights in the zoning of the surrounding area or does the local legislature retain the right to amend the rules when the public interest requires? Consider the objections of the plaintiff in the following case to the Village of Tarrytown's early adoption of floating zoning.

RODGERS V. VILLAGE OF TARRYTOWN

Court of Appeals of New York, 1951.
302 N.Y. 115, 96 N.E.2d 731.

FULD, JUDGE.

This appeal, here by our permission, involves the validity of two amendments to the General Zoning Ordinance of the Village of Tarrytown, a suburban area in the County of Westchester, within twenty-five miles of New York City.

Some years ago, Tarrytown enacted a General Zoning Ordinance dividing the village into seven district or zones Residence A for single family dwellings, Residence B for two-family dwellings, Residence C for multiple dwellings and apartment houses, three business districts and an industrial zone. In 1947 and 1948, the board of trustees, the village's legislative body, passed the two amendatory ordinances here under attack.

The 1947 ordinance creates a new district or class of zone * * * (to) be called 'Residence B–B', in which, besides one-and two-family dwellings, buildings for multiple occupancy of fifteen or fewer families were permitted. The boundaries of the new type district were not delineated in the ordinance but were to be 'fixed by amendment of the offical [sic] village building zone map, at such times in the future as such district or class of zone is applied, to properties in this village.' The village planning board was empowered to approve such amendments and, in case such approval was withheld, the board of trustees was authorized to grant it by appropriate resolution. In addition, the ordinance erected exacting standards of size and physical layouts for Residence B–B zones: a minimum of ten acres of land and a maximum building height of three stories were mandated; setback and spacing requirements for structures were carefully prescribed; and no more than 15% of the ground area of the plot was to be occupied by buildings.

A year and a half after the 1947 amendment was enacted, defendant Elizabeth Rubin sought to have her property, consisting of almost ten and a half acres in the Residence A district, placed in a Residence B–B classification. After repeated modification of her plans to meet suggestions of the village planning board, that body gave its approval, and, several months later, in December of 1948, the board of trustees, also approving, passed the second ordinance here under attack. In essence, it provides that the Residence B–B district 'is hereby applied to the (Rubin) property * * * and the district or zone of said property is hereby changed to 'Residence B–B' and the official Building Zone Map of the Village of Tarrytown is hereby amended accordingly (by specification of the various parcels and plots involved)'.

Plaintiff, who owns a residence on a six acre plot about a hundred yards from Rubin's property, brought this action to have the two amendments declared invalid and to enjoin defendant Rubin from constructing multiple dwellings on her property. The courts below, adjudging the amendments valid and the action of the trustees proper, dismissed the complaint. We agree with their determination.

While stability and regularity are undoubtedly essential to the operation of zoning plans, zoning is by no means static. Changed or changing conditions call for changed plans, and persons who own property in a particular zone or use district enjoy no eternally vested right to that classification if the public interest demands otherwise. Accordingly, the power of a village to amend its basic zoning ordinance in such a way as reasonably to promote the general welfare cannot be questioned. Just as clearly, decision as to how a community shall be zoned or rezoned, as to how various properties shall be classified or reclassified, rests with the local legislative body; its judgment and determination will be conclusive, beyond interference from the courts, unless shown to be arbitrary, and the burden of establishing such arbitrariness is imposed upon him who asserts it. In that connection, we recently said in *Shepard v. Village of Skaneateles*, 300 N.Y. 115, 118, 89 N.E.2d 619, 620: 'Upon parties who attack an ordinance * * * rests the burden of showing that the regulation assailed is not justified under the police power of the state by any reasonable interpretation of the facts. 'If the validity of the legislative classification for zoning purposes be fairly debatable, the legislative judgment must be allowed to control.' *Village of Euclid v. Ambler Realty Co.*, 272 U.S. 365, 388, 47 S.Ct. 114, 118, 71 L.Ed. 303; see, also, *Town of Islip v. F. E. Summers Coal & Lbr. Co.*, 257 N.Y. 167, 169, 170, 177 N.E. 409, 410; *Matter of Wulfsohn v. Burden*, 241 N.Y. 288, 296–297, 150 N.E. 120, 121–122, 43 A.L.R. 651.'

By that test, the propriety of the decision here made is not even debatable. In other words, viewing the rezoning in the case before us, as it must be viewed, in the light of the area involved and the present and reasonably foreseeable needs of the community, the conclusion is inescapable that what was done not only accorded with sound zoning principles, not only complied with every requirement of law, but was accomplished in a proper, careful and reasonable manner.

The Tarrytown board of trustees was entitled to find that there was a real need for additional housing facilities; that the creation of Residence B–B districts for garden apartment developments would prevent young families, unable to find accommodations in the village, from moving elsewhere; would attract business to the community; would lighten the tax load of the small home owner, increasingly burdened by the shrinkage of tax revenues resulting from the depreciated value of large estates and the transfer of many such estates to tax exempt institutions; and would develop otherwise unmarketable and decaying property.

The village's zoning aim being clear, the choice of methods to accomplish it lay with the board. Two such methods were at hand. It could amend the General Zoning Ordinance so as to permit garden apartments on any plot of ten acres or more in Residence A and B zones (the zones more restricted) or it could amend that Ordinance so as to invite owners of ten or more acres, who wished to build garden apartments on their properties, to apply for a Residence B–B classification. The board chose to adopt the latter procedure. That it called for separate legislative authorization for each project presents no obstacle or drawback and so we have already held. See, e.g., *Nappi v. La Guardia*, 184 Misc. 775, 781, 55 N.Y.S.2d 80, 86, per Froessel, J. *affirmed* 269 App.Div. 693, 54 N.Y.S.2d 722, *affirmed* 295 N.Y. 652, 64 N.E.2d 716; *Matter of Green Point Sav. Bank v. Board of Zoning Appeals*, 281 N.Y. 534, 539, 24 N.E.2d 319, 321. Whether we would have made the same choice is not the issue; it is sufficient that the board's decision was neither arbitrary nor unreasonable.

As to the requirement that the applicant own a plot of at least ten acres, we find nothing therein unfair to plaintiff or other owners of smaller parcels. The board undoubtedly found, as it was privileged to find, that garden apartments would blend more attractively and harmoniously with the community setting, would impose less of a burden upon village facilities, if placed upon larger tracts of land rather than scattered about in smaller units. Obviously, some definite acreage had to be chosen, and, so far as the record before us reveals, the choice of ten acres as a minimum plot was well within the range of an unassailable legislative judgment. See, e.g., *Nappi v. LaGuardia, supra*, 295 N.Y. 652, 64 N.E.2d 716, affirming 269 App.Div. 693, 54 N.Y.S.2d 722, affirming 184 Misc. 775, 55 N.Y.S.2d 80, wherein the qualifying acreage was also fixed at ten.

Nor did the board, by following the course which it did, divest itself or the planning board of power to regulate future zoning with regard to garden apartments. The mere circumstance that an owner possesses a ten-acre plot and submits plans conforming to the physical requirements precribed [sic] by the 1947 amendment will not entitle him, ipso facto, to a Residence B–B classification. It will still be for the board to decide, in the exercise of a reasonable discretion, that the grant of such a classification accords with the comprehensive zoning plan and benefits the village as a whole. And while no such question is here presented we note that the board may not arbitrarily or unreasonably deny applications of other owners for permission to construct garden apartments on their properties. The action of the board must in all cases be reasonable and, whether a particular application be granted or denied, recourse may be had to the courts to correct an arbitrary or capricious determination. See, e.g., *Nappi v. La Guardia, supra*, 184 Misc. 775, 781, 55 N.Y.S.2d 80, 86, affirmed 269 App.Div. 693, 54 N.Y.S.2d 722, affirmed 295 N.Y. 652, 64 N.E.2d 716; *Matter of Green Point Sav. Bank v. Board of Zoning Appeals, supra*, 281 N.Y. 534, 539, 24 N.E.2d 319; *Arverne Bay Const. Co. v. Thatcher*, 278 N.Y. 222, 232, 15 N.E.2d 587, 591, 117 A.L.R. 1110; *Dowsey v. Village of Kensington*, 257 N.Y. 221, 231, 177 N.E. 427, 430, 86 A.L.R. 642; *Matter of Larkin Co. v. Schwab*, 242 N.Y. 330, 334, 336, 151 N.E. 637, 638, 639; *City of Little Rock v. Joyner*, 212 Ark. 508, 206 S.W.2d 446; *Frink v. Orleans Corp.*, 159 Fla. 646, 32 So.2d 425.

The charge of illegal 'spot zoning' leveled at the creation of a Residence B–B district and the reclassification of defendant's property is without substance. Defined as the process of singling out a small parcel of land for a use classification totally different from that of the surrounding area, for the benefit of the owner of such property and to the detriment of other owners, see *Harris v. City of Piedmont*, 5 Cal.App.2d 146, 152, 42 P.2d 356; *Cassel v. Mayor & City Council of Baltimore, Md.*, 73 A.2d 486, 488–489; *Board of Co. Comrs. of Anne Arundel County v. Snyder*, 186 Md. 342, 345–346, 46 A.2d 689; *Leahy v. Inspector of Bldgs. of New Bedford*, 308 Mass. 128, 134, 31 N.E.2d 436; *Page v. City of Portland*, 178 Or. 632, 641, 165 P.2d 280; *Weaver v. Ham*, Tex.Sup., 232 S.W.2d 704, 709; see, also, Yokley, Zoning Law and Practice (1948), s 85; cf. *People v. Cohen*, 272 N.Y. 319, 5 N.E.2d 835, 'spot zoning' is the very antithesis of planned zoning. If, therefore, an ordinance is enacted in accordance with a comprehensive zoning plan, it is not 'spot zoning,' even though it (1) singles out and affects but one small plot see, e.g., *Shepard v. Village of Skaneateles, supra*, 300 N.Y. 115, 89 N.E.2d 619, or (2) creates in the center of a large zone small areas or districts devoted to a different use. *See Nappi v. LaGuardia, supra*, 295 N.Y. 652, 64 N.E.2d 716, affirming 269 App.Div. 693, 54 N.Y.S.2d 722, affirming 184 Misc. 775, 55 N.Y.S.2d 80–business area in residence zone; *Marshall v. Salt Lake City*, 105 Utah 111, 126–127, 141 P.2d 704, 149 A.L.R. 282 business district in residence zone; *Higbee v. Chicago, B. & Q. R. R. Co.*, 235 Wis. 91, 98–99, 292 N.W. 320, 128 A.L.R. 734 railraod station in residence zone; *see, also, Avery v. Village of La Grange*, 381 Ill. 432, 442,

45 N.E.2d 647; *Town of Marblehead v. Rosenthal*, 316 Mass. 124, 126, 55 N.E.2d 13; Rathkopf, Law of Zoning and Planning (2d ed. 1949), p. 72 et seq. Thus, the relevant inquiry is not whether the particular zoning under attack consists of areas fixed within larger areas of different use, but whether it was accomplished for the benefit of individual owners rather than pursuant to a comprehensive plan for the general welfare of the community. Having already noted our conclusion that the ordinances were enacted to promote a comprehensive zoning plan, it is perhaps unnecessary to add that the record negates any claim that they were designed solely for the advantage of defendant or any other particular owner. Quite apart from the circumstance that defendant did not seek the benefit of the 1947 amendment until eighteen months after its passage, the all-significant fact is that that amendment applied to the entire territory of the village and accorded each and every owner of ten or more acres identical rights and privileges.

By the same token, there is no basis for the argument that "what has been done by the board of trustees" constitutes a device for "the granting of a variance", opinion of Conway, J., 302 N.Y. p. 129, 96 N.E.2d 738. As we have already shown, the village's zoning aim, the statute's purpose, was not to aid the individual owner but to permit the development of the property for the general welfare of the entire community. That being so, the board of trustees followed approved procedure by changing the General Zoning Ordinance itself. See, e.g., *Matter of Clark v. Board of Zoning Appeals*, 301 N.Y. 86, 91, 92 N.E.2d 903, 905. Accordingly, when the board was called upon to consider the reclassification of the Rubin property under the 1947 amendment, it was concerned, not with any issue of hardship, but only with the question of whether the property constituted a desirable location for a garden apartment.

We turn finally to the contention that the 1947 ordinance is invalid because, in proclaiming a Residence B–B district, it set no boundaries for the new district and made no changes on the building zone map. The short answer is that, since the ordinance merely prescribed specifications for a new use district, there was no need for it to do either the one or the other. True, until boundaries are fixed and until zoning map changes are made, no new zone actually comes into being, and neither property nor the rights of any property owner are affected. But it was not the design of the board of trustees by that enactment to bring any additional zone into being or to affect any property or rights; the ordinance merely provided the mechanics pursuant to which property owners might in the future apply for the redistricting of their property. In sum, the 1947 amendment was merely the first step in a reasoned plan of rezoning, and specifically provided for further action on the part of the board. That action was taken by the passage of the 1948 ordinance which fixed the boundaries of the newly created zone and amended the zoning map accordingly. It is indisputable that the two amendments, read together as they must be, fully complied with the requirements of the Village Law and accomplished a rezoning of village property in an unexceptionable manner.

In point of fact, there would have been no question about the validity of what was done had the board simply amended the General Zoning Ordinance so as to permit property in Residence A and Residence B zones or, for that matter, in the other districts throughout the village to be used for garden apartments, provided that they were built on ten-acre plots and that the other carefully planned conditions and restrictions were met. It may be conceded that, under the method which the board did adopt, no one will know, from the 1947 ordinance itself, precisely where a Residence B–B district will ultimately be located. But since such a district is simply a garden apartment development, we find nothing unusual or improper in that circumstance. The same uncertainty as to the location of the various types of structures would be present if a zoning ordinance were to sanction garden apartments as well as one-family homes in a Residence A district and yet there would be no doubt as to the propriety of that procedure. *See Nappi v. LaGuardia, supra,* 295 N.Y. 652, 64 N.E.2d 716, affirming 269 App.Div. 693, 54 N.Y.S.2d 722, affirming 184 Misc. 775, 55 N.Y.S.2d 80. Consequently, to condemn the action taken by the board in effectuating a perfectly permissible zoning scheme and to strike down the ordinance designed to carry out that scheme merely because the board had employed two steps to accomplish what may be, and usually is, done in one, would be to exalt form over substance and sacrifice substance to form.

Whether it is generally desirable that garden apartments be freely mingled among private residences under all circumstances, may be arguable. In view, however, of Tarrytown's changing scene and the other substantial reasons for the board's decision, we cannot say that its action was arbitrary or illegal. While hardships may be imposed on this or that owner, 'cardinal is the principle that what is best for the body politic in the long run must prevail over the interests of particular individuals.' *Shepard v. Village of Skaneateles, supra*, 300 N.Y. 115, 118, 89 N.E.2d 619, 620.

The judgment of the Appellate Division should be affirmed, with costs.

CONWAY, JUDGE (dissenting).

The decision here made gives judicial sanction to a novel and unprecedented device whereby the board of trustees of a village may, in the exercise of its discretion, authorize the erection of multiple family dwellings on property, located wholly within established districts theretofore uniformly zoned for use as one- or two-family dwellings, by the simple expedient of declaring, upon the application of individuals owning a certain acreage, that henceforth such property shall constitute a new and separate zoning district. The device may have much to commend it in the way of administrative convenience, but it most assuredly is not 'zoning', as that term has previously been understood. We think the action of the board of trustees of the village of Tarrytown is unauthorized by the Village Law of this State, which is the sole source of the board's power to act. Moreover, we feel that the board's action, here approved, is completely at odds with all sound zoning theory and practice, and may well prove to be the opening wedge in the destruction of effective and efficient zoning in this State.

First of all, we think the board had no power to create the so-called 'Residence B–B' district by the basic ordinance of 1947. Section III of that ordinance provided as follows: 'The boundaries of said newly created district or class of zone will be fixed by amendment of the official village building zone map, at such times in the future as such district or class of zone is applied to properties in this village.' That language can, in no sense, be considered as validly creating a new district or class of zone. It is essential to the creation of a zoning district that its physical boundaries be established in advance; otherwise there is no 'district', there is merely the possibility that a district may one day be delineated. *Matter of Kensington–Davis Corp. v. Schwab*, 239 N.Y. 54, 58–59, 145 N.E. 738, 739. Section 176 of the Village Law, entitled 'Districts', provides that ' * * * the board of trustees may divide the village into districts of such number, shape and area as may be deemed best suited to carry out the purposes of this act * * *' (emphasis supplied). The plain import of that language is that after the board has exercised its power to 'divide the village into districts', there should result a number of physically ascertainable districts, each having a definite 'shape' and 'area'. Obviously, the board of trustees, in enacting the 1947 ordinance, did not 'divide' the village into district; the board merely assigned a name or title to a district which might some day be created. As a result of that ordinance, no one could tell whether there would ever be any 'Residence B–B districts', or, if so, what their number, shape and area might be. Thus, the reference in the ordinance to 'districts' or 'zones' is meaningless, for it is impossible to have a true 'district' or 'zone' without specified boundaries. As we said in the *Kensington* case, *supra*, 239 N.Y. at page 58, 145 N.E. at page 739, 'Power was given under that law 'to divide the city into districts.' This clearly contemplated fixed areas with defined boundaries.' The key to any zoning ordinance is the map showing the boundaries of the areas affected. No map showing the location of the new Residence B–B district was, or could have been, made and filed with the 1947 ordinance which was therefore defective. *Village of Williston Park v. Israel*, 301 N.Y. 713, 95 N.E.2d 208, affirming 276 App.Div. 968, 94 N.Y.S.2d 921, affirming 191 Misc. 6, 76 N.Y.S.2d 605. All that the language of the 1947 ordinance means is that, from time to time, in the future, the board may, upon the application of individuals owning ten acres, set aside certain property in the village and assign to it the 'Residence B–B' designation. That, we submit, is 'spot zoning', if it may be classified as zoning at all, and is unauthorized under our statutes.

Under the mandate of section 177 of the Village Law, the regulations of the board of trustees, including the division of the village into districts, 'shall be made in accordance with a comprehensive plan'. The action of the board in the case at bar cannot, under any view of the facts, be considered as taken 'in accordance with a comprehensive plan'. The board takes no action on its own initiative. It makes no investigation to determine which areas of the village are suitable for the erection of multiple family dwellings, and which are not. With relation to the type of construction here involved, the board has adopted no plan, comprehensive or otherwise. Under the ordinance, the board merely waits for some individual, owning ten acres of land or who has acquired ten acres of land, to make an application to have it declared a 'Residence B–B' district; then the board accepts or rejects the application. That is not comprehensive planning by the board; it is just the opposite. It is spot zoning at the request of landed interests who may happen to find favor with the board. As a result of this decision, it is possible that there will be found in the residential areas of Tarrytown multiple family dwellings scattered (or spotted) haphazardly throughout the village without any studied, overall plan. How may the board adopt a comprehensive plan with respect to these multiple family dwellings when it is impossible for it to know the names, number and location of individuals who own or who may acquire ten-acre parcels and who may wish to avail themselves of the ordinance. This is an ordinance which benefits those who can meet a property qualification and is thus undemocratic.

We are adjured by the prevailing opinion, 302 N.Y. p. 126, 96 N.E.2d 736, not 'to exalt form over substance and sacrifice substance to form', yet we think the decision of the majority has done just that. Essentially and basically, what has been done by the board of trustees in the instant case is to permit a nonconforming use in an established zone. Heretofore, such action has always been referred to as the granting of a 'variance', yet the board has here sought to cloak its ultimate objective under the label and form of 'rezoning'. In order to protect and preserve our zoning systems from the frequent and inevitable attacks of interested parties who seek to avoid zoning laws for their own purposes, this court has imposed strict and severe limitations upon the granting of variances. Two recent illustrations are *Matter of Taxpayers' Ass'n v. Board of Zoning Appeals*, 301 N.Y. 215, 93 N.E.2d 645, and *Matter of Clark v. Board of Zoning Appeals*, 301 N.Y. 86, 92 N.E.2d 903. It cannot be denied that the individual respondent here would never have been able to secure a variance permitting the erection of multiple family dwellings in Residence A or B districts under the rules stated in those two cases. Nevertheless, the identical result has here been reached by denominating the action of the board as 'rezoning'. In that fashion, the board of trustees, which, incidentally, does not even have the power to grant a variance, since that power resides in the board of appeals, Village Law, § 175, has successfully avoided the long-established and stringent limitations upon the granting of variances, merely by adopting a procedure under the name of 'rezoning'. Now, instead of making the required showing that (1) the land cannot yield a reasonable return if used only for a purpose allowed in that zone, (2) that the plight of the owner is due to unique circumstances and not to the general conditions of the neighborhood, and (3) that the use sought will not alter the essential character of the neighborhood *Matter of Taxpayers' Ass'n v. Board of Zoning Appeals, supra*, 301 N.Y. at page 218, 93 N.E.2d at page 647, all a property owner need do is to show that he possesses ten acres of land and the board becomes authorized to permit a nonconforming use thereon. That, we submit, is truly exalting form over substance.

The case of *Nappi v. LaGuardia*, 295 N.Y. 652, 64 N.E.2d 716, affirming 269 App.Div. 693, 54 N.Y.S.2d 722, affirming 184 Misc. 775, 55 N.Y.S.2d 80, is clearly distinguishable from the case at bar. In the *Nappi* case, the New York City zoning resolution did not purport to establish a new district; it merely added a further permitted use to the uses already authorized in certain residence districts in the city. The distinction is obvious and important. A person purchasing property in New York City in the designated residence districts would be on notice that the additional use was authorized. He may examine the zoning ordinance and discover, with certainty, all the permitted uses to which the adjoining property could be put. On the contrary, a person purchasing property in Tarrytown in a Residence A or B district to bring up his children now has no way of knowing whether the property next to his may or may not become the site of a multiple family dwelling with the attendant increases in population, traffic dangers, commerce and congestion.

Finally, it seems to us specious to argue that since the ultimate objective of the board might have been accomplished in a different and legal manner, that the procedure actually used should therefore be sustained. The question remains whether the particular method adopted by the board was in conformity with the legislative requirements found in the Village Law, and whether it accorded with sound, proper zoning theory and practice. In this case, we feel that the board's action must fall on both counts. That being so, it is of no moment that the same result might have been reached through the employment of approved legal procedures. Zoning methods are determined by the Legislature and not by the ingenuity of local boards of trustees or by the courts. In short, we think the end cannot here justify the means used.

The judgments below should be reversed and the case remitted to Special Term for the entry of a judgment in plaintiff's favor in accordance with this opinion.

LOUGHRAN, C.J., and LEWIS, DYE and FROESSELL, JJ., concur with FULD, J.

CONWAY, J., dissents in opinion in which DESMOND, J., concurs.

Judgment affirmed.

Notes

1. The New York Town, Village, and General City Law, in authorizing local legislatures to create zoning districts require that "[a]ll such regulations shall be uniform for each class or kind of buildings, throughout such district but the regulations in one district may differ from those in other

districts." See § 7–702 Village Law. How does the majority opinion in Rodgers square with this statutory requirement?

2. Why is the dissenting judge so upset? He says that what the village has done here is not zoning. In the process he calls the floating zoning mechanism "spot zoning," a "nonconforming use," and a "variance." Consider those terms carefully and compare them to the floating zone technique that is sustained by the majority opinion.

3. Consider the meaning of this quote from the majority opinion in Rodgers: "Changed or changing conditions call for changed plans, and persons who own property in a particular zone or use district enjoy no eternally vested right to that classification if the public interest demands otherwise." Imagine you are advising a client who has just found that she lives next to a 10 acre parcel that has just been rezoned for garden apartments under a floating zone provision of the zoning ordinance. Read these words to her and try to anticipate her reaction. What security does existing zoning give to a landowner or neighbor? What changes in circumstances are sufficient to authorize a legislative body to change zoning uses, for example, from single family to multi-family or from residential to industrial?

4. In Bellemeade Company v. Priddle, Ky., 503 S.W.2d 734 (1973), the Kentucky Supreme Court upheld the floating zone provision that resulted in the construction of a motel within a neighborhood zoned residential and in Cetrulo v. City of Park Hills, Ky., 524 S.W.2d 628 (1975), the same court upheld a planning commission's approval of a "Planned Unit Development" (PUD) consisting of a seven story condominium on a seven-and-a-half acre tract within a neighborhood zoned for single family residences.

5. A good discussion of the concept and the potential uses of the floating zone is contained in a Comment, Zoning—The Floating Zone: A Potential Instrument of Versatile Zoning, 16 Cath.U.L.Rev. 85 (1966). The writer points out that the floating zone in theory floats above the landscape in anticipation of being brought down to earth by an amendment rezoning the area in question. It is a use classification that is not employed until needed nor pinned down to any area until the necessity arises. Obviously, where such a use or category of uses may reasonably be anticipated, the floating zone device offers the planner some substantial flexibility in dealing with the problem as it arises. Moreover, there may be new kinds of uses which will arise and cannot be anticipated but which the planner will have to provide for. The beauty of the floating zone is that it "descends to earth" at the time and place desired. It thus frees the hands of the planner from some of the limitations of Euclidean-type zoning. To the contrary, however, the "floating zone" may be said to float over the heads of landowners somewhat like a dark rain cloud. Thus the argument against the floating zone is that it is unfair to property owners because the protection accruing to them as the result of the more traditional Euclidean zoning techniques has been substantially diminished. On this, see Comment, Zoning Change: Flexibility vs. Stability, 26 Md.L.Rev. 48, 60 (1966), as well as Haar and Hering, The Lower Gwynedd Township Case, 74 Harv.L.Rev. at 1573 (1961). The Maryland commentator points out that it has also been argued that a floating zone is simply another, perhaps more grandiose, form of spot zoning.

6. In Beall v. Montgomery County Council, 240 Md. 77, 212 A.2d 751 (1965), the Maryland Court of Appeals sustained the county council in rezoning 41.6 acres of land from single-family residential use to multiple-family, high rise residential use. Prior to the application for rezoning, the county council had created a new type of zone, known as the R–H zone. Its purpose was to provide suitable sites for high density residential development and to allow numerous types of commercial, recreational, and educational uses within the area. The court stated that no evidence of a mistake in the original zoning or of a substantial change in the character of the neighborhood was necessary or applicable "in view of the conclusion of the Technical Staff, adopted by the Planning Commission and the Council, that the applications complied with the purposes of the R–H zone, and of our decisions in Costello v. Sieling, 223 Md. 24, 161 A.2d 824 (1960) and in Huff v. Board of Zoning Appeals, 214 Md. 48, 133 A.2d 83 (1957)."

7. Recognizing that the city had numerous abandoned properties that were non-conforming uses in the neighborhoods where they were located, the City of Cumberland, Maryland, created a Rehabilitation and Redevelopment Floating Zone. The purpose of this floating zone is to "allow and provide incentives for the reuse, rehabilitation, and redevelopment of such structures in a manner that will allow them to be restored to the active tax roles and inventory of land in the City, while preserving the integrity of the neighborhood in which they are located." Zoning Ordinance of the City of Cumberland, Maryland, § 5.01.12. To ensure that proposed rehabilitation and redevelopment of such properties are compatible with adjacent residential areas, the city included protective performance standards. The requirements first establish that the floating zone may be located only in areas designated by the city's comprehensive plan, or within four specific zoning districts: Urban Residential, Residential–Office, Gateway–Commercial District, and Gateway–Industrial District. § 6.14.01. The property owner seeking to create the floating zone must submit a petition to the city's zoning administrator. The ordinance contains permitted and prohibited uses in the four designated districts. For example, in the Urban Residential District, although not normally permitted in the district, uses such as retail/accessory light manufacturing, food and beverage manufacturing, packaging, and processing are permitted where the property will be designated a Rehabilitation and Redevelopment Floating Zone. § 6.14.02. The ordinance protects adjacent properties through performance standards. § 6.14.04. These standards include regulations governing the preservation of natural site amenities; the control of smoke, dust, noise, fumes, and vibrations; proper lighting, waste management, and parking; and appropriate landscape buffers.

B. SMARTER SITE PLANNING: CLUSTERING AND ENVIRONMENTAL IMPACT REVIEW

One approach to smart growth is to do a better job of site planning. Euclidian zoning combined with typical subdivision regulations forces local planners to approve cookie-cutter subdivisions. Under the traditional approach, the entire parcel is divided into lots and a single-family home is built on each lot. Every home is sited in a similar fashion, a result achieved by applying uniform setback, lot coverage, and height requirements to its design, and requiring that all streets, curbs, gutters, lighting, and landscaping follow set standards. In many communities this results in monotonous uniformity, car dependent living, the disappearance of open space, and high cost housing.

Many states have adopted amendments to their zoning enabling laws that delegate authority to localities to permit clustering of their residential developments. Clustering is discussed in detail in Chapter V, as part of the residential subdivision process. We note it here as a smart growth technique because, in its application, clustering has been used to preserve open space, protect valuable agriculture soils, promote housing affordability, and avoid development of critical environmental areas: all objectives of smart growth land use strategies.

In a number of states, local governments are allowed by law to control the development of individual parcels by conducting environmental impact reviews and imposing conditions on land use approvals in order to mitigate environmental impacts. The state legislatures in California, Massachusetts, Minnesota, New York, and Washington have delegated express authority to local governments to conduct environmental impact reviews on proposed land use projects. This allows local land use agencies to require that subdivision and site plans take into consideration and mitigate the adverse impacts of the proposed development on environmental resources.

In other states, the authority to protect the environment while reviewing and approving development plans for individual sites is found to be implied in the zoning enabling act. This is the case in South Carolina where localities may adopt environmental review procedures as part of their land use review process. The legal situation in South Carolina illustrates how a broad view of local authority can help communities in their efforts to adopt smart growth land use and planning strategies.

South Carolina—Flexibility Provisions

In South Carolina, municipalities derive their land use powers from both home rule authority and enabling statutes. The South Carolina Constitution authorizes the legislature to provide for "the structure and organization, powers, duties, functions and responsibilities of the municipalities * * * by general law." S.C. Const. art. VIII, § 8. The constitution says that "[t]he provisions of [the] Constitution and all laws concerning local government shall be liberally construed in their favor," and that any powers granted local government by the constitution and laws "shall include those fairly implied and not prohibited by [the] Constitution." S.C. Const. art. VIII, § 17. See also *Southern Bell Telephone and Telegraph Co. v. City of Aiken*, 279 S.C. 269, 306 S.E.2d 220 (1983) (holding that Article VIII of the South Carolina Constitution was completely revised for the purpose of accomplishing home rule and granted renewed autonomy to local government).

This broad grant of local authority was statutorily implemented by the South Carolina Legislature by provisions such as the following: "All counties of the State * * * have authority to enact regulations, resolutions, and ordinances * * * respecting any subject as appears to them necessary and proper for the security, general welfare, and convenience of counties or for preserving health, peace, order, and good government in them." S.C. Code Ann. § 4–9–25. "State legislation provides that the powers of a municipality shall be liberally construed in favor of the municipality and the specific mention of particular powers shall not be construed as limiting in any manner the general powers of such municipalities." S.C. Code Ann. § 5–7–10, see *Williams v. Town of Hilton Head Island*, 311 S.C. 417, 429 S.E.2d 802 (1993) (holding that the South Carolina Legislature intended to abolish the former rule of strict construction when enacting S.C. Code Ann. §§ 5–7–10 et seq.).

These provisions enlarge the scope of local government authority. Under home rule, local governments in South Carolina "may enact regulations deemed necessary and proper for the general welfare unless such regulations are actually inconsistent with the Constitution or general law of the state." Douglas T. Kendall, Preserving South Carolina's Beaches: The Role of Local Planning in Managing Growth in Coastal South Carolina, 1 S.C. Envt'l L.J. 61, 68 (2000). For a general discussion of South Carolina Home Rule, see *Hospitality Ass'n v. County of Charleston,* 320 S.C. 219, 464 S.E.2d 113 (1995).

Local governments in South Carolina derive their express zoning and planning powers from the South Carolina Local Government Planning Enabling Act. S.C. Code Ann. § 6–29–310–1200. Enacted in 1994, the purpose of the Act was to consolidate the local planning and zoning statutes in a comprehensive law and recognize new planning and zoning powers. See Kendall, at 65. The Act provides that a local government may create a planning commission, whose duty and function is to create "plans and programs * * * designed to promote public health, safety, morals, convenience, prosperity, or the general welfare." S.C. Code Ann. § 6–29–340(A). Comprehensive plans must include, but are not limited to, seven elements: (1) population, (2) economic development, (3) natural resources, (4) cultural resources, (5) community facilities, (6) housing, and (7) land use. § 6–29–510. The Act notes that "specific planning elements must be based upon careful and comprehensive surveys and studies of existing conditions and probable future development and include recommended means of implementation." § 6–29–340. All zoning and land use regulations must be in accordance with the comprehensive plan. 6–29–720(B). The Act also authorizes specific zoning techniques such as cluster development, floating zones, and planned development districts. 6–29–720(C). However, it makes clear that "any other planning and zoning techniques may be used." When making revisions to the zoning ordinance, the municipality is authorized to consider "the protection of * * * ecologically sensitive areas." S.C. Code Ann. § 6–29–710.

The South Carolina Local Government Planning Act extends the planning and zoning authority of local governments and emphasizes protection of the environment. This specific authority, state rules indicating that local authority is to be interpreted broadly, and a deepening concern for the environment persuaded the town of Mount Pleasant to adopt a local environmental review ordinance. Mount Pleasant, South Carolina, Code of Ordinances, § 156.264.

The purpose of the ordinance is to provide a basis for assessing the impacts of significant development proposals on the "town's overall environment and infrastructure, natural ecology, and economic, historic, social, and related public resources." § 156.264(A). The ordinance requires an impact assessment for development projects that meet certain thresholds. The developer must provide a general description of the project, and identify data about the impacts upon municipal facilities, services, and resources. The town planning director reviews the impact assessment and may conduct independent field investigations for verification. If negative impacts are identified, the town council determines whether the impacts are "acceptable and in the public interest." § 156.264(G). If not, the council has the authority to request the developer to mitigate negative impacts.

The Mount Pleasant impact assessment process requires extensive review of the impacts of individual development projects. Developers must submit information concerning the impacts upon "public services and facilities, the environment, natural resources, historical and archaeological resources, local housing needs, the local economy and other areas affecting the health, safety, general welfare and quality of life in the town." § 156.264(E).

There is an extensive traffic impact assessment process, which requires the developer to submit a Transportation Impact Assessment Data Form. § 156.264(2)(d). The impact assessment must address the negative effects the development will have on marshes, creeks, rivers, plant and animal habitats, and buffer zones and must describe the steps taken to mitigate the negative effects and to protect the natural resources. This local law provides its local boards extensive authority to review and condition land development projects so that their adverse impacts on the environment are minimized.

C. SMARTER PATTERNS OF GROWTH: FLEXIBILITY TECHNIQUES

While better site planning is an important objective, the real flaw in Euclidian zoning, from the smart growth perspective, is that it allows development—usually at relatively low densities—throughout the community. The traditional zoning district map provides a downtown core district, some neighborhood commercial zones, industrial districts along rail lines, highways, or rivers, allows multi-family housing in or close to some of these districts, and then puts the majority of the land in single-family zoning districts with different minimum lot sizes, ranging from a quarter-acre to five-acre lots.

In developing suburban and fringe communities, smart growth advocates that the densities of land uses permitted by the Euclidian zoning ordinance be arranged differently. The suggestion is to identify growth districts, allow mixed-use higher density zoning at the core of such districts, and arrange a mix of housing types around the core in a sufficiently dense pattern so that residents can walk to shop, to recreate, and, for some, to work. As older suburbs develop their remaining vacant land or, with older cities, redevelop blighted, underdeveloped, or abandoned areas, smart growth suggests that similar planning principles be applied. How precisely to approach new development and redevelopment of large tracts of land in any particular community will, of course, depend on the idiosyncrasies of the place. The question is whether there are strategies available under state law that allow them to create new and different land use patterns. In all cases however local planners need to know whether they have the tools necessary to arrange development and conservation of the land in a cost-effective, environmentally-friendly, and affordable fashion. The remainder of this chapter describes and illustrates some of the smart growth techniques available to arrange development at the area-wide level.

D. PERFORMANCE ZONING

(Citations for the material in this section are available in John R. Nolon, *Golden* and Its Emanations: The Surprising Origins of Smart Growth, The Urban Lawyer, Vol. 35, No. 1, Winter, 2003.)

Performance zoning is a land use invention that emerged in the late 1960s. It gained widespread attention in 1973 in Bucks County, Pennsylvania, which advocated its use by localities to provide developers more flexibility in site and building design while protecting open space and natural resources. The model was adopted, at least in part and for a time, by most of the communities in Bucks County.

The Bucks County model regulates development not by using traditional dimensional and use standards but by reference to performance standards that measure the impact of a development on a particular site. In Bucks County, performance zoning was limited to housing development: all types of housing were permitted in all zoning districts and were regulated by impact measures regarding impervious coverage, retained open space, and protection of wetlands, watercourses, and other natural resources.

Some aspects of traditional zoning—such as zoning districts and certain use prescriptions—were retained in the Bucks County model. Each was governed, however, by performance standards: an open space ratio, intensity factors such as building volume, transportation impacts, impervious coverage, and landscaping. Dense buffering was required between incompatible uses, and a site capacity calculation was used to limit development impacts on each parcel and its surroundings. Traffic impact analyses were used, density transfers were allowed to prevent hardships, and bonus densities were allowed to encourage affordable housing.

Despite its promise and growing relevance due to current interest in smart growth, performance zoning has not gained wide acceptance. The approach is thought to be less predictable and somewhat harder to administer than the classic use-and-dimension-based approach. Its principal contribution to local land use practice has been to encourage the gradual insinuation of performance standards into traditional mechanisms such as zoning ordinances and subdivision regulations. Many localities have become accustomed to administering complex and flexible environmental reviews of their land use decisions and enforcing a growing number of standards that they have adopted. These developments challenge the criticisms of performance zoning as too complex and indeterminate. The gradual adoption of other Post–Euclidian techniques may have proceeded far enough to merit a fresh look at performance zoning and its practicality.

Hyde Park, New York—Performance Zoning

The Town of Hyde Park, in New York, took such a look and drafted an interesting set of performance standards capable of reshaping the development pattern prescribed by local zoning. The Hyde Park approach to performance-based land use regulation begins with a division of the town into six areas: a greenbelt, the Hudson River waterfront, 10 neighborhoods, four hamlets, a planned development district, and a town center. Within the neighborhood, hamlet, and town center districts, core areas are established where mixed-use, higher density development is encouraged. In the waterfront district, there are five landing districts where higher density development of water-related land uses is encouraged. The planned development district connects the nationally-known Franklin and Eleanor Roosevelt sites, a national park, and the Culinary Institute of America. The PDD encourages a mix of tourism-related development and open space amenities that aspire to attract a large number of visitors, fuel the local economy, and strengthen the tax base. Major subdivision of land is discouraged in the waterfront and greenbelt districts. This is the regulatory base on which the more specific performance standards rest. This overall community design appears in, and is taken from, the adopted comprehensive plan of the community.

The organizing principle of the proposed Hyde Park zoning ordinance is to encourage "organic growth in community centers." The ordinance establishes three additional "strategic directions": enhancement of community identity, economic expansion, and civic cohesion. The zoning is calculated to encourage a pattern of land use in which mixed uses and development with higher density, scale, and intensity of use occur in community centers supported by infrastructure and services. "Outlying areas" are reserved for lower density, scale, and intensity of use and for the maintenance of open space and natural resources. Among the purposes of the new zoning are pedestrian orientation, orderly expansion of existing centers, integrity of Hudson River views, historic preservation, affordable housing, and reduction of traffic congestion.

A trilogy of performance standards guides development permitting under the ordinance: density, intensity, and scale factors. "Density" refers to the relative compactness or closeness of a land use, expressed in dwelling units per acre or employment units per acre. An employment unit is one to three persons simultaneously engaged in the conduct of a business, trade, or occupation. A business employing six persons constitutes two employment units. "Intensity" references the amount of traffic caused by the proposed land use, expressed as the number of daily vehicle trips generated. "Scale" is the size or bulk of the proposed structures, calculated in gross square feet of floor area in all buildings, excluding parking.

A list of land uses is permitted in various districts; it includes six residential, 16 non-residential, and nine "community" uses. These 31 uses may be combined: the ordinance encourages mixed uses in the core areas of all districts "provided that the scale, density, and intensity of all uses" complies with the standards established for each district. Bulk regulations are established including height, size, lot coverage, and yards.

Site design requirements regulate parking, ingress and egress, separate pedestrian ways and bicycle paths, landscaping, architectural features, stormwater management, erosion control, lighting, and infrastructure. Central water and sewer systems are required for all major developments proposed in the neighborhood, hamlet, town center and landing districts, including their core areas. Site standards list a variety of environmental performance factors, including wetland, stream, and natural area protection. The segmentation of any significant natural habitat or wildlife corridor is to be avoided. Protected open space is to be contiguous with that on adjacent lots and designed as a cohesive whole. Historic and scenic overlay districts are created.

The Hyde Park zoning ordinance proposes the use of site plan review to achieve its four strategic objectives. In neighborhood core areas, for example, residential densities up to eight units per acre, multi-family residences, bed and breakfast establishments, and commercial and community uses serving the neighborhood are encouraged. Low-intensity industrial uses close to the center of the core are deemed appropriate, as are small front yards, and common and connected open space with associated commercial and community gathering places. Buildings should incorporate attractive bays, balconies, and porches, use traditional building forms and natural materials, and building facades should vary, but not dramatically. Design consistency along streets is encouraged.

In the four designated hamlet districts, residential uses at a density of up to six units per acre are permitted along with limited non-residential uses. In the hamlet core area, densities of up to 10 dwelling units per acre are allowed along with more extensive commercial uses. In the core, residential subdivision is limited to multi-family housing purposes. In the rest of the hamlet district, subdivision of land is encouraged, as is mixed residential development that gradually decreases density from the hamlet core areas outward to the district's edge. Expressed in performance terms, parcels in core areas of hamlets are limited to a maximum of 12,000 gross square feet, 10 dwelling units, 20 employment units, and 5,480 daily vehicle trips per acre. The preservation of contiguous open space is encouraged in hamlet districts. A variety of other provisions are included that protect the environment. Notable among them is a 500–foot wetland buffer within which land uses are to be limited to those that are consistent with high quality wetlands.

The Hyde Park zoning draft contains guidelines for site plan review in the designated town center. In the core of the town center, performance maximums are 32,000 gross square feet, 24 dwelling units, 50 employment units, and 10,970 daily vehicle trips per acre. Non-residential uses in the core are encouraged that serve the needs of local residents and the tourist trade the plan aspires to support. In this district, only multi-family residential development is allowed. Open space standards are aimed at creating a public realm—parks, commons, and plazas that serve as public and private sector gathering points and amenities. All development is to be pedestrian friendly and designed to incorporate landscaping and building separations that diminish the visual dominance of automobiles and stark paved spaces.

In the Bellefield planned development district, immediately to the south of the town center district, development is encouraged that promotes tourism-related businesses while complementing the Roosevelt park, library, and homes, including a non-vehicular trail linking these sites through an environmentally sensitive area that is to be preserved. All subdivision of land must be consistent with a comprehensive plan and vision for the roughly 1,000–acre district, clustering of development is required to create small centers of development, and no more than 50 percent of the gross floor area of all development may consist of residences. Together, the town center and Bellefield PDD promise sensitively sited economic development to serve the economic needs of the residents and build a significant tax base for the community. The Bellefield PDD is to be the gateway to the town as well as a regional hub serving the tourism industry.

The zoning map that accompanies the zoning proposals depicts the size and location of all these districts. It appears that approximately 70 percent of the land area of the town is located in the greenbelt and waterfront districts. In these two districts, the performance standards allow a maximum density of one dwelling unit per four acres, a relatively low density development pattern that assures a rural context for the well-defined districts and cores. A species of relief is offered to landowners in these low density districts, as well as the other districts, should they wish to exceed the scale, density, and intensity standards. The zoning draft contains a special exception permit provision. Applications for this permit must demonstrate how the proposed development conforms with the four strategic objectives of the ordinance. Approval authority for this special use permit is given to the Zoning Board of Appeals.

In accompanying subdivision regulations, it is strongly recommend that all land subdivision in the Greenbelt and Waterfront districts be clustered to maintain the rural appearance and environmental resources of the town. The objective of these cluster provisions is to leave "substantial portions" of subdivided land undeveloped. The planning board is authorized to mandate clustering for any particular subdivision that may have a significant adverse impact on the community's rural landscape or its natural resources. Interestingly, mixed uses are permitted, including non-residential development. A net acreage method of determining maximum allowable density on a particular parcel is provided that avoids the time-consuming process of analyzing how many units would be permitted under a conventional subdivision. The open space to be preserved must have a conservation value which insures that preserved land will serve specific ecological, recreational, or agricultural purposes. To the extent that these provisions exceed the authority localities have to permit and require clustering, the draft regulations express an intent to supersede the Town Law provisions, using authority to supersede generally applicable state law under Section 10 of the Municipal Home Rule Law.

The Hyde Park model can be understood as a community-wide smart growth strategy, transferring mixed-use higher density development rights to defined cores comprising approximately one third of the community and greatly restricting development in designated environmental areas. The use of detailed site plan standards and of three impact factors (density, intensity, and scale) serve the same purpose as project-by-project environmental reviews: they mitigate the environmental impact of specific developments. They accomplish more by allowing developers in designated districts and their cores great flexibility to mix uses, achieve multi-family housing development, and build at greater densities.

Notes

1. See Kendig, Performance Zoning (American Planning Ass'n 1980). The prototypical ordinance presented in this publication contains eight zoning districts, Agricultural, Rural, Estate, Development, Urban Core, Neighborhood Conservation, Commercial Conservation, and Holding. Five general use categories are either permitted, denied or conditionally permitted in these districts (the five categories are agriculture, residential, institutional, commercial, and industrial). The heart of the ordinance is the performance standards provisions which provide minimum standards for open space, density, impervious surface coverage, and lot area. The publication contains detailed illustrations as well as a model ordinance with commentary. Also see Porter, Phillips & Lassar, Flexible Zoning: How It Works (Urban Land Inst.1988).

2. Performance zoning can be used to ensure that individual projects do not have a negative environmental effect on surrounding properties. It is the lack of such standards in many zoning, subdivision, and site plan laws that limits the ability of land use approval agencies to approve development

proposals, while protecting surrounding properties. In DeCoals v. Board of Zoning Appeals of Westover, 168 W.Va. 339, 284 S.E.2d 856 (1981), the court upheld extensive performance standards that prevented the emanation of dust and noise from industrial sites. The ordinance prohibited the escape of dust of any kind from the property and noise was allowed to equal but not exceed the decibel level of traffic sounds in the street during a normal work day.

3. The Florida Growth Management Act, § 163.3202, encourages municipalities to adopt innovative land use techniques including performance zoning as well as planned-unit development, impact fees, incentive zoning, and the transfer of development rights.

E. PLANNED UNIT DEVELOPMENT ZONING

To achieve greater flexibility, some localities have adopted a planned unit development (PUD) ordinance as part of their zoning law. Under some PUD laws, the owners of several adjacent parcels may apply for a special permit to create a higher density, mixed-use development, with considerable design flexibility. This type of PUD provides for the development of new neighborhoods of different sizes and land uses. It also allows underutilized or deteriorated sites to be assembled and redeveloped in older communities. PUD ordinances may provide bonus density and design flexibility as incentives to developers and require that the developer provide infrastructure investments, affordable housing, or open space and environmental benefits in exchange.

The PUD device can be used to combine several smaller parcels into one large parcel and to locate improvements on appropriate portions of the larger parcel to provide more cost-effective development and to conserve the larger site's sensitive environmental features. This technique provides the economic and environmental benefits of clustering development, but on a larger scale.

Although the types and requirements of PUDs vary, there are three characteristics that are common to most PUD ordinances. First, PUDs must conform to the local comprehensive or master plan. In Bridger Canyon Property Owners' Association, Inc. v. Planning and Zoning Commission, 270 Mont. 160, 890 P.2d 1268 (1995) a local homeowners' association challenged the local planning and zoning commission's conditional approval of a PUD application. In overturning the commission's PUD approval, the Supreme Court of Montana determined that the commission exceeded its authority when it approved the PUD, which failed to comply with the community's general plan for zoning. Large-scale, mixed-use development with significant environmental benefits can easily be provided for in a comprehensive plan as a means of accommodating appropriate types of development.

Second, to create a PUD most local governments require that the land to be developed as a PUD be under single ownership or be controlled by a single entity. For example, the city of Robbinsdale, Minnesota, PUD provision states that the "property shall be in single ownership or under the management or supervision of a central authority or otherwise subject to such supervisory lease or ownership control." Code of the City of Robbinsdale, Minnesota, § 530.05(2)(a).

This requirement allows the community to impose responsibility for establishing and maintaining the site's environmental features on a reliable and durable entity.

Third, the PUD permits the relaxation of underlying density and area requirements by clustering development in certain areas while preserving other areas as open space. By permitting increased density in certain portions of the PUD property, housing, businesses, and other amenities, such as restaurants, may be combined near one another, permitting residents to walk from one destination to another and reducing dependence on automobiles. This larger-scale shift of development away from the environmentally sensitive portion of the site allows truly significant landscapes to be preserved.

Because the creation of a PUD usually effects a change in the expectations of the property owners in the nearby areas, legal challenges are brought claiming that PUDs violate the uniformity requirement of the zoning enabling act or are beyond the scope of municipal land use authority. Although most state courts hold that the PUD is itself a zoning district, or is an acceptable means of effecting the most appropriate use of the land, some states have amended their enabling acts to expressly authorize the use of PUDs. Recall that in Rodgers v. Tarrytown, found at the beginning of this section, the court reasoned that "[t]he village's zoning aim being clear, the choice of methods to accomplish it lay with the board."

Great Falls, Montana—PUD Ordinance

The PUD ordinance of the City of Great Falls, Montana, is an example of a PUD provision that gives significant design discretion to the PUD developer, while requiring that significant benefits be provided to the community. The purpose of Great Falls' PUD ordinance is "to allow and provide for the imaginative and efficient utilization of land through large-scale development, greater design flexibility, the consolidation of open spaces, the clustering of buildings, and the integration of compatible uses." Code of the City of Great Falls, Montana, § 17.63.010. The process begins with a pre-application conference between the developer and the city's planning director and appropriate city officials to review preliminary plans. Within two weeks after the pre-application conference, the planning director must furnish the developer with written comments regarding the proposed PUD and provide recommendations to inform and assist the developer in preparing the PUD application. The formal PUD process begins when the developer submits a preliminary development plan to the local planning board, which must include a description of the number and type of dwelling units, proposed lot coverage, total open space, usable open space, and the type and amount of nonresidential development planned. The preliminary development plan must also include a map showing the natural features of the PUD property.

The Great Falls PUD law does not prescribe specific design, density, and setback requirements. (In contrast to Great Fall's PUD provisions, the city of Robbinsdale, Minnesota, prescribes specific requirements such as minimum project size, required frontage, yard setbacks, height restrictions, and density bonuses. Code of the City of Robbinsdale, Minnesota, § 530.05(5).) Instead, such matters are left to be negotiated between the developer and the planning board. The PUD ordinance provides that "PUDs are characterized by cluster developments and common open space. Only by proper design can the traditional values of privacy, light, air and ventilation be preserved. It is not practical to set specific standards that would be applicable to all PUD's for these items, but it is incumbent upon the developer and the Planning Board to consider these items in the design and review of the PUD." § 17.63.140. By providing significant design discretion to the developer, the design and development of each PUD in Great Falls can conform to the physical, economic, and social character of the area where a PUD is to be located.

The Great Falls ordinance is more prescriptive regarding open space requirements and the incorporation of environmental design. To ensure that the required open space is preserved, the PUD ordinance requires that the open space be protected by restrictive covenants or other legal agreements acceptable to the City of Great Falls. With respect to environmental design, the ordinance requires the developer to submit a landscaping plan that protects existing natural features and vegetation by minimizing the impact of the PUD development on these resources. § 17.63.210. The planning board may require measures to mitigate the PUD's impact on natural resources. Finally, the ordinance requires that the developer provide financial guarantees to the city to ensure that the PUD is developed in accordance with the submitted plans and according to the construction schedule provided by the developer. If, for example, the approved environmental conservation plans are violated, the city can remedy the problem and charge the costs to the developer, using the financial guarantee.

F. TRADITIONAL NEIGHBORHOOD DISTRICTS

New urbanists, sometimes called neo-traditionalists, advocate zoning and land use regulations that allow for the creation of traditional urban neighborhoods. They point out that, under conventional zoning and subdivision laws, most traditional neighborhoods found in urban areas can no longer be replicated. The corner drugstore or deli in a residential neighborhood is not allowed, apartments cannot exist above stores, and houses cannot be built close to the sidewalk, nor cars parked in garages that front on alleys that kids use as playgrounds. If cookie-cutter subdivisions are the result of standards contained in zoning and subdivision ordinances, the new urbanists ask, why can't such regulations be modified to create different, more flexible neighborhoods? See Jonathan

Barnett, What's New About New Urbanism?, in Charter of the New Urbanism 5 (2000).

Neo-traditionalists and many smart growth advocates argue that a new type of land development pattern is needed—one that is more concentrated and that creates a quality of neighborhood in which residents feel comfortable living. One such approach is to create mixed-use neighborhoods where housing types are varied, retail and commercial services are available within walking distance of residences, public green space is provided, visual and recreational amenities exist nearby, and pedestrian and bicycle travel is actively encouraged. Houses in such a neighborhood district can be allowed on smaller lots, retail and commercial uses can be mixed with residential uses, a variety of housing types can be allowed, and accessible open space can be created and dedicated to the use of all the neighbors.

Traditional Neighborhood Development (TND) is a zoning mechanism that has emerged in recent years as a method of achieving such objectives and as a promising alternative to conventional zoning. TND zoning districts are more friendly than conventional zoning to environmental conservation, pedestrian movement, and compact development. This device is similar to Planned Unit Development, but is focused more closely on achieving traditional spatial relationships.

City of Austin, Texas—TND Ordinance

The City of Austin's zoning code contains a Traditional Neighborhood District (TND) that illustrates how the mechanism works. The purpose of the Austin TND ordinance is to "encourage mixed-use, compact development that is sensitive to the environmental characteristics of the land and facilitates the efficient use of services." (§ 13–9–2.) The organizing principle behind a TND district is the neighborhood, which is characterized by diverse and integrated land uses existing in close proximity to each other. The TND neighborhood contains several well-defined areas within walking distance of the neighborhood center (typically a quarter-mile or a five-minute walk) connected by a network of thoroughfares that service both cars and pedestrians. To create recognizable areas within the larger integrated neighborhood, TND provisions govern the type, location, and amount of particular land uses in each area with an eye toward how they interact. TNDs also closely regulate the design standards for streetscapes, landscapes, and architecture that foster a sense of place among the residents.

Conventional zoning generally divides a municipality into zones with predetermined use, dimension, and density requirements. In contrast, Austin's TND ordinance:

- creates neighborhoods that are modest in size and pedestrian-oriented;
- allows a diversity of housing types, jobs, shopping, services, and public facilities within the district;

- integrates residences, shops, workplaces, and civic buildings all within close proximity;
- designs a neighborhood that respects and preserves unique natural features and open spaces;
- coordinates a more equitable transportation system with facilities for pedestrians, bicycles, public transit, and cars;
- creates well-configured squares, plazas, greens, landscaped streets, preserves, greenbelts, and parks woven into the pattern of the neighborhood and dedicated to the collective social activity, recreation, and visual enjoyment of the populace;
- provides for civic buildings, open spaces, and other visual features that act as landmarks, symbols, and focal points for community identity;
- contains design standards to provide for compatible building arrangement, bulk, form, character, and landscaping to establish a livable, harmonious, and diverse environment;
- forms a distinct edge and defines the border between the public street and the private block interior; and
- provides for architecture and landscape that respond to the unique character of the region.

(§ 13–9–2(B))

While continuing to regulate size, dimension, and use, the primary concern of the TND is the harmonious integration of land uses within the neighborhood. The two essential areas of Austin's TND exemplify this concern with integrating uses:

1. Neighborhood Center Area: TND districts have one Neighborhood Center Area that is generally not less than 5% of the gross land area within the district and is within easy walking distance of most of the lots in the adjacent Mixed Residential Area. This Neighborhood Center Area serves as the focal point of the district and usually contains a central square adjacent to which are generally located retail, commercial, civic and public services. Within this area, land uses are allocated as follows:

not less than 20% to townhouse, condo, multi-family residential,

not less than 20% to commercial, and

not less than 5% to civic uses.

2. Mixed Residential Area: The adjacent Mixed Residential Area includes a variety of residential land uses and open spaces. Retail and commercial uses are allowed, but required to blend into the residential character of the neighborhood. Streets must be designed to promote pedestrian activity while providing for safe and efficient movement of vehicular traffic. The land in this area is allocated as follows:

not less than 50% and not more than 80% to single family residential,

not more than 10% to duplex housing,

not less than 10% to townhouse, condo, multi-family residential,

not less than 1% and not more than 2% to commercial uses, and

not less than 2% to civic uses.

A TND district in Austin can contain a Neighborhood Edge Area along the perimeter of the district that is less dense than the Mixed Residential Area and between 100–250 feet in width. Only single-family residential dwellings, with larger lots and setbacks, are permitted here. A TND can also include a Workshop and Employment Center Area of not more than 10% of gross land area, where commercial and light industrial uses not appropriate in a Neighborhood Center or Mixed Residential Area can be located. Austin's TND ordinance contains these areas. (§ 13–9–45 Land Use Allocations.) The Austin TND ordinance also pays close attention to civic uses, such as community halls and open space, as they relate to residential and commercial development.

Austin's TND develops land in a purposeful manner in order to create a "sustainable, long-term community that provides economic opportunity and environmental and social equity for the residents." (§ 13–9–2 (A).) Integration of uses, pedestrian scale of development, diversity of building types, social interactions, and environmental sensitivity are the principles that guide the TND ordinance. The TND approach to creating compact, mixed-use development allows for better natural resource protection. Because a TND is limited in size, it encourages infill rather than the "leap-frog" development characteristic of suburban land development. Open space provided in the TND can be situated to link with other green spaces within the community.

Notes

1. Traditional Neighborhood Districts have been enacted by local governments in several states, without express enabling legislation. Some states, especially those whose courts have narrowly interpreted the requirement that zoning provisions must be uniform within zoning districts, may need to pass TND enabling statutes before localities will attempt its use. TND enabling legislation in Connecticut, Pennsylvania, and Wisconsin provides support and guidance for local TND regulations. (Sitkowski, R.J. et al. "Enabling Legislation for Traditional Neighborhood Development Regulations" Land Use Law & Zoning Digest October 2001 p. 3.)

2. In 2000, the Pennsylvania state legislature amended its Municipalities Planning Code to add the authority for localities to adopt TND provisions. (Act 68 of 2000; Article VII–A of the Act contains TND enabling legislation.)

3. See Wis. Stat. § 66.034(3) for a more comprehensive approach to getting local governments to use the TND technique. The purpose of the law is to give developers an alternative and more sustainable approach to

development. Cities and villages may enact the TND as a zoning district designation, an overlay zone, a floating zone, or as a modified approach to PUDs. The Wisconsin law provides for the University of Wisconsin Extension to prepare a model traditional neighborhood development ordinance. Wis. Stat. § 66.034(2)(a).

4. The Belmont, North Carolina, Traditional Neighborhood Development law, § 4.11.1 et seq. states that its purpose "is to minimize traffic congestion, suburban sprawl, infrastructure costs, and environmental degradation." The ordinance contains design standards for public and civic areas and privately constructed or rehabilitated structures.

G. TRANSFER OF DEVELOPMENT RIGHTS

Like the other techniques explored in this section, the transfer of development rights provides a mechanism for channeling growth to those areas of a community where the infrastructure and services needed to support additional development may be provided cost-effectively. New York statutes define transfer of development rights (TDR) as "the process by which development rights are transferred from one lot, parcel, or area of land in a sending district to another lot, parcel, or area of land in one or more receiving districts." N.Y. Town Law § 261–a; N.Y. Village Law § 7–701; N.Y. Gen. City Law § 20–f.

A 1997 survey of 3,500 local governments and a review of planning literature found 107 TDR programs in 25 states. John B. Bredin, Transfer of Development Rights: Cases, Statutes, and a Model, 2000 APA National Planning Conference, http://www.asu.edu/caed/proceedings00/BREDIN/bredin.htm.

The programs have been established in rural communities and in some of the country's largest cities, including New York City and Chicago.

The comprehensive plan for the Long Island Pine Barrens, for example, allocates development credits to land in the fragile pine barrens aquifer, based on the land's development yield under local zoning, and greatly restricts development in these "sending districts." (Central Pine Barrens Comprehensive Land Use Plan, ch. 6 (adopted June 28, 1995)). The plan establishes "receiving districts" into which these development credits may be transferred. Developers who own land in these receiving districts may purchase credits from landowners in sending districts. Each purchased credit allows the developer to build one housing unit over that permitted by the receiving district's zoning.

There are three basic elements to a TDR program: the sending district, the receiving district, and the TDR credits themselves. The sending district consists of the area to be protected from development. The receiving district is located where additional density can be absorbed and supported with existing or expanded infrastructure and services. The TDR credits are a legal representation of the abstract development rights that will be severed from property in the sending district and grafted onto property in the receiving district. The TDR credits can traded in a free market or a TDR bank can be established to facilitate exchanges. When a TDR credit is purchased from a property owner in the sending district, that property owner records a deed restriction prohibiting development on the property. The TDR credit can then be applied to property in the receiving district as a density bonus. In New York's Long Island Pine Barrens' TDR program, a 52,500-acre sending district and a 47,500-acre receiving district were established that crossed the jurisdictions of three towns and two villages.

Sarasota, Florida—TDR Program

The TDR program in Sarasota County, Florida was enacted for the purpose of preventing sprawl and preserving open space, agricultural lands, and environmentally sensitive areas. County of Sarasota, Florida, Transfer of Development Rights Ordinance, Ordinance No. 82–61 (1982). Under the program, there are two sending overlay zones: a Residential Sending Zone (RSZ), and a Conservation Sending Zone (CSZ). For a property to be designated as an RSZ, the parcel must be: (i) in a platted subdivision and fail to conform to the county's development regulation because of a lack of paved streets or drainage, or some other deficiency; (ii) in an environmentally sensitive area, including lands identified by the county as having high ecological value; (iii) in an area which is needed for agricultural, open space, or other conservation use; (iv) have historical or archeological significance; or (v) be located on a barrier island. County of Sarasota, Florida, Zoning Ordinance, § 7.20(a)(1). For a property to be designated as a CSZ it must contain at least 500 acres and either (i) be designated by the county as a site of high ecological value; (ii) be in a flood hazard zone; (iii) be in a storm surge area; or (iv) contain an important watercourse with associated wetlands. Sarasota County's TDR ordinance established four receiving overlay zones which allow urban-style densities for landowners or developers who acquire development rights from the sending districts.

The owners of land in the sending districts must apply to have their parcels included in the program and must agree to grant a conservation easement to the county that limits property development to agricultural or open space. § 7.20(c)(4). If the application is approved by the county planning commission and the board of commissioners, the owner receives a transfer permit for a specified number of development rights. These rights may then be sold to the owners of land in a designated receiving district. To use the development rights, the purchaser must submit a copy of the transfer permit along with an application for a permit to develop the property. If the applicant receives approval for the proposed development, the applicant may use the transferred development rights in addition to the rights allowed under the existing zoning on the receiving parcel.

SUITUM v. TAHOE REGIONAL PLANNING AGENCY

Supreme Court of the United States, 1997.
520 U.S. 725, 117 S.Ct. 1659, 137 L.Ed.2d 980.

JUSTICE SOUTER delivered the opinion of the Court.

Petitioner Bernadine Suitum owns land near the Nevada shore of Lake Tahoe. Respondent Tahoe Regional Planning Agency, which regulates land use in the region, determined that Suitum's property is ineligible for development but entitled to receive certain allegedly valuable "Transferable Development Rights" (TDR's). Suitum has brought an action for compensation under Rev. Stat. § 1979, 42 U.S.C. § 1983, claiming that the agency's determinations amounted to a regulatory taking of her property. While the pleadings raise issues about the significance of the TDR's both to the claim that a taking has occurred and to the constitutional requirement of just compensation, we have no occasion to decide, and we do not decide, whether or not these TDR's may be considered in deciding the issue whether there has been a taking in this case, as opposed to the issue whether just compensation has been afforded for such a taking. The sole question here is whether the claim is ripe for adjudication, even though Suitum has not attempted to sell the development rights she has or is eligible to receive. We hold that it is.

In 1969, Congress approved the Tahoe Regional Planning Compact between the States of California and Nevada, creating respondent as an interstate agency to regulate development in the Lake Tahoe basin. See *Lake Country Estates, Inc. v. Tahoe Regional Planning Agency*, 440 U.S. 391, 394, 99 S.Ct. 1171, 1173, 59 L.Ed.2d 401 (1979). After the 1969 compact had proven inadequate for protection of the lake and its environment, the States proposed and Congress approved an amendment in 1980, requiring the agency to adopt a plan barring any development exceeding such specific "environmental threshold carrying capacities" as the agency might find appropriate. Pub.L. 96–551, Arts. I(b), V(b), V(g), 94 Stat. 3234, 3239–3241.

In 1987, the agency adopted a new Regional Plan providing for an "Individual Parcel Evaluation System" (IPES) to rate the suitability of vacant residential parcels for building and other modification. Tahoe Regional Planning Agency Code of Ordinances, ch. 37 (TRPA Code). Whereas any property must attain a minimum IPES score to qualify for construction, *id.*, § 37.8.E; App. 145, an undeveloped parcel in certain areas carrying runoff into the watershed (known as "Stream Environment Zones" (SEZ's)) receives an IPES score of zero, TRPA Code § 37.4.A(3). With limited exceptions not relevant here, the agency permits no "additional land coverage or other permanent land disturbance" on such a parcel. *Id.*, § 20.4.

Although the agency's 1987 plan does not provide for the variances and exceptions of conventional land-use schemes, it addresses the potential sharpness of its restrictions by granting property owners TDR's that may be sold to owners of parcels eligible for construction, *id.*, §§ 20.3.C, 34.0 to 34.3. There are three kinds of residential TDR's. An owner needs both a "Residential Development Right" and a "Residential Allocation" to place a residential unit on a buildable parcel, *id.*, §§ 21.6.C, 33.2.A; the latter permits construction to begin in a specific calendar year, but expires at year's end, *id.*, § 33.2.B(3)(b). An owner must also have "Land Coverage Rights" for each square foot of impermeable cover placed upon land. App. 145; see also TRPA Code, ch. 20. All owners of vacant residential parcels that existed at the effective date of the 1987 plan (July 1, 1987), including SEZ parcels, automatically receive one Residential Development Right, *id.*, § 21.6.A; owners of SEZ property may obtain and transfer bonus points equivalent to three additional Residential Development Rights, *id.*, §§ 35.2.C, 35.2.D. SEZ property owners also receive Land Coverage Rights authorizing coverage of an area equal to 1% of the surface area of their land. *Id.*, §§ 20.3.A, 37.11. Finally, SEZ owners, like other property owners, may apply for a Residential Allocation, awarded by local jurisdictions in random drawings each year. *Id.*, § 33.2.B; App. 98–99. All three kinds of TDR's may be transferred for the benefit of any eligible property in the Lake Tahoe region, subject to approval by the agency based on the eligibility of the receiving parcel for development. TRPA Code §§ 20.3.C, 34.1 to 34.3.

In 1972, Suitum and her late husband bought an undeveloped lot in Washoe County, Nevada, within the agency's jurisdiction, and 17 years later, after adoption of the 1987 Regional Plan, Suitum obtained a Residential Allocation through Washoe County's annual drawing. When she then applied to the agency for permission to construct a house on her lot, the agency determined that her property was located within a SEZ, assigned it an IPES score of zero, and denied permission to build. Suitum appealed the denial to the agency's governing board, which itself denied relief.

After the agency turned down the request for a building permit, Suitum made no effort to transfer any of the TDR's that were hers under the 1987 plan, and there is no dispute that she still has the one Residential Development Right that owners of undeveloped lots automatically received, plus the Land Coverage Rights for 183 square feet that she got as the owner of 18,300 square feet of SEZ land. It is also common ground that Suitum has the right to receive three "bonus" Residential Development Rights. Although Suitum has questioned the certainty that she would obtain a new Residential Allocation if she sought one, the agency has represented to this Court that she undoubtedly[sic] would, see n. 2, *supra*.

Instead, Suitum brought this 42 U.S.C. § 1983 action alleging that in denying her the right to construct a house on her lot, the agency's restrictions deprived her of "all reasonable and economically viable use" of her property, and so amounted to a taking of her property without just compensation in violation of the Fifth and Fourteenth Amendments. App. 15, 16. The agency responded by objecting, among other things, that Suitum's takings claim was not ripe due to her "failure to obtain a final decision by TRPA as to the amount of development * * * that may be allowed by" the agency. *Id.*, at 10. On cross-motions for summary judgment, the District Court ordered supplemental briefing on the nature of Suitum's TDR's, including "what [TDR's] can be transferred in [Suitum's] case and the procedures, prerequisites and value of such transfer as applicable in this case." *Id.*, at 89. The agency introduced an affidavit from a real estate appraiser, whose opinion was that the Residential Development Right that Suitum already has, and the three more to which she is entitled, have a market value between $1,500 and $2,500 each; that her Land Coverage Rights can be sold for $6 to $12 per square foot ($1,098–$2,196 total); and that her lot devoid of all TDR's would sell for $7,125 to $16,750. *Id.*, at 131–132. The appraiser also said that if Suitum were to obtain a Residential Allocation and sell it with a Development Right, together they would bring between $30,000 and $35,000. *Ibid.* As if in spite of the figures supplied by its own affidavit, however, the agency maintained that the "*actual* benefits of the [TDR] program for [Suitum] * * * can only be known if she pursues an appropriate [transfer] application," with the result that Suitum's claim was not ripe for adjudication. *Id.*, at 91. For her part, Suitum insisted that trying to transfer her TDR's would be an " 'idle and futile act' " because the TDR program is a "sham," and she supplied the affidavit of one of the agency's former employees whose view was that "there is little to no value to [Suitum's TDR's] at the present time as * * * either [there is] no market for them or the procedure for transferring one particular right would restrict the opportunity to transfer a remaining right." *Id.*, at 135.

* * *

The only issue presented is whether Suitum's claim of a regulatory taking of her land in violation of the Fifth and Fourteenth Amendments is ready for judicial review under prudential ripeness principles. * * *

The agency nonetheless argued below, and the lower courts agreed, see *supra*, at 1664, that there remains a "final decision" for the agency to make: action on a possible application by Suitum to transfer the TDR's to which she is indisputably entitled. This is not, however, the type of "final decision" required by our *Williamson County* precedents. Those precedents addressed the virtual impossibility of determining what development will be permitted on a particular lot of land when its use is subject to the decision of a regulatory body invested with great discretion, which it has not yet even been asked to exercise. No such question is presented here. The parties agree on the particular TDR's to which Suitum is entitled, and no discretionary decision must be made by any agency official for her to obtain them or to offer them for sale. The only decision left to the agency is approval of a particular transfer of TDR's to make certain that a given potential buyer may lawfully use them. But whether a particular sale of TDR's may be completed is quite different from whether TDR's are salable; so long as the particular buyer is not the only person who can lawfully buy, the rights would not be rendered unsalable even if the agency were to make a discretionary decision to kill a particular sale. And the class of buyers is not even arguably so limited here, where there is no question so far as the law is concerned that TDR's may be bought and used for the benefit of all sorts of land parcels and lots.

The agency's argument that Suitum's case is not ripe because no "'values attributable to [Suitum's TDR's] are known,'" Brief for Respondent 23 (quoting No. CV-N-91-040-ECR (D.Nev., Mar. 30, 1994, App. to Pet. for Cert. C-4), is just a variation on the preceding position, and fares no better. First, as to Suitum's rights to receive TDR's that she may later sell, we have already noted that little or no uncertainty remains. Although the value of a Residential Development Right may well be greater if it is offered together with a Residential Allocation, and although Suitum must still enter the lottery for the latter, there is no discretionary decision to be made in determining whether she will get one; in fact, the probability of her getting one is "100 percent" according to the agency, see Tr. of Oral Arg. 40, since there are fewer applications than available allocations, see *id.*, at 39–40. But even if that were not the case, as it probably will not always be, it would be unreasonable to require Suitum to enter the drawing in order to ripen her suit. The agency does not, and surely could not, maintain that if the odds of success in the allocation lottery were low, Suitum's takings claim could be kept at bay from year to year until she actually won the drawing; such a rule would allow any local authority to stultify the Fifth Amendment's guarantee. Rather, in such circumstances, the value attributable to the allocation Suitum might or might not receive in the drawing would simply be discounted to reflect the mathematical likelihood of her obtaining one.

Second, as to Suitum's right to transfer her TDR's, the only contingency apart from private market demand turns on the right of the agency to deny approval for a specific transfer on grounds that the buyer's use of the TDR's would violate the terms of the scheme or other local land-use regulation, and the right of a local regulatory body to deny transfer approval for the latter reason. See TRPA Code §§ 20.3.C, 34.2, 34.3. But even if these potential bars based on a buyer's intended use of TDR's should turn out to involve the same degree of discretion assumed in the *Williamson County* ripeness requirement, that discretion still would not render the value of the TDR's nearly as unknowable as the chances of particular development being permitted on a particular parcel in the absence of a zoning board decision that could quite lawfully be either yes or no. While a particular sale is subject to approval, salability is not, and the agency's own position assumes that there are many potential, lawful buyers for Suitum's TDR's, whose receipt of those rights would unquestionably be approved.

The valuation of Suitum's TDR's is therefore simply an issue of fact about possible market prices, and one on which the District Court had considerable evidence before it, see *supra*, at 1663–1664. Of course, as the agency appears to be saying, see, *e.g.*, Brief for Respondent 22–23, the very best evidence of the value of Suitum's TDR's might be their actual selling price (assuming, of course, that the sale were made in good faith and at arm's length). But similar determinations of market value are routinely made in judicial proceedings without the benefit of a market transaction in the subject property. See, *e.g., United States v. 819.98 Acres of Land, More or Less, Located in Wasatch and Summit Counties*, 78 F.3d 1468, 1469–1470 (C.A.10 1996) (upholding valuation of condemned land based on expert testimony relating to comparable sales and discounted cash flow); *United States v. L.E. Cooke Co.*, 991 F.2d 336, 338–339 (C.A.6 1993) (same with respect to valuation of mineral rights leases); see also 5 J. Sackman, Nichols' Law of Eminent Domain § 23–01, p. 23–6 (rev. 3d ed. 1997) ("[I]t is well established that the value of * * * land taken or injured by the exercise of the power of eminent domain may be shown by opinion evidence"); see generally 4 *id.*, § 12.02 (discussing establishment of market value of condemned land). While it is true that market value may be hard to calculate without a regular trade in TDR's, if Suitum is ready to proceed in spite of this difficulty, ripeness doctrine does not block her. In fact, the reason for the agency's objection is probably a concern that without much market experience in sales of TDR's, their market values will get low estimates. But this is simply one of the risks of regulatory pioneering, and the pioneer here is the agency, not Suitum.

* * *

Because we find that Suitum has received a "final decision" consistent with *Williamson County's* ripeness requirement, we vacate the judgment of the Court of Appeals and remand for further proceedings consistent with this opinion.

It is so ordered.

Notes

1. In Suitum, the regulatory agency prevented all development on the property owner's lot which was located in a critical environmental area of national importance. If this is found to be a regulatory taking, is it possible that the Court could find that the TDR credits to which Suitum is entitled are adequate compensation for that taking?

2. In Fred F. French Investing Co., Inc. v. City of New York, 39 N.Y.2d 587, 350 N.E.2d 381, 385 N.Y.S.2d 5 (1976), the Court of Appeals declared that the city was unable to use the transfer development rights (TDR) of airspace from the regulated parcel to other receiving areas as a means of validating the rezoning of the petitioner's land as a public park. The court noted that the development rights that were transferred had a "value so uncertain and contingent, as to deprive the property owner of their practical usefulness." Notwithstanding the ineffectiveness of the TDR mechanism in this context, the court held that a TDR provision "may not be disregarded in determining whether the ordinance has destroyed the economic value of the underlying property."

3. TDR is used in a number of smart growth contexts where the goal is to shift zoned development potential conservation areas, as in Suitum, to more appropriate areas for development. In 1999, an Oregon law was adopted that creates a transferable development credit. The statute allows municipalities to establish receiving locations for denser development using these credits to conform to land use planning goals of the Oregon growth management statute. Consider the Dover, Maryland, Zoning Code, § 170-27.2. Transfer of Development Rights enacted to protect areas of high conservation value by concentrating development in appropriate areas and protecting land in areas with high natural resource values. [Added 10-31-90 by Ord. No. 16-90; amended 01-22-03 by Ord. 35-02] The City of Seattle and King County, Washington, have entered into an interlocal agreement and adopted local laws to establish a program of transferring development rights from rural unincorporated King County to downtown Seattle. The agreement acknowledges that there are mutual benefits to the City and the County in preserving the natural environment in rural King County, particularly by helping protect salmon species which are a federally listed threatened species. King County Ordinance 13274 and Ordinance 13974 and Seattle Ordinance 119365.

H. OVERLAY ZONING DISTRICTS

Overlay zoning can be used to protect large-scale critical environmental areas from development or to promote growth in areas that support higher density development. A simple strategy for achieving smart growth in a community is to identify one or two conservation overlay zones and one or two development overlay zones and implement them at the same time.

Overlay zoning is a flexible alternative to traditional zoning. To create an overlay zone, a mapped district is superimposed on one or more established zoning districts. Property within the overlay district is then subject to two sets of regulations and stipulations: those contained in the underlying zoning district provisions and those provided for by the overlay zone itself. Communities may create overlay zones as a smart growth strategy both to encourage appropriate development in a designated development district and to protect critical natural resource areas, such as a watershed or a large landscape, or important natural features, such as steep slopes, wildlife habitats, or wetlands. Overlay districts can also be used to protect and enhance urban neighborhoods and historic districts in all communities.

In Franchise Developers, Inc. v. City of Cincinnati, 30 Ohio St.3d 28, 505 N.E.2d 966 (1987), the Supreme Court of Ohio upheld the denial of a permit for a Wendy's restaurant in a commercial neighborhood designated for preservation and enhancement. The city council had adopted an overlay zone, called an environmental quality district, with special standards designed to prevent businesses from locating in designated urban neighborhoods where the characteristics of the environment are of significant public value and are vulnerable to damage by development permitted under conventional zoning. The court found support for the denial in the city's adopted Urban Design Plan which provided that fast food restaurants were not appropriate in this district. By reading the underlying zoning provisions, the standards of the environmental quality district, and the adopted plan together, the court found that the property owner was put on notice of the restriction and that the restriction, plan, and ordinance accomplished a valid public purpose of preserving the quality of this urban neighborhood.

Albuquerque, New Mexico, created a Historic Overlay Zone and an Urban Conservation Overlay Zone as a means of preserving areas that have high artistic value. Areas in the Historical Overlay are suitable for preservation for historical, architectural, or cultural reasons. Areas in the Urban Conservation Overlay have "distinctive characteristics that are worthy of conservation." For both types of overlay district the ordinance requires that the city council identify the area's distinctive characteristics and general preservation guidelines. Specific development guidelines must be adopted by the landmarks and urban conservation commission, which must also issue a certificate of appropriateness before any development activity begins. An application for an Urban Conservation Overlay can be made only by property owners in the area where the overlay is applied. Fifty-one percent of those property owners must agree in writing to the application before it can be submitted.

Development overlay zones are targeted for infrastructure expansion, urban park development, incentive zoning, traditional neighborhood district zoning, transfer of development rights, floating zones, and other programs that support appropriate development patterns. Local zoning can designate these development zones as the receiving districts under a TDR program and as eligible areas for bonus densities under incentive zoning. Supplemental design regulations can be adopted and recreational facilities targeted to ensure the quality of the denser development districts.

The overlay district is most often used as a technique for conserving fragile natural resources. The underlying zoning may permit the subdivision of all land in such an area for residential purposes—a plan that, without further safeguards, might destroy the natural resource. To accomplish a more appropriate land use pattern, an overlay district can be adopted that contains special clustering, setback provisions, or other standards that protect environmentally constrained areas. In conservation overlay districts, additional standards must be met to protect identified environmental assets.

If wildlife habitat is to be protected in an overlay district, for example, the provisions of the overlay zone will require that habitat areas are to be designated and that development of an affected parcel is to be regulated to avoid harm to the habitat. Quite often this is done by requiring developments that affect protected resources to secure a special permit. The special permit will contain conditions that protect the natural features by the way that buildings and improvements are located on the site. Additional provisions can be added to the overlay district's standards that are not typically found in zoning ordinances, such as provisions for grading or for landscape restoration, or limitations on the development of steep slopes. Consider the approach taken by the municipal regulator in the next principal case.

GLISSON v. ALACHUA COUNTY

District Court of Appeal of Florida, First District, 1990.
558 So.2d 1030.

JOANOS, JUDGE.

This appeal concerns land use regulations adopted by the Alachua County Board of County Commissioners which will impact on appellants' future use of their property.

* * *

Pursuant to the provisions of its comprehensive plan, Alachua County designated the Cross Creek region as a special study area. The Cross Creek Special Study Area includes 3,100 acres lying on either side of Cross Creek, between Orange Lake and Lake Lochloosa in southeast Alachua County. The area contains the site of the Marjorie Kinnan Rawlings house (a State of Florida Historic Site). There is little development in the area, and it is surrounded by the Lochloosa Wildlife Management Area and the two lakes. The two lakes and the Cross Creek body of water have been designated as Outstanding Florida Waters. *See* § 403.061(27)(a), Fla.Stat. (1987).

Appellants are eighteen landowners in the Cross Creek Special Study Area. Their holdings range from less than one acre to 522 acres, held by Mr. Ernest Southward, as trustee for several investors in the property. Appellants Southward and Brown purchased property in the Cross Creek area for development purposes. Other appellants are long-term residents or property owners in or near Cross Creek.

On August 13, 1985, the Alachua County Board of County Commissioners adopted CPA–5–85 as an amendment to the Alachua County Comprehensive Plan. The amendment established specific development guidelines for the Cross Creek area, and was the culmination of the special study of the Cross Creek area. The study contained three general sets of guidelines or policies for the Village Center development area and the Village periphery development area, four resource protection areas, and general development guidelines. The resource protection areas are the wetlands, exceptional upland habitat, hammock zones, and active use zones.

The wetland areas are restricted from all construction activity, except minor accessory uses. Under the regulations, permitted density could be transferred at a rate of one unit per five acres, where there was appropriate contiguous property under the same ownership. Areas designated as exceptional upland habitat are considered conservation areas, where only one dwelling unit per five acres is permitted. Lot sizes are reduced to one acre and the remaining four acres of the area are to be protected in their natural state. Removal of the existing indigenous vegetation is discouraged, except for bona fide agricultural practices on existing farm lands. The hammock zones are designated as areas which will serve as wildlife habitats of secondary value and generally act as transitional zones to buffer the conservation areas. In the Village periphery, one dwelling unit per five acres is permitted on lot sizes of one acre, clustered so as to preserve the most sensitive or unique areas. The active use zones are designated as areas having comparatively little ecological value, and will be the focus of future development. No active use is permitted within a radius of 750 feet of an eagle nest. Within an additional 750 feet, all residential density has to be transferred to appropriate contiguous property under the same ownership.

CPA–5–85 existed without change or amplification until December 22, 1987, when the Commission adopted Ordinance 87–25. Ordinance 87–25 modified CPA–5–85 by adding provisions for variance applications and created a system for transfer of development rights (TDR's) within the study area to qualifying property within an urban cluster. Under CPA–5–85, if TDR's were issued, they could only be used outside the Cross Creek area, because no urban cluster is located in Cross Creek. With the passage of Ordinance 87–25 two years later, a property owner could transfer density in a restricted use zone to appropriate contiguous property under the same ownership, or to appropriate adjoining property not under the same ownership if all the affected properties were presented for development as a planned unit development (PUD).

Evidence adduced at trial indicated that the areas designated as exceptional upland habitat and hammock are found throughout Alachua County, and are not unique to the Cross Creek area. In addition, there was evidence that many of these areas had been disturbed, either by timbering or by agricultural activities, and that only six of the forty-five active eagles' nests in Alachua County are located in the Cross Creek area. Expert testimony indicated that farming, and cattle grazing are not economically feasible in the Cross Creek area. According to the expert witness, the restrictions imposed under Ordinance 87–25 and CPA–5–85 make it unlikely that a prospective buyer would consider purchasing the property for agricultural purposes. In addition, testimony from a land planner and developer indicated that the value of the individual parcels of property in Cross Creek had been seriously reduced as a result of Ordinance 87–25, and that individual property owners had been denied beneficial uses of their property. The record reflects that appellants Southward, Glisson, and Brown expended varying sums of money prior to passage of CPA–5–85 to prepare their land for residential development. Although Mr. Glisson's plan had received conceptual approval, after passage of CPA–5–85, he was advised by the County Attorney's office that conceptual approval did not entitle a property owner to obtain a permit of any kind. Due to the advice he received from the county attorney, and his personal knowledge of the unsuccessful development approval efforts of Mr. Southward and Mr. Brown, Mr. Glisson considered that any further expenditures for obtaining development permits would be futile.

The county agrees that appellants' property located in the special study area would be more valuable if appellants were free to develop it for use as recreational vehicle and mobile home parks, condominiums, or at suburban intensities. On the other hand, the record reflects that only one appellant has applied for development approval since the adoption of CPA-5-85, and that his application was approved, and the subdivided lots were sold for a substantial sum.

* * *

The first issue concerns appellants' contention that the land use regulations promulgated by the county constitute an attempt to exercise the power of eminent domain, disguised as an exercise of the police power. In support of this contention, appellants assert that the language of the comprehensive plan amendments and zoning ordinance 87-25, together with trial testimony concerning specific details of the regulations and their impact on appellants' property, demonstrate that the Cross Creek plan constitutes the creation of a "public benefit." Appellants further assert that the evidence demonstrates that the boundaries for application of the Cross Creek plan were drawn on the assumption that the state would buy and preserve the surrounding area, and restrictions were accordingly imposed in the Cross Creek area to conform land uses in the area to those uses in the surrounding areas which are under state ownership. In essence, appellants contend that as owners of property in the Cross Creek area, they are entitled to compensation because the regulations require them to maintain the status quo with regard to present uses of their property, in order to preserve an area as a benefit to be enjoyed by the public at large.

At the outset, it is well settled that the state may, by regulation or condemnation, restrict the use of private property. The fifth amendment was not designed "to limit the governmental interference with property rights per se, but rather to secure compensation in the event of otherwise proper interference amounting to a taking." *First English Evangelical Lutheran Church of Glendale v. County of Los Angeles, Cal.*, 482 U.S. 304, 107 S.Ct. 2378, 2386, 96 L.Ed.2d 250 (1987). *See also Department of Agriculture v. Mid–Florida Growers, Inc.*, 521 So.2d 101, 103 (Fla.), *cert. denied*, 488 U.S. 870, 109 S.Ct. 180, 102 L.Ed.2d 149 (1988). There is no set formula or test for determining where legitimate government regulation ends and taking begins, in the sense that the regulation has gone too far. *MacDonald, Sommer & Frates v. Yolo County*, 477 U.S. 340, 106 S.Ct. 2561, 2566, 91 L.Ed.2d 285 (1986); *Penn Central Transportation Co. v. New York City*, 438 U.S. 104, 124, 98 S.Ct. 2646, 2659, 57 L.Ed.2d 631 (1978); *Goldblatt v. Hempstead*, 369 U.S. 590, 594, 82 S.Ct. 987, 990, 8 L.Ed.2d 130 (1962); *Graham v. Estuary Properties, Inc.*, 399 So.2d 1374, 1380 (Fla.), *cert. denied, sub nom., Taylor v. Graham*, 454 U.S. 1083, 102 S.Ct. 640, 70 L.Ed.2d 618 (1981). Not surprisingly, the difficulty has always been in defining "too far," i.e., in distinguishing "the point at which regulation becomes so onerous that it has the same effect as an appropriation of the property through eminent domain or physical possession." *MacDonald, Sommer & Frates v. Yolo County,* 106 S.Ct. at 2566. "The general rule * * * is that while property may be regulated to a certain extent, if regulation goes too far it will be recognized as a taking." *Pennsylvania Coal Co. v. Mahon,* 260 U.S. 393, 43 S.Ct. 158, 160, 67 L.Ed. 322 (1922).

The propriety of a land use regulation which requires a property owner to maintain the status quo with respect to land use was decided adversely to appellants' position in *Graham v. Estuary Properties, Inc.* In *Graham,* the court reaffirmed the rule that the "exercise of the state's police power must relate to health, safety, and welfare of the public and may not be arbitrarily and capriciously applied." 399 So.2d at 1379. See also *Sarasota County v. Barg,* 302 So.2d 737, 741 (Fla.1974); *Davis v. Sails,* 318 So.2d 214, 217 (Fla. 1st DCA 1975); *City of Sunrise v. D.C.A. Homes, Inc.,* 421 So.2d 1084, 1085 (Fla. 4th DCA 1982); *Moviematic Industries Corp. v. Board of County Commissioners of Metropolitan Dade County,* 349 So.2d 667, 669 (Fla. 3d DCA 1977). The issue in *Graham* was whether the denial of an application for approval of a development of regional impact (DRI) constituted a taking. The permit was denied primarily to prevent the destruction of a large mangrove forest as called for by the development plan. The court reviewed the question primarily on the basis of a harm-benefit test involving the following factors:

(1) whether there has been a physical invasion of the property;

(2) the diminution in value of the property, i.e., whether the regulation precludes all economically reasonable use of the property;

(3) whether the regulation confers a public benefit or prevents a public harm;

(4) whether the regulation promotes the health, safety, welfare, or morals of the public;

(5) whether the regulation was applied arbitrarily and capriciously; and

(6) the extent to which the regulation has curtailed investment-backed expectations.

Graham, 399 So.2d at 1380–1381.

In *Graham,* the court held that the restrictions on development constituted a valid exercise of the police power. The court concluded that denial of a DRI permit prevented a public harm in that the proposed development would pollute the surrounding bays. While recognizing the public would be benefited because the bays would remain clean, the benefit was not deemed compensable because it was "in the form of maintaining the status quo." *Graham,* 399 So.2d at 1382.

The interests purportedly protected by the regulations at issue in this case are appropriate subjects for exercise of the police power. For example, among the interests deemed legitimate for exercise of the state's police power are such matters as: (1) protection of aesthetic interests, *City of Sunrise v. D.C.A. Homes,* 421 So.2d at 1085, *Moviematic v. County Commissioners,* 349 So.2d at 669; (2) preservation of residential or historical character of a neighborhood, *Moviematic,* 349 So.2d at 669; and (3) protection of environmentally sensitive areas and pollution control, *Graham v. Estuary Properties,* 399 So.2d at 1381; *Moviematic,* 349 So.2d at 669. Under certain circumstances, a regulation may meet the standards necessary for exercise of the police power, but still result in a taking which requires compensation. *See Department of Agriculture v. Mid–Florida Growers,* 521 So.2d at 103; *Dade County v. National Bulk Carriers, Inc.,* 450 So.2d 213, 215 (Fla.1984); *Joint Ventures v. Department of Transportation,* 519 So.2d 1069, 1070 (Fla. 1st DCA 1988).

To succeed in a regulatory taking claim, a property owner must demonstrate (1) that a regulation is unreasonable or arbitrary, or (2) that it denies a substantial portion of the beneficial use of the property. *Joint Ventures v. Department of Transportation,* 519 So.2d at 1070. *See also Nollan v. California Coastal Commission,* 483 U.S. 825, 107 S.Ct. 3141, 97 L.Ed.2d 677 (1987); *First English Evangelical Lutheran Church v. Los Angeles County,* 107 S.Ct. at 2386; *MacDonald, Sommer & Frates v. Yolo County,* 106 S.Ct. at 2566; *Herrington v. Sonoma County,* 834 F.2d 1488, 1497 (9th Cir.1987), *cert. denied,* 489 U.S. 1090, 109 S.Ct. 1557, 103 L.Ed.2d 860 (1989). A police power regulation is not invalid simply because it denies the highest and best use of the property, *Penn Central Transportation Co. v. New York City,* 438 U.S. 104, 125, 98 S.Ct. 2646, 2659–2660, 57 L.Ed.2d 631 (1978); *Goldblatt v. Town of Hempstead,* 369 U.S. 590, 82 S.Ct. 987, 8 L.Ed.2d 130 (1962); *Graham v. Estuary Properties,* 399 So.2d at 1382, or because it dramatically diminishes the value of the property. *Hadacheck v. Sebastian,* 239 U.S. 394, 36 S.Ct. 143, 60 L.Ed. 348 (1915); *Graham v. Estuary Properties,* 399 So.2d at 1382. Rather, "[i]f the regulation is a valid exercise of the police power, it is not a taking if a reasonable use of the property remains." *Agins v. City of Tiburon,* 447 U.S. 255, 100 S.Ct. 2138, 2141, 65 L.Ed.2d 106 (1980); *American Savings & Loan Association v. Marin County,* 653 F.2d 364, 368 (9th Cir.1981).

Courts considering the police power/taking dichotomy have held that a taking issue is not ripe for determination until such time as the property owner has received a final determination from the government as to the permissible uses of the property. *Joint Ventures v. Department of Transportation,* 519 So.2d at 1073–1074, J. Ervin, specially concurring; *Moviematic,* 349 So.2d at 671. *See also MacDonald, Sommer & Frates v. Yolo County,* 106 S.Ct. at 2566. In other words, "an essential prerequisite to a taking claim is a final decision by the government as to what use of the property will be allowed." *MacDonald, Sommer & Frates,* 106 S.Ct. at 2566; *Unity Ventures v. Lake County,* 841 F.2d 770, 774 (7th Cir.1988). A final decision may be shown by (1) a rejected development plan, and (2) a denial of a variance. *Unity Ventures,* 841 F.2d 770, 774 (7th Cir.1988); *Kinzli v. City of Santa Cruz,* 818 F.2d 1449

(9th Cir.1987), *cert. denied,* 484 U.S. 1043, 108 S.Ct. 775, 98 L.Ed.2d 861 (1988). Although the final decision prerequisite also may be satisfied by proof that attempts to comply would be futile, futility is not established until at least one meaningful application has been filed. *Unity Ventures,* 841 F.2d at 775; *Kinzli,* 818 F.2d at 1454.

Where, as in the instant case, a taking claim arises in the context of a facial challenge rather than in the context of a concrete controversy concerning the effect of a regulation on a specific parcel of land, the only issue is whether the mere enactment of the regulation constitutes a taking. *Keystone Bituminous Coal Association v. DeBenedictis,* 480 U.S. 470, 107 S.Ct. 1232, 1247, 94 L.Ed.2d 472 (1987); *Agins v. City of Tiburon,* 100 S.Ct. at 2141. The test to be applied in considering a facial challenge is relatively straightforward, i.e., "[a] statute regulating the uses that can be made of property effects a taking if it 'denies an owner economically viable use of his land. * * * ' " *Keystone Bituminous Coal Association v. DeBenedictis,* 107 S.Ct. at 1247, quoting *Hodel v. Virginia Surface Mining and Reclamation Assn., Inc.,* 452 U.S. 264, 101 S.Ct. 2352, 69 L.Ed.2d 1 (1981). In determining whether a development restriction denies a landowner economically viable use of his property, the focus is on the existence of permissible uses. *Hodel v. Virginia Surface Mining and Reclamation Act; Agins v. City of Tiburon; Lake Nacimiento Ranch Co. v. San Luis Obispo County,* 830 F.2d 977, 982 (9th Cir.1987). To prevail, the landowner must show that there is no available beneficial use of his property under the land use ordinance. *Nacimiento,* 830 F.2d at 982. *See also Penn Central,* 98 S.Ct. at 2662.

* * * Application of the test for determining the facial validity of a regulation demonstrates that in this case, the contested regulations substantially advance legitimate state interests, in that the regulations are directed to protection of the environment and preservation of historic areas. Furthermore, because the regulations permit most existing uses of the property, and provide a mechanism whereby individual landowners may obtain a variance or a transfer of development rights, the regulations on their face do not deny individual landowners all economically viable uses of their property. The county concedes that the regulations have diminished the value of appellants' property by restricting some of the more economically rewarding uses to which the property may be put. However, diminution in value of the property is not the test. Rather, it is incumbent upon appellants to demonstrate that they have been denied all or a substantial portion of the beneficial uses of their property, and this they have failed to do.

Furthermore, we note that the "status quo" test set forth in *Graham v. Estuary Properties* imposes a more stringent test for recovery than the traditional balancing test. *See,* generally, *Keystone Bituminous Coal Association v. DeBenedictis; City of Miami Beach v. Ocean & Inland Co.,* 147 Fla. 480, 3 So.2d 364 (1941). In *Graham,* the court determined that reducing the amount of the property to be developed by one-half, did not so diminish the value of the property or the owner's investment-backed expectations as to render the exercise of the police power unreasonable. On the basis of the record before us, even if a proposed development plan had been pursued to a final determination, it is arguable whether under *Graham,* appellants could show a sufficient diminution in value or loss of investment-backed expectations, to warrant a finding that the contested land use regulations are unreasonable, hence invalid.

* * *

In summary, we conclude that the challenged amendments and regulations are not facially unconstitutional, and that the amendments and regulations properly address conservation concerns, as mandated by section 163.3177(6)(d), Florida Statutes (1987). Furthermore, the new restrictions on their face do not constitute a taking. However, since the restrictions have not been applied to a specific land use proposal, the taking issue cannot be determined as a factual matter. Accordingly, the amended final judgment is affirmed in all respects.

ERVIN and BARFIELD, JJ., concur.

Notes

1. What precisely were the appellant landowners upset about in the principal case? How was their land zoned prior to the adoption of the 1985 and 1987 amendments of their land use plan and regulations? How did these amendments change their rights to develop their property? How are the standards created for protecting the special study area apply and how do they relate to the standards contained in the underlying zoning provisions?

2. In the principal case, notice how the County Commissioners, by adding variance and Transfer of Development Rights features, successfully anticipated the owners' claim that the establishment of the special study area and its implementing provisions constituted a regulatory taking.

3. The Upland Preservation Overlay district adopted by Brookfield, Wisconsin, is intended to preserve "all significant woodlands, wildlife habitat areas, areas of rough topography and related scenic areas." In addition to maintaining "the natural beauty of the city," the overlay is intended to control erosion and sedimentation and to maintain water quality. The ordinance contains a deed restriction on subdivision plats prohibiting the erection of structures, the removal of vegetation, and any filling or excavating of land within the overlay, which runs with the land in perpetuity. (Brookfield, WI, Municipal Code § 17.96).

4. Limington, Maine, includes an Endangered Species and Critical Areas Overlay in its zoning ordinance to protect plants, fish, and animals in areas identified by the state as habitat for endangered species and for certain waterfowl, wading birds, and shorebirds, as spawning areas for Atlantic salmon, and as deer wintering areas. Except for non-intensive recreational uses, new structures and uses within the overlay require a conditional use permit. A report by a wildlife biologist on the probable effects of the proposed use on habitat and species may be required with as part of the permit application. (Limington, ME, Zoning Ordinance § 6.6.1).

5. The Town of Wallingford, Connecticut's zoning regulations contain two overlay districts that protect hydrological features of the local environment. These include an Aquifer Protection District and a Watershed Protection District. The regulations state that the Aquifer Protection District "shall be superimposed over the primary and secondary recharge areas of the Quinnipiac River Aquifer and the Muddy River Aquifer and all regulations, requirements, and controls of this section shall be in addition to the standard regulations of the underlying zoning district." The Watershed Protection District provisions state that its purpose is "to provide for additional standards for permitted uses of the underlying district in order to protect and maintain the surface waters of the Wallingford Public Water Supply Watershed to a quality consistent with its use as a primary drinking water source for the Town." (Town of Wallingford, CT, Zoning Regulations, § 4.12 B and 4.13 A).

6. Douglas County, Oregon, has adopted a series of overlays to protect specific natural resources: a Mineral Resources Overlay Development Ordinance; a Riparian Vegetation Corridor Overlay; a Peripheral Big Game Habitat Overlay; a Columbian White–Tailed Deer Habitat Overlay; and a Special Bird Habitat Overlay. Douglas County, OR, Land Use and Development Ordinances § 3.32.100. In Benton County, Oregon, a Sensitive Fish and Wildlife Habitat Overlay was applied to areas not protected by other state or local programs where sensitive nesting, roosting, or watering sites have been identified. The overlay applies "to all northern bald eagle nests and roosts, spotted owl nests, osprey nests, great blue heron rookeries, and band-tailed pigeon mineral springs." (Benton County, OR, Development Code, ch. 87).

I. INCENTIVE ZONING

Under the law of several states, local legislatures may allow developers to build at densities greater than those permitted by the existing zoning in exchange for public benefits such as the provision of affordable housing or the preservation of open space. Incentives may also include waivers of setback, lot coverage, and height requirements. In some of these states, the public benefits that municipalities may receive in exchange for zoning are broadly defined. Some states, such as California, Florida, New Jersey, and Oregon, enable localities to provide incentives for affordable housing as part of a statewide housing program. Maryland's incentive zoning enabling statute, permits localities to encourage innovation and promote flexibility, economy, and ingenuity in development and, to this end, to award developers incentives in the form of increased density.

In New York, communities used the standard zoning enabling statute to award incentives for affordable housing years before the legislature adopted a broad enabling act making it clear that localities can use bonus density incentives and waive all dimensional requirements of zoning codes in exchange for a broad range of public benefits, including infrastructure, open space, day care, and affordable housing. The Town of LaGrange, New York for example, awards a 40 percent density bonus when a developer promises to preserve 80 percent of a site for farming purposes. LaGrange, New York, Code ch. 100, art. III, § 100–31C(3). Most often the public benefits received for the incentives awarded are provide directly by the developer as part of the development itself. The New York statute allows communities to receive cash payments in exchange for zoning incentives awarded a developer. This allows localities to use the cash to achieve the public benefit directly. Under this authority, it is possible for the community to purchase development rights, or conservation easements, on valuable open land with the cash contributed by a developer who is granted zoning incentives to build in an appropriate location that can absorb the development impacts.

The City of Suffolk, Virginia, uses incentive zoning to conserve natural resources. Located in the southeast corner of the state along the James River, the city contains 430 square miles of land that includes woods, lakes, rivers, and rolling terrain. Under the city's incentive zoning ordinance, developers may receive density bonuses—in some instances up to 140 percent of the existing density—in exchange for providing a variety of public amenities. Density bonuses may be provided for the creation of public parks; the preservation of open space, agricultural land, or critical environmental areas; the construction of retirement housing; the redevelopment of existing commercial strip centers; the construction of traditional neighborhood development; or clustering. Determination of the density bonus is based upon a formula established under the city's Unified Development Ordinance. Unified Development Ordinance of the City of Suffolk, Virginia, § 31–409.

To obtain the density bonuses provided for by the Unified Development Ordinance, the developer of a parcel must obtain a conditional use permit. § 31–409(a)(3). This requires that the developer submit a conditional use permit application to the city's planning commission. Once the application is complete, the planning commission reviews the application and provides its recommendation to the city council. The city council then holds a public hearing on the permit. Before granting approval for the permit, the city council must be satisfied that the increase in density will not adversely affect the health, safety, or comfort of persons living or working in the neighborhood and that it has no greater impact on the neighborhood than any other use generally permitted in the same district. § 31–306.

In two neighboring communities in New York, incentive zoning is being used as a means of encouraging development in appropriate locations while protecting valuable farmland. The Village and the Town of Warwick, which have independent zoning authority, have entered into an intermunicipal agreement regarding the annexation of land by the village, the use of floating zoning, and the provision of incentive zoning to preserve farmland in the town that lies in the village's watershed and viewshed. Under the agreement, land annexed by the village is brought into the village and its water and sewer district at the same density permitted by town's three-acre single-family zone. A floating zone, allowing densities up to three units per acre, is available upon application by the developer of the annexed land. The floating zone is created as an incentive zone; developers are required to pay $50,000 per unit for each bonus housing unit made possible by the application of the zone to the land. This money is paid into a dedicated trust fund, jointly administered by the village and town. Nearly all of the funds will be used to purchase development rights on farmland in the town, much of it in proximity to the village. This illustrates the creative combination of incentive zoning, annexation, intermunicipal cooperation, and floating zoning to meet the common interests of both communities.

Notes

1. Municipal Arts Society of New York v. Koch, 137 Misc.2d 832, 522 N.Y.S.2d 800, (Sup. Ct. N.Y. County 1987), determined that the cash sale of a zoning bonus was an unacceptable application of incentive zoning. "The Coliseum is located in a zone which permits construction as-of-right of floor space up to a maximum of 15 times the square footage of the lot. This [density] is subject to being increased by up to 20% in exchange for the developer agreeing to 'provide major improvements for the adjacent subway stations' provided that 'the zoning lot for the development * * * which a [density] bonus is requested shall be adjacent to the mezzanine or concourse of the subway station for which the improvement is proposed or an existing connecting passageway to the station.'" 137 Misc.2d at 833. Under the development agreement between the city and the developer, the city would be "obtaining not only $35 to $40 million of local subway improvements, but an additional $57 million to be employed for other purposes." Id., at 832. The court determined that the sale was inappropriate because the cash payment to be made to the city was to be employed for purposes other than local improvements. The court held that the "government may not place itself in the position of reaping a cash premium because one of its agencies bestows a zoning benefit upon a developer. Zoning benefits are not cash items." Id., at 838.

2. The court in Asian Americans for Equality v. Koch, 72 N.Y.2d 121, 531 N.Y.S.2d 782, 527 N.E.2d 265 (1988), upheld a zoning amendment that created a special use district. The new zoning provided that development in the Special Manhattan Bridge District would be "regulated by a system of bonus points permitting increased density in residential buildings for those developers who agree to: 1) donate space for community facilities such as senior citizen or day care centers, educational facilities; 2) construct low-income dwelling units; or 3) rehabilitate existing substandard housing." 72 N.Y.2d at 122. The plaintiffs argued that the incentive zoning scheme provided greater bonuses for educational and senior citizen facilities than it did for low-income housing. They argued that such housing was necessary to combat the effects of gentrification caused by the creation of the special district and that the zoning discouraged developers from building low-income housing. The court concluded that inducing private developers to provide public benefits involves a complex set of considerations. It held that the plaintiffs had not carried their burden of proving that the bonus scheme was clearly arbitrary or capricious or undertaken for an improper purpose.

Chapter VII

LOCAL ENVIRONMENTAL LAW

SECTION 1. HISTORICAL OVERVIEW

Environmental law was defined originally by federal statutes adopted in the early 1970's such as the Clean Water Act and the Clean Air Act. Within a few years, well over a dozen such laws were adopted and a new era of environmental cleanup and pollution prevention was launched. Uniform standards were created, aggressive enforcement practices were adopted, and federal and state agencies were employed to preserve threatened natural resources and to protect the public health.

The emphasis in the teaching and practice of environmental law has been on the central role of the federal government as the standard-setter and steward of a healthy environment. This focus all but obscures the importance of the role of local governments in environmental protection. Federal agencies have successfully reduced pollution that emanates from "point sources," such as smokestacks and water pipes. But most environmental damage today is caused by "nonpoint source" pollution that results from land uses that are the legal responsibility of municipal governments. Federal attempts to influence local land use control in the interest of abating nonpoint source pollution have been thwarted by a variety of legal, political, and practical obstacles.

During the last two decades, there has been a remarkable but little noticed trend among local governments to adopt laws that protect natural resources and lessen environmental pollution. These local environmental laws exhibit a number of forms. They include local comprehensive plans expressing environmental values, zoning districts created to protect critical environmental areas, environmental standards contained in subdivision and site plan regulations, and stand-alone environmental laws adopted to protect particular natural features such as ridgelines, wetlands, floodplains, stream banks, existing vegetative cover, and forests. Local governments have creatively used a variety of traditional and modern powers that their state legislatures have delegated to them to address locally occurring environmental problems. This phenomenon is seldom studied in environmental law classes despite the critical legal role that localities play in determining the use of the land.

As earlier chapters demonstrate, our nation's legal system gives local governments a key, if not the principal role, in land use regulation. Local governments may adopt master plans, zoning ordinances, and a variety of community-building regulations that provide for their future development. Comprehensive zoning began as a mechanism for protecting public health and safety by separating incompatible land uses from one another. In its application, zoning became design-oriented, focusing on the layout of streets and highways, the location of public buildings, the ability of fire trucks and firefighters to reach and fight fires, the size and bulk requirements that protect property values, and the infrastructure connections that create a workable community.

Subdivision and site plan regulations emerged to complement zoning and help localities implement their physical plans. Such regulations initially concentrated on the creation of safe intersections; the fluid movement of vehicles; the adequacy of road width, curbs, and sidewalks; the siting of buildings; and the prevention of off-site impacts such as flooding. In Golden v. Ramapo, the leading state court case sustaining local growth management ordinances, New York's highest court referred to subdivision control as a mechanism "to guide community development in the directions outlined here, while at the same time encouraging the provision of adequate facilities for the housing, distribution, comfort and convenience of local residents." Golden, 30 N.Y.2d 359, 334 N.Y.S.2d 138, 285 N.E.2d 291, 298 (1972). At their inception, regulatory tools such as subdivision and site plan regulation were not designed to protect natural resources from degradation. This is not to say that land use regulations designed to protect the health of residents do not achieve environmental benefits, as the following case demonstrates.

DE MARS v. TOWN OF BOLTON

Connecticut Supreme Court, 1955.
142 Conn. 580, 115 A.2d 653.

WYNNE, ASSOCIATE JUSTICE.

The zoning commission of the town of Bolton adopted certain changes of the zoning regulations which had been in effect in that town for more than two years. Six residents of the town have appealed from a judgment of the Court of Common Pleas. That court dismissed an appeal by them from the action of the commission in adopting the changes. The question before us is whether the court erred in holding that the commission did not act arbitrarily, illegally, or in abuse of its discretion.

Following is a summary of the facts: Zoning regulations were adopted in the town on August 1, 1951. They provided for a residence zone A, a residence zone B and business zones. Residence zone A includes almost the entire town. Residence zone B relates to that portion of the town known as the Lake Area. This is primarily a colony of summer cottages surrounding a lake in the town, although some of the cottages have been made suitable for all-the-year occupancy. The business zones are small in area, not yet affected by the surge of out-of-town pressures. On April 19, 1954, a hearing was held by the zoning commission on certain proposals which the commission itself had initiated. These had to do primarily with enlarging lot areas by increasing the minimum dimensions of lots, in residence zone A, from 150 feet in width and 200 feet in depth to 200 by 200 feet; in residence zone B, from 75 feet in width and 150 feet in depth to 150 by 150 feet; and in business zones, from 150 feet in width and 200 feet in depth to 200 by 200 feet.

The plaintiffs' appeal is predicated upon three claims: (1) The commission is without power to change existing regulations unless there has been a substantial change in circumstances and conditions since the adoption of the regulations. (2) Where the commission makes amendments or changes on its own initiative, it must introduce at the public hearing sufficient facts to substantiate a valid reason or reasons for the change. (3) The records of the commission must set forth the facts warranting the commission's finding that a change is necessary.

Section 837 of the General Statutes confers upon zoning commissions the power to adopt regulations among other purposes, 'to promote health and the general welfare.' These regulations must be made upon reasonable consideration of the character of the district and its peculiar suitability for particular purposes and with a view to conserving the value of buildings and encouraging the most appropriate use of land throughout the town. They may be amended and changed. Cum.Sup. 1953, § 282c. A zoning authority is endowed with a wide and liberal discretion. *Bartram v. Zoning Commission*, 136 Conn. 89, 96, 68 A.2d 308. This discretion is to be overruled only when the commission has not acted fairly, with proper motives and upon valid reasons. *Mallory v. Town of West Hartford*, 138 Conn. 497, 505, 86 A.2d 668. It is true that ordinarily a change of zone affecting a small area should be made only when there has been a change in conditions or new considerations have arisen since the previous zoning of the area. *Hills v. Zoning Commission*, 139 Conn. 603, 609, 96 A.2d 212, * * *. In the instant case, the change in the regulations affected a substantial part of the town of Bolton. Even if the requirement was applicable, it has been met adequately. Anticipating that the greatest residential use of land in the town was yet to come, the board concluded that larger lot sizes would provide greater area for the disposal of sewage and would increase the distances between sewage disposal areas and the residential water supply. We cannot say that this purpose of the change in the regulations affecting the size of building lots was so unrelated to the public health and welfare as to be unreasonable. *State v. Hillman*, 110 Conn. 92, 100, 105, 147 A. 294; *Strain v. Mims*, 123 Conn. 275, 286, 193 A. 754. Zoning regulations such as the one here concerned have generally been held valid. *Simon v. Town of Needham*, 311 Mass. 560, 564, 42 N.E.2d 516, 141 A.L.R. 688; 1 Yokley, Zoning Law & Practice (2d Ed.) p. 422. The first claim of the plaintiffs is without merit.

The plaintiffs' second and third claims may be considered together. Section 282c of the 1953 Cumulative Supplement provides that "[w]hen-ever a zoning commission shall make any change in a zoning regulation or the boundaries of a zoning district it shall state upon its records the reason why such change is made." See *Levine v. Zoning Board of Appeals*, 124 Conn. 53, 57, 198 A. 173; *Perdue v. Zoning Board of Appeals*, 118 Conn. 174, 179, 171 A. 26; *Grady v. Katz*, 124 Conn. 525, 530, 1 A.2d 137. However, as we pointed out in *Couch v. Zoning Commission*, 141 Conn. 349, 358, 106 A.2d 173, the members of a zoning commission may well be laymen and cannot be expected to set forth the reasons for their action in language which would satisfy the meticulous criticism of a legal expert. The record of the commission shows that the change was made in the light of expected residential growth, in order to provide larger areas for sewage disposal, and by so doing to lessen the danger to the residential water supply. While the reason for the change was not stated as specifically and in as much detail as it could have been, we cannot say that the commission wholly failed to meet the direction given in the statute. In adopting regulations, the commission acts in a legislative capacity. It is by no means confined to a consideration of only such evidence as may be presented to it, and it is not required to disclose at the public hearing the information upon which it will act. It is entitled to take into consideration facts which may have been learned through personal observation. *Jennings v. Connecticut Light & Power Co.*, 140 Conn. 650, 675, 103 A.2d 535; *Mrowka v. Board of Zoning Appeals*, 134 Conn. 149, 154, 55 A.2d 909. The second and third claims of the plaintiffs are without validity.

There is no error.

Notes

1. Note that the Connecticut Supreme Court mentions that one of the purposes of zoning is to "encourage the most appropriate use of land." That language is in the Connecticut state statutes that delegate the power to zone to cities and towns. It is also contained in the Standard Zoning Enabling Act promulgated by the Hoover Commission in the early 1920s—the model adopted by many of the fifty states. Is this language, by itself, broad enough to authorize local zoning provisions that protect environmental resources and functions such as wetlands and habitats?

2. In most states, it is understood that municipalities have no inherent powers, but can exercise only that authority granted or necessarily implied from, or incident to, the powers expressly granted by the state. Courts vary from state to state in how strictly they construe express delegations of power to municipalities. Some find a broader range of implied or incidental powers within the express language used; others do not. It is for this reason that the power to adopt zoning, subdivision, or site plan regulations may not be sufficient in some states to support a broad range of local environmental laws. Finding authority to adopt such laws requires a careful reading of the express language of existing statutes and an understanding of whether state courts take broad or strict approaches to interpretation. Section 7–148 (c)(8) of the Connecticut General Statutes, for example, delegates separate authority to cities and towns to pass laws that "provide for the protection and improvement of the environment * * *."

3. In De Mars, the court upheld amendments to zoning regulations based, in part, on protecting the residential water supply pursuant to the municipality's power to adopt zoning laws. How does this court's interpretation of local authority compare to the court's interpretation in the case below?

MORRIS COUNTY LAND IMPROVEMENT CO. v. TOWNSHIP OF PARSIPPANY–TROY HILLS

Supreme Court of New Jersey, 1963.
40 N.J. 539, 193 A.2d 232.

HALL, J.

The fundamental question in this case is the constitutional validity of provisions of defendant township's zoning ordinance which greatly restrict the use of swampland and have for their prime object the retention of the land substantially in its natural state, essentially for public purposes. The provisions not only control land uses in the district, but also strictly regulate any reclamation or improvement of land therein. The Law Division sustained the provisions in a prerogative writ action brought by the plaintiff, a land owner within the area. We certified its appeal on our own motion before it was heard in the Appellate Division.

Parsippany–Troy Hills is a large, sprawling township in Morris County, with a great quantity of vacant land, which has in late years undergone very considerable development activity, accompanied by concomitant increase in population, with the usually resultant problems of planning and zoning. * * *

The particular area here involved is a large swamp of 1500 or more acres known as Troy Meadows. It is located mostly in the southeasterly corner of the township extending to some extent easterly into East Hanover Township and to a slight degree southerly across the boundary of Hanover Township. It and other similar formations in nearby municipalities represent the remaining parts of what was once Lake Passaic, a huge body of water formed eons ago by action of the last glacier in blocking the original channel of the Passaic River. Now, Troy Meadows slowly drains, by means of small streams and man-made ditches running through it, into tributaries of the present Passaic River and forms a portion of that river's basin.

As might be expected, the elevation of the area is low in relation to the surrounding land and considerably below the grade of the roads encircling or running through it. The terrain is typical swampland, with a high water table and marsh grass and cattail vegetation. The surface soil is black or dark brown muck and peat, two to six feet deep, wet and very unstable. The second stratum, from two to four feet in thickness, consists of clay and silt materials which drain poorly and are highly compressible in nature. The bottom layer is composed of sand and gravel, found, on the average, seven or eight feet beneath the surface. The testimony in the case is uncontradicted that the two top layers will not bear structures, are unsuitable for fill and would have to be removed and the land filled with proper material before it could be used for any active purpose, except possibly the raising of fish or the growing of aquatic plants.

At the present time, there are practically no active land uses in the Parsippany–Troy Hills portion of the area. About 75% of it is owned by Wildlife Preserves, Inc. (Wildlife), a private noncommercial, but taxpaying corporation, interested in conservation and preservation of the natural state of the area as a public or quasi-public wildlife sanctuary and nature study refuge. This organization has been energetic and apparently quite influential in urging the local authorities to restrict use of all of the land accordingly. It has even opposed filling of any of the land on the basis that the effect of the fill on the water would be biologically adverse to the conservation of wildlife.

There is no doubt that the area in its present state, acting essentially as a sponge, constitutes a natural detention basin for flood waters in times of very heavy rainfall, which would otherwise run off more quickly and aggravate damaging flood conditions occurring with some frequency in municipalities farther down the Passaic River valley. During such periods, Troy Meadows itself is flooded to some extent, but apparently with little, if any, effect on surrounding higher land.

Plaintiff's property consists of 66 acres in the lower corner of the meadows, fronting several hundred feet on Perrine (or Troy) Road, a dirt highway which is the boundary line in this section with Hanover Township. This acreage is part of a large tract, the balance of which is located across the road in Hanover. The entire parcel was acquired in 1952. The Hanover portion consisted mostly of high land, with a small amount of swamp near the road. At the time of acquisition and since, it has been zoned for industrial use. Plaintiff operates a sand and gravel business at the location in Hanover and has filled in the swampy portion of its property in that township with overburden and other unusable material from the sand and gravel pit.

At the time of acquisition, plaintiff's 66 acres in Parsippany–Troy Hills, along with the rest of Troy Meadows, was zoned, like the high land to the west, in the most restrictive residential classification under the township's original zoning ordinance adopted in 1945. The validity of the inclusion of the swamp in such a zone is indeed most doubtful, but apparently it was never attacked and, since no one would build an expensive home in a marsh, it served the practical purpose of precluding all development.

In 1954 an amendment to the zoning ordinance established "The Indeterminate Zone Classification * * * to cover such parts of the Township as Troy Meadows, where the nature of the land is such that its most appropriate future use is dependent on decisions by others than the government of the Township, such as with respect to flood control, and any change of present use and condition should be subject to special and individual consideration." The amendment forbade any new use, or change in existing use except for agricultural purposes or the growing of fish, water fowl and water plants, and also forbade any dumping or other disposal of material or any change in the natural or existing grade of the land, without the obtaining of a special permit from the Township Committee. From the evidence in the instant case, it is apparent that these almost "freezing" regulations were enacted as a stopgap or interim measure with the expectation or hope that higher governmental authority might well acquire the area as part of a large and much discussed flood control project to benefit the entire Passaic Valley—a project which has not yet come to pass.

Plaintiff attempted no utilization whatever of its Parsippany–Troy Hills land from 1952 until June 1959 when it commenced to fill along the edge of the road with overburden and excess material from the gravel pit operation, without obtaining any permit. Wildlife made a complaint against it in the Municipal Court for violation of the indeterminate zone regulations. While the complaint was pending, plaintiff unsuccessfully applied to the governing body to rezone its property for industrial use. Thereafter, in January 1960, plaintiff was granted a limited permission by the Township Committee to place fill to a depth of 300 feet from Perrine Road at its own risk, since the matter of the revision of land uses in the area was then under study by the township. This permission was conditioned upon submission to, and approval by, the Township Engineer of a sketch showing grades. Plaintiff resumed filling, but did not submit the sketch.

In March 1960, after an extended consideration of the meadows area by planning consultants and township officials, the indeterminate zone provisions were repealed and a new zoning classification created for the area under the title "Meadows Development Zone." The first paragraph of the new regulations set forth the purpose:

> "The Meadows Development Zone classification is established to be applied to areas of the Township with a high water table. These areas can perform a function for the Township of Parsippany–Troy Hills, if they are properly regulated in their uses. Therefore, the following special regulations become necessary to provide for the most appropriate uses of land in the district which will permit development in harmony with its character and the regional requirements for the area."

The new regulations permitted the following uses as of right: agricultural uses; raising of woody or herbaceous plants; commercial greenhouses; raising of aquatic plants, fish and fish food (with a one-family dwelling as an adjunct to any of these uses, provided its lowest floor was a specified distance above flood level); outdoor recreational uses operated by a governmental division or agency; conservation uses "including drainage control, forestry, wildlife sanctuaries and facilities for making same available and useful to the public"; hunting and fishing preserves; public utility transmission lines and substations; radio or television transmitting stations, and antenna towers; and township sewage treatment plants and water supply facilities.

The section went on to provide for what were designated as "uses which may be permitted as special exceptions by the Board of Adjustment under R.S. 40:55–39(b)," with the following preamble:

" * * * In determining whether a special exception shall be granted, the Board shall apply the standards set forth for each particular use and, in addition, shall determine that in its development and operation the proposed use will conform to the general purposes for which the district is established, and will not impair present or potential use of adjacent properties, as may be permitted under the terms of this section."

These so-called permitted uses amounted, for the most part, to strict regulation of land reclamation in aid of uses allowed as of right. Thus, a special exception, with particular conditions, was required for any permitted use which involved a change in any drainage ditch, for the removal of earth products, such as gravel, sand, fill-dirt and peat, and for the diking, damming or filling of any land within the zone with an existing elevation of less than 175 feet above sea level (apparently this limitation would encompass practically all the land in the zone). The standards and conditions for exceptions to permit removal of earth products and filling included intricate site plan approval by the Planning Board together with studies and reports by other township officials and agencies before favorable action could be taken by the Board of Adjustment. Moreover, no filling was allowed except by the use of material taken from land within the zone. In addition, approval was required of ponds and lakes which would inevitably be created by a filling operation (since the fill had to come from within the zone and the only suitable material was the sand and gravel found below the first two strata of soil).

The removal of earth products from the zone, as a use in itself, previously permitted, became prohibited by an amendment of these provisions in June 1960. This forbade such removal on a commercial or profit basis and completely banned taking earth products beyond the boundaries of the zone.

Plaintiff continued to fill its lands after the adoption of the Meadows Development Zone provisions, without municipal authorization, until further complaints made by Wildlife put an end to the work. By that time the fill extended 1000 feet or more along the road to a depth of 150 feet or greater. It then applied to the Board of Adjustment in August 1960 for a special exception, allegedly in accordance with the ordinance, to fill its lands further as shown on a map submitted, to excavate for an 18–acre reservoir of unspecified depth, to use the material taken therefrom to supply the fill and to sell the excess to defray the cost of the operation. Since the application sought leave to do things forbidden by the ordinance, it amounted also to a request for variance. The application was ultimately denied in January 1961. This suit against the Township and the Board of Adjustment followed.

* * *

[The court first ruled adversely to the plaintiff on claims (1) that the board of adjustment abused its discretion; (2) the court erred in making a visit to the land unaccompanied by counsel; and (3) the plaintiff had established a nonconforming use. The court then continued:]

This brings us to the important and decisive question in the case—the matter of the validity of the 1960 Meadows Development Zone provisions. Plaintiff's attack is full-scale and is not confined to unconstitutional effect of the regulations as applied to its property.

* * *

There cannot be the slightest doubt from the evidence that the prime object of the zone regulations is to retain the land substantially in its natural state. As we have already said, the testimony is uncontradicted that the character of the surface soil is such that it is unsuited for any of the permitted active uses, except possibly the raising of fish and aquatic plants. The first two layers would have to be removed and replaced with proper fill which would support structures where the use involved the construction of buildings, and with appropriate top soil where agriculture and similar soil uses were contemplated. And land reclamation along these lines is, for all practical purposes, rendered impossible. Apart from the matter of having to obtain permission subject to exceedingly difficult conditions, the regulations absolutely prohibit not only the removal of the unusable top two layers of earth from the zone (and, indeed, even from the particular premises within the zone under the amendment to the soil removal ordinance), but also forbid the importation from outside the zone of suitable fill material or soil. As a practical matter, the only available method seems to be to dredge fill material from the bottom stratum of sand and gravel in some other portion of the premises (which, however, does not have the qualities of fertile top soil) and to fill the excavation as far as possible with the unusable upper layers from the area being excavated and filled. Even then it appears that a pond or lake would probably result in the unfilled portion of the excavation because of the high water table. And the regulations also require approval of such a formation. Moreover, the regulations further provide that earth removal will be permitted only if it "will not impair the present and potential use of adjacent properties." This might well become another block to any land reclamation since, it will be recalled, Wildlife has objected to any filling on the ground of an adverse biological effect on the water and the swamp creatures in its sanctuary.

In addition, it will be noted that many of the previously listed permitted uses in the zone are public or quasi-public in nature, rather than of the type available to the ordinary private landowner as a reasonable means of obtaining a return from his property, i.e., outdoor recreational uses to be operated only by some governmental unit, conservation uses and activities, township sewage treatment plants and water facilities and public utility transmission lines, substations and radio and television transmitting stations and towers. All in all, about the only practical use which can be made of property in the zone is a hunting or fishing preserve or a wildlife sanctuary, none of which can be considered productive.

One has to conclude that the uses to which a private landowner may put his property in the zone under the 1960 regulations are little more favorable to him than the almost "freezing" provisions which controlled the area when subject to the stop-gap Indeterminate Zone regulations. One also has the strong feeling that the ordinance changes made in 1960 were adopted essentially, not to benefit the landowner or to permit practical change in the natural state of the area, but rather because it was considered, and quite properly so, that the indeterminate zone provisions were or had become invalid for any number of reasons.

It is equally obvious from the proofs, and legally of the highest significance, that the main purpose of enacting regulations with the practical effect of retaining the meadows in their natural state was for a public benefit. This benefit is twofold, with somewhat interrelated aspects: first, use of the area as a water detention basin in aid of flood control in the lower reaches of the Passaic Valley far beyond this municipality; and second, preservation of the land as open space for the benefits which would accrue to the local public from an undeveloped use such as that of a nature refuge by Wildlife (which paid taxes on it).

This prime public, rather than private, utilization can be clearly implied from the purpose sections of the zone regulations previously quoted. And it is established beyond any question by the testimony of the township's own witnesses. * * * It is fair to conclude from the proofs that any other factors which were taken into consideration in arriving at the detailed regulations were clearly subordinate to these two public purposes.

Private property may not, of course, be taken for public use without just compensation. N.J. Const., Art. I, par. 20. The measures here adopted to accomplish public benefits do not amount to a direct or outright taking, as were those struck down in *Grosso v. Board of Adjustment of Millburn Township*, 137 N.J.L. 630, 61 A.2d 167 (Sup.Ct. 1948), where use of the plaintiff's property was precluded by placing the lot in the bed of a proposed street on the official map; in *Hager v. Louisville & Jefferson County Planning & Zoning Commission*, 261 S.W.2d 619 (Ky.Ct.App.1953), where the plaintiff's land was rendered useless by zoning it as ponding areas for temporary storage basins in accordance with a flood control plan; and in *Miller v. City of Beaver Falls*, 368 Pa. 189, 82 A.2d 34 (Sup.Ct.1951), where private utilization of the tract was inhibited for a period of years, pursuant to a statute, by its inclusion in a territory encompassed by an ordinance adopting a general plan for present and future parks.

* * *

While the issue of regulation as against taking is always a matter of degree, there can be no question but that the line has been crossed where the purpose and practical effect of the regulation is to appropriate private property for a flood water detention basin or open space. These are laudable public purposes and we do not doubt the high-mindedness of their motivation. But such factors cannot cure basic unconstitutionality. Nor is the situation saved because the owner of most of the land in the zone, justifiably desirous of preserving an appropriate area in its natural state as a wetland wildlife sanctuary, supports the regulations. Both public uses are necessarily so all-encompassing as practically to prevent the exercise by a private owner of any worthwhile rights or benefits in the land. So public acquisition rather than regulation is required. See Dunham, *"Flood Control Via the Police Power"*, 107 U.Pa.L.Rev. 1098 (1959); Krasnowiecki and Paul, *"The Preservation of Open Space in Metropolitan Areas"*, 110 U.Pa.L.Rev. 179, 184–189 (1961); Note, *"Techniques for Preserving Open Spaces"*, 75 Harv.L.Rev. 1622 (1962); and, generally, Dunham, *"A Legal and Economic Basis for City Planning"*, 58 Colum.L.Rev. 650, 658–670 (1958). *Cf. Alford v. Finch*, 155 So.2d 790 (Fla.Sup.Ct.1963). Our statutes empower the State and its subdivisions to purchase or condemn property needed for flood control, see e.g., N.J.S.A. 58:16A–1 et seq., and N.J.S.A. 40:69–4.1 et seq., and that found desirable for open-space, park, playground, conservation and recreation purposes, see e.g., R.S. 40:61–1, N.J.S.A. and N.J.S.A. 13:8A–1 et seq. (New Jersey Green Acres Land Acquisition Act of 1961). And the federal government has provided for grants to states in aid of open space programs. 42 U.S.C.A. §§ 1500–1500e.

We cannot agree with the trial court's thesis that, despite the prime public purpose of the zone regulations, they are valid because they represent a reasonable local exercise of the police power in view of the nature of the area and because the presumption of validity was not overcome. In our opinion the provisions are clearly far too restrictive and as such are constitutionally unreasonable and confiscatory. * * *

The judgment of the Law Division is reversed and the cause remanded for the entry of a judgment consistent with this opinion.

Notes

1. Read the court's description of the physical process that a developer would have to follow to prepare the marshland owned by the plaintiff for productive use. What would the effect of that massive activity be on the site and surrounding ecosystem?

2. The court in Morris County Land recognized that the township's purpose in preventing productive use of the plaintiff's property was "to provide for the most appropriate use of the land * * *." Why wasn't that enough to sustain the township's regulation? What public benefits did the

court understand the regulation to serve? Do you think that, after the loss of hundreds of thousands of acres of wetlands during the ensuing four decades, the courts now have a deeper and more serious understanding of the benefits of wetlands protection? Would this understanding affect the court's interpretation of the reasonable investment-backed expectations of those who purchase this marsh with its high water table, six-foot deep layers of muck and peat, and general unsuitability for productive development use?

SECTION 2. ADVENT OF LOCAL ENVIRONMENTAL LAW

In the modern era, New Jersey courts have disregarded the holding in Morris County Land. In Gardner v. New Jersey Pinelands Com'n, 125 N.J. 193, 593 A.2d 251 (1991), the court upheld a restriction placing most of an existing farm in a district restricting uses to agricultural with limited possibilities to develop the land. The court rejected the takings claim, finding a lack of investment-backed expectations, and in the course of the opinion disapproved of much of the language in the Morris County case:

> Plaintiff also cites *Morris County Land Improvement Co. v. Parsippany–Troy Hills Township*, 40 N.J. 539, 193 A.2d 232 (1963) (Morris County Land), to support his contention that preservation zoning can constitute a taking if it interferes too greatly with the landowner's use of its property. *Morris County Land* held that a zoning ordinance that maintained an entire swamp area in its natural state, permitting use only for raising fish and aquatic plants and as a flood water detention basin, constituted a taking because the landowner had been deprived of "any worthwhile rights or benefits in the land." *Id.* at 555–56, 193 A.2d 232. We find *Morris County Land* inapposite. Plaintiff does not deny that the uses allowed under the Act and the CMP are "worthwhile rights or benefits in the land." In contrast to the permitted uses in *Morris County Land*, agriculture in the pinelands region is an existing, indeed a longstanding, endeavor that is economically supported locally and nationally. Moreover, the vitality of Morris County Land has declined with the *emerging priority accorded to the ecological integrity of the environment* (emphasis added). The decision, now nearly thirty years old, arose in a time before the environmental and social harms of indiscriminate and excessive development were widely understood or acknowledged. That the same facts would occasion the same result today is by no means certain. See *AMG Assocs. v. Township of Springfield*, 65 N.J. 101, 112 n. 4, 319 A.2d 705 (1974). Indeed, many more recent decisions have overtly or tacitly failed to follow *Morris County Land* in environmental contexts. E.g., *Loveladies Harbor, Inc.*, supra, 176 N.J.Super. 69, 422 A.2d 107; *Usdin*, supra, 173 N.J.Super. 311, 414 A.2d 280; *New Jersey Builders Ass'n*, supra, 169 N.J.Super. 76, 404 A.2d 320; *Toms River Affiliates*, supra, 140 N.J.Super. 135, 355 A.2d 679; *Sands Point Harbor, Inc.*, supra, 136 N.J.Super. 436, 346 A.2d

612. For example, in *American Dredging Co. v. State*, 161 N.J.Super. 504, 391 A.2d 1265 (Ch.Div.1978), aff'd, 169 N.J.Super. 18, 404 A.2d 42 (App.Div.1979), the Department of Environmental Protection, acting pursuant to the Wetlands Act of 1970, N.J.S.A. 13:9A–1 to– 10, issued an order prohibiting the plaintiff from placing dredged material on a portion of its land. The court distinguished *Morris County Land* by explaining, "Where the effect of the governmental prohibition against use is not in furtherance of a governmental activity, such as flood control or preservation of land for a park or recreational area, but rather to preserve the land for ecological reasons in its natural environment without change, the consideration of the reasonableness of the exercise of the police power must be redetermined." *Id*. 161 N.J.Super. at 509, 391 A.2d 1265.

The Gardner case was decided in 1991, nearly 30 years after Morris County Land. The Gardner court states that regulations that preserve the land "for ecological reasons" may be more reasonable than those aimed at flood control or open space preservation. It was during this 30 year period that land use patterns rapidly sprawled beyond urban boundaries and that the damage done to ecosystems became manifest. There is a fundamental difference between the typical local zoning regulation designed to separate one land use from another and the regulation involved in Gardner. The court characterizes it as preserving agricultural land uses for ecological reasons. By the date of the Gardner case, it appears that a discernable environmental ethic had entered land use legislation and jurisprudence.

In the cases below, notice the shift of local regulations from simply Euclidian Zoning to a consideration of environmental protection for purposes of protecting the public's health and welfare.

JUST v. MARINETTE COUNTY

Supreme Court of Wisconsin, 1972.
56 Wis.2d 7, 201 N.W.2d 761.

HALLOWS, CHIEF JUSTICE.

Marinette county's Shoreland Zoning Ordinance Number 24 was adopted September 19, 1967, became effective October 9, 1967, and follows a model ordinance published by the Wisconsin Department of Resource Development in July of 1967. See Kusler, Water Quality Protection For Inland Lakes in Wisconsin: A Comprehensive Approach to Water Pollution, 1970 Wis.L.Rev. 35, 62–63. The ordinance was designed to meet standards and criteria for shoreland regulation which the legislature required to be promulgated by the department of natural resources under sec. 144.26, Stats. These standards are found in 6 Wis.Adm.Code, sec. NR 115.03, May, 1971, Register No. 185. The legislation, secs. 59.971 and 144.26, Stats., authorizing the ordinance was enacted as a part of the Water Quality Act of 1965 by ch. 614, Laws of 1965.

Shorelands for the purpose of ordinances are defined in sec. 59.971(1), Stats., as lands within 1,000 feet of the normal high-water elevation of navigable lakes, ponds, or flowages and 300 feet from a navigable river or stream or to the landward side of the flood plain, whichever distance is greater. The state shoreland program is unique. All county shoreland zoning ordinances must be approved by the department of natural resources prior to their becoming effective. 6 Wis.Adm. Code, sec. NR 115.04, May, 1971, Register No. 185. If a county does not enact a shoreland zoning ordinance which complies with the state's standards, the department of natural resources may enact such an ordinance for the county. Sec. 59.971(6), Stats.

There can be no disagreement over the public purpose sought to be obtained by the ordinance. Its basic purpose is to protect navigable waters and the public rights therein from the degradation and deterioration which results from uncontrolled use and development of shorelands. In the Navigable Waters Protection Act, sec. 144.26, the purpose of the state's shoreland regulation program is stated as being to "aid in the fulfillment of the state's role as trustee of its navigable waters and to promote public health, safety, convenience and general welfare." In sec. 59.971(1), which grants authority for shoreland zoning to counties, the same purposes are reaffirmed. The Marinette County shoreland zoning ordinance in secs. 1.2 and 1.3 states the uncontrolled use of shorelands and pollution of navigable waters of Marinette county adversely affect public health, safety, convenience, and general welfare and impair the tax base.

The shoreland zoning ordinance divides the shorelands of Marinette County into general purpose districts, general recreation districts, and conservancy districts. A "conservancy" district is required by the statutory minimum standards and is defined in sec. 3.4 of the ordinance to include "all shorelands designated as swamps or marshes on the United States Geological Survey maps which have been designated as the Shoreland Zoning Map of Marinette County, Wisconsin or on the detailed Insert Shoreland Zoning Maps." The ordinance provides for permitted uses and conditional uses. One of the conditional uses requiring a permit under sec. 3.42(4) is the filling, drainage or dredging of wetlands according to the provisions of sec. 5 of the ordinance. "Wetlands" are defined in sec. 2.29 as "(a)reas where ground water is at or near the surface much of the year or where any segment of plant cover is deemed an aquatic according to N.C. Fassett's 'Manual of Aquatic Plants.'" Section 5.42(2) of the ordinance requires a conditional-use permit for any filling or grading "Of any area which is within three hundred feet horizontal distance of a navigable water and which has surface drainage toward the water and on which there is: (a) Filling of more than five hundred square feet of any wetland which is contiguous to the water * * * (d) Filling or grading of more than 2,000 square feet on slopes of twelve per cent or less."

In April of 1961, several years prior to the passage of this ordinance, the Justs purchased 36.4 acres of land in the town of Lake along the south shore of Lake Noquebay, a navigable lake in Marinette county. This land had a frontage of 1,266.7 feet on the lake and was purchased partially for personal use and partially for resale. During the years 1964, 1966, and 1967, the Justs made five sales of parcels having frontage and extending back from the lake some 600 feet, leaving the property involved in these suits. This property has a frontage of 366.7 feet and the south one half contains a stand of cedar, pine, various hard woods, birch and red maple. The north one half, closer to the lake, is barren of trees except immediately along the shore. The south three fourths of this north one half is populated with various plant grasses and vegetation including some plants which N.C. Fassett in his manual of aquatic plants has classified as "aquatic." There are also non-aquatic plants which grow upon the land. Along the shoreline there is a belt of trees. The shoreline is from one foot to 3.2 feet higher than the lake level and there is a narrow belt of higher land along the shore known as a "pressure ridge" or "ice heave," varying in width from one to three feet. South of this point, the natural level of the land ranges one to two feet above lake level. The land slopes generally toward the lake but has a slope less than twelve per cent. No water flows onto the land from the lake, but there is some surface water which collects on land and stands in pools.

The land owned by the Justs is designated as swamps or marshes on the United States Geological Survey Map and is located within 1,000 feet of the normal high-water elevation of the lake. Thus, the property is included in a conservancy district and, by sec. 2.29 of the ordinance, classified as "wetlands." Consequently, in order to place more than 500 square feet of fill on this property, the Justs were required to obtain a conditional-use permit from the zoning administrator of the county and pay a fee of $20 or incur a forfeiture of $10 to $200 for each day of violation.

In February and March of 1968, six months after the ordinance became effective, Ronald Just, without securing a conditional-use permit, hauled 1,040 square yards of sand onto this property and filled an area approximately 20–feet wide commencing at the southwest corner and extending almost 600 feet north to the northwest corner near the shoreline, then easterly along the shoreline almost to the lot line. He stayed back from the pressure ridge about 20 feet. More than 500 square feet of this fill was upon wetlands located contiguous to the water and which had surface drainage toward the lake. The fill within 300 feet of the lake also was more than 2,000 square feet on a slope less than 12 percent. It is not seriously contended that the Justs did not violate the ordinance and the trial court correctly found a violation.

The real issue is whether the conservancy district provisions and the wetlands filling restrictions are unconstitutional because they amount to a constructive taking of the Justs' land without compensation. Marinette County and the state of Wisconsin argue the restrictions of the conservancy district and wetlands provisions constitute a proper exercise of the police power of the state and do not so severely limit the use or depreciate the value of the land as to constitute a taking without compensation.

To state the issue in more meaningful terms, it is a conflict between the public interest in stopping the despoliation of natural resources, which our citizens until recently have taken as inevitable and for granted, and an owner's asserted right to use his property as he wishes. The protection of public rights may be accomplished by the exercise of the police power unless the damage to the property owner is too great and amounts to a confiscation. The securing or taking of a benefit not presently enjoyed by the public for its use is obtained by the government through its power of eminent domain. The distinction between the exercise of the police power and condemnation has been said to be a matter of degree of damage to the property owner. In the valid exercise of the police power reasonably restricting the use of property, the damage suffered by the owner is said to be incidental. However, where the restriction is so great the landowner ought not to bear such a burden for the public good, the restriction has been held to be a constructive taking even though the actual use or forbidden use has not been transferred to the government so as to be a taking in the traditional sense. *Stefan Auto Body v. State Highway Comm.* (1963), 21 Wis.2d 363, 124 N.W.2d 319; *Buhler v. Racine County* (1966), 33 Wis.2d 137, 146 N.W.2d 403; *Nick v. State Highway Comm.* (1961), 13 Wis.2d 511, 109 N.W.2d 71, 111 N.W.2d 95; *State v. Becker* (1934), 215 Wis. 564, 255 N.W. 144. Whether a taking has occurred depends upon whether "the restriction practically or substantially renders the land useless for all reasonable purposes." *Buhler v. Racine County, supra*. The loss caused the individual must be weighed to determine if it is more than he should bear. As this court stated in *Stefan*, at pp. 369–370, 124 N.W.2d 319, p. 323, " * * * if the damage is such as to be suffered by many similarly situated and is in the nature of a restriction on the use to which land may be put and ought to be borne by the individual as a member of society for the good of the public safety, health or general welfare, it is said to be a reasonable exercise of the police power, but if the damage is so great to the individual that he ought not to bear it under contemporary standards, then courts are inclined to treat it as a 'taking' of the property or an unreasonable exercise of the police power."

Many years ago, Professor Freund stated in his work on The Police Power, sec. 511, at 546–547, "It may be said that the state takes property by eminent domain because it is useful to the public, and under the police power because it is harmful * * *. From this results the difference between the power of eminent domain and the police power, that the former recognizes a right to compensation, while the latter on principle does not." Thus the necessity for monetary compensation for loss suffered to an owner by police power restriction arises when restrictions are placed on property in order to create a public benefit rather than to prevent a public harm. Rathkopf, The Law of Zoning and Planning, Vol. 1, ch. 6, pp. 6–7.

This case causes us to reexamine the concepts of public benefit in contrast to public harm and the scope of an owner's right to use of his property. In the instant case we have a restriction on the use of a citizen's property, not to secure a benefit for the public, but to prevent a harm from the change in the natural character of the citizen's property. We start with the premise that lakes and rivers in their natural state are unpolluted and the pollution which now exists is man made. The state of Wisconsin under the trust doctrine has a duty to eradicate the present pollution and to prevent further pollution in its navigable waters. This is not, in a legal sense, a gain or a securing of a benefit by the maintaining of the natural status quo of the environment. What makes this case different from most condemnation or police power zoning cases is the interrelationship of the wetlands, the swamps and the natural environment of shorelands to the purity of the water and to such natural resources as navigation, fishing, and scenic beauty. Swamps and wetlands were once considered wasteland, undesirable, and not picturesque. But as the people became more sophisticated, an appreciation was acquired that swamps and wetlands serve a vital role in nature, are part of the balance of nature and are essential to the purity of the water in our lakes and streams. Swamps and wetlands are a necessary part of the ecological creation and now, even to the uninitiated, possess their own beauty in nature.

Is the ownership of a parcel of land so absolute that man can change its nature to suit any of his purposes? The great forests of our state were stripped on the theory man's ownership was unlimited. But in forestry, the land at least was used naturally, only the natural fruit of the land (the trees) were taken. The despoilage was in the failure to look to the future and provide for the reforestation of the land. An owner of land has no absolute and unlimited right to change the essential natural character of his land so as to use it for a purpose for which it was unsuited in its natural state and which injures the rights of others. The exercise of the police power in zoning must be reasonable and we think it is not an unreasonable exercise of that power to prevent harm to public rights by limiting the use of private property to its natural uses.

This is not a case where an owner is prevented from using his land for natural and indigenous uses. The uses consistent with the nature of the land are allowed and other uses recognized and still others permitted by special permit. The shoreland zoning ordinance prevents to some extent the changing of the natural character of the land within 1,000 feet of a navigable lake and 300 feet of a navigable river because of such land's interrelation to the contiguous water. The changing of wetlands and swamps to the damage of the general public by upsetting the natural environment and the natural relationship is not a reasonable use of that land which is protected from police power regulation. Changes and filling to some extent are permitted because the extent of such changes and fillings does not cause harm. We realize no case in Wisconsin has yet dealt with shoreland regulations and there are several cases in other states which seem to hold such regulations unconstitutional; but nothing in this court has said or held in prior cases indicates that destroying the natural character of a swamp or a wetland so as to make that location available for human habitation is a reasonable use of that land when the new use, although of a more economical value to the owner, causes a harm to the general public.

* * *

The Justs rely on several cases from other jurisdictions which have held zoning regulations involving flood plain districts, flood basins and wetlands to be so confiscatory as to amount to a taking because the owners of the land were prevented from improving such property for residential or commercial purposes. While some of these cases may be distinguished on their facts, it is doubtful whether these differences go to the basic rationale which permeates the decision that an owner has a right to use his property in any way and for any purpose he sees fit. In *Dooley v. Town Plan & Zon. Com. of Town of Fairfield* (1964), 151 Conn. 304, 197 A.2d 770, the court held the restriction on land located in a flood plain district prevented its being used for residential or business purposes and thus the restriction destroyed the economic value to the owner. The court recognized the land was needed for a public purpose as it was part of the area in which the tidal stream overflowed when abnormally high tides existed, but the property was half a mile from the ocean and therefore could not be used for marina or boathouse purposes. In *Morris County Land I. Co. v. Parsippany–Troy Hills Tp.* (1963), 40 N.J. 539, 193 A.2d 232, a flood basin zoning ordinance was involved which required the controversial land to be retained in its natural state. The plaintiff owned 66 acres of a 1,500–acre swamp which was part of a river basin and acted as a natural detention basin for flood waters in times of very heavy rainfall. There was an extraneous issue that the freezing regulations were intended as a stop-gap until such time as the government would buy the property under a flood-control project. However, the court took the view the zoning had an effect of preserving the land as an open space as a water-detention basin and only the government or the public would be benefited, to the complete damage of the owner.

In *State v. Johnson* (1970), Me., 265 A.2d 711, the Wetlands Act restricted the alteration and use of certain wetlands without permission. The act was a conservation measure enacted under the police power to protect the ecology of areas bordering the coastal waters. The plaintiff owned a small tract of a salt-water marsh which was flooded at high tide. By filling, the land would be adapted for building purposes. The court held the restrictions against filling constituted a deprivation of a reasonable use of the owner's property and, thus, an unreasonable exercise of the police power. In *MacGibbon v. Board of Appeals of Duxbury* (1970), 356 Mass. 635, 255 N.E.2d 347, the plaintiff owned seven acres of land which were under water about twice a month in a shoreland area. He was denied a permit to excavate and fill part of his property. The purpose of the ordinance was to preserve from despoilage natural features and resources such as salt marshes, wetlands, and ponds. The court took the view the preservation of privately owned land in its natural, unspoiled state for the enjoyment and benefit of the public by preventing the owner from using it for any practical purpose was not within the limit and scope of the police power and the ordinance was not saved by the use of special permits.

It seems to us that filling a swamp not otherwise commercially usable is not in and of itself an existing use, which is prevented, but rather is the preparation for some future use which is not indigenous to a swamp. Too much stress is laid on the right of an owner to change commercially valueless land when that change does damage to the rights of the public. It is observed that a use of special permits is a means of control and accomplishing the purpose of the zoning ordinance as distinguished from the old concept of providing for variances. The special permit technique is now common practice and has met with judicial approval, and we think it is of some significance in considering whether or not a particular zoning ordinance is reasonable.

A recent case sustaining the validity of a zoning ordinance establishing a flood plain district is *Turnpike Realty Co. v. Town of Dedham* (June, 1972), 362 Mass. 221, 284 N.E.2d 891. The court held the validity of the ordinance was supported by valid considerations of public welfare, the conservation of "natural conditions, wildlife and open spaces." The ordinance provided that lands which were subject to seasonal or periodic flooding could not be used for residences or other purposes in such a manner as to endanger the health, safety or occupancy thereof and prohibited the erection of structures or buildings which required land to be filled. This case is analogous to the instant facts. The ordinance had a public purpose to preserve the natural condition of the area. No change was allowed which would injure the purposes sought to be preserved and through the special-permit technique, particular land within the zoning district could be excepted from the restrictions.

The Justs argue their property has been severely depreciated in value. But this depreciation of value is not based on the use of the land in its natural state but on what the land would be worth if it could be filled and used for the location of a dwelling. While loss of value is to be considered in determining whether a restriction is a constructive taking, value based upon changing the character of the land at the expense of harm to public rights is not an essential factor or controlling.

We are not unmindful of the warning in *Pennsylvania Coal Co. v. Mahon* (1922), 260 U.S. 393, 416, 43 S.Ct. 158, 160, 67 L.Ed. 322:

> " * * * We are in danger of forgetting that a strong public desire to improve the public condition is not enough to warrant achieving the desire by a shorter cut than the constitutional way of paying for the change."

This observation refers to the improvement of the public condition, the securing of a benefit not presently enjoyed and to which the public is not entitled. The shoreland zoning ordinance preserves nature, the environment, and natural resources as they were created and to which the people have a present right. The ordinance does not create or improve the public condition but only preserves nature from the despoilage and harm resulting from the unrestricted activities of humans.

* * *

The Judgment in case number 106, dismissing the Justs' action, is modified to set forth the declaratory adjudication that the shoreland zoning ordinance of respondent Marinette County is constitutional; that the Justs' property constitutes wetlands and that particularly the prohibition in the ordinance against the filling of wetlands is constitutional; and the judgment, as so modified, is affirmed. * * *

Notes

1. Other cases that "look in the same direction" as the Just case are: Candlestick Properties, Inc. v. San Francisco Bay Conservation and Development Comm'n, 11 Cal.App.3d 557, 89 Cal.Rptr. 897 (1970) (denial of a permit to place fill in the bay was upheld); Potomac Sand & Gravel Co. v. Governor of Maryland, 266 Md. 358, 293 A.2d 241 (1972), certiorari denied 409 U.S. 1040, 93 S.Ct. 525, 34 L.Ed.2d 490 (1972) (upholding wetlands legislation which forbade dredging on plaintiff's property); In re Loveladies Harbor, Inc., 176 N.J.Super. 69, 422 A.2d 107 (1980) (upholding denial of permit for filling and dredging 51 acres for development of 108 homes); Chokecherry Hills Estates, Inc. v. Deuel County, 294 N.W.2d 654 (S.D.1980) (upholding a Natural Resources District which prevented development of homesites on a lake); State, Dept. of Ecology v. Pacesetter Constr. Co., Inc., 89 Wash.2d 203, 571 P.2d 196 (1977) (upholding an injunction against construction of two lakefront houses which would significantly block the view of other homeowners near the lake).

2. At the time of the Just decision, local governments were just beginning to enact laws to protect wetlands and surrounding buffer areas from the impacts of development. In the late 1960's, Massachusetts towns relied on their delegated land use authority to protect locally-defined wetlands. In the early 1970's, the state legislatures in both Massachusetts and Connecticut passed statutes directly authorizing localities to adopt wetland regulations. The Connecticut statute, in fact, obligated local governments to adopt wetlands laws as strict as or stricter than state promulgated standards and to establish local wetland review agencies. Conn. Gen. Stat. §§ 22a–36 et. seq. A 1981 state court decision held that a local wetlands agency has the right to regulate areas adjacent to established wetlands where activities occur that might adversely impact the wetlands themselves. Aaron v. Conservation Comm'n of Redding, 183 Conn. 532, 441 A.2d 30 (1981).

3. State and federal courts have upheld environmental regulations that severely limit the amount of development allowed against charges that they constitute regulatory takings. See Moskow v. Commissioner of the Department of Environmental Management, 384 Mass. 530, 427 N.E.2d 750 (1981). In this case, state inland wetland regulations prevented development on over half of a 297,000 square-foot parcel, prohibiting the development of all but one house on the site. "A single family house is a sufficient practical use to

prevent the wetland restrictions from constituting a taking * * *." This position is sustained in Palazzolo v. Rhode Island, 533 U.S. 606, 121 S.Ct. 2448, 150 L.Ed.2d 592 (2001). Palazzolo owned a 20–acre parcel, most of which was salt marsh subject to tidal flooding. Development would have required significant fill, up to six feet in some places, to support any development. Under the Rhode Island coastal wetland regulations, development on the tidal wetlands portion of this site was prohibited unless the owner secured a special exception permit for an activity that serves a compelling public purpose that benefits the public as a whole. Since the responsible state agency, in denying Palazzolo's application to fill 11 of 18 tidal wetland acres for a private beach club, made a determination that this type of private development of tidal lands was not eligible for a special use permit, the Court held that the matter was ripe. Palazzolo's property contained two unregulated upland acres and it was agreed that a substantial residence could be built on that land. The Court upheld the Rhode Island Supreme Court's determination that the coastal regulations did not constitute a total taking under Lucas v. South Carolina Coastal Council, 505 U.S. 1003, 112 S.Ct. 2886, 120 L.Ed.2d 798 (1992). Palazzolo presented evidence that the land was appraised at $3,150,000 under a 74–lot subdivision proposal he had submitted for approval before his private beach club application. The parties agreed that the upland acres had a value of $200,000 for residential development. The Court noted that the development rights on the upland area did not constitute a token interest. Therefore, the regulations did not leave the land economically idle as must be the case for the Lucas total taking rule to apply.

IN RE SPRING VALLEY DEVELOPMENT

Supreme Judicial Court of Maine, 1973.
300 A.2d 736.

WEATHERBEE, JUSTICE.

Raymond Pond is located in the town of Raymond and is slightly more than one mile in length. Lakesites, Inc. is the owner of a large tract of land containing about 92 acres located on one side of the Pond. Lakesites' development of this land into a residential subdivision has been interrupted by an order of the Environmental Improvement Commission directing it to cease the operation of this development until Lakesites has applied for and received the Commission's approval of its development.

The Commission claims to have derived its authority for this order from 38 M.R.S.A. §§ 481–488, Site Location of Development Law, hereinafter referred to as the Site Location Law. Lakesites' appeal attacks both the Commission's interpretation of the Act as including residential subdivisions and the Act's constitutionality. We conclude that the authority of the Commission does extend to residential subdivisions and that the statute represents a valid exercise of the police power. We deny the appeal.

The agreed statement of facts and the testimony presented at hearing before the Commission reveal that Lakesites' property extends along the shore of the Pond at least 3400 feet. Lakesites has subdivided this tract into 90 lots ranging in size from 20,000 square feet to 53,000 square feet with several other areas reserved from sale. It refers to this property as its Spring Valley Development.

Lakesites has cleared and graded portions of this land, has built a road for ingress and egress and has surveyed the property, marking off the boundaries of the individual lots. While it contemplates that purchasers will build year-round or part-time homes on their lots it does not intend to construct or participate in the construction of the buildings or to control the use of the lots "except insofar as there are any required deed restrictions." No action has been taken with respect to providing services for any of the lots.

Lakesites proposes that the selling of these lots be a profitable venture and it has placed their sale in the hands of licensed real estate brokers.

Lakesites submitted its subdivision plan to the Raymond Planning Board which, after some changes had been made, approved it as satisfying the only subdivision requirement then existing in the town ordinance—that of lot size. The subdivision plan was then recorded in the Cumberland County Registry of Deeds.

There was in effect at this time the Site Location Law the constitutionality of which is under attack. This law required persons intending to construct or operate a development which may substantially affect local environment to notify, before commencing the construction or operation, the Environmental Improvement Commission of their intent and the nature and location of the development. If the Commission determines it to be necessary, a hearing shall be held at which the developer has the burden of satisfying the Commission that the development will not substantially adversely affect the environment or pose a threat to the public's health, safety or general welfare. 38 M.R.S.A. §§ 483, 484.

The Legislature defined developments which may substantially affect environment as meaning

> " * * * [1] any commercial or industrial development which requires a license from the Environmental Improvement Commission, [2] or which occupies a land area in excess of 20 acres, [3] or which contemplates drilling for or excavating natural resources, excluding borrow pits for sand, fill or gravel, regulated by the State Highway Commission and pits of less than 5 acres, [4] or which occupies on a single parcel a structure or structures in excess of a ground area of 60,000 square feet." 38 M.R.S.A. § 482(2).

Although Lakesites' development did occupy a land area in excess of 20 acres, it did not notify the Commission of its intentions. However, the Commission eventually learned of Lakesites' plans and proceeded at once to schedule and conduct a hearing as it is authorized to do by section 485. Notice of the hearing was given Lakesites.

Lakesites was represented at the hearing by its attorney who challenged the Commission's jurisdiction to regulate Lakesites' activity contending that the mere subdivision of land does not constitute a "commercial or industrial development" within the scope of the Site Location Law. The attorney made a formal objection to all testimony other than that relating to jurisdiction. He elected to waive his right to contest as to the merits of the case although he was offered full opportunity to do so, choosing not to offer evidence or to cross-examine witnesses who testified regarding the proposed development.

These witnesses testified at length as to various aspects of the environment which they said would be substantially adversely affected by the proposed development. Later, after consideration of the matter, the Commission made findings of fact and held that Lakesites had failed in its burden to prove that its proposed development meets the standards for approval established by the Legislature in section 4845 and had failed to demonstrate that it had plans that would adequately protect the public's health, safety and general welfare. It issued an order denying Lakesites the right to proceed with its development until such time as it has made a proper application to the Environmental Improvement Commission and has received the Commission's approval.

From this decision of the Commission, Lakesites has appealed to the Supreme Judicial Court sitting as the Law Court, [38 M.R.S.A. § 487] raising specifically the issue as to whether the offering for sale of subdivided lots of the type owned by Lakesites is either a commercial or an industrial development subject to the provisions of 38 M.R.S.A. §§ 481–488 and, secondarily, if the Site Location Law is applied to this developer, are there constitutional violations of Equal Protection and Due Process.

* * *

The Legislature's concise statement of its Findings and Purpose makes clear to us the basis for its conclusion that state action was essential to insure that commercial and industrial developments, which because of their nature or their size, will impose unusually heavy demands upon the natural environment, shall not be located in areas where the environment does not have the capacity to withstand the impact of the development. But did the Legislature intend to bring residential developments within the application of the law? If so, did it intend to include mere subdivisions?

* * *

We think that the use of the word "commercial" was intended to describe the motivation for the development and not the type of activity to be performed on the property after it is developed. We consider that the Legislature chose to distinguish between commercial and non-commercial developments for a sound reason—it doubtless concluded that a greater need for supervision exists in the case of a commercially motivated development where the dominant factor is the hope for profit than in a non-commercial development where land is being prepared for public enjoyment or divided for family distribution or for some other purpose than profit. In other words, commercial residential developments have a propensity for being big, concentrated and exhausting to the resources of the environment.

It seems to us that the business of subdividing large tracts of land and selling the lots must be considered a commercial venture. The Legislature doubtless so viewed it. Certainly, this construction best accords with the purpose of the statute. *Strout v. Burgess*, 144 Me. 263, 275, 68 A.2d 241, 250 (1949).

This interpretation finds support in the history of the legislation we are examining.

* * *

We find it significant in our assessment of legislative intent that the 105th Legislature, aware that the Commission was interpreting the Act to include residential subdivisions, took no affirmative action to indicate a contrary intent, rejected two attempts to remove some residential subdivisions from the operation of the Act and finally acted to add the specific words "including subdivisions."

In our opinion the 104th Legislature intended to include commercial residential developments among those developments which may substantially affect environment. But did the Legislature intend the Act to affect commercial residential developments where the developer merely plots the tract, subdivides it into lots by plan and offers the lots for sale to the public?

* * *

The Appellant argues to us that it was the Legislature's intention to prevent acts being done to the land which would harm the land and that, therefore, the law is directed to the person who will do the act—such as the builder—and not to the person who merely subdivides and sells the land. With this we cannot agree. The Legislature intended the Commission to scrutinize the proposals before the harmful act could be done. The Act is a preventive measure and the injury sought to be avoided can best be prevented as soon as plans for development reveal the harm which will occur upon its completion. We would hardly expect that the Legislature intended to postpone the determination of suitability of an area for a residential development until the lots had been sold to purchasers who will, upon starting construction, discover that they are participants in—as well as victims of—a local environmental disaster.

Furthermore, if a subdivider has sold the lots to numerous individual purchasers each of whom, among other things, is to construct his own building, grade his own land, build his own driveway to the street, and provide for his own sanitary sewage disposal, there would be no one "intending to construct or operate a development" who could be held responsible under the statute. We do not ascribe to the Legislature an intention that legislation so important to the public welfare would suffer from such inherent futility.

We consider that both the legislative intent and the statutory language of the Act encompass residential developments in which the developer merely subdivides the land into lots and offers the lots for sale without any intention to construct buildings or to provide additional improvements or services on the lots. We do not find that the Act as so interpreted and applied is constitutionally impermissible. The subdividing is the initial step in such a development.

The Commission correctly ruled as fact that this particular residential development is a commercial development which may substantially affect environment requiring compliance with the provisions of the Site Location Law.

* * *

CONSTITUTIONALITY OF APPLICATION OF THE ACT TO ONE WHO ONLY SUBDIVIDES

Lakesites does not deny the power of the State to act properly under the police power to protect the environment but urges us that the application of the Act to one who merely subdivides is constitutionally forbidden. It argues that a remedial Act must be designed and applied rationally and reasonably to achieve the purposes for which the Act was devised. The evil to be avoided, the appellant contends, is the damaging impact of the development upon the environment and the impact occurs and the damage is sustained only with the construction and occupation of the premises—not when the land is only subdivided on plans and the lots are sold. Until such activity creating the impact occurs on the land, the appellant argues, there is no burden or impact which can affect the environment and so the application of the Act to a mere subdivider as a prerequisite to his selling his land is not directly related to the Act's purpose.

It is true that the Act and its application under the police power must have a clear, real and substantial relation to the purpose of the Act.

* * *

In our opinion such a connection between the purpose of the Act and its application to the subdivider is clear and reasonable. We have concluded earlier in this opinion that the Legislature intended to empower the Commission to prevent ecological damage before it occurs rather than to permit the occurrence of harm which can then be cured only at great public expense—if at all. It is not unreasonable to place upon the subdivider who plans the number, size and location of the lots to be offered for sale the responsibility for avoiding an inevitable large scale ecological calamity. The subdividing for sale is the first step in a commercial residential development and the Legislature reasonably concluded that the public welfare requires that control be exercised through the subdivider rather than attempting it through (in this case) 90 different purchasers whose properties can perhaps never at that later point—because of sheer weight and concentration of numbers—avoid environmental misadventure.

* * *

Lakesites protests that as it is only a subdivider it cannot accurately foresee the activity to be performed on the lots it sells and so cannot control the future adequacy of provisions relating to pollution control and maintenance of healthful water supplies. To be sure, the Act imposes upon the developer—including the mere subdivider—responsibilities which he has not had in the past. The Legislature has determined that an owner of a large tract of undeveloped land may no longer subdivide it, sell the lots and then walk away from the transaction indifferent to the local catastrophe that may result when construction and occupancy reveal the incapacity of the environment to withstand the impact of the development. It may be that this responsibility can more easily be met by a subdivider who is also a constructor of the buildings but it is equally the responsibility of the subdivider who chooses only to sell the bare lots. The duty is no doubt more burdensome as the land is less suitable and it may be impossible of compliance if the environment is of a type incapable of sustaining the proposed development. In the latter situation the public welfare demands that the land be used for another purpose or that the impact of the same use be diminished. In many situations the subdivider may be able to meet his burden of affirmatively demonstrating to the Commission that he has met the criteria through satisfactory conditions in his instruments of sale. We do not consider the burden to be unreasonable in view of the overriding public interest.

* * *

DOES THE ACT DENY THE DEVELOPER EQUAL PROTECTION OF THE LAW?

Finally, Lakesites argues that the Act denies a developer—and especially it—equal protection under the law. It argues that the subdivider of over 20 acres must receive the Commission's approval while the subdivider of under 20 acres faces no such requirements, and so it contends it is denied equal protection because size, it says, has no rational or reasonable correlation to the environmental impact. A 21 acre subdivision, it argues, may contain 5 residences while one of 19 acres may contain 19 residences. It is elementary that the Legislature may in its judgment create classifications so long as they are not arbitrary and are based upon actual differences in classes which differences bear a substantial rational relation to the public purpose sought to be accomplished by the statute. *In re Milo Water Company*, 128 Me. 531, 149 A. 299 (1930).

The purpose, as we have said, was to control the locations of those commercial and industrial developments which could substantially adversely affect the environment. The Legislature evidently concluded that the size of a development has a distinct relationship to the amount of its potential adverse impact upon the environment and concluded that at this time the public interest could best be served by applying the admittedly severe restrictions of the new law to large developments. The justification of the distinction as to size seems most clear in such legislation as this. For example, in an area with no municipal sewage disposal system, such as in Spring Valley Development, and where much of the soil has a high seasonal water table and is unsuitable for septic tank disposal of domestic sewage, the potential danger to the environment from the discharge of sewage from 90 residences must be greater than the discharge from 2 or from 19. Drawing the line at 20 acres is not a denial of equal protection. * * *

We see no irrational or arbitrary discrimination in the application of the Act to the large mere-subdivider. It is his act of subdividing that initially indicates the volume of the impact likely to fall upon the environment.

The distinction made by the Legislature does not appear to be unreasonable.

* * *

We find that the application of the Act to Lakesites does not offend the provisions of either the state or federal constitutions.

* * *

MOVIEMATIC INDUSTRIES CORP. v. BOARD OF COUNTY COM'RS

Florida Court of Appeal, Third District, 1977.
349 So.2d 667.

HAVERFIELD, JUDGE.

Appellant seeks review of an order denying its petition for writ of certiorari, and upholding the validity of Dade County resolution Z-115-75 rezoning petitioner's property from IU-2 to GU.

Over ten years ago Moviematic Industries Corporation purchased 1,200 acres of undeveloped real property located in a remote area of unincorporated west Dade County zoned for heavy industrial use (IU-2) with a special exception for business airport uses. The property overlies the Biscayne Aquifer which serves as a major source of the drinking water in the county. On March 19, 1974 the county commission imposed a building moratorium on an area consisting of approximately 323 square miles of west Dade County, including petitioner's property, for the express purpose of conducting and preparing a comprehensive study directed to the protection of the fresh water supply and the natural ecosystems which function in this part of the county. Following the study, on April 23, 1975 the county building and zoning department and the planning department jointly recommended to the commission that (1) petitioner's property be rezoned from IU-2 to GU (interim classification which permits single family residential use on minimum five acre lots), and (2) the previously approved special permit for business airport uses be terminated. At a public hearing on this matter, the commission heard expert testimony in support of the recommended GU zoning classification and petitioner's evidence in opposition thereto. At the conclusion of the hearing, the commissioners adopted resolution Z–115–75 which rezoned the subject property from IU–2 to GU and terminated the special permit for business airport uses. Petitioner by way of certiorari sought review of the zoning resolution in the circuit court and after a hearing, the court entered its order of denial.

Appellant basically argues that zoning resolution Z–115–75 is invalid because it bears no reasonable relationship to the public health, safety, morals and welfare and constitutes such an unreasonable restriction on petitioner's right to the beneficial use of its property that the resolution amounts to a taking of real property without compensation in violation of the United States and Florida Constitutions. We cannot agree.

A threshold question to a consideration of this appeal is whether preservation of an adequate drinking water supply and ecological system in a particular area are legitimate objectives of zoning resolutions and ordinances.

Zoning regulations which are reasonably related to the adequacy of governmental services fall within the established purpose of the public health, safety and welfare; water supply relates clearly to the public health. Therefore, zoning ordinances have been sustained because of their tendency to insure that such essential governmental services as water supply will be provided. See Anderson, R.M., American Law of Zoning s 7.26 (2d ed 1968). It is clear that the county commission is empowered under Article 1, Section 1.01(A)(9) and (12) of the Home Rule Charter of Metropolitan Dade County to enact zoning ordinances and resolutions to assure an adequate water supply for the protection of the public. See also Section 2–116.3 et seq. Code of Metropolitan Dade County, Section 23A–1, Code of Metropolitan Dade County.

With respect to the objective of preserving the ecological systems, zoning regulations which tend to preserve the residential or historical character of a neighborhood and/to enhance the aesthetic appeal of a community are considered valid exercises of the public power as relating to the general welfare of the community. *See City of Miami Beach v. Ocean & Inland Co.*, 147 Fla. 480, 3 So.2d 364 (1941); *Merritt v. Peters*, 65 So.2d 861 (Fla.1953); *Sunad, Inc. v. City of Sarasota*, 122 So.2d 611 (Fla.1960); *William Murray, Inc. v. Jacksonville*, 254 So.2d 364 (Fla. 1st DCA 1971); *City of Boca Raton v. Tradewind Hills, Inc.*, 216 So.2d 460 (Fla. 4th DCA 1968); *County of Brevard v. Woodham*, 223 So.2d 344 (Fla. 4th DCA 1969); *Watson v. Mayflower Property, Inc.*, 223 So.2d 368 (Fla 4th DCA 1969); *City of Coral Gables v. Wood*, 305 So.2d 261 (Fla. 3d DCA 1974) and *E. B. Elliot Advertising Co. v. Metropolitan Dade County*, 425 F.2d 1141 (5th Cir. 1970); *Stone v. City of Maitland*, 446 F.2d 83 (5th Cir. 1971); *Maher v. City of New Orleans*, 516 F.2d 1051 (5th Cir. 1975). The above being legitimate concerns within the category of the general welfare, then certainly the irreversible effect on the area's ecological balance as the result of urban development can be and should be considered and reflected in zoning codes. We find the inclusion of ecological considerations as a legitimate objective of zoning ordinances and resolutions is long overdue and hold that preservation of the ecological balance of a particular area is a valid exercise of the police power as it relates to the general welfare. We are not alone in this determination as courts in other jurisdictions have recognized the importance of considering the ecological objectives in zoning matters. See *Nattin Realty, Inc. v. Ludewig*, 67 Misc.2d 828, 324 N.Y.S.2d 668 (Sup.Ct.1971) and *Steel Hill Development, Inc. v. Town of Sanbornton*, 469 F.2d 956 (1st Cir. 1972). *In Nattin Realty, Inc., supra*, 67 Misc.2d 828, 324 N.Y.S.2d at 672, the court summarized this issue most appropriately as follows:

> "Respecting ecology as a new factor, it appears that the time has come if, indeed, it has not already irretrievably passed for the courts, as it were, to take 'ecological notice' in zoning matters."

> "(5)* * * the municipality has here presented sufficient evidence to warrant the rezoning of the petitioner's property, for it was prompted to do so by ecological considerations based not upon whim or fancy but upon scientific findings. The definition of 'public health, safety and welfare' surely must now be broadened to include and to provide for these belatedly recognized threats and hazards to the public weal. The Town's decision to forego what, undoubtedly, would be substantial additional tax revenue would appear to constitute a recognition that it as well as an owner must subordinate immediate to long-term interests."

> "The Court is not unmindful that zoning changes prompted by such environmental considerations may appreciably limit the uses and profitability of land; yet if both factors were to be placed upon the scales, the pro bono public considerations must prevail. If there is substantial evidence sustaining the municipality's determination to rezone because of ecology, the court should not void such legislative determination."

In view of our determination that ecological considerations are legitimate objectives of a zoning ordinance or resolution, the following summation of evidence presented to the commission substantiates the county's position that resolution Z–115–75 is reasonably related to the public health and welfare and will confer a public benefit upon the citizens of the county:

> "The subject property area overlies one of the most permeable aquifers in the world, the Biscayne Aquifer. This aquifer serves as the source of virtually all drinking water in Dade County and must be protected from contamination. Due to the unique area hydrology and geology, the Biscayne Aquifer, the inland drainage canals, and the conservation area in West Dade County are all directly intercon-

nected. As a result of this interconnection, the bodies must be considered as component parts of the same water supply system."

The composition of the Biscayne Aquifer is mostly limestone and sand. The generally high porosity of the sand and the many passages through the limestone offer very little resistance to flow. The result is that the aquifer responds quickly to slight differences in the water table, with the following consequences:

1. The water table is relatively flat.

2. The yields of wells are large.

3. The ground and surface water regimens have an uncommonly high interrelationship.

4. The water table reacts quickly to rainfall. There is a high rate of rainfall penetration and surface water infiltration and, although annual rainfall is high, there is relatively little runoff as compared with other localities.

5. The coastal areas, which are exposed to Biscayne Bay and the Atlantic Ocean, are highly susceptible to saltwater intrusion.

The property in question contains a blue-green algae mat or periphyton which filters out many pollutants from the ground water. The process, which is referred to as 'biological assimilation', is important in protecting the ground and surface water quality.

Before it may be developed or improved, the subject property must be filled by a minimum of three feet of earth or other suitable fill material to comply with federal flood control criteria. Thus, the natural state of the property would have to be substantially altered before any meaningful development thereon could occur.

Any excavation of the Petitioner's property would remove the natural periphyton 'filtering mat' and would expose the aquifer, from which the drinking water supplies of Dade County are drawn, to a whole range of pollutants. The algae mat involves biological, chemical and physical processes which maintain the area's water quality.

"Rainfall, which varies between 40 and 85 inches per year and averages about 59 inches per year, provides the major water resource of Dade County. Approximately 80% of the annual rainfall occurs during the six-month 'rainy season' from May through October. The sensitivity of the area is unchallenged."

* * *

We conclude that the restrictions imposed by resolution Z–115–75 are reasonable in light of the legislative intent to preserve as nearly as possible an adequate water supply and the ecological balance in the area. However, that is not to say petitioner would be precluded from compensation under the Constitution if at some future date, upon taking positive steps to develop its property, petitioner proves it has been so restricted in its development efforts by the County that it is being deprived of the beneficial use of the property for the purpose of conferring a public benefit.

Affirmed.

Environmental Impact Reviews

In 1970, the federal government adopted the National Environmental Policy Act (NEPA), 42 U.S.C. §§ 4321–4370 (2000), which required federal agencies to evaluate the impact of their decisions on the environment. NEPA instilled environmental values in the agencies' decision-making process by requiring the preparation of an environmental impact statement for all federal actions that significantly affect the quality of the human environment. The heart of NEPA is the requirement that federal agencies conduct an environmental impact review (EIR) prior to initiating their own capital projects, allocating funds to others, or taking other actions that might have environmental impacts. EIR is a process that requires government decision-makers to determine whether projects will have a significant environmental impact and to consider how such impacts can be ameliorated. Federal agencies must prepare a detailed statement on the environmental impact of the proposed action, evaluate any adverse environmental effects, and consider alternatives to the proposed action before undertaking it. 42 U.S.C. § 4332.

NEPA was followed by the enactment of state environmental policy acts (SEPAs) in about half the states. Like NEPA, the state statutes stress the importance of environmental protection and require state agencies to conduct an environmental impact review before undertaking actions that might affect the environment adversely. Most SEPAs apply only to state agency actions. However, in six states—California, New York, Washington, Minnesota, Massachusetts, and Hawaii—the state statutes' EIR requirement applies to the actions of local government agencies as well. This requirement affects a host of local planning and zoning decisions, including the adoption of zoning ordinances and amendments, the grant of zoning variances, subdivision and site plan approvals, issuance of special use permits, and the adoption of comprehensive plans.

Where local land use agencies are required to conduct environmental impact reviews, additional steps are added to the local land use approval process that can conflict with the procedures prescribed for traditional land use reviews. In 1975, New York enacted the State Environmental Quality Review Act (SEQRA). N.Y. ENVTL. CONSERV. LAW §§ 8–0101 to 8–0117 (McKinney 2003). SEQRA requires an environmental impact statement for all government actions that may have a "significant effect on the environment." SEQRA applies to all agencies and instrumentalities of the state, which includes local agencies such as legislatures, planning boards, and zoning boards of appeals. SEQRA gives local land use agencies independent authority to impose conditions on land use approvals to mitigate the potential adverse environmental impacts of proposed projects. It can also be used to extend significantly the time it takes to conduct local land use reviews.

The following case required the judiciary in New York to sort out the conflicting policies of state-enacted land use and environmental statutes and to balance the developer's right to a predictable and timely local review with the public interest in environmental protection expressed in SEQRA.

SUN BEACH REAL ESTATE DEVELOPMENT CORP. v. ANDERSON

New York Supreme Court Appellate Division, Second Department, 1983.
469 N.Y.S.2d 964, 98 A.D.2d 367.

Lazer, J.

Under the Town Law, a planning board which fails to act on a preliminary subdivision plat application within 45 days is deemed to have approved the preliminary plat (Town Law, § 276, subd. 3). What we now decide is how that rigorous mandate for prompt action interacts with the State Environmental Quality Review Act (SEQRA) (ECL 8–0101 et seq.) requirement that an application for a permit or authorization shall not be deemed complete until a draft environmental impact statement (DEIS) has been accepted by the agency principally responsible for the approval (ECL 8–0109, subd 5).

Having been found in violation of the Town Law time restriction in processing petitioner's 777–acre subdivision plat, East Hampton's Planning Board argues that the 45–day time limit did not even begin to run until the board accepted petitioner's DEIS and that 45 days was too short a time for the board to meet its SEQRA obligations. Victorious at Special Term, the petitioner disagrees, contending that the 45–day time limit is an absolute one and that it is unaffected by any provision of SEQRA. We believe that preliminary plat approval determines important design features of a subdivision and therefore SEQRA's mandate for early meaningful consideration of the environmental consequences of a project requires environmental review to be undertaken when a preliminary plat application is filed. Once the East Hampton Planning Board determined that a DEIS was necessary, the preliminary plat application was not complete until the DEIS was accepted by the board. As a consequence, the time requirements of the Town Law did not commence running until after that acceptance.

On July 29, 1982, Sun Beach Real Estate Development Corp., the owner of a 777–acre tract in the Town of East Hampton, applied to the planning board for preliminary approval of a subdivision plat which showed a proposed development of 188 one-family residences and 143 condominium units. Attached to the application was an environmental assessment form (EAF) intended to assist the planning board in determining the environmental significance of the application (see 6 NYCRR 617.2 [l]). By letter dated September 7, 1982, the planning board informed Sun Beach that its application would be processed when it was complete, i.e., when the board issued a determination that the preliminary approval was of no environmental significance or when it accepted a DEIS if it decided there was environmental significance. Relying on subdivision 3 of section 276 of the Town Law, on October 15, 1982, Sun Beach demanded a certificate from the town clerk granting preliminary plat approval because the planning board had failed to hold a hearing on the plat within 45 days after submission of the application. On October 27, 1982, 90 days after the application had been filed, the planning board determined that the subdivision might significantly affect the environment and accepted as satisfactory a DEIS the applicant had submitted in mid-September, more than 45 days after filing of the application. A hearing was scheduled for December 8, 1982 to consider both the DEIS and the preliminary plat approval application. In January, 1983, Sun Beach brought this proceeding pursuant to CPLR article 78 against the town, the town clerk and the planning board seeking judgment directing issuance of a certificate of preliminary plat approval. Special Term granted the petition and directed the town clerk to issue the certificate. That judgment is at issue here.

There can be no doubt that absent SEQRA's requirements, Sun Beach would have been entitled to the approval certificate because default statutes such as section 276 of the Town Law and similar provisions governing city and village planning authorities (see General City Law, § 32; Village Law, § 7–728) have been uniformly construed to require automatic approval upon the failure to act within the prescribed time limits (*see, e.g., Matter of Pekar v. Town of Veteran Planning Bd.*, 58 A.D.2d 703; *Matter of Wallkill Manor v. Coulter*, 40 A.D.2d 828, affd. 33 N.Y.2d 783; *Matter of Northern Operating Corp. v. Chamberlain*, 34 A.D.2d 686, affd. 31 N.Y.2d 704; *Matter of Fishman v. Arnzen*, 29 A.D.2d 954; *Matter of Scarsdale Meadows v. Smith*, 20 A.D.2d 906; *Matter of Levin v. Thornbury*, 2 A.D.2d 774). None of the cited cases dealt, however, with the co-ordination between existing subdivision approval procedures and the SEQRA process. Recognizing the impact of SEQRA, the town contends that when section 276 of the Town Law is harmonized with SEQRA, the time limits imposed by the Town Law do not commence to run until the planning board has accepted a DEIS.

It is a familiar canon of statutory construction that apparently conflicting statutory provisions should be harmonized in a manner that preserves the essential purposes of both (*Matter of Burger King v. State Tax Comm.*, 51 N.Y.2d 614; *Matter of Lumpkin v. Department of Social Servs.*, 59 A.D.2d 485, affd. 45 N.Y.2d 351; McKinney's Cons Laws of NY, Book 1, Statutes, § 98). Since Sun Beach claims there is no conflict, it is necessary to examine the requirements of SEQRA to see if they can be integrated into existing subdivision approval time limits, and if they cannot, to decide whether there is any reasonable method to reconcile the two statutes.

SEQRA's procedures are intended to minimize to the greatest degree possible the adverse environmental consequences of any project that is approved. In *Glen Head–Glenwood Landing Civic Council v. Town of Oyster Bay* (88 A.D.2d 484, 486–487) we summarized the procedure as follows:

> "As early as possible in the SEQRA process, the agency 'having principal responsibility for carrying out or approving' a given project or activity—the 'lead' agency (ECL 8–0111, subd 6)—must determine whether an environmental impact statement (EIS) should be prepared with reference to the proposal submitted (ECL 8–0109, subd 4; 8–0111, subd 6). If the lead agency determines that the project 'may have a significant effect on the environment', either the agency or the applicant—at the latter's option—must prepare a draft environmental impact statement (DEIS) (ECL 8–0109, subds 2, 4). If the draft statement is accepted by the agency 'as satisfactory with respect to scope, content and adequacy', it is then circulated to the DEC, other agencies having an interest in the proposal, and 'interested members of the public' (ECL 8–0109, subds. 4, 5; 6 NYCRR 617.8 [b]; 617.10). After allowing a period for comment, the lead agency must prepare a final environmental impact statement (FEIS) and circulate it in the same manner as the draft statement (ECL 8–0109, subds 4, 5, 6; 6 NYCRR 617.10 [h]). Finally, upon adoption of the environmental-affecting proposal by the lead agency, it is required to make explicit findings that (1) the requirements of SEQRA have been met, and (2) adverse environmental effects revealed in the EIS process will be minimized or avoided to the maximum extent possible (ECL 8–0109, subd 8; 6 NYCRR 617.9 [c])."

It is undisputed that development of petitioner's 777–acre tract will have environmental reverberations and that the instant subdivision process constitutes an "action" which invokes SEQRA's directives. An action is defined as "projects or activities involving the issuance to a person of a lease, permit, license, certificate or other entitlement for use or permission to act by one or more agencies" (ECL 8–0105, subd. 4, par [i]). By regulation, "actions" also encompass "planning activities of an agency that commit the agency to a definite course of future decisions" (6 NYCRR 617.2 [b] [2]). All of the activities or steps in a capital project (i.e., planning, design, contracting, construction and operation) constitute an action, but only one draft and one final environmental statement are necessary if the statement "address[es] each step at a level of detail sufficient for an adequate analysis of environmental effects" (6 NYCRR 617.2 [b]).

While the imprecision of the statutory language renders it difficult to identify the precise point when a DEIS must be prepared during an "action" (see *Matter of Tri–County Taxpayers Assn. v. Town Bd.*, 55 N.Y.2d 41, 45), the legislative intent is that environmental factors be given consideration "[a]s early as possible in the formulation of a proposal for an action" (ECL 8–0109, subd 4; see, also, 6 NYCRR 617.1 [c]). The emphasis on early consideration facilitates the underlying purposes of a DEIS—"to relate environmental considerations to the inception of the planning process, to inform the public and other public agencies as early as possible about proposed actions that may significantly affect the quality of the environment" (ECL 8–0109, subd 4). This is consistent with the requirement that the SEQRA process "run concurrently with other procedures relating to the review and approval of the action" (ECL 8–0109, subd 5). If the DEIS is not prepared at an early stage, modification of a project in light of subsequently discovered environmental problems may become difficult because nonenvironmental considerations may have already been transformed into an over-all proposal (see Orloff, SEQRA: New York's Reformation of NEPA, 46 Albany L. Rev. 1128, 1136). Not only will the sponsors of projects be more likely to resist alteration of proposals which already have received some processing and approval, but institutional bias may result because later governmental decisions may be influenced by prior governmental decisions or commitments (*see Matter of Tri–County Taxpayers Assn. v. Town Bd., supra*; Note, Program Environmental Impact Statements: Review and Remedies, 75 Mich. L. Rev. 107, 111–112; 4 Rohan, Zoning and Land Use Controls, § 27.02 [2]). Indeed, in *Tri–County* (supra, pp. 46–47), the Court of Appeals declared that: "[T]he dynamics and freedom of decision-making with respect to a proposal to rescind a prior action are significantly more constrained than when the action is first under consideration for adoption. Thus, although not legally conclusive the initiatory action by the town board might well have been practically determinative. In effect the purpose of SEQRA is to assure the preparation and availability of an environmental impact statement at the time any significant authorization is granted for a specific proposal."

It is thus apparent that the DEIS must be prepared at a point " 'where genuine flexibility remains before bureaucratic momentum strips [it] of any real influence on decision-making' " (*see Mount Sutro Defense Comm. v. Regents of Univ. of Cal.*, 77 Cal.App.3d 20, 34).

With these considerations in mind, we return to the parties' debate as to when it is during the subdivision approval process that the DEIS must be filed. We view preliminary plat approval as so significant a determination during the process that an environmental impact statement must be deemed a prerequisite to the approval. * * *

In determining the temporal position of the DEIS in the subdivision process, the holdings of our sister States are entitled to respect in view of the essential uniformity of environmental legislation (see Robinson, SEQRA's Siblings: Precedents from Little NEPA's in the Sister States, 46 Albany L. Rev. 1155, 1157). Interpreting Washington's State Environmental Policy Act of 1971 (Wash. Rev. Code Ann., ch. 43.21C; SEPA), a statute similar to our own, the Supreme Court of Washington held that preliminary approval of a subdivision requires the preparation of an environmental impact statement (*see Loveless v. Yantis*, 82 Wn.2d 754). The court reasoned that preliminary approval of a plat is a discretionary, non-duplicative decision and preparation of a statement at the time of preliminary approval would facilitate early and meaningful environmental review of the project because that is the stage when the planning body, the developer and the public should be made aware of the environmental consequences of the design matters revealed in the preliminary plat and investment costs would be minimized if the plat were to be abandoned or altered (*Loveless v. Yantis, supra*, pp. 765–766).

Our conclusion, then, is that when the planning agency has determined that development of the subdivision might significantly affect the environment, the application for preliminary approval is not complete until a DEIS has been filed and has been accepted by the agency as satisfactory in scope and content (see ECL 8–0109, subd 5; 6 NYCRR 617.3 [e]). The DEIS should be available when it is still practicable to modify the project so as to mitigate potentially adverse economic effects or to choose a less environmentally damaging alternative (see ECL 8–0109, subds 2, 8) and before it is too late to influence the basic design of a project already fixed at the preliminary stage (*see* ECL 8–0103, subd 7; *Glen Head–Glenwood Landing Civic Council v. Town of Oyster Bay*, 88 A.D.2d 484, supra; *Matter of Town of Henrietta v. Department of Environmental Conservation*, 76 A.D.2d 215).

Once the application is complete, the planning board must coordinate its subdivision approval procedures with SEQRA (ECL 8–0109, subd. 5; 8–0103, subd 6). The 30–day period of comment on the DEIS for involved agencies and the public (6 NYCRR 617.8 [c]) easily fits within the 45–day period for holding a preliminary plat hearing under subdivision 3 of section 276 of the Town Law and it is preferable that a joint hearing be held (6 NYCRR 617.8 [d]). The final environmental impact statement need not be prepared until after the final plat has been submitted since SEQRA requires only one DEIS and one final environmental impact statement to be prepared for a given action (6 NYCRR 617.2 [b]); preparation of a final environmental impact statement need only precede the agency's final decision to approve an action (6 NYCRR 617.9 [c]). Depending on whether significant new information is revealed in the final plat submission, the agency may require the filing of a supplemental DEIS (*see Glen Head–Glenwood Landing Civic Council v. Town of Oyster Bay*, 88 A.D.2d 484, 494–495, supra).

Where a DEIS is a requisite to preliminary approval, the 45–day deadline imposed by the Town Law seems too short for planning boards to fulfill their SEQRA requirements. While an agency may vary SEQRA's time limits for "preparation, review and public hearings to coordinate the environmental review process with other procedures relating to review and approval of an action" (ECL 8–0109, subd. 5), provided the periods as varied are "no less protective of environmental values" (6 NYCRR 617.4 [b]), the agency cannot take any further steps until the submission of a DEIS (see ECL 8–0109, subd. 4). If the application does not contain the DEIS, the 45–day period for Town Law action may elapse before the statement has been filed, leaving the agency with the option of granting approval without the DEIS and running the risk of legal challenge to its decision or of denying approval on the ground of inadequate environmental review (Sahm, Project Approval Under the California Environmental Quality Act: It Always Takes Longer Than You Think, 19 Santa Clara L.Rev. 579). Neither alternative is acceptable.

It is apparent that SEQRA's drafters did not take into account some of the idiosyncracies of subdivision procedures (see Marsh, Commentary—Unresolved Issues, 46 Albany L. Rev. 1298, 1304) and it has been left to the judiciary to attempt to co-ordinate the statutes. Resolution of the instant case depends on which statute has preeminence—the 45-day requirement enacted in 1966 to limit the depredations of dilatory planning boards (see *Matter of Mahopac Isle v. Agar*, 39 Misc.2d. 1, *supra*; 1 Anderson, N.Y. Zoning Law and Practice [2d ed.], § 15.07) or SEQRA enacted in 1975 to save the environment and preserve it for future generations (ECL 8–0101, 8–0103, subds. 1, 8). We have no difficulty in according priority to SEQRA because the legislative declaration of purpose in that statute makes it obvious that protection of "the environment for the use and enjoyment of this and all future generations" (ECL 8–0103, subd. 8) far overshadows the rights of developers to obtain prompt action on their proposals. Once SEQRA's priority is recognized, the statute must be read to mandate that a preliminary plat application is not complete until a DEIS has either been dispensed with or accepted and the 45-day limitation in the Town Law does not commence to run until the application is complete (see *Asarco Inc. v. Air Quality Coalition*, 92 Wn.2d 685, 710). Here, the East Hampton Planning Board conducted a hearing on the preliminary plat within 45 days of its acceptance of the DEIS and therefore it acted in a timely manner without default under subdivision 3 of section 276 of the Town Law.

In reaching our conclusion, we are quite aware that SEQRA and its regulations have set no time limits within which a planning board must accept a proposed DEIS (see *Matter of East Clinton Developers v. Town of Clinton*, 88 A.D.2d 416). The danger, of course, is that planning boards may utilize the absence of SEQRA time limitations to resume the type of bureaucratic delay that resulted in the enactment of the 45-day time limitation in 1966. If such consequences are to be avoided, the Legislature and the Commissioner of Environmental Conservation should turn their attention to the problem.

Whatever the future may hold in this respect, however, the instant judgment should be reversed, without costs or disbursements, and proceeding dismissed.

* * *

Notes

1. The California Environmental Quality Act (CEQA), like New York's SEQRA, applies to the granting or denial of permits to private developers. Pub.Res.C. § 2100 et. seq. For a complete discussion on state environmental review acts and corresponding court decisions, see Nicholas Robinson, SEQRA's Siblings: Precedents from Little NEPA's in the Sister States, 46 Alb. L. Rev. 1155 (1982) and Philip Weinberg, A Powerful Mandate: NEPA and State Environmental Review Acts in the Courts, 5 Pace Envtl. L. Rev. 1

(1987). For an overview of state environmental review statutes see Growing Smart Legislative Guidebook, Chapter 12, Appendix B, pp. 12–30–12–32 (American Planning Association 2002).

2. Most environmental impact review statutes require the assessment of the impact of government actions on the "environment." Should the "environment" be limited to flora and fauna? In Chinese Staff and Workers Association v. City of New York, 68 N.Y.2d 359, 502 N.E.2d 176, 509 N.Y.S.2d 499 (1986), community residents used SEQRA to challenge the approval of a special use permit for the construction of a high-rise luxury condominium. The petitioners argued that the city's environmental review was arbitrary and capricious because it failed to consider the possible displacement of low-income residents. The court held that it is clear from the express terms of the statute and the regulations that the term environment is broadly defined and expressly includes considerations such as "existing patterns of population concentration, distribution, or growth, and existing community or neighborhood characteristics." Therefore, the court stated that the impact that a proposed project may have on population patterns or community character is a relevant concern in an environmental analysis. In Jackson v. New York State Urban Dev. Corp., 67 N.Y.2d 400, 503 N.Y.S.2d 298, 494 N.E.2d 429 (1986), although the Court of Appeals focused on SEQRA's "attempt to strike a balance between social and economic goals and concerns about the environment," it indicated that "environment" is "defined broadly to include 'land, air, water, minerals, flora, fauna, noise, objects of historic or aesthetic significance, existing patterns of population concentration, distribution, or growth, and existing community or neighborhood character.'"

SECTION 3. RESOURCE–SPECIFIC LOCAL LAND USE REGULATIONS

The gradual evolution toward environmental sensitivity in local land use controls has proceeded far enough that a distinct environmental ethic, as opposed to an incidental one, is evident. Local governments have adopted a host of environmental regulations. Local laws addressing the following issues can now be found and studied: cluster development; environmentally sensitive area protection; erosion and sediment control; grading, excavations, and fill; floodplain control; groundwater/aquifer resource protection; landscaping; ridgeline protection; scenic resource protection; soil removal; solid waste disposal; stream and watercourse protection; steep slopes; stormwater management; timber harvesting; tree protection; vegetation removal; and wetlands. Interestingly, many of these ordinances deal with the prevention of nonpoint source pollution, an urgent problem that generally is conceded to be beyond the reach of federal environmental law.

Local governments derive their authority to adopt laws that protect the environment from land use enabling statutes, home rule laws, and special laws directly aimed at environmental protection. In New York, municipalities have been delegated additional authority to protect the environment under the state's home rule law. The home rule provisions of Article IX of the New York Constitution and legislation passed pursuant to it give local governments broad home rule powers. N.Y. CONST. Art. IX. The state legislature implemented Article IX with the enactment of the Municipal Home Rule Law (MHRL), the provisions of which are to be "liberally construed." Under the MHRL, localities are given the authority to adopt laws relating to their "property, affairs or government," for "the protection and enhancement of [their] physical and visual environment."

The MHRL has been regarded as a source of local authority to regulate land use, in addition to the zoning and planning enabling statutes. It also has been interpreted to permit the enactment of purely environmental laws. For example, in Ardizzone v. Elliott, 75 N.Y.2d 150, 551 N.Y.S.2d 457, 550 N.E.2d 906, 908 (1989), the court stated that the municipality had the "power to regulate the freshwater wetlands within its boundaries under the Municipal Home Rule Law." This broad authority is critical to enacting laws that protect resources such as wildlife and wildlife habitat that may not fit squarely within the ambit of traditional zoning laws. The grant of authority encompassed in the MHRL provides a safety net for communities desiring to enact extensive environmental laws. This, combined with the power of local governments to include environmental standards in their zoning and land use regulations, provides ample authority for the state's villages, towns, and cities to create an integrated set of land use laws. Environmental laws may be added to the municipality's suite of land use laws by adopting them under the MHRL, the zoning enabling act, the subdivision or site plan delegation statutes, and by referring to the broad language of the planning enabling acts.

A. WATER RESOURCE PROTECTION

The adverse impact of development on surface waters is dramatically described by the U.S. Supreme Court in Tahoe–Sierra Preservation Council, Inc., et. al. v. Tahoe Regional Planning Agency, 535 U.S. 302, 122 S.Ct. 1465, 152 L.Ed.2d 517 (2002). The case explains the effect of nonpoint source pollution on Lake Tahoe as follows:

> Lake Tahoe's exceptional clarity is attributed to the absence of algae that obscures the waters of most other lakes. Historically, the lack of nitrogen and phosphorous, which nourish the growth of algae, has ensured the transparency of its waters. Unfortunately, the lake's pristine state has deteriorated rapidly over the past 40 years; increased land development in the Lake Tahoe Basin (Basin) has threatened the " 'noble sheet of blue water' " beloved by Twain and countless others. 34 F.Supp.2d, at 1230. As the District Court found, "[d]ramatic decreases in clarity first began to be noted in the late 1950's/early 1960's, shortly after development at the lake began in earnest." *Id.* at 1231. The lake's unsurpassed beauty, it seems, is the wellspring of its undoing.

The upsurge of development in the area has caused "increased nutrient loading of the lake largely because of the increase in impervious coverage of land in the Basin resulting from that development." *Ibid.* "Impervious coverage—such as asphalt, concrete, buildings, and even packed dirt—prevents precipitation from being absorbed by the soil. Instead, the water is gathered and concentrated by such coverage. Larger amounts of waterflowing off a driveway or a roof have more erosive force than scattered raindrops falling over a dispersed area—especially one covered with indigenous vegetation, which softens the impact of the raindrops themselves." Ibid. Given this trend, the District Court predicted that "unless the process is stopped, the lake will lose its clarity and its trademark blue color, becoming green and opaque for eternity."

535 U.S. at 306–08.

Those areas in the Basin that have steeper slopes produce more runoff; therefore, they are usually considered "high hazard" lands. Moreover, certain areas near streams or wetlands known as "Stream Environment Zones" (SEZs) are especially vulnerable to the impact of development because, in their natural state, they act as filters for much of the debris that runoff carries. Because "[t]he most obvious response to this problem * * * is to restrict development around the lake—especially in SEZ lands, as well as in areas already naturally prone to runoff," id., at 1232, conservation efforts have focused on controlling growth in these high hazard areas.

The Tahoe–Sierra decision and the other cases in this section demonstrate how rapidly land use controls are evolving in order to protect water resources from the adverse impacts of land development.

(1) Aquifer/Groundwater Supplies

Some localities use their environmental authority to protect drinking water aquifers by imposing additional regulatory standards on development projects proposed in such areas. The aquifer protection ordinance of Wallingford, Connecticut, prohibits certain land uses in order to protect its groundwater resources. Landowners are not allowed to conduct businesses that use hazardous chemicals, or to use their land for solid waste disposal facilities, junk yards, septage lagoons, hazardous waste drum storage areas, bulk storage piles, surface impoundments, road salt storage, or pipelines that transmit oil, gasoline or other hazardous materials. Other more manageable uses are allowed but restricted, such as above-ground chemical and fuel storage, underground fuel storage, dry cleaning, and new or enlarged manure, fertilizer, pesticide, and herbicide storage sites.

QUICK v. AUSTIN
Supreme Court of Texas, 1999.
7 S.W.3d 109.

JUSTICE ABBOTT delivered the opinion of the Court.

* * *

Frustrated by their perception that the Austin City Council was failing to safeguard Barton Springs adequately, a group of Austin citizens interested in protecting the environment initiated the Save Our Springs Ordinance and placed it on the Austin municipal ballot for a local referendum election. In August 1992, the Austin citizens participating in the referendum election overwhelmingly approved the Ordinance. Two days after the voters approved the Ordinance, the Austin City Council enacted the Ordinance and incorporated it into the City Code.

The purpose of the Ordinance, according to its Declaration of Intent, is to insure water quality control in Barton Creek, Barton Springs, and the Barton Springs Edwards Aquifer. The provisions of the Ordinance apply to those areas within Austin and Austin's extraterritorial jurisdiction that contain watersheds contributing to Barton Springs. The Ordinance limits impervious or non-porous cover on land in the regulated areas to between 15% and 25% of the net site area. The Ordinance also requires that new developments be set back from streams and not contribute to an increase in the amount of pollution constituents commonly found in urban rainfall runoff water. Construction in the "critical water quality zone" of the Barton Creek watershed is prohibited by the Ordinance. The Ordinance provides for no waivers or exceptions unless necessary to avoid conflict with state and federal laws.

Petitioners Jerry J. Quick, Kaira G. Quick, John M. Bryant, Ruth E. Bryant, Joe Cox, Dolores Cox, Florence Turck, and Circle C Land Corporation all own land outside the city limits of Austin but within its extraterritorial jurisdiction. Because their land is within Austin's extraterritorial jurisdiction, any development of their property must comply with the Ordinance. The Petitioners sued the City in Hays County, seeking a declaratory judgment that the Ordinance was void because it was illegally enacted. Additionally, Petitioners challenged the Ordinance under section 26.177(d) of the Texas Water Code, which authorizes a party aggrieved by a water pollution control ordinance to appeal to district court to review whether the ordinance is invalid, arbitrary, unreasonable, inefficient, or ineffective.

Save Our Springs Alliance, Inc., an incorporated association of individuals led by the citizen initiators of the Ordinance, moved to intervene in the suit. The Alliance urged that the City was incapable of adequately advocating the Alliance's interest due to previous hostilities over the Ordinance. *See, e.g., City Council of Austin v. Save Our Springs Coalition*, 828 S.W.2d 340 (Tex.App.—Austin 1992, no writ)(citizens sued

City to force election on the Ordinance). The trial court, however, struck the plea in intervention, leaving the City to defend the Ordinance.

The Petitioners and the City proceeded to try the case to a jury. The jury answered "yes" to all the questions in the charge inquiring whether the Ordinance and its impervious cover limitations, its prohibition against increases in pollution constituents, and its failure to contain variances were an unreasonable, arbitrary, and inefficient attempt to control water quality. The jury also found that the Ordinance was not a proper subject for the initiative and referendum process and that the Ordinance regulated the number, use, and size of buildings in the City's extraterritorial jurisdiction (a violation of section 212.003 of the Texas Local Government Code).

Based on the jury's answers, the trial court rendered judgment for the Petitioners declaring the Ordinance null and void. The trial court's final judgment also contained conclusions of law, including that the Ordinance was ineffective because the Texas Natural Resource Conservation Commission had not approved it and that the Ordinance was void because it was enacted without a public hearing in violation of section 212.002 of the Local Government Code. The trial court further decreed that any permit required by Petitioner Circle C Land Corporation to develop its property would be subject only to the law in effect when the original application for preliminary subdivision approval was filed, which, in some cases, pre-dated the enactment of the Ordinance.

The court of appeals reversed and rendered in part and modified in part the trial court's judgment. 930 S.W.2d 678. The appellate court first determined that the trial court did not abuse its discretion in striking the Alliance's plea in intervention. 930 S.W.2d at 683. The court of appeals then concluded that the trial court erred in rendering judgment that the Ordinance was unreasonable, arbitrary, and inefficient pursuant to section 26.177(d) of the Texas Water Code because section 26.177(d) was unconstitutional under article II, section 1 of the Texas Constitution, the separation of powers provision. *Id.* at 685. The court of appeals further held that the Ordinance was not illegally enacted because (1) it did not require approval by the Texas Natural Resource Conservation Commission before it could become effective, (2) it was not subject to sections 212.002 and 212 .003 of the Local Government Code, and (3) it was a proper subject of the initiative and referendum process. *Id.* at 686–91. The appellate court accordingly reversed the trial court's judgment in part and rendered judgment that the Ordinance was a valid legislative act. The court of appeals also modified the trial court's judgment in part, holding that any permit required by Circle C would be considered only under the regulations and ordinances in effect when the original application for preliminary subdivision approval was filed, as long as the permit application was filed after September 1, 1987. *Id.* at 693–94.

Petitioners challenged the court of appeals' judgment by filing an application for writ of error with this Court. Petitioners allege that the court of appeals erred by holding (1) that section 26.177(d) of the Water

Code is unconstitutional as a violation of separation of powers, (2) that the Ordinance is not subject to sections 212.002 and 212.003 of the Local Government Code, (3) that the Ordinance is effective without the City first obtaining the Texas Natural Resource Conservation Commission's approval, (4) that the Ordinance was a proper subject of the initiative and referendum process, and (5) that only Circle C's permit applications filed after September 1, 1987 would be considered on the basis of the regulations and ordinances in effect at that time. The Alliance also filed its own application for writ of error, contending that the court of appeals erred in upholding the trial court's striking of its plea in intervention.

We first consider the constitutionality of section 26.177(d) of the Texas Water Code. Section 26.177(d) provides in pertinent part:

> Any person affected by any * * * ordinance * * * relating to water pollution control and abatement outside the corporate limits of such city adopted pursuant to this section or any other statutory authorization may appeal such action to the [Texas Natural Resource Conservation Commission] or district court * * *. The issue on appeal is whether the action or program is invalid, arbitrary, unreasonable, inefficient, or ineffective in its attempt to control water quality. The commission or district court may overturn or modify the action of the city.

Tex. Water Code § 26.177(d).

The trial court submitted several questions to the jury inquiring whether various provisions of the Ordinance were "unreasonable," "arbitrary," or "inefficient." Based on the jury's affirmative answers to these questions, the court then rendered judgment that the Ordinance was invalid under section 26.177(d).

The court of appeals, however, concluded that section 26.177(d) violates the separation of powers doctrine of the Texas Constitution because it requires a de novo review of a legislative act. The court of appeals reasoned that the trial court conducted a de novo review of the statute as evidenced by the court's charge asking the jury to determine, by a preponderance of the evidence, whether the jury thought the Ordinance was unreasonable, arbitrary, or inefficient. The court of appeals further ruled that section 26.177(d) authorized such an unconstitutional de novo review by permitting the reviewing court to "modify" a legislative act and to determine whether a legislative act was "inefficient" or "ineffective."

* * *

Petitioners urge that the Ordinance's invalidity under the *Comeau* standard is manifest. Petitioners rely upon evidence in the record that, before the passage of the Ordinance, the City already had the most stringent water quality standards in Texas. Moreover, a city engineer and the head of Austin's Environmental Services admitted during trial that no discernible trend of pollution existed in Barton Springs prior to the Ordinance's enactment. Accordingly, Petitioners maintain that the Ordinance was unnecessary and based on flawed data.

Petitioners also complain that it is impossible to comply with the Ordinance. The Ordinance requires that a development not increase annual pollution loadings of thirteen identified constituents. Petitioners contend that the rules implemented by the City of Austin to execute the Ordinance require runoff surface water from a development to have lower average concentrations of some of these constituents than was found in certain rain samples taken in Austin. In fact, Petitioners point out that the Ordinance requires that runoff surface water have less average nitrogen than contained in some name-brand bottled drinking water. Petitioners allege that the Ordinance's practical effect is therefore a preclusion of all development in the watershed areas.

Petitioners also attack the lack of variances in the Ordinance. For instance, even if a landowner could establish that no increase in pollution would result from constructing a greater percentage of impervious cover than allowed under the Ordinance, no variance is permitted.

Finally, Petitioners impugn the Ordinance's financial impact. The City's own expert economist concluded that the Ordinance would, over a fifteen-year period, decrease property values in the watershed areas in the range of $229 million to $379 million. The Petitioners introduced evidence at trial that some land lost ninety percent of its value because of the Ordinance.

The City presented evidence at trial that sharply contradicted the Petitioners' arguments. In response to the Petitioners' evidence regarding the effectiveness of the water control ordinances in place before the Save Our Springs Ordinance, the City provided testimony that the Ordinance was cheaper and easier to administer than earlier measures. Further, the evidence also established that eighty-six percent of all development applications received a variance under the water quality ordinance in effect immediately prior to the Save Our Springs Ordinance. This excessive grant of variances under the prior ordinance, according to the City, obviously undercut its effectiveness.

To rebut the Petitioners' claim that it is impossible to comply with the Ordinance because its rules require that runoff be purer than rain, the City elicited testimony from Stephen Stecher, the project director of the Barton Creek watershed study. He testified that soil and plants on the ground typically capture much of the nitrogen and some other constituents in urban rainfall before the constituents reach a creek or tributary. Accordingly, even assuming that the Petitioners' evidence regarding the rainfall samples was reliable, *see* ante at n. 3, the City contends that compliance with the technical rules is still possible because runoff is naturally less contaminated with certain pollutants than rainfall. In further support of its argument that it is not impossible to comply with the Ordinance, the City presented testimony from two developers that it is not only possible, but actually profitable to develop land in the watershed areas in compliance with the Ordinance. These developers both testified that they were anticipating sizable profits from their developments complying with the strictures of the Ordinance.

Finally, the City offered evidence that the impervious cover limitations in the Ordinance reduce polluting runoff and are a nationally-recognized method of protecting water quality. According to the City, the provisions restricting the pollutant constituents are only a small percentage of the 138 pollutants that the City is required to monitor under federal law. The restrictions on impervious cover and pollutant constituents, the City therefore urges, are clearly related to its goal of protecting the watershed from pollution in order to preserve water quality.

In light of the conflicting evidence presented at trial regarding the Ordinance, we cannot conclude that the Petitioners met their "extraordinary burden" of establishing that reasonable minds could not differ regarding whether the Ordinance was invalid, arbitrary, unreasonable, inefficient, or ineffective in its attempt to control water quality. While Petitioners presented evidence tending to establish that prior water control ordinances were sufficient such that the Ordinance was not necessary, the City's evidence regarding the excessive grant of variances under the prior measure precludes a determination that reasonable minds could not differ on the need for the Ordinance.

The trial testimony conflicts regarding a landowner's ability to comply with the Ordinance. The Petitioners offered scientific testimony attempting to establish that it was virtually impossible to comply with the Ordinance, but this testimony was refuted by the City. Moreover, the City also presented the testimony of two developers that, not only did the City approve their developments under the Ordinance, they actually anticipate profitable returns on their investments. The conflict in this evidence demonstrates that reasonable minds could indeed differ on whether compliance with the Ordinance is possible.

While the Petitioners decry the lack of a variance procedure in the Ordinance, the Ordinance does actually provide a limited variance to keep the Ordinance from running afoul of federal and state laws. Moreover, the Petitioners' complaint regarding the lack of a variance procedure ignores the evidence that the excessive grant of variances under prior water control measures had undercut their effectiveness.

We perceive that the real crux of the Petitioners' complaint is that the Ordinance unreasonably reduces property values and requires excessive expenditures in order to comply with its provisions. The Petitioners established that the Ordinance will result in at least a $225 million decrease in property values in regulated areas, and that the Ordinance has caused some parcels of land to lose ninety percent of their value. The City has not refuted this evidence.

However, in this case, the fact that the Ordinance severely impacts some property values does not make it invalid, arbitrary, unreasonable, inefficient, or ineffective in its attempt to control water quality. While the Ordinance's impervious cover limitations undoubtedly substantially affect the value of some property parcels, such limitations are a nationally-recognized method of preserving water quality. Further, it is indisputable that limiting pollutants in runoff water will aid in preserving water quality. We therefore conclude that the Ordinance's provisions are rationally related to its goal of protecting water quality.

Because we have concluded that the Ordinance is rationally related to the governmental interest in protecting water quality, the City has the right to significantly limit development in watershed areas in furtherance of this interest. *See Day–Brite Lighting, Inc. v. Missouri*, 342 U.S. 421, 424, 72 S.Ct. 405, 96 L.Ed. 469 (1952). * * *

The Petitioners next attack the court of appeals' conclusion that the Ordinance is not void under sections 212.002 and 212.003 of the Local Government Code. Local Government Code section 212.002 provides:

> After a public hearing on the matter, the governing body of a municipality may adopt rules governing plats and subdivisions of land within the municipality's jurisdiction to promote the health, safety, morals, or general welfare of the municipality and the safe, orderly, and healthful development of the municipality. Tex. Loc. Gov't Code § 212.002.

Local Government Code section 212.003 provides in pertinent part:

> (a) The governing body of a municipality by ordinance may extend to the extraterritorial jurisdiction of the municipality the application of municipal ordinances adopted under Section 212.002 and other municipal ordinances relating to access to public roads. However, unless otherwise authorized by state law, in its extraterritorial jurisdiction a municipality shall not regulate:
>
>> (1) the use of any building or property for business, industrial, residential, or other purposes;
>>
>> (2) the bulk, height, or number of buildings constructed on a particular tract of land;
>>
>> (3) the size of a building that can be constructed on a particular tract of land, including without limitation any restriction on the ratio of building floor space to the land square footage; or
>>
>> (4) the number of residential units that can be built per acre of land.

Id. § 212.003.

Petitioners argue that (1) sections 212.002 and 212.003 govern the Ordinance, (2) the Ordinance was enacted without a public hearing in violation of section 212.002, and (3) the Ordinance effectively violates the prohibitions in section 212.003 by regulating the use, bulk, height, number, or size of buildings. Petitioners accordingly advocate that the trial court correctly held that the Ordinance was void. The City responds that sections 212.002 and 212.003 do not apply because these sections are zoning statutes and the Ordinance is a water pollution control measure. We agree with the City.

By their express terms, sections 212.002 and 212.003 apply to ordinances that "govern plats and subdivisions of land." Further, the statutes' legislative history indicates that they govern a city's zoning authority, not a city's authority to apply water quality requirements. For instance, House Bill 3187, which amended section 212.003, "prohibits the application of zoning regulations in ETJ areas." COMMITTEE ON URBAN AFFAIRS, BILL ANALYSIS, Tex. H.B. 3187, 71st Leg., R.S. (1989). In fact, the Legislature made it clear that section 212.003 was not intended "to affect the ability of a municipality to apply water control requirements" in its extraterritorial jurisdiction. CONFERENCE COMMITTEE REPORT, Tex. H.B. No. 3187, 71st Leg., R.S. (1989). We therefore conclude that sections 212.002 and 212.003 apply only to zoning statutes, not water control measures such as the Ordinance.

Petitioners nevertheless assert that the Ordinance is, in effect, a zoning ordinance, not a water control ordinance. Petitioners argue that the Ordinance's impervious cover limitations effectively constitute a regulation on the use, bulk, height, number, and size of buildings in the City's extraterritorial jurisdiction in violation of section 212.003. Petitioners contend that we should consider the actual effect of the Ordinance, not its stated purpose, in determining whether the Ordinance must comply with these statutes.

However, we disagree with Petitioners' assertion that the Ordinance effectively constitutes a zoning regulation. The Ordinance's stated goal is to protect and preserve a "clean and safe drinking water supply" and "to prevent further degradation of the water quality in Barton Creek, Barton Springs, and the Barton Springs Edwards Aquifer." While the Ordinance clearly has effects on land use through its imposition of impervious cover limitations, these cover limitations are typical features in ordinances protecting water quality. Indeed, as discussed previously, such cover limitations are a nationally-recognized method of preserving water quality, and therefore we conclude that the cover limitations further the Ordinance's stated goal. On balance, the Ordinance is not a zoning regulation seeking to shape urban development, but rather is a measure designed to protect water quality. We accordingly hold that the requirements of sections 212.002 and 212.003 are not applicable to the Ordinance, and the Ordinance cannot be invalidated by these statutes.

* * *

For the foregoing reasons, we affirm the court of appeals' judgment holding that the Ordinance is a valid legislative act that need not be approved by the Texas Natural Resource Conservation Commission to become effective and enforceable. We dismiss Circle C's point of error regarding the court of appeals' modification of the trial court's judgment with regard to section 481.143 of the Government Code because Circle C did not obtain final relief prior to the repeal of section 481.143.

* * *

Notes

1. In the Moviematic case, supra, note that the Florida court held that the preservation of an adequate drinking water supply and the ecological system in a particular area are legitimate objectives of zoning laws.

2. Under the Clean Water Act, most local governments in urban areas have an obligation to enact laws that reduce pollutants contained in stormwater runoff. One way of accomplishing this objective is to limit the amount of impervious coverage allowed in new developments approved by local land use review boards. In Quick v. Austin, supra, note how the Austin aquifer protection ordinance uses impervious coverage limitations in the interest of aquifer protection. Consider the court's conclusion that this ordinance was not adopted under the city's delegated zoning authority. If the zoning authority were the source of its legislative authority, would impervious coverage limitations applicable to its extraterritorial jurisdiction have been within its authority to enact? Why?

3. Note how in defending its ordinance, the City of Austin referred to its legal obligations under federal environmental statutes. Did this argument work for the City in rebutting landowners' claims that the ordinance was unreasonable and arbitrary? Does this suggest a strategic link that can be forged between federal and municipal environmental laws?

CONNECTICUT RESOURCES RECOVERY AUTH. v. PLANNING & ZONING COMM'N

Supreme Court of Connecticut, 1993.
225 Conn. 731, 626 A.2d 705.

KATZ, ASSOCIATE JUSTICE.

* * *

The following relevant facts are undisputed. Since 1945, Meriden has owned a 138 acre tract of land in Wallingford. In 1958, Wallingford adopted zoning regulations that placed the tract in a rural district. At that time, a relatively small portion of the tract was being used for solid waste disposal. The largest use of the tract was for sewage lagoons to accommodate overflow from a sewage treatment plant located in Meriden. Other portions of the tract were being used for sand excavation, industrial waste disposal and sludge disposal. Much of the tract was vacant. The parties presented conflicting evidence as to whether one portion of the tract was used for stump and brush disposal or for a sawmill and lumber storage area. The parties agree that sewage treatment facilities and garbage dumps were not permitted uses under the 1958 Wallingford zoning regulations. These regulations provided that while nonconforming uses could be continued, they could not be changed or extended except in very limited circumstances. Wallingford Planning and Zoning Regs. § 11 (1958), "Non-Conforming Buildings and Uses."

By 1982, approximately sixty and one-half acres of the tract were being used for disposal of solid and bulky waste. In 1983, Wallingford adopted zoning regulations that established an aquifer protection district and specifically prohibited solid waste disposal in this district.[1] The district consists of the primary and secondary recharge areas of the Quinnipiac River Aquifer and the Muddy River Aquifer. Wallingford Zoning Regs. § 4.12.B (1985), "Aquifer Protection (APD) District." It includes the tract owned by Meriden. The aquifer protection regulations were codified in September, 1985, at which time they took effect.

In December, 1985, Meriden agreed to lease part of its tract to CRRA for use as a disposal site for ash residue, sludge, bulky waste and solid waste. On November 10, 1988, CRRA and Meriden applied to the commission to delete the regulation prohibiting solid waste disposal in an aquifer protection district. Following a public hearing on January 5, 1989, regarding the application, the commission voted to retain the regulation.

On January 29, 1989, the plaintiffs appealed the commission's decision to the Superior Court pursuant to General Statutes § 8–9. The court held a preliminary hearing on the issue of standing to determine whether CRRA and Meriden had been aggrieved by the commission's decision. The court was concerned that solid waste disposal might be a protected nonconforming use of the tract, in which case the plaintiffs could not be harmed by the regulation prohibiting solid waste disposal in an aquifer protection district. At the hearing, the plaintiffs filed a motion to continue the appeal until they could pursue with local zoning authorities the issue of whether solid waste disposal was a valid nonconforming use of the tract. * * * The court granted the motion.

On February 22, 1990, CRRA and Meriden requested a certificate of zoning compliance from Linda Bush, the Wallingford zoning enforcement officer. By a letter dated March 14, 1990, Bush informed CRRA and Meriden that she would not issue a certificate because use of the tract for solid waste disposal was a nonconforming use that had been unlawfully expanded. CRRA and Meriden appealed Bush's decision to the board. Following a May 21, 1990 public hearing, the board voted to sustain Bush's decision.

The plaintiffs appealed the board's decision to the Superior Court pursuant to General Statutes § 8–8(b). The court granted a motion made by CRRA and Meriden to consolidate this appeal with the first appeal and held a hearing on both appeals on June 11, 1991. In a lengthy memorandum of decision dated January 8, 1992, the trial court rendered judgment for CRRA and Meriden in each appeal. The defendants filed petitions for certification to appeal to the Appellate Court. The Appellate Court granted the petitions, and we transferred the appeals to this court pursuant to Practice Book § 4023 and General Statutes § 51–199(c).

* * *

---

1. Section 4.12.A of the Wallingford zoning regulations provides: "A major source of Wallingford's drinking water is the Quinnipiac River Aquifer. Protection of this resource is vital to ensure an adequate supply of safe drinking water. This protection can best be achieved by regulations that control pollution within the aquifer recharge area." Section 4.12.F lists nonpermitted uses, including solid waste disposal. Wallingford Zoning Regs. § 4.12.B (1985), "Aquifer Protection (APD) District."

II

We next consider the first case, *Connecticut Resources Recovery Authority v. Planning & Zoning Commission* (Docket No. 14584). The commission claims that the trial court incorrectly determined that: (1) the regulation prohibiting solid waste disposal over an aquifer is an invalid exercise of the town's police power; (2) the regulation is inconsistent with the plan of development; (3) the regulation is preempted by state solid waste and water quality statutes; and (4) the commission's decision was not supported by the record. We consider these arguments in turn.

A

The trial court held that the blanket prohibition of solid waste disposal in an aquifer protection zone is an invalid exercise of the police power. The plaintiffs argue that General Statutes § 8–2 empowers the commission only to regulate land use, not to prohibit certain uses, and that the prohibition of solid waste disposal over an aquifer lacks a reasonable relation to the public health, safety and welfare. We disagree.

To challenge an ordinance successfully, a party must establish the invalidity of the ordinance beyond a reasonable doubt. *Lizotte v. Conservation Commission*, 216 Conn. 320, 337, 579 A.2d 1044 (1990). Section 8–2 authorizes local authorities to regulate land use through zoning, and specifically requires them to do so "with reasonable consideration for the protection of existing and potential public surface and ground drinking water supplies." We have said that "when a statute authorizes a municipality to regulate a certain activity, a prohibition of that activity will be valid if it is rationally related to the protection of the community's public health, safety and general welfare." *Beacon Falls v. Posick*, 212 Conn. 570, 583, 563 A.2d 285 (1989); see also *Lizotte v. Conservation Commission, supra*, 216 Conn. at 336, 579 A.2d 1044.

In *Lizotte v. Conservation Commission, supra*, at 322–23, 579 A.2d 1044, the plaintiffs challenged the validity of a local regulation prohibiting the location of a septic system within 150 feet of an inland wetland or watercourse. They contended that the regulation was invalid because the enabling statute authorized only "necessary" regulations and the blanket prohibition was not necessary. *Id.*, at 336, 579 A.2d 1044. We held that prohibitions of activities are within the police power of a municipality if they are rationally related to the protection of the public health, safety and welfare, and that a municipality may rationally conclude that prohibition of a risky activity is more appropriate than case-by-case analysis. *Id.*, at 334, 337, 579 A.2d 1044. In *Beacon Falls v. Posick, supra*, 212 Conn. at 586, 563 A.2d 285 we concluded that a townwide ban of garbage dumps was a valid exercise of the police power.

The record before the trial court indicated that, at the time it adopted the solid waste prohibition, the commission was aware that the Meriden owned tract was a suspected source of contamination of Wallingford's water supply. A document issued by a regional planning authority in 1980 specifically recommended that solid waste disposal operations over the aquifer should be suspended.

We have long held that "[a]n agency which has the authority to enact regulations is vested with a large measure of discretion, and the burden of showing that the agency has acted improperly rests upon the one who asserts it." *Aaron v. Conservation Commission*, 183 Conn. 532, 537, 441 A.2d 30 (1981); *see also Lizotte v. Conservation Commission, supra*, 216 Conn. at 337, 579 A.2d 1044. Local commissions "are closest to the circumstances and conditions which create the problem and shape the solution * * *. [I]n determining claims of error in such matters, [c]ourts must be scrupulous not to hamper the legitimate activities of civic administrative boards by indulging in a microscopic search for technical infirmities in their action." (Citations omitted; internal quotation marks omitted.) *Frito-Lay, Inc. v. Planning & Zoning Commission*, 206 Conn. 554, 573, 538 A.2d 1039 (1988). We conclude that Wallingford's prohibition of solid waste disposal over an aquifer is a valid exercise of its police power that is rationally related both to protection of the groundwater and to the public health, safety and welfare. Accordingly, we reverse the trial court's holding to the contrary.

B

The trial court also held that the solid waste ordinance was invalid because it did not comply with Wallingford's plan of development. The trial court noted that the town planning document recommends that an aquifer protection district should be created and "[r]estricted to uses which do not present undue risk of groundwater contamination and prohibiting or controlling those which do, such as, the use, storage, treatment or disposal of hazardous materials including storage of road salts or de-icing compounds* * *." Town of Wallingford Proposed Plan of Development Update, Phase 1 and 2—Summary Report, July, 1983, p. 14. The trial court held that because this plan did not specifically list solid waste disposal as an unduly risky activity, and there was no evidence that the commission considered the Meriden tract a threat to the groundwater at the time it adopted the plan of development, there was nothing in the record to indicate that the prohibition complied with the town plan of development.

We reject the trial court's reasoning and the plaintiffs' concomitant claim on appeal that because the plan provision quoted above specifically lists storage of "road salts" and "de-icing compounds" as unduly hazardous uses, the prohibition of solid waste disposal is necessarily inconsistent with this plan. As the trial court noted, a "plan of development is properly called a master plan * * *. The master plan, in its designation of appropriate uses for various areas in a town, is merely advisory." (Citation omitted.) *Dooley v. Town Plan & Zoning Commission*, 154 Conn. 470, 473, 226 A.2d 509 (1967).

General Statutes § 8–2 directs local authorities to regulate land use through zoning "with reasonable consideration for the protection of existing and potential public surface and ground drinking water supplies." It is clear from the record before the trial court that the Wallingford zoning authorities were aware that the Meriden owned tract was a threat to the groundwater and public health at the time they adopted the solid waste prohibition. We conclude that the solid waste prohibition was consistent both with the plan of development and with the comprehensive plan, which is to be found in the scheme of the zoning regulations themselves. *See Protect Hamden/North Haven from Excessive Traffic & Pollution, Inc. v. Planning & Zoning Commission, supra,* 220 Conn. at 551, 600 A.2d 757.

C

The trial court also held that the regulation banning solid waste disposal over an aquifer is preempted by certain state solid waste and water protection statutes. We disagree.

General Statutes § 22a–208a(b), part of the Solid Waste Management Act, provides that "nothing in this chapter or chapter 446e shall be construed to limit the right of any local governing body to regulate, through zoning, land usage for solid waste disposal." In *Beacon Falls v. Posick, supra,* 212 Conn. at 577–79, 563 A.2d 285, we held that this language demonstrated that the legislature did not intend to preempt local zoning regulation of solid waste disposal.

The plaintiffs attempt to distinguish *Beacon Falls v. Posick, supra,* on the grounds that that case involved a private dump whereas this case involves CRRA, a public instrumentality. Their argument is unpersuasive, however, because § 22a–208a(b) references chapter 446e, which is the section of the General Statutes creating CRRA. Further, in Beacon Falls v. Posick, supra, we specifically held "that the legislature intended only to preempt local zoning authority to the extent that it conflicted with the operation of a CRRA facility on property owned by the CRRA prior to May 11, 1984 * * *." *Id.,* at 579, 563 A.2d 285. The lease agreement between CRRA and Meriden was not even formed until late 1985. The trial court therefore incorrectly concluded that the solid waste prohibition was preempted.

D

Finally, we consider the trial court's conclusion that the commission's decision not to delete the solid waste prohibition was not reasonably supported by the record. The commission furnished two reasons for its refusal to delete the solid waste prohibition: (1) compliance with the town plan of development; and (2) protection of the drinking water supply. The commission claims that the trial court, in rejecting both of these reasons, impermissibly weighed the evidence and substituted its judgment for that of the commission. We agree.

We have often said that "[t]he trial court may not substitute its judgment for the wide and liberal discretion vested in the local authority when acting within its prescribed legislative powers." (Internal quotation marks omitted.) *Frito-Lay, Inc. v. Planning & Zoning Commission, supra,* 206 Conn. at 572–73, 538 A.2d 1039; *see also Calandro v. Zoning Commission,* 176 Conn. 439, 442, 408 A.2d 229 (1979). "[I]t is not the function of the court to retry the case. Conclusions reached by the commission must be upheld by the trial court if they are reasonably supported by the record. The credibility of the witnesses and the determination of issues of fact are matters solely within the province of the agency." (Internal quotation marks omitted.) *Protect Hamden/North Haven from Excessive Traffic & Pollution, Inc. v. Planning & Zoning Commission, supra,* 220 Conn. at 542–43, 600 A.2d 757; *Calandro v. Zoning Commission, supra,* 176 Conn. at 440, 408 A.2d 229. "The commission ha[s] the task of weighing th[e] evidence and reaching a conclusion on the merits of the plaintiff's application." *Calandro v. Zoning Commission, supra,* at 441, 408 A.2d 229. "[T]he court may grant relief on appeal only where the local authority has acted illegally or arbitrarily or has abused its discretion." (Internal quotation marks omitted.) *Frito-Lay, Inc. v. Planning & Zoning Commission, supra,* 206 Conn. at 573, 538 A.2d 1039. "[T]he action of the commission should be sustained if even one of the stated reasons is sufficient to support it." *Id.,* at 576, 538 A.2d 1039.

The commission had before it evidence that the Meriden solid waste disposal site was a suspected source of contamination of Wallingford's water supply. Documents from the state department of environmental protection, expert consultants, and a regional planning authority, and testimony from a member of the legislature's environment committee, all recommended that solid waste disposal operations over the aquifer be suspended. There was also testimony that expansion of the solid waste operations might cause further contamination.

We have said that "a local legislative body may consider the effects that are likely to flow from proposed amendments to its zoning regulations, and may decide, within the proper statutory parameters, that it would be unwise policy for the town to countenance those effects." *Protect Hamden/North Haven from Excessive Traffic & Pollution, Inc. v. Planning & Zoning Commission, supra,* 220 Conn. at 548, 600 A.2d 757. The plaintiffs conceded at oral argument that, at most, the evidence they presented at the hearing showed that there was a possibility that a solid waste disposal site could be operated safely over an aquifer. The trial court ruled that because there was a possibility of compatibility between these two uses, it was irrational for the commission to refuse to delete the blanket prohibition. We disagree.

In *Lizotte v. Conservation Commission, supra,* we upheld a blanket prohibition of septic systems within 150 feet of a wetland. We stated: "The commission could reasonably have concluded that, regardless of whether a specific prohibited activity may or may not adversely affect the town's wetlands, the risk of pollution outweighed in all instances the benefits to be gained by allowing case-by-case analysis of each application for a regulated use." *Id.,* at 337, 579 A.2d 1044. In this case, the commission could reasonably have concluded that although there was a possibility that a landfill could be operated safely in the aquifer protection district, the risk to the town's water supply outweighed any possible benefits.

In sum, we conclude that the local zoning authorities acted properly in refusing to delete the solid waste prohibition and in refusing to issue a certificate of zoning compliance.

The judgments are reversed and the cases are remanded with direction to render judgments dismissing the plaintiffs' appeals.

Notes

1. In the Connecticut Resources Recovery case, did the court hold that the state zoning enabling act delegated authority to cities and towns to prohibit solid waste facilities over groundwater aquifer areas? What language is contained in the Connecticut zoning enabling act that is missing in the relevant delegating statute in Texas? How broadly does the Connecticut court interpret the authority granted to local governments under the relevant state enabling act? Can you pinpoint the precise language the court relies on to sustain the local law and can you understand the principles of statutory interpretation that the court followed?

2. The town of North Kingston, Rhode Island, enacted an ordinance whose purpose was to protect the "chemical, physical and biological integrity" of the groundwater from pollutants in order "to ensure the availability of safe and potable drinking water for present and future needs." North Kingston Revised Ord. § 8–120 (1992). Maximum discharge levels of specified inorganic, organic, radioactive, and biologic pollutants are proscribed in the town's regulations. Discharges exceeding these levels are prohibited in areas designated as groundwater reservoir and recharge areas.

(2) Stormwater Management

Stormwater management is the process of controlling and cleansing the excess stormwater runoff so it does not harm natural resources or human health. As more land is covered with impervious surfaces, such as roads, parking lots, and buildings, there is less surface area available for stormwater to infiltrate. Where storm basins do not exist or are not adequate, stormwater finds its way to the nearest water body. Impervious surfaces not only increase the volume and velocity of runoff, but also prevent the natural processing of nutrients, sediments, and other contaminants. Regulation of stormwater runoff through stormwater management also controls floods, reduces erosion and sedimentation, and aids ground water replenishment.

Stormwater runoff control is crucial to the success of the federal Clean Water Act (CWA), 33 U.S.C. §§ 1251–1387(2000). It is one of the most serious causes of water pollution in the United States, exceeding in many locales the contamination caused by sewage and industrial facility discharges. Stormwater runoff carries algae-promoting nutrients, floatable trash, used motor oil, suspended metals, sediments, raw sewage, pesticides, and other toxic contaminants. They flow with stormwater runoff from their source to streams, rivers, lakes, estuaries, and oceans.

The United States Environmental Protection Agency (EPA), pursuant to its authority under the Clean Water Act, promulgated regulations establishing its Stormwater Management Program. EPA set forth a two-phase program. Phase I began regulating medium and large operators of municipal separate storm sewer systems (MS4s) in 1990. Phase I regulations require large cities and municipalities to implement a stormwater management program as a means to control polluted discharges from their MS4s. Phase II of the program, which was established in 1999, extends this coverage to small municipalities that operate MS4s.

Phase II regulates small MS4s as well as small construction activities; *i.e.*, those activities disturbing between one and five acres of land. Pursuant to these rules, municipal operators of regulated MS4s (those operating within a designated urbanized area) are required to obtain either an individual or a general National Pollutant Discharge Elimination System (NPDES) permit. There are three requirements in Phase II of the Stormwater Program: (1) reduce pollution to the maximum extent possible (MEP); (2) protect water quality; and (3) comply with the applicable water quality requirements of the Clean Water Act.

Best management practices are utilized to achieve the goal of reducing pollutants in stormwater. To ensure that operators meet the MEP standard, EPA set forth six minimum control measures that must be included in a management plan, including public education and participation programs, pollution prevention programs, programs to detect and eliminate illicit discharges, and programs to address stormwater runoff from construction sites and post-construction land uses.

The effect on local land use autonomy is evident in the fine print of the regulations. Local governments that operate stormwater systems are required to adopt erosion and sediment control laws, establish site plan review procedures for projects that will impact water quality, inspect construction activities, and adopt enforcement measures. Post-construction runoff controls are also required for development and redevelopment projects. Redevelopment is defined to include any change in the footprint of existing buildings that disturbs more than one acre of land. EPA has specifically targeted post-construction activities because areas undergoing new development or redevelopment have been shown to significantly increase pollution in receiving water bodies. Developing and implementing programs that minimize pollution in stormwater discharges is an effective approach to stormwater quality management.

Non-structural best management practices noted in the federal regulations include comprehensive planning and zoning ordinances that guide growth away from sensitive areas and that restrict industrial and other intense land uses that compromise water quality. Zoning measures targeted by the regulations include the requirement of buffer strips, designation of riparian preservation zones, and maximization of open space.

This extensive effort by the federal government to influence local land use regulation raises a number of political and legal issues, not the least of which is whether it violates the sovereign right of state governments to control land use without federal interference.

The Ninth Circuit Court of Appeals upheld federal regulations mandating municipalities to obtain Clean Water Act permits for storm sewers. The case below describes the legislative and political tension between local, state, and federal regulations.

ENVIRONMENTAL DEFENSE CENTER, INC. v. UNITED STATES ENVIRONMENTAL PROTECTION AGENCY

United States Court Of Appeals, Ninth Circuit, 2003.
319 F.3d 398.

BROWNING, JAMES. R., CIRCUIT JUDGE.

Petitioners challenge a rule issued by the United States Environmental Protection Agency pursuant to the Clean Water Act, 33 U.S.C. §§ 1251–1387, to control pollutants introduced into the nation's waters by storm sewers.

Storm sewers drain rainwater and melted snow from developed areas into water bodies that can handle the excess flow. Draining stormwater picks up a variety of contaminants as it filters through soil and over pavement on its way to sewers. Sewers are also used on occasion as an easy (if illicit) means for the direct discharge of unwanted contaminants. Since storm sewer systems generally channel collected runoff into federally protected water bodies, they are subject to the controls of the Clean Water Act. In October of 1999, after thirteen years in process, the Environmental Protection Agency ("EPA") promulgated a final administrative rule (the "Phase II Rule" or "the Rule") under § 402(p) of the Clean Water Act, 33 U.S.C. § 1342(p), mandating that discharges from small municipal separate storm sewer systems and from construction sites between one and five acres in size be subject to the permitting requirements of the National Pollutant Discharge Elimination System ("NPDES"), 33 U.S.C. §§ 1311(a), 1342. EPA preserved authority to regulate other harmful stormwater discharges in the future.

In the three cases consolidated here, petitioners and intervenors challenge the Phase II Rule on twenty-two constitutional, statutory, and procedural grounds. We remand three aspects of the Rule concerning the issuance of notices of intent under the Rule's general permitting scheme. We affirm the Rule against all other challenges.

* * *

The Municipal Petitioners' primary contention is that the Phase II Rule compels small MS4s to regulate citizens as a condition of receiving a permit to operate, and that EPA lacks both statutory and constitutional authority to impose such a requirement. * * *

The Municipal Petitioners contend that the Phase II Rule on its face compels operators of small MS4s to regulate third parties in contravention of the Tenth Amendment. We note that a facial challenge must show that there are no circumstances under which the challenged provisions would be constitutional. *Legal Aid Soc'y v. Legal Servs. Corp.*, 145 F.3d 1017, 1023–24 (9th Cir.1998). We conclude that the Rule does not violate the Tenth Amendment, because it directs no unconstitutional coercion.

The Phase II Rule requires any operator of a small MS4 applying for an individual permit or submitting a notice of intent for coverage under a general permit to specify plans for compliance with a series of six minimum control measures designed to protect water quality. 40 C.F.R. § 122.34. These "Minimum Measures" require an applicant to propose programs for: (1) conducting public education and outreach on stormwater impacts, *id.* at § 122.34(b)(1); (2) engaging public participation in the development of stormwater management programs, *id.* at § 122.34(b)(2); (3) detecting and eliminating illicit discharges to the MS4, *id.* at § 122.34(b)(3); (4) reducing pollution to the MS4 from construction activities disturbing one acre or more, *id.* at § 122.34(b)(4); (5) minimizing water quality impacts from development and redevelopment activities that disturb one acre or more, *id.* at § 122.34(b)(5); and (6) preventing or reducing pollutant runoff from municipal activities, *id.* at § 122.34(b)(6).

The Municipal Petitioners contend that the measures regulating illicit discharges, small construction sites, and development activities interfere excessively with local government functions and unconstitutionally compel small MS4 operators to regulate third parties, i.e. upstream dischargers. The Illicit Discharge Detection and Elimination measure requires that a permit seeker prohibit non-stormwater discharges to the MS4 and implement appropriate enforcement procedures. 40 C.F.R. § 122.34(b)(3)(ii)(B). The Construction Site Stormwater Runoff Control measure requires a permit seeker to implement and enforce a program to reduce stormwater pollutants from small construction sites. *Id.* at §§ 122.34(b)(4)(i)–(ii). It mandates erosion and sedimentation controls, site plan reviews that take account of water quality impacts, site inspections, and the consideration of public comment, and requires that construction site operators implement erosion, sedimentation, and waste management best management practices. *Id.* The Post–Construction/New Development measure requires permit seekers to address post-construction runoff from new development and redevelopment projects disturbing one acre or more. *Id.* at § 122.34(b)(5)(ii)(B). Noting that most MS4s are operated by municipal governments, and that "[t]he drainage of a city in the interest of the public health and welfare is one of the most important purposes for which the police power can be exercised," *New Orleans Gas Light Co. v. Drainage Comm'n*, 197 U.S. 453, 460, 25 S.Ct. 471, 49 L.Ed. 831 (1905), the Municipal Petitioners argue that requiring Phase II permit applicants to enact "ordinances or other regulatory measures" amounts to federal commandeering in contravention of the Tenth Amendment. *See New York v. United States*, 505 U.S. 144, 188, 112 S.Ct. 2408, 120 L.Ed.2d 120 (1992).

EPA counters that nothing in the Phase II Rule violates the Tenth Amendment, because it extends to small MS4s a generally applicable regulatory scheme that does not excessively interfere with municipal functions. It argues that the Phase II Rule no more trespasses on state sovereignty than did the Driver's Privacy Protection Act ("DPPA") unanimously upheld in *Reno v. Condon*, 528 U.S. 141, 151, 120 S.Ct. 666, 145 L.Ed.2d 587 (2000), as a rule of general applicability that "incidentally" applied to States—even though the universe of entities to which the DPPA could in fact apply included *only* States. 528 U.S. at 151, 120 S.Ct. 666 (declining to address whether general applicability is a constitutional requirement "because the DPPA is generally applicable"). EPA contends that the federal government need not avoid all requirements that cause States and localities to engage their legislative or executive processes, but only those that would "excessively interfere" with the functioning of those governments. *Printz v. United States*, 521 U.S. 898, 932, 117 S.Ct. 2365, 138 L.Ed.2d 914 (1997). EPA argues that the federal government's great interest in preventing water pollution justifies the "minimal interference" with municipal functions that the Minimum Measures might occasion, and asserts that the Measures by definition could not interfere "excessively" with state or local governments, since MS4s are only required to reduce pollutants to the "maximum extent practicable." 40 C.F.R. § 122.34(a).

The Tenth Amendment provides that "all is retained [by the States] which has not been surrendered [to the federal government]." *New York*, 505 U.S. at 156, 112 S.Ct. 2408 (internal quotations omitted). If a power is delegated to Congress by the Constitution, the Tenth Amendment expressly disclaims any reservation of that power to the States, and Congress's exercise of that power does not intrude impermissibly on state sovereignty. *Id.*; *Garcia v. San Antonio Metro. Transit Auth.*, 469 U.S. 528, 549, 105 S.Ct. 1005, 83 L.Ed.2d 1016 (1985). But the Tenth Amendment also signals constitutional protection for our system of dual sovereignty, confirming "that the power of the Federal Government is subject to limits that may, in a given instance, reserve power to the States." *New York*, 505 U.S. at 157, 112 S.Ct. 2408. Among the most important limits implied by the Tenth Amendment are the circumstances under which the federal government may not conscript state and local governments to regulate on its behalf—as petitioners contend EPA has inappropriately done in the Phase II Rule.

* * *

The Tenth Amendment thus requires that we evaluate whether the Phase II Rule coerces state action (leaving a State no choice but to comply with a federal mandate), whether the mandated action forces the State to regulate third parties (as opposed to regulating state activities legitimately subject to generally applicable federal law), and, if the federal law is generally applicable, whether it nevertheless excessively interferes with the functioning of state government.

In conducting this inquiry, however, we are sensitive to the fact that solving pressing environmental problems may require the formation of partnerships between federal and state authorities that the Supreme Court has referred to as "program[s] of cooperative federalism." *Hodel*, 452 U.S. at 289, 101 S.Ct. 2352 ("[T]he Surface Mining Act establishes a program of cooperative federalism that allows the States, within limits established by federal minimum standards, to enact and administer their own regulatory programs, structured to meet their own particular needs * * * "). Although local governments have traditionally enjoyed broad authority over drainage activities, *New Orleans Gas Light Co.*, 197 U.S. at 460, 25 S.Ct. 471, they do not enjoy exclusive sovereign authority over actions that contribute pollutants to the nation's waters.

We conclude that even if the Individual and General Permit options of the Phase II Rule require operators of small MS4s to regulate third parties, the Phase II Rule entails no unconstitutional coercion because operators of small MS4s have two alternatives to the Individual and General Permit options: the option of not discharging and the Alternative Permit option.

* * *

Notes

1. In Environmental Defense Center, the municipal petitioners argued vehemently that the Phase II regulations give them no choice but to regulate construction and post-construction activity. The majority stated that municipalities have alternative means for disposing of collected stormwater, such as recycling it or constructing wetland collectors, and can chose not to accept stormwater discharges running off construction sites. The majority concludes that the requirements of the Phase II regulations involve "minimal interference" with municipal functions. It further calls the stormwater regulatory regime "cooperative federalism" requiring the formation of a partnership between the federal and state authorities. In the dissent, Circuit Judge Tallman vigorously disagreed stating, "The law of gravity is inflexible; the stormwater will run downhill through the municipalities into federal waters whether the sewer system is open or blocked. No matter how much we want to uphold EPA's regulatory scheme, we cannot change the law of gravity." Which side of this debate seems correct to you? Are recycling and wetlands construction adequate, cost-effective solutions to controlling the ravaging runoff of a storm? Can municipalities realistically stop construction site and post-construction runoff from entering their municipal stormwater systems? Is there a difference between "requiring" a partnership and "coercing" state action?

2. Colorado law permits local governments to adopt regulations limiting development in stormwater and floodwater runoff channels. "To the end that adequate safety may be secured, the county planning commission may include in said zoning plan provisions establishing, regulating, and limiting such uses on or along any storm or floodwater runoff channel or basin * * *." COLO. REV. STAT. § 30–28–111 (1986).

3. The city of Fitchburg, Massachusetts, adopted a stormwater management and erosion control ordinance to prevent and diminish property damage and flooding. *See* FITCHBURG, MASS. CODE § 154–1 (1999). The ordinance was adopted to prevent or diminish "property damage, flooding, the contamination of drinking water supplies, the loss of recreational opportunities, adverse impacts on fisheries and wildlife, the loss of wetlands, and * * * the loss of valuable agricultural soils."

4. Minneapolis, Minnesota, enacted its stormwater management ordinance "to minimize negative impacts on stormwater runoff rates, volumes, and quality on Minneapolis lakes, streams, wetlands, and the Mississippi River by guiding future significant development and redevelopment activity, and by assuring long-term effectiveness of existing and future stormwater management constructed activities." MINNEAPOLIS 99–Or–156, § 1 (1999). The ordinance requires all land-disturbing projects to follow an approved Stormwater Management Plan.

(3) *Floodplains*

Development activities can destroy floodplains, decrease flood storage, increase runoff, and decrease water quality. Local floodplain regulations can limit the extension of buildings and infrastructure into the flood areas, require that such buildings are built at certain elevations, prevent the obstruction of stream channels, and prohibit the construction of chemical or other hazardous materials storage facilities. The National Flood Insurance Program exerted an early and strong influence on the initiation of local environmental legislation. It required localities to adopt and enforce floodplain management programs as a prerequisite to the eligibility of local property owners for flood disaster insurance and payments.

Irvine, California adopted a Floodplain District Ordinance for the purpose of promoting the public health, safety, and general welfare, and to minimize public and private losses due to flood conditions in specific areas. IRVINE, CA. ZONING ORD. § 5–2–2 (2002). Its floodplain ordinance notes that the flood hazard areas of the city are subject to periodic water inundation, which results in loss of life and property, health and safety hazards, and extraordinary public expenditures. The Flood Hazard Area Ordinance adopted by the city of Detroit is aimed at maintaining stable development patterns that are not subject to the "blighting influence of flood damage." DETROIT, MI. ZONING ORD. § 49.0102(D) (2001). The Floodplain Protection District Ordinance of the town of Penfield, New York, contains extensive provisions to protect the environment and the public from the dangers of flooding. PENFIELD, NY ZONING ORD. §§ 3–14(A), (F)(1–4) (1987).

APRIL v. CITY OF BROKEN ARROW

Supreme Court of Oklahoma, 1989.
775 P.2d 1347.

DOOLIN, JUSTICE.

The question presented is whether the adoption of two municipal land-use ordinances on their face substantially interfered with landowner's use and enjoyment of his property so as to constitute a permanent "taking" of property without just compensation in violation of the United States and Oklahoma Constitutions. Put another way, the question is, does a taking result if the limitations on the use of owner's property do "not substantially advance legitimate state interests, or denies an owner economical, viable use of his land, [citations omitted]."

I.

Appellee Paul April, M.D., ("Owner"), purchased 40 acres of undeveloped agricultural land, for investment purposes, in the City of Broken Arrow, Tulsa County, Oklahoma ("City"). City is a suburban residential area south of the city of Tulsa. Owner's real property, used as pasture land, is located within an existing 100–year flood plain of Haikey Creek and its tributaries ("Haikey"). Haikey is a "natural water drainage system" in and around City.

Property adjacent to Haikey, including Owner's land which is transversed by three pre-existing wet-weather creeks converging in the flood plain, is naturally subject to flooding following periods of heavy rainfall. Haikey drains over "one square mile" of Owner's property, because the elevation of Owner's property is lower than the elevation of the periodic hundred year flood. City has not made any physical intrusions or entered upon Owner's property. Nor has City diverted any additional water into Haikey's drainage system, or erected any facilities upstream from Owner's property, or granted any building permits altering the natural water flow throughout the topography of the 100–year flood plain.

Owner, intending to sell his land to a developer, requested and was granted R–2 residential single family zoning for his property in 1975, after his previous request for R–6 high density multifamily apartment zoning was denied by City. When R–2 zoning was approved, allowing three family dwellings per acre (theoretically 120 homes), City's planning commission and planning commission staff informed Owner:

> the majority of (your) property is within the 100–year frequency flood and is also within the adopted Flood Hazard Area * * *, (therefore) the developer will be required to build all house pads at least one foot above the 100–year frequency flood elevation * * *.

This was City's only regulatory requirement for development of land within the flood plain. In October 1977, Owner requested his property be rezoned from 40 acres of R–2, residential single family to 20 acres of R–4, duplex and 20 acres of R–5, apartments. Owner's request was denied by City's planning commission and staff.

In January 1978, Owner made another application to the City's planning commission, requesting his property be re-zoned from R–2 single family to R–4, Duplex. City's planning commission and staff again denied Owner's petition for re-zoning, and Owner, for the first time, appealed to the City Council. "[I]n anticipation of the 'floodplain' ordinance being adopted * * *, (Owner) sought relief in the form of a 'waiver' or variance from the * * * City Council on March 13, 1978 which was, * * *, denied. * * *."

On March 20, 1978, the city council enacted "The Flood Damage Protection Ordinance, No. 735", regulating the development of land in Haikey's flood plain, and "The Earth Change Resolution Ordinance No. 736", controlling all excavations and earth modifications throughout the municipality (both hereinafter, "Land–Use Ordinances"). Both land-use ordinances became effective immediately. On May 1, 1978, the city council denied Owner's appeal for rezoning.

Owner initiated the present inverse condemnation suit in December of 1978, alleging, inter alia, City's "overt actions;" that is, adoption of its land-use ordinances, limiting his property to "Flood Tolerant Land Uses," and city's approval of building permits to other developers in the flood plain has resulted in the appropriation of Owner's property for "general public use" as "a detention pond as part of a municipal stormwater drainage system." Owner further alleges City's action prohibits construction on Owner's land by restricting its use to "public or semi-public purposes," that it effectively limits Owner's use of his land as a "horse pasture," and finally that it denies Owner beneficial use of his property by destroying his reasonable "investment-backed expectations." After various motions and pleadings, Owner dismissed three other causes of action.

At trial, Owner asserted his "property lies in the path of (City's) future plans for a public park, Haikey Creek detention reservoir, levee pump station and channel improvements." Owner argued City's land-use ordinance "goes too far," because his property is "economically worthless, as evidenced by the Report of Commissioners," appointed by the trial court. The commissioners' report found the value of Owner's property "taken and damaged," resulting from City's enactment of the land-use ordinances, amounted to $240,000.00.

Before and during trial, City insistently argued two propositions to support its contention that there was no basis in either fact or law for the trial court to determine the constitutionality of the ordinances as applied to Owner's property. One, City's mere enactment of its ordinance regulating the general use of land within the flood plain does not, as a matter of law, constitute substantial interference with nor amount to an overt action exercising dominion and control over Owner's property, because Owner's property floods as a result of a natural phenomenon beyond City's exercise of its police power. Two, Owner has never applied for or been denied a building permit, or a variance under the land-use ordinances, thus, Owner has an adequate remedy at law to determine the beneficial use of his property.

City urged dismissal of Owner's action because the trial court lacked a justiciable issue. However, the jury rendered a verdict in favor of Owner and against City for $240,000.00. Thereafter, the trial court awarded attorney fees, appraisers fees, city engineering-planning fees, and trial cost against City pursuant to 27 O.S.1981 § 12. Owner retains possession of the land in question.

II.

In resolving this appeal we are confronted, as we were in *Mattoon v. City of Norman*, with the following contentions: One, whether a municipality's adoption of a flood plain ordinance constitutes a taking of property without just compensation for which a landowner may seek damages under an action in inverse condemnation. Two, whether the doctrine requiring exhaustion of administrative remedies is applicable to preclude judicial review of the action.

City and its amici argue that opinion does not control the instant case, because *Mattoon* is significantly distinguishable. Owner argues *Mattoon* provides the applicable rule to govern the results of this appeal. Therefore, we deem it important to reiterate, and go further into the statement of our opinion and reasons for our *Mattoon* decision, because due to the procedural posture of that appeal, we found ourselves unable to address the merits of the "taking" question.

In *Mattoon*, city enacted a flood plain ordinance, reserving landowner's (and approximately 500 other similarly situated landowners') property for flood drainage purposes. Landowner filed a class action for inverse condemnation, alleging city adopted its flood plain ordinance unreasonably, neglected and refused to properly maintain its drainage system, and had diverted surface waters into tributaries which crossed and flooded landowner's property. The trial court sustained city's demurrer to landowner's petition by merely finding the ordinance was a valid exercise of city's police power. * * *

We recognized "a valid enactment of a flood plain ordinance is not per se a taking," because "acts done in the proper exercise of the police power which merely impair the use (or value) of property do not constitute a 'taking.' " We held "the test of whether there can be a recovery in inverse condemnation is whether there is a sufficient interference with the landowner's use and enjoyment to constitute a taking." More importantly, we acknowledged governmental land-use regulations may amount to an actual or de facto taking—"(i)f there is an overt act by the governmental agency resulting in an assertion of dominion and control over property." (Emphasis added.)

Two components were implicit in the taking claim advanced by landowner's petition in *Mattoon*. First, landowner had alleged city's unreasonable adoption of its flood plain ordinance had "taken" his property, that is, the ordinance "goes too far," and any proffered compensation was not "just." Thus, landowner's factual contentions adequately alleged a "regulatory taking" claim, by contending city's ordinance was an extreme regulation destroying a major portion of landowner's property value. Second, landowner alleged a "physical taking" of property, that is, city also overtly acted to flood landowner's property by unreasonably diverting surface water, and improperly maintaining its drainage channels.

Accordingly, we reversed and remanded the trial court's judgment with directions to reinstate landowner's action, because first, merely finding an ordinance was validly enacted within city's lawful exercise of its police power, without considering the general principles of due process, does not "absolutely preclude compensation for property taken or damaged by such exercise." Second, landowner's petition alleged a question of fact, the reasonableness of city's diversion of surface water over landowner's property, and such challenge was sufficient to withstand city's demurrer.

* * *

III.

In cases such as this, the nature of the government's action and the type of taking alleged are critical factors in our analysis. Without undertaking to survey the historical intricacies of regulatory zoning ordinances it is fair to say that any local government seeking to participate in the National Flood Insurance Program is required by federal law and authorized by state law to enact land use and regulatory control measures. Other provisions enforcing such measures, (including a building permit and appeal system), are also required in mitigating flood hazards. City's legitimate exercise of its police power, asserted for the public welfare, controls owner's use of his property.

In balancing the private and public interests herein, Owner's potential use of all property, under our system of government, is subordinate to the right of City's reasonable regulations, ordinances, and all similar laws that are clearly necessary and bear a rational relation to preserving the health, safety, and general welfare of the residents of Broken Arrow.

* * *

While asserted with great vigor, Owner's argument that City has appropriated his property for general public use as a detention reservoir, is quite simply untenable under the particular facts of this case. We find no evidence, or persuasive testimony, indicating City has adopted any recommendations with respect to appropriating Owner's land as a detention pond. City has acquired no property interest in Owner's land, has not physically invaded Owner's property, nor has his land been set aside for a public use.

Indeed, Owner stipulated City has not proposed or approved the building of any facilities or taken any action increasing the natural flow of water over Owner's property or flooding his land. We note that as a result of Pre Trial Conference, Sec. 9 thereof, the owner declared and admitted;

> "9. (1) That the City of Broken Arrow has *not* constructed or caused to be constructed *any* facilities upstream from plaintiff's

property which has increased the waterflow over plaintiff's property." Unlike the extreme factual circumstances found in Mattoon, in the instant case, Owner's property floods following periods of heavy rainfall, and such a natural phenomenon is definitely beyond City's ordinary exercise of its police power.

Furthermore, even if Owner's allegations were substantiated by the record, City's future plans for inclusion of his property for "potential" public use in a flood control plan would not give rise to a cause of action for inverse condemnation. For as Justice Stewart wrote in his concurring opinion in *Hughes v. Washington*: "[T]he Constitution measures a taking of property not by what a state says, or what it intends, but by what it does."

Accepting as we must the general proposition that local public officials must be afforded reasonable "elasticity" in planning and implementing legitimate land-use interests, and given the "particular facts" of this case; we hold such limitations substantially advance City's legitimate goals of; one, reducing risks of loss of life and property; two, protecting the public's interest in health; three, preserving the aesthetic environment and fiscal integrity of Haikey's flood prone areas; four, enabling landowners to develop their property located within the flood plain, as well as allowing landowners to purchase federally-sponsored flood hazard insurance to protect their investments.

Our conclusion that City's land-use ordinances are lawful and valid exercises of its police power does not conclude this matter; for as we explicitly held in *Mattoon*, such a mere finding does not "absolutely preclude compensation for property taken or damaged by such exercises." In this connection, we proceed then to a consideration of whether Owner has been denied economical viable use of his land.

IV

It is relevant at this juncture to recognize Owner merely alleges a "regulatory taking" of property. Given the absence of any administrative decision regarding the application of City's land-use ordinances to Owner's property, City and its amici challenge our appellate jurisdiction and the trial court's adjudicatory authority, arguing Owner's "regulatory taking" claim is premature, because "an essential prerequisite to its assertion is a final and authoritative determination of the type and intensity of development legally permitted on the subject property." We agree.

Owner is completely incorrect when he asserts he has no "adequate" remedy at law. Owner alleged the development of 120 homesites "was permitted by existing zoning" prior to City's adoption of its land-use ordinances. Owner asserts such development "is not consistent with the terms of the ordinance (and) if permitted would seriously undermine the purpose of the ordinances." Owner contends he requested a waiver or variance from the city council by agreeing to reduce the number of dwelling units from 120 to 88. Owner further asserts he asked City to repeal the effect of the ordinance as it pertains to his property. This argument is misleading, and inaccurate.

Owner has never submitted a plan or subdivision plat to use or improve his real property. Nor did he properly seek and receive any concrete and definitive statement from City as to how many single family dwelling units he could build on his land, if the floor of such dwelling units were built one foot above the existing 100–year flood elevation.

Regardless of how many homesites are erected, City's land-use ordinances neither prevent the present and presumably most beneficial use of Owner's property, "nor extinguish a fundamental attribute of ownership." The disputed property, as earlier requested by Owner, is still zoned for single residential family dwellings.

Furthermore, and most significant, Owner has never applied for a building permit to develop his property, or an earth change permit to raise his land out of the flood plain, nor has he ever properly requested a hardship variance under the "established" administrative procedures of the land-use ordinances. In summary, the record indicates Owner failed to submit a plan for development of his property prior to or subsequent to the City's adoption of its land-use ordinances.

* * *

We conclude the trial court was presented with no justiciable issue to hear Owner's regulatory taking claim, because Owner has never applied for a building or earth change permit, has failed to exhaust his administrative remedies, and has presented no competent evidence showing the pursuit of such remedies would be futile or inadequate. We hold there is as yet no concrete controversy regarding the application of City's land-use ordinances to Owner's property, because even though City has denied Owner's increased zoning intensity applications, there are other economically viable uses available to Owner.

Lastly, it is important to note that Owner purchased flood-prone property in Haikey Creek and its tributaries. Even if City had taken no action with regards to flood-damage prevention, Owner's property would continue to flood following periods of heavy rainfall.

The judgment of the trial court is REVERSED, and the cause is REMANDED to the district court WITH DIRECTIONS TO DISMISS Owner's complaint—for want of a justiciable issue.

Notes

1. The National Flood Insurance Act of 1968, 42 U.S.C.A. § 1601 *et seq.*, requires local governments to enact floodplain regulations prior to making flood insurance available to residents of the community. This act has had a widespread effect in spurring floodplain regulations. See Dinkins, The Federal Zoning Program: Regulation of Floodplain Use Under the National Flood Insurance Act, ABA Law Notes, Spring 1978, Vol. 14, No. 2. An excellent overview of the Act can be found in Weinstein, Revisiting the

National Flood Insurance Program, 48 Land Use Law No. 10 (Oct. 1996), pp. 3–8.

2. What if the owner in the principal case had shown that the city's floodplain regulations prevented all viable and economic use of its property? Do owners of environmentally constrained land have legitimate investment-backed expectations in their development? To what extent? Do owners have an obligation to notice environmental features on land they intend to purchase? How does one discover flood plains? Do 100–year floods leave visible, discoverable marks? How far beyond a physical inspection must a prospective purchaser go in conducting due diligence prior to acquiring a parcel? See Leonard v. Town of Brimfield, 423 Mass. 152, 666 N.E.2d 1300 (1996), where the court held that floodplain restrictions were not a taking; the case takes a hard look at the issue of investment-backed expectations. In Karches v. City of Cincinnati, 38 Ohio St.3d 12, 526 N.E.2d 1350 (1988), the court held a zoning ordinance invalid as applied to property in a floodplain which had been downzoned to Riverfront District, RF–1; the court found that none of the RF–1 uses were economically feasible.

3. Floodplain restrictions were one of the first types of local environmental law enacted by municipalities. The general trend of decisions is to uphold restrictions that prohibit building structures in the floodplain. See Dunham, Flood Control Via the Police Power, 107 U.Pa.L.Rev. 1098 (1959); U.S. Water Resources Council, Regulation of Flood Hazard Areas (1971); American Society of Planning Officials, Regulations for Floodplains, Planning Advisory Service Report No. 277 (1972). Also see Vartelas v. Water Resources Comm'n, 146 Conn. 650, 153 A.2d 822 (1959), upholding the setting of encroachment lines along a stream and a regulation forbidding the placing of buildings within the lines; Turner v. County of Del Norte, 24 Cal.App.3d 311, 101 Cal.Rptr. 93 (1972), upholding an absolute prohibition of structures in a floodplain along the Klamath River; Turnpike Realty Co. v. Town of Dedham, 362 Mass. 221, 284 N.E.2d 891 (1972), upholding floodplain restrictions in a swampy area; Dur–Bar Realty Co. v. City of Utica, 57 A.D.2d 51, 394 N.Y.S.2d 913 (1977), affirmed 44 N.Y.2d 1002, 408 N.Y.S.2d 502, 380 N.E.2d 328 (1978), upholding a "Land Conservation District" which limited uses to farming, marinas, recreational uses, and landfill operations. See generally, Comment, Various Aspects of Floodplain Zoning, 55 N.Dak.L.Rev. 429 (1980).

4. In New City Office Park v. Planning Bd., Town of Clarkstown, 144 A.D.2d 348, 533 N.Y.S.2d 786 (1988), the court upheld denial of final site approval for an office park development located within the 100–year floodplain. The specific basis for the denial was that the project would have required a considerable amount of fill to elevate the buildings above the floodplain and the developer was unable to provide sufficient land for compensatory storage of floodwaters in the event of a 100–year flood.

5. What do you make of the intergovernmental relationship involved in floodplain regulation? A federal law, the National Flood Insurance Program, impacts directly on local governments, denying them and their constituent landowners a federal incentive (flood insurance and payments). Should there be a state role in such matters? If so, what should it be? Is there any benefit to the federal government involving state governments and agencies in these

regulatory relationships? A typical state enabling statute authorizing floodplain regulation is ARIZ.REV.STAT. § 48–3601 et seq. (Floodplain Act of 1973). One possible weakness in such enabling acts is that floodplain regulation is not mandatory for local governments. In some states control of floodplain construction is vested in a state agency. Typical of this approach is the State of Wisconsin. See State v. Trudeau, 139 Wis.2d 91, 408 N.W.2d 337 (1987), cert. denied 484 U.S. 1007, 108 S.Ct. 701, 98 L.Ed.2d 652 (1988), where the state sued the developer and the local government for granting a floodplain variance. Also see City of La Crosse v. Wisconsin Dept. of Natural Resources, 120 Wis.2d 168, 353 N.W.2d 68 (1984). Some states require local governments to adopt regulations protecting floodplains. In Montana, the state legislature passed the Floodway Management Act, designating the Department of Natural Resources and Conservation as the lead agency. MCA § 76–5–301 states that local governments must adopt land use regulations that meet or exceed minimum standards of the department in controlling development in designated floodplains or floodways. If a local government fails to enact such ordinances, the department must enforce its own minimum standards through a state permit system.

(4) Wetlands

Local wetlands regulations restrict activities such as dredging and soil disposal, construction of roads, grading and soil removal, timber harvesting, and placement of buildings and infrastructure on wetlands and their buffer areas. Wetlands exist where there is sufficient water to saturate the soil long enough to support animals and plants suited to wetland environments. In nature, wetlands often include wildlife habitat areas adjacent to watercourses, upland slopes, wooded lands, and other critical environmental features. Some local wetlands laws recognize these connections and attempt to protect the complete ecosystem. The town of Lewisboro, New York, has adopted a local wetlands and watercourse law that contains extensive protections for these resources. LEWISBORO, NY CODE § 217–1(A) (1999). The city of Concord, New Hampshire, has created a Shoreline Protection District to maintain the quality of surface waters and groundwater, retain flood storage properties, protect wildlife habitat and feeding areas, and protect other unique natural resources. CONCORD, NH CODE ch. 28 § 3–3 (2002).

In Connecticut, state law defines a wetland as an area containing soil types "designated as poorly drained, very poorly drained, alluvial, and floodplain by the National Cooperative Soils Survey, as may be amended from time to time, of the Natural Resources Conservation Service of the United States Department of Agriculture." CONN. GEN. STAT. § 22a–38(15) (2001). Connecticut's Inland Wetlands and Watercourses Act requires all municipalities to establish an inland wetlands agency. CONN. GEN. STAT. § 22a–36 to 22a–45. The agency regulates activities within wetlands designated by the municipalities. A local wetlands agency has the right to regulate not only the land within the established boundaries of a wetland or watercourse, but also any adjacent area where activities might occur that would "use" the wetlands in a prohibited manner. The Act prohibits anyone from conducting a "regulated activity" on any inland wetland or watercourse without a permit. Regulated activities include almost all development and land use activities. The Commissioner of the State Department of Environmental Protection (DEP) may revoke the local wetlands agency's authority to regulate activity in the wetlands if the DEP determines that the local agency has failed to perform its duties. The Commissioner's regulations require that local agencies report to the DEP all permits issued and any other action they have taken. Local wetlands agencies are given the authority to adopt regulations that expand on the Commissioner's regulations, or to add to them if necessary to protect the wetlands.

FAFARD v. CONSERVATION COMMISSION OF BARNSTABLE

Supreme Judicial Court of Massachusetts, 2000.
432 Mass. 194, 733 N.E.2d 66.

ABRAMS, J.

The plaintiffs, Madlyn and Howard Fafard (Fafards), appeal from the Conservation Commission of Barnstable's (commission's) decision denying them permission to build a fixed pier on the Eel River. The commission grounded its decision on town bylaws and pier regulations that claim authority to protect "the interests of recreation and public trust rights."

Pursuant to G.L. c. 249, § 4, the plaintiffs sought review in the nature of certiorari in the Superior Court. The Superior Court judge denied the Fafards' motion for judgment on the pleadings and affirmed the decision of the commission.[2] We granted the Fafards' application for direct appellate review.

The Fafards assert that the bylaws and pier regulations of Barnstable are invalid. According to them, only the Commonwealth may act to further public trust rights. They also argue that G.L. c. 91, which provides for State licensing of structures on coastal lands, preempts the pier regulations on which the commission based its decision. The Fafards also raise the issue of arbitrary and capricious decision-making by the commission, but that issue is not properly before us because it is raised only in their reply brief. See Mass. R.A.P. 16(a)(4), as amended, 367 Mass. 921 (1975).

2. The judge noted in his decision that "[t]he record is unclear as to whether the [town of Barnstable] has been approved by the Department [of Environmental Protection (DEP)] to administer a local permitting program." This issue has been clarified on appeal: Barnstable was not authorized by the DEP to administer a DEP permitting program. Therefore, although we affirm the Superior Court judge's decision, we do so on different grounds.

We also note that a related action, which was consolidated with the instant case but decided separately, remains pending in Superior Court. That action, which is not before us, concerns whether the commission's denial of the Fafards' first notice of intent was untimely. We are concerned with the Fafards' second notice of intent to the commission.

We conclude that only the Commonwealth or its express designee may act to further public trust rights. Therefore, those portions of the bylaw that claim to enforce public trust rights are not a valid exercise of the town's power. Consequently, the town could not grant such authority to the commission. We also conclude that, after the portions of the bylaw that claim public trust authority are struck, the remaining portion of the bylaw and pier regulations are not preempted by State statute. Because the commission also acted under valid portions of the town bylaw, we conclude that the commission's denial of the Fafards' request for a proposed pier was an appropriate exercise of municipal powers. We affirm the decision of the Superior Court.

1. *Facts.* Barnstable enacted a wetlands protection bylaw (wetlands bylaw) in order to regulate work in and around wetlands more strictly than does the State's wetlands protection act. See G.L. c. 131, § 40 (Wetlands Protection Act); Barnstable Bylaws, c. III, art. XXVII, § 12. See generally art. 89, § 6, of the Amendments to the Constitution of the Commonwealth (Home Rule Amendment). The wetlands bylaw also purports to protect "public trust rights in trustlands." Chapter III, art. XXVII, § 1. The wetlands bylaw vests in the commission the authority to issue and to deny permits for a number of specified activities affecting wetlands resources.

Pursuant to its powers under the wetlands bylaw, the commission adopted regulations for private piers and docks (pier regulations). The relevant pier regulations specify that piers may not extend more than twenty per cent of the width of a waterway and that piers serving private interests may not interfere with various water-related activities. The pier regulations also specify that, "[t]hese regulations notwithstanding, the [commission] will consider any and all pier proposals on a site specific basis, disposing of each according to its merit and the degree to which statutory interests have been protected and preserved at the locus."

The trust owns property, which the Fafards use as a seasonal residence, on the Eel River. The Eel River is a narrow coastal tidal inlet, approximately 2,000 feet long, closed at one end. The Fafards' property lies toward the closed end of the river.

In May, 1997, Howard Fafard filed a notice of intent with the commission as required by the wetlands bylaw seeking permission to construct a fixed pier and to install a ramp and floats to provide access from the upland portion of the property to the water. The proposed pier would extend forty-two feet beyond the mean low water mark into an area of the river which is 161 feet wide. Therefore, the planned pier would occupy more than twenty per cent of the width of the river and would stand on "Commonwealth tidelands," or lands below the mean high water mark. See G.L. c. 91, § 1; 310 Code Mass. Regs. § 9.02 (1994). The Fafards also proposed to keep their fifty-five foot twin-screw power boat at the pier, which, with a beam of sixteen feet, would extend another sixteen feet beyond the pier.

The commission held two public hearings and, on September 16, 1997, denied the Fafards' application "in the interest of recreation and public trust rights." In support of the denial, the commission found, inter alia, that (1) the proposed pier did not conform with the pier regulations; (2) the proposed pier would interfere with an existing mooring that had been in continuous use for over ten years; (3) the pier "would pose significant adverse impacts to the interest of recreation (such as navigation) and public trust rights"; and (4) the Fafards had not met their burden of proving that the pier would not have an "unacceptable significant and cumulative effect upon the wetland[s]."

* * *

3. *Preemption.* The Fafards also argue that the unsevered portions of the bylaw, and the pier regulations enacted under those portions of the bylaw, are invalid because they are inconsistent with sections of G.L. c. 91. We disagree.

"Municipalities may not adopt bylaws or ordinances that are inconsistent with State laws." *Boston Gas Co. v. Somerville*, 420 Mass. 702, 703, 652 N.E.2d 132 (1995), and cases cited. As a starting point in determining "whether a local ordinance is inconsistent with a statute, this court has looked to see whether there was * * * an express legislative intent to forbid local activity on the same subject." *Id.* at 704, 652 N.E.2d 132. Nothing in G.L. c. 91 states expressly that municipalities may deny permission to construct piers such as the Fafards proposed or that they may grant permission to construct piers. Therefore, we are confronted with one of the "hard cases * * * in which it is asserted that a legislative intent to bar local action should be inferred in all the circumstances." *Wendell v. Attorney Gen.*, 394 Mass. 518, 524, 476 N.E.2d 585 (1985).

a. *Frustration of purpose.* Legislative intent to bar local action may be inferred where "the local regulation would somehow frustrate the purpose of the statute so as to warrant an inference that the Legislature intended to preempt the subject." *Boston Gas Co. v. Newton*, 425 Mass. 697, 699, 682 N.E.2d 1336 (1997). We examine whether the pier regulations frustrate the three sections of G.L. c. 91 that explicitly address the Commonwealth's powers and responsibilities with respect to the licensing and permitting of piers on Commonwealth tidelands. See G.L. c. 91, §§ 2, 14, 18.

General Laws c. 91, § 2, sets forth the general rubric to be used by the DEP in issuing State permits and licenses for pier construction: "In carrying out its duties * * * the department shall act to preserve and protect the rights in tidelands of the inhabitants of the [C]ommonwealth by ensuring that the tidelands are utilized only for water-dependent uses or otherwise serve a proper public purpose." Section 2 also states that, in issuing licenses and permits, the DEP shall "protect the interests of the [C]ommonwealth." *Id.*

In *Golden v. Selectmen of Falmouth*, 358 Mass. 519, 265 N.E.2d 573 (1970), we considered whether a local bylaw was inconsistent with the State wetlands protection act. See G.L. c. 138, § 27A, as amended through St.1969, c. 406. We concluded that, because the State statute "establishes minimum State-wide standards * * * local communities [are] free to adopt more stringent controls" than those embodied in State law. *Id.* at 526, 265 N.E.2d 573. See *Lovequist v. Conservation Comm'n of Dennis*, 379 Mass. 7, 393 N.E.2d 858 (1979).

Like the statute considered in *Golden v. Selectmen of Falmouth*, supra, G.L. c. 91, § 2, sets forth minimum standards. This section does not address the impact of pier construction on zoning regulations, public safety, the creation of nuisances, or other spheres traditionally within municipal authority. Rather, § 2 specifies that the department may allow construction on Commonwealth tidelands only if that construction would serve a "proper public purpose."

The pier regulations do not usurp the DEP's authority to deny licenses or permits to applicants who seek to build structures that do not serve such a purpose. Rather, the pier regulations require a local permit in addition to the State requirement that applicants obtain a State permit. The existence of a local permitting program alongside the State program in no way interferes with the mandate of § 2. See *Lovequist v. Conservation Comm'n of Dennis, supra*; *Golden v. Selectmen of Falmouth, supra*. Cf. *Crawford v. Building Inspector of Barnstable*, 356 Mass. 174, 180, 248 N.E.2d 488 (1969) ("No special rights accrue * * * because the pier was constructed under a license granted by the Commonwealth's Department of Public Works. The license was 'subject to all applicable Federal, State, County, and Municipal laws, ordinances and regulations' ").

We consider next whether the pier regulations are preempted by G.L. c. 91, §§ 14 and 18. Section 14 authorizes the DEP to "license and prescribe the terms for the construction or extension of [piers and other structures]." Section 14 specifies that the DEP may not permit structures unless they serve "a proper public purpose and * * * said purpose shall provide a greater public benefit than public detriment to the rights of the public." Section 14 thus requires that the DEP balance the public costs against the public benefits of a proposed project.

Section 18 specifies procedures for licensing programs administered by the DEP and provides for notice to local authorities when application for a DEP license is made. Section 18 requires the DEP to "take into consideration the recommendation of the local planning board in making its decision whether to grant a license."

The Fafards argue that, because §§ 14 and 18 authorize the DEP to grant and deny licenses with local authorities acting only in an advisory capacity, we should infer that the Legislature intended to preclude local permitting programs. We disagree.

"The existence of legislation on a subject * * * is not necessarily a bar to the enactment of local ordinances and bylaws exercising powers or functions with respect to the same subject." *Bloom v. Worcester*, 363 Mass. 136, 156, 293 N.E.2d 268 (1973). Even where a statute specifies that local authorities act only in an advisory capacity to State licensing authorities, we need not infer that the Legislature intended to preclude local regulation. See *Golden v. Selectmen of Falmouth, supra* at 525, 265 N.E.2d 573. There, we considered whether a Falmouth zoning bylaw was preempted by G.L. c. 130, § 27A. The State statute at issue required individuals planning to remove, fill, or dredge certain coastal areas to provide notice to local authorities. Municipalities were permitted to make recommendations to the department of public works, which retained ultimate authority over whether the proposed activities would be permitted. See G.L. c. 130, § 27A. We concluded that "[t]he fact that the [statute] confers upon a local board the advisory power to make recommendations concerning the installation of certain protective measures 'as may protect the public interest' does not, we think, preclude the authority of the local board acting under the zoning bylaw to initially authorize or bar a project." *Id.* at 525, 265 N.E.2d 573.

The same reasoning applies here. None of the language in either G.L. c. 91, § 14 or § 18, suggests that, because the statute allows municipalities to provide advice to the DEP, the Legislature intended to preclude local regulation of pier construction on Commonwealth tidelands. "The legislative intent to preclude local action must be clear." *Bloom v. Worcester, supra* at 155, 293 N.E.2d 268.

The bylaws further the interests the Legislature intended to protect in G.L. c. 91. As long as the DEP retains ultimate authority to reject projects for which the public costs do not outweigh the public benefits, Barnstable's local permitting program is not inconsistent with G.L. c. 91, §§ 14 and 18. See *Lovequist v. Conservation Comm'n of Dennis, supra* at 15, 393 N.E.2d 858. Barnstable's permitting program does not frustrate the purpose of the relevant sections of G.L. c. 91.

b. *Field preemption.* Local regulation also may be preempted even where such regulation does not conflict directly with an existing statute: "in some circumstances we can infer that the Legislature intended to preempt the field because legislation on the subject is so comprehensive that any local enactment would frustrate the statute's purpose." *Boston Gas Co. v. Newton*, 425 Mass. 697, 699, 682 N.E.2d 1336 (1997), quoting *Boston Gas Co. v. Somerville*, 420 Mass. 702, 703, 652 N.E.2d 132 (1995).

The sections of G.L. c. 91 that regulate pier construction are by no means comprehensive. As the preceding discussion of the relevant sections demonstrates, the Legislature provided only general principles to be used in regulating construction on Commonwealth tidelands. See G.L. c. 91, § 14. This distinguishes the instant case from those cited by the Fafards in support of their argument. See *Boston Gas Co. v. Newton, supra* (State regulation of public utilities industry, which has long been recognized as thoroughly regulated, see *Boston Edison Co. v. Boston*, 390 Mass. 772–774, 459 N.E.2d 1231 [1984], preempts local ordinance); *Boston Gas Co. v. Somerville, supra* (same).

The Fafards, however, argue that, even if the statutes themselves are not comprehensive, the bylaws and pier regulations frustrate the Legislature's intent to create a centralized authority for managing Commonwealth tidelands. The Fafards suggest that this legislative intent is implicit in regulations promulgated by the DEP. See 310 Code Mass. Regs. § 9.07 (1996). Although regulations adopted by a State agency are not dispositive on the question of the scope of authority granted an agency by statute, "[w]e must uphold the regulation if it can be interpreted in harmony with the act by any reasonable construction." *Massachusetts Auto Body Ass'n, Inc. v. Commissioner of Ins.*, 409 Mass. 770, 777, 570 N.E.2d 147 (1991).

Title 310 Code Mass. Regs. § 9.07(3) establishes procedures for cities or towns seeking to administer "a local permitting program for small structures accessory to residences." Cities or towns authorized by the DEP under this regulation may issue permits in lieu of the DEP, subject to appeal to the DEP. *Id.*

The bylaw and pier regulations do not purport to issue State permits in lieu of the DEP. The bylaw and pier regulations require a local permit in addition to the permit required by the DEP and are not inconsistent with DEP regulations allowing towns and cities to act as local surrogates for the DEP.

The Fafards also complain that the commission "attempts to avoid * * * administrative review of its permitting decisions by DEP." Nothing in G.L. c. 91 "grants to the [DEP] the authority to authorize a project which [a] local board has vetoed." *Golden v. Selectmen of Falmouth, supra* at 525, 265 N.E.2d 573. Further, an individual in the Fafards' position may seek review of the commission's decision. "Such a person has exactly the same remedy * * * as is available under any other * * * by-law[,] an action in the nature of certiorari under G.L. c. 249, § 4." *Lovequist v. Conservation Comm'n of Dennis, supra* at 16, 393 N.E.2d 858.

4. *The commission's decision.* Because the pier regulations are not preempted by State statute, we consider whether, after severing the portions of the bylaw purporting to grant the commission authority to act on behalf of the public trust, the commission had the authority to deny permission to construct the pier. We conclude that it did.

The Legislature has granted local conservation commissions the authority to act to prevent alteration of wetlands in order to preserve certain wetlands values. See G.L. c. 40, § 8C; G.L. c. 131, § 40. Conservation commissions acting under G.L. c. 131, § 40, may take regulatory action to protect, inter alia, the recreational value of wetlands. *Lovequist v. Conservation Comm'n of Dennis, supra* at 12–13, 393 N.E.2d 858. Coastal wetlands subject to municipal regulation under G.L. c. 131, § 40, include "any bank, marsh, swamp, meadow, flat or other lowland subject to tidal action or coastal storm flowage." Thus, local conservation commissions are authorized by the Legislature to protect recreation values by regulating construction on Commonwealth tidelands.

The wetlands bylaw authorizes the commission to act to protect various wetlands values, "including, but not limited to, * * * recreation." Barnstable Bylaws, c. III, art. XXVII, § 1. The pier regulations derive authority from this section of the bylaw, stating that "[t]he Bylaw protects each citizen's enjoyment of [tidelands and waters] by protecting the interests spelled out in [G.L. c. 131, § 40,] and Town of Barnstable Article XXVII," and establishing "performance standards for private piers and docks."

The Fafards' proposed pier and ramp would extend across Commonwealth tidelands, which municipalities may regulate under G.L. c. 131, § 40, into submerged lands seaward of the low water mark. "When analyzing a grant of power to a municipal government we must keep in mind that 'a grant of an express power carries with it all unexpressed, incidental powers necessary to carry it into effect.'" *Greater Boston Real Estate Bd. v. Boston*, 397 Mass. 870, 876–877, 494 N.E.2d 1301 (1986), quoting *Flynn v. Cambridge*, 383 Mass. 152, 158, 418 N.E.2d 335 (1981). Of course, as with other spheres of regulation that do not fall within a municipality's ordinary powers, "no local action may be taken without explicit legislative authorization," and we recognize "only those powers which are expressly conferred by statute or necessarily implied from those expressly conferred." *Greater Boston Real Estate Bd. v. Boston*, *supra* at 877, 494 N.E.2d 1301, quoting *Church v. Boston*, 370 Mass. 598, 601, 351 N.E.2d 212 (1976). Therefore, the commission was authorized to protect recreational values by denying a permit for the pier.

Because of the proposed pier's large size, the commission determined that the pier would have a negative effect on recreation. Specifically, the commission found that the "Eel River in the subject reach is enjoyed by many recreational boaters who cruise the river to its end point and return to West Bay." The commission determined that, "as proposed, the pier would pose significant adverse impact to the interest of recreation" and would interfere with an existing mooring. Based on these findings, the commission cited recreational values as one of the bases for its decision in addition to public trust rights.

The commission's denial of permission to build the pier because it would impair recreational values is supported by the record. The denial is also a legitimate exercise of the commission's authority consistent with powers to protect wetlands granted by the Legislature to municipal conservation commissions. See G.L. c. 131, § 40.

5. *Conclusion.* Although the bylaws and pier regulations are not preempted by G.L. c. 91, they are void insofar as they claim authority to protect public trust rights without a legislative grant of authority or a grant of authority from the DEP. However, because the bylaw was severable and the commission's decision also is sustainable on the basis of powers granted by the Legislature to local conservation commissions, we conclude that the commission did not "substantially err[ ] in a way that materially affected the rights of the parties." *Massachusetts Bay*

Transp. Auth. v. Auditor of the Commonwealth, 430 Mass. 783, 791, 724 N.E.2d 288 (2000).

Judgment affirmed.

Notes

1. Fafard held that only the State of Massachusetts, or its express designee (which did not include Barnstable), can enforce public trust rights. The public trust doctrine has its roots in the Institutes of Justinian in Roman Law. Under English law, the King—or Sovereign—held property rights in the air, running water, and the sea and its shores. British doctrine considered tidelands to be held by the King for the benefit of all commonwealth subjects. This doctrine did not translate precisely to the American federal system: states replaced the Crown as the trustee of community resources and the state legislatures and courts became the principal arbiters of what is held in trust for the people and what enters the realm of private property. At common law, the lands covered and influenced by tidal water were navigable-in-law and preserved in the public trust; navigation rights were held by the public, subjecting riparian owners to a servitude running to members of the public. Coastal state legislatures have enacted tidal wetlands acts to regulate private land uses on coasts, adjacent to tidal estuaries, and along other tidally-influenced areas, including land adjacent to coastal inlets and large water bodies subject to tidal fluctuations.

2. The Fafard court is one of many that interprets broadly the delegation of local wetlands authority. In Danzinger v. Conservation Com'n of Town of Newtown, 29 Conn. L. Rptr. 367 (Conn. Sup. Ct. 2001), plaintiff challenged the municipal agency's regulations that expanded the area around wetlands that was subject to regulation and added additional definitions to a list of regulated activities. The court was faced with the issue of whether the defendant acted within its statutory authority when it expanded the geographical area and the activities subject to wetlands regulations. "Acting in such a legislative capacity, the defendant has wide and liberal discretion * * * and is free to amend its regulations whenever time, experience, and responsible planning for contemporary or future conditions reasonably indicate the need for a change." The court found that there was sufficient evidence to support the amendments. See also Queach Corp. v. Inland Wetlands Commission of the Town of Branford, 258 Conn. 178, 779 A.2d 134 (2001) (upholding a municipality's amendment increasing a 50–foot buffer protection area to a 100–foot protection area).

B. LAND RESOURCE PROTECTIONS

(1) Erosion and Sedimentation Control

Soil erosion is a major source of nonpoint source pollution. Some erosion occurs naturally, but it is greatly accelerated by urbanization. Erosion control measures are a critical ingredient in local stormwater management plans and floodplain programs. Comprehensive wetland regulations aim to limit erosion in upland development to prevent the effects of sedimentation of wetlands which greatly impairs their function and value to the public and nature.

Local governments can adopt regulations to prevent soil erosion and the deposit of sediments in surface waters that land development projects cause. Undeveloped land contains organic particles that are biologically and chemically active and that, when disturbed and transported to surface waters, can cause serious water quality problems. One local soil protection ordinance observes that its purpose is to safeguard persons, protect property, prevent damage to the environment, and promote the public welfare by guiding, regulating, and controlling the design, use, and maintenance of any development or other activity that disturbs or breaks the surface of soil or results in the movement of earth on land situated in the town.

MARION RD. ASS'N v. WESTPORT PLANNING & ZONING COMMISSION

Connecticut Superior Court, 1994.
1994 WL 592221.

LEVIN, JUDGE.

The plaintiffs, homeowners and a neighborhood association, appeal from the action of the defendant Westport Planning & Zoning Commission (commission) granting with conditions and modifications the application of the defendants Conservative Synagogue and Three Hundred PRW Associates for a special permit and site plan approval to construct a synagogue building on a 4.7 acre parcel in a Residence AA zone. The plaintiffs' appeal enumerates over sixteen claims of error against the commission. In their brief, however, the plaintiffs claim that the commission erred by (1) approving an application which was substantially unchanged from a prior application which it had denied, (2) approving an application which violated the parking and/or coverage requirements in the regulations, (3) approving the application despite uncontroverted expert testimony that the synagogue would have an adverse impact on neighborhood property values, (4) necessarily finding that the application conformed to certain sections of the zoning regulations, (5) accepting and acting on an incomplete and inadequate application, and (6) imposing illegal and improper conditions of approval in its decision. "Issues that were raised in the appeal but not briefed by the plaintiff[s] * * * are considered abandoned." *Grace Community Church v. Planning & Zoning Commission*, 42 Conn.Sup. 256, 259, 615 A.2d 1092 (1992) (Fuller, J.).

* * *

IX

The plaintiffs contend that the commission erred in approving an application that failed to comply with § 37 of the regulations which require the filing of a sediment and control plan.

Section 37–1 states: "The purpose of these Sediment and Erosion Control Regulations is to reduce accelerated soil erosion; reduce the danger from stormwater runoff and to minimize nonpoint sediment pollution resulting from and being developed." In furtherance of that purpose, § 37-2 of the regulations provides that a sediment and erosion "[p]lan shall be submitted with any application for development when the disturbed area of such development is cumulatively more than one-half (1/2) acre." Section 37-6 of the regulations provides for the contents and "standards" of such a plan.[3] No such plan appears in the record.

The defendants counter that the record reflects that a "conceptual" plan was submitted to the Conservation Director who reviewed it and requested that the final plan be submitted together with a "narrative" before a zoning permit was issued. The Conservation Commission reviewed this "plan" and also required that a final plan be submitted prior to the issuance of a zoning permit. Section 37-4 does provide that "[a]ll S & E [sediment and control] Plans shall be submitted to the Conservation Director for *recommendation* prior to the filing of any application with either the Planning and Zoning Commission or the Zoning Board of Appeals, as applicable or prior to the issuance of a Zoning Permit. The Conservation Director shall review the plan to determine compliance with Section 37-5 below and shall inform the appropriate authority and the applicant of his/her *recommendation* within thirty (30) days of the date of receipt of said plan. Upon receipt of the Conservation Director's *recommendations* the Zoning Enforcement Officer shall certify that the plan complies with the requirements of this Section." (Emphasis added.)

The "conceptual" plan, alone, submitted by the applicant, did not comply with the regulations. This conclusion is supported by provisions in the General Statutes. Sediment and erosion control regulations are not unique to this municipality. They are mandated by General Statutes § 22a-329.[4] More, General Statutes § 22a-327(5) states what a soil

---

3. Section 37-6 of the regulations, entitled "Standards", provides that "[a]ny S & E [soil and erosion] Plan submitted pursuant to this Section shall include but not be limited to the following: a) the cumulative area(s) of disturbance, including areas of excavation, filling or stockpiling of earth material; b) existing and proposed grades or spot elevations; c) location of any inland wetlands, tidal wetlands, watercourses, existing or proposed drainage facilities on or adjacent to the site; d) anticipated start and completion dates; e) agent's name; f) sequence for institution of soil erosion and sediment control measures; g) the minimum Soil Erosion and Sediment Control Plans shall be developed using principles outlines in Chapters #3 & #4 of the Connecticut Guidelines for Soil Erosion and Sediment Control; h) a bond may be required in accordance with Section 43-13 of the Zoning Regulations."

4. General Statutes "Sec. 22a-329. Municipal land use. Regulations. (a) The regulations adopted by a municipality pursuant to sections 8-2 and 8-25, on and after July 1, 1985, shall require that: (1) Proper provision be made for soil erosion and sediment control; (2) a soil erosion and sediment control plan be submitted with any application for development when the disturbed area of such development is more than one-half acre; and (3) the municipality or the soil and water conservation district shall certify that the plan complies with regulations adopted pursuant to said sections. Prior to certification, any plan submitted to a municipality may be reviewed by the soil and water conservation districts which may make recommendations concerning such plan, provided such review shall be completed within thirty days of the receipt of such plan. The regulations shall include, but not be limited to, provisions for certification of a plan and inspection of measures being installed pursuant to such plan. A single-family dwelling that is not a part of a subdivision of land shall be exempt from such regulations. The soil and water conservation districts shall assist municipalities

Sec. 3   SPECIFIC LOCAL LAND USE REGULATIONS   777

erosion and sediment control plan is and shall contain: " 'Soil erosion and sediment control plan' means a scheme that minimizes soil erosion and sedimentation and includes, but is not limited to, a map and narrative. The map shall show topography, cleared and graded areas, proposed area alterations and the location of and detailed information concerning erosion and sediment measures and facilities. The narrative shall describe the project, the schedule of major activities on the land, the application of conservation practices, design criteria, construction details and the maintenance program for any erosion and sediment control facilities that are installed * * * " No such plan was filed by the applicant. To allow the applicant's "conceptual" plan to pass muster would trivialize these requirements into "a consciousness-raising exercise [rather] than as obligatory regulations." Tondro, Connecticut Land Use Regulation (2d Ed.1992), p. 335.

* * *

Notes

1. The Marion Road decision in footnote 4 mentions that Connecticut state law requires that local zoning ordinances "shall provide that proper provision be made for soil erosion and sediment control pursuant to Section 22a–329." Local zoning laws in Connecticut also must protect existing and potential public surface and groundwater drinking supplies. These substantive mandates illustrate how state legislatures can link federal and local environmental law. In an ideal system, federal environmental standards would be reflected in state law and, where local land use law authority is implicated, state legislatures would provide encouragement and incentives to localities to adopt corresponding standards or, where necessary, mandate local compliance. How would states enforce such mandates? One technique used in federal point source pollution control and coastal zone protection laws is for the state to step in and enforce the standards where localities fail to cooperate. Is it economically feasible for the states to enforce soil and erosion prevention standards, for example, in every one of its municipalities? What does your answer to this question imply about the practicalities of formulating intergovernmental policy?

2. Violations of municipal erosion and sedimentation ordinances can result in the assessment of heavy fines. In City of Asheville v. Woodberry Assoc., 114 N.C.App. 377, 442 S.E.2d 328 (1994), a developer was fined $90,910 for failure "to take protective action to control the erosion and sedimentation which was occurring."

(2) Steep Slopes/Ridgeline/Hilltop Protections

Ridgelines and hilltops are valuable for both their scenic and their ecological qualities. Surface runoff from ridgeline development can con-

which so request in developing regulations to comply with this section. Nothing in this section shall be construed as extending the time limits for the approval of any application under chapter 124 or 126.

"(b) Notwithstanding the provisions of subsection (a) of this section, the council may grant an extension of time for the adoption of the regulations on soil and sediment control required under sections 8–2 and 8–25, but not beyond June 30, 1986, to any municipality which makes application to the council before July 1, 1985."

taminate rivers and streams that supply drinking water downstream. Development of septic systems on ridges and hilltops can cause contamination of lower-lying properties. Buildings and roads can disrupt wildlife corridors and critical habitats. Hillsides and ridgelines are inherently unstable and care must be taken to prevent mudslides and other catastrophic movements of earth. Local laws can require that development on ridgelines and hilltop areas blend in with the natural environment and be buffered to preserve particularly valuable viewsheds in the community.

Steep slopes usually are associated with other environmental features such as rock outcrops, shallow soils, bedrock fractures, and groundwater seeps. Excavations or building construction can cause instability through loosening of the soil structure and the removal of trees, vegetation, and rocks. Grading, cutting, and filling—activities associated with preparation of construction sites—can compromise the stability of some slopes. Activities such as agriculture, road and railway construction, house building, and land drainage can be regulated to protect steep slopes. The town of Cortlandt, New York, has adopted a local law for the purpose of preventing the "improper alteration" of steep slopes. CORTLANDT, NY CODE § 259.1 (1992). Provisions of this kind can often be found in local ridgeline or hilltop protection ordinances throughout the nation.

The trend in local environmental law is to recognize natural connections on the land and waters by broadening the scope of natural protection laws. Steep slopes, like wetlands, are often found in association with other critical environmental features and perform multiple functions of community value ranging from providing breathtaking vistas, to harboring wildlife in their unique, horizontal ecosystems, to protecting down-slope landowners and water bodies from flooding, erosion, and sedimentation. In Harris v. Zoning Com'n of the Town of Milford, 259 Conn. 402, 788 A.2d 1239 (2002), the Connecticut Supreme Court sustained a town law that protected ridgelines in this broader context. The local law amended the zoning ordinance to exclude from the calculation for determining buildable lots all wetlands, watercourses, and land with a 25 percent slope or greater. The calculation was applicable only in residential districts and served to lower density in those districts by increasing the minimum lot size needed for single-family home construction. The plaintiffs' claims that the law lacked a rational basis and violated the uniformity requirement for zoning under Connecticut law were rejected by the court.

SELLON v. CITY OF MANITOU SPRINGS

Supreme Court of Colorado, En Banc, 1987.
745 P.2d 229.

KIRSHBAUM, JUSTICE.

* * *

In July of 1973, the City adopted a master plan for a parcel of property, referred to as "Crystal Hills," located adjacent to the City.

That plan provided that 194 home sites could be developed on the property. On September 1, 1981, the City annexed Crystal Hills. The landowners purchased the property in March 1982.

The City contains many areas characterized by hills of varying degrees of slope. Consequently, problems of erosion, drainage and access are of particular concern to property owners, residents and city planners. On May 4, 1982, after much debate and discussion, the City Council adopted the hillside ordinance in an effort to deal in a meaningful fashion with some of these concerns. The ordinance created a special hillside low density residential zone and established an equation for calculating the minimal lot sizes necessary for development of property placed in that zone.[5] When applied to steeply graded property, the equation requires in general that development plans be based on larger lot sizes than those required for properties not so steeply sloped. The equation also distinguishes between "platted" and "unplatted" land and requires larger lots for development of areas which are designated "unplatted" land at the time the property is zoned or rezoned hillside residential than in areas which are designated "platted" land.

On September 23, 1983, the City Council adopted a resolution placing Crystal Hills in a low density residential zone and authorizing the development of 108 residential units on the property. Many citizens disapproved of this decision, however, and the City Council decided to place the question of the rezoning of Crystal Hills before the voters of the City. In November of 1983, a majority of the City's voting electorate indicated approval for the rezoning of Crystal Hills as hillside low density residential property.

The City Council subsequently scheduled two public hearings to consider the question of the appropriate zoning for the Crystal Hills property. On November 18, 1983, the landowners were advised by City representatives that, based upon the hillside density equation, residential development of the Crystal Hills property would be limited to sixty units under hillside low density residential zoning.

Lengthy public hearings were held before the City Council on December 6, 1983, and January 3, 1984. Although one of the landowners attended the hearings and stated that he was opposed to the rezoning, the landowners offered no evidence at these hearings. At the conclusion of the January 1984 hearing, the City Council voted to rezone the Crystal Hills property as hillside low density residential.

---

5. That segment of the ordinance reads:

(3) Development Requirements

(a) Minimum Lot Size—Allowable lot size shall be based on the average percent of slope, defined as follows:

Average Percent of Slope shall mean the percent of slope as computed by the following formula—

$$S = \frac{100IL}{A}$$

Where S = average percent of slope
I = contour interval in feet
L = summation of length of all contour lines in feet
A = area in square feet of parcel being considered

The landowners appealed this decision to the El Paso County District Court. Following a two-day hearing, the district court affirmed the City Council's action.

The landowners assert that the hillside ordinance is insufficiently related to public health, safety and welfare objectives of the City and that its terms are impermissibly vague. They suggest that because of these alleged deficiencies the hillside ordinance violates the due process clauses of the United States and Colorado Constitutions. We disagree.

The principles applicable to a determination of whether a particular municipal legislative enactment violates constitutional due process standards are well settled. A presumption of validity attaches to zoning decisions of municipal zoning authorities. *Board of County Comm'rs v. Mountain Air Ranch*, 192 Colo. 364, 563 P.2d 341 (1977); *Wright v. City of Littleton*, 174 Colo. 318, 483 P.2d 953 (1971); *Baum v. City & County of Denver*, 147 Colo. 104, 363 P.2d 688 (1961). Thus, a party challenging a zoning ordinance on constitutional grounds assumes the burden of proving the asserted invalidity beyond a reasonable doubt. *Tri–State Generation & Transmission Co. v. City of Thornton*, 647 P.2d 670 (Colo.1982); *Holcomb v. City & County of Denver*, 199 Colo. 251, 606 P.2d 858 (1980); *Ford Leasing Dev. Co. v. Board of County Comm'rs*, 186 Colo. 418, 528 P.2d 237 (1974); *Baum v. City & County of Denver*, 147 Colo. 104, 363 P.2d 688.

For purposes of the United States Constitution, an ordinance containing provisions that bear a rational relationship to legitimate state concerns satisfies due process requirements. *Schad v. Borough of Mount Ephraim*, 452 U.S. 61, 101 S.Ct. 2176, 68 L.Ed.2d 671 (1981); *Village of Euclid v. Ambler Realty Co.*, 272 U.S. 365, 47 S.Ct. 114, 71 L.Ed. 303 (1926). The due process clause of article II, section 25, of Colorado's Constitution requires a reasonable relation between an ordinance and a valid interest, such as public health, safety, morals or general welfare. *Nopro Co. v. Town of Cherry Hills Village*, 180 Colo. 217, 504 P.2d 344 (1972); *Wright v. City of Littleton*, 174 Colo. 318, 483 P.2d 953. The hillside ordinance must be evaluated pursuant to these standards.

The record reflects that prior to the adoption of the hillside ordinance great attention had been directed by the City Council to problems that had developed after improvements were made to property containing relatively steep slopes. For example, the city manager testified that the development of single-family units on steeply graded plots of land continually forced the City to deal with erosion, drainage, maintenance and emergency access issues. The record also contains evidence that residents of various areas of the City historically had experienced significant difficulties with some or all of these problems. The adoption of the hillside ordinance reflected a considered effort by the City Council to deal with these very real problems. Viewed in light of these facts, the ordinance addresses significant issues directly affecting the health and welfare of the City's residents.

Sec. 3	SPECIFIC LOCAL LAND USE REGULATIONS	781

At the review hearing conducted by the district court the landowners introduced evidence to the effect that the hillside ordinance was not the best means available to address problems of erosion, drainage or emergency access associated with development of residential housing units in steep slope areas of the City. However, the question is not whether other solutions to a governmental problem are feasible or superior to the program actually adopted; the question is whether the decision made is itself reasonably and rationally related to the problem being addressed. *See Schad v. Borough of Mount Ephraim*, 452 U.S. 61, 101 S.Ct. 2176; *Nopro Co. v. Town of Cherry Hills Village*, 180 Colo. 217, 504 P.2d 344; *Wright v. City of Littleton*, 174 Colo. 318, 483 P.2d 953. In this case, it is abundantly clear that the provisions of the hillside ordinance are rationally and reasonably related to problems of erosion, drainage, maintenance and emergency access occurring on sloping terrain that affect the health and safety of the City's residents.

* * *

The landowners next contend that the hillside ordinance is confiscatory and therefore unconstitutional as applied to them because it, in effect, precludes the use of the Crystal Hills property for any reasonable purpose. It is true that a zoning ordinance that prohibits the use of property for any reasonable purpose will be deemed confiscatory and therefore violative of just compensation and due process protections afforded by Colorado's Constitution. *Nopro Co. v. Town of Cherry Hills Village*, 180 Colo. 217, 504 P.2d 344 (1972*); Bird v. City of Colo. Springs*, 176 Colo. 32, 489 P.2d 324 (1971); *Madis v. Higginson*, 164 Colo. 320, 434 P.2d 705 (1967). However, our decisions have consistently emphasized the principle that a landowner is not entitled to obtain maximum profits from the use of property, and that so long as the zoning ordinance leaves some reasonable use for the property, the ordinance does not violate state constitutional standards. *Nopro Co. v. Town of Cherry Hills Village*, 180 Colo.217, 504 P.2d 344; *see Bird v. City of Colo. Springs*, 176 Colo. 32, 489 P.2d 324; *Baum v. City & County of Denver*, 147 Colo. 104, 363 P.2d 688 (1961).

The evidence establishes that the hillside ordinance does not render the Crystal Hills property devoid of any reasonable use, and that the landowners may still build a minimum of sixty residential units on the land. They are not entitled to obtain maximum profits from the use of their land or to obtain the highest and best use for the property. *Nopro Co. v. Town of Cherry Hills Village*, 180 Colo. 217, 504 P.2d 344; *Wright v. City of Littleton*, 174 Colo. 318, 483 P.2d 953 (1971). The landowners failed to establish that as the result of the hillside ordinance they could not put their property to any reasonable use. They therefore failed to satisfy their burden of demonstrating beyond a reasonable doubt that the ordinance was confiscatory.

* * *

Finally, the landowners argue that the City Council's decision to rezone Crystal Hills was arbitrary, capricious and an abuse of discretion in violation of C.R.C.P. 106(a)(4). A trial court reviewing a quasi-judicial action pursuant to C.R.C.P. 106(a)(4) must uphold that decision unless there is no competent evidence in the record to support it. *E.g., Ross v. Fire & Police Pension Ass'n,* 713 P.2d 1304 (Colo.1986); *Corper v. City & County of Denver,* 191 Colo. 252, 552 P.2d 13 (1976). The record in this case reflects that the City Council adopted the hillside ordinance because of long-standing concern over problems of erosion, drainage, maintenance and emergency access affecting hilly property. The decision to place Crystal Hills in the zone established by the hillside ordinance was entirely consistent with prior actions of the City seeking to address these problems. The record also establishes that the sharply contrasting geographical configurations of Crystal Hills make it well-suited for the zoning requirements established in the hillside ordinance. The City Council's action represents a reasonable and responsible effort to reconcile the interests of property owners and residents in the context of the geographical realities of the City. It was not arbitrary and capricious.

For the foregoing reasons, the judgment of the district court is affirmed.

Notes

1. Does reducing allowed density of development, by itself, serve the public interest? How does it protect the environment to exclude wetlands, watercourses, and steep slopes from lot count calculations, for example? How are such calculations different from traditional wetlands laws that severely regulate what can be built in defined wetlands and their buffers? How much scientific justification of a land use regulation is needed to survive judicial scrutiny? In the Sellon case, the court cited evidence on the record that the city had difficulty with prior building on relatively steep slopes and the testimony of the city manager at trial. In Harris v. Zoning Com'n of the Town of Milford, the court wrote that "our search of the record leads us to conclude that the zoning commission reasonably could have believed that conservation would be a corollary effect [of the net buildable lot calculation] * * *." Sellon further establishes that the regulator need not select the best solution but need only show that its solution "is itself reasonably and rationally related to the problem being addressed." What incentive do these judicial standards create to encourage regulators to use clear and convincing environmental science in drafting and supporting local environmental laws?

2. Another case involving restrictions on hillside development is City of San Marcos v. R.W. McDonald Development Corp., 700 S.W.2d 674 (Tex.App. 3 Dist.1985). The court assumed the validity of an ordinance which restricted development of land "located on hillsides or in areas with soil subject to erosion," but the decision turns on whether the developer made serious misrepresentations to the city (the city initially approved developer's subdivision but sued when it learned of the misrepresentations). Also see Hensler v. City of Glendale, 8 Cal.4th 1, 32 Cal.Rptr.2d 244, 876 P.2d 1043 (1994), cert. denied 513 U.S. 1184, 115 S.Ct. 1176, 130 L.Ed.2d 1129 (1995), where the court dismissed a developer's inverse condemnation action for failure to

exhaust administrative remedies. The developer challenged a city ordinance that precluded the building of houses on ridgelines claiming that 40 percent of his land was taken by the regulation. Similarly, in Lake Shore Estates, Inc. v. Denville Twp. Planning Bd., 127 N.J. 394, 605 A.2d 1073 (1992), the court upheld the retroactive application of a steep slope ordinance that frustrated a developer's subdivision plan. In Anello v. Zoning Bd. of Appeals of Dobbs Ferry, 89 N.Y.2d 535, 678 N.E.2d 870, 656 N.Y.S.2d 184 (1997), the court held that denial of a variance to build a single-family dwelling under the city's steep slope ordinance was not a taking because the owner acquired her property after the enactment of the ordinance; thus, she was not deprived of any property interest under the rationale of the Lucas case.

3. An explanation of the rationale and planning considerations for hillside development can be found in Robert B. Olshansky, Planning for Hillside Development, in Environment & Development (American Planning Ass'n, Sept./Oct. 1995).

4. In Pomona Pointe Assoc. v. Village of Pomona, 185 Misc.2d 131, 712 N.Y.S.2d 275 (N.Y.Sup.Ct.2000), the lower court upheld a local law which regulated the development of steep slopes to protect their environmental function. Local site plan regulations are authorized by New York state law to include standards that provide for proper parking, access, landscaping, location of buildings, protection of "adjacent land uses and physical features" and "any additional elements" specified by the local legislature. The court interpreted "any additional elements" broadly to include environmental considerations. The plaintiff owned two lots with slopes of varying steepness. The village's steep slope law required the issuance of a special permit for the disturbance of a "very steep" or "extremely steep slope" as defined in the law. The plaintiff challenged the law, arguing that it granted authority to the planning board in excess of the authority contained in the state site plan statute. The court found that consideration of steep slope criteria was within the authority delegated to the village pursuant to the site plan review statute. It held that the protection of "adjacent land uses and physical features" authorizes the adoption of regulations to protect steep slopes. Such provisions "are directly related to the possible impact that disturbance of very/extremely steep slopes could have on water runoff and the stable cohesive integrity of the soil, rocks, trees and vegetation on such slopes." The court thought that it was clear that site plan review could include consideration of natural resource protection, especially when adjacent resources may be adversely affected.

5. Pennsylvania courts have also upheld ordinances regulating development on steep slopes as a reasonable method to promote preservation of environmental areas, decrease landslide, and prevent erosion problems. See, e.g., Fisher v. Viola, 789 A.2d 782 (Pa.Cmwlth.2001).

6. The town of Castle Rock, Colorado, has adopted a ridgeline protection law that allows certain ridgelines and hilltops to be designated for protection of the visual environments they create. Development permits are then conditioned on keeping buildings and other structures out of sight. CASTLE ROCK, CO. CODE ch. 17.14.060, No. 99–15 (2002). The regulation lists specific criteria:

C. Mitigation of Impacts. Within * * * minor ridgeline areas of the district, all primary and accessory structures shall be required to comply with the following measures designated to mitigate the visual impact of the structure prior to occupancy, unless explicitly exempted elsewhere in this chapter.

1. Colors. All occupied structures and accessory structures shall be constructed and maintained so that predominant exterior wall colors * * * and roof surfacing materials (a) repeat the colors most commonly in the land and vegetation around the building (earth tone), and (b) have a light reflective value of no more than forty percent.

2. Vegetation. The area around each primary structure and accessory structure shall include at least one tree of a species with a mature height of at least thirty-five feet for each 2500 square feet of a lot or parcel area * * *.

(3) Scenic Resources

As congestion of homes, traffic, and people has accompanied urban sprawl, a counter movement has begun focusing on one salient symptom: the disappearance of open space—the appearance that things are too crowded. Citizens and local voters notice and complain that their communities look different. They lobby for local laws that protect views and the visual environment. Local legislatures have responded by enacting laws that protect scenic resources and assets, including open views, country roads, panoramic landscapes, tree-lined streets, stone walls, and agricultural scenes. Local efforts to preserve scenic resources include the regulation of road construction and maintenance, land-clearing, architecture, and placement of utility lines and signage. Other requirements such as the maintenance of vegetative buffers, street trees, and other vegetation may be included to minimize the visual impact of development.

Municipalities may protect specific view corridors that have particular aesthetic or economic importance to the community. The town of Vail, Colorado, has adopted a View Corridors ordinance expressly because "[t]he protection and perpetuation of certain mountain views and other significant views from various pedestrian public ways" will "strengthen and preserve the Town's unique environmental heritage and attributes," and will "enhance the aesthetic and economic vitality and values of the Town." Focal points and prominent landmarks are protected which "contribute to the community's unique sense of place." (Ord. 18 (1992) § 1) In Landmark Land Co. v. City and County of Denver, 728 P.2d 1281 (Colo. 1986), the Colorado Supreme Court upheld a similarly worded ordinance as being well within a city's police powers. Kern County, California, has implemented a Scenic Corridor Combining District "to designate areas which contain unique visual scenic resources as viewed from a major highway or freeway wherein the siting of off-site advertising signs needs to be reviewed on a case-by-case basis." [Ch.

Sec. 3   SPECIFIC LOCAL LAND USE REGULATIONS   785

19.74.010] The district is intended "to safeguard the scenic qualities of the natural environment and the visual qualities of primary entranceways into the county." The district regulations are added to "the regulations of the base commercial or industrial zoning district with which the SC district is combined."

Scenic resources, of course, are part of the integrated mosaic of the landscape, and laws that protect them are beginning to respect these connections. The Upland Preservation Overlay district adopted by Brookfield, Wisconsin, is intended to preserve "all significant woodlands, wildlife habitat areas, areas of rough topography and related scenic areas." [Ch. 17.96.] In addition to maintaining "the natural beauty of the city," the overlay is intended to control erosion and sedimentation and to maintain water quality. The ordinance contains a deed restriction on subdivision plats prohibiting the erection of structures, the removal of vegetation, and any filling or excavating of land within the overlay, which runs with the land in perpetuity. [17.96.070.]

Local laws that protect scenic resources arise in other contexts, including the built environment. Albuquerque, New Mexico, has created a Historic Overlay Zone and an Urban Conservation Overlay Zone as a means of preserving areas that may have "high artistic value." Areas in the Historical Overlay are suitable for preservation for historical, architectural, or cultural reasons. Areas in the Urban Conservation Overlay have "distinctive characteristics that are worthy of conservation." [§ 14–16–2–28.] For both types of overlay, the ordinance requires that the city council identify the area's distinctive characteristics and general preservation guidelines. The following case arises in the context of preserving scenic assets in the context of an historic district as well as a coastal zone and demonstrates how scenic, historic, and coastal protection provisions are being built into the basic land use regulations and procedure of local governments.

SMITH v. ZONING BD. OF APPEALS OF TOWN OF GREENWICH

Supreme Court of Connecticut, 1993.
227 Conn. 71, 629 A.2d 1089.

KATZ, ASSOCIATE JUSTICE.

The dispositive issue in this appeal is whether the planning and zoning board of appeals for the town of Greenwich (board) is authorized, under the Greenwich town charter (charter) and the applicable subdivision regulations, to consider historical factors in determining whether to grant or deny an application to subdivide property located in a historic district. The defendants, the board, the Historical Society of the Town of Greenwich, Inc. (historical society), and Anita De Lesseps Keefe, a landowner within 100 feet of the property, appeal, upon our grant of certification, from the judgment of the Appellate Court. The Appellate Court concluded that the board had not been authorized to consider historical factors in reviewing a subdivision application and reversed the judgment of the trial court. *Smith v. Zoning Board of Appeals*, 29 Conn.App. 28, 35, 614 A.2d 464 (1992). We disagree with the Appellate Court and, accordingly, reverse the judgment.

The following relevant facts are undisputed. The plaintiffs, E. Don Smith and Eileen Smith, own property located at 35 Strickland Road in Greenwich (property). The property is situated in the Mill Pond Historic District (district), which was established under article 5 of the charter and General Statutes § 7–147b. The property is also in an R–7 zone classification, which encompasses single homes.

In January, 1987, the plaintiffs submitted a preliminary subdivision application to the planning and zoning commission of the town of Greenwich (commission), seeking to subdivide the property into three lots. After a hearing, the commission preliminarily approved the plaintiffs' application, subject to the resolution of fourteen issues prior to the submission of the final application. In particular, the commission required the plaintiffs to meet with the historic district commission "in order to determine an appropriate house location for lot 1." The commission further instructed that "[t]he preservation of significant trees shall be taken into consideration in determining house location, as well as conformity as nearby as possible to the existing setback/streetscape of house locations to the south."

Pursuant to the commission's requirement, the plaintiffs met with members of the historic district commission. Although, in the absence of a final, approved subdivision plan the historic district commission could not take any formal action concerning the appropriateness of the building on lot 1, the historic district commission did, nonetheless, express its opposition to the proposal.

The plaintiffs subsequently submitted a final subdivision application. On November 22, 1988, the commission denied the plaintiffs' final subdivision application because granting it would "permit construction of a house in the * * * significant open space, thereby disrupting the essential characteristic of the historic district."

The plaintiffs appealed from the decision of the commission to the board pursuant to § 103(a) of the charter. Pursuant to § 103(a), the board conducted a de novo review of the application and held a public hearing. The board found that the plaintiffs were seeking to subdivide the property into three lots. Lot 1 would contain the plaintiffs' residence; lot 2 would contain an existing barn; and lot 3, a presently unimproved area in front of the plaintiffs' residence, would contain a single family house. The proposed building on lot 3 is the focus of this dispute.

Following the public hearing, the board denied the plaintiffs' appeal. The board concluded that the proposed building on lot 3 would disrupt the "sweeping front lawn" and, therefore, would not be consistent with the district's historic streetscape. The board stated that "[t]he proposed subdivision did not meet the purposes of the Subdivision Regulations as provided in Section 6–260, thereof. It does not conform to the Town of

Greenwich Plan of Development in that it does not meet the basic objectives of preservation of historic and architectural resources. Furthermore, it does not preserve the natural features of the landscape; namely, the historic streetscape." The board also concluded that the plaintiffs' application was subject to review under the Coastal Area Management Act (act), General Statutes § 22a–90 et seq. Applying the standards in the act, the board found that the subdivision proposal "would have an adverse impact on coastal resources because of the alteration of natural features of vistas."

The plaintiffs appealed from the decision of the board to the trial court pursuant to § 104 of the charter and General Statutes § 8–8(2)(b). Although the trial court disagreed with the applicability of one of the statutes, the act, on which the board had relied, the court concluded that other statutes, as well as the town's own land use regulations, supported the board's action. The trial court therefore dismissed the plaintiffs' appeal.

The trial court concluded that the board had the authority to consider the historic streetscape for three reasons: the provisions of the town's subdivision regulations, the statutory and town policy in favor of historic preservation and a restriction contained in the plaintiffs' deed. Section 6–260 provides that the purpose of the subdivision regulations is to "[f]urther the orderly development of the Town in accordance with the Town Plan of Development." Because the town plan has "as one of its 'Basic Objectives' the preservation of historic resources," the trial court concluded that the board acted within its authority in considering the historic streetscape. Additionally, § 6–266(a)(20) of the Greenwich Land Use Regulations specifically permits an evaluation of historical factors, noted in § 6–266(a)(19), in subdivisions located "within the coastal zone." Furthermore, the town's subdivision regulations are consistent with public policy favoring historic preservation that is contained in General Statutes § 7–147a et seq. and § 6–307 of the Greenwich Land Use Regulations. Finally, a restriction in the plaintiffs' deed states that " '[s]aid premises are conveyed subject to * * * [r]egulations imposed by reason of the fact that the premises are part of a historic district as established by the Town of Greenwich * * *.' "

The trial court affirmed the board's conclusion that the plaintiffs' subdivision proposal would impair the historic streetscape. The trial court reasoned that "[t]he Smiths' side of Strickland Road is characterized by homes on lots with sweeping front lawns. The plaintiffs plan to convert their front lawn into a building lot and construct thereon a house with the thirty feet by forty feet footprint, and setbacks of twenty-five feet from the front property line, twenty feet from the south property line, and fifteen feet from a line of trees. These exhibits show that construction of a house on the front lawn would drastically alter the streetscape, and support the Board's conclusion in that regard."

Finally, the trial court considered the plaintiffs' argument that "the denial of their plan constitutes a taking of property without due process of law." The court noted, however, that "[t]he Board rejected this claim, concluding that because other alternatives for development of the property exist, the plaintiffs were not deprived of their development rights. The defendant Board argues that [the] plaintiffs have failed to establish a diminution in the value of their property as a result of the decision, and further, only one proposal has been rejected, not all proposals."

Upon a grant of certification, the plaintiffs appealed to the Appellate Court, from the trial court's dismissal of their appeal. The Appellate Court reversed the judgment of the trial court, concluding that the board did not have the authority to consider historical factors in deciding whether to grant or deny a subdivision application because: "(1) the enabling statutes on subdivisions did not give the board the authority to include historical factors in its regulations; (2) the terms 'town plan of development,' 'historic factors' and 'historic streetscape' are not known and fixed standards required for subdivision regulations; (3) the Greenwich town charter forbids the board from denying a subdivision application based on the plan of development; and (4) it is the duty of the historic district commission, not the planning and zoning commission or the board of appeals, to decide whether a building should be erected in a historic district." *Smith v. Zoning Board of Appeals*, supra, 224 Conn. at 35, 617 A.2d 167. Having ourselves granted certification for the defendants to appeal, we now reverse the judgment of the Appellate Court.

In reviewing an appeal from an administrative agency, the trial court must determine whether " 'the agency has acted unreasonably, arbitrarily, illegally or in abuse of its discretion.' " *Board of Education v. State Employees Retirement Commission*, 210 Conn. 531, 541, 556 A.2d 572 (1989); *Frito-Lay, Inc. v. Planning & Zoning Commission,* 206 Conn. 554, 573, 538 A.2d 1039 (1988). " 'The trial court may not retry the case or substitute its judgment for that of the agency * * *.' " *Board of Education v. State Employees Retirement Commission*, supra, 210 Conn. at 540, 556 A.2d 572; *Burnham v. Planning & Zoning Commission*, 189 Conn. 261, 265, 455 A.2d 339 (1983). The principal issue in this case, however, presents "questions of law turning upon the interpretation of statutes." *Board of Education v. State Employees Retirement Commission,* supra. The defendants dispute the Appellate Court's conclusion that no statutory or regulatory authority existed allowing the commission to consider historical factors. "[T]he construction of a statute on an issue that has not previously been subjected to judicial scrutiny is a question of law on which an administrative ruling is not entitled to special deference." (Internal quotation marks omitted.) *Id.*

The defendants claim initially that the Appellate Court incorrectly concluded that the commission lacked the authority to promulgate subdivision regulations that provide for the consideration of historical or architectural factors. We agree with the defendants.

"It has been said that the whole field of subdivision regulation is peculiarly a creature of legislation. It is therefore imperative that before subdivision regulations may be made operative, the necessary statutory authorization of such regulation must exist * * *. In other words, in order to determine whether the regulation in question was within the authority of the commission to enact, we do not search for a statutory prohibition against such an enactment; rather, we must search for statutory authority for the enactment." (Internal quotation marks omitted.) *Finn v. Planning & Zoning Commission*, 156 Conn. 540, 545, 244 A.2d 391 (1968). In determining whether the board had the authority to deny subdivision applications for historical reasons, we must first determine whether the commission has the authority to enact subdivision regulations that provide for such consideration. The town of Greenwich exercises its zoning power by virtue of a special act. 26 Spec. Acts 325, No. 469 (1951). "This act established the [Greenwich Town Charter], which is the source of authority" to enact and enforce subdivision regulations. *Norwich v. Norwalk Wilbert Vault Co.*, 208 Conn. 1, 8, 544 A.2d 152 (1988); *O'Meara v. Norwich*, 167 Conn. 579, 581, 356 A.2d 906 (1975). "The charter serves as an enabling act, both creating power and prescribing the form in which it must be exercised * * *." (Internal quotation marks omitted.) *West Hartford Taxpayers Assn., Inc. v. Streeter*, 190 Conn. 736, 742, 462 A.2d 379 (1983). "Agents of a city, including commissions, have no source of authority beyond the charter. *Perretta v. New Britain*, 185 Conn. 88, 92, 440 A.2d 823 (1981)." (Internal quotation marks omitted.) *Norwich v. Norwalk Wilbert Vault Co.*, supra, 208 Conn. at 8–9, 544 A.2d 152.

The charter is the source of authority governing subdivisions, except if there is a clear legislative intent that the General Statutes control. *Pizzola v. Planning & Zoning Commission*, 167 Conn. 202, 206, 355 A.2d 21 (1974). The power of the planning and zoning commission to adopt subdivision regulations is limited by the terms of the statute or special act. *Caldrello v. Planning Board*, 193 Conn. 387, 391, 476 A.2d 1063 (1984); *Bishop v. Board of Zoning Appeals*, 133 Conn. 614, 619, 53 A.2d 659 (1947); see, e.g., *Reed v. Planning & Zoning Commission*, 208 Conn. 431, 544 A.2d 1213 (1988). "The ordinance must rest primarily upon the enabling act and must not go beyond the power delegated by it." *Bishop v. Board of Zoning Appeals*, supra.

Section 83 of the charter established the planning and zoning commission. In addition to other powers granted to the commission by the charter, § 83 also conferred upon the commission "the powers and duties conferred upon zoning commissions under the General Statutes." Section 101 of the charter sets forth those areas that the commission's subdivision regulations are meant to control or regulate. Section 101(d) provides that "[t]he regulations shall provide that the land to be subdivided shall be of such character that it can be used for building purposes without danger to health or the public safety, that proper provision shall be made for water, drainage and sewerage, and, in areas contiguous to brooks, rivers or other bodies of water subject to flooding, including tidal flooding, that provision shall be made for protective flood control measures and that the proposed streets are in harmony with existing or proposed principal thoroughfares shown in the Plan of Development as described in Section 94, especially in regard to safe intersections with such thoroughfares, and so arranged and of such width, as to provide an adequate and convenient system for present and prospective traffic needs." General Statutes § 8–25, the applicable section of the General Statutes, is substantially the same.

The plaintiffs argue that neither § 101 of the charter nor any other section of the charter addressing subdivisions specifically refers to historical factors. By contrast, there is specific language authorizing the commission to regulate and make provisions for such matters as water, drainage, sewage, flood control, street layout and grading, public utilities and the provision of parks and playgrounds. Greenwich Town Charter § 101(d), (e) and (g). Thus, the plaintiffs maintain that because the charter specially refers to several items that must be provided for in the regulations, and does not expressly include the consideration of historical factors, the commission lacks the authority to enact subdivision regulations that allow consideration of historical factors.

The defendants claim, on the contrary, that the commission's authority to promulgate regulations that consider historical factors arises from § 101(d) of the charter, which provides that subdivision "regulations shall provide that the land to be subdivided shall be of such character that it can be used for building purposes without danger to *health or the public safety* * * *." (Emphasis added.) The defendants argue that public health and safety includes protecting the environment, which, in turn, includes historic preservation. We agree with the defendants.

Although neither the charter nor the General Statutes provides a specific definition of "public health and safety" in the context of zoning regulations, other related statutes establish that environmental conservation is a legitimate concern within this broad regulatory rubric. The Environmental Protection Act (EPA); General Statutes § 22a–1 et seq.; includes the environment as a facet of public health and safety. Section 22a–1 provides in part that "the policy of the state of Connecticut is to conserve, improve and protect its * * * environment * * * in order to enhance the health, safety and welfare of the people of the state." (Emphasis added.) In addition, the Inland Wetlands and Watercourses Act; General Statutes § 22a–28 et seq.; provides that "[t]he preservation and protection of the wetlands and watercourses * * * is essential to the health, welfare and safety of the citizens of the state * * *." General Statutes § 22a–36; see *Mario v. Fairfield,* 217 Conn. 164, 168, 585 A.2d 87 (1991). These statutes illuminate the statutory phrase before us in this case because they address generally related subjects that the legislature may be presumed to have considered in like manner. *Link v. Shelton,* 186 Conn. 623, 627, 443 A.2d 902 (1982). In light of these principles, we find a relationship between protecting the public health and safety and protecting the environment. Accordingly, we conclude that public health and safety includes consideration of the "environment."

Although this court has not defined the contours of the term "environment," we may look again to the meaning given to this term in other statutory provisions. *Link v. Shelton*, supra. Once it is established that "public health and safety" includes consideration of environmental concerns, the environmental statutes make it clear that historical factors are a recognized element of environmental law. The EPA in General Statutes § 22a–1c includes a broad definition of actions that significantly affect the environment: "activities * * * proposed to be undertaken by state departments, institutions or agencies * * * which could have a major impact on the state's * * * *historic structures* * * *." (Emphasis added.) Additionally, General Statutes § 22a–19a states in part that the EPA "shall be applicable to the unreasonable destruction of historic structures and landmarks of the state, which shall be those properties (1) listed or under consideration for listing as individual units on the National Register of Historic Places (16 USC [§] 470a, as amended) or (2) which are a part of a district listed or under consideration for listing on said national register and which have been determined by the state historic preservation board to *contribute* to the *historic significance of such district*." (Emphasis added.) The EPA recognizes that the protection of many environmental concerns, such as air and water, is essentially the preservation of the resource that is being used. These regulations " 'guarantee that important land functions continue to operate while the land is being used, no matter what the use.' " T. Tondro, Connecticut Land Use Regulation 2d Ed. (1992), p. 263. Similarly, the protection of historical factors is a preservation of the function of the resource being used. *Id.*; see *Penn Central Transportation Co. v. New York City*, 438 U.S. 104, 108, 98 S.Ct. 2646, 2651, 57 L.Ed.2d 631 (1978) ("[h]istoric conservation is but one aspect of the much larger problem, *basically an environmental one*, of enhancing * * * the quality of life for people" [emphasis added; internal quotation marks omitted]). We note, as well, that we have interpreted the power to protect the "general welfare" to include the authority to consider historical factors. *Figarsky v. Historic District Commission*, 171 Conn. 198, 207–209, 368 A.2d 163 (1976).

Accordingly, we conclude that because the phrase "public health and safety" includes environmental factors, it includes historical factors. The commission, therefore, had the authority to promulgate subdivision regulations that take into account historical factors.

* * *

Our conclusion that the board incorrectly denied the plaintiffs' application on the basis of noncompliance with the town plan would ordinarily require that we affirm the Appellate Court's judgment. On appeal to the Appellate Court, as well as on appeal to this court, however, the defendants raised alternative grounds in their briefs upon which the trial court's decision may be affirmed. After review of the defendants' arguments, we conclude that the Appellate Court incorrectly dismissed one of these alternate grounds. "[T]his court is authorized to rely upon alternative grounds supported by the record to sustain a judgment * * *. 'The * * * judgment will be affirmed, though based on erroneous grounds, if the same result is required by law.' " Henderson v. Department of Motor Vehicles, 202 Conn. 453, 461, 521 A.2d 1040 (1987); *Ivey, Barnum & O'Mara v. Indian Harbor Properties, Inc.*, 190 Conn. 528, 532, 461 A.2d 1369 (1983); *A & H Corporation v. Bridgeport*, 180 Conn. 435, 443, 430 A.2d 25 (1980); *Johnny Cake, Inc. v. Zoning Board of Appeals*, 180 Conn. 296, 301, 429 A.2d 883 (1980); C. Tait, Connecticut Appellate Practice and Procedure (1991) § 7.14. We conclude that the trial court correctly concluded that the board was authorized, under the subdivision regulations, to consider historical factors when it acted on the application.

In construing regulations, the general rules of statutory construction apply. *Schwartz v. Planning & Zoning Commission*, 208 Conn. 146, 153, 543 A.2d 1339 (1988) (applying rules of statutory construction to interpretation of zoning regulations); see *Ghent v. Planning Commission*, 219 Conn. 511, 518–19, 594 A.2d 5 (1991); *Sonn v. Planning Commission*, 172 Conn. 156, 159–60, 374 A.2d 159 (1976). The commission is limited by the power conferred upon it by the subdivision regulations. See *Reed v. Planning & Zoning Commission*, 208 Conn. 431, 544 A.2d 1213 (1988) (planning commission cannot exercise a power that has been admittedly delegated to it, unless its own regulations give it the right to exercise that power). Section 6–266(a)[6] of the Greenwich Land Use Regulations sets forth the information that should be included in a preliminary subdivision application. "The preliminary layout shall be considered as a helpful guide in the preparation of a subdivision plan and should include the information set out in Section 6–266." Greenwich Land Use Regs. § 6–265. Subsection (a) of § 6–266 states that "[t]he preliminary layout shall include as many of the following items of information as is practicable." This general statement, set forth at the

---

6. Section 6–266(a) of the Greenwich Land Use Regulations provides in pertinent part: 'The preliminary layout shall include as many of the following items of information as is practicable * * *.

"(19) For a subdivision of ten (10) lots or more or the subdivision of ten (10) or more acres, an environmental assessment by qualified environmental specialists shall be provided. The Commission may require said assessment for smaller subdivisions if deemed necessary. The assessment shall include an evaluation of the following:

"(a) Conformance with the Open Space Plan of Development

"(b) Significant wetlands

"(c) Steep Slopes

"(d) Stormwater Drainage

"(e) Soils capabilities

"(f) Vegetation including forested areas and the identification of trees over 10" in caliper when not part of forested areas

"(g) Significant geological formations

"(h) Historical and archaeological factors

"(i) Animal habitats

"(j) Water availability and quality

"(k) Aquifer protection in accordance with the Statutes of the State of Connecticut

"(*l*) Other data which the Commission deems appropriate.

"The environmental assessment shall be subject to a review, after the receipt of recommendations of the Conservation Commission, by the Planning and Zoning Commission including the mitigation measures for minimizing environmental impact before the applicant proceeds to final plan."

beginning of the regulation, indicates the commission's intent to require only the information that is pertinent to a particular subdivision application.

Section 6–266 (a)(19) permits the commission in its discretion to require an environmental assessment in the preliminary layout of subdivisions of fewer than ten lots or ten acres. Subsection (a)(19) lists twelve relevant considerations, including "[h]istorical and archaeological factors." Greenwich Land Use Regs. § 6–266(a)(19)(h). In this case, the commission requested an evaluation by the historic district commission of the historic implications of the subdivision application. It also requested an evaluation by the required experts of some of the other considerations listed in § 6–266(a)(19). It did not request that each and every one of these items be evaluated, presumably because it did not see such a need.

The plaintiffs argue that § 6–266 does not apply because the commission did not formally request an "environmental assessment." The consequence of the plaintiffs' argument is that, unless the commission formally requests each item of information by calling it an "environmental assessment," the commission cannot consider potentially relevant information. We decline to accept such a narrow construction of the regulation.

Regulations are to be construed as a whole. *Forest Construction Co. v. Planning & Zoning Commission*, 155 Conn. 669, 679, 236 A.2d 917 (1967). There is nothing in § 6–266(a) that specifically requires that the commission label its request for information an "environmental assessment." Rather, "environmental assessment" is a general label for the types of information that the commission is authorized to consider in its determination of subdivision applications. Further, the intent of the preliminary layout is to convey relevant information to the commission in order to facilitate the process. This intent is indicated by the overall description of what should be included in a layout in § 6–266(a), which states that the "preliminary layout shall include as many of the following items of information as is practicable."

The plaintiffs further argue that the commission did not consider a full environmental assessment as required by the language of § 6–266(a)(19), which states that "[t]he assessment *shall* include an evaluation of the following * * *." (Emphasis added.) The plaintiffs contend that this regulation makes it mandatory that each of the twelve factors listed be included in an assessment of the property to be subdivided. We disagree.

Although subsection (a)(19) of § 6–266 employs the word "shall," it does not make sense to require the commission to evaluate factors that are not relevant to a particular subdivision. Whether the word "shall" is mandatory or precatory depends upon its context. See, e.g., *Caron v. Inland Wetlands & Watercourses Commission*, 222 Conn. 269, 273, 610 A.2d 584 (1992). In construction of the words of a regulation, like those of a statute, common sense must be used. *Police Department v. State*

Board of Labor Relations, 225 Conn. 297, 303, 622 A.2d 1005 (1993). The items listed to be considered include some specific items that will not be implicated in every subdivision application. For example, in addition to historical and archaeological factors, the list includes animal habitats, significant geological formations and aquifer protection. Greenwich Land Use Regs. § 6–266(a)(19)(g), (i) and (k). Not every subdivision application will require the consideration of each of these factors. It would be a waste of time, money and energy for the participants involved to be required to gather information that is not relevant to the subdivision application.

In addition, § 6–296(d) of the Greenwich Land Use Regulations explicitly permits the commission to require a redesign of a subdivision plan "in order to protect environmental or historic resources" if the environmental assessment indicates the need for a redesign. Thus, the regulations specifically anticipate a situation, like the one at hand, where historical preservation requires the redesign of subdivision plans.

We also must look to the overall intent of the applicable regulations in considering subdivision applications. *Forest Construction Co. v. Planning & Zoning Commission*, supra. "Regulations, like statutes, do not exist in a vacuum." *Bombero v. Planning & Zoning Commission*, 218 Conn. 737, 743, 591 A.2d 390 (1991). As noted above, § 6–266(a) requires the consideration of only that information that is necessary. Additionally, the purpose of the subdivision regulation is to "[f]urther the orderly development of the Town in accordance with the Town Plan of Development." Greenwich Land Use Regs. § 6–260(a)(1). Although, as noted above, the town plan cannot itself support the denial of a subdivision application, its provisions can serve as an interpretative guide to the meaning of properly enacted regulations. The plan has as one of its basic objectives the preservation of historic resources. The plan also provides that "Greenwich has a rich * * * historical heritage that should be protected for the benefit and enlightenment of future generations," and that "[c]onserving the Town's * * * historical resources is a notably effective land use tool for preserving the essential character and spirit of the community."

Accordingly, we conclude that § 6–266(a)(19)(h) expressly permits the commission to consider historical factors.

II

The defendants next claim that the Appellate Court incorrectly concluded that the terms "historical factors" and "historic streetscapes" do not comply with the established rules requiring regulations to be reasonably precise, adequate and sufficient. We agree with the defendants.

The standard for determining the adequacy of subdivision regulations is whether they " 'are as reasonably precise as the subject matter requires and are reasonably adequate and sufficient to guide the commission and to enable those affected to know their rights and obligations.' "

Nicoli v. Planning & Zoning Commission, 171 Conn. 89, 93, 368 A.2d 24 (1976); *Forest Construction Co. v. Planning & Zoning Commission*, supra, 155 Conn. at 680, 236 A.2d 917. Although some standards may be general, the regulation must be " 'reasonably sufficient to identify the criteria to be evaluated in their enforcement in order to meet the many variables involved since it would be impossible to establish one standard which would adequately cover all future cases.' " *Nicoli v. Planning & Zoning Commission,* supra, 171 Conn. at 93, 368 A.2d 24.

In this case, the commission's subdivision regulations sufficiently apprised the plaintiffs that historical factors would be considered in evaluating their subdivision application. In evaluating the regulations, we must construe them "as a whole since particular words or sections of the regulations, considered separately, may be 'lacking in precision of meaning to afford a standard sufficient to sustain' them." *Forest Construction Co. v. Planning & Zoning Commission*, supra, 155 Conn. at 679, 236 A.2d 917. *Ghent v. Planning Commission*, supra, 219 Conn. at 517, 594 A.2d 5; *Sonn v. Planning Commission*, supra, 172 Conn. at 162, 374 A.2d 159. Although § 6–266(a)(19) does not specifically define the term historical factors, the general purpose of the regulations specifically references the town plan. Section 6–260(a)(1) states that "[t]he purposes of this Article shall be to (1) [f]urther the orderly development of the Town in accordance with the Town Plan of Development." This reference puts prospective subdivision applicants on notice that the town plan will help define the specific terms in the subdivision regulations.

The plan has as one of its basic objectives "[t]o preserve historic and architectural resources." In its further discussion of the preservation of historical resources, the plan specifically mentions historical "streetscapes and districts" as important aspects of Greenwich that the town wishes to preserve. In a subsequent section, the plan states that "[t]he following considerations should be the starting point for decisionmaking * * * [t]he goal is to sustain a climate where * * * historic streetscapes can be preserved." These specific references to streetscapes, the historical factor at issue in this case, define one aspect of "historical factors" and certainly apprised the plaintiffs that this would be a consideration in their subdivision application.

The consideration of historical factors does not occur in a vacuum. See *Bombero v. Planning & Zoning Commission*, supra. "It is unrealistic to demand detailed standards which are impracticable or impossible." *Forest Construction Co. v. Planning & Zoning Commission*, supra, 155 Conn. at 679, 236 A.2d 917. The term historic factors derives meaning from the physical environment of the historic district. See *A-S-P Associates v. Raleigh*, 298 N.C. 207, 223, 258 S.E.2d 444 (1979). In the context of a historic district, there are identifiable and sufficiently distinct historical standards by which the commission may be guided. These same characteristics also put property owners on notice of the types of historical factors that will be considered. "Although * * * discretion cannot be entirely eliminated because of the subjective nature of this process"; *Bellevue Shopping Center Associates v. Chase*, 574 A.2d 760,

764 (R.I.1990); the board is confined to the relevant historic period in its consideration of historical factors.

Accordingly, we conclude that the standards set forth in the regulations and the plan are reasonably precise and sufficient to guide the commission. Accord *Maher v. New Orleans*, 516 F.2d 1051, 1067 (5th Cir.1975), cert. denied, 426 U.S. 905, 96 S.Ct. 2225, 48 L.Ed.2d 830 (1976); *Bellevue Shopping Center Associates v. Chase*, supra, 574 A.2d at 764–65; see generally *Burnham v. Planning & Zoning Commission*, 189 Conn. 261, 263–64, 455 A.2d 339 (1983); *Figarsky v. Historic District Commission*, supra, 171 Conn. at 207–209, 368 A.2d 163 (implicitly endorsing the adequacy of "historical factors" to guide municipal agencies and applicants); see also *Carlson v. Fisher*, 18 Conn.App. 488, 506–507, 558 A.2d 1029 (1989) (referencing streetscape). The Appellate Court was, therefore, incorrect in concluding that the regulations did not support the action taken by the commission.

* * *

IV

The defendants next argue that the Appellate Court incorrectly concluded that the board's consideration of the subdivision regulations improperly encroached upon the applicable zoning regulations. The plaintiffs claim, to the contrary, that because it is undisputed that the application conformed with the zoning requirements of an R–7 zone, it could not be denied on the basis of nonconformance with subdivision regulations. *Smith v. Zoning Board of Appeals*, supra, 29 Conn.App. at 37, 614 A.2d 464. We agree with the defendants.

Citing *Cristofaro v. Burlington*, 217 Conn. 103, 107, 584 A.2d 1168 (1991), the Appellate Court concluded that the commission lacked the authority "to include historical factors in its regulations" because "[s]ubdivision regulations cannot impose minimum lot size, shape, width and depth requirements greater than those required under the zoning regulations for the zone where the property is to be subdivided or deny approval of lots that meet all zoning requirements." *Smith v. Zoning Board of Appeals*, supra, 29 Conn.App. at 36, 614 A.2d 464. *Cristofaro*, however, is inapposite. In *Cristofaro*, the planning and zoning commission enacted a regulation that directly intruded on a subject that was exclusively a zoning matter. See *Avonside, Inc. v. Zoning & Planning Commission*, 153 Conn. 232, 238–39, 215 A.2d 409 (1965) (fees in subdivision regulations in excess of fees in zoning regulations invalid). A subdivision regulation may not conflict with applicable zoning regulations.

Although subdivision regulations and zoning regulations have separate functions, landowners must comply with the requirements of each applicable regulation. *Vose v. Planning & Zoning Commission*, 171 Conn. 480, 483, 370 A.2d 1026 (1976); see *Cristofaro v. Burlington*, supra, 217 Conn. at 106, 584 A.2d 1168; *Sheridan v. Planning Board*, 159 Conn. 1, 9, 266 A.2d 396 (1969). Only if the commission enacts subdivision regulations that exclusively concern zoning power, or if the subdivision regulations directly conflict with a zoning power, will the subdivision regulation be invalid. *Cristofaro v. Burlington*, supra, 217 Conn. at 107, 584 A.2d 1168; *Avonside, Inc. v. Zoning & Planning Commission*, supra.

In this case, the subdivision regulations neither encroach upon an area that is uniquely a zoning power, nor directly conflict with applicable zoning regulations. As we discussed above, § 101(d) of the charter permits the commission to enact regulations that consider historical factors. Although General Statutes § 8–2 authorized the zoning commission to enact zoning regulations that consider historical factors, the parties have not pointed to any zoning regulation that does so. The record therefore does not indicate any conflict between the pertinent subdivision regulations and any of the applicable zoning regulations.

Accordingly, the zoning regulations in this case do not prevent the board's review of historical factors in considering whether to grant or deny the plaintiffs' subdivision application. The Appellate Court was mistaken in relying on a conceived conflict of regulations as a ground for sustaining the plaintiffs' appeal.

* * *

The judgment of the Appellate Court is reversed and the case is remanded to that court with direction to affirm the trial court's judgment dismissing the plaintiffs' appeal.

Notes

1. Note how the scenic standards enforced in Smith arise in the course of the review of an application for the subdivision of land. One trend among communities interested in protecting environmental assets such as scenic views is to add standards to their traditional land use regulations, instead of adopting stand-alone regulations. Can you identify the local regulations and standards used in Smith that were used to deny the plaintiff's application? Were these standards contained in the zoning law, site plan regulations, or other local law?

2. In Wal–Mart Stores Inc. v. Planning Board of the Town of North Elba, 238 A.D.2d 93, 668 N.Y.S.2d 774 (1998), the board denied the big box retailer's application for a special permit and site plan approval for a large retail store. The Town's special permit regulations required that projects "not have a materially adverse impact on adjoining and nearby properties" and "will not result in a clearly adverse aesthetic impact." The Town, additionally, had adopted a Scenic Protection Overlay District to protect the view of nearby Whiteface Mountain that was visible to all incoming travelers on the main gateway entrance highway into the tourist community. New York local land use agencies have an obligation under state law to review the impact of their actions on the environment and the authority to impose conditions on their approvals to protect aesthetic resources. (Env. Cons. Law. Art. 8) The court sustained the denial finding that the record of the planning board's deliberation on the matter showed that "despite all efforts

to screen the store and parking area from the road, their presence would nevertheless bring about noticeable change in the visual character of this cultural area."

3. The Smith and Wal–Mart cases raise the question of how local governments obtain their authority to regulate in the interest of the environment. Developers, applying for standard subdivision and site plan approvals, are sometimes baffled when they learn that aesthetic considerations can lead to a denial or significant alteration in their proposed projects. Trace the line of authority from the state legislature, to the local government, to the operative administrative board in these cases to understand the delegation of power that is found to sustain aesthetic regulations.

4. How broad is local authority to protect environmental assets? Does the Smith court hold that Connecticut localities can require that full environmental assessments be submitted with all major subdivision applications? If so, how does it come to that conclusion? For an interesting article discussing how far North Carolina courts will go in upholding local environmental laws, see David W. Owens, Local Government Authority to Implement Smart Growth Programs: Dillon's Rule, Legislative Reform, and the Current State of Affairs in North Carolina, 35 WAKE FOREST L. REV. 671, 701 (2000) (quoting N.C. GEN. STAT. §§ 153A–340(a), 160A–381 (1999)).

5. The Town of Mount Pleasant, South Carolina, enacted a local law that requires an environmental impact review of individual development projects. South Carolina's legislature has not adopted a statute that authorizes state and local agencies to conduct environmental reviews of their actions. The impact assessment that developers must submit under this local law must address the negative effect their developments will have on marshes, creeks, rivers, plant and animal habitats, and buffer zones, and must describe the steps that will be taken to mitigate these effects and protect natural resources. The state Constitution provides that its provisions and all laws concerning local government shall be liberally construed in their favor and that any powers granted local government shall include those fairly implied and not prohibited by the Constitution. A state statute empowers localities to enact regulations regarding any subject that appears necessary and proper for the general welfare or for preserving health and good government. The land use enabling statute in South Carolina delegates local governments the authority to enact comprehensive plans, zoning, floating zones, and planned unit developments and provides that any other planning and zoning techniques may be used. Localities are authorized to consider the protection of ecologically sensitive areas through zoning. S.C. CONST. Art. VIII, § 17; S.C. ANN. CODE § 6–29–710.

6. In Swan v. Inhabitants of the Town of Norway, 1989 Me. Super. Lexis 80 (Me. Sup. Ct. 1989), the Superior Court of Maine upheld a site plan ordinance containing standards that preserved landscapes and prevented "development that would have an undue adverse effect on the scenic or natural beauty of the area, aesthetics, historic sites, or rare and irreplaceable natural areas" as being a proper delegation of legislative authority to the planning board.

7. In Batchelder v. City of Seattle, 77 Wash.App. 154, 890 P.2d 25 (1995), the court approved a developer's plan to subdivide his waterfront parcel into four lots, rehabilitate an existing house, and build three new

houses. A neighbor challenged the proposed plat on the ground that the plan would diminish his view. Seattle has a Shoreline Substantial Development Permit procedure. The court cited with approval a regulation promulgated to protect views of Portgage Bay; however, the court found that the impact of the proposed development on the neighbor's view was relatively minor; after construction, he would retain 80 percent of his view. The court remanded the case with instructions to reinstate the developer's permit.

8. In Ross v. City of Rolling Hills Estates, 192 Cal.App.3d 370, 238 Cal.Rptr. 561 (1987), parcel owners were prohibited from expanding their home because it violated the City's viewshed protection ordinance. The plaintiffs claimed that the language used was unconstitutionally vague, failed to provide adequate guidance to the planning commission, and contained unintelligible concepts. The ordinance referenced the "needless destruction and impairment of views and discouragement of the blockage and misuse of [hillside view lots]." The court found that this language was definite enough to pass the California standard for legislative precision. The language must be definite enough to provide a standard for those whose conduct is prescribed, as well as a standard by which administrative agencies can ascertain compliance. How definite is this language? How much guidance does it provide? If the courts create such low thresholds for the standards that local laws must contain, are there other reasons to strive for greater precision and persuasion in adopting innovative land use laws that restrict private land use? The regulated parties in the Ross case were local homeowners who applied to construct an addition to their current home.

9. To what degree can the police power be used to achieve such objectives? When will it be necessary to turn to public purchase programs to protect aesthetic resources? Can regulation and purchase programs be combined to achieve these goals and if so how? The discussion about how far localities should go—and what techniques they should use—in protecting views and open space is not new. William H. Whyte vigorously urged programs for the purchase of development easements. See Whyte, Open Space Action (Outdoor Recreation Review Commission Study Rep. 15, 1962). This approach was criticized by a Comment, Control of Urban Sprawl or Securing Open Space: Regulation by Condemnation or by Ordinance, 50 Calif.L.Rev. 483 (1962). Krasnowiecki & Paul, The Preservation of Open Space in Metropolitan Areas, 110 U.Pa.L.Rev. 179 (1961), urged a combined police power, public purchase program. In general see Jordahl, Conservation and Scenic Easements: An Experience Resume, 39 Land Econ. 343 (1963); Siegel, The Law of Open Space (N.Y. Regional Plan Ass'n, Inc., 1960); and Proceedings, Conservation Easements and Open Space Conference. (Wis. Dep't Resource Development, Dec. 13–14, 1961); 5 Williams, American Land Planning Law, Chap. 159 (1988). For an unusual perspective on the open space problem, see Platt, Feudal Origins of Open Space Law, 4 Land Use Controls Q. 27 (No. 4, 1970). Also see Williams, Scenic Protection as a Legitimate Goal of Public Regulation, 38 Wash.U.J.Urb. & Contemp.L. 3 (1990).

(4) Tree and Forest Preservation/Timber Preservation

Tree Preservation

Tree preservation ordinances typically establish a permit system under which tree removal is allowed, but only upon a showing of necessity and compliance with certain conditions, such as the replacement of some or all of the trees to be removed. Tree preservation ordinances may consider views, pruning, trimming, and setbacks from curbs, sidewalks, and street intersections. A number of states, including Georgia, GA. CODE ANN. § 12–2–8(h)(8) (2001); Hawaii, HAW. REV. STAT. §§ 58–1 to 58–5 (2001); Maine, ME. REV. STAT. § 38.439–A(5) (2001); and Maryland, MD. CODE ANN., NAT. RES. I § 5–1603 (2000), have adopted statutes that either require or permit local governments to adopt tree preservation laws.

Some communities have adopted ordinances to protect native tree species, or "heritage trees," such as oak, sycamore, walnut, and eucalyptus. These ordinances require reports by professional arborists and practices to be followed to preserve such specimens from development activities, including additions to single-family homes. Steamboat Springs, Colorado, has adopted a Trees and Shrubs Ordinance. The purpose of this local law is to prescribe requirements "for the protection of plants, including * * * trees, shrubs, lawns, and all other landscaping located, standing, or growing within or upon city property, including * * * any city-owned street, alley, right-of-way, or other public place or city or mountain park, recreation area, or open space." STEAMBOAT SPRINGS, COLO., CODE § 24–1 (2002).

The case below presents a different situation. The California city involved in this litigation enacted an ordinance allowing neighbors to apply for a permit compelling an owner to trim/remove trees grown in excess of a certain height that impair the neighbors' view.

ECHEVARRIETA v. CITY OF RANCHO PALOS VERDES

California Court of Appeal, Second Appellate District, 2001.
86 Cal.App.4th 472, 103 Cal.Rptr.2d 165.

HASTINGS, J.

Jon Echevarrieta (appellant) appeals from a judgment entered in favor of respondents the City of Rancho Palos Verdes (the City) and the City of Rancho Palos Verdes City Council (the City Council) after the trial court denied appellant's petition for writ of mandate. At issue is a "view protection" ordinance of the City. We affirm the trial court's judgment.

Voters in the City approved Proposition M on November 7, 1989. It was codified in section 17.02.040 of the Rancho Palos Verdes Municipal Code (hereinafter referred to as the Ordinance), and was most recently amended in January 1997.

In pertinent part, the Ordinance prohibits residents of the City from significantly impairing a view by permitting foliage to grow in excess of certain height limitations. If foliage in existence already exceeds those height limitations, the person whose view is impaired must first attempt to informally resolve the matter with the person who owns the foliage, and if that fails, may apply for a "view restoration permit." Hearings on the application for the permit are conducted by a view restoration Commission (VRC), a committee of seven members appointed by the City Council. The VRC may grant the permit only if certain specified findings are made. If the VRC orders any foliage trimmed or removed, or replacement foliage is ordered planted, the costs are to be borne by the permit applicant. Any interested party may appeal the VRC's decision to the City Council.

Since 1966, Norbert Keilbach has lived on Greve Drive in the City. His home faces south towards the Pacific Ocean and Catalina Island. Appellant lives on Ganado Drive, on a slope directly below Keilbach's home. Appellant has several trees which are near the border of his property and Keilbach's, which purportedly block Keilbach's view of the ocean and Catalina Island. Appellant purchased his property in 1964. The trees did not exist prior to the establishment of either Keilbach's or appellant's lots.

In February 1997, Keilbach filed an application with the City in order to compel appellant to trim trees that interfered with his view.

On May 1, 1997, a public hearing was held in connection with the view restoration application. Both appellant and Keilbach appeared. At the conclusion of the hearing, the VRC adopted Resolution No. 97–5, requiring that appellant remove the three pine trees, and to trim the tops of five other trees, at the expense of the applicant, Keilbach.

On May 16, 1997, appellant appealed the VRC's decision to the City Council. The City Council heard the appeal at its public meeting on July 1, 1997, and remanded the matter to the VRC for further consideration of the effect that trimming the trees would have on appellant's privacy.

The VRC held another public hearing on the application on October 2, 1997. At the conclusion of this hearing, the VRC ordered its staff to prepare for adoption at the next meeting a resolution requiring appellant to trim his trees.

On November 6, 1997, the VRC approved Resolution No. 97–22. This resolution required appellant to trim eight of his trees but also required Keilbach to plant a barrier of no more than 20 to 25 low-growing shrubs between his property and appellant's to mitigate appellant's privacy concerns.

Appellant appealed this decision to the City Council. On March 17, 1998, the City Council heard the appeal during its public meeting.

On April 7, 1998, the City Council adopted Resolution No. 98–21, affirming the VRC's approval of the view restoration permit application and requiring appellant to trim eight of his trees. Appellant then filed this lawsuit in superior court.

* * *

On appeal, appellant makes the following contentions: (1) the trial court erred in relying upon *Kucera v. Lizza,* supra, 59 Cal.App.4th 1141;

(2) the ordinance violates the takings clause; (3) retroactive application of the ordinance deprives him of due process; (4) the ordinance is deceptive and uncertain; (5) as applied, the ordinance impermissibly expands the City's police power. We first address issues (1) and (5).

In *Kucera v. Lizza*, supra, 59 Cal.App.4th 1141, the Court of Appeal considered the validity of an ordinance of the Town of Tiburon similar to the ordinance presented here. The stated purpose of the Tiburon ordinance was to establish "the right of persons to preserve views or sunlight which existed at any time since they purchased or occupied a property from unreasonable obstruction by the growth of trees" and to establish a process to achieve restoration of views and sunlight. (Tiburon Mun. Code, former §§ 15–1.A & 15–1.B.) In accord with the provisions of the ordinance, the Kuceras petitioned for informal dispute resolution with respect to trees located on the downhill lot across the street, on property owned by Lizza. The Kuceras claimed the trees obstructed their views of the San Francisco Bay and the Marin County mainland. Lizza refused to participate in the process. The Kuceras filed a complaint in superior court seeking to compel restoration of their views and for abatement of a public nuisance. The trial court entered judgment in favor of Lizza concluding that the ordinance was unconstitutional and void because it was preempted by state law and was an arbitrary and unreasonable exercise of the police power.

The Court of Appeal reversed: "It is well settled that the state may legitimately exercise its police powers to advance aesthetic values * * *." The concept of the public welfare is broad and inclusive. The values it represents are spiritual as well as physical, aesthetic as well as monetary. "[Citations.] * * * [¶] * * * [¶] We hold the Tiburon ordinance is directed toward a valid police power goal—to preserve views and sunlight. Tiburon's choice of regulating obstructing trees and tree growth obviously bears a reasonable relationship to the achievement of those goals. [Citation.]" (59 Cal.App.4th at pp. 1148–1149.)

Here, appellant contends that the Ordinance does not state a valid purpose because it states only that "the peace, health, safety and welfare of the community will be served by the adoption of this section." We disagree.

The ballot measure which was approved by the voters states the purposes of the Ordinance as follows: "The hillsides of the City constitute a limited natural resource in their scenic value to all residents of and visitors to the City. The hillsides provide potential vista points and view lots. The City's General Plan recognizes these natural resources and calls for their protection. The public health, safety and welfare of the City require prevention of needless destruction and impairment of these limited vista points and view lots * * *. [¶] Specifically, this Ordinance: [¶] 1. Protects, enhances and perpetuates views available to property owners and visitors because of the unique topographical features of the Palos Verdes Peninsula. These views provide unique and irreplaceable assets to the City and its neighboring communities * * *.

[¶] 2. Defines and protects finite visual resources by establishing limits which construction and plant growth can attain before encroaching onto a view. [¶] 3. Insures that the development of each parcel of land or additions to residences or structures occur in a manner which is harmonious and maintains neighborhood compatibility and the character of contiguous sub-community development as defined in the General Plan." These purposes were reprinted in the View Restoration Permit Guidelines and Procedures issued by the City.

Enacting the Ordinance for these purposes is a clearly a legitimate exercise of the city's traditional police power. (*Ehrlich v. City of Culver City* (1996) 12 Cal.4th 854, 886 [50 Cal.Rptr.2d 242, 911 P.2d 429]; *Kucera v. Lizza, supra*, 59 Cal.App.4th at p. 1149.) To the extent that the trial court cited *Kucera* for this proposition, it did not err.

* * *

The judgment of the superior court is affirmed.

VOGEL (C. S.), P. J., and EPSTEIN, J., concurred.

Notes

1. In the Echevarrietta case, the local law that was upheld required the property owner to trim eight tall trees on his property. Consider the nature of the regulation approved by the city's voters. What objectives did the voters have in mind when they approved the proposition limiting foliage growth through a view restoration permit? Do you think that topping or trimming tall trees is recommended by arborists who have the health and longevity of the trees in mind? Do large trees with abundant growth serve any positive purpose or do they just block views? What do your answers suggest regarding the narrowness of some local laws enacted to protect one of many possible environmental objectives?

2. In Wheat Ridge, Colorado, the city forester, upon 30 days notice, can enter private property in order to inspect trees and other plants in order "to determine if any destructive or communicable disease or other pestilence exists which is detrimental or endangers the good health and well-being of trees * * *." WHEAT RIDGE, CO. CODE § 24–5 (2002).

3. Other cities require tree preservation plans. In the city of Carrollton, Texas, prior to construction or development of land, an owner must submit a tree preservation plan if one or more "protected trees" (one of 38 listed trees, 4 inches or more in diameter and at least 4 feet in height) will be affected. If the land does not contain any protected trees, a registered surveyor, engineer, architect, or landscape architect must submit a letter verifying the absence of protected trees; where protected ones exist, a permit must be obtained and the landowner must either avoid cutting them or replace them. CITY OF CARROLLTON, TEX. CODE ch.155 (2001).

4. In Hawaii a statute adopted in 1975, Hawaii Rev. Stat. § 58–1 et seq., commands each county to establish an arborist advisory committee to advise and recommend protective ordinances and review all actions deemed to endanger exceptional trees. Section 58–4 authorizes counties to enact protective regulations and to seek injunctions against removal or destruction

of exceptional trees. Exceptional trees are defined as "a tree or stand or grove of trees with historic or cultural value, or which by reason of its age, variety, location, size, esthetic quality, or endemic status has been designated by the county committee as worthy of preservation."

Timber Preservation

The regulation of timber harvesting can help maintain an ecological balance while still meeting present and future demand for lumber and pulp. Some factors considered by local harvesting regulations include the successional role of species regeneration, the effects of competing vegetation, and potential damaging agents such as insects and pathogens. Construction of access roads, timber products processing centers, and other permanent structures in heavily forested areas are development activities that may be regulated by timber harvesting laws. The town of Pawling, New York, adopted a Timber Harvesting Law that regulates tree clearing and harvesting to prevent sedimentation and drainage problems. PAWLING, NY CODE §§ 45–2, 45–9 (1993). There are a variety of ways of limiting timber harvests in the public interest as the principal case demonstrates.

RANCHO LOBO v. DEVARGAS
United States Court of Appeals, Tenth Circuit, 2002.
303 F.3d 1195.

BRISCOE, CIRCUIT JUDGE.

Defendants, all members of the Board of Commissioners of the County of Rio Arriba, New Mexico (hereinafter "the County") appeal from a decision of the district court holding that the Rio Arriba County Timber Harvest Ordinance is invalid because it is preempted by the New Mexico Forest Conservation Act, N.M.S.A.1978 §§ 68–2–1 *et seq.*, and also holding that the ordinance's provisions for requiring an environmental assessment are invalid because they delegate unlimited power to the county planning and zoning commission. The County contends that the Timber Harvest Ordinance is not preempted by the Act, but instead asserts there is room for concurrent jurisdiction. The County further contends that the Timber Harvest Ordinance's provisions for environmental assessment do not improperly delegate unlimited power to the Planning and Zoning Commission. We reverse and remand.

I.

The facts in this case are undisputed. The New Mexico Forest Conservation Act establishes the State Forestry Division, which is authorized to enforce all laws, rules and regulations relating to all forested, cutover or brushlands within the state under the following circumstances:

    A. prevention and suppression of fires;

    B. logging and timber operations and practices;

Sec. 3   SPECIFIC LOCAL LAND USE REGULATIONS   805

    C. trespass, waste and littering; and

    D. conservation of commercial forest lands and products.

N.M.S.A 1978, § 68–2–14. The Division is authorized to make and enforce rules and regulations "for the prevention and suppression of forest or brush fires, and for the control of forest pests and for the application of commercial forest practices within the state." *Id.*, § 68–2–16. Section 68–2–16 also provides:

> Nothing in the Forest Conservation Act [citation omitted] shall prevent a landowner hereafter from converting forest vegetative types to nonforest vegetative types for such purposes as range, wildlife habitat, farming, surface mining or subdivision development; provided, however, any slash resulting from such conversion shall be treated in a manner that will minimize the spread of forest fires and the possibility of insect epidemic.

Pursuant to its authority under the Forest Conservation Act, the Division has promulgated a series of regulations concerning tree harvesting and forest regeneration. 19 NMAC 20.2. The objective of this series of regulations is to "require appropriate forest resource management in order to assist in the prevention and suppression of forest fires, the control of forest pests and to maintain and enhance the economic benefits of forests and forest resources to New Mexico." 19 NMAC 20.2.6. The regulations require a state harvest permit for the harvest of commercial forest species in an area of twenty-five acres or more, and require submission of the method of harvesting and the treatment of skid trails and slash, as well as a forest regeneration plan. 19 NMAC 20.2.8–20.2.10.

In response to a threat to its watershed caused by erosion from timber harvesting on private lands, the County in 1998 enacted the Timber Harvest Ordinance under its zoning authority and power to provide for the general welfare. The purpose of the ordinance is:

> to protect, maintain and restore fully functional forests and streams, rivers, watersheds and acequias while permitting the harvest of forest goods; to protect against immediate and long range threats to the quality of the Rio Arriba County's water; to preserve local customs, culture and traditions; to preserve the bosques from harm and exploitation; to protect landowners and the property value of timberlands; to encourage the location of compatible uses of land; to promote sustainable logging practices; to encourage logging operations within Rio Arriba County; and to protect the health, safety and welfare of the citizens of Rio Arriba County.

Timber Harvest Ordinance, Article II.

The Timber Harvest Ordinance requires those who wish to harvest timber to obtain a county permit in most instances. If a permit is required, the applicant must present a timber harvest plan detailing the action, including a plan to control erosion. *Id.*, Article VI(B)(4). In evaluating a plan, the county planning and zoning department considers:

1) the sustainability of timber production; 2) economic development and local employment; 3) water quality and availability; 4) soil protection; 5) logging roads and hauling; 6) harvest selection, techniques, old growth management and reforestation; 7) archeological, historic and cultural resources; 8) abatement of noise, dust, smoke and traffic; 9) hours of operation; 10) compatibility with adjacent land uses; and 11) the effect of existing harvests on the application. *Id.*, Article VI(C). In some cases where the planning and zoning department finds that the proposed harvest would create a significant environmental impact, the applicant may be required to prepare an environmental assessment. Id., Article VI(H), (I).

The Timber Harvest Ordinance requires compliance with measures that are recommended but left voluntary under the state scheme. Erosion control plans, logging roads, drainage systems, buffer zones to protect riparian areas, and regeneration plans must comply with the best management practices recommended in the New Mexico Guidelines. *Id.*, Article VI(B), (C).

In 1991, plaintiff Rancho Lobo acquired property in Rio Arriba County for the purpose of establishing a hunting preserve. In February of 2000, Rancho Lobo applied for and was granted a permit by the Forestry Division to harvest trees in order to "[r]elease understory trees," "[i]mprove residual tree health and growth," "[e]nhance wildlife habitat and utilization in the areas," "[p]romote the Englemann spruce as a stand component and/or aspen regeneration," and "[p]repare future prescribed burn areas by removing white fir and mistletoed Douglas fir from ponderosa pine/Douglas fir stand types and enhance their establishment." Aplt.App. at 85.

In March 2000, the County informed Rancho Lobo that it needed to apply for a county timber harvest permit under the Timber Harvest Ordinance. Rancho Lobo refused to seek a permit, and instead filed an action arguing that the ordinance was invalid because it conflicted with and was preempted by the Forest Conservation Act, that enforcement of the ordinance constituted a taking in violation of the Fifth and Fourteenth Amendments, and that the ordinance illegally deprived Rancho Lobo of its property.

Both parties filed motions for summary judgment on the issue of the validity of the ordinance. In its motion, Rancho Lobo alleged that the Timber Harvest Ordinance was invalid because it was preempted by the Forest Conservation Act and was not a proper use of the County's zoning authority. In ruling on the cross-motions, the district court first determined there was sufficient controlling New Mexico law for it to decide the validity of the ordinance without certifying the question to the New Mexico Supreme Court. The district court held that the Timber Harvest Ordinance conflicted with the Forest Conservation Act because the Act allows clear-cutting while the ordinance prohibits clear-cutting without a variance being obtained. The district court also held that the ordinance conflicted with the Forest Conservation Act because the ordinance required a more extensive and stricter permitting process.

On the issue of preemption, the district court found that the statutory language of the Forest Conservation Act providing that the Forestry Division is authorized to make and enforce rules and regulations, and enforce all laws, rules and regulations relating to forestry, logging and timber operations indicated an express preemption of the Timber Harvest Ordinance. The district court further found that although the ordinance was a valid exercise of zoning authority, its provision for requiring an environmental assessment was not a valid exercise of authority because it gave the county planning and zoning department "unlimited power" to determine who would be required to prepare an environmental assessment. Ultimately, the district court held that the entire Timber Harvest Ordinance was expressly preempted by the Forest Conservation Act, and was therefore invalid. As a result, the district court granted partial summary judgment in favor of Rancho Lobo. The district court certified the partial summary judgment as a final judgment pursuant to Fed.R.Civ.P. 54(b).

II.

* * *

The district court erred in determining the Forest Conservation Act preempts the Timber Harvest Ordinance.

III.

We now turn to the County's contention that the district court erred in finding that the provisions of the Timber Harvest Ordinance concerning the requirement of an environmental assessment are invalid because they give the county planning and zoning department unlimited power to decide who will be required to prepare an environmental assessment. The County contends that language stating that an assessment is necessary upon a finding that the proposed harvest would have a "significant effect on watercourses or acequia systems, county or private property, other natural or historic resources, or the public health, safety or welfare" is sufficient guidance to restrict the Department's discretion.

The Timber Harvest Ordinance provisions in question provide that:

An applicant *may be* required to prepare an Environmental Assessment (EA) for a proposed harvest when the Planning and Zoning Department, upon review of the THP application, finds that the proposed harvest would cause a significant environmental impact. The department's findings shall be in writing and fully state the nature and significance of the environmental impact and the legal and factual basis for the finding. Timber Harvest Ordinance, Article VI(I) (emphasis added.)

The ordinance further defines a significant environmental impact as "a significant effect on watercourses or acequia systems, county or private property, other natural or historic resources, or the public health, safety and welfare." *Id.*, Article VI(H.2). Similarly, another portion of the ordinance provides that, where the proposed harvest is part of a combined harvest plan:

> The Planning and Zoning Department may order an applicant to prepare an Environmental Assessment pursuant to this ordinance upon a finding that the proposed and existing harvests, when assessed together, would have significant effects on the environment, public and private property and infrastructure, and the public health safety and welfare. *Id.*, Article VI(C)(11) (emphasis added.)

The district court found that these provisions were invalid because use of the word "may" granted the planning and zoning department the "unlimited power to decide which persons will be ordered to prepare an Environmental Assessment."

It is true that, under New Mexico law, a legislative body "may not vest unbridled or arbitrary power in an administrative agency but must furnish a reasonably accurate standard to guide it." *City of Santa Fe v. Gamble-Skogmo, Inc.*, 73 N.M. 410, 389 P.2d 13, 18 (1964). However, such standards "need not be specific" and broad, general standards are permissible as long as they are capable of a reasonable application and are sufficient to limit and define the agencies' discretionary powers. *Id*.

In this case, the authority of the planning and zoning department to order an environmental assessment is limited by the requirement that such an assessment will be required only in cases where there is a significant environmental impact or where the "proposed and existing harvests, when assessed together, would have significant effects on the environment, public and private property and infrastructure, and the public health safety and welfare." While this may be a broad standard, it is not an impermissible one. The New Mexico Supreme Court has upheld a law with an equally broad standard. *See Parker v. Bd. of County Comm'rs*, 93 N.M. 641, 603 P.2d 1098, 1099–1100 (1979). In *Parker*, the court upheld a zoning regulation providing that the board of county commissioners "may" suspend or revoke approval of a plat if the applicant did not submit "sufficient information." The court noted that what constituted "sufficient information" was left to the board, but held that it was a valid broad general standard. *Id.* at 1100.

Similarly, the Timber Harvest Ordinance at issue in this case contains a valid general standard for the exercise of discretion. Contrary to the holding of the district court, the ordinance does not vest the planning and zoning board with the "unlimited power to decide which persons will be ordered to prepare an Environmental Assessment." Order at 8. Rather, the board may order an environmental assessment only when it finds that the planned timber harvest will have a "significant environmental impact" or where the "proposed and existing harvests, when assessed together, would have significant effects on the environment, public and private property and infrastructure, and the public health, safety and welfare." Timber Harvest Ordinance, Article VI(C)(11). This power is capable of review and is not arbitrary.

Rancho Lobo argues that complying with an order to prepare an environmental statement is expensive and burdensome. This argument has no bearing on whether the provision requiring an environmental assessment is a valid delegation of legislative authority. The district court erred when it concluded the Timber Harvest Ordinance provision that requires preparation of an environmental assessment was not properly promulgated under the county's zoning authority.

We REVERSE the district court's conclusion that the Timber Harvest Ordinance is preempted by the Forest Conservation Act. We also REVERSE the district court's conclusion that the ordinance's provision for requiring an environmental assessment constituted an invalid delegation of legislative authority. We REMAND for further proceedings. Appellee's motion to certify question of state law is DENIED.

(5) Fish and Wildlife Protection

Habitat destruction, which can be caused by land development, is the most crippling threat to biodiversity. Habitats provide the elements that species need to survive: temperature, water, soil, sunlight, food sources, places of refuge, and safe reproduction areas. The U.S. Fish and Wildlife Service has listed more than 1,200 species as endangered or threatened. Eighty-five percent of these listed species are threatened because of habitat degradation and loss. Timothy Beatley, Preserving Biodiversity: Challenges for Planners, APA Journal, vol. 66, No. 1 (Winter 2000).

Poorly planned development in critical wildlife areas creates harmful borders around isolated habitats, limits the number of islands of habitat that remain, and prevents migration of species from one suitable habitat to another. "Development fragments habitat by dividing it into smaller, spatially disjointed landscape units. A highly fragmented landscape is less likely to have large, intact habitat units. Furthermore, fragmentation isolates species and inhibits movement and reduces the probability of recolonization in the event that a species disappears from a given patch of habitat." Theobald, David, James Miller, and N. Thompson Hobbs, "Estimating the Cumulative Effects of Development on Wildlife Habitat," Landscape and Urban Planning 39 (1997): 25–36. Conversely, land use planning can ensure the preservation of areas of habitat, open up the borders around them, and provide migration corridors sensitive to the needs of vulnerable species. Factors that determine the effect of development on particular habitats include slope, proximity to water, and vegetative cover characteristics.

Washington State has been at the forefront of protecting fish and wildlife habitats. The state's Growth Management Act of 1990 implements what the Washington Department of Fish and Wildlife (WDFW) calls "a bottom-up approach to land use planning." It requires all counties, cities, and towns in the state to classify and designate resource lands and critical areas, including fish and wildlife habitats, and to adopt development regulations for them. The WDFW has created detailed checklists to assess the wildlife potential of urban areas and to aid local governments in reviewing the elements of their development regulations and comprehensive plans.

Classifications in the Critical Fish and Wildlife Habitat ordinance created by Cowlitz County, Washington, include species and habitats of local importance; commercial and recreation shellfish areas; kelp and eelgrass beds; herring and smelt spawning areas; and naturally occurring ponds under 20 acres and their submerged aquatic beds. The county has established performance standards and requires developers to secure permits before developing in critical habitat areas. Development projects must protect habitat and vegetated open space in contiguous blocks, in order to create a continuous system or corridor of open space and habitat areas. Native species must be used in any landscaping of disturbed, undeveloped, or buffer areas, and landscaping plans must emphasize heterogeneity and structural diversity of vegetation. Cowlitz County, Washington Sec. 15.08.110 Fish and Wildlife Habitat.

Colorado statutes provide local governments with the authority to adopt local environmental laws that protect wildlife habitat. COLO. REV. STAT. §§ 29–20–101–107, 24–65–101–106 (2001). The purpose of the State's Local Government Land Use Control Enabling Act is to achieve orderly land development within the state that maintains a balance between the basic human needs of its changing population and "legitimate environmental concerns." Specifically, the Act empowers local governments

> to plan for and regulate the use of land by * * * [p]rotecting lands from activities which would cause immediate or foreseeable material danger to significant wildlife habitat and would endanger wildlife species * * * [and by] [o]therwise planning for and regulating the use of land so as to provide planned and orderly use of land and protection of the environment in a manner consistent with constitutional rights. COLO. REV. STAT. §§ 29–20–104(1)(b), (h) (2001).

Pursuant to this authority, Summit County, Colorado, protects wildlife through a Wildlife Habitat Overlay District that "seeks to fully protect wildlife habitats * * * from the significant adverse affects of development." SUMMIT COUNTY, COLO. DEV. CODE § 4203.01 (2002). The ordinance requires that all proposals for development within the district include a special wildlife impact report that the State Division of Wildlife is to review and approve. Adding protective provisions to subdivision or site plan regulations, or adopting a separate local habitat protection law, can achieve habitat conservation for threatened species and help maintain biodiversity.

FLORIDA WILDLIFE FEDERATION
v. COLLIER COUNTY
Florida District Court of Appeal, First District, 2002.
819 So.2d 200.

ERVIN, J.

The Florida Wildlife Federation and the Collier County Audubon Society, appellants, appeal from a final order of the Department of Community Affairs, appellee, which approved a recommended order from the Division of Administrative Hearings finding amendments to the Collier County comprehensive plan to be in compliance with state law. We affirm.

In 1997, appellee, Collier County, promulgated certain amendments to its comprehensive plan, but the Department of Community Affairs rejected those amendments as not in compliance with state law. Following an administrative challenge in which appellants intervened, the Governor and Cabinet, sitting as the Administration Commission, issued a final order directing the County to take specific remedial measures with regard to its plan, one of which was that the County designate certain specified areas within the county as Natural Resource Protection Areas (NRPAs). The principal purpose of this designation is to protect indigenous fauna and flora, especially the Florida panther, a highly endangered species. The final order provided further that the NRPAs "shall be refined as actual data and analysis is made available." The Commission finally directed that within the NRPAs "only agricultural and directly-related uses and one single family dwelling unit per parcel or lot created prior to June 22, 1999, shall be allowed."

Pursuant to the order, Collier County adopted certain interim amendments to its comprehensive plan, including amendments which designated as NRPAs those areas specifically identified in the Administration Commission's final order. The Department reviewed the amendments and determined that they were in compliance with state law. Appellants subsequently challenged that determination, and the matter proceeded to a formal hearing before the Division of Administrative Hearings.

In the recommended order which followed, the administrative law judge (ALJ) discussed in detail the mapping of the NRPAs. Appellants sought expansion of these areas, based upon telemetry data gathered regarding the movement of panthers and upon a 1994 report prepared by the Florida Fish and Wildlife Commission. In rejecting the argument that the NRPA boundaries were not sufficient to protect wildlife and were not based on a thorough assessment, the ALJ observed that "the 1999 Final Order [of the Administration Commission] contemplates that the Interim NRPAs are a necessary prelude to that very assessment." He added that appellants, in effect, had asked "the County to reach its conclusions as to the natural resource issues before it undertakes the

Assessment mandated by the Final Order * * * [and such a] request is impracticable." Appellants thereafter took exception to the ALJ's recommended conclusion that the agricultural usage of land was not subject to an intensity-of-use standard. The Department rejected this exception in its final order, which adopted the ALJ's findings of fact and conclusions of law.

On appeal, appellants argue, as they did before the Department, that the NRPAs, as designated in the interim amendments, do not comply with section 163.3177(6)(a), Florida Statutes (1999). More particularly, appellants maintain that this statute, case law, and the Department's rule require application of an "intensity" standard as to agricultural uses contained within the NRPAs. Appellants also claim that the record evidence does not establish, "beyond fair debate," that the NRPA's boundaries do not require further expansion to protect the Florida panther, as the ALJ found and as the Department accepted in its final order.

Turning to the first issue, appellants rely primarily on the following emphasized language in section 163.3177(6), which provides, in pertinent part:

> (6) In addition to the requirements of subsections (1)–(5), the comprehensive plan *shall* include the following elements:
>
> > (a) *A future land use plan element designating proposed future general distribution, location, and extent of the uses of land* for residential uses, commercial uses, industry, agriculture, recreation, conservation, education, public buildings and grounds, other public facilities, and other categories of the public and private uses of land. The *future land use plan shall include standards to be followed in the control and distribution of population densities and building and structure intensities.* The proposed distribution, location, and extent of the various categories of land use shall be shown on a land use map or map series which shall be supplemented by goals, policies, and measurable objectives. *Each land use category shall be defined in terms of the types of uses included and specific standards for the density or intensity of use.*

(Emphasis added.)

Appellants observe that the above statute explicitly requires a designation of the "extent of the uses of land for * * * agricultural * * * uses of land," and further that each land use, including agriculture, must be reviewed pursuant to "standards for the density or intensity of use." Because of this language, they contend the approved interim NRPA amendments are not in compliance with the statutory directives because there is no standard within them regulating the intensity of an agricultural use.

Appellants also point out that the Department's own rule, Florida Administrative Code rule 9J–5.003(60), requires designation of an intensity standard, because this rule defines "intensity" as:

> [A]n objective measurement of the extent to which land may be developed *or used*, including the consumption or use of the space above, on or below ground; the measurement of the use of or demand on natural resources; and the measurement of the use of or demand on facilities and services.

(Emphasis added.)

Appellants continue that the language in the rule clearly reflects that the use of the term "intensity" within the statute does not refer solely to buildings and structures, contrary to the Department's non-rule policy decision. Consequently, the Department's order violates not only the statute but its own rule in failing to apply an intensity-of-use standard to an agricultural land use category.

The Department of Community Affairs, Collier County and other appellees argue in response that the term "intensity" is applicable only to the presence of buildings and structures, as provided in subsection (a) of the statute. Moreover, because buildings and structures are incompatible with the agricultural use of land, there is no corresponding necessity for imposing an intensity standard on a land use designated agricultural within the NRPAs.

In that the legislature delegated to the Department the power to enforce section 163.3177, we note that we are required to be highly deferential to the agency's interpretation of such statute. As the supreme court recently reaffirmed in *Verizon Florida, Inc. v. Jacobs*, 810 So.2d 906 (Fla.2002), an "agency's interpretation of the statute it is charged with enforcing is entitled to great deference." *See also BellSouth Telecomms., Inc. v. Johnson*, 708 So.2d 594, 596 (Fla.1998). Moreover, a court will not depart from the contemporaneous construction of a statute by a state agency charged with its regulation unless the construction is "clearly erroneous." *PW Ventures, Inc. v. Nichols*, 533 So.2d 281, 283 (Fla.1988). *Accord Miles v. Fla. A & M Univ.*, 813 So.2d 242 (Fla. 1st DCA 2002).

The interpretation the Department has given section 163.3177(6)(a) is not clearly erroneous. Although certain isolated portions of the statute support appellants' argument that all land use categories must be subjected to an intensity-of-use standard, an established statutory maxim emphasizes that all parts of a statute should be given effect in order to achieve a harmonious whole. *See State v. Knight*, 98 Fla. 891, 124 So. 461 (1929). Not only do the provisions within section 163.3177(6)(a) undergird the Department's interpretation that an agricultural use of land is excluded from an intensity review, but other pertinent statutes do as well.

Section 163.3177 is included within the Local Government Comprehensive Planning and Land Development Regulation Act. A primary purpose of the Act is that it be carried out in conformity with and in furtherance of the Florida Environmental Land and Water Management Act of 1972, chapter 380, in order "to utilize and strengthen the existing role, processes, and powers of local governments in the establishment and implementation of comprehensive planning programs to guide and control future development." § 163.3161(2), Fla. Stat. (1999) (emphasis added). In implementing the legislative mandate, the Department, acting in its role as the state land planning agency, is required to review local governments' proposed plans for the purpose of determining whether they are in compliance with the Act. § 163.3184(8), Fla. Stat. (1999).

It is obvious, as the regulatory agency charged with enforcing the statutes, that the Department must conduct its review in accordance with the legislative mandate that a submitted plan comply with the Act's overarching concern that future development be subjected to objective standards of guidance and control. To that end, the appropriate land use elements of section 163.3177 are required to be set out in the local comprehensive plans.

* * *

Section 380.04, included within the provisions of the Florida Environmental Land and Water Management Act of 1972, was enacted to implement the stated purpose of the Act, which, similar to the goal of the Local Government Comprehensive Planning and Land Development Regulation Act, was designed to protect the natural resources of the state by, among other things, adequately planning for and guiding growth and development in the state § 380.021, Fla. Stat. (1999). This Act, which predated the Local Government Comprehensive Planning and Land Development Regulation Act by three years, was devised, as was the latter act, to provide for orderly developmental growth without endangering the state's finite natural resources. Under both acts, the Department, acting as the state land planning agency, is empowered to review a local government's developmental plans which may have an impact on the state's environment. Under chapter 380, part I, it has the responsibility of reviewing developments of regional impact, and under chapter 163, part II, of reviewing comprehensive plans.

The primary purpose of the review under both acts is to ensure that developmental uses comply with statutory standards for the conservation of the state's environment. It is obvious to us that if a land use can be excluded from review under chapter 380 because it does not meet the definition of a development, a use not involving development need not be reviewed for its intensity under chapter 163.

For the above reasons, the interpretation the Department placed on section 163.3177(6)(a) is not clearly erroneous. The interim amendments provide, consistent with the final order, that only agricultural and directly related uses, and one single family dwelling unit per parcel or lot, are permitted in NRPAs. Thus, the comprehensive plan, as amended, does provide a standard regarding the "extent of the uses of land," as required by section 163.3177(6)(a), and appellants have failed to show that the Department was obliged to require an intensity standard in order to certify the interim amendments in compliance with law.

* * *

As for the second issue raised on appeal, that the evidence does not support the finding that the approved NRPA boundaries were sufficient to protect the Florida panther, we also affirm. Appellants claim that such finding was erroneous because there was evidence that such wildlife frequented areas not included within the NRPAs' boundaries. Even if we were to accept this argument as established by the evidence, appellants have failed to demonstrate how such a fact makes the boundaries of the NRPAs erroneous. As the ALJ noted, the boundaries approved are only intended to be temporary, subject to additional adjustment as further studies indicate may be necessary.

AFFIRMED

Notes

1. The city of Tumwater, Washington, adopted a law that defines and protects wildlife habitat. TUMWATER, WASH. CODE §§ 16.32.050, 16.32.060, 16.32.090 (1991) ("Fish and Wildlife Protection"). The regulations require habitat protection plans and establish buffer zones to retain and protect adequate urban wildlife habitats. In Green River, Wyoming, the city designated conservation districts that require the protection of critical wildlife habitat. Where development occurs, adequate impact mitigation measures are required. GREEN RIVER, WY. CODE § 7–1 (2002).

2. In Department of Community Affairs v. Moorman, 664 So.2d 930 (Fla.1995), the Florida court addressed the protection of the Florida Key deer. The court described the issue:

> This case involves the validity of a land-use ordinance enacted to protect an endangered species, the miniature Florida Key deer. The regulation affects Big Pine Key where the deer now are largely concentrated. Human development on the Key has put the deer perilously close to extinction, and their numbers are estimated to be only 350 to 400 animals. The minimum number needed to sustain a viable species is considered 100 to 250 animals. The animals are further endangered by human attempts to feed them, by pet dogs that may kill them, and by automobiles.
>
> The ordinance in question prohibits the erection of fencing in portions of Big Pine Key, where the respondents own property. It was enacted because, in a natural environment, Key deer must roam freely over slash pinelands and wetlands in search of food and water. This necessarily means the deer also must roam over some privately owned lands. 664 So.2d at 931–32.

The court upheld the revocation of the landowner's permit to erect a six-foot high, 400–foot long fence on his property, holding that the state's police power included protection of the environment and that "environmental degradation threatens not merely aesthetic concerns vital to the State's economy but also the health, welfare, and safety of substantial numbers of

Floridians." Residents of the Florida Keys are sharply divided over whether the species is really declining and whether further development of property on the Keys should be severely restricted. See Mireya Navarro, Striking a Balance Between Deer and Residents in the Florida Keys, N.Y. TIMES, Mar. 18, 1997, p. A 12.

3. In Southview Associates, Ltd. v. Bongartz, 980 F.2d 84 (2d Cir. 1992), a developer purchased an 88–acre parcel of land near a ski resort in Vermont with the intent of developing 78 vacation homes. The Vermont Conservation Commission found that the proposed development was situated within a 280–acre deeryard; *i.e.*, a winter habitat for white-tailed deer. This deeryard is the sole remaining, active deeryard within a 10.7 square mile area. The Commission denied the development permit and, on appeal to the state Environmental Board, the decision was affirmed on the ground that the development, if allowed to proceed, would "destroy and significantly imperil wildlife habitat." Even though white-tailed deer are not endangered (and the Endangered Species Act was not implicated in the case), the court held that the developer had not suffered a physical taking and that the question of a regulatory taking was not ripe for review.

(6) The Public Trust Doctrine

The public trust doctrine holds that certain natural resources are held by the sovereign in trust for the benefit of the people. The doctrine arose in Roman law, was incorporated into British common law, and has been adopted or abandoned to various degrees in the 50 states. Lands adjacent to or under oceans, tidally-influenced waters, and navigable surface water are purchased by private owners subject to the public's right to use the waters for navigation. Beachfront property is purchased subject to the public's right to use the beach to a point determined by the common law and statutes of coastal states. One of the earliest cases involving the public trust doctrine held that a person could not maintain a trespass action against another person when the properties trespassed on were under navigable rivers. Arnold v. Mundy, 6 N.J.L. 1 (1821). The New Jersey Supreme Court explained that "[n]avigable rivers, where the tide ebbs and flows, the ports, bays, coasts of the sea, including both the waters and the land under the waters, for the purposes of passing and repassing, navigation, fishing, fowling, sustenance, and all other uses of the water and its products, are common to all the people of New Jersey." Id.

Later, in Illinois Central Railroad Co. v. Illinois, 146 U.S. 387, 13 S.Ct. 110, 36 L.Ed. 1018 (1892), the United States Supreme Court held that although land submerged under Lake Michigan could be owned and used privately, the use could not conflict with the public's interest. Illinois Central Railroad Company purchased 1000 acres in fee simple of land submerged under Lake Michigan from the State of Illinois. The Court held that the land could not be transferred in fee simple free of public trust interests. The state was allowed to sell the land in small parcels with the public trust burden attached to such property, and could condition any future use of the land to benefit the public. In more recent cases, the Supreme Court has extended the public trust doctrine to apply to any land "subject to the ebb and flow of the tide." Phillips Petroleum Co. v. Mississippi, 484 U.S. 469, 108 S.Ct. 791, 98 L.Ed.2d 877 (1988).

The public trust doctrine is flexible and subject to interpretation by modern legislatures and courts. For example, in New Jersey, the public trust doctrine was applied beyond the high tide mark to the dry upland area, if a municipality owned this area. Neptune City v. Avon-By-the-Sea, 294 A.2d 47, 61 N.J. 296 (1972). The court stated that "[t]he public trust doctrine, like all common law principles, should not be considered fixed or static, but should be molded and extended to meet changing conditions and the needs of the public it was created to benefit." Id. at 54. New Jersey has since expanded the reach of the doctrine by removing the restriction that a municipality must own the upland area. See Matthews v. Bay Head Improvement Ass'n, 471 A.2d 355, 95 N.J. 306 (1984).

Public trust principles affect the jurisprudence of regulatory takings. A government regulation that limits development on land that may not be developed because of public trust rights does not effect a taking, even where the limitation constitutes a total deprivation of the right to develop the land; the land was subject to a common law limitation that is simply mirrored in the regulation. Purchasers of property are subject to the doctrine of caveat emptor (buyer beware); they are obliged to inspect their properties and take title to all defects and limitations that are discoverable. Where customary uses of the land arise under public trust concepts, the public's use of the land is as discoverable as the activities of an adjacent owner who owns an affirmative easement over the conveyed parcel. This duty to discover—to know the land and its inherent qualities—is relevant to the investment-backed expectations so important to determining whether a land use regulation is a regulatory taking. When a permit is issued by a land use agency subject to the public rights to use the land or to enjoy its benefits, courts will inquire whether and to what extent public rights in the land preexisted the plaintiff's purchase. If a permit condition requires the owner to allow the public on the land, such an invasive condition is not a regulatory taking if the public enjoys that same right under the common law of the state.

Developers who apply to develop submerged lands, tidal wetlands, freshwater wetlands, and associated upland areas have development rights that may be limited by the public trust doctrine of the state. These notions reinforce the reach and reasonableness of federal, state, and local tidal and freshwater wetland regulations and development permit conditions that protect the right of the community under the public trust doctrine.

ESPLANADE v. SEATTLE

United States Court of Appeals, Ninth Circuit, 2002.
307 F.3d 978.

B. Fletcher, Circuit Judge.

Plaintiff Esplanade Properties, LLC ("Esplanade") challenges the legality of the City of Seattle's ("the City's") denial of its application to develop shoreline property on Elliot Bay in Seattle, Washington. Esplanade contends that the City's action resulted in a complete deprivation of economic use of its property, constituting an inverse condemnation in violation of federal and state constitutional law, and violating both federal and state substantive due process. Specifically, plaintiff appeals three decisions of the district court which, *in toto*, resulted in the dismissal of its claims against the defendant, *to wit*, granting summary judgment to the defendant on plaintiff's takings claim, granting summary judgment to the defendant on plaintiff's federal substantive due process claim, and dismissing plaintiff's state substantive due process claim. We have jurisdiction under 28 U.S.C. § 1291 and we affirm.

In 1992, Esplanade began a long, and ultimately unsuccessful, process of attempting to secure permission to construct single-family residential housing on and over tidelands located below Magnolia bluff, near both a large city park and a large marina. The property is classified as first class tide-land, and is submerged completely for roughly half of the day, during which time it resembles a large sand bar.

Esplanade purchased the property for $40,000 in 1991, and quickly retained a development team to design and secure permits for nine waterfront homes, each to be constructed on platforms supported by pilings. In June of 1992, Esplanade applied for building permits, as well as various use permits, variance permits, and special use permits. None of these applications were ever approved.[7]

After reviewing Esplanade's permit applications, the City's Department of Construction and Land Use ("DCLU") identified three significant code compliance issues related to the proposed project: (1) the size of the proposed piers and docks, (2) the design of the causeway access to the houses, and (3) lack of parking on dry land. The City notified Esplanade of its concerns in a Correction Notice. Esplanade responded to the City's concerns, and sought three formal code interpretations from the DCLU, each relating to the issues raised by the City. Central to the ongoing dispute, the City was asked, *inter alia*, to interpret the code with respect to parking. According to the City's interpretation, parking built over water in a single-family zone was prohibited, despite the general requirement that single-family homes be constructed *with* on-site parking. Esplanade appealed this interpretation, which was eventually affirmed by the Washington Court of Appeals on the ground that residential housing was not a water-dependent or water-related use.

---

7. Under Washington's Shoreline Management Act ("SMA"), RCW 90.58.010, enacted in 1971, localities are required to develop a set of regulations with respect to their shorelines. Before 1992, under the Seattle Shoreline Master Program ("SSMP"), developed pursuant to the dictates of the SMA, above-water residential construction was seemingly allowed where the lots had less than 30 feet of dry land. Though the Seattle City Council later amended that provision in the SSMP, instead allowing for such use only where a lot has at least 15 feet of dry land, Esplanade filed its building permit applications before this change took effect, thus vesting its application to the former provision. *West Main Assoc. v. City of Bellevue*, 106 Wash.2d 47, 720 P.2d 782, 786 (1986) ("A vested right merely establishes the ordinances to which a building permit and subsequent development must comply.").

Sec. 3 SPECIFIC LOCAL LAND USE REGULATIONS 819

At the end of the appeals process, in November of 1997, Esplanade was informed by the City that it had 60 days to submit formal alterations to its proposed plan, in light of the DCLU's code interpretations, without which the application would be cancelled. Esplanade, instead of altering its parking proposal, simply applied for a variance. Because Esplanade failed to modify its plans with respect to each of the three design concerns raised by the City, on April 13, 1998, the City cancelled Esplanade's application, and later refused to reconsider its unappealable decision.

On June 5, 2000, Esplanade served a letter on the City threatening to make an inverse condemnation claim as a result of the cancellation of its application. Without a response from the City, Esplanade made good on its threat and filed the current action against the City on August 22, 2000.

In its complaint, Esplanade alleges, (1) "inverse condemnation [ ] in violation of the federal and state constitutional provisions prohibiting the taking of private property without just compensation," and (2) "violat[ion][of] plaintiff's right to substantive due process, in violation of the state and federal constitutions." Plaintiff seeks "monetary damages" under 42 U.S.C. § 1983 and RCW 64.40.020.

The district court granted the defendant's motion for partial summary judgment, dismissing Esplanade's federal substantive due process claim based upon our holding in *Armendariz v. Penman,* 75 F.3d 1311 (9th Cir.1996), that federal substantive due process claims are precluded where the alleged violation is addressed by explicit textual provisions of the Constitution, specifically, the Fifth Amendment's "Takings Clause."

The district court, in its Order, did not resolve Esplanade's state substantive due process claim, but requested further briefing from the parties on the question whether the matter should be certified for review by the Washington Supreme Court.

Having received supplemental briefing from the parties, the district court dismissed Esplanade's state substantive due process claim on the ground that Washington state courts had authoritatively held that the Washington Constitution provides no greater substantive due process protection than that afforded by the United States Constitution.

Subsequently, the district court granted the defendant's motion for summary judgment on Esplanade's remaining claim, to wit, the City's alleged taking of its property without just compensation, in violation of the Fifth Amendment. The court held that because Esplanade failed to establish that the City's action was the "proximate cause" of its alleged damages, and alternatively, because the "background principles" of Washington state law would have precluded the development, under *Lucas v. South Carolina Coastal Council,* 505 U.S. 1003, 112 S.Ct. 2886, 120 L.Ed.2d 798 (1992), the City was not liable to Esplanade.

Esplanade appealed, challenging each of the district court's three decisions.

* * *

Here, the district court found no taking of plaintiff's property for two reasons. First, the court found that the City's interpretation of the SSMP and its ultimate cancellation of Esplanade's development applications were not the proximate cause of Esplanade's alleged damages. Second, the court found that the background principles of Washington law, specifically the public trust doctrine, burdened plaintiff's property and precluded Esplanade from prevailing in a takings action against the City.

We agree with the district court that under both federal and state law a plaintiff must make a showing of causation between the government action and the alleged deprivation. *See Tahoe–Sierra* (9th Cir. 2000), 216 F.3d at 783 & n. 33 (discussing requirement that "plaintiff [in takings claim] must establish both causation-in-fact and proximate causation," and noting that while "true that there is little discussion of a 'causation' requirement in any of the case law involving regulatory takings," despite a passing reference to proximate cause in *Penn Central*, 438 U.S. at 124, 98 S.Ct. 2646, "this is due to nothing more than the fact that, in most regulatory takings cases, there is no doubt whatsoever about whether the government's action was the cause of the alleged taking."); *Ventures N.W. Ltd. P'ship v. State*, 81 Wash.App. 353, 914 P.2d 1180, 1187 (1996) ("An owner claiming loss of the economically viable use of property must show that the challenged government regulation proximately caused the loss of all such use.") (Citing *Guimont v. Clarke*, 121 Wash.2d 586, 854 P.2d 1 (1993), *cert. denied*, 510 U.S. 1176, 114 S.Ct. 1216, 127 L.Ed.2d 563 (1994); *Orion Corp. v. State*, 109 Wash.2d 621, 747 P.2d 1062 (1987), *cert. denied*, 486 U.S. 1022, 108 S.Ct. 1996, 100 L.Ed.2d 227 (1988)). However, because we find that the background principles of Washington state law would have precluded development of the proposed project, and therefore that plaintiff's claimed property right never existed, we do not address the question of causation.

As discussed above, a deprivation by the government of all beneficial uses of one's property results in a taking unless, inter alia, the "background principles" of state law already serve to deprive the property owner of such uses. *Lucas*, 505 U.S. at 1029, 112 S.Ct. 2886. In *Lucas*, subsequent to plaintiff's purchase of two residential lots of shoreline property, the state of South Carolina passed a statute having the "direct effect of barring petitioner from erecting any permanent structures on his two parcels," rendering them "valueless." 505 U.S. at 1007, 112 S.Ct. 2886. In response, the plaintiff sued, alleging that the government effected a complete deprivation of his property. The Court held that "[a]ny limitation so severe cannot be newly legislated or decreed (without compensation), but must inhere in the title itself, in the restrictions that background principles of the State's law of property and nuisance already place upon land ownership," and remanded for a determination of whether such "background principles" would have prevented the proposed use of plaintiff's property. *Id.*, 505 U.S. at 1029, 112 S.Ct. 2886.

In this case, the "restrictions that background principles" of Washington law place upon such ownership are found in the public trust doctrine. As the Washington Supreme Court recently explained, the "state's ownership of tidelands and shorelands is comprised of two distinct aspects—the *jus privatum* and the *jus publicum*." *State v. Longshore*, 141 Wash.2d 414, 5 P.3d 1256, 1262 (2000). Relevant here, the "jus publicum, or public trust doctrine, is the right 'of navigation, together with its incidental rights of fishing, boating, swimming, water skiing, and other related recreational purposes generally regarded as corollary to the right of navigation and the use of public waters.'" *Id.* (quoting *Caminiti v. Boyle*, 107 Wash.2d 662, 732 P.2d 989, 994 (1987) (internal quotation marks and citation omitted)). The "doctrine reserves a public property interest, the jus publicum, in tidelands and the waters flowing over them, despite the sale of these lands into private ownership." *Weden v. San Juan County*, 135 Wash.2d 678, 958 P.2d 273, 283 (1998), (citing Ralph W. Johnson et al., *The Public Trust Doctrine and Coastal Zone Management in Washington State*, 67 Wash. L.Rev. 521, 524 (1992)). "The state can no more convey or give away this jus publicum interest than it can 'abdicate its police powers in the administration of government and the preservation of the peace.'" *Caminiti*, 732 P.2d at 994 (quoting *Illinois Cent. R.R. v. Illinois*, 146 U.S. 387, 453, 13 S.Ct. 110, 36 L.Ed. 1018 (1892)). Instead, the state may only divest itself of interests in the state's waters in a manner that does not substantially impair the public interest. *Id.* at 993–95.

It is beyond cavil that "a public trust doctrine has always existed in Washington." *Orion Corp.*, 747 P.2d at 1072 (citing *Caminiti*, 732 P.2d at 994). The doctrine is "partially encapsulated in the language of [Washington's] constitution which reserves state ownership in 'the beds and shores of all navigable waters in the state.'" *Rettkowski v. Dep't of Ecology*, 122 Wash.2d 219, 858 P.2d 232, 239 (1993) (quoting Wash. Const. art. 17, § 1). The doctrine is also reflected in Washington's Shoreline Management Act ("SMA"), adopted in 1971. RCW §§ 90.58.010–.930. Following a long history "favoring the sale of tidelands and shorelands," resulting in the privatization of approximately 60 percent of the tidelands and 30 percent of the shorelands originally owned by the state, *Caminiti*, 732 P.2d at 996, the Washington legislature found that the SMA was necessary because "unrestricted construction on the privately owned or public owned shorelines * * * is not in the best public interest." RCW 90.58.020.

The public trust doctrine, reflected in part in the SMA, unquestionably burdens Esplanade's property.

We agree with the district court that the Washington Supreme Court's decision in Orion controls the outcome of this case, and that Washington's public trust doctrine ran with the title to the tideland properties and alone precluded the shoreline residential development proposed by Esplanade.

In *Orion*, the plaintiff corporation, prior to the enactment of the SMA, purchased tideland property in Padilla Bay, the "most diverse, least disturbed, and most biologically productive of all major estuaries on Puget Sound." *Id.*, 747 P.2d at 1065. Orion Corp. proposed dredging and filling of the Bay to create a significant residential community. *Id.* In addressing plaintiff's challenge to subsequent local and state environmental regulations, which it alleged combined to completely deprive it of all economically viable use of its property, the court decided that the tidelands of the Bay were burdened by the public trust doctrine prior to the enactment of the SMA. *Id.* at 1072. At the time of Orion's purchase, "Orion could make no use of the tidelands which would substantially impair the [public] trust." *Id.* at 1073. Specifically, "Orion never had the right to dredge and fill its tidelands, either for a residential community or farmlands [s]ince a property right must exist before it can be taken, neither the SMA nor the SCSMMP effected a taking * * * " *Id.* (internal quotation marks and citation omitted).

We find that the development proposed by Esplanade would suffer the same fate under the public trust doctrine as the project proposed by Orion Corp.

* * *

Esplanade's contention that the proposed development *was* consistent with the SMA at the time his project vested in 1992 is similarly without merit. As the City concedes, at the time of the purchase, the SMA, theoretically, permitted single-family dwellings to be constructed on the property. As the district court noted, however, "[t]here are numerous limitations that the SMA places on developments of shorelines, even if those developments, like Esplanade's, are not categorically prohibited." (citing, *e.g.*, RCW 90.58.020(2)(requiring that shoreline developments "[p]reserve the natural character of the shoreline"), and RCW 90.58.020(4) (requiring that "[p]rojects protect the resources and ecology of the shoreline")). In this case, because Esplanade's tideland property is navigable for the purpose of public recreation (used for fishing and general recreation, including by Tribes), and located just 700 feet from Discovery Park, the development would have interfered with those uses, and thus would have been inconsistent with the public trust doctrine. Therefore, Esplanade's development plans never constituted a legally permissible use.

As the district court correctly noted, "Esplanade * * * took the risk," when it purchased this large tract of tidelands in 1991 for only $40,000, "that, despite extensive federal, state, and local regulations restricting shoreline development, it could nonetheless overcome those numerous hurdles to complete its project and realize a substantial return on its limited initial investment. Now, having failed * * *, it seeks indemnity from the City." The takings doctrine does not supply plaintiff with such a right to indemnification.

Esplanade's proposal to construct concrete pilings, driveways and houses in the navigable tidelands of Elliot Bay, an area regularly used by the public for various recreational and other activities, was inconsistent with the public trust that the State of Washington is obligated to protect.

For the reasons given, we affirm.

AFFIRMED.

Notes

1. In DeBeradinis v. Zoning Com'n of City of Norwalk, 228 Conn. 187, 635 A.2d 1220 (Conn. 1994), a landowner filed a coastal site plan in accordance with Gen. Statutes § 22a–94 to expand his existing recycling operation on an adjacent parcel of real estate that bordered the Norwalk river. The zoning commission approved plaintiff's coastal site plan, but imposed six conditions including a grant by plaintiff of an easement to provide public access along the river. Plaintiff appealed the commission's administrative decision to the Superior Court, which set aside approval of the site plan with conditions because of the statutory invalidity of one of the conditions. The commission had acted illegally by conditioning the approval of the plaintiff's application on the grant of a public access easement along the waterfront because this condition was not related to and did not mitigate the potential adverse impacts of the proposal. Having determined that the invalid condition was an "essential component" of the approval of the plaintiff's application, the court reversed the commission's decision, thereby voiding the approval of the plaintiff's application.

2. Other courts have also refused to expand the public trust doctrine to allow public access over private land. See Opinion of the Justices, 365 Mass. 681, 313 N.E.2d 561 (1974). This opinion invalidated a bill that declared that the 'reserved interests of the public' in coastal land included a public "on-foot free right-of-passage" along the shore of the coastline between the mean high water line and the extreme water line. The court stated that the Massachusetts Bay Colony Ordinance, specifically retains the public rights of fishing, fowling and navigation in privately owned coastal land and the public's " * * * right of passage over dry land at periods of low tide cannot be reasonably included as one of the traditional rights of navigation" 313 N.E.2d at 566. Also see Opinion of the Justices, 139 N.H. 82, 649 A.2d 604 (1994) (finding that a bill recognizing a public easement in "dry sand areas" between public trust areas and intersection of beach and high ground was unconstitutional taking).

3. The Public Trust doctrine provided some justification for the passage of certain federal environmental laws that delegate power to federal agencies to protect public property. Examples include the Wild Free–Roaming Horses and Burros Act, 16 U.S.C. §§ 1331–1340 (2000); the Federal Land Policy and Management Act, 43 U.S.C. §§ 1701–1784 (2000); the National Park Service Act, 16 U.S.C. §§ 1–460 (2000); the Comprehensive Environmental Response, Compensation and Liability Act, 42 U.S.C. §§ 9601–9657 (2000); the Wilderness Act, 16 U.S.C. §§ 1131–1136 (2000); and the Coastal Zone Management Act, 16 U.S.C. §§ 1457–1464 (2000).

4. A strong statement of the public trust doctrine is found in State ex rel. Thornton v. Hay, 254 Or. 584, 462 P.2d 671 (1969) which upheld the rights of the public to use beaches above the high tide line:

> The dry-sand area in Oregon has been enjoyed by the general public as a recreational adjunct of the wet-sand or foreshore area since the beginning of the state's political history. The first European settlers on these shores found the aboriginal inhabitants using the foreshore for clam-digging and the dry-sand area for their cooking fires. The newcomers continued these customs after statehood. Thus, from the time of the earliest settlement to the present day, the general public has assumed that the dry-sand area was a part of the public beach, and the public has used the dry-sand area for picnics, gathering wood, building warming fires, and generally as a headquarters from which to supervise children or to range out over the foreshore as the tides advance and recede. In the Cannon Beach vicinity, state and local officers have policed the dry sand, and municipal sanitary crews have attempted to keep the area reasonably free from man-made litter. 462 P.2d at 673.

* * *

> Until very recently, no question concerning the right of the public to enjoy the dry-sand area appears to have been brought before the courts of this state. The public's assumption that the dry sand as well as the foreshore was "public property" had been reinforced by early judicial decisions. See Shively v. Bowlby, 152 U.S. 1, 14 S.Ct. 548, 38 L.Ed. 331 (1894), which affirmed Bowlby v. Shively, 22 Or. 410, 30 P. 154 (1892). These cases held that landowners claiming under federal patents owned seaward only to the "high-water" line, a line that was then assumed to be the vegetation line. Id., at 674.

* * *

> Recently, however, the scarcity of oceanfront building sites has attracted substantial private investments in resort facilities. Resort owners like these defendants now desire to reserve for their paying guests the recreational advantages that accrue to the dry-sand portions of their deeded property. Consequently, in 1967, public debate and political activity resulted in legislative attempts to resolve conflicts between public and private interests in the dry-sand area * * *. Id., at 674.

> Because so much of our law is the product of legislation, we sometimes lose sight of the importance of custom as a source of law in our society. It seems particularly appropriate in the case at bar to look to an ancient and accepted custom in this state as the source of a rule of law. The rule in this case, based upon custom, is salutary in confirming a public right, and at the same time it takes from no man anything which he has had a legitimate reason to regard as exclusively his * * *. Id at 678.

Chapter VIII

PRESERVING AESTHETICS, HISTORIC PLACES AND CULTURAL INTERESTS

As we have seen in the previous chapters, zoning started out as a tool for segregating inconsistent land uses in the city and for regulating the height and size of structures and their placement on lots. As zoning became both acceptable and fashionable, the legal approval extended to zoning was seen as a convenient source of power to accomplish public objectives which had nothing to do with separating uses or regulating building bulk. In many respects the development was much like the expansion of federal regulation which took place in Congress in the twentieth century acting under the Commerce Clause of Article I of the Constitution. The zoning power was something of an empty vessel receptive to many land use regulations to accomplish multiple purposes. In this chapter, several different types of land use regulations are examined. Some of the cases deal with provisions in zoning ordinances, and many of the opinions talk in terms of zoning and the police power. However, the subject matter of the regulations is not, strictly speaking, consonant with the concept of zoning, and thus the editors feel that this material belongs in a separate chapter.

SECTION 1. AESTHETICS AND ARCHITECTURAL CONTROL

Until the mid 1950's courts would state almost routinely that aesthetic considerations in land use regulation, especially zoning, were not a sufficient basis for exercising the police power. This attitude was probably reflective of the notion that the law could not tolerate restrictions based on something as indefinable as aesthetic sense, as beauty, after all, lies in the eye of the beholder. However, when Justice Douglas wrote in 1954 in Berman v. Parker, 348 U.S. 26, 75 S.Ct. 98, 99 L.Ed. 27 that taking property for urban renewal was taking for a public use, and that aesthetic considerations formed a part of the valid public interest, state appellate courts began to reexamine the question of whether aesthetics were a legitimate basis for public regulation. The impact of Berman v. Parker is illustrated by the Wisconsin decision in State ex rel. Saveland Park Holding Corp. v. Wieland, which is reproduced in this chapter. Half a century later, the attitude of courts has shifted quite substantially on the issue. The main developments have come in two areas: Regulation of signs and billboards and regulation of the appearance of structures.

In considering the cases and materials in this chapter, a number of considerations must be taken into account. Among others, these include the particular policy of a jurisdiction as manifested in its statutes or judicial attitudes and how high aesthetic, environmental and related considerations rank on the scale of values in that jurisdiction; whether such concerns are or should be legitimately included within the police power without regard to whether tradition would exclude them unless joined with some other "legitimate" police power concern; whether the upholding and enforcement of such values, even if considered a valid police power exercise, so deprive an owner of his property rights as to constitute a taking which should require compensation; and whether the judicial or statutory approval of such considerations would ultimately permit the aesthetic sensibilities of a few individuals to force others to conform to their particular ideas to the point of oppression.

A. REGULATION OF SIGNS AND BILLBOARDS

STATE v. DIAMOND MOTORS, INC.

Supreme Court of Hawaii, 1967.
50 Hawaii 33, 429 P.2d 825.

LEVINSON, JUSTICE.

In 1957 the City and County of Honolulu enacted Ordinance No. 1557 which was codified, after the adoption in 1959 of the Charter of the City and County of Honolulu, as Article 26 (Signs Regulations) of Chapter 13 (Regulations Promoting General Welfare) of the Revised Ordinances of Honolulu 1961. The ordinance is comprehensive in nature and provides for the regulation and control of outdoor signs, the location, erection, maintenance and use of signs, and penalties for the violation thereof. It prohibits, among other things, the erection and the maintenance in industrial districts of ground signs exceeding 75 square feet in area or exceeding 16 feet in height from the ground.[1]

---

1. Findings and declarations contained in the ordinance include the following:

"(a) That the people of the City have a primary interest in controlling the erection, location and maintenance of outdoor signs in a manner designed to protect the public health, safety and morals and to promote the public welfare; and

"(b) That the rapid economic development of the City has resulted in a great increase in the number of businesses with a marked increase in the number and size of signs advertising such business activities; and

* * *

Sec. 1   **AESTHETICS AND ARCHITECTURAL CONTROL**   827

Appellant Alexander is the owner of a ground sign 40 feet high and more than 75 square feet in area, which he installed in 1965 upon the premises of appellant Diamond Motors, Inc., located in an industrial district on the main highway between Honolulu International Airport and downtown Honolulu and the Waikiki beach area. As provided in the ordinance, the City's Building Superintendent gave written notice to appellants to correct the violation by appropriately reducing the area and height of the sign within 20 days. Appellants failed to make the corrections.

Each of the appellants was, thereafter, charged by an information filed August 25, 1965 with a violation of the ordinance and, upon a consolidated trial by jury, was found guilty as charged. * * *

Appellants assert: (1) that the ordinance, including its application to appellants, is based exclusively upon aesthetic considerations; (2) that legislation based exclusively upon aesthetic considerations is outside the scope of police powers and therefore invalid; and (3) that application of the ordinance to appellants constitutes a taking of private property without the payment of compensation in violation of the Fifth Amendment to the Constitution of the United States and Article I, Section 18 of the Constitution of the State of Hawaii.

Appellee disputes the first assertion and argues that the ordinance was enacted for a number of purposes, among which was the preservation of aesthetics as a means to the end of protecting and promoting the general welfare of the people of the City and County of Honolulu, particularly by protecting and promoting the tourist trade and thereby the economic well-being of the City and County of Honolulu.

Appellee's answering brief admittedly "does not extend to supporting the proposition that aesthetics alone is a proper objective for the exercise of the City's police power." Perhaps, the "weight of authority" in other jurisdictions persuaded the City to present the more traditional arguments because it felt that it was safer to do so. However, the brief of The Outdoor Circle as amicus curiae presents, as we think, a more modern and forthright position.

"(g) That the natural beauty of landscape, view and attractive surroundings of the Hawaiian Islands, including the City, constitutes an attraction for tourists and visitors; and

"(h) That a major source of income and revenue of the people of the City is derived from the tourist trade; and

"(i) That the indiscriminate erection and maintenance of large signs seriously detract from the enjoyment and pleasure of the natural scenic beauty of the City which in turn injuriously affect the tourist trade and thereby the economic well-being of the City; and

"(j) That it is necessary for the promotion and preservation of the public health, safety and welfare of the people of the City that the erection, construction, location, maintenance of signs be regulated and controlled. (Sec. 13-26.1 R.O. 1957)."

Permissible ground signs on any lot or parcel of land in industrial districts are limited by the ordinance to "One ground sign, lighted or unlighted, not exceeding 75 square feet in area, relating to businesses conducted on the premises, and not exceeding 16 feet in height from the ground."

We accept beauty as a proper community objective, attainable through the use of the police power. We are mindful of the reasoning of most courts that have upheld the validity of ordinances regulating outdoor advertising and of the need felt by them to find some basis in economics, health, safety, or even morality. See Thomas Cusack Co. v. City of Chicago, 242 U.S. 526, 37 S.Ct. 190, 61 L.Ed. 472 (1917). We do not feel so constrained.

Hawaii's constitution provides:

The State shall have power to conserve and develop its natural beauty, objects and places of historic or cultural interest, sightliness and physical good order, and for that purpose private property shall be subject to reasonable regulation. (Article VIII, Section 5.)

Appellants argue that this constitutional provision has no application to this case because the offending sign is located in an industrial area. We do not agree. The natural beauty of the Hawaiian Islands is not confined to mountain areas and beaches. The term "sightliness and physical good order" does not refer only to junk yards, slaughter houses, sanitation, cleanliness, or incongruous business activities in residential areas as appellants argue.

* * *

Cromwell v. Ferrier, 19 N.Y.2d 263, 225 N.E.2d 749 (New York 1967) upheld the constitutionality of a town zoning ordinance which was a comprehensive and detailed plan for regulation of signs in the township. The court said:

" * * * Advertising signs and billboards, if misplaced, often are egregious examples of ugliness, distraction, and deterioration. They are just as much subject to reasonable controls, including prohibition, as enterprises which emit offensive noises, odors, or debris. The eye is entitled to as much recognition as the other senses, but, of course, the offense to the eye must be substantial and be deemed to have material effect on the community or district pattern. * * * " (p. 755.)

Oregon City v. Hartke, 240 Or. 35, 400 P.2d 255, decided in 1965, in holding that an ordinance wholly excluding automobile wrecking yards from Oregon City was a valid exercise of the police power, said:

" * * * there is a growing judicial recognition of the power of a city to impose zoning restrictions which can be justified solely upon the ground that they will tend to prevent or minimize discordant and unsightly surroundings. This change in attitude is a reflection of the refinement of our tastes and the growing appreciation of cultural values in a maturing society. The change may be ascribed more directly to the judicial expansion of the police power to include within the concept of 'general welfare' the enhancement of the citizen's cultural life." (pp. 46–47, 400 P.2d p. 261.)

Sec. 1   AESTHETICS AND ARCHITECTURAL CONTROL   829

"We join in the view 'that aesthetic considerations alone may warrant an exercise of the police power.' " (p. 49, 400 P.2d p. 262.)

* * *

We hold that the application of the ordinance to appellants constituted a regulation for the public welfare under the City's police power in a legitimate field for legitimate aesthetic reasons and that it does not constitute a taking of private property without the payment of compensation. Cromwell v. Ferrier, supra, 19 N.Y.2d 263, 225 N.E.2d 749 (New York 1967).

The remaining question raised by appellants is whether the application of the ordinance to appellants is an arbitrary, discriminatory and unreasonable deprivation and denial of due process and equal protection in violation of the Fifth and Fourteenth Amendments to the Constitution of the United States and Article I, Section 4 of the Constitution of the State of Hawaii.

Appellants argue that "the arbitrary limitation of height and size of signs cannot be considered reasonably necessary and appropriate for the accomplishment of the aesthetic objective set forth in the * * * Ordinance, which seeks to eliminate the 'indiscriminate erection and maintenance of large signs which seriously detract from the enjoyment and pleasure of the natural scenic beauty' of the community."

The City has said through its legislative body that the limitations placed by the ordinance on height and size of signs are necessary. Classifications are obviously required. The burden is upon the appellants to show that the limitations and classifications are unreasonable. State v. Safeway Stores, Inc., 106 Mont. 182, 76 P.2d 81. The record does not so show. Appellants say that whether a classification violates the equal protection clause of the Fourteenth Amendment to the Constitution of the United States is a judicial question. It was incumbent on them in invoking the protection of the Fourteenth Amendment "to show with convincing clarity" that the ordinance created against them the discrimination of which they complain. Corporation Comm'n of Oklahoma v. Lowe, 281 U.S. 431, 50 S.Ct. 397, 74 L.Ed. 945. They have not done so.

* * *

The judgments are affirmed.

MAYOR AND CITY COUNCIL OF BALTIMORE v. MANO SWARTZ, INC.

Court of Appeals of Maryland, 1973.
268 Md. 79, 299 A.2d 828.

SINGLEY, JUDGE.

For the second time we have before us an attack on the validity of Ordinance No. 663 of the Mayor and City Council of Baltimore (the City), approved 1 November 1965, now Baltimore City Code Art. 1, § 39

(1966) (the Ordinance), which was designed to regulate signs in the central business district of Baltimore.

There was testimony that the City had been so successful in limiting the size and design of signs in agreements for the sale of sites in the Charles Center renewal area that a decision was made to endeavor to achieve uniformity in the whole of the downtown district.

In City of Baltimore v. Charles Center Parking, 259 Md. 595, 271 A.2d 144 (1970), we affirmed a decree of the Circuit Court of Baltimore City which had found arbitrary and discriminatory and violative of Article 23 of Maryland's Declaration of Rights and of the Fourteenth Amendment to the Constitution of the United States § 1(e)(4) of the Ordinance, which had made unlawful the painting of a sign on an exterior wall of a building. We concluded that this result was mandated by the fact that § 1(j) of the Ordinance permitted billboards and poster boards, subject to zoning regulations, in the same area where painted signs were prohibited, particularly since the City offered no testimony which would support a rational distinction between painted signs and billboards.

In that case, we addressed ourselves to a narrow issue—the validity of § 1(e)(4)—and expressed no opinion as regards the validity of the Ordinance as a whole. The assault mounted in this case is of wider scope.

On 30 October 1970, just before the expiration of the five-year moratorium contained in § 1(g) of the Ordinance, Mano Swartz, Inc., and nine other firms doing business in the central business district (Swartz) filed a bill of complaint in the Circuit Court of Baltimore City against the City and the City's Director of Construction and Building Inspection seeking to enjoin the enforcement of § 1(e)(1) which proscribes signs projecting more than 12 inches "from the primary surface of the building to which it is attached * * *" and § 1(e)(4) which prohibits roof top signs.

Filed with the bill of complaint was the text of the Ordinance: * * *

(a) A Commission on Signs is created. It shall have three members appointed as of January 1, 1966, under the provisions of Article IV, Section 6, of the City Charter. One of the three members shall represent the retail merchants in the area defined in this section. Another member shall represent the sign industry. The third member of the Commission shall be a representative of the public at large. * * *

(b) The Commission may retain technical advisors, amongst which shall be included an architect, a graphic artist and a sign designer.

* * *

(d) The Commission, after public notice and hearing may adopt and promulgate rules and regulations establishing standards and requirements for commercial signs, billboards, and other advertising structures and devices within the area described in this section. Any such rules and regulations shall be designed and intended to provide for beauty, attrac-

Sec. 1 AESTHETICS AND ARCHITECTURAL CONTROL 831

tiveness, esthetics, and symmetry in the commercial signs, billboards, and other advertising structures and devices, and to relieve conditions of gaudiness and drabness in certain portions of the defined area.

* * *

The Ordinance had as its sole purpose the achievement of an aesthetically pleasing result, and we have held this not to be a permissible use of the police power, Feldstein v. Kammauf, 209 Md. 479, 484–489, 121 A.2d 716 (1956); Goldman v. Crowther, 147 Md. 282, 302–309, 128 A. 50 (1925); Byrne v. Maryland Realty Co., 129 Md. 202, 211, 98 A. 547 (1916); see, 1 Anderson, American Law of Zoning § 7.21 at 520–21 (1968); 2 Metzenbaum, The Law of Zoning 1577–1578 (2d ed. 1955); 1 Rathkopf, The Law of Zoning and Planning 11–1 (3d ed. 1972); 16 Am.Jr.2d Constitutional Law § 292 at 569 (1964).

While aesthetic goals may legitimately serve as an additional legislative purpose, if health, morals or safety or other ends generally associated with the concept of public welfare are being served, * * * they cannot be the only purpose of regulation, Byrne v. Maryland Realty Co., supra, 129 Md. at 211, 98 A. 547.

The City might well have prevailed had the legislative intent been the elimination of signs or pennants which distracted motorists, Kenyon Peck, Inc. v. Kennedy, 210 Va. 60, 168 S.E.2d 117 (1969) or the promotion of highway safety, Stevens v. City of Salisbury, 240 Md. 556, 567–568, 214 A.2d 775 (1965); see E.B. Elliott Adv. Co. v. Metropolitan Dade County, 425 F.2d 1141 (5th Cir.1970), petition for cert. dismissed, 400 U.S. 805, 91 S.Ct. 12, 27 L.Ed.2d 35; Village of Larchmont v. Sutton, 30 Misc.2d 245, 217 N.Y.S.2d 929 (1961); *approved and followed in,* Village of Larchmont v. Levine, Sup., 225 N.Y.S.2d 452 (1961). The fact that another result might have been one which was aesthetically pleasing would not necessarily have imported an element of constitutional infirmity.

The effort to eliminate what was referred to in argument before us as "visual pollution" by controlling signs and billboards through the exercise of the zoning power has been slowly developing, General Outdoor Adv. Co. v. Indianapolis, 202 Ind. 85, 172 N.E. 309, 72 A.L.R. 453 (1930); Opinion of the Justices to the Senate, 333 Mass. 773, 128 N.E.2d 557, 561 (1955); People v. Sterling, 128 Misc. 650, 220 N.Y.S. 315 (1927); State ex rel. Saveland Park Holding Corp. v. Wieland, 269 Wis. 262, 69 N.W.2d 217, 222 (1955); 58 Am.Jur. Zoning § 30 at 959 (1948); 1 Anderson, American Law of Zoning, supra, § 7.21 at 520–23; 1 Rathkopf, Law of Zoning and Planning, supra, at 11–9, 11–22; 1 Yokely, Zoning Law and Practice § 2–4 at 28 (3d ed. 1965); Dukeminier, Zoning for Aesthetic Objectives: A Reappraisal, 20 Law & Contemp.Prob. 218 (1955); Masotti & Selfon, Aesthetic Zoning and the Police Power, supra, 46 J.Urban L. 773, 779–86; Note, 47 Cornell L.Rev. 647, 651–652 (1962); Annot., Aesthetic Objectives or Considerations as Affecting Validity of Zoning Ordinance, 21 A.L.R.3d 1222, 1225 (1968). The principal difficulty is that other forms of pollution, stench and noise and the like, can be measured by more nearly objective standards. If beauty, however, lies in the eyes of the beholder, so does the tawdry, the gaudy and the vulgar—and courts have traditionally taken a gingerly approach to legislation which circumscribes property rights by applying what amounts to subjective standards, which may well be those of an idiosyncratic group. See discussion in, General Outdoor Advertising Co. v. Department of Public Works, supra, 193 N.E. at 815–816; Cromwell v. Ferrier, 19 N.Y.2d 263, 279 N.Y.S.2d 22, 225 N.E.2d 749, 755, 21 A.L.R.3d 1212 (1967); Dukeminier, Zoning for Aesthetic Objectives: A Reappraisal, 20 Law & Contemp.Prob., supra, at 224–229 (1955); Michelman, Toward a Practical Standard for Aesthetic Regulation, 15 Prac.Law. 36 (1969); Norton, Police Power, Planning and Aesthetics, 7 Santa Clara Law. 171, 183–185 (1967); Note, Aesthetic Considerations in Land Use Planning, 35 Albany L.Rev. 126, 131 (1970); Note, Zoning for Aesthetics—A Problem of Definition, 32 U.Cin.L.Rev. 367, 373 (1963).

We think Justice Cardozo had it about right when, speaking for the New York Court of Appeals in People v. Rubenfeld, 254 N.Y. 245, 172 N.E. 485, 486–487 (1930), he observed, by way of dicta:

> "The organs of smell and hearing, assailed by sounds and odors too pungent to be borne, have been ever favored of the law * * * more conspicuously, it seems, than sight, which perhaps is more inured to what is ugly or disfigured * * *. Even so, the test for all the senses, for sight as well as smell and hearing, has been the effect of the offensive practice upon the reasonable man or woman of average sensibilities * * *. One of the unsettled questions of the law is the extent to which the concept of nuisance may be enlarged by legislation so as to give protection to sensibilities that are merely cultural or aesthetic." [citations omitted]

Our predecessors recognized that this problem had long existed when in Byrne v. Maryland Realty Co., supra, 129 Md. at 211, 98 A. 547, they cited with approval the language of the Mississippi court which rejected an attempt through the exercise of the police power to exclude a market from a residential area in Quintini v. City of Bay St. Louis, 64 Miss. 483, 1 So. 625, 628 (1887):

> "The law can know no distinction between citizens because of the superior cultivation of the one over the other. It is with common humanity that courts and legislatures must deal; and that use of property which in all common sense and reason is not a nuisance to the average man cannot be prohibited because repugnant to some sentiment of a particular class."

Until now, only a minority of jurisdictions can be said to have validated regulatory schemes which were primarily or solely concerned with aesthetic considerations, Stone v. City of Maitland, 446 F.2d 83, 89 (5th Cir.1971); City of St. Paul v. Chicago, St. Paul, Minneapolis & Omaha Ry. Co., 413 F.2d 762, 767–768 (8th Cir.1969); Sunad, Inc. v. Sarasota, 122 So.2d 611, 614 (Fla.1960); State ex rel. Civello v. New Orleans, 154 La. 271, 97 So. 440, 444–445, 33 A.L.R. 260 (1923); Naegele

Sec. 1   AESTHETICS AND ARCHITECTURAL CONTROL   833

Outdoor Adv. Co. v. Village of Minnetonka, 281 Minn. 492, 162 N.W.2d 206, 212 (1968); Cromwell v. Ferrier, supra, 225 N.E.2d at 753–755; People v. Stover, 12 N.Y.2d 462, 240 N.Y.S.2d 734, 191 N.E.2d 272, 274–276 (1963), appeal dismissed, 375 U.S. 42, 84 S.Ct. 147, 11 L.Ed.2d 107; United Advertising Corp. v. Metuchen, 42 N.J. 1, 198 A.2d 447, 449 (1964); Oregon City v. Hartke, 240 Or. 35, 400 P.2d 255, 262–263 (1965); State ex rel. Carter v. Harper, 182 Wis. 148, 196 N.W. 451, 454–456, 33 A.L.R. 269 (1923); 1 Anderson, American Law of Zoning, supra §§ 7.15, 7.22 at 508, 526 and cases cited therein; Annot., Aesthetic Objectives or Considerations as Affecting Validity of Zoning Ordinance, supra, 21 A.L.R.3d, § 4(a) at 1235 and cases cited therein.

* * *

We do not wish to be understood as saying that aesthetic considerations cannot play a proper role in the zoning process, because they do. It has long been recognized that the police power may rightly be exercised to preserve an area which is generally regarded by the public to be pleasing to the eye or historically or architecturally significant. * * *

In Footnote 88 to his article, Maryland Zoning—The Court and Its Critics, 27 Md.L.Rev. 39, 53 (1967), George W. Liebmann concludes, and we think quite rightly, that our case law and statutes have followed the approach urged by Ernst Freund, Standards of American Legislation 115–16 (1917):

"[I]t is undesirable to force by law upon the community standards of taste which a representative legislative body may happen to approve of, and compulsion with that end in view would be justly resented as inconsistent with a traditional spirit of individualism. But it is a different question whether the state may not protect the works of nature or the achievements of art or the associations of history from being wilfully marred. In other words, emphasis should be laid upon the character of the place as having an established claim to consideration and upon the idea of disfigurement as distinguished from the falling short of some standard of beauty."

Because the purpose of the Ordinance was not the preservation or protection of something which was aesthetically pleasing, but rather was intended to achieve by regulation an aesthetically pleasing result, with no thought of enhancing the public welfare, we shall not disturb the result reached below.

Decree affirmed, costs to be paid by appellants.

METROMEDIA, INC. v. CITY OF SAN DIEGO

Supreme Court of the United States, 1981.
453 U.S. 490, 101 S.Ct. 2882, 69 L.Ed.2d 800.

[The City of San Diego enacted an ordinance which, in effect banned all off-site billboards while allowing on-site advertising signs. The California Supreme Court upheld the ordinance, 26 Cal.3d 848, 610 P.2d 407

(1980), although the court also held that removal of some existing billboards after the expiration of an amortization period would require compensation under the Federal Highway Beautification Act.]

JUSTICE WHITE announced the judgment of the Court and delivered an opinion in which JUSTICE STEWART, JUSTICE MARSHALL and JUSTICE POWELL join.

This case involves the validity of an ordinance of the city of San Diego, Cal., imposing substantial prohibitions on the erection of outdoor advertising displays within the city.

* * *

Early cases in this Court sustaining regulation of and prohibitions aimed at billboards did not involve First Amendment considerations. See Packer Corporation v. Utah, 285 U.S. 105, 52 S.Ct. 273, 76 L.Ed. 643 (1932); St. Louis Poster Advertising Co. v. St. Louis, 249 U.S. 269, 39 S.Ct. 274, 63 L.Ed. 599 (1919); Cusack Co. v. City of Chicago, 242 U.S. 526, 37 S.Ct. 190, 61 L.Ed. 472 (1917). Since those decisions, we have not given plenary consideration to cases involving First Amendment challenges to statutes or ordinances limiting the use of billboards, preferring on several occasions summarily to affirm decisions sustaining state or local legislation directed at billboards.

Suffolk Outdoor Advertising Co. v. Hulse, 439 U.S. 808, 99 S.Ct. 66, 58 L.Ed.2d 101 (1978), involved a municipal ordinance that distinguished between off-site and on-site billboard advertising, prohibiting the former and permitting the latter. We summarily affirmed a judgment sustaining the ordinance, thereby rejecting the submission, repeated in this case, that prohibiting off-site commercial advertising violates the First Amendment. The definition of "billboard," however, was considerably narrower in *Suffolk* than it is here: "A sign which directs attention to a business, commodity, service, entertainment, or attraction sold, offered or existing elsewhere than upon the same lot where such sign is displayed." This definition did not sweep within its scope the broad range of noncommercial speech admittedly prohibited by the San Diego ordinance. Furthermore, the New York ordinance, unlike that in San Diego, contained a provision permitting the establishment of public information centers in which approved directional signs for businesses could be located. This Court has repeatedly stated that although summary dispositions are decisions on the merits, the decisions extend only to "the precise issues presented and necessarily decided by those actions." Mandel v. Bradley, 432 U.S. 173, 176, 97 S.Ct. 2238, 2240, 53 L.Ed.2d 199 (1977); see also Hicks v. Miranda, 422 U.S. 332, 345, n. 14, 95 S.Ct. 2281, 2290, 45 L.Ed.2d 223 (1975); Edelman v. Jordan, 415 U.S. 651, 671, 94 S.Ct. 1347, 1359, 39 L.Ed.2d 662 (1974). Insofar as the San Diego ordinance is challenged on the ground that it prohibits noncommercial speech, the *Suffolk* case does not directly support the decision below.

The Court has summarily disposed of appeals from state-court decisions upholding state restrictions on billboards on several other occasions. Markham Advertising Co. v. Washington, 393 U.S. 316, 89 S.Ct. 553, 21 L.Ed.2d 512 (1969), and Newman Signs, Inc. v. Hjelle, 440 U.S. 901, 99 S.Ct. 1205, 59 L.Ed.2d 449 (1979), both involved the facial validity of state billboard prohibitions that extended only to certain designated roadways or to areas zoned for certain uses. The statutes in both instances distinguished between on-site commercial billboards and off-site billboards within the protected areas. Our most recent summary action was Lotze v. Washington, 444 U.S. 921, 100 S.Ct. 257, 62 L.Ed.2d 177 (1979), which involved an "as applied" challenge to a Washington prohibition on off-site signs. In that case, appellants erected, on their own property, billboards expressing their political and social views. Although billboards conveying information relating to the commercial use of the property would have been permitted, appellants' billboards were prohibited, and the state courts ordered their removal. We affirmed a judgment rejecting the First Amendment challenge to the ordinance.

* * *

Billboards are a well-established medium of communication, used to convey a broad range of different kinds of messages. As Justice Clark noted in his dissent below:

"The outdoor sign or symbol is a venerable medium for expressing political, social and commercial ideas. From the poster or 'broadside' to the billboard, outdoor signs have played a prominent role throughout American history, rallying support for political and social causes." 164 Cal.Rptr., at 533–534, 610 P.2d, at 430–431.

The record in this case indicates that besides the typical commercial uses, San Diego billboards have been used

"to publicize the 'City in motion' campaign of the City of San Diego, to communicate messages from candidates for municipal, state and national offices, including candidates for judicial office, to propose marriage, to seek employment, to encourage the use of seat belts, to denounce the United Nations, to seek support for Prisoners of War and Missing in Action, to promote the United Crusade and a variety of other charitable and socially-related endeavors and to provide directions to the traveling public."

But whatever its communicative function, the billboard remains a "large, immobile, and permanent structure which like other structures is subject to * * * regulation." 164 Cal.Rptr., at 522, 610 P.2d, at 419. Moreover, because it is designed to stand out and apart from its surroundings, the billboard creates a unique set of problems for land-use planning and development.

* * *

As construed by the California Supreme Court, the ordinance restricts the use of certain kinds of outdoor signs. That restriction is defined in two ways: first, by reference to the structural characteristics of the sign; second, by reference to the content, or message, of the sign. Thus, the regulation only applies to a "permanent structure constituting, or used for the display of, a commercial or other advertisement to the public." 164 Cal.Rptr., at 513, n. 2, 610 P.2d, at 410. Within that class, the only permitted signs are those (1) identifying the premises on which the sign is located, or its owner or occupant, or advertising the goods produced or services rendered on such property and (2) those within one of the specified exemptions to the general prohibition, such as temporary political campaign signs. To determine if any billboard is prohibited by the ordinance, one must determine how it is constructed, where it is located, and what message it carries.

Thus, under the ordinance (1) a sign advertising goods or services available on the property where the sign is located is allowed; (2) a sign on a building or other property advertising goods or services produced or offered elsewhere is barred; (3) noncommercial advertising, unless within one of the specific exceptions, is everywhere prohibited. The occupant of property may advertise his own goods or services; he may not advertise the goods or services of others, nor may he display most noncommercial messages.

* * *

* * * [I]n Central Hudson v. Public Service Comm'n, 447 U.S. 557, 100 S.Ct. 2343, 65 L.Ed.2d 341 (1980), we held that: "The Constitution * * * accords a lesser protection to commercial speech than to other constitutionally guaranteed expression. The protection available for a particular commercial expression turns on the nature both of the expression and of the governmental interests served by its regulation." Id., at 562–563, 100 S.Ct., at 2349–2350 (citation omitted). We then adopted a four-part test for determining the validity of government restrictions on commercial speech as distinguished from more fully protected speech. (1) The First Amendment protects commercial speech only if that speech concerns lawful activity and is not misleading. A restriction on otherwise protected commercial speech is valid only if it (2) seeks to implement a substantial governmental interest, (3) directly advances that interest, and (4) reaches no farther than necessary to accomplish the given objective. Id., at 563–566, 100 S.Ct., at 2350–2351.

Appellants agree that the proper approach to be taken in determining the validity of the restrictions on commercial speech is that which was articulated in *Central Hudson,* but assert that the San Diego ordinance fails that test. We do not agree.

There can be little controversy over the application of the first, second, and fourth criteria. There is no suggestion that the commercial advertising at issue here involves unlawful activity or is misleading. Nor can there be substantial doubt that the twin goals that the ordinance seeks to further—traffic safety and the appearance of the city—are substantial governmental goals. It is far too late to contend otherwise with respect to either traffic safety, Railway Express Agency, Inc. v. New York, 336 U.S. 106, 69 S.Ct. 463, 93 L.Ed. 533 (1949), or esthetics, see

Penn Central Transportation Co. v. New York City, 438 U.S. 104, 98 S.Ct. 2646, 57 L.Ed.2d 631 (1978); Village of Belle Terre v. Boraas, 416 U.S. 1, 94 S.Ct. 1536, 39 L.Ed.2d 797 (1974); Berman v. Parker, 348 U.S. 26, 33, 75 S.Ct. 98, 102, 99 L.Ed. 27 (1954). Similarly, we reject appellants' claim that the ordinance is broader than necessary and, therefore, fails the fourth part of the *Central Hudson* test. If the city has a sufficient basis for believing that billboards are traffic hazards and are unattractive, then obviously the most direct and perhaps the only effective approach to solving the problems they create is to prohibit them. The city has gone no farther than necessary in seeking to meet its ends. Indeed, it has stopped short of fully accomplishing its ends: It has not prohibited all billboards, but allows on-site advertising and some other specifically exempted signs.

The more serious question, then, concerns the third of the *Central Hudson* criteria: Does the ordinance "directly advance" governmental interests in traffic safety and in the appearance of the city? It is asserted that the record is inadequate to show any connection between billboards and traffic safety. The California Supreme Court noted the meager record on this point but held "as a matter of law that an ordinance which eliminates billboards designed to be viewed from the streets and highways reasonably relates to traffic safety." 164 Cal.Rptr., at 515, 610 P.2d, at 412. Noting that "billboards are intended to, and undoubtedly do, divert a driver's attention from the roadway," ibid., and that whether the "distracting effect contributes to traffic accidents invokes an issue of continuing controversy," ibid., the California Supreme Court agreed with many other courts that a legislative judgment that billboards are traffic hazards is not manifestly unreasonable and should not be set aside. We likewise hesitate to disagree with the accumulated, commonsense judgments of local lawmakers and of the many reviewing courts that billboards are real and substantial hazards to traffic safety.[2] There is nothing here to suggest that these judgments are unreasonable. As we said in a different context, Railway Express Agency, Inc. v. People of New York, 336 U.S. 106, 109, 69 S.Ct. 463, 465, 93 L.Ed. 533 (1949):

> "We would be trespassing on one of the most intensely local and specialized of all municipal problems if we held that this regulation had no relation to the traffic problem of New York City. It is the

---

2. See E.B. Elliott Advertising Co. v. Metropolitan Dade County, 425 F.2d 1141, 1152 (C.A.5 1970); Markham Advertising Co. v. Washington, 73 Wash.2d 405, 439 P.2d 248, 258 (1968); New York State Thruway Authority v. Ashley Motor Court, 10 N.Y.2d 151, 218 N.Y.S.2d 640, 642, 176 N.E.2d 566, 568 (1961); Ghaster Properties, Inc. v. Preston, 176 Ohio St. 425, 200 N.E.2d 328, 337 (1964); Newman Signs, Inc. v. Hjelle, 268 N.W.2d 741, 757 (N.D. 1978); Lubbock Poster Co. v. City of Lubbock, 569 S.W.2d 935, 939 (Tex.Civ.App. 1978); State v. Lotze, 92 Wash.2d 52, 593 P.2d 811, 814 (1979); Inhabitants, Town of Boothbay v. National Advertising Co., 347 A.2d 419, 422 (Me.1975); Stuckey's Stores, Inc. v. O'Cheskey, 93 N.M. 312, 600 P.2d 258, 267 (1979); In re Opinion of the Justices, 103 N.H. 268, 169 A.2d 762, 764 (1961); General Outdoor Advertising Co. v. Dept. of Public Works, 289 Mass. 149, 193 N.E. 799, 813–814 (1935). But see John Donnelly & Sons v. Campbell, 639 F.2d 6, 11 (C.A.1 1980); State ex rel. Dept. of Transportation v. Pile, 603 P.2d 337, 343 (Okla.1979); Metromedia, Inc. v. City of Des Plaines, 26 Ill.App.3d 942, 326 N.E.2d 59, 62 (1975).

judgment of the local authorities that it does have such a relation. And nothing has been advanced which shows that to be palpably false."

We reach a similar result with respect to the second asserted justification for the ordinance—advancement of the city's esthetic interests. It is not speculative to recognize that billboards by their very nature, wherever located and however constructed, can be perceived an "esthetic harm."[3] San Diego, like many other States and municipalities, has chosen to minimize the presence of such structures. Such esthetic judgments are necessarily subjective, defying objective evaluation, and for that reason must be carefully scrutinized to determine if they are only a public rationalization of an impermissible purpose. But there is no claim in this case that San Diego has as an ulterior motive the suppression of speech, and the judgment involved here is not so unusual as to raise suspicions in itself.

It is nevertheless argued that the city denigrates its interest in traffic safety and beauty and defeats its own case by permitting on-site advertising and other specified signs. Appellants question whether the distinction between on-site and off-site advertising on the same property is justifiable in terms of either esthetics or traffic safety. The ordinance permits the occupant of property to use billboards located on that property to advertise goods and services offered at that location; identical billboards, equally distracting and unattractive, that advertise goods or services available elsewhere are prohibited even if permitting the latter would not multiply the number of billboards. Despite the apparent incongruity, this argument has been rejected, at least implicitly, in all of the cases sustaining the distinction between off-site and on-site commercial advertising. We agree with those cases and with our own decisions in Suffolk Outdoor Advertising Co. v. Hulse, 439 U.S. 808, 99 S.Ct. 66, 58 L.Ed.2d 101 (1978); Markham Advertising Co. v. Washington, 393 U.S. 316, 89 S.Ct. 553, 21 L.Ed.2d 512 (1969); Newman Signs, Inc. v. Hjelle, 440 U.S. 901, 99 S.Ct. 1205, 59 L.Ed.2d 449 (1979).

In the first place, whether on-site advertising is permitted or not, the prohibition of off-site advertising is directly related to the stated objectives of traffic safety and esthetics. This is not altered by the fact that the ordinance is under-inclusive because it permits on-site advertising. Second, the city may believe that off-site advertising, with its periodically changing content, presents a more acute problem than does

---

3. See John Donnelly & Sons v. Campbell, supra, 639 F.2d at 11–12; E.B. Elliott Advertising Co. v. Metropolitan Dade County, supra, 425 F.2d at 1152; Newman Signs, Inc. v. Hjelle, supra, 268 N.W.2d at 757; Markham Advertising Co. v. Washington, supra, 439 P.2d at 259; Stuckey's Stores, Inc. v. O'Cheskey, supra, 600 P.2d at 267; Suffolk Outdoor Advertising Co. v. Hulse, 43 N.Y.2d 483, 402 N.Y.S.2d 368, 370, 373 N.E.2d 263, 265 (1977); John Donnelly & Sons, Inc. v. Outdoor Advertising Bd., 369 Mass. 206, 339 N.E.2d 709, 717 (1975); Cromwell v. Ferrier, 19 N.Y.2d 263, 279 N.Y.S.2d 22, 26, 225 N.E.2d 749, 753 (1967); State v. Diamond Motors, Inc., 50 Haw. 33, 429 P.2d 825, 827 (Haw.1967); United Advertising Corp. v. Metuchen, 42 N.J. 1, 198 A.2d 447, 449 (1964); In re Opinion of the Justices, supra, 169 A.2d at 764. But see State ex rel. Dept. of Transportation v. Pile, supra, 603 P.2d at 342; Sunad, Inc. v. Sarasota, 122 So.2d 611, 614–615 (Fla.1960).

on-site advertising. See *Railway Express,* supra, 336 U.S. at 110, 69 S.Ct. at 465. Third, San Diego has obviously chosen to value one kind of commercial speech—on-site advertising—more than another kind of commercial speech—off-site advertising. The ordinance reflects a decision by the city that the former interest, but not the latter, is stronger than the city's interests in traffic safety and esthetics. The city has decided that in a limited instance—on-site commercial advertising—its interests should yield. We do not reject that judgment. As we see it, the city could reasonably conclude that a commercial enterprise—as well as the interested public—has a stronger interest in identifying its place of business and advertising the products or services available there than it has in using or leasing its available space for the purpose of advertising commercial enterprises located elsewhere. See Railway Express v. New York, supra, 336 U.S., at 116, 69 S.Ct., at 468 (Jackson, J., concurring); Bradley v. Public Utilities Comm'n, 289 U.S. 92, 97, 53 S.Ct. 577, 579, 77 L.Ed. 1053 (1933). It does not follow from the fact that the city has concluded that some commercial interests outweigh its municipal interests in this context that it must give similar weight to all other commercial advertising. Thus, off-site commercial billboards may be prohibited while on-site commercial billboards are permitted.

The constitutional problem in this area requires resolution of the conflict between the city's land-use interests and the commercial interests of those seeking to purvey goods and services within the city. In light of the above analysis, we cannot conclude that the city has drawn an ordinance broader than is necessary to meet its interests, or that it fails directly to advance substantial government interests. In sum, insofar as it regulates commercial speech the San Diego ordinance meets the constitutional requirements of *Central Hudson,* supra.

It does not follow, however, that San Diego's general ban on signs carrying noncommercial advertising is also valid under the First and Fourteenth Amendments. The fact that the city may value commercial messages relating to on-site goods and services more than it values commercial communications relating to off-site goods and services does not justify prohibiting an occupant from displaying its own ideas or those of others.

As indicated above, our recent commercial speech cases have consistently accorded noncommercial speech a greater degree of protection than commercial speech. San Diego effectively inverts this judgment, by affording a greater degree of protection to commercial than to noncommercial speech. There is a broad exception for on-site commercial advertisements, but there is no similar exception for noncommercial speech. The use of on-site billboards to carry commercial messages related to the commercial use of the premises is freely permitted, but the use of otherwise identical billboards to carry noncommercial messages is generally prohibited. The city does not explain how or why noncommercial billboards located in places where commercial billboards are permitted would be more threatening to safe driving or would detract more from the beauty of the city. Insofar as the city tolerates billboards at all, it cannot choose to limit their content to commercial messages; the city may not conclude that the communication of commercial information concerning goods and services connected with a particular site is of greater value than the communication of noncommercial messages.

Furthermore, the ordinance contains exceptions that permit various kinds of noncommercial signs, whether on property where goods and services are offered or not, that would otherwise be within the general ban. A fixed sign may be used to identify any piece of property and its owner. Any piece of property may carry or display religious symbols, commemorative plaques of recognized historical societies and organizations, signs carrying news items or telling the time or temperature, signs erected in discharge of any governmental function, or temporary political campaign signs. No other noncommercial or ideological signs meeting the structural definition are permitted, regardless of their effect on traffic safety or esthetics.

Although the city may distinguish between the relative value of different categories of commercial speech, the city does not have the same range of choice in the area of noncommercial speech to evaluate the strength of, or distinguish between, various communicative interests. See Carey v. Brown, 447 U.S. 455, 462, 100 S.Ct. 2286, 2291, 65 L.Ed.2d 263 (1980); Police Department of Chicago v. Mosley, 408 U.S. 92, 96, 92 S.Ct. 2286, 2290, 33 L.Ed.2d 212 (1972). With respect to noncommercial speech, the city may not choose the appropriate subjects for public discourse: "To allow a government the choice of permissible subjects for public debate would be to allow that government control over the search for political truth." *Consolidated Edison Co.,* supra, 447 U.S., at 538, 100 S.Ct., at 2333. Because some noncommercial messages may be conveyed on billboards throughout the commercial and industrial zones, San Diego must similarly allow billboards conveying other noncommercial messages throughout those zones.[4]

4. Because a total prohibition of outdoor advertising is not before us, we do not indicate whether such a ban would be consistent with the First Amendment. But see Schad v. Borough of Mount Ephraim, 452 U.S. 61, 101 S.Ct. 2176, 68 L.Ed.2d 671, on the constitutional problems created by a total prohibition of a particular expressive forum, live entertainment in that case. Despite Justice Stevens' insistence to the contrary, post, at 1, 2, and 10, n. 14, we do not imply that the ordinance is unconstitutional because it "does not abridge enough speech."

Similarly, we need not reach any decision in this case as to the constitutionality of the federal Highway Beautification Act of 1965, Pub.L. 89–285, 79 Stat. 1028, 23 U.S.C.A. § 131. That Act, like the San Diego ordinance, permits on-site commercial billboards in areas in which it does not permit billboards with noncommercial messages. 23 U.S.C.A. § 131(c). However, unlike the San Diego ordinance, which prohibits billboards conveying noncommercial messages throughout the city, the federal law does not contain a total prohibition of such billboards in areas adjacent to the Interstate and primary highway systems. As far as the Federal Government is concerned, such billboards are permitted adjacent to the highways in areas zoned industrial or commercial under state law or in unzoned commercial or industrial areas. 23 U.S.C.A. § 131(d). Regulation of billboards in those areas is left primarily to the States. For this reason, the decision today does not determine the constitutionality of the federal statute. Whether, in fact, the distinction is constitutionally significant can only be determined on the basis of a record establishing the actual effect of the Act on billboards conveying noncommercial messages.

Finally, we reject appellee's suggestion that the ordinance may be appropriately characterized as a reasonable "time, place and manner" restriction. The ordinance does not generally ban billboard advertising as an unacceptable "manner" of communicating information or ideas; rather, it permits various kinds of signs. Signs that are banned are banned everywhere and at all times. We have observed that time, place and manner restrictions are permissible if "they are justified without reference to the content of the regulated speech * * * serve a significant governmental interest, and * * * leave open ample alternative channels for communication of the information." Virginia Pharmacy Board v. Virginia Consumer Council, 425 U.S. 748, 771, 96 S.Ct. 1817, 1830, 48 L.Ed.2d 346 (1976). Here, it cannot be assumed that "alternative channels" are available, for the parties stipulated to just the opposite: "Many businesses, politicians and other persons rely upon outdoor advertising because other forms of advertising are insufficient, inappropriate and prohibitively expensive." A similar argument was made with respect to a prohibition on real estate "For Sale" signs in Linmark Associates, Inc. v. Willingboro, 431 U.S. 85, 97 S.Ct. 1614, 52 L.Ed.2d 155 (1977), and what we said there is equally applicable here:

> "Although in theory sellers remain free to employ a number of different alternatives, in practice [certain products are] not marketed through leaflets, sound trucks, demonstrations, or the like. The options to which sellers realistically are relegated * * * involve more cost and less autonomy than * * * signs * * * are less likely to reach persons not deliberately seeking sales information * * * and may be less effective media for communicating the message that is conveyed by a * * * sign. * * * The alternatives, then, are far from satisfactory." 431 U.S., at 93, 97 S.Ct., at 1618.

It is apparent as well that the ordinance distinguishes in several ways between permissible and impermissible signs at a particular location by reference to their content.

* * *

Because the San Diego ordinance reaches too far into the realm of protected speech, we conclude that it is unconstitutional on its face. The judgment of the California Supreme Court is reversed and the case remanded to that court.

JUSTICE BRENNAN, with whom JUSTICE BLACKMUN joins, concurring in the judgment.

Believing that "a total prohibition of outdoor advertising is not before us," * * *, the plurality does not decide "whether such a ban would be consistent with the First Amendment." Instead, it concludes that San Diego may ban all billboards containing commercial speech messages without violating the First Amendment, thereby sending the signal to municipalities that bifurcated billboard regulations prohibiting commercial messages but allowing noncommercial messages would pass constitutional muster. * * * I write separately because I believe this case in effect presents the total ban question, and because I believe the plurality's bifurcated approach itself raises serious First Amendment problems and relies on a distinction between commercial and noncommercial speech unanticipated by our prior cases.

* * *

* * * In the case of billboards, I would hold that a city may totally ban them if it can show that a sufficiently substantial governmental interest is directly furthered by the total ban, and that any more narrowly drawn restriction, i.e., anything less than a total ban, would promote less well the achievement of that goal.

Applying that test to the instant case, I would invalidate the San Diego ordinance. The city has failed to provide adequate justification for its substantial restriction on protected activity. * * * First, although I have no quarrel with the substantiality of the city's interest in traffic safety, the city has failed to come forward with evidence demonstrating that billboards actually impair traffic safety in San Diego. Indeed, the Joint Stipulation of Facts is completely silent on this issue. Although the plurality hesitates "to disagree with the accumulated, common sense judgments of local lawmakers and of the many reviewing courts that billboards are real and substantial hazards to traffic safety," ante, at 17, I would not be so quick to accept legal conclusions in other cases as an adequate substitute for evidence *in this case* that banning billboards directly furthers traffic safety. Moreover, the ordinance is not narrowly drawn to accomplish the traffic safety goal. Although it contains an exception for signs "not visible from any point on the boundary of the premises," App. to Juris. Statement 111a, billboards not visible from the street but nevertheless visible from the "boundary of the premises" are not exempted from the regulation's prohibition.

Second, I think that the city has failed to show that its asserted interest in aesthetics is sufficiently substantial in the commercial and industrial areas of San Diego. I do not doubt that "[i]t is within the power of the [city] to determine that the community should be beautiful," Berman v. Parker, 348 U.S. 26, 33, 75 S.Ct. 98, 102, 99 L.Ed. 27 (1954), but that power may not be exercised in contravention of the First Amendment. * * *

It is no doubt true that the appearance of certain areas of the city would be enhanced by the elimination of billboards, but "it is not immediately apparent as a matter of experience" that their elimination in all other areas as well would have more than a negligible impact on aesthetics. See John Donnelly & Sons v. Campbell, 639 F.2d 6, 23 (C.A.1 1980), petition for cert. filed (Mar. 19, 1981) (Pettine, J., concurring in the judgment.) The Joint Stipulation reveals that

> "[s]ome sections of the City of San Diego are scenic, some blighted, some containing strips of vehicle related commercial uses, some contain new and attractive office buildings, some functional industrial development and some areas contain older but useful commer-

cial establishments." Joint Stipulation § 8, App. to Juris. Statement 121a.

A billboard is not *necessarily* inconsistent with oil storage tanks, blighted areas, or strip development. Of course, it is not for a court to impose its own notion of beauty on San Diego. But before deferring to a city's judgment, a court must be convinced that the city is seriously and comprehensively addressing aesthetic concerns with respect to its environment. Here, San Diego has failed to demonstrate a comprehensive coordinated effort in its commercial and industrial areas to address other obvious contributors to an unattractive environment. In this sense the ordinance is underinclusive. See Erznoznik v. City of Jacksonville, 422 U.S. 205, 214, 95 S.Ct. 2268, 2275, 45 L.Ed.2d 125 (1975). Of course, this is not to say that the city must address all aesthetic problems at the same time, or none at all. Indeed, from a planning point of view, attacking the problem incrementally and sequentially may represent the most sensible solution. On the other hand, if billboards alone are banned and no further steps are contemplated or likely, the commitment of the city to improving its physical environment is placed in doubt. By showing a comprehensive commitment to making its physical environment in commercial and industrial areas more attractive, and by allowing only narrowly tailored exceptions, if any, San Diego could demonstrate that its interest in creating an aesthetically pleasing environment is genuine and substantial. This is a requirement where, as here, there is an infringement of important constitutional consequence.

I have little doubt that some jurisdictions will easily carry the burden of proving the substantiality of their interest in aesthetics. For example, the parties acknowledge that a historical community such as Williamsburg, Va. should be able to prove that its interests in aesthetics and historical authenticity are sufficiently important that the First Amendment value attached to billboards must yield. And I would be surprised if the Federal Government had much trouble making the argument that billboards could be entirely banned in Yellowstone National Park, where their very existence would so obviously be inconsistent with the surrounding landscape. I express no view on whether San Diego or other large urban areas will be able to meet the burden. But San Diego failed to do so here, and for that reason I would strike down its ordinance.

* * *

[Dissenting opinions by CHIEF JUSTICE BURGER, JUSTICE REHNQUIST and JUSTICE STEVENS are omitted.]

Notes

1. A staggering amount of case law exists in the area of sign regulations. In the early years courts were sometimes quite inventive in conjuring up non-aesthetic reasons to justify regulation of billboards and other signs. See, e.g., City of Passaic v. Paterson Bill Posting, Advertising and Sign Painting Co., 72 N.J.L. 285, 62 A. 267 (1905), where the court said:

In cases of fire they [signs] often cause their spread and constitute barriers against their extinction; and in cases of high wind, their temporary character, frail structure and broad surface render them liable to be blown down and to fall upon and injure those who may happen to be in their vicinity. The evidence shows and common observation teaches us that the ground in the rear thereof is being constantly used as privies and dumping ground for all kinds of waste * * * that behind [them] the lowest form of prostitution and other acts of immorality are frequently carried on, almost under public gaze; they offer shelter and concealment for the criminal while lying in wait for his victim * * *

The trend of decision today is in the frank recognition of the aesthetic justification for sign regulation, and the more recent cases tend to follow the reasoning of the Diamond Motors case. However, the Mano Swartz case should serve as a caution to the quick assumption that sign regulation is presumptively valid under the police power. In connection with the Mano Swartz case, see Montgomery County v. Citizens Bldg. & Loan Ass'n, Inc., 20 Md.App. 484, 316 A.2d 322 (1974), and Donnelly Advertising Corp. v. City of Baltimore, 279 Md. 660, 370 A.2d 1127 (1977), where the court distinguished Mano Swartz and upheld sign regulations in the Old Baltimore urban renewal district. In the course of the opinion the court also held that the company was not entitled to compensation for two billboards located near Interstate 40 because their removal was dictated by the ordinance and not by the Highway Beautification Act. Also see Metromedia, Inc. v. Mayor and City Council of Baltimore, 538 F.Supp. 1183 (D.Md.1982) which held that the city restrictions against outdoor advertising signs in an urban renewal area were justified constitutionally by the city's interests in traffic safety and aesthetics, but the ordinance was invalid in its discrimination against noncommercial messages.

2. Do you agree with the manner in which the Court in Metromedia disposed of the argument dealing with the difference between regulation of signs (location, size, setbacks, etc.) and prohibition of all off-site signs? Do you agree with the principle that cities may rationally distinguish between off-site signs, totally prohibiting such signs, and on-site signs? Are not many on-site signs just as distracting and aesthetically offensive as billboards? Is the decision to ban billboards while allowing on-site signs really a political decision in the sense that local governments cannot get away with ordering all local businesses to remove on-site signs? How can a city meet the burden of proof, outlined in Justice Brennan's concurring opinion? On-site/off-site distinctions have been upheld in numerous cases. See, Infinity Outdoor, Inc. v City of New York, 165 F.Supp.2d 403 (E.D.N.Y.2001) and Marathon Outdoor, LLC v. Vesconti, 107 F.Supp.2d 355 (S.D.N.Y.2000) where prohibiting only off-site signs is likely to raise suspicion under Metromedia. In Long Island Bd. of Realtors, Inc. v. Incorporated Village of Massapequa Park, 277 F.3d 622 (2d Cir.2002) the court upheld regulations that prohibited off-site commercial signs in residential zoning districts.

3. For a case upholding regulation of *all* signs to a size of under four square feet, see People v. Goodman, 31 N.Y.2d 262, 338 N.Y.S.2d 97, 290 N.E.2d 139 (1972). Compare City of Fayetteville v. S & H, Inc., 261 Ark. 148, 547 S.W.2d 94 (1977), where a majority of the court held that a sign

ordinance requiring removal of non-conforming signs after an amortization period was an unconstitutional taking, to the extent that the signs were in connection with an ongoing business and were not in themselves traffic hazards. A plurality of the court opined that the device of amortization was itself invalid. In a later case, City of Fayetteville v. McIlroy Bank & Trust Co., 278 Ark. 500, 647 S.W.2d 439 (1983), the court upheld the same ordinance and approved the amortization scheme.

4. Since the decision in Metromedia, courts have continued to uphold sign ordinances which do not differentiate between commercial and noncommercial speech. Some courts, however, have gone beyond Metromedia and have held content-neutral sign ordinances invalid as violative of the first amendment. In Macdonald Advertising Co. v. City of Pontiac, 916 F.Supp. 644 (E.D.Mich.1995) the court found that a city ordinance requiring billboards to obtain special permits was invalid insofar as there were not standards to guide the discretion of the local government and that the absence of standards constituted a prior restraint on freedom of speech under the First Amendment. In Village of Schaumburg v. Jeep Eagle Sales Corp., 285 Ill.App.3d 481, 221 Ill.Dec. 679, 676 N.E.2d 200 (1996) the court held that a local sign ordinance that prohibited display of more than three "official" flags at any one business violated the automobile dealer's First Amendment rights in that the ordinance permitted an unlimited number of "banners." See, Brown v. California Dept. of Transportation, 321 F.3d 1217 (9th Cir.2003) striking down a prohibition of anti-war banners displayed on a highway overpass next to American flags; also see Flying J Travel Plaza v. Commonwealth, Transportation Cabinet, 928 S.W.2d 344 (Ky.1996) where a ban on flashing signs was invalidated because the local law made exceptions for time, date, and weather signs.

5. A federal judge in Florida thrice struck down content-neutral bans on portable signs despite city arguments of traffic safety and aesthetics. See Signs, Inc. of Florida v. Orange County, Florida, 592 F.Supp. 693 (M.D.Fla. 1983); All American Sign Rentals, Inc. v. City of Orlando, 592 F.Supp. 85 (M.D.Fla.1983); Harnish v. Manatee County, Florida, 597 F.Supp. 601 (M.D.Fla.1984). The Eleventh Circuit Court of Appeals reversed the latter case, upholding the county's aesthetic interest, 783 F.2d 1535 (11th Cir. 1986).

6. In Lorillard Tobacco Co. v Reilly, 533 U.S. 525, 121 S.Ct. 2404, 150 L.Ed.2d 532 (2001), the U. S. Supreme Court determined that the Federal Cigarette Labeling and Advertising Act does not restrict a state or locality's ability to enact generally applicable zoning restrictions. The Court stated, "We have recognized that state interests in traffic safety and esthetics may justify zoning regulations for advertising. See Metromedia, Inc. v. San Diego, 453 U.S. 490, 507–508, 101 S.Ct. 2882, 69 L.Ed.2d 800 (1981). See also St. Louis Poster Advertising Co. v. St. Louis, 249 U.S. 269, 274, 39 S.Ct. 274, 63 L.Ed. 599 (1919); Thomas Cusack Co. v. Chicago, 242 U.S. 526, 529–531, 37 S.Ct. 190, 61 L.Ed. 472 (1917). Although Congress has taken into account the unique concerns about cigarette smoking and health in advertising, there is no indication that Congress intended to displace local community interests in general regulations of the location of billboards or large marquee advertising..."

7. An unusual sign case is presented in Supersign of Boca Raton, Inc. v. City of Fort Lauderdale, 766 F.2d 1528 (11th Cir.1985), where the court upheld a local sign ordinance provision which prohibited advertising signs on watercraft and certain vehicles. Also see Solomon v. City of Gainesville, 763 F.2d 1212 (11th Cir.1985), striking as unconstitutionally vague, a city ordinance prohibiting signs or graphics with obscene words or illustrations. The plaintiff was the owner of a pizza parlor whose sign depicted a reproduction of Leonardo da Vinci's famous anatomical illustration. And see City of Ladue v. Gilleo, 512 U.S. 43, 114 S.Ct. 2038, 129 L.Ed.2d 36 (1994) where the Court held that application of the zoning ordinance sign provisions to a homeowner who placed a notebook-size sheet of paper in her window protesting the Gulf War, was a denial of her First Amendment right of free speech. Should government regulate the placement of home-made signs displayed in the windows, on a door or on the lawn of an individual's home? Is it a matter of size and location? See, Kroll v. Steere, 60 Conn.App. 376, 759 A.2d 541 (2000) where the Court upheld size limits on a residential sign protesting the killing of deer.

8. Many of the cases after Metromedia present the similar situation of billboard companies challenging city restrictions. Some of these cases worth consulting include National Advertising Co. v. City of Rolling Meadows, 789 F.2d 571 (7th Cir.1986); Naegele Outdoor Advertising, Inc. v. City of Durham, 844 F.2d 172 (4th Cir.1988); Rzadkowolski v. Village of Lake Orion, 845 F.2d 653 (6th Cir.1988); National Advertising Co. v. City of Orange, 861 F.2d 246 (9th Cir.1988); Ackerley Communications of Mass., Inc. v. City of Somerville, 878 F.2d 513 (1st Cir.1989); Major Media of Southeast, Inc. v. City of Raleigh, 621 F.Supp. 1446 (E.D.N.C.1985) cert. denied 479 U.S. 1102, 107 S.Ct. 1334, 94 L.Ed.2d 185 (1987); Jackson v. City Council of Charlottesville, Virginia, 659 F.Supp. 470 (W.D.Va.1987) affirmed in part 840 F.2d 10 (4th Cir.1988); National Advertising Co. v. Town of Babylon, 703 F.Supp. 228 (E.D.N.Y.1989) affirmed in part 900 F.2d 551 (2d Cir.1990).

9. Around Election Day every year, streets and lawns are filled with political signs. To what extent can and should government regulate political signs? Prior to Metromedia, Martin v. Wray, 473 F.Supp. 1131 (E.D.Wis. 1979) and Farrell v. Township of Teaneck, 126 N.J.Super. 460, 315 A.2d 424 (1974)[5] struck down ordinances which banned political signs in residential zones. City of Antioch v. Candidates' Outdoor Graphic Service, 557 F.Supp. 52 (N.D.Cal.1982), held that an ordinance which imposed a year-round ban on political signs except for 60 days prior to an election was unconstitutional because it was not the least drastic means of protecting visual amenities and aesthetics. In striking down a durational limit on political signs in Outdoor Systems, Inc. v City of Merriam, Kan., 67 F.Supp.2d 1258 (D.Kan.1999), the Court said, "[n]early every court to address the issue has held that the government interest in aesthetics and safety is insufficient to justify a durational restriction on political signs in residential districts." See also,

---

5. Also see two subsequent New Jersey cases, State v. J. & J. Painting, 167 N.J.Super. 384, 400 A.2d 1204 (1979), holding that the commercial speech doctrine did not require that defendants be allowed to place temporary advertising signs on the lawns of houses they were in process of painting or roofing, and State v. Miller, 83 N.J. 402, 416 A.2d 821 (1980), holding that free speech protected defendant's political expression in placing a large sign in his front yard welcoming prospective residents to "this flood hazard area."

Sec. 1   **AESTHETICS AND ARCHITECTURAL CONTROL**   847

Sugarman v. Village of Chester, 192 F.Supp.2d 282 (S.D.N.Y.2002) invalidating the sign regulations of more than 19 separate municipalities in the county as they applied to political signs. Also, compare Abel v. Town of Orangetown, 724 F.Supp. 232 (S.D.N.Y.1989) (upholding ordinance prohibiting candidates from posting signs on public property) with Klein v. Baise, 708 F.Supp. 863 (N.D.Ill.1989) (enjoining enforcement of a state law prohibiting advertising on bus shelters on behalf of a political candidate).

10. Local sign ordinances must contain sufficient criteria for the reviewing authority (e.g. the building inspector, planning director, etc.) to prevent an abuse of discretion. In Lamar Advertising Co. v. City of Douglasville, Georgia, 254 F.Supp.2d 1321 (N.D.Ga.2003) the Court said, "...City officials are to consider the value of the surrounding property, the environment of the surrounding property, the public good, and the purpose of the zoning ordinance before granting or denying a variance. Pursuant to *Lady J. Lingerie, [Inc. v City of Jacksonville*, 176 F.3d 1358 (11th Cir.1999),] the breadth of these criteria provides the City unbridled discretion in granting and denying the right to post signs..." See also, North Olmstead Chamber of Commerce v City of North Olmstead, 86 F.Supp.2d 755 (N.D.Ohio 2000); Lawson v City of Kankakee, Ill., 81 F.Supp.2d 930 (C.D.Ill.2000); and Young v. City of Roseville, 78 F.Supp.2d 970 (D.Minn.1999).

11. According to Scenic America and the Congressional Research Service, there are at least 425,000 to 450,000 billboards lining America's federal-aid highways, with an average growth of 5,000 to 15,000 signs annually. See, http://www.scenic.org/hba_facts.htm.

A Note on the Federal Highway Beautification Act

On October 22, 1965, the Federal Highway Beautification Act took effect. Some of the political and interpretive problems under this act are commented on by Netherton and Markham in Roadside Development and Beautification: Legal Authority and Methods 11–15 (Highway Research Board, 1966):

Public Policy and the Highway Beautification Act of 1965

Major efforts were made by both the Administration and the Congress to define the public policy on which the Highway Beautification Act of 1965 was based, and not since the mid–1950's, when the present multi-billion dollar highway program was launched, has as voluminous a legislative history been produced for a Federal-aid highway law. Commencing with the President's Message on Natural Beauty in February, 1965, the formulation of policy was continued in a White House Conference on Natural Beauty in May, Congressional hearings in July and August, legislative debates leading to enactment of a law in October, and a series of special briefings for state officials, industry and non-governmental groups in November and December.

It is therefore ironical that despite this background the governmental agencies responsible for enacting and administering this law, the industries and groups affected by it, and the general public were, at the close of 1965, still uncertain about the policy of the law and the extent to which they favored it. Strong minority views in Congress apparently remained unreconciled by perfecting amendments to the original bill, and affected industries and organizations adopted a wait-and-see attitude toward features of the new program on which they had reservations. To some degree this atmosphere was also reflected by the remark of the President, upon signing the Highway Beautification Act: "This bill does not represent everything that we wanted. It does not represent what we need. It does not represent what the national interest requires. But it is a first step, and there will be other steps."[6]

Examining the policy of the highway beautification law first in its most basic terms, a starting point is provided by the President's statement that:

> "In a nation of continental size, transportation is essential to the growth and prosperity of the national economy. But that economy, and the roads that serve it, are not ends in themselves. They are meant to serve the real needs of the people of this country. And those needs include the opportunity to touch nature and see beauty, as well as rising income and swifter travel. Therefore, we must make sure that the massive resources we now devote to roads also serve to improve and broaden the quality of American life."[7]

It is evident that in 1965 the Administration proposed and the Congress agreed to the addition of a new dimension to the national Federal-aid highway policy. This new dimension extended the public interest to include what the President called "a new conservation * * * to protect the countryside, save it from destruction, and restore what has been destroyed * * *. [T]his new conservation must not be just the classic conservation of protection and development, but a creative conservation of restoration and innovation."[8] It clearly implied that henceforth highways should be viewed not only as facilities of transportation but as features of the community and environment, and that environmental quality ranked with engineering quality in roadbuilding.

* * *

The evident intention of Congress to define the public interest in highway beautification in such a way that hardship on roadside industry and landowners would be minimized led to further changes in Federal highway policy. While excepting commercial and industrial areas from the prohibitory features of effective billboard control, the law did make permitted structures in these areas subject to standards for size, spacing and lighting to be promulgated by the Secretary of Commerce. However, prior to enactment of this bill, the Secretary of Commerce advised the Congress of his intention that "such regulations insofar as they are consistent with the purposes of this act, shall be helpful to the advertising industry, and that, for instance, standards of size which may be adopted would be insofar as possible consistent with standard size billboards in customary use."[12] The presence of

---

6. White House Press Release, "Remarks of the President at the Signing Ceremony of the Highway Beautification Act," October 22, 1965.

7. House Report 1084, 89th Cong., 1st Session, "Highway Beautification Act of 1965," September 22, 1965, p. 2.

8. Statement by the President in A Report on Natural Beauty to the President from the Secretaries of Interior, Agriculture, Commerce, H.E.W., the Administrator of HHFA and Director of Office of Equal Opportunity, October 1, 1965.

12. House of Representatives, Report No. 1048, 89th Cong., 1st Sess., September 22, 1965, p. 5.

this statement in the legislative history of the beautification law raises a question as to the extent that standards of control for outdoor advertising should, in effect, be those developed by the advertising industry for promotion of practices it may desire, as opposed to those which existing local zoning and public desires may call for.

A similar question arises with respect to the Federal law's requirement that states pay just compensation to landowners and billboard owners when signs lawfully placed prior to the establishment of controls are removed. The law's legislative history makes it clear that Congress felt that "equity and fairness" required that those who lose their signs should receive compensation for the economic distress which regulation may cause. By so providing, however, it would seem that Congress is voluntarily extending the concept of public responsibility for the economic consequences of the highway program to new limits, building upon precedents established earlier in authorizing use of Federal aid funds for payment of the cost of relocating utility facilities and displaced persons. In these earlier cases, however, the policy of Congress was limited to authorizing payment when required by state law; here the payment appears as a mandatory feature of Federal aid.

The Highway Beautification Act of 1965 further expanded the scope of the public interest to include the special needs of the motoring public for information regarding automotive services and accommodations during travel. As substantial segments of the Interstate System have been opened for use, experience with controlled-access highway travel has convinced many that additional information facilities were needed. Therefore, the 1965 legislation authorized state highway departments to maintain maps, and permit directories and advertising pamphlets to be made available to motorists at information centers in safety rest areas adjacent to the highway.

One further provision representing an addition to Federal-aid policy, which Congress considered to be among the most important features of the 1965 act, related to exercise of administrative authority delegated to the Secretary of Commerce. Under the law, the Secretary was called upon, in conjunction with the states, to take certain actions, including the designation of commercial and industrial zones and unzoned areas being used for commercial or industrial purposes, and promulgation of standards for certain aspects of outdoor advertising control and the screening of junk-yards within areas where their continued presence was permitted. In the event that the Secretary and a state failed to agree on one of these matters the determination of the Secretary overrode that of the state. Thus, for the protection of all concerned, Congress provided that any state affected by the controls required under the act was entitled to a "day in court"—the right to judicial review of any determination by the Secretary that a state has failed to effectively control roadside advertising or junkyards. Preliminary to judicial review, administrative procedures (involving notice, hearing, written records and orders) prescribed in the law must be complied with.

Statutory provision for state suits against the Secretary of Commerce to determine eligibility for funds apportioned under the Federal-aid program is unprecedented in the historic Federal–State partnership for highway construction. Only once before has a state resorted to judicial processes to settle its differences with the Federal government over such a matter, and in this case the state's standing to sue without specific statutory authorization was open to serious question. Little can be ventured as to the effect of this new statutory right of the states since no experience yet exists with respect to it. Certainly, however, subordination of the Secretary's administrative judgment to that of the courts for determination of a state's eligibility for Federal aid even on a limited range of issues opens the possibility for development of a new dimension to the working relationship of the states and Federal government in the Federal-aid highway program, and adds a quasi-judicial character to the administrative functions of the Secretary of Commerce under this program. * * *

The 1978 amendments to the Highway Beautification Act, are very specific in requiring compensation for removal of certain signs. To put the problem in perspective, as of Sept. 30, 1977, 463,724 billboards had been removed from along federal highways under the act, leaving 265,952. Compensation for the average billboard in 1978 was $1,500. The Federal Highway Administration estimated that about $40 million a year for 10 years would be necessary to complete removal of all billboards along federal highways. In 1978 Congress appropriated $18 million for sign removal. See Charlton, The Billboard Act is Taking Effect, Ever So Slowly, N.Y. Times, Mar. 26, 1978, p. 18E. According to a 1997 study lead by Scenic America, the 1978 amendments to the Highway Beautification Act derailed the removal of non-conforming billboards by failing to provide further federal funding for the removal of signs and pushing this expense off onto local governments. In fact, the group estimates that there are now 73,000 billboards that do not conform with Highway Beautification Act standards. See, http://www.ewg.org/reports/billboards/billboards.html.

B. THE APPEARANCE OF STRUCTURES AND OTHER AESTHETIC REGULATIONS

STATE EX REL. SAVELAND PARK HOLDING CORP. v. WIELAND

Supreme Court of Wisconsin, 1955.
269 Wis. 262, 69 N.W.2d 217, certiorari denied
350 U.S. 841, 76 S.Ct. 81, 100 L.Ed. 750.

[The lower court issued a preemptory writ of mandamus commanding defendant to issue a building permit on the ground that the ordinance under which such permit had been refused was unconstitutional and void.]

CURRIE, JUSTICE.

The sole issue on this appeal is the constitutionality of ordinance No. 129 of the village of Fox Point, adopted by the village board of said village on July 23, 1946.

Sec. 1 of such ordinance provides as follows:

"No building permit for any structure for which a building permit is required shall be issued unless it has been found as a fact by the Building Board by at least a majority vote, after a view of the site of the proposed structure, and an examination of the application papers for a building permit, which shall include exterior elevations of the proposed structure, that the exterior architectural appeal and functional plan of the proposed structure will, when erected, not be so at variance with either the exterior architectural appeal and functional plan of the structures already constructed or in the course of construction in the immediate neighborhood or the character of the applicable district established by Ordinance No. 117 [the general zoning ordinance of the village], or any ordinance amendatory thereof or supplementary thereto, as to cause a substantial depreciation in the property values of said neighborhood within said applicable district."

Subsequent sections of the ordinance provide that the Building Board shall consist of three residents of the village, two of whom shall be architects, and provide a method of appeal from the decision of the Building Board to the Board of Appeals of the village.

On this appeal it is conceded that relator's application for a building permit disclosed compliance with all provisions of the general zoning ordinance of the village, and the sole reason why the defendant building inspector refused to grant the permit was the failure of the Building Board to make the necessary finding prescribed by sec. 1 of ordinance No. 129 as a prerequisite to the issuance of the permit.

The village of Fox Point was incorporated in 1926. It consists of approximately two and one-half square miles, and the entire area has been zoned for residential use only. There is, however, a small business district and a relatively small institutional district permitting churches, lodges, and municipal buildings, but the vast majority of the territory in the village is devoted to residence purposes. The village has developed into a highly desirable residential village, almost entirely built up of single family residences.

The learned trial court held the ordinance unconstitutional on the following three grounds: (1) that the preservation of property values is not by itself a proper objective for the exercise of the police power in enacting a zoning ordinance; (2) that the ordinance essentially is concerned with aesthetics which also is not a proper basis for exercise of the police power; and (3) that the standards prescribed in the ordinance for governing the action and decision of the Building Board are so indefinite as to subject applicants for building permits to the unlimited and arbitrary discretion of such board.

* * *

We have no difficulty in arriving at the conclusion that the protection of property values is an objective which falls within the exercise of the police power to promote the "general welfare", and that it is immaterial whether the zoning ordinance is grounded solely upon such objective or that such purpose is but one of several legitimate objectives. Anything that tends to destroy property values of the inhabitants of the village necessarily adversely affects the prosperity, and therefore the general welfare, of the entire village. Just because, in the particular case now before us, property values in a limited area only of the village are at stake does not mean that such threatened depreciation of property values does not affect the general welfare of the village as a whole. If relator is permitted to erect a dwelling house on its land of such nature as to substantially depreciate the value of surrounding property, there is danger that this same thing may be repeated elsewhere within the village, thus threatening property values throughout the village.

The learned trial court held that the objective of the ordinance is grounded largely upon aesthetic considerations, which are insufficient to justify the exercise of the police power. While the ordinance does use the term "architectural appeal", a building permit is only authorized to be withheld in those cases where the architectural appeal of the proposed structure is so at variance with that of structures already constructed, or being constructed, "as to cause a substantial depreciation in the property values" in the immediate neighborhood. This court pointed out in Jefferson County v. Timmel, 261 Wis. 39, 61, 51 N.W.2d 518 (1952), that while the general rule is that the zoning power may not be exercised for purely aesthetic considerations, such rule was undergoing development. In view of the latest word spoken on the subject by the United States supreme court in Berman v. Parker, 348 U.S. 26, 75 S.Ct. 98, 99 L.Ed. 27 (1954), this development of the law has proceeded to the point that renders it extremely doubtful that such prior rule is any longer the law.

In Berman v. Parker the United States supreme court had before it the question of the constitutionality of an Act of Congress providing for slum clearance in the District of Columbia under which appellants' property was included within the boundaries of the district to be condemned for slum clearance purposes, although it was used for store purposes and in no sense constituted slum housing. Appellants urged that the act, insofar as it permitted its property to be taken for such purpose, could not be justified under the police power, but was in violation of the "due process" clause of the Fifth Amendment. The court in a unanimous opinion by Mr. Justice Douglas declared, 75 S.Ct. at pages 102, 103:

> "The concept of the public welfare is broad and inclusive. See Day-Brite Lighting Inc. v. State of Missouri, 342 U.S. 421, 424, 72 S.Ct. 405, 407, 96 L.Ed. 469. The values it represents are spiritual as well as physical, aesthetic as well as monetary. It is within the power of the legislature to determine that the community should be beautiful as well as healthy, spacious as well as clean, well-balanced as well as carefully patrolled. In the present case, the Congress and its authorized agencies have made determinations that take into account a wide variety of values. It is not for us to reappraise them. *If those*

who govern the District of Columbia decide that the Nation's capitol should be beautiful as well as sanitary, there is nothing in the Fifth Amendment that stands in the way." (Emphasis supplied.)

While the court in Berman v. Parker, supra, was dealing with the "due process" clause of the Fifth Amendment, which restricts the power of Congress, and it is the "due process" clause of the Fourteenth Amendment which is applicable to state action, we consider such distinction to be immaterial in considering the scope of the police power and its exercise to promote the general welfare.

We now come to the last issue presented, *viz.,* whether the standards set by ordinance No. 129 for governing the functioning of the Building Board of the village are so indefinite as to subject applicants for building permits to the arbitrary discretion of such board. It will be recalled that the ordinance specifically provides for an appeal from the decision of the Building Board to the village Board of Appeals, and, of course, timely court review by certiorari will always lie from the decision of the Board of Appeals.

In order for a building permit to be refused under the ordinance the Building Board must find, as a fact, that the exterior architectural appeal and the proposed plan of structure when erected shall not be so at variance with those of structures already constructed, or in the course of construction, "in the immediate neighborhood" * * * "as to cause a *substantial* depreciation in the property values of said *neighborhood.*" The two words of the ordinance which have been singled out as being most objectionable from the standpoint of indefiniteness are "*neighborhood*" and "*substantial*".

While several cases are cited in which courts have been called upon to define the term "*neighborhood*" we consider the decision of the Iowa court in Youtzy v. City of Cedar Rapids, 150 Iowa 53, 129 N.W. 351 (1911), as being the most helpful. That case involved the taking of land by condemnation, and complaint was made by the appellant land owner that witnesses had been permitted to testify as to sale prices of lands which were so far removed as to not be located in the neighborhood of the property being condemned. The Iowa court, in its opinion, conceded that property to be used by way of comparison or illustration "should be in the same neighborhood or so nearly similar to the one in question that knowledge of the former, and of its value, will afford some degree of aid to the intelligent and fair-minded juror in estimating the value of the latter." It then proceeded to define "*neighborhood*", and stated:

"The term neighborhood is one of quite indefinite meaning, and it may well be that in some cases the trial court will permit the inquiry to take a wider territorial range than it could allow in others. Certainly this court cannot attempt to fix a standard of measurement, and say as a matter of law that the similar property concerning which inquiry may be found within a given number of feet, yards, or blocks of the property condemned. Counsel for appellant argues, in effect, that, as the word has been used in cases of this class, 'neighborhood' has reference only to adjoining property, but we think that this cannot be. The reasonable proposition is that the trial court is vested with discretion to draw the line in each case as shall seem just under all the circumstances developed by the testimony, and that, unless abuse of such discretion is shown, its ruling will not be held reversible error."

While the court in Youtzy v. Cedar Rapids, supra, was defining the term *"neighborhood"* as used in a rule of the common law, instead of a statute or ordinance, we consider the foregoing quotation equally applicable to its use in the instant case in ordinance No. 129. Clearly *"neighborhood"*, as used in the ordinance, does extend further than adjoining property and may vary according to existing conditions. For example, in a section of the village where the average building lot comprises several acres, the limits of the neighborhood might well be held to extend farther than in the case of an area in the village where building lots average less than an acre each in area.

Although it is impossible for this court in this decision to establish, in terms of measurement of feet, the radius of the largest permissible area which would qualify as a neighborhood under the ordinance, there is undoubtedly in each case a point beyond which a court could hold as a matter of law, that certain property was not in the same neighborhood as applicant's property, and that it would be an abuse of discretion if the Building Board determined otherwise. In case of a court review some effect necessarily would have to be accorded the adjective *"immediate"* preceding the word *"neighborhood"* where the latter first appears in the ordinance.

Just because some discretion is necessarily accorded the board to determine the limits of a neighborhood, as applied to a particular applicant's property, does not render the ordinance void. City of Milwaukee v. Ruplinger, 155 Wis. 391, 145 N.W. 42 (1914), and Pinkerton v. Buech, 173 Wis. 433, 181 N.W. 125 (1921). In the first mentioned of said two cases, this court upheld an ordinance of the plaintiff city which prohibited anyone from carrying on a junk shop in the city without a license, and further provided [155 Wis. 391, 145 N.W. 43] " 'all applications for license under this ordinance shall be made to the mayor who may grant or refuse to grant such license as to him may seem best for the good order of the city.' " The court held the ordinance granting to the mayor the power to grant or refuse licenses " *'as to him may seem best for the good order of the city'* " set a sufficiently definite standard, and held the ordinance constitutional. In the Pinkerton case the constitutionality of a statute providing for the licensing of private detectives was upheld which required the approval of the application by the fire and police commission of the city and a finding by the secretary of state that the applicant was *"of good character, competency and integrity."*

Turning now to the word *"substantial"* which has also been attacked by relator as being too indefinite, we find that the Washington supreme court in In re Krause's Estate, 173 Wash. 1, 21 P.2d 268, 270

(1933), held that the term *"substantially"* was not so indefinite as to render a contract employing it to be unenforceable. The particular contract provided "neither party shall have the right to make a new will as to property which has pursuant hereto been *substantially* benefited by the other party," with respect to which the court stated:

> "Substantial" as an adjective means something worthwhile as distinguished from something without value, or merely nominal.

This court is frequently required to apply the wording of section 227.20(1)(d), Stats., "unsupported by substantial evidence in view of the entire record", in cases involving review of determinations by administrative agencies under our uniform Administrative Procedure Act. We do not recall of any litigant ever having raised the question that the word "substantial" therein rendered such quoted portion of the statute indefinite and void.

Determining whether or not a proposed structure will *"substantially"* depreciate property values in the area is simply the reverse of the common question that must be answered in the assessing of benefits resulting from a public improvement in levying a special assessment against the benefited property. There the question must be determined whether or not the public improvement benefits property, and if so what property and to what extent.

It is our considered judgment that ordinance No. 129 constitutes a valid exercise of the police power of the village of Fox Point, and its provisions are not so indefinite or ambiguous as to subject applicants for building permits to the uncontrolled arbitrary discretion or caprice of the Building Board.

Judgment reversed and cause remanded with directions to quash the proceedings.

Note

Compare the case of Waterfront Estates Development, Inc. v. City of Palos Hills, 232 Ill.App.3d 367, 173 Ill.Dec. 667, 597 N.E.2d 641 (1992) where the court found that the ordinance creating the city's appearance commission was an overbroad delegation of authority, and that the ordinance was unconstitutionally vague. The defendant unsuccessfully argued that the appearance commission only acted in an advisory capacity making recommendations to the city council.

STATE EX REL. STOYANOFF v. BERKELEY

Supreme Court of Missouri, Division No. 2, 1970.
458 S.W.2d 305.

PRITCHARD, COMMISSIONER.

Upon summary judgment the trial court issued a peremptory writ of mandamus to compel appellant to issue a residential building permit to respondents. The trial court's judgment is that the below-mentioned ordinances are violative of Section 10, Article I of the Constitution of

Missouri, 1945, V.A.M.S., in that restrictions placed by the ordinances on the use of property deprive the owners of their property without due process of law. Relators' petition pleads that they applied to appellant Building Commissioner for a building permit to allow them to construct a single family residence in the City of Ladue, and that plans and specifications were submitted for the proposed residence, which was unusual in design, "but complied with all existing building and zoning regulations and ordinances of the City of Ladue, Missouri."

It is further pleaded that relators were refused a building permit for the construction of their proposed residence upon the ground that the permit was not approved by the Architectural Board of the City of Ladue. Ordinance 131, as amended by Ordinance 281 of that city, purports to set up an Architectural Board to approve plans and specifications for buildings and structures erected within the city and in a preamble to "conform to certain minimum architectural standards of appearance and conformity with surrounding structures, and that unsightly, grotesque and unsuitable structures, detrimental to the stability of value and the welfare of surrounding property, structures and residents, and to the general welfare and happiness of the community, be avoided, and that appropriate standards of beauty and conformity be fostered and encouraged." It is asserted in the petition that the ordinances are invalid, illegal and void, "are unconstitutional in that they are vague and provide no standard nor uniform rule by which to guide the architectural board," that the city acted in excess of statutory powers (§ 89.020, RSMo 1959, V.A.M.S.) in enacting the ordinances, which "attempt to allow respondent to impose aesthetic standards for buildings in the City of Ladue, and are in excess of the powers granted the City of Ladue by said statute."

Relators filed a motion for summary judgment and affidavits were filed in opposition thereto. Richard D. Shelton, Mayor of the City of Ladue, deponed that the facts in appellant's answer were true and correct, as here pertinent: that the City of Ladue constitutes one of the finer suburban residential areas of Metropolitan St. Louis, the homes therein are considerably more expensive than in cities of comparable size, being homes on lots from three fourths of an acre to three or more acres each; * * * It is then pleaded that relators' description of their proposed residence as " 'unusual in design' is the understatement of the year. It is in fact a monstrosity of grotesque design, which would seriously impair the value of property in the neighborhood."

The affidavit of Harold C. Simon, a developer of residential subdivisions in St. Louis County, is that he is familiar with relators' lot upon which they seek to build a house, and with the surrounding houses in the neighborhood; that the houses therein existent are virtually all two-story houses of conventional architectural design, such as Colonial, French Provincial or English; and that the house which relators propose to construct is of ultramodern design which would clash with and not be in conformity with any other house in the entire neighborhood. It is Mr. Simon's opinion that the design and appearance of relators' proposed

Sec. 1   **AESTHETICS AND ARCHITECTURAL CONTROL**   **857**

residence would have a substantial adverse effect upon the market values of other residential property in the neighborhood, such average market value ranging from $60,000 to $85,000 each.

As a part of the affidavit of Russell H. Riley, consultant for the city planning and engineering firm of Harland Bartholomew & Associates, photographic exhibits of homes surrounding relators' lot were attached. * * * In substance Mr. Riley went on to say that the City of Ladue is one of the finer residential suburbs in the St. Louis area with a minimum of commercial or industrial usage. The development of residences in the city has been primarily by private subdivisions, usually with one main lane or drive leading therein (such as Lorenzo Road Subdivision which runs north off of Ladue Road in which relators' lot is located). The homes are considerably more expensive than average homes found in a city of comparable size. The ordinance which has been adopted by the City of Ladue is typical of those which have been adopted by a number of suburban cities in St. Louis County and in similar cities throughout the United States, the need therefor being based upon the protection of existing property values by preventing the construction of houses that are in complete conflict with the general type of houses in a given area. The intrusion into this neighborhood of relators' unusual, grotesque and nonconforming structure would have a substantial adverse effect on market values of other homes in the immediate area. According to Mr. Riley the standards of Ordinance 131, as amended by Ordinance 281, are usually and customarily applied in city planning work and are: "(1) whether the proposed house meets the customary architectural requirements in appearance and design for a house of the particular type which is proposed (whether it be Colonial, Tudor English, French Provincial, or Modern), (2) whether the proposed house is in general conformity with the style and design of surrounding structures, and (3) whether the proposed house lends itself to the proper architectural development of the City; and that in applying said standards the Architectural Board and its Chairman are to determine whether the proposed house will have an adverse affect on the stability of values in the surrounding area."

Photographic exhibits of relators' proposed residence were also attached to Mr. Riley's affidavit. They show the residence to be of a pyramid shape, with a flat top, and with triangular shaped windows or doors at one or more corners.

* * *

Section 89.020 provides: "For the purpose of promoting health, safety, morals or the general welfare of the community, the legislative body of all cities, towns, and villages is hereby empowered to regulate and restrict the height, number of stories, and size of buildings and other structures, the percentage of lot that may be occupied, the size of yards, courts, and other open spaces, the density of population, the preservation of features of historical significance, and the location and use of buildings, structures and land for trade, industry, residence or other purposes." Section 89.040 provides: "Such regulations shall be made in accordance with a comprehensive plan and designed to lessen congestion in the streets; to secure safety from fire, panic and other dangers; to promote health *and the general welfare;* to provide adequate light and air; to prevent the overcrowding of land; to avoid undue concentration of population; to preserve features of historical significance; to facilitate the adequate provision of transportation, water, sewerage, schools, parks, and other public requirements. *Such regulations shall be made with reasonable consideration, among other things, to the character of the district and its peculiar suitability for particular uses, and with a view to conserving the values of buildings and encouraging the most appropriate use of land throughout such municipality.*" (Italics added.)

Relators say that "Neither Sections 89.020 or 89.040 nor any other provision of Chapter 89 mentions or gives a city the authority to regulate architectural design and appearance. There exists no provision providing for an architectural board and no entity even remotely resembling such a board is mentioned under the enabling legislation." Relators conclude that the City of Ladue lacked any power to adopt Ordinance 131 as amended by Ordinance 281 "and its intrusion into this area is wholly unwarranted and without sanction in the law." As to this aspect of the appeal relators rely upon the 1961 decision of State ex rel. Magidson v. Henze, Mo.App., 342 S.W.2d 261. That case had the identical question presented. An Architectural Control Commission was set up by an ordinance of the City of University City. In its report to the Building Commissioner, the Architectural Control Commission disapproved the Magidson application for permits to build four houses. It was commented that the proposed houses did not provide for the minimum number of square feet, and "In considering the existing character of this neighborhood, the Commission is of the opinion that houses of the character proposed in these plans are not in harmony with and will not contribute to nor protect the general welfare of this neighborhood" (loc. cit. 264). The court held that § 89.020, RSMo1949, V.A.M.S., does not grant to the city the right to impose upon the landowner aesthetic standards for the buildings he chooses to erect.

As is clear from the affidavits and attached exhibits, the City of Ladue is an area composed principally of residences of the general types of Colonial, French Provincial and English Tudor. The city has a comprehensive plan of zoning to maintain the general character of buildings therein. The Magidson case, supra, did not consider the effect of § 89.040, supra, and the italicized portion relating to the character of the district, its suitability for particular uses, and the conservation of the values of buildings therein. These considerations, sanctioned by statute, are directly related to the general welfare of the community. That proposition has support in a number of cases cited by appellant. State ex rel. Carter v. Harper, Building Commissioner, 182 Wis. 148, 196 N.W. 451, 454, quotes Chicago B. & Q. Ry. Co. v. People of State of Illinois ex rel. Drainage Commissioners, 200 U.S. 561, 26 S.Ct. 341, 50 L.Ed. 596, 609, " 'We hold that the police power of a state embraces regulations designed to promote the public convenience or the general prosperity, as well as regulations designed to promote the public health, the public morals or the public safety.'" In Marrs v. City of Oxford (D.C.D.Kan.) 24 F.2d 541, 548, it was said, "The stabilizing of property values, and giving some assurance to the public that, if property is purchased in a residential district, its value as such will be preserved, is probably the most cogent reason back of zoning ordinances." See also People v. Calvar Corporation et al., Sup., 69 N.Y.S.2d 272, 279 (aff'd 286 N.Y. 419, 36 N.E.2d 644); Kovacs v. Cooper, Judge, 336 U.S. 77, 69 S.Ct. 448, 93 L.Ed. 513, 526; Wulfsohn v. Burden, 241 N.Y. 288, 150 N.E. 120, 122[3], 43 A.L.R. 651; and Price et al. v. Schwafel (Cal.), 92 Cal.App.2d 77, 206 P.2d 683, 685. The preamble to Ordinance 131, quoted above in part, demonstrates that its purpose is to conform to the dictates of § 89.040, with reference to preserving values of property by zoning procedure and restrictions on the use of property. This is an illustration of what was referred to in Deimeke v. State Highway Commission, Mo., 444 S.W.2d 480, 484, as a growing number of cases recognizing a change in the scope of the term "general welfare." In the Deimeke case on the same page it is said, "Property use which offends sensibilities and debases property values affects not only the adjoining property owners in that vicinity but the general public as well because when such property values are destroyed or seriously impaired, the tax base of the community is affected and the public suffers economically as a result."

Relators say further that Ordinances 131 and 281 are invalid and unconstitutional as being an unreasonable and arbitrary exercise of the police power. It is argued that a mere reading of these ordinances shows that they are based entirely on aesthetic factors in that the stated purpose of the Architectural Board is to maintain "conformity with surrounding structures" and to assure that structures "conform to certain minimum architectural standards of appearance." The argument ignores the further provisos in the ordinance: " * * * and that unsightly, grotesque and unsuitable structures, *detrimental to the stability of value and the welfare of surrounding property, structures, and residents,* and *to the general welfare and happiness of the community,* be avoided, and that appropriate standards of beauty and conformity be fostered and encouraged." (Italics added.) Relators' proposed residence does not descend to the " 'patently offensive character of vehicle graveyards in close proximity to such highways' " referred to in the Deimeke case, supra (444 S.W.2d 484). Nevertheless, the aesthetic factor to be taken into account by the Architectural Board is not to be considered alone. Along with that inherent factor is the effect that the proposed residence would have upon the property values in the area. In this time of burgeoning urban areas, congested with people and structures, it is certainly in keeping with the ultimate ideal of general welfare that the Architectural Board, in its function, preserve and protect existing areas in which structures of a general conformity of architecture have been erected. The area under consideration is clearly, from the record, a fashionable one. In State ex rel. Civello v. City of New Orleans, 154 La. 271, 97 So. 440, 444, the court said, "If by the term 'aesthetic considerations' is meant a regard merely for outward appearances, for good taste in the matter of the beauty of the neighborhood itself, we do not observe any substantial reason for saying that such a consideration is not a matter of general welfare. The beauty of a fashionable residence neighborhood in a city is for the comfort and happiness of the residents, and it sustains in a general way the value of property in the neighborhood." See also People v. Stover, 12 N.Y.2d 462, 240 N.Y.S.2d 734, 191 N.E.2d 272, 274[3]; State ex rel. Saveland Park Holding Corp. v. Wieland, 269 Wis. 262, 69 N.W.2d 217, 222; Reid v. Architectural Board of Review of the City of Cleveland Heights, 119 Ohio App. 67, 192 N.E.2d 74, 77; and Oregon City v. Hartke, 240 Or. 35, 400 P.2d 255, 261, for pronouncements of the principle that aesthetics is a factor to be considered in zoning matters.

* * * The denial by appellant of a building permit for relators' highly modernistic residence in this area where traditional Colonial, French Provincial and English Tudor styles of architecture are erected does not appear to be arbitrary and unreasonable when the basic purpose to be served is that of the general welfare of persons in the entire community.

In addition to the above-stated purpose in the preamble to Ordinance 131, it establishes an Architectural Board of three members, all of whom must be architects. Meetings of the Board are to be open to the public, and every application for a building permit, except those not affecting the outward appearance of a building, shall be submitted to the Board along with plans, elevations, detail drawings and specifications, before being approved by the Building Commissioner. The Chairman of the Board shall examine the application to determine if it conforms to proper architectural standards in appearance and design and will be in general conformity with the style and design of surrounding structures and conducive to the proper architectural development of the city. If he so finds, he approves and returns the application to the Building Commissioner. If he does not find conformity, or has doubt, a full meeting of the Board is called, with notice of the time and place thereof given to the applicant. The Board shall disapprove the application if it determines the proposed structure will constitute an unsightly, grotesque or unsuitable structure in appearance, detrimental to the welfare of surrounding property or residents. If it cannot make that decision, the application shall be returned to the Building Commissioner either with or without suggestions or recommendations, and if that is done without disapproval, the Building Commissioner may issue the permit. If the Board's disapproval is given and the applicant refuses to comply with recommendations, the Building Commissioner shall refuse the permit. Thereafter provisions are made for an appeal to the Council of the city for review of the decision of the Architectural Board. Ordinance 281 amends Ordinance 131 only with respect to the application initially being submitted to and considered by all members of the Architectural Board.

Relators claim that the above provisions of the ordinance amount to an unconstitutional delegation of power by the city to the Architectural

Board. It is argued that the Board cannot be given the power to determine what is unsightly and grotesque and that the standards, "whether the proposed structure will conform to proper architectural standards in appearance and design, and will be in general conformity with the style and design of surrounding structures and conducive to the proper architectural development of the City * * *" and "the Board shall disapprove the application if it determines that the proposed structure will constitute an unsightly, grotesque or unsuitable structure in appearance, detrimental to the welfare of surrounding property or residents * * *," are inadequate. * * * Ordinances 131 and 281 are sufficient in their general standards calling for a factual determination of the suitability of any proposed structure with reference to the character of the surrounding neighborhood and to the determination of any adverse effect on the general welfare and preservation of property values of the community. Like holdings were made involving Architectural Board ordinances in State ex rel. Saveland Park Holding Corp. v. Wieland, 269 Wis. 262, 69 N.W.2d 217, and Reid v. Architectural Board of Review of the City of Cleveland Heights, 119 Ohio App. 67, 192 N.E.2d 74, supra.

The judgment is reversed.

Notes

1. Do the two principal cases indicate that aesthetic considerations alone may not be sufficient to sustain the police power, and that support for architectural review boards must be also found in the general welfare aspect of the police power as used to sustain property values? On the point of whether aesthetic considerations affect the validity of the zoning ordinance see the annotation in 21 A.L.R.3d 1222, and on architectural design regulations, see the annotation in 41 A.L.R.3d 1397.

2. In Guinnane v. San Francisco City Planning Comm'n, 209 Cal. App.3d 732, 257 Cal.Rptr. 742 (1989), the court upheld the denial of a permit for a four-story house with five bedrooms, five bathrooms, and parking for two cars. Although the proposed house was in conformance with all the zoning and building regulations, the permit was denied because the height, length, bulk, and area of the planned house would not be in character with the surrounding residences which were significantly smaller. The court rejected the argument that there were no specific standards to guide the planning commission, stating that this was the type of decision properly left to the sound discretion of the agency.

In most jurisdictions courts require the issuance of permits when all requirements of the ordinance have been met.

3. Not all of the modern cases support the validity of architectural review. For example, in Anderson v. City of Issaquah, 70 Wash.App. 64, 851 P.2d 744 (1993), the City's "aesthetic zoning" ordinance was ruled unconstitutional for vagueness. The Building Design section of the City ordinance provided in part, "Monotony of design in single or multiple building projects shall be avoided. Efforts should be made to create an interesting project by use of complimentary details, functional orientation of buildings, parting and

access provisions and relating the development to the site." The Court found that the commissioners had no objective guidelines to follow and that they "...enforced not a building design code but their own arbitrary concept of the provision of an unwritten 'statement'... This is the very epitome of discretionary, arbitrary enforcement of the law." See, Paul J. Weinberg and Nola McGuire, "Design Regulations and Architecture: Collision Course?" 22 Zoning and Planning Law Report (November 1999).

4. Many municipalities have established architectural review boards. What should be the appropriate powers and duties of these boards? How should these boards work with respect to planning boards and zoning boards? See, Diller and Fisher Co., Inc. v. Architectural Review Board of Borough of Stone Harbour, 246 N.J.Super. 362, 587 A.2d 674 (1990) (holding that the local ordinance empowering the borough's architectural review board to examine, review, approve, or disapprove, because of location, quality, and appropriateness of design, applications for permits for signs in business and light industry districts was an improper arrogation of authority that was vested in borough's zoning board).

5. In an article entitled, "Billboards, Glass Houses, and the Law," which appeared in the April, 1966, edition of Harper's Magazine, Richard F. Babcock, member of the Illinois Bar, stated at page 30:[13]

> Artistic creativeness is a function of the individual, and we social scientists, concerned with the place of grace in urban design, will have either to choose government by a Borgia or, if we insist upon a government of burghers, to declare design off-limits, for the politicians. The rub is that if we opt for the dictator we may get Dr. Goebbels rather than a Renaissance prince. So my choice, even at the cultural level, is to go for democracy but insist that design is not the function of government, except in the following limited area:
>
> First, we should be heartened by the evidence that a representative government is concerned enough to encourage the untried and the different in design and in any of the other arts. This is a different breed of cat from a command by government, municipal or federal, that design must conform to the established order. Nor do I regard as inconsistent with my thesis governmental efforts to preserve, by eminent domain or by regulation, those features of the man-made landscape that by any definition are landmarks of our heritage. And I do not regard as difficult the distinction that must be made between a thousand homogeneous suburbs and a Beacon Hill; a Galena, Illinois; portions of San Antonio; or the unique nineteenth-century square in Woodstock, Illinois. I am even ready to concede that from this exception it must logically follow that we must be prepared to preserve one or perhaps two postwar suburbs * * * which proves beyond question my devotion to logic if not to beauty!
>
> Second, government cannot abdicate its duty to select which natural amenities shall be shielded from any scheme of man. (The only issue here is whether government must pay or can achieve the result by regulation.) The government, local and national, must play the domi-

---

13. Copyright © 1966, by Harper's Magazine, Inc. Reprinted from the April, 1966 issue of Harper's Magazine by permission of the author.

nant role in any debate over whether any construction shall be permitted along the Chicago lakefront; whether a hydroelectric project on the Hudson River should be constructed irrespective of the consequences to historic landmarks and natural beauty; whether the Allagash River in Maine or the Dinosaur Area or the Redwoods or the Dunes shall be preserved or sacrificed for the economic best interest of the country; and whether the public view of San Francisco Bay shall be spoiled.

Third, government can and should identify those circumstances where design in the private sector will have a demonstrable impact upon public services. Government must prescribe the perimeters of the choices allowed the designer in such cases. If, for example, one accepts the premise that building bulk and density do have an impact on the efficiency of public services such as streets, sanitation, and schools, then one can more readily accept regulation designed to protect these facilities that may limit freedom of choice by the designer.

Finally, the government should offer incentives to the builder to provide more open space than would otherwise be required. The Chicago zoning ordinance grants a bonus in the form of additional permitted floor area to the builder who will provide greater open space at ground level. Some suburban ordinances will permit a greater number of dwelling units per acre to the developer who clusters his houses, thereby creating more usable common open space. (Both are examples of what baseball vice presidents call the "natural trade." The developer gets increased gross revenues, the city gets additional open space.)

Beyond these limits I fear to go in the regulation of design.

6. Should government regulate the display of artwork placed on the lawn of individual homeowners? Does this raise First Amendment concerns? Should certain artwork be considered inappropriate for display in a neighborhood? See, Galina Krasilovsky, "A Sculpture is Worth a Thousand Words: The First Amendment Rights of Homeowners Publicly Displaying Art on Private Property," 20 Colum. VLA J. L. & Arts 521 (1996) [The author beings with a true story of a sculptor and art professor who placed several large sculptures of her own creating on the front lawn of her New Jersey home, including an 11–foot high steel and fiberglass memorial to the Holocaust depicting a father, mother and young son in a somber procession, suitcases in hand.] When the neighbors complain about the display of art, what should the appropriate courses of action? See, Russ Versteeg, "Iguanas, Toads and Toothbrushes: Land–Use Regulation of Art as Signage," 25 Ga. L. Rev. 437 (1991).

PEOPLE v. STOVER

Court of Appeals of New York, 1963.
12 N.Y.2d 462, 240 N.Y.S.2d 734, 191 N.E.2d 272, appeal dismissed
375 U.S. 42, 84 S.Ct. 147, 11 L.Ed.2d 107 (1963).

FULD, JUDGE.

The defendants, Mr. and Mrs. Stover, residents of the City of Rye since 1940, live in a 2½–story 1–family dwelling, located in a pleasant and built-up residential district, on the corner of Rye Beach and Forest

Avenues. A clothesline, filled with old clothes and rags, made its first appearance in the Stovers' front yard in 1956 as a form of "peaceful protest" against the high taxes imposed by the city. And, during each of the five succeeding years, the defendants added another clothesline to mark their continued displeasure with the taxes. In 1961, therefore, six lines, from which there hung tattered clothing, old uniforms, underwear, rags and scarecrows, were strung across the Stovers' yard—three from the porch across the front yard to trees along Forest Avenue and three from the porch across the side yard to trees along Rye Beach Avenue.

In August of 1961, the city enacted an ordinance prohibiting the erection and maintenance of clotheslines or other devices for hanging clothes or other fabrics in a front or side yard abutting a street (General Ordinances, § 4–3.7). However, the ordinance provides for the issuance of a permit for the use of such clotheslines if there is "a practical difficulty or unnecessary hardship in drying clothes elsewhere on the premises" and grants a right of appeal to the applicant if a permit is denied.[14]

Following enactment of the ordinance, Mrs. Stover, the record owner of the property, applied for a permit to maintain clotheslines in her yard. Her application was denied because, she was advised, she had sufficient other property available for hanging clothes and she was directed to remove the clotheslines which were in the yards abutting the streets. Although no appeal was taken from this determination and no permit ever issued, the clotheslines were not removed. Relying upon the ordinance, the city thereupon charged the defendants with violating its provisions. They were tried and convicted and their judgments of conviction have been affirmed by the County Court of Westchester County. Upon the trial the defendant Webster Stover disputed the sufficiency of the evidence to connect him with the erection or maintenance of the clotheslines but he does not do so here, urging instead that the ordinance, as it has been applied to him and his wife, is unconstitutional both as an interference with free speech and as a deprivation of property without due process.[15]

14. The full text of the ordinance reads in this way (General Ordinance, § 4–3.7):

"*Clothes lines.* No clothes lines, drying racks, poles or other similar devices for hanging clothes, rags or other fabrics shall be erected or maintained in a front yard or side yard abutting a street. If there is a practical difficulty or unnecessary hardship in drying clothes elsewhere on the premises, a permit shall be issued by the City Clerk permitting the use of said front or side yard for such purpose upon approval of and a finding by the Building Inspector that drying of clothes elsewhere on the premises would create a practical difficulty or unnecessary hardship. If a permit is denied, the applicant may appeal to the Board of Appeals of this city. The provisions of this section shall be applicable to existing conditions."

15. We merely note that the proof of Mr. Stover's participation is more than ample to support the conviction. He not only acknowledged, at a public hearing before the Rye City Council, that he had erected the lines as a protest against his taxes and was leaving them there "until he got some action on his assessment" but he alleged the same thing in a complaint in a declaratory judgment action which he and his wife had instituted against the city.

It is a fair inference that adoption of the ordinance before us was prompted by the conduct and action of the defendants but we deem it clear that, if the law would otherwise be held constitutional, it will not be stricken as discriminatory or invalid because of its motivation. Cf. Town of Hempstead v. Goldblatt, 9 N.Y.2d 101, 211 N.Y.S.2d 185, 172 N.E.2d 562, affirmed 369 U.S. 590, 82 S.Ct. 987, 8 L.Ed.2d 130. Our problem, therefore, is to determine whether the law violates First Amendment rights or otherwise exceeds the police power vested in a city on the ground that it was enacted without regard to considerations of public health, safety and welfare.

The People maintain that the prohibition against clotheslines in front and side yards was "intended to provide clear visibility at street corners and in driving out of driveways, and thus avoid and reduce accidents; to reduce distractions to motorists and pedestrians; and to provide greater opportunity for access in the event of fires". Although there may be considerable doubt whether there is a sufficiently reasonable relationship between clotheslines and traffic or fire safety to support an exercise of the police power, it is our opinion that the ordinance may be sustained as an attempt to preserve the residential appearance of the city and its property values by banning, insofar as practicable, unsightly clotheslines from yards abutting a public street. In other words, the statute, though based on what may be termed aesthetic considerations, proscribes conduct which offends sensibilities and tends to debase the community and reduce real estate values.

There are a number of early decisions, both in this State * * * and elsewhere * * *, which hold that aesthetic considerations are not alone sufficient to justify exercise of the police power. But since 1930 this court has taken pains repeatedly to declare that the issue is an open and "unsettled" one in New York. People v. Rubenfeld, 254 N.Y. 245, 248–249, 172 N.E. 485, 486–487; see, also, Perlmutter v. Greene, 259 N.Y. 327, 332, 182 N.E. 5, 6, 81 A.L.R. 1543; New York State Thruway Auth. v. Ashley Motor Ct., Inc., 10 N.Y.2d 151, 156–157, 218 N.Y.S.2d 640, 642–643, 176 N.E.2d 566, 568–569. In addition, we have actually recognized the governmental interest in preserving the appearance of the community by holding that, whether or not aesthetic considerations are in and of themselves sufficient to support an exercise of the police power, they may be taken into account by the legislative body in enacting laws which are also designed to promote health and safety. * * * "Aesthetic considerations", this court wrote in Dowsey v. Village of Kensington, 257 N.Y. 221, 230, 177 N.E. 427, 430, supra, "are, fortunately, not wholly without weight in a practical world."

Once it be conceded that aesthetics is a valid subject of legislative concern, the conclusion seems inescapable that reasonable legislation designed to promote that end is a valid and permissible exercise of the police power. If zoning restrictions "which implement a policy of neighborhood amenity" are to be stricken as invalid, it should be, one commentator has said, not because they seek to promote "aesthetic objectives" but solely because the restrictions constitute "unreasonable devices of implementing community policy." Dukeminier, Zoning for Aesthetic Objectives: A Reappraisal, 20 Law & Contemp.Prob. 218, 231. Consequently, whether such a statute or ordinance should be voided should depend upon whether the restriction was "an arbitrary and irrational method of achieving an attractive, efficiently functioning, prosperous community—and *not* upon whether the objectives were primarily aesthetic." Dukeminier, loc. cit. And, indeed, this view finds support in an ever-increasing number of cases from other jurisdictions which recognize that aesthetic considerations alone may warrant an exercise of the police power. * * *

Cases may undoubtedly arise, as we observed above, in which the legislative body goes too far in the name of aesthetics, cf. Matter of Mid-State Adv. Corp. v. Bond, 274 N.Y. 82, 8 N.E.2d 286; Dowsey v. Village of Kensington, 257 N.Y. 221, 177 N.E. 427, supra; Dukeminier, Zoning for Aesthetic Objectives: A Reappraisal, 20 Law & Contemp.Prob. 218, 231, but the present, quite clearly is not one of them. The ordinance before us is in large sense regulatory rather than prohibitory. It causes no undue hardship to any property owner, for it expressly provides for the issuance of a permit for clotheslines in front and side yards in cases where there is practical difficulty or unnecessary hardship in drying clothes elsewhere on the premises. Moreover, the ordinance imposes no arbitrary or capricious standard of beauty or conformity upon the community. It simply proscribes conduct which is unnecessarily offensive to the visual sensibilities of the average person. It is settled that conduct which is similarly offensive to the senses of hearing and smell may be a valid subject of regulation under the police power, see, e.g., People v. Rubenfeld, 254 N.Y. 245, 172 N.E. 485, supra, and we perceive no basis for a different result merely because the sense of sight is involved.

Nor is there any warrant or justification for a charge—which seems to have been abandoned on this appeal—that the ordinance is being enforced solely against the defendants or that there is a pattern of discrimination consciously being practiced against them. As the court below noted, the building superintendent testified, without contradiction, that all applications for permits were checked and investigated, that other applications for permits had been denied and that the defendants were the only persons who refused to remove clotheslines violative of the ordinance.

* * *

[The balance of the majority opinion, in which the court discusses the contention of the defendants that their freedom of speech had been denied them, is omitted. The court concluded that the prohibition against clotheslines had no necessary relationship to the dissemination of ideas or opinions.]

The judgment appealed from should be affirmed.

VAN VOORHIS, JUDGE (dissenting).

Sec. 1   AESTHETICS AND ARCHITECTURAL CONTROL   867

My concern in this case is not with limitation of free speech nor whether aesthetic considerations are enough in themselves to justify zoning regulations in prescribed instances, but with the extent to which a municipality can go in restricting the use of private property. The ordinance whose validity is now being upheld prohibits the erection and maintenance of clotheslines in a front or side yard abutting a street. Exceptions may be granted, and we were told upon the argument that 26 exceptions have been allowed in Rye, with the practical result that this ordinance is enforced against few others, if any, than the appellants. Even if that be held not to undermine the ordinance, it seems to me to exceed zoning powers for municipalities such as this to dictate to owners of houses and lots where they may put their clotheslines. The validity of ordinances may be tested in court according to whether the exercise of power delegated to the municipality is reasonable or arbitrary. People ex rel. City of Olean v. Western N.Y. & Pa. Traction Co., 214 N.Y. 526, 108 N.E. 847; Commissioners of Palisades Interstate Park v. Lent, 240 N.Y. 1, 147 N.E. 228. In the case last cited it was said that "What is reasonable is in large part tested by what is ordinary usage and common experience." 240 N.Y. p. 8, 147 N.E. p. 230. What has happened here is that these defendants conceived the unusual idea of hanging what the majority opinion describes as "tattered clothing, old uniforms, underwear, rags and scarecrows" across their yard as a form of protest against the amount of their taxes. The city, at the instance of other residents in the area, fought back by adopting this ordinance from the operation of which almost every other property owner applying for a permit has been excepted. Although the origin of this dispute is evidently political in nature, the validity of this ordinance is sought to be upheld entirely on the basis of aesthetic considerations, e.g., that the eye is offended by what hangs from these clotheslines. No cases have been cited from this or any other jurisdiction holding that a municipal corporation or political subdivision can direct house and lot owners where they shall hang their clothes. Aesthetic considerations, in a certain sense, underlie all zoning, usually in combination with other factors with which they are interwoven. Lot area, setback and height restrictions, for example, are based essentially on aesthetic factors. Occasionally public safety considerations are blended with aesthetics, such as the tendency of billboards to distract the attention of automobile drivers or of high hedges to block their view at street intersections. Aesthetic factors are given effect, in such cases, but have been limited to specific situations and not extended to anything which offends the taste of the neighbors or of the local legislature. One may assume, for example, that a clothesline ordinance would be invalid which permitted the hanging of white but not red blankets, or allowed shirts to be put out to dry after washing but not underwear. Probably, at least until the next step in zoning law, a municipality would be held unauthorized to direct house owners what colors their homes should be painted, or what kinds of trees or shrubbery they should be allowed to grow and where they should be planted. Nevertheless if they can be told where to hang their clothes in their yards, these items would be but a small step beyond the present holding, or to prescribe what architectural designs should be adopted so as to harmonize with the designs of the neighbors. To direct by ordinance that all buildings erected in a certain area should be one-story ranch houses would scarcely go beyond the present ruling as a question of power, or to lay down the law that they should be all of the same color, or of different colors, or that each should be of one or two or more color tones as might suit the aesthetic predilections of the city councillors or zoning boards of appeal.

This ordinance is unrelated to the public safety, health, morals or welfare except insofar as it compels conformity to what the neighbors like to look at. Zoning, important as it is within limits, is too rapidly becoming a legalized device to prevent property owners from doing whatever their neighbors dislike. Protection of minority rights is as essential to democracy as majority vote. In our age of conformity it is still not possible for all to be exactly alike, nor is it the instinct of our law to compel uniformity wherever diversity may offend the sensibilities of those who cast the largest numbers of votes in municipal elections. The right to be different has its place in this country. The United States has drawn strength from differences among its people in taste, experience, temperament, ideas, and ambitions as well as from differences in race, national or religious background. Even where the use of property is bizarre, unsuitable or obstreperous it is not to be curtailed in the absence of overriding reasons of public policy. The security and repose which come from protection of the right to be different in matter of aesthetics, taste, thought, expression and within limits in conduct are not to be cast aside without violating constitutional privileges and immunities. This is not merely a matter of legislative policy, at whatever level. In my view, this pertains to individual rights protected by the Constitution.

Aesthetic factors have always played an important part in zoning, as they have in the licensing of television and radio. Theatre and entertainment, as well as other forms of music, art, philosophy and literature are closely involved in aesthetics, which are not a veneer but are fundamental to the human mind and spirit. Nor are aesthetics confined to landscape gardening, tract development or architectural design. The avoidance by courts, sometimes seemingly to the point of evasion, of sustaining the constitutionality of zoning solely on aesthetic grounds has had its origin in a wholesome fear of allowing government to trespass through aesthetics on the human personality. In this instance, hanging tattered clothing, underwear, rags and scarecrows on a clothesline can scarcely be regarded as articulating a protest against excessive taxation, but to prohibit it by law upon the ground that it offends the aesthetic sensibilities of the neighbors or of the public officials of the municipality means—unless well defined and effectively enforced limits are placed upon this power to rule aesthetics by government—opening the door to the invasion by majority rule of a great deal of territory that belongs to the individual human being. It was once said of a famous lady of history that she had so much taste, and all of it so bad. Individual taste, good or bad, should ordinarily be let alone by government.

In authorizing the regulation of setback lines, yard areas, height of buildings and many permitted uses, the dominant factor has often been and should be aesthetic. But it is important not to allow general or unlimited power in government to regulate aesthetics in zoning or other departments of municipal administration. Extending aesthetic factors to the regulation of clotheslines suggests that zoning power, in the future, may extend to many other types of regulation also, since municipal boards and councils are being authorized in large degree to impose their ideas of aesthetics, and may be expected to do so on an expanding scale to placate the wishes of other property owners who constitute a large segment of the electorate. Unless clotheslines create traffic or health hazards, it seems to me that they should not be interfered with by law in suburban or rural areas. More important than this, however, does it seem that extensions of categories of local legislation for purely aesthetic purposes should be defined and limited, and, if they are to be enlarged, it should not be under reasoning which sets no ascertainable bounds to what can be done or attempted under this power.

The judgments of conviction of appellants should be reversed and the charges against them dismissed.

Notes

1. In City of Smyrna v. Parks, 240 Ga. 699, 242 S.E.2d 73 (1978), the court upheld a prohibition against chain link fences in front yards, finding that, in addition to aesthetic objectives, the ordinance was a safety measure in that fire fighters would be able to enter premises more easily when faced with a wood fence. Also see People v. Tolman, 110 Cal.App.3d Supp. 6, 168 Cal.Rptr. 328 (1980), upholding an ordinance prohibiting parking of vehicles over three tons on residential streets, as applied to a homeowner who had parked a 7½ ton truck tractor in front of her home continuously for ten years prior to enactment of the ordinance. Compare State v. Piemontese, 282 N.J.Super. 307, 659 A.2d 1385 (1995) where the court held that an ordinance requiring property owners to keep lawns, hedges and bushes from becoming "overgrown and unsightly" was vague and overly broad.

2. The theory of the Stover case does not necessarily mean that all aesthetic regulations in New York are free from attack. In Sackson v. Zimmerman, 103 A.D.2d 843, 478 N.Y.S.2d 354 (1984) the court held that a purely aesthetic regulation must be supported by a showing that the offense to the eye has a substantial and material effect on the community. The court struck down application of a local ordinance which applied an inordinate setback on a property owner to preserve neighbors' views of nearby mansions which would be obstructed by the presence of a smaller house.

Tennessee and North Carolina have joined the ranks of the states which hold that purely aesthetic considerations are within the police power. See State v. Smith, 618 S.W.2d 474 (Tenn.1981) and State v. Jones, 305 N.C. 520, 290 S.E.2d 675 (1982).

3. Good discussions of the problem of zoning for aesthetic purposes and the development of the concept can be found in Newsom, Zoning for Beauty, 3 Land Use Controls Q. 33 (No. 3, 1969); Comment, Zoning, Aesthetics and

the First Amendment, 64 Colum.L.Rev. 81 (1964); and Note, Aesthetic Zoning: A Current Evaluation of the Law, 18 U.Fla.L.Rev. 430 (1965). As both the Florida note writer and the Wisconsin court in the Wieland case point out, Berman v. Parker, 348 U.S. 26, 75 S.Ct. 98, 99 L.Ed. 27 (1954), changed things as far as zoning for aesthetics was concerned. The Supreme Court had said that the legal concept of the public welfare included aesthetic values, as well as monetary values. Before that, aesthetic zoning had paraded under the guise of elevating the commercial worth of the property involved. While many jurisdictions may consider aesthetics, there must be some other sustaining purpose present. Typical of this line of cases is Farley v. Graney, 146 W.Va. 22, 119 S.E.2d 833 (1960), stating that the great weight of authority is to the effect that aesthetic considerations alone will not justify the exercise of the police power for zoning purposes, but that these considerations may be given due weight along with other factors. This is the majority rule, but it seems unlikely to represent the trend. Over the long haul, Berman v. Parker is more likely to prevail.

PARKING ASSOCIATION OF GEORGIA, INC. v. CITY OF ATLANTA, GEORGIA

Supreme Court of Georgia, 1994.
264 Ga. 764, 450 S.E.2d 200.

THOMPSON, JUSTICE.

The City of Atlanta enacted a zoning ordinance aimed specifically at surface parking lots with 30 or more spaces in several downtown and midtown zoning districts. The ordinance requires minimum barrier curbs and landscaping areas equal to at least ten percent of the paved area within a lot, ground cover (shrubs, ivy, pine bark or similar landscape materials) and at least one tree for every eight parking spaces. Its stated purpose is to improve the beauty and aesthetic appeal of the City, promote public safety, and ameliorate air quality and water run-off problems. All costs of compliance with the ordinance are to be borne by the landowners; however, no landowner is required to reduce the number of parking spaces by more than three percent.

Plaintiffs, an association of companies managing or owning surface parking lots in the affected areas, as well as individual owners of affected parking lots, brought suit against the City seeking declaratory and injunctive relief on the grounds that the ordinance is unconstitutional and void. The superior court ruled in favor of the City and denied injunctive relief. Plaintiffs appealed.

* * *

Plaintiffs failed to present clear and convincing evidence that the ordinance presents a significant detriment. Plaintiffs may experience a loss of profits due to a reduction in the number of available parking spaces and the costs of compliance; however, a zoning ordinance does not exceed the police power simply because it restricts the use of property, diminishes the value of property, or imposes costs in connection with the property. * * * A loss of at most three percent of plaintiffs' parking spaces does not constitute a significant deprivation. * * *

Plaintiffs also failed to present clear and convincing evidence that the ordinance is unsubstantially related to the public health, safety, morality and welfare. The ordinance was designed to regulate aesthetics, crime, water run-off, temperature and other environmental concerns. The means adopted have a real and substantial relation to the goals to be attained.

An ordinance is not unreasonable even if designed only to improve aesthetics. * * *

Plaintiffs failed to meet either prong of this state's balancing test. The ordinance is constitutional and valid.

Plaintiffs assert the ordinance constitutes an unconstitutional denial of equal protection because it only applies to paved parking lots with 30 or more spaces in downtown and midtown zoning districts. We disagree.

A zoning ordinance does not offend the equal protection clauses of the State and Federal Constitutions if "it has some fair and substantial relation to the object of the legislation and furnishes a legitimate ground of differentiation. [Cit.]" Bailey Investment Co. v. Augusta–Richmond County Board of Zoning Appeals, 256 Ga. 186, 187, 345 S.E.2d 596 (1986). The larger lots have a far greater impact upon aesthetics, water run-off, temperature, pedestrian traffic and other health, safety and environmental concerns; the affected districts have the greatest concentration of parking lots. Thus, the ordinance rationally differentiates between larger and smaller parking lots and between affected and unaffected zoning districts. " 'If the validity of the legislative classification for zoning purposes be fairly debatable, the legislative judgment must be allowed to control.' " DeKalb County v. Chamblee Dunwoody Hotel Partnership, 248 Ga. 186, 190, 281 S.E.2d 525 (1981) (quoting Euclid v. Ambler Realty Co., 272 U.S. 365, 388, 47 S.Ct. 114, 118, 71 L.Ed. 303 (1926)).

Judgment affirmed.

All the Justices concur, except HUNT, C.J., and SEARS and CARLEY, JJ., who dissent.

SEARS, JUSTICE, dissenting. [Dissenting opinion omitted.]

C. UNDERGROUND UTILITIES

On May 5, 1968, the St. Louis Post Dispatch printed excerpts from an article in the National Civic Review which extolled the virtues of burying power lines and telephone lines. The article pointed out that the cost of undergrounding utility wires in an average residential subdivision in southern California was only about $130 per lot in 1966. It was further reported Southern California Edison Company had, in 1966, undergrounded more than 18,000 homes. Although the cost of undergrounding utility wires is usually passed on by the subdivider to the homeowner, in some communities the cost may be split between the utility and the homeowner and the city. In Minnesota and North Dakota and other areas served by the Northern States Power Company the cost of undergrounding to all-electric homes is borne entirely by the utility.

The greatest obstacle to utilization of the police power by cities to require underground utility wires is the question of cost. Also, a problem may arise over the jurisdiction a municipality may exercise over a state-regulated utility.

UNION ELECTRIC CO. v. CITY OF CRESTWOOD

Supreme Court of Missouri, Division No. 2, 1973.
499 S.W.2d 480.

FINCH, JUSTICE.

The issue presented herein is whether a municipal ordinance which prohibits thereafter any aboveground construction of utility transmission lines is valid. The trial court upheld the ordinance. We reverse.

The pertinent facts are these: Union Electric Company (UE) is an electric utility company serving a considerable area, including the City of St. Louis and the numerous municipalities located in St. Louis County. * * *

* * *

Sometime in 1968, officials of Crestwood had a conference with officials of UE relative to the possibility of placing all UE lines underground, but UE discouraged the idea on the basis of the additional cost involved. Subsequently, and before UE started construction of the proposed 138KV line, the Board of Aldermen of the City of Crestwood passed its Ordinance No. 1119, the ordinance here in question. This ordinance prohibited future aboveground construction of transmission lines in the City of Crestwood and made violation of the ordinance a misdemeanor. This declaratory judgment suit by UE followed adoption of that ordinance.

UE's petition in that action asserted that (1) the ordinance is ultra vires in that it exceeds the authority of the city and invades the field of regulation of utility companies which the state has vested in and reserved to the Public Service Commission; (2) the additional cost of placing these lines underground would be so much greater that it would prevent UE from performing its statutory duty to render adequate and safe service at a reasonable cost; (3) the ordinance exceeds the police power of the city in that it does not reasonably relate to the health, safety and welfare of the public; and (4) the ordinance results in a partial taking of UE's vested property and contract rights as granted to it by the existing 20-year franchise.

* * *

The validity of the foregoing conclusion is demonstrated by the evidence in this case. It disclosed that to construct the 1.8 miles of

Sec. 1   AESTHETICS AND ARCHITECTURAL CONTROL   873

138KV line aboveground would cost $217,000, and the 34KV line would cost $84,300. However, to place these underground for the 1.8 miles located in Crestwood, the cost would increase to $1,560,000 and $496,600, respectively. If Crestwood had the right by its ordinance to specify how UE should design and install its transmission lines or to require it to spend this substantially greater sum in constructing said lines, then other municipalities would have like authority. The record shows that UE serves the City of St. Louis and 99 municipalities in St. Louis County. In addition, it operates elsewhere, although that is not detailed in this record. If 100 such municipalities each had the right to impose its own requirements with respect to installation of transmission facilities, a hodgepodge of methods of construction could result and costs and resulting capital requirements could mushroom. As a result, the supervision and control by the Public Service Commission with respect to the company, its facilities, its method of operation, its service, its indebtedness, its investment, and its rates which the General Assembly obviously contemplated would be nullified. As the New Jersey court observed, "chaos would result" and neither UE nor the Public Service Commission could be assured that the company would be able to and would furnish uniform, adequate and reasonable service to all customers.[16]

We conclude and hold that Ordinance No. 1119 invades the area of regulation vested in the Public Service Commission by the General Assembly and hence that Crestwood, in adopting that ordinance, exceeded its authority. For this reason, the ordinance is invalid, and we so hold.

* * *

16. While not a part of the record on appeal or dispositive of this case, it is of interest to note, and we take judicial notice of the fact, that the Public Service Commission has taken action to establish a comprehensive statewide plan with reference to what shall be done with respect to undergrounding of electric transmission and distribution lines of certificated electric utility companies in this state.

On March 3, 1970, in Case No. 16,926, the Commission entered an order directing its Staff to immediately undertake an investigation of all factors relative to the undergrounding of electric transmission and distribution lines, and on completion of the investigation to report its findings and recommendations concerning "(1) the desirability of a uniform statewide tariff for the underground construction of electric distribution and transmission lines, (2) the economic feasibility of underground construction of electric distribution and transmission lines as opposed to overhead construction of such lines in light of the comparative costs of their construction and maintenance, and (3) the establishment of undergrounding priorities with accompanying guidelines to aid in future analysis and determination of such priorities."

Thereafter, the order was amended on September 22, 1970, to provide that the investigation should proceed in phases. It specified that Phase I should relate to underground distribution systems in new residential subdivisions, including the power lines from substations to said subdivisions, and Phase II was to relate to underground distribution systems in high density commercial areas.

Thereafter, on June 28, 1971, the Commission adopted General Order No. 52—Section I, which was thereafter amended on October 26, 1971, requiring undergrounding of electrical distribution systems in new residential subdivisions, and directing certificated electric companies to file tariffs to cover said undergrounding directed by that General Order. Thus, action relative to Phase I has already been implemented, with other reports and possible subsequent action to follow.

In view of the conclusions hereinabove set out, we deem it unnecessary to consider and decide the other contentions advanced by UE as reasons for declaring Ordinance No. 1119 invalid.

Judgment reversed.

Notes

1. Does the principal case suggest that the city officials of Crestwood had read the article in the St. Louis Post Dispatch in 1968, but that the supreme court judges had not? Is the essence of the case that undergrounding of utilities can only be accomplished by statewide regulation or special enabling legislation? Some evidence of the effect of the case is found in statutes later adopted in other states, undoubtedly through the efforts of the regulated utilities.

2. A number of cases have held that in the absence of clear legislative intent to preempt municipal authority to regulate streets and utility lines, zoning regulations which require undergrounding of utilities are valid. Kahl v. Consolidated Gas, Elec. Light & Power Co., 191 Md. 249, 60 A.2d 754 (1948); Benzinger v. Union Light, Heat & Power Co., 293 Ky. 747, 170 S.W.2d 38 (1943); Arizona Public Serv. Co. v. Town of Paradise Valley, 125 Ariz. 447, 610 P.2d 449 (1980). In Central Maine Power Co. v. Waterville Urban Renewal Auth., 281 A.2d 233 (Me.1971), the court recognized the aesthetic significance of requiring undergrounding in a renewal area, and held that the utility could be compelled to bear the cost. Also see Sleepy Hollow Lake, Inc. v. Public Serv. Comm'n, 43 A.D.2d 439, 352 N.Y.S.2d 274 (1974), which upheld the state agency order to underground utilities, which order was allegedly based solely on aesthetic and environmental preservation grounds. On the other hand, requiring a landowner to reinstall electric wiring underground in the course of a redevelopment project was held to be a taking in Redevelopment Authority of Oil City v. Woodring, 498 Pa. 180, 445 A.2d 724 (1982). And, in Bright Development v. City of Tracy, 20 Cal.App.4th 783, 24 Cal.Rptr.2d 618 (1993) the court held that a developer could not be required to bear the cost of placing off-site utilities underground in order to receive approval of his subdivision plat.

3. Where the state has clearly preempted utility regulation, as the court found in the principal case, then municipal authority to compel undergrounding may be limited to the use of subdivision exactions requiring the developer to pay the cost of undergrounding, if the utility is equipped to install underground lines. Some of the cases finding state preemption are Village of Carthage v. Central New York Tel. & Tel. Co., 185 N.Y. 448, 78 N.E. 165 (1906); In re Public Serv. Elec. and Gas Co., 35 N.J. 358, 173 A.2d 233 (1961); Cleveland Elec. Illuminating Co. v. City of Painesville, 10 Ohio App.2d 85, 226 N.E.2d 145 (1967). See 7 McQuillan, Municipal Corporations § 24.588 (3d Ed.1968).

4. Quite apart from the movement to place utility wires underground, based solely on aesthetic considerations, what about a reverse problem? When public parks or other open spaces are considered as routes for highways or other public works allegedly inconsistent with park purposes, can citizens successfully prevent the undertaking? For a classic example of this problem see the lengthy litigation involving the struggle of citizens of

Memphis, Tennessee, to prevent the construction of Interstate Highway 40 through Overton Park in Memphis: Citizens to Preserve Overton Park, Inc. v. Volpe, 309 F.Supp. 1189 (W.D.Tenn.1970), 432 F.2d 1307 (6th Cir.1970), 401 U.S. 402, 91 S.Ct. 814, 28 L.Ed.2d 136 (1971); after remand Citizens to Preserve Overton Park, Inc. v. Volpe, 335 F.Supp. 873 (W.D.Tenn.1972), affirmed sub nom. Citizens to Preserve Overton Park, Inc. v. Brinegar, 494 F.2d 1212 (6th Cir.1974), certiorari denied sub nom. Citizens to Preserve Overton Park, Inc. v. Smith, 421 U.S. 991, 95 S.Ct. 1997, 44 L.Ed.2d 481 (1975). Early in 1981, newspaper reports indicated that the city had finally abandoned the completion of Interstate 40 through Memphis. Also see Coalition for Responsible Regional Development v. Brinegar, 518 F.2d 522 (4th Cir.1975). For an overview of the several legal theories that can be raised in such cases, see Annot., Construction of Highway Through Park as Violation of Use to which Park Property May Be Dedicated, 60 A.L.R.3d 581 (1974).

SECTION 2. HISTORICAL LANDMARK AND CULTURAL PRESERVATION

A. FEDERAL GOVERNMENT'S ROLE IN HISTORICAL LANDMARK AND CULTURAL PRESERVATION

The following excerpts from a report of the Advisory Council on Historic Preservation (see, http://www.achp.gov/book/sectionI.html#IA) describes the development of historic preservation law and regulation in the United States (footnotes have been deleted):

> Thirty years after passage of the National Historic Preservation Act of 1966 (NHPA), Federal law clearly reflects the Nation's commitment to preserving and protecting its wealth of historic resources. This was not always the case. Although Federal statutes containing preservation policies have existed since the turn of the 20th century, these laws typically were limited in scope and lacked effective means of enforcement.
>
> The earliest Federal preservation statute was the Antiquities Act of 1906, which authorized the President to set aside historic landmarks, structures, and objects located on lands controlled by the United States as national monuments. It required permits for archeological activities on Federal lands, and established criminal and civil penalties for violation of the act. The Historic Sites Act of 1935 was the second major piece of Federal historic preservation legislation. This act declared it national policy to preserve for public use historic sites, buildings, and objects of national significance and directed the Secretary of the Interior to conduct various programs with respect to historic preservation. Although these statutes were significant, they did not create a national awareness of the need for preservation or provide a means to incorporate preservation concerns into Federal agency programs.
>
> In 1964, the United States Conference of Mayors undertook a study of historic preservation in the United States. The resulting

report, "With Heritage So Rich," revealed a growing public interest in preservation and the need for a unified approach to the protection of historic resources. This report influenced Congress to enact a strong new statute establishing a nationwide preservation policy: the National Historic Preservation Act of 1966.

The National Historic Preservation Act was a watershed in preservation law, for it created a means by which the Nation's preservation goals could be achieved. Recognizing that increased knowledge and better administration of historic resources would improve the planning and execution of Federal undertakings and benefit economic growth and development nationwide, the act promoted the use of historic properties to meet the contemporary needs of society. It directed the Federal Government, in cooperation with State and local governments, Native Americans, and the public, to take a leadership role in preservation. Since 1966, Congress has strengthened national preservation policy further by recognizing the importance of preserving historic aspects of the Nation's heritage in several other statutes, among them the National Environmental Policy Act and several transportation acts and by enacting statutes directed toward the protection and preservation of archeological resources. These laws require Federal agencies to consider historic resources in their planning and decisionmaking and, although they are not co-extensive with NHPA, often overlap with the provisions of NHPA.

The Executive Branch has expressed its support for preservation through several key Executive Orders. In 1971, for example, President Nixon signed Executive Order No. 11593, which instituted procedures Federal agencies must follow in their property management activities. In 1996, President Clinton signed another important Executive Order, this one setting forth the Administration's support for locating Federal offices and facilities in historic districts and properties in the Nation's inner cities: Executive Order No. 13006 directs Federal agencies to use and rehabilitate properties in such areas wherever feasible and reaffirms the commitment to Federal leadership in the preservation of historic properties set forth in NHPA thirty years before. Another 1996 Executive Order, No. 13007, expresses support for the protection of Native American sacred sites.

The National Historic Preservation Act and other preservation statutes, as well as the Executive Orders mentioned above, have clarified and refined the duties and responsibilities of Federal agencies with regard to the protection of America's cultural heritage. Federal compliance with these authorities, however, has not always been consistent, giving rise to a number of lawsuits brought primarily by citizens and preservation organizations. The resulting court opinions interpret and elucidate the historic preservation provisions of these laws.

* * *

1. Historical and Archeological Data Preservation Act of 1974 (HADPA) and Archeological Resources Protection Act of 1979 (ARPA)

HADPA provides for the preservation of historical and archeological data that might otherwise be lost as the result of alterations to the terrain caused by a Federal or federally licensed activity or program. To carry out the purposes of the act, HADPA allows for the transfer of up to one percent of the appropriations for the project to the Secretary of the Interior. Unlike Section 106, which mandates consideration of historic properties during Federal agency planning, HADPA guides the implementation of mitigation measures once an agency decision is reached.

ARPA is designed to protect archeological resources on Federal and Indian lands and to encourage the exchange of information pertaining to such properties between the Federal Government and the archeological community. ARPA strengthens its predecessor HADPA by providing specific permit procedures that all persons, including private applicants as well as State and Federal agencies, must follow prior to excavating or removing any archeological resource on Federal or Indian lands. Unlike NHPA, ARPA provides both civil and criminal penalties for failure to comply with the act. ARPA does contain a confidentiality provision similar to NHPA.

2. Native American Graves Protection and Repatriation Act of 1990 (NAGPRA)

NAGPRA requires Federal agencies and museums to inventory their holdings of Native American cultural items and return such items to Indian tribes and other Native American groups. The definition of "Indian tribe" in NAGPRA has been interpreted to include an Indian group or community of Indians that the Secretary does not acknowledge as an Indian tribe. However, this decision was reached prior to promulgation of NAGPRA regulations which generally define "Indian tribe" as those recognized by the Secretary of Interior. The act also provides that any intentional excavation and removal of Native American human remains and other cultural items from Federal or tribal lands be conducted only with a permit issued pursuant to the Archeological Resources Protection Act and after consulting with the appropriate tribe. If an inadvertent discovery is made of Native American remains or objects in connection with an activity on Federal or tribal lands, the activity must cease in the area of the discovery, a reasonable effort must be made to protect the items discovered before resuming activity, and the appropriate Federal agency or tribal authority must be notified. Activities may resume 30 days after receiving certification of notification from the appropriate Federal agency or tribal authority. NAGPRA requirements may overlay Section 106 when undertakings occur on Federal or tribal lands.

3. American Indian Religious Freedom Act of 1978 (AIRFA)

AIRFA protects the rights of Native Americans to exercise their traditional religions by ensuring access to sites, use and possession of sacred objects, and the freedom to worship through ceremonials and traditional rites. The intent of AIRFA has been interpreted as ensuring that Native Americans obtain First Amendment protection, but not to grant them rights in excess of the First Amendment. Because such sites may be eligible for inclusion in the National Register, any effects that may occur, as a result of providing access to them, may trigger Section 106 review under NHPA.

B. THE ROLE OF STATE GOVERNMENTS IN HISTORIC AND CULTURAL PRESERVATION

The 1966 Historic Preservation Act required, among other things, that each state establish a State Historic Preservation Office and that the governor of each state appoint an officer to oversee preservation activities. The National Conference of State Historic Preservation Officers summarizes the state role as follows (see, http://www.ncshpo.org/about/):

The State Historic Preservation Officers, pursuant to the National Historic Preservation act,

- locate and record historic properties,
- nominate significant historic properties to the National Register,
- foster historic preservation programs at the local government level and the creation of preservation ordinances,
- provide matching funds for preservation projects,
- comment upon preservation projects under consideration for the federal rehabilitation tax credit,
- review all federal projects for impact on historic properties under Section 106 of the Act and the regulations of the Advisory Council on Historic Preservation, and
- provide technical assistance on restoration and other preservation activities to federal agencies, state and local governments, and the private sector.

The National Conference of State Legislatures maintains comprehensive links to state preservation statutes at http://www.ncsl.org/programs/arts/statehist_intro.htm .

C. HISTORIC PRESERVATION AT THE LOCAL GOVERNMENT LEVEL

Historic preservation depends in large part on the commitment of local governments through the use of design regulations, historic districts and innovative zoning techniques to accomplish preservation goals. In 1997, the American Planning Association revised its policy on historic and cultural preservation. Calling upon planners to assume greater responsibility for historic preservation, the policy acknowledges the important role of local governments in planning for preservation and urges, "...the coordination of comprehensive planning programs and implementation tools (zoning, subdivision, and land development) with state preservation legislation (facade controls tax incentives, and other tools)... these programs should utilize a variety of tools which may include (but are not limited to): a) Transfer of development rights; b) Expansion of clustering and planned unit development to increase opportunities for landmarking, village preservation, and historic districts; and c) Preservation of village settlement patters as a desirable means to promote community character and diversity. See, http://www.planning.org/policyguides/historic.htm. Municipalities often create local historic preservation or review commissions. These commissions may be advisory in nature and they may issue necessary certifications to enable development and redevelopment projects to proceed.

(1) Historic Districts

OPINION OF THE JUSTICES TO THE SENATE
Supreme Judicial Court of Massachusetts, 1955.
333 Mass. 773, 128 N.E.2d 557.

On July 7, 1955, the Justices submitted the following answers to questions propounded to them by the Senate:

To the Honorable Senate of the Commonwealth of Massachusetts:

The Justices of the Supreme Judicial Court respectfully submit these answers to questions set forth in an order of the Senate dated June 14, 1955, and transmitted to us on June 21.

The questions relate to a proposed act known as House No. 775, now pending before the Senate, entitled "An Act establishing an historic districts commission for the town of Nantucket and defining its powers and duties, and establishing historic districts in the town of Nantucket."

The purpose of the act is stated to be to promote the general welfare of the inhabitants of the town "through the preservation and protection of historic buildings, places and districts of historic interest; through the development of an appropriate setting for these buildings, places and districts; and through the benefits resulting to the economy of Nantucket in developing and maintaining its vacation-travel industry through the promotion of these historic associations." § 1.

The act establishes a historic districts commission of five members, who shall be resident taxpayers of the town, to be appointed by the selectmen. § 2. It establishes by definite boundaries two districts in the town to be known as (1) Old and Historic Nantucket District, and (2) Old and Historic Siasconset District. § 3. It contains provisions applicable in those districts that "No building or structure shall hereafter be erected, reconstructed, altered or restored" until an application for a building permit "shall have been approved as to exterior architectural features which are subject to public view from a public street, way or place," and evidence of such approval shall be "a certificate of appropriateness" issued by the commission (§ 4); that no building or structure shall be raised (razed?) without a permit approved by the commission, which may be refused for any building or structure "the removal of which in the opinion of said commission would be detrimental to the public interest" of the town or the village of Siasconset (§ 5); that occupational or other signs exceeding two feet in length and six inches in width, or the erection or display of more than one such sign, irrespective of size, on any lot, building or structure must be approved and certified by the commission (§ 6); and that the commission may hold public or private hearings as it may deem advisable (§ 7). It shall be the function and duty of the commission "to pass upon the appropriateness of exterior architectural features of buildings and structures hereafter to be erected, reconstructed, altered or restored * * * wherever such exterior features are subject to public view from a public street or way" and also to pass upon the removal of buildings and the erection or display of signs according to §§ 5 and 6 (§ 8[a]). It is provided that the commission "in passing upon appropriateness of exterior architectural features in any case, shall keep in mind the purposes set forth" in § 1, and "shall consider among other things the general design, arrangement, texture, material and color of the building or structure in question, and the relation of such factors to similar features of buildings and structures in the immediate surroundings" (§ 8[b]). It is expressly provided that the commission shall not consider detailed designs, relative size of buildings, interior arrangement or building features not subject to public view, and shall make no recommendations or requirements except for the purpose of preventing developments obviously incongruous to the historic aspects of the surroundings and the Old and Historic Districts (§ 8[c]). Upon approval of plans the commission shall cause a certificate of appropriateness to be issued (§ 8[e]). There are provisions for a penalty for violations of the act and for appeal to the selectmen and ultimately to the Superior Court. §§ 9–11. Appeal to the Superior Court with "rights of appeal and exception as in other equity cases" is to be the final exclusive remedy. § 11. The provision for appeal to the court is in terms similar to those employed in statutes providing for appeal to the court from decisions of zoning boards of appeals, which in Pendergast v. Board of Appeals of Barnstable, 331 Mass. 555, 120 N.E.2d 916, were held to carry up questions of law. The act is to take effect upon acceptance by the voters of the town. § 14.

The act contains no provision for compensation as for property taken. The commission is to be "unpaid." § 2. But under § 7 it "may incur expenses necessary to the carrying on of its work within the amount of its annual appropriation."

* * *

If the proposed act is to be construed as a taking of the property of owners affected by it, manifestly it is unconstitutional, since no provision is made for compensation as required by art. 10 of the Declaration of Rights. On the other hand, there may be many regulations and restrictions upon the use of private property under the so called police power which do not amount to a taking of the property and which rest upon the general power to legislate for the public safety, health, morals, and welfare. We are of opinion that the proposed act is not a taking. There is no provision for a formal taking, and title will remain in the owner as will also the possession and usufruct for nearly all purposes, even though restricted in ways that conceivably may in occasional instances bear down heavily. See American Unitarian Association v. Commonwealth, 193 Mass. 470, 476–477, 79 N.E. 878.

The question then arises whether the proposed act can be supported without a taking and the paying of compensation as a police regulation in the interest of public safety, health, morals, or welfare. There are many regulations belonging in these categories too numerous and too familiar to require specific reference here. Those which in many respects most nearly resemble the proposed act are the zoning laws the constitutionality of which is in general thoroughly established. * * * Many zoning regulations are as severe in their operation upon landowners as any of the provisions of the proposed act would be likely to be.

But the zoning regulations are in general directly related to the public safety and health, and less directly to the public morals. The proposed act can hardly be said in any ordinary sense to relate to the public safety, health, or morals. Can it rest upon the less definite and more inclusive ground that it serves the public welfare? The term public welfare has never been and cannot be precisely defined. Sometimes it has been said to include public convenience, comfort, peace and order, prosperity, and similar concepts, but not to include "mere expediency." Opinion of the Justices, 234 Mass. 597, 603, 127 N.E. 525. And it has been held or stated that aesthetic considerations alone are not enough, but that they may be taken into account, if the primary objects of the regulation are sufficient to justify it. * * * There is reason to think that more weight might now be given to aesthetic considerations than was given to them a half century ago.

* * *

The definition of the purpose of the proposed act as set forth in § 1 is along these same lines and includes "the preservation and protection of historic buildings, places and districts of historic interest; through the development of an appropriate setting for these buildings, places and districts; and through the benefits resulting to the economy of Nantucket in developing and maintaining its vacation-travel industry through the promotion of these historic associations." In the case of City of New Bedford v. New Bedford, Woods Hole, Martha's Vineyard & Nantucket Steamship Authority, 330 Mass. 422, 114 N.E.2d 553, this court took judicial notice of the general characteristics of the island of Nantucket and of its great interest in the entertainment of summer visitors. We may also take judicial notice that Nantucket is one of the very old towns of the Commonwealth; that for perhaps a century it was a famous seat of the whaling industry and accumulated wealth and culture which made itself manifest in some fine examples of early American architecture; and that the sedate and quaint appearance of the old island town has to a large extent still remained unspoiled and in all probability constitutes a substantial part of the appeal which has enabled it to build up its summer vacation business to take the place of its former means of livelihood. In a general way much the same can be said of the village of Siasconset, which is a part of the town of Nantucket. There has been substantial recognition by the courts of the public interest in the preservation of historic buildings, places, and districts. Opinion of the Justices, 297 Mass. 567, 8 N.E.2d 753. General Outdoor Advertising Co., Inc. v. Department of Public Works, 289 Mass. 149, 187–189, 197–198, 200–201, 193 N.E. 799. United States v. Gettysburg Electric Railway, 160 U.S. 668, 16 S.Ct. 427, 40 L.Ed. 576. State v. Kemp, 124 Kan. 716, 261 P. 556. Flaccomio v. Mayor & City Council of Baltimore, 194 Md. 275, 71 A.2d 12. See art. 51 of the Amendments to the Constitution of this Commonwealth.

It is not difficult to imagine how the erection of a few wholly incongruous structures might destroy one of the principal assets of the town, and we assume that the boundaries of the districts are so drawn as to include only areas of special value to the public because of possession of those characteristics which it is the purpose of the act to preserve.

We think the requirements of the proposed act are not too indefinite or lacking in sufficient standards. The act does not require anything to be done to existing structures with the possible exception of signs (§ 6). With the same possible exception, it applies only to exterior architectural features subject to public view from a public place (§ 4). It does not apply to details of design or sizes of buildings or interior arrangement of building features not subject to public view, and requirements by the commission must be limited to the preventing of developments "obviously incongruous to the historic aspects of the surroundings" (§ 8[c]). This last provision is apparently intended to prevent decisions based upon peculiar individual tastes. All provisions must be interpreted with reference to the main purposes of the act. See § 8(b). In at least two very recent cases regulations based in part upon standards of architecture intended to comport with the established surroundings have been sustained. City of New Orleans v. Levy, 223 La. 14, 64 So.2d 798. State ex rel. Saveland Park Holding Corp. v. Wieland, 269 Wis. 262, 69 N.W.2d 217. See 64 U.S.Sts. at Large, p. 903, c. 984, relating to "Old Georgetown."

We are of opinion that in a general sense the proposed act would be an act for the promotion of the public welfare and would be constitutional, and we answer the questions on that basis. * * *

Notes

1. On the same day as the decision in the principal case, the justices rendered an opinion that a similar historic district to preserve Beacon Hill in

Boston would be constitutional. See Opinion of the Justices to the Senate, 333 Mass. 783, 128 N.E.2d 563 (1955). The court stated:

> In addition to the facts appearing from the proposed act itself there are other facts of common knowledge in relation to Beacon Hill. The area was closely built up for the homes of persons of taste and culture in the architectural style of urban residences prevailing a century or more ago. There is general uniformity in design and structure. Although the area is not far from the business center of Boston, commercial development has proceeded in other directions, and the Beacon Hill section, with some exceptions, has remained to this day rather surprisingly free from inharmonious intrusions. Its general appearance is substantially what it was several generations ago. The Bulfinch front, so called, of the State House, completed before the year 1800, is at the highest point of the hill. The famous Boston Common is located on the side of Beacon Street opposite the southerly boundary of the proposed district. The area has contained the homes of many persons of distinction in the life of the State and Nation. That it is a locality of historic significance can hardly be doubted.
>
> The announced purpose of the act is to preserve this historic section for the educational, cultural, and economic advantage of the public. If the General Court believes that this object would be attained by the restrictions which the act would place upon the introduction into the district of inappropriate forms of construction that would destroy its unique value and associations, a court can hardly take the view that such legislative determination is so arbitrary or unreasonable that it cannot be comprehended within the public welfare.
>
> In our answers to recent questions of the Senate pertaining to proposed historic districts in Nantucket we have discussed at some length the constitutional aspects of restrictions upon the character of building in areas set apart as such districts, whether or not there is involved any element of aesthetic considerations, and we cited authorities revealed by our research into the subject. We beg to refer to what we there said without repeating it here. In that instance the districts of historic interest intended to be preserved were in ancient villages that had survived into our day. In this instance it is an ancient section of the capital city of the Commonwealth. But the principles are the same. There are some other differences between the two proposed acts, but we think none is sufficient to render what we said in our discussion in the former instance inapplicable in this later instance.

2. In Gumley v. Board of Selectmen of Nantucket, 371 Mass. 718, 358 N.E.2d 1011 (1977), the court held that a decision of the Nantucket Historic District Commission denying a certificate of appropriateness to a developer was improper to the extent that it was based on incongruence with the open space aspect of Nantucket. The court said: "That decision did not relate to 'exterior architectural features.' It went beyond the statutory purpose of 'preventing developments obviously incongruous to the historic aspects of the surroundings' and the district. It therefore exceeded the authority of the commission * * *."

3. See also, City of Santa Fe v. Gamble–Skogmo, 73 N.M. 410, 389 P.2d 13 (1964), upholding zoning seeking to preserve "Old Santa Fe Style" architecture. Similar to the Santa Fe situation were the earlier efforts of New Orleans to preserve the distinctive character of the French Quarter. This effort was embodied in the "Vieux Carre Ordinance," discussed in 2 Anderson, American Law of Zoning § 8.54 (1986) and 3 Williams, American Land Planning Law §§ 71.05–71.10 (1988). The ordinance sought to exercise control over the architecture in the French Quarter, but was based on specific authorization by the Louisiana Constitution (Art. 14, § 22A). Construed on several occasions, it was held that the ordinance adopted by the city pursuant to the constitutional provision, which would result in preserving the Quarter, was not just "sentimental" but also for the purpose of preserving the commercial value of the Vieux Carre and thus was a valid exercise of the police power. See City of New Orleans v. Pergament, 198 La. 852, 5 So.2d 129 (1941), which stated that it was not a denial of equal protection to require a gasoline station owner to obtain a permit from the commission to erect or maintain an advertising sign. See also, City of New Orleans v. Levy, 223 La. 14, 64 So.2d 798 (1953); and City of New Orleans v. Impastato, 198 La. 206, 3 So.2d 559 (1941). Although the New Orleans cases were based on an ordinance adopted and a commission created pursuant to specific constitutional authority, they helped lay the groundwork for acceptance of the idea that municipalities (as in the Santa Fe case) could rely upon a general delegation of authority to sustain zoning for preservation purposes. In Williamsburg, Virginia, the zoning power was employed to protect a restored area, rather than to preserve an historic area in its existing state. See Agnor, Beauty Begins a Comeback: Aesthetic Considerations in Zoning, 11 J.Pub.L. 260, 274 (1962); and Note, Zoning: Aesthetics: The Chameleon of Zoning, 4 Tulsa L.J. 48, 56 (1967).

SOUTH OF SECOND ASSOCIATES v. GEORGETOWN

Supreme Court of Colorado, En Banc, 1978.
196 Colo. 89, 580 P.2d 807.

ERICKSON, JUSTICE.

Georgetown is a municipal corporation created by the Colorado territorial legislature in 1868. The town and surrounding area are rich in the culture and history of early Colorado. In 1966, the National Park Service of the U.S. Department of the Interior designated the Georgetown/Silver Plume area as a registered National Historic Landmark District.

On May 18, 1970, the Board of Selectmen of Georgetown enacted Ordinance No. 205. The ordinance amended Georgetown's existing zoning ordinance by creating a Historic Preservation District (District) and a seven-member Historic Preservation Commission (Commission). The District boundaries encompassed all real property within the municipal limits of Georgetown. * * *

South of Second Associates, one of the plaintiffs, owns approximately five acres of undeveloped real property in Georgetown located on

Leavenworth Mountain south of the developed portion of the municipality. The property, at all times relevant to this proceeding, was zoned for multi-family use. On December 18, 1972, the plaintiffs submitted an application for a certificate of appropriateness to construct 57 townhouses which would occupy approximately 30% of their property on Leavenworth Mountain. The Commission reviewed the application and unanimously decided not to issue the requested certificate. The Georgetown Board of Selectmen voted four to two not to overrule the Commission's decision.

* * *

The pertinent provisions of Ordinance No. 205 provide:

"Section VII. 'HP—Historic Preservation District'

"A) GENERAL DESCRIPTION

This District is intended to promote the educational, cultural, economic, and general welfare of the public through the protection, enhancement, and use of structures and areas of historical and/or architectural significance. In order to maintain the character and beauty of such structures, and areas, restrictive requirements governing both the use of land and the erection, moving, demolition, reconstruction, restoration, or alteration of structures thereon are provided.

* * *

"B) DEFINITIONS FOR THE HISTORICAL PRESERVATION DISTRICT

* * *

4. Historical and/or Architectural Significance. That which has a special historical or aesthetic interest or value as part of the development, heritage, or cultural character of the city, region, state, or nation.

5. Area. Any land or buildings having notable character qualities of historical and/or architectural significance as determined by the Historical Preservation Commission. An area may include structures or other physical improvements on, above, or below the surface of the earth.

* * *

"C) ROLE OF HISTORICAL PRESERVATION COMMISSION

* * *

"In determining the recommendation to be made concerning the issuance of a certificate of appropriateness, the Commission shall consider the following criteria:

(1) The effect of the proposed change upon the general historical and/or architectural character of the structure or area."

* * *

The trial court concluded that the ordinances were unconstitutionally vague:

> "After reviewing the ordinances and after hearing the testimony of numerous witnesses concerned with their enforcement (each of whom seemed to have a different opinion as to the meaning of the term 'historical and architectural significance') the Court is convinced that the ordinances do not contain sufficient standards to advise ordinary and reasonable men as to the conduct which they attempt to proscribe or direct."

The trial court seems to have based its decision upon a finding that the "historical and/or architectural significance" language of the ordinance was vague. We find such language sufficiently definite, but hold the ordinances unconstitutionally vague in failing to delineate the differently classified areas within the District.

* * *

Courts in other jurisdictions have found similar enactments, although somewhat uncertain in the abstract, to be sufficiently definite in the context of actual application. In Town of Deering v. Tibbetts, 105 N.H. 481, 202 A.2d 232 (1964), the Court declared:

> "While determination of what is compatible with the 'atmosphere' of the town may on first impression be thought to be a matter of arbitrary and subjective judgment, under consideration it proves not to be. As stated in Anderson, 'Architectural Controls,' 12 Syracuse L.Rev. 26, 45, the language 'takes clear meaning from the observable character of the district to which it applies.' See also, 1 Rathkopf, The Law of Zoning and Planning (3d ed. 1969) 11–29."

Our conclusion that the "historical and/or architectural" language in the Georgetown ordinance is sufficiently definite reflects the consensus of those courts which have considered similar provisions designed to preserve historical areas through the enactment of reasonable regulations. Figarsky v. Historic District Commission of the City of Norwich, 171 Conn. 198, 368 A.2d 163 (1976); Trustees of Sailors' Snug Harbor v. Platt, 29 A.D.2d 376, 288 N.Y.S.2d 314 (1968); Town of Deering v. Tibbetts, supra; City of Santa Fe v. Gamble–Skogmo, Inc., 73 N.M. 410, 389 P.2d 13 (1964); Opinion of the Justices to the Senate, 333 Mass. 773, 128 N.E.2d 557 (1955); City of New Orleans v. Levy, 223 La. 14, 64 So.2d 798 (1953); See also 1 Rathkopf § 15.01, The Law of Zoning and Planning (4th ed.).

We conclude that the "historical and/or architectural character" language of the ordinance, when considered in conjunction with the objective factors contained in the ordinance, and in the context of the public purposes to be achieved, is sufficiently definite to pass constitutional muster. The ordinance contains sufficient standards to advise ordinary and reasonable men as to the type of construction permitted, permits reasonable application by the Commission, and limits the Commission's discretionary powers.

* * *

Georgetown's historical preservation ordinance designates all property within the municipal limits as a historical preservation district. Most municipalities which have established similar historical preservation districts, however, specifically delineate those areas which possess such a unique character as to be entitled to preservation. See Figarsky v. Historical District Commission of the City of Norwich, supra; Maher v. City of New Orleans, 516 F.2d 1051 (5th Cir.1975); Rebman v. City of Springfield, 111 Ill.App.2d 430, 250 N.E.2d 282 (1969); Opinion of the Justices to the Senate, supra; Opinion of the Justices to the Senate, 333 Mass. 783, 128 N.E.2d 563 (1955); see also section 24–65.1–201(1)(c), C.R.S.1973 (1977 Supp.).

Although the ordinance contains standards sufficient to give substance to the "historical and/or architectural character" language of the ordinance by reference to the area in which the proposed construction or structural alteration is to occur, nowhere in the ordinance is a delineation of the relevant areas to be found. The ordinances' definition of area * * * fails to set forth sufficient criteria to enable the potential applicant to reasonably ascertain in which area his property is situated.

The record indicates that the Commission members divide Georgetown into two or three distinct areas. Several members testified that Georgetown was divided into northern and southern areas. Still others, while agreeing that the northern and southern areas exist, felt that a transitional or buffer area exists between the two larger areas. The Commission's unpublished and indefinite delineation of the areas is legally insufficient.

We conclude that Ordinance Nos. 205 and 206 vested unreviewable discretion in the Commission. Under the ordinances a property owner cannot reasonably ascertain which architectural designs would entitle him to a certificate of appropriateness. Areas entitled to protection must be clearly delineated in the ordinance. The ordinances, therefore, are void for vagueness.

* * *

The judgment is affirmed.

Notes

1. After the decision in this case the plaintiffs were denied a building permit and sought a declaratory judgment that they were entitled to immediate issuance of a permit and damages for the delay in issuing a permit. The supreme court held that the plaintiffs were entitled to declaratory relief and remanded the case for a hearing on the damages issue. South of Second Associates v. Georgetown, 199 Colo. 394, 609 P.2d 125 (1980). In Unruh v. City of Asheville, 97 N.C.App. 287, 388 S.E.2d 235, rev. denied 326 N.C. 487, 391 S.E.2d 813 (1990) the court held that the city's historic district ordi-

nance was invalid because the city did not follow the prescribed adoption procedures in the state enabling legislation.

2. Can historic districts be empowered to control development outside the district which might have a deleterious effect upon the district? In Rebman v. City of Springfield, 111 Ill.App.2d 430, 250 N.E.2d 282 (1969), the court upheld denial of a rezoning to permit a restaurant on a commercial street adjacent to a four block historic district containing one historical structure, the Abraham Lincoln home. Also see, Hall County Historical Soc., Inc. v. Georgia Dept. of Transp., 447 F.Supp. 741 (N.D.Ga.1978), where the county historical society sought to protect an established district from a highway widening project close to the district boundaries. After finding that the society had standing based on the allegation that several members resided in or owned property in the historical district, the court held that (1) the plaintiffs failed to meet their burden of proof that the defendants' decision not to file an environmental impact statement was unreasonable under the National Environmental Policy Act; (2) defendants had not violated Section 4(f) of the Transportation Act (23 U.S.C.A. § 138) mandating that the Secretary of Transportation not approve any project which requires the use of land from an historic site if there is a feasible alternative; (3) the Department of Transportation did violate the National Historic Preservation Act (16 U.S.C.A. § 470f) which requires the federal agency to take into account the effect of a project on historic sites, by merely "rubber stamping" the conclusions of the state highway department that the project would not affect the district. An injunction against completion of the project was granted. In Bellevue Shopping Center Associates v. Chase, 574 A.2d 760 (R.I.1990) the court upheld denial of a proposal to add a new building to an existing shopping center because the design of the building would seriously impair the historic or architectural value of the surrounding historic district.

3. In Globe Newspaper Co. v. Beacon Hill Architectural Comm'n, 100 F.3d 175 (1st Cir.1996) the Court held that the architectural commission for the Beacon Hill historic district did have power to regulate the placement of newsracks, and that the guidelines promulgated by the commission did not violate the First Amendment.

(2) Preserving Landmark Structures

KENT COUNTY COUNCIL FOR HISTORIC PRESERVATION v. ROMNEY

United States District Court, Western District, Michigan, 1969.
304 F.Supp. 885.

THORNTON, DISTRICT JUDGE.

"This is a case of first impression insofar as the National Historic Sites Act of 1966, 16 U.S.C.A. § 470 et seq. is concerned, certainly in its application to the urban renewal process. Plaintiff is unaware of any reported decisions construing this Act. Potentially, it is a landmark case. For as it is true of the Act itself, the issue at hand is the capacity of the American people to prevent improvidence in matters relating to the conservation of our natural and manmade heritage."

Sec. 2 HISTORICAL LANDMARK & CULTURAL PRESERVATION 889

Thus reads plaintiff's brief in support of its motions for preliminary injunction in the two cases before the Court (now consolidated for trial purposes). The defendants include George W. Romney, Secretary of the Department of Housing and Urban Development, the Mayor of the City of Grand Rapids and numerous City administration officials, and the Union Bank and Trust Company. The Court set down plaintiff's preliminary injunction motions for early hearing because of the imminence of the demolition (Old Grand Rapids City Hall), which plaintiff seeks to at least forestall, if not prevent entirely. Prior to the commencement of the hearing there were filed motions to dismiss by all defendants, lack of jurisdiction being a basis common to all. Also advanced are contentions of non-retroactivity of the applicable legislative enactments and lack of standing. The preliminary injunction hearing, therefore, was held in abeyance so as to give precedence to a hearing on and determination of the various motions to dismiss.

* * *

It should be clear from the above that the Old Grand Rapids City Hall is on a parcel which is only a small segment of a substantial renewal plan area, that the plan was adopted by the City on April 4, 1961 and that execution of the plan has been proceeding since that time. The Act which plaintiff seeks to take advantage of came into existence October 15, 1966. The section of said Act relied upon by plaintiff is as follows:

"16 U.S.C.A. § 470f. Effect of Federal undertakings upon property listed in the National Register; comment by Advisory Council on Historic Preservation.

"The head of any Federal agency having direct or indirect jurisdiction over a proposed Federal or federally assisted undertaking in any State and the head of any Federal department or independent agency having authority to license any undertaking shall, prior to the approval of the expenditure of any Federal funds on the undertaking or prior to the issuance of any license, as the case may be, take into account the effect of the undertaking on any district, site, building, structure, or object that is included in the National Register. The head of any such Federal agency shall afford the Advisory Council on Historic Preservation established under sections 470i–470m of this title a reasonable opportunity to comment with regard to such undertaking. Pub.L. 89–665, Title I, § 106, Oct. 15, 1966, 80 Stat. 917."

* * *

[W]e are concerned with a statute, 16 U.S.C.A. § 470f whose function is to provide the Advisory Council on Historic Preservation a reasonable opportunity to comment with regard to an undertaking and its effect on any district, site, building, structure or object that is included in the National Register, and further to provide that the undertaking conform to other requirements of the statute. The National Historic Preservation Act provides in part as follows:

"(a) The Secretary of the Interior is authorized—

"(1) to expand and maintain a national register of districts, sites, buildings, structures, and objects significant in American history, architecture, archeology, and culture, hereinafter referred to as the National Register, and to grant funds to States for the purpose of preparing comprehensive statewide historic surveys and plans, in accordance with criteria established by the Secretary, for the preservation, acquisition, and development of such properties;" 16 U.S.C.A. § 470a.

Thus we are concerned with a statute that has application to federal agencies, heads of federal departments or individual agencies and the Advisory Council on Historic Preservation, with the duties of each clearly spelled out. [The Advisory Council on Historic Preservation, composed of seventeen members (not to be confused with Kent County Council for Historic Preservation), is not a party to this suit, either as a plaintiff or a defendant.] We are concerned with inanimate objects such as districts, sites, buildings, structures, or objects that are included in the National Register, rather than with individuals, organizations or corporations. * * *

Plaintiff has failed to establish by proof, argument or citation that it has any interest that would give it the right to bring this action. Accordingly, it lacks standing to sue.

The motions to dismiss heretofore filed herein should be granted. The moving parties may submit orders in accordance with this Memorandum, for consideration by the Court, incorporating therein such proposed supplemental comments as they may find desirable.

Notes

1. Compare with the principal case, Edwards v. First Bank of Dundee, 393 F.Supp. 680 (N.D.Ill.1975), which allowed residents standing to challenge demolition of a building on the National Register on the theory that the structure was a bank and relocation of a bank is subject to approval by the Federal Deposit Insurance Corporation which has responsibilities under both the National Environmental Policy Act and the National Historical Preservation Act. (The court did not reach the merits.) Also see Hart v. Denver Urban Renewal Auth., 551 F.2d 1178 (10th Cir.1977).

2. The Aluli case, cited in the previous note, and Romero–Barcelo v. Brown, 478 F.Supp. 646 (D.Puerto Rico 1979), modified 643 F.2d 835 (1st Cir.1981), both involve attempts to enjoin the United States Navy from using archeologically and environmentally significant areas for bombing, shelling and other training operations. Although both courts found violations of NEPA and the National Historic Preservation Act, the district court in Barcelo refused to enjoin the Navy for reasons of national defense and the Ninth Circuit in Aluli reversed an injunction requiring the Navy to file annual environmental impact statements.

PENN CENTRAL TRANSP. CO. v. CITY OF NEW YORK

Court of Appeals of New York, 1977.
42 N.Y.2d 324, 397 N.Y.S.2d 914, 366 N.E.2d 1271, affirmed
438 U.S. 104, 98 S.Ct. 2646, 57 L.Ed.2d 631 (1978).

[The Supreme Court opinion in this case, which appears in Chapter IX, deals primarily with the "taking" issue.]

BREITEL, CHIEF JUDGE.

In broad terms, the problem in this case is determining the scope of governmental power, within the Constitution, to preserve, without resorting to eminent domain, irreplaceable landmarks deemed to be of inestimable social or cultural significance. In controversy is the constitutionality of regulation which would prohibit appellants, owner and proposed developer of the air rights above Grand Central Terminal, from constructing an office building atop the terminal.

* * *

Plaintiffs, Penn Central Transportation Company and its affiliates, who have a fee interest in Grand Central Terminal, and UGP Properties, Inc., lessee of the development rights over the terminal, seek a declaration that the landmark preservation provisions of the Administrative Code of the City of New York, as applied to the terminal property, are unconstitutional. They also seek to enjoin defendants, the City of New York and the City Landmarks Preservation Commission, from enforcing those provisions against the subject property. Trial Term granted the requested relief, but a divided Appellate Division reversed and granted judgment to defendants. Plaintiffs appeal.

The order of the Appellate Division should be affirmed. Although government regulation is invalid if it denies a property owner all reasonable return, there is no constitutional imperative that the return embrace all attributes, incidental influences, or contributing external factors derived from the social complex in which the property rests. So many of these attributes are not the result of private effort or investment but of opportunities for the utilization or exploitation which an organized society offers to any private enterprise, especially to a public utility, favored by government and the public. These, too, constitute a background of massive social and governmental investment in the organized community without which the private enterprise could neither exist nor prosper. It is enough, for the limited purposes of a landmarking statute, albeit it is also essential, that the privately created ingredient of property receive a reasonable return. It is that privately created and privately managed ingredient which is the property on which the reasonable return is to be based. All else is society's contribution by the sweat of its brow and the expenditure of its funds. To that extent society is also entitled to its due.

Moreover, in this case, the challenged regulation provides Penn Central with transferable above-the-surface development rights which, because they may be attached to specific parcels of property, some already owned by Penn Central or its affiliates, may be considered as part of the owner's return on the terminal property.

Thus, the regulation does not deprive plaintiffs of property without due process of law, and should be upheld as a valid exercise of the police power.

* * *

This is not a zoning case. In many ways, the restrictions imposed on the use of the property are similar to zoning restrictions, but the purposes are different, and in determining whether regulation is reasonable, the purposes behind the regulation assume considerable significance * * *. Zoning restrictions operate to advance a comprehensive community plan for the common good. Each property owner in the zone is both benefited and restricted from exploitation, presumably without discrimination, except for permitted continuing nonconforming uses. The restrictions may be designed to maintain the general character of the area, or to assure orderly development, objectives inuring to the benefit of all, which property owners acting individually would find difficult or impossible to achieve * * *.

Nor does this case involve landmark regulation of a historic district. Historic district regulation, like zoning regulation, may be designed to maintain the character, both economic and esthetic or cultural, of an area (see Maher v. City of New Orleans, 5 Cir., 516 F.2d 1051, esp. p. 1060, cert. den. 426 U.S. 905, 96 S.Ct. 2225, 48 L.Ed.2d 830; Opinion of the Justices to the Senate, 333 Mass. 773, 778–780, 128 N.E.2d 557). The difference, generally, is that zoning does this largely by regulating construction of new buildings, while historic district regulation concentrates instead on preventing alteration or demolition of existing structures. In each case, owners although burdened by the restrictions also benefit, to some extent, from the furtherance of a general community plan.

Nor does this case partake of the principles applicable to a taking in eminent domain. As noted earlier, there is no taking for which just compensation must be paid. And it is the concept of just compensation which is so integrally related to value based on return. Instead, landmark regulation is a limitation on exploitation of property, an attribute shared with the classifications of zoning and historic districting. Yet landmark regulation is different because the burden of limitation is borne by a single owner. He may or may not benefit from that limitation but his neighbors most likely will. In contrast both an owner and his neighbors benefit to some degree and in some manner from zoning and historic districting.

Restrictions on alteration of individual landmarks are not designed to further a general community plan. Landmark restrictions are designed to prevent alteration or demolition of a single piece of property. To this extent, such restrictions, resemble "discriminatory" zoning restrictions, properly condemned, affecting properties singled out in a zoning district for more restrictive or more liberal zoning limitations * * * There is, however, a significant difference. Discriminatory zoning is condemned because there is no acceptable reason for singling out one particular parcel for different and less favorable treatment. When landmark regulation is involved, there is such a reason: the cultural, architectural, historical, or social significance attached to the affected parcel. Even when regulation is designed to achieve such an acceptable purpose, however, the landowner must be allowed a reasonable return or equivalent private use of his property * * * That is, in the case of commercial property, the owner must be assured of a continued reasonable return on the property.

* * *

Grand Central Terminal is no ordinary landmark. It may be true that no property has economic value in the absence of the society around it, but how much more true it is of a railroad terminal, set amid a metropolitan population, and entirely dependent on a heavy traffic of travelers to make it an economically feasible operation. Without people Grand Central would never have been a successful railroad terminal, and without the terminal, a major transportation center, the proposed building site would be much less desirable for an office building.

Of course it may be argued that had Grand Central Terminal never been built, the area would not have developed as it has. Thus, the argument runs, construction of the terminal triggered growth of the area, and created much of the terminal property's current value. Indeed, the argument has some validity. But, in reality, it is of little moment which comes first, the terminal or the travelers. For it is the interaction of economic influences in the greatest megalopolis of the western hemisphere—the terminal initially drawing people to the area, and the society developing the area with shops, hotels, office buildings, and unmatched civil services—that has made the property so valuable. Neither factor alone accounts for the increase in the property's value; both, in tandem, have contributed to the increase.

* * *

To put the matter another way, the massive and indistinguishable public, governmental, and private contributions to a landmark like the Grand Central Terminal are inseparably joint, and for most of its existence, made both the terminal and the railroads of which it was an integral part, a great financial success for generations of stockholders and bondholders. Their investment has long been eliminated or impaired by the recent vicissitudes of the Penn Central complex. It is exceedingly difficult but imperative, nevertheless, to sort out the merged ingredients and to assess the rights and responsibilities of owner and society. A fair return is to be accorded the owner, but society is to receive its due for its share in the making of a once great railroad. The historical, cultural, and architectural resource that remains was neither created solely by the private owner nor solely by the society in which it was permitted to evolve.

* * *

The discussion thus far is in accord with the teachings of Lutheran Church in Amer. v. City of New York, 35 N.Y.2d 121, 359 N.Y.S.2d 7, 316 N.E.2d 305, supra. The Lutheran Church, owner of the landmark site, established, as plaintiffs here have not, that economic considerations did not permit maintenance of the landmark building in its existing form (id., p. 132, 359 N.Y.S.2d p. 16, 316 N.E.2d p. 312). Moreover, the Lutheran Church was a charitable institution which, over the years, did not and could not reap the same pecuniary benefits of massive governmental investment enjoyed by the railroads and Grand Central Terminal. Yet, the regulatory provisions prohibited replacement of the landmark building without any new ameliorative provisions, other than the pre-existing tax exemption to which it had always been entitled, to assure that the property remained capable of usefulness on a reasonable economic basis. The same problem was reached and discussed in Matter of Trustees of Sailors' Snug Harbor v. Platt, 29 A.D.2d 376, esp. p. 378, 288 N.Y.S.2d 314, 316. In recognizing the invalidity of the landmark regulation as applied to *Lutheran Church,* however, this court as had the court in the *Sailors' Snug Harbor* case, supra, declined to strike down the landmarks preservation provisions of the city administrative code * * *. In this case, by contrast, there has been no showing that the property, owned not by a charitable enterprise but by an entity existing to make a profit, is incapable in its economic context of producing a reasonable return, even if its development is limited.

Moreover, plaintiffs have not been wholly deprived of the development rights above the terminal. Those rights have been made transferable to other parcels of land in the vicinity, at least eight of them owned by Penn Central, including the sites of the Biltmore, Commodore, Barclay, and Roosevelt Hotels.

The many defects in New York City's program for development rights transfers have been detailed elsewhere (Costonis, The Chicago Plan: Incentive Zoning and the Preservation of Urban Landmarks, 85 Harv.L.Rev. 574, 585–589). The area to which transfer is permitted is severely limited, complex procedures are required to obtain a transfer permit, and the program, it has been said, has the unfortunate consequence of encouraging large, bulky buildings around landmarks which are dwarfed by comparison. But the possibility that a better program could have been devised does not preclude analysis and justification of the existing one in this particular application.

* * *

* * * Plaintiffs in this case have failed to meet that burden. In none of their analyses do they include the benefits provided to Penn Central's varied real estate holdings by the terminal's operation. These real, albeit indirect, benefits alone might suffice to provide Penn Central with a reasonable return. But there is more. The development rights above Grand Central Terminal have been made transferable, and could be transferred to several sites owned by Penn Central and suitable for office building construction. These substitute rights are valuable, and provide significant, perhaps "fair", compensation for the loss of rights above the terminal itself. Hence, no constitutional violation has been established.

In times of easy affluence, preservation of historic landmarks through use of the eminent domain power might be desirable, or even required. But when a less expensive alternative is available, especially when a city is in financial distress, it should not be forced to choose between witnessing the demolition of its glorious past and mortgaging its hopes for the future. The landmark preservation provisions of the Administrative Code represent an effort to take a middle way (Marcus, Mandatory Development Rights Transfer and the Taking Clause: The Case of Manhattan's Tudor City Parks, 24 Buff.L.Rev. 77, 78, 107–110). The statute needs improvement. In some cases it protects property owners inadequately * * *. But, in its generality and as applied to Grand Central Terminal, the statute does not deprive plaintiffs of due process of law.

* * *

Accordingly, the order of the Appellate Division should be affirmed, with costs.

Notes

1. As noted by Judge Breitel in the principal case, the court had, in 1974, found the landmarks ordinance unconstitutional as applied to the Lutheran Church in America insofar as the commission had refused a permit for demolition of the J.P. Morgan house owned by the church and used as its national headquarters. Judge Breitel was one of the two dissenters in the Lutheran Church case. Note that in Penn Central the court distinguished the Lutheran Church case by drawing a distinction between a charitable property owner which had not received the accumulated economic benefits enjoyed by commercial ventures through surrounding property development. Is that a sufficient distinction to demarcate a valid regulation from a taking? After the Supreme Court affirmed Penn Central, a New York Court upheld the landmark designation of a charitable corporation in a fact situation much like that in Lutheran Church. See Society for Ethical Culture v. Spatt, 68 A.D.2d 112, 416 N.Y.S.2d 246 (1979), affirmed 51 N.Y.2d 449, 434 N.Y.S.2d 932, 415 N.E.2d 922 (1980).

2. Some years after the Penn Central decision the developer of a building site a few blocks from Grand Central Terminal sought a permit for a 74–story office building utilizing TDRs from the railroad. Public opposition to the proposal was strong and the commission denied the TDR transfer on the ground that the developer's parcel was not adjacent to the landmarked terminal. In 383 Madison Associates v. City of New York, 193 A.D.2d 518, 598 N.Y.S.2d 180 (1993), appeal dismissed 82 N.Y.2d 748, 602 N.Y.S.2d 806,

622 N.E.2d 307, cert. denied 511 U.S. 1081, 114 S.Ct. 1830, 128 L.Ed.2d 459 (1994) the court sided in part with the commission, rejecting the commission's finding that the proposed building would have a disproportionate impact on the neighborhood, but upholding the finding that even though a pattern of common ownership once joined the parcel with the terminal, because of intervening sales of the parcel in question and also sales of intervening lots by Penn Central, the requisite "adjacency" was broken. The developer had argued that despite the sales of surface lots, underground tracks still connected the parcels.

3. The question of landmark designation for religious structures has been especially controversial. A controversy in New York City over granting air rights development permission to St. Bartholomew's Church on Park Avenue raged for several years with a number of celebrity residents taking sides. A federal district court upheld the landmark designation of the church and the denial of the permit in Rector, Wardens, and Members of the Vestry of St. Bartholomew's Church v. City of New York, 728 F.Supp. 958 (S.D.N.Y. 1989) affirmed 914 F.2d 348 (2d Cir.1990), cert. denied 499 U.S. 905, 111 S.Ct. 1103, 113 L.Ed.2d 214 (1991). In 1987 Chicago amended its landmark ordinance to give owners of religious property the right to veto landmarking of property used for religious worship.

4. The Religious Land Use and Institutionalized Persons Act of 2000 (discussed more fully in Chapter XI), may impact the ability of local governments to enforce historic preservation regulations on religious institutions. See, Noles, "Can Historic Preservation Coexist with Protections for Religious Land Uses?" 17 Nat. Resources & Env't 89 (Fall 2002) and Carnell, "Zoning Churches: Washington State Constitutional Limitations on the Application of Land Use Regulations to Religious Buildings," 25 Seattle U. L. R. 699 (Spring 2002).

5. A Pennsylvania court upheld landmark designation for the interior as well as the exterior of an art deco movie house in Sameric Corp. of Chestnut St., Inc. v. City of Philadelphia, 125 Pa.Cmwlth. 520, 558 A.2d 155 (1989). When the case got to the Pennsylvania supreme court, an opinion was rendered that rejected the landmark ordinance, United Artists Theater Circuit, Inc. v. City of Philadelphia, 528 Pa. 12, 595 A.2d 6 (1991). Shortly thereafter, and after much public criticism, the court granted a reargument in the case. After reargument, the court partially reversed itself and held that the designation of the theater as a historical landmark without the consent of the owners did not constitute a taking; however, the court also held that the Philadelphia ordinance did not authorize designation of the interior of the building as historical. 535 Pa. 370, 635 A.2d 612 (1993). Compare Teachers Insurance and Annuity Ass'n of America v. City of New York, 82 N.Y.2d 35, 603 N.Y.S.2d 399, 623 N.E.2d 526 (1993) (decided one month earlier than the Pennsylvania case) where the court held that designation of the Four Seasons Restaurant inside the Seagram Building as a landmark was within the powers of the Landmark Preservation Commission. The owners argued, without success, that the interior of a restaurant is not the same sort of public space as the interior of a railroad station, which is habitually and customarily open to the public at large, the standard prescribed by the ordinance.

FGL & L PROPERTY CORP. v. CITY OF RYE
Court of Appeals of New York, 1985.
66 N.Y.2d 111, 495 N.Y.S.2d 321, 485 N.E.2d 986.

MEYER, JUDGE.

* * *

Plaintiff is the owner in fee of a parcel of land situated in the City of Rye (City) of approximately 22 acres on which are located the Jay Mansion, built in 1838 by Peter Jay, son of John Jay, the first Chief Justice of the United States Supreme Court, and another building known as the Carriage House, built around 1912 in the Colonial Revival style. There is some dispute between the parties concerning the historic or landmark significance of the Carriage House, but for purposes of this opinion we assume that both buildings have such significance. * * *

* * * In June 1983, the City Council adopted Local Law No. 5–1983, which added a new section 197–13.2 to the City Code creating the Alansten Landmarks Preservation District (LPD–A). As the revised zoning map demonstrates, and defendants do not deny, the only property zoned LPD–A was plaintiff's 22 acres. Plaintiff then began the present action, which in seven causes of action sought an injunction against enforcement of the section, a declaration that it is invalid as ultra vires, unconstitutional, site specific, spot zoning and not in accordance with a well-considered zoning plan, and money damages under 42 U.S.C.A. § 1983. * * *

The section as enacted declares that in order to provide for flexibility in the City's zoning "so that the significant historic buildings, the Jay Mansion and the Carriage House, and site features which characterize this site * * * are preserved for the future and that new construction be undertaken with care and consideration for these features and the environment", the new district is adopted. Subdivision B establishes standards for the new district, which include that "[t]he lot as approved shall have a minimum area of twenty-two (22) acres and shall be and remain in single ownership"; that "[t]he exterior of the Jay Mansion and Carriage House shall be rehabilitated and the interiors converted to residential use", for the Jay Mansion not to exceed three units and for the Carriage House not to exceed six; that there be a trapezoidal view way 90 feet in width at the rear of the Jay Mansion and 300 feet in width at the southerly property line; that the new dwelling units may not be occupied until the exteriors of the Jay Mansion and the Carriage House have been restored and the interiors converted to residential use and available for occupancy and that a bond be posted to assure such rehabilitation and conversion; and that the application for site plan approval be accompanied by, among other things, a draft condominium offering statement together with a draft of an easement and/or agreement for perpetual maintenance of the exteriors of the Jay Mansion and the Carriage House. Neither the statutes authorizing enactment of zoning provisions nor those dealing with historic landmarks empower the City Council to adopt a local law with such provisions, nor does anything in the Landmarks Preservation chapter of the City Code support its so doing.

* * *

Authority to enact section 197–13.2 of the Code of the City of Rye does not exist, therefore, unless it can be found in the historical preservation provisions contained in section 96–a and article 5–K of the General Municipal Law or the Landmarks Preservation provision of the Rye City Code (ch. 117).

Section 96–a of the General Municipal Law reads as follows: "In addition to any power or authority of a municipal corporation to regulate by planning or zoning laws and regulations or by local laws and regulations, the governing board or local legislative body of any county, city, town or village is empowered to provide by regulations, special conditions and restrictions for the protection, enhancement, perpetuation and use of places, districts, sites, buildings, structures, works of art, and other objects having a special character of special historical or aesthetic interest or value. Such regulations, special conditions and restrictions may include appropriate and reasonable control of the use or appearance of neighboring private property within public view, or both. In any such instance such measures, if adopted in the exercise of the police power, shall be reasonable and appropriate to the purpose, or if constituting a taking of private property shall provide for due compensation, which may include the limitation or remission of taxes." Article 5–K is broader in scope, covering historic preservation not only by regulation but by governmental acquisition as well. Section 119–bb(4) defines "historic preservation" to mean "for the purposes of this article and notwithstanding any other provision of law, the study, designation, protection, restoration, rehabilitation and use of buildings, structures, districts, areas, sites or objects significant in the history, architecture, archeology or culture of this state, its communities, or the nation." The operative provisions of the article are contained in section 119–dd, which is set forth in full in the margin.[17]

---

17. The section, entitled "Local historic preservation programs," reads as follows:

"In addition to existing powers and authorities for local historic preservation programs including existing powers and authorities to regulate by planning or zoning laws and regulations or by local laws and regulations for preservation of historic landmarks and districts and use of techniques including transfer of development rights, the legislative body of any county, city, town or village is hereby empowered to:

"1. Provide by regulations, special conditions and restrictions for the protection, enhancement, perpetuation and use of places, districts, sites, buildings, structures, works of art and other objects having a special character or special historical, cultural or aesthetic interest or value. Such regulations, special conditions and restrictions may include appropriate and reasonable control of the use or appearance of neighboring private property within the public view, or both.

"2. Establish a landmark or historical preservation board of commission with such powers as are necessary to carry out all or any of the authority possessed by the municipality for a his-

Sec. 2 HISTORICAL LANDMARK & CULTURAL PRESERVATION 899

Of importance to the present issue is the fact that the regulation, special condition or restriction by which section 119–dd(1) authorizes control of private property is "for the protection, enhancement, perpetuation and use of places, districts, sites, buildings, structures". Nothing in the subdivision speaks to regulation of ownership. Noteworthy also is the fact that though section 119–bb(4) refers to "restoration" and "rehabilitation", those words are not to be found in section 119–dd(1), presumably because it was intended to permit a municipality acting under section 119–dd(3) after acquisition of a fee or lesser interest to restore and rehabilitate historic buildings and sites, but not to permit the municipality to impose an obligation to restore or rehabilitate such buildings or sites as remain in private ownership. Here the Code sections creating the Alansten Landmarks Preservation District not only mandate that the entire 22-acre district remain in single ownership but also impose upon the developer the duty of rehabilitating the exteriors of the Jay Mansion and the Carriage House, proscribe the use of any new dwelling unit until that has been done, thus effectively requiring that the cost of rehabilitation be shared by owners in the district of units other than the Jay Mansion and the Carriage House, and by dictating condominium ownership of the entire district impose the cost of maintenance of the exteriors of the Mansion and the Carriage House upon owners of such units as well.

The right to impose reasonable controls on the use and appearance of neighboring private property within public view, given by General Municipal Law §§ 96–a and 119–dd(1), cannot be stretched to cover payment of restoration and maintenance costs, for such a construction, which would impose those costs upon every unit in the district, not just those "within public view," would render meaningless the limitation intended by those words which appear in both sections. Yet there is no question that such was the Council's intention, for its findings with respect to the final environmental impact statement flatly stated that "[o]nly under [condominium] ownership can the cost of maintaining the exteriors of the historic buildings be shared by all the homeowners", and

toric preservation program, as the local legislative body deems appropriate.

"3. After due notice and public hearing, by purchase, gift, grant, bequest, devise, lease or otherwise, acquire the fee or any lesser interest, development right, easement, covenant or other contractual right necessary to achieve the purposes of this article, to historical or cultural property within its jurisdiction. After acquisition of any such interest pursuant to this subdivision, the effect of the acquisition on the valuation placed on any remaining private interest in such property for purposes of real estate taxation shall be taken into account.

"4. Designate, purchase, restore, operate, lease and sell historic buildings or structures. Sales of such buildings and structures shall be upon such terms and conditions as the local legislative body deems appropriate to insure the maintenance of the historic quality of the buildings and structures, after public notice is appropriately given at least thirty days prior to the anticipated date of availability and shall be for fair and adequate consideration of such buildings and structures which in no event shall be less than the expenses incurred by the municipality with respect to such buildings and structures for acquisition, restoration, improvement and interest charges.

"5. Provide for transfer of development rights for purposes consistent with the purposes of this article."

that theme is repeatedly emphasized in the City's brief to this court. While that may be true, clearer authorization to enact such provisions than are contained in the General Municipal Law sections referred to is essential before section 197–13.2 can be upheld against the argument that it was beyond the City's power to enact.

Noteworthy also, in view of the requirement that the Mansion and Carriage House be completely restored before any other unit can be occupied is the absence from the General Municipal Law sections of authority to require restoration, as distinct from maintenance. Landmark and historic preservation laws normally prevent alteration or demolition of existing structures unless the owner can demonstrate hardship (*Penn Cent. Transp. Co. v. City of New York,* 42 N.Y.2d 324, 330, 397 N.Y.S.2d 914, 366 N.E.2d 1271, *affd.* 438 U.S. 104, 98 S.Ct. 2646, 57 L.Ed.2d 631), but if they place an undue and uncompensated burden on the individual owner they may be held unconstitutional (*Lutheran Church in Am. v. City of New York,* 35 N.Y.2d 121, 129, 359 N.Y.S.2d 7, 316 N.E.2d 305) because "it forces the owner to assume the cost of providing a benefit to the public without recoupment" (*French Investing Co. v. City of New York,* 39 N.Y.2d 587, 596, 385 N.Y.S.2d 5, 350 N.E.2d 381; *see,* Dunham, *A Legal and Economic Basis For City Planning,* 58 Colum.L.Rev. 650, 665). Here, society at large bears no part of the cost of restoration, it is rather to be borne initially by plaintiff and ultimately by the purchasers of dwelling units within the district. Yet the City's expert appraiser agreed that restoration costs of approximately $627,000 for the Jay Mansion and $588,000 for the Carriage House would be required.

We do not hold that the General Municipal Law sections could not be drafted to impose restoration costs on an owner without violating the Constitution, nor need we reach the question whether as applied to plaintiff's property section 197–13.2 is constitutional. We hold rather that in light of the well-recognized rule that statutes are to be construed so as to avoid constitutional issues if such a construction is fairly possible * * * the General Municipal Law sections under consideration as presently written should be construed not to authorize imposition of restoration costs solely upon plaintiff and purchasers from plaintiff or maintenance costs upon purchasers of properties other than those to be preserved.

* * *

For the foregoing reasons, the order of the Appellate Division declaring Rye City Code § 197–13.2 invalid is affirmed, with costs.

WACHTLER, C.J., and JASEN, SIMONS, KAYE, ALEXANDER AND TITONE, JJ., concur.

Order affirmed, with costs.

Notes

1. After the decision in this case the county board of legislators voted to take the property by eminent domain, and the developer entered into

Sec. 2   HISTORICAL LANDMARK & CULTURAL PRESERVATION   901

negotiations to sell the property to the county. Although the developer purchased the Jay house and land for $1.1 million in 1983, she set a price of $13.6 million on the property. The county had appraised the property at $6.9 million in 1989 and did not want to pay much more than the appraisal. The county also figured that the cost to rehabilitate the buildings would range from $2 million to $2.5 million and annual maintenance would run about $185,000.

2. The use of the police power to designate individual buildings as landmarks has proven to be much more controversial than the designation of areas as historic districts. One obvious reason for the disparate treatment is the view that creation of an historic district usually enhances the value of all the property in the district while the designation of a single building as a landmark usually imposes uncompensated burdens on the property owner. The validity of landmark ordinances has been questioned in several states. The Texas courts have used the constitutional principles of vagueness and unlawful delegation of legislative powers to strike down landmark designation efforts at both the state and local levels. See Texas Antiquities Committee v. Dallas County Community College Dist., 554 S.W.2d 924 (Tex.1977) and Southern Nat'l Bank of Houston v. City of Austin, 582 S.W.2d 229 (Tex.Civ.App.1979). Other cases showing some hostility to landmark preservation (although they do not involve particular ordinances) are Galich v. Catholic Bishop of Chicago, 75 Ill.App.3d 538, 31 Ill.Dec. 370, 394 N.E.2d 572 (1979) and Hoboken Environment Committee, Inc. v. German Seaman's Mission of New York, 161 N.J.Super. 256, 391 A.2d 577 (1978). An intermediate appellate court upheld denial of a demolition permit for a church building in First Presbyterian Church of York v. City Council of City of York, 25 Pa.Cmwlth. 154, 360 A.2d 257 (1976), but a concurring opinion in the case made the following observation:

> * * * [T]he legislatures and courts are adding a new dimension which may do violence to constitutional private property rights, for now we hold that a private property owner must make his property available without compensation for public view. In effect, he must dedicate his property without compensation for public historical, aesthetic, educational, and museum purposes, which in reality are public uses. Under the provisions of the ordinance in question, the Church can permit the interior or rear portions of its property to rot or deteriorate in a burned condition in any manner it sees fit, but it can't touch that portion of its property viewable from the street without permission of the local governing body, which uses vague standards founded on aesthetics and historical values, two concepts upon which reasonable men can disagree. There are no state health or safety standards involved whatsoever, rather the standards are based solely upon the feelings or observations of people interested in protecting neighboring properties in the historical district in the name of public welfare. I am concerned that we have reached a constitutional precipice and that an advancement of even a fraction of an inch will result in excessive governmental encroachment upon private property rights.
>
> I want to make it clear that I agree with and applaud the scheme to protect, restore, and maintain places of historical value, but if the public wants to use, take, or apply a private property for that public purpose,

then the public should pay for that laudatory purpose through constitutional means, e.g., eminent domain. In the past we have accomplished these purposes through parks and museums provided by public funds or the benevolence of private donors. Today we change that trend by our holding and instead provide for the establishment of public museums through restrictions on private property owners' rights. The very thought that the next step may be a governmental regulation that all buildings in York's historical district must be painted colonial blue is to me repugnant to the Constitution, and if anything like that should develop, perhaps that will be the place to draw the line.

Also see Lafayette Park Baptist Church v. Board of Adjustment of City of St. Louis, 599 S.W.2d 61 (Mo.App.1980), which involved a church seeking a demolition permit for a run-down structure it had purchased in order to expand parking facilities. Although the case deals with an historic district rather than a landmark designation, the opinion discusses the just compensation issue and the economics of preservation in a useful manner. Compare: Committee to Save the Bishop's House, Inc. v. Medical Center Hosp. of Vermont, Inc., 137 Vt. 142, 400 A.2d 1015 (1979). Another interesting case is Shubert Organization, Inc. v. Landmarks Preservation Comm'n of the City of New York, 166 A.D.2d 115, 570 N.Y.S.2d 504, appeal denied 79 N.Y.2d 751, 579 N.Y.S.2d 651, 587 N.E.2d 289, cert. denied 504 U.S. 946, 112 S.Ct. 2289, 119 L.Ed.2d 213 (1992). In this case the commission designated 45 theaters in central Manhattan as landmarks. The plaintiffs challenged the designation on the ground that the mass designation had nothing to do with the individual architectural worth of the theater buildings but was, instead, a back-door effort to create a theater district and to preserve the industry rather than buildings. The court ruled in favor of the designations.

In Prentiss v. City of South Pasadena, 15 Cal.App.4th 85, 18 Cal.Rptr.2d 641 (1993) the court sided with a homeowner whose application for a permit to build an addition was denied because the city concluded the existing house was a "qualified historic structure" and that the city had discretion to require that alterations to the home be done in a manner best preserving the historical character of the architecture. The court agreed that the issuance of a building permit where the application showed compliance with all building codes was a ministerial act, negating any discretionary power to impose conditions on the permit.

(3) *Conservation Easements and Land Trusts*

A conservation easement is a voluntary agreement between a private landowner and a municipal agency or a qualified not-for-profit corporation to restrict the development, management, or use of the land. The owner of the real property deeds an interest in the land—a conservation easement—to a qualified public or private agency. That agency holds the interest and enforces its restrictions against the transferring owner and all subsequent owners of the land. The purpose of a conservation easement is to preserve or conserve the scenic, open, historic, archaeological, architectural, or natural condition of real property. The easement is used to preserve scenic viewsheds, wildlife habitats, ecosystems, forest land or farmland, historic buildings or districts, and open space as such.

In addition to restricting land use, conservation easements may permit public access, such as hiking over a trail on the property or biking along a designated path.

The conservation easement restricts the use of the property in such a way that its natural or man-made features are not altered or developed in a manner that is inconsistent with their conservation or preservation. Existing uses on the property and expansions of uses not inconsistent with the preservation or conservation of these features are allowed on the restricted parcel.

Conservation easements may be donated, sold at full-market value, or sold at below-market value by the owner of the land. If the easement is donated or is sold at below-market value, the landowner may qualify for an income tax deduction in the year of the donation or bargain sale. Subject to a conservation easement, the land may qualify for a lower estate tax valuation on the death of the owner, thereby reducing the tax burden on the beneficiaries of the owner's estate. Similarly, the local property tax assessments may be lowered, benefiting the landowner on an annual basis thereafter.

A land trust is a local or regional not-for-profit organization, private in nature, organized to preserve and protect the natural and man-made environment by, among other techniques, holding conservation easements that restrict the use of real property. Land trusts usually pursue their own organizational agendas. However, under contract with a local government, a land trust may agree to serve as a vehicle for the negotiation, acquisition, holding, and enforcement of conservation easements agreed to by, or imposed on, landowners as part of the local development review and approval process. The purpose of involving a private land trust in a municipal conservation program is to save the local government the expense and inconvenience of holding, monitoring, and enforcing conservation easements and to take advantage of the land trust's expertise in these matters.

Conservation easements are appropriate when either a local government or a land trust believes that natural or man-made features of real property need protection, in addition to that afforded by zoning and other land use regulations. By purchasing the development rights on agriculturally productive farmlands and subjecting them to a conservation easement, the community or land trust can perpetuate and allow the reasonable expansion of the current agricultural use of the land, while providing compensation to the farmers for forgoing the right to develop their land.

A municipality can contract with a private land trust to hold and enforce conservation easements in order to take advantage of the land trust's funding, staff, expertise, and ability to act more quickly and decisively than a public body.

Almost every state provides specific statutory authorization for the use of this popular easement. Between 1988 and 1998, land trusts protected approximately 1.4 million acres through conservation easements. In 1981 the Uniform Conservation Easement Act was adopted, influencing statutes in about half of the states. A copy of the Act is available at www.cals.ncsu.edu/wq/LandPreservationNotebook/uniform.htm

Conservation easements are assumed to be created in perpetuity. However, the term of any specific easement may be limited to a fixed period or ended upon the happening of a specific event, such as the extinction of a species for which the protected land serves as a habitat. The easement may give the parties the authority to modify its terms by mutual agreement. Where modifications are permitted and occur, the modified agreement must be in writing, filed, and recorded.

Chapter IX

CONSTITUTIONAL LIMITS ON LOCAL CONTROL OF LAND USES

SECTION 1. INTRODUCTION

As we have already seen, the web of local regulatory control over the development of land is comprehensive and detailed. Are there limits on local regulatory power? The purpose of this chapter is to explore a range of external doctrines that might provide limitations on local government controls on land uses. One important limitation is found in the *ultra vires* doctrine. Units of local government have always been considered to have only those powers granted to them by the state or the state constitution. Consequently, the delegation of power to local government must be examined closely in every state to see if a particular exercise of local power is consistent with the delegation. In many jurisdictions, the state constitutional structure supports what is known as "home rule," allowing cities to adopt charters authorizing control and power over activities that are considered to be of local concern. For example, in Ayres v. City Council of City of Los Angeles, 34 Cal.2d 31, 207 P.2d 1, 11 A.L.R.2d 503 (1949), the developer contended that conditions placed on his proposed subdivision were not expressly provided for either in the state legislation or in the local ordinance. The court upheld the conditions, stating:

> The status of an autonomous city, Const. Art. XI, sec. 6; West Coast Advertising Co. v. San Francisco, 14 Cal.2d 516, 95 P.2d 138 (1939); City of Oakland v. Williams, 15 Cal.2d 542, 103 P.2d 168 (1940), is recognized by express references to city ordinances in the Subdivision Map Act. Where as here no specific restriction or limitation on the city's power is contained in the Charter, and none forbidding the particular conditions is included either in the Subdivision Map Act, or the city ordinances, it is proper to conclude that conditions are lawful which are not inconsistent with the Map Act and the ordinances and are reasonably required by the subdivision type and use as related to the character of local and neighborhood planning and traffic conditions.

In considering the scope of local regulatory power, many state courts utilize the so-called Dillon's Rule (named for the author of a leading 19th century treatise on Municipal Corporations) to the effect that municipalities have only those powers expressly delegated by the state legislature, those that are fairly implied from the express delegations, and those that are necessary. In cases of doubt, the courts generally find against the existence of the power.

Another dimension to the delegation of powers problem is the basic constitutional notion that governmental power cannot be delegated to private citizens. This is illustrated by those cases dealing with the issue of whether zoning ordinances can require neighbor consent to particular land uses. In this regard see, for example, Town of Gardiner v. Stanley Orchards, Inc., 105 Misc.2d 460, 432 N.Y.S.2d 335 (1980), where the court held invalid a provision in an ordinance that prohibited mobile homes unless all landowners within 500 feet consented in writing, and Grendel's Den, Inc. v. Goodwin, 495 F.Supp. 761 (D.Mass.1980), affirmed sub nom. Larkin v. Grendel's Den, 459 U.S. 116, 103 S.Ct. 505, 74 L.Ed.2d 297 (1982), where the court struck down a state statute that provided no premises within 500 feet of a church or school could receive a liquor license if the church or school filed a written objection. In both cases the courts discussed the problem of delegating legislative authority to private landowners. Also, consider the following case.

EMMETT McLOUGHLIN REALTY, INC. v. PIMA COUNTY

Court of Appeals of Arizona, Division 2, Department A., 2002.
203 Ariz. 557, 58 P.3d 39.

BRAMMER, PRESIDING JUDGE.

* * *

In 1998, the legislature added subsection (F) to § 11–829. 1998 Ariz. Sess. Laws, ch. 55, § 1; 1998 Ariz. Sess. Laws, ch. 204, § 10. Subsection (F) provided:

> The legislature finds that a rezoning of land that changes the zoning classification of the land or that restricts the use or reduces the value of the land is a matter of statewide concern and such a change in zoning that is initiated by the governing body or zoning body shall not be made without the express written consent of the property owner. The county shall not adopt any change in a zoning classification to circumvent the purpose of this subsection.

In April 2000, the Pima County Board of Supervisors considered and approved a county-initiated rezoning of a parcel of land owned by Emmett McLoughlin Realty, Inc., and Quik–Mart Stores, Inc. (collectively, McLoughlin), from CB–1 to a combination of SR and CR–2 zoning. Although numerous business uses are permitted within the former zoning classification, the latter two permit only residential uses. McLoughlin did not consent to the rezoning and filed this action challenging Pima County's downzoning of the property. Pima County admits its "legislative act of downzoning [the property] was undertaken without the express written consent of the owners of the property, in contravention of" § 11–829(F), but contended in its motion for partial judgment on the pleadings, made pursuant to Rule 12(c), Ariz. R. Civ. P., 16 A.R.S., Pt. 1, that the subsection's consent provision is an unconstitutional delegation of legislative authority. The trial court agreed and, after finding that the consent provision had been the impetus for adopting subsection (F), held the subsection unconstitutional and, citing Rule 54(b), Ariz. R. Civ. P., 16 A.R.S., Pt. 2, entered partial judgment on the pleadings in the county's favor. This appeal followed.

* * *

In deference to the legislature's lawmaking authority, we begin with a presumption that the statute is constitutional. * * * Indeed, if a statute can be constitutionally construed, we must adopt that construction. *Blake v. Schwartz,* 202 Ariz. 120, 42 P.3d 6 (App.2002).

"The legislative authority of the State shall be vested in the Legislature...." Ariz. Const. art. IV, pt. 1, § 1(1). Our courts, however, have condoned the legislature's delegation of certain of its powers under appropriate circumstances. Among the examples of permissible delegation of powers by the legislature is the delegation of zoning powers to cities and counties found in A.R.S. §§ 9–462 through 9–462.08 and 11–801 through 11–876. *See Transamerica Title Ins. Co. v. City of Tucson,* 157 Ariz. 346, 757 P.2d 1055 (1988); *Anderson v. Pima County,* 27 Ariz.App. 786, 558 P.2d 981 (1976); *see also Village of Euclid v. Ambler Realty Co.,* 272 U.S. 365, 47 S.Ct. 114, 71 L.Ed. 303 (1926). The parties do not dispute that zoning decisions are legislative in nature, *see Mehlhorn v. Pima County,* 194 Ariz. 140, 978 P.2d 117 (App.1998), but disagree on whether those decisions, or the ability to frustrate them, may be delegated to private individuals.

McLoughlin first contends § 11–829(F) is not a delegation of authority to property owners but merely constitutes the legislature's withdrawal of a portion of the counties' zoning power. The county points out, however, that each county has "a statutory duty to create a comprehensive plan in coordination with municipalities and to zone in coordination with municipalities in urban areas." *See* A.R.S. §§ 11–806 and 11–825(C)(4). A county's planning power is not merely ancillary to its ability to rezone; the two powers are interdependent. Only with the authority to rezone property can a county effectively make the extensive planning determinations required of it, such as is contemplated by the Urban Planning–Growing Smarter Act. *See* 1998 Ariz. Sess. Laws, ch. 204, §§ 1, 6–10; § 11–806. When it enacted § 11–829(F), the legislature neither revested in itself the zoning authority over property within counties' jurisdictions nor withdrew the counties' planning powers. Because it did not withdraw portions of counties' zoning authority by enacting the subsection, the legislature cannot effectively exercise the counties' zoning powers McLoughlin argues it ostensibly withdrew.

In contrast to McLoughlin's suggestion, the subsection affirmatively grants property owners the ability to prevent counties from initiating downzoning of the owners' property, *see* § 11–829(F) (county-initiated downzoning prohibited "without the express written consent of the property owner"), thereby effectively delegating to those property owners the downzoning authority that formerly reposed in counties. However, "[i]t is a well established theory that a legislature may not delegate its authority to private persons over whom the legislature has no supervision or control." *Industrial Comm'n v. C & D Pipeline, Inc.,* 125 Ariz. 64, 66, 607 P.2d 383, 385 (App.1979); *see Washington ex rel. Seattle Title Trust Co. v. Roberge,* 278 U.S. 116, 122, 49 S.Ct. 50, 52, 73 L.Ed. 210, 214 (1928) (holding unconstitutional a zoning law that purported to give landowners who were "not bound by any official duty, but [we]re free to withhold consent for selfish reasons or arbitrarily and [could] subject [a neighboring landowner] to their will or caprice" authority to prevent a particular use on a neighbor's land); *People ex rel. Chicago Dryer Co. v. City of Chicago,* 413 Ill. 315, 109 N.E.2d 201, 206 (1952) ("The legislature cannot abdicate its functions or subject citizens and their interests to any but lawful public agencies, and a delegation of any sovereign power of government to private citizens cannot be sustained nor their assumption of it justified."); 8 Eugene McQuillan, *Municipal Corporations* § 25.35, at 111 (3d ed. 2000) ("[Z]oning powers may not be delegated to private parties or property owners."); 83 Am.Jur.2d *Zoning and Planning* § 615 (1992); *see also FM Properties Operating Co. v. City of Austin,* 22 S.W.3d 868, 877 (Tex.2000) (state law allowing certain landowners to exempt their properties from municipal water requirements unconstitutionally delegated legislative power to landowners whose "pecuniary interest in developing their land to realize profit may be inconsistent with or repugnant to the public interest").

McLoughlin contends, however, that, instead of delegating to owners the ability to legislate, the subsection merely allows owners to waive a restriction established by the legislature, that is, a general prohibition on county-initiated downzoning. As Pima County points out, this argument highlights the distinction between two historical lines of authority in this area. The first, the "waiver" line, is typified by *Thomas Cusack Co. v. City of Chicago,* 242 U.S. 526, 37 S.Ct. 190, 61 L.Ed. 472 (1917), in which the Court upheld a city ordinance allowing a majority of property owners to waive a general prohibition against the erection of billboards in residential neighborhoods. In doing so, the Court noted the statute did "not [constitute] a delegation of legislative power, but [wa]s ... a familiar provision affecting the enforcement of laws and ordinances." *Id.* at 531, 37 S.Ct. at 192, 61 L.Ed. at 476. Courts have generally distinguished such "waiver" regulations from ones requiring an owner to obtain the consent of neighboring property owners before taking land-use planning action. In *Eubank v. City of Richmond,* 226 U.S. 137, 33 S.Ct. 76, 57 L.Ed. 156 (1912), for example, the Court struck down a city ordinance allowing a majority of property owners to establish neighborhood setback requirements.

In the second line of authority, the "consent" line, the Illinois Supreme Court addressed the distinction in *Chicago Dryer Co.* The Illinois legislature had delegated to municipal corporations the authority to name streets. In response to *Hagerty v. City of Chicago,* 360 Ill. 97, 195 N.E. 652 (1935) (naming of streets a legislative function), the legislature had amended the street-naming statute to require a municipal corporation to change a street's name it if received a petition containing the signatures of sixty percent of the street's property owners. The court found the amended statute's effect was

> to give the property owners unbridled discretion of what the law shall be, and, once they have made that determination, the corporate authorities become a mere automatic register of their action and the will of the property owners is given the effect of law. Stated simply, here the provision in reference to the consent of the abutting owners affects the enactment of the law rather than its execution. Thus construed, the decision of a group of property owners, in an admittedly legislative field, is made to prevail over that of the corporate authorities who represent the entire population ... without regard for the necessity, beneficence or reasonableness of their action. 109 N.E.2d at 205 (citations omitted).

As such, the court said, the law constituted "legislative delegation in its most obnoxious form." *Id.*

The county also relies on *Brodner v. City of Elgin,* 96 Ill.App.3d 224, 51 Ill.Dec. 618, 420 N.E.2d 1176 (1981), which we find helpful to our discussion. There, the City of Elgin adopted a municipal ordinance requiring applications for rezoning to be accompanied by the written consent of the owner of the property to be rezoned. Over the protests of several property owners, the city filed and adopted applications to rezone the owners' parcels. The owners sought a judicial declaration that the zoning amendments were invalid because the city had failed to obtain their consent. In upholding the trial court's dismissal of the complaint, the Illinois appellate court held that the owner consent provision was an unconstitutional delegation of the city's legislative zoning authority because it "confer[red] upon the owner of the property the absolute discretion to decide that no rezoning shall ever occur ... despite the fact that the City [might] be effecting a comprehensive zoning plan in pursuit of the common good." *Id.* at 1178.

The central question under these cases in classifying whether a statute such as § 11–829(F) falls within the consent or waiver line of authority is whether the legislative body permissibly delegated its legislative authority. Because the owner consent provision in the subsection affects a rezoning's enactment as opposed to its execution, § 11–829(F) cannot be classified a waiver statute. *See Chicago Dryer Co.* Similar to the ordinance at issue in *Brodner* and the statute at issue in *Chicago Dryer Co.,* § 11–829(F) is a consent statute that unconstitutionally permits a property owner to withhold consent from such a proposed rezoning based solely on his or her self-interest. In doing so, the property owner is unaccountable for frustrating the public health, safety, or welfare because the county's board of supervisors has no recourse. *See* A.R.S. § 11–251(30); 11–802.

McLoughlin also argues, however, that the legislature intended § 11–829(F) to create a type of vested right in zoning classifications. Under the vested rights doctrine, a property owner who materially acts in reliance on an issued building or special use permit may continue to act in conformance therewith, notwithstanding arbitrary governmental withdrawal or cancellation of the permit. *Town of Paradise Valley v. Gulf Leisure Corp.,* 27 Ariz.App. 600, 557 P.2d 532 (1976). Although McLoughlin suggests no material reliance here and points to no occasion in which the legislature has by implication expanded this equitable doctrine, we need not decide the issue because the legislative history accompanying § 11–829(F)'s adoption contains no suggestion the subsection was intended to expand property owners' vested rights to include zoning classifications. As we have already discussed, the narrow breadth of the legislation instead demonstrates no legislative intent to withdraw counties' downzoning authority; by implication, as the trial court found, the legislature's central purpose in enacting § 11–829(F) was adoption of the owner consent provision. Moreover, we question whether expanding the vested rights doctrine in this manner could be upheld as being substantially related to the public's health, safety, and welfare, *see Euclid; Rotter,* because the subsection's restriction applies only to county-initiated downzonings. Under such a system, any rights the legislature arguably might have intended to vest by enacting § 11–829(F) would be abrogated upon either a municipality's annexation of the owner's property or the incorporation of a municipality including that property.

* * *

Affirmed.

Note

Some other cases that present a similar issue are Luger v. City of Burnsville, 295 N.W.2d 609 (Minn.1980) where the court reversed a local decision to grant the property owner a variance "subject to letters of approval by all abutting property owners." The court indicated that a local zoning agency could not avoid the political implications of its decisions by such a transfer of power to the neighbors; and Lakin v. City of Peoria, 129 Ill.App.3d 651, 84 Ill.Dec. 837, 472 N.E.2d 1233 (1984) where the court held that requiring the applicant for a variance to obtain the consent of adjoining and abutting neighbors was an unconstitutional delegation of legislative authority.

With these basic principles of state law that define the authority of municipalities in mind, we look next at the Constitution of the United States and how various provisions affect the ability of local government to regulate land uses.

SECTION 2. REGULATORY TAKINGS

A. THE BASIC CONSTITUTIONAL CONSIDERATIONS

MUGLER v. KANSAS

Supreme Court of the United States, 1887.
123 U.S. 623, 8 S.Ct. 273, 31 L.Ed. 205.

[The state had enacted legislation banning the sale and manufacture of spirituous beverages. Petitioner was owner of a brewery located in the state.]

MR. JUSTICE HARLAN:

* * *

Upon this ground—if we do not misapprehend the position of defendants—it is contended that, as the primary and principal use of beer is as a beverage; as their respective breweries were erected when it was lawful to engage in the manufacture of beer for every purpose; as such establishments will become of no value as property, or, at least, will be materially diminished in value, if not employed in the manufacture of beer for every purpose; the prohibition upon their being so employed is, in effect, a taking of property for public use without compensation, and depriving the citizen of his property without due process of law. In other words, although the State, in the exercise of her police powers, may lawfully prohibit the manufacture and sale, within her limits, of intoxicating liquors to be used as a beverage, legislation having that object in view cannot be enforced against those who, at the time, happen to own property, the chief value of which consists in its fitness for such manufacturing purposes, unless compensation is first made for the diminution in the value of their property, resulting from such prohibitory enactments.

This interpretation of the Fourteenth Amendment is inadmissible. It cannot be supposed that the States intended, by adopting that Amendment, to impose restraints upon the exercise of their powers for the protection of the safety, health, or morals of the community.

* * *

It is supposed by the defendants that the doctrine for which they contend is sustained by *Pumpelly v. Green Bay Co.*, 13 Wall. 168. But in that view we do not concur. That was an action for the recovery of damages for the overflowing of the plaintiff's land by water, resulting from the construction of a dam across a river. The defence was that the dam constituted a part of the system adopted by the State for improving the navigation of Fox and Wisconsin rivers; and it was contended that as the damages of which the plaintiff complained were only the result of the improvement, under legislative sanction, of a navigable stream, he was not entitled to compensation from the State or its agents. The case, therefore, involved the question whether the overflowing of the plaintiff's land, to such an extent that it became practically unfit to be used, was a taking of property, within the meaning of the constitution of Wisconsin, providing that "the property of no person shall be taken for public use without just compensation therefor." This court said it would be a very curious and unsatisfactory result, were it held that, "if the government refrains from the absolute conversion of real property to the uses of the public, it can destroy its value entirely, can inflict irreparable and permanent injury to any extent, can, in effect, subject it to total destruction, without making any compensation, because, in the narrowest sense of that word, it is not *taken* for the public use. Such a construction would pervert the constitutional provision into a restriction upon the rights of the citizen, as those rights stood at the common law, instead of the government, and make it an authority for the invasion of private right under the pretext of the public good, which had no warrant in the laws or practices of our ancestors." pp. 177, 178.

These principles have no application to the case under consideration. The question in *Pumpelly v. Green Bay Company* arose under the State's power of eminent domain; while the question now before us arises under what are, strictly, the police powers of the State, exerted for the protection of the health, morals, and safety of the people. That case, as this court said in *Transportation Co. v. Chicago*, 99 U.S. 635, 642, was an extreme qualification of the doctrine, universally held, that "acts done in the proper exercise of governmental powers, and not directly encroaching upon private property, though these consequences may impair its use," do not constitute a taking within the meaning of the constitutional provision, or entitle the owner of such property to compensation from the State or its agents, or give him any right of action. It was a case in which there was a "permanent flooding of private property," a "physical invasion of the real estate of the private owner, and a practical ouster of his possession." His property was, in effect, required to be devoted to the use of the public, and, consequently, he was entitled to compensation.

As already stated, the present case must be governed by principles that do not involve the power of eminent domain, in the exercise of which property may not be taken for public use without compensation. A prohibition simply upon the use of property for purposes that are declared, by valid legislation, to be injurious to the health, morals, or safety of the community, cannot, in any just sense be deemed a taking or an appropriation of property for the public benefit. Such legislation does not disturb the owner in the control or use of his property for lawful purposes, nor restrict his right to dispose of it, but is only a declaration by the State that its use by any one, for certain forbidden purposes, is prejudicial to the public interests. Nor can legislation of that character come within the Fourteenth Amendment, in any case, unless it is apparent that its real object is not to protect the community, or to promote the general well-being, but, under the guise of police regulation, to deprive the owner of his liberty and property, without due process of law. The power which the States have of prohibiting such use by individuals of their property as will be prejudicial to the health, the morals, or the safety of the public, is not—and, consistently with the existence and safety of organized society, cannot be—burdened with the condition that the State must compensate such individual owners for pecuniary losses they may sustain, by reason of their not being permitted, by a noxious use of their property, to inflict injury upon the community. The exercise of the police power by the destruction of property which is itself a public nuisance, or the prohibition of its use in a particular way, whereby its value becomes depreciated, is very different from taking property for public use, or from depriving a person of his property without due process of law. In the one case, a nuisance only is abated; in the other, unoffending property is taken away from an innocent owner.

PENNSYLVANIA COAL CO. v. MAHON

Supreme Court of the United States, 1922.
260 U.S. 393, 43 S.Ct. 158, 67 L.Ed. 322.

MR. JUSTICE HOLMES delivered the opinion of the Court.

* * *

The statute forbids the mining of anthracite coal in such way as to cause the subsidence of, among other things, any structure used as a human habitation, with certain exceptions, including among them land where the surface is owned by the owner of the underlying coal and is distant more than one hundred and fifty feet from any improved property belonging to any other person. As applied to this case the statute is admitted to destroy previously existing rights of property and contract. The question is whether the police power can be stretched so far.

Government hardly could go on if to some extent values incident to property could not be diminished without paying for every such change in the general law. As long recognized, some values are enjoyed under an implied limitation and must yield to the police power. But obviously the implied limitation must have its limits, or the contract and due process clauses are gone. One fact for consideration in determining such limits is the extent of the diminution. When it reaches a certain magnitude, in most if not in all cases there must be an exercise of eminent domain and compensation to sustain the act. So the question depends upon the particular facts. The greatest weight is given to the judgment of the legislature, but it always is open to interested parties to contend that the legislature has gone beyond its constitutional power.

This is the case of a single private house. No doubt there is a public interest even in this, as there is in every purchase and sale and in all that happens within the commonwealth. Some existing rights may be modified even in such a case. *Rideout v. Knox*, 148 Mass. 368. But usually in ordinary private affairs the public interest does not warrant much of this kind of interference. A source of damage to such a house is not a public nuisance even if similar damage is inflicted on others in different places. The damage is not common or public. *Wesson v. Washburn Iron Co.*, 13 Allen, 95, 103. The extent of the public interest is shown by the statute to be limited, since the statute ordinarily does not apply to land when the surface is owned by the owner of the coal. Furthermore, it is not justified as a protection of personal safety. That could be provided for by notice. Indeed the very foundation of this bill is that the defendant gave timely notice of its intent to mine under the house. On the other hand the extent of the taking is great. It purports to abolish what is recognized in Pennsylvania as an estate in land—a very valuable estate—and what is declared by the Court below to be a contract hitherto binding the plaintiffs. If we were called upon to deal with the plaintiffs' position alone, we should think it clear that the statute does not disclose a public interest sufficient to warrant so extensive a destruction of the defendant's constitutionally protected rights.

But the case has been treated as one in which the general validity of the act should be discussed. The Attorney General of the State, the City of Scranton, and the representatives of other extensive interests were allowed to take part in the argument below and have submitted their contentions here. It seems, therefore, to be our duty to go farther in the statement of our opinion, in order that it may be known at once, and that further suits should not be brought in vain.

It is our opinion that the act cannot be sustained as an exercise of the police power, so far as it affects the mining of coal under streets or cities in places where the right to mine such coal has been reserved. As said in a Pennsylvania case, "For practical purposes, the right to coal consists in the right to mine it." *Commonwealth v. Clearview Coal Co.*, 256 Pa.St. 328, 331. What makes the right to mine coal valuable is that it can be exercised with profit. To make it commercially impracticable to mine certain coal has very nearly the same effect for constitutional purposes as appropriating or destroying it. This we think that we are warranted in assuming that the statute does.

* * *

The rights of the public in a street purchased or laid out by eminent domain are those that it has paid for. If in any case its representatives have been so short sighted as to acquire only surface rights without the right of support, we see no more authority for supplying the latter without compensation than there was for taking the right of way in the first place and refusing to pay for it because the public wanted it very much. The protection of private property in the Fifth Amendment presupposes that it is wanted for public use, but provides that it shall not be taken for such use without compensation. A similar assumption is made in the decisions upon the Fourteenth Amendment. * * * When this seemingly absolute protection is found to be qualified by the police power, the natural tendency of human nature is to extend the qualification more and more until at last private property disappears. But that cannot be accomplished in this way under the Constitution of the United States.

The general rule at least is, that while property may be regulated to a certain extent, if regulation goes too far it will be recognized as a taking. It may be doubted how far exceptional cases, like the blowing up of a house to stop a conflagration, go—and if they go beyond the general rule, whether they do not stand as much upon tradition as upon principle. * * * In general it is not plain that a man's misfortunes or necessities will justify his shifting the damages to his neighbor's shoulders. * * * We are in danger of forgetting that a strong public desire to improve the public condition is not enough to warrant achieving the desire by a shorter cut than the constitutional way of paying for the change. As we already have said, this is a question of degree—and therefore cannot be disposed of by general propositions. But we regard this as going beyond any of the cases decided by this Court. * * *

We assume, of course, that the statute was passed upon the conviction that an exigency existed that would warrant it, and we assume that an exigency exists that would warrant the exercise of eminent domain. But the question at bottom is upon whom the loss of the changes desired should fall. So far as private persons or communities have seen fit to take the risk of acquiring only surface rights, we cannot see that the fact that their risk has become a danger warrants the giving to them greater rights than they bought.

Decree reversed.

Mr. Justice Brandeis, dissenting.

* * *

Every restriction upon the use of property imposed in the exercise of the police power deprives the owner of some right theretofore enjoyed, and is, in that sense, an abridgement by the State of rights in property without making compensation. But restriction imposed to protect the public health, safety or morals from dangers threatened is not a taking. The restriction here in question is merely the prohibition of a noxious use. The property so restricted remains in the possession of its owner. The State does not appropriate it or make any use of it. The State merely prevents the owner from making a use which interferes with paramount rights of the public. Whenever the use prohibited ceases to be noxious,—as it may because of further change in local or social conditions,—the restriction will have to be removed and the owner will again be free to enjoy his property as heretofore.

The restriction upon the use of this property cannot, of course, be lawfully imposed, unless its purpose is to protect the public. But the purpose of a restriction does not cease to be public, because incidentally some private persons may thereby receive gratuitously valuable special benefits. Thus, owners of low buildings may obtain through statutory restrictions upon the height of neighboring structures, benefits equivalent to an easement of light and air. * * * Furthermore, a restriction, though imposed for a public purpose, will not be lawful, unless the restriction is an appropriate means to the public end. But to keep coal in place is surely an appropriate means of preventing subsidence of the surface; and ordinarily it is the only available means. Restriction upon use does not become inappropriate as a means, merely because it deprives the owner of the only use to which the property can then be profitably put. The liquor and the oleomargarine cases settled that. *Mugler v. Kansas*, 123 U.S. 623, 668, 669, 8 S.Ct. 273, 31 L.Ed. 205; *Powell v. Pennsylvania*, 127 U.S. 678, 682, 8 S.Ct. 992, 1257, 32 L.Ed. 253. See also *Hadacheck v. Sebastian*, 239 U.S. 394, 36 S.Ct. 143, 60 L.Ed. 348; *Pierce Oil Corporation v. City of Hope*, 248 U.S. 498, 39 S.Ct. 172, 63 L.Ed. 381. Nor is a restriction imposed through exercise of the police power inappropriate as a means, merely because the same end might be effected through exercise of the power of eminent domain, or otherwise at public expense. Every restriction upon the height of buildings might be secured through acquiring by eminent domain the right of each owner to build above the limiting height; but it is settled that the State need not resort to that power. Compare *Laurel Hill Cemetery v. San Francisco*, 216 U.S. 358, 30 S.Ct. 301, 54 L.Ed. 515; *Missouri Pacific Ry. Co. v. Omaha*, 235 U.S. 121, 35 S.Ct. 82, 59 L.Ed. 157. If by mining anthracite coal the owner would necessarily unloose poisonous gasses, I suppose no one would doubt the power of the State to prevent the mining, without buying his coal fields. And why may not the State, likewise, without paying compensation, prohibit one from digging so deep or excavating so near the surface, as to expose the community to like dangers? In the latter case, as in the former, carrying on the business would be a public nuisance.

It is said that one fact for consideration in determining whether the limits of the police power have been exceeded is the extent of the resulting diminution in value; and that here the restriction destroys existing rights of property and contract. But values are relative. If we are to consider the value of the coal kept in place by the restriction, we should compare it with the value of all other parts of the land. That is, with the value not of the coal alone, but with the value of the whole property. The rights of an owner as against the public are not increased by dividing the interests in his property into surface and subsoil. The sum of the rights in the parts cannot be greater than the rights in the whole. The estate of an owner in land is grandiloquently described as extending *ab orco usque ad coelum*. But I suppose no one would contend that by selling his interest above one hundred feet from the surface he could prevent the State from limiting, by the police power, the height of structures in a city. And why should a sale of underground rights bar the State's power? For aught that appears the value of the coal kept in place by the restriction may be negligible as compared with the value of the whole property, or even as compared with that part of it which is represented by the coal remaining in place and which may be extracted despite the statute. * * *

* * *

Sec. 2   REGULATORY TAKINGS   917

A prohibition of mining which causes subsidence of such structures and facilities is obviously enacted for a public purpose; and it seems, likewise, clear that mere notice of intention to mine would not in this connection secure the public safety. Yet it is said that these provisions of the act cannot be sustained as an exercise of the police power where the right to mine such coal has been reserved. The conclusion seems to rest upon the assumption that in order to justify such exercise of the police power there must be "an average reciprocity of advantage" as between the owner of the property restricted and the rest of the community; and that here such reciprocity is absent. Reciprocity of advantage is an important consideration, and may even be an essential, where the State's power is exercised for the purpose of conferring benefits upon the property of a neighborhood, as in drainage projects, *Wurts v. Hoagland*, 114 U.S. 606, 5 S.Ct. 1086, 29 L.Ed. 229; *Fallbrook Irrigation District v. Bradley*, 164 U.S. 112, 17 S.Ct. 56, 41 L.Ed. 369; or upon adjoining owners, as by party wall provisions, *Jackman v. Rosenbaum Co.*, ante, 22. But where the police power is exercised, not to confer benefits upon property owners, but to protect the public from detriment and danger, there is, in my opinion, no room for considering reciprocity of advantage. There was no reciprocal advantage to the owner prohibited from using his oil tanks in 248 U.S. 498; his brickyard, in 239 U.S. 394, 36 S.Ct. 143, 60 L.Ed. 348; his livery stable, in 237 U.S. 171, 35 S.Ct. 511, 59 L.Ed. 900; his billiard hall, in 225 U.S. 623, 32 S.Ct. 697, 56 L.Ed. 1229; his oleomargarine factory, in 127 U.S. 678, 8 S.Ct. 992, 1257, 32 L.Ed. 253; his brewery, in 123 U.S. 623, 8 S.Ct. 273, 31 L.Ed. 205; unless it be the advantage of living and doing business in a civilized community. That reciprocal advantage is given by the act to the coal operators.

Notes

1. Pennsylvania Coal gave birth to the concept of a regulatory taking or police power taking, that is, a taking without physical occupation of the owner's land. The concept, however, has been troublesome both for the Supreme Court and the state courts. Soon after Pennsylvania Coal, the Supreme Court was faced with the question of the validity of comprehensive zoning ordinances that dictated the permissible land uses in zoning districts. In Village of Euclid v. Ambler Realty Co., 272 U.S. 365, 47 S.Ct. 114, 71 L.Ed. 303 (1926), the Court upheld comprehensive zoning, despite the owner's argument that placing some of its land in a residential district devalued it quite heavily as potential industrial land. Mr. Justice Sutherland, speaking for the Court, warned that " * * * where the equitable remedy of injunction is sought, as it is here, not upon the ground of a present infringement or denial of a specific right, or of a particular injury in process of actual execution, but upon the broad ground that the mere existence and threatened enforcement of the ordinance, by materially and adversely affecting values and curtailing the opportunities of the market, constitute a present and irreparable injury, the court will not scrutinize its provisions, sentence by sentence, to ascertain by a process of piecemeal dissection whether there may be, here and there, provisions of a minor character, or relating to matters of administration, or not shown to contribute to the

injury complained of, which, if attacked separately, might not withstand the test of constitutionality."

After the Euclid case, the Court, in a unanimous opinion by Mr. Justice Sutherland, reversed a judgment denying an injunction against the enforcement of a zoning ordinance as to a particular piece of property. In Nectow v. Cambridge, 277 U.S. 183, 48 S.Ct. 447, 72 L.Ed. 842 (1928), the property had been placed in a residential zone, and after reviewing the facts, Mr. Justice Sutherland noted: "It is made pretty clear that because of the industrial and railroad purposes to which the immediately adjoining lands to the south and east have been devoted and for which they are zoned, the locus is of comparatively little value for the limited uses permitted by the ordinance." The Nectow case became the basis for what is the customary manner of attacking zoning—that the ordinance as applied to a particular tract of land, is arbitrary and unreasonable and amounts to confiscation as a result. The tension between a "takings" analysis, and a denial of "substantive due process" analysis in land use disputes will be explored more fully in the next section of this chapter.

2. In Keystone Bituminous Coal Ass'n v. DeBenedictis, 480 U.S. 470, 107 S.Ct. 1232, 94 L.Ed.2d 472 (1987), the Court upheld the Pennsylvania Bituminous Mine Subsidence and Land Conservation Act, distinguishing Pennsylvania Coal in its opinion. Justice Steven's opinion for the Court stated that the 1922 decision did not implicitly overrule cases like Mugler, and that the Subsidence Act was a valid exercise of the police power:

> We reject petitioners' implicit assertion that *Pennsylvania Coal* overruled these cases which focused so heavily on the nature of the state's interest in the regulation. Just five years after the *Pennsylvania Coal* decision, Justice Holmes joined the Court's unanimous decision in Miller v. Schoene, 276 U.S. 272, 48 S.Ct. 246, 72 L.Ed. 568 (1928), holding that the Takings Clause did not require the State of Virginia to compensate the owners of cedar trees for the value of the trees that the State had ordered destroyed. The trees needed to be destroyed to prevent a disease from spreading to nearby apple orchards, which represented a far more valuable resource. In upholding the state action, the Court did not consider it necessary to "weigh with nicety the question whether the infected cedars constitute a nuisance according to common law; or whether they may be so declared by statute." Id., at 280, 48 S.Ct., at 247. Rather, it was clear that the State's exercise of its police power to prevent the impending danger was justified, and did not require compensation. See also Euclid v. Ambler Realty Co., 272 U.S. 365, 47 S.Ct. 114, 71 L.Ed. 303 (1926); Omnia Commercial Co. v. United States, 261 U.S. 502, 509, 43 S.Ct. 437, 438, 67 L.Ed. 773 (1923). Other subsequent cases reaffirm the important role that the nature of the state action plays in our takings analysis.

* * *

> The second factor that distinguishes this case from *Pennsylvania Coal* is the finding in that case that the Kohler Act made mining of "certain coal" commercially impracticable. In this case, by contrast, petitioners have not shown any deprivation significant enough to satisfy

the heavy burden placed upon one alleging a regulatory taking. For this reason, their takings claim must fail. * * *

Petitioners thus face an uphill battle in making a facial attack on the Act as a taking.

The hill is made especially steep because petitioners have not claimed, at this stage, that the Act makes it commercially impracticable for them to continue mining their bituminous coal interests in western Pennsylvania. Indeed, petitioners have not even pointed to a single mine that can no longer be mined for profit. * * *

Because our test for regulatory taking requires us to compare the value that has been taken from the property with the value that remains in the property, one of the critical questions is determining how to define the unit of property "whose value is to furnish the denominator of the fraction." Michelman, Property, Utility, and Fairness: Comments on the Ethical Foundations of "Just Compensation" Law, 80 Harv. L.Rev. 1165, 1192 (1967). * * *

The parties have stipulated that enforcement of the DER's 50% rule will require petitioners to leave approximately 27 million tons of coal in place. Because they own that coal but cannot mine it, they contend that Pennsylvania has appropriated it for the public purposes described in the Subsidence Act.

This argument fails for the reason explained in *Penn Central* and *Andrus*. The 27 million tons of coal do not constitute a separate segment of property for takings law purposes. Many zoning ordinances place limits on the property owner's right to make profitable use of some segments of his property. A requirement that a building occupy no more than a specified percentage of the lot on which it is located could be characterized as a taking of the vacant area as readily as the requirement that coal pillars be left in place. Similarly, under petitioners' theory one could always argue that a set-back ordinance requiring that no structure be built within a certain distance from the property line constitutes a taking because the footage represents a distinct segment of property for takings law purposes. Cf. Gorieb v. Fox, 274 U.S. 603, 47 S.Ct. 675, 71 L.Ed. 1228 (1927) (upholding validity of set-back ordinance) (per Holmes, J.). There is no basis for treating the less than 2% of petitioners' coal as a separate parcel of property. * * *

Pennsylvania property law is apparently unique in regarding the support estate as a separate interest in land that can be conveyed apart from either the mineral estate or the surface estate. Petitioners therefore argue that even if comparable legislation in another State would not constitute a taking, the Subsidence Act has that consequence because it entirely destroys the value of their unique support estate. It is clear, however, that our takings jurisprudence forecloses reliance on such legalistic distinctions within a bundle of property rights. * * *

Thus, in practical terms, the support estate has value only insofar as it protects or enhances the value of the estate with which it is associated. Its value is merely a part of the entire bundle of rights possessed by the owner of either the coal or the surface. Because petitioners retain the right to mine virtually all of the coal in their mineral estates, the burden the Act places on the support estate does not constitute a taking. Petitioners may continue to mine coal profitably even if they may not destroy or damage surface structures at will in the process.

But even if we were to accept petitioners' invitation to view the support estate as a distinct segment of property for "takings" purposes, they have not satisfied their heavy burden of sustaining a facial challenge to the Act. Petitioners have acquired or retained the support estate for a great deal of land, only part of which is protected under the Subsidence Act, which, of course, deals with subsidence in the immediate vicinity of certain structures, bodies of water, and cemeteries. See n. 6, supra. The record is devoid of any evidence on what percentage of the purchased support estates, either in the aggregate or with respect to any individual estate, has been affected by the Act. Under these circumstances, petitioners' facial attack under the takings clause must surely fail.

Justice Rehnquist's dissent (joined by Justices Powell, O'Connor and Scalia) stated that " * * * petitioner's interests in particular coal deposits have been completely destroyed. By requiring that defined seams of coal remain in the ground * * * the Subsidence Act has extinguished any interest one might want to acquire in this property. * * * Application of the nuisance exception in these circumstances would allow the State not merely to forbid one 'particular use' of property with many uses but to extinguish all beneficial uses of petitioners' property." Also see M & J Coal Co. v. United States, 47 F.3d 1148 (Fed.Cir.1995) where the court held the company did not suffer a taking when the Department of Interior, Office of Surface Mining Reclamation and Enforcement (OSM) issued an order prohibiting further mining in an area where there was considerable surface subsidence; even though many of the affected residents had conveyed away their right to support, the court held that the agency's actions were necessary to protect the public health and safety and that the mining company's actions posed a threat to the public in general: "That certain individuals or their predecessors may have unwisely deeded away their rights to surface support cannot estop OSM from exercising its authority to abate an imminent danger to the public health or safety. * * * Justice and fairness do not require that the community at large bear the 'burden' of M & J's inability to mine in a manner that is safe to the public."

GOLDBLATT v. TOWN OF HEMPSTEAD, N.Y.

Supreme Court of the United States, 1962.
369 U.S. 590, 82 S.Ct. 987, 8 L.Ed.2d 130.

Mr. Justice Clark delivered the opinion of the Court.

The Town of Hempstead has enacted an ordinance regulating dredging and pit excavating on property within its limits. Appellants, who engaged in such operations prior to the enactment of the ordinance, claim that it in effect prevents them from continuing their business and therefore takes their property without due process of law in violation of the Fourteenth Amendment. * * *

Appellant Goldblatt owns a 38–acre tract within the Town of Hempstead. At the time of the present litigation appellant Builders Sand and Gravel Corporation was mining sand and gravel on this lot, a use to which the lot had been put continuously since 1927. Before the end of the first year the excavation had reached the water table leaving a water-filled crater which has been widened and deepened to the point that it is now a 20–acre lake with an average depth of 25 feet. The town has expanded around this excavation, and today within a radius of 3,500 feet there are more than 2,200 homes and four public schools with a combined enrollment of 4,500 pupils.

The present action is but one of a series of steps undertaken by the town in an effort to regulate mining excavations within its limits. A 1945 ordinance, No. 16, provided that such pits must be enclosed by a wire fence and comply with certain berm and slope requirements. Although appellants complied with this ordinance, the town sought an injunction against further excavation as being violative of a zoning ordinance. This failed because appellants were found to be "conducting a prior nonconforming use on the premises. * * *" 135 N.Y.L.J., issue 52, p. 12 (1956). The town did not appeal.

In 1958 the town amended Ordinance No. 16 to prohibit any excavating below the water table[1] and to impose an affirmative duty to refill any excavation presently below that level. The new amendment also made the berm, slope, and fence requirements more onerous.

In 1959 the town brought the present action to enjoin further mining by the appellants on the grounds that they had not complied with the ordinance, as amended, nor acquired a mining permit as required by it.[2] Appellants contended, inter alia, that the ordinance was unconstitutional because (1) it was not regulatory of their business but completely prohibitory and confiscated their property without compensation, (2) it deprived them of the benefit of the favorable judgment arising from the previous zoning litigation, and (3) it constituted ex post facto legislation. However, the trial court did not agree, and the appellants were enjoined from conducting further operations on the lot until they had obtained a permit and had complied with the new provisions of Ordinance No. 16.

Concededly the ordinance completely prohibits a beneficial use to which the property has previously been devoted. However, such a characterization does not tell us whether or not the ordinance is unconstitutional. It is an oft-repeated truism that every regulation necessarily speaks as a prohibition. If this ordinance is otherwise a valid exercise of the town's police powers, the fact that it deprives the property of its most beneficial use does not render it unconstitutional. * * * Nor is it of controlling significance that the "use" prohibited here is of the soil itself

---

1. Specifically the ordinance provides that "[n]o excavation shall be made below two feet above the maximum ground water level at the site."

2. Under the ordinance the town may deny a permit if the proposed excavation will violate any of the provisions of the ordinance.

as opposed to a "use" upon the soil, *cf. United States v. Central Eureka Mining Co.*, 357 U.S. 155, 78 S.Ct. 1097, 2 L.Ed.2d 1228 (1958), or that the use prohibited is arguably not a common-law nuisance, *e.g., Reinman v. Little Rock, supra.*

This is not to say, however, that governmental action in the form of regulation cannot be so onerous as to constitute a taking which constitutionally requires compensation. Pennsylvania Coal Co. v. Mahon, 260 U.S. 393, 43 S.Ct. 158, 67 L.Ed. 322 (1922); *see United States v. Central Eureka Mining Co., supra.* There is no set formula to determine where regulation ends and taking begins. Although a comparison of values before and after is relevant, *see Pennsylvania Coal Co. v. Mahon, supra*, it is by no means conclusive, *see Hadacheck v. Sebastian, supra*, where a diminution in value from $800,000 to $60,000 was upheld. How far regulation may go before it becomes a taking we need not now decide, for there is no evidence in the present record which even remotely suggests that prohibition of further mining will reduce the value of the lot in question.[3] Indulging in the usual presumption of constitutionality, * * * we find no indication that the prohibitory effect of Ordinance No. 16 is sufficient to render it an unconstitutional taking if it is otherwise a valid police regulation.

The question, therefore, narrows to whether the prohibition of further excavation below the water table is a valid exercise of the town's police power. The term "police power" connotes the time-tested conceptional limit of public encroachment upon private interests. Except for the substitution of the familiar standard of "reasonableness," this Court has generally refrained from announcing any specific criteria. The classic statement of the rule in *Lawton v. Steele*, 152 U.S. 133, 137, 14 S.Ct. 499, 38 L.Ed. 385 (1894), is still valid today:

> "To justify the State in * * * interposing its authority in behalf of the public, it must appear, first, that the interests of the public * * * require such interference; and, second, that the means are reasonably necessary for the accomplishment of the purpose, and not unduly oppressive upon individuals."

Even this rule is not applied with strict precision, for this Court has often said that "debatable questions as to reasonableness are not for the courts but for the legislature. * * * " *E.g., Sproles v. Binford*, 286 U.S. 374, 388, 52 S.Ct. 581, 76 L.Ed. 1167 (1932).

The ordinance in question was passed as a safety measure, and the town is attempting to uphold it on that basis. To evaluate its reasonableness we therefore need to know such things as the nature of the menace against which it will protect, the availability and effectiveness of other less drastic protective steps, and the loss which appellants will suffer from the imposition of the ordinance.

---

3. There is a similar scarcity of evidence relative to the value of the processing machinery in the event mining operations were shut down.

A careful examination of the record reveals a dearth of relevant evidence on these points. One fair inference arising from the evidence is that since a few holes had been burrowed under the fence surrounding the lake it might be attractive and dangerous to children. But there was no indication whether the lake as it stood was an actual danger to the public or whether deepening the lake would increase the danger. In terms of dollars or some other objective standard, there was no showing how much, if anything, the imposition of the ordinance would cost the appellants. In short, the evidence produced is clearly indecisive on the reasonableness of prohibiting further excavation below the water table.

Although one could imagine that preventing further deepening of a pond already 25 feet deep would have a de minimis effect on public safety, we cannot say that such a conclusion is compelled by facts of which we can take notice. Even if we could draw such a conclusion, we would be unable to say the ordinance is unreasonable; for all we know, the ordinance may have a de minimis effect on appellants. Our past cases leave no doubt that appellants had the burden on "reasonableness." * * * This burden not having been met, the prohibition of excavation on the 20–acre–lake tract must stand as a valid police regulation.

We now turn our attention to the remainder of the lot, the 18 acres surrounding the present pit which have not yet been mined or excavated. Appellants themselves contend that this area cannot be mined. They say that this surface space is necessary for the processing operations incident to mining and that no other space is obtainable. This was urged as an important factor in their contention that upholding the depth limitation of the ordinance would confiscate the entire mining utility of their property. However, we have upheld the validity of the prohibition even on that supposition. If the depth limitation in relation to deepening the existing pit is valid, it follows a fortiori that the limitation is constitutionally permissible as applied to prevent the creation of new pits. We also note that even if appellants were able to obtain suitable processing space the geology of the 18–acre tract would prevent any excavation. The water table, appellants admit, is too close to the ground surface to permit commercial mining in the face of the depth restrictions of the ordinance. The impossibility of further mining makes it unnecessary for us to decide to what extent the berm and slope of such excavation could be limited by the ordinance.

Affirmed.

PENN CENTRAL TRANSP. CO. v. NEW YORK CITY

Supreme Court of the United States, 1978.
438 U.S. 104, 98 S.Ct. 2646, 57 L.Ed.2d 631.

[Under New York City's Landmarks Preservation Law, Grand Central Terminal, owned by Petitioner, was designated as a landmark. After the agency charged with enforcing the law denied permission to build a multi-story office building in the air rights over the existing structure (on grounds that the proposed tower would impair the aesthetic quality of the terminal's existing facade), Petitioner brought suit claiming that the application of the law constituted a taking of its property.]

MR. JUSTICE BRENNAN delivered the opinion of the Court.

* * *

Before considering appellants' specific contentions, it will be useful to review the factors that have shaped the jurisprudence of the Fifth Amendment injunction "nor shall private property be taken for public use, without just compensation." The question of what constitutes a "taking" for purposes of the Fifth Amendment has proved to be a problem of considerable difficulty. While this Court has recognized that the "Fifth Amendment's guarantee [is] designed to bar Government from forcing some people alone to bear public burdens which, in all fairness and justice, should be borne by the public as a whole," *Armstrong v. United States*, 364 U.S. 40, 49, 80 S.Ct. 1563, 1569, 4 L.Ed.2d 1554 (1960), this Court, quite simply, has been unable to develop any "set formula" for determining when "justice and fairness" require that economic injuries caused by public action be compensated by the Government, rather than remain disproportionately concentrated on a few persons. *See Goldblatt v. Hempstead*, 369 U.S. 590, 594, 82 S.Ct. 987, 990, 8 L.Ed.2d 130 (1962). Indeed, we have frequently observed that whether a particular restriction will be rendered invalid by the Government's failure to pay for any losses proximately caused by it depends largely "upon the particular circumstances [in that] case." *United States v. Central Eureka Mining Co.*, 357 U.S. 155, 168, 78 S.Ct. 1097, 1104, 2 L.Ed.2d 1228 (1958); *see United States v. Caltex, Inc.*, 344 U.S. 149, 156, 73 S.Ct. 200, 203, 97 L.Ed. 157 (1952).

In engaging in these essentially ad hoc, factual inquiries, the Court's decisions have identified several factors that have particular significance. The economic impact of the regulation on the claimant and, particularly, the extent to which the regulation has interfered with distinct investment backed expectations are of course relevant considerations. *See Goldblatt v. Hempstead, supra,* 369 U.S., at 594, 82 S.Ct., at 990. So too is the character of the governmental action. A "taking" may more readily be found when the interference with property can be characterized as a physical invasion by Government, *see, e.g., United States v. Causby*, 328 U.S. 256, 66 S.Ct. 1062, 90 L.Ed. 1206 (1946), than when interference arises from some public program adjusting the benefits and burdens of economic life to promote the common good.

"Government could hardly go on if to some extent values incident to property could not be diminished without paying for every such change in the general law," *Pennsylvania Coal Co. v. Mahon*, 260 U.S. 393, 413, 43 S.Ct. 158, 159, 67 L.Ed. 322 (1922), and this Court has accordingly recognized, in a wide variety of contexts, that Government may execute laws or programs that adversely affect recognized economic values. Exercises of the taxing power are one obvious example. A second are the decisions in which this Court has dismissed "taking" challenges on the ground that, while the challenged Government action caused economic harm, it did not interfere with interests that were sufficiently bound up with the reasonable expectations of the claimant to constitute "property" for Fifth Amendment purposes. * * *

More importantly for the present case, in instances in which a state tribunal reasonably concluded that "the health, safety, morals or general welfare" would be promoted by prohibiting particular contemplated uses of land, this Court has upheld land use regulations that destroyed or adversely affected recognized real property interests. *See Nectow v. City of Cambridge*, 277 U.S. 183, 188, 48 S.Ct. 447, 448, 72 L.Ed. 842 (1928). Zoning laws are of course the classic example, *see Euclid v. Ambler Realty Co.*, 272 U.S. 365, 47 S.Ct. 114, 71 L.Ed. 303 (1926) (prohibition of industrial use); *Gorieb v. Fox*, 274 U.S. 603, 608, 47 S.Ct. 675, 677, 71 L.Ed. 1228 (1927) (requirement that portions of parcels be left unbuilt); *Welch v. Swasey*, 214 U.S. 91, 29 S.Ct. 567, 53 L.Ed. 923 (1909) (height restriction), which have been viewed as permissible governmental action even when prohibiting the most beneficial use of the property. * * *

Zoning laws generally do not affect existing uses of real property, but taking challenges have also been held to be without merit in a wide variety of situations when the challenged governmental actions prohibited a beneficial use to which individual parcels had previously been devoted and thus caused substantial individualized harm.

* * *

In contending that the New York City law has "taken" their property in violation of the Fifth and Fourteenth Amendments, appellants make a series of arguments, which, while tailored to the facts of this case, essentially urge that any substantial restriction imposed pursuant to a landmark law must be accompanied by just compensation if it is to be constitutional. Before considering these, we emphasize what is not in dispute. Because this Court has recognized, in a number of settings, that States and cities may enact land use restrictions or controls to enhance the quality of life by preserving the character and desirable aesthetic features of a city, *see City of New Orleans v. Dukes*, 427 U.S. 297, 96 S.Ct. 2513, 49 L.Ed.2d 511 (1976); *Young v. American Mini Theatres, Inc.*, 427 U.S. 50, 96 S.Ct. 2440, 49 L.Ed.2d 310 (1976); *Village of Belle Terre v. Boraas*, 416 U.S. 1, 9–10, 94 S.Ct. 1536, 39 L.Ed.2d 797 (1974); *Berman v. Parker*, 348 U.S. 26, 33, 75 S.Ct. 98, 102, 99 L.Ed. 27 (1954); *Welch v. Swasey, supra*, 214 U.S., at 108, 29 S.Ct., at 571, appellants do not contest that New York City's objective of preserving structures and areas with special historic, architectural, or cultural significance is an entirely permissible governmental goal. They also do not dispute that the restrictions imposed on its parcel are appropriate means of securing the purposes of the New York City law. Finally, appellants do not challenge any of the specific factual premises of the decision below. They accept for present purposes both that the parcel of land occupied by Grand Central Terminal must, in its present state, be regarded as capable of earning a reasonable return, and that the transferable development rights afforded appellants by virtue of the Terminal's designation as a landmark are valuable, even if not as valuable as the rights to construct above the Terminal. In appellants' view none of these factors derogate from their claim that New York City's law has effected a "taking."

* * *

Stated baldly, appellants' position appears to be that the only means of ensuring that selected owners are not singled out to endure financial hardship for no reason is to hold that any restriction imposed on individual landmarks pursuant to the New York scheme is a "taking" requiring the payment of "just compensation." Agreement with this argument would of course invalidate not just New York City's law, but all comparable landmark legislation in the Nation. We find no merit in it.

It is true, as appellants emphasize, that both historic district legislation and zoning laws regulate all properties within given physical communities whereas landmark laws apply only to selected parcels. But, contrary to appellants' suggestions, landmark laws are not like discriminatory, or "reverse spot," zoning: that is, a land use decision which arbitrarily singles out a particular parcel for different, less favorable treatment than the neighboring ones. See 2 Rathkopf, The Law of Zoning and Planning 26–4 and 26–4–26–5, n. 6 (2d Ed.1977). In contrast to discriminatory zoning, which is the antithesis of land use control as part of some comprehensive plan, the New York City law embodies a comprehensive plan to preserve structures of historic or aesthetic interest wherever they might be found in the city, and as noted, over 400 landmarks and 31 historic districts have been designated pursuant to this plan.

Equally without merit is the related argument that the decision to designate a structure as a landmark "is inevitably arbitrary or at least subjective because it basically is a matter of taste" * * *. [A]ppellants not only did not seek judicial review of either the designation or of the denials of the certificates of appropriateness and of no exterior effect, but do not even now suggest that the Commission's decisions concerning the Terminal were in any sense arbitrary or unprincipled. But, in any event, * * * there is no basis whatsoever for a conclusion that courts will have any greater difficulty identifying arbitrary or discriminatory action in the context of landmark regulation than in the context of classic zoning or indeed in any other context.

Next, appellants observe that New York City's law differs from zoning laws and historic district ordinances in that the Landmarks Law does not impose identical or similar restrictions on all structures located in particular physical communities. It follows, they argue, that New York City's law is inherently incapable of producing the fair and equitable distribution of benefits and burdens of governmental action which is characteristic of zoning laws and historic district legislation and which they maintain is a constitutional requirement if "just compensation" is not to be afforded. It is of course true that the Landmarks Law has a more severe impact on some landowners than on others, but that in itself does not mean that the law effects a "taking." Legislation designed to promote the general welfare commonly burdens some more than others. The owners of the brickyard in *Hadacheck*, of the cedar trees in *Miller v. Schoene*, and of the gravel and sand mine in *Goldblatt v. Hempstead*, were uniquely burdened by the legislation sustained in those cases. Similarly, zoning laws often impact more severely on some property owners than others but have not been held to be invalid on that account. For example, the property owner in *Euclid* who wished to use his property for industrial purposes was affected far more severely by the ordinance than his neighbors who wished to use their land for residences.

In any event, appellants' repeated suggestions that they are solely burdened and unbenefited is factually inaccurate. This contention overlooks the fact that the New York City law applies to vast numbers of structures in the city in addition to the Terminal—all the structures contained in the 31 historic districts and over 400 individual landmarks, many of which are close to the Terminal. Unless we are to reject the judgment of the New York City Council that the preservation of landmarks benefit all New York citizens and all structures, both economically and by improving the quality of life in the city as a whole—which we are unwilling to do—we cannot conclude that the owners of the Terminal have in no sense been benefited by the Landmarks Law. Doubtless appellants believe they are more burdened than benefited by the law, but that must have been true too of the property owners in *Miller*, *Hadacheck*, *Euclid*, and *Goldblatt*.

Appellants' final broad-based attack would have us treat the law as an instance, like that in *United States v. Causby, supra*, in which Government, acting in an enterprise capacity, has appropriated part of their property for some strictly governmental purpose. Apart from the fact that *Causby* was a case of invasion of airspace that destroyed the use of the farm beneath and this New York City law has in no wise impaired the present use of the Terminal, the Landmarks Law neither exploits appellants' parcel for city purposes nor facilitates nor arises from any entrepreneurial operations of the city. The situation is not remotely like that in *Causby* when the airspace above the Terminal was in the flight pattern for military aircraft. The Landmarks Law's effect is simply to prohibit appellants or anyone else from occupying portions of the airspace above the Terminal, while permitting appellants to use the remainder of the parcel in a gainful fashion. * * *

Rejection of appellants' broad arguments is not however the end of our inquiry, for all we thus far have established is that the New York law is not rendered invalid by its failure to provide "just compensation" whenever a landmark owner is restricted in the exploitation of property interests, such as air rights, to a greater extent than provided for under applicable zoning laws. We now must consider whether the interference with appellants' property is of such a magnitude that "there must be an exercise of eminent domain and compensation to sustain [it]." *Pennsyl-*

vania Coal Co. v. Mahon, 260 U.S., at 413, 43 S.Ct., at 159. That inquiry may be narrowed to the question of the severity of the impact of the law on appellants' parcel, and its resolution in turn requires a careful assessment of the impact of the regulation on the Terminal site.

Unlike the governmental acts in *Goldblatt*, *Miller*, *Causby*, *Griggs*, and *Hadacheck*, the New York City law does not interfere in any way with the present uses of the Terminal. Its designation as a landmark not only permits but contemplates that appellants may continue to use the property precisely as it has for the past 65 years: as a railroad terminal containing office space and concessions. So the law does not interfere with what must be regarded as Penn Central's primary expectation concerning the use of the parcel. More importantly, on this record, we must regard the New York City law as permitting Penn Central not only to profit from the Terminal but to obtain a "reasonable return" on its investment.

Appellants, moreover, exaggerate the effect of the Act on its ability to make use of the air rights above the Terminal in two respects. First, it simply cannot be maintained, on this record, that appellants have been prohibited from occupying any portion of the airspace above the Terminal. While the Commission's actions in denying applications to construct an office building in excess of 50 stories above the Terminal may indicate that it will refuse to issue a certificate of appropriateness for any comparably sized structure, nothing the Commission has said or done suggests an intention to prohibit any construction above the Terminal. The Commission's report emphasized that whether any construction would be allowed depended upon whether the proposed addition "would harmonize in scale, material, and character with [the Terminal]." * * * Since appellants have not sought approval for the construction of a smaller structure, we do not know that appellants will be denied any use of any portion of the airspace above the Terminal.

Second, to the extent appellants have been denied the right to build above the Terminal, it is not literally accurate to say that they have been denied all use of even those pre-existing air rights. Their ability to use these rights has not been abrogated; they are made transferable to at least eight parcels in the vicinity of the Terminal, one or two of which have been found suitable for the construction of new office buildings. Although appellants and others have argued that New York City's transferable development rights program is far from ideal, the New York courts here supportably found that, at least in the case of the Terminal, the rights afforded are valuable. While these rights may well not have constituted "just compensation" if a "taking" had occurred, the rights nevertheless undoubtedly mitigate whatever financial burdens the law has imposed on appellants and, for that reason, are to be taken into account in considering the impact of regulation. *Cf. Goldblatt v. Hempstead, supra*, 369 U.S., at 594 n. 3, 82 S.Ct., at 990 n. 3.

On this record we conclude that the application of New York City's Landmarks Preservation Law has not effected a "taking" of appellants' property. The restrictions imposed are substantially related to the promotion of the general welfare and not only permit reasonable beneficial use of the landmark site but afford appellants opportunities further to enhance not only the Terminal site proper but also other properties.

Affirmed.

MR. JUSTICE REHNQUIST, with whom THE CHIEF JUSTICE and MR. JUSTICE STEVENS join, dissenting.

* * *

Appellees do not dispute that valuable property rights have been destroyed. And the Court has frequently emphasized that the term "property" as used in the Taking Clause includes the entire "group of rights inhering in the citizen's [ownership]." *United States v. General Motors Corp.*, 323 U.S. 373, 65 S.Ct. 357, 89 L.Ed. 311 (1945). The term is not used in the

> vulgar and untechnical sense of the physical thing with respect to which the citizen exercises rights recognized by law. [Instead, it] denotes the *group of rights* inhering in the citizen's relation to the physical thing, *as the right to possess, use and dispose of it.* * * * The constitutional provision is addressed to *every sort of interest* the citizen may possess. Id., at 377–378, 65 S.Ct., at 359 (emphasis added).

While neighboring landowners are free to use their land and "air rights" in any way consistent with the broad boundaries of New York zoning, Penn Central, absent the permission of appellees, must forever maintain its property in its present state. The property has been thus subjected to a nonconsensual servitude not borne by any neighboring or similar properties.

Appellees have thus destroyed—in a literal sense, "taken"—substantial property rights of Penn Central. While the term "taken" might have been narrowly interpreted to include only physical seizures of property rights, the construction of the phrase has not been so narrow. * * * Because "not every destruction or injury to property by governmental action has been held to be a 'taking' in the constitutional sense," *Armstrong v. United States*, 364 U.S. 40, 48, 80 S.Ct. 1563, 1568, 4 L.Ed.2d 1554 (1960), however, this does not end our inquiry. But an examination of the two exceptions where the destruction of property does *not* constitute a taking demonstrates that a compensable taking has occurred here.

As early as 1887, the Court recognized that the government can prevent a property owner from using his property to injure others without having to compensate the owner for the value of the forbidden use.

> "A prohibition simply upon the use of property for purposes that are declared, by valid legislation, to be *injurious to the health, morals, or safety of the community*, cannot in any just sense, be deemed a

taking or an appropriation of property for the public benefit. Such legislation does not disturb the owner in the control or use of his property for lawful purposes, nor restrict his right to dispose of it, but is only a declaration by the State that its use by any one, for certain forbidden purposes, is prejudicial to the public interests. * * * The power which the States have of prohibiting such use by individuals of their property as will be prejudicial to the health, the morals, or the safety of the public, is not—and, consistently with the existence and safety of organized society, cannot be—burdened with the condition that the State must compensate such individual owners for pecuniary losses they may sustain, *by reason of their not being permitted, by a noxious use of their property, to inflict injury upon the community.*" *Mugler v. Kansas*, 123 U.S. 623, 668–669, 8 S.Ct. 273, 301, 31 L.Ed. 205 (1887).

Thus, there is no "taking" where a city prohibits the operation of a brickyard within a residential city, *see Hadacheck v. Sebastian*, 239 U.S. 394, 36 S.Ct. 143, 60 L.Ed. 348 (1915), or forbids excavation for sand and gravel below the water line, *see Goldblatt v. Town of Hempstead*, 369 U.S. 590, 82 S.Ct. 987, 8 L.Ed.2d 130 (1962). Nor is it relevant, where the government is merely prohibiting a noxious use of property, that the government would seem to be singling out a particular property owner. *Hadacheck*, 239 U.S., at 413, 36 S.Ct., at 146.

* * *

Appellees are not prohibiting a nuisance. The record is clear that the proposed addition to the Grand Central Terminal would be in full compliance with zoning, height limitations, and other health and safety requirements. Instead, appellees are seeking to preserve what they believe to be an outstanding example of Beaux Arts architecture. Penn Central is prevented from further developing its property basically because it did *too good* of a job in designing and building it. The city of New York, because of its unadorned admiration for the design, has decided that the owners of the building must preserve it unchanged for the benefit of sightseeing New Yorkers and tourists.

Unlike in the case of land use regulations, appellees are not *prohibiting* Penn Central from using its property in a narrow set of noxious ways. Instead, appellees have placed an *affirmative* duty on Penn Central to maintain the Terminal in its present state and in "good repair." Appellants are not free to use their property as they see fit within broad outer boundaries but must strictly adhere to their past use except where appellees conclude that alternative uses would not detract from the Landmark. While Penn Central may continue to use the Terminal as it is presently designed, appellees otherwise "exercise complete dominion and control over the surface of the land," *United States v. Causby*, 328 U.S. 256, 262, 66 S.Ct. 1062, 1066, 90 L.Ed. 1206 (1946), and must compensate the owner for his loss. Ibid. "Property is taken in the constitutional sense when inroads are made upon an owner's use of it to an extent that, as between private parties, a servitude has been acquired." *United States v. Dickinson*, 331 U.S. 745, 748, 67 S.Ct. 1382, 1385, 91 L.Ed. 1789 (1947). See also *Dugan v. Rank*, 372 U.S. 609, 625, 83 S.Ct. 999, 1009, 10 L.Ed.2d 15 (1963).

Even where the government prohibits a noninjurious use, the Court has ruled that a taking does not take place if the prohibition applies over a broad cross section of land and thereby "secure[s] an average reciprocity of advantage." *Pennsylvania Coal Co. v. Mahon*, 260 U.S. 393, 415, 43 S.Ct. 158, 160, 67 L.Ed. 322 (1922). It is for this reason that zoning does not constitute a "taking." While zoning at times reduces *individual* property values, the burden is shared relatively evenly and it is reasonable to conclude that on the whole an individual who is harmed by one aspect of the zoning will be benefited by another.

Here, however, a multimillion dollar loss has been imposed on appellants; it is uniquely felt and is not offset by any benefits flowing from the preservation of some 500 other "Landmarks" in New York. Appellees have imposed a substantial cost on less than one one-tenth of one percent of the buildings in New York for the general benefit of all its people. It is exactly this imposition of general costs on a few individuals at which the "taking" protection is directed. * * *

As Justice Holmes pointed out in *Pennsylvania Coal Co. v. Mahon*, "the question at bottom" in an eminent domain case "is upon whom the loss of the changes desired should fall." 260 U.S., at 416, 43 S.Ct., at 160. The benefits that appellees believe will flow from preservation of the Grand Central Terminal will accrue to all the citizens of New York. There is no reason to believe that appellants will enjoy a substantially greater share of these benefits. If the cost of preserving Grand Central Terminal were spread evenly across the entire population of the city of New York, the burden per person would be in cents per year—a minor cost appellees would surely concede for the benefit accrued. Instead, however, appellees would impose the entire cost of several million dollars per year on Penn Central. But it is precisely this sort of discrimination that the Fifth Amendment prohibits.

Appellees in response would argue that a taking only occurs where a property owner is denied *all* reasonable value of his property. The Court has frequently held that, even where a destruction of property rights would not *otherwise* constitute a taking, the inability of the owner to make a reasonable return on his property requires compensation under the Fifth Amendment. *See, e.g., United States v. Lynah*, 188 U.S. 445, 470, 23 S.Ct. 349, 357, 47 L.Ed. 539 (1903). But the converse is not true. A taking does not become a noncompensable exercise of police power simply because the government in its grace allows the owner to make some "reasonable" use of his property. "[I]t is the character of the invasion, not the amount of damage resulting from it, so long as the damage is substantial, that determines the question whether it is a taking." * * *

Notes

1. Does the Penn Central case provide any guidance in discerning the line between a permissible regulation and an invalid taking? Does Justice Brennan's observation that the cases have been "essentially ad hoc, factual inquiries" mean that the line can never be drawn with the degree of certainty that would satisfy an attorney seeking to advise a client?

2. If proof of no reasonable economic use is one way to demonstrate a taking, how can such proof be made? While this is really a question for students of evidence, some suggestions of value might be gleaned from the case of Schwartz v. City of Flint, 92 Mich.App. 495, 285 N.W.2d 344 (1979), reversed 426 Mich. 295, 395 N.W.2d 678 (1986), since extensive portions of the record in that case are reproduced in the opinion.

3. The cases are clear in distinguishing proof of no reasonable permitted use from mere loss of value due to the regulation. State courts have followed the lead of the Supreme Court in Goldblatt in holding that loss of value alone is not indicative of a taking. See, e.g., Pennington v. Rockdale County, 244 Ga. 743, 262 S.E.2d 59 (1979). An excellent presentation of this view is also found in William C. Haas & Co., Inc. v. City and County of San Francisco, 605 F.2d 1117 (9th Cir.1979).

4. Sometimes a *regulation* can be characterized as a *physical occupation* of property. For example, in Seawall Associates v. City of New York, 74 N.Y.2d 92, 544 N.Y.S.2d 542, 542 N.E.2d 1059 (1989) the court held that a city ordinance establishing a five-year moratorium on conversion, alteration, or demolition of single-room occupancy housing and requiring restoration of such units to habitable condition and requiring them to be leased at controlled rents, constituted a physical occupation and was a per se compensable taking. The ordinance was aimed at curbing the rampant conversion of "welfare hotels" into other types of housing.

5. Can the local government counter an alleged taking by showing alternate possible uses of the land, even though such uses might be beyond the resources of the property owner? See the interesting case of Friedman v. City of Fairfax, 81 Cal.App.3d 667, 146 Cal.Rptr. 687 (1978), where the court noted that the rezoning of the property resulted in a designation that would allow successful operation of a private tennis club, "a currently popular recreational use." (The appellate court reversed a trial court judgment for $1,200,000 damages and $115,000 attorney fees.)

6. Where a property owner challenges a regulation under the theory that a taking has occurred, the procedural device most often used is "inverse condemnation." Inverse condemnation cases proceed on the basis that the property has been taken and the governmental body responsible has not paid compensation to the owner. More often, however, the property owner sues to have the regulation declared invalid, either on its face, or as applied to his situation. In such cases, if a court finds that the regulation is invalid, for whatever reason, should the property owner receive "just compensation" for that period of time that she could not utilize her property while the case was being litigated? In Agins v. City of Tiburon, 24 Cal.3d 266, 157 Cal.Rptr. 372, 598 P.2d 25 (1979), affirmed 447 U.S. 255, 100 S.Ct. 2138, 65 L.Ed.2d 106 (1980), the plaintiff in an inverse condemnation action alleged that a zoning regulation forbade substantially all use of the land and was a taking. The

California Supreme Court held the inverse condemnation remedy inappropriate in that such a remedy would hamper flexibility in land use planning, and would have a chilling effect on local regulation because of judicial control of expenditure of public funds which is basically a legislative responsibility. The California Supreme Court dealt with the issue of the application of the Pennsylvania Coal case by noting:

> In balancing the constitutional rights of the landowner against the legitimate needs of government we do not ignore well established precedent. In Pennsylvania Coal Co. v. Mahon, 260 U.S. 393, 43 S.Ct. 158, 67 L.Ed. 322 (1922), an injunction was sought to prevent a coal company from causing subsidence of property due to the company's underground mining activities. This Supreme Court opinion has generated some confusion and has even been cited erroneously for the proposition that inverse condemnation is readily available as a remedy in zoning cases because of Justice Holmes' statement that "The general rule at least is, that while property may be regulated to a certain extent, if regulation goes too far it will be recognized as a taking." (*Mahon,* supra, at p. 415, 43 S.Ct., at p. 160.) It is clear both from context and from the disposition in *Mahon,* however, that the term 'taking' was used solely to indicate the limit by which the acknowledged social goal of land control could be achieved by regulation rather than by eminent domain. The high court set aside the injunctive relief which had been granted by the Pennsylvania courts and declared void the exercise of police power which had limited the company's right to mine its land. The court did not attempt, however, to transmute the illegal governmental infringement into an exercise of eminent domain and the possibility of compensation was not even considered.

The court also held that the plaintiff failed to establish a case for invalidation of the ordinance as depriving him of substantially all use of the property because he could still, under the terms of the ordinance, build one to five dwellings on his five acre parcel. On appeal, the United States Supreme Court used the latter holding to avoid the issue of whether plaintiff could be denied the remedy of inverse condemnation, stating that since there was no taking, the question of the proper remedy did not have to be decided.

In San Diego Gas & Electric Co. v. City of San Diego, 450 U.S. 621, 101 S.Ct. 1287, 67 L.Ed.2d 551 (1981), the Supreme Court again skirted the issue of the inverse condemnation remedy for regulatory takings by dismissing the appeal on the ground that the California Supreme Court judgment denying damages was not a final judgment. In a dissenting opinion by Justice Brennan, joined by three other Justices, and approvingly referred to in Justice Rehnquist's concurring opinion, five Justices indicated that invalidation of a land use regulation so oppressive as to amount to a taking is an inadequate remedy and that a landowner in such a situation might be entitled to monetary relief for a "temporary taking" with damages to be measured from the time of the adoption of the oppressive regulation to the time of invalidation. Justice Brennan cited for support of this idea, Hagman & Misczynski, Windfalls for Wipeouts 296–297 (1978) and Bosselman, The Third Alternative in Zoning Litigation, 17 Zoning Dig. 113, 114–119 (1965). Also see Duerksen & Mantell, Interim Damages: A Remedy in Land Use Cases?, 33 Land Use Law & Zoning Dig. 6 (April 1981).

FIRST ENGLISH EVANGELICAL LUTHERAN CHURCH v. LOS ANGELES COUNTY

Supreme Court of the United States, 1987.
482 U.S. 304, 107 S.Ct. 2378, 96 L.Ed.2d 250.

CHIEF JUSTICE REHNQUIST delivered the opinion of the Court.

* * *

In 1957, appellant First English Evangelical Lutheran Church purchased a 21–acre parcel of land in a canyon along the banks of the Middle Fork of Mill Creek in the Angeles National Forest. The Middle Fork is the natural drainage channel for a watershed area owned by the National Forest Service. Twelve of the acres owned by the church are flat land, and contained a dining hall, two bunkhouses, a caretaker's lodge, an outdoor chapel, and a footbridge across the creek. The church operated on the site a campground, known as "Lutherglen," as a retreat center and a recreational area for handicapped children.

In July 1977, a forest fire denuded the hills upstream from Lutherglen, destroying approximately 3,860 acres of the watershed area and creating a serious flood hazard. Such flooding occurred on February 9 and 10, 1978, when a storm dropped 11 inches of rain in the watershed. The runoff from the storm overflowed the banks of the Mill Creek, flooding Lutherglen and destroying its buildings.

In response to the flooding of the canyon, appellee County of Los Angeles adopted Interim Ordinance No. 11,855 in January 1979. The ordinance provided that "[a] person shall not construct, reconstruct, place or enlarge any building or structure, any portion of which is, or will be, located within the outer boundary lines of the interim flood protection area located in Mill Creek Canyon * * *." The ordinance was effective immediately because the county determined that it was "required for the immediate preservation of the public health and safety * * *." The interim flood protection area described by the ordinance included the flat areas on either side of Mill Creek on which Lutherglen had stood.

The church filed a complaint in the Superior Court of California a little more than a month after the ordinance was adopted. As subsequently amended, the complaint alleged two claims against the county and the Los Angeles County Flood Control District. The first alleged that the defendants were liable under Cal.Gov't Code Ann. § 835 (West 1980) for dangerous conditions on their upstream properties that contributed to the flooding of Lutherglen. As a part of this claim, appellant also alleged that "Ordinance No. 11,855 denies [appellant] all use of Lutherglen." The second claim sought to recover from the Flood District in inverse condemnation and in tort for engaging in cloud seeding during the storm that flooded Lutherglen. Appellant sought damages under each count for loss of use of Lutherglen. * * *

Appellant asks us to hold that the Supreme Court of California erred in *Agins v. Tiburon* in determining that the Fifth Amendment, as made applicable to the States through the Fourteenth Amendment, does not require compensation as a remedy for "temporary" regulatory takings—those regulatory takings which are ultimately invalidated by the courts. Four times this decade, we have considered similar claims and have found ourselves for one reason or another unable to consider the merits of the *Agins* rule. *See MacDonald, Sommer & Frates v. Yolo County*, 477 U.S. 340 (1986); *Williamson County Regional Planning Comm'n v. Hamilton Bank*, 473 U.S. 172 (1985); *San Diego Gas & Electric Co., supra; Agins v. Tiburon, supra*. For the reasons explained below, however, we find the constitutional claim properly presented in this case, and hold that on these facts the California courts have decided the compensation question inconsistently with the requirements of the Fifth Amendment.

* * *

Consideration of the compensation question must begin with direct reference to the language of the Fifth Amendment, which provides in relevant part that "private property [shall not] be taken for public use, without just compensation." As its language indicates, and as the Court has frequently noted, this provision does not prohibit the taking of private property, but instead places a condition on the exercise of that power. *See Williamson County*, 473 U.S., at 194; *Hodel v. Virginia Surface Mining & Reclamation Assn., Inc.*, 452 U.S. 264, 297, n. 40 (1981); *Hurley v. Kincaid*, 285 U.S. 95, 104 (1932); *Monongahela Navigation Co. v. United States*, 148 U.S. 312, 336 (1893); *United States v. Jones*, 109 U.S. 513, 518 (1883). This basic understanding of the Amendment makes clear that it is designed not to limit the governmental interference with property rights per se, but rather to secure compensation in the event of otherwise proper interference amounting to a taking. Thus, government action that works a taking of property rights necessarily implicates the "constitutional obligation to pay just compensation." *Armstrong v. United States*, 364 U.S. 40, 49 (1960).

We have recognized that a landowner is entitled to bring an action in inverse condemnation as a result of " 'the self-executing character of the constitutional provision with respect to compensation * * *.' " *United States v. Clarke*, 445 U.S. 253, 257 (1980), quoting 6 P. Nichols, Eminent Domain § 25.41 (3d rev. ed. 1972). As noted in JUSTICE BRENNAN's dissent in *San Diego Gas & Electric Co.*, 450 U.S., at 654–655, it has been established at least since *Jacobs v. United States*, 290 U.S. 13 (1933), that claims for just compensation are grounded in the Constitution itself:

> "The suits were based on the right to recover just compensation for property taken by the United States for public use in the exercise of its power of eminent domain. That right was guaranteed by the Constitution. The fact that condemnation proceedings were not instituted and that the right was asserted in suits by the owners did

not change the essential nature of the claim. The form of the remedy did not qualify the right. It rested upon the Fifth Amendment. Statutory recognition was not necessary. A promise to pay was not necessary. Such a promise was implied because of the duty to pay imposed by the Amendment. The suits were thus founded upon the Constitution of the United States." Id., at 16. (Emphasis added.)

Jacobs, moreover, does not stand alone, for the Court has frequently repeated the view that, in the event of a taking, the compensation remedy is required by the Constitution. *See, e.g., Kirby Forest Industries, Inc. v. United States*, 467 U.S. 1, 5 (1984); *United States v. Causby*, 328 U.S. 256, 267 (1946); *Seaboard Air Line R. Co. v. United States*, 261 U.S. 299, 304–306 (1923); *Monongahela Navigation, supra*, at 327.

* * *

While the Supreme Court of California may not have actually disavowed this general rule in *Agins*, we believe that it has truncated the rule by disallowing damages that occurred prior to the ultimate invalidation of the challenged regulation. The Supreme Court of California justified its conclusion at length in the *Agins* opinion, concluding that:

"In combination, the need for preserving a degree of freedom in the land-use planning function, and the inhibiting financial force which inheres in the inverse condemnation remedy, persuade us that on balance mandamus or declaratory relief rather than inverse condemnation is the appropriate relief under the circumstances." *Agins v. Tiburon*, 24 Cal.3d, at 276–277, 598 P.2d, at 31.

We, of course, are not unmindful of these considerations, but they must be evaluated in the light of the command of the Just Compensation Clause of the Fifth Amendment. The Court has recognized in more than one case that the government may elect to abandon its intrusion or discontinue regulations. *See, e.g., Kirby Forest Industries, Inc. v. United States, supra; United States v. Dow*, 357 U.S. 17, 26 (1958). Similarly, a governmental body may acquiesce in a judicial declaration that one of its ordinances has effected an unconstitutional taking of property; the landowner has no right under the Just Compensation Clause to insist that a "temporary" taking be deemed a permanent taking. But we have not resolved whether abandonment by the government requires payment of compensation for the period of time during which regulations deny a landowner all use of his land.

* * *

These cases reflect the fact that "temporary" takings which, as here, deny a landowner all use of his property, are not different in kind from permanent takings, for which the Constitution clearly requires compensation. *Cf. San Diego Gas & Electric Co.*, 450 U.S., at 657 (BRENNAN, J., dissenting) ("Nothing in the Just Compensation Clause suggests that 'takings' must be permanent and irrevocable"). It is axiomatic that the Fifth Amendment's just compensation provision is "designed to bar Government from forcing some people alone to bear public burdens which, in all fairness and justice, should be borne by the public as a whole." *Armstrong v. United States*, 364 U.S., at 49. *See also Penn Central Transportation Co. v. New York City*, 438 U.S., at 123–125; *Monongahela Navigation Co. v. United States*, 148 U.S., at 325. In the present case the interim ordinance was adopted by the County of Los Angeles in January 1979, and became effective immediately. Appellant filed suit within a month after the effective date of the ordinance and yet when the Supreme Court of California denied a hearing in the case on October 17, 1985, the merits of appellant's claim had yet to be determined. The United States has been required to pay compensation for leasehold interests of shorter duration than this. The value of a leasehold interest in property for a period of years may be substantial, and the burden on the property owner in extinguishing such an interest for a period of years may be great indeed. *See, e.g., United States v. General Motors, supra*. Where this burden results from governmental action that amounted to a taking, the Just Compensation Clause of the Fifth Amendment requires that the government pay the landowner for the value of the use of the land during this period. *Cf. United States v. Causby*, 328 U.S., at 261 ("It is the owner's loss, not the taker's gain, which is the measure of the value of the property taken"). Invalidation of the ordinance or its successor ordinance after this period of time, though converting the taking into a "temporary" one, is not a sufficient remedy to meet the demands of the Just Compensation Clause.

* * *

Nothing we say today is intended to abrogate the principle that the decision to exercise the power of eminent domain is a legislative function " 'for Congress and Congress alone to determine.' " *Hawaii Housing Authority v. Midkiff*, 467 U.S. 229, 240 (1984), quoting *Berman v. Parker*, 348 U.S. 26, 33 (1954). Once a court determines that a taking has occurred, the government retains the whole range of options already available—amendment of the regulation, withdrawal of the invalidated regulation, or exercise of eminent domain. Thus we do not, as the Solicitor General suggests, "permit a court, at the behest of a private person, to require the * * * Government to exercise the power of eminent domain * * *." Brief for United States as Amicus Curiae 22. We merely hold that where the government's activities have already worked a taking of all use of property, no subsequent action by the government can relieve it of the duty to provide compensation for the period during which the taking was effective.

We also point out that the allegation of the complaint which we treat as true for purposes of our decision was that the ordinance in question denied appellant all use of its property. We limit our holding to the facts presented, and of course do not deal with the quite different questions that would arise in the case of normal delays in obtaining building permits, changes in zoning ordinances, variances, and the like which are not before us. We realize that even our present holding will undoubtedly lessen to some extent the freedom and flexibility of land-use planners and governing bodies of municipal corporations when enacting land-use regulations. But such consequences necessarily flow from any decision upholding a claim of constitutional right; many of the provisions of the Constitution are designed to limit the flexibility and freedom of governmental authorities, and the Just Compensation Clause of the Fifth Amendment is one of them. As Justice Holmes aptly noted more than 50 years ago, "a strong public desire to improve the public condition is not enough to warrant achieving the desire by a shorter cut than the constitutional way of paying for the change." *Pennsylvania Coal Co. v. Mahon*, 260 U.S., at 416.

Here we must assume that the Los Angeles County ordinance has denied appellant all use of its property for a considerable period of years, and we hold that invalidation of the ordinance without payment of fair value for the use of the property during this period of time would be a constitutionally insufficient remedy. The judgment of the California Court of Appeal is therefore reversed, and the case is remanded for further proceedings not inconsistent with this opinion.

JUSTICE STEVENS, with whom JUSTICE BLACKMUN and JUSTICE O'CONNOR join as to Parts I and III, dissenting. [Opinion omitted here, but is reproduced in the next section.]

Note

After remand the California Court of Appeals held that the property had not been "taken" in the first instance because the regulation was necessary to protect public health and safety, and the cause of action for inverse condemnation was properly dismissed. First English Evangelical Lutheran Church of Glendale v. County of Los Angeles, 210 Cal.App.3d 1353, 258 Cal.Rptr. 893, certiorari denied 493 U.S. 1056, 110 S.Ct. 866, 107 L.Ed.2d 950 (1990). The net result then, is that while a property owner may be constitutionally entitled to compensation for an interim or temporary taking, she must first establish that a taking has, in fact, occurred. The following cases focus our attention again on the definition of what is a regulatory taking.

LUCAS v. SOUTH CAROLINA COASTAL COUNCIL

Supreme Court of the United States, 1992.
505 U.S. 1003, 112 S.Ct. 2886, 120 L.Ed.2d 798.

JUSTICE SCALIA delivered the opinion of the Court.

In 1986, petitioner David H. Lucas paid $975,000 for two residential lots on the Isle of Palms in Charleston County, South Carolina, on which he intended to build single-family homes. In 1988, however, the South Carolina Legislature enacted the Beachfront Management Act, S.C.Code § 48–39–250 et seq. (Supp.1990) (Act), which had the direct effect of barring petitioner from erecting any permanent habitable structures on his two parcels. See § 48–39–290(A). A state trial court found that this prohibition rendered Lucas's parcels "valueless." This case requires us to decide whether the Act's dramatic effect on the economic value of

Lucas's lots accomplished a taking of private property under the Fifth and Fourteenth Amendments requiring the payment of "just compensation." U.S. Const., Amdt. 5.

I

A

South Carolina's expressed interest in intensively managing development activities in the so-called "coastal zone" dates from 1977 when, in the aftermath of Congress's passage of the federal Coastal Zone Management Act of 1972, 86 Stat. 1280, as amended, 16 U.S.C.A. § 1451 et seq., the legislature enacted a Coastal Zone Management Act of its own. See S.C.Code § 48–39–10 et seq. (1987). In its original form, the South Carolina Act required owners of coastal zone land that qualified as a "critical area" (defined in the legislation to include beaches and immediately adjacent sand dunes, § 48–39–10(J)) to obtain a permit from the newly created South Carolina Coastal Council (respondent here) prior to committing the land to a "use other than the use the critical area was devoted to on [September 28, 1977]." § 48–39–130(A).

In the late 1970's, Lucas and others began extensive residential development of the Isle of Palms, a barrier island situated eastward of the City of Charleston. Toward the close of the development cycle for one residential subdivision known as "Beachwood East," Lucas in 1986 purchased the two lots at issue in this litigation for his own account. No portion of the lots, which were located approximately 300 feet from the beach, qualified as a "critical area" under the 1977 Act; accordingly, at the time Lucas acquired these parcels, he was not legally obliged to obtain a permit from the Council in advance of any development activity. His intention with respect to the lots was to do what the owners of the immediately adjacent parcels had already done: erect single-family residences. He commissioned architectural drawings for this purpose.

The Beachfront Management Act brought Lucas's plans to an abrupt end. Under that 1988 legislation, the Council was directed to establish a "baseline" connecting the landward-most "point[s] of erosion ... during the past forty years" in the region of the Isle of Palms that includes Lucas's lots. § 48–39–280(A)(2) (Supp.1988). In an action not challenged here, the Council fixed this baseline landward of Lucas's parcels. That was significant, for under the Act construction of occupiable improvements was flatly prohibited seaward of a line drawn 20 feet landward of, and parallel to, the baseline, § 48–39–290(A) (Supp.1988). The Act provided no exceptions.

B

Lucas promptly filed suit in the South Carolina Court of Common Pleas, contending that the Beachfront Management Act's construction bar effected a taking of his property without just compensation. Lucas did not take issue with the validity of the Act as a lawful exercise of South Carolina's police power, but contended that the Act's complete extinguishment of his property's value entitled him to compensation regardless of whether the legislature had acted in furtherance of legitimate police power objectives. Following a bench trial, the court agreed. Among its factual determinations was the finding that "at the time Lucas purchased the two lots, both were zoned for single-family residential construction and ... there were no restrictions imposed upon such use of the property by either the State of South Carolina, the County of Charleston, or the Town of the Isle of Palms." The trial court further found that the Beachfront Management Act decreed a permanent ban on construction insofar as Lucas's lots were concerned, and that this prohibition "deprive[d] Lucas of any reasonable economic use of the lots, ... eliminated the unrestricted right of use, and render[ed] them valueless." The court thus concluded that Lucas's properties had been "taken" by operation of the Act, and it ordered respondent to pay "just compensation" in the amount of $1,232,387.50.

The Supreme Court of South Carolina reversed. It found dispositive what it described as Lucas's concession "that the Beachfront Management Act [was] properly and validly designed to preserve ... South Carolina's beaches." 304 S.C. 376, 379, 404 S.E.2d 895, 896 (1991). Failing an attack on the validity of the statute as such, the court believed itself bound to accept the "uncontested ... findings" of the South Carolina legislature that new construction in the coastal zone—such as petitioner intended—threatened this public resource. Id., at 383, 404 S.E.2d, at 898. The Court ruled that when a regulation respecting the use of property is designed "to prevent serious public harm," id., at 383, 404 S.E.2d, at 899 (citing, *inter alia, Mugler v. Kansas*, 123 U.S. 623, 8 S.Ct. 273, 31 L.Ed. 205 (1887)), no compensation is owing under the Takings Clause regardless of the regulation's effect on the property's value.

Two justices dissented. They acknowledged that our *Mugler* line of cases recognizes governmental power to prohibit "noxious" uses of property—i.e., uses of property akin to "public nuisances"—without having to pay compensation. But they would not have characterized the Beachfront Management Act's "*primary* purpose [as] the prevention of a nuisance." 304 S.C., at 395, 404 S.E.2d, at 906 (Harwell, J., dissenting). To the dissenters, the chief purposes of the legislation, among them the promotion of tourism and the creation of a "habitat for indigenous flora and fauna," could not fairly be compared to nuisance abatement. Id., at 396, 404 S.E.2d, at 906. As a consequence, they would have affirmed the trial court's conclusion that the Act's obliteration of the value of petitioner's lots accomplished a taking.

* * *

III

A

Prior to Justice Holmes' exposition in *Pennsylvania Coal Co. v. Mahon*, 260 U.S. 393, 43 S.Ct. 158, 67 L.Ed. 322 (1922), it was generally thought that the Takings Clause reached only a "direct appropriation" of property, *Legal Tender Cases*, 12 Wall. 457, 551, 20 L.Ed. 287 (1871), or the functional equivalent of a "practical ouster of [the owner's] possession." *Transportation Co. v. Chicago*, 99 U.S. 635, 642, 25 L.Ed. 336 (1879). *See also Gibson v. United States*, 166 U.S. 269, 275–276, 17 S.Ct. 578, 580, 41 L.Ed. 996 (1897). Justice Holmes recognized in *Mahon*, however, that if the protection against physical appropriations of private property was to be meaningfully enforced, the government's power to redefine the range of interests included in the ownership of property was necessarily constrained by constitutional limits. 260 U.S., at 414–415, 43 S.Ct., at 160. If, instead, the uses of private property were subject to unbridled, uncompensated qualification under the police power, "the natural tendency of human nature [would be] to extend the qualification more and more until at last private property disappear[ed]." Id., at 415, 43 S.Ct., at 160. These considerations gave birth in that case to the oft-cited maxim that, "while property may be regulated to a certain extent, if regulation goes too far it will be recognized as a taking." Ibid.

Nevertheless, our decision in *Mahon* offered little insight into when, and under what circumstances, a given regulation would be seen as going "too far" for purposes of the Fifth Amendment. In 70–odd years of succeeding "regulatory takings" jurisprudence, we have generally eschewed any " 'set formula' " for determining how far is too far, preferring to "engag[e] in ... essentially ad hoc, factual inquiries," *Penn Central Transportation Co. v. New York City*, 438 U.S. 104, 124, 98 S.Ct. 2646, 2659, 57 L.Ed.2d 631 (1978) (quoting *Goldblatt v. Hempstead*, 369 U.S. 590, 594, 82 S.Ct. 987, 990, 8 L.Ed.2d 130 (1962)). See Epstein, Takings: Descent and Resurrection, 1987 Sup.Ct. Rev. 1, 4. We have, however, described at least two discrete categories of regulatory action as compensable without case-specific inquiry into the public interest advanced in support of the restraint. The first encompasses regulations that compel the property owner to suffer a physical "invasion" of his property. In general (at least with regard to permanent invasions), no matter how minute the intrusion, and no matter how weighty the public purpose behind it, we have required compensation. For example, in *Loretto v. Teleprompter Manhattan CATV Corp.*, 458 U.S. 419, 102 S.Ct. 3164, 73 L.Ed.2d 868 (1982), we determined that New York's law requiring landlords to allow television cable companies to emplace cable facilities in their apartment buildings constituted a taking, id., at 435–440, 102 S.Ct., at 3175–3178, even though the facilities occupied at most only 1 1/2 cubic feet of the landlords' property, see id., at 438, n. 16, 102 S.Ct., at 3177. *See also United States v. Causby*, 328 U.S. 256, 265, and n. 10, 66 S.Ct. 1062, 1067, and n. 10, 90 L.Ed. 1206 (1946) (physical invasions of airspace); *cf. Kaiser Aetna v. United States*, 444 U.S. 164, 100 S.Ct. 383, 62 L.Ed.2d 332 (1979) (imposition of navigational servitude upon private marina).

The second situation in which we have found categorical treatment appropriate is where regulation denies all economically beneficial or productive use of land. *See Agins*, 447 U.S., at 260, 100 S.Ct., at 2141; *see also Nollan v. California Coastal Comm'n*, 483 U.S. 825, 834, 107 S.Ct. 3141, 3147, 97 L.Ed.2d 677 (1987); *Keystone Bituminous Coal Assn. v. DeBenedictis*, 480 U.S. 470, 495, 107 S.Ct. 1232, 1247, 94 L.Ed.2d 472 (1987); *Hodel v. Virginia Surface Mining & Reclamation Assn., Inc.*, 452 U.S. 264, 295–296, 101 S.Ct. 2352, 2370, 69 L.Ed.2d 1 (1981). As we have said on numerous occasions, the Fifth Amendment is violated when land-use regulation "does not substantially advance legitimate state interests *or denies an owner economically viable use of his land*." Agins, supra, 447 U.S., at 260, 100 S.Ct., at 2141 (citations omitted) (emphasis added).

We have never set forth the justification for this rule. Perhaps it is simply, as Justice Brennan suggested, that total deprivation of beneficial use is, from the landowner's point of view, the equivalent of a physical appropriation. *See San Diego Gas & Electric Co. v. San Diego*, 450 U.S., at 652, 101 S.Ct., at 1304 (Brennan, J., dissenting). "[F]or what is the land but the profits thereof[?]" 1 E. Coke, Institutes ch. 1, § 1 (1st Am. ed. 1812). Surely, at least, in the extraordinary circumstance when no productive or economically beneficial use of land is permitted, it is less realistic to indulge our usual assumption that the legislature is simply "adjusting the benefits and burdens of economic life," *Penn Central Transportation Co.*, 438 U.S., at 124, 98 S.Ct., at 2659, in a manner that secures an "average reciprocity of advantage" to everyone concerned. *Pennsylvania Coal Co. v. Mahon*, 260 U.S., at 415, 43 S.Ct., at 160. And the *functional* basis for permitting the government, by regulation, to affect property values without compensation—that "Government hardly could go on if to some extent values incident to property could not be diminished without paying for every such change in the general law," id., at 413, 43 S.Ct., at 159—does not apply to the relatively rare situations where the government has deprived a landowner of all economically beneficial uses.

On the other side of the balance, affirmatively supporting a compensation requirement, is the fact that regulations that leave the owner of land without economically beneficial or productive options for its use—typically, as here, by requiring land to be left substantially in its natural state—carry with them a heightened risk that private property is being pressed into some form of public service under the guise of mitigating serious public harm. *See, e.g., Annicelli v. South Kingstown*, 463 A.2d 133, 140–141 (R.I.1983) (prohibition on construction adjacent to beach justified on twin grounds of safety and "conservation of open space"); *Morris County Land Improvement Co. v. Parsippany–Troy Hills Township*, 40 N.J. 539, 552–553, 193 A.2d 232, 240 (1963) (prohibition on filling marshlands imposed in order to preserve region as water detention basin and create wildlife refuge). As Justice Brennan explained: "From the government's point of view, the benefits flowing to the public from preservation of open space through regulation may be equally great as from creating a wildlife refuge through formal condemnation or increasing electricity production through a dam project that floods private property." *San Diego Gas & Elec. Co., supra*, 450 U.S., at 652,

101 S.Ct., at 1304 (Brennan, J., dissenting). The many statutes on the books, both state and federal, that provide for the use of eminent domain to impose servitudes on private scenic lands preventing developmental uses, or to acquire such lands altogether, suggest the practical equivalence in this setting of negative regulation and appropriation. See, e.g., 16 U.S.C.A. § 410ff–1(a) (authorizing acquisition of "lands, waters, or interests [within Channel Islands National Park] (including but not limited to scenic easements)"); § 460aa–2(a) (authorizing acquisition of "any lands, or lesser interests therein, including mineral interests and scenic easements" within Sawtooth National Recreation Area); §§ 3921–3923 (authorizing acquisition of wetlands); N.C. Gen.Stat. § 113A–38 (1990) (authorizing acquisition of, inter alia, " 'scenic easements' " within the North Carolina natural and scenic rivers system); Tenn.Code Ann. §§ 11–15–101—11–15–108 (1987) (authorizing acquisition of "protective easements" and other rights in real property adjacent to State's historic, architectural, archaeological, or cultural resources).

We think, in short, that there are good reasons for our frequently expressed belief that when the owner of real property has been called upon to sacrifice *all* economically beneficial uses in the name of the common good, that is, to leave his property economically idle, he has suffered a taking.

B

The trial court found Lucas's two beachfront lots to have been rendered valueless by respondent's enforcement of the coastal-zone construction ban. Under Lucas's theory of the case, which rested upon our "no economically viable use" statements, that finding entitled him to compensation. Lucas believed it unnecessary to take issue with either the purposes behind the Beachfront Management Act, or the means chosen by the South Carolina Legislature to effectuate those purposes. The South Carolina Supreme Court, however, thought otherwise. In its view, the Beachfront Management Act was no ordinary enactment, but involved an exercise of South Carolina's "police powers" to mitigate the harm to the public interest that petitioner's use of his land might occasion. 304 S.C., at 384, 404 S.E.2d, at 899. By neglecting to dispute the findings enumerated in the Act or otherwise to challenge the legislature's purposes, petitioner "concede[d] that the beach/dune area of South Carolina's shores is an extremely valuable public resource; that the erection of new construction, inter alia, contributes to the erosion and destruction of this public resource; and that discouraging new construction in close proximity to the beach/dune area is necessary to prevent a great public harm." Id., at 382–383, 404 S.E.2d, at 898. In the court's view, these concessions brought petitioner's challenge within a long line of this Court's cases sustaining against Due Process and Takings Clause challenges the State's use of its "police powers" to enjoin a property owner from activities akin to public nuisances. *See Mugler v. Kansas*, 123 U.S. 623, 8 S.Ct. 273, 31 L.Ed. 205 (1887) (law prohibiting manufacture of alcoholic beverages); *Hadacheck v. Sebastian*, 239 U.S.

394, 36 S.Ct. 143, 60 L.Ed. 348 (1915) (law barring operation of brick mill in residential area); *Miller v. Schoene*, 276 U.S. 272, 48 S.Ct. 246, 72 L.Ed. 568 (1928) (order to destroy diseased cedar trees to prevent infection of nearby orchards); *Goldblatt v. Hempstead*, 369 U.S. 590, 82 S.Ct. 987, 8 L.Ed.2d 130 (1962) (law effectively preventing continued operation of quarry in residential area).

It is correct that many of our prior opinions have suggested that "harmful or noxious uses" of property may be proscribed by government regulation without the requirement of compensation. For a number of reasons, however, we think the South Carolina Supreme Court was too quick to conclude that that principle decides the present case. The "harmful or noxious uses" principle was the Court's early attempt to describe in theoretical terms why government may, consistent with the Takings Clause, affect property values by regulation without incurring an obligation to compensate—a reality we nowadays acknowledge explicitly with respect to the full scope of the State's police power. * * *

The transition from our early focus on control of "noxious" uses to our contemporary understanding of the broad realm within which government may regulate without compensation was an easy one, since the distinction between "harm-preventing" and "benefit-conferring" regulation is often in the eye of the beholder. It is quite possible, for example, to describe in *either* fashion the ecological, economic, and aesthetic concerns that inspired the South Carolina legislature in the present case. One could say that imposing a servitude on Lucas's land is necessary in order to prevent his use of it from "harming" South Carolina's ecological resources; or, instead, in order to achieve the "benefits" of an ecological preserve. Compare, e.g., *Claridge v. New Hampshire Wetlands Board*, 125 N.H. 745, 752, 485 A.2d 287, 292 (1984) (owner may, without compensation, be barred from filling wetlands because landfilling would deprive adjacent coastal habitats and marine fisheries of ecological support), with, e.g., *Bartlett v. Zoning Comm'n of Old Lyme*, 161 Conn. 24, 30, 282 A.2d 907, 910 (1971) (owner barred from filling tidal marshland must be compensated, despite municipality's "laudable" goal of "preserv[ing] marshlands from encroachment or destruction"). Whether one or the other of the competing characterizations will come to one's lips in a particular case depends primarily upon one's evaluation of the worth of competing uses of real estate. See Restatement (Second) of Torts § 822, Comment g, p. 112 (1979) ("[p]ractically all human activities unless carried on in a wilderness interfere to some extent with others or involve some risk of interference"). A given restraint will be seen as mitigating "harm" to the adjacent parcels or securing a "benefit" for them, depending upon the observer's evaluation of the relative importance of the use that the restraint favors. See Sax, Takings and the Police Power, 74 Yale L.J. 36, 49 (1964) ("[T]he problem [in this area] is not one of noxiousness or harm-creating activity at all; rather it is a problem of inconsistency between perfectly innocent and independently desirable uses"). Whether Lucas's construction of single-family residences on his parcels should be described as bringing "harm" to South

Carolina's adjacent ecological resources thus depends principally upon whether the describer believes that the State's use interest in nurturing those resources is so important that *any* competing adjacent use must yield.

When it is understood that "prevention of harmful use" was merely our early formulation of the police power justification necessary to sustain (without compensation) *any* regulatory diminution in value; and that the distinction between regulation that "prevents harmful use" and that which "confers benefits" is difficult, if not impossible, to discern on an objective, value-free basis; it becomes self-evident that noxious-use logic cannot serve as a touchstone to distinguish regulatory "takings"—which require compensation—from regulatory deprivations that do not require compensation. *A fortiori* the legislature's recitation of a noxious-use justification cannot be the basis for departing from our categorical rule that total regulatory takings must be compensated. If it were, departure would virtually always be allowed. The South Carolina Supreme Court's approach would essentially nullify *Mahon*'s affirmation of limits to the noncompensable exercise of the police power. * * *

Where the State seeks to sustain regulation that deprives land of all economically beneficial use, we think it may resist compensation only if the logically antecedent inquiry into the nature of the owner's estate shows that the proscribed use interests were not part of his title to begin with. This accords, we think, with our "takings" jurisprudence, which has traditionally been guided by the understandings of our citizens regarding the content of, and the State's power over, the "bundle of rights" that they acquire when they obtain title to property. It seems to us that the property owner necessarily expects the uses of his property to be restricted, from time to time, by various measures newly enacted by the State in legitimate exercise of its police powers; "[a]s long recognized, some values are enjoyed under an implied limitation and must yield to the police power." *Pennsylvania Coal Co. v. Mahon*, 260 U.S., at 413, 43 S.Ct., at 159. And in the case of personal property, by reason of the State's traditionally high degree of control over commercial dealings, he ought to be aware of the possibility that new regulation might even render his property economically worthless (at least if the property's only economically productive use is sale or manufacture for sale), *see Andrus v. Allard*, 444 U.S. 51, 66–67, 100 S.Ct. 318, 327, 62 L.Ed.2d 210 (1979) (prohibition on sale of eagle feathers). In the case of land, however, we think the notion pressed by the Council that title is somehow held subject to the "implied limitation" that the State may subsequently eliminate all economically valuable use is inconsistent with the historical compact recorded in the Takings Clause that has become part of our constitutional culture.

Where "permanent physical occupation" of land is concerned, we have refused to allow the government to decree it anew (without compensation), no matter how weighty the asserted "public interests" involved, *Loretto v. Teleprompter Manhattan CATV Corp.*, 458 U.S., at 426, 102 S.Ct., at 3171—though we assuredly would permit the government to assert a permanent easement that was a pre-existing limitation upon the landowner's title. Compare *Scranton v. Wheeler*, 179 U.S. 141, 163, 21 S.Ct. 48, 57, 45 L.Ed. 126 (1900) (interests of "riparian owner in the submerged lands ... bordering on a public navigable water" held subject to Government's navigational servitude), with *Kaiser Aetna v. United States*, 444 U.S., at 178–180, 100 S.Ct., at 392–393 (imposition of navigational servitude on marina created and rendered navigable at private expense held to constitute a taking). We believe similar treatment must be accorded confiscatory regulations, i.e., regulations that prohibit all economically beneficial use of land: Any limitation so severe cannot be newly legislated or decreed (without compensation), but must inhere in the title itself, in the restrictions that background principles of the State's law of property and nuisance already place upon land ownership. A law or decree with such an effect must, in other words, do no more than duplicate the result that could have been achieved in the courts—by adjacent landowners (or other uniquely affected persons) under the State's law of private nuisance, or by the State under its complementary power to abate nuisances that affect the public generally, or otherwise.

On this analysis, the owner of a lake bed, for example, would not be entitled to compensation when he is denied the requisite permit to engage in a landfilling operation that would have the effect of flooding others' land. Nor the corporate owner of a nuclear generating plant, when it is directed to remove all improvements from its land upon discovery that the plant sits astride an earthquake fault. Such regulatory action may well have the effect of eliminating the land's only economically productive use, but it does not proscribe a productive use that was previously permissible under relevant property and nuisance principles. The use of these properties for what are now expressly prohibited purposes was *always* unlawful, and (subject to other constitutional limitations) it was open to the State at any point to make the implication of those background principles of nuisance and property law explicit. See Michelman, Property, Utility, and Fairness, Comments on the Ethical Foundations of "Just Compensation" Law, 80 Harv.L.Rev. 1165, 1239–1241 (1967). In light of our traditional resort to "existing rules or understandings that stem from an independent source such as state law" to define the range of interests that qualify for protection as "property" under the Fifth (and Fourteenth) amendments, * * * this recognition that the Takings Clause does not require compensation when an owner is barred from putting land to a use that is proscribed by those "existing rules or understandings" is surely unexceptional. When, however, a regulation that declares "off-limits" all economically productive or beneficial uses of land goes beyond what the relevant background principles would dictate, compensation must be paid to sustain it.

The "total taking" inquiry we require today will ordinarily entail (as the application of state nuisance law ordinarily entails) analysis of, among other things, the degree of harm to public lands and resources, or adjacent private property, posed by the claimant's proposed activities, see, e.g., Restatement (Second) of Torts §§ 826, 827, the social value of the claimant's activities and their suitability to the locality in question, see, e.g., id., §§ 828(a) and (b), 831, and the relative ease with which the alleged harm can be avoided through measures taken by the claimant and the government (or adjacent private landowners) alike, see, e.g., id., §§ 827(e), 828(c), 830. The fact that a particular use has long been engaged in by similarly situated owners ordinarily imports a lack of any common-law prohibition (though changed circumstances or new knowledge may make what was previously permissible no longer so), see Restatement (Second) of Torts, supra, § 827, comment *g*. So also does the fact that other landowners, similarly situated, are permitted to continue the use denied to the claimant.

It seems unlikely that common-law principles would have prevented the erection of any habitable or productive improvements on petitioner's land; they rarely support prohibition of the "essential use" of land, *Curtin v. Benson*, 222 U.S. 78, 86, 32 S.Ct. 31, 33, 56 L.Ed. 102 (1911). The question, however, is one of state law to be dealt with on remand. We emphasize that to win its case South Carolina must do more than proffer the legislature's declaration that the uses Lucas desires are inconsistent with the public interest, or the conclusory assertion that they violate a common-law maxim such as *sic utere tuo ut alienum non laedas*. As we have said, a "State, by *ipse dixit*, may not transform private property into public property without compensation...." *Webb's Fabulous Pharmacies, Inc. v. Beckwith*, 449 U.S. 155, 164, 101 S.Ct. 446, 452, 66 L.Ed.2d 358 (1980). Instead, as it would be required to do if it sought to restrain Lucas in a common-law action for public nuisance, South Carolina must identify background principles of nuisance and property law that prohibit the uses he now intends in the circumstances in which the property is presently found. Only on this showing can the State fairly claim that, in proscribing all such beneficial uses, the Beachfront Management Act is taking nothing.

* * *

The judgment is reversed and the cause remanded for proceedings not inconsistent with this opinion.

JUSTICE KENNEDY, concurring in the judgment.

* * *

The finding of no value must be considered under the Takings Clause by reference to the owner's reasonable, investment-backed expectations. * * * The Takings Clause, while conferring substantial protection on property owners, does not eliminate the police power of the State to enact limitations on the use of their property. *Mugler v. Kansas*, 123 U.S. 623, 669, 8 S.Ct. 273, 301, 31 L.Ed. 205 (1887). The rights conferred by the Takings Clause and the police power of the State may coexist without conflict. Property is bought and sold, investments are made, subject to the State's power to regulate. Where a taking is alleged from regulations which deprive the property of all value, the test must be whether the deprivation is contrary to reasonable, investment-backed expectations.

There is an inherent tendency towards circularity in this synthesis, of course; for if the owner's reasonable expectations are shaped by what courts allow as a proper exercise of governmental authority, property tends to become what courts say it is. Some circularity must be tolerated in these matters, however, as it is in other spheres. * * * The definition, moreover, is not circular in its entirety. The expectations protected by the Constitution are based on objective rules and customs that can be understood as reasonable by all parties involved.

In my view, reasonable expectations must be understood in light of the whole of our legal tradition. The common law of nuisance is too narrow a confine for the exercise of regulatory power in a complex and interdependent society. *Goldblatt v. Hempstead*, 369 U.S. 590, 593, 82 S.Ct. 987, 989, 8 L.Ed.2d 130 (1962). The State should not be prevented from enacting new regulatory initiatives in response to changing conditions, and courts must consider all reasonable expectations whatever their source. The Takings Clause does not require a static body of state property law; it protects private expectations to ensure private investment. I agree with the Court that nuisance prevention accords with the most common expectations of property owners who face regulation, but I do not believe this can be the sole source of state authority to impose severe restrictions. Coastal property may present such unique concerns for a fragile land system that the State can go further in regulating its development and use than the common law of nuisance might otherwise permit.

The Supreme Court of South Carolina erred, in my view, by reciting the general purposes for which the state regulations were enacted without a determination that they were in accord with the owner's reasonable expectations and therefore sufficient to support a severe restriction on specific parcels of property. See 304 S.C. 376, 383, 404 S.E.2d 895, 899 (1991). The promotion of tourism, for instance, ought not to suffice to deprive specific property of all value without a corresponding duty to compensate. Furthermore, the means as well as the ends of regulation must accord with the owner's reasonable expectations. Here, the State did not act until after the property had been zoned for individual lot development and most other parcels had been improved, throwing the whole burden of the regulation on the remaining lots. This too must be measured in the balance. *See Pennsylvania Coal Co. v. Mahon*, 260 U.S. 393, 416, 43 S.Ct. 158, 160, 67 L.Ed. 322 (1922).

With these observations, I concur in the judgment of the Court.

JUSTICE BLACKMUN, dissenting.

Today the Court launches a missile to kill a mouse.

The State of South Carolina prohibited petitioner Lucas from building a permanent structure on his property from 1988 to 1990. Relying on an unreviewed (and implausible) state trial court finding that this restriction left Lucas' property valueless, this Court granted review to determine whether compensation must be paid in cases where the State prohibits all economic use of real estate. According to the Court, such an occasion never has arisen in any of our prior cases, and the Court imagines that it will arise "relatively rarely" or only in "extraordinary circumstances." Almost certainly it did not happen in this case.

Nonetheless, the Court presses on to decide the issue, and as it does, it ignores its jurisdictional limits, remakes its traditional rules of review, and creates simultaneously a new categorical rule and an exception (neither of which is rooted in our prior case law, common law, or common sense). I protest not only the Court's decision, but each step taken to reach it. More fundamentally, I question the Court's wisdom in issuing sweeping new rules to decide such a narrow case. Surely, as Justice KENNEDY demonstrates, the Court could have reached the result it wanted without inflicting this damage upon our Takings Clause jurisprudence.

My fear is that the Court's new policies will spread beyond the narrow confines of the present case. For that reason, I, like the Court, will give far greater attention to this case than its narrow scope suggests—not because I can intercept the Court's missile, or save the targeted mouse, but because I hope perhaps to limit the collateral damage.

* * *

The South Carolina Supreme Court found that the Beachfront Management Act did not take petitioner's property without compensation. The decision rested on two premises that until today were unassailable—that the State has the power to prevent any use of property it finds to be harmful to its citizens, and that a state statute is entitled to a presumption of constitutionality.

The Beachfront Management Act includes a finding by the South Carolina General Assembly that the beach/dune system serves the purpose of "protect[ing] life and property by serving as a storm barrier which dissipates wave energy and contributes to shoreline stability in an economical and effective manner." § 48–39–250(1)(a). The General Assembly also found that "development unwisely has been sited too close to the [beach/dune] system. This type of development has jeopardized the stability of the beach/dune system, accelerated erosion, and endangered adjacent property." § 48–39–250(4); see also § 48–39–250(6) (discussing the need to "afford the beach/dune system space to accrete and erode").

If the state legislature is correct that the prohibition on building in front of the setback line prevents serious harm, then, under this Court's prior cases, the Act is constitutional. "Long ago it was recognized that all property in this country is held under the implied obligation that the owner's use of it shall not be injurious to the community, and the Takings Clause did not transform that principle to one that requires compensation whenever the State asserts its power to enforce it." *Keystone Bituminous Coal Assn. v. DeBenedictis*, 480 U.S. 470, 491–492, 107 S.Ct. 1232, 1245, 94 L.Ed.2d 472 (1987) (internal quotations omitted); see also *id.*, at 488–489, and n. 18, 107 S.Ct., at 1244, n. 18. The Court consistently has upheld regulations imposed to arrest a significant threat to the common welfare, whatever their economic effect on the owner. * * *

* * *

Even if I agreed with the Court that there were no jurisdictional barriers to deciding this case, I still would not try to decide it. The Court creates its new taking jurisprudence based on the trial court's finding that the property had lost all economic value. This finding is almost certainly erroneous. Petitioner still can enjoy other attributes of ownership, such as the right to exclude others, "one of the most essential sticks in the bundle of rights that are commonly characterized as property." *Kaiser Aetna v. United States*, 444 U.S. 164, 176, 100 S.Ct. 383, 391, 62 L.Ed.2d 332 (1979). Petitioner can picnic, swim, camp in a tent, or live on the property in a movable trailer. State courts frequently have recognized that land has economic value where the only residual economic uses are recreation or camping. *See, e.g., Turnpike Realty Co. v. Dedham*, 362 Mass. 221, 284 N.E.2d 891 (1972) cert. denied, 409 U.S. 1108, 93 S.Ct. 908, 34 L.Ed.2d 689 (1973); *Turner v. County of Del Norte*, 24 Cal.App.3d 311, 101 Cal.Rptr. 93 (1972); *Hall v. Board of Environmental Protection*, 528 A.2d 453 (Me.1987). Petitioner also retains the right to alienate the land, which would have value for neighbors and for those prepared to enjoy proximity to the ocean without a house.

Yet the trial court, apparently believing that "less value" and "valueless" could be used interchangeably, found the property "valueless." The court accepted no evidence from the State on the property's value without a home, and petitioner's appraiser testified that he never had considered what the value would be absent a residence. Tr. 54–55. The appraiser's value was based on the fact that the "highest and best use of these lots ... [is] luxury single family detached dwellings." Id., at 48. The trial court appeared to believe that the property could be considered "valueless" if it was not available for its most profitable use. Absent that erroneous assumption, *see Goldblatt*, 369 U.S., at 592, 82 S.Ct., at 989, I find no evidence in the record supporting the trial court's conclusion that the damage to the lots by virtue of the restrictions was "total." Record 128 (findings of fact). I agree with the Court, that it has the power to decide a case that turns on an erroneous finding, but I question the wisdom of deciding an issue based on a factual premise that does not exist in this case, and in the judgment of the Court will exist in the future only in "extraordinary circumstance[s]."

* * *

IV

* * *

This Court repeatedly has recognized the ability of government, in certain circumstances, to regulate property without compensation no matter how adverse the financial effect on the owner may be. More than a century ago, the Court explicitly upheld the right of States to prohibit uses of property injurious to public health, safety, or welfare without paying compensation: "A prohibition simply upon the use of property for purposes that are declared, by valid legislation, to be injurious to the health, morals, or safety of the community, cannot, in any just sense, be deemed a taking or an appropriation of property." *Mugler v. Kansas*, 123 U.S. 623, 668–669, 8 S.Ct. 273, 301, 31 L.Ed. 205 (1887). On this basis, the Court upheld an ordinance effectively prohibiting operation of a previously lawful brewery, although the "establishments will become of no value as property." * * *

Mugler was only the beginning in a long line of cases. In *Powell v. Pennsylvania*, 127 U.S. 678, 8 S.Ct. 992, 32 L.Ed. 253 (1888), the Court upheld legislation prohibiting the manufacture of oleomargarine, despite the owner's allegation that "if prevented from continuing it, the value of his property employed therein would be entirely lost and he be deprived of the means of livelihood." Id., at 682, 8 S.Ct., at 994. In *Hadacheck v. Sebastian*, 239 U.S. 394, 36 S.Ct. 143, 60 L.Ed. 348 (1915), the Court upheld an ordinance prohibiting a brickyard, although the owner had made excavations on the land that prevented it from being utilized for any purpose but a brickyard. Id., at 405, 36 S.Ct., at 143. In *Miller v. Schoene*, 276 U.S. 272, 48 S.Ct. 246, 72 L.Ed. 568 (1928), the Court held that the Fifth Amendment did not require Virginia to pay compensation to the owner of cedar trees ordered destroyed to prevent a disease from spreading to nearby apple orchards. The "preferment of [the public interest] over the property interest of the individual, to the extent even of its destruction, is one of the distinguishing characteristics of every exercise of the police power which affects property." Id., at 280, 48 S.Ct., at 247. Again, in *Omnia Commercial Co. v. United States*, 261 U.S. 502, 43 S.Ct. 437, 67 L.Ed. 773 (1923), the Court stated that "destruction of, or injury to, property is frequently accomplished without a 'taking' in the constitutional sense." Id., at 508, 43 S.Ct., at 437.

More recently, in *Goldblatt*, the Court upheld a town regulation that barred continued operation of an existing sand and gravel operation in order to protect public safety. 369 U.S., at 596, 82 S.Ct., at 991. "Although a comparison of values before and after is relevant," the Court stated, "it is by no means conclusive." Id., at 594, 82 S.Ct., at 990. In 1978, the Court declared that "in instances in which a state tribunal reasonably concluded that 'the health, safety, morals, or general welfare' would be promoted by prohibiting particular contemplated uses of land, this Court has upheld land-use regulation that destroyed ... recognized real property interests." *Penn Central Transp. Co.*, 438 U.S., at 125, 98 S.Ct., at 2659. * * *

The Court recognizes that "our prior opinions have suggested that 'harmful or noxious uses' of property may be proscribed by government regulation without the requirement of compensation," but seeks to reconcile them with its categorical rule by claiming that the Court never has upheld a regulation when the owner alleged the loss of all economic value. Even if the Court's factual premise were correct, its understanding of the Court's cases is distorted. In none of the cases did the Court suggest that the right of a State to prohibit certain activities without paying compensation turned on the availability of some residual valuable use. Instead, the cases depended on whether the government interest was sufficient to prohibit the activity, given the significant private cost.

These cases rest on the principle that the State has full power to prohibit an owner's use of property if it is harmful to the public. "[S]ince no individual has a right to use his property so as to create a nuisance or otherwise harm others, the State has not 'taken' anything when it asserts its power to enjoin the nuisance-like activity." *Keystone Bituminous Coal*, 480 U.S., at 491, n. 20, 107 S.Ct., at 1245, n. 20. It would make no sense under this theory to suggest that an owner has a constitutionally protected right to harm others, if only he makes the proper showing of economic loss.

* * *

C

Finally, the Court justifies its new rule that the legislature may not deprive a property owner of the only economically valuable use of his land, even if the legislature finds it to be a harmful use, because such action is not part of the "long recognized" "understandings of our citizens." These "understandings" permit such regulation only if the use is a nuisance under the common law. Any other course is "inconsistent with the historical compact recorded in the Takings Clause." It is not clear from the Court's opinion where our "historical compact" or "citizens' understanding" comes from, but it does not appear to be history.

The principle that the State should compensate individuals for property taken for public use was not widely established in America at the time of the Revolution.

> "The colonists ... inherited ... a concept of property which permitted extensive regulation of the use of that property for the public benefit—regulation that could even go so far as to deny all productive use of the property to the owner if, as Coke himself stated, the regulation 'extends to the public benefit ... for this is for the public, and every one hath benefit by it.'" F. Bosselman, D. Callies & J. Banta, The Taking Issue 80 1 (1973), quoting *The Case of the King's Prerogative in Saltpetre,* 12 Co.Rep. 12–13 (1606) (hereinafter Bosselman). See also Treanor, The Origins and Original Significance of the Just Compensation Clause of the Fifth Amendment, 94 Yale L.J. 694, 697, n. 9 (1985).

Even into the 19th century, state governments often felt free to take property for roads and other public projects without paying compensation to the owners. See M. Horwitz, The Transformation of American

Law, 1780–1860, pp. 63–64 (1977) (hereinafter Horwitz); Treanor, 94 Yale L.J., at 695. As one court declared in 1802, citizens "were bound to contribute as much of [land], as by the laws of the country, were deemed necessary for the public convenience." McClenachan v. Curwin, 3 Yeates 362, 373 (Pa.1802). There was an obvious movement toward establishing the just compensation principle during the 19th century, but "there continued to be a strong current in American legal thought that regarded compensation simply as a 'bounty given ... by the State' out of 'kindness' and not out of justice." Horwitz 65 (quoting *Commonwealth v. Fisher*, 1 Pen. & W. 462, 465 (Pa.1830)). *See also State v. Dawson*, 3 Hill 100, 103 (S.C.1836).

Although, prior to the adoption of the Bill of Rights, America was replete with land use regulations describing which activities were considered noxious and forbidden, see Bender, The Takings Clause: Principles or Politics?, 34 Buffalo L.Rev. 735, 751 (1985); L. Friedman, A History of American Law 66–68 (1973), the Fifth Amendment's Takings Clause originally did not extend to regulations of property, whatever the effect. Most state courts agreed with this narrow interpretation of a taking. "Until the end of the nineteenth century ... jurists held that the constitution protected possession only, and not value." Siegel, Understanding the Nineteenth Century Contract Clause: The Role of the Property–Privilege Distinction and "Takings" Clause Jurisprudence, 60 S.Cal.L.Rev. 1, 76 (1986); Bosselman 106. Even indirect and consequential injuries to property resulting from regulations were excluded from the definition of a taking. See Bosselman 106; *Callender v. Marsh*, 1 Pick. 418, 430 (Mass.1823).

Even when courts began to consider that regulation in some situations could constitute a taking, they continued to uphold bans on particular uses without paying compensation, notwithstanding the economic impact, under the rationale that no one can obtain a vested right to injure or endanger the public. In the Coates cases, for example, the Supreme Court of New York found no taking in New York's ban on the interment of the dead within the city, although "no other use can be made of these lands." *Coates v. City of New York*, 7 Cow. 585, 592 (N.Y.1827). *See also Brick Presbyterian Church v. City of New York*, 5 Cow. 538 (N.Y.1826); *Commonwealth v. Alger*, 7 Cush. 53, 59, 104 (Mass.1851); *St. Louis Gunning Advertisement Co. v. St. Louis*, 235 Mo. 99, 145–146, 137 S.W. 929, 942 (1911), appeal dism'd, 231 U.S. 761, 34 S.Ct. 325, 58 L.Ed. 470 (1913). More recent cases reach the same result. *See Consolidated Rock Products Co. v. Los Angeles*, 57 Cal.2d 515, 20 Cal.Rptr. 638, 370 P.2d 342, appeal dism'd, 371 U.S. 36, 83 S.Ct. 145, 9 L.Ed.2d 112 (1962); *Nassr v. Commonwealth*, 394 Mass. 767, 477 N.E.2d 987 (1985); *Eno v. Burlington*, 125 Vt. 8, 209 A.2d 499 (1965); *Turner v. County of Del Norte*, 24 Cal.App.3d 311, 101 Cal.Rptr. 93 (1972).

In addition, state courts historically have been less likely to find that a government action constitutes a taking when the affected land is undeveloped. According to the South Carolina court, the power of the legislature to take unimproved land without providing compensation was sanctioned by "ancient rights and principles." *Lindsay v. Commissioners*, 2 S.C.L. 38, 57 (1796). "Except for Massachusetts, no colony appears to have paid compensation when it built a state-owned road across unimproved land. Legislatures provided compensation only for enclosed or improved land." Treanor, 94 Yale L.J., at 695 (footnotes omitted). This rule was followed by some States into the 1800s. See Horwitz 63–65.

With similar result, the common agrarian conception of property limited owners to "natural" uses of their land prior to and during much of the 18th century. See id., at 32. Thus, for example, the owner could build nothing on his land that would alter the natural flow of water. See id., at 44; *see also, e.g., Merritt v. Parker*, 1 Coxe 460, 463 (N.J.1795). Some more recent state courts still follow this reasoning. *See, e.g., Just v. Marinette County*, 56 Wis.2d 7, 201 N.W.2d 761, 768 (1972).

Nor does history indicate any common-law limit on the State's power to regulate harmful uses even to the point of destroying all economic value. Nothing in the discussions in Congress concerning the Takings Clause indicates that the Clause was limited by the common-law nuisance doctrine. Common law courts themselves rejected such an understanding. They regularly recognized that it is "for the legislature to interpose, and by positive enactment to prohibit a use of property which would be injurious to the public." *Tewksbury*, 11 Metc., at 57. Chief Justice Shaw explained in upholding a regulation prohibiting construction of wharves, the existence of a taking did not depend on "whether a certain erection in tide water is a nuisance at common law or not." *Alger*, 7 Cush., at 104; see also State v. Paul, 5 R.I. 185, 193 (1858); *Commonwealth v. Parks*, 155 Mass. 531, 532, 30 N.E. 174 (1892) (Holmes, J.) ("[T]he legislature may change the common law as to nuisances, and may move the line either way, so as to make things nuisances which were not so, or to make things lawful which were nuisances").

In short, I find no clear and accepted "historical compact" or "understanding of our citizens" justifying the Court's new taking doctrine. Instead, the Court seems to treat history as a grab-bag of principles, to be adopted where they support the Court's theory, and ignored where they do not. If the Court decided that the early common law provides the background principles for interpreting the Taking Clause, then regulation, as opposed to physical confiscation, would not be compensable. If the Court decided that the law of a later period provides the background principles, then regulation might be compensable, but the Court would have to confront the fact that legislatures regularly determined which uses were prohibited, independent of the common law, and independent of whether the uses were lawful when the owner purchased. What makes the Court's analysis unworkable is its attempt to package the law of two incompatible eras and peddle it as historical fact.

V

The Court makes sweeping and, in my view, misguided and unsupported changes in our taking doctrine. While it limits these changes to the most narrow subset of government regulation—those that eliminate all economic value from land—these changes go far beyond what is necessary to secure petitioner Lucas' private benefit. One hopes they do not go beyond the narrow confines the Court assigns them to today.

I dissent.

JUSTICE STEVENS, dissenting. [Dissent omitted.]

[Separate statement by Justice SOUTER omitted.]

Notes

1. After remand the South Carolina court held that the Coastal Council did not have the ability under the common law to prohibit Lucas from constructing houses on his land. Lucas v. South Carolina Coastal Council, 309 S.C. 424, 424 S.E.2d 484 (1992). Reportedly, the state paid Lucas about $1 million for the temporary taking, and subsequently sold the land to another developer, recouping most of what it had paid.

2. Does the Lucas decision mean Penn Central is no longer valid? Most courts, since the Lucas decision, have utilized an analytical approach that asks, first, whether the regulation at issue is a "categorical taking" as described by Justice Scalia in Lucas. If the answer is "no" because the property owner still has viable economic uses (though not the "highest and best" uses)—as happens in most cases—then the court will usually revert to the Penn Central factors in determining a regulatory taking. See, e.g., Taub v. Deer Park, 882 S.W.2d 824 (Tex.1994).

3. How should courts interpret the language in Lucas that permits restrictions on property that "inhere in the title itself," (restrictions that background principles of the State's law of property and nuisance already place upon land ownership in terms of the state law that defines title)?

Consider the case of Hunziker v. State, 519 N.W.2d 367 (Iowa 1994), cert. denied 514 U.S. 1003, 115 S.Ct. 1313, 131 L.Ed.2d 195 (1995). A developer sold a lot in his subdivision to a buyer who planned to build a home. Before construction could begin, the state archaeologist discovered a Native American burial mound on the property, and pursuant to a state statute, prohibited disinterment of the mound and required a buffer zone around the mound for protection. The developer refunded the price of the lot and took it back; he then brought an action for compensation for a regulatory taking. The court ruled against the developer, holding that, under Lucas, "the 'bundle of rights' the plaintiffs acquired by their fee simple title did not include the right to use the land contrary to the provisions [of the statutes denying permission to disinter human remains determined to have state and national significance from an historical or scientific standpoint]. * * * The plaintiffs took title to the land in question subject to the provisions of these sections. These sections and their resulting prohibitions concerning the use of the land ran—so to speak—with the land." In a dissenting opinion the dissenter said: "In this case, a dead bones doctrine has risen from the soil, like a phoenix, to consume the live marrow of land ownership. The history surrounding these ancient bones should be preserved by granting compensation for its resurrection."

Also see Kim v. New York City, 90 N.Y.2d 1, 659 N.Y.S.2d 145, 681 N.E.2d 312 (1997) where the court held that a property owner's duty to maintain lateral support for roads that abut his property was a prevailing rule of property law inhering in his title, so that placement of fill by the city on the private property was not a taking. The dissenting opinion declared that the placement of fill was a physical taking for a public use—to shore up a roadway. In Esplanade Properties, LLC v. City of Seattle, 307 F.3d 978 (9th Cir.2002), the court held that a developer who was denied permission to develop some shoreland houses on platforms did not suffer a taking because under Washington law the public trust doctrine regarding tidelands was inherent in the title to private property. Same, as to tidewater land, McQueen v. South Carolina Coastal Council, 354 S.C. 142, 580 S.E.2d 116 (2003).

4. The majority opinion in Lucas suggests that the common law of nuisance may also constitute an exception to the categorical taking. In this regard, see Benjamin, Rith Energy, Inc. v. United States "The Best of Both Worlds": Use of Common Law and Statutory Law Together in Applying the Nuisance Exception to Defend a Takings Claim, 11 Fed. Circuit B.J. 855 (2002).

5. What if the landowner has no viable economic use after the regulation, but when he purchased the property he knew or should have known of the impending regulation? If Lucas applies in this situation, one can see the implications as people make property investments—not for the purpose of development—but for the possibility of obtaining compensation for a taking. See, in this regard, Avenal v. United States, 100 F.3d 933 (Fed.Cir. 1996) where a lessee of oyster beds in Louisiana was denied compensation after a Corps of Engineers freshwater diversion project wiped out the oysters. The court found that at the time of the lease, the claimant had full knowledge of the possibility of the diversion project. The court said:

> Though as entrepreneurs they are entitled to capitalize on the opportunities afforded by government action, they cannot here insist on a guarantee of non-interference by government when they well knew or should have known that, in response to widely-shared public concerns, including concerns of the oystering industry itself, government actions were being planned and executed that would directly affect their new economic investments. * * * Assuming, as we must, that these plaintiffs did not invest in their leases until the 1970's, these plaintiffs, in the words of Penn Central, cannot have had reasonable investment-backed expectations that their oyster leases would give them rights protected from the planned freshwater diversion projects of the state and federal governments.

Also see Alegria v. Keeney, 687 A.2d 1249 (R.I. 1997), a Rhode Island supreme court decision holding that the denial of an application to develop wetlands was not a regulatory taking because at the time he purchased the property, the owner knew that the property contained wetlands subject to regulation under the Freshwater Wetlands Act. The court found the owner did not have reasonable investment-backed expectations. Accord: Leonard v. Brimfield, 423 Mass. 152, 666 N.E.2d 1300 (1996); and Gazza v. New York State Dept. of Environmental Conservation, 89 N.Y.2d 603, 657 N.Y.S.2d

555, 679 N.E.2d 1035 (1997). The Rhode Island supreme court again upheld denial of a wetland development permit in the year 2000, under the state's coastal management regime. This time, the Supreme Court granted certiorari and reversed and remanded:

PALAZZOLO v. RHODE ISLAND
Supreme Court of the United States, 2001.
533 U.S. 606, 121 S.Ct. 2448, 150 L.Ed.2d 592.

JUSTICE KENNEDY delivered the opinion of the Court.

Petitioner Anthony Palazzolo owns a waterfront parcel of land in the town of Westerly, Rhode Island. Almost all of the property is designated as coastal wetlands under Rhode Island law. After petitioner's development proposals were rejected by respondent Rhode Island Coastal Resources Management Council (Council), he sued in state court, asserting the Council's application of its wetlands regulations took the property without compensation in violation of the Takings Clause of the Fifth Amendment, binding upon the State through the Due Process Clause of the Fourteenth Amendment. Petitioner sought review in this Court, contending the Supreme Court of Rhode Island erred in rejecting his takings claim.

* * *

Petitioner filed an inverse condemnation action in Rhode Island Superior Court, asserting that the State's wetlands regulations, as applied by the Council to his parcel, had taken the property without compensation in violation of the Fifth and Fourteenth Amendments. The suit alleged the Council's action deprived him of "economically, beneficial use" of his property, resulting in a total taking requiring compensation under *Lucas v. South Carolina Coastal Council,* 505 U.S. 1003, 112 S.Ct. 2886, 120 L.Ed.2d 798 (1992). He sought damages in the amount of $3,150,000, a figure derived from an appraiser's estimate as to the value of a 74–lot residential subdivision. The State countered with a host of defenses. After a bench trial, a justice of the Superior Court ruled against petitioner, accepting some of the State's theories.

The Rhode Island Supreme Court affirmed. 746 A.2d 707 (2000). Like the Superior Court, the State Supreme Court recited multiple grounds for rejecting petitioner's suit. * * * In addition to holding petitioner could not assert a takings claim based on the denial of all economic use, the court concluded he could not recover under the more general test of *Penn Central Transp. Co. v. City New York,* 438 U.S. 104, 98 S.Ct. 2646, 57 L.Ed.2d 631 (1978). On this claim, too, the date of acquisition of the parcel was found determinative, and the court held he could have had "no reasonable investment-backed expectations that were affected by this regulation" because it predated his ownership, 746 A.2d, at 717; see also *Penn Central, supra,* at 124, 98 S.Ct. 2646.

* * *

We turn to the second asserted basis for declining to address petitioner's takings claim on the merits. When the Council promulgated its wetlands regulations, the disputed parcel was owned not by petitioner but by the corporation of which he was sole shareholder. When title was transferred to petitioner by operation of law, the wetlands regulations were in force. The state court held the postregulation acquisition of title was fatal to the claim for deprivation of all economic use, 746 A.2d, at 716, and to the *Penn Central* claim, 746 A.2d, at 717. While the first holding was couched in terms of background principles of state property law, see *Lucas,* 505 U.S., at 1015, 112 S.Ct. 2886, and the second in terms of petitioner's reasonable investment-backed expectations, see *Penn Central,* 438 U.S., at 124, 98 S.Ct. 2646, the two holdings together amount to a single, sweeping, rule: A purchaser or a successive title holder like petitioner is deemed to have notice of an earlier-enacted restriction and is barred from claiming that it effects a taking.

The theory underlying the argument that postenactment purchasers cannot challenge a regulation under the Takings Clause seems to run on these lines: Property rights are created by the State. See, *e.g., Phillips v. Washington Legal Foundation,* 524 U.S. 156, 163, 118 S.Ct. 1925, 141 L.Ed.2d 174 (1998). So, the argument goes, by prospective legislation the State can shape and define property rights and reasonable investment-backed expectations, and subsequent owners cannot claim any injury from lost value. After all, they purchased or took title with notice of the limitation.

The State may not put so potent a Hobbesian stick into the Lockean bundle. The right to improve property, of course, is subject to the reasonable exercise of state authority, including the enforcement of valid zoning and land-use restrictions. See *Pennsylvania Coal Co.,* 260 U.S., at 413, 43 S.Ct. 158 ("Government hardly could go on if to some extent values incident to property could not be diminished without paying for every such change in the general law"). The Takings Clause, however, in certain circumstances allows a landowner to assert that a particular exercise of the State's regulatory power is so unreasonable or onerous as to compel compensation. Just as a prospective enactment, such as a new zoning ordinance, can limit the value of land without effecting a taking because it can be understood as reasonable by all concerned, other enactments are unreasonable and do not become less so through passage of time or title. Were we to accept the State's rule, the postenactment transfer of title would absolve the State of its obligation to defend any action restricting land use, no matter how extreme or unreasonable. A State would be allowed, in effect, to put an expiration date on the Takings Clause. This ought not to be the rule. Future generations, too, have a right to challenge unreasonable limitations on the use and value of land.

Nor does the justification of notice take into account the effect on owners at the time of enactment, who are prejudiced as well. Should an owner attempt to challenge a new regulation, but not survive the process of ripening his or her claim (which, as this case demonstrates, will often take years), under the proposed rule the right to compensation may not be asserted by an heir or successor, and so may not be asserted at all. The State's rule would work a critical alteration to the nature of property, as the newly regulated landowner is stripped of the ability to transfer the interest which was possessed prior to the regulation. The State may not by this means secure a windfall for itself. See *Webb's Fabulous Pharmacies, Inc. v. Beckwith,* 449 U.S. 155, 164, 101 S.Ct. 446, 66 L.Ed.2d 358 (1980) ("[A] State, by *ipse dixit,* may not transform private property into public property without compensation"); cf. Ellickson, Property in Land, 102 Yale L.J. 1315, 1368–1369 (1993) (right to transfer interest in land is a defining characteristic of the fee simple estate). The proposed rule is, furthermore, capricious in effect. The young owner contrasted with the older owner, the owner with the resources to hold contrasted with the owner with the need to sell, would be in different positions. The Takings Clause is not so quixotic. A blanket rule that purchasers with notice have no compensation right when a claim becomes ripe is too blunt an instrument to accord with the duty to compensate for what is taken.

Direct condemnation, by invocation of the State's power of eminent domain, presents different considerations from cases alleging a taking based on a burdensome regulation. In a direct condemnation action, or when a State has physically invaded the property without filing suit, the fact and extent of the taking are known. In such an instance, it is a general rule of the law of eminent domain that any award goes to the owner at the time of the taking, and that the right to compensation is not passed to a subsequent purchaser. See *Danforth v. United States,* 308 U.S. 271, 284, 60 S.Ct. 231, 84 L.Ed. 240 (1939); 2 Sackman, Eminent Domain, at § 5.01[5][d][i] ("It is well settled that when there is a taking of property by eminent domain in compliance with the law, it is the owner of the property *at the time of the taking* who is entitled to compensation"). A challenge to the application of a land-use regulation, by contrast, does not mature until ripeness requirements have been satisfied, under principles we have discussed; until this point an inverse condemnation claim alleging a regulatory taking cannot be maintained. It would be illogical, and unfair, to bar a regulatory takings claim because of the post-enactment transfer of ownership where the steps necessary to make the claim ripe were not taken, or could not have been taken, by a previous owner.

* * *

We have no occasion to consider the precise circumstances when a legislative enactment can be deemed a background principle of state law or whether those circumstances are present here. It suffices to say that a regulation that otherwise would be unconstitutional absent compensation is not transformed into a background principle of the State's law by mere virtue of the passage of title. This relative standard would be incompatible with our description of the concept in *Lucas,* which is explained in terms of those common, shared understandings of permissible limitations derived from a State's legal tradition, see *id.,* at 1029–1030, 112 S.Ct. 2886. A regulation or common-law rule cannot be a background principle for some owners but not for others. The determination whether an existing, general law can limit all economic use of property must turn on objective factors, such as the nature of the land use proscribed. See *id.,* at 1030, 112 S.Ct. 2886 ("The 'total taking' inquiry we require today will ordinarily entail ... analysis of, among other things, the degree of harm to public lands and resources, or adjacent private property, posed by the claimant's proposed activities"). A law does not become a background principle for subsequent owners by enactment itself. *Lucas* did not overrule our holding in *Nollan,* which, as we have noted, is based on essential Takings Clause principles. * * *

[T]he state court will not find it necessary to explore these matters on remand in connection with the claim that all economic use was deprived; it must address, however, the merits of petitioner's claim under *Penn Central.* That claim is not barred by the mere fact that title was acquired after the effective date of the state-imposed restriction.

* * *

For the reasons we have discussed, the State Supreme Court erred in finding petitioner's claims were unripe and in ruling that acquisition of title after the effective date of the regulations barred the takings claims. The court did not err in finding that petitioner failed to establish a deprivation of all economic value, for it is undisputed that the parcel retains significant worth for construction of a residence. The claims under the *Penn Central* analysis were not examined, and for this purpose the case should be remanded.

The judgment of the Rhode Island Supreme Court is affirmed in part and reversed in part, and the case is remanded for further proceedings not inconsistent with this opinion.

It is so ordered.

JUSTICE O'CONNOR, concurring.

I join the opinion of the Court but with my understanding of how the issues discussed in Part II–B of the opinion must be considered on remand.

Part II–B of the Court's opinion addresses the circumstance, present in this case, where a takings claimant has acquired title to the regulated property after the enactment of the regulation at issue. As the Court holds, the Rhode Island Supreme Court erred in effectively adopting the sweeping rule that the preacquisition enactment of the use restriction *ipso facto* defeats any takings claim based on that use restriction. Accordingly, the Court holds that petitioner's claim under *Penn Central Transp. Co. v. City of New York,* 438 U.S. 104, 98 S.Ct. 2646, 57 L.Ed.2d 631 (1978), "is not barred by the mere fact that title was acquired after the effective date of the state-imposed restriction." *Ante,* at 2464.

The more difficult question is what role the temporal relationship between regulatory enactment and title acquisition plays in a proper *Penn Central* analysis. Today's holding does not mean that the timing of the regulation's enactment relative to the acquisition of title is immaterial to the *Penn Central* analysis. Indeed, it would be just as much error to expunge this consideration from the takings inquiry as it would be to accord it exclusive significance. Our polestar instead remains the principles set forth in *Penn Central* itself and our other cases that govern partial regulatory takings. Under these cases, interference with investment-backed expectations is one of a number of factors that a court must examine. Further, the regulatory regime in place at the time the claimant acquires the property at issue helps to shape the reasonableness of those expectations.

* * *

The Rhode Island Supreme Court concluded that, because the wetlands regulations predated petitioner's acquisition of the property at issue, petitioner lacked reasonable investment-backed expectations and hence lacked a viable takings claim. 746 A.2d 707, 717 (2000). The court erred in elevating what it believed to be "[petitioner's] lack of reasonable investment-backed expectations" to "dispositive" status. Investment-backed expectations, though important, are not talismanic under *Penn Central*. Evaluation of the degree of interference with investment-backed expectations instead is *one* factor that points toward the answer to the question whether the application of a particular regulation to particular property "goes too far." *Pennsylvania Coal Co. v. Mahon,* 260 U.S. 393, 415, 43 S.Ct. 158, 67 L.Ed. 322 (1922).

Further, the state of regulatory affairs at the time of acquisition is not the only factor that may determine the extent of investment-backed expectations. For example, the nature and extent of permitted development under the regulatory regime vis-a-vis the development sought by the claimant may also shape legitimate expectations without vesting any kind of development right in the property owner. We also have never held that a takings claim is defeated simply on account of the lack of a personal financial investment by a postenactment acquirer of property, such as a donee, heir, or devisee. Cf. *Hodel v. Irving,* 481 U.S. 704, 714–718, 107 S.Ct. 2076, 95 L.Ed.2d 668 (1987). Courts instead must attend to those circumstances which are probative of what fairness requires in a given case.

If investment-backed expectations are given exclusive significance in the *Penn Central* analysis and existing regulations dictate the reasonableness of those expectations in every instance, then the State wields far too much power to redefine property rights upon passage of title. On the other hand, if existing regulations do nothing to inform the analysis, then some property owners may reap windfalls and an important indicium of fairness is lost. As I understand it, our decision today does not remove the regulatory backdrop against which an owner takes title to property from the purview of the *Penn Central* inquiry. It simply restores balance to that inquiry. Courts properly consider the effect of existing regulations under the rubric of investment-backed expectations in determining whether a compensable taking has occurred. As before, the salience of these facts cannot be reduced to any "set formula." *Penn Central,* 438 U.S., at 124, 98 S.Ct. 2646 (internal quotation marks omitted). The temptation to adopt what amount to *per se* rules in either direction must be resisted. The Takings Clause requires careful examination and weighing of all the relevant circumstances in this context. The court below therefore must consider on remand the array of relevant factors under *Penn Central* before deciding whether any compensation is due.

JUSTICE SCALIA concurring. [Opinion omitted.]

JUSTICE STEVENS concurring in part and dissenting in part.

In an admirable effort to frame its inquiries in broadly significant terms, the majority offers three pages of commentary on the issue of whether an owner of property can challenge regulations adopted prior to her acquisition of that property without ever discussing the particular facts or legal claims at issue in this case. While I agree with some of what the Court has to say on this issue, an examination of the issue in the context of the facts of this case convinces me that the Court has oversimplified a complex calculus and conflated two separate questions. Therefore, while I join Part II–A of the opinion, I dissent from the judgment and, in particular, from Part II–B.

* * *

Much of the difficulty of this case stems from genuine confusion as to when the taking Palazzolo alleges actually occurred. According to Palazzolo's theory of the case, the owners of his Westerly, Rhode Island, property possessed the right to fill the wetland portion of the property at some point in the not-too-distant past. In 1971, the State of Rhode Island passed a statute creating the Rhode Island Coastal Resources Management Council (Council) and delegating the Council the authority to promulgate regulations restricting the usage of coastal land. See 1971 R.I. Pub. Laws, ch. 279, § 1 *et seq.* The Council promptly adopted regulations that, *inter alia,* effectively foreclosed petitioner from filling his wetlands. As the regulations nonetheless provided for a process through which petitioner might seek permission to fill the wetlands, he filed two applications for such permission during the 1980's, both of which were denied.

The most natural reading of petitioner's complaint is that the regulations in and of themselves precluded him from filling the wetlands, and that their adoption therefore constituted the alleged taking. This reading is consistent with the Court's analysis in Part II–A of its opinion (which I join) in which the Court explains that petitioner's takings claims are ripe for decision because respondents' wetlands regulations unequivocally provide that there can be "no fill for any likely or foreseeable use." *Ante,* at 2459. If it is the regulations themselves of which petitioner complains, and if they did, in fact, diminish the value of his property, they did so when they were adopted.

To the extent that the adoption of the regulations constitute the challenged taking, petitioner is simply the wrong party to be bringing this action. If the regulations imposed a compensable injury on anyone, it was on the owner of the property at the moment the regulations were adopted. Given the trial court's finding that petitioner did not own the property at that time, in my judgment it is pellucidly clear that he has no standing to claim that the promulgation of the regulations constituted a taking of any part of the property that he subsequently acquired.

* * *

The title Palazzolo took by operation of law in 1978 was limited by the regulations then in place to the extent that such regulations represented a valid exercise of the police power. For the reasons expressed above, I think the regulations barred petitioner from filling the wetlands on his property. At the very least, however, they established a rule that such lands could not be filled unless the Council exercised its authority to make exceptions to that rule under certain circumstances. Under the reading of the regulations most favorable to Palazzolo, he acquired no more than the right to a discretionary determination by the Council as to whether to permit him to fill the wetlands. As his two hearings before that body attest, he was given the opportunity to make a presentation and receive such a determination. Thus, the Council properly respected whatever limited rights he may have retained with regard to filling the wetlands. * * *

In the final analysis, the property interest at stake in this litigation is the right to fill the wetlands on the tract that petitioner owns. Whether either he or his predecessors in title ever owned such an interest, and if so, when it was acquired by the State, are questions of state law. If it is clear—as I think it is and as I think the Court's disposition of the ripeness issue assumes—that any such taking occurred before he became the owner of the property, he has no standing to seek compensation for that taking. On the other hand, if the only viable takings claim has a different predicate that arose later, that claim is not ripe and the discussion in Part II–B of the Court's opinion is superfluous dictum. In either event, the judgment of the Rhode Island Supreme Court should be affirmed in its entirety.

JUSTICE GINSBURG, with whom JUSTICE SOUTER and JUSTICE BREYER join, dissenting. [Opinion omitted.]

JUSTICE BREYER, dissenting. [Opinion omitted.]

TAHOE–SIERRA PRESERVATION COUNCIL, INC. v. TAHOE REGIONAL PLANNING AGENCY

Supreme Court of the United States, 2002.
535 U.S. 302, 122 S.Ct. 1465, 152 L.Ed.2d 517.

JUSTICE STEVENS delivered the opinion of the Court.

The question presented is whether a moratorium on development imposed during the process of devising a comprehensive land-use plan constitutes a *per se* taking of property requiring compensation under the Takings Clause of the United States Constitution. This case actually involves two moratoria ordered by respondent Tahoe Regional Planning Agency (TRPA) to maintain the status quo while studying the impact of development on Lake Tahoe and designing a strategy for environmentally sound growth. The first, Ordinance 81–5, was effective from August 24, 1981, until August 26, 1983, whereas the second more restrictive Resolution 83–21 was in effect from August 27, 1983, until April 25, 1984. As a result of these two directives, virtually all development on a substantial portion of the property subject to TRPA's jurisdiction was prohibited for a period of 32 months. Although the question we decide relates only to that 32-month period, a brief description of the events leading up to the moratoria and a comment on the two permanent plans that TRPA adopted thereafter will clarify the narrow scope of our holding.

I

The relevant facts are undisputed. The Court of Appeals, while reversing the District Court on a question of law, accepted all of its findings of fact, and no party challenges those findings. All agree that Lake Tahoe is "uniquely beautiful," 34 F.Supp.2d 1226, 1230 (D.Nev. 1999), that President Clinton was right to call it a " 'national treasure that must be protected and preserved,' " *ibid.*, and that Mark Twain aptly described the clarity of its waters as " 'not *merely* transparent, but dazzlingly, brilliantly so,' " *ibid.* (emphasis added) (quoting M. Twain, Roughing It 174–175 (1872)).

Lake Tahoe's exceptional clarity is attributed to the absence of algae that obscures the waters of most other lakes. Historically, the lack of nitrogen and phosphorous, which nourish the growth of algae, has ensured the transparency of its waters. Unfortunately, the lake's pristine state has deteriorated rapidly over the past 40 years; increased land development in the Lake Tahoe Basin (Basin) has threatened the " 'noble sheet of blue water' " beloved by Twain and countless others. 34 F.Supp.2d, at 1230. As the District Court found, "[d]ramatic decreases in clarity first began to be noted in the late 1950's/early 1960's, shortly after development at the lake began in earnest." *Id.*, at 1231. The lake's unsurpassed beauty, it seems, is the wellspring of its undoing.

The upsurge of development in the area has caused "increased nutrient loading of the lake largely because of the increase in impervious coverage of land in the Basin resulting from that development." *Ibid.*

"Impervious coverage—such as asphalt, concrete, buildings, and even packed dirt—prevents precipitation from being absorbed by the soil. Instead, the water is gathered and concentrated by such coverage. Larger amounts of water flowing off a driveway or a roof have more erosive force than scattered raindrops falling over a dispersed area—especially one covered with indigenous vegetation, which softens the impact of the raindrops themselves." *Ibid.*

Given this trend, the District Court predicted that "unless the process is stopped, the lake will lose its clarity and its trademark blue color, becoming green and opaque for eternity."

Those areas in the Basin that have steeper slopes produce more runoff; therefore, they are usually considered "high hazard" lands. Moreover, certain areas near streams or wetlands known as "Stream Environment Zones" (SEZs) are especially vulnerable to the impact of development because, in their natural state, they act as filters for much of the debris that runoff carries. Because "[t]he most obvious response to this problem ... is to restrict development around the lake—especially in SEZ lands, as well as in areas already naturally prone to runoff," *id.,* at 1232, conservation efforts have focused on controlling growth in these high hazard areas.

* * *

Given the complexity of the task of defining "environmental threshold carrying capacities" and the division of opinion within TRPA's governing board, the District Court found that it was "unsurprising" that TRPA failed to adopt those thresholds until August 26, 1982, roughly two months after the Compact deadline. Under a liberal reading of the Compact, TRPA then had until August 26, 1983, to adopt a new regional plan. 94 Stat. 3240. "Unfortunately, but again not surprisingly, no regional plan was in place as of that date." 34 F.Supp.2d, at 1235. TRPA therefore adopted Resolution 83–21, "which completely suspended all project reviews and approvals, including the acceptance of new proposals," and which remained in effect until a new regional plan was adopted on April 26, 1984. Thus, Resolution 83–21 imposed an 8–month moratorium prohibiting all construction on high hazard lands in either State. In combination, Ordinance 81–5 and Resolution 83–21 effectively prohibited all construction on sensitive lands in California and on all SEZ lands in the entire Basin for 32 months, and on sensitive lands in Nevada (other than SEZ lands) for eight months. It is these two moratoria that are at issue in this case.

* * *

II

Approximately two months after the adoption of the 1984 plan, petitioners filed parallel actions against TRPA and other defendants in federal courts in Nevada and California that were ultimately consolidated for trial in the District of Nevada. The petitioners include the Tahoe–

Sierra Preservation Council, Inc., a nonprofit membership corporation representing about 2,000 owners of both improved and unimproved parcels of real estate in the Lake Tahoe Basin, and a class of some 400 individual owners of vacant lots located either on SEZ lands or in other parts of districts 1, 2, or 3. Those individuals purchased their properties prior to the effective date of the 1980 Compact, primarily for the purpose of constructing "at a time of their choosing" a single-family home "to serve as a permanent, retirement or vacation residence." When they made those purchases, they did so with the understanding that such construction was authorized provided that "they complied with all reasonable requirements for building."

Petitioners' complaints gave rise to protracted litigation that has produced four opinions by the Court of Appeals for the Ninth Circuit and several published District Court opinions. For present purposes, however, we need only describe those courts' disposition of the claim that three actions taken by TRPA—Ordinance 81–5, Resolution 83–21, and the 1984 regional plan—constituted takings of petitioners' property without just compensation. Indeed, the challenge to the 1984 plan is not before us because both the District Court and the Court of Appeals held that it was the federal injunction against implementing that plan, rather than the plan itself, that caused the post–1984 injuries that petitioners allegedly suffered, and those rulings are not encompassed within our limited grant of certiorari. Thus, we limit our discussion to the lower courts' disposition of the claims based on the 2–year moratorium (Ordinance 81–5) and the ensuing 8–month moratorium (Resolution 83–21).

The District Court began its constitutional analysis by identifying the distinction between a direct government appropriation of property without just compensation and a government regulation that imposes such a severe restriction on the owner's use of her property that it produces "nearly the same result as a direct appropriation." 34 F.Supp.2d, at 1238. The court noted that all of the claims in this case "are of the 'regulatory takings' variety." *Id.*, at 1239. Citing our decision in *Agins v. City of Tiburon*, 447 U.S. 255, 100 S.Ct. 2138, 65 L.Ed.2d 106 (1980), it then stated that a "regulation will constitute a taking when either: (1) it does not substantially advance a legitimate state interest; or (2) it denies the owner economically viable use of her land." 34 F.Supp.2d, at 1239. The District Court rejected the first alternative based on its finding that "further development on high hazard lands such as [petitioners'] would lead to significant additional damage to the lake." *Id.*, at 1240. With respect to the second alternative, the court first considered whether the analysis adopted in *Penn Central Transp. Co. v. New York City*, 438 U.S. 104, 98 S.Ct. 2646, 57 L.Ed.2d 631 (1978), would lead to the conclusion that TRPA had effected a "partial taking," and then whether those actions had effected a "total taking."

Emphasizing the temporary nature of the regulations, the testimony that the "average holding time of a lot in the Tahoe area between lot purchase and home construction is twenty-five years," and the failure of petitioners to offer specific evidence of harm, the District Court concluded that "consideration of the *Penn Central* factors clearly leads to the conclusion that there was no taking." 34 F.Supp.2d, at 1240. In the absence of evidence regarding any of the individual plaintiffs, the court evaluated the "average" purchasers' intent and found that such purchasers "did not have reasonable, investment-backed expectations that they would be able to build single-family homes on their land within the six-year period involved in this lawsuit."

The District Court had more difficulty with the "total taking" issue. Although it was satisfied that petitioners' property did retain some value during the moratoria, it found that they had been temporarily deprived of "all economically viable use of their land." *Id.*, at 1245. The court concluded that those actions therefore constituted "categorical" takings under our decision in *Lucas v. South Carolina Coastal Council,* 505 U.S. 1003, 112 S.Ct. 2886, 120 L.Ed.2d 798 (1992). It rejected TRPA's response that Ordinance 81–5 and Resolution 83–21 were "reasonable temporary planning moratoria" that should be excluded from *Lucas'* categorical approach. The court thought it "fairly clear" that such interim actions would not have been viewed as takings prior to our decisions in *Lucas* and *First English Evangelical Lutheran Church of Glendale v. County of Los Angeles,* 482 U.S. 304, 107 S.Ct. 2378, 96 L.Ed.2d 250 (1987), because "[z]oning boards, cities, counties and other agencies used them all the time to 'maintain the status quo pending study and governmental decision making.'" 34 F.Supp.2d, at 1248–1249 (quoting *Williams v. Central,* 907 P.2d 701, 706 (Colo.App.1995)). After expressing uncertainty as to whether those cases required a holding that moratoria on development automatically effect takings, the court concluded that TRPA's actions did so, partly because neither the ordinance nor the resolution, even though intended to be temporary from the beginning, contained an express termination date. 34 F.Supp.2d, at 1250–1251. Accordingly, it ordered TRPA to pay damages to most petitioners for the 32–month period from August 24, 1981, to April 25, 1984, and to those owning class 1, 2, or 3 property in Nevada for the 8–month period from August 27, 1983, to April 25, 1984.

Both parties appealed. * * *

Contrary to the District Court, the Court of Appeals held that because the regulations had only a temporary impact on petitioners' fee interest in the properties, no categorical taking had occurred. It reasoned:

"Property interests may have many different dimensions. For example, the dimensions of a property interest may include a physical dimension (which describes the size and shape of the property in question), a functional dimension (which describes the extent to which an owner may use or dispose of the property in question), and a temporal dimension (which describes the duration of the property interest). At base, the plaintiffs' argument is that we should conceptually sever each plaintiff's fee interest into discrete segments in at least one of these dimensions—the temporal one—and treat each of those segments as separate and distinct property interests for purposes of takings analysis. Under this theory, they argue that there was a categorical taking of one of those temporal segments." *Id.,* at 774.

Putting to one side "cases of physical invasion or occupation," the court read our cases involving regulatory taking claims to focus on the impact of a regulation on the parcel as a whole. In its view a "planning regulation that prevents the development of a parcel for a temporary period of time is conceptually no different than a land-use restriction that permanently denies all use on a discrete portion of property, or that permanently restricts a type of use across all of the parcel." In each situation, a regulation that affects only a portion of the parcel—whether limited by time, use, or space—does not deprive the owner of all economically beneficial use.

The Court of Appeals distinguished *Lucas* as applying to the " 'relatively rare' " case in which a regulation denies all productive use of an entire parcel, whereas the moratoria involve only a "temporal 'slice' " of the fee interest and a form of regulation that is widespread and well established. 216 F.3d, at 773–774. It also rejected petitioners' argument that our decision in *First English* was controlling. According to the Court of Appeals, *First English* concerned the question whether compensation is an appropriate remedy for a temporary taking and not whether or when such a taking has occurred. 216 F.3d, at 778. Faced squarely with the question whether a taking had occurred, the court held that *Penn Central* was the appropriate framework for analysis. Petitioners, however, had failed to challenge the District Court's conclusion that they could not make out a taking claim under the *Penn Central* factors.

Over the dissent of five judges, the Ninth Circuit denied a petition for rehearing en banc. 228 F.3d 998 (C.A.9 2000). In the dissenters' opinion, the panel's holding was not faithful to this Court's decisions in *First English* and *Lucas,* nor to Justice Holmes admonition in *Pennsylvania Coal Co. v. Mahon,* 260 U.S. 393, 416, 43 S.Ct. 158, 67 L.Ed. 322 (1922), that " 'a strong public desire to improve the public condition is not enough to warrant achieving the desire by a shorter cut than the constitutional way of paying for the change.' " 228 F.3d, at 1003. Because of the importance of the case, we granted certiorari limited to the question stated at the beginning of this opinion. We now affirm.

III

Petitioners make only a facial attack on Ordinance 81–5 and Resolution 83–21. They contend that the mere enactment of a temporary regulation that, while in effect, denies a property owner all viable economic use of her property gives rise to an unqualified constitutional obligation to compensate her for the value of its use during that period. Hence, they "face an uphill battle," *Keystone Bituminous Coal Assn. v. DeBenedictis,* 480 U.S. 470, 495, 107 S.Ct. 1232, 94 L.Ed.2d 472 (1987), that is made especially steep by their desire for a categorical rule requiring compensation whenever the government imposes such a moratorium on development. Under their proposed rule, there is no need to evaluate the landowners' investment-backed expectations, the actual impact of the regulation on any individual, the importance of the public interest served by the regulation, or the reasons for imposing the temporary restriction. For petitioners, it is enough that a regulation imposes a temporary deprivation—no matter how brief—of all economically viable use to trigger a *per se* rule that a taking has occurred. Petitioners assert that our opinions in *First English* and *Lucas* have already endorsed their view, and that it is a logical application of the principle that the Takings Clause was "designed to bar Government from forcing some people alone to bear burdens which, in all fairness and justice, should be borne by the public as a whole." *Armstrong v. United States,* 364 U.S. 40, 49, 80 S.Ct. 1563, 4 L.Ed.2d 1554 (1960).

We shall first explain why our cases do not support their proposed categorical rule—indeed, fairly read, they implicitly reject it. Next, we shall explain why the *Armstrong* principle requires rejection of that rule as well as the less extreme position advanced by petitioners at oral argument. In our view the answer to the abstract question whether a temporary moratorium effects a taking is neither "yes, always" nor "no, never"; the answer depends upon the particular circumstances of the case. Resisting "[t]he temptation to adopt what amount to *per se* rules in either direction," *Palazzolo v. Rhode Island,* 533 U.S. 606, 636, 121 S.Ct. 2448, 150 L.Ed.2d 592 (2001) (O'CONNOR, J., concurring), we conclude that the circumstances in this case are best analyzed within the *Penn Central* framework.

IV

The text of the Fifth Amendment itself provides a basis for drawing a distinction between physical takings and regulatory takings. Its plain language requires the payment of compensation whenever the government acquires private property for a public purpose, whether the acquisition is the result of a condemnation proceeding or a physical appropriation. But the Constitution contains no comparable reference to regulations that prohibit a property owner from making certain uses of her private property. Our jurisprudence involving condemnations and physical takings is as old as the Republic and, for the most part, involves the straightforward application of *per se* rules. Our regulatory takings jurisprudence, in contrast, is of more recent vintage and is characterized by "essentially ad hoc, factual inquiries," *Penn Central,* 438 U.S., at 124, 98 S.Ct. 2646, designed to allow "careful examination and weighing of all the relevant circumstances." *Palazzolo,* 533 U.S., at 636, 121 S.Ct. 2448 (O'CONNOR, J., concurring).

When the government physically takes possession of an interest in property for some public purpose, it has a categorical duty to compensate the former owner, *United States v. Pewee Coal Co.,* 341 U.S. 114, 115, 71 S.Ct. 670, 95 L.Ed. 809 (1951), regardless of whether the interest that is taken constitutes an entire parcel or merely a part thereof. Thus, compensation is mandated when a leasehold is taken and the government occupies the property for its own purposes, even though that use is temporary. *United States v. General Motors Corp.*, 323 U.S. 373, 65 S.Ct. 357, 89 L.Ed. 311 (1945); *United States v. Petty Motor Co.*, 327 U.S. 372, 66 S.Ct. 596, 90 L.Ed. 729 (1946). Similarly, when the government appropriates part of a rooftop in order to provide cable TV access for apartment tenants, *Loretto v. Teleprompter Manhattan CATV Corp.*, 458 U.S. 419, 102 S.Ct. 3164, 73 L.Ed.2d 868 (1982); or when its planes use private airspace to approach a government airport, *United States v. Causby*, 328 U.S. 256, 66 S.Ct. 1062, 90 L.Ed. 1206 (1946), it is required to pay for that share no matter how small. But a government regulation that merely prohibits landlords from evicting tenants unwilling to pay a higher rent, *Block v. Hirsh*, 256 U.S. 135, 41 S.Ct. 458, 65 L.Ed. 865 (1921); that bans certain private uses of a portion of an owner's property, *Village of Euclid v. Ambler Realty Co.*, 272 U.S. 365, 47 S.Ct. 114, 71 L.Ed. 303 (1926); *Keystone Bituminous Coal Assn. v. DeBenedictis*, 480 U.S. 470, 107 S.Ct. 1232, 94 L.Ed.2d 472 (1987); or that forbids the private use of certain airspace, *Penn Central Transp. Co. v. New York City*, 438 U.S. 104, 98 S.Ct. 2646, 57 L.Ed.2d 631 (1978), does not constitute a categorical taking. "The first category of cases requires courts to apply a clear rule; the second necessarily entails complex factual assessments of the purposes and economic effects of government actions." *Yee v. Escondido*, 503 U.S. 519, 523, 112 S.Ct. 1522, 118 L.Ed.2d 153 (1992). See also *Loretto*, 458 U.S., at 440, 102 S.Ct. 3164; *Keystone*, 480 U.S., at 489, n. 18, 107 S.Ct. 1232.

This longstanding distinction between acquisitions of property for public use, on the one hand, and regulations prohibiting private uses, on the other, makes it inappropriate to treat cases involving physical takings as controlling precedents for the evaluation of a claim that there has been a "regulatory taking," and vice versa. For the same reason that we do not ask whether a physical appropriation advances a substantial government interest or whether it deprives the owner of all economically valuable use, we do not apply our precedent from the physical takings context to regulatory takings claims. Land-use regulations are ubiquitous and most of them impact property values in some tangential way—often in completely unanticipated ways. Treating them all as *per se* takings would transform government regulation into a luxury few governments could afford. By contrast, physical appropriations are relatively rare, easily identified, and usually represent a greater affront to individual property rights. "This case does not present the 'classi[c] taking' in which the government directly appropriates private property for its own use," *Eastern Enterprises v. Apfel*, 524 U.S. 498, 522, 118 S.Ct. 2131, 141 L.Ed.2d 451 (1998); instead the interference with property rights "arises from some public program adjusting the benefits and burdens of economic life to promote the common good," *Penn Central*, 438 U.S., at 124, 98 S.Ct. 2646.

Perhaps recognizing this fundamental distinction, petitioners wisely do not place all their emphasis on analogies to physical takings cases.

Instead, they rely principally on our decision in *Lucas v. South Carolina Coastal Council,* 505 U.S. 1003, 112 S.Ct. 2886, 120 L.Ed.2d 798 (1992)—a regulatory takings case that, nevertheless, applied a categorical rule—to argue that the *Penn Central* framework is inapplicable here. A brief review of some of the cases that led to our decision in *Lucas,* however, will help to explain why the holding in that case does not answer the question presented here.

As we noted in *Lucas,* it was Justice Holmes' opinion in *Pennsylvania Coal Co. v. Mahon,* 260 U.S. 393, 43 S.Ct. 158, 67 L.Ed. 322 (1922), that gave birth to our regulatory takings jurisprudence. In subsequent opinions we have repeatedly and consistently endorsed Holmes' observation that "if regulation goes too far it will be recognized as a taking." *Id.,* at 415, 43 S.Ct. 158. Justice Holmes did not provide a standard for determining when a regulation goes "too far," but he did reject the view expressed in Justice Brandeis' dissent that there could not be a taking because the property remained in the possession of the owner and had not been appropriated or used by the public. After *Mahon,* neither a physical appropriation nor a public use has ever been a necessary component of a "regulatory taking."

In the decades following that decision, we have "generally eschewed" any set formula for determining how far is too far, choosing instead to engage in " 'essentially ad hoc, factual inquiries.' " *Lucas,* 505 U.S., at 1015, 112 S.Ct. 2886 (quoting *Penn Central,* 438 U.S., at 124, 98 S.Ct. 2646). Indeed, we still resist the temptation to adopt *per se* rules in our cases involving partial regulatory takings, preferring to examine "a number of factors" rather than a simple "mathematically precise" formula. Justice Brennan's opinion for the Court in *Penn Central* did, however, make it clear that even though multiple factors are relevant in the analysis of regulatory takings claims, in such cases we must focus on "the parcel as a whole":

> " 'Taking' jurisprudence does not divide a single parcel into discrete segments and attempt to determine whether rights in a particular segment have been entirely abrogated. In deciding whether a particular governmental action has effected a taking, this Court focuses rather both on the character of the action and on the nature and extent of the interference with rights in the parcel as a whole—here, the city tax block designated as the 'landmark site.' " *Id.,* at 130–131, 98 S.Ct. 2646.

This requirement that "the aggregate must be viewed in its entirety" explains why, for example, a regulation that prohibited commercial transactions in eagle feathers, but did not bar other uses or impose any physical invasion or restraint upon them, was not a taking. *Andrus v. Allard,* 444 U.S. 51, 66, 100 S.Ct. 318, 62 L.Ed.2d 210 (1979). It also clarifies why restrictions on the use of only limited portions of the parcel, such as setback ordinances, *Gorieb v. Fox,* 274 U.S. 603, 47 S.Ct. 675, 71 L.Ed. 1228 (1927), or a requirement that coal pillars be left in place to prevent mine subsidence, *Keystone Bituminous Coal Assn. v. DeBenedic-*

tis, 480 U.S., at 498, 107 S.Ct. 1232, were not considered regulatory takings. In each of these cases, we affirmed that "where an owner possesses a full 'bundle' of property rights, the destruction of one 'strand' of the bundle is not a taking." *Andrus,* 444 U.S., at 65–66, 100 S.Ct. 318.

While the foregoing cases considered whether particular regulations had "gone too far" and were therefore invalid, none of them addressed the separate remedial question of how compensation is measured once a regulatory taking is established. In his dissenting opinion in *San Diego Gas & Elec. Co. v. San Diego,* 450 U.S. 621, 636, 101 S.Ct. 1287, 67 L.Ed.2d 551 (1981), Justice Brennan identified that question and explained how he would answer it:

> "The constitutional rule I propose requires that, once a court finds that a police power regulation has effected a 'taking,' the government entity must pay just compensation for the period commencing on the date the regulation first effected the 'taking,' and ending on the date the government entity chooses to rescind or otherwise amend the regulation." *Id.,* at 658, 101 S.Ct. 1287.

Justice Brennan's proposed rule was subsequently endorsed by the Court in *First English,* 482 U.S., at 315, 318, 321, 107 S.Ct. 2378. *First English* was certainly a significant decision, and nothing that we say today qualifies its holding. Nonetheless, it is important to recognize that we did not address in that case the quite different and logically prior question whether the temporary regulation at issue had in fact constituted a taking.

In *First English,* the Court unambiguously and repeatedly characterized the issue to be decided as a "compensation question" or a "remedial question." *Id.,* at 311, 107 S.Ct. 2378 ("The disposition of the case on these grounds isolates the remedial question for our consideration"); see also *id.,* at 313, 318, 107 S.Ct. 2378. And the Court's statement of its holding was equally unambiguous: "We merely hold that where the government's activities *have already worked a taking* of all use of property, no subsequent action by the government can relieve it of the duty to provide compensation for the period during which the taking was effective." *Id.,* at 321, 107 S.Ct. 2378 (emphasis added). In fact, *First English* expressly disavowed any ruling on the merits of the takings issue because the California courts had decided the remedial question on the assumption that a taking had been alleged. *Id.,* at 312–313, 107 S.Ct. 2378 ("We reject appellee's suggestion that . . . we must independently evaluate the adequacy of the complaint and resolve the takings claim on the merits before we can reach the remedial question"). After our remand, the California courts concluded that there had not been a taking, *First English Evangelical Church of Glendale v. County of Los Angeles,* 210 Cal.App.3d 1353, 258 Cal.Rptr. 893 (1989), and we declined review of that decision, 493 U.S. 1056, 110 S.Ct. 866, 107 L.Ed.2d 950 (1990).

To the extent that the Court in *First English* referenced the antecedent takings question, we identified two reasons why a regulation temporarily denying an owner all use of her property might not constitute a taking. First, we recognized that "the county might avoid the conclusion that a compensable taking had occurred by establishing that the denial of all use was insulated as a part of the State's authority to enact safety regulations." 482 U.S., at 313, 107 S.Ct. 2378. Second, we limited our holding "to the facts presented" and recognized "the quite different questions that would arise in the case of normal delays in obtaining building permits, changes in zoning ordinances, variances, and the like which [were] not before us." *Id.*, at 321, 107 S.Ct. 2378. Thus, our decision in *First English* surely did not approve, and implicitly rejected, the categorical submission that petitioners are now advocating.

Similarly, our decision in *Lucas* is not dispositive of the question presented. Although *Lucas* endorsed and applied a categorical rule, it was not the one that petitioners propose. Lucas purchased two residential lots in 1988 for $975,000. These lots were rendered "valueless" by a statute enacted two years later. The trial court found that a taking had occurred and ordered compensation of $1,232,387.50, representing the value of the fee simple estate, plus interest. As the statute read at the time of the trial, it effected a taking that "was unconditional and permanent." 505 U.S., at 1012, 112 S.Ct. 2886. While the State's appeal was pending, the statute was amended to authorize exceptions that might have allowed Lucas to obtain a building permit. Despite the fact that the amendment gave the State Supreme Court the opportunity to dispose of the appeal on ripeness grounds, it resolved the merits of the permanent takings claim and reversed. Since "Lucas had no reason to proceed on a 'temporary taking' theory at trial," we decided the case on the permanent taking theory that both the trial court and the State Supreme Court had addressed.

The categorical rule that we applied in *Lucas* states that compensation is required when a regulation deprives an owner of "*all* economically beneficial uses*" of his land. *Id.*, at 1019, 112 S.Ct. 2886. Under that rule, a statute that "wholly eliminated the value" of Lucas' fee simple title clearly qualified as a taking. But our holding was limited to "the extraordinary circumstance when *no* productive or economically beneficial use of land is permitted." *Id.*, at 1017, 112 S.Ct. 2886. The emphasis on the word "no" in the text of the opinion was, in effect, reiterated in a footnote explaining that the categorical rule would not apply if the diminution in value were 95% instead of 100%. *Id.*, at 1019, n. 8, 112 S.Ct. 2886. Anything less than a "complete elimination of value," or a "total loss," the Court acknowledged, would require the kind of analysis applied in *Penn Central*. *Lucas*, 505 U.S., at 1019–1020, n. 8, 112 S.Ct. 2886.

Certainly, our holding that the permanent "obliteration of the value" of a fee simple estate constitutes a categorical taking does not answer the question whether a regulation prohibiting any economic use of land for a 32-month period has the same legal effect. Petitioners seek to bring this case under the rule announced in *Lucas* by arguing that we can effectively sever a 32-month segment from the remainder of each landowner's fee simple estate, and then ask whether that segment has been taken in its entirety by the moratoria. Of course, defining the property interest taken in terms of the very regulation being challenged is circular. With property so divided, every delay would become a total ban; the moratorium and the normal permit process alike would constitute categorical takings. Petitioners' "conceptual severance" argument is unavailing because it ignores *Penn Central's* admonition that in regulatory takings cases we must focus on "the parcel as a whole." 438 U.S., at 130–131, 98 S.Ct. 2646. We have consistently rejected such an approach to the "denominator" question. See *Keystone,* 480 U.S., at 497, 107 S.Ct. 1232. See also *Concrete Pipe & Products of Cal., Inc. v. Construction Laborers Pension Trust for Southern Cal.,* 508 U.S. 602, 644, 113 S.Ct. 2264, 124 L.Ed.2d 539 (1993) ("To the extent that any portion of property is taken, that portion is always taken in its entirety; the relevant question, however, is whether the property taken is all, or only a portion of, the parcel in question"). Thus, the District Court erred when it disaggregated petitioners' property into temporal segments corresponding to the regulations at issue and then analyzed whether petitioners were deprived of all economically viable use during each period. The starting point for the court's analysis should have been to ask whether there was a total taking of the entire parcel; if not, then *Penn Central* was the proper framework.

An interest in real property is defined by the metes and bounds that describe its geographic dimensions and the term of years that describes the temporal aspect of the owner's interest. See Restatement of Property §§ 7–9 (1936). Both dimensions must be considered if the interest is to be viewed in its entirety. Hence, a permanent deprivation of the owner's use of the entire area is a taking of "the parcel as a whole," whereas a temporary restriction that merely causes a diminution in value is not. Logically, a fee simple estate cannot be rendered valueless by a temporary prohibition on economic use, because the property will recover value as soon as the prohibition is lifted. Cf. *Agins v. City of Tiburon,* 447 U.S., at 263, n. 9, 100 S.Ct. 2138 ("Even if the appellants' ability to sell their property was limited during the pendency of the condemnation proceeding, the appellants were free to sell or develop their property when the proceedings ended. Mere fluctuations in value during the process of governmental decisionmaking, absent extraordinary delay, are 'incidents of ownership. They cannot be considered as a "taking" in the constitutional sense'" (quoting *Danforth v. United States,* 308 U.S. 271, 285, 60 S.Ct. 231, 84 L.Ed. 240 (1939))).

Neither *Lucas,* nor *First English,* nor any of our other regulatory takings cases compels us to accept petitioners' categorical submission. In fact, these cases make clear that the categorical rule in *Lucas* was carved out for the "extraordinary case" in which a regulation permanently deprives property of all value; the default rule remains that, in the regulatory taking context, we require a more fact specific inquiry.

Nevertheless, we will consider whether the interest in protecting individual property owners from bearing public burdens "which, in all fairness and justice, should be borne by the public as a whole," *Armstrong v. United States,* 364 U.S., at 49, 80 S.Ct. 1563, justifies creating a new rule for these circumstances.

V

Considerations of "fairness and justice" arguably could support the conclusion that TRPA's moratoria were takings of petitioners' property based on any of seven different theories. First, even though we have not previously done so, we might now announce a categorical rule that, in the interest of fairness and justice, compensation is required whenever government temporarily deprives an owner of all economically viable use of her property. Second, we could craft a narrower rule that would cover all temporary land-use restrictions except those "normal delays in obtaining building permits, changes in zoning ordinances, variances, and the like" which were put to one side in our opinion in *First English,* 482 U.S., at 321, 107 S.Ct. 2378. Third, we could adopt a rule like the one suggested by an *amicus* supporting petitioners that would "allow a short fixed period for deliberations to take place without compensation—say maximum one year—after which the just compensation requirements" would "kick in." Fourth, with the benefit of hindsight, we might characterize the successive actions of TRPA as a "series of rolling moratoria" that were the functional equivalent of a permanent taking. Fifth, were it not for the findings of the District Court that TRPA acted diligently and in good faith, we might have concluded that the agency was stalling in order to avoid promulgating the environmental threshold carrying capacities and regional plan mandated by the 1980 Compact. Cf. *Monterey v. Del Monte Dunes at Monterey, Ltd.,* 526 U.S. 687, 698, 119 S.Ct. 1624, 143 L.Ed.2d 882 (1999). Sixth, apart from the District Court's finding that TRPA's actions represented a proportional response to a serious risk of harm to the lake, petitioners might have argued that the moratoria did not substantially advance a legitimate state interest, see *Agins* and *Monterey*. Finally, if petitioners had challenged the application of the moratoria to their individual parcels, instead of making a facial challenge, some of them might have prevailed under a *Penn Central* analysis.

As the case comes to us, however, none of the last four theories is available. The "rolling moratoria" theory was presented in the petition for certiorari, but our order granting review did not encompass that issue, 533 U.S. 948, 121 S.Ct. 2589, 150 L.Ed.2d 749 (2001); the case was tried in the District Court and reviewed in the Court of Appeals on the theory that each of the two moratoria was a separate taking, one for a 2–year period and the other for an 8–month period. And, as we have already noted, recovery on either a bad faith theory or a theory that the state interests were insubstantial is foreclosed by the District Court's unchallenged findings of fact. Recovery under a *Penn Central* analysis is also foreclosed both because petitioners expressly disavowed that theory, and because they did not appeal from the District Court's conclusion that the evidence would not support it. Nonetheless, each of the three *per se* theories is fairly encompassed within the question that we decided to answer.

With respect to these theories, the ultimate constitutional question is whether the concepts of "fairness and justice" that underlie the Takings Clause will be better served by one of these categorical rules or by a *Penn Central* inquiry into all of the relevant circumstances in particular cases. From that perspective, the extreme categorical rule that any deprivation of all economic use, no matter how brief, constitutes a compensable taking surely cannot be sustained. Petitioners' broad submission would apply to numerous "normal delays in obtaining building permits, changes in zoning ordinances, variances, and the like," as well as to orders temporarily prohibiting access to crime scenes, businesses that violate health codes, fire-damaged buildings, or other areas that we cannot now foresee. Such a rule would undoubtedly require changes in numerous practices that have long been considered permissible exercises of the police power. As Justice Holmes warned in *Mahon,* "[g]overnment hardly could go on if to some extent values incident to property could not be diminished without paying for every such change in the general law." A rule that required compensation for every delay in the use of property would render routine government processes prohibitively expensive or encourage hasty decisionmaking. Such an important change in the law should be the product of legislative rulemaking rather than adjudication.

More importantly, for reasons set out at some length by Justice O'CONNOR in her concurring opinion in *Palazzolo v. Rhode Island,* 533 U.S., at 636, 121 S.Ct. 2448, we are persuaded that the better approach to claims that a regulation has effected a temporary taking "requires careful examination and weighing of all the relevant circumstances." In that opinion, Justice O'CONNOR specifically considered the role that the "temporal relationship between regulatory enactment and title acquisition" should play in the analysis of a takings claim. We have no occasion to address that particular issue in this case, because it involves a different temporal relationship—the distinction between a temporary restriction and one that is permanent. * * *

In rejecting petitioners' *per se* rule, we do not hold that the temporary nature of a land-use restriction precludes finding that it effects a taking; we simply recognize that it should not be given exclusive significance one way or the other.

A narrower rule that excluded the normal delays associated with processing permits, or that covered only delays of more than a year, would certainly have a less severe impact on prevailing practices, but it would still impose serious financial constraints on the planning process. Unlike the "extraordinary circumstance" in which the government deprives a property owner of all economic use, moratoria like Ordinance 81–5 and Resolution 83–21 are used widely among land-use planners to preserve the status quo while formulating a more permanent development strategy. In fact, the consensus in the planning community appears to be that moratoria, or "interim development controls" as they are often called, are an essential tool of successful development. Yet even the weak version of petitioners' categorical rule would treat these interim measures as takings regardless of the good faith of the planners, the reasonable expectations of the landowners, or the actual impact of the moratorium on property values.

The interest in facilitating informed decisionmaking by regulatory agencies counsels against adopting a *per se* rule that would impose such severe costs on their deliberations. Otherwise, the financial constraints of compensating property owners during a moratorium may force officials to rush through the planning process or to abandon the practice altogether. To the extent that communities are forced to abandon using moratoria, landowners will have incentives to develop their property quickly before a comprehensive plan can be enacted, thereby fostering inefficient and ill-conceived growth. A finding in the 1980 Compact itself, which presumably was endorsed by all three legislative bodies that participated in its enactment, attests to the importance of that concern. 94 Stat. 3243 ("The legislatures of the States of California and Nevada find that in order to make effective the regional plan as revised by the agency, it is necessary to halt temporarily works of development in the region which might otherwise absorb the entire capability of the region for further development or direct it out of harmony with the ultimate plan").

* * *

Indeed, the interest in protecting the decisional process is even stronger when an agency is developing a regional plan than when it is considering a permit for a single parcel. In the proceedings involving the Lake Tahoe Basin, for example, the moratoria enabled TRPA to obtain the benefit of comments and criticisms from interested parties, such as the petitioners, during its deliberations. Since a categorical rule tied to the length of deliberations would likely create added pressure on decisionmakers to reach a quick resolution of land-use questions, it would only serve to disadvantage those landowners and interest groups who are not as organized or familiar with the planning process. Moreover, with a temporary ban on development there is a lesser risk that individual landowners will be "singled out" to bear a special burden that should be shared by the public as a whole. At least with a moratorium there is a clear "reciprocity of advantage," because it protects the interests of all affected landowners against immediate construction that might be inconsistent with the provisions of the plan that is ultimately adopted. "While each of us is burdened somewhat by such restrictions, we, in turn, benefit greatly from the restrictions that are placed on others." In fact, there is reason to believe property values often will continue to increase despite a moratorium. See, *e.g., Growth Properties, Inc. v. Klingbeil Holding Co.,* 419 F.Supp. 212, 218 (D.Md.1976) (noting that land values could be expected to increase 20% during a 5–year moratorium on development). Cf. *Forest Properties, Inc. v. United States,* 177 F.3d 1360, 1367 (C.A.Fed.1999) (record showed that market value of the entire parcel increased despite denial of permit to fill and develop lake-bottom property). Such an increase makes sense in this context because property values throughout the Basin can be expected to reflect the added assurance that Lake Tahoe will remain in its pristine state. Since in some cases a 1–year moratorium may not impose a burden at all, we should not adopt a rule that assumes moratoria always force individuals to bear a special burden that should be shared by the public as a whole.

It may well be true that any moratorium that lasts for more than one year should be viewed with special skepticism. But given the fact that the District Court found that the 32 months required by TRPA to formulate the 1984 Regional Plan was not unreasonable, we could not possibly conclude that every delay of over one year is constitutionally unacceptable. Formulating a general rule of this kind is a suitable task for state legislatures. In our view, the duration of the restriction is one of the important factors that a court must consider in the appraisal of a regulatory takings claim, but with respect to that factor as with respect to other factors, the "temptation to adopt what amount to *per se* rules in either direction must be resisted." There may be moratoria that last longer than one year which interfere with reasonable investment-backed expectations, but as the District Court's opinion illustrates, petitioners' proposed rule is simply "too blunt an instrument" for identifying those cases. We conclude, therefore, that the interest in "fairness and justice" will be best served by relying on the familiar *Penn Central* approach when deciding cases like this, rather than by attempting to craft a new categorical rule.

Accordingly, the judgment of the Court of Appeals is affirmed.

It is so ordered.

CHIEF JUSTICE REHNQUIST, with whom JUSTICE SCALIA and JUSTICE THOMAS join, dissenting. [Opinion omitted.]

JUSTICE THOMAS, with whom JUSTICE SCALIA joins, dissenting. [Opinion omitted.]

B. SUBSTANTIVE DUE PROCESS AND EXCESSIVE REGULATION

FIRST ENGLISH EVANGELICAL LUTHERAN CHURCH v. LOS ANGELES COUNTY

Supreme Court of the United States, 1987.
482 U.S. 304, 107 S.Ct. 2378, 96 L.Ed.2d 250.

[The facts of this case appear in the previous section, as does the majority opinion.]

JUSTICE STEVENS, with whom JUSTICE BLACKMUN and JUSTICE O'CONNOR join as to Parts I and III, dissenting.

One thing is certain. The Court's decision today will generate a great deal of litigation. Most of it, I believe, will be unproductive. But the mere duty to defend the actions that today's decision will spawn will undoubtedly have a significant adverse impact on the land-use regulatory process. The Court has reached out to address an issue not actually presented in this case, and has then answered that self-imposed question in a superficial and, I believe, dangerous way.

Four flaws in the Court's analysis merit special comment. First, the Court unnecessarily and imprudently assumes that appellant's complaint alleges an unconstitutional taking of Lutherglen. Second, the Court distorts our precedents in the area of regulatory takings when it concludes that all ordinances which would constitute takings if allowed to remain in effect permanently, necessarily also constitute takings if they are in effect for only a limited period of time. Third, the Court incorrectly assumes that the California Supreme Court has already decided that it will never allow a state court to grant monetary relief for a temporary regulatory taking, and then uses that conclusion to reverse a judgment which is correct under the Court's own theories. Finally, the Court errs in concluding that it is the Takings Clause, rather than the Due Process Clause, which is the primary constraint on the use of unfair and dilatory procedures in the land-use area.

* * *

There is, of course, a possibility that land-use planning, like other forms of regulation, will unfairly deprive a citizen of the right to develop his property at the time and in the manner that will best serve his economic interests. The "regulatory taking" doctrine announced in *Pennsylvania Coal* places a limit on the permissible scope of land-use restrictions. In my opinion, however, it is the Due Process Clause rather than that doctrine that protects the property owner from improperly motivated, unfairly conducted, or unnecessarily protracted governmental decisionmaking. Violation of the procedural safeguards mandated by the Due Process Clause will give rise to actions for damages under 42 U.S.C.A. § 1983, but I am not persuaded that delays in the development of property that are occasioned by fairly conducted administrative or judicial proceedings are compensable, except perhaps in the most unusual circumstances. On the contrary, I am convinced that the public interest in having important governmental decisions made in an orderly, fully informed way amply justifies the temporary burden on the citizen that is the inevitable by-product of democratic government. * * *

The policy implications of today's decision are obvious and, I fear, far reaching. Cautious local officials and land-use planners may avoid taking any action that might later be challenged and thus give rise to a damage action. Much important regulation will never be enacted, even perhaps in the health and safety area. Were this result mandated by the Constitution, these serious implications would have to be ignored. But the loose cannon the Court fires today is not only unattached to the Constitution, but it also takes aim at a long line of precedents in the regulatory takings area. It would be the better part of valor simply to decide the case at hand instead of igniting the kind of litigation explosion that this decision will undoubtedly touch off.

I respectfully dissent.

Note

Justice Steven's dissent in this case poses a difficult problem for lawyers. Challenges to land use regulations can be brought to court under multiple theories. Is a cause of action for inverse condemnation significantly different from a cause of action based on the 14th Amendment due process or equal protection clause? Many state courts have struggled with this problem as the following case indicates.

PRESBYTERY OF SEATTLE v. KING COUNTY

Supreme Court of Washington, 1990.
114 Wash.2d 320, 787 P.2d 907, certiorari denied 498
U.S. 911, 111 S.Ct. 284, 112 L.Ed.2d 238.

ANDERSEN, JUSTICE.

* * *

In 1978 the Presbytery of Seattle purchased a single family home located on approximately 4.5 acres of land in Federal Way for $60,000. The financing documents indicate the property was purchased for the construction of a church.

In 1979 the Presbytery informed the Federal Way Planning and Development Commission that in 1980 it intended to begin construction of a church. However, for financial reasons, that building plan fell through. The Presbytery continued to rent out the existing home located on the property and has never filed an application for a development permit for the property.

Part of the Presbytery's property contains a "wetland." * * * The record before us indicates that in 1981 King County conducted an inventory of wetlands and concluded that the wetlands involved in this case, Hylebos Wetland No. 18, was a "class 1" wetland. The County provided affidavits to show that this wetland is in excess of 12,000 years old, is one of the last major wetlands in the Federal Way area and is of major environmental significance to King County. It also contains one of the few old growth cedar bogs still in existence in the Pacific Northwest. For purposes of this appeal, the parties concur that Wetland No. 18 comprises approximately one-third of the Presbytery's property.

In 1986 the County enacted ordinance 7746 (hereafter the 1986 Wetland Ordinance). The ordinance includes prohibitions on creation of new construction within the wetland boundaries and creates a buffer zone around the wetland (which may be increased if endangered species exist within the buffer) and a native growth protection easement. It is the Presbytery's argument that the ordinance prohibits the development of a substantial portion of its property and thereby effects a taking of property without just compensation. The Presbytery's inverse condemnation action alleges that the County's wetland regulations prevent it from using its land for a church or for any other economically reasonable or profitable use.

* * *

The trial court granted the County's motion to dismiss based on the landowner's failure to exhaust its administrative remedies. The Court of Appeals affirmed in an unpublished opinion. We herein consider the two issues we have determined to be dispositive and affirm both the Superior Court and the Court of Appeals.

* * *

A land use regulation which prohibits development of one portion of an undivided parcel of property does not necessarily constitute a "taking" of the portion which must remain undeveloped. Mere regulation on the use of land has never constituted a "taking" or a violation of due process under federal or state law. The problem in any given case is to determine when such a regulation exceeds constitutional bounds. In order to determine whether such a regulation would be unconstitutional either as a "taking" or as a violation of substantive due process, it is necessary to follow the proper tests for inverse condemnation and for substantive due process violations due to excessive land use regulation.

* * *

The "tests" for over-regulation have until recently proved somewhat of a quagmire of constitutional theory vacillating between substantive due process and "takings" theory. Both this court and the United States Supreme Court have in the past struggled with the difficult determination of where a mere regulation ends and a "taking" commences.

* * *

In this state, a land use regulation which too drastically curtails owners' use of their property can cause a constitutional "taking" or can constitute a denial of substantive due process. These two constitutional theories are alternatives in cases where overly severe land use regulations are alleged. It is critical that these two grounds be separately considered and independently analyzed because the remedies for each of these types of constitutional violation are different.

To determine which of these two constitutional tests to utilize, the threshold inquiry a court must make is whether the challenged regulation safeguards the public interest in health, safety, the environment or the fiscal integrity of an area. A regulation which does that is to be contrasted with one that goes beyond preventing a public harm and actually enhances a publicly owned right in property. Secondly, the court should ask whether the regulation destroys one or more of the fundamental attributes of ownership—the right to possess, to exclude others and to dispose of property. If a regulation does not infringe upon a fundamental attribute of ownership, and if it protects the public from one of the foregoing listed harms, then no constitutional "taking" requiring just compensation exists.

However, even if the regulation protects the public from harm, and does not deny the owners a fundamental attribute of ownership (and is thus insulated from a "takings" challenge), it still must withstand the due process test of reasonableness. The inquiry here must be whether the police power (rather than the eminent domain power) has exceeded its constitutional limits. To determine whether the regulation violates due process, the court should engage in the classic 3–prong due process test and ask: (1) whether the regulation is aimed at achieving a legitimate public purpose; (2) whether it uses means that are reasonably necessary to achieve that purpose; and (3) whether it is unduly oppressive on the land owner. * * *

The "unduly oppressive" inquiry lodges wide discretion in the court and implies a balancing of the public's interest against those of the regulated landowner. We have suggested several factors for the court to consider to assist it in determining whether a regulation is overly oppressive, namely: the nature of the harm sought to be avoided; the availability and effectiveness of less drastic protective measures; and the economic loss suffered by the property owner. Another well regarded commentator in this area of the law, Professor William B. Stoebuck of the University of Washington Law School, has suggested a helpful set of nonexclusive factors to aid the court in effecting this balancing. On the public's side, the seriousness of the public problem, the extent to which the owner's land contributes to it, the degree to which the proposed regulation solves it and the feasibility of less oppressive solutions would all be relevant. On the owner's side, the amount and percentage of value loss, the extent of remaining uses, past, present and future uses, temporary or permanent nature of the regulation, the extent to which the owner should have anticipated such regulation and how feasible it is for the owner to alter present or currently planned uses. Stoebuck, San Diego Gas: Problems, Pitfalls and a Better Way, 25 J.Urb. & Contemp.L. 3, 33 (1983). Use of these factors can materially assist the court in determining whether or not the regulation on use is unduly oppressive to the landowner.

If the regulation is not aimed at a legitimate public purpose, or uses a means which does not tend to achieve it, or if it unduly oppresses the landowner, then the ordinance will be struck down as violative of due process and the remedy is invalidation of the regulation. No compensation (which properly belongs with a "taking" analysis) is warranted in the face of a due process violation.

Invalidation of the ordinance (instead of compensation) also avoids intimidating the legislative body, a situation about which we have previously expressed concern. For example, as commentators have observed in this connection,

> if local governments in the past had thought that enactment of a land use regulation might result in monetary awards, then "very

likely no one would have proposed the planned unit development, the cluster zone, or the floating zone and even if those efforts had received the prior blessing of developers, it is highly unlikely that environmental concerns or regulation of coastal and inland waterways would ever have been risked."

Sallet, Regulatory "Takings" and Just Compensation: The Supreme Court's Search for a Solution Continues, 18 Urb.Law. 635, 636 (1986) (quoting Wright, Exclusionary Land Use Controls and the Taking Issue, 8 Hastings Const. L.Q. 545, 583 (1981)). Accordingly, many challenges to land use regulations will most appropriately be analyzed under a due process formula rather than under a "taking" formula. This is not to say, however, that a certain class of cases will not have to face a "taking" challenge.

* * *

The "taking" analysis requires that the court first ask whether the regulation substantially advances legitimate state interests. If it does not, then it constitutes a "taking." If it does substantially advance a legitimate state interest, then it becomes necessary to look further and see if the challenge to the regulation is a facial challenge or one involving application of the regulation to specific property. It would not be necessary for the challengers to exhaust administrative remedies in a facial challenge because the allegation would be that application of the regulation to any property would constitute a "taking." If the case is a facial challenge, then the landowner must show that the regulation denies all economically viable use of any parcel of regulated property in order to constitute a taking.

* * *

Returning to our "taking" analysis, if the challenge to the regulation is a facial one, and if the landowner succeeds in showing that a regulation denies all economically viable use of any parcel of regulated property, then a constitutional taking has occurred. Practically, however, this should prove to be a relatively rare occurrence.

If the challenge involves an application of the regulation to specific property, then the court should consider: (1) the economic impact of the regulation on the property; (2) the extent of the regulation's interference with investment-backed expectations; and (3) the character of the government action.

If the court determines a "taking" has, in fact, occurred, then just compensation is mandated by the Fifth and Fourteenth Amendments and by Const. art. 1, § 16. If the taking was due to an overly severe land use regulation, and was temporary and reversible, the governmental unit involved has the option of curing the taking or maintaining the status quo by exercising its eminent domain power. Whichever it chooses, just compensation must be paid for the period during which the taking is effective.

As previously noted, exhaustion would be unnecessary if the landowner was engaging in a facial challenge to the ordinance. However, the record presented in this case demonstrates that the landowner has not carried the burden of showing that the regulation denies it all economically viable use of any parcel of regulated property. Therefore, we consider the landowner's exhaustion argument in the context of an "as applied" challenge.

Applying the analysis discussed above to the present case, we could arguably conclude that the challenged regulation seeks to safeguard the public interest in the environment and does not appear to enhance a publicly owned right in other property. However, it would be premature at this time to decide whether the regulation denies an essential attribute of ownership. Assuming without deciding, that the regulation should be scrutinized under the 3-prong due process analysis, we simply do not have all of the required facts needed in order for this court to apply that formula.

Although it might be possible to determine that the regulation was aimed at achieving a legitimate public purpose and that it used means to achieve that purpose, on the limited record here presented it is not possible to determine whether the regulation was unduly oppressive to this landowner. Without knowledge of the uses to which this property can legally be put, it is not feasible to consider the factors which help to determine "undue oppressiveness". Exhaustion of administrative remedies is, therefore, necessary in order for a court to have before it the facts necessary to make such a determination.

Although the landowners argue that exhaustion would be futile in this particular case, we disagree. Exhaustion of administrative remedies is generally required before resort to the courts, although exhaustion is excused if a resort to administrative procedures would be futile.

* * *

Our recent decision in *Estate of Friedman v. Pierce Cy.*, 112 Wash.2d 68, 768 P.2d 462 (1989) involved a challenge to a planned unit development (PUD) map which required that a substantial amount of land in the PUD remain "open space". The present case is similar in that some portion (perhaps one-third) of the owner's land will have to remain "open space" to protect the Hylebos wetland under present regulations. Estate of Friedman made clear that it will be the uncommon case where a landowner can show a constitutional violation without first exhausting available procedures in an attempt to secure a permit for possible use. As noted earlier herein, King County argues that resort to administrative channels would not have been futile because the Sensitive Area Ordinance does allow development of wetlands if application of the wetland ordinance "would deny all reasonable uses of a property". As also noted, the County further argues that it is entirely possible that the landowner may be permitted to build a church on its land under existing regulations.

Because the landowner has not as yet sought any development permits, it is not possible to know what effect SEPA and other applicable regulations might have on the property in question. The Court of Appeals appropriately observed that without engaging in the application process, there is no way to know what beneficial use may be made of Presbytery's property, nor any way to know what deprivation of beneficial use was proximately caused by the Hylebos Wetland Ordinance.

Affirmed.

Notes

1. The distinction between a takings claim and a denial of substantive due process claim has several dimensions; most important are the differences between the two theories in terms of ripeness and exhaustion of administrative remedies and the differing measures of damages, if damages are appropriate. The distinction has tempted lawyers to combine the causes of action, thus shifting to the courts the difficulty of determining an analytical framework for the case. See Thomas E. Roberts, Karen Edginton Milner and Robert I. McMurry, Land Use Litigation: Doctrinal Confusion Under the Fifth and Fourteenth Amendments, 28 The Urban Lawyer 765 (1996).

The temptation to combine inverse condemnation claims with due process claims not only makes for analytical problems for courts, but each claim generates different procedural considerations.

2. In Meighan v. U.S. Sprint Communications Co., 924 S.W.2d 632 (Tenn.1996) the court held that under the Tennessee statutory framework for inverse condemnation suits a landowner could alternatively sue the alleged taker on a trespass theory and seek punitive as well as compensatory damages. In this case, the telecommunications company struck a deal with a railroad to run fiber optic cable along the right-of-way across plaintiffs' lands. The plaintiffs brought a class action against U.S. Sprint alleging a taking of property and trespass; defendant moved to dismiss the trespass and punitive damages claim.

3. In Del Oro Hills v. City of Oceanside, 31 Cal.App.4th 1060, 37 Cal.Rptr.2d 677 (1995) the court held that a developer who sought taking damages from a city after the city's growth control ordinance was found invalid, could not simply allege an invalid regulation and claim per se damages. The court found that the developer had sold all of his development, albeit not at the highest price he might have obtained (according to the developer's allegations) and that his land had enjoyed viable economic uses during the period the invalid ordinance was in effect. And, in Ellison v. County of Ventura, 217 Cal.App.3d 455, 265 Cal.Rptr. 795 (1990) the court found that amendments to a zoning ordinance could not be a taking because the value of the property had doubled despite the more restrictive zoning provisions adopted after the owner had purchased the property. See Donald L. Elliott, Givings and Takings, Land Use Law (Jan. 1996) p. 3, for a proposal that courts look to the values added to property by governmental actions as a factor in measuring governmental takings.

4. How to measure the compensation damages for a temporary taking is left to the lower courts. Since the First English case, federal courts have struggled with the problem. Two cases are illustrative:

(a). In Joseph Wheeler v. City of Pleasant Grove, 896 F.2d 1347 (11th Cir.1990) the court found that the developer had suffered a temporary taking by virtue of a city ordinance that prohibited the construction of new apartment buildings. The trial court refused to award damages on a theory of qualified immunity. The court of appeals reversed and remanded; the district court again refused to award damages stating that the ordinance was not responsible for plaintiff's loss. Again the court of appeals reversed for a calculation of damages. This time, the district court concluded that the developer had shown some $206,000 in increased construction costs, but they still retained the property and could have sold it and the property had appreciated in value throughout the period of the temporary taking. Once more the appeals court reversed and specifically instructed the district court to award the market rate return computed over the period of the temporary taking on the difference between the property's fair market value with and without the regulation. The district court held a hearing and concluded that the fair market value of the land was not diminished by the ordinance and again awarded no damages. Finally, the appeals court calculated damages by finding that the fair market value of the proposed apartment complex was $2.3 million in 1978. After the city's prohibition, the owners only had the land, appraised at $200,000. In 1978 the loan-to-value ratio was 75 percent of the value of the project, meaning that the expected return was 25 percent, or $575,000. After the city withdrew the permit, the owner had 25 percent equity in the land, or $50,000. The loss in fair market value was $525,000 and the period of temporary taking was 14 months and 3 days; the market rate of return for that period was 9.77 percent which equalled damages of $59,841.23. That amount was awarded to the owners.

(b). Corn v. City of Lauderdale Lakes, 771 F.Supp. 1557 (S.D.Fla. 1991) involved a rezoning of the plaintiff's land to prohibit the construction of mini-warehouses. After a state court held the rezoning to be arbitrary, the property owner sought damages for a temporary taking. The federal district court applied the same formula as the Wheeler court and found temporary taking damages of $291,622.59 and after calculating interest, awarded the property owner $727,875.02. In a lengthy appendix to the opinion the court sets forth its worksheet of calculations illustrating the application of the fair market value/rate of return formula described by the Eleventh Circuit in Wheeler. The court of appeals reversed the award in 997 F.2d 1369 and remanded the case to the district court which then ruled that there was no taking. Another appeal followed, 95 F.3d 1066. The appellate court held that Corn failed to show "no viable economic uses" remaining, but remanded once again to the district court for further findings on the validity of a city moratorium that delayed the property owner's plans for a significant time, so that his competitors occupied the market for mini-warehouses.

5. A very unusual compensation problem was presented in Board of County Supervisors of Prince William County, Virginia v. United States, 48

F.3d 520 (Fed.Cir.1995). A real estate developer proposed to develop 550 acres of land adjacent to Manassas Battlefield Park, a historic Civil War site. As a part of the rezoning process the developer presented the local government with a proffer of amenities he would provide, including storm drains, a community trail system, a community center and swimming pool, tennis courts, a ballfield, and a commitment to contribute a sum of money to the county for school purposes, plus five acres for a fire station and commuter parking lot; in addition to the proffer, the developer deeded several acres of his land to the county for road improvements. After a public outcry about the potential harm to the battlefield site, Congress enacted a statute to take the 550 acres as an addition to the Manassas Battlefield National Park, and to pay just compensation to the owners of any property taken pursuant to the Act. The United States paid the developer, but the county sued in the Court of Claims demanding compensation for the value of the proffers accepted by the county, and for the 16 acres of land the developer had conveyed for road improvements in connection with the proposed development (the road improvements were no longer necessary due to the federal taking). The appellate court held that the proffers made to the county were not "property" for the purposes of the taking clause, but that the county was entitled to compensation for the land that the developer had previously conveyed to the county for road improvements, reasoning that even though the land was in reality dedicated for public roads that now would never be built, there was some residual value in the land; the case was remanded for determination of that value.

6. If a property owner challenges a local land use regulation in federal court she must utilize one of several possible jurisdictional statutes. The most common choice is § 1983 of Title 28, U.S. Code—a civil rights statute giving federal courts the power to redress denial of constitutional rights under color of state law. Does every local land use regulation afford the basis for a federal court to review the regulation? The next case may help shed light on the question.

PEARSON v. CITY OF GRAND BLANC

United States Court of Appeals, Sixth Circuit, 1992.
961 F.2d 1211.

BERTELSMAN, CHIEF DISTRICT JUDGE

* * *

Plaintiff Pearson is the owner of a parcel of property in the City of Grand Blanc, Michigan. Plaintiff alleges that there are two zoning classifications assigned to the property, Residential 2 in the rear and Business 1 in the front.

Early in 1989, plaintiff applied for a complete rezoning of the property to B–2. Plaintiff desired to take advantage of an opportunity to sell the parcel to McDonald's for one of its fast food restaurants. Plaintiff originally contended that the divided zoning completely negates any economically viable use of his property, but has withdrawn any taking claim he might have had.

Plaintiff's rezoning application was approved by both the county and city planning commissions. The final decision was up to the city council under state law, however. As it happened, the neighbors were less than enthusiastic concerning the advent of the golden arches in their neighborhood. The request was rejected by the City Council and remanded to the city planning commission.

Subsequently, plaintiff submitted an amended site plan and zoning request, which was similarly rejected by the city council, although approved by the planning commission. Plaintiff avers that the rejection was arbitrary and capricious, depriving him of substantive due process of law. Plaintiff filed this action based primarily on federal claims in the state court, but it was removed to the district court by the defendants. Plaintiff also asserts an equal protection claim, arguing that similar zoning changes have been granted in the past in virtually identical situations.

He contends that the foregoing factors raise issues of material fact which entitle him to have a jury review the decisions of the city council to decide whether they were arbitrary and capricious.

We disagree and affirm, but on the basis of an analysis somewhat at variance with that employed by the trial court.

Some circuits impose a ripeness requirement in zoning cases. This issue must be addressed first because it is jurisdictional. In cases where plaintiff claims that the zoning is so stringent as to constitute a taking without just compensation, the Supreme Court requires what amounts to exhaustion of state judicial remedies, including the bringing of an inverse condemnation action, if the state affords such a remedy. A deprivation of economic viability of the property is also a prerequisite for bringing such an action.

The rationale for these requirements in taking cases is that the federal court cannot know what has been taken or what compensation has been afforded until state remedies have been utilized. Until that time, the federal court cannot determine whether a taking has occurred, whether compensation is due, or, if it has been afforded, whether it is just. These prerequisites are not technically an exhaustion requirement, but "a product of the ripeness doctrine."

By holding that the taking theory subsumes all other theories in zoning cases, the trial court in the instant case would impose these stringent ripeness requirements on all zoning cases.

Some circuits do impose a less stringent ripeness requirement on non-taking zoning cases. For example, the Eleventh Circuit holds that cases such as the one now before us, which it denominates "as applied substantive due process" claims, are "not ripe until the decision denying commercial zoning has been finally made and applied to the property."

Under this approach until at least one meaningful application has been submitted to the local zoning authority, futility is not established and a constitutional challenge to local zoning may not be entertained.

The Ninth Circuit imposes an even more stringent ripeness requirement in non-taking zoning cases and requires that the landowner not only submit one meaningful application, but seek at least one variance if that application is denied, before coming to federal court.

Another panel of this court recently held that the very existence of an allegedly unlawful zoning action, without more, makes a substantive due process claim ripe for federal adjudication. Plaintiff's claim is, therefore, ripe under the law now prevailing in this circuit. We may observe that plaintiff also met the stricter Ninth Circuit criteria in that he did make an application for an alternate use.

Plaintiff's principal contention is that he was subjected to arbitrary and capricious state action in the denial of his rezoning request and thus deprived of substantive due process of law.

Before we address this argument, some background is required to place the discussion in context. First, let us look at the various kinds of constitutional violations typically asserted in federal zoning cases.

We find the categories of federal zoning cases devised by the Eleventh Circuit to be quite useful in promoting meaningful analysis in this area. Our adopting them will also promote much-needed uniformity among the federal courts on this subject.

These categories of federal zoning claims are:

1. *Just compensation takings claim.* Plaintiff claims that the zoning applied to his land constitutes a taking of his property without just compensation in contravention of the Fifth Amendment, the remedy sought being the just compensation.

2. *Due process takings claim.* Plaintiff claims that the zoning applied to his property goes too far and destroys the value of his property to such an extent that it amounts to a taking by eminent domain without due process of law. The remedy sought is invalidation of the zoning regulation.

3. *Arbitrary and capricious substantive due process claim.* Plaintiff claims that the zoning regulation is arbitrary and capricious in that it does not bear a substantial relation to the public health, safety, morals, or general welfare. Two further subcategories may be discerned under this heading: (a) facial and (b) as applied.

4. *Equal protection.* Either based on suspect class, invoking strict scrutiny, or mere economic discrimination.

5. *Procedural due process.* Although not discussed by the Eleventh Circuit, there is, of course, a fifth category where plaintiff claims deprivation of procedural due process.

6. *First Amendment.* A category may also be defined when plaintiff claims that a First Amendment right such as freedom of speech or religion is violated by the zoning ordinance.

The case at bar is an "as applied substantive due process" claim. Both kinds of taking theories have been abandoned by the plaintiff, and his equal protection claim is of the economic variety (no racial or other suspect class overtones), which tends to merge with the substantive due process argument. Plaintiff makes no procedural due process or First Amendment claim.

The trial court held that all arbitrary and capricious substantive due process claims are merged into the taking claims described in the first two categories. As we have said, this view has recently been rejected by this court in another case.

Although the term "substantive due process" is used in a variety of contexts in modern constitutional discussion, it is possible to state a general definition: [The opinion quotes from a law review comment, "The doctrine that governmental deprivations of life, liberty or property are subject to limitations regardless of the adequacy of the procedures employed has come to be known as substantive due process."]

Some of the many contexts in which the term "substantive due process" is used are:

    1. Application of one of the rights *enumerated* in the federal constitution, such as the First Amendment, to a state.

    2. Application of a right *unenumerated* in the federal constitution to a state, such as the right to live together as a family.

    3. An action of state or local government which "shocks the conscience" of the federal court, may violate substantive due process. This court has recently expressed the view that " '[a]pplying the "shock the conscience" test in an area other than excessive force . . . is problematic.' "

    4. The right not to be subject to "arbitrary or capricious" action by a state either by legislative or administrative action is commonly referred to as a "substantive due process right."

In the case at bar, the plaintiff asserts only an "arbitrary and capricious" substantive due process claim. The circuits are in substantial disagreement on the role of the federal courts in reviewing zoning claims of this kind. Although the Supreme Court has held that federal review of local zoning on arbitrary and capricious substantive due process grounds is valid in appropriate cases, it has never laid down definitive standards of review. * * *

The lack of uniformity among the circuits in dealing with zoning cases of the "arbitrary and capricious substantive due process" category is remarkable.

The First Circuit, it seems, shows a great reluctance to interject the federal courts into local zoning matters, holding that substantive due process is not violated by local zoning even when accompanied by claims of purposeful malicious obstruction of a landowner's rights. It considers a zoning ordinance as a legislative act that need only bear a *"conceivable* rational relationship" to "legitimate governmental ends." It precludes the trial court from inquiring into actual as opposed to the declared motives of the local legislative body in passing the ordinance.

The Second Circuit, while proclaiming that "purely local zoning disputes are generally matters which are best left to municipal and state agencies to resolve," at one time would grant relief in extreme cases, as where an applicant has a clear property right to a certificate of occupancy but the defendants refuse to issue it for political motives. Its most recent case, however, denies review of a zoning decision, where the zoning authority was vested with any discretion, on the ground that the applicant lacked a protected property right. The bottom line of this approach is even more hostile to federal zoning plaintiffs than the First Circuit approach.

The Third Circuit will grant relief on the basis of substantive due process where the zoning decision is irrational in the strict sense, or prompted by invidious political or discriminatory motives.

The Fourth Circuit agrees with the Third; the leading cases involve political or religious discrimination.

The Fifth Circuit, on the other hand, views with strong disfavor the idea of federal courts being drawn into local zoning disputes, and classifies all zoning actions, even those pertaining to an individual piece of property, as legislative. This means that such actions can be set aside only under criteria that would justify invalidating a statute. Also, factual issues are reviewed under the criteria for legislative facts.

Contrary to the Fifth and First Circuits, our own Sixth Circuit has recently classified even zoning enactments of a general nature as administrative/adjudicatory, where zoning changes to individual parcels of land, not reflected in the initial publication of the ordinance, occur. This criterion applies even where the ordinance involves adoption of map changes covering extensive geographic areas. This means that affected owners of individual parcels may be entitled to personal notice and a due process hearing, including an impartial decisionmaker and particularized findings of fact. Presumably, where the zoning of an individual parcel is at stake, the federal scope of review would be of an administrative decision rather than a legislative one. * * * A recent case of this court addressing substantive due process review holds that local zoning may be set aside by a federal court only if it "shocks the conscience."

The Seventh Circuit, similar to the First and Fifth Circuits, strongly disapproves of federal courts' reviewing local zoning matters. It holds, contrary to the Sixth Circuit, that any action by the local legislative body on a zoning matter—even one concerning only a site plan for a single piece of property—is legislative. This means that the action could be set aside only if "invidious or irrational." For the Seventh Circuit, the presence of protectionist or parochial motives does not render the decision irrational, so long as there is some relation to land use. Since the local legislative body is acting legislatively, it need not make findings of fact, even in rejecting an individual site plan, and review of factual determinations by the federal court is extremely deferential as with any legislative finding. The Seventh Circuit also requires the developer to demonstrate the inadequacy of state remedies before pursuing procedural and substantive due process claims.

The Eighth Circuit judges are in disagreement among themselves as to the correct approach to federal review of local zoning, and a concurring opinion in an *en banc* case opines that the succinct majority opinion overruled the leading Eighth Circuit case by stating: "whether a substantive due process claim may arise from a denial of a zoning permit is an open question in this circuit."

The Ninth Circuit will subject local zoning decisions to substantive due process review, but the scope of review is that for legislation, even as to an individual property owner's claim, and any relationship to a proper zoning goal, such as prevention of traffic congestion, will be sufficient.

The Tenth Circuit imposes a strict property right test similar to the Second Circuit. If that test is met, it will consider whether the zoning was arbitrary and capricious.

The Eleventh Circuit approach is similar to the Ninth. Indeed, the Ninth Circuit relied on an Eleventh Circuit decision.

In reviewing a denial of an application for conversion from rental apartments to condominiums, the District of Columbia Circuit applied a very deferential standard of review under substantive due process. It held that "[o]nly a substantial infringement of state law prompted by personal or group animus, or a deliberate flouting of the law that trammels significant personal or property rights, qualifies for relief under § 1983."

The Federal Circuit is fortunate in not having to deal with zoning cases.

We must now sort out the conflicting decisions summarized above and clarify the law on federal review of zoning now prevailing in this circuit.

On this appeal plaintiff makes only substantive due process and economic equal protection claims. No procedural due process or taking claim is asserted.

While there are undoubtedly theoretical difficulties with the concept of substantive due process, the existence of such a right is too well established to be gainsaid. The Supreme Court in recent years has at least thrice reaffirmed a general right of substantive due process, stating that "the Due Process Clause contains a substantive component that bars certain arbitrary, wrongful government actions 'regardless of the fairness of the procedures used to implement them.'"

* * *

As pointed out in the earlier portions of this opinion, the precedents are not harmonious. Some consider all zoning decisions legislative, subject to only the most limited scope of review. Some state a general review for irrationality, without differentiating between legislative or administrative actions. Some classify decisions by the local legislative body as legislative while denominating actions by administrative boards, such as the board of adjustments, as administrative. Even this is not a hard and fast rule.

Recently this circuit has stated that the legislative/administrative distinction is of little utility, holding that "when a relatively small number of persons are affected on individual grounds," the action is considered administrative, at least for procedural due process purposes, even though it was taken by the legislative body as part of a general map change.

It has also been said that the difference is between "prospective, legislative-type rules and ... enforcement." Some courts consider whether the act involves policymaking rather than mere application of existing policies, or whether the facts utilized in making the decisions are specific, rather than general in nature.

It may be safely said that there is " 'no bright line' " between the legislative and administrative functions.

As stated, this circuit recognizes the legislative/administrative distinction. It is a close question whether the zoning decision in the case at bar is legislative or administrative. The action was by the legislative body and made policy rather than enforced it, but the decision concerned a specific piece of property. This is an issue we need not decide, however, since we hold that the decision for which review is sought survives scrutiny under the administrative standard. Therefore, *a fortiori,* it must survive the more deferential review for legislative zoning action.

Where a substantive due process attack is made on state *administrative* action, the scope of review by the federal courts is extremely narrow. To prevail, a plaintiff must show that the state administrative agency has been guilty of "arbitrary and capricious action" in the *strict* sense, meaning "that there is no rational basis for the ... [administrative] decision."

The use of the term "arbitrary and capricious" in this context causes considerable confusion, because these same terms are also used to describe the scope of review by state courts of state administrative action. Therefore, it must be emphasized that the state court scope of review of a decision of a state administrative agency is far broader than the federal scope of review under substantive due process.

In some states, a state court may set aside state administrative action as being "arbitrary and capricious" on the ground, among others, that it is not supported by substantial evidence. No such ground may be used by the federal court in reviewing state administrative action in connection with a federal substantive due process attack, however. In the federal court the standard is a much narrower one. The administrative action will withstand substantive due process attack unless it " 'is not supportable on any rational basis' " or is " 'willful and unreasoning action, without consideration and in disregard of the facts or circumstances of the case.'"

The federal court may make only the most limited review of the *evidence* before the state administrative agency. This review is limited to determining whether the agency has paid attention to the evidence adduced and acted rationally upon it. The state decision may not be set aside as arbitrary and capricious if there is "some factual basis" for the administrative action. Plaintiff here would have a jury rehear the evidence. However, we hold that the application of this deferential standard of review is a matter of law for the court. Otherwise, federal juries would sit as local boards of zoning appeals.

In other words, the appropriate scope of substantive due process review for state and local land use actions is the same as that accorded by the Supreme Court for state academic actions. That is, the federal courts should "show great respect" for the local authority's "professional judgment. Plainly, they may not override it unless it is such a substantial departure from accepted ... norms as to demonstrate that the [decisionmaker] ... did not actually exercise professional judgment."

The reasons for adopting this deferential standard in land use cases are the same as in the field of academics. Federalism and comity demand a reluctance by federal courts "to trench on the prerogatives of state and local ... institutions."

When this court stated recently * * * that local zoning actions would fall to substantive due process attack only if they shocked the conscience, it referred to the deferential review of local administrative zoning actions delineated above.

Although the "shocks the conscience" terminology, as another panel later observed, is more apt for cases involving physical force, it is useful in the zoning context too, to emphasize the degree of arbitrariness required to set aside a zoning decision by a local authority—and to underscore the overriding precept that "arbitrary and capricious" in the federal substantive due process context means something far different than in state administrative law.

By its "shocks the conscience" terminology the court was referring to extreme irrationality—after all we would not expect a planning commission or board of adjustments to be pumping the landowner's stomach. * * *

Under the foregoing principles, it is extremely rare for a federal court properly to vitiate the action of a state administrative agency as a violation of substantive due process. The vast majority of such attacks may readily be disposed of on summary judgment, as in the case at bar, thus keeping interference by federal courts with local government to a salutary minimum. Review of state administrative action is primarily a matter for the state courts, which quite properly have a much broader scope of review under state law.

Where zoning *legislation* is subjected to substantive due process attack, the scope of review by the federal court is the same as for any other legislation—even more deferential than for state administrative action. This may be discerned from a statement by the Supreme Court of the United States:

> "The power of local governments to zone and control land use is undoubtedly broad and its proper exercise is an essential aspect of achieving a satisfactory quality of life in both urban and rural communities. But the zoning power is not infinite and unchallengeable; it 'must be exercised within constitutional limits.' ... Accordingly, it is subject to judicial review; and as is most often the case, the standard of review is determined by the nature of the right assertedly threatened or violated rather than by the power being exercised or the specific limitation imposed....
>
> "Where *property interests* are adversely affected by zoning, the courts generally have emphasized the breadth of municipal power to control land use and have sustained the regulation *if it is rationally related to legitimate state* concerns and does not deprive the owner of economically viable use of his property....
>
> "Beyond that, *as is true of other ordinances,* when a zoning law infringes upon a protected liberty, it must be narrowly drawn and must further a sufficiently substantial government interest." *Schad v. Borough of Mount Ephraim,* 452 U.S. 61, 68, 101 S.Ct. 2176, 2182, 68 L.Ed.2d 671 (1981) (emphasis added) (citations omitted).

In summary, Fourteenth Amendment substantive due process requires that both state legislative and administrative actions that deprive the citizen of "life, liberty or property" must have some rational basis. Federal court review of the two types of action differs in that in reviewing *administrative* action the federal court must make an extremely limited review of the evidence as described above, but in reviewing *legislative* acts, even that is not permitted, the only permissible inquiry—absent equal protection, First Amendment or other such considerations—being whether the legislative action is rationally related to legitimate state land use concerns.

A zoning ordinance that affects only property interests merely has to bear such rational relationship. Whatever the state standard for review of its zoning legislation by its own courts may be, federal court review of a zoning ordinance may only determine whether it is clearly arbitrary and unreasonable, in the very restricted sense that it has " 'no substantial relation to the public health, safety, morals or general welfare.' "

Under these standards, the denial of plaintiff's application for a zoning change for his property withstands substantive due process attack, whether the action here was legislative or administrative.

The city legislative body heard evidence and statements by citizens who were concerned about traffic problems and over-commercialization of the area. It entered written findings, although summary in nature, that the property was better left as it was because of these concerns. Thus, its action and the facts before it were rationally related to zoning. Plaintiff is not a practitioner of palmistry denied a permit on the basis of religious prejudice. Nor has he suffered persecution based on "impermissible political animus." He is a property owner who wanted to sell out to McDonald's.

Plaintiff asserts that the protesting neighbors are guilty of tunnel vision in not welcoming the restaurant to their neighborhood, but concerns about traffic and the deterioration of the neighborhood are rationally related to the goals of zoning. Even parochial motives, if not based on animosity toward a protected class or similar invidious purpose, will not invalidate local zoning.

Therefore, the decision of the trial court must be, and is, hereby AFFIRMED.

Notes

1. The court's extensive footnotes and citations have been omitted, but would be useful for further research in this area.

2. As noted in the principal case, the federal courts have, for the most part, recognized the theory of a Section 1983 action where land use decisions amount to a denial of procedural or substantive due process or constitute a "taking." A successful 1983 suit could produce compensatory damages, punitive damages in cases that warrant such damages, costs and attorney's fees. Although numerous cases recognize the cause of action, precious few examples of actual award of damages can be found in the reports, although a definite increase in the number can be detected since the mid 1990's. The hurdles of ripeness, exhaustion of remedies, and the issue of whether a development permit is a property right are frequently impediments. The ripeness doctrine, in particular, can be a severe impediment. Compare Long Beach Equities, Inc. v. County of Ventura, 231 Cal.App.3d 1016, 282 Cal. Rptr. 877 (1991), cert. denied 505 U.S. 1219, 112 S.Ct. 3027, 120 L.Ed.2d 898 (1992) with Mayhew v. Town of Sunnyvale, 964 S.W.2d 922 (Tex.1998), cert. denied 526 U.S. 1144, 119 S.Ct. 2018, 143 L.Ed.2d 1030 (1999). Also see Gregory M. Stein, Regulatory Takings and Ripeness in the Federal Courts, 48 Vand. L. Rev. 1 (1995); Michael K. Whitman, The Ripeness Doctrine in the Land Use Context: The Municipality's Ally and the Landowner's Nemesis, 29 The Urban Lawyer 13 (1997). The courts also closely examine allegations of disparate treatment of the plaintiff developer, that is, if a regulation seems to be neutral and applicable to all developers, the claim of a denial of constitutional rights is weaker.

3. Does the standard mentioned in the principal case—local action that shocks the conscience of the court—make more sense than other formulations, such as arbitrary and capricious, or irrational? In United Artists Theatre Circuit, Inc. v. Township of Warrington, 316 F.3d 392 (3d Cir.2003) the court adopted the shock the conscience standard and remanded the case to the trial court; the plaintiff claimed the local zoning authority purposely delayed his application for a movie theater complex and swiftly granted a

rival company application when the rival offered the township a $100,000 "impact fee," alleging "improper motives." The court said:

> We note that our holding today brings our Court into line with several other Courts of Appeals that have ruled on substantive due process claims in land-use disputes. *See, e.g., Chesterfield Development Corp. v. City of Chesterfield,* 963 F.2d 1102, 1104–05 (8th Cir.1992) (holding that allegations that the city arbitrarily applied a zoning ordinance were insufficient to state a substantive due process claim, and stating in dicta that the "decision would be the same even if the City had knowingly enforced the invalid zoning ordinance in bad faith.... A bad-faith violation of state law remains only a violation of state law."); *PFZ Properties, Inc. v. Rodriguez,* 928 F.2d 28, 32 (1st Cir.1991) ("Even assuming that ARPE engaged in delaying tactics and refused to issue permits for the Vacia Talega project based on considerations outside the scope of its jurisdiction under Puerto Rico law, such practices, without more, do not rise to the level of violations of the federal constitution under a substantive due process label.").
>
> Application of the "shocks the conscience" standard in this context also prevents us from being cast in the role of a "zoning board of appeals." *Creative Environments, Inc. v. Estabrook,* 680 F.2d 822, 833 (1st Cir.1982) (quoting *Village of Belle Terre v. Boraas,* 416 U.S. 1, 13, 94 S.Ct. 1536, 39 L.Ed.2d 797 (1974) (Marshall, J., dissenting)); *see also Nestor Colon Medina & Sucesores, Inc. v. Custodio,* 964 F.2d 32, 45–46 (1st Cir.1992) (disagreeing with *Bello* and stating that "we have consistently held that the due process clause may not ordinarily be used to involve federal courts in the rights and wrongs of local planning disputes"). The First Circuit in *Estabrook* observed that every appeal by a disappointed developer from an adverse ruling of the local planning board involves some claim of abuse of legal authority, but "[i]t is not enough simply to give these state law claims constitutional labels such as 'due process' or 'equal protection' in order to raise a substantial federal question under section 1983." *Estabrook,* 680 F.2d at 833. Land-use decisions are matters of local concern, and such disputes should not be transformed into substantive due process claims based only on allegations that government officials acted with "improper" motives.

Attorneys who represent developers are often frustrated in pursuing substantive due process claims because of the unsettled question of what standard to apply. Even in state courts, this same problem can be found. See, for example, a Florida state court case that may be in the Supreme Court in the near future, City of Pompano Beach v. Yardarm Restaurant, Inc., 834 So.2d 861 (Fla.App. 4 Dist., 2002).

4. Despite the federal courts reluctance to review local zoning decisions, the potential damages in such cases generate many Section 1983 suits in federal and state courts.

Resolution Trust Corp. v. Town of Highland Beach, 18 F.3d 1536, judgment vacated 42 F.3d 626 (11th Cir.1994): The developer, in 1974, received permission to develop his 24.8 acres as a Planned Unit Development for 846 units. Under local rules at the time of the rezoning in 1975, approval of the PUD required that work begin within one year and that the project be completed in ten years. The local rules were interpreted to mean that the ten-year completion period began to run at the time the first building permit was issued in 1980. The developer asked for and received a letter from the mayor stating that the PUD approval expired on August 8, 1990. Shortly thereafter, there was a turnover in local officials and a change in attitude toward dense condo development. Rejecting the advice of the city attorney who sought to educate the planning commission about estoppel, the new commission took the position that the developer's time period began in 1975 and an ordinance was passed to terminate the PUD on July 1, 1985. In 1985, the town notified the developer that the PUD project was "dead" and in 1987 the land was downzoned to permit eight units per acre. In 1990, the land was further downzoned to allow six units per acre. The developer filed suit in state court and the town removed the case to federal court. The district judge ruled as a matter of law that the developer possessed a vested property right to the PUD zoning until 1990 based on the mayor's letter. A jury assessed damages of $16,150,000 for a temporary taking, and $15,000,000 for a permanent taking; the district judge also awarded nearly $1.8 million in attorney's fees. The court of appeals affirmed the judgment, holding that developer's acts of reliance on the 1990 expiration date "created a reasonable expectation rising to the level of a property right." The court also held that ripeness defense was inapplicable because it was clear that the town's actions in 1985 and 1987 were final. On substantive due process, the court stated:

> Deprivation of a property interest rises to the level of a substantive due process violation if done for improper motives and achieved through means that are arbitrary and capricious, and lacking any rational basis. * * * The question before us then is whether the Town acted in an arbitrary and capricious manner when it reinterpreted Ordinance 282. We conclude that it did.
>
> The record demonstrates that the Commission knew that the joint venture was relying upon the mutual understanding with the Town, and committed substantial funds to develop the RPUD. In fact, on several occasions, the Town's own attorney warned the Commission about the repercussions of its unilateral actions. Specifically, the attorney and other public officials informed the Town that the joint venture was relying upon the Mayor's letter declaring the completion date as 1990. The town attorney further cautioned that changing the existing interpretation of Ordinance 282 would create an "estoppel." Likewise, the Town ignored the mayor's warning that the Town led the joint venture down the "primrose path" to rely upon the 1990 completion date. Additionally, after the RPUD lapsed, causing the property designation to revert to "no zoning," the Town took an extended period of time to rezone the site, denying the joint venture use of the property. Finally, the Town refused to accept applications for the reissuance of previous permits, even though it previously had promised such permits were forthcoming. This evidence supports the jury's finding that the Town acted in an arbitrary and capricious manner without respect to the joint venture's rights.

After the case was argued before the en banc court, the parties settled the case; the plaintiff's zoning permits were restored and damages of $5.5 million dollars were paid.

A similar case is Blanche Road Corp. v. Bensalem Twp., 57 F.3d 253 (3d Cir.1995). The township sought a new trial after a $2 million judgment; certiorari was denied by the Supreme Court. A new trial was ordered based on misconduct of one of the plaintiff's attorneys. After the new trial the federal judge held in 1996 WL 368347:

> After a 13–day third trial, the jury rendered a verdict in favor of the plaintiff and against the Township in the sum of $245,489, but found in favor of all of the [individual] defendant supervisors. * * * The principal thrust of the Township's motion for judgment as a matter of law is that, since the defendant supervisors were all exonerated, and since the Township could only be held liable on the basis of a policy or practice approved or ratified by a policy-maker, the verdict against the Township lacks adequate evidentiary support. I reject that argument, for two reasons. It is clear that a municipality may be held liable under § 1983 for actions taken by individuals who are themselves protected by qualified immunity. * * * Moreover, the evidence sufficed to enable the jury to find that persons other than the supervisors had been delegated authority to establish the policies and practices which caused the constitutional violations. There was, for example, ample evidence to support a finding that the township manager was a policy-maker, and the township engineer, as well, at least with respect to the stop-work orders, and the assessment of "impact fees," which triggered much of the harm sustained by plaintiff.

* * *

B. *Plaintiff's Application for Counsel Fees*

Having obtained a verdict against the Township in the sum of $245,489, plaintiff now seeks an award of counsel fees aggregating $1,553,324.56. Plaintiff does not seek reimbursement for counsel fees incurred between June 1992 and August 1993, or after the entry of judgment on the jury verdict after the third trial.

Although the relationship between the counsel fees sought, and the jury's verdict, is a potential cause for concern at first blush, there can be no doubt that the services for which reimbursement is claimed were, for the most part, reasonably necessary to the victory ultimately achieved. The case was defended vigorously and extensively by the Township. As a result, both sides spent an inordinate amount of time in discovery disputes, repetitive depositions, and a remarkable number of attempts by the Township to avoid a trial. When plaintiff appealed from the dismissal at the second trial, the Township cross-appealed, sought reargument of the panel decision before the court *en banc,* and petitioned the United States Supreme Court for *certiorari.* By delaying until after the first trial its realization that the same law firm could not properly represent both the Township and the individual defendants in their personal capacities, the Township necessitated re-deposing various witnesses. Additional duplicative efforts were also necessitated by the Township's adding new witnesses shortly before the third trial.

Plaintiff did not prevail on its claim for loss of reputation, its claim for violation of procedural due process, and its claim for denial of equal protection. But no discernible time was spent by counsel in pursuing the claim for loss of reputation, and virtually all of the discovery obtained in support of the due process and equal protection claims was also necessary, and useful, in the successful pursuit of the substantive due process claim.

Because the litigation has lasted more than six years, the turnover of personnel in the offices of plaintiff's counsel resulted in some inefficiencies, attributable to the need to familiarize newly assigned associates with the facts and the issues. But plaintiff's counsel represent to the court that they have conscientiously reviewed all time records, and have deleted all such arguably wasteful duplication of efforts. They state that they have deleted a total of $867,749.60 from their actual billing records.
* * *

Plaintiff is awarded counsel fees and expenses attributable to the services rendered by the law firm of Pepper, Hamilton & Scheetz, in the sum of $1,025,702.56, and attributable to services rendered by William Kozub, Esquire, in the sum of $27,622 (for a total of $1,052,324.56), in addition to the costs to be taxed by the Clerk.

Also see Del Monte Dunes at Monterey, Ltd. v. City of Monterey, 95 F.3d 1422 (9th Cir.1996) where the court upheld a $1,450,000 jury verdict in a § 1983 suit for a regulatory taking. That case finally reached the Supreme Court. In an opinion by Justice Kennedy the Court held that: (1) § 1983 does not by itself confer right to jury trial; but (2) action under § 1983 is an "action at law" within meaning of Seventh Amendment right to jury trial; and (3) issues of whether city's repeated rejections of development proposals deprived owner of all economically viable use of land, and whether city's decision to reject development plan bore a reasonable relationship to its proffered justifications, were properly submitted to jury.

5. In Freeman v. Planning Board of West Boylston, 419 Mass. 548, 646 N.E.2d 139 (1995) the Massachusetts Supreme Court held that a developer whose proposed subdivision was unduly delayed by repeated demands of the town planning board could not receive monetary relief under 42 U.S.C.A. § 1983 or under a state civil rights act except in a "truly horrendous situation." The opinion sets forth the trial court's jury instructions; they are worthy of note.

6. In Anastasio v. Planning Board, 197 N.J.Super. 457, 484 A.2d 1358 (1984) a developer submitted a site plan for a townhouse development in May of 1979, the planning board delayed action for several months and finally denied the plan. The developer sued and won a favorable judgment in October, 1982; in November, 1982, the board approved the plan but delayed signing off on it until December, 1983. By then the developer had lost so much money, he was forced to sell the property. A § 1983 suit resulted in compensatory damages of over $66,000 plus interest, punitive damages of $5,000 against each of the three planning board members, and attorney's fees. On appeal of the punitive damage claim, the individual defendants were

held to be immune. 209 N.J.Super. 499, 507 A.2d 1194 (1986), cert. denied 107 N.J. 46, 526 A.2d 136.

7. Some § 1983 cases are unusual. In Bodor v. East Coventry Twp., 325 F.Supp. 1102 (E.D.Pa.1971), the plaintiff successfully sued to restrain the township officials from preventing him from establishing a seventy foot by twelve foot mobile home as a permanent residence on a four acre tract of land. "Plaintiffs' complaint raises the substantial constitutional issues of due process of law and equal protection under the law in that in order for Plaintiffs to avail themselves of the administrative remedies provided in the township's zoning ordinance and building code ordinance, Plaintiffs would allegedly have to pay a $750.00 filing fee. * * * Plaintiffs have alleged facts which, if proved, establish a concerted effort by the Board of Supervisors of East Coventry Township to preclude the review of their Zoning and Building Code Ordinances through the establishment of a prohibitive filing fee. Such an allegation sets forth a claim upon which relief can be granted." In Minshew v. Smith, 380 F.Supp. 918 (N.D.Miss.1974), several homeowners sued the owner of a motel and city officials for compensatory and punitive damages on the theory that the defendants conspired to achieve an illegal amendment of the zoning ordinance to allow the motel to expand into the adjacent residential zone. The court found for the plaintiffs and awarded compensatory damages of $6,000 for diminution in value of the plaintiffs' property, costs and attorney's fees, but refused to award punitive damages.

8. Can a developer sue city officials for improper actions in a land use case under a contract or quasi-contract theory? In River Park, Inc. v. City of Highland Park, 281 Ill.App.3d 154, 217 Ill.Dec. 410, 667 N.E.2d 499 (1996) a developer whose zoning petition was not considered by the city successfully established a cause of action for tortious interference with a business expectancy and breach of contract (an implied contract to consider a petition where all fees were properly paid). The Illinois Supreme Court overruled this case in 2001 in Village of Bloomingdale v. CDG Enterprises, Inc., 196 Ill.2d 484, 256 Ill.Dec. 848, 752 N.E.2d 1090, 752 N.E.2d 1090 (2001), holding that the Illinois Constitution does not permit imposition of a common law "corrupt or malicious motives" exception to immunities afforded by the state's Local Governmental and Governmental Employees Tort Immunity Act. In other states a developer might have more success in the absence of an immunity statute.

C. THE EQUAL PROTECTION CLAUSE

Sometimes, property owners utilize 1983 to raise a denial of equal protection when local governments frustrate their development proposals. Of course, if a proper claim of discrimination against a suspect class of persons can be made, the federal courts will provide relief. For example, cases that allege selective application of land use regulations, harassment of the property owner, or discrimination are fairly common. See, Cutting v. Muzzey, 724 F.2d 259 (1st Cir.1984), alleging racial animus against the developer's purchasers, all of whom had Italian surnames; Sylvia Development Corp. v. Calvert County, Maryland, 48 F.3d 810 (4th Cir.1995), alleging discrimination against a developer because he was born in Czechoslovakia, or, in the alternative, that he was from outside the county; Rodrigues v. Village of Larchmont, New York, 608 F.Supp. 467 (S.D.N.Y.1985), the harassment of nurseryman by denying him access to the village dump and arbitrary denial of a variance. Also see DeBlasio v. Zoning Bd. of Adjustment for the Twp. of West Amwell, 53 F.3d 592 (3d Cir.1995) where the court reversed a summary judgment and remanded the case for a trial on a property owner's claim that he was denied a variance because the secretary of the board of adjustment had a personal financial interest in the resolution of the owner's zoning problems [this holding may be questionable in light of the United Artists case cited in the previous section].

Selective enforcement of land use regulations poses a more difficult equal protection issue. In Shelton v. City of College Station, 754 F.2d 1251 (5th Cir.1985), the property owner claimed the denial of a variance in a situation where every other like applicant received a variance violated the 14th Amendment. If the evidence supports such a claim, should the court order the issuance of a variance? In considering how to answer the question look at the following case.

VILLAGE OF WILLOWBROOK v. OLECH

Supreme Court of the United States, 2000.
528 U.S. 562, 120 S.Ct. 1073, 145 L.Ed.2d 1060.

PER CURIAM.

Respondent Grace Olech and her late husband Thaddeus asked petitioner Village of Willowbrook (Village) to connect their property to the municipal water supply. The Village at first conditioned the connection on the Olechs granting the Village a 33–foot easement. The Olechs objected, claiming that the Village only required a 15–foot easement from other property owners seeking access to the water supply. After a 3–month delay, the Village relented and agreed to provide water service with only a 15–foot easement.

Olech sued the Village, claiming that the Village's demand of an additional 18–foot easement violated the Equal Protection Clause of the Fourteenth Amendment. Olech asserted that the 33–foot easement demand was "irrational and wholly arbitrary"; that the Village's demand was actually motivated by ill will resulting from the Olechs' previous filing of an unrelated, successful lawsuit against the Village; and that the Village acted either with the intent to deprive Olech of her rights or in reckless disregard of her rights.

The District Court dismissed the lawsuit pursuant to Federal Rule of Civil Procedure 12(b)(6) for failure to state a cognizable claim under the Equal Protection Clause. Relying on Circuit precedent, the Court of Appeals for the Seventh Circuit reversed, holding that a plaintiff can allege an equal protection violation by asserting that state action was motivated solely by a " 'spiteful effort to "get" him for reasons wholly unrelated to any legitimate state objective.' " 160 F.3d 386, 387 (1998) (quoting *Esmail v. Macrane,* 53 F.3d 176, 180 (C.A.7 1995)). It determined that Olech's complaint sufficiently alleged such a claim. 160 F.3d, at 388. We granted certiorari to determine whether the Equal Protection Clause gives rise to a cause of action on behalf of a "class of one" where the plaintiff did not allege membership in a class or group

Our cases have recognized successful equal protection claims brought by a "class of one," where the plaintiff alleges that she has been intentionally treated differently from others similarly situated and that there is no rational basis for the difference in treatment. See *Sioux City Bridge Co. v. Dakota County,* 260 U.S. 441, 43 S.Ct. 190, 67 L.Ed. 340 (1923); *Allegheny Pittsburgh Coal Co. v. Commission of Webster Cty.,* 488 U.S. 336, 109 S.Ct. 633, 102 L.Ed.2d 688 (1989). In so doing, we have explained that " '[t]he purpose of the equal protection clause of the Fourteenth Amendment is to secure every person within the State's jurisdiction against intentional and arbitrary discrimination, whether occasioned by express terms of a statute or by its improper execution through duly constituted agents.' " *Sioux City Bridge Co., supra,* at 445, 43 S.Ct. 190 (quoting *Sunday Lake Iron Co. v. Township of Wakefield,* 247 U.S. 350, 352, 38 S.Ct. 495, 62 L.Ed. 1154 (1918)).

That reasoning is applicable to this case. Olech's complaint can fairly be construed as alleging that the Village intentionally demanded a 33–foot easement as a condition of connecting her property to the municipal water supply where the Village required only a 15–foot easement from other similarly situated property owners. See *Conley v. Gibson,* 355 U.S. 41, 45–46, 78 S.Ct. 99, 2 L.Ed.2d 80 (1957). The complaint also alleged that the Village's demand was "irrational and wholly arbitrary" and that the Village ultimately connected her property after receiving a clearly adequate 15–foot easement. These allegations, quite apart from the Village's subjective motivation, are sufficient to state a claim for relief under traditional equal protection analysis. We therefore affirm the judgment of the Court of Appeals, but do not reach the alternative theory of "subjective ill will" relied on by that court.

It is so ordered.

JUSTICE BREYER, concurring in the result.

The Solicitor General and the village of Willowbrook have expressed concern lest we interpret the Equal Protection Clause in this case in a way that would transform many ordinary violations of city or state law into violations of the Constitution. It might be thought that a rule that looks only to an intentional difference in treatment and a lack of a rational basis for that different treatment would work such a transformation. Zoning decisions, for example, will often, perhaps almost always, treat one landowner differently from another, and one might claim that, when a city's zoning authority takes an action that fails to conform to a city zoning regulation, it lacks a "rational basis" for its action (at least if the regulation in question is reasonably clear).

This case, however, does not directly raise the question whether the simple and common instance of a faulty zoning decision would violate the Equal Protection Clause. That is because the Court of Appeals found that in this case respondent had alleged an extra factor as well—a factor that the Court of Appeals called "vindictive action," "illegitimate animus," or "ill will." 160 F.3d 386, 388 (C.A.7 1998). And, in that respect, the court said this case resembled *Esmail v. Macrane*, 53 F.3d 176 (C.A.7 1995), because the *Esmail* plaintiff had alleged that the municipality's differential treatment "was the result not of prosecutorial discretion honestly (even if ineptly—even if arbitrarily) exercised but of an illegitimate desire to 'get' him." 160 F.3d, at 388.

In my view, the presence of that added factor in this case is sufficient to minimize any concern about transforming run-of-the-mill zoning cases into cases of constitutional right. For this reason, along with the others mentioned by the Court, I concur in the result.

Notes

1. The Olech case expands the possibility of federal review of local land use decisions. For a thorough discussion of this case and how lower federal courts have reacted to it see Michael S. Giaimo, Ill Will and Class of One: Equal Protection Claims after the *Olech* Decision, Land Use Law & Zoning Digest, Feb. 2003, p. 3.

2. In City of Cleburne, Texas v. Cleburne Living Center, 473 U.S. 432, 105 S.Ct. 3249, 87 L.Ed.2d 313 (1985), the city denied a special use permit for the operation of a group home for the mentally retarded, acting pursuant to a municipal zoning ordinance requiring permits for such homes. The Supreme Court held, in an opinion by Justice White, that the mentally retarded did not comprise a "suspect class" so as to trigger the highest level of equal protection scrutiny. However, applying the "traditional" equal protection analysis, White found that the special use permit denial was arbitrary and irrational because the "City does not require a special use permit in an R-3 zone for apartment houses, multiple dwellings, boarding and lodging houses, fraternity or sorority houses, dormitories, apartment hotels, hospitals, sanitariums, nursing homes for convalescents or the aged (other than for the insane or feeble-minded or alcoholics or drug addicts), private clubs or fraternal orders, and other specified uses." Also see Arrington v. Urban Redevelopment Authority of the City of Pittsburgh, 822 A.2d 135 (Pa.Cmwlth. 2003) where the court found that excluding owner-occupied housing and churches from an urban redevelopment taking in a blighted area did not violate the equal protection clause because rational reasons for the exceptions could be found; a dissenting opinion stated that no rational reasons for those exclusions existed.

Chapter X

STATUTORY CONTROL AND OTHER LIMITS ON LOCAL LAND USES

SECTION 1. FEDERAL PREEMPTION

The federal impact on state and local land use planning and zoning is most apparent where specific statutory language preempts local government's ability to make certain land use decisions. Beginning in the late 1980's, a series of federal laws addressing housing discrimination, discrimination based upon disability, discrimination based on religious beliefs, and access to the airwaves for the siting of cellular and wireless towers, have had a profound impact on local government's ability to control the location of various types of land uses, as well as to prohibit municipalities from excluding certain uses from their borders. There are a number of reasons why the federal government has inserted its power into the local land use process. Among these are the inability of many local officials to effectively respond to the concerns of the community that represent NIMBY (Not In My Back Yard) for uses often believed to be LULUs (Locally Unwanted Land Uses) and the attitudes of those in the community who take a BANANA (Build Absolutely Nothing Anywhere Near Anyone) perspective on future development around them. Perhaps it is because too many local officials adopted a NIMTOO (Not In My Term Of Office) approach to land use planning and zoning decisions that advocacy organizations and business leaders were successful in realizing strong federal legislation designed to limit local control. As you read through the cases and the notes in this chapter, consider whether the federal laws highlighted are necessary, whether they are accomplishing their stated purpose, and whether these laws have a positive or negative effect on community development in general.

In her article, Federalism and the Public Good: The True Story Behind the Religious Land Use and Institutionalized Persons Act, 78 Ind. L. J. 311 (2003), Professor Marci A. Hamilton sets forth an argument as to why state and local governance in land use is preferable to federal governance by using the Religious Land Use and Institutionalized Persons Act, enacted in October 2000, and its legislative history to make her point. Her article also demonstrates the effectiveness of the influence of lobbyists and special interest advocacy before Congress. Below is an excerpt from her article (citations omitted):

RLUIPA is the quintessential legislative product—it is a compromise bill, stripped of other elements, containing oddly paired issues: land use and institutionalized persons involving religious individuals and institutions. One cannot understand RLUIPA without also knowing what happened with its precursors, the Religious Freedom Restoration Act and the Religious Liberty Protection Act bills.

1. The Religious Freedom Restoration Act ("RFRA")

* * * This is not the Article to go into too many details, but in a nutshell, religious lobbyists prevailed upon Congress to expand religious liberty and civil rights guarantees beyond what the Court interpreted the Constitution to require in Smith. Thus, in effect, they argued that religious claimants should not be subject to the rule of law, and that a handful of cases preceding Smith that had instituted strict scrutiny in the unemployment context should be extended across all laws. Congress was eager to acquiesce, and enacted the RFRA of 1993, which instituted strict scrutiny of every law substantially burdening a religious individual or institution. It was invalidated less than four years later in City of Boerne v. Flores. * * *

No less than 405 pages of legislative history were devoted to castigating the Court for its decision in Smith. RFRA meant that state laws traditionally in the realm of the states, from family law, including adoption and medical neglect standards, to immunization exemptions to land use law, would be altered through its application. Neither state nor local officials were called in to consult on its impact. Nor was there any effort by Congress itself to assess the potential impact of RFRA on the states. The takeover of state authority was simply not part of the legislative calculus.

2. The Religious Liberty Protection Act Bills ("RLPA")

After City of Boerne v. Flores invalidated the Religious Freedom Restoration Act, Congress introduced the Religious Liberty Protection Acts of 1998 and 1999 * * * After it became clear that RLPA could not be passed—as a result primarily of lobbying by children's advocates, civil rights advocates concerned about fair housing laws, and conservative Christian organizations concerned about the principles of federalism—many believed that its momentum could not be revived. They were wrong. Those organizations lobbying for land use privileges, led by Rev. Gary Dobson, and for greater authority to thwart prison administrators, led by Charles Colson, head of Prison Ministries Fellowship, continued to push for their particular elements of the bill. The ACLU, along with the Department of Justice, drafted a land use/prison bill, which was transformed in the hands of the ACLU into a land use/institutionalized persons bill. No hearings were held on RLUIPA per se; rather, the hearings on RLPA generally addressing land use law were supposed to stand in as hearings in support of RLUIPA. There was little in the RLPA hearings addressing "institutionalized persons." * * *

The hearings for RLPA involving land use, which then became the sole legislative history for RLUIPA, did not even as a cursory matter take into account the law of land use. No land use expert, either in the government or in the universities, was asked to testify to explain either prevailing legal principles in the field or to analyze RLPA's potential impact in the field. Nor was there any attempt to investigate the existing principles applied to landowners and religious landowners in the land use process.

1. Land Use: A Tradition of Deference to State and Local Governments

Land use law has always been a creature of state and local law. The reason for this is three-fold. First, the permanent nature of land—its immovability—makes its uses far more relevant to those who are nearby than those who are far away. Second, how land is used is an essential ingredient for communities to develop their character and to pursue shared purposes. Land use law is one of the key ways that communities come together to set priorities, to establish their character, and to meet fiscal, aesthetic, and lifestyle needs. Third, by keeping land use law local, citizens have more direct access to their representative (than if those representatives were national) and a proportionally larger voice in the land use process that directly affects them. Land use law is enacted by the state and local governing bodies and implemented by locally elected or appointed boards, with publicized public hearings an integral component in altering the law and in applying it.

The Supreme Court has consistently recognized "the States' traditional and primary power over land and water use." There is no indication in the Court's case law that these principles become inapplicable when the landowner is a religious entity or individual. To the contrary, the Court dismissed an appeal as lacking a substantial federal question brought by a church claiming the right to locate in a residential district, and later characterized that dismissal as follows:

> When the effect of a statute or ordinance upon the exercise of First Amendment freedoms is relatively small and the public interest to be protected is substantial, it is obvious that a rigid test requiring a showing of imminent danger to the security of the Nation is an absurdity. We recently dismissed for want of substantiality an appeal in which a church group contended that its First Amendment rights were violated by a municipal zoning ordinance preventing the building of churches in certain residential areas.

The federal courts' recognition that land use law is a state and local power has meant that each state has been left to develop its own land use jurisprudence and that the federal courts have "emphasize[d their] reluctance to substitute [their] judgment for that of local decisionmakers, particularly in matters of such local concern as land-use planning...." * * *

The value of federalism as a means of permitting individual communities to shape their goals, and as a means of permitting experimentation in achieving the elusive public good, is crystal clear in land use law. The states do not share a monolithic set of principles regarding land use by religious landowners, or any other landowners for that matter. Instead, they have been permitted to develop a wide variety of land use approaches that are keyed to the values, land, and public good sought in each particular community. * * *

[T]here is no state that gives religious landowners complete carte blanche under land use laws. Every state applies at least some elements of its land use law to religious landowners, whether it is zoning or use restrictions, or both. * * * There is also more to land use law than the mere fact of 50 governing jurisdictions. Within each jurisdiction, there are many categories of land use permits and restrictions, from setback to height and dimensional requirements, to occupancy limitations, as well as zoning. Traffic and the requisite parking is a dominant concern, as is bringing together compatible uses. Fire safety requirements, noise abatement, water usage, and environmental concerns also must be factored in. Some jurisdictions emphasize some elements more than others, but there is in general an attempt to find the right mix of factors to maximize optimal and harmonious use. Thus, focusing on any one element or zoning district in any one jurisdiction will not do justice to the entire balance of landowner rights and responsibilities in that particular jurisdiction, or the possibilities for location within that jurisdiction.

The universe of land use law is quite impressive and complex, though utterly missing from the RLPA history. For example, there are approximately 122,955,000 housing units in the United States. There are also approximately 268,254 houses of worship, approximately 92,012 public elementary and secondary schools, and 27,223 private elementary and secondary schools in the United States, 21,334 of which are religious schools. These statistics do not include other potentially relevant numbers, for example, the number of day care centers, religiously affiliated or otherwise, the number of homeless shelters, the number of religious gatherings held in private residential homes, or the number of church-run activity centers and camps.

There is no suggestion in the RLPA history that the Supreme Court has ever addressed the issue of zoning and land use, though, of course, it had addressed it as early as 1926, where it accurately predicted the necessity of increasing land use regulation:

> Building zone laws are of modern origin.... Until recent years, urban life was comparatively simple; but, with the great increase and concentration of population, problems are developed, and constantly are developing, which require, and will continue to require, additional restrictions in respect of the use and occupation of private lands in urban communities. Regulations, the wisdom, necessity and validity of which, as applied to existing conditions, are so apparent that they are now uniformly sustained, a century ago, or even half a century ago, probably would have been rejected as arbitrary and oppressive. Such regulations are sustained, under the complex conditions of our day, for reasons analogous to those which justify traffic regulations, which, before the advent of automobiles and rapid transit street railways, would have been condemned as fatally arbitrary and unreasonable. And in this there is no inconsistency, for, while the meaning of constitutional guaranties never varies, the scope of their application must expand or contract to meet the new and different conditions which are constantly coming within the field of their operation.

Nor did Congress study the changing nature of houses of worship.

The traditional concept of a small church serving the immediately neighboring community undoubtedly had something to do with the idea that such use was an integral part of community life in "the best and most open localities." However the establishment of a modern church, not dependent upon local residents as its communicants, and in some instances attracting people from far distances, the inevitable use of the automobile in connection therewith and the increased activities of the church for social and community functions having only a remote connection with its primary function, all present a different zoning picture.

Religious landowners regularly submit plans for multi-use buildings in the tens of thousands of square feet—and some hundreds of thousands—offering not just worship, but also religious education, elementary and high school education, banquet halls for religious celebrations, including weddings and bar and bat mitzvahs, coffee houses, motion picture theaters, fitness centers, all-night volleyball courts, child and senior day care centers, and social services, such as homeless shelters, soup kitchens, and drug and alcohol abuse treatment. Indeed, this trend has culminated in a move toward all-inclusive religious communities, from megachurches that are on the scale of a sizable shopping mall to planned communities that encompass not just a house of worship, but many social services and even private homes. This is a trend toward buildings that have greater negative secondary effects on neighbors, whether residential or commercial, and that raises issues properly and regularly considered by land use authorities in creating Master Plans or in the day-to-day determination of permit and variance requests.

A. RELIGIOUS LAND USES

ELSINORE CHRISTIAN CENTER v. CITY OF LAKE ELSINORE

United States District Court, Central District of California, 2003.
270 F.Supp.2d 1163.

WILSON, DISTRICT J.

Plaintiffs Elsinore Christian Center and Church member Gary Holmes (collectively "Church" or "Plaintiffs") brought this action against Defendants the City of Lake Elsinore and five individual members of the City Council (collectively "City" or "Defendants") after the Lake Elsinore Planning Commission denied the Church's application for a conditional use permit ("CUP") to operate a church on 217 N. Main Street, Lake Elsinore, California (the "Subject Property," "Property," or "Site").

* * *

The Church is currently located in the downtown area of Lake Elsinore and believes that it has been called by God to minister in that area. The Church has been operating downtown for more than twelve years. The Church's current location lacks on-site parking, however, and church members are forced to park on the street. Certain events—the monthly Open Air Market and the annual Lake Elsinore Classic—involve closed roads and further exacerbate parking inadequacies; some congregants are often forced to park at a considerable distance from the Church. The Church complains that these parking issues pose particular difficulties for elderly Church members and those with disabilities, and that the current facility is too small to accommodate a growing congregation. As a result, the Church seeks to relocate to the Subject Property, situated three blocks away, which is larger and possesses more parking.

The Subject Property and Church are located in downtown Lake Elsinore, an economically depressed area characterized by urban blight. The current tenant of the Property, Food Smarts, is a discount food store and recycling business. Food Smarts leases the Property from its current owner, the Elsinore Naval Military School ("School"). Because Food Smarts is a month-to-month tenant, the School is legally entitled to evict Food Smart on thirty days' notice. The School is willing to sell the Property to the Church, and the Church has entered into a purchase agreement with the School.

Both the Subject Property and the Church are located in an area of the City zoned as C–1, or "Neighborhood Commercial." The following uses are among those that may be located in C–1 zones as a matter of right: apparel stores, appliance stores, bicycle shops, food stores, florists, general merchandise stores, hardware stores, health and exercise clubs, hobby supply stores, jewelry stores, media shops, music stores, personal service establishments, pet shops, restaurants, schools for dance and music, sporting goods stores, toy shops, and sellers of vehicle parts.

The following uses may be located in C–1 zones subject to a CUP: automatic car washes, bars, churches, drive-through or drive-in establishments, arcades, gas stations, hotels, mortuaries, motels, private clubs and lodges, restaurants with outside eating areas, small animal veterinary clinics, and any other use having similar characteristics and in accord with the zone's purposes.

Additionally, the Subject Property is located in an area classified as "blighted" by the Rancho Laguna Redevelopment Project, which acts as an overlay to the City's zoning provisions. After entering into a purchase agreement with the School, the Church applied for a CUP. City staff prepared a report recommending approval of the CUP, subject to twenty-six conditions, to which the Church consented. However, the City's Planning Commission denied the CUP, citing loss of a needed service (the grocery store and recycling business), loss of tax revenue, insufficient parking at the Subject Property, and the belief that denial of the CUP would not work a substantial burden on the Church, as it could continue to operate at its present downtown location.

The Church's appeal of the CUP denial was rejected unanimously by the City Council. During the Council's hearing on this matter, City residents spoke out on both sides of the appeal. Church members described their difficulties in attending church, while downtown residents and Food Smarts employees cited the need for a grocery store within walking distance and the loss of jobs that would result if Food Smarts were evicted. Other downtown residents claimed that the presence of the Church would benefit the area.

* * *

The Church alleges that (1) the City's entire zoning Ordinance, (2) the rules regarding the C–1 zones as applied to Plaintiffs, and (3) the City's denial of the Church's CUP application, violate (1) the Religious Land Use and Institutionalized Persons Act ("RLUIPA"), (2) the U.S. Constitution, and (3) the California Constitution. The Complaint thereby presents an intricate analytical challenge, consisting of claims at three levels of generality, brought under four sections of RLUIPA, four provisions of the U.S. Constitution, and one section of the California Constitution—a total of approximately two dozen discrete yet interrelated claims.

* * *

On September 22, 2000, President Clinton signed into law the Religious Land Use and Institutionalized Persons Act of 2000, 114 Stat. 803–807 (codified at 42 U.S.C. § § 2000cc et seq.).

RLUIPA represents the latest act in an ongoing tug-of-war between Congress and the Supreme Court. In 1990, the Supreme Court decided

Employment Division v. Smith, 494 U.S. 872, 110 S.Ct. 1595, 108 L.Ed.2d 876 (1990), which held that rights under the Free Exercise Clause do not "relieve an individual of the obligation to comply with a 'valid and neutral law of general applicability on the ground that the law proscribes (or prescribes) conduct that his religion prescribes (or proscribes).'" *Id.* at 879. The Court refused to apply the balancing test employed in *Sherbert v. Verner,* 374 U.S. 398, 83 S.Ct. 1790, 10 L.Ed.2d 965 (1963), which held that government actions that substantially burden a religious practice must be justified by a compelling governmental interest. *Smith,* 494 U.S. at 883–84. The Court concluded that *Sherbert* has been largely confined to the context in which it was decided—denial of unemployment compensation—and that, in any case, its rule does not apply to neutral laws of general applicability. *Id.* at 879.

In direct response to *Employment Division v. Smith,* Congress in 1993 enacted the Religious Freedom Restoration Act ("RFRA"), 107 Stat. 1488 (codified at 42 U.S.C. § § 2000bb et seq.). RFRA purported to codify the *Sherbert* test and to apply it to all government acts that "substantially burden" religious exercise, even if the burden results from a rule of general applicability. 42 U.S.C. § 2000bb–1; *see* 42 U.S.C. § 2000bb(b).

Four years later the Supreme Court struck down RFRA, at least as it relates to state and local governments, in *City of Boerne v. Flores,* 521 U.S. 507, 117 S.Ct. 2157, 138 L.Ed.2d 624 (1997). Although Congress may enforce constitutional rights pursuant to Section 5 of the Fourteenth Amendment, the Court in *City of Boerne* concluded that RFRA exceeded that limited authority by, in effect, defining rights instead of simply enforcing them.

RLUIPA was drawn in attempt to achieve a constitutional balance. The "general rule" of RLUIPA is the same as that provided by RFRA: state action that "substantially burden[s]" religious exercise must be justified as the "least restrictive means" of furthering a "compelling governmental interest." *See* 42 U.S.C. § § 2000cc(a)(1); 2000cc–1(a). However, RLUIPA's provisions are more narrowly directed than those of RFRA. First, RLUIPA by its terms applies only to governmental action regarding land use or institutionalized persons. *See* 42 U.S.C. § § 2000cc; 2000cc–1. Second, within those categories, RLUIPA applies only where the substantial burden is imposed 1) in connection with a federally-funded activity; 2) where the burden affects interstate commerce; or, with respect to land use decisions, 3) where the burden is imposed in the context of a scheme whereby the state makes "individualized assessments" regarding the property involved. *See* 42 U.S.C. § § 2000cc(a)(2); 2000cc–1(b).

The "general rule" of RLUIPA provides that:

> No government shall impose or implement a land use regulation in a manner that imposes a substantial burden on the religious exercise of a person, including a religious assembly or institution, unless the

government demonstrates that imposition of the burden on that person, assembly, or institution—

(A) is in furtherance of a compelling governmental interest; and

(B) is the least restrictive means of furthering that compelling governmental interest.

. . .

42 U.S.C. § 2000cc(a)(1).

By the terms of the statute, this rule applies in three contexts: (A) where the burden is imposed in a federally-funded program or activity; (B) where the burden affects, or removal of the burden would affect, interstate commerce; and (C) where the "burden is imposed in the implementation of a land use regulation or system of land use regulations, under which a government makes . . . individualized assessments of the proposed uses for the property involved." 42 U.S.C. § 2000cc(a)(2).

Plaintiffs allege that the City "has in place formal or informal procedures . . . to make individualized assessments of the proposed religious use of the Subject Property." (Compl.¶ 45.) Indeed, the City's denial of a conditional use permit is, presumably, precisely the type of "individualized assessment" contemplated by subsection (C). *See DiLaura v. Ann Arbor Charter Twp.,* 30 Fed. Appx. 501, 510 (6th Cir.2002) (subsection (C) "clearly applies" to procedure for a zoning variance).

Thus, the Court first considers whether the land use regulation, or its implementation, "imposes a substantial burden on the religious exercise" of Plaintiffs. 42 U.S.C. § 2000cc(a)(1).

RLUIPA defines "religious exercise" to include "any exercise of religion, whether or not compelled by, or central to, a system of religious belief." 42 U.S.C. § 2000cc–5(7)(A). Further, the statute expressly provides that the term "religious exercise" includes the "use, building, or conversion of real property for the purpose of religious exercise. . . ." 42 U.S.C. § 2000cc–5(7)(B).

Therefore, the effective statutory question in this regard is whether the challenged zoning regulations, or the application thereof, effect a "substantial burden" on Plaintiffs' "use of real property for the purpose of religious exercise." A claimant under RLUIPA bears the burden of persuasion on this question. 42 U.S.C. § 2000cc–2(b).

The Court begins by considering Plaintiffs' narrowest ground of attack: the City's denial of the CUP. With regard to this action, the substantial burden question is easily answered in the affirmative. The burden on the Church's use of land in this case is not only substantial, but entire. By denying the conditional use permit, the City has effectively barred *any* use by the Church of the real property in question. This is not a case where the Church's proposed use of land—equated with "religious exercise" by RLUIPA—is restricted in a minor or "unsubstantial" way (e.g., by limiting a building's size or occupancy). Rather, the denial of the CUP bars the Church's use altogether, thereby imposing the ultimate burden on the use of that land.

* * *

Because zoning regulations and decisions rarely bear upon central tenets of religious belief, those regulations and decisions have not generally been held under these standards to impose a substantial burden on religious exercise. *See, e.g., Christian Gospel Church, Inc. v. San Francisco,* 896 F.2d 1221, 1224 (9th Cir.1990); *Messiah Baptist Church v. County of Jefferson,* 859 F.2d 820, 824–25 (10th Cir.), *cert. denied,* 490 U.S. 1005, 109 S.Ct. 1638, 104 L.Ed.2d 154 (1989); *Lakewood, Ohio Congregation of Jehovah's Witnesses, Inc. v. Lakewood,* 699 F.2d 303, 306–7 (6th Cir.1983); *Grosz v. City of Miami Beach,* 721 F.2d 729 (11th Cir.1983).

Clearly, RLUIPA was intended to and does upset this test. By explicitly prescribing that the centrality of a religious belief is immaterial to whether or not that belief constitutes "religious exercise," *see* 42 U.S.C. § 2000cc–5(7)(A), and by definitionally equating land use with "religious exercise," *see* § 2000cc–5(7)(B), RLUIPA establishes an entirely new and different standard than that employed in prior Free Exercise Clause jurisprudence. *See DiLaura,* 30 Fed. Appx. at 508–9; *but see San Jose Christian College v. City of Morgan Hill,* 2002 U.S. Dist. LEXIS 4517, at *4–7 (N.D.Cal. March 8, 2002) (applying pre-RLUIPA "substantial burden" test to RLUIPA claim).

* * *

The Church having established a prima facie case of a violation of § 2000cc(a)(1) of RLUIPA, the burden of persuasion shifts to the government to justify its actions. 42 U.S.C. § 2000cc–2(b). To satisfy its burden, the City must demonstrate both that its denial of the CUP a) is in furtherance of a compelling government interest, and b) is the least restrictive means of furthering that interest. 42 U.S.C. § 2000cc(a)(1).

RLUIPA does not define "compelling governmental interest," though the legislative history indicates the phrase was taken directly from the Religious Freedom Restoration Act of 1993 ("RFRA"), and "was and is intended to codify the traditional compelling interest test." Statement of Rep. Charles T. Canady, sponsor, on the Religious Land Use and Institutionalized Persons Act of 2000, 146 Cong Rec E 1563 (2000). One of the stated purposes of RFRA was "to restore the compelling interest test as set forth in *Sherbert v. Verner,* 374 U.S. 398 [, 83 S.Ct. 1790] (1963) and *Wisconsin v. Yoder,* 406 U.S. 205 [, 92 S.Ct. 1526] (1972) . . . ." 42 U.S.C. § 2000bb(b).

In *Sherbert,* the Supreme Court considered South Carolina's denial of unemployment benefits to a Seventh Day Adventist who, in conformity with her religion's Sabbatarian beliefs, refused to work on Saturdays. 374 U.S. at 400. The Court concluded that the scheme effected a burden on the adherent's religious exercise, and that any interest in avoiding abuse of or fraud on the unemployment system did not represent a "compelling state interest." *Id.* at 405–409. "[I]n this highly sensitive constitutional area, 'only the gravest abuses, endangering paramount interests, give occasion for permissible limitation.'" *Id.* at 406.

Employing a similarly strict standard, the Court in *Yoder* held that Wisconsin's interest in an educated citizenry was not sufficient to warrant impinging upon Amish and Mennonite religious beliefs that militate against formal education after the eighth grade. 406 U.S. at 234–35. The Court observed that "only those interests of the highest order and those not otherwise served can overbalance legitimate claims to the free exercise of religion." *Id.* at 215.

Indeed, the Supreme Court has identified only a few circumstances manifesting interests that satisfy the compelling interest test when applied in the free exercise context. *See United States v. Lee,* 455 U.S. 252, 259–61, 102 S.Ct. 1051, 71 L.Ed.2d 127 (1982) (government's interest in maintaining social security system justifies requiring contribution even from those religiously opposed); *Gillette v. United States,* 401 U.S. 437, 462, 91 S.Ct. 828, 28 L.Ed.2d 168 (1971) (interests in enforcing military draft justify burden on religious objectors); *Braunfeld v. Brown,* 366 U.S. 599, 607, 81 S.Ct. 1144, 6 L.Ed.2d 563 (1961) (state interest in day of repose for all workers justifies Sunday closing law despite incidental burden on those who observe Saturday as day of rest). Even significant governmental interests will not necessarily rise to the requisite level. *See, e.g., Church of the Lukumi Babalu Aye v. Hialeah,* 508 U.S. 520, 546, 113 S.Ct. 2217, 124 L.Ed.2d 472 (1993) (free exercise interests of church that practices animal sacrifice warrant invalidating ban on the practice founded on city's proffered interests in protecting against health risks, animal cruelty, emotional injury to child witnesses, etc.).

* * *

During its hearing on this matter, the Lake Elsinore City Council articulated three principal bases for its denial of the conditional use permit: 1) maintaining needed services provided by the Site's current tenant (a discount food store and recycling center); 2) preventing a loss of property tax revenue by replacing a commercial tenant with a non-commercial user; and, 3) the possible inadequacy of on-site parking for the Church's proposed use, and potential adverse consequences on the parking needs of adjacent users. (*See* Compl., Exh. D, City Council Minutes—March 13, 2001 [hereinafter City Council Minutes], at 29.)

The City now offers a post hoc articulation of its interests as "curbing urban blight, preserving the sole food market in an underprivileged low-income area, preserving jobs in the same area, [and] generating tax revenue for the use [of] all [City residents]." (*See* Defs.' Opp. at 15.) Thus, the City no longer argues that avoidance of (speculative) parking difficulties constitutes a compelling interest, and the Court doubts that such a showing could be made. (*Id.*)

Nor does an interest in maintaining tax revenue justify the City's decision. The maintenance of property tax revenue is a potentially pretextual basis for decision-making that appears to have been a specific target of RLUIPA. *See* Report of the House Committee on the Judiciary (House Rep. 106–219) (July 1, 1999), at text accompanying n. 79 (cited in Hatch–Kennedy Statement, 146 Cong. Rec. S 7774, at 7775). The Act's drafters were concerned that where, as here, a church is required to seek a permit, "[t]he zoning board [does] not have to give a specific reason [for denying the permit]. They can say it is not in the general welfare, or they can say you are taking property off the tax rolls." *Id.* Indeed, if a city's interest in maintaining property tax levels constituted a compelling governmental interest, the most significant provision of RLUIPA would be largely moot, as a decision to deny a religious assembly use of land would almost always be justifiable on that basis.

Thus, the only potentially compelling interest is that characterized by the City as "curbing urban blight" (i.e., maintaining the only food market in an economically depressed area, and avoiding loss of jobs). The Supreme Court has long acknowledged the importance of municipal zoning objectives, including ensuring safety and security, limiting noise, and providing a favorable environment to raise children. *See Village of Euclid v. Ambler Realty Co.*, 272 U.S. 365, 394–95, 47 S.Ct. 114, 71 L.Ed. 303 (1926); *Members of City Council v. Taxpayers for Vincent*, 466 U.S. 789, 806, 104 S.Ct. 2118, 80 L.Ed.2d 772 (1984) (interest in avoiding visual clutter); *Agins v. Tiburon*, 447 U.S. 255, 261, 100 S.Ct. 2138, 65 L.Ed.2d 106 (1980) (controlling urban sprawl). More significantly, as the Court has recognized in the First Amendment context, "a city's 'interest in attempting to preserve the quality of urban life is one that must be accorded high respect.'" *Renton v. Playtime Theatres, Inc.*, 475 U.S. 41, 50, 106 S.Ct. 925, 89 L.Ed.2d 29 (1986) (quoting *American Mini Theaters, Inc.*, 427 U.S. 50, 71, 96 S.Ct. 2440, 49 L.Ed.2d 310 (1976)).

Of course, such observations do not equate to holdings that the interests are "compelling." *See Walnut Properties v. Whittier*, 808 F.2d 1331, 1335–36 (9th Cir.1986). It seems apparent, however, that concerns regarding the vitality of city life are of paramount importance in land use planning. *See Murphy v. Zoning Comm'n*, 148 F.Supp.2d 173, 190 (D.Conn.2001) ("local governments have a compelling interest [under RLUIPA] in protecting the health and safety of their communities....").

Moreover, the interests claimed here go beyond merely preserving the quality of urban life. Rather, the City's proffered interest is in combating the economic and social ravages of blight—an interest underscored by comprehensive federal and state legislation with related objectives. *See* Housing Act of 1954, Pub.L. No. 68–560, 68 Stat. 590 (1954) (amended by various enactments 1955–1987); California Community Redevelopment Law ("CRL"), Cal. Health and Safety Code § § 33000 et seq. In fact, the C–1 zone at issue is classified as "blighted" by the Rancho Laguna Redevelopment Project, a "legislative body" under the CRL, and is thus "conclusively presumed" to be a blighted area under California law. *See* Cal. Health and Safety Code § 33368. Among the conditions of blight identified by the California legislature are a lack of necessary facilities, including grocery stores, and an abnormally high proportion of business vacancies. *See* Cal. Health and Safety Code §§ 33031(b)(2–3).

"Indeed, the more desperate the endeavor the more economically attractive the area is to alternate land users and the more compelling the City's need to exclude them if it is to have any chance to succeed." *International Church of the Foursquare Gospel v. City of Chicago Heights,* 955 F.Supp. 878, 881 (N.D.Ill.1996) (upholding, against RFRA challenge, city's decision to deny special use permit to church seeking to occupy abandoned commercial structure).

However, even assuming, without deciding, that curbing urban blight is a "compelling interest" under RLUIPA, it is not sufficient for the City simply to identify a compelling interest. Rather, the City must show that the challenged decision was "in furtherance" of that interest. *See* 42 U.S.C. § 2000cc(a)(1).

As with the other elements of the test, the "in furtherance" phrase is not defined by RLUIPA. Nonetheless, the language presumably requires a causal nexus between the proffered interests and the action that purportedly advances them.

It is on this issue that there is a critical disjunction between the City's action and the relevant interests. Food Smarts is merely a month-to-month tenant of the Site's current owner, Elsinore Naval and Military School. In fact, the record indicates that the School does not intend to enter into a lease or long-term arrangement with Food Smarts, and, indeed, "will evict Food Smarts, if necessary, to sell the property." (*See* Pls.' Mot. for Preliminary Injunction, Dec. of Rose M. Moore, ¶ 3.) Thus, the only evidence on this point is that the City's denial of the CUP will almost assuredly not guarantee the services and jobs the City claims to be preserving by way of its decision. Given its burden with respect to this issue, the City has failed as a matter of law to establish that its decision was "in furtherance" of the purportedly compelling interests upon which it relies.

Moreover, even if the City could show its decision was in furtherance of compelling governmental interests, it also has the burden of demonstrating that the decision was "the least restrictive means of furthering" those interests. 42 U.S.C. § § 2000cc(a)(1); 2000cc–2(b).

This provision of RLUIPA also draws from pre-*Smith* jurisprudence. *See Thomas v. Review Bd. of Indiana Employment Sec. Div.,* 450 U.S. 707, 718, 101 S.Ct. 1425, 67 L.Ed.2d 624 (1981). In essence, the City must show that its interests could not be achieved by narrower state action that burdens the Church to a lesser degree. *Hialeah,* 508 U.S. at 546; *see Sherbert,* 374 U.S. at 408 (test is whether "no alternative forms of regulation" would serve the government's interests).

The City argues that the "Food Smart [sic] site is a unique parcel of property providing a specific needed service," and that the City's interests could not be furthered "absent the denial of the CUP to the plaintiff." (Def.'s Opp. at 10.) The City has failed as a matter of law to establish that this is the case.

The City has adduced no evidence that the loss of Food Smarts as a tenant at the current site will necessarily equate to the loss of Food Smarts—or a similar service—from the community. For instance, the City does not point the Court to any evidence that there are no other suitable or available lots to which Food Smarts could or would relocate, and the Court is not obligated to scour the record in search of such. *See Keenan v. Allan,* 91 F.3d 1275, 1279 (9th Cir.1996). Nor has the City demonstrated why a less burdensome alternative, such as offering alternative space to Food Smarts, would be impracticable. Nor does the City argue that it is seeking to preserve the economic utility of property uniquely suited to a specific purpose. *Cf. International Church of the Foursquare Gospel,* 955 F.Supp. at 881.

For the City to carry its burden, it must demonstrate that approval of the CUP would necessarily entail dislocation of the assertedly vital use from the area, and thus that denial of the CUP is the least restrictive means of preventing that dislocation. The City has not identified any evidence that this is the case here, and thus fails as a matter of law to show that the CUP denial is the "least restrictive means" of advancing its interests.

The City fails to carry its burden for an additional reason. As elucidated above, the relevant ground for denying the CUP was justified by the City Council based principally upon its conclusion that "replacement of the present retail use with [the Church] would result in the loss of a needed service and recycling center serving the general public." (City Council Minutes, at 29.) Even if the City had carried its burden or raised a material issue with respect to this contention, the City has adduced no evidence that this "needed service" is necessarily inferior to those services provided by the Church, and thus that denying the CUP is the least restrictive means of "curbing blight." (*See supra.*)

The City cites a provision of the California Redevelopment Law as evidence that preserving grocery stores is critical to curbing blight. That same law suggests, however, that unsafe and unhealthy buildings are also characteristic of blight. *See* Cal. Health and Safety Code § 33031(a)(1). And City staffers have acknowledged that the Church might improve the Subject Property upon occupying it, and is otherwise likely to ameliorate the area's condition:

> The proposed project could improve the appearance of this northern edge of the Historic District and could assist in revitalization of the area. Another possible, indirect economic benefit to the City could be the number of new persons brought to this section of the City that may not normally visit the area. These people could be potential customers for restaurants and retail shops on Main Street.

(Compl., Exh. A., City of Lake Elsinore Report to Planning Commission and Design Review Committee Meeting of February 21, 2001 [hereinafter Feb. 21 Planning Commission Report], at p. 4.)

At the subsequent Planning Commission meeting denying the CUP, one commissioner observed that the Commission "does not win tonight no matter what [we] decide," and agreed that "both [Food Smarts and the Church] provide valuable services." (*See* Feb. 21 Planning Commission Report, at 6.) Another concluded that "the church has done wonderful things, but so has Food Smarts." (*Id.*) Members of the City Council evinced similar ambivalence in their comments prior to denying the City's appeal. (*See* City Council Minutes, at 26–29.)

The Court need not opine on which is the better course for improving the area's vitality and curbing blight. Under RLUIPA, it is the City's burden to show that its regulation is the *least restrictive* means of advancing a compelling governmental interest. The undisputed facts indicate that, as between two users with services that City officials concede could both advance the same general interests, the City chose the alternative *most* burdensome on Plaintiffs' "religious exercise" under RLUIPA.

Therefore, the City's denial of a CUP in this instance fails the strict scrutiny analysis required by RLUIPA.

* * *

The City argues, however, that Section 2(a) of RLUIPA represents an unconstitutional exercise of congressional authority. "Under our Constitution, the Federal Government is one of enumerated powers. *McCulloch v. Maryland,* 17 U.S. 316, 4 Wheat. 316, 4 L.Ed. 579 (1819); *see also* The Federalist No. 45, p. 292 (C. Rossiter ed. 1961) (J. Madison). The judicial authority to determine the constitutionality of the laws, in cases and controversies, is based on the premise that the 'powers of the legislature are defined and limited; and that those limits may not be mistaken, or forgotten, the constitution is written.' *Marbury v. Madison,* 5 U.S. 137, 1 Cranch 137, 2 L.Ed. 60 (1803)." *City of Boerne,* 521 U.S. at 516.

* * *

The legislative history states that RLUIPA was intended to enforce the Free Speech and Free Exercise Clauses of the First Amendment. *See* 146 Cong. Rec. S 7774, 7775. Two arguments are made in this respect. First, Intervenor United States of America argues that RLUIPA merely codifies the standard of *Sherbert v. Verner, supra,* which purportedly applies strict scrutiny to "individualized assessments" that bear on religious practice. (*See* Intervenor United States of America's Supp. Memo. in Support of Constitutionality of RLUIPA, at 5–8.) Second, it is contended that, to the extent RLUIPA exceeds existing constitutional protections, it is a valid prophylactic enactment. (*Id.* at 16–18 .)

RLUIPA's legislative history reflects the United States's position that the Act codifies the "individualized assessment" doctrine of *Sherbert*. See 146 Cong. Rec. S 7774, 7775–76. At least three district courts have adopted this position. *See Cottonwood Christian Ctr. v. Cypress Redevelopment Agency*, 218 F.Supp.2d 1203, 1221 (C.D.Cal.2002); *Hale O Kaula Church v. The Maui Planning Commission*, 229 F.Supp.2d 1056, 1072 (D.Haw.2002); *Freedom Baptist Church v. Township of Middletown*, 204 F.Supp.2d 857, 868 (E.D.Pa.2002).

The United States is incorrect for two reasons.

First, the Supreme Court has never invalidated a governmental action on the basis of *Sherbert* outside the context in which it was decided: denial of unemployment compensation. *Smith*, 494 U.S. at 883; *see, e.g.*, *Hobbie v. Unemployment Appeals Comm'n of Florida*, 480 U.S. 136, 141, 107 S.Ct. 1046, 94 L.Ed.2d 190 (1987); *Thomas v. Review Bd. of Indiana Employment Sec. Div.*, 450 U.S. 707, 718, 101 S.Ct. 1425, 67 L.Ed.2d 624 (1981). *Sherbert's* compelling interest standard has only rarely been applied by the Supreme Court in other free exercise contexts, never (to this Court's knowledge) in a land use challenge, and has always been found satisfied. *See Smith*, 494 U.S. at 883 (citing *United States v. Lee*, 455 U.S. 252, 102 S.Ct. 1051, 71 L.Ed.2d 127 (1982) and *Gillette v. United States*, 401 U.S. 437, 91 S.Ct. 828, 28 L.Ed.2d 168 (1971)). Thus, there is simply no controlling Supreme Court authority that establishes what this law purports to "codify."

Second, even if *Sherbert* has occasionally been applied to free exercise cases outside the unemployment compensation field, it is inapposite to challenges of this type.

As an initial matter, *Sherbert* applies only where the governmental action at issue effects a "substantial burden" on "religious practice." *See Smith*, 494 U.S. at 883; *Sherbert*, 374 U.S. at 406 (compelling interest test applies to state's "substantial infringement" of free exercise rights). In *Sherbert*, the state's decision to deny unemployment benefits to a Seventh Day Adventist placed "unmistakable" pressure upon her to forego her Sabbatarian beliefs. 374 U.S. at 404. Likewise, in *Church of Lukumi Babalu Aye v. City of Hialeah*, 508 U.S. 520, 537, 113 S.Ct. 2217, 124 L.Ed.2d 472 (1993), the Supreme Court struck down a set of city ordinances that were clearly intended to bar animal sacrifice central to the adherents' religion. 508 U.S. at 534. As discussed *supra*, however, a burden on a religious assembly's use of land has not generally been held to amount to a "substantial burden" on central religious practice under the Free Exercise Clause. In short, the compelling interest test of *Sherbert* would not normally apply to a land use permit decision and, therefore, a statute so applying it could not in any sense effect a simple "codification" of precedent.

Furthermore, to the extent that there is a general rule derivable from *Sherbert*, it is that, "in circumstances in which individualized *exemptions* from a general requirement are available, the government 'may not refuse to extend that system to cases of 'religious hardship' without compelling reason.'" *Church of Lukumi,* 508 U.S. at 537 (quoting *Smith,* 494 U.S. at 844 and *Bowen v. Roy,* 476 U.S. at 708) (emphasis added). In *Church of Lukumi,* for instance, the Supreme Court decided that, by exempting certain nonreligious slaughter from a general prohibition against animal killing, while refusing to do so for cases of religious sacrifice, the city's actions were subject to, and failed, the compelling interest test of *Sherbert. Id.* at 537–38 (citing *Smith's* reference to the *Sherbert* principle).

Land use permitting is not an analogous case. In determining whether to issue a zoning permit, municipal authorities do not decide whether to exempt a proposed user from an applicable law, but rather whether the general law *applies* to the facts before it. If such quasi-judicial determinations were governed by *Sherbert,* many if not most governmental decisions affecting religious actors would be subject to strict scrutiny, and the rule of *Smith* would have virtually no effect.

Moreover, even if the City's conditional use permit process could be characterized as a system of "individualized exemptions" from the general zoning rules, there is simply no indication here that the City has "refuse[d] to extend that system to cases of 'religious hardship,'" thereby invoking the compelling interest test of *Sherbert. Church of Lukumi,* 508 U.S. at 537. The Church was not denied a CUP simply because it is a church, or because its reasons for seeking the CUP were religiously motivated. Rather, the City treated the Church as it would any similarly-situated entity: by balancing the public policy factors that inform municipal land use decisions. The Church seeks to relocate within an essentially commercial zone principally for secular reasons (better parking and more space), and the City denied the CUP for secular reasons (including the existing tenant's ability to provide specific commercial services to an economically depressed area). The record does not reflect any refusal by the City to consider religious factors in making the CUP determination, thereby invoking the concerns underlying *Sherbert.*

Nor is there any evidence that the City has used nonreligious factors to effect a de facto exclusion of religious land users from the zone or City, or that otherwise indicates the City's decision was motivated by religious bigotry. Rather, the City has granted twenty-three of twenty-six CUPs to churches seeking to locate in C–1 zones. Indeed, the Church itself was granted a CUP in a C–1 zone for use of the property it currently occupies, which is located a mere three blocks from that to which it seeks to relocate.

* * *

Rather than codifying precedent, RLUIPA mandates a sea change in the relevant standard of review. Under RLUIPA, a church's status as a religious institution entitles it to strict scrutiny review of any governmental action restricting its use of land, regardless of the degree to which that action is related to or impinges upon the church's central religious beliefs or mission, or is motivated by religious hostility.

* * *

Unlike the record attending the Voting Rights Act, which represents a valid exercise of Congress's Fourteenth Amendment enforcement powers, RFRA's legislative history was notably deficient in its failure to identify even a single generally applicable law passed because of unconstitutional bigotry. *City of Boerne,* 521 U.S. at 530. Apparently mindful of this deficiency, RLUIPA's sponsors stated that "the committees in each house have examined large numbers of cases, and the hearing record reveals a widespread pattern of discrimination against churches as compared to secular places of assembly...." 146 Cong. Rec. S 7774, 7775.

In fact, the hearing record consists of a relatively small number of anecdotal instances in which religious assemblies were dissatisfied with zoning decisions or regulations, few of which constitute state or municipal action of a clearly unconstitutional character. *Cf. Hibbs,* 2003 U.S. Lexis 4272, at 21–26 (identifying widespread pattern of discriminatory family leave laws, which favored female employees, in a decision upholding across-the-board provisions of federal Family and Medical Leave Act as applied to state employers). Nonetheless, Congress is the body constitutionally appointed to decide in the first instance "whether and what legislation is needed to secure the guarantees of the Fourteenth Amendment," and thus its conclusions are entitled to great deference. *Kimel,* 528 U.S. at 80–81 (quoting *City of Boerne,* 521 U.S. at 536).

* * *

Although the record supporting RFRA was scant, this was not the principal basis upon which *City of Boerne* was decided. 521 U.S. at 531 ("lack of support in the legislative record ... is not RFRA's most serious shortcoming"). Rather, RFRA was "so out of proportion to a supposed remedial or preventive object that it [could not] be understood as responsive to, or designed to prevent, unconstitutional behavior." *See City of Boerne,* 521 U.S. at 532. RLUIPA suffers precisely the same infirmity.

To be sure, RLUIPA is more narrowly directed than RFRA: it applies only to decisions and regulations affecting either land use or institutionalized persons. But as with RFRA, and in contrast to, e.g., provisions of the Voting Rights Act upheld by the Supreme Court, RLUIPA's effect is not confined to a specific type of law (or zoning regulation) "with a long history as a 'notorious means'" of effecting unconstitutional discrimination, nor is it limited in geographic breadth or duration. *Id.* at 533. While such limitations are not required, they "tend to ensure Congress' means are proportionate to ends legitimate under § 5." *Id.; see also Hibbs,* 2003 U.S. LEXIS 4272, at 30–32.

The failure to cabin RLUIPA's operation is exacerbated by the strict scrutiny standard it imposes. So searching is the judicial inquiry under this test that at least two Justices of the Supreme Court have questioned whether, or concluded that, it is "strict in theory, but fatal in fact." *Fullilove v. Klutznick,* 448 U.S. 448, 507, 519, 100 S.Ct. 2758, 65 L.Ed.2d 902 (1980) (Powell, J., concurring, and Marshall, J., concurring in the judgment). Whether or not this is modernly accurate, *see Adarand Constructors v. Pena,* 515 U.S. 200, 237, 115 S.Ct. 2097, 132 L.Ed.2d 158 (1995), RLUIPA's test places a virtually insuperable barrier before states and municipalities attempting to justify actions that, far more often than not, are neither motivated by religious bigotry nor burdensome on central religious practice or beliefs.

* * *

By vastly expanding the types of exercise protected by the most exacting standard of review, Congress has effectively redefined the First Amendment rights it is purporting to enforce. The result is likely to be, as in this case, that many land use decisions will be invalidated despite being legitimately motivated and generic in effect, simply because the aggrieved landowner is a religious actor. Even assuming Congress has identified an area where there is a persistent minority of unconstitutional rules and decisions, the landscape is not so pervaded by religious bigotry that this blunderbuss of a remedy can be described as "congruent and proportional" to the perceived injury.

Therefore, Section 2(a) of RLUIPA exceeds Congress's power under Section 5 of the Fourteenth Amendment.

* * *

Because 42 U.S.C. § 2000cc(a), as applied in § 2000cc(a)(2)(C), was enacted without the ambit of congressional authority, it is unconstitutional. The Court need not and does not consider Defendants' argument that this provision would, even if otherwise within Congress's powers, violate the Establishment Clause.

Therefore, Plaintiffs' Motion for Partial Summary Judgment is DENIED, and Defendants' Motion for Summary Judgment is GRANTED IN PART as to Plaintiffs' Second Cause of Action, under 42 U.S.C. § 2000cc(a). The Court will issue a separate Order addressing the remaining portions of Defendants' Motion for Summary Judgment and Plaintiffs' Motion under Rule 56(f).

IT IS SO ORDERED.

Notes

1. In August 2003 the judge agreed to reconsider his ruling and to also consider the commerce clause issues. Also see Freedom Baptist Church of Delaware County v. Township of Middletown, 204 F.Supp.2d 857 (E.D.Pa. 2002) where the court held RLUIPA constitutional and the parties entered into a consent decree. So far, the U.S. Supreme Court has not had occasion to review the constitutionality of the RLUIPA. How do you think the Court will decide when presented squarely with a constitutional challenge? For an account of all cases challenging the application of RLUIPA to planning and

decisions, *see* www.RLUIPA.org, a site maintained by The Beckett Fund, an organization that provides litigation support to organizations and individuals seeking to protect religious liberties.

2. What is the test to determine whether a zoning regulation imposes a "substantial burden" on religion? See, Grace United Methodist Church v. City of Cheyenne, 235 F.Supp.2d 1186 (D.Wyo.2002).

3. There is an increasing amount of litigation in the federal courts surrounding the applicability of RLUIPA to various planning and zoning decisions. Does RLUIPA give a congregation the right to intervene in land use proceeding to block the siting of a cellular tower where the congregation believes that the placement of the tower will block their view through the windows when they are in the sanctuary praying? See, Omnipoint Communications, Inc. v. City of White Plains, 175 F.Supp.2d 697 (S.D.N.Y.2001). Is the practice of allowing homeless individuals to sleep on the steps of the church a religious use protected under RLUIPA? See, Fifth Avenue Presbyterian Church v. City of New York, 293 F.3d 570 (2d Cir.2002) in Chapter XI.

4. How far does a municipality have to go in accommodating the development needs of a religious institution? See, Prater v City of Burnside, 289 F.3d 417 (6th Cir.2002) (holding that the City's decision to develop a previously laid-out roadway between two church-owned parcels did not give rise to a claim under RLUIPA). See, McGann v. Incorporated Village of Old Westbury, 293 A.D.2d 581, 741 N.Y.S.2d 75 (2nd Dept. 2002) (finding that a cemetery owned by the Roman Catholic Diocese is a religious use and that although it is entitled to preferential treatment, a proposed use of land as a 97 acre cemetery is subject to environmental review under state law). Are religious institutions always compatible with every other type of land use? See, Boyajian v Gatzunis, 212 F.3d 1 (1st Cir.2000) and Congregation Kol Ami v. Abington Township, 309 F.3d 120 (3rd Cir.2002) suggesting perhaps different answers.

B. FEDERAL FAIR HOUSING ACT AMENDMENTS OF 1988

The following excerpt from Professor Peter W. Salsich, Jr.'s article, Federal Influence on Local Land Use Decisions: The Fair Housing Act, 9 J. Affordable Housing & Community Dev. L. 228 (2000) explains the applicability of the Federal Fair Housing Act Amendments of 1988 to local land use planning and zoning decisions (citations omitted).

> The Fair Housing Act does not specifically refer to local land use laws. Section 3604(a), as amended, makes it unlawful to "refuse to sell or rent ... or otherwise make unavailable or deny, a dwelling to any person because of race, color, religion, sex, familial status, or national origin." The phrase "or otherwise make unavailable or deny" has long been held to include local land use regulations.
>
> In Huntington Branch NAACP v. Town of Huntington, the Second Circuit applied the disparate impact test of Title VII employment discrimination cases to strike down a refusal to rezone for multifamily housing. Under this test, discriminatory effect rather than discriminatory intent is the standard. If the plaintiff estab-

lishes a prima facie case that a land use regulation has a discriminatory effect, the burden shifts to the defendant municipality to "prove that its actions furthered, in theory and in practice, a legitimate, bona fide governmental interest and that no alternative would serve that interest with less discriminatory effect."

Applying the effect test, the court concluded that the refusal to rezone in order to enable a multifamily subsidized housing development to be located outside the urban renewal area to which such projects were restricted by the local zoning ordinance created "a strong prima facie showing of discriminatory effect" because of its "disproportionate impact" on minorities and its "segregative impact on the entire community." The court then reviewed the town's justifications for its decisions, dividing those reasons into "plan-specific" and "site-specific" reasons.

"Plan-specific" objections, such as parking and fire protection problems, proximity to a railroad station and a utility substation, inadequate recreation and play areas, and undersized and unrealistic units, "could presumably have been solved with reasonable design modifications ... and proper landscaping," the court asserted. "Site-specific" objections, such as traffic problems and health concerns relating to sewage disposal and proximity to a utility substation, are more problematic. However, the court dismissed these objections because town officials did not focus on these concerns at the land use regulatory stage, but only after the suit was filed. Thus, they amounted to "[p]ost hoc rationalizations by administrative agencies (that) should be afforded 'little deference' by the courts."

Fair Housing Amendments Act

The Fair Housing Amendments Act of 1988 added significant provisions to the Fair Housing Act that affect local land use regulations. The amendments expanded the protections against discrimination in the Fair Housing Act to persons with disabilities and families with children under the age of eighteen. * * *

Important definitions include "handicapped," which means "with respect to a person—(1) a physical or mental impairment which substantially limits one or more of such person's major life activities, (2) a record of having such an impairment, or (3) being regarded as having such an impairment, but such term does not include current, illegal use of or addiction to a controlled substance (as defined in section 102 of the Controlled Substances Act (21 U.S.C. § 802))."

"Familial status" means "one or more individuals (who have not obtained the age of eighteen years) being domiciled with—(1) a parent or another person having legal custody of such individual or individuals; or (2) the designee of such parent or other person having such custody, with the written permission of such parent or other person." The familial status protection also applies to pregnant women and persons securing legal custody of children under eighteen years of age.

Provisions Affecting Local Land Use Regulations

The amendments extend the § 3604 coverage to familial status and disabled status, which impact zoning through apartment and group home controversies.

The second way in which the Fair Housing Amendments Act is made applicable to local land use regulations is contained in the provision adding disabled status as a protective class. Prohibited discrimination against that class includes "... a refusal to make reasonable accommodations in rules, policies, practices, or services, when such accommodations may be necessary to afford such person equal opportunity to use and enjoy a dwelling."

Exemptions from Coverage

Important qualifications to the application of the Fair Housing Amendments Act to local land use regulations include: (a) a statement that the amendments are not intended to invalidate or limit any law that "requires dwellings to be designed and constructed in a manner that affords handicapped persons greater access than is required by this sub-chapter," and (b) a provision that dwellings do not have to be made available to individuals "whose tenancy would constitute a direct threat to the health and safety of other individuals or whose tenancy would result in substantial physical damage to the property of others."

The amendments also exempt from coverage "any reasonable local, State, or Federal restrictions regarding the maximum number of occupants permitted to occupy a dwelling." In addition, the amendments exempt housing for older persons from the familial status discrimination prohibitions. Finally, § 3607(b)(4) denies the protections of the Act to persons convicted of the illegal manufacture or distribution of a controlled substance. * * *

CITY OF EDMONDS v. OXFORD HOUSE, INC.

Supreme Court of the United States, 1995.
514 U.S. 725, 115 S.Ct. 1776, 131 L.Ed.2d 801.

JUSTICE GINSBURG delivered the opinion of the Court.

The Fair Housing Act (FHA or Act) prohibits discrimination in housing against, inter alios, persons with handicaps. Section 807(b)(1) of the Act entirely exempts from the FHA's compass "any reasonable local, State, or Federal restrictions regarding the maximum number of occupants permitted to occupy a dwelling." 42 U.S.C. § 3607(b)(1). This case presents the question whether a provision in petitioner City of Edmonds' zoning code qualifies for § 3607(b)(1)'s complete exemption from FHA scrutiny. The provision, governing areas zoned for single-family dwelling units, defines "family" as "persons [without regard to number] related by genetics, adoption, or marriage, or a group of five or fewer [unrelated] persons." Edmonds Community Development Code (ECDC) § 21.30.010 (1991).

The defining provision at issue describes who may compose a family unit; it does not prescribe "the maximum number of occupants" a dwelling unit may house. We hold that § 3607(b)(1) does not exempt prescriptions of the family-defining kind, i.e., provisions designed to foster the family character of a neighborhood. Instead, § 3607(b)(1)'s absolute exemption removes from the FHA's scope only total occupancy limits, i.e., numerical ceilings that serve to prevent overcrowding in living quarters.

I

In the summer of 1990, respondent Oxford House opened a group home in the City of Edmonds, Washington (City), for 10 to 12 adults recovering from alcoholism and drug addiction. The group home, called Oxford House–Edmonds, is located in a neighborhood zoned for single-family residences. Upon learning that Oxford House had leased and was operating a home in Edmonds, the City issued criminal citations to the owner and a resident of the house. The citations charged violation of the zoning code rule that defines who may live in single-family dwelling units. The occupants of such units must compose a "family," and family, under the City's defining rule, "means an individual or two or more persons related by genetics, adoption, or marriage, or a group of five or fewer persons who are not related by genetics, adoption, or marriage." ECDC § 21.30.010. Oxford House–Edmonds houses more than five unrelated persons, and therefore does not conform to the code.

Oxford House asserted reliance on the Fair Housing Act, 102 Stat. 1619, 42 U.S.C. § 3601 et seq., which declares it unlawful "[t]o discriminate in the sale or rental, or to otherwise make unavailable or deny, a dwelling to any buyer or renter because of a handicap of ... that buyer or renter." § 3604(f)(1)(A). The parties have stipulated, for purposes of this litigation, that the residents of Oxford House–Edmonds "are recovering alcoholics and drug addicts and are handicapped persons within the meaning" of the Act.

Discrimination covered by the FHA includes "a refusal to make reasonable accommodations in rules, policies, practices, or services, when such accommodations may be necessary to afford [handicapped] person[s] equal opportunity to use and enjoy a dwelling." § 3604(f)(3)(B). Oxford House asked Edmonds to make a "reasonable accommodation" by allowing it to remain in the single-family dwelling it had leased. Group homes for recovering substance abusers, Oxford urged, need 8 to 12 residents to be financially and therapeutically viable. Edmonds declined to permit Oxford House to stay in a single-family residential zone, but passed an ordinance listing group homes as permitted uses in multifamily and general commercial zones. * * *

II

The sole question before the Court is whether Edmonds' family composition rule qualifies as a "restrictio[n] regarding the maximum number of occupants permitted to occupy a dwelling" within the meaning of the FHA's absolute exemption. 42 U.S.C. § 3607(b)(1). In answering this question, we are mindful of the Act's stated policy "to provide, within constitutional limitations, for fair housing throughout the United States." § 3601. We also note precedent recognizing the FHA's "broad and inclusive" compass, and therefore according a "generous construction" to the Act's complaint-filing provision. *Trafficante v. Metropolitan Life Ins. Co.*, 409 U.S. 205, 209, 212, 93 S.Ct. 364, 366–367, 368, 34 L.Ed.2d 415 (1972). Accordingly, we regard this case as an instance in which an exception to "a general statement of policy" is sensibly read "narrowly in order to preserve the primary operation of the [policy]." *Commissioner v. Clark*, 489 U.S. 726, 739, 109 S.Ct. 1455, 1463, 103 L.Ed.2d 753 (1989).

A

Congress enacted § 3607(b)(1) against the backdrop of an evident distinction between municipal land-use restrictions and maximum occupancy restrictions.

Land-use restrictions designate "districts in which only compatible uses are allowed and incompatible uses are excluded." D. Mandelker, Land Use Law § 4.16, pp. 113–114 (3d ed.1993) (hereinafter Mandelker). These restrictions typically categorize uses as single-family residential, multiple-family residential, commercial, or industrial. See, e.g., 1 E. Ziegler, Jr., Rathkopf's The Law of Zoning and Planning § 8.01, pp. 8–2 to 8–3 (4th ed.1995); Mandelker § 1.03, p. 4; 1 E. Yokley, Zoning Law and Practice § 7–2, p. 252 (4th ed.1978).

Land use restrictions aim to prevent problems caused by the "pig in the parlor instead of the barnyard." *Village of Euclid v. Ambler Realty Co.*, 272 U.S. 365, 388, 47 S.Ct. 114, 118, 71 L.Ed. 303 (1926). In particular, reserving land for single-family residences preserves the character of neighborhoods, securing "zones where family values, youth values, and the blessings of quiet seclusion and clean air make the area a sanctuary for people." *Village of Belle Terre v. Boraas*, 416 U.S. 1, 9, 94 S.Ct. 1536, 1541, 39 L.Ed.2d 797 (1974); see also *Moore v. East Cleveland*, 431 U.S. 494, 521, 97 S.Ct. 1932, 1947, 52 L.Ed.2d 531 (1977) (Burger, C.J., dissenting) (purpose of East Cleveland's single-family zoning ordinance "is the traditional one of preserving certain areas as family residential communities"). To limit land use to single-family residences, a municipality must define the term "family"; thus family composition rules are an essential component of single-family residential use restrictions.

Maximum occupancy restrictions, in contradistinction, cap the number of occupants per dwelling, typically in relation to available floor space or the number and type of rooms. See, e.g., International Conference of Building Officials, Uniform Housing Code § 503(b) (1988); Building Officials and Code Administrators International, Inc., BOCA National Property Maintenance Code §§ PM–405.3, PM–405.5 (1993) (hereinafter BOCA Code); Southern Building Code Congress, International, Inc., Standard Housing Code §§ 306.1, 306.2 (1991); E. Mood, APHA–CDC Recommended Minimum Housing Standards § 9.02, p. 37 (1986) (hereinafter APHA–CDC Standards). These restrictions ordinarily apply uniformly to all residents of all dwelling units. Their purpose is to protect health and safety by preventing dwelling overcrowding. See, e.g., BOCA Code §§ PM–101.3, PM–405.3, PM–405.5 and commentary; Abbott, Housing Policy, Housing Codes and Tenant Remedies, 56 B.U.L.Rev. 1, 41–45 (1976).

We recognized this distinction between maximum occupancy restrictions and land-use restrictions in *Moore v. East Cleveland,* 431 U.S. 494, 97 S.Ct. 1932, 52 L.Ed.2d 531 (1977). In *Moore,* the Court held unconstitutional the constricted definition of "family" contained in East Cleveland's housing ordinance. East Cleveland's ordinance "select[ed] certain categories of relatives who may live together and declare[d] that others may not"; in particular, East Cleveland's definition of "family" made "a crime of a grandmother's choice to live with her grandson." Id., at 498–499, 97 S.Ct., at 1935 (plurality opinion). In response to East Cleveland's argument that its aim was to prevent overcrowded dwellings, streets, and schools, we observed that the municipality's restrictive definition of family served the asserted, and undeniably legitimate, goals "marginally, at best." Id., at 500, 97 S.Ct., at 1936 (footnote omitted). Another East Cleveland ordinance, we noted, "specifically addressed ... the problem of overcrowding"; that ordinance tied "the maximum permissible occupancy of a dwelling to the habitable floor area." Id., at 500, n. 7, 97 S.Ct., at 1936, n. 7; accord, id., at 520, n. 16, 97 S.Ct., at 1939, n. 16 (STEVENS, J., concurring in judgment). Justice Stewart, in dissent, also distinguished restrictions designed to "preserv[e] the character of a residential area," from prescription of "a minimum habitable floor area per person," id., at 539, n. 9, 97 S.Ct., at 1937, n. 9, in the interest of community health and safety.

Section 3607(b)(1)'s language—"restrictions regarding the maximum number of occupants permitted to occupy a dwelling"—surely encompasses maximum occupancy restrictions. But the formulation does not fit family composition rules typically tied to land-use restrictions. In sum, rules that cap the total number of occupants in order to prevent overcrowding of a dwelling "plainly and unmistakably," *see A.H. Phillips, Inc. v. Walling,* 324 U.S. 490, 493, 65 S.Ct. 807, 808, 89 L.Ed. 1095 (1945), fall within § 3607(b)(1)'s absolute exemption from the FHA's governance; rules designed to preserve the family character of a neighborhood, fastening on the composition of households rather than on the total number of occupants living quarters can contain, do not.

B

Turning specifically to the City's Community Development Code, we note that the provisions Edmonds invoked against Oxford House, ECDC

§§ 16.20.010 and 21.30.010, are classic examples of a use restriction and complementing family composition rule. These provisions do not cap the number of people who may live in a dwelling. In plain terms, they direct that dwellings be used only to house families. Captioned "USES," ECDC § 16.20.010 provides that the sole "Permitted Primary Us[e]" in a single-family residential zone is "[s]ingle-family dwelling units." Edmonds itself recognizes that this provision simply "defines those uses permitted in a single family residential zone."

A separate provision caps the number of occupants a dwelling may house, based on floor area:

> "Floor Area. Every dwelling unit shall have at least one room which shall have not less than 120 square feet of floor area. Other habitable rooms, except kitchens, shall have an area of not less than 70 square feet. Where more than two persons occupy a room used for sleeping purposes, the required floor area shall be increased at the rate of 50 square feet for each occupant in excess of two." ECDC § 19.10.000 (adopting Uniform Housing Code § 503(b) (1988)).

Edmonds nevertheless argues that its family composition rule, ECDC § 21.30.010, falls within § 3607(b)(1), the FHA exemption for maximum occupancy restrictions, because the rule caps at five the number of unrelated persons allowed to occupy a single-family dwelling. But Edmonds' family composition rule surely does not answer the question: "What is the maximum number of occupants permitted to occupy a house?" So long as they are related "by genetics, adoption, or marriage," any number of people can live in a house. Ten siblings, their parents and grandparents, for example, could dwell in a house in Edmonds' single-family residential zone without offending Edmonds' family composition rule.

Family living, not living space per occupant, is what ECDC § 21.30.010 describes. Defining family primarily by biological and legal relationships, the provision also accommodates another group association: Five or fewer unrelated people are allowed to live together as though they were family. This accommodation is the peg on which Edmonds rests its plea for § 3607(b)(1) exemption. Had the City defined a family solely by biological and legal links, § 3607(b)(1) would not have been the ground on which Edmonds staked its case. It is curious reasoning indeed that converts a family values preserver into a maximum occupancy restriction once a town adds to a related persons prescription "and also two unrelated persons."

Edmonds additionally contends that subjecting single-family zoning to FHA scrutiny will "overturn Euclidian zoning" and "destroy the effectiveness and purpose of single-family zoning." This contention both ignores the limited scope of the issue before us and exaggerates the force of the FHA's antidiscrimination provisions. We address only whether Edmonds' family composition rule qualifies for § 3607(b)(1) exemption. Moreover, the FHA antidiscrimination provisions, when applicable, require only "reasonable" accommodations to afford persons with handicaps "equal opportunity to use and enjoy" housing. §§ 3604(f)(1)(A) and (f)(3)(B).

* * *

The parties have presented, and we have decided, only a threshold question: Edmonds' zoning code provision describing who may compose a "family" is not a maximum occupancy restriction exempt from the FHA under § 3607(b)(1). It remains for the lower courts to decide whether Edmonds' actions against Oxford House violate the FHA's prohibitions against discrimination set out in §§ 3604(f)(1)(A) and (f)(3)(B). For the reasons stated, the judgment of the United States Court of Appeals for the Ninth Circuit is

Affirmed.

JUSTICE THOMAS, with whom JUSTICE SCALIA and JUSTICE KENNEDY join, dissenting. [Dissenting opinion omitted.]

HOWARD v. CITY OF BEAVERCREEK

United States Court of Appeals, Sixth Circuit, 2002.
276 F.3d 802.

SILER, CIRCUIT JUDGE.

Plaintiff Joseph L. Howard brought suit against the defendant City of Beavercreek ("Beavercreek") alleging that the denial of his request for a variance to Beavercreek's zoning law to accommodate his handicap violated 42 U.S.C. § 3604(f)(3)(B) of the Fair Housing Amendments Act of 1988 ("FHAA") and subsections 4112.02(H)(1), (4), (18), and (19) of the Ohio Revised Code. Howard appeals the district court's order granting summary judgment in favor of Beavercreek. For the reasons that follow, we AFFIRM the district court's judgment.

Howard owns a home in Beavercreek, Ohio, where he has lived with his wife and children since 1984. The home is located on a lot which is 255 feet deep and 110 feet wide. Howard's lot is separated from the adjacent lots on both sides by a split rail fence that is less than five feet eight inches in height. There is also a chain link fence, at least four feet high, that runs across the back of Howard's lot about thirty feet from the rear property line.

In 1996, Howard became concerned that the neighbors who lived on the west side of his property were spying on his family. Howard suffers from post traumatic stress disorder ("PTSD") and a heart condition. Because of the conditions at his home with regard to his neighbors, Howard felt that his medical and psychological conditions were being exacerbated. Thus, he wanted to erect a six-foot privacy fence along the west side of his property to block his neighbors' view. He believed that this would eliminate any undue stress on his medical and psychological conditions and, in addition, would block leaves from blowing into his yard which he no longer could rake due to his heart condition.

The fence Howard intended to construct would run seventy feet from the southwest corner of his property to the street. Under Beavercreek's zoning ordinance, Howard was prohibited from erecting a six-foot fence along the first forty feet of the west property line running from the right-of-way to his house without first obtaining a variance. The zoning ordinance, however, would permit him to build a six-foot fence along the remainder of his property without a variance. He applied for a variance in 1997. In support of his application, Howard provided a statement from his treating physician which detailed his medical and psychological conditions. After a public hearing in May 1998, the Board of Zoning Appeals for the City of Beavercreek denied Howard's request.

In December 1998, Howard filed suit against Beavercreek seeking damages under the FHAA, 42 U.S.C. § 3604(f)(3)(B), and damages, declaratory judgment and injunctive relief under Ohio law, Ohio Revised Code § 4112.02. He alleged that Beavercreek had discriminated against him, as a person who suffers from a handicap, by failing to consider his request for a reasonable accommodation to its zoning rules, when such an accommodation was necessary to afford him an equal opportunity to use and enjoy his dwelling.

The district court * * * granted summary judgment in favor of Beavercreek on Howard's claim under the FHAA and his state law claims for declaratory and injunctive relief. * * * The court went on to find that although fact issues existed as to whether Howard's request for a variance was a reasonable accommodation under the FHAA, the city's denial of his request did not deny him the right to live in the neighborhood of his choice and, thus, did not violate the FHAA. Since the applicable sections of the Ohio Revised Code had language similar to that of the FHAA, the court used the same analysis when it reviewed and rejected Howard's state law claims for declaratory and injunctive relief. The court also determined that there was a second basis for granting summary judgment in favor of Beavercreek on Howard's FHAA claim. Because the "uncontroverted evidence" showed that the six-foot fence would cause a threat to pedestrian and vehicular traffic, the court held that Beavercreek was not required under § 3604(f)(9) of the FHAA to grant Howard's request for a variance. See 42 U.S.C. § 3604(f)(9). * * *

The FHAA makes it unlawful to discriminate against a person with a handicap by refusing "to make reasonable accommodations in rules, policies, practices, or services, when such accommodations may be necessary to afford such person equal opportunity to use and enjoy a dwelling." 42 U.S.C. § 3604(f)(3)(B). This creates an affirmative duty on municipalities, like Beavercreek, to afford its disabled citizens reasonable accommodations in its municipal zoning practices if necessary to afford such persons equal opportunity in the use and enjoyment of their property. *See Smith & Lee Assocs., Inc. v. City of Taylor,* 102 F.3d 781, 794–795 (6th Cir.1996) (holding that city had violated the FHAA by failing to allow adult foster care homes to operate in areas zoned only for single-family neighborhoods); *City of Edmonds v. Washington State Bldg. Code Council,* 18 F.3d 802, 806 (9th Cir.1994), aff'd, 514 U.S. 725, 115

S.Ct. 1776, 131 L.Ed.2d 801 (1995) ("The FHAA imposes an affirmative duty to reasonably accommodate handicapped people.").

When analyzing whether an accommodation is required under this Act, the three operative elements are "reasonable," "equal opportunity" and "necessary." See Smith, 102 F.3d at 794. An accommodation is "reasonable" when it imposes no "fundamental alteration in the nature of the program" or "undue financial and administrative burdens." Id. at 795 (quoting *Southeastern Community College v. Davis,* 442 U.S. 397, 410, 412, 99 S.Ct. 2361, 60 L.Ed.2d 980 (1979)). "Equal opportunity" under the FHAA is defined as "giving handicapped individuals the right to choose to live in single-family neighborhoods, for that right serves to end the exclusion of handicapped individuals from the American mainstream." Id. at 794–95. Linked to the goal of equal opportunity is the term "necessary." Id. at 795. In order to prove that an accommodation is "necessary," "[p]laintiffs must show that, but for the accommodation, they likely will be denied an equal opportunity to enjoy the housing of their choice." Id. (citing *Bronk v. Ineichen,* 54 F.3d 425, 429 (7th Cir.1995) ("[T]he concept of necessity requires at a minimum the showing that the desired accommodation will affirmatively enhance a disabled plaintiff's quality of life by ameliorating the effects of the disability.")).

Howard argues that the district court erred when it held that the requested accommodation was not necessary under the FHAA, because Howard had enjoyed the housing of his choice without the fence since 1984, and he continued to live in his home after the problems with his neighbors began in 1996. Howard asserts that the requested variance would ameliorate the exacerbation of his handicap satisfying the necessity requirement in § 3604(f)(3)(B), as defined in Smith and Bronk. We conclude that the district court was correct in its decision that under the FHAA Howard failed to prove that his requested accommodation was necessary to afford him the equal opportunity to enjoy the housing of his choice.

In his deposition, Howard stated that because of his medical conditions he needed to avoid being upset. He explained that by erecting a six-foot fence, he could avoid being upset by precluding his neighbors from viewing his property from their lot. In addition, he felt that the fence would prevent leaves from blowing into his yard, which he could no longer rake because of his heart condition. Without the fence, Howard stated that he may be forced to move. In addition, one of his treating physicians stated only that "[i]t is feasible that the installation of the privacy fence may relieve this undue stress and allow Mr. Howard to return to his baseline status." This evidence combined with the fact that Howard has lived in his home for several years without the requested variance illustrates that the denial of Howard's variance request has not denied him an equal opportunity to enjoy the housing or community of his choice. See Robinson v. City of Friendswood, 890 F.Supp. 616, 622 (S.D.Tex.1995) ("The Plaintiff had the same disabilities and lived in the same house for years before he constructed the carport indicates that the ordinance did not prevent him from obtaining housing of his choice nor from living in the community of his choice.").

"The Act is intended to prohibit the application of special requirements through land-use regulations, restrictive covenants, and conditional or special use permits that have the effect of limiting the ability of [handicapped] individuals to live in the residence of their choice in the community." H.R.Rep. No. 100–711, at 24 (1988), U.S.Code Cong. & Admin.News 1988, p. 2173, 2185. Thus, local governments are prohibited from "applying land use regulations in a manner that will exclude people with disabilities entirely from zoning neighborhoods, particularly residential neighborhoods, or that will give disabled people less opportunity to live in certain neighborhoods than people without disabilities." *Smith,* 102 F.3d at 795 (citation omitted). Although the requested variance may have reduced some of the stress Howard reportedly was subjected to, Beavercreek's denial of Howard's variance request has neither excluded Howard from the neighborhood or residence of his choice, nor has it created less opportunity for Howard, as a handicapped person, to live in his neighborhood.

In sum, because Howard failed to present sufficient evidence to create a genuine issue of material fact as to whether the variance he requested was a necessary accommodation under § 3604(f)(3)(B), the district court correctly granted summary judgment in favor of Beavercreek on Howard's FHAA claim. Because we find that the district court correctly granted summary judgment based on the "necessary" prong of the Act, we need not address whether the district court was also correct in finding a second basis for granting summary judgment based on the safety hazard posed by the fence. * * *

AFFIRMED.

C. AMERICANS WITH DISABILITIES ACT

INNOVATIVE HEALTH SYSTEMS v. CITY OF WHITE PLAINS

United States Court of Appeals, Second Circuit, 1997.
117 F.3d 37.

HEANEY, SENIOR CIRCUIT JUDGE:

In December 1992, plaintiff-appellee Innovative Health Systems, Inc. ("IHS"), an outpatient drug- and alcohol-rehabilitation treatment center, began efforts to relocate to a building in downtown White Plains. After over a year of seeking permission from the city, IHS was ultimately denied the necessary building permit by the White Plains Zoning Board of Appeals ("ZBA"). On November 14, 1995, plaintiffs-appellees, IHS and five individual clients, initiated this action against the City of White Plains; Mayor S.J. Schulmann; the ZBA; Chair of the ZBA, Terrence Guerrier; the White Plains Planning Board; and Chair of the Planning Board, Mary Cavallero, (collectively, "the City"), alleging that the ZBA's zoning decision violated both Title II of the Americans with Disabilities Act, 42 U.S.C. §§ 12131–12165 (1994), and section 504 of the Rehabilitation Act of 1973, 29 U.S.C. § 794 (1994). The plaintiffs-appellees moved for a preliminary injunction to prevent the City from interfering with IHS's occupation of the new site. The City cross-moved to dismiss the complaint. In a detailed and thorough opinion, the United States District Court for the Southern District of New York (Barrington D. Parker, Jr., Judge) granted the preliminary injunction and denied the motion to dismiss, except with respect to Mayor Schulmann. *Innovative Health Sys. v. City of White Plains,* 931 F.Supp. 222 (S.D.N.Y.1996). The remaining defendants appeal. We affirm except with respect to one individual client, Martin A.

In 1992, Dr. Ross Fishman, Executive Director of IHS, decided that the program should move from its current facility to a building located in downtown White Plains. The new site was more than five times as large as the current site and was closer to a bus line and to other service providers that IHS clients frequently visit. Dr. Fishman planned to expand the services offered by IHS at the new site to include a program for children of chemically dependent persons. Therefore, IHS predicted an increase in the number of clients it would serve.

In December 1992, the Deputy Commissioner of Building for the City of White Plains informed IHS that its proposed use of the downtown site—counseling offices with no physicians on staff for physical examinations or dispensing of medication—qualified as a business or professional office under White Plains' zoning ordinance and thus would be permissible in the zoning district. In January 1994, Dr. Fishman signed a lease for the new space. IHS paid a monthly rent of $8,500 from July 1, 1994 to June 30, 1995 and has paid $6,000 per month since July 1995. The leased space includes a section that formerly had been used as retail space. Dr. Fishman initially intended to renovate the former retail space for the treatment program and sub-lease the remaining space, which had previously been used as an office. In April 1994, IHS filed an application with the White Plains Department of Building for a building permit. Because the application requested a change of use from "retail" to "office," the Commissioner of Building ("Commissioner") referred it to the Planning Board for approval as required by the local zoning ordinance.

The application provoked tremendous opposition from the surrounding community, including Cameo House Owners, Inc. ("Cameo House"), a co-operative association representing resident-owners who lived in the remainder of the downtown building in which IHS sought to relocate, and Fashion Mall Partners, L.P. ("Fashion Mall"), the owner of a shopping mall located near the proposed IHS site. The Planning Board held two public meetings on the proposed use at which the opponents expressed their concern about the condition and appearance of people who attend alcohol- and drug-dependence treatment programs and the effect such a program would have on property values. Opponents also argued that the proposed use constituted a "clinic" and that, therefore, under the zoning ordinance, the use was a "hospital or sanitarium," an impermissible use in the zoning district. In response to this argument, at the Planning Board's request, the Commissioner reconsidered and reaffirmed his previous determination that the proposed site constituted permitted "office" use.

Because continued opposition caused delay and additional costs, IHS withdrew its application from the Planning Board. It instead applied to the Commissioner for a permit to renovate the former retail section of the downtown site, which did not involve a change of use or the Planning Board's approval. Again, however, the application was vehemently opposed by members of the surrounding community.

To resolve the dispute, the Commissioner sought review of his decision by the White Plains Corporation Counsel. In his written opinion, the Corporation Counsel stated that, absent compelling authority to the contrary, the Commissioner's decision should stand. The Corporation Counsel considered the opponents' argument under the zoning ordinance and concluded that the Commissioner's interpretation was correct. Accordingly, the Commissioner issued his final determination that the use was permitted and the Department of Building issued the building permit to IHS.

Cameo House and Fashion Mall immediately appealed the Commissioner's decision to the ZBA, requesting an interpretation of the zoning ordinance that an alcohol-treatment facility is not permitted in the relevant zoning district. The ZBA conducted a two-day public hearing on the matter, at which community members continued to voice strong opposition to having a drug- and alcohol-dependency treatment center in the downtown location. They again focused largely on fears of jeopardized safety and falling property values. The opposition also pressed the same zoning arguments rejected by the Commissioner and the Corporation Counsel. IHS relied on the reasoning of the previous decisions and urged the ZBA to consider their consistency with already-permitted uses in the same zoning district. Specifically, IHS reminded the board that the zoning district of its former location also excludes "hospitals and sanitaria" and that several other mental health professionals and social workers practiced in the district of the proposed site.

On July 5, 1995, the ZBA voted four-to-one to reverse the Commissioner's decision. The Board did not issue a written resolution, as required by the zoning ordinance, but rather stated on the record that, based on its understanding of the services IHS provides, it is better classified as a clinic than an office. Absent in their discussion, however, was any reference to the zoning ordinance or the Commissioner's interpretation.

IHS and five individual clients initiated this action against the City, alleging that the revocation of the building permit constituted discrimination and differential treatment based on a disability as against both the individual clients and the program that assisted them. They also claimed that even if the zoning decision was not discriminatory, the City should have permitted the relocation as a reasonable accommodation. In February 1996, they moved for a preliminary injunction against the City to prevent it from interfering with the occupation of the downtown site.

The City opposed the motion and moved for dismissal, arguing: (1) zoning decisions do not fall within the scope of the ADA or the Rehabilitation Act, (2) the appellees lack standing under the ADA, (3) the federal statutes do not accord preferential treatment to persons with disabilities, and (4) neither IHS nor the individual clients have demonstrated irreparable harm or a likelihood of success on the merits. The district court granted the preliminary injunction and denied the motion to dismiss, except as against the Mayor. The City now appeals, raising essentially the same arguments.

* * *

B. Likelihood of Success on the Merits

The City also challenges the district court's determination that the appellees have demonstrated a likelihood of success on the merits, arguing primarily: (1) neither the ADA nor the Rehabilitation Act covers zoning decisions, (2) the appellees lack standing under both the ADA and the Rehabilitation Act, and (3) appellees have not stated a claim under either statute. We address each argument in turn.

1. Application of Discrimination Statutes to Zoning

Both Title II of the ADA and section 508 of the Rehabilitation Act prohibit discrimination based on a disability by a public entity. The ADA provides:

> [N]o qualified individual with a disability shall, by reason of such disability, be excluded from participation in or be denied the benefits of the services, programs, or activities of a public entity, or be subjected to discrimination by any such entity. 42 U.S.C. sec. 12132(1994).

The Rehabilitation Act contains the following similar prohibition:

> No otherwise qualified individual with a disability ... shall, solely by reason of her or his disability, be excluded from the participation in, be denied the benefits of, or be subjected to discrimination under any program or activity receiving Federal financial assistance.... 29 U.S.C. sec. 794(a)(1994).

It is undisputed that both anti-discrimination provisions govern the City. What the City contests is the application of either statute to its zoning decisions because it contends that zoning does not constitute a "service, program, or activity." We disagree.

The ADA does not explicitly define "services, programs, or activities." Section 508 of the Rehabilitation Act, however, defines "program or activity" as "all of the operations" of specific entities, including "a department, agency, special purpose district, or other instrumentality of a State or of a local government." 29 U.S.C. § 794(b)(1)(A) (1994).

Further, as the district court recognized, the plain meaning of "activity" is a "natural or normal function or operation." *Innovative Health Sys.*, 931 F.Supp. at 232 (quoting Webster's Third New International Dictionary (1993)). Thus, as the district court held, both the ADA and the Rehabilitation Act clearly encompass zoning decisions by the City because making such decisions is a normal function of a governmental entity. Id. Moreover, as the district court also noted, the language of Title II's anti-discrimination provision does not limit the ADA's coverage to conduct that occurs in the "programs, services, or activities" of the City. Rather, it is a catch-all phrase that prohibits all discrimination by a public entity, regardless of the context, and that should avoid the very type of hair-splitting arguments the City attempts to make here.

In its analysis, the district court also looked to the ADA's legislative history and the Department of Justice's regulations and Technical Assistance Manual, all of which support the court's interpretation of the plain language of the statute. With respect to Title II of the ADA, the House Committee on Education and Labor stated:

> The Committee has chosen not to list all the types of actions that are included within the term "discrimination", as was done in titles I and III, because this title essentially simply extends the anti-discrimination prohibition embodied in section 504 to all actions of state and local governments....
>
> Title II of the bill makes all activities of State and local governments subject to the types of prohibitions against discrimination against a qualified individual with a disability included in section 504 (nondiscrimination).

H.R.Rep. No. 101–485(II), at 84, 151 (1990), reprinted in 1990 U.S.C.C.A.N. 303, 367, 434 (emphasis added). As the preamble to the Department of Justice regulations explains, "[T]itle II applies to anything a public entity does.... All governmental activities of public entities are covered." 28 C.F.R. pt. 35, app. A at 456 (1996). The Department of Justice's Technical Assistance Manual, which interprets its regulations, specifically refers to zoning as an example of a public entity's obligation to modify its policies, practices, and procedures to avoid discrimination. The Americans with Disabilities Act: Title II Technical Assistance Manual § II–3.6100, illus. 1 (1993) ("TA Manual").

Although it gives lip service to the importance of looking to the statutory language to glean legislative intent, the City does not point to specific language in either statute to explain the exemption it seeks to create for zoning decisions. We decline to draw an arbitrary distinction—to prohibit public entities from discriminating against persons with disabilities in some of their activities and not in others—without a reasoned basis for such a distinction. The only authority for the City's interpretation of Title II are several lower court decisions that hold that the ADA does not apply to zoning decisions. After careful review of the cited authority, we agree with the district court that none of the cases adequately analyzed the language of the ADA. Similarly, we find no direction from any other circuit on this issue. Without persuasive authority to the contrary, we affirm the district court's sound and thorough analysis.

The City also challenges IHS's standing to sue under either the ADA or the Rehabilitation Act. Although the City does not contest that IHS can meet the constitutional standing requirements of injury-in-fact, causation, and redressability, see *Valley Forge Christian College v. Americans United for Separation of Church & State,* 454 U.S. 464, 472, 102 S.Ct. 752, 758, 70 L.Ed.2d 700 (1982) (setting forth the Article III requirements), it argues that prudential standing requirements bar IHS from asserting a claim under either statute. *See Warth v. Seldin,* 422 U.S. 490, 499, 95 S.Ct. 2197, 2205, 45 L.Ed.2d 343 (1975) (generally, a party "must assert his own legal rights and interests, and cannot rest his claim to relief on the legal rights or interests of third parties"). Specifically, the City argues that the discrimination statutes confer rights on a narrow class of persons, namely "qualified individual[s] with a disability," as set forth in both statutes' definitions of discrimination by public entities. See 42 U.S.C. § 12132; 29 U.S.C. § 794; see also *Kessler,* 876 F.Supp. at 653 (holding that an entity that serves the disabled lacks standing under the ADA).

At first blush, this argument has appeal. The City appropriately looks to the statutory language to determine whether Congress granted an express right of action to persons who otherwise would be barred by prudential standing rules. *See Warth,* 422 U.S. at 501, 95 S.Ct. at 2206 (as long as constitutional requirements met, Congress may grant standing to seek relief on the basis of the legal rights and interests of others). The City's analysis falls short, however, in its selective analysis of the statutes. It stops at the definitions of discrimination, which set forth a substantive, legal right of persons with disabilities to be free from discrimination. That IHS is not granted legal rights under the statutes, however, "hardly determines whether they may sue to enforce the ... rights of others." *See Gladstone, Realtors v. Village of Bellwood,* 441 U.S. 91, 103 n. 9, 99 S.Ct. 1601, 1609 n. 9, 60 L.Ed.2d 66 (1979). Rather, we must look to whether the statutes "grant [ ] persons in the plaintiff's position a right to judicial relief." *Warth,* 422 U.S. at 500, 95 S.Ct. at 2206.

Looking to the enforcement provisions of each statute, we agree with the district court that IHS has standing under both Title II of the ADA and the Rehabilitation Act. Title II's enforcement provision extends relief to "any person alleging discrimination on the basis of disability." 42 U.S.C. § 12133 (1994). Similarly, the Rehabilitation Act extends its remedies to "any person aggrieved" by the discrimination of a person on the basis of his or her disability. 29 U.S.C. § 794a(a)(2). As the district court noted, the use of such broad language in the enforcement provisions of the statutes "evinces a congressional intention to define standing to bring a private action under 504 [and Title II] as broadly as is permitted by Article III of the Constitution." See *Innovative Health Sys.,* 931 F.Supp. at 237 (quoting *Nodleman v. Aero Mexico,* 528 F.Supp. 475,

485 (D.C.Cal.1981) (citing *Trafficante v. Metropolitan Life Ins. Co.*, 409 U.S. 205, 209, 93 S.Ct. 364, 366–67, 34 L.Ed.2d 415 (1972))).

With respect to Title II, the City further argues that we should respect the different language Congress chose to employ in Titles I and III, which define discrimination to include conduct directed at an entity based on its relationship or association with disabled persons. See 42 U.S.C. § 12112(b)(4) (Title I); 42 U.S.C. § 12182(b)(1)(E) (Title III). According to the City, because Title II does not contain similar language, Congress intended to prevent standing based on association under this section. Although courts generally should be reluctant to conclude that the omission of language in one part of a statute that is included in another is unintentional, see e.g., *City of Chicago v. Environmental Defense Fund*, 511 U.S. 328, 337–38, 114 S.Ct. 1588, 1593, 128 L.Ed.2d 302 (1994), there is extensive support in this instance to read the specific examples of discrimination from the other two titles into Title II.

As a starting point, Title II sets out only a general definition of discrimination. By listing specific examples of discriminatory behavior in the other two titles, Congress surely did not intend to excuse similar discriminatory conduct by a public entity simply because such conduct is not spelled out in Title II. This common-sense interpretation of Title II is confirmed by the legislative history. The House Committee on Education and Labor indicated that Title II's prohibitions are to be "identical to those set out in the applicable provisions of titles I and III of this legislation." H.R.Rep. No. 101–485(II), at 84 (1990), reprinted in 1990 U.S.C.C.A.N. 303, 367. More specifically, the House Report on the ADA states that the prohibitions of discrimination on the basis of association from Titles I and III should be incorporated in the regulations implementing Title II. *Id.;* H.R.Rep. No. 485(III), at 51 (1990), *reprinted in* 1990 U.S.C.C.A.N. 445, 474; *see also Kinney v. Yerusalim*, 9 F.3d 1067, 1073 n. 6 (3d Cir.1993) (legislative history indicates that Titles II and III are to be read consistently).

As directed by the House Report, the regulations implementing Title II provide:

> A public entity shall not exclude or otherwise deny equal services, programs, or activities to an individual or entity because of the known disability of an individual with whom the individual or entity is known to have a relationship or association. 28 C.F.R. sec. 35.130(g).

The preamble to section 35 acknowledges that the regulation is based on the relevant sections from Titles I and III and that "[t]his paragraph was not contained in the proposed rule." 28 C.F.R. pt. 35, app. A at 470. Based on the inconsistency between the rule and the regulation, the City argues persuasively that we should not give the regulation "controlling weight." In light of the specific congressional mandate to include this paragraph in the regulations, however, and the fact that this particular construction of discrimination is not "manifestly contrary" to Title II's general discrimination prohibition, we give the regulation the weight to which it is due. See *Chevron,* 467 U.S. at 844, 104 S.Ct. at 2782–83. * * *

In any event, because we have already determined that Title II provides relief to "any person alleging discrimination," it is irrelevant whether Title II directly proscribes discrimination based on association with disabled persons. Accordingly, we affirm the district court's determination that IHS has standing to assert a claim under both the ADA and the Rehabilitation Act.

Assuming that the discrimination statutes apply to zoning decisions and that the appellees have standing, the City contends that the district court erred in concluding the appellees will likely be successful on the merits of their discrimination claims. The City argues that the appellees' claims will fail because (1) IHS's clients are not "qualified individuals with a disability" because they are not drug-free, (2) the appellees were not denied the benefits of the City's zoning activity, and (3) the City's zoning decision was not based on bias against chemically-dependent persons. We address each argument in turn.

The City claims that IHS has admitted that some of its clients are not drug-free and that therefore, under either statute the clients are excluded from the definition of "qualified individuals with a disability." See 42 U.S.C. § 12210(a) (term "does not include an individual who is currently engaging in the illegal use of drugs, when the covered entity acts on the basis of such use"); 29 U.S.C. § 706(8)(C)(i) (same). Although, we are not convinced that IHS has admitted that its clients are not drug-free, the program indisputably does not tolerate drug use by its participants. An inevitable, small percentage of failures should not defeat the rights of the majority of participants in the rehabilitation program who are drug-free and therefore disabled under both statutes. See 42 U.S.C. § 12210(b)(2); 29 U.S.C. § 706(8)(C)(ii)(II).

The City also argues that the appellees have not been denied the benefits of the City's zoning activity because they were able to participate in every step of the process: They were given full consideration by the Commissioner, the Corporation Counsel, the Planning Board, and the ZBA. In so arguing, the City has misconstrued the nature of the appellees' complaint. The appellees' claim is not premised on the denial of the right to participate in the zoning approval process. Rather, they allege that they have been denied the benefit of having the City make a zoning decision without regard to the disabilities of IHS's clients. They have therefore made a claim cognizable under both statutes of discrimination.

The City additionally contends that the appellees have not produced any evidence of the City's discriminatory motives in denying the building permit to IHS. There is little evidence in the record to support the ZBA's decision on any ground other than the need to alleviate the intense political pressure from the surrounding community brought on by the prospect of drug- and alcohol-addicted neighbors. The public hearings and submitted letters were replete with discriminatory comments about drug- and alcohol-dependent persons based on stereotypes and general, unsupported fears. * * * Although the City certainly may consider legitimate safety concerns in its zoning decisions, it may not base its decisions on the perceived harm from such stereotypes and generalized fears. As the district court found, a decision made in the context of strong, discriminatory opposition becomes tainted with discriminatory intent even if the decisionmakers personally have no strong views on the matter. *Innovative Health Sys.*, 931 F.Supp. at 243 (quoting *Association of Relatives & Friends of AIDS Patients v. Regulations & Permits Admin.*, 740 F.Supp. 95, 104 (D.P.R.1990)); see also *Support Ministries for Persons with AIDS, Inc. v. Village of Waterford, N.Y.*, 808 F.Supp. 120, 134 (N.D.N.Y.1992) (zoning officials who "bowed to political pressure" by those with animus against people with alcohol- and drug-related disabilities violated Fair Housing Act).

We also find the ZBA's decision to be highly suspect in light of the requirements set forth in the zoning ordinance. The Commissioner and the Corporation Counsel carefully reviewed IHS's application and gave detailed explanations for their approval. The Corporation Counsel analyzed the definition of "hospital or sanitaria" and concluded that because IHS was not an "institution for the purpose of serving general medical, surgical, psychiatric, physical therapy and rehabilitation purposes," it did not fall under this classification. The ZBA, on the other hand, simply stated, without explanation, that IHS was a clinic and thus an impermissible use in the downtown site. The ZBA ignored the requirements of the "hospital or sanitaria" classification and did not explain why it declined to follow the Corporation Counsel's straightforward analysis. Further, although made aware of other similar uses in the same district, the ZBA did not explain the distinction between IHS's proposed use and the other mental health professionals and social workers who do not work exclusively with chemically-dependent persons. On appeal, the City states that the ZBA's decision was "amply supported by legal arguments" without setting forth any of the supposed "legal arguments" for our consideration. The lack of a credible justification for the zoning decision raises an additional inference that the decision was based on impermissible factors, namely the chemical-dependent status of IHS's clients. Accordingly, we see no reason to disturb the district court's finding of likelihood of success on the merits.

* * *

Accordingly, we affirm the district court's grant of a preliminary injunction in favor of appellees, except with respect to Martin A., who lacks standing to pursue this claim.

Notes

1. Since the required accommodations are pretty much the same, plaintiffs tend to bring challenges alleging violations of the FHAA, the ADA and the Rehabilitation Act in their lawsuits. See, e.g., Dadian v. Village of Wilmette, 269 F.3d 831 (7th Cir.2001). Also see First Step, Inc. v. City of

New London, 247 F.Supp.2d 135 (D.Conn.2003) with facts very similar to the principal case.

2. It is often left to the Courts to figure out what constitutes a "reasonable accommodation" under the acts. In Regional Economic Community Action Program, Inc. v. City of Middletown, 294 F.3d 35 (2d Cir.2002) the Court said, "...a proper reasonable accommodation might assert that the zoning authority should have waived or modified its rule against elevators in residential dwellings to permit those who need them to use them and thereby have full access to and enjoyment of residences there." See, Oconomowoc Residential Programs v. City of Milwaukee, 300 F.3d 775 (7th Cir.2002) (a variance from the City zoning ordinance restricting group homes from operating within 2,500 feet of each other is a reasonable accommodation under both the ADA and the FHAA).

3. The requirement for a reasonable accommodation imposes an affirmative duty to modify local requirements when they discriminate against the handicapped. See, Liddy v. Cisneros, 823 F.Supp. 164, 176 (S.D.N.Y. 1993). The Courts have broadly defined what constitutes a "handicap" under the Act. For example, the following conditions have been found to be covered under the definition: alcoholism and drug addition (see, e.g., Oxford House v. Township of Cherry Hill, 799 F.Supp. 450 (D. N.J. 1991)); emotional problems and mental illness (see, e.g., Association for Advancement of the Mentally Handicapped, Inc. v City of Elizabeth, 876 F.Supp. 614 (D.N.J. 1994); old age (see, e.g., United States v. Commonwealth of Puerto Rico, 764 F.Supp. 220 (D.P.R. 1991)); AIDS and HIV (see, e.g., Support Ministries for Person With AIDS, Inc. v. Village of Waterford, 808 F.Supp. 120 (N.D.N.Y. 1992)); and homelessness (see, Stewart B. McKinney Foundation v. Town of Fairfield, 790 F.Supp. 1197 (D.Conn. 1992)).

D. TELECOMMUNICATIONS ACT OF 1996

The following introduction to Professor Carol A. Goforth's article, "A Bad Call: Preemption of State and Local Authority to Regulate Wireless Communication Facilities on the Basis of Radio Frequency Emissions," 44 N.Y. L. Sch. L. Rev. 311 (2001) provides a good overview of the status of local governments' ability to regulate the siting of wireless towers after the enactment of the Telecommunications Act of 1996 (citations omitted).

> Early in 1996, Congress enacted a complicated piece of federal legislation entitled the Telecommunications Act of 1996 (the "Telecom Act"). When President Clinton signed the Telecom Act into law on February 8, 1996, he characterized it as "truly revolutionary legislation that [would] bring the future to our doorstep." The legislation was promoted as being "pro-competitive," and "deregulatory," and supporters claimed that it would offer consumers lower prices, better service, and faster access to new technologies.
>
> The Telecom Act applies broadly to the entire telecommunications industry, and many of its provisions are of unquestioned benefit to the American public. However, buried among the many complicated provisions of the statute is a section which precludes

state and local governments from regulating the placement of "personal wireless facilities" on the basis of the "environmental effects" of radio-frequency emissions, to the extent that such emissions are within the Federal Communication Commission's safety guidelines. Although it may not be obvious, the technical phrase "personal wireless facilities" refers primarily to the towers which cellular and personal communications services (PCS) providers have been building in ever-increasing numbers. In addition, "environmental effects" is a euphemism which was apparently intended to encompass any impact that radio-frequency emissions may have on human health. Unfortunately, even though the FCC has promulgated exposure guidelines for such emissions, the Commission has never claimed to be an expert in human health matters and generally relies on industry to set the standards. The effects of radio-frequency (RF) emissions are only now being studied, and everyone acknowledges that the scientific data is far from complete.

As a practical matter, this seemingly trivial section in the massive Telecom Act removes from state and local governments power to make decisions about where cellular and PCS towers should be located in order to protect citizens from possible health risks. The potential magnitude of this problem becomes apparent when one considers the number of towers being built by the telecommunications industry.

By now, virtually every community in the country has been touched by the phenomenon which has been called "the pin-cushioning of America." Some commentators have complained that towers which provide space for the PCS and/or cellular antennas have been appearing "like mushrooms after the rain." It is predicted that 100,000 new towers will be needed in the next few years to accommodate the growing needs of these industries.

While state and local governments generally retain the ability to regulate the placement of such facilities on the basis of considerations such as aesthetics, they cannot promulgate zoning regulations or ordinances based on any potential health risks from the RF emissions from these towers. Moreover, in at least one state, the courts have found that the language in the Telecom Act also precludes individual citizens from presenting evidence about health risks in private litigation.

Industry claims such preemption is necessary in order to enable them to build out their systems, which they say everyone wants and needs. They argue that state and local regulation is both unnecessary and counter-productive because the FCC is already regulating RF exposure. On the other hand, critics complain that the Telecom Act, by preempting state and local regulation in this manner, has created "a serious threat to our health and environment in ways that Congress simply did not understand when they passed the Telecommunications Act of 1996." * * *

SPRINT SPECTRUM v. WILLOTH
United States Court of Appeals, Second Circuit, 1998.
176 F.3d 630.

JOHN M. WALKER, JR., CIRCUIT JUDGE:

* * *

On or about May 5, 1996, Sprint presented its proposal to build three cell sites to representatives from Ontario as part of its plan to provide PCS services to the town. * * * The Planning Board first considered Sprint's three applications at its public meeting on June 11, 1996. At the meeting, Sprint generally described the PCS technology and reviewed its plans. The Board decided to hold a public hearing on Sprint's application on July 9, 1996, and asked Sprint to submit a Full Environmental Assessment Form ("FEAF") and visual addendum for each application so that the Planning Board could determine whether Sprint was required to file an environmental impact statement ("EIS") pursuant to New York's State Environmental Quality Review Act ("SEQRA").

SEQRA requires agencies to evaluate whether pending actions have significant environmental consequences, and if so, requires the agency to go through an EIS procedure beginning with a draft EIS ("DEIS") and continuing through a final EIS ("FEIS") aimed at ferreting out the environmental consequences of approving a project as well as practicable mitigating measures.

Following the public hearing, the Board met to review Sprint's applications on August 13, 1996 in accordance with SEQRA's requirements. That meeting primarily revolved around alternative sites and network designs for the Town of Ontario which the Board had asked Sprint to consider. The discussions included whether two 250 foot towers located in the industrial or industrial transitional zone would meet Sprint's needs, and whether it would be feasible for Sprint's proposed towers to be lower.

At a special meeting held on September 3, 1996, the Board adopted a resolution "to declare a positive environmental impact" pursuant to SEQRA regarding the three proposed sites. The resolution indicated that there might be some potentially significant adverse environmental impact associated with Sprint's proposals, roughly described as impact on property values, visual impact and "cumulative impacts" of the proposed facilities and possible future facilities * * *

At its May 20, 1997 meeting, the Board accepted the DEIS as complete, and, after a public hearing on July 8, 1997, Sprint submitted a FEIS to the Board on August 8, 1997. * * *

On September 25, 1997, the Board, faced with a choice between three towers or none, concluded that Sprint had failed to mitigate the environmental impact to the largest extent practicable and denied the application.

Sprint challenged the Board's decision under the Telecommunications Act as well as under New York State law * * *

The Telecommunications Act of 1996 ("TCA"), codified at 47 U.S.C. § 151 et seq., is an omnibus overhaul of the federal regulation of communications companies, intended:

> to provide for a pro-competitive, de-regulatory national policy framework designed to accelerate rapidly private sector deployment of advanced telecommunications and information technologies and services ... by opening all telecommunications markets to competition....

H.R. Conf. Rep. No. 104–458, at 113 (1996). In furtherance of this goal, Congress enacted 47 U.S.C. § 332(c)(7) which limits the state and local government's authority to deny construction of wireless telecommunications towers, see id. § 332(c)(7)(B)(i), and regulates how such decisions must be made, see id. §§ 332(c)(7)(B)(ii)–(iv). Although the TCA preserves local zoning authority in all other respects over the siting of wireless facilities, id. § 332(c)(7)(A), "the method by which siting decisions are made is now subject to judicial oversight. Therefore, denials subject to the TCA are reviewed by this court more closely" than are other types of zoning decisions to which federal courts generally accord great deference.

The two principal limitations on local zoning authority, both of which are at issue in this case, are found in subsection B(i), which provides that state and local regulation of "the placement, construction, and modification of personal wireless service facilities ... (I) shall not unreasonably discriminate among providers of functionally equivalent services; and (II) shall not prohibit or have the effect of prohibiting the provision of personal wireless services." 47 U.S.C. § 332(c)(7)(B)(i).

A denial of a request to build wireless facilities must be "in writing and supported by substantial evidence contained in a written record," id. § 332(c)(7)(B)(iii), and not contrary to the limits on town authority set forth in id. § 332(c)(7)(B)(i). Whether a decision is supported by substantial evidence must be determined according to " 'the traditional standard used for judicial review of agency actions.' " *Cellular Tel. Co.,* 166 F.3d at 494. Substantial evidence requires evaluation of the entire record, including opposing evidence, and requires a decision to be supported by "less than a preponderance but more than a scintilla of evidence. 'It means such relevant evidence as a reasonable mind might accept as adequate to support a conclusion.' " *Cellular Tel. Co.,* 166 F.3d at 494.

Sprint claims it has been subjected to unreasonable discrimination in violation of subsection B(i)(I) because its application was treated less favorably than that of Frontier Corp., a cellular provider whose application for a single tower in the town's industrial area was approved by the Town Board in 1993. The record is sparse on this issue, but Sprint appears to base its claim on two grounds. First, Sprint asserts, and the Planning Board concedes, that Frontier did not have to undergo the extensive environmental review process with which Sprint had to contend. Second, Sprint points out that Frontier was permitted to construct a tower, consistent with its coverage plan, that allows it to provide in-building coverage, whereas Sprint's application for the three towers it requires to provide in-building coverage was denied.

Sprint has produced no direct evidence that Frontier provides greater coverage than Sprint would be able to if it were to site one or two towers in less sensitive parts of town. Sprint only points out that PCS systems (like Sprint's) require more towers than do analog cellular systems (like Frontier's) to provide the same level of service. * * *

We assume, arguendo, that the Board's treatment of Sprint's application could be construed as discriminatory because (1) Sprint, but not Frontier, was required to undergo a time-consuming and costly environmental quality review procedure, and (2) the Board's denial of Sprint's three tower application could disable Sprint from matching Frontier's level of coverage. Even so, we think that the Planning Board's actions still would not be "unreasonable" within the meaning of subsection B(i)(I). "[T]he Act explicitly contemplates that some discrimination among providers of functionally equivalent services is allowed. Any discrimination need only be reasonable." *AT & T Wireless PCS, Inc. v. City Council of Va. Beach,* 155 F.3d 423, 427 (4th Cir.1998). The legislative history of the TCA contemplated that the very form of discrimination asserted by Sprint would occur and should be permitted.

[T]he phrase "unreasonably discriminate among providers of functionally equivalent services" will provide localities with the flexibility to treat facilities that create different visual, aesthetic, or safety concerns differently to the extent permitted under generally applicable zoning requirements even if those facilities provide functionally equivalent services. For example, the conferees do not intend that if a State or local government grants a permit in a commercial district, it must also grant a permit for a competitor's 50–foot tower in a residential district.

In other words, local governments may reasonably take the location of the telecommunications tower into consideration when deciding whether: (1) to require a more probing inquiry, and (2) to approve an application for construction of wireless telecommunications facilities, even though this may result in discrimination between providers of functionally equivalent services. See *AT & T Wireless PCS,* 155 F.3d at 427 (discrimination based on traditional bases of zoning regulation such as preserving character of neighborhood and avoiding aesthetic blight is not unreasonable). As far as the record reveals, that is what occurred in this case. Thus, we reject Sprint's unreasonable discrimination claim.

Sprint claims that the Planning Board's refusal to approve its application to construct three towers "prohibit[s] or [has] the effect of prohibiting the provision of personal wireless services" in violation of subsection (B)(i)(II).

The essence of Sprint's argument is that it has the right under this provision of the TCA to construct any and all towers that, in its business judgment, it deems necessary to compete effectively with other telecommunications providers, wireless or not. Otherwise, Sprint argues in substance, the effect will be to "prohibit ... the provision of personal wireless services." This untenable position founders on the statutory language. Since Sprint admits it would never propose to build towers it deems unnecessary to compete successfully, a fact which undoubtedly will hold true for most service providers, such a rule would effectively nullify a local government's right to deny construction of wireless telecommunications facilities, a right explicitly contemplated in 47 U.S.C. § 332(c)(7)(B)(iii). See *AT & T Wireless PCS*, 155 F.3d at 428.

In support of its claim to provide services as it sees fit, Sprint points to the TCA's purposes "[t]o promote competition and reduce regulation in order to secure lower prices and higher quality services for American telecommunications consumers and encourage the rapid deployment of new telecommunications technologies." Pub.L. No. 104–104, 100 Stat. 56, preamble (1996). Sprint also argues correctly that some of the competition contemplated by the TCA may come from personal wireless services, since such services can be a substitute for traditional land-line based systems. See 47 U.S.C. § 332(c)(3)(A) (commercial mobile service providers not exempt from state-imposed universal availability requirements "where such services are a substitute for land line telephone exchange service for a substantial portion of the communications within such State").

We do not read the TCA to allow the goals of increased competition and rapid deployment of new technology to trump all other important considerations, including the preservation of the autonomy of states and municipalities. In the context of constructing a national wireless telecommunications infrastructure, Congress chose to preserve all local zoning authority "over decisions regarding the placement, construction, and modification of personal wireless service facilities," 47 U.S.C. § 332(c)(7)(A), subject only to the limitations set forth in section 332(c)(7)(B). Sprint's ability to compete with land-line based services simply is not part of the inquiry under subsection B. Subsection B(i)(I) speaks only to Sprint's ability to compete with "functionally equivalent services," which does not include land-line services. Because subsection B(i)(II) only considers whether a town's decision will have the effect of prohibiting personal wireless services in a given area, Sprint's reliance on that subsection to contend that it cannot be prohibited from competing effectively with land-line systems is misplaced.

* * *

The Planning Board's principal argument to the contrary is equally untenable. * * * Absent an explicit policy banning personal wireless services, the Board contends, courts can only consider whether in aggregate a town's repeated denials of applications have the effect of a general ban. Since Ontario does not have a general ban in effect, as evidenced by its earlier approval of Frontier's application and professed willingness to accept some level of PCS service, the Board insists its actions must necessarily be in conformance with subsection B(i)(II). We disagree with this reasoning.

The Planning Board's interpretation would essentially convert subsection B(i)(II) into a simple directive to consider applications on a case-by-case basis. * * * Since the Planning Board's interpretation would run counter to the TCA's stated goals, and since the plain language of the statute compels a solution that accommodates the TCA's purposes and that does not render any portion of subsection B(i)(II) superfluous, we refuse to adopt the Board's interpretation.

Construing subsection B(i)(II) to apply only to general bans would lead to the conclusion that, in the absence of an explicit anti-tower policy, a court would have to wait for a series of denied applications before it could step in and force a local government to end its illegal boycott of personal wireless services. That solution does not fit well or easily within the statutory scheme of expedited appeal set forth in subsection B(v) and the preferred remedy of imposing injunctive relief on local governments that impermissibly deny tower construction applications.

Interpreting subsection B(i)(II) as only prohibiting general bans also would lead to the untenable result that once personal wireless services are available somewhere within the jurisdiction of a state or local government, whether by virtue of a facility located outside or inside its borders, the state or local government could deny any further applications with impunity. * * * We believe that what is meant by the Act's proscription that local government regulation of wireless service facilities "shall not prohibit or have the effect of prohibiting the provision of personal wireless services" lies between the extreme positions argued by Sprint and the Planning Board. The question for us to resolve is what Congress meant by "personal wireless services." The plain statutory language of subsection B(i)(II) read in conjunction with the appropriate definitions set forth in the TCA provides the answer.

"It would be [a] gross understatement to say that the Telecommunications Act of 1996 is not a model of clarity." *AT & T Corp. v. Iowa Utils. Bd.*, 525 U.S. 366, 119 S.Ct. 721, 738, 142 L.Ed.2d 835 (1999). Our task, regrettably, requires a detailed parsing of the statutory language, including layers of highly technical definitions. From this exercise, however, we conclude that the parameters of the statutory proscription of local government's prohibition of "personal wireless services" in the context of this case depends upon a conception of "personal wireless services" that is the equivalent of the ability of mobile, handheld telephones to reach a cell site that provides access to a land-line exchange and allows phone calls to be made to and from the national telephone network.

"Personal wireless services" is defined, if somewhat opaquely, as "[1] commercial mobile services, [2] unlicensed wireless services, and [3] common carrier wireless exchange access services." 47 U.S.C. § 332(c)(7)(C)(i). Each of the three individual terms are further defined in the TCA, although some of the definitions are lacking in both clarity and apparent usefulness. Each will be considered in turn.

1. "Commercial mobile services" is essentially defined as mobile service for profit that makes interconnected service available to the public. See id. § 332(d)(1). "Interconnected service" is in turn defined as "service that is interconnected with the public switched network...." Id. § 332(d)(2). The FCC defines "public switched network," as "[a]ny common carrier switched network, whether by wire or radio, including local exchange carriers, interexchange carriers, and mobile service providers, that use the North American Numbering Plan in connection with the provision of switched services," 47 C.F.R. § 20.3, which in plain language means the public telephone network. See id. § 68.2. "Mobile service" is defined in pertinent part as "a radio communication service carried on between mobile stations or receivers and land stations." 47 U.S.C. § 153(27). "Commercial mobile services" therefore means a for profit radio communication services carried on between mobile stations or receivers and land stations that are connected to the national telephone network.

2. "Unlicensed wireless services," is defined as "the offering of telecommunications services using duly authorized devices which do not require individual licenses...." Id. § 332(c)(7)(C). Since Sprint's PCS network requires a license, that part of the definition is not relevant to this case.

3. "Common carrier wireless exchange access services," as with other definitions in this statutory maze, consists of several individually defined terms. Sprint is a "common carrier" as defined in id. § 153(10), because it offers its common carrier services for hire, and this definition therefore is pertinent to this case. "Exchange access" is defined as "the offering of access to telephone exchange services or facilities for the purpose of the origination or termination of telephone toll services." Id. § 153(16). In other words, this part of the definition of "personal wireless services" deals with the ability to make and receive telephone calls using wireless equipment.

For the reader who has chosen to follow this exercise, the end is near. Putting together the first and third components of the definition of "personal wireless services," those relevant to this case, we can conclude that the local government is proscribed from prohibiting for-profit radio communication services carried on between mobile stations or receivers and land stations that (1) are connected to the national telephone network and that (2) provide wireless phones with access to telephone exchange services or facilities for the purpose of the origination or termination of telephone toll services.

By speaking in terms of communications between land stations (cell sites that connect directly to land-lines) and mobile stations (wireless telephones) and access to facilities necessary to make and receive phone calls, the plain focus of the statute is on whether it is possible for a user in a given remote location to reach a facility that can establish connections to the national telephone network. In our view, therefore, the most compelling reading of subsection B(i)(II) is that local governments may not regulate personal wireless service facilities in such a way as to prohibit remote users from reaching such facilities. In other words, local governments must allow service providers to fill gaps in the ability of wireless telephones to have access to land-lines.

The Planning Board argues that our interpretation would render illusory the town's right to deny applications, a right contemplated in subsection B(iii). We disagree.

A local government may reject an application for construction of a wireless service facility in an under-served area without thereby prohibiting personal wireless services if the service gap can be closed by less intrusive means. There are numerous ways to limit the aesthetic impact of a cell site. It may be possible to select a less sensitive site, to use a preexisting structure or to camouflage the tower and/or antennae * * * A local government may also reject an application that seeks permission to construct more towers than the minimum required to provide wireless telephone services in a given area. A denial of such a request is not a prohibition of personal wireless services as long as fewer towers would provide users in the given area with some ability to reach a cell site.

Furthermore, once an area is sufficiently serviced by a wireless service provider, the right to deny applications becomes broader: State and local governments may deny subsequent applications without thereby violating subsection B(i)(II). The right to deny applications will still be tempered by subsection B(i)(I), which prohibits unreasonable discrimination. However, it is not unreasonably discriminatory to deny a subsequent application for a cell site that is substantially more intrusive than existing cell sites by virtue of its structure, placement or cumulative impact. We hold only that the Act's ban on prohibiting personal wireless services precludes denying an application for a facility that is the least intrusive means for closing a significant gap in a remote user's ability to reach a cell site that provides access to land-lines.

Turning to Sprint's application in this case, the evidence in the record establishes that two towers and possibly even a single tower would allow Sprint to provide in-vehicle coverage throughout the entire town of Ontario, and in-building coverage throughout most of it, including the more densely populated areas. Where the holes in coverage are very limited in number or size (such as the interiors of buildings in a sparsely populated rural area, or confined to a limited number of houses or spots as the area covered by buildings increases) the lack of coverage likely will be de minimis so that denying applications to construct towers necessary to fill these holes will not amount to a prohibition of service.

Because there is substantial evidence in the record to support the conclusion that virtually all of Ontario could be serviced with fewer than three towers, the Planning Board did not violate subsection B(i)(II)'s ban on prohibiting personal wireless services by rejecting Sprint's all or nothing application. See Town of Amherst, 173 F.3d at 14 (no prohibition of personal wireless services where "lower towers could be used (and possibly resited)").

The TCA imposes limits on the authority of state and local governments to restrict personal wireless services. The TCA itself does not provide the legal basis to deny an application to construct a personal wireless facility. That authority must be found in state or local law. In this case, it is state law that prescribes the Planning Board's obligation to deny a site plan that does not satisfy SEQRA's substantive and procedural requirements.

* * *

Aesthetics is generally a valid subject of municipal regulation and concern both under the Planning Board's review of a site plan. While there are times when "the inclusion of a permitted use in a local zoning ordinance is tantamount to a legislative finding that the permitted use is in harmony with the general zoning plan and will not adversely affect the local community," WEOK Broad. Corp., 79 N.Y.2d at 383, 583 N.Y.S.2d 170, 592 N.E.2d 778, the fact that the towers constitute a permitted use is "by no means determinative," id. A local zoning ordinance permitting a specific type of structure, such as radio or television towers, may give rise to a presumption "that the aesthetic visual impact of the towers was . . . considered at the time that radio and television towers were included as permitted uses in the . . . zone." Id. But no such presumption is warranted here because the pertinent zoning ordinance permits "utility substations," a term encompassing a multitude of structures. This general term does not support the inference that the Ontario Town Board considered and accepted the aesthetic impact of telecommunications towers. To the contrary, a natural reading of the applicable zoning ordinance is that the Town Board left open for future consideration by the Planning Board on a case-by-case basis the compatibility between a proposed structure and the affected neighborhood. Consequently, the Planning Board is neither precluded from evaluating the aesthetic impact of Sprint's proposal, nor must it overcome a presumption that Sprint's towers are in conformance with the neighborhood character.

The Board's decision to reject Sprint's application on aesthetic grounds will be impervious to attack in the courts where "the Board . . . has made a reasoned elaboration resulting from its 'hard look' pursuant to SEQRA review such that it can be concluded that its findings and determination are supported by substantial evidence," id. and is not otherwise "affected by an error of law, or its decision was not rational, or is arbitrary or capricious. . . ." Id.

* * *

Sprint's contrary assertions notwithstanding, the evidence in the record before us is more than adequate to support the Planning Board's conclusion that Sprint's three tower proposal would have a significant negative aesthetic impact. Sprint submitted information about minimum tower height requirements and photographic simulations, admitting that "[b]y necessity, the tower will be visible from a wide area surrounding the site." The real estate experts consulted by the Planning Board stated that the towers would have a stigmatizing effect based in part on aesthetics which would reduce the buyer pool, leading to a 10% to 25% reduction in property values. The stigmatizing effect is substantiated by a letter written by Sprint's attorney to the neighboring town of Walworth's planning board, explaining Sprint's difficulties in finding alternate property sites. A real estate expert hired by Sprint even admitted that "a diminished supply of potential buyers ... concededly may exist for a property which views or is in the vicinity of a nearby tower installation," but predicted that the property value would not be affected. The Planning Board was, of course, entitled to disregard that prediction where two of its own real estate experts concluded otherwise.

* * *

The Planning Board also found that approving Sprint's application would set a precedent that could "result [in] ... a large number of towers in the town," and concluded that "the cumulative impact of multiple towers would have a significant environmental impact on the Town of Ontario." Sprint challenges this analysis, arguing that the Planning Board could not consider the cumulative impact of future applicants because no applications were currently pending. We disagree. * * * Given the Planning Board's correct determination that it could not discriminate between providers, the nexus between Sprint's application and the identified cumulative effects is so close that the Planning Board acted well within its discretion in considering the cumulative effects of Sprint's application.

* * *

Affirmed.

Note

A large number of cases can be found interpreting the Telecommunications Act of 1996. See, for some representative examples, Independent Wireless One Corp. v. Town of Charlotte, 242 F.Supp.2d 409 (D.Vt. 2003); USCOC of Virginia RSA#3, Inc. v. Montgomery County, 245 F.Supp.2d 817 (W.D.Va. 2003).

Further Notes on Federal Preemption

Normally, we do not think of the federal government setting out to override local land use regulations, and indeed that issue is rarely discussed in the formulation of federal law or regulations. However, in recent years more and more instances appear to conflict—or apparently conflict—between local land use ordinances and federal statutes or regulations. Cataloging all such conflicts is impossible, however the previous sections highlighted the issues that are currently heavily litigated. Other examples of federal preemption in the land use arena include:

1. The Federal Railway Safety Act has been held to preempt all local railroad safety legislation (except state law in an area where the Secretary of Transportation has not issued a regulation or order, and stricter state law is necessary). CSX Transportation, Inc. v. City of Plymouth, 86 F.3d 626 (6th Cir.1996). In this case the court held that a local ordinance prohibiting trains from obstructing streets for more than five minutes was preempted by the federal act. The reasoning was that compliance with the local ordinance would require railroads to schedule shorter, more frequent trains, with a concomitant effect on train traffic accident rates. Many communities where railroads still operate have ordinances like the one held preempted.

2. In Payless ShoeSource, Inc. v. Town of Penfield, New York, 934 F.Supp. 540 (W.D.N.Y.1996), the court considered the application of a town sign ordinance that required all commercial signs in a particular area to be either yellow, red, or white. The owner of a retail shoe store claimed that the sign ordinance conflicted with a federally registered trademark. The trademarked sign was yellow with two orange-colored "O"s. The court held that the sign ordinance was not preempted by the federal Lanham Act provision prohibiting a state or one of its subdivisions from requiring "alteration" of a federally registered mark.

3. Local regulation of television satellite dishes and antennas was specifically preempted by FCC regulation. 47 C.F.R. § 25.104 et seq. This specific preemption came about as a result of widespread aesthetic concerns, particularly in suburban communities, when satellite receiving dishes became popular in the 1970's and thereafter. See Loschiavo v. City of Dearborn, 33 F.3d 548 (6th Cir.1994), holding that the FCC regulation precluding enforcement of zoning restrictions regulating satellite dishes created a private right of action under § 1983.

4. The National Manufactured Housing and Safety Standards Act, 42 U.S.C.A. §§ 5401–5426 has been held to preempt city ordinances imposing greater safety requirements for mobile or manufactured homes. Scurlock v. City of Lynn Haven, Florida, 858 F.2d 1521 (11th Cir.1988); but the act does not preempt zoning of mobile home locations, King v. City of Bainbridge, 276 Ga. 484, 577 S.E.2d 772 (2003).

5. The Stewart B. McKinney Homeless Assistance Act, 42 U.S.C.A. § 11301 et seq. requires federal agencies to make surplus and underutilized federal property available to lease to organizations wishing to provide housing for homeless persons. This act was held to preempt local zoning ordinances in United States v. Village of New Hempstead, New York, 832 F.Supp. 76 (S.D.N.Y.1993).

6. CERCLA (Comprehensive Environmental Response, Compensation and Liability Act) has been held to preempt conflicting state or local regulation ("conflict preemption"). See, e.g., United States v. Denver, 100 F.3d 1509 (10th Cir.1996). This case pitted a local zoning restriction on maintenance of hazardous waste in industrial zones against an EPA order requiring the owner of a site in the city to do on-site solidification of soils contaminated with radioactive waste.

7. Environmental Justice is the fair treatment and meaningful involvement of all people regardless of race, color, national origin, or income with respect to the development, implementation, and enforcement of environmental laws, regulations, and policies. Fair treatment means that no group of people, including a racial, ethnic, or a socioeconomic group, should bear a disproportionate share of the negative environmental consequences resulting from industrial, municipal, and commercial operations or the execution of federal, state, local, and tribal programs and policies. Meaningful involvement means that: (1) potentially affected community residents have an appropriate opportunity to participate in decisions about a proposed activity that will affect their environment and/or health; (2) the public's contribution can influence the regulatory agency's decision; (3) the concerns of all participants involved will be considered in the decision making process; and (4) the decision makers seek out and facilitate the involvement of those potentially affected. In sum, environmental justice is the goal to be achieved for all communities and persons across this Nation. Environmental justice is achieved when everyone, regardless of race, culture, or income, enjoys the same degree of protection from environmental and health hazards and equal access to the decision-making process to have a healthy environment in which to live, learn, and work. A federal Interagency Working Group on Environmental Justice (IWG) was established in 1994 pursuant to Executive Order 12898. The National Environmental Justice Advisory Council (NEJAC) is a federal advisory committee established by charter on September 30, 1993, to provide independent advice, consultation, and recommendations to the Administrator of the U.S. Environmental Protection Agency (EPA) on matters related to environmental justice. See, www.epa.gov/compliance/environmentaljustice.

Although there is no federal statute or specific regulation entitled "environmental justice," advocates successfully utilize the authority of the Civil Rights Act of 1964 to enforce environmental justice principles. A recent study by the National Academy of Public Administration, Addressing Community Concerns: How Environmental Justice Relates to Land Use Planning and Zoning (July 2003), clearly signals that planning and zoning decision makers need to be more aware of environmental concerns (the report is available at http://www.napawah.org/pubs/ej.pdf). There is likely to be a flurry of lawsuits over the next decade challenging the decisions and actions of local officials relative to land use matters and environmental justice. For an excellent summary of the various land use planning and zoning techniques that impact environmental justice concerns, see Craig Anthony Arnold, Planning Milagros: Environmental Justice and Land Use Regulation, 76 Denv. U. L. Rev. 1 (1998).

8. The Endangered Species Act of 1973, 16 U.S.C. secs. 1531–1544 provides "for conservation, protection and propagation of endangered species ... by Federal action and by encouraging the establishment of State endangered species conservation programs." S. Rep. No. 307, 93rd Cong., 1st Sess., 1, reprinted in 1973 U.S. Code Cong. & Admin, News 2989–90. Section 9 of the ESA prohibits "any person or agency" from "taking" an endangered species of fish or wildlife. This is where local land use decisionmaking is implicated. See, Comment, The Scope of Federal Authority Under the Endangered Species Act: Implications for Local Land Use Planning, 65 Alb.

L. Rev. 497 (2001) and Coggins & Russell, Beyond Shooting Snail Darters in Pork Barrels: Endangered Species and Land Use in America, 70 Geo. L.J. 1433 (1982).

SECTION 2. STATE PREEMPTION

The previous section demonstrated areas where the federal government has intervened through statute and/or regulation to preempt or limit local control over certain types of land uses. The state governments may also play a significant role in limiting or restricting local decision-making control in certain areas. Consider the cases below and the notes that follow.

A. MINING

GERNATT ASPHALT PRODUCTS, INC. v. TOWN OF SARDINIA

New York Court of Appeals, 1996.
87 N.Y.2d 668, 642 N.Y.S.2d 164, 664 N.E.2d 1226.

SIMONS, J.

Petitioner challenges the legality of amendments to the Town of Sardinia's Zoning Ordinance which eliminated mining as a permitted use throughout the Town. The principal issues presented are whether: (1) the Town violated various statutory provisions relating to referral and public notice of the amendments when it enacted some but not all of the amendments that were proposed; (2) the New York State Mined Land Reclamation Law supersedes the Town's authority to amend its Zoning Ordinance in a manner that eliminates mining as a permitted use throughout the Town; and (3) the Town's action constituted impermissible exclusionary zoning. * * *

The Town of Sardinia is a small rural community located in western New York. Farming is the economic mainstay but it is rich in deposits of extractable minerals. Eight mines, covering over 600 acres, are presently located within the Town. These mining uses were lawful under the Town Zoning Ordinance adopted in 1969, which permitted mining in all R–A districts and, by incorporation, in all other districts in the Town. Town Board approval of a mining site was required, however, and approval was conditioned on consideration of the possible nuisance to neighbors of the proposed site and the miner's plan to restore the land after mining operations ceased.

Petitioner Gernatt has conducted mining operations at several sites within the Town for many years and presently owns three operating mines. In 1989, it acquired a 400–acre parcel of land known as the Gabel Thomas property. It has applied to the Department of Environmental Conservation (DEC) for the necessary State permit to mine the site but has not yet received one. Following petitioner's purchase of the Gabel Thomas site, the Town became concerned about the effect its development might have on this rural community, and took a number of steps to regulate the expansion of mining within its borders.

This litigation focuses on three ordinances introduced by the Town Board at its meeting August 18, 1993. The first two were adopted. Section 6.02(A)(5) of the existing Zoning Ordinance made quarries, clay, sand and gravel pits permitted uses in R–A districts, and the first ordinance adopted at the August meeting repealed that section. The second ordinance repealed section 7.07 which required approval of the Town Board to excavate. The third proposal, which designated quarries, clay, sand and gravel pits as specially permitted uses but only at sites currently authorized by DEC, was tabled for further study.

It is important to note three points about the Town's actions and the three proposed amendments: (1) the amendments as enacted did not *prohibit* or terminate existing mining operations throughout the Town—they continued as lawful, but nonconforming uses; (2) the only functional difference between the amendments as proposed and as enacted is the legal status of currently operating mines: while mining on existing sites is now a nonconforming use under the Town's Zoning Ordinance, had the amendments been adopted as proposed mining on existing sites would have been a specially permitted use; and (3) even if all three proposed amendments had been enacted, *new* mining would not have been permitted in the Town, because proposed section 7.07 authorized special permits only for mining sites permitted by the DEC at the time the legislation was enacted.

Petitioner instituted this special proceeding seeking to annul the Board's adoption of the "repealer" amendments and to enjoin the Town from enforcing the nonconforming use provision of its Zoning Ordinance. * * * On appeal, the Appellate Division concluded * * * that the adopted amendments were inconsistent with and preempted by the New York State Mined Land Reclamation Law * * *.

II. THE MINED LAND RECLAMATION LAW

The Mined Land Reclamation Law (ECL 23–2701 et seq. [the MLRL]) is a comprehensive legislative scheme which broadly empowers the Department of Environmental Conservation to regulate the mining industry in this State. The policies underlying the statute are to foster and encourage an economically sound and stable mining and minerals industry, to manage well depletable mineral resources, and to provide for the reclamation of mined land (see, ECL 23–2703[1] [as originally enacted, L 1974, ch 1043, and as amended, L 1991, ch 166]). The Legislature sought to achieve those purposes by replacing the existing patchwork of local regulatory ordinances with "standard and uniform restrictions and regulations" and by addressing the environmental issues related to reclamation of abandoned mining sites (*Matter of Frew Run Gravel Prods. v. Town of Carroll,* 71 N.Y.2d 126, 131–133, 524 N.Y.S.2d 25, 518 N.E.2d 920). As originally enacted, the provisions of the statute expressly superseded "all other state and local laws relating to the extractive mining industry * * * [except] local zoning ordinances or other local laws which impose stricter mined land reclamation standards or requirements than those found herein" (ECL 23-2703 [former (2)]).

In *Frew Run,* we addressed whether the MLRL preempted a municipality's zoning ordinance when the DEC had issued a permit to operate a sand and gravel mine at a site that lay within a zoning district in which mining was not a permitted use. We noted that under the MLRL, the preemption question was one of statutory construction, not a search for implied preemption, because the Legislature included within the MLRL an express supersession clause. We concluded that the MLRL did not preempt the local zoning ordinance which limited mining activities to certain zoned districts (see, *Matter of Frew Run,* 71 N.Y.2d, at 130-131, 524 N.Y.S.2d 25, 518 N.E.2d 920, supra).

The supersession clause of the MLRL has since been amended (see, ECL 23-2703[2], amended by L 1991, ch 166, § 228), and we must now determine whether the amendments to the Zoning Ordinance of the Town of Sardinia which eliminated mining as a permitted use in all zoning districts are preempted by the Mined Land Reclamation Law. Relying on the amendment to the MLRL as a restatement of the policy in favor of fostering and promoting the mining industry in this State, and contending that our holding in Frew Run leaves municipalities with the limited authority to determine in which zoning districts mining may be conducted but not the authority to prohibit mining in all zoning districts, petitioner contends that the "repealer provisions" enacted by the Town of Sardinia are invalid because they are preempted by the Mined Land Reclamation Law. Neither the Mined Land Reclamation Law as amended nor the holding in *Frew Run* leads to that conclusion.

In *Frew Run,* we distinguished between zoning ordinances and local ordinances that directly regulate mining activities. Zoning ordinances, we noted, have the purpose of regulating land use generally. Notwithstanding the incidental effect of local land use laws upon the extractive mining industry, zoning ordinances are not the type of regulatory provision the Legislature foresaw as preempted by Mined Land Reclamation Law; the distinction is between ordinances that regulate property uses and ordinances that regulate mining activities (see, *Matter of Frew Run,* 71 N.Y.2d, at 131, 524 N.Y.S.2d 25, 518 N.E.2d 920, supra; see also, *Matter of Hunt Bros. v. Glennon,* 81 N.Y.2d 906, 597 N.Y.S.2d 643, 613 N.E.2d 549; compare, *Matter of Briarcliff Assocs. v. Town of Cortlandt,* 144 A.D.2d 457, 534 N.Y.S.2d 215, lv. denied 74 N.Y.2d 611, 546 N.Y.S.2d 555, 545 N.E.2d 869; *Matter of Northeast Mines v. State of New York Dept. of Envtl. Conservation,* 113 A.D.2d 62, 494 N.Y.S.2d 914, lv. denied 68 N.Y.2d 612, 510 N.Y.S.2d 1026, 503 N.E.2d 123). In *Frew Run,* we concluded that nothing in the plain language, statutory scheme, or legislative purpose of the Mined Land Reclamation Law suggested that its reach "was intended to be broader than necessary to preempt conflicting regulations dealing with mining operations and reclamation of mined lands" (id., at 133, 524 N.Y.S.2d 25, 518 N.E.2d 920 [emphasis added]), and that in the absence of a clear expression of legislative intent to preempt local control over land use, the statute could not be read as preempting local zoning authority.

The express supersession provision of the MLRL (ECL 23-2703), was amended in 1991. It now provides:

"For the purposes stated herein, this title shall supersede all other state and local laws relating to the extractive mining industry; provided, however, that nothing in this title shall be construed to prevent any local government from * * * enacting or enforcing local zoning ordinances or laws which determine permissible uses in zoning districts" (ECL 23-2703[2] [b]).

The patent purpose of the 1991 amendment was to withdraw from municipalities the authority to enact local laws imposing land reclamation standards that were stricter than the State-wide standards under the MLRL. The language of this amended provision accords with the distinction drawn in Frew Run between zoning ordinances and local ordinances that regulate mining activities, and there is nothing in the sparse legislative history of the amendment to the statute suggesting that the Legislature intended the MLRL to go further and limit municipalities' broad authority to govern land use.

Petitioner contends that the amendments to the Zoning Ordinance prohibit mining throughout the Town. In its view the amendments necessarily regulate mining and are therefore preempted by the MLRL because they conflict with the statute's stated purpose of fostering the mining industry in this State. It relies on this Court's observation in *Frew Run* that while the Town of Carroll prohibited mining in one district, it allowed mining by special permit in another. At bottom, petitioner's argument is that if the land within the municipality contains extractable minerals, the statute obliges the municipality to permit them to be mined somewhere within the municipality.

Nothing in the MLRL imposes that obligation on municipalities, nor has the Legislature broadened the preemptive reach of the statute to restrict municipal authority to regulate permissible uses of land within the municipality. Rather, in amending ECL 23-2703 in 1991, the Legislature expressly excluded that authority from its preemptive reach. Thus, we conclude that the MLRL does not preempt the Town's authority to determine that mining should not be a permitted use of land within the Town, and to enact amendments to the local zoning ordinance in accordance with that determination.

* * *

The municipality's authority to amend its Zoning Ordinance to eliminate mining as a permitted use in the municipality is not preempted by the Mined Land Reclamation Law, because that statute specifically exempts local zoning enactments from its preemptive reach. * * *

Accordingly, the order of the Appellate Division should be reversed, with costs, and the order and judgment of Supreme Court, Erie County, reinstated.

KAYE C.J., and TITONE, BELLACOSA, SMITH, LEVINE and CIPARICK, JJ., concur.

B. AGRICULTURAL USES

CRAIG v. COUNTY OF CHATHAM
Supreme Court of North Carolina, 2002.
356 N.C. 40, 565 S.E.2d 172.

LAKE, CHIEF J.

The issues raised here on review require the interpretation of the North Carolina General Statutes and application of North Carolina case law governing the question of preemption of county ordinances by the State. Specifically, the primary issues presented, defendants' first and second issues, relate to the validity of two Chatham County ordinances passed by the Chatham County Board of Commissioners and certain rules passed by the Chatham County Board of Health, all regulating swine farms.

On 6 April 1998, the Chatham County Board of Commissioners enacted the "Chatham County Ordinance Regulating Swine Farms" (the Swine Ordinance) and "An Ordinance to Amend the Chatham County Zoning Ordinance to Provide for Regulation of Swine Farms" (the Zoning Ordinance). The Swine Ordinance regulates swine farms "raising 250 or more animals of the porcine species," through a permitting system which affects currently existing farms and those which expand in the future. The Swine Ordinance is applicable to all such swine farms without regard to whether the farm is served by an animal waste management system having a design capacity of 600,000 pounds "steady state live weight" or greater. Under the Swine Ordinance, the owners of swine farms are assigned the financial responsibility for future contaminations that might occur, which responsibility is ensured through both a written agreement with the Chatham County Health Department and some form of financial security. The Swine Ordinance also provides requirements for setback distances and buffer zones for farms and sprayfields, and semiannual testing of wells on the farm.

The Zoning Ordinance is applicable only to swine farms that are "served by an animal waste management system having a design capacity of 600,000 pounds steady state live weight (SSLW) or greater." The Zoning Ordinance limits swine farms to areas of the county which are zoned either "Light Industrial" or "Heavy Industrial." The Zoning Ordinance further requires the swine farmer to obtain a conditional use permit, with issuance contingent upon a showing of compliance with the Swine Ordinance.

On 28 April 1998, the Chatham County Board of Health enacted the "Chatham County Board of Health Swine Farm Operation Rules" (Health Board Rules), which apply to all swine farms raising "250 or more animals of the porcine species," without regard to the design capacity of the farm's animal waste management system. The Health Board Rules are virtually identical to the Swine Ordinance.

On 2 September 1998, Timothy H. Craig and the Chatham County Agribusiness Council (CCAC) filed a complaint against defendants in superior court seeking a declaration that the Swine Ordinance, Zoning Ordinance and Health Board Rules were not legally valid. On 2 September 1999, CCAC filed a motion for partial summary judgment, and in September 1999, defendants filed an answer and a motion for summary judgment. The trial court granted defendants' motion for summary judgment and denied CCAC's motion for partial summary judgment. Plaintiffs appealed to the Court of Appeals, which affirmed in part and reversed in part the ruling of the trial court, holding that the Health Board Rules and the Swine Ordinance are preempted by state law but holding that the trial court was correct in granting summary judgment to defendants as to the Zoning Ordinance. This Court subsequently allowed defendants' petition for discretionary review and plaintiffs' conditional petition for discretionary review as to an additional issue.

Defendants first contend that the Court of Appeals erred in concluding that state law preempts the regulation of swine farms and thus prevents county commissioners and a local board of health from adopting an ordinance and rules regulating swine farms.

The enactment and operation of a general, statewide law does not necessarily prevent a county from regulating in the same field. However, preemption issues arise when it is shown that the legislature intended to implement statewide regulation in the area, to the exclusion of local regulation. See N.C.G.S. § 160A–174(b)(5) (2001). " '[M]unicipal by-laws and ordinances must be in harmony with the general laws of the State, and whenever they come in conflict with the general laws, the by-laws and ordinances must give way.' " *State v. Williams,* 283 N.C. 550, 552, 196 S.E.2d 756, 757 (1973) (quoting *Town of Washington v. Hammond,* 76 N.C. 33, 36 (1877)). The law of preemption is grounded in the need to avoid dual regulation. See, e.g., id. at 554, 196 S.E.2d at 759.

Counties are creatures of the General Assembly and have no inherent legislative powers. *High Point Surplus Co. v. Pleasants,* 264 N.C. 650, 654, 142 S.E.2d 697, 701 (1965); *DeLoatch v. Beamon,* 252 N.C. 754, 757, 114 S.E.2d 711, 714 (1960). They are instrumentalities of state government and possess only those powers the General Assembly has conferred upon them. *Harris v. Board of Comm'rs of Washington Cty.,* 274 N.C. 343, 346, 163 S.E.2d 387, 390 (1968); *High Point Surplus,* 264 N.C. at 654, 142 S.E.2d at 701. Hence, we look to the North Carolina General Statutes to see what powers the General Assembly has delegated broadly to counties on a statewide basis or more specifically to counties such as Chatham in the area of swine farm regulation.

The General Assembly, in N.C.G.S. § 153A–121, has delegated to counties the power and authority to enact ordinances. That statute provides in part:

A county may by ordinance define, regulate, prohibit, or abate acts, omissions, or conditions detrimental to the health, safety, or welfare of its citizens. N.C.G.S. § 153A–121(a) (2001).

However, N.C.G.S. § 160A–174, as interpreted and applied by our case law, provides limitations on the exercise of this power.

The relevant portions of N.C.G.S. § 160A–174 state:

> A city ordinance shall be consistent with the Constitution and laws of North Carolina and of the United States. An ordinance is not consistent with State or federal law when:
>
> * * *
>
> (5) The ordinance purports to regulate a field for which a State or federal statute clearly shows a legislative intent to provide a complete and integrated regulatory scheme to the exclusion of local regulation.

This Court has held that N.C.G.S. § 160A–174 is applicable to counties as well as cities. *State v. Tenore,* 280 N.C. 238, 185 S.E.2d 644 (1972).

N.C.G.S. § 130A–39 delegates power to the local board of health to adopt a more stringent rule in an area regulated by the Commission for Health Services or the Environmental Management Commission where, in the opinion of the local board of health, a more stringent rule is required to protect the public health. N.C.G.S. § 130A–39(b) (2001).

The Commission for Health Services and the Environmental Management Commission (EMC) are state agencies. The governor appoints all members serving on the EMC and a majority of the members serving on the Commission for Health Services. N.C.G.S. § 143B–283(a) (1999) (amended in 2001); N.C.G.S. § 130A–30(a) (2001). A local board of health is limited in its rule-making powers in that the regulation must be "related to the promotion or protection of health." *City of Roanoke Rapids v. Peedin,* 124 N.C.App. 578, 587, 478 S.E.2d 528, 533 (1996).

In holding that the Swine Ordinance and the Health Board Rules were preempted by state law, the Court of Appeals reasoned that the Chatham County Board of Commissioners and the Chatham County Board of Health sought to regulate an area in which the General Assembly had provided a "complete and integrated regulatory scheme" of swine farm regulations. *Craig v. County of Chatham,* 143 N.C.App. 30, 545 S.E.2d 455 (2001); see also N.C.G.S. § 160A–174(b)(5). We concur in this assessment.

In determining if the General Assembly intended to provide statewide regulation to the exclusion of local regulation, we must decide if it has shown a clear legislative intent to provide such a "complete and integrated regulatory scheme."

Defendants argue that when the General Assembly intends to preempt the field, it will do so through an express statement of intent.

Furthermore, they argue that without such an expression of intent, this Court would be merely imposing its own judgment for that of the General Assembly in finding that the General Assembly preempted the field. We disagree.

If the General Assembly were required to provide an express statement of intent, N.C.G.S. § 160A–174(b)(5) would be meaningless. The General Assembly can create a regulatory scheme which, though not expressly exclusory, is so complete in covering the field that it is clear any regulation on the county level would be contrary to the statewide regulatory purpose.

In determining the purpose and intent of the General Assembly in adopting the swine regulation statutes, we must primarily look to " 'the spirit of the act[ ] and what the act seeks to accomplish.' " *State v. Anthony,* 351 N.C. 611, 615, 528 S.E.2d 321, 323 (2000) (quoting *Taylor v. Taylor,* 343 N.C. 50, 56, 468 S.E.2d 33, 37 (1996)). Where legislative intent is not readily apparent from the act, it is appropriate to look at various related statutes in pari materia so as to determine and effectuate the legislative intent. *Brown v. Flowe,* 349 N.C. 520, 523–24, 507 S.E.2d 894, 896 (1998).

* * *

In *Greene v. City of Winston–Salem,* 287 N.C. 66, 213 S.E.2d 231 (1975), this Court found upon review of an ordinance enacted by the City of Winston–Salem that there was a legislative intent to preempt. The City of Winston–Salem enacted an ordinance which required sprinkler systems in high-rise buildings. Id. at 67, 213 S.E.2d at 232. The City referred to a state law which required sprinkler systems in certain buildings in support of its argument that state law did not give the State Building Code Council sole regulatory authority in the area. Id. at 75, 213 S.E.2d at 237. This Court noted that the General Assembly does not have to delegate all or sole authority in the particular regulatory field to one state agency in order to establish that there is a "complete and integrated regulatory scheme." Id.

There are two components to the statewide swine farm regulations found in the North Carolina General Statutes, the "Swine Farm Siting Act" and the "Animal Waste Management Systems." In examining each of these, we will look to any statement of "purpose" and "intent" in an effort to determine if the General Assembly has created a "complete and integrated system" for swine farm regulation in the state.

The Swine Farm Siting Act, N.C.G.S. §§ 106–800 to –805 (2001), governs the placement of swine farms and lagoons, and provides in its section designated "Purpose" the following:

> [C]ertain limitations on the siting of swine houses and lagoons for swine farms can assist in the development of pork production, which contributes to the economic development of the State, by lessening the interference with the use and enjoyment of adjoining property. N.C.G.S. § 106–801.

This expression of intent is significant in that it notes pork production is important to the economic stability of the state, yet recognizes that adjoining landowners have a right to the use and enjoyment of their land. This stated intent also shows that the General Assembly was trying to reach a balance between two very important interests, the economy of North Carolina and the right of a landowner to enjoy his land with minimal interference. If each of North Carolina's one hundred counties is free to create its own particularized regulations for swine farms, the overall balance which the General Assembly has reached within a uniform plan for the entire state will be lost. The result could well be that the rights of adjacent landowners in each individual county would be substantially elevated above the rights of swine farmers to workable, nonexcessive regulations. Swine farms would be forced to comply with both state and county regulations. Furthermore, a swine farmer with a large farm that crossed the boundaries of one or more counties in North Carolina conceivably would have to conform the farm to the regulations established by various counties and those established by the state. Ultimately, such farms could be forced to adapt to differing, even conflicting, regulations. Any such dual regulation would present an excessive burden on swine farmers and the pork production industry as a whole.

The Animal Waste Management Systems component of the statewide regulations, N.C.G.S. §§ 143–215.10A to 215.10M (2001) (§ 143–215.10C altered in 1999; § 143–215.10B altered in 2001), provides in pertinent part: "It is the intention of the State to promote a cooperative and coordinated approach to animal waste management among the agencies of the State." N.C.G.S. § 143–215.10A (emphasis added). This unequivocal statement makes it clear that the purpose for creating these statutes was to regulate animal waste management at the state level. If each county were allowed to enact its own waste management guidelines, there could be no statewide "coordinated approach." Notably also, the agencies designated to implement the Animal Waste Management Systems statutes are exclusively state agencies. N.C.G.S. §§ 143–215.10A to –215.10M (permitting, inspection, and enforcement are vested in the Division of Water Quality, while the Soil and Water Conservation Commission is in charge of designating the technical specialists responsible for inspecting the waste management plans). The expression of intent further provides that one of the goals of the Act is "minimizing the regulatory burden." N.C.G.S. § 143–215.10A. Certainly, the stated goal of limiting or minimizing the burden of the regulatory scheme for waste management systems on swine farms would not be attainable if counties could impose additional burdens on swine farmers to comply with varying regulations.

Thus, from our review of the expressed "purpose" and "intent" of the Swine Farm Siting Act and the Animal Waste Management statutes, we conclude that these two components of North Carolina's swine farm regulations show an intention to cover the entire field of swine farm regulation in North Carolina.

* * *

The Animal Waste Management Systems component regulates swine farms even more extensively than the Swine Farm Siting Act. The Animal Waste Management Systems component creates a "permitting program" which requires swine farm owners to obtain a permit before constructing or operating any waste management system. N.C.G.S. § 143–215.10C(a). An "animal waste management system" is defined as practices "that provide for the collection, treatment, storage, or land application of animal waste." N.C.G.S. § 143–215.10B(3). To obtain the necessary permit, swine farm owners must submit to the EMC their waste management system plan, which has been approved by a technical specialist. N.C.G.S. § 143–215.10C(d). The Animal Waste Management Systems has detailed specifications as to how each farm's animal waste management system shall be designed, constructed and operated so as to prevent pollution. N.C.G.S. § 143–215.10C. It also provides a time limit upon which the EMC must approve or deny the permit after a new permit has been applied for or a renewal permit is sought. N.C.G.S. § 143–215.10C(c). In the event the EMC does not act in the required ninety days, the permit is considered to be approved. Id. The Animal Waste Management Systems component provides an extensive list of necessary parts for all animal waste management plans, such as provisions regarding periodic testing of waste products used on the farm as nutrient sources and a checklist of potential odor sources and management practices which are designed to minimize the source of the odor. N.C.G.S. § 143–215.10C(e). Any established swine farm waste management plan must require at least annual testing of the soil at crop sites where the waste has been applied to the land. N.C.G.S. § 143–215.10C(e)(6).

We conclude from the foregoing specifications that North Carolina's swine farm regulations, the Swine Farm Siting Act and the Animal Waste Management Systems statutes are so comprehensive in scope that the General Assembly must have intended that they comprise a "complete and integrated regulatory scheme" on a statewide basis, thus leaving no room for further local regulation.

Turning now to the Health Board Rules enacted by the Chatham County Board of Health, we note that they contain more stringent rules than those established in the EMC regulations. However, N.C.G.S. § 130A–39 specifically grants local boards of health the power to enact rules which are more strict when they are "required to protect the public health." N.C.G.S. § 130A–39(b). In an effort to protect the environment, the EMC has created a system of permitting and inspection which regulates waste management systems on farms, including swine farms of more than 250 swine. See 15A NCAC 2H.0217(a)(1)(A) (Sept.2001).

* * *

When we look at the Swine Farm Siting Act, the Animal Waste Management Systems statutes, and the EMC's regulation together, as parts of an overall scheme, we conclude that the Swine Ordinance and the Health Board Rules are incompatible with state law in that they purport to regulate a field in which the State has provided a "complete and integrated regulatory scheme" to the exclusion of local regulation. We therefore affirm the Court of Appeals in this regard.

We next address the issue of the ordinance to amend the Zoning Ordinance, which is before us upon plaintiffs' petition for discretionary review as to an additional issue. Plaintiffs contend the Court of Appeals erred in upholding the Zoning Ordinance. We agree.

"Counties have no inherent authority to enact zoning ordinances." *Jackson v. Guilford Cty. Bd. of Adjust.*, 275 N.C. 155, 162, 166 S.E.2d 78, 83 (1969). N.C.G.S. § 153A–340 is the statutory grant of power which provides counties with the authority to zone. There is, however, a specific limitation on this grant of power as it relates to swine farms:

> A county may adopt zoning regulations governing swine farms served by animal waste management systems having a design capacity of 600,000 pounds steady state live weight (SSLW) or greater provided that the zoning regulations may not have the effect of excluding swine farms served by an animal waste management system having a design capacity of 600,000 pounds SSLW or greater from the entire zoning jurisdiction. N.C.G.S. § 153A–340(b)(3) (2001).

The Zoning Ordinance, as amended, enacted by Chatham County requires all swine farms served by an animal waste management system having a design capacity of 600,000 pounds SSLW or greater, regardless of the actual number of swine, to be located in either a "Light" or "Heavy Industrial" district. The Zoning Ordinance further compels applicants to obtain a Construction/Expansion permit "as required by the [Swine Ordinance]."

Plaintiffs contend that in light of the Court of Appeals' determination that the Swine Ordinance is invalid, the Zoning Ordinance's express incorporation of the Swine Ordinance causes the Zoning Ordinance to fail as well. Specifically, plaintiffs argue that state preemption of the Swine Ordinance, as it is incorporated in the Zoning Ordinance, invalidates the Zoning Ordinance.

The Zoning Ordinance is not per se invalid. However, in this case, as written, the Zoning Ordinance cannot stand.

The sole restriction on zoning swine farms is that they "may not have the effect of excluding swine farms served by an animal waste management system having a design capacity of 600,000 pounds SSLW or greater from the entire zoning jurisdiction." N.C.G.S. § 153A–340(b)(3). Chatham County's Zoning Ordinance does not exclude all farms with an animal waste management system of 600,000 SSLW or greater, but merely restricts these farms to "Light" or "Heavy Industrial" districts within the county. The Zoning Ordinance complies with the restrictions established in section 153A–340(b)(3).

However, the requirement in the Zoning Ordinance that the applicant must have a Construction/Expansion permit obtained through compliance with the Swine Ordinance proves to be fatal. The Zoning Ordinance requires compliance with only a portion of the Swine Ordinance; however, that specific portion of the Swine Ordinance requires compliance with all other sections of the Swine Ordinance, to the extent the other sections are applicable to swine farms.

As we noted above, the Swine Ordinance cannot stand because it seeks to impose regulations on swine farmers where the State has shown an intent to cover the field of swine farm regulation. The Zoning Ordinance's attempt to incorporate the Swine Ordinance prevents us from sustaining its validity. Accordingly, we conclude that the Zoning Ordinance's incorporation of the Swine Ordinance invalidates the Zoning Ordinance.

* * *

AFFIRMED IN PART; REVERSED IN PART.

C. GROUP HOMES FOR THE MENTALLY ILL

JENNINGS v. NEW YORK STATE OFFICE OF MENTAL HEALTH

Court of Appeals of New York, 1997.
90 N.Y.2d 227, 660 N.Y.S.2d 352, 682 N.E.2d 953.

SMITH, J.

New York State policy has long favored the establishment of residential housing facilities to deinstitutionalize the treatment of mentally disabled persons. However, some residents of the Pine Hills community in the City of Albany (the City) believed that their neighborhood was already overcrowded with such facilities. The present dispute arose when the City filed an objection to the siting of the newest housing residence proposed for the area pursuant to Mental Hygiene Law § 41.34. Following a hearing, the Acting Commissioner of the New York State Office of Mental Health (the Commissioner) found that the proposed facility would not substantially alter the nature or character of the neighborhood in question.[1] We conclude that the determination of the Commis-

---

1. Mental Hygiene Law § 41.34(c)(5) provides: "In the event the municipality objects to establishment of a facility in the municipality because to do so would result in such a concentration of community residential facilities for the mentally disabled or combination of such facilities and other facilities licensed by other state agencies that the nature and character of areas within the municipality would be substantially altered; or the sponsoring agency objects to the establishment of a facility in the area or areas suggested by the municipality; or in the event that the municipality and sponsoring agency cannot agree upon a site, either the sponsoring agency or the municipality may request an immediate hearing before the commissioner to resolve the issue. The commissioner shall personally or by a hearing officer conduct such a hearing

sioner is supported by substantial evidence and dismiss the City's CPLR article 78 petition against the Commissioner's decision.

In December of 1994, Rehabilitation Support Services, Inc. (RSS), a private sponsor of residential facilities for disabled adults, notified the City that it wished to renovate an abandoned structure at 117 South Lake Avenue and open a community residential facility for the mentally disabled at that location. Gerald D. Jennings, the Mayor of the City of Albany, wrote the Commissioner "to formally object to the siting of a community residence proposed for the premises located at 117 South Lake Avenue." Without suggesting an alternative site for the proposed facility, Mayor Jennings requested a hearing pursuant to Mental Health Law § 41.34(c)(5) to resolve the dispute. It was the first time that the City had objected "under the Mental Hygiene Law to [the] siting of a facility."

At the hearing, the Director of Program Development for RSS testified that the proposed facility would provide transitional housing for 10 mentally disabled adults who had been recently discharged from an institutional psychiatric hospital. The RSS representative testified that the facility would offer a "supportive natural setting" for the residents to organize their lives, set goals and prepare "for [a] more long-term housing setting where they would then continue their progress in their rehabilitation and using a variety of community services to help them do that." She testified that residents would attend school or work during the day. In the evenings, residents would dine together "family style" and engage in various activities, such as homework or household chores, before retiring.

Licensed by the New York State Office of Mental Health, the facility would be supervised around the clock by a nonresident staff working in shifts. At most times, one or two staff members would be on duty but up to three staff members could share supervisory responsibilities during the busiest part of the day. Persons who are in immediate danger to themselves or others, are chemically dependent upon drugs or alcohol or have acute medical needs that require on-site medical supervision would not be permitted to reside in the house.

A representative of the Albany County Department of Mental Health testified that according to the estimates of the Albany County Discharge Facilitation Program, there were around 90 people receiving inpatient care who were presently in need of a community residential placement such as the one proposed. There was also evidence that, at the time, there was "only one other similar residential program" providing a short-term placement option for the mentally disabled in the process of "reentering and integrating themselves into the community." The need for the proposed facility was apparently exacerbated by the mandated

within fifteen days of such a request. * * * The commissioner shall sustain the objection if he determines that the nature and character of the area in which the facility is to be based would be substantially altered as a result of establishment of the facility. The commissioner shall make a determination within thirty days of the hearing."

sufficient proof of substantial alteration which would result from the latter." The Commissioner found that such evidence was lacking in this case. In so holding, the Commissioner acknowledged the apprehensions of the City's witnesses as "subjectively genuine" but concluded that the residents' primary concern had to do with the behavior of persons who utilized the Alcoholism Receiving Center, just as the Hearing Officer had also noted. However, the Commissioner found that "the testimony that these behaviors may be continued and expanded on by individuals residing in the proposed program is wholly speculative and not convincing in any manner. Such conjectural testimony cannot support a conclusion that the proposed residence would substantially alter the area."

The City filed this article 78 proceeding seeking to annul the Commissioner's decision. The City's primary argument concerned the "area" examined. According to the City, the Commissioner arbitrarily excluded several facilities from consideration by limiting his analysis to the "neighborhood" rather than the "area."

The Appellate Division compared the 13–block area examined by the Commissioner with the maps prepared by the City that depicted the number of special needs housing within a three-fourths-mile radius of 117 South Lake Avenue. The Court found that the Commissioner's delineation of the affected area was arbitrary and capricious and annulled the Commissioner's approval of the residence: "Although we recognize there can be no precise definition of an 'area,' and the Commissioner's findings in this regard are entitled to great deference, in this unique situation where there is a high concentration of similar facilities that impact upon the subject area, we find that the Commissioner's delineation of the neighborhood boundaries to exclude a number of other residential facilities in close proximity to the site in question was arbitrary and capricious, and that an additional community residence would only serve to continue the substantial alteration of the nature and character of the area" (220 A.D.2d 148, 151–152, 644 N.Y.S.2d 844).

* * *

Mental Hygiene Law § 41.34 was enacted and designed "to facilitate the establishment of community residences" (Governor's Approval Mem., L. 1978, chs. 468, 469, 470, 1978 McKinney's Session Laws of N.Y., at 1821; see also, *Crane Neck Assn., Inc. v. New York City/Long Is. County Servs. Group*, 61 N.Y.2d 154, 472 N.Y.S.2d 901, 460 N.E.2d 1336). As Governor Carey wrote in approving the bill, the law was a legislative attempt "to encourage a process of joint discussion and accommodation between the providers of care and services to the mentally disabled and representatives of the community" (1978 McKinney's Session Laws of N.Y., at 1821). In creating a balance between these potentially competing interests, the Legislature set forth a specific mechanism for the resolution of disputes involving the placement of community residences for the mentally disabled. A sponsoring agency intending to establish or operate a community residential facility for the disabled must provide notice of such intention to the chief executive officer of the municipality (Mental Hygiene Law § 41.34[c][1]). The municipality, in turn, may either approve of the recommended site, suggest alternatives within the jurisdiction, or outright object to the proposal. The Commissioner of the department responsible for licensing the proposed facility must hold a hearing to resolve any dispute (Mental Hygiene Law § 41.34[c][5]).

In reviewing any objection to the facility, the Commissioner must consider the need for the facility and the concentration of similar facilities already established in the area (id.). Nevertheless, the only ground provided in the statute to justify sustaining the objection is if the Commissioner determines "that the nature and character of the area in which the facility is to be based would be substantially altered as a result of establishment of the facility" (Mental Hygiene Law § 41.34[c][5]). Thus, while over concentration is certainly relevant, whether the nature and character of an area will be substantially altered by the establishment of the proposed facility is the dispositive inquiry.

Here, the Commissioner's delineation of the area to be affected by the establishment of the proposed residence is rational and supported by the evidence adduced at the hearing. The Commissioner determined that the relevant "area" was the neighborhood beginning "at Morris Street * * * east to Robin Street, south to Myrtle Avenue, west to South Lake, south to its intersection with New Scotland and Woodlawn Avenues, west on Woodlawn Avenue to Ontario Street and north again to Morris Street." The larger area urged by the City is delineated by a circle within a three-fourths-mile radius from 117 South Lake. This boundary has no relation to physical or subjective neighborhood limits. In contrast, the Commissioner relied upon boundaries created by parks and main thoroughfares which residents were not likely to cross on foot.

The Commissioner's determination rationally adopts the boundaries of the neighborhood as defined by the City's own witnesses. It was the neighbors closest to 117 South Lake Avenue who testified about the boundaries of their neighborhood and it is in that neighborhood where the proposed facility would be located. Such evidence is of paramount importance under the State policy, which is geared towards incorporating the mentally disabled into "the life of the community which is expected to provide them with sustenance" (Governor's Approval Mem., 1978 McKinney's Session Laws of N.Y., at 1821). Accordingly, the Commissioner may properly focus on the potential impact upon direct "neighbors" (id.).

The Appellate Division's choice of a different area was simply that—a different choice. The record contains evidence relating to zoning districts, zip code districts and census districts as well as boundaries within concentric circles radiating out from the site of the proposed facility in varying one-fourth-mile increments. Although the relevant area might reasonably have been determined in a variety of ways, the dispositive inquiry is whether the establishment of the subject facility will substantially alter the nature or character of the area in which the facility will be located and there is little evidence of this beyond speculation. If the proposed facility would not "substantially alter" its immediate neighborhood, it is difficult to find fault with the conclusion that adjacent areas would be little affected. In sum, the Commissioner's decision to examine the potential impact of the proposed facility upon its immediately surrounding community is entitled to deference as rational and supported by the record.

The City argues primarily that, upon consideration of a larger area, more facilities would be encompassed within the analysis. That a larger area includes more facilities is not surprising. However, the inverse corollary is also true. More facilities would be found over a larger area. Here, there is no indication that the larger area considered by the Appellate Division would be any more "saturated" than the smaller neighborhood examined by the Commissioner. In fact, the maps prepared by the City support the opposite conclusion.

It should be noted that one of the goals of the statute is to avoid over concentration of such facilities in any one area. Nevertheless, as the Commissioner noted, the mere number of "special needs" facilities within an area is not dispositive.

Here, the evidence strongly supports the conceded need for the proposed residence and the City suggested no alternative site. The mere presence of other facilities already situated in a particular area cannot be the sole basis for denying the establishment of a similar new facility when such need for that facility is demonstrated. This is precisely the balance reached by the statute in which concentration is relevant but secondary to a determination that the nature and character of an area will be "substantially altered." Thus, it was reasonable for the Commissioner to require proof of more than a mere recitation of the number of other facilities located in the same area to sustain the City's objection.

Finally, the Commissioner's decision to limit his examination to certain facilities was not arbitrary. The Mental Hygiene Law only requires the Commissioner to consider

> "the existing concentration of such facilities and other similar facilities licensed by other state agencies in the municipality or in the area in proximity to the site selected and any other facilities in the municipality or in the area in proximity to the site selected providing residential services to a significant number of persons who have formerly received in-patient mental health services in facilities of the office of mental health or the office of mental retardation and developmental disabilities" (Mental Hygiene Law § 41.34[c][5] [emphasis supplied]).

Thus, under section 41.34, only facilities which are licensed by a State agency or which house former patients of OMH/OMRDD services must be considered. In contrast, the City argues that all "special needs" facilities should be taken into account regardless of licensing status, size or function. Such a sweeping position is not the one adopted by the

Legislature and the Commissioner's conclusions in this regard are rational.

Judging from the testimony of the residents, it appears that many of the concerns may be traced to the Alcoholism Receiving Center and the nonlicensed Oxford House. The proposed residence at issue, however, is for individuals who suffer from mental disabilities, not addiction. Concerns about behavior of those receiving treatment for addiction must not obfuscate the primary issue before us. The record supports the Commissioner's conclusion that the addition of a residence housing 10 mentally disabled adults would neither result in an over concentration of similar facilities nor substantially alter the nature and character of the neighborhood.

Accordingly, the judgment of the Appellate Division should be reversed, with costs, and the petition dismissed.

KAYE, C.J., and TITONE, BELLACOSA, LEVINE, CIPARICK and WESLEY, JJ., concur.

Notes

1. The first case in this section dealing with mining presents an example of how state governments may not entirely preempt local governments from controlling certain land uses, but rather how the state may regulate certain activities that occur on the land. In these situations, the local governments may, for example, decide whether to allow mining to occur in a particular zoning district, but once the activity is a permitted use, the state preempts local control regarding regulating how the mining operation is conducted. But see, San Pedro Mining Corp. v. Board of County Commissioners of Santa Fe County, 121 N.M. 194, 909 P.2d 754 (Ct.App. 1996) and River Springs Limited Liability Company v Board of County Commissioners of the County of Teton, 899 P.2d 1329 (Wyo.1995) where courts have held that the states' mining law did not preempt all local regulation of mining activities. What are the reasons why state government would want to regulate the mining industry? For a discussion of the preemption of local zoning control over mining activities on federal public lands see, South Dakota Min. Ass'n, Inc. v Lawrence, 155 F.3d 1005, 29 Envtl L. Rep. 20,043 (8th Cir.1998).

2. In his article, Local Land Use Regulation of Extractive Industries: Evolving Judicial and Regulatory Approaches, 14 UCLA J. Envtl. L. & Pol'y 41 (1995/96), Professor Bruce Kramer offers the following observation:

> Regulation of the extractive industries antedates the regulation of urban development through comprehensive zoning and planning. The trend towards not only suburban, but rur-urban, development will undoubtedly increase local political pressure to further regulate and restrict the extractive industries. In addition, counties are being empowered to engage in zoning and planning regulation. These two developments will undoubtedly lead to further confrontation between those who make their living extracting minerals and those who want a "quiet place to live." Traditional land use doctrines can be applied to the industry, but a number of courts have recognized the unique locational circumstances

of the industry. Other courts treat the extractive industry as any other use, subject to the police power, constrained only by constitutional limitations. The recent spate of appellate court opinions indicates that the confrontation between the various interests involved has become a reality and is likely to continue into the future.

Professor Kramer also discusses the overlapping and potentially conflicting state and local regulation of the industry. Can different levels of government effectively regulate different aspects of land use and activities that occur on land? If so, who benefits? What are the potential economic impacts of dual regulation?

3. Similar to the challenges of the confrontation between newer suburban and rural homeowners with the mining industries, farmers and agribusiness often face bitter NIMBY stand-offs with neighbors who may complain about odors, timing of farm operations and related noise, and farm related traffic. The growing political influence of the surrounding landowners, who often out-number the farmer in votes, has changed the landscape of local government regulation of agribusinesses. As a result, states have increasingly adopted regulations in the area of agricultural activities, sometimes supporting the farming industry (e.g., right to farm laws) and other times regulating farming operations out of public health and safety concerns. Which level of government is most appropriate to regulate the activities that occur on farms, the state government or the local government where the farming operation is located? See, Christopher A. Novack, Agriculture's New Environmental Battleground: The Preemption of County Livestock Regulations, 5 Drake J. A. L. 429 (2000).

4. Should state government require that local governments permit the siting of group homes for the mentally ill? While the Federal Fair Housing Act discussed in the previous section would cover group homes as well, why have state governments enacted their own preemptive regulations? Can and should local government officials ever get past the pressures of NIMBY when it comes to siting locally unwanted land uses? What would support a mayor's decision to oppose the siting of group homes on non-discriminatory grounds? Should local governments be required to permit somewhere within their borders all types of imaginable housing and uses?

5. When local governments fail to take reasonable decisive actions, which may be politically unpopular due to the "not in my back yard" ("NIMBY") syndrome, the private sector and non-profit advocacy organizations eventually plead to a higher level of government. Many local land use decisions are difficult. Millions of dollars may be at risk, as well as real or perceived public health and welfare issues. It is uncomfortable for zoning board members and local legislators to listen to their constituents, neighbors, and friends oppose proposed projects for what may amount to NIMBY and fail to support constituent desires. Although local officials could debate the differences between representative and delegate theories of governance, the bottom line is that progress is delayed, economic development is stalled, and needed housing alternatives to accommodate all members of the community are prohibited. When this happens, it naturally begs the point that, "There must be a better way." See, Patricia E. Salkin, The Politics of Land Use Reform in New York: Challenges and Opportunities, 73 St. John's L.

Rev. 1041 (1999). What level of government is most appropriate to regulate land use?

SECTION 3. INTERGOVERNMENTAL CONFLICTS

A. STATE–LOCAL CONFLICTS

BROWN v. KANSAS FORESTRY, FISH AND GAME COMM'N

Court of Appeals of Kansas, 1978.
2 Kan.App.2d 102, 576 P.2d 230.

FOTH, CHIEF JUDGE:

The issue presented in this appeal is whether, in the absence of any clear legislative direction one way or the other, a state agency must conform its land use to local zoning regulations. It is an issue which has not been squarely answered by the courts of this state.

The agency involved here is the state forestry, fish and game commission. In 1975 it purchased two lots in the middle of a twenty-three lot subdivision near Manhattan, Kansas, which had been zoned for single family residences. The commission intended to use the land for a public parking lot, complete with toilet facilities, for the convenience of its patrons using a fishing and recreation facility on the adjacent Big Blue River.

The plaintiffs own and reside on fourteen of the twenty-one other lots in the subdivision. They brought this action to enjoin the commission from its proposed use of its land, alleging that such use would violate both Riley county zoning regulations and certain restrictive covenants governing the subdivision. After a hearing, and upon the parties' stipulation that the commission's proposed use would violate the zoning regulations, the trial court temporarily enjoined the use. It further ordered that the injunction would be made permanent unless the commission promptly perfected an appeal or applied for rezoning. Rather than seek rezoning the commission elected to take this appeal.

In this court, as in the court below, the commission argues that it is exempt from local zoning regulations for two reasons. First it says that as an agency of the state itself, performing a governmental function, it is immune from regulation by a mere political subdivision in the absence of a legislative declaration to the contrary. Second, it relies on its possession of the power of eminent domain as indicating a legislative intent that its use of land not be subject to control by local authorities.

A concise review of the terms in which courts have traditionally analyzed conflicts between governmental agencies over land use regulations is found in City of Temple Terrace v. Hillsborough Ass'n, Etc., 322 So.2d 571 (Fla.App.1975), affirmed on opinion below, Hillsborough Ass'n,

Etc., v. City of Temple Terrace, 332 So.2d 610 (Fla.1976). The Florida Court of Appeals there noted:

"* * * In deciding this type of case, the courts have used varying tests. One approach utilized by a number of courts is to rule in favor of the superior sovereign. Thus, where immunity from a local zoning ordinance is claimed by an agency occupying a superior position in the governmental hierarchy, it is presumed that immunity was intended in the absence of express statutory language to the contrary. E.g., Aviation Services, Inc. v. Board of Adjustment, 1956, 20 N.J. 275, 119 A.2d 761. A second test frequently employed is to determine whether the institutional use proposed for the land is 'governmental' or 'proprietary' in nature. If the political unit is found to be performing a governmental function, it is immune from the conflicting zoning ordinance. E.g., City of Scottsdale v. Municipal Court, 1962, 90 Ariz. 393, 368 P.2d 637. On the other hand, when the use is considered proprietary, the zoning ordinance prevails. E.g., Taber v. City of Benton Harbor, 1937, 280 Mich. 522, 274 N.W. 324. Where the power of eminent domain has been granted to the governmental unit seeking immunity from local zoning, some courts have concluded that this conclusively demonstrates the unit's superiority where its proposed use conflicts with zoning regulations. E.g., Mayor of Savannah v. Collins, 1954, 211 Ga. 191, 84 S.E.2d 454. Other cases are controlled by explicit statutory provisions dealing with the question of whether the operation of a particular governmental unit is subject to local zoning. E.g., Mogilner v. Metropolitan Plan Commission, 1957, 236 Ind. 298, 140 N.E.2d 220.

"When the governmental unit which seeks to circumvent a zoning ordinance is an arm of the state, the application of any of the foregoing tests has generally resulted in a judgment permitting the proposed use. This has accounted for statements of hornbook law to the effect that a state agency authorized to carry out a function of the state is not bound by local zoning regulations. 2 Anderson, American Law of Zoning § 9.06 (1968); 8 McQuillin, Municipal Corporations § 25.15 (1965)." (p. 574.)

* * *

There being no "explicit statutory provision" applicable here, the commission relies on the other three common tests: in its first argument it combines the "superior sovereign" with the "governmental-proprietary" test; in its second it asserts the "eminent domain" test. All have been subject to scholarly criticism as too simplistic, avoiding the kind of analysis needed for rational resolution of the complex issues posed by land use problems in a modern, urban-oriented society. See, Comment, "The Applicability of Zoning Ordinances to Governmental Land Use," 39 Tex.L.Rev. 316 (1961); Note, "Municipal Power to Regulate Building Construction and Land Use by Other State Agencies," 49 Minn.L.Rev. 284 (1964); Comment, "The Inapplicability of Municipal Zoning Ordinances to Governmental Land Uses," 19 Syracuse L.Rev. 698 (1968);

Note, "Governmental Immunity From Local Zoning Ordinances," 84 Harv.L.Rev. 869 (1971).

Recent judicial pronouncements are increasingly in the same vein. Thus in State v. Kopp, 330 S.W.2d 882 (Mo.1960), the question was whether a city had to comply with county zoning ordinances in building a sewage disposal plant outside the city limits. The court viewed the question as one of legislative intent, "not to be resolved simply by applying the 'governmental vs. proprietary' test." (p. 887.) The court went on to find that the grant of eminent domain power to the city evinced a legislative intent that it not be subject to county zoning. Just two years later, however, the same court, in St. Louis County v. City of Manchester, 360 S.W.2d 638 (Mo.1962), found that a city's possession of eminent domain power did not grant automatic immunity from the county's zoning power in locating its disposal plant. Rather, the court sought to reconcile the two powers and held that the eminent domain statutes "do not purport to give the city the right to select the exact location in St. Louis County, and the public interest is best served in requiring it to be done in accordance with the zoning laws." (p. 642.) Missouri thus has abandoned as controlling both the governmental-proprietary and the eminent domain tests, looking instead to legislative intent and the public interest.

The Missouri court relied in part on City of Richmond v. County Board, 199 Va. 679, 101 S.E.2d 641 (1958), where a statute authorizing the city to establish a jail outside the city limits was held not to authorize a location in violation of the county's zoning regulation. Rather than rely on any automatic test, and specifically rejecting the "governmental-proprietary" test, the Virginia court also sought to reconcile the two enactments and give each full play. * * *

Pennsylvania has employed a similar analysis. In Wilkinsburg–Penn Jt. W.A. v. Churchill B., 417 Pa. 93, 207 A.2d 905 (1965), a municipal water authority sought to build a water tower in violation of borough zoning restrictions. When the borough refused a variance the authority brought suit to enjoin the borough from interfering with the proposed structure. The court viewed the question as one of statutory construction; the fact that the authority was given the power to determine its services "exclusively" did not make it immune from the zoning power of the borough. "The initial service decisions remain with the Authority, but they must be made within the framework of other applicable laws, unless the Legislature directs otherwise." (p. 101, 207 A.2d p. 909.) The two grants of authority—to build and to zone—could be reconciled. Should there be an improper exercise of the zoning power as to the authority's land use, the court said, it could be challenged in the same manner as other zoning decisions.

Later, in City of Pittsburgh v. Commonwealth, 468 Pa. 174, 360 A.2d 607 (1976), the same court decided a zoning dispute between the state's bureau of corrections and a city over the location of a pre-release center for women convicts. It commenced its analysis by observing:

"Resolving the conflict simply by saying that the 'state' agency must prevail because it is exercising the power of the sovereign overlooks that the zoning power the city seeks to exercise is also a sovereign power. Such a resolution ignores the interests the state seeks to promote by legislative grants of powers to municipalities. Interests such as those fostered by comprehensive land use planning statutes are too important not to be recognized as involving exercises of state power." (p. 180, 360 A.2d p. 610.)

The court resolved the question by again reconciling the grants of authority. The city's zoning, which would permit pre-release centers in other parts of the city, was held not to be arbitrary. Finding that "suitable alternatives exist to accommodate both the community's interest in maintaining the integrity of low-density, residential zoning and the needs of the Bureau" (p. 187, 360 A.2d p. 614), the court held that the state agency's use was subject to the city's zoning ordinance.

Pennsylvania's way in this area was indicated by the leading case in the new wave of intergovernmental zoning decisions, Rutgers v. Piluso, 60 N.J. 142, 286 A.2d 697 (1972). There the question was whether Rutgers, the state university, could build student housing units in excess of the maximum number permitted by a township zoning ordinance.
* * *

After recognizing the three common tests (asserted by the commission here) and reviewing its own prior decisions, the court formulated its own test:

"The rationale which runs through our cases and which we are convinced should furnish the true test of immunity in the first instance, albeit a somewhat nebulous one, is the legislative intent in this regard with respect to the particular agency or function involved. That intent, rarely specifically expressed, is to be divined from a consideration of many factors, with a value judgment reached on an overall evaluation. All possible factors cannot be abstractly catalogued. The most obvious and common ones include [1] the nature and scope of the instrumentality seeking immunity, [2] the kind of function or land use involved, [3] the extent of the public interest to be served thereby, [4] the effect local land use regulation would have upon the enterprise concerned and [5] the impact upon legitimate local interests. * * * In some instances one factor will be more influential than another or may be so significant as to completely overshadow all others. No one, such as the granting or withholding of the power of eminent domain, is to be thought of as ritualistically required or controlling. And there will undoubtedly be cases, as there have been in the past, where the broader public interest is so important that immunity must be granted even though the local interests may be great. The point is that there is no precise formula or set of criteria which will determine every case mechanically and automatically." (pp. 152–53, 286 A.2d p. 702. Numbers inserted.)

The court went on to find that the state university performed an essential governmental function for the benefit of all the people of the state, and that the legislature would not intend its growth to be subject to restriction or control by local land use regulation. After observing that the same reasoning would generally be true of all state functions and agencies, the court added the following caveat:

> "It is, however, most important to stress that such immunity in any situation is not completely unbridled. Even when it is found to exist, it must not, as this court said in Washington Township v. Village of Ridgewood, supra, 26 N.J. [578] at 584–586, 141 A.2d 308, be exercised in an unreasonable fashion so as to arbitrarily override all important legitimate local interests. This rule must apply to the state and its instrumentalities as well as to lesser governmental entities entitled to immunity. For example, it would be arbitrary, if the state proposed to erect an office building in the crowded business district of a city where provision for off-street parking was required, for the state not to make some reasonable provision in that respect. And, at the very least, even if the proposed action of the immune governmental instrumentality does not reach the unreasonable stage for any sufficient reason, the instrumentality ought to consult with the local authorities and sympathetically listen and give every consideration to local objections, problems and suggestions in order to minimize the conflict as much as possible. * * * " (pp. 153–54, 286 A.2d p. 703.)

The test applied in *Rutgers* has come to be known as the "balancing of interests" test. In Kunimoto v. Kawakami, 56 Haw. 582, 545 P.2d 684 (1976), the state university of Hawaii was permitted to condemn land for a use which would violate Honolulu's zoning ordinances. The finding of immunity was based on the overriding statewide concern for higher education expressed in the Hawaii constitution and the university's enabling legislation. The court, however, expressly reserved the question of whether the "balancing of interest" test expounded in *Rutgers* would apply to other state projects.

In another state university case, City of Newark v. University of Delaware, 304 A.2d 347 (Del.Ch.1973), the court reached the same result—i.e., the university's immunity—by expressly following the *Rutgers* rationale. A legislative intent that the university be immune from local zoning was inferred from the vital role it plays in the state's public mission, although such immunity would not prevail if the university's action were shown to be unreasonable or arbitrary in a given instance.

Minnesota adopted a "balancing of interests" test in Town of Oronoco v. City of Rochester, 293 Minn. 468, 197 N.W.2d 426 (1972), at about the same time as and apparently quite independently of the *Rutgers* decision, which was not cited. In that case the city's proposed sanitary landfill would violate a township zoning ordinance. The court recognized that under the "general rule" the city would be immune because it possessed eminent domain powers and would be exercising a governmental function. It declined to follow the general rule, saying:

"* * * However, the trend is to limit such freedom from regulation, a trend which we believe is well within the dictates of the public interest, principally because the pungent realities of urban sprawl and overpopulation have accentuated the need for land-use planning and control that serves as foundation for the exercise of police power in the area of zoning. Consequently, in order to support the principle of enlightened land-use control, we decline to adopt in Minnesota the general rule of governmental exemption from zoning regulation.

"The exigencies of the present matter, however, illustrate the core of wisdom in that general rule and the danger in too readily assuming enlightenment where none in fact may exist in the implementation of a particular local zoning policy. Therefore, we adopt a balancing-of-public-interests test for the resolution of conflicts which arise between the exercise by governmental agencies of their police power and their right of eminent domain. This is preferable to adherence to a less flexible 'general rule' based simply on the form of the opposing parties rather than the substance of their conflict." (p. 471, 197 N.W.2d p. 429. Footnotes omitted.)

Balancing the city's urgent need to replace its present disposal system against the marginal impact on the proposed area for the new facility, the court found immunity should prevail under the facts of that case.

The Florida Court of Appeals, in City of Temple Terrace v. Hillsborough Ass'n, Etc., supra, after describing the traditional tests in the language quoted above, rejected them one by one. It adopted in their stead the *Rutgers* "balancing of interests" test, justifying its decision by saying:

"The old tests were adopted at a time when state government was much smaller. The myriad of agencies now conducting the functions of the state have necessarily resulted in a diminution of centralized control. The decision of a person administering an outlying function of a state agency with respect to the site where this function should be performed is not necessarily any better than the decision of the local authorities on the subject of land use. The adoption of the balancing of interests test will compel governmental agencies to make more responsible land-use decisions by forcing them to consider the feasibility of other sites for the facility as well as alternative methods of making the use of the proposed site less detrimental to the local zoning scheme.

"Our burgeoning population and the rapidly diminishing available land make it all the more important that the use of land be intelligently controlled. This can only be done by a cooperative effort between interested parties who approach their differences with an open mind and with respect for the objectives of the other. When the state legislature is silent on the subject, the governmental unit seeking to use land contrary to applicable zoning regulations should have the burden of proving that the public interests favoring the proposed use outweigh those mitigating against a use not sanctioned by the zoning regulations of the host government." (322 So.2d at 578–79.)

In adopting the Court of Appeals opinion in that case as its own the Florida Supreme Court noted a further policy consideration:

"An ancillary benefit in resolving inter-governmental disputes results from our adoption of the City's view. By requiring state agencies to seek local approval for non-conforming uses, an administrative solution is always present in the form of zoning appeals. In contrast, if the state were not required to seek local approval, the city would always be forced to litigate its disagreement, as happened here. It serves the public's benefit to resolve these controversies in a way which does not mandate the most expensive and least expeditious way of settling intergovernmental disputes." (Hillsborough Ass'n, Etc. v. City of Temple Terrace, supra at 612, n. 3.)

Finally, among foreign cases, we note Matter of Suntide Inn Motel, 563 P.2d 125 (Okl.1977), cited to us by the commission at oral argument. It does not support the kind of automatic immunity urged on us by the commission. The issue in that case was whether the state department of corrections was required to have city planning commission approval for the location of a community treatment center. Three justices in the majority found that such approval was not necessary, basically because the state, as the superior sovereign, was not bound by local regulation in the absence of an express legislative declaration. Four justices dissented, urging that the *Rutgers* balancing test should be adopted, and that under such a test the state agency should seek local approval. * * *

Two justices were in between. They concurred in the finding of immunity, but only because they thought the result of balancing tipped in favor of the state agency. * * *

* * *

In our own analysis we start with the premise that the legislature has not spoken directly on the subject, any more than has our Supreme Court. * * * There is nothing in the statutes which says the commission is subject to local zoning, nor is there anything which grants it immunity.

We therefore regard the question as open in this state. Given the choice, we think this case aptly illustrates why the balancing of interests test better promotes the public's interest than any of the traditional mechanical tests.

* * * The real questions are where the decision-making authority should be lodged, and if a claim of arbitrariness is to be made who should have the presumption of reasonableness and who the burden of proof.

Dealing with the specifics of this case, we are not talking about establishing a public hunting or fishing facility in an area zoned for agriculture. The merits of such a case appear clear, at least on the surface. Here, we are dealing with an all-night parking lot with toilet facilities in the middle of a residential subdivision. The commission anticipates that the recreational facility will be used at a rate of 10,000 man days per year. At least some of those users will employ the proposed parking lot. The merits of this proposal are not nearly so clear. * * *

If we look at the factors suggested as relevant by the Rutgers court we find: (1) The instrumentality seeking immunity is a state agency, and its judgment is entitled to considerable deference. (2) The general function being performed—promoting recreation—is one of recognized public utility but hardly on a level of importance with public education. The specific use, providing parking space near but not in a recreation area, is of a more marginal public interest. (3) While there is public interest in the proposed use in that some people will find this parking lot more convenient than other available lots, the segment of the population affected is relatively small. (4) Regulation, if rezoning is refused, would have the effect of requiring the parking lot to be located in some area other than a residential subdivision. Such a move might make the lot less convenient, but would probably not substantially impair the usefulness of the recreation area. (5) The proposed use would, prima facie at least, have a substantial adverse impact on the surrounding householders and on the existing land use plan.

* * * [T]hese factors were not weighed on the basis of evidence either by a zoning body or by the court below, and our observations are based on a skimpy record and our own general knowledge. The commission simply asserted its immunity, without attempting to justify the reasonableness of its decision, while the court looked no further than the admitted violation of the zoning regulation.

It seems to us that, on balance, the initial decision on reasonableness in this case can be made more expeditiously and with greater discernment by the local zoning authority—here the county. That being so, we infer a legislative intent that the responsibility should be imposed on that body. If rezoning is arbitrarily denied, that decision can be reviewed by the courts at the commission's behest through normal channels. If, on the other hand, we were to hold that the commission's status as superior sovereign immunizes it from the normal zoning processes as it urges, then the burden of going forward with a lawsuit would fall on either the county or the affected landowners. In such a suit they would be required to show arbitrariness on the part of the commission. While it is true the landowners would have much the same burden if dissatisfied by an order *granting* rezoning, that would be because two administrative agencies at different levels have concurred in finding the proposed use appropriate. The zoning route strikes us as cheaper and faster, and it puts the local land use decision in local hands where, in this case, it belongs.

In this case the district court ordered the commission to seek rezoning. It can still do so. In our opinion that is the proper course for it to take, and the trial court properly so ordered.

Affirmed.

Notes

1. Two years after the principal case, the Supreme Court of Kansas was faced with the question of whether the state Board of Regents was required to obtain a building permit and follow city building codes in constructing a new facility at the University of Kansas Medical Center. In State ex rel. Schneider v. City of Kansas City, 228 Kan. 25, 612 P.2d 578 (1980), the court quoted extensively from the principal case, and then, enigmatically, stated: "Whatever may be the merits of such a balancing of interest approach to the use of land by a state agency under city or county zoning laws, we do not feel such a test would be feasible or practical as applied to local building codes and proposed construction by the Board of Regents." (A similar case involving local building codes and a state university is Regents of Univ. of California v. City of Santa Monica, 77 Cal.App.3d 130, 143 Cal.Rptr. 276 (1978). Compare Varnado v. Southern University at New Orleans, 621 So.2d 176 (La.App.1993) holding that the university was bound by the local zoning ordinance as to the use of off-campus property.) Ten years later the Kansas court felt that the balancing test should apply to a state agency charged with the construction of prisons. In Herrmann v. Board of County Comm'rs, 246 Kan. 152, 785 P.2d 1003 (1990) the court held the agency not to be immune from local zoning, but found that the balancing test favored the construction of a correctional facility because a prison is a major project of compelling state interest; moreover, a federal court had ordered a new prison or, if the state failed, court-ordered release of felons.

2. The Temple Terrace case from Florida, relied on by the court in the principal case, dealt with the issue of whether a non-profit corporation performing what would otherwise be a state function in operating a home for the mentally retarded, was immune from a local zoning ordinance. See City of Muskegon Heights v. Moseler, 178 Mich.App. 609, 444 N.W.2d 145 (1989), reversed without opinion 433 Mich. 918, 448 N.W.2d 721 (1989).

3. Courts in many states have taken up the question of which test to use in resolving intergovernmental zoning conflicts. Although the superior sovereign and eminent domain tests still appear to prevail, the trend of decisions is clearly in the direction of the balancing of interests approach. See, e.g., City of Ames v. Story County, 392 N.W.2d 145 (Iowa 1986). The issue in this case is becoming very common—whether a city is subject to county regulations in locating a waste disposal facility. See City of Fargo v. Harwood Twp., 256 N.W.2d 694 (N.D.1977); City of Everett v. Snohomish County, 112 Wash.2d 433, 772 P.2d 992 (1989). But see City of Washington v. Warren County, 899 S.W.2d 863 (Mo.banc 1995) where the court espoused the eminent domain test and held that a city was immune from the county's zoning ordinance in connection with an airport; Macon–Bibb County Hospital Authority v. Madison, 204 Ga.App. 741, 420 S.E.2d 586 (1992), holding

that the county hospital was immune from local zoning regulations as regards placement of roof signs on its medical center.

4. Several cases dealing with intergovernmental immunity involve the applicability of local zoning ordinances to construction of correctional facilities by state agencies. This type of public use is almost certain to provoke neighbors and local communities to protest and litigate the question. In Dearden v. City of Detroit, 403 Mich. 257, 269 N.W.2d 139 (1978), the court held that the state department of corrections was immune from local zoning ordinances, and to hold otherwise would thwart state policy to locate correctional facilities in community settings. To the same effect, see City of New Orleans v. State of Louisiana, 364 So.2d 1020 (La.1978); County Commissioners of Bristol v. Conservation Comm'n of Dartmouth, 380 Mass. 706, 405 N.E.2d 637 (1980); Lane v. Zoning Bd. of Adjustment of City of Talladega, 669 So.2d 958 (Ala.Civ.App.1995). With these cases, compare City of Pittsburgh v. Commonwealth of Pennsylvania, 468 Pa. 174, 360 A.2d 607 (1976) and Matter of Suntide Inn Motel, 563 P.2d 125 (Okl.1977) (overruled by Independent School Dist. No. 89 v. City of Oklahoma City, 722 P.2d 1212 (Okl.1986) (adopting balancing test)), both discussed in the principal case. In Peter Garrett Gunsmith v. City of Dayton, 98 S.W.3d 517 (Ky.App. 2002) the court held that a state statute prohibiting local control of guns did not preempt local zoning restrictions pertaining to location of gun shops.

Also see City of Hattiesburg v. Region XII Comm'n on Mental Health and Retardation, 654 So.2d 516 (Miss.1995); Taylor v. State, Dept. of Rehabilitation and Correction, 43 Ohio App.3d 205, 540 N.E.2d 310 (1988) where the court held the state should make "reasonable efforts" to comply with local land use restrictions in siting correctional facilities, but need not follow local zoning procedures. And in City of Louisville Bd. of Zoning Adjustment v. Gailor, 920 S.W.2d 887 (Ky.App.1996) the court held that a private corporation seeking to construct and operate a correctional facility in downtown Louisville enjoyed the same immunity from local zoning regulations as a public entity. Contra to the Kentucky decision is Freedom Ranch, Inc. v. Board of Adjustment of City of Tulsa, 878 P.2d 380 (Okl.App.1994), cert. denied 513 U.S. 1043, 115 S.Ct. 636, 130 L.Ed.2d 543.

5. What if the intergovernmental dispute involves a "foreign" government? In Town of Groton v. Laird, 353 F.Supp. 344 (D.Conn.1972) the court stated that the Navy was exempt from the local zoning ordinance. In Township of Middletown v. N/E Regional Office, United States Postal Service, 601 F.Supp. 125 (D.N.J.1985) the court held that the Postal Service was not subject to local zoning laws. And, in U.S. Postal Service v. Town of Greenwich, Connecticut, 901 F.Supp. 500 (D.Conn.1995) the court held that the state building code could not be applied to a post office construction project under the Supremacy Clause. Compare Pan American Health Organization v. Montgomery County, 338 Md. 214, 657 A.2d 1163 (1995) where the court held the international health organization was not exempt from the local zoning rules. This problem is discussed in 3 Williams, American Land Planning Law § 81.01 (1986).

6. If the ultimate issue in zoning conflicts between various levels of state government is that of legislative intent, do you think the best solution might be a statute spelling out the proper relationships? Along this line see

City and County of Denver v. Board of County Commissioners, 782 P.2d 753 (Colo.1989) discussing the 1974 Land Use Act which allows both state and local government to regulate land uses that might have an impact beyond the immediate scope of the project. The case involved site selection and construction of major water and sewage treatment systems.

In South Carolina, S.C. Code Ann. § 6–7–830 (Supp. 1991) provides: "All agencies, departments and subdivisions of this State that use real property, as owner or tenant, in any county or municipality in this State shall be subject to the zoning ordinance thereof." See City of Charleston v. South Carolina State Ports Authority, 309 S.C. 118, 420 S.E.2d 497 (1992) (ports authority had to obtain architectural approval by city board of architectural review before constructing a building).

7. Of course, a statutory solution might not be viable in heading off conflicts between two cities or two counties. Consider, for example, City of Kirkwood v. City of Sunset Hills, 589 S.W.2d 31 (Mo.App.1979) dealing with the issue of one municipality acquiring a municipal swimming pool in a neighboring town without complying with a zoning ordinance.

B. LOCAL–LOCAL CONFLICTS

CITY OF BRIDGETON v. CITY OF ST. LOUIS

Missouri Court of Appeals, E.D., 2000.
18 S.W.3d 107.

ROBERT G. DOWD, JR., JUDGE.

The City of Bridgeton (Bridgeton) appeals from a judgment in a court-tried civil case in an action for declaratory judgment and injunction which seeks to prevent the City of St. Louis (St. Louis) from proceeding with its plan, W–1W, for the expansion of Lambert–St. Louis International Airport (Lambert Airport) and St. Louis's counterclaim which seeks a declaration that St. Louis is not required to comply with Bridgeton's zoning ordinances.* * *

Bridgeton is a constitutional charter city under Missouri Constitution, Art. VI, Section 19, located in St. Louis County, Missouri. The City of St. Louis is a special constitutional charter city under Missouri Constitution, Art. VI, Section 31. St. Louis has owned and operated Lambert Airport since the 1920's. Lambert Airport is located outside of St. Louis, in Bridgeton and other adjacent cities in northwest St. Louis County.

In 1993, it was determined that the Master Plan for the airport needed to be updated. St. Louis proposed to add a runway and terminals to Lambert Airport. The proposed W–1W plan would extend the runway into an area of Bridgeton that is not zoned for an airport. The new runway is needed to allow for simultaneous landing of aircraft during inclement weather. The Federal Aviation Administration (FAA) requires runways to be 3,400 feet apart in order to have simultaneous instrument landings. Currently, the two major runways at Lambert Airport are less than 1,400 feet apart. At Lambert Airport, simultaneous instrument landings are not possible during inclement weather which creates delays to passengers in St. Louis and other destinations. The costs of these delays to the national economy is reflected in the FAA's Record of Decision which predicted a savings (based on the construction of the W–1W Project) of $1.9 billion at Lambert Airport and $5.1 billion to the National Air Transportation System during 2005 to 2015. There are also predicted savings to passengers from reduced delays of $1.4 billion at Lambert Airport and $9.5 billion nationally. The FAA, after considering several plans, approved the W–1W plan as the only possible, prudent and practicable alternative.

Bridgeton sued St. Louis to prevent the expansion of the airport into Bridgeton in contravention of Bridgeton's zoning laws. The trial court found for St. Louis. This appeal follows.

In its first point, Bridgeton claims the trial court erred when it held Section 305.200(3), did not prohibit St. Louis from expanding Lambert Airport in Bridgeton without first obtaining Bridgeton's zoning approval. Bridgeton argues the plain language of the statute prohibits the construction of the new runway in violation of Bridgeton's Zoning Ordinance.

This same issue was litigated and decided in *City of St. Louis v. City of Bridgeton*, 705 S.W.2d 524 (Mo.App. E.D.1985) (hereinafter *Bridgeton I*). In *Bridgeton I*, St. Louis wanted to construct an airport employee parking lot in Bridgeton on land St. Louis owned. The area was not zoned for this use. After the Bridgeton City Council unanimously rejected a proposed ordinance granting St. Louis permission to construct the lot under a section of the zoning ordinance applicable to off-street parking, St. Louis sought declaratory and injunctive relief seeking immunity from Bridgeton's zoning. In its opinion, this court analyzed Section 305.200(3). The pertinent part of Section 305.200(3) states:

> ... no airport or landing field shall be established or located in any county, city or city under special charter in violation of any plan or master airport plan or zoning regulation restricting the location of an airport or landing field adopted by the planning commission of any such county, city or city under special charter.

Judge Reinhard, writing for this court, found in analyzing this portion of Section 305.200(3) that "[t]his provision relates to the establishment of a new airport in a new location, not the operation of an existing one, and we find it inapplicable here." *Bridgeton I*, 705 S.W.2d at 528. We further note the absence of, or specific legislative silence related to, any statutory language regarding expansion or addition in Section 305.200(3). In Chapter 305, the term "establish" patently refers to an action undertaken at the outset of an airport's existence; wherein the act of establishing an airport or landing field is an act separate from acquiring, leasing or setting apart real property for such purpose. Section 305.210. Further, paragraph three of Section 305.200 states, "no airport or landing field shall be established or located in any county, city or city under special charter...."; whereas paragraph one of Section

305.200 provides that a county, city or special charter city can acquire property "for an airport or landing field or *addition* thereto...." (emphasis added.) It may be reasonably concluded that this language evinces a legislative intent to distinguish between a new airport and the expansion of existing facilities; thereby avoiding the situation where no surrounding municipalities would allow expansion within their boundaries; and thereby render expansion an impossibility and potentially, as a result, doom a viable airport, as well as the economic well-being of the dependent region.

The addition of a runway to Lambert Airport is not the establishment of a new airport in a new location; it is the operation and expansion of an existing airport. Lambert Airport is an established airport. The proposed runway addition would enhance facilities already located there. The runway is meant to be an addition to existing facilities. We find W–1W is the expansion of an existing and operating airport. We again find Section 305.200(3) is inapplicable to this case. Point denied.

In its second point, Bridgeton claims the trial court erred when it ruled a new runway was not a "landing field" under Section 305.200(3). Bridgeton argues the construction of a new runway is a "landing field" under Section 305.200(3), and it cannot be built without zoning approval.

The language of the statute prohibits the establishment or location of a landing field or airport. We found under Bridgeton's first point that St. Louis is expanding an existing airport. St. Louis is not establishing or locating an airport or a landing field. Section 305.200(3) again is inapplicable. Point denied.

In its third point, Bridgeton claims the trial court erred when it held St. Louis did not first have to apply to Bridgeton for zoning approval. Bridgeton argues the Bridgeton Zoning Ordinance and the Intergovernmental Zoning Immunity Ordinance are valid exercises of Bridgeton's authority and the evidence did not establish facts which would invalidate the ordinances. Bridgeton argues that even if Section 305.200(3) does not prohibit the airport expansion into Bridgeton, the basic principles of home rule embodied in Article VI, Section 19(a) of the Missouri Constitution should bar St. Louis from moving forward with W–1W. Bridgeton claims St. Louis must seek zoning approval from Bridgeton or establish that it is immune. St. Louis argues the determination of whether or not St. Louis is immune from Bridgeton's zoning regulations is a question of law for the courts, not a question for a city council to decide. Bridgeton argues St. Louis must exhaust administrative remedies by first seeking immunity under the Ordinance before seeking judicial relief. * * *

Here, the question is whether or not St. Louis is immune from Bridgeton's zoning ordinances—a question of law. We find it is not necessary for St. Louis to exhaust administrative remedies before asking the court in its counterclaim to determine immunity. If the question had been "Is the area zoned R–1 or R–2?," it would be a question requiring the special expertise within the scope of the administrative agency's responsibility. Bridgeton's City Council has special knowledge and expertise in determining the zoning in areas of Bridgeton. Instead the question to be resolved here is whether or not St. Louis is immune from Bridgeton's zoning ordinances. We find it is not necessary for St. Louis to exhaust administrative remedies. Point denied. * * *

Both parties pleaded facts which were relevant to a balancing of interests test. Bridgeton specifically pleaded the negative effects the airport expansion would have on the community of Bridgeton. Bridgeton was aware intergovernmental immunity was at issue if the court found the Intergovernmental Immunity Ordinance was invalid. St. Louis asserts in its counterclaim that Bridgeton's Zoning Ordinance cannot be applied to prevent St. Louis from proceeding with its planned expansion of the Airport under the W–1W Project. St. Louis also stated in its counterclaim that a justiciable controversy exists between the parties as to whether St. Louis is subject to Bridgeton's Zoning Ordinance in connection with St. Louis's plan to expand the airport under the W–1W Project. Consequently, St. Louis would not be subject to Bridgeton's Zoning Ordinance if it had intergovernmental immunity. We find this issue was sufficiently pleaded to put Bridgeton on notice that the balancing of interests test would be used to show St. Louis's intergovernmental immunity. Point denied. * * *

We also find the trial court properly applied the balance of interests test. The trial court heard evidence from both parties considering the impact of the Airport expansion. In resolving claims of governmental immunity from zoning regulations, Missouri courts have applied two tests: (1) the "power of eminent domain" test, and (2) the "balancing of interests" test. *City of Washington v. Warren County,* 899 S.W.2d 863, 865–66 (Mo.1995).

The court in Bridgeton I detailed factors to consider when evaluating immunity under the balancing of interests test. "The factors the court considered were the nature and scope of the instrumentality seeking immunity, the kind of function or land use involved, the extent of the public interest to be served thereby, the effect local land use regulation would have upon the enterprise concerned and the impact upon legitimate local interest." *Bridgeton I,* 705 S.W.2d at 529. "In some instances one factor will be more influential than another or may be so significant as to completely overshadow all others." Id. "And there will undoubtedly be cases, as there have been in the past, where the broader public interest is so important that immunity must be granted even though the local interests may be great." Id.

Here, the trial court evaluated the interests of the parties using the balancing of interests test. In its analysis, the trial court concluded St. Louis was immune from Bridgeton's zoning ordinances because the importance of expanding Lambert Airport pursuant to the W–1W plan outweighed Bridgeton's interest in enforcing its zoning ordinances as to St. Louis.

The trial court considered Lambert Airport's current inadequate capacity which might endanger its status as a hub airport. The trial court considered Lambert Airport's inability to accommodate traffic during inclement weather. The trial court also considered the savings to passengers because of reduced delays. There was also evidence of the regional and statewide importance of expanding Lambert Airport. Lambert Airport's location west of St. Louis provides important access to Jefferson City, the State capitol, and its location benefits the St. Louis region concentrated westward of St. Louis City. Delay or impediment to Lambert Airport's expansion would be detrimental to the economic development of the State of Missouri. Additionally, there was credible testimony that airports generate significant regional economic growth in terms of jobs and commercial activity, including in those communities in close proximity to the Airport.

The trial court also heard evidence of Bridgeton's interest in maintaining their community. The acquisition for the expansion would require over 18% of Bridgeton's total land area including more than 1,900 residential parcels, 6 schools, at least 2 parks, 6 churches and 75 businesses. After considering all of the evidence, the court found the expansion would benefit not only citizens of St. Louis, but citizens in Bridgeton, the entire metropolitan area, and the State of Missouri.

The trial court examined copious amounts of evidence and determined St. Louis is immune from Bridgeton's zoning ordinances using the balancing of interests test. The substantial benefits conferred by the operation of the airport on the public clearly outweigh the interests of Bridgeton. The expansion of Lambert Airport is essential to its survival. We find there was substantial evidence to support the trial court's finding, the finding was not against the weight of the evidence, and the trial court did not erroneously declare or apply the law. Point denied.

* * *

Judgment affirmed.

CITY OF NEW ROCHELLE v. TOWN OF MAMARONECK

United States District Court, Southern District of New York, 2000.
111 F.Supp.2d 353.

McMahon, District Judge.

For some months, two shore communities in lower Westchester County have been embroiled in debate over a proposal to build an IKEA, the Swedish home furnishings superstore, on a 16.4–acre area on the eastern border of the City of New Rochelle, New York. Within New Rochelle, the matter has generated an extraordinary amount of dissension. City officials view the proposal as vital to urban redevelopment, while residents of the stable working-class neighborhood that would be destroyed if the City acquired the property needed for construction of the store oppose the project. But the highly publicized debate is not confined to the City's borders. Fearing that the store would create serious traffic congestion on its nearby streets, the adjacent Town of Mamaroneck has actively opposed the IKEA project. When it became clear that New Rochelle intended to proceed with condemnation of the property, Mamaroneck's Town Board passed an ordinance, known as the Local Impact Review Law ("Local Law"), which requires that its Town Board review the impact of certain major development projects in an area outside of, but adjacent to, Mamaroneck. The Law provides that a permit must be granted upon a showing that the impact of the development on the Town will be mitigated.

New Rochelle commenced an action in the New York State Supreme Court for declaratory and injunctive relief and damages as a result of the passage of the Local Law. It asserts several constitutional and statutory claims under both Federal and State law. Defendants timely removed the action to this Court pursuant to 28 U.S.C. § 1441(b), on the ground that this Court has original jurisdiction over the federal claims in suit. Defendants now move to dismiss the complaint on various substantive grounds, including lack of standing, lack of ripeness and failure to state a federal claim. Plaintiff opposes that motion and has cross-moved to remand the action to state court.

For the reasons stated below, Defendants' motion is granted in part and denied in part. The state law claims are remanded to New York State Supreme Court. Plaintiff's remaining federal claim is stayed pending resolution of the issues of New York statutory and constitutional law that are paramount in this very local matter. * * *

"Whether a claimant has standing is 'the threshold question in every federal case, determining the power of the court to entertain the suit.'" *In re Gucci,* 126 F.3d 380, 387–88 (2d Cir.1997). To establish standing to bring a complaint, a plaintiff must allege a personal stake in the outcome of the case and a "distinct and palpable" injury by way of "specific, concrete facts." *Duke Power Co. v. Carolina Environmental Study Group, Inc.,* 438 U.S. 59, 72, 98 S.Ct. 2620, 57 L.Ed.2d 595 (1978). Mamaroneck argues that, because the Local Law imposes an environmental review requirement on "developers" and "development," but imposes no obligation on any municipal entities, including New Rochelle, New Rochelle lacks standing to challenge the law. Mamaroneck is wrong.

Contrary to Mamaroneck's contention, the Local Law does not limit its provisions to "developers" or "development," but rather applies to any "project" that is "undertaken" that "abuts, adjoins or is adjacent to a Town street." (Local Law at §§ 130–2, 130–3.) Nothing in the plain language of the statute limits its applicability to "developers." Nor does the Local Law explicitly exclude municipalities or municipally-sponsored projects from the permit requirements. It is thus reasonable to conclude that New Rochelle's current undertaking of a major urban renewal project within the Fifth Avenue Redevelopment Area involving the "physical alteration of 10 acres or more" would fall well within the Defendants' new Local Law. I therefore find that New Rochelle has sufficiently alleged an "injury in fact" or such a personal stake in the outcome of the litigation as to warrant invocation of the Court's jurisdiction.

New Rochelle shares a 3.5 mile border with Mamaroneck. The proposed Fifth Avenue Urban Renewal Area abuts Mamaroneck. New Rochelle is in the midst of a comprehensive environmental review and other deliberations involving the Urban Renewal Area and the adoption of an Urban Renewal Plan. Indeed, Defendants have on several occasions conceded that the passage of the Local Law and its timing was directed at forcing New Rochelle to abandon its redevelopment efforts in the Fifth Avenue Area, specifically, the assemblage of property necessary for the development of the IKEA site. For example, the Local Law was adopted after New Rochelle rejected Mamaroneck's request that Mamaroneck be granted "equal approver" status over the project under SEQRA. New Rochelle clearly has a sufficient legal interest and direct stake in being able to undertake redevelopment projects within its own borders without subjecting itself to the independent jurisdiction of the Town of Mamaroneck. And as Mamaroneck's efforts were specifically aimed at stalling New Rochelle's redevelopment plans, it is disingenuous, at best, for Mamaroneck to claim that New Rochelle is "attempting to assert the rights that actually belong, if at all, to the developer or owner of property that may be subject to the Local Law."

Aside from the Urban Renewal Plan, New Rochelle also alleges that it owns roads and other properties within the area affected by the Local Law. Even if the law were not aimed specifically at the IKEA project (which it clearly is), New Rochelle would have sufficient allegations of injury to its own real property to confer standing upon it in this matter.
* * *

Defendants further contend that, even if Plaintiff has standing to challenge the Local Law, New Rochelle's claims are speculative and premature because neither New Rochelle nor any developer has made an application under the Local Law. New Rochelle alleges that it suffered impairment of its state and federal rights at the moment the law was passed. To the extent that Count V of the complaint can be read to allege a taking of New Rochelle's real property in violation of the Due Process Clause, Defendants are correct; that claim is not ripe for review. All other claims, however, are ripe. * * *

Mamaroneck moves to dismiss Count IV on the ground that the Local Law is a local quality of life ordinance that has no identifiable impact on interstate commerce. New Rochelle counters that the complaint pleads a Commerce Clause violation by alleging that the Local Law will "[i]mpede the free flow of commerce and discriminate against businesses or developments desiring to locate in the City, thus causing it economic loss." New Rochelle also contends that its allegation that the "Local Law jeopardizes any major development in New Rochelle that borders Mamaroneck, specifically the Urban Renewal Project, provides a disincentive for any developer to come into New Rochelle, and has the potential of depressing the City's economy and harming the well-being of its residents," states a claim for violation of the Commerce Clause.

The Commerce Clause provides that "[t]he Congress shall have Power ... To regulate Commerce ... among the several States...." U.S. Const., Art. I, § 8, cl. 3. The so-called dormant Commerce Clause, the scope of which has been defined through judicial opinions, forbids States and their subdivisions to regulate interstate commerce. The Supreme Court has generally distinguished between two types of impermissible state or local regulations: (1) those that discriminate against out-of-state interests; and (2) those that do not discriminate against out-of-state interests, but have an incidental effect on interstate commerce. The first category of laws receive strict scrutiny, and are virtually per se violations of the Commerce Clause. *See Oregon Waste Sys., Inc. v. Department of Envtl. Quality,* 511 U.S. 93, 99, 114 S.Ct. 1345, 128 L.Ed.2d 13 (1994). In analyzing the second category of laws, courts balance the burden imposed on interstate commerce against the benefits provided to local interests. *See Pike v. Bruce Church, Inc.,* 397 U.S. 137, 142, 90 S.Ct. 844, 25 L.Ed.2d 174 (1970). Under this balancing test, the law will be held valid unless the burden on interstate commerce is clearly excessive in relation to the putative local benefits. See id. See also *C & A Carbone, Inc. v. Clarkstown,* 511 U.S. 383, 402, 114 S.Ct. 1677, 128 L.Ed.2d 399 (1994) (O'Connor, J. concurring) (internal citations omitted). But the Court has recognized that the line between per se violations and those that require a balancing of considerations is not always clear. Thus, the critical consideration in determining whether a statute is a constitutionally permissible regulation "is the overall effect of the statute on both local and interstate activity." *Brown–Forman Distillers Corp. v. New York State Liquor Authority,* 476 U.S. 573, 579, 106 S.Ct. 2080, 90 L.Ed.2d 552 (1986).

Turning first to whether the complaint alleges a per se violation of the Commerce Clause, I conclude that it does not. Mamaroneck asserts that the Local Law was enacted solely to protect the environment and living conditions in and around Mamaroneck. New Rochelle counters that the Law was intended and designed to impede the Urban Redevelopment Project. The complaint alleges discrimination against non-local, i.e. non-Mamaroneck, commerce. It does not, however, allege discrimination against out-of-state interests. * * *

A local ordinance that discriminates against non-local interests but does not explicitly discriminate against out-of-state economic interests may nonetheless implicate the dormant commerce clause. Legislation relating to "health and safety" and to the "protection of the environment and conservation of natural resources" is a legitimate exercise of state and local authority. *Gary D. Peake Excavating Inc. v. Town Bd. of Hancock,* 93 F.3d 68 (2d Cir.1996). Defendants contend that, because the Local Law concerns itself exclusively with environmental, health and safety matters, and because the benefits of the law redound to the locality and local residents, it cannot be said to violate the Commerce Clause. However, if there is any effect on interstate commerce, no matter how incidental, I am required to weigh the magnitude of the effect on interstate commerce against the local benefits. See *Pike,* 397 U.S. 137, 90 S.Ct. 844, 25 L.Ed.2d 174.

* * *

Because the Local Law is an economically protectionist law, New Rochelle argues that it represents an impediment to the free flow of goods in interstate commerce. I find Plaintiff's argument that the Local Law has an incidental effect on interstate commerce, because many of the builders and contractors who would be engaged in construction in the redevelopment zone come from out of state and use products that travel in interstate commerce, to be insufficient. This sort of "house that Jack built" argument is far too attenuated to support a conclusion of interference in interstate commerce and fails as a matter of law. (Indeed, accepting such an argument would be to accept that every nearly every municipal zoning regulation is a Commerce Clause violation.)

However, the Local Law may have other potential effects on interstate commerce. For example, discovery might reveal that the law was, in fact, aimed solely at preventing national or international retail "superstores" from being built in the area. Or it might be revealed that Mamaroneck was looking to keep out streams of shoppers from across the Connecticut border, which lies just ten miles from the redevelopment area.* * *

I therefore deny Defendants' motion to dismiss the Commerce Clause claim.

Counts V and VI allege due process and equal protection violations. Plaintiff's due process claim consists of three grounds: (1) the Local Law constitutes a taking of New Rochelle's property without due process; (2) the Local Law, on its face, represents an unlawful taking of New Rochelle's property interest in its own permitting process; and (3) the Local Law is unconstitutionally vague. New Rochelle's equal protection claim alleges that the Local Law "will inhibit new construction in the City of New Rochelle, and shift development away from the City and to [Mamaroneck], as well as cause economic benefit to existing businesses within [Mamaroneck] by stifling competition." Additionally, Plaintiff argues that the Local Law creates a statutory classification insofar as it applies to those properties that fall within the Local Law's parameters: (a) "the construction of 250 or more residential units," (b) "the physical alteration of ten acres or more," (c) "the construction of a facility with more than 100,000 square feet," of (d) a project that "involves parking for more than 1,000 vehicles," provided (e) said development project "abuts, adjoins or is adjacent to a Town street within or upon the border of the Town of Mamaroneck...." (citing Local law No. 4–2000.) Plaintiff contends that the Law is unconstitutional because such classification—which treats different property owners differently—lacks any rational justification.

The threshold issue, which neither party has addressed, is whether New Rochelle, a municipal corporation organized under the laws of New York State, can maintain a suit challenging the Local Law on the basis that its rights to due process and equal protection were infringed. While the Second Circuit has not yet spoken on this issue, I conclude that New Rochelle cannot maintain a claim under these Clauses.

It has long been the case that a municipality may not invoke the protections of the Fourteenth Amendment against its own state. *See City of Newark v. New Jersey,* 262 U.S. 192, 196, 43 S.Ct. 539, 67 L.Ed. 943 (1923). A municipality is thus prevented from attacking state legislation on the grounds that the law violates the municipality's own rights. See, e.g., *City of New Orleans v. New Orleans Water-Works Co.,* 142 U.S. 79, 89–91, 12 S.Ct. 142, 35 L.Ed. 943 (1891); *Hunter v. City of Pittsburgh,* 207 U.S. 161, 28 S.Ct. 40, 52 L.Ed. 151 (1907). Moreover, while municipalities or other state political subdivisions may challenge the constitutionality of state legislation on certain grounds and in certain circumstances, these do not include challenges brought under the Due Process or Equal Protection Clauses of the Fourteenth Amendment. See, e.g., *Rogers v. Brockette,* 588 F.2d 1057 (5th Cir.), cert. denied, 444 U.S. 827, 100 S.Ct. 52, 62 L.Ed.2d 35 (1979). This is because "a municipal corporation, in its own right, receives no protection from the Equal Protection or Due Process Clauses vis-a-vis its creating state." *South Macomb Disposal Authority v. Township of Washington,* 790 F.2d 500, 505 (6th Cir.1986). * * *

In *South Macomb,* the Sixth Circuit addressed the question of whether a municipal corporation could sue another township within the same state on the ground that the township imposed certain waste disposal permitting requirements in violation of the municipal corporation's right to due process and equal protection. Applying the same reasoning that has led federal courts to bar municipalities from bringing due process and equal protection claims against their own states, the Sixth Circuit concluded:

[T]he Fourteenth Amendment simply does not prescribe guidelines and impose restriction upon one political subdivision vis-a-vis another political subdivision. The relationship between the entities is a matter of state concern; the Fourteenth Amendment protections and limitations do not apply.

I agree with the holding of *South Macomb,* and dismiss Counts V and VI to the extent they allege a violation of New Rochelle's rights as a governmental entity.

* * *

In order to plead a violation of its due process rights under the Fifth and Fourteenth Amendments, a plaintiff must allege that it has a protectable property interest, that it was deprived of that property interest by the adoption of the Local Law; and that the deprivation occurred without due process of law or the payment of just compensation. See *Board of Regents v. Roth,* 408 U.S. 564, 576–77, 92 S.Ct. 2701, 33 L.Ed.2d 548 (1972); *Brady v. Town of Colchester,* 863 F.2d 205, 211 (1988).

As noted above, any real property takings claim is not presently justiciable because New Rochelle has not applied for approval through the Local Law. With its alternative theory, Plaintiff argues that Mamaroneck has interfered with its jurisdiction and control over the Urban Renewal project, and has thereby interfered with its ability as a sovereign municipality to bestow various "forms of largess"—including land use approvals and permits—upon private applicants within its own municipal boundaries. New Rochelle contends that it maintains a property interest in the power to grant permits, and that any derogation of that power is a deprivation of its property.

* * *

New Rochelle's claim that the Local Law represented a taking of that property in violation of the Fifth and Fourteenth Amendments, * * * would be non-justiciable until Mamaroneck actually rendered a final decision under the law. Second, the holding of Macomb compels me to conclude that, where the authority to grant "largess" is conferred by the state, it is matter of state law to resolve any alleged infringements on that authority. It is simply not a question of the property rights of a "person" as contemplated by the Due Process Clause.

Plaintiff's allegation of an equal protection violation likewise fails. Where a statute challenged under equal protection does not burden a fundamental right or draw a distinction based on suspect classification, the statute will be upheld if it is rationally related to a legitimate government purpose. See *Nicholas v. Tucker,* 114 F.3d 17, 20 (2d Cir.1997). * * * I find that Mamaroneck had a legitimate governmental purpose in determining that developments of a certain size and location required additional environmental review.

Plaintiff next argues that the Local Law distinguishes between "applicable projects that are adjoining or adjacent to a Town street, but not similar projects that are adjoining or adjacent to a State or County road located within the Town of Mamaroneck." It further argues that the Law impermissibly distinguishes between residents and non-residents of Mamaroneck. The first argument is silly, as the Law clearly states it is concerned about a specific area adjoining Mamaroneck's border; I do not read Mamaroneck's use of the terms "town road" as making any distinction between types of roads within Mamaroneck. In any event, neither of these arguments, however, is enough to meet the high threshold for equal protection challenges to economic regulations. The purposes of the Local Law are stated in the law itself and clearly establish the relationship between the law and Mamaroneck's interest in the health, safety, welfare, comfort and convenience of its residents.

* * *

The state law claims, Counts I, II, III, IV and VIII, are hereby remanded to the New York State Supreme Court. Counts V and VI are dismissed. Count IV, the Commerce Clause claim, is stayed pending resolution of the State law claims.

Notes

1. Can a local unit rule its provincial world and ignore the effects of its zoning upon "outsiders"? If not, how can these outside interests be heard and be protected? Note that these may be interests of immediate neighbors as in Borough of Cresskill v Borough of Dumont, 15 N.J. 238, 104 A.2d 441 (Sup. Ct.1954), or wider metropolitan regional interests as in State ex rel. Anshe Chesed Congregation v. Bruggemeier, 97 Ohio App. 67, 115 N.E.2d 65 (1953), where a satellite village of 1,800 was required to take a metropolitan-wide synagogue with 5,000 members. Or there may be state-wide interest as in the case of zoning affecting the state highways or the state's public waters. Or the interests might be national, as where local zoning has impact on national defense activities, national parks or forests or national transportation routes. See, e.g., MacDonald v. Board of County Comm'rs for Prince George's County, 238 Md. 549, 210 A.2d 325 (1965) which involved the national interest in protecting the view from Mt. Vernon from a proposed high-rise apartment building across the river in Maryland. Also see United States v. Board of Supervisors, 611 F.2d 1367 (4th Cir.1979), holding that the United States had standing to seek an injunction to restrain construction of high-rise office buildings across the Potomac from the capitol. The interest of the government was its proprietary interest in the capitol and protecting the symmetry of its skyline and the setting of its monuments. The gravamen of the complaint was the ultra vires action of defendant in granting a special use permit.

Will the courts always act to protect such interest? If so, on what substantive legal basis? The statutory requirement of a "comprehensive plan"? Due process and its prolific offspring, "general welfare"? Equal protection? And what about party-in-interest rules on the procedural side? Are these such that interested outside groups, local units, the state or the federal government can intervene in local zoning proceedings and insist on judicial review? Would an administrative appeals procedure to a state agency or to a joint local-state board be a better solution?

2. In Wrigley Properties, Inc. v. City of Ladue, 369 S.W.2d 397 (Mo. 1963), a city which lay in the path of better residential development and representing about the finest residential development in the entire St. Louis metropolitan area refused to change its residential zoning so as to authorize a 10–acre shopping center. The question, said the court, was fairly debatable. One of the reasons cited by the court as possibly sustaining the council's refusal to rezone was "that the proposed use as a shopping center appears to be *more for the benefit of other cities and towns than for the benefit of Ladue.*" (Emphasis supplied.) Compare this with Duffcon Concrete Products v. Cresskill, 1 N.J. 509, 64 A.2d 347, 9 A.L.R.2d 678 (1949), where the New Jersey court concluded that a densely settled suburb could properly exclude industry if it has some other place to go in the general area, but nevertheless, where the following general standard was announced:

What may be the most appropriate use of any particular property depends not only on all the conditions, physical, economic and social, prevailing within the municipality and its needs, present and reasonably prospective, but also on the nature of the entire region in which the municipality is located and the use to which the land in that region has been or may be put most advantageously. The effective development of a region should not and cannot be made to depend upon the adventitious location of municipal boundaries, often prescribed decades or even centuries ago and based in many instances on considerations of geography, of commerce, or of politics that are no longer significant with respect to zoning.

See Haar, Regionalism and Realism in Land Use Planning, 105 U.Pa. L.Rev. 5 (1957), and Note, Zoning Against the Public Welfare: Judicial Limitations on Municipal Parochialism, 71 Yale L.J. 720 (1962).

3. On this question of regional considerations, what about the following: A town in the state of New York adopted a law which rezoned part of the town, including an area contiguous to the New Jersey border, from a residential district of one-acre plots to an "office park" district. At the time the law was passed, the land which was rezoned was "mostly wooded" and sloped up from a river. The new zoning provision made possible the construction of a large office-research complex. A municipal corporation of the State of New Jersey brought an action in federal court complaining with respect to the action taken by the adjoining New York community. The New Jersey community argued that it would be injured by reduction in revenues which would result from depreciation in the value of its property and by the need for additional expenditures "to provide for adequate traffic and other related expenses." It sought damages in excess of $10,000 and declaratory relief. The New York town moved for summary judgment alleging that the complaint failed to state a cause of action. Aside from the merits of the claim, does the New Jersey township have standing to sue? See Township of River Vale v. Town of Orangetown, 403 F.2d 684 (2d Cir.1968). Compare Orange Fibre Mills, Inc. v. City of Middletown, 94 Misc.2d 233, 404 N.Y.S.2d 296 (1978). Also see Village of Barrington Hills v. Village of Hoffman Estates, 81 Ill.2d 392, 43 Ill.Dec. 37, 410 N.E.2d 37 (1980), certiorari denied, 449 U.S. 1126, 101 S.Ct. 943, 67 L.Ed.2d 112 (1981), where the court held that one municipality had standing to challenge another's zoning decision to allow construction of an open-air music theatre near the residential areas in the plaintiff village, and City of Thornton v. Board of County Comm'rs, 42 Colo.App. 102, 595 P.2d 264 (1979), where the city was allowed standing to challenge the county rezoning of property adjacent to city-owned land from agricultural to planned unit development. In Town of Mesilla v. City of Las Cruces, 120 N.M. 69, 898 P.2d 121 (1995) the court held that a town was a "person aggrieved" and had standing to challenge rezoning of the neighboring city that allegedly resulted in aesthetic and economic injury to the plaintiff town.

4. A common problem in recent years, involves the shopping center developer who secures relatively inexpensive undeveloped land near a city which is usually subject to less onerous county regulation and the developer proposes a "regional" shopping center which may have a harmful economic impact on city plans to either preserve or redevelop a viable downtown retail

Sec. 3   INTERGOVERNMENTAL CONFLICTS   1099

district or to establish a regional shopping center at a different location. Does the city have any basis for blocking the proposed development? Consider the following cases:

a. Save a Valuable Environment (SAVE) v. City of Bothell, 89 Wash.2d 862, 576 P.2d 401 (1978): The city rezoned a 141 acre farm to permit construction of a major regional shopping center. SAVE, a nonprofit environmental protection organization, challenged the rezoning as having a detrimental effect on both the environment and the economy of the area. After holding that SAVE had standing, the court stated:

> * * * Bothell may not act in disregard of the effects outside its boundaries. Where the potential exists that a zoning action will cause a serious environmental effect outside jurisdictional borders, the zoning body must serve the welfare of the entire affected community. If it does not do so it acts in an arbitrary and capricious manner. * * *
>
> The action was arbitrary and capricious [in this case] in that it failed to serve the welfare of the community as a whole. Specifically, adverse environmental effects and potentially severe financial burdens on the affected community have been completely disregarded. * * *
>
> We do not hold that a city proposing a rezone which will affect neighboring jurisdictions must engage in inter-jurisdictional planning. It is clear, however, that such coordinated planning is desirable and might have avoided the result in this case.

b. Carmel Estates, Inc. v. Land Conservation and Development Commission, 51 Or.App. 435, 625 P.2d 1367 (1981). The Board of County Commissioners approved rezoning 26.5 acres of agricultural land for the construction of a shopping center halfway between the cities of Sandy and Gresham. The city of Sandy and the Metropolitan Service District challenged the proposed rezoning as inconsistent with several goals of the existing comprehensive plan, most particularly the goal prohibiting conversion of agricultural land to urban uses without a showing of necessity. In the report of the hearing officer (which was adopted by the Commission), after stating that to allow this development would frustrate the very purpose of urban growth boundaries and render the plan useless in controlling urban sprawl, the following comment appears:

> According to the testimony, this development would seriously frustrate urban-level utilization of lands in Sandy. Mr. Roger Jordan, city manager, testified that ' * * * a development of this magnitude only three or four miles away from our incorporated boundaries, when we have made all the investments to accommodate growth within our boundaries, would have a drastic effect.' * * * Mr. Jack Hammond, the city attorney stated that a consultant hired by the city found that [the proposed] shopping center would reduce retail sales in Sandy by 17.7 percent * * * In response to this undisputed evidence, the Board of County Commissioners found:

"The City of Sandy has presented argument that it will suffer economic injury because of increased competition to its existing and planned commercial enterprises. The Board has weighed the detriment to the city against the public benefit of the proposed uses and finds that the proposed uses outweigh the detriment to the City of Sandy." Findings, p. 6.

This finding ignores applicable law. Proof that rural development will injure a city is proof of a Goal 14 violation. Cities and counties are not in competition for urban developments. Cities are the housing, employment, shopping, and service centers and providers. * * * The whole point of Goal 14 is that rural lands are not available to satisfy the state's housing, shopping, nonresource employment, and other non-farm and non-forest related needs.

5. Sometimes the shopping center dispute involves two cities which are vying for the large shopping center so as to increase the tax base. This problem is typified by the case of City of Rohnert Park v. Harris, 601 F.2d 1040 (9th Cir.1979), cert. denied sub nom. City of Rohnert Park v. Landrieu, 445 U.S. 961, 100 S.Ct. 1647, 64 L.Ed.2d 236 (1980). Here two towns, seven miles apart, each wanted to develop a regional shopping center. When one of the towns lined up a developer and anchor tenants, the other town sued alleging violation of antitrust laws, HUD regulations (selling urban renewal land at under market value to the developer) and the federal administrative procedure act. The court found no cause of action.

Chapter XI

ZONING AND DISCRIMINATION

The institution of zoning may be said to be inherently discriminatory because it is exclusionary by nature. The heart of the zoning process is to separate land uses by districts, which necessarily means that all uses will be excluded from a particular district except those that are specifically or conditionally permitted. If the zoning ordinance makes no provision for a specific use or for its inclusion as a conditional use, then the use is excluded from the entire jurisdiction.

Obviously, this situation presents several important considerations. An initial and basic issue is whether a zoning ordinance must provide, at least in one or more districts, for any or every type of land use that may be desired. If that question is answered in the affirmative, zoning would not prove to be a useful technique in eliminating or confining certain undesirable or troublesome land uses, such as boiler factories, rendering plants, other types of heavy industry, or automobile junkyards. If the answer is in the negative, however, and a city need not provide for every kind of land use, then carried to the extreme this could give rise to other serious legal considerations. To put it another way, if a city need not permit every type of land use, can it exclude all or practically all forms of land use except the very highest or most desirable? In such a situation, what legal principles can be applied to control the use of zoning to prevent discrimination resulting from economic disparities which, either obviously or inferentially, may include racial discrimination or which, in effect, may preserve racial segregation? What legal principles may be applied, and to what extent, to zoning limitations on opportunities for federally subsidized housing for persons of low and moderate incomes or relative to privately financed housing for persons of that status?

A more subtle form of exclusion results or may result from traditional zoning regulations that do not exclude uses, but which have an exclusionary effect through their impact on the cost of housing and the appearance of the community. These requirements include minimum lot size requirements, minimum house sizes, extraordinary setback requirements, and for that matter, subdivision exactions that affect the economics of land development and thereby create market limitations. Inquiry is appropriate as to the point at which the cumulative effect of unusual and expensive subdivision exactions, minimum zoning requirements and costs attributable to building code regulations may so promote segregated housing patterns as to amount to a misuse of the police power. Although most segregation is along economic lines, racial discrimination is also a persistent problem.

The exclusionary effect of zoning and land use controls in general has become one of the most discussed issues of the past few decades, although the question has been around for much longer than that as illustrated by articles extending back to the early and middle 1950's. The issue has heightened and become an increasing point of litigation in roughly the past twenty years. This chapter is intended to provide some insight into these difficult problems that constitute some of the most complex and sophisticated issues existing in the field of land use control.

SECTION 1. DISCRIMINATION AND HOUSING

A. INTRODUCTION

The nature of the housing industry has changed immensely in the past one hundred years. At the beginning of the 20th century single-family housing was built on a lot-by-lot basis. One would purchase a piece of land and hire someone, usually a skilled carpenter, to build the house in accordance with plans and specifications. One could even order all the components of a house from the Sears & Roebuck catalog; delivery would be by railroad and all the parts would be precut and numbered and put together on site. The first suburbs began to emerge along with the growing popularity of the automobile. In the cities, multi-family housing was mostly tenements, and the buildings and neighborhoods became crowded with immigrants.

Government first began to intervene in housing in the depression years. The first use of federal money to subsidize public housing emerged and during the 1930's the federal government helped build the "greenbelt" towns, such as Greenbelt, Maryland. Private housing was still mostly financed by bank mortgages on a house-by-house basis. Again, in the cities, upscale apartment buildings began to proliferate in the 1920's. Recall that Justice Sutherland in the 1926 Euclid case, upholding the concept of zoning, lamented the coming of apartments that destroyed the bucolic single-family structures in Washington, D.C.

After World War II, the pent up demand for housing by returning GIs and their growing families resulted in several changes in housing. The mass production of suburban housing, evidenced by Levittown on Long Island created almost instantaneous communities. The federal government subsidized mortgages through the Veterans Administration first, and then the Federal Housing Authority (FHA). Most importantly, federal money started pouring into highway construction. The suburbs were now linked to the central cities by multi-lane expressways and freeways. In the 1950's and 1960's we saw the strange sight of six lane expressways jammed with cars going toward the city in the morning hours while empty on the other side, only to see a reversal in the evening as commuters headed home. The early post-war years were marked by the so-called bedroom suburbs, containing only single-family dwellings, protected by zoning regimes from any discordant uses such as apartments, mobile home parks, and even first generation shopping centers. The central cities were mostly left to the poor and minority populations.

The next stage of change came about when the suburbs found the cost of maintaining the quality of life exceeded the willingness of homeowners to pay ever-rising property taxes to support municipal services. At first, the suburbs resorted to subdivision exactions and impact fees to pass the cost of new growth on to the newcomers. Then, the bedroom communities began to seek out industry (of the "clean" type) and office and shopping centers to bring in more tax revenue. When this began on a large scale, mostly in the 1970's, city residents sought to move to where the new jobs were to be found. The market demand for multi-family housing in the suburbs and other forms of less expensive housing forced many suburban communities to accommodate these formerly resented kinds of housing. A great deal of litigation emerged at this time, some challenging the zoning scheme, some using federal civil rights legislation, notably the Fair Housing Act. The federal government increased its efforts to subsidize low-interest mortgages and made many efforts to attain the post-war aspirational policy goal that every American is entitled to safe and decent housing. Zoning and its discriminatory effects as to housing represents a large percentage of the litigation over zoning.

In looking at the overall land use system in this country one truism is apparent—people vote with their feet. Residents of first-ring suburbs moved farther out to second-ring suburbs to seek better schools for their children, more space and a "higher" quality of life. City dwellers who could obtain mortgages on easier terms in the 1990's and currently bought the houses in the older suburbs. And then, a curious thing happened. The more affluent suburban dwellers who fled the city earlier, after their children finished high school, began to move back into the city into gentrified buildings near the center or into luxurious high-rise condominiums in the heart of the city. Developers and builders closely followed such trends and market forces played a large role in convincing local government to modify zoning restrictions and assumptions.

The larger policy issue that faces cities today is whether to allow market demand to dictate zoning distinctions or instead try to dictate and guide the housing arrangements. This issue is partly economic, partly political, and somewhat shaped by legal trends, through legislation and litigation. This chapter tries to guide students through the evolution of these developments on the ground and legal changes in the courts.

B. THE BEDROOM SUBURB

McDERMOTT v. VILLAGE OF CALVERTON PARK
Supreme Court of Missouri, En Banc, 1970.
454 S.W.2d 577.

[In their petition the McDermotts directed a three-pronged attack on the constitutionality and the validity of the Village's zoning ordinance, Ordinance No. 77. That ordinance, while it divided the municipality into four districts, restricted the use of land and buildings in all such districts to one-family dwellings, save for public parks and other uses not here material. Relying in the main on the decision of the Supreme Court in *City of Moline Acres v. Heidbreder*, Mo., 367 S.W.2d 568, the trial court held that under our zoning enabling statutes, §§ 89.010 to 89.140, inclusive, RSMo 1959, V.A.M.S., the Village did not have the statutory power and authority to adopt a zoning ordinance which restricted the use of all land and buildings to one-family dwellings, and declared Ordinance No. 77 invalid. Defendants' appeal followed.

* * *

Plaintiff's property comprises about 2½ acres, and fronts 280 feet on the west side of North Florissant Road between Connolly Drive and Barto Drive, in the Village of Calverton Park. It was subdivided into 19 lots in 1925. The McDermotts acquired the tract in June, 1946. On January 15, 1953, the Village adopted Ordinance No. 77. As stated the use of the land and buildings in all of the four districts into which the municipality is thereby divided is restricted by the ordinance to one-family dwellings, the differences in the zoning districts being the size of the lots, building lines, and building materials. On January 8, 1963, the McDermotts entered into a contract for the sale of their property to Larry Witzer or assigns for $58,500, conditioned upon the rezoning of the tract for the commercial use of the property as a shopping center, "at the expense of the seller"; and the procurement of all necessary building permits, based upon the purchaser's plans, which "shall be obtained by buyer at his expense." Thereafter, on May 27, 1967, the McDermotts as owners and William Goodman as their real estate agent filed with the Village an application for a change of zoning. The Board of Trustees of the Village denied the application on September 23, 1963. On January 21, 1964, the McDermotts filed with the Village's Building Commissioner an application for a building permit for the construction of a shopping center on their property, accompanied by a set of plans, which application the Building Commissioner denied. This action followed, instituted by the McDermotts on February 8, 1964. This statement of facts is from the intermediate appellate decision.]

HOLMAN, JUDGE.

* * *

Our first task is to re-examine the case of *City of Moline Acres v. Heidbreder, supra,* in which a zoning ordinance that placed all of the village in one district zoned for single-family dwellings was held to be invalid. Defendants have devoted a substantial portion of their brief in pointing out factual distinctions between that case and the one before us, and contend that Moline Acres is not here applicable. While these cases have many distinguishing features we think *Moline Acres*, unless overruled, would control the decision in the case before us. This because *Moline Acres* held that our zoning statutes did not give to a municipality the power to adopt a one-use district zoning ordinance encompassing the whole town; that the village had no authority to adopt such a zoning ordinance. While Calverton Park had four districts, all were restricted to a single use, i.e., "one-family dwellings," and hence we consider the Moline Acres case to be applicable.

We have carefully re-examined *Moline Acres* and have concluded that it is not sound and should therefore no longer be followed. We have read and reread the applicable statutes and find nothing therein to indicate a legislative intent that, *under all circumstances,* a municipality must provide for more than one use in its zoning ordinance. We recognize that a comprehensive plan of zoning would, in most cities, particularly isolated ones, require commercial zoning districts in order for the needs of the residents to be conveniently supplied. However, St. Louis County, which completely surrounds (except for the portion fronting on the Mississippi River) the large City of St. Louis, is in a rather unique situation. Many people who work in St. Louis City live in the County. That fact, coupled with its own growth, has caused a vast number of cities and villages to be formed in the County, many of which are primarily for residential purposes rather than commercial or manufacturing. Those are often referred to as "bedroom" municipalities. Many of those cities are completely surrounded by other cities and most of the others border on one or more cities. * * *

The purpose for zoning is to promote health, safety, morals, and the general welfare. Section 89.020, supra. Certainly, where commercial and professional services are conveniently available elsewhere, none of those purposes would be enhanced by multiple-use zoning as compared to one-family dwelling use. Moreover, § 89.040 provides that the zoning should be "designed to lessen congestion in the streets; to secure safety from fire, panic and other dangers; to promote health and the general welfare; to provide adequate light and air; to prevent the overcrowding of land; to avoid undue concentration of population * * *." Under circumstances such as exist in Calverton Park all of those objectives are promoted by the one-family dwelling requirement and would be more likely to be accomplished than would be the case if there were multiple-use zoning. Furthermore, the "comprehensive plan" required by that section "shall be made with reasonable consideration, among other things, to the character of the district and its peculiar suitability for particular uses, and with a view to conserving the values of buildings and encouraging the most appropriate use of land throughout such municipality." Those requirements can be met by a one-use zoning ordinance such as we have in this case. We see nothing therein which would require multiple-use zoning.

As heretofore stated, we find nothing in any of the statutes which would preclude one-use zoning.

There do not appear to be many cases that have considered this question. The case of *Valley View Village v. Proffett*, 6th Cir., 221 F.2d 412, and *Connor v. Township of Chanhassen*, 249 Minn. 205, 81 N.W.2d 789, support our view. The contrary view is indicated in *Dowsey v. Village of Kensington*, 257 N.Y. 221, 177 N.E. 427, 86 A.L.R. 642, and *Gundersen v. Village of Bingham Farms*, 372 Mich. 352, 126 N.W.2d 715. The *Gunderson* case followed the *Moline Acres* case. While we regret that situation, we cannot permit it to restrain us from making what we consider to be a correct decision at this time.

As indicated, we rule that Ordinance No. 77 is not invalid as a matter of law.

* * *

The question for our decision is whether the public interest and welfare is sufficient to outweigh the financial detriment to plaintiff. If the question is fairly debatable we cannot interfere and the ruling of the Board of Trustees must prevail.

We have concluded that, at the very least, the question is fairly debatable. It would appear to be contrary to the general welfare of the inhabitants to rezone this property for unnecessary commercial use in a village so obviously suitable for exclusive one-family dwellings. When we consider that no resident except plaintiff would receive a benefit, and that there would be the various detriments which we have heretofore outlined, it could hardly be said that the decision of the trustees was so arbitrary and unreasonable that it would infringe upon the rights of plaintiff under the various constitutional provisions mentioned.

* * *

The judgment is reversed and the cause is remanded with directions to the trial court to enter a judgment in accordance with the views herein expressed.

Notes

1. Also see Cadoux v. Planning and Zoning Commission, 162 Conn. 425, 294 A.2d 582 (1972), certiorari denied 408 U.S. 924, 92 S.Ct. 2496, 33 L.Ed.2d 335 (1972), and the annotation in 54 A.L.R.3d 1282. In addition to the New York (Dowsey v. Village of Kensington) and Michigan (Gunderson v. Village of Bingham Farms) cases cited in the principal case for the view that single use zoning is invalid, see Hobart v. Collier, 3 Wis.2d 182, 87 N.W.2d 868 (1958) and Matthews v. Board of Zoning Appeals of Greene County, 218 Va. 270, 237 S.E.2d 128 (1977). The Gunderson case in Michigan was modified when a later court explained that towns had to have a minimum of two zones, and in Countrywalk Condominiums, Inc. v.

Oakland Circuit Court City of Orchard Lake Village, 221 Mich.App. 19, 561 N.W.2d 405 (1997) the court upheld a zoning scheme allowing only single-family, professional offices, and local business. The total exclusion of apartments and condominiums was justified on the basis of an overburdened traffic system.

The Missouri courts have continued to follow the Calverton Park case. See, e.g., Clarkson Valley Estates, Inc. v. Village of Clarkson Valley, 630 S.W.2d 151 (Mo.App.1982).

2. The Calverton Park case seems to be a relic of the past—the exclusively residential suburb. The high cost of providing municipal services and the limits on property taxation have combined to inspire local government to increase income by welcoming commercial and industrial land uses.

C. NON–TRADITIONAL FAMILIES

Zoning, from the point of view of the average citizen, created a hierarchy of districts, culminating in the single-family residential district. This "highest" district was to be protected, not only from commercial and industrial incursions, but also from structures that might house more than one family, such as duplexes, townhouses, and apartments. Also, the single-family dwelling was understood to exclude mobile homes and manufactured housing. In carrying out this Euclidean view of zoning, cities and towns had to define "single-family" in order to insure protection for this highest zoning district. In the course of doing this, a legal problem soon emerged—to what extent could a definition of family be applied to unusual personal living arrangements in structures that were clearly built as single-family houses.

VILLAGE OF BELLE TERRE v. BORAAS
Supreme Court of the United States, 1974.
416 U.S. 1, 94 S.Ct. 1536, 39 L.Ed.2d 797.

MR. JUSTICE DOUGLAS delivered the opinion of the Court.

Belle Terre is a village on Long Island's north shore of about 220 homes inhabited by 700 people. Its total land area is less than one square mile. It has restricted land use to one-family dwellings excluding lodging houses, boarding houses, fraternity houses, or multiple dwelling houses. The word "Family" as used in the ordinance means, "One or more persons related by blood, adoption or marriage, living and cooking together as a single housekeeping unit, exclusive of household servants. A number of persons but not exceeding two (2) living and cooking together as a single housekeeping unit though not related by blood, adoption, or marriage shall be deemed to constitute a family."

Appellees (Dickmans) are owners of a house in the village and leased it in December, 1971 for a term of 18 months to Michael Truman. Later Bruce Boraas became a colessee. Then Anne Parish moved into the house along with three others. These six are students at nearby State University at Stony Brook and none is related to the other by blood, adoption, or marriage. When the village served the Dickmans with an

"Order to Remedy Violations" of the ordinance, the owners plus three tenants thereupon brought this action under 42 U.S.C.A. § 1983 for an injunction declaring the ordinance unconstitutional. The District Court held the ordinance constitutional and the Court of Appeals reversed, one judge dissenting. 2 Cir., 476 F.2d 806. The case is here by appeal, 28 U.S.C.A. § 1254(2); and we noted probable jurisdiction, 414 U.S. 907, 94 S.Ct. 234, 38 L.Ed.2d 145.

* * *

The present ordinance is challenged on several grounds: that it interferes with a person's right to travel; that it interferes with the right to migrate to and settle within a State; that it bars people who are uncongenial to the present residents; that the ordinance expresses the social preferences of the residents for groups that will be congenial to them; that social homogeneity is not a legitimate interest of government; that the restriction of those whom the neighbors do not like trenches on the newcomers' rights of privacy; that it is of no rightful concern to villagers whether the residents are married or unmarried; that the ordinance is antithetical to the Nation's experience, ideology and self-perception as an open, egalitarian, and integrated society.

We find none of these reasons in the record before us. It is not aimed at transients. Cf. Shapiro v. Thompson, 394 U.S. 618, 89 S.Ct. 1322, 22 L.Ed.2d 600. It involves no procedural disparity inflicted on some but not on others such as was presented by Griffin v. Illinois, 351 U.S. 12, 76 S.Ct. 585, 100 L.Ed. 891. It involves no "fundamental" right guaranteed by the Constitution, such as voting, *Harper v. Virginia State Board*, 383 U.S. 663, 86 S.Ct. 1079, 16 L.Ed.2d 169; the right of association, *NAACP v. Alabama ex rel. Patterson*, 357 U.S. 449, 78 S.Ct. 1163, 2 L.Ed.2d 1488; the right of access to the courts, *NAACP v. Button*, 371 U.S. 415, 83 S.Ct. 328, 9 L.Ed.2d 405; or any rights of privacy, cf. *Griswold v. Connecticut*, 381 U.S. 479, 85 S.Ct. 1678, 14 L.Ed.2d 510; *Eisenstadt v. Baird*, 405 U.S. 438, 453–454, 92 S.Ct. 1029, 1038–1039, 31 L.Ed.2d 349. We deal with economic and social legislation where legislatures have historically drawn lines which we respect against the charge of violation of the Equal Protection Clause if the law be "reasonable, not arbitrary" (quoting *F.S. Royster Guano Co. v. Virginia*, 253 U.S. 412, 415, 40 S.Ct. 560, 561, 64 L.Ed. 989) and bears "a rational relationship to a [permissible] state objective." Reed v. Reed, 404 U.S. 71, 76, 92 S.Ct. 251, 254, 30 L.Ed.2d 225.

It is said, however, that if two unmarried people can constitute a "family," there is no reason why three or four may not. But every line drawn by a legislature leaves some out that might well have been included. That exercise of discretion, however, is a legislative not a judicial function.

It is said that the Belle Terre ordinance reeks with an animosity to unmarried couples who live together. There is no evidence to support it; and the provision of the ordinance bringing within the definition of a "family" two unmarried people belies the charge.

The ordinance places no ban on other forms of association, for a "family" may, so far as the ordinance is concerned, entertain whomever they like.

The regimes of boarding houses, fraternity houses, and the like present urban problems. More people occupy a given space; more cars rather continuously pass by; more cars are parked; noise travels with crowds.

A quiet place where yards are wide, people few, and motor vehicles restricted are legitimate guidelines in a land use project addressed to family needs. This goal is a permissible one within Berman v. Parker, supra. The police power is not confined to elimination of filth, stench, and unhealthy places. It is ample to lay out zones where family values, youth values, and the blessings of quiet seclusion, and clean air make the area a sanctuary for people.

* * *

Reversed.

MR. JUSTICE MARSHALL, dissenting.

* * *

When separate but equal was still accepted constitutional dogma, this Court struck down a racially restrictive zoning ordinance. *Buchanan v. Warley*, 245 U.S. 60, 38 S.Ct. 16, 62 L.Ed. 149 (1917). I am sure the Court would not be hesitant to invalidate that ordinance today. The lower federal courts have considered procedural aspects of zoning, and acted to insure that land use controls are not used as means of confining minorities and the poor to the ghettos of our central cities. These are limited but necessary intrusions on the discretion of zoning authorities. By the same token, I think it clear that the First Amendment provides some limitation on zoning laws. It is inconceivable to me that we would allow the exercise of the zoning power to burden First Amendment freedoms, as by ordinances that restrict occupancy to individuals adhering to particular religious, political or scientific beliefs. Zoning officials properly concern themselves with the uses of land—with, for example, the number and kind of dwellings to be constructed in a certain neighborhood or the number of persons who can reside in those dwellings. But zoning authorities cannot validly consider who those persons are, what they believe, or how they choose to live, whether they are Negro or white, Catholic or Jew, Republican or Democrat, married or unmarried.

My disagreement with the Court today is based upon my view that the ordinance in this case unnecessarily burdens appellees' First Amendment freedom of association and their constitutionally guaranteed right to privacy. Our decisions establish that the First and Fourteenth Amendments protect the freedom to choose one's associates. *NAACP v. Button*, 371 U.S. 415, 430, 83 S.Ct. 328, 336, 9 L.Ed.2d 405 (1963). Constitutional protection is extended not only to modes of association that are political in the usual sense, but also to those that pertain to the social and economic benefit of the members. The selection of one's living companions involves similar choices as to the emotional, social, or economic benefits to be derived from alternative living arrangements.

The freedom of association is often inextricably entwined with the constitutionally guaranteed right of privacy. The right to "establish a home" is an essential part of the liberty guaranteed by the Fourteenth Amendment. *Meyer v. Nebraska*, 262 U.S. 390, 399, 43 S.Ct. 625, 626, 67 L.Ed. 1042 (1923); *Griswold v. Connecticut*, 381 U.S. 479, 495, 85 S.Ct. 1678, 1687, 14 L.Ed.2d 510 (1965). And the Constitution secures to an individual a freedom "to satisfy his intellectual and emotional needs within the privacy of his own home." *Stanley v. Georgia*, 394 U.S. 557, 564–565, 89 S.Ct. 1243, 1248, 22 L.Ed.2d 542 (1969); see *Paris Adult Theatre I v. Slaton*, 413 U.S. 49, 66–67, 93 S.Ct. 2628, 2640–2641, 37 L.Ed.2d 446 (1973). Constitutionally protected privacy is, in Mr. Justice Brandeis' words, "as against the government, the right to be let alone * * * the right most valued by civilized man." *Olmstead v. United States*, 277 U.S. 438, 478, 48 S.Ct. 564, 572, 72 L.Ed. 944 (1928) (dissenting opinion). The choice of household companions—of whether a person's "intellectual and emotional needs" are best met by living with family, friends, professional associates or others—involves deeply personal considerations as to the kind and quality of intimate relationships within the home. That decision surely falls within the ambit of the right to privacy protected by the Constitution.

The instant ordinance discriminates on the basis of just such a personal lifestyle choice as to household companions. It permits any number of persons related by blood or marriage, be it two or twenty, to live in a single household, but it limits to two the number of unrelated persons bound by profession, love, friendship, religious or political affiliation or mere economics who can occupy a single home. Belle Terre imposes upon those who deviate from the community norm in their choice of living companions significantly greater restrictions than are applied to residential groups who are related by blood or marriage, and comprise the established order with the community. The town has, in effect, acted to fence out those individuals whose choice of lifestyle differs from that of its current residents.

This is not a case where the Court is being asked to nullify a township's sincere efforts to maintain its residential character by preventing the operation of rooming houses, fraternity houses or other commercial or high-density residential uses. Unquestionably, a town is free to restrict such uses. Moreover, as a general proposition, I see no constitutional infirmity in a town limiting the density of use in residential areas by zoning regulations which do not discriminate on the basis of constitutionally suspect criteria. This ordinance, however, limits the density of occupancy of only those homes occupied by unrelated persons. It thus reaches beyond control of the use of land or the density of population, and undertakes to regulate the way people choose to associate with each other within the privacy of their own homes.

* * *

I respectfully dissent.

[A dissenting opinion by JUSTICE BRENNAN is omitted.]

Notes

1. Also see Palo Alto Tenants Union v. Morgan, 321 F.Supp. 908 (N.D.Cal.1970), affirmed 487 F.2d 883 (9th Cir.1973), certiorari denied 417 U.S. 910, 94 S.Ct. 2608, 41 L.Ed.2d 214 (1974).

2. In 1977, the Supreme Court was faced with another "single-family" case. In Moore v. City of East Cleveland, Ohio, 431 U.S. 494, 97 S.Ct. 1932, 52 L.Ed.2d 531 (1977), the ordinance contained a complex definition of family which had the effect of making Mrs. Moore's occupancy of her dwelling along with her son and two grandsons (who were first cousins) illegal. In a plurality opinion by Justice Powell, the Court distinguished Belle Terre by noting that the earlier case affected only unrelated individuals while the East Cleveland ordinance forbade the living together of certain categories of relatives. The Court thus gave "close scrutiny" to the ordinance because of the governmental intrusion into the "family" and found that the city could offer no acceptable justification for such intrusion. The city's argument that the objectives of the ordinance were to avoid overcrowding, traffic congestion and undue burdens on the school system was found by the Court to have, at best, a tenuous relationship to the definition of family and the effect of the ordinance on Mrs. Moore.

Justice Powell explained the Belle Terre case in the following statement:

The city argues that our decision in Village of Belle Terre v. Boraas, 416 U.S. 1, 94 S.Ct. 1536, 39 L.Ed.2d 797 (1974), requires us to sustain the ordinance attacked here. Belle Terre, like East Cleveland, imposed limits on the types of groups that could occupy a single dwelling unit. Applying the constitutional standard announced in this Court's leading land-use case, Village of Euclid v. Ambler Realty Co., 272 U.S. 365, 47 S.Ct. 114, 71 L.Ed. 303 (1926), we sustained the Belle Terre ordinance on the ground that it bore a rational relationship to permissible state objectives.

But one overriding factor sets this case apart from *Belle Terre*. The ordinance there affected only *unrelated* individuals. It expressly allowed all who were related by "blood, adoption, or marriage" to live together, and in sustaining the ordinance we were careful to note that it promoted "family needs" and "family values." 416 U.S., at 9, 94 S.Ct., at 1541. East Cleveland, in contrast, has chosen to regulate the occupancy of its housing by slicing deeply into the family itself. This is no mere incidental result of the ordinance. On its face it selects certain categories of relatives who may live together and declares that others may not. In particular, it makes a crime of a grandmother's choice to live with her grandson in circumstances like those presented here.

When a city undertakes such intrusive regulation of the family, neither *Belle Terre* nor *Euclid* governs; the usual judicial deference to the legislature is inappropriate. "This Court has long recognized that freedom of personal choice in matters of marriage and family life is one of the liberties protected by the Due Process Clause of the Fourteenth Amendment." * * * Of course, the family is not beyond regulation.

* * * But when the government intrudes on choices concerning family living arrangements, this Court must examine carefully the importance of the governmental interests advanced and the extent to which they are served by the challenged regulation.

3. After Belle Terre, would you expect the state courts to accept restrictive zoning ordinance definitions of "family" so as to exclude from the single-family district living arrangements other than the traditional family? Consider the following materials.

McMINN v. TOWN OF OYSTER BAY

Court of Appeals of New York, 1985.
66 N.Y.2d 544, 498 N.Y.S.2d 128, 488 N.E.2d 1240.

SIMONS, JUDGE.

Plaintiffs are the owners and tenants of a four-bedroom house in Massapequa in the Town of Oyster Bay, Long Island, which is in violation of the Town zoning ordinance. They commenced this action against defendants, the Town of Oyster Bay, the Town Council and its supervisor and building inspector, for a declaration that that portion of the ordinance restricting "single-family" housing to any number of persons related by blood, marriage or adoption or to two persons not so related but both of whom are 62 years of age or older violates the due process and equal protection clauses of the State Constitution (N.Y. Const., art. I, §§ 6, 11) and Human Rights Law § 296 (Executive Law § 296). Plaintiffs also sought an injunction against further enforcement of the ordinance. Following a trial, Supreme Court concluded that the age requirement for defining two unrelated individuals as a family violated the State constitutional guarantee of equal protection of the laws and that the ordinance also violated Executive Law § 296(5) to the extent it prohibited occupancy of a single-family house by two individuals on the ground of marital status but that the ordinance was in all other respects valid (111 Misc.2d 1046, 445 N.Y.S.2d 859). The combined effect of these rulings was to find the ordinance constitutional insofar as it restricted occupancy of a single-family home to any number of persons related by blood, marriage or adoption or two unrelated persons. On cross appeals, the Appellate Division modified the judgment and declared that the challenged portion of the ordinance was facially unconstitutional under the due process clause of our State Constitution insofar as it prohibits occupancy of one-family homes by persons unrelated by blood, marriage or adoption and that it was constitutional insofar as it limits occupancy of one-family homes to a single housekeeping unit (105 A.D.2d 46, 482 N.Y.S.2d 773).

* * *

Plaintiffs Robert and Joan McMinn purchased their house in 1973. It is in a D Residence district. On June 1, 1976, they leased the house to four unrelated young men between the ages of 22 and 25 who had grown up in the area and wanted to remain near their families but not reside with them. Shortly after the tenants moved in, a criminal information was filed against the McMinns in District Court, Nassau County, charging them with violating the zoning ordinance because the house was occupied by more than one family. The McMinns and the tenants then commenced this action seeking declaratory and injunctive relief and the criminal proceedings have been adjourned pending its disposition. In their complaint, plaintiffs assert only State constitutional and statutory claims and expressly reserve the right to litigate all Federal claims in a Federal forum pursuant to *England v. Medical Examiners,* 375 U.S. 411, 84 S.Ct. 461, 11 L.Ed.2d 440. They contend that the restrictive definition of "family" contained in the ordinance is facially invalid under Executive Law § 296 and the due process and equal protection clauses of the State Constitution (N.Y. Const., art. I, §§ 6, 11) or, in the alternative, that it violated these statutory and constitutional provisions as applied to them.

* * *

Indisputably, this ordinance was enacted to further several legitimate governmental purposes, including preservation of the character of traditional single-family neighborhoods, reduction of parking and traffic problems, control of population density and prevention of noise and disturbance. The dispute centers on whether the means the local legislature has chosen, the challenged ordinance and more specifically the definition of "family" contained in it, are reasonably related to the achievement of these legitimate purposes.

Manifestly, restricting occupancy of single-family housing based generally on the biological or legal relationships between its inhabitants bears no reasonable relationship to the goals of reducing parking and traffic problems, controlling population density and preventing noise and disturbance (*see, Moore v. East Cleveland,* 431 U.S. 494, 499–500, 97 S.Ct. 1932, 1935–1936, 52 L.Ed.2d 531; *id.,* at p. 520, n. 16, 97 S.Ct. at p. 1946, n. 16 [Stevens, J., concurring]; *City of Santa Barbara v. Adamson,* 27 Cal.3d 123, 164 Cal.Rptr. 539, 544, 610 P.2d 436, 441; *State v. Baker,* 81 N.J. 99, 405 A.2d 368, 373). Their achievement depends not upon the biological or legal relations between the occupants of a house but generally upon the size of the dwelling and the lot and the number of its occupants. Thus, the definition of family employed here is both fatally overinclusive in prohibiting, for example, a young unmarried couple from occupying a four-bedroom house who do not threaten the purposes of the ordinance and the underinclusive in failing to prohibit occupancy of a two-bedroom home by 10 or 12 persons who are related in only the most distant manner and who might well be expected to present serious overcrowding and traffic problems.

* * *

Defendants contend that the scope of protection accorded under the due process clause of our State Constitution is coextensive with the protection provided by the due process clause of the 14th Amendment and that the challenged portion of the ordinance would survive Federal due process scrutiny under *Village of Belle Terre v. Boraas,* 416 U.S. 1, 94 S.Ct. 1536, 39 L.Ed.2d 797, *supra.* Because the ordinance challenged in this case contains age limitations making it more restrictive than the *Belle Terre* ordinance and because the Supreme Court did not state in either *Belle Terre* or *Moore v. East Cleveland,* 431 U.S. 494, 97 S.Ct. 1932, 52 L.Ed.2d 531, *supra* what definition of family is minimally necessary to survive Federal due process scrutiny, those decisions are not determinative of whether the ordinance before us would withstand Federal constitutional analysis. We have no need to consider the issue, however, for it is clear that the definition of family contained in this ordinance is incompatible with our prior decisions in *White Plains* and *Group House.* Although those cases did not involve an explicit adjudication of the homeowner's constitutional rights, they also cannot reasonably be interpreted as relying upon the public policy favoring establishment of group homes found in the Social Services Law (Social Services Law § 374–c). Quite the contrary, in each case the court expressly disavowed any reliance on the homeowner's assertion that enforcement of the restrictive definitions of family contained in the challenged ordinance would contravene the State's Social Services Law and the public policy embodied in it (*see, Group House v. Board of Zoning & Appeals,* 45 N.Y.2d 266, 271, 408 N.Y.S.2d 377, 380 N.E.2d 207, *supra; City of White Plains v. Ferraioli,* 34 N.Y.2d 300, 306, 357 N.Y.S.2d 449, 313 N.E.2d 756, *supra; cf. Crane Neck Assn. v. New York City/Long Is. County Servs. Group,* 61 N.Y.2d 154, 472 N.Y.S.2d 901, 460 N.E.2d 1336). Thus, the reasoning employed in *White Plains* and *Group House* is equally applicable to the constitutional issue raised on this appeal and provides ample support for the conclusion reached today.

Accordingly, in view of our holding that the definition of family in article I, § 1 of the Building Zone Ordinance of the Town of Oyster Bay is facially unconstitutional under the due process clause of the New York State Constitution (art. I, § 6), the order of the Appellate Division should be affirmed, with costs.

KAYE, JUDGE (concurring).

[Concurring opinion omitted.]

Notes

1. Also see Baer v. Town of Brookhaven, 73 N.Y.2d 942, 540 N.Y.S.2d 234, 537 N.E.2d 619 (1989) where the court struck down a prohibition against more than four unrelated persons in the single family district. The defendants were five elderly women sharing a house.

2. Several case involve what has become known as the problem of "house stuffing" in college towns or cities. Residential areas near college campuses become crowded with numbers of students who share a house. Many cases review ordinances that seek to control the problem by limiting the number of non-related persons who can occupy a house. Some cases are:

a. Borough of Glassboro v. Vallorosi, 117 N.J. 421, 568 A.2d 888 (1990). The New Jersey Supreme Court struck down a single-family definition that was applied to a group of ten college sophomores leasing a house. The court noted that the ordinance was adopted after "a rowdy weekend celebration by Glassboro State College students." Because the students planned to live in the house for three years and shared housekeeping duties, the court found that they were the functional equivalent of a family.

b. College Area Renters and Landlord Ass'n v. City of San Diego, 43 Cal.App.4th 677, 50 Cal.Rptr.2d 515 (1996). Here the court held that an attempt by the city to restrict the number of unrelated occupants in apartments under a sliding scale relating to square footage, off-street parking, and number of bathrooms violated the state constitution's equal protection provision. Owner-occupied overcrowded housing was exempted from the ordinance, enacted to deal with the problem of "mini dorms" in neighborhoods near college campuses. Another "mini dorm" case is Kirsch v. Prince George's County, 331 Md. 89, 626 A.2d 372, cert. denied 510 U.S. 1011, 114 S.Ct. 600, 126 L.Ed.2d 565 (1993) (zoning ordinance restricting rental to student groups but not other groups of similar size violates Equal Protection Clause).

c. The Michigan Court of Appeals, on the other hand, upheld an ordinance in Ann Arbor limiting occupancy of single-family houses to not more than six unrelated individuals. Stegeman v. City of Ann Arbor, 213 Mich.App. 487, 540 N.W.2d 724 (1995). Perhaps college students in Michigan are different than a religious commune, because an earlier Michigan Supreme Court case, Charter Twp. of Delta v. Dinolfo, 419 Mich. 253, 351 N.W.2d 831 (1984) held that a ban against more than six unrelated individuals occupying a single-family house denied due process and was arbitrary as applied to members of The Work of Christ Community living together in a house. Also see Unification Theological Seminary v. City of Poughkeepsie, 201 A.D.2d 484, 607 N.Y.S.2d 383 (1994).

d. Dvorak v. City of Bloomington, 768 N.E.2d 490 (Ind.2002). The court struck down a limitation on the number of unrelated adults on the basis of the equal privileges and immunities clause of the state constitution.

3. Santa Barbara v. Adamson, 27 Cal.3d 123, 164 Cal.Rptr. 539, 610 P.2d 436 (1980) was an unusual situation. There the California Supreme Court struck down an ordinance that defined family to include as many as five unrelated people living together as a single housekeeping unit. The court based its decision primarily upon the provision in the California constitution protecting privacy. The facts in Adamson are somewhat unusual:

> The record shows that appellants are three residents of a house in a single-family zone where the minimum lot-size is one acre. They and other individuals form a group of 12 adults who live in a 24–room, 10–bedroom, 6–bathroom house owned by appellant Adamson. The occupants are in their late 20's or early 30's and include a business woman, a graduate biochemistry student, a tractor-business operator, a real estate woman, a lawyer, and others. They are not related by blood, marriage, or adoption.

They moved into the house after Adamson acquired it on December 1, 1977. On February 9, 1978, following warnings, the city attorney sued for a temporary restraining order, preliminary injunction, and permanent injunction. A restraining order was issued on March 7, 1978; a preliminary injunction on March 29, 1978.

Appellants' household illustrates the kind of living arrangements prohibited by the ordinance's rule-of-five. (Section 28.04.230, subd. 2, supra.) They chose to reside with each other when Adamson made it known she was looking for congenial people with whom to share her house. Since then, they explain, they have become a close group with social, economic, and psychological commitments to each other. They share expenses, rotate chores, and eat evening meals together. Some have children who regularly visit. Two (not including Adamson) have contributed over $2,000 each to improving the house and defraying costs of this lawsuit. Emotional support and stability are provided by the members to each other; they enjoy recreational activities such as a trip to Mexico together; they have chosen to live together mainly because of their compatibility.

Regarding physical environment, the house has 6,231 square feet of space and is hidden from the street by trees and a fence. It has off-street parking for at least 12 cars. Appellants have built a wall around part of the property and a new, private driveway to help isolate them from neighbors' houses. There is no evidence of overcrowding though, after appellants had arrived, some neighbors did notice a larger number of cars parked on the property and an understandable increase in the number of residents.

Another case, similar to the Adamson case, also rejected the Belle Terre rationale and found that an ordinance containing a restrictive definition of family violated the state constitutional provision recognizing the right of privacy. See State v. Baker, 81 N.J. 99, 405 A.2d 368 (1979). Also see City of Chula Vista v. Pagard, 115 Cal.App.3d 785, 171 Cal.Rptr. 738 (1981), where a claim of religious freedom to live communally was at issue; Holy Name Hospital v. Montroy, 153 N.J.Super. 181, 379 A.2d 299 (1977), where the court found that four nuns sharing a house constituted a harmless voluntary family; Children's Home of Easton v. City of Easton, 53 Pa.Cmwlth. 216, 417 A.2d 830 (1980), where the court held that a proposed foster home was the functional equivalent of a biological family and thus distinguishable from Belle Terre.

4. So far, the cases indicate that the problem of allowing unrelated persons to share a house revolves around issues of traffic, overcrowding, noise, and other environmental impacts. However, the next case illustrates that a "moral" component might be important.

CITY OF LADUE v. HORN

Missouri Court of Appeals, 1986.
720 S.W.2d 745.

CRANDALL, JUDGE.

Defendants, Joan Horn and E. Terrence Jones, appeal from the judgment of the trial court in favor of plaintiff, City of Ladue (Ladue), which enjoined defendants from occupying their home in violation of Ladue's zoning ordinance and which dismissed defendants' counterclaim. We affirm.

The case was submitted to the trial court on stipulated facts. Ladue's Zoning Ordinance No. 1175 was in effect at all times pertinent to the present action. Certain zones were designated as one-family residential. The zoning ordinance defined family as: "One or more persons related by blood, marriage or adoption, occupying a dwelling unit as an individual housekeeping organization." The only authorized accessory use in residential districts was for "[a]ccommodations for domestic persons employed and living on the premises and home occupations." The purpose of Ladue's zoning ordinance was broadly stated as to promote "the health, safety, morals and general welfare" of Ladue.

In July, 1981, defendants purchased a seven-bedroom, four-bathroom house which was located in a single-family residential zone in Ladue. Residing in defendants' home were Horn's two children (aged 16 and 19) and Jones's one child (age 18). The two older children attended out-of-state universities and lived in the house only on a part-time basis. Although defendants were not married, they shared a common bedroom, maintained a joint checking account for the household expenses, ate their meals together, entertained together, and disciplined each other's children. Ladue made demands upon defendants to vacate their home because their household did not comprise a family, as defined by Ladue's zoning ordinance, and therefore they could not live in an area zoned for single-family dwellings. When defendants refused to vacate, Ladue sought to enjoin defendants' continued violation of the zoning ordinance. Defendants counterclaimed, seeking a declaration that the zoning ordinance was constitutionally void. They also sought attorneys' fees and costs. The trial court entered a permanent injunction in favor of Ladue and dismissed defendants' counterclaim. Enforcement of the injunction was stayed pending this appeal.

* * *

Defendants posit that the term "family" is susceptible to several meanings. They contend that, since their household is the "functional and factual equivalent of a natural family," the ordinance may not preclude them from living in a single-family residential Ladue neighborhood. *See, e.g., McMinn v. Town of Oyster Bay,* 66 N.Y.2d 544, 498 N.Y.S.2d 128, 488 N.E.2d 1240 (Ct.App.1985). Defendants argue in their brief as follows:

> The record amply demonstrates that the private, intimate interests of Horn and Jones are substantial. Horn, Jones, and their respective children have historically lived together as a single family unit. They use and occupy their home for the identical purposes and in the identical manners as families which are biologically or maritally related.

To bolster this contention, defendants elaborate on their shared duties, as set forth earlier in this opinion. Defendants acknowledge the importance of viewing themselves as a family unit, albeit a "conceptual family" as opposed to a "true non-family," in order to prevent the application of the ordinance.

The fallacy in defendants' syllogism is that the stipulated facts do not compel the conclusion that defendants are living as a family. A man and woman living together, sharing pleasures and certain responsibilities, does not *per se* constitute a family in even the conceptual sense. To approximate a family relationship, there must exist a commitment to a permanent relationship and a perceived reciprocal obligation to support and to care for each other. *See, e.g., State ex rel. Ellis v. Liddle,* 520 S.W.2d 644, 650 (Mo.App.1975). Only when these characteristics are present can the conceptual family, perhaps, equate with the traditional family. In a traditional family, certain of its inherent attributes arise from the legal relationship of the family members. In a non-traditional family, those same qualities arise in fact, either by explicit agreement or by tacit understanding among the parties.

While the stipulated facts could arguably support an inference by the trial court that defendants and their children comprised a non-traditional family, they do not compel that inference. Absent findings of fact and conclusions of law, we cannot assume that the trial court's perception of defendants' familial status comported with defendants' characterization of themselves as a conceptual family. In fact, if a finding by the trial court that defendants' living arrangement constituted a conceptual family is critical to a determination in defendants' favor, we can assume that the court's finding was adverse to defendants' position. Ordinarily, given our deference to the decision of the trial court, that would dispose of this appeal. We decline, however, to restrict our ruling to such a narrow basis. We therefore consider the broader issues presented by the parties. We assume, *arguendo,* that the sole basis for the judgment entered by the trial court was that defendants were not related by blood, marriage or adoption, as required by Ladue's ordinance.

* * *

Ladue has a legitimate concern with laying out guidelines for land use addressed to family needs. "It is ample to lay out zones where family values, youth values, and the blessings of quiet seclusion and clean air make the area a sanctuary for people." [Citing the Belle Terre case.] The question of whether Ladue could have chosen more precise means to effectuate its legislative goals is immaterial. Ladue's zoning ordinance is rationally related to its expressed purposes and violates no provisions of the Constitution of the United States. Further, defendants' assertion that they have a constitutional right to share their residence with whomever they please amounts to the same argument that was made and found unpersuasive by the court in *Belle Terre.*

* * *

The essence of zoning is selection; and, if it is not invidious or discriminatory against those not selected, it is proper. *Town of Durham v. White Enterprises, Inc.*, 115 N.H. 645, 348 A.2d 706 (1975). There is no doubt that there is a governmental interest in marriage and in preserving the integrity of the biological or legal family. There is no concomitant governmental interest in keeping together a group of unrelated persons, no matter how closely they simulate a family. Further, there is no state policy which commands that groups of people may live under the same roof in any section of a municipality they choose.

The stated purpose of Ladue's zoning ordinance is the promotion of the health, safety, morals and general welfare in the city. Whether Ladue could have adopted less restrictive means to achieve these same goals is not a controlling factor in considering the constitutionality of the zoning ordinance. Rather, our focus is on whether there exists some reasonable basis for the means actually employed. In making such a determination, if any state of facts either known or which could reasonably be assumed is presented in support of the ordinance, we must defer to the legislative judgment. We find that Ladue has not acted arbitrarily in enacting its zoning ordinance which defines family as those related by blood, marriage or adoption. Given the fact that Ladue has so defined family, we defer to its legislative judgment.

The judgment of the trial court is affirmed.

PUDLOWSKI, P.J., and KAROHL, J., concur.

Notes

1. Another case like the Ladue case is Zavala v. City of Denver, 759 P.2d 664 (Colo.1988).

2. In the Wall Street Journal, Jan. 7, 1981, p. 21, an article describes the building of a new type of house in California, called a tandem house, containing two private areas of equal size with a bedroom and bathroom flanking a common area of living room, dining room and kitchen. This house is designed for buyers called "mingles" or "couplets" who may be unrelated persons (neither a traditional nor alternative family) who could not individually afford to buy a house and who by combining assets can share a house. The tandem house is obviously designed to meet the problem of inflationary mortgage and building costs. Should zoning ordinance definitions of family be allowed to inhibit such real estate marketing devices as the tandem house?

3. The single-family problem is important not only in the context presented in the previous cases—the traditional family as opposed to alternative styles of living—but is also an essential ingredient in the problem of exclusion of group homes and institutional uses in the single-family zoning district.

CITY OF WHITE PLAINS v. FERRAIOLI
Court of Appeals of New York, 1974.
34 N.Y.2d 300, 357 N.Y.S.2d 449, 313 N.E.2d 756.

BREITEL, CHIEF JUDGE.

In an action by the City of White Plains to enforce its zoning ordinance and enjoin use of a single-family house as a "group home" for 10 foster children, defendants, Abbott House, Inc. and the owners of the house, appeal. Abbott House, a private agency licensed by the State to care for neglected and abandoned children, leases the house in an "R–2" single-family zone. The city contends that the group home is not a single-family use, but either a philanthropic institution, allowed only by special permit, or a boarding house, wholly excluded from an "R–2" zone. The city obtained summary judgment in the courts below.

The issue is a narrow one: whether the "group home," consisting of a married couple and their two children, together with 10 foster children, qualifies as a single "family" unit, under the ordinance. It is concluded that the group home, set up in theory, size, appearance and structure to resemble a family unit, fits within the definition of family, for purposes of a zoning ordinance. Hence, the order of the Appellate Division should be reversed and summary judgment granted to defendants.

Abbott House as noted, is a not-for-profit membership corporation licensed by the State to care for neglected and abandoned children. In 1971, legislation was enacted permitting so-called "authorized agencies" like Abbott House to establish "group homes," under strict State regulation and inspection, where from 7 to 12 foster children might live in a simulated family atmosphere (Social Services Law, § 374–c, Consol. Laws, c. 55; L.1971, ch. 677). The group home concept is relatively new; instead of being institutionalized, neglected or abandoned youngsters are divided into small groups and placed in homes with an adult couple, approximating a normal family environment. In this way, it is thought, the children obtain many of the benefits of home life. Siblings may be kept together. Whatever other advantages there are to the group home, it is also less costly than institutionalized care. Abbott House also operates a traditional dormitory-style institution elsewhere in the State which houses over 100 children.

The particular group home in this case consists of an adult couple, the Seards, their two children, and 10 foster children. Of the 10, there are seven siblings, the Bell children ranging in age from 7 to 13, and three unrelated youngsters. The Seards are paid a salary to care for the children and all household expenses are paid by Abbott House, with substantial funding to it by the City of New York. Abbott House has a five-year lease on a house owned by the Ferraiolis who are also defendants. The children, natural and foster, live together as if they were brothers and sisters and the Seards were their common parents. The household is maintained as a family would be in a single housekeeping unit with kitchen facilities.

The Ferraioli house is in an R–2 zone of the city where the principal permitted uses are as a "Single family dwelling for one housekeeping unit only," fire houses, police stations, public schools and churches. As an accessory use, a resident family may include up to two roomers. Welfare uses, including philanthropic institutions, are special uses permitted in R–2 districts or other residential districts only at the discretion of the zoning board of appeals. Abbott House has not sought permission from the board. Rooming houses are permitted in certain residential districts of the city, but not in an R–2 zone.

The zoning ordinance defines a family:

A "family" is one or more persons limited to the spouse, parents, grandparents, grandchildren, sons, daughters, brothers or sisters of the owner or the tenant or of the owner's spouse or tenant's spouse living together as a single housekeeping unit with kitchen facilities.

It is significant that the group home is structured as a single housekeeping unit and is, to all outward appearances, a relatively normal, stable, and permanent family unit, with which the community is properly concerned. If that be true, the group home is no less qualified to occupy the Ferraioli house than are any of the neighboring families in their respective homes.

The group home is not, for purposes of a zoning ordinance, a temporary living arrangement as would be a group of college students sharing a house and commuting to a nearby school * * *. Every year or so, different college students would come to take the place of those before them. There would be none of the permanency of community that characterizes a residential neighborhood of private homes. Nor is it like the so-called "commune" style of living. The group home is a permanent arrangement and akin to a traditional family, which also may be sundered by death, divorce, or emancipation of the young. Neither the foster parents nor the children are to be shifted about; the intention is that they remain and develop ties in the community. The purpose is to emulate the traditional family and not to introduce a different "life style."

Of course, the Supreme Court of the United States, in the recent *Belle Terre* case, has held that it is a proper purpose of zoning to lay out districts devoted to "family values" and "youth values." Hence, toward that end those uses which conflict with a stable, uncongested single family environment may be restricted. High density uses, for example, may be restricted; so too those uses which are associated with occupancy by numbers of transient persons may be limited. By requiring single family use of a house, the ordinance emphasizes and ensures the character of the neighborhood to promote the family environment. The group home does not conflict with that character and, indeed, is deliberately designed to conform with it.

Thus the city has a proper purpose in largely limiting the uses in a zone to single-family units. But if it goes beyond to require that the relationships in the family unit be those of blood or adoption, then its definition of family might be too restrictive (see *Kirsch Holding Co. v. Borough of Manasquan*, 59 N.J. 241, 250, 281 A.2d 527; *City of Des Plaines v. Trottner*, 34 Ill.2d 432, 216 N.E.2d 116 [per Schaeffer, J.]; *Boston–Edison Protective Assn. v. Paulist Fathers*, 306 Mich. 253, 10 N.W.2d 847). Zoning is intended to control types of housing and living and not the genetic or intimate internal family relations of human beings.

Whether a family be organized along ties of blood or formal adoptions, or be a similarly structured group sponsored by the State, as is the group home, should not be consequential in meeting the test of the zoning ordinance. So long as the group home bears the generic character of a family unit as a relatively permanent household, and is not a framework for transients or transient living, it conforms to the purpose of the ordinance (see *Planning & Zoning Comm. v. Synanon Foundation*, 153 Conn. 305, 308, 216 A.2d 442). Moreover, in no sense is the group home an institutional arrangement, which would be another matter. Indeed, the purpose of the group home is to be quite the contrary of an institution and to be a home like other homes.

In short, an ordinance may restrict a residential zone to occupancy by stable families occupying single-family homes, but neither by express provision nor construction may it limit the definition of family to exclude a household which in every but a biological sense is a single family. The minimal arrangement to meet the test of a zoning provision, as this one, is a group headed by a householder caring for a reasonable number of children as one would be likely to find in a biologically unitary family.
* * *

Defendants contend, and the issue raised is not without trouble, that the zoning ordinance, if it prohibits a group home use in an R–2 district, absolutely or without a special permit, contravenes the State's Social Services Law. That law, as discussed above, authorizes licensed agencies to establish group homes in appropriate neighborhoods (Social Services Law, § 374–c). In somewhat analogous circumstances, courts have held local zoning ordinances void as contrary to State policy when they restricted an "agency boarding home," a day care center, and a center for delinquent youths (*Abbott House v. Village of Tarrytown*, 34 A.D.2d 821, 312 N.Y.S.2d 841; *Matter of Unitarian Universalist Church v. Shorten*, 63 Misc.2d 978, 980–981, 314 N.Y.S.2d 66 [Meyer, J.]; Nowack v. Department of Audit & Control, 72 Misc.2d 518, 520, 338 N.Y.S.2d 52). Certainly, by constitutional provision and State policy, the care of neglected and abandoned children is a paramount concern (N.Y.Const., art. VII, § 8, subd. 2; *Matter of Wiltwyck School v. Hill*, 11 N.Y.2d 182, 193, 227 N.Y.S.2d 655, 182 N.E.2d 268). Since it is concluded, however, that a group home is a family, this broader question need not now be resolved by this court.

* * *

Accordingly, the order of the Appellate Division should be reversed, with costs, and summary judgment granted to defendants dismissing the complaint.

Notes

1. The group home is an outgrowth of the principle of deinstitutionalization or normalization which is based on the policy of rejecting the large custodial institution as a method of dealing with those members of society who are dependent, such as the mentally handicapped, juvenile delinquents and neglected or orphaned children. The group home is designed to provide an environment that approximates that of normal society, which perforce includes the idea of family living. The public and private organizations that promote and operate group homes frequently seek locations in single-family zoning districts; often, a clash between local government or nearby neighbors and the proposed group home results in litigation. Because so many local governments have demonstrated hostility to the location of group homes in single-family districts, since the late 1970's, state legislation has become increasingly common as a device for preempting local zoning ordinances restrictive of group homes. For an overview of this problem, see Comment, 24 Kan.L.Rev. 677 (1976); Kressel, The Community Residence Movement: Land Use Conflicts and Planning Imperatives, 5 N.Y.U.Rev.L. & Soc.Change 137 (1975); Lippincott, A Sanctuary for People: Strategies for Overcoming Zoning Restrictions on Community Homes for Retarded Persons, 31 Stan.L.Rev. 767 (1979); Hopperton, A State Legislative Strategy for Ending Exclusionary Zoning of Community Homes, 19 Urb.L.Ann. 47 (1980).

2. The majority of cases dealing with zoning of group homes have favored their location in single-family districts. In most of the cases the courts utilize the approach of defining the word family so as to include the surrogate family implicit in the group home concept. See, e.g., Oliver v. Zoning Comm'n of Town of Chester, 31 Conn.Sup. 197, 326 A.2d 841 (1974) permitting a state-supervised group home for eight or nine employable adult retarded persons and two house-parents in the single-family district. In Eichlin v. Zoning Hearing Bd. of New Hope Borough, 671 A.2d 1173 (Pa.Cmwlth 1996) the court held that eight unrelated HIV-infected persons were the functional equivalent of a family. However, the courts are not always willing to treat every type of group home as a family situation:

In Planning and Zoning Commission of Town of Westport v. Synanon Foundation, Inc., 153 Conn. 305, 216 A.2d 442 (1966), the zoning ordinance provided for "one family per lot." The evidence showed that anywhere from eleven to thirty-four people were living on the premises. The court reversed a lower court decision denying an injunction, stating:

> The only remaining question is whether the phrase "one family," which is left undefined in the Westport zoning ordinance, is broad enough to encompass the group of persons residing at the premises leased by the defendant. The trial court concluded that the use of this property as found was not excluded by the zoning ordinance. The applicable provision of the ordinance, which is a permissive rather than a prohibitory ordinance, allows "[o]ne detached dwelling for occupancy by one family per lot." Westport Zoning Regs., c. 3, § 1(B)(1) (1958, as amended).

Obviously the use of this dwelling was not by one family, under any definition, since the trial court found that it was occupied over a long period of time by an everchanging aggregate of individuals. Such a group of individuals, who were sleeping, cooking, eating, working, and carrying on other activities at these premises, cannot be interpreted to come within the meaning of the word "family," either according to common usage or under the dictionary definitions, and the trial court's conclusion to the contrary, in the absence of a controlling definition in the ordinance, cannot be sustained. City of Schenectady v. Alumni Ass'n of Union Chapter, Delta Chi Fraternity, Inc., 5 A.D.2d 14, 15, 168 N.Y.S.2d 754; Cassidy v. Triebel, 337 Ill.App. 117, 127, 85 N.E.2d 461; 101 C.J.S. Zoning § 143. Indeed, if these occupants were held to constitute "one family," it is difficult to imagine any group or organization which would not be considered one family, and the phrase 'occupancy by one family per lot' would be rendered superfluous, in conflict with the well-established rule that, whenever feasible, the language of an ordinance will be construed so that no clause is held superfluous, void, or insignificant.

The same type of reasoning was used by the Supreme Court of Ohio in holding that a foster home with an average of seven foster children was not an integrated family unit and could not locate in a single-family zoning district. Carroll v. Washington Twp. Zoning Comm'n, 63 Ohio St.2d 249, 408 N.E.2d 191 (1980). Also see Civitans Care, Inc. v. Board of Adj., 437 So.2d 540 (Ala.Civ.App.1983). And, in Northern Maine General Hosp. v. Ricker, 572 A.2d 479 (Me.1990) the court held that a prerelease center for adult inmates could be excluded from a single-family district that permitted group homes because it was significantly more objectionable than other types of group homes.

3. Some courts have avoided the "single-family" problem by finding a group home to be a permitted educational facility in the single-family district, e.g., Fitchburg Housing Auth. v. Board of Zoning Appeals, 380 Mass. 869, 406 N.E.2d 1006 (1980); Campbell v. City Council of Lynn, 415 Mass. 772, 616 N.E.2d 445 (1993), or a permitted community center, e.g., Appeal of Fleming, 44 Pa.Cmwlth. 641, 405 A.2d 1309 (1979).

4. Some group home cases do not involve local hostility through the zoning ordinance but rather a conflict with restrictive covenants limiting use of the proposed group home to single-family dwelling purposes. Here again, the courts generally read the covenants so as to permit the group home. See, e.g., Bellarmine Hills Ass'n v. Residential Systems Co., 84 Mich.App. 554, 269 N.W.2d 673 (1978); Jayno Heights Landowners Ass'n v. Preston, 85 Mich.App. 443, 271 N.W.2d 268 (1978); Malcolm v. Shamie, 95 Mich.App. 132, 290 N.W.2d 101 (1980); Crowley v. Knapp, 94 Wis.2d 421, 288 N.W.2d 815 (1980); Annotation, 71 A.L.R.3d 693 (1976). In Berger v. State, 71 N.J. 206, 364 A.2d 993 (1976), the court dealt with both a covenant and a restrictive zoning ordinance and also discussed a state statute favoring establishment of group homes. In Clem v. Christole, Inc., 548 N.E.2d 1180 (Ind.App.1990), the court held that a state statute invalidating restrictive covenants which prohibit group homes constituted a taking.

5. Another approach to the group home problem is reflected in cases that find state-operated or state-sponsored group homes are immune from local zoning ordinances. See Hillsborough Ass'n for Retarded Citizens v. City of Temple Terrace, 332 So.2d 610 (Fla.1976); Township of South Fayette v. Commonwealth, 477 Pa. 574, 385 A.2d 344 (1978); City of Baltimore v. State Dept. of Health and Mental Hygiene, 38 Md.App. 570, 381 A.2d 1188 (1978); Region 10 Client Management, Inc. v. Town of Hampstead, 120 N.H. 885, 424 A.2d 207 (1980). Compare Brownfield v. State, 63 Ohio St.2d 282, 407 N.E.2d 1365 (1980).

6. In some cases the zoning ordinance is not exclusionary as to group homes, but such uses may require a special use permit or exception, or may be a conditional use in the single-family district. As to the standards to be applied in such cases, see Warren County Probation Ass'n v. Warren County Zoning Hearing Bd., 50 Pa.Cmwlth. 486, 414 A.2d 398 (1980). Also see State ex rel. Catholic Family & Children's Services v. City of Bellingham, 25 Wash.App. 33, 605 P.2d 788 (1979); Ayers v. Porter County Plan Comm'n, 544 N.E.2d 213 (Ind.App.1989). In City of Cleburne, Texas v. Cleburne Living Center, 473 U.S. 432, 105 S.Ct. 3249, 87 L.Ed.2d 313 (1985) the Court held that requiring a special use permit for a group home for the mentally retarded in the city's R–3 district was invalid because the same district did not require special use permits for nursing homes, sanitariums, hospitals, fraternity or sorority houses, boarding houses, dormitories and other similar uses.

7. More than one half of the states have adopted legislation since 1970 designed to overcome zoning barriers to establishment of group homes. The legislation is not uniform and the approach varies from state to state. Typically, the statutes may apply only to certain types of group homes, e.g., those for the developmentally disabled, and may impose maximum residency limits in language such as "up to six [or eight] persons." See Hopperton, A State Legislative Strategy for Ending Exclusionary Zoning of Community Homes, 19 Urban L.Ann. 47 (1980). Also see Adams County Ass'n for Retarded Citizens, Inc. v. City of Westminster, 196 Colo. 79, 580 P.2d 1246 (1978); State ex rel. Thelen v. City of Missoula, 168 Mont. 375, 543 P.2d 173 (1975). In Garcia v. Siffrin Residential Ass'n, 63 Ohio St.2d 259, 407 N.E.2d 1369 (1980), the court held the state statute permitting group homes in single-family districts could not operate to preempt a local home rule zoning ordinance excluding such uses.

8. One unusual case involving group homes is People v. St. Agatha Home for Children, 47 N.Y.2d 46, 416 N.Y.S.2d 577, 389 N.E.2d 1098 (1979), cert. denied 444 U.S. 869, 100 S.Ct. 145, 62 L.Ed.2d 94 (1979), where the plaintiffs charged the operators of a group home with operating a non-secure juvenile detention facility in violation of the criminal provisions of the zoning ordinance. The court held that the burden of proof requisite in a criminal proceeding had not been met and that the group home was operating under county aegis and was, therefore, immune from the city zoning ordinance.

9. The Fair Housing Amendments Act of 1988 (FHAA), P.L. 100–430 makes discrimination against the handicapped in the sale, lease, or construction of multi-family units a prohibited practice. In Baxter v. City of Belle-

ville, Ill., 720 F.Supp. 720 (S.D.Ill.1989) the court enjoined a city from refusing a special permit to remodel a building to house AIDS patients. In the same vein, see Association of Relatives and Friends of AIDS Patients v. Regulations and Permits Admn., 740 F.Supp. 95 (D.Puerto Rico 1990); Support Ministries for Persons with AIDS, Inc. v. Village of Waterford, New York, 808 F.Supp. 120 (N.D.N.Y.1992); Familystyle of St. Paul, Inc. v. City of St. Paul, 728 F.Supp. 1396 (D.Minn.1990). In Hill v. Community of Damien of Molokai, 121 N.M. 353, 911 P.2d 861 (1996) the court held that a group home for AIDS patients did not violate a restrictive covenant specifying single-family residential uses, and that even if the residents did not constitute a "family" and violated the covenant, the covenant would violate the Fair Housing Act. In United States v. City of Taylor, Michigan, 798 F.Supp. 442 (E.D.Mich.1992) the court found intentional discrimination against the proposed residents of an adult foster care home for 12 elderly disabled persons, and a violation of the Fair Housing Act. In Epicenter of Steubenville, Inc. v. City of Steubenville, 924 F.Supp. 845 (S.D.Ohio 1996) the court held that a city ordinance imposing a one-year moratorium against new adult care facilities violated the FHAA.

However, the Fair Housing Act does not provide a way to get around the separation of uses in a zoning ordinance. In Brandt v. Village of Chebanse, 82 F.3d 172 (7th Cir.1996) the court upheld denial of a variance for an apartment building with handicapped-accessible units to locate in a single-family residential district. The court found that because a permit had been previously denied for a similar non-accessible project, the denial in this case was not based on discrimination against the handicapped. Compare, however, Larkin v. State of Michigan Dept. of Social Services, 89 F.3d 285 (6th Cir.1996), where the court held that a Michigan statute prohibiting location of group homes within 1500 feet of existing group homes was preempted by the federal act. And in Association for Advancement of the Mentally Handicapped v. City of Elizabeth, 876 F.Supp. 614 (D.N.J.1994) the court held that a city ordinance and the authorizing provision of the state enabling act that automatically denied conditional use permits for group homes for developmentally disabled persons on certain conditions violated the FHAA.

10. In Culp v. City of Seattle, 22 Wash.App. 618, 590 P.2d 1288 (1979) the court found that a proposed home for up to 12 retarded children could not locate in a single-family district because the planned home would not have resident adult supervisors but rather would be staffed by rotating shifts of supervisors. The court said that such an arrangement made the home more of an institution than a group home. In Pemberton Township v. State, 171 N.J.Super. 287, 408 A.2d 832 (1979) the court enjoined location of a group home for juvenile delinquents in a residential area because it was an "institutional use" and thus did not come under the group home statute which defined group home as one operated by the state department of youth and family services (the proposed home was to be operated by the state department of corrections). On appeal the injunction was dissolved. 178 N.J.Super. 346, 429 A.2d 360 (1981).

In Taylor Home of Charlotte, Inc. v. City of Charlotte, 116 N.C.App. 188, 447 S.E.2d 438 (1994) neighbors succeeded in stopping a proposed group home for persons with full-blown AIDS. The court approved the local board interpretation of the state enabling legislation for group homes and the city ordinance to define group homes as "sheltered living arrangements primarily for rehabilitation." The court stated: "The Board interpreted that language to require that the residents of a group home be such that some day they could live normal lives. The Board found as a fact that that 'a dictionary commonly defines "rehabilitation" to mean the restoring of a handicapped or delinquent person to a useful life through education and therapy.'" Also see "K" Care, Inc. v. Town of Lac du Flambeau, 181 Wis.2d 59, 510 N.W.2d 697 (1993) where the court considered whether the denial of a permit to construct a facility for elderly residents violated the Fair Housing Act. The town argued that the federal statute only applied to discrimination against the handicapped and by definition the federal act was inapplicable to a home for the elderly. The court held: "We conclude that the proposed residents of the new facility * * * are handicapped within the meaning of the FHA. These residents obviously suffer from physical and mental impairments that substantially limit one or more major life activities. They are unable to eat, bathe, walk or use a toilet without assistance. In short, they are no longer able to live independently." Also see City of St. Joseph v. Preferred Family Healthcare, 859 S.W.2d 723 (Mo.App.1993) where the court found that persons recovering from alcohol and drug abuse were not mentally or physically handicapped within the meaning of the federal Rehabilitation Act of 1973, § 504 (29 U.S.C.A. § 794). Also see Daniel R. Mandelker, Zoning Discrimination Against Group Homes Under the Fair Housing Act, Land Use Law (Nov. 1994) p. 3.

11. What if group homes are specifically permitted in some zoning districts, but excluded from the single-family district? A rational approach to this problem would focus on whether the purpose and clientele of the group home requires a surrogate family setting. Courts seldom discuss this issue. See, e.g., Residential Management Systems v. Jefferson County Plan Comm'n, 542 N.E.2d 227 (Ind.App.1989).

D. MULTI–FAMILY HOUSING

APPEAL OF GIRSH
Supreme Court of Pennsylvania, 1970.
437 Pa. 237, 263 A.2d 395.

ROBERTS, JUSTICE. By agreement dated July 13, 1964, appellant contracted to purchase a 17½ acre tract of land, presently zoned R–1 Residential, in Nether Providence Township, Delaware County. Appellant agreed to pay a minimum of $110,000 (later changed by agreement to $120,000) for the property. He further agreed to request the Township Board of Commissioners to change the R–1 Residential zoning classification so that a high-rise apartment could be built on the property and to pay $140,000 if this request were granted.

Nether Providence is a first-class township with a population of almost 13,000 persons and an area of 4.64 square miles. Approximately 75% of the Township is zoned either R–1 or R–2 Residential, which permit the construction of single-family dwelling units on areas not less than 20,000 and 14,000 square feet, respectively. Multi-unit apartment buildings, although not *explicitly* prohibited, are not provided for in the ordinance. The Township contains the customary commercial and industrial districts, as well as two areas where apartments have been permitted and constructed only after variances were secured.

After the Board refused to amend the zoning ordinance, appellant sought a building permit to construct two nine-story luxury apartments, each containing 280 units. The permit was refused since the R–1 Residential classification does not permit multiple dwellings. Appellant appealed to the Zoning Board of Adjustment and announced that he would attack the constitutionality of the zoning ordinance in lieu of seeking a variance. The Zoning Board sustained the ordinance and denied relief. The Court of Common Pleas of Delaware County affirmed, and appellant took this appeal. We hold that the failure of appellee-township's zoning scheme to provide for apartments is unconstitutional and reverse the decree of the court below.

Initially, it is plain that appellee's zoning ordinance indeed makes no provision for apartment uses. Appellee argues that nonetheless apartments are not explicitly *prohibited* by the zoning ordinance. Appellee reasons that although only single-family residential uses are provided for, nowhere does the ordinance say that there shall be no apartments. In theory, an apartment use by variance is available, and appellee urges that this case thus is different from prior cases in which we severely questioned zoning schemes that did not allow given uses in an *entire* municipality. See *Exton Quarries, Inc. v. Zoning Board of Adjustment*, 425 Pa. 43, 228 A.2d 169 (1967); *Ammon R. Smith Auto Co. Appeal*, 423 Pa. 493, 223 A.2d 683 (1966); *Norate Corp. v. Zoning Board of Adjustment*, 417 Pa. 397, 207 A.2d 890 (1965).

Appellee's argument, although perhaps initially appealing, cannot withstand analysis. It is settled law that a variance is available *only* on narrow grounds, i.e., "where the property is subjected to an unnecessary hardship, unique or peculiar to itself, and where the grant thereof will not be contrary to the public interest. The reasons to justify the granting of a variance must be 'substantial, serious and compelling.'" *Poster Advertising Company, Inc. v. Zoning Board of Adjustment*, 408 Pa. 248, 251, 182 A.2d 521, 523 (1962). In light of this standard, appellee's land-use restriction in the case before us cannot be upheld against constitutional attack because of the *possibility* that an *occasional* property owner may carry the heavy burden of proving sufficient hardship to receive a variance. To be constitutionally sustained, appellee's land-use restriction must be reasonable. If the failure to make allowance in the Township's zoning plan for apartment uses is unreasonable, that restriction does not become any the more reasonable because once in a while, a developer may be able to show the hardship necessary to sustain a petition for a variance. At least for the purposes of this case, the failure to provide for apartments anywhere within the Township must be viewed as the legal equivalent of an explicit total prohibition of apartment houses in the zoning ordinance.

Were we to accept appellee's argument, we would encourage the Township in effect to spot-zone a given use on variance-hardship grounds. This approach distorts the question before us, which is whether appellee must provide for apartment living as part of its *plan* of development. Cf. *Eves v. Zoning Board of Adjustment*, 401 Pa. 211, 164 A.2d 7 (1960).

By emphasizing the possibility that a given land owner *could* obtain a variance, the Township overlooks the broader question that is presented by this case. In refusing to allow apartment development as part of its zoning scheme, appellee has in effect decided to zone *out* the people who would be able to live in the Township if apartments were available. Cf. *National Land and Investment Co. v. Easttown Twp. Board of Adjustment*, 419 Pa. 504, 532, 215 A.2d 597, 612 (1965): "The question posed is whether the township can stand in the way of the natural forces which send our growing population into hitherto undeveloped areas in search of a comfortable place to live. We have concluded not. A zoning ordinance whose primary purpose is to prevent the entrance of newcomers in order to avoid future burdens, economic and otherwise, upon the administration of public services and facilities can not be held valid."

We emphasize that we are not here faced with the question whether we can compel appellee to zone *all* of its land to permit apartment development, since this is a case where *nowhere* in the Township are apartments permitted. Instead, we are guided by the reasoning that controlled in *Exton Quarries,* supra. We there stated that "The constitutionality of zoning ordinances which totally prohibit legitimate businesses * * * from an entire community should be regarded with particular circumspection; for unlike the constitutionality of most restrictions on property rights imposed by other ordinances, the constitutionality of total prohibitions of legitimate businesses cannot be premised on the fundamental reasonableness of allocating to each type of activity a particular location in the community." 425 Pa. at 58, 228 A.2d at 179. In *Exton Quarries* we struck down an ordinance which did not allow quarrying anywhere in the municipality, just as in *Ammon R. Smith Auto Co. Appeal,* supra, we did not tolerate a total ban on flashing signs and in *Norate Corp.,* supra, we struck down a prohibition on billboards everywhere in the municipality. Here we are faced with a similar case, but its implications are even more critical, for we are here dealing with the crucial problem of population, not with billboards or quarries. Just as we held in *Exton Quarries, Ammon R. Smith,* and *Norate* that the governing bodies must make some provision for the use in question, we today follow those cases and hold that appellee cannot have a zoning scheme that makes no reasonable provision for apartment uses.

Appellee argues that apartment uses would cause a significant population increase with a resulting strain on available municipal services and roads, and would clash with the existing residential neighborhood. But we *explicitly* rejected both these claims in *National Land,* supra: "Zoning is a tool in the hands of governmental bodies which enables them to more effectively meet the demands of evolving and growing communities. It must not and can not be used by those officials as an instrument by which they may shirk their responsibilities. Zoning is a means by which a governmental body can plan for the future—it may not be used as a means to deny the future. * * * Zoning provisions may not be used * * * to avoid the increased responsibilities and economic burdens which time and natural growth invariably bring." 419 Pa. at 527–528, 215 A.2d at 610. Cf. *Delaware County Community College Appeal*, 435 Pa. 264, 254 A.2d 641 (1969); O'Hara's Appeal, 389 Pa. 35, 131 A.2d 587 (1957). That reasoning applies equally here. Likewise we reaffirm our holding in *National Land* that protecting the character—really the aesthetic nature—of the municipality is not sufficient justification for an exclusionary zoning technique. 419 Pa. at 528–529, 215 A.2d at 610–611.

This case presents a situation where, no less than in *National Land,* the Township is trying to "stand in the way of the natural forces which send our growing population into hitherto undeveloped areas in search of a comfortable place to live." Appellee here has simply made a decision that it is content with things as they are, and that the expense or change in character that would result from people moving in to find "a comfortable place to live" are for someone else to worry about. That decision is unacceptable. Statistics indicate that people are attempting to move away from the urban core areas, relieving the grossly over-crowded conditions that exist in most of our major cities. Figures show that most jobs that are being created in urban areas, including the one here in question, are in the suburbs. New York Times, June 29, 1969, p. 39 (City Edition). Thus the suburbs, which at one time were merely "bedrooms" for those who worked in the urban core, are now becoming active business areas in their own right. It follows then that formerly "outlying," somewhat rural communities, are becoming logical areas for development and population growth—in a sense, suburbs to the suburbs. With improvements in regional transportation systems, these areas also are now more accessible to the central city.

In light of this, Nether Providence Township may not permissibly choose to only take as many people as can live in single-family housing, in effect freezing the population at near present levels. Obviously if every municipality took that view, population spread would be completely frustrated. Municipal services must be provided *somewhere,* and if Nether Providence is a logical place for development to take place, it should not be heard to say that it will not bear its rightful part of the burden.[1] Certainly it can protect its attractive character by requiring apartments to be built in accordance with (reasonable) setback, open space, height, and other light-and-air requirements,[2] but it cannot refuse

---

[1]. Perhaps in an ideal world, planning and zoning would be done on a *regional* basis, so that a given community would have apartments, while an adjoining community would not. But as long as we allow zoning to be done community by community, it is intolerable to allow one municipality (or many municipalities) to close its doors at the expense of surrounding communities and the central city.

[2]. As appellants indicate, the apartments here in question would cover only 2.7 acres of a 17.7 acre tract, would be located

to make any provision for apartment living. The simple fact that someone is anxious to build apartments is strong indication that the location of this township is such that people are desirous of moving in, and we do not believe Nether Providence can close its doors to those people.

It is not true that the logical result of our holding today is that a municipality must provide for all types of land use. This case deals with the right of people to *live on land,* a very different problem than whether appellee must allow certain industrial uses within its borders.[3] Apartment living is a fact of life that communities like Nether Providence must learn to accept. If Nether Providence is located so that it is a place where apartment living is in demand, it must provide for apartments in its plan for future growth; it cannot be allowed to close its doors to others seeking a "comfortable place to live."

The order of the Court of Common Pleas of Delaware County is reversed.

BELL, C.J., files a concurring opinion.

JONES, J., files a dissenting opinion in which COHEN and POMEROY, JJ., join.

BELL, CHIEF JUSTICE (concurring).

This case poses for me a very difficult problem. One of the most important rights, privileges and powers which (at least until recently) has differentiated our Country from Communist and Socialist Countries, is the right of ownership and the concomitant use of property. The only limitation or restriction thereof was "sic utere tuo ut alienum non laedas"—a right to use one's property in any way and manner and for any purpose the owner desires, except and unless it injures the property of another, or endangers or seriously affects the health or morals or safety of others.

Then along came zoning with its desirable objectives. However, desirable or worthwhile objectives have too often been carried to an

---

far back from the road and adjacent properties, and would be screened by existing high trees. Over half of the trees now on the tract would be saved.

It should be pointed out that much of the opposition to apartment uses in suburban communities is based on fictitious emotional appeals which insist on categorizing all apartments as being equivalent to the worst big-city tenements. See Babcock and Bosselman, Suburban Zoning and the Apartment Boom, 111 U.Pa.L.Rev. 1040, 1051–1072 (1963), wherein the authors also convincingly refute the arguments that apartments necessarily will: not "pay their own way"; cut off light and air; become slums; reduce property values; be destructive to the "character of the community"; and bring in "low-class" people.

3. Even in the latter case, if the Township instituted a total ban on a given use, that decision would be open to at least considerable question under our decision in *Exton Quarries,* supra.

In addition, at least hypothetically, appellee could show that apartments are not appropriate on the site where appellant wishes to build, but that question is not before us as long as the zoning ordinance in question is fatally defective on its face. Appellee could properly decide that apartments are more appropriate in one part of the Township than in another, but it cannot decide that apartments can fit in *no* part of the Township.

unfair or unwise or unjustifiable extreme, or an extreme which makes the Act or Ordinance illegal or unconstitutional.

This Ordinance cannot be sustained under the theory or unwitting pretense that it is necessary for, or has a substantial relationship to the protection of the health or morals or safety of the people of that Township, and, as Justice Roberts points out, it cannot and should not be legalized or Constitutionalized under the theory of "general welfare" or "public interest or worthy objectives." Furthermore, Courts, Legislators, zoning bodies and most of the public have forgotten or rendered meaningless Article I, Section 1, of the Constitution of Pennsylvania, which provides: "All men are born equally free and independent, and have certain inherent and indefeasible rights, among which are those of * * * acquiring, possessing and protecting property * * *."

I believe that a County or Township can "reasonably" regulate the location, size, height, setbacks, light and air requirements, etc. of apartment houses or buildings, but that neither a County nor a Township can *totally prohibit* all apartment houses or buildings. Cf. *Exton Quarries Inc. v. Zoning Board of Adjustment*, 425 Pa. 43, 228 A.2d 169. Whether an ordinance which makes no provision for, or authorization of, apartment houses is equivalent to a total prohibition thereof raises (at least, for me) a difficult question. However, I have come to the conclusion that the present zoning ordinance (1) *in practical effect* amounts to a prohibition of apartment houses, and (2) cannot be saved or legalized by a right to a variance which is grantable only upon proof of (a) unnecessary hardship upon and which is unique or peculiar to the property involved, as distinguished from the hardship arising from the impact of the zoning ordinance upon the entire district, and (b) where the proposed variance will not be contrary to the public safety, health, morals or general welfare: *Di Santo v. Zoning Board of Adjustment*, 410 Pa. 331, 189 A.2d 135; *Sheedy v. Zoning Board of Adjustment*, 409 Pa. 655, 187 A.2d 907; *Brennen v. Zoning Board of Adjustment*, 409 Pa. 376, 187 A.2d 180; *Joseph B. Simon & Co. v. Zoning Board of Adjustment*, 403 Pa. 176, 168 A.2d 317.

For these reasons, I concur in the Opinion of the Court.

JONES, JUSTICE (dissenting).

* * *

The principles governing the disposition of cases involving a constitutional attack on a zoning ordinance have been oft-repeated in our case law. "The test of constitutionality of a zoning ordinance is whether it bears a substantial relation to the health, safety, morals or general welfare of the public: [Citing authority]. One who challenges the constitutionality of a zoning ordinance has no light burden and it is settled that before a zoning ordinance can be declared unconstitutional it must be shown that its provisions are clearly arbitrary and unreasonable, having no substantial relation to the public health, safety, morals or general welfare. If the validity of the legislative judgment is fairly debatable, the legislative judgment must be allowed to control: * * * "

* * *

I turn now to appellant's second contention, *viz.*, that the zoning ordinance permitting only single-family dwellings is unconstitutional as applied to the Duer Tract in particular. Appellant's first argument under this heading is that the ordinance has no relation to the public health, safety and welfare. I cannot agree. The proposed apartment complex would be the largest of its kind in Delaware County, housing an estimated 1,600 persons, and would increase the population of the township by 13%. We cannot refute the conclusion that such a large and rapid increase in population would place a strain on the township's limited municipal services and rural roads. Furthermore, except for the railroad tracks, the area surrounding the Duer Tract is composed exclusively of single-family dwellings. The proposed apartment towers would be incompatible with the existing residential neighborhood and would introduce a structure completely out of proportion to any other building in the township. Furthermore, the complex would present a density problem in this area of the township. The First Class Township Code specifically empowers local municipalities to zone for density; I conclude that the ordinance in question is a proper application of that power.

* * *

Therefore, I would hold that the Township is *not* constitutionally required to provide for multiple-unit apartment buildings in its zoning ordinance and that the ordinance in question is not unconstitutional as applied to the Duer Tract.

I dissent.

COHEN and POMEROY, JJ., join in this dissenting opinion.

Notes

1. Does the court's decision in the Girsh case fail to take into account the role of land values and market forces in affecting types of housing? How can a court—in reviewing allegedly exclusionary zoning practices—mandate housing for low and moderate income families? If a court is unable to give affirmative relief, is the community decision to exclude what, in reality, amounts to high priced apartments really arbitrary? In this connection, consider the Mt. Laurel case, infra, and see Slade, Mt. Laurel: A View From the Bridge, 27 Land Use & Zoning Digest No. 6, p. 15 (1975).

2. Recall the language Justice Sutherland used in the Euclid case when referring to apartments: " * * * [V]ery often the apartment house is a mere parasite, constructed in order to take advantage of the open spaces and attractive surroundings created by the residential character of the district. Moreover, the coming of one apartment house is followed by others * * *." Not only have attitudes about multi-family dwellings changed a great deal since 1926, the economics of development in recent years have forced developers out of single-family development into some form of multi-family

development. On the other hand, the prejudice Justice Sutherland exhibited toward mingling of apartment houses and single-family dwellings in the same district is still very much evident today.

3. In Berger v. Board of Supervisors of Whitpain Twp., 31 Pa.Cmwlth. 386, 376 A.2d 296 (1977), the court found a township zoning ordinance invalid in not allowing, as a matter of right, townhouse development; citing Girsh, the court said: " * * * the ordinance which fails entirely to provide for a needed and desired kind of residential use is exclusionary and as a consequence unconstitutional." In Application of Friday, 33 Pa.Cmwlth. 256, 381 A.2d 504 (1978), the court struck down a total exclusion of apartments despite the municipality's argument that it was not in the path of population expansion and that it was a participant in a regional planning effort. The Pennsylvania courts have not limited their holdings on exclusionary zoning to total exclusion of multi-family housing. In Township of Willistown v. Chesterdale Farms, Inc., 462 Pa. 445, 341 A.2d 466 (1975), the supreme court invalidated a zoning ordinance that permitted multi-family dwellings on 80 acres out of a total of 11,589 acres in the township, calling the ordinance an example of "tokenism" and "selective admission." Then, in Surrick v. Zoning Hearing Board of Township of Upper Providence, 476 Pa. 182, 382 A.2d 105 (1977), the supreme court announced a three part test for defining exclusionary zoning:

> The initial inquiry must focus upon whether the community in question is a logical area for development and population growth. * * * The community's proximity to a large metropolis and the community's and region's projected population growth figures are factors which courts have considered in answering this inquiry. * * *
>
> Having determined that a particular community is in the path of urban-suburban growth, the present level of development within the particular community must be examined. Population density data and the percentage of total undeveloped land and the percentage available for the development of multi-family dwellings are factors highly relevant to this inquiry.
>
> * * *
>
> Assuming that a community is situated in the path of population expansion and is not already highly developed, this Court has, in the past, determined whether the challenged zoning scheme effected an exclusionary result or, alternatively, whether there was evidence of a "primary purpose" or exclusionary intent to zone out the natural growth of population.

For a case applying the three factors, see Appeal of Abcon, Inc., 35 Pa. Cmwlth. 589, 387 A.2d 1303 (1978). In that case the court found that the township was not practicing de jure exclusion of townhouses because one of the seven residential districts did inferentially permit such development. However, when applying the Surrick factors the court found de facto exclusion in that Horsham Township, eight miles from the Philadelphia city limits, is a likely area for development and population growth, that only 124 acres or 1.16% of the total land area is zoned for multi-family housing, and that while no evidence of exclusionary intent is shown, the exclusionary impact is clear. Compare, H & R Builders, Inc. v. Borough Council, 124 Pa.Cmwlth. 88, 555 A.2d 948 (1989).

4. In Zelvin v. Zoning Board of Appeals of Town of Windsor, 30 Conn.Sup. 157, 306 A.2d 151 (1973), the court refused to hold unconstitutional a zoning amendment which had the effect of halting all apartment development. After noting the Girsh case, the court distinguished that case by pointing out that previous development of apartments in Windsor had been allowed to the extent that 19% of the total number of dwelling units in the town were in multi-family structures. Also see Moss v. Town of Winchester, 365 Mass. 297, 311 N.E.2d 555 (1974).

5. For an unusual case where a developer tried to attack a zoning ordinance as exclusionary because it permitted garden apartments but excluded high-rise luxury apartments, see Swiss Village Associates v. Municipal Council of Twp. of Wayne, 162 N.J.Super. 138, 392 A.2d 596 (1978).

McHENRY STATE BANK v. CITY OF McHENRY

Appellate Court of Illinois, Second District, 1983.
113 Ill.App.3d 82, 68 Ill.Dec. 615, 446 N.E.2d 521.

[The plaintiff bank was trustee of property having on it a seventeen unit apartment building which the beneficial owner, Peter Tutera, wanted to convert to condominiums. It was in an area zoned R–4 for multiple family dwellings. There was a minimum lot requirement of 2500 square feet per dwelling, and this property was non-conforming in only having 1882 square feet per dwelling. Condominiums were permitted only in R–5 and R–5A districts having larger square feet requirements. The city would not permit the conversion, denied rezoning and denied an area variance. The trial court granted defendant's motion to dismiss.]

HOPF, JUSTICE:

* * *

A zoning ordinance is presumed valid and a party attacking the ordinance must prove by clear and convincing evidence that the classification is arbitrary, unreasonable and without a substantial relationship to the public welfare. * * *

Plaintiff has challenged the facial validity of the ordinance, consequently we are required to review the ordinance itself.

Under the ordinance, condominiums are only permitted in districts R–5 and R–5A, and are the only permitted uses in those districts. Other residential zoning districts permit cumulative zoning; however, R–5 and R–5A do not. There further appears to be a wide disparity between the minimum lot requirements in the districts which permit condominiums as opposed to requirements in those zoned districts which permit apartments.

According to the city's zoning ordinance in general the city council may grant a variation in zoning only where the physical surroundings of the property would result in particular hardship if the zoning ordinance is applied strictly; the conditions on which the petition is based are unique; the petitioner's purpose is not solely financial gain; the alleged hardship has not been created by the present owner; granting the variation will not be materially detrimental to the public welfare or surrounding properties, and; the proposed variation will not impair an adequate supply of light and air to adjacent property, substantially increase fire hazards or traffic, endanger the public safety, or substantially impair the value of neighboring property. As one can see by simple review of the variations standards, procuring a variation is not compatible with apartment conversion.

Condominiums and condominium conversions are lawful operations (Ill.Rev.Stat.1981, ch. 30, pars. 301 *et seq.*), and they should not be prohibited entirely by a zoning ordinance unless doing so has a substantial relationship to the public welfare. *Village of Cahokia v. Wright* (1973), 11 Ill.App.3d 124, 296 N.E.2d 30, *aff'd* (1974), 57 Ill.2d 166, 311 N.E.2d 153; *High Meadows Park, Inc. v. City of Aurora* (1969), 112 Ill.App.2d 220, 250 N.E.2d 517.

Though condominiums are not prohibited entirely under the city's zoning ordinance, as condominium zones within the ordinance are provided, the practical effect of restricting condominiums to only condominium zones does constitute an impermissible discrimination against the conversion of existing apartment dwellings into condominium units. A disparate treatment of condominiums and apartments is constitutional only if there would be some basis for distinction. (*Village of Cahokia v. Wright* (1973) 11 Ill.App.3d 124, 296 N.E.2d 30, *aff'd* (1974), 57 Ill.2d 166, 311 N.E.2d 153.) Where no real difference exists between groups treated differently and there is no basis for the disparity of classification, the ordinance is invalid. If a zoning ordinance permits certain uses of property but excludes other uses which are not significantly different, the ordinance cannot be sustained. *City of Chicago v. Sachs* (1953), 1 Ill.2d 342, 115 N.E.2d 762.

A conversion of an apartment building into a condominium complex does not basically involve a change in the use of the property, but only a change in the ownership. (*Maplewood Village Tenants Association v. Maplewood Village* (1971), 116 N.J.Super. 372, 282 A.2d 428; *Bridge Park Co. v. Borough of Highland Park* (1971), 113 N.J.Super. 219, 273 A.2d 397.) The statute enabling a municipality to enact zoning ordinances is directed to the regulation of the use of the property. See Ill.Rev.Stat.1981, ch. 24, par. 11–13–1.

There appears to be no Illinois case precisely on this point, however a municipality should not be permitted to use its zoning power for the purpose of precluding condominiums or condominium conversions. *Maplewood Tenants Association v. Maplewood Village* (1971), 116 N.J.Super. 372, 282 A.2d 428; *Bridge Park Co. v. Borough of Highland Park* (1971), 113 N.J.Super. 219, 273 A.2d 397.

* * *

The plaintiff has made out a *prima facie* case that the city by restricting condominium use to a non-cumulative lower density zoning district has discriminated against the conversion of apartment buildings to condominiums in other zoning areas. The statute enabling a municipality to enact zoning ordinances is directed against the use of the property. (Ill.Rev.Stat.1981, ch. 24, par. 11–13–1.) The city may not use its zoning powers to differentiate between condominiums and apartments based solely on the form of ownership. *Maplewood Village Tenants Association v. Maplewood Village* (1971), 116 N.J.Super. 372, 282 A.2d 428; *Bridge Park Co. v. Borough of Highland Park* (1971), 113 N.J.Super. 219, 273 A.2d 397.

In the present posture of the case there has been no evidence of a distinction between use contemplated by the plaintiff for his apartment building in Zone R–4 and the permissible condominium use of R–5 and R–5A. In the absence of evidence showing any distinction between these uses, or that the zoning classifications bore any real and substantial relationship to the public health, safety or welfare (*City of Champaign v. Roseman* (1958), 15 Ill.2d 363, 155 N.E.2d 34), the case must be remanded for further proceedings.

The judgment of the trial court of McHenry County is reversed and this case is remanded for further proceedings.

Reversed and Remanded.

VAN DEUSEN and LINDBERG, JJ., concur.

Notes

1. In Boland v. City of Great Falls, 275 Mont. 128, 910 P.2d 890 (1996) the court upheld a rezoning to allow construction of a condominium complex on land previously zoned for single-family dwellings. The neighbors' allegation of impermissible spot zoning was dismissed by the court because the prior zoning allowed townhouses, which the court concluded were generally similar to the proposed condos. The court also held that the entire neighborhood would benefit from the elimination of eyesores on the undeveloped property.

2. Most courts faced with the question of zoning ordinances that allegedly discriminate against the condominium form of ownership have found such restrictions invalid, usually on the theory that the form of ownership or title-holding is not a legitimate zoning consideration. The problem of conversion of existing apartments to condominiums, however, involves a different set of problems. The existing structure remains the same (perhaps even refurbished and aesthetically more appealing), but the existing stock of rental housing is diminished. Many cities have sought to regulate such conversions. In City of Miami Beach v. Rocio Corp., 404 So.2d 1066 (Fla.App.1981) the court held that the city ordinance was preempted by state law. The California Supreme Court upheld a city ordinance which required a special use permit for conversion of apartments to condominiums, Griffin Development Co. v. City of Oxnard, 39 Cal.3d 256, 217 Cal.Rptr. 1, 703 P.2d 339 (1985). Also see, Leavenworth Properties v. City and County of San Francisco, 189 Cal.App.3d 986, 234 Cal.Rptr. 598 (1987); Claridge House

One, Inc. v. Borough of Verona, 490 F.Supp. 706 (D.N.J.1980), affirmed 633 F.2d 209 (3d Cir.1980); Hornstein v. Barry, 560 A.2d 530 (D.C.App.1989); Bannerman v. City of Fall River, 391 Mass. 328, 461 N.E.2d 793 (1984); Annotation, Validity and Construction of Law Regulating Conversion of Rental Housing to Condominiums, 21 A.L.R.4th 1083 (1983); Judson, Defining Property Rights: The Constitutionality of Protecting Tenants from Condominium Conversion, 18 Harv.Civ.Rts.Civ.Lib.L.Rev. 179 (1983).

3. In City of Portsmouth v. Schlesinger, 140 N.H. 733, 672 A.2d 712 (1996) the court considered the problem of whether a developer who sought to convert existing housing units to condominium ownership could be assessed an "impact fee" of $2.5 million in exchange for a rezoning. The developer made two payments and then stopped, leaving a balance of $1.7 million on its promissory note to the city. In a suit to collect, the developers asserted that the exaction was illegal and ultra vires. The city argued that the defense could not be raised because the developers did not timely appeal the original rezoning. When the case was originally heard in the federal district court, that court ruled for the developers. On appeal, the U.S. Court of Appeals for the First Circuit certified the question of timeliness to the New Hampshire Supreme Court. That court ruled that the defense was properly raised. Subsequently the First Circuit affirmed the original district court judgment for the developers. See 82 F.3d 547 (1st Cir.1996).

E. MOBILE HOMES AND MANUFACTURED HOUSING

TOWN OF GLOCESTER v. OLIVO'S MOBILE HOME COURT, INC.

Supreme Court of Rhode Island, 1973.
111 R.I. 120, 300 A.2d 465.

KELLEHER, JUSTICE.

The defendant corporation is the owner and operator of a mobile home park located in the town of Glocester on land which is situated on the easterly side of Chopmist Hill Road just north of the junction of that highway and Pound Road. The parcel contains approximately 38 acres. In this action, the town seeks to enjoin the corporation from violating a provision found in both its licensing and zoning ordinances which limits the number of mobile homes that can be parked in such a facility to 30. The defendant filed an answer which in essence challenges the constitutionality of the 30–unit limitation and asked that the town be restrained from interfering with "its right" to operate a mobile home park containing more than 30 units. A hearing was held before a justice of the Superior Court. The trial justice, in upholding the limitation, alluded to the public health problems which are not found in "conventional habitation." Judgment was entered ordering the defendant to reduce the number of units parked on its premises to 30 and to obtain the requisite license. This appeal ensued and to put it in its proper focus, we will set out just a few of the pertinent facts found in the record. * * *

In May, 1965, the council made several substantial changes in its mobile home ordinance. All mobile homes had to be located in a park.

The maximum number of mobile homes that could be serviced at any given time in any park was 30. About five months later, in October, 1965, the town council reinforced its restrictive efforts relative to the immobilized mobile home by enacting a zoning ordinance in which the use of mobile homes was prohibited except that any mobile home park then in existence could continue and expand so long as its expansion did not exceed the 30–unit limitation found in the licensing ordinance. There were at that time three such parks in the town. Any potential mobile home park operator who might wish to locate in Glocester now found himself in the same zoning category as the manufacturer of fertilizer, the distiller of tar, or the owner of a commercial piggery.

* * *

The common law permitted one to use his property in a manner and for such purposes as he chose so long as he did not maintain a nuisance or injure others. This right, however, has been made subject to regulations, restrictions and control by the state through the legitimate exercise of its police power. The test of legitimacy is the existence of a reasonable relationship between the exercise of this power and the public health, safety, morals and general welfare. A zoning limitation which is not so related represents a confiscation of private property without just compensation. *See Goldstein v. Zoning Board of Review*, 101 R.I. 728, 227 A.2d 195 (1967); *Buckminster v. Zoning Board of Review*, 69 R.I. 396, 33 A.2d 199 (1943); *Robinson v. Town Council*, 60 R.I. 422, 199 A. 308 (1938). When measured by these standards, the limitation of 30 mobile homes as applied to Olivo is patently unconstitutional. We have made this determination realizing full well that a duly enacted ordinance carries with it a presumption of constitutionality which will disappear only on a contrary showing beyond a reasonable doubt. *City of Providence v. Stephens*, 47 R.I. 387, 133 A. 614 (1926). However, such a principle does not permit us to adopt an ostrich-like stance by burying our heads in the sand and ignoring the obvious.

* * *

The restrictive steps taken by the Glocester Town Council give us an opportunity to examine the motives of those who call their mobile house a home. We are told that "Recent population increases, coupled with the apparent inability of the United States housing industry to overcome problems of tight money, galloping costs, and labor shortages, have resulted in a serious undersupply of new single family dwellings in the low to middle price ranges. These conditions have caused a rapid expansion of the mobile home industry. Derived from this is a demand for more mobile home parks, whose expansion has been frustrated by public pressure, municipal policies, and zoning restrictions which attempt to keep mobile homes and mobile home parks out of a given area." Van Iden, Zoning Restrictions Applied to Mobile Homes, 20 Clev. St.L.Rev. 196 (1970). It is believed that today one out of every five new single-family dwellings is a mobile home and that this fraction will increase. Note, The Community and the Park Owner Versus the Mobile

Home Park Resident: Reforming the Landlord–Tenant Relationship, 52 B.U.L.Rev. 810 (1972). It is obvious that a mobile home park can no longer be primarily classified as a gathering place for a group of nomads who wander hither, thither and yon over the highways and byways. We cannot assume that an occupant of a mobile home poses any greater threat to the public safety than the other inhabitants of a municipality who might live in a more conventional type of residence. Many years ago, this court observed that a gasoline filling station was not a nuisance *per se*. *Sundlun v. Zoning Board of Review*, 50 R.I. 108, 145 A. 451 (1929). Today, the same sentiments can be expressed about a mobile home park.

The municipality's contention, that its limitation of 30 units constitutes an effort to lessen congestion, seems to be a diplomatic way of expressing its real concern, that of finding some way to maintain the population of its schools at a point where a stable tax rate can be preserved. We do not believe that a zoning ordinance was ever intended to fulfill such a function. Rhode Island, like its sister states, has witnessed the exodus from the cities to the suburbs. Our state is often described as the "City–State." A motorist may, because of our modern expanded system of highways, travel from one end of Rhode Island to its extreme opposite end in the matter of just one hour. Glocester is a pleasant rural area. By automobile, it lies just about 25 minutes to the west of our capital city, Providence. Its 1965 zoning ordinance sets up four zones—agricultural, residential, commercial and industrial. The bulk of the town is zoned for agriculture. The commercial classification is subdivided into two categories—neighborhood commercial and highway commercial. Most commercial establishments are to be found along United States Route 44. Even though the council provided an industrial zoning classification, the zoning map, which is part of the ordinance, shows that no part of the town has been zoned industrial.

The 30–mobile home limit might be considered as one type of exclusionary zoning.

Even though we have stated that the location and use of a mobile home is subject to a valid exercise of the police power, the limitation of 30 mobile homes found in the Glocester zoning ordinance and its licensing counterpart, at least as it applies to Olivo's property, fails to satisfy the requisite constitutional standards.

* * *

The defendant's appeal is sustained. The judgment appealed from is vacated and the case is remanded to the Superior Court for entry of judgment in accordance with this opinion.

Notes

1. Compare the case of Clark v. County of Winnebago, 817 F.2d 407 (7th Cir.1987). The property owner sought to have a portion of his land rezoned to "Mobile Home District." When his request was denied, he brought a due process challenge in federal court on the theory that the requirements for the mobile home district were discriminatory and that the

ordinance unconstitutionally discriminated between site-built homes and mobile homes. The court upheld the ordinance, stating: "There was testimony at trial that, despite advances in the mobile home industry, distinctions between mobile homes and site-built homes still exist with respect to design, construction, and general appearance. While some mobile homes may compare favorably with conventional homes, zoning classifications necessarily require that generalizations be made. Mathematical certainty is not required for the ordinance to pass constitutional muster, so long as there is a reasonable basis for the classification chosen."

2. Because of the general recognition that manufactured housing is an essential method of meeting the housing needs of low and moderate income residents, courts have begun to question the validity of total exclusion of mobile homes or mobile home parks from the entire community. See, e.g., In re Shore, 524 Pa. 436, 573 A.2d 1011 (1990); Guy v. Brandon Twp., 181 Mich.App. 775, 450 N.W.2d 279 (1989); Taylor v. Shaw and Cannon Co., 236 Va. 15, 372 S.E.2d 128 (1988); Jensen's, Inc. v. City of Dover, 130 N.H. 761, 547 A.2d 277 (1988); Borough of Malvern v. Jackson, 108 Pa.Cmwlth. 248, 529 A.2d 96 (1987), settlement stipulation approved 521 Pa. 570, 559 A.2d 489 (1989). In Stahl v. Upper Southampton Twp. Zoning Hearing Bd., 146 Pa.Cmwlth. 659, 606 A.2d 960 (1992), appeal denied 533 Pa. 639, 621 A.2d 584 (1993), the court found a de facto exclusion of mobile home parks where the ordinance permitted such parks with minimum 9,000 square foot lots, density requirements of three units per acre, and a requirement that the park be in single ownership.

3. Congress, in P.L. 93–383, provided the basis for federal regulation of construction standards for manufactured homes. See 42 U.S.C.A. § 5401 et seq. and 24 C.F.R. § 3280 et seq. The federal certification of manufactured homes along with changes in style (such as pitched roofs and non-metal siding) and the advent of double-wide and triple-wide homes have contributed to more widespread acceptance of manufactured housing in communities around the country. See Colorado Manufactured Housing Ass'n v. Pueblo County, 857 P.2d 507 (Colo.App.1993); Tennessee Manufactured Housing Ass'n v. Metropolitan Government of Nashville, 798 S.W.2d 254 (Tenn.App. 1990); compare Duggins v. Walnut Cove, 63 N.C.App. 684, 306 S.E.2d 186 (1983). In Lauderbaugh v. Hopewell Township, 319 F.3d 568 (3d Cir.2003) the court held that the federal statute may preempt more restrictive local building regulations, but does not deal with location issues.

4. Not all mobile home parks are low and moderate income neighborhoods. The New York Times, Dec. 13, 1990, p. B 1, contains an illustrated article about the Point Dume Club in Malibu, California, a 297 unit mobile home park where units sell for as much as $300,000 and may have a Maserati or Rolls–Royce parked in the driveway. One insurance company that insures mobile homes has estimated that the percentage of mobile home owners with incomes above $40,000 increased from 2% in 1981 to 10% in 1990 to 15% in 1993. See Kevin Sack, Mobile Homes Go Upscale: One Pet Per Plot, Please, N.Y. Times, Feb. 23, 1997, p. E 3.

5. Modular housing is something that is quite different from the "mobile home" problem. In 1967 great interest was stirred at the Montreal World Exposition when a young architect, Moshe Safdie, who had studied at

McGill University, designed and built 158 "houses" by stacking 354 modular units that were built in a nearby factory and trucked to the site, an island in the St. Lawrence River. The complex, known as Habitat 67, is still considered a desirable place to live. A 1997 report describing life at Habitat 67: http://pages.infinit.net/westweb/Habitat.htm. A photograph of the complex is at http://www.GreatBuildings.com/buildings/Habitat_67.html.

6. The bulk of the litigation involving zoning and mobile homes or manufactured housing deals with the issue of whether such dwellings can be confined to parks or special districts and excluded from single-family zones. The next case and notes following it take up this issue.

BAHL v. CITY OF ASBURY

Supreme Court of Iowa, 2002.
656 N.W.2d 336.

Ternus, Justice.

The determinative issue in this case is one of statutory interpretation: does Iowa Code section 414.28A (1999) require that a city treat land-leased communities of manufactured housing the same as similar communities of site-built housing or does this statute merely require that a city allow land-leased communities of manufactured housing somewhere within the city limits? The district court held that section 414.28A requires equal treatment of manufactured housing developments and similar site-built housing projects. On the basis of this interpretation of the statute, the court ruled that the zoning ordinance of the appellee, City of Asbury, violated section 414.28A by relegating land-leased communities to R–4 zoning districts only when they contain manufactured homes. The court further held that the appellee, City Council of the City of Asbury, Iowa, acted illegally in denying a rezoning application filed by the appellants, Martin J. Bahl, Linda C. Bahl, and Terrence G. Bahl, because the Bahls planned to build a land-leased community of manufactured homes on their property.

* * *

The Bahls own property located in the city limits of Asbury, Dubuque County, Iowa. In 1997, they submitted a request to rezone their property from A–1 (agricultural) to R–4 (high density residential) to allow for the construction of a manufactured housing development. Rezoning was necessary because the Asbury city zoning ordinance allowed "mobile home parks" only in R–4 districts.

The Bahls' application proposed a phased development of manufactured homes known as Oak Meadows. The request for rezoning was supported by plans, drawings and other pertinent information. The plans submitted with the application showed the overall character of the development as well as anticipated landscaping, including evergreen screening on the perimeters of the property. Proposed development conditions for Oak Meadows, which set appearance standards and provided for methods of enforcement, were also set forth. Finally, the Bahls' application contained detailed specifications and photographs of the types of manufactured housing and mobile homes that would be permitted in the development, with none over three years old being allowed.

The City's planning and zoning commission held a public hearing in June 1998 on the application. *See generally* Iowa Code § 414.6 (providing for city council's appointment of a zoning commission to recommend changes in zoning district boundaries to the council). Opposition to the proposed "trailer park" was nearly universal. There was concern that the development would lower property values and ruin the beauty of the area. Some members of the public who spoke at the hearing expressed stereotypical views. A retired school principal asked whether the citizens of Asbury wanted their children to go to school with kids from a "trailer court"? He said, "[Trailer court kids] come to school with a lot of baggage. I know from experience. These kids tend to be hyperactive and easily distracted. Mainly, it's due to the confinement. They are confined in these small little houses for long periods of time. You let them out in the open spaces and they are going to run." Another person commented that the road fronting the development would "be a drag way all of the time" if the proposed plan were allowed. The predominant sentiment appeared to be "not in my back yard."

* * *

In November 1998, an updated land use plan prepared by an outside consultant was presented to the commission. At that time the proposed plan showed the Bahls' property as R–4, a designation that would permit manufactured housing developments. Again, opposition was widespread and again it was focused on the location of a manufactured housing community on the Bahls' property. The dominant view was that the City of Asbury did not need that type of housing. Repeated references were made to a recent housing study done at the city council's request that recommended demolishing the only trailer park in the city and creating upper-end, single-family housing. Speakers relying on the housing study emphasized that the study did not recommend the construction of trailer parks. Several residents pointed out the "upper-end" character of the city and its housing. In line with these observations was the statement of one person who cited statistics from the housing study that "Asbury has 58% higher median household income, 36% higher average household income, and 5% higher per capita income than the state" and that "[t]he percent of families and people living below the poverty level in Asbury is significantly lower than that of the county and the state."

Another citizen claimed the Asbury "blood line" was R–2 and asked why couldn't Asbury continue just as it had? A later speaker expressed a similar feeling: "We like this community the way it is." Assertions were also made that individuals who wanted to live in a mobile home park could live in Dubuque, but they didn't need those things "right here in Asbury." This sentiment was echoed by a subsequent resident who said that if people want to live in that type of housing, "then let them live in Dubuque." Many questioned whether there was a need for *any* R–4 districts in the community, regardless of location. One person said, "My first feeling is I don't believe this community needs to have that type of zoning. I understand the political structure and that if a community needs to have it, then it ought to be in a certain place * * *. It probably deserves to be more down * * * towards the industrial area." At the end of the hearing, a man accurately summarized the prevailing feeling: "I don't think there is one person here that is opposed to anything but trailer parks. I don't think anybody in this room wants trailers." Not surprisingly, a member of the commission then moved to amend the proposed plan in one particular: to change the zoning designation of the Bahls' farm from R-4 to R-3. After the unanimous approval of the amendment, the commission voted to recommend the new land use plan to the city council.

Two months later the city council met to consider adoption of the plan. The Bahls' attorney spoke at that meeting and urged the council to reconsider the proposed specification of the Bahls' property as R-3. He pointed out that the housing study had indicated a need for "housing for young families." He observed the same study stated that 75% of the houses in Asbury were valued at $100,000 or more, and 100% of the homes currently for sale had an asking price in excess of $100,000. Noting that such homes were not within the financial reach of many young people, the Bahls' attorney argued that the proposed manufactured housing development "would address the need for affordable housing" and "the need for housing for a variety of living environments," such as "low-to-moderate income housing, first-time homebuyers, and retirement [housing]." Notwithstanding these comments, the new land use plan was unanimously approved, including the designation of the Bahls' property as R-3.

Thereafter, in March 1999, the commission met to consider the Bahls' 1997 application to rezone their property to R-4. Despite the recently adopted land use plan showing this property as R-3, the commission voted to recommend to the council that the Bahls' rezoning application be granted. Notwithstanding this favorable recommendation, the city council denied the Bahls' request, concluding that R-4 zoning was not consistent with the City's land use plan. The Bahls thereafter filed an amended rezoning application that, among other changes, reduced the density of housing in the proposed development. This time, the planning and zoning commission recommended denial of the application, and that was the ultimate decision of the city council.

The City's denial of the Bahls' rezoning applications successfully shelved the Bahls' plan to build a manufactured housing development on their land because such developments, as noted previously, are restricted to R-4 districts by the Asbury zoning ordinance. The City does not dispute the effect of the council's decision, acknowledging in its brief that under the City's zoning ordinance "trailer parks" are excluded from districts other than R-4.

* * *

Section 414.28A, first enacted in 1997, currently provides in pertinent part:

> A city shall not adopt or enforce zoning or subdivision regulations or other ordinances which disallow or make infeasible the plans and specifications of land-leased communities because the housing within the land-leased community will be manufactured housing.

Iowa Code § 414.28A; *see* 1997 Iowa Acts ch. 86, § 4.

This statute is very similar to a related statute adopted by the Iowa legislature nearly twenty years ago. In 1984, the General Assembly passed a bill that added the following provision to chapter 414:

> A city shall not adopt or enforce zoning regulations or other ordinances which disallow the plans and specifications of a proposed residential structure solely because the proposed structure is a manufactured home. . . .

1984 Iowa Acts ch. 1238, § 2 (codified at Iowa Code § 414.28 (1985).

There appears to be very little difference between section 414.28 and section 414.28A with respect to the operative language. The primary distinction of course is that section 414.28 applies to "residential structure[s]" whereas section 414.28A governs "land-leased communities." Section 414.28A is also broader in scope, prohibiting subdivision regulations, as well as general zoning regulations. Originally section 414.28A, like section 414.28, only prohibited ordinances that "disallowed" manufactured housing developments "solely because" the homes were manufactured homes. 1997 Iowa Acts ch. 86, § 4 (codified at Iowa Code § 414.28A (1998)). Section 414.28A was soon amended, however, to enlarge the prohibition by barring regulations or ordinances that "make infeasible" manufactured housing developments, as well as those that outright disallow such developments. 1998 Iowa Acts ch. 1107, § 16 (codified at Iowa Code § 414.28A (Supp.1998)). In addition to this change, section 414.28A was also amended to strike the word "solely," *see id.*, again broadening the reach of the statute so as to eliminate the requirement that the disallowance or infeasibility occur only because manufactured housing is involved.

* * *

Although there is no legislative history explaining the legislature's objective in adopting section 414.28, it appears this statute was enacted in response to a perceived crisis in the supply of affordable housing. *See generally Brady v. City of Dubuque*, 495 N.W.2d 701, 705 (Iowa 1993) (noting that contemporary circumstances may be considered as an aid to interpretation of a statute); Iowa Code § 4.6(2) (stating that "the court, in determining the intention of the legislature, may consider . . . [t]he circumstances under which the statute was enacted"). In 1981, then-president Reagan established the President's Commission on Housing to study the housing industry and make recommendations for national policy to address the housing recession caused by inflation and high interest rates. *See* Exec. Order No. 12,310, 46 Fed.Reg. 31,869 (June 16, 1981) (directing Commission "to develop housing * * * options which strengthen the ability of the private sector to maximize opportunities for homeownership"); *see also* Proclamation No. 4988, 47 Fed.Reg. 46,837 (Oct. 19, 1982) (referencing the adverse impact on housing "from the twin afflictions of inflation and high interest rates" and the establishment of the Commission to study national housing policy).

One of the Commission's fundamental concerns was "the housing problems of low-income Americans," specifically the affordability of housing. Report of the President's Commission on Housing 3, 10–12 (1982). The Commission concluded that "[m]anufactured housing [was] a significant source of affordable housing for American families, particularly first-time homebuyers, the elderly, and low-and moderate-income families." *Id.* at 85. Nonetheless, it recognized that local action often impeded the ability of homebuyers from choosing this type of housing. *Id.* at 86. Therefore, the Commission recommended "removing zoning provisions that discriminate against manufactured housing." *Id.; see id.* at 203 ("States and localities should remove from their zoning laws all forms of discrimination against manufactured housing * * *."); *see also* Proclamation No. 4988, 47 Fed.Reg. 46,837 (Oct. 19, 1982) (noting Commission's report "reaffirmed our national commitment to equal housing choice"). The following explanation was given in support of this recommendation:

Because of sharply rising housing costs, manufactured housing today offers many households their only option for homeownership. Indeed, in 1980, manufactured ("mobile") homes amounted to 29 percent of all single-family homes sold. The marketplace demand for mobile homes has come from improvements in the product as well as from a competitive price.

Despite the increasing attractiveness of manufactured housing, *local zoning laws continued to discriminate against mobile homes. In many localities, mobile homes are segregated into special areas, often in disadvantageous locations set aside as "trailer parks."*

There is an increasing recognition that the quality of manufactured housing has improved. Since 1976, manufactured housing has been built under a national code, supervised by HUD, setting health and safety requirements. Vermont, California, and Indiana have enacted laws precluding discrimination against manufactured homes. The Michigan Supreme Court last year struck down a zoning law because it violated the State constitution: "The *per se* exclusion of mobile homes from all areas not designated as mobile home parks has no reasonable basis under the police power, and is therefore unconstitutional."

Manufactured housing can be as safe and healthy as comparable site-built housing. Housing systems or components satisfying a nationally recognized model code similarly should not be excluded from use in a locality. *Exclusionary zoning provisions based on type of manufacture are arbitrary and unrelated to legitimate zoning concerns.*

Report of the President's Commission on Housing 203–04 (emphasis added).

It was within this historical context that the Iowa legislature in 1984 adopted section 414.28.

Although this court has never interpreted section 414.28, Iowa's statute was discussed in a 1988 article appearing in Urban Lawyer. *See* Molly A. Sellman, *Equal Treatment of Housing: A Proposed Model State Code for Manufactured Housing,* 20 Urb. Law. 73, 84 (1988). Noting that one solution to the affordable housing problem is "state enabling legislation demanding comparable or equal treatment of all forms of housing," *id.* at 81, the author observes, "Three states—Iowa, Minnesota, and Vermont—have enacted progressive codes encouraging the utilization of manufactured housing *by mandating equal treatment of all forms of housing,*" *id.* at 82 (emphasis added). The author makes a similar statement later in discussing Iowa's specific statutory provisions, noting again that they "mandate *equal treatment* of manufactured housing with site-built housing." *Id.* at 84 (emphasis added) (citing Iowa Code Ann. § § 358A.30, 414.28 (West 1976 & Supp.1986)).

* * *

We think the commentators are correct. The historical context in which section 414.28 was enacted indicates that the statute was intended to prevent local zoning authorities from discriminating against manufactured housing. The same purpose logically must be ascribed to section 414.28A. *See* 2B Norman J. Singer, *Statutes and Statutory Construction* § 51.02, at 176–78 (6th ed.2000 revision) (stating that when a new provision is enacted that relates to the same subject matter as previous statutes, "the new provision is presumed in accord with the legislative policy embodied in those prior statutes"). More importantly, this interpretation of the statute is most consistent with the language of section 414.28 as well as the language of section 414.28A. Section 414.28 prohibits discrimination by providing that plans for a residential structure cannot be disallowed solely because the proposed structure is a manufactured home. Similarly, section 414.28A mandates equal treatment for manufactured housing developments by stating that plans for a land-leased community cannot be disallowed (or even made infeasible) because the proposed community contains manufactured homes. Nothing in the language of the statute supports the City's contention that section 414.28A simply prohibits a municipality from totally excluding manufactured housing developments from the community.

The Vermont Supreme Court reached the same conclusion that we reach here when it interpreted similar legislation enacted in that state. *See In re Appeal of Lunde,* 166 Vt. 167, 688 A.2d 1312 (1997). In *Lunde,* the city's zoning regulations restricted mobile homes to certain locations, a restriction that was not placed on site-built homes. 688 A.2d at 1313. A mobile home owner claimed the city ordinance violated a Vermont statute providing that "no zoning regulation shall have the effect of excluding mobile homes * * * from the municipality, except upon the same terms and conditions as conventional housing is excluded." *Id.* (quoting Vt. Stat. Ann. tit. 24, § 4406(4)(A)). The Vermont Supreme Court rejected an argument that the statute "was intended to prevent municipalities from excluding mobile homes 'from the municipality,' but to allow restricting mobile homes to mobile home parks or to a particular zone." *Id.* at 1314. Rather, the court concluded, the legislature "intended municipalities to treat mobile homes in the same manner as conventional housing." *Id.*

Although the Vermont statute is not worded precisely the same as Iowa's statute, it too is "equal treatment" legislation. *See* Sellman, *Equal Treatment of Housing: A Proposed Model State Code for Manufactured Housing*, 20 Urb. Law. at 82. The *Lunde* case is persuasive authority that "equal treatment" statutes prohibit ordinances that treat manufactured housing developments differently from conventional housing developments, even though manufactured housing developments are not entirely excluded from the municipality.

* * *

Turning to the facts of the case before us, we conclude the Asbury zoning ordinance contravenes section 414.28A by relegating "mobile home parks," not all condominium-type communities, to R–4 zoning districts. Without a doubt, this restrictive ordinance has made the Bahls' land-leased community infeasible because it contains manufactured housing, a clear violation of the statute. The facts of the present case present a classic example of exclusionary and discriminatory zoning regulations and decisions of the very type the President's Commission called on states to prevent. Moreover, the City's zoning ordinance is exactly the type of discriminatory treatment of manufactured housing projects our legislature intended to thwart when it enacted section 414.28A.

* * *

AFFIRMED.

All justices concur except STREIT, J., who dissents.

STREIT, JUSTICE (dissenting).

I agree with the majority that the ultimate issue in this case is a matter of statutory interpretation. However, I respectfully disagree with the majority's interpretation of Iowa Code section 414.28A. The majority interprets section 414.28A to mean mobile home parks must be allowed in any district in which "similar communities of site-built housing are allowed." Given this interpretation, it concludes the Asbury ordinance is illegal under 414.28A because the ordinance assigns mobile home parks to the high-density residential district. The majority adds meaning to this statute where the plain language shows it was not intended by the legislature.

The plain and unambiguous language of the statute is ignored under the guise of providing statutory interpretation. Where a statute is clear and unambiguous, resort to extrinsic aids is unwarranted. We need only look to the plain language of the statute to determine whether the ordinance, in assigning mobile home parks to R–4 districts, violates section 414.28A. The statute provides, in part,

> A city shall not adopt or enforce zoning or subdivision regulations or other ordinances which disallow or make infeasible the plans and specifications of land-leased communities because the housing within the land-leased community will be manufactured housing.

Iowa Code § 414.28A (1999).

Before we examine the meaning of this section, we must look to the terms of the statute to determine its scope. Namely, we look to what is a "land-leased community" and what constitutes "manufactured housing."

Iowa Code section 414.28 defines a manufactured home as,

> a factory-built structure which * * * is to be used as a place for human habitation, but which is not constructed or equipped with a permanent hitch or other device allowing it to be moved other than for the purpose of moving to a permanent site, and which does not have permanently attached to its body or frame any wheels or axles.

Iowa Code § 414.28.

A land-leased community is "any site, lot, field, or tract of land under common ownership upon which ten or more occupied manufactured homes are harbored, either free of charge or for revenue purposes...." Iowa Code § 414.28A. Given these statutory definitions, the simple reading of section 414.28A provides: a city shall not enforce zoning or subdivision regulations or other ordinances that prevent the construction of ten or more manufactured homes upon a site simply because the site will consist of factory-built, manufactured homes. By assigning mobile home parks to R–4 districts, the ordinance does allow—and does not disallow or make infeasible—the construction of mobile home parks in the City. The statute contains no other language of limitation upon the actions of a city in regulating the development of land-leased communities.

The plain language of this section supports the conclusion that it protects land-leased communities only in so far as a municipality cannot ban mobile home parks from its districts. The statute makes it illegal for a municipality to reject or make infeasible a proposed land-leased community because it will contain manufactured housing, including mobile home parks. This statute protects manufactured homes in a limited fashion because the City still has power to regulate or place reasonable restrictions upon manufactured housing developments. *See Huff v. City of Des Moines,* 244 Iowa 89, 94, 56 N.W.2d 54, 57 (1952) (regulation and restriction of mobile home parks is a "legitimate exercise of police power").

None of the language of this statute indicates that in order to comply with the section a city must allow mobile home parks in more than just the R–4 district. This section does not say the ordinance must allow mobile home *parks* in *every* zoning district. It does not say the ordinance must subject mobile home parks to the same conditions as it does all other "similar communities of site-built housing." It does not act as an absolute prohibition on the City's power to regulate the land under its control simply because a mobile home park is involved.

The majority avoids the simple reading of the statute and instead engages in an analysis of clear and unambiguous language. It attempts to characterize section 414.28A as a non-discriminatory or "equal treatment" statute that protects the civil rights of mobile home park developers. It does this by making a comparison between mobile home parks and "site-built houses in land-leased communities." Such a creature does not exist under this statute. The plain meaning does not support the majority's conclusion that the legislature intended that mobile home parks be treated in the same fashion as are site-built homes in similar communities. Rather the statute does nothing more than prevent a city from outright prohibiting mobile home parks.

The majority contends its holding does not mean the City must allow mobile home parks in *all* zoning districts, but only in some. Despite this declaration, it is not clear where the City can limit the placement of mobile home parks. In fact, the inescapable conclusion from the majority's opinion is that the City of Asbury must allow mobile home parks to be constructed in any and all of its districts. Such a result is beyond both the force of section 414.28A's prohibition and the legislative intent behind this statute.

* * *

I also disagree with the majority's finding that the city council denied Bahls' application for rezoning based upon the fact that the proposed development consisted of mobile homes. The majority bases its conclusion upon one factor only—the inflammatory comments of neighbors regarding the proposed mobile home park. Based only upon the neighbors' offensive language, the majority impermissibly ascribes bad motive to the city council's denial of Bahls' petition for rezoning. Other than the odious and sometimes loony comments themselves, there is no evidence in the record to indicate the city council made its decision based on the neighbors' comments.

* * *

In general, the city council had ample evidence to consider regarding the ultimate result of constructing the new housing units. The impact of putting 300 housing units on 110 acres of land would be significant. It would create substantial additional traffic and noise in the area. The size of the development would directly impact the City's fire, police, water, and sewer services. Moreover, the city council was told of claims of the Bahls' generally poor record of maintenance on their properties. As the Bahls proposed to complete the project in seven phases, the council could have found the project might ultimately fail and be left partially completed.

* * * Because the reasonableness of the denial of the rezoning application is fairly debatable, the city council's discretion in this matter is controlling. *See Perkins,* 636 N.W.2d at 67. I would reverse the district court's ruling that the Asbury zoning ordinance violates section 414.28A

Notes

1. In Cannon v. Coweta County, 260 Ga. 56, 389 S.E.2d 329 (1990), the Supreme Court of Georgia held that a per se exclusion of manufactured homes from single-family districts was unconstitutional. The court questioned the trial court's acceptance of the county argument that manufactured homes adversely affect the local tax base and that manufactured homes adversely affect the value of nearby site-built homes. In a footnote the court suggested that a local government could regulate manufactured homes in such ways as requiring attachment to a permanent foundation, appropriate lot sizes, and aesthetic standards. Compare, Grant v. County of Seminole, Fla., 817 F.2d 731 (11th Cir.1987).

2. Note that the court in the Bahl case did not address the issue of whether a "mobile home" can be construed to be a "single-family dwelling" and thus be permitted in the single-family residential district. A number of cases touch on this issue, which turns out to be a difficult one for courts. A series of cases in just two states well illustrates this difficulty. See Columbia County v. Kelly, 25 Or.App. 1, 548 P.2d 163 (1976); Clackamas County v. Dunham, 30 Or.App. 595, 567 P.2d 605 (1977) reversed 282 Or. 419, 579 P.2d 223 (1978) for the Oregon approach, and Courtland Twp. v. Cole, 66 Mich.App. 474, 239 N.W.2d 630 (1976); Robinson Twp. v. Knoll, 70 Mich. App. 258, 245 N.W.2d 709 (1976), affirmed, vacated, and remanded 410 Mich. 293, 302 N.W.2d 146 (1981); North Cherokee Village Membership v. Murphy, 71 Mich.App. 592, 248 N.W.2d 629 (1976) for the Michigan approach. Also see, Hansman v. Oneida County, 123 Wis.2d 511, 366 N.W.2d 901 (1985) (modular home permanently attached to a foundation held not to be a mobile home) and Fischer v. Driesen, 446 N.W.2d 84 (Iowa App.1989) (double-wide manufactured home set on concrete and steel piers held not to violate restrictive covenant against trailers).

3. In California a statute, Cal.Govt.Code § 65852.3, provides:

(a) A city, including a charter city, county, or city and county, shall allow the installation of manufactured homes certified under the National Manufactured Housing Construction and Safety Standards Act of 1974 (42 U.S.C.A. Sec. 5401 et seq.) on a foundation system, pursuant to Section 18551 of the Health and Safety Code, on lots zoned for conventional single-family residential dwellings. Except with respect to architectural requirements, a city, including a charter city, county, or city and county, shall only subject the manufactured home and the lot on which it is placed to the same development standards to which a conventional single-family residential dwelling on the same lot would be subject, including, but not limited to, building setback standards, side and rear yard requirements, standards for enclosures, access, and vehicle parking, aesthetic requirements, and minimum square footage requirements. Any architectural requirements imposed on the manufactured home structure itself, exclusive of any requirement for any and all additional enclosures, shall be limited to its roof overhang, roofing material, and siding material. These architectural requirements may be imposed on manufactured homes even if similar requirements are not imposed on conventional single-family residential dwellings. However, any architectural requirements for roofing and siding material shall not exceed those which would be required of conventional single-family dwellings constructed on the same lot. At the discretion of the local legislative body, the city or county may preclude installation of a manufactured home in zones specified in this section if more than 10 years have elapsed between the date of manufacture of the manufactured home and the date of the application for the issuance of a permit to install the mobilehome in the affected zone. In no case may a city, including a charter city, county, or city and county, apply any development standards which will have the effect of precluding manufactured homes from being installed as permanent residences.

Also see 30A Maine Rev.Stat.Ann. § 4358, and Paladac v. City of Rockland, 558 A.2d 372 (Me.1989). A number of states have adopted statutes similar to the one in California. In Tennessee Manufactured Housing Ass'n v. Metropolitan Govt. of Nashville, 798 S.W.2d 254 (Tenn.App.1990), the court construed a statute providing "* * * no power or authority granted by this Code to regulate zoning or land use planning shall be used to exclude the placement of a residential dwelling on land designated for residential use solely because the dwelling is partially or completely constructed in a manufacturing facility; provided, however, that the term 'residential dwelling' as used in this part shall not apply to factory-manufactured mobile homes constructed as a single self-contained unit and mounted on a single chassis * * *" The court held that the proviso did not apply to a double-wide manufactured home, reasoning that the word "and" in the proviso was intended as a conjunctive; thus a double-wide home was not one on a single chassis.

4. In Rolling Pines Ltd. Partnership v. City of Little Rock, 73 Ark.App. 97, 40 S.W.3d 828 (2001) the court upheld the city's denial of the developer's application for a conditional use permit to place manufactured homes in a portion of his subdivision (previous development in the subdivision had been modest site-built brick homes). The city relied on a provision in its conditional use permit standards that stated one factor to be considered is "compatibility with the neighborhood." The court said that the standard of compatibility was not too vague. Compare that holding with the following case:

MARION COUNTY v. DEPARTMENT OF COMMUNITY AFFAIRS

District Court of Appeal of Florida, Fifth District, 2002.
817 So.2d 1062.

PETERSON, J.

Marion County appeals a summary final judgment finding that its Ordinance 98–21 is "invalid insofar as it attempts to restrict manufactured housing within a residentially zoned area which otherwise permits on site construction."

On May 20, 1998, the Board of County Commissioners of Marion County enacted Ordinance 98–21 to discourage incompatible land uses. The operative section of the ordinance allowed manufactured buildings to be installed "in all zoning classifications which allow residential structures, except R–1 properties located in subdivisions." The ordinance clashed head-on with a pre-existing statute, section 553.38, Florida Statutes (1998), which provided:

> The department shall enforce every provision of this part and the rules adopted pursuant hereto, except that local land use and zoning requirements, fire zones, building setback requirements, side and rear yard requirements, site development requirements, property line requirements, subdivision control, and onsite installation requirements, as well as the review and regulation of architectural and aesthetic requirements, are specifically and entirely reserved to local authorities. *Such local requirements and rules which may be enacted by local authorities must be reasonable and uniformly applied and enforced without any distinction as to whether a building is a conventionally constructed or manufactured building.* A local government shall require permit fees only for those inspections actually performed by the local government for the installation of a factory-built structure. Such fees shall be equal to the amount charged for similar inspections on conventionally built housing.

(Emphasis added).

Manufactured housing was defined in section 553.36(11), Florida Statutes (1998), which provided:

> "Manufactured building" means a closed structure, building assembly, or system of subassemblies, which may include structural, electrical, plumbing, heating, ventilating, or other service systems manufactured in manufacturing facilities for installation or erection, with or without other specified components, as a finished building or as part of a finished building, which shall include, but not be limited to, residential, commercial, institutional, storage, and industrial structures. This part does not apply to mobile homes. Manufactured building may also mean, at the option of the manufacturer, any building of open construction made or assembled in manufacturing

facilities away from the building site for installation, or assembly and installation, on the building site.

Although there have been minor amendments to these sections, both are substantially in the same form. *See* § § 553.36(12); 553.38, Fla. Stat. (2001).

* * *

Marion County has made clear that the motive for enacting 98–21 was a response to the complaints by landowners in R–1 districts that manufactured buildings are not compatible with conventionally built homes for the reasons that:

    1. Manufactured homes are different in appearance, mostly due to shallow-pitched roof lines.

    2. Conventionally built homes are subject to strict building codes and undergo rigorous inspections by county officials during the building process while manufactured homes are inspected and approved by the FDCA.

    3. Manufactured homes burn quickly and are usually beyond saving by the time fire departments can respond.

The only argument that seems valid to us is the first of these. An extension of this argument is that the two types of buildings when placed side-by-side have incompatible appearances. This incompatibility has a detrimental effect on the value of the conventionally built home. The validity of the other reasons are suspect when it is recognized that Marion County has narrowed its exclusions to only subdivisions in R–1 districts. Manufactured housing is not restricted in any zoning classification except subdivisions zoned R–1 in unincorporated areas of the county.

The Florida Legislature has made it clear in section 553.38 that it is the policy of the state that manufactured buildings may not be the subject of discrimination by local authorities. The main complaint by Marion County appears to be that when a manufactured building is placed side-by-side with a conventional building, they are incompatible in appearance and undermine property values. The legislature seems to have recognized that appearance is important and has reserved the right to local authorities to enact architectural and aesthetic requirements uniformly applicable to all building methods. There has been no attempt by Marion County to exercise those rights reserved to local authorities in the statute. Instead, the county has chosen to do exactly that which the legislature prohibits. Obviously, the county, as a political subdivision of the state created by the legislature, must yield to the policy established by the legislature.

AFIRMED.

COBB AND GRIFFIN, JJ., concur.

Note

In Ettinger v. City of Lansing, 215 Mich.App. 451, 546 N.W.2d 652 (1996), the court upheld a zoning ordinance that permitted mobile homes in residential single-family districts but excluded mobile home parks in most such districts. The property owner unsuccessfully relied on a Michigan statute providing: "A local government ordinance shall not be designed as exclusionary to mobile homes generally whether the mobile homes are located inside or outside of mobile home parks or seasonal mobile home parks."

F. RACIAL DISCRIMINATION IN HOUSING

UNITED STATES v. CITY OF BLACK JACK, MISSOURI

United States Court of Appeals, Eighth Circuit, 1974.
508 F.2d 1179, certiorari denied 422 U.S. 1042,
95 S.Ct. 2656, 45 L.Ed.2d 694 (1975).

[In 1970 the Black Jack area was unincorporated, and was under the St. Louis County master plan. The plan designated 67 acres for multi-family housing, only 15 of which had been developed. In 1969, the Inter-Religious Center for Urban Affairs obtained an option on 12 acres for the purpose of creating housing for low and moderate income persons living in economically depressed and deteriorated areas of St. Louis. In 1970, the area residents succeeded in having Black Jack incorporated as a city. After its incorporation, an ordinance was passed prohibiting the construction of any new multiple-family dwellings and making existing ones nonconforming uses. The United States brought an action to enjoin enforcement of the ordinance under Title VIII of the Civil Rights Act of 1968, 42 U.S.C.A. § 3601 et seq. The District Court held the plaintiff had failed to establish a racially discriminatory purpose or effect and it dismissed the case. Further facts appear in the opinion.]

HEANEY, CIRCUIT JUDGE.

* * *

The racial composition of Black Jack and the surrounding area was set forth by the District Court in its opinion, and is not contested by the parties:

"Statistical information submitted shows that at the relevant time the area which is now the City of Black Jack was virtually all white, with a black population of between 1% and 2%. The area of St. Louis County north of Interstate Highway 270, which includes Black Jack, is approximately 99% white. * * *

"The virtually all-white character of Black Jack was in marked contrast to the racial composition of other parts of the St. Louis area. In 1970, the pupil population of the City of St. Louis School District was 65.6% black. * * * In 1970, the Kinloch School District, which is only two miles from the nearest boundary of the Hazelwood

School District [of which Black Jack is a part], had 1,245 students, all of whom were black.

"The percentage of blacks in St. Louis County has increased only slightly overall from 4.1% in 1950 to 4.8% in 1970. During the same period, the percentage of blacks in the City of St. Louis more than doubled from 17.9% to 40.9%.

"Between 1950 and 1970, the population of the city declined * * * [by] 27%, while the population of the county more than doubled * * *. From 1960 to 1970, there were approximately 102,298 new housing starts in the county, and 15,348 in the city, a ratio of almost 7 to 1. During the same period, the city had a net decrease of 24,548 housing units, while the county had a net increase of 84,169. * * *

"The concentration of blacks in the city and in pockets in the county is accompanied by the confinement of a disproportionate number of them in overcrowded or substandard accommodations. The 1970 census reveals that in St. Louis city and county approximately 40% of the black families, as compared with 14% of the white families, lived in overcrowded units. * * * "

United States v. City of Black Jack, Missouri, supra, 372 F.Supp. at 325.

The District Court further found that the average cost of a home in the City of Black Jack in 1970 was approximately $30,000, and that the average income of Black Jack families is approximately $15,000 per year. It found that Park View Heights was designed to meet the housing needs of families making between $5,528 and $10,143 per year.

* * *

We turn then to the merits of the decision below. Congress has declared that the purpose of the Fair Housing Act of 1968 is "to provide, within constitutional limitations, for fair housing throughout the United States." 42 U.S.C.A. § 3601. The Act was passed pursuant to congressional power under the Thirteenth Amendment to eliminate the badges and incidents of slavery. In construing the Civil Rights Act of 1866, also founded on that power, the Supreme Court has declared that

> * * * when racial discrimination herds men into ghettos and makes their ability to buy property turn on the color of their skin, then it too is a relic of slavery.

Jones v. Mayer Co., 392 U.S. 409, 442–443, 88 S.Ct. 2186, 2205, 20 L.Ed.2d 1189 (1968).

Title VIII is designed to prohibit "all forms of discrimination, sophisticated as well as simple-minded." *Williams v. Matthews Co.*, 499 F.2d 819, 826 (8th Cir.1974). Just as Congress requires

> * * * the removal of artificial, arbitrary, and unnecessary barriers to employment when the barriers operate invidiously to discriminate on the basis of racial or other impermissible classification[,]

Griggs v. Duke Power Co., 401 U.S. 424, 430–431, 91 S.Ct. 849, 853, 28 L.Ed.2d 158 (1971), such barriers must also give way in the field of housing. The discretion of local zoning officials, recently recognized in *Village of Belle Terre v. Boraas*, 416 U.S. 1, 94 S.Ct. 1536, 39 L.Ed.2d 797 (1974), must be curbed where "the clear result of such discretion is the segregation of low-income Blacks from all White neighborhoods." *Banks v. Perk*, 341 F.Supp. 1175, 1180 (N.D.Ohio, 1972), aff'd in part & rev'd in part without opinion, 473 F.2d 910 (6th Cir.1973).

The burden of proof in Title VIII cases is governed by the concept of the "prima facie case." *Williams v. Matthews Co., supra* 499 F.2d at 826. To establish a prima facie case of racial discrimination, the plaintiff need prove no more than that the conduct of the defendant actually or predictably results in racial discrimination; in other words, that it has a discriminatory effect. See id.; *United Farmworkers of Florida Housing Project, Inc. v. City of Delray Beach*, 493 F.2d 799, 808 (5th Cir.1974); *Hawkins v. Town of Shaw, Mississippi*, 461 F.2d 1171, 1172 (5th Cir.1972) (en banc); *Kennedy Park Homes Ass'n v. City of Lackawanna, supra* 436 F.2d at 114; *Dailey v. City of Lawton, Oklahoma*, 425 F.2d 1037, 1039 (10th Cir.1970); *Norwalk CORE v. Norwalk Redevelopment Agency*, 395 F.2d 920, 931 (2d Cir.1968). The plaintiff need make no showing whatsoever that the action resulting in racial discrimination in housing was racially motivated.[4] See *Williams v. Matthews Co., supra* 499 F.2d at 826; *United Farmworkers of Florida Housing Project, Inc. v. City of Delray Beach, supra* 493 F.2d at 808; *Kennedy Park Homes Ass'n v. City of Lackawanna, supra* 436 F.2d at 114; *Citizens Committee for Faraday Wood v. Lindsay, supra* 362 F.Supp. at 658; *Banks v. Park, supra* 341 F.Supp. at 1180. Effect, and not motivation, is the touchstone, in part because clever men may easily conceal their motivations, but more importantly, because

> * * * [w]hatever our law was once, * * * we now firmly recognize that the arbitrary quality of thoughtlessness can be as disastrous and unfair to private rights and the public interest as the perversity of a willful scheme.

---

4. The United States contends that the ordinance ought also be enjoined because it was enacted for the purpose of excluding blacks. There is evidence in the record to support that contention. Opposition to Park View Heights was repeatedly expressed in racial terms by persons whom the District Court found to be the leaders of the incorporation movement, by individuals circulating petitions, and by zoning commissioners themselves. Racial criticism of Park View Heights was made and cheered at public meetings. The uncontradicted evidence indicates that, at all levels of opposition, race placed a significant role, both in the drive to incorporate and the decision to rezone. We agree with the Tenth Circuit's conclusion that improper purpose may be shown circumstantially:

* * * If proof of a civil right violation depends on an open statement by an official of an intent to discriminate, the Fourteenth Amendment offers little solace to those seeking its protection. In our opinion it is enough for the complaining parties to show that the local officials are effectuating the discriminatory designs of private individuals. * * *

Dailey v. City of Lawton, 425 F.2d 1037, 1039 (10th Cir.1970).

Nevertheless, we do not base our conclusion that the Black Jack ordinance violates Title VIII on a finding that there was an improper purpose.

Hobson v. Hansen, 269 F.Supp. 401, 497 (D.D.C.1967), aff'd sub nom. *Smuck v. Hobson*, 132 U.S.App.D.C. 372, 408 F.2d 175 (1969) (en banc).

Once the plaintiff has established a prima facie case by demonstrating racially discriminatory effect, the burden shifts to the governmental defendant to demonstrate that its conduct was necessary to promote a compelling governmental interest.

The District Court concluded that the ordinance had no discriminatory effect. It based this conclusion on its finding that, because Park View Heights was designed to meet the needs of families earning between $5,000 and $10,000 per year—a class including 32 percent of the black population in the metropolitan area and 29 percent of the white population—the ordinance had no measurably greater effect on blacks than on whites. The court's conclusion was in error. It failed to take into account either the "ultimate effect" or the "historical context" of the City's action. See *United Farmworkers of Florida Housing Project, Inc. v. City of Delray Beach*, supra 493 F.2d at 810; *Kennedy Park Homes Ass'n v. City of Lackawanna*, supra 436 F.2d at 112. The ultimate effect of the ordinance was to foreclose 85 percent of the blacks living in the metropolitan area from obtaining housing in Black Jack, and to foreclose them at a time when 40 percent of them were living in substandard or overcrowded units.

The discriminatory effect of the ordinance is more onerous when assessed in light of the fact that segregated housing in the St. Louis metropolitan area was

> * * * in large measure the result of deliberate racial discrimination in the housing market by the real estate industry and by agencies of the federal, state, and local governments. * * *

United States v. City of Black Jack, Missouri, supra 372 F.Supp. at 326.

Black Jack's action is but one more factor confining blacks to low-income housing in the center city, confirming the inexorable process whereby the St. Louis metropolitan area becomes one that "has the racial shape of a donut, with the Negroes in the hole and with mostly Whites occupying the ring." *Mahaley v. Cuyahoga Metropolitan Housing Authority*, 355 F.Supp. 1257, 1260 (N.D.Ohio, 1973), rev'd, 500 F.2d 1087 (6th Cir.1974). See also *Crow v. Brown*, 332 F.Supp. 382, 384 (N.D.Ga., 1971), aff'd per curiam, 457 F.2d 788 (5th Cir.1972). Park View Heights was particularly designed to contribute to the prevention of this prospect so antithetical to the Fair Housing Act. The Board of Directors of the Park View Housing Corporation was one-half white and one-half black. Affirmative measures were planned to assure that members of the black community would be aware of the opportunity to live in Park View Heights. There was ample proof that many blacks would live in the development, and that the exclusion of the townhouses would contribute to the perpetuation of segregation in a community which was 99 percent white.

It having been established that the ordinance had a discriminatory effect, it follows that the United States had made out a prima facie case under Title VIII, and the burden shifted to the City to demonstrate that a compelling governmental interest was furthered by that ordinance. We turn to that question. The City asserted primarily the following governmental interests to justify the ban on further apartments:

(1) Road and traffic control;

(2) Prevention of overcrowding of schools;

(3) Prevention of devaluation of adjacent single-family homes.

Several other interests were also alluded to in the record, including exclusion of apartments where there were already too many and where there was no need for them.

In determining whether any of these rise to the level of a compelling governmental interest, we must examine: first, whether the ordinance in fact furthers the governmental interest asserted; second, whether the public interest served by the ordinance is constitutionally permissible[5] and is substantial enough to outweigh the private detriment caused by it;[6] and third, whether less drastic means are available whereby the stated governmental interest may be attained. See *Shapiro v. Thompson*, 394 U.S. 618, 637, 89 S.Ct. 1322, 22 L.Ed.2d 600 (1969); Note, Exclusionary Zoning and Equal Protection, 84 Harv.L.Rev. 1645, 1651 (1971).

We need not go beyond the first step in the inquiry, for we find that there is no factual basis for the assertion that any one of the three primary interests asserted by the City is in fact furthered by the zoning ordinance, and we find that the other asserted interests—at least on the facts of this case—are clearly not substantial in relation to the housing opportunities foreclosed. To paraphrase the Supreme Court in *Shapiro v. Thompson, supra* at 638, 89 S.Ct. 1322, we conclude that the City does not use and has no need to use the ordinance for the governmental purposes suggested.

* * *

We hold that Zoning Ordinance No. 12 of the City of Black Jack violates Title VIII, because it denies persons housing on the basis of race, in violation of § 3604(a), and interferes with the exercise of the right to equal housing opportunity, in violation of § 3617. The remedy for this violation of the Fair Housing Act is provided in § 3615:

5. This portion of the analysis is essentially a qualitative one. For example, *Shapiro v. Thompson, supra* 394 U.S. at 629–631, 89 S.Ct. 1322, 22 L.Ed.2d 600, held that it was constitutionally impermissible for a state to inhibit migration by needy persons into the state, because such migration was a constitutional right. That case further held that limiting payment of welfare benefits to those who had "contributed" to the state in the past through taxes was constitutionally impermissible. Id. at 633, 89 S.Ct. 1322.

6. This portion of the analysis is essentially quantitative. For example, preservation of the public peace and welfare by avoiding racial conflict was held insufficient to validate a zoning ordinance restricting racial integration in *Buchanan v. Warley*, 245 U.S. 60, 38 S.Ct. 16, 62 L.Ed. 149 (1917).

* * * any law of a State, a political subdivision, or other such jurisdiction that purports to require or permit any action that would be a discriminatory housing practice under this subchapter shall to that extent be invalid.

We, therefore, reverse and remand with instructions to the District Court to enter a permanent injunction upon receipt of this Court's order, enjoining the enforcement of the ordinance. The mandate of this Court shall be issued forthwith.

Reversed and remanded.

Note

The sponsors of the project in the principal case also sued the City of Black Jack. In Park View Heights Corp. v. City of Black Jack, 467 F.2d 1208 (8th Cir.1972) (pre-dating the principal case), the court found the zoning ordinance to be exclusionary, ordered reclassification of all land zoned for multi-family use prior to the offending ordinance to a multi-family designation, ordered affirmative action to permit the construction of the particular project, and, after the principal case, approved a consent settlement of $450,000 damages. The affirmative action portion of the decree was further litigated, and in Park View Heights Corp. v. City of Black Jack, 454 F.Supp. 1223 (E.D.Mo.1978), the district court denied injunctive relief requiring the city to ensure construction of the project and additional damages because the project had become economically infeasible due to inflation and new property standards established by HUD. The Eighth Circuit Court of Appeals reversed, 605 F.2d 1033 (8th Cir.1979), holding that notwithstanding the earlier damage settlement and the present economic infeasibility of the project, the city is subject to a continuing, enforceable duty to affirmatively promote moderately priced, interracial housing equivalent to that which would have been built but for the racially discriminatory zoning. In February, 1982, a consent decree was entered which permanently enjoins the city from engaging in discriminatory actions depriving persons of equal access to housing. At one point during the protracted Black Jack litigation, a local woman with a large number of children ran for mayor, campaigning in Ku Klux Klan regalia; she lost in the primary.

VILLAGE OF ARLINGTON HEIGHTS v. METROPOLITAN HOUSING DEVELOPMENT CORP.

Supreme Court of the United States, 1977.
429 U.S. 252, 97 S.Ct. 555, 50 L.Ed.2d 450.

Mr. Justice Powell delivered the opinion of the Court.

In 1971 respondent Metropolitan Housing Development Corporation (MHDC) applied to petitioner, the Village of Arlington Heights, Ill., for the rezoning of a 15-acre parcel from single-family to multiple-family classification. Using federal financial assistance, MHDC planned to build 190 clustered townhouse units for low-and moderate-income tenants. The Village denied the rezoning request. MHDC, joined by other plaintiffs who are also respondents here, brought suit in the United States District Court for the Northern District of Illinois. They alleged that the denial was racially discriminatory and that it violated, *inter alia,* the Fourteenth Amendment and the Fair Housing Act of 1968, 82 Stat. 81, 42 U.S.C.A. § 3601 et seq. Following a bench trial, the District Court entered judgment for the Village, 373 F.Supp. 208 (1974), and respondents appealed. The Court of Appeals for the Seventh Circuit reversed, finding that the "ultimate effect" of the denial was racially discriminatory, and that the refusal to rezone therefore violated the Fourteenth Amendment. 517 F.2d 409 (1975). We granted the Village's petition for certiorari, 423 U.S. 1030, 96 S.Ct. 560, 46 L.Ed.2d 404 (1975), and now reverse.

* * *

The planned development did not conform to the Village's zoning ordinance and could not be built unless Arlington Heights rezoned the parcel to R–5, its multiple-family housing classification. Accordingly, MHDC filed with the Village Plan Commission a petition for rezoning, accompanied by supporting materials describing the development and specifying that it would be subsidized under § 236. The materials made clear that one requirement under § 236 is an affirmative marketing plan designed to assure that a subsidized development is racially integrated. MHDC also submitted studies demonstrating the need for housing of this type and analyzing the probable impact of the development. To prepare for the hearings before the Plan Commission and to assure compliance with the Village building code, fire regulations, and related requirements, MHDC consulted with the Village staff for preliminary review of the development. The parties have stipulated that every change recommended during such consultations was incorporated into the plans.

During the spring of 1971, the Plan Commission considered the proposal at a series of three public meetings, which drew large crowds. Although many of those attending were quite vocal and demonstrative in opposition to Lincoln Green, a number of individuals and representatives of community groups spoke in support of rezoning. Some of the comments, both from opponents and supporters, addressed what was referred to as the "social issue"—the desirability or undesirability of introducing at this location in Arlington Heights low-and moderate-income housing, housing that would probably be racially integrated.

Many of the opponents, however, focused on the zoning aspects of the petition, stressing two arguments. First, the area always had been zoned single-family, and the neighboring citizens had built or purchased there in reliance on that classification. Rezoning threatened to cause a measurable drop in property value for neighboring sites. Second, the Village's apartment policy, adopted by the Village Board in 1962 and amended in 1970, called for R–5 zoning primarily to serve as a buffer between single-family development and land uses thought incompatible, such as commercial or manufacturing districts. Lincoln Green did not meet this requirement, as it adjoined no commercial or manufacturing district.

At the close of the third meeting, the Plan Commission adopted a motion to recommend to the Village's Board of Trustees that it deny the request. The motion stated: "While the need for low and moderate income housing may exist in Arlington Heights or its environs, the Plan Commission would be derelict in recommending it at the proposed location." Two members voted against the motion and submitted a minority report, stressing that in their view the change to accommodate Lincoln Green represented "good zoning." The Village Board met on September 28, 1971, to consider MHDC's request and the recommendation of the Plan Commission. After a public hearing, the Board denied the rezoning by a 6–1 vote.

* * *

[The Seventh Circuit Court of Appeals] first approved the District Court's finding that the defendants were motivated by a concern for the integrity of the zoning plan, rather than by racial discrimination. Deciding whether their refusal to rezone would have discriminatory effects was more complex. The court observed that the refusal would have a disproportionate impact on blacks. Based upon family income, blacks constituted 40% of those Chicago area residents who were eligible to become tenants of Lincoln Green, although they composed a far lower percentage of total area population. The court reasoned, however, that under our decision in James v. Valtierra, 402 U.S. 137, 91 S.Ct. 1331, 28 L.Ed.2d 678 (1971), such a disparity in racial impact alone does not call for strict scrutiny of a municipality's decision that prevents the construction of the low-cost housing.

There was another level to the court's analysis of allegedly discriminatory results. Invoking language from *Kennedy Park Homes Assn. v. City of Lackawanna*, 436 F.2d 108, 112 (C.A.2 1970), cert. denied, 401 U.S. 1010, 91 S.Ct. 1256 (1971), the Court of Appeals ruled that the denial of rezoning must be examined in light of its "historical context and ultimate effect." 517 F.2d, at 413. Northwest Cook County was enjoying rapid growth in employment opportunities and population, but it continued to exhibit a high degree of residential segregation. The court held that Arlington Heights could not simply ignore this problem. Indeed, it found that the Village had been "exploiting" the situation by allowing itself to become a nearly all-white community. Id., at 414. The Village had no other current plans for building low-and moderate-income housing, and no other R–5 parcels in the Village were available to MHDC at an economically feasible price.

Against this background, the Court of Appeals ruled that the denial of the Lincoln Green proposal had racially discriminatory effects and could be tolerated only if it served compelling interests. Neither the buffer policy nor the desire to protect property values met this exacting

Sec. 1 **DISCRIMINATION AND HOUSING** **1163**

standard. The court therefore concluded that the denial violated the Equal Protection Clause of the Fourteenth Amendment.

* * *

Our decision last Term in *Washington v. Davis*, 426 U.S. 229, 96 S.Ct. 2040, 48 L.Ed.2d 597 (1976), made it clear that official action will not be held unconstitutional solely because it results in a racially disproportionate impact. "Disproportionate impact is not irrelevant, but it is not the sole touchstone of an invidious racial discrimination." Id., at 242. Proof of racially discriminatory intent or purpose is required to show a violation of the Equal Protection Clause. * * *

* * * In making its findings on this issue, the District Court noted that some of the opponents of Lincoln Green who spoke at the various hearings might have been motivated by opposition to minority groups. The court held, however, that the evidence "does not warrant the conclusion that this motivated the defendants." 373 F.Supp., at 211.

On appeal the Court of Appeals focused primarily on respondents' claim that the Village's buffer policy had not been consistently applied and was being invoked with a strictness here that could only demonstrate some other underlying motive. The court concluded that the buffer policy, though not always applied with perfect consistency, had on several occasions formed the basis for the Board's decision to deny other rezoning proposals. "The evidence does not necessitate a finding that Arlington Heights administered this policy in a discriminatory manner." 517 F.2d, at 412. The Court of Appeals therefore approved the District Court's findings concerning the Village's purposes in denying rezoning to MHDC.

We also have reviewed the evidence. The impact of the Village's decision does arguably bear more heavily on racial minorities. Minorities constitute 18% of the Chicago area population, and 40% of the income groups said to be eligible for Lincoln Green. But there is little about the sequence of events leading up to the decision that would spark suspicion. The area around the Viatorian property has been zoned R–3 since 1959, the year when Arlington Heights first adopted a zoning map. Single-family homes surround the 80–acre site, and the Village is undeniably committed to single-family homes as its dominant residential land use. The rezoning request progressed according to the usual procedures. The Plan Commission even scheduled two additional hearings, at least in part to accommodate MHDC and permit it to supplement its presentation with answers to questions generated at the first hearing.

The statements by the Plan Commission and Village Board members, as reflected in the official minutes, focused almost exclusively on the zoning aspects of the MHDC petition, and the zoning factors on which they relied are not novel criteria in the Village's rezoning decisions. There is no reason to doubt that there has been reliance by some neighboring property owners on the maintenance of single-family zoning in the vicinity. The Village originally adopted its buffer policy long before

MHDC entered the picture and has applied the policy too consistently for us to infer discriminatory purpose from its application in this case. Finally, MHDC called one member of the Village Board to the stand at trial. Nothing in her testimony supports an inference of invidious purpose.

In sum, the evidence does not warrant overturning the concurrent findings of both courts below. Respondents simply failed to carry their burden of proving that discriminatory purpose was a motivating factor in the Village's decision. This conclusion ends the constitutional inquiry. The Court of Appeals' further finding that the Village's decision carried a discriminatory "ultimate effect" is without independent constitutional significance.

Respondents' complaint also alleged that the refusal to rezone violated the Fair Housing Act of 1968, 42 U.S.C.A. § 3601 et seq. They continue to urge here that a zoning decision made by a public body may, and that petitioners' action did, violate § 3604 or § 3617. The Court of Appeals, however, proceeding in a somewhat unorthodox fashion, did not decide the statutory question. We remand the case for further consideration of respondents' statutory claims.

Reversed and remanded.

[Concurring and dissenting opinions are omitted.]

Notes

1. The effect of the Arlington Heights decision was to alert attorneys that a statistical showing of discriminatory impact of land use decisions discouraging subsidized multi-family housing would not be enough to invoke the equal protection clause of the Fourteenth Amendment. However, as the Black Jack, Missouri case indicates and as the closing paragraph of Arlington Heights suggests, a statistical presentation might be sufficient to establish a violation of the Fair Housing Act. This distinction was taken up by the Seventh Circuit upon the remand of the Arlington Heights case. In Metropolitan Housing Development Corp. v. Village of Arlington Heights, 558 F.2d 1283 (7th Cir.1977), certiorari denied 434 U.S. 1025, 98 S.Ct. 752, 54 L.Ed.2d 772 (1978), the court held that Arlington Heights had a statutory obligation under the Fair Housing Act to refrain from zoning policies that had the effect of foreclosing construction of low-cost housing within its boundaries. The Court of Appeals remanded the case to the District Court. In 1978, MHDC and the Village of Arlington Heights reached a settlement that provided for construction of low-cost housing on an alternate 26–acre site in an unincorporated area abutting the village. A nearby suburb, Mount Prospect, and a civic association sought intervention to protest the approval of the consent decree. The Seventh Circuit upheld the decree in Metropolitan Housing Development Corp. v. Village of Arlington Heights, 616 F.2d 1006 (7th Cir.1980). Also see Creek v. Village of Westhaven, 80 F.3d 186 (7th Cir.1996).

The Seventh Circuit opinion was apparently adopted by the Supreme Court in Town of Huntington, New York v. Huntington Branch, NAACP, 488 U.S. 15, 109 S.Ct. 276, 102 L.Ed.2d 180 (1988) (per curiam opinion).

Sec. 1   **DISCRIMINATION AND HOUSING**   **1165**

2. Other important cases involving racially discriminatory zoning practices are Kennedy Park Homes Ass'n v. City of Lackawanna, N.Y., 436 F.2d 108 (2d Cir.1970), certiorari denied 401 U.S. 1010, 91 S.Ct. 1256, 28 L.Ed.2d 546 (1971); Joseph Skillken & Co. v. City of Toledo, 380 F.Supp. 228 (N.D.Ohio 1974), reversed 528 F.2d 867 (6th Cir.1975), vacated and remanded 429 U.S. 1068, 97 S.Ct. 800, 50 L.Ed.2d 786 (1977), after remand 558 F.2d 350 (6th Cir.1977), certiorari denied 434 U.S. 985, 98 S.Ct. 611, 54 L.Ed.2d 479 (1977), rehearing denied 434 U.S. 1051, 98 S.Ct. 904, 54 L.Ed.2d 805 (1978); Resident Advisory Bd. v. Rizzo, 564 F.2d 126 (3d Cir.1977), certiorari denied 435 U.S. 908, 98 S.Ct. 1457, 55 L.Ed.2d 499 (1978); United States v. City of Parma, Ohio, 494 F.Supp. 1049 (N.D.Ohio 1980); United States v. City of Birmingham, 538 F.Supp. 819 (E.D.Mich.1982). Also see Scott v. Greenville County, 716 F.2d 1409 (4th Cir.1983), holding that a developer who was denied a permit to build low-income housing that complied with all existing zoning regulations could sue the county for damages under Section 1983.

3. Is the import of the above cases that no city can make a zoning decision that is unfavorable to a developer of low income housing? May a city defend a negative decision by showing good faith use of traditional zoning principles plus no racially discriminatory motive plus other nearby opportunities for low income housing? For authority that the answer to the first question is no and the answer to the second question is yes, see Confederacion de la Raza Unida v. City of Morgan Hill, 324 F.Supp. 895 (N.D.Cal. 1971) and Ybarra v. Town of Los Altos Hills, 503 F.2d 250 (9th Cir.1974). Compare Southern Alameda Spanish Speaking Organization v. City of Union City, California, 424 F.2d 291 (9th Cir.1970).

Obviously, not every impediment placed in the path of the developer of racially integrated, low-income housing is a violation of equal protection or the Fair Housing Act. Not every denial of a building permit or refusal to rezone land for higher density development can be shown to be a case of exclusionary zoning based on race. See Cowart v. City of Ocala, 478 F.Supp. 774 (M.D.Fla.1979), where the developer failed to modify his plan to comply with local ordinances, resulting in official withdrawal of approval of the project and denial of a building permit. Also see Des Vergnes v. Seekonk Water Dist., 601 F.2d 9 (1st Cir.1979), vacated 454 U.S. 807, 102 S.Ct. 81, 70 L.Ed.2d 76 (1981); Angell v. Zinsser, 473 F.Supp. 488 (D.Conn.1979); Lake Bluff Housing Partners v. City of South Milwaukee, 197 Wis.2d 157, 540 N.W.2d 189 (1995). Also see Brandt v. Village of Chebanse, Illinois, 82 F.3d 172 (7th Cir.1996) where the court held that the Fair Housing Act was not applicable to a developer who wanted a variance to build four-unit apartment buildings with the first floor apartments wheelchair accessible. The court noted that developers are required to make apartments accessible to the handicapped:

> So what Brandt proposes to build is essentially the minimum required by federal law. If such a proposal obliges a government to waive its single-family zoning rules, then four (or more) unit buildings can be erected anywhere a developer pleases. Those who find zoning laws unjustifiable limitations on the use of property would be cheered; but it is unlikely that the Fair Housing Act was designed to abolish single-

family zoning for all developers who comply with the requirement that first-floor apartments be accessible to handicapped tenants.

4. The Fair Housing Act and the concomitant development of the discriminatory effect doctrine, and the Fourteenth Amendment suit alleging discriminatory intent, are not the only legal remedies available to rectify alleged acts of local officials that result in housing discrimination. A conspiracy theory under 42 U.S.C.A. § 1985(3) was recognized by a federal court in Fralin & Waldron, Inc. v. County of Henrico, Virginia, 474 F.Supp. 1315 (E.D.Va.1979). In that case the developers optioned a tract of land that was zoned to permit medium density residential development. After making extensive preparations to build a low-to moderate-income housing project, the county officials downzoned the land to exclude the type of project that was planned. The plaintiffs asked for injunctive and monetary relief and the court, in denying defendants' motion to dismiss, found sufficient allegations of conspiracy to deny constitutional rights. The court also discussed the extent of immunity which some of the individual defendants might claim under the civil rights statutes.

5. Virtually all the cases litigating the issue of housing discrimination under the Fair Housing Act involve municipal defendants and challenges to land use policies on the ground of their discriminatory intent or discriminatory effect. Does the Fair Housing Act apply to a private landlord who takes some action regarding his property that has the effect of reducing the available housing stock for minority persons within the community? See the case of Dreher v. Rana Management, Inc., 493 F.Supp. 930 (E.D.N.Y.1980), where tenants sued the landlord under the Fair Housing Act to enjoin conversion of the building into housing for college students. The plaintiffs alleged that 90 percent of the occupants were black and that after conversion 90 percent of the occupants would be white, thus reducing the housing stock available to black persons in the community. The court granted defendants' motion for a summary judgment.

A case striking down a private landlord's policy excluding families with children (the policy was to limit occupancy of one-bedroom apartments in the complex to one person) is United States v. Badgett, 976 F.2d 1176 (8th Cir.1992).

6. An interesting case involved a suit against a homeowners group for interfering with the purchase of a home for use as a group home. In United States v. Wagner, 930 F.Supp. 1148 (N.D.Tex.1996), the federal government sued several homeowners in a subdivision who had filed a lawsuit in state court seeking to prevent a neighbor from selling a house for use as a group home for mentally retarded children. The trial court held that the neighbors violated the Fair Housing Act and awarded damages to the intervening homeowner who had tried to sell for a group home ($7,500 for emotional distress and $8,000 in punitive damages). Also, the attorney for the homeowner was awarded over $46,000 in attorney's fees and expenses for the intervention in the federal suit to establish the FHA violation (he had already been awarded more than $3,500 for defending in the state court lawsuit).

A Note on Gentrification

In many cities the process of gentrification—rehabilitation of buildings in certain neighborhoods which opens housing opportunities to upscale tenants but, at the same time, displaces minorities and lower income residents—has resulted in conflict and litigation. Especially where the gentrifiers obtain government subsidies either by way of HUD grants or rehabilitation tax credits, representatives of the lower income displacees have tried to enjoin the subsidies. The case law in this area is not consistent; often the issue of standing is involved. Also the extent of HUD authority may be in question. City government generally endorses gentrification because it upgrades neighborhoods and fattens the tax base. On the other hand, the potential displacees frequently have some political voice in local government, and some cities have ordinances regulating gentrification. Following are some authorities that address the problems:

1. Law review articles: McDougall, Gentrification: The Class Conflict over Urban Space Moves into the Courts, 10 Fordham Urb.L.J. 177 (1981); LeGates & Hartman, Gentrification–Caused Displacement, 14 The Urban Lawyer 31 (1982); Henig, Neighborhood Response to Gentrification: Conditions of Mobilization, 17 Urb.Affairs Q. 343 (1982); Bryant & McGee, Gentrification and the Law: Combatting Urban Displacement, 25 Wash. U.J.Urb. & Contemp.L. 43 (1983); Cohen, San Francisco's Neighborhood Commercial Special Use District Ordinance: An Innovative Approach to Commercial Gentrification: 13 Golden Gate U.L.Rev. 367 (1983); Marcuse, To Control Gentrification: Anti–Displacement Zoning and Planning for Stable Residential Districts, 13 N.Y.U.Rev. of Law & Social Change 931 (1984); Marcuse, Gentrification, Abandonment, and Displacement: Connections, Causes, and Policy Responses in New York City, 28 Wash.U.J.Urb. & Contemp.L. 195 (1985).

2. Cases that touch on the problem of gentrification: Angell v. Zinsser, 473 F.Supp. 488 (D.Conn.1979); Alschuler v. Department of Housing and Urban Development, 515 F.Supp. 1212 (N.D.Ill.1981), affirmed and remanded 686 F.2d 472 (7th Cir.1982); Business Ass'n of University City v. Landrieu, 660 F.2d 867 (3d Cir.1981); Wicker Park Historic District Preservation Fund v. Pierce, 565 F.Supp. 1066 (N.D.Ill.1982); Munoz–Mendoza v. Pierce, 711 F.2d 421 (1st Cir.1983); NAACP v. Harris, 567 F.Supp. 637 (D.Mass.1983); Sansom Committee v. Lynn, 735 F.2d 1552, 1553 (3d Cir. 1984), cert. denied 469 U.S. 1017, 105 S.Ct. 431, 83 L.Ed.2d 358 (1984); Latinos Unidos De Chelsea v. Secretary of Housing, 799 F.2d 774 (1st Cir.1986).

G. AGE DISCRIMINATION IN HOUSING

COLONY COVE ASSOCIATES v. BROWN

California Court of Appeal, 1990.
220 Cal.App.3d 195, 269 Cal.Rptr. 234.

BOREN, ASSOCIATE JUSTICE.

Respondent, owner of a mobile home park, enacted a park rule restricting residency to senior citizens, age 55 or older. Respondent then sought to evict appellants, tenants in the park, because appellants' children, minors born after the park's enactment of its age restriction, were not "grandfathered" as were their parents, who had resided in the park prior to the rule. Appellants appeal following summary judgments granted in unlawful detainer actions brought by respondent. We hold that the enforcement of the mobile home park's senior citizen, age 55 or older, resident restriction does not run afoul of constitutional proscriptions, relevant state statutes, or the Fair Housing Amendments Act of 1988.

* * *

I. Constitutional Concerns

In *Schmidt v. Superior Court* (1989) 48 Cal.3d 370, 256 Cal.Rptr. 750, 769 P.2d 932, the Supreme Court held that a mobile home park rule limiting residence to adults 25 years or older was not unconstitutional. The *Schmidt* court assumed arguendo the existence of state action such as to warrant applying constitutional concerns to private conduct (*id.* at pp. 388–389, fn. 14, 389, 256 Cal.Rptr. 750, 769 P.2d 932), and concluded that the mobile home park rule was not, as or when applied, either irrational or arbitrary and did not violate the constitutional rights to equal protection or familial privacy. (*Id.* at pp. 390–391, 256 Cal.Rptr. 750, 769 P.2d 932.)

In sustaining the constitutionality of the mobile home park rule, the court reasoned as follows: "[A]lthough the constitutional right of 'familial privacy' undoubtedly encompasses a parent's right to live with his or her child (see, e.g., *Moore [v. East Cleveland* (1977)] 431 U.S. 494, 500–506 [97 S.Ct. 1932, 1936–1939, 52 L.Ed.2d 531]), the mobile home park's 25–years–or–older policy at issue here does not, of course, purport to compel the separation of parent and child or to preclude the family from living together in an entire city (cf., e.g., *Moore, supra,* 431 U.S. 494 [97 S.Ct. 1932]; *Molino v. Mayer and Council of Bor. of Glassboro* (1971) 116 N.J.Super. 195 [281 A.2d 401]) or neighborhood (cf. [*City of Santa Barbara v.*] *Adamson* [1980] 27 Cal.3d 123 [164 Cal.Rptr. 539, 610 P.2d 436]), but simply denies the family access to a limited number of housing units. In *Bynes v. Toll* (2d Cir.1975) 512 F.2d 252, 254–256, the Second Circuit upheld a state university regulation excluding married students with children from university housing, explaining that the students' unquestioned constitutional right to procreate and to bring up their children did not mean that the university was 'constitutionally mandated to provide them campus housing to perform their protected prerogatives' (512 F.2d at p. 255), and, on similar grounds, courts of other states which have considered the validity of age-based housing regulations comparable to the rule at issue here—in the absence of a legislative measure barring such age restrictions—uniformly upheld the general constitutional validity of such rules. [Citations.] Particularly in light of the distinct characteristics of mobile home parks—e.g., the generally greater percentage of older residents, the smaller size of the units, the more substantial potential lack of privacy and the greater expense that might have to be incurred in rendering such a park safe for children residents—we agree with the conclusion of the above cited cases that such an age-based regulation is neither irrational nor arbitrary or otherwise vulnerable to constitutional attack." (*Schmidt v. Superior Court, supra,* 48 Cal.3d at pp. 389–390, 256 Cal.Rptr. 750, 769 P.2d 932, fns. omitted.)

The reasoning in *Schmidt* is particularly compelling here in the context of not merely an adult-only but a senior citizen age restriction rule. In view of the recognized desirability of special living environments and services providing communal educational and recreational facilities which meet the physical and social needs of senior citizens (see Civ.Code, §§ 51.2, subd. (a) and 51.3, subd. (a); cf. *Huntington Landmark Adult Community Assn. v. Ross* (1989) 213 Cal.App.3d 1012, 1018–1019, 261 Cal.Rptr. 875), respondent's age-based discrimination is "neither irrational nor arbitrary or otherwise vulnerable to constitutional attack." (*Schmidt v. Superior Court, supra,* 48 Cal.3d at p. 390, 256 Cal.Rptr. 750, 769 P.2d 932.)

II. STATE STATUTORY PROVISIONS

Relevant California statutes do not preclude the establishment and enforcement of a senior citizen age qualification rule in a private mobile home park. In analyzing relevant state statutes, *Schmidt v. Superior Court, supra,* 48 Cal.3d 370, 256 Cal.Rptr. 750, 769 P.2d 932 held that a private mobile home park rule which limited residence in the park to persons 25 years or older, as permitted by Civil Code section 798.76,[7] did not violate the broad antidiscrimination policy embodied in the Unruh Civil Rights Act (Civ.Code, § 51 et seq.), even though the park rule operated to exclude families with children younger than 25 years of age. Most significantly, the amendments to the Unruh Act which address age-based discrimination in housing, Civil Code sections 51.2 and 51.3,[8] reflect a legislative intent specifically to exclude mobile home parks from the reach of the act. * * *

---

7. Civil Code section 798.76 provides as follows:

"The management may require that a purchaser of a mobile home which will remain in the park, comply with any rule or regulation limiting residence to adults only."

8. Civil Code section 51.2 provides, in pertinent part, as follows: "(a) Section 51 shall be construed to prohibit a business establishment from discriminating in the sale or rental of housing based upon age. Where accommodations are designed to meet the physical and social needs of senior citizens, a business establishment may establish and preserve such housing for senior citizens, pursuant to Section 51.3 of the Civil Code."

Civil Code section 51.3 provides, in pertinent part, as follows: "(a) The Legislature finds and declares that this section is essential to establish and preserve specially designed accessible housing for senior citizens. There are senior citizens who need special living environments and services, and find that there is an inadequate supply of this type of housing in the state. [¶](b) The Legislature finds and declares that different age limitations for senior citizens housing are appropriate in recognition of the size of a development in relationship to the community in which it is located. [¶](c) For the purposes of this section, the following definitions apply: * * * [¶](4) 'Dwelling unit' or 'housing' means any residential accommodation other than a mobile home."

The amendments to the Unruh Act were enacted in response to a prior judicial expression of the appropriateness of age-based discrimination favoring senior citizens. In *Marina Point, Ltd. v. Wolfson* (1982) 30 Cal.3d 721, 180 Cal.Rptr. 496, 640 P.2d 115, where the court held the general provisions of the Unruh Act prohibited an ordinary apartment complex from adopting a rule which excluded all families with children from the complex, the court emphasized that the age-based exclusionary policy which it proscribed was distinguishable from "the age-limited admission policies of retirement communities or housing complexes reserved for older citizens." (*Id.* at p. 742, 180 Cal.Rptr. 496, 640 P.2d 115.) As the court observed, "In light of the public policy reflected by [legislation allowing for adults-only housing in mobile home parks (Civ. Code, § 798.76)], age qualifications as to a housing facility reserved for older citizens can operate as a reasonable and permissible means under the Unruh Act of establishing and preserving specialized facilities for those particularly in need of such services or environment. [Citations.] Such a specialized institution designed to meet a social need differs fundamentally from the wholesale exclusion of children from an apartment complex otherwise open to the general public." (*Id.* at pp. 742–743, 180 Cal.Rptr. 496, 640 P.2d 115, fns. omitted.)

With the declared intent "to clarify the holdings in *Marina Point, Ltd. v. Wolfson [, supra]*" (Civ.Code, § 51.2, subd. (b)), and another related decision, the Legislature enacted Civil Code sections 51.2 and 51.3. (See *Schmidt v. Superior Court, supra,* 48 Cal.3d at pp. 383–384, 256 Cal.Rptr. 750, 769 P.2d 932.) * * *

III. The Fair Housing Amendments Act of 1988

The contention that the Fair Housing Amendments Act of 1988 (Pub.L. No. 100–430 (Sept. 13, 1988) 102 Stat. 1619, 1988 U.S.Code Cong. & Admin.News, No. 8), effective March 1989, invalidates respondent's adults-only policy and proscribes eviction proceedings on familial status grounds is unavailing. In applying federal legislation to the present situation (see *Gulf Offshore Co. v. Mobil Oil Corp.* (1981) 453 U.S. 473, 477–478, 101 S.Ct. 2870, 2874–2875, 69 L.Ed.2d 784), it is apparent that the Fair Housing Amendments Act makes it generally unlawful to discriminate in the sale or rental of housing or to make a "dwelling" otherwise unavailable on the basis of "familial status," as well as on the previously forbidden grounds of race, color, religion, sex or national origin. (42 U.S.C.A. § 3604.) The definition of the term "dwelling" in the Fair Housing Act includes mobile home sites. (See, e.g., *United States v. Warwick Mobile Home Estates, Inc.*(4th Cir.1976) 537 F.2d 1148; *United States v. Grooms* (M.D.Fla.1972) 348 F.Supp. 1130, 1133.) The term "familial status" is defined as families which include children under the age of 18. (42 U.S.C.A. § 3602(k).)

While the amendment to the Fair Housing Act thus generally bars discrimination in mobile home housing against families with children under 18, it also, however, creates an exception for "housing for older persons" in which discrimination on the basis of familial status is not prohibited. (42 U.S.C.A. § 3607(b)(1).) "Housing for older persons" is legislatively defined to include, in part, housing which is (1) "intended for, solely occupied by, persons 62 years of age or older," or (2) "intended and operated for occupancy by at least one person 55 years of age or older per unit." (42 U.S.C.A. § 3607(b)(2)(B) and (b)(2)(C).)

In determining whether "housing for older persons" qualifies within the meaning of the latter category involving "occupancy by at least one person 55 years of age or older per unit," the amendment to the Fair Housing Act requires that "the Secretary [of Housing and Urban Development (HUD)] shall develop regulations which include at least the following requirements: (i) the existence of significant facilities and services specifically designed to meet the physical or social needs of older persons, or if the provision of such facilities and services is not practicable, that such housing is necessary to provide important housing opportunities for older persons; and (ii) that at least 80 percent of the units are occupied by at least one person 55 years of age or older per unit; and (iii) the publication of, and adherence to, policies and procedures which demonstrate an intent by the owner or manager to provide housing for persons 55 years of age or older." (42 U.S.C.A. § 3607(b)(2)(C)(i to iii).)

The amendment further contains a "grandfather clause" in section 3607(b)(3)(A). That section provides that housing will not be disqualified as "housing for older persons" merely because "persons residing in such housing as of September 13, 1988," do not meet the requirements under either the 62 or 55 years of age or older categories, so long as any new occupants meet the age requirements under either of those two categories, as specified in section 3607(b)(2)(B) or (b)(2)(C).

* * *

It is sufficient for our purpose in reviewing the grant of a motion for summary judgment that the mobile home park, as indicated by its age restriction regulation, was "intended and operated for occupancy by at least one person 55 years of age or older per unit." (42 U.S.C.A. § 3607(b)(2)(C).) Moreover, as a matter of law, to the extent that units in the park are occupied by persons not in that category, "The act also contains a 'grandfather clause,' providing that persons under the applicable age limits who were residing in housing when the federal act was enacted will not disqualify the housing from the statutory exemption for housing for older persons so long as the applicable age requirements are applied to all new occupants. (42 U.S.C.A. § 3607(b)(3).)" (*Schmidt v. Superior Court, supra,* 48 Cal.3d at p. 375, fn. 4, 256 Cal.Rptr. 750, 769 P.2d 932.) Accordingly, there were no triable issues of material fact, and summary judgment was appropriate. (See *AARTS Productions, Inc. v. Crocker National Bank* (1986) 179 Cal.App.3d 1061, 1064–1065, 225 Cal.Rptr. 203; Code Civ.Proc., § 437c, subd. (c).)

* * *

IV. CONCLUSION

We are aware of the plight of young couples with children who seek affordable housing. We also recognize the unique difficulties which arise when a mobile home owner is forced to vacate a mobile home park rental space. The Legislature has also acknowledged the critical importance of adequate housing for families. (See Health & Saf.Code, §§ 50001, 50003, 50003.3, 50004; Gov.Code, § 65913; *Marina Point, Ltd. v. Wolfson, supra,* 30 Cal.3d at p. 743, 180 Cal.Rptr. 496, 640 P.2d 115.) Discrimination against children in housing is at odds with fundamental notions of humanity. "A society that sanctions wholesale discrimination against its children in obtaining housing engages in a suspect activity. Even the most primitive society fosters the protection of its young; such a society would hardly discriminate against children in their need for shelter * * *." (*Marina Point, Ltd. v. Wolfson, supra,* 30 Cal.3d at p. 744, 180 Cal.Rptr. 496, 640 P.2d 115.)

Nonetheless, as discussed above, our legislative bodies have also addressed the competing interests and housing needs of older persons in our society. Consistent with our constitutional and legislative analysis, appellants' legitimate housing needs cannot be satisfied by the present attack upon legislation which provides for the establishment of senior citizen mobile home parks.

Disposition

The judgments are affirmed. Respondent's request for sanctions is denied.

LUCAS, P.J., and ASHBY, J., concur.

Notes

1. Another case that gives a full discussion of the reasons for allowing mobile home parks dedicated to the elderly is Taxpayers Ass'n of Weymouth Twp., Inc. v. Weymouth Twp., 80 N.J. 6, 364 A.2d 1016 (1976), appeal dismissed 430 U.S. 977, 97 S.Ct. 1672, 52 L.Ed.2d 373 (1977). Also see Seifred v. Zabel, 369 N.W.2d 571 (Minn.App.1985); Metro. Dade County Fair Housing and Employment Appeals Bd. v. Sunrise Village Mobile Home Park, Inc., 485 So.2d 865 (Fla.App. 3 Dist.1986).

2. A leading case contrary to the position of allowing zoning for the elderly is Hinman v. Planning and Zoning Comm'n, 26 Conn.Sup. 125, 214 A.2d 131 (1965). The court ruled that a rural town of less than 5,000 population did not have authority under the enabling act to create a new zoning classification (Senior Citizen Planned Community District) for development on tracts of 400 or more acres. In New York, the courts have allowed such zoning. See Maldini v. Ambro, 36 N.Y.2d 481, 369 N.Y.S.2d 385, 330 N.E.2d 403 (1975), appeal dismissed 423 U.S. 993, 96 S.Ct. 419, 46 L.Ed.2d 367 (1975); Campbell v. Barraud, 58 A.D.2d 570, 394 N.Y.S.2d 909 (1977); Apfelbaum v. Town of Clarkstown, 104 Misc.2d 371, 428 N.Y.S.2d 387 (1980); but see the unusual case of Central Management Co. v. Town Bd. of Oyster Bay, 47 Misc.2d 385, 262 N.Y.S.2d 728 (1965), where the town board rejected a proposed high rise apartment building for the elderly because it

was to be built in an area remote from medical and shopping facilities on a plot of land which was virtually an island between two expressways, and the court held that the board could not take into account the age of the proposed residents and the rejection was thus arbitrary.

3. Prior to the decision in the principal case, the California legislature passed a resolution (S.J.R. 1, 1989) requesting that the President and the Congress amend the Fair Housing Act Amendments of 1988 to clarify the rules concerning mobile home parks for the elderly. The resolution states that most California mobile home parks have adults-only restrictions and that the HUD regulations are ambiguous as to what is required for a mobile home park to operate with age restrictions without violating the act. The resolution also notes that the cost of senior citizen housing in mobile home parks might be increased by the cost of installation of facilities to meet the physical or social needs of the residents as stated in the act. Federal courts have been reluctant to find exceptions for elder residences that lack special facilities. In Lanier v. Fairfield Communities, Inc., 776 F.Supp. 1533 (M.D.Fl.1990) the court held that the exception was not available where the residential community was two miles from the nearest shopping and medical facilities, provided no transportation, no emergency call buttons, and no congregate dining or health facilities. Also see Park Place Home Brokers v. P–K Mobile Home Park, 773 F.Supp. 46 (N.D.Ohio 1991) (off-site facilities and services could not be considered in determining whether the mobile home park could claim the exemption); Hooker v. Weathers, 990 F.2d 913 (6th Cir.1993) (burden of proof is on the owner of the residences to establish the older persons exemption). In 1995 Congress amended the act to strike out the section requiring significant facilities to serve the elderly as a condition for exemption, P.L. 104–76, § 2.

4. Perhaps the most controversial part of the Fair Housing Act Amendments of 1988 is the rule against discrimination in the rental of apartment housing on the basis of familial status (i.e., children under 18). The Congressional intent is clearly to prohibit adults-only apartment buildings, a widespread practice across the nation. This provision became effective in March, 1989. See, e.g., United States v. Badgett, 976 F.2d 1176 (8th Cir.1992); United States v. Tropic Seas, Inc., 887 F.Supp. 1347 (D.Haw.1995). Also, federal courts have seen a number of cases brought under the provision in the Fair Housing Act Amendments prohibiting discrimination in housing on the basis of handicap. See, e.g., Larkin v. State of Michigan Dept. of Social Services, 89 F.3d 285 (6th Cir.1996). Also see James Brooke, Young Unwelcome in Retirees' Haven, N.Y. Times, Feb. 16, 1997, p. 10.

5. In Betsey v. Turtle Creek Associates, 736 F.2d 983 (4th Cir.1984), the court found a violation of the Fair Housing Act where an adults-only rental policy had a disparate racial impact on minority tenants.

6. See Helen L. Edmonds and Dwight H. Merriam, Zoning and the Elderly: Issues for the 21st Century, Land Use Law (Mar. 1995), p. 3.

H. INDIRECT HOUSING DISCRIMINATION

The local zoning ordinance will usually prescribe a minimum lot size for industrial, commercial or residential use. In this section we look at cases involving such restrictions for residential use. In prescribing such minimal requirements the local legislative body may have in mind the need for a sufficiently fat real estate levy to pay pro rata costs of schools and municipal services; aesthetics, in the sense of an attractive estate type of neighborhood for pleasant living with substantial green space; protection of agricultural land from premature subdivision into small lots; development of a "snob appeal" neighborhood for the "right" people, or otherwise expressed, "preservation of the character of the neighborhood;" public health, especially where absence of public sewer and heavy soil requires a substantial area for effective private sewage disposal; protection from the spread of fire; traffic control and off-street parking; or, making certain that low cost housing does not penetrate the community. The zoning ordinance may also prescribe minimum house sizes.

Unlike most of the cases alleging that a zoning ordinance is exclusionary because no provision is made for a particular use, the cases below raise the housing discrimination problem because the particular requirement allegedly raises the cost of housing or renders economically infeasible housing types which might be within the means of low and moderate income families. Should the courts, or do the courts, apply different legal standards to this type of exclusion?

NATIONAL LAND AND INVESTMENT CO. v. KOHN

Supreme Court of Pennsylvania, 1965.
419 Pa. 504, 215 A.2d 597.

["Sweetbriar," an 85 acre residential development tract, was worth $260,000 when the lot minimum was one acre. Now that the minimum for the residential area of which "Sweetbriar" is a part has been changed to four acres, the most optimistic estimate is $175,000. The zoning amendment was held unconstitutional by the trial court. The Supreme Court first disposed of a variety of procedural questions to get to the substance of the constitutional issue. Part of the court's analysis of that issue is set out below. Two judges dissented.]

ROBERTS, JUSTICE. * * *

Easttown Township has an area of 8.2 square miles devoted almost exclusively to residential use * * * The township finds itself in the path of a population expansion approaching from two directions. From the east, suburbs closer to the center of Philadelphia are reaching capacity and residential development is extending further west to Easttown. In addition, a market for residential sites is being generated by the fast growing industrial-commercial complex in the King of Prussia–Valley Forge area to the north of Easttown Township.

Easttown's vital statistics provide a good indication of its character. At present, about 60% of the township's population resides in an area of about 20% of the township. The remaining 40% of the population occupies the balance of about 80% of its area. Privately imposed restrictions limit lot areas to four, five and ten acre minimums on approximately 10% of the total area of the township, consisting of land located in the southern and western sections. Of the total 5,157 acres in the township, some 898, or about 17%, have been restricted by the new zoning ordinance to minimum lots of two acres. Approximately 1,565 acres composing about 30% of the township are restricted by the zoning ordinance to lots of four acres minimum area. About 5% of the population live in the areas zoned for two and four acre sites which together constitute about 47% of the township. Some 1,835 acres, representing about 35% of the township, remain unaffected by the new zoning and continue, under the township's original zoning classification, to be zoned for building sites with a minimum area of one acre.

* * *

U.S. Census figures show that Easttown's population grew from 2,307 in 1920 to 6,907 in 1960. As of April, 1963, the population estimate was 8,400. Public school population through the sixth grade grew from 498 in the school year 1955–56 to 1,052 in the school year 1963–64 and, as projected, will be about 1,680 in 1969–70.

New residential construction from 1951 through the first eight months of 1963, a twelve year period, consisted of 1,149 units at an estimated cost of about $21,000,000, with an average of 100 building permits annually. At this rate of growth, allowing four persons per housing unit in Easttown, its population, related to new residences, would grow under the previous one acre minimum zoning at the rate of about 400 persons per annum.

* * *

The task of considering the Easttown Township zoning ordinance and passing upon the constitutionality of its four acre minimum area requirement as applied to appellees' property is not an easy one. In the span of years since 1926 when zoning received its judicial blessing, the art and science of land planning has grown increasingly complex and sophisticated. The days are fast disappearing when the judiciary can look at a zoning ordinance and, with nearly as much confidence as a professional zoning expert, decide upon the merits of a zoning plan and its contribution to the health, safety, morals or general welfare of the community. This Court has become increasingly aware that it is neither a super board of adjustment nor a planning commission of last resort * * * The zoning power is one of the tools of government which, in order to be effective, must not be subjected to judicial interference unless clearly necessary. For this reason, a presumption of validity attaches to a zoning ordinance which imposes the burden to prove its invalidity upon the one who challenges it. * * *

While recognizing this presumption, we must also appreciate the fact that zoning involves governmental restrictions upon a landowner's constitutionally guaranteed right to use his property, unfettered, except in very specific instances, by governmental restrictions. The time must never come when, because of frustration with concepts foreign to their legal training, courts abdicate their judicial responsibility to protect the constitutional rights of individual citizens. Thus, the burden of proof imposed upon one who challenges the validity of a zoning regulation must never be made so onerous as to foreclose, for all practical purposes, a landowner's avenue of redress against the infringement of constitutionally protected rights.

The oft repeated, although ill defined, limitation upon the exercise of the zoning power requires that zoning ordinances be enacted for the health, safety, morals or general welfare of the community. * * *

We turn, then, to the question of the constitutionality of four acre minimum in the factual context of the instant case. Quite obviously, appellees will be deprived of part of the value of their property if they are limited in the use of it to four acre lots. When divided into one acre lots as originally planned, the value of "Sweetbriar" for residential building was approximately $260,000. When the four acre restriction was imposed, the number of available building sites in "Sweetbriar" was reduced by 75% and the value of the land, under the most optimistic appraisal, fell to $175,000. The four acre minimum greatly restricts the marketability of this tract because, with fewer potential lots, the cost of improvements such as curbing, streets and other facilities is thus greater on each lot. In addition, each building lot being larger, the cost per lot is automatically increased. The desire of many buyers not to be burdened with the upkeep of a four acre lot also makes "Sweetbriar," so restricted, less desirable. Although there was some evidence in the record that lots of four acres or more could eventually be sold it is clear that there is not a readily available market for such offerings.

Against this deprivation of value, the alleged public purposes cited as justification for the imposition of a four acre minimum area requirement upon appellees' land must be examined. Appellants contend that the four acre minimum is necessary to insure proper sewage disposal in the township and to protect township water from pollution. * * *

We can not help but note also that the Second Class Township Code provides for establishing sanitary regulations which can be enforced by a "sanitary board" regardless of the zoning for the area. The Code also provides for the installation and maintenance of sewer systems but the township has made no plans in this regard. In addition, under the township subdivision regulations, the zoning officer may require lots larger than the minimum permitted by the zoning ordinance if the result of percolation tests upon the land show that a larger land area is needed for proper drainage and disposal of sewage. These legislatively sanctioned methods for dealing with the sewage problem compel the conclusion that a four acre minimum is neither a necessary nor a reasonable method by which Easttown can protect itself from the menace of pollution.

In addition to the alleged problem of sewage disposal as justifying the four acre minimum, appellants cite the inadequacy of township roads and the burden which continued one acre zoning for the entire township would impose upon that road system.

* * *

According to the experts produced for both sides, Easttown's present road network as a whole is capable, with normal maintenance and improvement, of serving a population up to 13,000. This is 4,600 more than the population of the township in April, 1963. On the basis of the former one acre zoning, resulting in a population increase of 400 persons per year, that figure would not be reached until after 1972 or later.

It can be seen, therefore, that the restriction to four acre lots, so far as traffic is concerned, is based upon possible future conditions. Zoning is a tool in the hands of governmental bodies which enables them to more effectively meet the demands of evolving and growing communities. It must not and can not be used by those officials as an instrument by which they may shirk their responsibilities. Zoning is a means by which a governmental body can plan for the future—it may not be used as a means to deny the future. * * *

It is not difficult to envision the tremendous hardship, as well as the chaotic conditions, which would result if all the townships in this area decided to deny to a growing population sites for residential development within the means of at least a significant segment of the people.

The third justification for rezoning, and one urged upon us most assiduously, deals with the preservation of the "character" of this area. The photographic exhibits placed in the record by appellants attest to the fact that this is an area of great beauty containing old homes surrounded by beautiful pasture, farm and wood land. It is a very desirable and attractive place in which to live.

Involved in preserving Easttown's "character" are four aspects of concern which the township gives for desiring four acre minimum zoning. First, they cite the preservation of open space and the creation of a "greenbelt" which, as most present day commentators impress upon us, are worthy goals. While in full agreement with these goals, we are convinced that four acre minimum zoning does not achieve the creation of a greenbelt in its technical sense and, to the limited extent that open space is so preserved, such zoning as is here involved is not a permissible means to that end.

* * *

If the preservation of open spaces is the township objective, there are means by which this can be accomplished which include authorization for "cluster zoning" or condemnation of development rights with compensation paid for that which is taken. A four acre minimum acreage requirement is not a reasonable method by which the stated end can be achieved.

Next, the township urges us to consider the historic sites in the township and the need to present them in the proper setting. We are unmoved by this contention since it appears to be purely and simply a makeweight. First, an examination of the map of historical sites in the township demonstrates that the overwhelming majority of such sites, located in areas of dense population, can hardly be provided with proper settings by four acre zoning elsewhere in the township. * * *

Closely related to the goal of protecting historic monuments is the expressed desire to protect the "setting" for a number of old homes in Easttown, some dating back to the early days of our Commonwealth. Appellants denominate this goal as falling within the ambit of promoting the "general welfare". Unfortunately, the concept of the general welfare defies meaningful capsule definition and constitutes an exceedingly difficult standard against which to test the validity of legislation. However, it must always be ascertained at the outset whether, in fact, it is the public welfare which is being benefited or whether, disguised as legislation for the public welfare, a zoning ordinance actually served purely private interests.

There is no doubt that many of the residents of this area are highly desirous of keeping it the way it is, preferring, quite naturally, to look out upon land in its natural state rather than on other homes. These desires, however, do not rise to the level of public welfare. This is purely a matter of private desire which zoning regulations may not be employed to effectuate.

* * *

The fourth argument advanced by appellants, and one closely analogous to the preceding one, is that the rural character of the area must be preserved. If the township were developed on the basis of this zoning, however, it could not be seriously contended that the land would retain its rural character—it would simply be dotted with larger homes on larger lots.

Appellants point to the fact that the surrounding townships have similar low density zoning provisions. Although the zoning of the surrounding area is frequently a relevant consideration in assessing the validity of a zoning regulation * * * it is not controlling on the issue presented. This is particularly so when we are dealing with a unique zoning classification such as is involved here. With most zoning classifications, there can be little question as to their suitability in any political subdivision; the only issue concerns their placement. With these classifications, the surrounding zoning is particularly relevant. As the classification itself becomes more questionable, however, similar classifications in surrounding districts become of less significance in supporting the validity of the restriction.

* * *

The township's brief raises (but, unfortunately, does not attempt to answer) the interesting issue of the township's responsibility to those who do not yet live in the township but who are part, or may become part, of the population expansion of the suburbs. Four acre zoning represents Easttown's position that it does not desire to accommodate those who are pressing for admittance to the township unless such admittance will not create any additional burdens upon governmental functions and services. The question posed is whether the township can stand in the way of the natural forces which send our growing population into hitherto undeveloped areas in search of a comfortable place to live. We have concluded not. A zoning ordinance whose primary purpose is to prevent the entrance of newcomers in order to avoid future burdens, economic and otherwise, upon the administration of public services and facilities can not be held valid. Of course, we do not mean to imply that a governmental body may not utilize its zoning power in order to insure that the municipal services which the community requires are provided in an orderly and rational manner.

The brief of the appellant-intervenors creates less of a problem but points up the factors which sometime lurk behind the espoused motives for zoning. What basically appears to bother intervenors is that a small number of lovely old homes will have to start keeping company with a growing number of smaller, less expensive, more densely located houses. It is clear, however, that the general welfare is not fostered or promoted by a zoning ordinance designed to be exclusive and exclusionary. * * *

In light of the foregoing, therefore, we are compelled to conclude that the board of adjustment committed an error of law in upholding the constitutionality of the Easttown Township four acre minimum requirement as applied to appellees' property. We therefore affirm the order of the Court of Common Pleas of Chester County.

Order affirmed.

Notes

1. The Wall Street Journal for August 15, 1966, reported that to avoid the expense of further litigation the town and the builder in the principal case finally compromised on two-acre lots.

2. Compare with the Kohn case, Bilbar Const. Co. v. Board of Adjustment, 393 Pa. 62, 141 A.2d 851 (1958), which notes that minimum lot areas cannot be so large as to be exclusionary and thereby serve private interests, but finds a one-acre requirement to be reasonable. This was in the same township.

3. See also, Board of County Supervisors v. Carper, 200 Va. 653, 107 S.E.2d 390 (1959), in which a two-acre minimum lot requirement was imposed on about two-thirds of a rapidly growing county. The Virginia court viewed the practical effect of the restriction as preventing low-income people from living in that part of the county and stated that this purpose bore no relation to a valid exercise of the police power. Apparently, it was intended to funnel the low-income population into the eastern one-third of the county "where the cost of operating government would be more economical."

4. The Pennsylvania court returned to the problem of large lot zoning in Appeal of Kit–Mar Builders, Inc., 439 Pa. 466, 268 A.2d 765 (1970). In this case the developer contracted to purchase 140 acres contingent on rezoning

to permit one-acre homesites, the existing zoning requiring two acre lots on roadways and three acre lots in the interior. The rezoning was denied on grounds of sewerage problems and the developer appealed. Justice Roberts again wrote the majority opinion, striking down the two and three acre restrictions, and reaffirming National Land: "We once again reaffirm our past authority and refuse to allow the township to do precisely what we have never permitted—keep out people, rather than make community improvements. * * * [C]ommunities must deal with the problems of population growth. They may not refuse to confront the future by adopting zoning regulations that effectively restrict population to near present levels." Justice Bell wrote a concurring opinion and two justices dissented. Justice Roberts keyed his opinion to a judicial stand against exclusionary zoning practices. Is a decision striking down two acre zoning to favor a developer who desires one acre sites a judicial blow against exclusionary zoning? Should not the real issue be whether the community is making provisions for low and moderate income housing? And further, if a community does provide in its zoning for a variety of housing types, then why does it matter that some zones are set aside for one, two, or five acre lots?

5. Consider also the case of County Comm'rs of Queen Anne's County v. Miles, 246 Md. 355, 228 A.2d 450 (1967), in which the Maryland Court of Appeals upheld a county zoning ordinance providing for five residential zones, one of which covered a substantial land area and imposed a five-acre minimum lot size. The ordinance was attacked on the basis that "the properties were so zoned in order that they could be disposed of only to 'substantial' people, of 'more than ample' financial resources." The court noted that "there were many criteria considered in the decision" including the fact that many historical sites were located in the area. Other testimony, which the court cited, was to the effect that it was desirable to attract persons "of means" to the community; that tourists could be attracted in this manner; that it was a reasonable use of zoning for a rural county to employ in an otherwise urbanized area to preserve the desired character of the county; and that it would contribute to the health and safety of the county by minimizing the sanitation problems, reducing the traffic and channeling the denser population growth into locations nearer the centers of public service, the established towns, etc. The court stated:

> We agree that if the primary purpose or effect of the ordinance is to benefit private interests, rather than the public welfare, the legislation cannot be held valid merely because some of its incidental effects may be for the general good. On the other hand, if the ordinance has a substantial relationship to the general welfare of the community in that it can fairly be taken as a reasonable effort to plan for the future within the framework of the County's economic and social life, it is not unconstitutional because under it some persons may suffer loss and others be benefited. Courts of other states have had occasion to balance these factors; the decisions, as we read them, turn on the various economic, physical and sociological factors involved in the particular case.

After reviewing a number of these cases, the Maryland court concluded that the ordinance was fair and reasonable and not arbitrary or capricious. The court further concluded that the ordinance did not treat like properties in ways that were unjustifiably dissimilar.

In County of Ada v. Henry, 105 Idaho 263, 668 P.2d 994 (1983) the court upheld a county ordinance requiring an 80–acre minimum lot size. A dissenting judge said: "It is a strange West which we now have where a man of industrious nature is by a bureaucratic ordinance deprived of the right to build his own house on a ten-acre tract. And for what reason? Because it has been thought better that the law should be that a single dwelling be not erected on less than 80 acres! The proposition is basically so monstrous as to be undeserving of further comment."

6. Coke and Liebman, Political Values and Population Density Control, 37 Land Econ. 347 (1961) conclude:

Large minimum lot size requirements have become an important focus of the suburban political process because they are thought to be instrumental in achieving three values: amenity, tax base, and neighborhood homogeneity. Realization of the tax base and homogeneity values depend in large part upon the correctness of the assumption that larger lots result in higher priced homes. The results of this study cast considerable doubt upon the wisdom of making the assumption. The correlation between lot size and selling price is so low that a municipality cannot automatically assure itself of expensive residential areas simply by adopting large lot zoning policies.

YBARRA v. TOWN OF LOS ALTOS HILLS

United States Court of Appeals, Ninth Circuit, 1974.
503 F.2d 250.

Before KILKENNY and WALLACE, CIRCUIT JUDGES, and SOLOMON, DISTRICT JUDGE.

OPINION

SOLOMON, DISTRICT JUDGE.

Appellants challenge the constitutionality of a large-lot zoning ordinance of the City of the Town of Los Altos Hills ["Los Altos" or "the town"], a California suburban community. The trial court held that the zoning ordinance was constitutional and dismissed the action. We affirm.

Appellants are two Mexican–Americans and the Confederacion de la Raza Unida, an unincorporated association of Mexican–American organizations. Neither of the named individual appellants are residents of Los Altos, but both qualify for federally assisted low-income housing. They brought this action on their own behalf and on behalf of all other persons of Mexican descent whose incomes qualify them for federally assisted housing.

In December, 1970, appellants obtained an option to buy certain lots in Los Altos. They paid a nominal amount for the option but agreed to pay $14,000 per acre if the option were exercised. The option could only be exercised if the land were rezoned for multifamily dwellings and if the

Federal Housing Administration approved a low-income housing project for that land.

The zoning ordinance provides that a housing lot shall contain not less than one acre and that no lot shall be occupied by more than one primary dwelling unit. Appellants have not applied for a zoning variance to allow construction of their proposed multifamily project.

Appellants brought this action against the town, its city manager, and the members of the town council. Appellants allege that the zoning ordinance prevents them from constructing a housing project and assert that the ordinance violates the supremacy, due process, and equal protection clauses of the United States Constitution. They seek declaratory and injunctive relief.

* * *

Appellants' principal contention is that the Los Altos zoning ordinance denies them equal protection of the laws. They assert that the ordinance discriminates against Mexican–Americans and the poor and that the town must show a compelling state interest to justify discrimination against "suspect classifications" based on ethnic background and wealth.

Appellants' evidence at trial showed that in Santa Clara County, in which Los Altos is located, there is a high statistical correlation between being Mexican–American and being poor. Mexican–Americans form only 2.1% of the town's population but comprise 17.59% of the county's population.

The trial court found that the ordinance prevented poor people from living in Los Altos. He also found that if Mexican–Americans did not live there, it was because of the poverty and not because of their race. Appellants concede that the ordinance does not bar wealthy Mexican–Americans from living in Los Altos. We agree that discrimination against the poor does not become discrimination against an ethnic minority merely because there is a statistical correlation between poverty and ethnic background.

Appellants also assert that they need not show racial discrimination to void the ordinance and that it is sufficient to show that the ordinance discriminates against the poor. They argue that the town must show a compelling interest to justify the ordinance because wealth is a suspect classification. *See *Harper v. Virginia Board of Elections*, 383 U.S. 663, 86 S.Ct. 1079, 16 L.Ed.2d 169 (1966); *Griffin v. Illinois*, 351 U.S. 12, 76 S.Ct. 585, 100 L.Ed. 891 (1956).

In *San Antonio School District v. Rodriguez*, 411 U.S. 1, 93 S.Ct. 1278, 36 L.Ed.2d 16 (1973), the court discussed the conditions under which poverty becomes a suspect classification under the equal protection clause:

> "The individuals, or groups of individuals, who constituted the class discriminated against in our prior cases shared two distinguishing

characteristics: because of their impecunity they were completely unable to pay for some desired benefit, and as a consequence, they sustained an absolute deprivation of a meaningful opportunity to enjoy that benefit. 411 U.S. at 20, 93 S.Ct. at 1290."

In our view these two criteria set forth the threshold requirements before a court using traditional tests may consider whether the classification is constitutionally impermissible.

Appellants meet the first criterion because the ordinance prevents them from living in Los Altos because of their poverty. They failed to meet the second criterion because they did not show that they had no "meaningful opportunity" to obtain low-cost housing. The evidence showed that no poor people live or work in Los Altos. Appellants failed to show that adequate low-cost housing was unavailable elsewhere in Santa Clara County in areas accessible to appellants' jobs and social services. In these circumstances the town need not show a compelling interest to justify a zoning ordinance which discriminates against the poor.

Since there is no suspect classification requiring a strict standard of review, the town need only show that the ordinance bears a rational relationship to a legitimate governmental interest. Id. at 40, 93 S.Ct. 1278. Here the ordinance is rationally related to preserving the town's rural environment. See *Village of Belle Terre v. Boraas*, 416 U.S. 1, 94 S.Ct. 1536, 39 L.Ed.2d 797 (1974). The ordinance does not violate the equal protection clause.

Appellants allege that the ordinance violates Section 65302 of the California Government Code, which requires towns to adopt housing plans which "make adequate provision for the housing needs of all economic segments of the community." We believe that the section requires a town to provide housing for its residents but does not require it to provide housing for non-residents, even though the non-residents may live in the broader urban community of which the town is a part.

Appellants' other contentions are without merit. The ordinance does not conflict with the National Housing Act, 42 U.S.C.A. §§ 1401 et seq., and does not violate the supremacy clause. *James v. Valtierra*, 402 U.S. 137, 140, 91 S.Ct. 1331, 28 L.Ed.2d 678 (1971). The ordinance is not arbitrary and does not deny appellants due process. See *Village of Euclid v. Ambler Realty Co.*, 272 U.S. 365, 47 S.Ct. 114, 71 L.Ed. 303 (1926).

The judgment of the district court dismissing the action is affirmed.

Note

Is the legal principle to be gleaned from the preceding case that large lot zoning is definitely exclusionary in regard to low income groups, but such exclusion is constitutionally legitimate as long as housing opportunities for lower income groups are provided elsewhere in the region? If you think otherwise, then what is the principle? An intermediate appellate court in New York, in Robert E. Kurzius, Inc. v. Incorporated Village of Upper Brookville, 67 A.D.2d 70, 414 N.Y.S.2d 573 (1979), reversed 51 N.Y.2d 338, 434 N.Y.S.2d 180, 414 N.E.2d 680 (1980), struck down a five acre minimum on the ground that the housing needs of low and moderate income persons were not being met within the village. The Court of Appeals rejected that reasoning, stating: "There was no proof that persons of low or moderate incomes were foreclosed from housing in the *general region* because of an unavailability of properly zoned land." (Emphasis supplied.)

HOME BUILDERS LEAGUE OF SOUTH JERSEY, INC. v. TOWNSHIP OF BERLIN

Supreme Court of New Jersey, 1979.
81 N.J. 127, 405 A.2d 381.

SCHREIBER, J.

At issue in this case is the validity of provisions in a municipal zoning ordinance which impose minimum floor area requirements for residential dwellings irrespective of the number of occupants living in the home and unrelated to any other factor, such as frontage or lot size. The challenge was initiated when the Home Builders League of South Jersey, Inc. (League) and three builders, Award Homes, Inc., Lincoln Property Co., N.E., Inc., and Chiusano Bros., Inc., filed a complaint in lieu of prerogative writ in the Superior Court seeking invalidation of the floor area minima in the zoning ordinances of four municipalities in Camden County—Voorhees Township, Berlin Township, and the Boroughs of Pine Hill and Stratford. The New Jersey Public Advocate, the Senior Citizens Advocate Center, the Gray Panthers of South Jersey, and the South Jersey Tenants Organization were permitted to intervene as plaintiffs. At the conclusion of an extended trial the trial court found defendants' "nonoccupancy based" floor area minima to be unrelated to the public health, safety or welfare and hence an arbitrary, capricious and unreasonable exercise of the municipal zoning power. Defendants were given 90 days to amend their ordinances to provide for occupancy-related floor area standards. 157 N.J.Super. 586, 385 A.2d 295 (Law Div.1978).

* * *

In support of its contention that the municipality has the authority to enact a provision setting forth floor space minima for residences, Voorhees relies upon two provisions in the Municipal Land Use Law. N.J.S.A. 40:55D–65(b) provides that a zoning ordinance may regulate the "size of buildings," "the percentage of lot" that may be occupied, and for these purposes "may specify floor area ratios and other ratios and regulatory techniques governing the intensity of land use and the provision of adequate light and air." Second, N.J.S.A. 40:55D–62(a) states that "[t]he zoning ordinance shall be drawn with reasonable consideration to the character of each district and its peculiar suitability for particular uses and to encourage the most appropriate use of land."

Even though N.J.S.A. 40:55D–65(b) might be read literally to include the power to impose minimum floor space (regulation of the size of a building), the end result must not be contrary to the general welfare and in fact must further the public health, safety, morals or general welfare. Almost inevitably restrictions on the use of land will have both salutary and detrimental effects. A provision which has some beneficial effect will not automatically be deemed valid and consonant with the general welfare. Attention must also be directed toward the detrimental effects that a particular provision has. A provision which has some relationship to promotion of the general welfare or any subpart thereof, such as public health, safety, or any of the other purposes designated in the Municipal Land Use Law, N.J.S.A. 40:55D–2, would be upheld if it does not at the same time promote ends which are contrary to the general welfare. Where, however, a zoning provision, in addition to promoting legitimate zoning goals, also has effects contrary to the general welfare, closer scrutiny of the provision and its effects must be undertaken. The fact that a provision may have some adverse effect is not determinative. Rather, the court is required to decide whether a proper legislative goal is being achieved in a manner reasonably related to that goal.

Consider, for example, minimum lot size. Such a restriction may be closely related to the goals of public health and safety, as well as preserving the characteristics of a neighborhood. Thus, such a restriction may be valid despite the exclusionary impact resulting from increased housing costs due to minimum lot size. Compare *Fischer v. Tp. of Bedminster*, 11 N.J. 194, 93 A.2d 378 (1952) (upholding validity of five-acre minimum lot size) with *Schere v. Tp. of Freehold*, 119 N.J.Super. 433, 292 A.2d 35 (App.Div.), certif. den. 62 N.J. 69, 299 A.2d 67 (1972), cert. den. 410 U.S. 931, 93 S.Ct. 1374, 35 L.Ed.2d 593 (1973) (invalidating minimum lot restriction of slightly less than one acre). Where, however, these adverse consequences become too predominant, the zoning provision cannot stand, despite the fact that it bears some relationship to legitimate zoning purposes.

Minimum floor area requirements bear a direct relationship to the cost of a house. The larger the house, the more likely its cost will be greater. Living in a more spacious house will be more expensive due to higher taxes, mortgage payments, and expenses for heat, maintenance, and insurance. * * *

* * * If the Township's sole purpose in setting up the minima was to provide for more costly residences so as to exclude lower or moderate income persons, we would strike down this direct form of economic segregation. See, e.g., Lefcoe, "The Public Housing Referendum Case, Zoning, and the Supreme Court," 59 Calif.L.Rev. 1384, 1438–1439 (1971); Sager, "Tight Little Islands: Exclusionary Zoning, Equal Protection, and the Indigent," 21 Stan.L.Rev. 767, 781 (1969); Williams, "Planning Law and Democratic Living," 20 Law & Contemp.Prob. 317, 343 (1955); Haar, "Zoning for Minimum Standards: The Wayne Township Case," 66 Harv.L.Rev. 1051, 1055 (1953).

A limitation on a person's right to expend whatever amount he desires to construct a house—unrelated to appropriate purposes such as health, safety or welfare—would transgress constitutional due process standards. See *Brookdale Homes, Inc. v. Johnson*, 123 N.J.L. 602, 606, 10 A.2d 477 (Sup.Ct.1940), aff'd o.b. 126 N.J.L. 516, 19 A.2d 868 (E. & A. 1941). (The holding in *Brookdale Homes* that an ordinance imposing minimum restrictions on the size of dwellings to protect the character of a community and property values therein was invalid was overruled in *Lionshead Lake, Inc. v. Tp. of Wayne*, 10 N.J. 165, 172, 89 A.2d 693 (1952), app. dism. 344 U.S. 919, 73 S.Ct. 386, 97 L.Ed. 708 (1953).) The few cases which touch on the validity of zoning ordinances prescribing minimum dollar cost of houses have indicated them to be unreasonable. See *Stein v. City of Long Branch*, 2 N.J.Misc. 121 (Sup.Ct), app. dism. 100 N.J.L. 413, 126 A. 924 (E. & A. 1924); *County Comm'rs v. Ward*, 186 Md. 330, 46 A.2d 684 (1946); Appeal from Ordinance, Borough of Speers, 28 Wash.Co. 221 (Pa.Quar.Sess.1948).

We have acknowledged that zoning restrictions and limitations may have some economic effect in elevating the cost of a house, but nothing in the Municipal Land Use Law sanctions such economic segregation in and of itself as a proper zoning goal. We hold that when it is shown that a municipality has adopted as part of its zoning ordinance a minimum size living area provision which is on its face unrelated to any other factor, it will be presumed to have acted for improper purposes. The burden is then on the municipality to establish that a valid basis does exist. * * * We hasten to add that the establishment of such a basis does not terminate the judicial inquiry. At that point it must be determined whether the provision furthers or is contrary to the general welfare. It is then that the court must weigh and balance, as previously discussed, the exclusionary and salutary effects of the provision.

The bases which Voorhees has advanced are that the minima will (1) promote public health and safety and (2) maintain the nature of residential neighborhoods and conserve property values.

A. Public Health and Safety

We agree with the trial court's factual findings that minimum floor area requirements are not *per se* related to public health, safety or morals. The record contains substantial evidence in this respect. Dr. Eric Mood, Associate Clinical Professor of Public Health in the Department of Epidemiology and Public Health in the Yale School of Medicine, testified that the Voorhees floor space requirements were not related to and did not serve the public health, safety and welfare. In his opinion such criteria could be so related only if they were based on occupancy. The same opinion was expressed by John Rahenkamp, who has been engaged in land planning for years, and Alan Mallach, who heads a consulting firm which works principally in the area of housing.

* * *

The ratio of occupants to space obviously can affect public health, family stability and emotional well being. 2 N. Williams, American Planning Law § 63.01 at 626 (1974). This interrelationship is found in standards fixed by the American Public Health Association which set a minimum residency requirement of 150 square feet for one person and 100 square feet for each additional occupant. These criteria are currently recommended by the U.S. Department of Housing and Urban Development (HUD). HUD has always prescribed occupancy-based standards in relation to space.

We have previously adverted to the different area minima in Voorhees' various residential zones. Since the minima necessary for public health, safety and morals in the R.R., RD–2 and other zones are unquestionably the same, it follows that the Township was not considering health, safety and morals when it enacted these provisions. As the trial court aptly commented, "It is ridiculous to suggest that an 1,100 square foot house may be 'healthful' in one part of town and not another." 157 N.J.Super. at 601, 385 A.2d at 302.

Nor can minimum floor areas be utilized to prevent over-crowding. In the absence of some relationship between living areas and the number of occupants, unless there is a ratio between the space and inhabitants, obviously the problem is not being alleviated. This is not to say that there is not a minimum below which any residence may not go without the risk of impairing the health of an inhabitant. * * *

* * *

Whether the size of a house alone has relevance to the quality or property value of neighboring homes is a troublesome question. This is brought into sharp focus when the decision in *Lionshead Lake, Inc. v. Tp. of Wayne, supra*, is compared with the expert testimony in this case. The experts testified without exception that smaller houses do not because of their size cause a decrease in the value of adjacent dwellings or adversely affect the character of the neighborhood. They pointed out that aesthetic qualities are best maintained through the use, *inter alia,* of lot size, setbacks, side yards, lot coverage ratios, topographical and landscaping requirements.

Williams and Wacks have expressed a similar thought:

"Increasing the size of houses has nothing to do with improving the appearance of an area. Topography has a lot to do with it, and the presence of trees has even more. (Landscaping and maintenance obviously are also important.) Perhaps most important of all is lot size, and particularly lot size in relation to house size; in fact, the present appearance of both the central plain and Lionshead Lake strongly suggests that an increase in house size can actually detract from the appearance of an area, unless lot sizes are increased proportionately. [Williams & Wacks, "Segregation of Residential Areas Along Economic Lines: Lionshead Lake Revisited," 1969 Wis. L.Rev. 827, 846]"

Professor Haar has written:

Certainly beauty has no relation to size. The ordinance, moreover, contains no guarantee of design or site planning. In addition, if the initial cost of building to meet the minimum size requirement is high, a family budget may not permit the additions to exteriors, such as planting and painting, which may be aesthetically desirable. [Haar, supra, 66 Harv.L.Rev. at 1057–1058]

The majority opinion in *Lionshead Lake, Inc. v. Tp. of Wayne, supra*, although referring to the fact that there are minima in housing below which the health of the occupants might be impaired, rested its conclusion in upholding several minimum living areas in the zoning ordinance on the protection of land values generally and of the character of the community[9] *Lionshead* recognized that

> [w]ith respect to every zoning ordinance, however, the question remains as to whether or not in the particular facts of the case and in the light of all of the surrounding circumstances the minimum floor-area requirements are reasonable. [10 N.J. at 174, 89 A.2d at 698]

The opinion did not discuss the impact of economic segregation, although Justice Oliphant in dissent referred to that factor when he wrote:

> "Zoning has its purposes, but as I conceive the effect of the majority opinion it precludes individuals in those income brackets who could not pay between $8,500 and $12,000 for the erection of a house on a lot from ever establishing a residence in this community as long as the 768 square feet of living space is the minimum requirement in the zoning ordinance. A zoning provision that can produce this effect certainly runs afoul of the fundamental principles of our form of government. [10 N.J. at 181, 89 A.2d at 701]"

Shortly after *Lionshead,* the Court acknowledged in *Pierro v. Baxendale*, 20 N.J. 17, 118 A.2d 401 (1955), that when conditions change, the dangers of economic segregation may warrant a reexamination of *Lionshead*. In that case Justice Jacobs wrote on behalf of the majority:

> "We are aware of the extensive academic discussion following the decisions in the *Lionshead* and *Bedminster* cases, supra, and the suggestion that the very broad principles which they embody may intensify dangers of economic segregation which even the more traditional modes of zoning entail. * * * In the light of existing population and land conditions within our State these [municipal zoning] powers may be fairly exercised without in anywise endangering the needs or reasonable expectations of any segments of our people. If and when conditions change, alterations in zoning restrictions and pertinent legislative and judicial attitudes need not be long delayed." [20 N.J. at 29, 118 A.2d at 407–409]

We have experienced that change in conditions which has been reflected in pertinent legislative and judicial attitudes. Zoning which

---

9. Some commentators have interpreted *Lionshead* as resting on public health grounds. See, e.g., 2 R. Anderson, American Law of Zoning, § 8.06 at 22 (2d ed. 1976); 6 P. Rohan, Zoning and Land Use Controls, § 42.05[2][b] at 79–82 (1978). If that were its basis, it would certainly no longer be sound. See *Kirsch Holding Co. v. Borough of Manasquan, supra.*

excludes low and moderate income families for fiscal purposes has been condemned as contrary to the general welfare. * * * As we have stated previously, once it is demonstrated that the ordinance excludes people on an economic basis without on its face relating the minimum floor area to one or more appropriate variables, the burden of proof shifts to the municipality to show a proper purpose is being served. This was a burden Wayne was not called upon to meet and Voorhees is. It is a burden which Voorhees has failed to meet.

In conclusion we hold that on its face the Voorhees zoning ordinance prescribes minimum floor areas for residences which are unrelated to legitimate zoning purposes. Voorhees has not directed our attention to anything in the ordinance which ties these requirements to public health or safety or preservation of the character of the neighborhood. Rather, the ordinance appears to be directed solely toward economic segregation. Under these circumstances and in the absence of proofs showing a connection between the minima and the legitimate purposes of zoning (public health, safety and welfare), such as would be established by an occupancy relationship, the provisions must fall.

The judgment declaring invalid those provisions of the Voorhees Township zoning ordinance requiring that residential units contain minimum area floor space is affirmed. We perceive no reason to stay the effectiveness of our adjudication of invalidity.

Notes

1. The Lionshead Lake decision, discussed in the principal case was the subject of a number of law review articles. The case was debated pro and con in the following series of articles: Haar, The Wayne Township Case: Zoning for Minimum Standards, 66 Harv.L.Rev. 1051 (1953); Nolan and Horack, How Small A House?—Zoning for Minimum Space Requirements, 67 Harv. L.Rev. 967 (1954); and Haar, Wayne Township: Zoning for Whom?—In Brief Reply, 67 Harv.L.Rev. 986 (1954). Haar's first article dissects the case pointing out in detail what he regarded to be defects in the court's reasoning and difficulties presented by the result. Professor Haar regarded the case as pointing up the need for regional planning to provide standards for the courts to follow in weighing individual zoning provisions. Professors Nolan and Horack disagreed somewhat sharply with Professor Haar's evaluation of the case. They felt that Haar's charge that zoning had been misused in this way to create economic segregation and permit the domination of real estate interests over legitimate planning was not supported by the facts or record in the case. After an extensive exploration of the facts, record and the opinion, Nolan and Horack concluded that the decision was justified and well-founded. Haar responded, again expressing his point of view, and stating his opposition to the social and economic stratification which he felt the decision encouraged.

2. Also see Appeal of Medinger, 377 Pa. 217, 104 A.2d 118 (1954), where the court struck down a sliding scale minimum scheme with greater square footage required in higher zoning districts than in lower residential districts. The plaintiffs in that case desired to construct a replica of a

colonial farmhouse using authentic materials painstakingly acquired over many years. In Frischkorn Constr. Co. v. Lambert, 315 Mich. 556, 24 N.W.2d 209 (1946), the court struck down a requirement of a minimum number of cubic feet for each house noting that compliance would do no more than irrationally expand attic space and not increase usable living space. Compare Foremost Life Ins. Co. v. Waters, 125 Mich.App. 799, 337 N.W.2d 29 (1983) upholding a 720 square foot minimum for mobile homes. Just the opposite of most cases, what about a local ordinance that restricts the maximum square footage of houses? In Bd. Of County Comm'rs v. Crow, 65 P.3d 720 (Wyo.2003) the court upheld a local ordinance restricting maximum house size to 8,000 square feet. The property owner who had four contiguous lots sought to build a 12,000 square foot house and argued that since the ordinance would permit him to build 4 8,000 square foot houses, he should be allowed to build the one larger home. The court said that the ordinance was valid on the following police power grounds: preservation of the county's colorful past; undue impact on the microeconomics of the county; land use compatibility; promotion of housing affordability; and mitigation of unworkable increase in the need for numbers of low wage employees to service and maintain large homes.

3. Consider this comment from Babcock, Classification and Segregation Among Zoning Districts, 1954 U.Ill.L.F. 186, 201–203:

> The control of house size has raised the cry of "economic segregation," amounting to snobbery or "aesthetics." There *is* economic segregation in such minimum controls, but this should not shock us unless we are shocked by the entire principle of zoning. Zoning is full of examples of "economic segregation," none of which appear to disturb the critics or the courts.
>
> The basic character of a zoning ordinance is classification, and, if you wish, segregation. The two-family residence is kept out of the single-family area, the corner grocery is kept out of both districts. It is apparent that such segregation does impose economic hardship upon individuals who may wish to augment their income by converting their house to two apartments or by erecting a store on the front of their living quarters. They are thereby kept out of a neighborhood they might otherwise occupy. Indeed, in the absence of pertinent decisions on the subject in Illinois, it is to such established practices that the proponent of these *new* standards must turn for precedent.
>
> The history of zoning ordinances is the history of an attempt to divide the municipality into districts not simply on the basis of *use* classifications but of other standards more akin to house and lot size than to use of land. Thus there are numerous Illinois ordinances in which residential districts have different yard and setback provisions. The use of these controls on a sliding scale appears to eliminate any rationale as a health or fire safety measure. The justification for a sliding scale of minimum yard provisions cannot be based alone upon providing adequate open spaces for recreation or fire safety. If so, the space should increase in direct ratio to an increase in density of occupancy; yet just the opposite ratio is customarily established. The justification for minimum setbacks varying with the district has no

exclusive basis in providing adequate traffic vision; otherwise the same setback would be applicable to all districts. Indeed, even the exclusion of two-family dwellings from single-family areas, though looked upon generally as a health and fire safety measure, has an apparent element of this same concept of protection to the existing character of a neighborhood.

The issue must, it would appear, be faced, first, on the basis of whether there *is* a relationship between relative uniformity of size of house and lot within a particular area *and* the preservation of property values and the tax base in that area; and second, if this relationship does exist, whether this "conservation" is a reasonable exercise of the police power, or simply a segregation scheme, at its best economic and at its worst racial in its implications.

There is much opinion (but few if any facts) that there is a clear relationship between the maintenance of adequate tax values and the maintenance of uniform standards of house size in a particular area. Certainly there is evidence that an area of large homes puts into the community far more in taxes than it takes out in cost of services. If such a relationship does exist it is hard to see where classification by maintenance of those standards has any less relationship to the 'public health, welfare, comfort, and morals' than the old customary classifications of districts by yards, setbacks, and, indeed, in some of its forms, height. * * *

Compare, Williams, Planning Law in the Supreme Court, Zoning Digest 107 (April 1961):

* * * The whole value structure of American democracy was heavily influenced by, and in fact was a natural outgrowth of, a particular type of society, widely prevalent in the colonial settlements along the Atlantic seaboard and recurring regularly on later frontiers and elsewhere: a small town or rural society where there were no great inequalities and everyone knew everyone else, so that mutual acquaintance and respect had a chance to develop. These values not only survived but had substantial influence in modifying the great social differences which arose in the nineteenth century. When the crisis of the Civil War came, the eventual result was the official restatement of these values in the thirteenth, fourteenth, and fifteenth amendments. There are of course all sorts of current complications in this connection. Among them, the current suburbanization of the nation raises a new set of problems. To the extent that the strong trend toward "homogeneous"—i.e. segregated—residential areas becomes the prevailing pattern, there is at least a substantial possibility of a gradual erosion of the living habits and attitudes that form the basis of such values. In a democratic society, committed to moving towards these ideals, serious questions are raised when the powers of government are used to exclude a minority from access to decent living conditions; and the situation is not improved when it is a small, relatively well-to-do minority trying to exclude the majority of the population. * * *

4. Although the courts discuss the lack of relationship between minimum house size and the number of occupants and hint that regulations

limiting occupancy might pass muster, do you think that a regulation limiting the number of persons who can live in a dwelling would be valid? Consider College Area Renters and Landlord Association v. City of San Diego, 43 Cal.App.4th 677, 50 Cal.Rptr.2d 515 (1996). In this case the city sought to alleviate problems caused by "mini dorms" described as apartments where several students lived in a small area. The regulation provided:

> It shall be unlawful for an owner of real property in the R–1–5000 zone and located within the area designated on Map C–841 on file in the office of the City Clerk to rent, lease or allow to be occupied or subleased, for any form of consideration, any one-family dwelling unit, or portion thereof, in violation of any of the following development regulations:
>
> 1. No such dwelling unit shall be occupied by more persons, over the age of eighteen (18), than is permitted by the most restrictive of the following regulations:
>
> a. Two (2) persons for each 70 square feet of shared bedroom area, plus one (1) additional person for each additional 50 square feet of bedroom area in bedrooms shared by more than two (2) persons, as provided for in Uniform Housing Code section 503; or
>
> b. Four (4) persons for each full or three-quarter bathroom and two (2) persons for each half bathroom; or
>
> c. One (1) person for each usable off-street parking space on the premises, developed, located and maintained in accordance with the provisions of Division 8 of this Article, plus one additional person; provided, however, that not more than two (2) parking spaces may be in tandem, nor more than one (1) curb cut per front yard, street side yard or alley be allowed for determining occupancy limits based on parking restrictions.
>
> 2. No such dwelling or portion thereof, may be rented if it does not have at least one room, other than a bedroom, with a minimum of 120 square feet of habitable net floor space.

The court found that the regulation violated equal protection because of the distinction between owner-occupied and rented dwellings.

I. JUDICIAL AND LEGISLATIVE OVERSIGHT OF DISCRIMINATORY ZONING

In exclusionary zoning cases where the nature of the issue is exclusion of a particular use from the community as a whole or from the single-family residential zoning district, the remedy to be applied by a court is rather easy to state. Usually the developer-plaintiff will be granted an injunction to allow the particular use desired. However, where the allegations of exclusionary zoning are directed at the community's failure to make provision for housing all segments of the population in need of housing, the remedies available to a court raise important legal and social questions. Does the concept of exclusionary zoning in the constitutional sense imply a duty of *inclusionary* zoning—affirmative action on the part of the community to meet the legitimate needs of all segments of the population? If the answer to this question is yes, then how is court to ensure that the duty is met? These troubling questions are addressed in the following materials.

SOUTHERN BURLINGTON COUNTY NAACP v. TOWNSHIP OF MOUNT LAUREL

Supreme Court of New Jersey, 1975.
67 N.J. 151, 336 A.2d 713, appeal dismissed 423
U.S. 808, 96 S.Ct. 18, 46 L.Ed.2d 28 (1975).

HALL, J.

This case attacks the system of land use regulation by defendant Township of Mount Laurel on the ground that low and moderate income families are thereby unlawfully excluded from the municipality. The trial court so found, 119 N.J.Super. 164 (Law Div.1972), and declared the township zoning ordinance totally invalid. Its judgment went on, in line with the requests for affirmative relief, to order the municipality to make studies of the housing needs of low and moderate income persons presently or formerly residing in the community in substandard housing, as well as those in such income classifications presently employed in the township and living elsewhere or reasonably expected to be employed therein in the future, and to present a plan of affirmative public action designed "to enable and encourage the satisfaction of the indicated needs." Jurisdiction was retained for judicial consideration and approval of such a plan and for the entry of a final order requiring its implementation.

The township appealed to the Appellate Division and those plaintiffs, not present or former residents, cross-appealed on the basis that the judgment should have directed that the prescribed plan take into account as well a fair share of the regional housing needs of low and moderate income families without limitation to those having past, present or prospective connection with the township. * * *

The implications of the issue presented are indeed broad and far-reaching, extending much beyond these particular plaintiffs and the boundaries of this particular municipality.

There is not the slightest doubt that New Jersey has been, and continues to be, faced with a desperate need for housing, especially of decent living accommodations economically suitable for low and moderate income families. The situation was characterized as a "crisis" and fully explored and documented by Governor Cahill in two special messages to the Legislature—A Blueprint for Housing in New Jersey (1970) and New Horizons in Housing (1972).

Plaintiffs represent the minority group poor (black and Hispanic)[10] seeking such quarters. But they are not the only category of persons

---

10. Plaintiffs fall into four categories: (1) present residents of the township residing in dilapidated or substandard housing; (2) former residents who were forced to move elsewhere because of the absence of suitable housing; (3) nonresidents living in central city substandard housing in the region who desire to secure decent housing

barred from so many municipalities by reason of restrictive land use regulations. We have reference to young and elderly couples, single persons and large, growing families not in the poverty class, but who still cannot afford the only kinds of housing realistically permitted in most places—relatively high-priced, single-family detached dwellings on sizeable lots and, in some municipalities, expensive apartments. We will, therefore, consider the case from the wider viewpoint that the effect of Mount Laurel's land use regulation has been to prevent various categories of persons from living in the township because of the limited extent of their income and resources. In this connection, we accept the representation of the municipality's counsel at oral argument that the regulatory scheme was not adopted with any desire or intent to exclude prospective residents on the obviously illegal bases of race, origin or believed social incompatibility.

As already intimated, the issue here is not confined to Mount Laurel. The same question arises with respect to any number of other municipalities of sizeable land area outside the central cities and older built-up suburbs of our North and South Jersey metropolitan areas (and surrounding some of the smaller cities outside those areas as well) which, like Mount Laurel, have substantially shed rural characteristics and have undergone great population increase since World War II, or are now in the process of doing so, but still are not completely developed and remain in the path of inevitable future residential, commercial and industrial demand and growth. Most such municipalities, with but relatively insignificant variation in details, present generally comparable physical situations, courses of municipal policies, practices, enactments and results and human, governmental and legal problems arising therefrom. It is in the context of communities now of this type or which become so in the future, rather than with central cities or older built-up suburbs or areas still rural and likely to continue to be for some time yet, that we deal with the question raised.

Extensive oral and documentary evidence was introduced at the trial, largely informational, dealing with the development of Mount Laurel, including the nature and effect of municipal regulation, the details of the region of which it is a part and the recent history thereof, and some of the basics of housing, special reference being directed to that for low and moderate income families. The record has been supplemented by figures, maps, studies and literature furnished or referred to by counsel and the *amici*, so that the court has a clear picture of land

and accompanying advantages within their means elsewhere; (4) three organizations representing the housing and other interests of racial minorities. The township originally challenged plaintiffs' standing to bring this action. The trial court properly held (119 N.J.Super. at 166) that the resident plaintiffs had adequate standing to ground the entire action and found it unnecessary to pass on that of the other plaintiffs. The issue has not been raised on appeal. We merely add that both categories of nonresident individuals likewise have standing. N.J.S.A. 40:55–47.1; cf. *Walker v. Borough of Stanhope*, 23 N.J. 657 (1957). No opinion is expressed as to the standing of the organizations.

use regulation and its effects in the developing municipalities of the state.

This evidence was not contradicted by the township, except in a few unimportant details. Its candid position is that, conceding its land use regulation was intended to result and has resulted in economic discrimination and exclusion of substantial segments of the area population, its policies and practices are in the best present and future fiscal interest of the municipality and its inhabitants and are legally permissible and justified. It further asserts that the trial court was without power to direct the affirmative relief it did.

I

THE FACTS * * *

[At this point Judge Hall presents an extensive physical description and history of the growth and development of the township.]

* * *

All this affirmative action for the benefit of certain segments of the population is in sharp contrast to the lack of action, and indeed hostility, with respect to affording any opportunity for decent housing for the township's own poor living in substandard accommodations, found largely in the section known as Springville (R–3 zone). The 1969 Master Plan Report recognized it and recommended positive action. The continuous official reaction has been rather a negative policy of waiting for dilapidated premises to be vacated and then forbidding further occupancy. An earlier non-governmental effort to improve conditions had been effectively thwarted. In 1968 a private non-profit association sought to build subsidized, multi-family housing in the Springville section with funds to be granted by a higher level governmental agency. Advance municipal approval of the project was required. The Township Committee responded with a purportedly approving resolution, which found a need for "moderate" income housing in the area, but went on to specify that such housing must be constructed subject to all zoning, planning, building and other applicable ordinances and codes. This meant single-family detached dwellings on 20,000 square foot lots. (Fear was also expressed that such housing would attract low income families from outside the township.) Needless to say, such requirements killed realistic housing for this group of low and moderate income families.

The record thoroughly substantiates the findings of the trial court that over the years Mount Laurel "has acted affirmatively to control development and to attract a selective type of growth" (119 N.J.Super. at 168) and that "through its zoning ordinances has exhibited economic discrimination in that the poor have been deprived of adequate housing and the opportunity to secure the construction of subsidized housing, and has used federal, state, county and local finances and resources solely for the betterment of middle and upper-income persons." (119 N.J.Super. at 178.)

There cannot be the slightest doubt that the reason for this course of conduct has been to keep down local taxes on *property* (Mount Laurel is not a high tax municipality) and that the policy was carried out without regard for non-fiscal considerations with respect to *people,* either within or without its boundaries. This conclusion is demonstrated not only by what was done and what happened, as we have related, but also by innumerable direct statements of municipal officials at public meetings over the years which are found in the exhibits. The trial court referred to a number of them. 119 N.J.Super. at 169–170. No official testified to the contrary.

This policy of land use regulation for a fiscal end derives from New Jersey's tax structure, which has imposed on local real estate most of the cost of municipal and county government and of the primary and secondary education of the municipality's children. The latter expense is much the largest, so, basically, the fewer the school children, the lower the tax rate. Sizeable industrial and commercial ratables are eagerly sought and homes and the lots on which they are situate are required to be large enough, through minimum lot sizes and minimum floor areas, to have substantial value in order to produce greater tax revenues to meet school costs. Large families who cannot afford to buy large houses and must live in cheaper rental accommodations are definitely not wanted, so we find drastic bedroom restrictions for, or complete prohibition of, multi-family or other feasible housing for those of lesser income.

This pattern of land use regulation has been adopted for the same purpose in developing municipality after developing municipality. Almost every one acts solely in its own selfish and parochial interest and in effect builds a wall around itself to keep out those people or entities not adding favorably to the tax base, despite the location of the municipality or the demand for varied kinds of housing. There has been no effective intermunicipal or area planning or land use regulation. * * *

II

The Legal Issue

The legal question before us, as earlier indicated, is whether a developing municipality like Mount Laurel may validly, by a system of land use regulation, make it physically and economically impossible to provide low and moderate income housing in the municipality for the various categories of persons who need and want it and thereby, as Mount Laurel has, exclude such people from living within its confines because of the limited extent of their income and resources. Necessarily implicated are the broader questions of the right of such municipalities to limit the kinds of available housing and of any obligation to make possible a variety and choice of types of living accommodations.

We conclude that every such municipality must, by its land use regulations, presumptively make realistically possible an appropriate variety and choice of housing. More specifically, presumptively it cannot foreclose the opportunity of the classes of people mentioned for low and moderate income housing and in its regulations must affirmatively afford that opportunity, at least to the extent of the municipality's fair share of the present and prospective regional need therefor. These obligations must be met unless the particular municipality can sustain the heavy burden of demonstrating peculiar circumstances which dictate that it should not be required so to do.

We reach this conclusion under state law and so do not find it necessary to consider federal constitutional grounds urged by plaintiffs. We begin with some fundamental principles as applied to the scene before us.

Land use regulation is encompassed within the state's police power. Our constitutions have expressly so provided since an amendment in 1927. That amendment, now Art. IV, § 6, par. 2 of the 1947 Constitution, authorized legislative delegation of the power to municipalities (other than counties), but reserved the legislative right to repeal or alter the delegation (which we take it means repeal or alteration in whole or in part). The legislative delegation of the zoning power followed in 1928, by adoption of the standard zoning enabling act, now found, with subsequent amendments, in N.J.S.A. 40:55–30 to 51.

It is elementary theory that all police power enactments, no matter at what level of government, must conform to the basic state constitutional requirements of substantive due process and equal protection of the laws. These are inherent in Art. I, par. 1 of our Constitution, the requirements of which may be more demanding than those of the federal Constitution. * * *

* * *

It is plain beyond dispute that proper provision for adequate housing of all categories of people is certainly an absolute essential in promotion of the general welfare required in all local land use regulation. Further the universal and constant need for such housing is so important and of such broad public interest that the general welfare which developing municipalities like Mount Laurel must consider extends beyond their boundaries and cannot be parochially confined to the claimed good of the particular municipality. It has to follow that, broadly speaking, the presumptive obligation arises for each such municipality affirmatively to plan and provide, by its land use regulations, the reasonable opportunity for an appropriate variety and choice of housing, including, of course, low and moderate cost housing, to meet the needs, desires and resources of all categories of people who may desire to live within its boundaries. Negatively, it may not adopt regulations or policies which thwart or preclude that opportunity.

* * *

We turn to application of these principles in appraisal of Mount Laurel's zoning ordinance, useful as well, we think, as guidelines for future application in other municipalities.

The township's general zoning ordinance (including the cluster zone provision) permits, as we have said, only one type of housing—single-family detached dwellings. This means that all other types—multi-family including garden apartments and other kinds housing more than one family, town (row) houses, mobile home parks—are prohibited. Concededly, low and moderate income housing has been intentionally excluded. While a large percentage of the population living outside of cities prefers a one-family house on its own sizeable lot, a substantial proportion do not for various reasons. Moreover, single-family dwellings are the most expensive type of quarters and a great number of families cannot afford them. Certainly they are not pecuniarily feasible for low and moderate income families, most young people and many elderly and retired persons, except for some of moderate income by the use of low cost construction on small lots.

As previously indicated, Mount Laurel has allowed some multi-family housing by agreement in planned unit developments, but only for the relatively affluent and of no benefit to low and moderate income families. And even here, the contractual agreements between municipality and developer sharply limit the number of apartments having more than one bedroom. * * *

Mount Laurel's zoning ordinance is also so restrictive in its minimum lot area, lot frontage and building size requirements, earlier detailed, as to preclude single-family housing for even moderate income families. Required lot area of at least 9,375 square feet in one remaining regular residential zone and 20,000 square feet (almost half an acre) in the other, with required frontage of 75 and 100 feet, respectively, cannot be called small lots and amounts to low density zoning, very definitely increasing the cost of purchasing and improving land and so affecting the cost of housing. As to building size, the township's general requirements of a minimum dwelling floor area of 1,100 square feet for all one-story houses and 1,300 square feet for all of one and one-half stories or higher is without regard to required minimum lot size or frontage or the number of occupants (see Sente v. Mayor and Municipal Council of City of Clifton, 66 N.J. 204, 208–209, 330 A.2d 321 (1974)). In most aspects these requirements are greater even than those approved in *Lionshead Lake, Inc. v. Township of Wayne, supra*, 10 N.J. 165, 89 A.2d 693, almost 24 years ago and before population decentralization, outer suburban development and exclusionary zoning had attained today's condition. See also Williams and Wacks, Segregation of Residential Areas Along Economic Lines: Lionshead Lake Revisited, 1969 Wis.L.Rev. 827. Again it is evident these requirements increase the size and so the cost of housing. The conclusion is irresistible that Mount Laurel permits only such middle and upper income housing as it believes will have sufficient taxable value to come close to paying its own governmental way. * * *

Without further elaboration at this point, our opinion is that Mount Laurel's zoning ordinance is presumptively contrary to the general welfare and outside the intended scope of the zoning power in the particulars mentioned. A facial showing of invalidity is thus established, shifting to the municipality the burden of establishing valid superseding reasons for its action and non-action. We now examine the reasons it advances.

* * *

[Judge Hall rejected the reasons advanced by the defendant, which were primarily fiscal and ecological.]

* * *

We have earlier stated that a developing municipality's obligation to afford the opportunity for decent and adequate low and moderate income housing extends at least to " * * * that municipality's fair share of the present and prospective regional need therefor." Some comment on that conclusion is in order at this point. Frequently it might be sounder to have more of such housing, like some specialized land uses, in one municipality in a region than in another, because of greater availability of suitable land, location of employment, accessibility of public transportation or some other significant reason. But, under present New Jersey legislation, zoning must be on an individual municipal basis, rather than regionally. So long as that situation persists under the present tax structure, or in the absence of some kind of binding agreement among all the municipalities of a region, we feel that every municipality therein must bear its fair share of the regional burden. (In this respect our holding is broader than that of the trial court, which was limited to Mount Laurel-related low and moderate income housing needs.)

The composition of the applicable "region" will necessarily vary from situation to situation and probably no hard and fast rule will serve to furnish the answer in every case. Confinement to or within a certain county appears not to be realistic, but restriction within the boundaries of the state seems practical and advisable. (This is not to say that a developing municipality can ignore a demand for housing within its boundaries on the part of people who commute to work in another state.) Here we have already defined the region at present as "those portions of Camden, Burlington and Gloucester Counties within a semicircle having a radius of 20 miles or so from the heart of Camden City." The concept of "fair share" is coming into more general use and, through the expertise of the municipal planning adviser, the county planning boards and the state planning agency, a reasonable figure for Mount Laurel can be determined, which can then be translated to the allocation of sufficient land therefor on the zoning map. See generally, New Jersey Trends, ch. 27, Listokin, Fair Share Housing Distribution: An Idea Whose Time Has Come?, p. 353. We may add that we think that, in arriving at such a determination, the type of information and estimates, which the trial judge (119 N.J.Super. at 178) directed the township to compile and furnish to him, concerning the housing needs of persons of low and moderate income now or formerly residing in the township in substandard dwellings and those presently employed or reasonably expected to be employed therein, will be pertinent.

There is no reason why developing municipalities like Mount Laurel, required by this opinion to afford the opportunity for all types of housing to meet the needs of various categories of people, may not become and remain attractive, viable communities providing good living and adequate services for all their residents in the kind of atmosphere which a democracy and free institutions demand. They can have industrial sections, commercial sections and sections for every kind of housing from low cost and multi-family to lots of more than an acre with very expensive homes. Proper planning and governmental cooperation can prevent over-intensive and too sudden development, insure against future suburban sprawl and slums and assure the preservation of open space and local beauty. We do not intend that developing municipalities shall be overwhelmed by voracious land speculators and developers if they use the powers which they have intelligently and in the broad public interest. Under our holdings today, they can be better communities for all than they previously have been.

III

THE REMEDY

As outlined at the outset of this opinion, the trial court invalidated the zoning ordinance *in toto* and ordered the township to make certain studies and investigations and to present to the court a plan of affirmative public action designed "to enable and encourage the satisfaction of the indicated needs" for township related low and moderate income housing. Jurisdiction was retained for judicial consideration and approval of such a plan and for the entry of a final order requiring its implementation.

We are of the view that the trial court's judgment should be modified in certain respects. We see no reason why the entire zoning ordinance should be nullified. Therefore we declare it to be invalid only to the extent and in the particulars set forth in this opinion. The township is granted 90 days from the date hereof, or such additional time as the trial court may find is reasonable and necessary to allow, to adopt amendments to correct the deficiencies herein specified. It is the local function and responsibility, in the first instance at least, rather than the court's, to decide on the details of the same within the guidelines we have laid down. If plaintiffs desire to attack such amendments, they may do so by supplemental complaint filed in this cause within 30 days of the final adoption of the amendments.

We are not at all sure what the trial judge had in mind as ultimate action with reference to the approval of a plan for affirmative public action concerning the satisfaction of indicated housing needs and the entry of a final order requiring implementation thereof. Courts do not build housing nor do municipalities. That function is performed by private builders, various kinds of associations, or, for public housing, by special agencies created for that purpose at various levels of government. The municipal function is initially to provide the opportunity through appropriate land use regulations and we have spelled out what Mount Laurel must do in that regard. It is not appropriate at this time, particularly in view of the advanced view of zoning law as applied to housing laid down by this opinion, to deal with the matter of the further extent of judicial power in the field or to exercise any such power. See, however, *Pascack Ass'n v. Mayor and Council of the Township of Washington*, 131 N.J.Super. 195, 329 A.2d 89 (Law Div.1974), and cases therein cited, for a discussion of this question. The municipality should first have full opportunity to itself act without judicial supervision. We trust it will do so in the spirit we have suggested, both by appropriate zoning ordinance amendments and whatever additional action encouraging the fulfillment of its fair share of the regional need for low and moderate income housing may be indicated as necessary and advisable. (We have in mind that there is at least a moral obligation in a municipality to establish a local housing agency pursuant to state law to provide housing for its resident poor now living in dilapidated, unhealthy quarters.) The portion of the trial court's judgment ordering the preparation and submission of the aforesaid study, report and plan to it for further action is therefore vacated as at least premature. Should Mount Laurel not perform as we expect, further judicial action may be sought by supplemental pleading in this cause.

The judgment of the Law Division is modified as set forth herein. No costs.

[Two concurring opinions are omitted.]

Note

Not long after Mount Laurel I the New York Court of Appeals, in Berenson v. Town of New Castle, 38 N.Y.2d 102, 378 N.Y.S.2d 672, 341 N.E.2d 236 (1975), held that zoning ordinances must give consideration to regional housing needs. After remand, the trial court found that the town was not meeting its fair share of regional housing needs and ordered, inter alia, that the town make provision for 3,500 units of multi-family housing by the year 1987. The town appealed the order, with the following result:

BERENSON v. TOWN OF NEW CASTLE

Supreme Court of New York, Appellate Division, 1979.
67 A.D.2d 506, 415 N.Y.S.2d 669.

GULOTTA, JUSTICE.

The plaintiffs have secured a declaratory judgment invalidating the zoning ordinance of the Town of New Castle to the extent that it fails to make adequate provision for multi-family housing. (At the time this action was commenced, the ordinance totally excluded multi-family residential housing from the list of permitted uses. A subsequent amendment, examined in proposal form at the trial and enacted prior to Special Term's decision, purports to provide for 100–150 units of multi-family housing, as a permitted use, in the central business district of Chappaqua.) The issue on appeal is *not* whether the Town of New Castle may permissibly exclude multi-family housing from within its borders. The town now concedes that its total exclusion was improper and contends that the interim amendment of its zoning ordinance "is just the beginning of a process of experimentation in accommodating alternative housing forms including multi-family housing." Rather, the issue before us is whether the far-reaching remedial provisions of the judgment may be sustained. We hold that, for the most part, they may not.

* * *

* * * That there does exist an unmet local and regional need for multi-family housing is not seriously contested by the town on appeal, and this finding is amply supported by the evidence. However, instead of merely declaring the ordinance unconstitutional and remanding the matter to the Town Board for passage of an amended zoning ordinance which would pass judicial muster, Special Term went further and awarded the plaintiffs comprehensive affirmative relief. Finding that the town had not merely "failed" to consider local and regional housing needs, but, on the contrary, had "continuously and actively opposed any planning or program that would suggest the assumption by it of any responsibility to meet local or regional housing needs", and that compliance with the standards for local government land use control would not be promoted if made to depend upon repetitive litigation of the basic substantive issues, Special Term promulgated "judicially established housing goals" by declaring that the construction of 3,500 units of multi-family housing over the next 10 years was "the most conservative estimate of what will be required of New Castle * * * to supply its own needs * * * [and] its share of the regional needs", and directed the town to amend its zoning ordinance, land use regulations and planning policies to accommodate the needed housing. The town was given six months within which to comply, and in the absence of timely and satisfactory compliance, Special Term decreed that the traditional presumption of validity attending zoning ordinances would be suspended and applications for rezoning would be granted on an *ad hoc* basis to individual developers whose proposals meet the judicially established housing goals, unless the town is able to establish compelling reasons for denial. Special Term also declared that the zoning ordinance was unconstitutional as it applied to the plaintiffs' property and directed the town to rezone that property for multi-family housing at a density of eight units per acre within six months. In its decision, Special Term stated that a building permit should be issued to the plaintiffs upon the advent of rezoning. To all of this broad, comprehensive relief the town objects, and rightfully so.

* * *

* * * Zoning and land use regulations were deemed to be legislative functions, to be exercised by and within the particular expertise of the *local* legislative body. Thus, with the single exception of discriminatory zoning of similarly situated parcels, in which case the obvious remedy was to treat like parcels alike, a judicial declaration that a zoning ordinance was invalid as applied to a particular piece of property was never accompanied by a declaration which actually rezoned that property or placed it within a particular use classification. * * *

More recently, however, court challenges to exclusionary zoning on behalf of those excluded from the community have come into being, spawned by tremendous economic and social changes and the deterioration of city life. These challenges have not been prompted by the mere growth of the suburbs as attractive, affluent, mainly white collar bedroom communities, for those have been with us for many years. Rather, the critical factor appears to have been the relatively recent flight of blue collar jobs to the suburbs, where housing for the employer, but not his employees, was willingly provided. Moreover, while the early judicial challenges to such exclusionary practices were brought by plaintiff-developers who wished to put their property to a more profitable, higher density use, it was soon recognized that the developers' rights could not realistically be separated from the rights of others, then nonresidents, " 'in search of a comfortable place to live' "(*Concord Township Appeal*, 439 Pa. 466, 474, n. 6, 268 A.2d 765, 768, n. 6) and the cases were decided accordingly. In these cases, the relief sought was generally a declaration of the unconstitutionality of the zoning ordinance and the relief, when granted, consisted of such a declaration and, in some of cases, in a departure from past practices, a direction, in effect, rezoning the plaintiff's land * * *.

[At this point the court reviewed the Pennsylvania and New Jersey exclusionary zoning cases.]

* * *

Turning back now to the case at bar, Special Term found, on the basis of the evidence adduced at the trial that "the most conservative estimate of what will be required of New Castle over the next ten years to supply its own needs for multi-family housing and to meet its share of the regional needs for such housing is not less than 3,500 multi-family housing units," a figure which the court determined was not speculative, but rather "a realistic planning goal that recognized the minimum needs established by the evidence." As previously noted, since it deemed the town to be resistant to the voluntary assumption of its responsibilities in this respect and considered a one-time detailed mandate of specified changes in the zoning ordinance to be superior to expensive and repetitive litigation to achieve zoning relief on a parcel by parcel basis, Special Term simply directed the town to amend its ordinance and accessory regulations to provide for the construction of at least 3,500 units of multi-family housing by the end of 1987. In our opinion, this mandate is unsupported by the evidence, contrary to law, and contrary to sound principles of planning.

As respects the evidence adduced at the trial, it is readily apparent that this case contains a most peculiar incongruity. Although the amended complaint does not challenge the town's ordinance as exclusionary with respect to low and moderate income housing (which, in fact, it certainly is), and plaintiffs themselves do not purport either to represent low and moderate income persons seeking housing within the town or to be interested in building multi-family housing affordable by such persons, evidence as to the housing needs of this particular income group (persons having an annual income of less than $10,000 in 1970, which by reason of inflation, translates into $14,613 in 1977) abounds in the record. Indeed, evidence as to the present housing needs of the town's residents and workers was quantified only as to this income group, although evidence as to regional housing needs was introduced both as to this lower income group and the population in general. As for the number of units it ordered to be provided, Special Term did not ascribe its 3,500 figure to any particular evidence or expert witness, but it is clear from the record that it was taken from the testimony of two particular experts, Levy and Raymond. Although one witness worked forward and the other backward, both estimated a "fair share" for the town to be about 3,500 units, based on a projected growth of the population of Westchester County, the number of housing units required to be constructed to keep pace with such growth, and New Castle's fair share of such units, figured on the basis of its percentage of the remaining land in the county suitable for such development. *However, neither estimate was geared to the needs of lower income groups in particular.* In fact, Levy's "target figure" was not meant to include only multi-family units, while Raymond admitted that it was preferable to satisfy present needs first, as future needs might change during the period between the advent of rezoning and completion of the finished units.

There was also evidence in the case (not relied on by Levy or Raymond) that the Tri-State Regional Planning Commission had estimated a housing deficit, based on the 1970 census, of over 2,000,000 units in the tri-state region, over 60,000 units in Westchester County, and about 6,000 units in the 13 communities of Northern Westchester, of which New Castle is a part. These figures were based exclusively on the needs of families earning less than $10,000 in 1970 and took into account those units necessary to replace housing which was presently substandard, overcrowded (more than 1.01 persons per room) or cost-imbalanced (rent being 25% or more of the family's income), as well as new units which would be necessary for those who wished to reside closer to their employment. However, the figures themselves are inherently inflated, as the categories of substandard, overcrowded and cost-imbalanced housing often overlap; they do not distinguish between single-and multi-family dwellings; and, more importantly, the appropriate remedy for the problem described is not necessarily the construction of new housing, since the emphasis today is on the rehabilitation of existing units and on rent subsidies. Moreover, the data is now more than eight years old, and the estimated shortfall of 6,000 units was calculated with reference to all 13 communities of Northern Westchester, most of which have similarly made little or no provision for multi-family or "least-cost" housing, but have not been joined as defendants in this action (cf. *Urban League of Greater New Brunswick v. Mayor,* 142 N.J.Super. 11, 359 A.2d 526).

In point of fact then, the multi-family housing quota of 3,500 units, adopted by Special Term as New Castle's "fair share" of regional housing needs is a highly abstract and speculative number, to which the trial court ultimately gave more weight than did its proponents, Levy and Raymond. Further, the court apparently failed to appreciate that the figure itself was referable to the housing market in general, both as to income groups and the type of housing (single-or multi-family) to be provided, and was not directly referable to the needs of the low income groups with which the court was primarily concerned. *The use of a "fair share" goal has never been judicially approved in the context of the housing needs of the population at large.* Its *raison d'etre* lies in the housing needs of the low and moderate income groups whose "circumstances of * * * economic helplessness * * * to find adequate housing * * * [combined with] the wantonness of foreclosing them therefrom by [exclusionary] zoning", impelled the New Jersey Supreme Court to adopt the "fair share" doctrine in the first instance (*Pascack Assn. v. Mayor & Council of Township of Washington, Bergen County,* 74 N.J. 470, 480, 379 A.2d 6, 11). Moreover, Special Term's judgment cannot and does not insure that any of the multi-family units to be constructed will be anything other than luxury condominiums, with which the market may already be saturated. While not sufficient to save the zoning ordinance from invalidation, the town's contention that multi-family rental housing (the type most affordable by persons of low and moderate income) cannot be constructed today even *with* governmental subsidies unless the land is publicly owned or figured at zero cost is not without some merit, especially if we are talking about providing lower income housing in sizeable quantities. Indeed, the New Jersey Supreme Court's subsequent focus upon "least-cost" housing as opposed to *low-income* housing is attributable to its recognition that it will be virtually impossible to provide large amounts of newly constructed housing for the economically less fortunate in the foreseeable future (*Oakwood at Madison v. Township of Madison,* 72 N.J. 481, 371 A.2d 1192 supra).

Aside from these evidentiary and practical problems, it is also abundantly clear that Special Term's declaration of a specific, mandatory "fair share" quota for the Town of New Castle is unsupported by case law and contrary to the public policy considerations embodied therein. It will be recalled that the "fair share" doctrine in Pennsylvania never encompassed the judicial specification of a particular number of higher density units to be built or the acreage to be devoted to such usage, and that even in New Jersey, where the doctrine is most highly developed, the Supreme Court has thus far refused to require judicial prescription of a mandatory "fair share" unit quota, concluding in essence, that such a course would be both inappropriate and impracticable. Nor is the decision of the Court of Appeals on the prior *Berenson* appeal (38 N.Y.2d 102, 378 N.Y.S.2d 672, 341 N.E.2d 236, supra) authority for the adoption of a "fair share" unit quota. Quite to the contrary, in holding that New Castle could validly exclude multi-family housing if its neighboring communities provided a sufficient number of such units, or the land upon which they could be built, to satisfy their own, New Castle's, and the regional needs, the Court of Appeals impliedly held that New Castle per se did not have to bear any "fair share" of any such housing burden. On the other hand, however, we cannot be blind to the fact that were the regional and local needs already being satisfied elsewhere, it is unlikely that we would be presented with the instant lawsuit, as the desire of developers and builders such as the plaintiffs to maximize their profits through more intensive land usage is, after all, dependent upon a market demand for that type of development. In any event, by holding that the courts had no choice, in the absence of meaningful regional planning, but to "assess the reasonableness of what the locality has done" (*Berenson v. Town of New Castle*, 38 N.Y.2d 102, 111, 378 N.Y.S.2d 672, 682, 341 N.E.2d 236, 243, supra), the Court of Appeals in our view, merely intended to have Special Term determine whether New Castle's exclusion of multi-family dwellings was reasonable in light of present and foreseeable local and regional needs. We do not perceive that the court intended that a finding of unreasonableness, i.e., that there was an *unmet* local or regional need for multi-family housing which the town had ignored by excluding such housing, would authorize the court to go even further and remedy the deficiency by specific judicial fiat.

Although we therefore find that Special Term erred in mandating a "fair share" unit goal, there is little doubt but that the record establishes an unsatisfied local and regional need for multi-family housing on the part of what we shall simply call the less affluent residents of the New York City metropolitan area. Indeed, the town does not argue to the contrary. And while multi-family zoning cannot insure that such units will actually be built, or that, if built, they will be affordable by families of modest means, the absence of such zoning, as noted by Special Term, surely precludes any such construction.

As a court of law, we cannot provide any lasting solution for the complex problems posed by cases such as this, but we can and must in appropriate cases require a developing municipality such as the Town of New Castle to cease its policy of immunizing itself from the ordinary incidents of growth and "confront the challenge of population growth with open doors" (*Golden v. Planning Bd. of Town of Ramapo*, 30 N.Y.2d 359, 379, 334 N.Y.S.2d 138, 153, 285 N.E.2d 291, 302, supra). The zoning ordinance thus having been properly declared unconstitutional for failure to make adequate provision for multi-family housing, the judgment should be modified so as to delete the 3,500 unit requirement, but direct that the matter be remanded to the Town Board to remedy its zoning deficiency within six months. Further, Special Term should retain jurisdiction for the purpose of allowing the plaintiffs to challenge the sufficiency of any amended ordinance by supplemental pleadings in this case. It is our expectation that the town will now set about its task with the utmost good faith. However, we feel compelled to note that the interim amendment here, characterized by one of plaintiffs' witnesses as having been drawn with such care as might be exercised if the town had to accept a leper colony into its midst, was not such a good-faith effort. Allegedly designed to provide 100–150 units of multi-family housing in the central business district of Chappaqua (an inadequate number in any event), plaintiffs presented uncontroverted proof that this estimated yield was based solely on spatial capacity and, as a general matter, could not be realized without the conversion of existing commercial space into residential space or the construction of a second floor on the tops of one-story commercial buildings, there being so little vacant land left to develop; as a practical matter, it was stated, the construction of no more than 27 units was realistically possible.

* * *

Judgment of the Supreme Court, Westchester County, entered December 30, 1977, modified, on the law, by deleting the third, fourth, fifth and sixth decretal paragraphs thereof and substituting therefor provisions (1) remanding the matter to the Town Board to remedy its zoning deficiency within a period of six months, (2) directing the Town Board to rezone plaintiffs' property for multi-family use and (3) directing that Special Term retain jurisdiction for the purpose of allowing plaintiffs to challenge the sufficiency and validity of any amended ordinance by supplemental pleadings in this case. As so modified, judgment affirmed, with costs to respondents payable by appellant.

* * *

SHAPIRO, JUSTICE (concurring in part and dissenting in part).

With one exception, I concur in the scholarly and comprehensive opinion of my brother MR. JUSTICE GULOTTA.

The amended zoning ordinance enacted by the Town of New Castle in response to the caveat of *Berenson v. Town of New Castle*, 38 N.Y.2d 102, 378 N.Y.S.2d 672, 341 N.E.2d 236, was a derisive mockery, verging on contempt. * * *

* * *

In a case such as this where the dilatory tactics of the town have prevented the plaintiffs from proceeding with their building project for more than five years, two strikes should be out. The conduct of the town fathers exhibits a flagrant and intentional and malicious policy of disregard for the law which was clearly intended to impede, if not entirely defeat, the rights of the plaintiffs. Thus, the zoning ordinance should be declared invalid with no period of grace. If there is no zoning until the town fathers shoulder their proper responsibilities—so be it. They should not be given leisure time to reform. Enough is enough.

Notes

1. The earlier decision in the Berenson case rejected a facial attack on the zoning ordinance, Berenson v. Town of New Castle, 38 N.Y.2d 102, 378 N.Y.S.2d 672, 341 N.E.2d 236 (1975).

2. The New York courts have, since the Berenson decision, continued to insist that fair share problems are for the legislature, and attempts to obtain judicial relief have, for the most part, failed. See, e.g., Suffolk Housing Services v. Town of Brookhaven, 70 N.Y.2d 122, 517 N.Y.S.2d 924, 511 N.E.2d 67 (1987) and Asian Americans for Equality v. Koch, 72 N.Y.2d 121, 531 N.Y.S.2d 782, 527 N.E.2d 265 (1988). Also see Strykers Bay Neighborhood Council v. City of New York, 695 F.Supp. 1531 (S.D.N.Y.1988); Spallone v. United States, 493 U.S. 265, 110 S.Ct. 625, 107 L.Ed.2d 644 (1990).

3. Pennsylvania has also taken an approach based on the Mt. Laurel doctrine. See Fernley v. Board of Supervisors of Schuylkill Township, 509 Pa. 413, 502 A.2d 585 (1985). The Fernley case was followed in Borough of Malvern v. Jackson, 108 Pa.Cmwlth. 248, 529 A.2d 96 (1987), remanded 521 Pa. 570, 559 A.2d 489 (1989) and H & R Builders, Inc. v. Borough Council of Norwood, 124 Pa.Cmwlth. 88, 555 A.2d 948 (1989).

4. Where a fully developed city has been found in violation of the Fair Housing Act or guilty of racially discriminatory zoning practices under the Equal Protection clause, the problem of fashioning judicial relief is almost as great as in cases involving developing municipalities. See United States v. City of Parma, Ohio, 494 F.Supp. 1049 (N.D.Ohio 1980).

TOLL BROTHERS, INC. v. TOWNSHIP OF WEST WINDSOR

Supreme Court of New Jersey, 2002.
173 N.J. 502, 803 A.2d 53.

PORITZ, C.J.

This is a second round *Mount Laurel* exclusionary zoning case brought by Toll Brothers, Inc. (Toll Brothers) against the Township of West Windsor, the Township Committee of the Township of West Windsor, and the Planning Board of the Township of West Windsor (collectively "West Windsor" or the "Township"). Toll Brothers, the owner of a 293 acre tract of land located in West Windsor, alleged below that the Township had engaged in exclusionary zoning in violation of the New Jersey Constitution and the Fair Housing Act of New Jersey (FHA), N.J.S.A. 52:27D–301 to–329, and sought a builder's remedy from the trial court. *Toll Bros., Inc. v. Township of West Windsor*, 303 N.J.Super. 518, 526–27, 697 A.2d 201 (Law Div.1996) (*West Windsor*). Following a bench trial, the court concluded that West Windsor was "not in compliance with the *Mount Laurel* mandate, and thus * * * [had] violat[ed] * * * the New Jersey Constitution and the New Jersey Fair Housing Act." *Id.* At 574, 697 A.2d 201. Based on that finding, the trial court held that Toll Brothers was entitled to a builder's remedy, the specifics of which were to be addressed at a later date. *Id.* At 575–76, 697 A.2d 201.

* * *

In 1975, this Court decided *Southern Burlington County NAACP v. Mount Laurel Township*, 67 N.J. 151, 336 A.2d 713, *cert. denied*, 423 U.S. 808, 96 S.Ct. 18, 46 L.Ed.2d 28 (1975) (*Mount Laurel I*). In that opinion, we held that developing municipalities are obligated under our State Constitution to provide a realistic opportunity for the development of low and moderate income housing.

Despite *Mount Laurel I* and the subsequent creation of the builder's remedy, the years that followed saw "many municipalities fail[ing] to comply with the clear mandate of *Mt. Laurel I*." *Holmdel Builders Ass'n v. Township of Holmdel,* 121 N.J. 550, 555, 583 A.2d 277 (1990). Thus, in *Southern Burlington County NAACP v. Mount Laurel Township,* 92 N.J. 158, 456 A.2d 390 (1983) (*Mount Laurel II*), "[w]e clarified and reaffirmed the constitutional mandate set forth in *Mt. Laurel I,* imposing an affirmative obligation on every municipality to provide its fair share of affordable housing." *Holmdel, supra,* 121 N.J. at 555, 583 A.2d 277 (citing *Mount Laurel II, supra,* 92 N.J. 158, 456 A.2d 390).

Most relevant to the instant matter, the Court also clarified the conditions under which a builder's remedy may be granted. We began by acknowledging that

"[b]uilder's remedies have been one of many controversial aspects of the *Mount Laurel* doctrine." *Mount Laurel II, supra,* 92 N.J. at 279, 456 A.2d 390. Notwithstanding that controversy, however, we found that "[e]xperience * * * has demonstrated to us that builder's remedies must be made more readily available to achieve compliance with *Mount Laurel*." *Ibid.* Yet, because of concerns about land use planning, we urged the trial courts when formulating a builder's remedy to "make as much use as * * * [possible] of the [municipal] planning board's expertise and experience so that the proposed project is suitable for the municipality." *Id.* at 279–80, 456 A.2d 390. We also cautioned that "[t]rial courts should guard the public interest carefully to be sure that plaintiff-developers do not abuse the *Mount Laurel* doctrine." *Id.* at 281, 456 A.2d 390.

On July 2, 1985, "the Legislature codified the *Mt. Laurel* doctrine, including its available compliance measures," by enacting the FHA. *Holmdel, supra,* 121 N.J. at 556, 583 A.2d 277. The FHA creates a new administrative agency, the Council on Affordable Housing (COAH), N.J.S.A. 52:27D–307, to oversee the development of low and moderate income housing throughout the state through a system of voluntary participation by municipalities in the COAH process. To carry out its function, the agency is authorized to adopt necessary rules and regulations.

Under the FHA, COAH serves as an alternative forum for the resolution of *Mount Laurel* disputes. Municipalities facing *Mount Laurel* challenges may use the COAH mediation and review process, *id.* at–316b, or independently may seek COAH review of their zoning and affordable housing regulations, *id.* at–314, in order to receive a measure of protection from future challenges. *See id.* at–317a. On a grant of substantive certification from COAH, *id.* at–314, a municipality's housing plan enjoys a ten-year presumption of validity that may be overcome in subsequent litigation only by clear and convincing evidence. *See id.* at–317a; *id.* at–313.

In *Hills Development Co. v. Bernards Township,* 103 N.J. 1, 25, 510 A.2d 621 (1986), this Court upheld the constitutionality of the FHA.

* * *

To meet its original obligation, West Windsor adopted a housing plan and various conforming zoning amendments. The amendments addressed issues such as common open space, density and residential-type distribution, affordable unit distribution and locational criteria, and expedited review of low and moderate income developments. New zones "EH" (Elderly Housing), and "R3A," "R4A," and "R4B" (Residence Districts) were added, and eleven sites were zoned for inclusionary development as follows: Sites 1 and 5A (120 affordable units), Sites 2 and 8 (312 affordable units), Site 3 (twenty affordable units), Site 4 (thirty-four affordable units), Site 5 (100 affordable units), Site 6 (the Toll Brothers property—527 affordable units), Site 7 (forty affordable units), Site A (102 affordable units), and Site B (206 affordable units).

Those eleven sites were to provide a realistic opportunity for the development of 1,461 affordable housing units. Also, under the compliance plan West Windsor agreed to rehabilitate thirty-seven existing dwellings that, in the main, consisted of multi-family units. In all, the plan provided for the potential development of 1,498 affordable units generally consisting of multi-family housing. As described by the trial court in the opinion below, the plan

> rel[ied] almost exclusively on multi-family housing as the vehicle for development of inclusionary projects. Conventional single-family detached housing [was] generally not permitted in the inclusionary zones. The single-family detached housing that [was] permitted either must be located in a specialty zone, or it must be a novel product, e.g., zero lot-line homes [,] * * * where one side of the house is windowless and lies directly on a side lot-line. [*Id.* at 554, 697 A.2d 201.]

* * *

On May 12, 1993, Toll Brothers filed this lawsuit alleging that West Windsor had engaged in a pattern of exclusionary zoning in violation of the New Jersey Constitution as interpreted in the *Mount Laurel* cases and the FHA. West Windsor's period of repose under the 1985 judgment had expired on July 21, 1991, and West Windsor had not applied to COAH for interim certification. If granted interim certification, West Windsor would have been required to continue implementing the terms of the 1985 judgment and would have continued to enjoy the same measure of protection from litigation that was provided by that judgment.

West Windsor nonetheless continued to implement the 1985 court-approved plan, which "remained in effect essentially unchanged, until late summer 1994." Of the eleven sites included in the 1985 judgment, however, only two actually had been developed by the time Toll Brothers instituted its *Mount Laurel* challenge—the Windsor Haven property (Site 3 from the 1985 judgment), which produced thirty-seven "for-sale" condominium units, and Steward's Watch (Site A from the 1985 judgment), which yielded 102 rental units. During roughly the same period (1982–1994), however, "a massive amount of development of conventional single-family detached homes ha[d] occurred in non-inclusionary zones." Specifically, "the number of houses in West Windsor Township more than doubled, increasing from 2,907 units to 6,115 units," with the purchasers generally moving into "high-priced, large-lot, single-family houses."

Toll Brothers argued that West Windsor's "poor" development rate for the construction of affordable housing was due to a variety of factors, including: (1) the severe impact of environmental constraints (*e.g.*, freshwater wetlands, freshwater wetlands buffers, and floodplain areas) on the developability of the sites zoned for affordable housing; (2) West Windsor's unduly cost-generative public sewer policies that required developers of inclusionary sites to provide and "front" the high costs of oversized and expensive gravity flow sewer systems; (3) public resistance to, and application processing delays regarding, development of sites zoned for affordable housing (highlighted by the testimony of plaintiff's expert, who also had been the planner for the former owner, that when attempting to obtain development approval from the West Windsor Planning Board the developer was subjected to over fifty public hearings in three-and-one-half years, a delay that the trial court, in October 1987, found to be "'unjustified,' 'purposeful or unexcusable'"); (4) West Windsor's failure, in its zoning of affordable housing sites, to include conventional single-family houses on small lots despite the demonstrated strong market demand for such units; and (5) West Windsor's other restrictive zoning standards and cost-generative ordinances, such as the requirement that 175 senior citizen affordable units be built on the Toll Brothers site "without regard to the number of market units built," as well as ordinances establishing the set-aside of an "unreasonable amount of common open and recreational space." As the trial court summarized,

> plaintiff asks this court to look beyond the face of defendant's assertedly inclusionary zoning. It asks for consideration of numerous factors—environment, infrastructure, market demand, municipal policy and other zoning-related factors—for a finding that defendant is deficient in its affirmative duty under the *Mount Laurel* cases. It asks for a builder's remedy to permit development of its property in a more cost-effective, market-responsive manner than defendant's current zoning allows. [*Id.* at 537, 697 A.2d 201.]

The builder's remedy sought by Toll Brothers would necessitate the rezoning of the Toll Brothers site. At the time, the site was zoned PRN–1, which requires a mix of three housing types with no one housing type accounting for more than eighty percent of the total units. The permitted types were townhouses, garden apartments, patio homes, two-family rentals, maisonettes and zero lot-line single-family units. The rezoning sought by Toll Brothers would allow it to construct 735 to 765 units, of which 625 to 650 would be conventional, market-rate, single-family detached houses on small lots and 110 to 115 units would be affordable rental housing. Eighty percent of the affordable rental units would be single-family detached zero lot-line housing, with the balance a mix of conventional single-family detached houses on small lots, as well as a second unidentified housing type.

* * *

When this Court decided *Mount Laurel I* in 1975 "[t]here [was] not the slightest doubt that New Jersey ha[d] been, and continue[d] to be, faced with a desperate need for housing, especially of decent living accommodations economically suitable for low and moderate income families." *Mount Laurel I, supra,* 67 N.J. at 158, 336 A.2d 713 (footnote omitted). Despite the documented lack of acceptable accommodations for those most in need, "the only kinds of housing realistically permitted in most places * * * [consisted of] relatively high-priced, single-family detached dwellings on sizeable lots and, in some municipalities, expensive apartments." *Id.* at 159, 336 A.2d 713. Although the plaintiffs in that case represented poor minorities who claimed that Mount Laurel's land use regulations unconstitutionally barred them from living in the township due to their limited income and resources, we recognized at the outset that "the issue * * * [was] not confined to Mount Laurel." *Id.* at 160, 336 A.2d 713. We said then:

> The same question arises with respect to any number of other municipalities of sizeable land area outside the central cities and older built-up suburbs of our North and South Jersey metropolitan areas (and surrounding some of the smaller cities outside those areas as well) which, like Mount Laurel, have substantially shed rural characteristics and have undergone great population increase since World War II, or are now in the process of doing so, but still are not completely developed and remain in the path of inevitable future residential, commercial and industrial demand and growth. [*Ibid.*]

* * *

Mount Laurel I thus established the contours of municipalities' constitutional obligation to provide a realistic opportunity for the development of low and moderate income housing. But, as we said in that case, "[c]ourts do not build housing nor do municipalities"—builders, private associations, and special governmental agencies do. Under *Mount Laurel I* and our subsequent exclusionary zoning cases, a municipality is responsible for promulgating appropriate land use ordinances under which a developer could be expected to construct the municipality's fair share of affordable housing. In *Madison, supra,* 72 N.J. at 549–51, 371 A.2d 1192, however, the Court created a judicial remedy for the enforcement of the *Mount Laurel* doctrine known generally as the builder's remedy. The builder's remedy was designed as an "incentive for the institution of socially beneficial but costly litigation * * * [in order to] get on with the provision of needed housing for at least some portion of the moderate income elements of the population." *Id.* at 550–51, 371 A.2d 1192. Without the inducement of such a remedy there was little reason for a private developer to challenge a municipality's zoning ordinances.

We also recognized in *Mount Laurel I, supra,* and *Mount Laurel II, supra,* that municipal zoning ordinances have a substantial impact beyond a municipality's borders implicating the general welfare "of those residing outside of the municipality but within the region that contributes to the housing demand within the municipality." 67 N.J. at 177, 336 A.2d 713; 92 N.J. at 208, 456 A.2d 390. For that reason, we determined in *Mount Laurel I* that a "developing" municipality has a presumptive constitutional obligation affirmatively to afford "a realistic opportunity for the construction of its fair share of the present and prospective regional need for low and moderate income housing." *Mount Laurel II, supra,* 92 N.J. at 204–05, 456 A.2d 390 (citing *Mount Laurel I, supra,* 67 N.J. at 174, 336 A.2d 713). At that time, the Court chose to limit its holding to a general notion of developing communities—land areas, outside of central cities and older suburbs, that are in the path of anticipated growth—because there was no "official guidance * * * as to the state's plans for its own future, its own determination of where development should occur and where it should not, and what kind of development * * *." *Id.* at 224–25, 456 A.2d 390. Yet, as we observed in *Mount Laurel II,* the concept was vague, at best, and endangered "prime agricultural land, open spaces, and areas of scenic beauty" in towns that fit within the category of a developing community but that "should *not* yield to 'inevitable future residential, commercial and industrial demand and growth.' " *Id.* at 224, 336 A.2d 713 (emphasis in original).

When, in 1980, the Legislature enacted the State Development Guide Plan (SDGP or Plan), "provid[ing] a statewide blueprint for future development," *id.* at 225, 336 A.2d 713, we embraced its use in exclusionary zoning cases. "[T]he SDGP discussed a variety of factors related to New Jersey's growth and development, including population distribution, natural resources, infrastructure, and the economy." *Van Dalen, supra,* 120 N.J. at 241, 576 A.2d 819 (citing *Mount Laurel II, supra,* 92 N.J. at 225, 456 A.2d 390). The maps developed as part of the Plan provided a framework for decision-making "[b]y clearly setting forth the state's policy as to where growth should be encouraged and discouraged." *Mount Laurel II, supra,* 92 N.J. at 226, 456 A.2d 390. Accordingly, we held that the *Mount Laurel* mandate should apply essentially in the areas marked for "growth" by the SDGP. *Id.* at 227, 456 A.2d 390. "We observed that the SDGP promoted sound statewide planning because it 'ensure[d] that the imposition of fair share obligations will coincide with the State's regional planning goals and objectives.' " *Van Dalen, supra,* 120 N.J. at 242, 576 A.2d 819 (quoting *Mount Laurel II, supra,* 92 N.J. at 225, 456 A.2d 390).

In respect of determining a municipality's fair share, and in the absence of legislative direction on this issue, *Mount Laurel II* established new procedures for the handling of exclusionary zoning litigation in the courts. We understood at that time that our failure to require the designation of a "region, its [present and prospective] need, and the fair share of the municipality" in each case had weakened the *Mount Laurel* mandate. *Mount Laurel II, supra,* 92 N.J. at 251, 456 A.2d 390. Consequently, we restricted those cases to three judges, each to be responsible for matters arising in his or her region of the State, with the expectation "that after several cases ha[d] been tried before each judge, a regional pattern for the area for which he or she is responsible [would] emerge." *Id.* at 254, 456 A.2d 390. We believed that the method for calculating a municipality's fair share would be consistent within the region, and that "[u]ltimately a regional pattern for the entire state [would] be established." *Ibid.* In rejecting our earlier approach, we stated: "What is required is the precision of a specific area and specific numbers. They are required not because we think scientific accuracy is possible, but because we believe the requirement is most likely to achieve the goals of *Mount Laurel.*" *Id.* at 257, 456 A.2d 390.

In *Mount Laurel II* we also provided guidance to municipalities regarding what it means to create a "realistic opportunity" for low and moderate income housing. We called for municipalities, "at the very least, [to] remove all municipally created barriers to the construction of their fair share of lower income housing." *Id.* at 258–59, 456 A.2d 390. But, because merely removing barriers to the construction of low income housing might not be sufficient to bring about that housing, we required affirmative measures "to make the opportunity real." *Id.* at 261, 456 A.2d 390. To induce builders to provide affordable housing we suggested "(1) encouraging or requiring the use of available state or federal housing subsidies, and (2) providing incentives for or requiring private developers to set aside a portion of their development for lower income housing." *Id.* at 262, 456 A.2d 390.

Our strong preference for legislative action enforcing the constitutional mandate could not have been more clearly stated than in *Mount Laurel II*, wherein we said that

> a brief reminder of the judicial role in this sensitive area is appropriate, since powerful reasons suggest, and we agree, that the matter is better left to the Legislature. We act first and foremost because the Constitution of our State requires protection of the interests involved and because the Legislature has not protected them. [*Id.* at 212, 456 A.2d 390.]

As discussed earlier, *supra* at 513, 803 A.2d at 59, the Legislature responded in July 1985 by enacting the FHA. Under that statute COAH was charged with, among other things, determining State housing regions, N.J.S.A. 52:27D–307a, estimating the State and regional present and prospective need for low and moderate income housing, *id.* at–307b, and adopting criteria and guidelines for a "[m]unicipal determination of its present and prospective fair share of [the region's] housing need." *Id.* at–307c(1).

* * *

The trial court found that Toll Brothers was entitled to a builder's remedy, concluding that "[t]here is no question that plaintiff-developer Toll Brothers has succeeded in this *Mount Laurel* litigation, and has proposed to develop its land in such a way as to produce a setaside of at least fifteen percent affordable units." *Id.* at 575, 697 A.2d 201. * * *

West Windsor asserts that Toll Brothers failed to satisfy the requirements of *Mount Laurel II* and therefore is not entitled to a builder's remedy. The Township claims that Toll Brothers (1) did not first seek approval for its development from the Township, thereby denying it the opportunity to hear the application; (2) should have been found unsuccessful at trial in challenging the Township's zoning ordinances; and (3) proposed a development that was not consonant with sound planning and did not provide a substantial number of affordable housing units.

Toll Brothers points to its success at trial in proving West Windsor's non-compliance with the Township's affordable housing obligations. Plaintiff cites as evidence of that success the numerous zoning amendments adopted by West Windsor during and after the commencement of this litigation. According to plaintiff, up to seventy percent of the fair share plan ultimately approved by the court was due to its lawsuit. In addition, plaintiff points to its success at trial in proving its claims regarding market demand, West Windsor's sewer policy, environmental limitations, and lot assemblage.

The courts below properly held that Toll Brothers satisfied the *Mount Laurel II* requirements for the grant of a builder's remedy. West Windsor has not established that Toll Brothers acted in bad faith. Both prior to commencing litigation and throughout the summer and fall of 1993, Toll Brothers communicated with the Planning Board, cautioning that zoning ordinances would have to be amended to implement its project and expressing its willingness to settle. Under the zoning in place at the time, Toll Brothers' plan necessarily would require variances. As the Appellate Division observed, the Toll Brothers site was not a good candidate for variances because of the "size of the property, its importance in the Township's compliance plan and the number of variances needed to build conventional single-family dwellings * * *." In those circumstances, it cannot be said that Toll Brothers acted in bad faith by not applying to the Planning Board.

We find that Toll Brothers succeeded at trial. West Windsor's claim that it was already compliant and had instituted amendments to its fair share plan at the time Toll Brothers initiated its lawsuit ignores the critical point—it was Toll Brothers that served as the catalyst for change and that successfully demonstrated West Windsor's *non*-compliance with its constitutional obligation. We also find that the Appellate Division properly rejected West Windsor's assertions that the Toll Brothers development does not accord with sound land use planning and does not provide a substantial number of affordable dwelling units. Indeed, Toll Brothers' development does not differ from development previously permitted except that a portion of the site will contain "marketable" detached single-family houses rather than "unmarketable" zero lot-line houses. In any case, the Toll Brothers development will produce affordable housing that, with a rental bonus, will satisfy 290 units of West Windsor's 688–unit obligation. Although as a general matter a twenty percent set-aside has been considered adequate, the trial court reasonably determined in this case that the fifteen percent set-aside was sufficient.

* * *

Concerned about "sound land use planning," we stressed that when formulating a specific builder's remedy, the trial courts should "make as much use as they can of the planning board's expertise and experience so that the proposed project is suitable for the municipality." *Id.* at 280, 456 A.2d 390. We further advised trial courts to take care to "guard the public interest" by ensuring that plaintiff-developers do not "abuse the *Mount Laurel* doctrine." *Id.* at 281, 456 A.2d 390.

* * *

Whether through COAH or as the result of litigation, since 1980 more than 28,855 affordable housing units have been constructed. *See* COAH Report at 4. That amount of housing is not likely to have a large impact on the municipal landscape. In contrast, as the dissent observes, *post* at 568, 803 A.2d at 93, there has been significant development statewide of market rate residential housing (more than 450,000 units since 1983). David N. Kinsey, *Reaffirm Mount Laurel*, N.J.L.J., Aug. 13, 2001, at 619. In West Windsor alone over 3,000 expensive single-family homes have been constructed on large lots during the 1980s and early 1990s when "only 139 low and moderate income units" were built. *West Windsor, supra*, 303 N.J.Super. at 531, 697 A.2d 201.

* * *

If municipalities believe, as the League of Municipalities contends, that the builder's remedy has become a developer's weapon, it is the municipalities that possess the shield of COAH-afforded protection to ward off builder's remedy litigation. Until practically all municipalities with a significant *Mount Laurel* obligation use the COAH process, however, the builder's remedy remains a necessary mechanism for the enforcement of constitutional values. Experience demonstrates that absent adequate enforcement, the *Mount Laurel* doctrine can deliver little more than a vague and hollow promise that a reasonable opportunity for the development of affordable housing will be provided. This case demonstrates that unfortunate fact.

The judgment of the Appellate Division is affirmed.

[Concurring and dissenting opinions omitted.]

Note

New Hampshire found the first Mt. Laurel case persuasive, and in Britton v. Town of Chester, 134 N.H. 434, 595 A.2d 492 (1991), the court struck down a two-acre minimum lot size restriction, and found that the ordinance had the effect of limiting the total area of the town available for affordable housing to 1.73% of the land in the town. The court said the ordinance violated the state zoning enabling legislation delegating zoning power for the "general welfare of the community." The court also approved of a builder's remedy as in Mt. Laurel II, but less drastic; the court ordered the town to revise its zoning ordinance, and face a builder's remedy if it did not do so. In addition to a builder's remedy, New Jersey courts have recognized other innovative remedies, zoning density bonuses, mandatory set asides, development fees linked to commercial development and fees in lieu of building inclusionary housing for the purpose of subsidizing low-cost housing. These were discussed in Holmdel Builders Association v. Township of Holmdel, 121 N.J. 550, 583 A.2d 277, certiorari denied sub. nom Morris Indus. Builders, Inc. v. Township of South Brunswick, 507 U.S. 1031, 113 S.Ct. 1848, 123 L.Ed.2d 472 (1993). In that case the court said:

> The [lower] court further concluded that ordinances requiring mandatory set-asides are valid only if accompanied by zoning incentives, such as a density bonus, that bear a reasonable relationship to the cost incurred in constructing the mandatory-set-aside housing. * * * The court ruled that a voluntary provision allowing a developer to choose between constructing affordable housing or paying an "in lieu" development fee into an affordable-housing trust fund is valid provided that the fee bears a reasonable relationship to the benefits conferred by the density bonus. * * *
>
> The Appellate Division ruled that the ordinances of the Townships of Chester and South Brunswick, which require payment of a mandatory development fee, were invalid because they imposed an unauthorized tax. Middletown Township's ordinance was held invalid because one section imposed a mandatory development fee, while another section required a mandatory set-aside without providing a compensating benefit. The court concluded that the voluntary nature of Holmdel's ordinance and its optional provision for an increase in density, giving the developer a compensating benefit, was facially valid; it remanded the *Holmdel* case for a plenary hearing with respect to the validity of Holmdel's ordinance as applied. The Appellate Division did not rule on intervenor Cherry Hill's ordinance.

* * *

This appeal raises two major substantive issues. One is whether there is statutory authority, derived from the FHA, the Municipal Land Use Law (MLUL), N.J.S.A. 40:55D-1 to-129, and the general police power of government, N.J.S.A. 40:48-2, that enables a municipality to impose affordable-housing development fees as a condition for development approval. That issue raises the related questions whether the development-fee ordinances constitute an impermissible taking of property or violate substantive due process or equal protection. The second major issue is whether affordable-housing development fees are an unconstitutional form of taxation. Finally, if these ordinances are invalid, the appeal presents the issue whether a trade organization has standing to seek a refund on behalf of its members.

* * *

In sum, the Townships of Chester and South Brunswick have enacted ordinances that impose a mandatory development fee on all new non-inclusionary developments as a condition for development approval. Their ordinances do not give developers a density bonus in exchange for the development fee. Middletown Township's ordinance imposes a mandatory development fee on all new commercial development as a condition for development approval. Non-inclusionary residential developers may choose between constructing the affordable housing or paying an in-lieu fee. Density bonuses do not accompany any of the options. Holmdel Township enacted an ordinance that gives developers a density bonus if they contribute to an affordable-housing trust fund. Cherry Hill Township's ordinance imposes a mandatory development fee on all new commercial developments and non-inclusionary residential developments of a sufficient size.

* * *

The principal mode of compliance suggested in *Mt. Laurel II* was mandatory set-asides. We flatly rejected claims that such inclusionary measures amount to a taking without just compensation and an impermissible socio-economic use of the zoning power, concluding that "the builder who undertakes a project that includes a mandatory set-aside voluntarily assumes the financial burden, if there is one, of that condition." * * * However, we never envisaged mandatory set-asides as the exclusive solution for the dearth of lower-income housing. In *Mt. Laurel II*, we encouraged municipalities "to create other devices and methods for meeting fair share obligations."

The solutions proposed in *Mt. Laurel II* to meet the critical shortage of affordable housing were strongly influenced by the Court's perception of the causes of that shortage. We noted that the flight of industry and commerce from urban to suburban areas is largely responsible for the social ill that the Mt. Laurel doctrine is intended to address. * * *

The phenomenon of unfettered non-residential development has exacerbated the need for lower-income housing, and has generated widespread efforts to link such needed residential development to non-residential development. Thus, nationwide, municipalities have attempted to shift the externalities of development to non-inclusionary developers. See, e.g., Alterman, "Evaluating Linkage and Beyond: Letting the Windfall Genie Out of the Exactions Bottle," 34 Wash. U.J. Urb. & Contemp. L. 3, 7 (1988).

The broad concept of linkage describes any of a wide range of municipal regulations that condition the grant of development approval on the payment of funds to help finance services and facilities needed as a result of development. In the context of developing affordable housing, linkage refers to any scheme that requires developers to mitigate the adverse effects of non-residential development upon the shortage of housing either indirectly, by contributing to an affordable-housing trust fund, or directly, by actually constructing affordable housing. See A. Mallach, Inclusionary Housing Programs: Policies and Practices (1985). The idea of linking community housing goals with non-residential real estate development has inspired new governmental efforts to address the lower-income housing crisis. See Smith, "From Subdivision Improvement Requirements to Community Benefit Assessments and Linkage Payments: A Brief History of Land Development Exactions," 50 Law & Contemp. Probs. 5 (1987); Gallogly, "Opening the Door for Boston's Poor: Will 'Linkage' Survive Judicial Review?", 14 Environmental Affairs 447 (1987).

Affordable-housing linkage ordinances are the most recent phenomenon in this area. See, e.g., Connors & High, "The Expanding Circle of Exactions: From Dedication to Linkage," 50 Law & Contemp. Probs. 69 (1987). Such ordinances link or couple the right to engage in non-residential development to the provision of affordable housing. The ordinances at issue in this appeal are all examples of linkage. Each requires certain developers to help finance the construction of affordable housing either as a condition for receiving permission to build or in order to obtain some type of density bonus. Only Holmdel's ordinance gives developers the option of actually constructing affordable-housing units.

The linkage trend has gained momentum during the past decade. See Symposium: Land–Use, Zoning, and Linkage Requirements Affecting the Pace of Urban Growth, 20 Urban Lawyer 513 (1988); Bauman & Ethier, "Development Exactions and Impact Fees: A Survey of American Practices," 50 Law & Contemp. Probs. 51 (1987). The fairness and legality of linkage have inspired much debate among legal scholars, the business community, and the judiciary. Proponents, including amicus curiae Princeton Township, forcefully argue that by attracting new residents to an area, commercial developments increase the need for housing in general and thus for affordable housing. To the extent that the additional need for housing is not met with increased supply, housing prices will be pushed upward, exacerbating both the need for, and unattainability of, lower-income housing. Therefore, it is appropriate for municipalities to charge commercial developers with a portion of the responsibility for creating more affordable-housing units. Gruen, "The Economics of Requiring Office–Space Development to Contribute to the Production and/or Rehabilitation of Housing," in D. Porter, Downtown Linkages (1985); cf. Surenian, "Mount Laurel II and the Fair Housing Act," 319–23 (NJICLE 1987) (advocating linkage fees in theory but cautioning against fees in practice due to "ineffectiveness of bureaucracy" and propensity of municipalities to evade fair-share obligations). In addition, linkage advocates stress the need to consider the effect of all development on the finite supply of land. Land must be viewed as an essential but exhaustible resource; any land that is developed for any purpose reduces the supply of land capable of being used to build affordable housing. See Major, "Linkage of Housing and Commercial Development: The Legal Issues," 15 Real Estate L.J. 328, 331 (1987). The scarcity of land as a resource bears on the opportunity and means to provide affordable housing. See *Hills Dev. Co. v. Bernards Township, supra,* 103 N.J. at 61, 510 A.2d 621; *Tocco v. New Jersey Council on Affordable Hous.,* 242 N.J.Super. 218, 221, 576 A.2d 328 (App.Div.), certif. denied, 122 N.J. 403, 585 A.2d 401 (1990).

Amicus curiae the Public Advocate argues that commercial developers ought not be exempt from the financial burden of Mt. Laurel compliance because their projects, like those of multifamily residential developers, consume land, water, and sewerage capacity that could otherwise be devoted to or held for the satisfaction of the municipality's lower-income-housing obligation. This Court has implicitly recognized that unrestrained nonresidential development can itself deepen the shortage of affordable housing. *Mt. Laurel II, supra,* 92 N.J. at 210 n. 5, 456 A.2d 390.

* * *

Plaintiffs argue that linkage fees constitute an impermissible form of exactions because they seek to require developers to provide for off-site public needs that have not been caused by their developments and furnish them no benefits. See *Divan Builders v. Planning Bd. of Wayne Township,* 66 N.J. 582, 598, 334 A.2d 30 (1975) (developer "could be compelled only to bear that portion of the cost [of off-site improvements] which bears a rational nexus to the needs created by and benefits conferred upon, the subdivision"); *New Jersey Builders Ass'n v. Mayor of Bernards Township,* 108 N.J. 223, 237, 528 A.2d 555 (1987) (municipal authority to charge developers limited "only to improvements the need for which arose as a direct consequence of the particular subdivision or development under review"); see also N.J.S.A. 40:55D–42 (developer can be required "to pay his pro rata share of the cost of providing only reasonable and necessary street improvements and water, sewerage and drainage facilities" located off-site). Because we have uniformly required a strong nexus between development and off-site improvements, plaintiffs contend that the development fees are prohibited. Although the Appellate Division found that N.J.S.A. 40:55D–42 does not specifically govern the development-fee ordinances at issue in this case, it determined that the development fees were variant forms of off-site exactions and invalid. 232 N.J.Super. at 198, 556 A.2d 1236.

In the context of off-site improvements, an exaction generally requires developers to supply or finance public facilities or amenities made necessary by proposed development. See Smith, supra, 50 Law & Contemp. Probs. 5. We have traditionally required a strong, almost but-for, causal nexus between off-site public facilities and private development in order to justify exactions. That nexus achieves two ends. First, it ensures that a developer pays for improvement that is necessitated by the development itself, *Divan Builders, supra,* 66 N.J. at 601, 334 A.2d 30, or is a "direct consequence" of the development, *New Jersey Builders Ass'n, supra,* 108 N.J. at 237, 528 A.2d 555. Second, it protects a developer from paying a disproportionate share of the cost of improvements that also benefit other persons. *Longridge Builders, Inc. v. Planning Bd. of Princeton Township,* 52 N.J. 348, 350, 245 A.2d 336 (1968); see also N.J.S.A. 40:56–27 (special assessments may be imposed on property owners only for unique or special benefits); *Meglino v. Township Comm. of the Township of Eagleswood*, 103 N.J. 144, 161, 510 A.2d 1134 (1986) (special assessments in excess of benefit to particular properties violate both enabling legislation and takings clause); *McNally v. Township of Teaneck, supra,* 75 N.J. 33, 43, 379 A.2d 446 (1977) (same).

Those commentators who believe that affordable-housing linkage measures are essentially a type of exaction for off-site improvements generally assume that a similar causal link is required and exists between new commercial space and an increased demand for lower-income housing. See Merriam & Andrews, "Defensible Linkage," 54 J. Am. Plan. A. 199 (1988); Bosselman & Stroud, "Mandatory Tithes: The Legality of Land Development Linkage," 17 Land Use and Envtl. L. Rev. 151 (1986). We do not believe, however, that the development-fee ordinances before us must be founded on a stringent nexus between commercial construction and the need for affordable housing. We find a sound basis to support a legislative judgment that there is a reasonable relationship between unrestrained nonresidential development and the need for affordable residential development. We do not equate such a reasonable relationship with the strict rational-nexus standard that demands a but-for causal connection or direct consequential relationship between the private activity that gives rise to the exaction and the public activity to which it is applied. Rather, the relationship is to be founded on the actual, albeit indirect and general, impact that such nonresidential development has on both the need for lower-income residential development and on the opportunity and capacity of municipalities to meet that need. Inclusionary zoning itself is based on that relationship. Such zoning measures are designed to reach all land development, to address the potential diminishment of affordable housing, and to encourage within the municipality, the region, and the state the creation of affordable housing. Such governmental measures are thus not analogous to specific off-site infrastructure improvements occasioned by a particular development.

We conclude that the rational-nexus test is not apposite in determining the validity of inclusionary zoning devices generally or of affordable-housing development fees in particular. * * *

The claims based on alleged violations of due process and equal protection standards by development-fee ordinances do not project new or additional substantive considerations [because plaintiffs do not allege that they are a member of a suspect class.] * * *

Further, central to those several claims is the allegation that development fees are confiscatory. The Appellate Division, believing that the fees were unfair or confiscatory, concluded that those constitutional violations would be rectified if developers received compensatory benefits. 232 N.J.Super. at 201, 556 A.2d 1236.

In response to similar claims in *Mt. Laurel II* that mandatory set-asides were confiscatory, this Court stated that "the builder who undertakes a project that includes a mandatory set-aside voluntarily assumes the financial burden, if there is any, of that condition." 92 N.J. at 267 n.

30, 456 A.2d 390. A developer may be made to bear the economic burdens of providing affordable housing so long as those burdens are not excessive and the project remains profitable. See id. at 279 n. 37, 456 A.2d 390 (a twenty-percent set-aside may be a "reasonable minimum"); N.J.A.C. 5:92–8.4(c); see also *In re Egg Harbor Assocs., supra*, 94 N.J. at 358, 464 A.2d 1115 (specific plan for inclusionary zoning involving a 20% set-aside is "neither arbitrary nor unreasonable," nor an unconstitutional taking). In *Mt. Laurel II*, we suggested that "[w]here practical, a municipality should use mandatory set-asides even where [federal] subsidies are not available," 92 N.J. at 268, 456 A.2d 390, and that mandatory set-asides would be legitimate as long as developers were assured "an adequate return on their investments," ibid.; no density bonuses, compensatory benefits, or subsidies were specifically required.

* * *

Plaintiffs' remaining major contention is that the affordable-housing development fees are a form of taxation and, as such, exceed delegated municipal revenue-raising authority in violation of the state constitutional command that all property taxes be levied uniformly. N.J. Const. of 1947 art. VIII, § 1, para. 1.

* * *

In *Mt. Laurel II*, however, we determined that mandatory set-asides as a form of inclusionary zoning were not analogous to a tax. We viewed them as legitimate regulatory measures suitably addressed to the broad goals of zoning. Development fees, to reiterate, perform an identical function.

* * *

Although we do not regard development fees as a form of taxation, we stress that mandatory set-asides do not transgress the uniformity provision by imposing the responsibility of addressing the municipality's affordable-housing problems on developers of residential property. Ordinances that impose that responsibility on developers of commercial property and non-inclusionary residential property stand on the same footing.

In sum, because the development fees are a form of inclusionary zoning and similar to other land-use and related exactions, they are regulatory measures, not taxes.

* * *

Notes

1. For a general view of the problems discussed in the Holmdel case, see Johnston, Schwartz, Wandeseforde–Smith & Caplan, Selling Zoning: Do Density Bonus Incentives for Moderate–Cost Housing Work?, 36 Wash. U.J.Urb. & Contemp.L. 45 (1989). In Villager Pond, Inc. v. Town of Darien, 56 F.3d 375 (2d Cir.1995) the developer of a condominium sued the town for damages in regard to an "exaction" of two units in the development to be conveyed to the town for low and moderate income people. The court rejected the argument that the developer had a property interest in receiving

his zoning permits under the Dolan v. City of Tigard case, but remanded to the trial court for a determination of the developer's property interest.

2. The issue of solving shortages of low cost housing through the use of mandatory set asides has stirred a great deal of debate. The next two cases illustrate both sides of the issue:

HOME BUILDERS ASSOCIATION OF NORTHERN CALIFORNIA v. CITY OF NAPA
California Court of Appeal, First District, Division 5, 2001.
90 Cal.App.4th 188, 108 Cal.Rptr.2d 60.

JONES, P.J.

* * *

City, like many other localities in California, has a shortage of affordable housing. This shortage has negative consequences for all of City's population, but causes particularly severe problems for those on the lower end of the economic spectrum. Manual laborers, some of whom work in the region's wine or leisure industries, are forced to live in crowded, substandard housing. There is a large, and growing population of homeless, including many families and teenagers. Workers from low income families increasingly are forced to live greater distances from their places of employment, which causes increased traffic congestion and pollution.

City formed the Napa Affordable Housing Task Force to address these problems. The task force was a broad based community group that included representatives from non-profit agencies, environmental groups, religious institutions, local industries, for-profit developers, and the local chamber of commerce. The purpose of the task force was to "study the issues surrounding affordable housing in the City of Napa and * * * make recommendations to the Housing Authority Commission."

The task force studied housing issues for several months. It formed subcommittees, conducted public hearings, and evaluated affordable housing solutions that had been enacted by other communities. Ultimately the task force recommended that City enact an inclusionary housing ordinance modeled after one that had been enacted by Napa county.

City responded by enacting the inclusionary zoning ordinance that is at issue in the present appeal. The ordinance applies to all development in the city, including residential and non-residential.

The primary mandate imposed by the ordinance on residential developers is a requirement that ten percent of all newly constructed units must be "affordable" as that term is defined. The ordinance offers developers two alternatives. First, developers of single-family units may, at their option, satisfy the so called inclusionary requirement through an "alternative equivalent proposal" such as a dedication of land, or the construction of affordable units on another site. Developers of multi-family units may also satisfy the 10 percent requirement through an "alternative equivalent proposal" if the City Council, in its sole discretion, determines that the proposed alternative results in affordable housing opportunities equal to or greater than those created by the basic inclusionary requirement.

As a second alternative, a residential developer may choose to satisfy the inclusionary requirement by paying an in-lieu fee. Developers of single-family units may choose this option by right, while developers of multi-family units are permitted this option if the City Council, again in its sole discretion, approves. All fees generated through this option are deposited into a housing trust fund, and may only be used to increase and improve the supply of affordable housing in City.

Developments that include affordable housing are eligible for a variety of benefits including expedited processing, fee deferrals, loans or grants, and density bonuses that allow more intensive development than otherwise would be allowed. In addition, the ordinance permits a developer to appeal for a reduction, adjustment, or *complete waiver* of obligations under the ordinance "based upon the absence of any reasonable relationship or nexus between the impact of the development and ... the inclusionary requirement."

HBA is a non-profit corporation and association of builders, contractors, and related trades and professionals involved in the residential construction industry. In September 1999, HBA filed a complaint against City seeking to have the inclusionary zoning ordinance declared facially invalid. * * *

HBA contends that City's inclusionary zoning ordinance is facially invalid because it violates the taking clauses of the Federal and State Constitutions.

* * *

Here, City's inclusionary zoning ordinance imposes significant burdens on those who wish to develop their property. However the ordinance also provides significant benefits to those who comply with its terms. Developments that include affordable housing are eligible for expedited processing, fee deferrals, loans or grants, and density bonuses. More critically, the ordinance permits a developer to appeal for a reduction, adjustment, or *complete waiver* of the ordinance's requirements. Since City has the ability to waive the requirements imposed by the ordinance, the ordinance cannot and does not, on its face, result in a taking.

HBA contends the ordinance's waiver clause does not preclude a facial challenge because that clause improperly places the burden on the developer to prove that a waiver would be appropriate when the City has not established a justification for the exactions mandated by the ordinance. According to HBA, allocating the burden in this way is inconsistent with *Dolan v. City of Tigard* (1994) 512 U.S. 374, 391, footnote 8,

114 S.Ct. 2309, 129 L.Ed.2d 304. HBA misreads *Dolan.* Quite to the contrary, the Supreme Court stated in *Dolan,* that when evaluating the validity of generally applicable zoning regulations, it is appropriate to place the burden on the party who is challenging the regulation. (*Ibid.*) As we will discuss below, City's inclusionary zoning ordinance is a generally applicable legislative enactment rather than an individualized assessment imposed as a condition of development. Thus, the burden shifting standard described in *Dolan* does not apply.

* * *

Here, HBA contends that City's inclusionary zoning ordinance * * * is invalid because it fails to substantially advance legitimate state interests. We are unpersuaded.

First, we have no doubt that creating affordable housing for low and moderate income families is a legitimate state interest. Our Supreme Court has said that the "assistance of moderate-income households with their housing needs is recognized in this state as a legitimate governmental purpose." (*Santa Monica Beach, Ltd. v. Superior Court* (1999) 19 Cal.4th 952, 970, 81 Cal.Rptr.2d 93, 968 P.2d 993.) This conclusion is consistent with repeated pronouncements from the state Legislature which has declared that "the development of a sufficient supply of housing to meet the needs of *all Californians* is a matter of statewide concern," (Gov.Code, § 65913.9, emphasis added) and that local governments have "a responsibility to use the powers vested in them to facilitate the improvement and development of housing to make adequate provision for the housing needs of *all economic segments of the community.*" (Gov.Code, § 65580, subd. (d), emphasis added.) Indeed, Witkin lists 12 separate statutes that are "designed to stimulate the construction of low and moderate income housing by the private sector." (4 Witkin, Summary of Cal. Law (9th ed. 1987) Real Property § 54, p. 275; *id.* (2000 Supp.) § 54, p. 134.)

Second, it is beyond question that City's inclusionary zoning ordinance will "substantially advance" the important governmental interest of providing affordable housing for low and moderate income families. By requiring developers in City to create a modest amount of affordable housing (or to comply with one of the alternatives) the ordinance will necessarily increase the supply of affordable housing. We conclude City's ordinance "substantially advance[s] legitimate state interests." (*Agins v. Tiburon, supra,* 447 U.S. at p. 260, 100 S.Ct. 2138.)

HBA's principal constitutional claim is that City's ordinance is invalid under *Nollan v. California Coastal Comm'n* (1987) 483 U.S. 825, 107 S.Ct. 3141, 97 L.Ed.2d 677, and *Dolan v. City of Tigard, supra,* 512 U.S. 374, 114 S.Ct. 2309, 129 L.Ed.2d 304.

In *Nollan* the court discussed the "substantially advance" test in the context of a governmental requirement that appellant property owners dedicate a portion of their beachfront property to the public as a condition for obtaining a rebuilding permit. In the course of its discussion, the court said there must be an "essential nexus" between a condition imposed on the use of land, and the impacts caused by the proposed use. (*Nollan v. California Coastal Comm'n, supra,* 483 U.S. at p. 837, 107 S.Ct. 3141.)

Dolan also involved dedications of property that were a condition for granting a development permit. There the court said that a "rough proportionality" standard "best encapsulates what we hold to be the requirement of the Fifth Amendment. No precise mathematical calculation is required, but the city must make some sort of individualized determination that the required dedication is related both in nature and extent to the impact of the proposed development." (*Dolan v. City of Tigard, supra,* 512 U.S. at p. 391, 114 S.Ct. 2309.)

HBA contends City's ordinance is invalid under *Nollan* and *Dolan* because there is no "essential nexus" or "rough proportionality" between the exaction required by the ordinance, and the impacts caused by development of property.

We reject this argument because *Nollan* and *Dolan* are inapplicable under the facts of this case. "[T]he intermediate standard of judicial scrutiny formulated by the high court in *Nollan* and *Dolan* is intended to address ... land use 'bargains' between property owners and regulatory bodies—those in which the local government conditions permit approval for a given use on the owner's surrender of benefits which *purportedly* offset the impact of the proposed development. It is in this paradigmatic permit context—where the individual property owner-developer seeks to negotiate approval of a planned development—that the combined *Nollan* and *Dolan* test quintessentially applies." (*Ehrlich v. City of Culver City* (1996) 12 Cal.4th 854, 868, 50 Cal.Rptr.2d 242, 911 P.2d 429.) "But a different standard of scrutiny [applies] to development fees that are generally applicable through legislative action 'because the heightened risk of the "extortionate" use of the police power to exact unconstitutional conditions is not present.' " (*Santa Monica Beach, Ltd. v. Superior Court, supra,* 19 Cal.4th at p. 966, 81 Cal.Rptr.2d 93, 968 P.2d 993, quoting *Ehrlich v. City of Culver City, supra,* 12 Cal.4th at p. 876, 50 Cal.Rptr.2d 242, 911 P.2d 429.) "[I]ndividualized development fees warrant a type of review akin to the conditional conveyances at issue in *Nollan* and *Dolan,* whereas generally applicable development fees warrant the more deferential review that the *Dolan* court recognized is generally accorded to legislative determinations." (*Santa Monica Beach, Ltd. v. Superior Court, supra,* 19 Cal.4th at pp. 966–967, 81 Cal.Rptr.2d 93, 968 P.2d 993.) The justification for these varying levels of scrutiny is founded in the nature of the two types of exactions. "It is one thing for courts to make a government agency adhere to its own justification for requiring the dedication of a particular portion of property as a condition of development; such adherence safeguards against the possibility that the justification is merely a pretext for taking the property without paying compensation * * *. But it is another thing for courts to require that a complex, generally applicable piece of economic legislation that will have many effects on many different persons and entities accomplish precisely the goals stated in a legislative preamble in order to preserve its constitutionality." (*Santa Monica Beach, Ltd. v. Superior Court, supra,* 19 Cal.4th at p. 972, 81 Cal.Rptr.2d 93, 968 P.2d 993.)

Here, we are not called upon to determine the validity of a particular land use bargain between a governmental agency and a person who wants to develop his or her land. Instead we are faced with a facial challenge to economic legislation that is generally applicable to *all* development in City. We conclude the heightened standard of review described in *Nollan* and *Dolan* is inapplicable under these facts.

* * *

HBA also contends that the inclusionary zoning ordinance is invalid because the lack of housing for low and moderate income families in City is the product of City's own prior restrictive land use policies.

HBA has not cited any authority to support the proposition that a zoning ordinance which tries to solve problems caused by prior legislative decisions is invalid, and case law is directly to the contrary. For example, in *Penn Central Transp. Co. v. New York City* (1978) 438 U.S. 104, the Supreme Court ruled that New York could enact a landmark preservation law that was designed to mitigate the effects of prior policies that permitted "large numbers of historic structures, landmarks, and areas" to be destroyed. (*Id.* at p. 108.) If New York can enact a landmark preservation law to remedy a shortage of historic buildings created by its prior policies, City can enact an inclusionary zoning ordinance even if its prior policies contributed to a scarcity of available land and a shortage of affordable housing.

HBA contends the inclusionary zoning ordinance is facially invalid under the due process clause of the Federal Constitution because it "requires property owners who develop residential housing to sell or rent 10% of their units at prices or rents that are based entirely upon certain fixed percentages of the income levels of lower and very low-income households." Imposing such a requirement violates the due process clause, HBA argues, because "the inclusionary zoning law provides no mechanism to make a fair return for property owners who are forced to sell or rent units at an amount unrelated to market prices."

We doubt seriously that HBA is entitled to a "fair return" under the due process clause. The "fair return" standard is commonly used to evaluate restrictions placed on historically regulated industries such as railroads and public utilities. (See, e.g., *Power Comm'n v. Pipeline Co.* (1942) 315 U.S. 575.) It has also been used to evaluate rent control ordinances. (See e.g. *Fisher v. City of Berkeley* (1984) 37 Cal.3d 644, 679.) However HBA has not cited, and we are not aware of, any case that holds a housing developer is entitled to *"fair return" on his or her investment.*

However we need not base our decision on this ground. First, it is not literally correct to say that City's ordinance "requires property owners who develop residential housing to sell or rent 10% of their units [to low income individuals]." Under the ordinance, any person who does not want to sell or rent a portion of his or her housing unites to low income individuals may choose one of the alternatives, such as donating vacant land or paying an in-lieu fee. Thus HBA's argument is based on an incorrect premise.

Second, and more importantly, HBA's facial due process challenge must necessarily fail. As we have said, " 'A claim that a regulation is *facially* invalid is only tenable if the terms of the regulation will not permit those who administer it to avoid an unconstitutional *application* to the complaining parties.' " (*San Mateo County Coastal Landowners' Assn. v. County of San Mateo, supra,* 38 Cal.App.4th at p. 547, internal citation omitted.) When an ordinance contains provision that allow for administrative relief, we must presume the implementing authorities will exercise their authority in conformity with the Constitution. (See *Fisher v. City of Berkeley, supra,* 37 Cal.3d at p. 684.)

Here, as we have noted, City's ordinance includes a clause that allows city officials to reduce, modify or waive the requirements contained in the ordinance "based upon the absence of any reasonable relationship or nexus between the impact of the development and * * * the inclusionary requirement." Since City has the authority to completely waive a developer's obligations, a facial challenge under the due process clause must necessarily fail.

HBA contends the waiver clause does not preclude a facial challenge because it does not state expressly that a waiver may be granted based on a lack of a "fair return." However the power of an agency to make adjustments to guarantee a fair return is "not limited to those literally granted by the ordinance * * *." (*City of Berkeley v. City of Berkeley Rent Stabilization Bd.* (1994) 27 Cal.App.4th 951, 962.) When this standard is not expressly stated, it is "present by implication." (*Ibid.*)

The judgment is affirmed.

BOARD OF SUPERVISORS OF FAIRFAX COUNTY v. DeGROFF ENTERPRISES, INC.

Supreme Court of Virginia, 1973.
214 Va. 235, 198 S.E.2d 600.

HARMAN, JUSTICE.

The question presented by this appeal is the validity of amendment 156 (the amendment) to the Fairfax County Zoning Ordinance (ordinance) which became effective on September 1, 1971.

When the amendment, which consists of 39 typewritten pages, is stripped of detail, it requires the developer of fifty or more dwelling units in five zoning districts (RT–5, RTC–5, RT–10, RTC–10 and RM–2G) to commit himself, before rezoning or site plan approval to build at least 15% of these dwelling units as low and moderate income housing within the definitions promulgated from time to time by the Fairfax County

Housing and Redevelopment Authority (FCHRA) and the United States Department of Housing and Urban Development (HUD). Under the amendment the housing units designated as low and moderate income units can be sold or rented only to persons of low and moderate income as defined by FCRHA and HUD regulations and the sale or rental price for such units cannot exceed the amount established as price guidelines by those agencies.

After a lengthy hearing the trial court found the amendment invalid on the grounds that the Board of Supervisors exceeded its authority under the zoning enabling act, Code § 15.1–486 et seq., that the amendment constituted an improper delegation of legislative authority, and that the amendment was arbitrary and capricious.

The hearing before the trial court clearly demonstrated both a demand and an urgent need for housing units for low and moderate income families in Fairfax County. Indeed, the uncontroverted evidence indicates that the need then existed there for 10,500 such dwelling units.

The Board of Supervisors of Fairfax County (Board) on the basis of this need, would have us hold the amendment valid on the ground that it "facilitates 'creation of a convenient * * * and harmonious community' and is essential to the 'health, safety, * * * [and] general welfare of the public.' " In support of this proposition the Board cites Code § 15.1–489 in which these purposes for zoning ordinances are enumerated.

That a problem exists in the need for low and moderate income housing has been recognized for many years. In 1937, in an effort to help meet this need, the Congress passed the United States Housing Act, Act of Sept. 1, 1937, c. 896, 50 Stat. 888.

The following year the General Assembly, to implement the low income housing provisions of this federal act, passed the Housing Authority Law, Acts of Assembly, 1938, c. 310, which now appears, as amended, as Code § 36–1 et seq. In *Mumpower v. Housing Authority*, 176 Va. 426, 11 S.E.2d 732 (1940), we considered the Housing Authorities Law and found it to be a constitutionally valid exercise of the police power. In doing so we recognized that slum eradication and the erection of low income public housing was "a matter of vital concern to the public and to the State." Id. at 437, 11 S.E.2d at 735.

Today, as a part of the nationwide effort to solve the housing problem upon which billions of dollars of public funds have been expended, redevelopment and housing authorities exist in most, if not all, of the urban areas of the Commonwealth and in many of the non-urban areas.

Thus it would appear that providing low and moderate income housing serves a legitimate public purpose. The question, then, becomes whether this public purpose can be accomplished by the amendment to the ordinance which rests upon the police power.

The principles of zoning law are well settled in Virginia. This court, speaking through Mr. Justice I'Anson, in *Board of Supervisors v. Carper*,

200 Va. 653, 107 S.E.2d 390 (1959), summarized these established principles as follows:

"The general principles applicable to a judicial review of the validity of zoning ordinances are well settled. The legislative branch of a local government in the exercise of its police power has wide discretion in the enactment and amendment of zoning ordinances. Its action is presumed to be valid so long as it is not unreasonable and arbitrary. The burden of proof is on him who assails it to prove that it is clearly unreasonable, arbitrary or capricious, and that it bears no reasonable or substantial relation to the public health, safety, morals, or general welfare. The court will not substitute its judgment for that of a legislative body, and if the reasonableness of a zoning ordinance is fairly debatable it must be sustained. * * * The exercise of the police power is subject to the constitutional guarantee that no property shall be taken without due process of law and where the police power conflicts with the Constitution the latter is supreme, but courts will not restrain the exercise of such power except when the conflict is clear." *West Bros. Brick Co. v. City of Alexandria, supra,* 169 Va. at page 281, 192 S.E. at page 885.

" * * * '[T]he purpose of zoning is in general twofold: to preserve the existing character of an area by excluding prejudicial uses, and to provide for the development of the several areas in a manner consistent with the uses for which they are suited. The regulations should be related to the character of the district which they affect; and should be designed to serve the welfare of those who own and occupy land in those districts.' See also I Yokley, Zoning Law and Practice, § 10, pp. 12, 13." 200 Va. at 660, 107 S.E.2d at 395.

In *Carper* we held invalid a zoning ordinance which had as its purpose the exclusion of low and middle income groups from the western areas of Fairfax County. The effect of this decision is to prohibit socio-economic zoning. We conclude that the legislative intent was to permit localities to enact only traditional zoning ordinances directed to physical characteristics and having the purpose neither to include nor exclude any particular socio-economic group.

* * *

More recently in *Fairfax County v. Columbia Pike Ltd.*, 213 Va. 437, 192 S.E.2d 778 (1972), we followed our earlier holding in *Mooreland v. Young*, 197 Va. 771, 91 S.E.2d 438 (1956), that the zoning enabling act does not authorize the governing body of a county to control compensation for the use of lands or the improvements thereon.

When the amendment is measured by these legal standards, we find it deficient.

The amendment, in establishing maximum rental and sale prices for 15% of the units in the development, exceeds the authority granted by the enabling act to the local governing body because it is socio-economic zoning and attempts to control the compensation for the use of land and the improvements thereon.

Of greater importance, however, is that the amendment requires the developer or owner to rent or sell 15% of the dwelling units in the development to persons of low or moderate income at rental or sale prices not fixed by a free market. Such a scheme violates the guarantee set forth in Section 11 of Article 1 of the Constitution of Virginia, 1971, that no property will be taken or damaged for public purposes without just compensation.

Affirmed.

Notes

1. In the Mt. Laurel II case the court specifically rejected the reasoning of the Virginia court. Do you see a parallel between mandatory set-asides in the housing field and the dispute over affirmative action in the employment and college admission areas? What do you think of the California court's reasoning?

2. The Napa case discusses some California statutes that encourage development of low cost housing. Some other states also have statutory mandates. In Board of Appeals of Hanover v. Housing Appeals Committee in Dept. of Community Affairs, 363 Mass. 339, 294 N.E.2d 393 (1973) the Supreme Judicial Court of Massachusetts upheld the validity of a Massachusetts statute, G.L. c. 40B, §§ 20–23, inserted by St.1969, c. 774, § 1 (c. 774). The statute allows the state Department of Community Affairs to override local zoning ordinances that preclude the construction and location of low cost housing. One interesting issue discussed by the court dealt with spot zoning:

> The amici curiae argue that when the committee exercises its power to override local zoning by-laws deemed inconsistent with local needs, it engages in illegal spot zoning because its act singles out a particular parcel of property in a community for treatment different from that given to similar surrounding land indistinguishable from it in character.
>
> However, we have frequently held that a spot zoning violation involves more than a mere finding that a parcel of property is singled out for less restrictive treatment than that of surrounding land of a similar character. If we accepted the amici curiae's test for spot zoning, the State could never exercise its undoubted power to override local zoning ordinances or by-laws for legitimate public purposes because there would always be a disparity of treatment between the area where the local ordinance or by-law is ignored and the rest of that zoning area where it is enforced. Moreover, zoning variances and amendments would also be subject to serious challenge on spot zoning grounds if the test were merely one of dissimilar treatment of similar parcels of property.
>
> * * * Chapter 774 reflects the Legislature's judgment that the special treatment accorded to a site proposed for the construction of low and moderate income housing and necessitated by exclusionary zoning practices serves the general welfare by promoting the construction of badly needed housing units in the suburbs. The statute's "consistent

with local needs" standard and its provisions for judicial review of the board's and committee's decisions insure that special treatment will be allowed only when it serves the public interest. Thus, we hold that the exercise of c. 774's power to override local zoning by-laws and ordinances deemed inconsistent with local needs does not constitute spot zoning.

Id., at 363 Mass. 360–63, 294 N.E.2d at 410–411.

3. In 1975, Massachusetts amended its enabling act to provide, *inter alia,* "zoning ordinances or by-laws may also provide for special permits authorizing increases in the permissible density of population or intensity of a particular use in a proposed development; provided that the petitioner or applicant shall, as a condition for the grant of said permit, provide certain open space, housing for persons of low or moderate income, traffic or pedestrian improvements, or other amenities." See Iodice v. City of Newton, 397 Mass. 329, 491 N.E.2d 618 (1986); Bonan v. City of Boston, 398 Mass. 315, 496 N.E.2d 640 (1986); Zoning Bd. of Appeals of Greenfield v. Housing Appeals Comm., 15 Mass.App.Ct. 553, 446 N.E.2d 748 (1983).

4. Also see Cal.Govt.Code § 65580 et seq., a 1980 statute that deals with planning for the housing needs of the community and the region, including the fair share concept. Of special interest is § 65589 which states, in part: "Nothing in this article shall require a city * * * to * * * expend local revenues for the construction of housing, housing subsidies, or land acquisition." Other relevant California statutes to consider are Cal. Govt.Code § 65302.8, § 65863.6, § 65913.1, § 65913.2, and § 66412.2.

5. Rhode Island has amended its zoning enabling legislation to provide, in R.I. Gen. L. § 45–24–30, that the purposes of zoning ordinances include:

* * *

(8) Promoting a balance of housing choices, for all income levels and groups, to assure the health, safety and welfare of all citizens and their rights to affordable, accessible, safe and sanitary housing.

(9) Providing opportunities for the establishment of low and moderate income housing.

* * *

(16) Providing opportunities for reasonable accommodations in order to comply with the Rhode Island Fair Housing Practices Act, the United States Fair Housing Amendments Act of 1988 (FHAA), the Rhode Island Civil Rights of Individuals with Handicaps Act, and the Americans with Disabilities Act of 1990 (ADA).

6. Also see Floyd v. New York State Urban Development Corp., 41 A.D.2d 395, 343 N.Y.S.2d 493 (1973), affirmed 33 N.Y.2d 1, 347 N.Y.S.2d 161, 300 N.E.2d 704 (1973), upholding the power of the Urban Development Corporation, a public entity, to override the zoning regulations of local municipalities. See Chapter VI and the discussion of the Affordable Housing Appeals Act.

7. Not very many states have enacted legislation allowing regional or state agencies to override local zoning, probably for the reason that local

municipal control of zoning is so entrenched and agencies like those created in in Massachusettsand elsewhere smack of regional government, a highly controversial political notion.

SECTION 2. DISCRIMINATION AGAINST PARTICULAR USES

A. INDUSTRIAL USES

GENERAL BATTERY CORP. v. ZONING HEARING BD. OF ALSACE TWP.
Commonwealth Court of Pennsylvania, 1977.
29 Pa.Cmwlth. 498, 371 A.2d 1030.

MENCER, JUDGE.

Nestled in the picturesque setting of a well-known valley, Alsace Township, Berks County, is in many ways removed from the metropolitan activities of the nearby City of Reading. The township's inhabitants enjoy a harmonious mix of rural and suburban uses in their "bedroom community" close to the city. It is not surprising, then, that they seek to perpetuate their township's seclusion. One method they have chosen is zoning: The Alsace Township zoning ordinance makes no provision for industry or industry-related uses anywhere in the township.

This ordinance has been attacked by General Battery Corporation (General Battery). General Battery, which generates waste as an incident of its lead-smelting operations in Muhlenberg Township, was denied a permit to construct waste disposal facilities on land it owned in an R–2 rural farm zone of Alsace Township. It appealed to the Alsace Township Zoning Hearing Board (Board), contending, *inter alia,* that the zoning ordinance embodied an unreasonable exercise of police power. The Board disagreed, and General Battery appealed to the Court of Common Pleas of Berks County. Without taking additional evidence, the court held the ordinance invalid. The Alsace Township Board of Supervisors appealed to this Court.

* * *

Initially, we note that, while a party challenging a zoning ordinance must overcome its presumed validity, the presumption is overcome by showing a total exclusion of an otherwise legitimate use. *Appeal of Green & White Copter, Inc.*, 25 Pa.Cmwlth. 445, 360 A.2d 283 (1976). Within this context, a legitimate use is one which is not so particularly objectionable and undesirable that its prohibition appears prima facie to be designed to protect the public interest. *Beaver Gasoline Company v. Osborne Borough,* 445 Pa. 571, 285 A.2d 501 (1971); *Green & White Copter,* supra; see, *Exton Quarries,* supra note 1. Thus, an activity "generally known to give off noxious odors, disturb the tranquility of a large area by making loud noises, have the obvious potential of poisoning the air or the water of the area, or similarly have clearly deleterious effects upon the general public" is not a legitimate use of land under this rule.

Once the presumption of validity is overcome, the burden of proof shifts to the municipality to establish the legitimacy of the prohibition by evidence establishing what interest is sought to be protected. *Beaver,* supra.

We hold that the total exclusion of industrial waste disposal facilities in Alsace Township shifts the burden of proof to the municipality. In this connection, we note the comprehensive role of an active and proficient department of this Commonwealth which has been entrusted with the duty of controlling and supervising the type of activity with which we are concerned. Under the authority of the Pennsylvania Solid Waste Management Act, the Pennsylvania Department of Environmental Resources is given broad power to regulate waste disposal systems. In addition, the Department is authorized to use a wide variety of methods to protect and preserve the quality of our water. Under these circumstances, we conclude that waste disposal facilities do not have the obvious potential for polluting air or water or otherwise creating uncontrollable health or safety hazards. Nor do common knowledge and experience suggest other clearly deleterious effects which would inevitably be visited upon the public in general. We therefore conclude that waste disposal facilities under the diligent control of the Department do not embody a use, the total exclusion of which appears prima facie to be designed to protect the public health, safety and welfare. Concomitantly, the burden shifts to Alsace Township to justify the exclusionary zoning ordinance.

We hold that Alsace Township has not carried its burden. In particular, we are unpersuaded that the township has established that by excluding the activity in issue it endeavored to protect those public interests which zoning statutes permit municipalities to protect. Before the Board, the township sought by cross-examination of General Battery's witnesses to establish that the specific disposal facility contemplated, a landfill with a liner and a system of tanks designed to protect against the possible leaching into the soil of compounds produced in General Battery's lead-smelting operations, might have detrimental effects. However, this evidence, dealing as it does with the application of the ordinance to General Battery's proposed use of its land, is not dispositive on the issue of the ordinance's facial invalidity. Obviously, a zoning ordinance may be invalid as a whole, although not in relation to specific property. *Exton Quarries,* supra note 1; accord, *Girsh Appeal,* supra note 1. We conclude that whether a possibility exists that General Battery's activity might have detrimental effects does not justify a total exclusion of all industrial waste disposal facilities.

Nor can we consider as other than specious the township's attitude that the prohibition protects township inhabitants from industrial waste generated in another municipality. Clearly, *where* the waste is generated has very little bearing on whether its disposal is harmful. See *Lutz v. Armour,* 395 Pa. 576, 151 A.2d 108 (1959). Having been unable to conclude that whatever effects might issue from waste disposal operations would be so prejudicial to the public health, safety and welfare as to support the total exclusion of those facilities, we decline to derive such prejudice from the origin of the waste to be disposed of.

We therefore hold that the Board committed an error of law when it concluded that Alsace Township had established a public interest in support of its total exclusion of industrial waste disposal facilities. We agree with the court below that the zoning ordinance is invalid.

Order affirmed.

Notes

1. In Beaver Gasoline Co. v. Zoning Hearing Board of Borough of Osborne, 445 Pa. 571, 285 A.2d 501 (1971), the court was confronted with an ordinance that created two residential zones and one commercial zone. The commercial zone specifically excluded gasoline service stations, resulting in a total ban on such uses in the borough. The court dealt with the problem of the opponent of a zoning classification having the burden of proof to establish invalidity by stating:

> In situations involving the total prohibition of otherwise legitimate land uses, which, by common experience, appear to be as innocuous as the land use here contested, the applicant has met his burden of overcoming the presumption of constitutionality by showing the total ban. Thereafter, if the municipality is to sustain the validity of the ban, it must present evidence to establish the public purpose served by the regulation. It is not inconceivable, of course, that the municipality could establish the validity of a total ban, but it is its responsibility to do so. In the instant case, the municipality offered no evidence to establish the validity of the regulation and has, consequently failed to show that the regulation bears a relationship to the public health, safety, morals and general welfare.

In Lambros, Inc. v. Town of Ocean Ridge, Fla., 392 So.2d 993 (Fla.App. 1981), the court rejected the Pennsylvania rule and held that the burden of proof remained with the property owner to establish that the ordinance (excluding all commercial use after an amortization period) was arbitrary.

Pennsylvania courts have regularly taken the position that the zoning power does not usually permit total exclusion of a particular use. In addition to the principal case and Beaver Gasoline, see Exton Quarries, Inc. v. Zoning Board of Adjustment, 425 Pa. 43, 228 A.2d 169 (1967) and Sullivan v. Board of Supervisors of Lower Makefield Twp., 22 Pa.Cmwlth. 318, 348 A.2d 464 (1975).

In Eveline Twp. v. H & D Trucking Co., 181 Mich.App. 25, 448 N.W.2d 727 (1989) the court held the local ordinance totally prohibited commercial port facilities within the township and was, therefore, unconstitutional.

2. In Marcus Associates, Inc. v. Town of Huntington, 45 N.Y.2d 501, 410 N.Y.S.2d 546, 382 N.E.2d 1323 (1978), the court upheld a zoning ordinance which limited the number of uses and the size of uses in the only zoning district designated for industrial uses. The property owner argued that the ordinance was invalid because its purpose was to preserve the

character of the district for "blue chip" industry, which exceeded the municipal power under the zoning enabling legislation. The court stated that the language of the enabling legislation "indicates that population density may be regulated in any setting, whether industrial or residential."

B. COMMERCIAL USES

A surprising array of ordinary commercial uses have found themselves excluded from communities by zoning provisions. Sometimes the exclusions may be based on aesthetics or lack of enthusiasm for the kind of business involved. Some state courts have considered the validity of zoning ordinances that exclude fast food or carry out restaurants from the retail business district. In Frost v. Village of Glen Ellyn, 30 Ill.2d 241, 195 N.E.2d 616 (1964), and La Salle Nat. Bank v. City of Park Ridge, 74 Ill.App.3d 647, 30 Ill.Dec. 587, 393 N.E.2d 623 (1979), the courts found such exclusions invalid. Also see A. Copeland Enterprises v. City of New Orleans, 372 So.2d 764 (La.App.1979). On bowling alleys and billiard rooms, see the annotation in 100 A.L.R.3d 252 (1980). Exclusion of video game parlors was upheld in Marshfield Family Skateland, Inc. v. Town of Marshfield, 389 Mass. 436, 450 N.E.2d 605 (1983) (contra as to pinball machines, People v. Palazzolo, 62 Mich.App. 140, 233 N.W.2d 216 (1975)). An intermediate appellate court in Connecticut upheld a town's prohibition of ice cream vending trucks in Blue Sky Bar v. Town of Stratford, 4 Conn.App. 261, 493 A.2d 908 (1985) affirmed 203 Conn. 14, 523 A.2d 467 (1987). A federal court, on the other hand, found a city's denial of a permit to operate a fortune telling and palmistry business violated substantive due process. Marks v. City Council of City of Chesapeake, Va., 723 F.Supp. 1155 (E.D.Va.1988). Also see Fox Valley Reproductive Health Care Center, Inc. v. Arft, 446 F.Supp. 1072 (E.D.Wis.1978); Bossier City Medical Suite, Inc. v. City of Bossier City, 483 F.Supp. 633 (W.D.La.1980); Genusa v. City of Peoria, 475 F.Supp. 1199 (C.D.Ill.1979), modified 619 F.2d 1203 (7th Cir.1980), all dealing with exclusion of abortion clinics.

Residents in middle and upper income suburbs often resist the so-called "big box" stores that are spreading around the country into suburban areas. In 1999 the California legislature adopted a bill (No. 84, 1999–00 Regular Sess.) that prohibited a public agency from authorizing a project or development that includes a retail store exceeding 100,000 square feet with over 15,000 square feet to be devoted to the sale of nontaxable merchandise. The bill was directed at the Wal–Mart supercenters (food items are nontaxable in California). The bill was vetoed by the governor on Sept. 22, 1999. However, some local governments have adopted ordinances that are like the vetoed California bill. Contra Costa, California and Tucson, Arizona are two such places. "Big box" stores regularly precipitate highly politicized zoning battles that often divide the populace. These battles are not confined to suburban areas. See, for example, Constance Hays, "For Wal–Mart, New Orleans Is Hardly the Big Easy," N.Y. Times, Apr. 27, 2003, Business Section, p. 1.

Sec. 2   DISCRIMINATION AGAINST PARTICULAR USES   1237

The exclusionary zoning argument may involve friction between an older, precisely worded zoning ordinance and a commercial proposal that does not quite fit the legislative mold. See, e.g., Edgemont Bank & Trust Co. v. City of Belleville, 85 Ill.App.3d 665, 40 Ill.Dec. 928, 407 N.E.2d 159 (1980), where the court held invalid a zoning classification that prohibited use of property for a walk-up banking facility in a light commercial zone. In Uni–Worth Enterprises, Inc. v. City of Cleveland, 412 F.Supp. 349 (N.D.Miss.1976), the court enjoined enforcement of the zoning ordinance to the extent it disallowed the plaintiff's business of replacing automobile windshields at the customers' homes (in residential zones). The court found that, as applied to plaintiff, the ordinance was an interference with interstate commerce.

By far, the greatest number of cases involving exclusion of commercial activities deal with sexually oriented businesses. Most of these cases involve First Amendment issues. The following cases are interesting examples.

SECRET DESIRES LINGERIE, INC. v. CITY OF ATLANTA

Supreme Court of Georgia, 1996.
266 Ga. 760, 470 S.E.2d 879.

THOMPSON, JUSTICE.

On October 4, 1993, the City of Atlanta enacted an ordinance to regulate lingerie modeling studios. Appellants challenged the constitutionality of the ordinance, seeking declaratory and injunctive relief. Following a trial, the superior court upheld the constitutionality of the ordinance. This appeal followed.

Appellants assert the City did not rely upon relevant evidence of the undesirable secondary effects of lingerie modeling studios when it enacted the ordinance and that, therefore, the ordinance cannot pass constitutional muster. We agree.

When a governing body enacts an ordinance regulating adult entertainment establishments because of their purported undesireable secondary effects, it must rely upon specific evidence showing a correlation between such establishments and the undesirable secondary effects the governing body seeks to control. *Chambers v. Peach County*, 266 Ga. 318, 320, 467 S.E.2d 519 (1996). The governing body can rely on evidence in the form of studies performed by other governmental units. *City of Renton v. Playtime Theatres*, 475 U.S. 41, 51, 106 S.Ct. 925, 930–31, 89 L.Ed.2d 29 (1986); *Discotheque v. City Council of Augusta*, 264 Ga. 623, 624, 449 S.E.2d 608 (1994). It can rely on evidence in the form of its own formal studies, see *World Famous Dudley's v. City of College Park*, 265 Ga. 618, 619, 458 S.E.2d 823 (1995), and it may rely on evidence not contained in formal studies. See *Parker v. Whitfield County*, 265 Ga. 829, 463 S.E.2d 116 (1995) (county relied upon studies of other communities as well as formal and informal meetings between members of the board, county sheriff's department, county residents and commissioners of other counties). The studies need not be perfect, *World Famous Dudley's v. City of College Park, supra*, but they must be considered before the ordinance is passed in order for the ordinance to be considered as one enacted for the purpose of combating the undesirable secondary effects of sexually explicit businesses. *Chambers v. Peach County, supra*. In a lawsuit challenging the constitutionality of an ordinance regulating adult business establishments, the governing body must be able to offer evidence of the studies it relied upon in enacting the ordinance. Id. If it cannot do so, the ordinance cannot be deemed constitutional.

At trial, the City introduced the testimony of three of its vice squad officers who opined that there is a correlation between lingerie modeling studios and prostitution. But the City did not even show that members of the city council were aware of the officers' conclusions, much less that the ordinance was enacted on the basis of those conclusions. And the ordinance itself sheds no light on this issue.

Compare *World Famous Dudley's v. City of College Park, supra*, in which the preamble of an ordinance regulating adult business establishments recited that it was based on the experiences of certain cities.

The City is unable to point to any evidence demonstrating that it considered specific studies of the pernicious secondary effects of lingerie modeling studios before enacting the ordinance. Although the trial court found that the City had knowledge of the police officers' conclusions prior to the enactment of the ordinance, the trial court's finding is clearly erroneous. There is not a scintilla of evidence demonstrating that the police officers (or their superiors) alerted the city council to the problems they uncovered.

The trial court erred in upholding the constitutionality of the ordinance. *Chambers v. Peach County, supra*.

Judgment reversed.

All the Justices concur, except FLETCHER, P.J., and HUNSTEIN, J., who dissent.

FLETCHER, PRESIDING JUSTICE, dissenting.

The trial court found that the City of Atlanta had knowledge of the secondary effects of lingerie modeling studios "prior to and at the time" the city council enacted the challenged ordinance. Because this factual finding is not clearly erroneous and the city's ordinance does not violate free speech, I dissent.

* * *

The police officers testified that they had investigated complaints of criminal activity in lingerie modeling studios; had seen acts of prostitution, simulated sex, and public indecency in the establishments; and had arrested one patron for engaging in sexual intercourse with an employee. The officers explained the difficulties they encountered in making arrests and their discussions with their supervisors about how best to curtail the crimes occurring in lingerie modeling shops and other adult entertainment establishments. This testimony shows that the city did not need to collect studies from other cities; it could rely on its own relevant experience in passing the ordinance to prevent crime. After two days of testimony, the trial court found that "acts of public indecency have been taking place in such establishments for several years" and the city was "aware of criminal activities taking place in lingerie modeling studios prior to and at the time the ordinance was enacted." A review of the record shows that the trial court was not clearly erroneous in finding the city relied on its own experience in enacting the ordinance.

In reversing, the majority opinion ignores the rationale for evaluating city ordinances to determine if they impermissibly infringe on free speech. Instead, it collapses federal first amendment law to a single test: whether the city council relied on "specific studies" of secondary effects before enacting the ordinance. Just as a governing body is not required to consider a "study" before adopting regulations that restrict leafletting at a state park or seeking an injunction that restricts demonstrations on public streets and sidewalks outside facilities offering abortions, a city is not required under either the United States Constitution or the Georgia Constitution to consider a "study" before enacting an ordinance that regulates lingerie modeling studios. All the first amendment requires is that a city rely on evidence that it reasonably believes is relevant to its important governmental interests. This court should not require more.

We have never addressed whether lingerie modeling is expressive conduct entitled to the protection of the free speech clause of the United States and Georgia Constitutions. Assuming that it is, this court must determine whether the law furthers an important government interest, the government interest is unrelated to the suppression of speech, and the incidental restriction of speech is no greater than is essential to further the government interest. The Atlanta ordinance meets this test. First, the trial court found that acts of public indecency had occurred in lingerie modeling establishments for years and that the city was aware of these criminal activities in enacting the ordinance. Second, the city's interest in preventing crime is unrelated to the suppression of expressive conduct. Third, the restrictions in the ordinance are no greater than is essential to further the city's interest in crime prevention. Unlike the total ban on private modeling sessions that was challenged in *Quetgles*, [264 Ga. at 708, 450 S.E.2d 677] the challenged ordinance here merely imposes reasonable regulations. The ordinance requires each establishment to obtain a license and employee permits, prohibits locking devices that hinder police inspection, and establishes reasonable closing hours. Because the city's ordinance does not restrict protected expression in violation of the federal or state constitutions, the trial court properly concluded that the ordinance was constitutional. Therefore, I would affirm.

I am authorized to state that JUSTICE HUNSTEIN joins in this dissent.

Note

Some sexually oriented uses may be considered so "obnoxious" that total exclusion will be upheld. See, e.g., Wigginess Inc. v. Fruchtman, 482 F.Supp. 681 (S.D.N.Y.1979), upholding a zoning ordinance provision prohibiting the operation of adult physical culture establishments offering massages by members of the opposite sex to their customers, and Northend Cinema, Inc. v. City of Seattle, 90 Wash.2d 709, 585 P.2d 1153 (1978), certiorari denied sub nom. Apple Theatre, Inc. v. City of Seattle, 441 U.S. 946, 99 S.Ct. 2166, 60 L.Ed.2d 1048 (1979), upholding a zoning ordinance prohibiting "adult movie" theaters in all neighborhoods but the downtown district.

An important Supreme Court case relating the exclusionary zoning issue to the First and Fourteenth Amendments is Young v. American Mini Theatres, Inc., 427 U.S. 50, 96 S.Ct. 2440, 49 L.Ed.2d 310 (1976), which upheld a Detroit zoning ordinance requiring dispersal of adult theaters and bookstores. The ordinance involved in that case is much like the one in the Northend Cinema case, supra, and has become a much-utilized device in larger cities plagued with complaints about the detrimental effects of sex-oriented businesses on both residential and commercial neighborhoods. See Annotation, Validity of "War Zone" Ordinances Restricting Location of Sex-Oriented Businesses, 1 A.L.R.4th 1297 (1980). However, courts do sometimes strike down locational zoning for adult businesses. See Topanga Press, Inc. v. City of Los Angeles, 989 F.2d 1524 (9th Cir.1993). And some adult business ordinances falter on the definitions that trigger restrictions. For example, in Triplett Grille, Inc. v. City of Akron, 816 F.Supp. 1249 (N.D.Ohio 1993) the ordinance was struck down as overbroad because it applied to performances which included nudity of any kind, not just erotic entertainment. Also see Barnes v. Glen Theatre, Inc., 501 U.S. 560, 111 S.Ct. 2456, 115 L.Ed.2d 504 (1991), and City of Renton v. Playtime Theatres, 475 U.S. 41, 106 S.Ct. 925, 89 L.Ed.2d 29 (1986), the source of the secondary effects doctrine discussed in the principal case.

VOYEUR DORM, L.C. v. CITY OF TAMPA

United States Court of Appeals, Eleventh Circuit, 2001.
265 F.3d 1232.

DUBINA, CIRCUIT JUDGE:

This appeal arises from Voyeur Dorm L.C.'s ("Voyeur Dorm") alleged violation of Tampa's City Code based on the district court's characterization of Voyeur Dorm as an adult entertainment facility. Because we conclude the district court misapplied Tampa's City Code when it erroneously found that Voyeur Dorm offered adult entertainment to the public at the residence in question, we reverse the judgment of the district court.

As alleged in its complaint, Voyeur Dorm is a Florida limited liability company that maintains offices and conducts its business in Hillsborough County, Florida. Voyeur Dorm operates an internet based web site that provides a 24 hour a day internet transmission portraying the lives of the residents of 2312 West Farwell Drive, Tampa, Florida.

Throughout its existence, Voyeur Dorm has employed 25 to 30 different women, most of whom entered into a contract that specifies, among other things, that they are "employees," on a "stage and filming location," with "no reasonable expectation of privacy," for "entertainment purposes." Subscribers to "voyeurdorm.com" pay a subscription fee of $34.95 a month to watch the women employed at the premises and pay an added fee of $16.00 per month to "chat" with the women. From August 1998 to June 2000, Voyeur Dorm generated subscriptions and sales totaling $3,166,551.35.

In 1998, Voyeur Dorm learned that local law enforcement agencies had initiated an investigation into its business. In response, counsel for Voyeur Dorm sent a letter to Tampa's Zoning Coordinator requesting her interpretation of the City Code as it applied to the activities occurring at 2312 West Farwell Drive. In February of 1999, Tampa's Zoning Coordinator, Gloria Moreda, replied to counsel's request and issued her interpretation of the City Code, concluding in relevant part:

The following generally describes the activities occurring on the property:

    1. 5 unrelated women are residing on the premises.

    2. 30 Internet cameras are located in various rooms in the house; such as the bedrooms, bathrooms, living rooms, shower and kitchen.

    3. For a fee, internet viewers are able to monitor the activities in the different rooms.

    4. The web page address is *http://www.voyeurdorm.com/*

    5. The web page shows various scenes from the house, including a woman with exposed buttocks. Statements on the page describe activities that can be viewed such as "the girls of Voyeur Dorm are fresh, naturally erotic and as young as 18. Catch them in the most intimate acts of youthful indiscretion."

The web page can be found by going to Yahoo! and entering "Voyeurdorm" on the search. The name of the website is, itself, advertising the adult nature of the entertainment. Voyeur is defined in the *American Heritage Dictionary,* Second College Edition as "A [sic] person who derives sexual gratification from observing the sex organs or sexual acts of others, especially from a secret vantage point."

It is my determination that the use occurring at 2312 W. Farwell Dr., as described in your letter, is an adult use. Section 27–523 defines adult entertainment as: "Any [sic] premises, except those businesses otherwise defined in this chapter, on which is offered to members of the public or any person, for a consideration, entertainment featuring or in any way including specified sexual activities, as defined in this section, or entertainment featuring the displaying or depicting of specified anatomical areas, as defined in this section; 'entertainment' as used in this definition shall include, but not be limited to, books, magazines, films, newspapers, photographs, paintings, drawings, sketches or other publications or graphic media, filmed or live plays, dances or other performances distinguished by their display or depiction of specified anatomical areas or specified anatomical activities, as defined in this section."

Please be aware that the property is zoned RS–60 Residential Single Family, and an adult use business is not permitted use. You should advise your client to cease operation at that location.

Thereafter, in April of 1999, Dan and Sharon Gold Marshlack appealed the Zoning Coordinator's decision to Tampa's Variance Review Board. On or about July 13, 1999, the Variance Review Board conducted a hearing. At the hearing, Voyeur Dorm's counsel conceded the following: that five women live in the house; that there are cameras in the corners of all the rooms of the house; that for a fee a person can join a membership to a web site wherein a member can view the women 24 hours a day, seven days a week; that a member, at times, can see someone disrobed; that the women receive free room and board; that the women are part of a business enterprise; and that the women are paid. At the conclusion of the hearing, the Variance Review Board unanimously upheld the Zoning Coordinator's determination that the use occurring at 2312 West Farwell Drive was an adult use. Subsequently, Mr. and Mrs. Marshlack filed an appeal from the decision of the Variance Review Board to the City Council. The Tampa City Council held a hearing in August of 1999, at the conclusion of which the City Council unanimously affirmed the decision of the Variance Review Board.

* * *

The threshold inquiry is whether section 27–523 of Tampa's City Code applies to the alleged activities occurring at 2312 West Farwell Drive. Because of the way we answer that inquiry, it will not be necessary for us to analyze the thorny constitutional issues presented in this case.

Section 27–523 defines adult entertainment establishments as

[a]ny premises, except those businesses otherwise defined in this chapter, on which is offered to members of the public or any person, for a consideration, entertainment featuring or in any way including specified sexual activities, as defined in this section, or entertainment featuring the displaying or depicting of specified anatomical areas, as defined in this section; "entertainment" as used in this definition shall include, but not be limited to, books, magazines, films, newspapers, photographs, paintings, drawings, sketches or other publications or graphic media, filmed or live plays, dances or other performances either by single individuals or groups, distinguished by their display or depiction of specified anatomical areas or specified sexual activities, as defined in this section.

Tampa argues that Voyeur Dorm is an adult use business pursuant to the express and unambiguous language of section 27–523 and, as such, cannot operate in a residential neighborhood. In that regard, Tampa points out: that members of the public pay to watch women employed on the premises; that the Employment Agreement refers to the premises as "a stage and filming location"; that certain anatomical areas and sexual activities are displayed for entertainment; and that the entertainers are paid accordingly. Most importantly, Tampa asserts that nothing in the City Code limits its applicability to premises where the adult entertainment is actually consumed.

In accord with Tampa's arguments, the district court specifically determined that the "plain and unambiguous language of the City Code * * * does not expressly state a requirement that the members of the public paying consideration be *on* the premises viewing the adult entertainment." *Voyeur Dorm, L.C., et al., v. City of Tampa, Fla.,* 121 F.Supp.2d 1373 (M.D.Fla.2000) (order granting summary judgment to Tampa). While the public does not congregate to a specific edifice or location in order to enjoy the entertainment provided by Voyeur Dorm, the district court found 2312 West Farwell Drive to be "a premises on which is offered to members of the public for consideration entertainment featuring specified sexual activities within the plain meaning of the City Code." *Id.*

Moreover, the district court relied on Supreme Court and Eleventh Circuit precedent that trumpets a city's entitlement to protect and improve the quality of residential neighborhoods. *See City of Renton v. Playtime Theatres, Inc.,* 475 U.S. 41, 50, 106 S.Ct. 925, 89 L.Ed.2d 29 (1986) ("'[A] city's 'interest in attempting to preserve the quality of urban life is one that must be accorded high respect.'") (quoting *Young v. American Mini Theatres, Inc.,* 427 U.S. 50, 71, 96 S.Ct. 2440, 2453, 49 L.Ed.2d 310 (1976)); *Sammy's of Mobile, Ltd. v. City of Mobile,* 140 F.3d 993, 996–97 (11th Cir.1998) (noting that it is well established that the regulation of public health, safety, and morals is a valid and substantial state interest); *Corn v. City of Lauderdale Lakes,* 997 F.2d 1369, 1375 (11th Cir.1993) (noting that the "Supreme Court has held [that] restrictions may be imposed to protect 'family values, youth values and the blessings of quiet seclusion'") (internal citations omitted).

In opposition, Voyeur Dorm argues that it is not an adult use business. Specifically, Voyeur Dorm contends that section 27–523 applies to locations or premises wherein adult entertainment is actually offered to the public. Because the public does not, indeed cannot, physically attend 2312 West Farwell Drive to enjoy the adult entertainment, 2312 West Farwell Drive does not fall within the purview of Tampa's zoning ordinance. We agree with this argument.

The residence of 2312 West Farwell Drive provides no "offer[ing] [of adult entertainment] to members of the public." The offering occurs when the videotaped images are dispersed over the internet and into the public eye for consumption. The City Code cannot be applied to a location that does not, itself, offer adult entertainment to the public. As a practical matter, zoning restrictions are indelibly anchored in particular geographic locations. Residential areas are often cordoned off from business districts in order to promote a State's interest. *See, e.g., City of Renton,* 475 U.S. at 50, 106 S.Ct. 925 ("A city's interest in attempting to preserve the quality of urban life is one that must be accorded high respect."). It does not follow, then, that a zoning ordinance designed to restrict facilities that offer adult entertainment can be applied to a particular location that does not, at that location, offer adult entertainment. Moreover, the case law relied upon by Tampa and the district court concerns adult entertainment in which customers *physically attend* the premises wherein the entertainment is performed. Here, the audience or consumers of the adult entertainment do not go to 2312 West Farwell Drive or congregate anywhere else in Tampa to enjoy the entertainment. Indeed, the public offering occurs over the Internet in "virtual space." While the district court read section 27–523 in a literal sense, finding no requirement that the paying public be *on the premises,* we hold that section 27–523 does not apply to a residence at which there is no public offering of adult entertainment. Accordingly, because the district court misapplied section 27–523 to the residence of 2312 West Farwell Drive, we reverse the district court's order granting summary judgment to Tampa. Since the resolution of this threshold issue obviates the need for further analysis, we do not reach the remaining issues regarding the constitutionality of Tampa's zoning restrictions as applied to Voyeur Dorm.

C. RELIGIOUS INSTITUTIONS AND PRIVATE SCHOOLS

STATE EX REL. LAKE DRIVE BAPTIST CHURCH v. VILLAGE OF BAYSIDE

Supreme Court of Wisconsin, 1961.
12 Wis.2d 585, 108 N.W.2d 288.

[Mandamus to compel rezoning to permit plaintiff to build a church. The lower court dismissed the action. Bayside, which grew from 553 residents in 1953, when the village was incorporated, to about 3,000 in 1958, is principally residential. In the first half of 1954, the village board indicated it would agree to the construction of the church but wanted to see plans. In mid–1954 the church incorporated, choosing its name in expectation that it would build on the proposed Lake Drive site. In July, 1954, the village adopted a zoning ordinance which excluded churches from the entire village. In 1956, this ordinance was amended and churches were permitted at several locations but, in spite of the recommendation of its planning consultant and its planning commission, the village board refused to rezone plaintiff's land so that a church could be built on it.]

FAIRCHILD, JUSTICE.

* * * With respect to use of land in residence districts for a church, zoning ordinances fall into three types: (1) Permitting churches in all; (2) permitting a church only upon special permit, after hearing; and (3) excluding churches, often, if not usually, from districts where residential use is itself restricted to certain types of dwellings.

It appears that most zoning ordinances fall into the first two types. The first presents no constitutional problem. Many of the cases on this subject arise from denials of permits under the second type of ordinance. Standards in ordinances of the second type appear to be vaguely defined or omitted, and that fact has given rise to some difficulty. A practical advantage of this method is that it permits administrative determination on a case-by-case basis of the suitability of particular sites for church use. We are urged to decide the matter before us on the principle that only the first or possibly the second type of ordinance is valid. Several courts, in considering whether to set aside a denial of a permit under an ordinance of the second type, have said that an ordinance of the third type would be invalid.

The supreme court of Texas had an ordinance of the third type before it, and held it invalid.

The supreme court of Florida held a similar ordinance valid. The court noted that the church bought the property with knowledge of the zoning restrictions; there were sites available in districts where churches would be permitted; church use would cause the value of the surrounding property to depreciate, and give rise to a genuine traffic problem. The court also pointed out that churches are now customarily used for many activities besides worship services and prayer meetings.

A California court of appeal held an ordinance of the third type valid. The court noted that the record did not indicate that the church could not be built in a district where churches would be permitted. The following reference to that decision was made by the supreme court of the United States:

"When the effect of a statute or ordinance upon the exercise of First-amendment freedoms is relatively small and the public interest to be protected is substantial, it is obvious that a rigid test requiring a showing of imminent danger to the security of the nation is an absurdity. We recently dismissed for want of substantiality an appeal in which a church group contended that its First-amendment rights were violated by a municipal zoning ordinance preventing the building of churches in certain residential areas."

Most of the decisions on this subject appear to involve denials of a special permit to build a church under the second type of ordinance. In a number, the denial has been set aside, sometimes with an accompanying statement that there is no valid basis for exclusion.

In a few cases, denials under the second type of ordinance have been upheld.

It is clear enough that a church has some attributes which tend to make it less desirable to its next-door neighbor than a one-family dwelling. It entails substantial gatherings of people, resulting disturbance, and the problem of parking automobiles. * * *

This court has recognized that the protection of property values is an objective upon which a zoning ordinance may be grounded. In the same decision, it referred to the general rule that zoning power may not be exercised for purely aesthetic considerations, but suggested great doubt whether this rule is still the law. Whether restriction of use of a district to strictly residential uses will protect property values is the type of question upon which the decision of the municipal board is accepted unless shown to be unreasonable.

A church, however, is not to be viewed merely as the owner of property complaining against a restriction on its use. It may also challenge an ordinance as an unwarranted burden upon, or interference with, the freedom of the adherents of the church to worship after the manner of their faith. We are familiar with the constitutional protection of freedom of religion from governmental interference.

An ordinance which excludes a church from a particular district must pass two tests:

(1) Can it reasonably be said that use for a church would have such an effect on the area that exclusion of such use will promote the general welfare, and

(2) Does the exclusion impose a burden upon freedom of worship which is not commensurate with the promotion of general welfare secured?

* * *

The test is whether a regulation is an *undue infringement*. Any restriction upon the opportunity to build a house of worship is at least a potential burden upon the freedom of those who would like to worship there. Whether the burden is slight or substantial will depend upon circumstances. In a community where adequate and accessible building sites are available in all districts, it might be a negligible burden to exclude churches from some of them. There must be many circumstances under which a religious group could demonstrate that an exclusion from a particular area would be a substantial burden.

The Bayside ordinance, since 1956, has excluded churches from "A," "B," and "C" districts, where one-family dwellings are permitted, has permitted dwellings, churches, and other institutions in several "E" districts, and has confined "D" districts to dwellings and certain business uses. We conclude that the exclusion of churches, of itself, does not render the ordinance invalid. To determine invalidity would require determination that the "E" districts do not afford reasonably suitable, accessible, and available sites as compared with those in other districts. While there was testimony questioning the suitability of sites in the "E" districts, and the court found that some of the land was overpriced, we do not find it necessary, in this case, to decide whether, as to a church first coming upon the scene after passage of the 1956 amendment, the exclusion of churches from all but "E" districts was an undue burden.

3. *Invalidity with respect to "C" districts.* The Bayside ordinance permits schools and municipal buildings in "C" districts, but excludes churches. Permitted schools are not limited to public schools. Some, at least, of the attributes of a church which annoy neighbors, are also characteristic of schools. It is at least arguable that it is arbitrary and capricious to exclude churches while permitting schools. Exclusion of churches has been held invalid where an ordinance permitted dwellings, schools, colleges, public libraries, public museums and art galleries, parks, etc., and farms and greenhouses and where an ordinance permitted homes, municipal buildings, railroad stations, public schools, and clubhouses. This court has upheld exclusion of private and parochial high schools from a district where public high schools are permitted, but considered it necessary to point out that while all high schools would present detrimental effects, public high schools presented certain advantages which the zoning authority could have considered compensating. In any event, little attention has been given to this issue in the briefs of the parties here, and we do not decide it. [The court then stated that the 1954 Bayside ordinance which excluded churches from the entire village had been clearly unconstitutional.]

5. *Presumption of validity.* "Under well-established rules, where a municipal body enacts regulations pursuant to authority expressly granted, all presumptions are in favor of its validity, and any person attacking it must make the fact of its invalidity clearly appear." Cases like the present, however, raise not only the questions usually raised by restriction upon an owner's right to use his property, but the additional question of whether religious freedom is being unduly impaired. We conclude that it is the duty of a court to give the closest scrutiny to the question whether the exclusion of a church from a district is justified.

The supreme court of Oregon has commented critically on a tendency "to cloak petitioning churches with a species of judicial favoritism under the zoning laws." It seems to us that the courts must be sensitive to any claim that an undue burden is put upon freedom of worship. This is true both because of the importance of this freedom, and because of the real possibility that an overgenerous reliance upon the presumption of validity may cloak discriminatory action against a religious group which is too small a minority in the community to have an effective voice.

6. *Vested rights.* Plaintiff argues that its action in reliance upon favorable intimations of the village board gave it a property right to construct a church on its site, or estopped the village board from preventing it. Counsel cites *Rosenberg v. Whitefish Bay*, 199 Wis. 214, 225 N.W. 838 (1929), and subsequent decisions. Plaintiff accepted the land (as a gift), chose its name, and prepared its first plans after the board manifested a favorable attitude and before the 1956 amendment. The record does not disclose the extent of any expenditure during that period, and we do not find that the principle of the Rosenberg Case is applicable.

7. *Arbitrary action of the board.* As we have heretofore noted, the Bayside ordinance of 1954 excluded churches from the village and therefore could not have prevented plaintiff from building on its site. Assuming that the 1956 amendment, by providing that churches might be erected in certain districts, made valid the parts of the ordinance excluding churches from other districts, was it arbitrary and capricious not to include plaintiff's site in a district where plaintiff could proceed with its building? While plaintiff's prior relationship with the village board and its various activities in reliance thereon are insufficient to give plaintiff a so-called "vested" right to build, they do provide strong equitable considerations for favorable zoning if at all reasonable.

In reaching the conclusion that the action of the village board was arbitrary and capricious, we have been persuaded by the following propositions: (a) Plaintiff is entitled to the benefit of equitable considerations arising out of its actions in reliance on the board's indication of agreement. (b) The board rejected not only its own original view, but the recommendation of the consultant it employed, and the repeated recommendation of the village plan commission. (c) It appears that the property is better suited for a church than for residences. (d) Any traffic hazard could be readily eliminated by the village. (e) The fact that other owners combined their lots in Pelham Heath has little significance. [The court then found the site was suitable for a church; that there would be no adverse effects on other lots; that traffic adjustments could easily be made and that the village was not morally committed to keep the zoning unchanged.]

* * *

Judgment reversed, cause remanded with directions to enjoin enforcement of the Bayside zoning ordinance against construction of a church on plaintiff's site, and to issue a peremptory writ of mandamus commanding the building inspector to issue the building permit applied for.

[The concurring and dissenting opinions which follow have been drastically edited.]

HALLOWS, JUSTICE (concurring). I concur with the result of the court's opinion and much of its reasoning. However, I would reverse also on the ground the exclusion of churches from residential districts is invalid and particularly the exclusion of churches from the "C" district which permits schools and municipal buildings as well as residences is invalid because such classification is arbitrary, unreasonable, and capricious.

* * *

Considering the nature of the zoning power of a municipality, I cannot agree the exercise of that power to exclude churches of itself does not render an ordinance invalid. The zoning power may only be exercised to promote the health, safety, morals, and general welfare of the community. * * *

The majority rule in this country is that churches may not, either by the express or implied language of the zoning ordinance, validly be excluded from residential areas as an absolute and an invariable rule. * * *

The church in our society has long been identified with family and residential life. Churches traditionally have been and should be located in that part of the community where people live. They should be easily and conveniently located to the home. Churches are not supermarkets, manufacturing plants, or commercial establishments and should not be restricted to such areas. How can the exclusion of churches from a residential area promote public morals or the general welfare? To so hold is a failure to understand the purpose and the influence of churches. * * *

CURRIE, JUSTICE (dissenting). I am in full accord with the holding of the opinion of the court written by MR. JUSTICE FAIRCHILD that zoning ordinances which exclude churches from residence districts do not violate the First amendment of the United States constitution as incorporated into the Fourteenth amendment, if suitable and sufficient locations for churches are provided in other use districts.

* * *

However, I must respectfully dissent from the holding of the opinion of the court that the zoning of the particular tract of land owned by the relator was arbitrary and capricious. * * *

In as much as the avoidance of traffic congestion in residence areas, and protection against depreciation of surrounding property values, are a sufficient basis to support the exercise of the police power to exclude churches from residence-use districts, it is not proper for a court to second-guess the municipal legislative body as to whether a church to be built in some particular location in a residence-use district would produce such harmful results. Therefore, in the instant case it is entirely immaterial what motives prompted the majority of the village board to vote not to include relator's property in a class "E" district so long as the motive was not to discriminate against a church as such.

* * *

The trial court's memorandum opinion, findings of fact, and conclusions of law, make it clear that the trial court found that the village board's action did not discriminate against the relator's property on grounds of religion. Such finding is not against the great weight and clear preponderance of the evidence, and, therefore, is conclusive upon this court.

I would affirm the judgment below.

Notes

1. Although the principal case is more than 40 years old, the principles discussed in the case are still current, and courts continue to struggle with

the problems of religious institutions and zoning. For a more current survey of the problem, see Shelley R. Saxer, When Religion Becomes a Nuisance: Balancing Land Use and Religious Freedom When Activities of Religious Institutions Bring Outsiders into the Neighborhood, 84 Kentucky L. J. 507 (1996). Also see Church, Regulations Excluding Churches from Residential Districts, 1962 Wis.L.Rev. 358; Comment, Churches and Zoning, 70 Harv. L.Rev. 1428 (1957); Reynolds, Zoning the Church: The Police Power Versus the First Amendment, 64 Boston U.L.Rev. 767 (1984). Also see Kola Tepee v. Marion County, 99 Or.App. 481, 782 P.2d 955, rev. denied 309 Or. 441, 789 P.2d 5 (1990), where a proposed church was excluded from a district zoned exclusively for agricultural use, and Cornerstone Bible Church v. City of Hastings, 740 F.Supp. 654 (D.Minn.1990), where a church was ordered to vacate a commercial building under a zoning ordinance that allowed churches in residential, but not commercial, districts.

2. If a community decides to regulate church location by special use permit, particular care should be taken in drafting the standards to be applied by the local administrators. Thus in State ex rel. Anshe Chesed Congregation v. Bruggemeier, 97 Ohio App. 67, 115 N.E.2d 65 (1953), the ordinance provided for a permit to build a church "when such location will substantially serve the public convenience and welfare and will not substantially and permanently injure the appropriate use of neighboring property." The court in overruling the denial of a permit for a very large synagogue stressed the absence of any reference in the standard to traffic and safety. The court also said: "It must be observed that a village, which is contiguous to and a part of a great metropolitan area from which it derives its very existence, cannot arbitrarily refuse within reasonable limits to contribute its share to the general welfare of the community as a whole." Compare Jewish Reconstructionist Synagogue of North Shore, Inc. v. Incorporated Village of Roslyn Harbor, 38 N.Y.2d 283, 379 N.Y.S.2d 747, 342 N.E.2d 534 (1975), where the court held that religious institutions have a preeminent status under the First Amendment and that status makes freedom of religion the dominant factor in considering the application of zoning restrictions that are detrimental to the religious institution. In this case the court held that a 100 foot setback ordinance could not be applied so as to exclude the institution. In a subsequent proceeding in the same case the court further held that the village could not require the synagogue to pay the costs of a transcript of the variance proceeding nor the cost of renting a hall for the hearing, 40 N.Y.2d 158, 386 N.Y.S.2d 198, 352 N.E.2d 115 (1976). But the "preeminent status" argument did not seem to sway the federal court in Holy Spirit Ass'n for the Unification of World Christianity v. Town of New Castle, 480 F.Supp. 1212 (S.D.N.Y.1979), where the court held that the town might make a limited inquiry into the bona fides of the institution's beliefs without violating its First Amendment rights.

3. Congress, in the Religious Freedom Restoration Act of 1993, 42 U.S.C.A. § 2000bb, et seq., provided that government shall not substantially burden a person's exercise of religion, even if the burden results from a rule of general applicability unless the government demonstrates that application of the burden is in furtherance of a compelling governmental interest and is the least restrictive means of furthering that interest. This statute was enacted in response to the Supreme Court's holding in the "Indian Peyote"

Sec. 2   **DISCRIMINATION AGAINST PARTICULAR USES**   1251

case, Employment Div. v. Smith, 494 U.S. 872, 110 S.Ct. 1595, 108 L.Ed.2d 876 (1990), that a facially neutral rule applies to religiously motivated conduct. In Flores v. City of Boerne, 73 F.3d 1352 (5th Cir.1996), the court upheld the validity of RFRA in a case challenging the inclusion of portions of a Roman Catholic cathedral in the city's historic district. The Supreme Court granted certiorari in the case late in 1996, and on June 25, 1997, the Court struck down the Act as exceeding the powers of Congress. 521 U.S. 507, 117 S.Ct. 2157, 138 L.Ed.2d 624 (1997). Although RFRA is no longer a factor in evaluating the validity of zoning ordinances as applied to religious uses, the First Amendment free exercise clause is still applicable.

In 2002 Congress passed and the President signed a replacement for RFRA that sought to cure the constitutional infirmities the Court found in the Flores case. This statute, The Religious Land Use and Institutionalized Persons Act of 2002, 42 U.S.C. § 2000cc, provides, in part: "No government shall impose or implement a land use regulation in a manner that imposes a substantial burden on the religious exercise of a person, including a religious assembly or institution, unless the government demonstrates that imposition of the burden * * * (A) is in furtherance of a compelling governmental interest; and (B) is the least restrictive means of furthering that compelling governmental interest." A significant number of cases have been progressing through the courts under RLUIPA. Many of them involve another portion of the act that prohibits religious discrimination against institutionalized persons; most of these cases attack prison regulations that affect religious practices of prisoners. The lower federal courts have divided on the constitutionality of the act, and it is likely that the validity of RLUIPA will be before the Supreme Court in the near future.

4. As the principal case suggests, most zoning ordinances establish a policy of finding churches compatible with the single-family residential district (albeit with some protection for surrounding residences by way of conditional use permits or some similar device). However, ancillary religious institutions such as convents or monasteries pose different problems. See Diakonian Soc'y v. City of Chicago Zoning Bd. of Appeals, 63 Ill.App.3d 823, 20 Ill.Dec. 634, 380 N.E.2d 843 (1978). Also see Missionaries of Our Lady of La Salette v. Village of Whitefish Bay, 267 Wis. 609, 66 N.W.2d 627 (1954) which involved the single family provisions of an ordinance as applied to three priests and two lay brothers living in a house owned by a religious order. Application of Laporte, 2 A.D.2d 710, 152 N.Y.S.2d 916, affirmed Laporte v. City of New Rochelle, 2 N.Y.2d 921, 161 N.Y.S.2d 886, 141 N.E.2d 917 (1957), considered *sixty* student members of a religious order as constituting a single family group where they occupied a Roman Catholic college building as a residence. The dissenting judge in the appellate division opinion pointed out that this was really a college dormitory not a one-family dwelling. In Damascus Community Church v. Clackamas County, 45 Or.App. 1065, 610 P.2d 273 (1980), appeal dismissed 450 U.S. 902, 101 S.Ct. 1336, 67 L.Ed.2d 326 (1981), the court held that a permit for a church in a residential area did not authorize establishment of an ancillary, full-time parochial school. Accord: Abram v. City of Fayetteville, 281 Ark. 63, 661 S.W.2d 371 (1983); Seward Chapel, Inc. v. City of Seward, 655 P.2d 1293 (Alaska 1982); Rhema Christian Center v. District of Columbia Bd. of Zoning Adj., 515 A.2d 189 (D.C.App.1986), subsequent decision, Towles v. District of Columbia Bd.

of Zoning Adj., 578 A.2d 1128 (D.C.App.1990). Contra: Alpine Christian Fellowship v. County Comm'rs of Pitkin County, 870 F.Supp. 991 (D.Colo. 1994).

In Needham Pastoral Counseling Center, Inc. v. Board of Appeals of Needham, 29 Mass.App.Ct. 31, 557 N.E.2d 43, rev. denied 408 Mass. 1103, 560 N.E.2d 121 (1990), the court found that a proposed 864 square foot addition to a church building for offices and counseling rooms for a psychological counseling center with a spiritual component was more like a mental health clinic than a religious activity, and that the building permit was properly denied.

In St. John's Evangelical Lutheran Church v. City of Hoboken, 195 N.J.Super. 414, 479 A.2d 935 (1983), the city sought to prevent the church from operating a shelter for 30 to 50 homeless persons on the ground that such a shelter is not a customary accessory use. The court granted an injunction in favor of the church. Contra are First Assembly of God of Naples, Florida, Inc. v. Collier County, 20 F.3d 419, (11th Cir.1994), modified, 27 F.3d 526, cert. denied 513 U.S. 1080, 115 S.Ct. 730, 130 L.Ed.2d 634 (1995); Daytona Rescue Mission, Inc. v. City of Daytona Beach, 885 F.Supp. 1554 (M.D.Fla.1995) (the court in this case also held that RFRA did not protect the church from a neutral and generally applicable zoning code). However, in Jesus Center v. Farmington Hills Zoning Bd. of Appeals, 215 Mich.App. 54, 544 N.W.2d 698 (1996) the court held that RFRA was applicable to a homeless shelter operated by a church on weekends; homeless persons were bussed to the church from poor neighborhoods in the region. Also see Western Presbyterian Church v. Board of Zoning Adjustment of District of Columbia, 862 F.Supp. 538 (D.D.C.1994). Many churches seek to aid homeless persons in various ways, and often run afoul of the zoning ordinance; the next case is a good example:

FIFTH AVENUE PRESBYTERIAN CHURCH v. CITY OF NEW YORK

United States Court of Appeals, Second Circuit, 2002.
293 F.3d 570.

STRAUB, CIRCUIT JUDGE.

Presbyterian is located at the corner of Fifth Avenue and 55th Street in Manhattan. For several years, homeless persons have chosen to sleep on the Church's outdoor property. In February 1999, the Church officially designated two areas on its outdoor property upon which homeless persons are permitted to sleep at night. The first of these areas encompasses the landings at the tops of the staircases leading into the Church's main sanctuary on Fifth Avenue and into its 55th Street entrance. The landings are contained within arched entryways and are recessed approximately five to ten feet from the sidewalk and raised approximately six feet above the sidewalk. The second designated area is a strip of land adjacent to the Church's southern wall that extends approximately five feet to the public sidewalk.

The Church views its outdoor space as a sanctuary for the service-resistant homeless who prefer not to sleep in shelters. Homeless persons

Sec. 2   **DISCRIMINATION AGAINST PARTICULAR USES**   1253

are welcome on the Church's outdoor property between 8:00 p.m. and 7:00 a.m. They are not permitted to set up their sleeping area or lie down until 9:00 p.m. Persons taking advantage of the Church's invitation to sleep on its outdoor property are given a list of rules, which includes instructions to clean up after themselves and a prohibition on begging, loud music, disruptive behavior, and foul language.

In November 2001, the City notified Presbyterian that it would no longer permit the homeless to sleep on the Church's outdoor property. Thereafter, on three occasions in early December 2001, city police removed the homeless from the Church's property during the night. Presbyterian claims that the police threatened the homeless with arrest if they refused to leave.

On December 17, 2001, Presbyterian brought suit under 42 U.S.C. § 1983, the First Amendment, the common law of trespass, the Religious Land Use and Institutionalized Persons Act of 2000 ("RLUIPA"), 42 U.S.C. § 2000cc, *et. seq.,* and for deprivation of due process and violation of Article 1, Section 3 of the New York State Constitution. Presbyterian sought injunctive relief preventing the City from entering onto Church property and dispersing the homeless. Focusing primarily on the Church's cause of action under the Free Exercise Clause of the First Amendment, the City argued that allowing the homeless to sleep on the sidewalk and on Church grounds does not constitute protected religious activity, and that the Church had violated applicable laws or regulations in four ways: (1) operating a shelter without a license; (2) creation of a public nuisance; (3) allowing persons to sleep on a sidewalk that is subject to City regulation; and (4) allowing the use of boxes, tents, and similar materials on the sidewalk in violation of City codes.

Following a hearing, the District Court issued a memorandum and order granting in part the Church's request for a preliminary injunction. In ruling on the Church's application, the District Court concluded that allowing homeless persons to sleep on the Church's private property constitutes protected religious activity because doing so enables the Church to interact with and assist the homeless in bettering their lives. The court rejected the City's arguments that the Church is operating a *de facto* shelter, and that the presence of the homeless amounts to a public nuisance. The court agreed with the City that it is permitted to regulate the presence of sleeping persons, as well as cardboard shelters and tents, on the Church's land adjacent to the sidewalk on 55th Street. Accordingly, the District Court entered a preliminary injunction prohibiting the City from interfering with homeless persons who are sleeping on the Church steps and landings above sidewalk level. The court denied the application with regard to those sleeping on Church property adjacent to the public sidewalk.

* * *

We agree with the District Court that on the present record, the Church has demonstrated a likelihood of success in establishing that its provision of outdoor sleeping space for the homeless effectuates a sincerely held religious belief and therefore is protected under the Free Exercise Clause. *Cf. Stuart Circle Parish v. Bd. of Zoning Appeals of the City of Richmond,* 946 F.Supp. 1225, 1236 (E.D.Va.1996); *Western Presbyterian Church v. Bd. of Zoning Adjustment of the District of Columbia,* 862 F.Supp. 538, 544–46 (D.D.C.1994). Further, we assume, without deciding, that the City's actions in dispersing the homeless substantially burden the Church's protected religious activity, a proposition with which the City has not argued. Accordingly, absent a demonstration that a neutral law of general applicability justifies the City's actions, the City must assert a compelling interest in preventing the homeless from sleeping on Church property that would suffice to overcome the Church's free exercise rights, and that the means it has adopted to fulfill that interest are narrowly tailored. *See Church of Lukumi Babalu Aye,* 508 U.S. at 546, 113 S.Ct. 2217; *Wisconsin v. Yoder,* 406 U.S. 205, 214–15, 92 S.Ct. 1526, 32 L.Ed.2d 15 (1972).

The City points to several laws or policies that it claims support its actions. First, the City argues that Presbyterian is operating a homeless shelter without a license and in contravention of state regulations. Pursuant to 18 N.Y.C.R.R. §§ 485.1 & 491.1, the operator of a shelter for adults must obtain certification from the New York State Department of Social Services and comply with its applicable regulations. A shelter is defined as "an adult care facility established and operated for the purpose of providing temporary residential care, room, board, supervision, information *and* referral...." *Id.* § 491.2 (emphasis added). We agree with the District Court that an invitation to the homeless to sleep on outdoor property does not fall within the ambit of these regulations, which contemplate an indoor facility and the provision of comprehensive social services for the homeless. *See, e.g., id.* § 491.10 (setting forth detailed requirements for shelters pertaining to building and fire codes, furniture, amenities and housekeeping).

As an alternative justification for its actions, the City argues that it is empowered to enforce minimum standards of habitability for privately-run shelters in the absence of applicable regulations. In support of this proposition, the City cites the New York Court of Appeals' decision in *McCain v. Koch,* 70 N.Y.2d 109, 517 N.Y.S.2d 918, 511 N.E.2d 62 (1987). *McCain* held that the New York Supreme Court has the equitable power to require a minimum standard of care for city-run emergency housing so long as the standard of care does not conflict with applicable state or city regulations. *McCain's* holding was premised on the principle that once the City has undertaken to provide emergency housing, it has a duty to ensure certain minimum standards of habitability. *Id.* at 119–20, 517 N.Y.S.2d 918, 511 N.E.2d 62. We decline to extend *McCain's* holding beyond the context of government-administered housing on these facts. Moreover, *McCain* addressed *a court's* equitable power to issue an injunction requiring the City to provide particular amenities; it did not address the City's power to devise and enforce equitable standards of its own making. Nor did the Court of Appeals in *McCain* express any opinion as to the substance of the injunction in that case—*i.e.,* whether the specific requirements in that injunction were in fact the minimum acceptable standards of habitability for a shelter.

The City argues that its power to enforce equitable standards of care for homeless shelters derives from its ability to enforce public nuisance laws. The District Court ruled below that the City had not established the existence of a nuisance, and the City does not challenge that particular holding on appeal. Therefore, we need not consider this argument. The City also claims, in its reply brief, that it has a "policy of regarding the provision of subminimal shelter as a nuisance." Not only is this argument untimely raised, *see Thomas v. Roach,* 165 F.3d 137, 145–46 (2d Cir.1999), but the City has not adequately demonstrated the existence or general applicability of such a policy, or that it applies to the Church's activities.

Finally, the City argues for the first time on appeal that the Church is in violation of New York City Zoning Resolution Section 12–10 because its outdoor sanctuary is not a permissible "accessory" use of its property. Because this argument was not raised below and refusing to consider it will not result in "manifest injustice" in light of the posture of the case, and because adjudication of zoning disputes over accessory uses entails an inherently factual inquiry, *see New York Botanical Garden v. Bd. of Standards & Appeals,* 91 N.Y.2d 413, 420, 671 N.Y.S.2d 423, 694 N.E.2d 424 (1998), we decline to consider the City's argument here. *See Coogan v. Smyers,* 134 F.3d 479, 486–87 (2d Cir.1998). Nor, therefore, need we express any opinion on the plaintiffs' argument, also raised for the first time on appeal, that the Religious Land Use and Institutionalized Persons Act of 2000 ("RLUIPA"), 42 U.S.C. § 2000cc, *et. seq.,* subjects the City's application of its Zoning Resolution to strict scrutiny.

Thus, at the present time, the City has not sufficiently shown the existence of a relevant law or policy that is neutral and of general applicability, and that would therefore justify its actions in dispersing the homeless from the Church's landings and steps. For the first time in its reply brief, the City argues that its dispersal of the homeless from Presbyterian's property is justified by a compelling state governmental interest, namely, "preventing the Church from providing inadequate shelter nightly and encouraging homeless persons to avoid a safer, more civilized alternative." Although arguments raised for the first time in a reply brief need not be considered, *see Thomas,* 165 F.3d at 145–46, we note that the homeless who take advantage of the Church's offer, ten of whom are plaintiffs in this action, do so voluntarily. Moreover, common sense, in addition to evidence put forth by the homeless plaintiffs, suggests that the majority of these homeless will not go to shelters if the City is permitted to disperse them; rather, they will find another place on the street upon which to sleep. Thus, it is doubtful that the "ends" support the City's "means," nor has the City attempted to show that police dispersal in the middle of the night is the least restrictive means of accomplishing its goal of ensuring that the homeless have appropriate sleeping quarters. *See Yoder,* 406 U.S. at 215, 92 S.Ct. 1526.

For the foregoing reasons, we find that the District Court did not abuse its discretion in concluding that Presbyterian has demonstrated a likelihood of success on the merits of its free exercise claim. The opinion and order of the District Court entering a preliminary injunction in favor of Presbyterian is hereby AFFIRMED.

Notes

1. In State v. Cameron, 100 N.J. 586, 498 A.2d 1217 (1985), the New Jersey Supreme Court held that an ordinance that excludes churches and similar places of worship from the single-family district was unconstitutionally vague as applied to a minister who held weekly services in his home for 25 people. Also see, Farhi v. Commissioners of the Borough of Deal, 204 N.J.Super. 575, 499 A.2d 559 (1985). Compare City of Colorado Springs v. Blanche, 761 P.2d 212 (Colo.1988). In LeBlanc–Sternberg v. Fletcher, 104 F.3d 355 (2d Cir.1996) the court upheld a district court's array of relief in a long dispute between groups of Orthodox Jews and the Village of Airmont, New York. The plaintiffs claimed that the zoning code of the village was discriminatory in purposefully inhibiting the rights of home worship and other religious expression. The district court opinion is in 922 F.Supp. 959 (S.D.N.Y.1996) and a previous appellate opinion is 67 F.3d 412 (2d Cir.1995), dealing with the federal government cause of action based on the Fair Housing Act. Prayer meetings and worship services in single-family houses in single-family zoning districts are a growing problem in many cities, and several of the current RLUIPA disputes involve that issue. Other homeowners in the vicinity of the home worship facility often complain about the nuisance-like aspects such as traffic, unusual numbers of people, noise, littering, and the like.

2. In Cochise County v. Broken Arrow Baptist Church, 161 Ariz. 406, 778 P.2d 1302 (App.1989), the church built a metal building containing 5,000 square feet with a concrete floor to contain a printing press and literature distribution center; there was no sanctuary in the building. The church neglected to obtain a permit and the trial court granted an injunction against occupying the building finding it a public nuisance. On appeal the court held that the building was obviously a manufacturing facility and not a church, and affirmed the injunction.

3. In Love Church v. City of Evanston, 671 F.Supp. 515 (N.D.Ill.1987) the court held that an ordinance requiring churches to obtain a special permit was a violation of equal protection because meeting halls, theatres and schools were not required to obtain special permits.

STATE EX REL. WISCONSIN LUTHERAN HIGH SCHOOL CONFERENCE v. SINAR

Supreme Court of Wisconsin, 1954.
267 Wis. 91, 65 N.W.2d 43, appeal dismissed 349 U.S.
913, 75 S.Ct. 604, 99 L.Ed. 1248 (1955).

[The zoning ordinance of Wauwatosa permitted public schools in the residential district and private elementary schools, but excluded private high schools.]

Sec. 2   DISCRIMINATION AGAINST PARTICULAR USES   1257

BROWN, JUSTICE.

* * *

* * * Appellants have made it abundantly clear that respondent's projected school has many features which seriously impair the social and economic benefits to the entire community which the zoning law is designed to preserve and promote. It will add to the congestion of the surrounding streets. Athletic events will bring noisy crowds and if the contests are held at night, there will be bright lights to interfere with the peace and comfort of the neighborhood. The school property will be taken from the tax roll, thus increasing the financial burden of the city's taxpayers. The presence of the school will lessen the taxable value of nearby homes and will deter the building of new homes in the area. Other detriments are easily thought of. But, as respondent points out, each such discordant feature attends the presence of a public school to an equal degree.

Respondent submits, therefore, that there is no difference in the effect on the community between the permitted public high school and the prohibited private one and hence the ordinance's discrimination between them is unreasonable, not founded on a difference in fact material to the object sought to be attained by building ordinances, and is a measure which denies to respondent the equal protection of the laws and deprives it of property without due process of law, contrary to the provisions of the Fourteenth Amendment of the United States Constitution. Therefore, it asserts, so far as this case is concerned, the ordinance is void.

* * * Respondent cites *Catholic Bishop of Chicago v. Kingery*, 371 Ill. 257, 20 N.E.2d 583, and City of Miami Beach v. State ex rel. Lear, 128 Fla. 750, 175 So. 537. These are cases whose facts are practically identical with the present one. In them the respective courts held that there was no substantial difference between public and private schools in relation to the object sought to be accomplished by the zoning ordinance and therefore, in so far as it prohibited the presence of a private school while allowing a public one, it was void. If these decisions were controlling authority upon us we would necessarily affirm the learned trial court for we can not distinguish them from ours in any material respect. But their authority is persuasive, only, and it fails to persuade.

* * *

[W]e decide the present appeal on the narrower ground that tangible differences material to the classifications of the ordinance can be readily pointed out which sustain the distinction made by the ordinance between the schools. To begin with, the term "public" is the antithesis of "private." The public school is not a private one. They serve different interests and are designed to do so. The private school is founded and maintained because it is different. Is that difference material to the purpose of zoning? In many respects the two schools perform like functions and in probably all respects concerning noise, traffic difficulties and the other objectionable features already mentioned they stand on an equality, so that in several of the objects of zoning ordinances,—the promotion of health, safety and morals, as laid down by sec. 62.23(7)(a), Stats., and developed by respondent's brief, we may not say that the two schools differ. But when we come to "the promotion of the general welfare of the community",—"Ay, there's the rub." The public school has the same features objectionable to the surrounding area as a private one, but it has, also, a virtue which the other lacks, namely, that it is located to serve and does serve that area without discrimination. Whether the private school is sectarian or commercial, though it now complains of discrimination, in its services it discriminates and the public school does not. Anyone in the district of fit age and educational qualifications may attend the public high school. It is his right. He has no comparable right to attend a private school. To go there he must meet additional standards over which the public neither has nor should have control. The private school imposes on the community all the disadvantages of the public school but does not compensate the community in the same manner or to the same extent. If the private school does not make the same contribution to public welfare this difference may be taken into consideration by the legislative body in framing its ordinances. If education offered by a school to the residents of an area without discrimination is considered by the council to compensate for the admitted drawbacks to its presence there, that school may be permitted a location which is denied to another school which does not match the offer, and we can not say that such a distinction is arbitrary or unreasonable or that such discrimination between the two schools lacks foundation in a difference which bears a "fair, substantial, reasonable and just relation;" to the promotion of the general welfare of the community, which is the statutory purpose of zoning laws in general and of the ordinance in question.

* * *

Orders and judgment reversed. Cause remanded with directions to quash the writ of mandamus.

[Two justices dissented. STEINLE, J.'s dissenting opinion is not given.]

Notes

1. The California court (3 judges dissenting) disagreed with the Sinar holding. Roman Catholic Welfare Corp. v. City of Piedmont, 45 Cal.2d 325, 289 P.2d 438 (1955). It relied on Catholic Bishop of Chicago v. Kingery, 371 Ill. 257, 20 N.E.2d 583 (1939), where the Illinois court stated: " * * * [S]uch a [Catholic] school, conducted in accordance with the educational requirements established by State educational authorities, is promotive of the general welfare." These would seem to be the better reasoned cases. It may be argued, among other things, that private schools, in this day of overcrowded public schools, serve a useful public purpose. But most important, where is the public interest served under the police power when public schools and private elementary schools are permitted in an area but private high schools are denied admittance? To compress the exclusion of private

Sec. 2   DISCRIMINATION AGAINST PARTICULAR USES   1259

high schools within the power to regulate for the health, safety, morals and welfare of the community, within such a context, is to strain at a gnat and develop a mental hernia in the process. See Annot., 74 A.L.R.3d 14 (1976).

The Michigan Court of Appeals, in Lutheran High School Ass'n of Greater Detroit v. City of Farmington Hills, 146 Mich.App. 641, 381 N.W.2d 417 (1985), appeal denied 425 Mich. 870 (1986), held that a parochial high school was not immune from the local zoning ordinance and that the city did not act improperly in denying a variance to build a gymnasium (apparently, public high schools are not subject to the zoning ordinance). Also see Cornell University v. Bagnardi, 68 N.Y.2d 583, 510 N.Y.S.2d 861, 503 N.E.2d 509 (1986); Father Ryan High School, Inc. v. City of Oak Hill, 774 S.W.2d 184 (Tenn.App.1988).

2. Just what is a "school?" A number of interesting cases tackle that definitional problem. The Town of Yorktown is an area consisting of fine homes. Its zoning permitted public elementary and high schools and private and parochial elementary and high schools. A school was defined as an institution "offering a comprehensive curriculum of study similar to that of a public school." Also permitted were accessory uses customarily incidental and subordinate to school use. Wiltwyck School for Boys is financed by public and private funds. It accepts free of charge about 100 delinquent, maladjusted or emotionally disturbed boys between ages 8 and 12, who are found to have potential for rehabilitation. The boys receive instruction in regular grammar school subjects by teachers employed by the City of New York. In addition, the school has a many faceted program of other activities—singing, sports, art, counseling, etc. After Wiltwyck had purchased 113 acres as a site for a new "school" in Yorktown, the town amended its zoning so as to prohibit any "charitable institution" unless it was using land prior to the date of the amendment. The majority of the appellate division said Wiltwyck was a charitable institution and properly excluded. In an elaborate dissent, Justice Kleinfeld disagreed saying that in his judgment Wiltwyck was a "school" permitted by the ordinance. He also said that if this was not so then the exclusion of Wiltwyck was invalid as being contrary to clearly enunciated state policy: "The town by its * * * Zoning Ordinance, and * * * its officials by their decisions construing it, have effectively thwarted and subverted the State's fundamental public policy to provide for the support and welfare of delinquent and neglected children. For if Yorktown may bar W[iltwyck], so may every other municipality in the State." Wiltwyck School for Boys, Inc. v. Hill, 14 A.D.2d 198, 219 N.Y.S.2d 161 (1961), reversed 11 N.Y.2d 182, 227 N.Y.S.2d 655, 182 N.E.2d 268 (1962). And see an excellent Comment, Zoning Against the Public Welfare: Judicial Limitations on Municipal Parochialism, 71 Yale L.J. 720 (1962).

3. In DeSisto College, Inc. v. Town of Howey–In–The–Hills, 706 F.Supp. 1479 (M.D.Fla.1989), the court held that a college for learning disabled students was not a school within the meaning of the zoning ordinance. Compare Visionquest National, Ltd. v. Pima County Bd. of Adj. Dist. No. 1, 146 Ariz. 103, 703 P.2d 1252 (App.1985), where the court held that a facility for juvenile offenders on a ranch was a private school. But see Visionquest National, Ltd. v. Board of Supervisors of Honey Brook Twp., 524 Pa. 107, 569 A.2d 915 (1990) holding the opposite.

4. Residential zoning permits "public and parochial schools." A missionary seminary was held not to be a "school" within the meaning of this ordinance. Only grammar and high schools to serve residents of the neighboring area were intended. Yanow v. Seven Oaks Park Inc., 11 N.J. 341, 94 A.2d 482, 36 A.L.R.2d 639 (1953). Is this justified? How does it correspond to the reasoning in the above cases?

5. For a note on preschools, day schools and summer camps, see Annot., 64 A.L.R.3d 1087 (1975). And consider Langbein v. Board of Zoning Appeals, 135 Conn. 575, 67 A.2d 5 (1949). A zoning ordinance permitted "schools" in a residential district. Mr. Borman applied for a permit to operate a summer day "school" for boys and girls between 5 and 14 years of age. Proposed activities included swimming, arts, crafts, boating, hiking, basketball, volleyball, softball, tetherball, badminton, horseshoes, story telling, photography, croquet, fishing and free play. The Connecticut court said Mr. Borman was entitled to a permit under the ordinance. Also see Mandelstam v. City Com'n of South Miami, 539 So.2d 1139 (Fla.App.1988) (gymnastics school).

6. Are day care centers schools? What about Montessori pre-schools? See Cohen v. City of Des Plaines, 742 F.Supp. 458 (N.D.Ill.1990), where day care centers were allowed to operate in church buildings but not elsewhere; the court found a denial of equal protection and an establishment clause violation. The Seventh Circuit reversed, 8 F.3d 484 (1993), cert. denied 512 U.S. 1236, 114 S.Ct. 2741, 129 L.Ed.2d 861 (1994). In City of Little Rock v. Infant–Toddler Montessori School, Inc., 270 Ark. 697, 606 S.W.2d 743 (1980), the Arkansas Supreme Court reversed a lower court finding that a proposed Montessori school for children one to three years in age was an "educational institution with curriculum equivalent to a public elementary school" which could locate as a matter of right under the zoning ordinance in the single-family district. The majority opinion stated: "The ages and accompanying capabilities of children as young as one year old are also evidence that the curriculum does not rise to the level of public elementary education." A dissenting opinion disagreed: "The Infant–Toddler Montessori School has a curriculum which includes instruction in language development, math, science, geography, botany, zoology, reading, and motor development. * * * The educational structure and method used are comparable to those of the beginning grades of the public elementary schools." Compare the case of Chicago v. Sachs, 1 Ill.2d 342, 115 N.E.2d 762 (1953), where the court struck down exclusion of a pre-kindergarten play school from an apartment district. Also see Hartman v. City of Columbia, 268 S.C. 44, 232 S.E.2d 15 (1977), where the court found a day care center to be the equivalent of a school. Accord: City of Richmond Heights v. Richmond Heights Presbyterian Church, 764 S.W.2d 647 (Mo. banc 1989). Contra: Seidita v. Board of Zoning Appeals of City of Scranton, 41 Pa.Cmwlth. 340, 399 A.2d 156 (1979) where a day care center was not allowed to occupy a former public elementary school building because the zoning district did not allow day care (a different district did). In Church of God of Louisiana, Inc. v. Monroe–Ouachita Regional Planning Comm'n, 404 F.Supp. 175 (W.D.La. 1975), the court found denial of a special exception for a day-care center to be operated by a black church to be racially discriminatory and found no compelling governmental interest to justify the discrimination.

Chapter XII

REVIEW BY THE PEOPLE, PARTIES, AND COURTS

SECTION 1. REVIEW BY THE PEOPLE—CONSENT, INITIATIVE AND REFERENDUM

A. INTRODUCTION

When parties are aggrieved by a land use decision, we normally think about their opportunity to seek redress from the courts. We readily understand that the land use decisions of public bodies are subject to judicial review. It is also possible for disgruntled neighbors, in some communities, to invoke consent requirements, for the public to subject legislative actions to popular referendum, and for the involved stakeholders to agree to mediate their disputes over land use decisions. Each of these forms of review is limited by the circumstances and the laws and practice of the state.

As we consider all of the options for reviewing the public body's decision, we are forced to review the nature of that decision, the characteristics of the decision-making entity, and the procedures that agencies follow. In this respect, our studies serve as a useful review of the preceding chapters. Whether the courts will review the legality of a land use decision will depend on whether the matter is ripe, the decision final, and the appeal timely. Were all administrative remedies pursued and exhausted? Was a variance requested? What standards do courts use in reviewing the actions of land use agencies? Does it matter if the decision is a legislative, quasi-judicial, or administrative one? Given the courts' standards of judicial review, am I likely to prevail if I chose the judicial route? Do state statutes provide me and my fellow citizens an opportunity to vote on the matter, that is to reconsider it via referendum? Do the procedures of the decision-making board allow us and other affected parties to mediate the matter? Once litigation has been initiated, can we still settle the dispute through mediation or other alternative methods of dispute resolution? Will we be required to do so?

The practice varies from state to state with respect to all of these modes of review. Courts exhibit varying degrees of deference to regulatory decisions, legislatures adopt a range of direct democracy options (consent, petition, initiative, referendum, etc.), and administrative procedures and court rules allow for different ADR techniques to be used as a land use application proceeds from its conception, through board decision, to final review and determination.

B. CONSENT BY THE NEIGHBORS

At common law, landowners can bring a private nuisance action to enjoin an offensive use of neighboring land. What happens then, when the zoning ordinance allows, and an administrative body approves, the placement of a use offensive to the neighbors, such as a gasoline station or billboard, in a residential neighborhood? What if the local legislature subjects specified land uses to a requirement that a certain percent of the neighbors consent before those land uses can be approved as a specially permitted use by the planning commission, for example? Is the legislature simply recognizing the common law nuisance rights of neighbors or is it unlawfully delegating its legislative prerogatives to the public in violation of the due process rights of the landowner who is denied the right to build the gasoline station or billboard? Does the zoning enabling law of the state allow this type of delegation of discretionary decision-making?

VALKANET v. CITY OF CHICAGO

Supreme Court of Illinois, 1958.
13 Ill.2d 268, 148 N.E.2d 767.

[Plaintiffs asked for a declaratory judgment in the trial court that they were entitled to a license to operate a home for the aged in an apartment zone. The ordinance required consent by a majority of owners on both sides of the street for the block in which a home for the aged was to be located. Plaintiffs contended this requirement was invalid and did not obtain such consent. The trial court found the requirement void and the city appealed].

DAVIS, CHIEF JUSTICE.

* * * From the complaint and the record of the proceedings below, it appears that the plaintiffs' theory is that the ordinance is void in that it is an illegal delegation of legislative power to private individuals, a deprivation of property without due process of law, and a denial of equal protection of the law.

The defendant contends that the restriction imposed on operating such homes by section 136–6 is a reasonable and proper exercise of police power, and that the consent provision for waiver of the restriction is valid.

Unaided by brief and argument of plaintiffs, we have examined the state of the law concerning the validity of "frontage consent" provisions, and, like McQuillin, have found "a decided difference of judicial view and sometimes of jurisdictional consistency as to the validity of municipal legislation of this character, not entirely explainable by varying provisions of the ordinances or by differing statutory or charter grants of authority." (8 McQuillin, Municipal Corporations, 3rd ed., p. 348.) * * *

An analysis of * * * [our] decisions reveals that we have sustained frontage-consent provisions where the effect was to permit the waiver of a prohibition of a structure, business, trade or occupation properly subject to the police power, such as livery stables, saloons, garages and billboards. Spies v. Board of Appeals, 337 Ill. 507, 513, 169 N.E. 220. Yet we have consistently held that a municipality cannot deprive a citizen of a valuable property right under the guise of prohibiting or regulating some business or occupation which has no tendency to injure the public health or morals, or interfere with the general welfare. Spies v. Board of Appeals, 337 Ill. 507, 169 N.E. 220; People ex rel. Deitenbeck v. Village of Oak Park, 331 Ill. 406, 163 N.E. 445; People ex rel. Friend v. City of Chicago, 261 Ill. 16, 103 N.E. 609.

The prevailing view concerning such consent provisions is illustrated by two leading decisions of the United States Supreme Court. The first, Eubank v. City of Richmond, 226 U.S. 137, 33 S.Ct. 76, 57 L.Ed. 156, held invalid an ordinance allowing two thirds of the abutting property owners in the block to establish a set-back line, on the ground that such enactment was, in effect, legislative action by the property owners without the benefit of any standard for the exercise of such power, and therefore an improper delegation of a legislative function. Cf. Gorieb v. Fox, 274 U.S. 603, 47 S.Ct. 675, 71 L.Ed. 1228. The second decision, Thomas Cusack Co. v. City of Chicago, 242 U.S. 526, 37 S.Ct. 190, 61 L.Ed. 472, involved a billboard ordinance in language similar to the ordinance before us. It absolutely prohibited billboards in certain districts, but permitted the restriction to be modified with the consent of the persons most affected. The court, at Thomas Cusack Co. v. City of Chicago, 242 U.S. 526, 531, 37 S.Ct. 190, 61 L.Ed. 472, 476, in distinguishing the Eubank case, said:

> "The one ordinance permits two thirds of the lot owners to impose restrictions upon the other property in the block, while the other permits one-half of the lot owners to remove a restriction from the other property owners. This is not a delegation of legislative power, but is, as we have seen a familiar provision affecting the enforcement of laws and ordinances."

While the Cusack decision has been criticized, (University of Illinois 1954 Law Forum, 309, 311–312,) it has been generally followed. And, even though it is impossible to lay down a hard-and-fast rule, we conclude that if an ordinance permits a certain percentage of the property owners to impose or create a restriction upon their neighbors' property by the device of consent provisions, such limitation constitutes an invalid delegation of legislative power, but if the consent provision merely waives or modifies a lawful and reasonable legislative restriction or prohibition, it is within constitutional limitations. (2 Metzenbaum, Law of Zoning, 2d ed., p. 1067; 8 McQuillin, Municipal Corporations, 3rd ed., page 348, sec. 25.151; 1 Yokley, Zoning Law, p. 201, sec. 89; Anno: 21 A.L.R.2d 551 et seq.) It follows that the consent provisions of section 136–6 of the code are not an invalid delegation of legislative power. However, this does not determine that its proscription of homes for the aged is a reasonable exercise of the police power. The cases in which we have upheld prohibitions that might be waived by consent provisions have dealt with uses the location of which have a strong tendency to injure public health or morals or affect the general welfare, and have the general characteristics of a nuisance, such as saloons, Swift v. People ex rel. Ferris Wheel Co., 162 Ill. 534, 44 N.E. 528, junk shops, Smolensky v. City of Chicago, 282 Ill. 131, 118 N.E. 410, garages, People ex rel. Busching v. Ericsson, 263 Ill. 368, 105 N.E. 315, and billboards, Thomas Cusack Co. v. City of Chicago, 267 Ill. 344, 108 N.E. 340, affirmed in 242 U.S. 526, 37 S.Ct. 190, 61 L.Ed. 472. There is no showing in this record that homes for the aged are offensive to the health, morals and welfare of the community. The property in question is located in the "apartment house" use district which includes "boarding or lodging house, hotels, hospital home for dependents or nursing home." Defendant urges that such homes are properly subject to the police power, citing Father Basil's Lodge, Inc. v. City of Chicago, 393 Ill. 246, 65 N.E.2d 805 but in that case we merely held that a municipality had the power to regulate and license the establishment of homes for the aged for the purpose of protecting the health and safety of the occupants thereof. We refrained from passing upon the validity of the frontage-consent provisions of the ordinance, since we found such provisions to be severable and without application to the appellant.

The case most analogous to the facts here is State of Washington ex rel. Seattle Title Trust Co. v. Roberge, 278 U.S. 116, 49 S.Ct. 50, 73 L.Ed. 210. There an ordinance, similar to the one before us, prohibited erection of homes for the aged in a "first residence district" unless two thirds of the property owners within 400 feet of the proposed site gave their consent in writing. The court held this restriction violative of due process, State of Washington ex rel. Seattle Title Trust Co. v. Roberge, 278 U.S. 116, 121, 49 S.Ct. 50, 73 L.Ed. 210, 213, and stated: "Legislatures may not, under the guise of the police power, impose restrictions that are unnecessary and unreasonable upon the use of private property or the pursuit of useful activities. * * * The facts disclosed by the record make it clear that the exclusion of the new home from the first district is not indispensable to the general zoning plan. And there is no legislative determination that the proposed building and use would be inconsistent with public health, safety, morals or general welfare. The enactment itself plainly implies the contrary. The grant of permission for such building and use, although purporting to be subject to such consents, shows that the legislative body found that the construction and maintenance of the new home was in harmony with the public interest and with the general scope and plan of the zoning ordinance."

In its opinion the court also distinguished Thomas Cusack Co. v. City of Chicago, 242 U.S. 526, 37 S.Ct. 190, 61 L.Ed. 472, relied on by defendant, on the ground that the facts there were sufficient to warrant the conclusion that billboards were liable to endanger the safety and decency of the district involved and held that a home for the aged is clearly distinguishable "from such billboards or other uses which by reason of their nature are liable to be offensive." 278 U.S. 122, 73 L.Ed. 214.

Similar results have been reached in cases involving an "old ladies home," Women's Kansas City St. Andrew Society v. Kansas City, Mo., 58 F.2d 593, a church, State ex rel. Roman Catholic Bishop of Reno v. Hill, 59 Nev. 231, 90 P.2d 217, a retail store, Spies v. Board of Appeals, 337 Ill. 507, 169 N.E. 220, and a school, Concordia Collegiate Institute v. Miller, 301 N.Y. 189, 93 N.E.2d 632, 21 A.L.R.2d 544. Defendant has not cited, nor have we found, any case upholding the exclusion of homes for the aged from a use district similar to the one in question, either by application of frontage-consent provisions or otherwise. Defendant, however, urges that Shepard v. City of Seattle, 59 Wash. 363, 109 P. 1067, is analogous to the case at bar. We cannot agree. The court there upheld an ordinance which declared insane asylums to be a public nuisance, and provided for their abatement as such, subject to the written consent of any property owner within 200 feet. Such ordinance, which contained a legislative finding that the proposed use is a public nuisance, is clearly inapposite here. State of Washington ex rel. Seattle Title Trust Co. v. Roberge, 278 U.S. 116, 122, 73 L.Ed. 210, 214.

In the case at bar there is neither legislative finding that the proposed use is a public nuisance, or that it is apt to be such when operated in an apartment-house use district, nor satisfactory evidence tending to show that the maintenance of the home will work an injury, annoyance or inconvenience to any property owner. On the contrary, the general zoning plan of the city of Chicago declares a nursing home to be appropriate in an apartment-house-use district. The record fails to disclose a rational basis for subjecting homes for the aged to the requirement of frontage consents and is without evidence to support a conclusion that the proposed use has any different effect on the public health, welfare, safety and morals than the other permitted uses in the district.

Since we find no basis for the exercise of the police power in prohibiting the home for the aged in the apartment-house-use district, the ordinance as applied to this proposed use is an unconstitutional deprivation of property without due process of law. Spies v. Board of Appeals, 337 Ill. 507, 169 N.E. 220; State of Washington ex rel. Seattle Title Trust Co. v. Roberge, 278 U.S. 116, 49 S.Ct. 50, 73 L.Ed. 210. Accordingly, the judgment of the trial court is affirmed.

Judgment affirmed.

Notes

1. In Cary v. City of Rapid City, 559 N.W.2d 891 (S.D. 1997), the Supreme Court of South Dakota held that a protest statute was unconstitutional which allowed 40 percent of neighboring property owners to file a written protest that would completely bar the rezoning of property. The court noted that the statute allowed "a potentially small number of neighboring property owners to make the ultimate determination of the public's best interest."

2. In Town of Gardiner v. Stanley Orchards, Inc., 105 Misc.2d 460, 432 N.Y.S.2d 335 (1980), the court held invalid a provision in an ordinance which prohibited mobile homes unless all landowners within 500 feet consented in writing, and in Grendel's Den, Inc. v. Goodwin, 495 F.Supp. 761 (D.Mass. 1980), affirmed sub nom. Larkin v. Grendel's Den, 459 U.S. 116, 103 S.Ct. 505, 74 L.Ed.2d 297 (1982), the court struck down a state statute which provided that no premises within 500 feet of a church or school could receive a liquor license if the church or school filed a written objection. In both cases the courts discussed the problem of delegating legislative authority to private landowners.

3. In Luger v. City of Burnsville, 295 N.W.2d 609 (Minn.1980), the court reversed a local decision to grant the property owner a variance "subject to letters of approval by all abutting property owners." The court indicated that a local zoning agency could not avoid the political implications of its decisions by such a transfer of power to the neighbors. Also, in Lakin v. City of Peoria, 129 Ill.App.3d 651, 84 Ill.Dec. 837, 472 N.E.2d 1233 (1984), the court held that requiring the applicant for a variance to obtain the consent of adjoining and abutting neighbors was an unconstitutional delegation of legislative authority.

4. New York's highest court struck down a village ordinance requiring the consent of 80 percent of the property owners in the neighborhood before a permit could be issued to an educational institution in a residential zoning district. The court held that the provision violated the Fourteenth Amendment of the Constitution of the United States because the neighbors could veto the as-of-right use by taking no action, unguided and unrestricted by legislative standards. Had the use in question been a potential nuisance, however, the court might have found otherwise. It said: "In the case now before us, we are not dealing with billboards or garages or other offensive uses in connection with which consent provisions may be proper." Concordia Collegiate Institute v. Miller, 301 N.Y. 189, 93 N.E.2d 632 (1950).

C. THE INITIATIVE AND REFERENDUM PROCESS

Constitutions of the 50 states delegate the police power to state legislatures. The elected representatives of the people of the state are given the authority to adopt laws necessary to protect the public health, safety, welfare, and morals. Zoning enabling laws are enacted as one example of the exercise of this police power. In some states, the legislature has seen fit to give some of this legislative authority back to the people. At the local level, citizens may be authorized to enact land use regulations by initiative or to subject local legislative zoning decisions to review by referendum. Both initiative and referendum proceedings are begun by voter petitions which must follow the procedural and time prescriptions of state law.

The judicial questions that arise in this context are whether state law allows local citizens initiative or referendum rights and, when the answer is yes, whether the particular objective of the initiative or referendum is within the authority granted to citizens to act on by direct democratic means. A key inquiry here is often whether it matters that the decision subjected to popular vote is a legislative one, such as the adoption of a zoning law or amendment, or one that is administrative or quasi-judicial in nature, such as the issuance of a variance, special use permit, or zoning interpretation. The cases examine a range of nuts and bolts issues, as well, such as whether the petitions were properly drafted, submitted in a timely fashion, signed by a sufficient number of registered voters, and properly presented to the electorate.

CITY OF EASTLAKE v. FOREST CITY ENTERPRISES, INC.

Supreme Court of the United States, 1976.
426 U.S. 668, 96 S.Ct. 2358, 49 L.Ed.2d 132.

MR. CHIEF JUSTICE BURGER delivered the opinion of the Court.

The question in this case is whether a city charter provision requiring proposed land use changes to be ratified by 55% of the votes cast violates the due process rights of a landowner who applies for a zoning change.

The City of Eastlake, Ohio, a suburb of Cleveland, has a comprehensive zoning plan codified in a municipal ordinance. Respondent, a real estate developer, acquired an eight-acre parcel of real estate in Eastlake zoned for "light industrial" uses at the time of purchase.

In May 1971, respondent applied to the City Planning Commission for a zoning change to permit construction of a multifamily, high-rise apartment building. The Planning Commission recommended the proposed change to the City Council, which under Eastlake's procedures could either accept or reject the Planning Commission's recommendation. Meanwhile, by popular vote, the voters of Eastlake amended the city charter to require that any changes in land use agreed to by the Council be approved by a 55% vote in a referendum.[1] The City Council

---

1. As adopted by the voters, Art. VIII, § 3, of the Eastlake City Charter provides in pertinent part:

"That any change to the existing land uses or any change whatsoever to any ordinance * * * cannot be approved unless and until it shall have been submitted to the Planning Commission, for approval or disapproval. That in the event the city council should approve any of the preceding changes, or enactments, whether approved or disapproved by the Planning Commission it shall not be approved or passed by the declaration of an emergency, and it shall not be effective, but it shall be mandatory that the same be approved by a 55% favorable vote of all votes cast of the qualified electors of the City of Eastlake at the next regular municipal election, if one shall occur not less than sixty (60) or more than one hundred and twenty (120) days after its passage, otherwise at a special election falling on the generally established day of the primary election * * *."

approved the Planning Commission's recommendation for reclassification of respondent's property to permit the proposed project. Respondent then applied to the Planning Commission for "parking and yard" approval for the proposed building. The Commission rejected the application, on the ground that the City Council's rezoning action had not yet been submitted to the voters for ratification.

Respondent then filed an action in state court, seeking a judgment declaring the charter provision invalid as an unconstitutional delegation of legislative power to the people. While the case was pending, the City Council's action was submitted to a referendum, but the proposed zoning change was not approved by the requisite 55% margin. Following the election, the Court of Common Pleas and the Ohio Court of Appeals sustained the charter provision.

The Ohio Supreme Court reversed. 41 Ohio St.2d 187, 324 N.E.2d 740 (1975). Concluding that enactment of zoning and rezoning provisions is a legislative function, the court held that a popular referendum requirement, lacking standards to guide the decision of the voters, permitted the police power to be exercised in a standardless, hence arbitrary and capricious manner. Relying on this Court's decisions in Washington ex rel. Seattle Title Trust Co. v. Roberge, 278 U.S. 116, 49 S.Ct. 50, 73 L.Ed. 210 (1928), Thomas Cusack Co. v. Chicago, 242 U.S. 526, 37 S.Ct. 190, 61 L.Ed. 472 (1917), and Eubank v. Richmond, 226 U.S. 137, 33 S.Ct. 76, 57 L.Ed. 156 (1912), but distinguishing James v. Valtierra, 402 U.S. 137, 91 S.Ct. 1331, 28 L.Ed.2d 678 (1971), the court concluded that the referendum provision constituted an unlawful delegation of legislative power.

We reverse.

The conclusion that Eastlake's procedure violates federal constitutional guarantees rests upon the proposition that a zoning referendum involves a delegation of legislative power. A referendum cannot, however, be characterized as a delegation of power. Under our constitutional assumptions, all power derives from the people, who can delegate it to representative instruments which they create. See, e.g., The Federalist No. 39 (J. Madison). In establishing legislative bodies, the people can reserve to themselves power to deal directly with matters which might otherwise be assigned to the legislature. Hunter v. Erickson, 393 U.S. 385, 392, 89 S.Ct. 557, 561, 21 L.Ed.2d 616 (1969).

The reservation of such power is the basis for the town meeting, a tradition which continues to this day in some States as both a practical and symbolic part of our democratic processes. The referendum, similarly, is a means for direct political participation, allowing the people the final decision, amounting to a veto power, over enactments of representative bodies. The practice is designed to "give citizens a voice on questions of public policy." James v. Valtierra, supra, 402 U.S., at 141, 91 S.Ct., at 1333.

In framing a state constitution, the people of Ohio specifically reserved the power of referendum to the people of each municipality within the State.

* * *

To be subject to Ohio's referendum procedure, the question must be one within the scope of legislative power. The Ohio Supreme Court expressly found that the City Council's action in rezoning respondent's eight acres from light industrial to high-density residential use was legislative in nature. Distinguishing between administrative and legislative acts, the court separated the power to zone or rezone, by passage or amendment of a zoning ordinance, from the power to grant relief from unnecessary hardship. The former function was found to be legislative in nature. * * *

The Ohio Supreme Court further concluded that the amendment to the city charter constituted a "delegation" of power violative of federal constitutional guarantees because the voters were given no standards to guide their decision. Under Eastlake's procedure, the Ohio Supreme Court reasoned, no mechanism existed, nor indeed could exist, to assure that the voters would act rationally in passing upon a proposed zoning change. This means that "appropriate legislative action [would] be made dependent upon the potentially arbitrary and unreasonable whims of the voting public." 41 Ohio St.2d, at 195, 324 N.E.2d, at 746. The potential for arbitrariness in the process, the court concluded, violated due process.

* * *

In basing its claim on federal due process requirements, respondent also invokes Euclid v. Ambler Realty Co., 272 U.S. 365, 47 S.Ct. 114, 71 L.Ed. 303 (1926), but it does not rely on the direct teaching of that case. Under *Euclid,* a property owner can challenge a zoning restriction if the measure is "clearly arbitrary and unreasonable, having no substantial relation to the public health, safety, morals, or general welfare." Id., at 395, 47 S.Ct., at 121. If the substantive result of the referendum is arbitrary and capricious, bearing no relation to the police power, then the fact that the voters of Eastlake wish it so would not save the restriction. * * *

But no challenge of the sort contemplated in Euclid v. Ambler Realty is before us. The Ohio Supreme Court did not hold, and respondent does not argue, that the present zoning classification under Eastlake's comprehensive ordinance violates the principles established in Euclid v. Ambler Realty. If respondent considers the referendum result itself to be unreasonable, the zoning restriction is open to challenge in state court, where the scope of the state remedy available to respondent would be determined as a matter of state law, as well as under Fourteenth Amendment standards. That being so, nothing more is required by the Constitution.

Nothing in our cases is inconsistent with this conclusion. Two decisions of this Court were relied on by the Ohio Supreme Court in invalidating Eastlake's procedure. The thread common to both decisions is the delegation of legislative power, originally given by the people to a legislative body, and in turn delegated by the legislature to a *narrow segment* of the community, not to the people at large. In Eubank v. Richmond, 226 U.S. 137, 33 S.Ct. 76, 57 L.Ed. 156 (1912), the Court invalidated a city ordinance which conferred the power to establish building setback lines upon the owners of two-thirds of the property abutting any street. Similarly, in Washington ex rel. Seattle Title Trust Co. v. Roberge, 278 U.S. 116, 49 S.Ct. 50, 73 L.Ed. 210 (1928), the Court struck down an ordinance which permitted the establishment of philanthropic homes for the aged in residential areas, but only upon the written consent of the owners of two-thirds of the property within 400 feet of the proposed facility.[2]

Neither *Eubank* nor *Roberge* involved a referendum procedure such as we have in this case; the standardless delegation of power to a limited group of property owners condemned by the Court in *Eubank* and *Roberge* is not to be equated with decisionmaking by the people through the referendum process. The Court of Appeals for the Ninth Circuit put it this way:

> "A referendum, however, is far more than an expression of ambiguously founded neighborhood preference. It is the city itself legislating through its voters—an exercise by the voters of their traditional right through direct legislation to override the views of their elected representatives as to what serves the public interest." Southern Alameda Spanish Speaking Organization v. Union City, California, 424 F.2d 291, 294 (1970).

Our decision in James v. Valtierra, upholding California's mandatory referendum requirement, confirms this view. Mr. Justice Black, speaking for the Court in that case, said:

> This procedure ensures that *all the people* of a community will have a voice in a decision which may lead to large expenditures of local governmental funds for increased public services * * *. 402 U.S., at 143, 91 S.Ct., at 1334 (emphasis added).

---

2. The Ohio Supreme Court also considered this Court's decision in Thomas Cusack Co. v. Chicago, 242 U.S. 526, 37 S.Ct. 190, 61 L.Ed. 472 (1917). In contrast to *Eubank* and *Roberge,* the *Cusack* Court *upheld* a neighborhood consent provision which permitted property owners to waive a municipal restriction prohibiting the construction of billboards. This Court in *Cusack* distinguished *Eubank* in the following way:

> "[The ordinance in *Eubank*] left the establishment of the building line untouched until the lot owners should act and then * * * gave to it the effect of law. The ordinance in the case at bar absolutely prohibits the erection of any billboards * * * but permits this prohibition to be modified with the consent of the persons who are to be most affected by such modification." 242 U.S., at 531, 37 S.Ct. at 192. Since the property owners could simply waive an otherwise applicable legislative limitation, the Court in *Cusack* determined that the provision did not delegate legislative power at all. Ibid.

Mr. Justice Black went on to say that a referendum procedure, such as the one at issue here, is a classic demonstration of "devotion to democracy * * *." Id., at 141. As a basic instrument of democratic government, the referendum process does not, in itself, violate the Due Process Clause of the Fourteenth Amendment when applied to a rezoning ordinance.[3] Since the rezoning decision in this case was properly reserved to the people of Eastlake under the Ohio Constitution, the Ohio Supreme Court erred in holding invalid, on federal constitutional grounds, the charter amendment permitting the voters to decide whether the zoned use of respondent's property could be altered.

The judgment of the Ohio Supreme Court is reversed, and the case is remanded for further proceedings not inconsistent with this opinion.

Reversed and remanded.

[A dissenting opinion by MR. JUSTICE POWELL is omitted.]

MR. JUSTICE STEVENS, with whom MR. JUSTICE BRENNAN joins, dissenting.

* * *

A zoning code is unlike other legislation affecting the use of property. The deprivation caused by a zoning code is customarily qualified by recognizing the property owner's right to apply for an amendment or variance to accommodate his individual needs. The expectancy that particular changes consistent with the basic zoning plan will be allowed frequently and on their merits is a normal incident of property ownership. When the governing body offers the owner the opportunity to seek such a change—whether that opportunity is denominated a privilege or a right—it is affording protection to the owner's interest in making legitimate use of his property.

The fact that an individual owner (like any other petitioner or plaintiff) may not have a legal right to the relief he seeks does not mean that he has no right to fair procedure in the consideration of the merits of his application. The fact that codes regularly provide a procedure for granting individual exceptions or changes, the fact that such changes are granted in individual cases with great frequency, and the fact that the particular code in the record before us contemplates that changes consistent with the basic plan will be allowed, all support my opinion that the opportunity to apply for an amendment is an aspect of property

---

3. The fears expressed in dissent rest on the proposition that the procedure at issue here is "fundamentally unfair" to landowners; this fails to take into account the mechanisms for relief potentially available to property owners whose desired land use changes are rejected by the voters. First, if hardship is occasioned by zoning restrictions, *administrative* relief is potentially available. Indeed, the very purpose of "variances" allowed by zoning officials is to avoid "practical difficulties and unnecessary hardship." 8 E. McQuillan, Municipal Corporations § 25.159, p. 511 (3d ed. 1965). As we noted, *supra,* at 677, remedies remain available under the Ohio Supreme Court's holding and provide a means to challenge unreasonable or arbitrary action. Euclid v. Ambler Realty Co., 272 U.S. 365, 47 S.Ct. 114, 71 L.Ed. 303 (1926).

ownership protected by the Due Process Clause of the Fourteenth Amendment.

* * *

Although this Court has decided only a handful of zoning cases, literally thousands of zoning disputes have been resolved by state courts. Those courts have repeatedly identified the obvious difference between the adoption of a comprehensive citywide plan by legislative action and the decision of particular issues involving specific uses of specific parcels. In the former situation there is generally great deference to the judgment of the legislature; in the latter situation state courts have not hesitated to correct manifest injustice.

* * *

Specialists in the practice of zoning law are unhappily familiar with the potential for abuse which exists when inadequate procedural safeguards apply to the dispensation of special grants. The power to deny arbitrarily may give rise to the power to exact intolerable conditions.[4] The insistence on fair procedure in this area of the law falls squarely within the purpose of the Due Process Clause of the Fourteenth Amendment.

* * *

As the Justices of the Ohio Supreme Court recognized, we are concerned with the fairness of a provision for determining the right to make a particular use of a particular parcel of land. In such cases, the state courts have frequently described the capricious character of a decision supported by majority sentiment rather than reference to articulable standards. Moreover, they have limited statutory referendum procedures to apply only to approvals of comprehensive zoning ordinances as opposed to amendments affecting specific parcels. This conclusion has been supported by characterizing particular amendments as "administrative" and revision of an entire plan as "legislative."

In this case the Ohio Supreme Court characterized the Council's approval of respondent's proposal as "legislative." I think many state courts would have characterized it as "administrative." The courts thus may well differ in their selection of the label to apply to this action, but I find substantial agreement among state tribunals on the proposition that

---

4. One expert on zoning matters has made the following comment:

"The freedom from accountability of the municipal governing body may be tolerable in those cases where the legislature is engaged in legislating but it makes no sense where the legislature is dispensing or refusing to dispense special grants. When the local legislature acts to pass general laws applicable generally it is performing its traditional role and it is entitled to be free from those strictures we place upon an agency that is charged with granting or denying special privileges to particular persons. When the municipal legislature crosses over into the role of hearing and passing on individual petitions in adversary proceedings it should be required to meet the same procedural standards we expect from a traditional administrative agency." R. Babcock, The Zoning Game 158 (1966). Compare this comment with the practice of another "zoning man." See United States v. Staszcuk, 517 F.2d 53, 56 (C.A.7 1975).

requiring a citywide referendum for approval of a particular proposal like this is manifestly unreasonable. Surely that is my view.

* * *

I have no doubt about the validity of the initiative or the referendum as an appropriate method of deciding questions of community policy. I think it is equally clear that the popular vote is not an acceptable method of adjudicating the rights of individual litigants. The problem presented by this case is unique, because it may involve a three-sided controversy, in which there is at least potential conflict between the rights of the property owner and the rights of his neighbors, and also potential conflict with the public interest in preserving the city's basic zoning plan. If the latter aspect of the controversy were predominant, the referendum would be an acceptable procedure. On the other hand, when the record indicates without contradiction that there is no threat to the general public interest in preserving the city's plan—as it does in this case, since respondent's proposal was approved by both the Planning Commission and the City Council and there has been no allegation that the use of this eight-acre parcel for apartments rather than light industry would adversely affect the community or raise any policy issue of citywide concern—I think the case should be treated as one in which it is essential that the private property owner be given a fair opportunity to have his claim determined on its merits.

As Justice Stern points out in his concurring opinion, it would be absurd to use a referendum to decide whether a gasoline station could be operated on a particular corner in the city of Cleveland. The case before us is not that clear because we are told that there are only 20,000 people in the city of Eastlake. Conceivably, an eight-acre development could be sufficiently dramatic to arouse the legitimate interest of the entire community; it is also conceivable that most of the voters would be indifferent and uninformed about the wisdom of building apartments rather than a warehouse or factory on these eight acres. The record is silent on which of these alternatives is the more probable. Since the ordinance places a manifestly unreasonable obstacle in the path of every property owner seeking any zoning change, since it provides no standards or procedures for exempting particular parcels or claims from the referendum requirement, and since the record contains no justification for the use of the procedure in this case, I am persuaded that we should respect the state judiciary's appraisal of the fundamental fairness of this decisionmaking process in his case.

I therefore conclude that the Ohio Supreme Court correctly held that Art. VIII, § 3, of the Eastlake charter violates the Due Process Clause of the Fourteenth Amendment, and that its judgment should be affirmed.

Notes

1. On remand, the Ohio Supreme Court found no state constitutional issues in the case and dismissed the proceedings. Forest City Enterprises v.

City of Eastlake, 48 Ohio St.2d 47, 356 N.E.2d 499 (1976). In Jurkiewicz v. Butler County Bd. of Elections, 85 Ohio App.3d 503, 620 N.E.2d 146 (1993), the court held that a change of zoning to planned unit development was a legislative act and thus subject to referendum.

2. The U.S. Supreme Court reinforced Eastlake in City of Cuyahoga Falls v. Buckeye Community Hope Foundation, 538 U.S. 188, 123 S.Ct. 1389, 155 L.Ed.2d 349 (2003). The city planning commission approved a site plan application for a multifamily, low-income housing complex, finding that the development was permitted under the zoning law of the city. The city council, by ordinance, approved the project, which was vigorously opposed by local citizens. After the council's approval, a group of citizens filed a formal petition with the city requesting that the ordinance be repealed or submitted to a popular vote. This had the effect, under Ohio law, of staying the approval and the non-profit developer was denied its application for a building permit. The approval was submitted to a local referendum that then passed. The Ohio Supreme Court held the referendum unconstitutional because the state constitution allows only legislative acts, not administrative acts, to be subject to referendums. The Supreme Court, Justice O'Connor, reversed stating:

> As a matter of federal constitutional law, we have rejected the distinction that respondents ask us to draw, and that the Ohio Supreme Court drew as a matter of state law, between legislative and administrative referendums. In *Eastlake v. Forest City Enterprises, Inc.*, 426 U.S., at 672, 675, 96 S.Ct. 2358, we made clear that because all power stems from the people, "[a] referendum cannot * * * be characterized as a delegation of power," unlawful unless accompanied by "discernible standards." The people retain the power to govern through referendum " 'with respect to any matter, legislative or administrative, within the realm of local affairs.' "*Id.*, at 674, n. 9, 96 S.Ct. 2358. Cf. *James v. Valtierra*, 402 U.S., at 137, 91 S.Ct. 1331. Though the "substantive result" of a referendum may be invalid if it is "arbitrary and capricious," *Eastlake v. Forest City Enterprises, supra*, at 676, 96 S.Ct. 2358, respondents do not challenge the referendum itself. The subjection of the site-plan ordinance to the City's referendum process, regardless of whether that ordinance reflected an administrative or legislative decision, did not constitute *per se* arbitrary government conduct in violation of due process.

In Land Use Law & Zoning Dig., July 2003 pp. 3–14 six commentators reflect on the Buckeye decision, under the general title, "The Tyranny of the Majority." Most of the commentaries are critical of the decision.

3. In James v. Valtierra, 402 U.S. 137, 91 S.Ct. 1331, 28 L.Ed.2d 678 (1971), relied on in the principal case, the Court upheld a California constitutional provision which provided that no low-rent public housing project could be developed unless approved by referendum in the community. The California Supreme Court held, in DeVita v. County of Napa, 9 Cal.4th 763, 38 Cal.Rptr.2d 699, 889 P.2d 1019 (1995), that voters could amend a comprehensive plan by use of the initiative and could, in that amended plan, provide that any land use designations enacted by initiative can only be changed during the following 30 years by majority vote of the county

electorate. The purpose and effect of the amended plan was to keep land designated as agricultural or open space in those categories for 30 years, unless voters agreed to change.

4. By holding that the federal constitution does not inhibit mandatory referenda in zoning cases, the Court is essentially leaving the issue to state law and state court determination. Some state courts have held that a zoning amendment is not subject to referendum because a zoning amendment is quasi-judicial or administrative in nature and is not a legislative act. See Leonard v. City of Bothell, 87 Wash.2d 847, 557 P.2d 1306 (1976). Also see Kelley v. John, 162 Neb. 319, 75 N.W.2d 713 (1956). Compare Arnel Development Co. v. City of Costa Mesa, 28 Cal.3d 511, 169 Cal.Rptr. 904, 620 P.2d 565 (1980), where the court held that the enactment or amendment of a zoning ordinance is a legislative act even if it affects only a small area or a few landowners and is subject to the initiative and referendum provisions of the state constitution. On remand, the Court of Appeals found the initiative arbitrary and discriminatory as it was directed at one developer. 126 Cal.App.3d 330, 178 Cal.Rptr. 723 (1981).

A majority of states find rezonings to be legislative. See State ex rel. Hickman v. City Council of Kirksville, 690 S.W.2d 799 (Mo.App.1985); Florida Land Co. v. City of Winter Springs, 427 So.2d 170 (Fla.1983); Wright v. City of Lakewood, 43 Colo.App. 480, 608 P.2d 361 (1979), cf. Margolis v. District Ct., County of Arapahoe, 638 P.2d 297 (Colo.1981); Schanz v. City of Billings, 182 Mont. 328, 597 P.2d 67 (1979) ("A rezoning ordinance, like a zoning ordinance is a legislative enactment"), Greens at Fort Missoula, LLC v. City of Missoula, 271 Mont. 398, 897 P.2d 1078 (1995) (rezoning ordinance subject to referendum); Albright v. City of Portage, 470 N.W.2d 657 (Mich. App.1991); R. G. Moore Building Corp. v. Committee for the Repeal of Ordinance R (C)–88–13, 239 Va. 484, 391 S.E.2d 587 (1990); Garvin v. Ninth Judicial District, 59 P.3d 1180 (Nev.2002) (sustaining the use of initiative for zoning amendments, and holding that a sustainable growth initiative measure was legislation, and not an administrative act). In Kirschenman v. Hutchinson County Board of Commissioners, 656 N.W.2d 330 (S.D.2003), the Supreme Court of South Dakota held that a conditional use permit allowing a hog confinement facility was a legislative rather than administrative act and thus subject to referendum. The court found that the lack of objective criteria for granting the permit in the county ordinance made the board's actions discretionary.

5. The application of initiative and referendum mechanisms to local land use decisions is offensive to some. After all, the law provides for the adoption of a comprehensive plan with citizen participation, the adoption of conforming zoning following public hearings, and public involvement in most site specific land use decisions. In 1991, the Urban, State and Local Government Law Section of the American Bar Association approved a recommendation to the ABA House of Delegates regarding the problem reflected in the City of Eastlake situation. Part A of the recommendation was that the ABA recommend: "That all state legislatures adopt legislation prohibiting the use of the initiative/referendum in 'site specific' zoning cases." Part B urged state legislatures in states with initiative and referendum provisions to adopt legislation prohibiting general land-use policy proposals from being submitted for initiative or referendum unless the proposal conforms with the

comprehensive plan or amends such plan. For an explanation of the reasons for the proposals see 14 Urban, State and Local Law Newsletter, No. 3, Spring 1991 (American Bar Association). Apparently, at the House of Delegates meeting, August 12–13, 1991, the section report (No. 111) on site-specific zoning referenda and initiatives (Part A) was withdrawn by the proponents. ABA, Summary of Action of the House of Delegates, 1991 Annual Meeting. Why do you suppose Part A was withdrawn? What are the pros and cons of the use of referenda to review land use decisions?

6. A distinction is frequently made between use of the initiative to adopt a zoning ordinance and the use of a referendum to subject a zoning decision to the electorate for approval or rejection. Many courts have held that an initiated zoning ordinance is improper because of conflict with the state zoning enabling legislation which usually requires notice and hearing prior to adoption of a zoning ordinance. However, in Oregon, a 1974 case holding the initiative process inapplicable to zoning, Tatum v. Clackamas County, 19 Or.App. 770, 529 P.2d 393 (1974), was overruled in Allison v. Washington County, 24 Or.App. 571, 548 P.2d 188 (1976). Ohio has long held that zoning ordinances or amendments are subject to initiative. Drockton v. Board of Elections, 16 Ohio Misc. 211, 240 N.E.2d 896 (1968). Also see Queen Creek Land & Cattle Corp. v. Yavapai County Bd. of Supervisors, 108 Ariz. 449, 501 P.2d 391 (1972), discussing initiative as a right under the state constitution.

Hawaii allows referenda on zoning ordinances: County of Kauai v. Pacific Standard Life Insurance, 65 Hawaii 318, 653 P.2d 766 (1982). However, the state Supreme Court has held that zoning by initiative is inconsistent with comprehensive planning: Kaiser Hawaii Kai Development Co. v. City and County of Honolulu, 70 Hawaii 480, 777 P.2d 244 (1989). New Jersey's Municipal Land Use Act prohibits zoning by initiative and referendum. N.J.S.A. 40:55D–62. A non-binding referendum to determine public sentiment about a proposed zoning amendment is permitted. See Great Atlantic & Pacific Tea Co. v. Borough of Point Pleasant, 137 N.J. 136, 644 A.2d 598 (1994). In I'On, L.L.C. v. Town of Mt. Pleasant, 338 S.C. 406, 526 S.E.2d 716 (S.C. 2000), the South Carolina Supreme Court quoted the New Jersey Supreme Court: "Zoning ordinances touch people where they live. Sensitive to the intense public interest in local land use development, the Legislature has developed an orderly structure for public participation in the process. That process also contemplates the rational development of land use, free from undue political influence." The South Carolina court held that, under the state's detailed comprehensive planning and enabling legislation, the state legislature "has not condoned—and we should not approve—a process by which voters could circumvent this deliberative process by deciding zoning matters in an initiative and referendum process."

SECTION 2. MEDIATION

A. AN INTRODUCTION TO LAND USE MEDIATION

As early as 1886, the New York Legislature recognized the importance of mediation in resolving conflicts in collective bargaining disputes. In this context, mediation was conceived not as an alternative to litigation but as a means of preventing labor strikes and the societal disruptions they cause. By 1925, mediation was being used in New York City in court-related conciliation programs as a cost-effective means of resolving cases through conciliation rather than adjudication.

In this early period, the lesson of mediation was that consensus-based compromise was an effective method of producing mutually satisfying results to critical disputes in society and to particular quarrels among individuals. By the 1970's, the field of alternative dispute resolution had emerged, sparked by the interest of jurists in caseload management. In 1982, Chief Justice Burger warned that we had "reached a period where our system of justice may literally break down before the end of the century..." He called for a "fresh, hard look" at alternative methods of dispute resolution.

At the time the Chief Justice spoke, community-based mediation programs were emerging as a productive method of resolving disputes among community members who had to live with one another in shared environments. More recently, mediation has been embraced by corporation counsel in large companies as a method of achieving settlement based on sound business practices rather than strict legal standards. Today, federal and state agencies are experimenting with mediation as a method of developing consensus on pending regulations and of resolving disputes that arise in the administrative process of issuing development and environmental permits. Mediation is beginning to be used at the local level in a variety of land use and environmental contexts.

The first significant land use dispute employing alternative dispute resolution took place in Washington State in 1974. In order to settle a dispute over the proposed location of a flood control dam on the Snoqualmie River, two mediators facilitated a discussion among opposing parties. Environmental advocates opposed the project's proponents because of their concern over the survival of the river's ecosystem; farmers were concerned about proposed reductions in water for irrigation; and citizens worried about the potential for uncontrolled suburban sprawl. Although the dam was never constructed, many of the land use recommendations that were agreed to among the parties were implemented, and a coordinating council formed by the stakeholders continued operating for 10 years.

As it has evolved, mediation has been defined in a variety of ways and has developed a range of applications and approaches about which there is vigorous debate. It has remained vibrant, however, as a voluntary, consensus-based conflict prevention and resolution strategy. It is a non-predictive method that leaves the outcomes to its participants. In essence, it is a negotiation-assisting process that works when the contestants believe that settlement is a better alternative than protracted hostility or the winner-take-all results of litigation.

The Consensus Building Institute (CBI) and the Lincoln Institute of Land Policy undertook a study in 1999 of mediated land use disputes based on interviews with participants in 100 cases in which a professional neutral assisted in the resolution of a land use dispute. This study indicated that 85 percent of participants had a positive view of assisted negotiation. Additionally, of respondents who participated in cases that were settled, 92 percent believed that their own interests were well served by the settlement and 86 percent believed that all parties' interests were served by the agreement reached.

(1) Land Use Approvals as Negotiations

When a landowner submits an application for a development permit to a local land use agency, an extended process of negotiation is initiated. The parties to this negotiation are the owner, the members of the local administrative agency with approval authority, other involved public agencies, and those affected by the proposed project: neighbors, taxpayers, and citizens of the community. Unlike commercial and personal negotiations, this process is not viewed by most of its participants as a negotiation, in the traditional sense. Local zoning ordinances give the landowner property rights that must be respected. State and local statutes prescribe standards and procedures that the agency members must follow. Affected neighbors and citizens receive notice of their right to attend and speak at one or more public hearings. This process is not organized, in most localities, as a structured negotiation in which the parties meet face-to-face, follow a self-determined process of decision-making, and arrive at a mutually acceptable agreement based on facts gathered in the process and compromise on all sides.

The local development approval process often costs the applicant significant sums of money, involves only indirect contacts among interested parties, and provides little opportunity to develop creative, win-win solutions. For most significant development proposals, the process is lengthy, inflexible, and frustrating. The outcomes are unpredictable and relationships among those involved are more often damaged than strengthened. Nonetheless, during the awkward journey of a development proposal through the local approval process, critical interests of many stakeholders in the matter are expressed, heard, considered, and disposed of by a decision rendered by a voluntary board of local citizens. This is, in the classic sense, a negotiation that resolves, if not satisfies, each participant's interests. When it is seen as such, methods of making it more productive, satisfying, and efficient seem obvious.

Although mediation is described as a dispute *resolution* technique, it is also an effective means of *avoiding* disputes in the land use area. Often, when a developer seeks approval of a project from a local board, the public may not become involved in the process until the public hearing stage. By this time, the developer may have invested substantial time, money, and energy in the proposal and have become highly invested in it. Due to this investment, the developer may resist suggested changes, more so than if those suggestions had been made earlier. Public hearings and public comment periods, which occur in the later stages of project review, often result in requests to modify the proposal significantly.

Mediation may be employed to bring the interested parties together much earlier in the process, so that a project's design accommodates the concerns of as many of the interested parties as possible. Introduced at this point, mediation influences the developer's application, resulting in early amendments to plans based on the results achieved in mediation. Disputes that arise later in the land use approval process may be resolved through mediation as well. When the local government allows the parties to mediate these differences as and when they occur, they are provided with an opportunity to explore a variety of ways of realizing the objectives of all interested parties.

(2) *Mediators and Facilitators*

Mediation is properly understood as negotiation assisted by a third party who is usually a neutral. Professional mediators can be called in when the parties to a dispute recognize that they have a dispute, understand the importance of mediated resolution, and can agree upon, and have the resources to pay, a neutral mediator. Where these conditions do not exist, someone involved in the local matter may come forward and attempt to structure a process that results in a facilitated decision, using the techniques of the experienced mediator. The alternative to traditional mediation or structured facilitation is for the parties to proceed at arms length through the local decision-making process and to risk litigation by those not satisfied by it.

Facilitators and mediators are process experts who carefully structure multi-party negotiations. They are skilled in effective negotiation and decision-making processes. They help by bringing involved parties together, building trust, clearly establishing the interests of those involved, serving as intermediaries, seeing that options to the resolution of the matter are generated, and working toward a settlement that is acceptable to all parties.

Mediated proceedings are usually informal and flexible, allow the parties to structure the decision-making process itself, and result in consensus-based settlements that are not binding on the participants or public bodies. When the agreement is based on the consensus of all affected parties, supported by credible facts, and consistent with regulatory standards, it can be highly influential in determining the administrative review body's decision on a development proposal.

(3) *Broader Applications*

Mediation has been used in recent years as a method of building consensus regarding public policies and formulating land use plans and regulations. In this context, mediation techniques assist parties with disparate interest to participate in a productive public decision-making process. In the land use field, this can involve the development of a comprehensive land use plan, the scope of an environmental impact study of a proposed project, determining how to rezone a community, a landscape, or a neighborhood, and coming to agreement regarding specific development proposals advanced by a land developer during the permit issuance process.

Illustrations of this use of mediation methods include the Negotiated Rulemaking Act (5 USC § 581), the Administrative Dispute Resolution Act (Pub. L. No. 101–552), and the U.S. Department of Labor's Negotiated Rulemaking Handbook (1992) at the federal level. Several state legislatures have adopted statutes establishing negotiated rulemaking processes. (Fla. Stat. § 120.54; Neb. Rev. Stat. §§ 84–919.01 et seq.; Idaho Code §§ 67–5206(3)(c), 67–5220; 1993 Or. Laws 647; Mont. Code Ann. § 2–5–101; Tex. Govt. Code ch. 2008).

B. KEY STEPS IN THE MEDIATION PROCESS

(This section is included with permission from Lawrence Susskind and Alexis Gensberg, *The Important Role of Consensus Building in Planning for Smart Growth* (Jan. 28, 2002).)

The consensus-building process by which such agreements can be negotiated has five basic steps. The first is called ***convening***. A sponsoring or convening body (usually a governmental agency) must initiate a discussion about whether or not to have a consensus building dialogue. This is best done by commissioning a mediator or some other "professional neutral" to talk privately with the obvious stakeholders to see if they have sufficient reason to support such an effort. Such consultations usually lead to the preparation of a draft conflict assessment (a written report) mapping the views and interests of all the relevant stakeholders. The stakeholders must be interviewed individually, but not for attribution. A summary of their interests (and the points of agreement and disagreement among them) will help to clarify whether it is worth trying to bring them all together in an extended (public) dialogue. In addition, if there appears to be sufficient interest in initiating a dialogue, the conflict assessment can then be used to generate a work plan, timetable, operating ground rules, budget, and an outline of the data or technical material that needs to be gathered. A conflict assessment also contains the neutral's suggestion regarding the categories of stakeholders that ought to be represented in the dialogue, as well as an indication of which groups or individuals might actually be invited (by the convenor) to participate. The neutral may also be called upon to caucus the various categories of stakeholders to help them choose their spokespeople. Finally, during Pre–Negotiations, the mediator may be asked to develop joint fact finding proposals, identify potential technical consultants or advisors to the full group, assist in fund raising, and even help to train the participants in negotiation techniques.

The tasks of the mediator stretch from the behind-the-scenes "Pre–Negotiation" work crucial to launching a consensus-building process, through the facilitation of face-to-face interaction when the parties finally come to the table, to the "Post–Negotiation" dynamics of helping to implement whatever agreement is reached. Only someone with the requisite skill, experience, and credibility can "add value" in such politically-charged circumstances.

The second step in the consensus-building process is ***clarifying responsibilities***. Assuming the parties decide to proceed, it will be necessary to select a facilitator or mediator as well as a recorder. The responsibilities of each of these "helpers' is usually spelled out in a contract between the neutral providing such services and the participants in the process. Face-to-face dialogue in a consensus building process usually takes place in a public forum. Thus, rules must be set regarding the participation (if any) of observers. The ground rules spelling out the role of each stakeholder representative must also be initialed by the participants and often by their organizational leadership. Technical consultants, selected to assist with any joint fact-finding, work for the group as a whole and are coordinated by the facilitator or the mediator.

The third step in the process involves ***deliberating***. This can be a daunting challenge for groups that involve 25 or more participants. It falls to the facilitator or mediator to ensure that each face-to-face session is professionally managed. An agenda (approved by all participants) must be prepared prior to each meeting. Often sub-committees of participants (assisted by external experts agreed to by everyone involved) prepare reports on specific issues laying out options or arguments for the full group to consider. Deliberations are most effective when the "invention" of options or packages spelling out possible ways of meeting the conflicting interests of the stakeholders are explored independently of any final decisions. Ultimately, what has come to be known as "a single text procedure" can be used to synthesize the views expressed during the "inventing" phase of deliberations as the parties seek to reach agreement on suggested actions. A single text procedure usually takes advantage of the neutral party who can introduce a working draft of an agreement for parties to discuss and revise.

When the parties are face-to-face, during the deliberation and decision-making phases of the consensus-building process, the mediator is expected to manage the brainstorming process, coordinate the drafting of options, and generate a single text that offers a draft written agreement that the group can work to enhance. Often, a mediator meets privately with each party to identify and test possible trades or "packages." A mediator can even help the participants present proposed agreements to their respective constituencies, ensuring that all representatives have been in touch with the groups or individuals they are supposed to represent. Finally, during this phase of the consensus-building process, a mediator may serve as a point of contact with the media or approach outsiders on behalf of the group, seeking assistance of various kinds.

The fourth step in a consensus building-process, ***deciding***, is handled quite differently from what most people are used to in public policy-making settings. The goals are to (1) maximize joint gains, not merely to find a minimally acceptable (i.e., lowest common denominator) agreement; (2) formulate a set of suggestions that can be adopted by consensus, rather than to vote on something that pleases only a majority; and (3) pursue a process of conversation that clarifies the reasons that people want or don't want to support a particular proposal, so that group problem-solving becomes easier. Consensus does not necessarily mean unanimity, but it does mean overwhelming agreement in response to the question, "Who can live with this?" In a consensus-building dialogue, participants are responsible not only for presenting their own views but for suggesting ways of meeting the interests of others as well.

The final step involves a focus on ***implementing agreements***. The product of most consensus-building efforts in the growth management field is a proposal that must still be approved by elected or appointed agencies or officials. It is not appropriate to substitute ad hoc decision-making for the formal (and accountable) judgment of duly appointed boards or officials. Yet, since officials are the ones serving as convenors of the consensus-building process, their staff often participate in the process and the mediator or facilitator routinely keeps the officials updated about the group's progress. The final product of the group is a proposal that is often sent to officials via the mediator or facilitator. Decision-makers are almost always eager to know what they could recommend that would satisfy all the stakeholders involved and to learn what the product of informed discussion and debate (as opposed to the emotion-laden outbursts at a traditional public hearing) might be.

The implementation phase of a consensus-building process involves finding ways of linking the informal agreement to the formal mechanisms of decision-making. For example, a negotiated agreement may still have to be acted upon by an administrative agency. A mediator may be asked to approach the relevant elected or appointed officials on behalf of the group (even if those agencies were represented at the staff level at the table). Mediators are often "written into" agreements to serve as monitors of on-going efforts at implementation or given a mandate to reassemble the participants if some aspect of the agreement goes awry.

C. MEDIATION STATUTES

Mediation may be used to address land use disputes regardless of whether there is specific legislative authorization. However, the existence of legislative authority serves several purposes. Among other things, statutory provisions provide guidance and encouragement for the appropriate use of mediation; offer a suggested framework and time frame; and inform the public of the right to request mediation. Laws authorizing or prescribing mediation can exist at either the local, state, or federal level.

Land use mediation of various types is authorized by statute in about two dozen states. Mediation may be authorized for very specific issues such as regional impact development projects, border disputes between local governments, or decisions on land use applications. The point at which mediation is encouraged or required varies under these laws from early in the development approval process until after a project decision is made and litigation has been initiated. At least twelve states[5] offer some type of mediation or dispute resolution services to assist parties mediate in the land use context. Some state mediation statutes use the word mediation but describe a process that it is not completely voluntary so is more akin to arbitration. About half of the statutes are directed to the resolution of a specific type of issue, an example being reuse of a military base.[6] Fourteen states authorize mediation for regional planning disputes.[7] These statutes define procedures for the adoption of plans such as a comprehensive plan, or a plan for growth management or for water quality. These statutes require notice to and authorize intervention by a neighboring government before a plan is adopted.

A number of states have statutes that recognize and define a mediation procedure for land use disputes between a private individual and a government body.[8] These procedures are voluntary and arise in the context of the application for a land use permit. The greatest distinction among the statutes that authorize mediation of land use applications is the point at which mediation is authorized. In Maine and Florida, mediation is authorized after a final decision on the application is rendered, and in California, Connecticut, and Oregon mediation is not expressly authorized until after a court action has been filed. Idaho, Pennsylvania, and Hawaii,[9] provide for mediation once an application for a land use proposal is submitted for approval; that is, before a final decision is rendered on the application. Under these proceedings, involved and affected parties have the opportunity to influence modifications to a project before it is approved by the governing authority.

Most of these statutes address several basic mediation issues:[10]

- How does a mediation proceeding affect the applicable time limits?
- Who qualifies to participate?
- What rules of evidence apply to the mediation proceedings?
- How are the costs allocated?

In California, Connecticut, and Oregon, the law provides for mediation only after a court action is filed. A notice of mediation stays the appeal. In Florida and Maine, mediation tolls the time for seeking

---

5. CO, DE, GA, ME, MN, NJ, NY, OR, PA, UT, VT, WA.

6. Cal. Gov't Code § 65050

7. CA, CO, DE, FL, GA, HI, MN, NJ, OK, OR, PA, TN, VT, WA.

8. CA, CT, FL, ID, ME, OR, PA. Utah and Virginia have dispute resolution procedures but are not included in the count because Utah's statute is purely for takings claims, and Virginia's statute was only adopted in 2002 legislation and so far there are no codified statutes that utilize such process.

9. Hawaii's statute is unique. It is listed as a regional planning statute because it applies specifically to applications for geothermal development, and not to development proposals in general. Hawaii's statute differs from the other regional planning statutes in that it allows a private person to participate in the mediation as a party. The Hawaii statute authorizes a mediation proceeding on a particular issue raised at a public hearing in the context of a geothermal development proposal.

10. The California statute does not mention cost allocation.

judicial review. The toll period is 165 days in Florida and the parties may extend the toll, while in Maine the maximum toll is 120 days. The deadlines regarding decisions on pending applications are tolled in Idaho and Pennsylvania. In Pennsylvania, the time limits are suspended as agreed by the parties, including the land use approval body.

Each of these statutes stipulates that representations and evidence obtained through the mediation proceedings are not admissible in subsequent litigation. Where a state or local agency is involved in an official way, open meetings laws may be triggered; in these proceedings statements made are not confidential and are admissible in litigation. In Oregon, the parties can overrule the default provision and agree that the proceedings are admissible. The statutes vary as to the admissibility of the final report of the mediator. In Connecticut and Maine, the final report can become part of the court's record. In Florida, the Special Master's report is a public record, and likewise in Pennsylvania the final written report is admissible.

Pennsylvania's statute is an example of a brief yet complete land use mediation statute.

PENNSYLVANIA STATUTES
TITLE 53. MUNICIPAL AND QUASI–MUNICIPAL CORPORATIONS
PART I. GENERAL MUNICIPAL LAW
CHAPTER 30. PLANNING AND DEVELOPMENT
ARTICLE IX. ZONING HEARING BOARD AND OTHER ADMINISTRATIVE PROCEEDINGS

53 P.S. § 10908.1 (2002)
§ 10908.1. Mediation option

(a) Parties to proceedings authorized in this article and Article X–A may utilize mediation as an aid in completing such proceedings. In proceedings before the zoning hearing board, in no case shall the zoning hearing board initiate mediation or participate as a mediating party. Mediation shall supplement, not replace, those procedures in this article and Article X–A once they have been formally initiated. Nothing in this section shall be interpreted as expanding or limiting municipal police powers or as modifying any principles of substantive law.

(b) Participation in mediation shall be wholly voluntary. The appropriateness of mediation shall be determined by the particulars of each case and the willingness of the parties to negotiate. Any municipality offering the mediation option shall assure that, in each case, the mediating parties, assisted by the mediator as appropriate, develop terms and conditions for:

(1) Funding mediation.

(2) Selecting a mediator who, at a minimum, shall have a working knowledge of municipal zoning and subdivision procedures and demonstrated skills in mediation.

(3) Completing mediation, including time limits for such completion.

(4) Suspending time limits otherwise authorized in this act, provided there is written consent by the mediating parties, and by an applicant or municipal decision making body if either is not a party to the mediation.

(5) Identifying all parties and affording them the opportunity to participate.

(6) Subject to legal restraints, determining whether some or all of the mediation sessions shall be open or closed to the public.

(7) Assuring that mediated solutions are in writing and signed by the parties, and become subject to review and approval by the appropriate decision making body pursuant to the authorized procedures set forth in the other sections of this act.

(c) No offers or statements made in the mediation sessions, excluding the final written mediated agreement, shall be admissible as evidence in any subsequent judicial or administrative proceedings.

The following California case illustrates how mediation provisions can be insinuated into the local land use decision-making and dispute resolution process by local law.

KUCERA v. LIZZA

Court of Appeal, First District, Division 2, California, 1997.
59 Cal.App.4th 1141, 69 Cal.Rptr.2d 582.

LAMBDEN, ASSOCIATE JUSTICE.

We consider the validity of an ordinance of the Town of Tiburon which preserves views and sunlight against unreasonable obstruction by tree growth. Gilbert and Heidi Kucera, owners of an apartment building, used the ordinance to attempt resolution of a dispute with neighboring apartment building owner Tiberio Lizza over eight Monterey Pines which had grown to obstruct their view. Reaching no resolution through less formal procedures dictated by the ordinance, they brought this superior court action against Lizza, also under the ordinance, to compel restoration of their views.

The case presented the trial court with issues of whether the obstruction was unreasonable under the ordinance and, more fundamentally, whether the ordinance was invalid. In a bifurcated trial on stipulated facts, the court gave judgment for Lizza on the latter ground. It held the ordinance unconstitutional and "void as (1) preempted by state law governing the creation of servitudes and land burdens, and (2) an arbitrary and unreasonable exercise of police power.

* * *

The ordinance, entitled "View and Sunlight Obstruction from Trees," comprises chapter 15 of the Tiburon Municipal Code. Its purpose is to establish "the right of persons to preserve views or sunlight which existed at any time since they purchased or occupied a property from unreasonable obstruction by the growth of trees" (§ 15–1.A.) and "a process" to seek "restoration" of views and sunlight (§ 15–1B).

* * *

The ordinance grants persons "the right to preserve and seek restoration of views or sunlight which existed at any time since they purchased or occupied a property, when such views or sunlight are from the primary living area or active use area and have subsequently been unreasonably obstructed by the growth of trees." (§ 15–3.) Concomitantly, "No person shall plant, maintain, or permit to grow any tree which unreasonably obstructs the view from, or sunlight reaching, the primary living area or active use area of any other parcel of property" within the town (§ 15–4(a)). Prescribed procedures must be followed to establish rights under the ordinance, but private parties also retain their "right to seek remedial action for imminent danger" caused by trees. (§ 15–3.)

The ordinance defines pertinent [criteria] for determining what constitutes an "unreasonable obstruction" [and guidance for appropriate] "Restorative Action" to resolve a tree dispute (§ 15–2). [T]he ordinance favors "aggressive action" for "Undesirable Trees": "By reason of their tall height at maturity, rapid growth, dense foliage, shallow root structure, flammability, break ability, or invasiveness, certain types of trees have been deemed 'undesirable' by the Town, including Blue Gum Eucalyptus, Coast Redwood, Monterey Pine, Monterey Cypress trees, or any other tree which generally grows more than 3 feet per year in height and is capable of reaching a height of over 35 feet at maturity. When considering restorative action for 'undesirable' trees, aggressive action is preferred." (§ 15–8.)

The ordinance imposes a progression of informal and alternative dispute resolution before resort to litigation. "Initial Reconciliation" calls for written notice to and personal discussions with the tree owner plus community association assistance, the aim being a mutually agreeable solution. Failing in that, the party must propose voluntary mediation, which is informal and cannot yield binding orders under the ordinance. (§ 15–9.) Should mediation fail or be declined by the tree owner, the party must present the owner with a written claim containing specified evidence and proposed restorative action (§ 15–10) and offer voluntary, binding arbitration. The aim is a written report by the agreed arbitrator containing findings on unreasonable obstruction and restorative action. (§ 15–11.) Costs of mediation and arbitration are shared equally unless the participants agree otherwise or empower the mediator or arbitrator to allocate costs. Costs of restorative action are set by mutual agreement, mediation or arbitration, as the case may be. (§ 15–13.)

Should the owner decline binding arbitration, "then civil action may be pursued by the Complaining Party for resolution of the view or sunlight obstruction dispute under the rights and provisions of this

Chapter." (§ 15–12) Copies of "the lawsuit" and any order or settlement are filed with the town attorney (§ 15–12), and costs of litigation and restorative action are determined by the court or by settlement (§ 15–13).

According to the stipulated facts, Lizza purchased his property in 1978 and the Kuceras theirs in 1990. Lizza's is across the street and downhill from the Kuceras', and trees on his property have grown, since the Kuceras purchased their property, to obstruct their views of San Francisco Bay and the Marin County mainland from primary living or active use areas. The ordinance was passed in December 1991. The Kuceras initiated the ordinance's informal dispute resolution process in June 1992 and have satisfied all of its procedures. Lizza refused to participate in mediation (or, evidently, arbitration). He had no use or building or other land entitlement applications pending in Tiburon.

* * *

The [trial court found the ordinance invalid and] gave judgment for Lizza. [After finding the locality could validly regulate views and sunlight using the means employed, the appellate court reversed. The validity of the mediation provisions was not challenged or discussed.]

Notes

1. Mediation can be encouraged and enabled by the local government through the creation of local land use mediation laws such as the Tiburon ordinance. In most states, there is no general state law that expressly permits or preempts the adoption of a local land use mediation law of this type. There are, however, general state laws that require local land use agencies to follow specific procedures and respect discrete timetables when an application for a land use approval is filed. A local mediation law modifies these timetables to accommodate effective mediation of the interests implicated by the proposal. For example, in New York, state statutes allow local governments to alter, or supersede, these procedures and the time requirements contained in state law or, with the consent of the parties, to suspend the deadlines involved in a specific land use proceeding.

2. Unlike Tiburon's view and sunlight protection ordinance, which *requires* the party seeking relief to propose mediation, most land use ordinances involving mediation encourage mediation as a *voluntary* technique for resolving land use disputes. For example, in Bainbridge Island, Washington, the Municipal Code provides that "[l]and use mediation is an optional, voluntary method for the resolution of contested land use applications and code enforcement." What are the advantages and disadvantages of requiring mediation versus incorporating mediation as an alternative option for resolving land use disputes? Are there certain situations where one method would be preferable to the other?

3. In City of New London v. University of Connecticut, 1994 WL 65316, 11 Conn. L. Rptr. 133, Sup. Conn. Super., (Feb. 24, 1994), the defendants sought to establish an HIV research project in New London, which had the third highest per capita AIDS rate in the state. When defendants met and discussed the project with members of New London's

planning and zoning commission they were informed that under the present zoning regulations the research facility was prohibited. Shortly thereafter the city obtained a temporary injunction against the defendants. In dissolving the temporary injunction and ordering the parties to prepare the case for the trial, the court noted that "it is both wasteful and doubly unfortunate for two governmental bodies to litigate this issue of great public significance; rather, the court urges them to earnestly pursue a resolution of this matter by way of negotiation and mediation."

D. MEDIATION BEFORE A LAND USE APPLICATION IS MADE

Mediation too soon or too late in the maturation of a dispute is problematic. Early in the land use development process, for example, the parties affected by a proposed development may not be identified or may not realize the nature of their affected interest. They are less likely, however, to have developed the distrust that plagues attempts to mediate disputes late in the process after the parties have developed rigid positions and a palpable dislike for one another. In the case that follows, the county land use authority successfully secured the participation of critical players and developed some consensus regarding a very dramatic development project even before an official application was made.

SANTA MARGARITA AREA RESIDENTS v. SAN LUIS OBISPO COUNTY BOARD OF SUPERVISORS

Court of Appeal, Second District, Division 6, California, 2000.
84 Cal.App.4th 221, 100 Cal.Rptr.2d 740.

PERREN, J.

* * *

The Santa Margarita Ranch (Ranch) consists of approximately 13,800 acres of real property in San Luis Obispo County. The owner of the Ranch, Santa Margarita Limited, has long desired to develop the Ranch. Santa Margarita Area Advisory Council, a community organization, has opposed the development. After Santa Margarita Limited sued the County to facilitate development by increasing the number of legal parcels in the Ranch, Santa Margarita Limited, the County, and representatives of the Santa Margarita Area Advisory Council agreed to mediate their differences over long-range development of the Ranch. The mediation achieved a consensus among most of the participants, including representatives from the Santa Margarita Area Advisory Council. A mediation report reflecting the consensus recommended approval of a project which would include 550 housing units and non-residential improvements in an 1,800 acre area, devote at least 8,400 acres to permanent open space easements, and place a minimum of 3,600 acres under 40–year Williamson Act contracts for preservation of agricultural land.[11] The report also

---

11. The Williamson Act, section 51200 et seq., permits local governments to enter into contracts limiting the use of land to agricultural purposes in return for prefer-

recommended use of a development agreement to guarantee that the 550 residential units would be "subject to applicable laws and regulations."

Shortly after the mediation, the County began preparing a development agreement with Santa Margarita Limited for the specific planning of a project which would include the improvements and other land uses specified in the mediation report and which also designated a golf course, guest lodge, equestrian center, bikeways, and parklands as non-residential improvements (Project). At the same time, the County amended part of its general plan, the Salinas River Area Plan, to describe the Project and establish certain criteria for its ultimate implementation.

After lengthy negotiations and a public hearing, the County enacted an ordinance authorizing it to enter into the development agreement (Agreement). The next day, the chairperson of the County's Board of Supervisors signed the Agreement.

In general, the Agreement freezes zoning on the Project property in return for the developer's commitment to submit a specific plan for construction in compliance with County land use requirements. Contingencies and further approvals remain, but the Agreement commits the County and Santa Margarita Limited to the Project, including its public improvements and amenities.

Specifically, the Agreement provides that Santa Margarita Limited will file a comprehensive application for approval of the Project, including a specific plan, a vesting tentative map, and an environmental impact report. The specific plan must incorporate the standards set forth in the Salinas River Area Plan. The application must state that Santa Margarita Limited will commit itself to develop the Project in its entirety and to engage in all necessary environmental review. The Agreement also provides that Santa Margarita Limited will dedicate land for a public swimming pool, sewer treatment plant, and cemetery expansion.

In return for these commitments, the County agrees to process, review, and approve or disapprove the specific plan, and to apply its current zoning and other land use regulations to the plan without change for up to five years during the review and approval period.[12] The Agreement is entered into under the authority of the Development Agreement Statute and satisfies its technical requirements.

The Agreement does not give Santa Margarita Limited a right to construct the Project or impose upon it an obligation to do so. Rather, the Agreement contemplates a second development agreement pertaining to the actual construction of the Project, and requires that the County and Santa Margarita Limited "will make a good faith effort to negotiate a Subsequent Development Agreement that shall, if agreed

---

ential tax treatment. (*Kelsey v. Colwell* (1973) 30 Cal.App.3d 590, 592, 106 Cal. Rptr. 420.)

12. The Agreement provides for a five-year term with a two-year extension in the event of litigation concerning the Agreement. Although this lawsuit may trigger the two-year extension, we will refer to the Agreement as having a five-year term.

upon, provide [Santa Margarita Limited] with a vested right to the benefits and burdens of the Project." It provides that the parties "ultimately seek to secure ... an enforceable arrangement" allowing construction, but neither party "obligates itself to benefit or burden the Project Site with the above-described Project until such time as a Final EIR is certified, the Specific Plan application is favorably acted upon by the County, [and] the Subsequent Development Agreement ... becomes binding on the parties...."

The development agreement statute permits a city or county to "enter into a development agreement" with any property owner "for the development of the property." (§ 65865, subd. (a).) In essence, the statute allows a city or county to freeze zoning and other land use regulation applicable to specified property to guarantee that a developer will not be affected by changes in the standards for government approval during the period of development. (*City of West Hollywood v. Beverly Towers, Inc.* (1991) 52 Cal.3d 1184, 1193, fn. 6, 278 Cal.Rptr. 375, 805 P.2d 329; *Citizens for Responsible Government v. City of Albany* (1997) 56 Cal.App.4th 1199, 1213, 66 Cal.Rptr.2d 102.) In the words of the statute, "[u]nless otherwise provided by the development agreement, rules, regulations, and official policies governing permitted uses of the land, governing density, and governing design, improvement, and construction standards and specifications, applicable to development of the property subject to a development agreement, shall be those rules, regulations, and official policies in force at the time of execution of the agreement." (§ 65866.)

The statute declares that "lack of certainty in the approval of development projects can result in a waste of resources, escalate the cost of housing and other development to the consumer, and discourage investment in and commitment to comprehensive planning which would make maximum efficient utilization of resources at the least economic cost to the public." (§ 65864, subd. (a).) The statute reflects the Legislature's conclusion that giving "[a]ssurance to the applicant for a development project that upon approval of the project, the applicant may proceed with the project in accordance with existing policies, rules and regulations, and subject to conditions of approval, will strengthen the public planning process, encourage private participation in comprehensive planning, and reduce the economic costs of development." (§ 65864, subd. (b).)

Particulars of the statute include requirements that a development agreement may be approved only after a public hearing (§ 65867) and must be consistent with the general plan and any specific plan (§ 65867.5), a provision permitting annual review by the governmental entity and termination for noncompliance (§ 65865.1), and a statement that the agreement is subject to referendum (§ 65867.5). The statute also specifies certain provisions which may or must be included in a development agreement. (§ 65865.2.)

Appellants contend that the Agreement is invalid under the statute because the statute permits a development agreement only after a project has been approved for actual construction. Appellants claim that, without a fully-designed and approved project, the Agreement is essentially a unilateral County agreement to freeze zoning without obtaining any public benefits in return.

Appellants interpret the statute and the Agreement too narrowly. The statute is best served through a liberal construction which encompasses agreements that substantially comply with its specific terms and conditions and achieve its essential objectives. (*National Parks & Conservation Assn. v. County of Riverside* (1996) 42 Cal.App.4th 1505, 1522, 50 Cal.Rptr.2d 339.) To interpret the statute and Agreement in any other manner would unduly restrict the County from working with a private landowner to plan and develop facilities which support public needs.

Moreover, the statement of legislative purpose in section 65864 encourages the creation of rights and obligations early in a project in order to promote public and private participation during planning, especially when the scope of a project requires a lengthy process of obtaining regulatory approvals. The statute recognizes that comprehensive planning is important in controlling the economic and environmental costs of development. It should be construed to allow development agreements as soon as the government and developer are required to make significant financial and personnel commitments to a project.

The Agreement conforms to this construction of the statute. Because it focuses on the planning stage of the Project, the Agreement meets, rather than evades, the purpose of the statute. The Agreement maximizes the public's role in the final development and control over the inclusion of public facilities and benefits in the project. It also permits the County to monitor the planning of the Project to effectively assure compliance with existing County land use regulations.

Additionally, environmental review is advanced by considering environmental issues at the earliest feasible time. (*Fullerton Joint Union High School Dist. v. State Bd. of Education* (1982) 32 Cal.3d 779, 797, 187 Cal.Rptr. 398, 654 P.2d 168.) The Agreement makes environmental review an integral part of the planning process, thus avoiding the sort of "*post hoc* rationalizations to support action already taken" which might occur if environmental review were deferred until later. (See *Laurel Heights Improvement Assn. v. Regents of University of California* (1988) 47 Cal.3d 376, 394, 253 Cal.Rptr. 426, 764 P.2d 278.)

While further agreement and discretionary approvals are necessary, every approval or denial permitted by the Agreement is designed to advance the project in accordance with the standards for Ranch development adopted by the County in the Salinas River Area Plan. As shown by the record, the County and the participants in the mediation which preceded the Agreement intend the Agreement to play a critical role in facilitating the completion of a large-scale real estate development.

There is nothing in the Development Agreement Statute inconsistent with this type of development agreement.

Finally, the Agreement was approved by an ordinance duly enacted by the County Board of Supervisors and we defer to that body in matters pertaining to the merits, usefulness and public advantages of the Agreement. One of the purposes of development agreements is to obtain benefits for the public, and the record shows that the County believed that an agreement was required as an incentive to the developer to engage in the comprehensive planning desired by the County, and also as an incentive to expand the public facilities and benefits included in the Project.

The Agreement also represents the resolution of a protracted dispute and balances the interests of all concerned parties. Santa Margarita Limited sought a more comprehensive agreement but, according to a planning commission staff report, the County decided to "lock-in" the Salinas River Area Plan standards while deferring construction approval. The record reveals that the County's decision resulted from careful assessment of the importance of the Ranch to the region.

The record also reveals that the Agreement resulted from a mediation by parties interested in the future of the Ranch. The mediation did not result in unanimity but produced an agreement among most participants, including representatives of the public. As such, the mediation and Agreement reflect an inclusive and open governmental process.

As well as arguing that the Agreement does too little to satisfy the statute, appellants argue that it does too much to avoid constitutional infirmity. Appellants contend that the freeze on Ranch zoning before a project that is ready for construction constitutes the contracting away of the County's zoning authority and, therefore, a surrender of the right to exercise its police power in the future. We disagree. If anything, case law concerning a municipality's "surrender" of its regulatory authority supports the conclusion that the Agreement, as well as the development agreement statute, satisfy all constitutional mandates concerning a city or county's exercise of its regulatory authority.

It is established that a city or county may not contract away its right to exercise police power in the future (*Avco Community Developers, Inc. v. South Coast Regional Com., supra,* 17 Cal.3d at p. 800, 132 Cal.Rptr. 386, 553 P.2d 546) and that the power to enact, modify, and amend zoning and other land use regulations constitutes a part of a county's police power. (*Alameda County Land Use Assn. v. City of Hayward* (1995) 38 Cal.App.4th 1716, 1724, 45 Cal.Rptr.2d 752.) Therefore, the development agreement statute must be construed in a manner that does not permit the County to surrender its police power in the name of planning efficiency. (See *Conway v. Pasadena Humane Society* (1996) 45 Cal.App.4th 163, 177, 52 Cal.Rptr.2d 777.)

The Agreement in this case presents no such constitutional infirmity. Land use regulation is an established function of local government and the County has authority to enter into contracts to carry out this function. (§ 23004, subd. (c); *Carruth v. City of Madera* (1965) 233 Cal.App.2d 688, 695, 43 Cal.Rptr. 855; see also *Professional Engineers v. Department of Transportation* (1993) 13 Cal.App.4th 585, 591–592, 16 Cal.Rptr.2d 599.) A contract which "appears to have been fair, just, and reasonable at the time of its execution, and prompted by the necessities of the situation or in its nature advantageous to the municipality at the time it was entered into, is neither void nor voidable merely because some of its executory features may extend beyond the terms of office of the members" of the legislative body which entered into the contract. (*Denio v. City of Huntington Beach* (1943) 22 Cal.2d 580, 590, 140 P.2d 392; *Carruth, supra,* at p. 695, 43 Cal.Rptr. 855.)

A governmental entity does not contract away its police power unless the contract amounts to the "surrender" or "abnegation" of a proper governmental function. (*Morrison Homes Corp. v. City of Pleasanton* (1976) 58 Cal.App.3d 724, 734, 130 Cal.Rptr. 196.) The zoning freeze in the Agreement is not such a surrender or abnegation. The Project must be developed in accordance with the County's general plan (§ 65867.5), and the Agreement does not permit construction until the County has approved detailed building plans. The Agreement retains the County's discretionary authority in the future and, in any event, the zoning freeze is for five years. It is not of unlimited duration.

Seventy-five years ago, the Supreme Court stated that the "police power, as such, is not confined within the narrow circumspection of precedents, resting upon past conditions which do not cover and control present-day conditions obviously calling for revised regulations to promote the health, safety, morals, or general welfare of the public. That is to say, as a commonwealth develops politically, economically, and socially, the police power likewise develops, within reason, to meet the changed and changing conditions." (*Miller v. Board of Public Works* (1925) 195 Cal. 477, 484, 234 P. 381.) If anything, the court's statement in *Miller* resonates more clearly today than when it was first made, and provides a framework for the analysis of this case. Here, the development agreement statute and the constitutional mandate requiring the County to retain its regulatory power intersect to permit the contemporary approach to land use regulation reflected in the Agreement.

It is true that local government may not surrender its regulatory power through ad hoc commitments. It may, however, act in partnership with private enterprise, as authorized by the development agreement statute and the Agreement. The Agreement addresses recurring land use issues without limiting the County's regulatory discretion. Through the Agreement, the County tailors the exercise of its legislative power to the complex issues involved in regulating a major real estate project in the public interest. By requiring expeditious Project planning and preserving future options, the Agreement enhances the County's power to regulate land use to achieve its Salinas River Area Plan and other land use goals.

The judgment is affirmed. Costs on appeal are awarded to Santa Margarita Limited.

Notes

1. In the principal case, the court noted that the California statute encourages the creation of rights and obligations early in a project to promote public and private participation during planning. This, it says, maximizes the public's role at the earliest feasible time. The court refers to benefits to the public that result and notes that the interests involved are balanced in the process. The court also noted that although the mediation did not result in unanimity on all issues, it did produce an agreement among the participants, including representatives of the public. As such, it concluded, the mediation reflects an inclusive and open governmental process. Despite this enthusiastic endorsement, can you think of any down side to an agreement of this type made so early in the planning process?

2. Section 65864 of California's Development Agreement Statute states: "The Legislature finds and declares that: (a) The lack of certainty in the approval of development projects can result in a waste of resources, escalate the cost of housing and other development to the consumer, and discourage investment in and commitment to comprehensive planning which would make maximum efficient utilization of resources at the least economic cost to the public." In what way do negotiated discussions between land use approval officials and developers contribute to the reduction of wasted costs and resources?

E. MEDIATION DURING THE DEVELOPMENT APPROVAL PROCESS

MERSON v. McNALLY

Court of Appeals of New York, 1997.
90 N.Y.2d 742, 665 N.Y.S.2d 605, 688 N.E.2d 479.

SMITH, JUDGE.

We hold that, under certain circumstances, a negative declaration may be issued under the State Environmental Quality Review Act (SEQRA) even where the project—a Type I action—has been modified during the initial review process to accommodate environmental concerns of the lead agency and other interested parties.

In the first case, *Matter of Merson v. McNally*, we conclude that the modifications made to the project in response to environmental concerns raised during the Planning Board's review, were a legitimate product of the process and did not implicitly convert the ultimate determination of nonsignificance into an improperly conditioned negative declaration. Thus, the order of the Appellate Division annulling the negative declaration should be reversed. Since that decision was relied upon by the Appellate Division to dismiss the project developer's petition in the second action, *Matter of Philipstown Indus. Park v. Town Bd.*, a reversal is also appropriate in that case. Each case must be remitted to the Appellate Division for a determination of issues raised but not decided on the appeal to that Court.

The cases before us represent two parts of one long story for which the relevant facts will be summarized herein. Philipstown Industrial Park, Inc. (PIP) is the owner of over 80 acres of real property located within an industrial zoning district in the Town of Philipstown, Putnam County, New York. PIP's development plans for the land included soil mining and reclamation on the southern portion of the parcel.

Prior to PIP's purchase of the land in 1987, the property had been extensively mined but had not been relandscaped. Under its proposal, about 9.8 acres would again be subject to surface mining which would consist of "sizing" gravel by sifting the material through a portable screen. Another area of about 7.5 acres would not be mined but would be regraded and reclaimed and a third area would be subject to various activities necessary to the operation of the mine. The mining project would result in an expansion of the pond located on the parcel which PIP claims would "yield environmental benefits and recreational opportunities."

PIP applied to the Department of Environmental Conservation (DEC) for a "mined land reclamation permit" pursuant to New York's Mined Land Reclamation Law (MLRL; ECL 23–2701—23–2727). PIP also applied to the Planning Board for a temporary Town Special Use Mining Permit pursuant to the Town Mining Law.

The Planning Board first determined that the mining project qualified as a Type I action under SEQRA because it "involve[d] the physical alteration of 10 acres" (6 NYCRR 617.12[b][6][i]). PIP then submitted a draft of a full Environmental Assessment Form (EAF) pursuant to the SEQRA regulations. During the review process, the Planning Board identified several "potentially large" environmental impacts from the proposed project. In response to concerns raised by the interested agencies, the Planning Board and community members during public meetings and hearings, PIP continually revised portions of its project plans. All of the modifications were discussed and considered by the Planning Board during these open meetings. The entire project proposal was reduced to a single bound volume (which included a completed EAF) and was finally submitted on May 4, 1993.

On May 18, 1993, the Planning Board received an opinion from the DEC that a determination of nonsignificance in the form of a negative declaration would be appropriate for the mining project. Two days later, on May 20, 1993, the Planning Board issued a negative declaration by unanimous vote. The Planning Board also granted the temporary special use permit (subject to the final approval of the Town Board) upon its finding that "the applicant has met or exceeded the performance standards outlined" in the Town Zoning Law. Soon afterward, a group of community residents filed a CPLR article 78 petition in Supreme Court seeking to annul the negative declaration of the Planning Board and PIP intervened.

Supreme Court dismissed the proceeding and concluded that the determination of the Planning Board was not improperly issued. In so holding, the court found that "the environmental assessment form adequately identified areas of environmental impact." The court stated that it would "defer to the planning board's discretion as to the * * * issuance of a negative declaration under SEQRA."

The Appellate Division reversed and annulled the negative declaration. The Court held (227 A.D.2d 487, 490, 643 N.Y.S.2d 129):

> "Inherent in the Planning Board's determination was a recognition of significant environmental impacts posed by the intervenor's project * * *. It is evident that the numerous measures proposed by the intervenor in mitigation of these impacts were conditional prerequisites for the issuance of the negative declaration * * *. Under these circumstances, we conclude that the Planning Board's negative declaration was the functional equivalent of a conditioned negative declaration" (citations omitted).

"SEQRA's fundamental policy is to inject environmental considerations directly into governmental decision making" (*Matter of Coca–Cola Bottling Co. v. Board of Estimate*, 72 N.Y.2d 674, 679, 536 N.Y.S.2d 33, 532 N.E.2d 1261). This policy is effectuated, in part, through strict compliance with the review procedures outlined in the environmental laws and regulations (see, *Matter of King v. Saratoga County Bd. of Supervisors*, 89 N.Y.2d 341, 347–348, 653 N.Y.S.2d 233, 675 N.E.2d 1185). A SEQRA review process conducted through closed bilateral negotiations between an agency and a developer would bypass, if not eliminate, the comprehensive, open weighing of environmentally compatible alternatives both to the proposed action and to any suggested mitigation measures.

However, we disagree with the Appellate Division's holding to the extent it can be read to bar *any* significant modification during the review process as a conditioned negative declaration. Instead, we adopt an analysis which allows for consideration of the legitimate maturation of a development project in accordance with the goals of environmental regulation. In exercising our judicial review function concerning the process at issue, we conclude that the determination of nonsignificance made by the lead agency was not improper.

The Regulatory Process Under SEQRA

Under the procedures set forth in the DEC regulations, when a developer first submits a proposal for a particular project, it is determined whether the project qualifies as a Type I, Type II or an unlisted action for purposes of SEQRA review (6 NYCRR 617.5[a][4]). For Type I actions, the developer must submit a full EAF which "must be used to determine the significance of such actions" (6 NYCRR 617.5[b]).[13]

The very purpose of an EAF is to assist an agency "in determining the environmental significance or nonsignificance of actions" (6 NYCRR

---

13. The agency may waive the requirement of an EAF if a draft EIS is submitted instead (6 NYCRR 617.6[a][4]).

617.2 [m]). As the form itself states, "[t]he full EAF is intended to provide a method whereby applicants and agencies can be assured that the determination process has been orderly, comprehensive in nature, yet flexible enough to allow introduction of information to fit a project or action" (6 NYCRR 617.20, appendix A). Part 2 of the EAF allows the lead agency to identify "the range of possible impacts" and "whether an impact can be mitigated or reduced" (6 NYCRR 617.20, appendix A). As stated on the required form, "[i]dentifying that an impact will be potentially large * * * does not mean that it is also necessarily significant. Any large impact must be evaluated in Part 3 to determine significance. Identifying an impact in column 2 simply asks that it be looked at further." This highlights the functional difference between an EAF and an Environmental Impact Statement (EIS). While an EAF is used to determine significance or nonsignificance, the purpose of an EIS is to examine the identified potentially significant environmental impacts which may result from a project (*Matter of Coca–Cola Bottling Co. v. Board of Estimate*, 72 N.Y.2d, at 680, 536 N.Y.S.2d 33, 532 N.E.2d 1261).[14]

To arrive at its determination of significance, the lead agency must identify "the relevant areas of environmental concern" and take a "hard look" at them (*Matter of Chemical Specialties Mfrs. Assn. v. Jorling*, 85 N.Y.2d 382, 397, 626 N.Y.S.2d 1, 649 N.E.2d 1145; see also, *Matter of Kahn v. Pasnik*, 90 N.Y.2d 569, 664 N.Y.S.2d 584, 687 N.E.2d 402 [decided today]). The agency must set forth a reasoned elaboration for its determination (*see, Matter of WEOK Broadcasting Corp. v. Planning Bd.*, 79 N.Y.2d 373, 381, 583 N.Y.S.2d 170, 592 N.E.2d 778; *Matter of Coca–Cola Bottling Co. v. Board of Estimate*, 72 N.Y.2d, at 680, 536 N.Y.S.2d 33, 532 N.E.2d 1261). As we have stated, "[w]here an agency fails to take the requisite hard look and make a reasoned elaboration, or its determination is affected by an error of law, or its decision was not rational, or is arbitrary and capricious or not supported by substantial evidence, the agency's determination may be annulled" (*Matter of WEOK Broadcasting Corp. v. Planning Bd.*, 79 N.Y.2d, at 383, 583 N.Y.S.2d 170, 592 N.E.2d 778). However, we have also cautioned that "[w]hile judicial review must be meaningful, the courts may not substitute their judgment for that of the agency for it is not their role to 'weigh the desirability of any action or [to] choose among alternatives'" (*Akpan v. Koch*, 75 N.Y.2d 561, 570, 555 N.Y.S.2d 16, 554 N.E.2d 53, quoting *Matter of Jackson v. New York State Urban Dev. Corp.*, 67 N.Y.2d 400, 416, 503 N.Y.S.2d 298, 494 N.E.2d 429).

14. As stated in the current regulations, "[a]n EIS provides a means for agencies, project sponsors and the public to systematically consider significant adverse environmental impacts, alternatives and mitigation" (6 NYCRR 617.2[n]). If the lead agency determines "that the action may include the potential for at least one significant environmental effect" (6 NYCRR 617.6[g][1][i]), the agency must issue a positive declaration (6 NYCRR 617.2[cc]; Matter of Coca–Cola Bottling Co. v. Board of Estimate, 72 N.Y.2d, at 680, 536 N.Y.S.2d 33, 532 N.E.2d 1261). However, when the agency determines that "the implementation of the action as proposed will not result in any significant environmental effects," the agency may issue an unqualified negative declaration (see, 6 NYCRR 617.2 [y]).

Although the parties presently contest issues such as whether the agency took a "hard look," the Appellate Division resolved these cases solely on the ground that modifications made to the project were an improper circumvention of the procedural requirements under the environmental regulations. Thus, that is the threshold critical issue that we must address.

The Impact of Modifications on the SEQRA Process

The dilemma is this—how to permit an evolving process for identification of environmental concerns and initiatives to meet those concerns yet, on the other hand, to guard against an avoidance of the EIS process through private bilateral negotiations between a developer and a lead agency when a project may have potentially significant environmental impacts which need full and open consideration.

To deal with this dilemma, we start with the definition of a conditioned negative declaration, permitted only in unlisted actions:

"a negative declaration issued by a lead agency for an unlisted action, involving an applicant, in which the action as *initially proposed may result in one or more significant adverse environmental effects; however, mitigation measures identified and required by the lead agency* * * * will modify the proposed action so that no significant environmental impacts will result" (6 NYCRR 617.2[h].

Applying this definition in the context of a Type I action, we prescribe a twofold inquiry to examine whether a negative declaration has been impermissibly conditioned: (1) whether the project, as initially proposed, might result in the identification of one or more "significant adverse environmental effects"; and (2) whether the proposed mitigating measures incorporated into part 3 of the EAF were "identified and required by the lead agency" as a condition precedent to the issuance of the negative declaration.

On the first point, if all areas of concern involve a minimal risk to the environment, no further inquiry is necessary and modifications in these areas would not impermissibly condition or invalidate an otherwise proper negative declaration. However, where the lead agency has identified potentially significant impacts (*see,Chinese Staff & Workers Assn. v. City of New York*, 68 N.Y.2d 359, 364–365, 509 N.Y.S.2d 499, 502 N.E.2d 176), or where the record supports the inference that the identified impacts would have to be considered potentially significant (*see, Inland Vale Farm Co. v. Stergianopoulos*, 104 A.D.2d 395, 397, 478 N.Y.S.2d 926, affd. 65 N.Y.2d 718, 492 N.Y.S.2d 7, 481 N.E.2d 547), or where the identified impacts fall within typically environmentally sensitive areas or locations, the second prong of the test must be examined.

At the second phase of analysis, a court must examine whether the proposed mitigating measures, incorporated as part of an open and deliberative process, negated the project's potential adverse effects. Under such circumstances, the proposal, as revised, could still result in a determination of nonsignificance and the issuance of a valid negative declaration. In this regard, mitigating measures could be viewed as part of the "give and take" of the application process, and would be less of a concern than those revisions or mitigation measures made after final submission of the EAF.

However, a lead agency clearly may not issue a negative declaration on the basis of conditions contained in the declaration itself. Nor could the lead agency achieve the same end by other means, such as supporting the negative declaration with a statement that conditions would be imposed only on an underlying special use permit to reduce environmental impacts; extracting concessions from the developer as necessary prerequisites to the issuance of the negative declaration (*Matter of Shawangunk Mtn. Envtl. Assn. v. Planning Bd.*, 157 A.D.2d 273, 277, 557 N.Y.S.2d 495); or requiring specific mitigation measures, and then approving a proposal that has been revised in compliance with the mandate of the lead agency.

The environmental review process was not meant to be a bilateral negotiation between a developer and lead agency but, rather, an open process that also involves other interested agencies and the public. Thus, there would ordinarily be no inherent problem in revising or modifying project plans to address concerns raised during the environmental review, particularly concerns raised by other agencies.

However, mitigating measures will not obviate the need for an EIS unless they clearly negate the continued potentiality of the adverse effects of the proposed action. Otherwise, the EIS process would be necessary to review the adequacy of the mitigating measures, and any environmentally compatible alternatives to the suggested mitigations. The lead agency's determination of the sufficiency of the proposed mitigation measures would of course be subject to a judicial examination of whether the lead agency took the requisite hard look (*see, e.g., Matter of Kahn v. Pasnik*, 90 N.Y.2d 569, 664 N.Y.S.2d 584, 687 N.E.2d 402, *supra* [decided today]); the more numerous and significant the environmental impacts identified at the outset, the greater possibility that mitigation measures would not suffice, and an EIS would be required.

Here, the Planning Board, in reviewing part 2 of the EAF identified a number of impacts as "potentially large." For example, the Town's planning consultant articulated his concern with "ambient noise level and access to a mining operation through a subdivision." Indeed, the consultant specifically stated that "the Board must consider the noise issue more in depth as it has been shown to be one of the most complex and important matters in connection with the application" bearing on SEQRA review.

Nevertheless, the agency's general concerns relating to noise levels were alleviated through the review process by the actions of, and open discussions with, the developer. In response to such concerns, PIP explained that it had taken several surveys and readings of the ambient noise in the area of the mining operation and, as a result of its analysis, PIP concluded that "an ambient noise level within the guidelines of the [local] zoning law will be maintainable by the mining operation." Additionally, in this regard, the agency suggested that Saturday hours and operations be limited only to the sale of materials and the developer agreed.

A similar open and deliberative process surrounded the concerns raised by the increased traffic stemming from the project. The Board suggested that the developer "consider" a separate access road and the mining plan was amended in response to such comments. PIP pursued a temporary access route onto Route 9 and other measures to lessen the traffic on residential streets.

Thus, the modifications here were not conditions unilaterally imposed by the lead agency, but essentially were adjustments incorporated by the project sponsor to mitigate the concerns identified by the public and the reviewing agencies, with only minor variations requested by the lead agency during the review process. Of distinguishing dispositive import here is that the modifications were examined openly and with input from all parties involved. This process comports with the overriding purposes of SEQRA.

The revisions thus came about as part of the review process and were submitted and publicly evaluated prior to the issuance of the negative declaration. Moreover, the lead agency properly sought the views of other interested agencies before making a final determination regarding significance. In fact, the DEC issued its recommendation of nonsignificance based upon the final revised project plans in accordance with the regulations (see, 6 NYCRR 617.3 [e]). These considerations combine to support the conclusion that the negative declaration in this case was not improperly conditioned.

This case illustrates the practical reality that a project, especially a large undertaking such as a Type I action, usually undergoes modifications from its initial specifications. Modifications made to a project during the review process should not necessarily be characterized as impermissible "conditions." Indeed, the SEQRA regulations themselves help to show that the purpose of identifying "potentially large" environmental impacts in the midst of the EAF process is to allow a developer the opportunity to address those potential impacts in the project proposal.

In sum, the mere circumstance that modifications may have been made to a proposal is an insufficient basis to nullify a negative declaration otherwise properly issued. What is dispositive is the character and source of the identified modifications. The SEQRA process here was conducted openly and deliberatively. Moreover, the agency's elaboration of the basis for its determination of nonsignificance is reasonable. Accordingly, in each case, the order of the Appellate Division should be reversed, with costs, and the matter remitted to the Appellate Division for further proceedings in accordance with this opinion.

Notes

1. Does the Merson case really involve a mediation? Who is the mediator? Need there be a mediator? Perhaps the sessions were simply skillfully conducted negotiations facilitated by a planning board chair who understood, intuitively or through training, the skills needed for effective dispute resolution. Note how, apparently, the interested parties were involved in an open and deliberative process organized by the review board. The court made clear that the process was not a bilateral negotiation, but part of the "give and take" of the review process. Modifications in the proposal, it said, were not unilaterally imposed, but were adjustments incorporated by the applicant to mitigate concerns identified by the public and the involved public agencies. What went wrong? Who sued? Why?

2. If, during the give and take of a mediation, the applicant agrees to modify the proposal to meet the interest of a party involved in the negotiations, is this the same as the review board imposing a condition on a project as part of the approval process? See In the Matter of Waste Management of New York v. Doherty, 267 A.D.2d 464 (1999): As stated by the Court of Appeals in Merson v. McNally, "modifications made to a project during the review process should not necessarily be characterized as impermissible 'conditions,' * * * the mere circumstance that modifications may have been made to a proposal is an insufficient basis to nullify a negative declaration otherwise properly issued."

3. Do you think the court struck the right balance between providing all parties a meaningful role in the environmental review and allowing flexibility in the project review stage? Note that New York has no statute authorizing or encouraging mediation of disputes over local land use applications. Neither did the town of Philipstown. How is it that the planning board (lead agency) had the authority to conduct a mediation of the interests involved among the parties involved in the application? The state regulations prescribing the rules for local environmental review allow all applicable time frames to be waived upon the consent of the parties. Do you think that taking time to conduct a mediation of the issues in such a case is a good reason for an applicant to agree to waive deadlines in the review process? What are the pros and cons?

4. Do interested parties have reason to complain that mediation sessions of the type held in the Merson case are not open to their full and effective participation. See In the Matter of Tarrytown v. Planning Board of Village of Sleepy Hollow, 741 N.Y.S.2d 44 (2002): "Where a developer works with the lead agency and other reviewing agencies in public and, as a result of open consultation, incorporates changes in the project which mitigate the potential environmental impacts, a negative declaration may be appropriate—provided that such declaration is not the product of closed-door negotiations or of the developer's compliance with conditions unilaterally imposed by the lead agency."

MEDEIROS v. HAWAII COUNTY PLANNING COMMISSION

Intermediate Court of Appeals of Hawaii, 1990.
8 Haw.App. 183, 797 P.2d 59.

HEEN, JUDGE.

Appellants Delan Perry, Jennifer Perry (the Perrys), and Nelson Ho (collectively Appellants) appeal from Appellee Hawaii County Planning Commission's (Commission) August 15, 1989 approval of a geothermal resource permit (the permit) authorizing Appellees Hawaii Natural Energy Institute and the Research Corporation of the University of Hawaii (Applicants) to drill four exploratory geothermal wells in the East Rift Zone of the Puna District on the Island of Hawaii. We affirm.

I.

The general procedures for considering geothermal resource permit applications by the counties are established by HRS [Hawaii Revised Statutes] § 205–5.1(e) and (f) which read as follows:

> (e) If geothermal development activities are proposed within agricultural, rural, or urban districts and such proposed activities are not permitted uses pursuant to county general plan and zoning ordinances, then after receipt of a properly filed and completed application, including all required supporting data, the appropriate county authority shall conduct a public hearing. Upon appropriate request for mediation from any party who submitted comment at the public hearing, the county authority shall appoint a mediator within five days. The county authority shall require the parties to participate in mediation. The mediator shall not be an employee of any county agency or its staff. The mediation period shall not extend beyond thirty days after mediation started, except by order of the county authority. Mediation shall be confined to the issues raised at the public hearing by the party requesting mediation. The mediator will submit a written recommendation to the county authority, based upon any mediation agreement reached between the parties for consideration by the county authority in its final decision. If there is no mediation agreement, the county authority may have a second public hearing to receive additional comment related to the mediation issues. Within ten days after the second public hearing, the county authority may receive additional written comment on the issues raised at the second public hearing from any party.
>
> The county authority shall consider the comments raised at the second hearing before rendering its final decision. The county authority shall then determine whether a geothermal resource permit shall be granted to authorize the geothermal development activities described in the application. The appropriate county authority shall grant a geothermal resource permit if it finds that applicant has demonstrated that:

(1) The desired uses would not have unreasonable adverse health, environmental, or socio-economic effects on residents or surrounding property;

(2) The desired uses would not unreasonably burden public agencies to provide roads and streets, sewers, water, drainage, school improvements, and police and fire protection; and

(3) That there are reasonable measures available to mitigate the unreasonable adverse effects or burdens referred to above.

Unless there is a mutual agreement to extend, a decision shall be made on the application by the appropriate county authority within six months of the date a complete application was filed; provided that the time limit may be extended by agreement between the applicant and the appropriate county authority.

(f) Requests for mediation shall be received by the board or county authority within five days after the close of the initial public hearing. Within five days thereafter, the board or county authority shall appoint a mediator. Any person submitting an appropriate request for mediation shall be notified by the board or county authority of the date, time, and place of the mediation conference by depositing such notice in the mail to the return address stated on the request for mediation. The notice shall be mailed no later than ten days before the start of the mediation conference. The conference shall be held on the island where the public hearing is held.

An authority's decision on a geothermal resource permit application pursuant to a public hearing or hearings is appealable directly to the supreme court for review in accordance with the provisions of HRS § 91–14(b) and (g) (1985). However, the decision is not subject to a contested case hearing. HRS § 205–5.1(g).[15]

III.

On January 31, 1989, Applicants applied to the Commission for permission to drill four Scientific Observation Holes (Holes), numbered 1 through 4, in the Subzone established by the Board within the Kilauea East Rift Zone. According to the application, each Hole will be approximately four inches in diameter and 4,000 feet deep, and will be located on approximately one quarter acre of land.

---

15. HRS § 205–5.1(g) (Supp.1989) provides:

(g) Any decision made by an appropriate county authority or the board pursuant to a public hearing or hearings under this section may be appealed directly on the record to the supreme court for final decision and shall not be subject to a contested case hearing. Sections 91–14(b) and (g) shall govern the appeal, notwithstanding the lack of a contested case hearing on the matter. The appropriate county authority or the board shall provide a court reporter to produce a transcript of the proceedings at all public hearings under this section for purposes of an appeal.

The public hearing began on April 11, 1989. At the public hearing a member of the staff of the Hawaii County Planning Department (Planning Department) recommended approval of the application with a number of conditions. Twenty-nine people, including Appellants, also spoke. All speakers, except the Planning Department's staff member, were limited to three minutes, and only Commission members were allowed to question any of the speakers. Mr. Harry Kim, Director of Civil Defense for Hawaii County, spoke and requested mediation. At the close of the proceedings, the Commission voted to continue the hearing at a later date.

When the hearing resumed on May 9, 1989, forty-five people spoke, including the Perrys. The speakers were limited to five minutes each and, again, the audience was not allowed to question any of the speakers. At the close of the hearing the Commission's chairman announced that all parties who wanted mediation should submit written requests within five days. Numerous persons, including the Perrys, requested mediation.

On May 19, 1989, the Commission appointed Dee Dee Letts (Letts), Assistant Director of the Program on Alternative Dispute Resolution of the State Judiciary, as mediator. Subsequently, Letts was joined by Dr. Kem Lowry of the University of Hawaii and Richard Spiegel of the West Hawaii Mediation Service as "co-mediators." The first mediation meeting was held on June 7, 1989, and the last on July 6. On July 10, 1989, the president of the Kapoho Community Association (Association) wrote a letter to the Commission pointing out that, during mediation, Applicants revealed there will be hydrogen sulfide emission from the wells, contrary to their statement in the application. The Association requested a contested case hearing. On July 13, 1989, the mediators submitted their final report, outlining the items of agreement and disagreement among the participants.

On August 15, 1989, the Commission approved the permit and Appellants appealed.

IV.

Appellants wage a four-pronged attack on the permit. First, they argue that HRS § 205–5.1(g)'s provision that the authority's decision "shall not be subject to a contested case hearing" violates their constitutional right to due process of law under Article I, § 5 of the Hawaii State Constitution. Second, they assert that the procedures employed by the Commission violated their due process rights. We find no merit in Appellants' arguments.

A.

HRS § 205–5.1 was enacted in 1983. Act 296, § 3, 1983 Haw.Sess. Laws 636, 637–38. In 1984, the statute was amended to provide for contested case hearings on applications submitted under the statute. Act 151, § 2, 1984 Haw.Sess.Laws 278, 280. In 1987, the legislature deleted the provisions for contested case hearings and substituted public hearings and a mediation process. Act 378, § 1, 1987 Haw.Sess.Laws 1198, 1200–01. The purpose of the change was "to provide for a simpler procedure to consider and act on permits for geothermal development before state and county agencies." Sen.Stand.Comm.Rep. No. 1118, in 1987 Senate Journal, at 1387.

Appellants argue that "[t]he ability to cross examine witnesses and the preservation of arguments for the reviewing body to assess are key to the most basic citizen rights as included in the Hawaii State Constitution Bill of Rights[.]" They contend that a contested case hearing is essential to the preservation of those rights.

Applicants argue that Appellants' interests are aesthetic and environmental and are not "property" in the context of due process. However, the record shows that the Perrys own and farm property abutting the land covered by the permit. It is at least arguable that the Perrys' use of their property might be so severely curtailed by Applicants' geothermal activities as to constitute a deprivation of property. In any event, we need not decide whether or not Appellants have a protectible property interest. This is for the reason that, even if Appellants do have a protectible property interest, HRS § 205–5.1 satisfies due process requirements.

A contested case hearing is not essential to the guarantee of due process. The legislature has inherent power to establish the procedure for a particular type of case. *See Marcello v. Bonds,* 349 U.S. 302, 75 S.Ct. 757, 99 L.Ed. 1107, *reh'g denied,* 350 U.S. 856, 76 S.Ct. 38, 100 L.Ed. 761 (1955).

In *Marcello,* the Court recognized that Congress often had good reasons for requiring different procedures for resolving different types of disputes because of the nature and context of the decisions to be made. Congress is free to establish different decision-making procedures for different agencies and different types of decisions as long as the procedures it establishes do not fall below the minimum procedures required by due process. Since *Marcello,* the Court determines the adequacy of the procedures used by an agency through independent analysis of the requirements of statutes and of the Constitution.

R. Pierce, S. Shapiro & P. Verkuil, *Administrative Law and Process* § 6.4, at 281 (1985).

Due process is not a fixed concept requiring a specific procedural course in every situation. "[D]ue process is flexible and calls for such procedural protections as the particular situation demands." *Morrissey v. Brewer,* 408 U.S. 471, 481, 92 S.Ct. 2593, 2600, 33 L.Ed.2d 484, 494 (1972). The full rights of due process present in a court of law, including presentation of witnesses and cross-examination, do not automatically attach to a quasi-judicial hearing. *See Goss v. Lopez,* 419 U.S. 565, 95 S.Ct. 729, 42 L.Ed.2d 725 (1975); *Arnett v. Kennedy,* 416 U.S. 134, 94 S.Ct. 1633, 40 L.Ed.2d 15 (1974). The basic elements of procedural due process of law require notice and an opportunity to be heard at a meaningful time and in a meaningful manner before governmental deprivation of a significant property interest. *Mathews v. Eldridge,* 424 U.S. 319, 333, 96 S.Ct. 893, 902, 47 L.Ed.2d 18, 32 (1976); *North Georgia Finishing, Inc. v. Di–Chem, Inc.,* 419 U.S. 601, 605–606, 95 S.Ct. 719, 722, 42 L.Ed.2d 751, 756–57 (1975).

Determination of the specific procedures required to satisfy due process requires a balancing of several factors: (1) the private interest which will be affected; (2) the risk of an erroneous deprivation of such interest through the procedures actually used, and the probable value, if any, of additional or alternative procedural safeguards; and (3) the governmental interest, including the burden that additional procedural safeguards would entail. *Mathews v. Eldridge,* 424 U.S. at 335, 96 S.Ct. at 903, 47 L.Ed.2d at 33; *Silver v. Castle Memorial Hosp.,* 53 Haw. [475,] 484, 497 P.2d [564,] 571 [1972]. *Sandy Beach Defense Fund v. City Council,* 70 Haw. 361, 378, 773 P.2d 250, 261 (1989).

Considering the factors set forth in *Sandy Beach,* we find that, even assuming Appellants have a property interest requiring protection under the due process clause, the procedures established by the statute are sufficient to protect Appellants' property from erroneous deprivation.

The state government is keenly interested in exploring and developing geothermal energy as a cheaper alternative to oil as a source of electrical energy for the general populace. The legislature has decided that geothermal energy development is so important that it should not be delayed by protracted contested case hearings. However, mindful of the potential adverse impact of geothermal energy development on the surrounding properties, the legislature has required the appropriate authority to provide notice, an opportunity to be heard, and a record of the proceedings for appellate review.

The public hearing, together with the mediation process, was viewed by the legislature as a reasonable alternative to the contested case. Indeed, since it allows the interested parties the opportunity to meet with the developers on a one-to-one basis and to attempt to resolve their differences, mediation may, as a practical matter, provide the residents and property owners with greater impact on the decision than a contested case. The fact that the differences between the Applicants and the affected property owners may not always be resolved in favor of the property owners does not mean that the process fails to pass constitutional muster. The constitution guarantees the right to be heard, not the right to have one's views adopted. Neither does the constitution establish the contested case as the only forum for ensuring a property owner's right to be heard. *See Sandy Beach, supra.*

Here, Appellants were afforded a hearing and an opportunity to present testimony and evidence. They have not convinced us that a contested case hearing would have given them any further protection, and we have no doubt that it would have considerably burdened the process.

In the final analysis, a geothermal permit proceeding is essentially a zoning matter. Historically, and universally, such matters have been decided after notice and a public hearing. We are not aware of any precedent for holding that the constitution requires a contested case hearing on a zoning change application.

Appellants further argue that, even if the statute meets due process requirements, the procedures actually employed by the Commission did not provide them with the opportunity to be heard in a meaningful manner:

Appellants assert the following as constitutional error:

(1) time limitations were imposed on the testimony at the public hearing;

(2) public comments on the procedures employed by the Commission were not accepted;

(3) the request for a second hearing was denied;

(4) the parties had no voice in selecting the mediator; and

(5) strict time constraints were imposed on the mediation process.

We find that the complained of Commission actions did not violate Appellants' due process rights.

The participants at the public hearing were allowed to speak and present written evidence. It was not unreasonable to limit the speaking time, since testimony at such large public hearings tends to be repetitious. *See In re Haw. Elec. Light Co.,* 67 Haw. 425, 690 P.2d 274 (1984).

Since the Commission's procedures were lawful, we do not think it was error to disallow public comment on them.

A second hearing was not necessary. Appellants argue that Applicants' revelation during the mediation process that the Holes would emit hydrogen sulfide gas should have prompted the Commission to hold a second hearing. However, one of the conditions of the permit is that, prior to the start of any drilling, Applicants will submit and get the Planning Department's approval for an air monitoring plan, which must be operational in all phases of the project. The condition is obviously meant by the Commission to address the issue of gaseous emissions, and a second hearing was not necessary.

The time constraints in the mediation process were in accord with the dictates of HRS § 205–5.1(e). However, Appellants argue that, although they were required to share the cost of mediation, they were not given a voice in the selection of the mediators. We do not believe it is essential to due process that Appellants participate in naming the mediator or mediators. Appellants' due process rights are protected so long as the selection process and the chosen mediator are unbiased. Appellants do not claim the mediators were biased or prejudiced and do not claim to have been prejudiced by the Commission's selection.

Affirmed.

Notes

1. In Pele v. Puna Geothermal, 797 P.2d 69 (1990), the appellants argued that HRS 205–5.1 violated their due process rights under the Fourteenth Amendment of the United States Constitution and Article I, Section 5 of the Hawaii State Constitution. The court disagreed, reaffirmed the Medeiros decision, and further concluded that for all the same reasons enumerated in Medeiros HRS § 205–5.1 satisfies the due process requirements of the United States Constitution.

2. Reflect again on the value of mediation of land use disputes. In Medeiros, the court enthusiastically endorsed mediation with these words: "[S]ince it allows the interested parties the opportunity to meet with the developers on a one-to one basis and to attempt to resolve their differences, mediation may, as a practical matter, provide the residents and property owners with greater impact on the decision than a contested case." The concurring opinion by Justice Bryson in Fasano v. Washington County, Bd. of County Comm'rs, 264 Or. 574, 507 P.2d 23 (1973), is also instructive: "The basic facts in this case exemplify the prohibitive cost and extended uncertainty to a homeowner when a government body decides to change or modify a zoning ordinance or comprehensive plan * * * No average homeowner or small business enterprise can afford a judicial process such as described above nor can the judicial system cope with or endure such a process in achieving justice. The number of controversies is ascending."

3. The Medieros case involves a state mediation statute related to a very specific topic: applications for geothermal resource permits. Other state mediation statutes that limit themselves to specific contexts include:

Housing:

- a. Mass General Law Chap. 40B—Mass. Office of Dispute Resolution established mediation program to resolve disputes arising under state anti-snob zoning act.
- b. RI Gen Laws § 45–34—Mediation before state housing appeal board renders decision.
- c. NJ—Under New Jersey Fair Housing Act, local governments are required to adopt housing plans, may choose to participate in mediation.

Growth Management/Regional Planning:

- a. New Jersey State Planning Act—"cross-acceptance" process—§ 52:18A–202
- b. The Washington State Growth Management Act—36.70A.190
- c. Vermont Growth Management Act—VT Stat. Ann. T. 24 § 4305(b)

Comprehensive Plans:

- a. Florida—F.S.A. § 163.3184
- b. Colorado—C.R.S. § 24–32–3209 (mandatory mediation between local governments)
- c. Delaware—Del.C. § 9103

d. Minnesota—M.S.A. § 572A.01

e. Oregon—O.R.S. § 197.633 (periodic review of comprehensive plans)

f. Tennessee—T.C.A. § 6–58–104 (comprehensive growth plans)

Other Contexts:

a. Hazardous Waste/Radiation Cleanup Statutes: CA, NJ, PN, WA, WV, WI

b. Annexation: GA, ND, TX. See also Higdon v. City of Senoia, 273 Ga. 83 (2000).

c. Coastal zone management (HI), natural gas pipelines(ME), watershed plans(MN), Hudson River Greenway(NY), Farmland tax assessment (NJ).

d. North Carolina (§ 7A–38.3) encourages the mediation of farmland nuisance disputes any time during the dispute, but requires that "prior to bringing a civil action involving a farm nuisance dispute, a farm resident or any other party shall initiate mediation pursuant to this section."

F. MEDIATION AFTER THE DEVELOPMENT APPROVAL PROCESS

SCOTT v. POLK COUNTY

District Court of Appeal of Florida, Second District, 2001.
793 So.2d 85.

THREADGILL, ACTING CHIEF JUDGE.

* * *

In March 1999, the Polk County Board of County Commissioners denied a Planned Unit Development (PUD) application submitted by Scott for the LKP property. The proposed PUD sought to convert the waterfront portion of the LKP's property into a marina and resort.

After the PUD application was denied [in April], pursuant to section 70.51(4), Florida Statutes (1999), [Scott] filed a letter with the county board, seeking alternative, nonjudicial review of the board's order by a special master, who, as provided by the statute, would be duly chosen by both Scott and the county board. Eight days later, Scott filed this lawsuit against Polk County, alleging that, with regard to his PUD application, his substantive due process rights were violated by unlawful, ex parte communications between county personnel and the South Florida Water Management District, which had a prospective interest in the LKP property. Scott claimed that those ex parte communications were improperly considered and were instrumental in the county board's denial of the subject PUD application. On October 19, 1999, Scott filed an amended complaint, alleging more specific due process violation claims against the county, pursuant to 42 U.S.C. § 1983 (1999). All efforts by the county to dismiss Scott's lawsuit were denied by the trial court.

On November 22, 1999, the special master filed a "Mediator's Report" in Scott's civil lawsuit, indicating that a proper section 70.51 special master proceeding had been conducted but had culminated in an impasse. The report went on to indicate that the special master was prepared to continue either "upon agreement of the parties or further direction of [the trial] court."

On February 10, 2000, the county filed—in the civil lawsuit—an amended motion to dismiss, abate, or stay the special master proceedings. After a hearing, the trial court entered an order, dismissing the special master proceedings. The trial court found that the special master proceedings were intended only as an alternative to judicial proceedings—of any kind, presumably—and that, once judicial proceedings were instituted, the right to a special master proceeding was waived.

On review, Scott, in essence, contends that the trial court departed from the essential requirements of the law in dismissing the special master proceedings, because it was without jurisdiction to do so. We agree.

The instant judicial action involves a § 1983 due process claim, which, in the context of a zoning case, may be viewed as an action independent and distinct from the judicial review process relating to the approval or denial of a zoning request. *See Jennings v. Dade County*, 589 So.2d 1337 (Fla. 3d DCA 1991) (holding that an original judicial action for declaratory and injunctive relief regarding due process violations in a quasi-judicial zoning proceeding before a county board can be maintained apart from the judicial review process of the board's actual zoning decision). On the other hand, the section 70.51 special master proceeding at issue herein is an alternative dispute resolution process instituted to resolve challenges to the actual merit of a zoning decision, in lieu of judicial review. This court reaches no conclusion as to whether, pursuant to *Jennings*, section 70.51 special master proceedings may be maintained simultaneously with a § 1983 judicial proceeding arising from the process employed by a governmental entity in evaluating a zoning request. We do conclude, however, that the trial court in this instance was without the legal authority to dismiss the special master proceeding. The statute provides for optional review by a special master of final zoning decisions issued by governmental entities. The option may be exercised before judicial review of a zoning decision is sought. § 70.51(10)(a). If the option is exercised, the time for filing a judicial challenge to a final zoning decision is tolled "until the special master's recommendation is acted upon by the local government." *Id.* The property owner's election to file for judicial review of a final zoning order prior to initiating a nonjudicial proceeding under the statute waives any right to a special master proceeding. *Id.* Judicial review of a final zoning order is obtained by certiorari in the circuit court and then, if necessary, by certiorari in the district court. *See ABG Real Estate Dev. Co. of Fla., Inc. v. St. Johns County*, 608 So.2d 59, 61–62 (Fla. 5th DCA 1992). In this instance, judicial review of the subject zoning order has not been initiated.

The plain language of section 70.51 indicates that the alternative proceedings contemplated by that section are informal and nonjudicial and are controlled strictly by the special master and the parties. No provision within section 70.51 confers jurisdiction on any court of law or otherwise authorizes judicial intervention or involvement in a special master proceeding, because judicial review of a zoning decision is an entirely separate formal process that may be initiated. *See* § 70.51(10)(a)-(b); *see also* ABG, 608 So.2d at 61–62. The trial court in this instance was therefore without the authority to intervene in the special master proceedings or to otherwise dismiss them. It thus departed from the essential requirements of the law in doing so.

Based on the foregoing, common law certiorari is granted. The trial court's order is quashed, and this cause is remanded for further proceedings consistent with this opinion.

Notes

1. In Maine's Land Use Mediation Statute (5 M.R.S.A.§ 3341), as in Florida's Land Use Mediation Statute (F.S.A. § 70.51), the application for mediation tolls the time to seek judicial review.

2. Unlike the Pennsylvania, Hawaii, and Idaho land use mediation statutes mentioned above, which encourage mediation during the permit approval process, the Florida mediation statute applicable in the principal case permits mediation only after a final decision on a permit approval has occurred. See also California (Cal. Gov. Code §§ 66030–66037), Connecticut (C.G.S.A. § 8–8), Oregon (O.R.S. § 197.860), and Maine (5 M.R.S.A. § 3341). In Brand v. Town of Brunswick, 1999 Me. Super. (unreported), the defendant filed a motion to dismiss the plaintiff's application for land use mediation under statute 5 M.R.S.A. § 3341. The plaintiff had violated a zoning ordinance by cutting down trees on her property and appealed that violation. However, prior to her application for land use mediation, the plaintiff had not requested any permit, variance, or special exception. The court found that the case was not ripe for mediation pursuant to § 3341.

G. MEDIATION AND LAWYERING

WILMINGTON HOSPITALITY v. NEW CASTLE COUNTY

Court of Chancery of Delaware, New Castle County, 2001.
788 A.2d 536.

LAMB, VICE CHANCELLOR

Plaintiff Wilmington Hospitality ("WH") moved to enforce a settlement agreement that it claims to have reached with plaintiff-in-intervention Republic Bank ("RB")—but not with the defendant, New Castle County ("County")—during the course of voluntary mediation. * * * I find that the mediation was subject to Court of Chancery Rule 174 and that the terms of that rule and the public policy underlying it require denial of WH's application. I also conclude that WH has failed to show that WH ever agreed to settle without the active agreement of the County. Thus, the motion to enforce a settlement that does not include the County must be denied.

This * * * [case] arise[s] out of the refusal of the County to issue a certificate of occupancy ("CO") and other necessary permits and licenses for the Wilmington Radisson Hotel to open for business. The County initially refused the CO when its inspectors discovered that the square footage of the hotel, as built, greatly exceeded the limits set in the record plan for the development. RB was allowed to intervene in the action to better protect its collateral interest in the property. On October 20 and November 3, 2000, I heard WH's applications for temporary and preliminary injunctive relief. * * * I denied the relief sought because WH failed to satisfy the standards for obtaining mandatory equitable relief.

At the time of the second hearing, there appeared to be two obstacles to opening the hotel. First, there were a number of health and safety issues that needed to be addressed and resolved before any CO could issue. These issues were more or less technical in nature and, while difficult to resolve in the context of a litigation, could be worked through by a well-designed and implemented program of mediation undertaken in good faith. Second, from a legal perspective, the continued financial and managerial involvement of the principals of WH in the project posed an obstacle to the ultimate ability of WH or RB to obtain the relief needed to open the hotel.

For these reasons, I suggested to the parties that they engage in a two-part mediation effort: one part aimed at eliminating (or at least minimizing) the health and safety issues, and the other at finding a solution to end WH's principals' continued involvement in the project. I suggested that Retired Resident Judge Bifferato serve as mediator. The parties agreed and met with Judge Bifferato on November 3, 2000. In connection with the mediation, I also scheduled trial.

As the mediation progressed, it became apparent that the arrangement to remove the WH principals from the deal, although dependent on the County's agreement to issue a CO, mostly involved a negotiation between WH and RB, who pursued those discussions with Judge Bifferato. The County's involvement in this aspect of the discussions was largely limited to reacting to structures proposed by the others and identifying conditions to its agreement to issue the CO and cooperate in opening the hotel in full.

Although not spelled out in detail in the record before me on this motion, I understand that the other aspect of the mediation made progress in addressing and narrowing the health and safety issues that stood in the way of issuing a CO. In particular, I understand that, assuming a satisfactory resolution of the other aspect of the mediation, the County was prepared to issue a temporary CO for a 102,000 square foot operation and to work cooperatively with a new owner to secure the permits necessary to open all 158,000 square feet of the building.

On November 27, 2000, the day before the scheduled trial, I met with counsel for all parties, at the request of RB's counsel. * * * [C]ounsel for both RB and WH indicated that their clients had reached an agreement in principle to resolve the financial and managerial aspect of the mediation and that, with a single exception, there was an overall agreement with the County. That exception related to the County's demand for the inclusion of a restrictive deed covenant relating to the involvement, directly or indirectly, of WH's principals and their affiliates and relatives in future ownership of the hotel. * * *

In what now appears to have been a gambit to force the County to come to terms on its deed restriction demand, counsel for RB and WH expressed a willingness to settle the issues between them without the County's agreement. * * *

RB's counsel quickly made clear, however, that it did not propose to move forward without the County's agreement. Instead, it proposed to delay the trial and to continue the mediation process with Judge Bifferato over the County's deed restriction demands. * * * I put the trial off without date and directed that the parties present a formal written settlement agreement on December 6, 2000.

Thereafter, counsel for RB prepared a draft three-party settlement agreement and circulated it to WH, but not the County. WH, through its counsel, objected to its terms and made a counter-proposal that was not acceptable to RB. Eventually, discussions broke down between RB and WH, leading to RB's decision to substitute new counsel. On December 6, 2000, the parties informed the court of the lack of progress. WH thereafter filed a motion to enforce the terms of a claimed two-party agreement to settle between it and RB.

WH contends that the terms of this settlement can be gleaned from a series of letters counsel for RB and WH exchanged between November 17 and 21, 2000. These letters were written in connection with the mediation and reflect the parties' efforts to reach a mediated settlement. WH also relies on several affidavits, including an affidavit of its counsel discussing at length the substance of the mediation.

[The court first finds that Court of Chancery Rule 174 ("Voluntary mediation in the Court of Chancery") governs the mediation at issue.] * * * [T]wo subparts of [Rule 174] are of particular importance. Subpart (g) provides that, if the parties to the mediation reach an agreement, "their agreement shall be reduced to writing and signed by the parties and the mediator. The agreement shall set forth the terms of the resolution of the issues and the future responsibility of each party." Subpart (d) provides that any "communication made in or in connection with the mediation that relates to the controversy being mediated, whether made to the mediator or a party, . . . is confidential" and is "not subject to disclosure in *any judicial or administrative proceeding*" (emphasis added). The only exceptions to this rule of confidentiality are where all the mediation parties agree in writing to waive confidentiality, or where the material was not prepared specifically for mediation and is otherwise subject to discovery. RB and the County argue that, taken together, these provisions preclude (i) WH's motion to enforce a mediated settlement not reduced to writing and signed by the parties and the mediator, and (ii) WH's introduction into the record and reliance on any communications between the parties to the mediation made in connection with it. * * *

WH [counters] that the confidentiality provisions of the rule only apply to communications made at a mediation conference and that the four letters it relies on as evidencing the terms of the settlement were exchanged outside the context of a specific mediation conference. This argument misreads the rule. The portion of Rule 174(d) WH relies on provides for the confidential treatment of communications made to *any person* "if made at a mediation conference." WH ignores the far broader confidential treatment accorded by the same subpart of the rule to communications to *the mediator or a party* "made *in or in connection with* the mediation that relates to the controversy being mediated." (Emphasis added.) This broader treatment plainly and unambiguously covers the series of letters WH relies on to prove the terms of the alleged settlement agreement. Those letters contain communications to parties to the mediation, were sent in connection with the mediation, and relate to the controversy being mediated. * * *

Confidentiality of all communications between the parties or among them and the mediator serves the important public policy of promoting a broad discussion of potential resolutions to the matters being mediated. Without the expectation of confidentiality, parties would hesitate to propose compromise solutions out of the concern that they would later be prejudiced by their disclosure. I have already concluded that the series of letters on which WH seeks to rely are entitled to confidential treatment in accordance with subpart (d) of the rule and, thus, "are not subject to disclosure in any judicial ... proceeding." For these reasons, I cannot rely on them to discover the terms of the settlement WH says it reached with RB [and WH's motion to enforce must be denied.]

Relatedly, it is consistent with the purpose of Rule 174 to interpret subpart (g) thereof as requiring that any settlement between the parties to the mediation be reduced to writing and signed by them and the mediator as a condition to its enforceability. As this proceeding itself well illustrates, it is reasonable to expect that such a bright-line rule is the best way to protect the confidentiality of the mediation when disputes arise over the terms of a putative settlement. Where, as here, there is *no* written settlement signed by *anyone,* it is impossible for the parties to litigate over the terms of the putative agreement without breaching the confidentiality of the mediation process in a substantial way. Indeed, WH argues that the terms of the settlement can be gleaned from a series of four letters each prepared and sent in connection with the mediation. [I recognize that a dispute could arise about the enforceability of a settlement memorialized in writing and signed by fewer than all the parties and do not decide the questions raised by that scenario. *See, e.g. Few v. Hammack Enterprises, Inc.,* 511 S E.2d 665 (N.C. Ct.

App. 1999). ("Mediated Settlement Agreement" prepared by mediator and, subsequently signed by plaintiff, could be enforced against non-signing defendant without invading privileged confidentiality of mediation).] * * *

I also conclude that the motion should be denied because the County is not a party to WH's putative agreement with RB. Yet, the object of the litigation and the mediation—opening the Wilmington Radisson Hotel—could not be accomplished by a settlement that did not include the County. While it is possible that WH and RB could have agreed to resolve some issues arising out of their lending relationship that were not even part of a litigation at the time, they could not have agreed to a settlement of this case without the participation of the County. * * *

For the reasons stated above, I deny plaintiff's motion for enforcement of settlement. I also conclude that all confidential mediation material that has been made part of the record in this proceeding and all other documents that reveal or discuss confidential information relating to the mediation should be sealed. Counsel for Republic Bank are to submit an order within 5 days of the date of this opinion.

Notes

1. The cases discuss agreements that are the result of mediations. Once an agreement has been reached, what is the role of the mediator in drafting the agreement? What is the role of counsel for the disputants? How does a mediation agreement differ, if at all, from an ordinary contract? What terms should a mediation agreement contain? How clearly must the mediation agreement, or contract, be drafted to guide the parties in the post-mediation phase? What happens if the mediation agreement isn't complete, clear, or comprehensive?

2. The case describes a breakdown in the mediation when the parties attempted to commit the agreement to paper. What practices within the mediation process could have helped avoid an impasse at this point?

3. In West Beach Marina, Ltd. v. Erdeljac, 94 S.W.3d 248 (Tex.App. 2002), one of the issues adjudicated was whether a mediation agreement was sufficiently detailed to be enforceable. The case involved a dispute that arose when West Beach Marina applied for a permit to build a marina which neighbors contended would interfere with their easement across the property. Following a lengthy mediation, the parties authorized their attorneys to prepare and sign an agreement. West Beach then repudiated the agreement. Although the agreement did not refer to or settle certain aspects of the dispute, the court found that it was definite enough to be enforceable. The agreement demonstrated that the parties intended to be bound by it and contained sufficient terms to bind the parties to the representations it contained. Compare Haghighi v. Russian–American Broadcasting Co., 577 N.W.2d 927 (Minn. 1998) (under the requirements of the Minnesota Civil Mediation Act, a handwritten agreement prepared by the parties' attorneys at the close of a mediation session was unenforceable where the document failed to state that the agreement was binding); Schwartz v. Adamson, 1999 WL 170676 (Minn.App. 1999, unpublished) (an oral agreement reached in a

mediation session was unenforceable where a written agreement prepared by the mediator a day after the mediation was never signed by the parties and failed to state that the agreement was binding); Environmental Abatement, Inc. v. Astrum R.E. Corp., 27 S.W.3d 530 (Tenn.Ct.App. 2000) (where a contractor was allowed to withdraw consent to a mediated agreement that was not made on the record or in open court, as defined by the rules of the state Supreme Court).

4. Plum Creek Timber Co., L.P. v. Hillman, 95 Wash.App. 1061 (1999) (settlement agreements are considered to be contracts and their construction is governed by contract law); Brown v. Brown 2002 WL 1343222 (Tex.App. 2002, not designated for publication) (a mediated settlement reserving mineral rights held enforceable as a binding contract under general contract law).

5. The American Bar Association's Model Rules of Professional Conduct contain interesting language regarding the lawyer's duty to advise clients regarding mediation and ADR. Model Rule 1.4(b) states: "A lawyer shall explain a matter to the extent reasonably necessary to permit the client to make informed decisions regarding the representation." Model Rule 1.2(a) states: "A lawyer shall abide by a client's decisions concerning the objectives of representation * * * and shall consult with the client as to the means by which they are to be pursued." The language of the Model Rules does not clearly require lawyers to allow clients to decide whether and how to pursue ADR. The Comment to Model Rule 2.1 states: "[W]hen a matter is likely to involve litigation it may be necessary * * * to inform the client of forms of dispute resolution that might constitute reasonable alternatives to litigation." State rules adopted by Arkansas, Colorado, Georgia, Hawaii, and Ohio encourage discussing ADR with clients; rules in Massachusetts, Michigan, Pennsylvania, and Virginia require lawyers to inform clients of ADR options. See Robert F. Cochran, Jr., Educating Clients on ADR Alternatives, Los Angeles Lawyer, October, 2002, and Professional Rules and ADR: Control of Alternative Dispute Resolution Under the ABA Ethics 2000 Committee Proposal and Other Professional Responsibility Standards, 28 Fordham Urb. L. J. 895 (2001).

SECTION 3. REVIEW BY THE COURTS

A. INTRODUCTION

We have been studying judicial review from the outset. Every land use case raises important questions about the role of the courts and the posture and attitude of the courts shed light on the land use decision-making process. The Standard Zoning Enabling Act established rules that govern judicial review of the decisions of zoning and planning boards. These bodies typically conduct hearings and keep a record of their proceedings. This record can be certified to a court issuing a writ of certiorari. Once again, statutes in each state define the matter and redress from administrative and quasi-judicial land use decisions varies according to the state law definitions. The definition of an aggrieved party, the statute of limitations for bringing an action, and the administrative remedies available prior to court review are built into most state land use enabling statutes. What happens, however, when the aggrieved party challenges a legislative decision, such as a rezoning of a parcel? The rights of individuals to challenge the legislative decisions of governments are governed by a different body of law, and other writs, statutes of limitation, standards of review, and remedies may apply.

In this section we encounter a variety of judicial review issues: standing, ripeness, finality, exhaustion, standards of review, burdens of proof, res judicata, and remedies, among other matters.

FRITTS v. CITY OF ASHLAND
Court of Appeals of Kentucky, 1961.
348 S.W.2d 712.

CULLEN, COMMISSIONER.

The Board of Commissioners of the City of Ashland rezoned from R-2 Residential to I-1 Light Industrial a tract of four acres which was in single ownership. A group of neighboring property owners brought action attacking the rezoning ordinance on the ground that it was arbitrary, capricious and unreasonable. The circuit court entered judgment upholding the ordinance and the plaintiffs have appealed.

Ashland adopted a comprehensive zoning ordinance in 1955, following a study with the assistance of state experts that began in 1951. The city bounds on the Ohio River on the northeast and extends to the south and west. The area along the river was zoned for industrial and commercial uses. Aside from this area only two other districts were zoned for light industry, one in the northwest quarter of the city and the other near the west boundary. The rest of the city was zoned residential, except for appropriately located small commercial districts and for necessary educational, institutional and recreational areas. The tract here in question, which is called the Wilson tract, is located near the geographical center of the city in a neighborhood that is residential in character. The tract is two blocks from a grade school accommodating 350 children and three blocks from the presently being constructed senior high school which will have an enrollment of some 1200 students. The nearest industrially zoned property is one and one-half miles away.

* * *

The Wilson tract was rezoned in September 1960. It is clear from the record that the zoning change was made because the owners of a garment factory, which had outgrown its existing location in the city, desired to build a new factory on the Wilson tract, and threatened to leave the city unless this tract was made available. There is no pretense that the zoning change was a step in any coordinated plan for establishment of industrial districts.

The contention of the appellants is, of course, that this is a case of spot zoning.

There was no evidence of any change in the neighborhood since the enactment of the original zoning ordinance in 1955, nor was there proof that the Wilson tract was by its situation distinguishable in character from the surrounding or adjoining property. Therefore, under the decision in Byrn v. Beechwood Village, Ky., 253 S.W.2d 395, the zoning change on its face was arbitrary, capricious and unreasonable, and the burden was on the city authorities to justify the change.

The city authorities have attempted to justify their action on two grounds. One is that the "general welfare" of the city will be promoted by reason of employment being provided for some 400 citizens in the relocated garment factory. The other is that zoning in Ashland was still in a formative state and therefore the city should be entitled to great latitude in modifying the original plan.

The argument with respect to the first ground points up a common fallacy that seems to exist in the minds of zoning agencies. It is that the particular use that a particular owner says he intends to make of a particular tract of land is a controlling factor. Here the Wilson tract was rezoned because the Wilsons said they intended to convey it to the owners of the garment factory who said they intended to build a new garment factory there. However, the ordinance did not rezone the tract for use by the Ashland Crafts Garment Factory but for any appropriate light industry use. There was no guaranty that either the Wilsons or the garment factory people would not change their minds, resulting in the tract being occupied by some light industry that would not have the appealing features of the proposed garment factory. * * * The point is that in establishing a light industry zone the only proper consideration is whether in the light of a comprehensive, coordinated zoning plan the particular area should be set aside for general light industry uses. See Pierson Trapp Co. v. Peak, Ky., 340 S.W.2d 456.

Regardless of the foregoing considerations, the general welfare argument is not sound. The providing of employment opportunities is merely one element of general welfare as that term relates to the zoning field. Sociological factors, protection of property values, traffic and safety considerations, preservation of health, providing adequate light and air, all enter into the question of general welfare. See KRS 100.066, 100.520. If the appellees' argument were carried to its logical conclusion the mere fact that employment would be provided through a particular use of land would overcome all other factors, and a boiler factory could be put in the middle of a beautiful residential neighborhood.

The appellees argue that it is essential to the welfare of the city that the garment factory be retained, and that there are not suitable light industry sites in the city other than the Wilson tract. Our answer to that is that if the lack of suitable industrial sites is due to the restrictions of the present zoning ordinance a study and survey of the situation should be made, suitable areas for industrial development selected, and changes made in the zoning ordinance in accordance with systematic planning. On the other hand, if lack of suitable sites is due to other factors no real solution to the long range problem is reached by momentarily satisfying one particular industry.

The proposition that zoning in Ashland is in the formative state is based upon a statement in the report of the consultants who prepared the 1959 *master plan,* to the effect that the work on the master plan was of limited scope and therefore should be considered subject to modification when additional studies were made, and that the "Land Use Plan" and the "Major Street Plan" were designated as "preliminary". As hereinbefore mentioned, the master plan relates only to *public facilities,* such as streets, sewers, parks, public utilities, airports, etc., and does not establish private use restrictions or districts. Accordingly, the fact that the master plan may have been in a formative state does not mean that the zoning ordinance establishing private use restrictions and districts was in any way preliminary or conditional. Furthermore, even if the zoning ordinance should be considered in a formative state it would not follow that modifications could be made without regard to any coordinated plan.

The circuit court found as a fact that the zoning change was "in accord with an orderly plan of zoning development." The evidence does not support that finding but on the contrary shows that the change was made solely to meet a particular exigency.

The circuit court further found that there was no evidence to show that the plaintiffs or other property owners would be injured by the rezoning, and that there was substantial proof that the neighborhood would be improved. However, as pointed out in Byrn v. Beechwood Village, Ky., 253 S.W.2d 395, Shemwell v. Speck, Ky., 265 S.W.2d 468, and Pierson Trapp Co. v. Peak, Ky., 340 S.W.2d 456, the effect of a zoning change on the value of neighboring property is only one factor to be considered, and the purpose of zoning is not to protect the value of the property of particular individuals but rather to promote the welfare of the community as a whole. The entire community is damaged by haphazard zoning because it causes insecurity of property values throughout the city. So the mere fact that the particular complaining parties may not suffer a decrease in the value of their property will not redeem a zoning change that is not related to proper zoning objects.

In our opinion we have here a clear case of spot zoning and the ordinance making the zoning change must be held invalid.

We feel impelled to express briefly our view of the proper theory of zoning as relates to the making of changes in an original comprehensive ordinance. We think the theory is that after the enactment of the original ordinance there should be a continuous or periodic study of the development of property uses, the nature of population trends, and the commercial and industrial growth, both actual and prospective. On the basis of such study, changes may be made intelligently, systematically, and according to a coordinated plan designed to promote zoning objectives. An examination of the multitude of zoning cases that have reached this court leads us to the conclusion that the common practice of zoning agencies, after the adoption of an original ordinance, is simply to wait until some property owner finds an opportunity to acquire a financial advantage by devoting his property to a use other than that for which it is zoned, and then struggle with the question of whether some excuse can be found for complying with his request for a rezoning. The result has been that in most of the rezoning cases reaching the courts there actually has been spot zoning and the courts have upheld or invalidated the change according to how flagrant the violation of true zoning principles has been. It is to be hoped that in the future zoning authorities will give recognition to the fact that an essential feature of zoning is *planning.*

The judgment is reversed, with directions to enter judgment holding the rezoning ordinance invalid.

Notes

1. Does the local legislative body, the Board of Commissioners in the principal case, have the legal authority to adopt a zoning amendment that does not conform with the comprehensive plan? If not, its action is *ultra vires*, beyond the city's legal authority. Is it a legitimate function for the judiciary to review whether municipal corporations act within their authority? What does this case tell us about the importance of having a comprehensive plan and using it as the predicate for subsequent legislative zoning decisions?

2. When a court considers the remedy available in a land use case, does it matter what type of body made the decision being reviewed? When will a court, for example, issue a writ of mandamus ordering a legislature to rezone a parcel? In Landgrave v. Watson, 593 S.W.2d 875 (Ky.App.1979), the local legislative authority refused to rezone property for use as a liquor store in an area where the factual setting prevented any realistic development for residential purposes. The trial court ordered the rezoning and the court of appeals reversed, stating: "The scope of the circuit court's inquiry in reviewing the action of a legislative body in a zoning case is limited. It can decide if the agency acted in excess of granted powers and if it afforded procedural due process to all parties * * *. Further, a de novo trial is impermissible." What does the court mean when it says a trial de novo is impermissible? Did the legislative body create a record of the facts it gathered on which its decision is based? Why should a court refrain from conducting a trial to discover and reassess the facts chosen by the legislative body to guide its discretion in deciding whether and how to act? Must a local legislature entertain any property owner's petition to rezone land or can it simply refuse to act as a method of ratifying its current comprehensive plan and zoning scheme? Also see State ex rel. Barber & Sons Tobacco Co., Inc. v. Jackson County, 869 S.W.2d 113 (Mo.App.1993), where the court affirmed the refusal to rezone a 12–acre parcel from residential to a zoning classification to permit construction of a concrete batch mixing plant despite the fact that the property was in the middle of a rock quarry, adjacent to an asphalt plant and rock crusher, and was used to store crushed rock and by-products.

3. Is the decision of the local legislature to rezone a parcel a legislative one or an administrative or quasi-judicial one? Do you think that a court will

act differently, using different standards of review, if it is reviewing a legislative rather than an administrative or quasi-judicial decision? One difficulty prominent in zoning cases is the uncertainty about whether to classify zoning decisions as legislative in character, which would dictate a narrow scope of review (arbitrary, irrational), or administrative or quasi-judicial, which would give the court more flexibility in considering the "reasonableness" of the zoning decision. Complicating the problem even more is the evident penchant of some courts to engage in what might be called "judicial zoning." For an analysis of the problem in one state, see Gitelman, Judicial Review of Zoning in Arkansas, 23 Ark.L.Rev. 22 (1969).

Consider the following expressions of judicial opinion:

a. City of Phoenix v. Beall, 22 Ariz.App. 141, 524 P.2d 1314 (1974):

> The plaintiffs concede that the enactment of an overall zoning ordinance is legislative action. They contend that the City Council, in enacting or declining to enact a zoning amendment of the type which the plaintiffs request, is acting more nearly in a judicial than in a legislative capacity. This contention appears to relate to the quantum of proof necessary for a court decision overturning the refusal to rezone. We do not agree. The United States Supreme Court in Village of Belle Terre v. Boraas, 416 U.S. 1, 94 S.Ct. 1536, 39 L.Ed.2d 797 (1974), stated:
>
> * * * But every line drawn by a legislature leaves some out that might well have been included. That exercise of discretion, however, is a legislative not a judicial function. [Footnote omitted.] 416 U.S. at 7, 94 S.Ct. at 1540, 39 L.Ed.2d at 803, 804.
>
> The Arizona Legislature in empowering cities to zone specifies that zoning and zoning changes be "by ordinance." The Arizona cases recognize that zoning is legislative and that there is a presumption of the validity of zoning enactments. * * * Zoning will be upheld unless it is clearly arbitrary and unreasonable and without a substantial relation to public health, safety, morals or general welfare. * * *
>
> If the evidence is fairly debatable the zoning or failure to change the zoning as requested will be upheld in the appellate courts. * * *
>
> The test to be used by the trial court is that zoning will be upheld unless it is clearly arbitrary and unreasonable and without substantial relation to public health, safety, morals or general welfare. Zoning ordinances are presumed valid, and where the reasonableness of the ordinance is fairly debatable, the trial court must uphold its validity.
>
> What is the applicable standard to be used by the appellate court in reviewing the trial court's decision to upset the zoning ordinance which in effect finds that the presumption of validity of zoning has been overcome? In one case, City of Phoenix v. Burke, 9 Ariz.App. 395, 452 P.2d 722 (1969), a case not presented to our Supreme Court for review, the majority of the Court used the usual standards of review in civil actions, namely, that the trial court will be upheld if there is evidence in support of its judgment. We hold that the test applied in Burke is not the law in Arizona. * * * The ruling of a trial court which upsets zoning will be upheld only if the zoning is clearly arbitrary and unreasonable

and without substantial relation to the public health, safety, morals or general welfare. Furthermore, if in a review of the record, the appellate court finds that it is fairly debatable as to whether the zoning is clearly arbitrary and unreasonable and without a substantial relation to the above factors, then the zoning or the failure to amend the zoning will be upheld and the trial court will be reversed. The fact that the property would be more valuable if zoned for a different use is not controlling.

b. Carter v. Adams, 928 S.W.2d 39 (Tenn.App.1996):

[Landowners sought a zoning change from A–1, Agriculture, Light Industry to M–2, Heavy Industry to operate a demolition landfill; the planning commission denied the request, but the county commission rezoned the land. The lower court held the zoning change to be unreasonable and arbitrary.] On appeal:

Zoning bodies are legislative in nature and the scope of judicial review for their actions is restricted. * * * Over time, the standards of "fairly debatable," "rational basis," and "arbitrary and capricious" have come to hold the same meaning * * *. Whichever term is applied, the level of scrutiny required of the court is to "refrain from substituting its judgment for that of a local governmental body * * * If any possible reason exists justifying the action, it will be upheld." [Citation omitted.]

c. MacDonald v. Board of County Comm'rs, 238 Md. 549, 210 A.2d 325 (1965) (dissenting opinion):

The majority states, in effect, that rezoning can only be sustained when there is "strong evidence of mistake" in the original zoning or where there is "a substantial change in conditions" in the neighborhood. This "mistake-change in conditions" rule came into the Maryland law by way of dicta of our predecessors and in a rather oblique way. The "change in conditions" concept seems to be first stated, without any supporting authority, in Northwest Merchants Terminal v. O'Rourke, 191 Md. 171, 60 A.2d 743 (1948). It was repeated in a restricted form in Cassel v. Mayor and City Council of Baltimore, 195 Md. 348, 358, 73 A.2d 486, 488 (1950). This *dictum* was then expanded by additional *dicta* in Kracke v. Weinberg, 197 Md. 339, 79 A.2d 387, 391 (1951) which added "mistake in original zoning" to a "change in the character of the neighborhood"—and so the Maryland Rule of "mistake-change in conditions" was born. It was entirely judicially conceived and delivered. It had no legislative assistance. It has had a rapid and, to my mind, unhealthy growth in the Maryland law. The formulae have become talismanic phrases now applied with Draconian severity to the rezoning efforts of the local legislative bodies, with unfortunate results. In my opinion, the time to re-examine the entire doctrine and its premises is long overdue. As it is entirely "judge-made," a change in, or broadening of, the doctrine would operate only prospectively and would in no way impair vested rights, inasmuch as it is not a rule of property. Under these circumstances, the doctrine of *stare decisis* is not a substantial obstacle in effecting a much-needed change. If my Brethren are reluctant to overrule or modify the "mistake-change" doctrine, I suggest with great respect, that the Legislative Council and ultimately the General Assembly give serious thought to a change by appropriate legislation.

In Buckel v. Board of County Commissioners, 80 Md.App. 305, 562 A.2d 1297 (1989), cert. denied 318 Md. 96, 566 A.2d 1112 (1989), the court, applying the same principles decried by the dissenter in the MacDonald case, held that a small increase in population, construction of a shopping center, and neighborhood rezonings did not constitute a substantial change. The planning staff and the board had both approved the rezoning of land zoned agricultural for the construction of a motel and the neighbors were the appellants.

NEUZIL v. CITY OF IOWA CITY

Supreme Court of Iowa, 1990.
451 N.W.2d 159.

LAVORATO, JUSTICE.

In this law action, the district court concluded a zoning amendment that downzoned undeveloped property was valid. The property owners appealed. We transferred the case to the court of appeals, which reversed. Because we think the district court was right, we vacate the decision of the court of appeals and affirm the judgment of the district court.

I. BACKGROUND FACTS AND PROCEEDINGS.

The Neuzil family owns an eight and one-half acre tract of land (tract) southwest of the University of Iowa Hospitals and Clinics in Iowa City. They have owned the tract since 1941. Mrs. Ella Neuzil and a son Gregory occupy houses on the tract. There also is a rental house there, but the remainder of the tract is undeveloped.

* * *

In 1962 Iowa City adopted a comprehensive zoning plan known as the Bartholomew Plan. Under the plan the tract was zoned R-3A. The R-3A zoning allowed multifamily dwellings and permitted up to forty-four units per acre.

In 1972 the tract was rezoned from R-3A to R-3. The R-3 zoning also allowed multifamily dwellings but limited the number of units per acre to fourteen.

In 1978 Iowa City adopted a new comprehensive plan. * * *

There was no new zoning concerning the tract pursuant to the 1978 Comprehensive Plan. However, this plan recommended that the tract be limited to residential development at a density of eight to sixteen dwellings per acre.

In 1983 Iowa City updated its comprehensive zoning plan. The tract was then zoned RM-12, a zoning that had the same limitations as the R-3 zoning. For all practical purposes the tract was under the same use restrictions as it was in 1972.

In 1985 after many requests from area residents, the tract was again downzoned, this time to RS–8. RS–8 zoning is for single-family or duplex dwellings and permits only eight units per acre.

The Neuzil family has consistently objected to the downzoning. Each time the family claimed that the proposed zoning would decrease the value of the tract. The family, however, had agreed not to sell or begin developing the tract for commercial purposes while Ella was still alive.

In the 1960s and 1970s much of the area surrounding the tract was highly developed. The tract borders University Heights on the north and west side. In fact, the only access to the tract is through streets from University Heights although the tract is in Iowa City. The land abutting the tract in University Heights is single-family residential. The land to the east and south of the tract consists of single-family dwellings. A ravine runs east and west on the tract and drains into Melrose Lake, which is on the land immediately east of the tract. The land * * * immediately east of the tract was also downzoned to RS–8 in 1985. But its owners did apply for, and received, a variance to permit multifamily occupancy.

Because the tract was undeveloped, the neighbors often used it for recreational purposes. In fact, residents in the area tried unsuccessfully to get University Heights and Iowa City to purchase the tract for a neighborhood park.

Shortly after the 1983 zoning ordinance was adopted, owners of the Smith land were making plans to develop their land as permitted under the then existing zoning ordinance. Residents from University Heights and Iowa City who lived close to the tract organized the Melrose Lake Association.

Because the association did not want more multifamily housing in the area, it petitioned the Iowa City Planning Commission to downzone the tract, as well as the Smith land to RS–8. When the commission refused, the association petitioned the city council of Iowa City to downzone the tract.

The city council held two public hearings on the petition in March and April 1985. Proponents and opponents of the proposed downzoning were heard. On June 4, 1985, the council voted to downzone the tract to RS–8.

The city council drafted its findings and reasons for approving the downzoning after the Neuzils filed the present lawsuit. The district court, however, found that the council had indeed relied on these reasons in downzoning the tract. These reasons included the following: 1. The Neuzil tract contains 8.5 acres of land, with direct access only into streets through residential neighborhoods. 2. The Neuzil tract is surrounded on three sides by single-family residential neighborhoods, those on the north and west being located in the Town of University Heights. On June 4, 1985, the property to the east of the Neuzil tract was also rezoned to RS–8. 3. The streets in the single-family neighborhood abutting the Neuzil tract were not designed to handle heavy amounts of traffic, and the other streets in the area are already heavily traveled. 4. Development of the Neuzil tract at the maximum density permitted in the RM–12 zone would allow construction of approximately 126 additional dwelling units raising the potential for generating approximately 1550 motor vehicle trips daily. 5. The allowable density on the Neuzil tract will reduce the potential increase to traffic congestion on the streets in the immediate area. 6. The area is shown on the City's Comprehensive Plan as being developed at 8 to 16 dwellings per acre, and the RS–8 zoning is consistent with that Plan. 7. Multifamily development of the tract, at the density permitted in the RM–12 zone, would have a negative impact on the value of property surrounding the tract. Development of the density permitted in the RS–8 zone should help maintain the value of neighboring properties. 8. The Neuzil tract contains a pond and two large, partially wooded ravines, and the property immediately to the east of the Neuzil tract contains Melrose Lake, an environmentally sensitive and important feature of the area. 9. Storm water runoff occasionally causes Melrose Lake to overflow, floods areas downstream, and contributes to pollution of the lake. 10. Development at a lower density will reduce the magnitude of the increase in Melrose Lake drainage, flooding and pollution problems, but will still permit development which is sensitive to the fragile environment.

Following the 1985 rezoning, the Neuzils brought this suit against Iowa City, seeking a declaratory judgment and damages. They wanted the 1985 downzoning declared void as unreasonable. They also sought damages based on claims of tortious interference with business opportunities, an unconstitutional taking without just compensation, and inverse condemnation. The suit was filed at law and tried to the court. On the day of trial, the Neuzils withdrew their inverse condemnation claim.

The district court found that the 1985 downzoning amendment was reasonable and that the Neuzils had not proven their claims of tortious interference or civil rights violation. The Neuzils appealed, raising one issue: Was the 1985 downzoning amendment valid under the circumstances?

The court of appeals, using a de novo review, reversed. We granted the city's petition for further review, and the case is now before us.

* * *

III. Validity of the 1985 Amendment Downzoning the Tract.

Zoning is an exercise of the police powers delegated by the State to municipalities. Iowa Code § 414.1 (1985). A zoning ordinance, including any amendments to it, carries a strong presumption of validity. This means that if the ordinance is facially valid and the reasonableness of the ordinance is fairly debatable, it must be allowed to stand. Anderson v. City of Cedar Rapids, 168 N.W.2d 739, 742 (Iowa 1969). Stated another way,

[t]he validity of an ordinance is said to be fairly debatable when for any reason it is open to dispute or controversy on grounds that make sense or point to a logical deduction that in no way involves its constitutional validity, and validity is fairly debatable where reasonable minds may differ, or where the evidence provides a basis for a fair difference of opinion as to the constitutionality of the ordinance or its application to particular property. 1 Anderson, American Law of Zoning 3d, § 3.20, at 137 (1986) (citations omitted).

So "if there is some basis for the ordinance . . . and there is room for two opinions, the challenged ordinance is valid." Id.

An ordinance is valid if it has any real, substantial relation to the public health, comfort, safety, and welfare, including the maintenance of property values. Anderson v. City of Cedar Rapids, 168 N.W.2d at 742; Iowa Code § 414.1. In applying this test, the court's prime consideration is the ordinance's general purpose and not the hardship of an individual case. Id.

Even though a challenged zoning ordinance adversely affects a property interest or prohibits the most beneficial use of the property, a court should not, for that reason alone, strike it down. Stone v. City of Wilton, 331 N.W.2d 398, 402 (Iowa 1983). This rule applies to the original zoning ordinance and amendments to it because we recognize that zoning is not static. Id. at 403.

Iowa law requires municipalities to pass all zoning ordinances in accordance with a comprehensive plan. Iowa Code § 414.3. Among other things, such ordinances should be designed to encourage efficient urban development patterns; to lessen congestion in the streets; to service the public from fire, flood, panic, and other dangers; to promote health and the general welfare; to provide adequate light and air; to prevent the overcrowding of land; and to avoid undue concentration of population. Id. In passing such ordinances a municipality is required by law to give reasonable consideration . . . to the character of the [area in question] and the peculiar suitability of [the area] for particular uses, and with a view to conserving the value of buildings and encouraging the most appropriate use of land throughout [the] city. Id.

A change in conditions sometimes calls for a change in plans. For this reason, a property owner has no vested right to continuity of zoning of the general area in which the owner resides. Likewise, the owners of property adjacent to a district which is restricted to a particular use have no vested right in the continuation of that use when the public interest dictates otherwise. Anderson, § 4.26, at 286.

A municipality's power to amend zoning ordinances does have some restrictions. Generally, the municipality may not "amend a comprehensive zoning law to remove or impose more or less onerous restrictions upon a small tract or lot similar in character and use to the surrounding property." Hermann v. City of Des Moines, 250 Iowa 1281, 1286–87, 97 N.W.2d 893, 896 (1959). A zoning amendment reflecting such a discrepancy in similarly-situated property is discriminatory. Id. This type of regulation is called spot zoning and should be upheld only if there are "substantial and reasonable grounds or basis" for the discriminatory treatment. Id. 97 N.W.2d at 897.

Nor may the municipality downzone property to the point that the property cannot be improved with any development that would be economically feasible. Kempf v. City of Iowa City, 402 N.W.2d 393, 400 (Iowa 1987). In these circumstances the downzoning amounts to an unconstitutional taking. Id. at 400–01. Such a result is another way of saying that the ordinance, as applied to the particular property, is unreasonable.

The Neuzils did not contend in the district court that the 1985 downzoning amendment constituted spot zoning. Although the Neuzils did claim the amendment constituted inverse condemnation, they withdrew that claim on the day of trial.

In the district court the Neuzils tried the case on the theory that the 1985 rezoning amendment was unreasonable, arbitrary, and capricious. In support of their theory the Neuzils urged a number of reasons why the amendment was unreasonable. We restrict our review to that theory and to those reasons.

The district court noted that for the Neuzils to prevail the court would have to adopt the Maryland rule on rezoning. The district court properly refused to do so, recognizing that it was bound to follow our pronouncements on the subject.

Under the Maryland rule once land is zoned it can only be rezoned to correct an original error or because of a change in circumstances. Northwest Merchants Terminal v. O'Rourke, 191 Md. 171, 189–193, 60 A.2d 743, 752–53 (1948). Undergirding the rule is the presumption of reasonableness as to the original ordinance. Id. Moreover, if the question of correctness or change is fairly debatable, the court will not substitute its judgment for that of the zoning authority. Wakefield v. Kraft, 202 Md. 136, 147, 96 A.2d 27, 29 (1953). Such an approach gives the original zoning regulation a greater presumption of correctness than the amendment.

After surveying cases concerning the Maryland rule, one writer observed that the greatest drawback in using the rule is that it completely thwarts the efforts of legislative or zoning authorities in the absence of satisfaction of [the "mistake or change" rule]; there are many circumstances where change is desirable, but impossible, due to the rule. H. Goldman, Zoning Change: Flexibility v. Stability, 26 Md.L.Rev. 48, 51 (1966) [hereinafter Goldman]. The facts in one Maryland case illustrate exactly what the writer means. See MacDonald v. Board of County Comm'rs for Prince George's County, 238 Md. 549, 210 A.2d 325 (1965). In MacDonald the property in question was zoned single family residential but had never been developed. As such there could be no showing of a change in condition. The developers wanted to build high-rise apartments on the land. The zoning board decided this might be a better use for the land, but no one had been able to prove the original zoning was erroneous when passed. As the writer concluded, [t]he reason for the change [in MacDonald] was evident—ideas had changed. A more modern jurisdiction would have allowed the change had the proponents shown the amendment to be reasonable and not arbitrary or capricious; the Maryland court, not able to satisfy the "mistake or change" test, had no choice but to strike down the amendment, no matter how reasonable and desirable it appeared to be. Goldman at 52.

In contrast our rule on amending zoning ordinances is considered more liberal and flexible. Under our approach we give the original zoning ordinance no greater presumption of validity than the amendment. The same standards used to justify original zoning are used in determining the propriety of amendatory ordinances. Id. at 53–54. We expressed our view on this point in Keller v. City of Council Bluffs, 246 Iowa 202, 207–08, 66 N.W.2d 113, 116–17 (1954):

> We are of the opinion the governing body of a municipality may amend its zoning ordinances anytime it deems circumstances and conditions warrant such actions, and such an amendment is valid if the procedural requirements of the statute are followed and it is not unreasonable or capricious nor inconsistent with the spirit and design of the zoning statute. The burden is upon the plaintiffs attacking the amendment to establish that the acts of the council were arbitrary, unreasonable, unjust and out of keeping with the spirit of the zoning statute. See also Iowa Code § 414.5 (municipality "may from time to time ... amend, supplement, change, modify, or repeal" zoning ordinances).

This liberality and flexibility expressed in Keller is consistent with the rule that in legislative matters a municipality may not bind its successors. Hanna v. Rathje, 171 N.W.2d 876, 880 (Iowa 1969). Such a rule is necessary because city council members are "trustees for the public." Id. So the determination of when the public's interest requires a change in zoning must be within the discretion of the municipality. Anderson, § 4.27 at 291. Because of this discretion, courts reviewing zoning amendments should not substitute their judgment as to the wisdom or propriety of the municipality's action when the reasonableness of the amendments is fairly debatable. Anderson v. City of Cedar Rapids, 168 N.W.2d at 742.

Here we need to review the written reasons the city gave for enacting the 1985 amendment that downzoned the tract. Only after such a review can we determine whether circumstances and conditions warranted the downzoning.

The district court found that the city had relied on the written reasons in downzoning the tract, that the reasons were proper ones to consider, and that the reasons were "debatably reasonable." The court concluded it could not, therefore, strike down the amendatory ordinance. For reasons that follow, we think there is substantial evidence to support the district court's findings.

The Neuzils cite their own reasons why the 1985 downzoning amendment is unreasonable, arbitrary, and capricious. They include the following: 1. The tract has proximity to the largest employer—The University of Iowa Hospitals and Clinics—in Johnson County, which is within walking distance. 2. City utilities are available. 3. The size of the tract will permit large-scale development and preserve open space. 4. Housing on this tract will help reduce the need for private automobile transportation. The city bus service is one block away. 5. Public schools are in the vicinity. 6. There are three access streets to the tract. 7. The tract is adjacent to other multifamily dwellings. 8. The area has been zoned for multifamily use since 1962. 9. Prior to the 1985 rezoning, there were no changes in the area or environment since the adoption of the most recent Iowa City Zoning Ordinance. All these reasons are arguments for developing the tract with multifamily units. However, balanced against Neuzils' reasons are the city's reasons for downzoning the tract. All the city's reasons are statutorily recognized. Moreover, there is substantial evidence to support each one.

While the tract was originally zoned for multifamily dwellings, the actual development of the surrounding area is mostly single-family and duplex dwellings. So the challenged amendment seeks to place the tract in conformity with other land in the same area. See Iowa Code § 414.3 (municipality is required to give reasonable consideration to the character of the area).

The city found that the prior zoning—RM-12—would increase the traffic flow in the area past its current accommodation. According to the city's thinking, the downzoning would reduce the potential for such burdensome traffic increases. Traffic considerations are reasonable grounds, under the city's police power, for amending zoning ordinances. See Iowa Code § 414.3 (zoning ordinances should be designed to lessen congestion in the streets).

Additionally, the city found that downzoning would help maintain the current property values in the area—a consideration that bears a substantial relationship to the public's health, safety, welfare and comfort. * * * Finally, the city considered the environmental impact of the current zoning. Consideration included both aesthetic impact and flood-pollution consequences of the prior RM-12 zoning. These two considerations take into account the safety and security of the area as well as the general public's comfort and welfare. * * *

One fact that bears on our analysis is that the 1978 Comprehensive Plan contemplated limiting development of the tract at eight to sixteen dwellings per acre. As the city recognized in its written reasons, the 1985 downzoning amendment is consistent with what the city had been contemplating since 1978. So the Neuzils should not have been surprised that what was contemplated in 1978 occurred in 1985. What the city did in 1985 was in keeping with the spirit of the 1978 Comprehensive Plan.

What immediately becomes apparent from our analysis is that there is a difference of opinion between the Neuzils and the city. Differing opinions are the crux of the "fairly debatable" rule—"if there is some basis for the ordinance ... and there is room for two opinions, the challenged ordinance is valid." Anderson, § 3.20, at 138.

The Neuzils' reasons boil down to this: the 1985 downzoning amendment prohibited the most beneficial use of the tract. As we said, this is not enough to brand a zoning ordinance as unreasonable, capricious or discriminatory. Stone v. City of Wilton, 331 N.W.2d at 402. The Neuzils offered no proof, as the plaintiffs did in Kempf, that the tract could not be improved with any development that would be economically feasible. See Kempf v. City of Iowa City, 402 N.W.2d at 400.

IV. DISPOSITION.

The Neuzils' burden on appeal is a heavy one: to establish, as a matter of law, that the 1985 downzoning amendment was unreasonable, capricious or discriminatory. We think they failed to do so. Under the facts as found by the district court, we are convinced that the city acted within its authorized police power in downzoning the tract in 1985.

Accordingly, we vacate the decision of the court of appeals and affirm the judgment of the district court.

DECISION OF COURT OF APPEALS VACATED; DISTRICT COURT JUDGMENT AFFIRMED.

All justices concur except SCHULTZ, J., who dissents.

SCHULTZ, JUSTICE (dissenting).

The fundamental justification for amending a zoning ordinance is a change in conditions making the amendment reasonably necessary to protect the public interest. 8 E. McQuillin, The Law of Municipal Corporations § 25.67b, at 170 (3d rev. ed. 1976). Here, the trial court found that there was no significant change in the general location from the 1983–84 zoning ordinance to the 1985 downzoning. Under the facts of this case, I would conclude that the action of the city council was unreasonable and should be declared invalid.

From the time this property was annexed by the city in 1956 until 1985, the city has never zoned the property in a manner that would prevent the construction of multifamily residences. In 1962 the city commissioned a comprehensive zoning plan which affected the property but allowed multifamily dwellings. In the 1960s and 1970s the surrounding property was highly developed. In 1978 the property was rezoned and a new comprehensive plan adopted. Following extensive studies a new ordinance was adopted in 1983. Because of a defect it was readopted during the spring of 1985. While the property was downzoned during this period, multi-resident dwellings were still allowed.

At the insistence of a group of neighbors and over the recommendation of its planning and zoning commission, the city council, four months after its latest ordinance, rezoned the property to a type of district which disallows multi-dwelling construction. Neighbors also use the land for recreational purposes, and their representatives had previously attempted to have the same undeveloped property made into a city park.

Because of its location near the stadium and the hospital, this property is best used as multifamily dwellings. The object of zoning is to put property to its best use.

I am aware that zoning is not static and existing ordinances are subject to reasonable revision as the need appears and that ordinances may be amended any time circumstances and conditions warrant such action. * * *

What was the reason for the ordinance amendment? After this action was filed, the city set forth the purported reasons for the rezoning. Traffic, pollution and congestion are not new to the area and were present both four months and two years earlier when the city studied this tract. This rezoning procedure was instituted by neighbors and not by the city or its planning staff. The obvious reason for the rezoning was neighborhood pressure. While I do not challenge or condemn the political process, I do not believe that the city council acted reasonably under the circumstances. It ignored the best use of the property and the interest of the general public in having housing convenient to Iowa City's largest employer. It bowed to a group who has enjoyed the use of this property and wishes to dictate its further use at the owners' expense. Without a careful restudy of the property in the area, the council had no legitimate reason to make changes.

I would reverse the trial court.

Notes

1. Neuzil is similar to many cases presented in the casebook. In this section, it permits the student to consider several aspects of the role of the courts in land use decision-making. What standard of review of the legislature's decision did the court use? Does that standard reflect a posture of deference on the part of the court to the legislative determination? If there is a fair difference of opinion about how a site should be zoned in one community in the state, which body—the local legislature or the state court—should decide which view prevails? Why? What remedies did the landowner petition the court to apply? Did it ask the court to rezone the property to a particular use or to declare that the allowed use was unreasonable under the circumstances? What would the effect be if a court determined that a rezoning decision was unreasonable? Who, then, would decide the use to which the land could be put?

2. Did the court in the principal case actually characterize the rezoning decision as a legislative one? Did the court treat it as one? Upon which party, the city or the landowner, did the court impose the burden of proof? Why?

FASANO v. BOARD OF COUNTY COMM'RS OF WASHINGTON COUNTY

Supreme Court of Oregon, In Banc, 1973.
264 Or. 574, 507 P.2d 23.

HOWELL, JUSTICE. The plaintiffs, homeowners in Washington county, unsuccessfully opposed a zone change before the Board of County Commissioners of Washington County. Plaintiffs applied for and received a writ of review of the action of the commissioners allowing the change. The trial court found in favor of plaintiffs, disallowed the zone change, and reversed the commissioners' order. The Court of Appeals affirmed, 489 P.2d 693 (1971), and this court granted review.

The defendants are the Board of County Commissioners and A.G.S. Development Company. A.G.S., the owner of 32 acres which had been zoned R–7 (Single Family Residential), applied for a zone change to P–R (Planned Residential), which allows for the construction of a mobile home park. The change failed to receive a majority vote of the Planning Commission. The Board of County Commissioners approved the change and found, among other matters, that the change allows for "increased densities and different types of housing to meet the needs of urbanization over that allowed by the existing zoning."

The trial court, relying on its interpretation of Roseta v. County of Washington, 254 Or. 161, 458 P.2d 405, 40 A.L.R.3d 364 (1969), reversed the order of the commissioners because the commissioners had not shown any change in the character of the neighborhood which would justify the rezoning. The Court of Appeals affirmed for the same reason, but added the additional ground that the defendants failed to show that the change was consistent with the comprehensive plan for Washington county.

According to the briefs, the comprehensive plan of development for Washington county was adopted in 1959 and included classifications in the county for residential, neighborhood commercial, retail commercial, general commercial, industrial park and light industry, general and heavy industry, and agricultural areas.

The land in question, which was designated "residential" by the comprehensive plan, was zoned R–7, Single Family Residential.

Subsequent to the time the comprehensive plan was adopted, Washington county established a Planned Residential (P–R) zoning classification in 1963. The P–R classification was adopted by ordinance and provided that a planned residential unit development could be established and should include open space for utilities, access, and recreation; should not be less than 10 acres in size; and should be located in or adjacent to a residential zone. The P–R zone adopted by the 1963 ordinance is of the type known as a "floating zone," so-called because the ordinance creates a zone classification authorized for future use but not placed on the zoning map until its use at a particular location is approved by the governing body. The R-7 classification for the 32 acres continued until April 1970 when the classification was changed to P-R to permit the defendant A.G.S. to construct the mobile home park on the 32 acres involved.

The defendants argue that (1) the action of the county commissioners approving the change is presumptively valid, requiring plaintiffs to show that the commissioners acted arbitrarily in approving the zone change; (2) it was not necessary to show a change of conditions in the area before a zone change could be accomplished; and (3) the change from R-7 to P-R was in accordance with the Washington county comprehensive plan.

We granted review in this case to consider the questions—by what standards does a county commission exercise its authority in zoning matters; who has the burden of meeting those standards when a request for change of zone is made; and what is the scope of court review of such actions?

Any meaningful decision as to the proper scope of judicial review of a zoning decision must start with a characterization of the nature of that decision. The majority of jurisdictions state that a zoning ordinance is a legislative act and is thereby entitled to presumptive validity. This court made such a characterization of zoning decisions in Smith v. County of Washington, 241 Or. 380, 406 P.2d 545 (1965):

> "Inasmuch as ORS 215.110 specifically grants to the governing board of the county the power to amend zoning ordinances, a challenged amendment is a legislative act and is clothed with a presumption in its favor. Jehovah's Witnesses v. Mullen et al., 214 Or. 281, 292, 330 P.2d 5, 74 A.L.R.2d 347 (1958), appeal dismissed and cert. denied, 359 U.S. 436, 79 S.Ct. 940, 3 L.Ed.2d 932 (1959)." 241 Or. at 383, 406 P.2d at 547.

However, in *Smith* an exception to the presumption was found and the zoning held invalid. Furthermore, the case cited by the *Smith* court, Jehovah's Witnesses v. Mullen et al., supra, at least at one point viewed the contested zoning in that case as an administrative as opposed to legislative act.

At this juncture we feel we would be ignoring reality to rigidly view all zoning decisions by local governing bodies as legislative acts to be accorded a full presumption of validity and shielded from less than constitutional scrutiny by the theory of separation of powers. Local and small decision groups are simply not the equivalent in all respects of state and national legislatures. There is a growing judicial recognition of this fact of life:

> "It is not a part of the legislative function to grant permits, make special exceptions, or decide particular cases. Such activities are not legislative but administrative, quasi-judicial, or judicial in character. To place them in the hands of legislative bodies, whose acts as such are not judicially reviewable, is to open the door completely to arbitrary government." Ward v. Village of Skokie, 26 Ill.2d 415, 186 N.E.2d 529, 533 (1962) (Klingbiel, J., specially concurring).

The Supreme Court of Washington, in reviewing a rezoning decision, recently stated:

> "Whatever descriptive characterization may be otherwise attached to the role or function of the planning commission in zoning procedures, e.g., advisory, recommendatory, investigatory, administrative or legislative, it is manifest * * * that it is a public agency, * * * a principle [sic] and statutory duty of which is to conduct public hearings in specified planning and zoning matters, enter findings of fact—often on the basis of disputed facts—and make recommendations with reasons assigned thereto. Certainly, in its role as a hearing and fact-finding tribunal, the planning commission's function more nearly than not partakes of the nature of an administrative, quasi-judicial proceeding, * * *." Chrobuck v. Snohomish County, 78 Wash.2d 858, 480 P.2d 489, 495–496 (1971).

Ordinances laying down general policies without regard to a specific piece of property are usually an exercise of legislative authority, are subject to limited review, and may only be attacked upon constitutional grounds for an arbitrary abuse of authority. On the other hand, a determination whether the permissible use of a specific piece of property should be changed is usually an exercise of judicial authority and its propriety is subject to an altogether different test. An illustration of an exercise of legislative authority is the passage of the ordinance by the Washington County Commission in 1963 which provided for the formation of a planned residential classification to be located in or adjacent to any residential zone. An exercise of judicial authority is the county commissioners' determination in this particular matter to change the classification of A.G.S. Development Company's specific piece of property. The distinction is stated, as follows, in Comment, Zoning Amendments—The Product of Judicial or Quasi–Judicial Action, 33 Ohio St.L.J. 130 (1972):

> " * * * Basically, this test involves the determination of whether action produces a general rule or policy which is applicable to an open class of individuals, interest, or situations, or whether it entails the application of a general rule or policy to specific individuals, interests, or situations. If the former determination is satisfied, there is legislative action; if the latter determination is satisfied, the action is judicial." 33 Ohio St.L.J. at 137.

We reject the proposition that judicial review of the county commissioners' determination to change the zoning of the particular property in question is limited to a determination whether the change was arbitrary and capricious.

In order to establish a standard of review, it is necessary to delineate certain basic principles relating to land use regulation.

* * *

In Oregon the county planning commission is required by ORS 215.050 to adopt a comprehensive plan for the use of some or all of the land in the county. Under ORS 215.110(1), after the comprehensive plan has been adopted, the planning commission recommends to the governing body of the county the ordinances necessary to "carry out" the comprehensive plan. The purpose of the zoning ordinances, both under our statute and the general law of land use regulation, is to "carry out" or implement the comprehensive plan. 1 Anderson, American Law of Zoning, § 1.12 (1968). Although we are aware of the analytical distinction between zoning and planning, it is clear that under our statutes the plan adopted by the planning commission and the zoning ordinances enacted by the county governing body are closely related; both are intended to be parts of a single integrated procedure for land use control. The plan embodies policy determinations and guiding principles; the zoning ordinances provide the detailed means of giving effect to those principles.

* * *

We believe that the state legislature has conditioned the county's power to zone upon the prerequisite that the zoning attempt to further the general welfare of the community through consciousness, in a prospective sense, of the factors mentioned above. In other words, except as noted later in this opinion, it must be proved that the change is in conformance with the comprehensive plan.

In proving that the change is in conformance with the comprehensive plan in this case, the proof at a minimum, should show (1) there is a public need for a change of the kind in question, and (2) that the need will be best served by changing the classification of the particular piece of property in question as compared with other available property.

* * *

Because the action of the commission in this instance is an exercise of judicial authority, the burden of proof should be placed, as is usual in judicial proceedings, upon the one seeking change. The more drastic the change, the greater will be the burden of showing that it is in conformance with the comprehensive plan as implemented by the ordinance, that there is a public need for the kind of change in question, and that the need is best met by the proposal under consideration. As the degree of change increases, the burden of showing that the potential impact upon the area in question was carefully considered and weighed will also increase. If other areas have previously been designated for the particular type of development, it must be shown why it is necessary to introduce it into an area not previously contemplated and why the property owners there should bear the burden of the departure.[16]

Although we have said in *Roseta* that zoning changes may be justified without a showing of a mistake in the original plan or ordi-

---

16. For example, if an area is designated by the plan as generally appropriate for residential development, the plan may also indicate that some high-density residential development within the area is to be anticipated, without specifying the exact location at which that development is to take place. The comprehensive plan might provide that

nance, or of changes in the physical characteristics of an affected area, any of these factors which are present in a particular case would, of course, be relevant. Their importance would depend upon the nature of the precise change under consideration.

By treating the exercise of authority by the commission in this case as the exercise of judicial rather than of legislative authority and thus enlarging the scope of review on appeal, and by placing the burden of the above level of proof upon the one seeking change, we may lay the court open to criticism by legal scholars who think it desirable that planning authorities be vested with the ability to adjust more freely to changed conditions. However, having weighed the dangers of making desirable change more difficult against the dangers of the almost irresistible pressures that can be asserted by private economic interests on local government, we believe that the latter dangers are more to be feared.

What we have said above is necessarily general, as the approach we adopt contains no absolute standards or mechanical tests. We believe, however, that it is adequate to provide meaningful guidance for local governments making zoning decisions and for trial courts called upon to review them. With future cases in mind, it is appropriate to add some brief remarks on questions of procedure. Parties at the hearing before the county governing body are entitled to an opportunity to be heard, to an opportunity to present and rebut evidence, to a tribunal which is impartial in the matter—i.e., having had no prehearing or ex parte contacts concerning the question at issue—and to a record made and adequate findings executed. Comment, Zoning Amendments—The Product of Judicial or Quasi–Judicial Action, 33 Ohio St.L.J. 130–143 (1972).

* * *

its goal for residential development is to assure that residential areas are healthful, pleasant and safe places in which to live. The plan might also list the following policies which, among others, are to be pursued in achieving that goal:

1. High-density residential areas should be located close to the urban core area.

2. Residential neighborhoods should be protected from any land use activity involving an excessive level of noise, pollution or traffic volume.

3. High trip-generating multiple family units should have ready access to arterial or collector streets.

4. A variety of living areas and housing types should be provided appropriate to the needs of the special and general groups they are to serve.

5. Residential development at urban densities should be within planned sewer and water service areas and where other utilities can be adequately provided.

Under such a hypothetical plan, property originally zoned for single family dwellings might later be rezoned for duplexes, for garden apartments, or for high-rise apartment buildings. Each of these changes could be shown to be consistent with the plan. Although in addition we would require a showing that the county governing body found a bona fide need for a zone change in order to accommodate new high-density development which at least balanced the disruption shown by the challengers, that requirement would be met in most instances by a record which disclosed that the governing body had considered the facts relevant to this question and exercised its judgment in good faith. However, these changes, while all could be shown to be consistent with the plan, could be expected to have differing impacts on the surrounding area, depending on the nature of that area. As the potential impact on the area in question increases, so will the necessity to show a justification.

As there has not been an adequate showing that the change was in accord with the plan, or that the factors listed in ORS 215.055 were given proper consideration, the judgment is affirmed.

BRYSON, JUSTICE (specially concurring).

The basic facts in this case exemplify the prohibitive cost and extended uncertainty to a homeowner when a governmental body decides to change or modify a zoning ordinance or comprehensive plan affecting such owner's real property.

This controversy has proceeded through the following steps:

1. The respondent opposed the zone change before the Washington County Planning Department and Planning Commission.

2. The County Commission, after a hearing, allowed the change.

3. The trial court reversed (disallowed the change).

4. The Court of Appeals affirmed the trial court.

5. We ordered reargument and additional briefs.

6. This court affirmed.

The principal respondent in this case, Fasano, happens to be an attorney at law, and his residence is near the proposed mobile home park of the petitioner A.G.S. No average homeowner or small business enterprise can afford a judicial process such as described above nor can a judicial system cope with or endure such a process in achieving justice. The number of such controversies is ascending.

In this case the majority opinion, in which I concur, adopts some sound rules to enable county and municipal planning commissions and governing bodies, as well as trial courts, to reach finality in decision. However, the procedure is no panacea and it is still burdensome.

It is solely within the domain of the legislative branch of government to devise a new and simplified statutory procedure to expedite finality of decision.

Notes

1. The Fasano doctrine was re-examined in a subsequent case and applied to a rezoning of a 600–acre tract for multifamily housing, Neuberger v. City of Portland, 37 Or.App. 13, 586 P.2d 351 (1978). On appeal, the Oregon Supreme Court modified the court of appeals' decision, but adhered to the application of Fasano to the rezoning in issue, and devoted considerable attention to the question of which land use decisions might be legislative in nature and which would be treated as quasi-judicial. Neuberger v. City of Portland, 288 Or. 155, 603 P.2d 771 (1979), rehearing denied 288 Or. 585, 607 P.2d 722. The court stated:

* * * [O]ur land use decisions indicate that when a particular action by a local government is directed at a relatively small number of identifiable persons, and when that action also involves the application

of existing policy to a specific factual setting, the requirement of quasi-judicial procedures has been implied from the governing law.

Although both of these factors are frequently present in the cases in which we have held or assumed that quasi-judicial functions were exercised, each is * * * a separate indicator of the possible need for adjudicatory procedures. The reasons, moreover, are different in each instance.

When specific facts must be determined in order that pre-existing criteria may be applied, procedures similar to those used in adjudications are important in order to assure that factual determinations will be made correctly. When the requirement of such procedures is implied because a relatively small number of persons is directly affected, even though the decision-maker is not entirely bound by pre-existing criteria but is empowered to exercise broad discretion the law may require a formal hearing procedure. * * *

A third consideration * * * is whether the process is bound to result in a decision. Although that factor is rarely discussed in the cases because in many contexts its presence is readily apparent, it was not so obvious in * * * the recent case of Henthorn v. Grand Prairie School Dist., 287 Or. 683, 601 P.2d 1243 (1979). In *Henthorn* the determination that the school board was required to make a decision on the basis of information produced at a hearing required by statute was important to our conclusion that the proceedings were quasi-judicial and, therefore subject to judicial review under the writ of review.

2. The Fasano court imposed the burden of proof on the legislative body, the Board of County Commissioners. Why? What precisely is the Board required to prove? Consider the following statement of the Fasano majority: "Because the action of the commission in this instance is an exercise of judicial authority, the burden of proof should be placed, as is usual in judicial proceedings, upon the one seeking change. The more drastic the change, the greater will be the burden of showing that it is in conformance with the comprehensive plan as implemented by the ordinance, that there is a public need for the kind of change in question, and that the need is best met by the proposal under consideration."

3. In Cooper v. Board of County Comm'rs of Ada County, 101 Idaho 407, 614 P.2d 947 (1980), the court held that a decision to not rezone 99 acres from low density residential (one unit per acre) to a density which would permit two to three units per acre, was a quasi-judicial decision, entitling the property owner to procedural due process, which, on the facts, the court found had been denied. Also see Golden v. City of Overland Park, 224 Kan. 591, 584 P.2d 130 (1978), where the city denied approval to a rezoning request from an office designation to permit a small shopping center, and the court also found the decision to be quasi-judicial and, on the facts, unreasonable.

4. The Supreme Court of Florida moved in the direction of Fasano and overruled some earlier cases in Board of County Comm'rs of Brevard County v. Snyder, 627 So.2d 469 (Fla.1993). In this case, the owner of a half-acre parcel located in a district zoned for single-family use applied for a rezoning to multifamily, intending to build four to six units. The planning director

indicated he approved of the rezoning as it was consistent with the comprehensive plan, but several citizens were opposed because of potential increase in traffic and the rezoning was denied. The court held that although earlier cases had applied the fairly debatable rule in rezonings as well as initial zoning efforts, rezoning actions which have an impact on a limited number of persons where the decision can be viewed as policy application rather than policy setting, should be viewed as quasi-judicial. The court delineated the following procedure:

> Upon consideration, we hold that a landowner seeking to rezone property has the burden of proving that the proposal is consistent with the comprehensive plan and complies with all procedural requirements of the zoning ordinance. At this point, the burden shifts to the governmental board to demonstrate that maintaining the existing zoning classification with respect to the property accomplishes a legitimate public purpose. In effect the landowners' traditional remedies will be subsumed within this rule, and the board will now have the burden of showing that the refusal to rezone the property is not arbitrary, discriminatory, or unreasonable. If the board carries its burden, the application should be denied.

5. Compare with the above cases, South Gwinnett Venture v. Pruitt, 491 F.2d 5 (5th Cir.1974), where the entire court, sitting en banc, overturned a panel decision and held "that local zoning is a quasi-legislative procedure, not subject to federal judicial consideration in the absence of arbitrary action. Moreover, we see no viable distinction between zoning board functions involved in the adoption of a comprehensive zoning plan and those exercised in reclassification of a piece of property under an existing plan * * *." This was in line with Higginbotham v. Barrett, 473 F.2d 745 (5th Cir.1973), in which the same court had stated that "the law is settled that the zoning of property, including the preparation of comprehensive land plans, involves the exercise of judgment which is legislative in character and is subject to judicial control only if arbitrary and without rational basis." The majority of the panel in the earlier version of South Gwinnett Venture v. Pruitt, 482 F.2d 389 (5th Cir.1973), certiorari denied 416 U.S. 901, 94 S.Ct. 1625, 40 L.Ed.2d 119 (1974), attempted to distinguish the legislative action of adopting a comprehensive zoning plan from "the adjudicative decision inherent in tract rezoning"—the latter situation deemed to require adherence to minimal standards of due process.

NOVA HORIZON, INC. v. CITY COUNCIL OF THE CITY OF RENO

Supreme Court of Nevada, 1989.
105 Nev. 92, 769 P.2d 721.

Per Curiam

Appellants are developers who planned to build a hotel/convention center (the Project) on land next to the Bally Grand in Reno. Prior to submitting an application for necessary approvals, appellants purchased the land in question. The plot consists of 2.9 acres, bordered on three sides by the Bally Grand. On August 29, 1984, appellants submitted to the Reno Planning Commission an application requesting:

1. a change of zoning, M–1 to C–3;
2. a Special Use Permit; and
3. acceptance of a tentative subdivision map,

to construct a twenty-eight story, 804–room hotel and casino. At that time, the property owned by appellants was zoned M–1 as defined and limited in Section 18.06.270 of the Reno Municipal Code. M–1 zoning allows commercial development but imposes height restrictions of sixty-five feet, which would not accommodate appellants' project as planned. Additionally, M–1 does not allow any residential use and the proposed project was planned to include the sale of 312 units on a time-share basis.

On November 7, 1984, the Reno Planning Commission, by a vote of four to three, recommended to the City Council that it approve the three separate requests. Appellants' application came before respondents on December 10, 1984. At that time, a public hearing was held wherein appellants presented their case and the community was given the opportunity to respond. After the conclusion of testimony, the City Council unanimously voted to deny all of appellants' requests.

* * *

We note, preliminarily, that the district court properly subjected the City's action to a substantial evidence standard of review. This court, in addressing the propriety of a district court ruling reversing a zone change approval by the appropriate governmental body, declared:

> Respondents recognize the general rule that a court is not empowered to substitute its judgment for that of a zoning board, in this case the board of county commissioners, when the board's action is supported by substantial evidence.

* * *

> The lower court had before it the same evidence as the board. Its function was not to conduct a trial de novo, but only to ascertain as a matter of law if there was any substantial evidence before the board which would sustain the board's action. The function of this court at this time is the same as that of the lower court. [Citation omitted.]

* * *

> Under the police power, zoning is a matter within sound legislative action and such legislative action must be upheld if the facts do not show that the bounds of that discretion have been exceeded.

McKenzie v. Shelly, 77 Nev. 237, 240–242, 362 P.2d 268, 269–70 (1961). In *Shelly,* we reversed the district court since the presumptive validity of the board's action was supported by substantial evidence and there was no showing that the board abused its discretion.

Numerous cases support the premise that zoning boards may not unreasonably or arbitrarily deprive property owners of legitimate, advantageous land uses. For example, the Supreme Court of Virginia affirmed a trial court decision holding an unduly restrictive zoning classification void. *Town of Vienna Council v. Kohler,* 218 Va. 966, 244 S.E.2d 542 (1978). The *Kohler* court concluded that "a denial of a rezoning request will not be sustained if under all the facts of the particular case, the denial is unreasonable, or is discriminatory, or is without substantial relationship to the public health, safety, morals and general welfare." *Id.* 244 S.E.2d at 548. *See also,* e.g., *Raabe v. City of Walker,* 383 Mich. 165, 174 N.W.2d 789 (1970) (invalidating rezoning of small enclave in midst of residential area to accommodate an industrial park); *City of Conway v. Housing Authority,* 266 Ark. 404, 584 S.W.2d 10 (1979) (City of Conway directed to rezone property, as the denial of the rezoning request was arbitrary and inconsistent with surrounding zoning); *Lowe v. City of Missoula,* 165 Mont. 38, 525 P.2d 551 (1974) (restrictive zoning impressed on landowner's property was so lacking in fact information as to constitute an abuse of discretion; rezoning held to be invalid). In the latter case, the Montana Supreme Court, quoting from an earlier case, stated:

> Under the guise of protecting the public or advancing its interest, the state may not unduly interfere with private business or prohibit lawful occupations, or impose unreasonable or unnecessary restrictions upon them. Any law or regulation which imposes unjust limitations upon the full use and enjoyment of property, or destroys property value or use, deprives the owner of property rights.

In the instant case, the requested change in zoning was in conformity with the long-range development plans adopted by the City of Reno. The zone change was requested at the suggestion of the Reno City Planning staff and is consistent with the zoning of the surrounding property. Moreover, it appears that appellants may have invested substantial sums of money (allegedly over $1,200,000.00) in land acquisition and project development costs in anticipation of the City's approval of their application.

At the public hearing in which appellants' application was considered, only one person presented opposition to the project and his objections were basically rebuffed by members of the Reno City Council. Nevertheless, the Council unanimously denied approval to what was described as an architecturally "superior" project on the specified grounds that approval would violate a campaign promise against locating new casinos outside the "downtown area" and a similar pledge to diversification that would pay higher employee wages.

In determining whether the action of the Council concerning the zone change was without substantial evidentiary support and, consequently, an abuse of discretion, it is essential to first consider the effect of the City's master plan, as amended, and land use/transportation guide on the Council's latitude in zoning matters.

Chapter 278 of the Nevada Revised Statutes governs many aspects of planning and zoning. It not only provides for the formation and compensation of planning commissions and the adoption of master plans, it also provides for zoning in accordance with an adopted master plan. NRS 278.250(2) provides, in pertinent part: "2. The zoning regulations shall be adopted in accordance with the master plan for land use * * *." (Emphasis supplied.) This suggests that municipal entities must adopt zoning regulations that are in substantial agreement with the master plan, including a land-use guide if one is also adopted by the city council. Other jurisdictions have construed their statutes as requiring strict conformity between master plans and zoning ordinances, even to the point of requiring changes in zoning after a modification in a master plan. *See Baker v. City of Milwaukie,* 271 Or. 500, 533 P.2d 772 (1975); *Fasano v. Board of County Comm'rs,* 264 Or. 574, 507 P.2d 23 (1973). While such a strict view of the invariable application of a master plan on zoning matters may lend a high degree of predictability to prospective land uses and facilitate usage planning by land owners, we do not perceive the legislative intent to be so confining and inflexible. We therefore choose to view a master plan as a standard that commands deference and a presumption of applicability, rather than a legislative straightjacket from which no leave may be taken. In pertinent part, the Montana Supreme Court analyzed the issue as follows:

> To require strict compliance with the master plan would result in a master plan so unworkable that it would have to be constantly changed to comply with the realities. The master plan is, after all, a plan. On the other hand, to require no compliance at all would defeat the whole idea of planning. Why have a plan if the local government units are free to ignore it at any time? The statutes are clear enough to send the message that in reaching zoning decisions, the local governmental unit should at least substantially comply with the comprehensive plan (or master plan).

Little v. Board of County Comm'rs, 631 P.2d 1282, 1293 (Mont.1981).

Having determined that master plans are to be accorded substantial compliance under Nevada's statutory scheme, and recognizing anew the general reluctance to judicially intervene in zoning determinations absent clear necessity, *Board of Comm'rs v. Dayton Dev. Co.,* 91 Nev. 71, 530 P.2d 1187 (1975), we turn now to the issue of respondents' zoning action in the instant case. It is clear on the record that no evidentiary basis exists for the Council's denial of appellants' zone change request. It is equally clear that no deference, let alone a presumptive applicability, was accorded Reno's master plan by the Council. In one instance, an expression of deference to a campaign promise was the stated basis for what was tantamount to a disregard for the master plan. The other expression offered as a specific basis for rejecting appellants' application was a pledge, presumably to constituents, to seek diversification in favor of higher employee wages. The latter point was equally untenable as a basis for zoning denial. Moreover, as noted above, the surrounding properties enjoyed the same zoning sought by appellants and no evidence, let alone reasoning, was presented to justify a denial of appellants' request for rezoning. We therefore are compelled to reverse the district court on this point.

We are not constrained to grant similar relief concerning appellants' request for a special use permit and acceptance of a tentative subdivision map. While the record provides no existing or prospective basis for denying the zone change, we are loathe to direct authorization for a project that may or may not be deserving of the Council's approval. The Council simply did not effectively address the effect of the impact of such a substantial project on the City of Reno. While it may be argued with considerable cogency from the record that appellants justified an approval of their entire application, and that it is unfair to subject them to further proceedings, we nevertheless conclude that it would be unwise and inappropriate for this court to accommodate an approval by forfeiture.

If appellants remain interested in the construction of their project, we will assume that, upon rehearing, the Council will exercise its judgment fairly and in accordance with the merits as reflected by the evidence and deliberations of record.

We realize that our ruling may appear to be inconsistent with our opinion in *City Council, Reno v. Travelers Hotel,* 100 Nev. 436, 683 P.2d 960 (1984), where we affirmed the issuance of a peremptory writ of mandamus requiring approval of a special use permit for a hotel-casino. In that case, however, rezoning was not an issue and the Council was able to focus directly on the project itself. Here, the only specified basis for rejecting appellants' application was essentially the project's location outside the downtown area, a reason which, if implemented, would constitute an inappropriate *de facto* amendment to the City's master plan and land use/transportation guide. We are simply unable to discern from the record that the Council adequately focused its attention on the merits of the project and its total impact on the community. Considerations of public health, safety and welfare demand both such a focused attention and the exercise of a fair and enlightened discretion by the Council based upon substantial evidence.

The judgment of the district court is reversed insofar as the zone change is concerned, and remanded with instructions to issue a peremptory writ of mandamus requiring respondents to grant appellants' application for zone change. The district court shall also modify its judgment to the extent of requiring respondents, upon application by appellants, to entertain anew the merits of appellants' application for special use permit and acceptance of tentative subdivision map, all in accordance with this opinion.

Notes

1. Compare with the Nevada decision, Tate v. Miles, 503 A.2d 187 (Del.1986). In the latter case, the planning commission held a hearing on a rezoning application and recommended approval to the county council; the

council held a public hearing and subsequently enacted a rezoning ordinance with no findings or statement of reasons, merely stating that change was in accord with the comprehensive plan and promoted public welfare. The trial court gave the neighbors a summary judgment and the supreme court affirmed, stating that although under Delaware law rezoning is a legislative act, it "resembles" a judicial determination because a zoning decision must be supported by a record sufficient to withstand judicial challenge. With no reasons for the change in the record, a court has no means to review the decision. The court held that a rezoning decision must be accompanied by findings and a statement of the reasons for the rezoning.

2. In addition to the question of the standard of review when rezoning is viewed as a quasi-judicial rather than a legislative act, other consequences may flow from the characterization of rezoning decisions. For example, in a judicial challenge to a city's decision not to rezone, may the plaintiff-property owner compel members of the city legislative body to testify as to their reasons or motivations for voting to deny the petition? In Wait v. City of Scottsdale, 127 Ariz. 107, 618 P.2d 601 (1980), the court held that the denial of a rezoning petition was a legislative act and that the motives of council members in denying the petition and the reasons they considered were beyond the scope of judicial inquiry. Similarly, in Sheffield Development Co. v. City of Troy, 99 Mich.App. 527, 298 N.W.2d 23 (1980), the court held that because rezoning was a legislative act, council members could not be compelled to answer questions regarding their motives in denying the rezoning application. The court did state that the motives of legislators could be examined when the complaint alleges fraud, personal interest, or corruption.

3. The particular method of reviewing zoning decisions varies from state to state. Some enabling acts and some zoning ordinances prescribe the method of seeking review. Where statutes or ordinances are silent, injunction suits and certiorari are quite common. See, e.g., Platte Woods United Methodist Church v. City of Platte Woods, 935 S.W.2d 735 (Mo.App.1996). In recent years attorneys have sometimes sought to utilize the federal courts to review zoning decisions, relying on civil rights legislation or other, more novel, theories of federal jurisdiction.

a. Bodor v. East Coventry Twp., 325 F.Supp. 1102 (E.D.Pa.1971). Plaintiff sued to restrain the township officials from preventing him from establishing a 70–foot-by–12–foot mobile home as a permanent residence on a four-acre tract of land. "Plaintiffs' complaint raises the substantial constitutional issues of due process of law and equal protection under the law in that in order for Plaintiffs to avail themselves of the administrative remedies provided in the township's zoning ordinance and building code ordinance, Plaintiffs would allegedly have to pay a $750.00 filing fee. * * * Plaintiffs have alleged facts which, if proved, establish a concerted effort by the Board of Supervisors of East Coventry Township to preclude the review of their Zoning and Building Code Ordinances through the establishment of a prohibitive filing fee. Such an allegation sets forth a claim upon which relief can be granted."

b. City of Miami v. Woolin, 387 F.2d 893 (5th Cir.1968). The city ordinances prohibited erection of gasoline filling stations within 350 yards of a church, hospital, or school, and within 750 feet of another filling station. The court held that the equal protection clause of the Fourteenth Amendment rendered the ordinance unconstitutional and upheld a permanent injunction.

c. Minshew v. Smith, 380 F.Supp. 918 (N.D.Miss.1974). Plaintiffs, homeowners and adjacent property owners, sued the owner of a motel and several city officials for compensatory and punitive damages on a theory that the defendants conspired to achieve an illegal amendment of the zoning ordinance to allow the motel to expand into the adjacent residential zone. The court found for the plaintiffs and ordered compensatory damages (the motel had already built), but refused to award punitive damages.

d. Walker v. State of North Carolina, 262 F.Supp. 102 (W.D.N.C.1966), affirmed 372 F.2d 129 (4th Cir.1967), certiorari denied 388 U.S. 917, 87 S.Ct. 2134, 18 L.Ed.2d 1360 (1967). Petitioner remodeled his house without securing a building permit. He was arrested and charged with a misdemeanor, receiving a thirty-day jail sentence which was suspended on the condition that he comply with the building code and pay court costs. Petitioner appealed to the state supreme court which upheld the validity of the building code. Petitioner is now in federal district court seeking a writ of habeas corpus. "Petitioner has failed to show a violation of any of his federal constitutional rights, and, for this reason, his petition will be, and hereby is, dismissed."

e. Bob Layne Contractor, Inc. v. Bartel, 504 F.2d 1293 (7th Cir.1974). The developer of a subdivision that included restrictive covenants for residential use only subsequently vacated a portion of the plat because of a new highway and sought to turn the vacated portion into commercial property. Residents in the subdivision sued in state court to enforce the covenant. The developer brought this action in federal court alleging that the actions of the defendants to oppose the commercial rezoning and to enforce the covenant were a violation of the federal antitrust laws. A summary judgment for defendants was upheld.

f. DeFalco v. Dirie, 923 F.Supp. 473 (S.D.N.Y.1996). Real estate developers sued town officials and others for extortion under RICO (Racketeer Influenced and Corrupt Organizations, 18 U.S.C.A. § 1962 (c). The court held that the plaintiffs stated a cause of action based on municipal employees' activities in extorting money in return for necessary permits. The court also held that a municipality could be considered as an "enterprise" for purposes of bringing a RICO claim. Also see Manor Healthcare Corp. v. Lomelo, 929 F.2d 633 (11th Cir.1991), a suit against the mayor and president of the city council under § 1983 alleging that the defendants extorted $30,000 from a nursing home in a rezoning matter. The court held that the city was properly dismissed as a party because the city neither adopted nor ratified the mayor's bribery and extortion.

4. Use of § 1983 to review zoning decisions has grown more popular since the Supreme Court ruled that cities are subject to suit under that provision in Monell v. Department of Social Services of the City of New York, 436 U.S. 658, 98 S.Ct. 2018, 56 L.Ed.2d 611 (1978). However, § 1983 suits may have limitations. First, the complaint must allege deprivation of a constitutional right, which can be difficult for the disappointed property

owner denied a rezoning; many federal courts have held that a zoning permit is not a property right. Second, the local legislators may have immunity. See T & M Homes, Inc. v. Township of Mansfield, 162 N.J.Super. 497, 393 A.2d 613 (1978); Gorman Towers, Inc. v. Bogoslavsky, 626 F.2d 607 (8th Cir. 1980); Creative Environments, Inc. v. Estabrook, 491 F.Supp. 547 (D.Mass. 1980); Robinson v. City of Raytown, 606 S.W.2d 460 (Mo.App.1980). However, in Dunmore v. City of Natchez, 703 F.Supp. 31 (S.D.Miss.1988), the court held that to the extent city officials were acting in a legislative capacity in denying a variance they were immune from personal liability, but to the extent that they may have participated in a conspiracy to deny a black female applicant a variance because of her race, they had no immunity.

5. Students should be aware that zoning disputes sometimes turn on the interpretation of words in the ordinance. For example, many zoning ordinances prohibit the keeping of "livestock" in residential districts. Persons who keep exotic pets often find themselves embroiled in a dispute over the issue of whether their pet is "livestock." See, e.g., Barnes v. City of Anderson, 642 N.E.2d 1004 (Ind.App.1994), where the court considered if "Sassy" the Vietnamese pot-bellied pig was a household pet or "livestock." Sometimes the ordinance uses the term "wild animal" thus placing pet lions, tigers, and bears in jeopardy when neighbors complain. Another example is Saurer v. Board of Zoning Appeals, 629 N.E.2d 893 (Ind.App.1994), where the court held that rusty trailers, building trusses, semi-trailers, hog roasters and tables kept outdoors in a rural area did not constitute "junk" under a zoning ordinance defining a junkyard as a lot for the storage or sale of junk, scrap metal, scrap vehicles, or scrap machinery. The court said that junk, like pornography, is difficult to define but that "we know them when we see them." Just because the items are unpleasant to view does not make them junk, and courts are not arbiters of aesthetics and good taste.

6. Courts often strictly interpret the language of land use regulations, resolving ambiguities in favor of landowners, because such regulations are said to be "in derogation of common law property rights." How does this general rule of interpretation square with the presumption of validity that courts afford the regulations themselves? Can you determine the difference between presuming that a land use law is valid and restrictively interpreting its meaning as applied?

Index

References are to Pages

ABANDONMENT
As basis for terminating nonconforming use, 378–388

ACCESSORY USES
See Zoning

AESTHETICS
Generally, 825–875
Architectural control, 850–863
As basis for injunction against nuisance, 74
As basis for regulating minimum lot sizes, 1173–74
Billboards, 826–847
Clotheslines, 863–69
Conservation easements, 902
Federal legislation, 875–78
Highway beautification, 847–850
Historic districts, 879–888
Land trusts, 903
Landmark structures, 888–902
Minimum lot sizes, 1173–74
Parking lots, 870
Police power, 850–55
Private property, protection of, 863–69
Residences, 850–874
Signs, 826–847
Underground utilities, 871–75

AGRICULTURE
Hog ranches, 1060–67
Nuisances conflicting with, 40
Swine control ordinance, 1060–67
Zoning for, 1060–67

AIRSPACE
Condominiums, 164–67
Construction in, 923–931
Development of, 891–95
Nuisance situations, 103
Taking by inverse condemnation, 103

AMORTIZATION
Limitations on, 397
Nonconforming uses, 390–97
Tests of validity of period, 391–96

ANTITRUST LAW
Shopping centers, 1100
Zoning and, 1098–1100

APARTMENTS
Compared with condominiums, 1135–37

APARTMENTS—Cont'd
Excluded by zoning, 1127–1135

ARCHITECTURAL CONTROLS
See Aesthetics

BILLBOARDS
Amortization of, 397
Highway beautification, 847–850
Nonconforming uses, amortization of, 397
Zoning for aesthetics, 826–845

BUILDING SIZE
See also, Exclusionary Zoning
Generally, 1184–1192

CEMETERIES
See also, Nuisances
Generally, 60–62
Compared with funeral parlors, 60–62, 114

CHURCHES
As conditional uses, 364–370, 1250
Exclusion through restrictive covenants, 167–170
Exclusion through zoning, 1244–1256
First Amendment issue, 1244–49
Impact on area, 1250
Religious Freedom Restoration Act, 1250
Religious Land Use and Institutionalized Persons Act, 1005–1024, 1251
Schools attached to, 1251

CLUSTER PLAN
Generally, 444–452

COMMERCE AND INDUSTRY
Exclusion by zoning, 1233–1244
Residence as nuisance in industrial area, 95–7

COMMON INTEREST COMMUNITY
Created by covenants, 11
Private government, and, 243–247

CONDOMINIUMS
As part of a planned unit development, 4
Conversion as subdivision, 443
Conversion of apartments to, 1135–38
Gentrification, 1167
Police power, in connection with, 1137
Restrictive covenants, effect on, 163

CONSENT PROVISIONS
As condition of granting variance, 1266

INDEX

CONSENT PROVISIONS—Cont'd
As delegation of police power, 906–910
Validity of, 1262–66

CONSERVATION
Trees, 799–809
Viewsheds, 784–799
Watersheds, 703–09

CONTRACT
As condition of rezoning, 332–349
For installation of subdivision amenities, 461

COVENANTS
See Restrictive Covenants

CREMATORIUM
As nuisance, 46–9

DAMAGES
Interim, in cases of temporary taking, 932–38
Section 1983 cases, 987–1001

DEDICATION FOR PUBLIC USE
Contracting to obtain, 490
Governmental power to regulate, 430–31
Off-site activities, 466–475
Payments in lieu of, 479–489
Schools and parks, 476–487
Subdivisions, 457–462

DEFEASIBLE ESTATES
    Generally, 111–123
Covenants compared to, 111
Determinable fee, 113
Easements distinguished, 115
Equitable servitudes distinguished, 114
Restrictions on subdivisions, use of to impose, 111
Reverter and conditions, rules and problems, 114
Types, 113–14
Uniform Reverter Act, 241

DEMOLITION OF HOUSE
As nuisance, 112
For violation of covenants, 178

DEVELOPER AGREEMENTS
    See also, Vested Rights
    Generally, 538–549
Impairment of contract, 545–48
Statutory authorization, 548–49

DRUG HOUSE
As nuisance, 75

ECONOMICS
Impact on land use regulation, 195–200

EMINENT DOMAIN
Conservation and rehabilitation programs, 629
Historic districts, 879–888
Inverse condemnation, 933
Minimum lot sizes, 1173–1184

EMINENT DOMAIN—Cont'd
Official map, relation to, 524–530
Police power, 18–27
Property, definition of, 16–18
Public use versus public purpose, 641
Taking, 911–978
    Historic Districts, 879–888
    Interim, 934–938
    Landmark structures, 923–932
    Zoning, 300–08
Urban renewal, 629

ENABLING ACT
Planning, 200–206
Zoning, 282–84

ENERGY CONSERVATION
Solar devices,
    Interference with as nuisance, 88–93
Windmills, 94

ENDANGERED SPECIES ACT
Generally, 1055–56

ENTERPRISE ZONES
Generally, 640–43

ENVIRONMENTAL CONTROLS
Floodplains, 758–766
Environmental justice, 1055
Impact reviews, 729–736
Hillsides, 777–784
Local environmental law,
    Generally, 699–824
    Erosion control, 774–77
    Fish and wildlife, 809–816
    History of, 699–710
    Protection of water supply, 746–758
    Scenic resources, 784–799
    Steep slopes, 777–784
    Stormwater management, 752–58
    Trees and forests, 799–809
    Water resources, 725–29, 737–752
Public trust doctrine, 816–824
Shorelands, 711–725
Subdivisions, 719–725
Wetlands, 703–710, 766–774
Wildlife protection, 809–816

EQUAL PROTECTION
Limitation on local regulation, 1001–04

EQUITABLE SERVITUDES
    Generally, 135–158
Conveyance or contract, 147
Ownership of benefited lands, 137
Reciprocal negative easements, 141

ESCAPING GASES
Nuisances, 69–70

ETHICS
Engineers, 228
Lawyers, 223–28
Local officials, 229

ETHICS—Cont'd
Planners, 220–23

EXCLUSIONARY ZONING
See also, Growth of Urban Areas; Inclusionary Zoning; Subdivision of Land; Zoning
Adult theaters and bookstores, 1240
Age discrimination, 1167–1173
Apartments, 1127–1135
Big box stores, 1236
Churches,
　First Amendment issue, 1244–49
　Impact on area, 1250
Commerce, 1236–1244
Condominiums, 1135–38
Convents or monasteries, 1251
Fast food outlets, 1236
Gasoline stations, 1235
Group homes,
　AIDS patients, 1126
　As institutional use, 1126
　Federal legislation, 1125
　Purpose of, 1123
　Single-family issue, 1104–1127
　State legislation, 1125
Housing discrimination,
　Generally, 1102–1233
　Affirmative relief for, 1193–1223
　Age as a factor, 1167–1173
　Compelling governmental interest, 1159
　Damages for, 1160
　Fair Housing Act, effect of, 1166
　"Fair share" concept, 1197–1208
　Fourteenth Amendment, 1155–1166
　Low and moderate income housing, 1193–1217
　Racial composition, 1155–1160
　Racially discriminatory effect, 1155–1160
　Racially discriminatory purpose or intent, 1160–64
　Single-family character, 1107–1119
Industry, 1233–36
Institutional uses, 1126
Massage parlors, 1240
Manufactured homes,
　Classification of, 1142–1155
　Number limitations, 1138–1140
One use limitations, 1104–07
Path of population growth, 1130
Schools,
　Generally, 1256–1260
　Invalid distinctions, 1259–1260
　Private versus public, 1256–58
Racial discrimination in zoning, 1155–1167
Sex-oriented businesses, 1237–1247
Video game establishments, 1236

"FAIR SHARE" PRINCIPLE
Generally, 1197–1208

FAMILY
Constitutional issues, 1107–1111
Defined, 1107

FAMILY—Cont'd
Group homes, 1120–1127
Religious groups, 1251
Unrelated people, 1107–1119

FILLING STATIONS
Exclusion of, 1235
Nuisances, 107

FINANCING
Subdivision requirements, 460–62
Tax increment, 630–640

FLOODPLAINS
　Generally, 758–766
Channel building lines, 765
Development restrictions, 6,
Insurance, 765
Zoning, 758–764

FORESTRY
Timber regulations, 804–09
Tree protection, 799–804

FUNERAL HOMES
See also, Nuisances
Compared with cemetery and crematory cases, 43

GASOLINE STATIONS
See Filling Stations

GENTRIFICATION
Generally, 1167

GROWTH OF URBAN AREAS
Effect of minimum building sizes, 1184–1192
Effect of minimum lot sizes, 1173–1184
Environmental concerns, 710–736
Freezing growth, 586–597
Regulation of, 12, 550–52
Smart growth defined, 550
Timed and sequential, 552–563

HARDSHIP
See Official Map; Zoning, Variance

HIGHWAYS AND STREETS
See Dedication for Public Use; Easements; Subdivision of Land

HISTORIC DISTRICTS
　Generally, 879–888
Beacon Hill, 882–83
Lincoln's home, 888
Nantucket Island, 879–882
Old Santa Fe, 884
Vieux Carre, 884
Williamsburg, 884

HISTORIC SITES
See Landmark Structures

HISTORICAL OVERVIEW
　Generally, 15–27
Nuisances, 32

HISTORICAL OVERVIEW—Cont'd
Private property, right of, 16–18

HOME FOR AGED
Consent provision, 1262–65

HOME RULE
Local government power, 905

HOMEOWNERS' ASSOCIATION
As private government, 187–191
Enforcement of restrictive covenant, 158–160
Standing to enforce affirmative covenant, 124–130

HOUSING
See Exclusionary Zoning, Housing discrimination; Publicly Financed Housing; Urban Renewal

HOUSING AND URBAN DEVELOPMENT
See Urban Renewal

HOUSING CODES
See Smart Growth

IMPACT FEES
To fund new infrastructure, 12, 525–535

INCENTIVE ZONING
Affordable housing, 1214
Growth management technique, 696–98

INCLUSIONARY ZONING
See also Exclusionary Zoning; Zoning
Generally, 1192–1232
Affirmative relief, 1193–1201
Builder's remedy, 1208–1217
"Fair share" concept, 1193–1208
Housing needs, consideration in, 1201–08
Judicial remedies for, 1193–1223
Legislative approaches, 1223, 1231–33
Linkage fees, 1217–1223
Regional considerations, 1283–1290, 1295
Requiring low income units, 1223–1231
Spot zoning to achieve, 1231–32

INITIATIVE AND REFERENDUM
Generally, 1266–1276
Constitutionality, 1267–1273
Difference, 1276
Initiative and zoning, 1276
Legislative act issue, 1274

INTERGOVERNMENTAL CONFLICTS IN ZONING
Generally, 1076–1100
City versus city, 1086–1100
Corrections facility, 1085
Federal preemption, 1005–1056
Group homes, effect on, 1067–1074
National interests, 1097
Regional considerations, 1098
State agency versus city, 1076–1084
State university, 1084
Statutory provisions, 1085–86

ZONING—Cont'd
Tests, 1076–1084

INVERSE CONDEMNATION
See Eminent Domain

JUDICIAL CONTROLS ON LAND USE
Generally, 15–16
Conflicting uses,
  Older settled areas, 70–93
  Open country, 37–45
  Suburban fringe, 55–70
Nuisance doctrines, 32–7

JUDICIAL REVIEW OF ZONING
Generally, 1316–46
Legislative test, 1320–1331
Quasi-judicial test, 1332–39

JUNKYARDS
Aesthetics, 70–74
Amortization, 396–97
As nuisances, 70–74
Zoning relative to, 1346

LAND DEVELOPMENT
See also, Subdivision of Land
Antitrust implications, 1100
Clustering, 444–452
Dedication of streets, 457
Defeasible estates, 111
Density transfer, 680–87
Energy conservation, 550–62
Equitable servitudes, 135–158
Floodplains and open lands, 758–766
Growth controls,
  See smart growth
Planned unit developments, 674–76
Restrictive covenants, 175–78
Shoreland controls, 767–774, 817–823
Subdivisions,
  Ecological considerations, 719–725
  Environmental controls, 729–736
  Exactions, 452–522
  Governmental power to regulate, 426
  Reasons for and nature of regulation, 416–426
Timed and sequential growth, 552–564
Urban growth, regulation of, 550–52
Wetlands, 703–710, 766–774, 956–964

LANDMARK STRUCTURES
Generally, 888–902
Constitutional problems, 923–932
Eminent domain issues, 923–932
Grand Central Terminal, 891–95
J.P. Morgan house, 895
Jay mansion, 897–900
National Register, effect of, 890
Old Grand Rapids City Hall, 888–890
Ordinances preventing demolition of, 901
Religious Land Use and Institutionalized Persons Act, 896
St. Bartholomew's Church, 896

LANDMARK STRUCTURES—Cont'd
Transfer of development rights, 891–905

LEGISLATIVE CONTROLS ON LAND USE
See also, Zoning
Early examples, 19–21
State preemption, 1056–1076,
Zoning,
    Enabling authority, 282–84
    Interim, 575–76

LOT SIZE
As indirect discrimination, 1173–1184

MARKETABILITY OF LAND
Master Plan, effect of, 243–49
Official map, effect of, 524–530

MASTER PLAN
Adoption of, 230–36
As basic planning device, 279
Consistency doctrine, 240–43
Content of, 230, 284–86–86
Effect of,
    Generally, 236–252, 281
    On governing bodies, 236
    On land subdivision, 241–42, 252
Marketability of land, effect on, 243–49, 252
Model Land Development Code, 231–33
Standard Planning Enabling Act, 230

MEDIATION
Generally, 1276–1316
After development approval process, 1309–1311
During development approval process, 1294–1309
Key steps, 1280–82
Lawyering and, 1311–16
Mediators, 1279
Negotiation, development approval and, 1278
Prior to land use application, 1288–1294
Statutes, 1282–85

METES AND BOUNDS
Sales of land by, 442

MINIMUM BUILDING SIZE
As exclusionary, 1184–1192

MINIMUM LOT SIZE
As exclusionary, 1173–1184

MOBILE HOMES
Age discrimination and, 1167–1173
Definition of in restrictive covenants, 160–63
Exclusion of, 1138–1155
    From community, 1141
    From single-family districts, 1142–1155

MODEL LAND DEVELOPMENT CODE
Areas of critical state concern, 203
Master plan, 287–289

MORATORIUM
As taking, 964–978

NAVIGATION, OBSTRUCTIONS TO
As nuisances, 45

NEIGHBORHOOD
Definition, 77–8

NONCONFORMING USES
Generally, 371–397
Abandonment of, 378–388
Amortization of, 390–97
As nuisances, 373
Destruction and rebuilding of, 388–390
Exemption of, 371–73
Expansion or enlargement, 373–78

NOTICE
Building scheme, 145–46
Equitable servitudes, 141–44
Subdivisions, 146
Variances, 364

NUISANCES
Generally, 32–37
Agriculture or livestock, uses in conflict with, 37
Balancing of hardships and equities, 35, 72
Billboards, 107
Brickyards, 98
Brothels, 102
Cement plants, 37, 65
Cemeteries, 43
Commercial and industrial areas, 95
Country club, 128–129
Crematories, 46
Demolition of house, 80
Drug house, 75
Escaping gases, 67–70
Feedlots, 57–64
Filling stations, 107
First Amendment, 108
Funeral homes, 47, 76–79
    Among commercial uses, 79
    In residential neighborhoods, 76
Golf course, 97
Gravel pits, 108
Historic background, 32
Interference with solar collectors, 88
Junkyards, 98–103, 107–8
Livery stables, 101
Motive, 36
Moving to, 35, 64
Navigation, obstructions to, 45
Noise, 49, 55
Odors, 42
Open country, 32–46
Ore reduction, 40
Per accidens, 36
Per se, 36
Piggeries, 52–55
Private nuisances, 33
Public nuisances, 33
Recreational uses, 77, 102

References are to Pages

NUISANCES—Cont'd
Rendering plants, 42
Residential uses, 70
    Recreational, 52
    Rural, 46
    Rururban fringe, 55
Rural residential use, 46
Rururban fringe, 83
Salvage yards, 70–74
Self-help, 103
Sic utere tuo ut alienum non laedas, 59
Sign, 88
Solar device, 88
Spite fence, 83–88
Substantial harm, 34
Supermarkets, 75
Television interference, 139
Trees, 80, 93
Ultrahazardous activities, 69
Windmills, 94
Zoned areas, 104–108

OFFICIAL MAP
    Generally, 522–538
Constitutionality, 524–530
Establishing building or set-back lines, other methods, 523
Hardship cases or provisions, 537
Master plan, comparison with, 533–36
Title encumbrance, 538

OPEN LANDS
Environmental controls on, 703–729
Flood plains, 758–766
Highway beautification and scenic easements, 847–850
Hillside protection, 777–784
Nuisances, 32–46
Shorelands, 816–824
View protection, 784–799
Wildlife preserves, 809–816

OVERLAY ZONING
As smart growth technique, 687–696

PARKS
See Dedication for Public Use, Schools and parks

PIGGERIES
As nuisance, 52–55

PLANNED UNIT DEVELOPMENT (PUD)
As a development choice, 4–5
Smart growth, and, 736–738

PLANNING
    See also, Master Plan; Zoning
    Generally, 200–230
Background, 200, 281
Enabling acts, 201
Failure to plan, 309–313
Federal legislation, 205, 252–58
Interstate compacts, 271–78
Planning commission, 7, 229
Planning profession, 206

PLANNING—Cont'd
Planning profession—Cont'd
    Ethical code, 220–23
    Legal status, 207
    Licensing of planners, 217
Regional, 269–271
State, 258–269
Zoning, relation to, 309–326
Zoning versus planning, 323–26

POLICE POWER
Basic rule, 24
Constitutional considerations, 911–1004
Delegation of powers, 905–911
Flood plains, 758–766
Hillsides, 777–784
Historic development, 21–25
Historic districts, 879–888
Official map, relation to, 522–538
Reservations of use, 566–571
Subdivision regulations, relation to, 431–32
Ultra vires doctrine, 969
Zoning, relation to, 281–84

PREEMPTION
Federal legislation, 1005–1056
    Americans With Disabilities Act, 1034–1043
    Fair housing, 1024–1034
    Religious Land Use and Institutionalized Persons Act, 1005–1024, 1251
    Telecommunications Act, 1043–1053
Intergovernmental conflicts,
    Local-local, 1086–1100
    State-local, 1076–1086
State preemption, 1056–1076
    Agricultural uses, 1060–67
    Group homes, mentally ill, 1067–1074
    Mining, 1056–1060

PRIVATE CONTROLS
See Easements; Equitable Servitudes; Restrictive Covenants

PRIVATE PROPERTY
Aesthetics, protection of, 850–871
Justification for, 16–18
Police power, effect on, 22–25, 286–88
Takings legislation, 27–32

PROPERTY
Equitable servitude or restrictive covenant as, 151–58
Property rights legislation, 27–32
Theory of right of ownership, 16–18

PUBLIC-PRIVATE COOPERATION
Enterprise zones, 640–42
Joint ventures, 630–642

PUBLIC SAFETY
As defense to taking, 938

RACIAL EXCLUSION
    Generally, 1155–1167

RACIAL EXCLUSION—Cont'd
Zoning,
    Exclusionary, 1155–1167
    Inclusionary, 1193–1201

RAILROADS
Right of way, conversion to trails, 121–23

RECIPROCAL NEGATIVE EASEMENTS
See Equitable Servitudes

RECREATIONAL USES
As nuisances, 49–52, 54, 97, 102–03

REGIONAL PLANNING
Flood plains or wetlands, 765–67
Interstate compacts, 271–78
Minnesota, 269–271
Timed and sequential growth, 552–564

REGULATION
Justification for, 18–27
Regulatory takings, 911–978

RENDERING PLANTS
See Nuisances, Rendering plants

RESIDENTIAL USES
See Nuisances, Residential uses

RESTRICTIVE COVENANTS
    Generally, 109–194
Alteration of, 178
As property, 147–158
Assessments, 175–181
Binding on land, 174–5
Change in neighborhood, effect on, 171
Churches, affected by, 167–170
Common building scheme, 145–47
Compensation for loss of, 151–58
Community associations, 187–191
Conditional use permit and, 175
Condominiums, 163–67
Drafting problems, 191–94
Enforcement of, 158–178
    Change in neighborhood, 181–85
    Effect of zoning, 171
    Homeowners' associations, 187–191
Equitable servitudes, creation of, 135–147
Notice of, 141–47
    Actual, 146
    Constructive, 141–44
Real covenants, 123–135
Right to release, 185–87
Tax deeds, effect on, 114
Termination, 181–87
Zoning, effect on, 171–74

SCENIC EASEMENTS
See Aesthetics; Easements

SCHOOLS
See Dedication for Public Use; Zoning

SERVITUDES
See Restrictive Covenants

SHOPPING CENTERS
Antitrust laws and, 1100
Effect on other local governments, 1098–1100

SHORELANDS,
See Environmental Controls: Land Development

SINGLE-FAMILY
As exclusionary, 1107–1119
Defined, 1107
Housing discrimination, based on, 1107–1127
Restrictive covenants, 159–163
Single use zoning, 1104–07

SLUMS
See Urban Renewal

SMART GROWTH
    Generally, 550–698
Brownfield redevelopment, 652
Competition, protection from, 643–653
Defined, 550
Growth centers,
    Generally, 622–653
    Enterprise zones, 640
    Housing codes, 623–29
    Parcelization, 640
    Public purpose doctrine, 641
    Tax increment financing, 630–640
    Urban development techniques, 641
Growth management,
    Generally, 576–622
    Access to infrastructure, 603–610
    Initiative by voters, 586–597
    Local regulation, 577–586
    Population cap, 596
    Recreation and resort area, 597
    State legislation, 610–622
Moratoria,
    Generally, 564–576
    Adoption of new plans or rules, 564–66, 575–76
    Public health or safety, 571–75
    Reservation for future acquisition, 566–571
Techniques, 653–698
    Cluster plans, 665
    Environmental impact review, 665–68
    Floating zones, 655–665
    Incentive zoning, 696–98
    Overlay zoning districts, 687–696
    Performance zoning, 669–674
    Planned unit development, 674–76
    Traditional neighborhood districts, 676–680
    Transfer of development rights, 680–87
Timed and sequential growth, 614–626

SPOT ZONING
See Zoning

STANDING
To challenge approval of subdivision, 582

STATE PLANNING
Generally, 258–269
Hawaii, 264–269
Vermont, 258–263

STATUTE OF FRAUDS
Effect on restrictive covenants, 147

STREETS AND HIGHWAYS
See Dedication for Public Use; Easements; Subdivision of Land

SUBDIVISION OF LAND
See also, Land Development; Restrictive Covenants
Generally, 416–522
Background, 416–421
Cluster plan, 444–452
Concept plat, 5
Condominiums, 443
Constitutionality of regulations, 491–511
Contracting for, 443
Controlling community growth, 416–421
Dedications to public use, 457–462
Defeasible estate, use of to restrict, 111
Enabling acts, 441–42
Environmental controls, 719–725
Exactions,
    Non-traditional, 476
    Off-site, 466
    Traditional, 453
Failure to approve and denial of plans, 513–522
Flood plains, 758–766
Growth controls, 552–566
Home rule, 457–59
Impact fees, 470
Improvements required, 5, 460–62
Interstate Land Sales Full Disclosure Act, 433–34
Laying out, 5
Metes and bounds sales, 442
Planning commission, 421–26
Plat, 5–7
Police power, effect on, 431–32
Retroactive regulation, 434–37
Schools and parks, dedication of land for,
    Generally, 476–490
    Authority to require, 479–486
    Contracting to obtain, 490
    Payment in lieu of, 479–486
Sewers, 461–62
Streets, 463–66
Surety bonds to insure improvements, 460
Testamentary devise, 443
Theories sustaining regulation, 426–433
    Conditional acceptance of street dedications, 430
    Conditioning recording, 426–29
    Protecting against fraud, 433
    Protecting health, safety and welfare, 431–33

SUBDIVISION OF LAND—Cont'd
Theories sustaining regulation—Cont'd
    Protecting right of communities to tax real estate, 431
Vested right, 436–37, 513–522

SUBSTANTIVE DUE PROCESS
Excessive regulation, 978–1001

SUPERMARKETS
As nuisances, 75

SURETY BONDS
Assuring installation of subdivision improvements, 461

TAKING
See Eminent Domain; Police Power

TANDEM HOUSE
Generally, 1119

TAX DEEDS
Equitable servitudes, effect on, 114
Restrictive covenants, effect on, 114

TAX INCREMENT FINANCING
See Financing

TAXATION
As affecting historic preservation, 879
Tax increment financing, 630–640

TRAILER PARKS
See Mobile Homes

TRANSFER OF DEVELOPMENT RIGHTS
Generally, 680–87
As a taking, 923–931
Historic sites, 891–96

TREES
As nuisance, 80–7, 93–4
Preservation, 6 , 799–809

UNDERGROUND UTILITIES
Aesthetic aspects, 874
Regulation of, 871–75
Subdivision exactions, 874

URBAN RENEWAL
Generally, 629–630
Background and history of, 629–630
Constitutionality, 629
Public use versus private purpose, 641–43

VARIANCE
See Zoning

VESTED RIGHTS
See also, Developer Agreements
Detrimental reliance, 437, 548–49
Statutes, 538–540
Under common law, 542
Zoning change, 437

INDEX

References are to Pages

WETLANDS
Generally, 6, 703–710, 766–774, 956–964

ZONING
See also, Aesthetics; Eminent Domain; Environmental Controls; Exclusionary Zoning; Flood Plains; Inclusionary Zoning; Master Plan; Nuisances; Planning; Police Power
Accessory uses, 398–408
Amendment,
    Generally, 332–349
    Change of conditions, 1322
    Contract or conditional rezoning, 332–349
    Judicial review, 1316–1346
    Mistake as basis for, 1322
    Spot zoning, 335
    Validity, 332–36
Amortization, 390–97
Architectural controls, 850–862
Billboards, 826–850
Churches, 1244–1256
Cluster plan, 444–452
Comprehensive or master plan,
    Generally, 282–86, 309–313
    As prerequisite to zoning, 310, 323–26
    Relation to spot zoning, 311
Conditional zoning, 332–349
Consent provisions,
    Generally, 1262–66
    Funeral homes, 79
    Manufactured homes, 1266
    Old folks home, 1262–65
Constitutionality, 291–307
County zoning, 318–323
Delegation of authority to administrative agencies, 349–351
Early cases, 291–307
Enabling acts, 282, 309
Exclusionary zoning,
    Generally, 1104–1260
    Apartments, 1127–1138
    Commerce and industry, 1233–1244
    Condominiums, 1135–38
    Housing, 1102–1233
    Institutions and group homes, 1120–27
    Minimum building sizes, 1184–1192
    Minimum lot sizes, 1174–1184
    Mobile homes, 1138–1155
    Single families, 1107–1119
    Timed and sequential growth, 552–563
Family, definition of, 1107
Flexibility in, 327–371
Floating zones, 655–665
Flood plains, 758–766
Highway beautification, 847–850
History of, 279
Home occupations, 408–415
Incentive, 696–98
Judicial review, 1316–1346
Junkyards, 1346

ZONING—Cont'd
Limitations on, 286–88
Livery stables, 101
Mediation, 1276–1316
Minimum building size,
    Generally, 1184–1192
    Economic segregation versus legitimate planning, 1190–91
    Police power, 1190
Minimum lot size,
    Generally, 1173–1184
    Police power, 1174–1184
    Values obtained by, 1173–74
Manufactured homes, 1138–1155
Neighbors,
    Consent by, 1262–66
Nonconforming uses,
    Generally, 371–398
    Abandonment of, 378–388
    Amortization, 390–97
    Destruction of, 388–390
    Expansion or enlargement, 373–78
Nuisances in zoned areas,
    Generally, 104–08
    Conforming uses, 106
    Nonconforming uses, 107–08
Ordinance as, 375–379
Overlay districts, 687–696
Performance zoning, 669–674
Planned unit development (PUD),
    Generally, 674–76
    As smart growth technique, 674–76
    Cluster plan, 444–452
Planning,
    Prerequisite to, 282–84
    Relation to, 282
Police power, 281–84
Post–Euclidian, 653–55
Regional considerations, 1197–1208
Restrictive covenants, effect on, 171–74
Schools, 1256–1260
Single-family limitations, 1107–1119
Special permits,
    Generally, 289, 364–371
    Churches, 364
    Conditional, 371
Spot zoning,
    Generally, 311–18
    Comprehensive plan, effect on and relation to, 311
    Defined, 311
Taking,
    Police power as, 911–1004
    Zoning amounting to, 300–07
Trailer parks, 1138–1140
Variance,
    Generally, 349–364
    Area versus use, 357–361
    Hardship as requirement, 351
    Nonconforming uses, 363